TOP

HAY

ENGLISH
AMERICAN SOUTH AFRICAN

TIMOTHY ALFALFA CLOVER RYEGRASS

SUPPLIERS TO LEADING TRAINERS AND STUD FARMS

J. & J. Ransley

AYR,
AINTREE,
YORK, EPSOM,
LINGFIELD, NAAS
NEWMARKET,
NEWBURY, HAYDOCK,
WOLVERHAMPTON,
CHEPSTOW, KELSO, RIPON
GOODWOOD,
SANDOWN PARK, LEICESTER,
CHEPSTOW, KEMPTON PARK
CHELTENHAM
HUNTINGDON, WETHERBY,
ASCOT, EXETER, RIPON
PLUMPTON, YAR... TH,
DONCASTER, ...PTON
CHESTER, HAM... PAR...
UTTOXETER, ...AST...
WAR...CK, ...
CHE...OWN
RE...

Seen winning in all the right places - **UNDER BOTH CODES!**

Baileys ®
HORSE FEEDS

MASTERS OF RACE NUTRITION

Baileys Horse Feeds Tel: 01371 850247 www.baileyshorsefeeds.co.uk

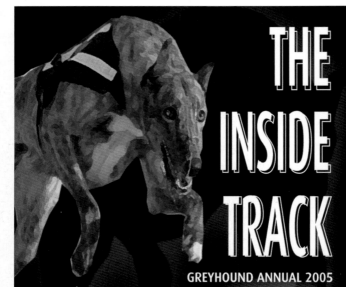

112th
YEAR OF PUBLICATION

Raceform

HORSES

in Training 2005

ISBN 1 904317 87 1

INDEX TO GENERAL CONTENTS

Editor; Simon Turner; Raceform Ltd, Compton, Newbury, Berkshire, RG20 6NL. Fax: 01635 578101 E-mail: simon.turner@mgn.co.uk

Assisstant Editor; Richard Lowther

Production Editor; Mark Knibbs; Bloodstock Services, Weatherbys Typesetting: Maggie Elvie; Production Servics, Weatherbys Sanders Road, Wellingborough, NN8 4BX.

Orders; Raceform Ltd., Compton, Newbury, Berkshire, RG20 6NL. Tel: 01635 578080 Fax: 01635 578101 E-mail: rfsubscription@mgn.co.uk

Advertisements; Alison Wheeler; Compton, Newbury, Berkshire, RG20 6NL. Tel: 01635 577610, Fax: 01635 578101

Printed by Woolnough Bookbinding Ltd., Irthlingborough, Northamptonshire, NN9 5SE.
Distributed to the Newstrade by MMC, Octagon House, White Hart Meadows, Ripley, Woking, Surrey, GU23 6HR. Tel: 01483 211222
Distributed in the booktrade by Orca Book Services, Stanley House, 3 Fleets Lane, Poole, Dorset BH15 3AJ. Tel: 01202 665432

© Raceform Ltd
Raceform Ltd is a wholly-owned subsidary of MGN Ltd
www.raceform.co.uk.

INDEX TO ADVERTISERS

2005

RACING FIXTURES

AND SALE DATES

(SUBJECT TO ALTERATION)

Flat fixtures are in **Black Type**; Jump in Light Type; Irish in *Italic*; French in ***Italic***; asterisk
(☆) indicates an evening meeting;
† indicates an All Weather meeting. Sale dates are at foot of fixtures

*Foalings dates are shown for two-year-olds where these are provided,
and the purchase price (in guineas) as a yearling.*

*Please note that the price published for two-year-olds is the official
recorded purchase price, and not the price used by the British
Horseracing Board for race entry purposes.*

JANUARY

Sun	Mon	Tues	Wed	Thur	Fri	Sat
30	**31**					**1**
Tramore *Punchestown*	Exeter Kempton **Wolverhampton†**					Catterick Cheltenham Fontwell **Southwell†** *Fairyhouse* *Tramore*
2	**3**	**4**	**5**	**6**	**7**	**8**
Plumpton **Southwell†** *Naas*	Exeter Folkestone **Southwell†** Wetherby *Cork*	Ayr **Lingfield†** **Wolverhampton†**	Hereford **Lingfield†** **Southwell†** ***Deauville***	Ludlow Wincanton **Wolverhampton†**	Musselburgh Towcester **Wolverhampton†**	Haydock **Lingfield†** Sandown Uttoxeter *Navan* ***Deauville***
9	**10**	**11**	**12**	**13**	**14**	**15**
Leopardstown	Newcastle Taunton **Wolverhampton†**	Leicester Sedgefield **Southwell†** ***Deauville***	**Lingfield†** Newbury **Wolverhampton†**	Catterick **Lingfield†** **Southwell†** *Limerick*	Huntingdon Kelso **Wolverhampton†** ***Deauville***	Kempton **Lingfield†** Warwick Wetherby *Punchestown*
	Keeneland Sales	Keeneland Sales	Keeneland Sales	Keeneland Sales	Keeneland Sales	Keeneland Sales
16	**17**	**18**	**19**	**20**	**21**	**22**
Cork *Fairyhouse*	Doncaster Plumpton **Wolverhampton†**	Folkestone **Southwell†** Towcester	Fakenham **Lingfield†** Newcastle	Ludlow **Southwell†** Taunton *Gowran Park*	Chepstow Musselburgh **Wolverhampton†**	Catterick Haydock **Lingfield†** Uttoxeter (from Ascot) Wincanton *Naas*
23	**24**	**25**	**26**	**27**	**28**	**29**
Leopardstown	Fontwell Southwell **Wolverhampton†**	Leicester Sedgefield **Southwell†**	Huntingdon **Lingfield†** Wetherby	Plumpton **Southwell†** Warwick *Thurles*	Doncaster Folkestone **Wolverhampton†**	Ayr Cheltenham Doncaster **Lingfield†** *Fairyhouse*
	Doncaster Sales	Doncaster Sales				

FEBRUARY

Sun	Mon	Tues	Wed	Thur	Fri	Sat
		1 **Lingfield**† **Southwell**† Taunton	**2** Leicester **Lingfield**† Newcastle	**3** Kelso **Southwell**† Towcester *Clonmel*	**4** Catterick Fontwell **Wolverhampton**†	**5** Chepstow **Lingfield**† Sandown Wetherby *Naas*
		Tattersalls (IRE) Sales	Tattersalls (IRE) Sales	Tattersalls Sales	Tattersalls Sales	
6 Hereford Musselburgh **Southwell**† *Leopardstown*	**7** Sedgefield **Southwell**† **Wolverhampton**†	**8** **Lingfield**† Market Rasen **Southwell**†	**9** Carlisle **Lingfield**† Ludlow *Punchestown*	**10** Huntingdon **Southwell**† Wincanton *Thurles*	**11** Bangor Kempton **Wolverhampton**†	**12** Ayr **Lingfield**† Newbury Warwick **Wolverhampton**†☆ *Gowran Park*
				Deauville Sales		
13 Ayr Exeter Hereford *Navan*	**14** **Lingfield**† Plumpton **Wolverhampton**† *Navan*	**15** Folkestone Newcastle **Southwell**†	**16** Leicester **Lingfield**† Musselburgh *Down Royal*	**17** Sandown **Southwell**† Taunton *Clonmel*	**18** Fakenham Sandown **Wolverhampton**†	**19** Haydock Lingfield (from Ascot) Haydock Uttoxeter Wincanton **Wolverhampton**† *Fairyhouse*
		Goffs Sales	Goffs Sales	Goffs Sales		
20 Fontwell Towcester *Naas*	**21** Carlisle **Lingfield**† **Wolverhampton**†	**22** **Lingfield**† Sedgefield **Southwell**†	**23** Doncaster **Lingfield**† Ludlow	**24** Haydock Huntingdon **Southwell**† *Thurles*	**25** Kempton Warwick **Wolverhampton**†	**26** Chepstow Kempton **Lingfield**† Newcastle *Fairyhouse*
		Ascot Sales				
27 Musselburgh **Southwell**† *Downpatrick* *Punchestown*	**28** **Lingfield**† Plumpton **Wolverhampton**†					

MARCH

Sun	Mon	Tues	Wed	Thur	Fri	Sat
		1 Leicester **Lingfield**† Catterick *Auteuil*	**2** Folkestone **Southwell**† Wetherby	**3** **Lingfield**† Ludlow Taunton *Limerick* \\ Goresbridge Sales	**4** Doncaster Newbury **Wolverhampton**† *Saint-Cloud*	**5** Doncaster Huntingdon Kelso Newbury *Navan*
6 Kempton Market Rasen *Clonmel* *Leopardstown* **Auteuil**	**7** Hereford **Lingfield**† **Wolverhampton**†	**8** Exeter Newcastle **Southwell**†	**9** Bangor-on-Dee Catterick Fontwell **Maisons-Laffitte**	**10** Carlisle Towcester Wincanton *Thurles* **Saint-Cloud**	**11** Ayr Leicester Sandown	**12** Ayr Chepstow Sandown **Southwell**† **Wolverhampton**† *Downpatrick* **Saint-Cloud**
13 **Southwell**† Warwick *Naas* **Auteuil**	**14** Plumpton Stratford Taunton	**15** Cheltenham Sedgefield **Southwell**† **Maisons-Laffitte**	**16** Cheltenham Huntingdon **Wolverhampton**†	**17** Cheltenham Hexham **Southwell**† *Down Royal* *Wexford* **Saint-Cloud**	**18** Cheltenham Fakenham **Lingfield**† **Maisons-Laffitte**	**19** Bangor **Lingfield**† Newcastle Uttoxeter **Wolverhampton**† *Tramore* **Saint-Cloud**
20 Carlisle Fontwell *Curragh* *Limerick* **Auteuil**	**21** Hereford **Lingfield**† **Southwell**†	**22** Exeter **Lingfield**† Wetherby **Maisons-Laffitte**	**23** Chepstow **Lingfield**† Towcester	**24** Ludlow Wincanton **Wolverhampton**† **Longchamp**	**25** **Maisons-Laffitte**	**26** Carlisle Haydock **Kempton** Newton Abbot **Wolverhampton**† *Cork* *Down Royal*
27 **Musselburgh** Plumpton Towcester *Cork* *Fairyhouse* **Auteuil**	**28** Fakenham Huntingdon **Kempton** Plumpton **Redcar** Sedgefield **Warwick** **Yarmouth** *Cork* *Fairyhouse* **Saint-Cloud**	**29** Chepstow **Pontefract** **Warwick** *Fairyhouse*	**30** Exeter **Folkestone** Fontwell **Auteuil** \\ Doncaster Sales	**31** **Doncaster** **Lingfield**† Ludlow *Clonmel* **Longchamp**		

30

APRIL

Sun	Mon	Tues	Wed	Thur	Fri	Sat
					1 Doncaster **Lingfield**† Newbury ***Msisons-Laffitte***	**2** Bangor **Doncaster** Kempton Newbury **Wolverhampton**†☆ *Navan* ***Auteuil***
3 Kelso Market Rasen Wincanton *Curragh* *Tramore* ***Longchamp***	**4** **Southwell**† **Wolverhampton**† Yarmouth ***Saint-Cloud***	**5** Folkestone Sedgefield **Southwell**† ***Maisons-Laffitte***	**6** **Catterick** **Lingfield**† Nottingham *Gowran Park*	**7** Aintree Leicester Taunton *Tipperary* ***Longchamp***	**8** Aintree **Lingfield**† **Southwell**† ***Auteuil***	**9** Aintree **Lingfield**† Hereford Newcastle
10 Hexham Newton Abbot Worcester *Leopardstown* *Limerick* ***Longchamp***	**11** Kelso **Lingfield**† **Southwell** ***Saint-Cloud***	**12** Exeter **Musselburgh** **Newmarket** ***Auteuil*** Doncaster Sales	**13** **Beverley** Cheltenham **Newmarket** *Fairyhouse* ***Saint-Cloud*** Doncaster Sales	**14** Cheltenham **Newmarket** Ripon *Tipperary*	**15** Ayr **Newbury** Taunton☆ **Thirsk** **Wolverhampton**†☆ ***Longchamp***	**16** Ayr Bangor **Newbury** **Nottingham**☆ **Thirsk** **Wolverahmpton**†☆ *Navan*
			Tattersalls Sales Ascot Sales	Tattersalls Sales	Goffs France Sales	Goffs France Sales
17 Carlisle Stratford Wincanton *Curragh* *Listowel* ***Auteuil***	**18** Hexham Plumpton **Pontefract** **Windsor**☆ **Wolverhampton**†☆	**19** **Brighton**☆ Folkestone Newcastle **Southwell** Towcester☆ ***Saint-Cloud*** Ascot Sales	**20** **Catterick** Epsom **Lingfield**†☆ Perth Worcester☆ *Gowran Park*	**21** **Bath**☆ **Beverley** Fontwell Perth **Southwell**†☆ *Gowran Park* ***Longchamp***	**22** Chepstow☆ Newton Abbot☆ Perth **Sandown (Mixed)** **Wolverhampton**† ***Auteuil***	**23** **Haydock**☆ **Leicester** Market Rasen **Sandown (Mixed)** Ripon **Wolverhampton**†☆ *Naas*
24 **Brighton** Ludlow Wetherby *Cork* *Leopardstown* ***Longchamp***	**25** Hamilton **Southwell**†☆ Towcester **Windsor**☆ **Wolverhampton**†☆ *Sligo*☆ ***Chantilly***	**26** Bath Newton Abbot **Southwell**† **Warwick**☆ Yarmouth☆ *Punchestown*	**27** Cheltenham☆ Exeter Kelso☆ **Lingfield (from Ascot)** **Pontefract** *Punchestown* ***Auteuil***	**28** Hereford Kelso☆ **Lingfield**†☆ **Redcar** **Southwell**† *Punchestown* ***Longchamp***	**29** Bangor☆ Fontwell☆ **Musselburgh** Nottingham Southwell *Punchestown* ***Chantilly***	**30** **Goodwood** Hexham☆ **Newmarket** **Thirsk** Uttoxeter Worcester☆ *Punchestown* ***Longchamp***

The photo-finish every jockey dreads

Few people realise that a National Hunt Jockey can expect to fall once in every ten races, and sustain serious injury once in every 250. A bad fall could end his career, or worse still, leave him paralysed for life. Another well kept secret is their pay. Only very famous jockeys get rich. Most are lucky to make a living wage. So when they are injured and unable to cope with their insurance, many are badly in need of a helping hand.

This is where the Injured Jockeys Fund comes in. We help pay for the specialist medical care the jockeys need and where necessary we provide financial assistance for their families.

So if you enjoy racing, send a donation to The Injured Jockeys Fund and help put a jockey back in the saddle.

Please send donations to:
The Injured Jockeys Fund,
1 Victoria Way, Newmarket CB8 7SH

MAY

Sun	Mon	Tues	Wed	Thur	Fri	Sat
1 Hamilton Newmarket Salisbury *Gowran Park* *Navan* **Saint-Cloud**	**2** Doncaster Kempton Newcastle Sedgefield Warwick *Curragh* *Down Royal* *Limerick* **Chantilly**	**3** Bath Catterick☆ Exeter☆ Leicester Ludlow **Auteuil**	**4** Chepstow Chester Fakenham *Ballinrobe☆* **Maisons-Laffitte**	**5** Chepstow☆ Chester Folkestone Newton Abbot *Wetherby☆* *Tipperary☆*	**6** Chester Hamilton☆ Lingfield Nottingham Wincanton☆ *Cork☆*	**7** Beverley Haydock (Mixed) Hexham Lingfield (from Ascot) Newmarket Thirsk☆ Warwick☆ *Kilbeggan☆*
8 Plumpton Uttoxeter Worcester Windsor *Killarney* *Leopardstown* **Auteuil**	**9** Kempton Redcar Towcester☆ Windsor☆ Wolverhampton† *Killarney* **Longchamp**	**10** Hereford Huntingdon☆ **Musselburgh** Newton Abbot☆ Yarmouth *Killarney* **Maisons-Laffitte**	**11** Brighton Exeter Newcastle☆ Perth☆ York **Chantilly**	**12** Carlisle☆ Ludlow☆ Perth Salisbury York *Clonmel☆* **Longchamp**	**13** Aintree☆ Hamilton☆ Newbury Nottingham York *Downpatrick☆* *Wexford☆* **Auteuil**	**14** Bangor Newbury Nottingham Thirsk Uttoxeter☆ Worcester *Naas☆*
15 Fakenham Market Rasen Ripon *Gowran Park* *Navan* **Longchamp**	**16** Bath Musselburgh☆ Newton Abbot Windsor☆ Wolverhampton†☆ *Roscommon☆* **Saint-Cloud**	**17** Beverley Leicester☆ Lingfield☆ Redcar Towcester **Auteuil** Ascot Sales Goresbridge Sales	**18** Folkestone☆ **Goodwood** Kelso Sedgefield☆ **Southwell**† *Fairyhouse☆* **Chantilly**	**19** Doncaster☆ Goodwood Kelso Newcastle Wetherby *Tipperary☆* **Longchamp**	**20** Bath☆ Goodwood Haydock Newmarket Stratford☆ *Cork☆* *Downpatrick☆* **Auteuil**	**21** Catterick Haydock Kempton☆ Lingfield (from Ascot) Newmarket☆ Stratford☆ *Curragh* **Maisons-Laffitte**
22 Brighton Hereford Southwell *Curragh* **Longchamp**	**23** Beverley Carlisle Leicester Thirsk☆ Windsor☆ *Kilbeggan☆* **Chantilly** Doncaster Sales	**24** Lingfield Nottingham Ripon Sedgefield☆ Worcester☆ *Sligo☆* Doncaster Sales	**25** Cartmel Fontwell Lingfield Kempton☆ Ripon☆ *Leopardstown☆* **Saint-Cloud** Doncaster Sales	**26** Ayr Bath Huntingdon☆ Newton Abbot *Wetherby☆* *Clonmel☆* **Longchamp** Doncaster Sales	**27** Brighton Catterick Pontefract☆ Towcester☆ Wolverhampton† *Limerick☆* *Wexford☆* **Chantilly** Doncaster Sales	**28** Cartmel☆ Doncaster Goodwood Hexham Lingfield☆ **Musselburgh** *Punchestown☆*
29 Fontwell **Newmarket** Uttoxeter *Gowran Park* *Listowel* **Auteuil**	**30** Cartmel Chepstow Leicester Redcar Sandown *Ballinrobe☆* **Saint-Cloud**	**31** Carlisle Hexham☆ Leicester Sandown☆ Redcar *Ballinrobe☆* **Maisons-Laffitte** Goffs Sales				

JUNE

Sun	Mon	Tues	Wed	Thur	Fri	Sat
			1 Beverley☆ Newcastle Nottingham Southwell†☆ Yarmouth *Leopardstown* **Longchamp**	**2** Brighton Hamilton Haydock Sandown *Uttoxeter☆* **Saint-Cloud**	**3** Epsom Goodwood☆ Haydock☆ Thirsk Wolverhampton† *Tramore☆* **Auteuil**	**4** Chepstow☆ Doncaster Epsom Haydock Lingfield☆ Worcester *Kilbeggan☆* **Chantilly**
			Goffs Sales	Goffs Sales	Goffs Sales	
5 Bath Perth Stratford *Navan Tralee* **Chantilly**	**6** Folkestone Newton Abbot Pontefract☆ Windsor☆ *Naas Tralee* **Saint-Cloud**	**7** Chester☆ Huntingdon☆ Redcar Salisbury *Tralee* **Auteuil**	**8** Beverley Hamilton☆ Hereford Market Rasen Newbury☆ *Leopardstown☆*	**9** Brighton☆ Ripon Southwell† Uttoxeter☆ Yarmouth *Tipperary☆* **Longchamp**	**10** Catterick Chepstow☆ Goodwood☆ Sandown Wolverhampton†☆ *Navan☆ Wexford☆*	**11** Bath Hexham Leicester☆ Lingfield☆ Ripon Sandown *Cork*
		Ascot Sales				
12 Doncaster Salisbury Stratford *Cork Roscommon* **Chantilly**	**13** Brighton Thirsk Warwick☆ Windsor☆ *Roscommon☆* **Saint-Cloud**	**14** Royal Ascot (York) Carlisle *Hereford☆* Newton Abbot☆ **Auteuil**	**15** Royal Ascot (York) Chepstow☆ Hamilton Kempton☆ Worcester *Leopardstown☆*	**16** Royal Ascot (York) Aintree☆ Beverley☆ Newbury Southwell† *Clonmel☆* **Longchamp**	**17** Royal Ascot (York) Ayr Goodwood☆ Newmarket☆ Redcar *Down Royal☆ Limerick☆* **Maisons-Laffitte**	**18** Royal Ascot (York) Ayr Lingfield☆ Newmarket Redcar☆ Warwick *Down Royal* **Auteuil**
19 Hexham Pontefract Warwick *Down Royal Gowran Park*	**20** Musselburgh Nottingham Ripon☆ Windsor☆ *Kilbeggan☆* **Saint-Cloud**	**21** Beverley Brighton Newbury☆ *Newton Abbot☆ Ballinrobe☆* **Longchamp**	**22** Bath☆ Carlisle Kempton☆ Salisbury Worcester *Naas☆* **Maisons-Laffitte**	**23** Hamilton☆ Leicester☆ Newcastle Salisbury Thirsk *Tipperary☆* **Chantilly**	**24** Folkestone Market Rasen Newcastle☆ Newmarket☆ Wolverhampton†☆ *Curragh☆ Limerick☆* **Auteuil**	**25** Chester Doncaster☆ Lingfield☆ Newcastle Newmarket Windsor *Curragh*
	Tattersalls (IRE) Sales	Tattersalls (IRE) Sales	Tattersalls (IRE) Sales	Tattersalls (IRE) Sales	Tattersalls (IRE) Sales	Goffs Sales
26 Uttoxeter Windsor *Curragh* **Saint-Cloud**	**27** Musselburgh☆ Pontefract Windsor☆ Wolverhampton† **Longchamp**	**28** Brighton Hamilton *Sligo☆* **Auteuil**	**29** Catterick Chepstow☆ Kempton☆ Perth Worcester *Bellewstown☆*	**30** Epsom☆ Haydock Newbury☆ Perth Yarmouth *Bellewstown☆ Tipperary☆*		
				Goffs France Sales		

36

JULY

Sun	Mon	Tues	Wed	Thur	Fri	Sat
31 Chester Market Rasen **Newbury** *Cork* *Galway* ***Deauville***					**1** Beverley☆ Haydock☆ **Sandown** Southwell† **Warwick** *Bellewstown☆* *Limerick☆*	**2** **Beverley** Carlisle☆ Haydock **Leicester** Nottingham☆ **Sandown** *Leopardstown☆* *Limerick☆*
						Goffs France Sales
3 **Brighton** Market Rasen ***Chantilly***	**4** **Bath** **Musselburgh** Ripon☆ Windsor☆ *Roscommon☆*	**5** **Newmarket** Pontefract Uttoxeter☆ Wolverhampton†☆ *Roscommon☆* ***Deauville***	**6** Catterick Kempton☆ **Lingfield** **Newmarket** Worcester☆ *Naas☆*	**7** Doncaster☆ **Epsom**☆ **Folkestone** Newmarket **Warwick** *Gowran Park☆* ***Deauville***	**8** Chepstow☆ **Chester**☆ Lingfield (from Ascot) Wolverhampton† **York** *Cork☆* *Wexford☆*	**9** **Chester** Hamilton☆ Lingfield (from Ascot) Nottingham Salisbury☆ **York** *Fairyhouse☆* ***Deauville***
		Tattersalls Sales	**Tattersalls Sales**	**Tattersalls Sales**		
10 **Haydock** Perth Stratford *Sligo* *Tipperary* ***Maisons-Laffitte***	**11** **Ayr** Newton Abbot Wolverhampton†☆ *Killarney☆* ***Chantilly***	**12** **Beverley** **Brighton** *Killarney☆*	**13** Catterick Kempton☆ **Lingfield** Uttoxeter Worcester☆ *Killarney☆* *Leopardstown☆* ***Maisons-Laffitte***	**14** Cartmel Doncaster☆ **Epsom**☆ **Hamilton** **Leicester** *Killarney* ***Longchamp***	**15** **Carlisle** Hamilton☆ Newmarket☆ Pontefract☆ Southwell **Warwick** *Kilbeggan☆* ***Chantilly***	**16** Haydock☆ Lingfield☆ Market Rasen **Newbury** Newmarket Ripon☆ *Curragh* ***Maisons-Laffitte***
17 Newton Abbot **Redcar** Stratford *Curragh*	**18** Ayr☆ **Beverley**☆ **Brighton** Windsor☆ *Ballinrobe☆*	**19** **Ayr** **Yarmouth** *Ballinrobe*	**20** Catterick **Leicester**☆ **Lingfield** Sandown☆ Worcester *Naas☆*	**21** **Bath** Doncaster☆ **Folkestone**☆ **Sandown** Uttoxeter	**22** Chepstow☆ Newbury (from Ascot) Newmarket☆ Wolverhampton† **York** *Fairyhouse☆* *Limerick☆*	**23** Lingfield☆ Newbury (from Ascot) **Newcastle** Nottingham Salisbury☆ **York** *Leopardstown☆*
		Ascot Sales **Goresbridge Sales**				
24 Newbury (from Ascot) **Newmarket** Pontefract *Wexford* ***Maisons-Laffitte***	**25** Sedgefield Southwell† Windsor☆ **Yarmouth**☆ *Galway☆* ***Chantilly***	**26** **Beverley** **Goodwood** *Galway☆*	**27** **Goodwood** Kempton☆ **Leicester**☆ **Musselburgh** Newton Abbot *Galway*	**28** **Carlisle** **Epsom**☆ **Goodwood** Musselburgh☆ Stratford *Galway*	**29** Bangor **Goodwood** Newmarket☆ **Nottingham**☆ **Thirsk** *Galway☆*	**30** Doncaster☆ **Goodwood** Hamilton☆ Lingfield☆ **Newmarket** **Thirsk** *Galway* ***Deauville***

RANSFORDS EQUESTRIAN
RIDING SURFACES

ALL WEATHER GALLOPS & ARENAS, SURFACED AND TOPPED UP
Full construction undertaken if required

- Ransfords equestrian bark free woodfibre – a favourite in racing.
- Carefully selected wood – a firm yet yielding all-weather surface.
- Kind to the horses' legs.
- We use only <u>one</u> type of wood chosen for its ground contact durability. This is paramount to the lifespan of an all-weather gallop or arena.
- We guarantee that we will never supply you with recycled wood waste such as shredded aged pallet wood which has low quality ground contact durability.
- Hardwood and softwood waste comes from the demolition and construction industries so we also guarantee that our surface contains no chipboard, MDF or plywood which "returns to source" when wet (sawdust) which ruins drainage. These chipboards also contain formaldehyde which increases respiratory problems in horses.
- 100% free of any form of contaminates or shrapnel (wood waste is passed under a magnet to try and extract nails and other shrapnel which is not always successful).
- Non freezing.

Chosing Ransfords equestrian bark free woodfibre will give you complete peace of mind for the safety of your owners' horses and their peak fitness. Many of our customers have won the Hennessey, Cheltenham Gold Cup and Grand National, so join the winners.

The ultimate equestrian woodfibre – at a competitive price

01588 638331

email pnoble@ransfords.co.uk
web site: http://www.ransfords.co.uk/equine

AUGUST

Sun	Mon	Tues	Wed	Thur	Fri	Sat
	1 Carlisle☆ Newton Abbot **Ripon** **Windsor**☆ *Cork* *Naas*	**2** Brighton Catterick *Roscommon*☆ ***Deauville***	**3** Brighton Kempton☆ Newcastle Pontefract Yarmouth☆ *Sligo*☆	**4** Brighton☆ Chepstow Folkestone☆ Haydock Yarmouth *Sligo*☆ *Tipperary*☆ ***Deauville***	**5** Haydock☆ Lingfield Newmarket☆ Sedgefield Worcester *Wexford*☆	**6** Ayr☆ Haydock Lingfield☆ Newmarket Redcar Windsor (from Ascot) *Kilbeggan*☆ ***Deauville***
			Doncaster Sales	Doncaster Sales	Doncaster Sales	
7 Leicester Lingfield Redcar *Curragh* *Downpatrick* ***Deauville***	**8** Southwell Thirsk☆ Windsor☆ Wolverhampton† *Ballinrobe*	**9** Bath Newton Abbot ***Deauville***	**10** Beverley Hamilton☆ Salisbury Sandown☆ Yarmouth *Gowran Park*☆ ***Deauville***	**11** Beverley Chepstow Haydock☆ Salisbury Sandown *Tramore*☆	**12** Catterick☆ Folkestone Newbury Newcastle Newmarket☆ *Tramore*☆	**13** Bangor **Goodwood**☆ Market Rasen☆ Newbury Newmarket Ripon *Tramore*☆ ***Deauville***
	Tattersalls (IRE) Sales	Tattersalls (IRE) Sales Fasig-Tipton Sales	Tattersalls (IRE) Sales Fasig-Tipton Sales	Tattersalls (IRE) Sales Fasig-Tipton Sales	Tattersalls (IRE) Sales	
14 Bath Pontefract Stratford *Leopardstown* *Tramore* ***Deauville***	**15** Brighton Nottingham Windsor☆ Yarmouth☆ *Roscommon*☆ ***Deauville***	**16** Hamilton York	**17** Carlisle Kempton☆ Nottingham☆ Worcester York *Bellewstown*☆ *Sligo*☆ ***Deauville***	**18** Chepstow Chester Fontwell☆ Wolverhampton† York *Bellewstown*☆ *Tipperary*☆	**19** Ayr Chester Salisbury☆ Sandown Wolverhampton† *Kilbeggan*☆	**20** Beverley Chester Lingfield☆ Newton Abbot Sandown Redcar *Curragh* ***Deauville***
Fasig Tipton Sales	Fasig Tipton Sales					
21 Folkestone Newton Abbot Southwell *Cork* *Gowran Park* ***Deauville***	**22** Hamilton Leicester Windsor☆ Wolverhampton†☆ *Tralee*	**23** Brighton Perth☆ Worcester☆ Yarmouth *Tralee* ***Deauville***	**24** Brighton Catterick Perth *Tralee*	**25** Bangor Lingfield Musselburgh *Tralee*	**26** Bath☆ Newcastle☆ Newmarket Salisbury Thirsk ***Deauville***	**27** Cartmel **Goodwood** Market Rasen Newmarket Windsor☆ York *Wexford*
Deauville Sales	Deauville Sales	Deauville Sales	Deauville Sales			
28 Beverley **Goodwood** Yarmouth *Ballinrobe* *Fairyhouse* ***Deauville***	**29** Cartmel Chepstow Epsom Huntingdon Newcastle Ripon Warwick *Downpatrick*	**30** Leicester **Ripon** Sedgefield ***Chantilly***	**31** Lingfield Newton Abbot York *Clonmel*			
		Fasig-Tipton Sales	Ascot Sales			

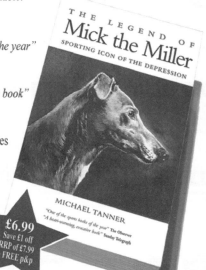

SEPTEMBER

Sun	Mon	Tues	Wed	Thur	Fri	Sat
				1 Carlisle Redcar Salisbury *Laytown* **Chantilly**	**2** Chepstow Haydock Kempton *Down Royal* **Auteuil**	**3** Folkestone Haydock Kempton Stratford **Thirsk** Wolverhampton†☆ *Down Royal*
					Baden-Baden Sales	Baden-Baden Sales
4 Fontwell Worcester **York** *Curragh* *Galway* **Longchamp**	**5** Bath Newcastle Warwick *Galway*	**6** Catterick Leicester Lingfield *Galway* **Auteuil**	**7** Doncaster Epsom Uttoxeter **Chantilly**	**8** Chepstow Doncaster Epsom **Longchamp**	**9** Bangor Doncaster Sandown *Kilbeggan* **Auteuil**	**10** Chester Doncaster Goodwood Musselburgh Wolverhampton†☆ *Leopardstown*
		Doncaster Sales	Doncaster Sales	Doncaster Sales	Doncaster Sales	
11 Carlisle Goodwood Stratford *Killarney* **Longchamp**	**12** Folkestone Musselburgh Redcar *Roscommon* **Chantilly**	**13** Salisbury Thirsk Yarmouth	**14** Beverley Sandown Yarmouth	**15** Ayr Pontefract Yarmouth *Tipperary* **Auteuil**	**16** Ayr Newbury Nottingham *Downpatrick* **Chantilly**	**17** Ayr Catterick Lingfield† Newbury Warwick Wolverhampton†☆ *Curragh* **Longchamp**
	Keeneland Sales	Keeneland Sales	Keeneland Sales	Keeneland Sales	Keeneland Sales	Keeneland Sales
18 Hamilton Plumpton Uttoxeter *Curragh* *Listowel*	**19** Chepstow Kempton Leicester *Listowel*	**20** Beverley Brighton Newmarket *Listowel* **Auteuil**	**21** Goodwood Redcar Perth *Listowel* **Maisons-Laffitte**	**22** Fontwell Perth Pontefract *Listowel*	**23** Haydock Lingfield (from Ascot) Worcester *Listowel* **Auteuil**	**24** Haydock Kempton Market Rasen Newmarket (from Ascot) Ripon *Fairyhouse* *Listowel* **Maisons-Laffitte**
Keeneland Sales	Keeneland Sales Tattersalls (IRE) Sales	Keeneland Sales Tattersalls (IRE) Sales	Keeneland Sales Tattersalls (IRE) Sales	Keeneland Sales Tattersalls (IRE) Sales	Keeneland Sales Tattersalls (IRE) Sales	Keeneland Sales
25 Huntingdon **Musselburgh** Newmarket (from Ascot)	**26** Bath Hamilton Wolverhampton† **Chantilly**	**27** Goodwood Nottingham Sedgefield **Saint-Cloud**	**28** Lingfield† Newcastle Salisbury *Downpatrick* **Auteuil**	**29** Ayr Hereford Newmarket *Thurles*	**30** Hexham Lingfield Newmarket **Maisons-Laffitte**	
	Goffs Sales	Goffs Sales	Goffs Sales	Goffs Sales	Goffs Sales	

OCTOBER

Sun	Mon	Tues	Wed	Thur	Fri	Sat
30 Ayr Carlisle **Lingfield†** *Galway* *Wexford* **Saint-Cloud**	**31** Plumpton Warwick **Wolverhampton†** *Galway* *Leopardstown* *Tattersalls (IRE) Sales*					**1** Epsom Fontwell **Newmarket** Redcar **Southwell†** **Wolverhampton☆** *Curragh* **Longchamp** *Goffs France Sales*
2 Kelso Market Rasen Uttoxeter *Tipperary* **Longchamp**	**3** **Brighton** **Pontefract** **Windsor** *Roscommon* *Tattersalls Sales*	**4** **Catterick** Huntingdon Leicester *Tattersalls Sales*	**5** Exeter **Nottingham** Towcester **Auteuil** *Tattersalls Sales*	**6** **Southwell†** Wincanton Worcester **Maisons-Laffitte** *Tattersalls Sales*	**7** Carlisle **Newbury** **York** *Gowran Park* **Chantilly** *Tattersalls Sales*	**8** Bangor Chepstow Hexham Salisbury (from Ascot) Warwick **York** *Gowran Park* **Saint-Cloud**
9 Bath Goodwood Newcastle *Curragh* *Limerick* **Auteuil**	**10** Ayr Windsor **Wolverhampton†☆** **Maisons-Laffitte**	**11** Ayr Leicester **Southwell†** *Ascot Sales* *Tattersalls Sales*	**12** **Lingfield†** Uttoxeter Wetherby *Navan* *Tattersalls Sales*	**13** Newmarket Ludlow **Southwell†** *Tramore* *Tattersalls Sales*	**14** Brighton Newmarket Redcar **Chantilly** *Tattersalls Sales*	**15** Catterick Kempton **Lingfield†** Newmarket Stratford *Cork* **Auteuil** *Tattersalls Sales*
16 Hereford Market Rasen **Musselburgh** *Cork* *Naas* **Longchamp**	**17** **Pontefract** Plumpton Windsor **Deauville** *Doncaster Sales* *Deauville Sales*	**18** Exeter **Southwell†** Yarmouth **Deauville** *Doncaster Sales* *Deauville Sales*	**19** Bath Newcastle Nottingham *Punchestown* **Deauville** *Doncaster Sales* *Deauville Sales*	**20** **Brighton** Haydock Ludlow *Punchestown* **Maisons-Laffitte** *Doncaster Sales* *Baden-Baden Sales*	**21** Doncaster Fakenham Newbury **Saint-Cloud** *Doncaster Sales* *Baden-Baden Sales*	**22** Aintree Chepstow **Doncaster** Kelso Newbury **Wolverhampton†** *Fairyhouse* **Auteuil**
23 Aintree Towcester Wincanton *Clonmel* *Curragh* **Longchamp**	**24** Leicester **Lingfield†** **Wolverhampton†** *Curragh* **Maisons-Laffitte** *Tattersalls Sales* *Goresbridge Sales* *Fasig-Tipton Sales*	**25** **Catterick** Cheltenham Yarmouth **Saint-Cloud** *Tattersalls Sales* *Goresbridge Sales* *Fasig-Tipton Sales*	**26** Cheltenham **Nottingham** Sedgefield *Navan* *Tattersalls Sales*	**27** **Lingfield†** Stratford Taunton **Auteuil** *Tattersalls Sales*	**28** Newmarket Uttoxeter Wetherby **Longchamp** *Goffs Sales*	**29** Ayr Lingfield **Newmarket** **Southwell†** Wetherby **Wolverhampton†☆** *Naas☆* *Wexford*

NOVEMBER

Sun	Mon	Tues	Wed	Thur	Fri	Sat
		1	**2**	**3**	**4**	**5**
		Catterick Exeter Worcester ***Maisons-Laffitte***	Kempton **Nottingham** *Punchestown* ***Saint-Cloud***	Haydock **Musselburgh** Towcester *Clonmel*	Fontwell Hexham **Yarmouth** *Down Royal* ***Saint-Cloud***	**Doncaster** Kelso Sandown Southwell† Wincanton Wolverhampton†☆ *Down Royal* ***Auteuil***
		Tattersalls (IRE) Sales	Tattersalls (IRE) Sales	Tattersalls (IRE) Sales	Tattersalls (IRE) Sales	Tattersalls (IRE) Sales
6	**7**	**8**	**9**	**10**	**11**	**12**
Ayr Hereford Market Rasen *Cork* *Leopardstown* ***Auteuil***	Carlisle Stratford **Wolverhampton†**	Huntingdon Sedgefield **Southwell†** ***Maisons-Laffitte***	Bangor Lingfield **Wolverhampton†** *Fairyhouse*	**Lingfield†** Ludlow Taunton *Thurles*	Cheltenham Newcastle **Wolverhampton†**	Cheltenham **Lingfield†** **Southwell†** Uttoxeter Wetherby **Wolverhampton†** *Naas* ***Saint-Cloud***
Tattersalls (IRE) Sales Keeneland Sales Fasig-Tipton Sales	Tattersalls (IRE) Sales Keeneland Sales	Tattersalls (IRE) Sales Keeneland Sales	Tattersalls (IRE) Sales Keeneland Sales Ascot Sales	Tattersalls (IRE) Sales Keeneland Sales	Tattersals (IRE) Sales Keeneland Sales	Tattersalls (IRE) Sales Keeneland Sales
13	**14**	**15**	**16**	**17**	**18**	**19**
Carlisle Cheltenham Fontwell *Limerick* *Navan* ***Auteuil***	Folkestone Leicester **Wolverhampton†**	Fakenham **Lingfield†** **Southwell†** ***Auteuil***	Hexham Kempton **Southwell†** *Downpatrick* ***Maisons-Laffitte***	Hereford Market Rasen Wincanton *Clonmel*	Exeter Kelso Windsor (from Ascot)	Haydock Huntingdon **Lingfield†** **Southwell†** Windsor **Wolverhampton†☆** *Punchestown*
Tattersalls (IRE) Sales Keeneland Sales	Doncaster Sales Keeneland Sales	Doncaster Sales Goffs Sales Keeneland Sales	Doncaster Sales Goffs Sales Keeneland Sales	Doncaster Sa;es Goffs Sales Keeneland Sales Goffs France Sales	Doncaster Sales Goffs Sales Keeneland Sales Goffs France Sales	Goffs Sales Keeneland Sales
20	**21**	**22**	**23**	**24**	**25**	**26**
Aintree Plumpton Towcester *Cork* *Punchestown* ***Auteuil***	**Lingfield†** Ludlow **Southwell†** ***Maisons-Laffitte***	Sedgefield **Southwell†** Warwick ***Saint-Cloud***	Chepstow Lingfield Wetherby ***Auteuil***	Carlisle Taunton Uttoxeter *Thurles*	Musselburgh Newbury **Wolverhampton†**	Newbury Newcastle **Lingfield†** Towcester **Wolverhampton†☆** *Gowran Park* ***Saint-Cloud***
Goffs Sales	Tattersalls Sales	Tattersalls Sales	Tattersalls Sales	Tattersalls Sales	Tattersalls Sales	Tattersalls Sales
27	**28**	**29**	**30**			
Doncster Leicester Newbury *Navan* ***Auteuil***	Folkestone **Southwell†** **Wolverhampton†**	Hereford **Lingfield†** **Southwell†** ***Maisons-Laffitte***	Catterick Plumpton **Wolverhampton†** ***Deauville***			
	Tattersalls Sales	Tattersalls Sales	Tattersalls Sales			

DECEMBER

Sun	Mon	Tues	Wed	Thur	Fri	Sat
				1 Leicester Market Rasen Wincanton *Thurles* ***Deauville*** Tattersalls Sales Goresbridge Sales	**2** Exeter Sandown **Wolverhampton†** Tattersalls Sales	**3** Chepstow Haydock Sandown Wetherby **Wolverhampton†☆** *Fairyhouse* Deauville Sales
4 Kelso **Southwell†** Warwick *Fairyhouse* **Autuil** Deauville Sales	**5** **Lingfield†** Newcastle **Wolverhampton†** Deauville Sales	**6** Fontwell Sedgefield **Southwell†** ***Maisons-Laffitte*** Goffs Sales	**7** Hexham Leicester **Lingfield†** Goffs Sales	**8** Huntingdon Ludlow Taunton *Clonmel* ***Deauville*** Goffs Sales	**9** Cheltenham Doncaster **Wolverhampton†** **Saint-Cloud** Doncaster Sales Goffs Sales	**10** Cheltenham Doncaster Lingfield **Southwell†** **Wolverhampton†☆** Goffs Sales
11 *Cork* *Punchestown*	**12** Plumpton **Southwell†** **Wolverhampton†** Tattersalls (IRE) Sales	**13** Folkestone **Southwell†** Warwick Ascot Sales Tattersalls (IRE) Sales	**14** Bangor **Lingfield** Newbury *Downpatrick* ***Deauville*** Tattersalls (IRE) Sales	**15** Catterick Exeter **Southwell†** *Gowran Park* Tattersalls (IRE) Sales	**16** Uttoxeter Windsor (from Ascot) **Wolverhampton†** Tattersalls (IRE) Sales	**17** Haydock **Lingfield†** Newcastle Windsor (from Ascot) *Fairyhouse*
18 Musselburgh **Southwell†** *Navan* *Thurles*	**19** Doncaster **Lingfield†** **Wolverhampton†**	**20** Fontwell **Lingfield†** **Southwell†**	**21** **Lingfield†** Ludlow **Wolverhampton†**	**22** Ayr Fakenham **Southwell†**	**23**	**24** ***Deauville***
25	**26** Huntingdon Kempton Market Rasen Sedgefield Towcester Wetherby Wincanton **Wolverhampton†** *Down Royal* *Leopardstown* *Limerick*	**27** Chepstow Kempton Leicester **Southwell†** Wetherby *Leopardstown* *Limerick*	**28** Catterick Newbury **Wolverhampton†** *Leopardstown* *Limerick* ***Deauville***	**29** **Lingfield†** Musselburgh Newbury *Leopardstown* *Limerick*	**30** Haydock **Lingfield†** Taunton ***Deauville***	**31** Lingfield (from Ascot) Uttoxeter Warwick **Wolverhampton†** *Punchestown* *Tramore*

INDEX TO TRAINERS
†denotes Permit to train under N.H. Rules only

Name	Team No.
BOUTFLOWER, MISS KIRSTIN	056
BOWEN, MR P.	057
BOWLBY, MRS A. J.	058
BOWRING, MR S. R.	059
BOYLE, MR J. R.	060
BRADBURNE, MRS S. C.	061
BRADLEY, MR J. M.	062
BRADSTOCK, MR M. F.	063
BRAVERY, MR G. C.	064
BRENNAN, MR OWEN	065
†BREWIS, MISS RHONA G.	066
BRIDGER, MR J. J.	067
†BRIDGES, MRS H. M.	068
BRIDGWATER, MR D. G.	069
BRIDGWATER, MR G. F.	070
BRISBOURNE, MR W. M.	071
BRITTAIN, MR C. E.	072
BRITTAIN, MR M. A.	073
†BROCKBANK, MR J. E.	074
†BROOKHOUSE, MR R. S.	075
BROOKSHAW, MR S. A.	076
BROTHERTON, MR R.	077
BROWN, MR G.	078
†BROWN, MR I. A.	079
†BROWN, MR I. R.	080
BROWNE, MISS G.	081
†BROYD, MISS A. E.	082
†BRYANT, MISS M. P.	083
BUCKLER, MR R. H.	084
BUCKLEY, MR M. A.	085
BURCHELL, MR W. D.	086
BURKE, MR K. R.	087
BURNS, MR JAMES G.	088
BURROUGH, MR S. C.	089
†BUTLER, MRS D. A.	090
BUTLER, MR P.	091

C

Name	Team No.
CALDWELL, MR T. H.	092
CALLAGHAN, MR N. A.	093
CAMACHO, MISS J. A.	094
CAMPION, MR A. M.	095
CANDLISH, MRS J.	096
CANDY, MR HENRY D. N. B.	097
CARROLL, MR A. W.	098
CARROLL, MR D.	099
†CARSON, MR R. M.	100
†CARTER, MR O. J.	101
CASE, MR B. I.	102
†CASTLE, MR J. M.	103
CECIL, MR H. R. A.	104
†CHADWICK, MR S. G.	105
CHAMBERLAIN, MR A. J.	106
CHAMINGS, MR P. R.	107
CHANCE, MR N. T.	108
CHANNON, MR M.	109
CHAPMAN, MR DAVID W.	110
CHAPMAN, MR M. C.	111
CHAPPLE-HYAM, MR P. W.	112
CHARLES-JONES, MR G. F. H.	113
CHARLTON, MR J. I. A.	114
CHARLTON, MR ROGER J.	115
CHUNG, MR G. C. H.	116
†CLARK, MR R. M.	117
†CLARK, MR S. B.	118
CLEMENT, MR NICOLAS	119
CLEMENT, MR T. T.	120
CLINTON, MR P. L.	121
CLUTTERBUCK, MR K. F.	122
COAKLEY, MR D. J.	123
COLE, MR P. F. I.	124
COLLET, MR R.	125
COLLINGRIDGE, MR H. J.	126
COLTHERD, MR W. S.	127
†CONNELL, LADY	128
COOMBE, MR M. J.	129
CORNWALL, MR J. R.	130
COTTRELL, MR L. G.	131
COWELL, MR R. M. H.	132
COX, MR C. G.	133
CRAGGS, MR R.	134
†CRESSWELL, MR J. K. S.	135

Name	Team No.
CROOK, MR A.	136
CUMANI, MR L. M.	137
CUNDELL, MR P. D.	138
CUNNINGHAM, MR M.	139
CUNNINGHAM, MR W. S.	140
CUNNINGHAM-BROWN, MR K.	141
CURLEY, MR B. J.	142
CURTIS, MR R.	143
CUTHBERT, MR T. A. K.	144

D

Name	Team No.
DACE, MR L. A.	145
DALTON, MRS H.	146
DALTON, MR P. T.	147
DALY, MR DECLAN	148
DALY, MR H. D. J.	149
DARTNALL, MR V. R. A.	150
DAVIS, MISS J. S.	151
DAVISON, MISS Z. C.	152
DE BEST-TURNER, MR W.	153
DE HAAN, MR B.	154
†DEAKIN, MR A. J.	155
†DENNIS, MR W. W.	156
DICKIN, MR R.	157
DICKINSON, MR MICHAEL W.	158
DICKMAN, MR A.	159
†DIXON, MR J. E.	160
DODS, MR M. J. K.	161
DOUMEN, MR FRANCOIS	162
DOW, MR S. L.	163
DOWN, MR C. J.	164
DOYLE, MS J. S.	165
DREW, MR C.	166
DREWE, MR C. J.	167
DUFFIELD, MRS A.	168
DUKE, MR B. W.	169
†DUNGER, MR N. A.	170
DUNLOP, MR E. A. L.	171
DUNLOP, MR J. L.	172
DUTFIELD, MRS P. N.	173
DWYER, MR C. A.	174

Name	Team No.
†DYSON, MISS C.	175

E

Name	Team No.
EARLE, MR S. A.	176
EASTERBY, MR M. W.	177
EASTERBY, MR T. D.	178
†ECKLEY, MR B. J.	179
EDDY, MR D.	180
†EDWARDS, MR G. F.	181
EGERTON, MR C. R.	182
†ELLIOTT, MR E. A.	183
ELLIOTT, MR R. P.	184
ELLISON, MR BRIAN	185
ELSWORTH, MR D. R. C.	186
EMBIRICOS, MS A. E.	187
EMMERSON, MR I.	188
†ENGLAND, MISS E. M. V.	189
ENNIS, MR A. M.	190
ENRIGHT, MR G. P.	191
EUSTACE, MR J. M. P.	192
EVANS, MS D. J.	193
†EVANS, MR H. J.	194
†EVANS, MRS M.	195
†EVANS, MR M. J. M.	196
EVANS, MR P. D.	197
†EWART, MR J. P. L.	198

F

Name	Team No.
FABRE, MR A.	199
FAHEY, MR R. A.	200
FAIRHURST, MR C. W.	201
FANSHAWE, MR J. R.	202
FEATHERSTONE, MS L. M.	203
FEEK, MR D. B.	204
FEILDEN, MISS J. D.	205
FFRENCH DAVIS, MR D. J. S.	206
†FIELDER, MR R.	207
FIERRO, MR G.	208
FISHER, MR R. F.	209
FITZGERALD, MR T. J.	210

Name	Team No.
†FLINT, MR J. L.	211
FLINT, MR R.	212
FLOOD, MR D. J.	213
FLOOD, MR F.	214
FORBES, MR A. L.	215
FORD, MRS P. M.	216
FORD, MR R.	217
†FORSTER, MR D. M.	218
FORSTER, MISS S. E.	219
FOSTER, MR B. R. J. P.	220
FOWLER, MR J. R. H.	221
FOX, MR J. C.	222
†FRANCIS, MR M. E. D.	223
FROST, MR J. D.	224

G

Name	Team No.
GALLAGHER, MR JOHN	225
GALPIN, MRS E. J.	226
GANDOLFO, MR D. R.	227
GARDNER, MRS S.	228
GEAKE, MR J. A.	229
†GEORGE, CAPT J. A.	230
GEORGE, MR T. R.	231
GIBSON, MR RICHARD	232
GIFFORD, MR N. J. G.	233
GILLIGAN, MR P. L.	234
GILMORE, MR S. J.	235
GINGELL, MR M. J.	236
GIVEN, MR JAMES	237
GLOVER, MR J. A.	238
GOLDIE, MR J. S.	239
†GOLDIE, MR R. H.	240
GOLDSWORTHY, MR K.	241
GOLLINGS, MR S.	242
GRAHAM, MRS H. O.	243
GRANT, MR C.	244
GRASSICK, MR L. P.	245
GRASSICK, MR M. J.	246
GRAY, MR C. J.	247
GREENWAY, MR V. G.	248
†GRIFFITHS, MR S. G.	249

Name	Team No.
GRIFFITHS, MR S. P.	250
GUEST, MR R.	251
GUEST, MR R. C.	252

H

Name	Team No.
HAGGAS, MR W. J.	253
HAIGH, MISS V.	254
HALDANE, MR J. S.	255
HALES, MR A. M.	256
HALL, MISS S. E.	257
HAM, MR G. A.	258
HAMBRO, MRS M. C.	259
HAMER, MRS D. A.	260
†HAMILTON, MRS A.	261
†HAMILTON, MRS A. C.	262
HAMILTON-FAIRLEY, MRS A. J.	263
HAMMOND, MR M. D.	264
HANNON, MR R.	265
HARKER, MR G. A.	266
†HARPER, MR R. C.	267
HARRINGTON, MRS JESSICA	268
HARRIS, MR J. A.	269
HARRIS, MR M. F.	270
HARRIS, MR RON	271
HASLAM, MR PATRICK	272
HAWKE, MR N. J.	273
HAYDEN, MR JOHN C	274
HAYDN JONES, MR D.	275
HAYNES, MR A. B.	276
HAYNES, MR H. E.	277
†HAYNES, MR J. C.	278
HEAD, MRS C.	279
HEDGER, MR P. R.	280
HEMSLEY, MR C. J.	281
HENDERSON, MR N. J.	282
HERRIES, LADY	283
HETHERTON, MR J.	284
HIATT, MR P. W.	285
†HILL, MISS E.	286
HILLS, MR B. W.	287
HILLS, MR J. W.	288

Name	Team No.	Name	Team No.
HOAD, MR M. R.	289	JONES, MR A. P.	325
HOBBS, MR P. J.	290	†JONES, MR G. ELWYN	326
HODGES, MR R. J.	291	†JONES, MR P. J.	327
†HOGAN, MR M. J.	292	JONES, MR T. M.	328
HOGAN, MR TOM	293	JORDAN, MR F. T. J.	329
†HOGARTH, MR H. P.	294	†JOSEPH, MR J.	330
†HOLDSWORTH, MR A. S. T.	295	JUCKES, MR A. G.	331
HOLLINGSWORTH, MR A. F.	296		
HOLLINSHEAD, MR R.	297		

K

Name	Team No.	Name	Team No.
HOLT, MR J. R.	298	KEANE, MR D. P.	332
HOURIGAN, MR M.	299	KEDDY, MR T.	333
HOWE, MR H. S.	300	KEIGHTLEY, MR S. L.	334
HOWLING, MR P.	301	KELLETT, MR C. N.	335
HUFFER, MR G. A.	302	KELLEWAY, MISS G. M.	336
HUGHES, MR D. T.	303	KELLY, MR G. P.	337
		†KELSALL, MR P.	338
		†KERR, MRS C. J.	339

I

Name	Team No.	Name	Team No.
INCISA, DON E.	304	KING, MRS A. L. M.	340
INGRAM, MR R.	305	KING, MR ALAN	341
IVORY, MR D. K.	306	KING, MR J. S.	342
		KING, MR N. B.	343
		†KIRBY, MR F.	344
		KIRK, MR S. A.	345

J

Name	Team No.	Name	Team No.
JAMES, MR L. R.	307	KITTOW, MR W. S.	346
JARVIS, MR A. P.	308	KNIGHT, MISS H. C.	347
JARVIS, MR M. A.	309	†KNIPE, MR R. F.	348
JARVIS, MR W.	310		
JAY, MR J.	311		

L

Name	Team No.	Name	Team No.
JEFFERSON, MR J. M.	312	LAFFON-PARIAS, MR C.	349
JENKINS, MR J. R. W.	313	LAMYMAN, MRS S.	350
JENKS, MR W. P.	314	LAVELLE, MISS E. C.	351
†JESSOP, MR A. E. M.	315	†LAY, MR B. L.	352
JEWELL, MRS L. C.	316	LE BROCQ, MRS J. L.	353
JOHNSON, MR B. R.	317	LEAHY, MR AUGUSTINE	354
JOHNSON HOUGHTON, MR R. F.	318	LEAVY, MR B. D.	355
JOHNSON, MR J. H.	319	LEE, MR R.	356
JOHNSON, MR P.	320	LELLOUCHE, MR ELIE	357
†JOHNSON, MR P. R.	321	†LEWIS, MISS H.	358
JOHNSON, MR ROBERT W.	322	LIDDERDALE, MR A. J. D.	359
JOHNSON, MRS S. M.	323	LIDDIARD, MRS STEF	360
JONES, MR A. E.	324		

The photo-finish every jockey dreads

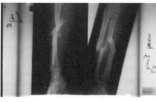

Few people realise that a National Hunt Jockey can expect to fall once in every ten races, and sustain serious injury once in every 250. A bad fall could end his career, or worse still, leave him paralysed for life. Another well kept secret is their pay. Only very famous jockeys get rich. Most are lucky to make a living wage. So when they are injured and unable to cope with their insurance, many are badly in need of a helping hand.

This is where the Injured Jockeys Fund comes in. We help pay for the specialist medical care the jockeys need and where necessary we provide financial assistance for their families.

So if you enjoy racing, send a donation to The Injured Jockeys Fund and help put a jockey back in the saddle.

Please send donations to:
The Injured Jockeys Fund,
1 Victoria Way, Newmarket CB8 7SH

Name	Team No.
LITTMODEN, MR N. P.	361
†LLEWELLYN, MR B.	362
LLEWELLYN, MR B. J.	363
†LLOYD, MR D. M.	364
†LLOYD, MR F.	365
LOCKWOOD, MR A. J.	366
LONG, MR J. E.	367
LUNGO, MR L.	368
LYONS, MR GER	369

M

Name	Team No.
MACAIRE, MR G.	370
MACAULEY, MRS N. J.	371
MACKIE, MR W. J. W.	372
MACTAGGART, MR A. B.	373
†MACTAGGART, MR A. H.	374
†MADDISON, MR P.	375
MADGWICK, MR M. J.	376
MAGNUSSON, MR M. A.	377
MAKIN, MR P. J.	378
MALZARD, MRS ALYSON	379
MANGAN, MR JAMES J.	380
MANN, MR C. J.	381
†MANN, MRS J. M. E.	382
MARGARSON, MR G. G.	383
MARVIN, MR R. F.	384
MCBRIDE, MR P. J.	385
MCCAIN, MR D.	386
†MCCORMACK, MR N. P.	387
MCGOVERN, MR T. P.	388
MCGREGOR, MRS J. C.	389
MCHALE, MISS D. A.	390
MCINNES, MR I. W.	391
MCKEOWN, MR W. J.	392
MCMAHON, MR E. S. A.	393
†MCMATH, MR I.	394
†MCMILLAN, MR M. D.	395
MEEHAN, MR B. J.	396
†MEEK, MARY	397
MIDGLEY, MR P. T.	398
MILLIGAN, MISS M. K.	399

Name	Team No.
MILLMAN, MR B. R.	400
MILLS, MR T. G.	401
†MITCHELL, MR C. W.	402
MITCHELL, MR N. R.	403
MITCHELL, MR PHILIP	404
MOFFATT, MR D. J.	405
MONTEITH, MR P.	406
MOORE, MR A. L.	407
MOORE, MR G. L.	408
MOORE, MR G. M.	409
MOORE, MR J. S.	410
MORGAN, MR K. A.	411
MORLOCK, MR C. P. H.	412
MORRIS, MR M.	413
MORRISON, MR H.	414
MOUNTAIN, MISS D.	415
MUGGERIDGE, MR M. P.	416
MUIR, MR WILLIAM R.	417
MULLINEAUX, MR M.	418
MULLINS, MR J. W.	419
MULLINS, MR WILLIAM P.	420
MURPHY, MR F.	421
MURPHY, MR P. G.	422
MURTAGH, MR F. P.	423
MUSSON, MR W. J.	424

N

Name	Team No.
NAYLOR, DR J. R. J.	425
†NEEDHAM, MR J. L.	426
†NEEDHAM, MR P.	427
†NELMES, MRS H. R. J.	428
NEWCOMBE, MR A. G.	429
NEWTON-SMITH, MISS A. M.	430
NICHOLLS, MR D.	431
NICHOLLS, MR P. F.	432
NIVEN, MR P. D.	433
†NIXON, MR G. R. S.	434
†NOCK, MRS S.	435
NOLAN, MR D. A.	436
NORMILE, MRS L. B.	437
NORTON, MR J. R.	438

Name	Team No.
NOSEDA, MR J. J.	439

O
Name	Team No.
O'GORMAN, MR W. A.	440
O'GRADY, MR E. J.	441
O'KEEFFE, MR J.	442
†O'NEILL, MR J. G.	443
O'NEILL, MR J. J.	444
O'NEILL, MR O.	445
O'SHEA, MR J. G. M.	446
O'SULLIVAN, MR EUGENE M.	447
OERTEL, MR E. R.	448
OLD, MR J. A. B.	449
OLIVER, MRS J. K. M.	450
OSBORNE, MR J. A.	451
†OWEN, MR H. G.	452

P
Name	Team No.
PALLING, MR BRYN	453
†PANVERT, MR J. F.	454
PARKER, MR ANDREW	455
PARKES, MR J. E.	456
†PAYNE, MR J. R.	457
PAYNE, MR J. W.	458
PEACOCK, MR R. E.	459
PEARCE, MR B. A.	460
PEARCE, MR J.	461
†PEARCE, MR K. E.	462
PEASE, MR J. E.	463
PERRATT, MISS L. A.	464
PERRETT, MRS A. J.	465
†PEWTER, MR G. R.	466
PHILLIPS, MR R. T.	467
†PIKE, MR S. L.	468
PINDER, MR ANTHONY D. W.	469
PIPE, C.B.E., MR M. C.	470
PITMAN, MR M. A.	471
†POGSON, MR C. T.	472
POLGLASE, MR M. J.	473
POLLOCK, MR B. N.	474

Name	Team No.
POMFRET, MR N. J.	475
POPHAM, MR C. L.	476
PORTMAN, MR J. G. B.	477
POULTON, MR J. C.	478
POULTON, MR J. R.	479
POWELL, MR B. G.	480
PRESCOTT BT, SIR MARK	481
†PRICE, MRS A.	482
PRICE, MR A. E.	483
PRICE, MR C. J.	484
†PRICE, MR J. K.	485
PRICE, MR RICHARD J.	486
PRITCHARD, DR P. L. J.	487
PRODROMOU, MR G.	488
†PUDD, MRS H.	489
PURDY, MR P. D.	490

Q
Name	Team No.
QUINLAN, MR M.	491
QUINN, MR J. J.	492

R
Name	Team No.
RAMSDEN, MRS J. R.	493
REED, MR W. T.	494
REES, MR D.	495
†REES, MRS H. E.	496
REID, MR A. S.	497
†RETTER, MRS J. G.	498
REVELEY, MR K. G.	499
RICH, MR P. M.	500
RICHARDS, MRS LYDIA	501
RICHARDS, MR N. G.	502
†RICHARDSON, MRS S. L.	503
RIMELL, MR M. G.	504
RITCHENS, MR P. C.	505
ROBERTS, MISS V. C.	506
ROBESON, MRS P.	507
†ROBSON, MR A.	508
ROBSON, MISS P.	509
ROHAUT, MR FRANCOIS	510

Name	Team No.	Name	Team No.
ROPER, MR W. M.	511	†SMITH, MS SUE	550
ROSSITER, MR N. I. M.	512	SMITH, MR V.	551
ROTHWELL, MR B. S.	513	SMYLY, MR G. R. I.	552
ROUGET, MR J-C	514	SOUTHCOMBE, MISS J. A.	553
ROWE, MR R.	515	SOWERSBY, MR M. E.	554
ROWLAND, MISS M. E.	516	SPEARING, MR J. L.	555
ROYER-DUPRE, MR A. DE	517	†SPOTTISWOOD, MR P.	556
RUSSELL, MRS L. V.	518	STACK, MR T.	557
RYALL, MR B. J. M.	519	†STIMPSON, MR J. T.	558
RYAN, MR K. A.	520	†STIRK, MRS M. K.	559
		†STODDART, MR D. R.	560
		STOREY, MR W.	561

S

Name	Team No.	Name	Team No.
SALAMAN, MR M. A.	521	STOUTE, SIR M.	562
SANDERS, MISS B.	522	STRONGE, MR R. M.	563
SAUNDERS, MRS J. A.	523	STUBBS, MRS L.	564
SAUNDERS, MR M. S.	524	SUPPLE, MR J. A.	565
SAYER, MRS H. D.	525	SWAN, MR CHARLIE	566
SCARGILL, DR J. D.	526	SWEETING, MRS H.	567
†SCOTT, MR D. D.	527	SWINBANK, MR G. A.	568
SCOTT, MISS V.	528	SWINBURN, MR W. R. J.	569
†SCRASE, MRS J. E.	529		
†SCRIVEN, MR B.	530		

T

Name	Team No.	Name	Team No.
SCUDAMORE, MR M. J.	531	TATE, MR T. P.	570
SEMPLE, MR I.	532	TAYLOR, MRS L. C.	571
SENIOR, MR A.	533	TEAGUE, MR COLIN	572
SHARPE, MRS N. S.	534	†TETLEY, MRS P. A.	573
SHAW, MR D.	535	†THOMAS, MRS D.	574
SHEPPARD, MR M. I.	536	†THOMAS, MR K. S.	575
SHERWOOD, MR O. M. C.	537	THOMPSON, MR D. W.	576
SHERWOOD, MR S. E. H.	538	THOMPSON, MR RONALD	577
SHIRLEY-BEAVAN, MR S. H.	539	THOMPSON, MR V.	578
SIDDALL, MISS L. C.	540	†THOMSON, MRS B. K.	579
SIMCOCK, MR D. M. I.	541	†THOMSON, MR R. W.	580
SLY, MRS P. M.	542	THORNTON, MR C. W.	581
SMAGA, MR D.	543	THORPE, MRS A. M.	582
SMART, MR B.	544	TINKLER, MR C.	583
SMITH, MR A. D.	545	TINNING, MR W. H.	584
SMITH, MR G. J.	546	TIZZARD, MR C.	585
SMITH, MR JULIAN SIMON	547	TODHUNTER, MR D. M.	586
SMITH, MRS NADINE	548	TOLLER, MR J. A. R.	587
SMITH, MISS S.	549	TOMPKINS, MR M. H.	588 TPDEL 12

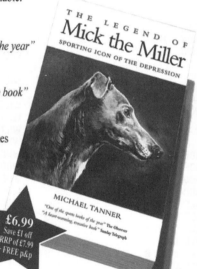

Name	Team No.
TOWNSLEY, MRS P	589
TREGONING, MR M. P.	590
TUCK, MR J. C.	591
†TUCKER, MR F. G.	592
TUER, MR E. W.	593
TURNELL, MR ANDREW	594
†TURNER, MR D. C.	595
†TURNER, MR D. T.	596
TURNER, MR J. R.	597
†TUTTY, MRS K. J.	598
TWISTON-DAVIES, MR N. A.	599

U

Name	Team No.
UNETT, MR J. W.	600
UPSON, MR J. R.	601
USHER, MR M. D. I.	602

V

Name	Team No.
VAUGHAN, MR E. F.	603
VON DER RECKE, MR C.	604

W

Name	Team No.
†WADE, MR J.	605
WADHAM, MRS L. A. M.	606
†WAGGOTT, MR N.	607
WAINWRIGHT, MR J. S.	608
†WALEY-COHEN, MR R. B.	609
WALFORD, MR T. D.	610
WALL, MR C. F.	611
†WALL, MRS S.	612
WALL, MR T. R.	613
WALLACE, MR MARK	614
WALTON, MRS K.	615
WARING, MRS BARBARA	616
†WARING, MR L.	617
†WATSON, LADY S.	618
†WATT, MRS S. A.	619

Name	Team No.
WEBBER, MR P. R.	620
WEEDEN, MR M. J.	621
WEGMANN, MR P.	622
WELLINGS, MR MARK	623
WELLS, MR L.	624
WEYMES, MR J. R.	625
WHEELER, MR E. A.	626
WHILLANS, MR A. C.	627
WHITAKER, MR R. M.	628
†WHITEHEAD, MR A. J.	629
WILESMITH, MR M. S.	630
WILLIAMS, MR D. L.	631
WILLIAMS, MR EVAN	632
WILLIAMS, MR IAN	633
WILLIAMS, MR N. S. L.	634
WILLIAMS, MR S. C.	635
WILLIAMS, MRS S. D.	636
WILLIAMS, MISS V. M.	637
WILLIAMSON, MRS L. V.	638
WILSON, MR A. J.	639
WILSON, MR C. R.	640
WILSON, MR N.	641
WILTON, MISS S. J.	642
WINKWORTH, MR P. L.	643
WINTLE, MR D. J.	644
WOOD, MR I. A.	645
WOODHOUSE, MR R. D. E.	646
†WOODROW, MRS A. M.	647
WOODWARD, MR G.	648
†WORMALL, MISS J.	649
WRAGG, MR GEOFFREY	650

Y

Name	Team No.
YORK, MR R. H.	651
†YOUNG, MR W. G.	652

PROPERTY OF HER MAJESTY

The Queen

Colours: Purple, gold braid, scarlet sleeves, black cap with gold fringe

Trained by **Sir M. Stoute,** Newmarket

    1 BORDER CASTLE, 4yo b c Grand Lodge (USA)-Tempting Prospect
    2 DESERT STAR, 5yo b g Green Desert (USA)-Phantom Gold
    3 PROMOTION, 5yo b g Sadler's Wells (USA)-Tempting Prospect

THREE-YEAR-OLDS

    4 AVIEMORE, b c Selkirk (USA)-Film Script
    5 FLAG LIEUTENANT, b c Machiavellian (USA)-Fairy Godmother

TWO-YEAR-OLDS

    6 DEAN'S YARD, b c 27/3 Machiavellian (USA)-Abbey Strand (USA) (Shadeed (USA))
    7 FLEETING MEMORY, b f 31/1 Danehill (USA)-Flight of Fancy (Sadler's Wells (USA))
    8 GLAMIS CASTLE (USA), b c 2/3 Selkirk (USA)-Fairy Godmother (Fairy King (USA))
    9 UPPERMOST, b f 24/2 Montjeu (IRE)-Zenith (Shirley Heights)
    10 WELL HIDDEN, b f 13/2 Sadler's Wells (USA)-Phantom Gold (Machiavellian (USA))

Trained by **Roger J. Charlton,** Beckhampton

THREE-YEAR-OLDS

    11 FREE LIFT, ch f Cadeaux Genereux-Step Aloft
    12 LIFE'S A WHIRL, b f Machiavellian (USA)-Spinning Top
    13 NAVY LARK, ch g Nashwan (USA)-Holly Blue
    14 OBVIOUS CHARM, b f Machiavellian (USA)-Clear Attraction (USA)
    15 VIRTUE, ch f Vettori (IRE)-Zenith

TWO-YEAR-OLDS

    16 FONDNESS, ch f 10/4 Dr Fong (USA)-Island Story (Shirley Heights)
    17 GELDER, b f 8/3 Grand Lodge (USA)-Purple Heather (USA) (Rahy (USA))
    18 RAINBOW'S EDGE, b f 22/3 Rainbow Quest (USA)-Film Script (Unfuwain (USA))
    19 REGENT'S PARK, b f 20/2 Green Desert (USA)-New Assembly (IRE) (Machiavellian (USA))
    20 STARLIT SKY, ch f 6/4 Galileo (IRE)-Starlet (Teenoso (USA))

Trained by **R. Hannon,** Marlborough

    21 TURNSTILE, 4yo gr c Linamix (FR)-Kissing Gate (USA)

THREE-YEAR-OLDS

    22 FORWARD MOVE (IRE), ch c Dr Fong (USA)-Kissing Gate (USA)
    23 MARCHING SONG, b c Royal Applause-Marl
    24 MONEY MARKET (IRE), b g Machiavellian (USA)-Trying for Gold (USA)
    25 TAKE IT THERE, ch f Cadeaux Genereux-Feel Free (IRE)
    26 THE COIRES (IRE), b c Green Desert (USA)-Purple Heather (USA)

PROPERTY OF HER MAJESTY

The Queen

R. Hannon-continued

TWO-YEAR-OLDS

27 **BLUE JEANS**, b g Zilzal (USA)—Royal Applause-Holly Blue (Bluebird (USA))
28 **DESERT FLAIR**, b f 24/1 Desert Style (IRE)-Celtic Cross (Selkirk (USA))
29 **FLOWER MARKET**, ch f 10/2 Cadeaux Genereux-Marl (Lycius (USA))
30 **GOOD TURN**, b f 5/3 Royal Applause-Gracious Gift (Cadeaux Genereux)
31 **PURE FICTION**, b f 3/4 Zilzal (USA)-Once Upon A Time (Teenoso (USA))
32 **SHINE BRIGHT**, ch f 11/3 Fantastic Light (USA)-Beyond Doubt (Belmez (USA))

Trained by **N. J. Henderson**, Lambourn

33 **BRIGHT SPIRIT**, 4yo b g Petoski-Lunabelle
34 **FAIRY SILVER**, 4yo gr f Silver Patriarch (IRE)-Bewitch
35 **FIRST LOVE**, 9yo br g Bustino-First Romance
36 **SEA CAPTAIN**, 5yo b g Oscar (IRE)-Calabria
37 **SHINING STRAND**, 6yo ch g Karinga Bay-First Romance

Trained by **A. M. Balding**, Kingsclere

THREE-YEAR-OLD

38 **BANKNOTE**, b c Zafonic (USA)-Brand

---

1 | **MR JONATHAN AKEHURST, Epsom**
Postal: **South Hatch Stables, 44 Burgh Heath Road, Epsom, Surrey, KT17 4LX.**
Contacts: **PHONE (01372) 745880 FAX (01372) 744231**

1 **AUDIENCE**, 5, b g Zilzal (USA)—Only Yours **Canisbay Bloodstock**
2 **CAPRICHO (IRE)**, 8, gr g Lake Coniston (IRE)—Star Spectacle **Canisbay Bloodstock**
3 **CAPTAIN MARRYAT**, 4, ch g Inchinor—Finlaggan **Canisbay Bloodstock**
4 **COMPETITOR**, 4, b c Danzero (AUS)—Ceanothus (IRE) **Who Cares Who Wins**
5 **DEEPER IN DEBT**, 7, ch g Piccolo—Harold's Girl (FR) **Tipp-Ex Rapid Racing II**
6 **DR COOL**, 8, b g Ezzoud (IRE)—Vayavaig **Canisbay Bloodstock**
7 **DR SYNN**, 4, br c Danzero (AUS)—Our Shirley **Canisbay Bloodstock**
8 **DUELLING BANJOS**, 6, ch g Most Welcome—Khadino **Tattenham Corner Racing 2**
9 **ESPERANCE (IRE)**, 5, ch g Bluebird (USA)—Dioscorea (IRE) **The Grass is Greener Partnership IV**
10 **FATHER ABRAHAM (IRE)**, 7, b g Idris (IRE)—Mothers Blessing **A. D. Spence**
11 **FREE WHEELIN (IRE)**, 5, b g Polar Falcon (USA)—Farhana **Canisbay Bloodstock**
12 **GLENCALVIE (IRE)**, 4, ch g Grand Lodge (USA)—Top of The Form (IRE) **Tattenham Corner Racing**
13 **GRIZEDALE (IRE)**, 6, ch g Lake Coniston (IRE)—Zabeta **Canisbay Bloodstock**
14 **HOLLYWOOD HENRY (IRE)**, 5, b g Bahhare (USA)—Takeshi (IRE) **Lonwin Partnership**
15 **LIGHT SCENT (USA)**, 6, b g Silver Hawk (USA)—Music Lane (USA) **A. D. Spence**
16 **MAC LOVE**, 4, b g Cape Cross (IRE)—My Lass **V. Khosla**
17 **MARNIE**, 8, ch m First Trump—Miss Aboyne **The Grass is Greener Partnership**
18 **MARSAD (IRE)**, 11, ch g Fayruz—Broad Haven (IRE) **Canisbay Bloodstock**
19 **ROBIN SHARP**, 7, ch h First Trump—Mo Stopher **Canisbay Bloodstock**
20 **ROWAN PURSUIT**, 4, b f Pursuit of Love—Golden Seattle (IRE) **C. C. Clarke**
21 **RYAN'S FUTURE (IRE)**, 5, b h Danetime (IRE)—Era **V. Khosla**
22 **SPIRIT'S AWAKENING**, 6, b g Danzig Connection (USA)—Mo Stopher **Canisbay Bloodstock**

MR JONATHAN AKEHURST—continued

23 STOLEN HOURS (USA), 5, b br h Silver Deputy (CAN)—Fasta (USA) **A. D. Spence**
24 TUNING FORK, 5, b g Alzao (USA)—Tuning **Canisbay Bloodstock**
25 UNLEADED, 5, ch m Danzig Connection (USA)—Mo Stopher **Canisbay Bloodstock**

THREE-YEAR-OLDS

26 GARPLE BURN, b c Zaha (CAN)—Skedaddle **V. Khosla**
27 MASTER COBBLER (IRE), b c Alhaarth (IRE)—Lady Joshua (IRE) **A. D. Spence**
28 MONTAGE (IRE), b g Montjeu (IRE)—Ocean View (USA) **A. D. Spence**
29 POLLY PERKINS (IRE), b f Pivotal—Prospering **V. Khosla**
30 TOURNEDOS (IRE), b c Rossini (USA)—Don't Care (IRE) **V. Khosla**

TWO-YEAR-OLDS

31 B c 26/4 College Chapel—Anastasia Venture (Lion Cavern (USA)) **Canisbay Bloodstock**
32 BIJLI (IRE), gr c 9/3 Key of Luck (USA)—More Magnanimous (King Persian) (30000) **V. Khosla**
33 Ch f 5/3 Komaite (USA)—Ramajana (USA) (Shadeed (USA)) (800) **A. Pitt**
34 SCOT LOVE (IRE), b c 3/2 Dansili—Fashion (Bin Ajwaad (IRE)) (85000) **V. Khosla**
35 SPICE RUN, b c 3/4 Zafonic (USA)—Palatial (Green Desert (USA)) (22000) **V. Khosla**
36 UANDI, b f 24/3 Singspiel (IRE)—Krajina (FR) (Hoist (USA)) (10000) **Streamhill Ltd**
37 B f 9/2 Dansili—Vettorina (IRE) (Vettori (IRE)) (28168) **Mr R. P. Tullett**
38 Ch c 21/4 Zaha (CAN)—Vrennan (Suave Dancer (USA)) **Canisbay Bloodstock**

Other Owners: N. Boyce, P. A. Allard, J. D. A. Gordon, G. B. Griffin, G. P. Harper, Mr R. G. Harrington, C. D. Jarvis, R. F. Kilby, Mr P. Rose, Miss M. E. Stopher.

Jockey (flat): C. Catlin, T. Quinn, S. Sanders. **Jockey (NH):** T. J. Murphy, S. Durack. **Amateur:** Mr S. Gascoyne.

---

2   **MR HAMISH H. ALEXANDER, York**
Postal: **Low House, Hanging Grimston, Kirby Underdale, York, Yorkshire, YO41 1QZ.**
Contacts: **PHONE (01759) 368484 MOBILE (07774) 214072**

1 COMFORTABLE CALL, 7, ch g Nashwan (USA)—High Standard **P. J. Dixon**
2 CRACKINGTON (FR), 5, gr g Linamix (FR)—Ta Awun (USA) **J. S. Dale**
3 DARK CUT (IRE), 5, b g Ali-Royal (IRE)—Prima Nox **Mrs B. Alexander**
4 MEDIC (IRE), 4, b c Dr Fong (USA)—Elupa (IRE) **Ms I. Bristow**
5 RED BLUFF (IRE), 5, b h Waky Nao—Reine Rouge (GER) **Mrs L. Lever**
6 ROYAL EXPOSURE (IRE), 8, b g Emperor Jones (USA)—Blue Garter **Mr N. Jarratt**
7 SHAMELESS, 8, ch g Prince Daniel (USA)—Level Edge **N. Baillie**
8 SIXTILSIX (IRE), 4, ch g Night Shift (USA)—Assafiyah (IRE) **Ms I. Bristow**
9 STAR OVATION (IRE), 8, ch g Fourstars Allstar (USA)—Standing Ovation **Double Jay Syndicate**

THREE-YEAR-OLDS

10 LOBENGULA (IRE), b g Spectrum (IRE)—Playwaki (USA) **Ms I. Bristow**
11 MAYNOOTH PRINCE (IRE), b g Spectrum (IRE)—Muffle **Ms I. Bristow**
12 TRIM IMAGE, br f Averti (IRE)—Altizaf **Ms I. Bristow**

Other Owners: J. Farrar, P. G. Haran, A. Kelly.

Assistant Trainer: Neil Baillie

Jockey (NH): R. McGrath. **Conditional:** J. P. Byrne. **Amateur:** Mr A. Alexander.

---

3   **MR N. W. ALEXANDER, Leslie**
Postal: **Kinneston, Leslie, Glenrothes, Fife, KY6 3JJ.**
Contacts: **PHONE (01592) 840774**
E-MAIL kinneston@aol.com

1 FEARLESS FOURSOME, 6, b g Perpendicular—Harrietfield **Alexander Family**
2 FOUNTAIN BRIG, 9, b br g Royal Fountain—Lillies Brig **Mr N. W. Alexander**
3 5, Ch h Primitive Rising (USA)—Harrietfield **Alexander Family**
4 JINFUL DU GRAND VAL (FR), 8, b g Useful (FR)—Marine (FR) **Mr Jamie Alexander**
5 LUCKY BRUSH (IRE), 11, b g Brush Aside (USA)—Luck Daughter **Mr Jamie Alexander**
6 MOON MIST, 7, gr m Accondy (IRE)—Lillies Brig **Alexander Family**

MR N. W. ALEXANDER—continued

7 **OLYMPIC STORM (IRE)**, 7, b g Glacial Storm (USA)—Philly Athletic **Mr Jamie Alexander**
8 5, B g Mister Lord (USA)—Rose Miller **Mrs S. R. Alexander**
9 **SEA OTTER (IRE)**, 8, b g King's Ride—Knockarctic **Mrs S. R. Alexander**
10 **VENTURE TO FLY (IRE)**, 11, ch g Roselier (FR)—Fly Run **Mr Jamie Alexander**
11 **WISE MAN (IRE)**, 10, ch g Mister Lord (USA)—Ballinlonig Star **Mr N. W. Alexander**

Other Owners: M. C. Alexander.

Assistant Trainer: Francesca Macmanaway

Amateur: Mr Jamie Alexander.

4

MR C. N. ALLEN, Newmarket
Postal: **Byerley House, Warrington Street, Newmarket, Suffolk, CB8 8BA.**
Contacts: **HOME (01638) 667870 FAX (01638) 561603 MOBILE (07802) 692621**
E-MAIL conrad@sportsdays.co.uk WEBSITE www.sportsdays.co.uk

1 **FRENCH GIGOLO**, 5, ch g Pursuit of Love—French Mist **N. L. Davies**
2 **MISTER QUICKSAND (USA)**, 6, ch h Sandpit (BRZ)—Get Friendly Quick (USA) **Mr P. Harper**
3 **PRINCE AARON (IRE)**, 5, b g Marju (IRE)—Spirito Libro (USA) **Black Star Racing**
4 **SUMMERISE**, 4, b f Atraf—Summerhill Special (IRE) **Mrs H. Charlet**
5 **WEECANDOO (IRE)**, 7, b m Turtle Island (IRE)—Romantic Air **Sportsdays Ltd**

TWO-YEAR-OLDS

6 **TITIAN SAGA (IRE)**, ch f 25/4 Titus Livius (FR)—
Nordic Living (IRE) (Nordico (USA)) (14754) **Arabian Shield 2004**

Other Owners: J. Kerly, MR C. N. Allen, J. R. Bamforth, J. Gunnell.

Assistant Trainer: Miss Bobbie Allen

5

MR R. H. ALNER, Blandford
Postal: **Locketts Farm, Droop, Blandford, Dorset, DT11 0EZ.**
Contacts: **PHONE (01258) 817271 MOBILE (07767) 436375**
E-MAIL robertalner@btopenworld.com

1 **AVAS DELIGHT (IRE)**, 7, b g Ajraas (USA)—Whothatis **P. M. De Wilde**
2 **BACK NINE (IRE)**, 8, b g Bob Back (USA)—Sylvia Fox **Old Moss Farm**
3 **BARNARDS GREEN (IRE)**, 7, ch g Florida Son—Pearly Castle (IRE) **T. H. Chadney**
4 **BOWLEAZE (IRE)**, 6, br g Right Win (IRE)—Mrs Cullen **M. Short**
5 **BRIGADIER BENSON (IRE)**, 5, b g Fourstars Allstar (USA)—Decent Enough **A. Hordle**
6 **CANSALRUN (IRE)**, 6, b m Anshan—Monamandy (IRE) **Mrs J. S. Stoner**
7 **COMMANCHE JIM (IRE)**, 9, b g Commanche Run—On A Dream **Mrs S. Lewis-Harris**
8 **CRACKING DAWN (IRE)**, 10, b g Be My Native (USA)—Rare Coin **P. A. Bonner**
9 **DELAWARE BAY**, 6, ch g Karinga Bay—Galacia (IRE) **A. P. Hedditch**
10 **DILETIA**, 8, b m Dilum (USA)—Miss Laetitia (IRE) **T. H. Chadney**
11 **DISTANT THUNDER (IRE)**, 7, b g Phardante (FR)—Park Breeze (IRE) **Old Moss Farm**
12 **DUNCLIFFE**, 8, b g Executive Perk—Ida Melba **Lady Cobham**
13 **EL HOMBRE DEL RIO (IRE)**, 8, ch g Over The River (FR)—Hug In A Fog (IRE) **Perpetual Publications Limited**
14 **EVEN MORE (IRE)**, 10, b g Husyan (USA)—Milan Moss **G. F. Keirle**
15 **FOX IN THE BOX**, 8, b gr g Supreme Leader—Charlotte Gray **P. A. Bonner**
16 **GATEJUMPER (IRE)**, 7, b g Zaffaran (USA)—Nelly Don **Pell-mell Partners**
17 **GENERAL O'KEEFFE**, 8, b g Alflora (IRE)—Rosie O'keeffe (IRE) **Mr R. H. Alner**
18 **GOTHAM (IRE)**, 8, gr g Gothland (FR)—Inchriver (IRE) **Pell-mell Partners**
19 **GOTTA GET ON**, 4, br f Emperor Fountain—Lonicera **Mrs S. A. Old**
20 **GUS DES BOIS (FR)**, 11, ch g Lampon (FR)—Fiacina (FR) **The CD Partnership**
21 **JONGLEUR COLLONGES (FR)**, 8, gr g Royal Charter (FR)—Soubrette Collonge (FR) **A. O. Wiles**
22 **KADARA (IRE)**, 6, b m Slip Anchor—Kadassa (IRE) **Mrs N. Kelly**
23 **KEEPERS MEAD (IRE)**, 7, ch g Aahsaylad—Runaway Pilot **J. C. Browne**
24 **KINGSCLIFF (IRE)**, 8, b g Toulon—Pixies Glen **A. J. Sendell**
25 **KOSMOS BLEU (FR)**, 7, ch g Franc Bleu Argent (USA)—Fee du Lac (FR) **P. M. De Wilde**
26 **LE ROCHELAIS (FR)**, 6, ch g Goldneyev (USA)—Olympiade de Brion (FR) **M. Short**
27 **LORD HALFNOTHIN (IRE)**, 9, b g Mandalus—Midnight Seeker **Exors of the Late H. V. Perry**

MR R. H. ALNER—continued

28 **MACMAR (FR)**, 5, b g Ragmar (FR)—Ex des Sacart (FR) **Mr E. W. Carnell**
29 **MAGOT DE GRUGY (FR)**, 5, b g Tzar Rodney (FR)—Hirlish (FR) **P. M. De Wilde**
30 **MIKO DE BEAUCHENE (FR)**, 5, b g Nashamaa—Chipie d'angron (FR) **A. O. Wiles**
31 **MOTCOMBE (IRE)**, 7, ch m Carroll House—Cooks Lawn **Lady Cobham**
32 **MY WORLD (FR)**, 5, b m Lost World (IRE)—Fortuna Jet (FR) **Nicky Turner, Penny Tozer, Lotte Schicht**
33 **NEW PARK (IRE)**, 5, b g Luso—Charleys Lane (IRE) **Mrs S. Lewis-Harris**
34 **PECCADILLO (IRE)**, 11, br g Un Desperado (FR)—First Mistake **D. W. Makins**
35 **PERFECT LIAISON**, 8, b g Afflora (IRE)—Connie's Pet **Neil & Susie Dalgren**
36 **PRAYERFUL**, 6, b m Syrtos—Pure Formality **Miss H. J. Flower**
37 **ROMAN COURT (IRE)**, 7, b g Witness Box (USA)—Small Iron **Club Ten**
38 **SILVER INNGOT (IRE)**, 6, gr g Gothland (FR)—
Hotel Saltees (IRE) **J. Browne, Mrs C. Robertson, Mrs E. Woodhouse**
39 **SIR REMBRANDT (IRE)**, 9, b g Mandalus—Sue's A Lady **A. Hordle**
40 **SPRING GROVE (IRE)**, 10, b g Mandalus—Lucy Lorraine (IRE) **Exors of the Late H. V. Perry**
41 **THE CAD (IRE)**, 5, b g Broken Hearted—Redondo Beach **P. M. De Wilde**
42 **THE LISTENER (IRE)**, 6, gr h Roselier (FR)—Park Breeze (IRE) **Old Moss Farm**
43 **TOMS GONE GREY (IRE)**, 6, gr g Gothland (FR)—Cpv Lady **T. H. Chadney**
44 **TOULOUSE (IRE)**, 8, b g Toulon—Neasham **Pell-mell Partners**
45 **TRUST FUND (IRE)**, 7, ch g Rashar (USA)—Tuney Blade **T. R. Collins**
46 **TWISTED LOGIC (IRE)**, 12, b g Tremblant—Logical View **P. M. De Wilde**
47 **UP THE PUB (IRE)**, 7, ch g Carroll House—Brave Ruby **Mr G. Keirle & Mr P. Cox**
48 **XYPHOR SEEKER (IRE)**, 5, b g Moonax (USA)—Vera Dodd (IRE) **Miss H. J. Flower**

Other Owners: J. Chromiak, D. J. Constant, R. W. Humphreys, Mrs S. Humphreys, R. J. Jenks, Mrs R. A. Jenks, Mrs P. J. Makins, S. McDonald, A. D. Old, Mrs F. A. Robertson, A. C. B. Thomas, Mrs P. Tozer, S. P. Trevor, Mrs N. C. Turner, H. Wellstead, Mrs S. M. D. Woodhouse.

Assistant Trainer: Mrs S Alner, Nick Mitchell & Mrs S A Old

Jockey (NH): A. Thornton. **Conditional:** R. Walford. **Amateur:** Mr D. Jacob.

---

6   MR E. J. ALSTON, Preston
Postal: **Edges Farm Stables, Chapel Lane, Longton, Preston, Lancashire, PR4 5NA.**
Contacts: **PHONE** (01772) 612120 **FAX** (01772) 619600 **MOBILE** (07879) 641660
E-MAIL eric1943@supanet.com

1 **ALLIED VICTORY (USA)**, 5, b h Red Ransom (USA)—Coral Dance (FR) **The Honest Traders Syndicate**
2 **CHAMPAIN SANDS (IRE)**, 6, b g Green Desert (USA)—Grecian Bride (IRE) **Mr G. Long**
3 **ELLENS ACADEMY (IRE)**, 10, b g Royal Academy (USA)—Lady Ellen **Mr K. Lee and Mr I. Davies**
4 **FLYING EDGE (IRE)**, 5, b g Flying Spur (AUS)—Day Is Dawning (IRE) **The Eric Alston Partnership**
5 **GOODBYE MR BOND**, 5, b g Elmaamul (USA)—Fifth Emerald **P. J. Davies**
6 **INTRICATE WEB (IRE)**, 9, b g Warning—In Anticipation (IRE) **Morris, Oliver, Pierce Partnership**
7 **JADAN (IRE)**, 4, b g Imperial Ballet (IRE)—Sports Post Lady (IRE) **D. Mossop**
8 **JOHNSTON'S DIAMOND (IRE)**, 7, b g Tagula (IRE)—Toshair Flyer **Mollington Golf Club Boys**
9 **MALAHIDE EXPRESS (IRE)**, 5, gr g Compton Place—Gracious Gretclo **The Steady Eddie Partnership**
10 **NAKWA (IRE)**, 7, b g Namaqualand (USA)—Cajo (IRE) **A. Dick**
11 **NIGHT PEARL (IRE)**, 4, b f Night Shift (USA)—Miss Pickpocket (IRE) **Mr & Mrs G. Middlebrook**
12 **NO GROUSE**, 5, b g Pursuit of Love—Lady Joyce (FR) **P. G. Buist**
13 **PICCLED**, 7, b g Piccolo—Creme de Menthe (IRE) **The Pain And Heartache Partnership**
14 **PICCOLO PRINCE**, 4, ch g Piccolo—Aegean Flame **The Burlington Partnership**
15 **PILGRIM PRINCESS (IRE)**, 7, b m Flying Spur (AUS)—Hasaid Lady (IRE) **Mrs P. O. Morris**
16 **RYMER'S RASCAL**, 13, b g Rymer—City Sound **Brian Chambers**
17 **TIME N TIME AGAIN**, 7, b g Timeless Times (USA)—Primum Tempus **Springs Equestrian Partnership**
18 **WEAKEST LINK**, 4, b g Mind Games—Sky Music **The Eric Alston Partnership**

THREE-YEAR-OLDS

19 **ALLSTAR PRINCESS**, b f Environment Friend—Turf Moor (IRE) **Valley Paddocks Racing Limited**
20 **MONDELLO (IRE)**, b f Tagula (IRE)—Teodora (IRE) **Liam & Tony Ferguson**
21 **NIKITA SUNRISE (IRE)**, ch f Namid—Shun **Beckfoot Farm, Laura & Steve Downs**
22 **ROBURY**, b g Robellino (USA)—Youdontsay **Whitehills Racing Syndicate**
23 **SECOND REEF**, b c Second Empire (IRE)—Vax Lady **Valley Paddocks Racing Limited**
24 **TIVISKI (IRE)**, b f Desert Style (IRE)—Mummys Best **The Selebians**

MR E. J. ALSTON—continued

TWO-YEAR-OLDS

25 **ALTESSA (IRE)**, b f 15/2 Desert Style (IRE)—
                  Savona (IRE) (Cyrano de Bergerac) (5500) **Edges Farm Racing Stables Ltd**
26 B f 21/2 Groom Dancer (USA)—
                  Catch The Flame (USA) (Storm Bird (CAN)) (4000) **Edges Farm Racing Stables Ltd**
27 **SECOND CITY**, ch f 25/4 Mark of Esteem (IRE)—Trefoil (FR) (Blakeney) (8000) **Brian Chambers**
28 **SEESAWMILU (IRE)**, b c 29/3 Almutawakel—
                  Clos de Tart (IRE) (Indian Ridge) **Mr John Jackson & Mr John Thompson**

Other Owners: Mrs S. Y. Alston, M. F. H. Brown, M. L. Ferguson, Mr C. A. Ferguson, J. W. D. R. Lightfoot, Anthony Scholes, Mrs A. E. Scholes.

Assistant Trainer: Mrs Sue Alston

Jockey (flat): D. Allan, K. Fallon, W. Supple. **Amateur:** Miss Kim E. Jones.

---

7   MR W. AMOS, Hawick
Postal: **Broadhaugh Farm, Newmill on Teviot, Hawick, Roxburghshire, TD9 0JX.**
Contacts: **PHONE (01450) 850323 MOBILE (07810) 738149**

1 **BOULTA (IRE)**, 11, ch g Commanche Run—Boulta View **Mrs C. Moore**
2 **COOL DESSA BLUES**, 6, br m Cool Jazz—Our Dessa **Mrs D. S. Alder, Stewart Bonney**
3 **COOLE ABBEY (IRE)**, 13, b g Viteric (FR)—Eleanors Joy **Mrs C. Moore**
4 **DOUBLE GIN**, 5, gr g Double Trigger (IRE)—Belmore Cloud **Mrs C. A. Warden**
5 **HIGH DELIGHT**, 5, b g Dancing High—Dunrowan **Mr W. Amos**
6 **NOBLE TEVIOT**, 7, b g Lithgie-Brig—Polly Peril **R. J. Kyle**
7 **REIVERS MOON**, 6, b br m Midnight Legend—Here Comes Tibby **J. W. McNeill**
8 **SHELEVEN (IRE)**, 6, ch g Accordion—Southcoast Gale (IRE) **J. E. Curry**
9 **TEVIOTINO**, 4, gr f Weldnaas (USA)—Dolitino **Teviot Racing**

Other Owners: Mrs S. M. Alder, S. Bonney, Mrs D. E. Smith, Mr A. D. Smith.

---

8   MR M. APPLEBY, Compton Verney
Postal: **Home Farm Racing Stables, Compton Verney, Warwick, CV35 7HJ.**
Contacts: **HOME (01926) 691122 MOBILE (07884) 366421**
E-MAIL appleby477@aol.com

1 **ATLANTIC JANE**, 5, b m Tamure (IRE)—Atlantic View **P. J. Hughes Developments Ltd**
2 **CELTIC VISION (IRE)**, 9, b g Be My Native (USA)—Dream Run **P. & P. J. Hughes**
3 **CLOUD CATCHER (IRE)**, 4, br f Charnwood Forest (IRE)—Notley Park **Mr E. P. Spain**
4 **DUNDONALD**, 6, ch g Magic Ring (IRE)—Cal Norma's Lady (IRE) **Mr M. Appleby**
5 **FLASHY SIR**, 6, ch g Weld—Manx Princess **M. S. Fentiman**
6 **GENTLE WARNING**, 5, b m Parthian Springs—Manx Princess **M. S. Fentiman**
7 **HENRY'S LUCK PENNY (IRE)**, 5, br g Muroto—Lady Sallyanna **P. J. Hughes Developments Ltd**
8 **HURLERS CROSS (IRE)**, 7, b g Jurado (USA)—Maid of Music (IRE) **P. J. Hughes Developments Ltd**
9 **JUST OFFALY (IRE)**, 8, b g Supreme Leader—Head of The Gang **Mr E. P. Spain**
10 **LA MUETTE (IRE)**, 5, b m Charnwood Forest (IRE)—Elton Grove (IRE) **Clovers**
11 **MUNNY HILL**, 5, b ro g Golden Heights—More Laughter **Mr E. P. Spain**

THREE-YEAR-OLDS

12 **WITCHY VIBES**, ch f Tomba—Risk The Witch **Mr M. Appleby**

Other Owners: Mr J. Hudson.

Assistant Trainer: Mr Lee Moulson

Jockey (flat): S. Righton. **Jockey (NH):** P. Flynn. **Conditional:** Ben Orde-Powlett. **Amateur:** Miss F. Turner.

9

MR D. W. P. ARBUTHNOT, Upper Lambourn
Postal: **Saxon Gate, Upper Lambourn, Hungerford, Berkshire, RG17 8QH.**
Contacts: **PHONE/FAX** (01488) 72383 **HOME** (01488) 72402 **MOBILE** (07836) 276464
E-MAIL arbo_saxongate@hotmail.com **WEBSITE** www.arbuthnotracing.co.uk

1 **BORDER ALLIANCE**, 5, ch g Selkirk (USA)—Regal Peace **D. C. Broomfield**
2 **BRAVO MAESTRO (USA)**, 4, b g Stravinsky (USA)—Amaranthus (USA) **D. C. Broomfield**
3 **EVEN HOTTER**, 4, b f Desert Style (IRE)—Level Pegging (IRE) **Lady Whent**
4 **GO GARUDA**, 4, b g Air Express (IRE)—Free As A Bird **The Arbo Partnership 1**
5 **GREEN MANALISHI**, 4, b g Green Desert (USA)—Silca-Cisa **D. C. Broomfield**
6 **LORD ZINC**, 4, b g Forzando—Zolica **P. Banfield**
7 **RINGMOOR DOWN**, 6, b m Pivotal—Floppie (FR) **Prof C. D. Green**
8 **ROMAN QUINTET (IRE)**, 5, ch g Titus Livius (FR)—Quintellina **Saxon Gate Partnership**

THREE-YEAR-OLDS

9 **HIGH BEECH (IRE)**, b f Tagula (IRE)—Belladera (IRE) **Prof C. D. Green**
10 **LORD OF DREAMS (IRE)**, ch g Barathea (IRE)—The Multiyorker (IRE) **N. D. Cronin & Mr P. Banfield**
11 **TANZANITE (IRE)**, b f Revoque (IRE)—Resume (IRE) **D. C. Broomfield & N. D. Cronin**

TWO-YEAR-OLDS

12 **BANOO (IRE)**, b f 3/3 Hernando (FR)—Toi Toi (IRE) (In The Wings) **N. D. Cronin**
13 **CALMING WATERS**, ch c 21/4 Dr Fong (USA)—Faraway Waters (Pharly (FR)) **Mr R. E. Crutchley**
14 Ro f 19/4 Soviet Star (USA)—Clotted Cream (USA) (Eagle Eyed (USA)) (10060) **Prof C. D. Green**
15 Ch c 16/4 Distant Music (USA)—Glen of Imaal (IRE) (Common Grounds) (12072)
16 B f 24/3 Danetime (IRE)—Gone With The Wind (IRE) (Common Grounds) (17000) **Prof C. D. Green**
17 B c 11/5 Fraam—Lana Turrel (USA) (Trempolino (USA)) (8000)
18 **MON PETITE AMOUR**, b f 21/4 Efisio—Food of Love (Music Boy) (15000) **N. D. Cronin**
19 B g 3/5 Agnes World (USA)—The Frog Lady (IRE) (Al Hareb (USA))

Other Owners: A. F. S. Haynes, P. Murphy, Mrs Sandra R. Murphy, N. A. Wyman.

Jockey (flat): T. Quinn. **Apprentice:** Shane Alan Crighton.

10

MR R. J. ARMSON, Melbourne
Postal: **Scotlands Farm, Burney Lane, Staunton-Harold, Melbourne, Derbyshire, DE73 1BH.**
Contacts: **HOME** (01332) 865383 **OFFICE** (01332) 865293 **MOBILE** (07811) 827678

1 **BLAZING FIDDLE (IRE)**, 6, b g Anshan—Second Violin (IRE) **Mr R. J. Armson**
2 **CALKE PARK**, 8, gr g Neltino—Karena Park **Mr R. J. Armson**
3 **EARL TOKEN**, 9, b g Primitive Rising (USA)—Lady Token **Mr R. J. Armson**
4 **EDGEMOOR PRINCESS**, 7, b m Broadsword (USA)—Stubbin Moor **Mr R. J. Armson**
5 5, B g Teenoso (USA)—Karina's Carbon **Mr R. J. Armson**
6 5, Br m Alderbrook—One of Those Days **Mr R. J. Armson**

Assistant Trainer: Mrs S Armson

Amateur: Mr R. J. Armson.

11

MR P. G. ATKINSON, Northallerton
Postal: **Yafforth Hill Farm, Yafforth, Northallerton, North Yorkshire, DL7 0LT.**
Contacts: **PHONE** (01609) 772598 **MOBILE** (07751) 131215

1 **GO NOMADIC**, 11, b g Nomadic Way (USA)—Dreamago **D. G. Atkinson**
2 **KERRS WHIN**, 5, b g Past Glories—Dreamago **D. G. Atkinson**
3 4, B g Florida Son—My Moona **D. G. Atkinson**
4 **NOMADIC BLAZE**, 8, b g Nomadic Way (USA)—Dreamago **D. G. Atkinson**

Jockey (NH): L. McGrath.

12   MR M. J. ATTWATER, Wysall
Postal: **Brooklands Racing Stables, Costock Road, Wysall, Nottinghamshire, NG12 5QT.**
Contacts: **PHONE (01509) 881048 MOBILE (07761) 072996**

1 **BELLA TUTRICE (IRE)**, 4, b f Woodborough (USA)—Institutrice (IRE) **Brooklands Racing**
2 **LA PUCE**, 4, b f Danzero (AUS)—Verbena (IRE) **Brooklands Racing**
3 **SHADOW JUMPER (IRE)**, 4, b g Dayjur (USA)—Specifically (USA) **Brooklands Racing**

THREE-YEAR-OLDS

4 **GAUDALPIN (IRE)**, b f Danetime (IRE)—Lila Pedigo (IRE) **Brooklands Racing**
5 **RUMAN (IRE)**, b g Fayruz—Starway To Heaven (ITY) **Brooklands Racing**
6 **WILFORD MAVERICK (IRE)**, b c Fasliyev (USA)—Lioness **Brooklands Racing**
7 **XAARA DOON (IRE)**, b f Xaar—Hill of Doon (IRE) **Brooklands Racing**
8 **YORKSHIRE LAD (IRE)**, b c Second Empire (IRE)—Villaminta (IRE) **Brooklands Racing**

TWO-YEAR-OLDS

9 B f 7/1 Rossini (USA)—Belmont Princess (IRE) (Carmelite House (USA)) (2681) **Brooklands Racing**
10 B c 20/5 Bluebird (USA)—Vol de Reve (IRE) (Nordico (USA)) (2145) **Brooklands Racing**

Other Owners: M. H. Bates, D. S. Lovatt, R. J. Robinson.

Jockey (flat): N. Callan, S. Righton. **Amateur:** Mr R. Morris.

13   MR JEAN-RENE AUVRAY, Upper Lambourn
Postal: **Frenchman's Lodge Stables, Upper Lambourn, Hungerford, Berkshire, RG17 8QT.**
Contacts: **PHONE/FAX (01488) 73740 MOBILE (07798) 645796**
E-MAIL **jr.auvray@lambournracing.com** WEBSITE **www.lambournracing.com**

1 **BOLD TRUMP**, 4, b g First Trump—Blue Nile (IRE) **M. J. Lewin & D. E. Grieve**
2 **COUNT DRACULA**, 4, b g Dracula (AUS)—Chipaya **Miss K. J. Keir**
3 **DELIGHTFULLY**, 4, b f Definite Article—Kingpin Delight **Mr Jean-Rene Auvray**
4 **EURADREAM (IRE)**, 7, ch g Eurobus—Its All A Dream **Lady Eliza Mays-Smith**
5 **HARNAGE (IRE)**, 10, b g Mujadil (USA)—Wilderness **R. T. Grant**
6 **IRISHKAWA BELLEVUE (FR)**, 7, b br g Irish Prospector (FR)—Strakawa (FR) **The Magpie Partnership**
7 **IT'S RUMOURED**, 5, ch g Fleetwood (IRE)—Etourdie (USA) **The Simpsons Partnership**
8 **L'ARTISTE BELLEVUE (FR)**, 6, b g Start Fast (FR)—Enus du Manoir (FR) **The Dragon Partnership**
9 **MEPHISTOS KICK**, 4, b g Kingmambo (USA)—Mempari **Mrs C. V. Fennell**
10 **ONE ALONE**, 4, b f Atraf—Songsheet **Realistic Racing**
11 **SAHARAN SONG (IRE)**, 4, ch f Singspiel (IRE)—Sahara Baladee (USA) **M. J. Lewin & D. E. Grieve**
12 **SPINNING SILVER**, 10, b g Nearly A Hand—Paid Elation **R. T. Grant**

THREE-YEAR-OLDS

13 **BLACK DRAFT**, b br g Josr Algarhoud (IRE)—Tilia **Mr Jean-Rene Auvray**
14 **POCKETWOOD**, b g Fleetwood (IRE)—Pocket Venus (IRE) **M. J. Lewin**

TWO-YEAR-OLDS

15 B c 30/4 Fleetwood (IRE)—Pocket Venus (IRE) (King's Theatre (IRE)) (7142) **M. J. Lewin**
16 B f 21/3 Kalanisi (IRE)—Towaahi (IRE) (Caerleon (USA))

Other Owners: Miss S. Collie, Mr K. Geering, Mr M. Van Oostrum, Miss C. Aldridge, Mr Pradip Jani, Mr H. Groves, Mr R. C. C. Gait, Mr D. W. Lord, S. McPhee, A. V. Roper, Mr S. Ross, D. M. Speker, J. Stark, Mrs J. M. Turner.

Jockey (NH): M. Foley. **Conditional:** D. Crosse. **Amateur:** Miss Laura Sleep.

14   MR N. G. AYLIFFE, Minehead
Postal: **Glebe Stables, Little Ham, Winsford, Minehead, Somerset, TA24 7JH.**
Contacts: **PHONE (01643) 851265 MOBILE (07786) 918447**

1 **A POUND DOWN (IRE)**, 8, b g Treasure Hunter—Ann's Queen (IRE) **M. J. Hayes & W. G. Winzer**
2 **ANNE'S BAND**, 6, b g Bandmaster (USA)—Fair Anne **Mrs M. A. Barrett**
3 **BLUES STORY (FR)**, 7, b g Pistolet Bleu (IRE)—Herbe Sucree (FR) **R. Allatt**
4 **FAIRLY HIGH (IRE)**, 5, b m Sri Pekan (USA)—Ecco Mi (IRE) **D. T. Hooper**

MR N. G. AYLIFFE—continued

5 **GRIFFIN'S LEGACY**, 6, b g Wace (USA)—Griffin's Girl **Mrs M. A. Barrett**
6 **RUBY GATE (IRE)**, 10, b g Rashar (USA)—Vam Cas (IRE) **D. T. Hooper**

Jockey (NH): J. Mogford. **Conditional:** D. Crosse.

---

15 MR J. W. F. AYNSLEY, Morpeth

Postal: **Rye Hill Farm, Thropton, Morpeth, Northumberland, NE65 7NG.**
Contacts: **PHONE (01669) 620271**

1 **OLD NODDY (IRE)**, 5, ch g Duky—General Run **Mr J. W. F. Aynsley**

Assistant Trainer: J R Aynsley

Jockey (NH): R. Hodge, C. McCormack, R. McGrath. **Amateur:** Mr J. R. Barlow, Mr J. B. Walton.

---

16 MR N. M. BABBAGE, Cheltenham

Postal: **The Deer Park, Brockhampton, Cheltenham, Gloucestershire, GL54 5SR.**
Contacts: **HOME (01242) 821097 OFFICE (01242) 821117 FAX (01242) 821147
MOBILE (07976) 262547**

1 **ATLANTIC TERN**, 4, b c Atraf—Great Tern **Mrs P. J. Cantrill**
2 **COTSWOLD ROSE**, 5, b m Sovereign Water (FR)—Rosehall **R. Coates**
3 **DRAGUT TORGHOUD (IRE)**, 9, b g Persian Mews—Artist's Jewel **B. Babbage**
4 **ENNEL BOY (IRE)**, 12, ch g Torus—Golden Symphony **Provex Products Ltd**
5 **FLYING FORTUNE (IRE)**, 9, b g Jolly Jake (NZ)—Dynamite Flyer (USA) **Mr & Mrs John & Pat Cantrill**
6 **HOMER (IRE)**, 8, b g Sadler's Wells (USA)—Gravieres (FR) **V. J. Tickel**
7 **JUST MIDAS**, 7, b g Merdon Melody—Thabeh **B. Babbage**
8 **LORD BROADWAY (IRE)**, 9, b g Shardari—Country Course (IRE) **D. G. & D. J. Robinson**
9 **MARINO WEST (IRE)**, 10, ch g Phardante (FR)—Seanaphobal Lady **Provex Products Ltd**
10 **PURE PLEASURE (NZ)**, 6, gr g Casual Lies (USA)—Pure Glory (NZ) **A. G. Craddock**
11 **QUEENS WOOD**, 6, br m Abzu—Fleur de Tal **A. G. Craddock**
12 **VETRANIO (IRE)**, 8, ch g Hubbly Bubbly (USA)—Cool Charm **Provex Products Ltd**
13 **WEDNESDAY CLUB**, 4, ch g Shahanndeh—Fleur de Tal **Provex Products Ltd**
14 **YOUNG ALEX (IRE)**, 7, ch g Midhish—Snipe Hunt (IRE) **D. G. & D. J. Robinson**

THREE-YEAR-OLDS

15 **PADDY'S TERN**, b c Fraam—Great Tern **Mrs P. J. Cantrill**

Assistant Trainer: Robin Craddock

Jockey (flat): Paul Eddery. **Jockey (NH):** Pat Brennan, Liam Cummings, B. Fenton. **Amateur:** Mrs K. Blanche, Mr G. Wigley, Miss D. Wilson.

---

17 MR A. BAILEY, Tarporley

Postal: **Sandybrow Stables, Forest Road, Cotebrook, Tarporley, Cheshire, CW6 9EG.**
Contacts: **PHONE (01829) 760762 FAX (01829) 760370 MOBILE (07808) 734223**

1 **ALLEZ MOUSSON**, 7, b g Hernando (FR)—Rynechra **Dr K. Kaye**
2 **BLADE'S EDGE**, 4, b c Daggers Drawn (USA)—Hayhurst **Mr A. Bailey**
3 **BODFARI ROSE**, 6, ch m Indian Ridge—Royale Rose (FR) **Mr A. Bailey**
4 **CAPE FAIRY (IRE)**, 4, b f Cape Cross (IRE)—Sharp Fairy **A. H. Bennett**
5 **COURAGEOUS DOVE**, 4, gr c Overbury (IRE)—Mazzelmo **Mr C. A. Oats**
6 **DANTE'S DEVINE (IRE)**, 4, b g Ashkalani (IRE)—Basilea (FR) **R. Gomersall**
7 **GLARAMARA**, 4, b g Nicolotte—Digamist Girl (IRE) **C. M. Martin**
8 **GOLDEN BOOT**, 6, ch g Unfuwain (USA)—Sports Delight **P. G. Freeman**
9 **INFIDELITY (IRE)**, 4, b f Bluebird (USA)—Madaniyya (USA) **www.mark-kilner-racing.com (20)**
10 **LADY MYTTON**, 5, ch m Lake Coniston (IRE)—The In-Laws (IRE) **G. Mytton**
11 **LENNEL**, 7, b g Presidium—Ladykirk **Mr A. Bailey**
12 **PRINCE OF THE WOOD (IRE)**, 5, ch g Woodborough (USA)—Ard Dauphine (IRE) **The Four Of Us**
13 **QUEENS RHAPSODY**, 5, gr g Baryshnikov (AUS)—Digamist Girl (IRE) **C. M. Martin**
14 **QUIBBLE**, 8, ch g Lammtarra (USA)—Bloudan (USA) **www.mark-kilner-racing.com (16)**
15 **SHARPCUT (IRE)**, 6, b g Alhaarth (IRE)—Safiya (USA) **www.mark-kilner-racing.com(21)**

MR A. BAILEY—continued

16 **SHOWTIME ANNIE**, 4, b f Wizard King—Rebel County (IRE) **Showtime Ice Cream Concessionaire**
17 **SPARTAN ODYSSEY**, 4, b g Overbury (IRE)—Spartan Native **George Maher**
18 **THE FAIRY FLAG (IRE)**, 7, ch m Inchinor—Good Reference (IRE) **Mrs V. Farrington**

THREE-YEAR-OLDS

19 **BALLYCROY GIRL (IRE)**, ch f Pennekamp (USA)—Hulm (IRE) **R. T. Collins**
20 **HIGH ARCTIC**, b g Pivotal—Ladykirk **North Cheshire Trading & Storage Ltd**
21 **ITS SO UNFAIR (IRE)**, ch c Night Shift (USA)—Majakerta (IRE) **Mr T. P. Ramsden**
22 **MICKLEDO**, b c Perryston View—Ever So Lonely **Mr D. J. P. Turner**
23 **MYTTON'S BELL (IRE)**, b f Bold Edge—Ionian Secret **G. Mytton**
24 **MYTTON'S DREAM**, br f Diktat—Courtisane **G. Mytton**
25 **OXFORD STREET PETE (IRE)**, b g Rossini (USA)—Thabeh **Mr P. Hughes**
26 **SHOWTIME FAYE**, b f Overbury (IRE)—Rebel County (IRE) **Showtime Ice Cream Concessionaire**
27 **WIZARDMICKTEE (IRE)**, b c Monashee Mountain (USA)—Epsilon **Mr D. J. P. Turner**
28 **XEIGHT EXPRESS (IRE)**, b f Ashkalani (IRE)—Believing **X8 Racing**

TWO-YEAR-OLDS

29 B c 6/3 Mujadil (USA)—Bryna (IRE) (Ezzoud (IRE)) (10000)
30 **CRESTA GOLD**, b f 17/2 Halling (USA)—Fleet Hill (IRE) (Warrshan (USA)) **P. T. Tellwright**
31 B f 21/3 Danehill Dancer (IRE)—Enthrone (USA) (Diesis) (17000) **X8 Racing**
32 B f 15/4 Beckett (IRE)—Fag End (IRE) (Treasure Kay) (10500)
33 Ch c 20/1 Beckett (IRE)—La Paola (IRE) (Common Grounds) (15000)
34 B c 24/4 Tagula (IRE)—Pictina (Petong) (12000)

Other Owners: Miss M. Archdeacon, Miss P. Cooper, Mr J. K. Ebbrell, R. Farrington, Mr M. F. Johnson, M. Kilner, Mr D. J. Lockwood, Mrs S. A. Martin, Mrs B. May.

Apprentice: Natalie Hassall.

---

18   MR K. C. BAILEY, Preston Capes
Postal: **Grange Farm, Preston Capes, Daventry, Northamptonshire, NN11 3TQ.**
Contacts: **PHONE** (01327) 361733 **FAX** (01327) 361703
E-MAIL kim@kcbaileyracing.com WEBSITE www.kcbaileyracing.com

1 **AH YEAH (IRE)**, 8, b g Roselier (FR)—Serena Bay **A Wing And A Prayer Partnership**
2 **AZURE WINGS (IRE)**, 5, ch m Karinga Bay—Minora **Mrs S. S. M. Bates**
3 **BAY KENNY**, 7, b g Karinga Bay—Erica Superba **I. F. W. Buchan**
4 **BLACK COLLAR**, 6, br m Bob's Return (IRE)—Rosemoss **W. J. Ives**
5 **BLANK CANVAS (IRE)**, 7, b g Presenting—Strong Cloth **D. C. R. Allen**
6 **CHANTICLIER**, 8, b g Alflora (IRE)—Cherry Crest **Mrs V. J. Lane**
7 **COUNTESS CAMILLA**, 8, br m Bob's Return (IRE)—Forest Pride (IRE) **The Fingers Crossed Partnership**
8 **EXTREMIST (USA)**, 6, b g Dynaformer (USA)—Strumming (IRE) **Be Lucky Partnership**
9 **FAMFONI (FR)**, 12, b g Pamponi (FR)—India Rosa (FR) **The Propelers Partnership**
10 **FRONT RANK (IRE)**, 5, b h Sadler's Wells (USA)—Alignment (IRE) **Off The Bridle Partnership**
11 **FULGERE (IRE)**, 7, b g Old Vic—Moppet's Last **The Shine On Partnership**
12 **GLENOGUE (IRE)**, 7, b m Hushang (IRE)—Glenamal **Big Hitters Racing Partnership**
13 **GRASIA (IRE)**, 6, b g Glacial Storm (USA)—Bar Flute (IRE) **A. N. Solomons**
14 **HEARTOFMIDLOTHIAN (IRE)**, 6, ch g Anshan—Random Wind **L. J. Haugh**
15 **KATY'S CLASSIC (IRE)**, 5, b g Classic Cliche (IRE)—Mrs Jennifer **W. J. Ives**
16 **KELANTAN**, 8, b g Kris—Surf Bird **Have Fun Racing Partnership**
17 **KING OF GOTHLAND (IRE)**, 6, gr g Gothland (FR)—Rose Deer **The Norfolk Neighbours**
18 **LONGSHANKS**, 8, b g Broadsword (USA)—Brass Castle **D. A. Halsall**
19 **LORD SEAMUS**, 10, b g Arctic Lord—Erica Superba **I. F. W. Buchan**
20 **LUCKY LUK (FR)**, 6, b g Lights Out (FR)—Citronelle II (FR) **Mrs E. A. Kellar**
21 **MALKO DE BEAUMONT (FR)**, 5, b br g Gold and Steel (FR)—Givry (FR) **Dream Makers Partnership**
22 **MARTOVIC (IRE)**, 6, b m Old Vic—Martomick **D. A. Halsall**
23 **METAL DETECTOR (IRE)**, 8, b g Treasure Hunter—Las-Cancellas **D. C. R. Allen**
24 **MORELUCK (IRE)**, 9, b g Roselier (FR)—Vulcan Belle **Graham and Alison Jelley**
25 **MOUNT PRAGUE (IRE)**, 11, br g Lord Americo—Celtic Duchess **W. J. Ives**
26 **MURPHY'S NAILS (IRE)**, 8, b g Bob's Return (IRE)—Southern Run **Major R. G. Wilson**
27 **ONYOURHEADBEIT (IRE)**, 7, b g Glacial Storm (USA)—Family Birthday **Mr and Mrs Giles Wilson**
28 **PIRANDELLO (IRE)**, 7, ch g Shalford (IRE)—Scenic Villa **Quicksilver Racing Partnership**
29 **PUTUP OR SHUTUP (IRE)**, 9, br g Religiously (USA)—Nights Crack **L. McLaughlin**
30 **RIFLE RYDE (IRE)**, 5, br g Needle Gun (IRE)—Nellsway **G. D. W. Swire**

MR K. C. BAILEY—continued

31 5, B m Sovereign Water (FR)—Sail On Sunday **The May Buddies**
32 **SIR BRASTIAS**, 6, b g Shaamit (IRE)—Premier Night **D. G. Churston**
33 **TERIVIC**, 5, br g Terimon—Ludoviciana **G. W. Paul**
34 **TERMINOLOGY**, 7, gr g Terimon—Rhyming Moppet **J. F. Perriss**
35 **THAROS**, 5, b g Sri Pekan (USA)—Rose Show **Sir Gordon Brunton**
36 **VERY SPECIAL ONE (IRE)**, 5, b m Supreme Leader—Bright News **D. C. R. Allen**
37 **WALKING SUNDAY (IRE)**, 7, b br g Denel (FR)—Blue Mount (IRE) **Dream Makers Partnership**
38 **WOODVIEW (IRE)**, 6, ch g Flemensfirth (USA)—Marys Bard **D. A. Halsall**
39 **ZAFFISFACTION**, 5, b m Zaffaran (USA)—Anaconda (IRE) **Mr And Mrs David Laing And Vicky Laing**

Other Owners: Mrs S. E. Acland, P. D. Ashdown, MR K. C. Bailey, Mrs C. Bailey, A. J. Baxter, A. H. Beck, A. J. Brettell, A. D. Brown, S. P. L. Christian, H. G. Davies, Mrs G. Dessain, S. M. Jaggard, Lord Leigh, Mrs J. L. Milton, P. A. C. Mordaunt, F. H. M. Reid, M. A. Sherwood, Lady St Clair-Ford, A. R. Tabony.

Jockey (NH): J. P. McNamara.

---

19 | **MRS L. P. BAKER, Maidstone**
Postal: **1 Big Allington, Pilgrims Way, Hollingbourne, Maidstone, Kent, ME17 1RD.**
Contacts: **PHONE (01622) 880655 MOBILE (07714) 264115**
E-MAIL lesley@bakerbloodstock.fsnet.co.uk

1 **BODIAM (IRE)**, 5, b m Mukaddamah (USA)—Partenza (USA) **Miss S. E. Baker**
2 **CATFISH HUNTER**, 5, b g Safawan—Secret Account **Mrs L. P. Baker**

Assistant Trainer: M W Baker

---

20 | **MR A. M. BALDING, Kingsclere**
Postal: **Park House Stables, Kingsclere, Newbury, Berkshire, RG20 5PY.**
Contacts: **PHONE (01635) 298210 FAX (01635) 298305 MOBILE (07774) 633791**
E-MAIL admin@kingsclere.com WEBSITE www.kingsclere.com

1 **ALBINUS**, 4, gr c Selkirk (USA)—Alouette **Miss K. Rausing**
2 **ARCTIC DESERT**, 5, b g Desert Prince (IRE)—Thamud (IRE) **Holistic Racing Ltd**
3 **BORDER MUSIC**, 4, b g Selkirk (USA)—Mara River **Kingsclere Stud**
4 **BOURGAINVILLE**, 7, b g Pivotal—Petonica (IRE) **Messrs J. C., J. R. and S. R. Hitchins**
5 **BRIAREUS**, 5, ch g Halling (USA)—Lower The Tone (IRE) **Miss E. Lambourne**
6 **CHAMBRAY (IRE)**, 4, b f Barathea (IRE)—Spurned (USA) **Kingsclere Stud**
7 **CONJUROR**, 4, b g Efisio—Princess Athena **Kennet Valley Thorougbreds I**
8 **COOL MONTY (IRE)**, 11, ch g Montelimar (USA)—Rose Ground **G. J. G. Luck**
9 **CROWN AGENT (IRE)**, 5, b g Mukaddamah (USA)—Supreme Crown (USA) **Miss A. V. Hill**
10 **DEEP PURPLE**, 4, b g Halling (USA)—Seal Indigo (IRE) **P. Green**
11 **DISTANT PROSPECT (IRE)**, 8, b g Namaqualand (USA)—
Ukraine's Affair (USA) **The Rae Smiths and Pauline Gale**
12 **DONASTRELA (IRE)**, 4, b f Tagula (IRE)—David's Star **G. J. G. Luck, Rosemary de Rougemont, Tom Cox**
13 **DUCHAMP (USA)**, 8, b g Pine Bluff (USA)—Higher Learning (USA) **Messrs J. C., J. R. and S. R. Hitchins**
14 **FLORIDA HEART**, 4, ch f First Trump—Miami Dancer (USA) **Park House Partnership**
15 **GREY ADMIRAL**, 4, gr g Cozzene (USA)—Remarkable Style (USA) **D. H. Caslon**
16 **GUNNER WELBURN**, 13, ch g Gunner B—Vedra (IRE) **W. A. Ritson/D. H. Hall/R. D. Ellis**
17 **IRONY (IRE)**, 6, gr g Mujadil (USA)—Cidaris (IRE) **John Nicholls Ltd/Mobley Homes**
18 **MR LAMBROS**, 4, ch g Pivotal—Magical Veil **Winterbeck Manor Stud Ltd**
19 **PENTECOST**, 6, ch g Tagula (IRE)—Boughtbyphone **Messrs J. C., J. R. and S. R. Hitchins**
20 **PHOENIX REACH (IRE)**, 5, b h Alhaarth (IRE)—Carroll's Canyon (IRE) **Winterbeck Manor Stud Ltd**
21 **PRINCE OF THEBES (IRE)**, 4, b g Desert Prince (IRE)—
Persian Walk (FR) **Mr N. H. Harris, Dr E. Harris, Miss M. Green**
22 **REDI (ITY)**, 4, b c Danehill Dancer (IRE)—Rossella **Thurloe Thoroughbreds XI**
23 **SAINT ETIENNE (IRE)**, 4, b f Robellino (USA)—Stop Out **G. W. Chong**
24 **SPANISH ACE**, 4, b g First Trump—Spanish Heart **The Farleigh Court Racing Partnership**
25 **THE PLAYER**, 6, b g Octagonal (NZ)—Patria (USA) **Action Bloodstock**
26 **VANDERLIN**, 6, ch g Halling (USA)—Massorah (FR) **Messrs J. C., J. R. and S. R. Hitchins**
27 **VOICE MAIL**, 6, b g So Factual (USA)—Wizardry **R. G. Parry**
28 **ZARGUS**, 6, b g Zamindar (USA)—My First Romance **Mrs M. V. Bruce Copp**

MR A. M. BALDING—continued

THREE-YEAR-OLDS

29 **ANGEL WING**, ch f Barathea (IRE)—Lochangel **J. C. Smith**
30 **ARRIVATO**, b f Efisio—Beloved Visitor (USA) **Mrs N. S. Tregaskes**
31 **BALLINGER VENTURE**, b f Vettori (IRE)—Branston Ridge **Mrs H. V. Barber**
32 **BANKNOTE**, b c Zafonic (USA)—Brand **Her Majesty The Queen**
33 **BAY HAWK**, b c Alhaarth (IRE)—Fleeting Vision (IRE) **Winterbeck Manor Stud Ltd**
34 **CAPE GREKO**, ro c Loup Sauvage (USA)—Onefortheditch (USA) **Holistic Racing Ltd**
35 **CASUAL GLANCE**, b f Sinndar (IRE)—Spurned (USA) **Kingsclere Stud**
36 **CHANTACU (USA)**, b c Bahri (USA)—Dominant Dancer **The Pink Hat Racing Partnership**
37 **COMPTON COURT**, b g Compton Place—Loriner's Lass **I. G. Burbidge**
38 **COUNTY CLARE**, ch f Barathea (IRE)—Input **T. W. Farmer**
39 **DELLA SALUTE**, gr f Dansili—Marie Dora (FR) **Lord Roborough**
40 **DIKTATORIAL**, br c Diktat—Reason To Dance **Tweenhills Thurloe**
41 **ELKHORN**, b c Indian Ridge—Rimba (USA) **George Strawbridge**
42 **FLYING RIDGE (IRE)**, ch f Indian Ridge—Jarrayan **E. N. Kronfeld**
43 **FOXY GWYNNE**, b f Entrepreneur—Nahlin **O. F. Waller**
44 **GREAT AUNT**, br f Dansili—Shebasis (USA) **R. D. McDougall & Partners**
45 **HEAT ALERT (USA)**, b br f Valid Expectations (USA)—Melt My Heart (USA) **W. S. Farish**
46 **HOH HOH HOH**, ch c Piccolo—Nesting **D. F. Allport**
47 **HOLBECK GHYLL (IRE)**, ch c Titus Livius (FR)—Crimada (IRE) **Holbeck Ghyll Partnership**
48 **HONEY NUT**, ch f Entrepreneur—Nocciola **Winterbeck Manor Stud Ltd**
49 **HOUSE MARTIN**, b f Spectrum (IRE)—Guignol (IRE) **J. T. Thomas**
50 **INTENDED**, b f Singspiel (IRE)—Introducing **George Strawbridge**
51 **KINGSHOLM**, ch c Selkirk (USA)—Putuna **Messrs J. C., J. R. and S. R. Hitchins**
52 **LIGHTED WAY**, b f Kris—Natchez Trace **Dr J. A. E. Hobby**
53 **MARAJUANA**, b f Robellino—Mara River **Lady C. S. Cadbury**
54 **MIDDLE EARTH (USA)**, ch c Dixieland Band (USA)—Lite Twilight (USA) **Blue Riband Partnership**
55 **NIGHTWING**, b c Lujain (USA)—Rasmalai **Holistic Racing Ltd**
56 **NORTHERN SECRET**, b f Sinndar (IRE)—Northern Goddess **N. H. Harris**
57 **OCEANCOOKIE (IRE)**, b f Dashing Blade—Sankaty Light (USA) **Miss C. V. Balding**
58 **PALACE WALK (FR)**, b c Sinndar (IRE)—Page Bleue **Winterbeck Manor Stud Ltd**
59 **PITTSBURGH**, ch c Nashwan (USA)—Oatey **Blue Riband Partnership**
60 **REGAL ATTIRE (USA)**, ch c Kingmambo (USA)—Style Setter (USA) **W. S. Farish**
61 **ROGUE**, b f Royal Applause—Mystique **Winterbeck Manor Stud Ltd**
62 **ROLLERBIRD**, b f Sinndar (IRE)—Speedybird (IRE) **George Strawbridge**
63 **ROMAN ARMY (IRE)**, b c Trans Island—Contravene (IRE) **Stamford Bridge Partnership**
64 **ROSECLIFF**, b c Montjeu (IRE)—Dance Clear (IRE) **M. Tabor**
65 **SAMSON QUEST**, b c Cyrano de Bergerac—Zenita (IRE) **Samson Centre Owners Group (JDRP)**
66 **SHADE COZY (USA)**, gr c Cozzene (USA)—Fire And Shade (USA) **Anthony & Valerie Hogarth**
67 **SILVER HIGHLIGHT (CAN)**, gr ro f Silver Charm (USA)—Rare Opportunity (USA) **D. H. Caslon**
68 **SPEED OF SOUND**, ch f Zafonic (USA)—Blue Siren **J. C. Smith**
69 **STAY CLOSE**, b g Belong To Me (USA)—Cymbala (FR) **W. S. Farish**
70 **STORM CENTRE**, ch g Pivotal—Long View **Pink Partnership**
71 **STRING BAND (USA)**, br f Spinning World (USA)—Our Wildirish Rose (USA) **W. S. Farish**
72 **SUKUMA (IRE)**, ch f Highest Honor (FR)—Selva (IRE) **M. A. L. Evans**
73 **SUN BIAN**, b c Makbul—Silken Dalliance **The C H F Partnership**
74 **TAPA**, b f Tagula (IRE)—Tweed Mill **D. H. Back**
75 **TASHYRA (IRE)**, b f Tagula (IRE)—Shiyra **Mr J. P. Robinson**
76 **TRYMORE (IRE)**, ch c Tagula (IRE)—Marimar (IRE) **G. L. Weston**
77 **TUVALU (GER)**, ch c Dashing Blade—Tepana (GER) **N. H. Harris**

TWO-YEAR-OLDS

78 **ALMANZORA BAY (IRE)**, ch f 1/3 Pivotal—Putuna (Generous (IRE)) **Messrs J. C., J. R. and S. R. Hitchins**
79 B f 3/4 Indian Lodge (IRE)—Almond Flower (IRE) (Alzao (USA)) (20000) **G. W. Chong**
80 **ANTIGONI (IRE)**, ch f 8/4 Grand Lodge (USA)—
　　　　　　　　　　　　　　　Butter Knife (IRE) (Sure Blade (USA)) **Winterbeck Manor Stud Ltd**
81 **APACHE ANGEL**, ch c 16/4 Indian Ridge—Lochangel (Night Shift (USA)) **J. C. Smith**
82 B f 12/2 Daggers Drawn (USA)—Appelone (Emperor Jones (USA)) (14000) **Park House Partnership**
83 **BALLINGER GOLD**, b c 11/4 Golden Snake (USA)—Branston Ridge (Indian Ridge) **Mrs H. V. Barber**
84 B f 20/3 Desert Prince (IRE)—Bathe In Light (USA) (Sunshine Forever (USA)) (20000) **Coriolan Partnership**
85 B c 8/5 Tagula (IRE)—Boughtbyphone (Warning) (28000)
86 **BROADWAY CALLING**, ch c 19/4 Dr Fong (USA)—
　　　　　　　　　　　　　　　Manhattan Sunset (USA) (El Gran Senor (USA)) (15000) **J. Gale**

MR A. M. BALDING—continued

 87 **CERTAIN CIRCLES (USA)**, b c 17/5 King Cugat (USA)—
Daily Special (USA) (Dayjur (USA)) **L. Register/W.S. Farish jr.**
 88 **COSTA PACKET (IRE)**, ch f 24/1 Hussonet (USA)—Costa Balena (CHI) (Great Regent (CAN)) **The Hon R. Hanson**
 89 **CRUSH ON YOU**, b f 2/3 Golden Snake (USA)—Mourir d'aimer (USA) (Trempolino (USA)) (666) **S. McPhee**
 90 **DARK MISSILE**, b f 14/1 Night Shift (USA)—Exorcet (FR) (Selkirk (USA)) **J. C. Smith**
 91 **DEEPWATER BAY (USA)**, b c 16/2 Chester House (USA)—Gem Treck (USA) (Java Gold (USA)) **E. N. Kronfeld**
 92 **EBONY LORD**, b c 2/2 Fraam—Dorissio (IRE) (Efisio) (3238) **Miss A. V. Hill**
 93 **FLY BY JOVE (IRE)**, b c 7/2 Fasliyev (USA)—Flyleaf (FR) (Persian Bold) (53655) **J. Robinson & D. Stubbs**
 94 **FREE TO AIR**, b c 25/4 Generous (IRE)—Petonica (IRE) (Petoski) (10000) **Miss C. V. Balding**
 95 **GENEROSIA**, b f 7/3 Generous (IRE)—Come On Rosi (Valiyar) **Winterbeck Manor Stud Ltd**
 96 Ch f 10/5 Alhaarth (IRE)—Ghayah (IRE) (Night Shift (USA)) (14000) **J. T. Thomas**
 97 **GRACEFUL EXIT (IRE)**, ch c 30/1 Hussonet (USA)—
La Sencilla (ARG) (Lookinforthebigone (USA)) **The Hon R. Hanson**
 98 **HIGHLAND BELLE**, b f 29/1 Robellino (USA)—Scottish Spice (Selkirk (USA)) **J. C. Smith**
 99 **HOH WOTANITE**, ch c 24/4 Stravinsky (USA)—West One (Gone West (USA)) **D. F. Allport**
100 **KALANKARI (IRE)**, b br c 15/3 Kalanisi (IRE)—
Stately Princess (Robellino (USA)) (31000) **Dubai Thoroughbred Racing**
101 **KALANTERA (IRE)**, b c 24/3 Kalanisi (IRE)—
Tintera (IRE) (King's Theatre (IRE)) (40240) **J. Robinson & D. Stubbs**
102 B c 29/4 Generous (IRE)—Kimba (USA) (Kris S (USA)) **George Strawbridge**
103 B f 18/2 Observatory (USA)—Lady Donatella (Last Tycoon) **Michael E. Wates**
104 **LOCH VERDI**, b f 15/2 Green Desert (USA)—Lochsong (Song) **J. C. Smith**
105 B f 6/4 Hernando (FR)—Mara River (Efisio)
106 **OVERLOOK**, b f 17/4 Generous (IRE)—Spurned (USA) (Robellino (USA)) **Kingsclere Stud**
107 **PALMISTRY**, br c 16/2 Lend A Hand—Divina Mia (Dowsing (USA)) (40000) **Kennet Valley Thoroughbreds III**
108 **PINCH OF SALT (IRE)**, b c 8/3 Hussonet (USA)—Granita (CHI) (Roy (USA)) **The Hon R. Hanson**
109 **RAG TAG (IRE)**, b c 5/3 Tagula (IRE)—Lovat Spring (USA) (Storm Bird (CAN)) (20120) **W. V. Robins**
110 **RAINBOWS GUEST (IRE)**, ch f 11/4 Indian Lodge (IRE)—
Maura's Guest (IRE) (Be My Guest (USA)) (10000) **Winterbeck Manor Stud Ltd**
111 B c 2/4 Selkirk (USA)—Red May (IRE) (Persian Bold) (70000) **George Strawbridge**
112 Ch f 24/3 Miswaki (USA)—S S Capote (USA) (Capote (USA)) **D. H. Caslon**
113 **SABAH**, ch f 8/4 Nashwan (USA)—Massorah (FR) (Habitat) (39000) **Sir R. J. Buckley**
114 **SANTIAGO STAR (IRE)**, ch c 15/1 Hussonet (USA)—Normandy (CHI) (Great Regent (CAN)) **The Hon R. Hanson**
115 Ch c 12/3 Rahy (USA)—Silver Fling (USA) (The Minstrel (CAN)) **George Strawbridge**
116 **SOUL BLAZER (USA)**, b c 14/3 Honour And Glory (USA)—
See You (USA) (Gulch (USA)) **Winterbeck Manor Stud Ltd**
117 **SPANISH STORY**, b f 16/2 Vettori (IRE)—Spanish Heart (King of Spain) **Farleigh Court Racing Partnership**
118 **SUN FIRE**, b c 3/2 Hernando (FR)—Venetian Red (USA) (Blushing Groom (FR)) (40000) **W. V. Robins**
119 B c 12/4 Fayruz—Super Zoe (Bustino) (9389) **Park House Partnership**
120 **TANGARITA**, b f 10/2 Tagula (IRE)—Santa Isobel (Nashwan (USA)) **J.C, J.R. & S.R. Hitchins**
121 Ch c 26/2 Fruits of Love (USA)—The Iron Lady (IRE) (Polish Patriot (USA)) (17000)
122 **THE JABR (IRE)**, gr c 25/2 Aljabr (USA)—Vital Laser (USA) (Seeking The Gold (USA)) (22802) **D. H. Caslon**
123 **THEATRE ROYAL**, b f 15/3 Royal Applause—
Rada's Daughter (Robellino (USA)) (100000) **Mrs Richard Plummer & Partners**
124 **TIME OUT (IRE)**, b c 2/3 Alhaarth (IRE)—Waif (Groom Dancer (USA)) (44000) **W. V. Robins**
125 **TIZ TIMELY (USA)**, b f 13/4 Tiznow (USA)—Delivery Day (USA) (Dayjur (USA)) **D. H. Caslon**
126 **TYPHOON LING LING (USA)**, ch f 16/3 Hennessy (USA)—
Lady In Waiting (USA) (Woodman (USA)) **E. N. Kronfeld**
127 **WAY TO THE STARS**, gr f 13/3 Dansili—Reason To Dance (Damister (USA)) (78000) **Mrs D. O. Joly**
128 **WELSH DRAGON**, b c 19/2 Cape Cross (IRE)—Blorenge (Prince Sabo) (21000)
129 B c 19/4 Fruits of Love (USA)—Where's Charlotte (Sure Blade (USA)) (10000) **Park House Partnership**
130 **WHITE HEATHER**, br f 21/1 Selkirk (USA)—Durrah Green (Green Desert (USA)) **Miss K. Rausing**
131 **WITH INTEREST**, b c 17/3 Selkirk (USA)—With Fascination (USA) (Dayjur (USA)) **George Strawbridge**
132 **YEOMAN SPIRIT (IRE)**, ch c 29/4 Soviet Star (USA)—
Hollywood Pearl (USA) (Phone Trick (USA)) (24144) **Mrs S. Dalton**
133 **YEOMAN'S GIRL**, b f 25/1 Slip Anchor—Rasmalai (Sadler's Wells (USA)) (9500) **Yeoman Homes Ltd**

Other Owners: S. Alansari, G. D. Anderson, I. A. Balding, Mrs E. A. M. Balding, P.R. Barter, Mr R. P. Beare, Mrs V. I. Beare, P.J. Box, Mr John Dunbar, Mr M. K. Elliott, J. A. Fergusson, K. H. Fischer, C. H. Fischer, Mrs C. M. Foster, Mrs P. C. Gale, J. N. Hambly, B. D. Heath, J. S. Hobhouse, Hoh Oilfield Services Limited, D. R. O. How, Mrs E. A. Ireland, G. R. Ireland, Ms L. La Plante, P. K. Lacy, Mr A. Loughran, Sir Nevil MacReady, R. P. B. Michaelson, Mr D. Nicholson, O. J. W. Pawle, Miss J. Philip-Jones, Mrs A. B. Plummer, Mrs M. A. Rae Smith, A. F. Rae Smith, Mr D. Redvers, N. J. F. Robinson, T. D. Rootes, S. L. Ross, R. A. Simmons, Mrs A. Stokes, T. J. D. Walker, Mrs E. M. Wechsler.

MR A. M. BALDING—continued

Assistant Trainer: I A Balding

Jockey (flat): M. Dwyer. **Apprentice:** N. Chalmers, L. Keniry, R. Killoran. **Amateur:** Mr A. Braithwaite.

---

21 MR J. BALDING, Doncaster
Postal: **Mayflower Stables, Saracens Lane, Scrooby, Doncaster, South Yorkshire, DN10 6AS.**
Contacts: **HOME (01302) 710096 FAX (01302) 710096 MOBILE (07816) 612631**
E-MAIL j.balding@mayflowerstables.freeserve.co.uk

1 **ABSENT FRIENDS**, 8, b g Rock City—Green Supreme **Mrs J. Hardy**
2 **ARMS ACROSSTHESEA**, 6, b g Namaqualand (USA)—Zolica **J. Carter**
3 **COMPTON MICKY**, 4, ch g Compton Place—Nunthorpe **J. M. Lacey**
4 **EFISTORM**, 4, b c Efisio—Abundance **Mrs J. Hardy**
5 **FIRST ECLIPSE (IRE)**, 4, b f Fayruz—Naked Poser (IRE) **J J D Partnership**
6 **HENRY TUN**, 7, b g Chaddleworth (IRE)—B Grade **T. Reffell**
7 **JACQUI EVANS**, 4, b f Komaite (USA)—Rudda Flash **Mrs J. R. Evans**
8 **JUSTALORD**, 7, b g King's Signet (USA)—Just Lady **Mr T. H. Heckingbottom**
9 **LADY PROTECTOR**, 6, b m Sri Pekan (USA)—Scared **Simon Mapletoft Racing II**
10 **LAKE EYRE (IRE)**, 6, b m Bluebird (USA)—Pooh Wee **Mr J. Balding**
11 **LARGS**, 5, ch m Sheikh Albadou—Madam Zando **Hollinbridge Racing**
12 **MARYSIENKA**, 4, b f Primo Dominie—Polish Romance (USA) **Simon Balding**
13 **MATTY TUN**, 6, b g Lugana Beach—B Grade **Mrs O. Tunstall**
14 **ROCKY REPPIN**, 5, b g Rock City—Tino Reppin **Sandown Park Stud**
15 **ROYAL NITE OWL**, 4, b g Royal Applause—Nite-Owl Dancer **J. Saul**
16 **SCARY NIGHT (IRE)**, 5, b g Night Shift (USA)—Private Bucks (USA) **D. Moss**
17 **SHORT CHORUS**, 4, ch f Inchinor—Strawberry Song **J. Bladen**
18 **SOBA JONES**, 8, b g Emperor Jones (USA)—Soba **R. L. Crowe**
19 **TOM TUN**, 10, b g Bold Arrangement—B Grade **Mrs O. Tunstall**

THREE-YEAR-OLDS

20 **AFTON**, ch f Bien Bien (USA)—Madam Zando **Mrs G. A. R. Jones**
21 **BORU**, ch f Silver Patriarch (IRE)—Muftuffenuf **Mrs J. Everitt**
22 **GIFTED LASS**, b f Bold Edge—Meeson Times **Bawtry Racing Partnership**
23 **GYFLYM**, b f Atraf—Bold Gift **Miss J. Wright**
24 **HAROLDINI (IRE)**, b g Orpen (USA)—Ciubanga (IRE) **Tykes And Terriers Racing Club**
25 **LUGANA POINT**, b g Lugana Beach—Raisa Point **J. J. Amass**
26 **SWING**, b g Dansili—Blues Indigo **Richard Watson**

TWO-YEAR-OLDS

27 **FERROLI**, b c 2/3 Efisio—Ordained (Mtoto) (16000) **T. Reffell**
28 **TATSTHETICKET**, b c 5/2 Diktat—Dekelsmary (Komaite (USA)) (11000) **D. Moss**

Other Owners: Mr R. Leach, Mr J. D. Evans, Mrs C. M. Beresford, D. C. Bichan, M. Carr, M. V. Firth, S. A. Mapletoft, Mrs J. Mapletoft, J. P. Severn, C. Wagstaff, Mrs E. Wagstaff, R. Wright.

Assistant Trainer: Claire Edmunds

Jockey (flat): J. Edmunds. **Apprentice:** K. Pierrepont.

---

22 MR M. C. BANKS, Sandy
Postal: **Manor Farm, Manor Farm Road, Waresley, Sandy, Bedfordshire, SG19 3BX.**
Contacts: **PHONE (01767) 650563 FAX (01767) 652988 MOBILE (07860) 627370**

1 5, Ch g Topanoora—High 'b' **Mr M. C. Banks**
2 **IRISH PREACHER (IRE)**, 6, br g Presenting—Cherl Bo-A **Mr M. C. Banks**
3 **KING CLAUDIUS (IRE)**, 9, b g King's Ride—Lepida **Mr M. C. Banks**
4 **POLY AMANSHAA (IRE)**, 13, b br g Nashamaa—Mombones **Mr M. C. Banks**

23 MR J. BARCLAY, Glenfarg
Postal: **St Serf's, The Cobbles, Kinnesswood, KY13 9HL.**
Contacts: **PHONE (01592) 840331 MOBILE (07709) 878676**
E-MAIL ccbarclay@btopenworld.com

1 **AUGUST ROSE (IRE)**, 5, b br m Accordion—Lockersleybay (IRE) **Mr Scott Rose**
2 **BLACKOUT (IRE)**, 10, b g Black Monday—Fine Bess **Mr J. Barclay**
3 **SILVER PEARL**, 14, gr g Insan (USA)—Vanishing Trick **Miss Linda Wood**
4 **SWORDS AT DAWN (IRE)**, 4, ch f Daggers Drawn (USA)—Caraway **Mr J. Barclay**

Assistant Trainer: Miss Caroline Barclay & James Barclay Jnr

24 MRS T. M. BARFOOT-SAUNT, Wotton-under-Edge
Postal: **Cosy Farm, Huntingford, Charfield, Wotton-under-Edge, Gloucestershire, GL12 8EY.**
Contacts: **PHONE (01453) 520312 MOBILE (07976) 360626**

1 **BAYOSS**, 9, b g Commanche Run—Baylough Lady (IRE) **Mrs T. M. Barfoot-Saunt**
2 **MIXSTERTHETRIXSTER (USA)**, 9, b g Alleged (USA)—Parliament House (USA) **Mrs T. M. Barfoot-Saunt**
3 **PENNYS FROM HEAVEN**, 11, gr g Generous (IRE)—Heavenly Cause (USA) **The Dando Consortium**
4 **TWENTY TO EIGHT**, 9, b g Faustus (USA)—Leilaway **T. S. Ide**

Other Owners: Mr M. R. Parker, Mr B. N. Scholfield.

Amateur: Mr Geoff Barfoot-Saunt.

25 MR D. W. BARKER, Richmond
Postal: **Tancred Grange, Scorton, Richmond, North Yorkshire, DL10 6AB.**
Contacts: **WORK (01325) 378266 HOME (01748) 811371 FAX (01325) 378266
MOBILE (07836) 260149 E-MAIL david.barker513@tesco.net**

1 **CELTIC MILL**, 7, b g Celtic Swing—Madam Millie **P. Asquith**
2 **ESREEN**, 4, ch f Bijou d'inde—Audeen **D. G. Clayton**
3 **FOX COVERT (IRE)**, 4, b g Foxhound (USA)—Serious Contender (IRE) **Mr D. W. Barker**
4 **MECCA'S MATE**, 4, gr f Paris House—Clancassie **D. T. J. Metcalfe**
5 **MR WOLF**, 4, b g Wolfhound (USA)—Madam Millie **P. Asquith**
6 **RED MOUNTAIN**, 4, b g Unfuwain (USA)—Red Cascade (IRE) **Burns Farm Racing**
7 **SIERRA VISTA**, 5, ch m Atraf—Park Vista **D. T. J. Metcalfe**
8 **SUMMER SPECIAL**, 5, b g Mind Games—Summerhill Special (IRE) **Alba Racing Syndicate**
9 **TANCRED IMP**, 4, b f Atraf—Tancred Mischief **Mr D. W. Barker**
10 **TANCRED MISS**, 6, b m Presidium—Mischievous Miss **Mrs S. J. Barker**
11 **WHINHILL HOUSE**, 5, ch g Paris House—Darussalam **J. J. Crosier**

THREE-YEAR-OLDS

12 **BRUT**, b g Mind Games—Champenoise **Mr D. W. Barker**
13 **DORN DANCER (IRE)**, b f Danehill Dancer (IRE)—Appledorn **The Ebor Partnership**
14 **HIGHLAND FAIR (IRE)**, b f Orpen (USA)—Fairy Highlands (IRE) **Mr D. W. Barker**
15 **MUARA**, ch f Wolfhound (USA)—Darussalam **Mr D. W. Barker**
16 **SPECIALISE**, b f Atraf—Summerhill Special (IRE) **Miss A. Cliff**
17 **STAR SIGN**, b f Robellino (USA)—Amid The Stars **G. N. Parker**
18 **TANCRED SPRITE**, b f Atraf—Tancred Mischief **Mr D. W. Barker**
19 **WOLFMAN**, ch g Wolfhound (USA)—Madam Millie **P. Asquith**

TWO-YEAR-OLDS

20 Ch f 31/3 Danzig Connection (USA)—Amid The Stars (Midyan (USA)) **P. Asquith**
21 **CAPE SYDNEY (IRE)**, b f 9/4 Cape Cross (IRE)—Lady At War (Warning) (21461) **Mr M. Sumner**
22 **CASH FLOW**, b f 15/4 Mtoto—Little Change (Grundy) **Mrs John Trotter**
23 Ch f 27/2 City On A Hill (USA)—Cat's Tale (Catrail (USA)) (6706) **The Ebor Partnership**
24 **CHOYSIA**, b f 24/4 Pivotal—Bonica (Rousillon (USA)) **Mrs John Trotter**
25 **FOX FLIGHT (IRE)**, b c 9/2 Brave Act—Danz Danz (Efisio) (8047) **Mr & Mrs W. Barker**
26 **HYPNOSIS**, b f 7/3 Mind Games—Salacious (Sallust) (3200) **Mr D. W. Barker**
27 B f 28/2 Bahamian Bounty—Tick Tack (Primo Dominie) **P. Asquith**

Other Owners: Mr W. R. Asquith, Mr P. Cartmell, Mr S. Williams.

Assistant Trainer: Pat Barker & Samantha Barker

26 MISS S. BARKER, Foston
Postal: **Foston Stud, Hay Lane, Foston, Derbyshire, DE65 5PJ.**
Contacts: **PHONE (01283) 585036 MOBILE (07720) 854997**

1 **PRINCE TARQUIN**, 5, br g Overbury (IRE)—Civiki **Miss S. Barker**

Assistant Trainer: W A Corten

27 SIR J. BARLOW, Nantwich
Postal: **Ash House, Brindley, Nantwich, Cheshire, CW5 8HX.**
Contacts: **OFFICE (01270) 524339 FAX (01270) 524047**

1 **IVERAIN (FR)**, 9, b g Le Riverain (FR)—Ursala (FR) **Sir John & Lady Barlow**
2 **LORD TIDDLYPUSH (IRE)**, 7, b g Lord Americo—Ag Rith Abhaile **Sir John & Lady Barlow**
3 **ROWAN CASTLE**, 9, ch g Broadsword (USA)—Brass Castle (IRE) **Sir John & Lady Barlow**
4 **SILENT VOICE (IRE)**, 8, ch g Unfuwain (USA)—Symeterie (USA) **Sir John & Lady Barlow**

28 MR M. A. BARNES, Brampton
Postal: **Tarnside, Farlam, Brampton, Cumbria, CA8 1LA.**
Contacts: **PHONE/FAX (01697) 746675**
E-MAIL anne.barnes1@btinternet.com

1 **ALCHEMYSTIC (IRE)**, 5, b g In The Wings—Kama Tashoof **Thirdtimelucky**
2 **CROFTON ARCH**, 5, b g Jumbo Hirt (USA)—Joyful Imp **Mrs E. M. Dixon**
3 **HAPPY BOY (IRE)**, 4, b g Victory Note (USA)—Pepper And Salt (IRE) **T. A. Barnes**
4 **PIKESTAFF (USA)**, 7, ch g Diesis—Navarene (USA) **J. M. Carlyle**
5 **REGAL LEADER**, 6, b g Mistertopogigo (IRE)—Princess Zena **Purple Patch Racing**
6 **ROY MCAVOY (IRE)**, 7, b g Danehill (USA)—Decadence **T. A. Barnes**
7 **SKIDDAW JONES**, 5, b g Emperor Jones (USA)—Woodrising **J. R. Wills**
8 **TORKIN WIND**, 4, ch g Chocolat de Meguro (USA)—Helm Wind **S. C. Brown**
9 **TORKINKING (IRE)**, 6, b g Supreme Leader—Nicola's News (IRE) **J. G. Graham**

THREE-YEAR-OLDS

10 **INDIAN WIND**, ch g Chocolat de Meguro (USA)—Helm Wind **Mr M. A. Barnes**

Other Owners: Mr J. Dixon, Mr N. Ricciopo, Mr Scott Lowther, S. Nightingale, Mr T. Yates.

Jockey (NH): Peter Buchanan, A. Thornton. **Conditional:** D. McGann.

29 MR R. E. BARR, Middlesbrough
Postal: **Carr House Farm, Seamer, Stokesley, Middlesbrough, Cleveland, TS9 5LL.**
Contacts: **PHONE (01642) 710687/713177 MOBILE (07711) 895309**
E-MAIL christinebar1@aol.com

1 **BORODINSKY**, 4, b g Magic Ring (IRE)—Valldemosa **Mrs C. Barr**
2 **DARK CHAMPION**, 5, b g Abou Zouz (USA)—Hazy Kay (IRE) **A. Suddes**
3 **DUMADIC**, 8, b g Nomadic Way (USA)—Duright **R. P. Willis**
4 **ERUPT**, 12, b g Beveled (USA)—Sparklingsovereign **Mrs C. Barr**
5 **FIRST BASE**, 6, ch g First Trump—Rose Music **M. O'Hair**
6 **FRIMLEY'S MATTERRY**, 5, b g Bluegrass Prince (IRE)—Lonely Street **Mrs C. Barr**
7 **IN GOOD FAITH**, 13, b g Beveled (USA)—Dulcidene **P. Cartmell**
8 **LOUGHLORIEN (IRE)**, 6, b g Lake Coniston (IRE)—Fey Lady (IRE) **P. Cartmell**
9 **MEHMAAS**, 9, b g Distant Relative—Guest List **Cloughton Racing Partnership**
10 **NEXT FLIGHT (IRE)**, 6, b g Woodborough (USA)—Sans Ceriph (IRE) **Mr Malcolm O'Hair, Mrs C. Barr**
11 **NOBLE PURSUIT**, 8, b g Pursuit of Love—Noble Peregrine **P. Cartmell**
12 **PAY TIME**, 6, ch m Timeless Times (USA)—Payvashooz **Mrs C. Barr**
13 **ROYAL AWAKENING (IRE)**, 4, b g Ali-Royal (IRE)—Morning Surprise **Mrs C. Barr**
14 **STRENSALL**, 8, b g Beveled (USA)—Payvashooz **Mr R. E. Barr**

MR R. E. BARR—continued

THREE-YEAR-OLDS

15 **BLACK EYED PEA**, gr f Grey Desire—Cheeky Pigeon **Mrs C. Barr**
16 **BORN FOR DIAMONDS (IRE)**, b f Night Shift (USA)—Kirri (IRE)
17 **NIGHT GUEST (IRE)**, b c Danehill Dancer (IRE)—Meadow Grass (IRE) **Mrs C. Barr**

Other Owners: Robert A. Atkinson, J. Pratt, Miss J. Sawney.

Assistant Trainer: Mrs C Barr

Amateur: Miss V. Barr.

---

30   **MR T. D. BARRON, Thirsk**
Postal: **Maunby House, Maunby, Thirsk, North Yorkshire, YO7 4HD.**
Contacts: **PHONE (01845) 587435**

1 **BLONDE STREAK (USA)**, 5, ch m Dumaani (USA)—Katiba (USA) **Mrs L. E. Jones**
2 **COALAMI (USA)**, 4, b g Bianconi (USA)—Luppiano (USA) **L. G. O'Kane**
3 **DISPOL KATIE**, 4, ch f Komaite (USA)—Twilight Time **W. B. Imison**
4 **DISPOL VELETA**, 4, b f Makbul—Foxtrot Pie **W. B. Imison**
5 **FAMILIAR AFFAIR**, 4, b g Intikhab (USA)—Familiar (USA) **N. R. Shields**
6 **FLIPANDO (IRE)**, 4, b g Sri Pekan (USA)—Magic Touch **Mrs J. Hazell**
7 **GIFTED FLAME**, 6, b g Revoque (IRE)—Little Lady Leah (USA) **R. C. Miquel**
8 **IMPERIAL ECHO (USA)**, 4, b g Labeeb—Regal Baby (USA) **J. W. Stephenson**
9 **LUALUA**, 4, ch g Presidium—Tawny **B. Hathaway**
10 **MISTRESS TWISTER**, 4, b f Pivotal—Foreign Mistress **D. Scott**
11 **NATHAN BRITTLES (USA)**, 5, ch g Cat's Career (USA)—Doc's Answer (USA) **S. Vickers**
12 **OFF BEAT (USA)**, 4, ch g Mister Baileys—Off Off (USA) **D. G. Pryde**
13 **OLD BAILEY (USA)**, 5, gr g Lit de Justice (USA)—Olden Lek (USA) **J. Baggott**
14 **PALACE THEATRE (IRE)**, 4, b g Imperial Ballet (IRE)—Luminary **Mr C. McHale**
15 **PARTNERS IN JAZZ**, 4, gr c Jambalaya Jazz (USA)—
                        Just About Enough (USA) **Sporting Occasions Racing No 2**
16 **PAWN IN LIFE (IRE)**, 7, b g Midhish—Lady-Mumtaz **L. G. O'Kane**
17 **PENWELL HILL (USA)**, 6, b g Distant View (USA)—Avie's Jili (USA) **Mrs E. Jones**
18 **QUINCANNON**, 4, b g Kayrawan—Sulalat **G. Houghton**
19 **RACCOON (IRE)**, 5, b g Raphane (USA)—Kunucu (IRE) **Mr P. D. Savill**
20 **RAFFERTY (IRE)**, 6, ch g Lion Cavern (USA)—Badawi (USA) **N. R. Shields**
21 **RISING SHADOW (IRE)**, 4, b g Efisio—Jouet **G. Morrill**
22 **SILVERHAY**, 4, b g Inchinnor—Moon Spin **D. C. Rutter, P. J. Huntbach**
23 **THORNABY GREEN**, 4, b g Whittingham (IRE)—Dona Filipa **Thornaby Racing Club**
24 **TRANCE (IRE)**, 5, ch g Bahhare (USA)—Lady of Dreams (IRE) **N. R. Shields**
25 **TYNE**, 4, b g Komaite (USA)—High Typha **B. Hathaway**
26 **UNDETERRED**, 9, ch g Zafonic (USA)—Mint Crisp (IRE) **Mr P. D. Savill**
27 **WAHOO SAM (USA)**, 5, ch g Sandpit (BRZ)—Good Reputation (USA) **Mr C. A. Washbourn**
28 **ZARIANO**, 5, b g Emperor Jones (USA)—Douce Maison (IRE) **N. R. Shields**
29 **ZERO TOLERANCE (IRE)**, 5, ch g Nashwan (USA)—Place de l'opera **The Hornsey Warriors Racing Syndicate**

THREE-YEAR-OLDS

30 **BALGARTH (USA)**, b g Zamindar (USA)—Vaguely Regal (IRE) **Mrs J. M. MacPherson**
31 **BRACE OF DOVES**, b g Bahamian Bounty—Overcome **Dovebrace Ltd**
32 **CARNIVORE**, ch c Zafonic (USA)—Ermine (IRE) **The Meat Eaters**
33 **COMMENDABLE COUP (USA)**, b br c Commendable (USA)—Bird Dance (USA) **Orchard Partnership**
34 **DAISY POOTER (IRE)**, b f Charnwood Forest (IRE)—Idrak **S. Woodall**
35 **DISPOL ISLE (IRE)**, gr f Trans Island—Pictina **W. B. Imison**
36 **GYPSY FAIR**, b f Compton Place—Marjorie's Memory (IRE) **Harrowgate Bloodstock Ltd**
37 **IMPERIAL DYNASTY (USA)**, b c Devil's Bag (USA)—Leasears (USA) **J. W. Stephenson**
38 **LADY PHANTASTICA (FR)**, b f Muhtathir—Phantastica (FR) **R. J. Searle**
39 **LAMH EILE (IRE)**, b f Lend A Hand—Mothers Footprints (IRE) **Oghill House Stud**
40 **LERIDA**, ch g Groom Dancer (USA)—Catalonia (IRE) **D. G. Pryde**
41 **LORD MAYFAIR (USA)**, b g Silic (FR)—Spring Wedding (USA) **Mr C. McHale**
42 **MELVINO**, b g Josr Algarhoud (IRE)—Safe Secret **Mr Theo Williams and Mr Charles Mocatta**
43 **NAMIR (IRE)**, b c Namid—Danalia (IRE) **U. K. Letterbox Marketing Ltd (N.L.M.)**
44 **NEPAL (IRE)**, ch f Monashee Mountain—Zetonic **Kevin Shaw**
45 **ONE GREAT IDEA (IRE)**, b g Night Shift (USA)—Scenaria (IRE) **U. K. Letterbox Marketing Ltd (N.L.M.)**

MR T. D. BARRON—continued

46 **PEDLAR OF DREAMS (IRE)**, b f Fayruz—Beautyofthepeace (IRE) **G. E. Griffiths**
47 **RANCHO CUCAMONGA (IRE)**, ch f Raphane (USA)—Kunucu (IRE) **Mr P. D. Savill**
48 **SWEET POTATO (IRE)**, b f Monashee Mountain (USA)—Villafranca (IRE) **Harrowgate Bloodstock Ltd**
49 **ULA GOODNIGHT (USA)**, b br f Elnadim (USA)—Ensoleille (USA) **T. D. Barron**
50 **VENETIAN LULLABY (USA)**, b br f Lear Fan (USA)—Wellomond (FR) **Mr C. A. Washbourn**

TWO-YEAR-OLDS

51 **AMY LOUISE (IRE)**, ch f 24/2 Swain (IRE)—Mur Taasha (USA) (Riverman (USA)) (18000) **Mr P. D. Savill**
52 B c 2/3 King of Kings (IRE)—Araza (USA) (Arazi (USA))
53 B c 2/5 Muhtarram (USA)—Ashover Amber (Green Desert (USA)) **Mrs L. E. Jones**
54 Ch f 3/4 Piccolo—Cardinal Press (Sharrood (USA)) **R. J. Searle**
55 Ch c 27/2 Lure (USA)—Catala (USA) (Northern Park (USA)) (18621)
56 Ch c 28/1 Running Stag (USA)—Flashy Cat (USA) (Mountain Cat (USA)) (11705)
57 B g 24/1 Piccolo—Flourish (Selkirk (USA)) (12000) **Mrs J. Hazell**
58 B c 16/4 Dansili—Fudge (Polar Falcon (USA)) (32000) **Mrs J. M. MacPherson**
59 **GIFTED GLORI**, ch c 6/3 Vettori (USA)—Azira (Arazi (USA)) (7500) **R. C. Miquel**
60 Ch f 2/3 Beckett (IRE)—High Demand (Sabrehill (USA)) (1400)
61 **HORSEFAIR DANCER**, b f 23/3 Almaty (IRE)—Minskip Miss (Lucky Wednesday)) (800) **Mrs A. E. Pallister**
62 **IMPERIAL SWORD**, b c 7/3 Danehill Dancer (IRE)—Hajat (Mujtahid (USA)) (42000) **J. W. Stephenson**
63 **IMPERIAL VENTURE (USA)**, ro c 14/4 Woodman (USA)—Be Elusive (USA) (With Approval (CAN)) (30327)
64 B br c 14/5 Arch (USA)—Inca Dove (USA) (Mr Prospector (USA)) (20750) **D. Scott**
65 B c 3/2 First Trump—Lady Caroline Lamb (IRE) (Contract Law (USA)) (5500) **S. Knighton**
66 Ch c 19/4 First Trump—Lily Missoula (USA) (Dayjur (USA))
67 B c 23/3 First Trump—Meeson Times (Enchantment) (1000)
68 B c 31/3 Jambalaya Jazz (USA)—Miss U Mama (USA) (Minshaanshu Amad (USA)) (3990)
69 B c 16/3 Komaite (USA)—On The Wagon (Then Again) (3500)
70 B c 14/3 Green Desert (USA)—Pure Misk (Rainbow Quest (USA)) (105000)
71 **ROYAL MOON (USA)**, ch c 5/3 Royal Academy (USA)—Wedding Gift (FR) (Always Fair (USA)) (10641)
72 B f 27/3 Soviet Star (USA)—Ruby Rose (Red Ransom (USA)) (3800)
73 **SCHERZO A LA RUSSE (USA)**, b br f 2/5 Stravinsky (USA)—Zadracarta (CAN) (Bold Ruckus (USA)) (7448)
74 **SEA SALT**, b c 9/2 Titus Livius (FR)—Carati (USA) (Green Desert (USA)) (12000)
75 **SIR ORPEN (IRE)**, gr c 3/3 Orpen (USA)—Yalciyna (Nishapour (FR)) (38000) **Mr O. Boyle**
76 **SKHILLING SPIRIT**, b c 15/3 Most Welcome—Calcavella (Pursuit of Love) (6200) **Mr I. Hill**
77 Ch c 5/5 Pivotal—Starring (FR) (Ashkalani (IRE)) (46000) **Mrs J. Hazell**
78 **SUNBOLT (IRE)**, b c 13/2 Barathea (IRE)—Sunset (IRE) (Polish Precedent (USA)) (30000) **Mrs J. Hazell**
79 **TEMPESTUOUS SEA (IRE)**, ch f 27/3 Tagula (IRE)—Mrs Siddons (IRE) (Royal Academy (USA)) (26000)
80 B c 22/4 Luhuk (USA)—Ursula (VEN) (Phone Trick (USA)) (11173)
81 Ch c 4/2 Compton Place—Wathbat Mtoto (Mtoto) (15000) **Harrowgate Bloodstock Ltd**
82 **WENSLEYDALE STAR**, b g 11/5 Alzao (USA)—
            Janiceland (IRE) (Foxhound (USA)) (15000) **Wensleydale Bacon Ltd**

Other Owners: K. J. Alderson, J. A. Bailie, T. D. Barron, Mrs T. D. Barron, E. Buck, Mrs D. Catlow, Mel Catlow, R. H. Coombe, T. C. Cox, P. M. Hobbs, Mr P. Hyland, Mr H. D. Hyland, J. Knotts, A. S. Kundi, J. M. Lamont, Mrs J. R. Lamont, Mr G. Marshall, Miss E. L. Murphy, R. Nolan.

Jockey (flat): D. Mernagh. **Apprentice:** Phillip Makin.

---

31   **MR F. M. BARTON, Tarporley**
Postal: **Radley Wood Farm, Whitchurch Road, Spurstow, Tarporley, Cheshire, CW6 9TD.**
Contacts: **PHONE (01829) 260453 MOBILE (07833) 960632**

1 **GENERAL CUSTER (IRE)**, 11, b g Buckskin (FR)—Cottage Theme **Mr F. M. Barton**

Amateur: Miss S. Sharratt.

---

32   **MR P. BARY, Chantilly**
Postal: **5 Chemin des Aigles, 60500 Chantilly, France.**
Contacts: **PHONE +33 (0) 3 44 57 14 03 FAX +33 (0) 3 44 67 20 15**
E-MAIL p-bary@wanadoo.fr

1 **ABAKILA (IRE)**, 4, b c Sadler's Wells (USA)—Angelica Tree (CAN) **Ecurie J. L. Bouchard**
2 **AMERICAN TRUST (USA)**, 4, b c Sadler's Wells (USA)—Lady of Glamour (USA) **Cash Asmussen**
3 **ATLANDO (IRE)**, 4, b c Hernando (FR)—Atlantic Blue (USA) **Sanremo '85 Srl**

MR P. BARY—continued

4 **BLUE CANARI (FR)**, 4, ch c Acatenango (GER)—Delicieuse Lady **Ecurie J. L. Bouchard**
5 **CASTLE RISING**, 4, b c Indian Ridge—Orford Ness **K. Abdulla**
6 **HELIKE (USA)**, 4, ch c Rahy (USA)—East of The Moon (USA) **The Niarchos Family**
7 **HIGH FLASH (IRE)**, 4, ch c Selkirk (USA)—Hint of Silver (USA) **Ecurie Stella Maris**
8 **LEDI**, 4, b c Night Shift (USA)—Napoli **The Niarchos Family**
9 **SENSIBLE (FR)**, 7, b h Sadler's Wells (USA)—Raisonnable **The Niarchos Family**

THREE-YEAR-OLDS

10 **BAZART**, b c Highest Honor (FR)—Summer Exhibition **K. Abdullah**
11 **BEYOND THE DREAM (USA)**, b f Fusaichi Pegasus (USA)—East of The Moon (USA) **The Niarchos Family**
12 **BLESSING**, b f Dubai Millennium—Hydro Calido (USA) **Lordship Stud**
13 **BLUE KITE**, b c Kingmambo (USA)—Black Penny (USA) **Skymarc Farm Inc.**
14 **CONNIVING**, b f Machiavellian (USA)—Bolas **K. Abdullah**
15 **DESERT CHILD**, b c Green Desert (USA)—Bedside Story **Grundy Bloodstock Ltd**
16 **DIVINE PROPORTIONS (USA)**, b f Kingmambo (USA)—Myth To Reality (FR) **The Niarchos Family**
17 **DIVINE REINE (USA)**, b f Bahri (USA)—Divinite (USA) **Mrs P. de Moussac**
18 **FAST ENOUGH (FR)**, b c Anabaa (USA)—Odalisque (IRE) **Ecurie J. L. Bouchard**
19 **FEE DU NORD**, b f Inchinnor—Fee Des Mers **Baron E. de Rothschild**
20 **FOUNTAIN OF PEACE (USA)**, ch f Kris S (USA)—Coup de Genie (USA) **The Niarchos Family**
21 **GESTURE**, b c Bahri (USA)—Stark Ballet (USA) **K. Abdullah**
22 **GLAZED FROST (FR)**, b f Verglas (IRE)—Vol Sauvage (FR) **D. Jacob**
23 **GREAT LOOP (USA)**, b c Seattle Slew (USA)—Turning Wheel (USA) **The Niarchos Family**
24 **HOUSEKEEPING**, b f Dansili—Houseproud (USA) **K. Abdullah**
25 **LATCHKEY**, ch f Unfuwain (USA)—Tarocchi (USA) **K. Abdullah**
26 **LONESOME ME (FR)**, b f Zafonic (USA)—Lone Spirit (IRE) **Skymarc Farm Inc.**
27 **LOVE ME WELL**, b c Sadler's Wells (USA)—Love Divine **Ecurie J. L. Bouchard**
28 **LUTIKAI**, b c Sadler's Wells (USA)—Lungta **The Niarchos Family**
29 **MACHINALE (USA)**, ch f Kingmambo (USA)—Gold Bust **Ecurie J. L. Bouchard**
30 **MARINE LIFE**, b c Unfuwain (USA)—Aquamarine **K. Abdullah**
31 **MARTINES (FR)**, gr f Linamix (FR)—Fracci **Grundy Bloodstock Ltd**
32 **MATERNELLE (FR)**, ro f Machiavellian (USA)—Mare Aux Fees **Ecurie J. L. Bouchard**
33 **MISDIRECT**, b f Darshaan—Miscast **Lady O'Reilly**
34 **MORLANA (USA)**, b f More Than Ready (USA)—Tuscolana (CHI) **Mr R. B. Newton**
35 **MUSKETIER (GER)**, gr c Acatenango (GER)—Myth And Reality **Ecurie J. L. Bouchard**
36 **MYSTERY TWAIN**, b f Unfuwain (USA)—Mystery Tune **Baron E. de Rothschild**
37 **NAIYO**, b f Diktat—Nokomis **Scuderia Vittadini SRL**
38 **NID D'ABEILLES (IRE)**, b c Green Desert (USA)—Massarossa **Skymarc Farm Inc.**
39 **NIGHT DHU**, gr f Montjeu (IRE)—Kenmist **Saini Fasanotti U.**
40 **ODIN (FR)**, ch c Lahint (USA)—Heliette (FR) **G. Sandor**
41 **PALOMAR (USA)**, b c Chester House (USA)—Ball Gown (USA) **K. Abdullah**
42 **PERFECT CROSS (FR)**, b c Cape Cross (IRE)—Wavy Paz (FR) **D. Jacob**
43 **PRIVATE BANKING (FR)**, b f Anabaa (USA)—Aka Lady (FR) **Ecurie des Monceaux**
44 **QUESTO**, b c Zafonic (USA)—Quest of Fire (FR) **Ecurie Chalhoub**
45 **REINE D'AVRIL (FR)**, ch f Le Triton (USA)—La Malombree (FR) **P. Bary**
46 **ROYAL HIGHNESS (GER)**, b f Monsun (GER)—Reem Dubai (IRE) **Ecurie des Monceaux**
47 **SABIA (FR)**, b f Sadler's Wells (USA)—Remote Romance (USA) **The Niarchos Family**
48 **SAHARA SNOW**, gr f Linamix (FR)—Sahara Sunrise (USA) **Lady O'Reilly**
49 **SANOR (FR)**, b c Machiavellian (USA)—Soul Dream **The Niarchos Family**
50 **SERANDINE (IRE)**, ch f Hernando (FR)—Serafica **Lady O'Reilly**
51 **SHE ANN (IRE)**, b f Anabaa (USA)—She's All Class **Laghi SNC**
52 **SHIPPING LANE**, b c Grand Lodge (USA)—Docklands (USA) **K. Abdullah**
53 **SILK ROAD**, b f Dansili—Bold Empress (USA) **K. Abdullah**
54 **SPEAR POINT**, b c Spectrum (IRE)—Seralia **Ecurie Chalhoub**
55 **SPECTRALIA (JPN)**, b f Dream Well (FR)—Rangoon Ruby **The Niarchos Family**
56 **SPRING PARTY (IRE)**, b f Anabaa (USA)—Party Zane **Ecurie J. L. Bouchard**
57 **STELLA BLUE (FR)**, b f Anabaa (USA)—Libanoor **Ecurie Stella Maris**
58 **TIMIAS (USA)**, b c Seeking The Gold (USA)—Dragonada (USA) **The Niarchos Family**
59 **URBAN SUMMER (USA)**, b c Red Ransom (USA)—Kamaina (USA) **The Niarchos Family**
60 **YELLOW PURPLE (JPN)**, b f Dream Well (FR)—Moon Is Up **The Niarchos Family**

TWO-YEAR-OLDS

61 B f 28/1 Grand Slam (USA)—Angela Serra (Arctic Tern (USA)) **Skymarc Farm & Incisa Della Rochetta**
62 **ANNA DEESSE (FR)**, b f 2/4 Anabaa (USA)—
                      Anna Edes (FR) (Fabulous Dancer (USA)) (93896) **Ecurie des Monceaux**
63 **ATTIMA**, b f 14/3 Zafonic (USA)—Guarded (Eagle Eyed (USA)) **Ecurie J. L. Bouchard**

MR P. BARY—continued

64 **AUDELA (IRE)**, b f 28/2 Dream Well (FR)—Metaphor (USA) (Woodman (USA)) (26827) **The Niarchos Family**
65 **BALOR (FR)**, ch c 3/2 Hernando (FR)—Visions On Space (IRE) (Lure (USA)) **The Niarchos Family**
66 **BELLEROPHON (USA)**, ch c 21/5 Giant's Causeway (USA)—Aviance (Northfields (USA)) **The Niarchos Family**
67 B f 23/5 Kingmambo (USA)—Black Penny (USA) (Private Account (USA)) **Skymarc Farm Inc.**
68 **BOROBUDUR (USA)**, b c 7/2 Kingmambo (USA)—
 Chimes of Freedom (Private Account (USA)) **The Niarchos Family**
69 **BREAKING DAWN**, b f 5/2 Rainbow Quest (USA)—Biosphere (Pharly (FR)) **Grundy Bloodstock S R L**
70 **BREATHE (FR)**, ch f 13/2 Ocean of Wisdom (USA)—Yogya (USA) (Riverman (USA)) **The Niarchos Family**
71 **CHANGER TOUT CA (FR)**, b c 22/4 Johann Quatz (FR)—Replace (FR) (Deploy) (16767) **Thomas Li Chu Kwan**
72 **FAMOUS ANGEL (FR)**, ch f 5/4 In The Wings—Fay Wray (FR) (Primo Dominie) (117370) **Ecurie J. L. Bouchard**
73 **FAMOUS PAINTER (FR)**, b c 13/2 Peintre Celebre (USA)—
 Far Distance (USA) (Distant View (USA)) (117370) **Ecurie J. L. Bouchard**
74 **FIVE LAKES (USA)**, ch f 27/1 Coronado's Quest (USA)—Shoogle (USA) (A P Indy (USA)) **K. Abdullah**
75 B f 25/3 Anabaa (USA)—Genuine (FR) (Generous (IRE)) (100603) **Jean-Paul Van Gysel**
76 **GRANDE MELODY (IRE)**, b f 29/3 Grand Lodge (USA)—
 Crystal Melody (Nureyev (USA)) (134138) **Ecurie J. L. Bouchard**
77 B c 1/1 Pivotal—Hadra (USA) (Dayjur (USA)) **Mr Jean-Claude Seroul**
78 **HURRICANE MIST (IRE)**, ch f 29/1 Spinning World (USA)—
 Mare Nostrum (Caerleon (USA)) **The Niarchos Family**
79 B c 26/2 Night Shift (USA)—Imbabala (Zafonic (USA)) **K. Abdullah**
80 **INSOR (IRE)**, ch c 22/2 Sinndar (IRE)—
 Tresor Russe (IRE) (Soviet Star (USA)) (43594) **Madame Lily Ades and Madame Dominique Ades-Hazan**
81 Gr c 18/3 Linamix (FR)—Kiss Me Goodknight (First Trump) (40241) **Thomas Li Chu Kwan**
82 **KRANJI**, ch f 8/3 Dr Fong (Kris)—Kelang (Kris) **Grundy Bloodstock Ltd**
83 **LA GUIDECCA**, b f 27/4 Anabaa (USA)—La Splendide (FR) (Slip Anchor) (46948) **D. Jacob**
84 B c 16/2 Barathea (IRE)—Lame De Fond (FR) (Darshaan) (83836) **Thomas Li Chu Kwan**
85 **LARME (IRE)**, b f 29/3 Soviet Star (USA)—Laramie (USA) (Gulch (USA)) **Lady O'Reilly**
86 **LETO (USA)**, b c 14/3 Diesis—Lingerie (Shirley Heights) **The Niarchos Family**
87 **LIKASI (FR)**, b c 3/2 Kalanisi (IRE)—Liwana (IRE) (Rainbow Quest (USA)) (30181) **Sanremo '85 Srl**
88 B c 8/2 Zafonic (USA)—Matinee (Sadler's Wells (USA)) **K. Abdullah**
89 **MIND SAILING (IRE)**, b c 23/2 Dream Well (FR)—Moon Is Up (USA) (Woodman (USA)) **The Niarchos Family**
90 **MINE EXCAVATION (FR)**, ch f 28/1 Galileo (IRE)—Whakilyric (USA) (Miswaki (USA)) **The Niarchos Family**
91 Ch c 25/2 Alhaarth (IRE)—Misbegotten (IRE) (Baillamont (USA)) **Lady O'Reilly**
92 **MISS CLEM'S (FR)**, b f 3/3 Barathea (IRE)—Erinys (FR) (Kendor (FR)) (23474) **G. Larrieu**
93 **MOUSQUETON (FR)**, gr c 24/3 Linamix (FR)—Caerau (Nashwan (USA)) (40241) **Ecurie J. L. Bouchard**
94 **MUSICAL HORIZON (USA)**, b f 29/4 Distant View (USA)—Musicanti (Nijinsky (CAN)) **K. Abdullah**
95 **NIBBANA (USA)**, ch f 26/1 Giant's Causeway (USA)—
 Piquetnol (USA) (Private Account (USA)) **The Niarchos Family**
96 **PARTICULIERE**, ch f 7/4 Spectrum (IRE)—Party Zane (Zafonic (USA)) **Ecurie J. L. Bouchard**
97 **PENDRAGON (FR)**, ch c 9/3 Rahy (USA)—
 Turning Wheel (USA) (Seeking The Gold (USA)) **The Niarchos Family**
98 B f 20/2 Anabaa (USA)—Phone West (USA) (Gone West (USA)) **K. Abdullah**
99 B f 31/1 Hernando (FR)—Rasha's Realm (USA) (Woodman (USA)) (40241) **Ecurie des Monceaux**
100 B c 20/2 Deputy Commander (USA)—Reine Amandine (FR) (Marignan (USA)) (30181) **Ecurie Saint-Martin**
101 **ROYAL MIRAGE (FR)**, b c 9/4 Zafonic (USA)—Tiara (Risk Me (FR)) (60362) **Ecurie J. L. Bouchard**
102 **SERACINA**, ch f 25/3 Nashwan (USA)—Seralia (Royal Academy (USA)) **Lady O'Reilly**
103 **SPECIAL VISION (FR)**, ch f 27/3 Vettori (IRE)—Special Gallery (IRE) (Tate Gallery (USA)) **Mr R. B. Newton**
104 **SPICY WINGS (FR)**, b br c 4/3 In The Wings—Spicy Girl (FR) (Marignan (USA)) (67069) **Ecurie Chalhoub**
105 **STELLA NOVA (FR)**, b f 21/3 Bering—Libanoor (FR) (Highest Honor (FR)) (6706) **Ecurie Stella Maris**
106 B f 1/2 Dansili—Tarocchi (USA) (Affirmed (USA)) **K. Abdullah**
107 **THE AU SAHARA (FR)**, ch c 21/3 Green Tune (USA)—
 Helvetica (FR) (Cricket Ball (USA)) (77129) **Ecurie J. L. Bouchard**
108 Gr ro f 20/5 Cozzene (USA)—To The Rainbow (FR) (Rainbow Quest (USA)) (39904) **Ecurie des Monceaux**
109 **WATERPAINT**, ch c 13/3 Observatory (USA)—Aquarelle (Kenmare (FR)) **K. Abdullah**
110 **WEST INDIAN (IRE)**, ch c 4/4 Indian Ridge—Stella Berine (FR) (Bering) (147551) **Ecurie J. L. Bouchard**

Jockey (flat): C. P. Lemaire, T. Thulliez. **Apprentice:** M. Legaillard.

---

33 | **MR R. BASTIMAN, Wetherby**
Postal: **Goosemoor Farm, Warfield Lane, Cowthorpe, Wetherby, West Yorkshire, LS22 5EU.**
Contacts: **PHONE (01423) 359397**

1 **CLASSIC JAZZ (NZ)**, 10, br g Paris Opera (AUS)—Johnny Loves Jazz (NZ) **Miss J. E. Foster**
2 **DESERT FURY**, 8, b g Warning—Number One Spot **Mr R. Bastiman**
3 **FILLE GRIS**, 4, gr f Double Trigger (IRE)—Cool Grey **J. E. Endersby**

MR R. BASTIMAN—continued

4 **MAROMITO (IRE)**, 8, b g Up And At 'em—Amtico **Mrs C. B. Bastiman**
5 **ON EVERY STREET**, 4, b g Singspiel (IRE)—Nekhbet **Mr R. Bastiman**
6 **ONE LAST TIME**, 5, b g Primo Dominie—Leap of Faith (IRE) **P. C. Beaton-Brown**
7 **OUTWARD (USA)**, 5, b g Gone West (USA)—Seebe (USA) **P. C. Beaton-Brown**
8 **PEPPER ROAD**, 6, ch g Elmaamul (USA)—Floral Spark **Mr P. Julian**
9 **SEMENOVSKII**, 5, b g Fraam—Country Spirit **P. C. Beaton-Brown**
10 **SENNEN COVE**, 6, ch g Bering—Dame Laura (IRE) **Border Rail & Plant Limited**
11 **SUNNYSIDE ROYALE (IRE)**, 6, b g Ali-Royal (IRE)—Kuwah (IRE) **S. Durkin, P. Earnshaw**
12 **TUSCAN FLYER**, 7, b g Clantime—Excavator Lady **J. E. Endersby**
13 **VALIANT ROMEO**, 5, b g Primo Dominie—Desert Lynx (IRE) **Mrs P. Bastiman**
14 **WALLY WONDER (IRE)**, 7, ch g Magical Wonder (USA)—Sally Gap **R. J. Long**
15 **WERE NOT STOPPIN**, 10, b g Mystiko (USA)—Power Take Off **I. B. Barker**

THREE-YEAR-OLDS

16 **BORDERLESCOTT**, b c Compton Place—Jeewan **Border Rail & Plant Limited**
17 **SMIDDY HILL**, b f Factual (USA)—Hello Hobson's (IRE) **I. B. Barker**

TWO-YEAR-OLDS

18 **CHARMING PRINCESS**, b f 28/4 Primo Valentino (IRE)—
Via Dolorosa (Chaddleworth (IRE)) (1500) **B Selective Partnership**
19 **IMMACULATE RED**, ch g 16/3 Woodborough (USA)—Primula Bairn (Bairn (USA)) (2500) **Partnership**
20 **LONGY THE LASH**, b c 2/4 Contract Law (USA)—Hello Hobson's (IRE) (Fayruz) **R. J. Long**
21 **MEGALO MANIAC**, b c 9/4 Efisio—Sharanella (Shareef Dancer (USA)) (20000) **Mr R. Bastiman**

Other Owners: K. R. Barker, Mrs W. A. D. Craven, Miss F. J. Gibson, R. Hartley, P. Harwood, Mr G. J. Smith.

Jockey (flat): R. Ffrench, H. Bastiman. **Jockey (NH):** H. Bastiman. **Amateur:** Miss R. Bastiman.

---

34   MR C. C. BEALBY, Grantham
Postal: **North Lodge, Barrowby, Grantham, Lincolnshire, NG32 1DH.**
Contacts: **OFFICE** (01476) 564568 **FAX** (01476) 572391 **MOBILE** (07831) 538689
E-MAIL trainer@northlodgeracing.co.uk **WEBSITE** www.northlodgeracing.co.uk

1 **AVANTI TIGER (IRE)**, 6, b br g Supreme Leader—Reign of Terror (IRE) **Mr C. L. Martin**
2 **BLAME THE REF (IRE)**, 8, ch g Aahsaylad—Nags Head (IRE) **Michael Hill**
3 **BURNSIDE PLACE**, 5, b m Alderbrook—Knowing **The Fernnash Partners**
4 **CAVENDISH KNIGHT (IRE)**, 5, b g Warcraft (USA)—All Alright **North Lodge Racing**
5 **CLASSIC SIGHT**, 5, ch m Classic Cliche (IRE)—Speckyfoureyes **Dr & Mrs Why & Miss A. Storrs**
6 **COLMCILLE (IRE)**, 5, ch g Desert Story (IRE)—Lasting Peace (IRE) **A. Boughen**
7 **COUNTBACK (FR)**, 6, b g Anabaa (USA)—Count Me Out (FR) **Blake Kennedy Partnership**
8 **COURAGE UNDER FIRE**, 10, b g Risk Me (FR)—Dreamtime Quest **A Ram, A Baggie And Two Reds**
9 **DALUS PARK (IRE)**, 10, b g Mandalus—Pollerton Park **The Northern Echo Partnership**
10 **DI'S DILEMMA**, 7, b m Teenoso (USA)—Reve En Rose **T. W. Readett Bayley**
11 **ESKIMO PIE (IRE)**, 6, ch g Glacial Storm (USA)—Arctic Verb **I. S. Naylor**
12 **EXTRA SMOOTH**, 4, gr g Cloudings (IRE)—Miss Ondee (FR) **Mr C. L. Martin**
13 **FARMER TOM (IRE)**, 5, br g Lord Americo—Churchtown Mist **Michael Hill**
14 **FOURBOYSTOY (IRE)**, 6, ch g Roselier (FR)—Little Twig (IRE) **Farmers, Foresters & Financiers**
15 **GOLDEN PARACHUTE (IRE)**, 4, b g Executive Perk—Ardfallon (IRE) **I. S. Naylor**
16 **INDIAN LABURNUM (IRE)**, 8, b g Alphabatim (USA)—St Cristoph **Mrs F. J. Martin**
17 **MARSH ORCHID**, 4, b g Lahib (USA)—Majalis **North Lodge Racing**
18 **MAYYAS**, 5, b g Robellino (USA)—Amidst **Michael Hill**
19 **MOUSTIQUE DE L'ISLE (FR)**, 5, gr g Dom Alco (FR)—Gratiene de L'isle (FR) **Michael Hill**
20 **POINT OF ORIGIN (IRE)**, 8, b g Caerleon (USA)—Aptostar (USA) **Get Em Off**
21 **RAINBOW TREE**, 5, b g Rainbows For Life (CAN)—Little Twig (IRE) **Michael Hill**
22 **RIVER MARSHAL (IRE)**, 7, b g Synefos (USA)—Marshallstown **A. Boughen**
23 **SILVER SNITCH (IRE)**, 5, gr g Supreme Leader—Banderole (IRE) **Mrs L. M. Lamyman**
24 **SMURFIT (IRE)**, 9, ch g Anshan—Williams Girl (IRE) **R. A. Jenkinson**
25 **TYCOON TIM**, 6, b g Alflora (IRE)—Padykin **T. P. Radford**
26 **UNA ROSA PARA TI**, 4, gr f Silver Patriarch (IRE)—Manzanilla **North Lodge Racing**

Other Owners: Mr C. C. Bealby, M. G. H. Adcock, R. J. Adcock, Mrs E. A. Bingley, D. R. Blake, P. M. Clarkson, Mr W. Ferrier, C. J. Grindal, M. J. Hazard, Mrs J. C. Holt, R. J. Nash, Mr M. D. Ogburn, Mr J. Roome, N. Skinner, Mr L. Stewart, Mrs S. J. Storer.

Assistant Trainer: Matthew Bond

Jockey (NH): N. Fehily. **Conditional:** D. Flavin. **Amateur:** Mr S. Morris.

35 MR P. BEAUMONT, Brandsby
Postal: **Foulrice Farm, Brandsby, York, YO61 4SB.**
Contacts: **PHONE (01347) 888208 FAX (01347) 889033 MOBILE (07801) 529783**
E-MAIL peterbeaumont@btconnect.com

1 **BRIGHT DAWN (IRE)**, 6, br m Norwich—Bright Day (IRE) **I. P. Drury**
2 **CIONN MHALANNA (IRE)**, 7, b g Corrouge (USA)—Pennyland **Mr D. R. Brown & Miss E. E. Toland**
3 **CLOUDLESS DAWN**, 5, b m Cloudings (IRE)—Charlotte's Emma **Us Lot**
4 5, B g Oscar (IRE)—Far And Deep (IRE) **T. J. Hemmings**
5 **FENCOTE (IRE)**, 8, b g Norwich—Primrose Forest **Mrs K. M. Richardson**
6 **FENCOTE GOLD**, 5, ch g Bob's Return (IRE)—Goldaw **Mrs K. M. Richardson**
7 **FLIGHT COMMAND**, 7, ch g Gunner B—Wing On **N. W. A. Bannister**
8 **HUNTERS TWEED**, 9, ch g Nashwan (USA)—Zorette (USA) **T. J. Hemmings**
9 **HUSSARD COLLONGES (FR)**, 10, b g Video Rock (FR)—Ariane Collonges (FR) **N. W. A. Bannister**
10 5, B h Rakaposhi King—I'm Fine **P. Beaumont**
11 4, B c Rakaposhi King—I'm Fine **P. Beaumont**
12 **I'M NO FAIRY**, 6, b g Efisio—Fairywings **L. H. B. Syndicate**
13 **ITALIANO**, 6, b g Emperor Jones (USA)—Elka (USA) **Mrs M. Turner**
14 **JODANTE (IRE)**, 8, ch g Phardante (FR)—Crashtown Lucy **T. J. Hemmings**
15 **KYLIE TIME (IRE)**, 8, ch g Good Thyne (USA)—Miss Kylogue (IRE) **Mr & Mrs Raymond Anderson Green**
16 **LORD RODNEY (IRE)**, 6, b g Hatim (USA)—Howcleuch **Estio Racing**
17 5, B g Presenting—Merry Watt **T. J. Hemmings**
18 **MOOR SPIRIT**, 8, b g Nomadic Way (USA)—Navos **Mrs C. M. Clarke**
19 **MOORAMANA**, 6, ch g Alflora (IRE)—Petit Primitive **Mrs K. Ratcliffe**
20 **MR PRICKLE (IRE)**, 5, ch g Carroll House—Auntie Prickle Pin (IRE) **W. L. Smith**
21 **OCEAN DANCER**, 8, b g Primitive Rising (USA)—Bally Small **Mrs S. C. Sunter**
22 4, Ch f Silver Patriarch (IRE)—Pinch **P. Beaumont**
23 **PROFOWENS (IRE)**, 7, b g Welsh Term—Cutty Sark **T. J. Hemmings**
24 5, B m Presenting—Relkissimo **D. N. Yeadon**
25 5, B g Paris House—Renshaw Wood **Mrs J. M. Plummer**
26 **ROSE D'ARPAL (FR)**, 8, gr g April Night (FR)—Rose De Hoc (FR) **Fellowship Of The Rose Partnership**
27 **ROSINA COPPER**, 5, ch m Keen—Emilymoore **Mrs A. E. Dixon**
28 **SHARP SINGLE (IRE)**, 9, b m Supreme Leader—Pollyville **W. L. Smith**
29 **UPHAM LORD (IRE)**, 12, b g Lord Americo—Top O The Mall **Mrs E. W. Wilson**
30 **YOUNG FALCON**, 5, ch m Young Ern—Northern Falcon **P. A. H. Hartley**

Other Owners: P. Allison, Mr L. Barker, Mrs R. M. Barker, D. S. Bowring, Mrs D. L. Holloway, L. W. Lawson, Miss D. Midwinter, C. R. Parker, J. Ratcliffe, D. W. Thompson, R. E. Turner, Mr P. R. Woodcock-Jones.

Assistant Trainer: Patrick Holmes

Jockey (NH): Russ Garrity. **Amateur:** Mr Guy Brewer.

36 MR R. M. BECKETT, Lambourn
Postal: **Windsor House Stables, Crowle Road, Lambourn, Hungerford, Berkshire, RG17 8NR.**
Contacts: **PHONE/FAX (01488) 71099 MOBILE (07802) 219022**
E-MAIL trainer@rbeckett.com

1 **ACCENDERE**, 4, b g Machiavellian (USA)—Littlewick (IRE) **A.W.A. Partnership**
2 **DANEHILL STROLLER (IRE)**, 5, b g Danetime (IRE)—Tuft Hill **The Classic Strollers Partnership**
3 **DARK EMPRESS (IRE)**, 4, br f Second Empire (IRE)—Good Reference (IRE) **Lady Marchwood**
4 **EUROPEAN (ARG)**, 5, br h Nugget Point—Enfeitada (ARG) **Mr M. Lynch & Mrs R. Lycett Green**
5 **FIVE YEARS ON (IRE)**, 4, b g Desert Sun—Snowspin **Surf N'Turf Racing**
6 **LIGHT HEARTED LILY**, 6, b m Deploy—Darling Splodge **The Foxons Fillies Partnership**
7 **LYES GREEN**, 4, gr g Bien Bien (USA)—Dissolve **Absolute Solvents Ltd**
8 **OUR MONOGRAM**, 9, b g Deploy—Darling Splodge **The Foxons Fillies Partnership**
9 **VAMP**, 4, b f Dracula (AUS)—Circe **A. D. G. Oldrey**

THREE-YEAR-OLDS
10 **BIRD AWAY**, b f Bien Bien (USA)—Grace Browning **Mrs Robert Langton**
11 **BIRD OVER**, b f Bold Edge—High Bird (IRE) **Mrs Robert Langton**
12 **COME ON JONNY (IRE)**, b c Desert King (IRE)—Idle Fancy **Mr A. E. Frost**
13 **EPITOMISE**, b f Mind Games—Yanomami (USA) **D. A. Lucie-Smith**
14 **GRASP**, b c Kayf Tara—Circe **A. D. G. Oldrey**
15 **HIGH DAWN (IRE)**, b g Namid—Highbrook (USA) **Mrs P. H. Frost**

MR R. M. BECKETT—continued

16 **JENNA STANNIS**, ch f Wolfhound (USA)—Darling Splodge **The Foxons Fillies Partnership**
17 **JOHNNY JUMPUP (IRE)**, ch c Pivotal—Clarice Orsini **Mr & Mrs A. Briars**
18 **LITTLE WARNING**, b f Piccolo—Iltimas (USA) **C. F. Colquhoun**
19 **MINNESINGER**, b f Fraam—Rose Alto **Mrs L. M. Aykroyd**
20 **PENKENNA PRINCESS (IRE)**, b f Pivotal—Tiriana **Mrs H. M. Chamberlain**
21 **PURPLE DOOR**, b f Daggers Drawn (USA)—Carreamia **The Don't Touch Partnership**
22 **RED RUDY**, ch g Pivotal—Piroshka **Winding Wheel Partnership**
23 **TOXIQUE (IRE)**, b f Orpen (USA)—Lady Donna **Absolute Solvents Ltd**

TWO-YEAR-OLDS

24 Ch f 28/4 Pivotal—
　　　　Antonia's Double (Primo Dominie) (28000) **Mrs R. Aykroyd, R. J. Cornelius & The Countryside Alliance**
25 **BANTIKHI (IRE)**, b c 4/4 Intikhab (USA)—Limited Option (IRE) (Mujadil (USA)) (20000) **Bantikhi Partnership**
26 Ch f 20/3 King's Best (USA)—Bareilly (USA) (Lyphard (USA)) (28000) **T. W. Bloodstock Ltd**
27 **CARLOMAN**, ch c 5/4 King Charlemagne (USA)—
　　　　Jarrayan (Machiavellian (USA)) (3333) **R. Jones & J. Blyth Currie**
28 **CELTIC SPIRIT (IRE)**, ch c 27/2 Pivotal—Cavernista (Lion Cavern (USA)) (58000) **Mrs H. M. Chamberlain**
29 **CHARLIE DELTA**, b c 6/4 Pennekamp (USA)—Papita (IRE) (Law Society (USA)) (1619) **Absolute Solvents Ltd**
30 Ch g 13/4 Dracula (AUS)—Circe (Main Reef) **A. D. G. Oldrey**
31 **CZAHRELLA**, b f 3/5 Zaha (CAN)—Queen of Cologne (IRE) (Brief Truce (USA)) **Equadox Racing**
32 B c 10/2 Princely Heir (IRE)—Easy Going (Hamas (IRE)) (15000) **P. Rosas**
33 **INGRATITUDE (IRE)**, ch c 28/4 Inchinor—Merci (IRE) (Cadeaux Genereux) (10000) **Young Guns**
34 **LOOKER**, b f 5/2 Barathea (IRE)—Last Look (Rainbow Quest (USA)) **J. H. Richmond-Watson**
35 **MIDDLETON MINX**, b f 24/3 Foxhound (USA)—Franica (IRE) (Inzar (USA)) **Ms M. A. Rowlands**
36 **MIMITEH (USA)**, ch f 17/5 Maria's Mon (USA)—
　　　　Green Minstrel (FR) (Green Tune (USA)) (40241) **Absolute Solvents Ltd**
37 **PEARLY POLL**, ch f 7/5 Prince Sabo—Bit of A Tart (Distant Relative) (800) **Mrs I. M. Beckett**
38 **PLAYFUL**, b f 5/3 Piccolo—Autumn Affair (Lugana Beach) (15000) **Mrs L. M. Aykroyd**
39 **SOUNDS SIMLA (IRE)**, b f 9/3 Indian Rocket—Evocative (IRE) (Double Schwartz) (5029) **Millennium Madness**
40 **SPINNING RUBY**, b f 15/4 Pivotal—Red Rabbit (Suave Dancer (USA)) (34000) **The Axis Partnership**
41 **SPUNGER**, b f 24/3 Fraam—
　　　　Complimentary Pass (Danehill (USA)) (15000) **Frost Williams and Tweenhills Racing**
42 **VEILED APPLAUSE**, b c 12/4 Royal Applause—Scarlet Veil (Tyrnavos) (19000) **Wright and Wrong Partnership**

Other Owners: A. McCorn, A. Adams, R. Pegum, Mrs E. Fenston, Mrs M. Turney, Mrs K. Adams, Mrs J. M Blyth-Currie, J. Singh, J. Lee, K. Lawrence, Miss J. Morritt, Lady Daventry, Mrs J. M. Kirkpatrick, E. Prosser, M. Mitchell, P Mason, P Moloney, J. Hormaeche, Larksborough Stud, P. Deal, B. Furneaux, A. Murchie, J. Lake, J. Burgess, J. Foley, C. Von Sijpesteijn, Mrs E. Benyon, Mrs C. M. Briars, K. J. Craddock, M. S. Edwards, G. C. Hartigan, S. F. Oldrey, A. Owen, G. R. Pooley, N. D. Simmons, Mrs H. L. Smyly, R. F. Whitehouse, Mrs P. H. Williams, A. Williams.

Amateur: Mr R. V. Moore.

37　MR KEVIN BELL, Wantage
Postal: **The Office, North Farm, Fawley, Wantage, Oxfordshire, OX12 9NJ.**
Contacts: **OFFICE (01488) 638243 MOBILE (07881) 814688**
E-MAIL grace.muir@virgin.net

1 **BLUE STREAK (IRE)**, 8, ch g Bluebird (USA)—Fleet Amour (USA) **Mrs A. B. Ellis**
2 **DEFERLANT (FR)**, 8, ch g Bering—Sail Storm (USA) **Mrs G. McNeela**
3 **KING AT LAST**, 6, b g Zamindar (USA)—Louis' Queen (IRE) **Wayne and Hilary Thornton**
4 **MISCHIEF**, 9, ch g Generous (IRE)—Knight's Baroness **Mrs A. B. Ellis**
5 **POWER TO BURN**, 4, b g Superpower—Into The Fire **Red Hot Partnership**
6 **PRINCE SHAAMAAL**, 7, b g Shaamit (IRE)—Princess Alaska **The Upshire Racing Partnership**
7 **STATE OF BALANCE**, 7, ch m Mizoram (USA)—Equilibrium **North Farm Stud**
8 **TINTAC**, 4, b f Intikhab (USA)—Susquehanna Days (USA) **M. A. Collins**
9 **TRIGGERS DOUBLE**, 4, ch g Double Trigger (IRE)—Princess Alaska **No Fools Only Horses Partnership**
10 **WHAT A MONDAY**, 7, b g Beveled (USA)—Raise Memories **North Farm Partnership**

THREE-YEAR-OLDS

11 **EDGE OF ITALY**, ch f Bold Edge—Brera (IRE) **The Sing When You're Winning Partnership**
12 **GREENACRE LEGEND**, b c Faustus (USA)—Alice Holt **Fielden Racing**
13 **YOUNG BOLDRIC**, b g Faustus (USA)—Bold Byzantium **The Herewegoagain Partnership**

MR KEVIN BELL—continued

Other Owners: Miss C. Bullard, Ms L. Clark, Mr Paul Couchman, Mr Terence Couchman, Mr T. Leach, Mrs Alison Moir, Mr B. Scarre, Mrs C. Wilesmith, Miss N. Wiesenthal, Mr P. Osborne, Miss G. E. Muir, Mr & Mrs L. A. E. Hopkins, Mrs B. Harding, Mr Timothy Couchman, A. G. Greenfield, A. Harding, N. J. Hubbard, David J. Muir, Mrs A. Muir, Mrs N. M. Russell, Mr J. R. Woodhouse, Mrs B. J. Woodhouse.

Assistant Trainer: Miss J Ellis

Jockey (flat): C. Catlin, D. R. McCabe. **Jockey (NH):** Sean Curran, C. Llewellyn. **Amateur:** Miss J. Ellis.

38

MR M. L. W. BELL, Newmarket

Postal: **Fitzroy House, Newmarket, Suffolk, CB8 0JT.**
Contacts: **PHONE (01638) 666567 FAX (01638) 668000 MOBILE (07802) 264514**
E-MAIL mlwbell.racing@virgin.net WEBSITE www.michaelbellracing.co.uk

1 **BARKING MAD (USA)**, 7, b br g Dayjur (USA)—Avian Assembly (USA) **Mr Christopher Wright**
2 **BRAZILIAN TERRACE**, 5, ch m Zilzal (USA)—
    Elaine's Honor (USA) **Mrs G. Rowland-Clark & M. L. W. Bell Racing Ltd**
3 **BREAD OF HEAVEN**, 4, b f Machiavellian (USA)—Khubza **Usk Valley Stud**
4 **MAGIC STING**, 4, ch g Magic Ring (IRE)—Ground Game **Mrs D. J. R. Fenwick**
5 **OLIHIDER (USA)**, 4, gr g Woodman (USA)—Ingot's Dance Away (USA) **Mrs D. J. Higgins**
6 **RIVER OF BABYLON**, 4, b f Marju (IRE)—Isle of Flame **Mr Christopher Wright & The Hon Mrs J. M. Corbett**
7 **SHABERNAK (IRE)**, 6, gr g Akarad (FR)—Salinova (FR) **Thurloe Thoroughbreds VII**
8 **SILVER SASH (GER)**, 4, gr f Mark of Esteem (IRE)—Salinova (FR) **Baron F. C. Oppenheim**
9 **SOVIET THREAT (IRE)**, 4, ch g Soviet Star (USA)—
    Veiled Threat (IRE) **Mr Billy Maguire & M.L.W.Bell Racing Ltd**
10 **TEMPLE PLACE (IRE)**, 4, b c Sadler's Wells (USA)—Puzzled Look (USA) **Mr M. B. Hawtin**
11 **WOODCRACKER**, 4, ch g Docksider (USA)—Hen Harrier **Sir Thomas Pilkington**
12 **WUNDERBRA (IRE)**, 4, b f Second Empire (IRE)—Supportive (IRE) **Fitzroy Thoroughbreds**
13 **ZILCH**, 7, ch g Zilzal (USA)—Bunty Boo **Mary Mayall, Linda Redmond, Julie Martin**

THREE-YEAR-OLDS

14 **ABERDOVEY**, b f Mister Baileys—Annapurna (IRE) **Usk Valley Stud**
15 **BOLD DESIRE**, b f Cadeaux Genereux—Polish Romance (USA) **Cheveley Park Stud**
16 **BRIGHT MOLL**, b f Mind Games—Molly Brown **A Buxton P Fenwick & Lostford Manor Stud**
17 **COLOUR BLIND (IRE)**, b c Spectrum (IRE)—Sarooh's Love (USA) **Mr Raymond Tooth**
18 **COMTESSE LALANDE (USA)**, ch f King of Kings (IRE)—
    Beyond the Realm (USA) **Mr Christopher Wright & The Hon Mrs J. M. Corbett**
19 **COOL PANIC (IRE)**, b c Brave Act—Geht Schnell (USA) **D. W. & L. Y. Payne**
20 **COUNTING BLESSINGS**, b f Compton Place—
    Banco Suivi (IRE) **Mr Christopher Wright & The Hon Mrs J. M. Corbett**
21 **GLEN IDA**, ch c Selkirk (USA)—Yanka (USA) **Mr Andrew Buxton & Mr B J Warren**
22 **GOLDEN GATE (IRE)**, b c Giant's Causeway (USA)—Bay Queen **Mr B. J. Warren**
23 **GOOSE CHASE**, b g Inchinor—Bronzewing **Sir Thomas Pilkington**
24 **HIGHER LOVE (IRE)**, b f Sadler's Wells (USA)—Dollar Bird (IRE) **DGH Partnership**
25 **HOH INTREPID (IRE)**, b f Namid—Bazaar Promise **Mr David Allport & Mr Michael Lynch**
26 **HOH MY DARLING**, br f Dansili—Now And Forever (IRE) **Mr David Allport & HOH Oilfield Services**
27 **KAHIRA (IRE)**, ch f King's Best (USA)—Sine Labe (USA) **L. Lillingston**
28 **KISSING LIGHTS (IRE)**, b f Machiavellian (USA)—Nasaieb (IRE) **Mr M. B. Hawtin**
29 **LANGSTON BOY**, b g Namid—Blinding Mission (IRE) **Exors of the late D. J. Higgins**
30 **MISS TRUANT**, b f Zaha (CAN)—Miss Runaway **The Funny Hahas**
31 **MOTIVATOR**, b c Montjeu (IRE)—Out West (USA) **The Royal Ascot Racing Club**
32 **MYSTERIOSA**, b f Mujahid (USA)—Mrs Gray **Waney Racing Group Inc**
33 **PATRONAGE**, b c Royal Applause—Passionate Pursuit **Highclere Thoroughbred Racing (XXII)**
34 **PEARL'S A SINGER (IRE)**, ch f Spectrum (IRE)—Cultured Pearl (IRE) **Mr Christopher Wright**
35 **PEPPERMINT TEA (IRE)**, b f Intikhab (USA)—Karayb (IRE) **DGH Partnership & M. L. W. Bell Racing Ltd**
36 **PLANET (IRE)**, b g Soviet Star (USA)—Laurentia (USA) **Highclere Thoroughbred Racing (XX)**
37 **RED JAPONICA**, b f Daylami (IRE)—Red Camellia **Cheveley Park Stud**
38 **RED SAM (IRE)**, ch g Desert King (IRE)—Mustique Dream **Mr T. Neill MBE & M. L. W. Bell**
39 **ROYAL GAME**, b g Vettori (IRE)—Ground Game **P. T. Fenwick OBE**
40 **ROYAL PARDON**, b f Royal Applause—Miss Mercy (IRE) **Mr Billy Maguire**
41 **SILBER MOND**, gr g Monsun (GER)—Salinova (FR) **Baron F. C. Oppenheim**
42 **SKIDROW**, b c Bachir (IRE)—Flourishing (IRE) **Mr Raymond Tooth & Miss Debbie Dove**
43 **TINCTURE**, b f Dr Fong (USA)—Miss d'ouilly (FR) **Lady Carolyn Warren & The Duke of Roxburghe**
44 **USHINDI (IRE)**, b f Montjeu (IRE)—Fern **Mrs G. E. Rowland-Clark**

MR M. L. W. BELL—continued

45 **WHATATODO,** b f Compton Place—Emerald Dream (IRE) **Mr M. Talbot-Ponsonby & Partners**
46 **WHISTLE BLOWING (IRE),** ch g Forzando—Philgwyn **Mr Jim Ratcliffe & M. L. W. Bell Racing Ltd**
47 **WINDERMERE ISLAND,** b f Cadeaux Genereux—Corndavon (USA) **Mrs J. M. M. Scott**

TWO-YEAR-OLDS

48 Ch c 25/4 Stravinsky (USA)—Altair (USA) (Alydar (USA)) (100000) **H. E. Sheikh Rashid Bin Mohammed**
49 B f 11/2 Observatory (USA)—Always On My Mind (Distant Relative) **Mascalls Stud**
50 B f 21/1 Kingmambo (USA)—
    Amethyst (IRE) (Sadler's Wells) (USA)) (159616) **Mr Christopher Wright & Mr Michael Watt**
51 **ASCENDING STAR,** b c 28/4 Pivotal—Ascendancy (Sadler's Wells (USA)) **Cheveley Park Stud**
52 **BEETHOVENS FIFTH (IRE),** b c 13/2 Marju (IRE)—
    Diaspora (Kris) (31521) **Mr Christopher Wright & The Hon Mrs J. M. Corbett**
53 **CASSAVA (IRE),** b f 27/3 Vettori (IRE)—Maycocks Bay (Muhtarram (USA)) **Lady Bamford**
54 **CHOREOGRAPHY,** ch c 14/4 Medicean—Stark Ballet (USA) (Nureyev (USA)) **Cheveley Park Stud**
55 **CHRIS CORSA,** b c 19/1 Mark of Esteem (IRE)—Risque Lady (Kenmare (FR)) (30000) **Mr George Houghton**
56 **CLOCKWISE,** ch f 16/4 Pivotal—Sparkling (Kris) **Cheveley Park Stud**
57 **CRITIC (IRE),** b c 30/4 Fasliyev (USA)—
    Scruple (IRE) (Catrail (USA)) (30000) **Highclere Thoroughbred Racing XXX**
58 B c 26/2 Singspiel (IRE)—Croeso Cariad (Most Welcome) **Usk Valley Stud**
59 **CULRANE,** ch c 4/3 Lomitas—Sleepless (Night Shift (USA)) (25000) **Mrs Audrey Scotney & Mr Malcolm Joyce**
60 B f 15/1 Dr Fong (USA)—Datura (Darshaan) **The Duke of Devonshire**
61 **DIRECT DEBIT (IRE),** b c 6/1 Dansili—Dimple (Fairy King (USA)) (28000) **Mr Billy Maguire & M. L. W. Bell**
62 B c 29/3 Tagula (IRE)—Easy Pop (IRE) (Shernazar) (46947) **H. E. Sheikh Rashid Bin Mohammed**
63 **ENTHUSIUS,** b c 13/2 Generous (IRE)—Edouna (FR) (Doyoun) **Baron F. C. Oppenheim**
64 **FONIC ROCK (IRE),** b f 28/1 Zafonic (USA)—Blue Crystal (IRE) (Lure (USA)) (16766) **Fitzroy Thoroughbreds I**
65 **FORCES SWEETHEART,** b f 11/1 Allied Forces (USA)—
    Talighta (USA) (Barathea (IRE)) (20120) **Mr Richard I. Morris Jnr**
66 **GHOSTLY PET (IRE),** b br c 10/3 Spectrum (IRE)—
    Fabulous Pet (Somethingfabulous (USA)) (26827) **Mr Tim Redman & Mr Peter Philipps**
67 B f 3/5 Montjeu (IRE)—Glenarff (USA) (Irish River (FR)) (20000) **Mr Michael Tabor**
68 **HOLLY ACRES,** b f 1/5 Kalanisi (IRE)—Bay Queen (Damister (USA)) **Mr B. J. Warren**
69 Ch c 27/3 Lomitas—India Atlanta (Ahonoora) (30000) **M. L. W. Bell Racing Ltd**
70 **ITALIAN ROMANCE,** b c 21/4 Medicean—Polish Romance (USA) (Danzig (USA)) **Cheveley Park Stud**
71 B c 17/4 Robellino (USA)—Jezyah (USA) (Chief's Crown) (USA)) (8000) **B. R. H. Burrough**
72 Ch c 24/2 Alhaarth (IRE)—L'amour (USA) (Gone West (USA)) (80000) **H. E. Sheikh Rashid Bin Mohammed**
73 **LES SOEURS (IRE),** b f 7/2 Indian Lodge (IRE)—Manazil (IRE) (Generous (IRE)) (12500) **Mrs Maureen Buckley**
74 **MALECH (IRE),** b c 28/1 Bahhare (USA)—
    Choral Sundown (Night Shift (USA)) (30000) **Lord Blyth & Mr R. P. B. Michaelson**
75 B c 21/2 Montjeu (IRE)—
    Midnight Fever (Sure Blade (USA)) (320000) **H. E. Sheikh Rashid Bin Mohammed**
76 **MY LOVELY LADY (IRE),** b f 23/4 Cape Cross (IRE)—Lace Flower (Old Vic) (46947) **Mrs Moira Gershinson**
77 **MYSTIC HALO,** ch f 30/4 Medicean—Aglow (Spinning World (USA)) **Cheveley Park Stud**
78 **PANIC STATIONS,** b f 24/1 Singspiel (IRE)—
    Fiddle-Dee-Dee (IRE) (Mujtahid (USA)) (42000) **D. W. & L. Y. Payne**
79 **POUND SIGN,** ch c 3/3 Singspiel (IRE)—Profit Alert (IRE) (Alzao (USA)) (52000) **Fitzroy Thoroughbreds I**
80 B c 28/4 Green Desert (USA)—Priory Belle (IRE) (Priolo (USA)) (160000) **H. E. Sheikh Rashid Bin Mohammed**
81 **PTOLEMAC COSMOLOGY,** b c 23/4 Galileo (IRE)—
    Crystal Ring (IRE) (Kris) **Lady Carolyn Warren & M. L. W. Bell Racing Ltd**
82 B f 15/4 Alhaarth (IRE)—Reactress (USA) (Sharpen Up) **The Duke of Devonshire**
83 **RED EVIE (IRE),** b f 1/3 Intikhab (USA)—
    Malafemmena (IRE) (Nordico) (58000) **Mr T. Neill MBE & M. L. W. Bell**
84 **ROYAL BUNTING,** b c 5/2 Royal Applause—Baby Bunting (Wolfhound (USA)) (16000) **Mrs P. D. Gray**
85 B c 12/2 Montjeu (IRE)—Sallanches (USA) (Gone West (USA)) (348759) **Mr Michael Tabor**
86 B f 3/4 Revoque (IRE)—Shajara (FR) (Kendor (FR)) (73775) **Mr M. B. Hawtin**
87 **SOUFFLEUR,** b c 21/2 In The Wings—Salinova (FR) (Linamix (FR)) **Baron F. C. Oppenheim**
88 **STAR JASMINE,** b f 27/2 Grand Lodge (USA)—Shalimar (IRE) (Indian Ridge) (55000) **Lady Bamford**
89 **TAY BRIDGE (IRE),** ch c 30/1 Tagula (IRE)—
    Wild Liffey (USA) (Irish River (FR)) (15425) **Mr Christopher Wright & The Hon Mrs J. M. Corbett**
90 Ch c 12/3 Danehill Dancer (USA)—Tumble (Mtoto) (70000) **H. E. Sheikh Rashid Bin Mohammed**
91 **TURN ME ON (IRE),** b c 2/5 Tagula (IRE)—
    Jacobina (Magic Ring (IRE)) (38000) **Mr Christopher Wright & Mr David Murrell**
92 B br c 1/4 Giant's Causeway (USA)—
    Woodland Orchid (IRE) (Woodman (USA)) (120000) **H. E. Sheikh Rashid Bin Mohammed**
93 B gr c 13/4 Daylami (IRE)—Woodwin (IRE) (Woodman (USA)) (45000) **H. E. Sheikh Rashid Bin Mohammed**
94 B c 18/3 Sinndar (IRE)—Zivania (IRE) (Shernazar) (110000) **H. E. Sheikh Rashid Bin Mohammed**

MR M. L. W. BELL—continued

Other Owners: Mr George Archer, Mr & Mrs Derek Asplin, Mr Tony Bianchi, Mr Rob Baker, Miss Heather Chellingworth, Mrs Linda Dyer, Mr David Hardisty, Mr Richard Holt, Mr Steve Leoni, Mr & Mrs Rob Hughes, Mrs Christopher Wright, Mr & Mrs Peter Waney, Mr Alistair Simpson, Mr Michael Scotney, Mr Charles Rhodes, Mrs Sue Mercer, Mr K. J. Mercer, Mr & Mrs Gerry Lynch, Mr Frank Hendry, Mr Michael Flynn, F. M. Conway Ltd, The Hon Mrs C. Corbett, Miss D. S. Dove, Mrs J. F. Feerick, V. Feerick, Mrs R. M. Gray, The Hon H. M. Herbert, Mr M. W. Joyce, W. Maguire, R. P. B. Michaelson, J. Ransley, Mrs P. R. Ransley.

Assistant Trainer: Amy Weaver

Jockey (flat): J. Mackay. **Apprentice:** Hayley Turner.

---

39 **MR S. B. BELL, Chathill**
Postal: **Tughall Grange, Chathill, Northumberland, NE67 5EN.**
Contacts: **PHONE (07974) 419368**
E-MAIL simonbell105@yahoo.co.uk

1 **BONNY BLINK (IRE)**, 5, b m Needle Gun (IRE)—Pas de Mot
2 **DIAMOND COTTAGE (IRE)**, 10, b g Peacock (FR)—Sea Bright (IRE) **C. H. P. Bell**
3 **DUSKY DAME**, 5, ch m Sir Harry Lewis (USA)—Red Dusk
4 **SHINING TYNE**, 11, b g Primitive Rising (USA)—Shining Bann **D. Blythe**
5 **UPSWING**, 8, b g Perpendicular—Moorfield Lady **C. H. P. Bell**

Other Owners: Mr J. L. Gledson.

---

40 **MR A. BERRY, Cockerham**
Postal: **Moss Side Racing Stables, Crimbles Lane, Cockerham, Lancaster, LA2 0ES.**
Contacts: **PHONE (01524) 791179 FAX (01524) 791958 MOBILE (07880) 553515**
E-MAIL office@mosssideracingstables.fsnet.co.uk

1 **BANANA GROVE (IRE)**, 4, b g Sesaro (USA)—Megan's Dream (IRE) **Mr A. Berry**
2 **CAMPBELLS LAD**, 4, b c Mind Games—T O O Mamma's (IRE) **Campbells Kingdom**
3 **CIRCUIT DANCER (IRE)**, 5, b g Mujadil (USA)—Trysinger (IRE) **D. T. Fish**
4 **COMMANDO SCOTT (IRE)**, 4, b g Danetime (IRE)—Faye **Mrs A. Morris**
5 **COMPTON DRAGON (USA)**, 8, ch g Woodman (USA)—Vilikaia (USA) **J. Connor**
6 **COUNTRYWIDE GIRL (IRE)**, 6, ch m Catrail (USA)—Polish Saga **Galaxy Moss Side Racing Clubs Limited**
7 **GARNOCK VENTURE (IRE)**, 4, b c Mujadil (USA)—Stay Sharpe (USA) **Robert Aird**
8 **GDANSK (IRE)**, 8, b g Pips Pride—Merry Twinkle **Mr A. Berry**
9 **INDIAN MUSIC**, 8, b g Indian Ridge—Dagny Juel (USA) **Mr A. Berry**
10 **KIRKBY'S TREASURE**, 7, gr g Mind Games—Gem of Gold **Kirkby Lonsdale Racing**
11 **LAVISH TIMES**, 4, ch c Timeless Times (USA)—Lavernock Lady **P. J. Dixon**
12 **LION'S DOMANE**, 8, b g Lion Cavern (USA)—Vilany **Mr A. Berry**
13 **LONGMEADOWS BOY (IRE)**, 5, b g Victory Note (USA)—Karoi (IRE) **John Wilding Promotions**
14 **OBE BOLD (IRE)**, 4, b f Orpen (USA)—Capable Kate (IRE) **Mr S. Lowthian & Mr A. Parr**
15 **OBE ONE**, 5, b g Puissance—Plum Bold **BDR Partnership**
16 **PETER'S IMP (IRE)**, 10, b g Imp Society (USA)—Catherine Clare **Mr. Ian Bolland**
17 **PHOENIX NIGHTS (IRE)**, 5, b g General Monash (USA)—Beauty Appeal (USA) **Mr A. Berry**
18 **TELEPATHIC (IRE)**, 5, b g Mind Games—Madrina **Mr A. Berry**
19 **THROWMEUPSOMETHING (IRE)**, 4, b g Cape Cross (IRE)—Hawksbill Special (IRE) **Mr A. Berry**
20 **TROODOS JET**, 4, b g Atraf—Costa Verde **A. R. White**
21 **TUSCAN DREAM**, 10, b g Clantime—Excavator Lady **Galaxy Moss Side Racing Clubs Limited**
22 **WALTZING WIZARD**, 6, b g Magic Ring (IRE)—Legendary Dancer **P. J. Dixon**
23 **WILSON BLYTH**, 7, b g Puissance—Pearls **J. Connor**

THREE-YEAR-OLDS

24 **ALEXIA ROSE (IRE)**, b f Mujadil (USA)—Meursault (IRE) **Pisani PLC**
25 **ANSELLS LEGACY (IRE)**, b g Charnwood Forest (IRE)—Hanzala (FR) **Mr A. Berry**
26 **BETWEEN FRIENDS**, b f Slip Anchor—Charisse Dancer **Mr Tom Bibby**
27 Ch c Dancing Spree (USA)—Charlies Bride (IRE)
28 **DEN PERRY**, ch c Tipsy Creek (USA)—Beverley Monkey (IRE) **Mr A. Berry**
29 **GEORDIE DANCER (IRE)**, b g Dansili—Awtaar (USA) **Goodoldfun**
30 **HAENERTSBURG (IRE)**, b f Victory Note (USA)—Olivia's Pride (IRE) **D. Hilton**
31 **HILLSIDE HEATHER (IRE)**, ch f Tagula (IRE)—Danzig Craft (IRE) **Hillside Racing**
32 **KATIE BOO (IRE)**, br f Namid—Misty Peak (IRE) **The Early Doors Partnership**

MR A. BERRY—continued

33 **KINKY,** b c Kingsinger (IRE)—Lucky Dip **P. J. Dixon**
34 **KRISTIKHAB (IRE),** ch g Intikhab (USA)—Alajyal (IRE) **Mr J. P. Smith**
35 **LOVE FROM RUSSIA,** b g Xaar—Heart **Bigwigs Bloodstock VII**
36 **MAKE US FLUSH,** b f Mind Games—Pearls **The Bath Tub Boys**
37 **MARLENES GIRL (IRE),** ro f Foxhound (USA)—Premier Place (USA) **Mrs A. Morris**
38 **NEE LEMON LEFT,** b f Puissance—Via Dolorosa **Mr A. Berry**
39 **OCEANICO DOT COM (IRE),** br f Hernando (FR)—Karen Blixen **The Red and The Green**
40 **OUR LITTLE SECRET (IRE),** ch f Rossini (USA)—Sports Post Lady (IRE) **J. Berry**
41 **PETER ROUGHLEY (IRE),** b g Indian Lodge (IRE)—Dahabiah **The Cinco Amigo's Partnership**
42 **PRIMARILY,** b g Mind Games—Prim N Proper **T. G. & M. E. Holdcroft**
43 B f Tagula (IRE)—Requena
44 **STEAL THE THUNDER,** br g Timeless Times (USA)—Lavernock Lady **W. Burns**
45 **STRATHTAY,** ch f Pivotal—Cressida **E. R. H. Nisbet**
46 **TEWITFIELD LASS,** b f Bluegrass Prince (IRE)—Madam Marash (IRE) **Longlands Racing**
47 **THE TERMINATOR (IRE),** b g Night Shift (USA)—Surmise (USA) **J. Connor**

TWO-YEAR-OLDS

48 B c 6/3 Diktat—Antonia's Folly (Music Boy) (2000) **Mr Adrian Parr**
49 Ch c 27/3 Night Shift (USA)—Arbaletta (GER) (Surumu (GER)) (17500)
50 B c 17/4 Fayruz—Bardia (Jalmood (USA))
51 Ch f 28/3 Perryston View—Bergliot (Governor General) (1400) **W. Burns**
52 B f 8/2 Carrowkeel (IRE)—Cajo (IRE) (Tirol) (10060)
53 B c 16/2 Foxhound (USA)—Classic Storm (Belfort (FR)) (5800) **Mr Derek Ayres**
54 B f 30/3 Makbul—Costa Verde (King of Spain) **Auldyn Stud Ltd**
55 B f 18/4 King Charlemagne (USA)—Day Star (Dayjur (USA)) (6000)
56 B c 24/3 Carrowkeel (IRE)—Deerussa (IRE) (Jareer (USA)) (9389)
57 B f 23/3 Trans Island—Embroidery (Lords (USA)) (4023)
58 Ch f 2/4 Rossini (USA)—Fureur de Vivre (IRE) (Bluebird (USA)) (2011)
59 Ch c 23/2 Titus Livius (FR)—Gleam (Green Desert (USA)) (5364)
60 B br c 28/4 Monashee Mountain (USA)—Hierarchy (Sabrehill (USA))
61 B f 28/1 Muhtarram (USA)—Ishaam (Selkirk (USA)) (6706)
62 B f 21/4 Shinko Forest (IRE)—Jayess Elle (Sabrehill (USA)) (6706)
63 **KIRKBYS BELLE (IRE),** b f 16/2 Namid—Saltwood (Mujtahid (USA)) (6706) **Kirkby Lonsdale Racing**
64 B f 16/1 Fasliyev (USA)—Luisa Demon (IRE) (Barathea (IRE)) (4694) **Mr Leslie Young**
65 Ch f 29/4 Beckett (IRE)—Ma Bella Luna (Jalmood (USA)) (2011)
66 B f 25/1 Foxhound (USA)—Milliscent (Primo Dominie) (2500)
67 Ch f 24/4 Titus Livius (FR)—Miss Body (IRE) (Hamas (IRE)) (8047)
68 Ch f 27/2 Daggers Drawn (USA)—Pecan Pie (IRE) (Sri Pekan (USA)) (1000)
69 B f 9/4 Tagula (IRE)—Pretty Sally (IRE) (Polish Patriot (USA)) (3688)
70 B c 1/2 Mull of Kintyre (USA)—Punta Gorda (IRE) (Roi Danzig (USA)) (7377)
71 Ch c 30/3 Observatory (USA)—Revoltosa (IRE) (Catrail (USA)) (2000)
72 B f 20/2 Tagula (IRE)—Sesame Heights (IRE) (High Estate) (1000)
73 Ch c 20/2 Danetime (IRE)—Seven Sisters (USA) (Shadeed (USA)) (2600)
74 B c 2/3 Tagula (IRE)—Shimla (IRE) (Rudimentary (USA)) (8047)
75 **THUMPERS DREAM,** b f 16/2 Cape Cross (IRE)—Perfect Peach (Lycius (USA)) **Mrs A. Morris**
76 **TRUE VALENTINE,** br f 28/4 Primo Valentino (IRE)—
                                        Prim N Proper (Tragic Role (USA)) (3500) **T. G. & M. E. Holdcroft**
77 **WEE ZIGGY,** b c 24/6 Ziggy's Dancer (USA)—Midnight Arrow (Robellino (USA)) **J. Connor**

Other Owners: Mr J. Aldridge, T. C. Barnfather, Mrs J. M. Berry, I. A. Bolland, Mr L. Carberry, G. J. Edmondson, Mr D. M. Fox, N. T. Gormley, Ms A. Hartley, Mr J. A. Hibbard, S. R. Lowthian, J. D. Mason, A. B. Parr, Barry Robinson.

Jockey (flat): Paul Bradley, F. Lynch, F. Norton. **Apprentice:** Patrick Mathers.

---

41 | MR J. A. BERRY, Blackwater
Postal: **Ballyroe, Blackwater, Co. Wexford, Ireland.**
Contacts: **PHONE +353 (0) 27205 MOBILE +353 (0) (8625) 57537**

1 **COCIEMBE (IRE),** 6, ch g Anshan—Lady Suntan **Manjana Syndicate**
2 **CORSTON JIGTHYME (IRE),** 7, br g Good Thyne—Corston Dancer (IRE) **A. S. Lyburn**
3 **CORSTONE BELLE (IRE),** 6, b br m Broken Hearted—Corston Dancer (IRE) **A. S. Lyburn**
4 **ESKIMO JILL (IRE),** 6, ch m Glacial Storm (USA)—Meadowell (USA) **J. P. Berry**
5 **FIDELE GALOPIN (FR),** 7, b g Comte du Bourg (FR)—Buff Beauty (FR) **R. Larkin**
6 **GALLOPING HOME (IRE),** 7, ch g Rashar (USA)—Gort Na Lynn (IRE) **N. O'Gorman**

MR J. A. BERRY—continued

  7 HE'S ON HIS WAY (IRE), 6, ch g Zaffaran (USA)—Soraway **J. P. Berry**
  8 KYLEGARRA LADY (IRE), 6, ch m Teamster—Eyre Street Lady **M. Parle**
  9 LORD OF THE FURZE (IRE), 9, b g Lord Americo—Furry Gran **M. Devine**
10 NO TAILS TOLD (IRE), 7, b m Glacial Storm—Askasilla **Ballyroe Syndicate**
11 PALMERS PEAK (IRE), 6, b g Arctic Lord—Shahreza **Ballyroe Syndicate**
12 READY FOR TAKEOFF (IRE), 8, br g Supreme Leader—Spread Your Wings (IRE) **J. P. Berry**
13 RIVER GROVE (IRE), 9, b m Over The River (FR)—Laurelann **Dr A. Cleary**
14 ROSE OF PORTRANE (IRE), 7, b m Hubbly Bubbly (USA)—Aingeal **P. Tyrell**
15 SNAPPER CREEK (IRE), 9, b g Castle Keep—Vultang Lady **Manjana Syndicate**
16 SUIL NA STOIRME (IRE), 6, b g Glacial Storm (USA)—Shuil Athasach (IRE) **N. Foley**
17 THE WRENS NEST (IRE), 6, ch m Shernazar—Approach The Dawn (IRE) **Mrs A. Berry**

Assistant Trainer: Dan Doyle

Jockey (NH): C. O'Dwyer. **Conditional:** J. Cullen. **Amateur:** Mr G. Davis, Mr R. M. Moran, Mr J. T. Rath.

---

42   MR J. C. DE P. BERRY, Newmarket
Postal: **Beverley House Stables, Exeter Road, Newmarket, Suffolk, CB8 8LR.**
Contacts: **PHONE (01638) 660663**

  1 A MONK SWIMMING (IRE), 4, br g Among Men (USA)—Sea Magic (IRE) **The 1997 Partnership**
  2 BIG BERTHA, 7, ch m Dancing Spree (USA)—Bertrade **Miss A. J. Rawding**
  3 BRIEF GOODBYE, 5, b g Slip Anchor—Queen of Silk (IRE) **J. McCarthy**
  4 DESIREE (IRE), 4, b f Desert Story (IRE)—Elba (IRE) **Mrs L. A. Thompson**
  5 DIAMOND MAXINE (IRE), 5, b m Turtle Island (IRE)—Kawther **Diamond Racing Ltd**
  6 JACK DAWSON (IRE), 8, b g Persian Bold—Dream of Jenny **The Premier Cru**
  7 ODABELLA (IRE), 5, b m Selkirk (USA)—Circe's Isle **Mr John Berry**
  8 SPARTAN SPEAR, 4, b g Sure Blade (USA)—Confection **J. A. Khan**
  9 TANAH MERA (AUS), 5, ch m Nediym—Wonder Road (AUS) **Mr M. Tidmarsh**

THREE-YEAR-OLDS

10 A FORTUNATE LIFE (IRE), b f Desert Sun—Pirie (USA) **Mr John Berry**
11 BE BOP ALOHA, b f Most Welcome—Just Julia **H. R. Moszkowicz**
12 BENEDICT, b c Benny The Dip (USA)—Abbey Strand (USA) **Mr P. J. Skinner**
13 BILKIE (IRE), ch g Polish Precedent (USA)—Lesgor (USA) **L. C. Wadey**
14 DIAMOND DAN (IRE), b g Foxhound (USA)—Kawther **Diamond Racing Ltd**
15 DIAMOND JOSH, ch g Primo Dominie—Exit **Diamond Racing Ltd**
16 GRANDMA RYTA, br f Cyrano de Bergerac—Tamara **J. B. J. Richards**
17 LA GESSA, gr f Largesse—En Grisaille **Mrs R. A. Moszkowicz**
18 LAST CHAPTER (IRE), b g Desert Story (IRE)—Dutosky **Miss J. V. May**
19 MY OBSESSION (IRE), b g Spectrum (IRE)—Little Love **Mr John Berry**
20 NGAURUHOE (IRE), b f Desert Sun—Snowcap (IRE) **Mr John Berry**
21 PICOT DE SAY, b g Largesse—Facsimile **H. R. Moszkowicz**
22 SERGEANT SMALL (IRE), b g Dr Devious (IRE)—Yavarro **Mr John Berry**

TWO-YEAR-OLDS

23 BY STORM, b f 10/3 Largesse—Polar Storm (IRE) (Law Society (USA)) (5000) **H. R. Moszkowicz**
24 B f 25/4 Mull of Kintyre (USA)—Dream of Jenny (Caerleon (USA)) (10060) **J. McCarthy**
25 LADY SUFFRAGETTE (IRE), b f 5/4 Mull of Kintyre (USA)—
                                   Miss Senate (IRE) (Alzao (USA)) (4023) **Mr John Berry**
26 LARGESSE NO LESS, b f 26/3 Largesse—Pleasure Dome (Most Welcome) **H. R. Moszkowicz**

Other Owners: Miss L. McCarthy, Mr J. Hathorn, Mr C. Stone, Mrs V. A. Ward, Golden Vale Stud, Mr L. C. Casey, W. F. Benter, K. R. Brown, W. Ginzel, G. E. Grimstone.

Jockey (flat): G. Baker, B. Doyle, T. E. Durcan, J. F. Egan, M. Fenton, Lisa Jones. **Jockey (NH):** J. Culloty, T. J. Murphy, C. Rafter, V. Slattery. **Amateur:** Mr R. Sims.

43

MR J. J. BEST, Wisborough Green
Postal: **Furnace Pond Cottage, Pallingham Manor Farm, Wisborough Green, Billingshurst, West Sussex, RH14 0EZ.**
Contacts: **PHONE/FAX (01403) 700945 MOBILE (07968) 743272**

1 **EAST HILL (IRE)**, 9, b g Satco (FR)—Sharmalyne (FR) **L. Best**
2 **GREENSMITH LANE**, 9, br g Greensmith—Handy Lane **L. Best**
3 **HAPPY CAMPER (IRE)**, 5, b g Pennekamp (USA)—Happy Dancer (USA) **L. Best**
4 **ORIENTAL STYLE (IRE)**, 11, ro g Indian Ridge—Bazaar Promise **L. Best**
5 **RIVER AMORA (IRE)**, 10, b g Willie Joe (IRE)—That's Amora **L. Best**
6 **STARS DELIGHT (IRE)**, 8, ch g Fourstars Allstar (USA)—Celtic Cygnet **L. Best**

Assistant Trainer: Mr T. Best

Jockey (NH): T. Best. **Amateur:** Mr Lee Hamilton, Mr Justin Morgan, Miss Katie Cuthbertson.

44

MR J. R. BEST, Maidstone
Postal: **Scragged Oak Farm, Scragged Oak Road, Hucking, Maidstone, Kent, ME17 1QU.**
Contacts: **PHONE (01622) 880276 FAX (01622) 880904 MOBILE (07889) 362154**
E-MAIL **john.best@johnbestracing.com** WEBSITE **www.johnbestracing.com**

1 **AVALANCHE (FR)**, 8, gr g Highest Honor (FR)—Fairy Gold **The Downhill Partnership**
2 **BEST DESERT (IRE)**, 4, b g Desert Style (IRE)—La Alla Wa Asa (IRE) **P. E. Hudson**
3 **BIG MYSTERY (IRE)**, 4, b f Grand Lodge (USA)—Mysterious Plans (IRE) **Mr A. A. Lyons**
4 **BURNT COPPER (IRE)**, 5, b g College Chapel—Try My Rosie **R. Blake**
5 **CHARLIES DOUBLE**, 6, b g Double Eclipse (IRE)—Pendil's Niece **The Highly Hopeful Club**
6 **DAVE (IRE)**, 4, b g Danzero (AUS)—Paradise News **M. Folan, A. Warner, D. Giles, C. Dennison**
7 **FOREVER MY LORD**, 7, b g Be My Chief (USA)—In Love Again (IRE) **S. F. Cook**
8 **HAYS MEWS (IRE)**, 7, b g Lion Cavern (USA)—Classic Design **R. Blake**
9 **HIGH DIVA**, 6, b m Piccolo—Gifted **Mr R. Sherratt**
10 **JALPREUIL MALTA (FR)**, 8, gr g Saint Preuil (FR)—Alzira (FR) **I. Marshall**
11 **JOEY PERHAPS**, 4, b g Danzig Connection (USA)—Realms of Gold (USA) **D. S. Nevison**
12 **JUPITERS PRINCESS**, 7, b m Jupiter Island—Capricious Lass **T. Morris**
13 **KALLISTA'S PRIDE**, 5, b m Puissance—Clan Scotia **G G Racing**
14 **KING OF DIAMONDS**, 4, b c Mtoto—Capricious Lass **D. M. Newland**
15 **MASTER BREW**, 7, b g Homo Sapien—Edithmead (IRE) **Mr G. J. Larby & Mr P. J. Smith**
16 **MERCATO (FR)**, 9, b g Mansonnien (FR)—Royal Lie (FR) **R. T. Sturgis**
17 **MIND HOW YOU GO (FR)**, 7, b g Hernando (FR)—Cos I Do (IRE) **A Fiver In Mind Partnership**
18 **MINE BEHIND**, 5, b g Sheikh Albadou—Arapi (IRE) **M. Folan, R. Lees, R. Crampton**
19 **MISTER COMPLETELY (IRE)**, 4, b g Princely Heir (IRE)—Blue Goose **G G Racing**
20 **MORTAR**, 6, b g Weld—Rockmount Rose **A. J. S. Palmer**
21 **NAUGHTY NOAH**, 7, b g Rakaposhi King—Rockmount Rose **A. J. S. Palmer**
22 **OTAGO (IRE)**, 4, b g Desert Sun—Martino **Mrs L. M. Askew**
23 **PALACE PETT**, 5, ch m Afflora (IRE)—Black H'penny **R. Blake**
24 **PAT'S NEMISIS (IRE)**, 4, b f Sri Pekan (USA)—Exemplaire (FR) **Mr A. A. Lyons**
25 **PRINCESS GALADRIEL**, 4, b f Magic Ring (IRE)—Prim Lass **Mrs P. Akhurst**
26 **RECOUNT (FR)**, 5, b g Sillery (USA)—Dear Countess (FR) **D. B. Howe**
27 **ROYAL RACER (FR)**, 7, b g Danehill (USA)—Green Rosy (USA) **Mr & Mrs R. Dawbarn**
28 **SMOKIN JOE**, 4, b g Cigar—Beau Dada (IRE) **G G Racing**
29 **SOMERSET WEST (IRE)**, 5, b g Catrail (USA)—Pizzazz **Mr J. P. Ferguson**
30 **STEELY DAN**, 6, b g Danzig Connection (USA)—No Comebacks **E. A. Condon**
31 **TEMPER TANTRUM**, 7, b g Pursuit of Love—Queenbird **The Little House Partnership**
32 **THREES COMPANY (IRE)**, 10, b g Torus—Doonaree Belle (IRE) **Mrs J. E. Omer**
33 **WHIPPASNAPPER**, 5, b g Cayman Kai (USA)—Give Us A Treat **Miss V. A. Church**
34 **WILLHEGO**, 4, ch g Pivotal—Woodrising **G G Racing**
35 **YOUNG KATE**, 4, b f Desert King (IRE)—Stardyn **M. F. Kentish**

THREE-YEAR-OLDS

36 B g Forzando—Broom Isle **D. S. Nevison**
37 **COMCATCHINI**, ch c Compton Place—Baileys Firecat **The Weak At The Knees Partnership**
38 **EXTRA MARK**, b g Mark of Esteem (IRE)—No Comebacks **Miss V. A. Church**
39 **GENERAL HAIGH**, b g Mujahid (USA)—Stygian (USA) **D. S. Nevison**
40 **KING AFTER**, b g Bahamian Bounty—Child Star (FR) **D. S. Nevison**
41 **KINGSGATE BAY (IRE)**, b g Desert Sun—Selkirk Flyer **J. H. Mayne**
42 **MONASHEE PRINCE (IRE)**, ch g Monashee Mountain—Lodema (IRE) **Richmond Thoroughbreds**
43 **WATERFRONT DANCER**, b g Groom Dancer (USA)—Azula **D. S. Nevison**

MR J. R. BEST—continued

TWO-YEAR-OLDS

44 Ch f 22/3 Desert Sun—Albaiyda (IRE) (Brief Truce (USA)) (30180)
45 Ch c 20/2 Barathea (IRE)—Calypso Run (Lycius (USA)) (15000) **Mr & Mrs F. P. Wood**
46 CAPE LATINA, b f 5/1 Cape Cross (IRE)—Latina (IRE) (King's Theatre (IRE)) (9000) **Mrs J. Grist**
47 DAUGHTERS WORLD, b f 18/2 Agnes World (USA)—Priluki (Lycius (USA)) (48000) **Mrs J. A. Schabacker**
48 EPINEUSE, b f 29/1 Gorse—Four-Legged Friend (Aragon) (10000)
49 MAGIDENE, b c 29/1 Magic Ring (IRE)—Everdene (Bustino) (16000) **The Little Tiny Partnership**
50 Ch c 8/3 Fraam—Medina de Rioseco (Puissance) (16000) **G G Racing**
51 MINE THE BALANCE (IRE), b c 18/3 Desert Style (IRE)—Dia (IRE) (Astronef) (25000) **M. Folan & R. Lees**
52 Ch c 31/3 Daggers Drawn (USA)—Racing Brenda (Faustus (USA)) (5364)
53 B br c 3/3 Bertolini (USA)—Salvezza (IRE) (Superpower) (16096)
54 B c 18/3 Groom Dancer (USA)—Sheila's Secret (IRE) (Bluebird (USA)) (15000)
55 SOUBRIQUET (IRE), b c 26/3 Daylami (IRE)—Green Lucia (Green Dancer (USA)) (26000) **Mrs L. M. Askew**
56 Bl f 21/3 Cape Cross (IRE)—Woodrising (Nomination) (13413)

Other Owners: G. K. Aldridge, Mrs B. G. Blake, T. J. E. Brereton, Mr B. Cains, P. A. M. Gazeley, F. K. Gilmour, Mrs D. Godmon, G. Godmon, Mr M. Hurd, P. M. Nelson, N. Newman, D. T. Norton, Mr R. Rooks.

Amateur: Miss L. Baldwin, Miss J. Ferguson, Miss K. Manser.

---

45 **MR J. D. BETHELL, Middleham**
Postal: **Clarendon House, Middleham, Leyburn, North Yorkshire, DL8 4NP.**
Contacts: **PHONE (01969) 622962 FAX (01969) 622157**
E-MAIL james@jamesbethell.co.uk WEBSITE www.jamesbethell.co.uk

1 DOMIRATI, 5, b g Emarati (USA)—Julia Domna **Exors of the Late D. A. Shirley**
2 FOSSGATE, 4, ch g Halling (USA)—Peryllys **Mrs S. Bethell**
3 GRANSTON (IRE), 4, b gr g Revoque (IRE)—Gracious Gretclo **Four Players Partnership**
4 KING HARSON, 6, b g Greensmith—Safari Park **C. J. Burley**
5 LITTLE BOB, 4, ch g Zilzal (USA)—Hunters of Brora (IRE) **R. F. Gibbons**
6 MASTER WELLS (IRE), 4, b g Sadler's Wells (USA)—Eljazzi **J. E. Lund**
7 MINE (IRE), 7, b h Primo Dominie—Ellebanna **Mr M. J. Dawson**
8 SCOTLAND THE BRAVE, 5, ch m Zilzal (USA)—Hunters of Brora (IRE) **R. F. Gibbons**
9 SCOTS GUARD (IRE), 4, b g Selkirk (USA)—Island Race **Car Colston Hall Stud**
10 SNOWED UNDER, 4, gr g Most Welcome—Snowy Mantle **Mrs G. Fane**
11 STRETTON (IRE), 7, br g Doyoun—Awayil (USA) **Mr M. J. Dawson**
12 TRUE MAGIC, 4, b f Magic Ring (IRE)—True Precision **T. R. Lock**

THREE-YEAR-OLDS

13 ABSTRACT FOLLY (IRE), b g Rossini (USA)—Cochiti **Queens House Management Services Ltd**
14 ANGELOFTHENORTH, b f Tomba—Dark Kristal (IRE) **J. Hamilton**
15 ASKWITH (IRE), b g Marju (IRE)—Hayward **Clarendon Thoroughbred Racing**
16 BOSCHETTE, b f Dansili—Secret Dance **C. J. Burley**
17 FLAXBY, b g Mister Baileys—Harryana **Clarendon Thoroughbred Racing**
18 INGLEBY CROSS, b f Cape Cross (IRE)—No Islands **Clarendon Thoroughbred Racing**
19 LOYALTY LODGE (IRE), ch g Grand Lodge (USA)—Gaily Grecian (IRE) **J. E. Lund**
20 STRAWBERRY DALE (IRE), b f Bering—Manchaca (FR) **Mr M. J. Dawson**
21 TEE EL CEE, b f Lujain (USA)—Dona Filipa **J. Hamilton**
22 TWICE NIGHTLY, b g Wolfhound (USA)—Dusty's Darling **Richard Whiteley, Clarendon Racing**

TWO-YEAR-OLDS

23 AZERLEY (IRE), b f 1/4 Desert Style (IRE)—
                Miss Indigo (Indian Ridge) (10000) **Clarendon Thoroughbred Racing**
24 B c 15/2 Hennessy (USA)—Coeur de La Mer (IRE) (Caerleon (USA)) (30000) **J. E. Lund**
25 GRAFTON (IRE), b c 25/4 Desert Style (IRE)—Gracious Gretclo (Common Grounds) (14754) **Mr & Mrs D. West**
26 Ch f 15/4 Lomitas—Latch Key Lady (Tejano (USA)) (6500) **D. Scott**
27 MARKINGTON, b c 11/4 Medicean—Nemesia (Mill Reef (USA)) (22000) **Clarendon Thoroughbred Racing**
28 MIDAS DEVA (IRE), b c 12/3 Barathea (IRE)—Trexenta (IRE) (Green Desert (USA)) (30000) **Mr G. Povey**
29 Ch f 29/3 Indian Ridge—Mora (IRE) (Second Set (IRE)) (30000)
30 NESNO (USA), ch c 22/2 Royal Academy (USA)—Cognac Lady (USA) (Olympio (USA)) (138334) **Mr J. A. Elliott**
31 OURS (IRE), b c 20/4 Mark of Esteem (IRE)—Ellebanna (Tina's Pet) (38000) **Mr M. J. Dawson**
32 STAINLEY (IRE), b c 30/3 Elnadim (USA)—Fizz Up (Alzao (USA)) (24000) **Clarendon Thoroughbred Racing**

Other Owners: N. J. Forman Hardy, Mrs J. M. Forman Hardy, R. T. Vickers, Mrs J. E. Vickers.

46 MR R. N. BEVIS, Malpas
Postal: **Upperwood Farm, Sarn Road, Threapwood, Malpas, Cheshire, SY14 7AW.**
Contacts: **PHONE/FAX (01948) 770427 MOBILE (07802) 446045**

1 **BARABASCHI**, 9, b g Elmaamul (USA)—Hills' Presidium **P. J. Doyle**
2 **BARTON SUN (IRE)**, 6, b g Indian Ridge—Sun Screen **Mr R. N. Bevis**
3 **COPPER COIN (IRE)**, 11, b br g Mandalus—Two-Penny Rice **Miss Nancy Taylor**
4 **ELEGANT CLUTTER (IRE)**, 7, b g Petorius—Mountain Hop (IRE) **J. K. Emmerson-Briggs**
5 **FREDDIE ED**, 4, b g Makbul—Miss Mirror **S. Corbett**
6 **HIGH JINKS**, 10, b g High Estate—Waffling **Mr R. N. Bevis**
7 **KILLALA (IRE)**, 5, b g Among Men (USA)—Hat And Gloves **R. J. Bevis**
8 **MAISIEBEL**, 7, ch m Be My Native (USA)—High 'b' **E. E. Williams**
9 **PARK LANE HARRY**, 6, b g Nalchik (USA)—Kathy's Role **Mrs Wendy Batho**

Other Owners: Mr T. Lloyd, Mr D. Davies, Mr M. Lyons, Mr A. Maddox, Mr N. Mustill, Mr G. Dewhurst.

Assistant Trainer: R J Bevis

Conditional: A Evans. **Amateur:** Mr S. Magee, Mr R. N. Bevis.

47 MR J. R. BEWLEY, Jedburgh
Postal: **Overton Bush Farm, Camptown, Jedburgh, Roxburghshire, TD8 6RW.**
Contacts: **PHONE (01835) 840273**
E-MAIL **overtonbush@aol.com**

1 **ABERDARE**, 6, b m Overbury (IRE)—Temple Heights **Mr J. R. Bewley**
2 5, B m Jumbo Hirt (USA)—Dipador (IRE) **Mr J. R. Bewley**
3 **FALCHION**, 10, b g Broadsword (USA)—Fastlass **Mr J. R. Bewley**

Assistant Trainer: Mrs K Bewley

Jockey (NH): K. Renwick. **Conditional:** Gary Berridge.

48 MRS P. F. BICKERTON, Market Drayton
Postal: **3 Pixley Cottage, Hinstock, Market Drayton, Shropshire, TF9 2TN.**
Contacts: **PHONE (01952) 550384 MOBILE (07966) 441001**

1 **PIXLEY**, 5, ch g Saxon Farm—Lady Renton **Mrs P. F. Bickerton**
2 **SAXON MILL**, 10, ch g Saxon Farm—Djellaba **Mrs P. F. Bickerton**

49 MR J. N. R. BILLINGE, Cupar
Postal: **Hilton Farm, Cupar, Fife, KY15 4QD.**
Contacts: **PHONE (01334) 655180 MOBILES (07971) 831495/(07974) 753430**
E-MAIL **billinge.hilton@virgin.net WEBSITE www.jbillingeracing.co.uk**

1 **ALBA ROSE**, 6, gr m Overbury (IRE)—Belle Rose (IRE) **Mrs V. J. Gilmour**
2 **BASIL**, 12, br g Lighter—Thrupence **Mrs H. R. Dunn**
3 **CLAWICK CONNECTION (IRE)**, 10, b g Torus—Katie Lowe (IRE) **Mr J. N. R. Billinge**
4 **DOCK COPPER'S GIRL**, 5, b m Thowra (FR)—Reeling **J. N. R. Billinge, David and John Cupit**
5 **HOLLOW FLIGHT (IRE)**, 7, b g Hollow Hand—Gers Pet (IRE) **J. A. Findlay**
6 **MOONZIE LAIRD (IRE)**, 7, b br g Good Thyne (USA)—Sweet Roselier (IRE) **Sceptre House Golf Society**
7 **SEA LAUGHTER (IRE)**, 7, gr m Presenting—Bruna Rosa **Mrs R. Linzee Gordon & Mrs M. M. Wilson**
8 **SHAZAL**, 8, b m Afzal—Isolationist **Lordscairnie Racing**
9 **TEST OF FAITH**, 8, b g Weld—Gold Pigeon (IRE) **Hilton Racing Partnership**
10 **TULLIMOSS (IRE)**, 10, b m Husyan (USA)—Ballynattin Moss **Mrs S.E. Billinge & Mrs C. Latilla-Campbell**

Other Owners: A. J. Comette, B. A. Cotton, Mr J. F. Cupit, J. G. H. Fenton, C. F. Hallett, Mr R. Scobbie, Mrs M. V. Wolseley Brinton, P. F. Wyborn, J. C. Wythe.

Assistant Trainer: Mrs S E Billinge

Jockey (NH): G. Lee. **Conditional:** D. C. Costello, F. King. **Amateur:** Mr E. Whillans.

50 MR K. BISHOP, Bridgwater
Postal: **Barford Park Stables, Spaxton, Bridgwater, Somerset, TA5 1AF.**
Contacts: **PHONE/FAX (01278) 671437 MOBILE (07821) 387342**

1 **ASHLEY BROOK (IRE),** 7, ch g Magical Wonder (USA)—Seamill (IRE) **Mrs E. K. Ellis**
2 **BARREN LANDS,** 10, b g Green Desert (USA)—Current Raiser **Mrs E. K. Ellis**
3 **CILLAMON,** 8, b m Terimon—Dubacilla **H. T. Cole**
4 **COMPTON AMICA (IRE),** 9, gr m High Estate—Nephrite **Mrs E. K. Ellis**
5 **DAME BEEZIL,** 6, b m Man Among Men (IRE)—Cuillin **J. M. Wingfield Digby**
6 **DAMIER BAY,** 8, b g Karinga Bay—Mountain Mear **Mr K. Bishop**
7 **DARE TOO DREAM,** 6, b g Thowra (FR)—Dubacilla **H. T. Cole**
8 **GRAVE DOUBTS,** 9, ch g Karinga Bay—Redgrave Girl **Bill Davies & Bernard Tottle**
9 **GUMLEY GALE,** 10, b g Greensmith—Clodaigh Gale **Portcullis Racing**
10 **MESSAGE RECU (FR),** 9, b g Luth Dancer (USA)—High Steppe **Mrs A. E. Baker**
11 **MONGER LANE,** 9, b m Karinga Bay—Grace Moore **Slabs And Lucan**
12 **MY BOLD BOYO,** 10, b g Never So Bold—My Rosie **Mr E. T. Roberts**
13 **PRIMROSE PARK,** 6, b m Thowra (FR)—Redgrave Rose **Mr K. Bishop**
14 **SACRIFICE,** 10, b g Arctic Lord—Kellyann **M. J. Cornish**
15 **SMART DESIGN (IRE),** 10, ch g Good Thyne—Polly's Cottage **Mr B. T. Youl**
16 **SUREFAST,** 10, ch g Nearly A Hand—Meldon Lady **B. A. Derrick**

Other Owners: R. C. Hicks, D. J. Jones, C. J. Macey, C. H. Roberts, Mr D. J. Starks, V. J. Thorne, R. J. Whatley.

Assistant Trainer: Heather Bishop

Jockey (NH): R. Greene. **Conditional:** P. J. Brennan.

51 MR A. G. BLACKMORE, Hertford
Postal: **'Chasers', Stockings Lane, Little Berkhamsted, Hertford.**
Contacts: **PHONE (01707) 875060 MOBILE (07803) 711453**

1 **COOL ROXY,** 8, b g Environment Friend—Roxy River **Mr A. G. Blackmore**
2 **FLAMING CHEEK,** 7, b g Blushing Flame (USA)—Rueful Lady **Mr A. G. Blackmore**
3 **NAKED FLAME,** 6, b g Blushing Flame (USA)—Final Attraction **Mr A. G. Blackmore**

Assistant Trainer: Mrs P M Blackmore

Conditional: C. Honour.

52 MR M. T. W. BLANSHARD, Upper Lambourn
Postal: **Lethornes Stables, Upper Lambourn, Newbury, Berkshire, RG17 8QP.**
Contacts: **PHONE (01488) 71091 FAX (01488) 73497 MOBILE (07785) 370093**
E-MAIL blanshard.racing@virgin.net

1 **CUMBRIAN PRINCESS,** 8, gr m Mtoto—Cumbrian Melody **D. Sykes**
2 **DREAM ALIVE,** 4, b g Unfuwain (USA)—Petite Sonnerie **The Dream Alive Syndicate**
3 **KINGSCROSS,** 7, ch g King's Signet (USA)—Calamanco **Mrs D. Ellis**
4 **PELLA,** 4, ch f Hector Protector (USA)—Norpella **Mr Philip Chakko**
5 **SEW'N'SO CHARACTER (IRE),** 8, b g Imperial Ballet (IRE)—Hope And Glory (USA) **Aykroyd and Sons Limited**
6 **SEWMORE CHARACTER,** 5, b h Hector Protector (USA)—Kyle Rhea **Aykroyd and Sons Limited**
7 **SEWMUCH CHARACTER,** 6, b g Magic Ring (IRE)—Diplomatist **Aykroyd and Sons Limited**
8 **THE JOBBER (IRE),** 4, b g Foxhound—Clairification (IRE) **A. R. B. Ward & Mrs C. J. Ward**
9 **THE TRADER (IRE),** 7, ch g Selkirk (USA)—Snowing **Mrs C. J. Ward & Mr D. Chambers**

THREE-YEAR-OLDS

10 **BOUNTIFUL,** gr f Pivotal—Kinsaile **Lady Bland**
11 **GRANITA,** b br f Machiavellian (USA)—Actualite
12 **LOW FOLD FLYER,** ch g Fraam—Maniere d'amour (FR) **J. M. Beever**
13 **MERRYMADCAP (IRE),** b g Lujain (USA)—Carina Clare **Mrs C. Young**
14 **MISSED A BEAT,** b f Mister Baileys—Lonely Heart **The First Timers**
15 **MULBERRY WINE,** b f Benny The Dip (USA)—Top Berry **Lady Bland**
16 **PIPER LILY,** b f Piccolo—Polly Golightly **D. Sykes**
17 **ROSIELLA,** b f Tagula (IRE)—Queen of Silk (IRE) **Mr T Wellman, B McAllister, D Hampson**
18 **THE COMPOSER,** b c Royal Applause—Superspring **Mrs C. J. Ward & Mrs G. Phillips**
19 **WEBSTER,** b g Kingsinger (IRE)—Worsted **Mrs D. Ellis**

MR M. T. W. BLANSHARD—continued

TWO-YEAR-OLDS

20 B c 27/2 Namid—Bayalika (IRE) (Selkirk (USA)) (12000)
21 B f 6/4 Marju—Briggsmaid (Elegant Air) (10000)
22 B f 6/4 Inchinor—Creme de Menthe (IRE) (Green Desert (USA)) (37000) **Mr Gordon Phillips**
23 B f 24/4 Polish Precedent (USA)—Demerger (USA) (Distant View (USA)) **G. Russell & J. Gale**
24 **DORA'S GREEN,** b f 9/4 Rambling Bear—Compradore (Mujtahid (USA)) (2285) **The Newchange Syndicate**
25 B f 29/3 Mozart (IRE)—Kayoko (IRE) (Shalford (IRE)) (14000) **Mrs C. Young**
26 **MACVEL (IRE),** b f 7/3 Mull of Kintyre—Velvet Appeal (IRE) (Petorius) (15000) **Hertford Offset**
27 B c 14/4 Kalanisi (IRE)—Mill Rainbow (FR) (Rainbow Quest (USA)) **Messrs Else, Oilver, Ward, Berg & Smith**
28 B c 11/3 Imperial Ballet (IRE)—Mysticism (Mystiko (USA)) (8047)
29 **PADDY'S PLACE (IRE),** b f 20/4 Compton Place—Lamarita (Emarati (USA)) **Mr T. Wellman & Mrs M. Payne**
30 B c 16/4 Sinndar (IRE)—Peony (Lion Cavern (USA)) (46948)
31 Ch c 13/4 Tagula (IRE)—Seymour (IRE) (Eagle Eyed (USA)) (21000) **J. M. Beever**
32 **THE COMBO,** gr c 20/4 Selkirk (USA)—Snowing (Tate Gallery (USA)) (100000) **A. R. B. Ward & Mrs C. J. Ward**
33 **THE SPREAD,** ch f 27/3 Alhaarth (IRE)—
Evie Hone (IRE) (Royal Academy (USA)) (19000) **A. R. B. Ward & Mrs C. J. Ward**
34 **UP AT DAWN,** b f 23/2 Inchinor—Up And About (Barathea (IRE)) **Mr P. Player**
35 B c 10/4 Kingsinger (IRE)—Worsted (Whittingham (IRE))

Other Owners: D. Sloan, Mrs S. M. Ward, MR M. T. W. Blanshard, A. J. Budd, T. K. Bullimore, K. C. Epps, Mr D. C. Hughes, C. McKenna, C. A. Philipson, R. A. Slater, Mrs S. M. Willey.

---

53 MR P. A. BLOCKLEY, Newport
Postal: **Cefn Llogel Racing Stables, Coedkernew, Newport, Gwent, NP10 8UD.**
Contacts: **PHONE (01633) 682849**

1 **AFTER LENT (IRE),** 4, b g Desert Style (IRE)—Yashville **Mrs J. F. Hughes**
2 **ALTITUDE DANCER (IRE),** 5, b g Sadler's Wells (USA)—Height of Passion **J. D. Cotterill**
3 **ANDURIL,** 4, ch c Kris—Attribute **R. W. Thorne**
4 **ARCTIC QUEEN,** 4, br f Linamix (FR)—Thamud (IRE) **Winterbeck Manor Stud Ltd**
5 **BEFRIEND (USA),** 5, ch m Allied Forces (USA)—Approcheer (USA) **Its Two Men In A Suit**
6 **BLUE EMPIRE,** 4, b g Second Empire (USA)—Paleria (USA) **N. R. Shields**
7 **BLUEBERRY RHYME,** 6, b g Alhijaz—Irenic **N. R. Shields**
8 **CHEERFUL GROOM (IRE),** 14, ch g Shy Groom (USA)—Carange **W. F. Cahill**
9 **CLANN A COUGAR,** 5, ch g Bahamian Bounty—Move Darling **Mrs S. Pidcock**
10 **DAUNTED (IRE),** 9, b g Priolo (USA)—Dauntess **Mrs J. F. Hughes**
11 **DELTA FORCE,** 6, b g High Kicker (USA)—Maedaley **Miss E. C. Shally**
12 **EL PALMAR,** 4, b g Case Law—Aybeegirl **C. A. F. Whiting**
13 **EMPEROR CAT (IRE),** 4, b g Desert Story (IRE)—Catfoot Lane **The Dilum Partnership**
14 **FRIENDS HOPE,** 4, ch f Docksider (USA)—Stygian (USA) **M. J. Wiley**
15 **GALLERY BREEZE,** 6, b m Zamindar (USA)—Wantage Park **N. R. Shields**
16 **GAME GURU,** 6, b g First Trump—Scarlett Holly **Mr C. Would**
17 **HIAWATHA (IRE),** 6, b g Danehill (USA)—Hi Bettina **N. R. Shields**
18 **HIDDEN DRAGON (USA),** 6, b g Danzig (USA)—
Summer Home (USA) **Jane, Victoria, Aimee & Thelma Whiting**
19 **HIT'S ONLY MONEY (IRE),** 5, br g Hamas (IRE)—Toordillon (IRE) **C. A. F. Whiting**
20 **INK IN GOLD (IRE),** 4, b g Intikhab (USA)—Your Village (IRE) **Mr K. Tyre**
21 **KEY PARTNERS (IRE),** 4, b g Key of Luck (USA)—Teacher Preacher (IRE) **T. J. Wardle**
22 **KNIGHT OF HEARTS (IRE),** 4, gr g Idris (IRE)—Heart To Heart (IRE) **Mrs A. M. O'Sullivan**
23 **LINDA GREEN,** 4, b f Victory Note (USA)—Edge of Darkness **S. Roots**
24 **LINNING WINE (IRE),** 9, b g Scenic—Zallaka (IRE) **N. R. Shields**
25 **MISARO (GER),** 4, b g Acambaro (GER)—Misniniski **Mrs K. E. Cross**
26 **MUSICAL GIFT,** 5, ch g Cadeaux Genereux—Kazoo **N. R. Shields**
27 **ON CLOUD NINE,** 4, ro f Cloudings (IRE)—Princess Moodyshoe **J. J. Ryan**
28 **ONLINE INVESTOR,** 6, b g Puissance—Anytime Baby **G. Flitcroft**
29 **ONLY IF I LAUGH,** 4, ch g Piccolo—Agony Aunt **Phones Direct Partnership**
30 **PENEL (IRE),** 4, b g Orpen (USA)—Jayess Elle **J. L. Guillambert**
31 **PREMIER DREAM (USA),** 4, ch c Woodman (USA)—Marina Ruff **J. J. Ryan**
32 **PRINCE DAYJUR (USA),** 6, b br g Dayjur (USA)—Distinct Beauty (USA) **C. A. F. Whiting**
33 **REGAL FANTASY (IRE),** 5, b m King's Theatre (IRE)—Threesome (USA) **M. J. Wiley**
34 **REPEAT (IRE),** 5, ch g Night Shift (USA)—Identical (IRE) **J. Billson**
35 **SENOR SET (GER),** 4, b g Second Set (IRE)—Shine Share (IRE) **R. R. H. Whiting**
36 **SHINJIRU (USA),** 5, b g Broad Brush (USA)—Kalwada (USA) **Phones Direct Partnership**
37 **SKIP OF COLOUR,** 5, b g Rainbow Quest (USA)—Minskip (USA) **Mrs J. F. Hughes**

MR P. A. BLOCKLEY—continued

38 **SMART STARPRINCESS (IRE)**, 4, b f Soviet Star (USA)—Takeshi (IRE) **Brooklands Racing**
39 **SMITH N ALLAN OILS**, 6, b g Bahamian Bounty—Grand Splendour **Mrs J. F. Hughes**
40 **TURN AROUND**, 5, b g Pivotal—Bemuse **C. A. F. Whiting**
41 **WAINWRIGHT (IRE)**, 5, b g Victory Note (USA)—Double Opus (IRE) **Miss D. E. Sarjantson**
42 **WEET WATCHERS**, 5, br g Polar Prince (IRE)—Weet Ees Girl (IRE) **Ed Weetman (Haulage & Storage) Ltd**
43 **WESSEX (USA)**, 5, ch g Gone West (USA)—Satin Velvet (USA) **N. R. Shields**
44 **YASHIN (IRE)**, 4, b g Soviet Star (USA)—My Mariam **N. R. Shields**
45 **YORKIE**, 6, b g Aragon—Light The Way **C. A. F. Whiting**
46 **ZALAM (IRE)**, 5, b g Alzao (USA)—Zarlana (IRE) **R. R. H. Whiting**

THREE-YEAR-OLDS

47 **BENTLEY BROOK (IRE)**, ch c Singspiel (IRE)—Gay Bentley (USA) **T. J. Wardle**
48 **BOGAZ (IRE)**, b c Rossini (USA)—Fastnet **P. Rosas**
49 **DRAGON SLAYER (IRE)**, ch c Night Shift (USA)—Arandora Star (USA) **Mr C. Would**
50 **EQUILIBRIA (USA)**, b c Gulch (USA)—Julie La Rousse (IRE) **Mrs K. E. Cross**
51 **FAIR ALONG (GER)**, b g Alkalde (GER)—Fairy Tango (FR) **J. L. Guillambert**
52 **GENEREUX JOS**, b g Josr Algarhoud (IRE)—Bright Fountain (IRE) **Team Eight**
53 **HITS ONLY CASH**, b c Inchinor—Persian Blue **Mrs Z. Scott**
54 **KUMALA OCEAN (IRE)**, ch f Blue Ocean (USA)—Kumala (IRE) **The One Over Par Partnership**
55 **LALMADAS**, b g Josr Algarhoud (IRE)—Primulette **J. L. Guillambert**
56 **MILL BY THE STREAM**, b g Lujain (USA)—Lonesome **J. L. Guillambert**
57 **MRS MILLIONS (IRE)**, b f Brave Act—Cappuchino (IRE) **J. Laughton**
58 **OH DARA (USA)**, b f Aljabr (USA)—Sabaah Elfull **Mr C. Would**
59 **PENNAUTIER (IRE)**, gr f Paris House—Traci's Castle (IRE) **Ashby & Blount Racing Partnership**
60 **PERCHERON (IRE)**, ch g Perugino (USA)—Silvery Halo (USA) **Mrs J. E. And Mr D. G. Bird**
61 **PLUNGINGTON TAVERN (IRE)**, b c Josr Algarhoud (IRE)—Hever Golf Lady **Mikado Syndicate**
62 **ROSSIN GOLD (IRE)**, b g Rossini (USA)—Sacred Heart (IRE) **J. P. Kok**
63 **TIFFIN DEANO (IRE)**, b g Mujadil (USA)—Xania **Joint Ownership Terminated**
64 **TOWN END TOM**, b g Entrepreneur—Prima Silk **J. L. Guillambert**
65 **WEET N MEASURES**, ch c Weet-A-Minute (IRE)—Weet Ees Girl (IRE) **Ed Weetman (Haulage & Storage) Ltd**
66 **WINDY PROSPECT**, ch c Intikhab (USA)—Yellow Ribbon (IRE) **Bell House Racing Limited**

TWO-YEAR-OLDS

67 **WEET FOR YOU**, gr f 29/4 Weet-A-Minute (IRE)—
              Weet Ees Girl (IRE) (Common Grounds) **Ed Weetman (Haulage & Storage) Ltd**

Other Owners: Mrs G. Ashby, M. H. Bates, Mrs J. E. Bird, Mr D. G. Bird, Mr S. A. Blount, R. C. Cox, A. C. Eaton, Mr R. A. Hunt, A. C. Kirkham, D. S. Lovatt, Mr J. Marshall, Mr M. J. Oxton, Mr D. Robinson, R. J. Robinson, Mr P. W. Stally, M. Sziler, Mrs J. Whiting, Miss V. J. Whiting, Miss A. L. Whiting, Mrs Joyce Wood, D. Wright.

Jockey (flat): K. Fallon, Dean McKeown, G. Parkin. **Apprentice:** D Nolan, Derek Nolan, S Yourston. **Amateur:** Miss S. L. Renwick.

MRS MYRIAM BOLLACK-BADEL, Lamorlaye

Postal: **20 Rue Blanche, 60260 Lamorlaye, France.**
Contacts: PHONE (33) 03 44 21 55 34 FAX (33) 03 44 21 33 67 MOBILE (33) 06 10 80 93 47
E-MAIL myriam.bollack@wanadoo.fr

1 **ADVALINE (FR)**, 5, gr m Highest Honor (FR)—Advalor (FR) **Mrs M. Bollack-Badel**
2 **COLLEGIENNE (FR)**, 5, b m Bering—Carole Dream (FR) **Patrick Fellous**
3 **CROIX DE LORRAINE (FR)**, 4, ch f Lord of Men—Rocade (IRE) **Scuderia Mirabella**
4 **DALAMINE (FR)**, 5, b m Sillery (USA)—Dalyane (FR) **Mrs M. Bollack-Badel**
5 **DESERT PLUS (IRE)**, 5, b h Desert King (IRE)—Welcome Break **Scuderia Mirabella**
6 **JARDIN BLEU**, 6, b h Diesis—Cask **Katsumi Yoshida**
7 **JOHN D'AO (FR)**, 4, b c Johann Quatz (FR)—Flutiskoa **Mrs M. Bollack-Badel & Mrs D. Taleb**
8 **KNOUT (FR)**, 4, gr f Kendor (FR)—Zita Blues (IRE) **Mrs G. de Chatelperron**
9 **TRES MERCI (FR)**, 4, ch f Take Risks (FR)—La Barbara (FR) **Mrs M. Bollack-Badel**

THREE-YEAR-OLDS

10 **AIGUILLE DU MIDI (FR)**, b f Fly To The Stars—Rocade (IRE) **Scuderia Mirabella**
11 **ANNA FRANCESCA (FR)**, b f Anabaa (USA)—Lanasara **Mrs G. de Chatelperron**
12 **DOCTOR ICE (FR)**, br c Cape Cross (IRE)—Blue Lure (USA) **J. C. Smith**
13 **HERMANCE**, b f Enrique—Heroine (FR) **Mrs Y. Seydoux de Clausonne**

MRS MYRIAM BOLLACK-BADEL—continued

14 **L'AN DEUX (FR)**, b c Revoque (IRE)—Lune Et L'autre **Scuderia Mirabella**
15 **L'ATLANTIQUE (FR)**, ch f Kaldounevees (FR)—Kachara (FR) **Serge Plot**
16 **MISS NELLA (FR)**, b f Trempolino (USA)—Miss Naelle (FR) **Mrs M. Bollack-Badel**
17 **MUSIC LEGEND**, gr f Highest Honor (FR)—Music Park (IRE) **J. C. Smith**
18 **ROBE DES CHAMPS**, b f Enrique—Blade of Grass **Mrs G. de Chatelperron**
19 **SAITAMA**, b f Pursuit of Love—Sea Ballad (USA) **Ian Goldsmith**
20 **TSE TSE (FR)**, b f Marchand de Sable (USA)—Lucia Novia (GER) **Scuderia Mirabella**
21 **VIE DE CHATEAU (IRE)**, b f Second Empire (IRE)—Voyage of Dreams (USA) **Peter Valentiner**
22 **ZERO ZERO SEPT (FR)**, ro g Take Risks (FR)—Zayine (IRE) **Scuderia Mirabella**

TWO-YEAR-OLDS

23 **ACHAEOS (FR)**, b c 10/3 Dashing Blade—Ma Lumiere (FR) (Niniski (USA)) (16096) **J. C. Smith**
24 **ALIX ROAD (FR)**, gr f 4/5 Linamix (FR)—
                    Life On The Road (IRE) (Persian Heights) (53655) **Mrs G. de Chatelperron**
25 B c 28/4.Highest Honor (FR)—Baino Bluff (Be My Guest (USA)) (48289) **Barry Stewart & Jenny Smith**
26 **DEHRADOUN**, b c 6/5 Primo Valentino (IRE)—
                    Pondicherry (USA) (Sir Wimborne (USA)) (8000) **Anne & Dwayne Woods**
27 Ch f 23/3 Desert Prince (IRE)—Lady Killeen (FR) (Marju (IRE)) (3700) **Jean Smolen**
28 B f 11/2 Grape Tree Road—Saiga (FR) (Baryshnikov (AUS)) (30181) **J. C. Smith**
29 **SANS FOLIE**, b f 14/1 Lahib (USA)—Sellette (IRE) (Selkirk (USA)) (11000) **Paul Mihalop**
30 **THE GREAT INDIAN (FR)**, b f 9/3 Indian Danehill (IRE)—
                    The Great Blasket (FR) (Saint Estephe (FR)) (18779) **Katsumi Yoshida**
31 **ZYTHON (FR)**, b f 30/3 Kabool—Zayine (IRE) (Polish Patriot (USA)) **Mrs M. Bollack-Badel**

---

55   MR M. R. BOSLEY, Wantage
Postal: Kingston Lisle Farm Stables, Kingston Lisle, Wantage, Oxfordshire, OX12 9QH.
Contacts: **OFFICE/FAX (01367) 820115 MOBILE (07778) 938040**
E-MAIL martin@bosrace.fsnet.co.uk

1 **ABSINTHE**, 8, b g Presidium—Heavenly Queen **Mrs J. M. O'Connor**
2 **BIJOU DANCER**, 5, ch g Bijou d'inde—Dancing Diana **The Blowingstone Partnership**
3 **CHARIOT (IRE)**, 4, ch g Titus Livius (FR)—Battle Queen **Mrs J. M. O'Connor**
4 **CLASSIC RUBY**, 5, b m Classic Cliche (IRE)—Burmese Ruby **Mrs J. M. O'Connor**
5 5, B g Supreme Leader—Jennys Castle **Mrs J. M. O'Connor**
6 **JUST A FLUKE (IRE)**, 4, b g Darshaan—Star Profile (IRE) **The Delta Line Racing Partnership**
7 **MAKARIM (IRE)**, 9, ch g Generous (IRE)—Emmaline (USA) **Mrs J. M. O'Connor**
8 **MIALYSSA**, 5, b m Rakaposhi King—Theme Arena **All On Top Racing**
9 **MIGHTY PIP (IRE)**, 9, b g Pips Pride—Hard To Stop **Mrs J. M. O'Connor**
10 **QOBTAAN (USA)**, 6, b g Capote—Queen's Gallery (USA) **Inca Financial Services**
11 **QUIET READING (USA)**, 8, b g Northern Flagship (USA)—Forlis Key (USA) **Mrs J. M. O'Connor**
12 **RAVEL (IRE)**, 4, b g Fasliyev (USA)—Lili Cup (FR) **Mrs J. M. O'Connor**
13 **ROKY STAR (FR)**, 8, b g Start Fast (FR)—Rosydolie (FR) **N Turner, D Kelly, D Merricks, R Jones**
14 **SILVER PROPHET (IRE)**, 6, gr g Idris (IRE)—Silver Heart **Mrs J. M. O'Connor**
15 **STONESFIELD CONEY**, 5, br g Sadler's Way—Rocquelle **Mrs H. M. Gaskell**

THREE-YEAR-OLDS

16 **SHAM RUBY**, ch f Tagula (IRE)—Bistro (USA) **F. Lewis**

Other Owners: Mrs S. M. Brotheron, G. H. Carson, Mrs P. M. Colson, Mrs N. C. Diment, P. W. Hunt, Mrs M. P. Johnson, F. Lewis, Mrs K. Whitaker.

Jockey (flat): G. Baker. **Jockey (NH):** S. Curran. **Amateur:** Mrs S. Bosley.

---

56   MISS KIRSTIN BOUTFLOWER, Blewbury
Postal: **White Shoot Stables, Woodway Road, Blewbury, Oxfordshire, OX11 9EY.**
Contacts: **PHONE (01235) 851161 MOBILE (07966) 730745**
E-MAIL kirstin.boutflower@virgin.net WEBSITE www.silver2racing.co.uk

1 **ALMARA**, 5, b m Wolfhound (USA)—Alacrity **Mara Racing**
2 **ARENAS (IRE)**, 6, b h Revoque (IRE)—Carroll's Canyon (IRE) **Greenites**
3 **CHASTE**, 5, br gr m Groom Dancer (USA)—Brilliant Timing (USA) **Silver2Racing**
4 **ISLAND PEARL (IRE)**, 6, ch m Definite Article—Iolanta (IRE) **Greenites**
5 **KILGWRRWG**, 10, b g Shaab—Watch Lady **Greenites**

MISS KIRSTIN BOUTFLOWER—continued

THREE-YEAR-OLDS

  6 FESTIVAL ROSE (IRE), b f Zafonic (USA)—Kerry Ring **Chris Beek Racing**
  7 PAVILION, b f Robellino (USA)—Chiltern Court (USA) **Silver2Racing**
  8 REGIS FLIGHT, b c Piccolo—Anthem Flight (USA) **Flight Racing**

TWO-YEAR-OLDS

  9 B f 25/2 Mujahid (USA)—Northern Bird (Interrex (CAN)) (1500) **The Rochester Group**

Other Owners: R. Rowe, P. Bird, P. Uniacke, Mrs S. Boutflower, M. Breen, B. O'Hanlon, M. Roper, M. V. S. Aram, R. A. Aram, Mr D. G. Archard, Miss Kirstin Boutflower, Mr W. S. Nichol, A. G. Taylor.

Assistant Trainer: Brain O'Hanlon

---

57   **MR P. BOWEN, Haverfordwest**
Postal: **Yet-Y-Rhug, Letterston, Haverfordwest, Pembrokeshire, SA62 5TB.**
Contacts: **PHONE (01348) 840118 MOBILE (07811) 111234**

  1 BALLYCASSIDY (IRE), 9, br g Insan (USA)—Bitofabreeze (IRE) **R Owen & P Fullagar**
  2 CELTIC BOY (IRE), 7, b g Arctic Lord—Laugh Away **Walters Plant Hire Ltd**
  3 DRAGON KING, 13, b g Rakaposhi King—Dunsilly Bell **C. E. R. Greenway**
  4 FAMOUS GROUSE, 5, b g Selkirk (USA)—Shoot Clear **G. J. Morris**
  5 FARLINGTON, 8, b g Alflora (IRE)—Annapuma **Ms J. Wells**
  6 FOOTBALL CRAZY (IRE), 6, b g Mujadil (USA)—Schonbein (IRE) **Ken Bevan, Stuart Brain**
  7 HIRVINE (FR), 7, ch g Snurge—Guadanella (FR) **Mr B. A. Crumbley**
  8 HOMEBRED BUDDY, 6, ch g Environment Friend—Royal Brush **Homebred Racing**
  9 HOMEBRED STAR, 4, ch g Safawan—Celtic Chimes **Homebred Racing**
10 IT'S DEFINITE (IRE), 6, b g Definite Article—Taoveret (IRE) **R Owen & P Fullagar**
11 MR ED (IRE), 7, ch g In The Wings—Center Moriches (IRE) **G. J. Morris**
12 OUH JAY, 7, ch m Karinga Bay—Creeping Jane **Mr K. C. Trotman**
13 QABAS (USA), 5, b g Swain (IRE)—Classical Dance (CAN) **Mr P. Bowen**
14 RIFLEMAN (IRE), 5, ch g Starborough—En Garde (USA) **The Galloping Punters**
15 SARASOTA (IRE), 10, b g Lord Americo—Ceoltoir Dubh **F. W. & E. P. Ridge**
16 SIENA STAR (IRE), 7, b g Brief Truce (USA)—Gooseberry Pie **P. A. N. Bailey**
17 SWANSEA BAY, 9, b g Jurado (USA)—Slave's Bangle **W. J. Evans**
18 THE STAND (IRE), 9, b g Witness Box (USA)—Denys Daughter (IRE) **The Courters**
19 WITHTHELADS (IRE), 7, b g Tidaro (USA)—Quayside Charm **Donttellthewife Partnership**
20 YES SIR (IRE), 6, b g Needle Gun (IRE)—Miss Pushover **Ms Y. M. Hill**

Other Owners: Mrs A. Allen, P. G. A. Bowling, Mr S. Brain, W. Bryan, Mr B. A. Crumbley, P. G. Fullagar, Mr J. A. Goldsobel, C. E. R. Greenway, K. Kisley, R. R. Owen, D. H. Richards, Mr F. W. Ridge, Mrs E. P. Ridge, D. J. Robbins, L. M. Rutherford, C. M. Wall, Mrs S. Wall, Ms J. Wells.

Assistant Trainer: K Bowen

Jockey (NH): S. Durack, R. Johnson, W. Marston, A. P. McCoy. **Amateur:** Mr Marc Barber.

---

58   **MRS A. J. BOWLBY, Wantage**
Postal: **Gurnsmead Farm, Kingston Lisle, Wantage, Oxfordshire, OX12 9QT.**
Contacts: **PHONE (01367) 820888 FAX (01367) 820880 MOBILE (07768) 277833**
E-MAIL mandy@mandybowlby.com

  1 ARICOVAIR (IRE), 5, ch g Desert Prince (IRE)—Linoise (FR) **The Reg Partnership**
  2 COTTON EASTER, 4, b f Robellino (USA)—Pluck **The Reg Partnership**
  3 CULTURED, 4, b f Danzero (AUS)—Seek The Pearl **The Stay Positive Partnership**
  4 DON ARGENTO, 4, gr g Sri Pekan (USA)—Grey Galava **The Lambourn Yankees**
  5 FINNFOREST (IRE), 5, ch g Eagle Eyed (USA)—Stockrose **Finnforest (UK) Ltd**
  6 HENRY ISLAND (IRE), 12, ch g Sharp Victor (USA)—Monterana **Mrs A. J. Bowlby**
  7 LADY RACQUET (IRE), 6, b m Glacial Storm (USA)—Kindly Light (IRE) **The Norman Partnership**
  8 LOOKSHARP LAD (IRE), 7, b g Simply Great (FR)—Merry Madness **J. Shaw**
  9 RIFFLES, 5, br m Alderbrook—Idiot's Lady **Mr David Houston**
10 SMOOTHLY DOES IT, 4, b g Efisio—Exotic Forest **Michael Bowlby Racing**
11 THAT'S FINAL, 4, b g Komaite (USA)—Fine Fettle **Dr Lesley-Anne Hatter**

MRS A. J. BOWLBY—continued

TWO-YEAR-OLDS

12 Ch f 10/5 Allied Forces (USA)—Cc Canova (Millkom)
13 B f 5/2 Mark of Esteem (IRE)—Royal Dream (Ardkinglass)

Other Owners: M. S. S. Bowlby, R. A. Cox, H. A. Elphick, Ms C. E. Elphick, D. J. Erwin, K. P. Jones.

Assistant Trainer: Michael Bowlby

Jockey (flat): E. Ahern.

---

59   **MR S. R. BOWRING, Edwinstowe**
Postal: **Fir Tree Farm, Edwinstowe, Mansfield, Nottinghamshire, NG21 9JG.**
Contacts: **PHONE (01623) 822451 MOBILE (07973) 712942**

1 ACE-MA-VAHRA, 7, b m Savahra Sound—Asmarina **S. J. Burgan**
2 ASCENMOOR, 5, b g Mistertopogigo (IRE)—Asmarina **Mr S. R. Bowring**
3 ASWAN (IRE), 7, ch g Ashkalani (IRE)—Ghariba **G. P. Bacon**
4 AVENTURA (IRE), 5, b g Sri Pekan (USA)—La Belle Katherine (USA) **A. Potts**
5 BARZAK (IRE), 5, b g Barathea (IRE)—Zakuska **Clark Industrial Services Partnership**
6 BREEZIT (USA), 4, b f Stravinsky (USA)—Sharka **A. Potts**
7 DUBAI DREAMS, 5, b g Marju (IRE)—Arndilly **A. Potts**
8 FAR NOTE (USA), 7, ch g Distant View (USA)—Descant (USA) **Mrs A. Potts**
9 FIR TREE, 5, b g Mistertopogigo (IRE)—Marina's Song **Mr S. R. Bowring**
10 FIRST MAITE, 12, b g Komaite (USA)—Marina Plata **Mr S. R. Bowring**
11 INMOM (IRE), 4, b f Barathea (IRE)—Zakuska **Clark Industrial Services Partnership**
12 KINGSMAITE, 4, b g Komaite (USA)—Antonias Melody **Mr S. R. Bowring**
13 KUSTOM KIT FOR HER, 5, b m Overbury (IRE)—Antonias Melody **Charterhouse Holdings Plc**
14 MARINAITE, 4, b f Komaite (USA)—Marina's Song **Mr S. R. Bowring**
15 PEACE TREATY (IRE), 4, b f Turtle Island (IRE)—Beautyofthepeace (IRE) **Mr S. R. Bowring**
16 WILL TELL, 7, b g Rainbow Quest (USA)—Guillem (USA) **A. Potts**
17 XPRES DIGITAL, 4, b c Komaite (USA)—Kustom Kit Xpres **Charterhouse Holdings Plc**

THREE-YEAR-OLDS

18 AMAZING GRACE MARY, b f Dancing Spree (USA)—Frisky Miss (IRE) **D. H. Bowring**
19 ANN'S DELIGHT (IRE), b f Imperial Ballet (IRE)—Najariya **Mrs A. Potts**
20 EASTFIELDS LAD, b g Overbury (IRE)—Honey Day **Mr S. R. Bowring**
21 TEMPLE BELLE XPRES, b f Overbury (IRE)—Kustom Kit Xpres **Charterhouse Holdings Plc**

TWO-YEAR-OLDS

22 B c 30/4 Komaite (USA)—Antonias Melody (Rambo Dancer (CAN)) **Mr S. R. Bowring**
23 Ch f 8/4 Rambling Bear—Cledeschamps (Doc Marten) **Mr S. R. Bowring**
24 B c 24/4 Tagula (IRE)—Highly Motivated (Midyan (USA)) (1800) **Mr S. R. Bowring**
25 B c 12/4 Carrowkeel (IRE)—Java Jive (Hotfoot) (3000) **Mr S. R. Bowring**
26 WHISTON LAD (IRE), b c 4/4 Barathea (IRE)—
                 Fille de Bucheron (USA) (Woodman (USA)) **Clark Industrial Services Partnership**

Other Owners: J. D. Clark, D. D. Clark.

Amateur: Mrs M. Morris.

---

60   **MR J. R. BOYLE, Epsom**
Postal: **South Hatch Stables, Burgh Heath Road, Epsom, Surrey, KT17 4LX.**
Contacts: **PHONE (01372) 748800 FAX (01372) 739410 MOBILE (07719) 554147**
E-MAIL info@jamesboyle.co.uk WEBSITE www.jamesboyle.co.uk

1 ADMIRAL COMPTON, 4, ch c Compton Place—Sunfleet **Inside Track Racing Club**
2 CEDAR MASTER (IRE), 8, b g Soviet Lad (USA)—Samriah (IRE) **R. M. J. Allen**
3 CHIMALI (IRE), 4, b g Foxhound (USA)—Mari-Ela (IRE) **Inside Track Racing Club**
4 CLEARING SKY (IRE), 4, gr f Exploit (USA)—Litchfield Hills (USA) **Clearing Sky Partnership**
5 DANCE ON THE TOP, 7, ch g Caerleon (USA)—Fern **J-P. Lim & John Hopkins**
6 DESERT CRISTAL (IRE), 4, ch f Desert King (IRE)—Damiana (IRE) **John Hopkins (T/A South Hatch Racing)**
7 FORZENUFF, 4, b c Mujadil (USA)—Sada **John Hopkins (T/A South Hatch Racing)**

MR J. R. BOYLE—continued

8 **IDLE POWER (IRE)**, 7, b g Common Grounds—Idle Fancy **The Idle B'S**
9 **JOY AND PAIN**, 4, b g Pursuit of Love—Ice Chocolate (USA) **E. Farncombe (T/A EWS Shavings)**
10 **LABELLED WITH LOVE**, 5, ch g Zilzal (USA)—Dream Baby **Inside Track Racing Club**
11 **PACKIN EM IN**, 7, b h Young Ern—Wendy's Way **City Industrial Supplies Ltd**
12 **PADDY BOY (IRE)**, 4, br g Overbury (IRE)—Arts Project (IRE) **B. McAtavey**
13 **PARISIEN STAR (IRE)**, 9, ch g Paris House—Auction Maid (IRE) **John Hopkins (T/A South Hatch Racing)**
14 **PERFIDIOUS (USA)**, 7, b g Lear Fan (USA)—Perfolia (USA) **Oxford Computer Consultants Partnership**
15 **SACHIN**, 4, b g Bijou d'inde—Dark Kristal (IRE) **Epsom Sorts**
16 **SINGLE TRACK MIND**, 7, b g Mind Games—Compact Disc (IRE) **John Hopkins (T/A South Hatch Racing)**
17 **SWELLMOVA**, 6, b g Sadler's Wells (USA)—Supamova (USA) **R. M. J. Allen**

THREE-YEAR-OLDS

18 **ARAMAT**, b f Cigar—Winze Kible **J. Michell**
19 **BELLE CHANSON**, b f Kingsinger (IRE)—Tallulah Belle **Inside Track Racing Club**
20 **BRIANNIE (IRE)**, b f Xaar—Annieirwin (IRE) **B. McAtavey**
21 B f Killer Instinct—Farrh Nouriya (IRE) **Miss Pippa Muggeridge**
22 **HEART OF ETERNITY (IRE)**, b f Namid—Kurfuffle **John Hopkins (T/A South Hatch Racing)**
23 **HUGO THE BOSS (IRE)**, ch g Trans Island—Heartland **John Hopkins (T/A South Hatch Racing)**
24 **LILY LENAT**, b f Josr Algarhoud (IRE)—Rushing River (USA) **Allen B. Pope, Andrew J. King**
25 **MUJIMAC (IRE)**, b g Mujadil (USA)—Cross Dall (IRE) **B. McAtavey**
26 **PATRONOFCONFUCIUS (IRE)**, b g Imperial Ballet (IRE)—Shefoog **Mr C. C. A. Kwok**

TWO-YEAR-OLDS

27 Ch c 28/4 Docksider (USA)—Bay Bay (Bay Express) (6036) **Mr C. C. A. Kwok**
28 **CINNAMON GIRL**, ch f 12/3 Erhaab (USA)—Distant Cheers (USA) (Distant View (USA)) (800) **D. E. Grieve**
29 B f 15/3 Mull of Kintyre (USA)—Lala Salama (IRE) (College Chapel) (670) **Mr J. Boyle & Miss Muggeridge**
30 B c 15/1 Tagula (IRE)—Naked Poser (IRE) (Night Shift (USA)) (13413) **Mr James Lau**
31 B c 27/2 Distant Music (USA)—Relankina (IRE) (Broken Hearted) (14754) **Allen B. Pope & Andrew J. King**
32 B f 10/4 Shinko Forest (IRE)—Samriah (IRE) (Wassl) (1333) **R. M. J. Allen**
33 B f 15/1 Imperial Ballet (IRE)—Sugar (Hernando (FR)) (4694) **South Hatch Racing & G. Swift**

Other Owners: Mrs N. D. A. Blatch, M. W. Boyle, A. J. Chambers, Mrs S. E. Crayden, Mr C. W. Eacott, J. Hopkins, M. Mathews, T. R. Pritchard, E. Sames.

Amateur: Mr M. Pattinson.

---

61 MRS S. C. BRADBURNE, Cupar
Postal: **Cunnoquhie Cottage, Letham, Cupar, Fife, KY15 7RU.**
Contacts: **PHONE (01337) 810325 FAX (01337) 810486 MOBILES (07769) 711064 (07768) 705722**
E-MAIL susanbradburne@aol.com

1 **ALMIRE DU LIA (FR)**, 7, ch g Beyssac (FR)—Lita (FR) **Hardie, Cochrane, Paterson & Steel**
2 **ARCTIC LAGOON (IRE)**, 6, ch g Bering—Lake Pleasant (IRE) **William Powrie & Strathpack Partnership**
3 **BODFARI SIGNET**, 9, ch g King's Signet (USA)—Darakah **Strath Pack Partnership**
4 **BODKIN BOY (IRE)**, 5, b g Darnay—Kristar **Noel-Paton, Thorburn, Stewart, Barber**
5 **CASE OF POTEEN (IRE)**, 9, b br m Witness Box (USA)—On The Hooch **Mrs P. Grant**
6 **CHERGAN (IRE)**, 12, b g Yashgan—Cherry Bright (IRE) **Copland, Hardie and Steel**
7 **KHARAK (FR)**, 6, gr g Danehill (USA)—Khariyda (FR) **Hardie, Robb, Copland & Steel**
8 **KIRKSIDE PLEASURE (IRE)**, 4, ch g Grand Plaisir (IRE)—Caledon Mist (IRE)
9 **NO HESITATION**, b g Terimon—Just A Minute **J. G. Bradburne**
10 **NO PICNIC (IRE)**, 7, ch g Be My Native (USA)—Emmagreen **Broad and Cochrane**
11 **NOBLE TIGER (IRE)**, 4, b f Tiger Hill (IRE)—Noble Conquest (USA) **Mark Fleming & Jane Cameron**
12 **NOT A TRACE (IRE)**, 6, b g Gothland (FR)—Copmenow (USA) **Mark Fleming & Jane Cameron**
13 **POWERLOVE (FR)**, 4, b f Solon (GER)—Bywaldor (FR) **Mark Fleming & Jane Cameron**
14 **SOUTH BRONX (IRE)**, 6, br g Anshan—Tender Tan **Mrs S. M. Irwin**
15 **SPEED KRIS (IRE)**, 6, b g Belmez (USA)—Pandia (USA) **Lord Cochrane And Partners**
16 **SUMMER SPECIAL**, 5, b g Mind Games—Summerhill Special (IRE) **Alba Racing Syndicate**
17 **TA TA FOR NOW**, 8, b g Ezzoud (IRE)—Exit Laughing **Mrs V. M. Stewart**
18 **TANDAVA (IRE)**, 7, ch g Indian Ridge—Kashka (USA) **Black & White Communication (Scotland) Ltd**

Other Owners: MR D. W. Barker, Mrs C. J. Broad, The Hon T. H. V. Cochrane, D. Copland, S. E. Kennedy, Mrs C. M. Kennedy, I. McLeod.

Assistant Trainer: J G Bradburne

Jockey (NH): M. Bradburne.

62 MR J. M. BRADLEY, Chepstow
Postal: **Meads Farm, Sedbury Park, Chepstow, Gwent, NP16 7HN.**
Contacts: **PHONE (01291) 622486 FAX (01291) 626939**
E-MAIL j.m.bradley@virgin.net

1 AINTNECESSARILYSO, 7, ch g So Factual (USA)—Ovideo **Miss S. A. Howell**
2 BILLY BATHWICK (IRE), 8, ch g Fayruz—Cut It Fine (USA) **Ms A. M. Williams**
3 BOANERGES (IRE), 8, br g Caerleon (USA)—Sea Siren **E. A. Hayward**
4 CAYMAN BREEZE, 5, b g Danzig (USA)—Lady Thynn (FR) **Mr G. & L. Johnson**
5 CORANGLAIS, 5, ch g Piccolo—Antonia's Folly **J. Brookman**
6 CORRIDOR CREEPER (FR), 8, ch g Polish Precedent (USA)—Sonia Rose (USA) **Mr G. & L. Johnson**
7 CURRENCY, 8, b g Sri Pekan (USA)—On Tiptoes **R. M. Bailey**
8 DEVIOUS AYERS (IRE), 4, br g Dr Devious (IRE)—Yulara (IRE) **Latona Leisure Limited**
9 FLEET ANCHOR, 4, b c Fleetwood (IRE)—Upping The Tempo **The Bourn Partners**
10 FLY MORE, 8, ch g Lycius (USA)—Double River (USA) **E. A. Hayward**
11 FRENCHMANS LODGE, 5, b g Piccolo—St Helena **Mr G. & L. Johnson**
12 FULL SPATE, 10, ch g Unfuwain (USA)—Double River (USA) **E. A. Hayward**
13 HIGH RIDGE, 6, ch g Indian Ridge—Change For A Buck (USA) **James Leisure Ltd**
14 JOHANNIAN, 7, b g Hernando (FR)—Photo Call **Ms A. M. Williams**
15 JUWWI, 11, ch g Mujtahid (USA)—Nouvelle Star (AUS) **Mr J. M. Bradley**
16 MUJKAH (IRE), 9, ch g Mujtahid (USA)—Hot Curry (USA) **R. M. Bailey**
17 NINAH, 4, b f First Trump—Alwal **R. M. Bailey**
18 ONE WAY TICKET, 5, ch h Pursuit of Love—Prima Cominna **Saracen Racing**
19 PARKSIDE PURSUIT, 7, b g Pursuit of Love—Ivory Bride **Mr J. M. Bradley**
20 PHECKLESS, 6, ch g Be My Guest (USA)—Phlirty **racingshares.co.uk**
21 PULSE, 7, b g Salse (USA)—French Gift **R. C. Tooth**
22 REGAL FLIGHT (IRE), 4, b g King's Theatre (IRE)—Green Belt (FR) **Ms A. M. Williams**
23 SABANA (IRE), 7, b g Sri Pekan (USA)—Atyaaf (USA) **E. A. Hayward**
24 SALVIATI (USA), 8, b g Lahib (USA)—Mother Courage **Mr J. M. Bradley**
25 SEVEN NO TRUMPS, 8, ch g Pips Pride—Classic Ring (IRE) **E. A. Hayward**
26 SNOW WOLF, 4, ch g Wolfhound (USA)—Christmas Rose **E. A. Hayward**
27 STARS AT MIDNIGHT, 5, b m Magic Ring (IRE)—Boughtbyphone **Ms A. M. Williams**
28 SUMMER RECLUSE (USA), 6, gr g Cozzene (USA)—Summer Retreat (USA) **C. M. Hunt**
29 TAPAU (IRE), 7, b m Nicolotte—Urtica (IRE) **Ms A. M. Williams**
30 THE TATLING (IRE), 8, b br g Perugino (USA)—Aunty Eileen **Dab Hand Racing**
31 TOMTHEVIC, 7, ch g Emarati (USA)—Madame Bovary **C. M. Hunt**
32 TOPPLING, 7, b g Cadeaux Genereux—Topicality (USA) **E. A. Hayward**
33 VLASTA WEINER, 5, b g Magic Ring (IRE)—Armaiti **Miss D. Hill**
34 WHITBARROW (IRE), 6, b g Royal Abjar (USA)—Danccini (IRE) **Seasons Holidays**
35 ZAMBEZI RIVER, 6, ch g Zamindar (USA)—Double River (USA) **Mr J. M. Bradley**

THREE-YEAR-OLDS

36 DANESCOURT (IRE), b c Danetime (IRE)—Faye **James Leisure Ltd**
37 DREAMER'S LASS, b f Pyramus (USA)—Qualitair Dream **Ken Lock Racing Ltd**
38 MS POLLY GARTER, br f Petong—Utopia **Delamere Cottage Racing Partners (1996)**
39 PEOPLETON BROOK, b g Compton Place—Merch Rhyd-Y-Grug **Mr G. S. Thompson & Mr P. Banfield**
40 QUATRE SAISONS, ch g Bering—Inseparable **Mrs B. V. Chennells**
41 SABO PRINCE, ch g Atraf—Moving Princess **Mr J. M. Bradley**
42 TIME FOR YOU, b f Vettori (IRE)—La Fija **Saracen Racing**

Other Owners: Mrs J. K. Bradley, G. W. Holland, G. T. Lever, S. McAvoy, D. Pearson, A. D. Pirie, Mrs V. M. Ralston, D. A. Shinton, Mr P. Sinfield, Mrs L. Sinfield.

Assistant Trainer: Miss Hayley Davies

Jockey (flat): P. Fitzsimmons. **Jockey (NH):** R. Johnson. **Conditional:** C. J. Davies. **Amateur:** Mr C. Davies.

63 MR M. F. BRADSTOCK, Wantage
Postal: **The Old Manor Stables, Letcombe Bassett, Wantage, Oxfordshire, OX12 9LP.**
Contacts: **PHONE (01235) 760780 FAX (01235) 760754 MOBILE (07887) 686697**
E-MAIL mark.bradstock@btinternet.com

1 AD ASTRA, 6, b g Alhijaz—So It Goes **Mrs M. Fitzpatrick**
2 ALMARAVIDE (GER), 9, ch g Orfano (GER)—Allerleirauh (GER) **P. J. Constable**
3 COSSACK DANCER (IRE), 7, b g Moscow Society (USA)—Merry Lesa **The United Front Partnership**

MR M. F. BRADSTOCK—continued

4 **GAELIC MUSIC (IRE),** 6, b g Accordion—Cuilin Bui (IRE) **P. J. Constable**
5 **GO WHITE LIGHTNING (IRE),** 10, gr g Zaffaran (USA)—Rosy Posy (IRE) **J. B. G. Macleod**
6 **INDESTRUCTIBLE (FR),** 6, b g Hero's Honor (USA)—Money Bag (FR) **The United Front Partnership**
7 **KING HARALD (IRE),** 7, b g King's Ride—Cuilin Bui (IRE) **Piers Pottinger and P B-J Partnership**
8 5, B br m Bob Back (USA)—Lady Bellaghy (IRE) **Mr P. A. Brewer**
9 **NEVER WONDER (IRE),** 10, b g John French—Mistress Anna **Ever The Optimists**
10 **NONANTAIS (FR),** 8, b g Nikos—Sanhia (FR) **The Frankly Intolerable**
11 4, B g Saddlers' Hall (IRE)—Rainbow Light **Ormonds Head Partnership**
12 **SILVER GHOST,** 6, gr g Alderbrook—Belmore Cloud **The Silver Cloud Partnership**
13 **SOMETHING CRISTAL (FR),** 4, b g Baby Turk—Something Fun (FR) **The Something's Up Partnership**
14 **SOMETHING GOLD (FR),** 5, gr g Baby Turk—Exiled (USA) **J. B. G. Macleod**
15 **STAR DIVA (IRE),** 9, b m Toulon—Kerris Melody **Dorchester On Thames Syndicate**

Other Owners: S. Holley, M. J. Bailey, P. Bennett-Jones, C. E. R. Greenway, Bill Hinge, P. D. Hunt, Mrs C. Leitch, Mr H. J. Leitch, J. B. G. Macleod, A. T. A. Manning, Miss J. M. Newell, M. S. Tamburro, C. A. Vernon.

Assistant Trainer: Sara Bradstock

Jockey (NH): M. Bachelor. **Conditional:** J. Bunsell.

MR G. C. BRAVERY, Newmarket
Postal: **Revida Place, Hamilton Road, Newmarket, Suffolk, CB8 7JQ.**
Contacts: **STABLES/FAX** (01638) 668985 **HOME** (01638) 666231 **MOBILE** (07711) 112345
E-MAIL Braverygc@aol.com

1 **BESTAM,** 6, b g Selkirk (USA)—Showery **K. A. Dasmal**
2 **EIJAAZ (IRE),** 4, b c Green Desert (USA)—Kismah **Marilyn Holt And Janet Currie**
3 **RICKY MARTAN,** 4, ch c Foxhound (USA)—Cyrillic **Blackfoot Bloodstock**

THREE-YEAR-OLDS

4 **FARTHING (IRE),** b f Mujadil (USA)—Neat Shilling (IRE) **The TT Partnership**
5 **HAYRAAN (IRE),** b c Bluebird (USA)—Alma Latina (IRE) **F. Nass**
6 **KAWACATOOSE (IRE),** b c Imperial Ballet (IRE)—Cree's Figurine **Hintlesham Cree Partners**
7 **NIGHT OUT (FR),** b f Night Shift (USA)—My Lucky Day (FR) **H. P. Carrington**
8 **UNCLE BULGARIA (IRE),** b c Alhaarth (IRE)—Istibshar (USA) **Orinoco Partnership**

TWO-YEAR-OLDS

9 B c 6/4 Bluebird (USA)—Alma Latina (IRE) (Persian Bold) (16766)
10 Ch f 4/2 Singspiel (IRE)—Blinding (IRE) (High Top) (21000)
11 B f 27/2 Mujadil (USA)—Croeso Cynnes (Most Welcome) (12000)
12 Ch f 19/4 Bertolini (USA)—Kara Sea (USA) (River Special (USA)) (800)
13 B f 21/1 King of Kings (IRE)—Sianema (Persian Bold) (19000)
14 B f 29/1 Royal Academy (USA)—Wild Vintage (USA) (Alysheba (USA)) (40000)

Other Owners: David Allan, MR G. C. Bravery, J. P. Carrington, Miss G. Dobson, T. Taniguchi, Mr A. P. D. Wyke.

Apprentice: Kevin Jackson.

MR OWEN BRENNAN, Worksop
Postal: **Sloswicks Farm, Broad Lane, Worksop, Nottinghamshire, S80 3NJ.**
Contacts: **PHONE** (01909) 473950

1 **AMBER WARRIOR (IRE),** 5, b br g College Chapel—Book Choice **Lady Anne Bentinck**
2 **AMERICAN PRESIDENT (IRE),** 9, br g Lord Americo—Deceptive Response **Lady Anne Bentinck**
3 **COMMON GIRL (IRE),** 7, gr m Roselier (FR)—Rumups Debut (IRE) **J. W. Hardy**
4 **DARIALANN (IRE),** 10, b g Kahyasi—Delsy (FR) **J. Sheridan**
5 **EXTRA CACHE (NZ),** 12, br g Cache of Gold (USA)—Gizmo (NZ) **Lady Anne Bentinck**
6 **FIREAWAY,** 11, b g Infantry—Handymouse **Mrs P. N. Brennan**
7 **GALE STAR (IRE),** 12, b g Strong Gale—Fairly Deep **Mr Owen Brennan**
8 **GOLDHORN (IRE),** 10, b g Little Bighorn—Stylish Gold (IRE) **Mr Owen Brennan**
9 **KING OF THE LIGHT,** 11, b g Rakaposhi King—Dawn Encounter **Lady Anne Bentinck**
10 **SUPERSHOT (IRE),** 7, b g Son of Sharp Shot (IRE)—One To Two (IRE) **Mr Owen Brennan**
11 **TACOLINO (FR),** 11, ch g Royal Charter—Tamilda (FR) **J. Sheridan**
12 **TIPP TOP (IRE),** 8, b g Brief Truce (USA)—Very Sophisticated (USA) **P. Stoner**

Jockey (NH): N. Fehily. **Conditional:** S. Carey.

66 MISS RHONA BREWIS, Belford
Postal: **Chester Hill, Belford, Northumberland, NE70 7EF.**
Contacts: **PHONE (01668) 213239/213281**

1 **CONCHITA**, 8, b m St Ninian—Carnetto **Mrs G. E. Brewis**
2 **CRACKADEE**, 6, b br g Alflora (IRE)—Carnetto **Miss Rhona Brewis**
3 **KEPPEL**, 5, b g Sir Harry Lewis (USA)—Kimberley Rose **Miss Rhona Brewis**
4 **PEPPERNICK**, 9, br g Alflora (IRE)—Nicolini **R. Brewis**
5 **TIMBERLEY**, 11, ch g Dancing High—Kimberley Rose **Miss Rhona Brewis**

67 MR J. J. BRIDGER, Liphook
Postal: **Upper Hatch Farm, Liphook, Hampshire, GU30 7EL.**
Contacts: **PHONE/FAX (01428) 722528 MOBILE (07785) 716614**

1 **BORDER EDGE**, 7, b g Beveled (USA)—Seymour Ann **Allsorts**
2 **CATCH THE FOX**, 5, b g Fraam—Versaillesprincess **Five For Fun**
3 **CROMARTY BAY**, 4, b f Victory Note (USA)—Cromarty **Mr Barry Webb**
4 **DUNCANBIL (IRE)**, 4, b f Turtle Island (IRE)—Saintly Guest **R. Reynolds**
5 **HARBOUR HOUSE**, 6, b g Distant Relative—Double Flutter **T. Ware**
6 **MUST BE SO**, 4, b f So Factual (USA)—Ovideo **Connaught Racing**
7 **MYTHICAL CHARM**, 6, b m Charnwood Forest (IRE)—Triple Tricks (IRE) **T. Ware**
8 **PIQUET**, 7, br m Mind Games—Petonellajill **Mr J. J. Bridger**
9 **ZAZOUS**, 4, b g Zafonic (USA)—Confidentiality (USA) **Miss Rachel Bridger**
10 **ZINGING**, 6, b g Fraam—Hi Hoh (IRE) **Mr J. J. Bridger**

THREE-YEAR-OLDS

11 **BRUSHWOOD (UAE)**, b g Timber Country (USA)—Sandova (IRE) **Mrs J. McInnes**
12 **BYRON BAY**, b c My Best Valentine—Candarela **I. M. Tough**
13 **ENTERTAIN**, b f Royal Applause—Darshay (IRE) **W. A. Wood**
14 **KEMPSEY**, ch c Wolfhound (USA)—Mockingbird **T. Thorn**
15 **ROBIN BANKES**, b c Shannon Cottage (USA)—Mistress Bankes (IRE) **Mr W. S. Ivens**
16 **WORTH A GRAND (IRE)**, br g Raise A Grand (IRE)—Ballykett Pride (IRE) **S. J. Taylor**

TWO-YEAR-OLDS

17 **DANNY THE DIP**, b g 12/4 Prince Sabo—Ann's Pearl (IRE) (Cyrano de Bergerac) (1238) **S. J. Taylor**
18 **FRATT'N PARK (IRE)**, b f 1/4 Tagula (IRE)—Bouffant (High Top) (10000) **R. Reynolds**
19 Gr f 14/4 Paris House—Tangerine (Primo Dominie) **N. S. Short**

Other Owners: P. J. Hague, Mr J. Jenner, Mrs J. E. Lunn, C. Marshall, C. R. Mussell, E. Treacy.

Assistant Trainer: Rachel Bridger

Amateur: Miss Donna Handley.

68 MRS H. M. BRIDGES, Shaftesbury
Postal: **Gears Mill, Shaftesbury, Dorset, SP7 0LT.**
Contacts: **PHONE (01747) 852825**

1 **APPACH (FR)**, 6, gr g Riche Mare (FR)—Simply Red (FR) **Mrs H. M. Bridges**
2 **BALKIRK**, 8, ch g Selkirk (USA)—Balenare **Mrs H. M. Bridges**
3 **DARCEY MAE**, 7, b m Afzal—Belhelvie **Mrs H. M. Bridges**
4 **KATTEGAT**, 9, b g Slip Anchor—Kirsten **Mrs H. M. Bridges**
5 **MASALARIAN (IRE)**, 10, b g Doyoun—Masamiyda **Mrs H. M. Bridges**
6 **SAFARI PARADISE (FR)**, 8, ch g Red Paradise—Safari Liz (USA) **Mrs H. M. Bridges**
7 **SOLO DANCER**, 7, ch m Sayaarr (USA)—Oiseval **Mrs H. M. Bridges**
8 **ST KILDA**, 8, b m Past Glories—Oiseval **Mrs H. M. Bridges**
9 **THERE IS NO DOUBT (FR)**, 4, b g Mansonnien (FR)—Ma Chance (FR) **Mrs H. M. Bridges**
10 **WAHIBA SANDS**, 12, b g Pharly (FR)—Lovely Noor (USA) **Mrs H. M. Bridges**

Other Owners: Mrs E. G. Hayward.

Assistant Trainer: Miss Lucy Bridges

Amateur: Miss Lucy Bridges.

69 MR D. G. BRIDGWATER, Stow-on-the-Wold
Postal: Wyck Hill Farm, Wyck Hill, Stow on the Wold, Cheltenham, Gloucestershire, GL54 1HT.
Contacts: PHONE (01242) 609086/609233 FAX (01242) 609086 MOBILE (07831) 635817

1 AMUSEMENT, 9, ch g Mystiko (USA)—Jolies Eaux **Daltagh Construction Ltd**
2 ASK AGAIN, 6, ch g Rakaposhi King—Boreen's Glory **D. A. Thorpe**
3 BOBBLE WONDER, 4, b f Classic Cliche (IRE)—Wonderfall (FR) **D. A. Thorpe**
4 BOSPHORUS, 6, b g Polish Precedent (USA)—Ancara **Led Astray Again Partnership**
5 CASSANOS (IRE), 4, b g Ali-Royal (IRE)—I'm Your Girl **A. A. Wright**
6 COLOURFUL ERA, 11, ch h Indian Ridge—Clare Celeste **Mr D. G. Bridgwater**
7 CONSANT (IRE), 8, ch g Barathea (IRE)—Dinalina (FR) **The Rule Racing Syndicate**
8 DARGO, 11, b g Formidable (USA)—Mountain Memory **Mr D. G. Bridgwater**
9 FLEURENKA, 7, br m Alflora (IRE)—Tochenka **Anita & Relton Minton**
10 FOREST STREAM, 5, b m Alderbrook—Drakes Adventure **Dr E. E. Hill**
11 HONOR ROUGE (IRE), 6, ch m Highest Honor (FR)—Ayers Rock (IRE) **Terry & Sarah Amos**
12 ICEY RUN, 5, b g Runnett—Polar Storm (IRE) **Miss V. B. H. Evans**
13 IRISH PLAYWRIGHT (IRE), 5, b g King's Theatre (IRE)—Marino Waltz **Brooklands Farms Ltd**
14 KIEV (IRE), 5, b g Bahhare (USA)—Badrah (USA) **Rother Garth Racing**
15 LASSER LIGHT, 5, b br g Inchinor—Light Ray **Miss M. S. Hill**
16 LUSHPOOL (IRE), 7, b m Supreme Leader—Dawn Hunt (IRE) **D. A. Thorpe**
17 MUROTOEVATION (IRE), 6, b g Muroto—Toevarro **N. D. Edden**
18 MY CARAIDD, 9, b m Rakaposhi King—Tochenka **Anita & Relton Minton**
19 PUCKS WAY, 6, b g Nomadic Way (USA)—Adventurous Lady **Dr E. E. Hill**
20 RUN ON, 7, b h Runnett—Polar Storm (IRE) **Miss V. B. H. Evans**
21 SLINKY MALINKY, 7, b m Alderbrook—Winnie The Witch **The Cats Whiskers**
22 SOCIETY PET, 6, b m Runnett—Polar Storm (IRE) **Miss V. B. H. Evans**
23 SPACE HOPPER (IRE), 10, ch g Mister Lord (USA)—Kilmalooda Lass **N. D. Edden**
24 STREET GAMES, 6, b g Mind Games—Pusey Street **Mrs L. Launchbury**
25 THE BEDUTH NAVI, 5, b g Forzando—Sweets (IRE) **R. W. Neale**
26 TRUMPINGTON, 7, ch m First Trump—Brockton Flame **R. P. Russell**
27 YAKAREEM (IRE), 9, b g Rainbows For Life (CAN)—Brandywell **Mrs M. A. Bridgwater**

THREE-YEAR-OLDS

28 ORTICA (FR), b g Subotica (FR)—Volniste (FR) **Terry & Sarah Amos**
29 OUR JAKE, b c Wizard King—Russian Project (IRE) **J. C. Bradbury**

TWO-YEAR-OLDS

30 Ch c 3/2 Forzando—Sweets (IRE) (Persian Heights) (10000) **R. Neale**

Other Owners: Ms L. M. Butcher, C. L. Chatwin, W. J. Joyce, D. J. Mills, G. P. D. Walker, Mr T. M. Wright.

Jockey (flat): S. Righton. **Jockey (NH):** R. Thornton. **Conditional:** S. Johnson. **Apprentice:** D. Nolan.

70 MR G. F. BRIDGWATER, Claverdon
Postal: The Rowans, 14 Shrewley Common, Shrewley, Warwickshire, CV35 7AP.
Contacts: PHONE (01926) 840137 MOBILE (07769) 894400
E-MAIL bridgwater9@aol.com

1 ELLAMYTE, 5, b m Elmaamul (USA)—Deanta In Eirinn **Mrs G. J. Bridgwater**
2 IMPERO, 7, b g Emperor Jones (USA)—Fight Right (FR) **See You Later Club**
3 IZZY GETS BUSY (IRE), 5, b m Flemensfirth (USA)—Builders Line (IRE) **Smallburns Stud**
4 LADY PREDOMINANT, 4, b f Primo Dominie—Enlisted (IRE) **City Racing Club**
5 MEIKLECANTLY CHARM, 6, b m White Sorrel—Forgotten Empress **Mr R. Kester**
6 ORO STREET (IRE), 9, b g Dolphin Street (FR)—Love Unlimited **Mrs G. J. Bridgwater**
7 WINNIE FLIES AGAIN, 9, b m Phardante—Winnie The Witch **Mrs M. A. Bridgwater**

Other Owners: K. W. Bradley, Mr A. Dowton, M. J. Lurcock, Mr G. F. Rowledge, R. Sidebottom, Ms L. Tomlin.

71 MR W. M. BRISBOURNE, Nesscliffe
Postal: Ness Strange Stables, Great Ness, Shrewsbury, Shropshire, SY4 2LE.
Contacts: PHONE (01743) 741536/741360 FAX (01743) 741285 MOBILE (07803) 019651

1 ACUZIO, 4, b c Mon Tresor—Veni Vici (IRE) **Derek Hartland**
2 ADOBE, 10, b g Green Desert (USA)—Shamshir **P. R. Kirk**

MR W. M. BRISBOURNE—continued

  3 6, Gr m Roselier (FR)—Afford **Mr C. Edwards**
  4 AL AWWAM, 6, b g Machiavellian (USA)—Just A Mirage **Hamerton, Twidle**
  5 BAYCHEVELLE (IRE), 4, ch f Bahamian Bounty—Phantom Ring **R. Bailey**
  6 BEAVER DIVA, 4, b f Bishop of Cashel—Beaver Skin Hunter **S. McPhee**
  7 BELLA PAVLINA, 7, ch m Sure Blade (USA)—Pab's Choice **The Cartmel Syndicate**
  8 BEN HUR, 6, b g Zafonic (USA)—Gayane **D. C. Rutter & H. Clewlow**
  9 BEVELLER, 6, ch g Beveled (USA)—Klairover **N. C. Jones**
10 BISH BASH BOSH (IRE), 4, b f Bien Bien (USA)—Eurolink Virago **Let's Live Racing**
11 BLACKIES ALL (USA), 7, b g Hazaam (USA)—Allijess (USA) **Mrs K. J. Oulton**
12 BRAVELY DOES IT (USA), 5, gr g Holy Bull (USA)—Vigors Destiny (USA) **Team Racing**
13 BUSCADOR (USA), 6, ch g Crafty Prospector (USA)—Fairway Flag (USA) **David Robson**
14 CALARA HILLS, 4, ch f Bluegrass Prince (IRE)—Atlantic Line **Mrs J. M. Russell**
15 CANTEMERE (IRE), 5, b m Bluebird (USA)—Legally Delicious **R. Bailey**
16 CASHNEEM (IRE), 7, b g Case Law—Haanem **Law Abiding Citizens**
17 CHARLIE CHAPEL, 6, b g College Chapel—Lightino **D. Shenton Syndicate**
18 DANETTIE, 4, b f Danzero (AUS)—Petite Heritiere **J. Oldknow**
19 DESERT ARC (IRE), 7, b g Spectrum (IRE)—Bint Albadou (IRE) **S. E. Roberts**
20 DISPOL VERITY, 5, b m Averti (IRE)—Fawley Mist **L. R. Owen**
21 DORANS LANE, 7, b m Gildoran—Snitton Lane **G. L. Porter**
22 DOUBLE TURN, 5, ch g Double Trigger (IRE)—Its My Turn **Mr G Critchley**
23 DUNN DEAL (IRE), 5, b g Revoque (IRE)—Buddy And Soda (IRE) **R. McNeill**
24 EASTERN SCARLET (IRE), 5, b g Woodborough (USA)—Cuddles (IRE)
25 ELLWAY HEIGHTS, 8, b g Shirley Heights—Amina
26 ESCALADE, 8, b g Green Desert (USA)—Sans Escale (USA) **D. F. Slingsby**
27 ETCHING (USA), 5, b m Groom Dancer (USA)—Eternity
28 FIRST TRUTH, 8, b g Rudimentary (USA)—Pursuit of Truth (USA) **R. Bailey**
29 FRENCH RISK (IRE), 5, b g Entrepreneur—Troyes **Mrs D. Tumman**
30 GIUNCHIGLIO, 6, ch g Millkom—Daffodil Fields **Mr J Scott**
31 GOLD FERVOUR (IRE), 6, b g Mon Tresor—Fervent Fan (IRE) **J. Tomlinson**
32 GOLDBRICKER, 5, b g Muhtarram (USA)—Sally Slade **K. Bennett**
33 GOLDEN COIN, 9, ch g St Ninian—Legal Coin **Mr R. Moseley**
34 GOT TO BE CASH, 6, ch m Lake Coniston (IRE)—Rasayel (USA) **Mrs B. Penton**
35 ICED DIAMOND (IRE), 6, b g Petardia—Prime Site (IRE) **P. J. Williams**
36 IFTIKHAR (USA), 6, b g Storm Cat (USA)—Muhbubh (USA) **L. R. Owen**
37 INSTANT HIT, 6, b g Indian Ridge—Pick of the Pops **M. M. Woods**
38 LIGHT THE DAWN (IRE), 5, ch m Indian Ridge—Flaming June (USA) **A. P. Burgoyne**
39 LOADED GUN, 5, ch g Highest Honor (FR)—Woodwardia (USA) **J. F. Thomas**
40 LUCKILY (IRE), 6, br m Key of Luck (USA)—Sarapaka (IRE) **M. M. Woods**
41 MAGARI, 4, b f Royal Applause—Thatcher's Era (IRE) **Startford Bards Racing**
42 MARAVEDI (IRE), 5, ch m Hector Protector (USA)—Manuetti (IRE) **Stratford Bards Racing**
43 5, B g Primitive Rising (USA)—Meole Brace **Mr J. Tomlinson**
44 MERDIFF, 6, b g Machiavellian (USA)—Balwa (USA) **Team Racing**
45 MERRYMAKER, 5, b g Machiavellian (USA)—Wild Pavane **The Blacktoffee Partnership**
46 MILLI WIZZ, 5, b m Wizard King—State of Love **S. V. Parry**
47 MILLY WATERS, 4, b f Danzero (AUS)—Chilly Waters **J. Oldknow**
48 MISKINA, 4, b f Mark of Esteem (IRE)—Najmat Alshemaal (IRE) **The Blacktoffee Partnership**
49 MORNING PAL (IRE), 6, br g Scribano—Morning Clare (IRE) **Mr F. Lloyd**
50 MOSCOW EXECUTIVE, 7, b m Moscow Society (USA)—Stylish Executive (IRE) **Over the Last Partnership**
51 OPPORTUNE (GER), 10, br g Shirley Heights—On The Tiles **The Ox Hill Flyers**
52 OSORNO, 5, ch g Inchinor—Pacifica **Mrs K. J. Oulton**
53 PAVEMENT GATES, 5, b m Bishop of Cashel—Very Bold **M. Wynne-Jones**
54 PHAR RIVER (IRE), 6, ch g Scribano—Down By The River **Mr F. Lloyd**
55 PRELUDE, 4, b f Danzero (AUS)—Dancing Debut **A. P. Burgoyne**
56 RANI TWO, 6, b m Wolfhound (USA)—Donya **Mr B. L. Loader**
57 RED SCORPION (USA), 6, ch g Nureyev (USA)—Pricket (USA) **Mrs E. M. Coquelin**
58 REDSTAR ATTRACTION, 7, ch g Nalchik (USA)—Star Gal **Magnate Racing**
59 REGENCY RED (IRE), 7, ch g Dolphin Street (FR)—Future Romance **Mrs J. M. Russell**
60 ROMAN MAZE, 5, ch g Lycius (USA)—Maze Garden (USA) **The Jenko and Thomo Partnership**
61 ROYAL INDULGENCE, 5, b g Royal Applause—Silent Indulgence (USA) **Mr P. G. Evans**
62 ROYAL UPSTART, 4, ch g Up And At 'em—Tycoon Tina **Mr W. M. Brisbourne**
63 SAFIRAH, 4, b f Singspiel (IRE)—Princess Haifa (USA) **J. Sankey**
64 SALTRIO, 7, b g Slip Anchor—Hills' Presidium **R. McNeill**
65 SAMUEL CHARLES, 7, b g Green Desert (USA)—Hejraan (USA) **J. F. Thomas**
66 SASPYS LAD, 8, b g Faustus (USA)—Legendary Lady **Mrs K. J. Oulton**
67 SIENNA SUNSET (IRE), 6, ch m Spectrum (IRE)—Wasabi (IRE) **R. Bailey**
68 SMIRFYS PARTY, 7, ch g Clantime—Party Scenes **Mrs D. Plant**

MR W. M. BRISBOURNE—continued

69 SMIRFYS SYSTEMS, 6, b g Safawan—Saint Systems **Mrs D. Plant**
70 SUMMER SHADES, 7, b m Green Desert (USA)—Sally Slade **K. Bennett**
71 SYLVIAJAZZ, 6, b m Alhijaz—Dispol Princess (IRE) **J. W. Jenkins**
72 TBM CAN, 6, b g Rock City—Fire Sprite **Golden Furlong Racing**
73 TOKEWANNA, 5, b m Danehill (USA)—High Atlas **Merryland Properties Ltd**
74 TRUSTED MOLE (IRE), 7, b g Eagle Eyed (USA)—Orient Air **Mr P. G. Evans**
75 TURNER, 4, gr g El Prado (IRE)—Gaily Royal (IRE) **Mr W. M. Clare**
76 WOOD FERN (UAE), 5, b g Green Desert (USA)—Woodsia
77 YORK CLIFF, 7, b g Marju (IRE)—Azm **Team Racing**
78 ZAHUNDA (IRE), 6, b m Spectrum (IRE)—Gift of Glory (FR) **The Nelson Pigs Might Fly Racing Club**
79 ZEN GARDEN, 4, b f Alzao (USA)—Maze Garden (USA) **Mrs E. M. Coquelin**

THREE-YEAR-OLDS

80 BARBIROLLI, b c Machiavellian (USA)—Blushing Barada (USA) **Team Racing**
81 BELLA PLUNKETT (IRE), ch f Daggers Drawn (USA)—Amazona (IRE) **Mr P. G. Evans**
82 BINT IL SULTAN (IRE), b f Xaar—Knight's Place (IRE) **Mr P. J. Salisbury**
83 CASCADE LAKES, ch f Fraam—Spring Flyer (IRE) **Swanvista Limited**
84 CONSIDER THIS, b f Josr Algarhoud (IRE)—River of Fortune (IRE) **Lostford Manor Stud**
85 DEWIN COCH, b g Wizard King—Drudwen **J. E. Lloyd**
86 DUNYA, b f Unfuwain (USA)—Tithcar **Mrs J. Minton**
87 B f Bettergeton—Flicker **Harry Clewlow**
88 Gr c Cloudings (IRE)—Hill Farm Dancer **M. E. Hughes**
89 IGNITION, ch f Rock City—Fire Sprite **M. F. Hyman**
90 INSIGNIA (IRE), b c Royal Applause—Amathea (IRE) **Mr W. M. Clare**
91 LIQUID LOVER (IRE), b c Night Shift (USA)—New Tycoon (IRE)
92 NEW ENGLAND, ch g Bachir (IRE)—West Escape **County Stairlift Ltd**
93 RAPID FLOW, b c Fasliyev (USA)—Fleet River (USA)
94 SHARP N FROSTY, b g Somayda (USA)—Wily Miss **M. A. Wood**
95 B c Prince Sabo—Sorridar
96 TONIGHT (IRE), b g Imperial Ballet (IRE)—No Tomorrow (IRE)
97 ZENDARO, b g Danzero (AUS)—Countess Maud **Zen Racing**

TWO-YEAR-OLDS

98 GAMESTERS LADY, br f 8/4 Almushtarak (IRE)—Tycoon Tina (Tina's Pet) (3200) **Gamesters Partnership**
99 Ch f 29/4 Rock City—Hill Farm Dancer (Gunner B) **M. E. Hughes**
100 B g 24/1 Observatory (USA)—Precocious Miss (USA) (Diesis) (7000) **Mr W. M. Brisbourne**
101 Ch c 11/3 Foxhound (USA)—Ragged Moon (Raga Navarro (ITY)) (800) **Mr Fairclough**
102 B c 2/4 Almushtarak (IRE)—Risk The Witch (Risk Me (FR)) **Mr C. Davies**
103 Ch c 28/4 Most Welcome—Spring Flyer (IRE) (Waajib) **Swanvista Limited**
104 THE FLYING PEACH, ch f 27/1 Observatory (USA)—Taffeta (IRE) (Barathea (IRE)) (2500) **Mr C. Peach**

Other Owners: D. Barnett, G. J. Baskott, Mr R. C. Carter, Mr P. Clare, Mr B. L. Clark, Mr G. Dewhurst, Mr R. C. Edwards, Mr C. J. Edwards, C. J. Fitch, P. G. Gradwell, J. N. Harper, P. M. Hill, S. J. Hill, J Scott Furnishers Ltd, H. R. Johnstone, A. S. Johnstone, Mr A. Jones, D. Musgrave, Miss S. A. Nicholls, Mr S. Petty, Mr M. J. Petty, N. Pharo, A. Pitt, Mrs J. B. Pye, Mr R. A. Sankey, D. W. Sibson, D. N. Smith, Mr D. R. Southworth, D. Sutton, P. T. Williams, S. M. Woodhall.

Assistant Trainer: Mrs Pam Brisbourne

Jockey (flat): G. Baker, K. Fallon, S. W. Kelly, R. Mullen. **Jockey (NH):** A. P. McCoy, R. Thornton. **Apprentice:** Ben Swarbrick.

MR C. E. BRITTAIN, Newmarket
Postal: **'Carlburg'**, 49 Bury Road, Newmarket, Suffolk, CB8 7BY.
Contacts: **HOME (01638) 663739 OFFICE (01638) 664347 FAX (01638) 661744**
MOBILE (07785) 302121
E-MAIL **carlburgst@aol.com**

1 ALBADI, 4, b g Green Desert (USA)—Lyrist **S. Manana**
2 AMPOULE, 6, b g Zamindar (USA)—Diamond Park (IRE) **R. A. Pledger**
3 BAHIANO (IRE), 4, ch c Barathea (USA)—Trystero **Mr C. E. Brittain**
4 BUZZ BUZZ, 4, b f Mtoto—Abuzz **Mrs C. E. Brittain**
5 FRAGRANT STAR, 4, gr f Soviet Star (USA)—Norfolk Lavender (CAN) **Mr C. E. Brittain**
6 MAZUNA (IRE), 4, b f Cape Cross (IRE)—Keswa **S. Manana**
7 MEMBERSHIP (USA), 5, ch h Belong To Me (USA)—Shamisen **S. Manana**

MR C. E. BRITTAIN—continued

8 MENHOUBAH (USA), 4, b f Dixieland Band (USA)—Private Seductress (USA) **S. Manana**
9 NASSIRIA, 4, b f Singspiel (IRE)—Naskhi **S. Manana**
10 SANTANDO, 5, b g Hernando (FR)—Santarem (USA) **Mrs J. M. Khan**
11 SHUSH, 7, b g Shambo—Abuzz **Mrs C. E. Brittain**
12 SIERRA, 4, ch f Dr Fong (USA)—Warning Belle **Wyck Hall Stud Ltd**
13 SYLVA ROYAL (IRE), 4, gr f Royal Applause—Trim Star **E. A. Grimstead & Son Ltd**
14 VAR (USA), 6, b br h Forest Wildcat (USA)—Loma Preata **Mr M. Rashid**
15 WARRSAN (IRE), 7, b h Caerleon (USA)—Lucayan Princess **S. Manana**

THREE-YEAR-OLDS

16 AKONA MATATA (USA), b c Seeking The Gold (USA)—
Oh What A Dance (USA) **Sheikh Hamdan Bin Mohammed Al Maktoum**
17 AMALIE (IRE), b f Fasliyev (USA)—Princess Amalie (USA) **S. Manana**
18 ANISSATI, ch f Machiavellian (USA)—Inchacooley (IRE) **Mr M. Al Shafar**
19 ASHARON, b c Efisio—Arriving **R. A. Pledger**
20 BAHAR SHUMAAL (IRE), b c Dubai Millennium—High Spirited **S. Manana**
21 CALIFORNIA GIRL, ch f Zafonic (USA)—Lady Georgia **A. J. Richards**
22 CARIBBEAN PEARL (USA), b f Silver Hawk (USA)—Ras Shaikh (USA) **Mohamed Obaida**
23 COUNTRY PURSUIT (USA), ch c Theatrical—Jade Flush (USA) **Sheikh Hamdan Bin Mohammed Al Maktoum**
24 CRIMSON YEAR (USA), ch f Dubai Millennium—Crimson Conquest (USA) **Marwan Al Maktoum**
25 DOCTOR'S CAVE, b c Night Shift (USA)—Periquitum **A. J. Richards**
26 EXCUSEZ MOI (USA), b c Fusaichi Pegasus (USA)—Jiving **Sheikh Hamdan Bin Mohammed Al Maktoum**
27 EXTREME BEAUTY (USA), ch f Rahy (USA)—Mediation (IRE) **Dr A. Ridha**
28 FOX, b c Diktat—Badawi (USA) **Marwan Al Maktoum**
29 GHASIBA (IRE), gr f Daylami (IRE)—Night Owl **S. Manana**
30 GIDAM GIDAM (IRE), b g King's Best (USA)—Flamands (IRE) **S. Ali**
31 HALLOWED DREAM (IRE), b f Alhaarth (IRE)—Salul **Minster Stud**
32 HASHIMA (USA), b f Kingmambo (USA)—Fairy Heights (IRE) **S. Manana**
33 HATTAN (IRE), ch c Halling (USA)—Luana **S. Manana**
34 IMPROVISE, b f Lend A Hand—Mellow Jazz **S. Ali**
35 KANDIDATE, b c Kabool—Valleyrose (IRE) **A. J. Richards**
36 LADY PILOT, b f Dansili—Mighty Flyer (IRE) **S. Manana**
37 LUCINA, b f Machiavellian (USA)—Lunda (IRE) **S. Manana**
38 LUNAR SKY (USA), b f Lemon Drop Kid (USA)—Celestial Bliss (USA) **S. Ali**
39 MANSIYA, ch f Vettori (IRE)—Bay Shade (USA) **S. Manana**
40 MARCH HEIR (USA), b c Deputy Minister (CAN)—
Advancing Star (USA) **Sheikh Hamdan Bin Mohammed Al Maktoum**
41 MINA A SALEM, b c Singspiel (IRE)—Amber Fizz (USA) **S. Manana**
42 NAIVETY, ch f Machiavellian (USA)—Innocence **S. Ali**
43 NICE TUNE, b f Diktat—Military Tune (IRE) **S. Manana**
44 PARTY BOSS, gr c Silver Patriarch (IRE)—Third Party **Michael Clarke**
45 PUNCTUATION, b c Groom Dancer (USA)—Shady Point (IRE) **Marwan Al Maktoum**
46 RANSACKER, b g Bahamian Bounty—Hazy Heights **A. J. Richards & S. A. Richards**
47 SAFFA GARDEN (IRE), b f King's Best (USA)—Allegheny River (USA) **S. Manana**
48 SAWARI, b f Zafonic (USA)—Nefeli **S. Manana**
49 SHRINE MOUNTAIN (USA), b c Distorted Humor (USA)—Fancy Ruler (USA) **WinStar Farm LLC**
50 SIGN OF LUCK (IRE), ch f Daylami (IRE)—Ascot Cyclone (USA) **Mohamed Obaida**
51 TAKRIT (IRE), b f Giant's Causeway—Mockery **S. Manana**
52 TANZANI (USA), b c Giant's Causeway (USA)—Aunt Pearl (USA) **S. Manana**
53 TAXMAN (IRE), ch g Singspiel (IRE)—Love of Silver (USA) **Ali Saeed**
54 TONY JAMES (IRE), b c Xaar—Sunset Ridge (FR) **A. J. Richards**
55 TREASURY (IRE), b f King's Best (USA)—Copious (IRE) **S. Ali**
56 TREBLE SEVEN (USA), b br f Fusaichi Pegasus (USA)—Nemea (USA) **S. Manana**
57 WOLF PACK, b c Green Desert (USA)—Warning Shadows (IRE) **Marwan Al Maktoum**

TWO-YEAR-OLDS

58 B f 7/3 Cape Cross (IRE)—Astuti (IRE) (Waajib) (50000) **Sultan Ali & Saeed Misleh**
59 AZIME (IRE), b c 19/3 Cape Cross (IRE)—Adjisa (IRE) (Doyoun) (36000) **S. Manana**
60 B f 29/4 Rahy (USA)—Bevel (USA) (Mr Prospector (USA)) **Marwan Al Maktoum**
61 B f 28/1 In The Wings—Blodwen (USA) (Mister Baileys) (24000) **S. Manana**
62 B br f 10/4 Kingmambo (USA)—Catinca (USA) (Storm Cat) (63846) **S. Manana**
63 B br f 7/1 King Cugat (USA)—Chaste (USA) (Cozzene) (53205) **S. Ali**
64 B f 17/3 Polish Precedent (USA)—Chiltern Court (USA) (Topsider (USA)) (6200) **Mr C. E. Brittain**
65 B br f 8/2 Cozzene (USA)—Cruisie (USA) (Assert) (66507) **S. Ali**
66 B br f 5/2 Machiavellian (USA)—Cymbala (FR) (Assert) (53205) **Sultan Ali (Jumeirah Racing)**

MR C. E. BRITTAIN—continued

67 **DALLMA (IRE)**, b f 25/3 Daylami (IRE)—Play With Fire (FR) (Priolo (USA)) **S. Manana**
68 B c 1/2 Xaar—Diamond Park (IRE) (Alzao (USA)) (19000) **S. Manana**
69 Ch c 26/1 Thunder Gulch (USA)—Dubian (High Line) **Mohamed Obaida**
70 Gr ro f 15/1 Giant's Causeway (USA)—Ela Athena (Ezzoud (IRE)) (100000) **Dr A. Ridha**
71 B br f 21/4 Forest Wildcat (USA)—Farrfesheena (USA) (Rahy (USA)) **Marwan Al Maktoum**
72 **FLY ME TO THE MOON (GER)**, b f 12/2 Galileo (IRE)—Four Roses (IRE) (Darshaan) (50000) **S. Ali**
73 B f 22/3 Diesis—Forest Storm (USA) (Woodman (USA)) (25000) **S. Manana**
74 **FORMAT**, b f 16/4 Mark of Esteem (IRE)—Forum (Lion Cavern (USA)) **Wyck Hall Stud Ltd**
75 B f 2/4 Sinndar (IRE)—Imelda (USA) (Manila (USA)) (28000) **S. Manana**
76 B f 20/2 Swain (IRE)—Impetuous Image (USA) (Mr Prospector (USA)) (53205) **S. Ali**
77 B f 30/3 Kingmambo (USA)—Isle de France (IRE) (Nureyev (USA)) (43594) **S. Manana**
78 Ch f 4/4 Singspiel (IRE)—Kameez (IRE) (Arazi (USA)) (11400) **Ali Saeed**
79 B f 8/5 Sadler's Wells (USA)—La Pepite (USA) (Mr Prospector (USA)) **S. Manana**
80 B br f 11/5 Dixie Union (USA)—Leading The Way (USA) (Septieme Ciel (USA)) **S. Ali**
81 B br f 8/2 Grand Slam (USA)—Lucky Lineage (USA) (Storm Cat (USA)) (37243) **S. Ali**
82 B f 17/2 Singspiel (IRE)—Lunda (IRE) (Soviet Star (USA)) **S. Manana**
83 Ch c 10/3 Galileo (IRE)—Lyric (Lycius (USA)) (57000) **Mr Salem Rashid**
84 Ch f 14/3 Fantastic Light (USA)—Maggi For Margaret (Shavian) (50000) **Sultan Ali (Jumeirah Racing)**
85 B f 27/2 Diktat—Magic Sister (Cadeaux Genereux) (27000) **S. Manana**
86 Ch f 8/4 Diesis—Min Elreeh (USA) (Danzig (USA)) (39904) **S. Manana**
87 B f 22/2 Mark of Esteem (IRE)—Mistle Song (Nashwan (USA)) **S. Manana**
88 B c 18/4 Mark of Esteem (IRE)—Mistook (USA) (Phone Trick (USA)) **Wyck Hall Stud Ltd**
89 **MY AMALIE (IRE)**, b f 26/4 Galileo (IRE)—Princess Amalie (USA) (Rahy (USA)) (42000) **S. Manana**
90 **NESHLA**, ch f 3/4 Singspiel (IRE)—Nordica (Northfields (USA)) (55000) **S. Manana**
91 B f 21/3 Green Desert (USA)—New Sayyedati (USA) (Shadeed (USA)) **Ali Saeed**
92 B f 12/3 Medicean—Opari (IRE) (Night Shift (USA)) (20000) **S. Manana**
93 **ORANGES AND LEMONS (FR)**, b f 3/2 Zafonic (USA)—
                                      Tarte Aux Pommes (USA) (Local Talent (USA)) **A. J. Richards**
94 B br f 27/3 Kingmambo (USA)—Ozena (USA) (Strawberry Road (AUS)) **WinStar Farm LLC**
95 **PARTY BELLE**, b f 12/3 Silver Patriarch (IRE)—Third Party (Lomond (USA)) **Michael Clarke**
96 **PRINQUET (USA)**, ch f 26/1 Marquetry (USA)—Princess Kris (Kris) (34583) **S. Ali**
97 B f 16/2 Rainbow Quest (USA)—Radiant (USA) (Foolish Pleasure (USA)) (52000) **S. Manana**
98 B c 15/4 Lujain (USA)—Rose Bay (Shareef Dancer (USA)) (10000) **S. Manana**
99 B f 10/2 Rahy (USA)—Sayyedati (Shadeed (USA)) **Mohamed Obaida**
100 **SEIGNEUR**, b c 14/3 Diktat—Hazy Heights (Shirley Heights) (USA) **Wyck Hall Stud Ltd**
101 B c 27/1 Lomitas—Sephala (USA) (Mr Prospector (USA)) **S. Manana**
102 Ch f 3/4 Fantastic Light (USA)—Shady Point (IRE) (Unfuwain (USA)) **Marwan Al Maktoum**
103 **SHAWL**, ch f 31/1 Shahrastani (USA)—Circlet (Lion Cavern (USA)) **Wyck Hall Stud Ltd**
104 B f 27/2 Xaar—Signs And Wonders (Danehill (USA)) (22000) **S. Manana**
105 B br f 6/3 Lujain (USA)—Slow Jazz (USA) (Chief's Crown (USA)) **S. Ali**
106 B f 8/2 Seeking The Gold (USA)—South of Saturn (USA) (Seattle Slew (USA)) (63846) **S. Manana**
107 B f 2/3 Marju (IRE)—St Bride's Bay (Caerleon (USA)) (60000) **Saeed Misleh**
108 B c 29/5 Sadler's Wells (USA)—Teggiano (IRE) (Mujtahid (USA)) (27000) **S. Ali**
109 B c 28/4 Fasliyev (USA)—Tiriana (Common Grounds) (32000) **S. Manana**
110 B f 6/2 Zafonic (USA)—Torgau (IRE) (Zieten (USA)) (42000) **Mr Saif Ali & Saeed Altayar**
111 B br f 13/4 War Chant (USA)—Valid Bonnet (USA) (Valid Appeal (USA)) **Shamsudeen**
112 B f 23/4 Giant's Causeway (USA)—Veil of Avalon (USA) (Thunder Gulch (USA)) (14365) **S. Manana**
113 Ch c 17/2 Singspiel (IRE)—Warning Shadows (IRE) (Cadeaux Genereux) **Marwan Al Maktoum**
114 B c 11/2 Diktat—Will You Dance (Shareef Dancer (USA)) (16000) **S. Manana**

Apprentice: J. P. Guillambert.

---

73 **MR M. A. BRITTAIN, Warthill**
Postal: **Northgate Lodge, Warthill, York, YO19 5XR.**
Contacts: **PHONE (01759) 371472 FAX (01759) 372915**
E-MAIL **email@melbrittain.co.uk** WEBSITE **www.melbrittain.co.uk**

1 **BLUE A FUSE (IRE)**, 5, b m Bluebird (USA)—Gleaming Heather (USA) **NEC Special Projects Ltd**
2 **CONSENSUS (IRE)**, 6, b m Common Grounds—Kilbride Lass (IRE) **Northgate Lodgers**
3 **DASAR**, 5, ch m Catrail (USA)—Rising of The Moon (IRE) **Northgate Lodge Racing Club**
4 **MEDALLA (FR)**, 5, gr h Medaaly—Sharp Cracker (IRE) **Mr M. A. Brittain**
5 **MELODIAN**, 10, b h Grey Desire—Mere Melody **Mr M. A. Brittain**
6 5, B m Factual (USA)—Mere Melody
7 **STORMVILLE (IRE)**, 8, b g Catrail (USA)—Haut Volee **Northgate Gold**
8 **TRINITY (IRE)**, 9, b h College Chapel—Kaskazi **Miss D. J. Woods**

MR M. A. BRITTAIN—continued

THREE-YEAR-OLDS

   9 **BAHAMIAN BAY,** b f Bahamian Bounty—Moly **Mr M. A. Brittain**
  10 **DANZAR,** b c Danzero (AUS)—Tarf (USA) **Northgate Blue**
  11 **GUADALOUP,** ch f Loup Sauvage (USA)—Rash **Northgate Red**
  12 **MELANDRE,** b f Lujain (USA)—Talighta (USA) **Mr M. A. Brittain**
  13 **SOWERBY,** b c Grey Desire—Brief Star (IRE) **Mr M. A. Brittain**

Other Owners: Mr R. Adams, Mr J. Allan, Mr D. Bennett, Mr E. Bentham, Mr N. Dobbs, Mrs A. Foster, Mr J. Gunn, Mr C. Knowles, Mr B. Leatherbarrow, Mrs H. Knowles, Mrs S. Sim, Mr J. Richardson, Mr B. Richards, Mr D. Rhodes, Mrs L. Redhead, Mr C. Parks, Mr D. Parker, Mr A. Pannett, Mr N. Wilson, Mrs C. J. Taylor, Mrs M. Matthews, Miss S. King, Mr J. Gardner, Mr M. Foster, Mrs E. Charlesworth, Mr P. Chambers, Mr L. Chambers, Mrs I. Battla, S. J. Box, Mr K. T. Chambers, J. Jarvis, G. N. Marshall, Mr G. Pritchard, Mr S. Taylor, D. B. White.

Assistant Trainer: Neil Jordan (Head Lad)

Apprentice: Marvin Cheung.

---

74 MR J. E. BROCKBANK, Carlisle
Postal: **Westward Park, Wigton, Cumbria, CA7 8AP.**
Contacts: **PHONE (01697) 342391**

   1 **DISTRACTING,** 8, b m Royal Fountain—Icelandic Poppy **J. E. Brockbank**
   2 **TRIVIAL (IRE),** 13, b m Rakaposhi King—Miss Rubbish **J. T. Brockbank**

Assistant Trainer: Mrs C M Fitzgerald

Amateur: Mr Luke Morgan, Mr R. Morgan.

---

75 MR R. S. BROOKHOUSE, Alcester
Postal: **Moor Hall Farm, Wixford, Alcester, Warwickshire, B49 6DL.**
Contacts: **PHONE/FAX (01789) 778244**

   1 **CITY VENTURE,** 8, ch g Pursuit of Love—City of Angels **Mr R. S. Brookhouse**
   2 **LEO'S LUCKYMAN (USA),** 6, b br g Woodman (USA)—Leo's Lucky Lady (USA) **Mrs S. J. Brookhouse**
   3 **MILLIE'S FORTUNE,** 4, b f Classic Cliche (IRE)—Millies Misfortune (IRE) **Mr R. S. Brookhouse**
   4 **ONE NATION (IRE),** 10, br g Be My Native (USA)—Diklers Run **Mr R. S. Brookhouse**
   5 **PRINCE OF PERSIA,** 5, b g Turtle Island (IRE)—Sianiski **Mr R. S. Brookhouse**
   6 **SHE'S THE LADY,** 5, b m Unfuwain (USA)—City of Angels **Mr R. S. Brookhouse**
   7 **SOL CHANCE,** 6, ch g Jupiter Island—Super Sol **Mr R. S. Brookhouse**
   8 **STAR OF GERMANY (IRE),** 5, b g Germany (USA)—Twinkle Bright (USA) **Mr R. S. Brookhouse**
   9 **THREE LIONS,** 8, ch g Jupiter Island—Super Sol **Mr R. S. Brookhouse**
  10 **WHISPERED PROMISES (USA),** 4, b g Real Quiet (USA)—Anna's Honor (USA) **Mrs S. J. Brookhouse**
  11 **WIXFORD VENTURE,** 6, b g Presidium—Forgiving **Mr R. S. Brookhouse**
  12 **WIZARDTREE,** 6, ch g Presidium—Snow Tree **Mr R. S. Brookhouse**

Assistant Trainer: Mr Brian Doran

---

76 MR S. A. BROOKSHAW, Telford
Postal: **Tarri-O, Wollerton, Market Drayton, Shropshire, TF9 3NX.**
Contacts: **PHONE/FAX (01630) 685371 MOBILE (07973) 959986**
E-MAIL steve@freeserve.co.uk

   1 **BUDE,** 6, gr g Environment Friend—Gay da Cheen (IRE) **Mr L. Briggs**
   2 **CASHEL DANCER,** 6, b m Bishop of Cashel—Dancing Debut **K. Edwards**
   3 **CASSIA HEIGHTS,** 10, b g Montelimar (USA)—Cloncoose (IRE) **Mr B. Ridge & Mr D. Hewitt**
   4 4, Br g I'm Supposin (IRE)—Cloncoose (IRE)
   5 4, B g Overbury (IRE)—Inch Maid
   6 **MAJOR BIT,** 9, b g Henbit (USA)—Cute Pam **Steven Brookshaw Racing Partnership I**
   7 **POLLENSA BAY,** 6, b g Overbury (IRE)—Cloncoose (IRE) **Mr S. A. Brookshaw**
   8 **SILVER SAMUEL (NZ),** 8, gr g Hula Town (NZ)—Offrande (NZ) **Redcroft Racing**
   9 **TALBOT LAD,** 9, b g Weld—Greenacres Girl **M. J. Talbot**
  10 **WELSH WHISPER,** 6, b m Overbury (IRE)—Grugiar **Mr S. A. Brookshaw**

Other Owners: Miss H. Brookshaw, W. B. R. Davies, Mrs S. A. Kenney, Mr A. Phillips, Mrs L. M. Powell.

77 MR R. BROTHERTON, Pershore
Postal: **Mill End Racing Stables, Netherton Road, Elmley Castle, Pershore, Worcestershire, WR10 3JF.**
Contacts: **PHONE/FAX (01386) 710772 MOBILE (07973) 877280**

1 **ARABIAN MOON (IRE)**, 9, ch g Barathea (IRE)—Excellent Alibi (USA) **Goldliner Racing West Midlands**
2 **BLAKESHALL QUEST**, 5, b m Piccolo—Corniche Quest (IRE) **Droitwich Jokers**
3 **BLUE MOON HITMAN (IRE)**, 4, ch g Blue Ocean (USA)—Miss Kookaburra (IRE) **Mrs N. K. Cambridge**
4 **BOJANGLES (IRE)**, 6, b g Danehill (USA)—Itching (IRE) **A. D. Solomon**
5 **FIREBIRD RISING (USA)**, 4, b f Stravinsky (USA)—Capable (USA) **J. R. Hall**
6 **KISS THE RAIN**, 5, b m Forzando—Devils Dirge **The Joiners Arms Racing Club Quarndon**
7 **MAGIC GLADE**, 6, b g Magic Ring (IRE)—Ash Glade **A. D. Solomon**
8 **NEUTRAL NIGHT (IRE)**, 5, b m Night Shift (USA)—Neutrality (IRE) **R. N. Auld**
9 **RED DELIRIUM**, 9, b g Robellino (USA)—Made of Pearl (USA) **The Joiners Arms Racing Club Quarndon**
10 **SAVILE'S DELIGHT (IRE)**, 6, b g Cadeaux Genereux—Across The Ice (USA) **A. D. Solomon**
11 **STAR LAD (IRE)**, 5, ch g Lake Coniston (IRE)—Simply Special (IRE) **Mr R. Austin & Mrs P. Austin**
12 **STRICTLY SPEAKING (IRE)**, 8, b g Sri Pekan (USA)—Gaijin **A. D. Solomon**

THREE-YEAR-OLDS

13 **BEECHES THEATRE (IRE)**, b f King's Theatre (IRE)—Sandpiper **R. N. Auld**
14 **FERRARA FLAME (IRE)**, b f Titus Livius (FR)—Isolette **A. D. Solomon**
15 **LITTLE INDY**, ch c Forzando—Indian Nectar **Mrs C. A. Newman**
16 **MAD MARTY WILDCARD**, b c Komaite (USA)—Done And Dusted (IRE) **A. D. Solomon**

Other Owners: MR R. Brotherton, Mr T. J. Dobson, A. Gandy, T. L. Martin, Mrs K. B. Powers, R. Smith, M. J. Whitehall.

Jockey (flat): I. Mongan. **Jockey (NH):** W. Marston. **Apprentice:** D. Nolan. **Amateur:** Mr Simon Walker.

78 MR G. BROWN, Hungerford
Postal: **The Lodge, Wallingtons Road, Kintbury, Hungerford, Berkshire, RG17 9SS.**
Contacts: **PHONE (01488) 670071 FAX (01488) 670175 MOBILE (07785) 757090**

1 **BALLYBROPHY (IRE)**, 10, gr g Roselier (FR)—Bavardmore **K. Berry**
2 **CAPTAIN HARDY (IRE)**, 5, b g Victory Note (USA)—Airey Fairy (IRE) **Mr A. B. Dix**
3 **GONDOLIN (IRE)**, 5, b g Marju (IRE)—Galletina (IRE) **Brian Palmer**
4 **LAND OF NOD (IRE)**, 4, b f Barathea (IRE)—Rafit (USA) **Mrs C. A. Brown**
5 **MISS RIDEAMIGHT**, 6, b m Overbury (IRE)—Nicolynn **Mrs C. A. Davies**

Other Owners: A. A. King.

79 MR I. A. BROWN, Nunnington
Postal: **2 Warren Cottage, Great Edstone, Kirkbymoorside, York.**
Contacts: **HOME (01751) 431066 YARD (01439) 748233**

1 **FLEMMING (USA)**, 8, ch g Green Dancer (USA)—La Groupie (FR) **Mr I. A. Brown**
2 **FORTUNE'S FOOL**, 6, b g Zilzal (USA)—Peryllys **Mr I. A. Brown**
3 **LADY LEXIE**, 4, b f Cape Cross (IRE)—Lady of The Land **Mrs J. Brown**
4 **PUCKS COURT**, 8, b g Nomadic Way (USA)—Miss Puck **W. Brown**

Amateur: Mrs J. Brown.

80 MR I. R. BROWN, Bucknell
Postal: **The Royal George, Lingen, Bucknell, Shropshire, SY7 0DY.**
Contacts: **PHONE/FAX (01544) 267322**
E-MAIL theroyalgeorge@lingen.fsbusiness.co.uk

1 **BOSCO (IRE)**, 4, br g Petardia—Classic Goddess (IRE) **Mr I. R. Brown**
2 **ORIGINAL SIN (IRE)**, 5, b g Bluebird (USA)—Majakerta (IRE) **Mr I. R. Brown**

Assistant Trainer: A. C. Brown

Amateur: Miss Sarah Jane Davies, Mr A. Brown.

81 MISS G. BROWNE, Kingston Lisle
Postal: **Blowing Stone Stables, Kingston Lisle, Wantage, Oxfordshire, OX12 9QL.**
Contacts: **PHONE (01367) 820966 MOBILE (07780) 951634**

1 **BARRACAT (IRE)**, 8, br g Good Thyne (USA)—Hendon Fashion (IRE) **D. C. G. Gyle-Thompson**
2 **COLORADO PEARL (IRE)**, 4, br f Anshan—Flying Silver **The Mill Emerald Partnership**
3 **DR MANN (IRE)**, 7, b br g Phardante (FR)—Shuil Le Laoi (IRE) **Mr And Mrs J. Allen And Brig C. K. Price**
4 **FELIX DARBY (IRE)**, 10, b g Buckskin (FR)—Cool Anne **Ms P. Treacy**
5 **LADY BLAZE**, 6, ch m Alflora (IRE)—Lady Elle (IRE) **Ms P. Treacy**
6 **LE GRIS (GER)**, 6, gr g Neshad (USA)—Lady Pedomade (GER) **Cistm Racing Club Ltd**
7 **LEROY'S SISTER (FR)**, 5, b m Phantom Breeze—Loumir (USA) **Mrs J. A. Stewart**
8 **MISSATTITUDE**, 4, gr f Silver Patriarch (IRE)—Phil's Folly **The Windrush Mob**
9 **NORTHERN LINK (IRE)**, 6, b g Distinctly North (USA)—Miss Eurolink **The Windrush Mob**
10 **NYCTEOS (FR)**, 4, ch g Chamberlin (FR)—Cynthia (FR) **Mrs J. Stewart**
11 **ONE OF THEM**, 6, ch g Pharly (FR)—Hicklam Millie **Cistm Racing Club Ltd**
12 **PEGGY LOU**, 5, b m Washington State (USA)—Rosemary Nalden **T. G. B. Racing Club**
13 **PHAR BLEU (FR)**, 4, b g Agent Bleu (FR)—Guilt Less (FR) **Mrs J. A. Stewart**
14 **POLISH ROSE**, 4, ch f Polish Precedent (USA)—Messila Rose **Blowing Stone Quartet**
15 **STONEY ROAD GIRL (IRE)**, 5, gr m Saddlers' Hall (IRE)—No Slow **Virac Marketing Ltd**
16 **THE BAR MAID**, 7, b m Alderbrook—Corny Story **Brig C. K. Price**
17 **THEATRE GROUP (USA)**, 6, ch g Theatrical—Model Bride **B. M. Mathieson**

Other Owners: Mr T. White, Mrs A. Jenkins, Mrs F. J. Browne, M. B. Catris, P. J. Foley, W. R. Jones.

Assistant Trainer: Miss E J Jones

Amateur: Miss E. J. Jones.

82 MISS A. E. BROYD, Crickhowell
Postal: **Penrhiw Farm, Llangenny, Crickhowell, Powys, NP8 1HD.**
Contacts: **PHONE (01873) 812292 MOBILE (07885) 475492**
E-MAIL alison.broyd@btopenworld.com

1 **MERITOCRACY (IRE)**, 7, b g Lahib (USA)—Merry Devil (IRE) **Miss A. E. Broyd**

83 MISS M. P. BRYANT, Lewes
Postal: **Bevern Bridge Farm Cottage, South Chailey, Lewes, East Sussex, BN8 4QH.**
Contacts: **PHONE/FAX (01273) 400638 MOBILE (07976) 217542**

1 **BRYANTS ROONEY**, 9, ch g Prince Rooney (IRE)—Forever Blushing **Miss M. P. Bryant**
2 **FIRESIDE LEGEND (IRE)**, 6, b g College Chapel—Miss Sandman **Miss M. P. Bryant**
3 **FOREVER ROONEY**, 8, b g Prince Rooney (IRE)—Forever Blushing **Miss M. P. Bryant**
4 **NASONE (IRE)**, 14, b g Nearly A Nose (USA)—Skateaway **Miss M. P. Bryant**
5 **SPRINGER THE LAD**, 8, ch g Carlton (GER)—Also Kirsty **Miss M. P. Bryant**
6 **VICTORY SIGN (IRE)**, 5, b g Forzando—Mo Ceri **Miss M. P. Bryant**

Amateur: Miss M. P. Bryant.

84 MR R. H. BUCKLER, Bridport
Postal: **Melplash Court Farm, Melplash, Bridport, Dorset, DT6 3UH.**
Contacts: **HOME (01308) 488318 FAX (01308) 488403 MOBILE (07785) 773957**

1 **ALFA SUNRISE**, 8, b g Alflora (IRE)—Gipsy Dawn **T. Fiorillo**
2 **CLOUDY BLUES (IRE)**, 7, ro g Glacial Storm (USA)—Chataka Blues (IRE) **Mrs R. L. Haskins**
3 **DERWENT (USA)**, 6, b br g Distant View (USA)—Nothing Sweeter (USA) **FF Racing Services Partnership XIX**
4 **DONTNOCK'ER (IRE)**, 7, br m Naheez (USA)—Castlemagner (FR) **Woodland Flowers**
5 **DOUBLE DIZZY**, 4, gr g Double Trigger (IRE)—Miss Diskin (IRE) **M. J. Forrester**
6 **ELFKIRK (IRE)**, 6, b m Zaffaran (USA)—Winter Sunset **Mrs D. A. La Trobe**
7 **FIVE ALLEY (IRE)**, 8, gr g Roselier (FR)—Panel Pin **K. C. B. Mackenzie & Mrs M. K. Graves**
8 **GLACIAL EVENING (IRE)**, 9, b br g Glacial Storm (USA)—Cold Evening (IRE) **The Deadly Sins Partnership**
9 **HE'S THE BOSS**, 8, b g Supreme Leader—Attykee (IRE) **M. J. Hallett**
10 **HE'S THE GUV'NOR (IRE)**, 6, b g Supreme Leader—Love The Lord (IRE) **M. J. Hallett**
11 **I HEAR THUNDER (IRE)**, 7, b g Montelimar (USA)—Carrigeen Gala **N. Elliott**

MR R. H. BUCKLER—continued

12 **KEEPTHEDREAMALIVE**, 7, gr g Roselier (FR)—Nicklup **Twentyman**
13 **KITIMAT**, 8, b g Then Again—Quago **The Eight Optimists**
14 **NATIVE CUNNING**, 7, b g Be My Native (USA)—Icy Miss **N. Elliott**
15 **OSCAR PERFORMANCE (IRE)**, 10, gr g Roselier (FR)—Miss Iverk **Twentyman**
16 **PALACE (FR)**, 9, b g Rahotep (FR)—La Musardiere (FR) **B. L. Blinman**
17 **PALOUSE (IRE)**, 9, gr g Toulon—Hop Picker (USA) **Woodland Flowers**
18 **PHAR CITY (IRE)**, 8, b g Phardante (FR)—Aunty Dawn (IRE) **Mrs F. S. Lewis**
19 **RIVER INDUS**, 5, b g Rakaposhi King—Flow **Mrs H. R. Dunn**
20 **ROYAL FONTENAILLES (FR)**, 6, ch g Tel Quel (FR)—Sissi Fontenailles (FR) **The Ever Smiling Partnership**
21 **RUM POINTER (IRE)**, 9, b g Turtle Island (IRE)—Osmunda **K. C. B. Mackenzie**
22 **TAKSINA**, 6, b m Wace (USA)—Quago **Mrs F. S. Lewis**
23 **THE SAWDUST KID**, 11, ch g River God (USA)—Susie's Money **Golden Cap**
24 **WOZZECK**, 5, b g Groom Dancer (USA)—Opera Lover (IRE) **Mrs P. J. Buckler**
25 **ZIGGY DAN**, 5, b g Slip Anchor—Nikatino **D. R. Fear**

Other Owners: Mrs P. J. Buckler, Mr L. G. Kimber, Mr H. E. Shane, M. A. Styles.

Assistant Trainer: Giles Scott (Head Lad)

Jockey (NH): B. Hitchcott. **Conditional:** P. Davey, A. Honeyball. **Amateur:** Mrs M. Roberts.

MR M. A. BUCKLEY, Stamford
Postal: **Potters Hill Stables, Morkery Lane, Castle Bytham, Stamford, Lincolnshire, NG33 4SP.**
Contacts: **OFFICE (01780) 411158 FAX (01780) 410481 MOBILE (07808) 360488**

1 **ALLUDE (IRE)**, 6, b g Darshaan—Ahliyat (USA) **Mr C. Hanley**
2 **ARMAGNAC**, 7, b g Young Ern—Arianna Aldini **C. C. Buckley**
3 **COME AWAY WITH ME (IRE)**, 5, b m Machiavellian (USA)—Vert Val (USA) **C. C. Buckley**
4 **CONVINCE (USA)**, 4, ch g Mt Livermore (USA)—Conical **C. C. Buckley**
5 **DISTANT COUSIN**, 8, b g Distant Relative—Tinaca (USA) **Mr M. A. Buckley**
6 **IN THE PINK (IRE)**, 5, gr m Indian Ridge—Norfolk Lavender (CAN) **Mrs D. J. Buckley**
7 **LAW MAKER**, 5, b g Case Law—Bo' Babbity **North Cheshire Trading & Storage Ltd**
8 **LORD LAHAR**, 6, b g Fraam—Brigadiers Bird (IRE) **X8 Racing**
9 **PEDRO JACK (IRE)**, 8, b g Mujadil (USA)—Festival of Light **North Cheshire Trading & Storage Ltd**

THREE-YEAR-OLDS

10 **BILLY'S BROTHER**, ch g Wolfhound (USA)—Chili Lass **The Roaring Partnership**
11 **CILLA'S SMILE**, b f Lake Coniston (IRE)—Tinkerbird **J. M. Cleeve**
12 Ch g Zaha (CAN)—Isabeau **J. M. Cleeve**
13 **JAAMID**, b g Desert Prince (IRE)—Strictly Cool (USA) **C. C. Buckley**
14 **PEVENSEY (IRE)**, b g Danehill (USA)—Champaka (IRE) **C. C. Buckley**

TWO-YEAR-OLDS

15 B f 4/4 Medicean—Charlecote (IRE) (Caerleon (USA)) (11000) **C. C. Buckley**
16 B g 17/3 Dansili—Strictly Cool (USA) (Bering) (17000) **C. C. Buckley**

Other Owners: Mr J. K. Ebbrell, Mr D. J. Lockwood.

MR W. D. BURCHELL, Ebbw Vale
Postal: **Drysiog Farm, Briery Hill, Ebbw Vale, Gwent, NP23 6BU.**
Contacts: **PHONE (01495) 302551 FAX (01495) 352464 MOBILE (07980) 482860**
E-MAIL www.burchelldairuth@aol.com

1 **BAKER OF OZ**, 4, b c Pursuit of Love—Moorish Idol **B. J. Williams**
2 **EYES TO THE RIGHT (IRE)**, 6, ch g Eagle Eyed (USA)—Capable Kate (IRE) **D. I. Gould**
3 **HERNE BAY (IRE)**, 5, b g Hernando (FR)—Charita (IRE) **T. R. Pearson**
4 **LUNAR LORD**, 9, b g Elmaamul (USA)—Cache **B. J. Williams**
5 **NICK'S CHOICE**, 9, b g Sula Bula—Clare's Choice **D. I. Gould**
6 **PADDY THE OPTIMIST (IRE)**, 9, b g Leading Counsel (USA)—Erne Duchess (IRE) **D. I. Gould, Mervyn Phillips**
7 **SCIENTIST**, 5, ch g Dr Fong (USA)—Green Bonnet (IRE) **D. I. Gould, W. Gorman**
8 **ST JEROME**, 5, ch g Danzig Connection (USA)—Indigo Dawn **Raglan Racing Club**
9 **TAFFRAIL**, 7, b g Slip Anchor—Tizona **Mr P. S. & Mrs N. G. Pritchard**

MR W. D. BURCHELL—continued

10 **THE VARLET**, 5, b g Groom Dancer (USA)—Valagalore **Raglan Racing Club**
11 **THREE WELSHMEN**, 4, b g Muhtarram (USA)—Merch Rhyd-Y-Grug **Mouse Racing**
12 **WESLEY'S LAD (IRE)**, 11, b r g Classic Secret (USA)—Galouga (FR) **B. J. Williams**

THREE-YEAR-OLDS

13 **COUNTESS FOLEY**, b f Wizard King—Princess Foley (IRE) **J. F. Tew**

Other Owners: C. T. Bevan, B. Collins, Mr T. R. Fooks, G. Mayo, Mrs D. Mccabe, Mr T. M. Phillips, G. Spilsbury, Mrs P. Williams.

Assistant Trainer: Ruth Burchell

Jockey (flat): R. Price. **Jockey (NH):** A. Scholes. **Conditional:** L. Stephens, Christian Williams. **Amateur:** Miss Emily Jones, Miss E. Tucker, Mr N. Williams.

---

87 MR K. R. BURKE, Leyburn

Postal: **Spigot Lodge, Middleham, Leyburn, North Yorkshire, DL8 4TL.**
Contacts: **PHONE (01969) 625088 FAX (01969) 625099 MOBILE (07778) 458777**
E-MAIL karl@karlburke.co.uk

1 **A LITTLE BIT YARIE**, 4, b g Paris House—Slipperose **Reds 4 Racing**
2 **ATLANTIC QUEST (USA)**, 6, b g Woodman (USA)—Pleasant Pat (USA) **Mr A. Polignone**
3 **BARRISSIMO (IRE)**, 5, b g Night Shift (USA)—Belle de Cadix (IRE) **Mrs L. Charge**
4 **BLUE POWER (IRE)**, 4, b g Zieten (USA)—La Miserable **Mr F. Jeffers**
5 **BLUE SKY THINKING (IRE)**, 6, b g Danehill Dancer (USA)—Lauretta Blue (IRE) **Triple Trio Partnership**
6 **BRIOS BOY**, 5, ch g My Best Valentine—Rose Elegance **Mr A. Polignone**
7 **DARING AFFAIR**, 4, b f Bien Bien (USA)—Daring Destiny **N. R. Shields**
8 **HE'S A ROCKET (IRE)**, 4, b g Indian Rocket—Dellua (IRE) **Spigot Lodge Partnership**
9 **HIGH VOLTAGE**, 4, ch g Wolfhound (USA)—Real Emotion (USA) **Mrs K. Halsall**
10 **HOPEFUL MISSION**, 4, b g Bien Bien (USA)—Tiama (IRE) **Mr F. Jeffers**
11 **IMPERIALISTIC (IRE)**, 4, b f Imperial Ballet (IRE)—Shefoog **Bigwigs Bloodstock II**
12 **KHANJAR (USA)**, 5, ch g Kris S (USA)—Alyssum (USA) **Mr A. Draper**
13 **MARCUS EILE (IRE)**, 4, b g Daggers Drawn (USA)—Sheranada (USA) **Spigot Lodge Partnership**
14 **MILLION PERCENT**, 6, b g Ashkalani (IRE)—Royal Jade **Champagne Racing**
15 **MUNAAWASHAT (IRE)**, 4, b f Marju (IRE)—Simaat (USA) **J. A. Duffy**
16 **PARTY PLOY**, 7, b g Deploy—Party Treat (IRE) **Mr I. McInnes**
17 **PLATINUM CHARMER (IRE)**, 5, b g Kahyasi—Mystic Charm **Spigot Lodge Partnership 1**
18 **PLATINUM PIRATE**, 4, b g Merdon Melody—Woodland Steps **Spigot Lodge Partnership 2**
19 **RADIANT BRIDE**, 5, ch m Groom Dancer (USA)—Radiancy (IRE) **Spigot Lodge Partnership**
20 **ROMIL STAR (GER)**, 8, b g Chief's Crown (USA)—Romelia (USA) **Mrs E. M. Burke**
21 **SHANK ON FOURTEEN (IRE)**, 4, b g Fayruz—Hever Rosina
22 **SILVER RHYTHM**, 4, ch f Silver Patriarch (IRE)—Party Treat (IRE) **Mr I. McInnes**
23 **TAKES TUTU (USA)**, 6, b g Afternoon Deelites (USA)—Lady Affirmed (USA) **Mr B. Baugh**
24 **TINIAN**, 7, b g Mtoto—Housefull **Spigot Lodge Partnership**
25 **WARES HOME (IRE)**, 4, b g Indian Rocket—Pepilin **Spigot Lodge Partnership**

THREE-YEAR-OLDS

26 **ASHES (IRE)**, b f General Monash (USA)—Wakayi **Bryce, Dower, Morgan**
27 **BALLETTO**, b f Robellino (USA)—Denial **M. Nelmes-Crocker**
28 **BOLD MARC (IRE)**, b g Bold Fact (USA)—Zara's Birthday (IRE) **Market Avenue Racing Club Ltd**
29 **BOO**, b g Namaqualand (USA)—Violet (IRE) **Mrs M. P. V. Gittins**
30 **CHISELLED (IRE)**, b g Rossini (USA)—Con Dancer **Mrs S. L. Jones**
31 **DANAATT (USA)**, b f Gulch (USA)—Agama (USA) **Mrs C de Stefano Vande Yar**
32 **DESPERATION (IRE)**, b g Desert Style (USA)—Mauras Pride (IRE) **J. C. S. Wilson**
33 **DICTION (IRE)**, br f Diktat—Waft (USA) **J. C. S. Wilson**
34 **DUROOB**, b g Bahhare (USA)—Amaniy (USA) **Mr K Burke**
35 B f Imperial Ballet (IRE)—Easter Girl
36 **EMINENCE GIFT**, b f Cadeaux Genereux—Germane **D. S. McMahon**
37 **HIGH MINDED**, b g Mind Games—Pips Way (IRE) **P. J. McCaughey**
38 **HOWS THAT**, ch f Vettori (IRE)—Royalty (IRE) **Mr D. Wigglesworth & Mr J. Harthen**
39 **LA VIOLA**, b f Fraam—Arasong **Mr A. Polignone**
40 **LADY ERICA**, b f Komaite (USA)—Zamarra (USA) **N. D. Ryan**
41 **LITTLE BISCUIT (IRE)**, ro f Indian Lodge (IRE)—Arjan (IRE)
42 **ORPHAN (IRE)**, b g Orpen (USA)—Ballinlee (IRE) **M. R. Johnson**

MR K. R. BURKE—continued

43 **ROCKBURST,** b f Xaar—Topwinder (USA) **Mrs S. L. Jones**
44 **SIMPLIFY,** b g Fasliyev (USA)—Simplicity **Mr K. Burke**
45 **SLATE GREY,** gr g Paris House—Slipperose **Mrs S. L. Jones**
46 **SPEED DIAL HARRY (IRE),** b g General Monash (USA)—Jacobina **N. R. Shields**
47 **TARTAN SPECIAL,** b g Fasliyev (USA)—Colchica **Mrs M. Bryce**
48 **TEQUILA SHEILA (IRE),** ch f Raise A Grand (IRE)—Hever Rosina **Mr L. Westwood & Mr D. Clarke**
49 **THUNDERWING (IRE),** b br c Indian Danehill (IRE)—Scandisk (IRE) **Market Avenue Racing Club Ltd**
50 **VANCOUVER GOLD (IRE),** b f Monashee Mountain (USA)—Forest Berries (IRE) **Bigwigs Bloodstock II**

TWO-YEAR-OLDS

51 **ANGEL VOICES (IRE),** b f 10/3 Tagula (IRE)—
Lithe Spirit (IRE) (Dancing Dissident (USA)) (14000) **Mr J. Cowan & Mrs M. Bryce**
52 B f 30/4 Elnadim (USA)—Arjan (IRE) (Paris House) (8000) **Mr K Burke**
53 **BAHAMIAN DUKE,** ch c 27/4 Bahamian Bounty—Madame Sisu (Emarati (USA)) (7000) **Mr D. Bowker**
54 B f 22/3 Alhaarth (IRE)—Beseeching (IRE)—Hamas (IRE)) (4023) **Mr J. Duffy**
55 B f 3/3 Mull of Kintyre (USA)—Canlubang (Mujtahid (USA)) (4000) **Mr K Burke**
56 **CITY FOR CONQUEST (IRE),** b f 22/3 City On A Hill (USA)—
Northern Life (IRE) (Distinctly North (USA)) (16000) **Mr P. Allen**
57 B c 16/3 City On A Hill (USA)—Cloche du Roi (FR) (Fairy King (USA)) (19000) **Mr K. Burke**
58 Ch f 10/3 Monashee Mountain (USA)—Dellua (IRE) (Suave Dancer (USA)) (4560) **P. A. Brazier**
59 B c 22/3 Bold Fact (USA)—Dungeon Princess (IRE) (Danehill (USA)) (20000) **Market Avenue Racing Club Ltd**
60 **FOOD FOR THOUGHT,** b f 21/2 Mind Games—Ladycake (IRE) (Perugino (USA)) (800) **Mr B. Baugh**
61 **HILL OF ALMHUIM (IRE),** b c 12/3 City On A Hill (USA)—
Kitty Kildare (Seattle Dancer (USA)) (10000) **Mr P. Allen**
62 Ch g 20/4 Indian Danehill (IRE)—In Behind (IRE) (Entitled) (6000) **Mr M. Johnson**
63 B c 6/3 Merdon Melody—Lady-Love (Pursuit of Love) (17000) **Mr N. Ryan**
64 Ch f 15/3 Primo Valentino (IRE)—Lake Mistassiu (Tina's Pet) (6500) **Mr J. Wilson**
65 **MISS LOPEZ (IRE),** br f 2/5 Key of Luck (USA)—Legit (IRE) (Runnett) (26827) **C. Bryce**
66 B f 14/2 Orpen (USA)—Morale (Bluebird (USA)) (23473) **Mr K Burke**
67 **MYRTLE BAY (IRE),** bl c 28/3 Pennekamp (USA)—Moneypenny (GER) (Neshad (USA)) (11000) **Mrs M. Bryce**
68 B f 14/2 Fraam—Nightingale Song (Tina's Pet) (15000) **Mr K Burke**
69 **PAB SPECIAL (IRE),** b c 22/4 City On A Hill (USA)—Tinos Island (IRE) (Alzao (USA)) (4000) **Mr K Burke**
70 B c 9/3 Intikhab (USA)—Quelle Celtique (FR) (Tel Quel (FR)) (26000) **Mr K Burke**
71 B f 9/2 Primo Valentino (IRE)—Sandblaster (Most Welcome) (4500) **Mr J. Wilson**
72 B c 1/2 Bertolini (USA)—Seren Teg (Timeless Times (USA)) (12000) **Mr Timmings & Mr Rhodes**
73 B c 22/4 Desert Style (IRE)—Sideloader Special (Song) (3500) **Mr R. Hoiles**
74 **SURELY TRULY (IRE),** b f 4/5 Trans Island—Londubh (Tumble Wind) (8718) **Mr J. Cowan & Mrs M. Bryce**
75 B f 6/3 Bluebird (USA)—Syringa (Lure) (9500) **Mr J. Duffy**
76 B f 15/3 Distant Music (USA)—Topwinder (USA) (Topsider (USA)) (21000) **Mrs S. L. Jones**
77 Ch c 23/3 Fruits of Love (USA)—Truly Flattering (Hard Fought) (9500) **Mr K Burke**
78 B c 27/1 Medicean—Warning Star (Warning) (20000) **Mr K Burke**

Other Owners: D. C. Clarke, S. A. Cleverley, Mrs M. Dower, R. S. Dufficy, M. Jones, Market Avenue Racing Club Ltd, S. P. Marley, D. H. Morgan, R. Preston.

Assistant Trainer: Mrs E Burke

Jockey (flat): Darren Williams. **Apprentice:** A. Elliott, S. Bushby. **Amateur:** Miss K. Burke, Mr S. Dobson.

---

88 MR JAMES G. BURNS, Curragh
Postal: Landfall Paddocks, The Curragh, Co. Kildare, Ireland.
Contacts: **PHONE** +353 (0) 45 441811 **FAX** (045) 441213 **MOBILE** +353 (0) 86 8201212
E-MAIL landfall@eircom.net

1 **ASTRILLE (IRE),** 4, b f Bahhare (USA)—Miss Dolly (IRE)
2 **CHARMED FOREST,** 4, b f Shinko Forest (IRE)—Charmed Lady **Sean O'Keeffe**
3 **CIRCE'S MELODY (IRE),** 4, b f Entrepreneur—Circe's Isle **C. Corrigan**
4 **DOLPHIN BAY (IRE),** 5, b h Dolphin Street (FR)—Stella Ann **Miss R. Tonson-Rye**
5 **EZIMIX (IRE),** 4, gr g Linamix (FR)—Ezilla (IRE) **Ms Mary McDonald**
6 **FIINA,** 4, ch f Most Welcome—Finlandaise (FR) **Janet Chaplin**
7 **GROUPETIME (USA),** 5, b m Gilded Time (USA)—La Groupie (FR)
8 **LEONE D'ORO (GER),** 5, b g Java Gold (USA)—Leventina (GER) **Enno Albert**
9 **LEPIDINA (IRE),** 5, b m Oscar (IRE)—Lepida **Miss R. Tonson-Rye**
10 **MRS ST GEORGE (IRE),** 4, b f Orpen (USA)—Tamarzana (IRE) **M. A. Kilduff**

MR JAMES G. BURNS—continued

11 4, B f Charnwood Forest (IRE)—Oare Linnet **Gerard Keane**
12 **PEAK FARE (IRE)**, 5, b m Sri Pekan (USA)—City Imp (IRE) **William Fenlon**
13 **ROCHETTO (IRE)**, 4, ch f Indian Rocket—Romangoddess (IRE) **Mrs J. A. Dene**
14 **TURGESIUS (USA)**, 5, b h Ghazi (USA)—Makati (USA) **Owen Kiernan**
15 **VICKY LANE (IRE)**, 4, b f Victory Note (USA)—City Imp (IRE) **Tim I. Naughton**

THREE-YEAR-OLDS

16 **ASK JENNY (IRE)**, b f Marju (IRE)—Waltzing Matilda **Mrs J. Costelloe**
17 Ch f Woodman (USA)—Brackish (USA) **Forenaghts Stud**
18 **BROSNA BELLE (IRE)**, b f Imperial Ballet (IRE)—Northumbrian Belle (IRE) **M. A. Kilduff**
19 **CHAMPAGNE SPARKLE (IRE)**, b f Sadler's Wells (USA)—Champagne Girl **John McEnery**
20 **FIZGIG (USA)**, b f Swain (IRE)—Benguela (USA) **Mr A. Rogers**
21 **FOOL'S PENNY**, b f Boundary (USA)—Abscond (USA) **Max Ervine**
22 **GALA STYLE (IRE)**, b f Elnadim (USA)—Style n' Elegance (USA) **Mr G. W. Jennings**
23 **GOLDEN DEW (IRE)**, b f Montjeu (IRE)—Golden Cat (USA) **Mr G. W. Jennings**
24 **GRAND CARE (IRE)**, gr f Raise A Grand (IRE)—Ikala **James Carey**
25 **ISLANDBANE (IRE)**, b f Orpen (USA)—Bayazida **C. J. Foy**
26 **KING OF THE DAY (IRE)**, b c King's Theatre (IRE)—Tertia (IRE) **Ms Stephanie Von Schilcher**
27 **LA PRIOLA (IRE)**, b f Priolo (USA)—Canadian Girl (IRE) **Marco Valade**
28 **LION'S FLIGHT (IRE)**, b f Tagula (IRE)—Summerhill **James G. Burns**
29 **LISCARRA LAD (IRE)**, ch c Night Shift (USA)—Virtue Rewarded (IRE) **Colm Gavin**
30 B f Rossini (USA)—Mafiosa **Mrs T. P. Burns**
31 **MAIGUE VIOLET (IRE)**, b f Night Shift (USA)—Dame's Violet (IRE) **Denis Brosnan**
32 **NOSE ONE'S WAY (IRE)**, b f Revoque (IRE)—Preponderance (USA) **Colman O'Flynn**
33 **OAKUM (IRE)**, b f Danehill Dancer (IRE)—Ship's Twine (USA) **Martin Cullinane**
34 **ON TIME ARRIVAL (USA)**, ch f Devil's Bag (USA)—St Agnes (USA) **James G. Burns**
35 **OUR BLUEBUTTON (IRE)**, ch c Indian Rocket—Bluebutton
36 **PELICAN BAY (IRE)**, ch f Night Shift (USA)—Capegulch (USA) **Mr G. W. Jennings**
37 **ROCKY RIDGE (IRE)**, b f Intikhab (USA)—Twin Logic (USA) **Jack Hamilton**
38 Br f Namid—Savona (IRE) **Edward Kent**
39 **SONG OF THE WIND (IRE)**, b f Rossini (USA)—Khawafi **Dolmen South East Syndicate**
40 **VINTAGE QUEST**, b f Diktat—Sadly Sober (IRE) **Max Ervine**

TWO-YEAR-OLDS

41 B f 1/6 Pleasant Tap (USA)—Alliage (USA) (Alleged (USA)) **Lady O'Reilly**
42 B c 10/2 Indian Danehill (IRE)—Beat It (USA) (Diesis) (12072)
43 **BROSNA LIVE (IRE)**, b c 20/4 Titus Livius (FR)—Fustanella (Mtoto) **M. A. Kilduff**
44 Ch f 8/3 Daylami (IRE)—Ezana (Ela-Mana-Mou) **Ms Mary McDonald**
45 B f 25/2 Definite Article—Jesting (Muhtarram (USA)) (3353)
46 B c 14/4 Observatory (USA)—Kadja Chenee (Spectrum (IRE)) (13413)
47 B c 5/5 Mark of Esteem (IRE)—Kasota (IRE) (Alzao (USA)) (13413)
48 B f 14/4 Cape Cross (IRE)—Marylou Whitney (USA) (Fappiano (USA)) (24144) **Lady O'Reilly**
49 Ch f 27/2 Docksider (USA)—Passing Beauty (Green Desert (USA)) (2011) **Mrs T. P. Burns**
50 Ch f 24/4 Definite Article—Romanylei (IRE) (Blues Traveller (IRE)) **Mrs J. A. Dene**
51 B f 28/4 Spectrum (IRE)—Siskin (IRE) (Royal Academy (USA)) (8047) **C. Corrigan**

Other Owners: Patrick Doyle, D. MacAbhaird, Sean O'Sullivan, Dermot Cantillon, Gerard Cullen, John McGuire, J. P. M. O'Connor MRCVS, Michael Tolan.

Assistant Trainer: Martin Brew (Head Man) & Neil Magee (Assistant Trainer)

Jockey (flat): D. J. Condon. **Jockey (NH):** P. A. Carberry.

---

89 MR S. C. BURROUGH, Wellington
Postal: **Gringles Farm, West Buckland, Wellington, Somerset, TA21 9LE.**
Contacts: **PHONE/FAX** (01823) 666837 **MOBILE** (07887) 958131

1 **ALGYMO**, 5, b m Tamure (IRE)—Red Point **Mrs M. S. Emery**
2 **BATTLING BUSTER (IRE)**, 8, b g Glacial Storm (USA)—Flutter (IRE) **G. J. P. Regan**
3 **BENNANABAA**, 6, b g Anabaa (USA)—Arc Empress Jane (IRE) **Mr & Mrs Charles Hill**
4 **BERENGARIO (IRE)**, 5, b g Mark of Esteem (IRE)—Ivrea **Mrs D. H. Potter**
5 **BOLD CENTURY**, 8, b g Casteddu—Bold Green (FR) **Mr & Mrs Charles Hill**
6 **CHARLIES FUTURE**, 7, b g Democratic (USA)—Faustelerie **M. L. Lewis-Jones**
7 **CHITA'S FLIGHT**, 5, gr m Busy Flight—Chita's Cone **I. M. Ham**

MR S. C. BURROUGH—continued

8 5, B m Opera Ghost—Country Magic **Mr Fred Tucker**
9 **DAISY DALE,** 7, gr m Terimon—Quetta's Girl **Mr N. K. Allin**
10 **FINAL BELLE,** 6, ch m Afflora (IRE)—B Final **Mr N. K. Allin**
11 **GOLDSEAM (GER),** 6, gr g Neshad (USA)—Goldkatze (GER) **D. W. E. Coombs**
12 **HERIOT,** 9, b g Hamas (IRE)—Sure Victory (IRE) **The Fullmoon Racing Partnership**
13 **HUW THE NEWS,** 6, b g Primo Dominie—Martha Stevens (USA) **H. J. W. Davies**
14 **IMTIHAN (IRE),** 6, ch g Unfuwain (USA)—Azyaa **P. J. Nunn**
15 **KALUGA (IRE),** 7, ch m Tagula (IRE)—Another Baileys
16 **MENDIP MANOR,** 7, b g Rakaposhi King—Broughton Manor **R. J. Croker**
17 **MINSTER PARK,** 6, b g Minster Son—Go Gipsy **The Three Diamonds Partnership**
18 **MONTROLIN,** 5, ch g Classic Cliche (IRE)—Charmed I'm Sure **M. A. F. Searle**
19 **MULAN PRINCESS (IRE),** 5, b m Mukaddamah (USA)—Notley Park **Hill, Kemp and Hill**
20 **NO SAM NO,** 7, b m Reprimand—Samjamalifran **G. J. P. Regan**
21 **SHE'S OUR DAISY (IRE),** 5, b m Supreme Leader—Tell A Tale **G. J. P. Regan**
22 **SIMONOVSKI (USA),** 4, b c Miswaki (USA)—Earthra (USA) **Mrs D. H. Potter**
23 **SWEET AZ,** 5, b m Averti (IRE)—Yen Haven (USA) **Mr & Mrs Enticott**
24 **THEBELLINNBROADWAY,** 5, b m El Conquistador—Ten Deep **Mr G. Knight**
25 **THEME PARK,** 5, b g Classic Cliche (IRE)—Arcady **The Three Diamonds Partnership**
26 6, Ch g Romany Rye—Tribal Solace **Mr D. Boscherini**
27 **TWOTENSFORAFIVE,** 12, b g Arctic Lord—Sister of Gold **Mr Stephen Priest**

THREE-YEAR-OLDS

28 **BRACKENORAH,** b f Double Trigger (IRE)—Little Preston (IRE) **Mr J. Beer & Mrs M. Daley**
29 **DOMPTEUR (FR),** gr g Marathon (USA)—Dompteuse (FR) **Mr R. Croker**
30 **TROUBLESOME GERRI,** b f Thowra (FR)—Sid's Pretence **Mr L. Browning & Mr L. Cornall**

Other Owners: Miss J. Bown, Mr M. T. Carter, C. C. Gaylard, Mrs C. A. Lewis-Jones, A. P. Smith, D. E. Tidball.

Jockey (NH): R. Greene. **Amateur:** Mr W. P. Kavanagh.

---

90 MRS D. A. BUTLER, Southam
Postal: **Springholm, Napton Road, Stockton, Southam, Warwickshire, CV47 8HT.**
Contacts: **PHONE (01926) 815366**
E-MAIL deborah@chapple-hyam.freeserve.co.uk

1 **THINKING DOUBLE,** 7, br g Homo Sapien—Sheppie's Double **Mrs D. A. Butler**
2 **VANDAL,** 5, b g Entrepreneur—Vax Star **Mrs D. A. Butler**

---

91 MR P. BUTLER, Lewes
Postal: **Homewood Gate Racing Stables, Novington Lane, East Chiltington, Lewes, East Sussex, BN7 3AU.**
Contacts: **PHONE/FAX (01273) 890124 MOBILE (07973) 873846**
E-MAIL homewoodgate@aol.com

1 **CANNI THINKAAR (IRE),** 4, b g Alhaarth (IRE)—Cannikin (IRE) **Homewoodgate Racing Club**
2 **FELLOW SHIP,** 6, b g Elmaamul (USA)—Genoa **E. H. Whatmough**
3 **GEOGRAPHY (IRE),** 5, ch g Definite Article—Classic Ring (IRE) **Homewoodgate Racing Club**
4 **L'ETANG BLEU (FR),** 7, gr g Graveron (FR)—Strawberry Jam (FR) **Mrs E. Lucey-Butler**
5 **RHETORICAL,** 4, b g Unfuwain (USA)—Miswaki Belle (USA) **Mrs E. Lucey-Butler**
6 **SALIX BAY,** 9, b g Karinga Bay—Willow Gale **Mrs E. Lucey-Butler**

THREE-YEAR-OLDS

7 **BUZZ MAITE,** b g Komaite (USA)—Scotland Bay **C. W. Wilson**

Other Owners: Mrs P. A. Wood.

Assistant Trainer: Mrs E Lucey-Butler

Conditional: R. Butler-Lucey.

92   MR T. H. CALDWELL, Warrington

Postal: Burley Heyes Cottage, Arley Road, Appleton, Warrington, Cheshire, WA4 4RR.
Contacts: PHONE/FAX (01565) 777275 MOBILE (07879) 455767

1 **BUTHAINA (IRE)**, 5, b m Bahhare (USA)—Haddeyah (USA) **Mr C. W. Mather**
2 **CLEOPATRAS THERAPY (IRE)**, 8, b g Gone Fishin—Nec Precario **Mr T. H. Caldwell**
3 **DISCORD**, 4, b g Desert King (IRE)—Lead Note (USA) **Mr T. H. Caldwell**
4 **DUMFRIES**, 4, ch g Selkirk (USA)—Pat Or Else **Mr T. H. Caldwell**
5 **FAIRLY GLORIOUS**, 4, b g Tina's Pet—Steamy Windows **Colin Mather & Stephen Tomkinson**
6 **FIRION KING (IRE)**, 5, b g Earl of Barking (IRE)—Miss Tan A Dee **Mr D. J. Raynor**
7 **GOLDEN SNOOPY (IRE)**, 8, ch g Insan (USA)—Lovely Snoopy (IRE) **S. H. Tomkinson**
8 **LORD LUPIN (IRE)**, 9, b g Sadler's Wells (USA)—Penza **Mr T. H. Caldwell**
9 **MISS COSPECTOR**, 6, ch m Emperor Fountain—Gypsy Race (IRE) **R. Cabrera-Vargas**

Other Owners: R. S. G. Jones, S. H. Tomkinson.

Assistant Trainer: Mrs P J Wharfe

Jockey (flat): J. Carroll, J. Fanning, A. Nicholls, P. Robinson. **Jockey (NH):** A. Dobbin, T. J. Murphy, J. P. McNamara.
Conditional: B. Wharfe. **Amateur:** Miss R. Bolton, Mrs P. Wharfe.

93   MR N. A. CALLAGHAN, Newmarket

Postal: 22 Hamilton Road, Newmarket, Suffolk, CB8 0NY.
Contacts: HOME (01638) 664040 FAX (01638) 668446 MOBILE (07768) 882606

1 **ANUVASTEEL**, 4, gr g Vettori (IRE)—Mrs Gray **Tipp-Ex Rapid Racing**
2 **HAZYVIEW**, 4, b c Cape Cross (IRE)—Euridice (IRE) **T. M. Mohan**

THREE-YEAR-OLDS

3 **BELLALOU**, b f Vettori (IRE)—Spinning Mouse **J. A. Bianchi**
4 **BIBI HELEN**, b f Robellino (USA)—Tarry **Mr J. Pearce**
5 **BLOOD MONEY**, b g Dracula (AUS)—Guinea **G. C. Hartigan**
6 **CARRAIG (IRE)**, b f Orpen (USA)—Rose of Mooncoin (IRE) **Cunningham Racing**
7 **CATCH A STAR**, ch f Giant's Causeway (USA)—Amy Hunter (USA) **M. Tabor**
8 **DANEHILL WILLY (IRE)**, b c Danehill Dancer (USA)—Lowtown **T. M. Mohan**
9 **FINALMENTE**, b g Kahyasi—Sudden Spirit (FR) **E. M. Kirtland**
10 **GOLDEN ASHA**, ch f Danehill Dancer (USA)—Snugfit Annie **Norcroft Park Stud**
11 **GURRUN**, b c Dansili—Mashmoon (USA) **T. S. M. S. Riley-Smith**
12 **HEIGHT OF GLORY (IRE)**, ch c Grand Lodge (USA)—Ghayah (IRE) **M. Tabor**
13 **LIBERTY RUN (IRE)**, ch c Grand Lodge (USA)—Bathe In Light (USA) **Mr Philip Green & Mr M. Tabor**
14 **LOLA SAPOLA (IRE)**, b f Benny The Dip (USA)—Cutpurse Moll **A. J. J. Gompertz**
15 **MY PRINCESS (IRE)**, b f Danehill Dancer (USA)—Shanoora (IRE) **T. M. Mohan**
16 **NEVER AWAY**, b f Royal Applause—Waypoint **Mrs P. A. Reditt**
17 **OLIGARCH (IRE)**, b c Monashee Mountain (USA)—Courtier **Team Havana**
18 **PENALTY KICK (IRE)**, b c Montjeu (IRE)—Dafrah (USA) **John Livock Bloodstock Limited**
19 **REBEL REBEL (IRE)**, b c Revoque (IRE)—French Quarter **Six Star Racing**
20 **SHADES OF GREEN**, b f Loup Sauvage (USA)—Green Light (FR) **Manor Farm Packers Ltd**
21 **TERMINATE (GER)**, ch g Acatenango (GER)—Taghareed (USA) **Gallagher Equine Ltd**
22 **VERBIER**, b f Fusaichi Pegasus (USA)—Oh Nellie (USA) **Mrs D. A. Tabor**

TWO-YEAR-OLDS

23 B c 27/1 Night Shift (USA)—Belle de Cadix (IRE) (Law Society (USA)) (190000) **M. Tabor**
24 **CATBANG (IRE)**, b c 25/4 Zafonic (USA)—Silky Dawn (IRE) (Night Shift (USA)) (75000) **R. K. Carvill**
25 B c 11/4 King Charlemagne (USA)—Cutpurse Moll (Green Desert (USA)) (21000) **The Carved Up Partnership**
26 B c 30/1 King Charlemagne (USA)—
                          Devil's Crown (USA) (Chief's Crown (USA)) **Mr R. O. Simpson & Mr A. Guinle**
27 B c 21/2 Danehill Dancer (IRE)—Fille Dansante (IRE) (Dancing Dissident (USA)) (130000) **M. Tabor**
28 B br c 23/1 Brahms (USA)—Georgian Bay (USA) (Storm Cat (USA)) (70000) **Team Havana**
29 **JOHN CLAUDE (IRE)**, b c 16/5 Night Shift (USA)—Koukla Mou (Keen) **Mr Alan Dee**
30 B f 25/4 Danehill Dancer (USA)—Kaguyahime (Distant Relative) (14000) **Mr D. Moss**
31 **KING MALACHI (IRE)**, b c 31/3 King Charlemagne (USA)—Sparky's Song (Electric) (50000) **Mrs June Powell**
32 **LOUIE LOUIE (IRE)**, b c 18/1 King Charlemagne (USA)—
                          Rose of Mooncoin (IRE) (Brief Truce (USA)) (31000) **Jack Banks Racing**
33 **LUSCINIA**, b f 19/4 Bluebird (USA)—Welsh Dawn (Zafonic (USA)) (12000) **G. C. Hartigan**

MR N. A. CALLAGHAN—continued

34 MACS RANSOM (USA), b f 7/4 Red Ransom (USA)—
Gaye's Express (USA) (Timeless Native (USA)) (36000) **M. McDonnell**
35 Br gr c 19/1 Kalanisi (IRE)—Perugia (IRE) (Perugino (USA)) (70000)
36 Gr c 28/1 Marju (IRE)—Purple Risks (FR) (Take Risks (FR)) (85000)
37 Ch c 27/2 Grand Lodge (USA)—Simacota (GER) (Acatenango (GER)) (50000) **M. Tabor**
38 Ch c 10/5 Pivotal—Sintenis (GER) (Polish Precedent (USA)) (78000) **M. McDonnell**
39 YELLOW CARD, ch c 25/2 Inchinor—Tranquillity (Night Shift (USA)) (72000) **John Livock Bloodstock Limited**

Other Owners: Paul & Jenny Green, Mr N. A. Callaghan, C. Batt, G. H. Beeby, P. Cunningham, P. M. Cunningham, Family Amusements Ltd, R. Farrington, Mrs T. A. Foreman, Lord Marchwood, M. C. Moutray-Read, A. D. G. Oldrey, A. J. Smith.

Assistant Trainer: Simon Callaghan

---

94 MISS J. A CAMACHO, Malton
Postal: Star Cottage, Welham Road, Norton, Malton, North Yorkshire, YO17 9QE.
Contacts: PHONE (01653) 696205 FAX (01653) 694901 MOBILE (07779) 318135/(07950) 356440
E-MAIL jacracing@starcottage.fsbusiness.co.uk

1 ALCAIDESA, 4, b g Charnwood Forest (IRE)—Calachuchi **Mrs S. Camacho**
2 ESTEPONA, 4, ch g Polar Falcon (USA)—Kingdom Ruby (IRE) **Mrs S. Camacho**
3 HIGHER STATE, 4, b c Danehill (USA)—High And Low **OA Racing**
4 LAGO D'ORO, 5, b m Slip Anchor—Salala **Mrs S. Camacho**
5 LAMPOS (USA), 5, b br g Southern Halo (USA)—Gone Private (USA) **L. A. Bolingbroke**
6 LAURO, 5, b m Mukaddamah (USA)—Lapu-Lapu **Shangri-La Racing Club**
7 MIND ALERT, 4, b g Mind Games—Bombay Sapphire **D. W. Armstrong**
8 ROYAL MELBOURNE (IRE), 5, ch g Among Men (USA)—Calachuchi **J. S. Spence**
9 SUPER REVO, 4, b g Revoque (IRE)—Kingdom Princess **G. B. Turnbull Ltd**
10 VAL DE MAAL (IRE), 5, ch g Eagle Eyed (USA)—Miss Bojangles **L. A. Bolingbroke**

THREE-YEAR-OLDS

11 B f Danzig Connection (USA)—Fairey Firefly **Mrs S. Camacho**
12 RIO RIVA, b c Pivotal—Dixie Favor (USA) **Rio Riva Partnership**
13 Ch f Polar Falcon (USA)—Silky Heights (IRE) **Mrs S. Camacho**
14 SIR NOD, b c Tagula (IRE)—Nordan Raider **Brian Nordan**

TWO-YEAR-OLDS

15 Ch f 9/5 Pivotal—Bayleaf (Efisio) (27000) **D. W. Armstrong**
16 B c 29/4 Lahib (USA)—Calachuchi (Martinmas) **Mrs S. Camacho**
17 B f 13/4 Bertolini (USA)—Dixie Favor (USA) (Dixieland Band (USA)) (23000) **D. W. Armstrong**
18 ENTRANCED, b f 23/2 Saddlers' Hall (IRE)—Vent d'aout (IRE) (Imp Society (USA)) **Elite Racing Club**
19 Ch f 21/4 Benny The Dip (USA)—Kingdom Ruby (IRE) (Bluebird (USA)) **Mrs S. Camacho**
20 Ch f 22/3 Timeless Times (USA)—Lapu-Lapu (Prince Sabo) **Shangri-La Racing Club**
21 SOLO STAR, ch f 17/2 Observatory (USA)—
Aura of Grace (USA) (Southern Halo (USA)) (10000) **G. B. Turnbull Ltd**
22 SPANISH LACE, b f 3/4 Hernando (FR)—Kabayil (Dancing Brave (USA)) **Elite Racing Club**

Other Owners: Miss J. A. Camacho, H. K. Gallagher, G. P. Howard, C. J. Murphy, T. S. Postill, W. Riley, M. R. Wainwright.

Assistant Trainer: Mr S Brown

Jockey (flat): A. Culhane, R. Winston.

---

95 MR A. M. CAMPION, Malton
Postal: Whitewell House Stables, Whitewall, Malton, North Yorkshire, YO17 9EH.
Contacts: PHONE (01653) 692729 FAX (01653) 600066 MOBILE (07973) 178311
E-MAIL info@markcampion-racing.com WEBSITE www.markcampion-racing.com

1 BRICKETSTOWN KING (IRE), 9, br g Mandalus—Laurel Walk **Wolfracing UK**
2 COMTE DE CHAMBORD, 9, gr g Baron Blakeney—Show Rose **Mr A. M. Campion**
3 COXWELL COSSACK, 12, ch g Gildoran—Stepout **F. S. W. Partnership**
4 MELOGRANO (IRE), 5, ch g Hector Protector (USA)—Just A Treat (IRE) **Faulkner West & Co Ltd**

Other Owners: Mr R. R. Bailey, R. N. Forman, Mr D. F. Henery, C. C. Straw, I. D. Woolfitt.

96 MRS J. CANDLISH, Leek
Postal: **Basford Grange Racing Stables, Basford, Leek, Staffordshire, ST13 7ET.**
Contacts: **PHONE (01538) 360324 FAX (01538) 361643 MOBILE (07976) 825134/(07977) 599596**
E-MAIL candlishracing@aol.com

1 **BALLYBAY DEMENSE (IRE)**, 9, b br g Bob Back (USA)—Coach Road **Racing For You Limited**
2 **BERKELEY HEIGHTS**, 5, b m Hector Protector (USA)—Dancing Heights (IRE) **A. J. Cartlich**
3 **BLACK BULLET (NZ)**, 12, br g Silver Pistol (AUS)—Monte d'oro (NZ) **M. R. Jump**
4 **CELTIC PRIDE (IRE)**, 10, gr g Roselier (FR)—Grannie No **M. R. Jump**
5 **COLUMBUS (IRE)**, 8, b g Sadler's Wells (USA)—Northern Script (USA) **Racing For You Limited**
6 **COMMONWEALTH (IRE)**, 9, b g Common Grounds—Silver Slipper **J. T. Summerfield**
7 **DONEGAL SHORE (IRE)**, 6, b h Mujadil (USA)—Distant Shore (IRE) **M. A. O'Donnell**
8 **DOWNING STREET (IRE)**, 4, b g Sadler's Wells (USA)—Photographie (USA) **Mr J. R. Candlish**
9 **FIELDINGS SOCIETY (IRE)**, 6, ch g Moscow Society (USA)—Lone Trail (IRE) **M. R. Jump**
10 **FIT TO FLY (IRE)**, 4, b g Lahib (USA)—Maid of Mourne **Mr P. And Mrs G. A. Clarke**
11 **GOLDEN FIELDS (IRE)**, 5, b m Definite Article—Quickstep Queen (FR) **Mrs J. M. Phillips**
12 **GREENCARD GOLF**, 4, b g Foxhound (USA)—Reticent Bride (IRE) **Racing For You Limited**
13 **HARDI DE CHALAMONT (FR)**, 10, gr g Royal Charter (FR)—Naita II (FR) **N. Heath**
14 **INCH' ALLAH (FR)**, 9, b g Royal Charter (FR)—Cadoudaline (FR) **Racing For You Limited**
15 **MAJOR SHARK (FR)**, 7, b g Saint Preuil (FR)—Cindy Cad (FR) **Greencard Golfers**
16 **OUR IMPERIAL BAY (USA)**, 6, b g Smart Strike (CAN)—Heat Lightning (USA) **Mrs J. M. Phillips**
17 **REGAL ACT (IRE)**, 9, ch g Montelimar (USA)—Portal Lady **Racing For You Limited**
18 **RICHIE BOY**, 4, b c Dr Fong (USA)—Alathezal (USA) **Mr J. R. Candlish**
19 **SOROKA (IRE)**, 6, b g Sadler's Wells (USA)—Ivy (USA) **A. J. Baxter**
20 **TWO RIVERS (IRE)**, 6, b g Over The River (FR)—Clarin River (IRE) **M. R. Jump**

Other Owners: Congleton Racing Club, Mr R. Wild, Mr G. Corbett, Mr R. Fielding, M. A. O'Donnell.

Assistant Trainer: Mr James Robbie Candlish

Jockey (flat): N. Callan, I. Mongan, A. Nicholls. **Jockey (NH):** S. Durak. **Conditional:** A. O'Keeffe.

97 MR HENRY D. N. B. CANDY, Wantage
Postal: **Kingston Warren, Wantage, Oxfordshire, OX12 9QF.**
Contacts: **PHONE (01367) 820276/820514 FAX (01367) 820500 MOBILE (07836) 211264**

1 **ALENUSHKA**, 4, b f Soviet Star (USA)—National Portrait (IRE) **Mrs F Gordon Mrs J Carter Mrs A Penfold**
2 **COLLOQUIAL**, 4, b f Classic Cliche (IRE)—Celia Brady **Mrs M. J. Blackburn**
3 **ELA PAPAROUNA**, 4, b f Vettori (IRE)—Pretty Poppy **P. J. L. Wright**
4 **FIREBIRD**, 4, b f Soviet Star (USA)—Al Corniche (IRE) **Mr Henry D. N. B. Candy**
5 **GOSLAR**, 4, ch f In The Wings—Anna of Brunswick **Major M. G. Wyatt**
6 **JAYER GILLES**, 5, br g Busy Flight—Jadidh **Mrs S. L. Brimble**
7 **JOHNNY PARKES**, 4, b g Wolfhound (USA)—Lucky Parkes **J. Heler**
8 **NIVERNAIS**, 6, b g Forzando—Funny Wave **M. J. M. Tricks**
9 **POLONIUS**, 4, b g Great Dane (IRE)—Bridge Pool **P. A. Deal**
10 **WIGGY SMITH**, 6, ch g Master Willie—Monsoon **Mrs V. M. F. Tricks**
11 **WILLOFCOURSE**, 4, b g Aragon—Willyet **Mr Henry D. N. B. Candy**
12 **WOODLAND GLADE**, 4, b f Mark of Esteem (IRE)—Incendio **Mr J. Thomas**

THREE-YEAR-OLDS

13 **ANNALS**, b f Lujain (USA)—Anna of Brunswick **Major M. G. Wyatt**
14 **BOLD ACT (IRE)**, b c Brave Act—Banco Solo **Mrs C. M. Poland**
15 **BOW WAVE**, b c Danzero (AUS)—Moxby **Henry Candy & Partners**
16 **CAESAR BEWARE (IRE)**, b g Daggers Drawn (USA)—Red Shareef **H. E. Sheikh Rashid Al Maktoum**
17 **DEVILS RIVER (IRE)**, b g Anabaa (USA)—Riviere du Diable **H. R. Mould**
18 **DRY ICE (IRE)**, b g Desert Sun—Snowspin **Simon Broke and Partners**
19 **ENTERTAINING**, b f Halling (USA)—Quaver **Girsonfield Ltd**
20 **GAMBLING SPIRIT**, ch f Mister Baileys—Royal Roulette **Simon Broke and Partners**
21 **GREAT ORATOR (USA)**, b g Bahri (USA)—Verbal Intrigue (USA) **Byrne, Billington & Penfold**
22 **IWUNDER (IRE)**, b f King's Best (USA)—Sweetest Thing (IRE) **J. Ellis**
23 **JUBILEE DAWN**, b f Mark of Esteem (IRE)—Eveningperformance **Mrs M. J. Blackburn**
24 **KHYBER KIM**, b g Mujahid (USA)—Jungle Rose **Mrs C. M. Mould**
25 **LOADERFUN (IRE)**, br g Danehill Dancer (IRE)—Sideloader Special **Paul & Linda Dixon**
26 B g Fraam—Monsoon **Mrs V. M. F. Tricks**
27 **MONTFLEUR**, b f Sadler's Wells (USA)—Mackie (USA) **Britton House Stud**

MR HENRY D. N. B. CANDY—continued

28 **PALATINATE (FR),** br g Desert Prince (IRE)—Dead Certain **Crichel Racing**
29 **PUYA,** b f Kris—Pervenche **Girsonfield Ltd**
30 **SEAMUS SHINDIG,** b g Aragon—Sheesha (USA) **Mr Henry D. N. B. Candy**
31 **SUDDEN EDGE,** b g Bold Edge—Surprise Surprise **Mrs J. E. L. Wright**
32 **THE ABBESS,** gr f Bishop of Cashel—Nisha **Girsonfield Ltd**
33 **WOODWOOL,** br f Benny The Dip (USA)—Woodcrest **Major M. G. Wyatt**
34 **ZIGGY ZAGGY,** b f Diktat—Gorgeous Dancer (IRE) **J. Strange**

TWO-YEAR-OLDS

35 Ch c 13/3 Dracula (AUS)—Anna Karietta (Precocious) **The Earl Cadogan**
36 **BAJAN PARKES,** b br c 25/2 Zafonic (USA)—My Melody Parkes (Teenoso (USA)) **J. Heler**
37 **CANDLE,** b f 29/5 Dansili—Celia Brady (Last Tycoon) **Mrs M. J. Blackburn**
38 **CANVAS (IRE),** b f 18/1 Dansili—Sampan (Elmaamul (USA)) **M. H. Dixon**
39 **CHENEY HILL,** b g 7/4 Compton Place—Catriona (Bustino) (22000) **C. J. Burley**
40 **COLINETTE,** b f 8/2 Groom Dancer (USA)—Collide (High Line) **Major M. G. Wyatt**
41 B f 19/2 Dansili—Common Consent (IRE) (Common Grounds) (1500) **Mrs F. M. Gordon**
42 **COSMIC GIRL,** b f 17/3 Gorse—Lotus Moon (Shareef Dancer (USA))
43 B c 2/4 Orpen (USA)—Courtier (Saddlers' Hall (IRE)) (25000) **Thurloe Thoroughbreds XVI**
44 **DANCEATDUSK,** b f 12/4 Desert Prince (IRE)—Ballet (Sharrood (USA)) (40000) **Mrs E. C. Roberts**
45 **EARLY EVENING,** b c 27/2 Daylami (IRE)—Regent Court (IRE) (Marju (IRE)) **Mrs S. Larkin**
46 **GOLD FLAME,** b c 15/3 Gorse—Uae Flame (IRE) (Polish Precedent (USA)) (7000) **Girsonfield Ltd**
47 **HOTHAM,** b c 20/4 Komaite (USA)—Malcesine (IRE) (Auction Ring (USA)) (30000) **Paul & Linda Dixon**
48 B f 11/3 Robellino (USA)—Hymne d'amour (USA) (Dixieland Band (USA)) **The Earl Cadogan**
49 **MAMONTA,** b f 29/3 Fantastic Light (USA)—Mamoura (IRE) (Lomond (USA)) (45000) **Major M. G. Wyatt**
50 B f 11/2 Horse Chestnut (SAF)—McCall (USA) (Shirley Heights) (19686) **Mrs B. D. Oppenheimer**
51 B gr c 23/5 Daylami (IRE)—Morina (USA) (Lyphard (USA)) (75000) **H. R. Mould**
52 **NIGHTSTRIKE (IRE),** b f 18/4 Night Shift (USA)—Come Together (Mtoto) (23000) **Henry Candy & Partners**
53 **PIPER'S SONG (IRE),** b g 24/4 Distant Music (USA)—
                              Dane's Lane (IRE) (Danehill (USA)) (7000) **Mr Henry D. N. B. Candy**
54 **QUINTRELL,** b f 12/5 Royal Applause—Peryllys (Warning) **Major M. G. Wyatt**
55 **SIGNOR PELTRO,** b c 24/2 Bertolini (USA)—Pewter Lass (Dowsing (USA)) (16000) **First of Many Partnership**
56 **SUMMER'S EVE,** gr f 19/5 Singspiel (IRE)—Early Rising (USA) (Grey Dawn II) (85000) **Mrs S. Lakin**
57 **SUMMERTIME PARKES,** ch f 20/3 Silver Patriarch (IRE)—Summerhill Spruce (Windjammer (USA)) **J. Heler**
58 **SUZIE FONG,** b f 2/3 Dr Fong—Limuru (Salse (USA)) (30000) **Mill House Partnership**
59 **THORNHILL,** ch g 26/4 Gorse—Red Hot Dancer (USA) (Seattle Dancer (USA)) (9000) **Mr Henry D. N. B. Candy**
60 B f 30/3 Mull of Kintyre (USA)—Velvet Slipper (Muhtafal (USA)) (22000) **A. H. Bennett**

Other Owners: J. B. Inverdale, Mrs S. Nash, S. Clayton, A. L. Deal, Major-Geng H. Watkins, Mr D. Moules, John & Sarah Haydon, Richard & Barbara Huckerby, Mrs S. Cowling, Mrs J. Graham, A. Frost, T. J. Billington, John Joseph Byrne, C. E. Trading Limited, Crichel Farms Ltd, J. S. Dale, P. J. Dixon, Mrs L. J. Dixon, T. A. F. Frost, R. W. Huggins, Mr P. Newton, Sir Arthur G. Norman, T. C. Norman, O. J. W. Pawle, Penfold Bloodstock, Mrs N. H. Stafford, Lady Whent.

Assistant Trainer: Miss Emma Candy

Jockey (flat): Dane O'Neill.

---

98 **MR A. W. CARROLL, Alcester**
Postal: **Moor Hall Stables, Alcester, Wixford, Warwickshire, B49 6DL.**
Contacts: **HOME** (01386) 793459 **OFFICE** (01789) 772808 **MOBILE** (07770) 472431
E-MAIL awcarrollracing@aol.com **WEBSITE** www.awcarrollracing.com

1 **ALDIRUOS (IRE),** 5, ch g Bigstone (IRE)—Ball Cat (FR) **Aramis Racing Syndicate**
2 **AMBERSONG,** 7, ch g Hernando (FR)—Stygian (USA) **Pursuit Media Limited**
3 **BACKLASH,** 4, b f Fraam—Mezza Luna **One Under Par Racing**
4 **BE WISE GIRL,** 4, ch f Fleetwood (IRE)—Zabelina (USA) **Group 1 Racing (1994) Ltd**
5 **BOWD LANE JOE,** 6, gr g Mazaad—Race To The Rhythm **R. H. Fox**
6 **BRUNSTON CASTLE,** 5, b g Hector Protector (USA)—Villella **Seasons Holidays**
7 **BUZ KIRI (USA),** 7, b g Gulch (USA)—White Corners (USA) **Mr S. Agodino**
8 **CHATSHOW (USA),** 4, br g Distant View (USA)—Galanty Show **D. J. Deacon**
9 **COMPTON ARROW (IRE),** 9, b g Petardia—Impressive Lady **A. G. Bloom**
10 **DARK SOCIETY,** 7, b g Imp Society (USA)—No Candles Tonight **Group 1 Racing (1994) Ltd**
11 **DVINSKY (USA),** 4, ch c Stravinsky (USA)—Festive Season (USA) **D. J. Deacon**
12 **ELA FIGURA,** 5, ch m The West (USA)—Chili Bouchier (USA) **Xunely Limited**
13 **ELLIE MOSS,** 7, b m Le Moss—Kayella **Mrs J. Cumiskey, M. Doocey & K. Doocey**

MR A. W. CARROLL—continued

14 **EMARADIA**, 4, ch f Emarati (USA)—Rewardia (IRE) **D. J. Deacon**
15 **FLAPDOODLE**, 7, b m Superpower—My Concordia **J. Halsey**
16 **FORTUNE POINT (IRE)**, 7, ch g Cadeaux Genereux—Mountains of Mist (IRE) **The T. J. Racing Partnership**
17 **HELLBENT**, 6, b g Selkirk (USA)—Loure (USA) **D. J. Deacon**
18 **HOOISE**, 8, b g Welsh Captain—The Last Tune **Lewis Robinson Partnership**
19 **KANZ WOOD (USA)**, 9, ch g Woodman (USA)—Kanz (USA) **T. J. Plant & Lifting Services Ltd**
20 **KETY STAR (FR)**, 7, b g Bojador (FR)—Danystar (FR) **Seasons Holidays**
21 **KIND SIR**, 9, b g Generous (IRE)—Noble Conquest (USA) **L. T. Cheshire**
22 **KING SOLOMON (FR)**, 6, gr h Simon du Desert (USA)—All Square (FR) **Seasons Holidays**
23 **LAKESIDE GUY (IRE)**, 4, b g Revouce (IRE)—Glen of Imaal (IRE) **D. J. Deacon**
24 **LE CHATELIER (FR)**, 6, b g Kadalko (FR)—Tulipp D'avril (FR) **Mr D. K. Pitt**
25 **LETSPLAY (IRE)**, 5, ch g Accordion—Pennine Sue (IRE) **M. Kelly**
26 **LUPIN (FR)**, 6, b g Luchiroverte (IRE)—Amarante II (FR)
27 **MIDSHIPMAN**, 7, b h Executive Man—Midler **Langwood Racing**
28 **MOKUM (FR)**, 4, b g Octagonal (NZ)—Back On Top (FR) **Xunely Limited**
29 **MOVING EARTH (IRE)**, 12, b g Brush Aside (USA)—Park Breeze (IRE) **Pursuit Media Limited**
30 **MR DIP**, 5, b g Reprimand—Scottish Lady **J. J. Smith**
31 **OLD MARSH (IRE)**, 9, b g Grand Lodge—Lolly Dolly **Seasons and Paradise**
32 **ORCHESTRATION (IRE)**, 4, ch g Stravinsky (USA)—Mora (IRE) **D. T. Shorthouse**
33 **OUR DESTINY**, 7, b g Mujadil (USA)—Superspring **D. J. Deacon**
34 **PLAUSABELLE**, 4, b f Royal Applause—Sipsi Fach **M. Kelly**
35 **ROBBIE CAN CAN**, 6, b g Robellino (USA)—Can Can Lady **K. F. Coleman**
36 **SOVEREIGN GIRL**, 4, b f Sovereign Water (FR)—The Quaker **R. W. Mitchell**
37 **SPECTESTED (IRE)**, 4, ch g Spectrum (IRE)—Nisibis **Bezwell Fixings Ltd**
38 **STOOP TO CONQUER**, 5, b g Polar Falcon (USA)—Princess Genista **Seasons Holidays**
39 **TUSCARORA (IRE)**, 6, b m Revouce (IRE)—Fresh Look (IRE) **Pursuit Media Limited**
40 **UP THE GLEN (IRE)**, 11, b g Tale Quale—Etrenne **Pursuit Media Limited**
41 **VALENTINE'S PET**, 5, b m My Best Valentine—Fabulous Pet **Bezwell Fixings Ltd**
42 **VIZULIZE**, 6, b m Robellino (USA)—Euridice (IRE) **Last Day Racing Partnership**
43 **WAVE ROCK**, 10, br g Tragic Role (USA)—Moonscape **Sterling Racing Syndicate**
44 **YOUNGS FORTH**, 5, b m Most Welcome—Pegs **D. J. Deacon**
45 **ZIET D'ALSACE (FR)**, 5, b m Zieten (USA)—Providenc Mill (FR) **D. J. Deacon**

THREE-YEAR-OLDS

46 **FIRE AT WILL**, b c Lugana Beach—Kahyasi Moll (IRE) **G. Bull & M. Bayley**
47 **FORTISZAMO**, b g Forzando—Flamingo Times **Bruce W. Wyatt, Michael J. Peacock**
48 **SAVOY CHAPEL**, br c Xaar—Royal Gift **D. J. Deacon**

Other Owners: A. Allright, Mrs M. Bayley, E. E. A. Buddle, K. E. Collins, Mrs K. T. Cumiskey, M. Doocey, K. P. Doocey, Mr R. Gibbs, Ms S. A. Kearney, Mr H. Lewis, Mr D. P. Robinson, Mr A. D. Rogers, R. A. Sansom, Mrs J. Shaw, G. Siden, J. H. Treadwell, A. E. Wool.

Jockey (flat): J. Fortune. **Jockey (NH):** T. J. Murphy. **Amateur:** Mr M. Smith.

---

99   MR D. CARROLL, Warthilll
Postal: **P.O. Box 691, York, YO32 9WY.**
Contacts: **HOME (01904) 400674 OFFICE (01759) 373083 FAX (01759) 373586**
MOBILE (07801) 553779
E-MAIL **declan@dcarrollracing.com** WEBSITE **www.dcarrollracing.com**

1 **BENBYAS**, 8, b g Rambo Dancer (CAN)—Light The Way **C. H. Stephenson & Partners**
2 **CARAMAN (IRE)**, 7, ch g Grand Lodge (USA)—Caraiyma (IRE) **Alan Mann**
3 **CLEVELAND WAY**, 5, b g Forzando—Fallal (IRE) **Mr Denis Hardy**
4 **DIAMOND SHANNON (IRE)**, 4, b f Petorius—Balgren (IRE) **Diamond Racing Ltd**
5 **GOLD GUEST**, 6, ch g Vettori (IRE)—Cassilis (IRE) **Diamond Racing Ltd**
6 **GRANDMA LILY (IRE)**, 7, b m Bigstone (IRE)—Mrs Fisher (IRE) **David Fravigar, Alan Mann, David Marshall**
7 **JOSHUA'S GOLD (IRE)**, 4, b g Sesaro (USA)—Lady of The Night (IRE) **K. H. Taylor Limited**
8 **LIVE AND DANGEROUS**, 4, b f Mark of Esteem (IRE)—Mazaya (IRE) **Mr Seamus Mannion**
9 **LONGSTONE LASS**, 5, b m Wizard King—Kamaress **L. Ibbotson**
10 **MEZEREON**, 5, b m Alzao (USA)—Blown-Over **Diamond Racing Ltd**
11 **MISTER SWEETS**, 6, ch g Nashwan (USA)—Keyboogie (USA) **Mr David Fravigar-Mr Alan Mann**
12 **PEARL FISHER**, 4, ch f Foxhound (USA)—Naivity (IRE) **Dreams**
13 5, B br m Dr Massini (IRE)—Port Alley **Mr Seamus Mannion**
14 **ROYAL SESSION (IRE)**, 5, b m Accordion—Mrs Keppel **Dreams**

MR D. CARROLL—continued

15 **RUSH'N'RUN**, 6, b g Kasakov—Runfawit Pet **K. Nicholson**
16 **RUST EN VREDE**, 6, b g Royal Applause—Souveniers **Alan Mann**
17 **SHE'S OUR LASS (IRE)**, 4, b f Orpen (USA)—Sharadja (IRE) **We-Know Partnership**
18 **SHIFTY**, 6, b g Night Shift (USA)—Crodelle (IRE) **WRB Racing 39 (wrbracing.com)**
19 **SOVIET JOY (IRE)**, 4, b br g Russian Revival (USA)—Danny's Joy (IRE) **A. Mann**
20 **TISN'T EASY (IRE)**, 7, b m Mandalus—Gemini Gale **Mr Seamus Mannion**
21 **TOMMYTYLER (IRE)**, 6, b g Goldmark (USA)—John's Ballad (IRE) **Mrs M. Behan**
22 **WINGS OF MORNING (IRE)**, 4, ch g Fumo di Londra (IRE)—Hay Knot **N. Green**

THREE-YEAR-OLDS

23 **EMERALD DESTINY (IRE)**, b g Key of Luck (USA)—Green Belt (FR) **WRB Racing 53 (wrbracing.com)**
24 **FIRST BOY**, b g Polar Prince (IRE)—Seraphim (FR) **Mrs B. Ramsden**
25 **LOVE ATTACK (IRE)**, b f Sri Pekan (USA)—Bradwell (IRE) **Diamond Racing Ltd**
26 **MING VASE**, b c Vettori (IRE)—Minstrel's Dance (CAN) **M. Ng**
27 **MISTER MINTY (IRE)**, b c Fasliyev (USA)—Sorb Apple (IRE) **David Fravigar, Kathy Dixon**
28 **ONE OF EACH (IRE)**, ch f Indian Lodge (IRE)—Indian City **We Know Partnership**

TWO-YEAR-OLDS

29 **AMES SOUER (IRE)**, b f 23/3 Fayruz—Taispeain (IRE) (Petorius) (10730) **Diamond Racing Ltd**
30 B c 27/2 Bold Fact (USA)—Balgren (IRE) (Ballad Rock) (8718) **Nine R' Us**
31 **FAIRYTALE OF YORK (IRE)**, b f 14/5 Imperial Ballet (IRE)—
Pekanski (IRE) (Sri Pekan (USA)) (4694) **Mr & Mrs K. Grogan**
32 B f 1/5 Averti (IRE)—Light of Aragon (Aragon) (800) **C. H. Stephenson & Partners**
33 Ch c 25/4 Elnadim (USA)—Madam Baileys (IRE) (Doulab (USA)) **Mrs M. Behan**
34 B c 7/6 Danetime (IRE)—Night Rhapsody (IRE) (Mujtahid (USA)) (9389)
35 B c 16/3 Imperial Ballet (IRE)—Sharadja (IRE) (Doyoun) (21461) **Claire King**
36 B f 25/1 Desert Style (IRE)—
Torretta (IRE) (Indian Ridge) (5029) **Martin J. Geraghty, Paul McGuinness & Tommy Campbell**

Other Owners: Sunpax Potatoes, Mr A. S. Scott, Mr Andrew Bates, Roger Peel, Mr Steve Goodwin, Mr Tony Yates, Mr David Thompson, Miss D. Allman, J. H. A. Hopkinson, E. Richmond, S. M. Scott, D. Scott, C. H. Stephenson, Mrs V. Stephenson, The Irish Sun, Wetherby Racing Bureau Ltd, Mrs S. J. Yates.

Apprentice: Danielle McCreery, Neil Brown, D. Tudhope. **Amateur:** Miss D. Allman.

---

100 **MR R. M. CARSON, Lambourn**
Postal: **58 Child Street, Lambourn, Hungerford, Berkshire, RG17 8NZ.**
Contacts: **PHONE (01488) 72080 MOBILE (07751) 440182**

1 **A RIGHT SET TWO**, 13, ch g Island Set (USA)—Super Sol **Mr R. M. Carson**
2 **HAIL THE KING (USA)**, 5, gr g Allied Forces (USA)—Hail Kris (USA) **Mrs P. Carson**

Assistant Trainer: Mrs P Carson

Jockey (NH): Mr J. A. McCarthy. **Conditional:** Mr R. Lucey-Butler.

---

101 **MR O. J. CARTER, Ottery St Mary**
Postal: **Wild Green, Metcombe, Ottery St Mary, Devon, EX11 1RS.**
Contacts: **PHONE (01404) 812607**

1 **ALLAHRAKHA**, 14, ch g Aragon—Bernigra Girl **Mr O. J. Carter**
2 **FIRST THOUGHT**, 7, b m Primitive Rising (USA)—Precis **Mr O. J. Carter**
3 **LOST DIRECTION**, 10, b m Heading North—Precis **Mr O. J. Carter**
4 **TIPTON RISE**, 9, b m Primitive Rising (USA)—Tipton Times **Mr O. J. Carter**
5 **VAGUE IDEA**, 12, gr g Tout Ensemble—Roodle Doodle **Mr O. J. Carter**
6 **VENN OTTERY**, 10, b g Access Ski—Tom's Comedy **Mr O. J. Carter**
7 **WATCH ME DOODLE**, 6, ch m Early Edition—Roodle Doodle **Mr O. J. Carter**

102 MR B. I. CASE, Banbury

Postal: **Edgcote House Stables, Edgcote, Chipping Warden, Banbury, Oxfordshire, OX17 1AG.**
Contacts: PHONE **(01295) 660909** FAX **(01295) 660908** MOBILE **(07808) 061223**
E-MAIL **info@bencaseracing.com** WEBSITE **www.bencaseracing.com**

1 BDELLIUM, 7, b m Royal Vulcan—Kelly's Logic **N. S. Hutley**
2 BODING, 4, b f Shambo—Pudding **Paul Rackham**
3 FLORAGALORE, 4, b f Dr Fong (USA)—Valagalore **Mrs A. D. Bourne**
4 HALF INCH, 5, b m Inchinor—Anhaar **Mrs M. A. Howlett**
5 HARRY COLLINS, 7, ch g Sir Harry Lewis (USA)—Run Fast For Gold **Case Racing Partnership**
6 HUNTER PUDDING, 5, b m Shambo—Pudding **Paul Rackham**
7 KINGS LINEN (IRE), 9, b g Persian Mews—Kings Princess **Dudley Moore**
8 LE JOYEUX (FR), 6, br g Video Rock (FR)—Agra (FR) **Dudley Moore**
9 MAGNETIC POLE, 4, b c Machiavellian (USA)—Clear Attraction (USA) **D. C. R. Allen**
10 RED KARINGA, 4, ch f Karinga Bay—Red Mirage (IRE) **Mrs J. Way**
11 SPECIAL CONSTABLE, 7, b br g Derrylin—Lavenham's Last **Case Racing Partnership**
12 TRUE MARINER (FR), 5, b g True Brave (USA)—Miss Above (FR) **D. C. R. Allen**

THREE-YEAR-OLDS

13 BAKKE, b g Danehill (USA)—Valagalore **Itchen Valley Stud**
14 B c Yaheeb (USA)—Lavenham's Last **Lady Jane Grosvenor**
15 SILVER BEAN, b f Silver Patriarch (IRE)—Beenaround (IRE) **Paul Rackham**
16 SWEET MATRIARCH, b f Silver Patriarch (IRE)—Pudding **Paul Rackham**

TWO-YEAR-OLDS

17 BENISON, ch c 16/4 Benny The Dip (USA)—Boojum (Mujtahid (USA)) **Itchen Valley Stud**
18 NAUGHTY MARIETTA, ch f 16/5 Mark of Esteem (IRE)—Valagalore (Generous (IRE)) **Itchen Valley Stud**

Other Owners: Mrs S. Harrison, Mrs A. Charlton, Mr & Mrs G. Nicholson, Mr J. Nowell-Smith, Mr & Mrs C. Nixey, Mrs J. Broughton, Mr & Mrs G. Rodenhurst, Mr P. Lush, Mr Payne, Mr & Mrs D. Sutton, Mr M. Turner, Mr J. Daffurn, L. Griffiths, Mrs P. Perriss, Mr A. Ringer, Lord Fellowes, Mrs K. Perrem, Mr & Mrs D. Baines, Mr A. Case, Mrs S. L. Case, Mr A. Jones.

Conditional: C. Honour.

103 MR J. M. CASTLE, Aylesbury

Postal: **Mottymead Farm, Long Crendon, Aylesbury, Buckinghamshire, HP18 9BE.**
Contacts: PHONE **(01844) 208107** FAX **(01844) 201107**
E-MAIL **mottymead@hotmail.com**

1 MONTY BE QUICK, 9, ch g Mon Tresor—Spartiquick **Mr J. M. Castle**

Assistant Trainer: Mrs S J Castle

104 MR H. R. A. CECIL, Newmarket

Postal: **Warren Place, Newmarket, Suffolk, CB8 8QQ.**
Contacts: OFFICE **(01638) 662192** FAX **(01638) 669005**

1 AKIMBO (USA), 4, b c Kingmambo (USA)—All At Sea (USA) **K. Abdulla**
2 DENOUNCE, 4, b c Selkirk (USA)—Didicoy (USA) **K. Abdulla**
3 FOCUS GROUP (USA), 4, b c Kris S (USA)—Interim **K. Abdulla**
4 INVASIAN (IRE), 4, ch c Desert Prince (IRE)—Jarrayan **Dr K. Sanderson**
5 SAYADAW (FR), 5, b h Darshaan—Vingt Et Une (FR) **The Niarchos Family**

THREE-YEAR-OLDS

6 AIR COMMODORE (USA), ch c Diesis—La Sky (IRE) **Lordship Stud Limited**
7 AWASH (USA), ch c Coronado's Quest (USA)—All At Sea (USA) **K. Abdulla**
8 CAMACHO, b c Danehill (USA)—Arabesque **K. Abdulla**
9 CUSTODIAN (IRE), b c Giant's Causeway (USA)—Desert Bluebell **Mr Robert Lanigan & Mrs John Magnier**
10 DOOIE DANCER, b c Entrepreneur—Vayavaig **www.KABIS.co.uk**
11 ECCENTRICITY (USA), ch f Kingmambo (USA)—Shiva (JPN) **The Niarchos Family**
12 ESTRELLE (GER), ch f Sternkoenig (IRE)—Enrica **Mr G. Schoeningh**
13 FLEECE, b f Daylami (IRE)—Gold Dodger (USA) **Bloomsbury Stud**
14 GEMS OF ARABY, b f Zafonic (USA)—Clepsydra **K. Abdulla**

Inspired Breeding

Airlie Stud have bred 7 Gr.1 winners of 11 Gr.1 races in the last 6 years, including in 2004: –

Airlie-bred BACHELOR DUKE wins the Gr.1 Irish 2000 Guineas at the Curragh defeating Azamour (Gr.1 St James's Palace Stakes and Gr.1 Irish Champion Stakes) and Grey Swallow (Gr.1 Irish Derby).

Airlie-bred CHELSEA ROSE runs on well to land the Gr.1 Moyglare Stud Stakes for two-year-old fillies, also at the Curragh.

Relatively speaking, one of the most successful breeders in the world

Yearlings consigned annually to Tattersalls Ireland, Goffs and Tattersalls Newmarket sales.

Also standing **DOCKSIDER** multiple Group winning miler by **Diesis** from the family of outstanding sires **Sadler's Wells**, **Nureyev** and **Fairy King**. Sire of 23 3-y-o winners of 40 races in 2004.

NB: Airlie can also offer breeders high quality boarding facilities for mares at their Grangewilliam headquarters and sales preparation for yearlings at the nearby Kilmacredock Stud.

AIRLIE STUD
Grangewilliam, Maynooth, Co Kildare, Ireland.
Enquiries to: **Anthony Rogers**
Tel: **+353 (0)1 6286336** or **6286038** *(yard)*
Mobile: **087 2450438** Fax: **+353 (0)1 6286674**
e-mail: **info@airliestud.com** web site: **www.airliestud.com**

MR H. R. A. CECIL—continued

15 **HACHITA (USA),** ch f Gone West (USA)—Choice Spirit (USA) **K. Abdulla**
16 **HALLIARD,** b f Halling (USA)—Felucca **K. Abdulla**
17 **KABIS AMIGOS,** ch c Nashwan (USA)—River Saint (USA) **Mr J. I. T. Patel**
18 **LA TRAVIATA (SWI),** ch f Grand Lodge (USA)—La Venta (USA) **J. Shack**
19 **LILAC MIST,** b f Spectrum (IRE)—L'ideale (USA) **J. Shack**
20 **LOUISE D'ARZENS,** br f Anabaa (USA)—Maidment **Mrs B.V. Chennells & Henry Cecil & Company Ltd**
21 **LOVE ME TENDER,** br f Green Desert (USA)—Easy To Love (USA) **Lordship Stud Limited**
22 **MADAME MOGAMBO (USA),** b f Kingmambo (USA)—Aqua Galinte (USA) **International Equities Holding Inc.**
23 **NEWTOWN VILLA,** b f Spectrum (IRE)—New Abbey **K. Abdulla**
24 **PARISETTE,** b f Dansili—Moulin Rouge **Mr & Mrs P. Homewood**
25 **POLITICAL INTRIGUE,** b c Dansili—Quandary (USA) **K. Abdulla**
26 **QUICK MOVE,** b c Selkirk (USA)—Flit (USA) **K. Abdulla**
27 **RATHOR (IRE),** b br c Machiavellian (USA)—Raisonnable **The Niarchos Family**
28 **SAVOIE,** ch f Grand Lodge (USA)—Spry **Plantation Stud Limited**
29 **SCOTCH HOUSE,** ch f Selkirk (USA)—Top Shop **Cliveden Stud Ltd**
30 **SHAMANA (USA),** b f Woodman (USA)—Yashmak (USA) **K. Abdulla**
31 **SONGBOOK,** b br f Singspiel (IRE)—Easy To Copy (USA) **Lordship Stud Limited**
32 **STAGECRAFT (USA),** b f Diesis—Eternity **Dr C. M. H. Wills**
33 **TEMPESTAD (IRE),** b f Giant's Causeway (USA)—Arutua (USA) **International Equities Holding Inc.**
34 **THE COOIE (IRE),** b c Sadler's Wells (USA)—Propensity **www.KABIS.co.uk**
35 **VIBRATO (USA),** b c Stravinsky (USA)—She's Fine (USA) **Henry Cecil & Company Ltd**
36 **VINTAGE FABRIC (USA),** b c Royal Anthem (USA)—Sandalwood (USA) **K. Abdulla**

TWO-YEAR-OLDS

37 **BIGGIN HILL (IRE),** b c 7/2 Alzao (USA)—Fire of London (Shirley Heights) (16000) **Mr H. Ponsonby**
38 **BORDER NEWS,** ch c 7/4 Selkirk (USA)—Flit (USA) (Lyphard (USA)) **K. Abdulla**
39 **CHALENTINA,** b f 25/4 Primo Valentino (IRE)—
                            Chantilly Myth (Sri Pekan (USA)) (20000) **Henry Cecil & Company Ltd**
40 **DANEWAY,** ch f 28/2 Danehill Dancer (IRE)—Scylla (Rock City) (23000) **Mrs A. Scott**
41 B f 15/3 Observatory (USA)—Didicoy (USA) (Danzig (USA)) **K. Abdulla**
42 Ch c 16/4 Barathea (IRE)—Granted (FR) (Cadeaux Genereux) (15500) **Pierre Van Belle**
43 **GRIEG,** b c 17/4 Generous (IRE)—Maidment (Insan (USA)) (22000) **Mrs B. V. Chennells**
44 **ISIS (USA),** b f 6/3 Royal Academy (USA)—Incredulous (FR) (Indian Ridge) **Dr C. M. H. Wills**
45 **LUCKY WISH,** b c 7/5 Alhaarth (IRE)—All The Luck (USA) (Mr Prospector (USA)) **K. Abdulla**
46 **MERLINS DREAMS,** b c 25/4 Dansili—Red Leggings (Shareef Dancer (USA)) (6000) **Mr I. Lindsay**
47 Ch f 26/3 Selkirk (USA)—Minority (Generous (IRE)) **K. Abdulla**
48 B f 25/4 Sadler's Wells (USA)—Modena (USA) (Roberto (USA)) **K. Abdulla**
49 **MOONSHADOW,** ch f 12/2 Diesis—La Sky (IRE) (Law Society (USA)) **Lordship Stud Limited**
50 **MULTIDIMENSIONAL (IRE),** b c 27/4 Danehill (USA)—Sacred Song (USA) (Diesis) **The Niarchos Family**
51 **OCEAN VALENTINE,** gr c 15/3 King Charlemagne (USA)—
                            Dolly Bevan (Another Realm) (26000) **Mr & Mrs C Thomas**
52 Ch f 10/2 Peintre Celebre (USA)—Quandary (USA) (Blushing Groom (FR)) **K. Abdulla**
53 **RAS TAFARII (FR),** ch c 5/2 Grand Lodge (USA)—Burning Sunset (Caerleon (USA)) **The Niarchos Family**
54 **TRAVEL GUIDE (USA),** ch c 29/1 Cozzene (USA)—Wandesta (Nashwan (USA)) **K. Abdulla**
55 Ch c 20/2 Barathea (IRE)—Tuning (Rainbow Quest (USA)) **K. Abdulla**
56 B c 19/4 Chester House (USA)—Yashmak (USA) (Danzig (USA)) **K. Abdulla**

Other Owners: G. M. Barnard, Dreamfields Inc., N. Gomersall, M. Tabor.

Assistant Trainer: David Lanigan

---

105 MR S. G. CHADWICK, Hayton
Postal: **Eskrigg, Hayton, Aspatria, Carlisle, Cumbria, CA7 2PD.**
Contacts: **PHONE (01697) 321226**

1 **BOSS MORTON (IRE),** 14, b g Tremblant—Sandy Kelly **Mr S. G. Chadwick**
2 **FAWN PRINCE (IRE),** 12, b g Electric—Regent Star **Mr S. G. Chadwick**
3 **HAYTON BOY,** 11, ch g Gypsy Castle—Young Christine VII **Mr S. G. Chadwick**
4 **JAMORIN DANCER,** 10, b g Charmer—Geryea (USA) **Mr S. G. Chadwick**
5 **MINSTER MEADOW,** 6, ch g Minster Son—Eddies Well **Mr S. G. Chadwick**
6 **MISS ARAGONT,** 6, b m Aragon—Uninvited **Mr S. G. Chadwick**
7 **MONTEYS CRYSTAL (IRE),** 7, b g Montelimar (USA)—Kindly Lass **Mr S. G. Chadwick**
8 **SCURRY DANCER (FR),** 9, b g Snurge—Fijar Dance (FR) **Mr S. G. Chadwick**

106 MR A. J. CHAMBERLAIN, Swindon

Postal: **North End Farm, Ashton Keynes, Swindon, Wiltshire, SN6 6QR.**
Contacts: **PHONE (01285) 861347 MOBILE (07941) 829976**

1 BEAUCHAMP RIBBON, 5, b m Vettori (IRE)—Beauchamp Kate **Mr A. C. Ledbury**
2 BOSWORTH BOY, 7, b g Deploy—Krill **F. J. Brennan**
3 DEVONICA, 6, br m Dr Devious (IRE)—Ann Veronica (IRE) **Mr R. J. Hall**
4 EXPENSIVE FOLLY (IRE), 7, b g Satco (FR)—Tarasandy (IRE) **N F B P L Racing**
5 FATHER PADDY, 10, ch g Minster Son—Sister Claire **F. J. Brennan**
6 FLYING SPUD, 4, ch g Fraam—Lorcanjo **Mr A. J. Chamberlain**
7 KARAKUM, 6, b g Mtoto—Magongo **Mr A. C. Ledbury**
8 REGAL REPOSE, 5, b m Classic Cliche (IRE)—Ideal Candidate **D. F. Bassett**
9 ROUGH CROSSING (IRE), 7, b g Houmayoun (FR)—Polocracy (IRE) **Mr A. J. Chamberlain**
10 STYLISH DANCER, 4, B F Muhtarram (USA)—Iltimas (USA)

THREE-YEAR-OLDS

11 WHITLAND, b g Namaqualand (USA)—Whittle Rock **Lord Goldicote**

Other Owners: M. Bishop, Mr N. R. Carter.

Assistant Trainer: B Brennan

Amateur: Mr D. Alers-Hankey, Mr S. Walsh.

107 MR P. R. CHAMINGS, Basingstoke

Postal: **Inhurst Farm Stables, Baughurst, Tadley, Hampshire, RG26 5JS.**
Contacts: **PHONE (01189) 814494 FAX (01189) 820454 MOBILE (07831) 360970**
E-MAIL chamingsracing@talk21.com

1 BINANTI, 5, b g Bin Ajwaad (IRE)—Princess Rosananti (IRE) **Mrs J. E. L. Wright**
2 DEPTFORD (IRE), 6, ch g Un Desperado (FR)—Katty London **Mrs V. K. Shaw**
3 DESERT DREAMER (IRE), 4, b g Green Desert (USA)—Follow That Dream **Patrick Chamings Sprint Club**
4 ENCORA BAY, 4, b f Primo Dominie—Brave Revival **Mr P. R. Chamings**
5 GIG HARBOR, 6, b g Efisio—Petonica (IRE) **Fraser Miller Racing**
6 GREY MISTRAL, 7, gr m Terimon—Winnowing (IRE) **Mrs V. K. Shaw**
7 LIFTED WAY, 6, b h In The Wings—Stack Rock **Mrs Alexandra J. Chandris**
8 LYRICAL WAY, 6, b g Vettori (IRE)—Fortunate **Mrs Alexandra J. Chandris**
9 MIDAS WAY, 5, ch g Halling (USA)—Arietta's Way (IRE) **Mrs Alexandra J. Chandris**
10 MOTU (IRE), 4, b g Desert Style (IRE)—Pink Cashmere (IRE) **Patrick Chamings Sprint Club**
11 NEPHETRITI WAY (IRE), 4, b f Docksider (USA)—Velvet Appeal (IRE) **Mrs Alexandra J. Chandris**
12 NIOBE'S WAY, 4, b f Singspiel (IRE)—Arietta's Way (IRE) **Mrs Alexandra J. Chandris**
13 PORT ST CHARLES (IRE), 8, b br g Night Shift (USA)—Safe Haven **Patrick Chamings Sprint Club**
14 RIO DE JANEIRO (IRE), 4, b c Sadler's Wells (USA)—Alleged Devotion (USA) **Fraser Miller Racing**
15 RUSSIAN APPLAUSE, 5, b g Royal Applause—Zeffirella **Inhurst Farm Stables Partnership**
16 SCOTISH LAW (IRE), 7, ch g Case Law—Scotia Rose **Inhurst Farm Stables Partnership**
17 SELF DEFENSE, 8, b g Warning—Dansara **Fraser Miller Racing**
18 SHAMBAR (IRE), 6, gr g Linamix (FR)—Shamawna (IRE) **Fraser Miller Racing**
19 SNOWY FORD (IRE), 8, b g Be My Native—Monalee Stream **R. V. Shaw**
20 STELLA MARAIS (IRE), 4, b f Second Empire (IRE)—Karakapa (FR) **J. C. Murphy**
21 TAKE A BOW, 4, b c Royal Applause—Giant Nipper **Mrs J. E. L. Wright**
22 THE LEADER, 12, b g Ardross—Leading Line **Inhurst Farm Stables Partnership**
23 USK VALLEY (IRE), 10, b g Tenby—Penultimate (USA) **Inhurst Farm Stables Partnership**
24 WOODLAND BLAZE (IRE), 6, b g Woodborough (USA)—Alpine Sunset **Patrick Chamings Sprint Club**

THREE-YEAR-OLDS

25 BOB BAILEYS, b g Mister Baileys—Bob's Princess **Mrs J. E. L. Wright**
26 FOXHAVEN, ch c Unfuwain (USA)—Dancing Mirage (IRE) **Mrs A. M. Jenkins**
27 GANACHE (IRE), ch c Halling (USA)—Granted (FR) **Mr E. D. Kessly & Mrs A. M. Jenkins**
28 OASIS WAY (IRE), b f Wadood (USA)—Northern Moon **Mrs Alexandra J. Chandris**
29 OBSTREPEROUS WAY, ch c Dr Fong (USA)—Fleet Key **Mrs Alexandra J. Chandris**
30 ONEIRO WAY (IRE), b g King's Best (USA)—Koumiss **Mrs Alexandra J. Chandris**
31 ORIENTAL WAY (IRE), b f Fascinating Way (GR)—Light Wind (GR) **Mrs Alexandra J. Chandris**
32 OSIRIS WAY, ch c Indian Ridge—Heady **Mrs Alexandra J. Chandris**
33 OVATION WAY (GR), ch c Military Fashion—Analampi (GR) **Mrs Alexandra J. Chandris**
34 OVERJOY WAY, b f Cadeaux Genereux—May Light **Mrs Alexandra J. Chandris**

MR P. R. CHAMINGS—continued

35 **OVERLORD WAY (GR)**, br c Tony Galvin (GR)—Fortunate Way (GR) **Mrs Alexandra J. Chandris**
36 **OVERTOP WAY (GR)**, b c Denebola Way (GR)—Dada (GR) **Mrs Alexandra J. Chandris**

TWO-YEAR-OLDS

37 Ch c 27/2 Apotheosis (USA)—Alkmini (GR) (Guy Butters (GR)) (7619) **Mrs Alexandra J. Chandris**
38 B c 10/5 Docksider (USA)—Arietta's Way (IRE) (Darshaan) (18000) **Mrs Alexandra J. Chandris**
39 **BENELLINO**, b c 12/4 Robellino (USA)—Benjarong (Sharpo) (5000) **Mrs J. E. L. Wright**
40 Ch c 31/3 Wadood (USA)—Evropi's Way (Sanglamore (USA)) (8571) **Mrs Alexandra J. Chandris**
41 **JAIN AIR**, b f 31/1 Lujain (USA)—Bellair (Beveled (USA)) (7000) **Mrs A. M. Jenkins**
42 B f 24/4 Fascinating Way (GR)—Misirlou (GR) (Lai Lai (GR)) (7619) **Mrs Alexandra J. Chandris**
43 B f 10/3 Apotheosis (USA)—Northern Moon (Ile de Bourbon (USA)) (9523) **Mrs Alexandra J. Chandris**
44 **PASIPINE'S WAY**, b f 30/1 Piccolo—Passiflora (Night Shift (USA)) (27000) **Mrs Alexandra J. Chandris**
45 **RICKETY BRIDGE (IRE)**, ch c 22/2 Elnadim (USA)—Kriva (Reference Point) (8500) **Mrs A. M. Jenkins**
46 **THOMAS A BECKETT (IRE)**, b c 11/4 Beckett (IRE)—Kenema (IRE) (Petardia) (46000) **Mrs A. M. Jenkins**
47 Ch f 19/4 Docksider (USA)—Waft (USA) (Topsider (USA)) (1000) **Mrs A. M. Jenkins**
48 **WOODCOTE PLACE**, b c 19/2 Lujain (USA)—
                                     Giant Nipper (Nashwan (USA)) (15000) **Mr E. D. Kessly & Mrs A. M. Jenkins**

Other Owners: Mr & Mrs P. Bennett, Mr W. Evans, Mr & Mrs D. Chammings, Mr & Mrs L. Attrill, Mr & Mrs R. Hadden-Wright, Mr R. Rosier, Mrs J. Miller, Mrs S. Gibbons, Mr & Mrs N. Patterson, Mrs P. Anders, Mr M. Lear, Mr & Mrs A. Clifford, Mrs J. Tag, Mr M. Herring, Mr T. Goswell, Mrs S. Trimble, Mrs J. Marshall, Mr J. Randall, Mrs D. Swallow, Mrs S. De Speville, Mrs J. R. Foster, Mr F. T. Lee, Mr B. G. Slade, Mr K. W. Tyrrell.

Jockey (flat): J. Quinn. **Conditional:** James Davies. **Amateur:** Mr D. Alers-Hankey.

108 MR N. T. CHANCE, Upper Lambourn
Postal: **Berkeley House Stables, Upper Lambourn, Hungerford, Berkshire, RG17 8QP.**
Contacts: OFFICE (01488) 73436 FAX (01488) 72296 MOBILE (07785) 300168
E-MAIL noel.chance@virgin.net

1 **ACCUMULUS**, 5, b g Cloudings (IRE)—Norstock **Ian Murray & Nick Quesnel**
2 **BEYOND THE PALE (IRE)**, 7, gr g Be My Native (USA)—Cyrano Imperial (IRE) **A. D. Weller**
3 **CIGARILLO (IRE)**, 7, br g Vestris Abu—Rose-Anore **C. C. Shand Kydd**
4 **CORPORATE PLAYER (IRE)**, 7, b g Zaffaran (USA)—Khazna **A. D. Weller**
5 **DANS PRIDE (IRE)**, 7, b g Presenting—Mindyourown (IRE) **B. T. Jacobs**
6 **DARK STORM**, 6, gr g Terimon—Norstock **Ian Murray & Nick Quesnel**
7 **DIRECT FLIGHT (IRE)**, 7, ch g Dry Dock—Midnight Mistress **Top Flight Racing**
8 **FLAME CREEK (IRE)**, 9, b g Shardari—Sheila's Pet (IRE) **Martin Wesson Partners**
9 **FREE RETURN (IRE)**, 10, ch g Magical Wonder (USA)—Free Reserve (USA) **Mrs J. D. Cox**
10 **GAELIC FLIGHT (IRE)**, 7, b br g Norwich—Ash Dame (IRE) **Top Flight Racing 3**
11 **GARDEN SHED REBEL**, 5, b g Tragic Role (USA)—Clare Island
12 **GOLD AGAIN (IRE)**, 7, b g Old Vic—Thomastown Girl **D. O'Sullivan**
13 4, B g Needle Gun (IRE)—Grange Park (IRE) **Mrs N. Kelly**
14 **GREAT MAN (FR)**, 4, b g Bering—Great Connection (USA) **The Cardinal Syndicate**
15 **KATY JONES**, 5, b m Alderbrook—Just Jodi (IRE) **Mrs R. F. Greener**
16 **KILLULTAGH STAR (IRE)**, 5, b g Oscar Schindler (IRE)—Rostrevor Lady **Mrs R. Boyd**
17 **KILLULTAGH STORM (IRE)**, 11, b g Mandalus—Rostrevor Lady **Mrs R. Boyd**
18 **LISSARA (IRE)**, 7, b g Glacial Storm (USA)—Bonnies Glory **Mrs R. Boyd**
19 **LORD OF BEAUTY (FR)**, 5, ch g Medaaly—Arctic Beauty (USA) **Warren, Upton & Chenkin & Townson**
20 **MAJESTIC FLIGHT (IRE)**, 4, br g In The Wings—Gracieuse Majeste (FR) **Top Flight Racing 4**
21 **MAKE IT A DOUBLE (IRE)**, 7, ch g Zaffaran (USA)—La Danse **A. D. Weller**
22 **MEGAPAC (IRE)**, 7, b g Supreme Leader—Mistress Gale **B. T. Jacobs**
23 **MIO CARO (FR)**, 5, ch g Bering—Composition (USA) **M. F. Browne**
24 **MORNING FLIGHT (IRE)**, 9, b m Supreme Leader—Morning Jane (IRE) **Top Flight Racing (2)**
25 **MURPHY'S CARDINAL (IRE)**, 9, b g Shernazar—Lady Swinford **Mr T. Conway & Mrs Conway**
26 **NEW MISCHIEF (IRE)**, 7, b g Accordion—Alone Party (IRE) **R. W. and J. R. Fidler**
27 **NO TURNING BACK (IRE)**, 6, b g Shernazar—Offaly Rose (IRE) **I. R. Murray**
28 **PERFECT MATCH (IRE)**, 7, b br g Un Desperado (FR)—Imperial Blue (IRE) **A. D. Weller**
29 **PLATINUM POINT (IRE)**, 6, b g Norwich—Blackhill Lass (IRE) **Gregor Shore Ltd**
30 **PRAIRIE LORD (IRE)**, 5, b g Lord of Appeal—Johara (USA) **Mrs S. Rowley-Williams**
31 **PREMIER FLIGHT (IRE)**, 5, br g Afzal—Hatherley **Mrs M. Chance**
32 **PRIDE OF FINEWOOD (IRE)**, 7, ch g Old Vic—Macamore Rose **Finewood Joinery Products Ltd**
33 **RED RUFFLES (IRE)**, 6, b g Anshan—Rosie Ruffles (USA) **T. F. C. Partnership**
34 **RIVER CITY (IRE)**, 8, b g Norwich—Shuil Na Lee (IRE) **Mrs S. Rowley-Williams & Partners**

MR N. T. CHANCE—continued

35 SINGLE PLAYER (IRE), 5, br g Accordion—Alone Party (IRE) **C. C. Shand Kydd**
36 6, Ch g Witness Box (USA)—Some Gossip
37 SUPREME OCEAN (IRE), 5, b m Supreme Leader—Shannon Spray **Mrs N. Kelly**
38 TRUE STAR (IRE), 5, ch g Fourstars Allstar (USA)—Scouts Honour (IRE) **T. F. C. Partnership**
39 TRUST ME (IRE), 6, gr g Roselier (FR)—Lady Owenette (IRE) **Mrs M. Chance and Mr T. Warner**
40 VICTOM'S CHANCE (IRE), 7, b g Old Vic—Lady Swinford **Mr T. Conway & Mrs Conway**
41 YOUWONTCATCHMENOW (IRE), 7, b m Old Vic—Sudden Decision **www.thrillofownership.co.uk**

Other Owners: R. Coates, J. P. Craughwell, George Creighton, R. J. Fairlie, M. A. Garraway, A. K. Gregory, S. B. Humbles, Mr K. A. McDonald, Mrs J. McKay, Dr M. M. Ogilvy, Miss Harriet Rochester, Mr D. A. Russell, A. M. Snow, P. Struthers, K. P. Trowbridge, T. G. Warren, Mr M. R. Wesson.

Assistant Trainer: Ian Yeates

Jockey (flat): J. F. McDonald. **Jockey (NH):** B. J. Crowley, T. Doyle, S. Durack. **Conditional:** W. Kennedy. **Amateur:** Mr R. F. Coonan, N. Harris.

---

109 MR M. CHANNON, West Ilsley

Postal: **West Ilsley Stables, West Ilsley, Newbury, Berkshire, RG20 7AE.**
Contacts: **PHONE (01635) 281166 FAX (01635) 281177**
E-MAIL mick@mick-channon.com

1 ALMIZAN (IRE), 5, b g Darshaan—Bint Albaadiya (USA) **Sheikh Ahmed Al Maktoum**
2 BEAUTY OF DREAMS, 4, b f Russian Revival (USA)—Giggleswick Girl **Mr M. Channon**
3 CHAMPION LION (IRE), 6, b g Sadler's Wells—Honey Bun **Mr M. Channon**
4 COMPTON'S ELEVEN, 4, gr g Compton Place—Princess Tara **PCM Racing**
5 DIGITAL, 8, ch g Safawan—Heavenly Goddess **W. G. R. Wightman**
6 FLOTTA, 6, ch g Elmaamul (USA)—Heavenly Goddess **W. G. R. Wightman**
7 HANA DEE, 4, b f Cadeaux Genereux—Jumairah Sun (IRE) **P. Trant**
8 JAZZ SCENE (IRE), 4, b c Danehill Dancer (IRE)—Dixie Jazz **P. Trant**
9 KEW THE MUSIC, 5, b g Botanic (USA)—Harmonia **Miss B. G Coyle**
10 LE TISS (IRE), 4, b g Croco Rouge (IRE)—Manarah **P. Trant**
11 MAJESTIC DESERT, 4, b f Fraam—Calcutta Queen **J. Abdullah**
12 MALAPOPISM, 5, ch g Compton Place—Mrs Malaprop **M. A. Foy**
13 MASTER ROBBIE, 6, b g Piccolo—Victoria's Secret (IRE) **A. J. Tuckerman**
14 MILLENNIUM FORCE, 7, b g Bin Ajwaad (IRE)—Jumairah Sun (IRE) **A. Merza**
15 MUZIO SCEVOLA (IRE), 4, ch g Titus Livius (FR)—Dancing Sunset (IRE) **Mrs T. Burns**
16 NAJEEBON (FR), 6, ch g Cadeaux Genereux—Jumairah Sun (IRE) **A. Merza**
17 ROYAL LOGIC, 4, b f Royal Applause—Lucie Edward **Mr M. Channon**
18 ROYAL MILLENNIUM (IRE), 7, b g Royal Academy (USA)—Galatrix **Jackie & George Smith**
19 SIGNORA PANETTIERA (FR), 4, ch f Lord of Men—Karaferya (USA) **Timberhill Racing Partnership**
20 TOP SEED (IRE), 4, b c Cadeaux Genereux—Midnight Heights **John Livock Bloodstock Limited**

THREE-YEAR-OLDS

21 ACTIVE ASSET (IRE), ch c Sinndar (IRE)—Sacristy **aAIM Racing Syndicate**
22 ARABIAN DANCER, b f Dansili—Hymne (FR) **J. Abdullah**
23 BALL BOY, b g Xaar—Tanz (IRE) **John Livock Bloodstock Limited**
24 BOLD CHEVERAK, b g Bold Edge—Curlew Calling (IRE) **Tim Corby**
25 BRIANNSTA (IRE), b c Bluebird (USA)—Nacote (USA) **B. R. Brooks**
26 CAPABLE GUEST (IRE), b br c Cape Cross (IRE)—Alexander Confranc (IRE) **J. D. Guest**
27 CHRYSANDER, b c Cadeaux Genereux—Jumairah Sun (IRE) **Jumeirah Racing**
28 CLASSIC GUEST, b f Xaar—My Lass **J. D. Guest**
29 CORNICHE DANCER, b f Marju (IRE)—Sellette (IRE) **Mrs A. M. Jones**
30 CROSS TIME (USA), b c Cape Cross (IRE)—Reine Maid (USA) **J. Abdullah**
31 DAHTEER (IRE), b g Bachir (IRE)—Reematna **Sheikh Ahmed Al Maktoum**
32 DESERT MOVE (IRE), b f Desert King (IRE)—Campestral (USA) **J. Abdullah**
33 DISOBEY, b f Machiavellian (USA)—Polisonne **Jumeirah Racing**
34 DOCTOR BAILEY, b c Mister Baileys—Frustration **J. Abdullah**
35 DREAM TONIC, b c Zafonic (USA)—Dream On Deya (IRE) **The National Stud Owner-Breeders' Club Ltd**
36 EVANESCE, b f Lujain (USA)—Search Party **Dave & Gill Hedley**
37 FADING AWAY, b f Fraam—Fading **P. Taplin**
38 FLYING HEART, ch f Bahamian Bounty—Flying Wind **Heart Of The South Racing**
39 FORCE IN THE WINGS (IRE), b f In The Wings—Cathy Garcia (IRE) **J. Abdullah**

MR M. CHANNON—continued

40 **GASPING (USA)**, b f Rahy (USA)—Millstream (USA) **Sheikh Ahmed Al Maktoum**
41 **GOLD MAJESTY**, b f Josr Algarhoud (IRE)—Calcutta Queen **J. Abdullah**
42 **GOLD QUEEN**, b f Grand Lodge (USA)—Silver Colours (USA) **J. Abdullah**
43 **HAATMEY**, b c Josr Algarhoud (IRE)—Raneen Alwatar **Sheikh Ahmed Al Maktoum**
44 **HALLHOO (IRE)**, gr c Indian Ridge—Nuit Chaud (USA) **Sheikh Ahmed Al Maktoum**
45 **IFIT (IRE)**, b f Inchinor—Robin **Tim Corby**
46 **JOINT ASPIRATION**, ch f Pivotal—Welcome Home **Ridgeway Downs Racing**
47 **KALMINI (USA)**, b br f Rahy (USA)—Kilma (USA) **Sheikh Ahmed Al Maktoum**
48 **KING MARRAKECH (IRE)**, b c King's Best (USA)—Tenue d'amour (FR) **J. Abdullah**
49 **LADY DORIS WATTS**, b f Emarati (USA)—Wrong Bride **Mrs J. Keegan**
50 **LIMIT (IRE)**, b f Barathea (IRE)—Orlena (USA) **Tim Corby**
51 **LOVE THIRTY**, b f Mister Baileys—Polished Up **John Livock Bloodstock Limited**
52 **MAGIC TREE (UAE)**, ch f Timber Country (USA)—Moyesii (USA) **Jumeirah Racing**
53 **MAHMJRA**, b c Josr Algarhoud (IRE)—Jamrat Samya (IRE) **Sheikh Ahmed Al Maktoum**
54 **MAJESTIC RANIA (IRE)**, ch f Giant's Causeway (USA)—Crystal Ring (IRE) **J. Abdullah**
55 **MARHABA MILLION (IRE)**, gr c Linamix (FR)—Modelliste **J. Abdullah**
56 **MASTER JOSEPH**, b g Komaite (USA)—Petit Peu (IRE) **A. J. Tuckerman**
57 **MIN ASL WAFI (IRE)**, b f Octagonal (NZ)—Shy Lady (FR) **J. Abdullah**
58 **MOLLY DANCER**, b f Emarati (USA)—Perfect Partner **Mrs J. Keegan**
59 **MOONMAIDEN**, ch f Selkirk (USA)—Top Table **Derek and Jean Clee**
60 **MUJAZAF**, b c Grand Lodge (USA)—Decision Maid (USA) **J. Abdullah**
61 **OBE GOLD**, b c Namaqualand (USA)—Gagajulu **BDR Partnership**
62 **PLATNIX (IRE)**, b f Perugino (USA)—Familiar Quest (IRE) **Phil Jen Racing**
63 **PROPRIOCEPTION (IRE)**, ch f Danehill Dancer (IRE)—Pepper And Salt (IRE) **Ridgeway Downs Racing**
64 **QUEEN'S DANCER**, b f Groom Dancer (USA)—Special Beat **Miss C. T. Wardley**
65 **RAIN STOPS PLAY (IRE)**, b c Desert Prince (IRE)—Pinta (IRE) **John Livock Bloodstock Limited**
66 **ROCAMADOUR**, b c Celtic Swing—Watch Me (IRE) **Salem Suhail**
67 **ROYAL JET**, b g Royal Applause—Red Bouquet **J. Abdullah**
68 **SADIE THOMPSON (IRE)**, b f King's Best (USA)—Femme Fatale **Sheikh Mohammed**
69 **SEA HUNTER**, b c Lend A Hand—Ocean Grove (IRE) **Jumeirah Racing**
70 **SMOOTH JAZZ**, b c Zafonic (USA)—Halska **Mr P. D. Savill**
71 **SPILL A LITTLE**, b c Zafonic (USA)—Lypharitissima (FR) **Greenfield Stud S A**
72 **STANBURY (USA)**, ch g Zamindar (USA)—Staffin **Sheikh Mohammed**
73 **STREAM OF PASSION**, ch f Vettori (IRE)—Between The Sticks **Mr S. Cunningham**
74 **SUFFRAGETTE**, b f Machiavellian (USA)—Risque Lady **Jumeirah Racing**
75 **SUNBLUSH (UAE)**, br f Timber Country (USA)—Tanami **Jumeirah Racing**
76 **SUNSET STRIP**, b c Josr Algarhoud (IRE)—Shady Street (USA) **Jumeirah Racing**
77 **TURNKEY**, br c Pivotal—Persian Air **Sheikh Mohammed**
78 **UMNIYA (IRE)**, b f Bluebird (USA)—Sparky's Song **Kuwait Racing Syndicate**
79 **VICTORY HYMN (IRE)**, b f Victory Note (USA)—Nordic Union (IRE) **Mr H. Ponsonby**
80 **VOOM**, b f Fraam—Natalie Jay **Mr M. Channon**
81 **WANSDYKE LASS**, b f Josr Algarhoud (IRE)—Silankka **Stan James Winners**
82 **WAR PENNANT**, b g Selkirk (USA)—Bunting **Mohammed Al Nabouda**
83 **WILLIAM TELL (IRE)**, b c Rossini (USA)—Livry (USA) **P. Taplin**
84 **YAJBILL (IRE)**, b c Royal Applause—Tee Cee **Sheikh Ahmed Al Maktoum**

TWO-YEAR-OLDS

85 Ch f 26/3 Fantastic Light (USA)—Abeyr (Unfuwain (USA)) **Sheikh Ahmed Al Maktoum**
86 **AJIGOLO**, ch c 17/1 Piccolo—Ajig Dancer (Niniski (USA)) **Timberhill Racing Partnership**
87 **AL BALADEEN**, b c 19/4 Danehill Dancer (IRE)—Reticent Bride (IRE) (Shy Groom (USA)) (26000) **J. Abdullah**
88 **ALMOST SPINNING (IRE)**, ch f 19/2 Spinning World (USA)—Almost A Lady (IRE) (Entitled) (35000) **Box 41**
89 B f 16/1 Diktat—Altaweelah (IRE) (Fairy King (USA)) **Sheikh Ahmed Al Maktoum**
90 B f 6/2 King's Best—Areydha (Cadeaux Genereux) **Sheikh Ahmed Al Maktoum**
91 **BA FOXTROT**, b c 10/2 Foxhound (USA)—Aunt Susan (Distant Relative) (12000) **The Highlife Racing Club**
92 Ch c 3/2 Rahy (USA)—Belle Genius (USA) (Beau Genius (CAN)) **Sheikh Ahmed Al Maktoum**
93 **BIBURY LODGE**, gr c 26/1 Indian Lodge (IRE)—
　　　　　　　　　　　　　　　　　　　Pearl Bright (FR) (Kaldoun (FR)) (32000) **Ridgeway Downs Racing**
94 **BINT AL HAMMOUR (IRE)**, b f 31/3 Grand Lodge (USA)—Forest Lair (Habitat) (46948) **J. Abdullah**
95 **BOLD CROSS (IRE)**, b c 9/4 Cape Cross (IRE)—Machikane Akaiito (IRE) (Persian Bold) (26827) **Box 41**
96 **BUSY SHARK (IRE)**, gr c 2/2 Shinko Forest (IRE)—Felicita (IRE) (Catrail (USA)) (70421) **J. Abdullah**
97 **CALL MY NUMBER (IRE)**, b c 9/3 Grand Lodge (USA)—
　　　　　　　　　　　　　　　　　　　Screen Idol (IRE) (Sadler's Wells (USA)) (31521) **J. Abdullah**
98 **CELESTIAL PRINCESS**, b f 5/3 Observatory (USA)—Affair of State (IRE) (Tate Gallery (USA)) (16000) **Box 41**

MR M. CHANNON—continued

  99 **CHAMPIONSHIP POINT (IRE)**, b c 3/2 Lomitas—
               Flying Squaw (Be My Chief (USA)) (85000) **John Livock Bloodstock Limited**
100 B c 28/1 Mujadil (USA)—Common Cause (Polish Patriot (USA)) (8047)
101 **CRABADABADOO**, b f 1/3 Tagula (IRE)—Kastaway (Distant Relative) (24000) **The Crab Partnership**
102 **CRIMSON (IRE)**, b f 28/4 Fasliyev (USA)—
               Fey Lady (IRE) (Fairy King (USA)) (44000) **Highclere Thoroughbred Racing Ltd**
103 **CRIMSON FLAME (IRE)**, b c 21/3 Celtic Swing—Wish List (IRE) (Mujadil (USA)) (32000) **Box 41**
104 B f 9/4 Night Shift (USA)—D D's Jakette (USA) (Deputy Minister (CAN)) (30000) **J. Abdullah**
105 **DEYAREE (IRE)**, ch c 20/1 Grand Lodge (USA)—Legende D'or (FR) (Diesis) **J. Abdullah**
106 **DREAM CHAMPION**, b c 19/3 Fraam—Forest Fantasy (Rambo Dancer (CAN)) **J. Abdullah**
107 **DREAM ROSE (IRE)**, b f 16/5 Anabaa (USA)—Hiddnah (Affirmed (USA)) **J. Abdullah**
108 Ch c 22/2 Observatory (USA)—Effie (Royal Academy (USA)) (5000)
109 **FIGARO FLYER (IRE)**, b c 21/2 Mozart (IRE)—Ellway Star (IRE) (Night Shift (USA)) (40000) **Box 41**
110 **FLASHY WINGS**, ch f 13/3 Zafonic (USA)—Lovealoch (IRE) (Lomond (USA)) (32000) **J. Abdullah**
111 B c 30/4 Royal Applause—Gorgeous Dancer (IRE) (Nordico (USA)) (160000) **Sheikh Ahmed Al Maktoum**
112 **GRACECHURCH (IRE)**, b c 22/2 Marju (IRE)—
               Saffron Crocus (Shareef Dancer (USA)) (47000) **aAIM Racing Syndicate**
113 **GRANTLEY ADAMS**, b c 17/3 Dansili—Noble Peregrine (Lomond (USA)) (18000) **Mrs Tania Trant**
114 **HISTORIC APPEAL (USA)**, b br c 10/2 Diesis—Karasavina (IRE) (Sadler's Wells (USA)) **Sangster Family**
115 B c 20/4 Mozart (IRE)—Hoh Dear (IRE) (Sri Pekan (USA)) (78000) **J. D. Guest**
116 **INDIAN WIZARD (IRE)**, b c 18/4 Indian Ridge—Ragtime Rumble (USA) (Dixieland Band (USA)) (62000) **Box 41**
117 B c 22/3 Josr Algarhoud (IRE)—Jamrat Samya (IRE) (Sadler's Wells (USA)) **Sheikh Ahmed Al Maktoum**
118 **JOINT ACQUISITION (IRE)**, b c 14/4 Mull of Kintyre (USA)—
               Vieux Carre (Pas de Seul) (30851) **Ridgeway Downs Racing**
119 **KALMINA (USA)**, b br f 11/4 Rahy (USA)—Kilma (USA) (Silver Hawk (USA)) **Sheikh Ahmed Al Maktoum**
120 B c 24/2 Mozart (IRE)—Kardelle (Kalaglow) (160000) **Sheikh Ahmed Al Maktoum**
121 **KASSIOPEIA (IRE)**, b f 10/3 Galileo (IRE)—Brush Strokes (Cadeaux Genereux) (195000) **Jackie & George Smith**
122 **KAYLIANNI**, b f 20/2 Kalanisi (IRE)—Vivianna (Indian Ridge) (19000) **Box 41**
123 Br f 25/2 Fraam—Kissing Time (Lugana Beach)
124 **KULSHE ZAIN**, b c 24/3 Hunting Lion (IRE)—Frampant (Fraam) **J. Abdullah**
125 B f 11/1 Galileo (IRE)—Lady Lahar (Fraam) **Barry Walters Catering**
126 B c 9/4 Zafonic (USA)—Llyn Gwynant (Persian Bold) (55000) **J. D. Guest**
127 **MAGICAL MUSIC**, b f 23/2 Fraam—Magical Flute (Piccolo) **P. Taplin**
128 B f 19/3 Marju (IRE)—Meshhed (USA) (Gulch (USA)) **Barry Walters Catering**
129 B f 13/2 Rahy (USA)—Millstream (USA) (Dayjur (USA)) **Sheikh Ahmed Al Maktoum**
130 B c 23/2 Kalanisi (IRE)—Miracle (Ezzoud (IRE)) (15500) **Tim Corby**
131 B f 17/3 Cadeaux Genereux—Mirage (Red Sunset) (87189) **John Livock Bloodstock Limited**
132 **MUSIC NOTE (IRE)**, b c 28/2 Indian Ridge—Samara Middle East (FR) (Marju (IRE)) **J. Abdullah**
133 B c 23/3 Polish Precedent (USA)—Nawaji (USA) (Trempolino (USA)) **T. Al-Mazeedi**
134 B c 10/5 Inchinor—Needwood Epic (Midyan (USA)) (100000) **Sheikh Ahmed Al Maktoum**
135 Gr f 28/1 Dansili—Night Haven (Night Shift (USA)) (26000) **Gainsborough Stud Management Ltd**
136 **NORAKIT**, b f 22/3 Mull of Kintyre (USA)—Thailand (Lycius (USA)) **Yeoman & Kenyon Partnership**
137 B f 4/3 Distant Music (USA)—Oklahoma (Shareef Dancer (USA)) (32192) **Tim Corby**
138 Ch c 13/3 Fantastic Light (USA)—One of The Family (Alzao (USA)) (100000) **Sheikh Ahmed Al Maktoum**
139 B c 25/2 Fantastic Light (USA)—Pagoda (FR) (Sadler's Wells (USA)) **Jackie & George Smith**
140 B c 21/5 Agnes World (USA)—Pass The Rose (IRE) (Thatching) (28000) **BDR Partnership**
141 **PUSKAS (IRE)**, b c 7/2 King's Best (USA)—Chiquita Linda (IRE) (Mujadil (USA)) (50300) **J. Breslin**
142 B c 13/2 Cape Cross (IRE)—Reematna (Sabrehill) (USA) **Sheikh Ahmed Al Maktoum**
143 **RIDGEWAY CROSS (IRE)**, gr f 12/4 Cape Cross (IRE)—
               Karatista (Nishapour (FR)) (28168) **Ridgeway Downs Racing**
144 **ROSE MUWASIM**, ch f 1/2 In The Wings—Muwasim (USA) (Meadowlake (USA)) **Mr A. Jaber**
145 **ROYAL POWER (IRE)**, b c 4/2 Xaar—Magic Touch (Fairy King (USA)) (30180) **J. Abdullah**
146 **RUNDEAR**, b f 17/1 Danehill Dancer (USA)—Comprehension (USA) (Diesis) (44000) **J. Breslin**
147 B c 4/4 Josr Algarhoud (IRE)—Saaryeh (Royal Academy (USA)) **Sheikh Ahmed Al Maktoum**
148 **SALUTE HIM (IRE)**, b c 15/4 Mull of Kintyre (USA)—Living Legend (ITY) (Archway (IRE)) (34000) **J. Abdullah**
149 **SAVERNAKE BLUE**, b c 19/4 Mtoto—Mrs Malaprop (Night Shift (USA)) (30000) **M. A. Foy**
150 Ch f 14/4 King of Kings (IRE)—Shamisen (Diesis) (30000) **J. Abdullah**
151 B c 27/3 Marju (IRE)—Shimna (Mr Prospector (USA)) (105000) **Sheikh Ahmed Al Maktoum**
152 **SILCA'S SISTER**, ch f 26/2 Inchinor—Silca-Cisa (Hallgate) **Aldridge Racing Ltd**
153 **SILVER TOUCH (IRE)**, b f 22/3 Dansili—Sanpala (Sanglamore) (40241) **J. Abdullah**
154 **SOUTH CAPE**, b c 6/3 Cape Cross (IRE)—Aunt Ruby (USA) (Rubiano (USA)) **Heart Of The South Racing**
155 B c 11/2 Stravinsky (USA)—Spirit In The Sky (USA) (Gulch (USA)) (110000) **Sheikh Mohammed**
156 **SPLINDA (USA)**, ch f 26/1 Southern Halo (USA)—Saabga (USA) (Woodman (USA)) **Sheikh Ahmed Al Maktoum**
157 **SPRING DREAM (IRE)**, gr f 26/4 Kalanisi (IRE)—Zest (USA) (Zilzal (USA)) (13413) **Mr H. Ponsonby**
158 Ch f 7/3 Fraam—Stride Home (Absalom) **P. Taplin**
159 **SUNCAR**, b c 31/3 Efisio—Diplomatist (Dominion) (34000) **J. Abdullah**

MR M. CHANNON—continued

160 B f 6/4 Fleetwood (IRE)—Sunley Sinner (Try My Best (USA)) **J. B. Sunley**
161 TRIMWAKI (USA), b c 9/4 Miswaki (USA)—My Trim (USA) (Trempolino (USA)) (43594) **Box 41**
162 B f 18/4 Royal Applause—Triple Joy (Most Welcome) (50000) **Kuwait Racing Syndicate**
163 TRUE DREAM, ch c 27/4 Mark of Esteem (IRE)—Crystal Cavern (USA) (Be My Guest (USA)) (45000) **Mr A. Jaber**
164 UPPER HAND, ch c 12/2 Mark of Esteem (IRE)—Pelagia (IRE) (Lycius (USA)) (20000) **Mr James Repard**
165 VENETO (IRE), ch c 17/4 Spinning World (USA)—Padua (IRE) (Cadeaux Genereux) **Mr P. D. Savill**
166 B f 23/3 Danehill (USA)—Wardat Allayl (IRE) (Mtoto) **Sheikh Ahmed Al Maktoum**
167 Ch f 4/3 Zafonic (USA)—Wedoudah (IRE) (Sadler's Wells (USA)) **Sheikh Ahmed Al Maktoum**
168 WEE CHARLIE CASTLE (IRE), b c 3/4 Sinndar (IRE)—
                             Seasonal Blossom (IRE) (Fairy King (USA)) (30000) **G. Love**
169 WOODHEDO, bl c 12/2 Hunting Lion (IRE)—Ernie's Girl (Fraam) **Woodentops Partnership**
170 B c 8/4 Cape Cross (IRE)—Yankee Dancer (Groom Dancer (USA)) (32192) **P. Taplin**
171 YOUMZAIN (IRE), b c 20/2 Sinndar (IRE)—Sadima (IRE) (Sadler's Wells (USA)) (30000) **J. Abdullah**
172 ZABEEL TOWER, b c 24/4 Anabaa (USA)—Bint Kaldoun (IRE) (Kaldoun (FR)) **M. Jaber**
173 ZAHARATH AL BUSTAN, ch f 9/4 Gulch (USA)—Cayman Sunset (IRE) (Night Shift (USA)) (100000) **J. Abdullah**
174 ZATO (IRE), ch c 17/2 Zafonic (USA)—Top Table (Shirley Heights) (28000) **Derek and Jean Clee**
175 ZIZOU (IRE), b c 27/4 Fantastic Light (USA)—
                             Search Committee (USA) (Roberto (USA)) (36887) **Patrick and Simon Trant**

Other Owners: Brian Brooks, Frank Adams, K. M. Al-Mudhaf, Mohammed Jasem Al-Qatami, G. Blackwell, N. S. G. Bunter, Mrs J. M. Channon, N. J. Hitchins, A. C. D. Ingleby-Mackenzie, Ms K. Lowe, Mike Channon Bloodstock Ltd, Mr P. M. Morris, Sir Arthur G. Norman, Dr R. P. Norwich, J. R. Penny, Mrs C. Penny, B. Robe, Mrs D. F. Robe, Ali Saeed, Mr R. D. Whitton.

Assistant Trainer: Joe Tuite

Jockey (flat): A. Culhane, S. Hitchcott, C. Catlin, T. E. Durcan. **Apprentice:** Eddie Creighton, Tom O'Brien, Tolley Dean, Leon Harman. **Amateur:** Mrs Tania Trant.

---

110 MR DAVID W. CHAPMAN, York
Postal: Mowbray House Farm, Stillington, York, YO61 1LT.
Contacts: **PHONE (01347) 821683 CAR PHONE (07966) 513866 FAX (01347) 821683**

1 DASHING DANE, 5, b h Danehill (USA)—Baldemara (FR) **Miss N. F. Thesiger**
2 DESERT OPAL, 5, ch h Cadeaux Genereux—Nullarbor **Miss N. F. Thesiger**
3 EARTHLING, 4, b g Rainbow Quest (USA)—Cruising Height **Mr David W. Chapman**
4 GEM BIEN (USA), 7, b g Bien Bien (USA)—Eastern Gem (USA) **J. M. Chapman**
5 GREENBELT, 4, b g Desert Prince (IRE)—Emerald (May) **Mr David W. Chapman**
6 HEADLAND (USA), 7, b br g Distant View (USA)—Fijar Echo (USA) **H. D. White**
7 MARABAR, 7, b m Sri Pekan (USA)—Erbaya (IRE) **Miss N. F. Thesiger**
8 ON THE TRAIL, 8, ch g Catrail (USA)—From The Rooftops (IRE) **J. M. Chapman**
9 PADDYWACK (IRE), 8, b g Bigstone (IRE)—Millie's Return (IRE) **T. S. Redman**
10 QUEEN OF NIGHT, 5, b m Piccolo—Cardinal Press **Michael Hill**
11 QUITO (IRE), 8, b r Machiavellian (USA)—Qirmazi (USA) **Michael Hill**
12 SHAMI, 6, ch h Rainbow Quest (USA)—Bosra Sham (USA) **Mr David W. Chapman**
13 SHARP HAT, 11, b g Shavian—Madam Trilby **Miss N. F. Thesiger**
14 ST PANCRAS (IRE), 5, b h Danehill Dancer (IRE)—Lauretta Blue (IRE) **Michael Hill**
15 TORRENT, 10, ch g Prince Sabo—Maiden Pool **Mr David W. Chapman**
16 ZARIN (IRE), 7, b g Inzar (USA)—Non Dimenticar Me (IRE) **J. M. Chapman**

THREE-YEAR-OLDS

17 AVONTUUR (FR), ch g Kabool—Ipoh (FR) **E. Rollinson**
18 CADOGEN SQUARE, ch f Takhlid (USA)—Mount Park (IRE) **Michael Hill**
19 DISPOL CHARM (IRE), br f Charnwood Forest (IRE)—Phoenix Venture (IRE) **E. Rollinson**

Assistant Trainer: Ruth Clark

Jockey (flat): A. Culhane. **Amateur:** Mr Richard Clark.

111   MR M. C. CHAPMAN, Market Rasen
Postal: **Woodlands Racing Stables, Woodlands Lane, Willingham Road, Market Rasen, Lincolnshire, LN8 3RE.**
Contacts: **PHONE/FAX (01673) 843663 MOBILE (07971) 940087**

1 **AMANDA'S LAD (IRE)**, 5, b g Danetime (IRE)—Art Duo **E. Knowles**
2 **BLUNHAM**, 5, b g Danzig Connection (USA)—Relatively Sharp **Twinacre Nurseries Ltd**
3 **CHEENEY BASIN (IRE)**, 7, ch g King's Signet (USA)—Gratclo **Ms G. E. Keal**
4 **DABUS**, 10, b g Kris—Licorne **J. C. Greenway**
5 **DALRIATH**, 6, b m Fraam—Alsiba **M. B. Gielty**
6 **DEVIL'S BITE**, 4, ch g Dracula (AUS)—Niggle **Coverscope Ductwork & Reedkleen Supplies**
7 **GOVERNMENT (IRE)**, 4, b g Great Dane (IRE)—Hidden Agenda (FR) **Mrs S. M. Richards**
8 **MR SPLIFFY (IRE)**, 6, b g Fayruz—Johns Conquerer (IRE) **Queens Head Racing Club**
9 **PROPER POSER (IRE)**, 9, b g Posen (USA)—Dahar's Love (USA) **Denis Robb**
10 **RAINBOW RIVER (IRE)**, 7, ch g Rainbows For Life (CAN)—Shrewd Girl (USA) **P. Darcy**
11 **SELF BELIEF**, 4, b f Easycall—Princess of Spain **K. D. Blanch**
12 **SHALAAL (USA)**, 11, b g Sheikh Albadou—One Fine Day (USA) **E. Knowles**
13 **SIEGFRIEDS NIGHT (IRE)**, 4, ch g Night Shift (USA)—Shelbiana (USA) **K. D. Blanch**
14 **TALPOUR (IRE)**, 5, ch g Ashkalani (IRE)—Talwara (USA) **Denis Robb**
15 **WIN ALOT**, 7, b g Aragon—Having Fun **Coverscope Ductwork & Reedkleen Supplies**

THREE-YEAR-OLDS

16 **AMANDERICA (IRE)**, b f Indian Lodge (IRE)—Striking Gold (USA) **E. Knowles**
17 **CHAMPAGNE ROSSINI (IRE)**, b g Rossini (USA)—Alpencrocus (IRE) **R. A. Gadd**
18 **ORPEN WIDE (IRE)**, b g Orpen (USA)—Melba (IRE) **Sir Clement Freud**

Other Owners: J. Deno, J. E. Reed, P. M. Sedgwick, Mrs J. Wiltschinsky, A. N. Wright.

Jockey (NH): A. C. Coyle. **Conditional:** D. Swan. **Apprentice:** G. Edwards.

112   MR P. W. CHAPPLE-HYAM, Newmarket
Postal: **St Gatien Stables, All Saints Road, Newmarket, Suffolk, CB8 8HJ.**
Contacts: **PHONE (01638) 560827 FAX (01638) 561908**
E-MAIL info@peterchapplehyam.com WEBSITE www.peterchapplehyam.com

1 **AFRICAN DREAM**, 4, b g Mark of Esteem (IRE)—Fleet Hill (IRE) **Franconson Partners**
2 **MATOURAKA (FR)**, 4, b br f Great Palm (USA)—Madragoa (FR) **The Comic Strip Heroes**
3 **MISS PORCIA**, 4, ch f Inchinor—Krista **C. A. McKechnie**
4 **PLECTRUM (USA)**, 4, b c Awesome Again (CAN)—Berceau (USA) **Mr David Heath**
5 **SENTINEL**, 6, ch g Hector Protector (USA)—Soolaimon (IRE) **Five Horses Ltd**
6 **THE CAT'S WHISKERS (NZ)**, 5, b m Tale of The Cat (USA)—Good Faith (NZ) **Bloomsbury Stud**
7 **TORONTO HEIGHTS (USA)**, 4, ch g King of Kings (IRE)—Revoltosa (IRE) **Mrs Jane Chapple-Hyam**
8 **WELLINGTON HALL (GER)**, 7, b g Halling (USA)—Wells Whisper (FR) **Allan Darke & Tom Matthews**

THREE-YEAR-OLDS

9 **ALTA PETENS**, b f Mujadil (USA)—Be Exciting (IRE) **The Hon Andrew Peacock**
10 **AZIZAM**, ch f Singspiel (IRE)—Perdicula (IRE) **Theobalds Stud**
11 **BILLY ONE PUNCH**, b c Mark of Esteem (IRE)—Polytess (IRE) **Norcroft Park Stud**
12 **BORACAY DREAM (IRE)**, ch c Grand Lodge (USA)—Mild Intrigue (USA) **Franconson Partners**
13 **CAPTAIN HURRICANE**, b c Desert Style (IRE)—Ravine **The Comic Strip Heroes**
14 **CLEAR IMPRESSION (IRE)**, b f Danehill (USA)—Shining Hour (USA) **Sangster Family**
15 **COURS DE LA REINE (IRE)**, b f Fasliyev (USA)—Society Queen (IRE) **Classic St Gatien Partnership**
16 **DIVINELY DECADENT (IRE)**, br f Turtle Island (IRE)—Divine Prospect (IRE) **Mrs S. P. Catt**
17 **EDICT**, br f Diktat—Pericardia **The Long Lunch Partnership**
18 **FRAMILY LOVE**, gr g Fraam—Asian Love **Mr John Sillet**
19 **HEAT OF THE NIGHT**, b f Lear Fan (USA)—Hot Thong (BRZ) **Miss K. Rausing**
20 **KING MARJU (IRE)**, b c Marju (IRE)—Katoushka (IRE) **B. Fry**
21 **KRULLINO (IRE)**, b g Rossini (USA)—Jemima Yorke **W. Grubmuller**
22 **LEIGHTON BUZZARD**, b g Cyrano de Bergerac—Winsome Wooster **Diamond Racing Ltd**
23 **LOS ORGANOS (IRE)**, br f Turtle Island (IRE)—Spicebird (IRE) **Bloomsbury Stud**
24 **MAMBO'S MELODY**, b g Kingmambo (USA)—Key Academy **Norcroft Park Stud**
25 **MINEKO**, b f Nashwan (USA)—Musetta (IRE) **B. H. Voak**
26 **MONTGOMERY'S ARCH (USA)**, b br c Arch (USA)—Inny River (USA) **Franconson Partners**
27 **MOON FOREST (IRE)**, br c Woodborough (USA)—Ma Bella Luna **Collins, Deal, Harrison-Allan, Chapple-Hyam**

MR P. W. CHAPPLE-HYAM—continued

28 **MR VEGAS (IRE)**, b c Montjeu (IRE)—Germignaga (ITY) **Vincenzo Covone**
29 **PERFORMING ART**, b c Sadler's Wells (USA)—Charming Life (NZ) **Bloomsbury Stud & Partners**
30 **PLAY ME**, b f Nashwan (USA)—Mrs Moonlight **Bloomsbury Stud**
31 **PRIZE FIGHTER (IRE)**, b g Desert Sun—Papal **Diamond Racing Ltd**
32 **RIVER ALHAARTH (IRE)**, b c Alhaarth (IRE)—Sudden Interest (FR) **R. J. Arculli**
33 **RIVER ROYALE**, b c Royal Applause—Trundley Wood **R. J. Arculli**
34 **SALINGER (USA)**, b c Lear Fan (USA)—Sharp Flick (USA) **Curtis, Dundon, Macklin, Mulvihill**
35 **SUBYAN DREAMS**, b f Spectrum (IRE)—Subya **Five Horses Ltd & Mrs Jane Chapple-Hyam**
36 **SUIVEZ MOI (IRE)**, ch c Daggers Drawn (USA)—Pamiers **Mr & Mrs Heywood & Mr & Mrs Bovingdon**
37 **SWALLOW SENORA (IRE)**, b f Entrepreneur—Sangra (USA) **Foreneish Racing**
38 **TI ADORA (IRE)**, b f Montjeu (IRE)—Wavy Up (IRE) **Charnwood Boy, Mrs Harris, Mr B. Reilly**
39 **VILLAROSI (IRE)**, b f Rossini (USA)—Trinida **C. A. McKechnie**
40 **VIRGIN'S TEARS**, b f Bishop of Cashel—Lola Mora **Peter Fenwick Partnership**

TWO-YEAR-OLDS

41 Ch f 13/2 Nashwan (USA)—Aliena (IRE) (Grand Lodge (USA)) (40000) **Mr S. J. Mear**
42 **ART CRITIC (USA)**, b br f 6/5 Fusaichi Pegasus (USA)—
Performing Arts (The Minstrel (CAN)) (106411) **Sangster Family & B. V. Sangster**
43 **BASILIKO (USA)**, ch c 14/3 Fusaichi Pegasus (USA)—
Shootforthestars (USA) (Seattle Slew (USA)) **Sangster Family**
44 **BITTER CHILL**, b c 6/3 Agnes World (USA)—Azula (Bluebird (USA)) **Dr J. Wilson**
45 B c 18/3 Monashee Mountain (USA)—
Chardania (IRE) (Rainbows For Life (CAN)) (12072) **Charnwood Boy Partnership & Mr A. W. Abdo**
46 **CORTESIA (IRE)**, ch f 23/2 Courteous—Cecina (Welsh Saint) (12000) **Mrs Yoshiko Allan**
47 **COZINNETA (USA)**, gr ro f 20/1 Cozzene (USA)—
Inny River (USA) (Seattle Slew (USA)) (133014) **Richard L Golden**
48 **DIZZY DREAMER (IRE)**, b f 22/2 Spinning World (USA)—
Divine Prospect (IRE) (Namaqualand (USA)) (28000) **Mrs S. P. Catt**
49 B c 17/3 Mull of Kintyre (USA)—Fancy Theory (USA) (Quest For Fame) (22000) **David Allan**
50 B c 18/2 Titus Livius (FR)—Gay's Flutter (Beldale Flutter (USA)) (24144) **Favourites Racing Ltd**
51 **GIANT DESTINY (USA)**, b c 2/6 Giant's Causeway (USA)—
Lilac Garden (USA) (Roberto (USA)) (25000) **Mr A. Abdo**
52 Ch c 12/4 Docksider (USA)—Green Moon (FR) (Shirley Heights) (20000) **Mrs P**
53 B f 27/4 Forest Wildcat (USA)—Hot Princess (Hot Spark) (39904) **Diamond Racing Ltd**
54 Ch f 4/4 Night Shift (USA)—Iyandas (ITY) (Love The Groom (USA)) **Emerald Bloodstock & Mr M. Bozzi**
55 **JOHNNY ALPHA (IRE)**, b c 15/3 Namid—
Green's Maud Earl (Night Shift (USA)) (40000) **The Comic Strip Heroes**
56 **KING CUGAT KID (USA)**, b br c 2/5 King Cugat (USA)—
Let's Dance (USA) (Thorn Dance (USA)) **Mr John Hawkins**
57 **MARAJEL (IRE)**, b c 30/4 Marju (IRE)—Idilic Calm (IRE) (Indian Ridge) (44000) **Nagy El Azar**
58 **ME**, b f 17/3 Green Desert (USA)—Myself (Nashwan (USA)) **Bloomsbury Stud**
59 B c 13/4 Foxhound (USA)—Miss Up N Go (Gorytus (USA)) (8000) **David Allan**
60 Ch f 21/3 Swain (IRE)—Oumaldaaya (USA) (Nureyev (USA)) (16000) **Mrs J. Magnier & Mrs P. Shanahan**
61 B c 27/2 Mark of Esteem (IRE)—Perdicula (IRE) (Persian Heights) (10000) **Theobalds Stud**
62 **PRINCE DARIUS**, br c 8/3 Efisio—Celt Song (IRE) (Unfuwain (USA)) **Five Horses Ltd**
63 **RAINBOW ZEST**, b c 22/2 Rainbow Quest (USA)—Original (Caerleon (USA)) (25000) **Mr Raymond Tooth**
64 **ROYAL RESERVATION**, b c 15/2 Royal Applause—Wig Wam (IRE) (Indian Ridge) (35000) **C. M. Mercer**
65 B c 24/5 Alhaarth (IRE)—Serpentara (Kris) (15000) **Mr W. Harrison-Allan**
66 B c 3/2 Compton Place—Sewards Folly (Rudimentary (USA)) (18000) **Byculla Thoroughbreds**
67 B c 14/3 Indian Ridge—Sheer Spirit (IRE) (Caerleon (USA)) (48000) **R. J. Arculli**
68 **THE STRUIE**, b f 17/1 Observatory (USA)—My Way (IRE) (Marju (IRE)) (16000) **Wood Hall Stud Limited**
69 Ch c 20/3 Spinning World (USA)—Wavy Up (IRE) (Brustolon) **Charnwood Boy Partnership & Mr B. Reilly**
70 B c 24/2 Foxhound (USA)—Yanomami (USA) (Slew O' Gold (USA)) (23000) **A. W. Darke & Partners**
71 B c 21/1 Medicean—Yasalam (IRE) (Fairy King (USA)) (1000) **Saleh Al Homaizi**

Other Owners: Mrs Margaret Parker, Mr J. Powell, Mr P. Powell, A. W. Black, A. K. Collins, R. M. A. Craddock, Mrs D. Curran, D. Curran, P. A. Deal, A. J. Hollis, M. D. Hollis, T. M. Matthews, Plantation Stud Limited, G. E. Sangster, Sir David Sieff, J. P. Wray.

113
MR G. F. H. CHARLES-JONES, Okehampton
Postal: **Millaton Farm, Bridestowe, Okehampton, Devon, EX20 4QG.**
Contacts: **PHONE (01837) 861100 CAR (07836) 275292**

1 **BLUE NUN**, 4, b f Bishop of Cashel—Matisse **Miss H. Wynne**
2 **KATZ PYJAMAS (IRE)**, 4, b f Fasliyev (USA)—Allepolina (USA) **Miss H. Wynne**

MR G. F. H. CHARLES-JONES—continued

3 **KERRISTINA**, 4, b f So Factual (USA)—Arch Angel (IRE) **Peter H. Wafford**
4 **RUPERT BRUSH**, 4, b g Thornberry (USA)—O K Sohfar **Mrs Lucy Lane-Fox**
5 **WHIPPERS DELIGHT (IRE)**, 17, ch g King Persian—Crashing Juno **Mrs J. K. Charles-Jones**

Assistant Trainer: Jessica Charles-Jones

Jockey (flat): Joanna Badger. **Jockey (NH):** O. Nelmes. **Amateur:** Mr A. Charles-Jones.

---

114 **MR J. I. A. CHARLTON, Stocksfield**
Postal: **Mickley Grange, Stocksfield, Northumberland, NE43 7TB.**
Contacts: **PHONE (01661) 843247 MOBILE (07850) 007415**

1 5, B m Oscar (IRE)—A'dhahirah **M. H. Walton**
2 **BYWELL BEAU (IRE)**, 6, b g Lord Americo—Early Dalus (IRE) **W. F. Trueman**
3 **CAPTAIN MURPHY (IRE)**, 7, b g Executive Perk—Laura Daisy **M. H. Walton**
4 **DOUBLE GEM (IRE)**, 6, ch g Grand Plaisir (IRE)—Thatilldofornow (IRE) **Mr J. I. A. Charlton**
5 **GAELIC JIG**, 6, ch g Dancing High—Gaelic Charm (IRE) **G. A. G. Charlton**
6 **HOT AIR (IRE)**, 7, b g Air Display (USA)—Lyraisa **Sydney Ramsey & Partners**
7 **KILLWILLIE (IRE)**, 6, b g Carroll House—Home In The Glen **Mr J. I. A. Charlton**
8 5, B g Flemensfirth (USA)—Laura Daisy **M. H. Walton**
9 **MILLERBURN (IRE)**, 6, b g Ajraas (USA)—Granalice **The Tyne and Rede Partnership**
10 **NO KIDDING**, 11, b g Teenoso (USA)—Vaigly Fine **Miss J. Palmer**
11 **RATHOWEN (IRE)**, 6, b g Good Thyne (USA)—Owenageera (IRE) **Mr J. I. A. Charlton**
12 **SISTER O'MALLEY (IRE)**, 6, b br m Religiously (USA)—Arctic Laura **M. H. Walton**
13 5, B g Milieu—Sister Seven (IRE) **M. H. Walton**
14 **SNOWY (IRE)**, 7, gr g Pierre—Snowy Gunner **Mr & Mrs Raymond Anderson Green**
15 **TOBESURE (IRE)**, 11, b g Asir—Princess Citrus (IRE) **Richard Nixon**

Other Owners: Ms J. M. Findlay, Ms J. Rutherford, J. T. Stobbs, J. W. Walton, M. J. Walton.

Assistant Trainer: George A Charlton

Conditional: B. Gibson. **Amateur:** Mr A. J. Findlay.

---

115 **MR ROGER J. CHARLTON, Beckhampton**
Postal: **Beckhampton House, Marlborough, Wilts. SN8 1QR.**
Contacts: **HOME (01672) 539330 OFFICE (01672) 539533 FAX (01672) 539456**
E-MAIL **r.charlton@virgin.net**

1 **ALDERNEY RACE (USA)**, 4, ch c Seeking The Gold (USA)—Oyster Catcher (IRE) **Britton House Stud**
2 **AVERSHAM**, 5, b h Averti (IRE)—Vavona **D. J. Deer**
3 **AVONBRIDGE**, 5, b h Averti (IRE)—Alessia **D. J. Deer**
4 **BALAVISTA (USA)**, 4, br c Distant View (USA)—Balabina (USA) **K. Abdulla**
5 **BLUE MONDAY**, 4, b g Darshaan—Lunda (IRE) **Mountgrange Stud Ltd**
6 **DOROTHY'S FRIEND**, 5, b g Grand Lodge (USA)—Isle of Flame **Mountgrange Stud Ltd**
7 **JOSEPHUS**, 4, ch c King of Kings (IRE)—Khulasah (USA) **Mountgrange Stud Ltd**
8 **KIND (IRE)**, 4, b f Danehill (USA)—Rainbow Lake **K. Abdulla**
9 **NIGHTSPOT**, 4, ch g Night Shift (USA)—Rash Gift **D. J. Deer**
10 **PANZER (GER)**, 4, b g Vettori (IRE)—Prompt **Lady Rothschild**
11 **PARC AUX BOULES**, 4, gr g Royal Applause—
                              Aristocratique **Mountgrange Stud Ltd & Beckhampton Stables Ltd**
12 **PATAVELLIAN (IRE)**, 7, b br g Machiavellian (USA)—Alessia **D. J. Deer**
13 **PRESUMPTIVE (IRE)**, 5, b g Danehill (USA)—Demure **Thurloe Thoroughbreds XV**
14 **SEEL OF APPROVAL**, 6, b g Polar Falcon (USA)—Petit Point (IRE) **Mrs A. E. Morgan**
15 **SONG OF VALA**, 4, ch g Peintre Celebre (USA)—Yanka (USA) **A. Parker**
16 **STRIKING AMBITION**, 5, b br h Makbul—Lady Roxanne **P. Webb**

THREE-YEAR-OLDS

17 **ALL IVORY**, ch c Halling (USA)—Ivorine (USA) **K. Abdulla**
18 **AQUILONIA**, b f Giant's Causeway (USA)—Leonila (IRE) **Britton House Stud**
19 **ASSAILANT (IRE)**, b g Zafonic (USA)—Greenvera (USA) **B. E. Nielsen**

MR ROGER J. CHARLTON—continued

20 **BALANCE OF POWER**, b c Sadler's Wells (USA)—Cattermole (USA) **K. Abdulla**
21 **BAVARICA**, b f Dansili—Blue Gentian (USA) **K. Abdulla**
22 **BLAISE HOLLOW (USA)**, b g Woodman (USA)—Castellina (USA) **D. J. Deer**
23 **BON BOUCHE**, ch f Cadeaux Genereux—Canis Star **A. E. Oppenheimer**
24 **CURRENT AFFAIRS**, ch f Selkirk (USA)—Topicality (USA) **K. Abdulla**
25 **DEEP SPELL (USA)**, b br c El Prado (IRE)—Deep Magic (USA) **K. Abdulla**
26 **DILMOUN (IRE)**, b c Darshaan—Mannakea (USA) **B. E. Nielsen**
27 **DRIVE ME WILD (IRE)**, b c Indian Ridge—Wild Bluebell (IRE) **Mountgrange Stud Ltd**
28 **FOR A DANCER (IRE)**, b g Unfuwain (USA)—Another Dancer (FR) **Mountgrange Stud Ltd**
29 **FREE LIFT**, ch f Cadeaux Genereux—Step Aloft **Her Majesty The Queen**
30 **GERMANICUS**, b g Desert King (IRE)—Simacota (GER) **M. Pescod**
31 **HEIDI'S DASH (IRE)**, b f Green Desert (USA)—Child Prodigy (IRE) **A. J. Yemm**
32 **INTERIM PAYMENT (USA)**, b f Red Ransom (USA)—Interim **K. Abdulla**
33 **JALISSA**, b f Mister Baileys—Julia Domna **Exors of the Late D. A. Shirley**
34 **KALIMA**, b f Kahyasi—Kerali **K. Abdulla**
35 **KATAMANDA (IRE)**, b c Danehill (USA)—Scruple (IRE) **Mountgrange Stud Ltd**
36 **LA BELLA GRANDE (IRE)**, ch f Giant's Causeway (USA)—
    La Belle Otero (USA) **Marston Stud And Mr R. Bonnycastle**
37 **LASSO**, ch f Indian Ridge—Rosse **A. E. Oppenheimer**
38 **LIFE'S A WHIRL**, b f Machiavellian (USA)—Spinning Top **Her Majesty The Queen**
39 **MACAULAY (IRE)**, ch c Zafonic (USA)—Wigging **M. Pescod**
40 **MARELLA**, b f Desert Prince (IRE)—Rainbow Lake **K. Abdulla**
41 **MEIKLE BARFIL**, b g Compton Place—Oare Sparrow **Mr H. Keswick**
42 **MY PORTFOLIO (IRE)**, b g Montjeu (IRE)—Elaine's Honor (USA) **Thurloe Thoroughbreds XII**
43 **NAVY LARK**, ch g Nashwan (USA)—Holly Blue **Her Majesty The Queen**
44 **OBVIOUS CHARM**, b f Machiavellian (USA)—Clear Attraction (USA) **Her Majesty The Queen**
45 **PIKE BISHOP (IRE)**, b c Namid—Pink Cashmere (IRE) **M. Pescod**
46 **PIPER'S ASH (USA)**, b f Royal Academy (USA)—Merida **K. Abdulla**
47 **ROMAN VILLA (USA)**, b c Chester House (USA)—Danzante (USA) **K. Abdulla**
48 **RUSTLER**, b c Green Desert (USA)—Borgia **Lady Rothschild**
49 **SEA WALL**, b c Giant's Causeway (USA)—Spout **Lady Rothschild**
50 **STAR WOOD (IRE)**, b f Montjeu (IRE)—Woodwin (IRE) **Lady Vestey**
51 **STRAWBERRY LEAF**, ch f Unfuwain (USA)—Satin Bell **N. M. H. Jones**
52 **VERONESE (USA)**, b f Bianconi (USA)—Just Juliet (USA) **D. J. Deer**
53 **VIRTUE**, ch f Vettori (IRE)—Zenith **Her Majesty The Queen**
54 **YAQOOT**, b f Pivotal—Princess Minnie **Hamdan Al Maktoum**

TWO-YEAR-OLDS

55 **ACROBATIC (USA)**, ch c 21/4 Storm Boot (USA)—Alvernia (USA) (Alydar (USA)) **K. Abdulla**
56 **ADVANCED**, b c 29/1 Night Shift (USA)—Wonderful World (GER) (Dashing Blade) (55000) **A. J. Yemm**
57 **ASHMOLIAN (IRE)**, b c 2/4 Grand Lodge (USA)—
    Animatrice (USA) (Alleged (USA)) (100000) **A. E. Oppenheimer**
58 **BRABAZON (IRE)**, b c 25/3 In The Wings—Azure Lake (USA) (Lac Ouimet (USA)) (105000) **M. Pescod**
59 **BRANCACCI (IRE)**, b c 23/3 Vettori (IRE)—Robsart (IRE) (Robellino (USA)) (50000) **Delaware Racing**
60 B br c 12/4 Black Minnaloushe (USA)—Castellina (USA) (Danzig Connection (USA)) **D. J. Deer**
61 **COUNTING HOUSE (IRE)**, ch c 19/4 King's Best (USA)—Inforapenny (Deploy) (120723) **Mountgrange Stud Ltd**
62 **DAYS OF MY LIFE (IRE)**, b c 12/2 Daylami (IRE)—
    Truly Yours (IRE) (Barathea (IRE)) (53655) **Mountgrange Stud Ltd**
63 **DORABIL (IRE)**, ch f 18/4 Grand Lodge (USA)—Phantom Rain (Rainbow Quest (USA)) (16766) **Mr J. Wolfensohn**
64 **FIRE OF LOVE**, ch f 14/3 Allied Forces (USA)—Princess Minnie (Mistertopogigo (IRE)) (35000) **Mr Peter Webb**
65 **FIRST MOVER (IRE)**, b c 25/2 Polish Precedent (USA)—
    Girl of My Dreams (IRE) (Marju (IRE)) (60000) **Hippodrome Racing**
66 **FONDNESS**, ch f 10/4 Dr Fong (USA)—Island Story (Shirley Heights) **Her Majesty The Queen**
67 **GELDER**, b f 8/3 Grand Lodge (USA)—Purple Heather (Rahy (USA)) **Her Majesty The Queen**
68 **GREEN EYES (IRE)**, b f 15/3 Green Desert (USA)—Karlafsha (Top Ville) (230000) **Mountgrange Stud Ltd**
69 **HANG LOOSE**, b c 29/4 Agnes World (USA)—My Cadeaux (Cadeaux Genereux) (40000) **A. J. Yemm**
70 B f 16/3 Alhaarth (IRE)—High And Low (Rainbow Quest (USA)) **K. Abdulla**
71 **HIS HONOUR (IRE)**, ch c 28/2 Grand Lodge (USA)—Knight's Baroness (Rainbow Quest (USA)) **B. E. Nielsen**
72 **JUPITERS MOON (IRE)**, b c 3/3 Galileo (IRE)—
    Dance Treat (USA) (Nureyev (USA)) (80000) **Mountgrange Stud Ltd**
73 **KING MAGNUS (IRE)**, b c 30/3 Mull of Kintyre (USA)—Sandystones (Selkirk (USA)) (33534) **M. Pescod**
74 **LETHAL WEAPON (USA)**, gr ro c 2/3 War Chant (USA)—
    La Gandilie (FR) (Highest Honor (FR)) (260000) **Mountgrange Stud Ltd**
75 **MATURIN**, b g 3/4 Dr Fong (USA)—
    Polish Lake (Polish Precedent (USA)) **Mr M. Pescod and Beckhampton Stables**

MR ROGER J. CHARLTON—continued

76 B c 27/4 Namid—Night Scent (IRE) (Scenic) (40240) **Thurloe Thoroughbreds XV**
77 B f 16/5 Distant View (USA)—Questonia (Rainbow Quest (USA)) **K. Abdulla**
78 B c 6/4 Zafonic (USA)—Rainbow Lake (Rainbow Quest (USA)) **K. Abdulla**
79 RAINBOW'S EDGE, b f 22/3 Rainbow Quest (USA)—Film Script (Unfuwain (USA)) **Her Majesty The Queen**
80 REGENT'S PARK, b f 20/2 Green Desert (USA)—
  New Assembly (IRE) (Machiavellian (USA)) **Her Majesty The Queen**
81 RIVAGE (USA), b f 1/5 Silver Hawk (USA)—Prima Centauri (USA) (Distant View (USA)) **Mr Trevor Stewart**
82 ROSE BRIAR (IRE), b f 27/2 Grand Lodge (USA)—My Branch (Distant Relative) **B. E. Nielsen**
83 Ch f 8/3 Fantastic Light (USA)—Rosse (Kris) **A. E. Oppenheimer**
84 Ch c 5/4 Silver Hawk (USA)—Royal Devotion (USA) (His Majesty (USA)) (50000) **B. E. Nielsen**
85 SALVIA, ch f 13/2 Pivotal—Satin Bell (Midyan (USA)) **N. M. H. Jones**
86 B c 7/3 Dansili—Seven Sing (USA) (Machiavellian (USA)) **K. Abdulla**
87 SHOUT (IRE), ch f 28/4 Halling (USA)—Spout (Salse (USA)) **Lady Rothschild**
88 Ch f 11/3 Miswaki (USA)—Skiable (IRE) (Niniski (USA)) **K. Abdulla**
89 SKIT, b c 30/4 In The Wings—Skew (Niniski (USA)) **Lady Rothschild**
90 STARLIT SKY, ch f 6/4 Galileo (IRE)—Starlet (Teenoso (USA)) **Her Majesty The Queen**
91 STRUT, ch f 2/3 Danehill Dancer (IRE)—Boast (Most Welcome) **Lady Rothschild**
92 THERMIDOR (USA), ch c 26/2 Giant's Causeway (USA)—
  Langoustine (AUS) (Danehill (USA)) (300000) **Mountgrange Stud Ltd**
93 THIRD SET (IRE), b c 17/2 Royal Applause—Khamseh (Thatching) (55000) **J. W. Livock**
94 UMOYA, b f 17/4 Nashwan (USA)—Ingozi (Warning) **A. E. Oppenheimer**
95 B f 30/1 Green Desert (USA)—Well Warned (Warning) **K. Abdulla**
96 Ch f 30/3 Singspiel (IRE)—Yanka (USA) (Blushing John (USA)) **A. Parker**
97 B c 18/2 Barathea (IRE)—Zorleni (Zafonic (USA)) **K. Abdulla**

Other Owners: R. H. Beevor, R. A. N. Bonnycastle, J. H. Flower, O. J. W. Pawle, J. Ratcliffe, E. S. Tudor-Evans, T. C. Wilson.

Assistant Trainer: Tom Grantham

Apprentice: Richard Kingscote.

---

116 | MR G. C. H. CHUNG, Newmarket

Postal: **Linden Lodge Stables, Rowley Drive, Newmarket, Suffolk, CB8 0NH.**
Contacts: **PHONE (01638) 664348/663833 FAX (01638) 660338 MOBILE (07802) 204281**
E-MAIL greg.chung@lineone.net

1 AVEIRO (IRE), 9, b g Darshaan—Avila **This Time Next Year Racing**
2 GLOBAL ACHIEVER, 4, b g Key of Luck (USA)—Inflation **Dr J. Hon**
3 LA CALERA (GER), 4, ch f Big Shuffle (USA)—La Luce **This Time Next Year Racing**
4 LUCEFER (IRE), 7, b g Lycius (USA)—Maharani (USA) **I. J. Pattle**
5 MANDARIN SPIRIT (IRE), 5, b g Primo Dominie—Lithe Spirit (IRE) **P. Tsim**
6 OEUF A LA NEIGE, 5, b g Danehill (USA)—Reine de Neige **Mr G. C. H. Chung**
7 THE NIBBLER, 4, b g General Monash (USA)—Spoilt Again **The Maybe This Time Partnership**

THREE-YEAR-OLDS

8 GLOBAL BANKER (IRE), b c Desert Prince (IRE)—Luisa Demon (IRE) **Dr J. Hon**
9 INDUSTRIAL SPIRIT, b c Chester House (USA)—Celibataire (FR) **Magus Equine Ltd**
10 LEFONIC, ch c Zafonic (USA)—La Adrada **Middleham Park Racing VI**
11 SHATIN STAR, b br c Killer Instinct—Anetta **P. Tsim**
12 VICTOR ROSSINI (IRE), ch c Rossini (USA)—Right To The Top **The Maybe This Time Partnership**

TWO-YEAR-OLDS

13 B c 6/4 Rainbow Quest (USA)—Gaily Royal (IRE) (Royal Academy (USA)) (20000) **Magus Equine Ltd**
14 Ch c 29/4 Zilzal (USA)—Miss Bussell (Sabrehill (USA)) (22000) **Magus Equine Ltd**
15 B c 21/4 Desert Prince (IRE)—Regal Peace (Known Fact (USA)) (25000) **Magus Equine Ltd**
16 B c 14/2 Indian Danehill (IRE)—Special Park (USA) (Trempolino (USA)) (15000) **Magus Equine Ltd**
17 B c 31/3 Daylami (IRE)—Swift Dispersal (Shareef Dancer (USA)) (42000) **Magus Equine Ltd**
18 Br c 15/2 Lend A Hand—Tart (FR) (Warning) (32000) **Magus Equine Ltd**

Other Owners: Mrs Coralie Chung, Mr H. C. Chung, Mrs S. Chung, Mr A. Tse, Mr J. Luk, Mr and Mrs T. Elliott, Mr P. Chung, Mr R. Grant, Mr S. Aledessi, O. Churchill, Mrs L. S. Churchill, W. Paterson, B. L. Stephens, K. E. Woollacott.

Jockey (flat): M. Henry, O. Urbina. **Apprentice:** Dean P. Williams. **Amateur:** Mr T. Thomas.

117 **MR R. M. CLARK, West Lothian**
Postal: **Bonnytoun Farm, Linlithgow, West Lothian, EH49 7LP.**
Contacts: **PHONE (01506) 842075 FAX (01506) 846745 MOBILE (07715) 121387**

1 **GOLDEN HAWK (USA)**, 10, ch g Silver Hawk (USA)—Crockadore (USA) **Michael Clark**
2 **HICKLETON CLUB**, 7, b g Aragon—Honest Opinion **Michael Clark**

118 **MR S. B. CLARK, Sutton-on-the-Forest**
Postal: **Ride Away, Stillington Road, Sutton-On-The-Forest, York.**
Contacts: **HOME (01347) 810700 CAR (07974) 383521 FAX (01347) 810746**

1 **ARJAY**, 7, b g Shaamit (IRE)—Jenny's Call **Mr S. B. Clark**
2 **MUHTADI (IRE)**, 12, br g Marju (IRE)—Moon Parade **Mr S. B. Clark**
3 **SPIDER MUSIC**, 9, ch g Orchestra—Muffet's Spider **Mr S. B. Clark**
4 **SUPREME OPTIMIST (IRE)**, 8, b g Supreme Leader—Armagale (IRE) **Mr S. B. Clark**

Amateur: Mr Richard Clark.

119 **MR NICOLAS CLEMENT, Chantilly**
Postal: **37, Avenue de Joinville, 60500 Chantilly, France.**
Contacts: **PHONE +33 (0) 3 44 57 59 60 FAX +33 (0) 3 44 57 70 84**
E-MAIL nicolas.clement7@wanadoo.fr

1 **DOLMA (FR)**, 4, b f Marchand de Sable (USA)—Young Manila (USA)
2 **NINGFIELD (FR)**, 5, b g Lost World (IRE)—Cyrning (FR)
3 **PANFILO**, 10, b g Thatching—Reveuse du Soir

THREE-YEAR-OLDS

4 **AGUA DE MAYO (USA)**, b f Mr Greeley (USA)—Madeleine's Blush (USA)
5 **BOA ESTRELA (IRE)**, b f Intikhab (USA)—Charita (IRE)
6 **CONGLEVE (IRE)**, ch c Ashkalani (IRE)—Freedom Flame
7 **CRESSON**, b c Kaldounevees (FR)—Balsamita (FR)
8 **EMOUNA**, ch f Cadeaux Genereux—Red Rabbit
9 **GLACE MAGIQUE (IRE)**, b f King's Best (USA)—Ghostly (IRE)
10 **INVISIBLE QUEST (IRE)**, b f Intikhab (USA)—Ribot's Guest (IRE)
11 **LUCKY NORWEGIAN (IRE)**, b f Almutawakel—Echoes (USA)
12 **MARCHE CONCLU (IRE)**, b f Lomitas—Lacatena (GER)
13 **MARINE BLEUE (IRE)**, b f Desert Prince (IRE)—Mirina (FR)
14 **MISS FRIME (IRE)**, b f Xaar—Remiss (IRE)
15 **NAMONA (IRE)**, b f Halling (USA)—Flawlessly (FR)
16 **NORWEGIAN PRIDE (FR)**, b br f Diktat—Tricorne
17 **PRIERE**, b f Machiavellian (USA)—Play Around (IRE)
18 **RIVER BRIDE (USA)**, b br f Kingmambo (USA)—Anklet (USA)
19 **SAINT FINIAN'S BAY (USA)**, b c Lure (USA)—Axe Creek (USA)
20 **SAMMI PAIGE (IRE)**, b f Key of Luck (USA)—Zsa Zsa (IRE)
21 **SPECIAL ENVOY (FR)**, gr c Linamix (FR)—Pawnee Dancer (IRE)
22 **STORM'S STORY**, ch f Giant's Causeway (USA)—Red Roses Story (FR)
23 **SWEET VENTURE (FR)**, b c Verglas (IRE)—Bitter Sweet (FR)
24 **USAGE DU MONDE (FR)**, gr f Highest Honor (FR)—Caslon (FR)
25 **VANISHING CAUSEWAY (IRE)**, ch c Giant's Causeway (USA)—Vanishing Prairie (USA)
26 **VRACCA**, ch f Vettori (IRE)—Crystal Cavern (USA)
27 **WAIA (IRE)**, b f Septieme Ciel (USA)—Gentian Blue (IRE)

TWO-YEAR-OLDS

28 **ANNA MONA (GER)**, ch f 16/2 Monsun (GER)—Anna Oleanda (IRE) (Old Vic) (70000)
29 Ch f 9/5 Smart Strike (CAN)—Artistic (USA) (Pirate's Bounty (USA)) (21282)
30 B f 16/3 Mt Livermore (USA)—Axe Creek (USA) (Gulch (USA))
31 **BERINGS EXPRESS (FR)**, b c 8/4 Bering—Ess Express (FR) (Subotica (FR))
32 B f 20/2 Dynaformer (USA)—Desert Angel (USA) (Desert Wine (USA)) (127693)
33 **EVERYBODY KNOWS (FR)**, b c 25/1 Enrique—Great Care (USA) (El Gran Senor (USA)) (11401)
34 B f 30/4 King's Best (USA)—Luminosity (Sillery (USA)) (87189)
35 **MAILLE ABAA (FR)**, b c 12/5 Anabaa (USA)—Bric Mamaille (FR) (Bricassar (USA)) (70422)
36 B f 16/3 Fantastic Light (USA)—Majestic Sister (IRE) (Last Tycoon) (33534)
37 **MARCHAND D'ARGENT (FR)**, b c 7/4 Marchand de Sable (USA)—Masslama (FR) (No Pass No Sale) (50301)

MR NICOLAS CLEMENT—continued

38 **N'LY DWAG (USA)**, b f 17/2 Lear Fan (USA)—Ly Dawg (Lyphard (USA))
39 B c 20/2 Gulch (USA)—Prevail (USA) (Danzig (USA)) (30181)
40 Br f 8/4 Grand Lodge (USA)—Princesse Bilbao (FR) (Highest Honor (FR))
41 **SENSITIVITE (FR)**, b f 13/2 Aptitude (USA)—Andora (USA) (Conquistador Cielo (USA)) (18621)
42 **STROUDY (FR)**, ch f 20/2 Green Tune (USA)—Damnation (FR) (Pistolet Bleu (IRE)) (13413)
43 **SUCRE BRUN (FR)**, b c 24/1 Keos (USA)—Sugar (FR) (Nashwan (USA)) (55667)
44 **THEATRE BUFF (USA)**, b f 28/3 Theatrical—If Angels Sang (USA) (Seattle Slew (USA)) (58526)
45 **VERGLAS BIO (FR)**, gr c 7/4 Verglas (IRE)—Miss Bio (FR) (River Mist (USA)) (40241)
46 **WILD KING (USA)**, b c 5/5 Kingmambo (USA)—Anklet (USA) (Wild Again (USA)) (111731)
47 B f 10/1 Anabaa (USA)—Zghorta (USA) (Gone West (USA)) (114017)

---

120 MR T. T. CLEMENT, Newmarket
Postal: **Calder Park, Hamilton Road, Newmarket, Suffolk, CB8 0NY.**
Contacts: **MOBILE (07885) 674474**

1 **ALMISQ (USA)**, 4, ch f Diesis—Inscrutable Dancer (USA) **P. Harper**
2 **BOOGIE MAGIC**, 5, b m Wizard King—Dalby Dancer **Mr C. M. Davies**
3 **CHARLOTTEBUTTERFLY**, 5, b m Millkom—Tee Gee Jay **Future Electrical Services Ltd**
4 **CRIMSON KING (IRE)**, 4, ch g Pivotal—Always Happy **Mr C. M. Davies**
5 **DANCE LIGHT (IRE)**, 6, b m Lycius (USA)—Embracing **Mrs J. M. Garland**
6 **EDIN BURGHER (FR)**, 4, br g Hamas (IRE)—Jaljuli **Mr C. M. Davies**
7 **EXTEMPORISE (IRE)**, 5, ch h Indian Ridge—No Rehearsal (FR) **Ms K. Sadler**
8 **FEED THE METER (IRE)**, 5, b m Desert King (IRE)—Watch The Clock **P. Harper**
9 **LEGACY (JPN)**, 5, b g Carnegie (IRE)—Idraak **Ms K. Sadler**
10 **LOOKOUTHEREICOME**, 4, b f Rudimentary (USA)—Sylvatica **Mrs C. Clement**
11 4, Ch f First Trump—Loriner's Lass **Mrs C. Clement**
12 **MEDUSA**, 5, b m Emperor Jones (USA)—Diebiedale **J. W. Barnard**
13 **TUSCAN TREATY**, 5, b m Brief Truce (USA)—Fiorenz (USA) **Future Electrical Services Ltd**
14 **UNPRECEDENTED (IRE)**, 4, br g Primo Dominie—Misellina (FR) **R. J. Francis**

THREE-YEAR-OLDS

15 **DANCING BEAUTY (IRE)**, b f Charnwood Forest (IRE)—Viennese Dancer **Mrs C. Clement**
16 **EIDSFOSS (IRE)**, b g Danehill Dancer (IRE)—Alca Egeria (ITY) **R. J. Francis**
17 **GENEVIEVE**, b f Mtoto—Eternal Flame **C. Rowlands**
18 **SILVER TIARA**, b f Kayf Tara—Braiding **I. N. Reis**

Jockey (flat): T. G. McLaughlin. **Apprentice:** M. Halford.

---

121 MR P. L. CLINTON, Doveridge
Postal: **Lordlea Farm, Marston Lane, Doveridge, Ashbourne, Derbyshire, DE6 5JS.**
Contacts: **PHONE (01889) 566356 MOBILE (07815) 142642**
E-MAIL **clintonracing@supanet.com**

1 **AITCH DOUBLEYOU (IRE)**, 5, ch g Classic Memory—Bucksreward (IRE) **In The Clear Racing**
2 **ALWAYS WAINING (IRE)**, 4, b c Unfuwain (USA)—Glenarff (USA) **Peter J. Douglas Engineering**
3 **BUNJERRY**, 7, b m Rock City—Strawberry Split **Mrs C. Burrows**
4 **IMPERIAL ROYALE (IRE)**, 4, ch g Ali-Royal (IRE)—God Speed Her **In The Clear Racing**
5 **PARADISE GARDEN (USA)**, 8, b g Septieme Ciel (USA)—Water Course (USA) **In The Clear Racing**
6 **ZAMYATINA (IRE)**, 6, br m Danehill Dancer (IRE)—Miss Pickpocket (IRE) **In The Clear Racing**

Other Owners: MR P. L. Clinton, P. J. Douglas, Mrs L. Douglas, G. Worrall.

Assistant Trainer: G Worrall

---

122 MR K. F. CLUTTERBUCK, Newmarket
Postal: **Pond House Stables, Church Lane, Exning, Newmarket, Suffolk, CB8 7HF.**
Contacts: **PHONE (01638) 577043 MOBILE (07868) 605995**

1 **BALLA D'AIRE (IRE)**, 10, b br g Balla Cove—Silius **Mr K. F. Clutterbuck**
2 **CLYDEONEEYED**, 6, b g Primitive Rising (USA)—Holly **The T Class Partnership**

MR K. F. CLUTTERBUCK—continued

3 **JOLLYS PRIDE**, 4, b g Orpen (USA)—Greek Night Out (IRE) **Mrs J. K. Hammond**
4 **LORD ROCHESTER**, 9, b g Distant Relative—Kentfield **Mr K. F. Clutterbuck**
5 **MISTER GRAHAM**, 10, b g Rock Hopper—Celestial Air **Mr K. F. Clutterbuck**

Other Owners: S. Hammond.

Assistant Trainer: Nick Hyde

---

123 MR D. J. COAKLEY, West Ilsley
Postal: **Keeper's Stables, West Ilsley, Newbury, Berkshire, RG20 7AH.**
Contacts: **PHONE (01635) 281622 FAX (01635) 281624 MOBILE (07768) 658056**
E-MAIL denis@coakley99.freeserve.co.uk

1 **ENYA**, 4, b f Orpen (USA)—Mystery Night (FR) **Exors of the Late J. J. Henderson**
2 **FARRIERS CHARM**, 4, b f In Command (IRE)—Carn Maire **A. Hall**
3 **KESHYA**, 4, b f Mtoto—Liberatrice (FR) **Finders Keepers Partnership**
4 **MOCCA (IRE)**, 4, b f Sri Pekan (USA)—Ewan (IRE) **Mocca Partnership**
5 **SWEET PICKLE**, 4, b f Piccolo—Sweet Wilhelmina **C. T. Van Hoorn**
6 **TROMP**, 4, ch c Zilzal—Sulitelma (USA) **C. T. Van Hoorn**

THREE-YEAR-OLDS

7 **MAZINDAR (USA)**, b br g Zamindar (USA)—Fantastic Bloom (VEN) **Keepers Racing II**
8 **PRINCE VETTORI**, b c Vettori (IRE)—Bombalarina (IRE) **Hurley, Pattinson**
9 **SIRCE (IRE)**, b f Josr Algarhoud (IRE)—Trading Aces **Dorothy & Ivan Topley**
10 **TRANQUILIZER**, b f Dr Fong (USA)—Tranquillity **Count Calypso Racing**

TWO-YEAR-OLDS

11 B c 7/3 Orpen (USA)—Moorfield Daisy (IRE) (Waajib) (25000) **Bolam, Hurley, Ross**
12 **SILKEN SKY**, b c 18/2 Septieme Ciel (USA)—Westwood (FR) (Anabaa (USA)) (20000) **C. T. Van Hoorn**
13 **STEPPE DANCER (IRE)**, b c 2/4 Fasliyev (USA)—Exemina (USA) (Slip Anchor) (50000) **C. T. Van Hoorn**

Other Owners: G. Callegari, P. M. Emery, R. D. Whitehead.

---

124 MR P. F. I. COLE, Whatcombe
Postal: **Whatcombe Estate, Whatcombe, Wantage, Oxfordshire, OX12 9NW.**
Contacts: **PHONE (01488) 638433 FAX (01488) 638609**
E-MAIL pfi.cole@virgin.net WEBSITE www.pficole.co.uk

1 **AKRITAS**, 4, b c Polish Precedent (USA)—Dazzling Heights **C. Shiacolas**
2 **ARCHDUKE FERDINAND (FR)**, 7, ch g Dernier Empereur (USA)—
Lady Norcliffe (USA) **Mr Christopher Wright & The Hon Mrs J. M. Corbett**
3 **BEEJAY**, 4, b f Piccolo—Letluce **A. H. Robinson**
4 **BLAZE OF COLOUR**, 4, ch f Rainbow Quest (USA)—Hawait Al Barr **SIV Corporation**
5 **BLUE TOMATO**, 4, b c Orpen (USA)—Ocean Grove (IRE) **Mrs S. A. Smith**
6 **BUKIT FRASER (IRE)**, 4, b g Sri Pekan (USA)—London Pride (USA) **H.R.H. Sultan Ahmad Shah**
7 **CAMBERLEY (IRE)**, 8, b g Sri Pekan (USA)—Nsx **H.R.H. Sultan Ahmad Shah**
8 **DR THONG**, 4, ch c Dr Fong (USA)—Always On My Mind **F. P. Stella**
9 **EISTEDDFOD**, 4, ch g Cadeaux Genereux—Ffestiniog (IRE) **Elite Racing Club**
10 **FINE SILVER (IRE)**, 4, gr c Intikhab (USA)—Petula **SIV Corporation**
11 **HARCOURT (USA)**, 5, b h Cozzene (USA)—Ballinamallard (USA) **Sir George Meyrick**
12 **KEEPERS KNIGHT (IRE)**, 4, b c Sri Pekan (USA)—Keepers Dawn (IRE) **P. F. I. Cole Ltd**
13 **MALTESE FALCON**, 5, b g Mark of Esteem (IRE)—Crime Ofthecentury **Mr Christopher Wright**
14 **MR DINOS (IRE)**, 6, b h Desert King (IRE)—Spear Dance **C. Shiacolas**
15 **MR TAMBOURINE MAN (IRE)**, 4, b g Rainbow Quest (USA)—
Girl From Ipanema **Mr Christopher Wright & The Hon Mrs J. M. Corbett**
16 **PETER PAUL RUBENS (USA)**, 4, ch c Belong To Me (USA)—Skybox (USA) **Richard Green (Fine Paintings)**
17 **PUTRA SAS (IRE)**, 4, b c Sri Pekan (USA)—Puteri Wentworth **H.R.H. Sultan Ahmad Shah**
18 **SARISTAR**, 4, b f Starborough—Sari **R. A. Instone**
19 **SECRETARY GENERAL (IRE)**, 4, b c Fasliyev (USA)—Katie McLain (USA) **The Blenheim Partnership**
20 **SOUND OF FLEET (USA)**, 4, ch c Cozzene (USA)—Tempo (USA) **Meyrick, Smith, Landis & Cole**
21 **SOVEREIGN DREAMER (USA)**, 5, b h Kingmambo (USA)—Spend A Dream (USA) **P. F. I. Cole Ltd**

MR P. F. I. COLE—continued

22 **SQUIRTLE TURTLE**, 5, ch g Peintre Celebre (USA)—Hatton Gardens **Mrs V. Cole**
23 **SWING WING**, 6, b g In The Wings—Swift Spring (FR) **M. Arbib**
24 **TOTAL TURTLE (IRE)**, 6, b g Turtle Island (IRE)—Chagrin d'amour (IRE) **W. J. Smith and M. D. Dudley**

THREE-YEAR-OLDS

25 **ANDRONIKOS**, ch c Dr Fong (USA)—Arctic Air **C. Shiacolas**
26 **AYLMER ROAD (IRE)**, b c Groom Dancer (USA)—Pekan's Pride **H.R.H. Sultan Ahmad Shah**
27 **BEAUTIFUL MARIA (IRE)**, b f Sri Pekan (USA)—Puteri Wentworth **H.R.H. Sultan Ahmad Shah**
28 **BELLY DANCER (IRE)**, gr f Danehill Dancer (IRE)—Persian Mistress (IRE) **A. J. Smith**
29 **BRECON BEACON**, b c Spectrum (IRE)—Ffestiniog (IRE) **Elite Racing Club**
30 **BRUNO LE TRUFFLE**, b g Dansili—Crime Ofthecentury **Mr & Mrs Christopher Wright**
31 **COURAGEOUSLY**, b c Aljabr (USA)—Eishin Eleuthera (IRE) **R. A. Instone**
32 **DEPUTY OF WOOD (USA)**, b br f Deputy Minister (CAN)—Wood of Binn (USA) **C. B. Singer**
33 **DUNMAGLASS (USA)**, ch g Cat Thief (USA)—Indian Fashion (USA) **Faisal Salman**
34 **FANTAISISTE**, b f Nashwan (USA)—Fantastic Belle (IRE) **SIV Corporation**
35 **FIGARO'S QUEST (IRE)**, b c Singspiel (IRE)—Seren Quest **The Fairy Story Partnership**
36 **FINNEGANS RAINBOW**, ch c Spectrum (IRE)—Fairy Story (IRE) **The Fairy Story Partnership**
37 **HALCYON EXPRESS (IRE)**, b c Mujadil (USA)—Hakkaniyah **The Blandford Partnership**
38 **IGOR PROTTI**, b c Opening Verse (USA)—La Busona (IRE) **V. De Siero**
39 **LEAGUE OF NATIONS (IRE)**, b c Indian Danehill (USA)—Athens Belle (IRE) **The Blandford Partnership**
40 **LEGALLY FAST (USA)**, b c Deputy Minister (CAN)—Earthly Angel (USA) **C. B. Singer**
41 **LOOK OF EAGLES**, b f Fraam—Dreamtime Quest **Mrs S. A. Smith**
42 **LUIS MELENDEZ (USA)**, ch c Horse Chestnut (SAF)—Egoli (USA) **Richard Green (Fine Paintings)**
43 **MATLOCK GREEN (IRE)**, b g Sadler's Wells (USA)—Whitesville (IRE) **W. J. Smith and M. D. Dudley**
44 **MY PUTRA (USA)**, b br c Silver Hawk (USA)—Petite Triomphe (USA) **H.R.H. Sultan Ahmad Shah**
45 **NANTON (USA)**, gr ro g Spinning World (USA)—Grab The Green (USA) **Sir George Meyrick**
46 **RAKATA (USA)**, b f Quiet American (USA)—Haleakala (IRE) **A. H. Robinson**
47 **RUSSIAN GENERAL (IRE)**, b c Soviet Star (USA)—Azra (IRE) **The Blandford Partnership**
48 **SONGTHRUSH (USA)**, gr ro f Unbridled's Song (USA)—
                                      Virgin Michael (USA) **Mr Christopher Wright & The Hon Mrs J. M. Corbett**
49 **SPECIAL LAD**, b g Spectrum (USA)—Oh Hebe (IRE) **Team Havana**
50 **SPEIGHTSTOWN**, gr c Grand Lodge—Farfala (FR) **M. Arbib**
51 **SRI LIPIS**, ch c Cadeaux Genereux—Katrina (IRE) **H.R.H. Sultan Ahmad Shah**
52 **STINGRAY (IRE)**, b c Danehill (USA)—Music And Dance (USA) **Mr M. Tabor & Mr Philip Green**
53 **STRATEGIC QUEST**, b f Rainbow Quest (USA)—Danlu (USA) **M. Arbib**
54 **SWELL LAD**, b g Sadler's Wells (USA)—Lydara (USA) **M. Arbib**
55 **SWINDON (USA)**, b f Kingmambo (USA)—Dance Design (IRE) **M. Arbib**
56 **THUNDER CALLING (USA)**, b f Thunder Gulch (USA)—Glorious Calling (USA) **C. B. Singer**
57 **TRAIANOS (USA)**, b br c Mt Livermore (USA)—Shiitake (USA) **C. Shiacolas**
58 **UNRESERVEDLY**, b f Cadeaux Genereux—Iberian Dancer (CAN) **Bernard Gover Bloodstock Trading Ltd**
59 **XEBEC (IRE)**, b c Xaar—Via Camp **The Blandford Partnership**

TWO-YEAR-OLDS

60 **ART MARKET (CAN)**, ch c 19/4 Giant's Causeway (USA)—
                                      Fantasy Lake (Salt Lake (USA)) (66507) **Richard Green (Fine Paintings)**
61 **ASMARADANA**, b c 15/2 Groom Dancer (USA)—Nsx (Roi Danzig (USA)) **H.R.H. Sultan Ahmad Shah**
62 B c 1/2 Bertolini (USA)—Coffee Cream (Common Grounds) (16000)
63 **GENARI**, b c 11/4 Generous (IRE)—Sari (Faustus (USA)) (12000) **R. A. Instone**
64 **HALCYON LODGE (IRE)**, ch f 23/2 Grand Lodge (USA)—
                                      Halcyon Daze (Halling (USA)) (25000) **Mr Christopher Wright**
65 **HIGH HEEL SNEAKERS**, b f 30/3 Dansili—Sundae Girl (USA) (Green Dancer (USA)) **Mr Christopher Wright**
66 **MARCELLO**, b c 22/4 Diktat—Girl From Ipanema (Salse (USA)) (45000) **Sir George Meyrick**
67 B f 2/3 Fasliyev (USA)—Nefeli (First Trump) (5000) **C. Shiacolas**
68 **OCEANS APART**, ch f 12/3 Desert Prince (IRE)—Ffestiniog (IRE) (Efisio) **Elite Racing Club**
69 Br f 4/4 Dansili—Only In Dreams (Polar Falcon (USA)) (20000) **SIV Corporation**
70 **POWER BROKER**, b c 13/2 Mark of Esteem (IRE)—Galatrix (Be My Guest (USA)) (67000) **Faisal Salman**
71 **PUTERI SAS (IRE)**, b f 16/2 Fasliyev (USA)—
                                      Puteri Wentworth (Sadler's Wells (USA)) **H.R.H. Sultan Ahmad Shah**
72 B c 31/3 Barathea (IRE)—Radhwa (FR) (Shining Steel) (35000)
73 B c 18/4 Mozart (IRE)—Sarah-Clare (Reach) (290000) **M. Tabor**
74 B c 5/3 Stravinsky (USA)—Sign Here (USA) (Private Terms) (36887) **SIV Corporation**
75 B c 8/2 Selkirk (USA)—Silly Goose (IRE) (Sadler's Wells (USA)) (25000)
76 B f 17/3 Chester House (USA)—Stormy Squab (USA) (Storm Bird (CAN)) (10109) **F. P. Stella**
77 **STRATEGIC MOUNT**, b c 5/5 Montjeu (IRE)—Danlu (USA) (Danzig (USA)) **Mr B. G. Arbib**

MR P. F. I. COLE—continued

78 STRATEGIC PRINCE (IRE), b c 16/4 Anabaa (USA)—
Miss Party Line (USA) (Phone Trick (USA)) (110000) **H.R.H. Sultan Ahmad Shah**
79 Ch c 30/3 Dr Fong (USA)—Superspring (Superlative) (33534) **SIV Corporation**
80 B c 2/4 Night Shift (USA)—Thermopylae (Tenby) (50300)
81 Ch f 12/3 Compton Place—Thundercloud (Electric) (9500)
82 Ch c 9/2 Mark of Esteem (IRE)—Verify (IRE) (Polish Precedent (USA)) (18779)
83 WHITE LADDER (IRE), bl c 8/3 Marju (IRE)—
Lady Rachel (IRE) (Priolo (USA)) (43594) **Mr Christopher Wright & The Hon Mrs J. M. Corbett**

Other Owners: T. M. Bird, C. M. Budgett, Sir Mervyn Dunnington-Jefferson, R. A. Esau, Gilridge Bloodstock Ltd, E. R. Goodwin, P. N. R. Green, A. J. Hill, C. V. L. Meyrick, Miss S. D. Meyrick, M. C. Moutray-Read, Miss M. Noden, Miss C. S. Scott-Balls, A. J. Smith.

Assistant Trainer: Oliver Cole

Amateur: Mrs H. Clubb, Mr O. Cole.

MR R. COLLET, Chantilly
Postal: 32, Avenue Marie Amelie, 60500 Chantilly, France.
Contacts: HOME +33 (0) 57 59 27 OFFICE +33 (0) 3 44 57 06 72
FAX +33 (0) 57 32 25 MOBILE +33 (0) 608 789709
E-MAIL collet-robert@wanadoo.fr

1 ALPUYECA (FR), 4, ch f Ashkalani (IRE)—Finir En Beaute (FR) **Mr Shen**
2 ASO ROCK (IRE), 7, b g King's Theatre (IRE)—Zelda (IRE) **Mr Shen**
3 AVENUE MONTAIGNE (FR), 6, b m Take Risks (FR)—Valley Road (FR) **Mr Collet**
4 BABOUCHE (FR), 4, b c Desert Prince (IRE)—Les Trois Lamas (IRE) **Mr Lamara**
5 CANTONESE BED (IRE), 4, b f Barathea (IRE)—Kansa (FR) **Ecurie Fabien O**
6 CIARA MO GRA (IRE), 6, b m Tagula (IRE)—Kyra Crown (IRE) **Mr Tromel**
7 DESERT THREAT (IRE), 5, b m Desert Prince (IRE)—Veiled Threat (IRE) **Haras de La Sas**
8 DREAM MACHINE (IRE), 4, b c Machiavellian (USA)—Truly A Dream (IRE) **Mr Strauss**
9 ETOILE ENCHANTEE (FR), 4, b f Zieten (USA)—France Enchantee (FR) **Mr De Moussac**
10 GOLDENPHEE (FR), 4, b f Gold Away (IRE)—Onphee (FR) **Mr Collet**
11 HEINSTEIN (IRE), 5, b h Night Shift (USA)—Crumpetsfortea (IRE) **Mr Collet**
12 HOUSE MUSIC (FR), 6, b h Desert King (IRE)—Laquifan (USA) **Mr Trichter**
13 LE BYZANTIN (USA), 4, gr c Dynaformer (USA)—Venize (IRE) **Mr Strauss**
14 MIKOS (FR), 5, b h Sicyos (USA)—Sex Pistol (IRE) **Mr Esposito**
15 MOCHAM GLEN (FR), 8, b g Midyan (USA)—Marsoumeh (USA) **Mr Andreani**
16 NITE TRIPPA (FR), 4, b c Exit To Nowhere (USA)—Nativelee (FR) **Mr Mayoz**
17 ON LINE (FR), 5, ch h Green Tune (USA)—Odwalla **Mr Keslassy**
18 SIMON LE MAGICIEN (FR), 4, gr c Simon du Desert (FR)—Crimson Shadows **M. Vidal**
19 SIN EL FIL (IRE), 4, b c Night Shift (USA)—Soeur Ti (FR) **Mr Fruchan**
20 SKYROCK (USA), 6, b h Sky Classic (CAN)—Landholder (USA) **Mr Shen**
21 TYCOON'S HILL (IRE), 6, b h Danehill (USA)—Tycoon's Drama (IRE) **Mr Strauss**
22 VETTORINA (FR), 4, ch f Vettori (IRE)—Last Mecene (FR) **Haras De La Sas**
23 WHIPPER (IRE), 4, b c Miesque's Son (USA)—Myth To Reality (FR) **Mr Strauss**
24 ZANYBOY (FR), 5, bl h Night Shift (USA)—Party Zane **Mr Maeder**
25 ZIPPING (IRE), 6, b h Zafonic (USA)—Zelda (IRE) **Mr Strauss**

THREE-YEAR-OLDS

26 BENODET (IRE), b c King's Best (USA)—Pont-Aven **Mr Strauss**
27 CANCALAISE (IRE), b f Entrepreneur—Basilea (FR) **Mr Strauss**
28 CARACOLA (IRE), b c Xaar—Caralina (IRE) **Ecurie Central**
29 CENTIFOLIA (FR), gr f Kendor (FR)—Djayapura (FR) **Mr Berland**
30 KAPPELMANN (FR), gr c Verglas (IRE)—Black Dalhia (FR) **Mr Vallin**
31 LA CROISETTE (FR), b f Starborough—Charming Quest (USA) **Mr Collet**
32 LEONINSKA (FR), b f Varxi (FR)—Quelle Classe (FR) **Mr Collet**
33 NEW LARGUE (USA), b f Distant View (USA)—New Story (USA) **Mr Strauss**
34 NIPPING (IRE), b f Night Shift (USA)—Zelda (IRE) **Mr Strauss**
35 PAPIER MACHE (IRE), b f Desert Prince (IRE)—Truly A Gift (IRE) **Mr Collet**
36 RADUGA, ch f Sinndar (IRE)—Volcania (FR) **Mr Larsson**
37 RUE DE LAPPE (FR), bl c Highest Honor (FR)—Kadouville (FR) **Mr Segura**
38 SALUT THOMAS (FR), ch c Adnaan (IRE)—Salut Bebs (FR) **Mr Jesus**
39 SINGAPORE PEARL (FR), b f Kendor (FR)—Beijaflor (FR) **Haras De La Sas**

MR R. COLLET—continued

40 **SINGAPORE SUN (FR)**, b c Goldmark (USA)—All For Hope (USA) **Haras De La Sas**
41 **TEAM DREAM (IRE)**, b c Giant's Causeway (USA)—Truly A Dream (IRE) **Mr Strauss**
42 **TOGAMBO (FR)**, b c Le Triton (USA)—Movin' Meghan (USA) **Mr Shen**
43 **TOO NICE (FR)**, gr c Kaldounevees (FR)—Toomixa (FR) **Mr Vallin**
44 **URIGUNDE (IRE)**, b f Daggers Drawn (USA)—Gloria Crown (IRE) **Mr Tromel**
45 **VERDERET (FR)**, b c Desert Style (IRE)—Honor The Coffee (FR)
46 **YIPPEE (FR)**, b f Orpen (USA)—Crumpetsfortea (IRE) **P. Vidal**

TWO-YEAR-OLDS

47 Ch c 20/4 Trempolino (USA)—Bardouine (USA) (Northern Baby (CAN)) (10060) **Mr Collet**
48 **BINIOU (IRE)**, b c 22/2 Mozart (IRE)—Cap Coz (IRE) (Indian Ridge) **Mr Strauss**
49 Ch c 13/3 Bering—Chiquelina (FR) (Le Glorieux) (13413) **Mr Collet**
50 **COLOUR OF DESTINY (FR)**, b f 25/4 Verglas (IRE)—Holdout (FR) (College Chapel) (6706) **Mr Strauss**
51 **CORENTIN (IRE)**, ch c 22/5 Desert Prince (IRE)—Pont-Aven (Try My Best (USA)) **Mr Strauss**
52 **CRAZY FLING (FR)**, b f 12/4 Night Shift (USA)—Trust In Love (IRE) (Exit To Nowhere (USA)) **Mr Strauss**
53 **CRYSTALLINE STREAM (FR)**, b f 20/3 Polish Precedent (USA)—
Cootamundra (FR) (Double Bed (FR)) (73775) **Mr Strauss**
54 **DAYLINA (IRE)**, gr f 31/3 Daylami (USA)—Caralina (IRE) (Caerleon (USA)) **Mr Strauss**
55 B c 10/2 Anabaa (USA)—Delicieuse Lady (Trempolino (USA)) (214621) **Mr Collet**
56 **DREAM IN BLUE (FR)**, b c 3/4 Munir—Kenny Glitters (FR) (Kendor (FR)) **M. Vidal**
57 **ECOS DE L'ORME (FR)**, ch c 27/3 Sabrehill (USA)—Ecossette (FR) (Ecossais (FR)) **Mr Collet**
58 **EMERALD WAVE (IRE)**, b c 5/3 Galileo (IRE)—Cerulean Sky (IRE) (Darshaan) **Mr Strauss**
59 **ESSEMMESSE (FR)**, b c 24/4 Victory Note (USA)—Diese Memory (USA) (Diesis) (6036) **M. Vidal**
60 B c 21/2 King's Best (USA)—Flawly (Old Vic) (110663) **Mr Collet**
61 B c 24/1 Alzao (USA)—Graten (IRE) (Zieten) (21000) **Stone Ridge Farm**
62 **KOCOONING (IRE)**, b f 24/1 King's Best (USA)—Zelding (IRE) (Warning) **Mr Strauss**
63 **NEW GIRLFRIEND (IRE)**, b f 21/4 Diesis—New Story (USA) (Dynaformer (USA)) **Mr Strauss**
64 **QUEENSALSA (FR)**, b f 4/3 Kingsalsa (USA)—Gandelia (FR) (Ganges (USA)) **Mr Strauss**
65 **RITZY BABY (IRE)**, b f 26/2 Mozart (IRE)—Side of Paradise (IRE) (Sadler's Wells (USA)) **Mr Strauss**
66 **SALUT MON HOMME (FR)**, b c 28/4 Marchand de Sable (USA)—Salut Bebs (FR) (Kendor (FR)) **Mr Jesus**
67 Br c 23/2 Night Shift (USA)—Terracotta Hut (Habitat) (80482) **Mr Collet**
68 B c 13/4 Simon du Desert (FR)—Terring (FR) (Bering) (50301) **Mr Larsson**
69 **TROUBLE FETE (IRE)**, b c 12/3 Fantastic Light (USA)—Truly Generous (IRE) (Generous (IRE)) **Mr Strauss**
70 Gr c 27/1 Woodman (USA)—Venize (IRE) (Kaldoun (FR)) **Kilfrush Stud**
71 B c 11/2 Zafonic (USA)—White Quartz (IRE) (Sadler's Wells (USA)) (100603) **Mr Collet**
72 **WORDS OF LOVE (FR)**, gr c 4/5 Kendor (FR)—Lethals Lady (Rudimentary (USA)) **Mr Vallin**

---

126 **MR H. J. COLLINGRIDGE, Newmarket**
Postal: **Harraton Court Stables, Chapel Street, Exning, Newmarket, Suffolk, CB8 7HA.**
Contacts: **PHONE/FAX (01638) 577288 MOBILE (07748) 614912**
E-MAIL hugh@headquartersracing.co.uk WEBSITE www.headquarterspartnership.co.uk

1 **BRIERY MEC**, 10, b g Ron's Victory (USA)—Briery Fille **N. H. Gardner**
2 **CONCERT HOUSE (IRE)**, 5, b m Entrepreneur—Classic Heights **The Headquarters Partnership Ltd**
3 **FOREST HEATH (IRE)**, 8, gr g Common Grounds—Caroline Lady (JPN) **Group 1 Racing (1994) Ltd**
4 **HELLO IT'S ME**, 4, ch g Deploy—Evening Charm (IRE) **Mrs P. A. L. Butler**
5 **KARA DOOT**, 4, b f Bijou d'inde—Meghdoot **P. Tong**
6 **MASTER THEO (USA)**, 4, b g Southern Halo (USA)—Lilian Bayliss (IRE) **Mr K. W. & Mrs L. A. Styles**
7 **MUST BE MAGIC**, 8, b g Magic Ring (IRE)—Sequin Lady **The Headquarters Partnership Ltd**
8 **NO CHANCE TO DANCE (IRE)**, 5, b g Revoque (IRE)—Song of The Glens **The Headquarters Partnership Ltd**
9 **THE VIOLIN PLAYER (USA)**, 4, b g King of Kings (IRE)—Silk Masque (USA) **P. Webb**
10 **TROFANA FALCON**, 5, b g Polar Falcon (USA)—Silk St James **Greenhills Partnership**
11 **VELOCITAS**, 4, b g Magic Ring (IRE)—Folly Finnesse **The Headquarters Partnership Ltd**
12 **VICTORIANA**, 4, b f Wolfhound (USA)—Silk St James **Mrs J. Ison and Partners**

THREE-YEAR-OLDS

13 **BLUE HEDGES**, b c Polish Precedent (USA)—Palagene **N. H. Gardner**
14 **MALDONIAN**, b f Mujahid (USA)—Bellateena **The Headquarters Partnership Ltd**
15 **MISS AMOUR**, b f Pivotal—Georgia Stephens (USA) **P. Webb**
16 **REACHING OUT (IRE)**, b f Desert Prince (IRE)—Alwiyda (USA) **P. Webb**
17 **RED APACHE (IRE)**, b c Namid—Special Dissident **The Headquarters Partnership Ltd**
18 **SMOKEY RIDGE**, b f Namid—Chimere (FR) **G. B. Amy**

MR H. J. COLLINGRIDGE—continued

19 **SUNDANCE (IRE)**, ch c Namid—Titchwell Lass **Mr Richard Farquhar**
20 **TOPOGRAPHER (IRE)**, b c Alhaarth (IRE)—Baddi Heights (FR) **The Headquarters Partnership Ltd**

Other Owners: Mr & Mrs I. Dell, B. Hughes, L. Audus, R. C. Corbett, Mr Roger J Durrant, G. V. Jukes, Ms L. M. A. Kent.

Jockey (flat): J. Quinn. **Jockey (NH):** S. Curran. **Amateur:** Miss A. L. Hutchinson.

---

127 MR W. S. COLTHERD, Selkirk
Postal: **Clarilawmuir Farm, Selkirk, TD7 4QA.**
Contacts: PHONE (01750) 21251 MOBILE (0780) 1398199
E-MAIL w.s.coltherd@aol.com

1 **BALIGRUNDLE**, 5, b g Moshaajir (USA)—Masirah **G. L. S. Limited**
2 **CASTERFLO**, 6, b m Primitive Rising (USA)—Celtic Sands **Alex And Janet Card**
3 **CORBIE LYNN**, 8, ch m Jumbo Hirt (USA)—Kilkenny Gorge **J. R. Cheyne**
4 **CROSBY DANCER**, 6, b g Glory of Dancer—Mary Macblain **B. Confrey**
5 **GEOFFREY BROUGHTON**, 8, b g Weldnaas (USA)—Broughton's Gold (IRE) **M. F. Edgar**
6 **KALIC D'ALM (FR)**, 7, b g Passing Sale (FR)—Bekaa II (FR) **Tweedside Racing**
7 **MIDLEM MELODY**, 9, b m Syrtos—Singing Hills **Mr W. S. Coltherd**
8 **OPAL'S HELMSMAN (USA)**, 6, b g Helmsman (USA)—Opal's Notebook (USA) **Mrs I. A. Forrest**
9 **THE SLEEPER**, 9, b g Perpendicular—Distant Cherry **M. F. Edgar**

Other Owners: M. J. Scott, Mr R. J. Wilson.

Jockey (NH): A. Dempsey, B. Harding, G. Lee.

---

128 LADY CONNELL, Brackley
Postal: **Steane Park, Brackley, Northamptonshire, NN13 6DP.**
Contacts: PHONE (01280) 705899

1 **BARON STEANE (IRE)**, 6, b g Lord Americo—Lottosprite (IRE) **Mrs L. A. Gregory**
2 **CABIN BOY**, 10, ch g Royal Vulcan—Maytide **Sir Michael Connell**
3 **COURT ADJOURN**, 8, b g North Col—Tapalong **Sir Michael Connell**
4 **COURT ALERT**, 10, b g Petoski—Banbury Cake **J. E. Connell**
5 **EXCEPTIONNEL (FR)**, 6, b g Subotica (FR)—The Exception (FR) **Lady Connell**
6 **MAESTRO PLEASE (IRE)**, 6, b g Old Vic—Greek Melody (IRE) **S. J. Connell**
7 **PRIVATE PETE**, 12, ch g Gunner B—Vedra (IRE) **Sir Michael Connell**
8 **WILL STEANE**, 6, ch g Master Willie—Deep Pier **S. M. Connell**
9 **YER FATHER'S YACHT (IRE)**, 5, b g Desert Story (IRE)—Alchiea **Sir Michael Connell**

---

129 MR M. J. COOMBE, Weymouth
Postal: **Sea Barn Farm, Fleet, Weymouth, Dorset, DT3 4ED.**
Contacts: PHONE (01305) 782218/761745 FAX (01305) 775396
E-MAIL wib@seabarn.fsnet.co.uk

1 **GO ON AHEAD (IRE)**, 5, b g Namaqualand (USA)—Charm The Stars **Mr Richard G. Cuddihy**
2 **JOE DEANE (IRE)**, 9, ch g Alphabatim (USA)—Craic Go Leor **Mr & Mrs D. A. Gamble**
3 **KESTLE MILL (IRE)**, 9, ch g Be My Guest (USA)—Tatisha **Mr & Mrs D. A. Gamble**
4 **MADAM FLEET**, 6, ch m Carroll House—Bucktan **J. D. Roberts**

Other Owners: MR M. J. Coombe.

Assistant Trainer: Mrs M Roberts

Amateur: Mrs M. Roberts.

---

130 MR J. R. CORNWALL, Melton Mowbray
Postal: **April Cottage, Pasture Lane, Hose, Melton Mowbray, Leicestershire, LE14 4LB.**
Contacts: PHONE (01664) 444453 MOBILE (07939) 557091

1 **BACK DE BAY (IRE)**, 5, b g Bob Back (USA)—Baybush **Mr J. R. Cornwall**
2 **BUZYBAKSON (IRE)**, 8, b br g Bob Back (USA)—Middle Verde (USA) **Mr J. R. Cornwall**

MR J. R. CORNWALL—continued

3 FANTASTIC CHAMPION (IRE), 6, b g Entrepreneur—Reine Mathilde (USA) **Mr J. R. Cornwall**
4 JUST JOLLY (IRE), 10, b g Jolly Jake (NZ)—Bulgaden Gypsy **Mr J. R. Cornwall**
5 KERCABELLEC (FR), 7, b br g Useful (FR)—Marie De Geneve (FR) **Mr J. R. Cornwall**
6 KONKER, 10, ch g Selkirk (USA)—Helens Dreamgirl **Mr J. R. Cornwall**
7 POLISH PILOT (IRE), 10, b g Polish Patriot (USA)—Va Toujours **Mr J. R. Cornwall**
8 RUNAWAY BISHOP (USA), 10, b br g Lear Fan (USA)—Valid Linda (USA) **Mr J. R. Cornwall**
9 STAND EASY (IRE), 12, b g Buckskin (FR)—Geeaway **Mr J. R. Cornwall**
10 STRONG MAGIC (IRE), 13, br g Strong Gale—Baybush **Mr J. R. Cornwall**

Other Owners: The Hon Lady Gibbings.

Conditional: G Horner.

---

131 MR L. G. COTTRELL, Cullompton
Postal: **Sprinters, Dulford, Cullompton, Devon, EX15 2DX.**
Contacts: **PHONE (01884) 266320**

1 GO GO GIRL, 5, ch m Pivotal—Addicted To Love **Henry C. Seymour**
2 HAWRIDGE PRINCE, 5, b g Polar Falcon (USA)—Zahwa **E. J. S. Gadsden**
3 JUST A GLIMMER, 5, b m Bishop of Cashel—Rockin' Rosie **Mrs P. A. Reditt**
4 TARTIRUGA (IRE), 4, b g Turtle Island (IRE)—Palio Flyer **Fourever Hopeful**

THREE-YEAR-OLDS

5 AGILETE, b g Piccolo—Ingerence (FR) **J Boswell, H Seymour, A Walsh, T Walsh**
6 ANGEL SPRINTS, b f Piccolo—Runs In The Family **Mrs L. M. Halloran**
7 HAWRIDGE SENSATION, ch g Polish Precedent (USA)—Looks Sensational (USA) **E. J. S. Gadsden**
8 INCHCAPE ROCK, ch c Inchinor—Washm (USA) **Mrs C. J. Walsh**
9 TAKE THE PLUNGE, br f Benny The Dip (USA)—Pearly River **Manor Farm Packers Ltd**

Other Owners: L. G. Albertini, M. J. Collins, Mr I. D. M. Fraser, P. J. Gorman, Mrs S. L. M. Von Maltzahn.

Assistant Trainer: Mrs P M Cottrell & Mr L Jefford

Jockey (flat): A. Daly, L. Dettori, J. F. Egan, I. Mongan, F. Norton, J. Quinn. **Amateur:** Mr L. Jefford.

---

132 MR R. M. H. COWELL, Newmarket
Postal: **Bottisham Heath Stud, Six Mile Bottom, Newmarket, Suffolk, CB8 0TT.**
Contacts: **PHONE (01638) 570330 FAX (01638) 570246 MOBILE (07785) 512463**
E-MAIL cowellracing@aol.com

1 CAPTAIN DARLING (IRE), 5, b g Pennekamp (USA)—Gale Warning (IRE) **A. Dunmore**
2 CHADWELL LAD, 4, b g Vettori (IRE)—Elle Reef **Hackberry Bloodstock**
3 CLAUREEN PRINCE (IRE), 6, ch g Prince of Birds (USA)—Arkadina's Million **Bottisham Heath Stud**
4 FOREVER PHOENIX, 5, b m Shareef Dancer (USA)—With Care **J. M. Greetham**
5 HUSKY (POL), 7, b g Special Power—Hallo Bambina (POL) **Mrs J. M. Penney**
6 MARY CARLETON, 4, ch f Halling (USA)—Anne Bonny **Bottisham Heath Stud**
7 OTYLIA, 5, ch m Wolfhound (USA)—Soba **Miss D. Birkbeck**
8 PRAGMATICA, 4, b f Inchinor—Isabella Gonzaga **Cyril Humphris**
9 RED LANTERN, 4, ch g Young Ern—Croft Sally **Miss V. Pratt**
10 SECRET VISION (USA), 4, ch f Distant View (USA)—Secret Angel **A. J. Rix**
11 SILVER ISLAND, 4, ch g Silver Patriarch (IRE)—Island Maid **J. A. Vowles**
12 STAR FERN, 4, br g Young Ern—Christening (IRE) **Miss V. Pratt**
13 TARKEEZ (USA), 4, b g Lear Fan (USA)—Mt Morna (USA) **Ryder Racing Ltd**
14 TREGENNA, 4, b f Forzando—Nineteenth of May **Mr & Mrs D. A. Gamble**
15 VINDICATION, 5, ch g Compton Place—Prince's Feather (IRE) **B & F Mechanical Services Ltd**

THREE-YEAR-OLDS

16 CANADIAN DANEHILL (IRE), b c Indian Danehill (IRE)—San Jovita (CAN) **Blue Metropolis**
17 DEFINITELY ROYAL (IRE), b f Desert Prince (IRE)—Specifically (USA) **K. A. Dasmal**
18 ETERNALLY, ch c Timeless Times (USA)—Nice Spice (IRE) **Bottisham Heath Stud**
19 FERN VALLEY, ch c Young Ern—Croft Sally **Miss V. Pratt**
20 HIAMOVI (IRE), b g Monashee Mountain (USA)—Dunfern **Blue Metropolis**
21 PRIDE OF POONA (IRE), b f Indian Ridge—Scandalous **K. A. Dasmal**

MR R. M. H. COWELL—continued

22 **ROWANBERRY**, b f Bishop of Cashel—Raintree Venture **A. G. Don**
23 **TAYLOR MAID**, b f First Trump—Island Maid **J. A. Vowles**
24 **VERY CLEAR**, b f Loup Sauvage (USA)—Shoot Clear **Bottisham Heath Stud**

TWO-YEAR-OLDS

25 B c 1/2 Mujahid (USA)—Admonish (Warning) **Blue Metropolis '05**
26 B c 14/4 Vettori (IRE)—Dust (Green Desert (USA)) (15000) **Blue Metropolis '05**
27 Ch f 15/4 Medicean—Fine Honor (FR) (Highest Honor (FR)) (25000) **J. A. Vowles**
28 **MAID FOR LOVE**, ch f 7/3 Pursuit of Love—Island Maid (Forzando) **J. A. Vowles**
29 **SMOOCH**, b f 22/2 Inchinor—Two Step (Mujtahid (USA)) (22000) **Bottisham Heath Stud**
30 **TAPSALTEERIE**, b f 30/3 Tipsy Creek (USA)—Croft Sally (Crofthall) **Miss V. Pratt**
31 **TIP THE SPIRIT**, b f 19/1 Tipsy Creek (USA)—Christening (IRE) (Lahib (USA)) **Miss V. Pratt**

Other Owners: Mr C. W. Cosham, Mr N. C. Zawoda.

---

133 **MR C. G. COX, Hungerford**
Postal: Beechdown Farm, Sheepdrove Road, Lambourn, Hungerford, Berkshire, RG17 7UN.
Contacts: **OFFICE** (01488) 73072 **FAX** (01488) 73500 **MOBILE** (07740) 630521
E-MAIL info@clivecox.co.uk

1 **BID FOR FAME (USA)**, 8, b br g Quest For Fame—Shroud (USA) **Elite Racing Club**
2 **DAYDREAM DANCER**, 4, gr f Daylami (IRE)—Dancing World (IRE) **The Grey Lady Partnership**
3 **IONIAN SPRING (IRE)**, 10, b g Ela-Mana-Mou—Well Head (IRE) **Elite Racing Club**
4 **KOSTAR**, 4, ch g Komaite (USA)—Black And Amber **Mrs P. Scott-Dunn And Mrs F. J. Ryan**
5 **NEW SEEKER**, 5, b g Green Desert (USA)—Ahbab (IRE) **Elite Racing Club**
6 **NOBLE BARON**, 9, gr g Karinga Bay—Grey Baroness **T. Y. Bissett**
7 **OUT AFTER DARK**, 4, b g Cadeaux Genereux—Midnight Shift (IRE) **The Night Owls**
8 **THYOLO (IRE)**, 4, ch g Bering—Topline (GER) **Mr Mike Watts and Mr Steve Woodhams**
9 **WEST END PEARL**, 4, ch f The West (USA)—Raghill Hannah **Collins Racing**

THREE-YEAR-OLDS

10 **CHINALEA (IRE)**, b c Danetime (IRE)—Raise-A-Secret (IRE) **Ascot Racing**
11 **COUNT KRISTO**, br c Dr Fong (USA)—Aryadne **Mr and Mrs P. Hargreaves**
12 **DANCING ROSE (IRE)**, b f Danehill Dancer (IRE)—Shinkoh Rose (FR) **The Eighteen Dreamers**
13 **DANSILI DANCER**, b c Dansili—Magic Slipper **The Troupers**
14 **FIGGY'S BREW**, ch f Ashkalani (IRE)—Marabela (IRE) **C. V. Cruden**
15 **FORMIDABLE WILL (FR)**, b g Efisio—Shewillifshewants (IRE) **The Ridgeway Rangers**
16 **GRECIAN GOLD (IRE)**, b g Lujain (USA)—Falconera (IRE) **Mr Mike Watts and Mr Steve Woodhams**
17 **INHERENT (IRE)**, ch f In The Wings—Serpentara **Elite Racing Club**
18 **LAY A WHISPER**, br f Night Shift (USA)—Waffle On **Mr W. F. Davis**
19 **LOOK AT THE STARS (IRE)**, b g Bachir (IRE)—Pizzazz **S.Barrow, A. Parsons, P. Stevenson**
20 **SECRET MOMENT**, b c Polar Prince (IRE)—Inchtina **Mrs C. A. Stevenson**
21 **SOUTHERN SHORE (IRE)**, ch g Erhaab (USA)—Intisab **D. Shaw**
22 **SURWAKI (USA)**, b c Miswaki (USA)—Quinella **D. Shaw**
23 **WOODCOTE (IRE)**, b c Monashee Mountain—Tootle **D. Shaw**
24 **ZALZAAR (IRE)**, b g Xaar—Zalamalec (USA) **The Beechdown Optimists**

TWO-YEAR-OLDS

25 B c 24/3 Royal Applause—Anne Bonny (Ajdal (USA)) (47000) **Mr Luk King Ting**
26 **ARCHON STAR (IRE)**, b c 3/5 Ashkalani (IRE)—Scandalous (Warning) (14083) **S. W. Barrow**
27 B br c 9/4 Desert Story (IRE)—Cindy's Star (IRE) (Dancing Dissident (USA)) (16766) **Partnership**
28 **DUNELIGHT (IRE)**, ch c 4/4 Desert Sun—Badee'a (IRE) (Marju (IRE)) (73775) **Mr and Mrs P. Hargreaves**
29 **FISOLA (IRE)**, b f 10/5 Fasliyev (USA)—Afisiak (Efisio) (35000) **Partnership**
30 **PEARLY WEY**, b c 16/3 Lujain (USA)—Dunkellin (USA) (Irish River (FR)) (34000) **D. Shaw**
31 B f 8/3 Mujadil (USA)—Repique (USA) (Sharpen Up) (33000)
32 B f 9/2 City On A Hill (USA)—Royal Baldini (USA) (Green Dancer (USA)) (14754)
33 **TRAVOLTA**, b c 27/2 Dansili—Generous Diana (Generous (IRE)) **Elite Racing Club**
34 **WADDON (IRE)**, b c 26/4 Green Desert (USA)—Baldemara (FR) (Sanglamore (USA)) (60361) **D. Shaw**

Other Owners: Mr N. M. Collins, Mr S. J. Collins, A. J. Hill, B. D. Makepeace, Mrs P. Makepeace, Miss M. Noden, G. E. Powell, P. N. Ridgers.

Jockey (flat): Richard Smith. **Jockey (NH):** Mark Bradburne. **Amateur:** Miss Nadine Forde.

134   MR R. CRAGGS, Sedgefield
Postal: **East Close Farm, Sedgefield, Stockton-On-Tees, Cleveland, TS21 3HW.**
Contacts: **PHONE (01740) 620239 FAX (01740) 623476**

1 **GALLEY LAW**, 5, ch g Most Welcome—Miss Blitz **Mr R. Craggs**
2 **HIGH SWAINSTON**, 4, ch g The West (USA)—Reamzafonic **Mr R. Craggs**
3 **MISS FLEURIE**, 5, b m Alzao (USA)—Miss Sancerre **Mr R. Craggs**
4 **PREMIER GRAND**, 5, ch g Case Law—Seamill (IRE) **Mr R. Craggs**
5 **SHAPE UP (IRE)**, 5, b g Octagonal (NZ)—Bint Kaldoun (IRE) **Mr R. Craggs**
6 **THINK AGAIN (IRE)**, 11, b g Long Pond—Either Or **Mr R. Craggs**
7 **WATERPARK**, 7, b m Namaqualand (USA)—Willisa **Mr R. Craggs**
8 **WITCHELLE**, 4, br f Wizard King—Tachelle (IRE) **Mr R. Craggs**

THREE-YEAR-OLDS

9 **CAYMAN KING**, b g Cayman Kai (IRE)—Distinctly Laura (IRE) **Mr R. Craggs**
10 **WATERLOO CORNER**, b g Cayman Kai (IRE)—Rasin Luck **Mr R. Craggs**

Assistant Trainer: Miss J N Craggs

Amateur: Miss Nicola Craggs.

135   MR J. K. S. CRESSWELL, Oakamoor
Postal: **Stoneydale Farm, Oakamoor, Stoke-On-Trent, Staffordshire, ST10 3AH.**
Contacts: **HOME (01538) 702362 OFFICE (01782) 324606 FAX (01782) 324410**

1 **BROTHER TED**, 8, b g Henbit (USA)—Will Be Wanton **Mr J. K. S. Cresswell**
2 **EARLS ROCK**, 7, b g Gunner B—Will Be Wanton **Mr J. K. S. Cresswell**
3 **GOOD FRIEND**, 6, b m Environment Friend—Gunner Be Good **Mr J. K. S. Cresswell**
4 4, Ch g Gunner B—Hazel Hill **Mr J. K. S. Cresswell**
5 **HEATHY GORE**, 6, ch m Environment Friend—Hazel Hill **Mr J. K. S. Cresswell**

Assistant Trainer: Mrs E M Cresswell

136   MR A. CROOK, Leyburn
Postal: **Lilac Cottage, Harmby, Leyburn, North Yorkshire, DL8 5PD.**
Contacts: **PHONE/FAX (01969) 640303 2ND PHONE (01969) 640302 MOBILE (07764) 158899**
E-MAIL andycrookracing@fsmail.net WEBSITE www.andrewcrookracing.co.uk

1 4, B g Wizard King—Dark Amber **Emma O'Gorman**
2 4, B f Tamure (IRE)—Gay Muse
3 **IRIS'S PRINCE**, 6, ch g Gunner B—Colonial Princess **Leeds Plywood And Doors Ltd**
4 **KALIYOUN (IRE)**, 4, b G Grand Lodge (USA)—Kaliana (IRE)
5 **LADIES FROM LEEDS**, 6, b m Primitive Rising (USA)—Keldholme **Stefanos Stefanou**
6 **MATMATA DE TENDRON (FR)**, 5, gr g Badolato (USA)—Cora des Tamarix (FR)
7 **PORNIC (FR)**, 11, b g Shining Steel—Marie De Geneve (FR) **John Sinclair (Haulage) Ltd**
8 **RYALUX (IRE)**, 12, b g Riverhead (USA)—Kings de Lema (IRE) **Mr W. A. Lomas**
9 5, B g Luso—Shuil Shell (IRE) **R. P. E. Berry**
10 **TROOPER**, 11, b g Rock Hopper—Silica (USA) **R. M. Bakes**

THREE-YEAR-OLDS

11 **GENERAL MAX (IRE)**, b c General Monash (USA)—Sawaki **Leeds Plywood And Doors Ltd**
12 **JUDGE DAMUSS (IRE)**, ch c Tagula (IRE)—Acicula (USA) **Leeds Plywood And Doors Ltd**
13 **KEYALZAO (IRE)**, b f Alzao (USA)—Key Partner **Leeds Plywood And Doors Ltd**
14 **KING HENRIK (USA)**, b g King of Kings (IRE)—Ma Biche (USA) **W. Graham & Leeds Plywood & Doors Ltd**

Jockey (NH): G. Lee, R. McGrath, P. Robson. **Conditional:** A. Brimble.

137 MR L. M. CUMANI, Newmarket

Postal: Bedford House Stables, Bury Road, Newmarket, Suffolk, CB8 7BX.
Contacts: PHONE (01638) 665432 FAX (01638) 667160 MOBILE (07801) 225300
E-MAIL luca.cumani@bedfordhousestables.co.uk

1 ALKAASED (USA), 5, b h Kingmambo (USA)—Chesa Plana Mr M. R. Charlton
2 BALLAST (IRE), 4, ch c Desert Prince (IRE)—Suedoise Mr R. C. Thompson
3 BATIK (IRE), 4, gr f Peintre Celebre (USA)—Dali's Grey Aston House Stud
4 COPPICE (IRE), 4, ch g Rainbow Quest (USA)—Woodwin (IRE) Lord Vestey
5 CROCODILE DUNDEE (IRE), 4, b c Croco Rouge (IRE)—Miss Salsa Dancer Mr R. C. Thompson
6 ETTRICK WATER, 6, ch g Selkirk (USA)—Sadly Sober (IRE) Mrs E. H. Vestey
7 HIGHLAND GAMES (IRE), 5, b g Singspiel (IRE)—Highland Gift (IRE) K. Bailey, P. Booth, D. Boorer
8 IDEALISTIC (IRE), 4, b f Unfuwain (USA)—L'ideale Fittocks Stud Ltd
9 KUSTER, 9, b g Indian Ridge—Ustka Mrs Luca Cumani
10 LE VIE DEI COLORI, 5, b h Efisio—Mystic Tempo (USA) Scuderia Archi Romani
11 LITERATIM, 5, b g Polish Precedent (USA)—Annie Albright (USA) Aston House Stud
12 LOST SOLDIER THREE (IRE), 4, b g Barathea (IRE)—Donya Sheikh Mohammed Obaid Al Maktoum
13 MANDATUM, 4, b g Mtoto—Reamur Aston House Stud
14 MINORITY REPORT, 5, b g Rainbow Quest (USA)—Queen Sceptre (IRE) G. Shiel
15 NEWNHAM (IRE), 4, ch g Theatrical—Brief Escapade (IRE) Ballygallon Stud Ltd
16 PRENUP (IRE), 4, ch f Diesis—Mutual Consent (USA) Fittocks Stud Ltd
17 PUKKA (IRE), 4, b c Sadler's Wells (USA)—Puce Fittocks Stud Ltd
18 SELEBELA, 4, ch f Grand Lodge (USA)—Risarshana (FR) Scuderia Rencati Srl
19 ZEITGEIST (IRE), 4, b c Singspiel (IRE)—Diamond Quest L. Marinopoulos

THREE-YEAR-OLDS

20 ALLIED CAUSE, ch f Giant's Causeway (USA)—Alligram (USA) Helena Springfield Ltd
21 CAMPLI (IRE), b g Zafonic (USA)—Sept A Neuf Mrs A. S. Silver
22 CROON, b c Sinndar (IRE)—Shy Minstrel (USA) De La Warr Racing
23 DASH TO THE TOP, b f Montjeu (IRE)—Millennium Dash Helena Springfield Ltd
24 DONYA ONE, b f Cadeaux Genereux—Fadhah Sheikh Mohammed Obaid Al Maktoum
25 EDAS, b c Celtic Swing—Eden (IRE) L. Marinopoulos
26 ELEMENT OF TRUTH (USA), ch f Atticus (USA)—My Shafy Mr Christopher Wright
27 FLAMAND (USA), ch f Miswaki (USA)—Sister Sorrow (USA) Lady Carolyn Warren
28 FRANNY, b f Selkirk (USA)—Frangy Fittocks Stud Ltd
29 GOLBAND, b f Cadeaux Genereux—Hatheethah (IRE) Sheikh Mohammed Obaid Al Maktoum
30 HAPGOOD (IRE), b c Sadler's Wells (USA)—Maria Isabella (USA) The Leigh Family
31 JAZRAWY, b c Dansili—Dalila di Mare (IRE) Sheikh Mohammed Obaid Al Maktoum
32 MASSARO PAPE (IRE), b c Intikhab (USA)—Megeve (IRE) Equibreed Srl.
33 METRICAL, b f Inchinor—Salligram Fittocks Stud Ltd
34 NASRAWY, b c Grand Lodge (USA)—By Charter Sheikh Mohammed Obaid Al Maktoum
35 NEUTRINO, b c Mtoto—Fair Seas Mr Philip F. Myerscough
36 PAMIR, b g Namid—Mijouter (IRE) Mrs E. H. Vestey
37 PINK SHOES (IRE), b f Sadler's Wells (USA)—Dangerous Diva (IRE) Mr Bob Lanigan
38 PRAKARA (IRE), ch f Indian Ridge—Prima Volta Lady Juliet Tadgell
39 PRIDE OF NATION (IRE), b c Danehill Dancer (USA)—Anita Via (IRE) Equibreed Srl.
40 QUEEN TOMYRA (IRE), b f Montjeu (IRE)—Kama Tashoof Equibreed Srl.
41 QUIZZICAL QUESTION (IRE), ch f Bob Back (USA)—Quality of Life Allevamento Gialloblu
42 SACRANUN, ch c Pivotal—Spanish Craft (USA) Scuderia Rencati Srl
43 SAMARAI, ch g Tagula (IRE)—Gandini Mrs Luca Cumani
44 SEFEMM, ch f Alhaarth (IRE)—Pennsylvania (USA) Scuderia Rencati Srl
45 SHARED DREAMS, b f Seeking The Gold (USA)—Coretta (IRE) The Leigh Family
46 SOHGOL (IRE), ch f Singspiel (IRE)—Arruhan (IRE) Sheikh Mohammed Obaid Al Maktoum
47 STAUNCHLY (IRE), b f Namid—Sidelined (IRE) Allevamento Gialloblu
48 SWAINS BRIDGE, b c Swain (USA)—Saraa Ree (USA) Mr Christopher Wright
49 TERENZIUM (IRE), br c Cape Cross (IRE)—Tatanka (ITY) Scuderia Rencati Srl
50 TIMOTHEUS (USA), b c Diesis—Lilian Bayliss (IRE) Allevamento La Nuova Sbarra SRL
51 ZALIMAR (IRE), b f Montjeu (IRE)—Zanella (IRE) Mr B. J. Goldsmith & Mr & Mrs J. Wigan
52 ZEEBA (IRE), b f Barathea (IRE)—Donya Sheikh Mohammed Obaid Al Maktoum

TWO-YEAR-OLDS

53 B c 4/3 Lend A Hand—America Lontana (FR) (King's Theatre (IRE)) (27000) Mrs A. S. Silver
54 Ch c 9/4 Desert Prince (IRE)—Ardisia (USA) (Affirmed (USA)) The Duke of Devonshire
55 B c 5/3 Marju (IRE)—Arruhan (IRE) (Mujtahid (USA)) Sheikh Mohammed Obaid Al Maktoum
56 B f 18/1 Vettori (IRE)—Aymara (Darshaan) The Duke of Devonshire
57 B c 30/4 Machiavellian (USA)—Balalaika (Sadler's Wells (USA)) (70000) Castle Down Racing

MR L. M. CUMANI—continued

58 B c 13/2 Bahri (USA)—Balancoire (USA) (Diesis) (72000) **L. Marinopoulos**
59 BURGUNDY LOVER, b c 3/1 Montjeu (IRE)—
Personal Love (USA) (Diesis) (85000) **Mr Tim Steel & The Hon. Mrs Steel**
60 B c 14/4 Shinko Forest (IRE)—Changing Partners (Rainbow Quest (USA)) (52000) **Mrs A. S. Silver**
61 Ch f 11/4 Indian Ridge—
Courtlandt Queen (USA) (Deputy Minister (CAN)) (46000) **Allevamento La Nuova Sbarra SRL**
62 CROSBY HALL, b c 13/3 Compton Place—Alzianah (Alzao (USA)) (30000) **Allevamento Gialloblu**
63 Br gr c 18/4 Halling (USA)—Dali's Grey (Linamix (FR)) **Aston House Stud**
64 B c 26/3 Danehill (USA)—Dathiyna (IRE) (Kris) (127430) **Sheikh Mohammed Obaid Al Maktoum**
65 DIVO NERO (IRE), br c 2/4 Black Minnaloushe (USA)—
Backgammon Becky (USA) (Irish River (FR)) (30180) **Ms Marie Drion**
66 B c 20/1 In The Wings—Donya (Mill Reef (USA)) **Sheikh Mohammed Obaid Al Maktoum**
67 B f 4/3 Lujain (USA)—Fadhah (Mukaddamah (USA)) **Sheikh Mohammed Obaid Al Maktoum**
68 FALMASSIM, b c 25/2 Mozart (IRE)—Scostes (Cadeaux Genereux) **Scuderia Rencati Srl.**
69 FAMCRED, b f 17/1 Inchinor—Sumingasefa (Danehill (USA)) **Scuderia Rencati Srl.**
70 FAMILY ALBUM, b c 1/4 Polish Precedent (USA)—Photogenic (Midyan (USA)) (50000) **Normandie Stud**
71 FLUORESCENT, b f 28/1 Fantastic Light (USA)—Frangy (Sadler's Wells (USA)) **Fittocks Stud Ltd**
72 FUTUN, b c 12/2 In The Wings—Svanzega (Sharpen Up) **Scuderia Rencati Srl.**
73 GREEN TOBASCO, b c 18/4 Green Desert (USA)—
Hyperspectra (Rainbow Quest (USA)) (80000) **Castle Down Racing**
74 GREENWICH VILLAGE, b c 27/2 Mtoto—
D'azy (Persian Bold) (20000) **Mr Christopher Wright & The Hon Mrs J. M. Corbett**
75 B f 13/2 Cadeaux Genereux—Hatheethah (IRE) (Machiavellian (USA)) **Sheikh Mohammed Obaid Al Maktoum**
76 HEART OFTHE MATTER, b f 19/2 Rainbow Quest (USA)—
Silver Colours (USA) (Silver Hawk (USA)) **Mr Christopher Wright**
77 B f 21/2 Mark of Esteem (IRE)—Jumaireyah (Fairy King (USA)) **Sheikh Mohammed Obaid Al Maktoum**
78 KIBARA, b f 20/3 Sadler's Wells (USA)—Kithanga (IRE) (Darshaan) **Fittocks Stud Ltd**
79 KYOTO SUMMIT, ch c 7/2 Lomitas—Alligram (USA) (Alysheba (USA)) (52000) **Castle Down Racing**
80 MAIL EXPRESS (IRE), b f 1/3 Cape Cross (IRE)—
Mystic Tempo (El Gran Senor (USA)) **Ronchalon Racing (UK) Ltd**
81 MASTER AT ARMS, ch c 4/5 Grand Lodge—L'ideale (USA) (Alysheba (USA)) (60000) **Drones Racing**
82 MEZZO, b f 24/4 Singspiel (IRE)—Real Time (Polish Precedent (USA)) **Aston House Stud**
83 B f 8/4 King's Best (USA)—Mrs Ting (USA) (Lyphard (USA)) (115000) **Nicola Mahoney**
84 B c 30/4 Green Desert (USA)—On Call (Alleged (USA)) (70421) **Sheikh Mohammed Obaid Al Maktoum**
85 B f 1/5 Green Desert (USA)—One So Wonderful (Nashwan (USA)) **Helena Springfield Ltd**
86 PENTATONIC, b f 3/3 Giant's Causeway (USA)—
Fascinating Rhythm (Slip Anchor) (200000) **Helena Springfield Ltd**
87 PHEBE, b f 23/4 Sadler's Wells (USA)—Puce (Darshaan) **Fittocks Stud Ltd**
88 B f 3/2 Grand Lodge (USA)—Posta Vecchia (USA) (Rainbow Quest (USA)) (53655) **Equibreed Srl.**
89 SALESIN, ch c 19/4 Lomitas—Elisita (ARG) (Ride The Rails (USA)) (42000) **Scuderia Rencati Srl.**
90 SCIATIN (IRE), b c 19/5 Alhaarth (IRE)—Robalana (USA) (Wild Again (USA)) (90000) **Scuderia Rencati Srl.**
91 SCULASTIC, b c 16/4 Galileo (IRE)—Mutual Consent (IRE) (Reference Point) **Scuderia Rencati Srl.**
92 SIN CITY, b c 3/3 Sinndar (IRE)—Turn of A Century (Halling (USA)) (40000) **Castle Down Racing**
93 SPACEMAN, b c 19/4 In The Wings—Souk (IRE) (Ahonoora) **Fittocks Stud Ltd**
94 SPIA (USA), b f 24/2 Diesis—Space Time (FR) (Bering) **Fittocks Stud Ltd**
95 SULARINA (IRE), br f 20/2 Alhaarth (IRE)—
Quiet Counsel (IRE) (Law Society (USA)) (150000) **Ronchalon Racing (UK) Ltd**
96 SUMMER STAGE, b f 17/5 In The Wings—Summer Sonnet (Baillamont (USA)) **The Leigh Family**
97 SWIFTMARC (IRE), b c 7/4 In The Wings—
Shimmer (FR) (Green Dancer (USA)) (90000) **Ronchalon Racing (UK) Ltd**
98 B f 18/4 Medicean—Throw Away Line (USA) (Assert) (80000) **Nicola Mahoney**
99 TOPJEU (IRE), b c 20/5 Montjeu (IRE)—
Arabian Lass (SAF) (Al Mufti (USA)) (125000) **Ronchalon Racing (UK) Ltd**
100 TORMES, b c 1/6 Zafonic (USA)—Harefoot (Rainbow Quest (USA)) (15000) **Dario Hinojosa**
101 TRAFALGAR DAY, b c 23/2 Mark of Esteem (IRE)—Rosy Sunset (IRE) (Red Sunset) **Bill Paton-Smith**
102 VALERIE, b f 17/3 Sadler's Wells (USA)—Horatia (IRE) (Machiavellian (USA)) **The Leigh Family**
103 Ch f 13/4 Pivotal—Wenge (USA) (Housebuster (USA)) (134138) **Ronchalon Racing (UK) Ltd**

Other Owners: Anne Lees-Jones, S. Cockrill, R .Stevenson, J. L. Megevand, D. B. Murrell, Sir Eric Parker, G. Robotti, The Duke Of Roxburghe, P. G. S. Silver, M. Weinfeld, Miss H. S. Weinfeld.

Assistant Trainer: Guillermo Arizkorreta

Jockey (flat): N. Mackay. **Apprentice:** A. Hamblett. **Amateur:** Mrs S. Cumani, Miss F. Cumani.

138 **MR P. D. CUNDELL, Compton**
Postal: **Roden House, Wallingford Road, Compton, Newbury, Berkshire, RG20 6QR.**
Contacts: **PHONE (01635) 578267 FAX (01635) 578267**

1 **ANDALUZA (IRE)**, 4, b f Mujadil (USA)—Hierarchy **P. Rosas**
2 **IFFY**, 4, b g Orpen (USA)—Hopesay **N. Johnson-Hill**
3 **LADY McNAIR**, 5, b m Sheikh Albadou—Bonita Bee **I. M. Brown**
4 **MAN THE GATE**, 6, b g Elmaamul (USA)—Girl At The Gate **J. G. Morley**
5 **NAWOW**, 5, b g Blushing Flame (USA)—Fair Test **I. M. Brown**
6 **TARANAKI**, 7, b h Delta Dancer—Miss Ticklepenny **E. D. Evers**
7 **THREE DAYS REIGN (IRE)**, 11, br g Camden Town—Little Treat **Entre-Nous**

THREE-YEAR-OLDS

8 **APHRODELTA**, b f Delta Dancer—Mouton (IRE) **E. D. Evers**
9 **FRIDA**, b f Lujain (USA)—Ishona **P. Rosas**
10 **KINTBURY CROSS**, b g Kylian (USA)—Cebwob **Miss M. C. Fraser**
11 **LOITOKITOK**, b g Piccolo—Bonita Bee **I. M. Brown**
12 **PAX ROMANA (IRE)**, b f Alzao (USA)—Forest Lair **N. Johnson-Hill**

TWO-YEAR-OLDS

13 **DON PIETRO**, b c 8/4 Bertolini (USA)—Silver Spell (Aragon) (14000) **P. Rosas**
14 **MCNAIROBI**, b f 12/4 Josr Algarhoud (IRE)—Bonita Bee (King of Spain) **I. M. Brown**

Other Owners: Mrs S. M. Booker, W. M. Dobson, M. R. Kent.

139 **MR M. CUNNINGHAM, Navan**
Postal: **Gormanstown Stables, Kildalkey, Navan, Co.Meath, Ireland.**
Contacts: **PHONE + 353 (0) 46 94 31672 FAX +353 (0) 46 94 31467**

1 **BAMPA (IRE)**, 6, b h Welsh Term—Bold Lillian (IRE) **Mr Herb M. Stanley**
2 **COCCINELLE (IRE)**, 7, b m Great Marquess—Nuit d'ete (USA) **Brendan Kelly**
3 **CRAIGTOWN BOY (IRE)**, 6, b g Oscar (IRE)—Yarra Glen **Mr John McKeague**
4 **CUPID'S BOW**, 5, b m Kris—Lady Cinders (IRE) **Mrs Paul Shanahan**
5 **FINSBURY PARK (IRE)**, 5, b g Executive Perk—Liscahill View (IRE)
6 **FREE SURFING (FR)**, 4, b br g Freedom Cry—Surfing France (FR)
7 **HARD TO HANDLE (IRE)**, 5, b g Dr Massini (IRE)—Lady Callianire (IRE) **Mr Herb M. Stanley**
8 **HOOKEDONAFEELING (IRE)**, 7, ch m Shernazar—Fireblends (IRE) **Mr M. Cunningham**
9 **INDIAN'S LANDING (IRE)**, 4, b c Barathea (USA)—
We've Just Begun (USA) **Herb M. Stanley & Mrs Michael Cunningham**
10 **INISHDUBH (IRE)**, 5, b g Turtle Island (IRE)—Bold Lillian (IRE) **Banagher Glen Syndicate**
11 **LAURELDEAN (IRE)**, 7, b g Shernazar—Power Run **Mr M. Cunningham**
12 **LEGENDSOFTHEFALL (IRE)**, 6, b m Arctic Lord—Glen Dieu **Mrs Michael Cunningham**
13 **NANCYS BRIDGE (IRE)**, 6, b br m Old Vic—St Cristoph **Canal Racing Syndicate**
14 **NORTHSIDE (IRE)**, 7, b g King's Ride—Atlantic Hope **F. Connon**
15 **ROCK SNOW DROP (IRE)**, 6, b m Oscar (IRE)—Pre-Let (IRE) **P. G. Molony & Charles O'Reill-Hyland**
16 **SAHARA PRINCE (IRE)**, 5, b g Desert King (IRE)—Chehana **Herb M. Stanley**
17 **SUPREME BEING (IRE)**, 8, b g Supreme Leader—Parsonetta **Mrs B. Lynch**
18 **TARA'S GIFT (IRE)**, 7, b m Midhish—Bold Lillian (IRE) **Miss Tara Cunningham**
19 **TIERNAN'S TRIX (IRE)**, 4, b c Orpen (USA)—Sherabi (IRE) **Herb M. Stanley**

THREE-YEAR-OLDS

20 **ABRAHAM (IRE)**, b g Orpen (USA)—We've Just Begun (USA) **Herb M. Stanley & Mrs Michael Cunningham**
21 B f Leading Counsel (USA)—Glen Dieu **Mrs Michael Cunningham**
22 **HAITI (IRE)**, b f Orpen (USA)—Bold Lillian (IRE) **Alan Townsend**
23 **LADY VAUGHAN (IRE)**, ch f Orpen (USA)—Holly's Gold (IRE) **Mrs Brian Lynch**
24 B c Leading Counsel (USA)—Noeleen's Delight (IRE) **Mrs Michael Cunningham**

TWO-YEAR-OLDS

25 B f 7/4 Orpen (USA)—Holly's Gold (IRE) (Mac's Imp (USA)) **Brian Lynch**
26 Ch f 29/5 Barathea (IRE)—
We've Just Begun (USA) (Huguenot (USA)) **Herb M. Stanley & Mrs Michael Cunningham**

Assistant Trainer: Tara Cunningham

140 **MR W. S. CUNNINGHAM, Yarm**
Postal: Embleton Farm, Garbutts Lane, Hutton Rudby, Yarm, Cleveland, TS15 0DN.
Contacts: **PHONE (01642) 701290 MOBILE (07885) 158703**

1 **AMALFI COAST**, 6, b g Emperor Jones (USA)—Legend's Daughter (USA) **Ann and David Bell**
2 **CAPPED FOR VICTORY (USA)**, 4, b g Red Ransom (USA)—Nazoo (IRE) **Ann and David Bell**
3 **PLAYFUL DANE (IRE)**, 8, b g Dolphin Street (FR)—Omicida (IRE) **Ann and David Bell**
4 **SOLINIKI**, 4, b g Danzero (AUS)—Pride of My Heart **Ann and David Bell**

Assistant Trainer: Vicky Cunningham

141 **MR K. CUNNINGHAM-BROWN, Stockbridge**
Postal: Danebury Place, Stockbridge, Hampshire, SO20 6JX.
Contacts: **PHONE (01264) 781061 FAX (01264) 781061 MOBILE (07802) 500059**
E-MAIL kcb@unicheq.com

1 **HERODOTUS**, 7, b g Zafonic (USA)—Thalestria (FR) **A. J. Richards**
2 **MANGUS (IRE)**, 11, b g Mac's Imp (USA)—Holly Bird **Danebury Racing Stables Ltd**
3 **WHIPLASH (IRE)**, 4, b g Orpen (USA)—La Colombari (ITY) **Danebury Racing Stables Ltd**

THREE-YEAR-OLDS

4 **EWAR FINCH (FR)**, b f Kayf Tara—Ewar Empress (IRE) **A. J. Richards**
5 **YELLOW JERSEY**, b f Mark of Esteem (IRE)—La Bicyclette (FR) **A. J. Richards**

TWO-YEAR-OLDS

6 **ESPECIALLY YOURS (IRE)**, ch f 26/4 Beckett (IRE)—Khaladja (IRE) (Akarad (FR)) (5000) **Danebury Racing Stables Ltd**

Assistant Trainer: Ricky Todd

Jockey (flat): C. Catlin, D. O'Neil. **Jockey (NH):** B. Fenton.

142 **MR B. J. CURLEY, Newmarket**
Postal: 104A Centre Drive, Newmarket, Suffolk, CB8 8AP.
Contacts: **PHONE (01638) 668755**

1 **BE TELLING (IRE)**, 6, b g Oscar (IRE)—Manhattan King (IRE) **P. A. Byrne**
2 **BOLD PHOENIX (IRE)**, 4, b c Dr Fong (USA)—Subya **Mrs B. J. Curley**
3 **CRISTOFORO (IRE)**, 8, b g Perugino (USA)—Red Barons Lady (IRE) **P. A. Byrne**
4 **LILLEBROR (GER)**, 7, b g Top Waltz (FR)—Lady Soliciti (GER) **P. A. Byrne**
5 **MAD MAURICE**, 4, ch g Grand Lodge (USA)—Amarella (FR) **P. A. Byrne**
6 **NDOLA**, 6, b g Emperor Jones (USA)—Lykoa **Mrs B. J. Curley**
7 **SANDOKAN (GER)**, 4, b g Tiger Hill (IRE)—Suivez (FR) **Mrs B. J. Curley**

Assistant Trainer: Andrew Stringer

Jockey (flat): T. P. Queally. **Jockey (NH):** Paul Maloney.

143 **MR R. CURTIS, Lambourn**
Postal: Delamere Stables, Baydon Road, Lambourn, Hungerford, Berkshire, RG17 8NT.
Contacts: **PHONE (01488) 73007 FAX (01488) 73909 MOBILE (07836) 320690**
E-MAIL rcurtislambourn@aol.com WEBSITE www.rogercurtis.com

1 **ALDERBROOK GIRL (IRE)**, 5, b br m Alderbrook—Trassey Bridge **IPO Racing Partnership**
2 **ALMA BAY**, 5, ch m Karinga Bay—Almanot **Guildings Racing Club**
3 **CANNY SCOT**, 8, b g Slip Anchor—Pomade **Studley Racing Partnership**
4 **COPPERMALT (USA)**, 7, b g Affirmed (USA)—Poppy Carew (USA) **Collective Dreamers**
5 **FRAMLINGHAM**, 10, gr g Out of Hand—Sugar Hall **Miss B. J. Crouch**
6 **KROISOS (IRE)**, 7, b g Kris—Lydia Maria **Mrs R. A. Smith**
7 5, B m Teenoso (USA)—Miss Muire **P. A. Sells**
8 **NORTH POINT (IRE)**, 7, b g Definite Article—Friendly Song **Heart Of The South Racing**
9 **PAULA LANE**, 5, b m Factual (USA)—Colfax Classic **Mrs R. A. Smith**

MR R. CURTIS—continued

10 **POPSI'S CLOGGS,** 13, ch g Joli Wasfi (USA)—Popsi's Poppet **Mrs K. M. Curtis**
11 **SAMOLIS (IRE),** 4, b g College Chapel—Joyful Music **D. Harper**
12 **WOTAN (IRE),** 7, ch g Wolfhound (USA)—Triple Tricks (IRE) **A J J Racing**

THREE-YEAR-OLDS

13 **CAPE VENUS (IRE),** b f Cape Cross (IRE)—Lady Helen (IRE) **Ms Daphne Downes**
14 **MISS DEFYING,** b f Shambo—Dugy **The Mystified Partnership**

Other Owners: Jim Stanton, Mrs C. Simms, P. New, R. Bedford, S. Stockdale, C. Dick, Mrs C. Stevens, T. Parker, E. Downer, P. Harty, A. Braybrook, J. Hewish, L. Sturrock, M. Watkins, Mrs F. Boland, D. Hampton, B. Chegwidden, Mrs E. Wall, A. Rawlinson, C. Line, A. Fenn, R. Dyett, R. Last, K. Williams, R. Hine, D. Hickman, R. Walter, N. Howe, D. Patton, J. Gray, O. Boylan, A. Boylan, G. Minshall, A. White, P. Walker, Mrs V. Roach, P. Burns, D. Cutler, Andy Smith, C. Winn, R. W. J. Davis, G. Horley, Mrs M. Andrews, D. Chandler, C. H. Foster, T. Weller, T. Wynne, J. Sweet, Mr S. M. Smith, Miss Z. Lee, Mrs R. Surman, R. Cook, R. Byerley, R. Crow, T. Coyne, Mrs B. Curtis, Ms L. M. Barton, M. Carr, K. P. Jeffs, J. Johnson, B. Newman, J. R. Penny, Mrs C. Penny.

Assistant Trainer: Dawn Gibbs

Jockey (NH): T. Doyle.

144
MR T. A. K. CUTHBERT, Carlisle
Postal: **26 Eden Grange, Little Corby, Carlisle, Cumbria, CA4 8QW.**
Contacts: **PHONE** (01228) 560822 **STABLES** (01228) 561328 **FAX** (01228) 560822
MOBILE (07747) 843344

1 **CEZZARO (IRE),** 7, ch g Ashkalani (IRE)—Sept Roses (USA) **Mrs J. Cuthbert**
2 **EXALTED (IRE),** 12, b g High Estate—Heavenward (USA) **Mrs Elva Maxwell & Mr Roy Thorburn**
3 **GIVUSACUDDLE,** 12, ch m Little Wolf—Royal Marie **Mr T. A. K. Cuthbert**
4 **HEBENUS,** 6, b g Hamas (IRE)—Stinging Nettle **Mrs J. Cuthbert**
5 **SIREN SONG (IRE),** 14, b g Warning—Nazwa **Mrs J. Cuthbert**
6 **WAFIR (IRE),** 13, b g Scenic—Taniokey **Mr T. A. K. Cuthbert**

Amateur: Miss H. Cuthbert.

145
MR L. A. DACE, Billingshurst
Postal: **Copped Hall Farm, Okehurst Lane, Billingshurst, West Sussex, RH14 9HR.**
Contacts: **OFFICE** (01403) 780889 **MOBILE** (07949) 401085

1 **ASCOOLASICE,** 7, b g Thethingaboutitis (USA)—Frozen Pipe **A. P. Brewer**
2 **BROOMERS HILL (IRE),** 5, b g Sadler's Wells—Bella Vitessa (IRE) **A. P. Brewer**
3 **FOXTROTROMEOYANKEE,** 5, b g Tragic Role (USA)—Hope Chest **The Not So Magnificent Seven**
4 **IT'S GOT BUCKLEYS,** 6, b g El Conquistador—Saucey Pup **Ms C. Storey**
5 **QUEL FONTENAILLES (FR),** 7, b g Tel Quel (FR)—Sissi Fontenailles (FR) **Let's Have Fun Syndicate**
6 **RED RETURN (IRE),** 8, ch g Bob's Return (IRE)—Kerrie's Pearl **Mrs Y. P. Davess**

Other Owners: Miss L. Brewer, Mr G. Collacott, MR L. A. Dace, C. R. Eden.

Assistant Trainer: Miss L Brewer

Conditional: Mr Derek Laverty. **Amateur:** Miss L. Brewer.

146
MRS H. DALTON, Shifnal
Postal: **Norton House, Norton, Shifnal, Shropshire, TF11 9ED.**
Contacts: **PHONE** (01952) 730322 **FAX** (01952) 730722 **MOBILE** (07785) 972131
E-MAIL heatherdalton@shropshire.fslife.co.uk

1 **ACTIVE ACCOUNT (USA),** 8, b br g Unaccounted For (USA)—Ameritop (USA) **Mrs H. Dalton**
2 **AVADI (IRE),** 7, b g Un Desperado (FR)—Flamewood **Mrs J. M. T. Martin**
3 **BEARAWAY (IRE),** 8, b g Fourstars Allstar (USA)—Cruiseaway **Paternosters Racing**
4 **BOBBY BROWN (IRE),** 5, b g Insan (USA)—Miss Sally Knox (IRE) **P. J. Hughes Developments Ltd**
5 **BRIDEPARK TWO,** 5, b m Rakaposhi King—Bridepark Rose (IRE) **T. J. Segrue**
6 **BROADBROOK LASS,** 11, ch m Broadsword (USA)—Netherbrook Lass **M. H. Ings**

MRS H. DALTON—continued

7 **BROKE ROAD (IRE)**, 9, b g Deploy—Shamaka **S. C. Appelbee**
8 **CHAPEL BAY**, 5, b m Afflora (IRE)—Jack It In **G. B. Davies & Miss Elizabeth S. Smith**
9 **CRACBOUMWIZ (FR)**, 5, b g Baby Turk—Ellapampa (FR) **J. R. Hales**
10 **FEARLESS MEL (IRE)**, 11, b g Mandalus—Milan Pride **The Leppington Partnership**
11 **HEHASALIFE (IRE)**, 8, b g Safety Catch (USA)—America River (IRE) **Norton House Racing**
12 **HENRY'S PRIDE (IRE)**, 5, ch g Old Vic—Hightown Girl (IRE) **P. J. Hughes Developments Ltd**
13 **JOUR DE MEE (FR)**, 8, ch g Beyssac (FR)—Une de Mee (FR) **D. M. Williams**
14 **L'ORAGE LADY (IRE)**, 7, ch m Glacial Storm (USA)—Commanche Glen (IRE) **Edwards, Simpson & Dalton**
15 **LAKE IMPERIAL (IRE)**, 4, b g Imperial Ballet (IRE)—Lakes of Killarney (IRE) **W. J. Swinnerton & Mr R. Edwards**
16 **LORD OF THE HILL (IRE)**, 10, b g Dromod Hill—Telegram Mear **T. J. Segrue**
17 **MAJOR BLADE (GER)**, 7, b g Dashing Blade—Misniniski **G. Lloyd, G. Allmond, R. Barrs**
18 **MALMO BOY (IRE)**, 6, gr g Roselier (FR)—Charming Mo (IRE) **M. B. Jones**
19 **MCQUEEN (IRE)**, 5, ch g Barathea (IRE)—Bibliotheque (USA) **Mr R. Edwards and Mr W. J. Swinnerton**
20 **NEWS MAKER (IRE)**, 9, b g Good Thyne (USA)—Announcement **Mrs C. L. Shaw**
21 **NITE FOX (IRE)**, 6, ch m Anshan—New Talent **Mrs A. Beard, Miss M. Knapper & Mr J. Dalton**
22 **NOT FOR DIAMONDS (IRE)**, 5, b g Arctic Lord—Black-Crash **M. J. Scott**
23 **OLLIJAY**, 4, b g Wolfhound (USA)—Anthem Flight (USA) **B. M. Fletcher**
24 **PRINCESS ISMENE**, 4, b f Sri Pekan (USA)—Be Practical **P. J. Hughes Developments Ltd**
25 **REVERSE SWING**, 8, b m Charmer—Milly Kelly **The Herons Partnership**
26 **SON OF LIGHT (IRE)**, 10, br g Hollow Hand—Leaney Kamscort **Mrs R. A. N. Bateman**
27 **SQUANTUM (IRE)**, 8, b g Roselier (FR)—Coole Eile (IRE) **The Leppington Partnership**
28 **TERRE DE JAVA (FR)**, 7, b g Cadoudal (FR)—Terre d'argent (FR) **Miss L. J. Hales**
29 **TEST OF FRIENDSHIP**, 8, br g Roselier (FR)—Grease Pot **Severn River Racing**
30 **WYCHWAY (USA)**, 4, ch g Swain (IRE)—Garden Rose (IRE) **Norton Natives**
31 **ZONIC BOOM (FR)**, 5, b br g Zafonic (USA)—Rosi Zambotti (IRE)

THREE-YEAR-OLDS

32 **RONSARD (IRE)**, b g Spectrum (IRE)—Touche-A-Tout (IRE) **Mr R. Edwards and Mr W. J. Swinnerton**

Other Owners: Mrs A. J. Beard, A. N. Dalton, W. D. Edwards, D. M. Hughes, Mrs C. A. Leppington, J. A. C. Leppington, W. D. Leppington.

Jockey (flat): J. F. Egan, I. Mongan, S. Sanders. **Jockey (NH):** R. Johnson. **Conditional:** P. Merrigan, T. Greenway. **Amateur:** Mr R. Burton, Richard Spate.

---

147 **MR P. T. DALTON, Burton-on-Trent**
Postal: **Dovecote Cottage, Bretby Park, Bretby, Burton-On-Trent, Staffordshire, DE15 0RB.**
Contacts: **HOME/OFFICE (01283) 221922 FAX (01283) 229657 MOBILE (07774) 240753**
E-MAIL daltonpauldalton@aol.co.uk

1 **BLAZING HILLS**, 9, ch g Shaab—Cottage Blaze **Mrs J. M. T. Martin**
2 **BOBBI ROSE RED**, 8, ch m Bob Back (USA)—Lady Rosanna **Mrs J. M. T. Martin**
3 **DONIE DOOLEY (IRE)**, 7, ch g Be My Native (USA)—Bridgeofallen (IRE) **Mrs J. M. T. Martin**
4 **SIR BOB (IRE)**, 13, br g Aristocracy—Wilden **Mrs L. Farmer**
5 **TONY'S PRIDE**, 5, b g Alderbrook—Lucia Forte **Mrs L. Farmer**

Other Owners: D. R. Martin.

Assistant Trainer: Susan Dalton

---

148 **MR DECLAN DALY, Newmarket**
Postal: **Machell Place, Old Station Road, Newmarket, Suffolk, CB8 8DW.**
Contacts: **OFFICE/FAX (01638) 603005 HOME (01638) 602926 MOBILE (07812) 084523**
E-MAIL daly580@hotmail.com

1 **HILLTOP RHAPSODY**, 4, b f Bin Ajwaad (IRE)—Saferjel
2 **LEOBALLERO**, 5, ch g Lion Cavern (USA)—Ball Gown
3 **NOUNOU**, 4, b c Starborough—Watheeqah (USA)
4 **ROYAL FLIGHT**, 4, b c Royal Applause—Duende
5 **SINGLET**, 4, ch c Singspiel (IRE)—Ball Gown
6 **TICTACTOE**, 4, b f Komaite (USA)—White Valley (IRE)

MR DECLAN DALY—continued

THREE-YEAR-OLDS

7 **ARNIE DE BURGH,** br c Amfortas (IRE)—Align
8 B c Alhaarth (IRE)—Charmed Lady
9 **ELOPEMENT (IRE),** ch f Machiavellian (USA)—Melanzane
10 **GLADS IMAGE,** ch f Handsome Ridge—Secret So And So
11 **GLINTING DESERT (IRE),** b f Desert Prince (IRE)—Dazzling Park (IRE)
12 **HARRY MAY,** b c Lujain (USA)—Mrs May
13 **MAGIC BRACELET,** b f Inchinor—Sharanella
14 **MINK MITTEN,** b f Polish Precedent (USA)—Trefoil (FR)
15 **MISSATACAMA (IRE),** b f Desert Style (IRE)—Delta Town (USA)
16 **PAR JEU,** b f Montjeu (IRE)—Musical Twist (USA)
17 **SINGALONG,** b f Singspiel (IRE)—No Frills (IRE)
18 **SWORDS,** b c Vettori (IRE)—Pomorie (IRE)
19 **THREE WRENS (IRE),** b f Second Empire (IRE)—Three Terns (USA)

TWO-YEAR-OLDS

20 **ATWIRL,** b f 30/4 Pivotal—Amidst (Midyan (USA))
21 B f 2/4 Mark of Esteem (IRE)—Ball Gown (Jalmood (USA)) (5500)
22 B c 17/1 Galileo (IRE)—Brigadiers Bird (IRE) (Mujadil (USA))
23 B f 20/3 Definite Article—Chloe (IRE) (Green Desert (USA)) (6036)
24 **FULFILL,** ch f 13/2 Insatiable (IRE)—Les Hurlants (IRE) (Barathea (IRE))
25 B f 5/4 Desert Style (IRE)—Hayward (Indian Ridge) (6706)
26 Br c 17/2 Mozart (IRE)—In Full Cry (USA) (Seattle Slew (USA)) (50000)
27 Ch f 18/4 Night Shift (USA)—Sainte Adresse (USA) (Steinlen)

Owners: Mr S. Monahan, Sue Cawthorn, Mrs C. White, Mr A. Visintin, Mr L. Fisher, Mr K. S. Chambers, Mr Ian Wood, Mr P. C. Turrell, Mr R. Moore, Miss K. Walsh, Mr Greg Forrest, Mr K. T. Chambers, MR Declan Daly, Miss A. J. Farrell, C. V. Lines, M. C. Mason, Mr G. Noble, Mrs Rosalynd Norman, Miss M. Smart, Mrs D. M. Swinburn, J. M. Troy, Mr R. Upton, Mr G. B. U. Way, G. S. Weir, James Wigan, Mrs A. Wigan, Sir Evelyn de Rothschild.

Assistant Trainer: C V Lines

Jockey (flat): S. W. Kelly, J. Murtagh. **Amateur:** Mr Matthew Smith.

---

149 **MR H. D. J. DALY, Ludlow**
Postal: **Downton Hall Stables, Ludlow, Shropshire, SY8 3DX.**
Contacts: **OFFICE (01584) 873688 FAX (01584) 873525 MOBILES (07710) 973042/(07720) 074544**
E-MAIL hdjdaly@aol.com

1 **ALDERBURN,** 6, b g Alderbrook—Threewaygirl **Mrs D. P. G. Flory**
2 **ANKLES BACK (IRE),** 8, b g Seclude (USA)—Pedalo **R. Bailey**
3 **BILLYVODDAN (IRE),** 6, b g Accordion—Derryclare **T. J. Hemmings**
4 **BONUS BRIDGE (IRE),** 10, b g Executive Perk—Corivia **Viscountess Knutsford**
5 **BRIERY FOX (IRE),** 7, ch g Phardante (FR)—Briery Gale **Vicky Jeyes, Helen Plumbly, Jane Trafford**
6 **CAMPAIGN CHARLIE,** 5, b g Rakaposhi King—Inesdela **P. J. H. Wills**
7 **CLEVER THYNE (IRE),** 8, b g Good Thyne (USA)—Clever Milly **Mrs A. Churton**
8 **COMBE FLOREY,** 6, ch m Alflora (IRE)—Celtic Slave **B. G. Hellyer**
9 **COURSING RUN (IRE),** 9, ch g Glacial Storm (USA)—Let The Hare Run (IRE) **The Hon Mrs M. J. Heber-Percy**
10 **FERIMON,** 6, gr g Terimon—Rhyming Moppet **Strachan, Myddleton, Gabb, Stoddart, Lawson**
11 **FIERY PEACE,** 8, ch g Tina's Pet—Burning Mirage **R. M. Kirkland**
12 **GREEN TANGO,** 6, br g Greensmith—Furry Dance (USA) **Mrs Strachan, Gabb, Lady Barlow & Harford**
13 **HAND INN HAND,** 9, b g Alflora (IRE)—Deep Line **Patrick Burling Developments Ltd**
14 **HAUNTED HOUSE,** 5, ch g Opera Ghost—My Home **Gibson, Goddard, Hamer & Hawkes**
15 **IN ACCORD,** 6, ch g Accordion—Henry's True Love **T. F. F. Nixon**
16 5, B m Moscow Society (USA)—Irene Good-Night (IRE) **Fire Height Ltd & M. O'Flynn**
17 **IRONSIDE (IRE),** 6, b g Mister Lord (USA)—The Helmet (IRE) **Mrs A Reid Scott & Mrs G Leigh**
18 **IT'S IN THE STARS,** 5, b g Teenoso (USA)—Sail By The Stars **T. F. F. Nixon**
19 **JAKARI (FR),** 8, b g Apeldoorn (FR)—Tartifume II (FR) **The Earl Cadogan**
20 **JAUNTY TIMES,** 5, b g Luso—Jaunty June **J. B. Sumner**
21 **JUDAIC WAYS,** 11, b g Rudimentary (USA)—Judeah **Mr D. Sandells & Mr T. Broderick**
22 **KNOCK DOWN (IRE),** 6, b m Oscar (IRE)—Bottle A Knock (IRE) **Patrick Burling Developments Ltd**
23 **LANCASTRIAN JET (IRE),** 14, b g Lancastrian—Kilmurray Jet **The Hon Mrs M. J. Heber-Percy**
24 **LIVERPOOL ECHO (FR),** 5, b g Poliglote—Miss Echo **Million in Mind Partnership**

MR H. D. J. DALY—continued

25 **LONG WALK (IRE)**, 8, br g King's Ride—Seanaphobal Lady **The Earl Cadogan**
26 **LOUGH DANTE (IRE)**, 7, b g Phardante (FR)—Shannon Lough (IRE) **M. Lowe**
27 4, B g Mister Mat (FR)—Maid of Glenduragh (IRE) **M. Lowe**
28 **MAKE HASTE SLOWLY**, 8, b g Terimon—Henry's True Love **T. F. F. Nixon**
29 **MARTHA'S KINSMAN (IRE)**, 6, b g Petoski—Martha's Daughter **Exors of the Late M. Ward-Thomas**
30 **MASTER SAM (IRE)**, 5, b g Supreme Leader—Basically (IRE) **T. J. Hemmings**
31 **MENPHIS BEURY (FR)**, 5, b g Art Bleu—Pampa Star (FR) **R. M. Kirkland**
32 **MIGHTY MAN (FR)**, 5, b m Saddlers' Hall (IRE)—Opera Hat (IRE) **Ladywood Farm**
33 **OPERA HALL**, 5, b m Saddlers' Hall (IRE)—Opera Hat (IRE) **Ladywood Farm**
34 **PALARSHAN (FR)**, 7, b br g Darshaan—Palavera (FR) **Mrs A. L. Wood**
35 **PORTHILLY BAY**, 5, b g Primitive Rising (USA)—Threewaygirl **Mrs D. P. G. Flory**
36 **PRINCIPE AZZURRO (FR)**, 4, b g Pistolet Bleu (IRE)—Massalia (GER) **W. J. Tolhurst**
37 **RASH MOMENT (FR)**, 6, b g Rudimentary (USA)—Ashura (FR) **W. J. Tolhurst**
38 **ROBERTY BOB (IRE)**, 10, ch g Bob Back (USA)—Inesdela **P. J. H. Wills**
39 **RUMBLING BRIDGE**, 4, ch g Air Express (IRE)—Rushing River (USA) **The Earl Cadogan**
40 **SAAFEND ROCKET (IRE)**, 7, b g Distinctly North (USA)—Simple Annie **Ludlow Racing Partnership**
41 **SADDLERS EXPRESS**, 4, b f Saddlers' Hall (IRE)—Swift Conveyance (IRE) **Mrs A. L. Wood**
42 **SALOPIAN**, 5, b g Rakaposhi King—Dalbeattie **The Shropshire Lads Syndicate**
43 **STAR ANGLER (IRE)**, 7, b g Supreme Leader—So Pink (IRE) **Viscountess Knutsford**
44 **SUPREME HOPE (USA)**, 6, b g Supreme Leader—Flaming Hope (IRE) **Mrs A. Churton**
45 **THIEVERY**, 4, gr g Terimon—Piracy **Mrs A. W. Timpson**
46 **THISISYOURLIFE (IRE)**, 7, b g Lord Americo—Your Life **The Earl Cadogan**
47 **TRANSATLANTIC (USA)**, 7, gr g Dumaani (USA)—Viendra (USA) **Mrs A. W. Timpson**
48 **TROODOS VALLEY (IRE)**, 6, b g Executive Perk—Valleymay (IRE) **D. Sandells**
49 **WATERBERG (IRE)**, 10, b g Sadler's Wells (USA)—Pretoria **R. M. Kirkland**
50 **WATERLOO SON (IRE)**, 5, b g Luso—Waterloo Sunset **T. J. Hemmings**

Other Owners: Susan Barlow, T. Broderick, A. R. Bromley, MR H. D. J. Daly, E. R. Hanbury, R. L. C. Hartley, Mrs D. J. G. Hellyer, Mr J. Lacey, Mrs J. Minton, Mr F. Perry, Mrs A. Reid Scott, D. Sandells, M. J. Saunders, Mrs J. Saunders, Mrs E. M. Strachan.

Assistant Trainer: Tom Gretton

Jockey (NH): M. Bradburne, R. Johnson. **Conditional:** J. P. Byrne. **Amateur:** Mr M. Barber.

---

150 MR V. R. A. DARTNALL, Barnstaple
Postal: Higher Shutscombe Farm, Charles, Brayford, Barnstaple, Devon, EX32 7PU.
Contacts: **PHONE** (01598) 710280 **FAX** (01598) 710708 **MOBILE** (07974) 374272
E-MAIL victor-dartnall@dartnall-racing.freeserve.co.uk **WEBSITE** victordartnall.co.uk

1 **BUSINESSMONEY JAKE**, 4, b g Petoski—Cloverjay **Business Money Limited**
2 **DUSIT DOWN (IRE)**, 6, b g Anshan—Windy Road **Nick Viney**
3 **HAWADETH**, 10, ch g Machiavellian (USA)—Ghzaalh (USA) **Bill Hinge & Paul Jackson**
4 **HERE'S JOHNNY (IRE)**, 6, ch g Presenting—Treble Base (IRE) **The Big Boys Toys Partnership**
5 **HIRED GUN (IRE)**, 6, b g Needle Gun (IRE)—Monahullen Rose (IRE) **The Hired Gun Partnership**
6 **HOLLYWOOD**, 4, b f Bin Ajwaad (IRE)—Raaha **A. Hordle**
7 **ISOU (FR)**, 9, ch g Dom Alco (FR)—Aghate de Saisy (FR) **The Isou Partnership**
8 **JOKE CLUB**, 4, b g Inchinor—Kicka **The Double P Partnership**
9 **KARANJA**, 6, b g Karinga Bay—Proverbial Rose **D. G. Staddon**
10 **LE BRIAR SOUL (IRE)**, 5, b g Luso—El Moss (IRE) **Cape Codders**
11 **LORD SAM (IRE)**, 9, b br g Supreme Leader—Russian Gale (IRE) **Plain Peeps**
12 **MOUNT CLERIGO (IRE)**, 7, b g Supreme Leader—Fair Ava (IRE) **S. Andrew**
13 **NOCTURNALLY**, 5, b g Octagonal (NZ)—Arletty **The Owl Society**
14 **PHILOMENA**, 6, b m Bedford (USA)—Mandalay Miss **Dorset Racing**
15 **RUSSIAN LORD (IRE)**, 6, b g Topanoora—Russian Gale (IRE) **Plain Peeps**
16 **SILKWOOD TOP (IRE)**, 6, b g Norwich—Brave Mum **Mr O. C. R. Wynne & Mrs S. J. Wynne**
17 **SPRINGFIELD BELLE**, 6, b m El Conquistador—Corrie's Girl **Mrs L. M. Northover**
18 **VINGIS PARK (IRE)**, 7, b g Old Vic—Lady Glenbank **Nick Viney**
19 5, Br m Oscar (IRE)—Walkers Lady (IRE) **Mr V. R. A. Dartnall**
20 **WEST HILL GAIL (IRE)**, 6, b m Roselier (FR)—V'soske Gale (IRE) **D. G. Staddon**
21 **YOUNG DANCER (IRE)**, 7, b g Eurobus—Misquested **D. G. Staddon**

Other Owners: G. A. Dove, Mrs V. A. Forbes, Mr C. W. Hannam, Mrs J. N. Hillary, S. R. James, Mr C. G. Lintott, D. Morgan, M. C. Smith, Mrs A. J. Vardey, Mr R. I. Walker, Mr D. C. Willis, Miss A. J. Woolley, Mr A. R. Wright, Mr J. R. de Meo.

Assistant Trainer: G A Dartnall

Jockey (NH): J. Culloty.

151 MISS J. S. DAVIS, Chipping Sodbury
Postal: **Mousewell Farm, Codrington, Chipping Sodbury, Bristol.**
Contacts: **PHONE/FAX (01454) 323838 MOBILE (07879) 811535**
E-MAIL davisjo_007@hotmail.com

1 **BOSWORTH BOURN (IRE)**, 5, b g Aahsaylad—Pastinas Lass **J. L. Marriott**
2 4, Ch f Aahsaylad—De-Veers Currie (IRE) **Mrs M. A. Davis**
3 **LOWE GO**, 5, b g First Trump—Hotel California (IRE) **Oldfield Business Services Ltd**
4 **LUDERE (IRE)**, 10, ch g Desse Zenny (USA)—White Jasmin **J. Heaney**
5 **MAXILLA (IRE)**, 5, b br m Lahib (USA)—Lacinia **Mr K. B. Hodges**
6 **MEEHAN (IRE)**, 5, b br g Spectrum (IRE)—Seeds of Doubt (IRE) **J. L. Marriott**
7 **PERHAPS THIS TIME (IRE)**, 6, b g Flemensfirth (USA)—Royal Chapeau (IRE) **Mrs L. J. Robins**
8 **TYUP POMPEY (IRE)**, 4, ch g Docksider (USA)—Cindy's Baby **David & Lesley Byrne**

THREE-YEAR-OLDS

9 **GLOWING DAWN (IRE)**, b f Definite Article—Alizee (IRE)

Other Owners: A. L. Marriott.

Jockey (NH): J. Goldstein.

152 MISS Z. C. DAVISON, East Grinstead
Postal: **Shovelstrode Racing Stables, Shovelstrode Lane, Ashurstwood, East Grinstead, West Sussex, RH19 3PN.**
Contacts: **PHONE (01342) 323153 MOBILE (07813) 321709**

1 **BACK IN THE GAME**, 9, ch g Phountzi (USA)—Chasmarella **Mrs J. A. Irvine**
2 **CODE (IRE)**, 4, b c Danehill (USA)—Hidden Meaning (USA) **Rags To Riches**
3 **DISTANT ROMANCE**, 8, br m Phardante (FR)—Rhine Aria **A. A. Goldson**
4 **DROUMLEIGH LAD (IRE)**, 10, b g Jurado (USA)—Myra Gaye **The Secret Circle**
5 **FIRST OF MAY**, 4, b f Halling (USA)—Finger of Light **The Secret Circle**
6 **HI LILY**, 9, b m Jupiter Island—By Line **R. A. Jones**
7 **LILIAN**, 5, b m First Trump—Lillibella **The Secret Circle**
8 **MAD LOUIE**, 5, b g Perpendicular—Miss Bordeaux (IRE) **A. Walder**
9 6, B g Phountzi (USA)—Miss Ark Royal **The Secret Circle**
10 **OCKLEY FLYER**, 6, b g Sir Harry Lewis—Bewails (IRE) **A. Walder**
11 **ROMAN RAMPAGE**, 10, b g Perpendicular—Roman Moor **B. Ward**
12 **SHIRLEY OAKS (IRE)**, 7, b m Sri Pekan (USA)—Duly Elected **The Secret Circle**
13 **SPIDER BOY**, 8, b g Jupiter Island—Great Dilemma **D. A. Ash**
14 **THE DANCING PHOUNZ**, 7, b g Phountzi (USA)—Lyne Dancer **Exors of the Late Mrs G. A. Davison**
15 **ZAFFRE (IRE)**, 6, gr m Mtoto—Zeferina (IRE) **Rags To Riches**

THREE-YEAR-OLDS

16 **JUST BEWARE**, b f Makbul—Bewails (IRE) **The Secret Circle**
17 B f Indian Lodge (IRE)—Spire **Feel The Tension**
18 B f Wizard King—Three Star Rated (IRE) **Shovelstrode Racing Club**

Other Owners: Miss Z. C. Davison, Miss L. J. Johnson, G. Morley, A. N. Waters.

Assistant Trainer: A Irvine

Amateur: Miss Gemelle Davison.

153 MR W. DE BEST-TURNER, Calne
Postal: **North Farm Stables, West Overton, Marlborough, Wiltshire, SN8 1QE.**
Contacts: **HOME (07977) 910779 PHONE (01249) 811944 FAX (01249) 811955**
E-MAIL william@debestracing.fsnet.co.uk

1 **BEAU JAZZ**, 4, br c Merdon Melody—Ichor **de Best Racing**
2 **BELTANE**, 7, b g Magic Ring (IRE)—Sally's Trust (IRE) **Mrs G. R. Swanton**
3 **ONYX**, 4, b g Bijou d'inde—Prime Surprise **Spanish Connection**
4 **TIME FLYER**, 5, b g My Best Valentine—Sally's Trust (IRE) **Mrs G. R. Swanton**
5 **TOM FROM BOUNTY**, 5, ch g Opera Ghost—Tempus Fugit **Seasons Holidays**
6 **ZARNEETA**, 4, br f Tragic Role (USA)—Compton Amber **Mr W. de Best-Turner**

MR W. DE BEST-TURNER—continued

THREE-YEAR-OLDS

7 **BEAU LARGESSE**, b g Largesse—Just Visiting **H. R. Moszkowicz**
8 **BELLE LARGESSE**, b f Largesse—Palmstead Belle (IRE) **Mrs R. A. Moszkowicz**

TWO-YEAR-OLDS

9 **LUGNASAD**, b c 16/4 Sir Harry Lewis (USA)—Sally's Trust (IRE) (Classic Secret (USA)) **Mrs G. R. Swanton**
10 Gr f 24/3 Lord of Men—Princess Maud (USA) (Irish River (FR)) (800) **Mrs J. de Best-Betist**
11 Br c 5/4 Prince Sabo—Silkstone Lady (Puissance) **Mr W. de Best-Turner**
12 B c 13/5 Prince Sabo—Sorrowful (Moorestyle) **de Best Racing**
13 B c 15/3 Double Trigger (IRE)—Sweet Egyptian (FR) (Snurge) **Seasons Holidays**
14 Ch c 6/4 Raise A Grand (IRE)—Teresian Girl (IRE) (Glenstal (USA)) (5000) **Seasons Holidays**

Assistant Trainer: Gillian Swanton

Amateur: Mrs I. De Best.

| 154 | **MR B. DE HAAN**, Lambourn
Postal: **Fair View, Long Hedge, Lambourn, Newbury, Berkshire, RG17 8NA.**
Contacts: **PHONE (01488) 72163 FAX (01488) 71306 MOBILE (07831) 104574**
E-MAIL ben@bdehaan.fsnet.co.uk

1 **AVERLLINE**, 4, b f Averti (IRE)—Spring Sunrise **Mrs D. Vaughan**
2 **BENGO (IRE)**, 5, b g Beneficial—Goforroad (IRE) **Willsford Racing Ltd**
3 **BOLD MOMENTO**, 6, b g Never So Bold—Native of Huppel (IRE) **W. A. Tyrer**
4 **CRIMSON PIRATE (IRE)**, 8, b g Phardante (FR)—Stroked Again **Flora Charlie Limited**
5 **DANCE TO THE BLUES (IRE)**, 4, br f Danehill Dancer (IRE)—Blue Sioux **Mrs D. Vaughan**
6 **DESERTMORE CHIEF (IRE)**, 6, b g Broken Hearted—Mangan Lane **Mrs D. Vaughan**
7 **ILE FACILE (IRE)**, 4, b c Turtle Island (IRE)—Easy Pop (IRE) **Mr B. De Haan**
8 **INDIAN SQUAW (IRE)**, 6, br m Supreme Leader—Kemchee **Fair View Racing**
9 **LORD DUNDANIEL (IRE)**, 8, b br g Arctic Lord—Killoskehan Queen **Willsford Racing Ltd**
10 **MASTER REX**, 10, ch g Interrex (CAN)—Whose Lady (USA) **Miss L. J. F. Challis**
11 **NEOPHYTE (IRE)**, 6, gr g Broken Hearted—Dunmahon Lady **The Neophyte Four**
12 **NORTHERN ENDEAVOUR**, 6, b g Alflora (IRE)—Northern Jinks **Mrs E. Smith**
13 **ORIGINAL THOUGHT (IRE)**, 5, b g Entrepreneur—Troyanos **W. A. Tyrer**
14 **REGENTS WALK (IRE)**, 7, b g Phardante (FR)—Raw Courage (IRE) **Mrs D. Vaughan**
15 **SCARAMOUCHE**, 5, b h Busy Flight—Laura Lye (IRE) **Flora Charlie Limited**
16 **THE GREY BUTLER (IRE)**, 8, gr g Roselier (FR)—Georgic **Mrs D. Vaughan**
17 **WHISTLING FRED**, 6, b g Overbury (IRE)—Megabucks **Mr M. J. & Mrs A. M. Hoodless**

THREE-YEAR-OLDS

18 **DOUBLE DAWN**, b f Double Trigger (IRE)—Spring Sunrise **Mrs D. Vaughan**
19 **LITTLE LAURITA**, b f Overbury (IRE)—Laura Lye (IRE) **Flora Charlie Limited**

Other Owners: D. M. Cafferty, B. D. Heath, D. A. Klein, C. D. Lyall, P. T. Mott, J. D. Murtagh, J. Simms.

Jockey (flat): D. Kinsella. **Conditional:** R. Cosgrave.

| 155 | **MR A. J. DEAKIN**, Cannock
Postal: **7 Hornbeam Crescent, Hazel Slade, Cannock, Staffordshire, WS12 5SU.**
Contacts: **PHONE (01543) 424262 MOBILE (07880) 666986**
E-MAIL tonydeakin@hornbeamracing.freeserve.co.uk

1 **BERNARDON (GER)**, 9, b g Suave Dancer (USA)—Bejaria (GER) **Mr A. J. Deakin**
2 **TURAATH (IRE)**, 9, b g Sadler's Wells (USA)—Diamond Field (USA) **Mr A. J. Deakin**

THREE-YEAR-OLDS

3 B f Overbury (IRE)—Gladys Emmanuel **Mr A. J. Deakin**

TWO-YEAR-OLDS

4 B c 29/4 Cyrano de Bergerac—Reina (Homeboy) (2190) **Mr A. J. Deakin**

Jockey (NH): P. J. Brennan, J. Culloty.

156 MR W. W. DENNIS, Bude
Postal: Thorne Farm, Bude, Cornwall, EX23 0LU.
Contacts: PHONE (01288) 352849 FAX (01288) 352849
E-MAIL thornefarm@btconnect.com

1 COME TO THE BAR (IRE), 6, b g Witness Box (USA)—Copper Hill (IRE) Mr W. W. Dennis
2 EARNEST (IRE), 5, b g Oscar (IRE)—Unassisted (IRE) T. W. Dennis
3 ONE MADISON SQUARE (IRE), 6, br g Fourstars Allstar (USA)—Stormy Sunset Mrs J. E. Dennis
4 OUR SEAFARER (IRE), 6, ch g King Luthier—Dundock Wood Mr W. W. Dennis
5 STARS'N'STRIPES (IRE), 7, b g Lord Americo—Drumdeels Star (IRE) Mr W. W. Dennis
6 STRATCO (IRE), 11, b br g Satco (FR)—No Slow Mr W. W. Dennis

Jockey (NH): D. R. Dennis. Amateur: Mr T. Dennis.

157 MR R. DICKIN, Stratford-on-Avon
Postal: Alscot Racing Stables, Alscot Park, Atherstone On Stour, Stratford-Upon-Avon,
Warwickshire, CV37 8BL.
Contacts: PHONE (01789) 450052 FAX (01789) 450053 MOBILES (07979) 518593 (07979) 518594
E-MAIL claire.dickin@tesco.net and r.dickin@virgin.net

1 ARCTIC SPIRIT, 10, b g Arctic Lord—Dickies Girl The Lordy Racing Partnership
2 BILL BROWN, 7, b g North Briton—Dickies Girl The Lordy Racing Partnership
3 BOBOSH, 9, b g Devil's Jump—Jane Craig H. Gott
4 BREEMA DONNA, 7, b m Sir Harry Lewis (USA)—Donna Del Lago M. MacCarthy
5 CEDAR, 8, gr g Absalom—Setai's Palace Stratford Members Club
6 CHANGE AGENT, 9, br g Royal Fountain—Flashy Looks M. W. Harris
7 CHANNAHRLIE (IRE), 11, gr g Celio Rufo—Derravarragh Lady (IRE) Mr J. C. Clemmow
8 ERINS LASS (IRE), 8, b m Erins Isle—Amative Stratford Members Club
9 GOLDEN TAMESIS, 8, b g Golden Heights—Escribana Tamesis & Partners
10 GULFOSS, 4, b f Gunner B—Ballintava D. A. N. Ross
11 GUZZLE, 5, b m Puget (USA)—Convamore Queen (IRE) Ian K. Beale
12 HANBRIN ROSE, 8, gr m Lancastrian—Rymolbreese John Hanley, John Brindley
13 ILONGUE (FR), 4, b f Nononito (FR)—Marie De Geneve (FR) Steve Webb And Gerry Parker
14 JACARADO (IRE), 8, b g Jurado (USA)—Lady Mearba (IRE) R. G. & R. A. Whitehead
15 JACDOR (IRE), 11, b g Be My Native (USA)—Bellalma Jackie Matthews & Doreen Evans
16 JACK OF SPADES (IRE), 9, b g Mister Lord (USA)—Dooney's Daughter E. R. C. Beech & B. Wilkinson
17 JACOPO (FR), 8, b g Grand Tresor (FR)—Qolombine (FR) Fairfield Flyers
18 JAYEMCEE BOY (IRE), 5, b g Kahyasi—Needwood Fortune Mr John Edwards
19 JESNIC (IRE), 5, b g Kahyasi—Fur Hat J. Hanna
20 KADITO, 9, b g Petoski—Kadastra (FR) A. P. Paton
21 KARIBLUE, 7, ch m Imp Society (USA)—Kadastra (FR) A. P. Paton
22 KELTIC BLUE (IRE), 6, b g Blues Traveller (IRE)—White Caps The Alscot Blue Group
23 KHADIJA, 4, ch f Kadastrof (FR)—Dark Sirona Miss C. A. B. Allsopp
24 LITTLE BEGGAR, 7, b g North Col—Beggars Lane B. E. Merriman
25 LITTLE TERN (IRE), 6, b m Terimon—Miss Fern R. T. S. Matthews
26 LOGGER RHYTHM (USA), 5, b g Woodman—Formidable Dancer (USA) The Six Fellers
27 LUCKY DO (IRE), 8, b g Camden Town—Lane Baloo D. A. N. Ross
28 LUCKYCHARM (FR), 6, ch g Villez (USA)—Hitifly (FR) Robin's Rebels
29 MAYBESEVEN, 11, gr g Baron Blakeney—Ninth of May The Diamond Seven Partnership
30 MISTER KINGSTON, 14, ch g Kinglet—Flaxen Tina Mrs C. M. Dickin
31 MISTER TRICKSTER (IRE), 4, b c Woodborough (USA)—Tinos Island (IRE) The Tricksters
32 NAUTIC (FR), 4, b g Apple Tree (FR)—Bella Dicta (FR) Scrumpy Jacks
33 NEWICK PARK, 10, gr g Chilibang—Quilpee Mai Newick Park Partnership
34 NOT TO BE MISSED, 7, gr m Missed Flight—Petinata Only Horses and Fools
35 PARSON JACK, 8, b g Bedford (USA)—Scobitora R. T. S. Matthews
36 PRAIRIE MINSTREL (USA), 11, b g Regal Intention (CAN)—Prairie Sky (USA) E. R. C. Beech & B. Wilkinson
37 RAZZAMATAZZ, 7, b g Alhijaz—Salvezza (IRE) Mrs M. A. Cooper
38 REGAL TERM (IRE), 7, b g Welsh Term—Regal Hostess R. G. & R. A. Whitehead
39 ROMANY DREAM, 7, b m Nomadic Way (USA)—Half Asleep The Snoozy Partnership
40 SAILING THROUGH, 5, b g Bahhare (USA)—Hopesay Red Star Racing
41 SIMPLE GLORY (IRE), 6, br m Simply Great (F)—Cabin Glory E. R. C. Beech & B. Wilkinson
42 SISSINGHURST STORM (IRE), 7, b br m Good Thyne (USA)—Mrs Hill B. D. Clifford
43 THAI NOE, 5, b g Gunner B—Ballintava D. A. N. Ross
44 TOP GALE (IRE), 6, b m Topanoora—Amy's Gale (IRE) Mr Graham Moses
45 TUDOR BUCK (IRE), 5, b br g Luso—Tudor Doe (IRE) C. E. Eden
46 VICOMTE THOMAS (FR), 5, b g Highest Honor (FR)—Vigorine (FR) Robin Dickin Racing

MR R. DICKIN—continued

47 **WANNA SHOUT,** 7, b m Missed Flight—Lulu **E. R. C. Beech & B. Wilkinson**
48 **WRENS ISLAND (IRE),** 11, br g Yashgan—Tipiton **Mr Allan Bennett**

THREE-YEAR-OLDS

49 **JOLIE (IRE),** b f Orpen (USA)—Arabian Dream (IRE) **Mrs C. S. Baylis**
50 **JOVE (IRE),** b g In The Wings—Propitious (IRE) **Mrs C. S. Baylis**
51 B f Bahhare (USA)—Westside Flyer **Mr C. J. Dickin**

TWO-YEAR-OLDS

52 Gr g 25/1 Jimble (FR)—Something Fun (FR) (Rusticaro (FR)) **Mr C. J. Dickin**

Other Owners: Mrs Joan Wood, Mr & Mrs Danaher, Mrs C. M. Weaver, Mr G. Barrington, P. R. Armour, Mrs S. Brown, Andrew Bull, Ms J. E. Clark, J. R. Cooper, P. A. J. Doyle, W. P. Evans, E. D. Fraser, Dr N. W. Imlah, Mrs A. D. Jelley, T. G. Jones, P. R. Matthews, W. L. Miles, J. A. M. Nicholls, C. P. Paton, N. J. Scotland, J. N. Simpson, Mr P. Venvell, B. P. Wilson.

Assistant Trainer: Claire Dickin

Jockey (NH): D. R. Dennis, B. Hitchcott. **Conditional:** J. Pritchard, J. Stevenson. **Apprentice:** J. Pritchard. **Amateur:** Mr R. McCaul.

---

158 **MR MICHAEL W. DICKINSON, Maryland**
Postal: **Tapeta Farm, 100 Piney Creek Lane, North East Maryland 21901, U.S.A..**
Contacts: **PHONE 410 287 4567 FAX 410 287 8410**
E-MAIL mwd@tapeta.com

1 **A HUEVO (USA),** 9, b g Cool Joe (USA)—Verabald (USA) **Mark Hopkins**
2 **COCKLESHELL (USA),** 4, b c Red Ransom (USA)—Jangada (USA) **Dr John Chandler**
3 **DYNAMIA (USA),** 4, b f Dynaformer (USA)—Shelly River (USA) **Dr John Chandler**
4 **FAR AFIELD (USA),** 4, ch f Distant View (USA)—Shoshaloza (USA) **Dr John Chandler**
5 **GIJIMA (USA),** 4, b br f Red Ransom (USA)—Hamba (USA) **Dr John Chandler**
6 **KOSADE (USA),** 5, b m Cozzene (USA)—Daad (USA) **H. E. Faisal Alhegelan**
7 **LADY MANNERS (USA),** 4, b f Montbrook (USA)—Bold Burst (CAN) **Mr Faisal Alhegelan**
8 **PADDINGTON (USA),** 4, ch c Saint Ballado (CAN)—Painted Portrait (USA) **Gallop, LLC**
9 **POLISH FLOWER (USA),** 4, b f Danzig (USA)—Flower Canyon (USA) **Gary Knapp**
10 **PRICELESS QUALITY (USA),** 5, ch m Elusive Quality (USA)—Catumbella (USA) **Cherokee River Ranch**
11 **SARIE MARAIS (USA),** 5, ch m Unbridled (USA)—Aletta Maria (USA) **Dr John Chandler**
12 **STORMY ARCTIC (USA),** 4, ch f Storm Broker (USA)—
Starkly Arctic (USA) **Mr Mark Hopkins & Mr Jonathan Blank**
13 **TAPIT (USA),** 4, gr c Pulpit (USA)—Tap Your Heels (USA) **Winchell Thoroughbreds, LLC**
14 **VALLERA (GER),** 4, b f Monsun (GER)—Val d'etoile (GER) **Amerman**
15 **WESTERN RANSOM (USA),** 4, b f Red Ransom (USA)—Western Wind (USA) **Dr John Chandler**

THREE-YEAR-OLDS

16 **ANEFEW (USA),** b c Anees (USA)—Chambolle (USA) **Ken Lowe**
17 **ANURA (IRE),** b f Giant's Causeway (USA)—Shastri (USA) **Shirley Taylor & Wlazyt Ltd**
18 **BELLAMY ROAD (USA),** b c Concerto (USA)—Hurry Home Hillary (USA) **Kinsman Farm**
19 **DYNAMIST (USA),** b f Dynaformer (USA)—Arjunand (USA) **Dr John Chandler**
20 **IMPORT (USA),** ch c Gone West (USA)—Sunyata (USA) **Mr Robert S. Evans**
21 **JENNY JOY (USA),** ch f Acceptable (USA)—The Relentless Cat (USA) **Kinsman Farm**
22 **KING'S INTEREST (USA),** b f Kingmambo (USA)—Shared Interest (USA) **Mr Robert S. Evans**
23 **METEOR WELLS (IRE),** b f Sadler's Wells (USA)—Meteor Stage (USA) **Mr Robert S. Evans**
24 **POINTSMAN (USA),** b c Mt Livermore (USA)—Paris Notion (USA) **Gallop, LLC**
25 **RUTLEDGE BALLADO (USA),** b f Saint Ballado (CAN)—Gold From the West (USA) **Mr Herman Greenberg**

---

159 **MR A. DICKMAN, Sandhutton**
Postal: **Breckenbrough House (2nd Yard), Sandhutton, Thirsk, North Yorkshire, YO7 4EL.**
Contacts: **HOME (01845) 587432 MOBILE (07977) 694777**

1 **EIGHT TRUMPS,** 5, ch g First Trump—Misty Silks **The Golden B's Racing Partnership**
2 **INTER VISION (USA),** 5, b g Cryptoclearance (USA)—Fateful (USA) **Mr A. Dickman**
3 **KENNY THE TRUTH (IRE),** 6, b g Robellino (USA)—Just Blink (IRE) **Moorland Racing**

MR A. DICKMAN—continued

TWO-YEAR-OLDS

4 **WHOZART (IRE),** b c 30/3 Mozart (IRE)—Hertford Castle (Reference Point) (30000)

Other Owners: M. D. Lodge, P. M. Lodge, S. A. Mace, A. P. Simmill.

Assistant Trainer: B Bennett

Jockey (flat): P. Hanagan, R. Winston. **Jockey (NH):** S. Stronge. **Apprentice:** A Beech.

---

160 **MR J. E. DIXON, Carlisle**
Postal: **Moorend, Thursby, Carlisle, Cumbria, CA5 6QP.**
Contacts: **PHONE (01228) 711019**

1 **HIRT LODGE,** 14, ch g Jumbo Hirt (USA)—Holly Lodge **Mrs S. F. Dixon**
2 **JOYFUL ECHO,** 6, ch m Jumbo Hirt (USA)—Joyful Star **Mrs E. M. Dixon**
3 **JUMBO'S DREAM,** 14, b g Jumbo Hirt (USA)—Joyful Star **Mrs E. M. Dixon**
4 **SWEET MILLY,** 10, b m Milieu—Another Joyful **Mrs S. F. Dixon**

---

161 **MR M. J. K. DODS, Darlington**
Postal: **Denton Hall Farm, Piercebridge, Darlington, Co. Durham, DL2 3TY.**
Contacts: **PHONE (01325) 374270 FAX (01325) 374020 MOBILE (07860) 411590/(07773) 290830**
E-MAIL dods@teesdale-online.co.uk WEBSITE www.michaeldodsracing.co.uk

1 **AAHGOWANGOWAN (IRE),** 6, b m Tagula (IRE)—Cabcharge Princess (IRE) **D. V. Roper**
2 **BALAKIREF,** 6, b g Royal Applause—Pluck **Septimus Racing Group**
3 **BEAMSLEY BEACON,** 4, ch g Wolfhound (USA)—Petindia **K. Kirkup**
4 **BUNDY,** 9, b g Ezzoud (IRE)—Sanctuary Cove **A. J. Henderson**
5 **COMMITMENT LECTURE,** 5, b m Komaite (USA)—Hurtleberry (IRE) **Mrs B. Riddell**
6 **DIVINE SPIRIT,** 4, b g Foxhound (USA)—Vocation (IRE) **A. Mallen**
7 **FLY BACK,** 6, ch g Fraam—The Fernhill Flyer (IRE) **A. F. Monk**
8 **HULA BALLEW,** 5, ch m Weldnaas (USA)—Ballon **Mrs J. W. Hutchinson & Mrs P. A. Knox**
9 **MICKLEDOR (FR),** 5, ch m Lake Coniston (IRE)—Shamasiya (FR) **D. B. Stanley**
10 **MONICA GELLER,** 7, b m Komaite (USA)—Rion River (IRE) **Mrs S. E. Barclay**
11 **MR BOUNTIFUL (IRE),** 7, b g Mukaddamah (USA)—Nawadder **Denton Hall Racing Ltd**
12 **POLISH CORRIDOR,** 6, b g Danzig Connection (USA)—Possibility **R. D. Mould**
13 **QUEEN'S ECHO,** 4, b f Wizard King—Sunday News'n'echo (USA) **D. C. Batey**
14 **ROTUMA (IRE),** 6, b g Tagula (IRE)—Cross Question (USA) **Denton Hall Racing Ltd**
15 **SIR BOBBY,** 4, b g Kylian (USA)—Ishona **Mr M. J. K. Dods**
16 **SON OF THUNDER (IRE),** 4, ch g Dr Fong (USA)—Sakura Queen (IRE) **R. D. Mould**
17 **SPRING BREEZE,** 4, ch g Dr Fong (USA)—Trading Aces **Sheridan Fabrications Ltd**
18 **ZHITOMIR,** 7, ch g Lion Cavern (USA)—Treasure Trove (USA) **Mr M. J. K. Dods**

THREE-YEAR-OLDS

19 **CONTINENTAL FLYER (IRE),** b f Piccolo—Sunshine Coast **Continental Finance UK Racing**
20 **MAJOR MAGPIE (IRE),** b g Rossini (USA)—Picnic Basket **A. F. Monk**
21 **MISCHIEF NIGHT,** ch g Lake Coniston (IRE)—On Till Morning (IRE) **D. B. Stanley**
22 **ROYAL FLYNN,** b g Royal Applause—Shamriyna (IRE) **J. A. Wynn-Williams**
23 **SADIE'S STAR (IRE),** b f Indian Lodge (IRE)—Nishiki (USA) **The Newcastle Racing Club**
24 **SERGEANT SHINKO (IRE),** ch g Shinko Forest (IRE)—Sea Modena (IRE) **V. J. Spinks**
25 **SOCIETY MUSIC (IRE),** b f Almutawakel—Society Fair (FR) **Mr M. J. K. Dods**
26 **SOUND AND VISION (IRE),** b g Fayruz—Lyrical Vision (IRE) **The Idol Partnership**
27 **SPANISH LAW,** b g Zaha (CAN)—Misty Moon **G. Spencer**

TWO-YEAR-OLDS

28 **BINGO ONE (IRE),** b f 15/2 Mujahid (USA)—Barque Bleue (USA) (Steinlen) (3800) **J. M. & Mrs E. E. Ranson**
29 **COOL EBONY,** br c 1/4 Erhaab (USA)—Monawara (IRE) (Namaqualand (USA)) (8500) **Wedgewood Estates**
30 B g 25/3 Lujain (USA)—Final Glory (Midyan (USA)) (8000)
31 **GLASSHOUGHTON,** b c 13/4 Dansili—Roseum (Lahib (USA)) (23000) **J. N. Blackburn & Partners**
32 B f 14/4 Orpen (USA)—Ionian Secret (Mystiko (USA)) (6500) **Mr D. Lee**
33 **L'ITALIANA (IRE),** b f 3/3 Rossini (USA)—Paganina (FR) (Galetto (FR)) (23000) **J. A. Wynn-Williams**
34 B c 26/4 Agnes World (USA)—La Brise (IRE) (Llandaff (USA)) (26000) **Mr A. Battison & Partners**

MR M. J. K. DODS—continued

35 **LOVELY ANUSKA (USA)**, gr ro f 8/2 Tactical Cat (USA)—
  I'll Flutter By (USA) (Concorde's Tune (USA)) (15961) **D. V. Roper**
36 Br f 20/2 Shinko Forest (IRE)—Machudi (Bluebird (USA)) (15425) **Mr M. J. K. Dods**
37 B c 17/4 Namaqualand (USA)—Nordico Princess (Nordico (USA)) (4500) **J. N. Harrison**
38 B g 26/4 College Chapel—Possibility (Robellino (USA)) (3000) **Denton Hall Racing Ltd**
39 **PRINCE EGOR (IRE)**, b g 29/4 Imperial Ballet (IRE)—Harifana (FR) (Kahyasi) (18779) **Harris & Wharton**
40 B g 12/3 Fruits of Love (USA)—Rachel Green (IRE) (Case Law) (8000)
41 B g 29/4 Pursuit of Love—Sharp Top (Sharpo) (10000) **N. A. Riddell**

Other Owners: S. A. Breakwell, P. J. Carr, P. M. Clarkson, D. M. Cooper, B. A. Forester, Mr D. W. B. Hughes, Mrs A. Iles, J. H. Marris, Mrs P. Monk, Mrs K. S. Pratt, R. Stokell, D. J. Stokell, F. Watson.

Assistant Trainer: C Dods

---

162 MR FRANCOIS DOUMEN, Bouce
Postal: **Le Gue, 61570 Bouce, France.**
Contacts: **HOME +33 (0) 2 33 26 91 46 OFFICE +33 (0) 2 33 67 11 59 FAX +33 (0) 2 33 67 82 37 MOBILE +33 (0) 6 07 42 33 58**
E-MAIL **doumenecouves@wanadoo.fr**

1 **ANABAA REPUBLIC (FR)**, 4, b f Anabaa (USA)—Gigawatt (FR)
2 **ARBOR VITAE (FR)**, 7, b h Double Bed (FR)—Gloire de Rose
3 **BARACOUDA (FR)**, 10, b g Alesso (USA)—Peche Aubar (FR)
4 **BEST BELOVED (FR)**, 8, b h Double Bed (FR)—Gloire de Rose
5 **BLUE CANYON (FR)**, 7, b g Bering—Nini Princesse (IRE)
6 **DANAW (FR)**, 4, b c Lomitas—Damanka (IRE)
7 **DANCEROY (FR)**, 4, b c Deploy—Dancereine (FR)
8 **DOUBLE CREME (FR)**, 4, ch g Double Bed (FR)—Chester County
9 **DOUBLE TONIC (FR)**, 6, b h Double Bed (FR)—Jimka (FR)
10 **ERINS LOVE (IRE)**, 4, b br f Double Bed (FR)—Erintante (IRE)
11 **FIRST GOLD (FR)**, 12, b g Shafoun (FR)—Nuit d'or II (FR)
12 **FRED ASTOR (FR)**, 4, b g Baryshnikov (AUS)—Mary Astor (FR)
13 **GATEWICK (IRE)**, 5, b h Sunday Silence (USA)—Greek Air (IRE)
14 **INNOX (FR)**, 9, b g Lute Antique (FR)—Savane IIi (FR)
15 **JEUX OLYMPIQUES (FR)**, 8, b g Scooter Bleu (IRE)—Banassa (FR)
16 **JURRASSIQUE (FR)**, 8, b g Trebrook (FR)—Veves (FR)
17 **KELAMI (FR)**, 7, b g Lute Antique (FR)—Voltige De Nievre (FR)
18 **L'AMI (FR)**, 6, ch g Lute Antique (FR)—Voltige De Nievre (FR)
19 **LAST DANCE (GER)**, 6, ch g Monsun (GER)—Lilian (GER)
20 **LUDRE (FR)**, 6, gr g True Brave (USA)—Ahhotep (FR)
21 **MARIE MADELAINE (FR)**, 4, ch f Lord of Men—The Trollop (FR)
22 **MATELOT (FR)**, 5, b g Epervier Bleu—Gloria IV (FR)
23 **MAYEUL (FR)**, 5, ch g Luchiroverte (IRE)—Elbe (FR)
24 **MIEUX MIEUX (IRE)**, 4, b f Mark of Esteem (IRE)—L'annee Folle (FR)
25 **MIG (FR)**, 5, ch g Ragmar (FR)—Edie (FR)
26 **MILLENIUM ROYAL (FR)**, 5, b h Mansonnien (FR)—Pink Champagne (FR)
27 **MILRANE (FR)**, 4, b c Rajpoute (FR)—Bulgaria (FR)
28 **MISS BEHAVIOUR (FR)**, 4, b f Dolpour—Guard's Gala
29 **MONZON (FR)**, 5, b g Kadalko (FR)—Queenly (FR)
30 **MOULIN RICHE (FR)**, 5, b g Video Rock (FR)—Gintonique (FR)
31 **NARUKHA RAJPUT (FR)**, 4, b f Rajpoute—French Kiss IV (FR)
32 **NEVADA (FR)**, 4, ch g Ragmar (FR)—Attualita (FR)
33 **NINAS (FR)**, 4, ch g Funny Baby (FR)—Elza III (FR)
34 **NITRAT (FR)**, 4, b g Brier Creek (USA)—Evane (FR)
35 **NOCTAMBULE (FR)**, 4, b g Subotica (FR)—Calvi IV (FR)
36 **NOMAD (FR)**, 4, b g Brier Creek (USA)—Fortune V (FR)
37 **NOTRE AMI (FR)**, 4, b g Subotica (FR)—Voltige De Nievre (FR)
38 **NOUVEAU MAIRE (FR)**, 4, b g Ragmar (FR)—Countess Fellow (FR)
39 **OUED (FR)**, 5, gr h Double Bed (FR)—Tibriza
40 **ROYAL BABY (FR)**, 13, b g Garde Royale—Babylonie (FR)
41 **SAMANDO (FR)**, 5, ch m Hernando (FR)—Samshu
42 **STAG PARTY (FR)**, 4, ch c Exit To Nowhere (USA)—Marital Bliss (FR)
43 **SUNRISE SPIRIT (FR)**, 4, b g Double Bed (FR)—Belle Chaumiere

MR FRANCOIS DOUMEN—continued

44 **TERENEZ (FR)**, 5, b h Desert King (IRE)—Dibenoise (FR)
45 **WALK ON SEAS (IRE)**, 10, b g Shardari—Over The Seas
46 **WHISPERER (GER)**, 6, b g Spectrum (IRE)—Well Known (GER)

THREE-YEAR-OLDS

47 **CARDOUN JIM (FR)**, b g Cardoun (FR)—Jolie Jim (FR)
48 **DESERT JIM (FR)**, ch c Desert King (IRE)—Jimshine (FR)
49 **EL BADIL (FR)**, b c Double Bed (FR)—Syvanie (FR)
50 **FERRARE (FR)**, b f Lute Antique (FR)—Fleur de Mad (FR)
51 **FUJAIRAH (SWI)**, b f Sri Pekan (USA)—Fresh Look (IRE)
52 **GIGOLINO (FR)**, ch c Trempolino (USA)—Gigawatt (FR)
53 **IRUNARRI (FR)**, gr f Kendor (FR)—Aristi (FR)
54 **KASBAH BLISS (FR)**, b c Kahyasi—Marital Bliss (FR)
55 **KING FORADAY (FR)**, ch c Vettori (IRE)—Zakota (IRE)
56 **MEDAILLE (FR)**, gr f Medaaly—Super Rose (FR)
57 **ORMELLO (FR)**, b c Cyborg (FR)—Galante V (FR)
58 **OSANA (FR)**, b c Video Rock (FR)—Voilette (FR)
59 **OUSTE (FR)**, ch g Ragmar (FR)—Elbe (FR)
60 **OZYMANDIAS (FR)**, b g Rajpoute (FR)—Delphes d'or (FR)
61 **REBOND (FR)**, ch c Trempolino (USA)—Lattaquie (FR)
62 **ROYAL ANTARTIQUE (FR)**, b g Antarctique (IRE)—Royale Miller (FR)
63 **SPECTROFOLLE (FR)**, b f Spectrum (IRE)—L'annee Folle (FR)
64 **STARLOVE (FR)**, b f Astarabad (USA)—Forty Love (FR)
65 **STEED (FR)**, b c Double Bed (FR)—River Tweed
66 **SUNRISE HAVELI (FR)**, ch f Rajpoute (FR)—Belle Chaumiere (FR)

TWO-YEAR-OLDS

67 **BASTRINGUE (FR)**, b c 31/1 Double Bed (FR)—Cabaret Club (FR) (Top Ville)
68 **DOUBLE FIL (FR)**, b c 13/5 Double Bed (FR)—Filmata (Vayrann) (7377)
69 **HERTZIENNE (FR)**, ch f 12/4 Hernando (FR)—Gigawatt (FR) (Double Bed (FR))
70 **JIM JAMS (FR)**, gr f 23/4 Kaldounevees (FR)—Jimshine (Shining Steel)
71 **KILOMETRE NEUF (FR)**, b c 11/2 Double Bed (FR)—Mary Astor (FR) (Groom Dancer (USA))
72 B c 9/3 Priolo (USA)—Lanaba (IRE) (Anabaa (USA)) (26827)
73 **LITTLE STORPING (FR)**, ch c 4/3 Vertical Speed (FR)—Chop And Change (FR) (Double Bed (FR))
74 **MAJIMOURIEN (FR)**, b f 18/3 Majorien—Jolie Jim (FR) (Double Bed (FR))
75 B f 11/4 Fasliyev (USA)—Mercedes (GER) (Nebos (GER)) (16767)
76 **PARADI (FR)**, b g 25/5 Video Rock (FR)—Gintonique (FR) (Royal Charter (FR))
77 **PARPAILLOT (FR)**, b g 5/5 Subotica (FR)—Voilette (FR) (Brezzo (FR))
78 **PARRAIN (FR)**, b g 10/4 Brier Creek (USA)—Grenelle II (FR) (Quart de Vin (FR))
79 **POMMEROL (FR)**, b g 10/4 Subotica (FR)—Irish Cofee (FR) (Video Rock (FR))
80 **PRINCE RODNEY (FR)**, ch g 15/4 Tzar Rodney (FR)—Infante III (FR) (Roi de Rome (USA))
81 **PRIORY ROSE (FR)**, b f 4/4 Priolo (USA)—Super Rose (FR) (Darshaan)
82 **STARTOFF (IRE)**, b f 13/2 Hernando (FR)—Startup (IRE) (Fairy King (USA)) (30181)
83 **SUAVE (FR)**, b c 8/5 Double Bed (FR)—Syvanie (FR) (Sicyos (USA))
84 **XANADU BLISS (FR)**, b f 20/3 Xaar—Marital Bliss (FR) (Double Bed (FR))

Owners: Comtesse Armand, Mrs Bernard Destremau, Mr Dominique Dormeuil, Haras d'Ecouves, Conte Beaudouin de la Motte Saint Pierre, Mr Gautier de la Selle, Mr P. H. Vogt, Mr H. P. Vogt, Mr Herve d'Armaille, Mr Nelson Radwan, Mr Jean-Francois Lambert, Mr Philippe Houdart, Haras de Saint Pair du Mont, Mr Fritz Von Ballmoos, Mr Michel Bessis, Mr Claude Botton, Mr Louis de Bourgoing, Mr Richard Britten-Long, Mr Marc de Chambure, Mr Melwyn Davies, F. F. Racing Limited, Mr Fraguier, Mr Dirk Grauert, Halewood International Ltd, Haras d'Etreham, Mrs Marie-Joelle Levesque, Mr J. A. McCarthy, Mr J. P. McManus, Marquise de Moratalla, Mrs Denela Platt, Mr Henri de Pracomtal, Mr Eric Puerari, Mr Jean-Claude Seroul, Mr Michael Somerset-Leeke, Mr Emmanuel Tassin, Mr Hubert Tassin, Uplifting Bloodstock Ltd, Mr Joerg Vasicek, Mr Hans Wirth.

Jockey (flat): Mlle Alexandrie Chevallier. **Jockey (NH):** Mr Arnaud Duchene. **Amateur:** Mr Robert Danloux, Mr H. Naggar.

---

163 **MR S. L. DOW, Epsom**
Postal: **Clear Height Stables, Derby Stables Road, Epsom, Surrey, KT18 5LB.**
Contacts: **PHONE (01372) 721490 FAX (01372) 748099 MOBILE (07860) 800109**
E-MAIL (S. Dow) clear.height1.com@virgin.net (Office) clear.height.com@virgin.net
WEBSITE www.simondow.co.uk

1 **BLACK OVAL**, 4, b f Royal Applause—Corniche Quest (IRE) **Sylvia Luckman & Lesley Shepherd**
2 **DURLSTON BAY**, 8, b g Welsh Captain—Nelliellamay **Sandbaggers Club**

MR S. L. DOW—continued

3 **FAIRLAND (IRE)**, 6, b g Blues Traveller (IRE)—Massive Powder **Mrs B. M. Cullis**
4 **GALLERY GOD (FR)**, 9, ch g In The Wings—El Fabulous (FR) **J. B. Etheridge**
5 **HEAD BOY**, 4, ch g Forzando—Don't Jump (IRE) **R. E. Anderson**
6 **LONDONER (USA)**, 7, ch g Sky Classic (CAN)—Love And Affection (USA) **P. McCarthy**
7 **MALIBU (IRE)**, 4, b g Second Empire (IRE)—Tootle **John Robinson and Derek Stubbs**
8 **NIGHT STORM**, 4, b f Night Shift (USA)—Monte Calvo **Anderson, Connolly and Thornton**
9 **PHAT PEOPLES BEACH**, 4, b f Pharly (FR)—Eclectic **T. G. Parker**
10 **QUANTUM LEAP**, 8, b g Efisio—Prejudice **Mrs M. E. O'Shea**
11 **REDBANK (IRE)**, 4, b g Night Shift (USA)—Bush Rose **Mrs M. E. O'Shea**
12 **SHADY MERLIN (IRE)**, 7, b g Shardari—Merillion **R. Gurney**
13 **SHOTGUN ANNIE**, 5, b m Double Trigger (IRE)—Coh Sho No **H. D. Nass**
14 **SOLDERSHIRE**, 8, b g Weld—Dishcloth **P. McCarthy**
15 **STAR MAGNITUDE (USA)**, 4, ch g Distant View (USA)—Stellaria (USA) **Mr S. L. Dow**
16 **WHITGIFT ROCK**, 4, b g Piccolo—Fly South **Lesley & Terry Shepherd**

THREE-YEAR-OLDS

17 **AMAYA SILVA**, b f Silver Patriarch (IRE)—Queen of Tides (IRE) **T. G. Parker**
18 **COOMBE CENTENARY**, b f Robellino (USA)—Shining Dancer **Coombe Wood Racing Syndicate**
19 **EMERGING LIGHT**, ch c Mark of Esteem (IRE)—Aurora Bay (IRE) **Aldis, Caunce & Dow**
20 **LOVE ALWAYS**, b f Piccolo—Lady Isabell **T. Staplehurst**
21 **TAIPAN TOMMY (IRE)**, ch g Shinko Forest (IRE)—Adieu Cherie (IRE) **John Robinson and Derek Stubbs**

TWO-YEAR-OLDS

22 **CAMP ATTACK**, b c 4/3 Fleetwood (IRE)—Queen of Tides (IRE) (Soviet Star (USA)) **T. G. Parker**
23 B f 5/4 Josr Algarhoud (IRE)—Eclectic (Emarati (USA)) **T. G. Parker**
24 **KING'S CHARTER (USA)**, b c 15/2 Red Ransom (USA)—Extry (USA) (Broad Brush (USA)) (35000) **J. R. May**

Other Owners: Mrs A. Aldis, Mr D. F. Ballheimer, S. A. Caunce, V. J. Collier, Mr J. M. Connolly, M. G. Mackenzie, J. N. Robinson, N. S. Scandrett, T. K. Shepherd, Dr D. Stubbs, W. Thornton.

Apprentice: L. Smith. **Amateur:** Mr D. Hutchison.

---

164   MR C. J. DOWN, Cullompton
Postal: **Upton, Cullompton, Devon, EX15 1RA.**
Contacts: **PHONE/FAX (01884) 33097**

1 **ANOTHER DIAMOND (IRE)**, 7, b m First Trump—Rockin' Rosie **G. R. Waterman**
2 **BE POSITIVE**, 5, b g Petoski—Go Positive **Mrs G. H. Leeves**
3 **BEAU SUPREME (IRE)**, 8, b g Supreme Leader—Miss Sabreur **Mrs R. E. Vicary**
4 **CITY AFFAIR**, 4, b g Inchinor—Aldevonie **Mr W. R. Baddiley**
5 **CLASSICAL LOVE**, 5, b m Classic Cliche (IRE)—Hard Love **The Retailers**
6 **CORNISH ORCHID (IRE)**, 4, ch g Be My Guest (USA)—Nilousha **G. R. Waterman**
7 **CRAFTY MISS (IRE)**, 6, b br m Warcraft (USA)—Mrs Rumpole (IRE) **Mr M. D. Rusden**
8 **ELHEBA (IRE)**, 6, b br g Elbio—Fireheba (ITY) **Three To One Syndicate**
9 **FLURRY**, 6, gr m Terimon—Queen's Favourite **Julian Selby**
10 **HAMADEENAH**, 7, ch m Alhijaz—Mahbob Dancer (FR) **Mr W. R. Baddiley**
11 **IRISH TOTTY**, 6, b m Glacial Storm (USA)—Elver Season **Mrs S. J. Cork**
12 **JACKS JEWEL (IRE)**, 8, b g Welsh Term—September Daydream (IRE) **K. W. Field**
13 5, Ch h Master Willie—Kingky's Cottage **Sarah Burton & Richard Ward**
14 **LADY ALDERBROOK (IRE)**, 5, b m Alderbrook—Madame President (IRE) **Clear Racing**
15 **LAGO DI LEVICO**, 8, ch g Pelder (IRE)—Langton Herring **J. B. Radford**
16 **LIKE A BREEZE**, 6, bl m Bob Back (USA)—Whatagale **G. M. Rowe**
17 **LINUS**, 7, b g Bin Ajwaad (IRE)—Land Line **G. Doel**
18 **LORD KERNOW (IRE)**, 5, b g Lord Americo—Bramble Ridge (IRE) **G. R. Waterman**
19 **MADAME LUSO (IRE)**, 5, b m Luso—Real Town (IRE) **T. R. Hall**
20 **MILLCROFT SEASCAPE (IRE)**, 6, b g Good Thyne (USA)—Dante's Ville (IRE) **J. Carter**
21 **MISS LEWIS**, 7, b m Sir Harry Lewis (USA)—Teelyna **Mrs J. May & Mrs L. M. Edwards**
22 **NATIVE DAISY (IRE)**, 10, b m Be My Native (USA)—Castleblagh **Mr W. R. Baddiley**
23 **NEARLY A BREEZE**, 5, b m Thowra (FR)—Nearly At Sea **Mrs F. Down**
24 **PROBUS LORD**, 10, b g Rough Stones—Decoyanne **E. G. M. Beard**
25 **SEA YOU MADAME**, 6, b m Sea Raven (IRE)—Mildame **Mrs F. Down**
26 4, B g Oscar (IRE)—Sister Stephanie (IRE) **Mr W. R. Baddiley**

MR C. J. DOWN—continued

27 **TEAM CAPTAIN**, 11, ch g Teamster—Silly Sausage **P. J. Hickman**
28 4, B f Classic Cliche (IRE)—Tree Frog (IRE)
29 **WILLIES WAY**, 5, ch g Nomadic Way (USA)—Willies Witch **Mrs A. Whitten**

THREE-YEAR-OLDS

30 Ch f Inchinor—Key West (FR) **Mr C. J. Down**

Other Owners: Mr W. H. Banfield, H. J. W. Davies, B. J. Greening, R. G. Peacock, Ms M. M. Richardson, Ms L. Stark.

Assistant Trainer: Richard Down

Jockey (NH): James Davies, R. Greene, T. Scudamore, J. Tizzard.

---

165   MS J. S. DOYLE, Upper Lambourn
Postal: Flemington, Uplands Lane, Upper Lambourn, Hungerford, RG17 8QH.
Contacts: **YARD** (01488) 72223 **HOUSE** (01488) 72222 **FAX** (01488) 72223
MOBILE (07831) 880678
E-MAIL doyleracing@Yahoo.co.uk

1 **CHINA JACK (IRE)**, 7, b g West China—Camp Bay (IRE) **Mrs R. E. A. Alexander**
2 **GENERALS LASTSTAND (IRE)**, 7, b g Little Bighorn—Our Dorcet **Mrs R. E. A. Alexander**
3 **SOMAYDA (IRE)**, 10, b g Last Tycoon—Flame of Tara **Ms J. S. Doyle**
4 **ZANAY**, 9, b g Forzando—Nineteenth of May **Mr T. E. Ford**

THREE-YEAR-OLDS

5 **AMIGRA (IRE)**, b f Grand Lodge (USA)—Beaming **Ms J. S. Doyle**

TWO-YEAR-OLDS

6 B f 22/4 Woodborough (USA)—Atemme (Up And At 'em) (952) **Mr T. E. Ford**
7 Ch f 8/3 Bluegrass Prince (IRE)—Nahla (Wassl) (2857) **Mr T. E. Ford**

Other Owners: A. W. Regan.

Assistant Trainer: Miss Sophie Doyle

Apprentice: J. W. Doyle. **Amateur:** Miss Sophie Doyle.

---

166   MR C. DREW, Rampton
Postal: Fox End Stables, 83 King Street, Rampton, Cambridgeshire, CB4 8QD.
Contacts: **PHONE/FAX** (01954) 250772

1 **CHICHELE COLLEGE**, 4, b g Komaite (USA)—Myumi **J. L. Burt**
2 **MADAME ROUX**, 7, b m Rudimentary (USA)—Foreign Mistress **Miss P. Drew**

THREE-YEAR-OLDS

3 **MONAD (IRE)**, b f General Monash (USA)—Moon River (FR) **Mr D. Bird & Miss P. Drew**

TWO-YEAR-OLDS

4 Ch c 29/4 Whittingham (IRE)—Admire (Last Tycoon) (857)
5 B c 9/4 Whittingham (IRE)—Don't Smile (Sizzling Melody) (900) **Mr A. Plumb & Mr C. Drew**

Assistant Trainer: Miss Polly Drew

Amateur: Miss P. Drew.

167 MR C. J. DREWE, Didcot
Postal: **Lower Cross Farm, Blewbury Road, East Hagbourne, Didcot, Oxfordshire, OX11 9ND.**
Contacts: **PHONE (01235) 813124 MOBILE (07787) 503709**

1 4, Ch f The West (USA)—Alvecote Lady **Mr C. J. Drewe**
2 **BRIGHT TIMES AHEAD (IRE)**, 7, ch m Rainbows For Life (CAN)—Just A Second **W. P. Long**
3 **TIME TO PARLEZ**, 14, b g Amboise—Image of War **Mrs J. R. Strange**
4 **ZAKTOO (IRE)**, 4, b g Sri Pekan (USA)—Alpine Symphony **Mr C. J. Drewe**

Assistant Trainer: Lorraine Drewe

Jockey (NH): B. Hitchcott, R. Thornton.

168 MRS A. DUFFIELD, Leyburn
Postal: **Sun Hill Racing Stables, Sun Hill Farm, Constable Burton, Leyburn, North Yorkshire, DL8 5RL.**
Contacts: **PHONE (01677) 450303 FAX (01677) 450993 MOBILE (07802) 496332**
E-MAIL ann.duffield1@virgin.net

1 **CONSTABLE BURTON**, 4, b g Foxhound (USA)—Actress **Middleham Park Racing XV**
2 **JUBILEE STREET (IRE)**, 6, b g Dr Devious (IRE)—My Firebird **Mr D. W. Holdsworth & Mr J. A. McMahon**
3 **NAMED AT DINNER**, 4, ch g Halling (USA)—Salanka (IRE) **Middleham Park Racing XVI**
4 **NOBLE HOUSE**, 8, ch g Gildoran—Trust To Luck **R. Renny**
5 **PRAIRIE SUN (GER)**, 4, b f Law Society (USA)—Prairie Flame (IRE) **Miss H. Wynne**
6 **SEALILY (IRE)**, 4, gr f Docksider (USA)—Hariyana (IRE) **Miss B. C. Duxbury**
7 **YOUNG TOT (IRE)**, 7, b g Torus—Lady-K (IRE) **North Briton Racing**

THREE-YEAR-OLDS

8 **BOLD PURSUIT (IRE)**, br c Bold Fact (USA)—Lyphard Belle **S. Adamson**
9 **CALAMARI (IRE)**, ch f Desert King (IRE)—Mrs Fisher (IRE) **G. D. Waters**
10 **FINLAND (UAE)**, b c Timber Country (USA)—Najm Al Bahar (FR) **S. Adamson**
11 **PRINCE NAMID**, b c Namid—Fen Princess (IRE) **S. Adamson**
12 **ROSE OF GLENSHEE (IRE)**, ch f Titus Livius (FR)—Scotia Rose **Miss H. Wynne**
13 **SOOYOU SIR (IRE)**, b br g Orpen (USA)—Naivement (IRE) **Mortgage Search UK**
14 **SUNCLIFF**, b g Most Welcome—Marjorie's Orchid **Mrs Doreen Addison**
15 **TAHLAL (IRE)**, b c Dr Fong (USA)—Chatterberry
16 **UNLIMITED**, b g Bold Edge—Cabcharge Blue **Mrs L. J. Tounsend**

TWO-YEAR-OLDS

17 B f 7/5 Soviet Star (USA)—Alriyaah (Shareef Dancer (USA)) (4694) **Middleham Park Racing XV**
18 B f 15/4 Danehill Dancer (IRE)—
        Bent Al Fala (IRE) (Green Desert (USA)) (8000) **The Midnight Millionaires Partnership**
19 **DONIA DUBAI (IRE)**, b f 29/4 Docksider (USA)—Dafrah (USA) (Danzig (USA)) **Bouresly Racing Syndicate**
20 B f 12/4 Mull of Kintyre (USA)—Gracious Imp (USA) (Imp Society (USA)) (10000)
21 **KALZAK**, b f 17/3 Kalanisi (IRE)—Zakuska (Zafonic (USA)) **Mr J. Clark**
22 Ch f 22/4 Zilzal (USA)—Last Result (Northern Park (USA)) (9389) **Miss H. Wynne**
23 **LOVELY DUBAI (IRE)**, b c 22/5 Desert Prince (IRE)—Filia Ardross (Ardross) (35000) **Bouresly Racing Syndicate**
24 B f 27/4 Primo Valentino (IRE)—Margarets First (Puissance) (6500) **Network Global Solutions**
25 **MIDGE'S GIRL (IRE)**, b f 13/4 Indian Lodge (IRE)—Blue Sky Lady (IRE) (Bluebird (USA)) (800) **Mrs N. Mideely**
26 B c 8/3 Tagula (IRE)—Notley Park (Wolfhound (USA)) (8500) **R. Renny**
27 Ch c 20/2 Compton Place—Palisandra (USA) (Chief's Crown (USA)) (14000) **The R.S.J. Partnership**
28 Ch f 17/3 Spectrum (IRE)—Phantom Ring (Magic Ring (IRE)) (1600) **Mr R. Bailey**
29 **SILVER MONT (IRE)**, b c 4/2 Montjeu (IRE)—Silvernus (Machiavellian (USA)) **Mr J. Clark**
30 B f 6/4 Mull of Kintyre (USA)—Tamasriya (IRE) (Doyoun) (10730) **Mr G. Harper**

Other Owners: Mrs J. Berry, Mr & Mrs B. Rivington, Mrs A. Stafford, Mr L. Shears, Mrs J. A. Armstrong, Mr J. Berry, Mr R. Bouresly, Mr F. Y. R. Bouresly, R. Brown, Mrs A. Duffield, Miss B. C. Duxbury, T. S. Palin, Mr P. Stafford.

Assistant Trainer: G Duffield

Jockey (flat): G. Duffield.

169 MR B. W. DUKE, Lambourn
Postal: **Coppington Stables, Greenways, Lambourn, Berkshire, RG17 7LG.**
Contacts: **PHONE (01488) 71888 MOBILE (07967) 252182**

1 **BAILAORA (IRE),** 4, b br g Shinko Forest (IRE)—Tart (FR) **Exors of the Late Mr R. M. J. Kingston**
2 **BEN LOMAND,** 5, ch g Inchinor—Benjarong **Brendan W. Duke Racing**
3 **COPPINGTON FLYER (IRE),** 5, ch m Eagle Eyed (USA)—Miss Flite (IRE) **Brendan W. Duke Racing**
4 **MOSCOW REBEL (IRE),** 8, ch g Moscow Society (USA)—Astrella **Miss A. C. Telling**
5 **OPENIDE,** 4, b g Key of Luck (USA)—Eyelet (IRE) **Brendan W. Duke Racing**
6 **OSCARS VISION (IRE),** 5, ch m Oscar Schindler (IRE)—Eyelet (IRE) **Brendan W. Duke Racing**
7 **TARANAI (IRE),** 4, ch f Russian Revival (USA)—Miss Flite (IRE) **The Southern Lights**

THREE-YEAR-OLDS

8 **GRAND GIRL,** b f Mark of Esteem (IRE)—Ayunli **Brendan W. Duke Racing**
9 **GRAND OPTION,** ch c Compton Place—Follow The Stars **The G. S. M. Group**
10 **IMPERIAL MISS (IRE),** b f Imperial Ballet (IRE)—Miss Flite (IRE) **Briton & Time Racing Partnership**
11 **SLEEP TIGHT,** b c Dracula (AUS)—Pillowing **Briton & Time Racing Partnership**

TWO-YEAR-OLDS

12 B f 10/2 Ordway (USA)—Chorus (USA) (Darshaan) (4694) **Miss A. C. Telling**
13 B c 17/4 Bertolini (USA)—Corn Dolly (IRE) (Thatching) (4023) **Miss A. C. Telling**

Other Owners: MR B. W. Duke, Mrs J. B. H. Goldswain, Mr G. A. Hancox, Mr M. I. Morris, Mr P. L. Murray, Mr M. O'Connor, Ms R. E. Tupper.

Assistant Trainer: A C Telling

Jockey (flat): A. Daly. **Jockey (NH):** Charles Studd.

170 MR N. A. DUNGER, Pulborough
Postal: **Generation House, Coombelands Stables, Pulborough, West Sussex, RH20 1BP.**
Contacts: **PHONE (01798) 872194 MOBILE (07790) 631962 & (07719) 478860**
E-MAIL **dunger@supanet.com**

1 **CLERIC,** 4, ch g Inchinor—St Clair **Mr N. A. Dunger**
2 **THE TEUCHTER,** 6, b g First Trump—Barefoot Landing (USA) **Mr N. A. Dunger**

Assistant Trainer: Mrs D Dunger

Conditional: D. Lavertey. **Amateur:** Mr J. Morgan.

171 MR E. A. L. DUNLOP, Newmarket
Postal: **Gainsborough Stables, Hamilton Road, Newmarket, Suffolk, CB8 0TE.**
Contacts: **PHONE (01638) 661998 FAX (01638) 667394**
E-MAIL **edunlop@gainsborough-stables.co.uk WEBSITE www.edunlop.com**

1 **APEX,** 4, ch g Efisio—Royal Loft **Patrick Milmo and Stuart Tilling**
2 **BLYTHE KNIGHT (IRE),** 5, ch h Selkirk (USA)—Blushing Barada (USA) **Maktoum Al Maktoum**
3 **COURT MASTERPIECE,** 5, b h Polish Precedent (USA)—Easy Option (IRE) **Maktoum Al Maktoum**
4 **ELBASAR (IRE),** 4, ch g Unfuwain (USA)—Ballet Shoes (IRE) **Hamdan Al Maktoum**
5 **GENTLEMAN'S DEAL (IRE),** 4, b c Danehill (USA)—Sleepytime (IRE) **Khalifa Sultan and M. Jaber**
6 **MITH HILL,** 4, b c Daylami (IRE)—Delirious Moment (IRE) **M. Jaber**
7 **OUIJA BOARD,** 4, b f Cape Cross (IRE)—Selection Board **The Earl Of Derby**
8 **POST AND RAIL (USA),** 4, b c Silver Hawk (USA)—Past The Post (USA) **Hesmonds Stud Ltd**
9 **SECRET PLACE,** 4, ch g Compton Place—Secret Circle **K. Sultan**
10 **TABADUL (IRE),** 4, b g Cadeaux Genereux—Amaniy (USA) **Hamdan Al Maktoum**

THREE-YEAR-OLDS

11 **BRIDEGROOM,** b c Groom Dancer (USA)—La Piaf (FR) **Cheveley Park Stud**
12 **CALL ME MAX,** b g Vettori (IRE)—Always Vigilant (USA) **ORS, Woods, Weatherby, Davies and Stone**
13 **CARPET RIDE,** ch c Unfuwain (USA)—Fragrant Oasis (USA) **Maktoum Al Maktoum**
14 **COME WHAT AUGUSTUS,** b g Mujahid (USA)—Sky Red **The Storm Again Syndicate**
15 **DESERT CLASSIC,** b f Green Desert (USA)—High Standard **Maktoum Al Maktoum**

MR E. A. L. DUNLOP—continued

16 **ETAAR**, b c Zafonic (USA)—Hawayah (IRE) **Hamdan Al Maktoum**
17 **FAJR (IRE)**, b c Green Desert (USA)—Ta Rib (USA) **Hamdan Al Maktoum**
18 **FORT AUGUSTUS (USA)**, b c Quiet American (USA)—Fife (IRE) **Maktoum Al Maktoum**
19 **GARHOUD**, b c Grand Lodge (USA)—Puce **M. Jaber**
20 **GHURRA (USA)**, b f War Chant (USA)—Futuh (USA) **Hamdan Al Maktoum**
21 **INNOCENT SPLENDOUR**, b f Mtoto—Maureena (IRE) **The Granite Partnership**
22 **INSHAAD (IRE)**, b f Alhaarth (IRE)—Jedwa (IRE) **Hamdan Al Maktoum**
23 **JUMLAH**, b f Unfuwain (USA)—Sumood **Hamdan Al Maktoum**
24 **KANAD**, b g Bold Edge—Multi-Sofft **I. M. S. Belselah**
25 **KING KASYAPA (IRE)**, b c Darshaan—Ezana **Gainsborough Stud**
26 **NADIRA (IRE)**, b f Nashwan (USA)—Doomna (IRE) **Hamdan Al Maktoum**
27 **NAMATHEJ**, ch f Halling (USA)—Badaayer (USA) **Hamdan Al Maktoum**
28 **PALATINE DANCER (IRE)**, ch f Namid—Esquiline (USA) **The Jaspar Partnership**
29 **POLISH EAGLE**, b c Polish Precedent (USA)—Tinashaan (IRE) **Hesmonds Stud Ltd**
30 **RED RACKETEER (USA)**, b c Red Ransom (USA)—Furajet (USA) **Maktoum Al Maktoum**
31 **ROAD RAGE (IRE)**, b f Giant's Causeway (USA)—Endorsement **Cliveden Stud Ltd**
32 **SEYAADI**, b g Intikhab (USA)—Sioux Chef **Hamdan Al Maktoum**
33 **SHARABY (IRE)**, b f Cadeaux Genereux—Shawanni **Maktoum Al Maktoum**
34 **TADLIL**, b c Pivotal—Pretty Poppy **Hamdan Al Maktoum**
35 **TARABUT**, b f Green Desert (USA)—Nabadhaat (USA) **Hamdan Al Maktoum**
36 **TESARY**, b f Danehill (USA)—Baldemara (FR) **K. Sultan**
37 **THARUA (IRE)**, b f Indian Danehill (IRE)—Peig Sayers (IRE) **Mrs R. S. Dunlop**
38 **TRIPLE TWO**, ch f Pivotal—Tara's Girl (IRE) **Cheveley Park Stud**
39 **WITHOUT A TRACE (IRE)**, b f Darshaan—Star Profile (IRE) **Maktoum Al Maktoum**
40 **ZAHEYAH**, gr f Dansili—Arinaga **M. Jaber**

TWO-YEAR-OLDS

41 **ADRAAJ (USA)**, b f 24/4 Sahm (USA)—Hachiyah (IRE) (Generous (IRE)) **Hamdan Al Maktoum**
42 **ALESSANDRIA**, b f 16/2 Sunday Silence (USA)—Tereshkova (USA) (Mr Prospector (USA)) **Maktoum Al Maktoum**
43 **APT TO RUN (USA)**, b br c 8/4 Aptitude (USA)—Tufa (Warning) (106411) **Hesmonds Stud Ltd**
44 **ARRADOUL (USA)**, b f 15/2 Dixieland Band (USA)—
                    Gold Rush Queen (USA) (Seeking The Gold (USA)) (202181) **Mr William McAlpin**
45 **ASARABACCA (FR)**, ch f 28/2 Halling (USA)—All Our Hope (USA) (Gulch (USA)) **Maktoum Al Maktoum**
46 B f 14/3 Desert Prince (IRE)—Ballet Society (FR) (Sadler's Wells (USA)) (52000) **K. Sultan**
47 **BEEPING**, b c 4/2 Halling (USA)—Chief Bee (Chief's Crown (USA)) **Mrs Mark Burrell & Mr Anthony Burrell**
48 **BLACKTOFT (USA)**, b br c 18/1 Theatrical—
                    Black Truffle (USA) (Mt Livermore (USA)) (63846) **Maktoum Al Maktoum**
49 **BLESSINGS COUNT (USA)**, ch f 12/4 Pulpit (USA)—
                    Topicount (USA) (Private Account (USA)) (79808) **Mr William McAlpin**
50 **BOLD ALASKA (IRE)**, b c 24/4 Cape Cross (IRE)—
                    Dramatic Entry (IRE) (Persian Bold) (180000) **Maktoum Al Maktoum**
51 **BOUBOULINA**, b f 14/4 Grand Lodge (USA)—Ideal Lady (IRE) (Seattle Slew (USA)) **Maktoum Al Maktoum**
52 B c 10/4 Montjeu (IRE)—Camp Fire (IRE) (Lahib (USA)) (45000) **K. Sultan**
53 B f 29/1 Royal Applause—Circle of Light (Anshan) **The Earl Of Derby**
54 **CNOC NA GAOITHE (USA)**, ch c 2/5 Rahy (USA)—
                    Momentous (USA) (Summer Squall (USA)) **Maktoum Al Maktoum**
55 **COFFS HARBOUR (USA)**, b c 13/3 Swain (USA)—Tethkar (Machiavellian (USA)) **Maktoum Al Maktoum**
56 **CONGESTION CHARGE**, b f 8/4 Diktat—Overdrive (Shirley Heights) **Cliveden Stud Ltd**
57 **COOL CUSTOMER (USA)**, b c 21/1 Gone West (USA)—
                    Radu Cool (USA) (Carnivalay (USA)) (146315) **Maktoum Al Maktoum**
58 B f 8/2 Grand Lodge (USA)—Coyote (Indian Ridge) (85000)
59 **CROSS CHANNEL (USA)**, ch f 18/3 Giant's Causeway (USA)—
                    Sterling Pound (USA) (Seeking The Gold (USA)) **Cliveden Stud Ltd**
60 **DAWR (IRE)**, b f 1/5 Sinndar (IRE)—Al Amlah (USA) (Riverman (USA)) **Hamdan Al Maktoum**
61 **DAY FILE (FR)**, ch c 11/2 Daylami (IRE)—Star Profile (IRE) (Sadler's Wells (USA)) **Maktoum Al Maktoum**
62 **DESERT FLORA (IRE)**, gr f 30/3 Green Desert (USA)—Requesting (Rainbow Quest (USA)) **Maktoum Al Maktoum**
63 **DIAMOND SHOWER (USA)**, b c 15/3 Swain (IRE)—Quality Gift (Last Tycoon) **Maktoum Al Maktoum**
64 **EASY AIR**, ch c 20/2 Zafonic (USA)—Easy Option (IRE) (Prince Sabo) **Maktoum Al Maktoum**
65 **EILEAN BAN (USA)**, ch f 2/5 Silver Hawk (USA)—Isla Del Rey (USA) (Nureyev (USA)) **Maktoum Al Maktoum**
66 **EKTIMAAL**, ch c 22/4 Bahamian Bounty—Secret Circle (Magic Ring (IRE)) (130000) **Hamdan Al Maktoum**
67 **ESCAPADO (USA)**, b f 1/2 Red Ransom (USA)—
                    Dubai Visit (USA) (Quiet American (USA)) **Maktoum Al Maktoum**
68 **ESDARAAT**, ch f 4/3 Pivotal—Dahlawise (USA) (Caerleon (USA)) (62000) **Hamdan Al Maktoum**
69 **FARAFRAN (IRE)**, b f 16/1 Rainbow Quest (USA)—Sahara Star (Green Desert (USA)) **Maktoum Al Maktoum**
70 **FORBIDDEN (IRE)**, ch c 28/3 Singspiel (IRE)—Fragrant Oasis (USA) (Rahy (USA)) **Maktoum Al Maktoum**

MR E. A. L. DUNLOP—continued

71 **FORDHILL (IRE)**, b f 13/3 Danehill (USA)—Ultra Finesse (USA) (Rahy (USA)) **Maktoum Al Maktoum**
72 B c 13/4 Red Ransom (USA)—Futuh (USA) (Diesis) **Hamdan Al Maktoum**
73 **FYVIE**, ch f 2/3 Grand Lodge (USA)—Island of Silver (USA) (Forty Niner (USA)) **Maktoum Al Maktoum**
74 **GALAXY BOUND (IRE)**, b g 11/2 Mark of Esteem (IRE)—
                    Diner de Lune (IRE) (Be My Guest (USA)) (130000) **Maktoum Al Maktoum**
75 **GHALLAB**, b c 16/5 Alhaarth (IRE)—Ta Rib (USA) (Mr Prospector (USA)) **Hamdan Al Maktoum**
76 **GIBBS CAMP**, b f 3/3 Marju (IRE)—Serengeti Bride (USA) (Lion Cavern (USA)) **Maktoum Al Maktoum**
77 **GIVE ME THE NIGHT (IRE)**, b f 13/2 Night Shift (USA)—
                    There With Me (USA) (Distant View (USA)) (10000) **The Sorcerers**
78 B c 19/3 Brahms (USA)—Good Going Gracie (USA) (State Dinner (USA)) (50000) **M. Jaber**
79 **GREEN VISION (IRE)**, b f 20/4 Green Desert (USA)—
                    Mighty Isis (USA) (Pleasant Colony (USA)) **Maktoum Al Maktoum**
80 **HANAGAN (USA)**, b c 8/2 Rahy (USA)—Night And Dreams (USA) (Fappiano (USA)) **Maktoum Al Maktoum**
81 **HIGH COMMAND**, b c 11/5 Galileo (IRE)—Final Shot (Dalsaan) (70000) **M. Jaber**
82 **ISLAND GREEN (USA)**, b c 25/2 Cozzene (USA)—Legend of Spring (Night Shift (USA)) **Maktoum Al Maktoum**
83 **ISLAND ODYSSEY**, b f 1/3 Dansili—Tetravella (IRE) (Groom Dancer (USA)) (14000) **Mrs J. M. Quy**
84 **JUICY FRUITS**, b f 6/2 King's Best (USA)—Fruit Punch (IRE) (Barathea (IRE)) **John Kunkel**
85 **JUST OBSERVING**, ch c 16/4 Observatory (USA)—
                    Just Speculation (IRE) (Ahonoora) (25000) **The Wily Partnership**
86 **KARIJINI (IRE)**, b f 1/4 Anabaa (USA)—Legaya (Shirley Heights) **Maktoum Al Maktoum**
87 **KAVACHI (IRE)**, b c 18/2 Cadeaux Genereux—Answered Prayer (Green Desert (USA)) **Maktoum Al Maktoum**
88 B f 15/5 Lujain (USA)—Kingdom Queen (IRE) (Night Shift (USA)) (7500) **The Serendipity Partnership**
89 **KITABAAT (IRE)**, ch f 28/2 Halling (USA)—Nabadhaat (USA) (Mr Prospector (USA)) **Hamdan Al Maktoum**
90 **LAKE BONNEVILLE (USA)**, b f 3/3 Diesis—Muneefa (USA) (Storm Cat (USA)) **Maktoum Al Maktoum**
91 **LAKE SHABLA (USA)**, b f 24/2 Silver Hawk (USA)—Miss Zafonic (FR) (Zafonic (USA)) **Maktoum Al Maktoum**
92 **LUCKY TOKEN (IRE)**, gr f 31/3 Key of Luck (USA)—Shawanni (Shareef Dancer (USA)) **Maktoum Al Maktoum**
93 **MALMOOS (USA)**, ch c 11/5 Gulch (USA)—Sedrah (USA) (Dixieland Band (USA)) **Hamdan Al Maktoum**
94 **MARACHI BAND (USA)**, b f 10/5 Dixieland Band (USA)—
                    Khamsin (USA) (Mr Prospector (USA)) **Maktoum Al Maktoum**
95 **MARINA GAMBA (IRE)**, b f 24/1 Galileo (IRE)—
                    Appreciatively (USA) (Affirmed (USA)) (150000) **Maktoum Al Maktoum**
96 **MARYMAS**, b f 17/3 Selkirk (USA)—Late Summer (USA) (Gone West (USA)) **Cliveden Stud Ltd**
97 **MEADOW MISCHIEF (FR)**, ch c 9/4 Halling (USA)—
                    Moonlight Saunter (USA) (Woodman (USA)) **Maktoum Al Maktoum**
98 **MOBSIR**, b c 4/2 Mozart (IRE)—Pretty Sharp (Interrex (CAN)) (150000) **Hamdan Al Maktoum**
99 **MONTPELLIER (IRE)**, b c 9/2 Montjeu (IRE)—
                    Ring of Esteem (Mark of Esteem (IRE)) (130000) **Maktoum Al Maktoum**
100 B f 18/2 Muhtathir—Moon Gorge (Pursuit of Love) (33534)
101 **MOSHAHED**, ch c 14/4 Nashwan (USA)—Nafhaat (USA) (Roberto (USA)) **Hamdan Al Maktoum**
102 **MOUNT SINAI**, b c 22/2 Green Desert (USA)—
                    Apache Song (Dynaformer (USA)) (45000) **The Earl of Derby & The Hon Mrs Peter Stanley**
103 **NIDHAAL (IRE)**, ch f 7/3 Observatory (USA)—Jeed (IRE) (Mujtahid (USA)) **Hamdan Al Maktoum**
104 **NOJOOM (IRE)**, b f 9/5 Alhaarth (IRE)—Elauyun (IRE) (Muhtarram (USA)) (52000) **M. Sultan**
105 **OFF MESSAGE (IRE)**, b f 21/3 In The Wings—Independence (Selkirk (USA)) **Cliveden Stud Ltd**
106 **OQUAWKA (USA)**, b br c 26/4 Quiet American (USA)—Yazeanhaa (USA) (Zilzal (USA)) **Maktoum Al Maktoum**
107 **PATITIRI (USA)**, ch f 24/4 Rahy (USA)—Dharma (USA) (Zilzal (USA)) **Maktoum Al Maktoum**
108 B c 9/4 Fraam—Periquitum (Dilum (USA)) (110000) **M. Jaber**
109 **POINT PLEASANT**, b c 13/5 Grand Lodge (USA)—Follow That Dream (Darshaan) **Maktoum Al Maktoum**
110 **PUY DE DOME (FR)**, b c 6/5 Priolo (USA)—Auratum (USA) (Carson City (USA)) **Maktoum Al Maktoum**
111 **QUIDI VIDI**, b c 11/4 Kahyasi—Canadian Mill (USA) (Mill Reef (USA)) **Maktoum Al Maktoum**
112 B br c 19/3 Seeking The Gold (USA)—Ranin (Unfuwain (USA)) **Hamdan Al Maktoum**
113 **SEA OF CALM**, b f 1/1 Quiet American (USA)—
                    Ocean Ridge (USA) (Storm Bird (CAN)) **Maktoum Al Maktoum**
114 **SIWA**, b f 21/5 Green Desert (USA)—Criquette (Shirley Heights) **Maktoum Al Maktoum**
115 **SONG OF SILENCE (USA)**, b f 19/5 Unbridled's Song (USA)—
                    State Secret (Green Desert (USA)) **Maktoum Al Maktoum**
116 **TAM LIN**, b c 21/2 Selkirk (USA)—La Nuit Rose (FR) (Rainbow Quest (USA)) **Maktoum Al Maktoum**
117 **TANTALLON**, b c 2/3 Anabaa (USA)—Entice (FR) (Selkirk (USA)) **Maktoum Al Maktoum**
118 **WAGTAIL**, b f 8/2 Cape Cross (IRE)—Dancing Feather (Suave Dancer (USA)) (120000) **Hesmonds Stud Ltd**
119 B f 6/2 Lujain (USA)—Watch Me (IRE) (Green Desert (USA)) (38228) **St Albans Bloodstock**
120 **WAVESKI**, b f 7/5 Rainbow Quest (USA)—Jet Ski Lady (Vaguely Noble) **Maktoum Al Maktoum**
121 B f 5/2 Galileo (IRE)—Wosaita (Generous (IRE)) **Eurostrait Ltd**

MR E. A. L. DUNLOP—continued

122 XINRAN (USA), b f 2/4 Mt Livermore (USA)—Regal Star (Sadler's Wells (USA)) **Maktoum Al Maktoum**
123 ZABEEL HOUSE, b c 7/4 Anabaa (USA)—Divine Quest (Kris) (57000) **M. Jaber**

Other Owners: Mr D. Gold, Mr J. Strauss, Mr D. Roberts, Mrs L. Channing, Ms D. Noble, Mrs G. Gurdon, Lord P. Spens, Mr I. Quy, Mr D. Clewley, Mr A. Manhood, Mrs C. Bell, Mr D. Stamper, Stanshore Ltd, Mr K. Stetzel, Mr J. Bavin, Mr P. Draper, Mr S. Pardoe, Mr S. Herbert, A. C. F. Sports Promotions, J. W. Fullick, R. T. Goodes, D. G. Raffel, B. Stewart.

Assistant Trainer: William Knight

---

172   MR J. L. DUNLOP, Arundel
Postal: **Castle Stables, Arundel, West Sussex, BN18 9AB.**
Contacts: **PHONE (01903) 882194 FAX (01903) 884173**
E-MAIL jldunlop@jldunlop.co.uk WEBSITE www.jldunlop.co.uk

1 **AJEEL (IRE)**, 6, b g Green Desert (USA)—Samheh (USA) **Hamdan Al Maktoum**
2 **BIG BAD BOB (IRE)**, 5, br h Bob Back (USA)—Fantasy Girl (IRE) **Windflower Overseas Holdings Inc**
3 **CAMROSE**, 4, ch c Zafonic (USA)—Tularosa **Nicholas Cooper**
4 **COVENTINA (IRE)**, 4, gr f Daylami (IRE)—Lady of The Lake **Capt J. Macdonald-Buchanan**
5 **FLYING ADORED**, 4, b f Polar Falcon (USA)—Shining High **Mrs M. Burrell**
6 **FOREVER FANTASY (IRE)**, 4, b g Daylami (IRE)—Gay Fantasy **Windflower Overseas Holdings Inc**
7 **HARLESTONE GREY**, 7, gr g Shaamit (IRE)—Harlestone Lake **Mr J.-L. Dunlop**
8 **HATHRAH (IRE)**, 4, gr f Linamix (FR)—Zivania (IRE) **Hamdan Al Maktoum**
9 **JEDBURGH**, 4, b c Selkirk (USA)—Conspiracy **The Earl Cadogan**
10 **KODIAC**, 4, b c Danehill (USA)—Rafha **Prince A. A. Faisal**
11 **MANGO MISCHIEF (IRE)**, 4, ch f Desert King (IRE)—Eurolink Mischief **Antoniades Family**
12 **MILLENARY**, 8, b h Rainbow Quest (USA)—Ballerina (IRE) **Mr L. N. Jones**
13 **MUKAFEH (USA)**, 4, b c Danzig (USA)—Bint Salsabil (USA) **Hamdan Al Maktoum**
14 **PERSIAN DAGGER (IRE)**, 4, b g Daylami (IRE)—Persian Fantasy **Windflower Overseas Holdings Inc**
15 **PERSIAN LIGHTNING (IRE)**, 4, b g Sri Pekan (USA)—Persian Fantasy **Windflower Overseas Holdings Inc**
16 **PROTECTING HEIGHTS (IRE)**, 4, br g Hector Protector (USA)—
                                     Height of Fantasy (IRE) **Windflower Overseas Holdings Inc**
17 **RACE THE ACE**, 4, b g First Trump—Princess Genista **I. H. Stewart-Brown**
18 **RAVE REVIEWS (IRE)**, 4, b f Sadler's Wells (USA)—Pieds de Plume (FR) **Prince A. A. Faisal**

THREE-YEAR-OLDS

19 **AHDAAF (USA)**, b f Bahri (USA)—Ashraakat (USA) **Hamdan Al Maktoum**
20 **ALPINE GOLD (IRE)**, b f Montjeu (IRE)—Ski For Gold **Windflower Overseas Holdings Inc**
21 **AROUS (FR)**, br f Desert King (IRE)—Moneefa **Prince A. A. Faisal**
22 **ASAATEEL (IRE)**, br c Unfuwain (USA)—Alabaq (USA) **Hamdan Al Maktoum**
23 **BADDAM**, b c Mujahid (USA)—Aude La Belle (FR) **Mr N. Martin**
24 **BEFORE TIME**, ch c Giant's Causeway (USA)—Original Spin (IRE) **R. Barnett**
25 **BERTROSE**, ch g Machiavellian (USA)—Tularosa **Nicholas Cooper**
26 **BUSACO**, b c Mister Baileys—War Shanty **Harry Dunlop Racing Partnership**
27 **CASSYDORA**, b f Darshaan—Claxon **Hesmonds Stud Ltd**
28 **COUP D'ETAT**, b c Diktat—Megdale (IRE) **Mrs Dan Abbott (Susan Abbott Racing)**
29 **DANCINGINTHECLOUDS (IRE)**, b f Rainbow Quest (USA)—Ballerina (IRE) **Mr L. N. Jones**
30 **DAWN'S LAST SHOT (IRE)**, b g Son of Sharp Shot (IRE)—Dawn Star **Windflower Overseas Holdings Inc**
31 **DOWNLAND (USA)**, gr f El Prado (IRE)—Quelle Affaire (USA) **Robin F. Scully**
32 **EBTIKAAR (IRE)**, b c Darshaan—Jawlaat (USA) **Hamdan Al Maktoum**
33 **EMPANGENI**, b g Mtoto—Shibui **Mr J. L. Dunlop**
34 **EVA SONEVA SO FAST (IRE)**, b c In The Wings—Azyaa **Eurostrait Ltd**
35 **FANTASTIC LUCK (IRE)**, b g Josr Algarhoud (IRE)—Fantastic Fantasy (IRE) **Windflower Overseas Holdings Inc**
36 **FARDI (IRE)**, b c Green Desert (USA)—Shuruk **Hamdan Al Maktoum**
37 **FLAG POINT (IRE)**, b c Indian Danehill (IRE)—Bianca Cappello (IRE) **Mrs J. P. R. Boscawen**
38 **GASSAAED (USA)**, gr f Aljabr (USA)—Histoire (FR) **Hamdan Al Maktoum**
39 **GIFTED MUSICIAN**, b c Sadler's Wells (USA)—Photogenic **Nicholas Cooper**
40 **GINGIEFLY**, b c Sinndar (IRE)—Native Ring (FR) **Mr N. Martin**
41 **GOLDEN FURY**, ch c Cadeaux Genereux—Galaxie Dust (USA) **Hesmonds Stud Ltd**
42 **GOODWOOD SPIRIT**, b c Fraam—Rechanit (IRE) **Goodwood Racehorse Owners Group (Ten) Ltd**
43 **GREY PLOVER (IRE)**, b f Alzao (USA)—Firecrest (IRE) **Sir Thomas Pilkington**
44 **GWYNETH**, b f Zafonic (USA)—Llyn Gwynant **Capt J. Macdonald-Buchanan**
45 **HADDAAF (USA)**, b c Kingmambo (USA)—Bint Salsabil (USA) **Hamdan Al Maktoum**
46 **HARLESTONE LINN**, ch g Erhaab (USA)—Harlestone Lake **Mr J. L. Dunlop**
47 **IN THE FAN (USA)**, b g Lear Fan (USA)—Dippers (USA) **O. Murphy**

MR J. L. DUNLOP—continued

48 **IN THE LEAD (USA),** b f Bahri (USA)—Air de Noblesse (USA) **O. Murphy**
49 **ISSA,** b f Pursuit of Love—Catawba **Plantation Stud Limited**
50 **JUNGLE DRUMS (IRE),** b c Nashwan (USA)—Conspiracy **The Earl Cadogan**
51 **KARLU (GER),** ch c Big Shuffle (GER)—Krim (GER) **Pat Eddery Racing (Rainbow Quest)**
52 **KOLYMA (IRE),** ch f Grand Lodge (USA)—Koniya (IRE) **Mr T. G. Roddick**
53 **KONG (IRE),** b c Sadler's Wells (USA)—Hill of Snow **Mr L. N. Jones**
54 **LADEENA (IRE),** b f Dubai Millennium—Aqaarid (USA) **Hamdan Al Maktoum**
55 **MASHONA,** b f Danzero (AUS)—Madurai **Mr J. L. Dunlop**
56 **MISS THE BOAT,** b f Mtoto—Missed Again **Capt J. Macdonald-Buchanan**
57 **MOKARABA,** ch f Unfuwain (USA)—Muhaba (USA) **Hamdan Al Maktoum**
58 **MOTARASSED,** b c Green Desert (USA)—Sayedati Eljamilah (USA) **Hamdan Al Maktoum**
59 **MPENZI,** b f Groom Dancer (USA)—Muschana **Nigel & Carolyn Elwes**
60 **MUNSEF,** b c Zafonic (USA)—Mazaya (IRE) **Hamdan Al Maktoum**
61 **MURAABET,** b c Dubai Millennium—Mahasin (USA) **Hamdan Al Maktoum**
62 **MUSEEB (USA),** b c Danzig (USA)—Elle Seule (USA) **Hamdan Al Maktoum**
63 **NAZAAHA (USA),** gr f Elnadim (USA)—Taatof (IRE) **Hamdan Al Maktoum**
64 **PILLARS OF WISDOM,** ch c Desert Prince (IRE)—Eurolink Mischief **Antoniades Family**
65 **QUEEN OF ICENI,** b f Erhaab (USA)—Princess Genista **I. H. Stewart-Brown**
66 **SABBIOSA (IRE),** b f Desert Prince (IRE)—Alla Marcia (IRE) **Mr N. C. Clark (Susan Abbott Racing)**
67 **SCARLET INVADER (IRE),** b g Indian Ridge—Scarlet Plume **P. L. Wroughton**
68 **SHORTBREAD,** ch c Selkirk (USA)—Breadcrumb **Sir David Sieff**
69 **SILVER SONG,** gr g Silver Patriarch (IRE)—Singing The Blues **Emmanuel and Neighbour Partnership**
70 B br f Irish River (FR)—Soaring Bay (USA) **O. Murphy**
71 **SOUFAH (IRE),** b g Desert Style (IRE)—Entracte **P. L. Wroughton**
72 **SPANISH RIDGE (IRE),** b c Indian Ridge—Spanish Lady (IRE) **Windflower Overseas Holdings Inc**
73 **TAWQEET (USA),** ch c Kingmambo (USA)—Caerless (IRE) **Hamdan Al Maktoum**
74 **TEEBA (IRE),** ch f Seeking The Gold (USA)—Shadayid (USA) **Hamdan Al Maktoum**
75 **THAKAFAAT (IRE),** b f Unfuwain (USA)—Frappe (IRE) **Hamdan Al Maktoum**
76 **THE NAWAB (IRE),** ch c Almutawakel—Eschasse (USA) **Mr J. L. Dunlop**
77 **UNFURLED (IRE),** ch c Unfuwain (USA)—Peony **Mrs H. I. Slade**
78 **USTAD (IRE),** br c Giant's Causeway—Winsa (USA) **Hamdan Al Maktoum**
79 **VELVET HEIGHTS,** b c Barathea (IRE)—Height of Fantasy (IRE) **Windflower Overseas Holdings Inc**
80 **YANTRA,** ch f Indian Ridge—Divine Quest **Plantation Stud Limited**

TWO-YEAR-OLDS

81 **AAMAAQ,** b c 11/4 Danehill (USA)—Alabaq (USA) (Riverman (USA)) **Hamdan Al Maktoum**
82 **ACTS OF GRACE (USA),** b f 26/1 Bahri (USA)—Ratha (Kris) **Prince A. A. Faisal**
83 **ARCHIESTOWN (USA),** b c 13/2 Arch (USA)—Second Chorus (IRE) (Scenic) (26000) **Mrs S. Abbott**
84 B c 1/1 Kingmambo (USA)—Ashraakat (USA) (Danzig (USA)) **Hamdan Al Maktoum**
85 **BAMBOO BANKS (IRE),** b c 30/1 Indian Lodge (IRE)—Emma's Star (ITY) (Darshaan) (17000) **Mr J. L. Dunlop**
86 B c 18/3 Storm Cat (USA)—Bint Salsabil (USA) (Nashwan (USA)) **Hamdan Al Maktoum**
87 **BOMBARDIER BUSH (IRE),** b c 11/3 Desert Prince (IRE)—
   Fantasy Girl (IRE) (Marju (IRE)) **Windflower Overseas Holdings Inc**
88 Ch c 13/2 Elnadim (USA)—Broadway Rosie (Absalom) (25485) **Tessona Racing Ltd**
89 **BUNOOD (IRE),** b f 8/2 Sadler's Wells (USA)—Azdihaar (USA) (Mr Prospector (USA)) **Hamdan Al Maktoum**
90 **DIPPED WINGS (IRE),** b f 3/4 In The Wings—
   Fantasy Wood (IRE) (Charnwood Forest (IRE)) **Windflower Overseas Holdings Inc**
91 **DOUBLE AGENT (FR),** ch c 21/3 Sinndar (IRE)—Conspiracy (Rudimentary (USA)) **The Earl Cadogan**
92 Ch f 17/4 In The Wings—El Jazirah (Kris) (16000) **Prince A. A. Faisal**
93 B c 29/1 Bahri (USA)—Elrehaan (Sadler's Wells (USA)) **Hamdan Al Maktoum**
94 **ESTIQRAAR (IRE),** b c 31/1 Alhaarth (IRE)—Hureya (USA) (Woodman (USA)) **Hamdan Al Maktoum**
95 **FEAR TO TREAD (USA),** ch f 31/1 Peintre Celebre (USA)—Pleine Lune (IRE) (Alzao (USA)) **Robin F. Scully**
96 B c 15/4 Namid—Fundraiser (Welsh Saint) (6000)
97 B f 2/3 Sinndar (IRE)—Gentle Thoughts (Darshaan) (20000) **Michael Watt**
98 **GOODWOOD MARCH,** b f 10/4 Foxhound (USA)—
   Military Tune (IRE) (Nashwan (USA)) (15000) **Goodwood Racehorse Owners Group (Eleven) Ltd**
99 B f 30/4 Mull of Kintyre (USA)—Heavenward (USA) (Conquistador Cielo (USA)) **O. Murphy**
100 **HEIGHT OF FURY (IRE),** b c 8/4 Sadler's Wells (USA)—
   Height of Fantasy (IRE) (Shirley Heights) **Windflower Overseas Holdings Inc**
101 **HOPE'S ETERNAL,** ro c 4/5 Highest Honor (FR)—
   Tennessee Moon (Darshaan) (11000) **Harry Dunlop Racing Partnership**
102 Ch f 23/4 Rahy (USA)—Istiqlal (USA) (Diesis) **Hamdan Al Maktoum**
103 **JASAD,** gr f 16/2 Erhaab (USA)—Labibeh (USA) (Lyphard (USA)) **Hamdan Al Maktoum**
104 B f 11/2 Seeking The Gold (USA)—Khazayin (USA) (Bahri (USA)) **Hamdan Al Maktoum**

MR J. L. DUNLOP—continued

105 **KRISTAL'S QUEEN (IRE)**, b f 22/2 Sendawar (IRE)—
Kristal's Paradise (IRE) (Bluebird (USA)) **Windflower Overseas Holdings Inc**
106 **LAQATAAT (IRE)**, b f 16/5 Alhaarth (IRE)—Jawlaat (USA) (Dayjur (USA)) **Hamdan Al Maktoum**
107 B f 26/2 Soviet Star (USA)—Last Drama (IRE) (Last Tycoon) (58000) **Capt J. Macdonald-Buchanan**
108 **LAYAZAAL (IRE)**, b c 14/4 Mujadil (USA)—Law Review (IRE) (Case Law) (50000) **Hamdan Al Maktoum**
109 **LEVIN (IRE)**, b c 5/2 Fantastic Light (USA)—Knight's Place (IRE) (Hamas (IRE)) (22000) **Mr J. L. Dunlop**
110 **LIGHT METER (IRE)**, ch c 10/4 Cadeaux Genereux—
Zoom Lens (IRE) (Caerleon (USA)) (16000) **Mrs P. G. M. Jamison**
111 **MANOUCHE**, b c 30/3 Highest Honor (FR)—Green Charter (Green Desert (USA)) **B. Andersson**
112 **MISWADAH (IRE)**, b f 25/2 Machiavellian (USA)—Khulan (Bahri (USA)) **Hamdan Al Maktoum**
113 **MORGHIM (IRE)**, b c 6/6 Machiavellian (USA)—Saleela (USA) (Nureyev (USA)) **Hamdan Al Maktoum**
114 **MOUNT KILIMANJARO (IRE)**, b c 27/4 Sadler's Wells (USA)—Hill of Snow (Reference Point) **Mr L. N. Jones**
115 B c 1/5 Royal Applause—Muffled (USA) (Mizaaya) (11000) **Mrs J. M. Khan**
116 **MUGHAAMER**, ch c 9/3 Medicean—Soolaimon (IRE) (Shareef Dancer (USA)) (50000) **Hamdan Al Maktoum**
117 **NAWAQEES**, b c 24/3 Danehill (USA)—Elrafa Ah (USA) (Storm Cat (USA)) **Hamdan Al Maktoum**
118 **NIMRANA FORT**, b c 16/3 Indian Ridge—Ninotchka (USA) (Nijinsky (CAN)) **Miss K. Rausing**
119 **NURDRAH**, b f 7/4 Green Desert (USA)—Sayedati Eljamilah (USA) (Mr Prospector (USA)) **Hamdan Al Maktoum**
120 **PAIRUMANI'S GIRL (IRE)**, b f 20/3 Pairumani Star (USA)—
Persian Fantasia (Alzao (USA)) **Windflower Overseas Holdings Inc**
121 **PERSIAN CONQUEROR (IRE)**, b c 9/4 Sinndar (IRE)—
Persian Fantasy (Persian Bold) **Windflower Overseas Holdings Inc**
122 **PLEASING**, b f 5/5 Dr Fong (USA)—Trounce (Barathea (USA)) (15000) **Minster Stud**
123 **QUEST FOR ETERNITY (IRE)**, b f 9/2 Sadler's Wells (USA)—
Head In The Clouds (IRE) (Rainbow Quest (USA)) **Mr L. N. Jones**
124 **QUSOOR (IRE)**, b f 9/5 Fasliyev (USA)—Winsa (USA) (Riverman (USA)) **Hamdan Al Maktoum**
125 **SENOR DALI (IRE)**, ch c 31/3 Peintre Celebre (USA)—
Far Fetched (IRE) (Distant Relative) (20000) **Mrs H. I. Slade**
126 B f 10/3 Sahm (USA)—Shuhrah (USA) (Danzig (USA)) **Hamdan Al Maktoum**
127 B c 19/1 Hernando (FR)—Sirdhana (Selkirk (USA)) (10000) **Mr R. Barnett**
128 **SMART GAL (IRE)**, ch f 23/1 Galileo (IRE)—Spring Easy (IRE) (Alzao (USA)) (26827) **Mr G. N. Clark**
129 **SPANISH REINA (IRE)**, ch f 27/3 Rainbow Quest (USA)—
Spanish Lady (Bering) **Windflower Overseas Holdings Inc**
130 **SPY GLASS**, gr c 8/4 Observatory (USA)—Heather Mix (Linamix (FR)) (6000) **Mr J. L. Dunlop**
131 **SYBELLA**, ch f 9/4 In The Wings—Samara (IRE) (Polish Patriot (USA)) (40000) **Nigel & Carolyn Elwes**
132 B f 1/1 Bahri (USA)—Tamgeed (USA) (Woodman (USA)) **Hamdan Al Maktoum**
133 **TAWAAFUR**, b f 16/4 Fantastic Light (USA)—Mahasin (USA) (Danzig (USA)) **Hamdan Al Maktoum**
134 **TELL**, b c 4/2 Green Desert (USA)—Cephalonie (USA) (Kris S (USA)) (50000) **Prince A. A. Faisal**
135 **TIME ON**, b f 27/2 Sadler's Wells (USA)—Time Away (IRE) (Darshaan) **R. Barnett**
136 **WANNABE POSH (IRE)**, b f 13/3 Grand Lodge (USA)—Wannabe (Shirley Heights) (200000) **Nicholas Cooper**
137 B c 9/3 Seeking The Gold (USA)—Wasnah (USA) (Nijinsky (CAN)) **Hamdan Al Maktoum**
138 **XENOPHILE**, ch c 15/1 Elnadim (USA)—Femme Femme (USA) (Lyphard (USA)) (3000)
139 **ZAMALA**, b f 3/3 King's Best (USA)—Ajayib (USA) (Riverman (USA)) **Hamdan Al Maktoum**

Other Owners: Will Armitage, Lord Balfour, Mr Derek Bingley, James Barber, Mr W. P. Church-Ward, Mr Nigel Clark, Mr P. Darling, Mrs A. Finn, Mr A. Gordon-Lennox, Mr G. Galazka, Mr E. Perry, Sir Philip Payne-Gallwey, M. J. Meacock, James Mayne, Guy Landau, The Hon. George Hyde, Mr A. Grazebrook, Mr N. Graham, Mr P. Townsend, Phil Swallow, Mr A. J. Struthers, Mr M. Stevenson, Miss Di Shirley, Mr H. Scott-Dalgleish, Mr T. Ricketts, Mr L. Reed, M. Broughton, Mrs B. Trafford, Mrs L. Godbere-Dooley, Mr I. De Wesselow, Antony Croker-Poole, The Earl & Countess of Clarendon, Mr Ian Cameron, Miss Julia Bradford, Miss E. C. Antoniades, Miss A. C. Antoniades, Mrs Carolyn Antoniades, J. O. R. Darby, R. M. Emmanuel, Miss E. Emmanuel, Sir Nevil MacReady, Capt A. Pratt, D. K. Thorpe.

Assistant Trainer: Robert Allcock & Harry Dunlop

173
MRS P. N. DUTFIELD, Seaton
Postal: **Crabhayne Farm, Axmouth, Seaton, Devon, EX12 4BW.**
Contacts: **PHONE (01297) 553560 FAX (01297) 551185**
E-MAIL nerys.dutfield@tiscali.co.uk WEBSITE www.nerysdutfield.com

1 **AONINCH**, 5, ch m Inchinor—Willowbank **Mrs C. J. Walsh**
2 **AVESOMEOFTHAT (IRE)**, 4, b g Lahib (USA)—Lacinia **K. J. Pike**
3 **CONVENT GIRL (IRE)**, 5, b m Bishop of Cashel—Right To The Top **Axminster Carpets Ltd**
4 **CURRAGH GOLD (IRE)**, 5, b m Flying Spur (AUS)—Go Indigo (IRE) **The Goldrush Partners**
5 **DEAR SIR (IRE)**, 5, ch g Among Men (USA)—Deerussa (IRE) **Unity Farm Holiday Centre Ltd**
6 **IN DEEP**, 4, b f Deploy—Bobbie Dee **T. J. Hawkins**
7 **LA PROFESSORESSA (IRE)**, 4, b f Cadeaux Genereux—Fellwah (IRE) **Mrs M. Dart**

MRS P. N. DUTFIELD—continued

    8 ROYAL AXMINSTER, 10, b g Alzao (USA)—Number One Spot **Axminster Carpets Ltd**
    9 TITIAN FLAME (IRE), 5, ch m Titus Livius (FR)—Golden Choice **P. J. Quinn**

THREE-YEAR-OLDS

   10 CELTIC SPA (IRE), gr f Celtic Swing—Allegorica (IRE) **Mr B. McCabe**
   11 B f Raise A Grand (IRE)—Ella-Mou (IRE) **Mrs P. N. Dutfield**
   12 MY GACHO (IRE), b c Shinko Forest (IRE)—Floralia **Mr Grant Mercer & Mr R. G. Toes**
   13 WITHERING LADY (IRE), b f Tagula (IRE)—Princess Oberon (IRE) **Salter, Wilson and Oakes**
   14 WOOD SPIRIT (IRE), b f Woodborough (USA)—Windomen (IRE) **Mrs C. J. Walsh**

TWO-YEAR-OLDS

   15 Ch c 2/3 Fruits of Love (USA)—Alpine Flair (IRE) (Tirol) (46947) **Mr Grant Mercer & Mr R. G. Toes**
   16 B c 13/3 Mujadil (USA)—Cookawara (IRE) (Fairy King (USA)) (16000)
   17 INDIAN LADY (IRE), b f 12/1 Namid—Lady Eberspacher (IRE) (Royal Abjar (USA)) (3047)
   18 Ch c 1/5 Shinko Forest (IRE)—Ivory Bride (Domynsky) (13413) **S. J. Dutfield**
   19 Ch f 26/4 City On A Hill (USA)—La Rochelle (IRE) (Salse (USA)) (2011)
   20 LUCKY APRIL, b f 2/4 Whittingham (IRE)—Lucky Dip (Tirol) (2285)
   21 MATTEROFACT (IRE), b f 20/3 Bold Fact (USA)—Willow Dale (IRE) (Danehill (USA)) (7712) **M S T Partnership**
   22 Ch f 22/3 Bold Edge—Noor El Houdah (IRE) (Fayruz) (40000) **G. Mercer**
   23 QUEEN OF DIAMONDS (IRE), b f 6/2 Fruits of Love (USA)—
                                          Royal Jubilee (IRE) (King's Theatre (IRE)) (14754) **Mrs M. Coxon**
   24 STAR OF SIAM (IRE), ch f 7/5 Elnadim (USA)—
                              Thoroughly (IRE) (Woodman (USA)) (18779) **Mr Patrick Toes & Mr R. G. Toes**
   25 SUNNY HAZE, ch f 21/3 Compton Place—
                          Sunrise Girl (King's Signet (USA)) (1714) **Unity Farm Holiday Centre Ltd**
   26 B c 14/3 Raise A Grand (IRE)—Theresa Green (IRE) (Charnwood Forest (IRE)) (10730) **Mrs J. Fuller**
   27 B f 6/3 Mull of Kintyre (USA)—Wisecrack (IRE) (Lucky Guest) (4023)

Other Owners: Michael Dalton, Mrs M. H. Sinanan, E. M. Thornton, Mrs S. Thornton, Mr P. M. Toes, A. J. White.

Assistant Trainer: Paul Holley

Jockey (NH): P. Holley. **Amateur:** Mr P. Kirkbride, Mr M. Saint, Miss A. Wallace.

---

174   MR C. A. DWYER, Newmarket
Postal: Cedar Lodge Racing Stables, Hamilton Road, Newmarket, Suffolk, CB8 0NQ.
Contacts: **FAX (01638) 667857 MOBILE (07831) 579844**
E-MAIL getadwyer@aol.com

   1 ARRY DASH, 5, b g Fraam—Miletrian Cares (IRE) **Mike & Denise Dawes**
   2 BELISCO (USA), 4, b g Royal Academy (USA)—A Mean Fit (USA) **Mrs J. A. Simpson**
   3 CANTERLOUPE (IRE), 7, b m Wolfhound (USA)—Missed Again **Mrs J. A. Simpson**
   4 DAGOLA (IRE), 4, b g Daggers Drawn (USA)—Diabola (USA) **Mrs J. A. Simpson**
   5 DANDOUN, 7, b h Halling (USA)—Moneefa **Mrs J. A. Simpson**
   6 DELLAGIO (IRE), 4, b c Fasliyev (USA)—Lady Ounavarra (IRE) **Mrs J. Parvizi**
   7 GOLDEN DIXIE (USA), 6, ch g Dixieland Band (USA)—Beyrouth (USA) **Mrs J. A. Simpson**
   8 MAN CRAZY (IRE), 4, b f Foxhound (USA)—Schonbein (IRE) **S B Components (International) Ltd**
   9 MEGABOND, 4, b g Danehill Dancer (IRE)—Apple Peeler (IRE) **M. M. Foulger**
   10 PETARDIAS MAGIC (IRE), 4, ch c Petardia—Alexander Confranc (IRE) **Miss S. D. Warren**
   11 PLUM, 5, br m Pivotal—Rose Chime (IRE) **Mrs J. A. Simpson**
   12 RASID (USA), 7, b g Bahri (USA)—Makadir (USA) **David L. Bowkett**
   13 SOUTHERN BAZAAR (USA), 4, ch c Southern Halo (USA)—Sunday Bazaar (USA) **Mrs J. A. Simpson**
   14 YAWMI, 5, ch h Zafonic (USA)—Reine Wells (IRE) **Mrs J. A. Simpson**

THREE-YEAR-OLDS

   15 BAILEYS APPLAUSE, b f Royal Applause—Thicket **Cedar Lodge 2000 Syndicate**
   16 BODDEN BAY, b g Cayman Kai (IRE)—Badger Bay (IRE) **G. Middlemiss**
   17 FAITHISFLYING, ch c Wolfhound (USA)—Niggle **Mrs S. Dwyer**

MR C. A. DWYER—continued

18 **JUSTENJOY YOURSELF,** b f Tipsy Creek (USA)—Habibi **Mrs S. Dwyer**
19 **LADY SUESANNE (IRE),** b f Cape Cross (IRE)—Lady At War **S B Components (International) Ltd**
20 **PROSPECT POINT,** ch f Cayman Kai (IRE)—Sassy Lady (IRE) **G. Middlemiss**

Other Owners: G. J. Darrall, N. J. Dobson, I. Dodd, Mrs C. Rawson.

Assistant Trainer: Shelley Dwyer

Jockey (NH): Matt Smith. **Apprentice:** D. Fox.

---

175 **MISS C. DYSON, Bromsgrove**
Postal: Britannia House, Lower Bentley, Bromsgrove, Worcestershire, B60 4JA.
Contacts: **PHONE/FAX (01527) 821493 MOBILE (07803) 720183**

1 **DEVOLUTION (IRE),** 7, b g Distinctly North (USA)—Election Special **Miss C. Dyson**
2 **DR CHARLIE,** 7, ch g Dr Devious (IRE)—Miss Toot **Miss C. Dyson**
3 **LOVE DIAMONDS (IRE),** 9, b g Royal Academy (USA)—Baby Diamonds **Miss C. Dyson**
4 **MARGHUB (IRE),** 6, b g Darshaan—Arctique Royale **Miss C. Dyson**
5 **MASTER TANNER,** 5, ch g Master Willie—Flaxen Tina **Miss C. Dyson**
6 **REGAL VISION (IRE),** 8, b g Emperor Jones (USA)—Shining Eyes (USA) **Miss C. Dyson**
7 **TANNERS COURT,** 8, b g Framlington Court—True Nell **Miss C. Dyson**
8 **TANNERS DEN,** 5, br g Abzu—Equilibrium **Miss C. Dyson**
9 **TRUE TANNER,** 7, b g Lyphento (USA)—True Nell **Miss C. Dyson**

Amateur: Miss C. Dyson.

---

176 **MR S. A. EARLE, Warminster**
Postal: The Beeches, Deverill Road, Sutton Veny, Warminster, Wiltshire, BA12 7BY.
Contacts: **PHONE (01985) 841166 FAX (01985) 840474 MOBILE (07850) 350116**
E-MAIL simon@simonearleracing.com WEBSITE www.simonearleracing.com

1 **BARTON BEAU (IRE),** 6, b g Kylian (USA)—Hetty Green **Mr N. A. Merritt**
2 **IMPULSIVO,** 5, ch g Millkom—Joytime
3 **LOYOLA,** 5, ch m New Reputation—Stay With Me Baby **Miss R. Wakeford**
4 **MISS WIZADORA,** 10, ch m Gildoran—Lizzie The Twig **Miss J. Grant**
5 **NORTHERN VALENTINE,** 7, b g Alflora (IRE)—Northern Jinks **Equine Health Centre Ltd**
6 **NOVICIATE (IRE),** 5, b g Bishop of Cashel—Red Salute **A.J. Moore, S. Faulkner, R.L. Dacombe**
7 **PARSONS FANCY,** 7, ch m Alflora (IRE)—Preachers Popsy **T. J. C. Seegar**
8 **PLAY IT AGAIN,** 5, b g Double Trigger (IRE)—Play For Time **Equine Health Centre Ltd**
9 **SAUCY NIGHT,** 9, ch g Anshan—Kiss In The Dark **Equine Health Centre Ltd**

Other Owners: E. Wilmott, Mrs O. J. Wilmott.

---

177 **MR M. W. EASTERBY, Sheriff Hutton**
Postal: New House Farm, Sheriff Hutton, York, North Yorkshire, YO60 6TN.
Contacts: **PHONE (01347) 878368 FAX (01347) 878204 MOBILE (07831) 347481**

1 **AMALFI STORM,** 4, b f Slip Anchor—Mayroni **The Lucky 5 Partnership**
2 **ARAWAN (IRE),** 5, b g Entrepreneur—Asmara (USA) **W. M. Johnstone**
3 **BELISARIO (IRE),** 11, b br g Distinctly North (USA)—River Gala **P. G. Jacobs**
4 **BLUE BUSTER,** 5, b g Young Buster (IRE)—Lazybird Blue (IRE) **J. Connor**
5 **BLUE SPINNAKER (IRE),** 6, b g Bluebird (USA)—Suedoise **G. H. Sparkes, G. Hart, S. Curtis & T. Dewhirst**
6 **BLUE WING,** 4, b c Bluebird (USA)—Warbler **The Woodford Group Limited**
7 **BROADWAY SCORE (USA),** 7, b g Theatrical—Brocaro (USA) **D. Scott**
8 **BUTTRESS,** 6, b h Zamindar (USA)—Furnish **G. H. Sparkes**
9 **CAT'S WHISKERS,** 6, b g Catrail (USA)—Haut Volee **The Four Legged Friends**
10 **CAULKLEYS BANK,** 5, b g Slip Anchor—Mayroni **S. Hull**
11 **CHARLIES MEMORY,** 6, b g Blushing Flame (USA)—Hat Hill **Mrs M. E. Curtis**
12 **COTTAM GRANGE,** 5, b h River Falls—Karminski **P. Easterby**
13 **DANCE PARTY (IRE),** 5, b m Charnwood Forest (IRE)—Society Ball **The Woodford Group Limited**
14 **DEE PEE TEE CEE (IRE),** 11, b g Tidaro (USA)—Silver Glimpse **Mr M. W. Easterby**
15 **DIX BAY,** 10, b g Teenoso (USA)—Cooks Lawn **Lord Daresbury**
16 **EGO TRIP,** 4, b g Deploy—Boulevard Rouge (USA) **Mr K. and Mrs J. Hodgson**

MR M. W. EASTERBY—continued

17 **EMPEROR'S WELL**, 6, ch g First Trump—Catherines Well **Mr M. W. Easterby**
18 **EVERYTIME**, 5, b g Vettori (IRE)—Flamingo Times **J. W. P. Curtis**
19 **EXPECT (USA)**, 6, b h Storm Cat (USA)—Personal Business **G. H. Sparkes**
20 **FUN TO RIDE**, 4, ch f Desert Prince (IRE)—Zafaaf **S. Hull**
21 **GALA SUNDAY (USA)**, 5, b g Lear Fan (USA)—
Sunday Bazaar (USA) **T. Dewhirst, R. Moore, F. Murphy, G. H. Sparkes**
22 **GARY'S PIMPERNEL**, 6, b g Shaddad (USA)—Pennine Star (IRE) **Lord Daresbury**
23 **GASTORNIS**, 7, ch g Primitive Rising (USA)—Meggies Dene **Lord Daresbury**
24 **GOHH**, 9, ch g Alflora (IRE)—Lavenham's Last **Mrs R. C. Hartley**
25 **GROUND BREAKER**, 5, b g Emperor Jones (USA)—Startino **The Woodford Group Limited**
26 **HANDA ISLAND (USA)**, 6, br g Pleasant Colony (USA)—Remote (USA) **Lee Bolingbroke & Partners I**
27 **HILLS OF GOLD**, 6, b g Danehill (USA)—Valley of Gold (FR) **G. Hart, D. Scott & G. H. Sparkes**
28 **KEY FACTOR**, 4, b f Defacto (USA)—Onemoretime **Mrs M. Lingwood**
29 **KINGS SQUARE**, 5, b g Bal Harbour—Prime Property **Mr A. G. Black & Mr J. E. H. Quickfall**
30 **MAJESTIC CLASS (USA)**, 5, b g Majestic Twoeleven (USA)—
Miss Count Fleet (USA) **The Handbrake Partnership**
31 **MARSH RUN**, 6, b m Presenting—Madam Margeaux (IRE) **Mrs M. E. Curtis**
32 **MEZUZAH**, 5, b g Barathea (IRE)—Mezzogiorno **The Woodford Group Limited**
33 **MIDDLETHORPE**, 8, b g Noble Patriarch—Prime Property (IRE) **Mr J. E. H. Quickfall & Mr A. G. Black**
34 **MOUNT HILLABY (IRE)**, 5, b m Mujadil (USA)—Tetradonna (IRE) **The Woodford Group Limited**
35 **MRS SPENCE**, 4, b f Mind Games—Maid O'cannie **Mr J. Wade**
36 **NARCISO (GER)**, 5, ch g Acatenango (GER)—Notturna **The Woodford Group Limited**
37 **NASSTAR**, 4, b c Bal Harbour—Prime Property (IRE) **A. G. Black**
38 **NEW WISH (IRE)**, 5, b g Ali-Royal (IRE)—False Spring (IRE) **E. A. Brook**
39 **NOWELL HOUSE**, 9, ch g Polar Falcon (USA)—Langtry Lady **J. Walsh**
40 **ONE FIVE EIGHT**, 6, b g Alflora (IRE)—Dark Nightingale **J. W. P. Curtis**
41 **ORION EXPRESS**, 4, b c Bahhare (USA)—Kaprisky (IRE) **L P S Racing**
42 **PARKNASILLA**, 5, b g Marju (IRE)—Top Berry **Lady Bland**
43 **PRINCES THEATRE**, 7, b g Prince Sabo—Frisson **Mr M. W. Easterby**
44 **REAL SHADY**, 8, b g Bob's Return (IRE)—Madam Margeaux (IRE) **Lord Daresbury**
45 **REVERSIONARY**, 4, b g Poyle George—Harold's Girl (FR) **Mr A. G. Black & Mr A. M. Hedley**
46 **ROSEDALE GARDENS**, 5, b g Fleetwood (IRE)—Freddie's Recall **D. M. Dudley**
47 **ROYAL DISTANT (USA)**, 4, ch f Distant View (USA)—
Encoronico (USA) **T Dewhirst, R Moore, F Murphy, G H Sparkes**
48 **SAUCY KING**, 5, b g Amfortas (IRE)—So Saucy **Lord Daresbury**
49 **SPORTING GESTURE**, 8, ch g Safawan—Polly Packer **S. Hull**
50 **STRONG HAND**, 5, b m First Trump—Better Still (IRE) **Mrs L. J. Turpin**
51 **SUPER NOMAD**, 10, b g Nomadic Way (USA)—Super Sue **Brian Hutchinson & David & Steven Dudley**
52 **THE NOMAD**, 9, b g Nomadic Way (USA)—Bubbling **Mr S. Brewer, Mr D. Sugars & Mr B. Parker**
53 **TICKTON FLYER**, 7, b g Sovereign Water (FR)—Contradictory **Mr T. D. Rose, Mr J. S. Dale & A. Foreman**
54 **TOP DIRHAM**, 7, ch g Night Shift (USA)—Miller's Melody **S. Hull**
55 **TRICK CYCLIST**, 4, b g Mind Games—Sabonis (USA) **Mr A. Menzies**
56 **TROUBLE MOUNTAIN (USA)**, 8, br g Mt Livermore (USA)—Trouble Free (USA) **Mrs L. J. Turpin**
57 **TRUST RULE**, 5, b g Selkirk (USA)—Hagwah (USA) **S. Hull**
58 **UHURU PEAK**, 4, ch g Bal Harbour—Catherines Well **Mr K. and Mrs J. Hodgson**
59 **WE'LL MEET AGAIN**, 5, ch g Bin Ajwaad (IRE)—Tantalizing Song (CAN) **Lord Daresbury**
60 **WESTCOURT DREAM**, 5, ch m Bal Harbour—Katie's Kitty **Mr K. and Mrs J. Hodgson**
61 **WILLIAM'S WELL**, 11, ch g Superpower—Catherines Well **Mr K. and Mrs J. Hodgson**

THREE-YEAR-OLDS

62 **CHAMPAGNE LUJAIN**, b g Lujain (USA)—Brief Glimpse (IRE) **Mr A. Hughes**
63 **ENEMIES OF JAZZ (USA)**, gr g Pioneering (USA)—Just About Enough (USA) **Mr P. Hobbs**
64 **FOLLY MOUNT**, b g Anabaa (USA)—Height of Folly **Mrs L. J. Turpin**
65 **HIGH PETERGATE (IRE)**, b f Mujadil (USA)—Anamara (IRE) **S. Hull**
66 **KING ZAFEEN (IRE)**, b c Lend A Hand—Groom Dancing **Mr J. Wright**
67 **LORD JOHN**, b g Piccolo—Mahbob Dancer (FR) **Mr R. Edmonds & Mr J. Wade**
68 **LOVELORN**, b g Mind Games—Love Letters **Giles W. Pritchard-Gordon**
69 **MARIAN'S GIFT**, ch f Bold Edge—Thimbalina **The Woodford Group Limited**
70 **NORTONTHORPE LAD (IRE)**, b g Charnwood Forest—Tisima (FR) **E. A. Brook**
71 **PEE JAY'S DREAM**, ch g Vettori (IRE)—Langtry Lady **Mr P. Bown, Mr J. Wade & Mr R. Edmonds**
72 **QUEEN NEFITARI**, b f Celtic Swing—Opalette **Lady Herries**
73 **SELKIRK STORM (IRE)**, b g Trans Island—Force Divine (FR) **Morecool Racing**
74 **SNOOKERED AGAIN**, b g Lujain (USA)—Highest Bid (FR) **Mr R. Edmonds & Mr J. Wade**
75 **WAYWARD SHOT (IRE)**, b g Desert Prince (USA)—Style Parade (USA) **R. Priestley Developments Co Ltd**
76 **WOODFORD CONSULT**, b f Benny The Dip (USA)—Chicodove **The Woodford Group Limited**

MR M. W. EASTERBY—continued

77 **WORD PERFECT,** b f Diktat—Better Still (IRE) **Mrs L. J. Turpin**
78 **ZAGREUS (GER),** gr g Fasliyev (USA)—Zephyrine (IRE) **T Dewhirst, R Moore & G H Sparkes**
79 **ZAROVA (IRE),** gr g Zafonic (USA)—Estarova (FR) **S. Hull**

TWO-YEAR-OLDS

80 **AVERTIBLE,** b g 3/5 Averti (IRE)—Better Still (IRE) (Glenstal (USA)) **Mrs L. J. Turpin**
81 **BEVERLEY POLO (IRE),** br c 17/3 Prince Sabo—Justfortherecord (Forzando) (2000) **Mr A. Foreman**
82 **B f** 24/5 Josr Algarhoud (IRE)—Boulevard Rouge (USA) (Red Ransom (USA)) **Mr K. and Mrs J. Hodgson**
83 **BOW BRIDGE,** br f 10/4 Bertolini (USA)—Bow Peep (IRE) (Shalford (IRE)) (6000) **Mrs A. Jarvis**
84 **Ch c** 23/5 Dashing Blade—Braissim (Dancing Brave (USA)) (8500)
85 **B c** 28/4 Piccolo—Carn Maire (Northern Prospect (USA))
86 **B c** 20/3 Pursuit of Love—Exotic Forest (Dominion) (8500) **Mr N. Gravett**
87 **B c** 16/4 Fasliyev (USA)—Flower O'cannie (IRE) (Mujadil (USA)) **Mrs E. Rhind**
88 **B f** 27/4 Averti (IRE)—Georgia (Missed Flight) **A. G. Black**
89 **GUIDELINE,** b g 19/4 Diktat—Polisonne (Polish Precedent (USA)) (3700) **Mrs L. J. Turpin**
90 **B c** 11/3 Night Shift (USA)—India (IRE) (Indian Ridge) (10000)
91 **Ch c** 21/3 Indian Lodge (IRE)—Jumairah Sunset (Be My Guest (USA)) **L. C. Welburn**
92 **LADY FAS (IRE),** b f 8/4 Fasliyev (USA)—Lady Sheriff (Taufan (USA)) **E. J. Mangan**
93 **LOOKING NORTH,** gr f 25/2 Paris House—Emma Amour (Emarati (USA)) (2800) **K. Wreglesworth**
94 **Ch f** 15/4 First Trump—Mahbob Dancer (FR) (Groom Dancer (USA)) (800)
95 **B c** 20/2 Orpen—Mimining (Tower Walk) (2000) **Mr M. Broad**
96 **MYSTICALLY,** b c 24/2 Diktat—Mystic Beauty (IRE) (Alzao (USA)) (10000) **Lee Bolingbroke & Partners**
97 **NICO'S GIRL,** ch f 23/3 Mark of Esteem (USA)—Naskhi (Nashwan (USA)) (800) **Mr J. Greenall**
98 **B c** 3/5 Timeless Times (USA)—Penny Hasset (Lochnager) **David & Stephen Dudley**
99 **B f** 10/4 Mull of Kintyre (USA)—Persian Flower (Persian Heights) (8000) **Mr David Scott**
100 **B f** 7/2 Foxhound (USA)—Prima Sinfonia (Fairy King (USA)) (1200) **Mr David Sugars & Mr R. Parker**
101 **Ch c** 20/1 Vettori (IRE)—Queen of Scotland (IRE) (Mujadil (USA)) (1800) **Lee Bolingbroke & Partners**
102 **B f** 10/2 Danehill Dancer (IRE)—Sangra (USA) (El Gran Senor (USA)) (6200) **Mr J. Wright**
103 **B c** 2/2 Compton Admiral—Sherrington (Thatching) **A. C. M. Spalding**
104 **SOTO,** b c 19/4 Averti (IRE)—Belle of The Blues (IRE) (Blues Traveller (IRE)) (2000) **D. Sugars and B. Parker**
105 **STING IN HER TAIL (IRE),** b f 29/1 Marju (IRE)—Barbizou (FR) (Selkirk (USA)) (5000) **Ballygallon Stud Ltd**
106 **THE HISTORY MAN (IRE),** b c 9/4 Titus Livius (FR)—
Handsome Anna (IRE) (Bigstone (IRE)) (8000) **Morecool Racing 2**
107 **B c** 7/3 Zilzal (USA)—Thea (Marju (USA)) (3600) **E. A. Brook**
108 **B c** 22/2 Arkadian Hero (USA)—Timoko (Dancing Spree (USA)) (3000) **L. C. Welburn**
109 **B c** 21/5 Averti (IRE)—Westcourt Pearl (Emarati (USA)) (1800) **Mr K. and Mrs J. Hodgson**

Other Owners: P. E. Bayley, S. R. Crowley, Mr P. A. Davies, Mr P. Davies, D. M. Gibbons, P. A. H. Hartley, Mr P. Lawton, D. Richardson, S. J. Smith, J. L. Southway, D. F. Spence, Mr P. Viner, R. M. Woodhall, Mr M. J. Worsnop.

Assistant Trainer: R O'Ryan

Jockey (flat): Dale Gibson, T. Lucas. **Jockey (NH):** A. Dempsey. **Apprentice:** Paul Mulrennan. **Amateur:** Mr T. Greenall.

---

178 **MR T. D. EASTERBY, Malton**
Postal: Habton Grange, Great Habton, Malton, North Yorkshire, YO17 6TY.
Contacts: **PHONE (01653) 668566 FAX (01653) 668621**

1 **ARTIE,** 6, b g Whittingham (IRE)—Calamanco **Mr A. Arton**
2 **BAY SOLITAIRE,** 4, b g Charnwood Forest (USA)—Golden Wings (USA) **D. A. West**
3 **BOLLIN ANNABEL,** 4, b f King's Theatre (IRE)—Bollin Magdalene **Sir Neil Westbrook**
4 **BOLLIN EDWARD,** 6, b g Timeless Times (USA)—Bollin Harriet **Sir Neil Westbrook**
5 **BOLLIN THOMAS,** 7, b g Alhijaz—Bollin Magdalene **Mr T. D. Easterby**
6 **BOURGEOIS,** 8, ch g Sanglamore (USA)—Bourbon Girl **C. H. Stevens**
7 **CHARNOCK BATES ONE (IRE),** 4, b f Desert Sun—Fleetwood Fancy **Charnock Bates**
8 **CLASSIC EVENT (IRE),** 4, ch g Croco Rouge (IRE)—Delta Town (USA) **C. H. Stevens**
9 **COUNTY CLASSIC,** 6, b m Noble Patriarch—Cumbrian Rhapsody **T. J. Benson**
10 **DAZZLING BAY,** 5, b g Mind Games—Adorable Cherub **GHMW Racing**
11 **DISTANT TIMES,** 4, b c Orpen (USA)—Simply Times (USA) **Times Of Wigan Ltd**
12 **DOE NAL RUA (IRE),** 8, b g Mister Lord (USA)—Phardante Girl (IRE) **The G-Guck Group**
13 **EBORACUM (IRE),** 4, b f Alzao (USA)—Fire of London **Mrs K Arton**
14 **EDMO HEIGHTS,** 9, ch g Keen—Bodham **Edmolift UK Ltd**
15 **EDMO YEWKAY (IRE),** 5, b br g Sri Pekan (USA)—Mannequin (IRE) **Edmolift UK Ltd**
16 **FAYR JAG (IRE),** 6, b g Fayruz—Lominda (IRE) **J. Gill**

MR T. D. EASTERBY—continued

17 **FLASH RAM**, 4, b g Mind Games—Just A Gem **L. Connolly**
18 **FLIGHTY FELLOW (IRE)**, 5, ch g Flying Spur (AUS)—Al Theraab (USA) **D. W. Armstrong**
19 **GO TECH**, 5, b g Gothenberg (IRE)—Bollin Sophie **Ryedale Partners No 4**
20 **JEEPSTAR**, 5, b g Muhtarram (USA)—Jungle Rose **Miss E. Jeeps and Partners**
21 **JEROME**, 4, b g Nicolotte—Mim **Mrs J. M. MacPherson**
22 **JONNY'S KICK**, 5, b g Revoque (IRE)—Prudence **Seven Up Partnership**
23 **JOY BOX**, 5, ch g Unfuwain (USA)—El Jazirah **C. H. Stevens**
24 **KENTUCKY BLUE (IRE)**, 5, b g Revoque (IRE)—Delta Town (USA) **C. H. Stevens**
25 **KENTUCKY EXPRESS**, 4, b c Air Express (IRE)—Hotel California (IRE) **C. H. Stevens**
26 **KING'S BOUNTY**, 9, b g Le Moss—Fit For A King **C. H. Stevens**
27 **KING'S PROTECTOR**, 5, b h Hector Protector (USA)—Doliouchka **J. Buzzeo**
28 **MOST DEFINITELY (IRE)**, 5, b g Definite Article—Unbidden Melody (USA) **B. Batey**
29 **MR ALBERT (IRE)**, 6, ch g Flemensfirth (USA)—Parkroe Lady (IRE) **Mrs J. P. Connew**
30 **MRS MOH (IRE)**, 4, b f Orpen (USA)—My Gray (FR) **Salifix**
31 **NISTAKI (USA)**, 4, ch c Miswaki (USA)—Brandywine Belle (USA) **The Nistaki Partnership**
32 **PAY ATTENTION**, 4, b f Revoque (IRE)—Catch Me **Ryedale Partners No 6**
33 **PRINCESS KIOTTO**, 4, b f Desert King (IRE)—Ferghana Ma **R. Matthews**
34 **RAREFIED**, 4, b g Danehill (USA)—Tenuous **C. H. Stevens**
35 **ROMAN THE PARK (IRE)**, 4, b f Titus Livius (FR)—Missfortuna **Middleham Park Racing II**
36 **RYHALL (IRE)**, 5, b m Saddlers' Hall (IRE)—Loshian (IRE) **Mr & Mrs W. J. Williams**
37 **SOMNUS**, 5, b g Pivotal—Midnight's Reward **Legard Sidebottom & Sykes**
38 **STONE COLD**, 8, ch g Inchinor—Vaula **Six Diamonds Partnership**
39 **SWAINSWORLD (USA)**, 4, b br g Swain (IRE)—Highest Dream (IRE) **Bigwigs Bloodstock**
40 **THE RIP**, 4, ch g Definite Article—Polgwynne **Major I. C. Straker**
41 **THEWHIRLINGDERVISH (IRE)**, 7, ch g Definite Article—Nomadic Dancer (IRE) **M. H. Easterby**
42 **TIMES REVIEW (USA)**, 4, b c Crafty Prospector (USA)—Previewed (USA) **Times Of Wigan Ltd**
43 **TOM FRUIT**, 8, b g Supreme Leader—Forever Mine (IRE) **David & Steven Dudley**
44 **TOUGH LOVE**, 6, ch g Pursuit of Love—Food of Love **The Gordon Partnership**
45 **TRIBAL DISPUTE**, 8, b g Primitive Rising (USA)—Coral Princess **Mrs J. E. Pallister**
46 **TRIPLE JUMP**, 4, ch g Inchinor—Meteoric **Mr and Mrs J. D. Cotton**
47 **TURGEONEV (FR)**, 10, gr g Turgeon (USA)—County Kerry (FR) **D. F. Sills**
48 **WING COLLAR**, 4, b g In The Wings—Riyoom (USA) **Mr and Mrs J. D. Cotton**
49 **YOUNG MR GRACE (IRE)**, 5, b h Danetime (IRE)—Maid of Mourne **N. A. Jackson**

THREE-YEAR-OLDS

50 **ARTIC FOX**, b g Robellino (USA)—Lets Be Fair **C. H. Stevens**
51 **BIG HASSLE (IRE)**, b c Namid—Night After Night **Lee Connolly and Jason Jones**
52 **BOLLIN BILLY**, b g Mind Games—Bollin Ann **Sir Neil Westbrook**
53 **BOLLIN MICHAEL**, b c Celtic Swing—Bollin Zola **Sir Neil Westbrook**
54 **BOLLIN RUTH**, gr f Silver Patriarch (IRE)—Bollin Roberta **Sir Neil Westbrook**
55 **BRAVE BEAR**, br f Bold Edge—Sarah Bear **Mr H. Ponsonby**
56 **BUST (IRE)**, b c Fraam—Purse **Weatherby, Hambury, McKey, Watts**
57 **CLASSIC STYLE (IRE)**, b f Desert Style—Classic Ring (IRE) **D. A. West**
58 **COLONIAL GIRL (IRE)**, b f Desert Style—Telemania (IRE) **P. C. J. Bourke**
59 **DARRINGTON**, b g Vitus—Masirah **The G-Guck Group**
60 **EBORARRY (IRE)**, b g Desert Sun—Aztec Princess **T. J. Benson**
61 **ELSIE HART (IRE)**, b f Revoque (IRE)—Family At War (USA) **C. H. Stevens**
62 **FIZZLEPHUT (IRE)**, b g Indian Rocket—Cladantom (IRE) **Mr & Mrs W. J. Williams**
63 **FIZZY EAU**, b f Efisio—Antonia's Dream **Slatch Farm Stud**
64 **GAME LAD**, b c Mind Games—Catch Me **Mrs J. B. Mountifield**
65 **GOLDEN SQUAW**, ch f Grand Lodge (USA)—Wig Wam (IRE) **Mr T. D. Easterby**
66 **GRANDOS (IRE)**, b c Cadeaux Genereux—No Reservations **Charnock Bates**
67 **HARVEST WARRIOR**, b g Mujahid (USA)—Lammastide **Mr & Mrs W. J. Williams**
68 **INDIAN FLYER (IRE)**, ch c Indian Ridge—Gazar **Mr and Mrs J. D. Cotton**
69 **IRISH PIPER**, b c Piccolo—Freddie's Recall **M. P. Lindsay**
70 **KAZAMATSU (IRE)**, ch c Grand Lodge (USA)—Anthis (IRE) **I. Henderson**
71 **MALCHEEK (IRE)**, br c Lend A Hand—Russland (GER) **Mrs S. Dicker**
72 **MIMI MOUSE**, br f Diktat—Shifty Mouse (USA) **Mrs J. P. Connew**
73 **MISS ROSIE**, b f Xaar—Disallowed (IRE) **Frickley Holdings Ltd**
74 **MIZZ TEE (IRE)**, b f Orpen (USA)—D D's Jakette (USA) **Salifix**
75 **NOODLES**, b c Mind Games—Salacious **Mrs J. M. MacPherson**
76 **PARIS BELL**, gr c Paris House—Warning Bell **Ryedale Partners No 8**
77 **RICH ALBI**, b g Mind Games—Bollin Sophie **The Albi Partnership**
78 **ROBINZAL**, b g Zilzal (USA)—Sulitelma (USA) **H. Tweddell**
79 **RYEDANE (IRE)**, b c Danetime (IRE)—Miss Valediction (IRE) **Ryedale Partners No 5**

MR T. D. EASTERBY—continued

80 SATIN ROSE, b f Lujain (USA)—Shamwari (USA) **Ryedale Partners No 3**
81 SPACE SHUTTLE, b c Makbul—Sky Music **Jennifer Pallister & Jonathan Gill**
82 TAGULA BAY (IRE), b f Tagula (IRE)—Nezool Almatar (IRE) **Mrs B. A. Tranmer**
83 TCHERINA (IRE), b f Danehill Dancer (IRE)—Forget Paris (IRE) **Mr & Mrs W. J. Williams**
84 TRIGONY (IRE), b g Brave Act—Lulu Island **Mrs J. M. MacPherson**

TWO-YEAR-OLDS

85 Gr c 18/4 Inchinor—African Light (Kalaglow) (21461) **Mr K. and Mrs J. Hodgson**
86 ALARM CALL, b f 2/5 Mind Games—Warning Bell (Bustino) **Mr A. Arton**
87 ARTIE'S BOY (IRE), b c 14/4 Fayruz—Lady Rath (IRE) (Standiford (USA)) **Mr A. Arton**
88 BEVERLEY BELL, b f 10/5 Bertolini (USA)—Lowrianna (IRE) (Cyrano de Bergerac) (21000) **D. W. Armstrong**
89 BOLDEN, ch c 29/1 Bold Edge—Enaam (Shirley Heights) (13000) **April Fools**
90 BOLLIN DAVID, b c 17/3 Golden Snake (USA)—Bollin Ann (Anshan) **Sir Neil Westbrook**
91 BOLLIN DENNIS, b grc 22/2 Silver Patriarch (IRE)—Bollin Harriet (Lochnager) **Sir Neil Westbrook**
92 BOLLIN DEREK, b c 4/4 Silver Patriarch (IRE)—Bollin Magdalene (Teenoso) (USA)) **Sir Neil Westbrook**
93 BOLLIN DOLLY, ch f 10/2 Bien Bien (USA)—Bollin Roberta (Bob's Return (IRE)) **Sir Neil Westbrook**
94 B f 7/5 Mister Baileys—Bombay Sapphire (Be My Chief (USA)) (15000) **1438 Group**
95 CARIBBEAN NIGHTS (IRE), b c 9/2 Night Shift (USA)—
                        Caribbean Knockout (IRE) (Halling (USA)) (11000) **N. A. Jackson**
96 B f 25/2 Almutawakel—Chancel (USA) (Al Nasr (FR)) (2346)
97 B f 13/4 Primo Valentino (IRE)—Charming Lotte (Nicolotte) (12000) **Swanland Racing**
98 CHASE THE ACE, b c 16/3 Foxhound (USA)—
                        Quiz Show (Primo Dominie) (7000) **Mr T. G. Holdcroft & Mr T. Herbert-Jackson**
99 B f 23/2 Groom Dancer (USA)—Classic Fan (USA) (Lear Fan (USA)) (33534) **Mr M. Fry**
100 COLLATERAL DAMAGE (IRE), b c 13/3 Orpen (USA)—
                        Jay Gee (IRE) (Second Set (IRE)) (30000) **Middleham Park Racing XXV**
101 CRUSADER'S GOLD (FR), b c 23/2 Lujain (USA)—
                        Rain And Shine (FR) (Rainbow Quest (USA)) (5000) **Miss C. Hodgetts**
102 DAMELZA (IRE), b f 28/1 Orpen (USA)—Damezao (Alzao (USA)) (8200) **Salifix**
103 DANCING DANE (IRE), ch c 29/4 Danehill Dancer (IRE)—
                        Tifosi (IRE) (Mujadil (USA)) (4694) **Dave Bramley & Philip Headon**
104 DOLLY BROWN, ch f 21/3 Bertolini (USA)—Birichino (Dilum (USA)) **Mr D. H. Brown**
105 EASY DANCER, ch c 12/2 Muhtarram (USA)—Sing And Dance (Rambo Dancer (CAN)) (3500) **The G-Guck Group**
106 B c 19/2 King's Best (USA)—Exactly Red (CHI) (Roy (USA)) (13413) **L. Connolly**
107 FURS N GEMS, ch f 7/1 Foxhound (USA)—Just A Gem (Superlative) (4000) **Mr T. G. & Mrs M. E. Holdcroft**
108 GALLERY GIRL (IRE), ch f 28/2 Namid—September Tide (IRE) (Thatching) (23473) **P. C. J. Bourke**
109 GAME OF LOVE, br f 20/4 Primo Valentino (IRE)—
                        Play The Game (Mummy's Game) (12000) **Mr T. G. & Mrs M. E. Holdcroft**
110 Br f 1/3 Bluebird (USA)—Golden Diamont (IRE) (Thatching) (9000)
111 GOODTIME GIRL (IRE), ch f 25/4 Shinko Forest (IRE)—
                        Titchwell Lass (Lead On Time (USA)) (8718) **P. C. J. Bourke**
112 GREEK SECRET, b c 27/3 Josr Algarhoud (IRE)—Mazurkanova (Song) (21000) **Mr M. Lindsay**
113 KING'S REVENGE, br c 31/1 Wizard King—Retaliator (Rudimentary (USA)) (21000) **Mr H. Ponsonby**
114 LA ESTRELLA (USA), b c 17/3 Theatrical—Princess Ellen (Tirol) (53205) **The G-Guck Group**
115 B c 30/4 Superior Premium—La Volta (Komaite (USA)) (4000)
116 LANTAU PEAK, b c 15/3 Observatory (USA)—
                        Shifty Mouse (Night Shift (USA)) (16000) **Ambrose Turnbull & John Sexton**
117 LITTLE SPARKLER, b f 22/3 Stravinsky (USA)—Idma (Midyan (USA)) (2000) **Mr M. Lindsay**
118 LYNDALEE (IRE), b f 4/2 Fasliyev (USA)—Itsibitsi (IRE) (Brief Truce (USA)) (20000) **Mrs J. P. Connew**
119 B c 13/5 Mark of Esteem (USA)—Mademoiselle Chloe (Night Shift (USA)) (15000)
120 MAKING MUSIC, b f 3/4 Makbul—Crofters Ceilidh (Scottish Reel) (18000) **Jonathan Gill & Jennifer Pallister**
121 Ch c 10/3 Intikhab (USA)—Matikanehanafubuki (IRE) (Caerleon (USA)) (25000) **Mr M. Fry**
122 Ch c 8/5 Zilzal (USA)—Moogie (Young Generation) (4000)
123 MULLAAD (IRE), b c 12/2 Mull of Kintyre (USA)—
                        Suaad (IRE) (Fools Holme (USA)) (17437) **Croft, Taylor & Stone**
124 MULLIGAN'S GOLD (IRE), b c 27/3 Fasliyev (USA)—
                        Magic Lady (IRE) (Bigstone (IRE)) (27000) **Mr C. H. Stevens**
125 MYTHS AND VERSES, b f 20/3 Primo Valentino (IRE)—
                        Romantic Myth (Mind Games) (85000) **Mr T. G. Holdcroft & Mr T. Herbert-Jackson**
126 B c 1/3 Namid—Nassma (IRE) (Sadler's Wells (USA)) (21000) **Bigwigs Bloodstock**
127 OBSERVATORY STAR (IRE), b c 1/2 Observatory (USA)—
                        Pink Sovietstaia (FR) (Soviet Star (USA)) (78000) **Mr & Mrs J. B. Cotton**
128 ONE MORE THAN TEN, b c 22/3 Piccolo—Julietta Mia (USA) (Woodman (USA)) (24000) **Mr L. Browne**
129 OPERA WRITER (IRE), b c 25/3 Rossini (USA)—Miss Flite (IRE) (Law Society (USA)) (12072) **N. A. Jackson**
130 B c 9/3 Royal Applause—Passe Passe (USA) (Lear Fan (USA)) (7000) **Ryedale Partners No 4**

MR T. D. EASTERBY—continued

131 B c 19/3 Bertolini (USA)—Plie (Superlative) (20000) **D. W. Armstrong**
132 **PONTY CARLO (IRE),** b c 10/4 Mujadil (USA)—
Distant Shore (IRE) (Jareer (USA)) (16096) **The Lapin Blanc Racing Partnership**
133 **PRINCESS CLEO,** ch f 14/3 Mark of Esteem (IRE)—
Classy Cleo (IRE) (Mujadil (USA)) (24000) **Widdop Wanderers**
134 **QUEEN JEAN,** ch f 1/5 Pivotal—Composition (Wolfhound (USA)) (25000) **Mr M. J. Dawson**
135 **QUINTIN,** ch f 27/1 Spinning World (USA)—Quadri (Polish Precedent (USA)) (30000) **Lady Legard**
136 **RAROTONGA,** b f 15/2 Mind Games—Bollin Sophie (Efisio) **A. G. Chappell**
137 Ch c 17/2 Vettori (IRE)—Reservation (IRE) (Common Grounds) **Dicker, Lowrey & Tindall**
138 **RIVER CROSSING,** b f 1/4 Zafonic (USA)—Vax Star (Petong) (35000) **Mr C. H. Stevens**
139 **ROYAL PUNCH,** b f 27/2 Royal Applause—Macina (IRE) (Platini (GER)) (32000) **Charnock Bates**
140 **SAMBERTINI,** b f 14/2 Bertolini (USA)—Samadilla (IRE) (Mujadil (USA)) **W. T. Whittle**
141 **SEMELE (IRE),** b f 17/3 Muhtarram (USA)—Pasithea (IRE) (Celtic Swing) (5000) **Legard, Titcombe & Lees**
142 B f 10/4 Mull of Kintyre (USA)—Sharpe's Lady (Prince des Coeurs (USA)) (6000)
143 B c 2/3 Trans Island—Sherna Girl (IRE) (Desert Story (IRE))
144 **SILVER NUN,** b f 13/2 Mind Games—Sapphire Mill (Petong) (6600) **Mr P. Baillie**
145 B f 14/5 Dansili—Simply Times (USA) (Dodge (USA)) **Times Of Wigan Ltd**
146 B c 19/1 Beckett (IRE)—Skerries Bell (Taufan (USA)) (12500) **B. Batey**
147 B f 13/3 Dansili—Song of Skye (Warning) (22000) **D. W. Armstrong**
148 **STANLEY BAY (IRE),** ch f 24/4 Namid—Joy St Clair (Try My Best (USA)) (10730) **Mr Ambrose Turnbull**
149 Ch c 22/4 Raise A Grand (IRE)—Stoneware (Bigstone (IRE)) (9389) **Mr D. Armitage & Mr A. Heley**
150 **TRAPPER YORK,** b c 24/1 Foxhound (USA)—Chlo-Jo (Belmez (USA)) (3000) **Mr D. Armitage**
151 **TRUMPITA,** b g 8/3 Bertolini (USA)—Trump Street (First Trump) (17000) **Jonathan Gill & Jennifer Pallister**
152 **TURKISH SULTAN (IRE),** b c 17/3 Anabaa (USA)—
Odalisque (IRE) (Machiavellian (USA)) (24000) **Sir Tatton Sykes & Lady Legard**
153 B f 15/4 Polar Prince (IRE)—We're Joken (Statoblest) (2500)

Other Owners: G. Aldus, T. Atkinson, D. F. Bramley, S. D. Brearley, S. I. Charnock-Bates, N. Collins, L. Connolly, C. Cook, D. Currie, P. J. Dixon, Mrs L. J. Dixon, D. M. Dudley, S. M. Dudley, G. S. Duncan, D. J. Evans, Sir A. C. Ferguson, Mrs M. Forsyth, D. Frame, G. Gill, J. M. Gosse, S. D. Gray, B. H. Hague, R. I. Hambury, Mr P. F. Hebdon, T. J. Hemmings, Mrs M. E. Holdcroft, A. D. Hollinrake, J. J. Jones, P. F. Jordan, J. M. Lamont, Mrs J. R. Lamont, J. Laughton, Mrs M. Lyons, G. Martin, S. Massey, D. J. P. McWilliams, P. S. Mulligan, T. S. Palin, D. M. Parsons, A. H. Raby, Miss K. Revitt, Mrs F. C. Saint Jean, V. Shields, Mrs J. C. Short, R. Sidebottom, D. Smith, Mrs R. A. Straker, D. G. Sutherland, D. Turner, R. T. Vickers, Mr T. Vickers, G. H. M. Walker, Mr A. M. F. Walker, J. R. Weatherby, Ms M. F. White, C. E. Whiteley, W. K. G. Whitfield, H. M. Wilson.

Jockey (NH): R. Garritty.

---

179 MR B. J. ECKLEY, Brecon
Postal: **Closcedi Farm, Llanspyddid, Brecon, Powys, LD3 8NS.**
Contacts: **PHONE (01874) 622422**

1 **ABRAHAM SMITH,** 5, b g Lord Americo—Alice Smith **Mr B. J. Eckley**
2 **OLYMPIAN TIME,** 5, b m Luso—Little Time **Mr B. J. Eckley**
3 **SMITH'S TRIBE,** 7, gr g Homo Sapien—Alice Smith **Mr B. J. Eckley**
4 **WITNESS TIME (IRE),** 9, b g Witness Box (USA)—Lisnacoilla **Mr B. J. Eckley**

---

180 MR D. EDDY, Newcastle Upon Tyne
Postal: **The Byerley Stud, Ingoe, Newcastle Upon Tyne, Tyne and Wear, NE20 0SZ.**
Contacts: **PHONE (01661) 886356 FAX (01661) 886484**

1 **A FEW BOB BACK (IRE),** 9, b g Bob Back (USA)—Kottna (USA) **B. Chicken**
2 **DONNA'S DOUBLE,** 10, ch g Weldnaas (USA)—Shadha **James R. Adams**
3 **DUNASKIN (IRE),** 5, b g Bahhare (USA)—Mirwara (IRE) **Mrs I. Battla**
4 **FAIR SHAKE (IRE),** 5, b g Sheikh Albadou—Shamrock Fair **I. R. Clements**
5 **FLOWING RIVER (IRE),** 7, ch g Over The River (FR)—Minature Miss **Mrs H. Scotto**
6 **HAULAGE MAN,** 7, ch g Komaite (USA)—Texita **James R. Adams**
7 **KRISTENSEN,** 6, ch g Kris S (USA)—Papaha (FR) **Equiname Ltd**
8 **LORD MORLEY (IRE),** 5, br g Lord Americo—Minature Miss **Mrs H. Scotto**
9 6, B g Treasure Hunter—The Long Bill (IRE) **P. Lishman**

MR D. EDDY—continued

THREE-YEAR-OLDS

 10 **EASTERN MANDARIN,** b g Tipsy Creek (USA)—Hotel Street (USA) **D. V. Tate**
 11 B c Fayruz—Miss Nutwood (IRE) **Equiname Ltd**

Other Owners: K. R. Elliott.

Assistant Trainer: Karen McLintock

---

181 **MR G. F. EDWARDS, Minehead**
Postal: **Summering, Wheddon Cross, Minehead, Somerset, TA24 7AT.**
Contacts: **PHONE (01643) 831549 MOBILE (07970) 059297**
E-MAIL dazjock001@hotmail.com

 1 **ACKHURST (IRE),** 6, br g Anshan—Sassy Sally (IRE) **Mr G. F. Edwards**
 2 **CEDAR RANGERS (USA),** 7, b g Anabaa (USA)—Chelsea (USA) **Mr G. F. Edwards**
 3 **DEVITO (FR),** 4, ch g Trempolino (USA)—Snowy (FR) **Mr G. F. Edwards**
 4 **HOPE VALUE,** 10, b g Rock City—Folle Idee (USA) **Mr G. F. Edwards**
 5 **IACACIA (FR),** 9, b br g Silver Rainbow—Palencia (FR) **Mr G. F. Edwards**

Amateur: Mr D. Edwards.

---

182 **MR C. R. EGERTON, Chaddleworth**
Postal: **Heads Farm Stables, Chaddleworth, Newbury, Berkshire, RG20 7EU.**
Contacts: **HOME (01488) 638454 OFFICE (01488) 638771 FAX (01488) 638832**
MOBILE (07795) 220630
E-MAIL charles.egerton@virgin.net

 1 **ABSOLUT POWER (GER),** 4, ch c Acatenango (GER)—All Our Dreams **Dr G. Madan Mohan**
 2 **ADMIRAL PEARY (IRE),** 9, b br g Lord Americo—Arctic Brief **M. G. Haynes**
 3 **AURAZURE (IRE),** 7, gr g Roselier (FR)—Siul Currach **Mrs S. A. Roe**
 4 **BALLYROBERT (IRE),** 8, b br g Bob's Return (IRE)—Line Abreast **The Saxon Partnership**
 5 **BALLYWALTER (IRE),** 9, ch g Commanche Run—Call Me Honey **B. R. Marsden**
 6 **CARDENAS (GER),** 6, b g Acatenango (GER)—Cocorna **Dr G. Madan Mohan**
 7 **DARKNESS,** 6, ch g Accordion—Winnowing (IRE) **Lady Lloyd-Webber**
 8 **DRUIDS CONFEDERACY (IRE),** 7, ch m Great Marquess—Winsome Blends (IRE) **Bush Syndicate**
 9 **EDGEHILL (IRE),** 4, b g Ali-Royal (IRE)—Elfin Queen (IRE) **Mrs E. A. Hankinson**
10 **EXECUTIVE PARK (IRE),** 9, br g Executive Perk—Brave Park **C. P. Kilgour**
11 **GALLANT APPROACH (IRE),** 6, ch g Roselier (FR)—Nicks Approach (IRE) **Byrne Bros (Formwork) Limited**
12 **GRAPHIC APPROACH (IRE),** 7, b g King's Ride—Sharp Approach **Mr & Mrs Peter Orton**
13 **HIGH TECH MADE (FR),** 5, b g Nononito (FR)—Home Made (FR) **R. F. Bailey**
14 **HOBBS HILL,** 6, b g Alflora (IRE)—Rim of Pearl **Mr & Mrs Peter Orton**
15 **IT'S JUST HARRY,** 8, b g Tragic Role (USA)—Nipotina **J. J. Blackshaw**
16 **LIGHT DES MULOTTES (FR),** 6, gr g Solidoun (FR)—Tango Girl (FR) **R. K. Carvill**
17 **MR POINTMENT (IRE),** 6, b g Old Vic—Bettyhill **Stockton Heath Racing**
18 **OUR MEN,** 6, b g Classic Cliche (IRE)—Praise The Lord **Mr N. W. Alexander**
19 **PRE EMINANCE (IRE),** 4, b c Peintre Celebre (USA)—Sorb Apple (IRE) **Sangster Family & B. V. Sangster**
20 **ROMANTIC HERO (IRE),** 9, g g Supreme Leader—Right Love **Miss F. M. Fletcher**
21 **RUBBERDUBBER,** 5, b g Teenoso (USA)—True Clown **Mr & Mrs Peter Orton**
22 **RUSSIAN SYMPHONY (USA),** 4, ch g Stravinsky (USA)—Backwoods Teacher (USA) **Mrs E. A. Hankinson**
23 **SILJAN (GER),** 8, b g Darshaan—Schwarzmeer (GER) **Seven Wayward Lads**
24 **STAGE BY STAGE (USA),** 6, ch g In The Wings—Lady Thynn (FR) **Mrs E. A. Hankinson**
25 **THE BAILLIE (IRE),** 6, b g Castle Keep—Regular Dolan (IRE) **Mrs D. E. H. Turner**
26 **THE LOCAL,** 5, b g Selkirk (USA)—Finger of Light **B. R. Marsden**
27 **TYPHOON TILLY,** 8, b g Hernando (FR)—Meavy **Mrs E. A. Hankinson**
28 **VALANCE (IRE),** 5, br g Bahhare (USA)—Glowlamp (IRE) **M. Haynes, A. & J. Allison, J. Weatherby**
29 **VINANDO,** 4, ch c Hernando (FR)—Sirena (GER) **Mrs E. A. Hankinson**
30 **WINDING RIVER (IRE),** 8, b g Montelimar (USA)—Bellora (IRE) **Elite Racing Club**

THREE-YEAR-OLDS

31 **HOMME DANGEREUX,** b c Royal Applause—Happy Lady (FR) **Team Havana**

MR C. R. EGERTON—continued

TWO-YEAR-OLDS

32 **ALICE AMELIA**, b f 28/1 Alhaarth (IRE)—Wondrous Maid (GER) (Mondrian (GER)) **Mrs J. Martin**
33 **ART DECO (IRE)**, ch c 30/3 Peintre Celebre (USA)—
Sometime (IRE) (Royal Academy (USA)) (140000) **Mrs E. A. Hankinson**
34 **BUFFY BOO**, b br f 3/2 Agnes World (USA)—Bunty Boo (Noalto) (40000) **Julie Martin/Linda Redmond**
35 **CREME BRULEE**, b f 11/4 College Chapel—Balinsky (IRE) (Skyliner) **Mrs J. Martin**
36 B br c 12/5 Galileo (IRE)—Fontemar (ARG) (Babor (ARG)) (100602) **Mrs E. A. Hankinson**
37 **GRAND ENTRANCE (IRE)**, b c 30/1 Grand Lodge (USA)—Alessia (IRE) (Warning) (93896) **Mrs E. A. Hankinson**
38 **HUMUNGOUS (IRE)**, ch c 27/3 Giant's Causeway (USA)—
Doula (USA) (Gone West (USA)) (380000) **Mrs E. A. Hankinson**
39 **KAPELLMEISTER (IRE)**, b c 5/3 Mozart (IRE)—
March Hare (Groom Dancer (USA)) (105000) **Mrs E. A. Hankinson**
40 B c 22/3 Danehill (USA)—Loire Valley (IRE) (Sadler's Wells (USA)) (160000) **Sangster Family**
41 **WELL GUARDED (IRE)**, b c 11/5 Sadler's Wells (USA)—
En Garde (USA) (Irish River (FR)) (170000) **Mrs E. A. Hankinson**

Other Owners: Mr B. Gover, J. Allsopp, J. Byrne, S. Davies, A. Buller, Lady Julia Fraser, W. Gibbs, M. Grimsey, A. Johnson, I. Holloway, C. Taylor-Young, C. Pomford, M. Osbourne, M. Mitchell, P Mills, A. Miller, D. Kinsella, R. Jones, G. Triefus, S. K. Thompson, J. Jones, T. Gray, M. Frost, Lady Aitken, The Hon W. Astor, Mrs R. W. S. Baker, Mrs P. G. Boddington, C. R. Buttery, P. Byrne, J. P. Cavanagh, A. Drummond, P. T. Fenwick, Miss F. M. Fletcher, S. R. Harrap, A. J. Hill, R. Johnson, Mrs P J. M. McCarthy, R. E. Morris-Adams, M. C. Moutray-Read, Miss M. Noden, Mrs S. K. Perkins, B. G. Pomford, A. J. Smith, I. R. Taylor, D. Thomas, Mrs P. T. Walwyn.

Assistant Trainer: David Plunkett

Jockey (flat): S. Drowne. **Jockey (NH):** J. A. McCarthy, A. P. McCoy. **Conditional:** A. Tinkler.

---

183 **MR E. A. ELLIOTT, Rushyford**
Postal: **Planting House, Windlestone Park, Rushyford, Ferryhill, Co. Durham, DL17 0LZ.**
Contacts: **PHONE (01388) 720383 FAX (01388) 722355 MOBILE (07968) 352177**

1 5, B g Warcraft (USA)—Gallic Flame **Mr E. A. Elliott**
2 **PLACE ABOVE (IRE)**, 9, b g Alphabatim (USA)—Lucky Pit **Mr E. A. Elliott**
3 **SHAKWAA**, 6, ch m Lion Cavern (USA)—Shadha (USA) **Mrs A. E. Elliott**
4 **TWO STEPS TO GO (USA)**, 6, b g Rhythm (USA)—Lyonushka (CAN) **Mr E. A. Elliott**

---

184 **MR R. P. ELLIOTT, Formby**
Postal: **South Moss Racing, South Moss Stud, Pasture Lane, Formby, Merseyside, L37 0AP.**
Contacts: **PHONE (01704) 830668 FAX (01704) 834329 MOBILE (07715) 000796**
E-MAIL peter@graysonsh-e.fsnet.co.uk WEBSITE www.southmossracing.com

1 **LILLY GEE (IRE)**, 4, b f Ashkalani (IRE)—Welsh Mist **Mrs S. L. Grayson**
2 **PETANA**, 5, gr m Petong—Duxyana (IRE) **Mrs S. E. Barclay**
3 **PLATTOCRAT**, 5, b g Dancing Spree (USA)—No Comebacks **Mrs S. E. Barclay**
4 **VAUDEVIRE**, 4, b g Dancing Spree (USA)—Approved Quality (IRE) **The Gazetters**
5 **WENDY'S GIRL (IRE)**, 4, b f Ashkalani (IRE)—Mrs Evans (IRE) **Mr E. Grayson**

THREE-YEAR-OLDS

6 **ANKUDHEPLAY**, b g Groom Dancer (USA)—Another Fantasy (IRE) **Mrs S. L. Grayson**
7 **CARMANIA (IRE)**, b g Desert Sun—Scatter Brain **John Wilding Promotions**
8 **ETERNAL SUNSHINE (IRE)**, b f Rossini (USA)—Sweet As A Nut (IRE) **Mrs Anita Tomlinson, Mr Ernie Duo**
9 **HEATHERS FURIO (IRE)**, b f Spectrum (IRE)—Almi Ad (USA) **Mrs S. L. Grayson**
10 **HOUDINI BAY (IRE)**, b f Indian Lodge (IRE)—Do The Right Thing **Mr E. Grayson**
11 **LADY HOPEFUL (IRE)**, b f Lend A Hand—Treble Term **The Haydock Hopefuls**
12 **LUCKY LUCKY (IRE)**, ch f Lil's Boy (USA)—Join The Party **John Wilding Promotions**
13 **NIBBLES (IRE)**, b g Soviet Star (USA)—Tumbleweed Pearl **Paladin Racing**
14 **SPACE TO RUN**, ch f Dancing Spree (USA)—Approved Quality (IRE) **Mr J. P. McGing**
15 **TURN ON THE STYLE**, ch g Pivotal—Elegant Rose **The Haydock Badgeholders**
16 **ZANTERO**, b c Danzero (AUS)—Cruinn A Bhord **Mrs Sarah Grayson and Mrs Ann Wall**

MR R. P. ELLIOTT—continued

TWO-YEAR-OLDS

17 Ch c 28/3 Atraf—Approved Quality (IRE) (Persian Heights) (5000) **Mrs S. E. Barclay**
18 BELLALINI, b f 4/2 Bertolini (USA)—Primum Tempus (Primo Dominie) **Springs Equestrian Partnership**
19 Ch c 10/3 Bold Edge—Calypso Lady (IRE) (Priolo (USA)) (20000) **Mrs S. L. Grayson**
20 B f 14/4 Elnadim (USA)—Chocolate (IRE) (Brief Truce (USA))
21 B f 10/4 Elnadim (USA)—Do The Right Thing (Busted) (6706)
22 Br c 16/3 Lend A Hand—Election Special (Chief Singer) (20120)
23 B c 12/4 Tagula (IRE)—Eveam (IRE) (Mujadil (USA)) (6000)
24 Br c 9/3 Benny The Dip (USA)—Golconda (IRE) (Lahib (USA))
25 Ch g 23/2 Bahamian Bounty—Golden Panda (Music Boy) (5500)
26 IMAGINE THAT, b f 28/3 Bertolini (USA)—
                             Rythm N Time (Timeless Times (USA)) **Springs Equestrian Partnership**
27 KEY OF MAGIC (IRE), b c 15/4 Key of Luck (USA)—Desirous of Peace (Forzando) (5029) **21st Century Racing 3**
28 OGGY OGGY OGGY, ch f 10/4 Fraam—Princess Poquito (Hard Fought) (3000) **L. Ogburn**
29 Ch f 10/2 Rossini (USA)—Settle Petal (IRE) (Roi Danzig (USA))
30 SPIRIT OF CONISTON, b c 28/3 Lake Coniston (IRE)—Kigema (IRE) (Case Law) (5200)
31 STONEACRE GIRL (IRE), ch f 26/3 Rossini (USA)—Ring of Light (Auction Ring (USA)) (5364)
32 STONEACRE LAD (IRE), b c 21/2 Bluebird (USA)—Jay And-A (IRE) (Elbio) (10730)
33 STONEACRE LIL (IRE), b f 20/4 Fasliyev (USA)—Lady Ounavarra (IRE) (Simply Great (FR)) (10730)

Other Owners: A. W. Catterall, Mrs B. Catterall, P. M. Clarkson, Mr A. P. Dawson, Anthony Scholes, Mrs A. E. Scholes, J. Wilding, Mrs J. M. Wilding.

Assistant Trainer: Peter Grayson

---

185   MR BRIAN ELLISON, Malton
Postal: **Spring Cottage Stables, Langton Road, Norton, Malton, North Yorkshire, YO17 9PY.**
Contacts: **HOME (01653) 690005 OFFICE (01653) 690004 FAX (01653) 690008**
MOBILE (07785) 747426
E-MAIL ellisonracing@aol.com WEBSITE www.brianellison.co.uk

1 ARTISTIC STYLE, 5, b h Anabaa (USA)—Fine Detail (IRE) **Mr & Mrs D. A. Gamble**
2 ASH BOLD (IRE), 8, ch g Persian Bold—Pasadena Lady **Harvey Ashworth**
3 BERGAMO, 9, b g Robellino (USA)—Pretty Thing **Rasen Goes Racing**
4 BETHANYS BOY (IRE), 4, ch g Docksider (USA)—Daymoon (USA) **Get Into Racing**
5 CARTE DIAMOND (USA), 4, ch c Theatrical—Liteup My Life (USA) **A. Carr**
6 CD FLYER (IRE), 8, ch g Grand Lodge (USA)—Pretext **K. Middleton**
7 CLARADOTNET, 5, b m Sri Pekan (USA)—Lypharitissima (FR) **Get Into Racing**
8 COLEMANSTOWN, 5, b g Charnwood Forest (IRE)—Arme Fatale (IRE) **Get Into Racing**
9 COMPTON ECLAIRE (IRE), 5, ch m Lycius (USA)—Baylands Sunshine (IRE) **S. V. Rutter**
10 COURT OF APPEAL, 8, ch g Bering—Hiawatha's Song (USA) **Spring Cottage Syndicate**
11 DARING GAMES, 4, b f Mind Games—Daira **R. McCulloch**
12 DORIC (USA), 4, ch c Distant View—Doree (USA) **Mr & Mrs D. A. Gamble**
13 EVEREST (IRE), 8, ch g Indian Ridge—Reine d'beaute **Mr I. S. Sandhu and Partners**
14 FORT CHURCHILL (IRE), 4, b g Barathea (IRE)—Brisighella (IRE) **Benton and Partners**
15 FOURSWAINBY (IRE), 4, b g Foxhound (USA)—Arena **K. Middleton**
16 GEORGE STUBBS (USA), 7, b br g Affirmed (USA)—Mia Duchessa (USA) **P. J. Dixon**
17 GINGERBREAD, 4, ch g Pharly (FR)—Gay Sarah **The Half Moon Club**
18 GREAT AS GOLD (IRE), 6, b g Goldmark (USA)—Great Land (USA) **K. Middleton**
19 HOPE SOUND (IRE), 5, b g Turtle Island (IRE)—Lucky Pick **Raymond Wagner**
20 HUE, 4, ch c Peintre Celebre (USA)—Quandary (USA) **Get Into Racing**
21 JIMMY BYRNE (IRE), 5, ch g Red Sunset—Persian Sally (IRE) **K. Middleton**
22 KING EIDER, 6, b br g Mtoto—Hen Harrier **Angela Rix & Partners**
23 LEWIS ISLAND (IRE), 6, b g Turtle Island (IRE)—Phyllode **A. S. Williamson**
24 MISTER ARJAY (USA), 5, b h Mister Baileys—Crystal Stepper (USA) **K. Middleton**
25 PROUD WESTERN (USA), 7, b br g Gone West (USA)—Proud Lou (USA) **B. Ellison**
26 SEIFI, 6, b g Hector Protector (USA)—Garconniere **A. Carr**
27 SIR NORTHERNDANCER (IRE), 6, b h Danehill Dancer (IRE)—Lady At War **K. Middleton**
28 TIZZY MAY (FR), 5, ch h Highest Honor (FR)—Forentia (IRE) **Rita Wenmen**
29 TORRID KENTAVR (USA), 8, b g Trempolino (USA)—Torrid Tango (USA) **Get Into Racing**
30 TRANSIT, 6, b g Lion Cavern (USA)—Black Fighter (USA) **Get Into Racing**

MR BRIAN ELLISON—continued

31 UNTIDY DAUGHTER, 6, b m Sabrehill (USA)—Branitska **Alderclad Roofing, S. V. Rutter, G. Hamilton**
32 VANISHING DANCER (SWI), 8, ch g Llandaff (USA)—
Vanishing Prairie (USA) **Mr E. J. Berry & Mr Raymond Wagner**
33 ZIBELINE (IRE), 8, b g Cadeaux Genereux—Zia (USA) **A. Carr**

THREE-YEAR-OLDS

34 ASHKAL WAY (IRE), ch c Ashkalani (IRE)—Golden Way (IRE) **A. Carr**
35 JOHN FORBES, b c High Estate—Mavourneen (USA) **Mrs C. L. Ellison & Mr Raymond Wagner**
36 JUN FAN (USA), br c Artax (USA)—Ringside Lady (NZ) **Mrs C. L. Ellison**
37 MR MARUCCI (USA), b c Miner's Mark (USA)—Appealing Style (USA) **Spring Cottage Syndicate**
38 SENTIERO ROSSO (USA), b c Intidab (USA)—Kheyrah (USA) **Get Into Racing**
39 SPRING TIME GIRL, b f Timeless Times (USA)—Daira **R. McCulloch**
40 VICTOR BUCKWELL, br c Pivotal—Lonely Shore **A. Carr**

TWO-YEAR-OLDS

41 B c 25/2 King of Kings (IRE)—Al Saqiya (USA) (Woodman (USA)) (20000) **Get Into Racing**
42 B c 20/3 City On A Hill (USA)—Alkariyh (USA) (Alydar (USA)) (36000) **Get Into Racing**
43 B c 11/3 Elnadim (USA)—Brittas Blues (IRE) (Blues Traveller (IRE)) (19000) **Get Into Racing**
44 B c 29/3 Bertolini (USA)—Charlie Girl (Puissance) (24000) **Get Into Racing**
45 B c 22/1 Foxhound (USA)—Classy Relation (Puissance) (17000) **Get Into Racing**
46 Br c 4/5 Xaar—Decatur (Deploy) (15000) **Get Into Racing**
47 B c 10/3 Groom Dancer (USA)—Finlandaise (FR) (Arctic Tern (USA)) (15000) **Get Into Racing**
48 Ch c 12/4 Compton Place—Floral Spark (Forzando) (14000) **Get Into Racing**
49 Ch f 22/2 Tagula (IRE)—La Alla Wa Asa (IRE) (Alzao (USA)) (20000) **Get Into Racing**
50 Ch c 17/3 Tagula (IRE)—Limerick Princess (IRE) (Polish Patriot (USA)) (9000) **Get Into Racing**
51 B f 15/4 Bahhare (USA)—Nesting (Thatching) (16000) **Get Into Racing**
52 B br c 24/2 Dayjur (USA)—Ra'a (Diesis) (50000) **Get Into Racing**
53 B f 30/4 Dansili—Vilany (Never So Bold) (6000) **Get Into Racing**

Other Owners: Miss C. L. C. Adams, P. M. Clarkson, Mr J. Curry, P. J. Jacobs, A. Marucci, Mrs V. McGee, G. J. Price, Mrs C. Richardson, H. J. Rix, Mrs A. M. Rix.

Assistant Trainer: L Ellison

Jockey (flat): T. Eaves. **Jockey (NH):** V. T. Keane. **Apprentice:** T. Hamilton. **Amateur:** Miss L. Ellison, Mr C. Lidster.

---

186 MR D. R. C. ELSWORTH, Whitsbury
Postal: Whitsbury Manor Racing Stables, Whitsbury, Fordingbridge, Hampshire, SP6 3QB.
Contacts: OFFICE (01725) 518889 HOME (01725) 518274 FAX (01725) 518747
MOBILE (07771) 804828
E-MAIL david.elsworth@virgin.net

1 ALFRIDINI, 4, ch g Selkirk (USA)—Vivre En Paix **A. Heaney**
2 BACKBEAT (IRE), 8, ch g Bob Back (USA)—Pinata **W.V. & Mrs E.S. Robins**
3 BALKAN KNIGHT, 5, b h Selkirk (USA)—Crown of Light **R. C. Tooth**
4 BARRY ISLAND, 6, b g Turtle Island (IRE)—Pine Ridge **M. R. Green**
5 BLACK DE BESSY (FR), 7, b g Perrault—Emerald City **Mrs Derek Fletcher & Mrs B. P. Hall**
6 CALEDONIAN (IRE), 4, b g Soviet Star (USA)—Supercal **The Caledonian Racing Society**
7 CAUGHNAWAGA (FR), 7, b g Indian Ridge—Wakria (IRE) **R. J. Cohen**
8 ELZEES, 4, b g Magic Ring (IRE)—White Flash **Mr D. R. C. Elsworth**
9 FIRST BALLOT (IRE), 9, br g Perugino (USA)—Election Special **M. R. Green**
10 FOODBROKER FOUNDER, 5, ch g Groom Dancer (USA)—Nemea (USA) **Mr D. R. C. Elsworth**
11 GAY GLADYS, 5, b m Ridgewood Ben—Ovideo **Mr D. R. C. Elsworth**
12 GULF (IRE), 6, ch g Persian Bold—Broken Romance (IRE) **R. C. Tooth**
13 HI HUMPFREE, 5, b g Thowra (FR)—White Flash **Mr D. R. C. Elsworth**
14 HIGH BRAY (GER), 4, b c Zieten (USA)—Homing Instinct **Gestut Gorlsdorf**
15 HIGHLAND REEL, 8, ch g Selkirk (USA)—Taj Victory **Sir Gordon Brunton**
16 INDIAN TRAIL, 5, ch g Indian Ridge—Take Heart **The Trail Blazers**
17 ISLAND SOUND, 8, b g Turtle Island (IRE)—Ballet **Mrs M. F. Meredith**
18 KATHOLOGY (IRE), 8, b g College Chapel—Wicken Wonder (IRE) **McDowell Racing Ltd**
19 MASSIF CENTRALE, 4, ch c Selkirk (USA)—Madame Dubois **R. C. Tooth**
20 MICHAJO (IRE), 4, b g Robellino (USA)—Mole Creek **Mrs M. F. Meredith**
21 NORSE DANCER (IRE), 5, b h Halling (USA)—River Patrol **J. C. Smith**
22 RIVER GYPSY, 4, b c In The Wings—River Erne (USA) **J. C. Smith**

MR D. R. C. ELSWORTH—continued

23 **SAN HERNANDO,** 5, b g Hernando (FR)—Sandrella (IRE) **The Madding Crowd**
24 **SKIDMARK,** 4, b g Pennekamp (USA)—Flourishing (IRE) **R. C. Tooth**
25 **SPANISH DON,** 7, b g Zafonic (USA)—Spanish Wells (IRE) **R. J. Cohen**
26 **TOPKAT (IRE),** 4, b g Simply Great (FR)—Kitty's Sister **R. Standring**
27 **WAVERTREE BOY (IRE),** 5, ch g Hector Protector (USA)—Lust **Wavertree Racing Club (2002) Ltd**
28 **WHITSBURY CROSS,** 4, b c Cape Cross (IRE)—Vallauris **McDowell Racing Ltd & Mr D. R. C. Elsworth**

THREE-YEAR-OLDS

29 **ART EYES (USA),** ch f Halling (USA)—Careyes (IRE) **M. R. Green**
30 **BENIGHTED,** b f Benny The Dip (USA)—Premier Night **The Churston Family**
31 **BRECON,** ch f Unfuwain (USA)—Welsh Valley (USA) **Mr K. J. & Mrs S. Mercer**
32 **CALY DANCER (IRE),** ch g Entrepreneur—Mountain Dancer (IRE) **The Caledonian Racing Society**
33 **CANARY ISLAND (IRE),** b g Polar Falcon (USA)—Yellow Trumpet **Mrs A. J. K. Dunn**
34 **CAPE COLUMBINE,** b br f Diktat—Cape Merino **Old Peartee Stud**
35 **DARLING DEANIE (IRE),** ch f Sinndar (IRE)—
                                   Blushing Melody (IRE) **Mrs D. M. Solomon & Mr D. R. C. Elsworth**
36 **GARIBALDI (GER),** ch c Acatenango (GER)—Guanhumara **The Bramfield Racing Syndicate**
37 **GULCHINA (USA),** b f Gulch (USA)—Harda Arda (USA) **J. C. Smith**
38 **JOHN CHARLES (IRE),** b c Fraam—Norwegian Queen **M. J. Davies**
39 **JUBILEE DREAM,** b g Bluebird (USA)—Last Dream (IRE) **W.V. & Mrs E.S. Robins**
40 **MISSIE BAILEYS,** ch f Mister Baileys—Jilly Woo **Mrs J. Wotherspoon**
41 **NOTA BENE,** b c Zafonic (USA)—Dodo (IRE) **W.V. & Mrs E.S. Robins**
42 **OCEAN GIFT,** b g Cadeaux Genereux—Sea Drift (FR) **J. C. Smith**
43 Ch c Rainbow Quest (USA)—Ridgewood Pearl **Mrs A. M. Coughlan**
44 **SALFORD ARTIST,** ch g Zafonic (USA)—Highland Rhapsody (IRE) **M. R. Green**
45 **SELMA,** ch f Selkirk (USA)—Mish Mish **Miss K. Rausing**
46 **SHIRE (IRE),** br c Trans Island—Trebles (IRE) **Mr D. R. C. Elsworth**
47 **SIMPLY SUNSHINE (IRE),** b f Desert Sun—Summer Fashion **Dr D. B. Davis**
48 **SOMETHING EXCITING,** ch f Halling (USA)—Faraway Waters **Mr M. Watson**
49 **THE GEEZER,** ch c Halling (USA)—Polygueza (FR) **J. C. Smith**
50 **TOP GEAR,** b c Robellino (USA)—Bundle **Mrs P. J. Sheen**
51 **TUCKER,** b c Inchinor—Tender Moment (IRE) **R. K. Richards**
52 **WAVERTREE ONE OFF,** b g Diktat—Miss Clarinet **Wavertree Racing Club Syndicate C**
53 **WHITSBURY COMMON,** b f Lujain (USA)—Vallauris **Mr D. R. C. Elsworth**
54 **ZAMBOOZLE (IRE),** ch c Halling (USA)—Blue Sirocco **R. C. Tooth**

TWO-YEAR-OLDS

55 **BUNDLE UP,** b f 16/3 Diktat—Bundle (Cadeaux Genereux) (24000) **Mrs P. J. Sheen**
56 **CLASSIC PUNCH (IRE),** b c 23/2 Mozart (IRE)—Rum Cay (USA) (Our Native (USA)) (22000) **J. C. Smith**
57 B c 22/4 Almutawakel—Colourful (FR) (Gay Mecene (USA)) (21461) **Miss R. Wakeford**
58 **COMPTON EXPRESS,** gr f 7/4 Compton Place—Jilly Woo (Environment Friend) (5000) **Mrs J. Wotherspoon**
59 **DEGAS ART (IRE),** b c 18/3 Danehill Dancer (IRE)—Answer (Warning) (60000) **M. R. Green**
60 **DIMELIGHT,** b f 28/4 Fantastic Light (USA)—Dime Bag (High Line) (4250) **J. C. Smith**
61 **DOCTOR DASH,** ch c 25/1 Dr Fong (USA)—Dashiba (Dashing Blade) **J. C. Smith**
62 Ch f 19/4 Generous (IRE)—Duende (High Top) **Mr C. J. Harper**
63 **FAIR CATERINA,** b f 4/3 Vettori (IRE)—Memsahib (Alzao (USA)) **Sir Gordon Brunton**
64 **FOREST LODGE (IRE),** ch f 24/4 Indian Lodge (IRE)—Folkboat (Kalaglow) **W.V. & Mrs E.S. Robins**
65 Ch c 14/2 Lear Spear (USA)—French Gift (Cadeaux Genereux) (50000) **R. C. Tooth**
66 **GOWER SONG,** b f 19/4 Singspiel (IRE)—Gleaming Water (Kalaglow) (17000) **Mr K. J. & Mrs S. Mercer**
67 B c 9/5 Galileo (IRE)—Highshaan (Pistolet Bleu (IRE)) (120000) **M. Tabor**
68 **HILL SPIRIT,** b c 11/2 Polish Precedent (USA)—
                                   Homing Instinct (Arctic Tern (USA)) (15000) **Mr D. R. C. Elsworth**
69 Ch f 14/4 Pursuit of Love—Impulsive Decision (IRE) (Nomination) (21000) **Mr D. R. C. Elsworth**
70 Ch f 11/5 Singspiel (IRE)—Kalata (Assert) **Lordship Stud Limited**
71 **KINETIC POWER (IRE),** gr c 4/4 Alhaarth (USA)—Nichodoula (Doulab (USA)) (48000) **G. W. Y. Li**
72 **LOYAL ROYAL (IRE),** b c 6/3 King Charlemagne (USA)—
                                   Supportive (IRE) (Nashamaa) (67068) **W.V. & Mrs E.S. Robins**
73 **NAINI TAL,** ch f 26/3 Inchinor—Royal Patron (Royal Academy (USA)) **Sir Gordon Brunton**
74 B c 7/5 Compton Place—Ovideo (Domynsky) (12072) **Mr D. R. C. Elsworth**
75 **PENRYN,** ch c 31/1 Selkirk (USA)—Camcorder (Nashwan (USA)) (62000) **W.V. & Mrs E.S. Robins**
76 **PERMANEX PRIDE (IRE),** ch c 14/4 Ashkalani (IRE)—
                                   Lycia (Targowice (USA)) (22802) **Davies, Sunley, Coombs, Cox**
77 Ch c 15/4 Daylami (IRE)—River Erne (USA) (Irish River (FR)) (18108) **J. C. Smith**
78 **SALISBURY WORLD (IRE),** ch c 22/2 Spinning World (USA)—
                                   Dinka Raja (USA) (Woodman (USA)) (30180) **M. R. Green**

MR D. R. C. ELSWORTH—continued

79 **SNOQUALMIE BOY,** b c 23/4 Montjeu (IRE)—Seattle Ribbon (USA) (Seattle Dancer (USA)) **J. C. Smith**
80 Ch f 6/3 Selkirk (USA)—Solo Performance (IRE) (Sadler's Wells (USA)) (12072) **Mr D. R. C. Elsworth**
81 Ch f 16/2 Sinndar (IRE)—Spot Prize (USA) (Seattle Dancer (USA)) **J. C. Smith**
82 B f 20/5 Titus Livius (FR)—Summer Fashion (Moorestyle) (20000) **Mr D. R. C. Elsworth**
83 Ch f 30/1 Spinning World (USA)—Summer Style (IRE) (Indian Ridge) (14754) **Mrs A. M. Coughlan**
84 **WIZARDS DREAM,** b c 25/3 Silver Wizard (USA)—Last Dream (IRE) (Alzao (USA)) **W.V. & Mrs E.S. Robins**

Other Owners: Mrs J. Brown, Mrs N. M. Booth, T. N. Chick, Ms A. Dawson, J. Dwyer, Miss C. A. Green, R. Haim, C. J. Harper, D. Alastair Hodge, S. McPhee, Michael O'Rourke, D. Sutherland, Mrs R. G. H. Vivian, T. V. Wilkinson.

Assistant Trainer: Mrs Jeannie Brown

Jockey (flat): T. Quinn. **Jockey (NH):** R. Young. **Conditional:** O. Nelmes. **Apprentice:** L. Keniry.

---

187 MS A. E. EMBIRICOS, Newmarket
Postal: **2 Homefarm Cottage, Moulton Paddocks, Newmarket, Suffolk, CB8 8QJ.**
Contacts: PHONE **(01638) 660048** MOBILE **(07876) 592308**
E-MAIL **alexembiricos@fsmail.net**

1 5, Ch g Master Willie—Ardent Bride **Mrs S. N. J. Embiricos**
2 4, Ch f Silver Patriarch (IRE)—Ardent Bride **Mrs S. N. J. Embiricos**
3 **KEN'S DREAM,** 6, b g Bin Ajwaad (IRE)—Shoag (USA) **M. R. Underwood**
4 **MOLLY MAY,** 5, ch m Most Welcome—Merryhill Maid (IRE) **Mr Fred & Mrs Jane May**
5 **PLACID MAN (IRE),** 11, br g Un Desperado (FR)—Sparkling Gale **Tim Jones and Partners**
6 **PUNJABI BOY,** 5, b g Charmer—Punjabi Rose **Mr Fred & Mrs Jane May**
7 **ZELDA PLONK,** 5, b m Most Welcome—Zelda Zonk **Mr Fred & Mrs Jane May**

Other Owners: Mr S. N. J. Embiricos, Mrs P. A. Underwood.

Assistant Trainer: Tim Bryce

Amateur: Ms A. E. Embiricos.

---

188 MR I. EMMERSON, Chester-Le-Street
Postal: **Holmside Park, Holmside, Edmondsley, Co. Durham, DH7 6EY.**
Contacts: PHONE **(0191) 3710507** MOBILE **(07866) 682162**

1 **AIR OF ESTEEM,** 9, b g Forzando—Shadow Bird **Mr I. Emmerson**
2 **BEST LEAD,** 6, b g Distant Relative—Bestemor **Mr I. Emmerson**
3 **BRANSTON TIGER,** 6, b g Mark of Esteem (IRE)—Tuxford Hideaway **Mr I. Emmerson**
4 **DISPOL PETO,** 5, gr g Petong—Plie **Mr I. Emmerson**
5 **FAYRWAY RHYTHM (IRE),** 8, b g Fayruz—The Way She Moves **Ms J. Swinburn**
6 **TURF PRINCESS,** 4, b f Wizard King—Turf Moor (IRE) **Mr I. Emmerson**

Assistant Trainer: Josie Swinburn

Jockey (flat): A. Nicholls. **Jockey (NH):** M. Bradburne. **Conditional:** N. Hannity. **Apprentice:** D. Fentiman.

---

189 MISS E. M. V. ENGLAND, Rugby
Postal: **Grove Cottage, Priors Hardwick, Southam, Warwickshire, CV47 7SN.**
Contacts: PHONE **(01327) 260437**

1 **ANDY GIN (FR),** 6, b g Ski Chief (USA)—Love Love Kate (FR) **Miss E. M. V. England**

---

190 MR A. M. ENNIS, Dorking
Postal: **Henfold House Stables, Henfold Lane, Beare Green, Dorking, Surrey, RH5 4RW.**
Contacts: HOME/OFFICE/FAX **(01306) 631529** MOBILE **(07970) 424017**
E-MAIL **albert@henfoldstables.co.uk** WEBSITE **www.henfoldstables.co.uk**

1 **ANOTHER RALEAGH (IRE),** 11, b g Be My Native (USA)—Caffra Mills **A. T. A. Wates**
2 **DOWN THE STRETCH,** 5, b g Rakaposhi King—Si-Gaoith **The A T P Racing Partnership**
3 **GENERAL TANTRUM (IRE),** 8, b g Ilium—Barna Havna **J. G. M. Wates**

MR A. M. ENNIS—continued

4 **HOUSE WARMER (IRE)**, 6, ch g Carroll House—Under The Duvet (IRE) **A. T. A. Wates**
5 **MOSSAR (FR)**, 5, b g Passing Sale (FR)—Beatty's (FR) **A. T. A. Wates**
6 **NAGAM (FR)**, 4, b g Denham Red (FR)—Gamaytoise (FR) **A. T. A. Wates**
7 **ULTIMATE LIMIT**, 5, b g Bonny Scot (IRE)—Second Call **Lady Wates**
8 **WALCOT LAD (IRE)**, 9, b g Jurado (USA)—Butty Miss **Camis, Burke, Middleton, Heaps**
9 **WESTCRAFT (IRE)**, 5, b g Warcraft (USA)—Copperhurst (IRE) **West Coast Haulage Limited**

Other Owners: Mr J. A. Burke, F. D. Camis, Mr M. J. Heaps, A. J. McClafferty, P. W. Middleton, P. J. O'Grady, T. A. Parker.

---

191   **MR G. P. ENRIGHT, Lewes**
Postal: **The Oaks, Old Lewes Racecourse, Lewes, East Sussex, BN7 1UR.**
Contacts: **PHONE/FAX (01273) 479183**
E-MAIL enright@btinternet.com

1 **BRASILIA PRINCE**, 6, ch g Karinga Bay—Cappuccino Girl **Mrs E. M. J Gray**
2 **CORTON DENHAM**, 4, ch g Wolfhound (USA)—Wigit **A. A. Etheridge**
3 **DUTCH STAR**, 6, b m Alflora (IRE)—Double Dutch **McManus/Fuller**
4 **GRAN CLICQUOT**, 10, gr m Gran Alba (USA)—Tina's Beauty **Mrs M. Enright**
5 **HIGH POINT (IRE)**, 7, b g Ela-Mana-Mou—Top Lady (IRE) **The Aedean Partnership**
6 **HOME RULE**, 5, b m Wizard King—Pastures Green **Homebred Racing**
7 **MAAREES**, 4, b f Groom Dancer (USA)—Shemaleyah **Mr G. P. Enright**
8 **PEPPERSHOT**, 5, b g Vettori (IRE)—No Chili **R. Gurney**
9 **ROME (IRE)**, 6, br g Singspiel (IRE)—Ela Romara **G. R. Macdonald, K. Fitchie, M. Enright**
10 **WELSH ASSEMBLY**, 9, ch g Presidium—Celtic Chimes **Mr G. P. Enright**

THREE-YEAR-OLDS

11 **COMMANCHE DAWN**, b f Commanche Run—Charlycia **A. O. Ashford**

Other Owners: Mrs M. E. Etheridge, L. Fuller, Ms A. McManus, C. M. Wall, Mrs S. Wall.

Assistant Trainer: Mrs M Enright

Jockey (NH): R. Thornton. **Amateur:** Mrs M. Enright, Mr J. Pemberton.

---

192   **MR J. M. P. EUSTACE, Newmarket**
Postal: **Park Lodge Stables, Park Lane, Newmarket, Suffolk, CB8 8AX.**
Contacts: **PHONE (01638) 664277 FAX (01638) 664156 MOBILE (07802) 243764**
E-MAIL james@parklodgestables.demon.co.uk WEBSITE www.jameseustace.com

1 **CHIGORIN**, 4, b g Pivotal—Belle Vue **D. A. Rosenbaum**
2 **CONSIDINE (USA)**, 4, b c Romanov (IRE)—Libeccio (NZ) **E. Haloute**
3 **DUNOWEN (IRE)**, 10, b g Be My Native (USA)—Lucky Buck **Mrs P. H. Matthews**
4 **EIGHT (IRE)**, 9, ch g Thatching—Up To You **C. Z. Curtis**
5 **ORCADIAN**, 4, b g Kirkwall—Rosy Outlook (USA) **J. C. Smith**
6 **WELCOME STRANGER**, 5, b g Most Welcome—Just Julia **H. R. Moszkowicz**

THREE-YEAR-OLDS

7 **ARIODANTE**, b g Groom Dancer (USA)—Maestrale **The MacDougall Partnership**
8 **CETSHWAYO**, ch g Pursuit of Love—Induna **Mrs J. S. Wootton**
9 **DEMI TASSE**, b f Largesse—Not A Word **H. R. Moszkowicz**
10 **ELMS SCHOOLBOY**, ch g Komaite (USA)—Elms Schoolgirl **J. D. Moore**
11 **GENEROUS MEASURE**, b g Largesse—Stormy Heights **Upperwood Farm Stud Alliance**
12 **HIGH CARD**, b g So Factual (USA)—High Cut **J. C. Smith**
13 **HIGHLAND CASCADE**, ch f Tipsy Creek (USA)—Highland Hannah (IRE) **J. M. Ratcliffe**
14 **INNPURSUIT**, b g Inchinor—Quest For The Best **G. N. Carstairs**
15 **MISSED TURN**, b f Mind Games—Miss Beverley **Park Lodge Racing**
16 **MISTER AZIZ (IRE)**, b g Mister Baileys—Aziz Presenting (IRE) **Park Lane Racing**
17 **MOONSTRUCK**, ch g Fraam—Easter Moon (FR) **The MacDougall Partnership**
18 **RAFFISH**, ch g Atraf—Valadon **Blue Peter Racing 5**
19 **ROMANTIC GIFT**, b f Cadeaux Genereux—Last Romance (IRE) **Far Afield**
20 **ROYAL SAILOR (IRE)**, b g Bahhare (USA)—Old Tradition (IRE) **Mr R. O. Simpson**
21 **ROYAL WISH**, b f Royal Applause—Be My Wish **J. C. Smith**
22 **RUBY WINE**, b f Kayf Tara—Cribella (USA) **Mrs R. M. Wilson**

MR J. M. P. EUSTACE—continued

23 **TRANSACTION (IRE)**, ch g Trans Island—Meranie Girl (IRE) **T. G. Darling**
24 **WESTER LODGE (IRE)**, ch c Fraam—Reamzafonic **Mr and Mrs R. H. Brewer**

TWO-YEAR-OLDS

25 B f 29/3 Largesse—Alo Ez (Alzao (USA)) (3500) **H. R. Moszkowicz**
26 B c 4/2 Robellino (USA)—Ancient Secret (Warrshan (USA)) **J. C. Smith**
27 **AT THE MONEY**, b c 1/5 Robellino (USA)—Coh Sho No (Old Vic) (7000) **H. D. Nass**
28 **DICTATRIX**, gr f 8/3 Diktat—Apennina (USA) (Gulch (USA)) (27000) **Stephen Hodge & Peter Hillman**
29 **FAST BOWLER**, b c 5/3 Intikhab (USA)—Alegria (Night Shift (USA)) **J. C. Smith**
30 **FLASHING FLOOZIE**, ch f 11/2 Muhtarram (USA)—High Habit (Slip Anchor) **J. C. Smith**
31 **FLYING VISITOR**, b f 26/3 Magic Ring (IRE)—Just Visiting (Superlative) (1000) **Mrs R. A. Moszkowicz**
32 Ch f 6/5 Pursuit of Love—High Sevens (Master Willie) **Major M. G. Wyatt**
33 **KAPIOLANI (USA)**, ch f 15/2 Mr Greeley (USA)—Iolani (Alzao (USA)) (10641) **P. J. Hillman**
34 **LADY GALADRIEL (USA)**, ch f 2/2 Woodman (USA)—Dramatically (USA) (Theatrical) (48000) **J. C. Smith**
35 **LOCAL FANCY**, b f 6/3 Bahamian Bounty—Local Abbey (IRE) (Primo Dominie) **G. S. Shropshire**
36 Ch c 17/3 Fruits of Love (USA)—Meranie Girl (IRE) (Mujadil (USA)) (10000) **T. G. Darling**
37 B c 26/2 Zilzal (USA)—Picot (Piccolo) **Major M. G. Wyatt**
38 **TOFFEE TREAT**, b f 19/1 Mujahid (USA)—Toffolux (Sharpo) **J. C. Smith**
39 **WHISTLEUPTHEWIND**, b f 1/3 Piccolo—The Frog Queen (Bin Ajwaad (IRE)) (10500) **Blue Peter Racing 6**

Other Owners: S. C. Appelbee, Mr D. F. Ballheimer, I. P. Blance, Mr R. H. Brewer, Mrs P. E. M. Brewer, Mrs D. C. Cooper, Mrs G. R. Eustace, R. R. Fuller, S. J. Gibson, Miss R. M. Hatley, P. J. Hillman, S. M. G. Hodge, Mr C. I. Jackson, Mrs L. R. Lawson, Mrs K. A. McGladdery, A. M. Mitchell, Mr Greg Parsons, J. Riches.

Amateur: Miss Joanna Rees.

---

193 MS D. J. EVANS, Lydiate

Postal: **Oaklea Racing Stables, Southport Road, Lydiate, Merseyside, L31 4HH.**
Contacts: **HOME (01515) 260093 PARTNER (07748) 630685 FAX (01515) 200299
MOBILE (07860) 599101**

1 **AMBER LEGEND**, 4, b f Fraam—Abstone Queen **I. P. Mason**
2 **BEE MINOR**, 4, b f Barathea (IRE)—Bee Off (IRE) **P. Green**
3 **CARNT SPELL**, 4, b g Wizard King—Forever Shineing **P. Green**
4 **DOLLIVIUS (IRE)**, 4, b f Titus Livius (FR)—Dollar Magic **P. Green**
5 **EXTRA COVER (IRE)**, 4, b g Danehill Dancer (IRE)—Ballycurrane (IRE) **P. Green**
6 **JILLY WHY (IRE)**, 4, b f Mujadil (USA)—Ruwy **P. Green**
7 **RED SKELTON (IRE)**, 4, ch g Croco Rouge (IRE)—Newala **P. Green**
8 **SHAYMEE'S GIRL**, 4, b f Wizard King—Mouchez Le Nez (IRE) **B. & B. Hygiene Limited**
9 **SUITCASE MURPHY (IRE)**, 4, b g Petardia—Noble Rocket **P. Green**
10 **THEATRE BELLE**, 4, b f King's Theatre (IRE)—Cumbrian Rhapsody **Divson Bell Partnership**
11 **YORKER (USA)**, 7, b g Boundary (USA)—Shallows (USA) **Men Behaving Badly**

THREE-YEAR-OLDS

12 **AZA WISH (IRE)**, b f Mujadil (USA)—Kilcsem Eile (IRE) **Cannon, Grundy & Harris**
13 **COIS NA TINE EILE**, br f Cois Na Tine (IRE)—Water Pixie (IRE) **B. T. O'Sullivan**
14 **DEMATRAF (IRE)**, gr f Atraf—Demolition Jo **P. Green**
15 **DESERT FERN (IRE)**, b f Desert Style (IRE)—Lady Fern **A. Williams**
16 **FORPETESAKE**, ch g Primo Dominie—Showcase **Mr T. P. Cummins**
17 **GINGER FOR PLUCK**, b f Revoque (IRE)—Naughty Pistol (USA) **C. G. R. Booth**
18 **MISSIN MARGOT**, b f Fraam—Abstone Queen **J. E. Abbey**
19 **SOUMILLON**, gr f Benny The Dip (USA)—Kembla **P. Green**

TWO-YEAR-OLDS

20 B c 16/5 Foxhound (USA)—Anytime Baby (Bairn (USA)) (8000) **P. Green**
21 B c 21/2 Zilzal (USA)—Daanat Nawal (Machiavellian (USA)) (8500) **P. Green**
22 B f 31/3 Foxhound (USA)—Fizzy Fiona (Efisio) (15000) **P. Green**
23 B f 10/2 Wizard King—Hallowed Ground (IRE) (Godswalk (USA)) (500) **P. Green**

MS D. J. EVANS—continued

24 B c 14/2 Tagula (IRE)—Miraculous (IRE) (Marju (IRE)) (1200) **P. Green**
25 B f 3/3 Afternoon Deelites (USA)—Simona (CHI) (Dancing Groom (USA)) **Cannon, Grundy & Harris**

Other Owners: Mr S. Cannon, J. Ennis, Mr D. P. Grundy, R. Kent, A. Meale, M. F. Nolan, I. T. Smethurst.

Assistant Trainer: Mr Paul Green

Conditional: Antony Evans. **Amateur:** Mr C. Ellingham.

---

194 MR H. J. EVANS, Honeybourne
Postal: Poden, Mickleton Road, Honeybourne, Worcestershire, WR11 7PS.
Contacts: PHONE (01386) 438241

1 BONNY GROVE, 5, b g Bonny Scot (IRE)—Binny Grove **Mrs Jane Evans**
2 TIME FOR ACTION (IRE), 13, b g Alzao (USA)—Beyond Words **Mrs Jane Evans**

Assistant Trainer: Mrs Jane Evans

Jockey (NH): J. Pritchard.

---

195 MRS M. EVANS, Haverfordwest
Postal: Hengoed, Clarbeston Road, Pembrokeshire, SA63 4QL.
Contacts: PHONE (01437) 731336

1 FLORANZ, 9, br m Afzal—Tuesday Member **W. J. Evans**

Assistant Trainer: W J Evans

Amateur: Mr E. Williams.

---

196 MR M. J. M. EVANS, Kidderminster
Postal: The Hawthorns, Hurcott Lane, Kidderminster, Worcestershire, DY10 3PJ.
Contacts: PHONE (01562) 60970 MOBILE (07814) 631731
E-MAIL martinjohnmorgan@aol.com

1 ADVANCE EAST, 13, b g Polish Precedent (USA)—Startino **Mrs J. Z. Munday**
2 BAIE DES SINGES, 11, b g Royal Vulcan—Mikey's Monkey **Mr M. J. M. Evans**
3 BEETLE BUG, 5, br m Robellino (USA)—Special Beat **Mr M. J. M. Evans**
4 GIUST IN TEMP (IRE), 6, b h Polish Precedent (USA)—Blue Stricks **Mrs J. Z. Munday**
5 LUNAR LORD, 9, b g Elmaamul (USA)—Cache **Mrs J. Z. Munday**
6 MICHIGAN BLUE, 13, b g Rakaposhi King—Starquin (IRE) **Mrs J. Z. Munday**
7 QUEENSBERRY, 6, b g Up And At 'em—Princess Poquito **Mr M. J. M. Evans**
8 SPECIAL AGENDA (IRE), 11, b g Torus—Easter Blade (IRE) **Mrs J. Z. Munday**

Assistant Trainer: Jeanette Zoe Munday

Jockey (NH): O. McPhail. **Conditional:** S. J. Craine, Antony Evans.

---

197 MR P. D. EVANS, Abergavenny
Postal: Ty Derlwyn Farm, Pandy, Abergavenny, NP7 8DR.
Contacts: PHONE (01873) 890837

1 ALAFZAR, 7, b g Green Desert (USA)—Alasana (IRE) **Waterline Racing Club**
2 BEST BEFORE (IRE), 5, b g Mujadil (USA)—Miss Margate (IRE) **Waterline Racing Club**
3 BOAVISTA (IRE), 5, b m Fayruz—Florissa (FR) **D. Healy**
4 BONNY GREY, 7, gr m Seymour Hicks (FR)—Sky Wave **Mr P. D. Evans**
5 COMPTON BANKER (IRE), 8, br g Distinctly North (USA)—Mary Hinge **Waterline Racing Club**
6 CROSSWAYS, 7, b g Mister Baileys—Miami Dancer (USA) **Mr & Mrs T. Gallienne**
7 DARGHAN (IRE), 5, b g Air Express (IRE)—Darsannda (IRE) **S. Rudolf**
8 DOCTORED, 4, ch g Dr Devious (IRE)—Polygueza (FR) **Treble Chance Partnership**
9 FEN GYPSY, 7, b g Nashwan (USA)—Didicoy (USA) **Miss S. Howells**

MR P. D. EVANS—continued

10 **GALLANT BOY (IRE)**, 6, ch g Grand Lodge (USA)—Damerela (IRE) **M. W. Lawrence**
11 **GO GREEN**, 4, ch f Environment Friend—Sandra Mac **J. R. Pugh**
12 **GO YELLOW**, 4, b g Overbury (IRE)—Great Lyth Lass (IRE) **G. R. Price**
13 **HAZEWIND**, 4, gr g Daylami (IRE)—Fragrant Oasis (USA) **Waterline Racing Club**
14 **IZMAIL (IRE)**, 6, b g Bluebird (USA)—My-Lorraine (IRE) **G. M. McGuinness**
15 **LADY BLADE (IRE)**, 4, b f Daggers Drawn (USA)—Singhana (IRE) **M. W. Lawrence**
16 **LIGNE D'EAU**, 4, ch c Cadeaux Genereux—Miss Waterline **M. W. Lawrence**
17 **MELODY KING**, 4, b g Merdon Melody—Retaliator **Treble Chance Partnership**
18 **MORITAT (IRE)**, 5, b g Night Shift (USA)—Aunty Eileen **Mr P. D. Evans**
19 **NASHAAB (USA)**, 8, b g Zafonic (USA)—Tajannub (USA) **M. W. Lawrence**
20 **NAUGHTY GIRL (IRE)**, 5, b m Dr Devious (IRE)—Mary Magdalene **Mrs S. J. Lawrence**
21 **ODDSMAKER (IRE)**, 4, b g Barathea (IRE)—Archipova (IRE) **Mr D. Maloney & Mr S. Rudolf**
22 **PAS DE SURPRISE**, 7, b g Dancing Spree (USA)—Supreme Rose **D. Healy**
23 **PONT NEUF (IRE)**, 5, b m Revoque (IRE)—Petite Maxine **Mrs S. J. Lawrence**
24 **RISK FREE**, 8, ch g Risk Me (FR)—Princess Lily **Mr P. D. Evans**
25 **SERJEANT AT ARMS (IRE)**, 6, b g Bluebird (USA)—Curiously **M. W. Lawrence**
26 **STRIDER**, 4, ch g Pivotal—Sahara Belle (USA) **M. W. Lawrence**
27 **SUDDEN FLIGHT (IRE)**, 8, b g In The Wings—Ma Petite Cherie (USA) **Norbury Ten**
28 **SUPER SONG**, 5, b g Desert Prince (IRE)—Highland Rhapsody (IRE) **M. W. Lawrence**
29 **THE KIDDYKID (IRE)**, 5, b g Danetime (IRE)—Mezzanine **Mrs C. Massey**
30 **THREEZEDZZ**, 7, ch g Emarati (USA)—Exotic Forest **Mr B. McCabe**
31 **TOP OF THE CLASS (IRE)**, 8, b m Rudimentary (USA)—School Mum **Mr P. D. Evans**
32 **UNDER MY SPELL**, 4, b f Wizard King—Gagajulu **J. R. Salter**
33 **ZAFARSHAH (IRE)**, 6, b g Danehill (USA)—Zafarana (FR) **Waterline Racing Club**

THREE-YEAR-OLDS

34 **BRANSTON LILY**, ch f Cadeaux Genereux—Indefinite Article (IRE) **M. W. Lawrence**
35 **BRANSTON PENNY**, ch f Pennekamp (USA)—Branston Jewel (IRE) **Partnership**
36 **CHAMPAGNE BRANDY (IRE)**, ch f Spectrum (IRE)—Petite Liqueurelle (IRE) **Miss D L Wisbey & Mr R J Viney**
37 **DARTANIAN**, b g Jurado (USA)—Blackpool Mamma's **G. K. Gardiner**
38 **GLASSON LODGE**, b f Primo Dominie—Petrikov (IRE) **Supreme Corner Gang**
39 **GUINEA A MINUTE (IRE)**, ch f Raise A Grand (IRE)—Repique (USA) **Mrs S. J. Lawrence**
40 **I'M AIMEE**, ch f Timeless Times (USA)—Marfen **D. Hilton**
41 **LATERAL THINKER (IRE)**, b f Desert Sun—Miss Margate (IRE) **Colin G. R. Booth And Patricia Hughes**
42 **LITTLE WIZZY**, b f Wizard King—Little Unknown **E. A. R. Morgans**
43 **MISS CUISINA**, b f Vettori (IRE)—Rewardia (IRE) **Treble Chance Partnership**
44 **ON THE WATERLINE (IRE)**, b f Compton Place—Miss Waterline **M. W. Lawrence**
45 Ch c Bold Edge—Rainbow Chaser (IRE) **T. H. Gallienne**
46 **THE CROOKED FOX**, b g Magic Ring (IRE)—My Bonus **J. R. Salter**
47 **THE CROSS FOX**, gr g Wizard King—Megs Pearl **J. R. Pugh**
48 **TRACKATTACK**, ch g Atraf—Verbena (IRE) **Mr P. D. Evans**
49 **WATERLINE LOVER**, ch f Efisio—Food of Love **M. W. Lawrence**

TWO-YEAR-OLDS

50 B c 23/2 Wizard King—Choral Dancer (USA) (Night Shift (USA)) (2681) **Mr P. D. Evans**
51 Br f 25/4 Primo Valentino (IRE)—Cumbrian Concerto (Petong) (2011)
52 **DANETTE (IRE)**, bl f 11/2 Danehill Dancer (IRE)—
Jet Lock (USA) (Crafty Prospector (USA)) (14083) **E. A. R. Morgans**
53 B f 22/4 Elnadim (USA)—Dazzling Fire (USA) (Bluebird (USA)) (2011) **M. W. Lawrence**
54 Ch f 27/4 Monashee Mountain (USA)—Las Bela (Welsh Pageant) (4694) **Mr P. D. Evans**
55 Ch f 1/3 Raise A Grand (IRE)—Lindas Delight (Batshoof) (3353) **Mr W. Clifford**
56 **LIONAIRE (IRE)**, ch c 18/4 Royal Academy (USA)—
Higher Circle (USA) (Diesis) (14083) **Mr S. Rudolf & Mr P. D. Evans**
57 B f 17/5 Spectrum (IRE)—Mary Magdalene (Night Shift (USA))
58 **MULLZIMA (IRE)**, b f 19/3 Mull of Kintyre (USA)—Habaza (IRE) (Shernazar) (3018) **E. A. R. Morgans**
59 B c 16/3 Mind Games—Nom Francais (First Trump) (11000)
60 B g 23/4 Fraam—Rewardia (IRE) (Petardia) (1600) **Treble Chance Partnership**
61 **SIRBRIT**, b c 12/3 Cadeaux Genereux—Evening Promise (Aragon) (38000) **S. Rudolf**
62 B f 9/2 Indian Danehill (IRE)—Taisho (IRE) (Namaqualand (USA)) (8047) **M. W. Lawrence**
63 B f 11/5 Danetime (IRE)—Unfortunate (Komaite (USA)) (2346) **Mrs S. J. Lawrence**
64 **WIZBY**, b f 21/4 Wizard King—
Diamond Vanessa (IRE) (Distinctly North (USA)) **Miss D. L. Wisbey & Mr R. J. Viney**

Other Owners: G. M. L. Weaver.

Jockey (flat): Fran Ferris. **Conditional:** Antony Evans. **Apprentice:** S. Donohue. **Amateur:** Miss A. Bevan, Miss E. Folkes.

198 MR J. P. L. EWART, Langholm
Postal: **Burn Cottage, Westerkirk, Langholm, Dumfriesshire, DG13 0NZ.**
Contacts: **PHONE (01387) 370274 FAX (01387) 370720 MOBILE (07770) 937232**
E-MAIL jamesewartracing@fsmail.net

1 COGOLIE (FR), 5, ch m Cyborg (FR)—Concinna (FR) **Mr J. P. L. Ewart**
2 INDIENNE EFI (FR), 9, b m Passing Sale (FR)—Udine Bowl Efi (FR) **Mr R. Underwood & Mr J. P. L. Ewart**
3 KIMBAMBO (FR), 7, gr g Genereux Genie—Contessina (FR) **Mr N. M. L. Ewart**
4 NEMENCHA (FR), 4, bl f Princeton (FR)—Laurenza (FR) **Mr J. P. L. Ewart**
5 PURE SPEED (FR), 4, ch f Hamas (IRE)—Nexia (FR) **Mr J. P. L. Ewart**
6 RUN JUNIOR (FR), 4, b br g Concorde Jr (FR)—Run For Laborie (FR) **Mr D. A. Norris**
7 TANGOROCH (FR), 4, b br g Rochesson (FR)—Fitanga (FR) **Mr A. Shedden & Mr J. P. L. Ewart**

THREE-YEAR-OLDS

8 AZTURK (FR), b f Baby Turk—Pocahontas (FR) **Mr C. W. Ewart**
9 NASSIM (FR), b g Turgeon (USA)—Sweet Cashmere (FR) **Mr C. W. Ewart**
10 NUMBER ONE DE SOLZEN (FR), b g Passing Sale (FR)—
Tiffany's (FR) **N. M. L. Ewart/Mr P. Lockhart-Smith/Pierre de Mailessye**
11 OLEOLAT (FR), ch g Art Bleu—Contessina (FR) **Mr C. W. Ewart**
12 ORANG OUTAN (FR), b g Baby Turk—Ellapampa (FR) **Mr & Mrs J. D. Cotton**

Assistant Trainer: Mr G Nichol

199 MR A. FABRE, Chantilly
Postal: **14 Avenue de Bourbon, 60500 Chantilly, France.**
Contacts: **PHONE +33 (0) 3 44 57 04 98 FAX +33 (0) 3 44 58 14 15**

1 ADVICE, 4, b c Seeking The Gold (USA)—Anna Palariva (IRE) **Sheikh Mohammed**
2 APSIS, 4, b c Barathea (IRE)—Apogee **Prince Khalid Abdullah**
3 ART MASTER (USA), 4, b c Royal Academy (USA)—True Flare (USA) **Prince Khalid Abdullah**
4 BOLIVAR (GER), 4, b c Sadler's Wells (USA)—Borgia (GER) **Gestut Ammerland**
5 CACIQUE (IRE), 4, b c Danehill (USA)—Hasili (IRE) **Prince Khalid Abdullah**
6 DIAMOND GREEN (FR), 4, b br c Green Desert (USA)—Diamonaka (FR) **SNC Lagardere Elevage**
7 DIAMOND TANGO (FR), 4, b f Acatenango (GER)—Diamond Dance (FR) **SNC Lagardere Elevage**
8 FEU INDIEN, 4, b c Machiavellian (USA)—Danse Indienne (USA) **Mr E. Rothschild**
9 FRACASSANT (IRE), 4, gr c Linamix (FR)—Fragrant Hill **J. L. Lagardere**
10 GREY LILAS (IRE), 4, b f Danehill (USA)—Kenmist **Gestut Ammerland**
11 GROSGRAIN (USA), 4, b f Diesis—Green Lady (IRE) **Mme Fabre**
12 MY SPECIAL (IRE), 4, b f Peintre Celebre (USA)—My Secret (GER) **Gestut Ammerland**
13 REEFSCAPE, 4, gr c Linamix (FR)—Coraline **Prince Khalid Abdullah**
14 RUSSIAN HILL, 5, ch m Indian Ridge—Dievotchka **Mr E. Rothschild**
15 SHORT PAUSE, 6, b h Sadler's Wells (USA)—Interval **Prince Khalid Abdullah**
16 STAFF NURSE (USA), 4, b f Arch (USA)—Medicine Woman (USA) **Sheikh Mohammed**
17 VALIXIR (IRE), 4, b c Trempolino (USA)—Vadlamixa (FR) **SNC Lagardere Elevage**

THREE-YEAR-OLDS

18 ALHARMINA, gr f Linamix (FR)—Alharir (USA) **SNC Lagardere Elevage**
19 ANABAA BOY (IRE), b c Anabaa (USA)—Sweet Story (IRE) **Mr E. Rothschild**
20 ANTIQUE (IRE), ch f Dubai Millennium—Truly Generous (IRE) **Sheikh Mohammed**
21 ARCHANGE D'OR (IRE), b c Danehill (USA)—Dievotchka **Mr E. Rothschild**
22 BAKERMAN, b c Singspiel (IRE)—Patacake Patacake (USA) **Sheikh Mohammed**
23 BALLROOM (USA), b f Seeking The Gold (USA)—Colorado Dancer **Sheikh Mohammed**
24 BELLAMY CAY, b c Kris—Trellis Bay **Prince Khalid Abdullah**
25 BERNABEU (USA), ch c Kris S (USA)—Set In Motion (USA) **Maktoum Al Maktoum**
26 BIMINI, b f Sadler's Wells (USA)—Wemyss Bight **Prince Khalid Abdullah**
27 CARLIX (FR), gr c Linamix (FR)—Carlitta (USA) **SNC Lagardere Elevage**
28 CASTLE HOWARD (IRE), b c Montjeu (IRE)—Termania (IRE) **Sheikh Mohammed**
29 CHANGEABLE, br f Dansili—High And Low **Prince Khalid Abdullah**
30 CLOVERTE (IRE), b f Green Desert (USA)—Clodora (FR) **SNC Lagardere Elevage**
31 CRAFT FAIR (IRE), b c Danehill (USA)—Brush Strokes **Sheikh Mohammed**
32 CRAZY RHYTHM (IRE), ch c Grand Lodge (USA)—Goodwood Blizzard **Bob Lalemant**
33 CRIMSON AND GOLD, b br c Singspiel (IRE)—Rosia (IRE) **Sheikh Mohammed**
34 DANCE FOR JOY, ch f Halling (USA)—Wajd (USA) **Sheikh Mohammed**
35 DESIDERATUM, b c Darshaan—Desired **Sheikh Mohammed**
36 DIAMOND REEF, b f Alzao (USA)—Coraline **Prince Khalid Abdullah**

MR A. FABRE—continued

37 **DILAG (IRE)**, b f Almutawakel—Terracotta Hut **Anne Springer**
38 **DOCUMENTARY (USA)**, b c Storm Cat (USA)—Honest Lady (USA) **Prince Khalid Abdullah**
39 **EARL'S COURT**, b c King's Best (USA)—Reine Wells (IRE) **Sheikh Mohammed**
40 **FADING LIGHT**, b f King's Best (USA)—Fade **Sheikh Mohammed**
41 **FAIRWUALA (IRE)**, b f Unfuwain (USA)—Fairly Grey **SNC Lagardere Elevage**
42 **FRALOGA (FR)**, b f Grand Lodge (USA)—Fragrant Hill **SNC Lagardere Elevage**
43 **GALILANI (USA)**, b f Storm Creek (USA)—Cognac Lady (USA) **Mme Fabre**
44 **GRAND BAHAMA (IRE)**, b c Singspiel (IRE)—Rum Cay (USA) **Sheikh Mohammed**
45 **HAWKSMOOR (IRE)**, b c In The Wings—Moon Cactus **Sheikh Mohammed**
46 **HIGH IS THE MOON (FR)**, gr c Highest Honor (FR)—Ambassadrice (FR) **Bob Lalemant**
47 **HOME CALL (USA)**, b c Chester House (USA)—Call Account (USA) **Prince Khalid Abdullah**
48 **HURRICANE RUN (IRE)**, b c Montjeu (IRE)—Hold On (GER) **Gestut Ammerland**
49 **IVORY BLACK**, b c Fasliyev (USA)—Sinueuse (FR) **Mr E. Rothschild**
50 **JUMP FOR YOU (FR)**, b c Montjeu (IRE)—Polly's Wika (USA) **Bob Lalemant**
51 **KITTY FEVER (FR)**, b f Gold Fever (USA)—Kitty Be Wild (USA) **SNC Lagardere Elevage**
52 **KOCAB**, b c Unfuwain (USA)—Space Quest **Prince Khalid Abdullah**
53 **KRIEGSPIEL**, b br g Singspiel (IRE)—Karlaya (IRE) **Sheikh Mohammed**
54 **LAKE TOYA (USA)**, b f Darshaan—Shinko Hermes (IRE) **Sheikh Mohammed**
55 **MAGNUM OPUS (IRE)**, b c Sadler's Wells (USA)—Summer Breeze **Prince Khalid Abdullah**
56 **MATHEMATICIAN (IRE)**, br c Machiavellian (USA)—Zibilene **Sheikh Mohammed**
57 **MINIMIZE (USA)**, b c Chester House (USA)—Jolypha (USA) **Prince Khalid Abdullah**
58 **MIRABILIS (USA)**, b f Lear Fan (USA)—Media Nox **Prince Khalid Abdullah**
59 **NO GREATER LOVE (FR)**, b c Take Risks (USA)—Desperate Virgin (BEL) **Bob Lalemant**
60 **NUBIAN DIGNITARY (FR)**, b br c Highest Honor (FR)—Numidie (FR) **Sheikh Mohammed**
61 **OISEAU RARE (FR)**, ch f King's Best (USA)—Oiseau de Feu (USA) **SNC Lagardere Elevage**
62 **ORBIT O'GOLD (USA)**, ch c Kingmambo (USA)—Lily o'gold (USA) **Sheikh Mohammed**
63 **PACHELLO (IRE)**, b c Priolo (USA)—Most Charming (FR) **Maktoum Al Maktoum**
64 **POEMOANA**, br gr f Dansili—Proud Douna (FR) **Mme Fabre**
65 **RAINBOW ARCH**, b f Rainbow Quest (USA)—Dream Ticket (USA) **Maktoum Al Maktoum**
66 **RAZZLE (USA)**, b f Danzig (USA)—Razyana (USA) **Prince Khalid Abdullah**
67 **ROSAWA (FR)**, gr f Linamix (FR)—Rose Quartz **SNC Lagardere Elevage**
68 **ROUNDEL (USA)**, b f Kingmambo (USA)—Ring of Music **Sheikh Mohammed**
69 **RUNAWAY**, b c King's Best (USA)—Anasazi (IRE) **Prince Khalid Abdullah**
70 **SAILOR KING (IRE)**, b c King's Best (USA)—Manureva (USA) **Sheikh Mohammed**
71 **SCARTARA (FR)**, gr f Linamix (FR)—Scarlet Raider (USA) **SNC Lagardere Elevage**
72 **SELKIS (FR)**, b f Darshaan—Irish Order (USA) **Mme P. De Moussac**
73 **SHADUF (USA)**, b f Pleasant Tap (USA)—Shade Dance (USA) **Sheikh Mohammed**
74 **SHARE OPTION**, b f Polish Precedent (USA)—Quota (USA) **Prince Khalid Abdullah**
75 **SPRING RAIN (JPN)**, b f Dubai Millennium—Storm Song (USA) **Sheikh Mohammed**
76 **STOP MAKING SENSE**, b c Lujain (USA)—Freeway (FR) **Anne Springer**
77 **TALK SHOW**, b f Diktat—High Hawk **Sheikh Mohammed**
78 **TERRA VERDE (IRE)**, ch c Indian Ridge—Vituisa **Sheikh Mohammed**
79 **THRIFT (IRE)**, b f Green Desert (USA)—Fawaayid (USA) **Maktoum Al Maktoum**
80 **VADAWINA (IRE)**, b f Unfuwain (USA)—Vadaza (FR) **SNC Lagardere Elevage**
81 **VADORGA (FR)**, b f Grand Lodge (USA)—Vadsa Honor (FR) **SNC Lagardere Elevage**
82 **VAGAMIXA (FR)**, gr f Sagamix (FR)—Vadsa (USA) **SNC Lagardere Elevage**
83 **VALIMA (FR)**, gr f Linamix (FR)—Vadlawysa (FR) **SNC Lagardere Elevage**
84 **WELL SPOKEN (IRE)**, b f Sadler's Wells (USA)—Saintly Speech (USA) **Mr S. Mulryan**
85 **WINNING SEQUENCE (FR)**, b f Zafonic (USA)—Cracovie **Anne Springer**
86 **WINTER SILENCE**, b f Dansili—Hunt The Sun **Prince Khalid Abdullah**

TWO-YEAR-OLDS

87 **ALHAMARK (IRE)**, b c 14/4 Mark of Esteem (IRE)—Alharir (USA) (Zafonic (USA)) **SNC Lagardere Elevage**
88 **ALL THAT JAZZ (FR)**, b c 18/4 Desert Prince (IRE)—Udina (USA) (80482) **Anne Springer**
89 B f 22/3 Nashwan (USA)—All Time Great (Night Shift (USA)) **Gestut Ammerland**
90 **AMEN DESERT (FR)**, b f 12/3 Green Desert (USA)—Amen (USA) (Alydar (USA)) **SNC Lagardere Elevage**
91 Ch c 9/4 Rainbow Quest (USA)—Anka Britannia (USA) (Irish River (USA)) **Sheikh Mohammed**
92 **ARRIVEE (FR)**, bl f 7/1 Anabaa (USA)—Quiet Dream (USA) (Seattle Slew (USA)) **Wertheimer et Frere**
93 **AUTUMN PROMISE (IRE)**, b c 17/4 Montjeu (IRE)—
Seasonal Pleasure (USA) (Graustark) (187793) **Maktoum Al Maktoum**
94 B f 15/2 War Chant (USA)—Basking (USA) (Alydar (USA)) (159616) **Mr S. Mulryan**
95 **BEAUTY OF A TIGER (GER)**, b f 11/4 Tiger Hill (IRE)—
Bandeira (GER) (Law Society (USA)) (60362) **Anne Springer**
96 **BERINGOER (FR)**, ch c 6/4 Bering—Charmgoer (USA) (Nureyev (USA)) **Wertheimer et Frere**
97 Ch c 12/3 Rainbow Quest (USA)—Bina Ridge (Indian Ridge) **Prince Khalid Abdullah**

MR A. FABRE—continued

98 BLACK OPAL, b f 17/3 Machiavellian (USA)—Gold Field (IRE) (Unfuwain (USA)) (200000) **Sheikh Mohammed**
99 B c 21/3 Rahy (USA)—Blush Damask (USA) (Green Dancer (USA)) **Gestut Ammerland**
100 BREMEN, b c 25/2 Sadler's Wells (USA)—Anka Germania (Malinowski (USA)) **Sheikh Mohammed**
101 BRIDGEWATER (USA), b f 22/1 Chester House (USA)—Bristol Channel (Generous (IRE)) **Prince Khalid Abdullah**
102 CARLOTAMIX (FR), gr c 22/3 Linamix (FR)—Carlitta (USA) (Olympio (USA)) **SNC Lagardere Elevage**
103 CELEBRE FRAGANCE (FR), b f 30/4 Peintre Celebre (USA)—
                                    Fragrant Hill (Shirley Heights) **SNC Lagardere Elevage**
104 CELEBRE VADALA (FR), b f 24/5 Peintre Celebre (USA)—
                                    Vadlamixa (FR) (Linamix (FR)) **SNC Lagardere Elevage**
105 CHAMBORD (IRE), gr c 27/2 Green Desert (USA)—Kenmist (Kenmare (FR)) (290000) **Mr U. Saini-Fasanotti**
106 CHARMINAMIX (IRE), gr c 17/4 Linamix (FR)—Cheeky Charm (USA) (Nureyev (USA)) **Maktoum Al Maktoum**
107 B f 6/2 Anabaa (USA)—China Moon (USA) (Gone West (USA)) (207914) **Anne Springer**
108 B c 23/2 Sadler's Wells (USA)—Colza (USA) (Alleged (USA)) (87189) **Mr S. Mulryan**
109 Ch f 21/2 Grand Lodge (USA)—Coraline (Sadler's Wells (USA)) **Prince Khalid Abdullah**
110 DAY OFF (USA), b f 17/3 Dynaformer (USA)—Super Staff (USA) (Secretariat (USA)) **Prince Khalid Abdullah**
111 DEMI VOIX, ch f 18/2 Halling (USA)—Quarter Note (Danehill (USA)) **Sheikh Mohammed**
112 DIAMOGRANDE (FR), gr c 16/4 Grand Lodge (USA)—Diamonaka (FR) (Akarad (FR)) **SNC Lagardere Elevage**
113 B c 8/3 Sadler's Wells (USA)—Elegant As Always (USA) (Nashwan (USA)) (107310) **Gestut Ammerland**
114 FOR WOOLLY (FR), b c 18/2 Soviet Star (USA)—Fine And Mellow (FR) (Lando (GER)) **Bob Lalemant**
115 FUNMAKER (IRE), br c 30/3 Xaar—Indian Imp (Indian Ridge) **Sheikh Mohammed**
116 GABRIELI (IRE), b c 25/1 Sadler's Wells (USA)—Moselle (Mtoto) **Sheikh Mohammed**
117 GENTLEWAVE (IRE), b c 18/3 Monsun (GER)—Saumareine (FR) (Saumarez) (36887) **Bob Lalemant**
118 GRAND VADLA (FR), b f 28/2 Grand Lodge (USA)—Vadlava (FR) (Bikala) **SNC Lagardere Elevage**
119 GREENVADOR (FR), b c 7/5 Green Desert (USA)—
                                    Vadsa Honor (FR) (Highest Honor (FR)) **SNC Lagardere Elevage**
120 GRIGORIEVA (IRE), ch f 4/3 Woodman (USA)—Elbaaha (Arazi (USA)) (187793) **Mr S. Mulryan**
121 GULDIMIX (USA), gr ro c 6/2 Thunder Gulch (USA)—Diamilina (FR) (Linamix (FR)) **SNC Lagardere Elevage**
122 B c 21/3 Danehill (USA)—Hasili (IRE) (Kahyasi) **Prince Khalid Abdullah**
123 HEAD WAITER (IRE), b c 5/2 Lend A Hand—Anno Luce (Old Vic) **Sheikh Mohammed**
124 Ch f 9/5 Peintre Celebre (USA)—Hold On (GER) (Surumu (GER)) **Gestut Ammerland**
125 INFINITE CHARM (IRE), b c 2/1 Peintre Celebre (USA)—
                                    Tenue d'amour (FR) (Pursuit of Love) (214621) **Maktoum Al Maktoum**
126 INTERNATIONAL, b c 19/3 Poliglote—Green Bend (USA) (Riverman (USA)) **Wertheimer et Frere**
127 ISOBEL BAILLIE, ch f 18/2 Lomitas—Dubai Soprano (Zafonic (USA)) **Sheikh Mohammed**
128 KILDA (IRE), b f 14/3 Night Shift (USA)—Khatela (IRE) (Shernazar) (63715) **Mme Fabre**
129 KITTYMIX (FR), gr c 22/5 Linamix (FR)—Kitty Be Wild (USA) (Storm Cat (USA)) **SNC Lagardere Elevage**
130 MADAME ARCATI (IRE), b f 4/2 Sinndar (IRE)—Most Charming (FR) (Darshaan) **Maktoum Al Maktoum**
131 MAZARINI, b c 20/2 Singspiel (IRE)—Sweet Willa (USA) (Assert) **Sheikh Mohammed**
132 MEDIA BARON (USA), gr ro c 15/2 Maria's Mon (USA)—Media Nox (Lycius (USA)) **Prince Khalid Abdullah**
133 MOON MIX (FR), gr c 15/2 Linamix (FR)—Cherry Moon (USA) (Quiet American (USA)) **SNC Lagardere Elevage**
134 B c 10/2 Anabaa (USA)—Mosogna (IRE) (Last Tycoon) **Gestut Ammerland**
135 B c 8/5 Halling (USA)—Muscadel (Nashwan (USA)) **Sheikh Mohammed**
136 B c 25/3 Hennessy (USA)—My Dream Castles (USA) (Woodman (USA)) **Mr E. Rothschild**
137 NANTES (GER), b f 31/3 Night Shift (USA)—Nevskij Prospekt (IRE) (Acatenango (GER)) **Mr U. Saini-Fasanotti**
138 ONLY HIM, b c 11/5 Seeking The Gold (USA)—Only Seule (Lyphard (USA)) **Wertheimer et Frere**
139 OVERSHADOW (IRE), ch c 2/3 Desert Prince (IRE)—Raincloud (Rainbow Quest (USA)) **Sheikh Mohammed**
140 PHANTOM ROSE (USA), b f 5/2 Danzig (USA)—
                                    Honest Lady (USA) (Seattle Slew (USA)) **Prince Khalid Abdullah**
141 POLYSHEBA (FR), b f 15/4 Poliglote—Ganasheba (USA) (Alysheba (USA)) **Wertheimer et Frere**
142 POWWAW (FR), b c 15/4 Dansili—Proud Douna (FR) (Kaldoun (FR)) **Mme Fabre**
143 QUESTION OF TIME (IRE), b c 10/2 Singspiel (IRE)—
                                    Questina (FR) (Rainbow Quest (USA)) (60000) **Sheikh Mohammed**
144 QUIET WATERS (USA), b f 28/1 Quiet American (USA)—
                                    Zawaahy (USA) (El Gran Senor (USA)) **Maktoum Al Maktoum**
145 RHENUS, b c 23/4 Montjeu (IRE)—Roseate Wood (FR) (Kaldoun (FR)) (46948) **Haras de la Perelle**
146 B c 3/3 King's Best (USA)—Rising Spirits (Cure The Blues (USA)) (239425) **Mr S. Mulryan**
147 B c 23/4 Theatrical—Saudia (USA) (Gone West (USA)) (154296) **Mr S. Mulryan**
148 SCARMIX, gr c 19/3 Linamix (FR)—Scarlet Raider (USA) (Red Ransom (USA)) **SNC Lagardere Elevage**
149 SLIPLOGE (FR), b c 4/4 Grand Lodge (USA)—
                                    Slipstream Queen (USA) (Conquistador Cielo (USA)) **SNC Lagardere Elevage**
150 SPECTACULAIRE, ch c 6/2 Spectrum (IRE)—Gold Round (IRE) (Caerleon (USA)) **Wertheimer et Frere**
151 B f 28/3 Sadler's Wells (USA)—Summer Breeze (Rainbow Quest (USA)) **Prince Khalid Abdullah**
152 SWEET SHOP, b f 6/2 Grand Lodge (USA)—Candice (IRE) (Caerleon (USA)) **Maktoum Al Maktoum**
153 SWEET TRAVEL (IRE), b f 15/2 Danzig (USA)—Raise A Beauty (USA) (Alydar (USA)) **Wertheimer et Frere**
154 TIME AND TIDE (USA), ch c 25/4 Diesis—Reams of Verse (USA) (Nureyev (USA)) **Prince Khalid Abdullah**
155 VADLIX (FR), gr c 14/3 Linamix (FR)—Vadlawysa (IRE) (Always Fair (USA)) **SNC Lagardere Elevage**

MR A. FABRE—continued

156 **VISINDAR**, ch c 9/3 Sinndar (IRE)—Visor (USA) (Mr Prospector (USA)) **SNC Lagardere Elevage**
157 **VISON CELEBRE (IRE)**, gr c 28/3 Peintre Celebre (USA)—
Visionnaire (FR) (Linamix (FR)) **SNC Lagardere Elevage**
158 **WATCH WHAT HAPPENS (FR)**, b c 21/3 Stravinsky (USA)—
Eaton Place (IRE) (Zafonic (USA)) (97250) **Bob Lalemant**
159 **WILD SUNDAY**, ch c 21/1 Sunday Silence (USA)—Danzigaway (USA) (Danehill (USA)) **Wertheimer et Frere**
160 **WINGSPAN (USA)**, b f 21/4 Silver Hawk (USA)—Broad Pennant (USA) (Broad Brush (USA)) **Wertheimer et Frere**
161 **WIZARD OF OZ**, b c 7/2 Singspiel (IRE)—Red Slippers (USA) (Nureyev (USA)) **Sheikh Mohammed**
162 Gr f 23/2 Machiavellian (USA)—Zafadola (IRE) (Darshaan) **Sheikh Mohammed**

---

200 **MR R. A. FAHEY, Malton**
Postal: RF Racing Ltd, Mews House, Musley Bank, Malton, North Yorkshire, YO17 6TD.
Contacts: PHONE (01653) 698915 FAX (01653) 699735 MOBILE (07713) 478079
E-MAIL richard.fahey@virgin.net

1 **ABELARD (IRE)**, 4, b g Fasliyev (USA)—Half-Hitch (USA) **A. J. Ryan**
2 **ALRIDA (IRE)**, 6, b g Ali-Royal (IRE)—Ride Bold (USA) **Mark Russell & Friends**
3 **ALTAY**, 8, b g Erins Isle—Aliuska (IRE) **Mr R. M. Jeffs & Mr J. Potter**
4 **BALL O MALT (IRE)**, 9, b g Star Quest—Vera Dodd (IRE) **Mr Declan Kinahan**
5 **BESEIGED (USA)**, 8, ch g Cadeaux Genereux—Munnaya (USA) **M. J. Caulfield**
6 **BO MCGINTY (IRE)**, 4, ch g Fayruz—Georges Park Lady (IRE) **Paddy McGinty & Bo Turnbull**
7 **BOPPYS PRINCESS**, 4, b f Wizard King—Laurel Queen (IRE) **Mrs S. Bond**
8 **BRAMANTINO (IRE)**, 5, b g Perugino (USA)—Headrest **Mrs Kenyon, A Rhodes Haulage, P Timmins**
9 **BUTTERWICK CHIEF**, 8, b g Be My Chief (USA)—Swift Return **P. S. Cresswell**
10 **CHEVIN**, 6, ch m Danzig Connection (USA)—Starr Danias **D. M. Beresford**
11 **CLASSICAL BEN**, 7, ch g Most Welcome—Stoproveritate **J. D. Clark and Partners**
12 **DANELOR (IRE)**, 7, b g Danehill (USA)—Formulate **M. A. Leatham**
13 **DARK CHARM (FR)**, 6, b g Anabaa (USA)—Wardara **M. A. Leatham**
14 **DEFINITE GUEST (IRE)**, 7, gr g Definite Article—Nicea (IRE) **Partnership**
15 **DOITNOW (IRE)**, 4, b g Princely Heir (IRE)—Tonys Gift **Hi-Tech Racing Club**
16 **ELVERYS (IRE)**, 6, b g Lord Americo—Paddy's Babs **J. J. Staunton**
17 **EMPRESS OF IRELAND (IRE)**, 6, b m King's Ride—My Lovely Rose (IRE) **H. Magill Hurst**
18 **EXSTOTO**, 8, b g Mtoto—Stoproveritate **J. D. Clark and Partners**
19 **FLYING BANTAM (IRE)**, 4, b g Fayruz—Natural Pearl **The Matthewman Partnership**
20 **FONTHILL ROAD (IRE)**, 5, ch g Royal Abjar (USA)—Hannah Huxtable (IRE) **Mrs U. Towell**
21 **GHANTOOT**, 4, ch c Inchinor—Shall We Run **Peter & Richard Foden Racing Partnership**
22 **HARRISON'S FLYER (IRE)**, 4, b g Imperial Ballet (IRE)—Smart Pet **P. D. Smith Holdings Ltd**
23 **HOUT BAY**, 8, ch g Komaite (USA)—Maiden Pool **Northumbria Leisure Ltd**
24 **HUMID CLIMATE**, 5, ch g Desert King (IRE)—Pontoon **J. E. M. Hawkins Ltd**
25 **INSTRUCTOR**, 4, ch g Groom Dancer (USA)—Doctor's Glory (USA) **Yorkshire Racing Club Owners Group 1990**
26 **KAMENKA**, 4, ch f Wolfhound (USA)—Aliuska (IRE) **Mr R. M. Jeffs & Mr J. Potter**
27 **KING'S SILVER (IRE)**, 4, b g King of Kings (IRE)—Almi Ad (USA) **Let's Go Racing 2**
28 **KINGS COLLEGE BOY**, 5, b g College Chapel—The Kings Daughter **The Cosmic Cases**
29 **LINCOLN DANCER (IRE)**, 8, b g Turtle Island (IRE)—Double Grange (IRE) **The Gardening Partnership**
30 **LITTLE JIMBOB**, 4, b g Desert Story (IRE)—Artistic Licence **Dale Scaffolding Co Ltd**
31 **MAKEABREAK (IRE)**, 6, ch m Anshan—Nilousha **A. Rhodes (Haulage) Limited**
32 **MARKET AVENUE**, 6, b m Factual (USA)—The Lady Vanishes **Market Avenue Racing Club Ltd**
33 **MARSHALLSPARK (IRE)**, 6, b g Fayruz—Lindas Delight **J. J. Staunton**
34 **MOBANE FLYER**, 5, b g Groom Dancer (USA)—Enchant **Mr P. N. Devlin**
35 **MR LEAR (USA)**, 6, b g Lear Fan (USA)—Majestic Mae (USA) **Christine Townley & Ms Laura Townley**
36 **MR LEWIN**, 4, ch g Primo Dominie—Fighting Run **Market Avenue Racing Club Ltd**
37 **NAMROUD (USA)**, 8, b g Irish River (FR)—Top Line (FR) **The Yorkshire Lancashire Alliance**
38 **NECKAR VALLEY (IRE)**, 6, b g Desert King (IRE)—Solar Attraction (IRE) **G. Morrill**
39 **OLDENWAY**, 6, b g Most Welcome—Sickle Moon **Richard Abbott & Mario Stavrou**
40 **OPERA SINGER**, 4, b g Ali-Royal—Wheeler's Wonder (IRE) **R. Cowie**
41 **PENDLE FOREST (IRE)**, 5, gr m Charnwood Forest (IRE)—Pride of Pendle **Mrs L. Miller**
42 **PERTEMPS MAGUS**, 5, b m Silver Wizard (USA)—Brilliant Future **The Spinal Injuries Association**
43 **PHILHARMONIC**, 4, b g Victory Note (USA)—Lambast **R. Cowie**
44 **POLLY WHITEFOOT**, 6, b m Perpendicular—Cream O The Border **Mrs J. Cowan**
45 **RICHTEE (IRE)**, 4, ch f Desert Sun—Santarene (IRE) **Terence Elsey and Richard Mustill**
46 **RIPNTEAR**, 6, b g Sabrehill (USA)—Sea of Clouds **J. J. Staunton**
47 **RISKA KING**, 5, b g Forzando—Artistic Licence **Market Avenue Racing Club Ltd**
48 **SHAMROCK TEA**, 4, b g Imperial Ballet (IRE)—Yellow Ribbon (IRE) **Keith Brown Properties (Hull) Ltd**
49 **SHAROURA**, 9, ch m Inchinor—Kinkajoo **Manor House Partnership**

MR R. A. FAHEY—continued

50 **SIR SANDROVITCH (IRE),** 9, b g Polish Patriot (USA)—Old Downie **W. G. Moore & G. Winton**
51 **SKI JUMP (USA),** 5, gr g El Prado (IRE)—Skiable (IRE) **P. D. Smith Holdings Ltd**
52 **STARCROSS VENTURE,** 4, b f Orpen (USA)—Maculatus (USA) **D. M. Beresford**
53 **SUALDA (IRE),** 6, b g Idris (IRE)—Winning Heart **J. H. Tattersall**
54 **SWAN KNIGHT (USA),** 9, b br g Sadler's Wells (USA)—Shannkara (IRE) **J. J. Staunton**
55 **TIME TO REMEMBER (IRE),** 7, b g Pennekamp (USA)—Bequeath (USA) **The Knavesmire Alliance**
56 **TURN OF PHRASE (IRE),** 6, b g Cadeaux Genereux—Token Gesture (IRE) **Jacksons Transport (West Riding) Ltd**
57 **WATCHING,** 8, ch g Indian Ridge—Sweeping **M.A.Leatham, G.H.Leatham & R.G.Leatham**
58 **WING COMMANDER,** 6, b g Royal Applause—Southern Psychic (USA) **S. P. Ryan**
59 **WONDER WOLF,** 4, b f Wolfhound (USA)—Wrangbrook **The Tom Mix Partners**
60 **WRENLANE,** 4, ch g Fraam—Hi Hoh (IRE) **K. Taylor**
61 **WYATT EARP (IRE),** 4, b g Piccolo—Tribal Lady **Byculla Thoroughbreds**
62 **XPRESSIONS,** 4, b g Turtle Island (IRE)—Make Ready **J. C. Parsons**
63 **ZEALAND,** 5, ch g Zamindar (USA)—Risanda **J. J. Staunton**

THREE-YEAR-OLDS

64 **ANDY MAL,** b f Mark of Esteem (IRE)—Sunflower Seed **Mrs A. M. Mallinson**
65 **BLISSPHILLY,** b f Primo Dominie—Majalis **P. J. Lawton**
66 **BOLTON HALL (IRE),** b g Imperial Ballet (IRE)—Muneera (USA) **J. J. Staunton**
67 **BOPPYS DREAM,** ch f Clan of Roses—Laurel Queen (IRE) **Mrs S. Bond**
68 **BREAKING SHADOW (IRE),** br g Danehill Dancer (IRE)—Crimbourne **G. Morrill**
69 **BURNLEY AL (IRE),** ch g Desert King (IRE)—Bold Meadows **The Matthewman Partnership**
70 **CHOREOGRAPHIC (IRE),** b c Komaite (USA)—Lambas! **Galaxy Racing**
71 **CLARET AND AMBER,** b g Forzando—Artistic Licence **The Matthewman Partnership**
72 **COCONUT MOON,** b f Bahamian Bounty—Lunar Ridge **Valley Paddocks Racing Limited**
73 **ENBORNE AGAIN (IRE),** ch c Fayruz—Sharp Ellie (IRE) **G. & K. Murray**
74 **FAVOURING (IRE),** ch c Fayruz—Peace Dividend (IRE) **The Rumpole Partnership**
75 **GOLDEN LEGACY (IRE),** b f Rossini (USA)—Dissidentia **Mr P. N. Devlin**
76 **KARASHINO (IRE),** ch f Shinko Forest (IRE)—Karisal (IRE) **J. E. M. Hawkins Ltd**
77 **KNOT IN WOOD (IRE),** b c Shinko Forest (IRE)—Notley Park **Rhodes, Kenyon & Gill**
78 **KOMREYEV STAR,** b c Komaite (USA)—L'ancressaan **Mr G. Whittaker**
79 **MASTER BEAR (IRE),** b g Bluebird (USA)—Kunuz **J. A. & Kay Campbell**
80 **PAPARAAZI (IRE),** b c Victory Note (USA)—Raazi **Mr & Mrs A. R. Nemazee**
81 **PASSIONATELY ROYAL,** b c Royal Applause—Passionelle **W. J. Dobson**
82 **PETERS DELITE,** b c Makbul—Steadfast Elite (IRE) **Peter & Richard Foden Racing Partnership**
83 **PLENTY CRIED WOLF,** b g Wolfhound (USA)—Plentitude (FR) **G. J. Paver**
84 **SECOND REEF,** b c Second Empire (IRE)—Vax Lady **Valley Paddocks Racing Limited**
85 Br b g Desert Sun—Shifting Shadow (IRE) **Mrs M. W. Kenyon**
86 **SIOUX FLYTE (IRE),** gr f Daylami (IRE)—Street Lina (FR) **Mrs U. Towell**
87 **SUMMER SILKS,** ch f Bahamian Bounty—Sadler's Song **Falcon Assets/Kestrel**
88 **SUPERIOR HAND (IRE),** b c Lend A Hand—Cantata (IRE) **J. C. Parsons**
89 **TAGULA SUNRISE (IRE),** ch f Tagula (IRE)—Lady From Limerick (IRE) **Mr David M. Knaggs & Mel Roberts**
90 **TELEGRAM SAM (IRE),** b c Soviet Star (USA)—She's The Tops **Market Avenue Racing Club Ltd**
91 **TRIFFID,** b g Dracula (AUS)—Rockfest (USA) **Mr R. A. Fahey**
92 **WISE WAGER (IRE),** b f Titus Livius (FR)—Londubh **P. Timmins & J. Rhodes**

Other Owners: D. Barnett, R. G. W. Brown, J. Browne, I. T. Buchanan, Mrs P. A. Farr, J. Fieldus, F. Fitzmaurice, Miss C. Foster, C. R. Galloway, Dr A. J. F. Gillespie, J. J. Gilmartin, The Hon R. T. A. Goff, P. J. Greaves, M. L. Green, J. P. Hames, K. Hind, Lady Howard De Walden, Mr A. Jones, A. J. Keating, Mrs P. A. Morrison, Mrs E. A. Murray, R. W. North, G. R. Ralph, R. C. V. Stimson, M. A. Stoker, A. Tattersall, R. Teeman, P. J. Towell, R. S. Turnbull, T. A. H. Wake, R. Wardlaw, M. Wassall, T. Watts, Mr G. V. Williams.

Assistant Trainer: Pat Brilly

Jockey (flat): T. Hamilton, P. Hanagan. **Conditional:** J. Clare, P. Whelan. **Apprentice:** N. Lawes. **Amateur:** Miss V. Tunnicliffe, Mr D. Cottle.

201 MR C. W. FAIRHURST, Middleham
Postal: **Glasgow House, Middleham, Leyburn, North Yorkshire, DL8 4QG.**
Contacts: **PHONE/FAX (01969) 622039 MOBILE (07889) 410840**
E-MAIL cfairhurst@tiscali.co.uk WEBSITE www.chrisfairhurstracing.com

1 ABBAJABBA, 9, b g Barrys Gamble—Bo' Babbity **North Cheshire Trading & Storage Ltd**
2 HEZAAM (USA), 4, b c Red Ransom (USA)—Ashraakat (USA) **Six Iron Partnership**
3 LUCKY PISCEAN, 4, b g River Falls—Celestine **Grace Arnold Partnership**
4 M FOR MAGIC, 6, ch g First Trump—Celestine **Grace Arnold Partnership**
5 NETWORK OSCAR (IRE), 4, b g Oscar (IRE)—Just Wonderful (IRE) **N. Gravett**
6 PASSION FRUIT, 4, b f Pursuit of Love—Reine de Thebes (FR) **G. H. & S. Leggott**
7 QUINN, 5, ch g First Trump—Celestine **Grace Arnold Partnership**
8 RINGSIDE JACK, 9, b g Batshoof—Celestine **M. J. G. Partnership**
9 RIVER LINE (USA), 4, b g Keos (USA)—Portio (USA) **Mrs B. J. Boocock**
10 SILVER HILL LAD, 4, gr g Petoski—Miss Madelon **Mrs A. M. Leggett**
11 TICKHILL TOM, 5, ch g First Trump—Tender Loving Care **Tickhill Racing Partnership**
12 YORKE'S FOLLY (USA), 4, b f Stravinsky (USA)—Tommelise (USA) **Mrs A. M. Leggett**

THREE-YEAR-OLDS
13 BURNING THOUGHTS, ch g Rock City—Rama de Oro **Mrs B. J. Boocock**
14 DANCING SHIRL, b f Dancing Spree (USA)—Shirl **Mrs S. France**
15 TRUCKLE, b c Vettori (IRE)—Proud Titania (IRE) **W. H. Hill**

TWO-YEAR-OLDS
16 GOLDEN GROOM, b c 6/3 Groom Dancer (USA)—Reine de Thebes (FR) (Darshaan) **G. H. and Simon Leggott**
17 NIMBLE STAR, b f 16/2 Foxhound (USA)—Deerlet (Darshaan) (1000) **Coleraine Racing**
18 THE THRIFTY BEAR, ch g 24/2 Rambling Bear—Prudent Pet (Distant Relative) **Mrs C. Arnold**

Other Owners: Roseland Racing Partnership, Derek Latham, Mr M. Williams, Mr B. M. Saumtally, Mrs P. J. Taylor-Garthwaite, H. Taylor & Son, D. M. Gardner, M. J. Grace, Mrs D. Grace.

Jockey (flat): J. Fanning. **Conditional:** N. Hannity.

202 MR J. R. FANSHAWE, Newmarket
Postal: **Pegasus Stables, Snailwell Road, Newmarket, Suffolk, CB8 7DJ.**
Contacts: **PHONE (01638) 664525/660153 FAX (01638) 664523**
E-MAIL james.fanshawe@virgin.net WEBSITE www.jamesfanshawe.com

1 ABLE BAKER CHARLIE (IRE), 6, b g Sri Pekan (USA)—Lavezzola (IRE) **David Croft & Partners**
2 AZAROLE (IRE), 4, b g Alzao (USA)—Cashew **Lord Vestey**
3 CASHBAR, 4, b f Bishop of Cashel—Barford Sovereign **Lord Vestey**
4 CESARE, 4, b g Machiavellian (USA)—Tromond **Cheveley Park Stud**
5 CRUZSPIEL, 5, br g Singspiel (IRE)—Allespagne (USA) **P. Garvey**
6 DEFINING, 6, b g Definite Article—Gooseberry Pie **Mrs V. M. Shelton**
7 ETERNAL SPRING (IRE), 8, b g Persian Bold—Emerald Waters **P. C. Green**
8 FIRENZE, 4, ch f Efisio—Juliet Bravo **Mrs J. P. Hopper**
9 FLING, 4, b f Pursuit of Love—Full Orchestra **Cheveley Park Stud**
10 HIGH CHARTER, 4, b g Polish Precedent (USA)—By Charter **Mrs J. M. J. Fanshawe**
11 HIGH RESERVE, 4, b f Dr Fong (USA)—Hyabella **Helena Springfield Ltd**
12 I'LL FLY, 5, ch g Polar Falcon (USA)—I'll Try **Mrs K. Fraser, Mrs D. Strauss, Mrs R. Hambro**
13 LADY GEORGINA, 4, gr f Linamix (FR)—Georgia Venture **Byerley Turf**
14 MOLLYPUTTHEKETELON (USA), 4, b f Rainbow Quest (USA)—Nemea (USA) **Kilboy Estate**
15 MUSICANNA, 4, b f Cape Cross (IRE)—Upend **Ne'er Do Wells II**
16 PERSIAN WATERS (IRE), 9, b g Persian Bold—Emerald Waters **P. C. Green**
17 POLAR BEN, 6, b g Polar Falcon (USA)—Woodbeck **Mr Simon Gibson**
18 POLAR MAGIC, 4, ch c Polar Falcon (USA)—Enchant **R. C. Thompson**
19 POLAR SUN, 4, b g Polar Falcon (USA)—Barford Lady **Barford Bloodstock**
20 POLE STAR, 7, b br g Polar Falcon (USA)—Ellie Ardensky **P. C. Green**
21 PRINS WILLEM (IRE), 6, b g Alzao (USA)—American Garden (USA) **C. T. Van Hoorn**
22 REVEILLEZ, 6, gr g First Trump—Amalancher (USA) **Mr John P. McManus**
23 ROYAL PRINCE, 4, gr c Royal Applause—Onefortheditch (USA) **Gainsborough Stud Management Ltd**
24 SOLAR POWER (IRE), 4, b f Marju (IRE)—Next Round (IRE) **Deln Ltd**
25 SOVIET SONG (IRE), 5, b m Marju (IRE)—Kalinka (IRE) **Elite Racing Club**
26 SOVIET TIMES (IRE), 4, ch f Soviet Star (USA)—Ridge The Times (USA) **Ballylinch Stud**
27 SPRING JIM, 4, b g First Trump—Spring Sixpence **Andrew & Julia Turner**

MR J. R. FANSHAWE—continued

28 **STROLLER (IRE),** 4, b f Sadler's Wells (USA)—Gravieres (FR) **Ballylinch Stud**
29 **TRAYTONIC,** 4, b c Botanic (USA)—Lady Parker (IRE) **Clipper Group Holdings Ltd**
30 **UNSCRUPULOUS,** 6, ch g Machiavellian (USA)—Footlight Fantasy (USA) **The Unscrupulous Partnership**

THREE-YEAR-OLDS

31 **AZUCAR (IRE),** b f Desert Prince (IRE)—Cap Coz (IRE) **Mrs C. C. Regalado-Gonzalez**
32 **BAMZOOKI,** b f Zilzal (USA)—Cavernista **Three Ladies Partnership**
33 **BAYARD (USA),** gr c Lord Avie (USA)—Mersey **Mr & Mrs G. Middlebrook & Mr & Mrs P. Brain**
34 **BOUQUET,** b f Cadeaux Genereux—Bayadere (USA) **Mrs D. M. Haynes**
35 **BRACKLINN,** b f Deploy—Blane Water (USA) **C.I.T. Racing Ltd**
36 **BUSTER HYVONEN (IRE),** b c Dansili—Serotina (IRE) **Mr Simon Gibson**
37 **CYCLONIC,** br c Pivotal—Rainy Day Song **C. T. Van Hoorn**
38 **DAWN AT SEA,** b f Slip Anchor—Finger of Light **B. J. Mcallister**
39 **DREADNOUGHT,** b c Slip Anchor—Fleet Amour (USA) **Mrs D. M. Haynes**
40 **EGERIA (IRE),** gr f Daylami (IRE)—Spring **Lord Halifax**
41 **EMBARK,** b f Soviet Star (USA)—Shore Line **Cheveley Park Stud**
42 **GALLANT GUEST (IRE),** b f Be My Guest (USA)—Next Round (IRE) **Deln Ltd**
43 **GANDALF,** b c Sadler's Wells (USA)—Enchant **R. C. Thompson**
44 **INCHLOCH,** ch g Inchinor—Lake Pleasant (IRE) **Lord Vestey**
45 **INFATUATE,** b g Inchinor—First Fantasy **Nigel & Carolyn Elwes**
46 **JAMAAR,** ch c Nashwan (USA)—Kissogram **Lancen Farm Partnership**
47 **KAZATZKA,** ch f Groom Dancer (USA)—Kalinka (IRE) **Elite Racing Club**
48 **KRISTINOR (FR),** ch g Inchinor—Kristina **J. H. Richmond-Watson**
49 **LIGHTNING FLASH,** br c Docksider (USA)—Threatening **Mr N. G. Kairis**
50 **MANTLE,** b f Loup Sauvage (USA)—Kyle Rhea **Lady Wills**
51 **NOBELIX (IRE),** gr g Linamix (FR)—Nataliana **R. N. Hambro**
52 **NOR'WESTER,** br c Inchinor—Princess Nawaal (USA) **Dr C. M. H. Wills**
53 **PENNY WEDDING (IRE),** b f Pennekamp (USA)—Eilean Shona **Dr C. M. H. Wills**
54 **PRIMONDO (IRE),** b g Montjeu (IRE)—Tagiki (IRE) **Mr N. G. Kairis**
55 **RARE CROSS (IRE),** b f Cape Cross (IRE)—Hebrides **Lael Stable Syndicate**
56 **RIVER MIST IMAGE (USA),** ch f Swain (IRE)—Cat's Image (CAN) **The River Mist Image Partnership**
57 **SHESTHEBISCUIT,** b f Diktat—Selvi **The Hobnobs**
58 **SIR BERNARD,** ch g Benny The Dip (USA)—Viewfinder (USA) **Mr A. P. Thompson**
59 **SOAR,** b f Danzero (AUS)—Splice **Cheveley Park Stud**
60 **SPECTRAL STAR,** b f Unfuwain (USA)—Hyperspectra **Helena Springfield Ltd**
61 B g Singspiel (IRE)—Thea (USA) **T. R. G. Vestey**
62 **TILT,** b g Daylami (IRE)—Tromond **Cheveley Park Stud**
63 **TOOTSY,** b f Dansili—Totom **C. T. Van Hoorn**
64 B c Green Desert (USA)—Twilight Walk (USA) **Mr Yue Yun Hing**
65 **VIRGIL,** b c Machiavellian (USA)—Mystic Goddess (USA) **Cheveley Park Stud**
66 **ZIDANE,** b c Danzero (AUS)—Juliet Bravo **Mrs J. P. Hopper**

TWO-YEAR-OLDS

67 B f 4/2 Alhaarth (IRE)—Aguinaga (IRE) (Machiavellian (USA)) **Mr Frank Cosgrove**
68 B f 9/2 In The Wings—Allegheny River (USA) (Lear Fan (USA)) (42000) **Mrs C. C. Regalado-Gonzalez**
69 **AND AGAIN (USA),** b f 3/2 In The Wings—Garah (Ajdal (USA)) (20000) **Prince A. A. Faisal**
70 **APHORISM,** b f 12/3 Halling (USA)—Appiecross (Glint of Gold) **Dr C. M. H. Wills**
71 **BRIGYDON (IRE),** b c 24/5 Fasliyev (USA)—
　　　　　　　　　　　　　Creme Caramel (Septieme Ciel (USA)) (60000) **Mr Simon Gibson**
72 **BRONZE STAR,** b f 28/4 Mark of Esteem (IRE)—White House (Pursuit of Love) **J. M. Greetham**
73 **CAPE,** b f 11/2 Cape Cross (IRE)—Rubbiyati (Cadeaux Genereux) **Wyck Hall Stud Ltd**
74 B f 13/1 Spinning World (USA)—Carambola (IRE) (Danehill (USA)) (55000) **Mrs Martin Armstrong**
75 **CARESSED,** b f 14/2 Medicean—Embraced (Pursuit of Love) **Cheveley Park Stud**
76 B f 5/4 Woodman (USA)—Cois Cuain (IRE) (Night Shift (USA)) **Mr Frank Cosgrove**
77 **CONKERING (USA),** ch c 5/3 Horse Chestnut (SAF)—
　　　　　　　　　　　　　Nunbridled (USA) (Unbridled (USA)) **Mrs Harry Oppenheimer & Mrs Mary Slack**
78 **DANCE A DAYDREAM,** b f 12/4 Daylami (IRE)—Dance A Dream (Sadler's Wells (USA)) **Cheveley Park Stud**
79 **DETENTE,** b f 2/2 Medicean—Truce (Nashwan (USA)) **Cheveley Park Stud**
80 **DIK DIK,** b c 29/4 Diktat—Totom (Mtoto) (6000) **Mrs F. M. Russell**
81 **FONT,** b c 16/3 Sadler's Wells (USA)—River Saint (USA) (Irish River (FR)) **Cheveley Park Stud Ltd**
82 B f 27/2 Fasliyev (USA)—Georgia Venture (Shirley Heights)
83 **HAZELNUT,** b f 21/4 Selkirk (USA)—Cashew (Sharrood (USA)) **The Hon W. G. Vestey**
84 **IMPOSTOR (IRE),** b c 1/5 In The Wings—Princess Caraboo (IRE) (Alzao (USA)) (18500) **Mrs V. M. Shelton**
85 **KARTIKEYA (USA),** b br c 23/2 War Chant (USA)—Egoli (USA) (Seeking The Gold (USA)) **Bloomsbury Stud**
86 **KINGSCAPE (IRE),** br c 14/2 King Charlemagne (USA)—Cape Clear (Slip Anchor) (49000) **Mrs V. M. Shelton**

MR J. R. FANSHAWE—continued

87 B c 20/2 Medicean—Lishaway (FR) (Polish Precedent (USA)) (77128) **Ivan Allan**
88 B c 29/4 King's Best (USA)—Lyrical Dance (USA) (Lear Fan (USA)) (110000) **Clipper Group Holdings Ltd**
89 **MISS BRUSH,** b f 1/4 Foxhound (USA)—Tattinger (Prince Sabo) (800) **Mrs J. M. J. Fanshawe**
90 Ch f 3/5 Compton Place—Miss Rimex (USA) (Ezzoud (IRE)) **Park Farm Racing**
91 **PARADISE STREET (IRE),** b f 2/2 Machiavellian (USA)—Tani (USA) (Theatrical) (150000) **Kilboy Estate**
92 **PEPPERTREE,** b f 24/1 Fantastic Light (USA)—
                                    Delauncy (Machiavellian (USA)) (214621) **Wood Hall Stud Limited**
93 **PORTAL,** b f 10/2 Hernando (FR)—White Palace (Shirley Heights) **Cheveley Park Stud**
94 **QUEEN ISABELLA,** gr f 21/3 El Prado (IRE)—Ausherra (USA) (Diesis) (100000) **Lord Vestey**
95 **RHINEBIRD,** b c 24/3 Lomitas—Twitcher's Delight (Polar Falcon (USA)) (31000) **C. T. Van Hoorn**
96 **ROYAL FANTASY (IRE),** b br f 9/3 King's Best (USA)—Dreams (Rainbow Quest (USA)) **Nigel & Carolyn Elwes**
97 **RUSE,** b f 23/2 Diktat—Reuval (Sharpen Up) **Dr C. M. H. Wills**
98 **SANCTITY,** ch f 16/5 Pivotal—Blessed Honour (Ahonoora) **Cheveley Park Stud**
99 **SASETTI (IRE),** ch f 17/2 Selkirk (USA)—My Potters (USA) (Irish River (FR)) **Lady Clague**
100 **SHOTFIRE RIDGE,** ch c 7/4 Grand Lodge (USA)—Darya (USA) (Gulch (USA)) (50000) **Wood Hall Stud Limited**
101 **SOUTHPORT STAR (IRE),** b c 15/2 King's Best (USA)—
                                    Danzig's Girl (Danzig (USA)) (40240) **The Southport Star Partnership**
102 B f 24/2 Dansili—Tinashaan (IRE) (Darshaan) **Mr Bruce McAllister**
103 **TOP AWARD,** b c 22/4 Mark of Esteem (IRE)—First Fantasy (USA) (26000) **Nigel & Carolyn Elwes**
104 B f 21/2 Mozart (IRE)—Villa Carlotta (Rainbow Quest (USA)) **Mr J. H. Richmond Watson**
105 B f 19/2 Royal Applause—Wiener Wald (USA) (Woodman (USA)) **Car Colston Hall Stud & Mr & Mrs K. Hamill**

Other Owners: Mr Peter Bickmore, Mr T. Carroll, Mrs H. S. Ellinsen, Mr T. Hill, Mr R. Jackson, Mr T. I. Handscombe, Mrs C. Handscombe, Mrs G. Jackson, Mr Nigel Lewis, Mrs Heather Lewis, Mr J. D. Younger, Mrs S. Willson, Mr E. J. Williams, Mr M. Weinfeld, Mrs G. Thompson, Mrs A. Tate, Mrs Doreen M. Swinburn, Mr S. D. Swaden, Mr J. Kennedy, Mrs J. King, Mr D. King, Mr R. Gough, Mrs T. Underwood, Mrs S. Leach, Mr P. Leach, Mr W. G. R. Younger, Mrs K. Deane, Mr J. Norton, Mrs D. Nunn, Mr N. Nunn, Mr B. McGregor, Mrs G. M. Beller, Mrs A. J. Brudenell, Mr N. Cobby, D. M. B. Croft, S. M. De Zoete, Mrs E. Fanshawe, The Hon Mrs K. Fraser, Mrs M. R. Hambro, A. J. Hill, Mrs P. Morrell, Miss M. Noden, D. I. Russell, Mrs Derek Strauss, Miss H. S. Weinfeld.

Assistant Trainer: Emma Candy

---

203 MS LUCINDA FEATHERSTONE, Abberley
Postal: **Worsley Racing Stables, Abberley, Worcestershire, WR6 6BQ.**
Contacts: **MOBILE (07767) 067423 or (07946) 403147**
WEBSITE www.largessevirgin.net

1 4, B g Jumbo Hirt (USA)—A Sharp **J. Roundtree**
2 **BID SPOTTER (IRE),** 6, b g Eagle Eyed (USA)—Bebe Auction (IRE) **Heart Of England Racing**
3 **COURANT D'AIR (IRE),** 4, b g Indian Rocket—Red River Rose (IRE) **J. Billson**
4 **KINGS ROCK,** 4, ch g Kris—Both Sides Now (USA) **J. Billson**
5 **RIVER IRIS,** 4, ch f Riverhead (USA)—Barkston Singer **Heart Of England Racing**
6 **ROMAN CANDLE (IRE),** 9, b g Sabrehill (USA)—Penny Banger (IRE) **Largesse Racing**
7 **STORMDANCER (IRE),** 8, ch g Bluebird (USA)—Unspoiled **Largesse Racing**
8 4, B f Riverhead (USA)—Tallulah **J. Roundtree**

TWO-YEAR-OLDS

9 Ch c 19/2 Arkadian Hero (USA)—Flighty Dancer (Pivotal) **Blujon**

Other Owners: The Hon Cherry King, E. A. Buckley, Ms Lucinda Featherstone, Ms D. F. Wilder.

Assistant Trainer: Matthew Jones

Jockey (NH): T. J. Murphy, J. P. McNamara. **Apprentice:** David Nolan. **Amateur:** Miss Katie James.

---

204 MR D. B. FEEK, Brightling
Postal: **2 Street Cottage, Brightling, Robertsbridge, East Sussex, TN32 5HH.**
Contacts: **PHONE (01424) 838557 MOBILE (07884) 387798**
E-MAIL dfeek@brightlingracing.co.uk WEBSITE www.brightlingracing.co.uk

1 **ACE COMING,** 4, b g First Trump—Tarry **D. M. Grissell**
2 **BUCKLAND GOLD (IRE),** 5, b g Lord Americo—Beann Ard (IRE) **Mrs R. M. Hepburn**
3 **ELLAS RECOVERY (IRE),** 5, b g Shernazar—Nancys Wood (IRE) **D. R. Hunnisett**

MR D. B. FEEK—continued

  4 GREEN GAMBLE, 5, gr g Environment Friend—Gemma's Wager (IRE) **Mr Barry & Baroness Noakes**
  5 MR BILL, 5, ch g Cosmonaut—Latch On (IRE) **Mrs I. Y. Taylor**
  6 MR DINGLAWI (IRE), 4, b g Danehill Dancer (IRE)—Princess Leona (IRE) **Brightling Folly Partnership**
  7 MR TWINS (ARG), 4, ch g Numerous (USA)—Twins Parade (ARG) **N. J. Jones**
  8 MYSON (IRE), 6, ch g Accordion—Ah Suzie (IRE) **R. Winchester & Son**
  9 PRINCE VALENTINE, 4, b g My Best Valentine—Affaire de Coeur **D. R. Hunnisett**
10 TARTAN FLYER, 5, b g Bonny Scot (IRE)—Run Pet Run **R. J. Dyer**

THREE-YEAR-OLDS

11 DREAM OF LOVE, b f Pursuit of Love—Affaire de Coeur **D. R. Hunnisett**

Other Owners: J. T. Brown, A. J. Feek, Mr J. Hills, Baroness Noakes, C. B. Noakes, B. Spiby, R. F. Winchester, M. D. Winchester.

Conditional: James Davies.

---

205 | MISS J. D. FEILDEN, Newmarket
Postal: **Harraton Stables, Chapel Street, Exning, Newmarket, Suffolk, CB8 7HA.**
Contacts: **PHONE (01638) 577470 MOBILE (07974) 817694**
E-MAIL hoofbeatstours@aol.com

  1 BLAKE HALL LAD (IRE), 4, b g Cape Cross (IRE)—Queen of Art (IRE) **Eventmaker Partnership**
  2 DANCE WORLD, 5, b g Spectrum (IRE)—Dansara **Stowstowquickquickstow Partnership**
  3 ESSEX STAR (IRE), 4, b f Revoque (IRE)—Touch of White **Essex Partnership**
  4 GET TO THE POINT, 4, ch g Daggers Drawn (USA)—Penny Mint **Hoofbeats Racing Club**
  5 KING FLYER (IRE), 9, b g Ezzoud (IRE)—Al Guswa **J. W. Jenkins**
  6 LEVANTINE (IRE), 8, b g Sadler's Wells (USA)—Spain Lane (USA) **City Racing Club**
  7 LOVE YOU ALWAYS (USA), 5, ch g Woodman (USA)—Encorenous (USA) **Mr H. Thompson - Mr P. Thompson**
  8 LOVE'S DESIGN (IRE), 8, b br g Pursuit of Love—Cephista **City Racing Club**
  9 MISTY MAN (USA), 7, ch g El Gran Senor (USA)—Miasma (USA) **R. J. Creese**
10 NAJAABA (USA), 5, b m Bahhare (USA)—Ashbilya (USA) **A. K. Sparks**
11 ROAD KING (IRE), 11, b g Supreme Leader—Ladies Gazette **Miss J. D. Feilden**
12 SHAABAN (IRE), 4, b g Woodman (USA)—Ashbilya (USA) **DD & N Associates**
13 TEAM-MATE (IRE), 7, b g Nashwan (USA)—Ustka **Mrs P. Gooden and Mr G. F. Gooden**
14 THREE SHIPS, 4, ch g Dr Fong (USA)—River Lullaby (USA) **Ocean Trailers Ltd**

THREE-YEAR-OLDS

15 LADY HEN, b f Efisio—Royale Rose (FR) **R. J. Creese**
16 ORPEN ANNIE (IRE), b f Orpen (USA)—Nisibis **Hoofbeats Racing Club**
17 SAND REPEAL (IRE), b g Revoque (IRE)—Columbian Sand (IRE) **The Sultans of Speed**
18 SCISSORS (IRE), ch f Desert King (IRE)—Clipping **Mrs G. S. Fawsitt**
19 SILVER VISAGE (IRE), b g Lujain (USA)—About Face **Rosewood Racers**
20 WELSH TOUCH (IRE), b f Second Empire (IRE)—Touch of White **A. K. Sparks**

TWO-YEAR-OLDS

21 B c 26/5 Fasliyev (USA)—Clipping (Kris) (11000)
22 CRYSTAL AIR (IRE), b f 21/3 Distant Music (USA)—
                         Columbian Sand (IRE) (Salmon Leap (USA)) (5800) **Mr Michael Jennee**
23 Ch f 17/4 King Charlemagne (USA)—Persian Mistress (IRE) (Persian Bold) (10000)
24 Ch f 12/3 Beckett (IRE)—Sunlit Ride (Ahonoora)

Other Owners: Mr A. Dee, Miss J. D. Feilden, Ms J. L. Feilden, M. J. Lurcock, Mr P. Newman, Mr M. Newman, C. M. Page, R. Sidebottom, D. Sutherland, Mrs N. Sutherland.

Assistant Trainer: Poppy Feilden

Apprentice: K. Milczarek, Brian Reilly. **Amateur:** Miss V. Ferguson.

206 MR D. J. S. FFRENCH DAVIS, Lambourn
Postal: **Gordon Cottage, Parsonage Lane, Lambourn, Hungerford, Berkshire, RG17 8PA.**
Contacts: **HOME (01488) 72342 YARD (01488) 73675 MOBILE (07831) 118764**
E-MAIL ffrenchdavis@supanet.com WEBSITE www.ffrenchdavis.com

1 BLESSED PLACE, 5, ch g Compton Place—Cathedra **S. J. Edwards**
2 BREATHING SPACE (USA), 4, b br f Expelled (USA)—Summer Retreat (USA) **Miss Alison Jones**
3 CAPPANRUSH (IRE), 5, gr g Medaaly—Introvert (USA) **Mrs B. Keogh**
4 CRAFTY FANCY (IRE), 4, ch f Intikhab (USA)—Idle Fancy **Mrs F. Houlihan**
5 ENGLISH ROCKET (IRE), 4, b g Indian Rocket—Golden Charm (IRE) **Hargood Limited**
6 HEAD TO KERRY (IRE), 5, b g Eagle Eyed (USA)—The Poachers Lady (IRE) **Blueprint Construction Supplies Ltd**
7 MAJIK, 6, ch g Pivotal—Revoke (USA) **A. D. Stimpson**
8 MISTER RIGHT (IRE), 4, ch g Barathea—Broken Spirit (IRE) **Miss Alison Jones**
9 NASSAU STREET, 5, gr g Bahamian Bounty—Milva **Mrs P. J. M. McCarthy**
10 NIGHT EXPLOSION (IRE), 7, ch g Night Shift (USA)—Voodoo Rocket **Miss M. A. M. Turner**
11 TEORBAN (POL), 6, b g Don Corleone—Tabaka (POL) **Sheedy Scrap Metals (1976) Ltd**
12 THENFORD LAD (IRE), 4, b g Saddlers' Hall (IRE)—Lady Leona **A. C. H. Bond**

THREE-YEAR-OLDS

13 FLYING PASS, b g Alzao (USA)—Complimentary Pass **Woodview Racing**
14 GORTUMBLO, b g Sri Pekan (USA)—Evergreen (IRE) **Mr K. Corrigan**
15 KING GABRIEL (IRE), b g Desert King (IRE)—Broken Spirit (IRE) **Woodview Racing**
16 SWANKY STAR (IRE), b f Orpen (USA)—Haajra (IRE) **Hyperion Bloodstock**
17 TIPSY LAD, b g Tipsy Creek (USA)—Perfidy (FR) **S. J. Edwards**

TWO-YEAR-OLDS

18 B c 7/1 Danetime (IRE)—Alexander Eliott (IRE) (Night Shift (USA)) (10500) **P. B. Gallagher**
19 Ch f 23/2 Zaha (CAN)—Amber Rose (IRE) (Royal Academy (USA)) (5000) **Zaha Racing Syndicate**
20 FISHING INSTRUCTOR, gr g 16/4 Silver Patriarch (IRE)—Super Malt (IRE) (Milk of The Barley) **A. C. H. Bond**
21 Ch f 16/4 Atticus (USA)—Nunatak (USA) (Bering) (20000) **Miss Alison Jones**
22 THENFORD RYDE, b g 4/5 Emperor Fountain—Glenlyon Ryde (Fearless Action (USA)) **A. C. H. Bond**

Other Owners: D. M. Beresford, R. J. C. Brown, MR D. J. S. Ffrench Davis, P. Kilkenny, J. Kilkenny, R. A. Major, J. S. Mhajan, M. L. Pearl, Robin Sharp, R. J. Sheen.

Assistant Trainer: Avery Ffrench Davis

Jockey (flat): T. Quinn.

207 MR R. FIELDER, Cranleigh
Postal: **15 Clappers Meadow, Alfold, Cranleigh, Surrey, GU6 8HH.**
Contacts: **PHONE (01403) 752144 MOBILE (07711) 024054**
E-MAIL valerie.h.fielder@talk21.com

1 MY RETREAT (USA), 8, b g Hermitage (USA)—My Jessica Ann (USA) **Mr R. Fielder**

Amateur: Mr P. York.

208 MR G. FIERRO, Hednesford
Postal: **"Woodview", Hazel Slade Racing Stables, Rugeley Road, Hazel Slade, Hednesford, Staffordshire, WS12 0PH.**
Contacts: **HOME/YARD (01543) 879611 MOBILE (07976) 321468**

1 ABBIEJO (IRE), 8, b m Blues Traveller (IRE)—Chesham Lady (IRE) **Mr G. Fierro**
2 GO ON JACK, 7, ch g Saint Keyne—Swift Messenger **Mr G. Fierro**
3 GREEN CONVERSION (IRE), 4, ch g Desert King (IRE)—Blue Bangor (IRE) **P. Daykin**
4 JUST BETH, 9, ch m Carlingford Castle—One For The Road **Mr G. Fierro**
5 SILVER GIFT, 8, b m Rakaposhi King—Kellsboro Kate **Mr G. Fierro**
6 YES SES LES, 6, b g El Conquistador—Kellsboro Queen **Mr G. Fierro**

Assistant Trainer: M Fierro

Conditional: S. Lycett.

209 MR R. F. FISHER, Ulverston

Postal: **Great Head House, Priory Road, Ulverston, Cumbria, LA12 9RX.**
Contacts: **PHONE (01229) 585664 FAX (01229) 585079 MOBILE (07779) 609068**
E-MAIL elliefisher@btinternet.com WEBSITE www.roger-fisher.com

1 EURYALUS (IRE), 7, ch g Presenting—New Talent **Great Head House Estates Ltd**
2 KYBER, 4, ch g First Trump—Mahbob Dancer (FR) **Great Northern Partnership**
3 LAZY BUT LIVELY (IRE), 9, br g Supreme Leader—Oriel Dream **S. P. Marsh**
4 LOUIS CSASZAR (IRE), 7, b g Arctic Lord—Satlan's Treasure (IRE) **Great Head House Estates Ltd**
5 MENAI STRAIGHTS, 4, ch g Alhaarth (IRE)—Kind of Light **M. Maclennan**
6 MIKASA (IRE), 5, b g Victory Note (USA)—Resiusa (ITY) **Great Head House Estates Ltd**
7 RARE COINCIDENCE, 4, ch g Atraf—Green Seed (IRE) **Mr A. M. Kerr**
8 STOIC LEADER (IRE), 5, b g Danehill Dancer (IRE)—Starlust **A. Willoughby**
9 TEUTONIC (IRE), 4, b f Revoque (IRE)—Classic Ring (IRE) **Great Head House Estates Ltd**
10 TONI ALCALA, 6, b g Ezzoud (IRE)—Etourdie (USA) **A. Willoughby**
11 ZYGOMATIC, 7, ch g Risk Me (FR)—Give Me A Day **S. P. Marsh**

THREE-YEAR-OLDS

12 BECKERMET (IRE), b g Second Empire (IRE)—Razida (IRE) **Bishopthorpe Racing Two**
13 ESKDALE (IRE), b g Perugino (USA)—Gilding The Lily (IRE) **Great Head House Estates Ltd**
14 GRIZEBECK (IRE), b g Trans Island—Premier Amour **Great Head House Estates Ltd**
15 HARDKNOTT (IRE), ch g Intikhab (USA)—Danita (IRE) **Great Head House Estates Ltd**
16 MOUNT EPHRAM (IRE), b g Entrepreneur—Happy Dancer (USA) **Great Head House Estates Ltd**
17 NO COMMISSION (IRE), b g General Monash (USA)—Price of Passion **Bishopthorpe Racing Two**
18 PROCRASTINATE (IRE), ch g Rossini (USA)—May Hinton **Great Head House Estates Ltd**
19 VERSTONE (IRE), b f Brave Act—Golden Charm (IRE) **Great Head House Estates Ltd**

TWO-YEAR-OLDS

20 BACHARACH (IRE), b g 7/2 Indian Lodge (IRE)—
　　　　　Katherine Gorge (USA) (Hansel (USA)) (14754) **Great Head House Estates Ltd**
21 BARRAQUITO (IRE), b g 2/2 Titus Livius (FR)—
　　　　　Lacinia (Groom Dancer (USA)) (14754) **Great Head House Estates Ltd**
22 BESPOKE TRADER (IRE), b g 7/4 Beckett (IRE)—
　　　　　Social Butterfly (USA) (Sir Ivor (USA)) (18779) **Great Head House Estates Ltd**
23 HIGHLAND SONG (IRE), ch g 28/3 Fayruz—
　　　　　Rose 'n Reason (IRE) (Reasonable (FR)) (8718) **Great Head House Estates Ltd**
24 KEY TO CAIUS (IRE), b g 25/4 Shinko Forest (IRE)—Alpine Lady (IRE) (Tirol) (13413) **A. Willoughby**
25 MUNCASTER CASTLE (IRE), b g 8/4 Raise A Grand (IRE)—
　　　　　Sunrise (IRE) (Sri Pekan (USA)) **Great Head House Estates Ltd**
26 NEXT NESS (IRE), b g 20/3 Indian Lodge (IRE)—
　　　　　Fauna (IRE) (Taufan (USA)) (16096) **Great Head House Estates Ltd**
27 SPARKBRIDGE (IRE), b g 3/4 Mull of Kintyre (USA)—
　　　　　Persian Velvet (IRE) (Distinctly North (USA)) (14754) **Great Head House Estates Ltd**

Other Owners: Mr A. L. Gregg, J. K. S. Law, Mrs D. Miller, P. Morrell.

Jockey (flat): J. Fanning, R. Ffrench, P. Hanagan. **Jockey (NH):** D. Elsworth. **Conditional:** K. J. Mercer, Miles Seston.
Apprentice: L Fletcher, D. Nolan.

210 MR T. J. FITZGERALD, Malton

Postal: **Norton Grange, Norton, Malton, North Yorkshire, YO17 9EA.**
Contacts: **OFFICE (01653) 692718 MOBILE (07950) 356437**
E-MAIL fitzgeraldracing@aol.com

1 COY LAD (IRE), 8, ch g Be My Native (USA)—Don't Tutch Me **Mr & Mrs Raymond Anderson Green**
2 INCHNADAMPH, 5, b g Inchinor—Pelf (USA) **R. N. Cardwell**
3 KINGSDON (IRE), 8, b g Brief Truce (USA)—Richly Deserved (IRE) **M. F. Browne**
4 LA FONTEYNE, 4, b f Imperial Ballet (IRE)—Baliana
5 LAWGIVER (IRE), 4, b c Definite Article—Marylou Whitney (USA) **Mr P. Mina**
6 MOMENT OF MADNESS (IRE), 7, ch g Treasure Hunter—Sip of Orange **Mrs R. Haggie**
7 MUQARRAR (IRE), 6, ch h Alhaarth (IRE)—Narjis (USA) **Kramo Racing**
8 NAVELINA, 5, b m Presidium—Orange Imp **Mrs R. Haggie**
9 PATRIXTOO (FR), 4, gr c Linamix (FR)—Maradadi (USA) **Fudge Jeans Ltd**
10 RANDOM NATIVE (IRE), 7, br g Be My Native (USA)—Random Wind **J. T. Ennis**
11 SAYRIANNA, 4, br f Sayaarr (USA)—Arianna Aldini **Mrs J. A. Gawthorpe**

MR T. J. FITZGERALD—continued

12 **SEAPIN,** 4, b g Double Trigger (IRE)—Four-Legged Friend **Marquesa De Moratalla**
13 **SOVIET COMMITTEE,** 5, b g Presidium—Lady Magician **Mr T. J. Fitzgerald**
14 **VICENTIO,** 6, br g Vettori (IRE)—Smah **Shaw Thing Partnership**

THREE-YEAR-OLDS

15 **BOWHILL LADY,** b f Princely Heir (IRE)—Akola Angel **Mrs J. A. Gawthorpe**
16 **BREEDER'S FOLLY,** b f Mujahid (USA)—Wynona (IRE) **M. F. Browne**
17 **NORTON ROSE,** ch f Dr Fong (USA)—Bonica **The Rose Partnership**
18 Br gr c Deploy—Smooth Princess (IRE)
19 **WITH HONOURS,** b f Bien Bien (USA)—Fair Test **Mr T. J. Fitzgerald**

TWO-YEAR-OLDS

20 B c 12/4 Desert Story (IRE)—Arianna Aldini (Habitat) (1523) **Mrs J. A. Gawthorpe**
21 **RIVER DANUBE,** b c 5/4 Dansili—Campaspe (Dominion) **Mr A. Huddlestone**
22 Gr f 3/5 Danehill Dancer (IRE)—Smooth Princess (IRE) (Roi Danzig (USA))
23 Ch c 24/3 Distant Music (USA)—Sunny Slope (Mujtahid (USA)) (5000)

Other Owners: Mrs M. C. Corbett, Mr P. D. Grant, Mr P. R. Hunt, L. Milligan, J. S. Murdoch, Mr P. Popplewell.

---

211 MR J. L. FLINT, Bridgend
Postal: **Cherry Tree, 71 Woodlands Park, Kenfig Hill, Bridgend, Mid-Glamorgan, CF33 6EB.**
Contacts: **PHONE (01656) 744347 MOBILE (07713) 053626 or (07968) 044487 (Mrs Martine Flint)**
E-MAIL john@flint38fsnet.co.uk

1 **DANCINGINTHESTREET,** 5, b g Groom Dancer (USA)—Usk The Way **Mr J. L. Flint**
2 **SENNA DA SILVA,** 5, gr m Prince of Birds (USA)—Impulsive Decision (IRE) **Mr J. L. Flint**
3 **SIGWELLS CLUB BOY,** 5, b g Fayruz—Run With Pride **Mr J. L. Flint**

Assistant Trainer: Mrs Martine Louise Flint

---

212 MR R. FLINT, Bridgend
Postal: **6 Tyle Glas, Broadlands, North Cornelly, Bridgend, Mid-Glamorgan.**
Contacts: **PHONE (01656) 745827 MOBILE (07814) 797376**

1 **SOU'WESTER,** 5, b g Fleetwood (IRE)—Mayfair **R. Flint**

---

213 MR D. J. FLOOD, Hungerford
Postal: **Top Yard, Uplands, Upper Lambourn, Hungerford, Berkshire, RG17 8QJ.**
Contacts: **PHONE (01488) 686558 FAX (01488) 686109 MOBILE (07747) 806309**
E-MAIL floody682154111@aol.com

1 **AMYROSEISUPPOSE,** 6, b m Classic Cliche (IRE)—Fishki **Rowfield Racing**
2 **AUENTRAUM (GER),** 5, br h Big Shuffle (USA)—Auenglocke (GER) **Mr N. Ahmad**
3 **BOUNDLESS PROSPECT (USA),** 6, b g Boundary (USA)—Cape (USA) **Peace up a town Partnership**
4 **CONFUZED,** 5, b g Pivotal—Times of Times (IRE) **A. Smith**
5 **DESERT LORD,** 5, b h Green Desert (USA)—Red Carnival (USA) **K C Partnership II**
6 **DISSIDENT (GER),** 7, b h Polish Precedent (USA)—Diasprina (GER) **Mrs R. M. Serrell**
7 **FAIR OPTIONS,** 4, gr g Marju (IRE)—Silver Singing (USA) **Mrs R. M. Serrell**
8 **HANDEL (IRE),** 5, b g Sadler's Wells (USA)—Purchasepaperchase
9 **HURRICANE COAST,** 6, b g Hurricane Sky (AUS)—Tread Carefully **Mrs R. M. Serrell**
10 **HURRICANE FLOYD (IRE),** 7, ch g Pennekamp (USA)—Mood Swings (IRE) **W. Powrie**
11 **JONNY EBENEEZER,** 6, b g Hurricane Sky (AUS)—Leap of Faith (IRE) **Mrs R. M. Serrell**
12 **NIGHT WARRIOR (IRE),** 5, b g Alhaarth (IRE)—Miniver (IRE) **Rowfield Racing & The Warriors**
13 **ROLEX FREE (ARG),** 7, ch g Friul (ARG)—Karolera (ARG) **Mrs R. M. Serrell**
14 **SPINETAIL RUFOUS (IRE),** 7, b g Prince of Birds (USA)—Miss Kinabalu **Miss J. H. Wickens**
15 **TAG TEAM (IRE),** 4, ch g Tagula (IRE)—Okay Baby (IRE) **Peace up a town Partnership**
16 **TIPO (GER),** 4, ch c Big Shuffle (USA)—Triple Transe (USA) **The Regulate Partnership**
17 **TOSCO (GER),** 5, b h Second Set (IRE)—Tosca Rhea **Michiekei**

THREE-YEAR-OLDS

18 **CHINA BEACH (IRE),** b g Sadler's Wells (USA)—Musk Lime (USA)

MR D. J. FLOOD—continued

19 **COEUR COURAGEUX (FR),** b c Xaar—Linoise (FR) **Classic Racing I**
20 **GRAMADA (IRE),** b f Cape Cross (IRE)—Decatur **P. Rosas**
21 **HIGGYS PRINCE,** b g Prince Sabo—Themeda **I. Higginson**
22 **IM SPARTACUS,** b g Namaqualand (USA)—Captivating (IRE) **The Regulate Partnership**
23 **MOSSMANN GORGE,** b g Lujain (USA)—North Pine **Mrs R. M. Serrell**
24 **WILTSHIRE (IRE),** br g Spectrum (IRE)—Mary Magdalene **Lyttelton Racing Club**

Other Owners: Mr L. M. S. Bell, Mr J. Graham, Mr R. A. Halifax, Mr C. Hall, Mr S. J. Houghton, Mr S. Lang, P. R. Leeper, Mrs J. A. Leeper.

Assistant Trainer: Mrs Cheryl Flood

Jockey (flat): L. Dettori. **Jockey (NH):** A. P. McCoy.

---

214 MR F. FLOOD, Grangecon
Postal: **Ballynure, Grangecon, Co. Wicklow, Ireland.**
Contacts: **PHONE** +353 (0) 45 403136 **FAX** +353 (0) 45 403214 **MOBILE** +353 (0) 872 590919
E-MAIL fjflood1@eircom.net

1 **ACACIA AVENUE (IRE),** 5, b g Shardari—Ennel Lady (IRE) **Mrs F. Flood**
2 **ADONIA (IRE),** 7, b m Beneficial—Suny Castle (IRE) **Mr S. Reilly**
3 **AIMEES MARK (IRE),** 9, br g Jolly Jake (NZ)—Wee Mite **Mr R. McConn**
4 **ANNA OG (IRE),** 4, b f Saddlers' Hall (IRE)—Annadot (IRE) **L. Kelly**
5 **BE MY LEADER (IRE),** 6, b m Supreme Leader—Try Your Case **Mr P. Costigan**
6 **BESSINA (IRE),** 5, b m King's Theatre (IRE)—Ballycuirke **Mrs H. McParland**
7 **CARA MO CHROI (IRE),** 6, b g Broken Hearted—Kambaya (IRE) **Mr C. Falls**
8 **CHARM LORD (IRE),** 6, b g Arctic Lord—Danny's Charm (IRE) **Mr S. Murphy**
9 **COLDWELLS (IRE),** 5, b m Presenting—Coolmoonan **Thomas McParland**
10 **COLONEL GUN (IRE),** 5, ch g Catrail (USA)—Return Again (IRE) **Mr G. Martin**
11 **COURT STORM (IRE),** 6, b g Flemensfirth (USA)—Storm Court (IRE) **Batsheri Syndicate**
12 **DANNY'S DREAM (IRE),** 5, b br g Naheez (USA)—Gemma's Fridge **L. Kelly**
13 **DANSE MACABRE (IRE),** 6, b g Flemensfirth (USA)—My Romance **Mr R. P. Behan**
14 **FOXY FRED (IRE),** 5, b g Key of Luck (USA)—Winning Sally (IRE) **Mr D. Reddan**
15 **G V A IRELAND (IRE),** 7, br g Beneficial—Dippers Daughter **Mr D. O'Buachalla**
16 **GEORGES GIRL (IRE),** 7, b m Montelimar (USA)—Keshia **Mr G. Martin**
17 **GIOLLA DE (IRE),** 6, b g Glacial Storm (USA)—Deep Inagh **Mr C. Falls**
18 **GONE DANCING (IRE),** 5, b g Key of Luck (USA)—French Lady (IRE) **Mr D. Reddan**
19 **GRANGEBEG (IRE),** 6, b g Shernazar—Coolmoonan **Mrs H. McParland**
20 **HEEZ A WONDER (IRE),** 6, b g Naheez (USA)—Honey Wonder **Striding Snail Syndicate**
21 **HUDSON HOPE (IRE),** 7, b m Topanoora—Be My Hope (IRE) **Mr G. Mannion**
22 **JOAN'S GIRL (IRE),** 5, b m Supreme Leader—Keshia **Mr G. Martin**
23 **LANMIRE GLEN (IRE),** 8, b g Jurado (USA)—Cool Glen **Mr W. A. Browne**
24 **LIS NA GRENA (IRE),** 6, b m Broken Hearted—Tor-Na-Grena **Miss C. Byrne**
25 **LORNA'S STAR (IRE),** 6, b m Fourstars Allstar—Lorna's Beauty (IRE) **Mr J. M. O'Brien**
26 **MAGIC MARK (IRE),** 7, b g King's Ride—South Quay Lady **Mr R. McConn**
27 **MIJAS LADY (IRE),** 6, b m Jolly Jake (NZ)—South Quay Lady **Mr A. Doyle**
28 **MONTE SOLARO (IRE),** 5, br m Key of Luck (USA)—Footsteps (IRE) **Mr P. Behan**
29 **NUTSPREE (IRE),** 5, b g Taipan (IRE)—Super Tune (IRE) **Ten Heirs Syndicate**
30 **OUR FELLA (IRE),** 7, b g Be My Native (USA)—Bon Retour **Mr C. McDonnell**
31 **POM FLYER (FR),** 5, b g Broadway Flyer (USA)—Pomme D'emeraude (FR) **Madfish Syndicate**
32 **REKOPAC (IRE),** 9, gr g Ala Hounak—Ashford Doll **Kilronan Syndicate**
33 **SANDY LIE (IRE),** 5, b g Flemensfirth (USA)—Blake's Ride (IRE) **Boot Him Home Syndicate**
34 **SATOHA (IRE),** 7, b g Zaffaran (USA)—Whackers World **Never Despair Syndicate**
35 **SHIVERMETIMBER (IRE),** 7, b m Arctic Lord—Cherry Dancer **Abbey Rose Syndicate**
36 **STAR STORM (IRE),** 11, br g Glacial Storm (USA)—Star Whistler **Mr H. James**
37 **STRIKE RATE (IRE),** 6, b g Jurado (USA)—Tattens **J. D. Flood**
38 **SUPREME PEACE (IRE),** 7, b m Supreme Leader—Peace Time Girl (IRE) **Mr L. Kelly & Mr P. McAteer**
39 **THE CULDEE (IRE),** 9, ch g Phardante (FR)—Deep Inagh **Mr C. Falls**
40 **THE PENITENT MAN (IRE),** 7, b g Corrouge (USA)—Swift Glider (IRE) **Mr M. Holly**
41 **TOKPELA (IRE),** 6, ch g Shujan (USA)—Kokopelli (IRE) **Mrs N. O'Reilly**
42 **TONENILI (IRE),** 5, b m Old Vic—Kokopelli (IRE) **Mrs N. O'Reilly**
43 **WALK OVER (IRE),** 7, b g Welsh Term—Black-Crash **Mr J. P. McManus**
44 **WEST WICKLOW (IRE),** 5, ch g Shernazar—Graffogue (IRE) **Thomas McParland**
45 **WESTERN FLYER (IRE),** 6, b g Priolo (USA)—The Third Sister (IRE) **Mr F. Reynolds**
46 **WINDMILL FLYER (IRE),** 7, ch g Old Vic—Clahada Rose (IRE) **Elphin Racing Syndicate**

MR F. FLOOD—continued

THREE-YEAR-OLDS

  47 SEEYALATER (IRE), b f Definite Article—Brookhouse Lady (IRE) **Part of Us Syndicate**

Assistant Trainer: F J Flood

Jockey (NH): F. J. Flood. **Conditional:** K. T. Coleman, A. B. Joyce. **Apprentice:** T. J. Harvey. **Amateur:** Mr A. P. Keatley, Mr D. Macauley.

---

215 **MR A. L. FORBES, Uttoxeter**
Postal: **Hill House Farm, Poppits Lane, Stramshall, Uttoxeter, Staffordshire, ST14 5EX.**
Contacts: **PHONE (01889) 568145 FAX (01782) 599041 MOBILE (07812) 350991**
E-MAIL tony@thimble.net

  1 ASCARI, 9, br g Presidium—Ping Pong **Mr A. L. Forbes**
  2 DIAMOND ORCHID (IRE), 5, gr m Victory Note (USA)—Olivia's Pride (IRE) **Mr R. S. Blurton**
  3 DOUCEUR DES SONGES (FR), 8, b m Art Francais (USA)—Ma Poetesse (FR) **A. S. Ward**
  4 ICARE D'OUDAIRIES (FR), 9, ch g Port Etienne (FR)—Vellea (FR) **Mr R. S. Blurton**
  5 MINSTER SKY, 5, ch m Minster Son—Nicola's Princess **A. S. Ward**
  6 NONA'S LASS, 8, b m Clantime—Festive Lassie
  7 SAIF SAREEA, 5, b g Atraf—Slipperose **M. L. Green**
  8 VITELLI, 5, b g Vettori (IRE)—Mourne Trix **Mr R. S. Blurton**

Other Owners: J. E. Jackson.

Assistant Trainer: Mr Tim Eley

Jockey (NH): O. McPhail.

---

216 **MRS P. M. FORD, Hereford**
Postal: **Stone House Stables, Preston Wynne, Hereford, Herefordshire, HR1 3PB.**
Contacts: **HOME/FAX (01532) 820604 MOBILE (07733) 152051**
E-MAIL pam@fordracing.fsnet.co.uk

  1 ALWAYS BELIEVE (USA), 9, b g Carr de Naskra (USA)—Wonder Mar (USA) **R. S. Herbert**
  2 BEN KENOBI, 7, ch g Accondy (IRE)—Nour El Sahar (USA) **K. Marritt**
  3 DIEQUEST (USA), 4, ch g Diesis—Nuance (IRE) **Mr K. Ford**
  4 ELEGANT ACCORD (IRE), 7, b m Accordion—Swan Bridge (IRE) **J. T. Jones**
  5 HAYLEY'S PEARL, 6, b m Nomadic Way (USA)—Pacific Girl (IRE) **P. Martin**
  6 LITTLETON AMETHYST (IRE), 6, ch m Revoque (IRE)—Sept Roses (USA) **Mr K. Ford**
  7 5, B g Darnay—Mumtaz Queen (IRE) **Mr B. Coughlan**
  8 NEW DIAMOND, 6, ch g Bijou d'inde—Nannie Annie **R. S. Herbert**
  9 OUR MAN DENNIS, 11, b g Arzanni—Pendocks Polly **Mrs S. J. Williams**
 10 RIVARRIVED, 6, b g Riva Marquee—Pearly White **Miss C. M. Caden-Parker**

Assistant Trainer: Mr K Ford

Jockey (flat): R. Ffrench, Lisa Jones. **Jockey (NH):** R. Young. **Conditional:** Richard Spate. **Amateur:** Mr K. Ford.

---

217 **MR R. FORD, Tarporley**
Postal: **Folly Farm, Forest Road, Little Budworth, Tarporley, Cheshire, CW6 9ES.**
Contacts: **PHONE (01829) 760095 FAX (01829) 760895 MOBILE (07976) 522768**
E-MAIL richardfordracing.co.uk

  1 BLACKTHORN, 6, ch g Deploy—Balliasta (USA) **A. Eyres & D. F. Price**
  2 5, B g Millkom—Blossomville **W. J. Warner**
  3 BROWN TEDDY, 8, b g Afzal—Quadrapol **G. B. Barlow**
  4 BUCHANAN STREET (IRE), 4, b c Barathea (IRE)—Please Believe Me **Forge Bloodstock**
  5 CAMBO (FR), 4, b br g Mansonnien (FR)—Royal Lie (FR) **D. W. Watson**
  6 CHABRIMAL MINSTER, 8, b g Minster Son—Bromley Rose **B. Mills, C. Roberts, Miss M. Burrows**
  7 FOREST GUNNER, 11, ch g Gunner B—Gouly Duff **J. Gilsenan**
  8 5, Br m Supreme Leader—Frankly Native (IRE) **Mr O. Eaton**
  9 GOLDENAVOUR (FR), 6, b g Endeavour (USA)—Golden Moon (FR) **Miss M. Burrows and Partners**

MR R. FORD—continued

10 **GOOD OUTLOOK (IRE),** 6, b g Lord Americo—I'll Say She Is **The Good Outlook Partnership**
11 **JOSS NAYLOR (IRE),** 10, b g Be My Native (USA)—Sister Ida **D. C. Mercer**
12 **LANTERN LAD (IRE),** 9, b g Yashgan—Lantern Lass **Tarporley Turf Club**
13 **LASCAR DE FERBET (FR),** 6, br g Sleeping Car (FR)—Belle De Ferbet (FR) **Miss A. L. Lakin**
14 **LUCKY NOMAD,** 9, br g Nomadic Way (USA)—Daleena **N. A. Morgan**
15 **MCCRACKEN (IRE),** 9, b g Scenic—Sakanda (IRE) **N. A. Morgan, M. Beavan**
16 **MILL EMERALD,** 8, b m Old Vic—Millinetta **Bull, Bills & Beer**
17 **OCEAN TIDE,** 8, b g Deploy—Dancing Tide **A. Eyres & D. F. Price**
18 **PISTE BLEU (FR),** 5, b m Pistolet Bleu (IRE)—Thamissia (FR) **Mr M. Dunlevy & Mr N. A. Morgan**
19 **PRESENTFORYOU (IRE),** 6, b g Presenting—Killonerry **G. B. Barlow**
20 **RIVERBANK RAINBOW,** 4, b f Overbury (IRE)—Riverbank Rose **Mr G. Whieldon**
21 **ROYAL WHISPER,** 6, b g Prince of Birds (USA)—Hush It Up **Carrie Ford**
22 **SAMSON DES GALAS (FR),** 7, b br g Agent Bleu (FR)—Sarema (FR) **J & G Sporting Partners**
23 **SENDONTHECHEQUE (IRE),** 10, b g Torus—Miss Riversfield (IRE) **Barking Mad Syndicate 2**
24 **STONED (IRE),** 5, b g Bigstone (IRE)—Lady Celina (FR) **L. A. E. Hopkins**
25 **SUPER DOLPHIN,** 6, ch g Dolphin Street (FR)—Supergreen **N. A. Morgan**
26 **TOPINAMBOUR (FR),** 5, gr g Turgeon (USA)—La Deviniere (IRE) **D. W. Watson & Miss M. Burrows**
27 **TREGASTEL (FR),** 10, b g Tel Quel (FR)—Myrtlewood (FR) **D. W. Watson**

THREE-YEAR-OLDS

28 **MS THREE,** b f Josr Algarhoud (IRE)—Swing Along **A. Eyres & D. F. Price**

TWO-YEAR-OLDS

29 B c 10/2 Polar Prince (IRE)—Eastern Firedragon (IRE) (Shalford (IRE)) **D. Lyons**
30 B c 18/2 Polar Prince (IRE)—Ecaterina (NZ) (March Legend (NZ)) **D. Lyons**

Other Owners: R. Barber, D. C. Bostock, G. J. Darrall, I. Dodd, K. G. Ellison, V. Harvey, T. Hocking, C. P. Jones, Mr S. Ledbrooke, S. A. Stokes, Mr M. Waterfall, C. G. Wilson, D. A. Wilson.

Assistant Trainer: Carrie Ford

Jockey (NH): G. Lee, J. M. Maguire, R. McGrath. **Conditional:** Caroline Hurley, G. R. Thomas.

MR D. M. FORSTER, Darlington
Postal: **Todd Fall Farm, Heighington, Darlington, Co. Durham, DL2 2XG.**
Contacts: **PHONE (01388) 772441**

1 **ATOMIC BREEZE (IRE),** 11, b br g Strong Gale—Atomic Lady **Mr D. M. Forster**
2 5, B g Zaffaran (USA)—Blue Rinse **Mr D. M. Forster**
3 6, B g Accordion—Cool Virtue (IRE) **Mr D. M. Forster**
4 **JIMMYS DUKY (IRE),** 7, b g Duky—Harvey's Cream (IRE) **Mr D. M. Forster**
5 **OSSMOSES (IRE),** 8, gr g Roselier (FR)—Sugartown **Mr D. M. Forster**
6 4, B g Zaffaran (USA)—Parson's Run **Mr D. M. Forster**

Jockey (NH): R. McGrath.

MISS S. E. FORSTER, Kelso
Postal: **Halterburn Head, Yetholm, Kelso, Roxburghshire, TD5 8PP.**
Contacts: PHONE/FAX (01573) 420615 MOBILE (07880) 727877 or (07976) 587315
E-MAIL c.storey.pt-to-pt@tinyworld.co.uk

1 **AMERAS (IRE),** 7, b b m Hamas (IRE)—Amerindian **Mr A. G. & Mrs E. J. Bell**
2 **BROMLEY ABBEY,** 7, ch m Minster Son—Little Bromley **Mrs H. N. Eubank**
3 **BROMLEY MOSS,** 6, ch g Le Moss—Little Bromley **A. Eubank**
4 **COMPTON PRINCESS,** 5, b m Compton Place—Curlew Calling (IRE) **Mr C. Storey**
5 **FORTINO,** 4, ch g Abou Zouz (USA)—Blazing Sunset **Mr C. Storey**
6 4, B g Cloudings (IRE)—Glen Morvern **Mr R. Colvin & Mr J. Harrison**
7 **KATIE KAI,** 4, b f Cayman Kai (IRE)—Yemaail (IRE) **Mr A Dawson & Miss K Dawson**
8 **LADY JANAL,** 7, gr m Sir Harry Lewis (USA)—Mrs Dawson **Mr A. G. & Mrs E. J. Bell**
9 **PERSIAN POINT,** 9, ch g Persian Bold—Kind Thoughts **Mr C. Storey**
10 **RADAR (IRE),** 10, b g Petardia—Soignee **Mr C. Storey**
11 **ROMAN WAY,** 9, ch g Gildoran—Olympian Princess **R. Powell**
12 **RUBYLUV,** 6, ch m Rock Hopper—Hunting Cottage **Mrs J. Cadzow**

MISS S. E. FORSTER—continued

13 **SKENFRITH**, 6, b g Atraf—Hobbs Choice **J M & Miss H M Crichton, Miss S Forster**
14 **STAR TROOPER (IRE)**, 9, b br g Brief Truce (USA)—Star Cream **Mr C. Storey**
15 **THE MINER**, 7, ch g Hatim (USA)—Glen Morvern **Mr C. Storey & Mr D. Skeldon**
16 **TREASURED MEMORIES**, 5, b m Cloudings (IRE)—Glen Morvern **Mr C. Storey**
17 **UNEVEN LINE**, 9, b m Jurado (USA)—Altovise **D. Simpson**
18 **WELSH DREAM**, 8, b g Mtoto—Morgannwg (IRE) **Should Be Fun Racing**

Other Owners: Mr P. Innes, Mr F. Berry, Mr R. Armaston, Mr A. Black.

Assistant Trainer: C Storey

Jockey (NH): J. Crowley. **Conditional:** D. C. Costello. **Amateur:** Miss C. Frater, Mr C. Storey.

---

220 **MR B. R. J. P. FOSTER, Oswestry**
Postal: **Llwyntidmon Hall, Llwyntidmon, Maesbrook, Oswestry.**
Contacts: **OFFICE (01691) 839930 HOUSE (01978) 710553 MOBILE (07780) 644024**

1 **BABARULLAH**, 7, ch g Lucky Wednesday—Hantergantic **M. J. Brownrigg**
2 **BALALAIKA TUNE (IRE)**, 6, b m Lure (USA)—Bohemienne (USA) **M. J. Brownrigg**
3 **BE OFF WITH YOU**, 6, b m Nalchik (USA)—Tilstock Maid **M. J. Brownrigg**
4 **BOBE BRICK**, 4, b g Dervish—Tilstock Maid **M. J. Brownrigg**
5 **CROMARTY RULES**, 8, b g Anshan—Cromarty **M. J. Brownrigg**
6 **DOUBLE EMBLEM (IRE)**, 8, ch m Weld—Sultry **M. J. Brownrigg**
7 **GEBORA (FR)**, 6, ch g Villez (USA)—Sitapanoki (FR) **Mrs A. Brook**
8 **RIVELLI (IRE)**, 6, b m Lure (USA)—Kama Tashoof **M. J. Brownrigg**
9 **RUBIC**, 8, ch m Rubicund—La Leeza **Miss C. E. Ormrod**

TWO-YEAR-OLDS

10 B c 21/4 Dervish—Boulabas (IRE) (Nashamaa) **M. J. Brownrigg**

Jockey (NH): R. Greene. **Conditional:** R. Lucey-Butler. **Amateur:** Mrs Andy Brook, Mr B. R. Foster.

---

221 **MR J. R. H. FOWLER, Summerhill**
Postal: **Rahinston, Summerhill, Co. Meath, Ireland.**
Contacts: **PHONE +353 (0) 46 9557014 FAX +353 (0) 46 9557537**

1 **ALLEGED TO RHYME (IRE)**, 6, b m Leading Counsel (USA)—Fortunes Cast **Mrs Elizabeth Fletcher**
2 **BACK ON CONCORDE (IRE)**, 7, br g Executive Perk—Kitty Cullen **James McQuaid**
3 **BALLYRONAN (IRE)**, 8, ch g Be My Native (USA)—Blue Rainbow **S.P. Tindall**
4 **DOLLY OF DUBLIN (IRE)**, 7, br m Be My Native (USA)—Ar Ais Aris (IRE) **Miss D. Duggan**
5 **FIERY RING (IRE)**, 10, b g Torus—Kakemona **S. P. Tindall**
6 4, B f Presenting—Fine de Claire **S. P. Tindall**
7 **FREEMANTLE DOCTOR (IRE)**, 5, b m Luso—Lottobuck **T. A. Bruton**
8 **HEARTBREAK HILL (IRE)**, 6, b m Synefos (USA)—Knockea Hill **Lady J. Fowler**
9 **HOUDUNNIT (IRE)**, 10, br g Houmayoun (FR)—Super Leg **B. D. Smith**
10 4, B g Supreme Leader—Janet Lindup **J. R. H. Fowler**
11 **JENNIFERS DIARY (IRE)**, 7, b m Supreme Leader—Chattering **Lady J. Fowler**
12 **LA MARIANNE**, 5, b m Supreme Leader—Belle Magello (FR) **Mrs R. Chugg & Lady J. Fowler**
13 **MARMALADE SKY (IRE)**, 7, ch g Be My Native (USA)—Armagale (IRE) **Miss D. Duggan**
14 **NATIVE BEAT (IRE)**, 10, b g Be My Native (USA)—Deeprunonthepound (IRE) **Miss D. Duggan**
15 **RENVYLE SOCIETY (IRE)**, 7, ch m Moscow Society (USA)—Great Outlook (IRE) **March Hares Syndicate**
16 **SELOUS SCOUT (IRE)**, 8, ch g Be My Native (USA)—Lady Leona **Lady J. Fowler**
17 **SHIMINNIE (IRE)**, 6, b m Bob Back (USA)—Shining Willow **S. P. Tindall**
18 **SUMMERBING BLUES (IRE)**, 6, b m Blues Traveller (IRE)—Ennel Lady (IRE) **Mrs C. A. Waters**
19 **TENA TENA (IRE)**, 8, b g Fourstars Allstar (USA)—Ballybree **Mrs C. A. Waters**
20 **TSARETTA (IRE)**, 6, b m Supreme Leader—Pharetta (IRE) **Lady J. Fowler**

Jockey (NH): R. Geraghty. **Conditional:** A. P. Fagan. **Amateur:** Mr R. H. Fowler, Mr S. Burke.

222 MR J. C. FOX, Marlborough
Postal: **Highlands Farm Racing Stables, Herridge, Collingbourne Ducis, Marlborough, Wiltshire, SN8 3EG.**
Contacts: **PHONE (01264) 850218 MOBILE (07702) 880010**
E-MAIL jcfoxtrainer@aol.com

1 **BALLYBAWN HOUSE**, 4, b f Tamure (IRE)—Squeaky Cottage **ROL Construction Ltd**
2 **COLTSCROFT**, 5, b g Teenoso (USA)—Marquesa Juana **Metropolitan Masonry Limited**
3 **DEEWAAR (IRE)**, 5, b g Ashkalani (IRE)—Chandni (IRE) **Metropolitan Masonry Limited**
4 **JIMMY HAY**, 4, b g Bluegrass Prince (IRE)—Priory Bay **Mrs J. A. Cleary**
5 **KILMEENA LAD**, 9, b g Minshaanshu Amad (USA)—Kilmeena Glen **Mrs J. A. Cleary**
6 **KILMEENA ROSE**, 5, ch m Compton Place—Kilmeena Glen **Mrs J. A. Cleary**
7 **KILMEENA STAR**, 7, b g So Factual (USA)—Kilmeena Glen **Mrs J. A. Cleary**
8 **MAGIC WARRIOR**, 5, b g Magic Ring (IRE)—Clarista (USA) **Miss H. J. Flower**
9 **NEPTUNE**, 9, b g Dolphin Street (FR)—Seal Indigo (IRE) **S J V Construction**
10 **SAORSIE**, 7, b g Emperor Jones (USA)—Exclusive Lottery **Lord Mutton Racing Partnership**
11 **SHALATI PRINCESS**, 4, b f Bluegrass Prince (IRE)—Shalati (FR) **S J V Construction**
12 **SILVER WOOD**, 5, b m Silver Wizard (USA)—Eastwood Heiress **Mrs J. A. Cleary**
13 **SUNSET KING**, 5, b h King of Kings (IRE)—Sunset River (USA) **Mr B. J. Weddle**

THREE-YEAR-OLDS
14 **CABIN FEVER**, b f Averti (IRE)—Julietta Mia (USA) **James Horgan**

TWO-YEAR-OLDS
15 B c 15/3 Inchinor—Holy Smoke (Statoblest) (2200) **Lord Mutton Racing Partnership**
16 Ch c 3/1 Tomba—Nannie Annie (Persian Bold) (3500)
17 Ch f 30/4 Fleetwood (IRE)—On Request (IRE) (Be My Guest (USA)) (1000) **Miss Sarah-Jane Durman**

Other Owners: Mr C. Fiford, S. Kearns, J. Kearns, Miss A. Poplar.

Assistant Trainer: Sarah-Jane Durman

Jockey (NH): S. Fox. **Apprentice:** Vicky Hill. **Amateur:** Miss Sarah-Jane Durman.

223 MR M. E. D. FRANCIS, Lambourn
Postal: **Folly House, Upper Lambourn Road, Lambourn, Hungerford, Berkshire, RG17 8QG.**
Contacts: **PHONE (01488) 71700 MOBILE (07836) 244988**
E-MAIL merrick@lrtltd.demon.co.uk

1 **FARD DU MOULIN MAS (FR)**, 12, b br g Morespeed—Soiree d'ex (FR) **Mrs Merrick Francis III**
2 **ICE CREAM (FR)**, 4, ch f Cyborg (FR)—Icone (FR) **Mrs Merrick Francis III**

224 MR J. D. FROST, Buckfastleigh
Postal: **Hawson Stables, Buckfastleigh, Devon, TQ11 0HP.**
Contacts: **HOME (01364) 642332 YARD (01364) 642267**
FAX (01364) 643182 MOBILE (07860) 220229

1 **BALOO**, 9, b g Morpeth—Moorland Nell **Cloud Nine-Premier Cru**
2 **BEBE FACTUAL (GER)**, 4, b c So Factual (USA)—Bebe Kamira (GER) **Ifji Rochjobi**
3 **BROCHRUA (IRE)**, 5, b m Hernando (FR)—Severine (USA) **Ms H. M. Vernon-Jones**
4 **CRITICAL STAGE (IRE)**, 6, b g King's Theatre (IRE)—Zandaka (FR) **Le Rochjobi Partnership**
5 **DEER DANCER**, 5, b g Tamure (IRE)—Anatomic **Mrs J. Bury**
6 **DMITRI**, 5, b g Emperor Jones (USA)—Shining Cloud **Dmitri Club**
7 **DUN AN DORAS (IRE)**, 9, br g Glacial Storm (USA)—Doorslammer **Cloud Nine-Premier Cru**
8 **FIRE RANGER**, 9, ch m Presidium—Regal Flame **P. A. Tylor**
9 **GIN 'N' FONIC (IRE)**, 5, ch g Zafonic (USA)—Crepe Ginger (IRE) **Mr C. Johnston**
10 **INSURRECTION (IRE)**, 8, b g Un Desperado (FR)—Ballycahan Girl **Mrs J. McCormack**
11 **KILDEE LASS**, 6, gr m Morpeth—Pigeon Loft (IRE) **J. F. O'Donovan**
12 **KING'S TRAVEL (FR)**, 9, gr g Balleroy (USA)—Travel Free **Mr C. Johnston**
13 **KNIGHT OF SILVER**, 8, gr g Presidium—Misty Rocket **Mr C. Johnston**
14 **LADY MISPRINT**, 9, ch m Classic—Miss Primrose **W. J. Jordan**
15 **LATIN QUEEN (IRE)**, 5, b br m Desert Prince (IRE)—Atlantic Dream (USA) **Mr B. S. Williams**
16 **LESDREAM**, 8, b g Morpeth—Lesbet **Mrs E. S. Carlson**
17 **LONGSTONE LADY (IRE)**, 8, b m Mister Lord (USA)—Monamandy (IRE) **Mrs J. R. Bastard**

MR J. D. FROST—continued

18 **MEVAGISSEY (BEL)**, 8, b br g Sula Bula—Fowey **Miss V. A. Cunningham**
19 **MISS LEHMAN**, 7, ch m Beveled (USA)—Lehmans Lot **P. A. Tylor**
20 **MISS WOODPECKER**, 8, b m Morpeth—Pigeon Loft (IRE) **R. G. Frost**
21 **MOORLAND MONARCH**, 7, b g Morpeth—Moorland Nell **Peninsula Racegoers**
22 **OJAYS ALIBI (IRE)**, 9, b g Witness Box (USA)—Tinkers Lady **Mrs C. K. Irish**
23 **PRIDE OF PENLEE**, 5, b g Pontevecchio Notte—Kindly Lady **D. C. & Mrs T. M. Fisher**
24 **RIGHT PROUD**, 5, gr g Morpeth—Pigeon Loft (IRE) **Mr C. Johnston**
25 **SAFFRON SUN**, 10, b g Landyap (USA)—Saffron Bun **Mrs J. Bury**
26 **SARENA SPECIAL**, 8, b g Lucky Guest—Lariston Gale **Sarena Mfg Ltd**
27 **SILENT GUEST (IRE)**, 12, b g Don't Forget Me—Guest House **R. C. Burridge**
28 **SILVER SISTER**, 4, gr f Morpeth—Pigeon Loft (IRE) **The Silver Stars**
29 **STATTIN ISLAND (IRE)**, 6, b g Great Marquess—Push Over Lass **Mrs C. K. Irish**
30 **TREFOILALIGHT**, 6, b m Morpeth—Imalight **Dr D. Edwards**
31 **WRAGS TO RICHES (IRE)**, 8, b g Tremblant—Clonea Lady (IRE) **No Illusions Partnership**

THREE-YEAR-OLDS

32 **THEFLYINGSCOTTIE**, gr g Paris House—Miss Flossa (FR) **P. M. Tosh**

Other Owners: J. E. Blake, I. B. Carruth, Mr R. P. K. Clarkson, Mr C. V. Coward, W. A. Edgington, D. C. Fisher, Mrs T. M. Fisher, MR J. D. Frost, R. G. Frost, Mrs J. Lenaghan, Mrs M. Mitchell, Mrs D. M. Philpott, D. P. Pope, R. G. Pritchard, Mrs M. A. Simpson, Mrs M. P. Smallbone, G. Thompson, A. Watling, T. R. Watts, Mrs J. A. Williams.

Assistant Trainer: G Frost

Conditional: C. Honour.

---

225 MR JOHN GALLAGHER, Moreton-in-the-Marsh
Postal: **Little Grove, Chastleton, Moreton-in-the-Marsh, Gloucestershire, GL56 0SZ.**
Contacts: **PHONE/FAX (01608) 674492 MOBILE (07780) 972663**
E-MAIL **gallagher.racing@virgin.net** WEBSITE **www.gallagherracing.com**

1 **ARCHIE CLARKE (GER)**, 5, b g Taishan (GER)—Anthela (GER) **www.network-racing.com**
2 **CAROUBIER (IRE)**, 5, ch g Woodborough (USA)—Patsy Grimes **C. R. Marks (Banbury)**
3 **HOOBER**, 4, b g Mind Games—Chlo-Jo **Mr and Mrs R. Newman**
4 **KILLING ME SOFTLY**, 4, b g Kingsinger (IRE)—Slims Lady **S. R. Prior**
5 **MAKE MY HAY**, 6, b g Bluegrass Prince (IRE)—Shashi (IRE) **Mrs I. L. Clifford**
6 **MURZIM**, 6, b g Salse (USA)—Guilty Secret (IRE) **C. R. Marks (Banbury)**
7 **MY SHARP GREY**, 6, gr m Tragic Role (USA)—Sharp Anne **C. R. Marks (Banbury)**
8 **START OF AUTHORITY**, 4, ch g Muhtarram (USA)—Heiden's Delight (USA) **Adweb Ltd**
9 **TRESOR SECRET (FR)**, 5, b g Green Desert (USA)—Tresor (USA) **M. C. S. D. Racing Ltd**

THREE-YEAR-OLDS

10 **GOGETTER GIRL**, b f Wolfhound (USA)—Square Mile Miss (IRE) **Mr and Mrs R. Newman**
11 **SORCERESS**, b f Wizard King—Aonia **C. Rashbrook**

TWO-YEAR-OLDS

12 **GAELIC COLLEEN**, b f 12/4 Bertolini (USA)—Peruvian Jade (Petong) (1714) **M. C. S. D. Racing Ltd**
13 B c 22/3 My Best Valentine—Sandkatoon (IRE) (Archway (IRE)) (1333) **Mrs I. L. Clifford**
14 B f 19/4 My Best Valentine—Shashi (IRE) (Shaadi (USA)) (571) **Mrs I. L. Clifford**

Other Owners: J. F. Long, Mrs B. A. Long, C. Mitchell, Mrs D. A. Mitchell.

Assistant Trainer: Mrs R J Gallagher

Jockey (flat): J. Quinn. **Jockey (NH):** R. Johnson, J. Mogford.

---

226 MRS E. J. GALPIN, Wincanton
Postal: **Church Farm, Bratton Seymour, Wincanton, Somerset, BA9 8BY.**
Contacts: **HOME (01963) 32179 YARD (01963) 33276 FAX (01963) 32179 MOBILE (07929) 184132**

1 **LUSHES RUN**, 4, gr g Commanche Run—Lady Blakeney **Mrs B. A. Rading**
2 5, B m Accordion—Maid of Glenduragh (IRE) **Ms Gillian Metherell**

MRS E. J. GALPIN—continued

3 **MISTER MAMBO**, 5, b g Afzal—Elver Season **Mr J. Barnes**
4 **ORREZZO (GER)**, 5, br g Zinaad—Ordessa (GER) **D. J. Bridger**
5 **SIR FRANK GIBSON**, 4, b g Primo Dominie—Serotina (IRE) **Mrs E. J. Galpin**

THREE-YEAR-OLDS

6 **ZOLASH (IRE)**, b c General Monash (USA)—Zolba (IRE) **Mrs E. J. Galpin**

Assistant Trainer: Stephanie Smith

Jockey (flat): C. Catlin, A. Nicholls. **Jockey (NH):** S. Stronge, R. Young. **Amateur:** Mr J. Barnes.

---

227 | MR D. R. GANDOLFO, Wantage
Postal: **Downs Stables, Manor Road, Wantage, Oxfordshire, OX12 8NF.**
Contacts: **PHONE (01235) 763242 FAX (01235) 764149**
E-MAIL david.gandolfo@virgin.net

1 **CANDARLI (IRE)**, 9, ch g Polish Precedent (USA)—Calounia (IRE) **Mr A. E. Frost**
2 **COULDN'T BE PHAR (IRE)**, 8, ch g Phardante (FR)—Queenford Belle **D. R. Gandolfo Ltd**
3 **DIPLOMATIC DAISY (IRE)**, 6, b m Alflora (IRE)—Landa's Counsel **J. J. Blackshaw**
4 **FLEURETTE**, 5, b m Alflora (IRE)—Miss Wrensborough **G. C. Hartigan**
5 **FOLLOW THE BEAR**, 7, ch g Weld—Run Lady Run **J. T. Warner**
6 5, B m Primitive Rising (USA)—Foxtrot Pie **D R Gandolfo Ltd**
7 **GLENGARRA (IRE)**, 8, ch g Phardante (FR)—Glengarra Princess **Starlight Racing**
8 **GRAY'S EULOGY**, 7, b g Presenting—Gray's Ellergy **M. A. Dore**
9 **LEAD ROLE (IRE)**, 7, b g Supreme Leader—Surely Madam **D. R. Gandolfo Ltd**
10 4, B f Silver Patriarch (IRE)—Lotschberg Express **A. W. F. Clapperton**
11 4, B g Shaamit (IRE)—Manhunt **D R Gandolfo Ltd**
12 **PERCIPIENT**, 7, b g Pennekamp (USA)—Annie Albright (USA) **N. J. Stafford**
13 **PHAR FAR AWAY**, 7, b m Phardante (FR)—Shannon Juliette **Stephen Freud & Friends**
14 **PROVERBIAL GRAY**, 8, ro m Norton Challenger—Clove Bud **D. R. Gandolfo Ltd**
15 **QUATRAIN (IRE)**, 5, ch g Anshan—Gray's Ellergy **Starlight Racing**
16 **RAINBOWS AGLITTER**, 8, ch g Rainbows For Life (CAN)—Chalet Waldegg **M. F. Cartwright**
17 **READY TO LAND (IRE)**, 7, ch g Phardante (FR)—Spread Your Wings (IRE) **Mr A. E. Frost**
18 **RED SOCIALITE (IRE)**, 8, ch g Moscow Society (USA)—Dees Darling (IRE) **Starlight Racing**
19 **ROOSTER'S REUNION (IRE)**, 6, gr g Presenting—Court Town **J. T. Warner**
20 **ROYAL BUBBEL (IRE)**, 7, ch m Hubbly Bubbly (USA)—Last Royal **Starlight Racing**
21 **SHIRAZI**, 7, b g Mtoto—Al Shadeedah (USA) **Starlight Racing**
22 **SIYARAN (IRE)**, 4, ch c Grand Lodge (USA)—Sinndiya (IRE) **Mr A. E. Frost**
23 **TAKE THE OATH (IRE)**, 8, b g Big Sink Hope (USA)—Delgany Chimes (IRE) **Starlight Racing**
24 **UNTWIST (IRE)**, 6, b g Un Desperado (FR)—Pearltwist **G. C. Hartigan**

THREE-YEAR-OLDS

25 B g Kayf Tara—Lotschberg Express **A. W. F. Clapperton**
26 **MIGHTYMULLER (IRE)**, b g Montjeu (IRE)—Anazara (USA) **Mr A. E. Frost**

Other Owners: Mr P. Pritchard, Mrs J. Snell, Mr P. Renahan, Mr A. Chalmers, Mr V R Vyner-Brooks, Mr P. Slade, Mr J. P. Carrineton, Mr M. L. Fisher, Mr N. J. Stafford, Mr C. G. MacKenzie, Mr S. Florey, Mr O. Pierce, Mr G. Clarice, Mr J. Webb, Mrs P. Melotti, Mr H. J. M. Webb, T. J. Whitley.

Assistant Trainer: Miss E A Gandolfo

---

228 | MRS S. GARDNER, Longdown
Postal: **Woodhayes Farm, Longdown, Exeter.**
Contacts: **PHONE/FAX (01392) 811213 MOBILE (07971) 097936**

1 **BAK TO BILL**, 10, b g Nicholas Bill—Kirstins Pride **D. V. Gardner**
2 5, B g Fourstars Allstar (USA)—Brandy Hill Girl **D. V. Gardner**
3 **DARJEELING (IRE)**, 6, b m Presenting—Afternoon Tea (IRE) **D. V. Gardner**
4 **LURID AFFAIR (IRE)**, 4, b f Dr Massini (IRE)—Miss Good Night **D. V. Gardner**
5 5, Br g Dr Massini (IRE)—Parsons Storm (IRE) **D. V. Gardner**
6 4, B g Dr Massini (IRE)—Tina Torus (IRE) **D. V. Gardner**

MRS S. GARDNER—continued

THREE-YEAR-OLDS

7 B f Zaffaran (USA)—Windy Walls (IRE) **D. V. Gardner**

Assistant Trainer: D V Gardner

Jockey (NH): S. Durack. **Amateur:** Miss L. Gardner.

---

229 **MR J. A. GEAKE, Andover**
Postal: **Kimpton Down Stables, Kimpton Farm, Andover, Hampshire, SP11 8PQ.**
Contacts: **PHONE (01264) 772278/771815 FAX (01264) 771221 MOBILE (07768) 350738**
E-MAIL serena@baldingstrainings.fsnet.co.uk or lesley@kimptonstables.com
WEBSITE www.jonathan.geake.co.uk

1 **ACCIPITER,** 6, b g Polar Falcon (USA)—Accuracy **Miss B. E. Swire**
2 **BALLYVADDY (IRE),** 9, gr g Roselier (FR)—Bodalmore Kit **Lady G. Wates**
3 **BILIVERDIN (IRE),** 11, b g Bob Back (USA)—Straw Beret (USA) **Mr Theo Waddington and Mr Bernard Keay**
4 **BLACK HILLS,** 6, b g Dilum (USA)—Dakota Girl **The Kingfisher Partnership**
5 **BLUEGRASS BOY,** 5, b g Bluegrass Prince (IRE)—Honey Mill **Supreme Team**
6 **BREEZER,** 5, b g Forzando—Lady Lacey **Kimpton Down Racing Club**
7 **CA'D'ORO,** 12, ch g Cadeaux Genereux—Palace Street (USA) **Miss B. E. Swire**
8 **CALUSA LADY (IRE),** 5, ch m Titus Livius (FR)—Solas Abu (IRE) **Baldings (Training) Ltd**
9 **CAPTAIN VALIANT (IRE),** 7, b g Supreme Leader—Anna Valley **Miss B. E. Swire**
10 **COUNT BORIS,** 4, b g Groom Dancer (USA)—Bu Hagab (IRE) **The P. J. Partnership**
11 **CUGINA NICOLA,** 4, b f Nicolotte—Cugina **Miss B. E. Swire**
12 **DANCE DIRECTOR (IRE),** 8, b g Sadler's Wells (USA)—Memories (USA) **Dr G. Madan Mohan**
13 **DESAILLY,** 11, ch g Teamster—G W Superstar **The Team**
14 **DICKIE DEADEYE,** 8, b g Distant Relative—Accuracy **Miss B. E. Swire**
15 **DREAM WITH ME (FR),** 8, b g Johann Quatz (FR)—Midnight Ride (FR) **Dr G. Madan Mohan**
16 **DUKE OF MODENA,** 8, ch g Salse—Palace Street (USA) **Miss B. E. Swire**
17 **FORMALISE,** 5, b g Forzando—Esilam **Mrs Julie Palmer and Mr Simon Balding**
18 **GLACIAL VALE (IRE),** 6, b m Glacial Storm (USA)—Anna Valley **Miss B. E. Swire**
19 **GOLD RING,** 5, ch g Groom Dancer (USA)—Indubitable **Miss B. E. Swire**
20 **GOLDEN BAY,** 6, ch m Karinga Bay—Goldenswift (IRE) **Goldie's Friends**
21 **GOLDEN CREW,** 5, b h Busy Flight—Goldenswift (IRE) **Goldie's Friends 2**
22 **HARAMBEE (IRE),** 5, b m Robellino (USA)—Hymenee (USA) **J. T. Brown**
23 **HISTORIC PLACE (USA),** 5, b g Dynaformer (USA)—Captive Island **Miss G. Bishop & Mr Bernard Keay**
24 **JUSTINO,** 7, b g Bustino—Jupiter's Message **Argent Racing**
25 **KELTIC ROCK,** 6, ch g Bigstone (IRE)—Sibley **D J Erwin Bloodstock & Tony Geake**
26 **KING'S CAPRICE,** 4, ch g Pursuit of Love—Palace Street (USA) **Miss B. E. Swire**
27 **LATIMER'S PLACE,** 9, b g Teenoso (USA)—Pennethorne Place **Sir Christopher Wates**
28 **LUSIMUS,** 4, ch g Piccolo—Bob's Princess **Dr & Mrs Peter Leftley**
29 **M'LORD,** 7, b g Mister Lord (USA)—Dishcloth **Dr G. Madan Mohan**
30 **MARKER,** 5, ch g Pivotal—Palace Street (USA) **Miss B. E. Swire**
31 **MORGAN LEWIS (IRE),** 4, b g Orpen (USA)—Party Piece **Mrs G. K. Smith**
32 **PARNASSIAN,** 5, ch g Sabrehill (USA)—Delphic Way **Miss B. E. Swire**
33 4, B c Classic Cliche (IRE)—Pennethorne Place **Sir Christopher Wates**
34 **PENNEYROSE BAY,** 6, ch m Karinga Bay—Pennethorne Place **Sir Christopher Wates**
35 **PERSIAN GENIE (IRE),** 4, br f Grand Lodge (USA)—Persia (IRE) **R. L. Mead**
36 **PEVERIL PRIDE,** 7, b g Past Glories—Peveril Princess **Mrs E. A. Haycock**
37 **PINE MARTEN,** 6, b g Karinga Bay—Rakaposhi Queen **Mrs D. J. Hues**
38 **POLDEN MILKMAID,** 4, b f Atraf—Maid of Mischief **Mrs P. R. Barnett & Mr G. B. Balding**
39 **POMPEY CHIMES,** 5, b g Forzando—Silver Purse **C. Warner**
40 **PRIZEMAN (USA),** 7, b g Prized (USA)—Shuttle (USA) **The Prize Winners**
41 **RED RAPTOR,** 4, ch c Polar Falcon (USA)—Star Precision **Miss B. E. Swire**
42 4, Ch c Piccolo—Ring of Love **Baldings (Training) Ltd**
43 **ROSE THYNE (IRE),** 5, ch m Good Thyne (USA)—Leading The Act (IRE) **Double Kings Partnership**
44 **SABRINA BROWN,** 4, br f Polar Falcon (USA)—So True **Miss B. E. Swire**
45 **SILVER REIGN,** 4, gr g Prince Sabo—Primo Donna Magna **Mr & Mrs K. Finch**
46 **SIMPLYFORPLEASURE,** 6, b g Simply Great (FR)—Jupiter's Message **The P. K. Partnership**
47 **SPARTAN PLACE,** 5, b g Overbury (IRE)—Pennethorne Place **Sir Christopher Wates**
48 **SPRING DEW (FR),** 4, b f Starborough—Penniless (IRE) **J. T. Brown**
49 **THE REAL BOSS (IRE),** 7, b g Grand Plaisir (IRE)—White Beau **A. W. Sutcliffe**
50 **TIBURCE (FR),** 4, b g Signe Divin (USA)—Ferlia (FR) **Baldings (Training) Ltd**
51 **TURBO (IRE),** 6, b g Piccolo—By Arrangement (IRE) **P. M. Richardson**

MR J. A. GEAKE—continued

52 **UNCLE BERNON**, 6, ch g Pivotal—Magical Veil **Seabright Five**
53 **WATERLOO LILY**, 4, gr f Thethingaboutitis (USA)—Dumps **Richard & Mrs Gillian Clutterbuck**
54 **WINDMILL LANE**, 8, b m Saddlers' Hall (IRE)—Alpi Dora **R. Blanchard**
55 **ZUBROWSKO (FR)**, 4, b c Nikos—Tinozakia (FR) **Baldings (Training) Ltd**

THREE-YEAR-OLDS

56 **ARRIMAN**, ch c Bien Bien (USA)—Spellbinder (IRE) **The Dancing Partners**
57 **BENEDICT BAY**, b c In The Wings—Persia (IRE) **Dr & Mrs Peter Leftley**
58 **CAMERONS FUTURE (IRE)**, b c Indian Danehill (IRE)—
Wicken Wonder (IRE) **Messrs Keay, Waddington & Bishop**
59 **FINAL PROMISE**, b c Lujain (USA)—Unerring **Sideways Racing**
60 **JUBILEE COIN**, ch f Fumo di Londra (IRE)—Money Supply **Kimpton Down Racing Club**
61 **LA LUPA**, b f Loup Sauvage (USA)—Cugina **Miss B. E. Swire**
62 **MIRACLE BABY**, b f Atraf—Musica **Bouncebackability Partnership**
63 **MISTER TROUBRIDGE**, ch c Mister Baileys—So True **Miss B. E. Swire**
64 **MOONSIDE**, gr f Docksider (USA)—Moon Magic **Q. J. Jones**
65 **PALAIS POLAIRE**, ch f Polar Falcon (USA)—Palace Street (USA) **Miss B. E. Swire**
66 **QUALITY STREET**, ch f Fraam—Pusey Street Girl **The Rumble Racing Club**
67 **TILLY FLOSS**, ch f Piccolo—Lv Girl (IRE) **P. M. Richardson**

TWO-YEAR-OLDS

68 **CHANGIZ**, b c 27/4 Foxhound (USA)—Persia (IRE) (Persian Bold) (2000) **Dr Peter Leftley**
69 **COLLATERAL**, ch f 20/2 Groom Dancer (USA)—Cugina (Distant Relative) **Miss B. E. Swire**
70 **B c 12/3** Observatory (USA)—Dancing Fire (USA) (Dayjur (USA)) (18000) **Baldings (Training) Ltd**
71 **DANCING MELODY**, b f 27/1 Dr Fong (USA)—
Spring Mood (FR) (Nashwan (USA)) (5000) **Tony Geake & Mr D. Tribe**
72 **FOREVER THINE**, ch f 24/2 Groom Dancer (USA)—Indubitable (Sharpo) **Miss B. E. Swire**
73 **HOLLYWOOD DANCER**, b f 14/2 Woodborough (USA)—Fayre Holly (IRE) (Fayruz) (2857) **Mr & Mrs K. Finch**
74 **LITTLE MISS VERITY**, b f 7/5 Danzig Connection (USA)—Little White Lies (Runnett) **Redenham Racing Group**
75 **PARTHENOPE**, gr f 31/3 Namid—Twosixtythreewest (FR) (Kris) **Dr and Mrs John Merrington**
76 **B c 4/4** King Charlemagne (USA)—Party Piece (Thatch) (26000) **Baldings (Training) Ltd**
77 **B f 17/3** Kayf Tara—Pennethorne Place (Deep Run) **Sir Christopher Wates**
78 **RIPPLES**, b f 10/5 Dansili—Rivers Rhapsody (Dominion) **R. L. Mead**
79 **B f 15/4** Kayf Tara—Spellbinder (IRE) (Magical Wonder (USA)) **Mr G. B. Balding**
80 **Ch c 13/4** Groom Dancer (USA)—Unerring (Unfuwain (USA)) (3000) **Sideways Racing**

Other Owners: Fledglings Bloodstock, The Cleric Partnership, Mrs. S.A. Addington-Smith, Mr M. Aitken, Mr M. Bowman, Mr K. F. Chittock, Mr J. Coggan, Mr S. Cooke, Mr W. Craig, Mr M. Cuddigan, Mr M. Davies, Mr P.S. Dove, Miss P. Downing, Mr D. J. Erwin, Mrs E. Estall, Mrs M. R. Geake, Mrs S. A. Geake, Mr R. George, Mr P. Green, Mrs P.D. Gulliver, Mr W. Hackney, Mrs P. Haliday, Mr B. Harding, Mr J. Harris, Mr S. Hilcox, Mrs C. Hobbs, Mrs E. J. Hopkins, Mrs W. Hart, Mr A. Johnson, Mr S. M. Little, Sir Brian McGarth, Mr S. Miller, Mrs S. Oxlade, Mr M. Painter, Mrs C. Parry, Mrs K. L. Perrin, Mr C. J. Piper, Mr J. Robson, Mrs G. Schley, Mr J. Schley, Mr N. Sinfield, Mr G. S. Small, Mr R. J. Spencer, Mr A. Stone, Mrs S. Thayer, Mr J. Walker, Mr J. L. Walters, Mrs J. M. Walters, Mr R. C. Watts, Mrs S. D. Watts, Mr D. J. Wray, Mr N. Yeatman.

Assistant Trainer: Mr G B Balding

Jockey (flat): Steve Drowne, Robert Havlin, Steve Carson. **Jockey (NH):** Mark Bradburne, Seamus Durack, Brian Crowley. **Conditional:** Simon Elliott. **Apprentice:** Richard Thomas, Miss Frances Harper. **Amateur:** Mr Jamie Jenkinson.

230 CAPT J. A. GEORGE, Stroud
Postal: **Down Farm, Slad, Stroud, Gloucestershire, GL6 7QE.**
Contacts: **PHONE (01452) 813487 FAX (01452) 814293**

1 **MOYLISCAR**, 6, b m Terimon—Annie Kelly **Mrs J. A. George**

Conditional: W. McCarthy.

231 MR T. R. GEORGE, Slad
Postal: **Springbank, Slad, Stroud, Gloucestershire, GL6 7QE.**
Contacts: **PHONE (01452) 814267 FAX (01452) 814246 MOBILE (07850) 793483**

1 **BAR GAYNE (IRE)**, 6, ch g Good Thyne (USA)—Annie's Alkali **M. R. C. Opperman**
2 **BATON CHARGE (IRE)**, 7, b g Gildoran—Frizzball (IRE) **J. W. Dyson**

MR T. R. GEORGE—continued

3 **BE MY ROYAL (IRE)**, 11, b g Be My Native (USA)—Royal Rehearsal **Dr D. Chapman-Jones**
4 **BEE AN BEE (IRE)**, 8, b g Phardante (FR)—Portia's Delight (IRE) **W. S. Moore**
5 **BISCAY WIND (IRE)**, 5, ch m Anshan—La Bise **Silkword Racing Partnership**
6 **BURWOOD BREEZE (IRE)**, 9, b g Fresh Breeze (USA)—Shuil Le Cheile **David & Lesley Byrne**
7 **CALVIC (IRE)**, 7, ch g Old Vic—Calishee (IRE) **The Alchabas Partnership**
8 **CARTHYS CROSS (IRE)**, 6, ch g Moscow Society (USA)—Sweet Tarquin **T. N. Chick**
9 **COBBET (CHR)**, 9, b g Favoured Nations (IRE)—Creace (CZE) **T. N. Chick**
10 **CURTINS HILL (IRE)**, 11, b g Roi Guillaume (FR)—Kinallen Lady (IRE) **Mrs E. M. A. Pitman**
11 **DANTE CITIZEN (IRE)**, 7, ch g Phardante (FR)—Boreen Citizen **Ryder Racing Ltd**
12 **EGGMOUNT (IRE)**, 7, b g Riberetto—Brigade Leader (IRE) **R. P. Foden**
13 **EL HAMRA (IRE)**, 7, gr g Royal Abjar (USA)—Cherlinoa (FR) **Porthilly Partners**
14 **FLOWER OF PITCUR**, 8, b g Alflora (IRE)—Coire Vannich **Strachan,L-Palmer,Parkinson,Shakerley**
15 **GARRYVOE (IRE)**, 7, b g Lord Americo—Cottage Theme **Lady H. J. Clarke**
16 **GOOD CITIZEN (IRE)**, 5, b g Good Thyne (USA)—Citizen Levee **M. J. Hoskins**
17 **HISTORIC (IRE)**, 9, b g Sadler's Wells (USA)—Urjwan (USA) **Mrs R. E. R. Rumboll**
18 **IDLE TALK (IRE)**, 6, br g Hubbly Bubbly (USA)—Belon Breeze (IRE) **Mrs M. J. George**
19 **ISHKA BAHA (IRE)**, 6, ch m Shernazar—Brionglóid **Ms J. D. Wilson**
20 **JULIES BOY (IRE)**, 8, b g Toulon—Chickmo (IRE) **R. P. Foden**
21 **LAUGHERNE BANK (IRE)**, 5, b g Zaffaran (USA)—Cyrano Imperial (IRE) **John Tainton and Graham Townsend**
22 **LORD OF ILLUSION (IRE)**, 8, b g Mister Lord (USA)—Jellaride (IRE) **P. Kennedy**
23 **MAMIDEOS (IRE)**, 8, br g Good Thyne (USA)—Heavenly Artist (IRE) **Silkword Racing Partnership**
24 **MANDICA (IRE)**, 7, br g Mandalus—Mawtvica **R. A. Dalton**
25 **MANQUE PAS D'AIR (FR)**, 5, br m Kadalko (FR)—Chantalouette (FR) **Mrs S. B. Lockhart**
26 **MASTER FOX**, 7, b br g Puissance—Hill Vixen **Mrs A. D. Williams**
27 **MIGHTY MATTERS (IRE)**, 6, b g Muroto—Hasaway (FR) **Slad Valley Racing Partnership**
28 **MISS CHIPPY (IRE)**, 5, ch m Mister Lord (USA)—My Alanna **T. N. Chick**
29 **MOORLANDS AGAIN**, 10, b g Then Again—Sandford Springs (USA) **W. J. Odell**
30 **MYSTERY (GER)**, 7, br g Java Gold (USA)—My Secret (GER) **P. Kennedy**
31 **PETER'S DEBT**, 6, gr g Arzanni—Another Debt **Miss J. Semple**
32 **POLISH CLOUD (FR)**, 8, gr g Bering—Batchelor's Button (FR) **Mrs Grace Frankel & Partners**
33 **ROSETOWN (IRE)**, 7, gr g Roselier (FR)—Railstown Cheeky (IRE) **T. N. Chick**
34 **STACK THE PACK (IRE)**, 8, ch g Good Thyne (USA)—Game Trix **Mrs C. M. Davies**
35 **SWIFT THYNE (IRE)**, 5, b g Good Thyne (USA)—Firey Comet (IRE) **Thoroughbred Ladies**
36 **SWIFTS HILL (IRE)**, 7, ch g Executive Perk—Tudor Lady **Thoroughbred Ladies**
37 **THENAMEESCAPESME**, 5, b g Alderbrook—Gaygo Lady **Mrs S. C. Nelson**
38 **TOULOUSE-LAUTREC (IRE)**, 9, ch g Toulon—Bucks Slave **J. A. R. R. French**
39 **TREMALLT (IRE)**, 14, b g Henbit (USA)—Secret Romance **Mr T. R. George**
40 **TRENANCE (IRE)**, 8, b g Alflora (IRE)—Carmel's Joy (IRE) **Mr & Mrs D. A. Gamble**
41 **TURTLE SOUP (IRE)**, 9, b g Turtle Island (IRE)—Lisa's Favourite **M. K. George**

Other Owners: Mr A. Bamboye, Mrs L. W. Byrne, D. Byrne, B. C. Corrigan, R. A. Dalton, M. A. Evans, Mrs A. Gamble, D. A. Gamble, Mrs S. P. George, H. S. Harford, Mr C. J. D. Hodges, Mrs C. L. Llewellen Palmer, J. B. Lawson, A. R. Lewers, W. E. Moore, Mrs S. C. Nelson, Mr J. R. S. Newiss, Mrs C. L. Parkinson, P. T. Petrie, Mrs L. C. Shakerley, Mrs E. M. Strachan, Mr J. S. Tainton, T. G. Townsend, R. F. Tromans, A. M. Waller.

Jockey (NH): J. M. Maguire. **Conditional:** W. J. McCarthy, Zoe Owen.

---

232 ## MR RICHARD GIBSON, Chantilly
Postal: **7, avenue Montpensier, 60500 Chantilly, France.**
Contacts: PHONE +33 (0) 3 44 57 53 00 FAX +33 (0) 3 44 58 15 48 MOBILE +33 (0) 608 61 57 88
E-MAIL richard.gibson@wanadoo.fr

1 **AUSTRALIE (IRE)**, 4, b f Sadler's Wells (USA)—Asnieres (USA) **Mrs B. Strudwick**
2 **CATTIVA GENEROSA**, 4, b f Cadeaux Genereux—Signorina Cattiva (USA) **Haras De Saint Pair Du Mont**
3 **COMMON REQUEST (USA)**, 4, b f Lear Fan (USA)—Questonia **Mr P. Holm Lassen**
4 **DROP SHOT**, 4, ch c Groom Dancer (USA)—Three Greens **Mr J. Livock**
5 **LISIEUX ORCHID (IRE)**, 4, b f Sadler's Wells (USA)—Clear Issue (USA) **Mr A. Krishnan**
6 **LUNE D'OR (FR)**, 4, b f Green Tune—Luth d'or (FR) **Mrs P. de Moussac**
7 **PETIT CALVA (FR)**, 4, b f Desert King (IRE)—Jimkana (FR) **Mrs A. G. Kavanagh**
8 **SHEMRANA (USA)**, 4, b f Woodman (USA)—Shemaya (IRE) **Meridian Bloodstock**
9 **SWEDISH SHAVE (FR)**, 7, b g Midyan (USA)—Shavya **Mr S. Thynell**
10 **VERTE VALLEE (FR)**, 4, b f Septieme Ciel (USA)—Valleyrose (IRE) **M. O. Lecerf**
11 **VOCATINE (IRE)**, 4, b f Royal Applause—Voltage (IRE) **Mr W. Baumann**

MR RICHARD GIBSON—continued

THREE-YEAR-OLDS

12 **AMMO (IRE)**, b f Sadler's Wells (USA)—Animatrice (USA) **Mr A. E. Oppenheimer**
13 **AMOROSA BRI**, b f Bering—Ampelopsis (FR) **Mr J. Crowley**
14 **ANESTASIA (IRE)**, b f Anabaa (USA)—Spectacular Joke (USA) **Mr E. Mordukhovitch**
15 **ANNEE LUMIERE (IRE)**, ch f Giant's Causeway (USA)—Luminosity **Mrs G. Forlen**
16 **APACHE HOGAN (FR)**, ch c Indian Lodge (IRE)—Lisheba (USA) **Mr J. Wallinger**
17 **ARABIAN SPELL (IRE)**, ch f Desert Prince (IRE)—Truly Bewitched (USA) **Mr J. Brennan**
18 **CREME DE LA CREME (FR)**, b f Vettori (IRE)—Salvinaxia (FR) **Mr L. Robbins**
19 **CROISIERE (USA)**, b f Capote (USA)—Glasgow's Gold (USA) **Skymarc Farm**
20 **DOCTOR DINO (FR)**, ch c Muhtathir—Logica (IRE) **Mr J. Martinez Salmean**
21 **EGYPT MOON**, b f Zieten (USA)—Ile Mamou (IRE) **Mr. E. Soderberg**
22 **FILIMEALA (IRE)**, b f Pennekamp (USA)—Birdsong (IRE) **Mrs A. G. Kavanagh**
23 **HIDEAWAY (FR)**, b f Cape Cross (IRE)—Hint of Silver (USA) **Skymarc Farm**
24 **HIGHEST LOVER (FR)**, gr c Highest Honor (FR)—DISTANT LOVER **Mr E. Mordukhovitch**
25 **INCENSE**, b f Unfuwain (USA)—Blessed Honour **Mrs A. G. Kavanagh**
26 **LADY RAGAZZA (IRE)**, b f Bering—Mrs Ting (USA) **Mr H. de Burgh**
27 **LE TIGRE D'OR (FR)**, ch c Indian Ridge—La Panthere (USA) **Mr J. Livock**
28 **LEVENTINA (IRE)**, b f Anabaa (USA)—Perugina (FR) **Mr G. A. Oldham**
29 **LOVE FIFTEEN (IRE)**, ch f Grand Lodge (USA)—Tresor Russe (IRE) **Mr J. Livock**
30 **LUCERA (IRE)**, b f Fasliyev (USA)—Lunata (IRE) **Mr J. L. Bouchard**
31 **LYNNWOOD CHASE (USA)**, b f Horse Chestnut (SAF)—Lady Ilsley (USA) **Mr A. E. Oppenheimer**
32 **NARNIA**, b f Entrepreneur—Narola (GER) **Dr C. Berglar**
33 **NOVOSIBIRSK (USA)**, ch f Distant View (USA)—Nunatak (USA) **Ecurie Wildenstein**
34 **PACHANGA**, b f Inchinor—GAI BULGA **Mr A. E. Oldham**
35 **PARIS AT NIGHT (FR)**, b f In The Wings—Rigoureuse (USA) **Mr R. Barnes**
36 **PRETREVAL (FR)**, ch c Barathea (IRE)—Touville (USA) **Mr O. Lecerf**
37 **SAFEN (FR)**, b c Septieme Ciel (USA)—Champion's Sister (USA) **Mrs F. Woerth**
38 **SALTINO (IRE)**, b c Daylami (USA)—Mahalia (IRE) **Mr G. A. Oldham**
39 **SEGESTA (IRE)**, b f Vettori (IRE)—Mistra (IRE) **Mr G. A. Oldham**
40 **SOURCE OF LIFE (IRE)**, b f Fasliyev (USA)—Asnieres (USA) **Sangster Family**
41 **TAMRA DELIGHT (USA)**, b f Diesis—Danemarque (AUS) **Mr W. de Burgh**
42 **THE JEWEL (FR)**, b f Octagonal (NZ)—The Blade (GER) **Mr D. Stein**
43 **VOVAN (IRE)**, ch c Indian Ridge—Mistreat **Mr E. Mordukhovitch**
44 **WITHOUT SHOES (FR)**, b f Highest Honor (FR)—Lady Winner (FR) **Skymarc Farm**

TWO-YEAR-OLDS

45 **ALIVERA (FR)**, b f 26/4 Danehill (USA)—
Spectacular Joke (USA) (Spectacular Bid (USA)) (201207) **Mr E. Mordukhovitch**
46 **ANABAA INDY (IRE)**, b f 21/3 Anabaa (USA)—
Chanteleau (USA) (A P Indy (USA)) (77129) **Haras de Saint Pair du Mont**
47 **ANGLONA (IRE)**, b f 23/2 Anabaa (USA)—Pescia (IRE) (Darshaan) **Mr G. A. Oldham**
48 B f 6/2 Bahhare (USA)—Anoukit (Green Desert (USA)) (8047) **Mrs A. Gibson**
49 **ARBOREA (IRE)**, b f 8/2 Fantastic Light (USA)—Campiglia (IRE) (Fairy King (USA)) **Mr G. A. Oldham**
50 **ARTISTA (FR)**, b c 6/5 Highest Honor (FR)—Miss Alleged (USA) (Alleged (USA)) (33534) **Stromboli Farm Ltd**
51 Ch f 21/4 Grand Lodge (USA)—Asnieres (USA) (Spend A Buck (USA)) (67069) **Sangster Family**
52 B f 2/4 Red Ransom (USA)—Becolina (USA) (Tabasco Cat (USA)) (42564) **Ecurie Monceaux**
53 **BONORVA (IRE)**, b f 3/4 Grand Lodge (USA)—Cortona (IRE) (Caerleon (USA)) **Mr G. A. Oldham**
54 Ch f 9/2 Zafonic (USA)—Brownie (USA) (Tabasco Cat (USA)) (55000) **Ecurie Wildenstein**
55 Ch f 13/5 Night Shift (USA)—Caffe (USA) (Mr Prospector (USA)) **M. Cahan**
56 **CALLALONGA (FR)**, b f 15/2 Almutawakel—Private Party (FR) (Fabulous Dancer (USA)) **Mr J. L. Bouchard**
57 Gr c 1/3 Marju (IRE)—Coolgrape (USA) (Suave Dancer (USA)) (30851) **Mr J. Martinez Salmean**
58 B f 12/5 Lemon Drop Kid (USA)—Coral Sea (USA) (Rubiano (USA)) (101090) **Haras de Saint Pair du Mont**
59 B f 18/2 Royal Applause—Crohal di San Jore (Saddlers' Hall (IRE)) (30180) **Aleyrion Bloodstock Ltd**
60 B c 2/4 Sadler's Wells (USA)—Dalawara (IRE) (Top Ville) (110000) **Mr K. F. Leung**
61 Ch f 17/4 Bering—Dancing Rose (FR) (Dancing Spree (USA)) (43594) **Mr R. Barnes**
62 **DARINGA (FR)**, b f 21/3 Bering—Darema (IRE) (Kahyasi) (21462) **Sir Robert Ogden C.B.E., LLD**
63 **DIBA (GER)**, b f 24/4 Big Shuffle (USA)—Diandrina (Mondrian (GER)) (53655) **Ecurie Monceaux**
64 Ch c 16/1 King Charlemagne (USA)—Dreamwriter (USA) (Hennessy (USA)) **Mrs M. Cahan**
65 B f 17/3 Mozart (IRE)—Dwell (USA) (Habitat) (USA) **Mrs P. Jamison**
66 **ELLE GALANTE (FR)**, b f 26/2 Galileo (USA)—Elle Danzig (GER) (Roi Danzig (USA)) **Dr C. Berglar**
67 **ERICUS (FR)**, b c 4/2 Highest Honor (FR)—Aka Lady (FR) (Sanglamore (USA)) (73775) **Mr E. Soderberg**
68 **FARBENSPIEL (IRE)**, b f 16/2 Desert Prince (IRE)—Flanders (IRE) (Common Grounds) (62000) **Dr C. Berglar**
69 Gr f 31/3 Linamix (FR)—Fascinating Hill (FR) (Danehill) (USA) **A. E. Oppenheimer**
70 **FIRE GIRL (FR)**, b f 13/4 Stravinsky (USA)—Spectatrice (USA) (Nijinsky (CAN)) (40241) **Mr E. Soderberg**

MR RICHARD GIBSON—continued

71 **GREEN STORM (FR)**, ch f 20/4 Green Tune (USA)—Ella Nico (IRE) (Archway (IRE)) (22132) **Mr S. Thynell**
72 **HIDDEN MOONLIGHT**, b f 6/3 Desert Style (IRE)—Hidden Meaning (Cadeaux Genereux) **Mr R. Rauscher**
73 **IL CATTIVO (FR)**, b c 15/1 Mark of Esteem (IRE)—
            Signorina Cattiva (USA) (El Gran Senor (USA)) **Haras de Saint Pair du Mont**
74 B f 6/3 Anabaa (USA)—Kate Marie (USA) (Bering) (34875) **J. W. Livock**
75 **LA VALLIERE (FR)**, b f 29/4 Anabaa (USA)—Touville (USA) (Shadeed (USA)) (26827) **Mr O. Lecerf**
76 B f 21/3 Mozart (IRE)—Lady Emmaline (IRE) (Charnwood Forest (IRE)) (25000) **Mrs V. Riva**
77 **LADY WASHINGTON**, b f 27/3 Xaar—Mainmise (USA) (Septieme Ciel (USA)) (23474) **Mr P. Holm Lassen**
78 **LUJEANNE (FR)**, b f 21/3 Lujain (USA)—
            Agnes For Ransom (USA) (Red Ransom (USA)) **Haras de Saint Pair du Mont**
79 **MATTAHORN (IRE)**, b c 17/3 In The Wings—Francfurter (Legend of France (USA)) (120000) **Sangster Family**
80 **MAXIMO (GER)**, b c 10/5 Orpen—Maltage (USA) (Affirmed (USA)) (40000) **Dr C. Berglar**
81 **MEDNAYA (IRE)**, b f 21/2 Anabaa (USA)—Sopran Dandy (IRE) (Doyoun) (93896) **Mr E. Mordukhovitch**
82 B g 1/1 Loup Solitaire (USA)—Meduse (FR) (Kendor (FR)) **Mr P. Basquin**
83 **MOUNT LASSEN (USA)**, ch c 11/4 Mt Livermore (USA)—
            Crockadore (USA) (Nijinsky (CAN)) (33534) **Mr P. Holm Lassen**
84 B f 11/3 Agnes World (USA)—Muramixa (FR) (Linamix (FR)) (33534) **Mrs A. Gibson**
85 Ch c 11/4 Galileo (IRE)—Ocean View (USA) (Gone West) (100602) **Mr E. Mordukhovitch**
86 **PEINTRE MODERN**, ch c 31/1 Peintre Celebre (USA)—
            Spring Haven (USA) (Lear Fan (USA)) (40241) **Mr E. Soderberg**
87 **PIETEN BERE (FR)**, b c 9/3 Zieten (USA)—Shadeed Vallee (USA) (Shadeed) (40241) **Mrs A. Gibson**
88 B c 16/2 Danehill Dancer (IRE)—Provisoire (USA) (Gone West (USA)) (6706) **Mr K. F. Leung**
89 Ch c 25/2 Lomitas—Rekindled Affair (IRE) (Rainbow Quest (USA)) (43594) **Aleyrion Bloodstock Ltd**
90 **ROSALIE**, ch f 9/4 Fantastic Light (USA)—Tularosa (In The Wings) **Mrs P. Cooper**
91 **SALILA (IRE)**, b f 24/2 Sadler's Wells—Love For Ever (IRE) (Darshaan) (117370) **Mr A. Krishnan**
92 **SAMSA (FR)**, b f 29/1 Zafonic (USA)—Everlasting Love (Pursuit of Love) (53655) **Mr E. Mordukhovitch**
93 **SEASONS (FR)**, gr f 15/3 Pennekamp (USA)—Desert Mixa (FR) (Linamix (FR)) (20120) **Mrs A. Gibson**
94 Ch f 19/2 Elnadim (USA)—Shadow Casting (Warning) (26827) **Aleyrion Bloodstock Ltd**
95 Ch f 17/4 Observatory (USA)—Shavya (Shavian) (53655) **Skymarc Farm**
96 **SKY CHART (FR)**, ch f 6/2 Diesis—Veiled Wings (FR) (Priolo) (USA)) **Mrs V. Riva**
97 B f 9/2 Inchinor—So Admirable (Suave Dancer (USA)) (60000) **Skymarc Farm**
98 **STAR DANCING**, ch f 30/1 Danehill Dancer (IRE)—Streak of Silver (USA) (Dynaformer (USA)) **Skymarc Farm**
99 B c 24/1 Anabaa (USA)—Style For Life (IRE) (Law Society (USA)) (301810) **Mr R. Barnes**
100 **SWEDISH DANCER (SWE)**, ch c 1/5 Danehill Dancer (IRE)—
            Eko Normandy (IRE) (Midyan (USA)) (14788) **Mr S. Thynell**
101 **THOR'S HAMMER**, b c 16/1 Boundary (USA)—
            Thunder Queen (USA) (Thunder Gulch (USA)) (33534) **Mr P. Holm Lassen**
102 B c 30/4 King's Best (USA)—Time For Pearls (USA) (Time For A Change (USA)) **Mr Peurari**
103 **TOMBOUCTOU (FR)**, b f 1/4 Neverneyev (USA)—Caslon (FR) (Deep Roots) (11401) **Mrs A. Gibson**
104 **TONNARA (FR)**, gr f 5/2 Linamix (FR)—Mahalia (IRE) (Danehill (USA)) **Mr G. A. Oldham**
105 **VICTOP (FR)**, b c 24/3 Victory Note (USA)—Top Speed (FR) (Wolfhound (USA)) (10060) **Mme G. Forien**
106 Ch f 14/4 Trempolino (USA)—Wavy Kris (IRE) (Persian Bold) (23474) **Mrs A. G. Kavanagh**

Other Owners: Mr J. R. O'Connor, Mr M. Lind, Mrs J. Sanders, Mr R. Stephenson.

Assistant Trainer: Eric Gandon.

Jockey (flat): T. Jarnet. **Apprentice:** T. Richer.

---

233 **MR N. J. G. GIFFORD, Findon**
Postal: **The Downs, Stable Lane, Findon, West Sussex, BN14 0RR.**
Contacts: **OFFICE** (01903) 872226 **FAX** (01903) 877232 **MOBILE** (07940) 518077
E-MAIL downs.stables@btconnect.com

1 **ALPINE SLAVE**, 8, ch g Alflora (IRE)—Celtic Slave **Mrs J. T. Gifford**
2 **ALPINE STAR**, 8, ch g Alflora (IRE)—Northwood Star (IRE) **S. N. J. Embiricos**
3 5, Ch g Fourstars Allstar (USA)—Ath Dara **P. H. Betts**
4 4, B g Petong—Beau's Delight (USA) **J. Dunsdon**
5 **DIAMOND SONG (IRE)**, 6, gr m Carroll House—April Gold **R. A. Gadd**
6 **DUSKY LORD**, 6, b g Lord Americo—Red Dusk **The American Dream**
7 **FOLLOW YOUR HEART**, 5, b br g Broken Hearted—Souled Out (IRE) **Mr John P. McManus**
8 **GALAXY SAM (USA)**, 6, ch g Royal Academy—Istiska **S. E. Munir**
9 **JOLY BEY (FR)**, 8, ch g Beyssac (FR)—Rivolie (FR) **Mr D. H. Dunsdon**
10 **JUST A SPLASH (IRE)**, 5, ch g Synetos (USA)—Guitane Lady (FR) **Mrs T. J. Stone Brown**
11 **MAJOR CATCH (IRE)**, 6, b g Safety Catch (USA)—Inch Tape **Martin & Valerie Slade**

MR N. J. G. GIFFORD—continued

12 **MONSIEUR ROSE (IRE)**, 9, gr g Roselier (FR)—Derring Slipper **Martin & Valerie Slade**
13 **MOONHAMMER**, 6, ch g Karinga Bay—Binny Grove **Mr C. Keeley**
14 **MOORESINI (IRE)**, 5, b g Dr Massini (IRE)—Mooreshill (IRE) **Unstable Companions**
15 **MR NICK (IRE)**, 5, b g Naheez (USA)—Brave Express **Felix Rosenstiel's Widow & Son Ltd**
16 **MULLIGATAWNY (IRE)**, 11, b g Abednego—Mullangale **Pell-mell Partners**
17 **POUNSLEY MILL (IRE)**, 12, b g Asir—Clonroche Abendego **Mrs A. S. Shipley**
18 **SAFE ENOUGH (IRE)**, 9, ch g Safety Catch (USA)—Godfreys Cross (IRE) **D. S. Norden & R. S. Norden**
19 **SAFE OASIS**, 5, b g Hector Protector (USA)—Desert Maiden **D. G. Trangmar**
20 **SENOR SEDONA**, 6, b g Royal Vulcan—Star Shell **Felix Rosenstiel's Widow & Son Ltd**
21 **SISTER GRACE**, 5, b m Golden Heights—Black Spring (IRE) **B. J. White**
22 **SOLEIL FIX (FR)**, 4, b g Mansonnien (FR)—Ifaty (FR) **J. Dunsdon**
23 **SPANISH SCRIBE (IRE)**, 6, b g Scribano—Give Her Thyne (IRE) **Mrs J. T. Gifford**
24 **ST VITA (FR)**, 8, ch m Vettori (IRE)—St Isadora **Mrs M. M. Fox-Pitt**
25 **WEE ROBBIE**, 5, b g Bob Back (USA)—Blast Freeze (IRE) **P. H. Betts (Holdings) Ltd**
26 **YUFO (IRE)**, 5, ch g Invited (USA)—Smart Lass **Mrs M. C. Sweeney**

Other Owners: G. H. L. Bird, J. Chromiak, R. F. Eliot, Mrs S. N. J. Embiricos, R. J. Gilder, Mrs C. E. Jeanne.

Jockey (NH): L. Aspell, P. Hide. **Amateur:** Mr D. H. Dunsdon.

MR P. L. GILLIGAN, Newmarket
234
Postal: **Sackville House, Sackville Street, Newmarket, Suffolk, CB8 8DX.**
Contacts: **PHONE (01638) 669151 FAX (01638) 605107 MOBILE (07981) 754901/(07931) 857611**
E-MAIL patrick.gilligan@ntlworld.com

1 **AMETHYST ROCK**, 7, b g Rock Hopper—Kind Lady **John A. Peters**
2 **AVIT (FR)**, 5, ch m General Monash (USA)—Breakfast Boogie **Treasure Seekers 2000**
3 **CAERPHILLY GAL**, 5, b m Averti (IRE)—Noble Lustre (USA) **T. Williams**
4 **DREAM EASY**, 4, b g Pyramus (USA)—Hush Baby (IRE) **John A. Peters**
5 **FAIRLIGHT EXPRESS (IRE)**, 5, ch g Carroll House—Marble Fountain **Mr Martin Cahill**
6 **GARDEN SOCIETY (IRE)**, 8, ch g Caerleon (USA)—Eurobird **R. Marks**
7 **GREAT FOX (IRE)**, 4, b c Foxhound (USA)—Good Enough (IRE) **John A. Peters**
8 **JUSTE POUR L'AMOUR**, 5, ch g Pharly (FR)—Fontaine Lady **Ian Neville Marks**
9 **KIND EMPEROR**, 8, br g Emperor Jones (USA)—Kind Lady **John A. Peters**
10 **REDWOOD STAR**, 5, b m Piccolo—Thewaari (USA) **Best Futures**

THREE-YEAR-OLDS

11 **GORGEOUS BOY (IRE)**, ch c Forzando—Instil **Treasure Seekers 2000**
12 **HIGHEST REGARD**, b c Mark of Esteem (IRE)—Free As A Bird **Mr Harvey Bell**
13 **WELSH GALAXY (IRE)**, b f Pennekamp (USA)—Jamaiel (IRE) **T. Williams**

TWO-YEAR-OLDS

14 **BRUNELLESCHI**, ch c 1/3 Bertolini (USA)—Petrovna (IRE) (Petardia) **Dr Susan Barnes**
15 B c 27/2 Golden Snake (USA)—Fontaine Lady (Millfontaine) **Ian Neville Marks**
16 B c 6/4 Pyramus (USA)—Nordesta (IRE) (Nordico (USA)) (3800) **Mr Patrick Gilligan**

Other Owners: Mr F. B. Barnes, Mr Alan Fletcher, Mr Dean Fletcher, Mr E. Prosser, Mr D. Griffiths, J. M. Southgate.

MR S. J. GILMORE, Banbury
235
Postal: **1 Spinners Cottages, Magpie Road, Sulgrave, Banbury.**
Contacts: **PHONE (01295) 768384 MOBILE (07786) 586418**

1 **MAJOR EURO (IRE)**, 8, b g Lord Americo—Gold Bank **Miss J. A. Frost**
2 **MNASON (FR)**, 5, gr g Simon du Desert (FR)—Mincing (FR) **Gane, Kingston, Wilshire**
3 **PLENTY**, 6, b m Terimon—Mrs Moneypenny **M. Watt**
4 **SYLVAN SHACK (IRE)**, 7, b br g Grand Plaisir (IRE)—Caddy Shack **The Wellies**

Other Owners: P. T. Fenwick, Mrs D. Gane, MR S. J. Gilmore, R. A. Jeffery, Mr I. W. Kingston, Mr M. J. Swain, S. N. Wilshire.

Amateur: Mr P. Cowley.

236 MR M. J. GINGELL, Kings Lynn

Postal: **Runcton Hall Racing Stables, North Runcton, Kings Lynn, Norfolk, PE33 0RB.**
Contacts: HOME (01553) 842420 YARD (01553) 840676
MOBILE (07831) 623624 or (07770) 533488
E-MAIL gingell@ukonline.co.uk

1 **ALFHALA (IRE)**, 4, b f Acatenango (GER)—Maid of Kashmir (IRE) **Cambridge and Stanstead Coursing Club**
2 **DAWN FROLICS**, 4, gr f Silver Patriarch (IRE)—Mighty Frolic **Two's Up Partnership**
3 **DRIZZLE**, 4, ch g Hector Protector (USA)—Rainy Sky **Webtack Racing**
4 **GLADYS GERTRUDE**, 4, ch f Double Trigger (IRE)—Nour El Sahar (USA) **Dr T. Alexander and Dr G. S. Plastow**
5 **HARRY THE HOOVER (IRE)**, 5, b g Fayruz—Mitsubishi Style **Stanger, P. Whittall and Dr G. S. Plastow**
6 **IMPERATIVE (USA)**, 5, ch g Woodman (USA)—Wandesta **Webtack Racing**
7 **MA BURLS**, 5, b m Perpendicular—Isabeau **Fare Dealing Partnership**
8 **MAJOR BELLE (FR)**, 6, ch m Cyborg (FR)—Mistine Major (FR) **Bar Snacks Partnership**
9 **NEW PERK (IRE)**, 7, b g Executive Perk—New Chello (IRE) **A. J. White**
10 **NORTON SAPPHIRE**, 6, ch m Karinga Bay—Sea of Pearls (IRE) **Gentlemen Don't Work on Mondays**
11 **OULTON BROAD**, 9, b g Midyan (USA)—Lady Quachita (USA) **M. A. Reeder**
12 **PRINCESS STEPHANIE**, 7, b m Shaab—Waterloo Princess (IRE) **The Real Tadzio Partnership**
13 **RAY MOND**, 4, b g Midnight Legend—Kinsale Florale (IRE) **A. J. White**
14 **URBAN KNIGHT**, 4, br g Dracula (AUS)—Anhaar **Webtack Racing**
15 **VICKY BEE**, 4, b m Alflora (IRE)—Mighty Frolic **Fare Dealing Partnership**
16 **YEOMAN LAD**, 5, b g Groom Dancer (USA)—First Amendment **Two's Up Partnership**

Other Owners: Mr P. Bromfield, Ms F. H. Brunton, P. A. Burling, MR M. J. Gingell, Mr K. J. Hewitt, Mrs J. Kerr, P. Morrison, Mrs W. J. M. Stanger, Miss S. L. White, J. M. Williams.

Assistant Trainer: Mrs A Gingell

237 MR JAMES GIVEN, Gainsborough

Postal: **Mount House Stables, Long Lane, Willoughton, Gainsborough, Lincolnshire, DN21 5SQ.**
Contacts: PHONE (01427) 667618 FAX (01427) 667734 MOBILE (07801) 100496
E-MAIL james.given@bigfoot.com WEBSITE www.jamesgivenracing.com

1 **BURLEY FLAME**, 4, b g Marju (IRE)—Tarsa **Burley Appliances Ltd**
2 **CHANTRY FALLS (IRE)**, 5, b g Mukaddamah (USA)—Woodie Dancer (USA) **White Rose Poultry Ltd**
3 **DAKOTA BLACKHILLS**, 4, b c Singspiel (IRE)—Lady Blackfoot **M. S. Anderson & R.S.G. Jones**
4 **DAME DE NOCHE**, 5, b m Lion Cavern (USA)—Goodnight Kiss **The G-Guck Group**
5 **EUIPPE**, 4, b f Air Express (IRE)—Myth **Mr C. Rowles Nicholson**
6 **FREDDIE FRECCLES**, 4, ch g Komaite (USA)—Leprechaun Lady **The Secret Seven Partnership**
7 **GRAMPIAN**, 6, b h Selkirk (USA)—Gryada **Mr M. J. Dawson**
8 **HARRY UP**, 4, ch c Piccolo—Faraway Lass **Mr J. E. Rose**
9 **HUGS DESTINY (IRE)**, 4, b g Victory Note (USA)—Embracing **Mr J. G. White & Mr D. Maloney**
10 **LAKE DIVA**, 4, ch f Docksider (USA)—Cutpurse Moll **Mr P. B. Doyle**
11 **LISTEN TO REASON (IRE)**, 4, b g Mukaddamah (USA)—Tenalist (IRE) **Mike Beadle and John Furness**
12 **MARITIME BLUES**, 5, b g Fleetwood (USA)—Dixie d'oats **Downlands Racing**
13 **MOUNT COTTAGE**, 4, b f Cape Cross (IRE)—Brecon Beacons (IRE) **Mrs G. Jennings**
14 **MUNGO JERRY (GER)**, 4, b g Tannenkonig (IRE)—Mostly Sure (IRE) **Mrs Ann Harrison**
15 **NESSEN DORMA (IRE)**, 4, b g Entrepreneur—Goldilocks (IRE) **Hokey Cokey Partnership**
16 **OMAN GULF (USA)**, 4, b g Diesis—Dabaweyaa **Mrs J. Hardy**
17 **PROTECTIVE**, 4, ch c Hector Protector (USA)—You Make Me Real (USA) **Mr P. Onslow**
18 **QUEEN LUCIA (IRE)**, 4, b f Pursuit of Love—Inquirendo (USA) **Mr H. J. P. Farr**
19 **RILEY BOYS (IRE)**, 4, ch g Most Welcome—Scarlett Holly **Paul Riley**
20 **ROCK LOBSTER**, 4, b g Desert Sun—Distant Music **Andy Clarke**
21 **SAINT LAZARE (IRE)**, 4, b c Peintre Celebre—Height of Passion **Chris Watson**
22 **SILK SUIVANTE (IRE)**, 4, b f Danehill (USA)—White Satin (IRE) **David Eiffe**
23 **SIR SIDNEY**, 5, b g Shareef Dancer (USA)—Hattaafeh (IRE) **Becky and Sidney Stones**
24 **SKYE'S FOLLY (USA)**, 5, b g Kris S (USA)—Bittersweet Hour (USA) **Audrey Scotney & Malcolm Joyce**
25 **SONG KOI**, 4, b f Sri Pekan (USA)—Eastern Lyric **Mr R. Meredith**
26 **SUMMITVILLE**, 5, b m Grand Lodge (USA)—Tina Heights **Mountain High Partnership**
27 **TRUE TO YOURSELF (USA)**, 4, b g Royal Academy (USA)—Romilly **Mike Beadle**

THREE-YEAR-OLDS

28 **AFRICAN GIFT**, b f Cadeaux Genereux—African Light **Mr & Mrs G. Middlebrook**
29 **BAYREUTH**, ch f Halling (USA)—South Shore **Mr H. J. P. Farr**
30 **BESTBYFAR (IRE)**, b c King's Best (USA)—Pippas Song **Pentakan Ltd**

MR JAMES GIVEN—continued

31 **BOLD EPPIE**, b f Cyrano de Bergerac—So Ambitious **Skeltools Ltd**
32 **BOWNESS**, b f Efisio—Dominio (IRE) **Mr & Mrs G. Middlebrook**
33 **BURTON ASH**, b br f Diktat—Incendio **Mrs Susan Lee**
34 **CAVA BIEN**, b g Bien Bien (USA)—Bebe de Cham **Lovely Bubbly Racing**
35 **CRIMSON BOW (GER)**, ch f Night Shift (USA)—Carma (IRE) **Peter Swann**
36 **DEGREE OF HONOR (FR)**, ch f Highest Honor (FR)—Sheba Dancer (FR) **Peter Swann**
37 **E BRIDE (USA)**, gr ro f Runaway Groom (CAN)—Fast Selection (USA) **Anthony Warrender & Rosemary Morley**
38 **EASTWELL MAGIC**, b f Polish Precedent (USA)—Kinchenjunga **Eastwell Manor Racing Ltd**
39 **ELLERAY (IRE)**, b f Docksider (USA)—Saint Ann (USA) **Mr & Mrs G. Middlebrook**
40 **EPICUREAN**, ch f Pursuit of Love—Arminda **Mr H. J. P. Farr**
41 **FOLGA**, b f Atraf—Desert Dawn **Mr P. Onslow**
42 **FREEST**, b f Fraam—Libretta **Mr P. Onslow**
43 **GIVEN A CHOICE (IRE)**, b c Trans Island—Miss Audimar (USA) **The G-Guck Group**
44 **GLOVED HAND**, b f Royal Applause—Fudge **Mrs M. V. Chaworth-Musters**
45 **GREATCOAT**, ch g Erhaab (USA)—Vaula **Mrs M. V. Chaworth-Musters**
46 **HIGH TREASON (USA)**, ch c Diesis—Fabula Dancer (USA) **Mr S. Rudolf**
47 **KRISTALCHEN**, b f Singspiel (IRE)—Crystal Flite (IRE) **The Wheet Partnership**
48 **MISTERS SISTER**, b f Robellino (USA)—Baileys On Line **G. R. Bailey Ltd**
49 **MONTCALM (IRE)**, b f Montjeu (IRE)—Autumn Fall (USA) **Mr & Mrs G. Middlebrook**
50 **MONTLOBRE (IRE)**, b f Petardia—Fall of The Hammer (IRE) **One Stop Partnership**
51 **NELLIE GWYN**, b f King's Best (USA)—On Tiptoes **Mr C. Rowles Nicholson**
52 **QUEUE UP**, b g Royal Applause—Faraway Lass **Mr J. E. Rose**
53 **SCOTTENDALE**, ch f Zilzal (USA)—Mountain Lodge **Lord Halifax**
54 **SHAMROCK BAY**, b f Celtic Swing—Kabayil **Elite Racing Club**
55 **SHARP DIVERSION (USA)**, ch f Diesis—Jamie de Vil (USA) **Peter Swann**
56 **SHEBOYGAN (IRE)**, ch f Grand Lodge (USA)—White Satin (IRE) **David Eiffe**
57 **SONG FINCH**, b f Inchinor—Eastern Lyric **Mr R. Meredith**
58 **SUNNYDALE (IRE)**, ch f Shahrastani (USA)—Golden Cay **Mr David Allan**
59 **TRES BIEN**, b c Bien Bien (USA)—Zielana Gora **Skeltools Ltd**
60 **TRYLKO (USA)**, ch f Diesis—Gossamer (USA) **Willoughton Racing Club**
61 **UNION JACK JACKSON (IRE)**, b c Daggers Drawn (USA)—Beechwood Quest (IRE) **Andy Clarke**
62 **VANADIUM**, b c Dansili—Musianica **Bolton Grange**
63 **VETTORIOUS**, ch c Vettori (IRE)—Sleepless Scotney **Audrey Scotney, Malcolm Joyce & Partners**
64 **WHIRLING**, ch f Groom Dancer (USA)—Supersonic **Mr C. Rowles Nicholson**
65 **WOOD SPRITE**, b f Mister Baileys—Woodbeck **Mr B. H. Farr**
66 **ZORIPP (IRE)**, b g Spectrum (IRE)—Allspice **Mr P. Horton & Mr A. Britcliffe**

TWO-YEAR-OLDS

67 **ARCANGELA**, b f 25/2 Galileo (IRE)—Crafty Buzz (USA) (Crafty Prospector (USA)) (19000) **Mr Paul Moulton**
68 Ch c 18/3 Mister Baileys—Arminda (Blakeney) (12000) **Peter Swann**
69 B f 8/2 Mujahid (USA)—Bangles (Chilibang) **Mrs Susan Lee**
70 **CARRIETAU**, b c 24/2 Key of Luck (USA)—Carreamia (Weldnaas (USA)) (8500) **Mr J. Ellis**
71 B f 5/3 Royal Applause—Faraway Lass (Distant Relative) **Mr J. E. Rose**
72 **GIGS MAGIC (USA)**, ch c 19/4 Gulch (USA)—Magic of Love (Magic Ring (IRE)) (74487) **Mr John Barson**
73 B c 18/2 Pivotal—Hard Task (Formidable (USA)) **Limestone Stud**
74 Br c 3/3 Key of Luck (USA)—Haysong (IRE) (Ballad Rock) (6706) **Limestone & Tara Stud**
75 **HIGH AMBITION**, b c 26/4 High Estate—So Ambitious (Teenoso (USA)) **Skeltools Ltd**
76 B c 2/4 Singspiel (IRE)—Inanna (Persian Bold) (16000) **John Reid & James Given**
77 **JEU D'ESPRIT (IRE)**, b f 2/5 Montjeu (IRE)—
Cielo Vodkamartini (USA) (Conquistador Cielo (USA)) (43000) **Mr Paul Moulton**
78 **KHORKINA (IRE)**, b f 20/4 Soviet Star (USA)—Philgwyn (Milford) **Living Legend Racing Partnership**
79 **LAMBENCY (IRE)**, b f 27/3 Daylami (IRE)—Triomphale (USA) (Nureyev (USA)) (28000) **Mr Paul Moulton**
80 B f 18/4 Inchinor—Lochbelle (Robellino (USA)) **Mr H. J. P. Farr**
81 B f 14/2 Zaha (CAN)—Misty Moon (Polar Falcon (USA)) (6000) **Zaha Racing Syndicate**
82 B c 23/1 Halling (USA)—Molomo (Barathea (IRE)) (17500) **Chris Watson**
83 B c 21/4 Bold Fact (USA)—Mountain Hop (IRE) (Tirol) (5000) **Bruce Coulthard**
84 B f 28/3 Key of Luck (USA)—Mylania (Midyan (USA)) (5500) **Mr J. Ellis**
85 **PADDY MOON**, b c 18/2 Lujain (USA)—Tara Moon (Pivotal) (7000) **Mr & Mrs M. Tourle**
86 B c 21/4 Mark of Esteem (IRE)—Robellino Miss (Robellino (USA)) **Car Colston Hall Stud**
87 B c 6/4 Rainbow Quest (USA)—Shastri (USA) (Alleged (USA)) (40000) **Mr M. J. Dawson**
88 **SONG HUNTRESS**, b f 23/3 Foxhound (USA)—Eastern Lyric (Petong) (7000) **Mr R. Meredith**
89 Ch f 14/3 Singspiel (IRE)—South Shore (Caerleon (USA)) **Mr B. H. Farr**
90 **STACCATO BLUES (IRE)**, br f 12/4 Piccolo—Dixie d'oats (Alhijaz) **Downlands Racing**
91 **THE PREACHER**, b c 7/3 Namaqualand (USA)—Bustling Around (Bustino) **Mick Horner**
92 **TRICK OR TREAT**, b f 25/4 Lomitas—Trick of Ace (USA) (Clever Trick (USA)) (11000) **Mr P. Onslow**

MR JAMES GIVEN—continued

93 **TROOP THE COLOUR (USA)**, b br c 17/4 Theatrical—Winsome (Kris) (133014) **Mr John Barson**
94 **WHOOPEE (USA)**, b br f 10/4 Mozart (IRE)—Time For A Wedding (USA) (Manila (USA)) (61186) **Mr John Barson**
95 **XENIA**, b f 20/2 Labeeb—
   Known Class (USA) (Known Fact (USA)) (12000) **M. S. Anderson, R. Jones & R. England**

Other Owners: M. J. Beadle, Mrs M. E. Ellis, J. A. Ellis, B. H. Farr, Mrs J. M. Frew, D. Maloney, A. S. Robertson, D. A. Smeaton, Miss B. Stones, S. Stones, Mrs A. M. Sturges.

Assistant Trainer: Chris Nash

---

238 MR J. A. GLOVER, Worksop
Postal: **Pinewood Stables, Carburton, Worksop, Nottinghamshire, S80 3BT.**
Contacts: **OFFICE (01909) 475962 FAX (01909) 470936 MOBILE (07802) 362909**

1 **ALLINJIM (IRE)**, 6, b g Turtle Island (IRE)—Bounayya (USA) **Advanced Brickwork Ltd**
2 **FIELD SPARK**, 5, b g Sillery (USA)—On The Top **G. Taylor & J. P. Burton**

THREE-YEAR-OLDS

3 **BEDTIME BLUES**, b f Cyrano de Bergerac—Boomerang Blade **Mr A. J. Swingler**
4 **DIAMOND HERITAGE**, ch g Compton Place—Eccolina **Mr I & Mrs J Beckett & Dr J A Gawthorpe**
5 **DISCOMANIA**, b g Pursuit of Love—Discomatic (USA) **D. E. Jenkins**
6 **INSIDER**, ch f Docksider (USA)—Inquirendo (USA) **R. W. Metcalfe**
7 B f High Estate—Our Aisling **A. K. Smeaton**
8 **STEVMARIE STAR**, b f Muhtarram (USA)—Cabaret Artiste **S. J. Beard**

TWO-YEAR-OLDS

9 B g 12/4 Josr Algarhoud (IRE)—Dreamtime Quest (Blakeney) (7000) **Mr A. J. Swingler**
10 B f 3/4 Primo Valentino (IRE)—Go Tally-Ho (Gorytus (USA)) (4000) **P. A. Jarvis**
11 **MINI BLUE (IRE)**, b f 29/4 Distant Music (USA)—Sylviani (Ashkalani (IRE)) (8047) **K. P. Beecroft**
12 **PRINCE EVELITH (GER)**, b g 12/2 Dashing Blade—Peace Time (GER) (Surumu (GER)) (11401) **A. Stennett**

Assistant Trainer: Stewart Parr

---

239 MR J. S. GOLDIE, Glasgow
Postal: **Libo Hill Farm, Uplawmoor, Glasgow, Renfrewshire, G78 4BA.**
Contacts: **PHONE (01505) 850212 FAX (01505) 850054 MOBILE (07778) 241522**

1 **BALLYHURRY (USA)**, 8, b g Rubiano (USA)—Balakhna (FR) **J. Breslin**
2 **COSMIC CASE**, 10, b m Casteddu—La Fontainova (IRE) **The Cosmic Cases**
3 **DOUBLE YOU CUBED**, 11, b g Destroyer—Bright Suggestion **Mrs D. I. Goldie**
4 **GARGOYLE GIRL**, 8, b m Be My Chief (USA)—May Hills Legacy (IRE) **Mrs C. Brown**
5 **GLENCAIRN STAR**, 4, b c Selkirk (USA)—Bianca Nera **Mr Frank Brady**
6 5, Ch m Bijou d'inde—Harrken Heights (IRE) **Mr Frank Brady and J. S. Goldie**
7 4, B f Destroyer—Harrken Heights (IRE) **Mr J. S. Goldie**
8 **HIGHLAND WARRIOR**, 6, b h Makbul—Highland Rowena **Frank & Annette Brady**
9 **HOWARDS ROCKET**, 4, ch g Opening Verse (USA)—Houston Heiress (USA) **Miss G. H. Wilson**
10 **INCH HIGH**, 7, ch g Inchinor—Harrken Heights (IRE) **Mr J. S. Goldie**
11 **INDIAN SPARK**, 11, ch g Indian Ridge—Annes Gift **Mr Frank Brady**
12 **INSUBORDINATE**, 4, ch g Subordination (USA)—Manila Selection (USA) **Edinburgh Racing Club Limited**
13 **JALLASTEP (FR)**, 8, b g Boston Two Step (USA)—Balladine (FR) **Mr & Mrs Raymond Anderson Green**
14 **JEXEL (FR)**, 8, b g Video Rock (FR)—Siesta (FR) **Mr & Mrs Raymond Anderson Green**
15 **KELUCIA (IRE)**, 4, ch f Grand Lodge (USA)—Karachi (SPA) **B. Scanlon & F. Brady**
16 **KID'Z'PLAY (IRE)**, 9, b g Rudimentary—Saka Saka **Mr L. J. McGuigan**
17 **KYLE OF LOCHALSH**, 5, gr g Vettori (IRE)—Shaieef (IRE) **Loch Ness Racing Club**
18 **MIDDLEMARCH (IRE)**, 5, ch h Grand Lodge (USA)—Blanche Dubois **W. M. Johnstone**
19 **MUSIOTAL**, 4, ch c Pivotal—Bemuse **F. Brady, E. Bruce & S. Bruce**
20 **ORIENTOR**, 7, b h Inchinor—Orient **F. Brady, E. Bruce & S. Bruce**
21 **REGENT'S SECRET (USA)**, 5, br g Cryptoclearance (USA)—Misty Regent (CAN) **Mrs M. Craig**
22 **RIVER FALCON**, 5, b g Pivotal—Pearly River **F. Brady, E. Bruce & S. Bruce**
23 **STAR APPLAUSE**, 5, b m Royal Applause—Cominna **Edinburgh Racing Club Limited**
24 **STELLITE**, 5, ch g Pivotal—Donation **Mr S. Bruce**
25 **STING LIKE A BEE (IRE)**, 6, b g Ali-Royal (IRE)—Hidden Agenda (FR) **Mrs C. Brown**
26 **TONY TIE**, 9, b g Ardkinglass—Queen of The Quorn **Mr Frank Brady**

MR J. S. GOLDIE—continued

THREE-YEAR-OLDS

27 COMPTON CLASSIC, b c Compton Place—Ayr Classic **Edinburgh Racing Club Limited**
28 COMPTON SPARK, ch g Compton Place—Rhinefield Beauty (IRE) **Mr Frank Brady**
29 GEOJIMALI, ch c Compton Place—Harrken Heights (IRE) **Mr Frank Brady**
30 RAINBOW TREASURE (IRE), ch f Rainbow Quest (USA)—Gaily Royal (IRE) **B. Scanlon & F. Brady**
31 THORNTOUN PICCOLO, ch f Groom Dancer (USA)—Massorah (FR) **W. M. Johnstone**

TWO-YEAR-OLDS

32 Ch c 18/3 Compton Place—Class Wan (Safawan) **Mr Frank Brady**
33 B c 29/3 Compton Place—Harrken Heights (IRE) (Belmez (USA)) **Mr J. S. Goldie**
34 Ch f 16/1 Dr Fong (USA)—Lost In Lucca (Inchinor) (35000) **Mr D. Power**
35 B c 17/3 Bluebird (USA)—Masakira (IRE) (Royal Academy (USA)) (34000) **F. Brady, E. Bruce and S. Bruce**
36 B f 24/2 Red Ransom (USA)—Pappa Reale (Indian Ridge) (65000) **Mr Frank Brady**
37 B f 12/5 Lujain (USA)—Rhinefield Beauty (IRE) (Shalford (IRE)) **Mr Frank Brady**

Other Owners: Mr E. Robertson, T. C. Barnfather, I. T. Buchanan, W. Shanks, F. T. Steele, M. Wassall.

Assistant Trainer: James And George Goldie

Jockey (flat): T. Eaves, K. Fallon, N. Mackay, W. Supple. **Jockey (NH):** A. Dempsey, A. Dobbin, G. Lee, R. McGrath, K. Renwick. **Conditional:** P. Whelan. **Apprentice:** Tony Hamilton, Jonathan Currie, Paul Mulrennan. **Amateur:** Mr G. Goldie, Mrs Carol Williams.

---

240 MR R. H. GOLDIE, Kilmarnock
Postal: **Harpercroft, Old Loans Road, Dundonald, Kilmarnock, Ayrshire, KA2 9DD.**
Contacts: **PHONE (01292) 317222 FAX (01292) 313585 MOBILE (07801) 922552**

1 BATTLE OF SONG (IRE), 5, b g Warcraft (USA)—Waajib's Song (IRE) **Mr R. H. Goldie**
2 4, B f Old Vic—Easter Oats **Mr R. H. Goldie**
3 4, B f Florida Son—Ice Nel **Mr R. H. Goldie**
4 4, B c Florida Son—Miss Cavo **Mr R. H. Goldie**
5 SUNY HENRY, 8, ch g Henbit (USA)—Suny Zeta **Mr R. H. Goldie**

THREE-YEAR-OLDS

6 B f Rakaposhi King—Easter Oats **Mr R. H. Goldie**
7 B f Terimon—Ice Nel **Mr R. H. Goldie**
8 B c Terimon—Miss Cavo **Mr R. H. Goldie**

TWO-YEAR-OLDS

9 B c 22/6 Insan (USA)—Easter Oats (Oats) **Mr R. H. Goldie**
10 B f 14/4 Alflora (IRE)—Ice Bavard (Le Bavard (FR)) **Mr R. H. Goldie**
11 B f 8/7 Winged Love (IRE)—Miss Cavo (Ovac (ITY)) **Mr R. H. Goldie**

Assistant Trainer: Mrs R H Goldie

---

241 MR K. GOLDSWORTHY, Kilgetty
Postal: **Grumbly Bush Farm, Yerbeston, Kilgetty, Pembrokeshire, SA68 0NS.**
Contacts: **PHONE/FAX (01834) 891343 MOBILE (07796) 497733**
E-MAIL grumbly@supanet.com

1 BEAUCHAMP QUEST, 6, b g Pharly (FR)—Beauchamp Kate **City Racing Club**
2 BLUE LEADER (IRE), 6, b g Cadeaux Genereux—Blue Duster (USA) **Ms Diane Morgans**
3 CHARLIE BEAR, 4, ch c Bahamian Bounty—Abi **Mr R. A. Hughes**
4 CRACOW (IRE), 8, b g Polish Precedent (USA)—Height of Secrecy **The Landsker Line Partnership**
5 EAGLE'S LANDING, 7, b m Eagle Eyed (USA)—Anchorage (IRE) **Tenby Optimists**
6 ICE CRYSTAL, 8, b g Slip Anchor—Crystal Fountain **Mrs L. A. Goldsworthy**
7 MR DOW JONES (IRE), 13, b g The Bart (USA)—Roseowen **Mrs L. A. Goldsworthy**

Other Owners: Mrs A. Allen, Mr N. Edwards, Mr M. Evans, Mr J. Evenden, Greenacre Racing Partnership Ltd, M. J. Lurcock, R. Sidebottom.

Assistant Trainer: Mrs L A Goldsworthy

242 MR S. GOLLINGS, Louth
Postal: Highfield House, Scamblesby, Louth, Lincolnshire, LN11 9XT.
Contacts: HOME/FAX (01507) 343213 YARD (01507) 343204 MOBILE (07860) 218910
E-MAIL stevegollings@aol.com

1 ALL MARQUE (IRE), 5, b m Saddlers' Hall (IRE)—Buzzing Beauty R. Jones
2 ALMNADIA (IRE), 6, b m Alhaarth (IRE)—Mnaafa (IRE) J. Hennessy
3 BEYOND BORDERS (USA), 7, b br g Pleasant Colony (USA)—Welcome Proposal Holmes Court Securities Ltd
4 4, B f Shaddad (USA)—Bustling Around Mr G. N. Dyson
5 CASTLESHANE (IRE), 8, b g Kris—Ahbab (IRE) W. Hobson, J. King, G. King, P. Winfrow
6 CITY PALACE, 4, ch g Grand Lodge (USA)—Ajuga (USA) J. B. Webb
7 COLLEGE QUEEN, 7, b m Lugana Beach—Eccentric Dancer D. J. Butler
8 FREYDIS (IRE), 7, b m Supreme Leader—Lulu Buck The Highfield House Partnership
9 HIGH WINDOW (IRE), 5, b g King's Theatre (IRE)—Kayradja (IRE) J. B. Webb
10 IBERUS (GER), 7, b g Monsun (GER)—Iberica (GER) R. G. Gibney
11 JACK MARTIN (IRE), 8, ch g Erins Isle—Rolling Penny (IRE) J. B. Webb
12 JIDIYA (IRE), 6, b g Lahib (USA)—Yaqatha (IRE) Holmes Court Securities Ltd
13 KING'S THOUGHT, 6, b h King's Theatre (IRE)—Lora's Guest Mrs E. P. Houlton
14 KITSKI (FR), 7, b g Perrault—Macyrienne (FR) J. B. Webb
15 LANMIRE TOWER (IRE), 11, b g Celio Rufo—Lanigans Tower Mrs D. Dukes
16 MOVIE KING (IRE), 6, ch g Catrail (USA)—Marilyn (IRE) The High Five Partnership
17 PETROVKA (IRE), 5, b m King's Theatre (IRE)—Adjacent (IRE) P. Winfrow
18 ROCKET FORCE (USA), 5, ch g Spinning World (USA)—Pat Us (USA) J. B. Webb
19 ROYAL SHAKESPEARE (FR), 6, b g King's Theatre (IRE)—Persian Walk (FR) J. B. Webb
20 RUTLAND CHANTRY (USA), 11, b g Dixieland Band (USA)—Christchurch (FR) Mrs J. M. Gollings
21 SALHOOD, 6, b g Capote (USA)—Princess Haifa (USA) J. B. Webb
22 SEANIETHESMUGGLER (IRE), 7, b g Balla Cove—Sharp Shauna J. B. Webb
23 SEATTLE PRINCE (USA), 7, gr g Cozzene (USA)—Chicken Slew (USA) D. J. Butler
24 SENOR EDUARDO, 8, gr g Terimon—Jasmin Path Mrs J. B. Webb
25 SILENT AGE (IRE), 4, b g Danehill (USA)—Set Fair (USA) P. Winfrow
26 STONEYFORD BEN (IRE), 6, b g Beneficial—Rosie Rock J. B. Webb
27 THE FISIO, 5, b g Efisio—Misellina (FR) John Crow Holdings Ltd
28 VIGOUREUX (FR), 6, b g Villez (USA)—Rouge Folie (FR) Ian Hesketh & J. B. Webb
29 WICKED UNCLE, 6, b g Distant Relative—The Kings Daughter Wunckle Partnership
30 WILL HE WISH, 9, b g Winning Gallery—More To Life Mrs D. Dukes

Other Owners: Mrs A. E. Allen, J. D. Chilton, Mrs V. Chilton, Mr L. G. Cockerill, M. J. Quickfall, P. Whinham, R. Wilson.

Assistant Trainer: Mrs J M Gollings

Jockey (flat): D. Holland, I. Mongan. Jockey (NH): J. Culloty, T. Doyle, S. Durack, M. A. Fitzgerald, T. J. Murphy, T. Scudamore. Amateur: Mr T. Woodside, Mrs J. M. Gollings.

243 MRS H. O. GRAHAM, Jedburgh
Postal: Brundeanlaws Cottage, Camptown, Jedburgh, Roxburghshire, TD8 6NW.
Contacts: PHONE (01835) 840354 MOBILE (07843) 380401
E-MAIL hgrahamracing@aol.com WEBSITE www.horseracing.freeservers.com

1 ALICE'S OLD ROSE, 8, b m Broadsword (USA)—Rosie Marchioness C. J. Pickering
2 HARRY HOOLY, 10, b g Lithgie-Brig—Drummond Lass Mrs H. O. Graham
3 INDY MOOD, 6, ch g Endoli (USA)—Amanta (IRE) Girsonfield Stud Racing
4 LOFTY LEADER (IRE), 6, b g Norwich—Slaney Jazz L. H. Gilmurray
5 NUCLEAR PROSPECT (IRE), 5, ch g Nucleon (USA)—Carraigbyrne (IRE) Mr S. Huggan
6 ROSALYONS (IRE), 11, gr g Roselier (FR)—Coffee Shop Mrs H. O. Graham
7 RUSSIAN SKY, 6, gr g Endoli (USA)—Anzarna H G Racing
8 THEPUBHORSE, 5, ch g Endoli (USA)—Lady Insight The Ancrum Pointer

Other Owners: D. Arnold, T. A. Burnham, Mrs S. Corbett, R. D. Graham.

Assistant Trainer: R D Graham

Jockey (NH): J. McCarthy. Conditional: C. Eddery. Amateur: Miss R. Davidson.

244 MR C. GRANT, Billingham

Postal: **Low Burntoft Farm, Wolviston, Billingham, Cleveland, TS22 5PD.**
Contacts: **PHONE/FAX** (01740) 644054 **MOBILE** (07860) 577998
E-MAIL chris@chrisgrantracing.fsnet.co.uk **WEBSITE** www.chrisgrantracing.com

1 **BARON MONTY (IRE)**, 7, b g Supreme Leader—Lady Shoco **T. J. Hemmings**
2 **BRIAR'S MIST (IRE)**, 8, gr g Roselier (FR)—Claycastle (IRE) **T. J. Hemmings**
3 **CRUISE LEADER (IRE)**, 10, b g Supreme Leader—Ormskirk Mover **T. J. Hemmings**
4 4, Gr g Theatrical Charmer—Handmaiden **Lord Daresbury**
5 **KALOU (GER)**, 7, br g Law Society (USA)—Kompetenz (IRE) **W. Raw**
6 **MASTER WOOD**, 14, b g Wonderful Surprise—Miss Wood **Mr C. Grant**
7 **MINSTER SHADOW**, 6, b g Minster Son—Polar Belle **Anne Cairns And Partners**
8 **OVER FLO**, 6, b m Overbury (IRE)—Flo-Jo (DEN) **The Highly Sociable Syndicate**
9 **OVER TO JOE**, 5, br g Overbury (IRE)—Flo-Jo (DEN) **Anne Cairns & Partners II**
10 **ROOBIHOO (IRE)**, 6, b g Norwich—Griffinstown Lady **Mrs H. E. Aitkin**
11 **TIME SPIN**, 5, b g Robellino (USA)—Chiltern Court (USA) **Mr J. C. Garbutt, Mr B. Woods, Mrs L. Swainston**
12 **WASHINGTON PINK (IRE)**, 6, b g Tagula (IRE)—Little Red Rose **Mr C. Grant**
13 **WEB MASTER (FR)**, 7, b g Arctic Tern (USA)—Inesperada **The Hon Mrs D. Faulkner**

TWO-YEAR-OLDS

14 **IL DIVO**, b g 1/4 Tipsy Creek (USA)—Be My Hattie (Be My Chief (USA)) (800) **Mr C. Grant**

Other Owners: A. Cairns, R. Kent, I. T. Smethurst.

Assistant Trainer: Mrs S Grant

Jockey (NH): R. McGrath. **Amateur:** Mr T. Greenall, Mr P. Kinsella.

245 MR L. P. GRASSICK, Cheltenham

Postal: **Postlip Racing Stables, Winchcombe, Cheltenham, Gloucestershire, GL54 5AQ.**
Contacts: **HOME** (01242) 603124 **YARD** (01242) 603919
FAX (01242) 603602 **MOBILE** (07816) 930423
E-MAIL billy.grassick@btopenworld.com

1 **ALPHA LEATHER**, 14, gr g Zambrano—Harvey's Choice
2 **FELONY (IRE)**, 10, ch g Pharly (FR)—Scales of Justice **Baskerville Racing Club**
3 **MIDNIGHT GOLD**, 5, ch g Midnight Legend—Yamrah **Nettleton Harts**
4 **MIKE SIMMONS**, 9, b g Ballacashtal (CAN)—Lady Crusty **Mr L. P. Grassick**
5 **MUIR COTTAGE**, 4, b g Chaddleworth (IRE)—Lady Crusty **Mr L. P. Grassick**
6 **PROTECTION MONEY**, 5, ch g Hector Protector (USA)—Three Piece **Baskerville Racing Club**
7 **SANDYWELL GEORGE**, 10, ch g Zambrano—Farmcote Air **David Lloyd & Mrs Carole Lloyd**
8 **SIMON THE POACHER**, 6, br g Chaddleworth (IRE)—Lady Crusty **Mr N. G. Goodger & Postlip Racing**

TWO-YEAR-OLDS

9 Br c 1/5 Chaddleworth (IRE)—Lady Crusty (Golden Dipper)

Other Owners: P. F. D. Badham, Ms G. E. Morgan, N. R. Stephens.

Jockey (flat): V. Slattery. **Conditional:** D. Laverty. **Amateur:** Mr T. Malone.

246 MR M. J. GRASSICK, Curragh

Postal: **Fenpark Stables, Pollardstown, Curragh, Co. Kildare, Ireland.**
Contacts: **HOME** +353 (0) 45 436956 **YARD** +353 (0) 45 434483
FAX +353 (0) 45 437895 **MOBILE** +353 (0) 87 2431923
E-MAIL mjgrassick2@eircom.net

1 **BOCACCIO (IRE)**, 7, b g Brief Truce (USA)—Idara **Mrs C. Grassick**
2 **CATILINE (IRE)**, 4, b c Nashwan (USA)—Mild Intrigue (USA) **S. Rogers**
3 **CAYTEVA**, 5, ch m Hernando (FR)—Cupira (GER) **A. Bish**
4 **CUMBRIA**, 4, b f Singspiel (IRE)—Whitehaven **Mrs S. Grassick**
5 **DESERT OF GOLD (IRE)**, 4, ch f Desert Prince—Camisha (IRE) **M. Duffy**
6 **ECKBEAG (USA)**, 6, b m Trempolino (USA)—Stormin Jane (USA) **J. Clarke**
7 **EL GUERROUJ (USA)**, 4, b g Seeking The Gold (USA)—Dearest (USA) **Mrs C. Grassick**
8 **FINEENA (IRE)**, 4, br f Titus Livius (FR)—Silhouette (IRE) **S. Mullins**

MR M. J. GRASSICK—continued

9 **GEMINI DIAMOND (IRE)**, 5, b br m Desert King (IRE)—Wakria (IRE) **Mrs A. Higgins**
10 **GOLOVIN (GER)**, 8, b h Bering—Guilinn (IRE) **Mrs H. Focke**
11 **GRAVIERES**, 7, ch g Mujtahid (USA)—Jumairah Sunset **Mrs S. Grassick**
12 **INDIAN'S FEATHER (IRE)**, 4, ch f Indian Ridge—Mashmoum **Ms C. Tsui**
13 **LA GAMBA (IRE)**, 4, b f Alhaarth (IRE)—Aglaia (SWI) **R. Weiss**
14 **LAKE TAHOE (IRE)**, 4, ch f Grand Lodge (USA)—Ar Hyd Y Knos **M. C. Grassick**
15 **LORD PATCHY (USA)**, 5, b br g Lord Avie (USA)—Teeming Shore (USA) **Mrs C. Grassick**
16 **MADAME MARJOU (IRE)**, 5, b m Marju (IRE)—Sudeley **Mrs S. Grassick**
17 **MAJOR TITLE (IRE)**, 6, b g Brief Truce (USA)—Dariyba (IRE) **Tour Syndicate**
18 **MOORE'S LAW (USA)**, 7, b g Technology (USA)—Brass Needles (USA) **Mrs S. Grassick**
19 **MR SMOOTH (USA)**, 5, b g Diesis—Recoleta (USA) **A. Bish**
20 **NIGHT FAIRY (IRE)**, 4, b f Danehill (USA)—Sassenach (IRE) **Ms C. Tsui**
21 **PELAGIAS STAR (IRE)**, 4, b f Darshaan—Wakria (IRE) **J. Higgins**
22 **PINE VALLEY (IRE)**, 4, ch f Entrepreneur—Blue Valley (FR) **T. O'Donnell**
23 **POETICAL (IRE)**, 4, ch f Croco Rouge (IRE)—Abyat (USA) **Mrs S. Grassick**
24 **PRINCESS DARIYBA (IRE)**, 5, b m Victory Note (USA)—Dariyba (IRE) **Mr Andrew S. Bradley**
25 **RED BELLS**, 4, b g Magic Ring (IRE)—Redgrave Devil **A. Bish**
26 **SIDECAR (IRE)**, 4, gr f Spectrum (IRE)—Streetcar (USA) **D. Grant**
27 **SISSY SLEW (USA)**, 5, b m Unbridled's Song (USA)—Missy Slew (USA) **J. Higgins**
28 **SOUTHERN COMMAND (IRE)**, 5, b g In Command (IRE)—Pretoria **Mrs M. J. Grassick**
29 **SOUTHERN STYLE (IRE)**, 5, b m Southern Halo (USA)—Stately Bid (USA) **Mrs M. J. Grassick**
30 **SPRING OPERA (IRE)**, 4, b f Sadler's Wells (USA)—Spring Easy (USA) **J. Higgins**
31 **ST GEORGE'S DAY**, 5, gr g Sir Harry Lewis (USA)—Steel Typhoon **A. Bish**
32 **SUNSHINE GUEST (IRE)**, 5, b m Be My Guest (USA)—Arrow Field (USA) **H. Sweeney**
33 **TIME DISCLOSES ALL**, 5, b g Polar Falcon (USA)—Take Charge **Mrs S. Grassick**
34 **TRIKIRK (IRE)**, 4, b g Selkirk (USA)—Shastri (USA) **S. Taylor**

THREE-YEAR-OLDS

35 **ASHDALI (IRE)**, b f Grand Lodge (USA)—Sidama (FR) **M. Quirke**
36 **C C GILES (USA)**, b br c Labeeb—Shamsbitebaba (USA) **Dr Charles S. Giles**
37 **CARNBRIDGE (IRE)**, b c Giant's Causeway (USA)—Mayenne (USA) **Miss P. F. O'Reilly**
38 **CROCODILE ROSE (IRE)**, ch f Intikhab (USA)—Miss Salsa Dancer **M. O'Flynn**
39 **FLAME'S LAST (IRE)**, b f Montjeu (USA)—Flame of Tara **Miss P. F. O'Kelly**
40 B c Namid—Giadamar (IRE) **J. Dolan**
41 **GRANDFIELD (IRE)**, b f Fasliyev (USA)—Vernonhills **B. Cooke**
42 **LISCUNE (IRE)**, b f King's Best (USA)—Royal Lorna (USA) **Bernard Cooke**
43 **LITTLE NYMPH**, ch f Emperor Fountain—Light On Her Toes **S. Fox**
44 **MAKUTI (IRE)**, b f Monashee Mountain (USA)—Lady Anna Livia **T. Ward**
45 **NAKISKA**, b f Darshaan—Star Crystal (IRE) **J. Higgins**
46 **NIGHT CRY (IRE)**, b f Night Shift (USA)—Dariyba (IRE) **Andrew Bradley**
47 **PORTO VENERE (IRE)**, ch f Ashkalani (IRE)—Feather River (USA) **Mr A. Clarke**
48 **RAKITA (IRE)**, b f Rainbow Quest (USA)—Akarita (IRE) **Barouche Stud**
49 **RED VINTO**, ch c Vettori (IRE)—Redgrave Devil **A. Bish**
50 **SAPELE (USA)**, ch f Marquetry (USA)—River Fairy (USA) **D. Dundon**
51 **SEBASTENE (IRE)**, ch f Machiavellian (USA)—Spring Easy (USA) **J. Higgins**
52 **SECOND NATIVE (IRE)**, b f Second Empire (IRE)—Native Magic **R. Arculli**
53 **SEHOYA (IRE)**, br f Second Empire (IRE)—Blue Jazz (IRE) **M. C. Grassick**
54 **SLEEPLESS RAIN (USA)**, br f Gone West (USA)—Seattle Summer (USA) **D. Swan**
55 **STYLISH BID (IRE)**, gr f Desert Style (IRE)—Stately Bid (USA) **A. Finney**
56 **TARIANA (IRE)**, b f Revoque (IRE)—Traumerei (GER) **Miss S. Von Schilcher**
57 **THICK AND EASY (IRE)**, b f Welsh Lion (IRE)—Fast And Straight (IRE) **D. Sheahan**
58 **TURICUM (IRE)**, b g Turtle Island (IRE)—Aglaia (SWI) **R. Weiss**
59 **VALLEE BLANCHE (IRE)**, b f Zafonic (USA)—Grail (USA) **J. Higgins**
60 **WESTERN BRAVE (IRE)**, b g Intikhab (USA)—Ghassak (USA) **Tour Syndicate**
61 **ZACCHEUS (IRE)**, b g Zafonic (USA)—SUDELEY **D. Swan**

TWO-YEAR-OLDS

62 B br f 19/5 Hennessy (USA)—Dancin' On Water (USA) (Salt Lake (USA)) (6706) **Mrs M. J. Grassick**
63 B f 22/2 Desert Sun—Darabaka (IRE) (Doyoun) (14000) **Mr J. Nally**
64 **HONOR LOVE (FR)**, b f 4/3 Pursuit of Love—Honor Kicks (FR) (Highest Honor (FR)) **Mr D. Dundon**
65 Br f 23/2 Giant's Causeway (USA)—Lizanne (USA) (Theatrical) **Mrs B. Facchino**
66 B f 27/3 Mozart (IRE)—Molasses (FR) (Machiavellian) **Miss P. F. O'Kelly**
67 B f 6/4 Elusive Quality (USA)—Naazeq (Nashwan (USA)) (70000) **Mr T. Pabst**
68 B f 3/4 Desert Story (IRE)—Pride In Me (Indian Ridge) **Mrs S. Grassick**
69 B c 15/5 Desert Story (IRE)—Sarah Stokes (IRE) (Brief Truce (USA)) (4023) **Mrs M. J. Grassick**

MR M. J. GRASSICK—continued

70 Br gr c 11/3 Key of Luck (USA)—Stately Bid (USA) (Stately Don (USA)) **Albert Finney**
71 B f 18/4 Bahri (USA)—Tulipe Noire (USA) (Alleged (USA)) **Mrs S. Taylor**
72 Ch f 19/2 Alhaarth (IRE)—Tycooness (IRE) (Last Tycoon) (25000) **Mr K. Campbell**
73 B f 17/4 Zafonic (USA)—Urban Sky (FR) (Groom Dancer (USA)) **Miss C. Tsui**
74 B f 21/2 King's Best (USA)—Wakria (IRE) (Sadler's Wells (USA)) **Mr J. Higgins**
75 B c 9/4 Bahri (USA)—Zakiyya (USA) (Dayjur (USA)) **Mrs S. Grassick**

Assistant Trainer: Mr M C Grassick

Jockey (flat): N. G. McCullagh. **Apprentice:** D. Cannon.

---

247 MR C. J. GRAY, Bridgwater
Postal: **Horlake, Moorland, Bridgwater, Somerset, TA7 0AT.**
Contacts: **HOME (01278) 691359 MOBILE (07989) 768163**

1 **CHARM OFFENSIVE**, 7, b m Zieten (USA)—Shoag (USA) **Mr A P Helliar and Mr A J W Hill**
2 **FIELD MASTER (IRE)**, 8, ch g Foxhound (USA)—Bold Avril (IRE) **K. A. Mantyk**
3 **KING'S MOUNTAIN (USA)**, 5, b g King of Kings (IRE)—Statistic (USA) **G. Doel**
4 **LE FOREZIEN (FR)**, 6, b g Gunboat Diplomacy (FR)—Diane du Forez (FR) **S. C. Botham**
5 **MISSED A NOTE**, 5, br g Missed Flight—Out of Harmony **P. F. Popham**
6 **PEEJAY HOBBS**, 7, ch g Alhijaz—Hicklam Millie **Mrs C. M. L. Gray**
7 **PERFECT HINDSIGHT (IRE)**, 4, b g Spectrum (IRE)—Vinicky (USA) **G. Doel**
8 **RED GENIE**, 7, ch g Primitive Rising (USA)—Marsden Rock **The Hilltop Seven Partnership**
9 **VANORMIX (FR)**, 6, gr g Linamix (FR)—Vadsa Honor (FR) **S. C. Botham**

Other Owners: Mr S. Gregory, F. D. Popham.

Assistant Trainer: Mrs C M L Gray

---

248 MR V. G. GREENWAY, Taunton
Postal: **Manor Farm House, Fitzhead, Taunton, Somerset, TA4 3JZ.**
Contacts: **PHONE (01823) 400091**

1 **JOIZEL (FR)**, 8, b g Fill My Hopes (FR)—Anne de Boizel (FR) **Mr V. G. & Mrs M. M. Greenway**
2 **POLKA**, 10, b g Slip Anchor—Peace Dance **Mr V. G. Greenway**
3 **VEXFORD DELTIC**, 10, b m Deltic (USA)—Suchong **Mr V. G. Greenway**

Other Owners: M. G. Greenway.

---

249 MR S. G. GRIFFITHS, Carmarthen
Postal: **Rwyth Farm, Nantgaredig, Carmarthen, Dyfed, SA32 7LG.**
Contacts: **PHONE (01267) 290321/290120**

1 **SOLVE IT SOBER (IRE)**, 11, b g Carefree Dancer (USA)—Haunted Lady **Mr S. G. Griffiths**
2 **TIRIKUMBA**, 9, ch m Le Moss—Ntombi **Mr S. G. Griffiths**
3 **YOUNG WILL**, 6, b g Keen—Barkston Singer **Mr S. G. Griffiths**

Assistant Trainer: Martyn Roger Griffiths

---

250 MR S. P. GRIFFITHS, Easingwold
Postal: **Longbridge House Farm, Stillington Road, Easingwold, York.**
Contacts: **PHONE (01347) 823589 MOBILE (07967) 039208**
E-MAIL elizabeth@gusl.net

1 **COUNT COUGAR (USA)**, 5, b g Sir Cat (USA)—Gold Script (USA) **M. Grant**
2 **DIAMOND VEIN**, 6, b g Green Dancer (USA)—Blushing Sunrise (USA) **Mrs C. Grant**
3 **HOT GIRL**, 7, b m State Diplomacy (USA)—Hundred Islands **M. Grant**
4 **MISS CEYLON**, 5, b m Brief Truce (USA)—Five Islands **Jumbo Racing**
5 **MISS CHANCELOT**, 4, b f Forzando—Suedoro **Vixen Racing Partnership**
6 **WHITKIRK STAR (IRE)**, 4, b g Alhaarth (IRE)—Three Stars **M. Grant**

MR S. P. GRIFFITHS—continued

THREE-YEAR-OLDS

7 **TORRENS (IRE),** b c Royal Anthem (USA)—Azure Lake (USA) **Mr C. Reynard**

Other Owners: Ms J. M. Grant, Mr J. Horsfall, Ms P. A. McDonnell.

Assistant Trainer: Elizabeth Grant

---

251 | **MR R. GUEST, Newmarket**
Postal: **Chestnut Tree Stables, Hamilton Road, Newmarket, Suffolk, CB8 0NY.**
Contacts: **PHONE (01638) 661508 FAX (01638) 667317 MOBILE (07711) 301095**
E-MAIL raeguest@totalise.co.uk WEBSITE www.raeguest.co.uk

1 **AFTER THE SHOW,** 4, b c Royal Applause—Tango Teaser **Mr M. Ng & Miss L. Thompson**
2 **BRIGHT ANGEL,** 5, b m Alderbrook—Sharp Move **Mrs C. Spurrier**
3 **KENSINGTON (IRE),** 4, b g Cape Cross (IRE)—March Star (IRE) **M. Sakal**
4 **LIGHT OF MORN,** 4, gr f Daylami (IRE)—My Emma **Matthews Breeding And Racing Ltd**
5 **MALUTI,** 4, ch g Piccolo—Persian Blue **Mrs J. A. M. Poulter**
6 **MILLINSKY (USA),** 4, ch f Stravinsky (USA)—Millyant **C. J. Mills**
7 **MIMIC,** 5, b m Royal Applause—Stripanoora **C. J. Mills**
8 **MISS INKHA,** 4, b f Intikhab (USA)—Santi Sana **Mrs J. E. Lury and Mr O. T. Lury**
9 **MONTECRISTO,** 12, br g Warning—Sutosky **Mr Rae Guest**
10 **RIVER OF DIAMONDS,** 4, b g Muhtarram (USA)—City Gambler **J. J. May**
11 **SIR DESMOND,** 7, gr g Petong—I'm Your Lady **Davies, Guest & McCabe**
12 **YOMALO (IRE),** 5, ch m Woodborough (USA)—Alkariyh (USA) **F. C. Nowell**

THREE-YEAR-OLDS

13 **ALRIGHT MY SON (IRE),** b c Pennekamp (USA)—Pink Stone (FR) **J. R. Crickmore**
14 **BAHIA BREEZE,** b f Mister Baileys—Ring of Love **F. C. Nowell**
15 **CREEK DANCER,** b f Josr Algarhoud (IRE)—Dance Land (IRE) **Mrs S. R. Wadman**
16 **CUP OF LOVE (USA),** ch f Behrens (USA)—Cup Of Kindness (USA) **Adrian Smith**
17 **DANIELLA,** b f Dansili—Break Point **Mr & Mrs B. Cooper**
18 **DIAMOND KATIE (IRE),** b f Night Shift (USA)—Fayrooz (USA) **Matthews Breeding And Racing Ltd**
19 **EASY MOVER (IRE),** ch f Bluebird (USA)—Top Brex (FR) **Wendals Herbs Ltd**
20 **FANTASTIC NIGHT (DEN),** ch f Night Shift (USA)—Gaelic's Fantasy (IRE) **Mr P. K. Rolin**
21 **GO LIKE THE WIND,** br f Cape Cross (IRE)—Fly Like The Wind **Cosmic Greyhound Racing Partnership III**
22 **GRAND COURSE (IRE),** ch f Grand Lodge (USA)—
　　　　　　　　　　Star of The Course (USA) **Matthews Breeding And Racing Ltd**
23 **GRANDMA'S GIRL,** b f Desert Style (IRE)—Sakura Queen (IRE) **B. Stewart**
24 Ch f Selkirk (USA)—Midnight Shift (IRE) **C. J. Mills**
25 **MISS RUBY,** ch f Tagula (IRE)—Ruby Heights **Mrs J. E. Lury and Mr O. T. Lury**
26 **PHI PHI (IRE),** b f Fasliyev (USA)—Council Rock **Mr A. Hirschfeld**
27 **PRETTY AS CAN BE,** b f Giant's Causeway (USA)—Pato **Matthews Breeding And Racing Ltd**
28 **ROMA VALLEY (FR),** gr f Sagamix (FR)—Lois (FR) **Mrs J. A. M. Poulter**
29 **SPARTAN ENCORE,** ch g Spartan Monarch—Debs Review **Broomdown Racing 4**
30 B f Lake Coniston (IRE)—Sylvan Dancer (IRE) **J. J. May**
31 **TRAFALGAR SQUARE,** b c King's Best (USA)—Pat Or Else **Matthews Breeding And Racing Ltd**

TWO-YEAR-OLDS

32 **ALL CLUED UP (IRE),** b f 3/3 King Charlemagne (USA)—Clunie (Inchinor)
33 **CHERISH,** br f 15/2 Nashwan (USA)—Chere Amie (USA) (Mr Prospector (USA)) **Miss K. Rausing**
34 **COME WHAT SEPTIMUS (IRE),** ch c 27/3 Shinko Forest (IRE)—
　　　　　　　　Uffizi (IRE) (Royal Academy (USA)) **Storm Again Syndicate**
35 B f 2/4 Woodborough (USA)—Crackling (Electric) (17000) **C. J. Mills**
36 B f 24/4 Xaar—Dicentra (Rambo Dancer (CAN)) (6000)
37 Ch c 17/4 Halling (USA)—Marguerite de Vine (Zilzal (USA)) **Mr Rae Guest**
38 B c 11/3 Intikhab (USA)—Misellina (FR) (Polish Precedent (USA))
39 B f 22/4 Groom Dancer (USA)—Oriel Girl (Beveled (USA)) (1500) **Cinder Farm Stud Syndicate**
40 B f 12/3 Inchinor—Pie In The Sky (Bishop of Cashel) (8000)
41 **PRIMROSE QUEEN,** b f 16/2 Lear Fan (USA)—Primrose Place (USA) (Dayjur (USA)) **Mr Eugene Lismonde**
42 **ROYAL LASS,** b f 28/2 Fraam—Sabotini (Prince Sabo) (1500) **Royal Arms Racing Club**

MR R. GUEST—continued

43 **SUNSET RIDGE (IRE),** b f 3/4 Indian Ridge—Barbara Frietchie (IRE) (Try My Best (USA)) (7500) **DDB Racing**
44 **TEIDE LADY,** ch f 9/1 Nashwan (USA)—Oshiponga (Barathea (IRE)) **Mr E. Duggan**

Other Owners: Mr Ted Dale, Mr D. Moore, Mr M. Willis, Mr D. Willis, Mr S. Balfour, Mr S. A. Sprenger, Ms L. Dorling, Mr Bob Goodes, Mr Bob Young, Mr N. Elsass, Mrs Bridget Rickaby, Mr & Mrs D. J. Veasey, Mr C. Thompson, Mr C. M. Irish, Mr F. Briggs, Mr Terry Jennings, Mr John Wilson, Mr Jim Leyton, Mr A. Davies, Mr S. Russell, Mr P. McQueen, Mr D. Churchman, P. P. Thorman, L. J. M. J. Vaessen.

Assistant Trainer: Colin Campbell

Apprentice: R. Mills. **Amateur:** Ms Rachel Flynn.

252	**MR R. C. GUEST,** Brancepeth

Postal: **Brancepeth Manor Farm, Brancepeth, Nr Crook, Durham, Co. Durham, DL15 9AS.**
Contacts: **PHONE (0191) 373 5220 FAX (0191) 373 9655 MOBILE (07860) 883303**
E-MAIL richard.guest@richardguestracing.co.uk WEBSITE www.richardguestracing.co.uk

1 **ADMIRAL (IRE),** 4, b c Alhaarth (IRE)—Coast Is Clear (IRE) **W. McKay**
2 **APADI (USA),** 9, ch g Diesis—Ixtapa (USA) **Mrs A. Kenny**
3 **ASSUMETHEPOSITION (FR),** 5, gr g Cyborg (FR)—Jeanne Grey (FR) **Mr T. Delaney**
4 **BEAUGENCY (NZ),** 7, br g Prized (USA)—Naiades (NZ) **Gryffindor (www.racingtours.co.uk)**
5 **BEAVER (AUS),** 6, b g Bite The Bullet (USA)—Mahenge (AUS) **P. W. Beck**
6 **BERGERAC (NZ),** 7, b g Just A Dancer (USA)—Guiding Star (NZ) **P. W. Beck**
7 **BLACK SMOKE (IRE),** 8, gr g Ala Hounak—Korean Citizen (IRE) **R & H Burridge and Bard Entertainments**
8 **BLUSHING PRINCE (IRE),** 7, b g Priolo (USA)—Eliade (IRE) **Mr R. C. Guest**
9 **BURNS BELLE,** 4, b f Hawkstone (IRE)—Thorntoun Belle (IRE) **Burns Partnership**
10 **CARIBBEAN COVE (IRE),** 7, gr g Norwich—Peaceful Rose **P. W. Beck**
11 **CASH ON FRIDAY,** 4, b g Bishop of Cashel—Til Friday **Mr R. C. Guest**
12 **CERESFIELD (NZ),** 9, br m Westminster (NZ)—Audrey Rose (NZ) **K. Middleton**
13 **COLLEGE CITY (IRE),** 6, b g College Chapel—Polish Crack (IRE) **Mrs A. Kenny**
14 **DAN DE LION,** 6, b g Danzig Connection (USA)—Fiorini **M. N. Imray**
15 **DARGAVILLE (NZ),** 6, br bl g Sakti (NZ)—Oak Invasion (NZ) **P. W. Beck**
16 **DIAMOND CUTTER (NZ),** 6, br g Strike Diamonds (NZ)—Lough Allen (NZ) **C & G Racing**
17 **DONOVAN (NZ),** 6, b g Stark South (USA)—Agent Jane (NZ) **Concertina Racing Too**
18 **DUB DASH (USA),** 5, b g Siphon (BRZ)—Thesky'sthelimit (USA) **J. S. Kennerley**
19 **FLINTOFF (USA),** 4, ch g Diesis—Sahibah (USA) **Andrew Flintoff & Paul Beck**
20 **GABLA (NZ),** 9, b g Prince of Praise (NZ)—Dynataine (NZ) **T. N. Siviter**
21 **GATORADE (NZ),** 13, ch g Dahar (USA)—Ribena (NZ) **P. W. Beck**
22 **GHADAMES (FR),** 11, b g Synefos (USA)—Ouargla (FR) **Mr R. C. Guest**
23 **GO PETE (NZ),** 6, ch g Senor Pete (USA)—Lillibet (NZ) **P. W. Beck**
24 **HE'S HOT RIGHT NOW (NZ),** 6, b g Pentire—Philadelphia Fox (NZ) **P. W. Beck**
25 **ISELLIDO (IRE),** 6, b br m Good Thyne (USA)—Souled Out (IRE) **C. J. Cookson**
26 **JERICHO III (FR),** 8, b g Lute Antique (FR)—La Salamandre (FR) **P. W. Beck**
27 **LES ARCS (USA),** 5, br g Arch (USA)—La Sarto (USA) **W. McKay**
28 **MAGICO (NZ),** 7, b g Casual Lies (USA)—Majica (NZ) **P. W. Beck**
29 **MANA-MOU BAY (IRE),** 8, b g Ela-Mana-Mou—Summerhill **G. B. Roberts**
30 **MERSEY MIRAGE,** 8, b g King's Signet (USA)—Kirriemuir **The Friar Tuck Racing Club**
31 **MR BIGGLESWORTH (NZ),** 7, ch g Honor Grades (USA)—Panza Anne (NZ) **Bache Silk**
32 **NORTHERN FRIEND,** 5, b g Distinctly North (USA)—Pharaoh's Joy **P. W. Beck**
33 **OUR ARMAGEDDON (NZ),** 8, b g Sky Chase (NZ)—Monte d'oro (NZ) **L. J. Garrett**
34 **PAGE POINT (AUS),** 7, b g Supremo (USA)—She's Fun (NZ) **P. W. Beck**
35 **PAPAWALDO (IRE),** 6, ch g Presenting—Another Bless **Nicholas & Sean Kelly**
36 **POLISHED,** 6, ch g Danzig Connection (USA)—Glitter (FR) **The Cherry Blossom Partnership**
37 **PRIVATE JESSICA,** 4, ch f Cadeaux Genereux—Rose Bay **Blaydon Racers Partnership**
38 **READY TO RUMBLE (NZ),** 8, ch g Danasinga (AUS)—Regal Odyssey (NZ) **P. W. Beck**
39 **RED PERK (IRE),** 8, b g Executive Perk—Supreme View **D. V. Tate**
40 **RED STRIKER,** 11, ch g Gunner B—Cover Your Money **N. B. Mason**
41 **REEDSMAN (IRE),** 4, ch g Fayruz—The Way She Moves **Mr R. C. Guest**
42 **RISKY RHYTHM,** 6, b m Primitive Rising (USA)—Heatheridge (IRE) **Miss A. C. Croxford-Adams**
43 **SCONCED (USA),** 10, ch g Affirmed (USA)—Quaff (USA) **James S. Kennerley And Miss Jenny Hall**
44 **SHEM DYLAN (NZ),** 6, ch g Stark South (USA)—Khozaderry (NZ) **Mr R. C. Guest**
45 **SOVIET SOCIETY (IRE),** 7, b g Moscow Society (USA)—Catchmenot (IRE) **R. W. Smith**
46 **STAN (NZ),** 6, b g Super Imposing (NZ)—Take Care (NZ) **P. W. Beck**
47 **TIGER TALK,** 9, ch g Sabrehill (USA)—Tebre (USA) **P. W. Beck**
48 **TIME TO REFLECT (IRE),** 6, ch g Anshan—Castlemitchle (IRE) **Concertina Racing Three**

MR R. C. GUEST—continued

49 **TUA (NZ)**, 6, br bl g Rainbow Myth (NZ)—Wayside Inn (NZ) **Mr R. C. Guest**
50 **TYNEANDTHYNEAGAIN**, 10, b g Good Thyne (USA)—Radical Lady **N. B. Mason**
51 **VULCAN LANE (NZ)**, 8, ch g Star Way—Smudged (NZ) **Blaydon Racers Partnership**
52 **WHAT'S A FILLY**, 5, b m Bob's Return (IRE)—Pearly-B (IRE) **The Don't Tell Pat Partnership**
53 **WHY THE BIG PAWS**, 7, ch m Minster Son—Springdale Hall (USA) **Blaydon Racers Partnership**
54 **WHY THE LONG FACE**, 8, ch g Grosvenor (NZ)—My Charm (NZ) **J. M. Rogers**
55 **XAIPETE (IRE)**, 13, b g Jolly Jake (NZ)—Rolfete (USA) **N. B. Mason**
56 **YORK RITE (AUS)**, 9, ch g Grand Lodge (USA)—Amazaan (NZ) **P. W. Beck**

Other Owners: Mr S. Alderson, Mrs B. Alderson, P.A. Bache, Miss Frances Baker, C.K. Byers, Miss G. J. Charrington, J. E. S. Colling, Mrs F. R. Colling, P.S. Davies, P.J. F. Goldie, Peter G. Gorvin, Mr P. Hodgkinson, Mr P. J. Kelly, Mr N. Lennon, Mr J. F. McKeon, Miss C. Metcalfe, E. O'Sullivan, J. W. Ryan, Mr G. H Silk., Mr C. K. Siu, J. Tyrrell, L. Vettraino.

Assistant Trainer: Jane Hedley

Jockey (NH): L. McGrath, H. Oliver. **Conditional:** Darren Harold. **Amateur:** Mr J. Moorman, Miss C. Metcalfe.

---

253   MR W. J. HAGGAS, Newmarket
Postal: **Somerville Lodge, Fordham Road, Newmarket, Suffolk, CB8 7AA.**
Contacts: **PHONE (01638) 667013 FAX (01638) 660534**
E-MAIL william@somerville-lodge.co.uk

1 **BONUS (IRE)**, 5, b g Cadeaux Genereux—Khamseh **Highclere Thoroughbred Racing VII**
2 **BRUNEL (IRE)**, 4, b c Marju (IRE)—Castlerahan (IRE) **Highclere Thoroughbred Racing X**
3 **BYGONE DAYS**, 4, ch g Desert King (IRE)—May Light **J. Hanson**
4 **CHOIR LEADER**, 4, b g Sadler's Wells (USA)—Choir Mistress **Cheveley Park Stud**
5 **DEL MAR SUNSET**, 6, b g Unfuwain (USA)—City of Angels **R. A. Dawson**
6 **FYODOR (IRE)**, 4, b g Fasliyev (USA)—Royale Figurine (IRE) **The Fyodor Partnership**
7 **MAJESTIC MISSILE (IRE)**, 4, b c Royal Applause—Tshusick **Flying Tiger Partnership**
8 **MALVERN LIGHT**, 4, b f Zieten (USA)—Michelle Hicks **Tweenhills Racing (Summerhill)**
9 **OBRIGADO (USA)**, 5, b g Bahri (USA)—Glorious Diamond (USA) **J. B. Haggas**
10 **PERLE D'OR (IRE)**, 4, b f Entrepreneur—Rose Society **The Perle d'Or Partnership**
11 **POLAR BEAR**, 5, ch g Polar Falcon (USA)—Aim For The Top (USA) **J. B. Haggas**
12 **RAMPAGE**, 4, ch f Pivotal—Noor El Houdah (IRE) **Cheveley Park Stud**
13 **SUGGESTIVE**, 7, b g Reprimand—Pleasuring **Mrs B. Bassett**

THREE-YEAR-OLDS

14 **AILSA**, b f Bishop of Cashel—Mindomica **Mrs A. H. Daniels & Mr G. Reed**
15 **ALABAMA TWIST**, b c Magic Ring (IRE)—Glass **A.Duke/J.Netherthorpe/B.Smith/J.Guthrie**
16 **ALGHARB**, b br c Mujahid (USA)—Actress **Hamdan Al Maktoum**
17 **ARTFUL WHISPER (USA)**, b br f Machiavellian (USA)—Speak Softly To Me (USA) **C. C. Buckley**
18 **BLUFF**, b g Bluebird (USA)—Show Off **Mr and Mrs A. Peskin**
19 **BROCKHOLE (IRE)**, gr g Daylami (IRE)—Free Spirit (IRE) **Mr & Mrs G. Middlebrook**
20 **CALIFORNIA LAWS**, b g Pivotal—Noor El Houdah (IRE) **Rupert Bear Racing**
21 **CLUELESS**, b c Royal Applause—Pure **W. J. Gredley**
22 **CONFETTI**, ch f Groom Dancer (USA)—Fabulous **Cheveley Park Stud**
23 **CRETE (IRE)**, b c Montjeu (IRE)—Paesanella **Highclere Thoroughbred Racing XXI**
24 **DIG DEEP (IRE)**, b g Entrepreneur—Diamond Quest **G. Roberts/F. Green/Tessona Racing**
25 **DOONEQ**, b c Diktat—Apennina (USA) **Hamdan Al Maktoum**
26 **ELATED (IRE)**, b c Erhaab (USA)—Elauyun (IRE) **Gibson, Goddard, Hamer & Hawkes**
27 **ESKIMO'S NEST**, b f Polar Falcon (USA)—White House **J. M. Greetham**
28 **FIRST GENERATION**, b c Primo Dominie—My Cadeaux **P. S. Jensen**
29 **FLORINO**, b f Polish Precedent (USA)—Flourish **Wyck Hall Stud Ltd**
30 **GINGER SPICE (IRE)**, ch f Cadeaux Genereux—Pop Queen **B. Trew/R. Shead/D. Scott/W. Haggas**
31 **LANGDALE**, ch g Dr Fong (USA)—Ciboure **Mr & Mrs G. Middlebrook**
32 **LUCIDUS**, b g Danzero (AUS)—Lady In Colour (IRE) **Mrs J. J. Dye**
33 **NOVELINA (IRE)**, b f Fusaichi Pegasus (USA)—Novelette **Wentworth Racing (Pty) Ltd**
34 **PINGUS**, b f Polish Precedent (USA)—Maramba **Wood Hall Stud Limited**
35 **REQUIEM (USA)**, b f Royal Anthem (USA)—Bonus (USA) **Dachel Stud**
36 **ROWAN WARNING**, b c Diktat—Golden Seattle (IRE) **Rowan Stud Partnership**
37 **SAN MICHELE**, b f Vettori (IRE)—La Piazza (IRE) **Jolly Farmers Racing & Steve De Martino**
38 **SEAMLESS**, b c Gold Away (IRE)—Failara (FR) **Flying Tiger Partnership**
39 **SHARPLAW STAR**, b f Xaar—Hamsah (IRE) **Miss T. L. Miller**
40 **SOUTH CLUB HILL**, b f Danehill (USA)—Chantereine (USA) **Lael Stable**

MR W. J. HAGGAS—continued

41 **SQUAW DANCE**, ch f Indian Ridge—Likely Story (IRE) **A. Hirschfeld & D. Scott**
42 **STARGAZER JIM (FR)**, br g Fly To The Stars—L'americaine (USA) **N. J. Hughes**
43 **VERY WISE**, b c Pursuit of Love—With Care **J. M. Greetham**
44 **WHISPERING DEATH**, br c Pivotal—Lucky Arrow **G. Roberts/F. M. Green**

TWO-YEAR-OLDS

45 **ABANDON (USA)**, ch f 24/4 Rahy (USA)—Caerless (IRE) (Caerleon (USA)) **Cheveley Park Stud**
46 **ABWAAB**, b c 1/3 Agnes World (USA)—Flitteriss Park (Beldale Flutter (USA)) (60000) **Hamdan Al Maktoum**
47 Br f 9/3 Diktat—Agrippina (Timeless Times (USA))
48 **APPRECIATED**, b f 20/4 Most Welcome—Align (Petong) **Wyck Hall Stud Ltd**
49 **AVELIAN (IRE)**, b c 19/4 Cape Cross (IRE)—
      Mashoura (Shareef Dancer (USA)) (38000) **Highclere Thoroughbred Racing Ltd**
50 B f 8/3 Dansili—Bombalarina (IRE) (Barathea (IRE)) (4000) **Shortgrove Manor Stud**
51 **COMMENTARY**, b f 21/2 Medicean—Eloquent (Polar Falcon (USA)) **Cheveley Park Stud**
52 **DESERVING**, b f 4/3 Grand Lodge (USA)—Superstar Leo (IRE) (College Chapel) **Lael Stable**
53 **DINNER DANCE**, b f 4/4 Groom Dancer (USA)—Misleading Lady (Warning) **J. M. Greetham**
54 **EDAARA (IRE)**, ch f 26/1 Pivotal—Green Bonnet (IRE) (Green Desert (USA)) (130000) **Hamdan Al Maktoum**
55 **FORTRESS**, b f 8/4 Generous (IRE)—Imperial Bailiwick (IRE) (Imperial Frontier (USA)) **Mr & Mrs G. Middlebrook**
56 **FREGATE ISLAND (IRE)**, b g 24/4 Daylami (IRE)—Briery (Salse (USA)) **Mr & Mrs G. Middlebrook**
57 B c 30/5 Averti (IRE)—
      Green Run (USA) (Green Dancer (USA)) (5500) **The Countryside Alliance Racing Partnership**
58 **HEAVEN KNOWS**, ch c 23/4 Halling (USA)—Rambling Rose (Cadeaux Genereux) (50000) **J. B. Haggas**
59 **HENCHMAN**, b c 5/2 Anabaa (USA)—Gay Heroine (Caerleon (USA)) **Cheveley Park Stud**
60 **HOPEFUL PURCHASE (IRE)**, ch c 3/2 Grand Lodge (USA)—Funoon (IRE) (Kris) (67068) **J. Hanson**
61 **IN REALITY**, ch f 17/2 Fantastic Light (USA)—Poppadam (Salse (USA)) (85000) **W. J. Gredley**
62 **JEUDI**, b c 23/1 Montjeu (IRE)—Portorosa (USA) (Irish River (FR)) **J. B. Haggas**
63 B f 21/4 Giant's Causeway (USA)—June Moon (IRE) (Sadler's Wells (USA)) **Wentworth Racing (Pty) Ltd**
64 **LOVE OR MONEY**, b f 20/2 In The Wings—Lafite (Robellino (USA)) (50000) **Wood Hall Stud Limited**
65 **MILITARY CROSS**, b c 20/2 Cape Cross (IRE)—Tipsy (Kris) **Cheveley Park Stud**
66 **MONT ETOILE (IRE)**, b f 10/4 Montjeu (IRE)—Troyes (Troy) **A. Hirschfeld & D. Scott**
67 **NAQI**, ch f 18/2 Cadeaux Genereux—Farha (USA) (Nureyev (USA)) **Hamdan Al Maktoum**
68 **NATIONAL HEALTH**, b c 3/2 Medicean—Precious (Danehill (USA)) (45000) **Wentworth Racing (Pty) Ltd**
69 **NUSOOR (IRE)**, b c 25/2 Fasliyev (USA)—Zulfaa (USA) (Bahri (USA)) **Hamdan Al Maktoum**
70 **PEARL'S GIRL**, gr f 18/2 King's Best (USA)—Karsiyaka (IRE) (Kahyasi) (21000) **Winterbeck Manor Stud Ltd**
71 B f 8/2 Indian Danehill (IRE)—Poetry In Motion (IRE) (Ballad Rock) (12000) **Peter Ebdon**
72 B c 27/1 Barathea (IRE)—Poleaxe (Selkirk (USA)) (23000) **It Doesn't Matter**
73 **QUTONG**, ch c 17/2 Dr Fong (USA)—Ravine (Indian Ridge) (105000) **J. D. Ashenheim**
74 **RAVISH**, b f 9/5 Efisio—
      Looks Sensational (USA) (Majestic Light (USA)) (40240) **Highclere Thoroughbred Racing Ltd**
75 **RED DIADEM**, b f 27/3 Pivotal—Red Tiara (USA) (Mr Prospector (USA)) **Cheveley Park Stud**
76 Ch f 10/3 Groom Dancer (USA)—Remarkable (Wolfhound (USA)) **Don Magnifico Partnership**
77 **SECRET BLEND**, b f 4/3 Pivotal—It's A Secret (Polish Precedent (USA)) **Cheveley Park Stud**
78 **SHARPLAW AUTUMN (USA)**, b f 10/3 Red Ransom (USA)—
      Hawzah (Green Desert (USA)) (71827) **Miss T. L. Miller**
79 B f 27/2 Zafonic (USA)—Showering (Danehill (USA)) (20000) **B. N. Wallace**
80 **SOCIAL CALL**, b f 22/3 Danehill Dancer (IRE)—Society Rose (Saddlers' Hall (IRE)) **Cheveley Park Stud**
81 **SOFIE**, ch f 29/3 Efisio—Krista (Kris) (10000) **Mrs J. J. Dye**
82 **STARSHIP (IRE)**, b f 11/4 Galileo (IRE)—Council Rock (General Assembly (USA)) **A. Hirschfeld**

Other Owners: I. Brown, C. G. Ferrett, MR W. J. Haggas, The Hon H. M. Herbert, R. Jackson, Mrs G. S. Jackson, Mrs S. J. Jensen, Ms E. Murphy, R. J. Rendell, Mrs R. Ridout, J. E. Stringer, J. Waddington, A. W. D. Wright.

---

254 MISS V. HAIGH, Bawtry
Postal: **Martin Grange, Bawtry, Doncaster, South Yorkshire, DN10 6DD.**
Contacts: **PHONE** (01302) 714981/711018 **FAX** (01302) 711018 **MOBILE** (07816) 772451
E-MAIL vhaighracing01@aol.com

1 **BINT ROYAL (IRE)**, 7, ch m Royal Abjar (USA)—Living Legend (USA) **Miss V. Haigh**
2 **LOTTIE**, 4, b f Robellino (USA)—Montserrat **Miss V. Haigh**
3 **ROAN RAIDER (USA)**, 5, gr ro g El Prado (IRE)—Flirtacious Wonder (USA) **Tomlinson, Shelley, Haigh**

THREE-YEAR-OLDS

4 **BRUT FORCE (IRE)**, b g Desert Style (IRE)—La Foscarina **Miss V. Haigh**

MISS V. HAIGH—continued

TWO-YEAR-OLDS

5 B c 9/4 Fasliyev (USA)—Festive Season (USA) (Lypheor) (12072) **W. McKay**
6 B f 26/2 Definite Article—Key To Paris (ARG) (Profit Key (USA)) (8047) **W. McKay**
7 B f 2/2 Shinko Forest (IRE)—Phylella (Persian Bold) (13413) **Pisani PLC**
8 B f 3/4 Night Shift (USA)—Seduce (Pursuit of Love) (8382) **W. McKay**
9 B f 9/4 Danehill Dancer (IRE)—Simla Bibi (Indian Ridge) (20120) **W. McKay**
10 B c 11/3 King of Kings (IRE)—Statistic (USA) (Mr Prospector (USA)) (13413) **Pisani PLC**
11 B f 22/2 Mull of Kintyre (USA)—Sunset Park (IRE) (Red Sunset) (6706) **W. McKay**

Other Owners: D. J. Shelley, M. J. Tomlinson.

Jockey (flat): M. Henry. **Apprentice:** Robert Miles. **Amateur:** Miss V. Haigh.

---

255 | **MR J. S. HALDANE, Mindrum**
Postal: **The Yard Cottage, Mindrum, Northumberland, TD12 4QN.**
Contacts: **PHONE (01890) 850382**

1 **BIG LUGS,** 9, ch g Rakaposhi King—Winnowing (IRE) **Mr J. S. Haldane**
2 **BLACK BOB (IRE),** 8, b g Good Thyne (USA)—Midsummer Blends (IRE) **John & Mary Stenhouse**
3 **BURNING QUESTION,** 7, ch g Alderbrook—Give Me An Answer **Mrs Hugh Fraser**
4 **CAMP HILL,** 11, gr g Ra Nova—Baytino **Mrs Hugh Fraser**
5 **DARK MANDATE (IRE),** 7, b br m Mandalus—Ceoltoir Dubh **Mrs Hugh Fraser**
6 **HIGH EXPECTATIONS (IRE),** 10, ch g Over The River (FR)—Andy's Fancy (IRE) **John & Mary Stenhouse**
7 **ORANGINO,** 7, b g Primo Dominie—Sweet Jaffa **Mr J. S. Haldane**
8 **PRINCE OF PERILS,** 11, b g Lord Bud—Kumari Peril **John & Mary Stenhouse**
9 **THEATRE RIGHTS (IRE),** 5, ch g Old Vic—Deep Perk (IRE) **John & Mary Stenhouse**

Jockey (flat): P. McKewon. **Jockey (NH):** M. Bradburne. **Conditional:** N. Hannity. **Apprentice:** D. Fentiman.

---

256 | **MR A. M. HALES, Aylesbury**
Postal: **Ladymead Farm, Quainton, Aylesbury, Buckinghamshire, HP22 4AN.**
Contacts: **OFFICE (01296) 655255 FAX (01296) 651319 MOBILE (07771) 511652**
E-MAIL alex@alexhalesracing.com

1 **BUFFALO BILL (IRE),** 9, ch g Be My Native (USA)—Sylvia Fox **The West One Partnership**
2 **FULL ON,** 8, b g Le Moss—Flighty Dove **Coach House Racing**
3 **GO CLASSIC,** 5, b m Classic Cliche (IRE)—Edraianthus **It'll Be Fine Partnership**
4 **HELLO STRANGER (IRE),** 9, gr g Roselier (FR)—Emily Bishop (IRE) **Coach House Racing**
5 **HERMANO (IRE),** 8, b br g Malmsey (USA)—Ballyhornan VII **Mrs M. Logan**
6 **LOTS OF MAGIC,** 9, b g Magic Ring (IRE)—Pounelta **G. R. P. N. Valentine**
7 **PLEASED TO RECEIVE (IRE),** 5, ch g Beneficial—Cheeney's Gift **The Halestones Partnership**
8 **SALTANGO (GER),** 6, b g Acatenango (GER)—Salde (GER) **Cohen, Cleary, Kaplan, Minns, Payne, Wilson**
9 **SEAL OF OFFICE,** 6, ch g Mark of Esteem (IRE)—Minskip (USA) **The West One Partnership**
10 **SHARP RIGGING (IRE),** 5, b g Son of Sharp Shot (IRE)—In The Rigging (USA) **The Sharpshooters**
11 **STRATHCLYDE (IRE),** 6, b g Petong—It's Academic **A. M. Spargo**
12 **THYNE SUPREME (IRE),** 6, b g Good Thyne (USA)—Lisfuncheon Adage **Mrs S. E. Lindley**
13 **TIASFOURTH,** 4, b f Contract Law (USA)—Nordic Crown (USA) **J. C. Smith**
14 **VIVA FOREVER (FR),** 6, br m Lando (GER)—Very Mighty (FR) **P. A. Deal**
15 **WAGES,** 5, b g Lake Coniston (IRE)—Green Divot **Coach House Racing**

THREE-YEAR-OLDS

16 **MAGDELAINE,** b f Sinndar (IRE)—Crystal Drop **Wood Hall Stud Limited**
17 **MAURO (IRE),** b f Danehill Dancer (IRE)—Stop The Traffic (IRE) **Wood Hall Stud Limited**
18 **OUR WILDEST DREAMS,** b f Benny The Dip (USA)—Imperial Scholar (IRE) **Mr N. D. Byrne**
19 **SASTRE (IRE),** b f Bluebird (USA)—No Rehearsal (FR) **Wood Hall Stud Limited**

Other Owners: A. L. Cohen, Mr B. J. Coulter, M. Dragisic, Mr M. Gould, MR A. M. Hales, P. J. Minns, T. D. O'Sullivan, J. E. Payne, G. R. Poole, Mr J. Tyndall, Mrs T. Yates.

Amateur: Mr D. Lowe.

257 MISS S. E. HALL, Middleham

Postal: **Brecongill, Coverham, Leyburn, North Yorkshire, DL8 4TJ.**
Contacts: PHONE **(01969) 640223** FAX **(01969) 640567**
E-MAIL sally@brecongill.co.uk

1 **FRENCH TUNE (FR),** 7, ch g Green Tune (USA)—Guerre de Troie **Colin Platts**
2 **KATY O'HARA,** 6, b m Komaite (USA)—Amy Leigh (IRE) **Colin Platts**
3 **SIR LAMB,** 9, gr g Rambo Dancer (CAN)—Caroline Lamb **Colin Platts**
4 **ZERO POINT,** 4, b g Danzero (AUS)—Uniform **Colin Platts**

THREE-YEAR-OLDS

5 **BLUE OPAL,** b f Bold Edge—Second Affair (IRE) **Colin Platts**
6 **BOLD HAZE,** ch g Bold Edge—Melody Park **Mrs J. Hodgson**
7 B f Kayf Tara—Caroline Lamb **Miss S. E. Hall**

TWO-YEAR-OLDS

8 **HUNTING HAZE,** b g 15/3 Foxhound (USA)—Second Affair (IRE) (Pursuit of Love) (8500) **Mrs J. Hodgson**
9 Gr c 19/4 Classic Cliche (IRE)—Lizzy Lamb (Bustino) **Miss S. E. Hall**

Other Owners: Miss S. E. Hall, Colin Platts.

Assistant Trainer: Colin Platts

Jockey (NH): R. Johnson.

258 MR G. A. HAM, Axbridge

Postal: **Rose Farm, Rooksbridge, Axbridge, Somerset, BS26 2TH.**
Contacts: HOME **(01934) 750331** FAX **(01934) 751341** MOBILE **(07732) 979962**
E-MAIL info@rosefarmdevelopents.co.uk

1 **BLACK SWAN (IRE),** 5, b g Nashwan (USA)—Sea Spray (IRE) **C. B. Taylor**
2 **BOSS ROYAL,** 8, ch g Afzal—Born Bossy **The Holmes Office Limited**
3 **BROADWAY BAY,** 7, b g Karinga Bay—Brownscroft **Mrs W. D. Smith**
4 **CODY,** 6, ch g Zilzal (USA)—Ibtihaj (USA) **P. A. Dales**
5 **FIZZY LIZZY,** 5, b m Cool Jazz—Formidable Liz **Rose Farm Developments (UK) Ltd**
6 **GEORGIC BLAZE,** 11, b g Petoski—Pooka **E. Simmons**
7 **GORDY'S JOY,** 5, b m Cloudings (IRE)—Beatle Song **Sally & Tom Dalley**
8 **IDEAL JACK (FR),** 9, b g Agent Bleu (FR)—Nuit des Fanges (FR) **The Liskey Partnership**
9 **JACK DURRANCE (IRE),** 5, b g Polish Precedent (USA)—Atlantic Desire (IRE) **The Jack Durrance Partnership**
10 **MILK AND SULTANA,** 5, b m Millkom—Premier Princess **D. M. Drury**
11 **MILLKOM ELEGANCE,** 6, b m Millkom—Premier Princess **Rose Farm Developments (UK) Ltd**
12 **PENNY'S CROWN,** 6, b m Reprimand—Two And Sixpence (USA)
13 **REELINGA,** 6, b m Karinga Bay—Reeling **Mrs S. M. Fletcher**
14 **RESISTANCE (IRE),** 8, br g Phardante (FR)—Shean Hill (IRE) **Rose Farm Developments (UK) Ltd**
15 **SAXE-COBURG (IRE),** 8, b g Warning—Saxon Maid
16 **SNINFIA (IRE),** 5, b m Hector Protector (USA)—Christmas Kiss **Rose Farm Developments (UK) Ltd**
17 **UNDER CONSTRUCTION,** 7, b g Pennekamp (USA)—Madame Nureyev (USA) **Sally & Tom Dalley**

THREE-YEAR-OLDS

18 **INDIAN SAGE,** b c Awesome—Angharad Lyn **Mr J. Thomas**
19 **MILLQUISTA D'OR,** b f Millkom—Gild The Lily **Razzle Racing Partnership**
20 **ROOKS BRIDGE (IRE),** ch g General Monash (USA)—Lisa's Pride (IRE) **Rose Farm Developments (UK) Ltd**

Other Owners: Mr J. Broomfield, P. R. Masters, Mrs K. E. Masters, Mr K. Shaw, P. A. Terrett.

Jockey (flat): A. Daly, J. Quinn. **Jockey (NH):** R. Greene, V. Slattery. **Conditional:** E. Dehdashti, D. Cosgrave. **Apprentice:** J. F. McDonald.

259 MRS M. C. HAMBRO, Moreton-in-the-Marsh
Postal: **Cotswold Stud, Sezincote, Moreton-in-the-Marsh, Gloucestershire, GL56 9TB.**
Contacts: **PHONE (01386) 700700 FAX (01386) 700701 MOBILE (07860) 632990**
E-MAIL **maryhambro@cotswoldstud.com**

1 **BEECHY BANK (IRE)**, 7, b m Shareef Dancer (USA)—Neptunalia **Richard A. Hambro**
2 **BRUERN (IRE)**, 8, b g Aahsaylad—Bob's Girl (IRE) **Richard A. Hambro**
3 **DOVEDALE**, 5, b m Groom Dancer (USA)—Peetsie (IRE) **Richard A. Hambro**
4 **KINGHAM**, 5, ch g Desert Prince (IRE)—Marie de Flandre (FR) **Richard A. Hambro**
5 **KITEBROOK**, 4, b f Saddlers' Hall (IRE)—Neptunalia **Richard A. Hambro**
6 **OAT HILL**, 4, b g Mtoto—Chaloupe **Richard A. Hambro**
7 **STANWAY**, 6, b g Presenting—Nicklup **Cotswold Stud**

THREE-YEAR-OLDS

8 **DIDBROOK**, b f Alzao (USA)—Nedaarah **Richard A. Hambro**
9 **DORN HILL**, b f Lujain (USA)—Benedicite **Richard A. Hambro**

TWO-YEAR-OLDS

10 B f 14/4 Pivotal—Nedaarah (Reference Point) **Richard A. Hambro**

Jockey (flat): Vince Slattery.

260 MRS D. A. HAMER, Carmarthen
Postal: **Bryngors Uchaf, Nantycaws, Carmarthen, Dyfed, SA32 8EY.**
Contacts: **HOME (01267) 234585 MOBILE (07870) 643185**

1 **ALESSANDRO SEVERO**, 6, gr g Brief Truce (USA)—Altaia (FR) **M. I. Thomas**
2 **COUNT TONY**, 11, ch g Keen—Turtle Dove **B. E. Collett**
3 **DERE LYN**, 7, b g Awesome—Our Resolution **W. L. Phillips**
4 **GRIMSHAW (USA)**, 10, ch g St Jovite (USA)—Loa (USA) **W. J. Cole**
5 **POWER UNIT**, 10, ch g Risk Me (FR)—Hazel Bee **Mr C. A. Hanbury**
6 **RED MOOR (IRE)**, 5, gr g Eagle Eyed (USA)—Faakirah **Hanford's Chemist Ltd**
7 **THAT'S FOR SURE**, 5, b br g Forzando—Sure Flyer (IRE) **D. T. Davies**
8 **TREBERTH POLLY**, 8, b m Mon Tresor—Solbella **Treberth Partnership**

Assistant Trainer: Mr M P Hamer

261 MRS A. HAMILTON, Newcastle Upon Tyne
Postal: **Claywalls Farm, Capheaton, Newcastle Upon Tyne, NE19 2BP.**
Contacts: **PHONE (01830) 530219**

1 **DIVET HILL**, 11, b g Milieu—Bargello's Lady **I. Hamilton**
2 **HEDCHESTER**, 4, b g Missed Flight—Lady Manello **I. Hamilton**
3 **LUCKY DUCK**, 8, ch g Minster Son—Petroc Concert **I. Hamilton**
4 **MISS ROYELLO**, 8, b m Royal Fountain—Lady Manello **I. Hamilton**
5 **MR HAWKEYE (USA)**, 6, ch g Royal Academy (USA)—Port Plaisance (USA) **I. Hamilton**
6 **PRIMITIVE POPPY**, 6, b m Primitive Rising (USA)—Lady Manello **I. Hamilton**
7 **TYNEDALE (IRE)**, 6, b g Good Thyne (USA)—Book of Rules (IRE) **I. Hamilton**

Assistant Trainer: Ian Hamilton

262 MRS A. C. HAMILTON, Minto
Postal: **Old Orchard Cottage, Cavers, Hawick.**
Contacts: **PHONE (01450) 376399 MOBILE (07808) 763507**

1 **RED GAUNTLET**, 12, b g Wonderful Surprise—Border Minstrel **Mrs M. A. Bowie**
2 **WHAT A NIGHT**, 6, gr g Environment Friend—Misty Night **Mr & Mrs J. Hamilton & Mr J. Bowie**

Assistant Trainer: Mr G Hamilton

263 **MRS A. J. HAMILTON-FAIRLEY, Hook**
Postal: **Moor Place, Plough Lane, Bramshill, Hook, Hampshire, RG27 0RF.**
Contacts: **PHONE (0118) 932 6269 FAX (0118) 932 6085 MOBILE (07798) 577761**
E-MAIL **mouse@hamilton-fairley.co.uk**

1 **FFIZZAMO GO**, 4, b g Forzando—Lady Lacey **Hamilton-Fairley Racing**
2 **FRENCH MANNEQUIN (IRE)**, 6, b br m Key of Luck (USA)—Paris Model (IRE) **Runs In The Family**
3 **HATCH A PLAN (IRE)**, 4, b g Vettori (IRE)—Fast Chick **Hamilton-Fairley Racing**
4 **MOUNT BENGER**, 5, ch g Selkirk (USA)—Vice Vixen (CAN) **Hamilton-Fairley Racing**
5 **ROCK GARDEN (IRE)**, 6, br m Bigstone (IRE)—Woodland Garden **Mrs A. J. Hamilton-Fairley**
6 **THESPIAN LADY**, 4, b br f Kirkwall—Drama School **Ann Plummer & Friends**
7 **TILLA**, 5, b m Bin Ajwaad (IRE)—Tosca **Mrs C. M. Hurst-Brown**

Other Owners: Mr G. N. Hamilton-Fairley.

264 **MR M. D. HAMMOND, Middleham**
Postal: **Oakwood Stables, East Witton Road, Middleham, Leyburn, North Yorkshire, DL8 4PT.**
Contacts: **PHONE (01969) 625223 FAX (01969) 625224**
E-MAIL **mdhammondracing@aol.com**

1 **A MILLION FRANKS (IRE)**, 4, b g Insan (USA)—Copper Hill (IRE) **F. Hanson**
2 **ARCHIRONDEL**, 7, b g Bin Ajwaad (IRE)—Penang Rose (NZ) **The Archi Partnership**
3 **ASTON LAD**, 4, b c Bijou d'inde—Fishki **Mr S. T. Brankin & Mr M. D. Hammond**
4 **BORIS THE SPIDER**, 4, b g Makbul—Try Vickers (USA) **The Adbrokes Partnership**
5 **CHARLOTTE VALE**, 4, ch f Pivotal—Drying Grass Moon **P. J. Davies**
6 **DANNY LEAHY (FR)**, 5, b g Danehill (USA)—Paloma Bay (IRE) **Mr D. Green**
7 **DARK DAY BLUES (IRE)**, 4, ch g Night Shift (USA)—Tavildara (IRE) **Mr M. D. Hammond**
8 **DEEP WATER (USA)**, 11, b g Diesis—Water Course (USA) **The County Set**
9 **DIVEX (IRE)**, 4, b g Taipan (IRE)—Ebony Countess (IRE) **The County Set (Two)**
10 **FAIR SPIN**, 5, ch g Pivotal—Frankie Fair (IRE) **L. Thomas**
11 **GEORGE THE BEST (IRE)**, 4, b g Imperial Ballet (IRE)—En Retard (IRE) **Mr M. D. Hammond**
12 **GREEN 'N' GOLD**, 5, b m Cloudings (IRE)—Fishki **Mr E. Whalley**
13 **HEIDI III (FR)**, 10, b g Bayolidaan (FR)—Irlandaise (FR) **J. McAllister**
14 **HIGH COUNTRY (IRE)**, 5, b g Danehill (USA)—Dance Date (IRE) **F. Hanson**
15 **HOMBRE**, 10, ch g Shernazar—Delray Jet (USA) **R. D. Bickenson**
16 **KARO DE VINDECY (FR)**, 7, b g Mollicone Junior (FR)—Preves du Forez (FR) **Racing Management & Training Ltd**
17 **KETTONG (IRE)**, 5, b m Among Men (USA)—Kettenblume **Mr J. H. Eckersall**
18 **LATE ARRIVAL**, 8, b g Emperor Jones (USA)—Try Vickers (USA) **Mrs A. J. Findlay**
19 **LIONHEART (IRE)**, 5, ch g Rashar (USA)—Greyford River **Mrs H. E. Aitkin**
20 **MANBOW (IRE)**, 7, b g Mandalus—Treble Base (IRE) **Hope Springs Eternal**
21 **MEXICAN (USA)**, 6, b g Pine Bluff (USA)—Cuando Quiere (USA) **M. T. Mccarthy**
22 **RECTANGLE (IRE)**, 5, ch g Fayruz—Moona (USA) **The Rectangle Partnership**
23 **RICH CHIC (IRE)**, 4, b br f Sri Pekan (USA)—Ring Side (IRE) **S. C. B. Ltd & Mr G. Shiel**
24 **ROYAL WINDMILL (IRE)**, 6, b g Ali-Royal (IRE)—Salarya (FR) **Oakwood Racing Partnership**
25 **SIMONSTOWN**, 5, ch g Pivotal—Watership (USA) **Paul & Anne Sellars**
26 **TEE-JAY (IRE)**, 9, ch g Un Desperado (FR)—N T Nad **T. J. Equestrian Ltd**
27 **TIDY (IRE)**, 5, b h Mujadil (USA)—Neat Shilling (IRE) **Mr P. Davies**
28 **TITUS SALT (USA)**, 4, ch g Gentlemen (ARG)—Farewell Partner (USA) **Oakwood Racing Partnership**
29 **TRAFALGAR MAN**, 4, b br g Scribano—Call Over **J. M. Newbould**
30 **TRAVEL SUPREME**, 5, b g Makbul—Celtic Lady **"Travel Cruiser" Concessionaires Ltd**
31 **WASHBROOK**, 4, b g Royal Applause—Alacrity **Pentland Times Partnership**
32 **WEST POINT**, 8, ch g Unfuwain (USA)—Western Reel (USA) **Turner Technology Ltd**
33 **YOUNG WARRIOR (IRE)**, 4, b g Desert Style (IRE)—Arctic Splendour (USA) **Paul & Anne Sellars**

THREE-YEAR-OLDS

34 **CALFRAZ**, b br g Tamure (IRE)—Pas de Chat **J. McAllister**
35 **EL REY ROYALE**, b g Royal Applause—Spanish Serenade **A. Walker**
36 **MCCORMACK (IRE)**, b c Desert Story (IRE)—La Loba (IRE) **R. D. Bickenson**
37 **MISTER BUZZ**, b c Mind Games—Compact Disc (IRE) **J. Buzzeo**
38 **NOW AND ZEN**, b g Whittingham (IRE)—Uae Flame (USA) **Mr G. Yeung**
39 **PREMIER TIMES**, ch g Timeless Times (USA)—Lady Magician **Pentland Times Partnership**
40 **RASSEEM (IRE)**, b f Fasliyev (USA)—Yorba Linda (IRE) **I. B. Ender**
41 **RECTANGLE BLUE**, b g Atraf—Golden Decoy **The Rectangle Partnership**
42 **SCORPIO SALLY (IRE)**, b f Mujadil (USA)—Clear Procedure (USA) **Racing Management & Training Ltd**

MR M. D. HAMMOND—continued

TWO-YEAR-OLDS

43 B c 30/4 Desert Story (IRE)—She-Wolff (IRE) (Pips Pride) (17000) **A. Walker**

Other Owners: R. D. Anderson, J. Bell, G. Godsman, D. Godsman, E. D. Haggart, A. Harding, Mrs G. Mackintosh, Mr R. Marks, R. Morrice, Mrs M. E. Powney-Jones, B. Raper, P. Sellars, Mrs P. A. Sellars, J Thomson, H. W. Voigt, O. R. Weeks.

Assistant Trainer: Ernie Patterson

---

265 **MR R. HANNON, Marlborough**
Postal: **East Everleigh Stables, Everleigh, Marlborough, Wiltshire, SN8 3EY.**
Contacts: **PHONE (01264) 850 254 FAX (01264) 850 820**

1 BOHOLA FLYER (IRE), 4, b f Barathea (IRE)—Sharp Catch (IRE) **W. Durkan**
2 BOOGIE STREET, 4, b c Compton Place—Tart And A Half **Hippodrome Racing**
3 CAVERAL, 4, ch f Ashkalani (IRE)—Melting Gold (USA) **A. L. Stalder**
4 CELLO, 4, gr c Pivotal—Raffelina (USA) **L. S. A. Stalder**
5 CORKY (IRE), 4, b g Intikhab (USA)—Khamseh **Robert Whitworth & Jane Whitworth**
6 DAFORE, 4, b c Dr Fong (USA)—Aquaglow **Fieldspring Racing Syndicate**
7 DESERT HAWK, 4, b c Cape Cross (IRE)—Milling (IRE) **D. Boocock**
8 DORIS SOUTER (IRE), 5, b br m Desert Story (IRE)—Hope And Glory (USA) **A. F. J. Merritt**
9 ENFORD PRINCESS, 4, b f Pivotal—Expectation **Major A. M. Everett**
10 FAREWELL GIFT, 4, b g Cadeaux Genereux—Daring Ditty **Lady Whent and Friends**
11 FUEL CELL (IRE), 4, b c Desert Style (IRE)—Tappen Zee **A. F. M. (Holdings) Ltd**
12 HABANERO, 4, b c Cadeaux Genereux—Queen of Dance (IRE) **Waney Racing Group Inc**
13 HURRICANE ALAN (IRE), 5, b br h Mukaddamah (USA)—Bint Al Balad (IRE) **I. A. N. Wight**
14 IF PARADISE, 4, b c Compton Place—Sunley Stars **Mrs J. Wood**
15 LORD LINKS (IRE), 4, ch g Daggers Drawn (USA)—Lady From Limerick (IRE) **Coriolan Links Partnership VI**
16 LUCAYAN LEGEND (IRE), 4, b c Docksider (USA)—Capo di Monte **Lucayan Stud Ltd**
17 LUCKY SPIN, 4, b f Pivotal—Perioscope **G. C. Scudder**
18 MISSUS LINKS (USA), 4, b f Lure (USA)—Cozisaidso (USA) **Coriolan Partnership II**
19 MOONLIGHT MAN, 4, ch c Night Shift (USA)—Fleeting Rainbow **J. A. Lazzari**
20 PRESTO SHINKO (IRE), 4, b g Shinko Forest (IRE)—Swift Chorus **Major A. M. Everett**
21 PSYCHIATRIST, 4, ch g Dr Devious (IRE)—Zahwa **R. C. Tooth**
22 RED SPELL (IRE), 4, ch c Soviet Star (USA)—A-to-Z (IRE) **Mrs N. F. Lee**
23 RIDGE BOY (IRE), 4, b c Indian Ridge—Bold Tina (IRE) **Mrs C. Harrington**
24 SGT PEPPER (IRE), 4, b c Fasliyev—Amandine (IRE) **Mr A. T. Macdonald**
25 TREGARRON, 4, br g Efisio—Language of Love **J. R. Good**

THREE-YEAR-OLDS

26 ABIDE (FR), ch f Pivotal—Ariadne (GER) **Highclere Thoroughbred Racing XVIII**
27 AIGUILLE (USA), b c Royal Academy (USA)—Premier Peak (USA) **Fieldspring Racing Syndicate**
28 AMAZIN, b c Primo Dominie—Aegean Blue **K. Panos**
29 AUNT JULIA, b f In The Wings—Original **Justin Dowley & Michael Pescod**
30 BALTIC DIP (IRE), b f Benny The Dip (USA)—Drei (USA) **Thurloe Thoroughbreds VIII**
31 BENTLEY'S BUSH (IRE), ch f Barathea (IRE)—Veiled Threat (IRE) **Off Trak Partnership**
32 BORN TO BE BOLD, ch c Bold Edge—Birthday Venture **Julian Horn-Smith and Terry Barwick**
33 CAYMAN COLONY (IRE), b c Namid—Imperialist (IRE) **I. A. N. Wight**
34 CHALISON (IRE), b c Anabaa (USA)—Raincloud **N. R. Hodges**
35 CHAPTER (IRE), ch c Sinndar (IRE)—Web of Intrigue **Highclere Thoroughbred Racing XXII**
36 CORNUS, ch c Inchinor—Demerger (USA) **D. M. D. Mort**
37 COUNCELLOR (FR), b c Gilded Time (USA)—Sudden Storm Bird (USA) **Highclere Thoroughbred Racing XX**
38 CRESCENT LADY, ch f Kris—Prima Cominna **Exors of the Late Mrs J. A. Daniels**
39 CUEVAS BAY, b f Robellino (USA)—Down The Valley **J. R. Shannon**
40 EASY FEELING (IRE), b f Night Shift (USA)—Talena **Speedlith Group**
41 EDGE OF BLUE, b g Bold Edge—Blue Goddess **Lady Whent and Friends**
42 ELGIN MARBLES, b g Lujain (USA)—Bold Gem **Jumeirah Racing**
43 GALEOTA (IRE), b c Mujadil (USA)—Refined (IRE) **J. A. Lazzari**
44 GEOMETRIC, b c Octagonal (NZ)—Liska's Dance (USA) **The Royal Ascot Racing Club**
45 GOLDEN DYNASTY, ch c Erhaab (USA)—Ajeebah (IRE) **Mrs E. A. Judd**
46 HALLUCINATE, b c Spectrum (IRE)—Swift Spring (FR) **I. T. S. Racing**
47 HE'S A STAR, ch g Mark of Esteem (IRE)—Sahara Belle (USA) **Mrs J. P. E. Cunningham**
48 JAMAARON, ch c Bachir (IRE)—Kentmere (FR) **N. A. Woodcock**
49 JEWEL IN THE SAND (IRE), b f Bluebird (USA)—Dancing Drop **Sand Associates**

MR R. HANNON—continued

50 **JUST A TRY (USA)**, ch c Lure (USA)—Boubasis (USA) **R. Barby**
51 **KAMAKIRI (IRE)**, b c Trans Island—Alpine Flair (IRE) **M. Pescod**
52 **KINGS QUAY**, b c Montjeu (IRE)—Glen Rosie (IRE) **J. R. May**
53 **LOVE AFFAIR (IRE)**, b f Tagula (IRE)—Changing Partners **Speedlith Group**
54 **MADHAVI**, gr f Diktat—Grey Galava **White Beech Farm**
55 **NORTH SHORE (IRE)**, b c Soviet Star (USA)—Escape Path **D. Boocock**
56 **OAKLEY ABSOLUTE**, ch c Bluegrass Prince (IRE)—Susie Oakley VII **B. C. Oakley**
57 **PRINCE SAMOS (IRE)**, b c Mujadil (USA)—Sabaniya (FR) **Mrs S. M. Costello-Haloute**
58 **SCREWDRIVER**, b c Entrepreneur—Lust **R. C. Tooth**
59 **SERENADE BLUE**, gr f Linamix (FR)—Bimbola (FR) **Bob Lalemant**
60 **SOLANICH**, ch g Inchinor—Gussy Marlowe **N. R. Hodges**
61 **SOLENT (IRE)**, b c Montjeu (IRE)—Stylish **Mrs J. Wood**
62 **SPREE (IRE)**, gr f Dansili—Ibiza (GER) **A. F. Merritt & Partners**
63 **ST ANDREWS STORM (USA)**, b c Storm Creek (USA)—L'amour Toujours (USA) **Mr A. T. Macdonald**
64 **SWIFT DAME (IRE)**, b f Montjeu (IRE)—Velvet Appeal (IRE) **Mrs S. A. F. Brendish**
65 **TOP THE CHARTS**, b g Singspiel (IRE)—On The Tide **P. T. Tellwright**
66 **TRANSGRESS (IRE)**, b c Trans Island—Ned's Contessa (IRE) **R. C. Tooth**
67 **VALENTIN (IRE)**, ch f King of Kings (IRE)—Slip Ashore (IRE) **Mrs Valerie Hubbard & Mr A. J. Ilsley**
68 **WORTH ABBEY**, b g Mujadil (USA)—Housefull **J. Palmer-Brown & Mrs M. Jordan**
69 **XACOBEO (IRE)**, b c Montjeu (IRE)—Afisiak **Mr A. T. Macdonald**

TWO-YEAR-OLDS

70 B c 20/2 Daylami (IRE)—Aegean Dream (IRE) (Royal Academy (USA)) (34000) **Theobalds Stud**
71 B f 11/3 Danehill (USA)—Ahdaab (USA) (Rahy (USA)) **T. Hyde & Partners**
72 B c 24/4 Stravinsky (USA)—Alashir (Alysheba (USA)) (55000) **Danny Durkan**
73 **ARMINIUS (IRE)**, b c 11/2 Shinko Forest (IRE)—Tribal Rite (Be My Native (USA)) (30180) **M. Pescod**
74 **ASSERTIVE**, ch c 18/2 Bold Edge—Tart And A Half (Distant Relative) (36000) **A J Ilsley, K T Ivory & Lady Whent**
75 **ASSET (IRE)**, b c 9/3 Marju—Snow Peak (Arazi (USA)) (70000) **Highclere Thoroughbred Racing XXVI**
76 **BARBAR**, b c 3/5 Anabaa (USA)—Prends Ca (IRE) (Reprimand) **B. Bull**
77 **BAY DIAMOND**, b c 28/2 Lujain (USA)—La Nureyeva (USA) (Nureyev (USA)) (3000) **The Hon. Mrs D. Joly**
78 B c 13/2 Red Ransom (USA)—Bielska (USA) (Deposit Ticket (USA)) (214621) **Fieldspring Racing**
79 **BILLY BLING (IRE)**, b c 11/3 Enrique—Shewillshewants (IRE) (Alzao (USA)) (4800) **Miss V. O'Sullivan**
80 B f 23/2 Orpen (USA)—Bint Al Balad (IRE) (Ahonoora) (40000) **Thurloe Thoroughbreds XVI**
81 B f 25/4 Mozart (IRE)—Blew Her Top (USA) (Blushing John (USA)) (28000) **Knockainey Stud**
82 B f 31/1 Namid—Bold Fashion (FR) (Nashwan (USA)) (24000) **Fergus Jones**
83 **BON VIVEUR**, b c 29/3 Mozart (IRE)—Fantazia (Zafonic (USA)) (75000) **Mrs J. Wood**
84 **CAAN**, b c 25/4 Averti (IRE)—Bellifontaine (FR) (Bellypha) (9000) **K. T. Ivory & A. J. Ilsley**
85 **CHARLIE TOKYO (IRE)**, b c 30/4 Trans Island—Ellistown Lady (Red Sunset) (11400) **M. Pescod**
86 B f 14/4 Woodborough (USA)—Child Star (FR) (Bellypha) (5000) **B. C. Oakley**
87 **CHINA PEARL**, ch c 4/4 Benny The Dip (USA)—Seek The Pearl (Rainbow Quest (USA)) (22000) **Noodles Racing**
88 **COOL CREEK (IRE)**, b c 5/4 Desert Style (IRE)—
Shining Creek (CAN) (Bering) (34875) **Mr Michael Pescod & Mr Justin Dowley**
89 B c 23/3 Danetime (IRE)—Cotton Grace (IRE) (Case Law) (35545) **Coriolan Links Partnership IX**
90 B f 26/4 Medicean—Darling Lover (USA) (Dare And Go (USA)) (6036) **Fergus Jones**
91 Ch c 15/4 Beckett (IRE)—Date Mate (USA) (Thorn Dance (USA)) (22000) **Louis Stalder**
92 **ELLA MAE**, b f 23/3 Mozart (IRE)—Sareb (IRE) (Indian Ridge) **B. Bull**
93 **ENVISION**, b c 26/3 Pivotal—Entwine (Primo Dominie) (66000) **Mrs J. Wood**
94 **FALCON DIVE (USA)**, ch c 10/2 Diesis—Yanaseeni (USA) (Trempolino (USA)) **J. Abdullah**
95 B c 8/5 Stravinsky (USA)—Fife (USA) (Lomond (USA)) (38900) **Lucayan Stud & Major A. M. Everett**
96 **GAMBLE IN GOLD (IRE)**, b f 3/3 Monashee Mountain (USA)—
Starisa (IRE) (College Chapel) (15000) **Ms R. Z. Stephenson**
97 **GIN JOCKEY (FR)**, b c 23/4 Soviet Star (USA)—Singing Lark (FR) (Pampabird) (23474) **Bob Lalemant**
98 **GODFREY STREET**, ch c 21/4 Compton Place—
Tahara (IRE) (Caerleon (USA)) (6000) **J. A. Leek, T. Dale & J. Perry**
99 **GOLDEN ACER (IRE)**, ch c 21/2 Elnadim (USA)—Shifty Lady (Night Shift (USA)) (20000) **David Mort**
100 **GOLDEN SURF (IRE)**, b f 8/1 Gold Away (IRE)—
Silvery Surf (USA) (Silver Deputy (CAN)) (40000) **K. T. Ivory & A. J. Ilsley**
101 **GREEN PARK (IRE)**, b c 25/2 Shinko Forest (IRE)—
Danccini (IRE) (Dancing Dissident (USA)) (45000) **G. Battocchi, A. J. Ilsley & K. T. Ivory**
102 **GREEN PRIDE**, b c 18/4 Piccolo—Little Greenbird (Ardkinglass) (10000) **R. E. Greatorex & Partners**
103 B f 20/2 Kalanisi (IRE)—Hawksbill Special (IRE) (Taufan (USA)) (43594) **W. Durkan**
104 **HOT (IRE)**, b c 20/3 Xaar—Solar Display (USA) (Diesis) (12000) **Mrs J. Wood**
105 **INCIDENTALLY (IRE)**, ch c 2/2 Inchinor—Top Sauce (Hector Protector (USA)) (40000) **A. J. Ilsley & K. T. Ivory**
106 Br c 4/3 Zafonic (USA)—Irish Teen (USA) (Irish River (FR)) (40000) **Edmund Lee**
107 B f 11/5 Mujadil (USA)—Islandagore (IRE) (Indian Ridge) (30180) **Fergus Jones**

MR R. HANNON—continued

108 B f 10/1 Xaar—Jet Cat (IRE) (Catrail (USA)) (46947) **W. Durkan**
109 Ch c 30/4 Spinning World (USA)—Kafayef (USA) (Secreto (USA)) (35000) **Thurloe Bears**
110 KINGS CAVALIER (USA), b c 27/1 Stormin Fever (USA)—
                              Port of Silver (USA) (Silver Hawk (USA)) (75000) **J. R. May**
111 LA FANCIULLA, b f 22/3 Robellino (USA)—Molly Brown (Rudimentary (USA)) (40000) **R. Barby**
112 LADY LIVIUS (IRE), b f 17/4 Titus Livius (FR)—Refined (IRE) (Statoblest) (21000) **Mrs N. F. Lee**
113 LESTER LEAPS IN (USA), b br c 18/4 Red Ransom (USA)—
                              Rose Aurora (USA) (Majestic Light (USA)) (37000) **Bob Lalemant**
114 B g 18/4 Mark of Esteem (IRE)—Mayaro Bay (Robellino (USA)) **J. R. Shannon**
115 MIRTH, b f 30/3 Alhaarth (IRE)—
                              Justine Au Jardin (USA) (Black Tie Affair) (103957) **Highclere Thoroughbred Racing XXVII**
116 MONTANA SKY (IRE), b c 11/3 Peintre Celebre (USA)—Catch The Lights (Deploy) **Johnsey Estates (1990) Ltd**
117 MR CHAD, b c 4/5 Mujahid (USA)—Robanna (Robellino (USA)) **Green Pastures Partnership**
118 NED LUDD (IRE), b c 25/3 Montjeu (IRE)—Zanella (IRE) (Nordico (USA)) **Ben Goldsmith & Partners**
119 NEWPORT BOY (IRE), b c 19/3 Montjeu (IRE)—Dream Chaser (Record Token) **Johnsey Estates (1990) Ltd**
120 NIVELLE (IRE), b f 8/2 Imperial Ballet (IRE)—Funny Wave (Lugana Beach) (1000) **The 1917 Partnership**
121 OCEAN PRIDE (IRE), b c 2/2 Lend A Hand—
                              Irish Understudy (ITY) (In The Wings) (10000) **D. Churston & Partners**
122 B c 25/3 Mull of Kintyre (USA)—Petite Liqueurelle (IRE) (Shernazar) (30000) **J. B. R. Leisure Ltd**
123 PLUM PUDDING (IRE), b c 8/5 Elnadim (USA)—Karayb (IRE) (Last Tycoon) (52000) **Hyde Sporting Promotions**
124 PUNTA GARCIA (IRE), br c 3/3 Zafonic (USA)—Kobalt Sea (IRE) (Akarad (FR)) (130000) **J. A. Lazzari**
125 Ch f 24/2 Pursuit of Love—Radiant (Machiavellian (USA)) (5000) **K. Panos & C. J. Jones**
126 RAHY'S CROWN (USA), b c 26/4 Rahy (USA)—Inca Princess (USA) (Big Spruce (USA)) **J. Abdullah**
127 RED PRIDE (IRE), b c 2/3 Fasliyev (USA)—True Love (Robellino (USA)) (15425) **Terry Neill & Partners**
128 ROLL THE DICE (IRE), b c 7/3 Sinndar (IRE)—Piffle (Shirley Heights) (13413) **A. P. Patey**
129 B c 13/4 Mujadil (USA)—Sabaniya (FR) (Lashkari) (23473) **Des Kavanagh & Partners**
130 B c 8/2 Cape Cross (USA)—Samhat Mtoto (Mtoto) (31521) **Major A. M. Everett & Lucayan Stud**
131 SAVANNAH PRIDE (IRE), b f 1/4 Namid—
                              Milady Lillie (IRE) (Distinctly North (USA)) (9000) **R. E. Greatorex & Partners**
132 SENSUOUS, b f 9/2 Royal Applause—Zafaaf (Kris) (24000) **Mrs J. Wood**
133 SHE WHISPERS (IRE), b f 5/2 Royal Applause—
                              Zariyba (IRE) (In The Wings) (15000) **Paul J. Dixon & Simon Leech**
134 SILVER BLUE (IRE), ch c 15/3 Indian Lodge—Silver Echo (Caerleon (USA)) (23473) **Mrs S. A. F. Brendish**
135 B f 20/4 Xaar—Snoozeandyoulose (IRE) (Scenic) (9000) **L. S. A. Stalder**
136 SONNY SANTINO, b c 7/3 Bertolini (USA)—Irish Impulse (USA) (Irish River (FR)) (55000) **F. Sines**
137 B br c 24/3 Black Minnaloushe (USA)—Splendid (IRE) (Mujtahid (USA)) (50000) **Edmund Lee**
138 STORM ON THE RUN (IRE), b c 4/4 Desert Prince (IRE)—
                              Happy Dancer (USA) (Seattle Dancer (USA)) (42000) **J. Abdullah**
139 SUN CATCHER (IRE), b c 26/2 Cape Cross (USA)—Taalluf (USA) (Hansel (USA)) (37000) **A. F. J. Merritt**
140 B f 10/4 Royal Academy (USA)—Support The Arts (USA) (Taylor's Falls (USA)) (71827) **Kildare Stud**
141 SURF CITY, ch c 10/2 Distant Music (USA)—Tolyatti (Green Desert (USA)) (19000) **M. Pescod**
142 SWEET BOULANGERE, ch f 21/1 Grand Lodge (USA)—
                              Cybinka (Selkirk (USA)) (50000) **The Mystery Partnership**
143 Ch c 20/4 Giant's Causeway (USA)—Sweet Times (Riverman (USA)) (50000) **Cathal M. Ryan**
144 B c 14/2 Imperial Ballet (IRE)—Tancholo (So Factual (USA)) (22000) **Speedith Group**
145 THE SNATCHER (IRE), b c 17/4 Indian Danehill (IRE)—Saninka (IRE) (Doyoun) (10000) **Mrs R. Ablett**
146 THORNFIELD CLO (IRE), gr f 27/3 Zafonic (USA)—Flounce (Unfuwain (USA)) (20000) **Dr M. A. Dunleavy**
147 B br c 21/3 Mirardi (USA)—Time For The Show (USA) (Academy Award (USA)) (30180) **Mrs Dermot O'Rourke**
148 TUSCANY QUEEN (IRE), b f 11/2 Titus Livius (FR)—
                              Queen Molly (Emarati (USA)) (20790) **McDowell Racing Ltd**
149 B f 19/4 King's Best (USA)—Your Village (IRE) (Be My Guest (USA)) (26827) **Fergus Jones**

Assistant Trainer: Richard Hannon Jnr

Jockey (flat): Ryan Moore, P. Dobbs, R. Hughes, Dane O'Neill, R. Smith. **Apprentice:** Wayne Burton.

---

266 MR G. A. HARKER, Middleham
Postal: **The Winning Post, Bolton Hall, Wensley, Leyburn, North Yorkshire, DL8 4UF.**
Contacts: **PHONE** (01969) 624507 **MOBILE** (07803) 116412 or (07930) 125544
E-MAIL gandjhome@aol.com

1 BOLTON CASTLE, 8, b g Royal Fountain—Elegant Mary **P. I. Harker**
2 CUSTOM DESIGN, 4, ch g Minster Son—Scotto's Regret **Mr G Aldred Mr G Steel**
3 CYBORG DE SOU (FR), 7, b g Cyborg (FR)—Moomaw **J. J. Maguire**
4 ENZO DE BAUNE (FR), 8, b g En Calcat (FR)—Pure Moon (FR) **Lord Bolton**

MR G. A. HARKER—continued

5 **FAIRY SKIN MAKER (IRE)**, 7, ch g Nomadic Way (USA)—Malvern Madam **Partnership**
6 **FARNE ISLE**, 6, ch m Midnight Legend—Biloela **Steer Arms Belton Racing Club**
7 **JAY BE JUNIOR**, 5, br g J B Quick—Staggering (IRE) **Steve & Trish Wilson/Phillip & Tor Yuill**
8 **JETHRO TULL (IRE)**, 6, b g Witness Box (USA)—Country Project (IRE) **J. J. Maguire**
9 **MASTER SPEAKER**, 7, b g Presidium—Miss Ritz **Mrs D. R. Schreiber & Mr G. A. Harker**
10 **MYOSS (IRE)**, 6, b g Arctic Lord—Lake Garden Park **R. G. Makin**
11 **NOTAPROBLEM (IRE)**, 6, b g Oscar (IRE)—Smashed Free (IRE) **J. J. Maguire**
12 **OAKAPPLE EXPRESS**, 5, b g Alflora (IRE)—Royal Scarlet **Mr P. Taylor**
13 **RAJAM**, 7, b g Sadler's Wells (USA)—Rafif (USA) **Mr G. A. Harker**
14 **RED POKER**, 5, ch g Alflora (IRE)—Scarlet Ember **R. Brewis**
15 **SCARLET MEMORY**, 6, b m Dancing High—Scarlet Ember **R. Brewis**
16 **STARMIX**, 4, br g Linamix (FR)—Danlu (USA) **P. I. Harker**
17 **THE MASARETI KID (IRE)**, 8, b g Commanche Run—Little Crack (IRE) **Mr G. A. Harker**
18 **ZAFFIE PARSON (IRE)**, 4, b f Zaffaran (USA)—Katie Parson **Mr David Adair**

Other Owners: Miss Rhona Brewis, Mrs G. E. Brewis, S. Costello, J. G. Knibb.

Assistant Trainer: Jenny Harker

Conditional: N. Hannity.

---

267 **MR R. C. HARPER, Banbury**
Postal: **Home Farm, Kings Sutton, Banbury, Oxfordshire, OX17 3RS.**
Contacts: **PHONE (01295) 810997 FAX (01295) 812787 MOBILE (07970) 223481**
E-MAIL rharper@freeuk.com

1 **CASH 'N CARROTS**, 6, b g Missed Flight—Rhiannon **Mr R. C. Harper**
2 **CHEEKY LAD**, 5, b g Bering—Cheeky Charm (USA) **Mr R. C. Harper & Miss L. C. Clothier**
3 **LITTLE TRETHEW**, 6, ch m Presidium—Sister Claire **Mr R. C. Harper**
4 **MAJOR RENO (IRE)**, 8, b g Little Bighorn—Make Me An Island **Mr R. C. Harper**
5 **NAFSIKA (USA)**, 5, b m Sky Classic (CAN)—Exotic Beauty (USA) **Mr R. C. Harper**

Other Owners: Miss L. C. Clothier.

---

268 **MRS JESSICA HARRINGTON, Kildare**
Postal: **Commonstown Stables, Moone, Co. Kildare, Ireland.**
Contacts: **PHONE +353 (0) 598624153 FAX +353 (0) 598624292 MOBILE +353 (0) 872566129**
E-MAIL jessicaharrington@eircom.net WEBSITE www.jharringtonracing.com

1 5, Gr g Moscow Society (USA)—Abigail's Dream **Thomas Doran & Sarah Kelly**
2 **ANOTHER DOLLAR (IRE)**, 7, br m Supreme Leader—Deep Dollar **Godfrey Deacon**
3 **ATELIOS (USA)**, 4, ch g Royal Academy (USA)—Attrape (USA) **Kevin Mulligan**
4 **BACKSIDEUP (IRE)**, 5, b br m Bob Back—Relic Image (IRE) **The K. P. Syndicate**
5 **BADGERLAW (IRE)**, 5, b g Accordion—Beglawella **Lynn Wilson**
6 **BALLYBRACK LAD (IRE)**, 5, b g Brief Truce (USA)—Trace (USA) **Emma Harrington**
7 **BASANIO (IRE)**, 7, b g Jackson's Drift (USA)—Leinster Lady (IRE) **Joe O'Flaherty**
8 **BOB'S VISION (IRE)**, 8, b g Bob's Return (IRE)—Rare Dream **Richard Upton/David Attwood**
9 **BRASYA (FR)**, 6, gr m Baryshnikov (AUS)—La Toscanella (FR) **Commonstown Syndicate**
10 **BUNMAHON (IRE)**, 5, b br g Broken Hearted—Glenpatrick Peach (IRE) **Mrs E. Queally & Miss E Harrington**
11 **BUST OUT**, 9, ch g Bustino—Nordic Beauty (USA) **BB Racing Club**
12 **CARRIGEEN VICTOR (IRE)**, 7, b g Old Vic—Carrigeen Kerria (IRE) **Richard Doyle**
13 **CLASSIC VIC (IRE)**, 5, ch g Old Vic—Grangeclare Rose (IRE) **Malcolm Graham**
14 **CLONEY LORD (IRE)**, 8, b g Lord Americo—Dillrock Damsel **Mr M. Cloney**
15 **CLOSED ORDERS (IRE)**, 8, b g Phardante (FR)—Monks Lass (IRE) **Brian Smith & James Osbourne**
16 **COLCA CANYON (IRE)**, 8, br g Un Desperado (FR)—Golden Flats **P. Myerscough**
17 **COLOUR CARDS (IRE)**, 6, b g Warcraft (USA)—Polly's Cacador **Padraic Kierans**
18 5, B br h Scribano—Coolafinka (USA) **Paid Thru The Nose Syndicate**
19 **CORRAN ARD (IRE)**, 4, b g Imperial Ballet (IRE)—Beeper The Great (USA) **Mr E. Salmon**
20 **DERRYINVER BAY (IRE)**, 6, b g Religiously (USA)—You Name It (IRE) **Joe McBreen**
21 **DESIGN TO WIN (IRE)**, 6, b m Flemensfirth (USA)—Miss Brecknell (IRE) **The Thomas House Syndicate**
22 **DJANGO (IRE)**, 6, ch g Glacial Storm (USA)—Rathrim **K K Construction**
23 **ESHMORE BLUE (IRE)**, 5, b g Needle Gun (IRE)—BUNINOO (IRE) **Eshmore Racing Syndicate**
24 **EXPERT FOREVER (IRE)**, 7, b m Sharifabad (IRE)—Roam Forever (IRE) **Mervin Fox**
25 **EXPRESS EXIT**, 7, b h Exit To Nowhere (USA)—Jasminola (FR) **The Shiners Syndicate**

MRS JESSICA HARRINGTON—continued

26 **EXTRA PICKINS (IRE)**, 5, b h Sri Pekan (USA)—Extra Time **Oliver Murphy**
27 **FOUR ACES**, 8, b g Forzando—Anhaar **Lakeside Racing Syndicate**
28 **FRANK MOSS BENNETT (IRE)**, 5, b g Bahhare (USA)—Despondent (IRE) **DJMP Syndicate**
29 **GEMINI LUCY (IRE)**, 5, ch m Glacial Storm (USA)—Jodi (IRE) **Queens Prices Syndicate**
30 **GOOD NICK (IRE)**, 5, b g Saddlers' Hall (IRE)—Southern Run **The Seafield Syndicate**
31 **GREEN BELT FLYER (IRE)**, 7, b g Leading Counsel (USA)—Current Liability **The Green Belter Syndicate**
32 **HARD TO GET TEN (IRE)**, 5, b br m Rashar (USA)—Shuil Sionnach (IRE) **Sam Flemming Syndicate**
33 **HARPER'S PRIDE**, 5, b g Deploy—Lamees (USA) **Michael Harper**
34 **HIDDEN COMMOTION (IRE)**, 5, b g Great Commotion (USA)—Hidden Picture (IRE) **Click Syndicate**
35 **HOULDYURWHIST (IRE)**, 6, b m Supreme Leader—Don't Waste It (IRE) **BB Racing Club**
36 **HUME CASTLE (IRE)**, 8, b g Religiously (USA)—Clyde Avenue **Castle Hume Syndicate**
37 **HUME THEATRE (IRE)**, 6, b g Old Vic—Carrig Conn (IRE) **Castle Hume Syndicate**
38 **I'LL CALL YOU BACK (IRE)**, 6, b g Zaffaran (USA)—Ben Tack **Mighty Macs Syndicate**
39 **IMAZULUTOO (IRE)**, 5, b h Marju (IRE)—Zapata (IRE) **Mr E. Salmon**
40 **INCIDENTIAL (IRE)**, 5, b g Needle Gun (IRE)—Guernsey Girl **James Parkinson**
41 **INDIAN PRESENCE (IRE)**, 5, b m Presenting—Shequanah (IRE) **Jim McCabe**
42 **JEFF DE CHALAMONT (FR)**, 8, b g Abary (GER)—Clio de Chalamont (FR) **D. G. Q. Syndicate**
43 **KASAKOV PARK**, 5, b m Kasakov—Baladiya **Paddy Byrne**
44 **KNIGHT LEGEND (IRE)**, 6, b g Flying Legend (USA)—Well Trucked (IRE) **Lynn Wilson & Martin St Quinton**
45 **LA DEARG (IRE)**, 5, ch g Grand Plaisir (IRE)—Lady Dee **Pharma Syndicate**
46 **LAKE TACKER (IRE)**, 5, b m Lake Coniston (IRE)—Mystery Night (FR) **Francis Hughes**
47 **LIFFEY (IRE)**, 5, b h Desert Prince (IRE)—Toujours Irish (USA) **The River Syndicate**
48 **LUGANTE (IRE)**, 5, b m Luso—Bargante (IRE) **Mrs Helga Crowley**
49 **MACS JOY (IRE)**, 6, b g Religiously (USA)—Snob's Supreme (IRE) **The Macs J Syndicate**
50 **ME TOO SAN (IRE)**, 6, b g Carroll House—Smooth Leader (USA) **Joe McBreen**
51 5, B br m Norwich—Miss Ranova **Arthur McCooly**
52 **MISTER VIRGINIAN (IRE)**, 6, ch h Mister Lord (USA)—Ardglass Mist **The Round Up Syndicate**
53 **MOMMA MIA (IRE)**, 5, b br m Luso—Sacajawea **Mr John P. McManus**
54 **MOSCOW COURT (IRE)**, 7, b g Moscow Society—Hogan Stand **James Parkinson**
55 **MOSCOW FLYER (IRE)**, 11, b g Moscow Society (USA)—Meelick Lady (IRE) **Brian Kearney**
56 **MOUNT PROSPECT (IRE)**, 6, ch g Anshan—Rustic Court (USA) **Brian Kearney**
57 **MOYNALVEYLAD (IRE)**, 5, b g Taipan (IRE)—Tirol's Luck (IRE) **Vincent Walsh**
58 **MRS WOMAN (IRE)**, 5, b m Oscar (IRE)—Sakonnet (IRE) **Liam Quinn**
59 **NAN CHERO (IRE)**, 8, b h Jurado (USA)—Monksville **Mark O'Reilly & David Gough**
60 **NOONEWANTSME (IRE)**, 5, b g Topanoora—Cut No Ice **John Harrington**
61 **NOTHING YET (IRE)**, 6, b g Zaffaran (USA)—Windy Bop (IRE) **D. Lavin, G O'Flynn, J. Hayes & J. Hussey**
62 **NULLARBOR PLAIN (USA)**, 5, b g Quest For Fame—Tiff (USA) **Joe O'Flaherty**
63 **OLD VAL (IRE)**, 7, b g Old Vic—Kilkilrun **Seamus Murphy**
64 **ONLY ALYMER (IRE)**, 7, b g Be My Native (USA)—Castle-Etta (IRE) **Two Chances Syndicate**
65 **OUTONACALL (IRE)**, 6, b m King Persian—E-Augh (IRE) **N. Floyd**
66 **PAY IT FORWARD**, 7, b g Anshan—Kellsboro Kate **Paid Thru The Nose Syndicate**
67 **PEARL LAKE (IRE)**, 5, b m Charente River (IRE)—Petite Port (IRE) **The Shiners Syndicate**
68 **PENNYHILL THYNE (IRE)**, 5, br g Good Thyne (USA)—Baylough Lady (IRE) **Pennyhill Punters Club**
69 **PERSUE A HEAD (IRE)**, 6, b h Moonax (USA)—Forest Jem **The Dedham Syndicate**
70 **PRIVATE BEN (IRE)**, 7, b g Ridgewood Ben—Timeless **Seven Good Reasons Syndicate**
71 **QUARRYLAND MAGIC (IRE)**, 9, b m Toulon—Last Act **Gerry O'Malley**
72 **QUARTINO**, 4, b c Dynaformer (USA)—Qirmazi (USA) **The Midas Syndicate**
73 **QUEST FOR A STAR (IRE)**, 8, b h Rainbow Quest (USA)—Ridgewood Pearl **Mr Albert Crowley**
74 **QUIETLY DOES IT (IRE)**, 6, b m Old Vic—Tulip (IRE) **Gervaise Maher**
75 **RATHGANLEY LASS (IRE)**, 5, b br m Taipan (IRE)—Cotton Call (IRE) **Mick Pender**
76 **RIAL STAR (IRE)**, 5, b h Fourstars Allstar (USA)—Mullintoura Lady (IRE) **Commonstown Syndicate**
77 **RIGA LAD (IRE)**, 5, bl g Anshan—Yvonnes Princess **Paid Thru The Nose Syndicate**
78 **SADDLERS' SPIRIT (IRE)**, 4, b f Saddlers' Hall (IRE)—El Pina **Dil Thompson**
79 **SATCO'S LADY (IRE)**, 8, b m Satco (FR)—Back To Black (IRE) **Martin White**
80 5, Ch g Moscow Society (USA)—Scarlet River (IRE) **Cool Ring Syndicate**
81 **SEPTEMBER BLISS (IRE)**, 5, br g Norwich—Down The Garden (IRE) **B. Smith**
82 **SLANEY EAGLE (IRE)**, 5, b g Eagle Eyed (USA)—Mean To Me **Favourites Racing Ltd**
83 **SOCIETY BREEZE (IRE)**, 6, ch m Moscow Society (USA)—Just A Breeze (IRE) **Empty Pockets Syndicate**
84 **SPANISH GUEST (IRE)**, 5, b g Be My Guest (USA)—Cabcharge Princess (IRE) **The Dunboy Syndicate**
85 **SPORTEEN (IRE)**, 6, b g Un Desperado (FR)—Providence Lodge **Vincent Walsh**
86 **STANAFOSS (IRE)**, 6, b g Synefos (USA)—Northern Elation (IRE) **Favourites Racing Ltd**
87 **STAR HORSE (IRE)**, 7, b g Toulon—Clerical Lady **Des O'Connell**
88 **STRAIGHT'N'NARROW (IRE)**, 5, ch h Presenting—Blooming Rose **N. Moore, W. Smith, P. Dwyer & M. Green**
89 **STRIKE BACK (IRE)**, 7, b g Bob Back (USA)—First Strike (IRE) **Commonstown Syndicate**
90 **STUDMASTER**, 5, ch g Snurge—Danlu (USA) **Mothership Racing Club**
91 **SUPREME INVITE (IRE)**, 5, b m Supreme Leader—Sharp Invite **Brian Quinlan**

MRS JESSICA HARRINGTON—continued

 92 TRAGUMNA (IRE), 5, ch g Presenting—Billys Pet **Brian Kearney**
 93 TURN THE CORNER (IRE), 6, b g Bob Back (USA)—Tabu Lady (IRE) **Maynard Hamilton**
 94 TYCOON HALL (IRE), 5, ch h Halling (USA)—Tycooness (IRE) **Cathal M. Ryan**
 95 ULAAN BAATAR (IRE), 8, b g Jackson's Drift (USA)—Leinster Lady (IRE) **Joe O'Flaherty**
 96 UNDER N OVER (IRE), 6, b m Accordion—Laban Lady (IRE) **Conor Rafferty & Eric Callanan**
 97 UNDER OATH, 4, b g Selkirk (USA)—Wosaita **David Lawlor**
 98 USNOOZEULOSE (IRE), 5, b br g Grand Plaisir—Delnac **Gerry Byrne & Brian Fitzgerald**
 99 WAKE UP HENRY, 4, ch g Nashwan (USA)—River Saint (USA)
100 WATERLILY (IRE), 6, b m Revoque (IRE)—Cochineal (USA) **Dermot Cox & James Osbourne**
101 WELL PRESENTED (IRE), 7, b g Presenting—Casualty Madame **BB Racing Club**
102 WILLIE THE SHOE, 8, b g Pyramus (USA)—Me Neither **Thomas Doran & Sarah Kelly**
103 WOODHOUSE (IRE), 6, b g Glacial Storm (USA)—Alices Run **Mrs Noone**
104 YOUGHAL (IRE), 5, br g Bob Back (USA)—One Swoop (IRE) **Cathal M. Ryan**
105 YOUNG CUTHBERT, 7, b h Homo Sapien—Deirdres Dream **Gareth Read Racing Syndicate**
106 4, B c Ridgewood Ben—Zinovia (USA) **David Fenlon**

THREE-YEAR-OLDS

107 BLUE HAWAIIAN (IRE), br f Fasliyev (USA)—Julianne (IRE) **D. Nagle, A. Gurney, A. Nicholl & S. Collins**
108 FLAMING SHOT (IRE), b c Son of Sharp Shot (IRE)—Brockton Flame **Anamoine Ltd**
109 JAZZ PRINCESS (IRE), b br f Bahhare (USA)—Jazz Up **Tom Curran**
110 MAREDA (FR), b f Revoque (IRE)—Darema (IRE) **P. Myerscough**
111 OSSIANA (IRE), ch f Polish Precedent (USA)—Diavolina (USA) **Marguerite Clifford Racing LLC**
112 WOODLAND DREAM (IRE), b f Charnwood Forest (IRE)—Fantasy Girl (IRE) **Anamoine Ltd**

TWO-YEAR-OLDS

113 Ch f 15/2 Bahhare (USA)—Kindred Spirit (IRE) (Cadeaux Genereux) (63715) **Tom Curran**
114 Ch f 28/3 Bahhare (USA)—Town Girl (IRE) (Lammtarra (USA)) (10730) **Tom Curran**

---

269 **MR J. A. HARRIS, Melton Mowbray**
Postal: **Eastwell Hall Stables, Eastwell, Melton Mowbray, Leicestershire, LE14 4EE.**
Contacts: **HOME (01400) 282819 YARD/FAX (01949) 860671 MOBILE (07989) 941712**
E-MAIL annharris@stables007.wannadoo.co.uk

 1 BROTHER CADFAEL, 4, ch g So Factual (USA)—High Habit **Mrs A. E. Harris**
 2 CROSBY WALTZER, 5, b m Terimon—Mary Macblain **D. Jackson**
 3 ESTIMATE, 5, b m Mark of Esteem (IRE)—Mistle Thrush **Mrs A. E. Harris**
 4 FOREST RAIL (IRE), 5, b m Catrail (USA)—Forest Heights **D. Pettifor**
 5 HAUNT THE ZOO, 10, b m Komaite (USA)—Merryhill Maid (IRE) **Mrs A. E. Harris**
 6 HUMDINGER (IRE), 5, b m Charnwood Forest (IRE)—High Finish **K. Nicholls**
 7 KAPAROLO (USA), 6, ch g El Prado (IRE)—Parliament House (USA) **Mrs A. E. Harris**
 8 LADY LUCINDA, 4, b f Muhtarram (USA)—Lady Phyl **Mr W. A. Gonsalves**
 9 PALAIS (IRE), 10, b g Darshaan—Dance Festival **J. South**
10 RUIN, 7, b g Polish Precedent (USA)—Trojan Desert **P. E. Barrett**
11 SES SELINE, 4, b f Salse (USA)—Absentee **J. H. Henderson**
12 SHEER GUTS (IRE), 6, b g Hamas (IRE)—Balakera (FR) **Cleartherm Ltd**

Assistant Trainer: Miss Vicki M Harris, Mrs A E Harris

Jockey (flat): Dean McKeown, S. Sanders. **Jockey (NH):** P. Flynn.

---

270 **MR M. F. HARRIS, Banbury**
Postal: **Trafford Bridge Stables, Edgcote, Banbury, Oxfordshire, OX17 1AG.**
Contacts: **PHONE (01295) 660713 FAX (01295) 660767 MOBILE (07879) 634308**
E-MAIL info@miltonharrisracing.com WEBSITE www.miltonharrisracing.com

 1 BRINGONTHECLOWNS (IRE), 6, b g Entrepreneur—Circus Maid (IRE) **Joking Around Partnership**
 2 CONTAS (GER), 5, b h Lomitas—Cocorna **Three Off The Tee Partnership**
 3 5, Ch g Alflora (IRE)—Dorazine **The Virtual Partnership**
 4 EL CORREDOR (IRE), 6, b h Sadler's Wells (USA)—Meteor Stage (USA) **Mr M. F. Harris**
 5 FAIRLY SMART, 6, b m Good Thyne (USA)—Smart Chick **C. J. Courage**
 6 FAYR FIRENZE (IRE), 4, b g Fayruz—Shillay **Mr M. F. Harris**
 7 IOWA (IRE), 5, b g Sadler's Wells (USA)—Puzzled Look (USA) **Lord Bolton**
 8 LEOPOLD (SLO), 4, b g Solarstern (FR)—Lucera (GER) **A. J. Duffield**

MR M. F. HARRIS—continued

9 **LORD ATTICA (IRE)**, 6, b g Mister Lord (USA)—Brief Pace (IRE) **Mr D. K. Watkins**
10 **MAGUIRE (GER)**, 4, gr g Medaaly—Mayada (USA) **Mr M. F. Harris**
11 **MONDUL (GER)**, 5, b g Colon (GER)—Morgenrote (EG) **Partners In Crime**
12 **MONGINO (GER)**, 4, b g In A Tiff (IRE)—Mondalita (GER) **Prevention & Detection (Holdings) Limited**
13 **MONTECORVINO (GER)**, 4, ch g Acatenango (GER)—Manhattan Girl (USA) **W. Craig**
14 **NEWTOWN**, 6, b g Darshaan—Calypso Run **Mr M. F. Harris**
15 **PARDINI (USA)**, 6, b g Quest For Fame—Noblissima (IRE) **Prevention & Detection (Holdings) Limited**
16 **PAXFORD JACK**, 9, ch g Alflora (IRE)—Rakajack **Mrs R. E. Nelmes**
17 **PAXFORD TROOPER**, 11, b g Gunner B—Say Shanaz **Mr M. F. Harris**
18 **RATTINA (GER)**, 9, b m Motley (USA)—Rottara (GER) **Mrs S. E. Brown**
19 **REGENCY MALAYA**, 4, b f Sri Pekan (USA)—Paola (FR) **Mrs J. C. Webb**
20 **SALINAS (GER)**, 6, b g Macanal (USA)—Santa Ana (GER) **Prevention & Detection (Holdings) Limited**
21 **THE HAIRY LEMON**, 5, b g Eagle Eyed (USA)—Angie's Darling **The Hairy Lemon Partnership**
22 **TRAVELLING WARRIOR**, 6, b g Emperor Fountain—Gipsy Princess **The Golden Anorak Partnership**
23 **TRAVELLO (GER)**, 5, b g Bakharoff (USA)—Travista (GER) **Milton Harris Racing Club**
24 **VOLCANO SNOW**, 5, ch m Zilzal (USA)—Ash Glade **B. Morton**
25 **WATER QUIRL (GER)**, 6, ch g Dr Devious (IRE)—Water Quest (IRE) **Mr M. F. Harris**
26 **ZELOSO**, 7, b g Alzao (USA)—Silk Petal **The Paxford Optimists**

THREE-YEAR-OLDS

27 **BLACKCOMB MOUNTAIN (USA)**, b br f Royal Anthem (USA)—Ski Racer (FR) **Mr D. K. Watkins**
28 **CROSS MY SHADOW (IRE)**, b g Cape Cross (IRE)—Shadowglow **The Piranha Partnership**
29 **FORFEITER (USA)**, ch g Petionville (USA)—Picabo (USA) **Forfeit It All Partnership**
30 **MOONFLEET (IRE)**, b f Entrepreneur—Lunasa (IRE) **Moonfleet Racing**

TWO-YEAR-OLDS

31 Ch c 5/5 Nashwan (USA)—Balwa (USA) (Danzig (USA)) (11400) **Prevention & Detection (Holdings) Limited**
32 Ch c 5/3 Spinning World (USA)—Individual (USA) (Gulch (USA)) (3353) **A. J. Duffield**
33 B c 2/3 Lujain (USA)—Michelle's Ella (IRE) (Ela-Mana-Mou) (6706) **Mr M. F. Harris**
34 B c 16/4 Indian Danehill (IRE)—Rachel Pringle (IRE) (Doulab (USA)) (6706) **Mr M. F. Harris**
35 Ch c 18/3 Fruits of Love (USA)—Verusa (IRE) (Petorius) (20000) **L. R. Cross**

Other Owners: Mr S. A. Albiston, Mr C. W. Arrand, Mr M. S. Bresh, Mrs H. Courage, W. Craig, N. Farrell, Mrs A. Frampton, Mrs K. M. Graham, R. Hart, T. Hart, Miss C. M. Haworth, Mr C. Kelly, Mr C. Lee, Mr E. M. Leighton, Mr B. R. Martin, Mr R. A. McNeish, Mr A. Miles, Mr J. J. Murray, A. D. Potts, Mr M. G. R. Stapleton, Mr R. C. Tozer.

Assistant Trainer: Sam Geffray

Jockey (NH): O. McPhail.

271
MR RON HARRIS, Chepstow

Postal: Ridge House Stables, Earlswood, Chepstow, Monmouthshire, NP16 6AN.
Contacts: PHONE (01291) 641689/641462 FAX (01291) 641992 MOBILE (07831) 770899
E-MAIL ridgehousestables.ltd@virgin.net

1 **ATTORNEY**, 7, ch g Wolfhound (USA)—Princess Sadie **Mrs M. Harris**
2 **AUDIOSTREETDOTCOM**, 8, ch g Risk Me (FR)—Ballagarrow Girl **Mrs M. Harris**
3 **BACK AT DE FRONT (IRE)**, 4, b f Cape Cross (IRE)—Bold Fashion (FR) **Leeway Group Limited**
4 **BLAU GRAU (GER)**, 8, gr g Neshad (USA)—Belle Orfana (GER) **Topline Equestrian Ltd**
5 **CLUB ROYAL**, 8, b g Alflora (IRE)—Miss Club Royal **Topline Equestrian Ltd**
6 **COOLFORE JADE (IRE)**, 5, ch m Mukaddamah (USA)—Cashel Princess (IRE) **Leeway Group Limited**
7 **EL PEDRO**, 6, b g Piccolo—Standard Rose **Leeway Group Limited**
8 **FIZZY LADY**, 4, b f Efisio—The Frog Lady (IRE) **Leeway Group Limited**
9 **GWYN'S CHOICE**, 4, b g Faustus—Shalholme **B. T. Price**
10 **INDIAN BAZAAR (IRE)**, 9, ch g Indian Ridge—Bazaar Promise **Leeway Group Limited**
11 **LADY FRANPALM (IRE)**, 5, b m Danehill Dancer (IRE)—Be Nimble **Mrs M. Harris**
12 **MINE'S A MURPHYS**, 9, b g Broadsword—Sparkling Time (USA) **Mrs M. E. Horton**
13 **MISS AMAZER**, 6, b m Shaamit (IRE)—Kiss On Time **Ms A. M. Williams**
14 **NABOKOV**, 6, ch g Nashwan (USA)—Ninotchka (USA) **Mr Hicks**
15 **NETTLETON FLYER**, 4, b g Ajraas (USA)—Mybella Ann **Paul & Ann de Weck**
16 **PANJANDRUM**, 7, b g Polar Falcon (USA)—Rengaine (FR) **Leeway Group Limited**
17 **RUMOUR MILL (IRE)**, 4, b c Entrepreneur—Pursuit of Truth (USA) **Leeway Group Limited**
18 **TAPPIT (IRE)**, 6, b g Mujadil (USA)—Green Life **Mrs J. E. F. Adams**
19 **THE GAIKWAR (IRE)**, 6, b h Indian Ridge—Broadmara (IRE) **Leeway Group Limited**

MR RON HARRIS—continued

20 **THOMO (IRE)**, 7, b g Faustus (USA)—Dawn O'er Kells (IRE) **A. J. Cook**
21 **TURNING THE TIDE**, 6, b g Lugana Beach—Robert's Daughter **Ms A. M. Williams**
22 **VONADAISY**, 4, b f Averti—Vavona **Mr & Mrs I. D. Evans**
23 **YAHESKA (IRE)**, 8, b m Prince of Birds (USA)—How Ya Been (IRE) **Ms A. M. Williams**
24 **YORKIES BOY**, 10, gr g Clantime—Slipperose **Paul & Ann de Weck**

THREE-YEAR-OLDS

25 **FLYING DANCER**, b f Danzero (AUS)—Alzianah **Leeway Group Limited**
26 **FLYING HIGHEST**, b f Spectrum (IRE)—Mainly Sunset **Leeway Group Limited**

Assistant Trainer: Mrs Michelle Harris

Apprentice: M. Savage. **Amateur:** Mr Josh Harris.

---

272 **MR PATRICK HASLAM, Middleham**
Postal: Manor House Stables, Middleham, Leyburn, North Yorkshire, DL8 4QL.
Contacts: PHONE (01969) 624351 FAX (01969) 624463
E-MAIL haslamracing@rapidial.co.uk WEBSITE www.patrickhaslamracing.com

1 **ALPINE SPECIAL (IRE)**, 4, gr g Orpen (USA)—Halomix **L. Buckley**
2 **DALIDA**, 4, ch f Pursuit of Love—Debutante Days **Mrs C. Barclay**
3 **DIFFERENTGEAR**, 4, b g Robellino (USA)—Garconniere **P. C. Haslam**
4 **FIORI**, 9, b g Anshan—Fen Princess (IRE) **Wilson Imports I**
5 **KING REVO (IRE)**, 5, b g Revoque (IRE)—Tycoon Aly (IRE) **Dick Renwick & Mrs C. Barclay**
6 **KINNAIRD (IRE)**, 4, ch f Dr Devious (IRE)—Ribot's Guest (IRE) **Mrs R. J. Jacobs**
7 **MAUNBY RAVER**, 4, ch g Pivotal—Colleen Liath **Maunby Investment Management**
8 **MIDDLEHAM PARK (IRE)**, 5, b g Revoque (IRE)—Snap Crackle Pop (IRE) **Middleham Park Racing**
9 **MIDDLEHAM ROSE**, 4, b f Dr Fong (USA)—Shallop **Middleham Park Racing III**
10 **MR MISCHIEF**, 5, b g Millkom—Snow Huntress **Middleham Park Racing I & Mrs C Barclay**
11 **NOCATEE (IRE)**, 4, b g Vettori (IRE)—Rosy Sunset (IRE) **Middleham Park Racing & Middleham Turf**
12 **POSITIVE PROFILE (IRE)**, 7, b g Definite Article—Leyete Gulf (IRE) **Chelgate Public Relations Ltd**
13 **RED FLYER (IRE)**, 6, br g Catrail (USA)—Marostica (ITY) **Mrs C. Barclay & Gordon Craig**
14 **RESTART (IRE)**, 4, b g Revoque (IRE)—Stargard **J. D. Roundtree**
15 **TURKS AND CAICOS (IRE)**, 4, b br g Turtle Island (IRE)—Need You Badly **Chepstow Racing Club**
16 **YANKEEDOODLEDANDY (IRE)**, 4, b g Orpen (USA)—Laura Margaret **K. Tyre & Mrs C. Barclay**
17 **YOU'RE SPECIAL (USA)**, 8, b g Northern Flagship (USA)—Pillow Mint (USA) **L. Buckley**

THREE-YEAR-OLDS

18 **BLUSHING RUSSIAN (IRE)**, b g Fasliyev (USA)—Ange Rouge **Blue Lion Racing V**
19 **CANARY DANCER**, b f Groom Dancer (USA)—Bird of Time (IRE) **Kary-On Racing**
20 **CIRCUMSPECT (IRE)**, b g Spectrum (IRE)—Newala **Blue Lion Racing IV**
21 **COMICAL ERRORS (USA)**, b g Distorted Humor (USA)—Fallibility (USA) **Mrs C. Barclay**
22 **DAN'S HEIR**, b g Dansili—Million Heiress **Blue Lion Racing V**
23 **DENNICK**, b g Nicolotte—Branston Dancer **D. Browne**
24 **DRAMATIC REVIEW (IRE)**, b g Indian Lodge (IRE)—Dramatic Shift (IRE) **M. Cook**
25 **ETOILE RUSSE (IRE)**, b g Soviet Star (USA)—To The Skies (USA) **S. A. B. Dinsmore**
26 **FRANSISCAN**, ch g Fraam—Ordained **Northern Lights Racing**
27 **GILDAS FORTUNA**, b f Fort Wood (USA)—Gleaming Sky (SAF) **Mrs R. J. Jacobs**
28 **GOOD INVESTMENT**, b g Silver Patriarch (IRE)—Bundled Up (USA) **P. C. Haslam**
29 **GRACIE'S GIFT (IRE)**, b g Imperial Ballet (IRE)—Settle Petal (IRE) **Middleham Park Racing XXVII**
30 **IMPASSE CARRAIRE**, ch f Piccolo—Magical Dancer (IRE) **A. Peachey**
31 **JEUNE LOUP**, b g Loup Sauvage (USA)—Secret Waters **Blue Lion Racing IV**
32 **KERRY'S BLADE (IRE)**, ch g Daggers Drawn (USA)—Treasure (IRE) **G. Chapman**
33 **LIGHTNING PROSPECT**, ch f Zaha (CAN)—Lightning Blaze **Middleham Park Racing**
34 **LILLAS FOREST**, b g Forestry (USA)—Lines of Beauty (USA) **Mr M. T. Buckley**
35 **MAUNBY REVELLER**, b g Benny The Dip (USA)—Aunt Tate **Maunby Investment Management**
36 **MIDDLEHAM PRINCESS (IRE)**, ch f Grand Lodge (USA)—Merci (IRE) **Blue Lion Racing IV**
37 **MIDNIGHT IN MOSCOW (IRE)**, b g Soviet Star (USA)—Solar Display (USA) **Middleham Park Racing**
38 **MIST OPPORTUNITY (IRE)**, b g Danetime (IRE)—Lady of the Mist (IRE) **Blue Lion Racing V**
39 **PATXARAN (IRE)**, b f Revoque (IRE)—Stargard **D. H. Morgan**
40 **RUSSIAN RIO (IRE)**, b g Imperial Ballet (IRE)—L'harmonie (USA) **Rio Stainless Engineering Limited**
41 **SINNBARA**, b f Sinndar (IRE)—Souk (IRE) **Mrs C. Barclay**
42 **TETRA SING (IRE)**, b f Sinndar (IRE)—Tetralogy (USA) **Middleham Park Racing XV**
43 **TIFFIN BROWN**, br g Erhaab (USA)—Cockatrice **Lord Clyde Racing**

MR PATRICK HASLAM—continued

44 **VOCATIVE (GER)**, gr f Acatenango (GER)—Vadinaxa (FR) **Middleham Park Racing XXX**
45 **ZANDO**, b g Forzando—Rockin' Rosie **Blue Lion Racing IV**

TWO-YEAR-OLDS

46 **ALTO VERTIGO**, b g 7/4 Averti (IRE)—Singer On The Roof (Chief Singer) **Middleham Park Racing**
47 **BEAUTY ONE**, b g 25/2 Josr Algarhoud (IRE)—Beauty (IRE) (Alzao (USA)) (10060) **Vyas Ltd**
48 **BEDOUIN BLUE (IRE)**, b g 10/3 Desert Style (IRE)—
    Society Fair (FR) (Always Fair (USA)) (7377) **Blue Lion Racing V**
49 **DRAWN OUT (IRE)**, ch g 27/4 Daggers Drawn (USA)—Fastnet (Forzando) (12072) **Blue Lion Racing V**
50 B f 25/1 Hernando (FR)—Empress Dagmar (Selkirk (USA)) (9000) **P. Tomlinson**
51 **FITZSIMONS (IRE)**, b c 14/4 Carrowkeel (IRE)—Our Pet (Mummy's Pet) (7500) **D. Browne**
52 B f 28/2 Mtoto—Flower Princess (Slip Anchor) (2000) **P. C. Haslam**
53 **FREEDOM FLYING**, b f 24/3 Kalanisi (IRE)—Free Spirit (IRE) (Caerleon (USA)) (13500) **Middleham Park Racing**
54 **GOLDA SEEK (USA)**, b f 24/4 Seeking The Gold (USA)—
    Golightly (USA) (Take Me Out (USA)) (25000) **Mrs R. J. Jacobs**
55 **HOLY NORMA**, b f 5/5 Nashwan (USA)—Holy Nola (USA) (Silver Deputy (CAN)) (16000) **Mrs R. J. Jacobs**
56 **IMPECCABLE GUEST (IRE)**, b f 6/4 Orpen (USA)—Perfect Guest (What A Guest) **Middleham Park Racing**
57 **INCHDHUAIG**, ch g 28/1 Inchinor—Be Thankfull (IRE) (Linamix (FR)) (25000) **S. A. B. Dinsmore**
58 **INDIAN RUNNER (IRE)**, b f 10/4 Indian Danehill (IRE)—
    Sama Veda (IRE) (Rainbow Quest (USA)) (10060) **Blue Lion Racing V**
59 **KATRINA BALLERINA (IRE)**, b f 18/4 Imperial Ballet (IRE)—
    Sheznice (IRE) (Try My Best (USA)) (3018) **Middleham Park Racing**
60 **LUCKY BAMBLUE (IRE)**, b c 16/3 Key of Luck (USA)—Bamboo (IRE) (Thatching) (12742) **Blue Lion Racing V**
61 **MAROUSSIES WINGS (IRE)**, b f 3/5 In The Wings—Maroussie (FR) (Saumarez) **Mrs R. J. Jacobs**
62 B f 18/2 Spectrum (IRE)—Night Owl (Night Shift (USA)) (8000) **Mrs C. Barclay**
63 B f 28/3 Mujadil (USA)—Rahwah (Northern Baby (CAN)) (10000) **P. C. Haslam**
64 **RED IRIS (IRE)**, ch f 22/3 Soviet Star (USA)—Last Rolo (Mark of Esteem (IRE)) (9000) **Mrs I. Gibson**
65 B f 9/2 Royal Applause—Red Ryding Hood (Wolfhound (USA)) **D. H. Morgan**
66 **SCARLET PASTORALE**, b f 5/4 Vettori (IRE)—
    Show Me Genius (USA) (Beau Genius (CAN)) (5000) **S. A. B. Dinsmore**
67 B g 25/4 Bertolini (USA)—Snow Eagle (IRE) (Polar Falcon (USA)) (4000) **P. C. Haslam**
68 **TIFFIN JO (IRE)**, b f 16/4 Fruits of Love (USA)—Kick The Habit (Habitat) (11000) **Lord Clyde Racing**
69 **TILTILI (IRE)**, ch f 6/4 Spectrum (IRE)—
    Alexander Confranc (IRE) (Magical Wonder (USA)) (14000) **Mrs S. V. Milner**

Other Owners: J. Corbally, H. Guss, P. Ebdon, J. D. Briscoe, P. J. Curson, A. Gleadall, P. A. Hill-Walker, M. C. Mason, Sir George Meyrick, Mr M. Ryan, R. Young.

Assistant Trainer: Carol Williams

Jockey (NH): F. Keniry, A. P. McCoy. **Conditional:** T. Burton-Pye. **Apprentice:** Mark Flynn, G. Bartley, F. Pickard. **Amateur:** Mr B. Haslam, Miss J. Riding, Ms C. Williams.

---

273   MR N. J. HAWKE, Woolminstone

Postal: **Blackmore Farm, Woolminstone, Crewkerne, Somerset, TA18 8QP.**
Contacts: **PHONE (01635) 578101 MOBILE (07899) 922827**

1 **DEBATABLE**, 6, ch g Deploy—Questionable **T. O. Hearns**
2 **FRIENDLY GIRL (IRE)**, 6, b m King's Ride—Royal Patrol (IRE) **Mr N. J. Hawke**
3 **HARDRADA (IRE)**, 6, b g Entrepreneur—Alamiya (IRE) **T. O. Hearns**
4 **HONNEUR FONTENAIL (FR)**, 6, ch g Tel Quel (FR)—Fontanalia (FR) **Wags To Riches Partnership**
5 **JAVELIN**, 9, ch g Generous (IRE)—Moss **Mr C. Handford**
6 **JENAVIVE**, 5, b m Danzig Connection (USA)—Promise Fulfilled (USA) **T. O. Hearns**
7 **KIM FONTENAIL (FR)**, 5, b m Kaldounevees (FR)—Fontanalia (FR) **B. Fry**
8 **KING'S CHAMBERS**, 9, ch g Sabrehill (USA)—Flower Girl **C. G. Newman**
9 **LI'L LEES (IRE)**, 4, ch g Lake Coniston (IRE)—Kayrava **C. E. Handford**
10 **OPPORTUNITY KNOCKS**, 5, gr g Wace (USA)—Madame Ruby (FR) **Mrs D. A. Wetherall**
11 **PAPUA**, 11, ch g Green Dancer (USA)—Fairy Tern **N. Quesnel**
12 **PEN-ALMOZON**, 9, ch h Almoojid—Cornish Mona Lisa **P. A. Mann**
13 **RONALD**, 6, ch g Karinga Bay—Hy Wilma **M. J. Disney**
14 **RUDE HEALTH**, 5, b m Rudimentary (USA)—Birsay **D. R. Mead**
15 **RUNNING HOT**, 7, b g Sunley Builds—Running Cool **C. G. Newman**
16 **SILVER CRYSTAL (IRE)**, 5, b m Among Men (USA)—Silver Moon **N. J. McMullan**

MR N. J. HAWKE—continued

17 **SOEUR FONTENAIL (FR)**, 8, b m Turgeon (USA)—Fontanalia (FR) **La Connection Francaise**
18 **TARZAN DU MESNIL (FR)**, 4, ro g Turgeon (USA)—Ladies View (FR) **Mr T. O. Heayns**
19 **THE LAST OVER**, 4, b f Overbury (IRE)—Little Serena **W. E. Donohue**
20 **TWENTYTWOSILVER (IRE)**, 5, gr ro g Emarati (USA)—St Louis Lady **C. E. Handford**
21 **TWO TEARS**, 11, gr g Silver Owl—Vomero (NZ) **M. J. Disney**
22 **ZIMBABWE (FR)**, 5, b g Turgeon (USA)—Razzamatazz (FR) **R. J. & Mrs J. A. Peake**

Other Owners: S. W. Delve, M. J. Hallett, S. M. Lambert, A. J. Leech.

Assistant Trainer: Mrs S Hawke

Amateur: Miss T. Newman.

---

274 **MR JOHN C HAYDEN, Kildare**
Postal: **Castlemartin Abbey House Stables, Kilcullen, Co. Kildare, Ireland.**
Contacts: **PHONE/FAX +353 (0) 45 481598 MOBILE +353 (0) 86 8226717**
E-MAIL hayden-jj@yahoo.com WEBSITE www.jchayden.com

1 **ALONE HE STANDS (IRE)**, 5, b g Flying Spur (AUS)—Millennium Tale (FR)
2 **LILLY HAWK (IRE)**, 4, b f Shernazar—Bloomfield (IRE)
3 4, B g Desert Style (IRE)—Millennium Tale (FR)
4 **QUAKER GIRL (IRE)**, 6, b m Mujadil (USA)—Roundstone Dancer (IRE)

THREE-YEAR-OLDS

5 Ch f Almutawakel—Ilia (USA)
6 **NIGHT PRAYERS (IRE)**, ch c Night Shift (USA)—Eleanor Antoinette (IRE)
7 B f Lahib (USA)—Roundstone Dancer (IRE)
8 **SIGHTSEER (USA)**, b f Distant View (USA)—Lady of Vision

TWO-YEAR-OLDS

9 Ch c 31/3 Carrowkeel (IRE)—Golden Leap (Salmon Leap (USA)) (5029)
10 B c 27/3 Distant Music (USA)—Kirri (IRE) (Lycius (USA)) (3353) **Francis J. O'Toole**
11 **MONSIEUR HENRI (USA)**, b c 13/3 Chester House (USA)—Lady of Vision (Vision (USA)) (40000)
12 B f 10/4 Carrowkeel (IRE)—Roundstone Dancer (IRE) (Dancing Dissident (USA)) (1340) **Francis J. O'Toole**

Other Owners: F. Campbell, Castlemartin Racing Club, Mr P. Crimin, Mr J. Hardiman, Mr S. Hayden, Mr J. Keeling, Mr S. Kistler, Lady O'Reilly, Mr E. McAllister, Mr P. McCutcheon, Sir A. J. O'Reilly, Mr S. Ridgeway.

Assistant Trainer: J J Hayden

Jockey (flat): N. McCullagh, M. J. Kinane, J. P. Spencer. **Jockey (NH):** D. J. Casey. **Amateur:** Mr S. Ryder.

---

275 **MR D. HAYDN JONES, Pontypridd**
Postal: **Garth Paddocks, Efail Isaf, Pontypridd, Mid-Glamorgan, CF38 1SN.**
Contacts: **PHONE (01443) 202515 FAX (01443) 201877 MOBILE (07967) 680012**

1 **ARDKEEL LASS (IRE)**, 4, ch f Fumo di Londra (IRE)—Wot-A-Noise (IRE) **Merthyr Motor Auctions**
2 **BROWN DRAGON**, 4, ch g Primo Dominie—Cole Slaw **Jack Brown (Bookmaker) Ltd**
3 **CHICKADO (IRE)**, 4, b f Mujadil (USA)—Arcevia (IRE) **Monolithic Refractories Ltd**
4 **ERMINE GREY**, 4, gr g Wolfhound (USA)—Impulsive Decision (IRE) **L. M. Baker**
5 **FINE THANKS**, 4, b f Danzig Connection (USA)—Dim Ots **Mrs D. J. Hughes**
6 **HEATHERS GIRL**, 6, ch m Superlative—Kristis Girl **Trio Racing**
7 **KELTIC RAINBOW (IRE)**, 4, b f Spectrum (IRE)—Secrets of Honour **Miss G. M. Byrne**
8 **PASS THE PORT**, 4, ch g Docksider (USA)—One of The Family **The Porters**

THREE-YEAR-OLDS

9 **A LITTLE TIPSY**, b g Tipsy Creek (USA)—My Hearts Desire **G. J. Hicks**
10 **ALVARINHO LADY**, b f Royal Applause—Jugendliebe (IRE)
11 **HIGH DYKE**, b g Mujahid (USA)—Gold Linnet **L. M. Baker**
12 **HONORARY CITIZEN**, b g Montjoy (USA)—Heart So Blue **G. J. Hicks**
13 **IS THAT RIGHT**, b f Josr Algarhoud (IRE)—Dim Ots **Mrs D. J. Hughes**
14 **MISS SUDBROOK (IRE)**, ch f Daggers Drawn (USA)—Missed Opportunity (IRE) **L. M. Baker**

MR D. HAYDN JONES—continued

15 MONTE MAYOR BOY, b g First Trump—Risalah **Mr R. Phillips**
16 PRIORINA (IRE), b f Priolo (USA)—Strina (IRE) **J. E. Keeling**
17 ROYAL ORISSA, b c Royal Applause—Ling Lane **Llewelyn, Runeckles**
18 VISCOUNT ROSSINI, b br g Rossini (USA)—Spain **L. M. Baker**

TWO-YEAR-OLDS

19 B f 19/4 Night Shift (USA)—Avigail (USA) (Miswaki (USA)) (16766) **Mrs D. J. Hughes**
20 CHIA (IRE), ch f 25/4 Ashkalani (IRE)—Motley (Rainbow Quest (USA)) (16096) **G. I. D. Llewelyn**
21 B f 30/4 Xaar—Idle Chat (USA) (Assert) (12072) **Monolithic Refractories Ltd**
22 IN SOME STYLE (IRE), ch f 8/5 Grand Lodge (USA)—
                            Lovisa (USA) (Gone West (USA)) (13413) **Mrs D. J. Hughes**
23 B g 5/3 Mull of Kintyre (USA)—Monte Mayor Golf (IRE) (Case Law) (22000) **Mr R. Phillips**
24 B f 28/2 Key of Luck (USA)—Rainbow Melody (IRE) (Rainbows For Life (CAN)) (8718) **Mrs D. J. Hughes**
25 Gr f 18/4 Monashee Mountain (USA)—Siva (FR) (Bellypha) (6371) **K. Kynaston**

Other Owners: R. T. Drage, R. Hacker, G. I. D. Llewelyn, J. F. Runeckles.

Assistant Trainer: Mrs E M Haydn Jones

Apprentice: L. Brewer.

MR A. B. HAYNES, Marlborough
Postal: **Fairmile Stables, Herridge, Collingbourne Ducis, Wiltshire, SN8 3EG.**
Contacts: **PHONE (01264) 850088 FAX (01264) 850912 MOBILE (07796) 256060**
E-MAIL andyhaines7@hotmail.com WEBSITE www.ahaynesracingltd.co.uk

1 ASH HAB (USA), 7, b g A P Indy (USA)—Histoire (FR) **B. Comer**
2 FRANK'S QUEST (IRE), 5, b g Mujadil (USA)—Questuary (IRE) **Fun & Fantasy & Andrew Haynes Racing Ltd**
3 KINGS TOPIC (USA), 5, ch g Kingmambo (USA)—Topicount (USA) **Topics Tarts**
4 MAGICO, 4, ch g Magic Ring (IRE)—Silken Dalliance **Andrew Haynes Racing Ltd**
5 NOBLE MOUNT, 4, b g Muhtarram (USA)—Our Poppet (IRE) **G. S. Robinson**

THREE-YEAR-OLDS

6 ARDASNAILS (IRE), b g Spectrum (IRE)—Fey Lady (IRE) **Topics Tarts**
7 BANSHA BANDIT (IRE), b c Imperial Ballet (IRE)—Lagta **The Moonrakers**
8 B g Rossini (USA)—In The Mind (IRE)
9 ITZAWRITE, b f Fumo di Londra (IRE)—Canadian Jive **Mrs C. Macrae**
10 JUST COLIN (IRE), b g Shinko Forest (IRE)—Peaches And Cream (FR) **D. G. J. Fuller**
11 LITTLE GOLDMINE (IRE), ch f Raise A Grand (IRE)—State Treasure (USA) **The Moonrakers**
12 LITTLE MISS GRACIE, gr f Efisio—Circled (USA) **Abacus Employment & Alicia Harden**
13 SILVER MORGAN, gr g Silver Patriarch (IRE)—Liberatrice (FR) **Mr J. M. Sancaster**
14 STAN LEA MOORE, b g Josr Algarhoud (IRE)—Spriolo **Andrew Haynes Racing Ltd**
15 VICTIMISED (IRE), b g Victory Note (USA)—Eurolink Virago **Abacus Employment**
16 YOU'RE MY SON, b g Bold Edge—Sheer Nectar

TWO-YEAR-OLDS

17 B c 26/2 Carrowkeel (IRE)—Cindy's Baby (Bairn (USA)) (1800)
18 LITTLE MISS DAISY, br f 10/2 Zilzal (USA)—Jimgareen (IRE) (Lahib (USA)) (4500) **D. G. J. Fuller**
19 Ch c 31/3 Beckett (IRE)—Olympic Rock (IRE) (Ballad Rock) (4694)
20 PICCOSTAR, b f 20/4 Piccolo—Anneliina (Cadeaux Genereux) (5200) **Mr K. Corke & Mr M. L. Brett**
21 B f 7/3 Namid—Swan Lake (IRE) (Waajib) (3353)
22 Ch c 7/5 Titus Livius (FR)—Trojan Tale (USA) (Critique (USA)) (2011)

Other Owners: Ms C. Berry, Mr M. L. Brett, Mr K. Corke, Mr C. Reeder-Thomas, Mrs D. Robinson.

MR H. E. HAYNES, Highworth
Postal: **Red Down Farm, Highworth, Wiltshire, SN6 7SH.**
Contacts: **PHONE/FAX (01793) 762437**

1 CHOISTY (IRE), 15, ch g Callernish—Rosemount Rose **Mr H. E. Haynes**
2 COUSIN NICKY, 4, ch g Bob Back (USA)—Little Red Spider **The Reddown High Explosive Partnership**
3 FREDERICK JAMES, 11, b g Efisio—Rare Roberta (USA) **Miss S. R. Haynes**

MR H. E. HAYNES—continued

4 **GOT ALOT ON (USA)**, 7, b br g Charnwood Forest (IRE)—Fleety Belle (GER)
5 **IRISH CHAPEL (IRE)**, 9, b g College Chapel—Heart of Flame **Miss S. R. Haynes**
6 **MR JAKE**, 12, b g Safawan—Miss Tealeaf (USA) **Mrs F. Haynes**
7 **RICKHAM GLORY**, 7, b g Past Glories—Rickham Bay **Miss A. L. Joy**
8 **SOMETHING SPECIAL**, 7, b g Petong—My Dear Watson **The Reddown High Explosive Partnership**
9 **WORTH A GAMBLE**, 7, ch g So Factual (USA)—The Strid (IRE) **Miss S. R. Haynes**

TWO-YEAR-OLDS

10 Br c 22/3 Petrizzo—Fly Home (Skyliner)
11 Ch c 3/6 Sure Blade (USA)—Locket (Precocious)
12 B f 29/4 Petrizzo—Rupert's Princess (FR) (Prince Rupert (FR))
13 B f 19/5 Kayf Tara—Stormworthy Miss (IRE) (Glacial Storm (USA))
14 B c 21/4 Manhal—Viola (Extra)

Other Owners: P. Beach, M. Oliver, P. Beach (Snr), Clive Heatherington, R. H. Trotman, T. M. Hunt.

Assistant Trainer: Sally R Haynes

Jockey (flat): D. Allan, R. Winston. **Conditional:** D. Crosse. **Amateur:** Miss F. Haynes.

---

278 MR J. C. HAYNES, Brampton
Postal: **Cleugh Head, Low Row, Brampton, Cumbria, CA8 2JB.**
Contacts: **PHONE (01697) 746253 MOBILE (07771) 511471 (08451) 249715**

1 **FIFTEEN REDS**, 10, b g Jumbo Hirt (USA)—Dominance **Mr J. C. Haynes**
2 **FLASHY FILLY**, 5, b m Puissance—Tempted (IRE) **Mr J. C. Haynes**
3 **NORTHERN FLASH**, 11, b g Rambo Dancer (CAN)—Spinster **Mr J. C. Haynes**

THREE-YEAR-OLDS

4 B f Polar Prince (IRE)—Tempted (IRE) **Mr J. C. Haynes**

TWO-YEAR-OLDS

5 B f 31/1 Mull of Kintyre (USA)—Collision (Wolfhound (USA)) **Mr J. C. Haynes**

Jockey (NH): F. Keniry.

---

279 MRS C. HEAD, Chantilly
Postal: **32 Avenue du General Leclerc, 60500 Chantilly, France.**
Contacts: **PHONE +33 (0) 3 44 57 01 01 FAX +33 (0) 3 44 58 53 33 MOBILE +33 (0) 6 07 31 05 05**
E-MAIL christiane.head@wanadoo.fr

1 **EXIMIUS**, 4, ch f Atticus (USA)—Gorgeous (USA) **Wertheimer et Frere**
2 **FABULOUS SPEED (USA)**, 4, b f Silver Hawk (USA)—Fabulous Hostess (USA) **Wertheimer et Frere**
3 **LA POTERIE (FR)**, 4, b f Bering—River Ried (FR) **Mrs A. Head**
4 **LINDA REGINA (FR)**, 4, gr f Linamix (FR)—Altamira (FR) **G. B. Torrealba**
5 **LIVING ON MY OWN (GER)**, 4, b f Rainbow Quest (USA)—Lea (GER) **Mrs Focke**
6 **LONDRA (IRE)**, 4, b f Sadler's Wells (USA)—Lady Ambassador **Mme Hildegard Focke**
7 **MAXWELL (FR)**, 5, b h Anabaa (USA)—Malaisie (USA) **Mr Alec Head**
8 **MILIKAYA (FR)**, 4, ch f Green Tune (USA)—Mamamia (FR) **Mrs A. Head**
9 **POLYFIRST (FR)**, 4, b f Poliglote—First Turn (USA) **Wertheimer et Frere**
10 **PREMIER PAS (FR)**, 8, b h Sillery (USA)—Passionnee (USA) **Mr Alec Head**
11 **RED MO (USA)**, 4, b c Red Ransom (USA)—Moiava (USA) **Wertheimer et Frere**
12 **RED RUNNER (USA)**, 4, ch c Storm Cat (USA)—Blushing Away (USA) **Wertheimer et Frere**
13 **RED TUNE (FR)**, 4, ch c Green Tune (USA)—Born Gold (USA) **Wertheimer et Frere**
14 **SALYDORA (FR)**, 5, b m Peintre Celebre (USA)—Silwana (FR) **Wertheimer et Frere**
15 **SILVER RAIN (FR)**, 5, b m Rainbow Quest (USA)—Riviere d'argent (USA) **Wertheimer et Frere**
16 **SOFT PLEASURE (USA)**, 4, b f Diesis—Vintage (CAN) **Wertheimer et Frere**
17 **STAR BAND (USA)**, 4, b f Dixieland Band (USA)—Spenderella (FR) **Mrs A. Head**

MRS C. HEAD—continued

18 **TOUT SEUL (USA)**, 5, b h Gone West (USA)—Only Seule (USA) **Wertheimer et Frere**
19 **VILLADOLIDE (FR)**, 4, bl f Anabaa (USA)—Vassia (USA) **Mrs A. Head**

THREE-YEAR-OLDS

20 **ABUNDANCE (USA)**, b f Anabaa (USA)—Gorgeous (USA) **Robert Clay**
21 **ALDAMA (USA)**, ch f Theatrical—Ixtapa (USA) **Prince Khalid Abdulla**
22 **ANYNAME (IRE)**, b c Danehill (USA)—Anysheba (USA) **Wertheimer et Frere**
23 **ARABICA (USA)**, b f Red Ransom (USA)—Moiava (FR) **Wertheimer et Frere**
24 **ARTIC SAND (USA)**, ch c Dixieland Band (USA)—Hostessante (USA) **Wertheimer et Frere**
25 **ATTIRINA**, ch f Atticus (USA)—Ring Beaune (USA) **Wertheimer et Frere**
26 **BABBLING ON (FR)**, b f Poliglote—Sky Bibi (FR) **Wertheimer et Frere**
27 **BATTLESTAR**, b c Bering—Pan Galactic (USA) **Prince Khalid Abdulla**
28 **BLOW THE LOT (USA)**, b c Stravinsky (USA)—Night Risk (USA) **Bettina Jenney**
29 **BOLITHO (FR)**, b c Poliglote—Red Vintage (USA) **Wertheimer et Frere**
30 **BORN FRIENDLY (IRE)**, ch c Selkirk (USA)—Gold Round (IRE) **Wertheimer et Frere**
31 **BROAD SMILE**, b f Anabaa (USA)—Xaymara (USA) **Prince Khalid Abdulla**
32 **CELINDE (FR)**, b f Anabaa (USA)—Carelaine (USA) **Ecurie des Charmes**
33 **COMMANDEER**, b c Halling (USA)—I Will Lead (USA) **Prince Khalid Abdulla**
34 **EARLY MARCH**, br c Dansili—Emplane (USA) **Prince Khalid Abdulla**
35 **EIGHTY SIX (FR)**, b f Octagonal (NZ)—Sound Hill (FR) **Wertheimer et Frere**
36 **ELLE ET TOI (FR)**, bl f Octagonal (NZ)—Toi Et Moi (FR) **Wertheimer et Frere**
37 **FIREJACK (USA)**, b c Dixieland Band (USA)—Partygoer (USA) **Wertheimer et Frere**
38 **FLAMENBA (USA)**, b f Kingmambo (USA)—Sadler's Flag (IRE) **Wertheimer et Frere**
39 **GANAGO (FR)**, ch c Kingmambo (USA)—Ganasheba (USA) **Wertheimer et Frere**
40 **GOLDEN PALACE (USA)**, ch c Chester House (USA)—Doree (USA) **Prince Khalid Abdulla**
41 **GOLDINA (USA)**, b f Rahy (USA)—Natural Gold (FR) **Wertheimer et Frere**
42 **HAIRBALL**, b c Highest Honor (FR)—Sail Storm (USA) **Wertheimer et Frere**
43 **HAWKSBURY HEIGHTS**, ch c Nashwan (USA)—Gentle Dame **Maktoum Al Maktoum**
44 **JOLIE ETOILE (USA)**, ch f Diesis—Willstar (USA) **Prince Khalid Abdulla**
45 **KICKAHEAD (USA)**, b c Danzig (USA)—Krissante (USA) **Wertheimer et Frere**
46 **KLAIRONNETTE (FR)**, bl f Goldneyev (USA)—Sainte Gig (FR) **Wertheimer et Frere**
47 **LE REVEUR (USA)**, b c Machiavellian (USA)—Brooklyn's Dance (FR) **Wertheimer et Frere**
48 **LYFORDMIX (FR)**, gr c Linamix (FR)—Lady Carlotta (IRE) **Mr Alec Head**
49 **MENEUR (FR)**, gr g Septieme Ciel (USA)—Mamamia (FR) **Mr Alec Head**
50 **MYDARSHAAN**, b f Darshaan—Mypreciousprospect (USA) **Wertheimer et Frere**
51 **MYTHOMANE (FR)**, b br c Anabaa (USA)—Mythologie (FR) **Mr Alec Head**
52 **NAISSANCE ROYALE (IRE)**, ch f Giant's Causeway (USA)—Net Worth (USA) **Ecurie des Charmes**
53 **NANABANANA (IRE)**, b f Anabaa (USA)—Tanabata (FR) **Mr P. D. Savill**
54 **NIPPY (FR)**, bl f Anabaa (USA)—Neeran (USA) **Mrs A. Head**
55 **NO DANZIG (USA)**, b c Danzig (USA)—Juvenia (USA) **Wertheimer et Frere**
56 **PARAMOUNT (FR)**, b c Octagonal (NZ)—Passionnee (USA) **Wertheimer et Frere**
57 **PAROLE DE STAR (USA)**, b f King of Kings (IRE)—Statistic (USA) **Ecurie des Charmes**
58 **POLIGLOTTI (FR)**, b c Poliglote—Loretta Gianni (FR) **Wertheimer et Frere**
59 **RANELAGH (FR)**, b c Anabaa (USA)—Riziere (FR) **Mr Alec Head**
60 **REFLEX (FR)**, bl c Octagonal (NZ)—Roanne (FR) **Mr Alec Head**
61 **SABLONNE (USA)**, b f Silver Hawk (USA)—Desert Jewel (USA) **Wertheimer et Frere**
62 **SAPHIRE (USA)**, ch f Silver Hawk (USA)—Fabulous Hostess (USA) **Wertheimer et Frere**
63 **SENAT (FR)**, b c Octagonal (NZ)—Silvermine (FR) **Mr Alec Head**
64 **SILENT NAME (JPN)**, b c Sunday Silence (USA)—Danzigaway (USA) **Wertheimer et Frere**
65 **SILVER FASHION (IRE)**, b f Unfuwain (USA)—Silver Fun (FR) **Wertheimer et Frere**
66 **SOUTHERN SUNSET**, b f Polish Precedent—Due South **Maktoum Al Maktoum**
67 **SPECIALE (USA)**, b f War Chant (USA)—Spenderella (FR) **Mrs A. Head**
68 **SPIRIT GUIDE (FR)**, b c Anabaa (USA)—Shining Molly (FR) **Prince Khalid Abdulla**
69 **SPLENDIDE (FR)**, ch g Bering—Sienne (FR) **Mr Alec Head**
70 **STORM AVERTED (USA)**, b f Summer Squall (USA)—Averti (USA) **Prince Khalid Abdulla**
71 **STRADIVARI (USA)**, b c Silver Hawk (USA)—Vibrant **Robin Swily**
72 **STRETCHING (USA)**, b f Red Ransom (USA)—Broad Pennant (USA) **Wertheimer et Frere**
73 **SWINGSKY (IRE)**, b f Indian Ridge—Plissetskaia (FR) **Wertheimer et Frere**
74 **TAKENDO**, b c Acatenango (GER)—Tiyi (FR) **Wertheimer et Frere**
75 **TEEM (IRE)**, b f Xaar—Deluge **Prince Khalid Abdulla**
76 **TEMPERATURE**, ch c Bering—Thermal Spring **Prince Khalid Abdulla**
77 **TOUT ROUGE (USA)**, b c Red Ransom (USA)—Ecoute (USA) **Wertheimer et Frere**
78 **VIOLET LANE**, b f Danzero (AUS)—Banafsajee (USA) **Maktoum Al Maktoum**

MRS C. HEAD—continued

79 **VITTEL (FR)**, b c Highest Honor (FR)—Vassia (USA) **Mr Alec Head**
80 **WOMAN SECRET (IRE)**, b f Sadler's Wells (USA)—Monevassia (USA) **Ecurie des Charmes**
81 **ZIZARING**, b c Bering—Arazina **Wertheimer et Frere**

TWO-YEAR-OLDS

82 B c 4/4 Grand Lodge (USA)—Altamira (FR) (Highest Honor (FR)) **G. B. Torrealba**
83 B c 22/4 Zafonic (USA)—Bright Spells (USA) (Alleged (USA)) **Prince Khalid Abdulla**
84 **CATCH THE BLUE HAT (USA)**, ch f 29/4 Storm Cat (USA)—Catchascatchcan (Pursuit of Love) **T. A. Ryan**
85 **CHIMICHANGA (FR)**, b f 7/3 Garuda (IRE)—Convent Guest (IRE) (Be My Guest (USA)) **Jean Pierre Ribes**
86 B c 15/4 Emperor Jones (USA)—Composition (Sillery) **C. Head**
87 **CREE (FR)**, b c 12/4 Ski Chief (USA)—Church Mixa (FR) (Linamix (FR)) (14755) **Gilles Maarek**
88 **DAYANIGUAS (FR)**, bl f 27/1 Commands (AUS)—Diatara (FR) (Sillery) **Mrs A. Head**
89 B c 21/3 Anabaa (USA)—Flamenco Red (Warning) **Prince Khalid Abdulla**
90 B f 8/2 Danzig (USA)—Hidden Lake (USA) (Quiet American (USA)) **T. Farmer & R. Clay**
91 **INDIANA ANNIE (IRE)**, b f 2/3 Indian Ridge—Annex (Anabaa (USA)) (90543) **Mr P. D. Savill**
92 Ch f 19/1 Rainbow Quest (USA)—Jubilee Trail (Shareef Dancer (USA)) **Prince Khalid Abdulla**
93 **KARSCH (USA)**, b c 8/5 Red Ransom (USA)—Moiava (FR) (Bering) **Wertheimer et Frere**
94 B f 19/2 Kalanisi (IRE)—Kinetic Force (USA) (Holy Bull (USA)) **Prince Khalid Abdulla**
95 **LEMONETTE (USA)**, ch f 19/1 Lemon Drop Kid (USA)—Believability (USA) (Southern Halo (USA)) **T. A. Ryan**
96 B f 19/1 Grand Lodge (USA)—Light Ballet (Sadler's Wells (USA)) **Prince Khalid Abdulla**
97 **MAGIE FRANCAISE (FR)**, b f 11/2 Anabaa (USA)—Magical Hawk (Silver Hawk (USA)) (90543) **T. A. Ryan**
98 **MALAIS (FR)**, b c 21/4 Emperor Jones (USA)—Malaisie (USA) (Bering) **Mr Alec Head**
99 **MANADOUNA (FR)**, b f 3/3 Kaldounevees (FR)—
　　　　　　　　　　　　　　　　　　　Mana Margaeux (IRE) (Ela-Mana-Mou) (13413) **Jean Pierre Ribes**
100 B f 26/2 Rahy (USA)—Market Booster (USA) (Green Dancer (USA)) (71827) **Ecurie des Monceaux**
101 B f 18/2 Galileo (IRE)—Miss Lorilaw (FR) (Homme de Loi (IRE)) **James Wigan**
102 B f 27/2 Sahm (USA)—Nabahah (FR) (Rainbow Quest (USA)) (10731) **Mrs Cyril Morange**
103 **OMITAS**, b c 28/1 Lomitas—Featherquest (Rainbow Quest (USA)) **Wertheimer et Frere**
104 **PASSAGER (FR)**, b c 8/3 Anabaa (USA)—Passionnee (USA) (Woodman (USA)) **Wertheimer et Frere**
105 **POLLYPINK (FR)**, b f 10/5 Poliglote—Ring Pink (USA) (Bering) **Wertheimer et Frere**
106 Gr ro f 18/4 Silver Hawk (USA)—Quelle Affaire (USA) (Riverman (USA)) **Robin F. Scully**
107 **QUIET ROYAL (USA)**, b f 10/2 Royal Academy (USA)—Wakigoer (USA) (Miswaki (USA)) **Wertheimer et Frere**
108 **RING HILL**, ch f 21/5 Bering—Sound Hill (FR) (Green Tune (USA)) **Wertheimer et Frere**
109 **RING QUEST (FR)**, ch c 22/2 Spectrum (IRE)—Pinkai (IRE) (Caerleon (USA)) **Wertheimer et Frere**
110 **ROUGE (FR)**, b f 16/5 Red Ransom (USA)—Natural Gold (FR) (Mr Prospector (USA)) **Wertheimer et Frere**
111 **ROUGEOLE (USA)**, b f 19/2 Red Ransom (USA)—
　　　　　　　　　　　　　　　　　　　Dance With Grace (USA) (Mr Prospector (USA)) **Wertheimer et Frere**
112 B f 27/2 Barathea (IRE)—Serene View (Distant View (USA)) **Prince Khalid Abdulla**
113 **SET ALIGHT (USA)**, b c 11/2 Hennessy (USA)—Proflare (USA) (Mr Prospector (USA)) **Prince Khalid Abdulla**
114 **SILVER POINT (FR)**, b br c 26/3 Commands (AUS)—Silver Fame (USA) (Quest For Fame) **Mr Alec Head**
115 **SISTER JONES (FR)**, b f 9/2 Emperor Jones (USA)—Silverware (FR) (Polish Precedent (USA)) **Gilles Maarek**
116 **SOMETHINGSPANISH**, b c 29/3 Lomitas—Golden Party (USA) (Seeking The Gold (USA)) **Wertheimer et Frere**
117 **SWANG SONG (USA)**, b c 15/5 Dixieland Band (USA)—
　　　　　　　　　　　　　　　　　　　Hostessante (USA) (Pleasant Colony (USA)) **Wertheimer et Frere**
118 **THEORIQUE (FR)**, b br c 10/3 Highest Honor (FR)—Theorie (FR) (Anabaa (USA)) **Mr Alec Head**
119 **TREMPOLINISSIME (FR)**, b f 18/4 Trempolino—
　　　　　　　　　　　　　　　　　　　Red Vintage (USA) (Red Ransom (USA)) **Wertheimer et Frere**
120 **TRIENNALE (FR)**, b f 10/2 War Chant (USA)—Tresoriere (USA) (Lyphard (USA)) **Mr Alec Head**
121 **TRIUMVIRAT (FR)**, b c 9/3 Bering—Tremiere (FR) (Anabaa (USA)) **Mr Alec Head**
122 **TWINSPOT (USA)**, b br f 21/1 Bahri (USA)—Stormy Gold (USA) (Storm Cat (USA)) **Wertheimer et Frere**
123 **VAGUELY SURE (USA)**, b c 3/2 Diesis—Vintage (CAN) (Foolish Pleasure (USA)) **Wertheimer et Frere**
124 **VENITIEN**, ch c 20/3 Highest Honor (FR)—Vassia (USA) (Machiavellian (USA)) **Mr Alec Head**
125 B c 21/5 Dansili—West Dakota (USA) (Gone West (USA)) **Prince Khalid Abdulla**

Assistant Trainer: D Boulard

Jockey (flat): N. Guesdon, O. Peslier, R. Thomas. **Amateur:** Mrs I. Got.

---

280 **MR P. R. HEDGER, Chichester**
Postal: **Eastmere Stables, Eastergate Lane, Eastergate, Chichester, West Sussex, PO20 3SJ.**
Contacts: **PHONE (01243) 543863 FAX (01243) 543913 MOBILE (07860) 209448**

1 **DREAMS FORGOTTEN (IRE)**, 5, b m Victory Note (USA)—Sevens Are Wild **Mrs J. A. Tanswell**
2 **GATHERING STORM (IRE)**, 7, gr g Roselier (FR)—Queen of The Rock (IRE) **Mr H. Q. Spooner**

MR P. R. HEDGER—continued

3 JACK FULLER (IRE), 8, b g Be My Native (USA)—Jacks Sister (IRE) The Brightling Club 1997
4 KILDARE CHILLER (IRE), 11, ch g Shahrastani (USA)—Ballycuirke C. W. Broomfield
5 MICKLEY (IRE), 8, b g Ezzoud (IRE)—Dawsha (IRE) Mr P. R. Hedger
6 MISSION TO MARS, 6, b g Muhtarram (USA)—Ideal Candidate I. Hutchins
7 SNEEM'S ROCK, 4, br c Daylami (IRE)—Urchin (IRE) J. J. Whelan
8 SYSTEM, 6, ch g Nashwan (USA)—Vivid Imagination (USA)
9 WAIMEA BAY, 6, b m Karinga Bay—Smart In Sable C. J. Silverthorne

Other Owners: S. P. Cross, Mrs D. M. Grissell, M. M. Hooker, C. J. Newport.

Jockey (flat): S. Whitworth. Jockey (NH): L. Aspell, M. A. Fitzgerald. Amateur: Miss E. Kemp.

281 **MR C. J. HEMSLEY, Witney**
Postal: **Watermans Lodge Stables, Cornbury Park, Charlbury, Oxon, OX7 3HN.**
Contacts: HOME/FAX (01993) 844554 YARD (01608) 810455
MOBILES (07971) 205503 (07831) 641434
E-MAIL daijones@countryside-inter.net

1 AEGEAN PIRATE (IRE), 8, b g Polykratis—Rusheen Na Corra (IRE) K. I. McKay
2 ARADNAK (IRE), 5, b m Son of Sharp Shot (IRE)—Kandara (IRE) Mr A. King
3 BOBAWAY (IRE), 8, br g Bob Back (USA)—Baybush (IRE) K. I. McKay
4 HIPPY DIPPY DREAMS, 5, b m Dreams End—Virginia Stock Mrs S. S. Chandler
5 OUR SION, 5, b g Dreams End—Millfields Lady R. D. Evans
6 WESTCORK (IRE), 8, ch g Executive Perk—Cute Play Mr A. King

Assistant Trainer: Mr D S Jones

Jockey (NH): B. Fenton, J. Mogford, S. Stronge.

282 **MR N. J. HENDERSON, Lambourn**
Postal: **Seven Barrows, Lambourn, Hungerford, Berkshire, RG17 8UH.**
Contacts: PHONE (01488) 72259 FAX (01488) 72596

1 AFRAD (FR), 4, gr g Linamix (FR)—Afragha (IRE) The Not Afraid Partnership
2 ALL STAR (GER), 5, b g Lomitas—Alte Garde (FR) L. A. Wilson, Nick Wilson, Martin Landau
3 ALPHA GIOCONDA (IRE), 8, b g Alphabatim (USA)—Rio Dulce Mr N. J. Henderson
4 ANTINOMY (IRE), 5, ch m Anshan—Ardentinny Mr P. E. Clinton
5 ANTIQUARIAN (IRE), 5, b g Bob Back (USA)—Sudden Decision Mr & Mrs Peter Orton
6 ARCTIC SKY (IRE), 8, b g Arctic Lord—Lake Garden Park Mrs P. J. Pugh
7 ARISTOXENE (FR), 5, b g Start Fast (FR)—Petite Folie T. J. Hemmings
8 ASTYANAX (IRE), 5, b h Hector Protector (USA)—Craigmill A. Taylor
9 BACK TO BEN ALDER (IRE), 8, b br g Bob Back (USA)—Winter Fox Mrs B. A. Hanbury
10 BERNINI (IRE), 5, b g Grand Lodge (USA)—Alsahah (IRE) Mrs M. Buckley
11 BONCHESTER BRIDGE, 4, b f Shambo—Cabriole Legs Mr H. Ponsonby
12 BRANKLEY BOY, 7, ch g Afzal—Needwood Fortune G. J. Stewart
13 BRIGHT SPIRIT, 4, b c Petoski—Lunabelle Her Majesty The Queen
14 BRILLIANT CUT, 5, b gr g Terimon—Always Shining Mr H. Ponsonby
15 BUGLE MAJOR (IRE), 6, b g Anshan—Pit Runner Mrs E. L. Curling
16 CALLING BRAVE (IRE), 9, ch g Bob Back (USA)—Queenie Kelly Sir Robert Ogden C.B.E., LLD
17 CANDELLO, 7, b m Supreme Leader—Oubava (FR) R. D. Chugg
18 CAPITANA (GER), 4, ch f Lando (GER)—Capitolina (FR) P. J. D. Pottinger
19 CAPTAIN MILLER, 9, b g Batshoof—Miller's Gait Mr H. Ponsonby
20 CARACCIOLA (GER), 8, b g Lando (GER)—Capitolina (FR) P. J. D. Pottinger
21 CEANANNAS MOR (IRE), 11, b br g Strong Gale—Game Sunset Major C. Hanbury
22 CHAUVINIST (IRE), 10, b g Roselier (FR)—Sacajawea Mrs E. Roberts & Nick Roberts
23 COPSALE LAD, 8, ch g Karinga Bay—Squeaky Cottage Swallow Partnership
24 CRAVEN (IRE), 5, b g Accordion—Glen Dieu Sir Robert Ogden C.B.E., LLD
25 CUNNING PURSUIT, 4, b g Pursuit of Love—Mistitled (USA) Mrs M. Buckley
26 CUPBOARD LOVER, 9, ch g Risk Me (FR)—Galejade Mrs Lesley Lockwood and Mrs Judy Mihalop
27 DANCING BAY, 8, b g Suave Dancer (USA)—Kabayil Elite Racing Club
28 DEMARCO (IRE), 7, ch g Old Vic—Peas (IRE) R. A. Bartlett
29 DUNGARVANS CHOICE (IRE), 10, ch g Orchestra—Marys Gift Elite Racing Club
30 ETENDARD INDIEN (FR), 4, b c Selkirk (USA)—Danseuse Indienne (IRE) Mrs B. L. Harvey
31 FAIRY SILVER, 4, gr f Silver Patriarch (IRE)—Bewitch Her Majesty The Queen

MR N. J. HENDERSON—continued

32 **FIRST LOVE**, 9, br g Bustino—First Romance **Her Majesty The Queen**
33 **FOLLOW UP**, 7, b g Phardante (FR)—Dashing March **B. T. Stewart-Brown Esq**
34 **FONDMORT (FR)**, 9, b g Cyborg (FR)—Hansie (FR) **W. J. Brown**
35 **FOXCHAPEL QUEEN (IRE)**, 7, b br m Over The River (FR)—Glencairn Lass **P. C. Green**
36 **FOXTON BROOK (IRE)**, 6, br g Presenting—Martins Times (IRE) **L. A. Wilson**
37 **GEOS (FR)**, 10, b br g Pistolet Bleu (IRE)—Kaprika (FR) **Thurloe Finsbury**
38 **GO FOR BUST**, 6, b g Sabrehill (USA)—Butsova **Mrs E. Roberts & Nick Roberts**
39 **GRANDE JETE (SAF)**, 8, ch g Jallad (USA)—Corps de Ballet (SAF) **L. Westwood A. Chandler J. J. Hindley**
40 **GREENHOPE (IRE)**, 7, b g Definite Article—
                    Unbidden Melody (USA) **L. A. Wilson, Giles Wilson, Martin Landau**
41 **HAPPY SHOPPER (IRE)**, 5, b g Presenting—Reach Down (IRE) **Heli-Beds Racing**
42 **HUE AND CRY**, 4, br g Monsun (GER)—So Rarely (USA) **Mr N. J. Henderson**
43 **IAMBE DE LA SEE (FR)**, 9, b m Useful (FR)—Reine Mati (SWI) **Elite Racing Club**
44 **IN GOOD FAITH (USA)**, 4, b br f Dynaformer (USA)—Healing Hands **R. C. Tooth**
45 **IRISH HUSSAR (IRE)**, 9, b g Supreme Leader—Shuil Ard **Major C. Hanbury**
46 **ITS A DREAM (IRE)**, 5, b g Oscar (IRE)—Gra-Bri (IRE) **Mrs R. Murdoch & David Murdoch**
47 **JOHANN DE VONNAS (FR)**, 8, b g Cadoudal (FR)—Diana de Vonnas (FR) **B. T. M. Racing**
48 **JOYE DES ILES (FR)**, 8, b g Mont Basile (FR)—Titjana (FR) **Killinghurst Park Stud**
49 **JUVEIGNEUR (FR)**, 8, ch g Funny Baby (FR)—Azurea (FR) **Trevor Hemmings**
50 **KENZO III (FR)**, 7, ch g Agent Bleu (FR)—Kelinda (FR) **Killinghurst Park Stud**
51 **KYPER DISCO (FR)**, 7, b g Epervier Bleu—Disconea (FR) **Newbury Racehorse Owners Group**
52 **LADY OF FORTUNE (IRE)**, 6, b m Sovereign Water (FR)—Needwood Fortune **G. J. Stewart**
53 **LANDING LIGHT (IRE)**, 10, b g In The Wings—Gay Hellene **Mr & Mrs John Poynton**
54 **LIBERIA (IRE)**, 6, b g Kadalko (FR)—Unica Iv (FR) **Mrs T. J. Stone Brown**
55 **LIBERTHINE (FR)**, 6, b m Chamberlin (FR)—Libertina (FR) **Mr R. B. Waley-Cohen**
56 **LILIUM DE COTTE (FR)**, 6, b g Ragmar (FR)—Vanille de Cotte (FR) **Mr John P. McManus**
57 **LORD BUCKINGHAM**, 7, ch g Carroll House—Lady Buck **Mrs H. Maitland-Jones**
58 **LORD JOSHUA (IRE)**, 7, b g King's Theatre (IRE)—Lady Joshua (IRE) **Mrs W. S. Farish & Lady Lloyd Webber**
59 **LORD OF THE RIVER (IRE)**, 13, br g Lord Americo—Well Over **B. T. Stewart-Brown Esq**
60 **LUSTRAL DU SEUIL (FR)**, 8, b g Sassanian (USA)—Bella Tennise (FR) **W. J. Brown**
61 **MAGIC MISTRESS**, 6, b m Magic Ring (IRE)—Sight'n Sound **Brian Twojohns Partnership**
62 **MAHARBAL (FR)**, 5, b g Assessor (IRE)—Cynthia (FR) **The Pheasant Inn Partnership**
63 **MAJOR MILLER**, 4, b g Opera Ghost—Millers Action **Mr H. Ponsonby**
64 **MAMBO (FR)**, 7, b g Ashkalani (IRE)—Bold Tango (FR) **Mrs B. L. Harvey**
65 **MARLBOROUGH (IRE)**, 13, br g Strong Gale—Wrekenogan **Sir Robert Ogden C.B.E., LLD**
66 **MENCHIKOV (FR)**, 5, br g Garde Royale—Caucasie (FR) **Sir Robert Ogden C.B.E., LLD**
67 **MIGHTY STRONG**, 11, b g Strong Gale—Muffet's Spider **Henderson Family**
68 **MONTY'S SALVO (USA)**, 6, b g Supreme Leader—Likashot **Mr H. Ponsonby**
69 **NAS NA RIOGH (IRE)**, 6, b m King's Theatre (IRE)—Abstraite **Brian Twojohns Partnership**
70 **NIGHTWATCHMAN (IRE)**, 6, b g Hector Protector (USA)—Nightlark (IRE) **Sir Eric Parker & Mary Anne Parker**
71 **NIKOLAIEV (FR)**, 4, b g Nikos—Faensa (FR) **Killinghurst Park Stud**
72 **NO REGRETS (FR)**, 4, b g Nononito—Betty Royale **J. D. Cotton**
73 **NO SHENANIGANS (IRE)**, 8, b g King's Ride—Melarka **Mrs Christopher Hanbury**
74 **NON SO (FR)**, 7, b g Definite Article—Irish Woman (FR) **ROA Dawn Run Partnership**
75 **NUIT SOMBRE (IRE)**, 5, b g Night Shift (USA)—Belair Princess (USA) **Mrs M. Pett**
76 **OLD ROWLEY**, 6, br g Supreme Leader—Teeno Nell **Gibson, Goddard, Hamer & Hawkes**
77 **PAPINI (IRE)**, 4, ch g Lomitas—Pariana (USA) **Newbury Racehorse Owners Group**
78 **PERLE DE PUCE (FR)**, 6, b m Snurge—Ma Puce (FR) **Mr R. B. Waley-Cohen**
79 **PROMISE TO BE GOOD**, 4, b g Unfuwain (USA)—Kshessinskaya **W. J. Gredley**
80 **REGAL EXIT (FR)**, 9, ch g Exit To Nowhere (USA)—Regalante **B. Buckley**
81 **RICO HOMBRE (FR)**, 6, b g Cadoudal (FR)—Lady Carolina (FR) **Sir Robert Ogden C.B.E., LLD**
82 **RIVER PIRATE (IRE)**, 8, b g Un Desperado (FR)—Kigali (IRE) **Riverwood Racing II**
83 **ROI DE L'ODET (FR)**, 5, b g Grape Tree Road—Fanfare du Roi **Elite Racing Club**
84 **ROYAL KATIDOKI (FR)**, 5, b g Rochesson (FR)—Miss Coco (FR) **Anthony Speelman**
85 **SAINTSAIRE (FR)**, 6, b g Apeldoorn (FR)—Pro Wonder (FR) **Anthony Speelman**
86 **SCOTS GREY**, 10, gr g Terimon—Misowni **Mr H. Ponsonby**
87 **SEA CAPTAIN**, 5, b g Oscar (IRE)—Calabria **Her Majesty The Queen**
88 **SHINING STRAND**, 6, ch g Karinga Bay—First Romance **Her Majesty The Queen**
89 **SLEEP BAL (FR)**, 6, b g Sleeping Car (FR)—Balle Six (FR) **Mrs M. O. Bryant**
90 **SLICK (FR)**, 4, br g Highest Honor (FR)—Seven Secrets **Riverwood Racing II**
91 **SLOOGHY (FR)**, 9, br g Missolonghi (USA)—Lady Charrecey (FR) **P. A. Deal**
92 **SPREAD THE DREAM**, 7, ch g Alflora (IRE)—Cauchemar **Mrs N. S. Tregaskes**
93 **STAR PRIZE (IRE)**, 8, b g Fourstars Allstar (USA)—Dipper's Gift (IRE) **Mr R. J. Green**
94 **STARELLO**, 6, b m Supreme Leader—Oubava (FR) **Mr R. A. Ballin**
95 **SUNLEY FUTURE (IRE)**, 6, b g Broken Hearted—The Wicked Chicken (IRE) **J. B. Sunley**
96 **TANIKOS (FR)**, 6, b g Nikos—Tamana (USA) **Studwell Two Partnership**

MR N. J. HENDERSON—continued

97 **TESSANOORA**, 4, b f Topanoora—Club Sandwich **Tessa Henderson**
98 **THAMES (IRE)**, 7, b g Over The River (FR)—Aon Dochas (IRE) **T. J. Hemmings**
99 **THE GROCERS CURATE (IRE)**, 5, b g Anshan—Shining Willow **Lady Lloyd Webber & Terry Wogan**
100 **THE MARKET MAN (NZ)**, 5, ch g Grosvenor (NZ)—Eastern Bazzaar (IRE) **Sir Robert Ogden C.B.E., LLD**
101 **THE THUNDERER**, 6, gr g Terimon—By Line **T. C. Wilson**
102 **TRABOLGAN (IRE)**, 7, b g King's Ride—Derrella **T. J. Hemmings**
103 **TWIST OF FAITH (IRE)**, 6, b g Fresh Breeze (USA)—Merry And Bright **Studwell Three Partnership**
104 **TYSOU (FR)**, 8, b br g Ajdayt (USA)—Pretty Point **W. J. Brown**
105 **VAL DU DON (FR)**, 5, b g Garde Royale—Vallee Normande (FR) **Million in Mind Partnership**

Other Owners: Mr J. Allison, Mr P. A. G. Banes-Walker, R. H. Beevor, A. R. Bromley, M. F. Broughton, T. G. S. Busher, B. Cartmell, A. Charity, G. I. Charlton, Mr N. C. Clark, A. K. Collins, Mr M. J. Collins, P. J. Cornell, W. A. Cummings, P. A. Deal, Mr P. F. Dennett, Mrs D. M. Douglas-Pennant, R. Drewett, Mrs G. J. Edwards, A. T. Eggleton, P. F. Ellick, Mrs Judy England, J. G. Ferrand, Mr P. Finnegan, The Hon Lady Gibbings, Sir Peter Gibbings, C. B. Gibson, A. Goddard, G. F. Goode, Mrs N. J. G. Green, B. J. Griffiths, C. M. Hamer, R. V. Harding, M. J. C. Hawkes, Mrs C. Henderson, Miss S. L. Henderson, A. J. Hill, J. Hornsey, E. J. Hounslow, D. J. Howse, D. Humphreys, Mrs N. Jones, Mr B. J. Kimmins, Miss E. A. Lake, Mrs L. A. Lockwood, Mrs J. F. Maitland-Jones, Mr B. Marett, Mr I. C. Marr, E. McCormack, W. D. C. Minton, C. J. L. Moorsom, D. S. Mossman, Mrs R. Murdoch, Mr D. Murdoch, P. Murphy, I. R. Murray, David Nicholson, J. M. Nicholson, Miss M. Noden, D. R. Painter, J. Palmer-Brown, A. C. Parker, O. J. W. Pawle, T. Penniket, M. T. Penniket, J. Poynton, Mrs A. Poynton, Mrs J. S. Reed, Mrs E. C. Roberts, N. W. Roberts, Mrs F. C. Saint Jean, R. R. Shand, R. M. Siddle, Mrs H. I. Slade, J. A. B. Stafford, J. Studd, Mrs B. A. M. Studd, Studwell Two Partnership, D. F. Sumpter, Mr D. G. Tate, B. A. Taylor, P. Truman, M. R. Waley-Cohen, T. J. Whitley, M. J. F. T. Wilson, G. T. Wilson.

Jockey (NH): M. A. Fitzgerald, M. Foley. **Conditional:** S. Curling, A. Tinkler. **Amateur:** Mr B. King.

---

283 LADY HERRIES, Littlehampton
Postal: Angmering Park, Littlehampton, West Sussex, BN16 4EX.
Contacts: HOME (01903) 871421 YARD (01903) 871460 FAX (01903) 871609
MOBILE (07785) 282996

1 **ARGENTUM**, 4, b g Sillery (USA)—Frustration **Lady Herries and Friends**
2 **AUTHORITY (IRE)**, 5, b g Bluebird (USA)—Persian Tapestry **Seymour Racing Partnership**
3 **CLEAVER**, 4, ch g Kris—Much Too Risky **Lady Herries**
4 **HERON'S WING**, 4, ch g Hernando (FR)—Celtic Wing **Angmering Park Stud**
5 **ILE MICHEL**, 8, b g Machiavellian (USA)—Circe's Isle **Lady Herries**
6 **KIPSIGIS (IRE)**, 4, b g Octagonal (NZ)—Kisumu **Lady Sarah Clutton**
7 **LADY KORRIANDA**, 4, ch f Dr Fong (USA)—Prima Verde **P. J. Naughton**
8 **LASANGA**, 6, ch g Zamindar (USA)—Shall We Run **Mr Charles Green And Lady Herries**
9 **LUNAR EXIT (IRE)**, 4, gr g Exit To Nowhere (USA)—Moon Magic **Angmering Park Stud**
10 **MARIDAY**, 4, br g Trifolio—Classic Hand **C. E. Hardy**
11 **MURPHY'S QUEST**, 9, ch g Sir Harry Lewis (USA)—Rondeau **Lady Herries and Friends**
12 **POLAR TRYST**, 6, ch m Polar Falcon (USA)—Lovers Tryst **Lady Herries and Friends**
13 **RUDOOD (USA)**, 5, b g Theatrical—Kardashina (FR) **Lady Herries**
14 **TARTOUCHE**, 4, b f Pursuit of Love—Megan's Flight **Lady Herries**
15 **WARNINGCAMP (GER)**, 4, b g Lando (GER)—Wilette (GER) **Lady Sarah Clutton**
16 **WUNDERWOOD (USA)**, 6, b g Faltaat (USA)—Jasoorah (IRE) **A. J. Perkins**
17 **ZONERGEM**, 7, ch g Zafonic (USA)—Anasazi (IRE)

THREE-YEAR-OLDS

18 **HONOUR HIGH**, gr g Cloudings (IRE)—Meant To Be **Lady Mary Mumford and Sir Roger Gibbs**
19 **MOLEM**, br g Green Desert (USA)—Injaad **Seymour Racing Partnership**
20 **MUTAMAASEK (USA)**, b br c Swain (IRE)—Tamgeed (USA) **L. G. Lazarus**
21 **NERETONA**, b f Zieten (USA)—Golconda (IRE) **The Hon D. K. R. Oliver**
22 **RAFELITE**, b f Fraam—Megan's Flight **Lady Herries**
23 **STAND READY**, b f Perryston View—Leave It To Lib **C. E. Hardy**

TWO-YEAR-OLDS

24 Ch g 7/5 Indian Ridge—Moon Carnival (Be My Guest (USA)) (17000) **Angmering Park Stud**
25 Gr c 28/4 Daylami (IRE)—Moon Magic (Polish Precedent (USA)) (21000) **Angmering Park Stud**
26 B c 4/2 Medicean—Mrs Nash (Night Shift (USA)) (25000)
27 B g 1/4 Kalanisi (IRE)—Silly Mid-On (Midyan (USA)) (5000) **Angmering Park Stud**

Other Owners: Sir Roger G. Gibbs, C. Green, M. E. L. Melluish, Lady Mary Mumford, Seymour Bloodstock (Uk) Ltd, R. A. Turner.

284 MR J. HETHERTON, Malton
Postal: **The Old Farmhouse, Highfield, Beverley Road, Malton, North Yorkshire, YO17 9PJ.**
Contacts: **OFFICE/FAX (01653) 696778 MOBILE (07801) 441991**

1 ACE CLUB, 4, ch g Indian Rocket—Presently **K. C. West**
2 BLUE MAEVE, 5, b g Blue Ocean (USA)—Louisville Belle (IRE) **R. G. Fell**
3 COME ON, 6, b g Aragon—All On **N. Hetherton**
4 CYBER SANTA, 7, b g Celtic Swing—Qualitair Ridge **Qualitair Holdings Ltd**
5 DIAMOND JOSHUA (IRE), 7, b g Mujadil (USA)—Elminya (IRE) **Diamond Racing Ltd**
6 ENCOUNTER, 9, br g Primo Dominie—Dancing Spirit (IRE) **Qualitair Holdings Ltd**
7 HEVERSHAM (IRE), 4, b c Octagonal (NZ)—Saint Ann (USA) **K. C. West**
8 INITIATIVE, 9, ch g Arazi (USA)—Dance Quest (FR) **Mr F. E. Reay**
9 MELROSE, 6, b br m Past Glories—Meltonby **Mr J. Hetherton**
10 OWN LINE, 6, b g Classic Cliche (IRE)—Cold Line **N. Hetherton**
11 PHASE EIGHT GIRL, 9, b m Warrshan (USA)—Bugsy's Sister **P. W. Urquhart**
12 QUALITAIR PLEASURE, 5, b m Slip Anchor—Qualitair Ridge **Qualitair Holdings Ltd**
13 QUALITAIR WINGS, 6, b g Colonel Collins (USA)—Semperflorens **Qualitair Holdings Ltd**
14 THAT'S RACING, 5, ch g Classic Cliche (IRE)—All On **N. Hetherton**
15 VALEUREUX, 7, ch g Cadeaux Genereux—La Strada **Eureka Racing**
16 WARREN PLACE, 5, ch g Presidium—Coney Hills **Mrs S. Johnson**

THREE-YEAR-OLDS

17 DESERT BUZZ (IRE), b c Desert Story (IRE)—Sugar **21st Century Racing I**
18 MANGROVE CAY (IRE), b c Danetime (IRE)—Art Duo **K. C. West**

TWO-YEAR-OLDS

19 LITTLE WHITESOX, ch f 8/4 Arkadian Hero (USA)—Due West (Inchinor) (3500) **D. Gladwin**
20 Gr f 6/4 Silver Patriarch (IRE)—Meltonby (Sayf El Arab (USA)) **Mr J. Hetherton**

Other Owners: A. W. Catterall, Mrs B. Catterall.

Assistant Trainer: John Bottomley

285 MR P. W. HIATT, Banbury
Postal: **Six Ash Farm, Hook Norton, Banbury, Oxfordshire, OX15 5DB.**
Contacts: **PHONE (01608) 737255 FAX (01608) 730641 MOBILE (07973) 751115**

1 ALQAAYID, 4, b g Machiavellian (USA)—One So Wonderful **S. F. Holder**
2 BLUE HILLS, 4, br g Vettori (IRE)—Slow Jazz (USA) **Mr T. J. Pratt**
3 BUNDABERG, 5, b g Komaite (USA)—Lizzy Cantle **B. D. Cantle**
4 DANCING KING (IRE), 9, b g Fairy King (USA)—Zariysha (IRE) **Mr P. W. Hiatt**
5 DIDOE, 6, br m Son Pardo—My Diamond Ring **Mrs M. E. Wickham**
6 IPHIGENIA (IRE), 4, b br f Orpen (USA)—Silver Explosive **C. C. H. Roberts**
7 ISA'AF (IRE), 6, b g Darshaan—Shauna's Honey (IRE) **Miss M. McKinney**
8 KINGCOMBE LANE, 5, b g Superpower—Starlight Wonder **P. J. R. Gardner**
9 LAZZAZ, 7, b g Muhtarram (USA)—Astern (USA) **P. Kelly**
10 MEXICAN PETE, 5, b g Atraf—Eskimo Nel (IRE) **First Chance Racing**
11 MOONSHINE BEACH, 7, b g Lugana Beach—Monongelia **Ken Read And Jill Harmsworth**
12 MOONSHINE BILL, 6, ch g Master Willie—Monongelia **Mrs L. Stockley**
13 MY FRIEND FRITZ, 5, ch g Safawan—Little Scarlett **Mr P. W. Hiatt**
14 NORTHERN DESERT (IRE), 6, b g Desert Style (IRE)—Rosie's Guest (IRE) **Clive, Vince And Guy**
15 PRIMROSE COLLAR, 5, b m Superpower—Little Gift **P. J. R. Gardner**
16 SENIOR MINISTER, 7, b g Lion Cavern (USA)—Crime Ofthecentury **P. Kelly**
17 SHANNON'S DREAM, 9, gr m Anshan—Jenny's Call **Mr P. W. Hiatt**
18 SUNDRIED TOMATO, 6, b g Lugana Beach—Little Scarlett **C. C. H. Roberts**
19 TERMONFECKIN, 6, b g Runnett—Crimson Sol **P. Kelly**
20 TIGHT SQUEEZE, 8, br m Petoski—Snowline **A. Harrison**
21 TINSTRE (IRE), 7, ch g Dolphin Street (FR)—Satin Poppy **M. Wennington**
22 TRICKY VENTURE, 5, gr g Linamix (FR)—Ukraine Venture **Mr P. W. Hiatt**

MR P. W. HIATT—continued

THREE-YEAR-OLDS

23 **THE PLAINSMAN**, b g Atraf—Mylania **Mr P. W. Hiatt**

Other Owners: G. P. Convert, J. D. Groves, G. E. Patching, H. E. Peachey, Miss J. L. Peachey, K. L. Read, J. S. Sterry, M. Walker, R. Walker, V. J. Walsh.

Assistant Trainer: Mrs E Hiatt

Jockey (flat): Joanna Badger, R. Winston. **Apprentice:** D. Allan, L. Fletcher. **Amateur:** Miss E. J. Jones, Mrs Marie King, Miss Natasha McKim.

---

286 MISS E. HILL, Malvern
Postal: **Dobbins Farm, Colwall Road, Mathon, Malvern, Worcestershire, WR13 5PH.**
Contacts: **PHONE (01684) 540407 MOBILE (07866) 532722**

1 4, Ch f Simply Great (FR)—Rapid Ground **Mr R. Langley**
2 **RIVER GROUND (IRE)**, 10, br g Lord Americo—Rapid Ground **Mr R. Langley**
3 5, Ch m Executive Perk—Rosie Ring (IRE) **Mr R. Langley**
4 4, B f Flemensfirth (USA)—Rosie Ring (IRE) **Mr R. Langley**
5 **SEA SQUIRT (IRE)**, 8, b g Fourstars Allstar—Polynesian Goddess (IRE) **Mr R. Langley**
6 **TANK BUSTER**, 5, b g Executive Perk—Macfarly (IRE) **Mr R. Langley**
7 **WAVE BACK (IRE)**, 9, b m Bob Back (USA)—Stormy Wave **Mr R. Langley**

Assistant Trainer: Mr R Langley

Jockey (NH): V Slattery. **Amateur:** Mr R. Langley.

---

287 MR B. W. HILLS, Lambourn
Postal: **Wetherdown House, Lambourn, Hungerford, Berkshire, RG17 8UB.**
Contacts: **OFFICE (01488) 71548 FAX (01488) 72823**
E-MAIL info@barryhills.com WEBSITE www.barryhills.com

1 **ALFONSO**, 4, ch g Efisio—Winnebago **Mr Guy Reed**
2 **CALCUTTA**, 9, b h Indian Ridge—Echoing **The Hon Mrs J. M. Corbett & Mr Christopher Wright**
3 **DUBAI SUCCESS**, 9, b h Sadler's Wells (USA)—Crystal Spray **Maktoum Al Maktoum**
4 **FLAMBOYANT LAD**, 4, ch c Nashwan (USA)—Cheeky Charm (USA) **Maktoum Al Maktoum**
5 **KAMANDA LAUGH**, 4, ch g Most Welcome—Kamada (USA) **Mr John Sillett**
6 **LA CUCARACHA**, 4, b f Piccolo—Peggy Spencer **Mr Guy Reed**
7 **MOORS MYTH**, 4, b g Anabaa (USA)—West Devon (USA) **Gryffindor (www.racingtours.co.uk)**
8 **MOSS VALE (IRE)**, 4, b c Shinko Forest (IRE)—Wolf Cleugh (IRE) **Mr John C Grant & Cheveley Park Stu**
9 **PRIMO WAY**, 4, b c Primo Dominie—Waypoint **Derek M. James**

THREE-YEAR-OLDS

10 **ALL THAT AND MORE (IRE)**, ch c Unfuwain (USA)—Ideal Lady (IRE) **Maktoum Al Maktoum**
11 **ALMANSOOR (IRE)**, b c Sadler's Wells (USA)—Groom Order **Hamdan Al Maktoum**
12 **ALUMNI**, ch f Selkirk (USA)—Ajuga (USA) **Khalid Abdulla**
13 **AMIRA**, b f Efisio—Princess Athena **The Athenians**
14 **ANCHOR DATE**, b c Zafonic (USA)—Fame At Last (USA) **Khalid Abdulla**
15 **ART ELEGANT**, b c Desert Prince (IRE)—Elegant (IRE) **Matthew R. Green**
16 **ASK FOR RAIN**, gr f Green Desert (USA)—Requesting **Maktoum Al Maktoum**
17 **ASTRONOMICAL (IRE)**, b c Mister Baileys—Charm The Stars **John Hanson**
18 **BABE MACCOOL (IRE)**, ch c Giant's Causeway (USA)—Kotama (USA) **Ronald J. Arculli**
19 **BAIE DES FLAMANDS (USA)**, b c Kingmambo (USA)—Isle de France (USA)
20 **BALLETOMAINE (IRE)**, b f Sadler's Wells (USA)—Ivy (USA) **Mr & Mrs Peter Orton & Partner**
21 **BASSERAH (IRE)**, b f Unfuwain (USA)—Blueberry Walk **Hamdan Al Maktoum**
22 **BOBO**, ch f Efisio—Taza **Mr Guy Reed**
23 **BON BON**, b f Efisio—Polo **Mr Guy Reed**
24 **BORN FOR DANCING (IRE)**, b f Fasliyev (USA)—Fancy Boots (IRE) **Mrs Helen W. Polito**
25 **BRANDEXE (IRE)**, b f Xaar—Tintara (IRE) **R. A. N. Bonnycastle**
26 **C'EST LA VIE**, ch f Bering—Action de Grace (USA) **Mr Guy Reed**
27 **CEIRIOG VALLEY**, b f In The Wings—Bodfari Quarry **Robert J. McAlpine**
28 **CESAR MANRIQUE (IRE)**, ch c Vettori (IRE)—Norbella **Philip G. Harvey**

MR B. W. HILLS—continued

29 **CIEL BLEU**, ch f Septieme Ciel (USA)—Valthea (FR) **The Hon Mrs J. M. Corbett & Mr Christopher Wright**
30 **CLARA BOW (IRE)**, b f Sadler's Wells (USA)—Brigid (USA) **Lady Bamford**
31 **CLOVE (USA)**, b f Distant View (USA)—Nidd (USA) **Khalid Abdulla**
32 **DABBERS RIDGE (IRE)**, b c Indian Ridge—Much Commended **Maurice L. Mogg**
33 **DESERT DEMON (IRE)**, b c Unfuwain (USA)—Baldemosa (FR) **Maktoum Al Maktoum**
34 **DESERT IMP**, b f Green Desert (USA)—Devil's Imp (IRE) **Maktoum Al Maktoum**
35 **DHAULAR DHAR (IRE)**, b c Indian Ridge—Pescara (IRE) **Maktoum Al Maktoum**
36 **DIAMOND CIRCLE**, br f Halling (USA)—Canadian Mill (USA) **Maktoum Al Maktoum**
37 **DILALA (IRE)**, b f Barathea (IRE)—Deyaajeer (USA) **Hamdan Al Maktoum**
38 **DISGUISE**, b c Pursuit of Love—Nullarbor **Khalid Abdulla**
39 **DIXIEANNA**, ch f Night Shift (USA)—Dixielake (IRE) **Charlie G. P. Wyatt**
40 **ETLAALA**, ch c Selkirk (USA)—Portelet **Hamdan Al Maktoum**
41 **FASHIONABLE**, ch f Nashwan (USA)—Fine Detail (IRE) **Khalid Abdulla**
42 **FOLLOW MY LEAD**, b f Night Shift (USA)—Launch Time (USA) **Derek M. James**
43 **FOREST OF LOVE**, br f Charnwood Forest (IRE)—Touch And Love (IRE) **Maktoum Al Maktoum**
44 **FORTUNATE ISLE (USA)**, ch c Swain (IRE)—Isla Del Rey (USA) **Maktoum Al Maktoum**
45 **FRITH (IRE)**, b c Benny The Dip (USA)—Melodist (USA) **William J. Gredley**
46 **GOLDEN GRIMSHAW (IRE)**, b c Grand Lodge (USA)—
                         Daftina (IRE) **Matthew Green&Enton Thoroughbred Racing2**
47 **GRANDE ROCHE (IRE)**, b c Grand Lodge (USA)—Arabian Lass (SAF) **Ronald J. Arculli**
48 **GRIGOROVITCH (IRE)**, b c Fasliyev (USA)—Hasty Words (IRE) **William J. Gredley**
49 **GRINGO**, gr c Alzao (USA)—Glen Falls **Mr Guy Reed**
50 **GROUND RULES (USA)**, b c Boundary (USA)—Gombeen (USA) **Khalid Abdulla**
51 **GUADIARO (USA)**, b c El Prado (IRE)—Splendid (IRE) **P Savill, R Bonnycastle, Sangster Family**
52 **HEART STOPPING**, b f Chester House (USA)—Clog Dance **Khalid Abdulla**
53 **HEWARAAT (IRE)**, b g Fasliyev (USA)—Maraatib (IRE) **Hamdan Al Maktoum**
54 **HOLIDAY CAMP (USA)**, b c Chester House (USA)—Arewehavingfunyet (USA) **Khalid Abdulla**
55 **JACK THE GIANT (IRE)**, b c Giant's Causeway (USA)—State Crystal (IRE) **Hanbury Syndicate**
56 **KENMORE**, b c Compton Place—Watheeqah (USA) **John C. Grant**
57 **KING OF NEWBURY (IRE)**, b c Indian Lodge (IRE)—
                         Priyanka **SMJ Racing, Enton Thoroughbred Racing 2, Grant**
58 **MADEMOISELLE**, b f Efisio—Shall We Dance **Mr Guy Reed**
59 **MAIDS CAUSEWAY (IRE)**, b f Giant's Causeway (USA)—Vallee des Reves (USA) **Martin S. Schwartz**
60 **MAY MORNING (IRE)**, b f Danehill (USA)—Golden Digger (USA) **Maktoum Al Maktoum**
61 **MIDCAP (IRE)**, b f Entrepreneur—Tis Juliet (USA) **Mr & Mrs Peter Orton & Partner**
62 **MISS PARTICULAR (IRE)**, b f Sadler's Wells (USA)—Viz (USA) **Maktoum Al Maktoum**
63 **NAWAAEM (USA)**, b br f Swain (USA)—Alattrah (USA) **Hamdan Al Maktoum**
64 **ORANMORE CASTLE (IRE)**, b c Giant's Causeway (USA)—
                         Twice The Ease **Sangster Family, R Bonnycastle, P Savill**
65 **PAPER TALK (USA)**, b c Unbridled's Song (USA)—Journalist (IRE) **Maktoum Al Maktoum**
66 **PERFECT BLEND**, gr f Linamix (FR)—Picture Princess **Maktoum Al Maktoum**
67 **POSTMASTER**, b c Dansili—Post Modern (USA) **Khalid Abdulla**
68 **PRIME CONTENDER**, b c Efisio—Gecko Rouge **Derek M. James, SMJ Racing, Nick Pearce**
69 **RAINBOW SKY**, b f Rainbow Quest (USA)—Safayn (USA) **Derek M. James**
70 **RIGHTFUL RULER**, b c Montjoy (USA)—Lady of The Realm **George J. Hicks**
71 **SASSO**, b g Efisio—Sioux **Mr Guy Reed**
72 **SELF DISCIPLINE**, b c Dansili—Cosh (USA) **Khalid Abdulla**
73 **SEVERELY (FR)**, b f Cape Cross (IRE)—Sevres (USA) **R. A. N. Bonnycastle**
74 **SHANNON SPRINGS (IRE)**, b c Darshaan—Our Queen of Kings **Mr John C. Grant & Mr A. L. R. Morton**
75 **SHAREB (USA)**, b c El Prado (IRE)—My Hansel (USA) **Hilal Salem**
76 **SILENT SPRING (USA)**, b f Honour And Glory (USA)—Polar Bird (USA) **Sangster Family & Lady Bamford**
77 **SINCERELY**, b f Singspiel (IRE)—Noble Form **Mr Guy Reed**
78 **SPARKWELL**, b c Dansili—West Devon (USA) **Khalid Abdulla**
79 **TAHRIR (IRE)**, gr f Linamix (FR)—Miss Sacha (IRE) **Hamdan Al Maktoum**
80 **TOUCH OF SILK (IRE)**, ch f Night Shift (USA)—Blew Her Top (USA) **Richard F. Barnes**
81 **UNREAL**, b f Dansili—Illusory **Khalid Abdulla**
82 **WHAZZAT**, b f Daylami (IRE)—Wosaita **William J. Gredley**
83 **WITWATERSRAND (IRE)**, b f Unfuwain (USA)—Valley of Gold (FR) **Maktoum Al Maktoum**

TWO-YEAR-OLDS

84 **AUCTION ROOM (USA)**, b f 21/1 Chester House (USA)—Didina (Nashwan (USA))
85 **BEST LADY (IRE)**, b f 28/1 King's Best (USA)—Sassenach (IRE) (Night Shift (USA)) (67068)
86 **BONNIE PRINCE BLUE**, ch c 17/4 Tipsy Creek (USA)—Heart So Blue (Dilum (USA))
87 **BORDELLO**, b c 20/2 Efisio—Blow Me A Kiss (Kris)
88 B c 31/1 Bahri (USA)—Captive Island (Northfields (USA))

MR B. W. HILLS—continued

89 Ch f 19/4 With Approval (CAN)—Conical (Zafonic (USA))
90 **DISTANT DRUMS (IRE)**, ch f 29/3 Distant Music (USA)—No Hard Feelings (IRE) (Alzao (USA)) (23473)
91 **DON'T TELL SUE**, ch c 26/2 Bold Edge—Opopmil (IRE) (Pips Pride) (26000)
92 **DUBLIN DICE (IRE)**, b c 20/2 Orpen (USA)—Cullinan Diamond (IRE) (Bigstone (IRE)) (30180)
93 **FANCY DAY**, b f 23/4 Zafonic (USA)—Hiwaayati (Shadeed (USA))
94 **FIRST APPROVAL**, b f 14/3 Royal Applause—Gaijin (Caerleon (USA))
95 **GALILEO'S STAR (IRE)**, ch f 11/4 Galileo (IRE)—Anazara (USA) (Trempolino (USA)) (85000)
96 **GILT LINKED**, b f 13/2 Compton Place—Copy-Cat (Lion Cavern (USA)) (47000)
97 **GLOBAL GENIUS**, gr c 25/1 Galileo (IRE)—Vadsagreya (FR) (Linamix (FR)) (55000)
98 **GUS**, b c 29/3 Dr Fong (USA)—Tender Moment (IRE) (Caerleon (USA))
99 **HUNTING PARTY (IRE)**, ch c 25/4 Grand Lodge (USA)—Delilah (IRE) (Bluebird (USA)) (85000)
100 Ch c 3/5 Danehill Dancer (IRE)—Illusory (Kings Lake (USA))
101 B f 11/4 Bahri (USA)—Istikbal (USA) (Kingmambo (USA)) (26827)
102 **JAMIESON GOLD (IRE)**, b c 15/3 Desert Style (IRE)—Princess of Zurich (IRE) (Law Society (USA)) (67068)
103 **JIHAAZ (IRE)**, ch c 8/3 Elnadim (USA)—Gazar (Kris)
104 **KILLYBEGS (IRE)**, b c 27/3 Orpen (USA)—Belsay (Belmez (USA)) (43594)
105 **LADY ATHENA**, ch f 27/3 Tipsy Creek (USA)—Lady of The Realm (Prince Daniel (USA))
106 **LAITH (IRE)**, b c 7/3 Royal Applause—Dania (GER) (Night Shift (USA)) (200000)
107 **LISFANNON**, ch f 30/1 Bahamian Bounty—Amazed (Clantime) (60000)
108 **MABADI (USA)**, b f 9/3 Sahm (USA)—Barakat (Bustino)
109 B c 15/4 Bahri (USA)—Mamlakah (IRE) (Unfuwain (USA))
110 **MARIE (IRE)**, gr f 1/1 Observatory (USA)—Marie de Bayeux (FR) (Turgeon (USA)) (40000)
111 **MASHAAHED**, b c 6/3 In The Wings—Patacake Patacake (USA) (Bahri (USA)) (150000)
112 **MASHAAIR (IRE)**, ch c 23/2 King's Best (USA)—Al Bahathri (USA) (Blushing Groom (FR))
113 **MO CHROI**, ch f 7/4 Observatory (USA)—Away To Me (Exit To Nowhere (USA)) (15000)
114 **MOSHARREF (IRE)**, b c 7/2 Alhaarth (IRE)—Murjana (IRE) (Pleasant Colony (USA))
115 **MR SANDICLIFFE**, b c 27/3 Mujahid (USA)—Crinkle (IRE) (Distant Relative) (20000)
116 **MUZHER (IRE)**, ch c 15/2 Indian Ridge—Almurooj (Zafonic (USA))
117 B f 14/3 Mr Greeley (USA)—Mystic Lure (Green Desert (USA)) (140000)
118 **OLYMPIAN ODYSSEY**, b c 19/4 Sadler's Wells (USA)—Field of Hope (IRE) (Selkirk (USA)) (75000)
119 **PIROUETTING**, b f 18/2 Pivotal—Jitterbug (IRE) (Marju (IRE)) (52000)
120 **PORTLAND**, b c 10/2 Zafonic (USA)—Bayswater (Caerleon (USA))
121 **PRIVATE BUSINESS (USA)**, gr ro c 9/2 Cozzene (USA)—Privity (USA) (Private Account (USA))
122 **PROWESS (IRE)**, ch f 7/2 Peintre Celebre (USA)—Yawl (Rainbow Quest (USA))
123 **QUIET EMBRACE**, ch f 24/2 Sunday Silence (USA)—Flying Kiss (IRE) (Sadler's Wells (USA))
124 **RED ASH (USA)**, ch c 10/4 Woodman (USA)—Bermuda Girl (USA) (Danzig (USA))
125 **RED CLUBS (IRE)**, br c 17/1 Red Ransom (USA)—Two Clubs (First Trump) (40000)
126 **RIVER KINTYRE**, b c 31/3 Mull of Kintyre (USA)—Our Pleasure (Lake Coniston (IRE)) (40000)
127 **RODEO**, ch c 8/2 Pivotal—Flossy (Efisio)
128 **ROYAL ENVOY (IRE)**, b c 13/1 Royal Applause—Seven Notes (Zafonic (USA)) (110000)
129 **SAFQA**, b f 10/2 Singspiel (IRE)—Shamah (Unfuwain (USA))
130 B f 11/3 Mozart (IRE)—Shanty (Selkirk (USA))
131 **SHORT DANCE (USA)**, b f 19/3 Hennessy (USA)—Clog Dance (Pursuit of Love)
132 Ch c 17/3 Giant's Causeway (USA)—Shy Princess (USA) (Irish River (FR)) (120723)
133 **SICILIAN (IRE)**, b c 26/1 Sadler's Wells (USA)—Hula Angel (USA) (Woodman (USA))
134 **SILVER DIP**, gr f 2/3 Gulch (USA)—Silver Bandana (USA) (Silver Buck (USA)) (67000)
135 Ch c 7/4 Grand Lodge (USA)—Soviet Artic (FR) (Bering) (140000)
136 **SPINNING QUEEN**, ch f 27/3 Spinning World (USA)—Our Queen of Kings (Arazi (USA)) (42000)
137 B f 1/1 Dixieland Band (USA)—Tabheej (IRE) (Mujtahid (USA))
138 **TAKDEEM**, b c 3/5 Green Desert (USA)—Alshakr (Bahri (USA))
139 **TAWAAFUD**, b f 5/2 Nashwan (USA)—Intimaa (IRE) (Caerleon (USA))
140 **TEACH TO PREACH (USA)**, ch c 26/2 Pulpit (USA)—Chateaubaby (USA) (Nureyev (USA)) (146315)
141 **THE LAST DROP (IRE)**, b c 2/5 Galileo (IRE)—Epping (Charnwood Forest (IRE)) (80000)
142 Gr c 8/5 Linamix (FR)—Time Will Show (FR) (Exit To Nowhere (USA)) (100000)
143 **TOMMY TOOGOOD (IRE)**, b c 5/5 Danehill (USA)—On The Nile (IRE) (Sadler's Wells (USA)) (160965)
144 B f 6/5 Sadler's Wells (USA)—Upper Circle (Shirley Heights)
145 **VEBA (USA)**, ch c 12/2 Black Minnaloushe (USA)—Make Over (USA) (Time For A Change (USA)) (50300)
146 Ch f 6/3 Singspiel (IRE)—West Devon (USA) (Gone West (USA))

MR B. W. HILLS—continued

147 B c 13/3 Distant Music (USA)—Xaymara (USA) (Sanglamore (USA))
148 YANDINA (IRE), b f 6/4 Danehill (USA)—Lughz (USA) (Housebuster (USA)) (167672)

Other Owners: Mr Steven Falle, Mr Matthew Franklin, Mr James Sumsion, Mr M. H. Dixon, Brighthelm Racing, Mr Henry Barton, Mr J. R. Fleming, Marston Stud, Mr Ray Richards, Mrs David Nagle, Mr S. P. Tindall, Mr M. C. & Mrs D. A. Throsby, Mr Paul Shanahan, Mrs E. Roberts, Mrs Belinda Haruty, N. N. Browne, Burton Agnes Bloodstock, R. C. Dollar, R. Gruber, Mrs F. M. Lane, Mrs S. Magnier, K. P. McNamara, D. F. Powell, B. V. Sangster, G. E. Sangster, G. M. Tregaskes, Mr G. M. Tricks, Wickfield Stud and Hartshill Stud.

Assistant Trainer: K Mooney, C Hills, T Sturgis & S Savva

Apprentice: A. Medeiros, K May.

---

288 MR J. W. HILLS, Lambourn
Postal: **The Croft, Upper Lambourn, Newbury, Berkshire, RG17 8QH.**
Contacts: **PHONE (01488) 73144 FAX (01488) 73099 MOBILE (07836) 283091**
E-MAIL john@johnhills.com

1 **CARRY ON DOC**, 4, b g Dr Devious (IRE)—Florentynna Bay **Stuart Whitehouse & Abbott Racing Partners**
2 **DANCING LYRA**, 4, b g Alzao (USA)—Badaayer (USA) **N. N. Browne**
3 **FIGHTER COMMAND**, 4, ch g Docksider (USA)—Rose Alto **Mr J. W. Hills**
4 **FREELOADER (IRE)**, 5, b g Revoque (IRE)—Indian Sand **Scott Hardy Partnership**
5 **GOLDEN LEGEND (IRE)**, 4, ch f Selkirk (USA)—Daftiyna (IRE) **Mr D. M. Kerr and Mr N. Brunskill**
6 **LANDUCCI**, 4, b g Averti (IRE)—Divina Luna **R. J. Tufft**
7 **MASKED (IRE)**, 4, b g Soviet Star (USA)—Moon Masquerade (IRE) **The Phantom Partnership**

THREE-YEAR-OLDS

8 **BEAUSITE**, b f Grand Lodge (USA)—Stardance (USA) **Mr J. W. Hills**
9 **BEAUTIFUL MOVER (USA)**, ch f Spinning World (USA)—
　　　　Dancer's Glamour (USA) **Whitehouse, Morrison and Christie**
10 **CAPE ENTERPRISE (USA)**, b c Cape Canaveral (USA)—Principessa (USA) **Mr D. M. Kerr and Mr N. Brunskill**
11 **CLINET (IRE)**, b f Docksider (USA)—Oiche Mhaith **Wood Hall Stud Limited**
12 **DESERT SECRETS (IRE)**, b f Almutawakel—Shaping Up (USA) **The Scarecrows Partnership**
13 **DIAMOND HOMBRE (USA)**, gr c Two Punch (USA)—Flowing (USA) **Mr D. M. Kerr and Mr N. Brunskill**
14 **DOCK TOWER (IRE)**, b g Docksider (USA)—Thakhayr **Sir J. W. Robb**
15 **FLAMING WEAPON**, b g Unfuwain (USA)—Flame Valley (USA) **Mr Gary Woodward And Partners**
16 **NOBBLER**, ro gr c Classic Cliche (IRE)—Nicely (IRE) **Mrs C. M. Smith**
17 **REGAL DREAM (IRE)**, b c Namid—Lovely Me (IRE) **Mr Paul Saunders and Partners**
18 **SALTBURN LAD (IRE)**, b c Sadler's Wells (USA)—Highest Accolade **Mr Ray Empson & Partners**
19 **STAGBURY HILL (USA)**, ch c Woodman (USA)—Shalabia **Mr Nick Hubbard and Partners**
20 **SWEET NAMIBIA (IRE)**, ch f Namid—Almond Flower (IRE) **Mountgrange Stud**
21 **SWIFT OSCAR**, b c Mark of Esteem (IRE)—Surf Bird **M. J. Smith**
22 **TOFFEE VODKA (IRE)**, b f Danehill Dancer (IRE)—Vieux Carre **Mr G. and Mrs L. Woodward**
23 **TRANSVESTITE (IRE)**, b g Trans Island—Christoph's Girl **Mr Ken Wilkinson And Partners**
24 **WINDWOOD (IRE)**, b g Piccolo—Presently **Mr Ken Wilkinson And Partners**
25 **WINGMAN (IRE)**, b c In The Wings—Precedence (IRE) **D. M. Kerr**

TWO-YEAR-OLDS

26 **APRES SKI (USA)**, b br f 1/4 Stravinsky (USA)—
　　　　Dawn Aurora (USA) (Night Shift (USA)) (13301) **Mr G. and Mrs L. Woodward**
27 Gr c 7/3 Bluebird (USA)—Blanche Neige (USA) (Lit de Justice (USA)) (15000) **Dan Abbott Racing Partnership**
28 **BOMBER COMMAND (USA)**, b c 19/3 Stravinsky (USA)—
　　　　Parish Manor (USA) (Waquoit (USA)) (5000) **Mr J. W. Hills**
29 **CALYPSO KING**, gr c 20/3 Agnes World (USA)—T G's Girl (Selkirk (USA)) (26000) **Mr J. W. Hills**
30 **CATOMINE (USA)**, b f 3/2 Black Minnaloushe (USA)—
　　　　Kinetigal (USA) (Naskra (USA)) (42564) **N. Brunshill and D. M. Kerr**
31 B c 4/5 Fasliyev (USA)—Classic Design (Busted) **Mr J. W. Hills**
32 **CROFT (IRE)**, b c 20/3 Mull of Kintyre (Most Welcome) (18000) **H. C. Hardy**
33 **DAGGER (USA)**, b c 4/3 Diesis—Quittance (USA) (Riverman (USA)) (18779) **The Phantom Partnership**
34 **DARK ISLANDER (IRE)**, b c 29/1 Singspiel (IRE)—Lamanka Lass (USA) (Woodman (USA)) (26000) **D. M. Kerr**
35 **FOLLOW THE COLOURS (IRE)**, b c 28/3 Rainbow Quest (USA)—
　　　　Gardenia (IRE) (Sadler's Wells (USA)) **M. Wauchope, Sir Simon Dunning, R. Cottam**
36 **GIVERNY SPRING**, b f 20/3 Lujain (USA)—
　　　　Matisse (Shareef Dancer (USA)) (15000) **3rd Pheasant Inn Partnership**

MR J. W. HILLS—continued

37 **LADY ZANZARA (USA)**, ch f 16/5 Lion Cavern (USA)—
                Pace (USA) (Indian Ridge) (10000) **Mrs Jackie Ward Ramos**
38 **LE COLOMBIER**, ch c 7/4 Alhaarth (IRE)—Wide Range (IRE) (Spectrum (IRE)) (33534) **Mr N. N. Browne**
39 **LIMEGREEN BOW**, b f 9/2 Efisio—Sioux Chef (Be My Chief (USA)) **Mountgrange Stud Ltd**
40 B c 9/3 Orpen (USA)—Miss Kinabalu (Shirley Heights) (15000) **Mr J. W. Hills**
41 B c 14/5 Cape Town (USA)—New Account (USA) (Private Account (USA)) (42564) **Hubbard, Empson, Woodward**
42 **NUT (IRE)**, b f 5/2 Fasliyev (USA)—La Rosetta (IRE) (Alzao (USA)) (52000) **The Phantom Partnership**
43 B c 3/2 Sadler's Wells (USA)—Oriental Mystique (Kris) (73775) **Mr J. W. Hills**
44 **REFLECTING (IRE)**, gr f 12/2 Daylami (IRE)—Church Light (Caerleon (USA)) (26827) **Wyck Hall Stud Ltd**
45 **SCROLL**, b c 23/2 Mark of Esteem (IRE)—Bella Bellisimo (IRE) (Alzao (USA)) (10000) **Wyck Hall Stud Ltd**
46 **SEVEN SAMURAI**, b c 1/2 Mark of Esteem (IRE)—
             Eishin Eleuthera (IRE) (Sadler's Wells (USA)) (25000) **Amity Finance & Partners**
47 **STANLEY GOODSPEED**, ch c 29/3 Inchinor—Flying Carpet (Barathea (IRE)) (13000) **R. J. Tufft**
48 **STORMY MONDAY**, b f 10/4 Cadeaux Genereux—Hasta (USA) (Theatrical) (20000) **Mr J. W. Hills**
49 **TEMPSFORD FLYER (IRE)**, b c 1/3 Fasliyev (USA)—Castellane (FR) (Danehill (USA)) (32192) **Mrs M. Kingham**
50 **VINSKA (USA)**, b br f 27/1 Stravinsky (USA)—Konvincha (USA) (Cormorant (USA)) (10641) **Mrs C. M. Smith**

Other Owners: Mrs P. Caroe, Mrs S. Richards, Amity Finance Ltd, T. W. Bailey, A. H. Bartlett, P. J. Bolam, W. D. Eason, M. Kerr-Dineen, D. A. Klein, Mrs T. A. Maitland, Mrs M. A. Moore, Mountgrange Stud Ltd, C. New, M. J. Pallett, C. Ross, G. C. Rothwell, A. G. Scott, M. A. Styles, Mr R. P. Tullett, F. C. W. Whitehouse.

Assistant Trainer: Colin Gorman

Jockey (flat): E. Ahern, R. Hills, M. Hills, S. Whitworth.

---

289   **MR M. R. HOAD, Lewes**
Postal: Windmill Lodge Stables, Spital Road, Lewes, East Sussex, BN7 1LS.
Contacts: **PHONE (01273) 477124/(01273) 480691 MOBILE (07742) 446168**

1 **ADELPHIE LASS**, 5, b m Theatrical Charmer—Miss Adventure **Mrs J. E. Hoad**
2 **COCO DE CARA**, 4, gr g Terimon—Guardian Angel VII
3 **CORONADO FOREST (USA)**, 6, b g Spinning World (USA)—Desert Jewel (USA) **K. J. Webb**
4 **PACE STALKER (USA)**, 9, b g Lear Fan (USA)—In The Habit (USA) **P. C. Collins**
5 **THE STAGGERY BOY (IRE)**, 9, b g Shalford (IRE)—Murroe Star **Foray Racing**
6 **WILOM (GER)**, 7, ch g Lomitas—Whispering Willows **Mrs J. E. Hoad**

THREE-YEAR-OLDS

7 **A QUI LE TOUR**, b g Pyramus (USA)—Dolphin Beech (IRE) **Mrs J. E. Taylor**
8 **JUSTCALLMEHANDSOME**, ch g Handsome Ridge—Pearl Dawn (IRE) **Mrs J. E. Taylor**
9 B c Pyramus (USA)—Nordesta (IRE) **R. W. Townsend**

TWO-YEAR-OLDS

10 Ch c 6/3 College Chapel—Pearl Dawn (IRE) (Jareer (USA)) (1142) **Mrs J. E. Taylor**

Other Owners: R. E. G. Barnett, G. C. Brice, D. J. Dunworth, N. D. Potter, A. M. Styles, Mrs J. E. Taylor, C. S. Van't Hoff.

Jockey (flat): Dane O'Neill. **Jockey (NH):** L. Aspell.

---

290   **MR P. J. HOBBS, Minehead**
Postal: Sandhill, Bilbrook, Minehead, Somerset, TA24 6HA.
Contacts: **PHONE (01984) 640366 CAR (07860) 729795 FAX (01984) 641124**
E-MAIL racing@pjhobbs.freeserve.co.uk WEBSITE www.pjhobbs.co.uk

1 **ALEKHINE (IRE)**, 4, b g Soviet Star (USA)—Alriyaah **Mr J. Burley**
2 **ALL FOR A REASON (IRE)**, 6, gr g Zaffaran—Cyrano Imperial (IRE) **A. L. Cohen**
3 **ALLUMEE**, 6, ch g Alflora (IRE)—Coire Vannich **High Spirits**
4 **ALWAYS IN DEBT (IRE)**, 6, b g Norwich—Forever In Debt **Mrs K. V. Vann**
5 **AMARULA RIDGE (IRE)**, 4, b c Indian Ridge—Mail Boat **Mr John P. McManus**
6 **BE MY GUIDE (IRE)**, 7, b g Good Thyne (USA)—St Cristoph **The Country Side**
7 **BIG BONE (FR)**, 5, b g Zayyani—Bone Crasher (FR) **R Triple H**
8 **CAMERON BRIDGE (IRE)**, 9, b g Camden Town—Arctic Raheen **The Country Side**
9 **CASTLEBOY (IRE)**, 7, b g King's Ride—Bissie's Jayla **Mrs D. L. Whateley**
10 **CASTLEMORE (IRE)**, 7, b g Be My Native (USA)—Parsonetta **Castlemore Securities Limited**

MR P. J. HOBBS—continued

11 **CHILLING PLACE (IRE)**, 6, ch g Moscow Society (USA)—Ethel's Dream **M. J. Tuckey**
12 **CHIVITE (IRE)**, 6, b g Alhaarth (IRE)—Laura Margaret **I. Russell**
13 **CHRISTOPHER**, 8, gr g Arzanni—Forest Nymph (NZ) **A. Stennett**
14 **CLARENDON (IRE)**, 9, ch g Forest Wind (USA)—Sparkish (IRE) **The Plus Fours**
15 **CODE SIGN (USA)**, 6, b g Gulch (USA)—Karasavina (IRE) **Denise Winton and Elizabeth Hodgson**
16 **CROIX DE GUERRE (IRE)**, 5, gr g Highest Honor (FR)—Esclava (USA) **Mr J. Joseph**
17 **CUTTHROAT**, 5, ch g Kris—Could Have Been **Capt E. J. Edwards-Heathcote**
18 **DAMARISCO (FR)**, 5, b g Scribe (USA)—Blanche Dame (FR) **The Kingpins**
19 **DO L'ENFANT D'EAU (FR)**, 6, ch g Minds Music (USA)—L'eau Sauvage **J. T. Warner**
20 **DOUBLE HONOUR (FR)**, 7, gr g Highest Honor (FR)—Silver Cobra (USA) **The 4th Middleham Partnership**
21 **DREAM ALLIANCE**, 4, ch g Bien Bien (USA)—Rewbell **The Alliance Partnership**
22 **DRUMBEATER (IRE)**, 5, b g Supreme Leader—Ballydrummund (IRE) **D. C. R. Allen**
23 **DUNSTER CASTLE**, 10, ch g Carlingford Castle—Gay Edition **Mrs D. L. Whateley**
24 **ELENAS RIVER (IRE)**, 9, br g Over The River (FR)—Elenas Beauty **Ian David Limited**
25 **FAME**, 5, ch g Northern Amethyst—First Sapphire **Ms E. Reffo & Mr B. Cooper**
26 **FARMER JACK**, 9, b g Alflora (IRE)—Cheryls Pet (IRE) **P. Partridge**
27 **FLAGSHIP UBERALLES (IRE)**, 11, br g Accordion—Fourth Degree **Mr John P. McManus**
28 **FOOL ON THE HILL**, 8, b g Reprimand—Stock Hill Lass **Louisville Syndicate**
29 **FORDINGBRIDGE (USA)**, 5, b g Diesis—Souffle **Colin Brown Racing IV**
30 **FOREVER DREAM**, 7, b g Afzal—Quadrapol **Mr W. McKibbin & Mr A. Stevens**
31 **FROM DAWN TO DUSK**, 6, b g Afzal—Herald The Dawn **C. G. M. Lloyd-Baker**
32 **GENTLE BEAU**, 7, b g Homo Sapien—Tapua Taranata (IRE) **R. Hamilton**
33 **GREENHILL BRAMBLE (IRE)**, 5, b g Supreme Leader—Green Thorn (IRE) **J & B Gibbs & Sons Ltd**
34 **GREY BROTHER**, 7, gr g Morpeth—Pigeon Loft (IRE) **Christine and Aubrey Loze**
35 **GREY REPORT**, 8, gr g Roselier (FR)—Busters Lodge **Mrs D. A. La Trobe**
36 **GUNTHER MCBRIDE (IRE)**, 10, b g Glacial Storm (USA)—What Side **M. J. Tuckey**
37 **HARRY'S DREAM**, 8, b g Alflora (IRE)—Cheryls Pet (IRE) **P. Partridge**
38 **HOW GREAT THOU ART**, 9, b g Almoojid—Mamamere **D. R. Walsh**
39 **ILE DE PARIS (FR)**, 6, b g Cadoudal (FR)—Sweet Beauty (FR) **Sir Robert Ogden C.B.E., LLD**
40 **IN CONTRAST**, 9, b br g Be My Native (USA)—Ballinamona Lady (IRE) **A. P. Staple**
41 **ITALIAN COUNSEL (IRE)**, 8, b g Leading Counsel (USA)—Mullaghroe **Mr B. V. Ward & Mr C. Feeney**
42 **KALCA MOME (FR)**, 7, b g En Calcat (FR)—Belle Mome (FR) **Miss I. D. Du Pre**
43 **KOQUELICOT (FR)**, 7, ch g Video Rock (FR)—Ixia Des Saccarts (FR) **A. E. Peterson**
44 **LA DOLFINA**, 5, b m Pennekamp (USA)—Icecapped **Miss I. D. Du Pre**
45 **LACDOUDAL (FR)**, 6, gr g Cadoudal (FR)—Belfaster (FR) **Mrs C. Skan**
46 **LEAD ON (IRE)**, 4, b g Supreme Leader—Dressed In Style (IRE) **B. K. Peppiett**
47 **LIMERICK LEADER (IRE)**, 7, b g Supreme Leader—View of The Hills **D. R. Peppiatt**
48 **LINCOLN PLACE (IRE)**, 10, ch g Be My Native (USA)—Miss Lou **A. J. Scrimgeour**
49 **LORD HENRY (IRE)**, 6, b g Lord Americo—Auntie Honnie (IRE) **Mrs K. V. Vann**
50 **LORD STRICKLAND**, 12, b g Strong Gale—Lady Rag **Miss H. L. Cope**
51 **LOUP BLEU (USA)**, 7, b g Nureyev (USA)—Louve Bleue (USA) **Richard Green (Fine Paintings)**
52 **MADE IN JAPAN (JPN)**, 5, b g Barathea (IRE)—Charmante **T. M. Evans**
53 **MAHARAAT (USA)**, 4, b c Bahri (USA)—Siyadah (USA) **Belinda Harvey**
54 **MASTER D'OR (FR)**, 5, b g Cyborg (FR)—Une Pomme d'or (FR) **J. T. Warner**
55 **MCBAIN (USA)**, 6, br g Lear Fan (USA)—River City Moon (USA) **Hill, Trembath, Bryan and Outhart**
56 **MILLARDS LAD (IRE)**, 6, b g Flemensfirth (USA)—Toransha **T. M. Evans**
57 **MISTER CHATTERBOX (IRE)**, 4, b g Presenting—Lotta Talk (IRE) **The Royal Oak Syndicate**
58 **MISTER FLINT**, 7, b g Petoski—National Clover **A. E. Peterson**
59 **MONKERHOSTIN (FR)**, 8, b g Shining Steel—Ladoun (FR) **M. G. St Quinton**
60 **MONTICELLI (GER)**, 5, b g Pelder (IRE)—Marcelia (GER) **Mrs M. Findlay**
61 **MOSCOW WHISPER (IRE)**, 8, b g Moscow Society (USA)—Native Woodfire (IRE) **Ms F. Nasir**
62 **MOUNSEY CASTLE**, 8, ch g Carlingford Castle—Gay Ticket **A. E. Peterson**
63 **MR FLUFFY**, 8, br g Charmer—Hinton Bairn **The Cockpit Crew**
64 **MRS PHILIP**, 6, b m Puissance—Lightning Legacy (USA) **Mrs S. L. Hobbs**
65 **NOBLE REQUEST (FR)**, 4, gr g Highest Honor (FR)—Restless Mixa (IRE) **Mrs K. V. Vann**
66 **O'TOOLE (IRE)**, 6, b g Toulon—Legs Burke (IRE) **Mrs L. R. Lovell**
67 **OLIMPO (FR)**, 4, ch c Starborough—Emily Allan (IRE) **Christine and Aubrey Loze**
68 **ONE KNIGHT (IRE)**, 9, ch g Roselier (FR)—Midnights Daughter (IRE) **H. R. Gibbs**
69 **ORSWELL CREST**, 11, b g Crested Lark—Slave's Bangle **The Mane Chance Partnership**
70 **PAK JACK (FR)**, 5, ch g Pitchounet (FR)—Miss Noir Et Or (FR) **Sir Robert Ogden C.B.E., LLD**
71 **PARSONS LEGACY (IRE)**, 7, b g Leading Counsel (USA)—The Parson's Girl (IRE) **R. A. S. Offer**
72 **QUIET WATER (IRE)**, 9, br g Lord Americo—Sirana **Hill, Trembath, Bryan and Outhart**
73 **RAOUL DUFY (USA)**, 5, gr g El Prado (IRE)—Parrish Empress (USA) **Richard Green (Fine Paintings)**
74 **RED SOCIETY (IRE)**, 7, ch g Moscow Society (USA)—Allendara (IRE) **Mrs A. M. Taylor**
75 **RIFT VALLEY (IRE)**, 10, b g Good Thyne (USA)—Necochea **Mrs K. A. Stuart**
76 **ROLLO (IRE)**, 7, gr g Roselier (FR)—Comeragh Queen **A. E. Peterson**

MR P. J. HOBBS—continued

77 ROOSTER BOOSTER, 11, gr g Riverwise (USA)—Came Cottage **J. T. Warner**
78 ROSCHAL (IRE), 7, gr g Roselier (FR)—Sunday World (USA) **B. Walsh**
79 ROSS RIVER, 9, gr g Over The River (FR)—Solo Rose **Mr S. Ross**
80 ROYAL TIR (FR), 9, b br g Royal Charter (FR)—Tirtaine (FR) **Sir Robert Ogden C.B.E., LLD**
81 SABY (FR), 7, b b g Sassanian (USA)—Valy Flett (FR) **Setsquare Recruitment**
82 SALUTE (IRE), 6, b g Muhtarram (USA)—Alasib **Ian David Ltd & Byrne Bros (FWK) Ltd**
83 SANDMARTIN (IRE), 5, b g Alflora (IRE)—Quarry Machine **D. C. R. Allen**
84 SAVANNAH BAY, 6, ch g In The Wings—High Savannah **B. Walsh**
85 SERPENTINE ROCK, 5, ch g Hernando (FR)—Serpentara **C. de P. Berry, C. Moore, P. Rowe**
86 SHADOW RIVER (IRE), 7, b g Over The River (FR)—Society Belle **Ian David Ltd & Byrne Bros (FWK) Ltd**
87 SHALAKO (USA), 7, ch g Kingmambo (USA)—Sporades **D. J. Jones**
88 STICKY WICKET, 6, b m Petoski—Avec Le Vent (IRE) **Mrs E. A. Prowting**
89 STORM OF APPLAUSE (IRE), 4, b g Accordion—Dolce Notte (IRE) **R P Racing**
90 SUNNYLAND, 6, b m Sovereign Water (FR)—Quadrapol **David H. Smith**
91 SUPREME PIPER (IRE), 7, b g Supreme Leader—Whistling Doe **Mrs K. V. Vann**
92 SUPREME PRINCE (IRE), 8, b g Supreme Leader—Strong Serenade (IRE) **Mrs K. V. Vann**
93 SUPREME SERENADE (IRE), 6, b m Supreme Leader—Strong Serenade (IRE) **Mrs K. V. Vann**
94 SWEET BIRD (FR), 8, ch g Epervier Bleu—Sweet Virginia (FR) **A. L. Cohen**
95 TOI EXPRESS (IRE), 9, ch g Phardante (FR)—Toi Figures **D. F. P. Racing**
96 TRESOR PREZINIERE (FR), 7, b br g Grand Tresor (FR)—Rose de Martine (FR) **R. W. S. Jevon**
97 UNLEASH (USA), 6, ch g Benny The Dip (USA)—Lemhi Go (USA) **Cheveley Park Stud**
98 VILLAGE KING (IRE), 12, b g Roi Danzig (USA)—Honorine (USA) **Capt E. J. Edwards-Heathcote**
99 VIRTUS, 5, ch g Machiavellian (USA)—Exclusive Virtue (USA) **P. R. Bateman**
100 WELLBEING, 8, b g Sadler's Wells (USA)—Charming Life (NZ) **Plantation Stud**
101 WILLIE JOHN DALY (IRE), 8, b g Mister Lord (USA)—Murphy's Lady (IRE) **D. R. Peppiatt**
102 WOULD YOU BELIEVE, 9, gr g Derrylin—Ramelton **D. C. R. Allen**
103 XELLANCE (IRE), 8, b g Be My Guest (USA)—Excellent Alibi (USA) **The Five Nations Partnership**
104 ZABENZ (NZ), 8, b g Zabeel (NZ)—In The Country (NZ) **Michael Watt**
105 ZALDA, 4, ch f Zilzal (USA)—Gold Luck (USA) **Mrs L. H. Field**

Other Owners: J. Bateman, The Hon. J. R. Drummond, George Moore, Geoff Price, James Walle, Guy Faber, Peter Corrigan, Colin Rowlands, A. Allright, K. Barker, Mr J. Bateman, Claude Berry, J. N. W. Brookes, C. E. N. Brown, D. F. P. Callaghan, A. M. Carding, Mr J. P. Cooper, B. A. Cooper, P. A. Corrigan, H. B. Davies, Mrs J. N. Edwards-Heathcote, C. Feeney, Mr A. French, Mr D. A. Gascoigne, Mrs J. E. Gibbs, W. R. Gibson, Mrs G. D. Giles, I. Gould, T. M. Hailstone, J. R. Hall, J. F. Hanna, M. Hill, R. W. Hills, Mrs E. P. Hodgson, J. R. Holmes, Mrs B. J. House, R. B. Huckerby, R. W. Huggins, Ian David Limited, Mr B. R. Ingram, R. M. Kellow, S. C. Lee, A. Loze, Mrs C. Loze, D. P. J. Lyons, B. J. Malone, W. McKibbin, C. Moore, Dr R. D. P. Newland, Mrs L. M. Northover, M. J. Ogborne, J. H. Parslow, N. D. Peppiatt, R. G. Pritchard, Mrs E. N. Reed-Daunter, Ms E. M. B. A. Reffo, Mrs J. E. Richards, Sir J. W. Robb, Ms N. Rossa, P. H. B. Rowe, N. C. Savery, T. Sharman, Mrs B. Shaw, D. G. Sheldon, R. K. Simmons, C. D. Smith, A. G. Stevens, George Strawbridge, C. R. Trembath, S. R. Trow, M. J. Tuckey, Mr B. J. Tuckey, C. J. M. Walker, Mr A. J. A. Waller, B. V. Ward, Miss L. C. Whateley, P. R. Wiles, Mrs D. A. Winton, D. J. Wood.

Assistant Trainer: Richard White & Alex Elliott

Jockey (NH): P. J. Brennan, P. Flynn, R. Johnson. **Conditional:** S. Pateman, R. Stephens. **Amateur:** Mr T. O'Brian.

---

291 MR R. J. HODGES, Somerton
Postal: Footsteps, Cedar Lodge, Charlton Adam, Somerton, Somerset, TA11 7AR.
Contacts: **PHONE** (01458) 223922 **FAX** (01458) 223969 **MOBILE** (07770) 625846

1 BY DEGREE (IRE), 9, gr g Roselier (FR)—Decent Enough **Fieldspring Racing Syndicate**
2 CHANCE FLIGHT, 5, b m Busy Flight—Castle Maid **R. T. Sercombe**
3 COMPTON STAR, 5, ch g Compton Place—Darakah **A. M. Midgley**
4 DREAM FALCON, 5, b g Polar Falcon—Pip's Dream **P. E. Axon**
5 GOLDBROOK, 7, b g Alderbrook—Miss Marigold **John & Greer Norman**
6 HIGH BOUNCE (USA), 5, ch g Trempolino (USA)—Top Hope **R. G. Andrews**
7 JUPON VERT (FR), 8, b g Lights Out (FR)—Danse Verte (FR) **Mrs A. P. M. Jenkins**
8 JUST JIMBO, 9, ch g Karinga Bay—Ruby Green VII **R. J. Hart**
9 JUST PERCY, 5, b g Then Again—Persistent Gunner **Miss R. J. Dobson**
10 LODGER (FR), 5, ch g Grand Lodge (USA)—Light River (USA) **Fieldspring Racing Syndicate**
11 MASTER MAHOGANY, 4, b g Bandmaster—Impropriety **Villagers Five**
12 MOBO-BACO, 8, ch g Bandmaster (USA)—Darakah **Forme Racing**
13 MOUNTS BAY, 6, ch m Karinga Bay—Sweet On Willie (USA) **D. F. P. Racing**
14 NOBLE CALLING (FR), 8, b h Caller I D (USA)—Specificity (USA) **Nineways**
15 ON A DEAL, 7, b g Teenoso (USA)—Gale Spring (IRE) **Unity Farm Holiday Centre Ltd**
16 OVER TO YOU BERT, 6, b g Overbury (IRE)—Silvers Era **Mr R. J. Hodges**

MR R. J. HODGES—continued

17 **PENTHOUSE MINSTREL**, 11, b br g Seven Hearts—Pentameron **R. G. Andrews**
18 **PHAR JEFFEN (IRE)**, 10, ch g Phardante (FR)—Clever Milly **Fieldspring Racing Syndicate**
19 **POST IT**, 4, b f Thowra (FR)—Cream By Post **J. M. Dare**
20 **POWRA**, 5, b g Thowra (FR)—Lake Mariner **Mrs L Brafield**
21 **ROYAL PRODIGY (USA)**, 6, ch g Royal Academy (USA)—
                                    Prospector's Queen (USA) **The Gardens Entertainments Ltd**
22 **SAMMY SAMBA**, 7, b g Be My Chief (USA)—Peggy Spencer **D. Charlesworth**
23 **TENDER FALCON**, 5, br g Polar Falcon (USA)—Tendresse (FR) **P. E. Axon**
24 **TENSILE (IRE)**, 10, b g Tenby—Bonnie Isle **D. Charlesworth**
25 **THE GENE GENIE**, 10, b g Syrtos—Sally Maxwell **K. H. Small**
26 **WIZARD OF EDGE**, 5, b g Wizard King—Forever Shineing **D. Charlesworth**

TWO-YEAR-OLDS

27 **IN FASHION**, b f 4/3 Bertolini (USA)—Dress Design (IRE) (Brief Truce (USA)) (8800) **Miss R. J. Dobson**
28 **SAFARI**, b f 12/4 Namaqualand (USA)—Breakfast Creek (Hallgate) (7000) **Miss R. J. Dobson**
29 B f 4/3 Pyramus (USA)—Tenderetta (Tender King) (1400) **A. S. Hodges**

Other Owners: C. Bowen, K. J. Corcoran, Mrs A. M. Doyle, P. J. Doyle, R. G. Morgan, Miss J. E. Murray-Playfair, J. F. Newsome, R. G. Pritchard, Mrs J. E. Richards, J. P. Seviour, Mrs C. P. Taylor, R. V. Taylor, Mrs P. J. Taylor.

Amateur: Mr J. White.

---

292 MR M. J. HOGAN, Findon
Postal: **2 New Cottages, Gallops Farm, Findon, West Sussex, BN14 0RQ.**
Contacts: **PHONE (01903) 873348 MOBILE (07850) 441891**

1 **GREAT CRUSADER**, 13, ch g Deploy—Shannon Princess **Mrs B. E. Hogan**
2 **ISAM TOP (FR)**, 9, b g Siam (USA)—Miss Sic Top (FR) **Mrs B. E. Hogan**
3 **KINGS SIGNAL (USA)**, 7, b g Red Ransom (USA)—Star of Albion **Mrs B. E. Hogan**
4 **MYSTICAL STAR (FR)**, 8, b g Nicolotte—Addaya (IRE) **Mrs B. E. Hogan**

---

293 MR TOM HOGAN, Nenagh
Postal: **Fattheen House, Nenagh, Co. Tipperary, Ireland.**
Contacts: **HOUSE +353 (0) 67 33924 YARD +353 (0) 67 32846 FAX +44 (0) 1635 578101 & +353 (0) 67 33989 MOBILE +353 (0) 87 2332111**

1 **BEST AWAY (IRE)**, 7, ch m Un Desperado (FR)—Line Up (IRE) **Moving On Syndicate**
2 **CULMORE LADY (IRE)**, 7, b m Insan (USA)—Kemaldor **J. M. Ryan**
3 **FAYRLY LIVELY (IRE)**, 4, b f Fayruz—Pounding Beat **Moving On Syndicate**
4 **GREEN MAGICAL (IRE)**, 8, ch m Magical Strike (USA)—Green Legend (IRE)
5 **HASTY SECOND (IRE)**, 7, b m Aristocracy—Hasty Days **Troy Murphy**
6 **INDIAN TOM (IRE)**, 11, b br g Cataldi—Dame Sue **Mrs B. Cunningham**
7 **JACKAPPLE JOE (IRE)**, 7, gr g Warcraft (USA)—Steel Mariner **Frank Wallace**
8 **KYLEBEG DANCER (IRE)**, 4, ch f General Monash (USA)—Glamour Stock (USA) **N. Gleeson**
9 **NARROW WATER (IRE)**, 12, b g Mazaad—Miss Doogles **M. L. Masterson**
10 **NEWTOWN DANCER (IRE)**, 6, b m Danehill Dancer (IRE)—Patience of Angels (IRE) **Cool Out Syndicate**
11 **NO FRONTIER (IRE)**, 7, ch m Imperial Frontier (USA)—Poly Dancer **R. Gill & J. Hogan**
12 **PASCALI BOY (IRE)**, 8, b g Beau Sher—James Rose **Charlie Malone Syndicate**
13 **PENNY RICH (IRE)**, 11, br g Little Bighorn—Musical Puss **Mrs J. Hogan**
14 **PREMIER REBEL (IRE)**, 7, b g Borovoe—Gorazhire **Cork & Tipp Syndicate**
15 **ROOFTOP PROTEST (IRE)**, 8, b g Thatching—Seattle Siren (USA) **M. Byrne**
16 **ROSNAGOWLOGE (IRE)**, 7, b g Houmayoun (FR)—Ave Lira **John Carroll**
17 **SAND N SEA (IRE)**, 4, b f Desert Story (IRE)—Poscimur (IRE) **Mrs J. Hogan**
18 **TAKING SILK (IRE)**, 8, ch m Mister Lord (USA)—Yes Your Honour **M. L. O'Keeffe**
19 4, Ch c College Chapel—Tiger Wings (IRE) **T. Hogan**

Jockey (flat): R. M. Burke, F. Berry. **Jockey (NH):** K. Hadnett. **Conditional:** E. F. Power. **Apprentice:** E. McCutcheon, R. Celary. **Amateur:** Mr J. J. Ryan, Mr Mark Rogan, Mr A. J. Hogan, Mr W M Hayes.

294 **MR H. P. HOGARTH, Stillington**
Postal: **New Grange Farm, Stillington, York.**
Contacts: **PHONE (01347) 811168**

1 ALLFRIENDS, 6, b br g Alflora (IRE)—Three Friends (IRE) **Hogarth Racing**
2 CAPYBARA (IRE), 7, b g Commanche Run—The Pledger **Hogarth Racing**
3 CHERRY'S ECHO, 5, gr m Keen—Distant Cherry **Hogarth Racing**
4 ENCORE CADOUDAL (FR), 7, b g Cadoudal (FR)—Maousse (FR) **Hogarth Racing**
5 IMPERIAL DREAM (IRE), 7, b g Roselier (FR)—Royal Nora (IRE) **Hogarth Racing**
6 JURALAN (IRE), 10, b g Jurado (USA)—Boylan **Hogarth Racing**
7 KEIRAN (IRE), 11, b g Be My Native (USA)—Myra Gaye **Hogarth Racing**
8 LIBERTINE LADY, 8, b m Perpendicular—Distant Cherry **Hogarth Racing**
9 PRIMITIVE REBEL, 6, gr g Primitive Rising (USA)—Distant Cherry **Hogarth Racing**
10 RED RAMPAGE, 10, b g King's Ride—Mighty Fly **Hogarth Racing**
11 TINA'S SCALLYWAG, 8, br m Baron Blakeney—Southend Scallywag **Hogarth Racing**
12 TWO TONYS SHAM (IRE), 6, b g Fourstars Allstar (USA)—Millies Girl (IRE) **Hogarth Racing**

Other Owners: MR H. P. Hogarth, P. H. Hogarth, J. Hogarth, J. L. Hogarth.

Assistant Trainer: Mr P H Hogarth

Jockey (NH): D. O'Meara.

295 **MR A. S. T. HOLDSWORTH, Ogwell**
Postal: **Holbeam Mill, Ogwell, Devon, TQ12 6LX.**
Contacts: **HOME (01626) 365547 MOBILE (07791) 619037**

1 OFF MY TOES, 5, b m Relief Pitcher—On My Toes **N. J. W. A. Holdsworth**

THREE-YEAR-OLDS

2 BARHAM BROOK, b f Bandmaster (USA)—Time To Move (IRE) **N. J. W. A. Holdsworth**

Assistant Trainer: E M Vince

Jockey (NH): G. Supple. **Amateur:** Mr D. Alers-Hanky.

296 **MR A. F. HOLLINGSWORTH, Feckenham**
Postal: **Lanket House, Crofts Lane, Feckenham, Redditch, Worcestershire, B96 6PU.**
Contacts: **PHONE (01527) 68644/892054 FAX (01527) 60310 MOBILE (07775) 670644**

1 BLACKANBLUE, 6, b g Alflora (IRE)—Emmabella **Kombined Motor Services Ltd**
2 CENTREFOLD, 5, b h Sea Raven (IRE)—Gemmabel **Kombined Motor Services Ltd**
3 GALLIK DAWN, 7, ch g Anshan—Sticky Money **P. Adams**
4 GEMSTER, 7, b m Alflora (IRE)—Gemmabel **Kombined Motor Services Ltd**
5 LOOSE NUT, 7, b m Alflora (IRE)—Emmabella **Kombined Motor Services Ltd**
6 MAKE IT PLAIN, 6, b m Alflora (IRE)—Gemmabel **Mr A. F. Hollingsworth**
7 STROLLING, 8, br g Alflora (IRE)—Emmabella **Kombined Motor Services Ltd**

Assistant Trainer: Sharon Smith

Jockey (NH): D. R. Dennis, M. A. Fitzgerald, A. Thornton. **Amateur:** Mr G. Hanmer, Mr T. Stephenson.

297 **MR R. HOLLINSHEAD, Upper Longdon**
Postal: **Lodge Farm, Upper Longdon, Rugeley, Staffordshire, WS15 1QF.**
Contacts: **PHONE (01543) 490298 FAX (01543) 490490**

1 BOSWORTH GYPSY (IRE), 7, b m Aahsaylad—Googly **J. L. Marriott**
2 CAPER, 5, b g Salse (USA)—Spinning Mouse **C. W. Wardle**
3 CASTLE RING, 6, b g Sri Pekan (USA)—Understudy **Mr R. Hollinshead**
4 CHESTALL, 4, b g Polar Prince (IRE)—Maradata (IRE) **Mr R. Hollinshead**
5 CHICKASAW TRAIL, 7, ch m Be My Chief (USA)—Maraschino **Mr R. Hollinshead**
6 CROSS ASH (IRE), 5, ch g Ashkalani (IRE)—Priorite (IRE) **E. T. D. Leadbeater**
7 DANGER BIRD (IRE), 5, ch m Eagle Eyed (USA)—Danger Ahead **Mr R. Hollinshead**

MR R. HOLLINSHEAD—continued

8 **DANUM**, 5, b g Perpendicular—Maid of Essex **Lawrence And Hollinshead**
9 **DORA CORBINO**, 5, b m Superpower—Smartie Lee **Mrs M. E. Hill**
10 **FOOLISH GROOM**, 4, ch g Groom Dancer (USA)—Scared **J. D. Graham**
11 **GILDED COVE**, 5, b h Polar Prince (IRE)—Cloudy Reef **M. A. N. Johnson**
12 **GOLDEVA**, 6, gr m Makbul—Gold Belt (IRE) **Mr M. Pyle & Mrs T. Pyle**
13 **HEATHYARDS JOY**, 4, ch f Komaite (USA)—Heathyards Lady (USA) **L. A. Morgan**
14 **HEATHYARDS PRIDE**, 5, b g Polar Prince (IRE)—Heathyards Lady (USA) **L. A. Morgan**
15 **HEATHYARDSBLESSING (IRE)**, 8, b g Unblest—Noble Nadia **L. A. Morgan**
16 **MARGOLD (IRE)**, 5, ch m Goldmark (USA)—Arcevia (IRE) **L. & R. Roadlines Ltd**
17 **MR MIDASMAN (IRE)**, 4, b g Entrepreneur—Sifaara (IRE) **E. T. D. Leadbeater**
18 **NANNA (IRE)**, 4, b f Danetime (IRE)—Pre Catelan **Mrs G. A. Weetman**
19 **NORMA HILL**, 4, b f Polar Prince (IRE)—Smartie Lee **Mr G. Lloyd**
20 **NORTHERN NYMPH**, 6, b g Makbul—Needwood Sprite **E. T. D. Leadbeater**
21 **PRINCE OF GOLD**, 5, b h Polar Prince (IRE)—Gold Belt (IRE) **Horne, Hollinshead, Johnson**
22 **RED ROCKY**, 4, b f Danzero (AUS)—Post Mistress (IRE) **Mr R. Hollinshead**
23 **ROYAL CAVALIER**, 8, b g Prince of Birds (USA)—Gold Belt (IRE) **The Three R's**
24 **SAFFRON RIVER**, 4, b c Polar Prince (IRE)—Cloudy Reef **M. A. N. Johnson**
25 **SASHAY**, 7, b m Bishop of Cashel—St James's Antigua (USA)
26 **STRAVMOUR**, 9, ch h Seymour Hicks (FR)—La Stravaganza **E. Bennion**
27 **SUPER DOMINION**, 8, ch g Superpower—Smartie Lee **Mrs M. E. Hill**
28 **THEATRE TINKA (IRE)**, 6, b g King's Theatre (IRE)—Orange Grouse (IRE) **E. T. D. Leadbeater**
29 **THINK QUICK (IRE)**, 5, b m Goldmark (USA)—Crimson Ring **J. L. Marriott**
30 **VERMILION CREEK**, 6, b m Makbul—Cloudy Reef **M. A. N. Johnson**
31 **WEET A HEAD (IRE)**, 4, b g Foxhound (USA)—Morale **T. E. Weetman**

THREE-YEAR-OLDS

32 **BARACHOIS GAUDY**, br f Nomination—Barachois Princess (USA) **J. D. Graham**
33 **CHILLY CRACKER**, ch f Largesse—Polar Storm (IRE) **J. L. Marriott**
34 **CLEVELAND**, b c Pennekamp (USA)—Clerio **Connop And Hollinshead**
35 **CUTLASS GAUDY**, br c Nomination—Cutlass Princess (USA) **J. D. Graham**
36 **HARRY'S SIMMIE (IRE)**, ch f Spectrum (IRE)—Minstrels Folly (USA) **D. Coppenhall**
37 **JOEY**, b f Polar Prince (IRE)—Understudy **Mr R. Hollinshead**
38 **KEON (IRE)**, b c Rossini (USA)—Lonely Brook (USA) **Chasetown Civil Engineering Ltd**
39 **LEGAL LOVER (IRE)**, b c Woodborough (USA)—Victoria's Secret (IRE) **E. T. D. Leadbeater**
40 **MALAIKA**, b f Polar Prince (IRE)—Gold Belt (IRE) **Mr M. Pyle & Mrs T. Pyle**
41 **MENNA**, b f Mark of Esteem (IRE)—Pounelta **J. D. Graham**
42 **PAULINE'S PRINCE**, b c Polar Prince (IRE)—Etma Rose (IRE) **N. Chapman**
43 **POLAR PASSION**, b f Polar Prince (IRE)—Priorite (IRE) **E. T. D. Leadbeater**
44 **SISTER GEE (IRE)**, b f Desert Story (IRE)—My Gloria (IRE) **J. D. Graham**
45 **WHITBY ECHO (IRE)**, b c Entrepreneur—Nom de Plume (USA) **N. Chapman**

TWO-YEAR-OLDS

46 B c 29/3 Makbul—Flying Flip (Rolfe (USA))
47 **HIGH MEADOW GIRL**, b f 27/2 Pursuit of Love—Immaculate (Mark of Esteem (IRE))
48 **OCHRE BAY**, b c 1/3 Polar Prince (IRE)—Cloudy Reef (Cragador)
49 Br f 21/1 Namid—Otter's Field (IRE) (First Trump) **E. T. D. Leadbeater**
50 **ROYLE DANCER**, b g 12/3 Makbul—Foxtrot Pie (Shernazar) (7619) **R. Robinson**
51 **SAHARA STYLE**, b c 16/4 Desert Style (IRE)—Scapavia (FR) (Alzao (USA)) **Mrs D. E. Edwards**
52 B c 20/4 Kayf Tara—Stravsea (Handsome Sailor) **E. Bennion**
53 **WEET FOR YOU**, gr f 29/4 Weet-A-Minute (IRE)—
                         Weet Ees Girl (IRE) (Common Grounds) **Ed Weetman (Haulage & Storage) Ltd**

Other Owners: Miss B. Connop, D. R. Horne, A. L. Marriott, Mrs J. E. Wardle.

Assistant Trainer: A N Hollinshead

Conditional: A. Hawkins. **Apprentice:** R. Kennemore, H. Fellows, Stephanie Hollinshead. **Amateur:** Mrs Jane Galpin.

298 **MR J. R. HOLT, Peckleton**
Postal: Hall Farm, Church Road, Peckleton, Leicester.
Contacts: PHONE/FAX (01455) 821972 MOBILE (07850) 321059
E-MAIL john.holt@hallfarmracing.co.uk WEBSITE www.hallfarmracing.co.uk

1 FIESTY FROSTY (IRE), 7, b m Glacial Storm (USA)—Smashed Free (IRE) Mrs E. S. Holt
2 5, B m Commanche Run—Forgiving Me (IRE) Mr J. R. Holt
3 SILVER STYX, 6, gr g Terimon—Sconie's Poppet R. D. J. Swinburne
4 TEXAS BELLE (IRE), 7, b m Glacial Storm (USA)—Cloncannon Bell (IRE) Mrs M. D. Sharland

Assistant Trainer: Ellen Holt

299 **MR M. HOURIGAN, Limerick**
Postal: Lissaleen, Patrickswell, Limerick, Ireland.
Contacts: PHONE +353 (0) 61 396603
FAX +353 (0) 61 396812 MOBILE +353 (0) 86 8226655
E-MAIL info@mhourigan.ie WEBSITE www.mhourigan.ie

1 A GEM OF A STORY (IRE), 5, b br m Presenting—Graeme's Gem Storys Over Syndicate
2 A NEW STORY (IRE), 7, b g Fourstars Allstar (USA)—Diyala (FR) Storys Over Syndicate
3 ADDICTION (IRE), 8, b g Woods of Windsor (USA)—Star Cream I Remember It Well Syndicate
4 ALMIER (IRE), 7, gr g Phardante (FR)—Stepfaster C. Maune
5 ALPHA LIMA (IRE), 5, b br h Son of Sharp Shot (IRE)—Maidstown Lady (IRE) Conor Clarkson
6 APRIL ELEVENTH (IRE), 5, b g Naheez (USA)—Maeve's Magic (IRE) J. Keogh
7 ARTEEA (IRE), 6, b g Oscar (IRE)—Merric (IRE) M. O'Flaherty
8 AVERARD (IRE), 6, ch m Flemensfirth (USA)—Satula Frank Burke
9 BEEF OR SALMON (IRE), 9, ch g Cajetano (USA)—Farinella (IRE) B. J. Craig
10 BLACK N WHITE (IRE), 5, b g Simply Great (FR)—Silent Shot Mrs J. Stewart
11 BLANCO (IRE), 5, ch g First Trump—Balance The Books M. Hennessy
12 CENTRAL BILLING (IRE), 10, b g Ore—Guelder Rose D. Sperian
13 CHEVAUX LOCO (IRE), 8, b g Jolly Jake (NZ)—Kilbane Lass (IRE) Carwash Syndicate
14 CHURCH ISLAND (IRE), 6, ch g Erins Isle—Just Possible B. J. Craig
15 CLARIDGE (IRE), 6, b g Aahsaylad—Bucks Serenade (IRE) The Plough Syndicate
16 CLOCK HOUSE (IRE), 5, b g Mohaajir (USA)—Risk-A-Dinge (IRE)
17 CLONBOO BOY (IRE), 7, b g Eurobus—Clonboo Princess (IRE) Brendan Corbett
18 CRATLOE CASTLE (IRE), 7, b g Aahsaylad—Miss Paleface J. O'Gorman
19 DASHER'S CHOICE, 5, b m Defacto (USA)—Skiddaw Bird Dasher Syndicate
20 DASHER'S GIFT, 6, b m Overbury (IRE)—Amber's Image Dasher Syndicate
21 DR JULIAN (IRE), 5, b g Sesaro (USA)—Toda Enda Hunston
22 DROMHILL (IRE), 5, ch m Ajraas (USA)—Cruising Speed (IRE) P. Ward
23 EASY CASH (IRE), 6, b m Topanoora—Lantern Line Mrs M. Farrell
24 EMER'S CHOICE (IRE), 5, b m Moscow Society (USA)—Time O'day (IRE) F. Roche
25 EURO FLYER (IRE), 7, b m Muharib (USA)—Que Tranquila Euro Syndicate
26 GARSINGTON (IRE), 8, ch m Over The River (FR)—Apicat W. Neville
27 GREENWOOD TREE, 5, b m Keen—Sublime Racing Focus Racing Club
28 HANDY CASH (IRE), 6, b m Flemensfirth (USA)—Lantern Lass Mrs M. Farrell
29 HI CLOY (IRE), 8, b g Be My Native (USA)—Thomastown Girl Mrs S. McCloy
30 HORNER ROCKS (IRE), 9, b g Phardante (FR)—Horner Water (IRE) Prior-Wandesforde
31 INDIAN SAPPHIRE (IRE), 4, ch f Bijou d'inde—Capriati (USA) Bayside Racing Club
32 JUST (IRE), 6, ch g Great Marquess—Gerdando Lady (IRE) J & N Syndicate
33 KERRYHEAD WINDFARM (IRE), 7, br g Bob Back (USA)—Kerryhead Girl (IRE) J. Browne
34 KILBEGGAN BLADE, 6, b g Sure Blade (USA)—Moheli Frank Doyle
35 KILBEGGAN LAD (IRE), 7, b g Doyoun—Parnala (USA) Golf At Ballyneety Syndicate
36 KILFINNY CROSS (IRE), 6, b m Broken Hearted—Polls Joy Jay & Jay Syndicate
37 KING CAREW (IRE), 7, b h Fairy King (USA)—Kareena J. Carey
38 KNOCKNABROGUE (IRE), 7, b m Afzal—Just Precious
39 MARIKANA (IRE), 5, b m Rainbows For Life (CAN)—Brandywell M. Toomey
40 MAVERICK DANCER (IRE), 7, ch g Goldmark (USA)—Lili Bengam Four Maverick Syndicate
41 MOSCOW PARADE (IRE), 7, b g Moscow Society (USA)—Corrie Lough (IRE) Four Borders Syndicate
42 MOSS BAWN (IRE), 9, b g Jurado (USA)—Boylan Mrs S. McCloy
43 MOUNT LEITRIM (IRE), 6, gr g Ala Hounak—Monteleck Tom Morrison
44 MR RED VIC (IRE), 5, ch g Old Vic—Clive's Choice (IRE) Mr J. Barry
45 OLD KILMINCHY (IRE), 9, b br g Cashel Court—Janeyway Enda Hunston
46 OLYMPIC GOLD, 5, b m Thowra (FR)—Sharp Dance Come In For One Syndicate
47 ORCHESTRAL DREAM (IRE), 5, ch g Flying Legend—Mill Dancer (IRE) C. McGuinness
48 PUSH OR PULL (IRE), 6, b g Weldnaas (USA)—Clodagh River (IRE) Enda Hunston
49 SABRE'S EDGE (IRE), 4, b c Sadler's Wells (USA)—Brave Kris (IRE) Lady Bamford

MR M. HOURIGAN—continued

50 **SARGON**, 6, b h Oscar (IRE)—Syrian Queen **Miss M. O'Carroll**
51 **SHE'LL BE LUCKY (IRE)**, 7, ch m Arctic Cider (USA)—Johnnys Girl **G. Cummins**
52 **SIMON VAUGHAN (IRE)**, 7, ch g Montelimar (USA)—Arakeepa **M. Hourigan**
53 **SOCIETY TIME (IRE)**, 5, ch m Moscow Society (USA)—Vesper Time **Pin Two Racing Syndicate**
54 **SPIN IN THE WIND (IRE)**, 7, ch m Moscow Society (USA)—Turbulent Wind **Lady Petersham**
55 **STEVIE JAY (IRE)**, 5, ch g Oscar Schindler (IRE)—Mantlepiece (IRE) **S. Fahey**
56 **SURPRISE MILLION (IRE)**, 6, b g Semillon—Surprise Packet **Laune Syndicate**
57 **THE PARISHIONER (IRE)**, 7, ch m Glacial Storm (USA)—Phairy Miracles (IRE) **Fergus Syndicate**
58 **THE REAL SOLARA (IRE)**, 8, b g Aahsaylad—Arctic Brief **Foundation Syndicate**
59 **THE SHAM**, 5, b g Perpendicular—Our Aisling **Robert Butler Racing**
60 **THE SPACER (IRE)**, 7, ch g Florida Son—Tacova's Gift (IRE) **Enda Hunston**
61 **THE TAILOR CAREY (IRE)**, 6, b g Kadeed (IRE)—Secret Tryst (IRE) **J. Carey**
62 **VIC VILLE (IRE)**, 6, b g Old Vic—N T Nad **D. O'Connor**
63 **WHOWOULDYOUASK (IRE)**, 5, ch g Ridgewood Ben—Generali Contadini **Sneaky Boo Syndicate**
64 **WILLIESDREAM (IRE)**, 6, b g Kadeed—Eye In The Sky **W. Kavanagh**

Assistant Trainer: Kay Hourigan

Conditional: David F. Flannery. **Amateur:** Miss L. A. Hourigan, Mr M. J. O'Hare.

300
MR H. S. HOWE, Tiverton
Postal: **Ringstone Stables, Oakford, Tiverton, Devon, EX16 9EU.**
Contacts: **PHONE (01398) 351224 FAX (01398) 351153 MOBILE (07802) 506344**
E-MAIL stuarthoweracing@yahoo.co.uk

1 **DELAWARE**, 8, b g Alzao (USA)—Ballymac Girl **Horses Away Racing Ltd**
2 **PENSTRUMBLY FLOWER**, 5, b m Wild Law—Princess Poppy **Miss M. Robertson**
3 **SILVER CHARMER**, 6, b m Charmer—Sea Dart **J. Bull**
4 **STRAIGHT TALKER (IRE)**, 6, b g Warcraft (USA)—The Mighty Midge **Horses Away Racing Ltd**
5 **UIG**, 4, ch f Bien Bien (USA)—Madam Zando **B. P. Jones**

THREE-YEAR-OLDS

6 **MYSTERY MAID (IRE)**, b f King's Theatre (IRE)—Duly Elected **R. J. Parish**
7 **SILVER DREAMER (IRE)**, b f Brave Act—Heads We Called (IRE) **Mr J. Bull & Mr Michael Moore**

TWO-YEAR-OLDS

8 B f 6/2 Mujahid (USA)—Amy G (IRE) (Common Grounds) (4023) **Mr H. S. Howe**
9 B c 24/4 Namid—Balois (IRE) (Harnas (IRE)) (3688) **Mr B. P. Jones & Mr H. S. Howe**
10 B f 9/4 Beckett (IRE)—Coppelia (IRE) (Mac's Imp (USA)) (3486) **Mr H. S. Howe**
11 B f 13/2 King's Theatre (IRE)—Light-Flight (IRE) (Brief Truce (USA)) (3353) **Mr H. S. Howe**
12 B f 19/3 Mozart (IRE)—Markova's Dance (Mark of Esteem (IRE)) **Howard Barton Stud**
13 B c 18/4 Danetime (IRE)—
                           Raise-A-Secret (USA) (Classic Secret (USA)) **Mr & Mrs M. O'sullivan & Mr S. O'Sullivan**
14 B c 7/4 Wizard King—Roonah Quay (IRE) (Soviet Lad (USA)) (7377) **B. P. Jones**
15 B c 23/4 Bandmaster (USA)—Sheilas Dream (Inca Chief (USA)) **Mr George Searle**
16 B f 10/4 Danetime (IRE)—Tolomena (Tolomeo) (6371) **B. P. Jones**

Other Owners: Mrs V. W. Jones, M. J. Moore.

Jockey (flat): S. Drowne, D. Kinsella. **Jockey (NH):** P. Flynn, R. P. McNally.

301
MR P. HOWLING, Newmarket
Postal: **Wellbottom Lodge, Moulton Paddocks, Bury Road, Newmarket, Suffolk, CB8 7PJ.**
Contacts: **PHONE (01638) 668503 MOBILE (07866) 674469**
E-MAIL billichang@aol.com

1 **A TEEN**, 7, ch h Presidium—Very Good **Mrs A. K. Petersen**
2 **ANOTHER CON (IRE)**, 4, b f Lake Coniston (IRE)—Sweet Unison (USA) **D. C. Patrick**
3 **ANOUSA (IRE)**, 4, b c Intikhab (USA)—Annaletta **Arkland International (UK) Ltd**
4 **BELLS BEACH (IRE)**, 7, b m General Monash (USA)—Clifton Beach **R. P. Berenson**
5 **BLUE KNIGHT (IRE)**, 6, ch g Bluebird (USA)—Fer de Lance (IRE) **Mr M. Barber**
6 **CHARLIE MASTERS**, 4, b g Polar Falcon (USA)—Bowden Rose **M. L. Boreham**
7 **COBALT RUNNER (IRE)**, 4, b c Fayruz—Bui-Doi (IRE) **Mr M. Barber**

MR P. HOWLING—continued

8 **DIAL SQUARE**, 4, b g Bluegrass Prince (IRE)—Honey Mill **R. Murphy**
9 **DISCO DIVA**, 4, ch f Spectrum (IRE)—Compact Disc (IRE) **Mr P. Howling**
10 **LEAH'S PRIDE**, 4, b f Atraf—First Play **Mr M. Barber**
11 **MADIBA**, 6, b g Emperor Jones (USA)—Priluki **Eastwell Manor Racing Ltd**
12 **MY PENSION (IRE)**, 4, b g Orpen (USA)—Woodenitbenice (USA)
13 **NADIR**, 4, b c Pivotal—Amid The Stars **L. Sheridan**
14 **NANTUCKET SOUND (USA)**, 4, b g Quiet American (USA)—Anna **D. C. Patrick**
15 **NEARLY A FOOL**, 7, b g Komaite (USA)—Greenway Lady **Mrs D. R. Sawyer**
16 **PENWAY**, 4, b c Groom Dancer (USA)—Imani **Mrs J. M. Khan**
17 **RIQUEWIHR**, 5, ch m Compton Place—Juvenilia (IRE) **Eastwell Manor Racing Ltd**
18 **SHAMROCK CITY (IRE)**, 8, b g Rock City—Actualite **L. Sheridan**
19 **SIMON'S SEAT (USA)**, 6, ch g Woodman (USA)—Spire (USA) **Mrs E. M. Reid**
20 **SURDOUE**, 5, b g Bishop of Cashel—Chatter's Princess **Les Amis Partners**
21 **TOPTON (IRE)**, 11, b g Royal Academy (USA)—Circo **L. Sheridan**
22 **WARLINGHAM (IRE)**, 7, b g Catrail (USA)—Tadjnama (USA) **D. Brown**
23 **ZORN**, 6, br h Dilum (USA)—Very Good **Mrs A. K. Petersen**

THREE-YEAR-OLDS

24 B g Komaite (USA)—Blossoming **M. L. Boreham**
25 **CAVAN GAEL (FR)**, b c Dansili—Time Will Show (FR) **L. Sheridan**
26 B g Lugana Beach—Double Rock **Mr P. Howling**
27 **OUR KES (IRE)**, gr f Revoque (IRE)—Gracious Gretclo **Mr M. Entwistle**
28 **TIGER HUNTER**, b g Lake Coniston (IRE)—Daynabee **Mr T. S. Clifford**
29 **VENETIAN PRINCESS (IRE)**, b f Desert Style (IRE)—Dance With Care **Mr M. Barber**

TWO-YEAR-OLDS

30 B c 20/3 Forzando—Rain Splash (Petong) (5000) **Mr M. Entwistle**

Other Owners: Christopher N. Wright, Mr T. Baker, Mr P. Barker, R. H. Carey, C. Hammond, P. Hart.

Assistant Trainer: Mrs J Howling

Jockey (flat): K. Fallon, I. Mongan, R. Winston. **Amateur:** Miss F. Guillambert.

---

302 | **MR G. A. HUFFER, Newmarket**
Postal: **Grange House Stables, Hamilton Road, Newmarket, Suffolk, CB8 0TE.**
Contacts: **PHONE (01638) 561207 FAX (01638) 561603 MOBILE (07880) 706696**
E-MAIL geoffreyhuffer@hotmail.com

1 **FEAST OF ROMANCE**, 8, b g Pursuit of Love—June Fayre **Mr R. J. Stevens**
2 **MUSICAL GIFT**, 5, ch g Cadeaux Genereux—Kazoo **Mr T. P. Ramsden**
3 **ROYAL ATALZA (FR)**, 8, gr g Saint Preuil (FR)—Crystalza (FR) **Mr T. P. Ramsden**

THREE-YEAR-OLDS

4 **BANJO PATTERSON**, b c Green Desert (USA)—Rumpipumpy **Mr T. P. Ramsden**
5 **BOBSKI (IRE)**, b c Victory Note (USA)—Vivid Impression **Mr R. J. Thomson**
6 **DAYBREAK DANCER (IRE)**, b c Fasliyev (USA)—Darkling (IRE) **Mrs H. Wargen**
7 **OBEZYANA (USA)**, ch c Rahy (USA)—Polish Treaty (USA) **Mr T. P. Ramsden**
8 **RAZA CAB (IRE)**, b g Intikhab (USA)—Laraissa **Alan Brazil Racing Club**
9 **REVIEN (IRE)**, b c Rossini (USA)—Kazimiera **Mr T. P. Ramsden**
10 **SONNY PARKIN**, b g Spinning World (USA)—No Miss Kris (USA)
11 **STEPHANIE'S MIND**, b f Mind Games—Adorable Cherub (USA) **Alan Brazil Racing Club**

TWO-YEAR-OLDS

12 Br f 3/4 Namid—Kazimiera (IRE) (Polish Patriot (USA)) (5000) **Mr T. P. Ramsden**
13 Ch f 27/4 Namid—Krayyalei (IRE) (Krayyan) (46947) **Mr T. P. Ramsden**
14 B f 16/2 Agnes World (USA)—Maureena (IRE) (Grand Lodge (USA)) (28000) **Mr T. P. Ramsden**
15 B f 16/3 Xaar—Miss Mercy (IRE) (Law Society (USA)) (39000) **Alan Brazil Racing Club**
16 B g 20/4 Josr Algarhoud (IRE)—Persian Fortune (Forzando) (13413) **Mr T. P. Ramsden**

Assistant Trainer: M. Miller

303 MR D. T. HUGHES, Kildare
Postal: Osborne Lodge, Kildare, Co. Kildare, Ireland.
Contacts: PHONE +353 (0) 45 521490 FAX +353 (0) 45 521643 MOBILE +353 (0) 862 534098

1 **ADMIRAL BROWN (IRE)**, 9, b g Supreme Leader—Light The Lamp **K. McNulty**
2 **AKHTARI (IRE)**, 5, b h In The Wings—Akishka **Michael O'Leary**
3 **ALEXANDER NEVILLE**, 5, b g Unfuwain (USA)—Sports Delight **K. McNulty**
4 **ARDAN GLAS (IRE)**, 8, ch g Safety Catch (USA)—Jude's Hollow (IRE) **James J. Gleeson**
5 **BAMMERS (IRE)**, 7, ch m Zaffaran (USA)—Glaskerbeg Lady (IRE) **Mrs K. Leech**
6 **CARRICKFERGUS (USA)**, 6, gr g Benny The Dip—Stately Bid (USA) **Cathal M. Ryan**
7 **CELESTIAL LIGHT (IRE)**, 8, b m Archway (IRE)—Lady Heather **Michael B. Moore**
8 **CENTRAL ARCH**, 6, b m Dilum (USA)—Fantasy World **John Kenny**
9 **CENTRAL HOUSE**, 8, b g Alflora (IRE)—Fantasy World **Francis G. Kenny**
10 **CHAIN**, 8, b g Last Tycoon—Trampship **Mrs. Debra Merriman**
11 **COLUMBA (IRE)**, 9, b g Lord America—Jackson Miss **Brian MacMahon**
12 **CROCK A DOYLE (IRE)**, 6, b g Supreme Leader—Marie's Pride (IRE) **D. L. Doyle**
13 **CUPLA CAIRDE**, 5, b h Double Eclipse (IRE)—Four Legged Friend **Ceathrar Le Ceile Syndicate**
14 **DEMOPHILOS**, 7, b g Dr Devious (IRE)—Graecia Magna (USA) **Athos Christodoulou**
15 **DON AMECHIE (IRE)**, 7, gr g Roselier (FR)—Miss Pitpan **T. J. Culhane/Brian McMahon**
16 **DUBLIN HUNTER (IRE)**, 9, b g Treasure Hunter—Cutty Sark **Woodland Racing Syndicate**
17 **DUE RESPECT (IRE)**, 5, b g Danehill (USA)—Stylish **Fieldspring Racing Syndicate**
18 **DULGODTI BOB (IRE)**, 5, b g Bob Back (USA)—Trimar Gold **James J. Gleeson**
19 **FOREST LEAVES (IRE)**, 5, bl g Charnwood Forest (IRE)—Premier Code (IRE) **Legal Access Syndicate**
20 **GANDY (IRE)**, 8, b g Bob Back (USA)—Bramdean **Frank Ward**
21 **GONEFORALLTIME (IRE)**, 7, b m Lord America—Jackson Miss **Mrs Nancy Doyle**
22 **GUILT**, 5, b g Mark of Esteem (IRE)—Guillem (USA) **T C D D Syndicate**
23 **HANDY JACK (IRE)**, 6, b h King's Ride—Mossey Tune **H. A. Campbell**
24 **HAPRO (IRE)**, 5, b g Taipan (IRE)—Lara (USA) **Peter Brady**
25 **HARD WINTER (IRE)**, 8, b g Arctic Lord—Lucycello **D. A. Pim**
26 **HARDY DUCKETT (IRE)**, 6, br g Key of Luck (USA)—Bramdean **Laurence Byrne**
27 **HARDY EUSTACE (IRE)**, 8, b g Archway (IRE)—Sterna Star **Laurence Byrne**
28 **HARDY OLIVER (IRE)**, 6, b h Flemensfirth (USA)—Lucky Appeal **Laurence Byrne**
29 **HEADS ONTHE GROUND (IRE)**, 8, br g Be My Native (USA)—Strong Wings **Mr John P. McManus**
30 **IRISH STREAM (USA)**, 7, ch g Irish River (FR)—Euphonic (USA) **James T. Barton**
31 **IRON HAGUE (IRE)**, 4, b g Among Men (USA)—Conditional Sale (IRE) **John Duignam**
32 **JUSTPOURIT (IRE)**, 6, b h Glacial Storm (USA)—Gale Choice (IRE) **Hanged Mans Five Syndicate**
33 **KILDARE (IRE)**, 8, b g Supreme Leader—Fairly Deep **Cathal M. Ryan**
34 **KILDARE MINOR (IRE)**, 6, b g Old Vic—Fairly Deep **Cathal M. Ryan**
35 **LEINSTER (IRE)**, 8, b g Supreme Leader—Jennycomequick **Cathal M. Ryan**
36 **LISCANNOR LAD (IRE)**, 7, b g Nicolotte—Tinerana Memories (IRE) **C. P. O'Brien**
37 **LORNA'S LADY (IRE)**, 9, b m Be My Native (USA)—Gales Chariot **M. P. Whelan**
38 **MARK THE SHARK (IRE)**, 5, b g Entrepreneur—Danse Royale (IRE) **D. T. Hughes**
39 **MARKET MARINER (IRE)**, 6, ch g Bob Back (USA)—Bawnanell **Racing Management Services**
40 **MERRIE CHAPEL (IRE)**, 6, b g College Chapel—Merrie Moment **Three To One Syndicate**
41 **MR FITZER**, 6, b g Robellino (USA)—Tiszta Sharok **L. Fitzpatrick**
42 **MUTINEER (IRE)**, 6, gr g Highest Honor (FR)—Miss Amy R (USA) **Seven To Eleven Syndicate**
43 **NIGHT BUSKER (IRE)**, 7, b g Accordion—Toca Time (IRE) **Gigginstown House Stud**
44 **O'DRISCOLL (IRE)**, 7, b g Bob Back (USA)—Winter Fox **Cathal M. Ryan**
45 **ONE SMALL STEP (IRE)**, 4, b f Kahyasi—Nikki's Groom **Ms. Cynthia Maharaj**
46 **OULART**, 6, ch g Sabrehill (USA)—Gaye Fame **G. T. Piere**
47 **OUR HANDYMAN (IRE)**, 7, b g Nucleon (USA)—Burnished Gold **Peter S. Thompson**
48 **PHIL'S THUNDER (IRE)**, 5, br g Carroll House—Fairogan **Flower Pot Syndicate**
49 **POKER PAL (IRE)**, 8, b g Hollow Hand—Lady Dee **Lyreen Syndicate**
50 **POR CHABLIS (IRE)**, 6, b g Key of Luck (USA)—State Princess (USA) **K. McNulty**
51 **PUNTA CANA (IRE)**, 6, b h Moonax (IRE)—Aliceion **Pakie Cummins**
52 **ROBERT (IRE)**, 6, ch g Bob Back (USA)—Mother Imelda (IRE) **Robert L. Evans**
53 **TACITUS (IRE)**, 5, ch g Titus Livius (FR)—Idara **Nozzie Boys Syndicate**
54 **TAILS ONTHE GROUND (IRE)**, 5, b g Luso—Glencairn Lass **Mr John P. McManus**
55 **TATENDA (IRE)**, 7, b g Accordion—Loughloone (IRE) **Night Before Morning After Syndicate**
56 **THE HARROW (IRE)**, 6, b g Un Desperado (FR)—Royal Rosy (IRE) **Harrow Syndicate**
57 **THE JESUIT (IRE)**, 6, b g Key of Luck (USA)—Henrietta Street (IRE) **Cathal M. Ryan**
58 **THEATRE HOUSE (IRE)**, 6, b h Carroll House—Matinee Theatre **Matinee Syndicate**
59 **TIMBERA (IRE)**, 11, br g Commanche Run—Morry's Lady **Mrs J. M. Breen**
60 **TIMUCUA (IRE)**, 6, b br g Commanche Run—Morry's Lady **Mrs J. M. Breen**
61 **WALKIN AISY**, 5, b g Rudimentary (USA)—Lady Shipley **B. C. Marshall**

MR D. T. HUGHES—continued

  62 WINE MERCHANT (IRE), 7, b g Montelimar (USA)—Fly Fuss **James Nicholson**
  63 ZULULAND (IRE), 5, gr h Linamix (FR)—Zafadola (IRE) **H. A. Campbell**

Conditional: Patrick Flood. **Apprentice:** Paul Gallagher. **Amateur:** Mr Robert Hennessy, Mr R. Loughran.

---

304 DON E. INCISA, Middleham
Postal: **Thorngill House, Coverham, Middleham, Leyburn, North Yorkshire, DL8 4TJ.**
Contacts: **PHONE (01969) 640653 FAX (01969) 640694**

  1 ARCHERFIELD (IRE), 4, ch f Docksider (USA)—Willow River (CAN) **Don E. Incisa**
  2 CHEVERAK FOREST (IRE), 4, ch g Shinko Forest (IRE)—Meranie Girl (IRE) **Don E. Incisa**
  3 CRIPSEY BROOK, 7, ch g Lycius (USA)—Duwon (IRE) **Don E. Incisa**
  4 EAST CAPE, 8, b g Bering—Reine de Danse (USA) **Don E. Incisa**
  5 FRANCESCHIELLA (ITY), 4, gr f Beat of Drums—Filicaia **Razza Dormello Olgiata S.P.A.**
  6 JESSIE, 6, ch m Pivotal—Bold Gem **Don E. Incisa**
  7 LUFERTON LANE (IRE), 8, b m Ela-Mana-Mou—Saddle 'er Up (IRE) **Don E. Incisa**
  8 MICKLEGATE, 4, b f Dracula (AUS)—Primulette **Don E. Incisa**
  9 SIMPLE IDEALS (USA), 11, b g Woodman (USA)—Comfort And Style **Don E. Incisa**
  10 SIMPLY THE GUEST (IRE), 6, b g Mujadil (USA)—Ned's Contessa (IRE) **Don E. Incisa**
  11 SPEED RACER, 4, b f Zieten (USA)—Sharenara (USA) **Don E. Incisa**
  12 TURFTANZER (GER), 6, b g Lomitas—Tower Bridge (GER) **Don E. Incisa**
  13 UNO MENTE, 6, b m Mind Games—One Half Silver (CAN) **Don E. Incisa**

THREE-YEAR-OLDS

  14 CALA FONS (IRE), b f Alhaarth (IRE)—Lemon Tree (USA) **Don E. Incisa**
  15 CUT TO THE CHASE, b g Fraam—Chasetown Cailin **Don E. Incisa**
  16 LIABILITY (IRE), b f Bluebird (USA)—Madaniyya (USA) **Don E. Incisa**

TWO-YEAR-OLDS

  17 CECINA MARINA, b f 24/3 Sugarfoot—Chasetown Cailin (Suave Dancer (USA)) (3000) **Don E. Incisa**

Jockey (flat): Kim Tinkler. **Apprentice:** Janice E. Webster. **Amateur:** Mrs R. Howell.

---

305 MR R. INGRAM, Epsom
Postal: **Wendover Stables, Burgh Heath Road, Epsom, Surrey, KT17 4LX.**
Contacts: **PHONE (01372) 748505 or (01372) 749157 MOBILE (0777) 3665980**
E-MAIL roger.ingram.racing@virginnet.com

  1 BALERNO, 6, b g Machiavellian (USA)—Balabina (USA) **The Three Amigos**
  2 BOULE D'OR (IRE), 4, b c Croco Rouge (IRE)—Saffron Crocus **Friends and Family**
  3 DEVINE COMMAND, 4, b g In Command (IRE)—Adriya **L. Devine**
  4 HIGH PADDY, 6, b g Master Willie—Ivy Edith **G. A. Antill**
  5 ITSONLYAGAME, 5, b h Ali-Royal (IRE)—Mena **Mrs G. B. Brown**
  6 LYSANDER'S QUEST (IRE), 7, br g King's Theatre (IRE)—Haramayda (FR) **Mrs E. N. Nield**
  7 MAJORCA, 4, b c Green Desert (USA)—Majmu (USA) **Bill Hinge**
  8 MR HULLABALOU (IRE), 4, b g Princely Heir (IRE)—Lomalou (IRE) **Hullbran Bros**
  9 MY MAITE (IRE), 6, b g Komaite (USA)—Mena **The Stargazers 2nd XI**
  10 PRINCESS KAI (IRE), 4, b f Cayman Kai (IRE)—City Princess **Brannigan Bros**
  11 QUEEN CHARLOTTE, 6, ch m Tagula (IRE)—Tisima (FR) **P. W. Colley**
  12 QUIET MILLFIT (USA), 9, b g Quiet American (USA)—Millfit (USA) **Racing Marbles**
  13 ROYALE PEARL, 5, gr m Cloudings (IRE)—Ivy Edith **G. A. Antill**
  14 WILD WILD WES, 5, ch g The West (USA)—Dam Certain (IRE) **Global Trio Partnership**

THREE-YEAR-OLDS

  15 NAN JAN, b f Komaite (USA)—Dam Certain (IRE) **The Waltons**
  16 SKY CRUSADER, b c Mujahid (USA)—Red Cloud (IRE) **Pillar To Post Racing (IV)**
  17 SPANISH MUSIC, b f Piccolo—Raffelina (USA) **K. R. Steeper**
  18 VAGUE STAR (ITY), b c Soviet Star (USA)—Simova (USA) **L. Devine**

MR R. INGRAM—continued

TWO-YEAR-OLDS

19 Ch f 21/2 Primo Valentino (IRE)—Charlottevalentina (IRE) (Perugino (USA)) **Ellangowan Racing Partners**
20 Ch f 1/1 Primo Valentino (IRE)—Dam Certain (IRE) (Damister (USA)) **Mr R. Ingram**

Other Owners: Mr J. E. Bunyer, G. F. Chesneaux, A. J. Cousins, J. Dwight, L. E. Edwards, Mr D. R. Hull, Mr V. J. Hull, International Mortgage Plans, M. W. Joy, H. G. Newell, P. M. Overington, Mr D. Ross-Watt, K. M. Santana, G. Scott, P. C. Thompkins, Mr K. H. Walton, Mrs J. R. Walton.

Assistant Trainer: Sharon Ingram

Jockey (flat): N. Day. **Apprentice:** J. Loveridge.

---

306 **MR D. K. IVORY, Radlett**
Postal: **Harper Lodge Farm, Harper Lane, Radlett, Hertfordshire, WD7 7HU.**
Contacts: **PHONE (01923) 855337 FAX (01923) 852470 MOBILE (07785) 118658**
E-MAIL deanivoryracing.horses@virgin.net WEBSITE www.deanivoryracing.co.uk

1 **AZREME,** 5, ch h Unfuwain (USA)—Mariette **Halcyon Partnership**
2 **BERESFORD BOY,** 4, b g Easycall—Devils Dirge **Beresford Pumps Ltd**
3 **BUCKS,** 8, b g Slip Anchor—Alligram (USA) **M. Murphy**
4 **DUXFORD,** 4, ch g Young Ern—Marsara **J. B. Waterfall**
5 **EL CHAPARRAL (IRE),** 5, b g Bigstone (IRE)—Low Line **K. T. Ivory**
6 **FURTHER OUTLOOK (USA),** 11, gr g Zilzal (USA)—Future Bright (USA) **K. T. Ivory**
7 **GLENDALE,** 4, ch g Opening Verse (USA)—Kayartis **Mrs J. A. Cornwell**
8 **GUNS BLAZING,** 6, b g Puissance—Queen of Aragon **R. D. Hartshorn & Mike Smith**
9 **HARD TO CATCH (IRE),** 7, b g Namaqualand (USA)—Brook's Dilemma **Mrs K. B. Graham**
10 **JOOLS,** 7, b g Cadeaux Genereux—Madame Crecy (USA) **A. W. Parsons**
11 **KINDLELIGHT DEBUT,** 5, b m Groom Dancer (USA)—Dancing Debut **Kindlelight Ltd**
12 **KUMAKAWA,** 7, ch g Dancing Spree (USA)—Maria Cappuccini **R. D. Hartshorn**
13 **LOYAL TYCOON (IRE),** 7, br g Royal Abjar (USA)—Rosy Lydgate **A. W. Parsons**
14 **MIRASOL PRINCESS,** 4, ch f Ali-Royal (IRE)—Yanomami (USA) **A. W. Parsons**
15 **MISTER CLINTON (IRE),** 8, ch g Lion Cavern (USA)—Thewaari **J. B. Waterfall**
16 **RADLETT LADY,** 4, ch f Wolfhound (USA)—Royal Dream **Radlett Racing**
17 **SAPPHIRE SKY,** 4, b br f Compton Place—Jewel (IRE) **H. D. Shaw**
18 **SILVER PRELUDE,** 4, gr g Prince Sabo—Silver Blessings **Mrs A. Shone**
19 **SUMMER JOY,** 4, b f Myfontaine—Marycee (IRE) **D. O'Connor**
20 **SUPREME SALUTATION,** 9, ch g Most Welcome—Cardinal Press **Mrs K. B. Graham**

THREE-YEAR-OLDS

21 **BALTIC BOY,** ch g Bachir (IRE)—Sparkling Isle **Baltic Stone Ltd**
22 **BEAUFORT,** b g Yaheeb (USA)—Royal Blaze **R & M Bright**
23 **BENS GEORGIE (IRE),** ch f Opening Verse (USA)—Peperonata (IRE) **Marcoe Electrical**
24 **EDEN STAR (IRE),** b f Soviet Star (USA)—Gold Prospector (IRE) **Mrs A. Shone**
25 **JENNVERSE,** b f Opening Verse (USA)—Jennelle **Mrs J. A. Cornwell**
26 **LADY LONDRA (IRE),** b f Fumo di Londra (IRE)—Lady Phyl **Mr G. F. Jenkins**
27 **LIFE IS ROSIE (IRE),** ch f Rossini (USA)—Rachcara **Mrs K. B. Graham**
28 **LIMONIA (GER),** b f Perugino (USA)—Limoges (GER) **M. Murphy**
29 **LIVVIES LADY (IRE),** b f Opening Verse (USA)—Indian Wardance (ITY) **Marcoe Electrical And Dean Ivory**
30 **READY TEDDY GO,** b g Danzig Connection (USA)—Mariette **The Racy Ladies Club**

TWO-YEAR-OLDS

31 **ALLSUSSEDUP,** b g 4/4 Bertolini (USA)—Beau Duchess (FR) (Bering) (4500) **The Vine Associates**
32 **ANSELLS JOY,** b f 6/2 Primo Valentino (IRE)—
Eastern Ember (Indian King (USA)) (7800) **Ansells of Watford (Bookmakers)**
33 **ANSELLS PRIDE (IRE),** b c 15/4 King Charlemagne (USA)—
Accounting (Sillery (USA)) (26000) **Ansells of Watford (Bookmakers)**
34 **AT THE BAR,** ch c 2/2 Compton Place—Miss Tress (IRE) (Salse (USA)) (3500) **K. T. Ivory**
35 **BURFORD LASS (IRE),** b f 27/3 Quws—Dancing Willma (IRE) (Dancing Dissident (USA)) (7000) **M. F. Bourke**
36 **DYNAMITE DEANO,** b g 23/2 Dracula (AUS)—Katy Ivory (IRE) (Night Shift (USA)) **Mr D. K. Ivory**
37 Br f 10/5 Silver Wizard (USA)—I Have A Dream (SWE) (Mango Express) **J. A. & D. S. Dewhurst**
38 **LADY AMBITIOUS,** ch f 31/3 Pivotal—Ambitious (Ardkinglass) (22000) **Mr D. K. Ivory**
39 **MUJELLE,** b c 23/3 Mujahid (USA)—Jennelle (Nomination) (13000) **Mrs J. A. Cornwell**
40 Ch f 8/5 Silver Wizard (USA)—Myhat (Factual (USA)) **Mr D. K. Ivory**

MR D. K. IVORY—continued

  41 **PRIDE OF JOY**, ch f 10/3 Pursuit of Love—Ivory's Joy (Tina's Pet) (18000) **K. T. Ivory**
  42 Ch c 8/2 Efisio—Thatcher's Era (IRE) (Never So Bold) (5000) **P. M. Mooney**

Other Owners: Mr C. H. Bell, Mr M. S. Crilley, Dean Ivory Racing Ltd, Mr A. G. L. Evans, Ms B. A. Goodwin, Miss L. Grover, Mrs L. A. Ivory, Miss Helen Mary Ann Omersa, Mr R. E. Webb.

Assistant Trainer: Chris Scally

Apprentice: Mark Howard. **Amateur:** Mr David Collier.

---

307 **MR L. R. JAMES, Malton**
Postal: **The Seven, Norton Grange Stables, Park Road, Norton, Malton, N. Yorks, YO17 9EA.**
Contacts: **PHONE (01653) 691455 MOBILE (07732) 556322**

  1 **ATTACK MINDED**, 4, ch g Timeless Times (USA)—French Ginger **Mrs Carol Lloyd James**
  2 **KERRY MAGIC**, 5, b g Vettori (IRE)—Cailin Ciarrai (IRE) **Mrs Carol Lloyd James**
  3 **MARAUD**, 11, ch g Midyan (USA)—Peak Squaw (USA) **D. H. Dyer**
  4 **MISS TIDDLYPUSH**, 4, gr f Defacto (USA)—Misty Rocket **Mrs L. M. Lingwood**
  5 **MODULOR (FR)**, 13, gr g Less Ice—Chaumontaise (FR) **L. R. James Limited**
  6 **SECRET OF SECRETS**, 4, b g Timeless Times (USA)—Sophisticated Baby **C. E. Raine**
  7 **SHE WHO DARES WINS**, 5, b m Atraf—Mirani (IRE) **Nelson Unit Ltd**
  8 **TIOGA GOLD (IRE)**, 6, b g Goldmark (USA)—Coffee Bean **Nelson Unit Ltd**

Other Owners: Mrs C. L. Owen, MR L. R. James.

Assistant Trainer: Carol James

---

308 **MR A. P. JARVIS, Twyford**
Postal: **Twyford Mill, Mill Lane, Twyford, Buckinghamshire, MK18 4HA.**
Contacts: **PHONE (01296) 730707 FAX (01296) 733572 MOBILE (07770) 785551**
E-MAIL alan@alanjarvis.co.uk

  1 **DESERT REIGN**, 4, ch g Desert King (IRE)—Moondance **A. B. Pope**
  2 **EFFECTIVE**, 5, ch g Bahamian Bounty—Efficacy **Eurostrait Ltd**
  3 **JARDINES LOOKOUT (IRE)**, 8, b g Fourstars Allstar (USA)—
  Foolish Flight (IRE) **Morton, Bamford, Caird & Jarvis Partners**
  4 **LATIN REVIEW (IRE)**, 4, ch f Titus Livius (USA)—Law Review (IRE) **Mrs Ann Jarvis**
  5 **ON THE WING**, 4, b f Pivotal—Come Fly With Me **Grant & Bowman Limited**
  6 **SPRING GODDESS (IRE)**, 4, b f Daggers Drawn (USA)—Easter Girl **Grant & Bowman Limited**
  7 **SWEEP THE BOARD (IRE)**, 4, b g Fasliyev (USA)—Fun Board (FR) **Eurostrait Ltd**
  8 **WINNERS DELIGHT**, 4, ch g First Trump—Real Popcorn (IRE) **Breckland Cinema Company**

THREE-YEAR-OLDS

  9 B f Fumo di Londra (IRE)—Acebo Lyons (IRE) **Terence P. Lyons**
 10 B f Danzero (AUS)—Audition **Mrs Ann Jarvis**
 11 **BELLE ENCORE**, b f Prince Sabo—Frisson
 12 **CROSS THE LINE (IRE)**, b c Cape Cross (IRE)—Baalbek **Eurostrait Ltd**
 13 **DANEHILL DAZZLER (IRE)**, b f Danehill Dancer (IRE)—Finnegans Dilemma (IRE) **Wellmet Partners**
 14 **EDWARD (IRE)**, b g Namid—Daltak **A. L. R. Morton**
 15 **FOR LIFE (IRE)**, b c Bachir (IRE)—Zest (USA) **B. C. Oakley**
 16 B c Barathea (IRE)—Handora (IRE) **Morton, Bamford, Caird & Jarvis Partners**
 17 **LADY DIKTAT**, b f Diktat—Scared **Richard Aston Associates**
 18 **LADY LAKOTA (IRE)**, b f Indian Lodge—Milady Lillie (IRE) **The Aston Partnership**
 19 **LUNAR PROMISE (IRE)**, b g Mujadil (USA)—Lunadine (FR) **Mrs Ann Jarvis**
 20 **NEW PROPOSAL (IRE)**, b c Orpen (USA)—Woodenitbenice (USA) **Steam On Partnership**
 21 **OAKBRIDGE (IRE)**, b c Indian Ridge—Chauncy Lane (IRE)
 22 **OPEN VERDICT (IRE)**, b g Mujadil (USA)—Law Review (IRE) **Mrs Ann Jarvis**
 23 **OPERA BELLE**, b f Dr Fong (USA)—Opera Lover (IRE)
 24 B c Barathea (IRE)—Starlight Smile (USA) **Richard Aston Associates**
 25 **STORM CHASE (USA)**, b br g Awad (USA)—Night Duja (USA) **Quadrillian Partnership**
 26 **TAMORA**, ch f Dr Fong (USA)—Tahara (IRE) **Eurostrait Ltd**

MR A. P. JARVIS—continued

27 TRIPLE ZERO (IRE), b f Raise A Grand (IRE)—Locorotondo (IRE) **Quadrillian Partnership**
28 TURTLE BAY, ch f Dr Fong (USA)—My Valentina **Quadrillian Partnership**
29 WISE DENNIS, b g Polar Falcon (USA)—Bowden Rose **Quadrillian Partnership**

TWO-YEAR-OLDS

30 Ch f 22/2 Bertolini (USA)—Antonia's Choice (Music Boy) (36000)
31 B f 22/2 Lujain (USA)—Berliese (IRE) (High Estate) (14000)
32 Ch f 8/2 Observatory (USA)—Defined Feature (IRE) (Nabeel Dancer (USA)) (22000)
33 B f 15/4 Fumo di Londra (IRE)—Dulzie (Safawan)
34 B c 18/2 Distant Music (USA)—Itkan (IRE) (Marju (IRE)) (125000) **Mrs Ann Jarvis**
35 Ch f 2/5 Barathea (IRE)—Lioness (Lion Cavern (USA)) (22000)
36 Ch c 22/5 Dr Fong (USA)—Mad Annie (Anabaa (USA))
37 B br f 1/3 Lujain (USA)—Marjorie's Memory (IRE) (Fairy King (USA)) (17000)
38 NAMID REPROBATE (IRE), br c 18/4 Namid—Morning Surprise (Tragic Role (USA)) **Richard Aston Associates**
39 B c 14/3 Daggers Drawn (USA)—Oumaladia (IRE) (Waajib) (16000) **Mrs Ann Jarvis**
40 B br c 9/5 Spinning World (USA)—Pretty Procida (IRE) (Procida (USA)) (20000)
41 B f 9/3 Diktat—Real Popcorn (IRE) (Jareer (USA)) (9000)
42 RIGHT AGAIN, b c 7/4 Lujain (USA)—Doliouchka (Saumarez) (18000) **C. H. Shankland**
43 Ch c 23/2 Trans Island—Sankaty Light (USA) (Summer Squall (USA)) (28000) **Mrs Ann Jarvis**
44 SALSPERELLA, ch f 11/2 Observatory (USA)—Eau Rouge (Grand Lodge (USA)) (14000)
45 B f 22/4 Woodborough (USA)—Speed Queen (Goldmark (USA))
46 B c 25/1 Foxhound (USA)—Surrealist (ITY) (Night Shift (USA)) (25000)
47 B c 21/2 Tagula (IRE)—Taoveret (IRE) (Flash of Steel) (30000)
48 Ch c 14/1 Beckett (IRE)—Villa Nova (IRE) (Petardia) (44000)
49 WOODLANDS FLOWER, b f 5/4 Mujahid (USA)—Glascoed (Adbass (USA)) (6000) **C. H. Shankland**

Other Owners: R. A. Aston, Mrs P. E. Aston, T. H. Bambridge, N. A. Grover, MR A. P. Jarvis, A. J. King, M. L. Pepper.

Assistant Trainer: T O Jarvis, M A Jarvis, S E Simmons

Jockey (flat): N. Callan, K. Fallon, J. Quinn. **Apprentice:** Leon Harman, Ben Nishart.

---

309 MR M. A. JARVIS, Newmarket
Postal: **Kremlin House Stables, Fordham Road, Newmarket, Suffolk, CB8 7AQ.**
Contacts: **HOME** (01638) 662519 **OFFICE** (01638) 661702
FAX (01638) 667018 **MOBILE** (07836) 649280
E-MAIL majarvis@hotmail.com

1 DIVINE GIFT, 4, b c Groom Dancer (USA)—Child's Play (USA) **B. E. Nielsen**
2 IFFRAAJ, 4, b c Zafonic (USA)—Pastorale **Sheikh Ahmed Al Maktoum**
3 NEW MORNING (IRE), 4, b f Sadler's Wells (USA)—Hellenic **Mr N. R. A. Springer**
4 PEAK OF PERFECTION (IRE), 4, b g Deploy—Nsx **H.R.H. Sultan Ahmad Shah**
5 PUTRA KUANTAN, 5, b h Grand Lodge (USA)—Fade **H.R.H. Sultan Ahmad Shah**
6 PUTRA PEKAN, 7, b h Grand Lodge (USA)—Mazarine Blue **H.R.H. Sultan Ahmad Shah**
7 RAKTI, 6, b h Polish Precedent (USA)—Ragera (IRE) **G. A. Tanaka**
8 RUFFED, 4, br g First Trump—Maristax **T. G. Warner**
9 SHAHZAN HOUSE (IRE), 6, b h Sri Pekan (USA)—Nsx **H.R.H. Sultan Ahmad Shah**
10 ST ANDREWS (IRE), 5, b h Celtic Swing—Viola Royale (IRE) **Team Havana**
11 TOPWELL, 4, b g Most Welcome—Miss Top Ville (FR) **T. G. Warner**

THREE-YEAR-OLDS

12 A THOUSAND SMILES (IRE), b f Sadler's Wells (USA)—Bluffing (IRE) **Mr N. R. A. Springer**
13 ALBAHJA, b f Sinndar (IRE)—Eshq Albahr (USA) **Sheikh Ahmed Al Maktoum**
14 ALFAASIL, b c Darshaan—Bright Halo (IRE) **Hamdan Al Maktoum**
15 ANAAMIL (IRE), b f Darshaan—Noushkey **Sheikh Ahmed Al Maktoum**
16 AYAM ZAMAN (IRE), b f Montjeu (IRE)—Kardashina (FR) **S. Ali**
17 CAMERON ORCHID (IRE), b f Sri Pekan (USA)—London Pride (USA) **H.R.H. Sultan Ahmad Shah**
18 CHARADE (IRE), b f Danehill (USA)—Actoris (USA) **Sheikh Hamdan Al Maktoum**
19 CHEERLEADER, ch f Singspiel (IRE)—India Atlanta **Sheikh Hamdan Al Maktoum**
20 COST ANALYSIS (IRE), ch g Grand Lodge (USA)—Flower Girl **Mr A. D. Bly**
21 DONYANA, b f Mark of Esteem (IRE)—Albarsha **Sheikh Ahmed Al Maktoum**
22 ESWARAH, b f Unfuwain (USA)—Midway Lady **Hamdan Al Maktoum**
23 GOLD GUN (USA), b c Seeking The Gold (USA)—Possessive Dancer **Sheikh Ahmed Al Maktoum**
24 GOLO GAL, b c Mark of Esteem (IRE)—Western Sal **Sheikh Ahmed Al Maktoum**

MR M. A. JARVIS—continued

25 GONE FISHING (IRE), ch f Cadeaux Genereux—Dabbing (USA) **Mr N. R. A. Springer**
26 HAUNTING MEMORIES (IRE), b c Barathea (IRE)—King of All (IRE) **Mr L. Wosskow**
27 HELEN SHARP, ch f Pivotal—Sunny Davis (USA) **Cheveley Park Stud**
28 HINTERLAND (IRE), b br c Danzig (USA)—Electric Society (IRE) **Sheikh Hamdan Al Maktoum**
29 JOSH, b c Josr Algarhoud (IRE)—Charlie Girl **Mr T. G. & Mrs M. E. Holdcroft**
30 KARRNAK, b c Hernando (FR)—Maiden Aunt (IRE) **Sheikh Ahmed Al Maktoum**
31 KHE SANH, b f Mtoto—Hoh Chi Min **Mr N. R. A. Springer**
32 LAKE CHINI (IRE), b c Raise A Grand (IRE)—Where's The Money **H.R.H. Sultan Ahmad Shah**
33 MURHEF, b c Royal Applause—Petit Point (USA) **Hamdan Al Maktoum**
34 NATIVE AMERICAN, b g Indian Lodge (IRE)—Summer Siren (USA) **A. D. Spence**
35 NEWSROUND, ch c Cadeaux Genereux—Ring The Relatives **Sheikh Hamdan Al Maktoum**
36 NIGHT OF JOY (IRE), b f King's Best (USA)—Gilah (IRE) **S. Ali**
37 NOTABILITY, b c King's Best (USA)—Noble Rose (IRE) **Sheikh Hamdan Al Maktoum**
38 ONE PUTRA (IRE), b c Indian Ridge—Triomphale (USA) **H.R.H. Sultan Ahmad Shah**
39 PACE SHOT (IRE), b g Montjeu (IRE)—Pacific Grove **M. Tabor**
40 PEARL KING (IRE), gr c Daylami (IRE)—Regal Opinion (USA) **Sheikh Hamdan Al Maktoum**
41 PEKAN ONE, ch c Grand Lodge (USA)—Ballet **H.R.H. Sultan Ahmad Shah**
42 PRINCELET (IRE), b c Desert Prince (IRE)—Soeur Ti (FR) **B. E. Nielsen**
43 QAADMAH (IRE), b f Dubai Millennium—Zahrat Dubai **Sheikh Ahmed Al Maktoum**
44 SAADIGG (IRE), b g Indian Danehill (USA)—White Caps **Sheikh Ahmed Al Maktoum**
45 TAAKEED, b c Mark of Esteem (IRE)—Walimu (IRE) **Sheikh Hamdan Al Maktoum**
46 TARGGIS, b f Mtoto—Fair Shirley (IRE) **Sheikh Ahmed Al Maktoum**
47 VISTA BELLA, b f Diktat—Cox Orange (USA) **Sheikh Hamdan Al Maktoum**
48 WELL ESTABLISHED (IRE), b c Sadler's Wells (USA)—Riveryev (USA) **A. D. Spence**
49 YAMEELL, b g King's Best (USA)—Maid of Kashmir (IRE) **Sheikh Ahmed Al Maktoum**
50 ZAYN ZEN, ch f Singspiel (IRE)—Roshani (IRE) **Sheikh Ahmed Al Maktoum**

TWO-YEAR-OLDS

51 B f 2/3 Sadler's Wells (USA)—Aim For The Top (USA) (Irish River (FR)) (280000) **B. E. Nielsen**
52 Br f 12/2 Lujain (USA)—Akhira (Emperor Jones (USA)) **Mr D. A. Yardy**
53 B f 19/2 Intikhab (USA)—Ameerat Jumaira (USA) (Alydar (USA)) **Sheikh Ahmed Al Maktoum**
54 B f 3/4 Sadler's Wells (USA)—Antiguan Jane (Shirley Heights) (110000) **S. H. Altayer**
55 Ch c 22/3 Galileo (IRE)—Arctic Hunt (IRE) (Bering) (230000) **Sheikh Hamdan Al Maktoum**
56 BALTIC RHAPSODY, b f 8/3 Polish Precedent (USA)—
Rensaler (Stop The Music (USA)) (60000) **Mr W. J. P. Jackson**
57 BELLA BERTOLINI, b f 14/2 Bertolini (USA)—Fly Like The Wind (Cyrano de Bergerac) (14000) **R. V. Young**
58 B c 24/3 Giant's Causeway (USA)—Brightest Star (Unfuwain (USA)) (250000) **M. Tabor**
59 B c 23/2 Daylami (IRE)—Brogan's Well (IRE) (Caerleon (USA)) **Sheikh Hamdan Al Maktoum**
60 CELTIC SUNSET (IRE), b f 2/4 Celtic Swing—Hishmah (Nashwan (USA)) (37558) **Mr P. D. Savill**
61 B c 23/2 Grand Lodge (USA)—Champaka (IRE) (Caerleon (USA)) **Sheikh Hamdan Al Maktoum**
62 B c 7/2 Xaar—Common Rumpus (IRE) (Common Grounds) (134138) **Sheikh Hamdan Al Maktoum**
63 B c 2/3 Agnes World (USA)—Crime Ofthecentury (Pharly (FR)) (130000) **Sheikh Ahmed Al Maktoum**
64 DHEKRAA (IRE), b f 26/4 Fasliyev (USA)—White Heat (Last Tycoon) (90000) **Hamdan Al Maktoum**
65 B c 13/3 Green Desert (USA)—Felawnah (USA) (Mr Prospector (USA)) **Sheikh Hamdan Al Maktoum**
66 B f 12/3 Indian Ridge—Felona (Caerleon (USA)) **Sheikh Ahmed Al Maktoum**
67 GALIENT (IRE), b c 26/2 Galileo (IRE)—Endorsement (Warning) (75000) **Mr & Mrs Kevan Watts**
68 B f 1/4 Grand Lodge (USA)—Gilah (IRE) (Saddlers' Hall (IRE)) (80000) **Sheikh Hamdan Al Maktoum**
69 Gr f 10/3 Daylami (IRE)—Hawayih (IRE) (Shareef Dancer (USA)) (30000) **Jumeirah Racing**
70 HOUNDED, b c 1/4 Foxhound (USA)—Cyclone Flyer (College Chapel) (28000) **Mr T. G. & Mrs M. E. Holdcroft**
71 KING'S HEAD (IRE), b c 1/3 King's Best (USA)—Ustka (Lomond (USA)) (65000) **A. D. Spence**
72 Ch c 26/2 Indian Rocket—La Fille de Cirque (Cadeaux Genereux) (40000)
73 Br f 16/4 Diktat—Maid of Kashmir (IRE) (Dancing Brave (USA)) **Sheikh Ahmed Al Maktoum**
74 B f 20/4 Halling (USA)—Marienbad (FR) (Darshaan) (170000) **S. Ali**
75 B f 2/2 Sadler's Wells (USA)—Masskana (Darshaan) (240000) **S. Ali**
76 MEKYAAS, ch f 4/4 Pivotal—Land Ahead (USA) (Distant View (USA)) (260000) **Hamdan Al Maktoum**
77 MINISTER OF STATE, ch c 23/4 Machiavellian (USA)—
Mystic Goddess (USA) (Storm Bird (CAN)) **Cheveley Park Stud**
78 Br c 20/2 Key of Luck (USA)—Music Khan (Music Boy) (50300)
79 B c 19/3 Pivotal—My-Lorraine (IRE) (Mac's Imp (USA)) **Sheikh Hamdan Al Maktoum**
80 B c 28/4 Halling (USA)—Place de L'opera (Sadler's Wells (USA)) (300000) **Sheikh Ahmed Al Maktoum**
81 POSSESSED, b f 20/2 Desert Prince (IRE)—Obsessive (USA) (Seeking The Gold (USA)) **Cheveley Park Stud**
82 B c 18/2 King's Best (USA)—Prima Volta (Primo Dominie) (52000) **H.R.H. Sultan Ahmad Shah**
83 Ch c 10/4 Selkirk (USA)—Pump (USA) (Forli (ARG)) (120723) **Sheikh Hamdan Al Maktoum**
84 B c 14/4 Fantastic Light (USA)—Push A Button (Bold Lad (IRE)) **Sheikh Hamdan Al Maktoum**
85 B c 22/3 Averti (IRE)—Rivermead (USA) (Irish River (FR)) (23000) **R. P. Marchant**

MR M. A. JARVIS—continued

86 B f 6/2 Singspiel (IRE)—Roshani (IRE) (Kris) **Sheikh Ahmed Al Maktoum**
87 B f 4/3 Green Desert (USA)—Saeedah (Bustino) **Sheikh Ahmed Al Maktoum**
88 B c 5/3 Danehill Dancer (IRE)—Salul (Soviet Star (USA)) **Sheikh Hamdan Al Maktoum**
89 B f 25/3 Celtic Swing—Shabby Chic (USA) (Red Ransom (USA)) (58000) **Thurloe Thoroughbreds XV**
90 B br c 8/3 Seeking The Gold (USA)—Sheroog (USA) (Shareef Dancer (USA)) **Sheikh Ahmed Al Maktoum**
91 B c 10/3 Kalanisi (IRE)—Shesasmartlady (IRE) (Dolphin Street (FR)) **Sheikh Hamdan Al Maktoum**
92 **SOUL SOCIETY (IRE)**, ch f 30/4 Inchinor—Marika (Marju (IRE)) (30000) **Mr N. R. A. Springer**
93 B c 7/4 Marju (IRE)—Sweetest Thing (IRE) (Prince Rupert (FR)) (100000) **Sheikh Ahmed Al Maktoum**
94 **TEATRO (IRE)**, gr c 22/4 Daylami (IRE)—Star of The Course (USA) (Theatrical) (80000) **S. Dartnell**
95 B c 2/3 Mull of Kintyre (USA)—Tropicana (IRE) (Imperial Frontier (USA)) (115000) **H.R.H. Sultan Ahmad Shah**
96 B f 10/2 Fasliyev (USA)—Wild Missy (USA) (Wild Again (USA)) **Mr N. R. A. Springer**
97 B c 20/1 Mark of Esteem (IRE)—Winning Girl (Green Desert (USA)) (65000) **Sheikh Hamdan Al Maktoum**
98 Ch c 8/2 King's Best (USA)—Yorba Linda (IRE) (Night Shift (USA)) **Sheikh Hamdan Al Maktoum**
99 **ZAMALIK (USA)**, b br c 26/2 Machiavellian (USA)—Ashbilya (USA) (Nureyev (USA)) **Sheikh Ahmed Al Maktoum**
100 B f 29/3 Galileo (IRE)—Zibilene (Rainbow Quest (USA)) (360000) **Sheikh Ahmed Al Maktoum**

Other Owners: Mrs H. Holmes, M. C. Moutray-Read, O. J. W. Pawle, A. J. Smith, Mr K. Watts, Mrs P. M. L. Watts, D. G. A. E. Woods.

Assistant Trainer: Roger Varian

---

310   MR W. JARVIS, Newmarket
Postal: **Phantom House, Fordham Road, Newmarket, Suffolk, CB8 7AA.**
Contacts: **HOME (01638) 662677 OFFICE (01638) 669873 FAX (01638) 667328**
E-MAIL william.jarvis@virgin.net WEBSITE www.williamjarvis.com

1 COQUIN D'ALEZAN (IRE), 4, ch g Cadeaux Genereux—Nwaahil (IRE) **Mr Richard McDonnell**
2 FUSS, 4, b f Unfuwain (USA)—First Sapphire **Mr Brian Cooper & Elaine Reffo**
3 LA PERSIANA, 4, gr f Daylami (IRE)—La Papagena **Plantation Stud Limited**
4 MACARONI GOLD (IRE), 5, b g Rock Hopper—Strike It Rich (FR) **Dr J. Walker**
5 MOMTIC (IRE), 4, ch c Shinko Forest (IRE)—Uffizi (IRE) **Heath, Keenan & Verrier**
6 NAMAT (IRE), 4, b f Daylami (IRE)—Masharik (IRE) **G. B. Turnbull Ltd**
7 NOORA (IRE), 4, ch f Bahhare (USA)—Esteraad (IRE) **P. G. Jacobs & Partners**
8 RESHUFFLE, 4, ch f Compton Place—Prince's Feather (IRE) **Mr W. Jarvis**
9 TASS HEEL (IRE), 6, b g Danehill (USA)—Mamouna (IRE) **Tattersalls Ltd**
10 TAWNY WAY, 5, b m Polar Falcon (USA)—Ma Petite Anglaise **Rams Racing Club**
11 TORQUEMADA (IRE), 4, ch c Desert Sun—Gaelic's Fantasy (IRE) **Canisbay Bloodstock**

THREE-YEAR-OLDS

12 BABA GHANOUSH, ch f Zaha (CAN)—Vrennan **Canisbay Bloodstock**
13 BACHELOR AFFAIR, b c Bachir (IRE)—Profit Alert (IRE) **The Bachelor Affair Partnership**
14 BEDLAM, b f Dracula (AUS)—La Tiziana **The Bedlam Partnership**
15 CHILLIN OUT, ch c Bahamian Bounty—Steppin Out **Canisbay Bloodstock**
16 DINNER DATE, ch c Groom Dancer (USA)—Misleading Lady **J. M. Greetham**
17 DIZZY FUTURE, b g Fraam—Kara Sea (USA) **Mr W. Jarvis & Partners**
18 FIRST ACE, b f First Trump—Zinzi **Mr Raymond Tooth**
19 FOLLOWING FLOW (USA), b br g King of Kings (IRE)—Sign Here (USA) **Sales Race 2001 Syndicate**
20 FORT ASSOS, b c Grand Lodge (USA)—Cephalonia **Plantation Stud Limited**
21 GIMASHA, b f Cadeaux Genereux—First Waltz (FR) **Z. A. Galadari**
22 KILLENA BOY (IRE), b g Imperial Ballet (IRE)—Habaza (IRE) **Capel (CS) Ltd**
23 LET SLIP, b f Second Empire (IRE)—Loose Talk **Mrs S. J. Davis**
24 MISSTURNER (IRE), b f Danehill Dancer (IRE)—It's Academic **Mr Richard McDonnell**
25 MIXING, gr c Linamix (FR)—Tuning **Canisbay Bloodstock**
26 Ch c Zaha (CAN)—Mo Stopher **Canisbay Bloodstock**
27 PAPALITY, b f Giant's Causeway (USA)—Papabile (USA) **Plantation Stud Limited**
28 PATTERNMAKER (USA), b br g Elnadim (USA)—Attasliyah (IRE) **Dr J. Walker**
29 RESISTANCE HEROINE, b f Dr Fong (USA)—Odette **Mr M. C. Banks**
30 SLIP CATCH (IRE), b f Intikhab (USA)—Buckle (IRE) **Noodles Racing**
31 SUMMER CHARM, b f Dansili—Regent's Folly (IRE) **Mr W. Jarvis**
32 THREE BOARS, ch g Most Welcome—Precious Poppy **J. M. Greetham**
33 VALIANT SHADOW (GER), b g Winged Love (IRE)—Vangelis **Ian David Ltd & Mr P. Byrne**

MR W. JARVIS—continued

TWO-YEAR-OLDS

34 B c 17/4 College Chapel—Among Women (Common Grounds) (10000) **Mr Robert Percival**
35 **BLING,** ch c 12/3 Mark of Esteem (IRE)—Show Off (Efisio) (20000) **Mr & Mrs John Davis**
36 B c 5/4 Dansili—Break Point (Reference Point) **Mr Brian Cooper & Elaine Reffo**
37 **CICCONE,** ch c 21/4 Singspiel (IRE)—Untold Riches (USA) (Red Ransom (USA)) (27000) **A. Foster**
38 **DISEUSE,** b f 9/2 Diktat—
　　　　　Arletty (Rainbow Quest (USA)) (1500) **Miss H C Scrope, Julie Cecil & The Hon Benjamin Leigh**
39 **GAZE,** b f 19/2 Galileo (IRE)—Gryada (Shirley Heights) (50000) **E. A. J. Lismonde**
40 **GOLD DRAGON,** ch c 28/1 Piccolo—Fredora (Inchinor) (30000) **N. S. Young, N. Collins, E. Randall & G Whyatt**
41 B c 21/3 Matty G (USA)—Kalinka (USA) (Mr Prospector (USA)) (8000) **Sales Race 2001 Syndicate**
42 B c 14/4 Mull of Kintyre (USA)—Miss Willow Bend (USA) (Willow Hour (USA)) (20000) **Boysdayout Partnership**
43 **PEEL HOUSE,** ch c 22/4 Grand Lodge (USA)—Ice House (Northfields (USA)) (40000) **N. S. Yong**
44 **RIFF RAFF,** b f 7/3 Daylami (IRE)—Rafiya (Halling (USA)) (37000) **A. Foster**
45 B f 10/3 Komaite (USA)—Royal Girl (Kafu) (8000) **Mr Paul Malone**
46 **SAN GIMIGNANO (IRE),** ch f 14/4 City On A Hill (USA)—
　　　　　A La Longue (GER) (Mtoto) (22132) **Byculla Thoroughbreds**
47 Ch f 14/2 Lake Coniston (IRE)—Steppin Out (First Trump) **Canisbay Bloodstock**
48 B c 18/1 Mull of Kintyre (USA)—Total Aloof (Groom Dancer (USA)) (60000) **A Partnership**

Other Owners: Mr John Davis, R. C. C. Villiers, Una O'Brian Thring, C. G. Thring, Philip Hawkins, N. J. Donald, A. Donald, Christopher Miller, John Rowe, A. M. Briam, G. B. Turnbull Ltd, A. C. Grundy, Mrs F. M. Hallett, D. P. Heath, P.G. Jacobs, P. M. Keenan, R. F. Kilby, P. H. Marsh, W. R. Milner, D. J. G. Murray Smith, D. B. Murrell, J. W. Osborne, Mrs V. H. Pakenham, N. M. S. Rich, P. E. Selway-Swift, Miss M. E. Stopher, A. N. Verrier.

Assistant Trainer: Mrs J Cecil

311　MR J. JAY, Newmarket
Postal: **Exeter House Stables, 33 Exeter Road, Newmarket, Suffolk, CB8 8LP.**
Contacts: PHONE **(01638) 666928** MOBILE **(07711) 147071**
E-MAIL jjay@jce.co.uk WEBSITE www.exeterhousestables.co.uk

1 **ADORATA (GER),** 4, b f Tannenkonig (IRE)—Adora (GER) **Fremel and Friends**
2 **BILL BENNETT (FR),** 4, b g Bishop of Cashel—Concert **Mr & Mrs Jonathan Jay**
3 **BLUE MARINER,** 5, b g Marju (IRE)—Mazarine Blue **Graham & Lynn Knight**
4 **GAELIC ROULETTE (IRE),** 5, b m Turtle Island (IRE)—Money Spinner (USA) **Graham & Lynn Knight**
5 **INDIAN WARRIOR,** 9, b g Be My Chief (USA)—Wanton **Ali, Andrew and Johnston**
6 **RING OF DESTINY,** 6, b g Magic Ring (IRE)—Canna **The Ringleaders**
7 **SCOTT,** 4, gr g Polar Falcon (USA)—Circled (USA) **K. R. Wills**
8 **THE BONUS KING,** 5, b g Royal Applause—Selvi **Mrs Mo Done & Mrs Janet Martin**
9 **TREASURE HOUSE (IRE),** 4, b g Grand Lodge (USA)—Royal Wolff **J. M. Beever**
10 **WOOLSTONE BOY (USA),** 4, ch g Will's Way (USA)—My Pleasure **Neil Rodway & Carol Cope**
11 **ZAK ATTACK,** 4, ch g Young Ern—Premiere Moon **Mr D. Casserly**

THREE-YEAR-OLDS

12 **ALCOTT (FR),** ch g Medaaly—Louisa May (IRE) **Mrs S. J. Jay**
13 **BAILANDA (GER),** b f Mondrian (GER)—Brasilia (GER) **Miss Kim Bartlett**
14 **BEE SHARP,** ch f Twice As Sharp—Bee Gee **J. M. Beever**
15 **JERRY JOSLYN (IRE),** b f General Monash (USA)—Princess of Dance (IRE) **Mr K. G. Gooch**
16 **LYRIC DANCES (FR),** ch f Sendawar (IRE)—Romanche (FR) **A. D. Jones**
17 **PACIFIC BREEZE (IRE),** b f Turtle Island (IRE)—C'est Grand (IRE) **Exeter House Party**
18 **RHAPSODY IN SILVER (FR),** gr c Medaaly—Concert **Silver Quartet**
19 **SO ELEGANT (IRE),** b f Bahhare (USA)—Soignee **The Prospectors**
20 **TIDAL FURY (IRE),** b c Night Shift (USA)—Tidal Reach (USA) **Twelfth Night**

TWO-YEAR-OLDS

21 **ELLI LEWTIA,** ch f 21/3 Tomba—Troia (IRE) (Last Tycoon)

Other Owners: A. Ali, R. J. Andrew, Miss M. A. Carnell, J. Dixon, D. P. Fremel, Mrs M. L. Garrett, Mr D. Goult, D. J. Gregory, C. J. King, C. Phillips, Mr B. M. V. Williams.

Apprentice: Liam Jones. **Amateur:** Mr Troy Thomas.

312 MR J. M. JEFFERSON, Malton
Postal: **Newstead Cottage Stables, Norton, Malton, North Yorkshire, YO17 9PJ.**
Contacts: **PHONE (01653) 697225 MOBILE (07710) 502044**

1 **ANOTHER CHANCE**, 10, b g Golden Heights—Lapopie **North South Partnership**
2 5, B m Good Thyne (USA)—Another Grouse **Mrs K. S. Gaffney**
3 **BERTIE ARMS**, 5, b m Cloudings (IRE)—Pugilistic **P. F. Birch**
4 **BOXCLEVER**, 4, b g Accordion—Pugilistic **R. G. Marshall & Partners**
5 **BROOKLYN BROWNIE (IRE)**, 6, b g Presenting—In The Brownies (IRE) **P. Gaffney & J. N. Stevenson**
6 **CALATAGAN (IRE)**, 6, ch g Danzig Connection (USA)—Calachuchi **Mr & Mrs J. M. Davenport**
7 **CAYMAN CALYPSO (IRE)**, 4, ro g Danehill Dancer (IRE)—Warthill Whispers **T. R. Pryke**
8 **CLARINCH CLAYMORE**, 9, b g Sabrehill (USA)—Salu **J. Donald**
9 **CLASSIC CAPERS**, 6, ch g Classic Cliche (IRE)—Jobiska **R. Collins**
10 **CLEAR DAWN (IRE)**, 10, b g Clearly Bust—Cobra Queen **Mr & Mrs J. M. Davenport**
11 **CUMBRIAN KNIGHT (IRE)**, 7, b g Presenting—Crashrun **Mrs J. E. Pallister**
12 **DEWASENTAH (IRE)**, 6, b m Supreme Leader—Our Sioux (IRE) **Mrs J. U. Hales & Mrs L. M. Joicey**
13 **DUSKY DAWN (IRE)**, 4, b g Desert Style (USA)—Kaaba **Mrs J. E. Pallister**
14 **ELVIS RETURNS**, 7, b g Alhaatmi—Buckmist Blue (IRE) **J. M. Cleeve**
15 **HILLS OF VIEW**, 7, b g Sea Raven (IRE)—Hardwick Sun **R. G. Marshall**
16 **HONEST ENDEAVOUR**, 6, b g Alflora (IRE)—Isabeau **Warren Butterworth & Terry Pryke**
17 **I'LL DO IT TODAY**, 4, b g Mtoto—Knayton Lass **Mr & Mrs J. M. Davenport**
18 **JACK WEIGHELL**, 6, b g Accordion—Magic Bloom **P. Nelson**
19 **KIDS INHERITANCE (IRE)**, 7, b g Presenting—Princess Tino (IRE) **Mr & Mrs J. M. Davenport**
20 **KOKOPELLI MANA (IRE)**, 5, b m Saddlers' Hall (IRE)—Kachina (IRE) **Capt M. S. Bagley**
21 **LOI DE MARTIALE (IRE)**, 7, br g Presenting—Thresa-Anita (IRE) **R. G. Marshall**
22 **MOSS HARVEY**, 10, ch g Le Moss—Wings Ground **J. R. Salter**
23 **OSCAR THE BOXER (IRE)**, 6, b g Oscar (IRE)—Here She Comes **The New Phoenix Racing Club**
24 **PERTINO**, 9, b g Terimon—Persian Fountain (IRE) **W. Fouracres, T. Pryke & D. Willis**
25 **POLAR GUNNER**, 8, b g Gunner B—Polar Belle **Mrs M. E. Dixon**
26 **PORTAVADIE**, 6, b g Rakaposhi King—Woodland Flower **Ashleybank Investments Limited**
27 **ROMAN ARK**, 7, gr g Terimon—Larksmore **R. Collins**
28 **RUTLEDGE RED (IRE)**, 9, gr g Roselier (FR)—Katebeaujolais **Ashleybank Investments Limited**
29 **RYMON**, 5, br g Terimon—Rythmic Rymer **Mrs M. Barker**
30 **SCHINKEN OTTO (IRE)**, 4, ch c Shinko Forest (IRE)—Athassel Rose (IRE) **J. Donald**
31 **SHUIL TSARINA (IRE)**, 7, b m King's Ride—Shuil Realt (IRE) **Mrs K. S. Gaffney & Mrs Alix Stevenson**
32 **SILVER BOW**, 4, b f Silver Patriarch (IRE)—Isabeau **T. R. Pryke**
33 **STAMPARLAND HILL**, 10, b g Gildoran—Woodland Flower **J. R. Salter**
34 **SURE RHYTHM**, 4, b f Keen—Rythmic Rymer **Mrs M. Barker**
35 **THE FROSTY FERRET**, 7, b g Zaffaran (USA)—Frostbite **Ashleybank Investments Limited**
36 **THE MANSE BRAE (IRE)**, 9, b g Roselier (FR)—Decent Preacher **Ashleybank Investments Limited**
37 **THE YELLOW EARL (IRE)**, 5, b g Topanoora—Sweet Innocence (IRE) **Boundary Garage (Bury) Limited**
38 **VITAL SPARK**, 6, b g Primitive Rising (USA)—Enkindle **Ashleybank Investments Limited**

THREE-YEAR-OLDS

39 **DOUBLE ELLS**, b f Yaheeb (USA)—Knayton Lass **Mr & Mrs J. M. Davenport**

Other Owners: Mr S. R. Caley, Mrs K. M. Campey, Mrs M. J. Hales, H. E. St Quinton, M. Thompson, R. G. Tilbrook, R. E. Williams.

Jockey (NH): G. Lee. **Conditional:** F. King.

313 MR J. R. W. JENKINS, Royston
Postal: **Kings Ride, Baldock Road, Royston, Hertfordshire, SG8 9NN.**
Contacts: **PHONE (01763) 241141 HOME (01763) 246611 FAX (01763) 248223
MOBILE (07802) 750855**
E-MAIL john@johnjenkinsracing.co.uk WEBSITE www.johnjenkinsracing.co.uk

1 **AMIR ZAMAN**, 7, ch g Salse (USA)—Colorvista **Mrs W. A. Jenkins**
2 **AMWELL BRAVE**, 4, b g Pyramus (USA)—Passage Creeping (IRE) **Amwell Racing**
3 **CHARA**, 4, ch f Deploy—Subtle One (IRE) **Michael Ng**
4 **DAFFODIL TIME (IRE)**, 6, ch m Good Thyne (USA)—Mandys Gale (IRE) **N. Trevithick**
5 **DAVIDS MARK**, 5, b g Polar Prince (IRE)—Star of Flanders **Miss C. Roylance**
6 **DOMENICO (IRE)**, 7, b g Sadler's Wells (USA)—Russian Ballet (USA) **Skullduggery**
7 **EMPRESS JOSEPHINE**, 5, b m Emperor Jones (USA)—Valmaranda (USA) **Mrs O. Meddle**
8 **EZZ ELKHEIL**, 6, b g Bering—Numidie (FR) **K. Hudson**

MR J. R. W. JENKINS—continued

9 **FRUIT OF GLORY**, 6, b m Glory of Dancer—Fresh Fruit Daily **R. B. Hill**
10 **HILLY BE**, 4, b f Silver Patriarch (IRE)—Lolita (FR) **S. C. Finance Limited**
11 **HOLLOW JO**, 5, b g Most Welcome—Sir Hollow (USA) **J. McCarthy**
12 **IMTALKINGGIBBERISH**, 4, b g Pursuit of Love—Royal Orchid (IRE) **The Groovy Gang**
13 **JACK DORAN**, 5, ch g Gildoran—Faustelerie **Nolan's Bar Racing Syndicate**
14 **JAGGED (IRE)**, 5, b g Sesaro (USA)—Latin Mass **The Jagged Partnership**
15 **JAWWALA (USA)**, 6, b m Green Dancer (USA)—Fetch N Carry (USA) **Skullduggery**
16 **JOSHUA'S BAY**, 7, b g Karinga Bay—Bonita Blakeney **Mr & Mrs Leon Shack**
17 **MADDIE'S A JEM**, 5, b m Emperor Jones (USA)—Royal Orchid (IRE) **Mrs W. A. Jenkins**
18 **MAGIC AMIGO**, 4, ch g Zilzal (USA)—Emaline (FR) **N. Trevithick**
19 **MOON EMPEROR**, 8, b g Emperor Jones (USA)—Sir Hollow (USA)
20 **MUY BIEN**, 4, ch c Daggers Drawn (USA)—Primula Bairn **K. J. Reddington**
21 **PICK OF THE CROP**, 4, ch g Fraam—Fresh Fruit Daily **Bookmakers Index Ltd**
22 **PRINCE DU SOLEIL (FR)**, 9, b g Cardoun (FR)—Revelry (FR) **Mrs I. Leitendorfa-Lines**
23 **QUEST ON AIR**, 6, b g Star Quest—Stormy Heights **T. H. Ounsley**
24 **REN'S MAGIC**, 7, gr g Petong—Bath **Mrs T. McCoubrey**
25 **SECOND USER**, 4, b g Zilzal (USA)—Glossary **The Dough Boys**
26 **SIR HAYDN**, 5, ch g Definite Article—Snowscape **Ms Ellen R.M. Sowle & Mr Alan Sowle**
27 **ST GEORGE'S GIRL**, 4, b f Muthahb (IRE)—Nickelodeon **R. Smith**
28 **THUNDERING SURF**, 8, b g Lugana Beach—Thunder Bug (USA) **Mr C. N. & Mrs J. C. Wright**
29 **VANILLA MOON**, 5, b m Emperor Jones (USA)—Daarat Alayaam (IRE) **Mrs I. C. Hampson**
30 **VELVET TOUCH**, 4, b f Danzig Connection (USA)—Soft Touch (GER) **Kingsland Bloodstock**
31 **WESTMEAD ETOILE**, 5, b m Unfuwain (USA)—Glossary **Westmead**
32 **WHO CARES WINS**, 9, ch g Kris—Anne Bonny **Lea Valley Colour Laboratories Ltd**

THREE-YEAR-OLDS

33 **ANFIELD DREAM**, b c Lujain (USA)—Fifth Emerald **The Saints Partnership**
34 **APPLE OF MY EYE**, b f Fraam—Fresh Fruit Daily **R. B. Hill**
35 **BRADDERS**, b g Silver Patriarch (IRE)—Lolita (FR) **S. C. Finance Limited**
36 **FEI MAH**, b f Vettori (IRE)—Bluewain Lady **The Byerley Turk**
37 **LIGHTHORNE LAD**, ch c Hornbeam—Give Me A Day **K. C. Payne**
38 **POLISH INDEX**, b c Polish Precedent (USA)—Glossary **Mrs S. Peirce**
39 **TOUCH OF SPICE**, ch g Lake Coniston (IRE)—Soft Touch (GER) **Kingsland Bloodstock**

TWO-YEAR-OLDS

40 Ch c 25/4 Pursuit of Love—Fresh Fruit Daily (Reprimand)
41 **LATVIAN PRINCESS**, b f 12/3 Silver Patriarch (IRE)—Berzoud (Ezzoud (IRE)) **Mrs I. Leitendorfa-Lines**
42 Ch g 12/3 Zaha (CAN)—Soft Touch (GER) (Horst-Herbert) (2200) **Kingsland Bloodstock**
43 B c 14/4 Killer Instinct—Thewaari (USA) (Eskimo (USA))

Other Owners: Mr P. Austin, S. A. Barningham, J. C. Buchanan, J. Buffenbarger, W. E. Cockman, J. Dunn, Mrs P. Edwards, R. M. Ellis, M. A. Francis, R. V. Hall, Mr J. Hanson, R. M. Inman, Mrs B. J. Inman, P. J. Kirkpatrick, B. Lewis, W. E. D. Morris, T. G. Nolan, B. W. Parren, A. R. M. Peirce, Mr G. Strang, D. J. Tattersall, H. J. P. Thomas, G. P. Townsend.

---

314 MR W. P. JENKS, Bridgnorth
Postal: **Wadeley Farm, Glazeley, Bridgnorth, Shropshire, WV16 6AD.**
Contacts: **OFFICE (01746) 789288 FAX (01746) 789535**

1 **CHAGA**, 4, b f Hector Protector (USA)—Santarem (USA) **Mr W. P. Jenks**
2 **FENNEY SPRING**, 5, b m Polish Precedent (USA)—Sliprail (USA) **M. C. Stoddart**
3 **FULL PITCH**, 9, ch g Cadeaux Genereux—Tricky Note **Mr W. P. Jenks**
4 **GWUNGY**, 5, b g Mind Games—Kinlet Vision (IRE) **Mr W. P. Jenks**
5 **MAGICAL LIAISON (IRE)**, 7, b g Mujtahid (USA)—Instant Affair (USA) **The Glazeley Partnership 2**
6 **MUSALLY**, 8, ch g Muhtarram (USA)—Flourishing (IRE) **The Glazeley Partnership**
7 **PERCY JAY (NZ)**, 6, ch g Rainbow Myth (NZ)—Zillah Grace (NZ) **M. C. Stoddart**
8 **POINT**, 8, b g Polish Precedent (USA)—Sixslip (USA) **Mrs C. A. Jenks**
9 **SLEIGHT**, 6, ch m Bob's Return (IRE)—Jolejester **The Wadeley Partnership**
10 **TOM TUG (NZ)**, 5, b g Flying Pegasus (IRE)—Flight Judge (AUS) **Mr W. P. Jenks**

THREE-YEAR-OLDS

11 **ILLUMINATI**, b g Inchinor—Selection Board **M. J. Ephgrave**

Other Owners: Dr W. B. Alexander, Mrs M. A. Gabb, A. R. Mapp.

Jockey (NH): C. Llewellyn, W. Marston. **Apprentice:** Miss K. Harris. **Amateur:** Mr R. Burton.

315   MR A. E. M. JESSOP, Chelmsford
Postal: Flemings Farm, Warren Road, South Hanningfield, Chelmsford, Essex, CM3 8HU.
Contacts: PHONE (01268) 710210 MOBILE (07718) 736482

1 **BROADWAY LADY**, 5, b m Old Vic—Sailors Joy **Mrs G. Jessop**
2 4, B f Lord Americo—Flemings Delight
3 **LIVRET BLEU (FR)**, 6, b g Panoramic—Azur Bleue (FR) **Mrs G. Jessop**
4 **MISS COLMESNIL (FR)**, 5, b m Dear Doctor (FR)—Princesse Dolly (FR) **Mrs G. Jessop**
5 **MOSS RUN (IRE)**, 11, b g Commanche Run—Glenreigh Moss **Mrs G. Jessop**
6 **THE BOSUN**, 8, b g Charmer—Sailors Joy **A. Jessop**

Assistant Trainer: Alison Jessop

316   MRS L. C. JEWELL, Sutton Valence
Postal: Southfield Stables, South Lane, Sutton Valence, Maidstone, Kent, ME17 3AZ.
Contacts: PHONE (01622) 842788 MOBILE (07714) 239100
E-MAIL lindajewell@hotmail.com

1 **BAHAMA BELLE**, 4, b f Bahamian Bounty—Barque Bleue (USA) **Mrs A. Greengrow**
2 **BEENABOUTABIT**, 7, b m Komaite (USA)—Tassagh Bridge (IRE) **Miss L. S. McIntosh**
3 **CASPIAN LAKE (IRE)**, 4, ch g Lake Coniston (IRE)—Hardtimes (IRE) **K. Johnson, K. Jessup**
4 **COYOTE LAKES**, 6, ch g Be My Chief—Oakbrook Tern (USA) **Gallagher Equine Ltd**
5 **ENHANCER (IRE)**, 7, b g Zafonic (USA)—Ypha (USA) **Gallagher Equine Ltd**
6 **FAIRY QUEST (IRE)**, 6, b m Air Quest—Fairy Glade (IRE) **The Fairy Quest Partnership**
7 **IRON MOUNTAIN (IRE)**, 10, b g Scenic—Merlannah (IRE) **Mrs A. Greengrow**
8 4, B f Keen—Katie Jo **Mr R. B. Morton**
9 **LA CONCHA (IRE)**, 4, b g Kahyasi—Trojan Crown (IRE) **Gallagher Equine Ltd**
10 **MONSAL DALE (IRE)**, 6, ch g Desert King (IRE)—Zanella (IRE) **Mrs A. Greengrow**
11 **MY NATIVE MISS (IRE)**, 7, b m Be My Native (USA)—Explosive Missile (IRE) **The Red White and Blues**
12 **PRESTON HALL**, 4, b g Accordion—Little Preston (IRE) **Gallagher Equine Ltd**
13 **RED ENSIGN**, 8, b g Lancastrian—Medway Queen **Mrs S. M. Stanier, Mrs C. Diplock & Mr R. Young**
14 **ROCKLEY BAY (IRE)**, 4, b g Mujadil (USA)—Kilkee Bay (IRE) **Mrs A. Greengrow**
15 **SILISTRA**, 6, gr g Sadler's Wells—Dundel (IRE) **Mrs P. S. Donkin**
16 **SMART GUY**, 13, ch g Gildoran—Talahache Bridge **Mrs P. S. Donkin**
17 **STOPWATCH (IRE)**, 10, b g Lead On Time (USA)—Rose Bonbon (FR) **The Stopwatch Partnership**

THREE-YEAR-OLDS

18 **CONTENTED (IRE)**, b c Orpen (USA)—Joyfullness (USA) **J. Shannon & L. Beasley**

Other Owners: Mr J. Costello, John Dunleavy, P. Jones, P. A. Oppenheimer.

Assistant Trainer: Karen Jewell

Amateur: Mr Craig Messenger.

317   MR B. R. JOHNSON, Epsom
Postal: Little Woodruffe Racing Stables, Headley Road, Epsom, Surrey, KT18 6BH.
Contacts: YARD (01372) 270199 MOBILE (07768) 697141

1 **BEYOND THE POLE (USA)**, 7, b g Ghazi (USA)—North of Sunset (USA) **Tann Racing**
2 **GENTLE RESPONSE**, 5, b m Puissance—Sweet Whisper **Mr B. R. Johnson**
3 **JOHNNY ROOK (IRE)**, 4, ch g Woodman (USA)—Tani (USA) **Tann Racing**
4 **LAWAAHEB (IRE)**, 4, b g Alhaarth (IRE)—Ajayib (USA) **C. Lefevre**
5 **MONASH GIRL (IRE)**, 4, b f General Monash (USA)—Maricica (USA) **Mrs B. R. Williams**
6 **SPRING SURPRISE**, 4, b f Hector Protector (USA)—Tender Moment (IRE) **Tann Racing**
7 **TREETOPS HOTEL (IRE)**, 6, ch g Grand Lodge (USA)—Rousinette **Tann Racing**
8 **WHAT'S THE COUNT**, 9, gr g Theatrical Charmer—Yankee Silver **The Twenty Five Club**
9 **WORCESTER LODGE (IRE)**, 4, ch g Grand Lodge (USA)—Borgia **S. J. Townsend**

Other Owners: Miss N. J. Holmwood, P. Morley, B. A. Rolls, G. Tann, Mrs E. Tann, B. A. Whittaker.

Assistant Trainer: Julie Reeves

318 MR R. F. JOHNSON HOUGHTON, Didcot
Postal: **Woodway, Blewbury, Didcot, Oxfordshire, OX11 9EZ.**
Contacts: PHONE **(01235) 850480** FAX **(01235) 851045** MOBILE **(07836) 599232**
E-MAIL **fulke@johnsonhoughton.com**

1 **PHLUKE**, 4, b g Most Welcome—Phlirty **Mrs R. F. Johnson Houghton**
2 **REMINISCENT (IRE)**, 6, b g Kahyasi—Eliza Orzeszkowa (IRE) **Mr R. F. Johnson Houghton**
3 **VELVET WATERS**, 4, b f Unfuwain (USA)—Gleaming Water **Mr R. E. Crutchley**

THREE-YEAR-OLDS
4 **ASTEEM**, b g Mark of Esteem (IRE)—Amidst **Eden Racing (III)**
5 **BEAVER PATROL (IRE)**, ch c Tagula (IRE)—Erne Project (IRE) **G. C. Stevens**
6 **BRIDGE T'THE STARS**, b f Josr Algarhoud (IRE)—Petra's Star **Mrs Z. C. Campbell-Harris**
7 **DAYBREAKING (IRE)**, br c Daylami (USA)—Mawhiba (USA) **Anthony Pye-Jeary And Mel Smith**
8 **INTOXICATING**, b c Mujahid (USA)—Salalah **Anthony Pye-Jeary And Mel Smith**
9 **JUDD STREET**, b g Compton Place—Pudding Lane (IRE) **Mr R. F. Johnson Houghton**
10 **LOOKING GREAT (USA)**, b g Gulch (USA)—Shoofha (IRE) **S. Posford & R. E. Crutchley**
11 **PEACE LILY**, b f Dansili—Shall We Run **Mrs R. F. Johnson Houghton**
12 **PEEWIT (IRE)**, b f Namid—Petomi **Eden Racing (III)**
13 **PHLAUNT**, b f Faustus—Phlirty **Mrs R. F. Johnson Houghton**
14 **PICKAPEPPA**, ch f Piccolo—Cajole (IRE) **Mrs C. J. Hue Williams**
15 **ROODEYE**, b f Inchinor—Roo **Mrs G. T. Johnson Houghton**
16 **RUBIES**, ch f Inchinor—Fur Will Fly **Mrs G. M. McCalmont**
17 **THORNY MANDATE**, b g Diktat—Rosa Canina **R. C. Naylor**

TWO-YEAR-OLDS
18 **BELLANORA**, b f 25/1 Inchinor—Barberello (IRE) (Bigstone (IRE)) (20120) **G. C. Stevens**
19 **CALYPSO TIME**, b f 10/3 Josr Algarhoud (IRE)—Cajole (IRE) (Barathea (IRE)) **Mrs C. J. Hue Williams**
20 B f 23/2 Tagula (IRE)—Felin Special (Lyphard's Special (USA))
21 B c 14/4 Observatory (USA)—Honeyspike (IRE) (Chief's Crown (USA)) (24000) **C. W. Sumner**
22 B c 20/2 Namid—Madame Claude (IRE) (Paris House) (10730)
23 B c 17/3 Robellino (USA)—Pontressina (USA) (St Jovite (USA)) (10000)
24 **REBELLING (IRE)**, ch c 17/3 Peintre Celebre (USA)—
    El Divino (IRE) (Halling (USA)) (35000) **Anthony Pye-Jeary And Mel Smith**
25 **REVIVING (IRE)**, b c 21/3 Fasliyev (USA)—
    Hartstown House (IRE) (Primo Dominie) (23473) **Anthony Pye-Jeary And Mel Smith**
26 **TOUS LES DEUX**, b c 1/3 Efisio—Caerosa (Caerleon (USA)) (10000) **R. Grenville-Webb**
27 B c 13/5 Mujahid (USA)—Waqood (USA) (Riverman (USA)) (11000) **Mr R. F. Johnson Houghton**

Other Owners: Miss E. Johnson Houghton.

Assistant Trainer: Eve Johnson Houghton

Jockey (flat): S. Carson. **Jockey (NH):** M. Bradburne. **Amateur:** Miss E. Johnson Houghton.

319 MR J. H. JOHNSON, Crook
Postal: **White Lea Farm, Crook, Co. Durham, DL15 9QN.**
Contacts: PHONE **(01388) 762113** CAR **(07914) 691017** FAX **(01388) 768278**
MOBILE **(07714) 691016/691017**
E-MAIL **lucy@directroute1.co.uk**

1 **ABBEY PRINCESS**, 5, b m Prince Daniel (USA)—Riveran **Ken Roper, Elinor M. Roper, Norman Furness**
2 **ABBOTSFORD (IRE)**, 5, gr g Arzanni—Cloughan Girl (IRE) **W. M. G. Black**
3 4, Br g Taipan (IRE)—Abstemious **Andrea & Graham Wylie**
4 **AKILAK (IRE)**, 4, br c Charnwood Forest (IRE)—Akilara (IRE) **ADA Partnership**
5 **ALBANY (IRE)**, 5, ch g Alhaarth (IRE)—Tochar Ban (USA) **Andrea & Graham Wylie**
6 **ALDERCLAD LAD (IRE)**, 5, ch g Anshan—Novelist **Alderclad Roofing Ltd**
7 **ANOTHER DUDE (IRE)**, 8, br g Shardari—Gemma's Fridge **M. Hutchinson**
8 **ARCALIS**, 5, gr g Lear Fan (USA)—Aristocratique **Andrea & Graham Wylie**
9 **ARDYNAGH (IRE)**, 6, b g Aahsaylad—Night Matron (IRE) **Andrea & Graham Wylie**
10 **ASTRONOMIC**, 5, b g Zafonic (USA)—Sky Love (USA) **Andrea & Graham Wylie**
11 **BALLYBOUGH RASHER (IRE)**, 10, b g Broken Hearted—Chat Her Up **BDR Partnership**
12 **BALYAN (IRE)**, 4, b c Bahhare (USA)—Balaniya (USA) **Andrea & Graham Wylie**
13 **BEAU ARTISTE**, 5, ch g Peintre Celebre (USA)—Belle Esprit **G. F. Bear**
14 **BEAUCHAMP GIGI (IRE)**, 7, b m Bob Back (USA)—Beauchamp Grace **Andrea & Graham Wylie**

MR J. H. JOHNSON—continued

15 **BEST ACCOLADE**, 6, b g Oscar (IRE)—Made of Talent **Andrea & Graham Wylie**
16 **BEWLEYS BERRY (IRE)**, 7, ch g Shernazar—Approach The Dawn (IRE) **Andrea & Graham Wylie**
17 **BLAIRGOWRIE (IRE)**, 6, b g Supreme Leader—Parsons Term (IRE) **Transcend Bloodstock LLP**
18 **BOHEMIAN BROOK (IRE)**, 4, ch g Alderbrook—Bohemian Return (IRE) **The Son Of Alderbrook Partnership**
19 **BOY'S HURRAH (IRE)**, 9, b g Phardante (FR)—Gorryelm **Woolpack Farm Partnership**
20 **CALIN ROYAL (FR)**, 4, ch g Garde Royale—Caline de Froment (FR) **Andrea & Graham Wylie**
21 **CAN CAN FLYER (IRE)**, 4, ch c In The Wings—Can Can Lady **M. McKernan**
22 **CHEVET BOY (IRE)**, 7, b g Welsh Term—Sizzle **D. M. Gibbons**
23 **CHIVALRY**, 6, b g Mark of Esteem (IRE)—Gai Bulga **Andrea & Graham Wylie**
24 **COAT OF HONOUR (USA)**, 5, gr g Mark of Esteem (IRE)—Ballymac Girl **Andrea & Graham Wylie**
25 **COMEONSHE**, 4, ch f Commanche Run—Zajira (IRE) **Zajira Racing**
26 **COOL CARROLL (IRE)**, 7, b m Carroll House—Sohot Whyknot (IRE) **Miss B. Sykes**
27 **COTTY'S ROCK (IRE)**, 6, ch g Beneficial—Its Good Ere **Andrea & Graham Wylie**
28 **COVENT GARDEN**, 7, b g Sadler's Wells (USA)—Temple Row **Joint Ownership Terminated**
29 **CREDIT (IRE)**, 4, ch c Intikhab (USA)—Tycooness (IRE) **Andrea & Graham Wylie**
30 **CROSSMAGLEN (IRE)**, 4, ch g Shernazar—Gender Gap (USA) **M. McKernan**
31 **DALARAM (IRE)**, 5, b g Sadler's Wells (USA)—Dalara (IRE) **Andrea & Graham Wylie**
32 **DEJA VU (IRE)**, 6, b g Lord Americo—Khalkeys Shoon **The SGS Partnership**
33 **DIAMOND SAL**, 7, b m Bob Back (USA)—Fortune's Girl **Andrea & Graham Wylie**
34 **DIX HUIT CYBORG (FR)**, 4, ch g Cyborg (FR)—Dix Huit Brumaire (FR) **Mrs M. W. Bird**
35 **DORIS'S GIFT**, 4, gr g Environment Friend—Saxon Gift **Elliott Brothers**
36 4, B c Executive Perk—Down The Garden (IRE) **Andrea & Graham Wylie**
37 **EBAC (IRE)**, 4, ch g Accordion—Higher Again (IRE) **Elliott Brothers**
38 **FACTOR FIFTEEN**, 6, b g Hector Protector (USA)—Catch The Sun **M. McKernan**
39 **FIELDS OF HOME (IRE)**, 7, b m Synefos (USA)—Homefield Girl (IRE) **Roy Campion And J. Howard Johnson**
40 **FORTUNA FAVENTE (IRE)**, 5, b m Supreme Leader—La Grande Dame **Andrea & Graham Wylie**
41 **GALERO**, 6, b g Overbury (IRE)—Rare Luck **Andrea & Graham Wylie**
42 **GIULIANI**, 5, b g Sadler's Wells (USA)—Anka Germania **J. R. McAleese**
43 **GRATTAN LODGE (IRE)**, 8, gr g Roselier (FR)—Shallow Run **W. M. G. Black**
44 **GREY ABBEY (IRE)**, 11, gr g Nestor—Tacovaon **Ken Roper,Elinor M. Roper,Norman Furness**
45 **HAADEF (IRE)**, 4, b c Sadler's Wells (USA)—Taqreem (IRE) **Andrea & Graham Wylie**
46 **HOCKENHEIM (FR)**, 4, b g Kadalko (FR)—L'inka (FR) **Andrea & Graham Wylie**
47 **INCHING CLOSER**, 8, b g Inchinor—Maiyaasah **Andrea & Graham Wylie**
48 **INGLIS DREVER**, 6, b g In The Wings—Cormorant Creek **Andrea & Graham Wylie**
49 **INTERSKY NATIVE (IRE)**, 9, ch g Be My Native (USA)—Creative Music **Interskyracing.com**
50 **IRON MAN (FR)**, 4, ch g Video Rock (FR)—Key Figure (USA) **Andrea & Graham Wylie**
51 **ISIDORE BONHEUR (IRE)**, 4, b c Mtoto—Way O'gold (USA) **Andrea & Graham Wylie**
52 **ISLAND FAITH**, 8, b g Turtle Island (IRE)—Keep The Faith **M. K. Lee**
53 **JEALOUS MEAD (IRE)**, 4, ro g I'm Supposin (IRE)—Spindle's **Mr A. S. Smith**
54 **JEREMIAH JOHNSON (IRE)**, 5, b g Saddlers' Hall (USA)—Glenkess (IRE) **Mr Paul Shannahan**
55 **JULIUS CAESAR**, 5, b g Sadler's Wells (USA)—Stiletta **Jack Coupe and John Thompson**
56 **KASTHARI (IRE)**, 6, gr g Vettori (IRE)—Karliyka (IRE) **Elliott Brothers**
57 **KINBURN (IRE)**, 6, gr g Roselier (FR)—Leadaro (IRE) **W. M. G. Black**
58 **KINGS HILL LEADER (IRE)**, 6, b g Supreme Leader—Mary Kate Finn **J. R. McAleese**
59 **LA PERROTINE (FR)**, 5, b m Northern Crystal—Haratiyna **Mrs M. W. Bird**
60 **LADE BRAES (IRE)**, 4, b g Luso—Madamme Highlights **W. M. G. Black**
61 **LASTING LADY (IRE)**, 9, b br m Supreme Leader—Lasting Legacy **Mr J. H. Johnson**
62 **LE CID (FR)**, 8, b g Mansonnien (FR)—Dona Rahotep (FR) **Andrea & Graham Wylie**
63 **LENNON (IRE)**, 5, b br g Beneficial—Stradbally Bay **Andrea & Graham Wylie**
64 **LOG ON INTERSKY (IRE)**, 9, ch g Insan (USA)—Arctic Mo (IRE) **Interskyracing.com**
65 **LORD CAPITAINE (IRE)**, 11, b br g Mister Lord (USA)—
Salvation Sue **The Scottish Steeplechasing Partnership**
66 **LORD CHESTERS (IRE)**, 4, b g Lord of Appeal—Cherry Chase **Transcend Bloodstock LLP**
67 **LORD TRANSCEND (IRE)**, 8, gr g Aristocracy—Capincur Lady **Andrea & Graham Wylie**
68 **LOUSTIC COLLONGES (FR)**, 6, b g Kadalko (FR)—Altesse Collonges (FR) **Andrea & Graham Wylie**
69 4, Ch c Zaffaran (USA)—Lucky Daisy (IRE) **J. Howard Johnson**
70 **LUTHELLO (FR)**, 6, b g Marchand de Sable (USA)—Haudello (FR) **Mr J. H. Johnson**
71 **MELMOUNT STAR (IRE)**, 7, b br g Rashar (USA)—Bucktina **Nigel and Lucy Forbes**
72 **MEPHISTO (IRE)**, 6, b g Machiavellian (USA)—Cunning **Andrea & Graham Wylie**
73 **MONTMARTRE (IRE)**, 5, br m Grand Lodge—French Quarter **Andrea & Graham Wylie**
74 **MOSCOW BLUE**, 4, ch g Soviet Star (USA)—Aquamarine **G. Houghton**
75 **MOTIVE (FR)**, 4, ch g Machiavellian (USA)—Mistle Song **Andrea & Graham Wylie**
76 **NAMELESS WONDER (IRE)**, 9, b g Supreme Leader—Miss Kylogue (IRE) **Ellenvalley Optimists**
77 **NILE MOON (IRE)**, 4, b g Simply Great (FR)—Reasonable Time (IRE) **Transcend Bloodstock LLP**
78 **NO REFUGE (IRE)**, 5, ch g Hernando (FR)—Shamarra (IRE) **Andrea & Graham Wylie**
79 **OBE ONE**, 5, b g Puissance—Plum Bold **B & D Partnership**

MR J. H. JOHNSON—continued

80 **ONLY ONCE**, 10, b g King's Ride—Rambling Gold **Group Capt J. A. Prideaux**
81 **PERCUSSIONIST (IRE)**, 4, b c Sadler's Wells (USA)—Magnificent Style (USA) **Andrea & Graham Wylie**
82 **RAYSHAN (IRE)**, 5, b g Darshaan—Rayseka (IRE) **Andrea & Graham Wylie**
83 **REGAL SETTING (IRE)**, 4, br g King's Theatre (IRE)—Cartier Bijoux **Andrea & Graham Wylie**
84 **ROGUES GALLERY (IRE)**, 5, b g Luso—Sarah May (IRE) **Andrea & Graham Wylie**
85 **ROYAL ROSA (FR)**, 6, ch g Garde Royale—Crystalza (FR) **Andrea & Graham Wylie**
86 **SAN PEIRE (FR)**, 8, b g Cyborg (FR)—Shakapoura (FR) **Mr J. Howard Johnson**
87 **SCOTMAIL (IRE)**, 4, b g Old Vic—Snipe Singer **Gordon Brown/Bert Watson**
88 **SCOTMAIL TOO (IRE)**, 4, b g Saddlers' Hall (IRE)—Kam Slave **Gordon Brown/Bert Watson**
89 **SILVER DOLLARS (FR)**, 4, gr g Great Palm (USA)—Marie Olga (FR) **Transcend Bloodstock LLP**
90 4, Ch g Karinga Bay—Strawberry Split **Andrea & Graham Wylie**
91 **SUPREME LEISURE (IRE)**, 8, b g Supreme Leader—Maid of Leisure **Mrs Mary Bird & Mr J. Howard Johnson**
92 **TEME VALLEY**, 11, br g Polish Precedent (USA)—Sudeley **Mr Chris Heron & Mr J. Howard Johnson**
93 **THE LAIRD'S ENTRY (IRE)**, 10, b g King's Ride—Balancing Act **Ellenvalley Optimists**
94 **THE REVEREND (IRE)**, 5, b br g Taipan (IRE)—Sounds Classical (IRE) **Andrea & Graham Wylie**
95 **THEATRE KNIGHT (IRE)**, 7, b g Old Vic—Musical View (IRE) **Andrea & Graham Wylie**
96 **THISTLE**, 4, ch c Selkirk (USA)—Ardisia (USA) **Andrea & Graham Wylie**
97 **TOLLBRAE (IRE)**, 8, gr g Supreme Leader—Miss Henrietta (IRE) **Mr J. Howard Johnson**
98 **TOP STYLE (IRE)**, 7, ch g Topanoora—Kept In Style **T. F. Harty**
99 **TREYBOR (IRE)**, 6, br g Bob Back (USA)—Ballyvooney **Andrea & Graham Wylie**
100 **VALLEY HENRY (IRE)**, 10, b g Step Together (USA)—Pineway VII **Andrea & Graham Wylie**
101 **WISEGUY (IRE)**, 6, b g Darshaan—Bibliotheque (USA) **Andrea & Graham Wylie**
102 4, B c Zaffaran (USA)—Witchy Native (IRE) **Mr J. Howard Johnson**
103 **YOUNG SCOTTON**, 5, b g Cadeaux Genereux—Broken Wave **Elliott Brothers**

THREE-YEAR-OLDS

104 Ch c Carroll House—Ashie's Friend (IRE) **Mr J. Howard Johnson**
105 **BUDDY BROWN**, b c Lujain (USA)—Rose Bay **Andrea & Graham Wylie**
106 B g Sea Raven (IRE)—Commanche Glen (IRE) **Mr J. Howard Johnson**
107 B c Pistolet Bleu (IRE)—Di's Wag **Mr J. Howard Johnson**
108 B f Keen—Dominuet **Mr Frank Murphy**
109 **JACKADANDY (USA)**, b g Lear Fan (USA)—Chandra (CAN) **Andrea & Graham Wylie**
110 **MELODY QUE (IRE)**, b f Sadler's Wells (USA)—Bex (USA) **Andrea & Graham Wylie**
111 **NEGAS (IRE)**, b g Titus Livius (FR)—Alzeam (IRE) **Mrs M. W. Bird**
112 **PARCHMENT (IRE)**, ch g Singspiel (IRE)—Hannalou (FR) **Andrea & Graham Wylie**
113 Ch c Pistolet Bleu (IRE)—Peas (IRE) **Mr J. Howard Johnson**
114 **POIROT**, b g Montjeu (IRE)—Opari (IRE) **Andrea & Graham Wylie**
115 **RAINBOW RISING (IRE)**, b br g Desert King (IRE)—Fantastic Bid (USA) **Andrea & Graham Wylie**
116 **RENADA**, b f Sinndar (IRE)—Asterita **Andrea & Graham Wylie**
117 **ROCKPILER**, b g Halling (USA)—Emma Peel **Andrea & Graham Wylie**
118 **SANDYSNOWING (FR)**, b g Sendawar (USA)—Snow White **Andrea & Graham Wylie**
119 **TSAROXY (IRE)**, b g Xaar—Belsay **Andrea & Graham Wylie**
120 **VENETIAN KING (USA)**, b g King of Kings (IRE)—Vena (IRE) **Andrea & Graham Wylie**
121 **WOLF HAMMER (USA)**, ch g Diesis—Polly's Link (USA) **Andrea & Graham Wylie**

TWO-YEAR-OLDS

122 Bl gr c 3/6 Dansili—Aristocratique (Cadeaux Genereux) (40000) **Transcend Bloodstock LLP**
123 Gr f 27/2 Mozart (IRE)—Attachment (USA) (Trempolino (USA)) (53655) **Transcend Bloodstock LLP**
124 B c 27/2 King Charlemagne (USA)—Canary Bird (IRE) (Catrail (USA)) (32000) **Transcend Bloodstock LLP**
125 B c 8/3 Distant Music (USA)—Dark Albatross (USA) (Sheikh Albadou) (14000) **Transcend Bloodstock LLP**
126 B br f 10/3 Woodman (USA)—Elegant Ridge (IRE) (Indian Ridge) (93896) **Andrea & Graham Wylie**
127 B f 26/3 Orpen (USA)—Fantastic Bid (USA) (Auction Ring (USA)) (21461) **Transcend Bloodstock LLP**
128 B c 26/4 Fasliyev (USA)—Grey Again (Unfuwain (USA)) (37000) **Transcend Bloodstock LLP**
129 Ch c 10/2 Dr Fong (USA)—Heckle (In The Wings) (93896) **Andrea & Graham Wylie**
130 B f 19/3 Night Shift (USA)—Iktidar (Green Desert (USA)) (110000) **Andrea & Graham Wylie**
131 B f 5/3 Danetime (IRE)—Lady Ingabelle (IRE) (Catrail (USA)) (10000) **Transcend Bloodstock LLP**
132 Ch c 14/3 Giant's Causeway (USA)—
          Music House (USA) (Sadler's Wells (USA)) (201206) **Andrea & Graham Wylie**
133 B c 8/2 Cape Cross (IRE)—Ninth Wonder (USA) (Forty Niner (USA)) (174379) **Andrea & Graham Wylie**
134 B c 7/2 Compton Place—Only Yours (Aragon) (88000) **Andrea & Graham Wylie**
135 B c 14/5 Robellino (USA)—Running Tycoon (IRE) (Last Tycoon) (27000) **Transcend Bloodstock LLP**
136 B br c 2/1 King Charlemagne (USA)—
          Shining Desert (IRE) (Green Desert (USA)) (54000) **Transcend Bloodstock LLP**
137 B c 27/3 Mujadil (USA)—Silver Arrow (USA) (Shadeed (USA)) (50000) **Transcend Bloodstock LLP**
138 B c 23/3 Orpen (USA)—Siraka (FR) (Grand Lodge (USA)) (38000) **Transcend Bloodstock LLP**

MR J. H. JOHNSON—continued

139 B c 19/4 Distant Music (USA)—Space Travel (Dancing Dissident (USA)) (26000) **Transcend Bloodstock LLP**
140 B c 7/3 Stravinsky (USA)—Storm West (USA) (Gone West (USA)) (154258) **Andrea & Graham Wylie**
141 Gr c 27/4 Shinko Forest (IRE)—Thatchabella (IRE) (Thatching) (15000) **Transcend Bloodstock LLP**
142 B c 22/4 Mull of Kintyre (USA)—Thrill Seeker (IRE) (Treasure Kay) (30180) **Transcend Bloodstock LLP**
143 B c 14/3 Imperial Ballet (IRE)—Two Magpies (Doulab (USA)) (35000) **Transcend Bloodstock LLP**
144 B c 18/2 City On A Hill (USA)—Victoria's Secret (IRE) (Law Society (USA)) (38000) **Transcend Bloodstock LLP**
145 **WHO HA (USA)**, b c 27/3 Stravinsky (USA)—
        I Don't Know (USA) (Star de Naskra (USA)) (60361) **Transcend Bloodstock LLP**

Other Owners: G. Brown, J. Buchanan, Mrs F. Buchanan, F. J. Bush, J. Coupe, Mr J. A. Elliott, C. R. Elliott, Mr J. M. Elliott, Mrs T. Gaunt, R. Gurney, R. M. Kirkland, Terry McDermott, Mr W. Murphy, Mrs J. M. Newsome, D. Parry, B. C. Rafferty, B. Robe, Mrs D. F. Robe, A. Shearer, D. Taylor, Mr J. Thompson, R. D. P. Watson.

Jockey (flat): R. Winston. **Jockey (NH):** G. Lee. **Conditional:** Declan McGann, Matty Roe.

| 320 | **MR P. JOHNSON, Stanley**
Postal: **Low Wyndways Farm, White-le-Head, Stanley, Co. Durham, DH9 9SF.**
Contacts: **PHONE/FAX** (01207) 282246 **MOBILE** (07850) 752957
WEBSITE www.pauljohnsonracing.com |

1 **CASH**, 7, b g Bishop of Cashel—Ballad Island **Dr P. and Mrs D. M. Johnson**
2 **DIZZY IN THE HEAD**, 6, b g Mind Games—Giddy **Dr P. and Mrs D. M. Johnson**
3 **HOH'S BACK**, 6, b g Royal Applause—Paris Joelle (IRE) **Dr P. and Mrs D. M. Johnson**
4 **HORMUZ (IRE)**, 9, b g Hamas (IRE)—Balqis (USA) **Dr P. and Mrs D. M. Johnson**
5 **MOYNE PLEASURE (IRE)**, 7, b g Exit To Nowhere (USA)—Ilanga (IRE) **Dr P. and Mrs D. M. Johnson**
6 4, B f Polar Prince (IRE)—Patina **Dr P. and Mrs D. M. Johnson**
7 **THE GAMBLER**, 5, ch g First Trump—Future Options **Dr P. and Mrs D. M. Johnson**

THREE-YEAR-OLDS

8 B f Royal Applause—Arboretum (IRE) **Dr P. and Mrs D. M. Johnson**

TWO-YEAR-OLDS

9 Ch f 20/3 Compton Place—Hi Nicky (High Kicker (USA)) (800) **Dr P. and Mrs D. M. Johnson**
10 B c 30/3 Compton Place—La Perla (Royal Applause) (1000) **Dr P. and Mrs D. M. Johnson**
11 B f 27/2 Compton Place—Lost In Hook (IRE) (Dancing Dissident (USA)) (800) **Dr P. and Mrs D. M. Johnson**

Other Owners: Mr C. Johnson, Mr D. B. White, Mr J. Williams, Mrs M. Williams, Mr N. Ahier, MR P. Johnson.

Assistant Trainer: D M Johnson

Amateur: Mr P Evans.

| 321 | **MR P. R. JOHNSON, Cannock**
Postal: **Pinetrees Farm, Stafford Road, Huntington, Cannock, Staffordshire, WS12 4PX.**
Contacts: **PHONE** (01543) 502962 **MOBILE** (07812) 216786 |

1 **HOPESARISING**, 6, b g Primitive Rising (USA)—Super Brush (IRE) **Mr P. R. Johnson**
2 **KANSAS CITY (FR)**, 7, b br m Lute Antique (FR)—Tenacity (FR) **Mr P. R. Johnson**
3 **LADY DYNAMITE**, 5, b m Glacial Storm (USA)—Lady Elle (IRE) **Mrs L. V. Durnall**

Assistant Trainer: Ian Hooper

Jockey (NH): D. Verco.

| 322 | **MR ROBERT W. JOHNSON, Newcastle Upon Tyne**
Postal: **Grange Farm, Newburn, Newcastle Upon Tyne.**
Contacts: **PHONE** (0191) 2674464 **MOBILE** (07774) 131133 |

1 **AELRED**, 12, b g Ovac (ITY)—Sponsorship **Mr J. L. Gledson**
2 **ALLEGEDLY RED**, 6, ch m Sabrehill (USA)—Tendency **Mr Robert W. Johnson**
3 **BOB'S BUSTER**, 9, b g Bob's Return (IRE)—Saltina **Mrs G. Jones**
4 **BUCKSAREBACK (IRE)**, 9, b g Buckskin (FR)—Town of Trees (IRE) **Mr Robert W. Johnson**

MR ROBERT W. JOHNSON—continued

5 **DENNIS THE MENNIS (IRE)**, 6, b g Fourstars Allstar (USA)—Farm Approach **J. L. Armstrong**
6 **DERAINEY (IRE)**, 6, b g Farhaan—Hurricane Hazel **Mr R. H. Docchar**
7 **JACCOUT (FR)**, 7, b g Sheyrann—Jacottiere (FR) **Mr Robert W. Johnson**
8 **NA BAC LEIS**, 5, ch g Bijou d'inde—Risk The Witch **Peter & Paul Kelly**
9 **PIRAEUS (NZ)**, 6, b g Beau Zam (NZ)—Gull Mundur (NZ) **Mr J. E. Rogers**
10 **SANDS RISING**, 8, b g Primitive Rising (USA)—Celtic Sands **T. L. A. Robson**
11 **SEAFIRE LAD (IRE)**, 4, b g Portrait Gallery (IRE)—Act The Fool (IRE) **Mr Robert W. Johnson**
12 **STAFF NURSE (IRE)**, 5, b m Night Shift (USA)—Akebia (USA) **Mr L. G. Aldsworth**
13 **STORMY BEECH**, 9, b g Glacial Storm (USA)—Cheeny's Brig **Peter & Paul Kelly**
14 **THE LEATHER WEDGE (IRE)**, 6, b h Hamas (IRE)—Wallflower **C. P. Grindell**
15 **THORNBIRD LASS**, 9, b m Alflora (IRE)—Burling Moss **J. W. Thornton**
16 **VALUABLE (IRE)**, 8, b m Jurado (USA)—Can't Afford It (IRE) **The Jolly Boys Partnership**
17 **VINCERE**, 6, b g Tigani—Katy Keys **G. Pickering**

THREE-YEAR-OLDS

18 **MONTRACHET BELLE**, ch f Kadeed (IRE)—Swiss Hat **K. Eichler**

Other Owners: B. Weir, D. Weir.

Jockey (NH): K. Johnson. **Amateur:** Mr P. Johnson.

---

323 **MRS S. M. JOHNSON, Madley**
Postal: Carwardine Farm, Madley, Hereford.
Contacts: **PHONE** (01981) 250214 **FAX** (01981) 251538

1 **ABER GALE**, 6, br m Thethingaboutitis (USA)—Twablade (IRE) **G. I. Isaac**
2 **CALL ME BOBBI**, 6, b m Executive Perk—Call-Me-Dinky **C. A. Fuller**
3 **DON'T MATTER**, 5, b m Petong—Cool Run **Celtic Racing**
4 **JACK'S LAD (IRE)**, 6, ch g High Roller (IRE)—Captain's Covey **Mrs M. E. Mason**
5 **MENINA**, 6, b m Alflora (IRE)—Just Lynn **D. H. Cowgill**
6 **OVER BRIDGE**, 7, b g Overbury (IRE)—Celtic Bridge **I. K. Johnson**
7 **STILL RUNS DEEP**, 6, b m Karinga Bay—Millers Action **M. J. Langdell**
8 **THREEPENNY BIT**, 7, b m Safawan—Tuppence In Clover **J. P. and Mrs M. A. Skues**

Other Owners: J. Blain, J. Robinson.

Jockey (NH): R. Johnson. **Amateur:** Miss S. Beddoes, Mr R. Burton.

---

324 **MR A. E. JONES, Tiverton**
Postal: Steart House Racing Stables, Stoodleigh, Tiverton, Devon, EX16 9QA.
Contacts: **MOBILE** (07901) 505064
E-MAIL wannahorse@heritageracing.co.uk

1 **ALEEMDAR (IRE)**, 8, b g Doyoun—Aleema **J. Spence**
2 **DANGEROUSDANMAGRU (IRE)**, 9, b g Forest Wind (USA)—Blue Bell Girl **N. F. Glynn**
3 **GALANT EYE (IRE)**, 6, ch g Eagle Eyed (USA)—Galandria **R. C. Palmer**
4 **GILDED ALLY**, 5, b g Gildoran—Allyfair **G. Molen**
5 **ISLEOFHOPEANTEARS (IRE)**, 6, b g College Chapel—Fontaine Lodge (IRE) **N. F. Glynn**
6 **JOHNYYOURONLYJOKEN (IRE)**, 9, gr g Roselier (FR)—Badsworth Madam **N. F. Glynn**
7 **JUBILEE PRINCE**, 5, b g Petong—Efficacious (IRE) **G. P. Brown**
8 4, B c Thowra (FR)—Kolyas Girl (IRE) **G. P. Brown**
9 **MIGHTY MINSTER**, 8, ch m Minster Son—Mighty Fly **J. Spence**
10 **PAST HERITAGE**, 6, b g Past Glories—Norman's Delight (IRE) **J. Spence**
11 **RED JESTER**, 4, b c Thowra (FR)—Red Ebrel (IRE) **J. Spence**
12 **REDSWAN**, 10, ch g Risk Me (FR)—Bocas Rose **G. P. Brown**
13 **SAMMAGEFROMTENNESSE (IRE)**, 8, b g Petardia—Canoora **N. F. Glynn**
14 **THAI TOWN**, 6, br g Afzal—Koo-Ming **G. P. Brown**
15 **THRASHING**, 10, b g Kahyasi—White-Wash **G. P. Brown**
16 **TIGER ISLAND (USA)**, 5, b h Grand Slam (USA)—Paris Wild Cat (USA) **N. F. Glynn**
17 **TOTHEROADYOUVGONE**, 11, b g Carlingford Castle—Wild Rosie **N. F. Glynn**
18 **WUN CHAI (IRE)**, 6, b g King's Theatre (IRE)—Flower From Heaven **G. P. Brown**

MR A. E. JONES—continued

THREE-YEAR-OLDS

19 B f Kayf Tara—Norman's Delight (IRE) **G. P. Brown**
20 **PARSLEY'S RETURN**, b g Danzero (AUS)—The Frog Queen **G. Molen**
21 B c Kayf Tara—Red Ebrel (IRE) **G. P. Brown**

Assistant Trainer: Miss A Bartelink

Jockey (flat): K. Fallon. **Jockey (NH):** R. Johnson. **Amateur:** Mr K. Culligan, Miss S. Parmentier.

---

325 MR A. P. JONES, Upper Lambourn
Postal: Hillhouse Stables, Sherwood, Folly Road, Lambourn, Berkshire, RG17 8QE.
Contacts: **OFFICE/FAX** (01488) 670245 **MOBILE** (07771) 553242
E-MAIL apjonesracing@aol.com.uk

1 **BETTERWARE BOY**, 5, ch g Barathea (IRE)—Crystal Drop **Lambourn Racing**
2 **BUSINESS**, 6, br g Bluegrass Prince (IRE)—Dancing Doll (USA) **Mr C. Willett-Wills Dyer**
3 **DAISY FOREVER**, 5, b m My Best Valentine—Seymour Ann **Mrs K. Hitchins**
4 **DARK RAIDER (IRE)**, 4, br gr f Definite Article—Lady Shikari **T. G. N. Burrage**
5 **FIN BEC (FR)**, 12, b g Tip Moss (FR)—Tourbrune (FR) **P. T. Newell**
6 **GOOD ARTICLE (IRE)**, 4, b g Definite Article—Good News (IRE) **T. G. N. Burrage**
7 **HARRY'S GAME**, 8, gr g Emperor Jones (USA)—Lady Shikari **T. G. N. Burrage**
8 **IDEAL OPPORTUNITY**, 4, b f The West (USA)—Ninotchka **Mr C. Willett-Wills Dyer**
9 **INTRICAT**, 5, ch g Bluegrass Prince (IRE)—Noble Soul **B. W. Bedford**
10 **JESSINCA**, 9, b m Minshaanshu Amad (USA)—Noble Soul **The Lambourn Racing Club**
11 **LOUISVILLE PRINCE**, 4, ch g Bluegrass Prince (IRE)—Noble Soul **The Lambourn Racing Club**
12 **MR WHIZZ**, 8, ch g Manhal—Panienka (POL) **The Milk Sheiks**
13 **RUBY RAINNE**, 6, gr m Perugino (USA)—Lady Shikari **T. G. N. Burrage**
14 **SHADES OF THE WEST**, 5, b m The West (USA)—Spanish Luck **Mrs K. Hitchins**
15 **THE BEES KNEES**, 5, b g Bijou d'inde—Dismiss **T. G. N. Burrage**

THREE-YEAR-OLDS

16 **CHESTMINSTER GIRL**, ch f Tomba—Nannie Annie **Mr Roger & Robert Beadle**
17 **DEBBIES DILEMMA**, b g Bluegrass Prince (IRE)—Total Truth **Mr C. Willett-Wills Dyer & Mr A. McGuinness**
18 **EEEYORE**, b c El Conquistador—Jane Herring **Mrs K. Hitchins**
19 **GREGS GIRL**, b f Bluegrass Prince (IRE)—Ninotchka **Mrs K. Hitchins**
20 Ch g Fumo di Londra (IRE)—Noble Soul **Longhedge Gallops**
21 Ch g Bluegrass Prince (IRE)—Valetta **Mr C. Willett-Wills Dyer & Mr A. McGuinness**

TWO-YEAR-OLDS

22 Ch c 3/4 Bluegrass Prince (IRE)—Ballystate (Ballacashtal (CAN)) **Mrs K. Hitchins**
23 Ch f 24/3 Bluegrass Prince (IRE)—Martian Melody (Enchantment) **Mrs K. Hitchins**
24 Ch g 23/3 Fumo di Londra (IRE)—Misinterrex (Interrex (CAN)) **Mr C. Willett-Wills Dyer & Mr A. McGuinness**
25 Ch c 11/4 Bold Edge—Noble Soul (Sayf El Arab (USA)) (3238) **Longhedge Gallops**

Other Owners: Mr Keith Mailey, Mr Benny Bennet, Mr Doug McDonald, Mr Craig Anger, Mr G. Ciesco, Mr Ezan, MR A. P. Jones, K. D. Linsley, D. R. Mead.

Assistant Trainer: Christopher Willet, Wills Dyer

Jockey (flat): F. Norton, D. Sweeney, S. Whitworth. **Jockey (NH):** L. Aspell, T. Doyle, M. Foley, A. Thornton. **Conditional:** Derek Laverty. **Apprentice:** Derek Nolan, Jason Letherby, Liam Keniry. **Amateur:** Mr Emil Imelov.

---

326 MR G. ELWYN JONES, Lampeter
Postal: **Lluestnewydd, Bettws, Lampeter, Dyfed, SA48 8PB.**
Contacts: **PHONE** (01570) 493261 **MOBILE** (07817) 885504

1 **BLUE CASCADE (IRE)**, 6, b g Royal Academy (USA)—Blaine (USA) **Mr G. Elwyn Jones**
2 **DESERT SPA (USA)**, 10, b g Sheikh Albadou—Healing Waters (USA) **Mr G. Elwyn Jones**
3 **PRIME MINISTER**, 11, ch g Be My Chief (USA)—Classic Design **Mr G. Elwyn Jones**

Amateur: Mr David Turner.

327 MR P. J. JONES, Marlborough
Postal: **Fox Twitchen, East Kennett, Marlborough, Wiltshire, SN8 4EY.**
Contacts: **PHONE (06782) 861427**

1 **HARRY HARESTONE**, 10, b g Miner's Lamp—Slipalong **Mrs A. H. Jones**
2 **LADY BLING BLING**, 4, b f Midnight Legend—Slipmatic **Mr P. J. Jones**
3 **LUCKY PETE**, 8, b g Lyphento (USA)—Clare's Choice **Mr P. J. Jones**

328 MR T. M. JONES, Guildford
Postal: **Brook Farm, Albury, Guildford, Surrey, GU5 9DJ.**
Contacts: **PHONE (01483) 202604/203749 FAX (01483) 202604 MOBILE (07785) 915762**
E-MAIL buck@brookfarmalbury.freeserve.co.uk WEBSITE www.brookfarmracing.com

1 **ENNA (POL)**, 6, ch m Don Corleone—Elba (POL) **Mr T. M. Jones**
2 **ICANNSHIFT (IRE)**, 5, b g Night Shift (USA)—Cannikin (IRE) **Mrs S. Wynne**
3 **JASMINE PEARL (IRE)**, 4, b f King of Kings (IRE)—Tumbleweed Pearl **Mr T. M. Jones**
4 **MADISON AVENUE (GER)**, 8, b g Mondrian (GER)—Madly Noble (GER) **R. L. Page**

TWO-YEAR-OLDS

5 **ERHGENT SEA**, gr g 28/5 Erhaab (USA)—Gentle Gypsy (Junius (USA)) (3000) **Mrs S. Wynne**
6 Ch c 4/3 Presidium—Inonder (Belfort (FR)) (1500) **R. L. Page**
7 **SKEZAHRA**, b f 19/4 Zaha (CAN)—Skedaddle (Formidable (USA)) (800) **Mr T. M. Jones**
8 **YALLINGUP**, b f 16/4 Muhtarram (USA)—Boomerang Blade (Sure Blade (USA)) (900) **Mrs R. A. Jennings**

Other Owners: MR T. M. Jones.

Assistant Trainer: Miss K. Windsor-Luck

329 MR F. T. J. JORDAN, Towcester
Postal: **Highfields Stables, Adstone, Towcester, Northamptonshire, NN12 8DS.**
Contacts: **HOME (01327) 861162 OFFICE (01327) 860840 FAX (01327) 860810**
MOBILE (07831) 101632
E-MAIL jordyracer27@hotmail.com

1 **BLOW ME DOWN**, 6, b m Overbury (IRE)—Chinook's Daughter (IRE) **Mrs K. Roberts-Hindle**
2 **BUALADHBOS (IRE)**, 6, b g Royal Applause—Goodnight Girl (IRE) **F. K. Jennings**
3 **CAPTAINS TABLE**, 12, b g Welsh Captain—Wensum Girl **L. Pike**
4 **CONROY**, 6, b g Greensmith—Highland Spirit **D. I. Ancil**
5 **FIRSTFLOR**, 6, b m Alflora (IRE)—First Crack **Mr F. T. J. Jordan**
6 **FORBEARING (IRE)**, 8, b g Bering—For Example (USA) **Mr L. J. A. Griffiths**
7 **HIGH VIEW (USA)**, 4, ch c Distant View (USA)—Disco Doll (USA) **Mr F. T. J. Jordan**
8 **IRISH BLESSING (USA)**, 8, b g Ghazi (USA)—Win For Leah (USA) **The Bhiss Partnership**
9 **JUST RUBY**, 4, ch f Gunner B—First Crack **D. Pugh**
10 **KITTE OU DOUBLE (FR)**, 7, b g Agent Bleu (FR)—Briffault (FR) **Le Tricolore**
11 **LABELTHOU (FR)**, 6, b m Saint Preuil (FR)—Suzy de Thou (FR) **Le Tricolore**
12 **LERUBIS (FR)**, 6, b g Ragmar (FR)—Perle de Saisy (FR) **Mr F. T. J. Jordan**
13 **LET'S CELEBRATE**, 5, b g Groom Dancer (USA)—Shimmer **Mr F. T. J. Jordan**
14 **LIBRE**, 5, b g Bahamian Bounty—Premier Blues (FR) **Mr L. J. A. Griffiths**
15 **LUBINAS (IRE)**, 6, b g Grand Lodge (USA)—Liebesgirl **P. Ratcliffe**
16 **MARON**, 8, b g Puissance—Will Be Bold **G. E. Gibson**
17 **MEDKHAN (IRE)**, 8, ch g Lahib (USA)—Safayn (USA) **Miss L. M. Rochford**
18 **MISS TROOPER**, 5, b m Infantry—Mountain Glen **A. J. Mobley**
19 **MONSIEUR GEORGES (FR)**, 5, b g Kadalko (FR)—Djoumi (FR) **Near & Far Racing**
20 **POSH CRACK**, 5, b m Rakaposhi King—First Crack **Mr F. T. J. Jordan**
21 **ROBBIE WILL**, 4, b g Robellino (USA)—Life's Too Short (IRE) **Mr F. T. J. Jordan**
22 **SHADY ANNE**, 7, ch m Derrylin—Juno Away (IRE) **D. Pugh**
23 **SUCHWOT (IRE)**, 4, b g Intikhab (USA)—Fairy Water **Graham Parker**
24 **SUMMER BOUNTY**, 9, b g Lugana Beach—Tender Moment (IRE) **Mr T. Powell**
25 **THE LAST MOHICAN**, 6, b g Common Grounds—Arndilly **Mr L. J. A. Griffiths**
26 **TURTLE RECALL (IRE)**, 6, b g Turtle Island (IRE)—Nora Yo Ya **Mr F. T. J. Jordan**
27 **WELSH MAIN**, 8, br g Zafonic (USA)—Welsh Daylight **M. A. Reeder**

MR F. T. J. JORDAN—continued

THREE-YEAR-OLDS

28 **COME TO DADDY (IRE)**, ch g Fayruz—Forgren (IRE) **Mr F. T. J. Jordan**
29 **DANTE'S DIAMOND (IRE)**, b c Orpen (USA)—Flower From Heaven **The Goodfellas**
30 **HIDDEN STAR**, br c Lujain (USA)—Inimitable **A. Cocum**

Other Owners: R. K. Betts, D. A. Charlesworth, Mrs H. Charlet, A. Cocum, R. A. Hancocks, Mrs S. J. Le Gros, Mr J. Sleightholme, Mr A. D. Sleightholme, D. M. Thornton.

Assistant Trainer: Miss L Jordan

Amateur: Mr P. Cowley.

---

330 **MR J. JOSEPH, Amersham**
Postal: **Cherry Tree Farm, Tower Road, Coleshill, Amersham, Buckinghamshire, HP7 0LE.**
Contacts: **PHONE (01494) 722239 FAX (01494) 432992 MOBILES (07836) 219268 (07836) 219268**

1 **ADALIE**, 11, b m Absalom—Allied Newcastle **Mr J. Joseph**
2 **AMICELLI (GER)**, 6, b g Goofalik (USA)—Arratonia (GER) **Mr J. Joseph**
3 **COLESHILL LAD**, 5, br g Wizard King—Hallowed Ground (IRE) **Mr J. Joseph**
4 **DUNKERRON**, 8, b g Pursuit of Love—Top Berry **Mr J. Joseph**
5 **ELJUTAN (IRE)**, 7, b g Namaqualand (USA)—Camarat **Mr J. Joseph**
6 **KALAMBARI (IRE)**, 6, b g Kahyasi—Kalamba (IRE) **Mr J. Joseph**
7 **RAGDALE HALL (USA)**, 8, b g Bien Bien (USA)—Gift of Dance (USA) **Mr J. Joseph**
8 **SHAMSAN (IRE)**, 8, ch g Night Shift (USA)—Awayil (USA) **Mr J. Joseph**
9 **TEMPER LAD (USA)**, 10, b g Riverman (USA)—Dokki (USA) **Mr J. Joseph**

Assistant Trainer: Miss T Crossley

---

331 **MR A. G. JUCKES, Abberley**
Postal: **Cherry Ash, Worsley Farm, Abberley, Worcester.**
Contacts: **PHONE (01299) 896471/896522 MOBILE 07970 141246**

1 **ASADOR (FR)**, 9, ch g Kadounor (FR)—Apos (FR) **Mr A. G. Juckes**
2 **DHAUDELOUP (FR)**, 10, ch g Mister Sicy (FR)—Debolouve (FR) **Mr A. G. Juckes**
3 **DRAMATIC QUEST**, 8, b g Zafonic (USA)—Ultra Finesse (USA) **C. Rosbottom**
4 **ELSINORA**, 4, b f Great Dane (IRE)—Deanta In Eirinn **R. T. Juckes**
5 **HOLLY WALK**, 4, ch f Dr Fong (USA)—Holly Blue **Mr A. G. Juckes**
6 **I TINA**, 9, b m Lycius (USA)—Tintomara (IRE) **Whistlejacket Partnership**
7 **KEY OF GOLD (IRE)**, 4, b g Key of Luck (USA)—Damaslin **Whispering Winds**
8 **LORD MELBOURNE (IRE)**, 6, b g Lycius (USA)—Adana (IRE) **Whispering Winds**
9 **MANTLES PRINCE**, 11, ch g Emarati (USA)—Miami Mouse **Emlyn Hughes' Cleobury Golfers**
10 **MOON SHOT**, 9, gr g Pistolet Bleu (IRE)—La Luna (USA) **Whistlejacket Partnership**
11 **PRINCE NASSEEM (GER)**, 8, b h Neshad (USA)—Penola (GER) **Whispering Winds**
12 **QUEEN EXCALIBUR**, 6, ch m Sabrehill (USA)—Blue Room **R. T. Juckes**
13 **RED GALAXY (IRE)**, 5, b m Tagula (IRE)—Dancing Season **Mr A. G. Juckes**
14 **WINGED LADY (GER)**, 6, b m Winged Love (IRE)—Wonderful Lady (GER) **Whistlejacket Partnership**
15 **YOUNG OWEN**, 7, b g Balnibarbi—Polly Potter **D. Skinner**

Other Owners: N. I. P. Brown, Mrs E. J. Duggan, Exors of the Late Emlyn Hughes, Dr D. R. S. Woodhouse, J. C. S. Woodhouse.

Assistant Trainer: N R Juckes

Jockey (flat): D. Sweeney. **Jockey (NH):** O. McPhail, J. Mogford. **Apprentice:** G. Bartley.

---

332 **MR D. P. KEANE, Limpley Stoke**
Postal: **Conkwell Grange Stud, Limpley Stoke, Bath, Avon, BA2 7FD.**
Contacts: **PHONE (01225) 722806 MOBILE (07764) 200012**
E-MAIL conkwell@aol.com

1 5, B g Humbel (USA)—Adelinas Leader (IRE) **Avon Thoroughbreds Ltd**
2 **ALL IN THE STARS (IRE)**, 7, ch g Fourstars Allstar (USA)—Luton Flyer **Mrs H. R. Cross**
3 **BARTON BARON (IRE)**, 7, b g Phardante (FR)—Boolavogue (IRE) **Exors of the Late S. W. Clarke**

MR D. P. KEANE—continued

4 BARTON FLOWER, 4, br f Danzero (AUS)—Iota **Exors of the Late S. W. Clarke**
5 BARTON GATE, 7, b g Rock Hopper—Ruth's River **Exors of the Late S. W. Clarke**
6 BARTON HILL, 8, b g Nicholas Bill—Home From The Hill (IRE) **Exors of the Late S. W. Clarke**
7 BARTON MAY, 6, ch m Midnight Legend—Yamrah **Exors of the Late S. W. Clarke**
8 BARTON NIC, 12, b g Nicholas Bill—Dutch Majesty **Proverbial Optimists**
9 BARTON PARK, 5, b g Most Welcome—William's Bird (USA) **Exors of the Late S. W. Clarke**
10 BARTON STAR, 4, b f Midnight Legend—Home From The Hill (IRE) **Lady H. J. Clarke**
11 BATHWICK ANNIE, 9, ch m Sula Bula—Lily Mab (FR) **H. M. W. Clifford**
12 4, B g Mister Lord (USA)—Belmount Star (IRE) **Mrs S. Clifford**
13 BILL OWEN, 9, ch g Nicholas Bill—Pollys Owen **Tim/Mary Barton & Wadswickcountrystore**
14 5, B m Hubbly Bubbly (USA)—Coolteen Lass (IRE) **Avon Thoroughbreds Ltd**
15 DANCE WITH WOLVES (IRE), 5, ch g Tel Quel (FR)—La Florian (FR) **Lady H. J. Clarke**
16 ESPLENDIDOS (IRE), 6, b m Beneficial—Index Lady **Proverbial Optimists**
17 5, Ch m Anshan—Glacial Run (IRE) **Avon Thoroughbreds Ltd**
18 GREY SHARK (IRE), 6, gr g Roselier (FR)—Sharkezan (IRE) **R. M. Fear**
19 GUN'N ROSES II (FR), 11, gr g Royal Charter (FR)—Offenbach II (FR) **Lady H. J. Clarke**
20 5, B g Midnight Legend—Home From The Hill (IRE) **Lady H. J. Clarke**
21 ISLAND OF MEMORIES (IRE), 5, ch m Beneficial—Coronea Sea Queen (IRE) **Avon Thoroughbreds Ltd**
22 JOSEPH BEUYS (IRE), 6, ch g Flemensfirth (USA)—Final Countdown **Avon Thoroughbreds Ltd**
23 LATZOD'ALM (FR), 6, b g Passing Sale (FR)—Enea d'alm (FR) **R. D. J. Swinburne**
24 LIZZIE BATHWICK (IRE), 6, b m Glacial Storm (USA)—Protrial **H. M. W. Clifford**
25 MAGALINA (IRE), 6, br m Norwich—Pike Review **Dajam & Damian Burbidge**
26 MAORI LEGEND, 4, b f Midnight Legend—Hinemoa (USA) **Mrs H. R. Cross**
27 OYSTERHAVEN (IRE), 5, b g Mister Lord (USA)—Haven's Glory (IRE) **Lady H. J. Clarke**
28 4, B f Midnight Legend—Panda Shandy **R. M. Fear**
29 5, B m Oscar (IRE)—Protrial **Mrs S. Clifford**
30 PUFF AT MIDNIGHT, 5, b m Midnight Legend—Sulapuff **Dajam Ltd**
31 ROOFING SPIRIT (IRE), 7, b g Beneficial—Vulcash (IRE) **F. J. Matthews**
32 5, Ch g Flemensfirth (USA)—Sandy Ash (IRE) **Avon Thoroughbreds Ltd**
33 SEMI PRECIOUS (IRE), 7, ch g Semillon—Precious Petra **R. D. Stainer**
34 5, B g Fourstars Allstar—Solar Jet **Mr C. Pugsley**
35 5, B g Flemensfirth (USA)—Stillbyherself (IRE) **Paul Keane**
36 4, Ch c Midnight Legend—Sulapuff **Dajam Ltd**
37 WIZARD OF THE WEST, 5, b g Wizard King—Rose Burton **N. E. Webb**

THREE-YEAR-OLDS

38 NAPAPIJRI (FR), gr f Highest Honor (FR)—Les Marettes (FR) **The George Hotel Longbridge Deverill**

Other Owners: P. Barratt, I. Barton.

---

333 ### MR T. KEDDY, Newmarket
Postal: Heyward Place, Hamilton Road, Newmarket, Suffolk, CB8 7JQ.
Contacts: PHONE (01638) 561498 FAX (01638) 561498 MOBILE (07710) 450982
E-MAIL tkracing@aol.com

1 ABBEYGATE, 4, b g Unfuwain (USA)—Ayunli **Mrs H. Keddy**
2 FIDDLERS FORD (IRE), 4, b g Sadler's Wells (USA)—Old Domesday Book **J. H. Fielding**
3 HEYWARD PLACE, 5, b m Mind Games—Ginny Binny **Abbeygate Estates Limited**
4 HOH BLEU DEE, 4, b g Desert Style (IRE)—Ermine (IRE) **The T K Racing Partnership**
5 LITTLE FLUTE, 4, b c Piccolo—Nordic Victory (USA) **Mrs H. Keddy**
6 MISTER CHALK, 4, gr c Silver Patriarch (IRE)—B B Glen **OK Partnership**
7 MUTASSEM (FR), 4, b c Fasliyev (USA)—Fee Eria (FR) **Mr J. Ferguson**
8 ODDLYDODD (IRE), 9, b g Tremblant—Poor Times (IRE) **Mrs H. Keddy**
9 PETERS PLOY, 5, ch g Deploy—Alpi Dora **OK Partnership**
10 SILVALINE, 6, gr g Linamix (FR)—Upend **A. J. Duffield**
11 TAJAR (USA), 13, b g Slew O' Gold (USA)—Mashaarif (USA) **Mrs H. Keddy**
12 URSA MAJOR, 11, b g Warning—Double Entendre **NewmarketConnections.com**

THREE-YEAR-OLDS

13 ATHENS (IRE), b c Saddlers' Hall (IRE)—Athene (IRE) **A. J. Duffield**
14 BLACK WADI (IRE), br f Desert King (IRE)—Tamelia (USA)
15 CROSS MY MIND, b g Cape Cross (IRE)—Dynamic Dream (USA) **Dynamic Duo**

MR T. KEDDY—continued

16 **GINA TRIBBIANI,** br f Diktat—Black Fighter (USA) **newmarketconnections.com**
17 B f Sri Pekan (USA)—Malwiya (USA) **newmarketconnections.com**
18 **WIZ IN,** gr g Wizard King—Great Intent **Team Supreme**

TWO-YEAR-OLDS

19 **SUPREME KISS,** b f 31/1 Barathea Guest—Kiss Me Again (IRE) (Cyrano de Bergerac) (7500) **Team Supreme**

Other Owners: Eclipse Management (Newmarket) Ltd, J. Horgan, P. Karanjia, P. W. Newman, J. R. O'Leary, Mrs S. F. O'Leary, Mr J. Stevens.

Assistant Trainer: Hayley Keddy

Apprentice: Colin Haddon. **Amateur:** Miss Lynsey Hanna.

---

334 MR S. L. KEIGHTLEY, Melton Mowbray
Postal: **Racecourse Farm Stables, Bescaby Lane, Waltham on the Wolds, Melton Mowbray, Leicestershire, LE14 4AB.**
Contacts: **OFFICE (01664) 464251 FAX (01664) 464564 MOBILE (07989) 322654**

1 **ALASTAIR SMELLIE,** 9, ch g Sabrehill (USA)—Reel Foyle (USA) **Rothmere Racing Limited**
2 **BOISDALE (IRE),** 3, b g Common Grounds—Alstomeria **Ms S. Gray & Mr M. F. Galvin**
3 **IT MUST BE SPEECH,** 4, b g Advise (FR)—Maiden Speech **The Speech Partnership**
4 **OCTAGONAL (NZ),** 13, br h Zabeel (NZ)—Eight Carat **S. L. Keightley**
5 **PENNEECK,** 5, ch g Pennekamp (USA)—Orange Hill **Mrs A. W. Turner**

THREE-YEAR-OLDS

6 **IT'S PEGGY SPEECH,** b f Bishop of Cashel—Marsara **The Speech Partnership**
7 **JOYEAUX,** b f Mark of Esteem (IRE)—Divine Secret **Mrs C. C. Regalado-Gonzalez**
8 **MAKE IT HAPPEN NOW,** b br f Octagonal (NZ)—Whittle Woods Girl
9 **RED HUSSAR,** ch g Muhtarram (USA)—Miss Bussell **Rothmere Racing Limited**
10 **SAND IRON (IRE),** b f Desert Style (IRE)—Mettlesome **Rothmere Racing Limited**

TWO-YEAR-OLDS

11 B c 25/2 Benny The Dip (USA)—Polish Belle (Polish Precedent (USA)) **Mrs C. C. Regalado-Gonzalez**

Other Owners: Miss C. A. Salmon, Miss K. C. Salmon.

Jockey (flat): E. Ahern, R. Havlin, R. Fitzpatrick, A. Culhane. **Jockey (NH):** R. Garrity. **Amateur:** Miss A. L. Turner.

---

335 MR C. N. KELLETT, Burton-on-Trent
Postal: **Stoneyford Croft, Barton under Needwood, Burton-on-Trent, Staffordshire, DE13 8BW.**
Contacts: **PHONE/FAX (01283) 575646 MOBILE (07966) 097989**

1 **ASTORMYDAYISCOMING,** 7, b g Alhaatmi—Valentine Song **Out Of The Frying Pan Partnership**
2 **COUNTRYWIDE STAR (IRE),** 7, ch g Common Grounds—Silver Slipper **J. E. Titley**
3 **DOES IT MATTER,** 8, b g Carlingford Castle—Flopsy Mopsy
4 **FAIRMORNING (IRE),** 6, b g Ridgewood Ben—The Bratpack (IRE) **T. Morning**
5 **FAITES VOS JEUX,** 4, b f Foxhound (USA)—Desert Bloom (FR) **Mr S. Kitching & Mrs K. Taylor**
6 **GREEN GINGER,** 9, ch g Ardkinglass—Bella Maggio **T. Farrow**
7 **IROQUOIS CHIEF (USA),** 6, b g Known Fact (USA)—Celtic Shade **R. & S. Smith**
8 **LORD OF THE FENS,** 5, b g Danzig Connection (USA)—Zizi (IRE) **D. H. & Mrs R. E. Muir**
9 **MOUSEMAN,** 4, b g Young Ern—Scottish Royal (IRE) **J. E. Titley**
10 **NUTLEY QUEEN (IRE),** 6, b m Eagle Eyed (USA)—Secret Hideaway (USA) **A. M. Egan**
11 **PAULS PLAIN,** 4, b g Young Buster (IRE)—On The Wagon **Dachel Stud**
12 **PERUVIAN PRINCESS,** 6, gr m Missed Flight—Misty View **Mrs Maria Del Rosario Stimpson**
13 **RIVER OF FIRE,** 7, ch g Dilum (USA)—Bracey Brook **J. E. Titley**
14 **ROOKERY LAD,** 7, b g Makbul—Wayzgoose (USA) **Mr S. Kitching & Mrs K. Taylor**
15 **RUDY'S PRIDE (IRE),** 4, ch g Anshan—Lisa's Pride **D. H. Muir**
16 **SHANNKARA'S QUEST (USA),** 4, b br c Coronado's Quest (USA)—Shannkara (IRE) **Quest Racing**
17 **STILETTO LADY (IRE),** 4, b f Daggers Drawn (USA)—Nordic Pride **The JJP Partnership**

MR C. N. KELLETT—continued

18 **STRAWMAN**, 8, b g Ela-Mana-Mou—Oatfield **J. E. Titley**
19 **SUPER FELLOW (IRE)**, 11, b g Shy Groom (USA)—Killough **A. M. Egan**
20 **UNDERTHEINFLUENCE (IRE)**, 6, b m Great Commotion (USA)—Katie Craig (IRE) **A. M. Egan**

THREE-YEAR-OLDS

21 **POLESWORTH**, b f Wizard King—Nicholas Mistress **A. Fairfield**

Other Owners: Mr C. Bartley, R. Campbell, Mrs J. M. Campbell, P. A. Creighton, Mr M. A. Ewen, Miss S. J. Ewen, Mr M. W. Ewen, G. Pickering, D. J. Ward.

Assistant Trainer: L Muller

---

336 | **MISS G. M. KELLEWAY, Newmarket**
Postal: **House 1, Charnwood Stables, Hamilton Road, Newmarket, Suffolk, CB8 7JQ.**
Contacts: **PHONE (01638) 663187 FAX (01638) 662003 MOBILE (07974) 948768**
E-MAIL gay@gaykelleway.com WEBSITE www.gaykelleway.co.uk

1 **BALLYGRIFFIN KID**, 5, gr g Komaite (USA)—Ballygriffin Belle **T. C. Breen**
2 **BIENHEUREUX**, 4, b g Bien Bien (USA)—Rochea **Countrywide Classics Ltd**
3 **BROUGHTON KNOWS**, 8, b g Most Welcome—Broughtons Pet (IRE) **A. J. Clarke**
4 **CZARINA WALTZ**, 6, b m Emperor Jones (USA)—Ballerina Bay **The Leading Ladies**
5 **EIGHT ELLINGTON (IRE)**, 4, b g Ali-Royal (IRE)—Where's Charlotte **R. Grenville-Webb**
6 **FIVEOCLOCK EXPRESS (IRE)**, 5, gr g Woodborough (USA)—Brooks Masquerade **The Gay Kelleway Syndicate**
7 **FOREST KNIGHT (IRE)**, 4, b c Charnwood Forest (IRE)—Kristabelle (IRE) **N. A. Crahan**
8 **FORTHRIGHT**, 4, b g Cadeaux Genereux—Forthwith **Mrs B. Quinn**
9 **GERONIMO**, 8, b g Efisio—Apache Squaw **Mr A. P. Griffin**
10 **GLORY QUEST (USA)**, 8, b g Quest For Fame—Sonseri **WRB Racing 40 (wrbracing.com)**
11 **IAMBACK**, 5, b m Perugino (USA)—Smouldering (IRE) **Mr M D Banks**
12 **INTIMATE FRIEND (USA)**, 4, b f Expelled (USA)—Intimate (USA) **Black Horse Racing Club**
13 **LABRETT**, 8, b g Tragic Role (USA)—Play The Game **Mr A. P. Griffin**
14 **LAKE VERDI (IRE)**, 6, ch g Lake Coniston (IRE)—Shore Lark (USA) **Miss G. M. Kelleway**
15 **LYGETON LAD**, 7, b g Shaamit (IRE)—Smartie Lee **J McGonagle, B J McGonagle & E Oertel**
16 **MILLENIO (GER)**, 5, ch g Big Shuffle (USA)—Molto In Forma (GER) **Mr D. S. Hickling**
17 **MUGEBA**, 4, b f Primo Dominie—Ella Lamees **M. M. Foulger**
18 **MULTAHAB**, 6, b br g Zafonic (USA)—Alumisiyah (USA) **Mr P J Burke and Dave Anderson**
19 **PRINCESS BANKES**, 4, b f Vettori (IRE)—Lady Bankes (IRE) **T. Lightbowne**
20 **ROMANY NIGHTS (IRE)**, 5, b g Night Shift (USA)—Gipsy Moth **John Farley,Brian Eastwick,Jean-Paul Lim**
21 **SHIELALIGH**, 4, ch f Aragon—Sheesha (USA) **N. R. Shields**
22 **TE QUIERO**, 7, gr g Bering—Ma Lumiere (FR) **Mr A. P. Griffin**
23 **TRICKSTEP**, 4, b g Imperial Ballet (IRE)—Trick of Ace (USA) **Market Avenue Racing Club Ltd**
24 **VAMOSE (IRE)**, 4, ro g Victory Note (USA)—Narrow Band (IRE) **D. Downes R. Levitt M. Parsons J. Hanna**
25 **VITTORIOSO (IRE)**, 4, b g Victory Note (USA)—Miss Anita (IRE) **Mrs R. J. Simms**
26 **VORTEX**, 6, b g Danehill (USA)—Roupala (USA) **Coriolis Partnership**

THREE-YEAR-OLDS

27 **ATRIFFIC STORY**, ch g Atraf—Composition **WRB Racing 54 (wrbracing.com)**
28 **JE SUIS BELLE**, ch f Efisio—Blossom **JAYESSBEE Partnership**
29 **MY PLACE OR YOURS**, gr f Tagula (IRE)—Absalla (IRE) **J. Billson**
30 **SEATTLE ROBBER**, b g Robellino (USA)—Seattle Ribbon (USA) **J. Billson**
31 **VENEER (IRE)**, b g Woodborough (USA)—Sweet Lass **Mr J. Farley**
32 **WANDERING ACT (IRE)**, b g Brave Act—Cwm Deri (IRE) **Mrs B. Quinn**
33 **WASALAT (USA)**, b f Bahri (USA)—Saabga (USA) **Miss D. Downes**

Other Owners: A. W. A. Bates, Miss P. F. Crook, T. A. Edwards, P. H. Ewing, Mr D. Howe, Mrs J. V. Kier, Mr A. Lisney, T. W. Mortimer, A. J. Sullivan, Wetherby Racing Bureau Ltd, Mrs C. A. Whitwood, C. J. Wilkinson, Mrs A. P. Wilkinson.

Assistant Trainer: Michelle Button

Apprentice: Adam Kirby. **Amateur:** Miss Anna Wallace.

337 MR G. P. KELLY, Sheriff Hutton
Postal: **3 Church End Cottages, Sheriff Hutton, North Yorkshire, YO60 6SY.**
Contacts: **HOME (01347) 878770/878994 MOBILE (07866) 285187**

1 DERRY ANN, 9, b m Derrylin—Ancat Girl **C. I. Ratcliffe**
2 HOWSHAM LAD, 6, b g Perpendicular—Sherwood Hope **S. Fox**
3 MISS PRIM, 4, ch f Case Law—Calamanco
4 PARISI PRINCESS, 4, ch f Shaddad (USA)—Crambella (IRE)
5 WAHCHI (IRE), 6, ch g Nashwan (USA)—Nafhaat (USA) **Mr G. P. Kelly**

THREE-YEAR-OLDS
6 Ch c Doubletour (USA)—Morcat **C. M. Ratcliffe**

TWO-YEAR-OLDS
7 SHERIFF STAR, b f 20/2 Killer Instinct—Westcourt Ruby (Petong) **A. C. Barrett**

Other Owners: Mrs S. M. Oakes.

Assistant Trainer: Ian Ratcliffe

Jockey (flat): Dale Gibson, T. Lucas. **Conditional:** G. Carenza. **Apprentice:** Paul Mulrennan. **Amateur:** Miss S. Brotherton, Mr T. Greenall, Mr C. Mulhall, Mr M. Walford.

338 MR P. KELSALL, Risbury
Postal: **Gallop View House, Risbury, Herefordshire, HR6 0NQ.**
Contacts: **PHONE (01568) 760396 FAX (01568) 760673 MOBILE (07802) 160584**

1 ALL SONSILVER (FR), 8, b g Son of Silver—All Licette (FR) **Mr P. Kelsall**
2 FASHION SHOOT, 4, b f Double Trigger (IRE)—Paris Fashion (FR) **Mr P. Kelsall**
3 RUFIUS (IRE), 12, b g Celio Rufo—In View Lass **Mr P. Kelsall**
4 SHAH (IRE), 12, b g King Persian—Gay And Sharp **Mr P. Kelsall**
5 TUMBLEWEED GLEN (IRE), 9, ch g Mukaddamah (USA)—Mistic Glen (IRE) **Mr P. Kelsall**

THREE-YEAR-OLDS
6 B g Double Trigger (IRE)—Paris Fashion (FR) **Mr P. Kelsall**

Assistant Trainer: Miss J Kelsall

Jockey (NH): C. Llewelyn.

339 MRS C. J. KERR, Aberfeldy
Postal: **Balnacraig Farm, Fortingall, Aberfeldy, Perthshire, PH15 2LJ.**
Contacts: **PHONE (01887) 830354 MOBILE (07768) 682841**

1 ATHOLLBROSE (USA), 4, b g Mister Baileys—Knightly Cut Up (USA) **Mrs C. J. Kerr**
2 FISHER STREET, 10, gr g Tigani—Pricket Walk **Mrs C. J. Kerr**
3 MACKENZIE (IRE), 9, b g Mandalus—Crinkle Lady **Mrs C. J. Kerr**
4 MCCRINKLE (IRE), 8, br g Mandalus—Crinkle Lady **Mrs C. J. Kerr**
5 MISS ELLIE, 9, b m Elmaamul (USA)—Jussoli **Mrs C. J. Kerr**
6 PHARAGON (IRE), 7, b g Phardante (FR)—Hogan (IRE) **Mrs C. J. Kerr**

340 MRS A. L. M. KING, Stratford-upon-Avon
Postal: **Ridgeway House, Moor Farm, Wilmcote, Stratford-upon-Avon, Warwickshire, CV37 9XG.**
Contacts: **HOME (01789) 298346 OFFICE (01789) 205087 FAX (01789) 263260**
E-MAIL anabelking.racing@virgin.net

1 ARFINNIT (IRE), 4, b g College Chapel—Tidal Reach (USA) **All The Kings Horses**
2 ASTRAC (IRE), 14, b g Nordico (USA)—Shirleen **C. J. Titcomb**
3 CHASING THE DREAM (IRE), 4, b f Desert Sun—Dream of Jenny **Mrs L. R. Lovell**
4 CONVICTION, 4, b g Machiavellian (USA)—Beldarian (IRE) **H. A. Murphy**
5 GREAT VIEW (IRE), 6, b g Great Commotion (USA)—Tara View (IRE) **All The Kings Horses**
6 IMPERIAL ROCKET (USA), 8, b br g Northern Flagship (USA)—

Starsawhirl (USA) **Lynda Lovell and Aiden Murphy**

MRS A. L. M. KING—continued

7 **JACARANDA (IRE),** 5, ch g Bahhare (USA)—Near Miracle **Touchwood Racing**
8 **JEWEL OF INDIA,** 6, ch g Bijou d'inde—Low Hill **Touchwood Racing**
9 **OPEN ARMS,** 9, ch g Most Welcome—Amber Fizz (USA) **Touchwood Racing**
10 **RABBIT,** 4, b f Muhtarram (USA)—Ninia (USA)
11 **SUPERCLEAN,** 5, ch m Environment Friend—Star Mover **Ms D. Holloway**
12 **TSHUKUDU,** 4, ch f Fleetwood (IRE)—Pab's Choice **C. Papaioannou**

THREE-YEAR-OLDS

13 **GOLDEN APPLAUSE (FR),** b f Royal Applause—Golden Circle (USA) **Mrs L. H. Field**
14 **ROSIE MUIR,** br f Mind Games—Step On Degas **All The Kings Horses**
15 **TIEGS (IRE),** ch f Desert Prince (IRE)—Helianthus **Mrs L. H. Field**

TWO-YEAR-OLDS

16 **HAHNS PEAK,** b g 31/3 Mujahid (USA)—Fille Genereux (Cadeaux Genereux) (23000) **Mrs L. H. Field**
17 Ch f 16/3 Foxhound (USA)—Step On Degas (Superpower) (5000) **Mrs P. J. Muir**
18 **ZIRKEL (IRE),** br c 6/4 Highest Honor (FR)—Mythical Creek (USA) (Pleasant Tap (USA)) (9000) **Mrs L. H. Field**

Other Owners: R. S. Field, Mrs A. L. M. King, Mrs G. Titcomb, P. E. Whiting.

---

341   **MR ALAN KING, Barbury Castle**
Postal: **Barbury Castle Stables, Wroughton, Wiltshire, SN4 0QZ.**
Contacts: **PHONE (01793) 815009 FAX (01793) 845080 MOBILE (07973) 461233**
E-MAIL alanking.racing@virgin.net WEBSITE www.alankingracing.co.uk

1 **ADJAMI (IRE),** 4, b g Entrepreneur—Adjriyna **Let's Live Racing**
2 **AFAIR PROMISE (NZ),** 5, br g Vain Promise (AUS)—Diamond Fair (NZ) **Sir Robert Ogden C.B.E., LLD**
3 **ALF LAUREN,** 7, b g Alflora (IRE)—Gokatiego **Helen Loggin & Richard Preston**
4 **ALFASONIC,** 5, b g Alflora (IRE)—Lady Solstice **Mrs S. Warren**
5 **ALLEGED SLAVE (IRE),** 10, ch g Husyan (USA)—Lek Dawn **Mrs E. A. Prowting**
6 **ANSHABIL (IRE),** 6, br g Anshan—Billeragh Thyne (IRE) **J. Wright**
7 **ATAHUELPA,** 5, b g Hernando—Certain Story **Let's Live Racing**
8 **ATTITUDE,** 4, ch f Riverwise (USA)—Came Cottage **Mrs M. C. Sweeney**
9 **BALLISTIGO (IRE),** 6, br g Executive Perk—Herballistic **Mrs S. B. Lockhart**
10 **BARBURY HILL,** 9, b g Rashar (USA)—Supreme Rehearsal (USA) **Mrs D. Shutes**
11 **BELL LANE LAD (IRE),** 8, b g Wakashan—Busti Lass (IRE) **J. Mcgrath**
12 **BEN'S TURN (IRE),** 4, b f Saddlers' Hall (IRE)—Christines Gale (IRE) **C. B. Brookes**
13 **BORN LEADER (IRE),** 7, b g Supreme Leader—Real Lace **Nigel Bunter & Jules Sigler**
14 **BOURBON MANHATTAN,** 7, b g Alflora (IRE)—Vanina II (FR) **A Longman, T. Warner, R Devereux & Ptnrs**
15 **CALCOT FLYER,** 4, b g Anshan—Lady Catcher **Miss J. M. Bodycote**
16 **CALCOT LASS,** 4, b f Shambo—Lady Catcher **Miss J. M. Bodycote**
17 **CHICAGO BULLS (IRE),** 7, b g Darshaan—Celestial Melody (USA) **Mrs A. L. Davies**
18 **CRACKLEANDO,** 4, ch g Forzando—Crackling **P. Webb**
19 **CRYSTAL D'AINAY (FR),** 6, b g Saint Preuil (FR)—Guendale (FR) **Mr Tony Fisher & Mrs Jeni Fisher**
20 **D'ARGENT (IRE),** 8, gr g Roselier (FR)—Money Galore (IRE) **N. S. G. Bunter**
21 **DARYAL (IRE),** 4, b c Night Shift (USA)—Darata (IRE) **Let's Live Racing**
22 **DIAMOND MERCHANT,** 6, ch g Vettori (IRE)—Tosca **Mr T. J. & Mrs H. Parrott**
23 **DOCE VIDA (IRE),** 7, b m Montelimar (USA)—Miss The Post **Mrs C. Skan**
24 **EPITRE (FR),** 8, b g Common Grounds—Epistolienne **Let's Live Racing**
25 **FIRST DE LA BRUNIE (FR),** 4, ch g Mansonnien (FR)—Samisti (BEL) **Mr and Mrs F. C. Welch**
26 **FIVE COLOURS (IRE),** 5, b br g Lord Americo—Thousand Springs (IRE) **Knightsbridge Bc & Mr J. Sigler**
27 **FLEETWOOD FOREST,** 5, b g Fleetwood (IRE)—Louise Moillon **Mr Tony Fisher & Mrs Jeni Fisher**
28 **FORK LIGHTNING (IRE),** 9, gr g Roselier (FR)—Park Breeze (IRE) **Mr and Mrs F. C. Welch**
29 **FOUR FOR A LAUGH (IRE),** 6, b g Fourstars Allstar (USA)—She's No Laugh Ben (USA) **J. Wright**
30 **GLIMMER OF LIGHT (IRE),** 5, b g Marju (IRE)—Church Light **The Norf 'N' Sarf Partnership**
31 **GUTHRIE (IRE),** 7, ch g Mister Lord (USA)—Nephin Far (IRE) **Mrs J. K. Powell**
32 **HALCON GENELARDAIS (FR),** 5, ch g Halcon—Francetphile (FR) **Ian Payne & Kim Franklin**
33 **HALF AN HOUR,** 8, b g Alflora (IRE)—Country Mistress **C. W. Lane**
34 **HALLAND,** 7, ch g Halling (USA)—Northshiel **The Headquarters Partnership Ltd**
35 **HANDY MONEY,** 8, b g Imperial Frontier (USA)—Cryptic Gold **W. G. Dixon**
36 **HEATHERLEA LAIRD (NZ),** 5, ch g His Royal Highness (NZ)—Misty Gleam (NZ) **Sir Robert Ogden C.B.E., LLD**
37 **HIGH ALTITUDE (IRE),** 4, b g Alhaarth (IRE)—Delphini **N. S. G. Bunter**
38 **HOME JAMES (IRE),** 8, b g Commanche Run—Take Me Home **Mrs Stewart Catherwood**
39 **HOWLE HILL (IRE),** 5, b g Ali-Royal (IRE)—

Grandeur And Grace (USA) **Mrs J.Brown,R.Benton,R.Devereux,R.Lucas**

MR ALAN KING—continued

40 **IL DUCE (IRE)**, 5, br g Anshan—Glory-Glory (IRE) **Mrs E. A. Prowting**
41 **INCURSION**, 4, b g Inchinor—Morgannwg (IRE) **N. S. G. Bunter**
42 **INNOCENT REBEL (USA)**, 4, ch g Swain—Cadeaux d'amie (USA) **P. A. Deal & J. S. Dale**
43 **ITSA LEGEND**, 6, b g Midnight Legend—Onawing Andaprayer **The We're A Legend Partnership**
44 **JACKSON (FR)**, 8, b g Passing Sale (FR)—Tynia (FR) **C. B. Brookes**
45 **JAHASH**, 7, ch g Hernando—Jalsun **J. Hawkins**
46 **JET MAGIC (FR)**, 5, b g Semillon—Kerry Minstrel **Mr T. J. & Mrs H. Parrott**
47 **JUST KATE**, 6, b m Bob's Return (IRE)—M I Babe **C. B. Brookes**
48 **KADOUNT (FR)**, 7, b g Our Account (USA)—Une de Lann (FR) **Elite Racing Club**
49 **KANDJAR D'ALLIER (FR)**, 7, gr g Royal Charter (FR)—Miss Akarad (FR) **Let's Live Racing**
50 **KEN'TUCKY (FR)**, 7, b g Video Rock (FR)—La Salamandre (FR) **Sir Robert Ogden C.B.E., LLD**
51 **KIMONO ROYAL (FR)**, 7, b br g Garde Royale—Alizane (FR) **N. S. G. Bunter**
52 **KING LUSKIN (NZ)**, 6, ch g Kingsttenham (USA)—Luskin Lass (NZ) **Sir Robert Ogden C.B.E., LLD**
53 **KNIGHTON LAD (IRE)**, 5, b g Supreme Leader—Tarqueen (IRE) **Mrs M. M. Stobart**
54 **KNIGHTSBRIDGE TICH**, 4, b g Sovereign Water (FR)—

Shahdjat (IRE) **Knightsbridge Business Centre (Glos) Ltd**

55 **KOBAI (IRE)**, 6, b g Florida Son—Helens Birthday **Mrs M. C. Sweeney**
56 **LALAGUNE (FR)**, 6, b m Kadalko—Donatella II (FR) **J. A. H. West**
57 **LAMP'S RETURN**, 6, ch m Bob's Return (IRE)—Lampstone **Mr and Mrs F. C. Welch**
58 **LANTAUR LAD (IRE)**, 11, b g Brush Aside (USA)—Gleann Oge **Mrs D. Shutes**
59 **LE GALACTICO (FR)**, 4, br g Sleeping Car (FR)—Guendale (FR) **Mrs M. C. Sweeney**
60 **LORDS BEST (IRE)**, 9, b g Mister Lord—Ballinlonig Star **Jerry Wright, Peter Smith & Jules Sigler**
61 **MANSION SPECIAL (FR)**, 5, b g Mansonnien (FR)—Edition Speciale (FR) **J. T. Warner**
62 **MIKADO MELODY (IRE)**, 6, b g Supreme Leader—Double Symphony (IRE) **Mrs M. C. Sweeney**
63 **MISTRESS BANJO**, 5, b m Start Fast (FR)—Temperance (FR) **The Banjo Players**
64 **MUGHAS (IRE)**, 6, b g Sadler's Wells (USA)—Quest of Passion (FR) **B. Winfield, C. Fenton & A. Longman**
65 **MY WAY DE SOLZEN (FR)**, 5, b g Assessor (FR)—

Agathe de Solzen (FR) **B Winfield, A Longman, J Wright & C Fenton**

66 **NATTERJACK (IRE)**, 7, gr g Roselier (FR)—Hansel's Lady (IRE) **Elite Racing Club**
67 **NORTH LODGE (GER)**, 5, b g Grand Lodge (USA)—Nona (GER) **PRD Holdings Limited**
68 **NYRCHE (FR)**, 5, b g Medaaly—Thoiry (USA) **Mr Tony Fisher & Mrs Jeni Fisher**
69 **PANGBOURNE (FR)**, 4, b g Double Bed (FR)—Valgrija (FR) **P. E. Atkinson**
70 **PEARLY STAR**, 4, b g Bob's Return (IRE)—Pearly-B (IRE) **Let's Live Racing**
71 **PEDDARS WAY**, 6, b g Nomadic Way (USA)—Deep Selection (IRE) **Mrs Valerie Mason**
72 **PEEL ME A GRAPE**, 5, b m Gunner B—Dans Le Vent **Mrs E. A. Prowting**
73 **PENZANCE**, 4, ch g Pennekamp (USA)—Kalinka (IRE) **Elite Racing Club**
74 **PRECIOUS MYSTERY (IRE)**, 5, ch m Titus Livius (FR)—Ascoli **The Dunnkirk Partnership**
75 **PRETTY STAR (GER)**, 5, b h Lando (GER)—Pretty Ballerina **Exterior Profiles Ltd**
76 **RATHCANNON MAN (IRE)**, 5, b g Anshan—Miss Fern **Mrs P. Andrews**
77 **ROWLEY HILL**, 7, b g Karinga Bay—Scarlet Dymond **Mrs J. E. Brown & Mrs S. Faccenda**
78 **RUTLAND (IRE)**, 6, b g Supreme Leader—I Remember It Well (IRE) **Sir Robert Ogden C.B.E., LLD**
79 **SAINT PAR (FR)**, 7, gr g Saint Preuil (FR)—Paris Or (FR) **A. Stennett**
80 **SAMANDARA (FR)**, 5, b m Kris—Samneeza (USA) **Miss J. M. Bodycote**
81 **SAXON MIST**, 6, b g Slip Anchor—Ruby Venture **C. W. Lane**
82 **SEA THE LIGHT**, 5, b g Blue Ocean (USA)—Lamper's Light **Mr and Mrs F. C. Welch**
83 **SEAL HARBOUR (FR)**, 5, b g Vertical Speed (FR)—Maraxalou (FR) **W. A. Harrison-Allan**
84 **SENORITA RUMBALITA**, 4, b f Alflora (IRE)—Lavenham's Last **Let's Get Ready To Rumble Partnership**
85 **SENTO (IRE)**, 7, ch g Persian Bold—Esclava (USA) **Mrs M. C. Sweeney**
86 **SHAADIVA**, 7, b m Shaamit (IRE)—Kristal Diva **Cheltenham Racing Ltd**
87 **SHARAJAN (IRE)**, 5, b g Desert King (IRE)—Balakera (FR) **Mr Tony Fisher & Mrs Jeni Fisher**
88 **SHAREEF (FR)**, 8, b g Port Lyautey (FR)—Saralik **Mr Tony Fisher & Mrs Jeni Fisher**
89 **SILENCIO (IRE)**, 4, b g Sillery (USA)—Flabbergasted (FR) **Let's Live Racing**
90 **SOLAR SON**, 6, gr g Roselier (FR)—Polly Washdish **Mrs Bridget Chesney**
91 **SPECIAL RATE (IRE)**, 8, br g Grand Plaisir (IRE)—

Clerical Artist (IRE) **Mrs J.Brown,P.Bunter,M.Deeley,S.Faccenda**

92 **SUPREME RETURN**, 6, b g Bob's Return (IRE)—Supreme Wonder (IRE) **The Silhouettes**
93 **TELIMAR PRINCE (IRE)**, 9, b g Montelimar—Blakica **Mrs A. M. Brodie**
94 **TRIBAL KING**, 10, b br g Be My Native (USA)—Island Bridge **Mrs P. Andrews**
95 **TROUBLE AT BAY (IRE)**, 5, b g Slip Anchor—Fight Right (FR) **N. S. G. Bunter**
96 **VOY POR USTEDES (FR)**, 4, b g Villez (USA)—Nuit D'ecajeul (FR) **Million in Mind Partnership**
97 **WHISPERING STORM (IRE)**, 7, br g Good Thyne (USA)—Ballybride Gale (IRE) **Mrs A.Shutes, & Mr A.Humbert**
98 **WOOD NORTON (IRE)**, 5, br m Norwich—Money Galore (IRE) **Mickleton Racing Club**

MR ALAN KING—continued

THREE-YEAR-OLDS

99 **COMPTON QUAY**, ch c Compton Place—Roonah Quay (IRE) **The Bawtry Boys**
100 **COPPER BAY (IRE)**, b c Revoque (IRE)—Bahia Laura (FR) **Four Mile Racing**
101 **GITCHE MANITO (IRE)**, b c Namid—Chasing Rainbows **Mrs J. K. Powell**
102 **GRAPHEX**, b br c Inchinor—Allegra **Four Mile Racing**
103 **KNIGHTSBRIDGE HILL (IRE)**, b c Raise A Grand (IRE)—Desert Gem **Knightsbridge Business Centre (Glos) Ltd**
104 **LE CORVEE (IRE)**, b c Rossini (USA)—Elupa (IRE) **D. M. Mason**
105 **MYSTERY LOT (IRE)**, b f Revoque (IRE)—Mystery Bid **Four Mile Racing**
106 **PENNY ISLAND (IRE)**, b c Trans Island—Sparklingsovereign **Ford Associated Racing Team II**
107 **PINE CONE (IRE)**, ch f Dr Fong (USA)—Pine Needle **Ms J. H. Menzies**
108 **PRINCE VECTOR**, b c Vettori (IRE)—The In-Laws (IRE) **Nigel Bunter & Jules Sigler**
109 **RUSSIAN CONSORT (IRE)**, ch c Groom Dancer (USA)—Ukraine Venture **Four Mile Racing**
110 **SECRET AFFAIR**, b c Piccolo—Secret Circle **Four Mile Racing**
111 **SHINY THING (USA)**, br f Lear Fan (USA)—Juliet's Jewel (USA) **Mr H. F. Morris**
112 **SOLARIAS QUEST**, b g Pursuit of Love—Persuasion **A. Longman**

TWO-YEAR-OLDS

113 B c 5/4 Slip Anchor—Bramosia (Forzando) (17437) **N. S. G. Bunter**
114 **BRAVE FIGHT**, b c 31/3 Kalanisi (IRE)—Baalbek (Barathea (IRE)) (48000) **Four Mile Racing**
115 B c 27/4 Imperial Ballet (IRE)—Fallacy (Selkirk (USA)) (17000) **T. J. Parrott**
116 B f 6/5 Revoque (IRE)—Febrile (USA) (Trempolino (USA)) **J. Hawkins**
117 **LEVERA**, b c 7/4 Groom Dancer (USA)—Prancing (Prince Sabo) (28000) **Four Mile Racing**
118 B br c 13/5 Pine Bluff (USA)—One Great Lady (USA) (Fappiano (USA)) **J. Hawkins**
119 **SHIPMASTER**, b c 6/2 Slip Anchor—Cover Look (SAF) (Fort Wood (USA)) (44000) **N. S. G. Bunter**
120 **SHOGUN PRINCE (IRE)**, b c 9/2 Shinko Forest (IRE)—
    Lady of Dreams (IRE) (Prince Rupert (FR)) (31000) **Four Mile Racing**
121 **URBAN TIGER (GER)**, b c 12/1 Marju (IRE)—Ukraine Venture (Slip Anchor) (27000) **Four Mile Racing**
122 **XENIAM (IRE)**, b c 8/2 Rossini (USA)—Rose Tint (IRE) (Salse (USA)) (25000) **D. M. Mason**
123 **ZILCASH**, b g 7/4 Mujahid (USA)—Empty Purse (Pennine Walk) (11000) **Mr Alan King**

Other Owners: F. J. Allen, A. M. Armitage, H. R. F. Arthur, Mr P. J. Barrett, A. R. Bromley, Mrs S. R. Brown, Mrs P. S. Bunter, M. T. Cleary, M. R. Deeley, R. V. Dunnett, J. R. Edwards, Mr D. A. Heffer, A. J. Hill, P. M. Hill, S. J. Hill, D. W. Holpin, Mr R. Holt, V. Kerrigan, I. Kirkham, W. D. C. Minton, David Nicholson, Miss M. Noden, J. O'Grady, Mrs V. J. Powell, G. M. Powell, John P. L. Reynolds, Mr J. P. Smith, G. S. Spurling, Mrs K. J. Tudor, A. J. Viall, D. A. Wallace, Mrs S. H. West, A. P. Wyer.

Assistant Trainer: Noel Williams

Jockey (NH): R. Thornton. **Conditional:** P. Stringer, W. Hutchinson. **Amateur:** Mr G. Tumelty.

342 MR J. S. KING, Swindon

Postal: **Elm Cross House, Broad Hinton, Swindon, Wiltshire, SN4 9PF.**
Contacts: **PHONE** (01793) 731481 **FAX** (01793) 739001 **MOBILE** (07890) 444135
E-MAIL trishking1@hotmail.com

1 **BREAKING BREEZE (IRE)**, 10, b g Mandalus—Knockacool Breeze **V. Askew**
2 **CAPTAIN MACHELL (IRE)**, 7, b br g King's Ride—Flying Silver **R. B. Denny**
3 **FOXTROT YANKEE (IRE)**, 6, b g Lord Americo—Derby Fox (IRE) **Mrs R. M. Hill**
4 **GOODENOUGH MOVER**, 9, ch g Beveled (USA)—Rekindled Flame (IRE) **D. Goodenough Removals & Transport**
5 **LORD NELLSSON**, 9, b g Gunner Lord—Miss Petronella **Dajam Ltd**
6 **ROOD BOY (IRE)**, 4, b c Great Commotion (USA)—Cnocma (IRE) **Dajam Ltd**
7 **SILENT GUNNER**, 7, ch g Gunner B—Quiet Dawn **T. L. Morshead**
8 **TINO (IRE)**, 9, ch g Torus—Delphic Thunder **R. Skillen**
9 **TOOMEBRIDGE (IRE)**, 7, b g Warcraft (USA)—The Foalicule **Miss S. Douglas-Pennant**
10 **TRADINGUP (IRE)**, 6, b g Arctic Lord—Autumn Queen **Miss S. Douglas-Pennant**
11 **TUDOR KING (IRE)**, 11, br g Orchestra—Jane Bond **J. R. Kinloch**

Other Owners: W. H. Booty, M. P. Hill, Mrs P. M. King, J. McCarthy, P. W. Murphy, N. M. S. Rich.

Assistant Trainer: Mrs P M King

343 MR N. B. KING, Newmarket
Postal: **St Gatien Cottage, Vicarage Road, Newmarket, Suffolk, CB8 8HP.**
Contacts: **PHONE/FAX** (01638) 666150 **MOBILE** (07880) 702325
E-MAIL neil@neil-king.co.uk **WEBSITE** www.neil-king.co.uk

1 CHROMBOY (GER), 5, ch g Kornado—Chroma (GER) **St Gatien Racing Club**
2 DELLOVER, 4, br g Overbury (IRE)—Mrs Wumpkins (IRE) **Mr M. Clarke**
3 ETHAN SNOWFLAKE, 6, b g Weld—Snow Child **St Gatien Racing Club**
4 FESTIVE CHIMES (IRE), 4, b f Efisio—Delightful Chime (IRE) **Mr A. Spalding**
5 GOT NO SHADOW, 6, b g Terimon—Run On Stirling **Mr J. Rowsell & Mr P. Brannigan**
6 LAHOB, 5, ch g First Trump—Mystical Song **Mr T. S. Clifford**
7 MEM SCYLLA, 6, b br m Occatillo—Mrs F. P. J. Coole
8 PANGERAN (USA), 13, ch g Forty Niner (USA)—Smart Heiress (USA) **P. C. Cornwell**
9 PERERIN, 4, b g Whittingham (IRE)—Antithesis (IRE) **Mr N. B. King**
10 STARSHIPENTERPRISE, 7, b g The Star of Orion VII—Lequest **St Gatien Racing Club**

Other Owners: R. O. Oliver-Smith.

Assistant Trainer: Caroline Fryer.

Jockey (flat): Jamie Mackay. **Jockey (NH):** C. Rafter. **Amateur:** Mr M. Smith, Miss P. Gundry.

344 MR F. KIRBY, Northallerton
Postal: **High Whinholme Farm, Danby Wiske, Northallerton, North Yorkshire, DL7 0AS.**
Contacts: **PHONE/FAX** (01325) 378213 **MOBILE** (07891) 858088

1 FOREST DANTE (IRE), 12, ch g Phardante (FR)—Mossy Mistress (IRE) **Mr F. Kirby**
2 MAGIC BENGIE, 6, b g Magic Ring (IRE)—Zinzi **Mr F. Kirby**
3 MOUNT CLARA (IRE), 5, b br g Norwich—Show M How **Mr F. Kirby**
4 SOUND OF CHEERS, 8, br g Zilzal (USA)—Martha Stevens (USA) **Mr F. Kirby**
5 TOPPING TIME (IRE), 7, b g Topanoora—Vampirella (FR) **Mr F. Kirby**
6 VIKING SONG, 5, b g Savahra Sound—Relikon **Mr F. Kirby**
7 ZABADOU, 4, b g Abou Zouz (USA)—Strapped **Mr F. Kirby**

Assistant Trainer: N A Kirby

Jockey (NH): K. Johnson. **Conditional:** J. P. Byrne.

345 MR S. A. KIRK, Upper Lambourn
Postal: **Cedar Lodge Stables, Upper Lambourn, Hungerford, Berkshire, RG17 8QT.**
Contacts: **PHONE** (01488) 73215 **FAX** (01488) 73826 **MOBILE** (07768) 855261

1 BLUE TROJAN (IRE), 5, b g Inzar (USA)—Roman Heights (IRE) **The Ex Katy Boys**
2 CHANTELLE (IRE), 5, b m Lake Coniston (IRE)—Kristabelle (IRE) **Mr S. J. Murphy**
3 CLARE GALWAY, 4, b f Compton Place—Oublier L'ennui (FR) **Mrs M. Devine**
4 DELPHIE QUEEN (IRE), 4, ch f Desert Sun—Serious Delight **N. Hartery**
5 FISBY, 4, ch g Efisio—Trilby **G. R. P. N. Valentine**
6 GENERAL FEELING (IRE), 4, b g General Monash (USA)—Kamadara (IRE) **The So Long Partnership**
7 JUST FLY, 5, b g Efisio—Chrysalis **Ascot Brew Racing**
8 KARAOKE (IRE), 5, b g Mujadil (USA)—Kayoko (IRE) **Speedlith Group**
9 MERSEY SOUND (IRE), 7, b g Ela-Mana-Mou—Coral Sound (IRE) **A. Heaney**
10 MUSTANG ALI (IRE), 4, ch g Ali-Royal (IRE)—Classic Queen (IRE) **Ascot Brew Racing**
11 PREGNANT PAUSE (IRE), 4, b g General Monash (USA)—Dissidentia (IRE) **A. W. Nielsen**
12 REGAL PERFORMER (IRE), 4, b g Ali-Royal (IRE)—Khatiynza **I. A. N. Wight**
13 SRI DIAMOND, 5, b g Sri Pekan (USA)—Hana Marie **Ascot Brew Racing**
14 UNCLE JOHN, 4, b g Atraf—Bit O' May **Mrs John Lee**
15 VILLA MARA (IRE), 5, b g Alflora (IRE)—Claudia Electric (IRE) **M. M. Matalon**
16 WEE DINNS (IRE), 4, b f Marju (IRE)—Tir-An-Oir (IRE) **F. B. O. T. Racing**

THREE-YEAR-OLDS

17 AFRICAN STORM (IRE), b g Fasliyev (USA)—Out of Africa (IRE) **Cathal M. Ryan**
18 ALI THE MINX, b f King's Theatre (IRE)—Sarah's Dream (IRE) **Mr S. J. Murphy**
19 ALLEGRETTO (FR), b c Anabaa (USA)—Aimores (IRE) **M. G. White & S. Kirk**
20 CLEO COLLINS (IRE), b f General Monash (USA)—Madrina **Mr T. Collins**

MR S. A. KIRK—continued

21 **CLONARD (IRE)**, b g Revoque (IRE)—Belleclaire (IRE) **Mr S. J. Murphy**
22 **DASH OF LIME**, b f Bold Edge—Green Supreme **P. M. Crane**
23 **DON PELE (IRE)**, b c Monashee Mountain (USA)—Big Fandango **P. Rosas**
24 **FEATHERGRASS (IRE)**, b f Fasliyev (USA)—Jamaican Punch (IRE) **Thurloe Thoroughbreds XII**
25 **FIRESONG**, b c Dansili—Leaping Flame (USA) **Pat Eddery Racing (El Gran Senor)**
26 **GO MO (IRE)**, b g Night Shift (USA)—Quiche **Alan Merritt and Friends**
27 **GROUP CAPTAIN**, b c Dr Fong (USA)—Alusha **Speedlith Group**
28 **GUYANA (IRE)**, b c Lend A Hand—Romora (FR) **J. Breslin**
29 **HOH HEDSOR**, ch f Singspiel (IRE)—Ghassanah **D. Allport, R. P. B. Michaelson, T. Lock**
30 **IVANA ILLYICH (IRE)**, ch f Tipsy Creek (USA)—Tolstoya **N. Pickett**
31 **MAXAMILLION (IRE)**, b c Mujadil (USA)—Manazil (USA) **J. Dewberry**
32 **MONTJEU BABY (IRE)**, b f Montjeu (IRE)—Catch The Lights **Johnsey Estates (1990) Ltd**
33 **MY DREAM (IRE)**, b f King's Theatre (IRE)—Dream Chaser **Johnsey Estates (1990) Ltd**
34 **OPHISTROLIE (IRE)**, b c Foxhound (USA)—Thoughtful Kate **Fletchers Bar Partnership**
35 **SALAMANCA**, ch f Pivotal—Salanka (IRE) **Wood Street Syndicate**
36 **SEA MAP**, ch g Fraam—Shehana (USA) **The WWW.MORTGAGES.TV PARTNERSHIP**
37 **SISTER EUGENIE (IRE)**, b f Indian Lodge (IRE)—Skerray **Frank Brady and Robert Whitworth**
38 **STRIKE GOLD**, b c Mujahid (USA)—Gracious Beauty (USA) **A. W. Nielsen**
39 **VERITABLE**, br f So Factual (USA)—Madam Trilby **J. C. Smith**
40 **VOLITIO**, b g Mind Games—Millie's Lady (IRE) **Pat Eddery Racing (Alvaro)**
41 **YARDSTICK**, ch c Inchinor—Fair Verona (USA) **M. Nicolson, G. Doran, A. Wilson**

TWO-YEAR-OLDS

42 B f 10/4 Bertolini (USA)—Bethania (Mark of Esteem (IRE)) (30000) **Thurloe Thoroughbreds XVI**
43 B f 26/3 Mind Games—Blessed Lass (HOL) (Good Times (ITY)) (5000) **The C. J. Partnership**
44 B c 13/4 Monashee Mountain (USA)—Blue Sioux (Indian Ridge) (21000)
45 Ch c 7/4 Groom Dancer (USA)—Captivating (IRE) (Wolfhound (USA)) (12000) **Mrs John Lee**
46 B f 3/3 Pivotal—Coffee Ice (Primo Dominie) (16000) **Vernon C. Matalon & M. Matalon**
47 B f 12/4 Diktat—Decorous (IRE) (Runnett) (3000) **Ray Moore**
48 **DONA VITORIA**, b f 25/1 Diktat—Salanka (IRE) (Persian Heights) (42000) **Wood Street Syndicate**
49 **EL HOGAR (IRE)**, ch c 25/3 Namid—Fussing (IRE) (Persian Bold) (26000) **M. F. Browne**
50 Ch f 3/3 Pivotal—Elaine's Honor (USA) (Chief's Crown (USA)) (84000) **N. Hartery**
51 B f 21/3 Bertolini (USA)—Fair Kai (IRE) (Fayruz) (3000) **D. Boocock & R. Brennan**
52 B c 25/1 Barathea (IRE)—Green Life (Green Desert (USA)) (36000) **J. Breslin**
53 **HOH BLA DAA**, b c 11/2 Cape Cross (IRE)—
Monte Calvo (Shirley Heights) (37000) **Mr David Allport & HOH Oilfield Services**
54 B c 14/4 Danehill Dancer (IRE)—K S Sunshine (USA) (Sunshine Forever (USA)) (16000)
55 Ch c 26/4 Bahhare (USA)—Khawater (USA) (Silver Hawk (USA)) (3000) **J. C. Smith**
56 Ch c 16/4 Fruits of Love (USA)—Moonlight Partner (IRE) (Red Sunset) (11400) **P. Rosas**
57 **OPERA CAPE**, b c 31/3 Barathea (IRE)—Optaria (Song) **J. C. Smith**
58 B f 12/4 Namid—Preponderance (IRE) (Cyrano de Bergerac) (40000) **The Mystery Partnership**
59 B f 21/3 Danehill Dancer (IRE)—Promising Lady (Thunder Gulch (USA)) (40000) **Cregg House Stud**
60 B c 10/3 Night Shift (USA)—Ride Bold (USA) (J O Tobin (USA)) (16766) **I. A. N. Wight**
61 Br gr f 30/4 Robellino (USA)—Silver Charm (Dashing Blade) **J. C. Smith**
62 **SPECIALISED LADY**, b f 1/2 Labeeb—Eurolink Cafe (Grand Lodge (USA)) (10000) **Brick Kiln Stud**
63 **TEMPERANCE (IRE)**, b f 11/2 Orpen (USA)—Alberjas (IRE) (Sure Blade (USA)) (21000) **Lady Davis**
64 Ch f 2/4 Zafonic (USA)—Up On Points (Royal Academy (USA)) (3500) **V. C. Matalon**
65 Ch c 27/2 Soviet Star (USA)—Walnut Lady (Forzando) (11400) **D. Potter, J. Sanders, S McCay**
66 B c 9/5 Galileo (IRE)—Well Bought (IRE) (Auction Ring (USA)) (28000) **M. Browne**

Other Owners: K. P. Dunleavy, M. Dunleavy, D. Kavanagh, A. East, Miss E. Power, J. Sanders, Martin Leather, M. East, Hon. J. Lambton, D. Ravell, S. McKay, Mrs S. Z. Bates, Mrs D. Crow, P. D. Guntrip, J. Horgan, W. K. Jones, Mrs M. Jones, Mrs M. Kavanagh, Mrs P. McHugh, D. Potter, R. Scott.

Assistant Trainer: Fanny Kirk

Apprentice: Jon Daly, Joey Walsh.

---

346 **MR W. S. KITTOW, Cullompton**
Postal: **Hayneyfield Farm, Blackborough, Cullompton, Devon, EX15 2JD.**
Contacts: **HOME (01823) 680183 FAX (01823) 680601 MOBILE (07714) 218921**
E-MAIL stuartkittowracing@hotmail.com

1 **ABBEY HILL**, 8, b m Then Again—Galley Bay **J. A. Aldworth**
2 **ARCTIC MAGIC (IRE)**, 5, b m Saddlers' Hall (IRE)—Arctic Verb **Midd Shire Racing**

MR W. S. KITTOW—continued

3 **KARLINE LADY**, 5, b m Thowra (FR)—Logical Lady **Mrs R. C. Perry**
4 **LILY OF THE GUILD (IRE)**, 6, ch m Lycius (USA)—Secreto Bold **The Racing Guild**
5 **ONLY FOR SUE**, 6, ch g Pivotal—Barbary Court **Mrs S. G. Arnesen**
6 **SKYLARKER (USA)**, 7, b g Sky Classic (CAN)—O My Darling (USA) **Midd Shire Racing**
7 **TOP TREES**, 7, b g Charnwood Forest (IRE)—Low Line **Mrs P. E. Hawkings**

THREE-YEAR-OLDS

8 **DOVE COTTAGE (IRE)**, b g Great Commotion (USA)—Pooka **R. S. E. Gifford**
9 **GOODLEIGH GENERAL**, b g Prince of Peace—Blue-Bird Express **W. G. Kittow**
10 **HAWRIDGE KING**, b g Erhaab (USA)—Sadaka (USA) **E. J. S. Gadsden**
11 **HAWRIDGE STAR (IRE)**, b g Alzao (USA)—Serenity **E. J. S. Gadsden**
12 **IN THE SHADOWS**, b f Lujain (USA)—Addicted To Love **The Sheldonians**
13 B c Double Trigger (IRE)—Nour El Sahar (USA) **Dr G. S. Plastow**
14 **PINK BAY**, b f Forzando—Singer On The Roof **T. A. Jones**

TWO-YEAR-OLDS

15 **GUILDED WARRIOR**, b c 28/4 Mujahid (USA)—Pearly River (Elegant Air) (29000)
16 **HEMBURY FORT (IRE)**, b c 28/4 Mujahid (USA)—
                        Overcome (Belmez (USA)) (12000) **J.Hopkins,J.Boswell,R.Perry,I.Fraser**
17 **JOY IN THE GUILD (IRE)**, b f 20/4 Mull of Kintyre (USA)—About Face (Midyan (USA)) (7000)
18 **POLE DANCER**, b c 3/5 Polish Precedent (USA)—Pounelta (Tachypous) (10000)
19 **RYDAL MOUNT (IRE)**, b f 11/4 Cape Cross (IRE)—Pooka (Dominion) (46000) **R. S. E. Gifford**
20 **SUE'S SYMPHONY**, b g 9/2 Mozart (IRE)—Speremm (Sadler's Wells (USA)) (10000) **Mrs S. G. Arnesen**

Other Owners: D. W. Arnesen, D. C. Fraser, Mrs J. C. Hopkins, B. G. Middleton, Mrs H. M. Morgan, Mrs R. J. M. Perry, A. J. Shire, Miss D. M. Stafford, Mrs W. A. Stoker, R. A. Stoker.

Assistant Trainer: Mrs Judy Kittow

Jockey (flat): N. Callan, M. Fenton, I. Mongan. **Jockey (NH):** R. Johnson. **Amateur:** Mr L. Jefford.

---

347 MISS H. C. KNIGHT, Wantage
Postal: **West Lockinge Farm, Wantage, Oxfordshire, OX12 8QF.**
Contacts: **PHONE (01235) 833535 CAR (07808) 290898 FAX (01235) 820110**
MOBILE (07860) 110153

1 **ALTO FICO (IRE)**, 5, ch g Un Desperado (FR)—Barberstown's Last **Mr T. Cole & Mr A. Finney**
2 4, B g Darazari (IRE)—Annie's Glen (IRE) **Martin Broughton & Partners**
3 **AZTEC WARRIOR (IRE)**, 4, b g Taipan (IRE)—Eurocurrency (IRE) **Mrs C. M. Radford**
4 **BALLADEER (IRE)**, 7, b g King's Theatre (IRE)—Carousel Music **Scott Hardy Partnership**
5 **BANALUSO (IRE)**, 5, b g Luso—Trembling Lass (IRE) **Mrs N. L. M. Moores**
6 **BEST MATE (IRE)**, 10, b g Un Desperado (FR)—Katday (FR) **F. E. J. Lewis**
7 **BLAZING GUNS (IRE)**, 6, ch g Un Desperado (FR)—Quefort **F. E. J. Lewis**
8 **BOYTJIE (IRE)**, 5, b g Un Desperado (FR)—Miss Cali **F. E. J. Lewis**
9 **BURRINGBAR BELLE (IRE)**, 5, ch m Zaffaran (USA)—Castlemartin (IRE) **Miss M. Turner**
10 **BYNACK MHOR (IRE)**, 4, b g Taipan (IRE)—Pride of Poznan (IRE) **Mrs David Gardiner & Family**
11 **CADTAURI (FR)**, 4, b g Alpha Tauri (FR)—Cadmina (FR) **Winter Madness**
12 **CAPTAIN FLINDERS (IRE)**, 8, b g Satco (FR)—Auburn Queen **P. M. Warren**
13 **CHARMING FELLOW (IRE)**, 5, b g Taipan (IRE)—Latest Tangle **Blott, Newby & Brooks**
14 **CHASE THE SUNSET (IRE)**, 7, ch g Un Desperado (FR)—Cherry Chase (IRE) **F. E. J. Lewis**
15 **CHELSEA BRIDGE (IRE)**, 7, b g Over The River (FR)—Anguillita (IRE) **The Earl Cadogan**
16 **CRUISING RIVER (IRE)**, 6, b g Over The River (FR)—Jellaride (IRE) **Martin Broughton & Partners**
17 **DARETOBEDIFFERENT (IRE)**, 7, ch g Aristocracy—Telmary **Willsford Racing Ltd**
18 **EAREST PRESENT (IRE)**, 6, br g Presenting—Spring Fiddler (FR) **Mrs M. A. Humphries**
19 **EDREDON BLEU (FR)**, 13, b g Grand Tresor (FR)—Nuit Bleue III (FR) **F. E. J. Lewis**
20 **EL VAQUERO (IRE)**, 7, ch g Un Desperado (FR)—Marble Fontaine **T. M. Curtis**
21 **ESPRESSO FORTE (IRE)**, 6, ch g Anshan—Symphony Express (IRE) **The Hon Mrs V. M. A. Tower**
22 **EVA SO CHARMING**, 7, ch g Karinga Bay—Charming Gale **Eva so Charming Partnership**
23 **EVER AN OPTIMIST**, 8, b g Afflora (IRE)—Sweet Optimist **Mrs P. Glenn**
24 **FLINDERS BAY (IRE)**, 5, b br g Luso—McMufins Princess **P. M. Warren**
25 **GENERAL GREY (IRE)**, 5, gr g Fourstars Allstar (USA)—Tara The Grey (IRE) **Martin Broughton & Friends**
26 **GLASHEDY ROCK (IRE)**, 8, b g Shernazar—Classical Lady (IRE) **Flora Lane & Gwen Meacham**
27 **GLASKER MILL (IRE)**, 5, b g Old Vic—Lucey Allen **T. J. Hemmings**

MISS H. C. KNIGHT—continued

28 **GREAT BENEFIT (IRE)**, 6, ch g Beneficial—That's Lucy (IRE) **Senate Racing Partnership**
29 **HARRINGAY**, 5, b m Sir Harry Lewis (USA)—Tamergale (IRE) **Mrs R. I. Vaughan**
30 **HARRIS BAY**, 6, b g Karinga Bay—Harristown Lady **Mrs G. M. Sturges & H. Stephen Smith**
31 **HOWRWENOW (IRE)**, 7, b g Commanche Run—Maythefifth **T. Cole**
32 **ICE BUCKET (IRE)**, 5, ch g Glacial Storm (USA)—Tranbu (IRE) **Mrs A. J. Jamieson**
33 **IMPEK (FR)**, 9, b g Lute Antique (FR)—Attualita (FR) **F. E. J. Lewis**
34 **IRISH GROUSE (IRE)**, 6, b g Anshan—Another Grouse **Mrs M. A. Humphries**
35 **IT'S A PLEASURE (IRE)**, 5, b g Lord Americo—Kiria Mou (USA) **It's A Pleasure Racing**
36 **IT'S BLUE CHIP**, 4, b g Polar Falcon (USA)—Bellateena **Blue Chip Feed Ltd**
37 **JOHN DIAMOND (IRE)**, 4, b g Un Desperado (FR)—Lessons Lass (IRE) **Mrs Denise Winton**
38 **KICASSO**, 6, b g Environment Friend—Merry Jane **Mr D. J. Smith and Mr D. J. Ellis**
39 **KING KILLONE (IRE)**, 5, b g Moonax (IRE)—Killone Brae **Hogarth Racing**
40 **LARCH (IRE)**, 5, b g Luso—Riah **The Vestey Family Partnership**
41 **LORD JAY JAY (IRE)**, 5, b g Lord of Appeal—Mesena **Mrs J. M. Johnson**
42 **LOUGH RYNN (IRE)**, 7, b g Beneficial—Liffey Lady **Carfield.Baxter**
43 **LOUP CHARTER (FR)**, 6, gr g Royal Charter (FR)—Easy Ili (FR) **T. J. Hemmings**
44 **LUCENT (IRE)**, 4, b g Luso—Allenswood Girl (IRE) **Lord Vestey**
45 **MA FURIE (FR)**, 5, gr m Balleroy (USA)—Furie de Carmont (FR) **The Hon Mrs V. M. A. Tower**
46 **MAGNIFICENT SEVEN (IRE)**, 6, ch g Un Desperado (FR)—Seven Hills (FR) **Lady Vestey**
47 **MALJIMAR (IRE)**, 5, b g Un Desperado (FR)—Marble Miller (IRE) **F. E. J. Lewis**
48 **MARADO (IRE)**, 4, ch g Un Desperado (FR)—Hi Marble (IRE) **Martin Broughton**
49 **MELFORD (IRE)**, 7, br g Presenting—Echo Creek (IRE) **Mr J. Melville**
50 **MIDLAND FLAME (IRE)**, 10, b g Un Desperado (FR)—Lathanona **T. J. Hemmings**
51 **MILLER'S BAY**, 7, ch g Karinga Bay—Millers Action **Carfield Partners**
52 **MUHTENBAR**, 5, b g Muhtarram (USA)—Ardenbar **T. J. Wyatt**
53 **MY PAL VAL (IRE)**, 5, br g Classic Cliche (IRE)—Lessons Lass (IRE) **H. S. Winton**
54 **NO COLLUSION (IRE)**, 9, b g Buckskin (FR)—Miss Ironside **Mr T. Collins**
55 **ONLY VINTAGE (IRE)**, 5, b g Diesis—Wild Vintage (USA) **Lady Bamford & Alice Bamford**
56 **OPENING HYMN**, 5, b m Alderbrook—Hymne d'amour (USA) **The Earl Cadogan**
57 **PERFECT FELLOW**, 11, b g Teamster—G W Supermare **The Unlucky For Some Partnership**
58 **PIN HIGH (IRE)**, 6, b g Needle Gun (IRE)—Eva's Fancy **M.B.J.Kimmins & Mr & Mrs D.Anderson**
59 **PORTAVO (IRE)**, 5, b g Luso—Inchriver (IRE) **Mr N. C. Clark**
60 **POSH ACT**, 5, b g Rakaposhi King—Balancing Act **W. Shand Kydd**
61 **QUEEN SORAYA**, 7, b m Persian Bold—Fairlead **Mrs M. M. Fox-Pitt**
62 **RACING DEMON (IRE)**, 5, b g Old Vic—All Set (IRE) **Mrs C. M. Radford**
63 **RATHBAWN PRINCE (IRE)**, 13, ch g All Haste (USA)—Ellis Town **Miss S. L. Samworth**
64 **REACH FOR THE TOP (IRE)**, 4, br g Topanoora—Burren Gale (IRE) **F. E. J. Lewis**
65 **RED DAWN (IRE)**, 6, ch g Presenting—West Tour **F. E. J. Lewis**
66 **REGAL BANDIT (IRE)**, 7, b g Un Desperado (FR)—Rainbow Alliance (IRE) **The Bandits**
67 **RINGAROSES**, 4, b g Karinga Bay—Rose Ravine **Mrs Nicholas Jones/Martin Broughton**
68 **RIVER TRAPPER (IRE)**, 6, b g Over The River (FR)—Mousa **Mrs C. A. Waters**
69 **ROBBER BARON (IRE)**, 8, ch g Un Desperado (FR)—N T Nad **The Radicals Partnership**
70 **ROMANTIC AFFAIR (IRE)**, 8, ch g Persian Bold—Broken Romance (IRE) **The Earl Cadogan**
71 **SMART MOVER**, 6, b g Supreme Leader—Rachel C (IRE) **Rendezvous Racing**
72 **STAR FEVER (IRE)**, 4, b g Saddlers' Hall (IRE)—Phenics Allstar (IRE) **F. E. J. Lewis**
73 **STONEY DROVE (FR)**, 5, b g Exit To Nowhere (USA)—Miss Naelle (FR) **T. M. Curtis**
74 **SUPREME CATCH (IRE)**, 8, b g Supreme Leader—Lucky Trout **Bucknall Street Partnership**
75 **SUPREME MISSILE (IRE)**, 5, b g Shernazar—Explosive Missile (IRE) **Willsford Racing Ltd**
76 **TALIKOS (FR)**, 4, b g Nikos—Talaya (FR) **Carfield Partners**
77 **THE HOLY BEE (IRE)**, 6, ch g Un Desperado (FR)—Ballycahan Girl **H. S. Winton**
78 **THE TROJAN HORSE (IRE)**, 5, b g Ilium—Miss Cynthia **The Trojan Horse Partnership**
79 **TOPOL (IRE)**, 7, br g Topanoora—Kislev (IRE) **Top Brass Partnership**
80 **TUESDAY'S CHILD**, 6, b g Un Desperado (FR)—Amazing Silks **F. E. J. Lewis**
81 **TUSK**, 5, ch g Fleetwood (IRE)—Farmer's Pet **Hogarth Racing**
82 **VALUSO (IRE)**, 5, b g Luso—Regal Grove (IRE) **Mrs V. Griffiths**
83 **VICTOR GEORGE**, 5, b g Entrepreneur—National Treasure **West Mercia Fork Trucks Ltd**
84 **WATER JUMP (IRE)**, 8, b g Suave Dancer (USA)—Jolies Eaux **The Earl Cadogan**
85 **WENCESLAS (IRE)**, 5, b g Un Desperado (FR)—Lady of The West (IRE) **F. E. J. Lewis**
86 **WIDEMOUTH BAY (IRE)**, 7, br g Be My Native (USA)—Lisaleen River **Mrs J. F. Deithrick**
87 **YARDBIRD (IRE)**, 6, b g Moonax (IRE)—Princess Lizzie (IRE) **Gilco**

MISS H. C. KNIGHT—continued
88 ZAFFAMORE (IRE), 9, ch g Zaffaran (USA)—Furmore **Martin Broughton**
89 ZAFFINELLO (IRE), 6, ch g Zaffaran (USA)—Satin Sheen **Mrs A. J. Jamieson**

Other Owners: The Hon. William Vestey, Mrs Nicholas Vetch, A. G. & S. M. Carter Bloodstock, B. M. Barrett, Mrs V. J. Baxter, D. G. Blott, Mrs C. Bothway, S. G. Boyle, Mr W. Brooks, S. W. Broughton, A. R. F. Buxton, R. G. Carter, G. M. Carty, J. Cooper, Mrs C. D. E. Davies, Lord Donoughue, A. B. Greenfield, L. T. Hare, B. M. Hartigan, D. F. Hill, MR H. P. Hogarth, P. H. Hogarth, J. Hogarth, J. L. Hogarth, Lord D. L. Lipsey, J. G. G. Mason, Mrs S. E. McCathie, Jeremy Mitchell, K. Monk, G. J. Murrell, N. Mustoe, Mr A. Newby, Mrs S. D. Pasteur, Miss J. Pimblett, Dr J. R. Powney, Mrs M. E. Powney-Jones, W. S. Rogers, D. J. Wells.

Jockey (NH): J. Culloty. **Amateur:** Mr. J. Jarrett.

---

348 **MR R. F. KNIPE, Allensmore**
Postal: **Cobhall Court Stud, Millennium House, Allensmore, Herefordshire, HR2 9BG.**
Contacts: **PHONE (01432) 277245 MOBILE (07774) 866547**

1 4, Br f Supreme Leader—Frankly Native (IRE) **Mr R. F. Knipe**

Assistant Trainer: Mrs S D Knipe

---

349 **MR C. LAFFON-PARIAS, Chantilly**
Postal: **38, Avenue du General Leclerc, 60500 Chantilly, France.**
Contacts: **PHONE +33 (0) 3 44 57 53 75 FAX +33 (0) 3 44 57 52 43**
E-MAIL claffon@club-internet.fr

1 ANTIOQUIA, 4, ch f Singspiel (IRE)—Royale Rose (FR) **F. Hinojosa**
2 ARISTI (IRE), 4, b f Dr Fong (USA)—Edessa (IRE) **Stilvi Compania Financiera S A**
3 BERISSIMO (FR), 4, ch g Bering—Tetravella (IRE) **J. Gonzalez**
4 DELFOS (IRE), 4, ch c Green Tune (USA)—Akhla (USA) **Stilvi Compania Financiera S A**
5 KELTOS (FR), 7, gr h Kendor (FR)—Loxandra **Stilvi Compania Financiera S A**
6 NAPPING (FR), 4, gr c Linamix (FR)—Nany's Affair (USA) **Stilvi Compania Financiera S A**
7 PONY GIRL (IRE), 4, b f Darshaan—Mypreciousprospect (USA) **Wertheimer et Frere**
8 PRIMAXIS (IRE), 4, gr c Linamix (FR)—Ring Pink (USA) **Wertheimer et Frere**
9 PROSPECT PARK, 4, b c Sadler's Wells (USA)—Brooklyn's Dance (FR) **Wertheimer et Frere**
10 REVERIE SOLITAIRE (IRE), 4, b f Nashwan (USA)—Cloud Castle **Stilvi Compania Financiera S A**
11 SIMPLEX (FR), 4, b c Rainbow Quest (USA)—Russyskia (USA) **Wertheimer et Frere**
12 YORIK, 4, b c Danehill (USA)—Silver Fun (FR) **Wertheimer et Frere**

THREE-YEAR-OLDS

13 AGIEL (FR), b f Bering—Summery (USA) **Stilvi Compania Financiera S A**
14 AL ALBA (USA), 4, b f Distant View (USA)—Noblissima (IRE) **Almagro De Actividades Comerciales S. A.**
15 ALCALA (IRE), b c Marju (IRE)—Cunning **F. Hinojosa**
16 ALMAGUER, b c Spectrum—Cerita (IRE) **F. Hinojosa**
17 AQUAMARINA (IRE), b f Groom Dancer (USA)—On The Top **F. Hinojosa**
18 ARISTOCRATIC LADY (USA), b f Kris S (USA)—American Dynasty (USA) **R. Newton**
19 ARONDIGHT (IRE), b c Zafonic (USA)—Eriza **Stilvi Compania Financiera S A**
20 ASI SIEMPRE (USA), gr f El Prado (IRE)—Siempre Asi (USA) **Almagro De Actividades Comerciales S. A.**
21 ATICA (IRE), ch f Southern Halo (USA)—Princess Dixieland (USA) **F. Hinojosa**
22 BILINGUE (IRE), b c Poliglote—Irika (USA) **Wertheimer et Frere**
23 BLUE SILK (FR), b f Intikhab (USA)—Edessa (IRE) **Stilvi Compania Financiera S A**
24 BOUNCE (FR), b f Trempolino (USA)—Russyskia (USA) **Wertheimer et Frere**
25 CAROLINA MOON, ch f Cadeaux Genereux—Crescent Moon **Gainsborough Stud Management Ltd**
26 COMBLOUX (USA), ch f Southern Halo (USA)—Company (USA) **R. Radwan**
27 DWYN (IRE), b c Diktat—Diotima **Stilvi Compania Financiera S A**
28 ERMANOS (FR), b c Daylami (IRE)—Epagris **Stilvi Compania Financiera S A**
29 FELLINIA (USA), b f War Chant (USA)—Fairy West (USA) **R. Radwan**
30 FRIGILIANA, b f Red Ransom (USA)—Pharatta (IRE) **Darpat S L**
31 GANDIA (IRE), b f Danehill (USA)—Al Galop (USA) **F. Hinojosa**
32 GOLD SOUND (FR), ch c Green Tune (USA)—Born Gold (USA) **Wertheimer et Frere**
33 GUADALMEDINA (IRE), ch f Zafonic (USA)—Fast Riot (USA) **Darpat S. L.**
34 HIGH WIRE, b c Grand Lodge (USA)—Hill Silver (USA) **Bering S. L.**
35 HISTORIX (FR), gr f Linamix (FR)—Sallivaria (IRE) **Wertheimer et Frere**
36 HOUSE BLEND (IRE), ch f Filandros (GR)—Alanis **Stilvi Compania Financiera S A**
37 ISHINCA (USA), ch f Mt Livermore (USA)—Nazoo (IRE) **Gainsborough Stud**

MR C. LAFFON-PARIAS—continued

38 ISTAN (USA), b c Gone West (USA)—Ronda **Darpat S. L.**
39 KAVAFI (IRE), br c Zafonic (USA)—Loxandra **Stilvi Compania Financiera S A**
40 KUGELHOF (FR), b c Kahyasi—Planoise (FR) **Stilvi Compania Financiera S A**
41 LARIOS, b c Danehill (USA)—Private River (USA) **F. Hinojosa**
42 LASGO (IRE), b f King's Best (USA)—Selfish **Stilvi Compania Financiera S A**
43 LAVEROCK (IRE), b c Octagonal (NZ)—Sky Song (IRE) **Gainsborough Stud**
44 LOCH KATRINE, b f Selkirk (USA)—Wilayif (USA) **Gainsborough Stud**
45 LOPE, b c Green Desert (USA)—Algaira (USA) **F. Hinojosa**
46 LORD OF TURF (FR), ch c Lord of Men—Peche de Nuit (FR) **Stilvi Compania Financiera S A**
47 MAZEA (IRE), b f Montjeu (IRE)—Filly Mignonne (IRE) **Stilvi Compania Financiera S A**
48 MONTECARMELO (USA), b c Lear Fan (USA)—Yafill (USA) **Gainsborough Stud**
49 MY MAN (FR), b c Anabaa (USA)—Monitrice (USA) **A. Head**
50 OAKEN, b c Efisio—Exotic Forest **Stilvi Compania Financiera S A**
51 OPHTALMO (IRE), b c Spectrum (IRE)—Pinkai (IRE) **Wertheimer et Frere**
52 PAXAMOS, b c Entrepreneur—My Darlingdaughter **Stilvi Compania Financiera S A**
53 SAHEL (GER), b f Monsun (GER)—Sacarina **Wertheimer et Frere**
54 SEULEMENT (USA), ch c Rahy (USA)—Only Seule (USA) **Wertheimer et Frere**
55 SINTRA (IRE), ch f Kris—Gracious Line (FR) **F. Hinojosa**
56 SPAINBOROUGH (FR), ch c Starborough—Terring (FR) **J. Gonzalez**
57 SPECIAL HONOR (FR), ch c Highest Honor (USA)—Secret Wells (USA) **Wertheimer et Frere**
58 STYLUS (FR), bl c Anabaa (USA)—Sibylla (FR) **A. Head**
59 SUNANA, b f Anabaa (USA)—Like The Sun (USA) **Gainsborough Stud**
60 THEATRALE (USA), b f Theatrical—West Brooklyn (USA) **Wertheimer et Frere**
61 VERY GREEN (FR), b c Barathea (IRE)—Green Bend (USA) **Wertheimer et Frere**
62 WELLSAID (FR), b c Sadler's Wells (USA)—Ring Pink (USA) **Wertheimer et Frere**

TWO-YEAR-OLDS

63 ALCOR, ch f 21/1 Danehill Dancer (IRE)—Askri (Lion Cavern (USA)) **Stilvi Compania Financiera S A**
64 ALKIA, b f 12/3 Daylami (IRE)—Testaruda (IRE) (Caerleon (USA)) **Stilvi Compania Financiera S A**
65 ALYZEA (FR), b f 25/2 King Charlemagne (USA)—
Moivouloirtoi (USA) (Bering) (23474) **Stilvi Compania Financiera S A**
66 ARCHIDONA (FR), b f 1/3 Bluebird (USA)—Gembira (USA) (Alysheba (USA)) **Darpat S. L.**
67 BALIUS (IRE), b c 28/4 Mujahid (USA)—Akhla (USA) (Nashwan (USA)) **Stilvi Compania Financiera S A**
68 BAZATHA, b f 28/4 Bahamian Bounty—Gibaltarik (IRE) (Jareer (USA)) **Stilvi Compania Financiera S A**
69 Ch c 31/1 Generous (IRE)—Blue Charm (GER) (Kings Lake (USA)) (14755) **J. Gonzalez**
70 CARTAMA, b f 1/2 Mark of Esteem (IRE)—Tanz (IRE) (Sadler's Wells (USA)) (21461) **Darpat S. L.**
71 CASARES (USA), b c 11/3 Rahy (USA)—Ronda (Bluebird (USA)) **Darpat S. L.**
72 DIANGO (FR), ch c 11/3 Spinning World (USA)—Diotima (High Estate) **Stilvi Compania Financiera S A**
73 DROSIA (IRE), b f 8/3 King's Best (USA)—Eriza (Distant Relative) **Stilvi Compania Financiera S A**
74 EKLEKTOS (FR), b c 15/3 Bahhare (USA)—
Baddi Heights (FR) (Shirley Heights) **Stilvi Compania Financiera S A**
75 ELLE ET MOI (USA), b f 20/2 Trempolino (USA)—Toi Et Moi (USA) (Deputy Minister (CAN)) **Wertheimer et Frere**
76 FIRE FLYER (FR), ch c 23/2 Priolo (USA)—Flyer (FR) (Highest Honor (USA)) (21462) **J. Gonzalez**
77 B c 15/4 Bering—Fontanina (IRE) (Lake Coniston (IRE)) (8048) **J. Gonzalez**
78 B br c 15/3 Zafonic (USA)—Gentilesse (Generous (IRE)) (26156) **Mr Lomba**
79 GWENSEB (FR), ch f 16/4 Green Tune (USA)—La Popesse (USA) (St Jovite (USA)) (26827) **Wertheimer et Frere**
80 IMPRESSIONNANTE, b f 28/2 Danehill (USA)—Occupandiste (IRE) (Kaldoun (FR)) **Wertheimer et Frere**
81 INDIANSKI (IRE), br c 16/4 Indian Ridge—Plissetskaia (FR) (Caerleon (USA)) **Wertheimer et Frere**
82 JARL (FR), b c 28/2 Mozart (IRE)—Selfish (Bluebird (USA)) **Stilvi Compania Financiera S A**
83 KAKOFONIC (FR), b c 25/1 Zafonic (USA)—Brooklyn Gleam (FR) (Caerleon (USA)) **Wertheimer et Frere**
84 KEZIA (FR), b f 18/3 Spectrum (IRE)—Kresna (FR) (Distant Relative) **Stilvi Compania Financiera S A**
85 LADY OF VENICE (FR), ch f 9/4 Loup Solitaire (USA)—
Lacewings (USA) (Forty Niner (USA)) (36887) **Stilvi Compania Financiera S A**
86 LUCKY NAME (FR), b c 17/3 Anabaa (USA)—Seattle's Wood (USA) (Woodman (USA)) **Wertheimer et Frere**
87 B c 15/2 Singspiel (IRE)—Musical Twist (USA) (Woodman (USA)) (18500) **Bering S. L.**
88 OBRIGADO (FR), b c 22/3 Enrique—Banakill (FR) (Funambule (USA)) (14755) **Stilvi Compania Financiera S A**
89 PAKTOLOS (FR), b c 17/2 Dansili—Pithara (GR) (Never So Bold) **Stilvi Compania Financiera S A**
90 B f 15/3 Nashwan (USA)—Pharatta (IRE) (Fairy King (USA)) **Darpat S. L.**
91 RINGBOW (IRE), br c 26/3 Rainbow Quest (USA)—Ring Beaune (USA) (Bering) **Wertheimer et Frere**
92 Ch c 22/4 Mark of Esteem (IRE)—Rowat Arazi (Arazi (USA)) (12072) **Darpat S. L.**
93 Gr ro f 25/3 El Prado (USA)—Runaway Cherokee (USA) (Runaway Groom (CAN)) (35000) **F. Hinojosa**
94 SAN MARINO (FR), ch c 16/3 Bering—Sienne (FR) (Nureyev (USA)) **A. Head**
95 SCAMOT, ch c 10/4 Observatory—Eowyn (Distant Relative) **Mr Ferrer**
96 SHANDAR (FR), ch c 24/3 Observatory—Shikasta (IRE) (Kris) **Stilvi Compania Financiera S A**
97 SILVA (FR), b f 9/5 Anabaa (USA)—Silverqueen (FR) (Alydar (USA)) **A. Head**

MR C. LAFFON-PARIAS—continued

98 **STORM WATCH (IRE)**, ro c 28/2 Highest Honor (FR)—
Storm Card (Zalazl (USA)) **Stilvi Compania Financiera S A**
99 B c 25/2 Rossini (USA)—Sweet Adenine (IRE) (Fairy King (USA)) (10730) **Stilvi Compania Financiera S A**
100 **TOP WEST (IRE)**, b c 28/3 Priolo (USA)—Tossup (USA) (Gone West (USA)) (25486) **J. Gonzalez**
101 B c 28/1 Polish Precedent (USA)—Vissinia (Belmez (USA)) **Stilvi Compania Financiera S A**
102 **WANDERING SPIRIT (GER)**, b f 28/4 Dashing Blade—
Wells Whisper (FR) (Sadler's Wells (USA)) (174379) **Wertheimer et Frere**
103 **YRRAS (FR)**, b c 6/5 Danehill Dancer (USA)—Alanis (Warning) **Stilvi Compania Financiera S A**
104 **ZAQAR (FR)**, b c 20/4 Anabaa (USA)—Epagris (Zalazl (USA)) **Stilvi Compania Financiera S A**
105 **ZYLIG (IRE)**, b c 10/2 Lend A Hand—Red Shareef (Marju (IRE)) **Stilvi Compania Financiera S A**

Assistant Trainer: Charles Peck

Jockey (flat): Miguel Blancpain, O. Peslier.

---

350 MRS S. LAMYMAN, Louth
Postal: **Ruckland Manor, Louth, Lincolnshire, LN11 8RQ.**
Contacts: **PHONE (01507) 533260 FAX (01507) 534236 MOBILE (07733) 165721**

1 **ALL BLEEVABLE**, 8, b g Presidium—Eve's Treasure **Mike & Tony Blee and Roy Allerston**
2 **GIVEN A CHANCE**, 4, b b g Defacto (USA)—Milly Molly Mango **D. S. Arnold and M. W. Horner**
3 **GREEN FALCON**, 4, b c Green Desert (USA)—El Jazirah **D. C. Pierce and D. A. Morgan**
4 **JAMAICAN FLIGHT (USA)**, 12, b h Sunshine Forever (USA)—Kalamona (USA) **Mr P. E. L. Lamyman**
5 **JUST POSIN**, 4, ch f I'm Supposin (IRE)—We're In The Money **Double Ten Racing**
6 **KEEN WARRIOR**, 5, gr g Keen—Briden
7 **MIGRATION**, 9, b g Rainbow Quest (USA)—Armeria (USA) **Just Good Fun Club**
8 **MRS RITCHIE**, 8, b m Teenoso (USA)—Material Girl **Just Good Fun Club**
9 **PROTOCOL (IRE)**, 11, b g Taufan (USA)—Ukraine's Affair (USA) **Mr P. E. L. Lamyman**
10 **SINJAREE**, 7, b g Mark of Esteem (IRE)—Forthwith **Mr P. E. L. Lamyman**
11 **TRUE (IRE)**, 4, ch f Barathea (IRE)—Bibliotheque (USA) **The Underlaws**
12 **VICARS DESTINY**, 7, b m Sir Harry Lewis (USA)—Church Leap **T. A. Deal**
13 **VICTORY QUEST (IRE)**, 5, b g Victory Note (USA)—Marade (USA) **Mr P. E. L. Lamyman**
14 **WORLABY DALE**, 9, b g Terimon—Restandbethankful **Mr P. E. L. Lamyman**

Other Owners: Mrs S. M. Arnold, M. J. Blee, A. E. Blee, Mrs A. J. Chinn, P. W. Foster, Mrs S. Lamyman, D. C. Pierce, Sotby Farming Company Limited, Mrs S. J. Underwood, Mr N. Underwood.

Assistant Trainer: P Lamyman

Jockey (NH): L. Vickers.

---

351 MISS E. C. LAVELLE, Andover
Postal: **Cottage Stables, Hatherden, Andover, Hampshire, SP11 0HY.**
Contacts: **PHONE (01264) 735509 OFFICE (01264) 735412 FAX (01264) 735529**
MOBILE (07774) 993998
E-MAIL emma@elavelle.freeserve.co.uk WEBSITE www.emmalavelle.co.uk

1 **BANJO HILL**, 11, b g Arctic Lord—Just Hannah **J. B. Hobbs**
2 5, Br g Supreme Leader—Black Wind (IRE) **N. Collison**
3 **BOARDROOM FIDDLE (IRE)**, 6, ch g Executive Perk—Opera Time (IRE) **The Friday Night Racing Club**
4 6, B m Karinga Bay—Bolt Hole **W. A. Harrison-Allan**
5 **CELEBRATION TOWN (IRE)**, 8, b br g Case Law—Battle Queen **F. S. Williams**
6 **CHATEAU ROSE (IRE)**, 9, b g Roselier (FR)—Claycastle (IRE) **The Southern Set**
7 **CLOUDY GREY (IRE)**, 8, gr g Roselier (FR)—Dear Limousin **Mrs J. R. Lavelle & Mrs A. Hepworth**
8 **DEBRIS (IRE)**, 6, b br g Norwich—Tipperary Star **The Yellow Brick Road Partnership**
9 **FREAK OCCURENCE (IRE)**, 6, b g Stravinsky (USA)—Date Mate (USA) **Lots of Luck Gentlemen Syndicate**
10 **GLACIAL DELIGHT (IRE)**, 6, b g Glacial Storm (USA)—Annagh Delight **The Friday Night Racing Club**
11 **GOLDEN CHALICE (IRE)**, 6, ch g Selkirk (USA)—Special Oasis **Mr T. G. Smith**
12 **HERNANDITA**, 7, b m Hernando (FR)—Dara Dee **P. J. Clarke**
13 **IMMOLA (FR)**, 9, b bay g Quart de Vin (FR)—Jessica (FR) **Mrs S. V. M. Stevens**
14 **KILINDINI**, 4, gr g Silver Patriarch (IRE)—Newlands Corner **C. N. H. Foster**
15 **LAHARNA**, 5, b g Overbury (IRE)—Royal Celt **N. Mustoe**
16 **LIBERTY BEN (IRE)**, 5, b g Beneficial—Silver Fairy (IRE) **The Friday Night Racing Club**
17 **LIGHTIN' JACK (IRE)**, 7, ch g Beneficial—Cillrossanta (IRE) **Exors of the Late H. A. Watton**

MISS E. C. LAVELLE—continued

18 **LION HUNTER (USA)**, 6, b g Quest For Fame—Prodigious (FR) **Fraser Miller Racing**
19 **LUFTIKUS (GER)**, 8, ch g Formidable (USA)—La Paz (GER) **Furnish With Abbey**
20 **MADISON DE VONNAS (FR)**, 5, b br g Epervier Bleu—Carine de Neuvy (FR) **N. Mustoe**
21 **MARJINA**, 6, b m Classic Cliche (IRE)—Cavina **P. G. Jacobs**
22 **NO WAY BACK (IRE)**, 5, b g Eve's Error—Janeyway **Mr G. P. MacIntosh**
23 **NONE SO PRETTY**, 4, b f Tamure (IRE)—Sweet Memory
24 **ODAGH ODYSSEY (IRE)**, 11, ch g Ikdam—Riverside Willow **R. J. Lavelle**
25 **PALUA**, 8, b g Sri Pekan (USA)—Reticent Bride (IRE) **R. J. Lavelle**
26 **PENNY STALL**, 4, b f Silver Patriarch (IRE)—Madiyla **Bloomsbury Stud**
27 **PHAR OUT PHAVORITE (IRE)**, 6, b g Beneficial—Phar From Men (IRE) **Favourites Racing Ltd**
28 **POCKET SEVENS (IRE)**, 5, b g Supreme Leader—Flutter (IRE) **Remenham Racing**
29 **PRESENCE OF MIND (IRE)**, 7, ch g Presenting—Blue Rose (IRE) **M. L. Coghlan**
30 **PRESENTING EXPRESS (IRE)**, 6, b g Presenting—Glenbane Express (IRE) **N. Mustoe**
31 **PRIORS DALE**, 5, br g Lahib (USA)—Mathaayl (USA) **Mrs L. M. Alexander**
32 **QUILLS (IRE)**, 6, b g Scribano—The Potwalluper **Favourites Racing Ltd**
33 **SIR LAUGHALOT**, 5, b g Alzao (USA)—Funny Hilarious (USA) **Fraser Miller Racing**
34 **STAGE SECRET (IRE)**, 4, ch c Zilzal (USA)—Tuxford Hideaway **D. M. Bell**
35 **STARK RAVEN**, 5, b g Sea Raven (IRE)—Hilly Path **The Castlebar Partnership**
36 **STARLIGHT EXPRESS (FR)**, 5, b m Air Express (IRE)—Muramixa (FR) **D. M. Bell**
37 **STERN (IRE)**, 6, b br g Executive Perk—Christian Lady (IRE) **Adams, Payne, O'Connor, Gilchrist**
38 **STOCKS 'N SHARES**, 9, b m Jupiter Island—Norstock **The Norstock Partnership**
39 **TANA RIVER (IRE)**, 9, b g Over The River (FR)—Home In The Glen **The Frisky Fillies**
40 **TARTAN BELLE**, 5, ch m Classic Cliche (IRE)—Elusive **The Elusive Partnership**
41 **THE BANDIT (IRE)**, 8, b g Un Desperado (FR)—Sweet Friendship **R. J. Lavelle**
42 **THE BAY BRIDGE (IRE)**, 6, b br g Over The River (FR)—Alamo Bay **Frisky Fillies 2**
43 **TOMINA**, 5, b g Deploy—Cavina **P. G. Jacobs**
44 **VICTORY ROLL**, 9, b g In The Wings—Persian Victory (IRE) **Sir Gordon Brunton**
45 **WAKEUP SMILING (IRE)**, 7, b g Norwich—Blackmiller Lady **Wakeup**
46 **WICHWAY NOW (IRE)**, 6, b g Norwich—Proverb's Way **Telluride Racing**
47 **YESYES (IRE)**, 10, b g Supreme Leader—Barton Bay (IRE) **The Yomali Partnership**

THREE-YEAR-OLDS

48 **RUBY MUJA**, b f Mujahid (USA)—Ruby Julie **P. G. Jacobs & Partners**
49 **TIMBERLAKE**, b f Bluegrass Prince (IRE)—Ambience Lady **First Impressions Racing Group**
50 **TRITONVILLE LODGE (IRE)**, b g Grand Lodge (USA)—Olean **Mr P. McKiernan**

Other Owners: S. P. Adams, P. R. Attwater, Lady Bevan, N. A. Brimble, Mrs A. L. Davies, M. B. Davies, Mrs P. A. Deal, J. Dwyer, S. C. P. East, Mrs J. R. Foster, Mr N. K. Gilchrist, P. N. Gray, R. Hatchard, Mrs S. C. Hepworth, M. A. Imi, Mrs A. C. Lavelle, Mrs E. Lavelle, J. M. Layton, S. T. Marsh, P. B. Mitford-Slade, I. R. Murray, Mrs J. K. Newton, Mr R. A. O'Connor, Mr C. O'Grady, Mrs J. S. S. Page, Mr R. Page, T. Payne, Mrs A. J. Peel Cross, N. Quesnel, D. G. Quesnel, N. Scanlan, S. W. Shepherd, Sir David Sieff, Mr B. G. Slade, P. Stamp, Mrs A. W. Timpson, A. W. Turland, M. J. Yeomans.

Jockey (flat): S. Drowne. **Jockey (NH):** B. Fenton.

---

352 **MR B. L. LAY, Chipping Norton**
Postal: **Rest Hill Farm, Over Worton, Chipping Norton, Oxfordshire, OX7 7EW.**
Contacts: **PHONE (01608) 683608**
E-MAIL lawrence.lay@zoom.co.uk

1 **5**, Gr m Moonax (IRE)—Artanagh Rosa (IRE) **Mr B. L. Lay**
2 **4**, Ch g Manhal—Taffidale **Mr B. L. Lay**

Assistant Trainer: L Lay

Amateur: Mr L. Lay.

---

353 **MRS J. L. LE BROCQ, Jersey**
Postal: **St Etienne, Rue D'Elysee, St Peters, Jersey, JE3 7DT.**
Contacts: **PHONE/FAX (01534) 481461 MOBILE (07797) 750823**

1 **ARRY MARTIN**, 10, b g Aragon—Bells of St Martin **Mrs J. Le Brocq**
2 **CHEEKY GIRL**, 5, b m College Chapel—Merry Rous **Miss J. V. May & Mrs A. Richardson**
3 **DARMONT (FR)**, 14, b g Carmont (FR)—Tirole d'or (FR) **Mrs J. Le Brocq**

MRS J. L. LE BROCQ—continued

  4 DOBERMAN (IRE), 10, br g Dilum (USA)—Switch Blade (IRE) **The Barking Mad Partnership**
  5 HAKAM (USA), 6, ch g Woodman (USA)—Haniya (IRE) **Miss J. V. May**
  6 JOHAYRO, 12, ch g Clantime—Arroganza **Mr Frank Brady**
  7 MARTIN'S SUNSET, 7, ch g Royal Academy (USA)—Mainly Sunset **Miss J. V. May**
  8 PRINCESS DANIELLE, 13, b m Prince Daniel (USA)—Bells of St Martin **Miss J. V. May, Mrs J. Le Brocq**
  9 ROYAL STARLET, 4, b f Royal Applause—Legend **Miss J. V. May**
10 SATINEYEVA (FR), 6, b m Goldneyev (USA)—Sataga (FR) **Mrs J. Le Brocq**
11 SKY OF HOPE (FR), 9, b g Zieten (USA)—Rain Or Shine (FR) **The Sky Partnership**
12 TWIST, 8, b g Suave Dancer (USA)—Reason To Dance **Miss J. V. May**
13 WALL STREET RUNNER, 4, ch f Kirkwall—Running Tycoon (IRE) **The Press Gang**
14 WILDMOOR, 11, ch g Common Grounds—Impropriety **Miss J. V. May**

Other Owners: M. Naylor, D. Barrons, C. Benest, Mrs J. Bentley, N. Blake, Mr Allan Butler, Mr & Mrs Colin Casey, Mr & Mrs R Champion, J. Davies, Mick Druce, Zoe Jones, A. Langois, Joe Quinn.

Assistant Trainer: Martin Edwards

Jockey (flat): Joanna Badger, M. Edwards, A. Proctor, V. Slattery. **Jockey (NH):** M. Edwards, A. Proctor, V. Slattery.
Amateur: Mr R. Hodson, Mr M. Brint, Mr M. Burrows, Miss E. Folkes, Mrs J. Le Brocq.

---

354   MR AUGUSTINE LEAHY, Kilmallock
Postal: **"Lorien"**, Clogher, Kilmallock, Co. Limerick, Ireland.
Contacts: **PHONE** +353 (0) 63 90676/87 2580296 87 2725627 **FAX** +353 (0) 63 90676
E-MAIL susanleahy@eircom.net

  1 ALL FIRST (IRE), 5, b m Alhaarth (IRE)—Nafzira (IRE) **Dr Eithne Murphy**
  2 CELTIC WAVE (IRE), 7, gr m Spanish Place (USA)—Mexican Wave **R. Quinns**
  3 CLIPPER CHEYENNE (IRE), 9, b g Beau Sher—Hurricane Hattie **J. Leahy**
  4 DECLAN BROWNE (IRE), 4, b g Danetime (IRE)—WHISPERING DAWN **W. Kelly**
  5 FLYING BOAT (IRE), 8, b m Desert Style (IRE)—Keep Bobbin Up (IRE) **J. B. Fitzgerald**
  6 GANE MARIE (IRE), 4, b f Danehill Dancer (IRE)—Beech Bramble (IRE) **Daniel Crowley**
  7 GERARD'S GIRL (IRE), 6, b m High Roller (IRE)—Hotel du Lac **Martin Gaughan**
  8 4, Ch f Goldmark (USA)—Great Land (USA)
  9 HUMBEL BAIRD (IRE), 4, b g Humbel (USA)—Zoe Baird **Toms Top Ten Syndicate**
10 HUMBLE KATE (IRE), 4, b f Humbel (USA)—Dangerosa
11 KOMPRESSOR (IRE), 5, b g Petorius—Danny's Joy (IRE) **Mrs E. Leahy**
12 LADY SARELLE (IRE), 4, b f Tagula (IRE)—Lady Loire **Ballintlea Syndicate**
13 LAKE MILLSTATT (IRE), 10, b m Magical Strike (USA)—Repeat Addition (IRE) **Irish Equine Syndicate**
14 LIFE CLASS (IRE), 4, b f Orpen (USA)—Beguiled (IRE) **R. M. Lewis**
15 MUNROC DANCER (USA), 10, br g Show Dancer (USA)—Jessica's Spring (USA) **Kory Cornum**
16 SUITS ME FINE (IRE), 5, b g Saddlers' Hall (IRE)—She's Tough **J. P. McManus**
17 WALK IN MY SHADOW (IRE), 4, b f Orpen (USA)—Be My Folly (IRE) **Irish Equine Syndicate**

THREE-YEAR-OLDS

18 ENTICED (IRE), b f Alzao (USA)—Beguiled (IRE) **G. Harris**
19 INFOZOID (IRE), ch f Barathea (IRE)—Alazima (USA) **J. B. Fitzgerald**
20 KABLE KAR (IRE), b f Sri Pekan (USA)—Be My Folly (IRE) **Irish Equine Syndicate**
21 B f Indian Danehill (IRE)—Sunset Island (IRE)

TWO-YEAR-OLDS

22 B f 1/3 Machiavellian (USA)—Grapevine (IRE) (Sadler's Wells (USA)) **M. V. Prentiss**
23 B br f 10/2 Mull of Kintyre (USA)—Lake Poopo (IRE) (Persian Heights) (3353)
24 Ch f 6/4 Beckett (IRE)—Maxime (IRE) (Mac's Imp (USA)) (3486)
25 B br c 10/4 City On A Hill (USA)—Naivement (IRE) (Doyoun) (2011)
26 Ch f 30/3 City On A Hill (USA)—Queen of Sweden (IRE) (Solid Illusion (USA)) (401)

Other Owners: Miss M. McGrath, J. I. Madden, T. G. Curtin, S. J. Leahy, R. M. Lewis, Alan Lillingston, Lady Virginia Petersham, Hugh Williams, Ian Williams, Winners Circle Racing Club.

Assistant Trainer: Susan Leahy

Apprentice: Helen Keohane. **Amateur:** Miss S. Leahy.

355 MR B. D. LEAVY, Stoke-on-Trent
Postal: **Cash Heath Farm, Cash Heath, Forsbrook, Stoke on Trent.**
Contacts: **HOME/FAX** (01782) 398591 **MOBILE** (07855) 401154
E-MAIL bdlracing@cashheath.fsnet.co.uk

1 CAPRICORN PRINCESS, 11, b m Nicholas Bill—Yamrah **Mr B. D. Leavy**
2 DEBBIE, 6, b m Deploy—Elita **Bevan Holmes Underwood and Partners**
3 LA SOURCE A GOLD (IRE), 6, br g Octagonal (NZ)—Coral Sound (IRE)
4 MABEL RILEY (IRE), 5, b m Revoque—Mystic Dispute (IRE) **Keith O. Warner**
5 MANOR STAR, 6, b m Weld—Call Coup (IRE) **Manor Racing Club**
6 MY GOOD LORD (IRE), 6, br g Mister Lord (USA)—Glenstal Forest (IRE) **Mrs A. M. O'Sullivan**
7 NEVER CAN TELL, 9, ch g Emarati (USA)—Farmer's Pet **Mrs R. Farrington-Kirkham**
8 SON OF MAN (IRE), 6, b g Turtle Island (IRE)—Zagreb Flyer **Mrs R. A. N. Bateman**
9 TSUNAMI, 9, b m Beveled (USA)—Alvecote Lady **S. H. Riley**
10 TURTLE LOVE (IRE), 6, b m Turtle Island (IRE)—A Little Loving **Mrs R. Farrington-Kirkham**
11 ZULETA, 4, ch f Vettori (IRE)—Victoria **The Mighty Plotters**

THREE-YEAR-OLDS

12 RANDALLS TOUCH, b g Mind Games—L A Touch **Mrs H. M. Lipscomb**

Other Owners: Mrs P. J. Bevan, Capricorn Promotions Ltd, H. Kirkham, D. E. Simpson, Mrs M. M. Underwood.

Assistant Trainer: Miss L Cottam

Conditional: R. Hobson, W. A. Worthington.

356 MR R. LEE, Presteigne
Postal: **The Bell House, Byton, Presteigne.**
Contacts: **PHONE** (01544) 267672 **FAX** (01544) 260247 **MOBILE** (07836) 537145
E-MAIL rleeracing@hotmail.com **WEBSITE** www.rleeracing.com

1 ALMAYDAN, 7, b g Marju (IRE)—Cunning **George Brookes & Family**
2 BORORA, 6, gr g Shareef Dancer (USA)—Bustling Nelly **Mrs E. M. Clarke**
3 BRIGHT EAGLE (IRE), 5, ch g Eagle Eyed (USA)—Lumiere (USA) **Rex Norton and Mr & Mrs C. R. Elliott**
4 BUDLE BAY, 9, b g Gran Alba (USA)—Sunylyn **Mrs A.Scotney,D.Nightingale,C.Harrison**
5 BUNKUM, 7, b g Robellino (USA)—Spinning Mouse **John Jackson and Maggie Pope**
6 CINNAMON LINE, 9, ch g Derrylin—Cinnamon Run **R. J. Jenks**
7 COSMOCRAT, 7, b g Cosmonaut—Bella Coola **M. L. Shone**
8 EL BANDITO (IRE), 11, ch g Un Desperado (FR)—Red Marble **The Another Comedy Partnership**
9 GOLA SUPREME (IRE), 10, gr g Supreme Leader—Coal Burn **Mr J. P. Smith**
10 HARRY BRIDGES, 6, ch g Weld—Northern Quay **Mrs R. M. McFarlane**
11 KAID (IRE), 10, b g Alzao (USA)—Very Charming (USA) **Richard Lee And M. J. Bevan**
12 LEN ROSS, 6, b g Bob's Return (IRE)—Instabene **P. E. Atkinson**
13 MACGEORGE (IRE), 15, b g Mandalus—Colleen Donn **Mr & Mrs J. H. Watson**
14 MACNANCE (IRE), 9, b m Mandalus—Colleen Donn **Mrs S. B. Lowry**
15 MARKED MAN (IRE), 9, b g Grand Plaisir—Teazle **Mr & Mrs C. R. Elliott**
16 MORE HANKY PANKY (IRE), 7, b g King's Ride—Melarka **The Three Tees**
17 MYTHICAL KING (IRE), 8, b g Fairy King—Whatcombe (USA) **J. R. Edwards**
18 NO REMORSE, 7, b g Alflora (IRE)—G'ime A Buzz **G. E. Leech**
19 POTTS OF MAGIC, 6, b g Classic Cliche (IRE)—Potter's Gale (IRE) **J. E. Potter**
20 RED CHIEF (IRE), 5, b g Lahib (USA)—Karayb (IRE) **G. Samuel**
21 RUNNER BEAN, 11, b br g Henbit (USA)—Bean Alainn **H F P Foods Limited**
22 SAMUEL WILDERSPIN, 13, b g Henbit (USA)—Littoral **S. Smith**
23 SOUTHERNDOWN (IRE), 12, ch g Montelimar (USA)—Country Melody (IRE) **Mrs Bill Neale and John Jackson**
24 THE GLEN, 7, gr g Mtoto—Silver Singer **W. Roseff and Partners**
25 VANDANTE (IRE), 9, b g Phardante (FR)—Vanessa's Princess **John & Ros Fifield**
26 WOODENBRIDGE DREAM (IRE), 8, b g Good Thyne (USA)—Local Dream **Mrs E. O'Brien**
27 WOODENBRIDGE NATIF (IRE), 10, b g Be My Native (USA)—Wintry Shower **Mr W. J. O'Brien**

THREE-YEAR-OLDS

28 GENERAL NUISANCE (IRE), ch g General Monash (USA)—Baywood **Richard Lee**

Other Owners: N. Abbott, F. J. Allen, Mrs S. Archdale, A. J. Compton, C. R. Elliott, T. L. Greig, D. N. Harris, R. L. C. Hartley, W. Roseff, J. H. Watson, Mrs H. E. Watson.

Jockey (NH): T. Doyle, S. Durack, R. Johnson, J. P. McNamara, R. Thornton. **Amateur:** Mr R. Burton, Mr S. Morris.

357 MR ELIE LELLOUCHE, Lamorlaye

Postal: **23 Rue Charles Pratt, 60260 Lamorlaye, France.**
Contacts: **PHONE +33 (0) 3 44 21 99 16 FAX +33 (0) 3 44 21 46 14**
E-MAIL elielellouche@wanadoo.fr

1 **ANGHIARA (FR)**, 5, b m Poliglote—Artic Blue (FR) **Ecuire Etoiles du Galop**
2 **AQUADONA (FR)**, 6, ch m Cardoun (FR)—Aquatinte (FR) **Victor Azoulai, Elie Lellouche & Sauveur Lellouche**
3 **ARTISTE ROYAL (IRE)**, 4, b c Danehill (USA)—Agathe (USA) **Ecurie Wildenstein**
4 **BACK BACK BERO (FR)**, 4, b c Fasliyev (USA)—La Monalisa (FR) **Jean Zorbibe**
5 **BEBESEC (IRE)**, 6, b h Revoque (IRE)—Lunatica (FR) **Jean Zorbibe**
6 **CHAMPION DU MONDE (FR)**, 4, b c Lost World (IRE)—Silver Dime (FR) **Elie Lellouche**
7 **CHIP AND CHARGE (FR)**, 4, b c Goldneyev—Fair Cap (FR) **Elie Lellouche & Ecurie Passing**
8 **CONTEMPORAIN (FR)**, 5, b h Nicolotte—Layal (USA) **Edgar Zorbibe**
9 **DALVA (FR)**, 5, br m Johann Quatz (FR)—Sudaka (FR) **Claude Cohen**
10 **EQUADOR (FR)**, 11, b h Yuushun (BEL)—Kalasinger (FR) **Florence Brami & Elie Lellouche**
11 **FORTUNADO (FR)**, 4, ch c Green Tune (USA)—Alta Badia (IRE) **Frederic Bianco**
12 **HONOR STAR (FR)**, 4, b c Highest Honor (FR)—Ted Tide (USA) **Ecurie Etoiles du Galop**
13 **JAMAIS TROP TARD (FR)**, 5, b h Tot Ou Tard (IRE)—Minnehaha (FR) **Alain Decrion & Elie Lellouche**
14 **JUST DANCE ME (FR)**, 4, gr f Linamix (FR)—Reine de La Ciel (USA) **M. Teboul**
15 **KIWI DES MOTTES (FR)**, 7, b h Africanus (FR)—Princess Crystel (FR) **Elie Lellouche**
16 **LOUP MAGIQUE (FR)**, 4, b c Red Ransom (USA)—Louveterie (USA) **Ecurie Wildenstein**
17 **MISTER PACHA PACHA (FR)**, 7, ch h Pistolet Bleu (IRE)—Lady Rad (FR) **Edgar Zorbibe**
18 **OSTANKINO (FR)**, 4, b c Zieten (USA)—Otaiti (FR) **Ecurie Wildenstein**
19 **PETROGRAD (IRE)**, 4, b c Peintre Celebre (USA)—Palmeraie (USA) **Ecurie Wildenstein**
20 **PIERRE BONNARD (FR)**, 6, b h Danzig (USA)—Peinture Bleue (USA) **Ecurie Wildenstein**
21 **POINTING (FR)**, 4, b f Take Risks (FR)—Pointelle **Eric Andres**
22 **POLICY MAKER (IRE)**, 5, b h Sadler's Wells (USA)—Palmeraie (USA) **Ecurie Wildenstein**
23 **POUSSIN (IRE)**, 7, b h Alzao (USA)—Paix Blanche (USA) **Ecurie Wildenstein**
24 **PRETTY TOUGH (IRE)**, 5, b h Desert King (IRE)—Poughkeepsie (IRE) **Ecurie Wildenstein**
25 **RISK SEEKER (FR)**, 5, b h Elmaamul (USA)—Robertet (USA) **Ecurie Wildenstein**
26 **STARAMIX (FR)**, 4, gr c Linamix (FR)—Sectarine (FR) **Daniel Malingue**
27 **SVEDOV (FR)**, 4, ch c Exit To Nowhere (USA)—Carla (FR) **Claude Cohen**
28 **VALLEE ENCHANTEE (FR)**, 5, b m Peintre Celebre (USA)—Verveine (USA) **Ecurie Wildenstein**
29 **VASSILIEVSKY (IRE)**, 4, ch c Peintre Celebre (USA)—Verveine (USA) **Ecurie Wildenstein**
30 **VLADIVOSTOK (FR)**, 4, b c Nashwan (USA)—Victoire Bleue (USA) **Ecurie Wildenstein**
31 **WESTERNER (FR)**, 6, b h Danehill (USA)—Walensee **Ecurie Wildenstein**
32 **ZUPPA INGLESE (FR)**, 5, b m Le Balafre (FR)—Zayine (IRE) **Francis Teboul**

THREE-YEAR-OLDS

33 **ACQUA VERDE**, b f King's Best (USA)—En Public (FR) **Frederic Bianco & Francois Lazar**
34 **ADELANTE (GER)**, b f Surako (GER)—Arousal (GER) **Simon Springer**
35 **AKHMATOVA (USA)**, b br f Saint Ballado (CAN)—Action Francaise (USA) **Ecurie Wildenstein**
36 **ALL NIGHT (FR)**, b c Waky Nao—All Over (GER) **Simon Springer**
37 **ALTAREJOS (IRE)**, b f Vettori (IRE)—Ange Bleu (USA) **Ecurie Wildenstein**
38 **ANNENKOV (IRE)**, b c Danehill (USA)—Agathe (USA) **Ecurie Wildenstein**
39 **ARGENTINA (IRE)**, b f Sadler's Wells (USA)—Airline (USA) **Ecurie Wildenstein**
40 **ARTIST'S CHOICE (IRE)**, b f Giant's Causeway (USA)—Astorg (USA) **Ecurie Wildenstein**
41 **ASSASSINO (FR)**, b c Kaboo—Bleu Ciel Et Blanc (FR) **Elie Lellouche & Dominique Pelat**
42 **AZAY LE RIDEAU (USA)**, b br c Miswaki (USA)—Albertine (USA) **Ecurie Wildenstein**
43 **AZAZELLO (FR)**, ch c Selkirk (USA)—Amarige (FR) **Ecurie Wildenstein**
44 **BANC DE SABA (FR)**, ch f Grape Tree Road—Silver Dime (FR) **Elie Lellouche**
45 **BASTET (IRE)**, b f Giant's Causeway (USA)—Benediction **Ecurie Wildenstein**
46 **BEDAMIX (FR)**, gr c Double Bed (FR)—Hesse (FR) **Serge Fradkoff**
47 **BRULOV (IRE)**, b c Green Desert (USA)—Blue Cloud (IRE) **Ecurie Wildenstein**
48 **BULGAKOV (IRE)**, b c Loup Solitaire (USA)—Bright Moon (USA) **Ecurie Wildenstein**
49 **COHITA (GER)**, b f Sharp Prod (USA)—Christine Herme (USA) **Simon Springer**
50 **DOLPHIN STAR (FR)**, b br f Dolphin Street (FR)—Hariti (IRE) **Francis Teboul**
51 **FLYING KING (GER)**, b c Waky Nao—Flamingo Queen (GER) **Simon Springer**
52 **FRANC BOURGEOIS (FR)**, br c Alhaarth (IRE)—Partie de Dames (USA) **Fernand Krief**
53 **GRAND OPENING (FR)**, ch f Desert King (IRE)—Gamine (FR) **Ecurie Wildenstein**
54 **HARLEM DANCER (FR)**, br f Dr Devious (IRE)—Hymenee (USA) **Ecurie Wildenstein**
55 **IDAHO DREAM (FR)**, gr c Vettori (IRE)—Old Beino (FR) **Claude Cohen**
56 **JAYMITO (FR)**, b c Fasliyev (USA)—Jemifa (FR) **Simon Springer**
57 **KAMILLO (GER)**, b c Tiger Hill (IRE)—Kaiserlilie (GER) **Simon Springer**
58 **L'ESPION (FR)**, ch c Kaboo—Abigaila (FR) **Elie Lellouche & Sauveur Lellouche**
59 **L'ESTRANGE (FR)**, b c Green Tune (USA)—Alta Badia (IRE) **Frederic Bianco**

MR ELIE LELLOUCHE—continued

60 **LA REINE MAMBO (USA)**, b f High Yield (USA)—Zappeuse (USA) **Woodcote Stud Ltd**
61 **LABEGO (FR)**, b g Grape Tree Road—Jance (FR) **Elie Lellouche & Claude Cohen**
62 **LIVE LIFE (FR)**, gr f Linamix (FR)—Reine de La Ciel (USA) **John-Henri Metzger**
63 **LOUVE DES RÊVES (IRE)**, b f Sadler's Wells (USA)—Louve (USA) **Ecurie Wildenstein**
64 **LOUVE SECRETE (IRE)**, b f Fasliyev (USA)—Louve Sacree (USA) **Ecurie Wildenstein**
65 **MANDALEY (FR)**, ch f Goldneyev (USA)—Carla (FR) **Claude Cohen**
66 **MAORI KING (IRE)**, b c Spectrum (IRE)—Miss Tahiti (IRE) **Ecurie Wildenstein**
67 **MAVIALEVA (FR)**, b f Marchand de Sable (USA)—Luna Rossa (FR) **Jean-Jacques Taieb**
68 **MONA DES SABLES (IRE)**, b f Marchand de Sable (USA)—La Monalisa (FR) **Jean Zorbibe**
69 **MOSCOW SQUARE (IRE)**, b c Sadler's Wells (USA)—Moonlight Dance (USA) **Ecurie Wildenstein**
70 **OLYMPIC SKATER (IRE)**, b f Loup Solitaire (USA)—Otaiti (IRE) **Ecurie Wildenstein**
71 **OVIDIE (FR)**, gr f Gold Away (IRE)—Linaving (FR) **Claude Cohen**
72 **PACIENCIA (IRE)**, b f Cape Cross (IRE)—Palm Springs **Simon Springer**
73 **PEINTURE ANCIENNE (USA)**, b br f Seeking The Gold (USA)—Peinture Bleue (USA) **Ecurie Wildenstein**
74 **PEREDOVOI (FR)**, b c Fasliyev (USA)—Prairie Runner (IRE) **Ecurie Wildenstein**
75 **PERFECT MURDER (IRE)**, ch c Desert King (IRE)—Pine Chip (USA) **Ecurie Wildenstein**
76 **PHILADELPHIE (IRE)**, b br f Anabaa (USA)—Printaniere (IRE) **Ecurie Wildenstein**
77 **PLEIN D'ESTIME (FR)**, b c Mark of Esteem (IRE)—Jurata (IRE) **Fernand Krief**
78 **POPULAR TUNE (IRE)**, ch f Grand Lodge (USA)—Peace Signal (USA) **Ecurie Wildenstein**
79 **PRINCE DE CURTIS (IRE)**, b c Danehill (USA)—Mousse Glacee (FR) **Frederic Bianco**
80 **SAVAGE GARDEN (GER)**, b c Waky Nao—Superlativa (GER) **Simon Springer**
81 **SOUPCON (FR)**, b c Enrique—Topira (FR) **Elie Lellouche & Claude Cohen**
82 **STARANABAA (FR)**, b c Anabaa—Folle Envie (FR) **Francis Teboul**
83 **SUPERIOR OFFICER (FR)**, b c Anabaa—Supergirl (USA) **Ecurie Wildenstein**
84 **THE FLAYING CARPET (IRE)**, b f Septieme Ciel (USA)—Ile de Paques (IRE) **Frederic Bianco**
85 **TIGRESSE AFRICAINE (FR)**, b f Tiger Hill (IRE)—Tanzania (IRE) **Ecurie Wildenstein**
86 **TODMAN AVENUE (USA)**, b br c Lear Fan (USA)—Three Wishes **Paul Makin**
87 **VENETIAN DANCER (IRE)**, ch c Saint Ballado (CAN)—Venise (USA) **Ecurie Wildenstein**
88 **VENITIENNE**, ch f Giant's Causeway (USA)—Victory Cry (USA) **Ecurie Wildenstein**
89 **VIEILLE VILLE (FR)**, b f Sinndar (IRE)—Veleni (IRE) **Ecurie Wildenstein**
90 **VOLPONE (IRE)**, b c Fasliyev (USA)—Vahine (USA) **Ecurie Wildenstein**
91 **VOLTMETER (IRE)**, ch c Giant's Causeway (USA)—Verveine (USA) **Ecurie Wildenstein**
92 **WARNING SIGN (IRE)**, ch c Loup Solitaire (USA)—Wild Life (FR) **Ecurie Wildenstein**
93 **WHISPERING (FR)**, b f Xaar—Spring Quest **Fernand Krief**
94 **WOLAND (IRE)**, br c Loup Sauvage (USA)—War Game (FR) **Ecurie Wildenstein**
95 **YAYA GOLD (FR)**, b c Gold Away (IRE)—Shiguerlienne (FR) **Nicole Sarmant-Piau**

TWO-YEAR-OLDS

96 **ACTRICE FRANCAISE (USA)**, b br f 5/5 Dynaformer (USA)—
Action Francaise (USA) (Nureyev (USA)) **Ecurie Wildenstein**
97 **ANGELITA (IRE)**, b f 3/4 Alzao (USA)—Ange Bleu (USA) (Alleged (USA)) **Ecurie Wildenstein**
98 **ASCARI (FR)**, b c 31/5 Distant View (USA)—Albertine (FR) (Irish River (FR)) **Ecurie Wildenstein**
99 **AZALEE (IRE)**, b f 8/5 Peintre Celebre (USA)—Astorg (USA) (Lear Fan) **Ecurie Wildenstein**
100 **BARTHOLDI (IRE)**, b c 18/2 Kalanisi (IRE)—Buffalo Dance (IRE) (Sadler's Wells (USA)) **Ecurie Wildenstein**
101 **BATIAN (FR)**, b c 23/2 Desert Prince (IRE)—Blue Cloud (USA) (Nashwan (USA)) **Ecurie Wildenstein**
102 **BLUEGRASS (FR)**, b f 1/6 Sadler's Wells (USA)—Benediction (Day Is Done) **Ecurie Wildenstein**
103 **BRIGHT SUN (FR)**, ch c 24/5 Peintre Celebre (USA)—Bright Moon (USA) (Alysheba (USA)) **Ecurie Wildenstein**
104 **CAUCASIENNE (FR)**, b f 7/5 Galileo (IRE)—Carousel Girl (Gulch (USA)) **Ecurie Wildenstein**
105 B c 14/2 Zafonic (USA)—En Public (FR) (Rainbow Quest (USA)) (67069) **Frederic Bianco**
106 **GET THE RING (FR)**, gr f 26/4 Linamix (FR)—
Reine de La Ciel (USA) (Conquistador Cielo (USA)) **John-Henri Metzger**
107 **GREAT ARTIST (FR)**, b f 11/2 Desert Prince (IRE)—Gamine (IRE) (High Estate) **Ecurie Wildenstein**
108 **IN SOLIDUM (FR)**, b f 8/5 Peintre Celebre (USA)—Ile de Paques (IRE) (Turtle Island (IRE)) **Frederic Bianco**
109 B br c 8/5 Grape Tree Road—Jance (FR) (Agent Bleu (FR)) **Claude Cohen**
110 **LENANA (FR)**, b f 23/2 Peintre Celebre (USA)—Louve Sereine (FR) (Sadler's Wells (USA)) **Ecurie Wildenstein**
111 **LOUP MYSTERIEUX (FR)**, b c 26/5 Sadler's Wells (USA)—Louve (USA) (Irish River (FR)) **Ecurie Wildenstein**
112 **LOUVE DE SIBERIE (FR)**, b f 19/5 Vettori (IRE)—Lunareva (FR) (Nureyev (USA)) **Ecurie Wildenstein**
113 **LOUVE POLAIRE (IRE)**, b f 28/2 Fasliyev (USA)—
Louve Sacree (USA) (Seeking The Gold (USA)) **Ecurie Wildenstein**
114 **MARCH VIOLET (IRE)**, b f 18/3 Rainbow Quest (USA)—
Hidalguia (IRE) (Barathea (IRE)) (38229) **Frederic Bianco**
115 **MISS SIBERIA (USA)**, ch f 21/1 Giant's Causeway (USA)—
Miss Tobacco (USA) (Forty Niner (USA)) **Ecurie Wildenstein**
116 **MOON EXPLORER (IRE)**, br c 13/5 Linamix (FR)—Moonlight Dance (USA) (Alysheba (USA)) **Ecurie Wildenstein**
117 **MOUNTAIN FAIRY (IRE)**, ch f 12/4 Daylami (IRE)—Mountain Spirit (IRE) (Royal Academy (USA)) **Ecurie Wildenstein**

MR ELIE LELLOUCHE—continued

118 **NOUVELLE LUNE**, ch f 17/4 Fantastic Light (USA)—Sarah Georgina (Persian Bold) **Woodcote Stud Ltd**
119 **OBSERVER (FR)**, ch c 31/1 Peintre Celebre (USA)—Odessa (IRE) (Sadler's Wells (USA)) **Ecurie Wildenstein**
120 **OLD WOLFF (FR)**, gr c 27/2 Loup Solitaire (USA)—Old Beino (FR) (Highest Honor (FR)) **Claude Cohen**
121 **ORIENTAL LADY (IRE)**, b f 21/3 King's Best (USA)—Otaiti (IRE) (Sadler's Wells (USA)) **Ecurie Wildenstein**
122 **PARACHUTISTE**, b c 8/5 Danehill (USA)—Pine Chip (USA) (Nureyev (USA)) **Ecurie Wildenstein**
123 **PERSTROVKA (IRE)**, b f 14/5 Sadler's Wells (USA)—Palmeraie (USA) (Lear Fan (USA)) **Ecurie Wildenstein**
124 **PLACE D'ARMES (IRE)**, ch f 29/3 Spinning World (USA)—
                                   Peace Signal (USA) (Time For A Change (USA)) **Ecurie Wildenstein**
125 **POINTILLISTE (USA)**, ch c 22/4 Giant's Causeway (USA)—
                                   Peinture Bleue (USA) (Alydar (USA)) **Ecurie Wildenstein**
126 **POKOT (IRE)**, b c 19/2 Poliglote—Pont Audemer (USA) (Chief's Crown (USA)) **Ecurie Wildenstein**
127 **PONTREMOLI (FR)**, b c 10/3 Zieten (USA)—Carla (FR) (Cardoun (FR)) **Claude Cohen**
128 **POPOVA (FR)**, b f 7/5 Kahyasi—Prairie Runner (IRE) (Arazi (USA)) **Ecurie Wildenstein**
129 **PRESTIGE BLEU (IRE)**, ch c 17/4 Galileo (IRE)—Printaniere (IRE) (Thatching) **Ecurie Wildenstein**
130 **SEA KNIGHT (FR)**, b c 1/4 Bering—Seductrice (USA) (Kingmambo (USA)) **Ecurie Wildenstein**
131 **SNOWSTREAM (USA)**, ch f 25/3 Diesis—Three Wishes (Sadler's Wells (USA)) (21282) **Paul Makin**
132 **SUDAN (IRE)**, ch c 23/1 Peintre Celebre (USA)—Sarabande (USA) (Woodman (USA)) **Ecurie Wildenstein**
133 **SUREYYA (GER)**, b f 29/3 Monsun (GER)—Sankt Johanna (GER) (High Game) **Ecurie Wildenstein**
134 B c 19/2 Kingsalsa (USA)—Tender To Love (Old Vic) **Elie Lellouche & Bertrand Clin**
135 **VANTAGE POINT (FR)**, ch c 7/5 Zafonic (USA)—Victory Cry (IRE) (Caerleon (USA)) **Ecurie Wildenstein**
136 **VENDANGEUR (IRE)**, b c 2/2 Galileo (IRE)—Vahine (USA) (Alysheba (USA)) **Ecurie Wildenstein**
137 **VESTALE BLEUE**, b f 8/4 Anabaa (USA)—Veleni (IRE) (Doyoun) **Ecurie Wildenstein**
138 **WARDEN**, b c 23/2 Halling (USA)—War Game (FR) (Caerleon (USA)) **Ecurie Wildenstein**

Jockey (flat): S. Pasquier, O. Peslier. **Apprentice:** E. Lacaille, Ph. Lelorrian.

---

358 | **MISS H. LEWIS, Crickhowell**
Postal: Sugar Loaf Stables, Penrhiw Farm, Llangenny, Crickhowell, Powys, NP8 1HD.
Contacts: **MOBILE (07730) 387991**

1 **CELTIC PRINCE (IRE)**, 7, gr g Old Vic—No Slow **Miss H. Lewis**
2 **HAYDENS FIELD**, 11, b g Bedford (USA)—Releta **Miss H. Lewis**

Amateur: Mr J. Cook.

---

359 | **MR A. J. D. LIDDERDALE, Hungerford**
Postal: Eastbury Cottage Stables, Eastbury, Hungerford, Berkshire, RG17 7JJ.
Contacts: **PHONE (01488) 73694 FAX (01488) 670443 MOBILE (07785) 785375**
E-MAIL alastairlidderdale@btinternet.com

1 **BALTIC BLAZER (IRE)**, 5, b g Polish Precedent (USA)—Pine Needle
2 **BARCLAY BOY**, 6, b g Terimon—Nothings Forever **The MacToms**
3 **DALPE**, 4, ch g Siphon (BRZ)—Double Stake (USA) **Mrs S. J. Doyle**
4 **EVEN FLO**, 4, b f River Falls—Re-Spin **Mrs Linda Court**
5 **HE'S A RASCAL (IRE)**, 7, b g Fumo di Londra (IRE)—Lovely Ali (IRE) **Mrs A. Lidderdale**
6 **MISTRESS NELL**, 5, b m Thethingaboutitis (USA)—Neladar **A. J. H. Hallows**
7 **MR BELVEDERE**, 4, b g Royal Applause—Alarming Motown **Entertainments Committee**
8 **REGGAE RHYTHM (IRE)**, 11, b g Be My Native (USA)—Invery Lady **Mrs A. Lidderdale**
9 **TRUE VENTURE**, 5, b m Un Desperado (FR)—Millers Venture **Mrs Linda Court**

THREE-YEAR-OLDS

10 B f Zaha (CAN)—Appelania
11 **CASTLE VALENTINE**, b c Erhaab (USA)—Bassmaat (USA) **Mark Warwick And Partners**

TWO-YEAR-OLDS

12 Ch f 26/2 Compton Place—Flore Fair (Polar Falcon (USA)) (2000)
13 **NIGHT RAINBOW (IRE)**, ch f 13/4 Night Shift (USA)—Teresita (Rainbow Quest (USA)) **Damiem Brown**

Other Owners: D. V. Lidderdale, Mr W. H. Macklin, Mr J. H. Thompson.

360 MRS STEF LIDDIARD, Hungerford
Postal: **Shefford Valley Stud, Great Shefford, Hungerford, Berkshire, RG17 7EF.**
Contacts: **FAX (01488) 648939 MOBILE (07887) 991292**
E-MAIL **stef@svstud.co.uk** WEBSITE **www.stef-liddiard.co.uk**

1 AGUILA LOCO (IRE), 6, ch g Eagle Eyed (USA)—Go Likecrazy **Mr & Mrs L. Harris**
2 ARC EL CIEL (ARG), 7, b g Fitzcarraldo (ARG)—Ardoise (USA) **Shefford Valley Stud**
3 BANNISTER, 7, ch g Inchinor—Shall We Run **Mrs Stef Liddiard**
4 CERTAIN JUSTICE (USA), 7, gr g Lit de Justice (USA)—Pure Misk **Four Sure Partners**
5 EASTBOROUGH (IRE), 6, b g Woodborough (USA)—Easter Girl **C. H. Shankland**
6 EFRHINA (IRE), 5, ch m Woodman (USA)—Eshq Albahr (USA) **J. Liddiard**
7 FLYINGWITHOUTWINGS, 6, b g Komaite (USA)—Light Slippers (IRE) **L. McGarrigle**
8 FOLEY PRINCE, 4, b g Makbul—Princess Foley (IRE) **Threekay Racing**
9 GIVEMETHEMOONLIGHT, 6, ch m Woodborough (USA)—Rockin' Rosie **Valley Fencing**
10 IMPERIUM, 4, b g Imperial Ballet (IRE)—Partenza (USA) **The Cross Keys Racing Club**
11 INDALO GREY (IRE), 9, b gr g Toca Madera—Pollyfaster **Mrs E. Dolan**
12 LAKOTA BRAVE, 11, ch g Anshan—Pushkinia (FR) **Valley Fencing**
13 LOVE TRIANGLE (IRE), 4, ch g Titus Livius (FR)—Kirsova **Simon Mapletoft Racing II**
14 MALARKEY, 8, b g Mukaddamah (USA)—Malwiya (USA) **A. Liddiard**
15 MARIA BONITA (IRE), 4, b f Octagonal (NZ)—Nightitude **A. P. Grinter**
16 MISTRAL SKY, 6, b g Hurricane Sky (AUS)—Dusk In Daytona **Shefford Valley Stud**
17 MOLINIA, 4, b f Nicolotte—Themeda **Simon Mapletoft Racing I**
18 ONE UPMANSHIP, 4, ch g Bahamian Bounty—Magnolia **Mr F. Jeffers**
19 PARADISE VALLEY, 5, b g Groom Dancer (USA)—Rose de Reve (IRE) **Valley Fencing**
20 ROMAN BOY (ARG), 6, ch h Roy (USA)—Roman Red (USA) **Mr James Lau**
21 SWEETWATER (GER), 5, b m Goofalik (USA)—Safrane (GER) **KJB Investments Ltd**
22 TENDER (IRE), 5, b m Zieten (USA)—Jayess Ele **Mrs F. Ashfield**
23 TEXT, 4, b g Atraf—Idle Chat (USA) **N. Quesnel**
24 TREASON TRIAL, 4, b g Peintre Celebre (USA)—Pampabella (IRE) **Simon Mapletoft Racing I**
25 WEBBSWOOD LAD (IRE), 4, b g Robellino (USA)—Poleaxe **Mr H. J. Webb & Son**

THREE-YEAR-OLDS

26 CARA SPOSA (IRE), b c Lend A Hand—Charlton Spring (IRE) **Mrs E. Dolan**
27 COCONUT SQUEAK, b f Bahamian Bounty—Creeking **Mrs Stef Liddiard**
28 B f Mind Games—Polgwynne **Mr R. House**
29 SON OF BATHWICK (IRE), b c Dr Fong (USA)—Bathwick Babe (IRE) **Mr W. Clifford**
30 SPACED (IRE), b c Indian Rocket—Tolomena **Mr James Lau**

TWO-YEAR-OLDS

31 B f 29/4 Orpen (USA)—Actress (Known Fact (USA)) (12000) **Mr Richard Webb**
32 B c 26/4 Mull of Kintyre (USA)—Miss Siham (IRE) (Green Forest (USA)) (10000) **Mr W. Clifford**
33 Ch c 30/4 Woodborough (USA)—Supreme Rose (Frimley Park) (10000) **Mrs Stef Liddiard**

Other Owners: Mrs N. Booth, Mr A. Slattery, Mr P. Kennedy, Mr J. Webb, Mr M. McAuley, Mrs Alice Woo, Mrs S. Clifford, Mrs V. Harris, S. A. Mapletoft, Mrs J. Mapletoft.

Assistant Trainer: Mr Andrew Liddiard

Jockey (flat): S. Drowne, F. Norton. **Amateur:** Mrs Stef Liddiard.

361 MR N. P. LITTMODEN, Newmarket
Postal: **Southgate, Hamilton Road, Newmarket, Suffolk, CB8 0WY.**
Contacts: **PHONE (01638) 663375 FAX (01638) 661948 MOBILE (07770) 964865**
E-MAIL **nicklittmoden@btinternet.com**

1 ANOTHER CHOICE (IRE), 4, ch g Be My Guest (USA)—Gipsy Rose Lee (IRE) **A. A. Goodman**
2 BENNY THE BALL (USA), 4, b br g Benny The Dip (USA)—Heloise (USA) **Miss V. A. Church**
3 BERRY RACER (IRE), 4, ch f Titus Livius (FR)—Opening Day **Berry Racing**
4 CELADON (IRE), 4, b g Fasliyev (USA)—Dancing Drop **Mr J. Caplan**
5 COLOUR CODE (IRE), 4, b g Spectrum (IRE)—Viendra Nur **Mr I. Allan**
6 COUNTRYWIDE LUCK, 4, b g Inchinor—Thelma **Countrywide Steel & Tubes, Mr N. P. Littmoden**
7 CRETAN GIFT, 14, ch g Cadeaux Genereux—Caro's Niece **Mr N. P. Littmoden**
8 DOLLY WOTNOT (IRE), 4, b f Desert King (IRE)—Riding School (IRE) **Mrs Emma Littmoden**
9 GARRIGON, 4, b g Hector Protector (USA)—Queen of The Keys **Mrs A. M. Upsdell**
10 HOT LIPS PAGE (FR), 4, b f Hamas (IRE)—Salt Peanuts (IRE) **Elliott & Brown Racing**

MR N. P. LITTMODEN—continued

11 **INDIAN GEM,** 4, ch f Bijou d'inde—Cayla **Mrs A. M. Upsdell**
12 **IRISH DISTINCTION (IRE),** 7, b g Distinctly North (USA)—Shane's Girl (IRE) **Ryder Racing Ltd**
13 **JARVO,** 4, b g Pursuit of Love—Pinkie Rose (FR) **V and J Properties**
14 **JOELY GREEN,** 8, b g Binary Star (USA)—Comedy Lady **P. J. Dixon**
15 **JUST WIZ,** 9, b g Efisio—Jade Pet **Turf 2000 Limited**
16 **MANIATIS,** 8, b g Slip Anchor—Tamassos **N. R. Shields**
17 **MOAYED,** 6, b g Selkirk (USA)—Song of Years (IRE) **N. R. Shields**
18 **OH GOLLY GOSH,** 4, ch g Exit To Nowhere (USA)—Guerre de Troie **Mrs G. Curley**
19 **ORINOCOVSKY (IRE),** 6, ch g Grand Lodge (USA)—Brillantina (FR) **N. R. Shields**
20 **PERUVIAN STYLE (IRE),** 4, b g Desert Style (IRE)—Lady's Vision (IRE) **M. C. S. D. Racing Ltd**
21 **SMOKIN BEAU,** 8, b g Cigar—Beau Dada (IRE) **Broadstone Racing Limited**
22 **TALLDARK'N'ANDSOME,** 6, b g Efisio—Fleur du Val **Mrs G. Curley**
23 **TIBER TIGER (IRE),** 5, b g Titus Livius (FR)—Genetta **M. Harniman**
24 **TOP DANCER (IRE),** 5, ch g Danehill Dancer (IRE)—Shygate **Mr J. M. Ratcliffe**
25 **TREE ROOFER,** 6, b g King's Signet (USA)—Armaiti **Mrs Emma Littmoden**
26 **TROUBLE NEXT DOOR (IRE),** 7, b g Persian Bold—Adjacent (IRE) **Mrs L. M. Francis**
27 **TRUE COMPANION,** 6, b g Brief Truce (USA)—Comanche Companion **S. J. Simmons**
28 **VALJARV (IRE),** 4, gr f Bluebird (USA)—Iktidar **V and J Properties**
29 **WHAT-A-DANCER (IRE),** 8, b g Dancing Dissident (USA)—Cool Gales **N. R. Shields**
30 **ZAFFEU,** 4, ch g Zafonic (USA)—Leaping Flame (USA) **Mrs Emma Littmoden**

THREE-YEAR-OLDS

31 **CEREBUS,** b f Wolfhound (USA)—Bring On The Choir **P. J. Dixon**
32 **CRY OF THE WOLF,** ch c Loup Sauvage (USA)—Hopesay **Mrs Emma Littmoden**
33 **DANCE WITH DESTINY (IRE),** b f Key of Luck (USA)—Society Ball **C. McCarthy**
34 **DARTH VADER,** ch c Killer Instinct—Liebside Lass (IRE) **Turf 2000 Limited**
35 **FLOOSIE (IRE),** b f Night Shift (USA)—German Lady **Mrs L. M. Francis**
36 **HIS MAJESTY,** ch c Case Law—Eternal Triangle (USA) **Turf 2000 Limited**
37 **MOON MISCHIEF (IRE),** b f Desert Sun—Moonlight Path (IRE) **Miss V. A. Church**
38 **NOVA TOR (IRE),** b f Trans Island—Nordic Living (IRE) **N. R. Shields**
39 **OUR CHOICE (IRE),** b c Indian Danehill (IRE)—Spring Daffodil **A. A. Goodman**
40 **ROYAL COMPANION,** b c Royal Applause—Comanche Companion **S. J. Simmons**
41 B f Almutawakel—Shadia (USA) **C. McCarthy**
42 **WATCHMYEYES (IRE),** ch g Bold Fact (USA)—Shadow Smile (IRE) **V and J Properties**
43 **WAVERTREE WARRIOR,** br c Indian Lodge (IRE)—Karamana **Wavertree Racing Club Syndicate C**
44 **WESTFIELD BOY,** b g Unfuwain (USA)—Pick of the Pops **V and J Properties**
45 **WHITTINGHAM FAIR,** ch f Whittingham (IRE)—Shalyah (IRE) **Ms P. Ferguson**

TWO-YEAR-OLDS

46 B g 26/4 Alhaarth (IRE)—Alla Marcia (IRE) (Marju (IRE)) (8000) **Mr Matthew Green**
47 Gr f 13/2 Desert Style (IRE)—Chamonis (USA) (Affirmed (USA)) **Mr J. Caplan**
48 **CORTINA,** b f 22/3 Cigar—Dorothea Sharp (IRE) (Foxhound) (6000) **Turf 2000 Limited**
49 B c 18/1 City On A Hill (USA)—Fahan (IRE) (Sri Pekan (USA)) (40240) **Mr I. Allan**
50 **FANTASY LEGEND (IRE),** ch c 12/4 Beckett (IRE)—Sianiski (Niniski (USA)) (38000) **Mrs M. O. Goodman**
51 B f 20/5 Night Shift (USA)—German Lady (Mon Tresor) (17000) **Mr N. P. Littmoden**
52 B f 4/3 Whittingham (IRE)—Highland Blue (Never So Bold) **Mr J. M. Ratcliffe**
53 **KATSUMOTO,** ch g 28/4 Muhtarram (USA)—Self Assured (IRE) (Ahonoora) **Mr N. P. Littmoden**
54 **KISSIMEE,** br f 27/3 Whittingham (IRE)—Shalyah (IRE) (Shalford (IRE))
55 B f 25/4 Mujadil (USA)—Lalique (IRE) (Lahib (USA)) (5000) **Mrs A. M. Upsdell**
56 B g 15/4 Compton Place—Loveless Carla (Pursuit of Love) (3000) **Berry Racing**
57 B f 27/3 Namid—Serenity (Selkirk (USA)) (13000) **Mrs A. M. Upsdell**
58 B c 29/4 Imperial Ballet (IRE)—Some Merit (Midyan (USA)) (34875) **Mr I. Allan**
59 **SPINNING DANCER (IRE),** b f 5/2 Spinning World (USA)—
    Fair McLain (IRE) (Fairy King (USA)) (18108) **Elliott and Brown Racing**
60 **SYMPHONIA (IRE),** br f 3/3 Zafonic (USA)—Simplicity (Polish Precedent (USA)) (72000) **Mr P. Clinton**

Other Owners: Mr A. Highfield, Mr B. Cunningham, Mr D. Palmer, T. J. E. Brereton, Ms J. Brown, Mr M. W. Elliott, Mrs S. V. E. Jarvis, J. H. Jarvis, Richard Green (Fine Paintings).

Assistant Trainer: Matt Salaman

Jockey (flat): P. Cosgrave, T. G. McLaughlin. **Jockey (NH):** Paul Moloney. **Apprentice:** S. Harrison. **Amateur:** Mrs Emma Littmoden.

362 MR B. LLEWELLYN, Swansea
Postal: **Abergelli Farm, Felindre, Swansea, West Glamorgan, SA5 7NN.**
Contacts: **PHONE (01792) 776174**

1 BELLINO EMPRESARIO (IRE), 7, b g Robellino (USA)—The Last Empress (IRE) **Mrs M. Llewellyn**
2 CHEVRONNE, 5, b g Compton Place—Maria Isabella (FR) **Mrs M. Llewellyn**
3 KILMINCHY LADY (IRE), 4, b f Cape Cross (IRE)—Lace Flower **Mrs M. Llewellyn**

363 MR B. J. LLEWELLYN, Bargoed
Postal: **Ffynonau Duon Farm, Pentwyn, Fochriw, Bargoed, Mid-Glamorgan, CF81 9NP.**
Contacts: **PHONE (01685) 841259 FAX (01685) 843838 MOBILE (07971) 233473/(07971) 283262**

1 ALVA GLEN (USA), 8, b g Gulch (USA)—Domludge (USA)
2 ALVARO (IRE), 8, ch g Priolo (USA)—Gezalle **Caerphilly Building Supplies Ltd**
3 ANFLORA, 8, b m Alflora (IRE)—Ancella **Maenllwyd Racing Club**
4 BAILEYS PRIZE (USA), 8, ch g Mister Baileys—Mar Mar (USA) **Mrs E. A. Heal**
5 BARANOOK (IRE), 4, b c Barathea (IRE)—Gull Nook **J. T. Warner**
6 BISCAR TWO (IRE), 4, b g Daggers Drawn (USA)—Thoughtful Kate **Maenllwyd Racing Club**
7 BRISBANE ROAD (IRE), 8, b g Blues Traveller (IRE)—Eva Fay (IRE) **Mr C. R. Howell**
8 FABREZAN (FR), 6, b g Nikos—Fabulous Secret (FR) **B. W. Parren**
9 FINE PALETTE, 5, ch g Peintre Celebre (USA)—Filly Mignonne (IRE) **Mr C. R. Howell**
10 FRONTIER, 8, b g Indian Ridge—Adatiya (IRE) **Mr F. Jeffers**
11 GREAT COMPTON, 5, b g Compton Place—Thundercloud **Mr Greg Robinson and Mr A. N. Jay**
12 MAJLIS (IRE), 8, b g Caerleon (USA)—Ploy **J. T. Warner**
13 MONKSFORD, 6, b g Minster Son—Mortify **B. W. Parren**
14 RANDOM QUEST, 7, b g Rainbow Quest (USA)—Anne Bonny **J. T. Warner**
15 RILEYS DREAM, 6, b m Rudimentary (USA)—Dorazine **Mr Greg Robinson and Mr A. N. Jay**
16 TAFAAHUM (USA), 4, b g Erhaab (USA)—Makadir (USA) **Mr B. J. Llewellyn**
17 WHALEEF, 7, br g Darshaan—Wilayif (USA) **J. Parfitt**

THREE-YEAR-OLDS

18 ROBMANTRA, b c Prince Sabo—Eliza Jane **Mrs S. Geen**

Other Owners: J. N. W. Brookes, A. N. Jay, Mrs P. J. Lee, MR B. J. Llewellyn, G. Robinson.

Assistant Trainer: J L Llewellyn

Jockey (flat): R. Havlin. **Jockey (NH):** O. McPhail, Christian Williams.

364 MR D. M. LLOYD, Bridgend
Postal: **Avalon, Brynmenyn, Bridgend, Mid-Glamorgan, CF32 9LL.**
Contacts: **PHONE (01656) 724654**

1 GUARD DUTY, 8, b g Deploy—Hymne d'amour (USA) **Mr D. M. Lloyd**

Assistant Trainer: C Lewis

365 MR F. LLOYD, Bangor-on-Dee
Postal: **Bryn Hovah, Bangor-On-Dee, Wrexham, Clwyd, LL13 0DA.**
Contacts: **PHONE (01978) 780356 FAX (01978) 660152**

1 ASK ME NOT (IRE), 7, b m Shernazar—Cabin Glory **Mr F. Lloyd**
2 OVER THE CLOUDS, 4, gr f Cloudings (IRE)—Althrey Flame (IRE) **Mr F. Lloyd**
3 POSH KING, 4, b g Rakaposhi King—Althrey Princess (IRE) **Mr F. Lloyd**
4 SECRET'S OUT, 9, b g Polish Precedent (USA)—Secret Obsession (USA) **Mr F. Lloyd**

366 MR A. J. LOCKWOOD, Malton
Postal: **Fleet Cross Farm, Brawby, Malton, North Yorkshire, YO17 6QA.**
Contacts: **PHONE (01751) 431796 MOBILE (07747) 002535**

1 **DALYAN (IRE)**, 8, b g Turtle Island (IRE)—Salette **Mr A. J. Lockwood**
2 **FRANKINCENSE (IRE)**, 9, gr g Paris House—Mistral Wood (USA) **A. L. Bosomworth**
3 **FUSILLADE (IRE)**, 5, ch g Grand Lodge (FR)—Lili Cup (FR) **Highgreen Partnership**
4 **ONLY WORDS (USA)**, 8, ch g Shuailaan (USA)—Conversation Piece (USA) **Mrs L. Lumley**
5 **PADDY GEORGE (IRE)**, 4, ch g Houmayoun (FR)—Pennine Way (IRE) **J. L. Holdroyd**
6 **POMPEII (IRE)**, 8, b g Salse (USA)—Before Dawn (USA) **J. B. Slatcher**

THREE-YEAR-OLDS

7 Ch f Paris House—Peep O Day **Mrs L. Lumley**

Other Owners: Mr D. Wilson, Mr J. Richardson.

367 MR J. E. LONG, Woldingham
Postal: **Main Yard, Tillingdowns, Woldingham, Caterham, Surrey, CR3 7JA.**
Contacts: **PHONE (01883) 340730 MOBILE (07958) 296945/(07815) 186085**
E-MAIL winalot@aol.com

1 **CULMINATE**, 8, ch g Afzal—Straw Blade **J. King**
2 **EASTERN SPIRIT**, 6, ch g Arrasas (USA)—Straw Blade **J. L. Nicholson**
3 **FORTUNES FAVOURITE**, 5, ch m Barathea (IRE)—Golden Fortune **Amaroni Racing**
4 **INDEPENDENCE HALL (IRE)**, 8, b g Sadler's Wells (USA)—Fruition **M. J. Robinson**
5 **JUST DASHING**, 6, b g Arrasas (USA)—Smitten **Amaroni Racing**
6 **LADY TAVERNER**, 4, b f Marju (IRE)—Prompting **The Chantilly Partnership**
7 **SUSSEX MIST**, 6, b m Phountzi (USA)—Dumerica **Amaroni Racing**
8 **UNSUITED**, 6, b m Revoque (IRE)—Nagnagnag (IRE) **Amaroni Racing**

THREE-YEAR-OLDS

9 **APRIL SHANNON**, b f Tipsy Creek (USA)—Westering **P. R. Saxon**

TWO-YEAR-OLDS

10 **EFISIO PRINCESS**, br f 25/1 Efisio—Hardiprincess (Keen) (800) **Miss M. B. Fernandes**
11 B f 10/3 Kahyasi—Kris Mundi (Kris) (2200) **P. R. Saxon**

Other Owners: Neil Ward, Pauline Ward, D. Foster, David Ward, V. V. Advani, A. Advani, R. B. Root, Mrs J. P. Root.

Assistant Trainer: Miss S Cassidy

Jockey (flat): R. Havlin. **Conditional:** R. Lucey-Butler. **Apprentice:** Natalia Gemelova, R. Thomas. **Amateur:** Miss S. Cassidy.

368 MR L. LUNGO, Carrutherstown
Postal: **Hetland Hill Farm, Carrutherstown, Dumfriesshire, DG1 4JX.**
Contacts: **PHONE (01387) 840691 FAX (01387) 840323 MOBILE (07850) 711438**
E-MAIL office@lenlungo.com

1 5, B g Topanoora—Andros Dawn (IRE)
2 **ANOTHER DECKIE (IRE)**, 7, b g Naheez (USA)—Merry Friends **Mrs T. K. O'Hare**
3 **ARMAGUEDON (FR)**, 7, b g Garde Royale—Miss Dundee (FR) **Ashleybank Investments Limited**
4 **ASHLEYBANK HOUSE (IRE)**, 8, b g Lord Americo—Deep Perk (IRE) **Ashleybank Investments Limited**
5 **BAFFLING SECRET (IRE)**, 5, gr g Kizitca (FR)—Kadroulienne (FR) **Mrs B. Lungo**
6 **BOGUS DREAMS (IRE)**, 8, ch g Lahib (USA)—Dreams Are Free (IRE) **Mrs T. K. O'Hare**
7 **BRANDY WINE (IRE)**, 7, b g Roselier (FR)—Sakonnet (IRE) **Ashleybank Investments Limited**
8 **BRAVE LORD (IRE)**, 8, ch g Mister Lord (USA)—Artic Squaw (IRE) **Solway Stayers**
9 **BROOKLYN BREEZE (IRE)**, 8, b br g Be My Native (USA)—Moss Gale **Ashleybank Investments Limited**
10 **CAPTAIN'S LEAP (IRE)**, 9, ch g Grand Plaisir (IRE)—Ballingowan Star **Mrs B. Lungo**
11 **CARAPUCE (FR)**, 6, ch g Bigstone (IRE)—Treasure City (FR) **Mr & Mrs Raymond Anderson Green**
12 **CHEF DE COUR (FR)**, 4, b g Pistolet Bleu (IRE)—Cour de Rome (FR) **Ashleybank Investments Limited**
13 **CONTRACT SCOTLAND (IRE)**, 10, br g Religiously (USA)—Stroked Again **Contract Scotland Limited**
14 **CORRIB LAD (IRE)**, 7, b g Supreme Leader—Nun So Game **L. Mulryan**

MR L. LUNGO—continued

15 **CRAZY HORSE (IRE)**, 12, b g Little Bighorn—Our Dorcet **Ashleybank Investments Limited**
16 **EARL SIGURD (IRE)**, 7, ch g High Kicker (USA)—My Kind **W. Jardine**
17 **EBINZAYD (IRE)**, 9, b g Tenby—Sharakawa (IRE) **R. J. Gilbert**
18 **ERISKAY (IRE)**, 9, b g Montelimar (USA)—Little Peach **Mrs A.R. Wood And Col. D.C. Greig**
19 **FOUR MELONS (IRE)**, 6, b g Anshan—Four Shares **Ashleybank Investments Limited**
20 **FREETOWN (IRE)**, 9, b g Shirley Heights—Pageantry **Miss S. Blumberg & Mr R. Nairn**
21 **FULL IRISH (IRE)**, 9, ch g Rashar (USA)—Ross Gale **Mr D. Stronach**
22 **HETLAND HILL**, 9, ch g Secret Appeal—Mohibbah (USA) **Mrs B. Lungo**
23 **HUKA LODGE (IRE)**, 8, gr g Roselier (FR)—Derrella **Mrs J. M. Jones**
24 **ITSDEDFAST (IRE)**, 9, ch g Lashkari—Amazing Silks **Mrs B. Lungo**
25 **JOLIKA (FR)**, 8, b m Grand Tresor (FR)—Unika II (FR) **Dr K. S. Fraser**
26 **JUPITER DE BUSSY (FR)**, 8, b br g Silver Rainbow—Tosca de Bussy (FR) **Ayr Racehorse Owners Circle**
27 **KUPKA**, 6, ch g Rakaposhi King—Re-Spin **R. A. Bartlett**
28 **L'OISEAU (FR)**, 6, br g Video Rock (FR)—Roseraie (FR) **Ashleybank Investments Limited**
29 **LE BIASSAIS (FR)**, 6, b g Passing Sale (FR)—Petite Fanfan (FR) **Ashleybank Investments Limited**
30 **LOSCAR (FR)**, 6, b g General Holme (USA)—Unika II (FR) **W. J. E. Scott**
31 **LOST BOY (IRE)**, 6, ch g Roselier (FR)—Stranger Still **Ashleybank Investments Limited**
32 **LUTIN DU MOULIN (FR)**, 6, br g Saint Preuil—Emeraude du Moulin (FR) **K. L. Foster**
33 **MACONNOR (IRE)**, 8, b g Religiously (USA)—Door Belle **Mr D. B. O'Connor**
34 **MALT DE VERGY (FR)**, 5, br g Sleeping Car (FR)—Intense (FR) **Ashleybank Investments Limited**
35 **, ch g Deploy—Marlousion (IRE) **Contract Scotland Limited**
36 **MAUNSELL'S ROAD (IRE)**, 6, b g Desert Style (IRE)—Zara's Birthday (IRE) **C. Boon**
37 **MER BIHAN (FR)**, 5, b m Port Lyautey (FR)—Unika II (FR) **The Hookers**
38 **MIRJAN (IRE)**, 5, b g Tenby—Mirana (IRE) **Mrs B. Lungo**
39 **MONOLITH**, 7, b g Bigstone (IRE)—Ancara **Elite Racing Club**
40 **MR AUCHTERLONIE (IRE)**, 8, b g Mister Lord (USA)—Cahernane Girl **Ashleybank Investments Limited**
41 **MR TIM (IRE)**, 7, br g Naheez (USA)—Ari's Fashion **Ashleybank Investments Limited**
42 **, ch gr g Accordion—Mrs Jones (IRE)
43 **MY BEST SECRET**, 6, ch g Secret Appeal—Mohibbah (USA) **Mrs B. Lungo**
44 **NOBLEFIR (IRE)**, 7, b g Shernazar—Chrisali (IRE) **P. Gaffney & J. N. Stevenson**
45 **PADDY THE PIPER (IRE)**, 8, b g Witness Box (USA)—Divine Dibs **Mr & Mrs Raymond Anderson Green**
46 **PLUTOCRAT**, 9, b g Polar Falcon (USA)—Choire Mhor **A. W. Jack**
47 **RASHARROW (IRE)**, 6, ch g Rashar (USA)—Fleeting Arrow (IRE) **Ashleybank Investments Limited**
48 **REHEARSAL**, 4, b g Singspiel (IRE)—Daralaka (IRE) **Elite Racing Club**
49 **ROBERT THE BRUCE**, 10, ch g Distinct Native—Kawarau Queen **G. G. Fraser**
50 **SAGARDIAN (FR)**, 6, b g Mister Mat (FR)—Tipnik (FR) **Mrs S. J. Matthews**
51 **SARA MONICA (IRE)**, 8, ch m Moscow Society (USA)—Swift Trip (IRE) **R. J. Gilbert**
52 **SILKEN PEARLS**, 9, b m Leading Counsel (USA)—River Pearl **P. E. Truscott**
53 **SILVERTOWN**, 10, b g Danehill (USA)—Docklands (USA) **R J Gilbert & SW Transport (Swindon) Ltd**
54 **SKIPPERS CLEUCH (IRE)**, 11, b g Be My Native (USA)—Cloughoola Lady **Ashleybank Investments Limited**
55 **SOLWAY BOB**, 6, b g Bob's Return (USA)—Solway Moss (IRE) **David A. Harrison**
56 **SOLWAY GALE (IRE)**, 8, b m Husyan (USA)—Some Gale **David A. Harrison**
57 **TERRAMARIQUE (IRE)**, 6, b g Namaqualand (USA)—Secret Ocean **Mr & Mrs Sandy Orr**
58 **THE BAJAN BANDIT (IRE)**, 10, b g Commanche Run—Sunrise Highway VII **Ashleybank Investments Limited**
59 **THE WEAVER (FR)**, 6, b g Villez (USA)—Miss Planette (FR) **P. Gaffney & J. N. Stevenson**
60 **THOUTMOSIS (USA)**, 6, ch g Woodman (USA)—Toujours Elle (USA) **The Border Reivers**
61 **TROLL (FR)**, 4, b g Cadoudal (FR)—Miss Dundee (FR) **Ashleybank Investments Limited**
62 **VILLON (IRE)**, 6, b g Topanoora—Deep Adventure **R. A. Bartlett**
63 **WILD CANE RIDGE (IRE)**, 6, gr g Roselier (FR)—Shuil Na Lee (IRE) **Ashleybank Investments Limited**
64 **WORD GETS AROUND (IRE)**, 7, b g King's Ride—Kate Fisher (IRE) **Mr & Mrs Raymond Anderson Green**
65 **YANKEE JAMIE (IRE)**, 11, b g Strong Gale—Sparkling Opera **Mr & Mrs Sandy Orr**
66 **YOU DO THE MATH (IRE)**, 5, b g Carroll House—Ballymave (IRE) **Garden Shed Racing 1**

Other Owners: Mrs Sandra G. E. Arkwright, Mr P. Corson, Mrs K. Corson, Mrs C. M. T. Cunningham-Jardine, P. M. Curry, Lady Duncan, J. J. Elliot, N. Ender, A. J. Hill, R. C. Hyndman, K. G. Knox, A. C. Mack, P. Maddison, R. T. Merhi, Miss M. Noden, Mrs C. R. Orr, Mr J. A. M. Orr, R. Paisley, Dr R. A. Palmer, C. Paterson, Mrs M. A. Scott, Mrs S. M. Wood.

Jockey (NH): W. Dowling, A. Dobbin, B. Gibson. **Conditional:** G. Berridge, L. Berridge. **Amateur:** M. J. McAllister.

369 MR GER LYONS, Dunsany
Postal: Glenburnie Stables, Dunsany, Co. Meath, Ireland.
Contacts: PHONE +353 (0) 46 9025666 FAX +353 (0) 46 9026364 MOBILE +353 (0) 868 502439
E-MAIL gerlyons@iol.ie

1 **AMOURALLIS (IRE)**, 4, b f Dushyantor (USA)—Motley **Paul Kiernan**
2 **BAHAMAMIA (IRE)**, 5, b m Vettori (IRE)—Daleside Ladybird **Eugene McDermott**
3 **BENWILT GOLD (IRE)**, 4, b f Goldmark (USA)—Image of Truce (IRE) **Annalee Syndicate**
4 **BLACKZAL**, 4, b g Zilzal (USA)—Kirsten **Ger Lyons Racing**
5 **CARRAMANAGH LADY (IRE)**, 4, b f Anshan—Lady Claire (IRE) **Peter Tonery**
6 **CAT FIVE**, 6, b h Catrail (USA)—Wassl This Then (IRE) **Lady Mount Charles**
7 **FLASHY BEAU (IRE)**, 5, ch g Fumo di Londra (IRE)—Flash Donna (USA) **Brendan Murray**
8 **FROOT LOOP (IRE)**, 4, b f Mujadil (USA)—Millie's Return (IRE) **Jack Of Trumps Syndicate**
9 **GALWAY ADVERTISER (IRE)**, 4, ch g Woods of Windsor (USA)—Tacheo **Peter Timmins**
10 **HURRICANE ALLEY (IRE)**, 4, b c Ali-Royal (IRE)—Trumped (IRE) **Ger Lyons Racing**
11 **HURRY STAR (IRE)**, 5, b g Good Thyne (USA)—Dawn Scarlet (IRE) **Alive-A-5-0 Syndicate**
12 **IN THEORY**, 6, b h Ezzoud (IRE)—Little Black Dress (USA) **GS Racing Club**
13 **INCH ISLAND (IRE)**, 5, b g Turtle Island (IRE)—Persian Light (IRE) **John Devine**
14 **ITSONLYAPUPPET (IRE)**, 6, ch g Houmayoun (FR)—Adala (IRE) **Mrs Ann Smurfit**
15 **JEMMY JOHN (IRE)**, 5, b g College Chapel—Moscow Tycoon (IRE) **Mr S. Jones**
16 **JEMMY'S FLAME (IRE)**, 4, ch f Grand Lodge (USA)—Sophrana (USA) **Sean Jones**
17 **KELLS STAR (IRE)**, 4, ch f Oscar Schindler (IRE)—Indiana Bride (IRE) **DHJS Syndicate**
18 4, B f Un Desperado (FR)—Killycluggan (IRE) **Mr Dermot Conlon**
19 **LILY'S GIRL (IRE)**, 5, b br m Hamas (IRE)—Sheryl Lynn **Frank Gleeson**
20 **LUCKY SPIRIT (IRE)**, 4, br g Lucky Guest—Ezilana (IRE) **Sharon Murnaghan**
21 **MASRIYNA'S HEIRESS (IRE)**, 4, b f Princely Heir (IRE)—Masriyna (IRE) **Sport Racing Club**
22 **MER D'ARAL (FR)**, 5, gr m Balleroy (USA)—Sandsea (FR) **Martin Carr**
23 **MIGHTY MIST (IRE)**, 7, gr g Paris House—Morgiana **Phil Kennedy**
24 **MOY JOY (IRE)**, 4, b f Orpen (USA)—Berhala (IRE) **John Quinn**
25 4, B c Definite Article—Nice Spice (IRE) **Ger Lyons Racing**
26 **NORBORNE BANDIT (IRE)**, 4, b c Croco Rouge (IRE)—Saninka (IRE) **GS Racing Club**
27 **NUTLEY FLYER (IRE)**, 4, b f Marju—Society Fair (FR) **Tom Jones**
28 **PEDINA (IRE)**, 7, b g Toulon—Bilberry **Third Avenue Syndicate**
29 **ROCKAZAR**, 4, b c Opening Verse (USA)—Final Rush **Barry Dobbin & Vincent Gaul**
30 **ROISIN'S STAR (IRE)**, 5, b m Accordion—Lightning Bolt (IRE) **James Cummins**
31 **ROYAL CANYON (IRE)**, 4, b f Royal Applause—Carroll's Canyon (IRE) **Paul Kiernan**
32 **SHE'S SUPERSONIC (IRE)**, 5, ch m Accordion—Clasical Influence **Eddie Campbell**
33 **TIA WANA (IRE)**, 9, b g Toulon—Tempo Rose **Third Avenue Syndicate**
34 **WINDSOR DANCER (IRE)**, 7, ch m Woods of Windsor (USA)—Theatral **Mr Eddie Campbell**

THREE-YEAR-OLDS

35 **ABBEY SMOKE (IRE)**, ch f Flying Chevron (USA)—Smoke Lady (IRE) **John Burke**
36 **BENWILT BREEZE (IRE)**, b c Mujadil (USA)—Image of Truce (IRE) **Sean Shields**
37 **COILL CRI (IRE)**, b f Shinko Forest (IRE)—Carroll's Canyon (IRE) **Paul Kiernan**
38 **DIOSPER (USA)**, ch f Diesis—Prosper (USA) **Michael Daly**
39 **GALDO (IRE)**, b c Indian Lodge (IRE)—Bush Rose **PST Syndicate**
40 **GOLDSTAR DANCER (IRE)**, b c General Monash (USA)—Ravensdale Rose (IRE) **Double Eight Syndicate**
41 **JEMMY'S GIRL (IRE)**, b f Pennekamp (USA)—Cimeterre (IRE) **Sean Jones**
42 **JEMMY'S LAD (IRE)**, b c Namid—Gino Lady (IRE) **Sean Jones**
43 **KLEINOVA (IRE)**, b f Trans Island—Desert Bride (USA) **Tom Jones**
44 **LEAN ON ME (IRE)**, b c Lend A Hand—Tifosi (IRE) **Peter Kelly**
45 **NOT CRAFTY (USA)**, ch f Crafty Prospector (USA)—Lady Regency (CAN) **Michael Daly**
46 **ODDSHOES (IRE)**, b c Mujadil (USA)—Another Baileys **T-Shock Syndicate**
47 **OMACHAUN (IRE)**, ch c Soviet Star (USA)—Jilted (IRE)
48 **ORIHUELA FELLA (IRE)**, ch c Indian Lodge (IRE)—Grafton Girl (IRE) **John Thomson**
49 **PACKIE TAM (IRE)**, b c Tipsy Creek (USA)—Blonde Goddess (IRE) **Brian McMahon**
50 **RAIN CHANT (USA)**, b c Key of Luck (USA)—Tropical Rain **Rain Chant Syndicate**
51 **RAINTOWN (IRE)**, ch c Raise A Grand (IRE)—Lorella (IRE) **Vincent Gaul**
52 **XAARINSHKI (IRE)**, b f Xaar—Blushing Minstrel (IRE) **Paul Kiernan**

TWO-YEAR-OLDS

53 Ch f 17/3 In The Wings—Blushing Minstrel (IRE) (Nicholas (USA)) **Paul Kiernan**
54 B f 20/4 Lend A Hand—Carroll's Canyon (IRE) (Hatim (USA)) **Paul Kiernan**
55 B f 4/2 Xaar—Daunting Lady (IRE) (Mujadil (USA)) (60361) **Mrs Marguerite Clifford**
56 B f 30/4 Desert Prince (IRE)—Decant (Rousillon (USA)) (22000) **Jack Of Trumps Syndicate**
57 B f 22/1 Honour And Glory (USA)—Desert Digger (USA) (Mining (USA)) (15961)

MR GER LYONS—continued

58 B br f 26/5 Houmayoun (FR)—Hiltons Executive (IRE) (Petorius) (1340)
59 Ch c 25/3 Danehill Dancer (IRE)—Imperial Graf (USA) (Blushing John (USA)) (45606)
60 B f 23/2 Royal Applause—Kerasana (IRE) (Kahyasi) (26156)
61 B f 14/3 Key of Luck (USA)—Kutaisi (IRE) (Soviet Star (USA)) (4023) **MGK and JD Racing**
62 B f 17/2 Gulch (USA)—Lynneseemeplease (USA) (Avies Copy (USA)) (7980) **Fonsie O'Byrne**
63 **MABEL (IRE),** b f 16/1 In The Wings—Ma N'ieme Biche (USA) (Key To The Kingdom (USA)) **Mr Ryan Bailey**
64 B c 29/4 City On A Hill (USA)—Pontivy (IRE) (Last Tycoon) (14083) **Sharon Murnaghan**
65 B f 20/2 Mujadil (USA)—Probable (IRE) (Selkirk (USA)) (1676) **Ger Lyons Racing**
66 B f 15/2 Key of Luck (USA)—Questing Star (Rainbow Quest (USA)) (9389)
67 B f 1/3 King Charlemagne (USA)—Silly Imp (IRE) (Imperial Frontier (USA)) (7377) **Brian Eivers**
68 B c 25/3 Halling (USA)—Tithcar (Cadeaux Genereux) (13413) **Vincent Gaul**

Jockey (flat): P. Cosgrave. **Conditional:** R. Colgan. **Apprentice:** Mark J. Flynn. **Amateur:** Nina Carberry.

---

370 MR G. MACAIRE, Les Mathes

Postal: **Hippodrome de la Palmyre, 17570 Les Mathes, France.**
Contacts: **PHONE +33 (0) 546 236254/225855 FAX +33 (0) 546 225438**
MOBILE +33 (0) 607 654992 E-MAIL entrainement-g.macaire@wanadoo.fr

1 ALPHABIRD (FR), 4, b g Alpha Tauri (FR)—Arabird (USA) **Mr A. Faucheux**
2 AMAZONE DU BERLAIS (FR), 4, b f Indian River (FR)—Phedre Du Berlais (FR) **Mr C. Cohen**
3 APPLES JUICE (FR), 5, ch g Saint Cyrien (FR)—Une Joy (FR) **Mr R. Laffitte**
4 BALKO (FR), 4, b c Pistolet Bleu (IRE)—Ella Royale (FR) **Mr G. Blain**
5 BANDIT MANCHOT (FR), 4, b g Saint Cyrien (FR)—Murakala (FR) **Mr G. Baratoux**
6 BELISAMA (FR), 4, ch f Mansonnien (FR)—Ellapampa (FR) **Mr P. De Maleissye Melun**
7 BEN VETO (FR), 4, ch g Perrault—Sainte Lea (FR) **Mrs R. Waley-Cohen**
8 BICA (FR), 5, b g Cadoudal (FR)—Libertina (FR) **Mr R. Waley-Cohen**
9 BIELO VIESA (FR), 5, b g Mansonnien (FR)—Gold Or Silver (FR) **Mr F. Lazar**
10 BRIDGE OF STARS (FR), 5, b g Roakarad—Hersilia (FR) **Mr M. Bessis**
11 CALIKOSA (FR), 4, b f Nikos—Dhaucali (USA) **Mr O. Delegue**
12 CALISSON (FR), 4, ro c Mansonnien (FR)—Dona Cali (FR) **Mr O. Delegue**
13 CARIGNAN (FR), 4, b g Garde Royale—Cardoudalle (FR) **Mr R. Fougedoire**
14 CARLYSSAR (FR), 4, b f Bricassar (USA)—Carlynie (FR) **Mrs A. M. Roux**
15 CHANTEGRIL (FR), 5, b h Hasa (FR)—Mazzina (FR) **Mr J. M. Reillier**
16 CHEPSTOW (FR), 4, b g Marathon (USA)—Sterling Love (FR) **Mr J. C. Audry**
17 CYRIEN DEUX MILLE (FR), 5, b g Saint Cyrien (FR)—Top Chiz (FR) **Ecurie Guillaume Macaire**
18 DE CABO A RABO (IRE), 4, b g Sassanian (USA)—Inherited Lute (IRE) **Palmyr Racing**
19 DOLCE DU BERLAIS (FR), 4, b f Saint Preuil (FR)—Cadouly (FR) **Mr C. Cohen**
20 DOMIROME (FR), 7, b g Roi de Rome (USA)—Bold Senorita (IRE) **Mrs Y. Shen**
21 DOUZE DOUZE (FR), 9, ch g Saint Cyrien (FR)—Kitkelly (FR) **Mr F. Videaud**
22 ESPRIT SAINT (FR), 4, b g Mansonnien (FR)—Escopette (FR) **Mr R. Fougedoire**
23 FAUCON DU CERCLE (FR), 6, b h Faucon Noir (FR)—Corthalia (FR) **Mr R. Fougedoire**
24 GO ON MY SON (FR), 4, b c Pistolet Bleu (FR)—Shannondore (FR) **Mr J. C. Audry**
25 GOLDEN FLIGHT (FR), 6, b g Saint Cyrien (FR)—Sunday Flight (FR) **Mr J. Cotton**
26 GRIVERY (FR), 9, b g Nikos—Lady Segrave **Mr J. C. Audry**
27 HARTANY (GER), 4, b c Lavirco (GER)—Harasava (FR) **Mrs F. Montauban**
28 HUNORISK (FR), 4, b f Mansonnien (FR)—La Vie Immobile (USA) **Mr J. Cotton**
29 JAPHET (FR), 8, b g Perrault—Una Volta (FR) **Mr J. C. Audry**
30 JOE JEAN (FR), 4, b g Saumarez—Shabby Bleue (FR) **Ecurie Rib**
31 KADISCO (FR), 4, b g Perrault—Katikala (FR) **Mrs Vanden Broele**
32 KAMI DES OBEAUX (FR), 7, b g Saint Preuil (FR)—Ulisa II (FR) **Mme P. Papot**
33 KATIKI (FR), 8, b g Cadoudal (FR)—Tikiti Dancer (FR) **Mrs A. Poisot-Gantes**
34 KAUTO RAY (FR), 4, b g Saint Cyrien (FR)—Kautorette (FR) **Mr J. C. Audry**
35 L'AS DE PEMBO (FR), 6, b g Panoramic—Lumiere Du Porh (FR) **Mr A. Faucheux**
36 LADY DANCER (FR), 6, b m Lesotho (USA)—Lady Thatch (FR) **Mr G. Morosini**
37 LANCOME DE SOLZEN (FR), 6, b g Passing Sale (FR)—Tipperary II (FR) **Mr P. de Maleissye**
38 LAURIER DE COTTE (FR), 6, b g Kadalko (FR)—Rafale de Cotte (FR) **Mr R. Fougedoire**
39 LE PERO (FR), 7, b g Perrault—Nuit D'ecajeul (FR) **Ecurie Guillaume Macaire**
40 LE RIBARDON (FR), 5, b g Freedom Cry—Shabby Bleue (FR) **Ecurie Rib**
41 LE THEIL (FR), 6, b g Bayolidaan (FR)—Mazzina (FR) **Mr J. M. Reillier**
42 LEADER DU COCHET (FR), 6, b g Byzantium (FR)—Voiture Du Cochet (FR) **Mrs F. Montauban**
43 LEON DES OBEAUX (FR), 6, gr g Panoramic—Diese d'estruval (FR) **Mme N. Devilder**
44 LEVI DES OBEAUX (FR), 6, b g Royal Charter—Valse Des Obeaux (FR) **Mme N. Devilder**
45 LIBERDAL (FR), 7, b g Cadoudal (FR)—Libertina (FR) **Mrs B. Gabeur**

MR G. MACAIRE—continued

46 **LINGOT DE L'ISLE (FR)**, 6, b g Ragmar (FR)—Ceres de L'isle (FR) **Mr M. Froissard**
47 **LITTLE BRUERE (FR)**, 6, b g Villez (USA)—Divine Bruere (FR) **Mr R. Fougedoire**
48 **LOOK COLLONGES (FR)**, 6, gr g Dom Alco (FR)—Tessy Collonges (FR) **Mr C. Cohen**
49 **LOR WEEN (FR)**, 6, ch g Beyssac (FR)—Asterie L'ermitage (FR) **Mme P. Papot**
50 **LUCKI LUKE (FR)**, 6, b g Luchiroverte (IRE)—Birgonde (FR) **Mr X. Papot**
51 **LUSAKA DE PEMBO (FR)**, 6, b h Funny Baby (FR)—Crackeline (FR) **Mrs G. Genetay**
52 **MAD EO (FR)**, 5, b g Port Lyautey (FR)—Dans Dro (FR) **Mr A. Faucheux**
53 **MADISON DU BERLAIS (FR)**, 4, b g Indian River (FR)—Anais Du Berlais (FR) **Mr C. Cohen**
54 **MAGE D'ESTRUVAL (FR)**, 5, b g Sheyrann—Ivresse D'estruval (FR) **Mr B. Le Gentil**
55 **MALANDRIN (FR)**, 10, ch g Albert du Berlais (FR)—Maieta (FR) **Mr J. M. Reillier**
56 **MALCO MALTA (FR)**, 5, ch g Dom Alco (FR)—Alinda (FR) **Mr A. Faucheux**
57 **MARIUS DES OBEAUX (FR)**, 5, b g Grand Tresor (FR)—Diese D'estruval (FR) **Mme N. Devilder**
58 **MARS DES OBEAUX (FR)**, 5, b g Panoramic (FR)—Ceres Des Obeaux (FR) **Mme N. Devilder**
59 **MASKA (FR)**, 4, b f Kadalko (FR)—Fulgina (FR) **Mr R. Waley Cohen**
60 **MEISIR DU LUC (FR)**, 5, b h Chamberlin (FR)—Acca Du luc (FR) **Mr C. Dumeau**
61 **MEUTAC (FR)**, 4, b c Mansonnien (FR)—La Musardiere (FR) **Haras Du Reuilly**
62 **MICADOU (FR)**, 5, b g Cadoudal (FR)—Minouche (FR) **Mr F. Videaud**
63 **MINABELLA (FR)**, 5, b m Mister Mat (FR)—Migakash (FR) **Mr D. Powell**
64 **MINOS DES OBEAUX (FR)**, 5, gr g Saint Preuil (FR)—Alpaga (FR) **Mme N. Devilder**
65 **MINUIT DE COTTE (FR)**, 5, b g Kadalko (FR)—Rafale De Cotte (FR) **Mr R. Fougedoire**
66 **MISTRAL BOY (FR)**, 5, b g Port Lyautey (FR)—Une de Mai IV (FR) **Mrs A. Mahe**
67 **MITHRA DES OBEAUX (FR)**, 5, b m Panoramic—Brune de Cotte (FR) **Mme N. Devilder**
68 **MOKA DE L'ISLE (FR)**, 5, ch g Video Rock (FR)—Ceres de L'isle (FR) **Mrs S. A. Bramall**
69 **MONT MISERE (FR)**, 9, b g Mont Basile (FR)—Pique Flamme (FR) **Mr A. Chiche**
70 **MOUILLEURDEPONGES (FR)**, 4, b g Saumarez—Royale Flamby (FR) **Mr R. Fougedoire**
71 **MOUSSU LESCRIBAA (FR)**, 4, b g Panoramic—Mona Lisaa (FR) **Mrs F. Montauban**
72 **MUST ORIGNY (FR)**, 5, b br g Sleeping Car (FR)—Coralline (FR) **Mr R. Fougedoire**
73 **MUTIN DE COTTE (FR)**, 5, ch g Iris Noir (FR)—Kariantique (FR) **Mr R. Fougedoire**
74 **NACHO DES UNCHERES (FR)**, 4, b g Bulington (FR)—Radieuse Gamine (FR) **Mr Terry Amos**
75 **NAGGING (FR)**, 5, b g Nikos—Fassonwest (FR) **Mr D. Massias**
76 **NARVAL D'AVELOT (FR)**, 4, b g Video Rock (FR)—Reine Des Planches (FR) **Mr J. M. Robin**
77 **NASDACK (FR)**, 4, b g Epervier Bleu—Gribiche (FR) **Mr S. Benaroche**
78 **NASDACQ DELAB (FR)**, 4, b g Chamberlin (FR)—Berenice de Frosse (FR) **Mr De La Bassetiere**
79 **NATHALIE BLEU (FR)**, 4, ch f Epervier Bleu—Grace de Vonnas (FR) **Mrs M. Bryant**
80 **NAYAS (FR)**, 4, ch g Kaldou Star—Rigolette (FR) **Mr E. Van Haeran**
81 **NECTAR DES BROSSES (FR)**, 4, b g Epervier Bleu—Suzana Des Brosses (FR) **Mme P. Papot**
82 **NEILAND (FR)**, 4, ch f Cyborg (FR)—Vindhy (FR) **Mme P. Papot**
83 **NEMOSSUS (FR)**, 4, b g Mont Basile (FR)—Ephyra (FR) **Mr J. M. Robin**
84 **NEOPOLIS (FR)**, 4, ch g Ragmar (FR)—Apside (FR) **Mr R. Fougedoire**
85 **NEW ILLUSION (FR)**, 4, b f Solid Illusion (USA)—Madame Nathalie (FR) **Mr R. Waley-Cohen**
86 **NEW ROCK (FR)**, 4, b g Video Rock (FR)—Agathe de Beard (FR) **Mr J. C. Audry**
87 **NEWHORSE (FR)**, 4, b g Village Star (FR)—Canonniere (FR) **Mr R. Fougedoire**
88 **NEWTON D'AVELOT (FR)**, 4, b g Epervier Bleu—Unaria (FR) **Mr J. M. Robin**
89 **NICKEL DU COCHET (FR)**, 4, b g Ambroise (FR)—Diva Du Cochet (FR) **Mrs M. Bryant**
90 **NIKAIDO (FR)**, 4, b g Nikos—Zamsara (FR) **Palmyr Racing**
91 **NINI MALTA (FR)**, 4, ch f Cyborg (FR)—Miss Thann (FR) **Mrs M. Bryant**
92 **NIRVANA SWING (FR)**, 4, b g Chamberlin (FR)—Ukrainia II (FR) **Mr G. Morosini**
93 **NOIR SUR BLANC (FR)**, 4, ch f Mansonnien (FR)—Echarpe Noir (BRZ) **Mr R. Fougedoire**
94 **NOLWENN (FR)**, 4, b f Lute Antique (FR)—Asterie L'ermitage (FR) **Mr Terry Amos**
95 **NOMINALE (FR)**, 4, gr g Perrault—Caline De Sienne (FR) **Mrs Vanden Broele**
96 **NOTEZ LE (FR)**, 4, gr g Saint Preuil (FR)—Gibelotte (FR) **Mr R. Fougedoire**
97 **NOUED PAPILLLON (FR)**, 4, b g Video Rock (FR)—Samara IV (FR) **Mr R. Fougedoire**
98 **NOUVEA (FR)**, 4, ch c Perrault—Umea IV (FR) **Mrs S. Bramall**
99 **NOUVELLE DONNE (FR)**, 4, b f Sleeping Car (FR)—Nocha (FR) **Mr R. Fougedoire**
100 **NOZIC (FR)**, 4, b g Port Lyautey (FR)—Grizilh (FR) **Mr A. Faucheux**
101 **NUAGE DE COTTE (FR)**, 4, b g Sleeping Car (FR)—Kariantique (FR) **Mr R. Fougedoire**
102 **NUIT DES CHARTREUX (FR)**, 5, b m Villez (USA)—Nuit D'ecajeul (FR) **Mr F. Picoulet**
103 **NUMERO SPECIAL (FR)**, 4, b g Nikos—Ribalina (FR) **Mr R. Fougedoire**
104 **NUMITOR DES OBEAUX (FR)**, 4, gr g Balleroy (USA)—Castellia (FR) **Mme N. Devilder**
105 **OUBLIES CA (FR)**, 4, ch c Starborough—Okocha (GER) **Mr H. Rapp**
106 **PANTHEISTE (FR)**, 5, b g Panoramic—Azilal (FR) **Mr F. Lazar**
107 **PEINTRE CELESTE (FR)**, 4, b g Cricket Ball (USA)—Harmonie Celeste (FR) **Mr R. Fougedoire**
108 **PRINCE DES IFS (FR)**, 4, b g Sleeping Car (FR)—Miss Brodie (FR) **Mr R. Fougedoire**
109 **PRINCE TATANE (FR)**, 6, b g Agent Bleu (FR)—Sainte Astrid (FR) **Mme P. Papot**
110 **REXLOR (FR)**, 4, b g Port Lyautey (FR)—Isle du Tresor (FR) **Mr R. Fougedoire**
111 **RIB PILE (FR)**, 8, b g Garde Royale—Doll Poppy (FR) **Ecurie Rib**

MR G. MACAIRE—continued

112 **RIGOUREUX (FR)**, 5, b g Villez (USA)—Rouge Folie (FR) **Mr R. Fougedoire**
113 **ROBIN DE NONANT (FR)**, 5, ch g Garde Royale—Relayeuse (FR) **Mr R. Fougedoire**
114 **SAMANSONNIENNE (FR)**, 4, ch f Mansonnien—Sanhia (FR) **Mr O. Delegue**
115 **SEPT ET NEUF (FR)**, 5, b g Esprit Du Nord (USA)—Peau D'or **Mrs F. Montauban**
116 **SIKI (FR)**, 8, b g Chamberlin (FR)—Cerianthe (FR) **Mr J. Belzung**
117 **SUBEHARGUES (FR)**, 10, b g Mansonnien (FR)—Grande Yepa (FR) **Mr X. Papot**
118 **TALYSKER (FR)**, 4, b g Cadoudal (FR)—Miss Amande (FR) **Mr J. Cotton**
119 **TEMPO D'OR (FR)**, 7, b g Esprit du Nord (USA)—Peau d'or (FR) **Mrs F. Montauban**
120 **TIKI DE LUNE (FR)**, 4, gr g Cadoudal (FR)—Tikidoun (FR) **Mr R. W. Denechere**
121 **TYSSAC (FR)**, 4, ch g Beyssac (FR)—Aktia (FR) **Mr A. M. Chiche**
122 **VESUVE (FR)**, 6, b g Villez (USA)—Razzamatazz **Mrs H. Devin**
123 **VINDESROIS (FR)**, 6, b g Saint Cyrien (FR)—Orlight (FR) **Ecurie Guillaume Macaire**
124 **VISITE PRINCIERE (FR)**, 4, ch f Villez (USA)—Notabilite (FR) **Mrs M. Bryant**
125 **WESTOS (FR)**, 4, b g Nikos (GR)—Fassonwest (FR) **Mr J. C. Audry**
126 **ZEPHYR DES OBEAUX (FR)**, 4, ch g Franc Bleu (FR)—Zaouia (FR) **Mme N. Devilder**

THREE-YEAR-OLDS

127 **BAODAI (FR)**, b c Cadoudal—Royale Aube (FR) **Mr J. C. Audry**
128 **BEAUTIFUL NIGHT (FR)**, b f Sleeping Car (FR)—Doll Night (FR) **Mrs F. Montauban**
129 **CARSON (FR)**, b g Sleeping Car (FR)—Sunmania (FR) **Mr R. Fougedoire**
130 **CHANT DE LUNE (FR)**, gr g Cadoudal (FR)—Tikidoun (FR) **Mr R. W. Denechere**
131 **CHINKAPIN (FR)**, ch f Cyborg (FR)—Coralisse Royale (FR) **Mr R. Waley-Cohen**
132 **CRIDAC (FR)**, b f Cadoudal (FR)—Criade (FR) **Mrs B. Gabeur**
133 **CROISETTE (FR)**, ch f Mansonnien (FR)—Fouinette (FR) **Mrs B. Gabeur**
134 **DAVENTRY**, b c Kahyasi—Perfect Sister (USA) **Mr J. Detre**
135 **FIRST WONDER (FR)**, ch f Mansonnien (FR)—Eightwonder (FR) **Mr J. P. Garcon**
136 **GOOD SPIRIT (FR)**, b c Smadoun (FR)—Haute Tension (FR) **Mr J. C. Audry**
137 **KAUTO DANCER (FR)**, b g Jeune Homme (USA)—Kauto Relka (FR) **Mr C. Cohen**
138 **LADY CAD (FR)**, b f Cadoudal (FR)—Lady Corteira (FR) **Mr R. Green**
139 **MOON SIR (GER)**, b c Surako (GER)—Moonlit Water **Mr R. Fougedoire**
140 **O DE MONTOT (FR)**, b g Lights Out (FR)—Deep Turple (FR) **Mr F. Lazar**
141 **OBLAT PIERJI (FR)**, b c Epervier Bleu—Fanfare (FR) **Mme P. Papot**
142 **OCEANY (FR)**, b c Mansonnien (FR)—Infancy (FR) **Mrs M. Bryant**
143 **OEDIPE (FR)**, b g Chamberlin (FR)—Massada (FR) **Mr R. Fougedoire**
144 **OEIL POUR OEIL (FR)**, b g Take Risks (FR)—Ribalina (FR) **Mr R. Fougedoire**
145 **OFFICIER DE RESERVE (FR)**, b g Sleeping Car (FR)—Royaute (FR) **Mr R. Fougedoire**
146 **OISEAU BAI (FR)**, b c Cadoudal (FR)—Biolaine (FR) **Mme P. Papot**
147 **OLD WHISKY (FR)**, b c Epervier Bleu—Vodka Tonique (FR) **Mr M. Froissard**
148 **OLYMPE MALTA (FR)**, ch f Alesso (GER)—Creme Royale (FR) **Mr R. Fougedoire**
149 **ONCLE D'AMERIQUE (FR)**, ch g Robin des Champs (FR)—Nocha (FR) **Mr R. Fougedoire**
150 **ONDIN DE THAIX (FR)**, b g Ungaro (GER)—Gaite De Thaix (FR) **Mr R. Fougedoire**
151 **ONIGHT (FR)**, b g April Night (FR)—Canonniere (FR) **Mr R. Fougedoire**
152 **ONIX (FR)**, ch c Ragmar (FR)—Hase (FR) **Mr M. Bessis**
153 **ONYX BRUERE (FR)**, gr g Mansonnien (FR)—Hervine Bruere (FR) **Mr R. Fougedoire**
154 **OPIPARO (FR)**, ch g Valanjou (FR)—Quick Frisco (FR) **Mme P. Papot**
155 **OPIUM DE COTTE (FR)**, b g Apple Tree (FR)—Vanille de Cotte (FR) **Mr R. Fougedoire**
156 **OR EN BARRE (FR)**, ch f Video Rock (FR)—Chantalouette (FR) **Mr R. Fougedoire**
157 **ORAGE DE COTTE (FR)**, b g Apple Tree (FR)—Rafale de Cotte (FR) **Mr R. Fougedoire**
158 **ORGANIZ (FR)**, b g Mansonnien (FR)—Madame Illusion (FR) **Mrs M. Bryant & Mr R. Waley-Cohen**
159 **ORGUEUIL DES DIMES (FR)**, b c Rahotep (FR)—Fiduciaire (FR) **Mrs F. Montauban**
160 **OROCK (FR)**, b g Video Rock (FR)—Quatia du Rocher (FR) **Mr J. C. Audry**
161 **ORPHEE DE VONNAS (FR)**, b f Jimble (FR)—Grace de Vonnas (FR) **Mr R. Fougedoire**
162 **ORPHICA DE THAIX (FR)**, b g Video Rock (FR)—Jessica de Thaix (FR) **Mr R. Fougedoire**
163 **OSCARD MALTA (FR)**, b g Robin des Champs (FR)—Miss Thann (FR) **Mr R. Fougedoire**
164 **OUBLIONS LES (FR)**, b g Kahyasi—Shardazar **Mr R. Fougedoire**
165 **OUT OF REACH (FR)**, b g Saint Cyrien (FR)—Anabelle d'aumont (FR) **Mr J. M. Robin**
166 **OUVRONS LE FEU (FR)**, ch g Mansonnien (FR)—Gibelotte (FR) **Mr R. Fougedoire**
167 **OUZBEK (FR)**, b f Video Rock (FR)—Biblos (FR) **Mr F. Lazar**
168 **OVOMALTHINE (FR)**, b f Saint Preuil (FR)—Friandise II (FR) **Mr J. C. Audry**
169 **OWARD (FR)**, b c Mansonnien (FR)—Violette D'avril (FR) **Mr J. C. Audry**
170 **PRIMEIRA (GER)**, ch f Acatenango (GER)—Pretty Blue (GER) **Mrs F. Montauban**
171 **RICH ROMEO (GER)**, b c Greinton—Richgorl (GER) **Mr J. Detre**
172 **ROBIN DE BRUYERES (FR)**, ch g Robin des Champs (FR)—Arche Perdue (FR) **Mr R. Fougedoire**
173 **ROCK AUSSI (FR)**, b g Cyborg (FR)—Rosa Carola (FR) **Mrs M. Bryant**

MR G. MACAIRE—continued

174 **SEGRE (FR)**, gr f Fragrant Mix (IRE)—Stenoree (FR) **Mr R. Robert**
175 **SENSUALITE (FR)**, ch f Mansonnien (FR)—Creme Pralinee (FR) **Mr R. Y. Simon**
176 **SORAMIC (FR)**, gr f Panoramic—Sonight (FR) **Mrs F. Montauban**
177 **STOWAY (FR)**, b c Broadway Flyer (USA)—Stowe (FR) **Mr J. Detre**
178 **TIERSDESOU (FR)**, b g Adnaan (FR)—Culoth (FR) **Mr J. C. Audry**
179 **TITITONI (FR)**, b c Nikos—Fassonwest (FR) **Mr J. C. Audry**
180 **TWIST MAGIC (FR)**, b c Winged Love (IRE)—Twist Scarlett (GER) **Mrs F. Montauban**
181 **UN NONONITO (FR)**, b g Nononito (FR)—Basket Girande (FR) **Mme P. Papot**
182 **UNE SAINTE (FR)**, b f Ungaro (GER)—Sainte Astrid (FR) **Mme P. Papot**
183 **VILLENTIN (FR)**, b c Villez (USA)—Cadence Vite (FR) **Mr J. Detre**
184 **VINTOX (GER)**, b c Oxalagu (GER)—Vinca (GER) **Mrs F. Montauban**
185 **ZANORAMIC (FR)**, gr g Panoramic—Idylle d'estruval (FR) **Mr J. C. Audry**

TWO-YEAR-OLDS

186 **ALIFIERI (GER)**, b c 11/4 Surako (GER)—Anjou (GER) (Surumu (GER)) **Mr F. Fernandez**
187 **BEST OF THE WEST (FR)**, b c 4/4 Nikos—Fassonwest (FR) (Dom Pasquini (FR)) **Mrs B. Gabeur**
188 **BET ON ME (GER)**, b c 13/3 Second Set (IRE)—Bella Vista (GER) (Konigsstuhl (GER)) (6706) **Mr Terry Amos**
189 **BUONTALENTI (GER)**, b c 10/2 Winged Love (IRE)—
　　　　　　　　　　　　　　　　　　Bagana (GER) (Acatenango (GER)) (14755) **Mr S. Benaroche**
190 **EN LA CRUZ (FR)**, b f 27/3 Robin des Champs (FR)—Nuit D'ecajeul (FR) (Matahawk) **Mr F. Picoulet**
191 **FUELA PASS (FR)**, b f 30/1 Astarabad (USA)—Picoletta (FR) (Galetto (FR)) (6706) **Mr J. P. Bellaiche**
192 **KATRIA (GER)**, ch f 9/4 Protektor (GER)—Kelly's Diamond (Snurge) **Mr J. M. Robin**
193 **KHE DIVAT (FR)**, b f 9/3 Baby Turk—Kainja (FR) (Garde Royale) (10060) **Mr P. Coudert**
194 **LET'S ROLL (FR)**, ch c 24/2 Cadoudal (FR)—Battle Quest (FR) (Noblequest (FR)) **Mrs M. Bryant**
195 **MASTER MINDED (FR)**, b c 14/4 Nikos—Haute Tension (FR) (Garde Royale) **Mrs B. Gabeur**
196 **NADAL (FR)**, b c 1/6 Cadoudal (FR)—Libertina (FR) (Balsamo (FR)) **Mrs Nadal**
197 **PEAU AIME (FR)**, b c 1/1 Passing Sale (FR)—Carvine d'or (FR) (Pot d'or (FR)) **Mr J. M. Robin**
198 **PENVERN (FR)**, b c 1/1 Nononito (FR)—Fest Noz (FR) (Port Ettienne (FR)) **Mrs M. Bryant**
199 **PETIT PRINCE SUN (FR)**, b c 7/6 Vertical Speed (FR)—Five Rivers (FR) (Cadoudal (FR)) **Mr Audry**
200 **PORT GAUGAIN (FR)**, b c 21/3 Port Lyautey (FR)—Jobereine (FR) (Joberan (FR)) **Mr A. Faucheux**
201 **POWYS (FR)**, gr c 3/5 Silver Patriarch (IRE)—Humoriste (FR) (Saint Cyrien (FR)) (8048) **Mr G. Laroche**
202 **PRETTY BRUERE (FR)**, ch f 1/1 Villez (USA)—Hervine Bruere (FR) (Dom Pasquini (FR)) **Mrs M. Bryant**
203 **THE KALDOW (FR)**, b c 3/5 The Shadow (FR)—La Calotterie (FR) (Highest Honor (FR)) **Mrs M. Bryant**

Jockey (NH): B. Gicquel, Jacques Ricou. **Amateur:** Mr Adam Jones.

---

371 MRS N. J. MACAULEY, Melton Mowbray

Postal: **The Sidings, Saltby Road, Sproxton, Melton Mowbray, Leicestershire, LE14 4RA.**
Contacts: **HOME (01476) 860578 OFFICE (01476) 860090 FAX (01476) 860611
MOBILE (07741) 004444**

1 **BUNKHOUSE**, 5, ch g Wolfhound (USA)—Maid Welcome **Mrs N. J. Macauley**
2 **COME WHAT JULY (IRE)**, 4, b g Indian Rocket—Persian Sally (IRE) **R. Milward**
3 **COMETE DU LAC (FR)**, 8, ch m Comte du Bourg (FR)—Line du Nord (FR) **A. J. Peake**
4 **DIL**, 10, b g Primo Dominie—Swellegant **Mrs N. J. Macauley**
5 **MARIA MARIA (IRE)**, 4, ch f Among Men (USA)—Yiayia's Girl **Mrs E. A. M. Nelson**
6 **MI ODDS**, 9, b g Sure Blade (USA)—Vado Via (Brimardon Racing)
7 **MOON ROYALE**, 7, ch m Royal Abjar (USA)—Ragged Moon **B. Batey**
8 **MYSTIC PROMISE (IRE)**, 4, gr g Among Men (USA)—Ivory's Promise **Mrs E. A. M. Nelson**
9 **NOPLEAZINU**, 5, ch m Sure Blade (USA)—Vado Via **G. Wiltshire**
10 **OCKER (IRE)**, 11, br g Astronef—Violet Somers **Mrs N. J. Macauley**
11 **PUP'S PRIDE**, 8, b g Efisio—Moogie **West Indies Capital Company Limited**
12 **ROPPONGI DANCER**, 6, b m Mtoto—Ice Chocolate (USA) **A. J. Peake**
13 **SION HILL (IRE)**, 4, b g Desert Prince (IRE)—Mobilia **Mr Peter Smith**
14 **SORBIESHARRY (IRE)**, 6, gr g Sorbie Tower (IRE)—Silver Moon **Mrs E. A. M. Nelson**
15 **SPANISH STAR**, 8, b g Hernando (FR)—Desert Girl **Mrs N. J. Macauley**
16 **ST IVIAN**, 5, b g Inchinor—Lamarita **G. Horsford**
17 **WESTERN COMMAND (GER)**, 9, b g Saddlers' Hall (IRE)—Western Friend (USA) **A. J. Peake**

MRS N. J. MACAULEY—continued

THREE-YEAR-OLDS

18 **DANCING MOONLIGHT (IRE)**, b f Danehill Dancer (IRE)—Silver Moon **Mrs E. A. M. Nelson**
19 **LA CYGNE BLANCHE (IRE)**, gr f Saddlers' Hall (IRE)—Ivory's Promise **Mrs E. A. M. Nelson**
20 **PRESKANI**, b g Sri Pekan (USA)—Lamarita **G. Horsford**

TWO-YEAR-OLDS

21 **MONASHEEMINI (IRE)**, gr f 31/1 Monashee Mountain (USA)—
Ivory's Promise (Pursuit of Love) **Mrs E. A. M. Nelson**
22 **ORPHIR (IRE)**, b c 23/1 Orpen (USA)—Silver Moon (Environment Friend) **Mrs E. A. M. Nelson**

Jockey (flat): A. Culhane. **Apprentice:** Colin Haddon, S. Sayer. **Amateur:** Mrs M. Morris.

---

372 **MR W. J. W. MACKIE, Church Broughton**
Postal: **The Bungalow, Barton Blount, Church Broughton, Derby.**
Contacts: **PHONE (01283) 585604/585603 FAX (01283) 585603 MOBILE (07799) 145283**
E-MAIL jmackie@bartonblount.freeserve.co.uk

1 **ACCEPTING**, 8, b g Mtoto—D'azy **Mr M. T. Bloore & Mrs J. E. Lockwood**
2 **ALICE JONES (IRE)**, 7, b br m King's Ride—Alice Brennan (IRE) **G. A. Greaves**
3 **ASTRAL DANCER (IRE)**, 5, b g Fourstars Allstar (USA)—Walk n'dance (IRE) **The Festival Dream Partnership**
4 **BOLSHOI BALLET**, 7, b g Dancing Spree (USA)—Broom Isle **The M. A. S. Partnership**
5 **CANTARNA (IRE)**, 4, ch f Ashkalani (IRE)—Lancea (IRE) **Gwen K. Dot.Com**
6 **DANEBANK (IRE)**, 5, b g Danehill (USA)—Snow Bank (IRE) **Ms L. A. Machin**
7 **HADITOVSKI**, 9, b g Hatim (USA)—Grand Occasion **Mrs S. P. Adams**
8 **HAVING A PARTY**, 7, b m Dancing High—Lady Manello **Wall Racing Partners**
9 **HIGH RANK**, 6, b g Emperor Jones (USA)—Hotel Street (USA) **Trying to Buy Fun Partnership**
10 **HOT PRODUXION (USA)**, 6, ch g Tabasco Cat (USA)—Princess Harriet (USA) **A. J. Winterton**
11 **IMPISH JUDE**, 7, b m Imp Society (USA)—Miss Nanna **J. W. H. Fryer**
12 **JEROPINO (IRE)**, 7, b g Norwich—Guillig Lady (IRE) **Mr J. C. White**
13 **KATIE SAVAGE**, 5, b m Emperor Jones (USA)—Coax Me Molly (USA)
14 **KNOCK LORD (IRE)**, 8, b g Mister Lord (USA)—Sister Duke **M. J. Parr**
15 **MERCURIOUS (IRE)**, 5, ch m Grand Lodge (USA)—Rousinette **Gwen K. Dot.Com**
16 **RED FOREST (IRE)**, 6, b g Charnwood Forest (IRE)—High Atlas **P. Riley**
17 **RED SUN**, 8, b g Foxhound (USA)—Superetta **Bulls Head Racing Club**
18 **SILK TRADER**, 10, b g Nomadic Way (USA)—Money Run **The Festival Dream Partnership**
19 **SPEED VENTURE**, 8, b g Owington—Jade Venture **Wall Racing Partners**
20 **THYNE MAN (IRE)**, 7, br g Good Thyne (USA)—Showphar (IRE) **M. J. Parr**
21 **TIGER FROG (USA)**, 6, b g French Deputy (USA)—Woodyoubelieveit (USA) **Fools Who Dream**
22 **WELKINO'S BOY**, 4, ch g Most Welcome—Khadino **Scattered Friends Partnership**

THREE-YEAR-OLDS

23 **NE OUBLIE**, b c Makbul—Parkside Prospect **J. M. Graham**

Other Owners: M. A. Bates, R. A. Coleman, R. F. J. Coppack, P. G. Dawson, F. A. Dickinson, J. J. Dickson, D. J. Emsley, J. J. Finnegan, L. T. Foster, Mrs M. Foster, Mrs O. Harrison, R. H. Jackson, N. R. Jennings, Mrs E. Jordan, T. P. Keville, A. D. Miller, M. Morgan, R. J. Nash, A. J. L. Paterson, Mr A. Scholefield, B. Smith, A. J. Wall, C. J. Wall, R. T. Wall, Mrs S. J. Woolley.

Conditional: H. Gemberlu. **Amateur:** Mr Michael Ritchie.

---

373 **MR A. B. MACTAGGART, Hawick**
Postal: **Greendale, Hawick, Roxburghshire, TD9 7LH.**
Contacts: **PHONE/FAX (01450) 372086 MOBILE (07764) 159852/(07718) 920072**
E-MAIL brucemct@btinternet.com

1 **BLUE VENTURE (IRE)**, 5, ch g Alhaarth (IRE)—September Tide (IRE) **The Potassium Partnership**
2 **BORDER CRAIC (IRE)**, 5, ch g Glacial Storm (USA)—Clare Maid (IRE) **Kelso Members Lowflyers Club**
3 **BUFFY**, 5, b m Classic Cliche (IRE)—Annie Kelly **Harlequin Racing**
4 **CONOR'S PRIDE (IRE)**, 8, ch g Phardante (FR)—Surely Madam **Harlequin Racing**

MR A. B. MACTAGGART—continued

5 **CORBIE ABBEY (IRE)**, 10, b g Glacial Storm (USA)—Dromoland Lady **Mrs H. A. M. Mactaggart**
6 **CRUMBS**, 5, b m Puissance—Norska **In The Pink Syndicate**
7 **DANTE'S BROOK (IRE)**, 11, ch g Phardante (FR)—Arborfield Brook **Mr J. & Mr B. Jeffrey**
8 **EYZE (IRE)**, 9, b g Lord Americo—Another Raheen (IRE) **Stoneage Paving**
9 **JOHN O'GROATS (IRE)**, 7, b g Distinctly North (USA)—Bannons Dream (IRE) **Miss E. Johnston**
10 **LADY GODSON**, 6, ch m Bold Arrangement—Dreamy Desire **Mrs H. A. M. Mactaggart**
11 **MELAINA**, 4, b f Whittingham (IRE)—Oh I Say **Miss E. Johnston**
12 **MOUNTHOOLEY**, 9, ch g Karinga Bay—Gladys Emmanuel **Ashleybank Investments Limited**
13 **OLD NOSEY (IRE)**, 9, b g Muharib (USA)—Regent Star **The Potassium Partnership**
14 **THE MAYSTONE (IRE)**, 5, b br g Thowra (FR)—Peg O The Wood (IRE) **Stoneage Paving**

THREE-YEAR-OLDS

15 **HANSOMELLE (IRE)**, b f Titus Livius (FR)—Handsome Anna (IRE) **Corsby Racing**

Other Owners: H. G. Beeby, R. K. Bruce, Mrs F. M. Godson, Miss D. Haynes, D. Lamb, Mrs M. Marshall, Mr D. J. Pearce.

Assistant Trainer: Mrs H Mactaggart

Jockey (NH): A. Dempsey, G. Lee.

---

374 **MR A. H. MACTAGGART, Hawick**
Postal: **Wells, Denholm, Hawick, Roxburghshire, TD9 8TD.**
Contacts: **PHONE (01450) 870060 MOBILE (07711) 200445**

1 5, B m Alflora (IRE)—Poppea (IRE) **Alan & Marty Mactaggart**
2 5, B g Supreme Leader—Regal Spark **Alan & Marty Mactaggart**
3 **RUNNING MOSS**, 13, ch g Le Moss—Run'n Fly **Mrs A. H. Mactaggart**

Assistant Trainer: Mrs M A Mactaggart

Amateur: Mr J. Mactaggart, Mr C. Storey.

---

375 **MR P. MADDISON, Skewsby**
Postal: **5 West End Cottages, Skewsby, York, YO61 4SG.**
Contacts: **PHONE (01347) 888385**

1 **BANANA RIDGE**, 7, ch m Primitive Rising (USA)—Madison Girl **Mr P. Maddison**
2 **LOTHIAN FALCON**, 6, b g Relief Pitcher—Lothian Rose **Mr P. Maddison**
3 **SOLEMN VOW**, 4, b f Zaffaran (USA)—Quick Quick Sloe **Mr P. Maddison**

---

376 **MR M. J. MADGWICK, Denmead**
Postal: **Forest Farm, Forest Road, Denmead, Waterlooville, Hampshire, PO7 6UA.**
Contacts: **PHONE/FAX (02392) 258313 MOBILE (07835) 964969**

1 **CAPTAIN CLOUDY**, 5, b g Whittingham (IRE)—Money Supply **The Portsmouth Syndicate**
2 **DUNDRIDGE NATIVE**, 7, b m Be My Native (USA)—Fra Mau **C. L. Hood**
3 **ELLE ROSEADOR**, 6, b m El Conquistador—The Hon Rose **Mrs M. I. Yates**
4 **I WISH**, 7, ch m Beveled (USA)—Ballystate **All Four Corners**
5 **JAHIA (NZ)**, 6, br m Jahafil—Lana (NZ) **DDB Racing**
6 **LADY LAKSHMI**, 5, ch m Bahhare (USA)—Polish Honour (USA) **DDB Racing**
7 **LOCH LAIRD**, 10, b g Beveled (USA)—Daisy Loch **Miss E. M. L. Coller**
8 **MAXIMINUS**, 5, b g The West (USA)—Candarela **DDB Racing 1**
9 **MONTESINO**, 6, b g Bishop of Cashel—Sutosky **DDB Racing**
10 **PERSEPHONE HEIGHTS**, 5, br m Golden Heights—Jalland **Persephone Heights Racing**
11 **RICHMOND LODGE**, 5, br g Sesaro (USA)—Richmond Lillie **DDB Racing**
12 **SHARP SEAL**, 11, b g Broadsword (USA)—Little Beaver **Mr M. J. Madgwick**
13 **SWEET MINUET**, 8, b m Minshaanshu Amad (USA)—Sweet N' Twenty **W. E. Baird**
14 **SWEET SHOOTER**, 5, ch m Double Trigger (IRE)—Sweet N' Twenty **W. E. Baird**
15 **WAVERLEY ROAD**, 8, ch g Pelder (IRE)—Lillicara (FR) **W. V. Roker**

MR M. J. MADGWICK—continued

THREE-YEAR-OLDS

16 **BLUE LINE**, gr f Bluegrass Prince (IRE)—Out Line **Miss E. M. L. Coller**
17 **PIE CORNER**, ch c Fumo di Londra (IRE)—Ballystate

TWO-YEAR-OLDS

18 **WATCH OUT JESS**, gr f 4/4 Averti (IRE)—Out Line (Beveled (USA)) **Miss E. M. L. Coller**

Other Owners: F. W. J. Buckett, R. C. Denton, Mrs E. J. Harton-Carter, G. E. Heard, Mrs R. Luton, Mrs M. A. Luton, D. O'Sullivan, D. J. Willis.

Assistant Trainer: David Madgwick

Jockey (flat): G. Baker, T. Quinn. **Jockey (NH):** J. Goldstein. **Conditional:** R. Lucey-Butler.

---

377 **MR M. A. MAGNUSSON, Upper Lambourn**
Postal: **The Old Manor, Upper Lambourn, Hungerford, Berkshire, RG17 8RG.**
Contacts: **OFFICE (01488) 73966 FAX (01488) 71702 MOBILE (07775) 556306**
E-MAIL mikael.magnusson@virgin.net

1 **BACK IN ACTION**, 5, b g Hector Protector (USA)—Lucca **East Wind Racing Ltd and Martha Trussell**
2 **KHALIDIA (USA)**, 4, b g Boundary (USA)—Maniches Slew (USA) **East Wind Racing Ltd**
3 **MUTAWAQED (IRE)**, 7, ch g Zafonic (USA)—Waqood (USA) **East Wind Racing Ltd**
4 **SPINDOR (USA)**, 6, ch g Spinning World (USA)—Doree (USA) **East Wind Racing Ltd**
5 **UNAVAILABLE (IRE)**, 4, b f Alzao (USA)—Maid of Killeen (IRE) **East Wind Racing Ltd and Martha Trussell**

THREE-YEAR-OLDS

6 **KING OF BLUES (IRE)**, ch c Bluebird (USA)—Highly Respected (IRE) **East Wind Racing Ltd**
7 **MAGNATE (IRE)**, b c Entrepreneur—Hilbys Brite Flite (USA) **East Wind Racing Ltd**
8 **PERFECT TONE (USA)**, ch f Silver Hawk (USA)—Copper Cachet (USA) **East Wind Racing Ltd**
9 **SINNMORE (IRE)**, ch c Sinndar (IRE)—Demure **East Wind Racing Ltd**
10 **TUTU MUCH (IRE)**, b f Sadler's Wells (USA)—Filia Ardross **East Wind Racing Ltd and Martha Trussell**

TWO-YEAR-OLDS

11 B br f 10/2 Zafonic (USA)—Bank On Her (USA) (Rahy (USA)) (115000) **East Wind Racing Ltd**
12 Ch f 23/1 Fantastic Light (USA)—Muschana (Deploy) (57008) **East Wind Racing Ltd**
13 **SMART ENOUGH**, gr c 25/4 Cadeaux Genereux—
Good Enough (FR) (Mukaddamah (USA)) (78000) **East Wind Racing Ltd**
14 B br c 23/2 Mt Livermore (USA)—Swan River (USA) (Hennessy (USA)) (75000) **East Wind Racing Ltd**

Other Owners: Alain Falourd, Robert Trussell.

---

378 **MR P. J. MAKIN, Marlborough**
Postal: **Bonita Racing Stables, Ogbourne Maisey, Marlborough, Wiltshire, SN8 1RY.**
Contacts: **PHONE (01672) 512973 FAX (01672) 514166**
E-MAIL hq@petermakin-racing.com

1 **EMPIRE OF THE SUN**, 4, b f Second Empire (IRE)—Splicing **The Highly Sociable Syndicate**
2 **GREENSLADES**, 6, ch h Perugino (USA)—Woodfield Rose **Four Seasons Racing Ltd**
3 **HEAVENS WALK**, 4, ch c Compton Place—Ghost Dancing **Mrs P. J. Makin**
4 **INCH BY INCH**, 6, b m Inchinor—Maid Welcome **Mrs A. M. Sanders**
5 **NATHAN DETROIT**, 5, b g Entrepreneur—Mainly Sunset **Mrs J. M. Carrington**
6 **NOT SO DUSTY**, 5, b g Primo Dominie—Ann's Pearl (IRE) **Mrs S. A. Levinson**
7 **PIVOTAL POINT**, 5, b g Pivotal—True Precision **R. A. Bernard**
8 **SOUL DANCE**, 4, b f Imperial Ballet (IRE)—Piccante **D. A. Poole**
9 **STRIKE LUCKY**, 5, ch g Millkom—Lucky Flinders **Mrs P. J. Makin**
10 **WATAMU (IRE)**, 4, b g Groom Dancer (USA)—Miss Golden Sands **R. A. Henley**

MR P. J. MAKIN—continued

THREE-YEAR-OLDS

11 **CASEMATE**, b g Efisio—Flying Carpet **Four Seasons Racing Ltd**
12 **DR ZALO**, ch g Dr Fong (USA)—Azola (IRE) **Mrs Moore With Ahier Carrington Marchant**
13 **EDGED IN GOLD**, ch f Bold Edge—Piccante **Weldspec Glasgow Limited**
14 **JOHN BRATBY (USA)**, b br c Royal Academy (USA)—Side Saddle (IRE) **J. R. Hartnoll**
15 **KINRANDE (IRE)**, b c Sri Pekan (USA)—Pipers Pool (IRE) **G & R Marchant Ahier Carrington & Moore**
16 **KITCHEN SINK (IRE)**, ch g Bold Fact (USA)—Voodoo Rocket **Julian Hartnoll And Nick Pearce**
17 **KYLES PRINCE (IRE)**, b g In The Wings—Comprehension (USA) **Weldspec Glasgow Limited**
18 **LOUPHOLE**, ch g Loup Sauvage (USA)—Goodwood Lass (IRE) **Ten Of Hearts**
19 **SMALL STAKES (IRE)**, b g Pennekamp (USA)—Poker Chip **J P Carrington with Ahier Marchant Moore**
20 **SUN GOD**, b c Kayf Tara—Ghost Dancing **Mrs P. J. Makin**
21 **ZIPADEEDOODAH**, b c Bluebird (USA)—River Divine (USA) **Lady Davis, Beryl Lake, Richard Simmonds**

TWO-YEAR-OLDS

22 Ch c 1/3 Bluebird (USA)—
  Always True (USA) (Geiger Counter (USA)) (25000) **Martin Holland, John Gale, T. Wellard**
23 B c 27/3 Mozart (IRE)—Bold As Love (Lomond (USA)) (50000) **Thurloe Thoroughbreds XV**
24 B c 16/5 Bertolini (USA)—Cold Blow (Posse (USA)) (30000) **Alberto Panetta**
25 B c 6/5 Polish Precedent (USA)—Fanfare (Deploy) (10500) **R. A. Henley**
26 B c 19/3 Dansili—Manila Selection (USA) (Manila (USA)) (20000) **Camamile Hessert Scott Partnership**
27 B c 19/3 Bahamian Bounty—Mouchez Le Nez (IRE) (Cyrano de Bergerac) (10000) **Duncan Ritchie & Partners**
28 **PEEPHOLE**, ch c 4/4 Pursuit of Love—Goodwood Lass (IRE) (Alzao (USA)) (4700) **Ten Horsepower**
29 B f 31/3 Josr Algarhoud (IRE)—Piccante (Wolfhound) (USA) **Mrs P. J. Makin**
30 Br f 19/4 Beat All (USA)—Plum Bold (Be My Guest (USA)) (5000) **Lady Lonsdale**
31 Ch f 9/3 Spinning World (USA)—Royal Bounty (IRE) (Generous (IRE)) (21461) **Bakewell Bloodstock**
32 B c 10/3 Generous (IRE)—Sans Diablo (IRE) (Mac's Imp (USA)) (8000) **Countess Badeni**
33 B c 1/4 Inchinor—Savannah Belle (Green Desert (USA)) (8000) **Mrs A. M. Sanders**
34 **SNARK (IRE)**, b c 6/4 Cape Cross (IRE)—Agoer (Hadeer) (28000) **Darius Anderson**
35 **SUSSEX STAR (IRE)**, b c 17/2 Elnadim (USA)—Crystal Springs (IRE) (Kahyasi) (15000) **D. Ladhams & Partners**

Other Owners: D. M. Ahier, Mrs Monica Townsend-Moore, Peter Lycett, Chas Taylor, Mrs Keith Goodwin, Kevin Carl, Leigh Rosen, Chris J. Smith, J. J. Blackshaw, K. Brackpool, B. A. W. Brackpool, J. G. D. Brocklehurst, A. C. D. Hollingworth, R. Kent, Mr P. G. Melotti, E. J. Perry.

Jockey (flat): S. Sanders, D. Sweeney. **Amateur:** Mr S. Walker.

---

379 MRS ALYSON MALZARD, Jersey
Postal: **Les Etabl'yes, Grosnez, St Ouen, Jersey, JE3 2AD.**
Contacts: **PHONE (01534) 483773 MOBILE (07797) 738128**
E-MAIL themalzards@localdial.com

1 **CROSSWAYS**, 7, b g Mister Baileys—Miami Dancer (USA) **Mr & Mrs T. Gallienne**
2 **KEEP ON RUNNING (FR)**, 7, ch g Beyssac (FR)—Kiruna V (FR) **Keep on Running Racing**
3 **KHUZDAR (IRE)**, 6, ch g Definite Article—Mariyda (IRE) **Mrs Y. Burnett, Mr H. England & Mr D. Le Poidevin**
4 **NOBLE REEF**, 8, b g Deploy—Penny Mint **Mrs A. Malzard**
5 **PALALA RIVER**, 12, ch m Colmore Row—Express Edition **Miss J. Edgar & Mr J. Mercier**
6 **PERFECT PORTRAIT**, 5, ch g Selkirk (USA)—Flawless Image (USA) **Mrs P. Somers**
7 **REGAL ALI (IRE)**, 6, ch g Ali-Royal (IRE)—Depeche (FR) **Mr N. Ahier**
8 **TIME TO WYN**, 9, b g Timeless Times (USA)—Wyn-Bank **Westward Racing**
9 **UNVEIL**, 7, ch m Rudimentary (USA)—Magical Veil **Mr R. Theaker**
10 **WARRIORS PATH (IRE)**, 6, b g Namaqualand (USA)—Azinter (IRE) **Mr B. Le Prevost & Ms O. Liepina**

Jockey (flat): Ross Studholme. **Jockey (NH):** Ross Studholme. **Amateur:** Mr D. Cuthbert, Mrs G. Poingdestre.

---

380 MR JAMES J. MANGAN, Mallow
Postal: **Curraheen, Conna, Co. Cork, Ireland.**
Contacts: **PHONE/FAX +353 (0) 58 59116 MOBILE +353 (0) 87 2684611**

1 **BOBBAWN (IRE)**, 5, b g Bob Back (USA)—Bawnanell **Dr D. O'Sullivan**
2 **CARMELS COTTAGE (IRE)**, 7, b m Riberetto—Shoubad Melody **Mary Mangan**
3 **CONNA CASTLE (IRE)**, 6, b g Germany (USA)—Mrs Hegarty **The Kings Syndicate**
4 **MILL BANK (IRE)**, 10, b g Millfontaine—Mossy Bank (IRE) **The Maddock Syndicate**

MR JAMES J. MANGAN—continued

  5 **MONTY'S PASS (IRE)**, 12, b g Montelimar (USA)—Friars Pass **Dee Racing Syndicate**
  6 **SEE MORE BILLS**, 10, b g Seymour Hicks (FR)—Squawbil **Mary Mangan**
  7 **WE HAVE TIME (IRE)**, 6, b g Lord Americo—Floppy Disk **Mr A. Kenny**

Assistant Trainer: Mary Mangan

---

381 | **MR C. J. MANN**, Upper Lambourn
Postal: **Whitcoombe House Stables, Maddle Road, Upper Lambourn, Hungerford, Berkshire, RG17 8RA.**
Contacts: **PHONE** (01488) 71717/73118 **FAX** (01488) 73223 **MOBILE** (07721) 888333
E-MAIL charlie.mann@virgin.net **WEBSITE** www.charliemann.com

  1 **AFRO MAN**, 7, b g Commanche Run—Lady Elle (IRE) **Mrs J. E. Brown, R. A. Lucas & R. E. Good**
  2 **ALLBORN LAD (IRE)**, 5, b g Fourstars Allstar (USA)—Billeragh Girl **A. W. Stapleton**
  3 **ALROYAL (GER)**, 6, ch g Royal Solo (IRE)—Alamel (USA) **P. Cook**
  4 **AMMONIAS (GER)**, 6, b g Monsun (GER)—Augreta (GER) **Mrs J. E. Brown & P. A. Randall**
  5 **ANALOGY (IRE)**, 5, ch g Bahhare (USA)—Anna Comnena (IRE) **H. E. C. Villiers**
  6 **ANOTHER NATIVE (IRE)**, 7, b g Be My Native (USA)—Lancastrians Wine (IRE) **The Sport Of Kings Partnership**
  7 **BAGAN (FR)**, 6, b br h Rainbow Quest (USA)—Maid of Erin **F F Racing Services Limited**
  8 **BARMAN (USA)**, 6, ch g Atticus (USA)—Blue Tip (FR) **The Sport of Kings Partnership**
  9 **BLAZING THE TRAIL (IRE)**, 5, ch g Indian Ridge—Divine Pursuit **Mr C. J. Mann**
 10 **CA NA TRONA (IRE)**, 6, b g Accordion—Sterna Star **Mr M. Rowland & The Dunnkirk Partnership**
 11 **CAGED TIGER**, 6, b g Classic Cliche (IRE)—Run Tiger (IRE) **Mr C. J. Mann**
 12 **CAPITOLE (IRE)**, 4, b g Imperial Ballet (IRE)—Blue Glass **The Safest Syndicate**
 13 **CASH IN HAND (IRE)**, 5, b g Charente River (IRE)—Fern Fields (IRE) **Celtic Bloodstock Ltd**
 14 **CERTAIN FACT (USA)**, 4, b c Sir Cat (USA)—Pure Misk **Mr C. J. Mann**
 15 **CRUISING CLYDE**, 6, ch g Karinga Bay—Bournel **Abbott Racing Limited**
 16 **CYRIUM (IRE)**, 6, b g Woodborough (USA)—Jarmar Moon **Colin & Pauline Sturgeon**
 17 **DEARSON (IRE)**, 4, b g Definite Article—Petite Maxine **The Whitcoombe Four**
 18 **DEMI BEAU**, 7, b g Dr Devious (IRE)—Charming Life (NZ) **H. E. C. Villiers**
 19 **DEVIL'S TEARDROP**, 5, ch g Hernando (FR)—River Divine (USA) **The Happy Go Lucky Partnership**
 20 **EMPERORS GUEST**, 7, b g Emperor Jones (USA)—Intimate Guest **The Life Of Riley Partnership**
 21 **FANDANI (GER)**, 5, b g Lomitas—Fainting Spell (FR) **Mr N. Kempner & Mr C. J. Mann**
 22 **FIFTY QUID SHORT (IRE)**, 5, ch g Glacial Storm (USA)—Park Princess (IRE) **Celtic Bloodstock Ltd**
 23 **FLINDERS CHASE**, 10, gr g Terimon—Proverbial Rose **P. M. Warren**
 24 **FLOREANA (GER)**, 4, b f Acatenango (GER)—Frille (FR) **Mr M. Lynch**
 25 **GAORA BRIDGE (IRE)**, 7, b g Warcraft (USA)—Miss Good Night **Mr Robert Tompkins & Mrs Lynda Lovell**
 26 **GROUVILLE**, 4, b g Groom Dancer (USA)—Dance Land (IRE) **Roger Bender & Ray Bender**
 27 **HECKLEY CLARE GLEN**, 7, b m Dancing High—Heckley Spark **Mr M. Rowland & The Dunnkirk Partnership**
 28 **HEY BOY (IRE)**, 6, b g Courtship—Make Me An Island **Mrs J. E. Brown & R. E. Good**
 29 **HOH NELSON**, 4, b g Halling (USA)—Birsay **Mr David Allport & Mr Michael Lynch**
 30 **HOH VISS**, 5, b g Rudimentary (USA)—Now And Forever (IRE) **D. F. Allport**
 31 **INFIDEL (IRE)**, 5, b g Spectrum (IRE)—Implicit View **Mrs D. L. Mosley**
 32 **KALEXANDRO (FR)**, 7, b g Michel Georges—Dalexandra (FR) **T. E. Grove**
 33 **KELTIC BARD**, 8, b g Emperor Jones (USA)—Broughton Singer (IRE) **Mr M. Rowland, M. Collins & P. Cox**
 34 **LAWOOD (IRE)**, 5, gr g Charnwood Forest (IRE)—La Susiane **J. Davies, A. Merritt & W. Hagon**
 35 **LORIKO D'AIRY (FR)**, 6, b g Oblat (FR)—Ursali d'airy (FR) **Mrs J. M. Mayo**
 36 **MAKULU (IRE)**, 5, b g Alzao (USA)—Karinski (USA) **Matham Investments**
 37 **MERCHANTS FRIEND (IRE)**, 10, b g Lord Americo—Buck Maid **Magic Moments**
 38 **MONTYS ISLAND (IRE)**, 8, b g Montelimar (USA)—Sea Island **The Safest Syndicate**
 39 **MR FERNET**, 8, b g Mtoto—Francfurter **L Bolingbroke S Cannon N Gravett B Walsh**
 40 **MYSTIC FOREST**, 6, b g Charnwood Forest (IRE)—Mystic Beauty (IRE) **Lee Bolingbroke & Partners II**
 41 **NADOVER (FR)**, 4, br g Cyborg (FR)—Djerissa (FR) **Mr Tony Hayward & Partners**
 42 **NATHOS (GER)**, 8, b g Zaizoom (USA)—Nathania (GER) **John Davies & John Trickett**
 43 **POLAR SCOUT (IRE)**, 8, b g Arctic Lord—Baden (IRE) **Exors Of The Late Mrs L. G. Turner**
 44 **PRAIRIE MOONLIGHT (GER)**, 5, b m Monsun (GER)—Prairie Princess (GER) **Celtic Bloodstock Ltd**
 45 **PROPER SQUIRE (USA)**, 8, b g Bien Bien (USA)—La Cumbre **The Icy Fire Partnership**
 46 **ROTHERAM (USA)**, 5, b g Dynaformer (USA)—Out of Taxes (USA) **The Icy Fire Partnership**
 47 **SECOND (IRE)**, 4, b g Zaffaran (USA)—Slighter **H. E. C. Villiers**
 48 **SENESCHAL**, 4, b g Polar Falcon (USA)—Broughton Singer (IRE) **Mr C. J. Mann**
 49 **SLYBOOTS (USA)**, 6, gr g Neshad (USA)—Shanice (USA) **Mr C. J. Mann**
 50 **SONNANT (FR)**, 6, ch g Cyborg (FR)—Schwarzente (USA) **H. E. C. Villiers**
 51 **SUPREME HILL (IRE)**, 8, br g Supreme Leader—Regents Prancer **Mrs J. E. Brown & R. A. Lucas**
 52 **TWO HOOTS**, 7, b m Dancing High—Farm Track **M. T. Myers**
 53 **VERSUS (GER)**, 5, gr g Highest Honor (FR)—Very Mighty (FR) **The Safest Syndicate**

MR C. J. MANN—continued

54 VILLAGO (GER), 5, b g Laroche (GER)—Village (GER) **The Sport Of Kings Partnership**
55 VILLAIR (IRE), 10, b g Valville (FR)—Brackenair **The Safest Syndicate**
56 YOUNG PATRIARCH, 4, b g Silver Patriarch (IRE)—Mortify **The Little Ireland Syndicate**
57 ZIGGY ZEN, 6, br g Muhtarram (USA)—Springs Welcome **All For One & One For All Partnership 2**
58 ZOUAVE (IRE), 4, b g Spectrum (IRE)—Lady Windley **H. E. C. Villiers & The Stamford Bridge Partnership**

Other Owners: T. Woodward, D. Young, D. Price, D. Sottor, Mr G. I. Bowman, D. A. Burgess, B. R. H. Burrough, Mr P. R. Cooney, M. S. Hunter, Mr P. J. Kilgannon, I. Kirkham, Mrs C. J. Mann, R. P. B. Michaelson, M. J. Morrison, Mr M. C. O'Sullivan, A. M. Tolhurst.

Assistant Trainer: James Barrett

Jockey (NH): Noel Fehily. **Conditional:** S. J. Craine, D. Crosse. **Amateur:** Mr M. Deady.

---

382 **MRS J. M. E. MANN, Leamington Spa**
Postal: **Hill Farm, Ufton, Leamington Spa, Warwickshire, CV33 9PP.**
Contacts: **PHONE (01926) 612208**

1 FLAX HILL, 4, ch f Zaffaran (USA)—Annicombe Run **Mrs J. M. E. Mann**
2 KILLARNEY PRINCE (IRE), 6, b g Lord Americo—Henry Woman (IRE) **Mrs J. M. E. Mann**

THREE-YEAR-OLDS

3 B g Sovereign Water (FR)—Candle Glow **Mrs J. M. E. Mann**

TWO-YEAR-OLDS

4 JUST MALT, b g 7/5 Sir Harry Lewis (USA)—G-And-T (Gildoran) **Mrs J. M. E. Mann**

Amateur: Mr Peter Mann, Mr J. Owen.

---

383 **MR G. G. MARGARSON, Newmarket**
Postal: **Graham Lodge, Birdcage Walk, Newmarket, Suffolk, CB8 0NE.**
Contacts: **HOME/FAX (01638) 668043 MOBILE (07860) 198303**
E-MAIL george.margarson@btinternet.com

1 ATAVUS, 8, b h Distant Relative—Elysian **Stableside Racing Partnership II**
2 BERTOCELLI, 4, ch c Vettori (IRE)—Dame Jude **Stableside Racing Partnership**
3 DELCIENNE, 4, b f Golden Heights—Delciana (IRE) **The Del Boys**
4 GINGER ICE, 5, ch g Bahamian Bounty—Sharp Top **Mr G. G. Margarson**
5 HONEY'S GIFT, 6, b m Terimon—Honeycroft **Wrightway Construction/G. Margarson**
6 LADY MO, 4, b f Young Ern—Just Run (IRE) **The Gunnicks Partnership**
7 LENWADE, 4, gr f Environment Friend—Branitska **The Lenwade Partnership**
8 POLAR JEM, 5, b m Polar Falcon (USA)—Top Jem **Norcroft Park Stud**
9 SEA HOLLY (IRE), 5, b g Barathea (IRE)—Mountain Holly **P. E. Axon**
10 STAR OF NORMANDIE (USA), 6, b m Gulch—Depaze **Norcroft Park Stud**
11 TAMARELLA (IRE), 5, b m Tamarisk (IRE)—Miss Siham (IRE) **The Tamarisk Partnership**
12 TARANDOT (IRE), 4, b f Singspiel (IRE)—Rifada **Norcroft Park Stud**
13 THREE SECRETS (IRE), 4, b f Danehill (USA)—Castilian Queen (USA) **Norcroft Park Stud**
14 WOOLFALL PRINCESS, 6, b m Double Eclipse (IRE)—Emerald Dawn **Finaplan Ltd**

THREE-YEAR-OLDS

15 GREZIE, gr f Mark of Esteem (IRE)—Lozzie **G. Boyer**
16 KRUMPET, b f Mujahid (USA)—Dame Jude **Stableside Racing Partnership 9**
17 MAPLE BRANCH (USA), b f Stravinsky (USA)—Galanty Show **Peter Price**
18 RED AFFLECK (USA), b g Nicholas (USA)—Lucie Mon Amour (USA)
19 WOOLFALL JOANNA, gr f Petong—Real Princess **Finaplan Ltd**
20 YOUNG MICK, br g King's Theatre (IRE)—Just Warning **M. F. Kentish**

TWO-YEAR-OLDS

21 B f 5/2 Vettori (IRE)—Assertive Dancer (USA) (Assert)
22 Ch g 30/3 Zilzal (USA)—Dame Jude (Dilum (USA))
23 GENEROUS JEM, b f 21/3 Generous (IRE)—Top Jem (Damister (USA)) **Norcroft Park Stud**
24 JOLIS TARA, b f 24/2 Kayf Tara—Jolis Absent (Primo Dominie) **Norcroft Park Stud**

MR G. G. MARGARSON—continued

25 **LADY'S LAW**, b f 21/2 Diktat—Snugfit Annie (Midyan (USA)) **Norcroft Park Stud**
26 B c 21/3 Tiger Hill (IRE)—Lauren (GER) (Lightning (FR)) (12000)
27 B f 10/3 Zaha (CAN)—Little Miss Rocker (Rock Hopper)
28 Ch c 3/4 Danzig Connection (USA)—Roisin Clover (Faustus (USA))
29 Ch f 11/3 Danehill Dancer (IRE)—Saibhreas (IRE) (Last Tycoon) (34000) **J. D. Guest**
30 Ch c 17/4 Stravinsky (USA)—Saucy Blondy (USA) (Gilded Time (USA)) (40000) **J. D. Guest**
31 **SOVIET PROMISE (IRE)**, b c 11/3 Soviet Star (IRE)—Akarita (IRE) (Akarad (FR)) (24000) **Norcroft Park Stud**
32 **WOOLFALL BLUE (IRE)**, gr c 6/2 Bluebird (USA)—Diamond Waltz (IRE) (Linamix (FR)) (10000)
33 **WOOLFALL KING (IRE)**, b c 1/4 King Charlemagne (USA)—Bazaar Promise (Native Bazaar)

Other Owners: A J Hollis, M D Hollis, Dr M Lancaster-Smith, M F Kentish, D. Lancaster-Smith, H. W. Thommes.

Assistant Trainer: Frank Stribbling & Daniel Lancaster-Smith

Jockey (flat): A. McCarthy, J. Mackay, P. Robinson. **Apprentice:** Sally Adams. **Amateur:** Miss Katie Margarson.

---

384 MR R. F. MARVIN, Melton Mowbray
Postal: **Glebe Farm Stables, Saxelbye, Melton Mowbray, Leicestershire, LE14 3PQ.**
Contacts: **MOBILE (07903) 314614**

1 **ABOVE BOARD**, 10, b g Night Shift (USA)—Bundled Up (USA) **W. I. Bloomfield**
2 **DEMOLITION MOLLY**, 4, b f Rudimentary (USA)—Persian Fortune **D. G. Blott**
3 **EAGER ANGEL (IRE)**, 7, b m Up And At 'em—Seanee Squaw **J. F. Pitchford**
4 **JUDDA**, 4, b g Makbul—Pepeke **D. G. Blott**
5 **LOUTASHA**, 4, gr f Atraf—Petinata **D. G. Woods**
6 **MATHMAGICIAN**, 6, ch g Hector Protector (USA)—Inherent Magic (IRE) **Mrs M. A. Marvin**
7 **MELFORD RED (IRE)**, 5, b g Sri Pekan (USA)—Sunflower (IRE) **W. I. Bloomfield**
8 **SAMBA BEAT**, 6, ch m Efisio—Special Beat

THREE-YEAR-OLDS

9 **CHOICE CONNECTION**, b c Danzig Connection (USA)—Funny Choice (IRE) **Colin Alton**
10 Ch g Bluegrass Prince (IRE)—Persian Fortune

Other Owners: E. Atkinson, S. M. Deeman.

Assistant Trainer: M A Marvin

Jockey (flat): T. G. McLaughlin. **Amateur:** Mrs M. Morris.

---

385 MR P. J. MCBRIDE, Newmarket
Postal: **8 Ashley Road, Newmarket, Suffolk, CB8 8DA.**
Contacts: **PHONE/FAX (01638) 667841 MOBILE (07929) 265711**
E-MAIL charlie@pjmcbride.fsnet.co.uk

1 **ARGAMIA**, 9, br m Orfano (GER)—Arkona (GER) **P. J. McBride**
2 **DOVEDON HERO**, 5, ch g Millkom—Hot Topic (IRE) **M. C. Whatley**
3 **KINGSTON ROSE (GER)**, 4, b f Robellino (USA)—Kingston Avenue (USA) **Miss Kim Bartlett**
4 **PIRI PIRI (IRE)**, 5, b br m Priolo (USA)—Hot Curry (USA) **P. J. McBride & T. J. Wells**
5 **POMPEY BLUE**, 4, b f Abou Zouz (USA)—Habla Me (IRE) **Mrs J. M. Langmead**
6 **STRATHSPEY**, 6, ch m Dancing Spree (USA)—Diebiedale (USA) **P. J. McBride**

THREE-YEAR-OLDS

7 **BOWLED OUT (GER)**, b f Dansili—Braissim **The Silver-Lining Cricketers Syndicate**
8 **CHIEF DIPPER**, b c Benny The Dip (USA)—Cuban Reef **P. F. Charter**
9 **LA MUSIQUE**, b c Merdon Melody—Daleside Ladybird **P. J. McBride**
10 **ROSE BIEN**, b f Bien Bien (USA)—Madame Bovary **P. J. McBride**

TWO-YEAR-OLDS

11 **SARAH LAURELLE**, b f 16/3 Bertolini (USA)—Eldina (Distant Relative) (5000) **Mrs Julie King**
12 B c 1/4 Xaar—Swallowtailed Kite (USA) (Silver Hawk (USA)) **The Silver-Lining Cricketers Syndicate**

Other Owners: Mrs W. M. Chapman, R. P. Dix, Miss V. J. Mallalieu, Ms P. A. Mallalieu.

Jockey (flat): Seb Saunders, Tom Queally, Liam Kenairy. **Jockey (NH):** Jim Cullotty. **Apprentice:** Kevin Jackson.

386 MR D. MCCAIN, Cholmondeley

Postal: Bankhouse, Cholmondeley, Malpas, Cheshire, SY14 8AL.
Contacts: PHONE (01829) 720352 FAX (01829) 720475 MOBILES (07939) 126544/(07947) 583961
E-MAIL gingermccain@cholmondeley.fsbusiness.co.uk

1 **AMBERLEIGH HOUSE (IRE)**, 13, br g Buckskin (FR)—Chancy Gal **Halewood International Ltd**
2 4, B g Sir Harry Lewis (USA)—Analogical **Mr D. McCain**
3 **BALMORAL QUEEN**, 5, br m Wizard King—Balmoral Princess **Mrs B. McCain**
4 **BANNISTER LANE**, 5, b g Overbury (IRE)—Miss Club Royal **Shawhill Golf Club/Mr R. Rossiter/Mr D. McCain**
5 **CALOMERIA**, 4, b f Groom Dancer (USA)—Calendula **B. Dunn/Mr J. Hutchinson/Mrs J. Nolan**
6 5, B g Dr Massini (IRE)—Chancy Gal **Halewood International Ltd**
7 5, B m Overbury (IRE)—Chapel Hill (IRE) **Helshaw Grange**
8 **CHICKAPEAKRAY**, 4, b f Overbury (IRE)—Nevermind Hey **Champ Chicken Co Ltd**
9 **COMING AGAIN (IRE)**, 4, b g Rainbow Quest (USA)—Hagwah (USA) **Mr J. M. Glews**
10 4, Ch g Pursuit of Love—Constant Delight **Mr D. McCain**
11 **DOWN TO THE WOODS (USA)**, 7, ch g Woodman (USA)—Riviera Wonder (USA) **Mr J. Hutchinson**
12 **EBONY LIGHT (IRE)**, 9, br g Buckskin (FR)—Amelioras Daughter **R. Bellamy**
13 **FLAME PHOENIX**, 6, b br g Quest For Fame—Kingscote **Mr J. M. Glews**
14 **HARBEN (FR)**, 6, ch g Luchiroverte (IRE)—Dixia (FR) **Mr D. McCain**
15 4, B f Classic Cliche (IRE)—Hard Love **Mr D. McCain**
16 **HEAVENLY STRIDE**, 9, b g Karinga Bay—Chapel Hill (IRE) **Helshaw Grange/Mr E. O'Malley/D. McCain**
17 **INVESTMENT AFFAIR (IRE)**, 5, b g Sesaro (USA)—Superb Investment (IRE) **R. N. Fuller**
18 **IRIS'S QUEEN**, 5, b m Bob's Return (IRE)—Colonial Princess **R. Lester**
19 **ITSDOWNTOBEN**, 4, b g Karinga Bay—Martins Lottee **Mr D. Proos**
20 **ITSUPTOHARRY (IRE)**, 6, b g Old Vic—Celtic Gale **Mr D. Proos**
21 5, B m Double Eclipse (IRE)—Let Me Finish **Mr D. McCain**
22 5, Gr m Warcraft (USA)—Misty Joy **Mr D. McCain**
23 **MOORLAW (IRE)**, 4, b g Mtoto—Belle Etoile (FR) **Market Avenue Racing Club/Mr M. Hill**
24 **PINK HARBOUR**, 7, b m Rakaposhi King—Let Me Finish **W. Heys/D. McCain**
25 4, B g Zaffaran (USA)—Quinag **Mr D. McCain**
26 **RED LION (FR)**, 8, ch g Lion Cavern (USA)—Mahogany River **D. R. McCain**
27 **REEM TWO**, 4, b f Mtoto—Jamrat Samya (IRE) **Mr D. Ellis/D. McCain**
28 4, B g Grand Plaisir (IRE)—Regal Hostess **Mrs J. Heler**
29 5, Ch g King Persian—Sara Jane (IRE) **Mr D. McCain**
30 **SEVENS DELIGHT**, 5, b m Karinga Bay—Dante's Delight **Ms M. Adamson/Helshaw Grange**
31 4, B br g Overbury (IRE)—Slip A Coin **Mr D. McCain**
32 4, B f Classic Cliche (IRE)—Sovereign Belle **Mr D. McCain**
33 **SUBADAR MAJOR**, 8, b g Komaite—Rather Gorgeous **Major P. Bailey**
34 **TRIPLE MINT (IRE)**, 4, b g Flemensfirth (USA)—Bucktina **Mrs J. Heler**
35 **TUNES OF GLORY (IRE)**, 9, b g Symboli Heights (FR)—Coxtown Queen (IRE) **R. Pattison/T. Crehan/D. McCain**
36 **TWEED**, 8, ch g Barathea (IRE)—In Perpetuity **Mr J. Hutchinson**
37 **TWIST N TURN**, 5, b m Sir Harry Lewis (USA)—Gaye Gordon **R. Pattison/D. McCain**
38 4, B f Sir Harry Lewis (USA)—Tyrilda (FR) **Mr D. McCain**
39 **VICARIO**, 4, gr g Vettori (IRE)—Arantxa **Mr J. M. Glews**
40 **WEST HILL (IRE)**, 4, b c Gone West (USA)—Altamura (USA) **Mr J. M. Glews**

THREE-YEAR-OLDS

41 B f Environment Friend—Heathyards Gem **L. A. Morgan**
42 **PROPRIETOR (UAE)**, ch g Timber Country (USA)—Potentille (IRE) **Mr D. McCain**
43 **SWALLOW FALLS (IRE)**, b f Lake Coniston (IRE)—Common Cause **Mr D. McCain**
44 **TITUS ROCK (IRE)**, b f Titus Livius (FR)—Cossack Princess (IRE) **Mr D. McCain**
45 **YANKEY**, b g Amfortas (IRE)—Key **Mr D. Proos**

Assistant Trainer: Mrs B McCain, D R McCain (Jnr)

Jockey (NH): G. Lee. **Conditional:** G. Grogan. **Amateur:** Mr D. F. Williams.

387 MR N. P. MCCORMACK, Rowlands Gill

Postal: The Cottage, Southfield Farm, Hamsterley Mill, Rowlands Gill, Tyne and Wear, NE39 1NQ.
Contacts: HOME (01207) 549700 MOBILE (07961) 540173

1 **DIDIFON**, 10, b g Zafonic (USA)—Didicoy (USA) **Mrs D. McCormack**
2 **THE COLLECTOR (IRE)**, 6, ch g Forest Wind (USA)—Glowing Reeds **Mrs D. McCormack**

Assistant Trainer: Mrs D McCormack

388 **MR T. P. MCGOVERN, Lewes**
Postal: **Grandstand Stables, Old Lewes Racecourse, Lewes, East Sussex, BN7 1UR.**
Contacts: **PHONE (01273) 487813 MOBILE (07710) 123145**
E-MAIL monicamcgovern@tiscal.co.uk

1 DANCING SHIRLEY, 7, b m Dancing Spree (USA)—High Heather **S. J. Major**
2 ENGLISH JIM (IRE), 4, b g Saddlers' Hall (IRE)—Royal Folly (IRE) **J W P Sullivan & Quaystone Construction**
3 FALMER FOR ALL (IRE), 7, b g Warcraft (USA)—Sunset Walk **Tom Gilligan**
4 MISBEHAVIOUR, 6, b g Tragic Role (USA)—Exotic Forest **Lewes Racing**
5 PRINCE SLAYER, 9, b g Batshoof—Top Sovereign **A. A. Abdel-Khaleq**
6 SEE RED BILLDAN (IRE), 9, br g Riverhead (USA)—Sweet Mayo (IRE) **Mr R. Mackenzie**
7 WEST ASIDE (IRE), 11, b g Brush Aside (USA)—Chancy Belle **B. C. J. Enterprise**

Other Owners: R. A. Clark, P. C. Collins, P Hempenstall, Mrs B. L. Hillary, C. G. Hosmer, Mrs J. L. Hosmer, J. Noonan, J. W. P. Sullivan.

Assistant Trainer: Nigel Benstead

Conditional: Christopher Murray.

389 **MRS J. C. MCGREGOR, Milnathort**
Postal: **Tillyrie House, Milnathort, Kinross, KY13 0RW.**
Contacts: **PHONE (01577) 865071 FAX (01577) 863418 MOBILE (07764) 464299**
E-MAIL equijeanmcg@aol.com

1 ANTHEMION (IRE), 8, ch g Night Shift (USA)—New Sensitive **On The Level**
2 BLUE MORNING, 7, b m Balnibarbi—Bad Start (USA) **Mrs D. Pease**
3 DALAWAN, 6, b g Nashwan (USA)—Magdala (IRE) **Discounted Cashflow**
4 FEELING FIZZICAL, 7, b g Feelings (FR)—Stepdaughter **Mrs D. Thomson**
5 GEMINI LADY, 5, b m Emperor Fountain—Raunchy Rita **Mrs D. Thomson**
6 GOODANDPLENTY, 7, b g Sovereign Water (FR)—Our Wilma **The Kelsae Selection**
7 GOODBADINDIFERENT (IRE), 9, b br g Mandalus—Stay As You Are **The Good To Soft Firm**
8 KING'S ENVOY (USA), 6, b g Royal Academy (USA)—Island of Silver (USA) **Mrs D. Thomson**
9 LINGHAM BRIDESMAID, 9, b m Minster Son—Lingham Bride **Tillyrie Racing Club**
10 4, B f Rock City—More Champagne
11 5, Ch m Emperor Fountain—Our Wilma **Mrs J. C. McGregor**
12 PENNILLION, 5, b g Pennekamp (USA)—Brave Princess **Mrs J. C. McGregor**
13 SAFE SHOT, 6, b g Salse (USA)—Optaria **The Boozers Brigade**
14 SALVAGE, 10, b g Kahyasi—Storm Weaver (USA) **Mrs E. R. Sneddon**

THREE-YEAR-OLDS

15 B c Entrepreneur—College Night (IRE)

Other Owners: Mrs S. Coutts, Mr K. Trail, Mrs R. Trail, Mr M. O'Conner, Mr J. Black, Mr D. Faskin, Mr & Mrs E. Harper-Gow, Mrs L. Hessay, Mr J. Thomson, Mr & Mrs J. Ivory, Mr M. Croan, Mr B. Hazeldean, Mr G. Newstead, P. Byrne, Mr S. Taylor.

Jockey (flat): D. McGaffin. **Jockey (NH):** J. Crowley, B. Hitchcock, B. Harding, G. Lee. **Conditional:** D. Costello, F. King, P. Robson. **Apprentice:** T. Eaves.

390 **MISS DENISE MCHALE, Newmarket**
Postal: **Calder Park Stables (Goldacre), Hamilton Road, Newmarket, Suffolk.**
Contacts: **FAX (01142) 421508 MOBILE (07753) 675180**
E-MAIL nab743d@aol.com WEBSITE www.goldacreracing.com

1 BALLYRUSH (IRE), 5, ch g Titus Livius (FR)—Mandoline (IRE) **Mrs B. Keogh**
2 CHISEL, 4, ch g Hector Protector (USA)—Not Before Time (IRE) **Pi Lawyers**
3 GRAVARDLAX, 4, ch g Salse (USA)—Rubbiyati **Gravity Group**
4 HUM (IRE), 4, ch f Cadeaux Genereux—Ensorceleuse (FR) **N. Bashir**
5 JADEERON, 8, b g Green Desert (USA)—Rain And Shine (FR) **Miss D. McHale & K & D Racing**
6 SKELTHWAITE, 4, b g Desert Story (IRE)—Skip To Somerfield **N.Bashir/www.goldacreracing.com**
7 VANBRUGH (FR), 5, ch g Starborough—Renovate **N. Bashir**
8 ZAK FACTA (IRE), 5, b g Danetime (IRE)—Alexander Goddess (IRE) **N. Bashir**

MISS DENISE MCHALE—continued

THREE-YEAR-OLDS

9 **GOLD STRIKE (IRE)**, ch f Rainbow Quest (USA)—Turban **A. Smith**
10 B c City Honours (USA)—Huldine **Pi Lawyers**
11 **PROPHET'S CALLING (IRE)**, b g Brave Act—Arbitration (IRE) **N.Bashir/www.goldacreracing.com**

TWO-YEAR-OLDS

12 **SOLOMANS PROSPECT**, b c 30/5 Hazaaf (USA)—Our Stella (Petong) **N. Onofriou**
13 Gr c 24/4 Compton Place—Swissmatic (Petong) **A. Smith**
14 B c 18/2 Inchinor—Top (Shirley Heights) **A. Smith**

Other Owners: Miss D. A. McHale, Mr R. Helm & Mrs D. Helm, K. White, J. Puddick, P. McDonald, D. Cruickshank, A. Jackson.

Assistant Trainer: N Bashir

Jockey (flat): Darren Williams. **Apprentice:** Miss Stephanie Bancroft. **Amateur:** Miss Katie Stubbs.

---

391 MR I. W. MCINNES, Catwick
Postal: **Ivy House Farm, Main Street, Catwick, Beverley, East Yorkshire, HU17 5PJ.**
Contacts: **HOME/FAX** (01964) 542115 **MOBILE** (07720) 451233

1 **ALL ON MY OWN (USA)**, 10, ch g Unbridled (USA)—Some For All (USA) **Mr I. W. McInnes**
2 **DARING GAMBLE**, 8, b m Barrys Gamble—Rachel Sharp **Mr I. W. McInnes**
3 **H HARRISON (IRE)**, 5, b g Eagle Eyed (USA)—Penrose (IRE) **Ivy House Racing**
4 **HEALEY (IRE)**, 7, ch g Dr Devious (IRE)—Bean Siamsa **Mrs R. Auchterlounie**
5 **IZZET MUZZY (FR)**, 7, ch g Piccolo—Texanne (BEL) **Ivy House Racing**
6 **LAUREL DAWN**, 7, gr g Paris House—Madrina **Ivy House Racing**
7 **MACCHIATO**, 6, b f Inchinor—Tereyna **D. R. E. McDuffie**
8 **MAJHOOL**, 6, b g Mark of Esteem (IRE)—Be Peace (USA) **A. M. McArdle - Pamela McArdle**
9 **MAZRAM**, 6, b m Muhtarram (USA)—Royal Mazi **A. M. McArdle**
10 **MOLOTOV**, 5, b g Efisio—Mindomica **Cloak And Dagger Racing Club**
11 **NOW AND AGAIN**, 6, b g Shaamit (IRE)—Sweet Allegiance **M. C. Shirley**
12 **PILCA (FR)**, 5, ch g Pistolet Bleu (IRE)—Caricoe **M. C. Shirley**
13 **PRINCE RENESIS**, 4, b g Mind Games—Stoneydale **Brooklands Racing**
14 **ROCK CONCERT**, 7, b m Bishop of Cashel—Summer Pageant **Ivy House Racing**
15 **ROYAL FASHION (IRE)**, 5, b m Ali-Royal (IRE)—Fun Fashion (IRE) **The Weatherer Grain Partnership**
16 **SHAMWARI FIRE (IRE)**, 5, ch g Idris (IRE)—Bobby's Dream **Neptune Sonar Ltd**
17 **SHEER FOCUS**, 7, b g Eagle Eyed (USA)—Persian Danser (IRE) **Mrs R. Auchterlounie**
18 **SPOT IN TIME**, 5, br m Mtoto—Kelimutu **I. D. Woolfitt**
19 **TOJONESKI**, 6, b g Emperor Jones (USA)—Sampower Lady **M. C. Shirley**
20 **WESTERN ROOTS**, 4, ch g Dr Fong (USA)—Chrysalis **M. C. Shirley**

THREE-YEAR-OLDS

21 **IN RHUBARB**, ch g Piccolo—Versami (USA) **Rhubarb Racing Club**

Other Owners: Mr F. Wood, M. H. Bates, H. A. Grain, D. S. Lovatt, R. J. Robinson, D. Watts, M Weatherer, Mrs G. Wood, Mr B. Yeadon.

Assistant Trainer: Mr Ian McInnes (Senior)

Jockey (flat): R. Ffrench. **Jockey (NH):** C. Rafter, L. Vickers. **Apprentice:** N. Gemelova, J. F. McDonald. **Amateur:** Mr T. Gardham.

---

392 MR W. J. MCKEOWN, Newcastle
Postal: **East Wideopen Farm, Wideopen, Newcastle Upon Tyne, NE13 6DW.**
Contacts: **PHONE** (0191) 236 7545 **FAX** (0191) 236 2959 **MOBILE** (07931) 505593

1 **ACES FOUR (IRE)**, 6, ch g Fourstars Allstar (USA)—Special Trix (IRE) **J. G. Molloy**
2 **BRANMORE JACK (IRE)**, 5, b g Luso—Blue Approach (IRE) **Branmore Investments**
3 **CAPRICORN**, 7, b g Minster Son—Loch Scavaig (IRE) **I. E. Ives**
4 **MAN MURPHY (IRE)**, 9, b g Euphemism—Been About (IRE) **W. Manners**

MR W. J. MCKEOWN—continued

TWO-YEAR-OLDS

  5 Ch c 26/1 Shinko Forest (IRE)—Carpet Lady (IRE) (Night Shift (USA)) (12000) **Branmore Investments**
  6 Br c 7/4 Distant Music (USA)—Charitable (IRE) (Mujadil (USA)) (6371) **Mrs L. E. McKeown**
  7 SIULA GRANDE (IRE), ch c 22/4 Raise A Grand (IRE)—Starry Skies (USA) (Diesis) (4023) **Mrs L. E. McKeown**

Other Owners: Dr A. Branley, A. Mordain.

<table><tr><td>**393**</td><td>**MR EDWARD SYDNEY ARTHUR MCMAHON, Lichfield**
Postal: **Horsley Brook Farm, Tamworth Road, Swinfen, nr Lichfield, Staffordshire, WS14 9PT.**
Contacts: **PHONE/FAX (01543) 481224**
E-MAIL comeracing@horsleybrook.fsnet.co.uk</td></tr></table>

  1 BACK IN SPIRIT, 5, ch g Primo Dominie—Pusey Street Girl **The Oakley**
  2 BAND, 5, b g Band On The Run—Little Tich **D. J. Allen**
  3 CLASSIC EXPRESSION, 4, ch f Classic Cliche (IRE)—Breezy Day **R. L. Bedding**
  4 DESERT LEADER (IRE), 4, b g Green Desert (USA)—Za Aamah (USA) **J. C. Fretwell**
  5 INDIAN CALL, 4, ch g Classic Cliche (IRE)—Crees Sqaw **M. J. Sturgess**
  6 KEEPER'S LODGE (IRE), 4, ch f Grand Lodge (USA)—Gembira (USA) **W. D. McClennon**
  7 LOCAL POET, 4, b c Robellino (USA)—Laugharne **J. C. Fretwell**
  8 RAHJEL SULTAN, 7, b g Puissance—Dalby Dancer **Mrs J. McMahon**
  9 ROYAL CASCADE (IRE), 11, b g River Falls—Relative Stranger **Mrs J. McMahon**

THREE-YEAR-OLDS

10 ALLIZAM, b c Tragic Role (USA)—Mazilla **M. Rhodes**
11 AUTHENTICATE, b f Dansili—Exact Replica **J. C. Fretwell**
12 AZEEZAH, ch f Hernando (FR)—Brave Vanessa (USA) **K. A. Dasmal**
13 EL POTRO, b c Forzando—Gaelic Air **R.J.H. Ltd, G.Pickering & J.P.Hames**
14 LOOK HERE'S MAY, b f Revoque (IRE)—Where's Carol **S. L. Edwards**
15 MONKSTOWN ROAD, b c Makbul—Carolside **J. J. Staunton**
16 PIVOTAL FLAME, b c Pivotal—Reddening **R. L. Bedding**
17 PIVOTAL'S PRINCESS (IRE), ch f Pivotal—Art Princess (IRE) **R. L. Bedding & Mrs J. McMahon**
18 SUPERSTITIOUS (IRE), b c Bluebird (USA)—Stellar Empress (USA) **J. C. Fretwell**

TWO-YEAR-OLDS

19 ASBURY PARK, b c 26/1 Primo Valentino (IRE)—Ocean Grove (IRE) (Fairy King (USA)) (34000) **J. C. Fretwell**
20 CHARLLEN, ch f 6/4 Band On The Run—Breezy Day (Day Is Done) (4000) **R. Butler**
21 CURTAIL (IRE), b c 4/4 Namid—Nipitinthebud (USA) (Night Shift (USA)) (32000) **J. C. Fretwell**
22 FILM CRITIC (IRE), ch c 1/3 King of Kings (IRE)—
                                     Starlight Dreams (USA) (Black Tie Affair) (21000) **J. C. Fretwell**
23 GEE FOUR (IRE), br c 15/5 Bold Fact (USA)—Hay Knot (Main Reef) (6706) **Mrs J. McMahon**
24 OUT THE ORDINARY, b c 16/2 Whittingham (IRE)—Special One (Aragon) (30000) **J. C. Fretwell**
25 PENNY THOUGHTS, b f 25/2 Prince Sabo—United Passion (Emarati (USA)) (8200) **J. C. Fretwell**
26 ROMANTIC EVENING (IRE), ch c 30/3 Dr Fong (USA)—
                              By Candlelight (IRE) (Roi Danzig (USA)) (30000) **J. C. Fretwell**
27 ROSTHWAITE (IRE), b f 2/3 Desert Style (IRE)—Thirlmere (Cadeaux Genereux) (1000) **J. C. Fretwell**
28 SILVER CREST, gr c 12/4 Zilzal (USA)—Red Typhoon (Belfort (FR)) (6500) **Mrs J. McMahon**
29 TALBOT STREET, ch c 13/2 Compton Place—Roxy (Rock City) (36000) **J. C. Fretwell**
30 YA LATE MAITE, ch f 28/2 Komaite (USA)—Plentitude (FR) (Ela-Mana-Mou) (4000) **Mrs J. McMahon**

Other Owners: Mrs H. C. Abel, J. P. Hames, G. Pickering, R J H Limited, D. Spalding.

Assistant Trainer: Bryan Arthur McMahon

Jockey (flat): G. Gibbons. **Apprentice:** Richard Hodson. **Amateur:** Miss E. George, Miss S. Phizacklea.

<table><tr><td>**394**</td><td>**MR I. MCMATH, Carlisle**
Postal: **Thornedge, Station Road, Cumwhinton, Carlisle, Cumbria, CA4 8DJ.**
Contacts: **PHONE (01228) 560007 FAX (01228) 560053**
E-MAIL ianmcmath@aol.com</td></tr></table>

  1 ANAKA FLIGHT, 4, b f Missed Flight—Hamanaka (USA) **Mrs A. J. McMath**
  2 CALAMITYCHARACTER, 6, b m Tragic Role (USA)—Shaa Spin **Mrs A. J. McMath**

MR I. MCMATH—continued

3 **CHOCOLATCHANT,** 8, ch m Chocolat de Meguro (USA)—Secret Chant **Mrs A. J. McMath**
4 4, Ch g Mister Lord (USA)—Dalua River (IRE) **Mrs A. J. McMath**
5 **DOCKERSBOY (USA),** 5, b g Majestic Twoeleven (USA)—Star of Talisman (USA) **Mrs A. J. McMath**
6 **FASTAFFARAN (IRE),** 4, b g Zaffaran (USA)—Break Fast **Mrs A. J. McMath**
7 **MID SUMMER LARK (IRE),** 9, b g Tremblant—Tuney Blade **Mrs A. J. McMath**
8 4, B ro g Chocolat de Meguro (USA)—Miss Lakeland **Mrs A. J. McMath**
9 **SOUTHBOUND (IRE),** 6, ch g Zaffaran (USA)—Soxess (IRE) **Mrs A. J. McMath**

THREE-YEAR-OLDS

10 B g Relief Pitcher—Drumkilly Lilly (IRE) **Mrs A. J. McMath**

TWO-YEAR-OLDS

11 B g 13/4 Namaqualand (USA)—Hamanaka (USA) (Conquistador Cielo (USA)) **Mrs A. J. McMath**

Assistant Trainer: Miss Lynsey Kendall

Amateur: Miss L. Kendall.

395

MR M. D. MCMILLAN, Cheltenham
Postal: Pindrup Moor, Fossebridge, Cheltenham, Gloucestershire, GL54 3JR.
Contacts: PHONE (01285) 721050 FAX (01285) 721040 MOBILE (07973) 543272
E-MAIL md.mcm@btinternet.com

1 **MADAME BAVARDE,** 8, b m Henbit (USA)—La Princesse **Mr M. D. McMillan**
2 **TACITA,** 10, ch m Gunner B—Taco **Mr M. D. McMillan**
3 **TENKO,** 6, ch m Environment Friend—Taco **Mr M. D. McMillan**

396

MR B. J. MEEHAN, Upper Lambourn
Postal: Newlands Stables, Upper Lambourn, Hungerford, Berkshire, RG17 8QX.
Contacts: OFFICE (01488) 73656/73636 FAX (01488) 73633 MOBILE (07836) 754254
E-MAIL brian@brianmeehan.com WEBSITE www.brianmeehan.com

1 **ATTUNE,** 4, br f Singspiel (IRE)—Arriving **Wyck Hall Stud Ltd**
2 **CAPE FEAR,** 4, b c Cape Cross—Only In Dreams **Kennet Valley Thoroughbred II**
3 **CRYSTAL (IRE),** 4, b f Danehill (USA)—Solar Crystal (IRE) **F. C. T. Wilson**
4 **DENVER (IRE),** 4, b c Danehill (USA)—Born Beautiful (USA) **Gigginstown House Stud**
5 **DOLCE PICCATA,** 4, ch f Piccolo—Highland Rhapsody (IRE) **Mr H. Ponsonby**
6 **FAST HEART,** 4, b c Fasliyev (USA)—Heart of India (IRE) **Mr & Mrs D. Brown/Mr S. Dartnell**
7 **FONG'S THONG (USA),** 4, ch c Dr Fong (USA)—Bacinella (USA) **J. L. Allbritton**
8 **GJOVIC,** 4, br g Singspiel (IRE)—Photo Call **J. R. Good**
9 **HERMITAGE COURT (USA),** 4, ch g Out of Place (USA)—Russian Act (USA) **Gallagher Equine Ltd**
10 **HILBRE ISLAND,** 5, b h Halling (USA)—Faribole (IRE) **Paul & Jenny Green**
11 **INDIAN COUNTRY,** 6, ch g Indian Ridge—Arethusa **H. Rosenblatt**
12 **KAIETEUR (USA),** 6, b h Marlin (USA)—Strong Embrace (USA) **Mrs S. T. McCarthy**
13 **LEITRIM HOUSE,** 4, ch c Cadeaux Genereux—Lonely Heart **Gallagher Equine Ltd**
14 **STAR OF LIGHT,** 4, b g Mtoto—Star Entry **J. H. Widdows**
15 **THURLESTONE ROCK,** 5, ch g Sheikh Albadou—Don't Smile **Mr N. Attenborough & Mrs L. Mann**
16 **VIOLET PARK,** 4, b f Pivotal—Petonellajill **Mr & Mrs D. Cash**

THREE-YEAR-OLDS

17 **ABIENTOT (IRE),** b g Danetime (IRE)—Clandolly (IRE) **Clipper Group Holdings Ltd**
18 **ADMIRAL'S CRUISE,** b c A P Indy (USA)—Ladies Cruise (USA) **J. L. Allbritton**
19 **ALONG CAME MOLLY,** ch f Dr Fong (USA)—Torrid Tango (USA) **Kilboy Estate**
20 **ALPHUN (IRE),** b g Orpen (USA)—Fakhira (IRE) **J. S. Threadwell**
21 **BENTINCK (IRE),** b c In The Wings—Bareilly (USA) **T. W. Bloodstock Ltd**
22 **BLINIS (IRE),** ch g Danehill Dancer (IRE)—Richly Deserved (IRE) **Gravity Group II**
23 **BLUEBERRY TART (IRE),** b f Bluebird (USA)—Tart (IRE) **S. McCready, T. Clinton, D. Hicks**
2. **BORTHWICK GIRL (IRE),** b f Cape Cross (IRE)—Shannon Dore (IRE) **Mrs W. M. English**
   ..NEMORE (IRE), b c Diesis—Private Indy (USA) **Mrs S. M. Roy**
   ..SPERANZA (IRE), b f King's Best (USA)—Snow House (IRE) **Ms C. E. Musgrave**
   ..OUT, br c Tomba—Princess Zara **J. R. Good**
   ..IA (IRE), ch g Desert Prince (IRE)—Irish Celebrity (USA) **David Allan**

MR B. J. MEEHAN—continued

29 **CITY ZONE (IRE)**, gr f Zafonic (USA)—City Fortress **Ballymacoll Stud Farm Ltd**
30 **DAVID JUNIOR (USA)**, ch c Pleasant Tap (USA)—Paradise River (USA) **Roldvale Ltd**
31 **EUPHORIA**, b f Unfuwain (USA)—Maria Isabella (FR) **Miss G. J. Abbey**
32 **FIRST ROW (IRE)**, b c Daylami (IRE)—Ballet Society (FR) **J. L. Allbritton**
33 **HUMBLE OPINION**, b c Singspiel (IRE)—For More (FR) **Paul & Jenny Green**
34 **INDIAN PASSAGE**, br c Diktat—Heart of India (IRE) **J. L. Allbritton**
35 **LEGEND OF DANCE**, b f Dansili—Hard Task **Mr H. Ponsonby**
36 **MAGGIE JORDAN (USA)**, b f Fusaichi Pegasus (USA)—Pharapache (USA) **A. J. Smith**
37 **MAGICAL ROMANCE (IRE)**, b f Barathea (IRE)—Shouk **F. C. T. Wilson**
38 **MANGO GROOVE (IRE)**, b f Unfuwain (USA)—Solar Crystal (IRE) **T. W. Bloodstock Ltd**
39 **MUSICAL DAY**, ch f Singspiel (IRE)—Dayville (USA) **T. G. Holdcroft**
40 **PARK ROMANCE (IRE)**, b f Dr Fong (USA)—Park Charger **F. C. T. Wilson**
41 **PERFECT CHOICE (IRE)**, gr c Daylami (IRE)—Fairy Contessa (IRE) **Mrs S. M. Roy**
42 **POKER PLAYER (IRE)**, ch g Raise A Grand (IRE)—Look Nonchalant (IRE) **Ms C. E. Musgrave**
43 **PUGILIST**, b g Fraam—Travel Mystery **Rascals Racing**
44 **REBUTTAL (USA)**, b c Mr Greeley (USA)—Reboot (USA) **P. Minikes**
45 **RUBY MURRAY**, b f Zafonic (USA)—Poppadam **Team Havana**
46 **SHAHEER (IRE)**, b g Shahrastani (USA)—Atmospheric Blues (IRE) **David Crichton-Watt**
47 **SHOSOLOSA (IRE)**, b f Dansili—Hajat **Mr & Mrs David Brown**
48 **SIENA GOLD**, br b f Key of Luck (USA)—Corn Futures **J. W. Rowles**
49 **STEDFAST MCSTAUNCH (IRE)**, gr g Desert Style (IRE)—Aneydia (IRE) **The Comic Strip Heroes**
50 **TAKE A MILE (IRE)**, ch c Inchinor—Bu Hagab (IRE) **Kennet Valley Thoroughbreds VII**
51 **TOPIARY TED**, ch g Zafonic (USA)—Lovely Lyca **S. Dartnell**
52 **ZOHAR (USA)**, b c Aljabr (USA)—Dafnah (USA) **E. H. Jones (Paints) Ltd**

TWO-YEAR-OLDS

53 **ABBIELOU**, ch f 16/2 Bertolini (USA)—
　　　　　　　　Rockstine (IRE) (Ballad Rock) (12500) **Mr N. Attenborough & Mrs L. Mann**
54 **ADVENTURESS**, b f 24/1 Singspiel (IRE)—Arriving (Most Welcome) **Wyck Hall Stud Ltd**
55 **ANEMONE**, gr f 8/4 Arkadian Hero (USA)—Noble Haven (Indian King (USA)) (10000) **Mrs L. I. Howard-Spink**
56 B f 6/2 Singspiel (IRE)—Annapurna (IRE) (Brief Truce (USA)) **K. J. Mercer**
57 B g 26/2 Fraam—Annie Hall (Saddlers' Hall (IRE)) (16000) **Mackey Family Limited**
58 B c 10/3 Giant's Causeway (USA)—Autumn Leaf (USA) (Gone West (USA)) **J. L. Allbritton**
59 **BAKLAWA**, b f 27/2 Zafonic (USA)—Baked Alaska (Green Desert (USA)) **Cliveden Stud Ltd**
60 **BLUE CHIC (IRE)**, b br f 15/2 Bluebird (USA)—Fun Fashion (IRE) (Polish Patriot (USA)) (11000) **M. F. B. Peart**
61 **BRENDA MEOVA**, b f 6/4 Dr Fong (USA)—Iberian Dancer (CAN) (El Gran Senor (USA)) (8000) **Mr D. Barnard**
62 Ch c 12/2 Namid—Bumble (Rainbow Quest (USA)) (34875) **Clipper Group Holdings Ltd**
63 Ch c 22/3 Indian Ridge—Bye Bold Aileen (IRE) (Warning) (43594) **Gallagher Equine Ltd**
64 **CAPE MAYA**, b f 18/2 Cape Cross (IRE)—Incatinka (Inca Chief (USA)) (30000) **Abbott Racing Limited**
65 **CHEAP N CHIC**, ch f 20/4 Primo Valentino (IRE)—Amber Mill (Doulab (USA)) (40000) **S. Dartnell**
66 Br f 5/4 Bertolini (USA)—Comme Ca (Cyrano de Bergerac) (20000) **Pat Eddery Racing (Silver Patriarch)**
67 Gr c 16/2 Fantastic Light (USA)—Crepe Ginger (IRE) (Sadler's Wells (USA)) (130000) **T. W. Bloodstock Ltd**
68 **DANCE SPIRIT (IRE)**, ch g 24/4 Namid—
　　　　　　　　Phantom Act (USA) (Theatrical) (13000) **Mr N. Attenborough & Mrs L. Mann**
69 **DONNA BLINI**, ch f 27/3 Bertolini (USA)—
　　　　　　　　Cal Norma's Lady (IRE) (Lyphard's Special (USA)) (20000) **Mrs J. P. E. Cunningham**
70 B br f 2/3 Namid—Easter Heroine (IRE) (Exactly Sharp (USA)) **The Racegoers Club**
71 B c 26/1 Most Welcome—Ewenny (Warrshan (USA)) (26000) **The Second Pheasant Inn Partnership**
72 Ch c 11/4 Singspiel (IRE)—For More (FR) (Sanglamore (USA)) **Paul & Jenny Green**
73 **GLOBAL GUARDIAN**, ch c 10/5 Dr Fong (USA)—Penmayne (Inchinor) (10000) **The Top Banana Partnership**
74 B g 4/5 Desert Prince (IRE)—Gold Mist (Darshaan)
75 B br f 1/3 Singspiel (IRE)—Green Rosy (USA) (Green Dancer (USA)) (60362) **T. W. Bloodstock Ltd**
76 B c 5/5 Dr Fong (USA)—Heart of India (IRE) (Try My Best (USA)) **Mr & Mrs D. Brown**
77 B br f 10/3 Grand Slam (USA)—Indian Fashion (USA) (General Holme (USA)) (69167) **P. Minikes**
78 **INDIGENE**, b c 20/3 Pivotal—River City Moon (USA) (Riverman (USA)) **Wood Hall Stud Limited**
79 Ch c 21/2 Desert Prince (IRE)—Interpose (Indian Ridge) (26000) **J. S. Threadwell**
80 B f 5/3 Cape Cross (IRE)—L'accolade (IRE) (Seattle Dancer (USA)) (26000) **Clipper Group Holdings Ltd**
81 B f 30/1 Green Desert (USA)—Le Montrachet (Nashwan (USA)) (97000) **T. W. Bloodstock Ltd**
82 **LEDA**, ch f 19/4 Bertolini (USA)—Western Horizon (USA) (Gone West (USA)) **Wyck Hall Stud Ltd**
83 B c 26/4 Mujadil (USA)—Lonely Heart (Midyan (USA)) (46000) **Ed McCormack & J. McCarthy**
84 **LOPINOT (IRE)**, br g 28/2 Pursuit of Love—La Suquet (Puissance) (13500) **R. A. Bernard**
85 **MADAM MAC (IRE)**, b f 24/4 Royal Applause—
　　　　　　　　Wild Woman (Polar Falcon (USA)) (40000) **Mackey Family Limited**
86 B f 3/2 In The Wings—Midsummernitedream (GER) (Thatching) (14000) **The Racegoers Club**

MR B. J. MEEHAN—continued

87 **MORETASTIC (USA)**, ch g 29/1 Mt Livermore (USA)—
Brave New Boundary (USA) (Boundary (USA)) (40000) **S. Dartnell**
88 **MUSICAL ROMANCE (IRE)**, b f 2/2 Mozart (IRE)—Dear Jul (IRE) (Fairy King (USA)) (130000) **F. C. T. Wilson**
89 B f 16/3 Erhaab (USA)—My Preference (Reference Point) **J. H. Widdows**
90 **MYSTIC ROLL**, b c 9/4 Medicean—Pain Perdu (IRE) (Waajib) (26000) **Kennet Valley Farms Ltd**
91 B c 8/4 Galileo (IRE)—Pharmacist (IRE) (Machiavellian (USA)) (87189) **E. H. Jones (Paints) Ltd**
92 Ch f 20/3 Bertolini (USA)—Pretiosa (IRE) (Royal Abjar (USA)) (761) **Joy and Valentine Feerick**
93 B c 16/2 Danehill Dancer (IRE)—Price of Passion (Dolphin Street (FR)) (50000) **J. S. Threadwell**
94 B c 16/3 Tomba—Princess Zara (Reprimand) **J. R. Good**
95 B f 6/4 Storm Cat (USA)—Prospect Dalia (USA) (Mr Prospector (USA)) **P. Minikes**
96 B f 21/2 Green Desert (USA)—Queen's Music (USA) (Dixieland Band) (78000) **S. Dartnell**
97 **QUESTRIST**, b f 8/4 Halling (USA)—Arctic Air (Polar Falcon (USA)) (100000) **Wyck Hall Stud Ltd**
98 B f 26/3 Key of Luck (USA)—Radiancy (IRE) (Mujtahid (USA)) (12000) **Grays, Jaye & Connolly**
99 **ROMANTIC TOUCH (IRE)**, ch f 21/3 King's Best (USA)—
Glancing Touch (Nashwan (USA)) (150000) **F. C. T. Wilson**
100 B c 30/4 Royal Applause—Romoosh (Formidable (USA)) (32000) **Ed McCormack & Mrs S. Tucker**
101 B f 27/1 Galileo (IRE)—Rubies From Burma (USA) (Forty Niner (USA)) **T. W. Bloodstock Ltd**
102 B c 4/4 Pivotal—Sea Drift (FR) (Warning) (130000) **D. O'Rourke**
103 B f 13/3 Alhaarth (IRE)—Shamriyna (IRE) (Darshaan) (5500) **Mrs K. Meehan/Mrs S. McKeever**
104 B c 14/4 Xaar—Shona (USA) (Lyphard (USA)) (32000)
105 B f 27/1 Josr Algarhoud (IRE)—Silk Law (USA) (Barathea (IRE)) (10000)
106 **SIR ALFONS (FR)**, b c 23/1 Pivotal—Source de Reve (FR) (Kaldoun (FR)) (40000)
107 **SLEEPING STORM (IRE)**, b f 5/3 Danehill Dancer (IRE)—Caribbean Escape (Pivotal) (30000) **Miss J. Semple**
108 **SMARTWAY**, b c 25/2 Mozart (IRE)—Dayville (USA) (Dayjur (USA)) (62000) **B. A. Schroder**
109 B f 13/3 Docksider (USA)—Spring Symphony (IRE) (Darshaan) **Ballymacoll Stud Farm Ltd**
110 B f 6/3 Mtoto—Star Entry (In The Wings) (15000) **J. H. Widdows**
111 B f 14/3 Tiznow (USA)—Surprise Girl (USA) (Time For A Change (USA)) **P. Minikes**
112 B c 8/5 Indian Ridge—Tafrah (IRE) (Sadler's Wells (USA)) (46947) **Mrs W. M. English**
113 B c 12/4 Marju (IRE)—Tathkara (USA) (Alydar (USA)) **The Tumbleweed Partnership**
114 B f 3/4 Lion Cavern (USA)—Trophy Bride (USA) (Broad Brush (USA)) **A. Rosen**
115 **TWILIGHT AVENGER (IRE)**, b g 10/1 Dr Fong (USA)—
Asterita (Rainbow Quest (USA)) (25000) **The Comic Strip Heroes**
116 B f 16/4 Namid—Violet Spring (IRE) (Exactly Sharp (USA)) **The Racegoers Club**

Other Owners: The Dowager Duchess Of Bedford, T. S. M. Cunningham, Mr W. O'Donnell, Mr D. Margolis, Mrs P. Shananhan, Mr P. Burrell, Mr J. Rowan, Mr M. Morrison, Gold Group International, Mr D. Murray, Mr D. Lucie-Smith, Mrs Y. Allan, G. D. Anderson, A. W. Black, P. J. J. Eddery, Family Amusements Ltd, Mrs P. Good, Mr G. McDonald, M. C. Moutray-Read, N. J. F. Robinson, The Hon Mrs Frances Stanley, Mr P. M. Varty, J. P. Wray.

Assistant Trainer: J Allison

Jockey (flat): J Fortune. **Apprentice:** J. F. McDonald. **Amateur:** Miss J. Allison.

---

397 **MARY MEEK, Eastbury**
Postal: Castle Piece Racing Stables, Grange Road, Eastbury, Hungerford, Berkshire, RG17 7JR.
Contacts: PHONE (01488) 670100 MOBILE (07810) 866992

1 **BALLOCH**, 4, ch f Wootton Rivers (USA)—Balayer **Mary Meek**
2 **BEZWELL PRINCE**, 6, ch g Bluegrass Prince (IRE)—Money Supply **Mary Meek**
3 **CASISLE**, 4, ch f Wootton Rivers (USA)—Isle Maree **Miss L. Meek**
4 **DARK ISLAND**, 10, b g Silver Season—Isle Maree **Mary Meek**

---

398 **MR P. T. MIDGLEY, Westow**
Postal: Sandfield Farm, Westow, York.
Contacts: PHONE (01653) 658309 MOBILE (07976) 965220

1 **BOND DIAMOND**, 8, gr g Prince Sabo—Alsiba **P. J. Mee**
2 **CALL ME SUNSHINE**, 5, b m Robellino (USA)—Kirana **D. Mann**
3 **CLIP ON**, 4, b f Past Glories—Scalby Clipper **A. R. Dimmock**
4 **FAIRY MONARCH (IRE)**, 6, b g Ali-Royal (IRE)—Cookawara (IRE) **M. E. Elsworthy**
5 **RED HOT RUBY**, 4, ch f Komaite (USA)—Gleam of Gold **The Definitely Maybe Partnership**
6 **SEDGE (USA)**, 5, b g Lure (USA)—First Flyer (USA) **P. J. Mee**
7 **VESTA FLAME**, 4, b f Vettori (IRE)—Ciel de Feu (USA) **Church Lane Stud**
8 **WINSABONUS**, 5, b g Defacto (USA)—Heart Broken **Enjoy A Day Out Partnership**

MR P. T. MIDGLEY—continued

THREE-YEAR-OLDS

9 **AGREAT DAYOUTWITHU**, ch f Defacto (USA)—Lonely Lass **Enjoy A Day Out Partnership**
10 **FANTASY FEELING**, b g Easycall—Priceless Fantasy **M. E. Elsworthy**
11 **GRACEFUL FLIGHT**, gr f Cloudings (IRE)—Fantasy Flight **Mrs Grace Ng**

TWO-YEAR-OLDS

12 **BEST OF FRIENDS**, ch f 16/2 Silver Wizard (USA)—Feiticeira (USA) (Deposit Ticket (USA)) **Church Lane Stud**
13 B f 14/2 Whittingham (IRE)—Bint Baddi (FR) (Shareef Dancer (USA)) (1000) **Mr W. B. Imison**
14 B f 3/2 Bahamian Bounty—Bogus Mix (IRE) (Linamix (FR)) (1500) **Mr W. B. Imison**
15 B f 28/4 Namaqualand (USA)—Felinwen (White Mill) **Mrs K. L. Midgley**
16 **KELLYS DOUBLE GOLD (IRE)**, ch f 24/1 Spinning World (USA)—
Delighting (USA) (Boundary (USA)) (2700) **P. J. Mee**
17 B c 4/5 Easycall—Lady Susan (Petong)
18 **LORD LOVEROCKET**, ch c 25/4 Woodborough—Bowden Rose (Dashing Blade) (2000) **M. E. Elsworthy**
19 B c 17/3 Beckett (IRE)—No Shame (Formidable (USA)) (4000) **Mr W. B. Imison**
20 B f 21/4 Foxhound (USA)—River of Fortune (Lahib (USA)) (1600) **Mr W. B. Imison**
21 **SOBA FELLA**, b g 21/2 Puissance—Cedar Jeneva (Muhtarram (USA)) (2800)
22 **STORMING NORMAN**, ch g 6/4 Allied Forces (USA)—
Pleasant Memories (Danehill (USA)) (1200) **The Prize Guys**
23 B f 8/2 Woodborough (USA)—Tinker Osmaston (Dunbeath (USA)) (1500) **Mr W. B. Imison**
24 B f 21/4 Easycall—Whiting Bay (Contract Law (USA)) **Church Lane Stud**

Other Owners: MR P. T. Midgley, G. J. Paver, E. I. Pruchniewicz, N. A. Swales.

Jockey (flat): R. Fitzpatrick, L. Enstone, G. Parkin. **Jockey (NH):** V. T. Keane, V. Slattery. **Amateur:** Mr S. Walker.

---

399 **MISS M. K. MILLIGAN, Middleham**
Postal: **Castle Stables, Middleham, Leyburn, North Yorkshire, DL8 4QQ.**
Contacts: **HOME (01969) 624105 OFFICE (01969) 623221 FAX (01969) 623221**
MOBILE (07721) 529857 E-MAIL kate@mkmracing.fsnet.co.uk

1 **DARK BEN (FR)**, 5, b g Solar One (FR)—Reine D'auteuil (FR) **J. D. Gordon**
2 **INGLEWOOD**, 5, ch g Fleetwood (IRE)—Preening **The Aunts**
3 4, B g Cayman Kai (IRE)—Jamimo (IRE) **J. D. Gordon**
4 **KARYON (IRE)**, 5, b m Presidium—Stealthy **S. J. Ward**
5 **LORD PAT (IRE)**, 14, ch g Mister Lord (USA)—Arianrhod **Dr R. A. Palmer**
6 **MIDDLEWAY**, 9, b g Milieu—Galway Gal **Mrs J. M. L. Milligan**
7 **SAVANNAH RIVER (IRE)**, 4, b f Desert King (IRE)—Hayward **Mrs P. Monk**
8 **TAIPO PRINCE (IRE)**, 5, b g Entrepreneur—Dedicated Lady (IRE) **Mr E. Whalley**

Other Owners: Mrs D. L. Barrett, Miss M. K. Milligan, Mrs J. A. Robson.

Amateur: Miss T. Jackson.

---

400 **MR B. R. MILLMAN, Cullompton**
Postal: **The Paddocks, Kentisbeare, Cullompton, Devon, EX15 2DX.**
Contacts: **PHONE/FAX (01884) 266620 MOBILE (07885) 168447**
E-MAIL brmillman@tinyworld.co.uk

1 **ADANTINO**, 6, b g Glory of Dancer—Sweet Whisper **Tarka Two Racing**
2 **BALEARIC STAR (IRE)**, 4, b c Night Shift (USA)—La Menorquina (USA) **G. W. Dormer**
3 **BATHWICK BILL (USA)**, 4, ch g Stravinsky (USA)—Special Park (USA) **Mrs S. Clifford**
4 **BATHWICK BRUCE (IRE)**, 7, b g College Chapel—Naivity (IRE) **H. M. W. Clifford**
5 **BENNY BATHWICK (IRE)**, 4, b g Midyan (USA)—Sweet Pavlova (USA) **Mrs S. Clifford**
6 **CHORUS**, 8, b m Bandmaster (USA)—Name That Tune **Mrs L. S. Millman**
7 **FACTUAL LAD**, 7, b g So Factual (USA)—Surprise Surprise **Tarka Racing**
8 **FROMSONG (IRE)**, 7, b g Fayruz—Lindas Delight **Mrs E. Nelson, Mr Gary Dormer**
9 **JAZZY MILLENNIUM**, 3, ch g Lion Cavern (USA)—Woodcrest **Millennium Millionaires Partnership**
10 **LEAPING BRAVE (IRE)**, 4, b g Indian Rocket—Island Heather (IRE) **The Links Partnership**
11 **NINA FONTENAIL (FR)**, 4, gr f Kaldounevees (FR)—Ninon Fontenail (FR) **The Links Partnership**
12 **PASO DOBLE**, 7, b g Dancing Spree—Delta Tempo (USA) **Mr J. Millman**
13 **POLISH SPIRIT**, 10, b g Emarati (USA)—Gentle Star **Mrs I. T. M. Palmer**

MR B. R. MILLMAN—continued

14 **PRINCE NUREYEV (IRE)**, 5, b g Desert King (IRE)—Annaletta **H. G. T. Gooding**
15 **SERGEANT CECIL**, 6, ch g King's Signet (USA)—Jadidh **T. E. Cooper**
16 **STEVEDORE (IRE)**, 4, ch c Docksider (USA)—La Belle Katherine (USA) **Mrs S. Clifford**
17 **THETHREERONNIES**, 5, b g Classic Cliche (IRE)—Polly Leach **The Willey Win Partnership**

THREE-YEAR-OLDS

18 **ARBORS LITTLE GIRL**, b f Paris House—Arbor Ealis (IRE) **Dr I. R. Shenkin**
19 **AUWITESWEETHEART**, b f Josr Algarhoud (IRE)—Miss Kirsty (USA) **D. R. Windebank**
20 **BACKSTREET LAD**, b c Fraam—Forest Fantasy **David Lyons Racing Syndicate 4**
21 **BATHWICK FINESSE (IRE)**, b f Namid—Lace Flower
22 **COLONEL BILKO (IRE)**, b g General Monash (USA)—Mari-Ela (IRE) **Ray Gudge, Colin Lewis, Malcolm Calvert**
23 **DAVENPORT (IRE)**, b g Bold Fact—Semence D'or (FR)
24 **EDGE FUND**, b c Bold Edge—Truly Madly Deeply **Mrs G. Austen Smith, Colin Lewis, Malcolm Calvert**
25 B f Key of Luck (USA)—Gaelic Foray (IRE) **Dr I. R. Shenkin**
26 **HAPPY EVENT**, b c Makbul—La Belle Vie **V. R. S. Lawson**
27 **INDIAN SKY (IRE)**, b c Indian Lodge (IRE)—Bolero **Avalon Surfacing And Construction Co Ltd**
28 **MABELLA (IRE)**, b f Brave Act—Wee Merkin (IRE) **M S T Partnership**
29 **POLAR DAWN**, b f Polar Falcon (USA)—Leave At Dawn **T. E. Pocock**
30 **SEASONS ESTATES**, b f Mark of Esteem (IRE)—La Fazenda
31 **STAR DUSTER**, gr f Paris House—To The Stars (IRE) **Mrs M. Shenkin**
32 **TIGGERS TOUCH**, b f Fraam—Beacon Silver **R. L. Croft**
33 **WINTER MOON**, b f Mujadil (USA)—Crofters Ceilidh **Inter Property Consultancy Ltd**

TWO-YEAR-OLDS

34 B c 15/2 King Charlemagne (USA)—Anabaa's Music (Anabaa (USA)) (18000)
35 B f 7/3 Piccolo—Barnacla (IRE) (Bluebird (USA)) (9000) **T. E. Cooper**
36 B c 16/4 Beckett (IRE)—Bathwick Babe (IRE) (Sri Pekan (USA)) (3800) **H. M. W. Clifford**
37 B c 14/4 Josr Algarhoud (IRE)—Beryl (Bering) (16000)
38 B c 3/3 Carrowkeel (IRE)—Byproxy (IRE) (Mujtahid (USA)) (20000) **Mrs S. Clifford**
39 B f 19/2 Mark of Esteem (IRE)—Ciel de Feu (IRE) (Blushing John (USA)) (10000) **Mrs S. Clifford**
40 B c 15/3 Forzando—Clashfern (Smackover) (36000) **The Links Partnership**
41 B c 19/3 Fantastic Light (USA)—El Hakma (Shareef Dancer (USA)) (34000) **Seasons Holidays**
42 Ch c 21/3 Foxhound (USA)—Flag (Selkirk (USA)) (5000)
43 B c 27/3 Superior Premium—Gay Ming (Gay Meadow) (2000) **H. M. W. Clifford**
44 B c 18/2 Makbul—La Belle Vie (Indian King (USA)) (5000) **G. W. Dormer**
45 Ch c 13/4 Namid—Latest (IRE) (Bob Back (USA)) (11000)
46 B c 3/2 Makbul—Victoria Sioux (Ron's Victory (USA)) (20000) **M S T Partnership**
47 B c 14/3 Imperial Ballet (IRE)—Yahe (IRE) (Alzao (USA)) (5000) **David Lyons Racing Syndicate 3**

Other Owners: P. Banham, T. L. D. Blake, A. J. Conway, Mrs T. A. Dormer, Mrs A. A. Gooding, E. J. Grigg, R. Hewitt, V. B. Lewer, D. A. Little, D. P. J. Lyons, MR B. R. Millman, V. G. Palmer, C. Tayler, E. M. Thornton, Mrs S. Thornton, D. T. Whitefield, M. G. Willey.

Assistant Trainer: Louise Millman

Jockey (flat): G. Baker, S. Drowne. **Amateur:** Mr J. Millman.

---

401 **MR T. G. MILLS, Epsom**
Postal: **Loretta Lodge, Tilley Lane, Headley, Epsom, Surrey, KT18 6EP.**
Contacts: **PHONE** (01372) 377209 **FAX** (01372) 386578

1 **CAMBERWELL**, 4, b g Royal Applause—Into Orbit **Welcocks Skips Limited**
2 **DONT WORRY BOUT ME (IRE)**, 8, b g Brief Truce (USA)—Coggle **Mr T. G. Mills**
3 **EVALUATOR (IRE)**, 4, b g Ela-Mana-Mou—Summerhill **Mrs L. M. Askew**
4 **HERE TO ETERNITY (IRE)**, 4, b g In The Wings—Amnesty Bay **Mrs L. M. Askew**
5 **HIGH REACH**, 5, b g Royal Applause—Lady of Limerick (IRE) **Four M's**
6 **KEEP ON MOVIN' (IRE)**, 4, b f Danehill Dancer (IRE)—Tormented **J. E. Harley**
7 **LET ME TRY AGAIN (IRE)**, 5, b g Sadler's Wells (USA)—Dathiyna (IRE) **Mr T. G. Mills**
8 **NORTON (IRE)**, 8, ch g Barathea (IRE)—Primrose Valley **Mr T. G. Mills**
9 **OK PAL**, 5, b g Primo Dominie—Sheila's Secret (IRE) **Sherwoods Transport Ltd**
10 **RESPLENDENT KING (USA)**, 4, b g King of Kings (IRE)—Sister Fromseattle (USA) **Resplendent Racing Limited**
11 **RESPLENDENT ONE (IRE)**, 4, b g Marju—Licentious **Resplendent Racing Limited**
12 **ROYAL STARDUST**, 4, b g Cloudings (IRE)—Ivy Edith **G. A. Antill**
13 **SAVIOURS SPIRIT**, 4, ch g Komaite (USA)—Greenway Lady **J. E. Harley**

MR T. G. MILLS—continued

14 **SETTLEMENT CRAIC (IRE),** 4, b g Ela-Mana-Mou—Medway (IRE) **Buxted Partnership**
15 **SOMEWHERE MY LOVE,** 4, br f Pursuit of Love—Grand Coronet **Miss J. Leighs**
16 **TENDER TRAP (IRE),** 7, b g Sadler's Wells (USA)—Shamiyda (USA) **Mr T. G. Mills**
17 **THE WAY WE WERE,** 4, ch g Vettori (IRE)—Pandrop **Mrs C. Stephens**

THREE-YEAR-OLDS

18 **ENGLISH VICTORY,** ch c Grand Lodge (USA)—Amandine (IRE) **J. E. Harley**
19 **GIBRALTAR BAY (IRE),** b f Cape Cross (IRE)—Secrets of Honour **Mr Dennis Russell and Mrs Yvonne Norris**
20 **HE'S A DIAMOND,** ch g Vettori (IRE)—Azira **Ms T. Barker**
21 **HIGH CHART,** b f Robellino (USA)—Bright Spells **Mr Dennis Russell and Mrs Yvonne Norris**
22 **I HAVE DREAMED (IRE),** b c Montjeu (IRE)—Diamond Field (USA) **Mr T. G. Mills**
23 **LORD SODEN (IRE),** b g Namid—Arab Scimetar (IRE) **Albert Soden Ltd**
24 **PAPER DOLL,** ch f Mister Baileys—Grand Coronet **Ms T. Barker**
25 **PITCH UP (IRE),** b g Cape Cross (IRE)—Uhud (IRE) **Mr B. G. Chamley**
26 **RESPLENDENT GLORY (IRE),** ch c Namid—Aoife (IRE) **Resplendent Racing Limited**
27 **RESPLENDENT NOVA,** b c Pivotal—Santiburi Girl **Resplendent Racing Limited**
28 **RESPLENDENT PRINCE,** ch c Primo Dominie—Last Result **Resplendent Racing Limited**
29 **SNOW TEMPEST (USA),** b g Theatrical—January's Storm (USA) **Mr I. West**
30 **SOMETHING (IRE),** b c Trans Island—Persian Polly **John Humphreys (Turf Accountants) Ltd**
31 **SOUTH O'THE BORDER,** b g Wolfhound (USA)—Abbey's Gal **Mr T. G. Mills**
32 **SWEET LORRAINE,** b f Dashing Blade—Royal Future (IRE) **Mr P. C. Ryan**
33 **THEBESTISYETTOCOME,** b c Montjeu (IRE)—French Quartet (IRE) **John Humphreys (Turf Accountants) Ltd**
34 **TREMAR,** b c Royal Applause—Sabina **Mr Trevor Jacobs**

TWO-YEAR-OLDS

35 **BEFORE YOU GO (IRE),** b c 12/1 Sadler's Wells (USA)—
    Here On Earth (USA) (Mr Prospector (USA)) (100000) **Tina Smith**
36 **BERTI BERTOLINI,** b c 30/4 Bertolini (USA)—
    Cosmic Countess (IRE) (Lahib (USA)) **Cosmic Greyhound Racing Partnership III**
37 B c 27/3 Shinko Forest (IRE)—Maritana (Rahy (USA)) (40000) **Mr T. G. Mills**
38 B c 23/3 Mujadil (USA)—Non Dimenticar Me (IRE) (Don't Forget Me) (30000) **Mr T. G. Mills**
39 B c 8/5 Inchinor—Sabina (Prince Sabo) (40000) **J. E. Harley**
40 **THEY ALL LAUGHED,** ch c 1/4 Zafonic (USA)—Royal Future (IRE) (Royal Academy (USA)) (43594) **Mr T. G. Mills**

Other Owners: T. Crawley, M. R. Evans, J. P. Hanifin, T. Jacobs, G. F. Meek, T. F. Moxon, Mrs J. Ruthven.

Assistant Trainer: R A Mills

Apprentice: R. Keogh.

MR C. W. MITCHELL, Dorchester
402
Postal: **White House, Buckland Newton, Dorchester, Dorset, DT2 7DE.**
Contacts: **PHONE (01300) 345276**

1 **JASPER ROONEY,** 6, b g Riverwise (USA)—Miss Secret **Mr C. W. Mitchell**
2 **RIVER OF WISHES,** 7, b m Riverwise (USA)—Wishful Dream **Mr C. W. Mitchell**
3 **WALTER'S DESTINY,** 13, ch g White Prince (USA)—Tearful Sarah **Mr C. W. Mitchell**

MR N. R. MITCHELL, Dorchester
403
Postal: **East Hill Stables, Piddletrenthide, Dorchester, Dorset, DT2 7QY.**
Contacts: **PHONE/FAX (01300) 348739 MOBILE (07775) 843136**

1 **ASK ANDREA,** 5, ch m Busy Flight—Craberi Flash Foot **D. V. Stevens**
2 **DUN LOCHA CASTLE (IRE),** 10, b g Cataldi—Decent Preacher **Dunplush**
3 **KITTENKAT,** 11, b m Riverwise (USA)—Cut Above The Rest **P. S. Butler**
4 **LUCKY LEADER (IRE),** 10, b g Supreme Leader—Lucky House **M. A. Green**
5 **PANHANDLE,** 11, b m Riverwise (USA)—Pallanda **Mrs E. Mitchell**
6 **PETER PARKGATE,** 6, gr g Kuwait Beach (USA)—Nellie's Joy VII **Mrs R. O. Hutchings**
7 **RINGS OF POWER (IRE),** 8, ch g Mister Lord—Rainbow Gurriers (IRE) **M. A. Green**
8 **SILKIE PEKIN,** 6, gr m Riverwise (USA)—Came Cottage **Mrs E. Mitchell**

Other Owners: Mr N. P. I. Harrison, Mr P. J. Hiscock.

Assistant Trainer: Mrs E Mitchell

404 MR PHILIP MITCHELL, Epsom
Postal: **Downs House, Epsom Downs, Surrey, KT18 5ND.**
Contacts: PHONE **(01372) 273729** FAX **(01372) 278701** MOBILE **(07836) 231462**
E-MAIL **philip@downshouse.com**

1 **BURGUNDY,** 8, b g Lycius (USA)—Decant **Mrs S. Sheldon**
2 **CORRIOLANUS (GER),** 5, b h Zamindar (USA)—Caesarea (GER) **R. J. Cohen**
3 **COURT CHANCELLOR,** 4, b g Primo Dominie—Welcome Home **W. R. Mann & Georgia Partnership**
4 **DREAM OF DUBAI (IRE),** 4, b f Vettori (IRE)—Immortelle **Ransom Family & Friends**
5 **FOREVER FREE (GER),** 5, ch g Platini (GER)—Forever Nice (GER) **Ransom Family & Friends**
6 **FREE STRIKE (NZ),** 8, ch g Straight Strike (USA)—Ansellia (NZ) **Roger Cheetham**
7 **JOE BEAR (IRE),** 5, ch h Peintre Celebre (USA)—Maharani (USA) **Christopher Ransom**
8 **LORD OF THE SEA (IRE),** 4, b g Perugino (USA)—Sea Mistress **Barrie & Shirley Sancto**
9 **MARGALITA (IRE),** 5, b m Sesaro (USA)—Mamma Luigi (IRE) **The Harris Gore Partnership**
10 **MONTOSARI,** 6, ch g Persian Bold—Sartigila **Caterham Racing (jdrp)**
11 **MY LILLI (IRE),** 5, b m Marju (IRE)—Tamburello (IRE) **Mr M. Vickers**
12 **RAHEEL (IRE),** 5, ch g Barathea (IRE)—Tajawuz **Mrs S. Sheldon**
13 **RUSSIAN COUNT (USA),** 4, b c King of Kings (IRE)—Shriving (USA) **Georgia Partnership**
14 **SHOLAY (IRE),** 6, b g Bluebird (USA)—Splicing **Mrs P. A. Mitchell**
15 **SUNSET DREAMER (USA),** 4, ch f Boundary (USA)—Quaff (USA) **Georgia Partnership**
16 **SWAINSON (USA),** 4, br c Swain (USA)—Lyphard's Delta (USA) **R. J. Cohen**
17 **WILD PITCH,** 4, ch g Piccolo—Western Horizon (USA) **Mrs J. Auletta & Mrs P. Mitchell**

THREE-YEAR-OLDS

18 B c Miswaki (USA)—Ocean Jewel (USA) **Marquesa De Moratalla**
19 **RED SANS,** b c Rainbow Quest (USA)—Sarah Georgina **G. F. Sanders**
20 **WORLD SERIES (IRE),** b c Almutawakel—Mezzanine **G. W. Y. Li**

TWO-YEAR-OLDS

21 **BILLY WIZZ (IRE),** b c 20/4 Namid—Mareha (IRE) (Cadeaux Genereux) (11000) **Christopher Ransom**
22 Ch c 29/3 Spinning World—Intellectuelle (Caerleon (USA)) (20000) **Alyenian Racing Partnership**
23 B f 15/2 Barathea (IRE)—King of All (IRE) (King of Clubs) (40000) **Mr M. Vickers**
24 B c 3/2 Daylami (IRE)—Luana (Shaadi (USA)) (30000) **Christopher Ransom**
25 **SCARLET KNIGHT,** b c 28/2 Lujain (USA)—Gem (Most Welcome) (11000) **W. R. Mann**

Other Owners: Mr John Dunbar, Prof M. E. Gore, G. R. Harris, Mrs Y. J. Ray, J. Ray, J. R. Stephens.

Assistant Trainer: Roger Teal

Amateur: Mr Jack Mitchell.

405 MR D. J. MOFFATT, Cartmel
Postal: **Pit Farm Racing Stables, Cartmel, Grange Over Sands, Cumbria, LA11 6PJ.**
Contacts: PHONE **(01539) 536689** MOBILE **(07767) 367282**

1 **AMBER GO GO,** 8, ch m Rudimentary (USA)—Plaything **Stableline.com Ltd**
2 **BALL GAMES,** 7, b g Mind Games—Deb's Ball **Jennie Moffatt, Evan Munro**
3 **CAYMAN MISCHIEF,** 5, b m Cayman Kai (IRE)—Tribal Mischief **Greengate Lease Syndicate**
4 **CODY,** 6, ch g Zilzal (USA)—Ibtihaj (USA) **The Vilprano Partnership**
5 **FARAWAY ECHO,** 4, gr f Second Empire (IRE)—Salalah **Alfred Chadwick**
6 **FLAME OF ZARA,** 6, ch m Blushing Flame (USA)—Sierra Madrona (USA) **L. N. Sloan, James Varley**
7 **FORUM CHRIS (IRE),** 8, ch g Trempolino—Memory Green (USA) **Mrs J. Conroy**
8 **FRABROFEN,** 4, b f Mind Games—Oh My Oh My **Stableline.com Ltd**
9 **HAYSTACKS (IRE),** 9, b g Contract Law (USA)—Florissa (FR) **Mr & Mrs A. G. Milligan**
10 **INCHINNAN,** 8, b m Inchinor—Westering **The Sheroot Partnership**
11 **LA FOLICHONNE (FR),** 6, b m Useful (FR)—Allure Folle (FR) **Woodburn, Gallagher & Friends**
12 **LAGO,** 7, b g Maelstrom Lake—Jugendliebe (IRE) **Bernard Bargh, Jeff Hamer, Steve Henshaw**
13 **LANZLO (FR),** 8, b br g Le Balafre (FR)—L'eternite (FR) **The Sheroot Partnership**
14 **LOCH TORRIDON,** 6, b g Syrtos—Loch Scavaig (IRE) **Mrs G. A. Turnbull**
15 **OCOTILLO,** 5, b g Mark of Esteem (IRE)—Boojum **Alfred Chadwick**
16 **ONLY MILLIE,** 4, b f Prince Daniel (USA)—Deb's Ball **Mr & Mrs A. G. Milligan**
17 **PAVEY ARK (IRE),** 7, b g King's Ride—Splendid Run **Mr & Mrs A. G. Milligan**
18 **PETROLERO (ARG),** 6, gr g Perfect Parade—Louise (ARG) **P. Kiely & DJM**
19 **SPRING JOY,** 4, ch f Captain Maverick (USA)—Sciacca **Mrs L. Dyer**

MR D. J. MOFFATT—continued

THREE-YEAR-OLDS

20 **FERN HOUSE (IRE)**, b c Xaar—Certain Impression (USA) **J. W. Barrett**
21 **GLOBE TREKKER (USA)**, gr f Aljabr (USA)—Amazonia (USA) **J. W. Barrett**
22 **MITCHELLAND**, b f Namaqualand (USA)—Precious Girl **R. R. Whitton**

Other Owners: K. Bowron, J. Conroy, Mr M. Gallagher, Ms G. K. Humpage, A. R. Mills, MR D. J. Moffatt, G. R. Parrington, F. A. Woodburn.

Assistant Trainer: Dudley Moffatt Snr

Jockey (flat): Royston Ffrench, R. Winston. **Jockey (NH):** J. Crowley, A. Dobbin. **Conditional:** P. A. Aspell.

---

406 **MR PETER MONTEITH, Rosewell**
Postal: **Whitebog Farm, Rosewell, Midlothian, EH24 9AY.**
Contacts: PHONE **(0131) 4402309 FAX (0131) 4402226 MOBILE (07885) 060296**
E-MAIL pmonteith945@aol.com

1 **ALAM (USA)**, 6, b g Silver Hawk (USA)—Ghashtah (USA) **G. M. Cowan**
2 **ANDRE CHENIER (IRE)**, 4, b g Perugino (USA)—Almada (GER) **D. A. Johnson**
3 **BRAVE THOUGHT (IRE)**, 10, b g Commanche Run—Bristol Fairy **Hamilton House Ltd**
4 **BRIDGE PAL**, 5, ch m First Trump—White Domino **Miss E. G. Macgregor**
5 **CHARLIE GEORGE**, 4, ch g Idris (IRE)—Faithful Beauty (IRE) **J. D. Baxter**
6 **COMPADRE**, 7, gr g Environment Friend—Cardinal Press **J. W. Stephenson**
7 **CULCABOCK (IRE)**, 5, b g Unfuwain (USA)—Evidently (USA) **Mrs E. B. Ferguson**
8 **GONE TOO FAR**, 7, b g Reprimand—Blue Nile (IRE) **D. A. Johnson**
9 **IDEAL DU BOIS BEURY (FR)**, 9, b br g Useful (FR)—Pampa Star (FR) **G. M. Cowan**
10 **JORDAN'S RIDGE (IRE)**, 9, b br g Indian Ridge—Sadie Jordan (USA) **W. W. Stewart**
11 **LEADING FAIRY (IRE)**, 5, b g Flemensfirth (USA)—Woodland Fairy (IRE) **P. Monteith**
12 **LIBERTY SEEKER (FR)**, 6, ch g Machiavellian (USA)—Samara (IRE) **M. Sawers**
13 **MILLENNIUM HALL**, 6, b g Saddlers' Hall (IRE)—Millazure (USA) **Mrs E. B. Ferguson**
14 **MISTER MAGNUM (IRE)**, 7, b g Be My Native (USA)—Miss Henrietta (IRE) **P. Monteith**
15 **MOSCOW DANCER (IRE)**, 8, ch g Moscow Society (USA)—Cromhill Lady **J. W. Stephenson**
16 **NERONE (GER)**, 4, gr g Sternkoenig (IRE)—Nordwahl (GER) **D. A. Johnson**
17 **OLD BARNS (IRE)**, 5, b g Nucleon (USA)—Surfer Katie (IRE) **M. Sawers**
18 **POLYPHON (FR)**, 7, b g Murmure (FR)—Petite Folie **Mr & Mrs Raymond Anderson Green**
19 **SHARES (IRE)**, 5, b g Turtle Island (IRE)—Glendora **The Dregs Of Humanity**
20 **SPREE VISION**, 9, b g Suave Dancer (USA)—Regent's Folly (FR) **I. W. Bell**
21 **TERLAN (GER)**, 7, b g Medicus (GER)—Taxodium (GER) **I. W. Bell**
22 **THE BIKER (IRE)**, 8, br g Arctic Lord—Glenravel **W. W. Stewart**
23 **THE MIGHTY FLYNN**, 6, ch g Botanic—Owdbetts (IRE) **J. W. D. Campbell**
24 **TIGER KING (GER)**, 4, b g Tiger Hill (IRE)—Tennessee Girl (USA) **Mr & Mrs Raymond Anderson Green**
25 **TORGIANO (IRE)**, 4, b g Cadeaux Genereux—Delimara (IRE) **P. Monteith**
26 **WINSLOW BOY (USA)**, 4, b br g Expelled (USA)—Acusteal (USA) **P. Monteith**
27 **WYN DIXIE (IRE)**, 6, b g Great Commotion (USA)—Duchess Affair (IRE) **D. A. Johnson**
28 **ZAMAT**, 9, b g Slip Anchor—Khandjar **I. W. Bell**

Other Owners: R. M. S. Allison, A. G. Guthrie.

Assistant Trainer: Doreen Monteith

Jockey (flat): P. Fessey. **Conditional:** D. Da Silva. **Amateur:** Mr D. Blacker, Mr S. Waley-Cohen.

---

407 **MR A. L. MOORE, Naas**
Postal: **Dereens, Naas, Co. Kildare, Ireland.**
Contacts: HOME **+353 (0) 45 876292 FAX +353 (0) 45 899247 MOBILE +353 (0) 872 552535**

1 **BALLYNATTIN BUCK (IRE)**, 9, b g Buckskin (FR)—Dikler Gale (IRE) **M. O'Connor**
2 **BE MY BETTER HALF (IRE)**, 10, b g Be My Native (USA)—The Mrs **J. P. McManus**
3 **BLANC C'EST BLANC (FR)**, 8, ch g Royal Charter (FR)—Tamilda (FR) **F. Conroy**
4 **BON TEMPS ROULER (FR)**, 6, b g Hero's Honor (USA)—Top Nue (FR) **F. Clarke**
5 **BRAVE VILLA (FR)**, 6, b g Villez (USA)—Brave Lola (FR) **Lyreen Syndicate**
6 **COCK ROBIN (IRE)**, 6, b g Pierre—Burton Rose (IRE) **S. Mulryan**
7 **DERAWAR (IRE)**, 6, b g Kahyasi—Denizliya (IRE) **Mrs J. J. McGettigan**

MR A. L. MOORE—continued

8 **ESKIMO JACK (IRE)**, 9, ch g Glacial Storm (USA)—Covette **J McKinney**
9 **FATHOM IT OUT**, 6, b g Karinga Bay—Atlantic View
10 **FEICHEAD GHRA (IRE)**, 6, b g Goldmark (USA)—Semiramide (IRE) **Valentines Day Syndicate**
11 **FRIENDLY CONFLICT (IRE)**, 9, b g Jolly Jake (NZ)—Deep Rival **Mrs A. L. T. Moore**
12 **GLENELLY GALE (IRE)**, 11, b g Strong Gale—Smart Fashion **F. Bradley**
13 **GREEN FINGER**, 7, b g Environment Friend—Hunt The Thimble (FR) **Mrs M. Donnelly**
14 **GUESS (IRE)**, 5, b br g Executive Perk—Fiery Finch **Mrs A. L. T. Moore**
15 **IN TECHNICOLOR (IRE)**, 6, b g Germany (USA)—Light Argument (IRE) **Dominic J. Jones**
16 **INCAS (FR)**, 9, b g Video Rock (FR)—Amarante II (FR) **Incas Syndicate**
17 **JAQUOUILLE (FR)**, 8, b g Agent Bleu (FR)—Topeka (FR) **F. Clarke**
18 **JIRLAN (FR)**, 8, b g Fill My Hopes (FR)—Belle Brune (FR) **M. Bailey**
19 **JUNIOR FONTAINE (FR)**, 8, b g Silver Rainbow—Blanche Fontaine (FR) **W. W. Dennison**
20 **KILT D'ESTRUVAL (FR)**, 7, b g Cyborg (FR)—Vapeur (FR) **Mrs A. L. T. Moore**
21 **KRANJI (FR)**, 5, b g Take Risks (FR)—Vertevoie (FR) **Sir A. J. O'Reilly**
22 **LE ROI D'ANJOU (FR)**, 5, b g Nononito (FR)—Royalla (FR) **R. A. Keogh**
23 **LEINSTER HOUSE (IRE)**, 6, br g Grand Lodge (USA)—Overruled (IRE) **Mrs A. L. T. Moore**
24 **LEWIS DU MONTCEAU (FR)**, 6, b g Kadalko (FR)—Pam II (FR) **J. Fennelly**
25 **LUCKY STAR (IRE)**, 6, b g Luchiroverte (IRE)—Lady Pat Pong (FR) **T. Bailey**
26 **MAHDI DE COEUR (FR)**, 5, ch g Port Lyautey (FR)—Fete de Coeur (FR) **Wee Remy Syndicate**
27 **MANSONY (FR)**, 6, b g Mansonnien (FR)—Hairly (FR) **M. Mulholland**
28 **MARCUS DU BERLAIS (FR)**, 8, gr g Saint Preuil (FR)—Rosacotte (FR) **M. Beresford**
29 **MARMOT D'ESTRUVAL (FR)**, 5, b g Epervier Bleu—Alrose (FR) **Seven Deadly Syndicate**
30 **MINOR RUMPUS**, 6, b g Roselier (FR)—Avena **Mrs A. L. T. Moore**
31 **MONTOMAR (FR)**, 5, b g Panoramic—Fleur de Mar (FR) **G. Kinahan**
32 **MUNSTER (IRE)**, 8, b g Zaffaran (USA)—Delway **C. Ryan**
33 **NATIVE JACK (IRE)**, 11, br g Be My Native (USA)—Dorrha Daisy **Mrs F. Carroll**
34 **NATIVE UPMANSHIP (IRE)**, 12, ch g Be My Native (USA)—Hi' Upham **Mrs J. Magnier**
35 **NOADIBOU (FR)**, 8, b g Cadoudal (FR)—Bahia De Chalamont (FR) **Mr V. Keady**
36 **POLLY ANTHUS**, 6, b m Kahyasi—Bayariyka (IRE) **T. Ryan**
37 **RAPIDE PLAISIR (FR)**, 7, b g Grand Plaisir (IRE)—Royal Well **Glenavet Racing Syndicate**
38 **RHEINDROSS (IRE)**, 10, gr g Ala Hounak—Ardcarn Girl **C. Jones**
39 **ROB THE FIVE (IRE)**, 8, b g Supreme Leader—Derravarragh Lady (IRE) **J. P. McManus**
40 **SYROCO (FR)**, 6, b g Homme de Loi (IRE)—La Pommeraie (FR) **V. Kennedy**
41 **THE GATHERER (IRE)**, 11, b g Be My Native (USA)—Reaper's Run **J. P. McManus**
42 **THE RAILWAY MAN (IRE)**, 6, b g Shernazar—Sparky Sue (IRE) **C. Ryan**
43 **THEATRE LANE**, 8, b g Old Vic—Snitton Lane **Mrs S. Hickey**
44 **TIGER CRY (IRE)**, 4, b g Germany (USA)—Dream Academy **C. Jones**
45 **TOU CHARMING (IRE)**, 7, b g Toulon—Lucky Charm (IRE) **Tom Charming Syndicate**
46 **WAKI BAKI (IRE)**, 6, b g High Roller (USA)—Turbulent Wind **Virginia Viscountess Petersham**
47 **WESTERN ROAD (GER)**, 5, b m King's Theatre (IRE)—Walkona (IRE) **Mrs M. Cahill**
48 **WHAT PERK (IRE)**, 6, b g Executive Perk—Milford Run **Lyreen Syndicate**

Jockey (NH): B. M. Cash, C. O'Dwyer. **Conditional:** R. T. Dunne, D. Howard. **Amateur:** Mr P. J. King, Mr J. D. Moore.

---

408 **MR G. L. MOORE, Brighton**
Postal: **4 Downland Close, Woodingdean, Brighton, Sussex, BN2 6DN.**
Contacts: **HOME (01273) 620106 MOBILE (07753) 863123**

1 **ACORAZADO (IRE)**, 6, b g Petorius—Jaldi (IRE) **D T L Limited**
2 **ADECCO (IRE)**, 6, b g Eagle Eyed (USA)—Kharaliya (FR) **N. J. Jones**
3 **ADOPTED HERO (IRE)**, 5, b g Sadler's Wells (USA)—Lady Liberty (NZ) **N & J Racing Stables SL**
4 **ALFRED THE GREY**, 8, gr g Environment Friend—Ranyah (USA) **Mr Richard Muddle**
5 **ALI BRUCE**, 5, b g Cadeaux Genereux—Actualite **N. R. Shields**
6 **ALRAFID (IRE)**, 6, ch g Halling (USA)—Ginger Tree **Mr Graham Gillespie**
7 **AMNESTY**, 6, ch g Salse (USA)—Amaranthus **Mr G.A.Jackman, Mr J.F.Jackman**
8 **ARCTIC RAINBOW (IRE)**, 7, b g King's Ride—Arctic Chatter **The Hon Mrs C. Cameron**
9 **ASSOON (IRE)**, 6, b g Ezzoud (IRE)—Handy Dancer **B. V. Pennick**
10 **ATLANTIS (HOL)**, 6, ch g No Ski—File Moon (HOL) **S. Packham**
11 **AVESSIA**, 4, b f Averti (IRE)—Alessia **D. J. Deer**
12 **BANK ON HIM**, 10, b g Elmaamul (USA)—Feather Flower **Vetlab Supplies Ltd**
13 **BARRANCO (IRE)**, 4, b c Sadler's Wells (USA)—Belize Tropical (IRE) **Mr Russell Henderson**
14 **BATSWING**, 10, b g Batshoof—Magic Milly **Ashley Carr Racing**
15 **BRAVE CARADOC (IRE)**, 7, b g Un Desperado (FR)—Drivers Bureau **M. K. George**
16 **BRAVURA**, 7, ch g Never So Bold—Sylvan Song **R. Kiernan**
17 **BROWN FOX (FR)**, 4, b f Polar Falcon (USA)—Garmeria (FR) **M. R. Charlton**

MR G. L. MOORE—continued

18 **CHAMPAGNE SHADOW (IRE)**, 4, b c Kahyasi—Moet (IRE) **Mr D. R. Hunnisett & G. L. Moore**
19 **CHARING CROSS (IRE)**, 4, ch c Peintre Celebre (USA)—Charlotte Corday **K. Higson**
20 **CHARLIEMOORE**, 9, ch g Karinga Bay—Your Care (FR) **B. V. Pennick**
21 **CHEESE 'N BISCUITS**, 5, b m Spectrum (IRE)—Bint Shihama (USA) **D T L Limited**
22 **CHEROKEE BAY**, 5, b m Primo Dominie—Me Cherokee **D T L Limited**
23 **CHOCOLATE BOY (IRE)**, 6, b g Dolphin Street (FR)—Kawther **Sigma Estates**
24 **COLD TURKEY**, 8, b g Polar Falcon (USA)—South Rock **A. P. Grinter**
25 **CONSTANTINE**, 5, gr g Linamix (FR)—Speremm (IRE) **Mr Brendan Ward & Mr John Quinn**
26 **DANDYGREY RUSSETT (IRE)**, 4, gr f Singspiel (IRE)—Christian Church (IRE) **Bill Gibson & Partners**
27 **DANGEROUSLY GOOD**, 7, b g Shareef Dancer (USA)—Ecologically Kind **N. J. Jones**
28 **DARK PARADE (ARG)**, 4, b c Parade Marshal (USA)—Charming Dart (ARG) **N. J. Jones**
29 **DHARKAN (USA)**, 5, b g King of Kings (IRE)—Meritorious (USA) **N. J. Jones**
30 **DIEGO CAO (IRE)**, 4, b g Cape Cross (IRE)—Lady Moranbon **Vetlab Supplies Ltd**
31 **DOLZAGO**, 5, b g Pursuit of Love—Doctor's Glory (USA) **R. Kiernan, Paul Chapman**
32 **DUNDRY**, 4, b g Bin Ajwaad (IRE)—China's Pearl **D. J. Deer**
33 **DUSKY WARBLER**, 6, b g Ezzoud (IRE)—Bronzewing **Rodger Sargent**
34 **EARLSFIELD RAIDER**, 5, ch g Double Trigger (IRE)—Harlequin Walk (IRE) **Mr R. J. Doorgachum**
35 **EAU PURE (FR)**, 8, b m Epervier Bleu—Eau de Nuit **T. J. Painting**
36 **EHAB (IRE)**, 6, b g Cadeaux Genereux—Dernier Cri **The Go For Brokers Partnership**
37 **FLYING PATRIARCH**, 4, gr g Silver Patriarch (IRE)—Flying Wind **Heart Of The South Racing**
38 **FLYING SPIRIT (IRE)**, 4, b g Flying Spur (AUS)—All Laughter **Richard Green (Fine Paintings)**
39 **GABOR**, 6, b g Danzig Connection (USA)—Kiomi **Leydens Farm Stud**
40 **GEMI BED (FR)**, 10, b g Double Bed (FR)—Gemia (FR) **B. L. Lennard**
41 **GIN PALACE (IRE)**, 7, gr g King's Theatre (IRE)—Ikala **Mrs P. Gilmore**
42 **GRAND PRAIRIE (SWE)**, 9, b g Prairie—Platonica (ITY) **N. J. Jones**
43 **GROUND PATROL**, 4, b g Ashkalani (IRE)—Good Grounds (USA) **D. J. Deer**
44 **GURU**, 7, b g Slip Anchor—Ower (IRE) **Will Bennett, Thomas Cox & Geoff Brain**
45 **HAAFEL (USA)**, 8, ch g Diesis—Dish Dash **D. R. Hunnisett**
46 **HARIK**, 11, ch g Persian Bold—Yaqut (USA) **The Best Beech Partnership**
47 **HATHLEN (IRE)**, 4, b g Singspiel (IRE)—Kameez (IRE) **Vetlab Supplies Ltd**
48 **HIGH HOPE (FR)**, 7, ch g Lomitas—Highness Lady (GER) **RDM Racing**
49 **I D TECHNOLOGY (IRE)**, 9, ch g Commanche Run—Lady Geeno (IRE) **T. Keogh**
50 **IDRIS (GER)**, 4, ch c Generous (USA)—Idraak **RDM Racing**
51 **KRYSSA**, 4, ch f Kris—Alessandra **D. J. Deer**
52 **LIGHTNING STAR (USA)**, 10, b g El Gran Senor (USA)—Cuz's Star (USA) **Mr Mike Blossom**
53 **LOGSDAIL**, 5, b g Polish Precedent (USA)—Logic **D T L Limited**
54 **LORD HECCLES (IRE)**, 6, b g Supreme Leader—Parsons Lae **P. C. Collins**
55 **LUCKY VALENTINE**, 5, b m My Best Valentine—Vera's First (IRE) **The Laurels Stud Farm**
56 **MACLEAN**, 4, b g Machiavellian (USA)—Celtic Cross
57 **MAD CAREW (USA)**, 6, ch g Rahy—Poppy Carew (IRE) **Mr David Allen**
58 **MASTER T (USA)**, 6, b g Trempolino (USA)—Our Little C (USA) **Lancing Racing Syndicate**
59 **MID SUSSEX SPIRIT**, 6, b g Environment Friend—Ranyah (USA) **Mr Richard Muddle**
60 **MINI SADDLER (IRE)**, 6, b m Oscar (IRE)—Winnie Wumpkins (IRE) **M.Lee - L.Fogarty - J.Hills - D.Wolff**
61 **MOSTARSIL (USA)**, 7, ch g Kingmambo (USA)—Naazed **G. A. Jackman**
62 **MR BOO (IRE)**, 6, b g Needle Gun (IRE)—Dasi **The Hon Mrs C. Cameron**
63 **MR EX (ARG)**, 4, b c Numerous (USA)—Express Toss (ARG) **N. J. Jones**
64 **NATION STATE**, 4, b c Sadler's Wells (USA)—Native Justice (USA) **Mr D. G. Brownrigg**
65 **NAWAMEES (IRE)**, 7, b g Darshaan—Truly Generous (IRE) **P. Stamp**
66 **NEW ENTIC (FR)**, 4, b g Ragmar (FR)—Entiqua des Sacart (FR) **H. Hunt**
67 **OPERASHAAN (IRE)**, 5, b g Darshaan—Comic Opera (IRE) **Brightelm Racing**
68 **OPTIMO (GER)**, 4, b g Kahyasi—Onanga (GER) **Mr Trevor Painting**
69 **ORTHODOX**, 6, gr g Baryshnikov (AUS)—Sancta **R. Kiernan**
70 **OUR SAMSON (IRE)**, 5, b g Old Vic—Strong Gale Pigeon (IRE) **Mr Graham Gillespie**
71 **PANGLOSS (IRE)**, 4, ch g Croco Rouge (IRE)—Kafayef (USA) **Mr R N Martin Mr B V Pennick**
72 **PARDISHAR (IRE)**, 7, b g Kahyasi—Parapa (IRE) **Mr D. R. Hunnisett & G. L. Moore**
73 **PARTY GAMES (IRE)**, 8, b g King's Ride—Shady Miss **Goldfingers Syndicate**
74 **PHONE BACK (IRE)**, 6, b g Bob Back (USA)—Will Phone **Mrs P. Gilmore**
75 **PORAK (IRE)**, 8, ch g Perugino (USA)—Gayla Orchestra **Allen, Manley, Prichard, Russell**
76 **PRIME POWERED (IRE)**, 4, b g Barathea (IRE)—Caribbean Quest **Prime Power (GB) Ltd & G. L. Moore Racing**
77 **RESSOURCE (FR)**, 6, b g Broadway Flyer (USA)—Rayonne **Miss S. M. Eastes**
78 **ROB LEACH (IRE)**, 8, b g Robellino (USA)—Arc Empress Jane (IRE) **Richard Green (Fine Paintings)**
79 **ROUND THE BAY**, 6, b g Karinga Bay—Marty's Round **Mr K. Higson**
80 **SALUT SAINT CLOUD**, 5, b g Primo Dominie—Tiriana **A. P. Grinter**
81 **SESAME RAMBLER (IRE)**, 6, gr g Roselier (FR)—Sesame Cracker **Mr Graham Gillespie**
82 **SHAMAN**, 8, b g Fraam—Magic Maggie **P. R. Chapman**

MR G. L. MOORE—continued

83 **SON OF GREEK MYTH (USA)**, 4, b g Silver Hawk (USA)—Greek Myth (IRE) **P. Iron Ltd**
84 **SPACE COWBOY (IRE)**, 5, b h Anabaa (USA)—Lady Moranbon (USA) **Mr Michael Platt**
85 **STANCE**, 6, b g Salse (USA)—De Stael (USA) **N. J. Jones**
86 **STORMY SKYE (IRE)**, 9, b g Bluebird (USA)—Canna **Mrs J. Moore, Mrs J. Agnew & Mr T. Pollock**
87 **THOMAS LAWRENCE (IRE)**, 4, ch g Horse Chestnut (SAF)—Olatha (USA)
88 **TICERO**, 4, ch g First Trump—Lucky Flinders **Mr David Allen**
89 **TIKRAM**, 8, ch g Lycius (USA)—Black Fighter (USA) **Mike Charlton And Rodger Sargent**
90 **TIOMAN (IRE)**, 6, b br g Dr Devious (IRE)—Tochar Ban (USA) **N. R. Shields**
91 **TWENTY DEGREES**, 7, ch g Beveled (USA)—Sweet N' Twenty **W. E. Baird**
92 **UNUSUAL SUSPECT**, 6, b g Syrtos—Sally Maxwell **The Tsar Partnership/Mr Terry Kyriacou**
93 **VERASI**, 4, b g Kahyasi—Fair Verona (USA) **F. Ledger J. Bateman**
94 **WAIT FOR THE WILL (USA)**, 9, ch g Seeking The Gold (USA)—You'd Be Surprised (USA) **RDM Racing**
95 **WATERSIDE (IRE)**, 6, ch g Lake Coniston (IRE)—Classic Ring (IRE) **N. R. Shields**
96 **WAYWARD MELODY**, 5, b m Merdon Melody—Dubitable **BHW Partnership**
97 **WE'LL MAKE IT (IRE)**, 7, b g Spectrum (IRE)—Walliser **Wayne Barr,John & Paul Ripley, D. Goff, S. Moss**
98 **WESTERN (IRE)**, 5, ch g Gone West (USA)—Madame Est Sortie (FR) **H. Hunt**
99 **WHAT A MAN (IRE)**, 8, b g Beau Sher—Cactus Wren (IRE) **P. C. Green**
100 **ZIMBABWE**, 5, b g Kahyasi—Zeferina (IRE) **Rodger Sargent**

THREE-YEAR-OLDS

101 **ALESSANO**, ch c Hernando (FR)—Alessandra **D. J. Deer**
102 **AMICA**, b f Averti (IRE)—Friend For Life **D. J. Deer**
103 **ART CLASS**, b f Mtoto—Arpello **Hesmonds Stud & Mr Goulandris**
104 **BOLD MAGGIE**, ch f Bold Edge—Vera's First (IRE) **The Laurels Stud Farm**
105 **CAVALLINI (USA)**, b br g Bianconi (USA)—Taylor Park (USA) **D. J. Deer**
106 **CUSOON**, b c Dansili—Charming Life **The Winning Hand**
107 **DUKES POINT**, b c Sinndar (IRE)—Dimakya (USA) **N. J. Jones**
108 **ELECTION SEEKER (IRE)**, b g Intikhab (USA)—Scottish Eyes (USA) **Mr Michael Platt**
109 **INGLETON**, b c Komaite (USA)—Dash Cascade **Mr Graham Gillespie**
110 **JOSTLING**, b f Josr Algarhoud (IRE)—Arpero **Hesmonds Stud & Mr Goulandris**
111 **KEEP BACCKINHIT (IRE)**, b f Raise A Grand (IRE)—Taispeain (IRE) **Pleasure Palace Racing**
112 **KRASIVI'S BOY (USA)**, b br c Swain (IRE)—Krasivi (USA) **Mr R. Kiernan & Mr Paul Chapman**
113 **NINJA STORM (IRE)**, b c Namid—Swan Lake (IRE) **Pleasure Palace Racing**
114 **PRIMED UP (IRE)**, b g Rainbow Quest (USA)—Cape Mist (USA) **Prime Power GB Ltd**
115 **SOLE AGENT (IRE)**, b g Trans Island—Seattle Siren (USA) **Mr B. & Mr J. Crainey**
116 **TRIGGER GUARD**, ch g Double Trigger (IRE)—Harlequin Walk (IRE) **Mrs R. J. Doorgachurn & C. Stedman**

TWO-YEAR-OLDS

117 Ch f 19/4 Observatory (USA)—Brave Princess (Dancing Brave (USA)) (2800) **Roy Martin & Peter Pennick**
118 B c 18/1 Sadler's Wells (USA)—Goncharova (USA) (Gone West (USA)) (80000) **Gillespie Brothers**

Other Owners: M. Avery, Mr G. P. Ash, Dr C. A. Barnett, W. Barr, Mr E. J. Bateman, C. Bond, Mrs C. S. Braga, R. S. Briggs, Mrs M. A. Briggs, R. Brown, Mrs S. K. Bush, J. M. Bush, P. C. Collins, Mr B. Crainey, Mr J. Crainey, S. Danahar, R. De Giovanni, B. Donoghue, Mrs B. Farncombe, L. C. Fogarty, Mr L. G. Frankum, W. R. Gibson, T. G. Gillespie, Mrs D. Goff, I. Goldsmith, Mrs M. R. Goldsmith, L. A. Hambrook, J. Hinds, D. P. Hinds, R. Kiernan, S. D. King, T. Kyriacou, Mrs F. J. U. Ledger, M. J. Lee, H. N. Lund, K. G. Manley, Mrs V. A. Mason, Mrs J. Moore, D. Morgan, Mrs C. A. Painting, Mrs J. Peel, J. R. Penny, Mrs C. Penny, A. Pook, B. Prichard, J. Ripley, Mr P. Ripley, W. Russell, W. Russell, Prof A. R. Sanderson, W. P. Smith, M. H. Spong, C. E. Stedman, Mr D. H. Steel, Mrs K. E. Thorbes, Mr R. E. Thorbes, Vogue Development Company (Kent) Ltd, D. M. White.

Assistant Trainer: David Wilson

Jockey (flat): R. L. Moore, I. Mongan. **Jockey (NH):** M. Batchelor, P. Hide, A. P. McCoy, J. E. Moore. **Conditional:** E. Dehdashti. **Apprentice:** J. Marshall, H. Poulton. **Amateur:** Mr W. Russell, Mr Lee Hamilton.

---

409 MR G. M. MOORE, Middleham

Postal: **Warwick Lodge Stables, Middleham, Leyburn, North Yorkshire, DL8 4PB.**
Contacts: **PHONE** (01969) 623823 **FAX** (01969) 623823
E-MAIL carolmoore@tinyworld.co.uk WEBSITE www.george-moore-racing.co.uk

1 **AGNESE**, 5, ch m Abou Zouz (USA)—Efizia **Mrs H. I. S. Calzini**
2 **ALMENARA**, 6, ch m Weld—Dishcloth **The Three Socks Partnership**
3 **ALPHA JULIET (IRE)**, 4, b f Victory Note (USA)—Zara's Birthday (IRE) **A. J. Racehorses**
4 **APSARA**, 4, br f Groom Dancer (USA)—Ayodhya (IRE) **Mrs Mary and Miss Susan Hatfield**

MR G. M. MOORE—continued

5 **ARGENTO**, 8, b g Weldnaas (USA)—Four M's **J. B. Wallwin**
6 **ASHNAYA (FR)**, 7, b m Ashkalani (IRE)—Upend **B. P. Bradshaw**
7 5, ch m Prince Daniel (USA)—Audrina **Garry E. West**
8 **BATTO**, 5, b g Slip Anchor—Frog **Mrs I. I. Plumb**
9 **BEAMISH PRINCE**, 6, ch g Bijou d'inde—Unconditional Love (IRE) **Geoff & Sandra Turnbull**
10 **BLACK TORRINGTON (IRE)**, 7, b g Norwich—Sylvies Missiles (IRE) **Mrs S. C. Moore**
11 **CASTLE RICHARD (IRE)**, 8, gr g Sexton Blake—Miss McCormick (IRE) **Mrs Mary and Miss Susan Hatfield**
12 **CIARA'S RUN (IRE)**, 5, ch m Topanoora—Rugged Run **D. J. Bushell**
13 **FUTOO (IRE)**, 4, b g Foxhound (USA)—Nicola Wynn **M. K. Roddis**
14 **GLENDEVON GREY**, 6, gr g Karinga Bay—Sandy Etna (IRE) **Mrs J. M. Gray**
15 **IRON EXPRESS**, 9, b g Teenoso (USA)—Sylvia Beach **D. Parker**
16 **IRON WARRIOR (IRE)**, 5, b g Lear Fan (USA)—Robalana (USA) **D. Parker**
17 **JUNGLE JINKS (IRE)**, 10, b g Proud Panther (FR)—Three Ladies **Mrs Mary and Miss Susan Hatfield**
18 **KEALSHORE LAD**, 4, b g Supreme Leader—Our Aisling **Mr J. Pickavance**
19 **LAGOSTA (SAF)**, 5, ch g Fort Wood (USA)—Rose Wine **Mrs A. Roddis**
20 **LOOKING FORWARD**, 9, br g Primitive Rising (USA)—Gilzie Bank **Mrs G. Handley**
21 **LORD ROSSKIT (IRE)**, 5, b br g Lord Americo—Redstone Lady (IRE) **Mrs S. C. Moore**
22 **MAJOR OAK (IRE)**, 4, b g Deploy—Mahaasin **The Little Acorn Partnership**
23 **MICHAELS JOY (IRE)**, 6, br g Presenting—Scarteen Lower (IRE) **John Robson**
24 **ONEFORBERTANDHENRY (IRE)**, 6, b g Rashar (USA)—Roi Vision **J. B. Partnership**
25 **PAGAN RIVER**, 4, br g River Falls—Pagan Star **Richard J. Phizacklea**
26 **PLANTERS PUNCH (IRE)**, 4, b c Cape Cross (IRE)—Jamaican Punch (IRE) **D. Neale**
27 **PREMIER DRIVE (IRE)**, 12, ch g Black Minstrel—Ballyanihan **A. W. Sergeant**
28 **PRESUMPTUOUS**, 5, ch g Double Trigger (IRE)—T O O Mamma's (IRE) **C. Bradford-Nutter**
29 **PRINCE ADJAL (IRE)**, 5, b g Desert Prince (IRE)—Adjalisa (IRE) **J. W. Andrews**
30 **PRIZE RING**, 6, ch g Bering—Spot Prize (USA) **Gordon Brown/Bert Watson**
31 **SHOW NO FEAR**, 4, b c Groom Dancer (USA)—La Piaf (FR) **Gordon Brown/Bert Watson**
32 **SIR STORM (IRE)**, 9, b g Ore—Yonder Bay (IRE) **J. R. F. (Management Consultants) Ltd**
33 **SPRING GAMBLE (IRE)**, 6, b g Norwich—Aurora Run (IRE) **J. B. Wallwin**
34 **STEP PERFECT (USA)**, 4, b g Royal Academy (USA)—Gossiping (USA) **J. Lishman**
35 **SYLVIESBUCK (IRE)**, 8, b g Kasmayo—Sylvies Missiles (IRE) **Mrs I. I. Plumb**
36 **THE LONGFELLA**, 4, b g Petong—Miss Tri Colour **Mrs D. N. B. Pearson**
37 **THE LOOSE SCREW (IRE)**, 7, b g Bigstone (IRE)—Princess of Dance (IRE) **Sykes Distribution Ltd**

THREE-YEAR-OLDS

38 **FROGS' GIFT (IRE)**, gr f Danehill Dancer (IRE)—Warthill Whispers **Mrs I. I. Plumb**
39 **MERCARI**, ch f Bahamian Bounty—Aonach Mor **Mrs S. C. Moore**
40 **NUMERO DUE**, b c Sinndar (IRE)—Kindle **Valueplace Limited**
41 **SERENE PEARL (IRE)**, b f Night Shift (USA)—Shanjah **Mrs Mary and Miss Susan Hatfield**
42 **TOLDO (IRE)**, gr g Tagula (IRE)—Mystic Belle (IRE) **J. Armstrong**

TWO-YEAR-OLDS

43 Ch c 18/3 Alhaarth (IRE)—Abir (Soviet Star (USA)) **Mr J. Lishman**
44 B f 6/5 Bahamian Bounty—Aldevonie (Green Desert (USA)) (2000) **Geoff and Sandra Turnbull**
45 B f 21/3 Bahamian Bounty—Aonach Mor (Anabaa (USA)) (1000)
46 B c 2/4 Diesis—Desert Jewel (USA) (Caerleon (USA)) (42000) **Geoff and Sandra Turnbull**
47 B c 26/2 Allied Forces (USA)—Dusty Shoes (Shareef Dancer (USA)) **Mr J. Pickavance**
48 **FLYING DOCTOR**, b c 29/3 Mark of Esteem (IRE)—
    Vice Vixen (CAN) (Vice Regent (CAN)) (10000) **Mr John Robson**
49 B f 19/4 Fantastic Light (USA)—Putout (Dowsing (USA)) **Geoff and Sandra Turnbull**
50 B f 6/5 Alhaarth (IRE)—Thamud (IRE) (Lahib (USA))

Other Owners: J. Berry, A. C. Birkle, A. J. Coupland, Mr J. Heald, Mr H. Lonsdale, Mr G. L. Moore, J. P. Moulden, Mr D. J. Raynor, S. Smith, M. A. Tebbutt, Mrs J. A. Whitwham, A. S. Whitwham.

Jockey (NH): R. Garritty, F. Keniry, A. Ross. **Conditional:** Colin Moulden. **Amateur:** Mr G. Hardisty.

410 MR J. S. MOORE, Hungerford
Postal: Parsonage Farm Racing Stables, Newbury Road, East Garston,
Hungerford, Berkshire, RG17 7ER.
Contacts: PHONE (01488) 648822 FAX (01488) 648185
MOBILE (07860) 811127/(07900) 402856 E-MAIL jsmoore.racing@btopenworld.com

1 BARATHEA DREAMS (IRE), 4, b c Barathea (IRE)—Deyaajeer (USA) **Mrs F. H. Hay**
2 BRITESAND (IRE), 5, ch g Humbel (USA)—
The Hollow Beach (IRE) **Mr Tom Yates, Mrs Evelyn Yates, J. S. Moore**
3 CITY GENERAL (IRE), 4, ch g General Monash (USA)—Astra (IRE) **A. D. Crook**
4 COOLEYCALL STAR (IRE), 4, b g Foxhound (USA)—Ozwood (IRE) **Cooleycall Star Syndicate**
5 GARSTON STAR, 4, ch g Fleetwood (IRE)—Conquista **East Garston Racing**
6 GEMS BOND, 5, b g Magic Ring (IRE)—Jucinda **Mrs F. H. Hay**
7 HILITES (IRE), 4, ch f Desert King (IRE)—Slayjay (IRE) **Mr Tom Yates, Mrs Evelyn Yates, J.S.Moore**
8 LACONIA (IRE), 4, br g Orpen (USA)—Mislead (IRE) **Mrs F. H. Hay**
9 LARAD (IRE), 4, br g Desert Sun—Glenstal Priory **A. P. Crook**
10 OH SO ROSIE (IRE), 5, b m Danehill Dancer (USA)—Shinkoh Rose (FR) **Miss Karen Theobald**
11 REDSPIN (IRE), 5, ch g Spectrum (IRE)—Trendy Indian (IRE) **Mrs F. H. Hay**
12 SCARPIA, 5, ch g Rudimentary (USA)—Floria Tosca **Mr M. S. Block**
13 STAMFORD BLUE, 4, b g Bluegrass Prince (IRE)—Fayre Holly (IRE) **Miss Karen Theobald**
14 WHENWILLITWIN, 4, b g Bluegrass Prince (IRE)—Madam Marash (IRE) **A. D. Crook**

THREE-YEAR-OLDS

15 ARMATRADING (IRE), ch f Rossini (USA)—Queenfisher **Miss Karen Theobald**
16 DANEHAY (IRE), b g Danehill Dancer (IRE)—Popcorn **Mrs F. H. Hay**
17 DON'T TELL TRIGGER (IRE), b f Mujadil (USA)—Ordinate **Bigwigs Bloodstock Racing Club V**
18 ENCANTO (IRE), ch f Barathea (USA)—Born To Glamour **Mr Tom Yates, Mrs Evelyn Yates, J. S. Moore**
19 FOSROC (USA), ch g Royal Anthem (USA)—Stellar Blush **Mrs F. H. Hay**
20 MONASHEE ROSE (IRE), br f Monashee Mountain (USA)—Thorn Tree **The Fairway Connection**
21 PIPER GENERAL (IRE), br g General Monash (USA)—Pipewell (IRE) **A. J. Speyer**
22 SPERRIN VALLEY (IRE), ch f Rossini (USA)—Astra (IRE) **Mr J. McCullagh**
23 B g Beccari (USA)—Who Told Vicky (IRE) **A. Gorrie**

TWO-YEAR-OLDS

24 B c 27/4 In The Wings—Ann's Annie (IRE) (Alzao (USA)) (1904) **Mr J. S. Moore**
25 BINCRAFTY, b g 1/3 Benny The Dip (USA)—Spanish Craft (Jareer (USA)) **A. D. Crook**
26 BLUE MINX (IRE), b f 14/3 Darnay—Sea Idol (IRE) (Astronef) **Miss Karen Theobald**
27 DARUSSO, ch c 21/5 Daylami (IRE)—Rifada (Ela-Mana-Mou) (7377) **Mr Tom Yates and Mrs Evelyn Yates**
28 DONT DILI DALI, b f 6/4 Dansili—Miss Meltemi (IRE) (Miswaki Tern (USA)) (7500) **The Fairway Connection**
29 DUNE MELODY (IRE), b f 9/2 Distant Music (USA)—Desert Gift (Green Desert (USA)) (3018) **Mr J. S. Moore**
30 EMBRACEABLE (IRE), b f 19/2 Mull of Kintyre (USA)—
Embracing (Reference Point) (10060) **Mr Tom Yates and Mrs Evelyn Yates**
31 Ch c 20/5 Magic Ring (IRE)—I'll Try (My Best (USA)) **Mr D. Strauss**
32 B c 3/5 Compton Place—Kintara (Cyrano de Bergerac) (800)
33 MACEDON, b c 21/3 Dansili—Hypnotize (Machiavellian (USA)) (27000) **Mrs F. H. Hay**
34 B c 14/4 Desert Prince (IRE)—Pool Party (USA) (Summer Squall (USA)) (5500) **Mr M. Keogh**
35 B br g 23/2 City On A Hill (USA)—Prague Spring (Salse (USA)) (4000) **Mr J. S. Moore**
36 PUNTAMISS (IRE), b f 16/4 Tipsy Creek (USA)—
Blonde Goddess (IRE) (Godswalk (USA)) (1005) **Mr Tom Yates and Mrs Evelyn Yates**
37 STAMFORD STREET (IRE), ch c 3/2 Distant Music (USA)—
Exemplaire (FR) (Polish Precedent (USA)) (3353) **Miss Karen Theobald**
38 Ch f 29/4 Tagula (IRE)—Trading Aces (Be My Chief (USA)) (1340) **Mr J. S. Moore**
39 TWINNED (IRE), ch c 26/4 Soviet Star (USA)—Identical (IRE) (Machiavellian (USA)) (7377) **A. D. Crook**

Other Owners: G. L. C. Hodgson, J. Laughton, Mr D. P. Lee, Mr R. K. Lee, P. R. Webb.

Assistant Trainer: Mrs S Moore

Jockey (flat): M. Dwyer. **Jockey (NH):** S. Durack. **Apprentice:** Amy Parsons, Derek Nolan, Laura Reynolds. **Amateur:** Mrs S. Moore.

411 MR K. A. MORGAN, Melton Mowbray

Postal: Hall Farm Stables, Waltham On The Wolds, Melton Mowbray, Leicestershire, LE14 4AJ.
Contacts: PHONE (01664) 464711/464488 FAX (01664) 464492 MOBILE (07768) 996103

1 BURNING MOON, 4, b c Bering—Triple Green **D. S. Cooper**
2 BYLAND, 5, b g Danzig (USA)—Coxwold (USA) **Mrs G. J. Bradley**
3 COLOPHONY (USA), 5, ch g Distant View (USA)—
Private Line (USA) **H.A.Blenkhorn,C.J.Blenkhorn,Wentdale Ltd**
4 COURT OF JUSTICE (USA), 9, b g Alleged (USA)—Captive Island **Mrs P. A. L. Butler**
5 CRAZY MAZIE, 8, b m Risk Me (FR)—Post Impressionist (IRE) **Le Tricolore**
6 DR FOX (IRE), 4, b g Foxhound (USA)—Eleonora d'arborea **TSL Racing Ltd**
7 ELSUNDUS (USA), 7, b g Gone West (USA)—Aljawza (USA)
8 EMKANAT (IRE), 4, ch f Unfuwain (USA)—Raaqiaya (USA) **TSL Racing Ltd**
9 FLYOFF (IRE), 8, b g Mtoto—Flyleaf (FR) **Harmer Personal Care Ltd**
10 GREEK STAR, 4, b g Soviet Star (USA)—Graecia Magna (USA) **D. S. Cooper**
11 JAZIL, 10, b g Nashwan (USA)—Gracious Beauty (USA) **Mrs P. A. L. Butler**
12 JEBAL SURAAJ (USA), 5, b g Gone West (USA)—Trishyde (USA) **D. S. Cooper**
13 KIM BUCK (FR), 7, b g Ambroise (FR)—Darling Jouve (FR) **D. S. Cooper**
14 KINGKOHLER (IRE), 6, b g King's Theatre (IRE)—Legit (IRE) **Jo Champion, H. Morgan, E. Barlow**
15 LIFERAFT, 4, b f Kahyasi—Pontoon **Mr J. C. Carr**
16 MACREATER, 7, b m Mazaad—Gold Caste (USA) **J. N. Stokes**
17 MARKO JADEO (IRE), 7, b g Eagle Eyed (USA)—Fleeting Quest **J. Sheridan**
18 MAUNBY ROLLER (IRE), 6, b g Flying Spur (AUS)—Brown Foam **D. S. Cooper**
19 MUNAAHEJ (IRE), 4, b c Soviet Star (USA)—Azyaa **P. Doughty**
20 PENALTY CLAUSE (IRE), 5, b g Namaqualand (USA)—Lady Be Lucky (IRE) **TSL Racing Ltd**
21 PLAY MASTER (IRE), 4, b g Second Empire (USA)—Madam Waajib (IRE) **Mr J. Weston**
22 PRIMATECH (IRE), 4, b f Priolo (USA)—Ida Lupino (IRE) **Mr K. A. Morgan**
23 PROSPECT HILL (IRE), 7, ch g Nucleon (USA)—Ann Hill (IRE) **M. Di Murro**
24 SELKIRK GRACE, 5, b g Selkirk (USA)—Polina **D. S. Cooper**
25 URBAN FREEWAY (IRE), 6, b g Dr Devious (IRE)—Coupe d'hebe **D. S. Cooper**
26 WALTHAM DOVE, 10, b g Gypsy Castle—Dovetail **M. J. Harmer**

THREE-YEAR-OLDS

27 IVORY FAIR (USA), ch c Daylami (IRE)—Ivziza (IRE) **D. S. Cooper**

Other Owners: H. A. Blenkhorn, Miss C. J. Blenkhorn, Mrs J. Champion, D. A. Charlesworth, Mrs H. Charlet, P. N. Davis, MR K. A. Morgan, H. Morgan, Roemex Ltd, Partnership, Wentdale Limited.

412 MR C. P. H. MORLOCK, Wantage

Postal: Raceyard Cottage Stables, Kingston Lisle, Wantage, Oxfordshire, OX12 9QH.
Contacts: HOME/FAX (01367) 820510 MOBILE (07768) 923444
E-MAIL morlock@raceyard.freeserve.co.uk

1 AIRGUSTA (IRE), 4, b g Danehill Dancer (IRE)—Ministerial Model (IRE) **J. A. Lawless**
2 BOBALONG (IRE), 8, b g Bob's Return (IRE)—Northern Wind **Pell-mell Partners**
3 COMMANCHE KATE, 5, ch m Commanche Run—Spardante (IRE) **Mr R. J. And Mrs K. S. Lee**
4 DIVIDEND, 5, gr g Alderbrook—Rymolbreese **The Trogs**
5 FAIR TOUCH (IRE), 6, b g Air Display (IRE)—Anns Touch (IRE) **The Shouting Men**
6 4, B f Sure Blade (USA)—Game Domino **Mr Michael Padfield & Mr Philip Dean**
7 GIFTNEYEV (FR), 6, b br g Goldneyev (USA)—Girl's Gift (FR) **Pell-mell Partners**
8 HENRY'S HAPPINESS, 6, b m Bob's Return (IRE)—Irish Mint **W. R. Morlock**
9 KYNANCE COVE, 6, b g Karinga Bay—Excelled (IRE) **Mrs J. W. Melbourne**
10 LADY OF LISLE, 7, ch m Afzal—Holy Times (IRE) **A. F. Sawyer**
11 LAND ROVER LAD, 7, ch g Afflora (IRE)—Fililode **Mc Coy's Neighbours**
12 LIN D'ESTRUVAL (FR), 6, b g Cadoudal (FR)—Recolte D'estruval (FR) **Pell-mell Partners**
13 LISMEENAN (IRE), 11, ch g Be My Native (USA)—Sakanda (IRE) **Mr D. and Mrs H. Woodhall**
14 LORD GREYSTOKE (IRE), 4, b g Petardia—Jungle Story (IRE) **The Greystoke Partnership**
15 ROYAL BELUGA (IRE), 8, b g Rahy (USA)—Navratilovna (USA) **M. S. Lilly**
16 SEVEN UP (IRE), 6, b g Executive Perk—Rare Picture **Temple Dean**
17 SUNDAWN LADY, 7, b m Faustus (USA)—Game Domino **Mr Michael Padfield & Mr Philip Dean**

THREE-YEAR-OLDS

18 B f Rakaposhi King—Threads **C. Morlock and B. McNamee**

Other Owners: J. C. Berry, J. Chromiak, P. R. Fisher, R. J. Gilder, Mrs D. G. Patterson, S. R. C. Philip, S. M. Polley.

Jockey (NH): T. Doyle, J. A. McCarthy.

413 MR M. MORRIS, Fethard
Postal: Everardsgrange, Fethard, Co. Tipperary, Ireland.
Contacts: PHONE +353 (0) 52 31474 FAX +353 (0) 52 31654
E-MAIL mouse@eircom.net WEBSITE www.mousemorris.com

1 ALCAPONE (IRE), 11, b g Roselier (FR)—Ann's Cap (IRE) **Mrs Ann Daly**
2 BAILY BREEZE (IRE), 6, b g Zaffaran (USA)—Mixed Blends **Mr A. Scott**
3 BAILY MIST (IRE), 8, b m Zaffaran (USA)—Mixed Blends **Mr A. Scott**
4 BILLY BUSH (IRE), 6, b g Lord Americo—Castle Graigue (IRE) **Mr W. Crowe**
5 BROWNIE RETURNS (IRE), 12, b g Dry Dock—What A Brownie **Mrs Ann Daly**
6 BUACHAILL HAZE (IRE), 6, b g Great Marquess—Claudette **M. F. Morris**
7 FOTA ISLAND (IRE), 9, b g Supreme Leader—Mary Kate Finn **J. P. McManus**
8 GREAT ALTOGETHER (IRE), 7, b g Beneficial—Tacky Lady (IRE) **M. F. Morris**
9 KEEPATEM (IRE), 9, ch g Be My Native (USA)—Ariannrun **J. P. McManus**
10 LORD RED, 6, ch g Presenting—My Adventure (IRE) **M. A. Kilduff & Partners**
11 MEDIANOCHE (IRE), 5, b g Spanish Place (USA)—Midnights Daughter (IRE) **M. O'Leary**
12 MICK DIVINE (IRE), 7, b g Roselier (FR)—Brown Forest **M. O'Flynn**
13 NO TOAST (IRE), 6, ch g Great Marquess—Bright Diamond **No Butter Syndicate**
14 SEAFORDE (IRE), 5, ch g Titus Livius (FR)—Rosy Affair (IRE) **Sir A. J. O'Reilly**
15 SHANNAHYDE (IRE), 7, ch g Shernazar—Fernhill (IRE) **M. F. Morris**
16 SKIBB (IRE), 8, b g Be My Native (USA)—Inch Lady **Mrs Ann Daly**
17 SPAINNASH (IRE), 5, b g Nashwan (USA)—Agreed **Sir A. J. O'Reilly**
18 THE GALLANTJOHNJOE (IRE), 7, ch m Beneficial—Better Thana Brief (IRE) **Ms Catherine White**
19 THE KAYMAN (IRE), 5, ch g Zaffaran (USA)—Glaskerbeg Lady (IRE) **S. Keohane**
20 THREE STEPS (IRE), 7, b m Torus—Joes Nightmare **M. F. Morris**
21 VELVET HUXLEY (IRE), 7, b m Fourstars Allstar (USA)—Gentle Leader (IRE) **M. F. Morris**
22 WAR OF ATTRITION (IRE), 6, br g Presenting—Una Juna (IRE) **M. O'Leary**
23 ZERO TO HERO (IRE), 7, b g Lord Americo—Sea Island **D. Desmond**

Jockey (NH): D. J. Casey.

414 MR H. MORRISON, East Ilsley
Postal: Summerdown, East Ilsley, Newbury, Berkshire, RG20 7LB.
Contacts: PHONE (01635) 281678 FAX (01635) 281746 MOBILE (07836) 687799
E-MAIL hughie@hughiemorrison.co.uk

1 ALCAZAR (IRE), 10, b g Alzao (USA)—Sahara Breeze **J. Repard, F. Melrose, O. Pawle, M. Stokes, R. Black**
2 BALTIC KING, 5, b h Danetime (IRE)—Lindfield Belle (IRE) **Thurloe Thoroughbreds VIII**
3 BLUE JAVA, 4, ch g Bluegrass Prince (IRE)—Java Bay **Pangfield Partners**
4 BOBSLEIGH, 6, b g Robellino (USA)—Do Run Run **Mr A. Ogilvy and Mrs F. Ogilvy**
5 BOX BUILDER, 8, ch g Fraam—Ena Olley **M. A. Hutchinson**
6 BROUGH SUPREME, 4, b f Sayaarr (USA)—Loriner's Lady **Mrs J. A. M. Willment**
7 CAPE ST VINCENT, 5, gr g Paris House—Cape Merino **Barbara Jamet and Templeton Stud**
8 DESERT QUEST (IRE), 5, b g Rainbow Quest (USA)—Jumilla (USA) **Ballygallon Stud Ltd**
9 EVA JEAN, 4, b f Singspiel (IRE)—Go For Red (IRE) **Dr & Mrs John Wilson**
10 FLETCHER, 11, b g Salse (USA)—Ballet Classique (USA) **Lady Margadale**
11 FLINT RIVER, 7, b g Red Ransom (USA)—She's All Class (USA) **The Firm**
12 FRENCHMAN'S CREEK, 11, b g Emperor Fountain—Hollow Creek **Rory Sweet & Panda Christie**
13 GENTLEMAN JIMMY, 5, b g Alderbrook—Irish Orchid **Gentleman Jimmy**
14 HIHO SILVER LINING, 4, gr f Silver Patriarch (IRE)—By Line **Lady Blyth**
15 KINGS BAY, 6, ch m Beveled (USA)—Storm of Plenty **P. J. Doherty**
16 KYLKENNY, 10, b g Kylian (USA)—Fashion Flow **Mr H. Morrison**
17 LITTLE RIDGE (IRE), 4, b g Charnwood Forest (IRE)—Princess Natalie **Lady Margadale**
18 MARBLE ARCH, 9, b g Rock Hopper—Mayfair Minx **M. S. Wilson,R. Sweet,Mrs Mary Morrison**
19 MOLDAVIA (GER), 4, b f Lagunas—Moricana (GER) **Sir Clement Freud**
20 NOUVEAU RICHE (IRE), 4, ch f Entrepreneur—Dime Bag **N. G. Cooper**
21 ODIHAM, 4, b g Deploy—Hug Me **Odiham Partnership**
22 PADDINGTON GREEN, 7, b g Primitive Rising (USA)—
            Mayfair Minx **R. Sweet, Mrs M. Morrison, F. Flynn, R. Madden**
23 PANGO, 6, ch g Bluegrass Prince (IRE)—Riverine **Pangfield Partners**
24 PASTORAL PURSUITS, 4, b c Bahamian Bounty—Star **The Pursuits & National Stud Partnership**
25 RUBY ROCKET (IRE), 4, b f Indian Rocket—Geht Schnell **Thurloe Thoroughbreds IX**
26 SANGIOVESE, 6, b g Piccolo—Kaprisky (IRE) **Kentisbeare Quartet**
27 SECRET PLOY, 5, b g Deploy—By Line **A. M. Carding**
28 SOLO FLIGHT, 8, gr g Mtoto—Silver Singer **Lady Hardy**
29 STARZAAN (IRE), 6, b g Darshaan—Stellina (IRE) **Mr B. G. Arbib**

MR H. MORRISON—continued

30 **THE LAST CAST,** 6, ch g Prince of Birds (USA)—Atan's Gem (USA) **D. P. Barrie**
31 **THIEVES'GLEN,** 7, b g Teenoso (USA)—Hollow Creek **Panda Christie & Rory Sweet**
32 **TRAFALGAR NIGHT,** 4, b g Emperor Fountain—Hollow Creek **Ingrid Carding and Mary Morrison**
33 **WAVERLEY (IRE),** 6, b g Catrail (USA)—Marble Halls (IRE) **Exors of the Late Lord Margadale**
34 **WAZIRI (IRE),** 4, b g Mtoto—Euphorie (GER) **Ashley House Racing**
35 **ZANZIBAR BOY,** 6, gr g Arzanni—Bampton Fair **Lady Lewinton**
36 **ZOROASTER,** 5, gr g Linamix (FR)—Persian Walk (FR) **Mr & Mrs James Wigan**

THREE-YEAR-OLDS

37 **CASTANZA,** b f Bachir—Sylhall **Mr D. P. Barrie & Mr M. J. Rees**
38 **DR FLIGHT,** b g Dr Fong (USA)—Bustling Nelly
39 **EMERALD DANCER,** b f Groom Dancer (USA)—Green Bonnet (IRE) **Taheh Partnership**
40 **ESTANCIA,** b f Groom Dancer (USA)—Donostia **H. Scott-Barret, J. P. Repard, M. Kerr-Dineen**
41 **FIDRA (IRE),** gr f Vettori (IRE)—Doon Point **Team Havana**
42 **GROOMSMAN,** b g Groom Dancer (USA)—Trois Heures Apres **Wood Street Syndicate**
43 **GUILDENSTERN (IRE),** b c Danetime (IRE)—Lyphard Abu (IRE) **Scott-Barrett, Kerr-Dineen, Tufnell, Burley**
44 **HAWK ARROW (IRE),** ch c In The Wings—Barbizou (FR) **Noodles Racing**
45 **HIGH LIFE,** br f Kayf Tara—By Line **Mrs N. Jones**
46 **INTREPID JACK,** b c Compton Place—Maria Theresa **Mr M. Lynch**
47 **KEY OF SOLOMON (IRE),** ch c Machiavellian (USA)—Minerva (IRE) **Ballygallon Stud Ltd**
48 **KIAMA,** b f Dansili—Catriona **Ashley House Racing II**
49 **KITTY,** b f Kayf Tara—Dancing Bluebell (IRE) **Mr & Mrs W. G. B. Hungerford**
50 **LUJAIN ROSE,** b f Lujain (USA)—Rose Chime (IRE) **M T & A Bevan, P W Saunders, E T Farmer**
51 **MUSIC TEACHER,** ch f Piccolo—Duena **Thurloe Thoroughbreds X**
52 **NAVAL FORCE,** b g Forzando—Barsham **H. Scott-Barret, M. Kerr-Dineen, S. Dibb**
53 **NOTJUSTAPRETTYFACE (USA),** b br f Red Ransom (USA)—Maudie May (USA) **Loddington Bloodstock**
54 **PINAFORE,** ch f Fleetwood (IRE)—Shi Shi **Mrs J. A. M. Willment**
55 **POSTGRADUATE (IRE),** b c Almutawakel—Institutrice (IRE) **Thurloe Thoroughbreds XII**
56 **PRINCE OF THE MAY,** ch g Bluegrass Prince—Maytime **Ian Cameron**
57 **SCUBA (IRE),** b c Indian Danehill—March Star (IRE) **Team Havana**
58 **TANNING,** b f Atraf—Gerundive (USA) **Mrs M. D. W. Morrison**
59 **TOP MARK,** b g Mark of Esteem (IRE)—Red White And Blue **A. J. Richards**
60 **TOQUE,** ch f King's Best—Barboukh **WRB Racing 59 (wrbracing.com)**
61 **UNTIMELY,** ch f Inchinor—All The Time **Capt J. Macdonald-Buchanan**
62 **WOOLSACK (USA),** ch c Spinning World (USA)—Rich And Famous (FR) **De La Warr Racing**
63 **WUJOOD,** b g Alzao (USA)—Rahayeb **D. J. Donner**

TWO-YEAR-OLDS

64 Ch f 12/2 Galileo (IRE)—Anniversary (Salse (USA)) (70000) **Loddington Bloodstock**
65 **APPLY DAPPLY,** b f 4/4 Pursuit of Love—Daring Destiny (Daring March) (6500) **Mrs L. A. Garfield**
66 **BOMBAY DUCK,** b f 1/3 Mark of Esteem (IRE)—Lady Georgia (Arazi (USA)) (5000) **A. J. Richards**
67 B f 26/3 Anabaa (USA)—Dolydille (IRE) (Dolphin Street (FR)) **D. Hardisty**
68 B f 18/1 Pursuit of Love—Duena (Grand Lodge (USA)) **Michael E. Wates**
69 B c 17/2 Royal Academy (USA)—Garden Folly (USA) (Pine Bluff (USA)) (18000) **M S T Partnership**
70 **HERNANDO ROYAL,** b c 21/2 Hernando—Louis' Queen (Tragic Role (USA)) (6500) **A. N. Solomons**
71 **JEANMAIRE (IRE),** b f 19/4 Dansili—Lovely Lyca (Night Shift (USA)) **Turf Club Racing Syndicate (2004)**
72 **KASUMI,** ch f 10/2 Inchinor—Raindrop (Primo Dominie) (5000) **Viscountess Trenchard**
73 **KENTUCKY WARBLER (IRE),** b f 24/3 Spinning World (USA)—Dollar Bird (Kris) **Sir Thomas Pilkington**
74 Ch c 29/4 Barathea (IRE)—Khafaya (Unfuwain (USA)) (45000) **De La Warr Racing**
75 Ch c 23/3 Dracula (AUS)—La Notte (Factual (USA)) **Mr N. Horn**
76 **LEOPOLDINE,** br f 24/2 Desert Prince (IRE)—Beaming (Mtoto) **Normandie Stud & Richard Grossman**
77 **LOURDES (IRE),** b f 12/4 Spectrum (IRE)—Loure (Lyphard (USA)) **Ballygallon Stud Ltd**
78 **MARCH GOLD (IRE),** ch f 30/3 Rich Man's Gold (USA)—

         Dog Wood (SAF) (Fort Wood (USA)) **Mrs B. Oppenheimer**
79 **MASTEROFTHECOURT (USA),** ch c 12/2 Horse Chestnut (SAF)—

         Great Verdict (AUS) (Christmas Tree (AUS)) **Mrs B. Oppenheimer**
80 B f 10/3 Indian Rocket—Miss Sabre (Sabrehill (USA)) (24144) **Phantom Partnership**
81 **ORANGE DANCER (IRE),** b f 19/1 Danehill Dancer (IRE)—

         Strelitzia (SAF) (Fort Wood (USA)) **Mrs B. Oppenheimer**
82 **PLATINUM HOUND (IRE),** b f 14/2 Vettori (IRE)—Dog Rose (SAF) (Fort Wood (USA)) **Mrs B. Oppenheimer**
83 B c 16/2 Mozart (IRE)—Premiere Dance (IRE) (Loup Solitaire (USA)) (40000) **Thurloe Finsbury II**
84 **REHEARSED (IRE),** ch f 8/4 In The Wings—Emilia Romagna (GER) (Acatenango (GER)) **Peggy Maxwell**
85 Ch c 17/4 Lujain—Roma (Second Set (IRE)) (20120) **Scott-Barrett, Dibb, Eavis, Morrison**
86 B c 9/1 Josr Algarhoud (IRE)—Shi Shi (Alnasr Alwasheek) (3000) **Mrs J. A. M. Willment**
87 **SQUIRTLE (IRE),** ch f 5/5 In The Wings—Manilia (FR) (Kris) **Ballygallon Stud Ltd**

MR H. MORRISON—continued

88 B c 9/4 Mozart (IRE)—Stop Out (Rudimentary (USA)) (50000) **H. Scott-Barrett & Lord Margadale**
89 SUPASEUS, b c 15/3 Spinning World (USA)—
                     Supamova (USA) (Seattle Slew (USA)) (42000) **Ben & Sir Martyn Arbib**
90 SUZUKI (IRE), ch f 22/3 Barathea (IRE)—Nishan (Nashwan (USA)) (77000) **Phantom Partnership**
91 Ch c 15/2 Bertolini (USA)—Urania (Most Welcome) (45000) **Glen Swire & Partners**
92 WINGS OF SPEED, b f 23/2 Pursuit of Love—Fleeting Vision (IRE) (Vision (USA)) (1500) **Melksham Craic**

Other Owners: J. Burridge, S. Burridge, G. Pilkington, H. Rutland, A. R. Bavin, J. Bernstein, J. H. Flower, Miss C. A. Green, Mrs F. M. Hallett, B. P. Hammond, J. A. Knight, M. C. Moutray-Read, Mrs G. E. Renwick, N. M. S. Rich, P. E. Selway-Swift, M. A. F. Shenfield, A. J. Smith, J. A. B. Stafford, J. P. M. Sullivan, R. W. Swallow, I. J. Wassell.

Assistant Trainer: Gerry Gracey

Apprentice: Luke Fletcher. **Amateur:** Miss Gemma Gracey-Davison, Mr J. Rees.

---

415 MISS D. MOUNTAIN, Newmarket
Postal: Flat 2, 44 Old Station Road, Newmarket, Suffolk, CB8 8DW.
Contacts: **PHONE/FAX** (01638) 660820 **MOBILES** (07765) 964402 (07717) 532299
E-MAIL saharastables@aol.com **WEBSITE** www.saharastables.co.uk

1 AFRICAN SAHARA (USA), 6, br h El Gran Senor (USA)—Able Money (USA) **Miss D. Mountain**
2 BILLY FLYNN (IRE), 4, b c General Monash (USA)—Word of Honor (FR)
3 MARINO MOU (IRE), 5, b h Darshaan—Lia's Dance **M. Ioannou**
4 SOVIET SCEPTRE (IRE), 4, ch c Soviet Star (USA)—Princess Sceptre **D. P. Fremel**
5 VRISAKI (IRE), 4, b g Docksider (USA)—Kingdom Queen (IRE) **R. Dixon**

THREE-YEAR-OLDS

6 HIGH AUTHORITY (IRE), b c Soviet Star (USA)—Moon Masquerade (IRE) **A. J. Cavanagh**
7 B f Mark of Esteem (IRE)—La Puce Volante
8 LAKESDALE (IRE), b f Desert Style (IRE)—Option (IRE) **A. J. Cavanagh**
9 MISS CUE, b f Polish Precedent (USA)—Sharp Girl (FR) **Mickey Flynns Racing Partnership**
10 SLITE, gr f Mind Games—Sapphire Mill **G. Wilson**

TWO-YEAR-OLDS

11 B br c 10/3 Diktat—Abundance (Cadeaux Genereux) (13000)
12 B f 11/2 Xaar—Hannalou (FR) (Shareef Dancer (USA)) (4000)
13 Ch c 13/1 King Charlemagne (USA)—Maytpleasethecourt (IRE) (Persian Heights) (25000)
14 OCTOBER SUN, b c 7/2 Dansili—Autumn Pride (Lear Fan (USA)) (7000) **D. P. Fremel**
15 B br c 8/1 Catienus (USA)—Theyrplayinoursong (USA) (Seattle Dancer (USA)) (13000)

Other Owners: Parr Racing Partnership, Mr M. Khawaja, Mr D. Murray.

Assistant Trainer: Ahmad Kobeissi

---

416 MR M. P. MUGGERIDGE, Crawley Down
Postal: Oakfield Stables, Hophurst Lane, Crawley Down, Crawley, West Sussex, RH10 4LN.
Contacts: **PHONE** (01342) 717825 **FAX** (01342) 715814 **MOBILE** (07850) 203881/(07712) 897613
E-MAIL mpmuggeridge@hotmail.com

1 HARLYN DEED, 18, b g Henricus (ATA)—Dunedin Lass **R. W. Vincent**
2 INDIAN OAK (IRE), 4, b f Indian Rocket—Marathon Maid **R. W. Vincent**
3 PENNY CHASE, 4, b f Bien Bien (USA)—Fullfilling (IRE) **R. W. Vincent**
4 ROCKWELDA, 10, b m Weld—Hill's Rocket **R. W. Vincent**

Assistant Trainer: Miss S M Vincent

Jockey (NH): Sean Curran.

417 MR WILLIAM R. MUIR, Lambourn

Postal: Linkslade, Wantage Road, Lambourn, Hungerford, Berkshire, RG17 8UG.
Contacts: HOME (01488) 73748 OFFICE (01488) 73098 FAX (01488) 73490
MOBILE (07831) 457074 E-MAIL williamr.muir@virgin.net

1 **BUY ON THE RED,** 4, b c Komaite (USA)—Red Rosein
2 **CHANCE FOR ROMANCE,** 4, ch f Entrepreneur—My First Romance
3 **CHORISTAR,** 4, ch g Inchinor—Star Tulip
4 **HIGH FREQUENCY (IRE),** 4, ch g Grand Lodge (USA)—Freak Out (FR)
5 **IMPELLER (IRE),** 6, ch g Polish Precedent (USA)—Almaaseh (IRE)
6 **MATERIAL WITNESS (IRE),** 8, b g Barathea (IRE)—Dial Dream
7 **MISS JUDGEMENT (IRE),** 4, b f Revoque (IRE)—Mugello
8 **PRINCIPAL WITNESS (IRE),** 4, b g Definite Article—Double Eight (IRE)
9 **REBEL LEADER,** 8, br g Ezzoud (IRE)—Haitienne (FR)
10 **TEXAS GOLD,** 7, ch g Cadeaux Genereux—Star Tulip
11 **THE CLOWN,** 4, b g Russian Revival (USA)—Fashion Bride (IRE)
12 **TOTALLY YOURS (IRE),** 4, b f Desert Sun—Total Aloof

THREE-YEAR-OLDS

13 **BARBARY COAST (FR),** b c Anabaa (USA)—Viking's Cove (USA)
14 **BOLD DIKTATOR,** b c Diktat—Madam Bold
15 **CREE,** b g Indian Ridge—Nightitude
16 **ELOQUENT KNIGHT (USA),** b br c Aljabr (USA)—Matinee Mimic (USA)
17 **ENFORCER,** b c Efisio—Tarneem (USA)
18 **JUST CLIFF,** b c Handsome Ridge—Justfortherecord
19 **KATHRYN JANEWAY (IRE),** b f In The Wings—Freak Out (FR)
20 **LATIN EXPRESS (IRE),** b c Marju (IRE)—Sea Port
21 **MISTER GENEPI,** b c Mister Baileys—Ring Queen (USA)
22 **MULBERRY LAD (IRE),** b g Entrepreneur—Taisho (IRE)
23 **PIPPA'S DANCER (IRE),** b f Desert Style (IRE)—Soreze (IRE)
24 **SAN DENG,** gr g Averti (IRE)—Miss Mirror
25 B g Tagula (IRE)—Simply Sooty
26 **STOLEN,** b c Groom Dancer (USA)—Jezyah (USA)
27 **SUTURIA,** b f Cadeaux Genereux—Cream Tease
28 **TRAPPETO (IRE),** b c Barathea (IRE)—Campiglia (IRE)

TWO-YEAR-OLDS

29 Ch c 7/5 Cadeaux Genereux—Aoife (IRE) (Thatching) (134138)
30 **CARMENERO (GER),** b c 5/4 Barathea (IRE)—Claire Fraser (USA) (Gone West (USA)) (12000)
31 B c 25/4 Sinndar (IRE)—Crodelle (IRE) (Formidable (USA)) (12000)
32 **CROONER (IRE),** b c 21/3 Titus Livius (FR)—John's Ballad (IRE) (Ballad Rock) (34000)
33 B c 22/4 Mister Baileys—Cultural Role (Night Shift (USA)) (16000)
34 Ch c 7/5 Giant's Causeway (USA)—Dellagrazia (USA) (Trempolino (USA)) (90000)
35 Gr f 14/4 Sagamix (FR)—Dial Dream (Gay Mecene (USA)) (30181)
36 **KAHLUA KISS,** b f 30/4 Mister Baileys—Ring Queen (USA) (Fairy King (USA)) (36000)
37 **KANSAS GOLD,** b c 23/1 Alhaarth (IRE)—Star Tulip (Night Shift (USA))
38 **LADY CREE (IRE),** b f 17/3 Medicean—Nightitude (Night Shift (USA)) (18000)
39 B c 13/4 Daggers Drawn (USA)—Lypharden (IRE) (Lyphard's Special (USA)) (25000)
40 B c 19/2 Piccolo—Miletrian Cares (Hamas (IRE)) (24000)
41 **MILLION ALL DAY (IRE),** gr c 18/4 Daylami (IRE)—Madame Nureyev (USA) (Nureyev (USA))
42 **MOON EMPRESS (FR),** gr f 8/2 Rainbow Quest (USA)—Diamoona (FR) (Last Tycoon) (100603)
43 **RED WARNING,** b c 30/4 Diktat—Red Rosein (Red Sunset) (26000)
44 Ch f 20/2 Medicean—Rosewood Belle (USA) (Woodman (USA)) (45000)
45 **SAHARA SUN (IRE),** b f 12/4 Desert Sun—Perfect Rainbow (Rainbow Quest (USA)) (21461)
46 **SALUTE THE GENERAL,** ch c 17/2 Mark of Esteem (IRE)—Oiselina (FR) (Linamix (FR)) (10000)
47 **XALUNA BAY (IRE),** br f 23/4 Xaar—Lunadine (FR) (Bering) (12000)

418 MR M. MULLINEAUX, Tarporley
Postal: **Southley Farm, Alpraham, Tarporley, Cheshire, CW6 9JD.**
Contacts: PHONE **(01829) 261440 or 261622 FAX (01829) 261622 MOBILE (07753) 650263**
E-MAIL southleyfarmracing@aol.com WEBSITE www.cheshiretrainer.co.uk

1 BENTYHEATH LANE, 8, b g Puissance—Eye Sight **The Hon Mrs S. Pakenham**
2 BLUE WATER, 5, b m Shaamit (IRE)—November Song **T. M. Clarke**
3 BODFARI DREAM, 4, ch f Environment Friend—Al Reet (IRE) **www.mark-kilner-racing.com**
4 CHARLIE PARKES, 7, ch g Pursuit of Love—Lucky Parkes **J. Heler**
5 COMIC TALES, 4, b g Mind Games—Glorious Aragon **Mega Micks Racing Partnership**
6 DOUBLE SPREAD, 6, b g Afflora (IRE)—Flora Louisa **Mrs Caroline Wilson**
7 GREENACRES BOY, 10, b g Roscoe Blake—Deep Goddess **G. A. Probin**
8 ILLUSTRIOUS DUKE, 7, b g Dancing Spree (USA)—Killick **Miss M. J. L. Mullineaux**
9 KIMOE WARRIOR, 7, ch g Royal Abjar (USA)—Thewaari (USA) **D. Ashbrook**
10 LEWSHER, 5, b m Sir Harry Lewis (USA)—Sheraton Girl **Happy Times Ahead Partnership**
11 MARBURYANNA, 5, ch m Classic Cliche (IRE)—Lake Mistassiu **P. T. Hollins, S. K. Evans**
12 MIDNIGHT STAR, 4, b g Cloudings (IRE)—Blueberry Parkes **J. Heler**
13 MS FREEBEE, 6, ch m Gunner B—Luckifosome **Bluestone Partnership**
14 PHOENIX EYE, 4, b c Tragic Role (USA)—Eye Sight **J. R. Williamson**
15 PRINCE OF BLUES (IRE), 7, b g Prince of Birds (USA)—Reshift **T. M. Clarke**
16 SAILOR A'HOY, 9, b g Handsome Sailor—Eye Sight **J. R. Williamson**
17 SUSAN BE QUICK, 5, b m Sir Harry Lewis (USA)—Safeasthat **Mrs S. J. Mullineaux**
18 TALBOT AVENUE, 7, b g Puissance—Dancing Daughter **Mrs Caroline Wilson**
19 WIZARD OF US, 5, b g Wizard King—Sian's Girl **P. Currey**
20 YOUNG ROONEY, 5, b g Danzig Connection (USA)—Lady Broker **Esprit De Corps Racing**

THREE-YEAR-OLDS

21 B c Lake Coniston (IRE)—Killick **Mr S. Pritchard & Mr G. Gibson**
22 LAKE WAKATIPU, b f Lake Coniston (IRE)—Lady Broker **Esprit De Corps Racing**
23 LAYED BACK ROCKY, ch c Lake Coniston (IRE)—Madam Taylor **Esprit De Corps Racing**
24 LIRAGE, b f Wizard King—Diamond Rouge **P. Boyers**
25 ROYAL SPELL, b f Wizard King—Manadel **P. Currey**
26 SYDNEYROUGHDIAMOND, b g Whittingham (IRE)—November Song **T. M. Clarke**
27 WHERETHERES A WILL, gr c Wizard King—Sian's Girl **P. Currey**

TWO-YEAR-OLDS

28 ALWAYS OPTIMISTIC, b c 12/2 Puissance—Glorious Aragon (Aragon) **Mrs Caroline Wilson**
29 SUNNY PARKES, ch f 19/2 Arkadian Hero (USA)—Janette Parkes (Pursuit of Love) **J. Heler**

Other Owners: Mr M. Mullineaux, Mr M. Aspinwall, P. C. Burgess, J. D. Evans, Mr E. A. Griffiths, I. W. Jones, M. Kilner, K. A. Pratt, M. J. Pugh, G. T. Ruff, T. S. Wallace, Mrs C. A. Wallace, Mr R.G. Woolley.

Assistant Trainer: Susan Mullineaux

Amateur: Miss M. J. L. Mullineaux, Mr S. Ross.

419 MR J. W. MULLINS, Amesbury
Postal: **Wilsford Stables, Wilsford-Cum-Lake, Amesbury, Salisbury, Wiltshire, SP4 7BL.**
Contacts: PHONE/FAX **(01980) 626344 MOBILE (07802) 559634**
E-MAIL seamus@jwmullins.co.uk WEBSITE www.jwmullins.co.uk

1 ANOTHER CONQUEST, 6, b m El Conquistador—Kellys Special **F. G. Matthews**
2 AU LAC, 11, b g North Col—Janlarmar **D. E. Hazzard**
3 BALLYHOO (IRE), 5, b m Supreme Leader—Ballyhouraprincess (IRE) **I. M. McGready**
4 BOB'S FINESSE, 5, ch m Gran Alba (USA)—High Finesse **Miss C. A. James**
5 BROOKLANDS LAD, 8, b g North Col—Sancal **B. R. Edgeley**
6 CLASSIC CHINA, 8, ch m Karinga Bay—Chanelle **P. C. and Mrs S. I. Fry**
7 CON TRICKS, 12, b g El Conquistador—Dame Nellie **Shildon Racing**
8 CORRECT AND RIGHT (IRE), 6, b m Great Commotion (USA)—Miss Hawkins **Mr J. W. Mullins**
9 DEEP KING (IRE), 10, b b g King's Ride—Splendid Run **Miss D. J. Wilkins**
10 EARLY START, 7, ch m Husyan (USA)—Gipsy Dawn **A. M. Day**
11 FALLOUT (IRE), 4, b f Goldmark (USA)—Tearful Reunion **Mrs H. J. Pike**
12 FOREST FAUNA, 5, b m El Conquistador—Busy Mittens **New Forest Racing Partnership**
13 GOLDEN CRUSADER, 8, b g Gildoran—Pusey Street **First Impressions Racing Group**
14 HANSAN BUOY (IRE), 5, b br g Anshan—Miss Tagalie (IRE) **I. M. McGready**

MR J. W. MULLINS—continued

15 **HILL FORTS HENRY**, 7, ch g Karinga Bay—Maggie Tee **Mrs J. C. Scorgie**
16 **JOCKSER (IRE)**, 4, b g Desert Story (IRE)—Pupa Fiorini (ITY) **The D. M. L. Partnership**
17 **KAWAGINO (IRE)**, 5, b g Perugino (USA)—Sharakawa (IRE) **K. J. Pike**
18 **KELLYS FABLE**, 5, b g Thowra (FR)—Kellys Special **F. G. Matthews**
19 **KENTFORD GREBE**, 6, b m Teenoso (USA)—Notinhand **D. I. Bare**
20 **KENTFORD LADY**, 4, b f Emperor Fountain—Kentford Duchess **D. I. Bare**
21 **KJJIMMY**, 8, ch g Sunley Builds—Cavity **K. J. Pike**
22 **LETS GET BUSY (IRE)**, 5, ch m Presenting—Mindyourown (IRE) **Mrs M. Rayner**
23 **MCSNAPPY**, 8, ch g Risk Me (FR)—Nannie Annie **Cum-Lake Racing**
24 5, b m Anshan—Milan Moss **Mr J. W. Mullins**
25 **MINNIE THE MOOCHER**, 5, b m Karinga Bay—Slippery Fin **Woodmarsh Racing**
26 **MISS DOUBLET**, 4, ch f Double Trigger (USA)—Bournel **N. R. Bowden**
27 **MISTIFIED (IRE)**, 4, b g Ali-Royal (IRE)—Lough N Uisce (IRE) **Cum-Lake Racing**
28 **OUR JOLLY SWAGMAN**, 10, b g Thowra (FR)—Queens Dowry **F. G. Matthews**
29 **RADBROOK HALL**, 6, b g Teenoso (USA)—Sarah's Venture **Andrew Cocks And Tara Johnson**
30 5, b g Ala Hounak—Red Moth (IRE) **Mr J. W. Mullins**
31 **RI NA REALTA (IRE)**, 10, b g King's Ride—Realteen **Mrs S. A. Mullins**
32 **RUBY FLARE**, 9, b m Nader—Ruby Flame **Dr R. Jowett**
33 **SEAN NOS (IRE)**, 4, b g Sri Pekan (USA)—Coolaba Princess (IRE) **Mr J. W. Mullins**
34 **SEE ME THERE**, 5, b g Busy Flight—See-A-Rose **J. A. G. Meaden**
35 **SEE YOU AROUND**, 10, b g Sharp Deal—Seeborg **The Infamous Five**
36 **SEE YOU MAN**, 7, b g Young Freeman (USA)—Shepani **J. A. G. Meaden**
37 **SEE YOU SOMETIME**, 10, b g Sharp Deal—Shepani **J. A. G. Meaden**
38 **SEEADOR**, 6, b g El Conquistador—Shepani **J. A. G. Meaden**
39 **SHAMBOLINA**, 4, b f Shambo—Game Dilemma **Mrs S. White**
40 **SPECIAL CONQUEST**, 7, b g El Conquistador—Kellys Special **F. G. Matthews**
41 **SPECTACULAR HOPE**, 5, b m Marju (IRE)—Distant Music **Woodford Valley Racing**
42 **SPECULATIVE**, 11, b g Suave Dancer (USA)—Gull Nook **K. A. Hicks**
43 **SUSPICIOUS MINDS**, 4, b f Anabaa (USA)—Paloma Bay (IRE) **I. F. Sandell**
44 **TANO (CZE)**, 4, b g Sapano—Talci (CZE) **Mrs S. A. Mullins**
45 **TERRIBLE TENANT**, 6, gr g Terimon—Rent Day **D. I. Bare**
46 **THE GREY MAN**, 4, gr g Muhtarram (USA)—Lavender Della **M. N. Jenkins**
47 **TRUE LOVER (GER)**, 8, b g Winged Love (IRE)—Truneba (GER) **First Impressions Racing Group 3**

TWO-YEAR-OLDS

48 B f 1/2 Tipsy Creek (USA)—Hush It Up (Tina's Pet) (1500) **Mr S. Kennedy**

Other Owners: P. R. Attwater, M. A. Barrett, W. J. Brockway, R. E. Gray, R. Hatchard, Mrs M. J. Henry, Mrs A. M. Kley, Mr J. Moran, Mrs K. P. Steemson, J. H. Young.

Assistant Trainer: Miss S Young

Jockey (NH): S Curran, M. A. Fitzgerald, A. Thornton, J. Tizzard, R. Young. **Conditional:** J. Lindberg.

MR WILLIAM P. MULLINS, Carlow
420
Postal: Closutton, Bagenalstown, Co. Carlow, Ireland.
Contacts: **PHONE** +353 (0) 59 97 21786 **FAX** +353 (0) 59 97 21786 **MOBILE** +353 (0) 87 2564940
E-MAIL wpmullins@eircom.net **WEBSITE** www.wpmullins.com

1 **ADAMANT APPROACH (IRE)**, 11, b g Mandalus—Crash Approach **Greenstar Syndicate**
2 **ALEXANDER BANQUET (IRE)**, 12, b g Glacial Storm (USA)—Black Nancy **Mrs N. O'Callaghan**
3 **ALEXANDER TAIPAN (IRE)**, 5, b g Taipan (IRE)—Fayafi **Mrs N. O'Callaghan**
4 **ASIAN ALLIANCE (IRE)**, 4, ch f Soviet Star (USA)—Indian Express **Decagan Syndicate**
5 **AVOCA MIST (IRE)**, 5, b br m Luso—Apicat **T. Merrigan**
6 **BALLYAMBER (IRE)**, 10, b g Glacial Storm (USA)—El Scarsdale **Sean Mulyran**
7 **BALLYGOE (IRE)**, 6, b g Flemensfirth (USA)—Handy Lady **Mrs R. Boyd**
8 **BALTIMORE HILL (IRE)**, 5, b g Mister Lord (USA)—Culfadda Girl (IRE) **Ilen Syndicate**
9 **BASSETT TIGER (IRE)**, 9, b g Shardari—Bassett Girl **Tom Gilligan**
10 **BELINKIN**, 5, b h Robellino—Kintail **D. Flynn**
11 **BLACKCURRANT (FR)**, 5, b g Cadoudal—Double Spring (FR) **T. J. Hemmings**
12 **BONEYARROW (IRE)**, 9, ch g Over The River (FR)—Apicat **J. Comerford**
13 **BOTHAR NA (IRE)**, 6, ch g Mister Lord (USA)—Country Course (IRE) **Mrs M. O'Dwyer**
14 **BUNKERS HILL (IRE)**, 5, b h Lahib (USA)—Ela's Gold (IRE) **D. Flynn**
15 **CENTER FIELD (IRE)**, 7, b g Montelimar (USA)—Late Call (IRE) **Greenstar Syndicate**

MR WILLIAM P. MULLINS—continued

16 **COUSIN PETER (IRE)**, 6, ch g Over The River (FR)—Leafy Moss **J. Comerford**
17 **CRAANFORD MILL**, 6, b h Vettori (IRE)—Northern Bird **Oilean Ciarrai Syndicate**
18 **DAVENPORT DEMOCRAT (IRE)**, 7, ch g Fourstars Allstar (USA)—Storm Court (IRE) **PM Racing Syndicate**
19 **DAVENPORT MILENIUM (IRE)**, 9, b g Insan (USA)—Society Belle **Mrs N. O'Callaghan**
20 **DETONANTE (IRE)**, 5, ch m Cardoun (FR)—Cardwell (FR) **The Red Roosters Syndicate**
21 **DIACONATE (IRE)**, 4, b f Cape Cross (IRE)—Shadowglow **J. J. Brennan**
22 **DIEGO GARCIA (IRE)**, 5, b h Sri Pekan (USA)—Chapel Lawn **J. J. Brennan**
23 **EARLY HOURS (IRE)**, 8, b m Un Desperado (FR)—Call Me Anna **Macashbu Syndicate**
24 **ELLY JANE (IRE)**, 5, b m Luso—Casey Jane (IRE) **J. Comerford**
25 **EURO LEADER (IRE)**, 8, b g Supreme Leader—Noreaster (IRE) **J. Cox**
26 **FIRE OF KEN (FR)**, 4, b c Kendor (FR)—Terre de Feu (FR) **D. Flynn**
27 **FLORIDA BELLE (IRE)**, 6, b m Florida Son—Life of A Lady (IRE) **Holy Racing Syndicate**
28 **FRANKLINS TRAIL (IRE)**, 4, b c Imperial Ballet (IRE)—Nettle **J. J. Brennan**
29 **GALARINI (IRE)**, 4, b c King's Theatre (IRE)—Nordic Pageant (IRE) **F. Doyle**
30 **GAYLE ABATED (IRE)**, 6, b g Moscow Society (USA)—Hurricane Girl (IRE) **Sean Dunne**
31 **GLACIAL MOSS (IRE)**, 7, ch g Glacial Storm (USA)—Garrenroe **D. O'Connor**
32 **GOODNIGHT DICK (IRE)**, 5, b br g Luso—Morning Susan **J. Comerford**
33 **GRAVELY PINT (IRE)**, 5, b g Carroll House—Sharnad (IRE) **M D Syndicate**
34 **HEDGEHUNTER (IRE)**, 9, b g Montelimar (USA)—Aberedw (IRE) **T. J. Hemmings**
35 **HEEZAPISTOL (FR)**, 7, b g Pistolet Bleu (FR)—Strictly Cool (USA) **Heritage Syndicate**
36 **HOLY ORDERS (IRE)**, 8, b h Unblest—Shadowglow **A. McLuckie**
37 **HOMER WELLS (IRE)**, 7, b g Arctic Cider (USA)—Run And Shine **Mrs M. McMahon**
38 **JASMIN D'OUDAIRIES (FR)**, 8, b g Apeldoorn (FR)—Vellea (FR) **The Deise and Dubs Syndicate**
39 **JOUEUR D'ESTRUVAL (FR)**, 8, gr g Perrault—Alrose (FR) **Mrs V. O'Leary**
40 **KEAVENEY (IRE)**, 6, ch g Simply Great (FR)—Hogan Stand **Peter Garvey**
41 **KELLY'S CRAFT (IRE)**, 8, b g Warcraft (USA)—Kelly's Bridge **PM Racing Syndicate**
42 **KIM FONTAINE (FR)**, 7, b g Silver Rainbow—Blanche Fontaine (FR) **B. Doyle**
43 **KNOCKNABOOLY (IRE)**, 6, ch g John French—Valiyist (IRE) **Margaret O'Rourke**
44 **KOME BACK (FR)**, 7, b g Trebrook (FR)—Vaderetro II (FR) **Mrs J. M. Mullins**
45 **LA FISARMONICA (IRE)**, 5, b m Accordion—Moycullen **Mrs J. M. Mullins**
46 **LADY ACCORD (IRE)**, 5, b m Accordion—Lady of Tara **Mrs J. M. Mullins**
47 **LANJOU ROUGE (IRE)**, 6, b g Start Fast (FR)—Raika (FR) **Road Runner Syndicate**
48 **LASQUINI DU MOULIN (FR)**, 6, gr g Saint Preuil (FR)—Api (FR) **Sunny Bank Syndicate**
49 **LIVINGSTONEBRAMBLE (IRE)**, 9, b g Supreme Leader—Killiney Side **Favorites Racing Syndicate**
50 **LOVELY LAD (IRE)**, 6, b g Alphabatim (USA)—Lovely Still (IRE) **T. Allen**
51 **MACS GILDORAN**, 11, b g Gildoran—Shamrock Bridge **Mrs M. McManus**
52 **MAJOR BURNS (IRE)**, 7, b g Aahsaylad—Night Matron (IRE) **Festival Syndicate**
53 **MAJOR VERNON (IRE)**, 6, b g Flemensfirth (USA)—Rainys Run **B. Doyle**
54 **MALAHIDE MARINA**, 6, b g Teenoso (USA)—Marina Bird **Tom Gilligan**
55 **MAN ON THE NILE (IRE)**, 5, b h Snurge—Spirit of The Nile (FR) **D. Flynn**
56 **MARKS MEDICO (IRE)**, 8, gr g Roselier (FR)—Born Lucky **Sport Racing Club**
57 **MARTATOMIC (IRE)**, 7, b g Vestris Abu—Oonagh's Teddy **Greenstar Syndicate**
58 **MILKAT (IRE)**, 7, b g Machiavellian (USA)—Desert Victory **J. Comerford**
59 **MISSED THAT**, 6, b g Overbury (IRE)—Not Enough **Mrs V. O'Leary**
60 **MOSSY GREEN (IRE)**, 11, b g Moscow Society (USA)—Green Ajo **Greenstar Syndicate**
61 **MOUNTAIN SNOW (IRE)**, 5, ch h Barathea (IRE)—Mountains of Mist (IRE) **A. Fanning**
62 **MR BABBAGE (IRE)**, 7, ch g Carroll House—Winsome Doe **George Creighton**
63 **MUNCHY MIKE (IRE)**, 5, b g Presenting—Menedreams (IRE) **J. Kenny**
64 **NAY (FR)**, 4, b g Ragmar (FR)—Elysea (FR) **Mrs J. M. Mullins**
65 **NORTH ATLANTIC (IRE)**, 6, b g Arctic Lord—Cherry Avenue **North Atlantic Syndicate**
66 **OF COURSE (IRE)**, 7, ch g Montelimar (USA)—Linda's Course (IRE) **Mr Michael Whelan**
67 **OUR BEN**, 6, ch g Presenting—Forest Pride (IRE) **T. J. Hemmings**
68 **RAIKKONEN (IRE)**, 5, b g Lake Coniston (IRE)—Jour Ferie (IRE) **A. Fanning**
69 **REVE DE ROSE**, 6, b m Emperor Jones (USA)—Rose de Reve (FR) **Mrs M. McMahon**
70 **ROUNDSTONE LADY (IRE)**, 5, b br m Anshan—Young Preacher **MMD Syndicate**
71 **ROYAL ALPHABET (IRE)**, 7, b g King's Theatre—A-To-Z (IRE) **Ballylinch Stud**
72 **ROYAL HERITAGE (IRE)**, 6, b h Carroll House—Call Me Anna **Heritage Syndicate**
73 **RULE SUPREME (IRE)**, 9, b g Supreme Leader—Book of Rules (IRE) **John Fallon**
74 **SADLERS WINGS (IRE)**, 7, b h In The Wings—Anna Comnena (IRE) **J. J. Brennan**
75 **SCOFFYS BUSH (IRE)**, 5, ch g Old Vic—Leafy Moss **J. Comerford**
76 **SHANDON STAR (IRE)**, 6, b m Priolo (USA)—Noble Choice **W. P. Roche**
77 **SHANNONS CROSS (IRE)**, 6, b g Fourstars Allstar (USA)—Collopy's Cross **Tom Gilligan**
78 **SHERBERRY (IRE)**, 6, b m Shernazar—Bilberry **Does Size Matter Syndicate**
79 **SILK SCREEN (IRE)**, 5, b h Barathea (IRE)—Sun Screen **J. J. Brennan**
80 **SONNE CINQ (IRE)**, 6, b br m Old Vic—Ring Four (USA) **Scone Syndicate**
81 **SPIRITUAL SOCIETY (IRE)**, 5, b g Moscow Society (USA)—Sniggy **G. Mullins**

MR WILLIAM P. MULLINS—continued

82 **SUNAMI STORM (IRE)**, 7, b m Glacial Storm (USA)—Live It Up **W. P. Roche**
83 **SUPREME OBSESSION (IRE)**, 7, br g Supreme Leader—Death Or Glory **Tree Tops Syndicate**
84 **SUPREME PEARL**, 6, b g Supreme Leader—Vi's Delight **Mrs J. M. Mullins**
85 **TEMPLELUSK (IRE)**, 7, ch g Over The River (FR)—Leafy Moss **J. Comerford**
86 **VERROCCHIO (IRE)**, 5, b h Entrepreneur—Our Hope **J. J. Brennan**
87 **WARRENS CASTLE (IRE)**, 8, b g Fourstars Allstar (USA)—Jerusalem Cruiser (IRE) **J. J. Brennan**
88 **WATER STORM (IRE)**, 7, ch g Glacial Storm (USA)—Water Sprite **Mrs J. M. Mullins**

THREE-YEAR-OLDS

89 B c Spectrum (IRE)—Gipsy Anna (IRE) **Mrs J. M. Mullins**
90 B f King's Theatre (IRE)—Niamh Cinn Oir (IRE) **Mrs J. M. Mullins**

Jockey (NH): R. Walsh. **Apprentice:** David Condon. **Amateur:** Mr J. J. Codd, Mr J. A. Nash.

---

421 MR F. MURPHY, Leyburn
Postal: **Wynbury Stables, West Witton, Leyburn, North Yorkshire, DL8 4LR.**
Contacts: **PHONE** (01969) 622289 **FAX** (01969) 625278 **MOBILE** (07703) 444398
E-MAIL office@wynburystables.fsnet.co.uk **WEBSITE** www.ferdymurphyracing.com

1 5, B m Desert Style (IRE)—Aliyna (FR) **A. O'Gorman**
2 **BALLINCLAY KING (IRE)**, 11, b g Asir—Clonroche Artic **I. Guise, B. Leatherday, R. Spence**
3 **BARROW (SWI)**, 8, br g Caerleon (USA)—Bestow **Miss J. V. Morgan**
4 **BASILEA STAR (IRE)**, 8, b g Fourstars Allstar (USA)—Swiss Castle (IRE) **Mr B. J. O'Rourke**
5 **BE UPSTANDING**, 10, ch g Hubbly Bubbly (USA)—Two Travellers **F. M. Holmes**
6 **BLUE RISING**, 4, gr g Primitive Rising (USA)—Pollytickle **Mrs E. A. Kettlewell**
7 **BOWES CROSS**, 5, b g Environment Friend—Fenian Court (IRE) **Mr F. Murphy**
8 **CAIPIROSKA**, 6, b g Petoski—Caipirinha (IRE) **T. J. Hemmings**
9 **CALLINGWOOD (IRE)**, 5, ch g Pierre—Clonroche Artic **Mrs J. Morgan**
10 **CANAVAN (IRE)**, 6, gr g Bob Back (USA)—Silver Glen (IRE) **J. Duddy**
11 **CAPTAIN BUNGLE**, 4, b g Presenting—Minerstown (IRE) **S. L. Rodwell**
12 **CARLYS QUEST**, 11, ch g Primo Dominie—Tuppy (USA) **Ms L. Neville**
13 **CAVEMAN**, 5, b g Primitive Rising (USA)—Ferneyhill Lady **Mrs T. H. Barclay/Mrs F. D. McInnes Skinner**
14 **CHANCERS DANTE (IRE)**, 9, b g Phardante (FR)—Own Acre **Mrs P. B. Symes**
15 **CHARLY JACK**, 6, b g Alderbrook—Reperage (USA) **Mr L. M. Symes**
16 **CHICAGO BREEZE (IRE)**, 8, b m Lord Americo—Anguillita (IRE) **Mr W Winlow, Mrs C Seymour, Mr E Whalley**
17 5, B g Fourstars Allstar (USA)—Collopy's Cross **Chemipetro Limited**
18 **DAGUYDA (FR)**, 6, b g Northern Crystal—La Domizia (FR) **David Awty & David Williams**
19 **DARK THUNDER (IRE)**, 8, br g Religiously (USA)—Culkeern **A. O'Gorman**
20 **DOLMUR (IRE)**, 5, b br g Charnwood Forest (IRE)—Kawanin **Sean J. Murphy**
21 **DOUBLE LEO (FR)**, 4, b br g Double Bed (FR)—Miss Planette (FR) **Mrs F. D. McInnes Skinner**
22 **EUROPA**, 9, b g Jupiter Island—Dublin Ferry **T. J. Hemmings**
23 **EWE BEAUTY (FR)**, 5, b m Phantom Breeze—Baie de Chalamont (FR) **Mr and Mrs Neil Iveson**
24 **FAMILY VENTURE (IRE)**, 8, br g Montelimar (USA)—Well Honey **The Family Venture Partnership**
25 **FASHIONS MONTY (IRE)**, 9, ch m Montelimar (USA)—Fashions Side **B. F. Mulholland**
26 **FROM LITTLE ACORNS**, 9, b g Denel (FR)—Mount Gawn
27 **GARDE BIEN**, 8, br g Afzal—May Lady **Mrs M. B. Scholey**
28 **GRANIT D'ESTRUVAL (FR)**, 11, b g Quart de Vin (FR)—Jalousie (FR) **W. J. Gott**
29 **GRANITE STEPS**, 9, gr g Gran Alba (USA)—Pablena **Mrs T. H. Barclay/Mrs F. D. McInnes Skinner**
30 **GREEN IDEAL**, 7, b g Mark of Esteem (IRE)—Emerald (USA) **Mrs J. Morgan**
31 **HAS SCORED (IRE)**, 7, b g Sadler's Wells (USA)—City Ex **The Has Scored Partnership**
32 **HAUT DE GAMME (FR)**, 10, ch g Morespeed—Chantalouette (FR) **The Haut De Gamme Partnership**
33 **HISTORG (FR)**, 10, b g Cyborg (FR)—Kalliste (FR) **J. McCarthy**
34 **HOT WELD**, 6, b g Weld—Deb's Ball **S. L. Rodwell**
35 **HOWABOYS QUEST (USA)**, 8, b g Quest For Fame—Doctor Black (USA) **Winlow Brothers**
36 **JACK LYNCH**, 9, ch g Lancastrian—Troublewithjack **Mrs H. A. Lynch**
37 **JOES EDGE (IRE)**, 8, b br g Supreme Leader—Right Dark **Chemipetro Limited**
38 **JUST FOR FUN (IRE)**, 7, br g Kahyasi—Copper Breeze (IRE) **Northumberland Jumpers**
39 **KA ROSE (FR)**, 7, b g Missolonghi (USA)—Quelle Etoile V (FR) **A. O'Gorman**
40 **KING OF CONFUSION (IRE)**, 6, br g Topanoora—Rich Desire **J. Taqvi**
41 **KIPPOUR (FR)**, 7, b g Luchiroverte (IRE)—Obole III (FR) **T. J. Hemmings**
42 **LANICENE (IRE)**, 6, b g Moon Madness—Ocylla (FR) **Hill, Trembath, Bryan and Outhart**
43 **LEADING MAN (IRE)**, 5, b g Old Vic—Cudder Or Shudder (IRE) **Mrs Catriona M. McKeane**
44 **LEYLAND COMET (IRE)**, 7, b br g Roselier (FR)—Firey Comet **T. J. Hemmings**
45 **LUZCADOU (FR)**, 12, b g Cadoudal (FR)—Luzenia (FR) **A. G. Chappell**

MR F. MURPHY—continued

46 **MAC'S SUPREME (IRE)**, 13, b g Supreme Leader—Merry Breeze **B. McEntaggart**
47 **MIJICO (IRE)**, 9, b g Lord Americo—Mijette **Mrs R. D. Cairns**
48 **MISSOUDUN (FR)**, 5, b g Esteem Ball (FR)—Lisiana (FR) **P. T. J. Murphy**
49 **NATIVE LEGEND (IRE)**, 10, b g Be My Native (USA)—Tickhill **J. D. Gordon**
50 **NOBODYS PERFECT (IRE)**, 5, br m Heron Island (IRE)—Likeness **N. Gravett**
51 **ORNELLA SPEED (IRE)**, 5, b m Vertical Speed (FR)—Macyrienne (FR) **P. T. J. Murphy**
52 **RELIX (FR)**, 5, gr g Linamix (FR)—Resleona **Stuart Taylor, David Hardy, Lee Seaton**
53 **SAFFRONTO (IRE)**, 6, b g Muroto—Saffron Holly (IRE) **Sean J. Murphy**
54 **SPIDERS WEB**, 5, gr g Linamix (FR)—Cattermole (USA) **The Spiders Web Partnership**
55 **SUPREME DEVELOPER (IRE)**, 8, b g Supreme Leader—Bettys The Boss (IRE) **Mrs A. N. Durkan**
56 **SWALLOW MAGIC (IRE)**, 7, b g Magic Ring (IRE)—Scylla **J. D. Gordon**
57 **TOULON ROUGE (IRE)**, 8, b m Toulon—Master Nidee **Racegoers Club Owners Group**
58 **TRIBAL VENTURE (IRE)**, 7, gr g Dom Alco (FR)—Babacha (FR) **Hill, Trembath, Bryan and Outhart**
59 **TRUCKERS TAVERN (IRE)**, 10, ch g Phardante (FR)—Sweet Tulip **Mrs M. B. Scholey**
60 **ULUSABA**, 9, b g Alflora (IRE)—Mighty Fly **Dorothy Clinton, Chris McHugh, Jon King**
61 **UNION DEUX (FR)**, 6, ch g Nikos—Sanhia (FR) **Mrs M. B. Scholey**
62 **WATER TAXI**, 4, ch g Zafonic (USA)—Trellis Bay **Mr F. Murphy**
63 **WORLD VISION (IRE)**, 8, ch g Denel (FR)—Dusty Lane (IRE) **R. & M. J. Partnership**
64 **WYNBURY FLYER**, 10, ch g Risk Me (FR)—Woolcana **Mrs G. Seymour**
65 **YANKEE CROSSING (IRE)**, 7, b g Lord Americo—Ath Leathan **T. J. Hemmings**
66 **YOUR A GASSMAN (IRE)**, 7, b g King's Ride—Nish Bar **W. J. Gott**

Other Owners: W. M. Aitchison, Mrs J. Barclay, Ms R. Chapman, Miss D. M. Clinton, C. W. Cooper, Mr D. J. Hardy, M. Hill, Mr J. M. C. King, Ms M. J. Kitson, Miss J. M. Murray, D. Neale, D. Parry, Ms L. Y. Schofield, R. H. Scholey, Mrs C. Seymour, Mr R. J. Spence, R. Taylor, S. J. Taylor, C. R. Trembath, Mr E. Whalley, Mr W. H. Winlow.

Assistant Trainer: Janet Morgan

Jockey (NH): A. Dobbin, B. Harding, T. J. Murphy. **Conditional:** K. Mercer, N. Mulholland. **Amateur:** Mr N. Terry, Mr T. J. Dreaper, Miss Z. Morgan-Murphy.

---

422 | **MR P. G. MURPHY, Hungerford**
Postal: **Mabberleys, Front Street, East Garston, Hungerford, Berkshire, RG17 7EU.**
Contacts: **OFFICE (01488) 648473 FAX (01488) 649775 MOBILE (07831) 410409**
E-MAIL pat@mabberleys.freeserve.co.uk

1 **BIG BRADFORD**, 4, b g Tamure (IRE)—Heather Honey **A. N. Brackley**
2 **BLUE PLANET (IRE)**, 7, b g Bluebird (USA)—Millie Musique **Miss J. Collison**
3 **CROGHAN LOCH (IRE)**, 8, br g Mister Lord (USA)—Croghan Katie **Mrs D. E. Murphy**
4 **ESTERS BOY**, 7, b g Sure Blade (USA)—Moheli **J. Cooper**
5 **GREENWOOD**, 7, ch g Emarati (USA)—Charnwood Queen **The Golden Anorak Partnership**
6 **KNIGHT OF THE ROAD (IRE)**, 6, b br g Lord Americo—Trolly Dolly (IRE) **Mrs P. J. K. Spielman**
7 **LIGHT REFLECTIONS**, 12, b g Rainbow Quest (USA)—Tajfah (USA) **Miss J. Collison**
8 **MEIJIN (IRE)**, 5, b br g Desert King (IRE)—Fortitude (IRE)
9 **NOBLE MIND**, 4, b g Mind Games—Lady Annabel **Mr P. G. Murphy**
10 **PALMAC'S PRIDE**, 5, ch g Atraf—Nashwanah **The Virtual Partnership**
11 **PETWICK (IRE)**, 6, b br g Flemensfirth (USA)—Scottish Minnie (IRE) **Gilco**
12 **SUPREME GLORY (IRE)**, 12, b g Supreme Leader—Pentlows **C. J. L. Moorsom**
13 **SUPREME SIR (IRE)**, 7, b g Supreme Leader—Sirrah Madam **C. J. L. Moorsom**

Other Owners: Mrs R. B. Brackley, Mr T. Collins, J. W. Dyson, N. A. Gill, Mrs K. M. Graham, R. Hart, A. D. Potts.

Assistant Trainer: Mrs Dianne Murphy

Jockey (flat): S. Drowne, D. Kinsella. **Jockey (NH):** L. Aspell. **Conditional:** J. Quintin.

---

423 | **MR F. P. MURTAGH, Carlisle**
Postal: **Hurst Farm, Ivegill, Carlisle, Cumbria, CA4 0NL.**
Contacts: **PHONE (017684) 84649 MOBILE (0771) 4026741**
E-MAIL finbar@murtaghs.fsnet.co.uk

1 **BOBSOUROWN (IRE)**, 6, b g Parthian Springs—Suir Queen **Mr E. Chapman**
2 **BULLIES ACRE (IRE)**, 5, b g Arctic Cider (USA)—Clonminch Lady **Mr J. M. Murtagh**
3 **CELIA'S HIGH (IRE)**, 6, br g Hymns On High—Celia's Fountain (IRE) **Mr E. Chapman**

MR F. P. MURTAGH—continued

4 **CREED (IRE)**, 5, ch g Entrepreneur—Ardent Range (IRE) **Hurst Farm Racing**
5 4, B g Kris—Flower Fairy (FR) **Mr F. P. Murtagh**
6 **GIOCOMO (IRE)**, 7, ch g Indian Ridge—Karri Valley (USA) **Mugsrus**
7 **GLOBE PEARL (IRE)**, 5, b m Oscar (IRE)—Wolver Top **G. & P. Barker Ltd**
8 **HIGH CLASS PET**, 5, b m Petong—What A Pet **R. Millican**
9 **HOLLOWS MILL**, 9, b g Rudimentary (USA)—Strawberry Song **The Great Expectations Sporting Club**
10 **HOLLOWS MIST**, 7, b g Missed Flight—Joyfulness (FR) **The Great Expectations Sporting Club 2**
11 **I'M A DARK HORSE**, 4, b g Alzao (USA)—Romoosh **R. Millican**
12 **MAGENKO (IRE)**, 8, ch g Forest Wind (USA)—Bebe Auction (IRE) **R & J Wharton**
13 **MAGS TWO**, 8, b g Jumbo Hirt (USA)—Welsh Diamond **David A. Harrison**
14 **MATTHEW MY SON (IRE)**, 5, ch g Lake Coniston (IRE)—Mary Hinge **R. Millican**
15 **MINSTER BLUE**, 7, b m Minster Son—Elitist **J. M. Elliott**
16 **MINSTER BRIG**, 6, b g Minster Son—Royal Brig **R. S. Hamilton**
17 **MINSTREL'S DOUBLE**, 4, ch g Jumbo Hirt (USA)—Hand On Heart (IRE) **Minstrel's Double Racing**
18 **NORTHERN MINSTER**, 6, b g Minster Son—Hand On Heart (IRE) **Mr L. Irving & Mr T. Littleton**
19 **SPECTACULAR (IRE)**, 6, b g Spectrum (IRE)—Azra (IRE) **Spectacular Partnership**
20 **SPECTRUM STAR**, 5, b g Spectrum (IRE)—Persia (IRE) **D. O'Connor**
21 7, Ch m Rakaposhi King—Spicey Cut **David A. Harrison**
22 **TEAM RESDEV (IRE)**, 5, b m Zaffaran (USA)—Crabtreejazz (IRE) **N. M. Wright**
23 **THE COUNT (FR)**, 6, b g Sillery (USA)—Dear Countess (FR) **Jack The Lads**

Other Owners: G. J. Dowds, Mrs M. E. James, B. M. Johnson, Mrs B. Roger, E. Roger, T. D. Watson, T. W. Wilson.

Assistant Trainer: S A Murtagh

Jockey (NH): A. Dobbin, B. Harding, C. McCormack.

424
MR W. J. MUSSON, Newmarket
Postal: **Saville House, St Mary's Square, Newmarket, Suffolk, CB8 0HZ.**
Contacts: **PHONE (01638) 663371 FAX (01638) 667979**
E-MAIL williemusson@btconnect.com

1 **ANNAKITA**, 5, b m Unfuwain (USA)—Cuban Reef **Mr N. A. Rooney And Mr K. L. West**
2 **BROUGHTON BUZZER**, 4, b f Rudimentary (USA)—Broughtons Lure (IRE) **Broughton Thermal Insulation**
3 **BUON AMICI**, 4, b f Pivotal—Supreme Rose **Broughton Thermal Insulation**
4 **CRUISE DIRECTOR**, 5, b g Zilzal (USA)—Briggsmaid **Mr K. A. Cosby**
5 **DORCHESTER**, 8, b g Primo Dominie—Penthouse Lady **The Square Table**
6 **DUMARAN (IRE)**, 7, b g Be My Chief (USA)—Pine Needle **Propak Sheet Metal Limited**
7 **FINISHED ARTICLE (IRE)**, 8, b g Indian Ridge—Summer Fashion **Propak Sheet Metal Limited**
8 **FOLIO (IRE)**, 5, b g Perugino (USA)—Bayleaf **Broughton Thermal Insulation & Partner**
9 **FREE OPTION (IRE)**, 10, ch g Indian Ridge—Saneena **Mr W. J. Musson**
10 **JAIR OHMSFORD (IRE)**, 6, b g Hamas (IRE)—Harry's Irish Rose (USA) **Mr K. A. Cosby**
11 **KAREEB (FR)**, 8, b g Green Desert (USA)—Braari (USA) **The Finos Partnership**
12 **KRUGERRAND (USA)**, 6, ch g Gulch (USA)—Nasers Pride (USA) **The Square Table II**
13 **LARKING ABOUT (USA)**, 5, ch m Silver Hawk (USA)—Milly Ha Ha **Mr Christopher P. Ranson**
14 **LONGHOPE BOY**, 6, b g Rock Hopper—Always A Pleasure **R. D. Musson**
15 **PRINCE CYRANO**, 6, b g Cyrano de Bergerac—Odilese **I. K. Johnson**
16 **ROYAL PAVILLION (IRE)**, 4, b g Cape Cross—Regal Scintilla **Mr Howard Spooner**
17 **SAINTE JUST (IRE)**, 6, b g Polish Precedent (USA)—Charlotte Corday **Broughton Thermal Insulation**
18 **SISTER SOPHIA (USA)**, 5, b br m Deputy Commander (USA)—Sophia's Choice (USA) **Suffolk Racing**
19 **STAR WELCOME**, 4, ch f Most Welcome—My Greatest Star **Mrs N. A. Ward**
20 **STREET LIFE (IRE)**, 7, ch g Dolphin Street—Wolf Cleugh (IRE) **R. L. Tappin and Mrs M. Cowell**
21 **SWEET INDULGENCE (IRE)**, 4, ch g Inchinor—Silent Indulgence (USA) **Broughton Thermal Insulation**
22 **VIENNA'S BOY (IRE)**, 4, b g Victory Note (USA)—Shinkoh Rose (FR) **McGregor Bloodstock**

THREE-YEAR-OLDS

23 **BIRTHDAY STAR (IRE)**, b g Desert King (IRE)—White Paper (IRE) **Mr F. Al Tamimi**
24 **BOLODENKA (IRE)**, b g Soviet Star (USA)—My-Lorraine (IRE) **Spoons, Weaves, Jamie, Dukey**
25 **BREATHING FIRE**, b g Pivotal—Pearl Venture **Mr Howard Spooner**
26 **BROUGHTON REVIVAL**, b f Pivotal—Ella Lamees **Broughton Thermal Insulation**
27 **DEBS BROUGHTON**, b f Prince Sabo—Coy Debutante (USA) **Broughton Thermal Insulation**
28 **DESERT BAY (IRE)**, b g Desert Style (USA)—Petite Maxine **Mrs Rita Brown**
29 B f Groom Dancer (USA)—Hetra Heights (USA) **K. L. West**
30 **HIGH (IRE)**, b g Desert Story (IRE)—Sesame Heights (IRE) **Mr I. K. Johnson**

MR W. J. MUSSON—continued

31 **JEBEL AL TARIQ (IRE)**, b g Desert Style (IRE)—Song of The Glens **Mr W. J. Musson**
32 **OUTSIDE HALF (IRE)**, ch g Raise A Grand (IRE)—Lindas Delight **C. Bryce, S. Barker, N. Dower, H. Scott**

TWO-YEAR-OLDS

33 Gr f 26/2 Zaha (CAN)—Brillante (FR) (Green Dancer (USA)) (7000) **K. L. West & P. Bland**
34 **BUSKER ROYAL**, ch c 27/3 Shahrastani (USA)—Close Harmony (Bustino) **Mrs Rita Brown**
35 B f 19/3 Groom Dancer (USA)—Cressida (Polish Precedent (USA)) (3000) **Broughton Thermal Insulation**
36 B f 21/3 Bahamian Bounty—Quite Happy (IRE) (Statoblest) (2000) **Broughton Thermal Insulation**
37 Br c 27/3 Groom Dancer (USA)—Rainy Day Song (Persian Bold) (3000) **Broughton Thermal Insulation**
38 Ch f 19/3 Cadeaux Genereux—Tuxford Hideaway (Cawston's Clown) (50000) **Broughton Thermal Insulation**

Other Owners: Mr Richard Beare, Mr Peter Burke, Mr Con Dower, Mr P. C. Cornwell, Mr John Gunnell, Mr Brendan Rooney, Mrs A. Imrie, Mr Bryan Taylor, Mr David Lobban, Mr M. W. Goodey, M. E. Broughton, Mrs C. J. Broughton, Mrs D. C. Cooper, C. J. Cooper, A. J. Duke, T. M. Horsley, Mr D. McGregor, Mrs C. McGregor, J. F. Netherthorpe, I. L. Weaver.

Jockey (flat): Lisa Jones. **Apprentice:** Laura Pike, A. Rutter.

---

425 DR J. R. J. NAYLOR, Shrewton
Postal: **Cleeve Stables, Elston, Shrewton, Wiltshire, SP3 4HL.**
Contacts: **PHONE (01980) 620804 FAX (01980) 621999 MOBILE (07771) 740126**

1 **ANNIES THEME**, 7, b m Weld—Metannee **Mrs B. Bishop**
2 **AVANTI**, 9, gr h Reprimand—Dolly Bevan **Mrs S. P. Elphick**
3 **AWARDING**, 5, ch g Mark of Esteem (IRE)—Monaiya **Mrs S. P. Elphick**
4 **BELLAPORT GIRL**, 7, b m Supreme Leader—Derry Nell **Gallery Racing**
5 4, Gr g Hernando (FR)—Chambre Separee (USA)
6 **CHRISTON CANE**, 7, b g El Conquistador—Dancing Barefoot **Mrs M. Heritage**
7 **GALANDORA**, 5, b m Bijou d'inde—Jelabna **Mr M. C. Olpin**
8 **HEART SPRINGS**, 5, b m Parthian Springs—Metannee **Mrs B. Bishop**
9 **HILARIOUS (IRE)**, 5, b m Petorius—Heronwater (IRE) **Miles Electronics Ltd**
10 5, B g Dr Massini (IRE)—Icy Miss
11 **INDIAN CHANCE**, 11, b g Teenoso (USA)—Icy Miss **Chris and Stella Watson and Jock Cullen**
12 **INDIAN CHASE**, 8, b g Terimon—Icy Gunner **The Indian Chase Partnership**
13 **INDIAN GUNNER**, 12, b g Gunner B—Icy Miss **Mrs S. P. Elphick**
14 **JIM LAD**, 5, b g Young Ern—Anne's Bank (IRE) **Chris and Stella Watson**
15 **RURAL REPRIMAND**, 6, br g Reprimand—Lady Gwenmore **H. A. Smith**
16 **SEE MORE JOCK**, 7, b g Seymour Hicks (FR)—Metafan **Mrs B. Bishop**
17 **SPEARIOUS (IRE)**, 4, b g Tagula (IRE)—Gloria Crown (IRE) **Miles Electronics Ltd**
18 **WATCHFUL WITNESS**, 5, ch h In The Wings—Eternal **Mrs S. P. Elphick**

THREE-YEAR-OLDS

19 **LAUROLLIE**, b f Makbul—Madonna da Rossi **J. P. Lloyd**
20 B f Victory Note (USA)—Paddys Cocktail (IRE)

Other Owners: Mr G. A. Harrison, Mrs J. Cayford, Mrs T. Galton, Mr W. Miles, N. W. Boyd, Mrs S. R. N. Shepherd, Ms A. J. B. Smalldon, N. E. Webb.

---

426 MR J. L. NEEDHAM, Ludlow
Postal: **Gorsty Farm, Mary Knoll, Ludlow, Shropshire, SY8 2HD.**
Contacts: **PHONE (01584) 872112/874826 FAX (01584) 873256 MOBILE (07811) 451137**

1 **ANOTHER JOKER**, 10, b g Commanche Run—Just For A Laugh **Miss J. C. L. Needham**
2 **BELLASSINI**, 5, b m Dr Massini (IRE)—Carlingford Belle **Mr J. L. Needham**
3 **CLASSIC FABLE (IRE)**, 13, b m Lafontaine (USA)—Rathmill Syke **Mr J. L. Needham**
4 **FLASH HENRY**, 8, b g Executive Perk—Running Valley **Mr J. L. Needham**
5 **FOUR BELLES**, 6, ch m Fourstars Allstar (USA)—Carlingford Belle **Mr J. L. Needham**
6 6, B m Supreme Leader—Just For A Laugh **Miss J. C. L. Needham**
7 **KIRKFIELD (IRE)**, 10, b m Commanche Run—Another Grange **Mr J. L. Needham**
8 7, B g Supreme Leader—Leinthall Fox **Miss J. C. L. Needham**
9 **LUNAR FOX**, 6, b m Roselier (FR)—Leinthall Fox **Miss J. C. L. Needham**

MR J. L. NEEDHAM—continued

10 **ONE MORE NATIVE (IRE)**, 8, ch g Be My Native (USA)—Romany Fortune **Miss J. C. L. Needham**
11 **OVERAMOROUS**, 4, b f Overbury (IRE)—Random Romance **Mr J. L. Needham**

Assistant Trainer: P Hanly

Jockey (NH): T. Doyle, J. M. Maguire. **Conditional:** T. J. Phelan. **Amateur:** Mr A. Hanly.

427

MR P. NEEDHAM, Barnard Castle
Postal: **Woolhouse Farm, Marwood, Barnard Castle, Co. Durham, DL12 8RG.**
Contacts: **PHONE (01833) 690155**

1 **CHEERY MARTYR**, 7, b m Perpendicular—Kate O'kirkham **Mr P. Needham**
2 **CLASSIC LASH (IRE)**, 9, b g Classic Cheer (IRE)—Khaiylasha (IRE) **Mr P. Needham**
3 **PERCY BECK**, 9, ch g Minster Son—Kate O'kirkham **Mr P. Needham**

Assistant Trainer: Sally Richardson

Jockey (NH): C. McCormack.

428

MRS H. R. J. NELMES, Dorchester
Postal: **Warmwell Stables, 2 Church Cottages, Warmwell, Dorchester, Dorset, DT2 8HQ.**
Contacts: **PHONE/FAX (01305) 852254**
E-MAIL warmwellstud@tiscali.co.uk WEBSITE www.warmwellstud.com

1 **ARTHUR-K**, 8, ch g Greensmith—Classy Miss **K. A. Nelmes**
2 **BRAD**, 7, b g Deploy—Celia Brady **K. A. Nelmes**
3 **JUDY'S LAD**, 6, ch g Master Willie—Flexwing **K. A. Nelmes**
4 **OK SO (IRE)**, 12, ch g Naheez (USA)—Flowering Moss (IRE) **K. A. Nelmes**
5 **WEST BAY STORM**, 5, br m Relief Pitcher—West Bay Breeze **K. A. Nelmes**
6 **WILD POWER (GER)**, 7, b g Turtle Island (IRE)—White On Red (GER) **K. A. Nelmes**

Jockey (NH): O. Nelmes.

429

MR TONY NEWCOMBE, Barnstaple
Postal: **Lower Delworthy, Yarnscombe, Barnstaple, Devon, EX31 3LT.**
Contacts: **PHONE/FAX (01271) 858554 MOBILE (07785) 297210**

1 **AMONG DREAMS**, 4, ch f Among Men (USA)—Russell Creek **Dreams United**
2 **CREWES MISS ISLE**, 4, b f Makbul—Riviere Rouge **A. McRoberts**
3 **DAN DI CANIO (IRE)**, 4, b g Bahri (USA)—Khudud **Mr A. Newby**
4 **DINE 'N' DASH**, 4, ch g Komaite (USA)—Instinction **Mr A. Newby**
5 **DREAMS JEWEL**, 5, b g Dreams End—Jewel of The Nile **A. Ashcroft**
6 **ELVINA**, 4, b f Mark of Esteem (IRE)—Pharaoh's Joy **Patel, Thomas, Eagle & Capel**
7 **FIERY ANGEL (IRE)**, 4, ch f Machiavellian (USA)—Flaming June (USA) **M. K. F. Seymour**
8 **GAELIC PRINCESS**, 5, b m Cois Na Tine (IRE)—Berenice (ITY) **M. K. F. Seymour**
9 **INTO MISCHIEF**, 5, ch m Elegant Monarch—Enchanted Goddess **Mr R. John**
10 **INVER GOLD**, 8, ch h Arazi (USA)—Mary Martin **M. Patel**
11 **KENTUCKY BULLET (USA)**, 9, b g Housebuster (USA)—Exactly So **Mrs E. M. Sherwin**
12 **KNICKYKNACKIENOO**, 4, b g Bin Ajwaad (IRE)—Ring Fence **Mr Tony Newcombe**
13 **KNOCKTOPHER ABBEY**, 8, ch g Pursuit of Love—Kukri **Mr Tony Newcombe**
14 **MASTER OF STAFFORD**, 9, b g Salse (USA)—Artist's Glory **Lavis Medical Systems Ltd**
15 **MIDDLETON GREY**, 7, gr g Ashkalani (IRE)—Petula **Mr B. Ryan**
16 **MISS SKIPPY**, 6, b m Saddlers' Hall (IRE)—Katie Scarlett **Steadshaw Partnership**
17 **MONTGOMERY**, 4, b g In Command (IRE)—Lightening Reef **A. Beard**
18 **MOSCOW MARY**, 4, b f Imperial Ballet (IRE)—Baileys Firecat **A. Beard**
19 **MUFREH (USA)**, 7, br g Dayjur (USA)—Mathkurh (USA) **M. K. F. Seymour**
20 **NIMELLO (USA)**, 9, b g Kingmambo (USA)—Zakota (IRE) **Ms G. P. O'Reilly**
21 **NUKHBAH (USA)**, 4, b f Bahri (USA)—El Nafis (USA) **Mr A. G. Newcombe**
22 **ONETHREESIXSQADRON**, 7, b g Bandmaster (USA)—Paprika (IRE) **Lavis Medical Systems Ltd**
23 **RESONATE (IRE)**, 7, b h Erins Isle—Petronelli (USA) **S. D. Langridge**
24 **SAMARA SOUND**, 4, b c Savahra Sound—Hosting **S. F. Turton**
25 **TETCOTT (IRE)**, 4, ch f Definite Article—Charlene Lacy (IRE) **Bramhill, Holbrooke & Patel**
26 **THE BEST YET**, 7, ch h King's Signet (USA)—Miss Klew **Mr A. G. Newcombe**

MR TONY NEWCOMBE—continued

27 THE KING OF ROCK, 4, b c Nicolotte—Lv Girl (IRE) **Ms G. P. O'Reilly**
28 WIND CHIME (IRE), 8, ch h Arazi (USA)—Shamisen **M. K. F. Seymour**
29 WISHIN AND HOPIN, 4, b g Danzig Connection (USA)—Trina's Pet **Mr A. G. Newcombe**

THREE-YEAR-OLDS

30 BAILEYS HONOUR, b f Mark of Esteem (IRE)—Kanz (USA) **Mr D. Bramhill**
31 BEFORE THE DAWN, b f Lugana Beach—Chayanee's Arena (IRE) **Steadshaw Partnership 2**
32 BLENDON BELLE (FR), f Lugana Beach—Palace Green (IRE) **Blendon Communications**
33 BLENDON BOY (IRE), b g Brave Act—Negria (IRE) **Blendon Communications**
34 PRINCESS ZARA, b f Zaha (CAN)—Otaru (IRE) **M. K. F. Seymour**
35 RIBBONS OF GOLD, b f Primo Dominie—In Love Again (IRE) **Mr D. Bramhill**
36 SOLAR FALCON, ch f Polar Falcon (USA)—Beryl **Steadshaw Partnership**
37 Ch c Mark of Esteem (IRE)—Subtle One (IRE) **A. Beard**

TWO-YEAR-OLDS

38 BARNEY GOLD, br c 27/2 Superior Premium—Cyber Babe (IRE) (Persian Bold) **Mrs J. Bramhill**
39 Ch c 28/2 Zaha (CAN)—Cats Bottom (Primo Dominie) **M. K. F. Seymour**
40 B c 28/1 Superior Premium—Chayanee's Arena (IRE) (High Estate) (1000) **M. K. F. Seymour**
41 B f 18/2 Superior Premium—Fortuitious (IRE) (Polish Patriot (USA)) **Mr A. G. Newcombe**
42 Gr f 1/4 Superior Premium—Goody Four Shoes (Blazing Saddles (AUS)) **Mr A. G. Newcombe**
43 Br c 17/2 Hamas (IRE)—Kaliala (FR) (Pharly (FR)) **Mr C. Bradbury**
44 B f 22/3 Superior Premium—Lundy Lady (Rudimentary (USA)) **Mr A. G. Newcombe**
45 Ch f 3/3 Zaha (CAN)—Parisian Lady (IRE) (Paris House) **M. K. F. Seymour**
46 Br c 7/3 Superior Premium—Quartermark (IRE) (General Monash (USA)) (800) **Mr A. G. Newcombe**
47 Ch c 28/2 Zaha (CAN)—Victoriet (Hamas (IRE)) (2000) **Mr A. G. Newcombe**

Other Owners: N. S. Shaw, Mr M. D. Stead, H. Wetter.

Assistant Trainer: John Lovejoy

Jockey (flat): D. O'Neill, C. Catlin, S. Whitworth. **Jockey (NH):** B. J. Crowley, A. Thornton. **Apprentice:** L. Keniry. **Amateur:** Miss C. Hannaford.

---

430 **MISS A. M. NEWTON-SMITH, Polegate**
Postal: Bull Pen Cottage, Jevington, Polegate, East Sussex, BN26 5QB.
Contacts: PHONE (01323) 488354 FAX (01323) 482525 MOBILE (07970) 914124
E-MAIL charlestonracing.hotmail.com

1 COME BYE (IRE), 9, b g Star Quest—Boreen Dubh **PPS Racing**
2 COPPER SHELL, 11, ch g Beveled (USA)—Luly My Love **Brighton Racing Club**
3 DOUBLE AGENT, 12, ch g Niniski (USA)—Rexana **E. J. Farrant**
4 HURDLE (FR), 10, gr g Dadarissime (FR)—Ulisa II (FR) **F. G. Wilson**
5 HURRICANE DIPPER (IRE), 7, b g Glacial Storm (USA)—Minnies Dipper **Mrs S. B. S. Grist**
6 JAYCEE STAR (IRE), 4, ch f Idris (IRE)—Shantung (IRE) **Mrs J. C. Coombs**
7 JOLLYSHAU (IRE), 7, b g Jolly Jake (NZ)—Escheat **M. O. Coates**
8 SINTOS, 7, b br g Syrtos—Sindur **Mrs S. B. S. Grist**
9 SONDERBORG, 4, b f Great Dane (IRE)—Nordico Princess **H. F. Le Fanu**
10 TOMICH (IRE), 10, b br g Lord Americo—Gilt Course **J. P. Smith**

Other Owners: R. Delacroix, His Honour Judge A. Patience, J. R. Peppitt, A. K. Walker.

Jockey (flat): Lisa Jones, Hayley Turner. **Jockey (NH):** M. Batchelor. **Conditional:** C. Bolger. **Amateur:** Mr C. Gordon.

---

431 **MR D. NICHOLLS, Thirsk**
Postal: Tall Trees Racing Ltd, Tall Trees, Sessay, Thirsk, North Yorkshire, YO7 3ND.
Contacts: PHONE (01845) 501470 FAX (01845) 501666 MOBILE (07971) 555105
E-MAIL david.nicholls@btconnect.com WEBSITE www.davidnichollsracing.com

1 ALBASHOOSH, 7, b g Cadeaux Genereux—Annona (USA) **M. J. Pipe**
2 AMERICAN COUSIN, 10, b g Distant Relative—Zelda (USA) **Middleham Park Racing XIV**
3 APERITIF, 4, ch g Pivotal—Art Deco Lady **Mr D. Nicholls**
4 ARTIE'S LAD (IRE), 4, ch g Danehill Dancer (IRE)—Bold Avril (IRE) **The McCauley Boys**
5 ATLANTIC VIKING (IRE), 10, b g Danehill (USA)—Hi Bettina **Paul Kinane, Daily Mail**

MR D. NICHOLLS—continued

6 **AWAKE**, 8, ch g First Trump—Pluvial **Lucayan Stud & D. Nicholls**
7 **BAHAMIAN PIRATE (USA)**, 10, ch g Housebuster (USA)—Shining Through (USA) **Lucayan Stud Ltd**
8 **BAILIEBOROUGH (IRE)**, 6, b g Charnwood Forest (IRE)—Sherannda (USA) **Middleham Park Racing XVIII**
9 **BALLYBUNION (IRE)**, 6, ch g Entrepreneur—Clarentia **Mr I Blakey, Mr M Gosse, Mr D Nicholls**
10 **BANJO BAY (IRE)**, 7, b g Common Grounds—Thirlmere **Middleham Park Racing XXIII**
11 **BLACKHEATH (IRE)**, 9, ch g Common Grounds—
　　　　　　　　　　　　　　Queen Caroline (USA) **Middleham Park Racing XX & Streamhill**
12 **BRAVE BURT (IRE)**, 8, ch g Pips Pride—Friendly Song **Lucayan Stud Ltd**
13 **CANDLERIGGS (IRE)**, 9, ch g Indian Ridge—Ridge Pool (IRE) **Mr D. Nicholls**
14 **CAPTAIN CLIPPER**, 5, b g Royal Applause—Collide **Clipper Group Holdings Ltd**
15 **COLONEL COTTON (IRE)**, 6, b g Royal Applause—Cutpurse Moll **A A Bloodstock Ltd**
16 **CONTINENT**, 8, ch g Lake Coniston (IRE)—Krisia **Lucayan Stud Ltd**
17 **DANZIG RIVER (IRE)**, 4, b g Green Desert (USA)—Sahara Breeze **Mrs J. Graves**
18 **ETON (GER)**, 9, ch g Suave Dancer (USA)—Ermione **The McCauley Boys**
19 **FANLING LADY**, 4, gr f Highest Honor (FR)—Pain Perdu (IRE) **A. R. Turnbull**
20 **FIRE UP THE BAND**, 6, b h Prince Sabo—Green Supreme **Mr P. Crane, Mr A. Barker & Mr S. Short**
21 **FOUR AMIGOS (USA)**, 4, b g Southern Halo (USA)—Larentia **A A Bloodstock Ltd**
22 **FOURTH DIMENSION (IRE)**, 6, b g Entrepreneur—Isle of Spice (USA) **The McCauley Boys**
23 **FREMEN (USA)**, 5, ch g Rahy (USA)—Northern Trick (USA) **Claire King**
24 **FULL AS A ROCKET (IRE)**, 4, b g Foxhound—Taysala (IRE) **H W Racing**
25 **FUNFAIR WANE**, 6, b g Unfuwain (USA)—Ivory Bride **Mrs Jean Keegan & Mr D. Nicholls**
26 **GIFT HORSE**, 5, ch g Cadeaux Genereux—Careful Dancer **Alfi and Partners**
27 **GOLDEN SPECTRUM (IRE)**, 6, ch g Spectrum (IRE)—Plessaya (USA) **T. G. Meynell**
28 **GROWLER**, 4, ch g Foxhound—Femme Femme (USA) **Turf 2000 Limited**
29 **HAMAASY**, 4, b g Machiavellian (USA)—Sakha **J. P. Honeyman**
30 **HICCUPS**, 5, b g Polar Prince (IRE)—Simmie's Special **J. M. & Mrs E. E. Ranson**
31 **ICE PLANET**, 4, b c Polar Falcon (USA)—Preference **David Faulkner**
32 **ISLANDS FAREWELL**, 5, b g Emarati (USA)—Chief Island **H. G. W. Brown**
33 **LA VIE EST BELLE**, 4, b f Makbul—La Belle Vie **I. J. Blakey**
34 **LAFI (IRE)**, 6, ch g Indian Ridge—Petal Girl **Alfi and Partners**
35 **LAGO D'ORTA (IRE)**, 5, ch g Bahhare—Maelalong (IRE) **Chalfont Foodhalls Ltd**
36 **LORD OF THE EAST**, 6, b g Emarati (USA)—Fairy Free **The Wayward Lads**
37 **LUCAYAN DANCER (IRE)**, 5, b g Zieten (USA)—Tittle Tattle (IRE) **Lucayan Stud Ltd**
38 **MACHINIST (IRE)**, 5, br g Machiavellian (USA)—Athene (IRE) **M. J. Pipe**
39 **MAREN (USA)**, 4, b g Gulch (USA)—Fatina **V. P. Greaves**
40 **MERLIN'S DANCER**, 5, b g Magic Ring (IRE)—La Piaf (FR) **Chalfont Foodhalls Ltd**
41 **NATIVE TITLE**, 7, b g Pivotal—Bermuda Lily **C. McKenna**
42 **NEMO FUGAT (IRE)**, 6, b g Danehill Dancer (USA)—Do The Right Thing **J. A. Hair**
43 **ONLYTIME WILL TELL**, 7, ch g Efisio—Prejudice **Mr D. Faulkner & Mr J. Hair**
44 **PAX**, 8, ch g Brief Truce (USA)—Child's Play **Mr D. Nicholls**
45 **PIETER BRUEGHEL (USA)**, 6, b g Citidancer (USA)—Smart Tally (USA) **David Faulkner**
46 **PLATEAU**, 6, b g Zamindar (USA)—Painted Desert **A A Bloodstock Ltd**
47 **PRIMUS INTER PARES (IRE)**, 4, b g Sadler's Wells (USA)—Life At The Top **A A Bloodstock Ltd**
48 **PROUD BOAST**, 7, b m Komaite (USA)—Red Rosein **Mr P. D. Savill**
49 **ROYAL DIGNITARY (USA)**, 5, br g Saint Ballado (CAN)—Star Actress (USA) **Middleham Park Racing**
50 **RUDI'S PET (IRE)**, 11, ch g Don't Forget Me—Pink Fondant **Miss A. J. Watson**
51 **SAWWAAH (IRE)**, 8, b g Marju (IRE)—Just A Mirage **Fayzad Thoroughbred Ltd**
52 **SCOTTY'S FUTURE (IRE)**, 7, b g Namaqualand (USA)—Persian Empress (IRE) **Lucayan Stud Ltd**
53 **SELECTIVE**, 6, b g Selkirk (USA)—Portelet **A A Bloodstock Ltd**
54 **SERIEUX**, 6, b g Cadeaux Genereux—Seranda (IRE) **A A Bloodstock Ltd**
55 **SIR DON (IRE)**, 6, b g Lake Coniston (IRE)—New Sensitive **Mrs D. Plant**
56 **SMIRFYS PARTY**, 7, ch g Clantime—Party Scenes **Mrs D. Plant**
57 **SUSIEDIL (IRE)**, 4, b f Mujadil (USA)—Don't Take Me (IRE) **Dream On**
58 **TRINCULO (IRE)**, 8, b g Anita's Prince—Fandangerina (USA) **N. R. Shields**
59 **TRUE NIGHT**, 8, b g Night Shift (USA)—Dead Certain **Mrs L. Scaife, Mrs S. Radford**
60 **TURTLE DANCER (IRE)**, 7, b g Turtle Island (IRE)—Love Me Please (IRE) **Mr D. Nicholls**
61 **VICIOUS KNIGHT**, 7, b g Night Shift (USA)—Myth **The McCauley Boys**
62 **WANCHAI LAD**, 4, b c Danzero (AUS)—Frisson **A. R. Turnbull**
63 **WISTMAN (UAE)**, 4, br g Woodman (USA)—Saik (USA) **Fayzad Thoroughbred Ltd**
64 **ZIETZIG (IRE)**, 8, b g Zieten (USA)—Missing You **Mrs C. L. Swiers**

MR D. NICHOLLS—continued

THREE-YEAR-OLDS

65 **CHAIRMAN RICK (IRE)**, b c Danehill Dancer (IRE)—Come Together **Lucayan Stud Ltd**
66 **DESERT LOVER (IRE)**, b g Desert Prince (IRE)—Crystal Flute **Lucayan Stud Ltd**
67 **EXIT SMILING**, ch c Dr Fong (USA)—Away To Me **Mrs L. Scaife, Mrs S. Radford**
68 **KEYS OF CYPRUS**, ch g Deploy—Krisia **Lucayan Stud Ltd**
69 **MAYS DREAM**, b f Josr Algarhoud (IRE)—Amber Mill **D. S. & W. L. Armstrong Ltd**
70 B g Desert Style (IRE)—Nomadic Dancer (IRE) **A A Bloodstock Ltd**
71 **ON THE BRIGHT SIDE**, b f Cyrano de Bergerac—Jade Pet **The Oak Tree Syndicate**
72 **SONIC ANTHEM (USA)**, b g Royal Anthem (USA)—Whisperifyoudare (USA) **Middleham Park Racing XVII**
73 **STANLEY ARTHUR**, b g Mind Games—Midnight Orchid (IRE) **A A Bloodstock Ltd**
74 **STRAFFAN (IRE)**, b br f Shinko Forest (IRE)—Katherine Gorge (USA) **G G N Bloodstock Ltd**
75 **TAX FREE (IRE)**, b c Tagula (IRE)—Grandel **I. Hewitson**
76 **THEATRE OF DREAMS**, b g Averti (IRE)—Loch Fyne **Mr D. Nicholls**
77 **VICTORIA PEEK (IRE)**, b f Cape Cross (IRE)—Night Spirit (IRE) **A. R. Turnbull**

TWO-YEAR-OLDS

78 **CAPITAL LASS**, b br f 3/4 Forzando—Fair Test (Fair Season) (3500)
79 **CHING CHING (IRE)**, b c 12/5 Desert Prince (IRE)—Sudeley (Dancing Brave (USA)) **Mr M. Pipe**
80 **IMPERIAL LUCKY (IRE)**, b f 24/4 Desert Story (IRE)—Irina (IRE) (Polar Falcon (USA)) (3000) **D. Cohen**
81 **IMPERIAL SOLDIER (IRE)**, b c 10/2 Fasliyev (USA)—Hopping Higgins (IRE) (Brief Truce (USA)) (11000) **D. Cohen**
82 B c 17/3 Grand Lodge (USA)—Licorne (Sadler's Wells (USA)) (25000) **Chalfont Foodhalls Ltd**
83 **PRINCE ZAFONIC**, ch c 14/2 Zafonic (USA)—Kite Mark (Mark of Esteem (IRE)) (25000) **Mr A. Saha**
84 **STRIKE UP THE BAND**, b c 13/2 Cyrano de Bergerac—
Green Supreme (Primo Dominie) (42000) **The Oak Apple Syndicate**

Other Owners: M. Dixon, H.E. Lhendup Dorji, D. Frame, J. D. Gains, J. A. Hair, P.J. Jacobs, G. H. Leatham, M. A. Leatham, T. S. Palin, H. J. Rix, Mrs D. P. Sanders, P. B. Sanders, M. J. Waite, H. J. Walker, K. R. Wills.

Assistant Trainer: Ben Beasley, Ernie Greaves

Jockey (flat): Alex Greaves. **Apprentice:** P. J. Benson. **Amateur:** Miss Kelly Harrison, Mrs N. Wilson.

---

432 MR P. F. NICHOLLS, Shepton Mallet
Postal: **Manor Farm Stables, Ditcheat, Shepton Mallet, Somerset, BA4 6RD.**
Contacts: **PHONE** (01749) 860656 **FAX** (01749) 860523
E-MAIL info@paulnichollsracing.com

1 **AD HOC (IRE)**, 11, b g Strong Gale—Knockarctic **Sir Robert Ogden C.B.E., LLD**
2 **AIDE DE CAMP (FR)**, 6, b g Saint Preuil (FR)—Baraka De Thaix II (FR) **Sir Robert Ogden C.B.E., LLD**
3 **AIN'T THAT A SHAME (IRE)**, 5, ch g Broken Hearted—Alvinru **Ashleybank Investments Limited**
4 **ALBUHERA (IRE)**, 7, b g Desert Style (IRE)—Morning Welcome (IRE) **D. J. & F. A. Jackson**
5 **ALEXANDERTHEGREAT (IRE)**, 7, b g Saddlers' Hall (IRE)—Sandy Jayne (IRE) **The Irish Connection**
6 **ALMOST BROKE**, 8, ch g Nearly A Hand—Teletex **A. G. Fear**
7 **ANDREAS (FR)**, 5, b g Marchand de Sable (USA)—Muscova Dancer (FR) **M. Tincknell**
8 **ARMARIVER (FR)**, 5, ch g River Mist (USA)—Armalita (FR) **B. Millard**
9 **ARMATURK (FR)**, 8, ch g Baby Turk—Armalita (FR) **B. C. Marshall**
10 **ASK HENRY (IRE)**, 9, b br g Jolly Jake (NZ)—Pineway VII **Mrs M. G. Barber**
11 **ASPIRING ACTOR (IRE)**, 5, b g Old Vic—Stasias Dream (IRE) **Mrs J. A. Stewart**
12 **AZERTYUIOP (FR)**, 8, b g Baby Turk—Temara (FR) **J. R. Hales**
13 **AZZEMOUR (FR)**, 6, ch g Morespeed—Tarde (FR) **Tony Hayward and Barry Fulton**
14 **BANCHORY TWO (IRE)**, 5, b g Un Desperado (FR)—Theyllallwin (IRE) **B. C. Marshall**
15 **BE BE KING (IRE)**, 6, b g Bob Back (USA)—Trimar Gold **Mr C. G. Roach**
16 **BEEHAWK**, 6, b g Gunner B—Cupids Bower **R. D. Cox**
17 **BLUE AMERICO (IRE)**, 7, br g Lord Americo—Princess Menelek **Mrs A. Tincknell**
18 **BLUE BROOK**, 6, ch g Alderbrook—Connaught's Pride **Mrs A. Tincknell**
19 **BLUE BUSINESS**, 7, br g Roselier (FR)—Miss Redlands **Mrs A. Tincknell**
20 **BLUE ENDEAVOUR (IRE)**, 7, b g Endeavour (USA)—Jingle Bells (FR) **Mrs A. Tincknell**
21 **BLUSHING BULL**, 6, b g Makbul—Blush **Blushing Bull Partnership**
22 **BUNRATTY CASTLE (IRE)**, 10, b g Supreme Leader—Shannon Foam **T.J. Hawkins, D.J. Nichols, A.J. White**
23 **CENKOS (FR)**, 11, ch g Nikos—Vincenza **Mrs J. A. Stewart**
24 **CERIUM (FR)**, 4, b g Vaguely Pleasant (FR)—Tantatura (FR) **B Fulton, T Hayward, S Fisher, L Brady**
25 **CHAMOSS ROYALE (FR)**, 5, ch m Garde Royale—Chamoss (FR) **Mrs K. A. Stuart**
26 **CHEF TARTARE (FR)**, 5, b g Nikos—Rive Tartare (FR) **Million in Mind Partnership**

MR P. F. NICHOLLS—continued

27 **CHOCKDEE (FR)**, 5, b g King's Theatre (IRE)—Chagrin d'amour (IRE) **Mr and Mrs J. D. Cotton**
28 **COLOURFUL LIFE (IRE)**, 9, ch g Rainbows For Life (CAN)—Rasmara **Andy Peake & David Jackson**
29 **COMANCHE WAR PAINT (IRE)**, 8, b g Commanche Run—Galeshula **Tony Fear & Tim Hawkins**
30 **CORNISH REBEL (IRE)**, 8, br g Un Desperado (FR)—Katday (FR) **C. G. Roach**
31 **CORNISH SETT (IRE)**, 6, b g Accordion—Hue 'n' Cry (IRE) **Formpave Ltd**
32 **DARRIAS (GER)**, 4, b g Sternkoenig (IRE)—Dark Lady (GER) **Formpave Ltd**
33 **DUSTY BANDIT (IRE)**, 7, ch g Un Desperado (FR)—Marble Miller (IRE) **Mrs J. A. Stewart**
34 **EARTH MAN (IRE)**, 8, b g Hamas (IRE)—Rajaura (IRE) **Mr R. M. Penny**
35 **EARTHMOVER (IRE)**, 14, ch g Mister Lord (USA)—Clare's Crystal **Mr R. M. Penny**
36 **EAST LAWYER (FR)**, 6, b g Homme de Loi (IRE)—East Riding (FR) **Champneys Partnership**
37 **EMANIC (FR)**, 5, b g Video Rock (FR)—Una Volta (FR) **D. J. & F. A. Jackson**
38 **ESCAYOLA (IRE)**, 5, b g Revoque (IRE)—First Fling (IRE) **Mrs M. Findlay**
39 **EUROTREK (IRE)**, 9, ch g Eurobus (IRE)—Orient Jewel **P. C. Green**
40 **EXIT TO WAVE (FR)**, 9, ch g Exit To Nowhere (USA)—Hereke **Mr Malcolm Pearce & Mr Gerry Mizel II**
41 **FASGO (IRE)**, 10, b g Montelimar (USA)—Action Plan **F. A. Smith**
42 **FRENCH EXECUTIVE (IRE)**, 10, br g Beau Sher—
                                            Executive Move (IRE) **T.Chappell,R.Eddy,Mrs Jackson,Mrs Solman**
43 **GALAPIAT DU MESNIL (FR)**, 11, b g Sarpedon (FR)—Polka De Montrin (FR) **Mel Fordham**
44 **GENERAL CLAREMONT (IRE)**, 12, gr g Strong Gale—Kasam **K. G. Manley**
45 **GET MY DRIFT (FR)**, 6, b g Beneficial—Boreen Bro **Mr Tony Ambler & Mr Paul K. Barber**
46 **GIVE ME LOVE (FR)**, 5, ch g Bering—Cout Contact (USA) **C. Harriman**
47 **GOBLET OF FIRE (USA)**, 6, b g Green Desert (USA)—Laurentine (USA) **Mrs A. Tincknell**
48 **GORTNAVARNOGUE (IRE)**, 7, br g Phardante (FR)—Strong-Galeforce (IRE) **J. Duggan**
49 **GRANDE CREOLE (FR)**, 6, b g Byzantium (FR)—Sclos (FR) **Sir Robert Ogden C.B.E., LLD**
50 **GREAT TRAVEL (FR)**, 6, b g Great Palm (USA)—Travel Free **Mrs J. A. Stewart**
51 **HARAPOUR (FR)**, 7, b g Valanour (IRE)—Haratiyna **Mrs J. Smith**
52 **HEROS COLLONGES (FR)**, 10, b g Dom Alco (FR)—Carmen Collonges (FR) **J. R. Hales**
53 **HO HO HILL (IRE)**, 7, b g Beneficial—Bale Out **Mrs Mary Coburn & Mr Paul K Barber**
54 **HOT 'N' HOLY**, 6, b g Supreme Leader—Clonmello **Paul K. Barber & C. G. Roach**
55 **HOWDYDOODY (IRE)**, 9, b g Hawkstone (IRE)—Larry's Law (IRE) **Brian Blinman**
56 **IBAL (FR)**, 9, b g Balsamo (FR)—Quart D'hekla (FR) **T. Hayward & B. Fulton**
57 **INCA TRAIL (IRE)**, 9, br g Un Desperado (FR)—Katday (FR) **Mrs Susie Chown & Mrs Kathy Stuart**
58 **INDIEN ROYAL (FR)**, 6, b g Dauphin du Bourg (FR)—Royale Nabeysse (FR) **Mrs K. A. Stuart**
59 **KADAM (IRE)**, 5, b g Night Shift (USA)—Kadassa (IRE) **Notalotterry**
60 **KADARANN (IRE)**, 8, b g Bigstone (FR)—Kadassa (IRE) **Notalotterry**
61 **KAROO**, 7, b g Karinga Bay—Cupids Bower **R. D. Cox**
62 **KAUTO STAR (FR)**, 5, br g Village Star (FR)—Kauto Relka (FR) **C. D. Smith**
63 **KJETIL (USA)**, 5, b g King of Kings (IRE)—I Wich (FR) **C. D. Smith**
64 **L'ANGE AU CIEL (FR)**, 6, b g Agent Bleu (FR)—Epopee II (FR) **B. C. Marshall**
65 **L'AVENTURE (FR)**, 6, b m Cyborg (FR)—Amphitrite (FR) **C. J. Harriman**
66 **L'OUDON (FR)**, 4, ch g Alamo Bay (USA)—Stella Di Corte (FR) **Gerry Mizel & Terry Warner**
67 **LADALKO (FR)**, 6, b g Kadalko (FR)—Debandade (FR) **Mr Paul K Barber & Mrs M Findlay**
68 **LAYASAR**, 5, br g Wizard King—Rasayel (USA) **Mr A. W. Penton**
69 **LE DUC (FR)**, 6, b g Villez (USA)—Beberova (FR) **Mrs J. A. Stewart**
70 **LE JAGUAR (FR)**, 5, b g Freeland (FR)—Fee La Maline (FR) **The Connaught "Le Jaguar" Syndicate**
71 **LE PASSING (FR)**, 6, b g Passing Sale (FR)—
                                            Petite Serenade (FR) **The Hon Mrs C. A. Townshend & Mr J. R. Townshend**
72 **LE ROI MIGUEL (FR)**, 7, b g Point of No Return (FR)—Loumir (USA) **Mrs J. A. Stewart**
73 **LE SEYCHELLOIS (FR)**, 5, ch g Mansonnien (FR)—Adjirah (FR) **C. D. Smith**
74 **LORD LINGTON (FR)**, 6, b g Bulington (FR)—Tosca de Bussy (FR) **Mr Paul K Barber & Mrs M Findlay**
75 **LORD OF THE ROAD (FR)**, 6, b g Gildoran—Ethels Course **The Eight Amigos Racing Syndicate**
76 **LOU DU MOULIN MAS (FR)**, 6, b g Sassanian (USA)—Houf (FR) **The Eight Amigos Racing Syndicate**
77 5, B g Supreme Leader—Luminous Girl **Mrs J. A. Stewart**
78 **LUNCH WAS MY IDEA (IRE)**, 5, b br g Tawrrific (NZ)—Equity Law (IRE) **D. J. Nichols**
79 **LUNERAY (FR)**, 6, b m Poplar Bluff—Casandre (FR) **Sandicroft Stud**
80 **MADE IN MONTOT (FR)**, 5, b g Video Rock (FR)—Deep Turple (FR) **The Hon Mrs C. A. Townshend**
81 **MAIFUL (FR)**, 5, b g Useful (FR)—Shailann (FR) **Hill Fuels Limited**
82 **MANLY MONEY**, 7, b g Homo Sapien—Susie's Money **Mrs S. Chown**
83 **MONTE CINTO (FR)**, 5, br g Bulington (FR)—Algue Rouge (FR) **Mrs M. Hackett**
84 **MONTI FLYER**, 7, b g Terimon—Coole Pilate **www.thrillofownership.co.uk**
85 **MONTIFAULT (FR)**, 10, ch g Morespeed—Tarde (FR) **Mrs A. Fulton**
86 **MORSON BOY (USA)**, 5, b g Lear Fan (USA)—Esprit d'escalier (USA) **G. A. Mason**
87 **MOUSESKI**, 11, b g Petoski—Worth Matravers **M. H. Dare**
88 **MY WILL (FR)**, 5, b g Saint Preuil (FR)—Gleep Will (FR) **Mrs J. A. Stewart**
89 **NANGA PARBAT (FR)**, 4, b g True Brave (USA)—Celeste (FR) **Mrs K. A. Stuart**
90 **NAPOLITAIN (FR)**, 4, b g Ajdayt (USA)—Domage II (FR) **Mrs J. A. Stewart**

MR P. F. NICHOLLS—continued

91 **NIPPY DES MOTTES (FR)**, 4, b c Useful (FR)—Julie des Mottes (FR) **Mr Paul Green**
92 **NOLAND**, 4, b g Exit To Nowhere (USA)—Molakai (USA) **Mr John Hales and Miss Lisa Hales**
93 **NOTRE CYBORG (FR)**, 4, ch g Cyborg (FR)—Cate Bleue (FR) **G. Roach**
94 **ORACLE DES MOTTES (FR)**, 6, b g Signe Divin (USA)—Daisy des Mottes (FR) **M. Tincknell**
95 **PARSON PLOUGHMAN**, 10, br g Riverwise (USA)—Pretty Pantoes **A. W. Wadsworth**
96 **PATCHES (IRE)**, 6, b br g Presenting—Ballykilleen **Mrs M. G. Barber**
97 **PEARLY BAY**, 7, b m Karinga Bay—Marina Bird **Sandicroft Stud**
98 **PEROUSE**, 7, ch g Alderbrook—Track Angel **J. Dickson & S. McVie**
99 **PIRATE FLAGSHIP (FR)**, 6, b g River Mist—Sacadu **C. G. Roach**
100 **PITMINSTER**, 7, b g Karinga Bay—Eleanora Muse **R. H. Dunn**
101 **QUID PRO QUO (FR)**, 6, b g Cadoudal (FR)—Luzenia (USA) **Sir Robert Ogden C.B.E., LLD**
102 **RED DEVIL ROBERT (IRE)**, 7, ch g Carroll House—Well Over **Barry Marshall & Paul K Barber**
103 **REFLECTED GLORY (IRE)**, 6, b g Flemensfirth (USA)—Clashdermot Lass **D. G. Millard**
104 **RIGMAROLE**, 7, b g Fairy King (USA)—Cattermole (USA) **Mr & Mrs Mark Woodhouse**
105 **ROBYN ALEXANDER (IRE)**, 7, ch m Sharifabad (IRE)—Flagship Ahoy (IRE) **J. G. Hordle**
106 **ROYAL AUCLAIR (FR)**, 8, ch g Garde Royale—Carmonera (FR) **C. D. Smith**
107 **SHOTGUN WILLY (IRE)**, 11, ch g Be My Native (USA)—Minorettes Girl **C. G. Roach**
108 **SILENCE REIGNS**, 11, b g Saddlers' Hall (IRE)—Rensaler (USA) **The Madness Prevails Partnership**
109 **SILVER BIRCH (IRE)**, 8, b g Clearly Bust—All Gone **D. J. Nichols**
110 **SILVER JEWEL (IRE)**, 6, gr g Roselier (FR)—Martin's Pet (IRE) **Mr & Mrs Mark Woodhouse**
111 **SLEEPING MARGOT (IRE)**, 9, b g Sleeping Car (FR)—Doll Night (FR) **D. J. Jackson**
112 **SMUDGE (IRE)**, 8, br g Be My Native (USA)—Crash Call **Mrs B. P. Siddall**
113 **SPRING MARGOT (FR)**, 9, b g Kadalko (FR)—La Brunante (FR) **Sir Robert Ogden C.B.E., LLD**
114 **STAR DE MOHAISON (FR)**, 4, b g Beyssac (FR)—Belle De Mohaison (FR) **Sir Robert Ogden C.B.E., LLD**
115 **STRONG FLOW (IRE)**, 8, br g Over The River (FR)—Stormy Skies **B. C. Marshall**
116 **SWEET DIVERSION (IRE)**, 6, b g Carroll House—Serocco Wind **I. Marshall**
117 **TARANIS (FR)**, 4, ch g Mansonnien (FR)—Vikosa (FR) **Mrs A. Yeoman**
118 **THE BAG MAN**, 6, b g Alflora (IRE)—Lady Claudia (IRE) **J. Dickson & S. McVie**
119 **THE PERSUADER (IRE)**, 5, b g Sadler's Wells (USA)—Sister Dot (USA) **D. J. & F. A. Jackson**
120 **THISTHATANDTOTHER (IRE)**, 9, b g Bob Back (USA)—Baden (IRE) **C. G. Roach**
121 **TORDUFF EXPRESS (IRE)**, 14, b g Kambalda—Marhabtain **Two Plus Two**
122 **UN JOUR A VASSY (FR)**, 10, b g Video Rock (FR)—Bayalika (FR) **Mrs A. M. Millard**
123 **WERE IN TOUCH (IRE)**, 7, b g Old Vic—Winterland Gale (IRE) **Paul Barber,Malcolm Calvert,Colin Lewis**
124 **WHITENZO (FR)**, 9, b g Lesotho (USA)—Whitenzy (FR) **Mr Malcolm Pearce & Mr Gerry Mizel II**
125 **WHITFORD DON (IRE)**, 7, b g Accordion—Whitford Breeze **J. R. Hales**
126 **WILD CHIMES (IRE)**, 6, b g Oscar (IRE)—Jingle Bells **D. Chown**

Other Owners: R. Barber, I. Bewley, J. P. Blakeney, A. R. Bromley, Miss K. S. Buckley, R. V. S. Castle, Mr J. L. Coombs, J. G. Crumpler, D. R. Febry, J. M. French, G. F. Goode, A. P Green, Miss L. J. Hales, J. S. Middleton, W. D. C. Minton, M. Morgan, C. J. Nelson, David Nicholson, T. H. Northwood, S. J. Purdew, Mrs C. L. Solman, P. G. Stockdale, W. C. Tincknell.

Assistant Trainer: Daniel Skelton

Jockey (NH): J. Tizzard, R. Walsh. **Conditional:** Colm Sharkey, Christian Williams. **Amateur:** Mr N. Williams, Miss Rilly Goschen, Mr L. Heard, Miss C. Roddick, Miss C. Tizzard.

---

433 MR P. D. NIVEN, Malton
Postal: Clovafield, Barton-Le-Street, Malton, North Yorkshire, YO17 6PN.
Contacts: (01653) 628176 MOBILE (07860) 260999
E-MAIL willmary@onetel.net.uk

1 **ACTUAL**, 5, b g Factual (USA)—Tugra (FR)
2 **ADIOS (GER)**, 6, b g Lagunas—Aerope **I. G. M. Dalgleish**
3 **ANTIGONE'S FIRE**, 6, b m Lycius (USA)—Buzzbomb **J. P. Wise**
4 **BALLYHALE (IRE)**, 7, br g Mister Lord (USA)—Deep Inagh **R. A. Bartlett**
5 **BATTIES DEN (IRE)**, 5, br g Corrouge (USA)—Miners Society **Kinloch Arms (Carnoustie) Ltd**
6 **CANTERBURY BELL**, 5, b m Bishop of Cashel—Old Flower **Mrs J. A. C. Lundgren**
7 **CLASSIC CALVADOS (FR)**, 6, b br g Thatching—Mountain Stage (IRE) **David H. Cox**
8 **DALMARNOCK (IRE)**, 4, ch g Grand Lodge (USA)—Lochbelle **C. D. Carr**
9 **FRIEDHELMO (GER)**, 9, ch g Dashing Blade—Fox For Gold **The Cattlemen Syndicate**
10 **HURRICANE BAY**, 9, ch g Karinga Bay—Clodaigh Gale **I. G. M. Dalgleish**
11 **NO GLOATING (IRE)**, 6, b g King's Ride—Arctic Gale (IRE) **IBT Racing**
12 **SIMPLY MYSTIC**, 5, ch m Simply Great (FR)—Mystic Memory **Mrs J. A. Niven**

MR P. D. NIVEN—continued
13 STOLEN MOMENTS (FR), 4, gr g Villez (USA)—Brave Lola (FR) **L. M. Rutherford**
14 TALARIVE (USA), 9, ch g Riverman (USA)—Estala **I. G. M. Dalgleish**

Other Owners: Mr J. J. Fildes, Mr C. Lishman, Mr A. Needham, MR P. D. Niven, Mr G. A. S. Reid, I. Simpson, Mr J. S. Watson.

434 **MR G. R. S. NIXON, Selkirk**
Postal: Oakwood Farm, Ettrickbridge, Selkirk, Selkirkshire, TD7 5HJ.
Contacts: PHONE (01750) 52245

1 ALLEZ SCOTIA, 6, ch m Minster Son—Allez **Mr G. R. S. Nixon**
2 4, Ch g Minster Son—Delightfool
3 JANSUE CHARLIE, 11, ch g Ardar—Kincherinchee **Mr G. R. S. Nixon**
4 JUST SAL, 9, b m Silly Prices—Hanim (IRE) **Mr G. R. S. Nixon**
5 KEMPSKI, 5, b g Petoski—Little Katrina **Mr G. R. S. Nixon**
6 MILL TOWER, 8, b g Milieu—Tringa (GER) **Mr G. R. S. Nixon**
7 POLITICAL CRUISE, 7, b g Royal Fountain—Political Mill **Mr G. R. S. Nixon**
8 4, Br f Moshaajir (USA)—Political Mill
9 POLITICAL SOX, 11, br g Mirror Boy—Political Mill **Mr G. R. S. Nixon**

Other Owners: Mrs S. Nixon.

Assistant Trainer: Mrs S Nixon

435 **MRS S. NOCK, Stow-on-the-Wold**
Postal: Smenham Farm, Icomb, Stow On The Wold, Cheltenham, Gloucestershire, GL54 1JQ.
Contacts: PHONE (01451) 831688 FAX (01451) 831404

1 5, Ch g Zaffaran (USA)—Alavie (FR) **Camilla & Rosie Nock**
2 BALLYALBANY (IRE), 7, b g Lord Americo—Raisin Turf (IRE) **G. Nock**
3 DENADA, 9, ch g Bob Back (USA)—Alavie (FR) **Camilla & Rosie Nock**
4 DICTUM (GER), 7, ch g Secret 'n Classy (CAN)—Doretta (GER) **Camilla & Rosie Nock**
5 MISTER FELIX (IRE), 9, b g Ore—Pixies Glen **G. Nock**
6 MOLOSTIEP (FR), 5, b g Video Rock (FR)—Unetiepy (FR) **Camilla & Rosie Nock**
7 ROSS LEADER (IRE), 8, b g Supreme Leader—Emmagreen **Camilla & Rosie Nock**
8 TOM COSTALOT (IRE), 10, gr g Black Minstrel—Hop Picker (USA) **Camilla & Rosie Nock**

Other Owners: Mrs A. Olivier, Mr A. Duncanson.

436 **MR D. A. NOLAN, Wishaw**
Postal: Riverside Racing Stables, 227a Bonkle Road, Newmains, Wishaw, Lanarkshire, ML2 9QQ.
Contacts: PHONE (01698) 383850 FAX (01698) 383850

1 ALFIE LEE (IRE), 8, ch g Case Law—Nordic Living (IRE) **Miss M. Mcfadyen-Murray**
2 ANNETTES STAR, 4, b f Captain Maverick (USA)—Miss Hostess **Miss M. Mcfadyen-Murray**
3 AVESA, 5, br m Averti (IRE)—Andahlah **Miss M. Mcfadyen-Murray**
4 BILLY BELL (IRE), 12, b g Montelimar (USA)—Seymour Bay **Mr I. Young**
5 7, Ch m Sir Harry Lewis (USA)—Burmese Ruby **Mr I. Young**
6 EYES DONT LIE (IRE), 7, b g Namaqualand (USA)—Avidal Park **Miss M. Mcfadyen-Murray**
7 GLADYS AYLWARD, 5, b m Polar Falcon (USA)—Versami (USA) **Mr W. Prentice**
8 GO THUNDER (IRE), 11, b g Nordico (USA)—Moving Off **Miss M. Mcfadyen-Murray**
9 HOWARDS DREAM (IRE), 7, b g King's Theatre (IRE)—Keiko **Miss M. Mcfadyen-Murray**
10 KUNDALILA, 7, b m River Falls—Kalou **Miss E. Johnston**
11 LADY TILLY, 8, b m Puissance—Lady of Itatiba (BEL) **Miss E. Johnston**
12 LAS RAMBLAS (IRE), 8, b g Thatching—Raise A Warning **Miss M. Mcfadyen-Murray**
13 LORD ADVOCATE, 17, br g Law Society (USA)—Kereolle
14 MUTAYAM, 5, b g Compton Place—Final Shot **Miss M. Mcfadyen-Murray**
15 NORTHERN SVENGALI (IRE), 9, b g Distinctly North (USA)—Trilby's Dream (IRE) **Miss M. Mcfadyen-Murray**
16 REEDS RAINS, 7, b m Mind Games—Me Spede **Miss M. Mcfadyen-Murray**
17 SECOND WIND, 10, ch g Kris—Rimosa's Pet **Miss M. Mcfadyen-Murray**
18 SOKOKE, 4, ch g Compton Place—Sally Green (IRE) **Miss M. Mcfadyen-Murray**
19 SQUARE DANCER, 9, b g Then Again—Cubist (IRE) **Miss M. Mcfadyen-Murray**
20 STRAVONIAN, 5, b g Luso—In The Evening (IRE) **J. A. Cringan**

MR D. A. NOLAN—continued

21 **TAILI**, 4, b f Taipan (IRE)—Doubtfire **Mrs K. S. Dow**
22 **THE ANGEL GABRIEL**, 10, ch g My Generation—Minsk **Miss M. Mcfadyen-Murray**
23 **WOOLFE**, 8, ch m Wolfhound (USA)—Brosna (USA) **Miss M. Mcfadyen-Murray**

TWO-YEAR-OLDS

24 B f 3/6 Captain Maverick (USA)—Miss Hostess (Petong) **Miss M. Mcfadyen-Murray**
25 B f 2/5 Captain Maverick (USA)—Valley of Time (FR) (In Fijar (USA)) **Miss M. Mcfadyen-Murray**

Other Owners: Mr James Davidson.

Assistant Trainer: Miss M McFadyen-Murray

Jockey (flat): J. McAuley, P. Mathers, P. Fessey.

---

437 **MRS L. B. NORMILE, Glenfarg**
Postal: Duncrievie, Glenfarg, Perthshire, PH2 9PD.
Contacts: PHONE (01577) 830330 FAX (01577) 830658 MOBILES (07721) 454818/(07968) 585395
E-MAIL lucy@normileracing.co.uk WEBSITE www.normileracing.co.uk

1 **ABA GOLD (IRE)**, 5, b m Darnay—Abadila (IRE)
2 **ALFIE BRIGHT**, 7, ch g Alflora (IRE)—Candlebright **Mr J.M. Crichton and Mrs D.A. Whitaker**
3 **ARIJAZ**, 8, b g Teenoso (USA)—Zajira (IRE) **L B N Racing Club**
4 **BALINAHINCH CASTLE (IRE)**, 8, b g Good Thyne (USA)—Emerald Flair **K. J. Fehilly**
5 **BALLYNURE (IRE)**, 7, b br g Roselier (FR)—Fresh Partner (IRE) **Mrs J. M. Fraser**
6 **BELLA LIANA (IRE)**, 5, b m Sesaro (USA)—Bella Galiana (ITY) **J. Clements**
7 **BINT SESARO (IRE)**, 4, b f Sesaro (USA)—Crazed Rainbow (USA) **L B N Racing Club**
8 **CAMBRIAN DAWN**, 11, b g Danehill (USA)—Welsh Daylight **Out The Box Racing**
9 **CAMPING SITE**, 5, br g Desert King (IRE)—House Hunting **A. K. Collins**
10 4, B c Busy Flight—Candlebright **Mrs Joanna Cross**
11 **CHRIS AND RYAN (IRE)**, 7, b g Goldmark (USA)—Beautyofthepeace (IRE) **A. Grant**
12 **CLAN LAW (IRE)**, 7, b g Danehill (USA)—My-O-My (IRE) **Mrs L. B. Normile**
13 **DALKEYS LAD**, 5, b g Supreme Leader—Dalkey Sound **G. S. Brown**
14 **DALKEYS LASS**, 4, gr f Wolfhound (USA)—Dalkey Sound **G. S. Brown**
15 **ENDLESS POWER (IRE)**, 5, b g Perugino (USA)—Charroux (IRE) **Fyffees**
16 **FATHOM**, 7, ch g Zafonic (USA)—River Lullaby (USA) **K. J. Fehilly**
17 **FLAMING HECK**, 8, b g Dancing High—Heckley Spark **D. A. Whitaker**
18 5, B g Oscar (IRE)—Gale **G. S. Brown**
19 4, B g Wolfhound (USA)—Gale **G. S. Brown**
20 **GANDILOO GULLY**, 4, ch f Master Willie—Happydrome **R. F. Gibbons**
21 **GHOST BUSTER**, 6, ch g Opera Ghost—Venetian Storm **J. M. Crichton**
22 **HUTCH**, 7, b g Rock Hopper—Polly's Teahouse **R. F. Gibbons**
23 **JUST IN TIME**, 10, b g Night Shift (USA)—Future Past (USA) **J. Clements**
24 **LOCHIEDUBS**, 10, br g Cragador—Linn Falls **B. Thomson**
25 **MAJED (FR)**, 9, b g Fijar Tango (FR)—Full of Passion (USA) **Mr A. J. Neill**
26 **MASTER CORROUGE (IRE)**, 7, b g Corrouge (USA)—Ballyseskin **Mrs L. B. Normile**
27 **MOFFIED (IRE)**, 5, b g Nashwan (USA)—Del Deya (IRE) **Fyffees**
28 **MR COONEY (IRE)**, 11, b g Van Der Linden (FR)—Green Orchid **J. Clements**
29 **PACIFIC HIGHWAY (IRE)**, 6, b g Sadler's Wells (USA)—Obeah **Red Rock Racing**
30 4, B f Busy Flight—Pejawi **Mrs Joanna Cross**
31 **RATTY'S BAND**, 11, ch g Gunner B—Arctic Ander **Perth Racers**
32 **RODDER (USA)**, 9, ch g Rodrigo de Triano (USA)—Berceau (USA) **Mr K. J. Fehilly and Mr A. K. Collins**
33 **SAYOUN (IRE)**, 6, gr g Primo Dominie—Sarafia **Red Rock Racing**
34 **SCALLYWAGS RETURN**, 6, b m Bob's Return (USA)—Bee-A-Scally **Roberts Racing**
35 **SHAZANA**, 4, gr f Key of Luck (USA)—Shawanni **R. F. Gibbons**
36 **TANDAWIZI**, 8, b m Relief Pitcher—Arctic Ander **Mrs F. M. Whitaker**
37 **THE HONEY GUIDE**, 9, gr g Homo Sapien—The Whirlie Weevil **Mrs V. R. Olivier**
38 7, Ro gr g Alflora (IRE)—The Whirlie Weevil **Mrs L. B. Normile**
39 4, Gr f Alflora (IRE)—The Whirlie Weevil **Mrs D. A. Whitaker & Mrs C. Mitchell**
40 **TOAD HALL**, 11, b g Henbit (USA)—Candlebright **Mrs L. B. Normile**
41 **TRISONS STAR (IRE)**, 7, b g Roselier (FR)—Delkusha **Taylor, Martin, Scoular & White**

MRS L. B. NORMILE—continued

THREE-YEAR-OLDS

42 B g Silver Patriarch (IRE)—Dalkey Sound **G. S. Brown**
43 Br g Silver Patriarch (IRE)—Gale **G. S. Brown**
44 **LUTINE BELL (IRE)**, b f Darnay—Adjamiya (USA) **Ms Alison Mcfarlane**

Other Owners: Mrs L. Dyer, J. Fyffe, Mr S. Fyffe, L. H. Gilmurray, D. J. Hindmarsh, Mr R. Martin, Mr K. Scoular, Mrs F. M. Whitaker.

Assistant Trainer: Alan Normile

Conditional: D. Flavin.

---

438 **MR J. R. NORTON, Barnsley**
Postal: **Globe Farm, High Hoyland, Barnsley, South Yorkshire, S75 4BE.**
Contacts: **PHONE/FAX (01226) 387633 MOBILE (07970) 212707**
E-MAIL johnrnorton@hotmail.com

1 **ABZUSON**, 8, b g Abzu—Mellouise **Abzuson Syndicate**
2 **CASAS (IRE)**, 8, b g Tenby—Clodagh **H. Kidd**
3 **FISHER'S DREAM**, 4, b g Groom Dancer (USA)—Cremets **J. Norton**
4 **IRELAND'S EYE (IRE)**, 10, b b g Shareef Dancer (USA)—So Romantic (IRE) **Ejam Connection**
5 **JUNGLE LION**, 7, ch g Lion Cavern (USA)—Star Ridge (USA) **M. Rowley**
6 5, B m Flemensfirth (USA)—Philly Athletic **J. R. Norton Ltd**
7 **PRINTSMITH (IRE)**, 8, br m Petardia—Black And Blaze **Mrs H. Tattersall**
8 **QUAY WALLOPER**, 4, b g In Command (IRE)—Myrrh **Jaffa Racing Syndicate**
9 **RED RIVER REBEL**, 7, b g Inchinor—Bidweaya (USA) **J. Slaney**
10 **ROMARIC (USA)**, 4, b g Red Ransom (USA)—Eternal Reve (USA) **The Matthewman Partnership**
11 **SAM THE SORCERER**, 4, b g Wizard King—Awham (USA) **M. R. and T. Simcox**
12 **SECRET BLOOM**, 4, b g My Best Valentine—Rose Elegance **Reddal Racing**
13 **SQUANDAMANIA**, 12, b g Ela-Mana-Mou—Garden Pink (FR) **Jaffa Racing Syndicate**
14 **SQUARE DEALER**, 4, b g Vettori (IRE)—Pussy Foot **J. Norton**
15 **TARWIN**, 5, b g Danzig Connection (USA)—Persian Blue **Miss A. J. Hurst**

THREE-YEAR-OLDS

16 **FRAGILE WITNESS**, b g Fraam—Heavenly Abstone **J. R. Norton Ltd**
17 **KAGGAMAGIC**, ch g Abou Zouz (USA)—Meadmore Magic **The Kaggamagic Partners**

TWO-YEAR-OLDS

18 B c 17/4 First Trump—Efficacy (Efisio) (1800) **J. R. Norton Ltd**
19 B c 11/2 Dansili—Glamorous (Sanglamore (USA)) (8000) **The Matthewman Partnership**
20 B f 23/1 Xaar—Lough Erne (Never So Bold) (800) **J. R. Norton Ltd**
21 **MIGHTY DUEL**, b c 11/3 Daggers Drawn (USA)—
Runs In The Family (Distant Relative) (22000) **Woodcock Electrical Limited**
22 **NORTHERNER (IRE)**, b c 31/1 Mark of Esteem (IRE)—
Ensorceleuse (FR) (Fabulous Dancer (USA)) (14000) **Woodcock Electrical Limited**
23 B gr c 5/4 Arkadian Hero (USA)—Rising of The Moon (IRE) (Warning) (2600) **J. R. Norton Ltd**
24 **TROMBONE TOM**, b c 30/3 Superior Premium—Nine To Five (Imp Society (USA)) (1200) **Mrs H. Tattersall**

Other Owners: R. M. Firth, C. R. Green, P. J. Marshall, I. D. Mcewen, K. Mcewen, MR J. R. Norton, G. R. Ralph, P. Scholefield, A. Tattersall.

Jockey (NH): N. Hannity, C. Rafter. **Amateur:** Mr S. F. Magee.

---

439 **MR J. J. NOSEDA, Newmarket**
Postal: **Shalfleet, 17 Bury Road, Newmarket, Suffolk, CB8 7BX.**
Contacts: **PHONE (01638) 664010 FAX (01638) 664100 MOBILE (07710) 294093**
E-MAIL jeremy.noseda@virgin.net WEBSITE www.jeremynoseda.com

1 **BALMONT (USA)**, 4, b c Stravinsky (USA)—Aldebaran Light (USA)
2 **COURAGEOUS DUKE (USA)**, 6, b g Spinning World (USA)—Araadh (USA)
3 **ECOMIUM (IRE)**, 4, b c Sadler's Wells (USA)—Encens
4 **JUST JAMES**, 6, b g Spectrum (IRE)—Fairy Flight (IRE)

MR J. J. NOSEDA—continued

5 **MAJORS CAST (IRE)**, 4, b c Victory Note (USA)—Ziffany
6 **PEAK TO CREEK**, 4, b c Royal Applause—Rivers Rhapsody
7 **SOLDIER'S TALE (USA)**, 4, ch c Stravinsky (USA)—Myrtle

THREE-YEAR-OLDS

8 **ALMAVARA (USA)**, b br c Fusaichi Pegasus (USA)—Name of Love (IRE)
9 **ALMENDRADOS (IRE)**, b f Desert Prince (IRE)—Sevi's Choice (USA)
10 **AMERIGO VESPUCCI**, b c Zafonic (USA)—Amellnaa (IRE)
11 **ARTUSHOF (USA)**, b c Danzig (USA)—Maidee (USA)
12 **BALDASSARRE**, ch c Grand Lodge (USA)—Royal York
13 **BLUE DAKOTA (IRE)**, b c Namid—Touraya
14 **BRIDGE LOAN**, ch c Giant's Causeway (USA)—Credit-A-Plenty
15 **BRONWEN (IRE)**, b f King's Best (USA)—Tegwen (USA)
16 **DARING RANSOM (USA)**, b c Red Ransom (USA)—Young and Daring (USA)
17 **DESERT LIGHTNING (IRE)**, ch c Desert Prince (IRE)—Saibhreas (IRE)
18 **DOMINATING VISTA**, b f Diktat—Colorvista
19 **EMERALD LODGE**, b c Grand Lodge (USA)—Emerald Peace (IRE)
20 **FIRST SHOW**, b c Cape Cross (IRE)—Rose Show
21 **FOR SCARLETT (USA)**, br f Red Ransom (USA)—Lady Dixie (USA)
22 **IMLAAK**, ch c Giant's Causeway (USA)—Karen S (USA)
23 **INDEBTED**, b f Royal Applause—Briggsmaid
24 **INSIDE STORY (IRE)**, b c Rossini (USA)—Sliding
25 **JAMEHIR (IRE)**, gr c Machiavellian (USA)—Crodelle (IRE)
26 **KEYLIME (IRE)**, b f Green Desert (USA)—Comme d'habitude (USA)
27 **KHARISH (IRE)**, b c Desert Prince (IRE)—Moy Water (IRE)
28 **KING FOREVER**, b c King's Best (USA)—Elude
29 **LAKE CAREZZA (USA)**, b c Stravinsky (USA)—May Wedding (USA)
30 **MARLOWE (IRE)**, b c Sadler's Wells (USA)—Minnie Habit
31 **NAN SCURRY (FR)**, b f Danehill (USA)—Prends Ca (IRE)
32 **ONE TO WIN (IRE)**, b f Cape Cross (IRE)—Safe Exit (FR)
33 **PERSONA (IRE)**, b f Night Shift (USA)—Alonsa (IRE)
34 **POMPADOUR**, b f King's Best (USA)—Tanzilla
35 **PROCLAMATION (IRE)**, gr c King's Best (USA)—Shamarra (FR)
36 **PURITANICAL (IRE)**, ch f Desert King (IRE)—Zariysha (IRE)
37 **RASHIDA**, b f King's Best (USA)—Nimble Lady (AUS)
38 **SELF RESPECT (USA)**, b c Lear Fan (USA)—Cap of Dignity
39 **SPANKY'S LADDER (IRE)**, br c Zafonic (USA)—Blasted Heath
40 **STAGELIGHT (IRE)**, b c Montjeu (IRE)—Zivania (IRE)
41 **VICTORY DESIGN (IRE)**, b c Danehill (USA)—Sun Silk (USA)
42 **WRIGHTY ALMIGHTY (IRE)**, b c Danehill Dancer (IRE)—Persian Empress (IRE)

TWO-YEAR-OLDS

43 B c 26/3 Alhaarth (IRE)—Actualite (Polish Precedent (USA)) (97249)
44 **AIRMAN (IRE)**, b c 20/2 Danehill (USA)—Jiving (Generous (IRE))
45 **AITCH (IRE)**, b f 19/2 Alhaarth (IRE)—Sevi's Choice (USA) (Sir Ivor (USA)) (40000)
46 B c 26/1 Royal Applause—Amber Tide (IRE) (Pursuit of Love) (48000)
47 B c 24/3 Machiavellian (USA)—Amellnaa (IRE) (Sadler's Wells (USA))
48 **ANASTASIA STORM**, b f 27/3 Mozart (IRE)—Royal York (Bustino)
49 B f 31/1 Elusive Quality (USA)—April In Kentucky (USA) (Palace Music (USA)) (28000)
50 **BALANCED BUDGET**, b c 25/4 Mark of Esteem (IRE)—Credit-A-Plenty (Generous (IRE))
51 B c 3/2 Stravinsky (USA)—Belle Sultane (USA) (Seattle Slew (USA)) (117052)
52 **CAAMORA (IRE)**, b f 3/4 Cape Cross (IRE)—Tarafiya (USA) (Trempolino (USA)) (75000)
53 Ch c 28/1 Spinning World (USA)—Classic Park (Robellino (USA)) (110663)
54 B f 24/1 Zafonic (USA)—Claustra (FR) (Green Desert (USA)) (36887)
55 B c 23/2 Montjeu (IRE)—Cordon Bleu (USA) (D'accord (USA))
56 B c 8/4 Cadeaux Genereux—Desert Lynx (IRE) (Green Desert (USA)) (70000)
57 **DYNAMIC RHYTHM (USA)**, b c 9/3 Kingmambo (USA)—Palme d'or (IRE) (Sadler's Wells (USA)) (87000)
58 B c 16/4 Kingmambo (USA)—Easy Now (USA) (Danzig (USA))
59 B c 3/3 Royal Applause—Elsie Plunkett (Mind Games) (75000)
60 **HILL OF GRACE**, ch f 12/4 Desert Prince (IRE)—Tycoon's Dolce (IRE) (Rainbows For Life (CAN)) (35000)
61 **IN THE FASHION (IRE)**, b f 16/1 In The Wings—Tropical Lass (IRE) (Ballad Rock) (65000)
62 Ch f 13/3 Danehill Dancer (IRE)—Juno Madonna (IRE) (Sadler's Wells (USA)) (140000)
63 **JUST LOGIC (IRE)**, b br c 2/4 Desert Prince (IRE)—Tiavanita (USA) (J O Tobin (USA)) (46947)
64 **KORIKANCHA (IRE)**, b f 10/4 Fasliyev (USA)—Amravati (IRE) (Project Manager)
65 B f 13/4 Seeking The Gold (USA)—Korveya (USA) (Riverman (USA))

MR J. J. NOSEDA—continued

66 B c 25/2 Cape Cross (IRE)—Lady Moranbon (USA) (Trempolino (USA)) (100000)
67 LADY WORTH (USA), ch f 23/2 Spinning World (USA)—Net Worth (USA) (Forty Niner (USA))
68 LITTLEDODAYNO (IRE), b f 26/2 Mujadil (USA)—Perfect Welcome (Taufan (USA)) (55000)
69 B c 16/2 Galileo (IRE)—Love Divine (Diesis) (230000)
70 B c 18/3 Montjeu (IRE)—Lucy In The Sky (IRE) (Lycius (USA)) (140000)
71 B c 9/2 Arkadian Hero (USA)—Lyna (Slip Anchor) (24000)
72 B c 7/2 Inchinor—Margot (Sadler's Wells) (100000)
73 B f 8/2 King's Best (USA)—Maskunah (IRE) (Sadler's Wells (USA)) (75000)
74 MUSICAL MAGIC, b f 10/3 Mozart (IRE)—Kirk (Selkirk (USA)) (13000)
75 NANDO'S DREAM, ch f 10/5 Hernando (FR)—Dream Quest (Rainbow Quest (USA))
76 Ch c 5/5 High Yield (USA)—Nikita Moon (USA) (Secret Hello (USA)) (53205)
77 OTELCALIFONI (USA), b f 15/1 Gulch (USA)—Ive Gota Bad Liver (USA) (Mt Livermore (USA)) (200000)
78 PARK ESTEEM (IRE), b f 21/2 Singspiel (IRE)—Park Special (Relkino)
79 B f 1/3 Diesis—Pent (USA) (Mr Prospector (USA))
80 Ch c 27/1 Grand Lodge (USA)—Rainbow Lyrics (IRE) (Rainbow Quest (USA)) (105000)
81 B c 8/4 Mull of Kintyre (USA)—Resurgence (Polar Falcon (USA)) (150000)
82 Ch c 3/3 Grand Lodge (USA)—River Fantasy (USA) (Irish River (FR)) (135000)
83 SHOW WINNER, b c 9/5 Mtoto—Rose Show (Belmez (USA))
84 SILKY OAK (IRE), b f 14/1 Green Desert (USA)—Forest Express (AUS) (Kaaptive Edition (NZ))
85 B f 12/5 Rahy (USA)—Sister Crown (Danzig (USA))
86 STARS ARE OUT (IRE), b f 1/3 Spectrum (IRE)—Crystal Land (Kris) (14000)
87 B c 10/1 Danehill Dancer (IRE)—Suave Lady (FR) (Suave Dancer (USA)) (80000)
88 B c 29/4 King Charlemagne (USA)—Tadkiyra (IRE) (Darshaan) (200000)
89 B f 22/1 Gulch (USA)—True Life (USA) (El Gran Senor (USA)) (40000)
90 Ch f 11/5 Barathea (IRE)—Western Heights (Shirley Heights)
91 B c 11/4 Cape Cross (IRE)—Winter Tern (USA) (Arctic Tern (USA)) (60361)

Owners: Mr M. Al Shafar, I. J. Al-Sagar, S. Ali, Arashan Ali, S. H. Altayer, Mr Syd Belzberg, C. Bowen, Sir Gordon Brunton, Mrs S. Burns, P. Byrne, Mr L. Calvente, Mrs A. M. Doyle, Mr P. Doyle, Mrs P. Duffin, Fieldspring Racing Syndicate, C. E. S. Fox, Gigginstown House Stud, P. G. Goulandris, Mrs J. Harris, Mr A. Harris, Mr A. M. Hayes, Helena Springfield Ltd, Hesmonds Stud Ltd, C. E. Holt, Saleh Al Homeizi, M. H. Ings, Jayeff B. Stables, Jeremy Noseda Racing Ltd, Jumeirah Racing, M. Kelly, Mr E. Kelly, G. Lansbury, R. G. Levin, R. M. Levitt, Lucayan Stud Ltd, Mr B McAllister, Meon Valley Stud, Newgate Stud, Mr J. Newsome, Mr R. B. Newton, Miss K. Nikkel, Mr A. Nolan, Sir Robert Ogden C.B.E., LLD, Razza Pallorsi, Pat Eddery Racing Limited, O. J. W. Pawle, Mr P. A. Pritchard, G. J. Prussin, A. Purvis, Sattar Quresh, Mr M. Rashid, H. E. Shiekh Rashid Bin Mohammed, Mrs S. M. Roy, Mr P. Roy, Dr T. A. Ryan, Mrs J. M. Ryan, Abdullah Saeed Belhab, Mr Sanford Robertson, R. T. Santulli, Mrs K. Sellars, Mrs J. Magnier & Mrs P. Shanahan, A. J. Smith, P. J. Smith, M. Tabor, Thoroughbred Farms Ltd, Thurloe Thoroughbreds XII, Wood Hall Stud Limited, Woodcote Stud Ltd, Mr J. Wright.

Assistant Trainer: Dave Bradley

Jockey (flat): E. Ahern.

MR W. A. O'GORMAN, Newmarket

440

Postal: **Seven Springs, Hamilton Road, Newmarket, Suffolk, CB8 7JQ.**
Contacts: **PHONE (01638) 663330 FAX (01638) 663160**
E-MAIL billogorman@btopenworld.com WEBSITE www.emmaogorman.co.uk

1 GALLOWAY MAC, 5, ch h Environment Friend—Docklands **W. A. O'Gorman**
2 IMPERIAL DRAGON (USA), 5, b g Meadowlake—South Cove **P. J. O'Gorman**

TWO-YEAR-OLDS

3 B f 3/4 Diktat—Blackpool Belle (The Brianstan)
4 B c 2/5 Agnes World (USA)—Galine (Most Welcome) **S. Fustok**
5 GOLD EXPRESS, b c 13/4 Observatory (USA)—
Vanishing Point (USA) (Caller I D (USA)) (20000) **S. Fustok & N. S. Yong**

Assistant Trainer: P J O'Gorman

Jockey (flat): D. Holland.

441 **MR E. J. O'GRADY, Thurles**
Postal: Killeens, Ballynonty, Thurles, Co. Tipperary, Ireland.
Contacts: PHONE +353 (0) 52 56156 FAX +353 (0) 52 56466
E-MAIL edwardogrady@eircom.net

1 ACCORDING TO BILLY (IRE), 6, b g Accordion—Graphic Lady (IRE) **Mr Patsy Byrne**
2 AIR GUITAR (IRE), 5, b g Blues Traveller (IRE)—Money Talks (IRE) **Mr Liam Mulryan**
3 AKILANA (IRE), 4, b f Mark of Esteem (IRE)—Akishka **Mr John P. McManus**
4 APAIROFDUCKS (IRE), 5, b g Saddlers' Hall (IRE)—Distant Gale (IRE) **M.A.L.M. Syndicate**
5 BACK IN FRONT (IRE), 8, b g Bob Back (USA)—Storm Front (IRE) **Nelius Hayes & Dermot Cox**
6 BACKFOREMORE (IRE), 5, b g Bob Back (USA)—Letterfore **Mr Edward Wallace**
7 BEST GREY, 9, gr h Ezzoud (IRE)—Best Girl Friend **Mr Edward Wallace**
8 CASH AND CARRY (IRE), 7, b g Norwich—Little And Often (IRE) **Mr Edward Wallace**
9 COAST TO COAST (IRE), 6, ch g Moscow Society (USA)—Madame Vitesse **Seamus Carroll**
10 COLONEL MONROE (IRE), 8, b g Lord Americo—Fairy Blaze (IRE) **G. F. Mahony**
11 COPPET (IRE), 5, ch g Pennekamp (USA)—Esquiline (USA) **T. M. Dolan**
12 DALTON (IRE), 4, ch c Bering—Divination (FR) **M.A.L.M. Syndicate**
13 DAME O'NEILL (IRE), 5, br m Dr Massini (IRE)—Chroma (IRE) **Alec Bond**
14 DAN THE LIBERATOR (IRE), 5, b g Anshan—Serjitak **Mr J. J. King**
15 ENDLESS MAGIC (IRE), 10, br g Zaffaran (USA)—Merillion **J. O'Grady**
16 EXCELSIOR (IRE), 5, b g Luso—Sorimak Gale (IRE) **M. O'Leary**
17 FIND THE KING (IRE), 7, b g King's Theatre—Undiscovered **J. S. Gutkin**
18 FORTY LICKS (IRE), 8, b g Supreme Leader—Bridevalley **Mr John P. McManus**
19 GENERAL MONTCALM (IRE), 7, b g Roselier (FR)—Pamela's Princess **Mr G. F. Mahony**
20 GO ROGER GO (IRE), 13, b g Phardante (FR)—Tonto's Girl **Mr John P. McManus**
21 GRAPEVINE SALLY (IRE), 4, b f Saddlers' Hall (IRE)—Mrs Battleaxe **Mrs Patricia Wallace**
22 HEAR ME OUT (IRE), 5, b g Rock Hopper—Kindly Princess (IRE) **Mr John P. McManus**
23 HEART AFFAIR, 5, b m Cloudings (IRE)—Dara's Course (IRE) **Dermot Cox**
24 HOW IS THINGS (IRE), 7, b m Norwich—Deep Green **Time Will Tell Syndicate**
25 IT'S SHOWTIME (IRE), 7, gr g Roselier (FR)—Princess Crack (IRE) **Mr J. J. King**
26 JACK INGHAM (IRE), 5, b g Supreme Leader—Silent Run **Mrs J. Magnier**
27 KENTUCKY CHARM (FR), 4, gr g Linamix (FR)—Kentucky Kaper (USA) **J. P. O'Shea**
28 KICKHAM (IRE), 9, b g Supreme Leader—Knocknagow **Mr John P. McManus**
29 LARAGH HOUSE (IRE), 6, b br g Hubbly Bubbly (USA)—Black Valley (IRE) **Gone West Racing Syndicate**
30 LEONARDO DE VINCI (IRE), 5, b g Sadler's Wells (USA)—Andromaque (USA) **Mr Eamonn Ryan**
31 LEPIDUS (IRE), 8, br g Bob's Return (IRE)—Lepida **Miss Rosaleen Tonson-Rye**
32 LETTERMAN (IRE), 5, br g Presenting—Papoose (IRE) **S. P. Tindall**
33 LORD AJUS (IRE), 8, b g Lord Americo—Another Coup **Ms Nicola Meaden**
34 LORD SNOW (IRE), 4, br g Mister Lord (USA)—Snowdrifter **S. P. Tindall**
35 LULLABY (FR), 5, b br g Marchand de Sable (USA)—Tune (IRE) **W. A. Barrett**
36 LUNAR SEA (IRE), 5, ch g Beneficial—Moonvoy (USA) **Usual Suspects Syndicate**
37 LYSTER (IRE), 6, b g Oscar (IRE)—Sea Skin **Mr Brian Walsh**
38 MAJOR HAYWARD (IRE), 4, br g Anshan—Miss Euroflink **Mrs Susan Mahony**
39 MAMOUNA GALE (IRE), 7, b m Fairydel (IRE)—Stealth **Victoria Syndicate**
40 MARKTIC FASHION (IRE), 6, br m Arctic Lord—Sparkling Fashion **C. Hamilton**
41 MUTTIAH, 5, ch g Muhtarram (USA)—Loving Around (IRE) **S. P. Tindall**
42 NED KELLY (IRE), 9, ch g Be My Native (USA)—Silent Run **Mrs J. Magnier**
43 O'MUIRCHEARTAIGH (IRE), 5, b g Accordion—Brian's Delight (IRE) **Mrs W. T. O'Grady**
44 OH SO LIVELY (IRE), 7, b g King's Ride—Borgina **Mr K. T. Clancy**
45 OVER THE BAR (IRE), 9, b br g King's Ride—Merry Madness **Mr John P. McManus**
46 OVERBURY AFFAIR, 6, b g Overbury (IRE)—Dara's Course (IRE) **Mr John P. McManus**
47 PANA (IRE), 5, b g Broken Hearted—Charlies Rising (IRE) **Live In Hope Syndicate**
48 PASTARELLA (IRE), 4, b f Pasternak—Miss San Siro (IRE) **Germano Terrinoni**
49 PIZARRO (IRE), 8, ch g Broken Hearted—Our Swan Lady **Mr Edward Wallace**
50 PROUD ANDEES (IRE), 6, ch g Un Desperado (FR)—Whimsey **Mr R. MacDonald**
51 REDNECK GIRL (IRE), 6, b m Oscar (IRE)—Flamewood **Alec Bond**
52 RIDE THE STORM (IRE), 8, ch g Glacial Storm—Reach Down (IRE) **Nelius Hayes**
53 RINCESHANE (IRE), 6, ch g Anshan—Inse Na Rince (IRE) **Rule Four Syndicate**
54 RIVERSIDE PROJECT (IRE), 7, ch g Montelimar (USA)—Ballyweather Lady **Mr Seamus Carroll**
55 SHORT AND SWEET (IRE), 6, b m Fourstars Allstar (USA)—Lady Claire (IRE) **Star Syndicate**
56 4, b c Oscar (IRE)—Silent Supreme (IRE) **Mrs J. Magnier**
57 SKY'S THE LIMIT (FR), 4, gr c Medaaly—Highness Lady (GER) **R. Rooney**
58 SOME LEGEND (IRE), 5, b g Flying Legend (USA)—Albeit **The Tir Conaill Syndicate**
59 4, b g Saddlers' Hall (IRE)—Strong Profit (IRE) **M.A.L.M. Syndicate**
60 TAKAGI (IRE), 10, b g Husyan (USA)—Ballyclough Gale **Dermot Cox**
61 TENGO AMBRO, 6, b g Jupiter Island—Loving Around (IRE) **The Duke of Bedford**
62 THENFORD SNIPE (IRE), 4, b g Clerkenwell (USA)—Peas (IRE) **Alec Bond**

MR E. J. O'GRADY—continued

63 **THENFORD TROUT (IRE)**, 4, b g Midhish—Monteanna (IRE) **Alec Bond**
64 **THENFORD WOODCOCK (IRE)**, 4, b g Moonax (IRE)—American Flier (IRE) **Alec Bond**
65 **TOWER OF STEEL (IRE)**, 7, b g Executive Perk—Pineway VII **Tom Radley**
66 **TURTLEBACK (IRE)**, 7, b g Turtle Island—Mimicry **D. F. Desmond**
67 **VATIRISK (FR)**, 8, gr h Take Risks (FR)—Vatipan (FR) **Mr Edward Wallace**
68 **VICTOR ROYALE (IRE)**, 5, b g Old Vic—Sable Royale (USA) **Octagon Syndicate**
69 **VICTOR VICTORIOUS (IRE)**, 5, ch g Old Vic—Badsworth Madam **Mr E. P. King**
70 **YOU'VEGOTMEROCKING (IRE)**, 5, b g Saddlers' Hall (IRE)—Stormy Miss (IRE) **Mr Paul Shanahan**

---

442 MR J. O'KEEFFE, Leyburn
Postal: **Highbeck, Brecongill, Coverham, Leyburn, North Yorkshire, DL8 4TJ.**
Contacts: **PHONE (01969) 640330 FAX (01969) 640397 MOBILE (07710) 476705**
E-MAIL jeddokeeffe@compuserve.com

1 **BEAT THE HEAT (IRE)**, 7, b g Salse (USA)—Summer Trysting (USA) **R. P. E. Berry**
2 **FACE THE LIMELIGHT (IRE)**, 6, b g Quest For Fame—Miss Boniface **Highbeck Racing**
3 **HABITUAL DANCER**, 4, b g Groom Dancer (USA)—Pomorie (IRE) **The Country Stayers**
4 **IMPULSIVE BID (IRE)**, 4, b f Orpen (USA)—Tamburello (IRE) **Only For Fun Partnership**
5 **IRUSAN (IRE)**, 5, br g Catrail (USA)—Ostrusa (AUT) **Highbeck Racing**
6 **MAGIC CHARM**, 7, b m Magic Ring (IRE)—Loch Clair (IRE) **WRB Racing 46 (wrbracing.com)**
7 **MISSION TO BE**, 6, ch g Elmaamul (USA)—All The Girls (IRE) **J. E. Lund**
8 **MYSTERINCH**, 5, b g Inchinor—Hakone (IRE) **Colin and Melanie Moore**
9 **PARISIAN PLAYBOY**, 5, gr g Paris House—Exordium **Playboy Partnership**
10 **ROUTE SIXTY SIX (IRE)**, 9, b m Brief Truce (USA)—Lyphards Goddess (IRE) **WRB Racing 47 (wrbracing.com)**
11 **SIR NIGHT (IRE)**, 5, b g Night Shift (USA)—Highly Respected (IRE) **Highbeck Racing**
12 **SNOW BUNTING**, 7, ch g Polar Falcon (USA)—Marl **WRB Racing 49 (wrbracing.com)**
13 **STRAIT TALKING (FR)**, 7, b g Bering—Servia **B. E. Rider**
14 **TIYOUN (IRE)**, 7, b g Kahyasi—Taysala (IRE) **Miss S. Long**
15 **UNITED SPIRIT (IRE)**, 4, b f Fasliyev (USA)—Atlantic Desire (IRE) **Colin and Melanie Moore**
16 **WYOMING**, 4, ch f Inchinor—Shoshone **Mr J. O'Keeffe**

THREE-YEAR-OLDS

17 **ALANI (IRE)**, b f Benny The Dip (USA)—Toi Toi (IRE) **Miss S. Long**
18 **LADY MISHA**, b f Mister Baileys—Hakone (IRE) **Allen, Kelly & Moore**
19 **MADAME FATALE (IRE)**, br f Daggers Drawn (USA)—Taajreh (IRE) **Mr J. O'Keeffe**
20 **RELUCTANT SUITOR**, b c Singspiel (IRE)—Belle Esprit **Chippenham Lodge Stud Ltd**

TWO-YEAR-OLDS

21 B c 12/4 Second Empire (IRE)—Celtic Guest (IRE) (Be My Guest (USA)) (4200) **Wrbracing.com**
22 Ch c 14/3 Allied Forces (USA)—Macca Luna (IRE) (Kahyasi) (1500) **Mr J. O'Keeffe**
23 B c 3/2 Fruits of Love (USA)—Teodora (IRE) (Fairy King (USA)) (26000) **A. Walker**
24 Ch f 4/2 Halling (USA)—Zarma (FR) (Machiavellian (USA)) (12000) **Wood Farm Stud (Waresley)**

Other Owners: A. W. A. Bates, M. Chapman, P. F. Charter, Miss C. L. Hewson, B. Hickson, E. R. D. Johnson, Mrs J. E. Moule, R. W. Tunstall, Wetherby Racing Bureau Ltd.

Assistant Trainer: Andrea O'Keeffe

Jockey (NH): B. Harding. **Apprentice:** Leanne Kershaw. **Amateur:** Miss Jenna Waring.

---

443 MR J. G. O'NEILL, Bicester
Postal: **Hall Farm, Stratton Audley, Nr Bicester, Oxfordshire, OX27 9BT.**
Contacts: **PHONE (01869) 277202 FAX (01869) 227096 MOBILE (07785) 394128**
E-MAIL jgoneill@lineone.net

1 **SHOWBIZ FLOOZIE**, 5, b m Infantry—Laced Up (IRE)

444 MR J. J. O'NEILL, Cheltenham

Postal: Jackdaws Castle, Temple Guiting, Cheltenham, Gloucestershire, GL54 5XU.
Contacts: PHONE (01386) 584209 FAX (01386) 584219
E-MAIL jonjo@jonjooneillracing.com WEBSITE www.jonjooneillracing.com

1 ALRIGHT NOW M'LAD (IRE), 5, b g Supreme Leader—Chattering Mr John P. McManus
2 BALLYLUSKY (IRE), 8, b g Lord Americo—Blackbushe Place (IRE) Black Sheep Racing
3 BLACK JACK KETCHUM (IRE), 6, b g Oscar (IRE)—Cailin Supreme (IRE) Mrs G. K. Smith
4 BOLD BISHOP (IRE), 8, b g Religiously—Ladybojangles (IRE) Mrs G. K. Smith
5 BOLD INVESTOR, 8, b g Anshan—Shirlstar Investor Mrs A. R. Thompson
6 BRONCO CHARLIE (IRE), 7, b g Be My Native (USA)—Cockney Bug Mrs J. Magnier
7 BUCK WHALEY (IRE), 5, ch g Fleetwood (IRE)—Kayzarana (IRE) Mr Barry Connell
8 BUTLER'S CABIN (FR), 5, b g Poliglote—Strictly Cool (USA) Mr John P. McManus
9 CAMPAIGN TRAIL (IRE), 7, b g Sadler's Wells (USA)—Campestral (USA) Mr M. Tabor
10 CANON BARNEY (IRE), 10, b br g Salluceva—Debbies Candy Mr John P. McManus
11 CELTIC MAJOR (IRE), 7, gr g Roselier (FR)—Dun Oengus (IRE) Walters Plant Hire Ltd
12 CHAMPION'S DAY (GER), 4, ch g Valanour (IRE)—Courtly Times Mrs M. Done
13 CHERUB (GER), 5, b g Winged Love (IRE)—Chalkidiki (GER) Atlantic Joinery Limited
14 CLAN ROYAL (IRE), 10, b g Chef de Clan II (FR)—Allee Du Roy (FR) Mr John P. McManus
15 CLASSIC NATIVE (IRE), 7, b br g Be My Native (USA)—Thats Irish Ray & Sue Dodd Partnership
16 CLAUDE GREENGRASS, 9, ch g Shalford (IRE)—Rainbow Brite (BEL) Mr John P. McManus
17 CONFLUENCE (IRE), 4, gr c Linamix (FR)—River Swan Mrs G. K. Smith
18 CORTON (IRE), 6, gr g Definite Article—Limpopo Mrs B. L. Harvey
19 CREON, 10, b g Saddlers' Hall (IRE)—Creake Mr John P. McManus
20 DARK ROOM (IRE), 8, b g Toulon—Maudlin Bridge (IRE) Mr John P. McManus
21 DELGAY LAD, 7, b g Homo Sapien—Sloe Hill Mrs G. K. Smith
22 DON'T PUSH IT (IRE), 5, b g Old Vic—She's No Laugh Ben (USA) Mr John P. McManus
23 DOUBLE ASPECT (IRE), 4, b g Dr Fong (USA)—Spring Mrs G. K. Smith
24 EAST TYCOON (IRE), 6, ch g Bigstone (IRE)—Princesse Sharpo (USA) Mrs G. K. Smith
25 EXOTIC DANCER (IRE), 5, b g Turgeon (USA)—Northine (FR) Sir Robert Ogden C.B.E., LLD
26 FEEL THE PRIDE (IRE), 7, b m Persian Bold—Nordic Pride Mrs M. Liston
27 FIBRE OPTICS (IRE), 5, b g Presenting—Hooch Mrs G. K. Smith
28 FIRE DRAGON (IRE), 4, b g Sadler's Wells (USA)—Cattermole (USA) Mrs G. K. Smith
29 FUNDAMENTAL, 6, ch g Rudimentary (USA)—I'll Try Mr D. N. Green
30 GLOBAL CHALLENGE (IRE), 6, b g Sadler's Wells (USA)—Middle Prospect (USA) Mrs J. S. T. O'Neill
31 GOLDEN RAMBLER (IRE), 9, br g Roselier (FR)—Goldiyana (FR) Messrs J. C., J. R. and S. R. Hitchins
32 GOOD JUDGEMENT (IRE), 7, b g Good Thyne (USA)—Loch Na Mona (IRE) Mr John P. McManus
33 GOSS, 8, gr g Linamix (FR)—Guillem (USA) Mr John P. McManus
34 GOSS HAWK (NZ), 5, gr g Senor Pete (USA)—Stapleton Row (NZ) Mr P. Piller
35 HALEXY (FR), 10, b g Iron Duke (FR)—Tartifume II (FR) Sir Robert Ogden C.B.E., LLD
36 HASTY PRINCE, 7, ch g Halling (USA)—Sister Sophie (USA) Mr John P. McManus
37 HAUTCLAN (FR), 8, b g Chef de Clan II (FR)—Haute Tension (FR) Mr T. J. Hemmings
38 HAWK'S LANDING (IRE), 8, gr g Peacock (FR)—Lady Cheyenne Mr John P. McManus
39 HERE WE GO (IRE), 6, b g Bob Back (USA)—Bold Lyndsey Mr D. N. Green
40 INTERSKY FALCON, 8, ch g Polar Falcon (USA)—I'll Try interskyracing.com & Mrs Jonjo O'Neill
41 IRIS'S GIFT, 8, gr g Gunner B—Shirley's Gift Mr R. Lester
42 IT WOULD APPEAR (IRE), 6, b g Un Desperado (FR)—Toi-Dante (IRE) Mrs Anita Huber
43 KEEN LEADER (IRE), 9, b g Supreme Leader—Keen Gale (IRE) Mrs Stewart Catherwood
44 KINGSCOURT LAD (IRE), 7, b g Norwich—Mrs Minella Mrs J. S. T. O'Neill
45 KNIFE EDGE (USA), 10, b br g Kris S (USA)—My Turbulent Miss Mr John P. McManus
46 LINGO (IRE), 6, b g Poliglote—Sea Ring (FR) Mr John P. McManus
47 LONG ROAD HOME (IRE), 6, b g Supreme Leader—Chelsea Native Mrs J. S. T. O'Neill
48 MAC HINE (IRE), 8, b g Eurobus—Zoe Baird Mr John P. McManus
49 MANNERS (IRE), 7, b g Topanoora—Maneree Mr M. Tabor
50 MILLENAIRE (IRE), 6, b br g Mister Mat—Mille Perles (FR) The Risky Partnership
51 MINI SENSATION (IRE), 12, b g Be My Native (USA)—Minorettes Girl Mr John P. McManus
52 MONTE VISTA (IRE), 8, b g Montelimar (USA)—Targogan's Rose Mr John P. McManus
53 MONTEVIDEO, 5, b g Sadler's Wells (USA)—Montessori Mr John P. McManus
54 MULTEEN RIVER (IRE), 9, b g Supreme Leader—Blackwater Mist (IRE) Mr John P. McManus
55 NATIVE EMPEROR, 9, br g Be My Native (USA)—Fiona's Blue Messrs J. C., J. R. and S. R. Hitchins
56 NEW TIME (IRE), 8, b g Topanoora—Fast Time (IRE) Mr John P. McManus
57 OLASO (GER), 6, b g Law Society (USA)—Olaya (GER) Mr John P. McManus
58 OLD FEATHERS (IRE), 8, b g Hernando (FR)—Undiscovered Mr J. Connor
59 PERSONAL ASSURANCE, 8, b br g Un Desperado (FR)—Steel Typhoon Mr C. Johnston
60 PREDATOR (GER), 4, b g Protektor (GER)—Polish Affair (FR) Glencoe Plant Hire
61 PREDICAMENT, 6, ch g Machiavellian (USA)—Quandary (USA) Sir Robert Ogden C.B.E., LLD
62 PROGRESSIVE (IRE), 7, ch g Be My Native (USA)—Move Forward Mr John P. McManus

MR J. J. O'NEILL—continued

63 **PROKOFIEV (USA)**, 9, br g Nureyev (USA)—Aviara (USA) **Mrs S. M. Darlington**
64 **QUAZAR (IRE)**, 7, b g Inzar (USA)—Evictress (IRE) **Mr C. D. Carr**
65 **REFINEMENT (IRE)**, 6, b m Oscar (IRE)—Maneree **Mr M. Tabor**
66 **RENVYLE (IRE)**, 7, b br g Satco (FR)—Kara's Dream (IRE) **The Four Exiles**
67 **RHINESTONE COWBOY (IRE)**, 9, b g Be My Native (USA)—Monumental Gesture **Mrs J. Magnier**
68 **SELVAS (GER)**, 5, ch g Lomitas—Subia (GER) **Getjar Limited**
69 **SH BOOM**, 7, b g Alderbrook—Muznah **T. G. K. Construction Ltd**
70 **SHAMAWAN (IRE)**, 10, b g Kris—Shamawna (IRE) **Mr John P. McManus**
71 **SHE'S NO MUPPET**, 5, b m Teenoso (USA)—Persian Dream (IRE) **Mr and Mrs Andrew May**
72 **SHERKIN ISLAND (IRE)**, 7, b g Shernazar—Tullerolli (IRE) **Mr John P. McManus**
73 **SIMPLY GIFTED**, 10, b g Simply Great (FR)—Souveniers **Mr S. Hammond**
74 **SPECULAR (AUS)**, 9, b g Danehill (USA)—Spyglass (NZ) **Mr John P. McManus**
75 **SPIRIT OF NEW YORK (IRE)**, 6, b g Topanoora—Fiona's Blue **Mr John P. McManus**
76 **STEPPES OF GOLD (IRE)**, 8, b g Moscow Society (USA)—Trysting Place **Mrs G. K. Smith**
77 **STONEWALL GEORGE (NZ)**, 7, ch g Stark South (USA)—Mother's Word **Ray & Sue Dodd Partnership**
78 **TAKE FIVE (IRE)**, 12, br g Satco (FR)—Shan's Moss **Mr John P. McManus**
79 **TEN PRESSED MEN (FR)**, 5, b g Video Rock (FR)—Recolte D'estruval (FR) **Mrs V. F. Burke**
80 **THE RISING MOON (IRE)**, 6, br g Anshan—I'm So Happy (IRE) **Mr John P. McManus**
81 **THE SISTER**, 8, b m Alflora (IRE)—Donna Farina **Mrs R. H. Thompson**
82 **THEPRIDEOFEIREANN (IRE)**, 6, b g Toulon—Slaney Queen **Byrne Bros (Formwork) Limited**
83 **THYNE FOR INTERSKY (IRE)**, 6, ch g Good Thyne (USA)—One Last Chance **interskyracing.com**
84 **TIGERS LAIR (IRE)**, 6, b br g Accordion—Eadie (IRE) **Mrs G. K. Smith**
85 **TOMMY JAY (NZ)**, 7, b g Gold Brose (AUS)—Hey Paula (NZ) **Mr P. Piller**
86 **TREATY STONE (IRE)**, 6, b g Bigstone (IRE)—Quiet City **Mrs U. McElroy**
87 **URSIS (FR)**, 4, b c Trempolino (USA)—Bold Virgin (USA) **Mr C. H. McGhie**
88 **VERY OPTIMISTIC (IRE)**, 7, b g Un Desperado (FR)—Bright Future (IRE) **Mrs G. K. Smith**
89 **WILD IS THE WIND (FR)**, 4, ch g Acatenango (GER)—Whirlwind (FR) **Mr T. M. Mohan**
90 **WILFRED (IRE)**, 4, b g Desert King (USA)—Kharaliya (FR) **Mr C. Johnston**
91 **WORLD WIDE WEB (IRE)**, 9, b g Be My Native (USA)—Meldrum Lass **Mr John P. McManus**
92 **YEOMAN'S POINT (IRE)**, 9, b g Sadler's Wells (USA)—Truly Bound (USA) **Mr John P. McManus**
93 **YOULBESOLUCKY (IRE)**, 6, b g Accordion—Gaye Humour (IRE) **Mrs G. K. Smith**
94 **YOUNG DUDE (IRE)**, 6, b g Oscar (IRE)—Shuil Realt (IRE) **Mrs P. Shanahan**

Other Owners: Mr P. Hickey, Mr J. Rowan, Mr G. Hopkins, Mr J. Power, Mr M. Masterton, Mr P. Beighton, T. G. Coughlan, A. C. Eaves, Mr J. D. Hancock, T. C. Marshall, J. C. McGrath, Terry McDermott, Mr W. Murphy, Mr D. Murray, Mr W. J. Norton, P. J. Surtees, Mr G. R. Taylor.

---

445 **MR O. O'NEILL, Cheltenham**
Postal: **Cleeve Lodge, Cleeve Hill, Cheltenham, Gloucestershire, GL52 3PW.**
Contacts: **PHONE/FAX (01242) 673275 MOBILE (07733) 210177**

1 **ALLNITE**, 5, b g Bonny Scot (IRE)—Gold Nite **I. G. Potter**
2 **CASTLE RIVER (USA)**, 6, b g Irish River (FR)—Castellina (USA) **H C T Racing**
3 **DARING NEWS**, 10, b g Risk Me (FR)—Hot Sunday Sport **M. J. Brown**
4 **FOREST GREEN FLYER**, 9, b m Syrtos—Bolton Flyer **K. G. Boulton**
5 **MEMORIES OF GOLD (IRE)**, 5, b m Carroll House—Sweet Harmony (IRE) **J. A. Danahar**
6 **RICARDO'S CHANCE**, 6, b g Alflora (IRE)—Jims Sister **J. A. Atkin**
7 **SYLCAN EXPRESS**, 12, b g Sylvan Express—Dercanny **R. N. Fletcher**
8 **WILL YOU COME ON (IRE)**, 7, br m Carroll House—Tengello **J. A. Danahar**

Other Owners: M. J. Hurley, D. Teevan.

Assistant Trainer: John C Gilbert

Jockey (NH): V. Slattery.

---

446 **MR J. G. M. O'SHEA, Westbury on Severn**
Postal: **Tudor Racing Stables, Elton, Westbury on Severn, Gloucestershire, GL14 1JN.**
Contacts: **OFFICE/FAX (01452) 760835 MOBILE (07917) 124717**
WEBSITE www.johnoshearacing.co.uk

1 **BESTSELLER**, 5, ch m Selkirk (USA)—Top Shop **KJB Investments Ltd**
2 **BONJOUR BOND (IRE)**, 4, ro g Portrait Gallery (IRE)—Musical Essence **C. B. Beck**
3 **BRADY BOYS (USA)**, 8, b g Cozzene (USA)—Elvia (USA) **Mr D. Cound and Mr R. Davies**

MR J. G. M. O'SHEA—continued

4 **CULLIAN**, 8, b m Missed Flight—Diamond Gig **KJB Investments Ltd**
5 **DENARIUS (USA)**, 10, b g Silver Hawk (USA)—Ambrosine (USA) **KJB Investments Ltd**
6 **DUBAI LIGHTNING (USA)**, 5, br g Seeking The Gold (USA)—Heraklia (USA) **J. J. Ryan**
7 **HONEST INJUN**, 4, b c Efisio—Sioux **J. J. Ryan**
8 **JIM BELL (IRE)**, 10, br g Supreme Leader—Mightyatom **K. W. Bell**
9 **KIMBERLEY**, 10, b g Shareef Dancer (USA)—Willowbank **K. W. Bell & Son Ltd**
10 **LADY RADMORE**, 6, b m Overbury (IRE)—Val's Jem **J. R. Salter**
11 **LITZINSKY**, 7, b g Muhtarram (USA)—Boulevard Girl **Mrs R. E. Nelmes**
12 **LUCKY ARTHUR**, 4, ch f Grand Lodge (USA)—Soltura (IRE) **A. Watling**
13 **MAJOR BLUE**, 4, ch g Scallywag—Town Blues **Mrs Ruth Nelmes, C L Dubois, P Smith**
14 **MEANDMRSJONES**, 6, ch m Alderbrook—Dunbrody Abbey **Mrs M. E. Jones**
15 **MUFFLER**, 7, b h Next Boom (USA)—Public Offering **The Dog & Muffler Syndicate**
16 **MY NATIVE OGAN (IRE)**, 10, ch g Be My Native (USA)—Cooleogan **The Cross Racing Club**
17 **NORDIC PRINCE (IRE)**, 14, b g Nordance (USA)—Royal Desire **Blue Shirts**
18 **RABITATIT (IRE)**, 4, b f Robellino (USA)—Coupled **G. C. Roberts**
19 **RAVENGLASS (USA)**, 6, b h Miswaki (USA)—Urus (USA) **K. W. Bell**
20 **SHOW OF HANDS (IRE)**, 5, b g Zaffaran (USA)—New Technique (FR) **K. W. Bell**
21 **SO SURE (IRE)**, 5, b g Definite Article—Zorilla **Premier-Racing.Net (2)**
22 **ST BARCHAN (IRE)**, 4, ch g Grand Lodge (USA)—Moon Tango (IRE) **G. C. Roberts**
23 **STAFFORD KING (IRE)**, 8, b h Nicolotte—Opening Day **N. G. H. Ayliffe**
24 **TAM O'SHANTER**, 11, gr g Persian Bold—No More Rosies **N. M. Lowe**
25 **TOM BELL (IRE)**, 5, b g King's Theatre (USA)—Nordic Display (USA) **K. W. Bell**
26 **TUDOR BELL (IRE)**, 4, b c Definite Article—Late Night Lady (IRE) **K. W. Bell & Son Ltd**
27 **VALUABLE GIFT**, 8, ch g Cadeaux Genereux—Valbra **The Cross Racing Club**

THREE-YEAR-OLDS

28 **ARTHURS DREAM (IRE)**, b c Desert Prince (IRE)—Blueprint (USA) **A. Watling**
29 **BOB'S FLYER**, br f Lujain—Gymcrak Flyer **J. J. Ryan**
30 **BRADS HOUSE (IRE)**, b c Rossini (USA)—Gold Stamp **The Cross Racing Club**
31 **LORNA DUNE**, b f Desert Story (IRE)—Autumn Affair **G. C. Roberts**
32 **MICKEY PEARCE (IRE)**, b c Rossini (USA)—Lucky Coin **The Lovely Jubbly's**
33 **MISTER BELL**, gr c Lujain (USA)—Zaragossa **K. W. Bell**
34 **SONGGARIA**, b f Kingsinger (IRE)—Paula's Joy **G. C. Roberts**
35 **VALET**, b c Kayf Tara—Val de Fleurie (GER) **Mrs M. E. M. Konig**

Other Owners: N. G. H. Ayliffe, K. Batchelor, C. L. Dubois, Mr A. J. Eyles, G. Gwynne, M. P. James, P. Smith, W. Tyler, Mrs M. J. Whitehead.

Jockey (flat): R. Havlin, D. Sweeney. **Conditional:** G. Richards.

---

447 MR EUGENE M. O'SULLIVAN, Mallow
Postal: "Millwood", Currabower, Lombardstown, Mallow, Co. Cork, Ireland.
Contacts: PHONE +353 (0) 22 47304/47116 FAX +353 (0) 22 47588
MOBILE +353 (0) 86 2541398
E-MAIL eugenemosullivan@eircom.net

1 **ARCTIC TIMES (IRE)**, 9, ch g Montelimar (USA)—Miss Penguin **Trevor Hemmings**
2 **ARISTOCRATIC YANK (IRE)**, 6, b g Lord Americo—Dixons Dutchess (IRE) **Anne O'Sullivan**
3 **BANDON VALLEY (IRE)**, 11, b g Montelimar (USA)—Chattering **Bandon Valley Syndicate**
4 4, Br g Presenting—Be My Citizen **Trevor Hemmings**
5 **BILL DICK (IRE)**, 5, b g Topanoora—Dazmaz (IRE) **P. Byrne**
6 **BLACK LORD (IRE)**, 7, b g Mister Lord (USA)—Deruma Lady (IRE) **J. Fitzpatrick**
7 **CARAS CHOICE (IRE)**, 6, b g Mister Lord—Deruma Lady (IRE) **J. Fitzpatrick**
8 **CHAPEL CROSS (IRE)**, 7, b g Old Vic—Desert Flight (IRE) **E. M. O'Sullivan**
9 **COME HEER TO ME (IRE)**, 7, b m Supreme Leader—Easy Run (IRE) **E. J. O'Sullivan**
10 4, Ch g Anshan—Curra Citizen (IRE) **E. J. O'Sullivan**
11 **DORAN'S DAY (IRE)**, 8, b g Gildoran—Inverdonan **Trevor Hemmings**
12 **EVA BRAUN (IRE)**, 5, gr m Germany (USA)—Zodiac Lady **E. J. O'Sullivan**
13 4, g g Blue Ocean (USA)—Fern Fields (IRE) **Mr J. P. McManus**
14 **FOUR EAGLES (USA)**, 7, b g Lear Fan—Bloomingly (ARG) **Oliver McDowell**
15 **FRUITFULL CITIZEN (IRE)**, 5, ch m Anshan—Sweet Peach (IRE) **E. J. O'Sullivan**
16 **HANG SENG (IRE)**, 7, b g Phardante (FR)—Portia's Delight (IRE) **John White & Dermot Grumley**
17 **IAMHERE (IRE)**, 7, b g Mister Lord (USA)—Angie's Delight **J. Fitzpatrick**
18 **ISLAND PASS (IRE)**, 5, ch m Among Men (USA)—Ceremony **D. B. Riordan**

MR EUGENE M. O'SULLIVAN—continued

19 **JOHN STORM (IRE)**, 7, b g Glacial Storm (USA)—Johns Rose (IRE) **E. M. O'Sulivan & M. Foley**
20 **LOVE OF CLASSICS**, 5, b g Classic Cliche (IRE)—Ardent Love (IRE) **P. Byrne**
21 **LUBY (IRE)**, 7, b g Be My Native (USA)—Foxed (IRE) **E. M. O'Sullivan**
22 **MIDNIGHT RUN (IRE)**, 5, b g Lord Americo—Shannon Amber (IRE) **M. O'Flynn**
23 4, Ch g Classic Memory—Monkey Wench (IRE) **John G. Linehan**
24 **MONTREAL (IRE)**, 8, b br m Marju (IRE)—Porto Alegre **E. M. O'Sullivan**
25 **NIGHT BILLIARDS (IRE)**, 7, b g Distinctly North (USA)—Harp Song **Kate Jarvey**
26 **PASERELLA (IRE)**, 7, b g Persian Mews—Knockavilla **Eamon Murray & Maura Moylan**
27 **PEACH OF A CITIZEN (IRE)**, 6, b m Anshan—Sweet Peach (IRE) **E. J. O'Sullivan**
28 **PRIME LEADER (IRE)**, 6, b g Supreme Leader—Coole Eile (IRE) **Trevor Hemmings**
29 **TEO PERUGO (IRE)**, 6, b g Perugino (USA)—Teodosia **Camden Racing Syndicate**
30 **THE ALTER BOY (IRE)**, 7, b g Executive Perk—Beyond It **T.Cremin, J. Quaid, C. O. Crualaoi**
31 **TIME TO SELL (IRE)**, 6, b br g Executive Perk—Town of Trees (IRE) **Trevor Hemmings**
32 **TUBA (IRE)**, 10, b g Orchestra—Princess Paula **Kilshannig Racing Syndicate**
33 **TWO EXCUSES (IRE)**, 7, ch g Germany (USA)—Argideen Diver (IRE) **John G. Linehan**
34 4, Gr f Moonax (IRE)—Zodiac Lady **E. J. O'Sullivan**

Other Owners: A. Ahern, Kevin Dennehy, Aidan Foley, John Hickey, Mr Denis A. Linehan, Paul McDowell, Sean O'Donovan, Mrs M. C. O'Sullivan, Ger Stack.

Conditional: M. J. Ferris. **Apprentice:** D. G. O'Shea. **Amateur:** Mr E. Power, Mr J. Dullea, Mr W. M. O'Sullivan, Mr Justin Rea.

---

448 MR E. R. OERTEL, Newmarket
Postal: **Carriageway Stables, Hamilton Road, Newmarket, Suffolk, CB8 7JQ.**
Contacts: **PHONE (01638) 664292 FAX (01638) 561186 MOBILE (07833) 722655**
E-MAIL eoertel@hotmail.com WEBSITE www.eoertel.com

1 **ARMATORE (USA)**, 5, b g Gone West (USA)—Awesome Account (USA) **The Wandering Worfe Partnership**
2 **HARRY TU**, 5, b g Millkom—Risky Tu **Mr E. R. Oertel**
3 **MISS GLORY BE**, 7, b m Glory of Dancer—Miss Blondie (USA) **Mr E. R. Oertel**
4 **PIROUETTES (IRE)**, 5, b m Royal Applause—Dance Serenade (IRE) **Mr E. R. Oertel**
5 **RAGASAH**, 7, b m Glory of Dancer—Slight Risk **Mr E. R. Oertel**
6 **THE BARONESS (IRE)**, 5, b m Blues Traveller (IRE)—Wicken Wonder (IRE) **Mr E. R. Oertel**

Other Owners: R. Sedgley, Friends Of The Turf Racing.

---

449 MR J. A. B. OLD, Wroughton
Postal: **Upper Herdswick Farm, Hackpen, Burderop, Wroughton, Swindon, Wiltshire, SN4 0QH.**
Contacts: **OFFICE (01793) 845200 CAR (07836) 721459 FAX (01793) 845201**

1 **ALMUTASADER**, 5, b h Sadler's Wells (USA)—Dreamawhile **W. E. Sturt**
2 **ATTORNEY GENERAL (IRE)**, 6, b g Sadler's Wells (USA)—Her Ladyship **W. E. Sturt**
3 **BACK AMONG FRIENDS**, 7, b g Bob Back (USA)—Betty's Gold **Mrs J. A. Fowler**
4 **BARRYS ARK (IRE)**, 7, b br g Commanche Run—Hand Me Down **W. E. Sturt**
5 **BOTHERED (IRE)**, 5, ch g Anshan—Inamuddle (IRE) **W. E. Sturt**
6 **BOUNDARY HOUSE**, 7, ch g Afflora (IRE)—Preacher's Gem **Mrs P. V. Antrobus**
7 **BRODICK CASTLE**, 6, gr g Arzanni—Celtic Comma **Antrobus Britten Dacey Partnership**
8 **BRONZE KING**, 5, b g Rakaposhi King—Bronze Sunset
9 **CAPTAIN AUBREY (IRE)**, 6, b g Supreme Leader—Hamers Girl **W. E. Sturt**
10 **COLLINE DE FLEURS**, 5, b m Afflora (IRE)—B Greenhill **The Wheels Have Come Off**
11 **DUNSHAUGHLIN (IRE)**, 8, b g Supreme Leader—Russian Gale (IRE) **W. E. Sturt**
12 **DURANTE (IRE)**, 7, ch g Shernazar—Sweet Tune **W. E. Sturt**
13 **FLEXIBLE CONCIENCE (IRE)**, 10, br g Glacial Storm (USA)—Philly Athletic **Old Fools Partnership**
14 **FUTURE LEGEND**, 4, ch g Lomitas—Proudy (IRE) **W. E. Sturt**
15 **GLIDE**, 4, ch g In The Wings—Ash Glade **W. E. Sturt**
16 **KILDONNAN**, 6, b g Bob's Return (IRE)—Celtic Tore (IRE) **W. E. Sturt**
17 **KINGTOBEE (IRE)**, 7, b g King's Ride—Zephyrelle (IRE) **W. E. Sturt**
18 **LITTLE HERMAN (IRE)**, 9, b g Mandalus—Kilbricken Bay **W. E. Sturt**
19 **LITTLE SALTEE (IRE)**, 5, ch g Anshan—Shuil Na Mhuire (IRE) **W. E. Sturt**
20 **MAJESTIC BAY (IRE)**, 9, b g Unfuwain (USA)—That'll Be The Day (IRE) **W. J. Smith and M. D. Dudley**
21 **MISS MAILMIT**, 8, b m Rakaposhi King—Flora Louisa **P. D. Guntrip**
22 **MONTEFORTE**, 7, b g Afflora (IRE)—Double Dutch **W. E. Sturt**
23 **PARACHUTE**, 6, ch g Hector Protector (USA)—Shortfall **W. E. Sturt - Osborne House II**

MR J. A. B. OLD—continued

24 **PHYSICAL GRAFFITI (USA)**, 8, b g Mister Baileys—Gleaming Water (USA) **Old Fools Partnership**
25 **PIP MOSS**, 10, ch g Le Moss—My Aisling **Mrs A. M. Old**
26 **QUARRYMOUNT**, 4, b g Polar Falcon (USA)—Quilt **W. E. Sturt**
27 **ROUND THE HORN (IRE)**, 5, ch g Master Willie—Gaye Fame **W. E. Sturt**
28 **SARGASSO SEA**, 8, gr g Greensmith—Sea Spice **W. E. Sturt**
29 **SHERNATRA (IRE)**, 6, b g Shernazar—Miss Nancy **W. E. Sturt**
30 **SIR TALBOT**, 11, b g Ardross—Bermuda Lily **W. E. Sturt**
31 5, B g Bob Back (USA)—Skiddaw Samba **W. E. Sturt**
32 **SMEATHE'S RIDGE**, 7, b g Rakaposhi King—Mrs Barty (IRE) **P. D. Guntrip**
33 **SMOKESTACK (IRE)**, 9, b g Lord Americo—Chiminee Fly **C. J. Jenkins**
34 **STEVE THE FISH (IRE)**, 9, ch g Dry Dock—Country Clothing **The Old Boys Partnership**
35 **THE DUCKPOND (IRE)**, 8, ch g Bob's Return (IRE)—Miss Gosling **W. E. Sturt**
36 **THEDREAMSTILLALIVE (IRE)**, 5, ch g Houmayoun (FR)—State of Dream (IRE) **W. E. Sturt**
37 **TOP RAM (IRE)**, 5, ch g Topanoora—Aries Girl **W. E. Sturt**
38 4, ch g Shernazar—Toposki (FR) **Mr J. A. B. Old**
39 **TUESDAY CLUB (IRE)**, 6, ch g Old Vic—Asfreeasthewind (IRE) **W. J. Smith and M. D. Dudley**
40 **WAIN MOUNTAIN**, 9, b g Unfuwain (USA)—Mountain Memory **W. J. Smith and M. D. Dudley**
41 **WHOSETHATFOR (IRE)**, 5, b g Beneficial—Native Craft (IRE) **W. E. Sturt**
42 **YOUNG COLLIER**, 6, b g Vettori (IRE)—Cockatoo Island **W. E. Sturt**

THREE-YEAR-OLDS

43 **SIDNEY CHARLES (IRE)**, br g Mister Baileys—Distant Music **P. D. Guntrip**

Other Owners: A. J. Britten, Mrs J. B. Dacey, MR J. A. B. Old.

Jockey (NH): W. Hutchinson, C. Llewellyn.

---

450 **MRS J. K. M. OLIVER, Hawick**
Postal: **The Stables Cottage, Hassendean Bank, Hawick, Roxburghshire, TD9 8RX.**
Contacts: **PHONE/FAX (01450) 870216 MOBILE (07774) 426017**

1 **HE'S MY UNCLE**, 10, ch g Phardante (FR)—Red Dusk **Mrs J. K. M. Oliver**
2 **LADY HOWE**, 5, br m Lord Americo—Howcleuch **Miss J. S. Peat**
3 **LUCKEN HOWE**, 6, b g Keen—Gilston Lass **Mrs J. K. M. Oliver**
4 **MINSGILL GLEN**, 9, b m Minster Son—Gilmanscleuch (IRE) **Miss J. S. Peat**
5 **PRINCESS GILLIE**, 6, br m Prince Daniel (USA)—Gilmanscleuch (IRE) **Miss J. S. Peat**

---

451 **MR J. A. OSBORNE, Upper Lambourn**
Postal: **Kingsdown, Upper Lambourn, Hungerford, Berkshire, RG17 8QX.**
Contacts: **PHONE (01488) 73139 FAX (01488) 73084 MOBILE (07860) 533422**
E-MAIL jamieosborne@dial.pipex.com WEBSITE www.jamieosborne.com

1 **ANGELO'S PRIDE**, 4, ch g Young Ern—Considerable Charm **Mr J. A. Osborne**
2 **BOBBY KENNARD**, 6, b g Bobinski—Midnight Break **Mr J. A. Osborne**
3 **DESPERATE DAN**, 4, b g Danzero (AUS)—Alzianah **Mountgrange Stud Ltd**
4 **LAAWARIS (USA)**, 4, b g Souvenir Copy (USA)—Seattle Kat (USA) **Mr J. A. Osborne**
5 **MILK IT MICK**, 4, b c Millkom—Lunar Music **P. J. Dixon**
6 **MORSE (IRE)**, 4, b g Shinko Forest (IRE)—Auriga **Turf 2000 Limited**
7 **OKOBOJI (IRE)**, 4, ch c Indian Ridge—Pool Party (USA) **M. A. Collins**
8 **OVERDRAWN (IRE)**, 4, b g Daggers Drawn—In Denial (IRE) **P. J. Dixon**
9 **RED WINE**, 6, b g Hamas (IRE)—Red Bouquet **P. J. Dixon**
10 **TODLEA (IRE)**, 5, b g Desert Prince (IRE)—Imelda (USA)
11 **VANDENBERGHE**, 6, b g Millkom—Child Star (FR) **D. Marks**

THREE-YEAR-OLDS

12 **BEFITTING**, b g Inchinor—Ellebanna **The Befitting Partnership**
13 **BELLAMANDA (IRE)**, b f Soviet Star (USA)—Alriyaah **R. S. Leslie**
14 **BERKHAMSTED (IRE)**, b c Desert Sun—Accounting **R. S. Leslie**
15 **BLADE OF GOLD (IRE)**, ch f Daggers Drawn (USA)—Be Prepared (IRE) **Dr & Mrs R. Norwich & O. Hegarty**
16 **CHICKEN SOUP**, br c Dansili—Radiancy (IRE) **A. L. Cohen**
17 **CLAP**, b f Royal Applause—Devastating **M. Kerr-Dineen**
18 **CLOONAVERY (IRE)**, b g Xaar—Hero's Pride (FR) **David Reynolds & Chris Watkins**

MR J. A. OSBORNE—continued

19 **COLD PLAY**, ch g Inchinor—Ice House **Mountgrange Stud Ltd**
20 **CROCODILE KISS (IRE)**, b f Rossini (USA)—Pipe Opener **Home House**
21 **CUMMISKEY (IRE)**, b c Orpen (USA)—Ansariya (USA) **M. Tabor**
22 **DALDINI**, b g Josr Algarhoud (IRE)—Arianna Aldini **P. J. Dixon**
23 **FASYLITATOR (IRE)**, b c Fasliyev (USA)—Obsessed **Mountgrange Stud Ltd**
24 **GLAD BIG (GER)**, b c Big Shuffle (USA)—Glady Sum (GER) **Mountgrange Stud Ltd**
25 **ISSY BLUE**, b f Inchinor—Mountain Bluebird (USA) **Mr & Mrs I. Bendelow**
26 **LACONICOS (IRE)**, ch c Foxhound (USA)—Thermopylae **Pat Eddery Racing (Grundy)**
27 **LOWICZ**, b f Polish Precedent (USA)—
        Eldina **Amanda Brudenell, Clemmie Myers, Anthea Gibson Fleming, Gibson Flemming**
28 **MAJOR FAUX PAS (IRE)**, b g Barathea (IRE)—Edwina (IRE) **M. A. Collins**
29 **MOMENT OF CLARITY**, b c Lujain (USA)—Kicka **L. Turland**
30 **MR AITCH (IRE)**, ch c Soviet Star (USA)—Welsh Mist **Studwell Four**
31 **MR MAYFAIR (IRE)**, ch g Entrepreneur—French Gift **R. C. Tooth**
32 **MR REIN (IRE)**, b g Indian Danehill (IRE)—Lady's Vision (IRE) **Studwell Four**
33 **MY TURN NOW (IRE)**, ch g In The Wings—Wishful (IRE) **Mountgrange Stud Ltd**
34 **NITELITE**, ch f Bahamian Bounty—By Candlelight (IRE) **M. Kerr-Dineen**
35 **ORLAR (IRE)**, b f Green Desert (USA)—Soviet Maid (IRE) **W. Durkan**
36 **PERSIAN KHANOOM (IRE)**, b f Royal Applause—Kshessinskaya **Karmaa Racing Limited**
37 **PERSIAN ROCK (IRE)**, b g Namid—Cairo Lady (IRE) **Waney Racing Group Inc & Karmaa Racing**
38 **PHANTOM SONG (IRE)**, gr g Shinko Forest (IRE)—Natural Pearl **Mr & Mrs I. Bendelow**
39 **PIROETTA**, b f Averti (IRE)—Bint Albadou (IRE) **Chris & Antonia Deuters**
40 **RAISE A TUNE (IRE)**, ch c Raise A Grand (IRE)—Magic Melody **H. Rosenblatt and D. Margolis**
41 **ROSIE PAM (IRE)**, b f Lend A Hand—The Iron Lady (IRE) **F. Jones**
42 **SAN TELMO PROSPECT**, b f Royal Applause—Piney River **White Mouse Racing**
43 **SCROOBY BABY**, b f Mind Games—Lunar Music **P. J. Dixon**
44 **SECRET CAVERN (USA)**, b g Lion Cavern (USA)—River Dyna (USA) **Favourites Racing Ltd**
45 **SERGEANT LEWIS**, gr c Mind Games—Silver Blessings **Turf 2000 Limited**
46 **SINGHALESE**, ch f Singspiel (IRE)—Baize **P. J. Dixon**
47 **SOFT FOCUS (IRE)**, b f Spectrum (IRE)—Creme Caramel **WRB Racing 51 (wrbracing.com)**
48 **TEE REX**, ch g Loup Sauvage (USA)—Jeanne Avril **R. C. Tooth**
49 **VISIONIST (IRE)**, b c Orpen (USA)—Lady Taufan (IRE) **Pat Eddery Racing (Alvaro)**

TWO-YEAR-OLDS

50 Ch c 11/3 Royal Applause—Almost Amber (USA) (Mt Livermore (USA)) (32000)
51 B c 27/2 Compton Place—Anatase (Danehill (USA)) (20000)
52 Ch c 27/4 Alhaarth (IRE)—Balladonia (Primo Dominie) (30000) **Cavendish Racing**
53 B f 24/3 Elnadim (USA)—Believing (Belmez (USA)) (2000)
54 B f 15/4 Marju (IRE)—Braari (USA) (Gulch (USA)) (43594) **John Livock Bloodstock Limited**
55 B c 29/3 Distant Music (USA)—Cheeky Weeky (Cadeaux Genereux)
56 B f 22/4 Mozart (IRE)—Chelsea (IRE) (Miswaki (USA)) **Mountgrange Stud Ltd**
57 **CIGGI**, gr c 30/4 Cigar—Silver Blessings (Statoblest) (7000) **Turf 2000 Limited**
58 B f 13/3 Desert Style (IRE)—Cover Girl (IRE) (Common Grounds) (24000)
59 Ch c 1/3 Desert Sun—Daintree (IRE) (Tirol) (24000) **R. S. Leslie**
60 Gr f 21/3 Sinndar (IRE)—Dazzlingly Radiant (Try My Best (USA)) (26000) **Cavendish Star Racing**
61 B c 28/3 Generous (IRE)—Denial (Sadler's Wells (USA)) (26000) **L. Wilson & M. Landau**
62 **DIFFERENT (IRE)**, b c 20/2 Montjeu (IRE)—Zariysha (IRE) (Darshaan) (46947) **Mountgrange Stud Ltd**
63 B c 2/4 Desert Style (IRE)—Double Eight (IRE) (Common Grounds) (52000) **R. S. Leslie & Partners**
64 B c 25/1 Carrowkeel (IRE)—First Degree (Sabrehill (USA)) (58000) **Mountgrange Stud Ltd**
65 **FRENCH OPERA (IRE)**, b c 4/4 Bering—
        On Fair Stage (IRE) (Sadler's Wells (USA)) (52000) **L. Wilson & M. Landau**
66 **ILLUSTRIOUS BLUE**, b brc 29/3 Dansili—Gipsy Moth (Efisio) (28000) **Mr & Mrs I. Bendelow**
67 Br c 3/3 Mujadil (USA)—Karen Blixen (Kris) (22802)
68 B c 5/2 Bertolini (USA)—Leading Princess (IRE) (Double Schwartz) (22000) **Pat Eddery Racing (Danehill)**
69 **MILKOMOVITCH (FR)**, b c 14/4 Millkom—Verrokia (FR) (Always Fair (USA)) (4000)
70 **MIND OUT (USA)**, b c 7/4 Minardi (USA)—
        Tapped Twice (USA) (Pleasant Tap (USA)) (50300) **Mountgrange Stud Ltd**
71 Ch c 11/3 Pivotal—Mint Royale (IRE) (Cadeaux Genereux) (18000)
72 **MISS LACEY**, b f 21/2 Diktat—Launch Time (USA) (Relaunch (USA)) (28000) **Mountgrange Stud Ltd**
73 **MR EXCEL (IRE)**, b c 10/4 Orpen (USA)—Collected (IRE) (Taufan (USA)) (50000) **A. Taylor**
74 B c 13/4 Namid—Mrs Evans (IRE) (College Chapel) (26827)
75 **NIGHT CRUISE (IRE)**, b c 10/4 Docksider (USA)—Addaya (IRE) (Persian Bold) **G. Middlebrook**
76 Ch f 4/5 Priolo—Ostrusa (AUT) (Rustan (HUN)) (16096)
77 B c 24/2 Danehill (USA)—Paper Moon (IRE) (Lake Coniston (IRE)) (190000) **M. Tabor**

MR J. A. OSBORNE—continued

78 PARADISE ROOM (USA), gr ro c 6/3 Lure (USA)—
Dazzling Dancer (USA) (Green Dancer (USA)) (50000) **Mrs J. Flynn & Mrs J. Mulhern**
79 B c 11/2 Indian Ridge—Perfect Plum (IRE) (Darshaan) (40240) **L. Wilson, M. Laudau & M. St Quinton**
80 B c 20/4 Mozart (IRE)—Persian Song (Persian Bold) (15000) **Mrs R. D. Peacock**
81 PIANO PLAYER, b c 23/4 Mozart (IRE)—Got To Go (Shareef Dancer (USA)) (90000) **Mountgrange Stud Ltd**
82 Br c 21/3 Xaar—Prada (GER) (Lagunas) (70422) **R. S. Leslie**
83 B f 28/4 Rossini (USA)—Prima (Primo Dominie) (30180)
84 B br c 22/4 Woodman (USA)—Rhumba Rage (USA) (Nureyev (USA)) (15000) **ITPR**
85 Ch c 15/4 Bertolini (USA)—River Abouali (Bluebird (USA)) (26000)
86 ROCK OF CLOONERY (IRE), b c 13/3 Desert Prince (IRE)—
Mackla (Caerleon (USA)) (33534) **David Reynolds & Chris Watkins**
87 B f 20/2 Mujadil (USA)—Romanovna (Mummy's Pet) (31521)
88 B c 26/4 Daggers Drawn (USA)—Sacred Heart (IRE) (Catrail (USA)) (12072) **John Livock & Partners**
89 B f 3/4 Mull of Kintyre (USA)—Sail Away (GER) (Platini (GER)) (20120)
90 B c 14/3 Key of Luck (USA)—Scene (IRE) (Scenic) **P. J. Dixon**
91 SERGHEYEV, b c 27/2 King's Best (USA)—Schezerade (USA) (Tom Rolfe) (67069) **Mountgrange Stud Ltd**
92 TASK COMPLETE, ch f 3/2 Bahamian Bounty—Taskone (Be My Chief (USA)) **Task Training Limited**
93 TEARS OF A CLOWN (IRE), b c 23/2 Galileo (IRE)—
Mood Swings (IRE) (Shirley Heights) (150904) **Mountgrange Stud Ltd**
94 TOMJOS, br c 15/4 Diktat—Lucky Flinders (Free State) (28000) **A. Taylor**
95 TRYANDSTOPME, b f 3/1 Fraam—
Heavenly Abstone (Interrex (CAN)) (26827) **The Countryside Alliance Racing Partnership**
96 B f 23/4 Daggers Drawn (USA)—Vitality (Young Generation) (35000)
97 WEFT, b c 15/3 Barathea (IRE)—Lighthouse (Warning) (105000) **Mountgrange Stud & Watership Down Stud**
98 Br f 27/1 Key of Luck (USA)—Zoudie (Ezzoud (IRE)) (18000)

Other Owners: Jim McGrath, Ian Morgan, Paul Kemsley, Harry Red Knapp, Gary Middlebrook, Giles Wilson, Clive Owen, Lord De La Warr, Countess De La Warr, P. J. J. Eddery, G. A. Lucas, A. D. Miller, R. Newark, S. J. Piper, B. T. Stewart-Brown Esq, Surrey Laminators Ltd.

---

452 MR H. G. OWEN, Bicester
Postal: **Laurell Farm, Piddington, Bicester, Oxfordshire, OX25 1PY.**
Contacts: **(01844) 237094 (07919) 623375**

1 BARBILYRIFLE (IRE), 4, b g Indian Rocket—Age of Elegance **D. P. Owen**
2 EXCLUSIVE AIR (USA), 6, ch g Affirmed (USA)—Lac Dessert (USA) **Mr H. G. Owen**
3 FINAL LAP, 9, b g Batshoof—Lap of Honour **Mr H. G. Owen**

Other Owners: Mr J. Owen.

Amateur: Mr J. Owen.

---

453 MR BRYN PALLING, Cowbridge
Postal: **Ty-Wyth-Newydd, Tredodridge, Cowbridge, South Glam.**
Contacts: **PHONE (01446) 760122 FAX (01446) 760067 MOBILE (07831) 422492**

1 AMONG FRIENDS (IRE), 5, b g Among Men (USA)—Anita's Contessa (IRE) **P. H. Morgan**
2 CONCHONITA, 5, b m Bishop of Cashel—Cactus Road (FR) **Mrs M. M. Palling**
3 CYFRWYS (IRE), 4, b f Foxhound—Divine Elegance (IRE) **Derek and Jean Clee**
4 DANE RHAPSODY (IRE), 4, b f Danetime (IRE)—Hil Rhapsody **B. Reynolds**
5 DANIELLE'S LAD, 9, b g Emarati (USA)—Cactus Road (FR) **Mrs M. M. Palling**
6 ELIDORE, 5, b m Danetime (IRE)—Beveled Edge **N. Thomas**
7 GIOCOSO (USA), 5, b h Bahri (USA)—Wing My Chimes (USA) **Mr W. Devine & Mr P. Morgan**
8 GOJO (IRE), 4, b f Danetime (IRE)—Pretonic **A. J. Yemm**
9 JAKARMI, 4, b f Merdon Melody—Lady Ploy **Mrs M. M. Palling**
10 KINISKA, 4, b f Merdon Melody—Young Whip **Mrs M. M. Palling**
11 MY MICHELLE, 4, b f Ali-Royal—April Magic **P. H. Morgan**
12 PRINCIPESSA, 4, b f Machiavellian (USA)—Party Doll **Derek and Jean Clee**
13 SINGITTA, 4, b f Singspiel (IRE)—Ferber's Follies (USA) **Mr W. Devine & Mr P. Morgan**
14 SWOON, 4, b f Night Shift (USA)—Rock The Boat **Mr W. Devine & Mr P. Morgan**
15 TEEHEE (IRE), 7, b g Anita's Prince—Regal Charmer **Mrs M. M. Palling & Mr Paul Young**

MR BRYN PALLING—continued

THREE-YEAR-OLDS
16 **CARCINETTO (IRE)**, b f Danetime (IRE)—Dolphin Stamp (IRE) **A. J. Yemm**
17 **CHICKS BABE**, br f Chickawicka (IRE)—Ballasilla **Mrs M. M. Palling**
18 **CHICKS GIRL**, ch f Chickawicka (IRE)—Princess Kelly **Mrs M. M. Palling**
19 **CRYSTAL MYSTIC (IRE)**, b g Anita's Prince—Out On Her Own **Los Cabelleros**
20 **DANITA DANCER (IRE)**, b f Barathea (IRE)—Carranita (IRE) **Mrs A. J. Quinn**
21 **GRANARY GIRL**, b f Kingsinger (IRE)—Highland Blue **T. M. Clarke**
22 **INKA DANCER (IRE)**, ch f Intikhab (USA)—Grannys Reluctance (IRE) **Mrs A. J. Quinn**
23 **LUCKY EMERALD (IRE)**, b f Lend A Hand—Anita's Love (IRE) **T. M. Clarke**
24 **MIGHTY MOVER (IRE)**, ch c Bahhare (USA)—Ericeira (IRE)
25 **RINGVAUXHALL**, b g Magic Ring (IRE)—Beveled Edge **Mr R. Edwards & Steve Hughes**
26 **ROYAL COZYFIRE (IRE)**, b g Revoque (IRE)—Mystic Thoughts (IRE) **Crosslee PLC**

TWO-YEAR-OLDS
27 **COLD CURE**, b c 14/4 Averti (IRE)—Forest Song (Forzando) (3000) **A. J. Yemm**
28 **MISS MAXI (IRE)**, b f 24/4 Bold Fact (USA)—Beautyofthepeace (IRE) (Exactly Sharp (USA)) (8000) **A. J. Yemm**
29 B f 4/4 Montjeu (IRE)—Shirley Blue (IRE) (Shirley Heights) (21000)

Other Owners: J. R. Edwards, Mr S. J. Hughes, F. J. Lalies, R. Lewis, M. Lloyd, K. A. Morris, K. M. Rideout, P. A. Young.

---

454 **MR J. F. PANVERT, Tonbridge**
Postal: **Willow Tree Stables, Vines Lane, Hildenborough, Kent, TN11 9LT.**
Contacts: **HOME/FAX (01732) 834467 MOBILES (07764) 579175/(07732) 273837**
E-MAIL willowtreeracingstables.fsnet.co.uk

1 **COMMANCHE GENERAL (IRE)**, 8, b g Commanche Run—Shannon Amber (IRE) **Mr J. F. Panvert**
2 **GLOWING EMBER**, 5, b m Blushing Flame (USA)—California Dreamin **Mr J. F. Panvert**
3 **MIDNIGHT MARINE**, 4, b g Midnight Legend—The Bizzo **Mr J. F. Panvert**
4 **MR MCDELLON (IRE)**, 8, ch g Duky—Erin Brownie **Mr J. F. Panvert**
5 **ROYAL ACCENT**, 8, gr m Norton Challenger—Glebes Scallywag VII **Mr J. F. Panvert**
6 **SECRET EARNINGS**, 6, br g Young Ern—Secret Account **Mr J. F. Panvert**

THREE-YEAR-OLDS
7 **SUPERIOR DREAM**, b g Superpower—California Dreamin **Mr J. F. Panvert**

Assistant Trainer: Miss J Clark

Jockey (NH): O. McPhail. **Conditional:** C. Murray.

---

455 **MR ANDREW PARKER, Lockerbie**
Postal: **Parker Racing, Douglas Hall Farm, Lockerbie, Dumfriesshire, DG11 1AD.**
Contacts: **PHONE (01576) 510232/300238 FAX (01576) 510232 MOBILE (07968) 325650**

1 **BEHAVINGBADLY (IRE)**, 10, b g Lord Americo—Audrey's Turn **H. Henderson**
2 **CAYMANAS BAY**, 5, ch g Karinga Bay—Carribean Sound **Hamilton House Ltd**
3 **EM'S GUY**, 7, b g Royal Fountain—Gaelic Empress **J. J. Paterson**
4 **EM'S ROYALTY**, 8, b g Royal Fountain—Gaelic Empress **J. J. Paterson**
5 **FOREVER EYESOFBLUE**, 8, b g Leading Counsel (USA)—Forever Silver (IRE) **Mrs W. Wright**
6 **GANGSTERS R US (IRE)**, 9, br g Treasure Hunter—Our Mare Mick **J. Bagwell-Purefoy**
7 **HARLOV (FR)**, 10, ch g Garde Royale—Paulownia (FR) **Mr & Mrs Raymond Anderson Green**
8 **HUGO DE GREZ (FR)**, 10, b g Useful (FR)—Piqua des Gres (FR) **Mr & Mrs Raymond Anderson Green**
9 **JACKSONVILLE (FR)**, 8, b g Petit Montmorency (USA)—
　　　　　　　　　　　　　　　　　　Quinine Des Aulnes (FR) **Mr & Mrs Raymond Anderson Green**
10 **LAMPION DU BOST (FR)**, 6, b g Mont Basile (FR)—Ballerine du Bost (FR) **The Dodoz Partnership**
11 **LEADAWAY**, 6, b g Supreme Leader—Annicombe Run **Mr & Mrs Raymond Anderson Green**
12 **MAJOR ROYAL (FR)**, 5, ch g Garde Royale—Majorica Queen (FR) **Mr & Mrs Raymond Anderson Green**
13 **OKAYMAN (FR)**, 4, b g Mansonnien (FR)—Aykoku Saky (FR) **Mr & Mrs Raymond Anderson Green**

MR ANDREW PARKER—continued

14 **OVERSERVED**, 6, b br g Supreme Leader—Divine Comedy (IRE) **Mr & Mrs Raymond Anderson Green**
15 **TO THE FUTURE (IRE)**, 9, ch g Bob Back (USA)—Lady Graduate (IRE) **Mr & Mrs Raymond Anderson Green**
16 **TULACH ARD (IRE)**, 10, b g Erdelistan (FR)—Noon Hunting **Mr and Mrs M. C. MacKenzie**

Other Owners: Mrs S. E. Bagwell-Purefoy, Mr B. Dodds, Mr C. Moore, Mrs J. Parker.

Assistant Trainer: Mrs J Parker & G Kerrr

Conditional: P. Robson.

---

456 **MR J. E. PARKES, Malton**
Postal: **Garth Cottage, Upper Helmsley, North Yorkshire, YO41 1JY.**
Contacts: **PHONE/FAX** (01759) 372258 **MOBILE** (07866) 566499
E-MAIL llynnjade@aol.com

1 **APPETINA**, 4, b f Perugino (USA)—Tina Heights **P. J. Sweeney**
2 **CHAMPAGNE LOU LOU**, 7, b m Supreme Leader—Highfrith **D. Mossop**
3 **GRUB STREET**, 9, b g Barathea (USA)—Broadmara (IRE) **Mrs B. J. Sands**
4 **KING NICHOLAS (USA)**, 6, b g Nicholas (USA)—Lifetime Honour (USA) **M. Wormald**
5 **NEWTONIAN (USA)**, 6, ch g Distant View (USA)—Polly Adler (USA) **R. J. Flegg**
6 **SPY MASTER**, 7, b g Green Desert (USA)—Obsessive (USA) **Miss J. E. Frank**
7 **WALKMILL (IRE)**, 4, ch f Perugino (USA)—Simply Marilyn (IRE) **D. Mossop**
8 **ZAP ATTACK**, 5, b g Zafonic (USA)—Rappa Tap Tap (FR) **H. J. Bousfield**

THREE-YEAR-OLDS

9 **STARLIGHT RIVER (IRE)**, b f Spectrum (IRE)—Prosaic Star (IRE) **P. J. Sweeney**

Other Owners: D. E. Furman, Mrs L. M. Parkes.

Assistant Trainer: Mrs L Parkes

---

457 **MR J. R. PAYNE, Dulverton**
Postal: **Lower Holworthy Farm, Brompton Regis, Dulverton, Somerset, TA22 9NY.**
Contacts: **HOME/FAX** (01398) 371244

1 **ATHNOWEN (IRE)**, 13, b g Lord Americo—Lady Bluebird **R. J. Payne**
2 6, B g Puissance—Jennies' Gem **Mr J. R. Payne**
3 5, B m Wimbleball—Spirit Level **R. J. Payne**
4 5, B g Wimbleball—Toll Bridge **R. J. Payne**

---

458 **MR J. W. (PIP) PAYNE, Newmarket**
Postal: **Frankland Lodge, Hamilton Road, Newmarket, Suffolk, CB8 7JQ.**
Contacts: **PHONE** (01638) 668675 **FAX** (01638) 668675 **MOBILE** (07850) 133116
E-MAIL pip.payne@virgin.net

1 **CAPTAIN SMOOTHY**, 5, b g Charmer—The Lady Captain **Mr & Mrs P. Cranney**
2 **DARLA (IRE)**, 4, b f Night Shift (USA)—Darbela (IRE) **Mrs R. A. C. Vigors**
3 **FITTING GUEST (IRE)**, 4, ch g Grand Lodge (USA)—Sarah-Clare **T. W. Morley**
4 **KOMENA**, 7, b m Komaite (USA)—Mena **The Frankland Lodgers**
5 **NIGHT PROSPECTOR**, 5, b h Night Shift (USA)—Pride of My Heart **Mrs R. A. C. Visors**
6 **NISR**, 8, b g Grand Lodge (USA)—Tharwa (IRE) **Mrs L. M. Payne**
7 **POINT MAN (IRE)**, 5, b g Pivotal—Pursuit of Truth (USA) **Mrs J. W. Payne**
8 **TABOOR (IRE)**, 7, b g Mujadil (USA)—Christoph's Girl **T. W. Morley**
9 **TAIYO**, 5, b m Tagula (IRE)—Tharwa (IRE) **Mrs M. J. Morley**
10 **VICIANA**, 6, b m Sir Harry Lewis (USA)—Ludoviciana **G. W. Paul**

THREE-YEAR-OLDS

11 **COLLECT**, b f Vettori (IRE)—Ring Fence **David Thom**
12 **HILL OF CLARE (IRE)**, gr f Daylami (IRE)—Sarah-Clare **Mrs C. McGinn**
13 **LADRO VOLANTE (IRE)**, b br c Benny The Dip (USA)—Genoa **M. H. Dixon**

MR J. W. (PIP) PAYNE—continued

14 **MORETONS,** b c Sir Harry Lewis (USA)—Ludoviciana **G. W. Paul**
15 B f Primo Dominie—Sartigila **S. Gollogly**
16 **SUNNY TIMES (IRE),** b f Raise A Grand (IRE)—Dragon Star **T. H. Barma**

TWO-YEAR-OLDS

17 Gr f 14/3 Silver Patriarch (IRE)—Lady Coldunell (Deploy) (5500) **David Thom**

Apprentice: Brian Reilly.

---

459 **MR R. E. PEACOCK, Malmesbury**
Postal: **Oliver House Stud, Chedglow, Malmesbury, Wiltshire, SN16 9EZ.**
Contacts: **PHONE (01666) 577238 MOBILE (07748) 565574**

1 **CALL MY GUEST (IRE),** 15, b g Be My Guest (USA)—Overcall **Derek and Jean Clee**
2 **CANDY ANCHOR (FR),** 6, b m Slip Anchor—Kandavu **Mr R. E. Peacock**
3 **HERALDRY (IRE),** 5, b g Mark of Esteem (IRE)—Sorb Apple (IRE) **Mrs A. M. O'Sullivan**
4 **WHITE LEDGER (IRE),** 6, ch g Ali-Royal (IRE)—Boranwood (IRE) **Mr R. E. Peacock**

Assistant Trainer: Mrs C Peacock

Jockey (flat): V Slattery, S. Sanders. **Jockey (NH):** V Slattery.

---

460 **MR B. A. PEARCE, Lingfield**
Postal: **Sheridan Farm, West Park Road, Newchapel, Lingfield, Surrey, RH7 6HT.**
Contacts: **PHONE (01342) 713437 MOBILE (07710) 513913**

1 **BARABELLA (IRE),** 4, gr f Barathea (IRE)—Thatchabella (IRE) **M. P. Merwood**
2 **BRETTON,** 4, b g Polar Prince (IRE)—Understudy **N. J. B. Lawless**
3 **CARGO,** 6, b g Emarati (USA)—Portvasco **N. J. B. Lawless**
4 **LEYAALY,** 6, ch m Night Shift (USA)—Lower The Tone (IRE) **M. P. Merwood**
5 **MANTEL MINI,** 6, b m Reprimand—Foretell **M. J. Gibbs**
6 **NO MERCY,** 9, ch g Faustus (USA)—Nashville Blues (IRE) **P. M. Barter**
7 **SHAAMIT'S ALL OVER,** 6, br m Shaamit (IRE)—First Time Over **R. J. Gray**
8 **TOP PLACE,** 4, b f Compton Place—Double Top (IRE) **Kilmacanogue Racing Syndicate**

Other Owners: M. Rees, Mr P. Daly, R. D. John, T. D. Reed, J. Salter.

Jockey (flat): T. P. Queally. **Jockey (NH):** P. J. Brennan. **Apprentice:** P. Makin. **Amateur:** Mr G. Gallagher.

---

461 **MR J. PEARCE, Newmarket**
Postal: **Wroughton House, 37 Old Station Road, Newmarket, Suffolk, CB8 8DT.**
Contacts: **PHONE (01638) 664669/669891 MOBILE (07876) 444456/(07787) 517876**
E-MAIL jeffreypearce@apiserve.com

1 **DOCTOR DENNIS (IRE),** 8, b g Last Tycoon—Noble Lustre (USA)
2 **ELLINA,** 4, b f Robellino (USA)—Native Flair **The Exclusive Two Partnership**
3 **POLAR HAZE,** 8, ch g Polar Falcon (USA)—Sky Music **M. M. Foulger**
4 **REAP,** 7, b g Emperor Jones (USA)—Corn Futures **S. Robinson & D. F. Sills**
5 **SEEJAY,** 5, b m Bahamian Bounty—Grand Splendour **A. J. Holder**
6 **STARGEM,** 4, b f Compton Place—Holy Smoke **Mrs M. Miller & Mr C. Tulip**
7 **SUPER CANYON,** 7, ch g Gulch (USA)—Marina Park
8 **THE FUN MERCHANT,** 4, b g Mind Games—Sinking **J. Laughton & B & G Racing**
9 **WAVET,** 5, b m Pursuit of Love—Ballerina Bay **B. J. Goldsmith**

THREE-YEAR-OLDS

10 Ch g Compton Place—Ballerina Bay **Mr J. Pearce**
11 **CAPTAIN MARGARET,** b f Royal Applause—Go For Red (IRE) **Mrs M. A. Baxter & Mr & Mrs Matthews**
12 **DIVANI (IRE),** b f Shinko Forest (IRE)—Supreme Crown (USA) **Mr D. Leech & Mr A. Watford**
13 **FANTASY RIDE,** b c Bahhare (USA)—Grand Splendour **J. P. Hayes & Mr A. Puddick**
14 **GOLDEN ANTHEM (USA),** ch f Lion Cavern (USA)—Bacinella (USA) **S. Birdseye**

MR J. PEARCE—continued

15 **RAISON DETRE**, b c Mtoto—Kelimutu **J. R. Furlong**
16 **RUSSIAN SERVANA (IRE)**, b f Rossini (USA)—Ring of Light **Mr J. Pearce**
17 **YELDHAM LADY**, b f Mujahid (USA)—Future Options **Mrs E. M. Clarke**

TWO-YEAR-OLDS

18 **ALCESTES SELECTION**, b f 12/2 Selkirk (USA)—Attitre (FR) (Mtoto) **Newsells Park Stud (Limited)**
19 **GLASNAS GIANT**, b f 26/2 Giant's Causeway (USA)—
Gleefully (USA) (Septieme Ciel (USA)) **Newsells Park Stud (Limited)**
20 **UNASUMING (IRE)**, b f 22/3 Orpen (USA)—Untold (Final Straw) (17000) **J. Hayes**

Assistant Trainer: Mr Simon Pearce

Jockey (flat): J. Quinn. **Amateur:** Mr Simon Pearce.

462
MR K. R. PEARCE, Carmarthen
Postal: **The Brambles, Laugharne, Carmarthen, Carmarthenshire, SA33 4QP.**
Contacts: **HOME (01994) 427486 WORK (01994) 427868 FAX (01994) 427967**
MOBILE (07884) 184417
E-MAIL sandra.pearce@tiscali.co.uk

1 **BLACK LEGEND (IRE)**, 6, b g Marju (IRE)—Lamping **Mr K. R. Pearce**
2 **RAJATI (USA)**, 10, b g Chief's Crown (USA)—Charming Life (NZ)
3 **SCULPTOR**, 6, b g Salse (USA)—Classic Colleen (IRE) **Mr K. R. Pearce**
4 **SHANNON GALE BOY (IRE)**, 6, ch g Old Vic—Jemma's Gold (IRE) **Mr K. R. Pearce**

Amateur: Mr David S. Jones, Mrs Lucy Rowsell.

463
MR J. E. PEASE, Chantilly
Postal: **Villa Primerose, Chemin des Aigles, 60500 Chantilly, France.**
Contacts: **PHONE +33 (0) 3 44 58 19 96/03 44 57 23 09 FAX +33 (0) 3 44 57 59 90**
E-MAIL jpease8639@aol.com

1 **ALNITAK (USA)**, 4, b c Nureyev (USA)—Very True (USA) **The Niarchos Family**
2 **BAGO (FR)**, 4, b c Nashwan (USA)—Moonlight's Box (USA) **The Niarchos Family**
3 **BOXGROVE (FR)**, 4, gr g Trempolino (USA)—Little Emily **A. J. Richards**
4 **COOL BRITANNIA (IRE)**, 4, b c Rainbow Quest (USA)—Anka Britannia (USA) **The Leigh Family**
5 **HIGHLAND DANCER (FR)**, 4, ch c Kendor (FR)—Zarzaya (USA) **L. Roy/ D. How**
6 **HOUSTON CALLING (USA)**, 4, b c Rahy (USA)—Earth To Jackie (USA) **George Strawbridge**
7 **IMAGO MUNDI (FR)**, 5, b h Spinning World (USA)—Turning Wheel (USA) **The Niarchos Family**
8 **LILLA CREEK (USA)**, 5, b m Quest For Fame—Alice Springs (USA) **George Strawbridge**
9 **SECRET SLOPE (USA)**, 5, b h Quest For Fame—Kerulen **George Strawbridge**
10 **STARNEVEES (FR)**, 4, b c Kaldounevees (FR)—Stadia (FR) **R. C. Thompson**

THREE-YEAR-OLDS

11 **ALICE TOWN**, b f Darshaan—Cape Grace (IRE) **George Strawbridge**
12 **ALL THAT GLITTERS**, gr g Highest Honor (FR)—Ekaterina (USA) **George Strawbridge**
13 **BASEMAH (FR)**, b f Lemon Drop Kid (USA)—Attractive Crown (USA) **Baron F. C. von Oppenheim**
14 **BAVARIA STREET (FR)**, b f Dolphin Street (FR)—Silicon Bavaria (FR) **W. Wolf**
15 **CELTIC SEA (IRE)**, b f Celtic Swing—Sismique **N. J. Forman Hardy**
16 **DREAM STORY (FR)**, ch c Green Tune (USA)—Ella Nico (FR) **L. Roy, P. Tham, D. How & J. E. Pease**
17 **FINAL RANSOM (USA)**, b f Red Ransom (USA)—Last Approach (USA) **George Strawbridge**
18 **LATONA (FR)**, gr f Kendor (FR)—Silicon Lady (USA) **J. Goelet**
19 **METEBANI (FR)**, b c Lahib (USA)—Izenina **Sheik Faisal Seddiq Al Mutawa**
20 **MILLION WISHES**, b f Darshaan—Moonlight's Box **The Niarchos Family**
21 **MONTARE (IRE)**, b f Montjeu (IRE)—Contare **George Strawbridge**
22 **RIDDLE (FR)**, gr g Turgeon (USA)—Labyrinth (USA) **J. E. Pease**
23 **SAPAS (USA)**, ch f Kingmambo (USA)—Very True (USA) **The Niarchos Family**
24 **SCOTTISH HEIGHTS (IRE)**, b f Selkirk (USA)—Dazzling Heights **Peter Pritchard**
25 **SECOND HAPPINESS (USA)**, b f Storm Cat (USA)—Miesque (USA) **The Niarchos Family**
26 **SEMARANG**, b c Hernando (FR)—Obscura (USA) **The Niarchos Family**
27 **SUKAR (FR)**, b g Sendawar (IRE)—Marsakara (IRE) **George Strawbridge**
28 **TOP SPINNER (FR)**, b c Spinning World (USA)—Flurry (FR) **J. E. Pease**
29 **WITH REGARDS**, b c Selkirk (USA)—With Fascination (USA) **George Stawbridge**

MR J. E. PEASE—continued

TWO-YEAR-OLDS

30 B c 6/4 Grand Lodge (USA)—All Glory (Alzao (USA)) **Peter Pritchard**
31 **ALL POWER (FR)**, b c 20/4 Ocean of Wisdom (USA)—Solitaire (FR) (Sadler's Wells (USA)) **The Niarchos Family**
32 **AMAETHON (USA)**, ch c 26/3 Woodman (USA)—Aqua Galinte (USA) (Kris S (USA)) **The Niarchos Family**
33 Ch c 17/2 Selkirk (USA)—Amaryllis (IRE) (Sadler's Wells (USA)) **George Strawbridge**
34 B f 31/3 Daylami (IRE)—Antics (USA) (Unbridled (USA)) (279329) **George Strawbridge**
35 B f 6/5 Zafonic (USA)—Attractive Crown (USA) (Chief's Crown (USA)) **Sheik Faisal Seddiq Al Mutawa**
36 **BLUE SONG (FR)**, b c 4/3 Poliglote—Meduse Bleue (Salmon Leap (USA)) (40241) **L. Roy/D. How/P. Tham**
37 **BRESCELLO (FR)**, b c 31/3 Danehill Dancer (IRE)—Balouchina (IRE) (Rainbow Quest (USA)) (57008) **Mark Fisch**
38 B c 13/2 Mtoto—Cape Grace (IRE) (Priolo (USA)) **George Strawbridge**
39 **CLOUDS OF MAGELLAN (USA)**, b f 17/2 Dynaformer (USA)—
Witching Hour (FR) (Fairy King (USA)) **The Niarchos Family**
40 B c 27/5 Galileo (IRE)—Contare (Shirley Heights) **George Strawbridge**
41 B f 27/3 Alhaarth (IRE)—Fleeting Rainbow (Rainbow Quest (USA)) (90000) **George Strawbridge**
42 B c 24/2 Cozzene (USA)—Gabacha (USA) (Woodman (USA)) **George Strawbridge**
43 B c 16/2 Hernando (FR)—Golden Wings (USA) (Devil's Bag (USA)) (67069) **George Strawbridge**
44 B f 5/2 Hennessy (USA)—Gotablush (Nashwan (USA)) **George Strawbridge**
45 B br f 31/1 Cozzene (USA)—Kool Kat Katie (IRE) (Fairy King (USA)) **George Strawbridge**
46 **MANICLOWN**, ch c 11/4 Hernando (FR)—Gwydion (USA) (Raise A Cup (USA)) **The Niarchos Family**
47 B f 12/3 Commands (AUS)—No Exit (FR) (Exit To Nowhere (USA)) (43594) **Giacomo Algranti**
48 B c 17/4 King's Best (USA)—Petronilla (USA) (Lyphard (USA)) **George Strawbridge**
49 B c 5/3 Kingmambo (USA)—Recording (USA) (Danzig (USA)) **George Strawbridge**
50 **SILHOUETTING**, b c 1/3 Hernando (FR)—Moonlight's Box (USA) (Nureyev (USA)) **The Niarchos Family**
51 B f 30/4 Starborough—Silicon Lady (FR) (Mille Balles (FR)) **John Goelet**
52 B c 9/4 In The Wings—Texinadress (USA) (Copelan (USA)) (16767) **Sheik Faisal Seddiq Al Mutawa**
53 **TOWER OF BABEL**, b c 5/3 Poliglote—Flurry (FR) (Groom Dancer (USA)) **J. E. Pease**
54 B c 9/4 King's Best (USA)—Tricorne (Green Desert (USA)) (36887) **Sheik Faisal Seddiq Al Mutawa**
55 **TUMULTUEUX**, b c 2/3 Cadeaux Genereux—Folle Tempete (USA) (Fabulous Dancer (USA)) (26827) **Ecurie Defer**
56 **UP RIVER**, b f 17/2 Kaldounevees (FR)—Uplifting (Magic Ring (IRE)) **H. Seymour/Mrs R. M. Pease**
57 B c 12/5 Kingmambo (USA)—Valentine Waltz (IRE) (Be My Guest (USA)) (480000) **George Strawbridge**
58 **VERDANDI (FR)**, b f 19/2 Kahyasi—Phlizz (FR) (Kaldoun (FR)) **John Goelet**
59 B c 29/1 Spectrum (IRE)—With Fervour (USA) (Dayjur (USA)) **George Strawbridge**

Jockey (flat): T. Gillet, C. Stefan.

---

464 **MISS L. A. PERRATT, Ayr**
Postal: **Cree Lodge, 47 Craigie Road, Ayr, KA8 0HD.**
Contacts: **PHONE/FAX** (01292) 266232 **PHONE** (01292) 286958 **MOBILE** (07931) 306147
E-MAIL linda.perratt@ntlworld.com

1 **ARGENT**, 4, b g Barathea (IRE)—Red Tiara (USA) **P. Tsim**
2 **BALWEARIE (IRE)**, 4, b g Sesaro (USA)—Eight Mile Rock **N. J. Angus**
3 **CHAMPAGNE CRACKER**, 4, ch f 1 Up And At 'em—Kiveton Komet **Mr J. McLaren**
4 **FRIAR TUCK**, 10, ch g Inchinor—Jay Gee Ell **Cree Lodge Racing Club**
5 **LUCKY LARGO (IRE)**, 5, b br g Key of Luck (USA)—Lingering Melody (IRE) **Miss L. McFadzean**
6 **MADRA RUA (IRE)**, 4, b g Foxhound (USA)—Fun Fashion (IRE) **Mr John & Mrs Eva Peet**
7 **PAYS D'AMOUR (IRE)**, 8, b g Pursuit of Love—Lady of The Land **Miss L. McFadzean**
8 **PIRLIE HILL**, 5, b m Sea Raven (IRE)—Panayr **The Hon Miss Heather Galbraith**
9 **PROCREATE (IRE)**, 5, b g Among Men (USA)—Woodbury Princess **A. Irvine**
10 **PTARMIGAN RIDGE**, 9, b h Sea Raven (IRE)—Panayr **The Hon Miss Heather Galbraith**
11 **ROSTI**, 5, b g Whittingham (IRE)—Uae Flame (IRE) **Mrs L. B. K. Bone**
12 **SEAFIELD TOWERS**, 5, ch g Compton Place—Midnight Spell **N. J. Angus**
13 **STRAWBERRY PATCH (IRE)**, 6, b g Woodborough (USA)—Okino (USA) **Mrs L. B. K. Bone**
14 **THE SPOOK**, 5, b g Bin Ajwaad (IRE)—Rose Mill **The Jimmy Mac Partnership**
15 **XANADU**, 9, ch g Casteddu—Bellatrix **D. R. Sutherland**
16 **ZANDEED (IRE)**, 7, b g Inchinor—Persian Song **Miss L. A. Perratt**

THREE-YEAR-OLDS

17 **BORSCH (IRE)**, b g Soviet Star (USA)—Cheese Soup (USA) **N. J. Angus**
18 **DANCE NIGHT (IRE)**, b c Danehill Dancer (IRE)—Tiger Wings (IRE) **J. C. Fretwell**
19 **JERRY'S GIRL (IRE)**, ch f Danehill Dancer (IRE)—Lurgoe Lady (IRE) **J. Ryan**
20 **MYSTICAL AYR (IRE)**, br f Namid—Scanno's Choice (IRE) **Ayr Racehorse Owners Circle**
21 **NEIL'S LEGACY (IRE)**, br f Second Empire (IRE)—Eliade (IRE) **Mrs P. Harrison**

MISS L. A. PERRATT—continued

22 **PRESS EXPRESS (IRE)**, ch c Entrepreneur—Nawaji (USA) **Mrs L. B. K. Bone**
23 **QUICK GRAND (IRE)**, br f Raise A Grand (IRE)—Rose 'n Reason (IRE) **J. Ryan**
24 **SHATIN LEADER**, b f Atraf—Star Dancer **P. Tsim**
25̶ **TEE IT UP**, b g Josr Algarhoud (IRE)—Merry Mary **A. G. R. Cowan**

TWO-YEAR-OLDS

26 **CITY MISS**, br f 1/5 Rock City—Miss Pigalle (Good Times (ITY)) (800) **The Hon Miss Heather Galbraith**
27 Br c 6/3 Beckett (IRE)—Dacian (USA) (Diesis) (5000) **Mr Tim Finch**
28 Ch f 30/4 Inchinor—Dawn Alarm (Warning) (5500)
29 Br f 16/3 Mull of Kintyre (USA)—Gilding The Lily (IRE) (High Estate) (7377) **Mr John & Mrs Eva Peet**
30 **PENSATA**, b f 7/2 Compton Place—Artistic Merit (Alhaarth (IRE)) (22000) **Mrs Gill Khosla**
31 B f 26/3 Raise A Grand (IRE)—Playa Del Sol (Alzao (USA)) (2346)
32 Ch f 4/5 Compton Place—Sabre Lady (Sabrehill (USA)) (1800) **D. R. Sutherland**
33 Ch c 1/2 Night Shift (USA)—Secreto Bold (Never So Bold) (8000) **Mr John & Mrs Eva Peet**
34 Br gr f 21/4 King Charlemagne (USA)—Shamneez (IRE) (Pharly (FR)) (3353)
35 Ch c 20/4 Titus Livius (FR)—Two Thousand (IRE) (Polish Patriot (USA)) (3353)

Other Owners: Mr P. Corson, Mrs K. Corson, T. Hughes.

Assistant Trainer: Mr George Perratt

Jockey (flat): Nicky Mackay, K. Dalgleish, K. Darley, M. J. Kinane, F. Lynch, R. Winston. **Jockey (NH):** A. Dobbin, G. Lee.
Apprentice: T. Eaves. **Amateur:** Mr J. McLaren.

---

465 MRS A. J. PERRETT, Pulborough
Postal: **Coombelands Racing Stables, Pulborough, West Sussex, RH20 1BP.**
Contacts: **HOME** (01798) 874894 **OFFICE** (01798) 873011 **FAX** (01798) 875163
MOBILE (07803) 088713 **E-MAIL** aperrett@coombelands-stables.com

1 **AUDITORIUM**, 4, b c Royal Applause—Degree **Cheveley Park Stud**
2 **AUTUMN WEALTH (IRE)**, 4, ch f Cadeaux Genereux—Prickwillow (USA) **D. J. Burke**
3 **BARON'S PIT**, 5, b h Night Shift (USA)—Incendio **J. T. & K. M. Thomas**
4 **BATTLE CHANT (USA)**, 5, b g Coronado's Quest—Appointed One (USA) **Cheveley Park Stud**
5 **BIG MOMENT**, 7, ch g Be My Guest (USA)—Petralona (USA) **R Doel,A Black,Dr J Howells,R & P Scott**
6 **COLISAY**, 6, b g Entrepreneur—La Sorrela (IRE) **Mrs A. J. Perrett**
7 **DAY CARE**, 4, gr c Daylami (IRE)—Ancara **K. Abdulla**
8 **FUNFAIR**, 6, b g Singspiel (IRE)—Red Carnival (USA) **Cheveley Park Stud**
9 **GREY BOY (GER)**, 4, gr g Medaaly—Grey Perri **Sir Eric Parker**
10 **IT'S THE LIMIT (USA)**, 6, b g Boundary (USA)—Beside (USA) **J. E. Bodie**
11 **LITTLE GRACE**, 4, b f Fleetwood (IRE)—Everdene **S. P. Tindall**
12 **LOOK AGAIN**, 4, ch g Zilzal (USA)—Last Look **J. H. Richmond-Watson**
13 **ORANGE TOUCH (GER)**, 5, b h Lando (GER)—Orange Bowl **Cheveley Park Stud**
14 **PAGAN DANCE (IRE)**, 6, b g Revoque (IRE)—Ballade D'ainhoa (FR) **The Gap Partnership**
15 **POLAR WAY**, 6, b g Polar Falcon (USA)—Fetish **K. Abdulla**
16 **PORTHCAWL**, 4, b f Singspiel (IRE)—Dodo (IRE) **Usk Valley Stud**
17 **ROYAL STORM (IRE)**, 4, b h Royal Applause—Wakayi **The Cloran Family**
18 **SIMONDA**, 4, ch f Singspiel (IRE)—Jetbeeah (IRE) **S. P. Tindall**
19 **SOULACROIX**, 4, b c Kylian (USA)—California Dreamin **G. C. Stevens**
20 **SUSSEX LAD**, 8, b g Prince Sabo—Pea Green **Mrs A. J. Perrett**
21 **TABLEAU (USA)**, 4, ch c Marquetry (USA)—Model Bride (USA) **Mrs S. L. Whitehead**
22 **TAMINOULA (IRE)**, 4, b f Tagula (IRE)—Taormina (IRE) **Tandridge Racing (jdrp)**
23 **TEN CARAT**, 5, ch g Grand Lodge (USA)—Emerald (USA) **K. Abdulla**
24 **TORINMOOR (USA)**, 4, ch g Intikhab (USA)—Tochar Ban (USA) **Mr & Mrs R. Scott**
25 **TUNGSTEN STRIKE (USA)**, 4, ch g Smart Strike (CAN)—Bathilde (IRE) **J. P. Connolly**
26 **TURTLE PATRIARCH (IRE)**, 4, b c Turtle Island (IRE)—La Doyenne (IRE) **D. P. Angell**
27 **VAUGHAN**, 4, b c Machiavellian—Labibeh (USA) **Mr J. E. Bodie and Mr R. Wells**
28 **WEIGHTLESS**, 4, ch g In The Wings—Orford Ness **M. B. Hawtin**
29 **WESTMORELAND ROAD (USA)**, 5, b g Diesis—Tia Gigi (USA)
30 **WHIRLY BIRD**, 4, b f Nashwan (USA)—Inchyre **Woodcote Stud Ltd**
31 **WRIGHT**, 10, ch g Broadsword (USA)—Princess Florine (USA) **S. P. Tindall**

MRS A. J. PERRETT—continued

THREE-YEAR-OLDS

32 **ALFIE NOAKES**, b c Groom Dancer (USA)—Crimson Rosella **G. C. Stevens**
33 **ALWAYS MINE**, ch f Daylami (IRE)—Mamoura (IRE) **J. G. Davis**
34 **ART MODERN (IRE)**, ch g Giant's Causeway (USA)—Sinead (USA) **Sir Eric Parker & Mr M. Green**
35 **ART ROYAL (USA)**, b c Royal Academy (USA)—Chelsea Green (USA) **M. R. Green**
36 **BAYEUX DE MOI (IRE)**, b c Barathea (IRE)—Rivana **Lady Clague**
37 **BLUE TORPEDO (USA)**, ch g Rahy (USA)—Societe Royale **A. D. Spence**
38 **BREAMORE**, b c Dansili—Maze Garden (USA) **K. Abdulla**
39 **BULWARK (IRE)**, b c Montjeu (IRE)—Bulaxie **Hesmonds Stud Ltd**
40 **CHOCOLATE CARAMEL (USA)**, b c Storm Creek (USA)—Sandhill (BRZ) **Mrs P. S. Graham**
41 **CORCORAN**, b f Lear Fan (USA)—Corsini **K. Abdulla**
42 **DANGER ZONE**, b c Danzero (AUS)—Red Tulle (USA) **The Masqueraders (jdrp)**
43 **DANIEL THOMAS (IRE)**, b c Dansili—Last Look **J. H. Richmond-Watson**
44 **DREAM ALONG**, b c Sinndar (IRE)—Dream Quest **Hesmonds Stud Ltd**
45 **FULL OF ZEST**, ch f Pivotal—Tangerine **Hesmonds Stud Ltd**
46 **GREAT PLAINS**, b c Halling (USA)—West Dakota (USA) **K. Abdulla**
47 **ICE OF BATTLE (USA)**, b c Diesis—Dance Gaily (USA) **J. E. Bodie**
48 **KIRKBRIDE**, ch f Selkirk (USA)—Radiant Bride (USA) **K. Abdulla**
49 **LIAKOURA (GER)**, b g Royal Academy (USA)—Lady Member (FR) **M. Tracey**
50 **LINNET (GER)**, b f Dr Fong (USA)—Lauderdale (GER) **Highclere Thoroughbred Racing XXI**
51 **LOCH QUEST (IRE)**, ch g Giant's Causeway (USA)—Taibhseach (USA) **A. D. Spence**
52 **MEL'S MOMENT (USA)**, b c Storm Creek (USA)—One Moment In Time (USA) **Mrs P. S. Graham**
53 B f King of Kings (IRE)—Miss Twinkletoes (IRE) **S. P. Tindall**
54 **OVER THE LIMIT (IRE)**, b f Diktat—Premiere Cuvee **D. A. Hicks**
55 **PAGAN SWORD**, b c Selkirk (USA)—Vanessa Bell (USA) **The Gap Partnership**
56 **PHYSICAL (IRE)**, b c Efisio—St Clair **Fred And Sacha Cotton**
57 **PROUD SCHOLAR (USA)**, br f Royal Academy (USA)—Proud Fact (USA) **K. Abdulla**
58 **REGISTRAR**, ch c Machiavellian (USA)—Confidante (USA) **Cheveley Park Stud**
59 **ROSS MOOR**, b c Dansili—Snipe Hall **Mr & Mrs R. Scott**
60 **SALINJA (USA)**, b c Boundary (USA)—Lasha **Mrs P. S. Graham**
61 **SIR MONTY (USA)**, ch g Cat's Career (USA)—Lady of Meadowlane (USA) **Lingfield Breakfast Club**
62 **SKYSCAPE**, b f Zafonic (USA)—Aquarelle **K. Abdulla**
63 **STAGE MANAGER (IRE)**, ch c In The Wings—Evangola **Cheveley Park Stud**
64 **TAMALAIN (IRE)**, b f Royal Academy (USA)—Woodland Orchid (IRE) **Mr & Mrs R. Scott**
65 **THIS IS MY SONG**, b f Polish Precedent (USA)—Narva **Woodcote Stud Ltd**
66 **TRICK OF LIGHT**, b f Dansili—Stardom **K. Abdulla**
67 **TURNER'S TOUCH**, ch g Compton Place—Chairmans Daughter **M. R. Green**
68 **WATER PISTOL**, b g Double Trigger (IRE)—Water Flower **F Cotton S Cotton A Brooke P Silvester**
69 **WEDDING PARTY**, ch f Groom Dancer (USA)—Ceanothus (USA) **Cheveley Park Stud**
70 **WESTLAND (USA)**, gr c Cozzene (USA)—Cherie Yvonne (USA) **Mr & Mrs R. Scott**
71 **WINDS OF TIME (IRE)**, b c Danehill (USA)—Windmill **Mr & Mrs R. Scott**
72 **ZABADANI**, ch f Zafonic (USA)—Bloudan (USA) **K. Abdulla**

TWO-YEAR-OLDS

73 **ART INVESTOR**, b c 24/2 Sinndar (IRE)—Maid For Romance (Pursuit of Love) (80000) **M. R. Green**
74 **ART MAN**, b c 22/2 Dansili—Persuasion (Batshoof) (56000) **M. R. Green**
75 **ARTIST'S MUSE (USA)**, b f 28/1 Royal Academy (USA)—Atelier (Warning) **K. Abdulla**
76 **BANDAMA (IRE)**, b c 11/2 Green Desert (USA)—Orinoco (IRE) (Darshaan) **Lady Clague**
77 **CHEVIOT HEIGHTS**, b f 20/2 Intikhab (USA)—Cheviot Hills (Gulch (USA)) **Cheveley Park Stud**
78 **CLEAR VISION**, b f 30/3 Observatory (USA)—Claxon (Caerleon (USA)) **Hesmonds Stud Ltd**
79 **CONSTABLES ART**, b c 22/2 Royal Applause—Social Storm (USA) (Future Storm (USA)) (65000) **M. R. Green**
80 Ch c 5/2 Zafonic (USA)—Division Bell (Warning) **K. Abdulla**
81 **EMPHASIS**, ch f 28/1 Pivotal—Matoaka (USA) (A P Indy (USA)) **Cheveley Park Stud**
82 **FORTIFICATION (USA)**, b c 20/4 With Approval (CAN)—Palisade (USA) (Gone West (USA)) **K. Abdulla**
83 **HIMBA**, b c 25/4 Vettori (IRE)—Be My Wish (Be My Chief (USA)) (21000) **D. M. Slade**
84 **IT'S BASIL**, b c 10/1 Foxhound (USA)—Marabela (Shernazar) (20000) **G. C. Stevens**
85 **ITALIC**, ch f 6/4 Medicean—Ink Pot (USA) (Green Dancer (USA)) **Cheveley Park Stud**
86 **JUMBAJUKIBA**, b c 12/2 Barathea (IRE)—Danseuse du Soir (IRE) (Thatching) **Mrs S. G. Tait**
87 B c 18/2 Grand Lodge (USA)—Kardashina (FR) (Darshaan) (60000) **A. D. Spence**
88 B f 29/4 Fantastic Light (USA)—Khubza (Green Desert (USA))
89 B c 7/3 Elusive Quality (USA)—Love To Fight (USA) (Fit To Fight (USA)) **J. P. Connolly**
90 B c 20/4 Quiet American (USA)—Math (USA) (Devil's Bag (USA)) (47885)
91 B c 21/4 Elusive Quality (USA)—My Sister Sarah (USA) (Dr Geo Adams (USA)) (69167) **M. R. Green**
92 B c 14/3 Slip Anchor—Nanouche (Dayjur (USA)) (16000)

MRS A. J. PERRETT—continued

93 **NEVADA FLAME,** b f 13/5 Desert Prince (IRE)—Flame Valley (USA) (Gulch (USA)) **Cheveley Park Stud**
94 B br c 11/4 Diesis—Night Fax (USA) (Known Fact (USA)) (34583) **J. P. Connolly**
95 **NOS FERATU (IRE),** b c 7/3 In The Wings—Gothic Dream (IRE) (Nashwan (USA)) **Lady Clague**
96 B c 18/5 Singspiel (IRE)—One Beautiful Lady (Broad Brush (USA)) (159616) **Mr & Mrs R. Scott**
97 **PAGAN CREST,** ch c 6/5 Indian Ridge—Maria Theresa (Primo Dominie) (45000)
98 **REAL BECKHAM (USA),** b c 28/4 Lear Fan (USA)—Maria Dolores (USA) (Prized (USA)) (27666) **G. C. Stevens**
99 **RED COUNTESS,** b f 4/2 Pivotal—Red Empress (Nashwan (USA)) **Cheveley Park Stud**
100 **RITSI (IRE),** b c 22/3 Marju (IRE)—Anna Comnena (IRE) (Shareef Dancer (USA)) (42000) **Sir David Sieff**
101 **RUBILEO,** b f 16/2 Galileo (IRE)—Ruby Affair (IRE) (Night Shift (USA))
102 **SALVESTRO,** b c 3/3 Medicean—Katy Nowaitee (Komaite (USA)) **J. H. Richmond-Watson**
103 **SILKEN ACT (CAN),** b f 24/2 Theatrical—Silca Key Service (Bering) (117052) **Hesmonds Stud Ltd**
104 Ch f 7/3 College Chapel—Snowy Mantle (Siberian Express (USA)) **Homebred Racing**
105 **SOFT CENTRE,** ch f 1/3 Zafonic (USA)—Foodbroker Fancy (IRE) (Halling (USA)) (150000) **N. G. Cooper**
106 B c 25/2 Mozart (IRE)—Talena (Zafonic (USA)) (20120) **A. D. Spence**
107 B c 17/2 Spectrum (IRE)—Tomanivi (Caerleon (USA)) (12000)
108 **TRIPLE BEND,** b c 7/3 Singspiel (IRE)—Triple Green (Green Desert (USA)) **Hesmonds Stud Ltd**
109 **TRIPLE BLUFF,** b c 12/3 Medicean—Trinity Reef (Bustino) **Hesmonds Stud Ltd**

Other Owners: P. R. Anders, Mr S. W. Barnett, A. M. Black, A. J. N. Bray, A. W. Brooke, S. Cloran, B. J. Cloran, Mrs G. V. Cloran, Mrs Z. F. Cloran, F. G. Cotton, Mrs S. H. Cotton, Mrs R. J. Doel, Mr John Dunbar, The Hon H. M. Herbert, Highclere Thoroughbred Racing Ltd, J. T. Hill, Dr J. B. Howells, G. D. P. Materna, K. J. Mercer, Mrs S. Mercer, Mrs M. Parker, R. Scott, Mrs P. M. Scott, P. Silvester, Tessona Racing Ltd, J. T. Thomas, Mrs K. M. Thomas, C. M. Wall, Mrs S. Wall, J. R. L. Wells.

Apprentice: Liam Treadwell. **Amateur:** Miss L. J. Harwood.

---

466 MR G. R. PEWTER, Halstead
Postal: Great Lodge Farm, Castle Hedingham, Halstead, Essex, CO9 3AJ.
Contacts: PHONE (01787) 460964 FAX (01787) 462150 MOBILE (07966) 489541

1 **DALLIGAN (IRE),** 11, b g Executive Perk—Comeragh Queen **N. J. Pewter**
2 **FORT ROYAL (IRE),** 6, b g Commanche Run—Grainne Geal **N. J. Pewter**
3 **GREAT EXPENSE,** 6, b g Shambo—Zoes Pet **N. J. Pewter**

---

467 MR R. T. PHILLIPS, Moreton-in-the-Marsh
Postal: Adlestrop Stables, Adlestrop, Moreton-in-the-Marsh, Gloucestershire, GL56 0YN.
Contacts: PHONE (01608) 658710 FAX (01608) 658713 MOBILE (07774) 832715
E-MAIL info@richardphillipsracing.com WEBSITE www.richardphillipsracing.com

1 **ADLESTROP,** 5, ch m Alderbrook—Lady Buck **The Listeners**
2 **AFEEF (USA),** 6, b br g Dayjur (USA)—Jah (USA) **Ellangowan Racing Partners II**
3 **ALASKAN FIZZ,** 4, ch f Efisio—Anchorage (IRE) **Mrs C. M. Smith**
4 **ALDERMAN ROSE,** 5, b g Alderbrook—Rose Ravine **Mrs Nicholas Jones/Martin Broughton**
5 **ANOTHER GENERAL (IRE),** 10, b g Glacial Storm (USA)—
                           Whats In A Name (IRE) **Paul Duffy, Alan Beard, Brian Beard**
6 **ARCTIC RING,** 7, b m Karinga Bay—Arctic Advert **Mrs R. E. Hambro**
7 **ARNOLD LAYNE (IRE),** 6, gr g Roselier (FR)—Cotton Gale **Mr & Mrs R. Scott**
8 **ASSUMPTALINA,** 5, b m Primitive Rising (USA)—New Broom (IRE) **M. R. Barnes**
9 **BALLYBOLEY (IRE),** 7, b g Roselier (FR)—Benbradagh Vard (IRE) **Mr R. J. Spence**
10 **BARNEY MCALL (IRE),** 5, b g Grand Lodge (USA)—Persian Song **Mr & Mrs R. Scott**
11 **BAUHAUS (IRE),** 4, b g Second Empire (IRE)—Hi Bettina
12 **BROOKING (IRE),** 7, b g Roselier (FR)—Kilkil Pin **Annapurna Partnership**
13 **CAESAREAN HUNTER (USA),** 6, ch g Jade Hunter (USA)—Grey Fay (USA) **Mr A. A. Wickham**
14 **CASH AND NEW (IRE),** 6, b m Supreme Leader—Shannon Lough (IRE) **The 23rd Floor**
15 **CASH CONVERTER (IRE),** 7, ch g Houmayoun (FR)—Golden Symphony **Thurloe Thoroughbreds XI**
16 **CENTRAL COMMITTEE (IRE),** 10, ch g Royal Academy (USA)—Idle Chat (USA) **The Escape Committee**
17 **CHASTLETON BOY (IRE),** 6, b g Muroto—Noon Hunting **Garry and Catriona Braybrooke Jones**
18 **CHEEKY TRUCKER,** 4, ch f Atraf—Cheeky Monkey (USA) **S. F. Benton**
19 **CHOPNEYEV (FR),** 7, b g Goldneyev (USA)—Pierre de Soleil (FR) **Mrs C. M. Smith**
20 **CORALS LAUREL,** 6, b g Accordion—Bold Tipperary (IRE) **R. & P. Scott & I. Payne & K. Franklin**
21 **CREAGH BAY (IRE),** 6, b g Tidaro (USA)—Martha Anne (IRE)
22 **DARK'N SHARP (GER),** 10, b g Sharpo—Daytona Beach (GER) **Ascot Five Plus One**
23 **DATITO (IRE),** 10, b g Over The River (FR)—Crash Call **G. Lansbury**
24 **DEFINITE APPROACH (IRE),** 7, b g Presenting—Crash Approach **Ascot Five Plus One**
25 **EIGHT FIFTY FIVE (IRE),** 5, gr g Wood Chanter—Electric View (IRE) **The After Eights**

MR R. T. PHILLIPS—continued

26 FIVE PENCE, 9, b g Henbit (USA)—Le Saule d'or **W. Naylor**
27 FOREST MILLER, 6, b g Classic Cliche (IRE)—Its My Turn **The Old Foresters Partnership**
28 FOREST SPRITE, 5, b m Sir Harry Lewis (USA)—Formal Affair **The Old Foresters Partnership**
29 GEE AKER MALAYO (IRE), 9, b g Phardante (FR)—Flying Silver **Mr Darren Bloom & Mr Matthew Miller**
30 GENERAL DUROC (IRE), 9, ch g Un Desperado (FR)—Satula **S. F. Benton**
31 GENERAL GOSSIP (IRE), 9, b b g Supreme Leader—Sno-Sleigh **The Early Birds**
32 GEORGIAN HARRY (IRE), 8, b g Warcraft (USA)—Solo Player **Gale, Golden and Martin**
33 GINGERBREAD HOUSE (IRE), 7, b g Old Vic—Furun (IRE) **Mrs J. A. Stewart**
34 GIOVANNA, 4, b f Orpen (USA)—Red Leggings **Dozen Dreamers Partnership**
35 GLASSON HOUSE (IRE), 6, b m Supreme Leader—Nasowas (IRE) **Supreme Corner Gang**
36 GO HARVEY GO (IRE), 6, b g Supreme Leader—Python Wolf (IRE) **Mrs S. J. Harvey**
37 GREAT OVATION (FR), 6, ch m Boston Two Step (USA)—Baldiloa **Mrs C. M. Smith**
38 GREENFIELD (IRE), 7, ch g Pleasant Tap (USA)—No Review (USA) **Mrs S. J. Harvey**
39 GRENFELL (IRE), 6, br m Presenting—Arumah **Mrs J. K. Powell**
40 INLAND RUN (IRE), 9, b g Insan (USA)—Anns Run **A Beard, B Beard, P Doble, T Pearce**
41 JESPER (FR), 8, b g Video Rock (FR)—Belle des Airs (FR) **Mrs C. Skan**
42 KAFRI D'AIRY (FR), 7, b m Sheyrann—Afrika d'airy (FR) **Mrs C. M. Smith**
43 LATE CLAIM (IRE), 5, ch g King of Kings (IRE)—Irish Flare (USA) **Pertemps Ltd**
44 LONESOME MAN (IRE), 9, ch g Broken Hearted—Carn-Na-Ros **P. Docherty**
45 MANDINGO CHIEF (IRE), 6, b g Flying Spur (AUS)—Elizabethan Air **R. S. Williams**
46 MINIBALLIST (IRE), 7, b m Tragic Role (USA)—Herballistic **The Donnington Drinkers**
47 MORGANS MONEY, 6, ch g Karinga Bay—Another Rumour **R. & P. Scott & I. Payne & K. Franklin**
48 MR PHIPPS, 9, b g Shareef Dancer (USA)—Frost In Summer **W. Naylor**
49 MR RHUBARB (IRE), 7, ch g Shardari—Gale Griffin (IRE) **Mr & Mrs C. Schwick**
50 MRS FIZZIWIG, 6, b m Petoski—Dans Le Vent **Mrs E. A. Prowting**
51 ON Y VA (FR), 7, b g Goldneyev (USA)—Shakna (FR) **ROA Red Alligator Partnership**
52 PARTHIAN SHOT, 5, b m Parthian Springs—Lavenham's Last **Ford Associated Racing Team**
53 PEACHY (IRE), 10, b g Un Desperado (FR)—Little Peach **C. Pocock**
54 RAVEN'S LAST, 6, b g Sea Raven (IRE)—Lavenham's Last **Mrs Stewart Catherwood**
55 RESEDA (IRE), 8, b g Rock Hopper—Sweet Mignonette **R. S. Williams**
56 ROARINGWATER (IRE), 6, b g Roselier (FR)—Supreme Cherry **Rip-Roarers**
57 ROYAL CLICHE, 6, b g Classic Cliche (IRE)—Princess Hotpot (IRE) **The New Club Partnership**
58 SHARP JACK (IRE), 7, b g Be My Native (USA)—Polly Sharp **Mrs C. M. Smith**
59 SILK ROPE (IRE), 5, br m Presenting—Osiery Girl (IRE) **Mr & Mrs R. Johnson**
60 SOVIET SCEPTRE (IRE), 4, ch c Soviet Star (USA)—Princess Sceptre **J. E. Mills**
61 SUPREME TOSS (IRE), 9, b g Supreme Leader—Sleemana **The Coin Tossers**
62 TAWEELL (IRE), 6, b g Mtoto—Kronengold (USA) **Nut Club Partnership**
63 THE MICK WESTON, 6, b g North Col—Zalina **M. Weston**
64 THRILLING PROSPECT (IRE), 8, b m King's Ride—Bail Out **H. Fowler**
65 TOG GO BOGE (IRE), 7, b br g Erins Isle—Vision of Spring **Redmade Limited**
66 WIMBLEDONIAN, 6, b m Sir Harry Lewis (USA)—Ardent Love (IRE) **OWRC Partnership No 1**
67 YANN'S (FR), 9, b g Hellios (USA)—Listen Gyp (USA) **Mr Darren Bloom & Mr Matthew Miller**

THREE-YEAR-OLDS

68 ALANA'S GIFT, b f Montjeu (IRE)—Impatiente (USA) **Mrs C. M. Smith**
69 ASHWELL ROSE, b f Anabaa (USA)—Finicia (USA) **Mr & Mrs C. Schwick**

Other Owners: Mrs S. E. Acland, F. J. Allen, H. R. F. Arthur, M. R. Barnes, Mrs P. A. Bates, Alan Beard, B. M. Beard, A. Bird, Mrs L. M. A. Bird, D. Blake, M. L. Blake, Mr D. J. Bloom, M. F. Bourke, Mrs C. M. Braybrooke Jones, M. F. Broughton, S. W. Broughton, J. S. Cantrill, M. T. Cleary, K. P. Cullen, N. R. P. Dempster, Mr P. G. J. Devlin, D. P. Duffy, I. Dunbar, D. Gale, A. Golden, Mrs C. S. Heber-Percy, J. R. Hulme, Mrs N. Jones, G. P. Jones, G. J. King, G. Love, J. Martin, Mrs C. A. Maryan Green, D. M. Mason, Miss S. M. McHale, R. J. Meaney, C. C. Merson, M. Miller, T. H. Milson, G. Myers, T. Neill, C. F. Newman, C. J. Newport, P. Nichols, J. S. Palfreyman, O. J. W. Pawle, MR R. T. Phillips, M. T. Phillips, S. J. Popple, P. Porter, M. D. Poulton, J. H. Rosbotham, C. Schwick, Mrs C. V. Schwick, R. Scott, Mrs P. M. Scott, M. A. F. Shenfield, W. L. Smith, Mrs C. J. Smith, C. B. Smith, Mrs C. M. Smith, N. Tafuro, Mrs R. B. Weaver, N. J. Whitfield, T. C. Wilson, A. W. D. Wright, A. P. Wyer.

Jockey (NH): R. Johnson, W. Marston.

MR S. L. PIKE, Sidmouth
Postal: **Synderborough Farm, Sidbury, Sidmouth, Devon, EX10 0QJ.**
Contacts: **PHONE/FAX (01395) 597485 MOBILE (07836) 335293**
E-MAIL monique@pikes.eclipse.co.uk

1 BLUE MAGNUM (FR), 5, b g Pistolet Bleu (IRE)—Dalticia (FR) **Mr S. L. Pike**

MR S. L. PIKE—continued

2 **PRIVATE NOTE**, 5, b g Accordion—Lady Geneva **Mr S. L. Pike**
3 **SOVIETICA (FR)**, 4, b f Subotica (FR)—Vieille Russie **Mr S. L. Pike**

Assistant Trainer: Mrs M P Pike

Conditional: Ben Hitchcott. **Amateur:** Miss P. Gundry.

---

469 **MR ANTHONY D. W. PINDER, Wantage**
Postal: Little Farm, Fawler Road, Kingston Lisle, Wantage, Oxfordshire, OX12 9QH.
Contacts: PHONE (01367) 820280 MOBILE (07711) 396191
E-MAIL davidpinderracing@ukonline.co.uk

1 **DANISH MONARCH**, 4, b g Great Dane (IRE)—Moly **Little Farm Partnership II**
2 **DEXILEOS (IRE)**, 6, b g Danehill (USA)—Theano (IRE) **Mrs A. M. Pinder**
3 **KINDNESS**, 5, ch m Indian Ridge—Kissing Gate (USA) **Ms R. V. Richards**
4 **LOGISTICAL**, 5, b h Grand Lodge (USA)—Magic Milly **The Little Farm Partnership**

THREE-YEAR-OLDS

5 **PRO TEMPORE**, b f Fraam—Record Time **Mrs A. M. Pinder**

Other Owners: C. Cavanagh, Ms L. Burns, Ms L. Barber, Mr J. M. R. Pinder, P. J. Barnes.

Amateur: Miss L. Griffiths.

---

470 **MR M. C. PIPE, C.B.E., Wellington**
Postal: Pond House, Nicholashayne, Wellington, Somerset, TA21 9QY.
Contacts: OFFICE (01884) 840715 FAX (01884) 841343
E-MAIL martin@martinpipe.co.uk WEBSITE www.martinpipe.co.uk

1 **AKARUS (FR)**, 10, b g Labus (FR)—Meris (FR) **A. J. White**
2 **ALIKAT (IRE)**, 4, b f Alhaarth (IRE)—Be Crafty (USA) **D. A. Johnson**
3 **ALTESSE DE SOU (FR)**, 5, gr m Saint Preuil (FR)—Pretty Point **David Manning Associates**
4 **ANATAR (FR)**, 7, b g Caerleon (USA)—Anaza **Eminence Grise Partnership**
5 **BANNOW STRAND (IRE)**, 5, b g Luso—Bid For Fun (IRE) **D. A. Johnson**
6 **BERTIEBANOO (IRE)**, 7, ch g Be My Native (USA)—Gemeleks Gem (IRE) **P. A. Newey**
7 **BONGO FURY (FR)**, 6, b m Sillery (USA)—Nativelee (FR) **Lord Donoughmore & Countess Donoughmore**
8 **BOUNCE AGAIN (FR)**, 5, b g Jeune Homme (USA)—Lattaquie (FR) **Mrs B. L. Harvey**
9 **BOUNCE BACK (USA)**, 9, ch g Trempolino (USA)—Lattaquie (FR) **Mrs B. L. Harvey**
10 **BUENA VISTA (IRE)**, 4, b g In The Wings—Park Special **Mr Matt Archer & Miss Jean Broadhurst**
11 **BUMPER (FR)**, 4, b g Cadoudal (FR)—Dame Blonde (FR) **A. J. White**
12 **CALAMINTHA**, 5, b m Mtoto—Calendula **M. D. C. Jenks**
13 **CANTGETON (IRE)**, 5, b g Germany (USA)—Lahana (IRE) **D. A. Johnson**
14 **CARRYONHARRY (IRE)**, 11, gr g Roselier (FR)—Bluebell Avenue **Drs' D. Silk, J. Castro, M. Gillard, P. Walker**
15 **CASTLETOWN LAD**, 5, b g Afzal—Once Bitten **D. A. Johnson**
16 **CELESTIAL GOLD (IRE)**, 7, br g Persian Mews—What A Queen **D. A. Johnson**
17 **CELTIC SON (FR)**, 6, b g Celtic Arms (FR)—For Kicks (FR) **D. A. Johnson**
18 **CHICUELO (IRE)**, 9, b g Mansonnien (FR)—Dovapas (FR) **Mrs B. L. Harvey**
19 **CIMMAROON (IRE)**, 6, b g Synefos (USA)—Bayalika (FR) **B. A. Kilpatrick**
20 **CLASSIFIED (IRE)**, 9, b g Roselier (FR)—Treidlia (FR) **D. A. Johnson**
21 **COMMERCIAL FLYER (IRE)**, 6, ch g Carroll House—Shabra Princess **D. A. Johnson**
22 **COMPLY OR DIE (IRE)**, 6, b g Old Vic—Madam Madcap **D. A. Johnson**
23 **CONTRABAND**, 7, b g Red Ransom (USA)—Shortfall **D. A. Johnson**
24 **CONTROL MAN (IRE)**, 7, ch g Glacial Storm (USA)—Got To Fly (IRE) **D. A. Johnson**
25 **COPELAND**, 10, b g Generous (IRE)—Whitehaven **Dr D. Silk & Mrs Heather Silk**
26 **DANGEROUS DAN MCGO (IRE)**, 7, b g Un Desperado (FR)—Sharnad (IRE) **Mr J. Whelan**
27 **DESERT AIR (JPN)**, 6, b g Desert King (IRE)—Greek Air (IRE) **Mrs B. L. Harvey**
28 **DINARELLI (FR)**, 6, gr g Linamix (FR)—Dixiella (FR) **Lord Donoughmore & Countess Donoughmore**
29 **DON'T ASK ME (IRE)**, 4, b g Spectrum (IRE)—Ediyrna (IRE) **Mr J. Ennis**
30 **DOOF (IRE)**, 5, b g Old Vic—Ashpark Rose (IRE) **D. A. Johnson**
31 **DOWNTHEREFORDANCIN (IRE)**, 5, b g Groom Dancer (USA)—Merlin's Fancy **The Reims Partnership**
32 **DREAMING AWAY (IRE)**, 5, b g Un Desperado (FR)—Little Treat **D. A. Johnson**
33 **EARN OUT**, 4, b g Sovereign Water (FR)—Tudor Spartan **D. A. Johnson**
34 **ESCOMPTEUR (FR)**, 5, b g Poliglote—Escopette (FR) **D. A. Johnson**

MR M. C. PIPE, C.B.E.—continued

35 **FARCEUR (FR)**, 6, b br g Anabaa (USA)—Fabulous Account (USA) **Mr M. C. Pipe, C.B.E.**
36 **FAST MIX (FR)**, 6, gr g Linamix (FR)—Fascinating Hill (FR) **J. R. W. Weeden**
37 **FIELD ROLLER (IRE)**, 5, ch g High Roller (IRE)—Cathedral Road **D. A. Johnson**
38 **FIGARO DU ROCHER (FR)**, 5, ch g Beyssac (FR)—Fabinou (FR) **Mr M. C. Pipe, C.B.E.**
39 **FONTANESI (IRE)**, 5, b g Sadler's Wells (USA)—Northern Script (USA) **D. A. Johnson**
40 **FORTUNE ISLAND (IRE)**, 6, b g Turtle Island (IRE)—Blue Kestrel (IRE) **J. M. Brown & M. J. Blackburn**
41 **GETON (IRE)**, 5, b g Glacial Storm (USA)—Monavale (IRE) **D. A. Johnson**
42 **GNILLISH**, 5, b g Bob's Return (IRE)—Spring Flyer (IRE) **M. B. Jones**
43 **GOLD FOR ME (FR)**, 6, b g Solar One (FR)—Volcania (FR) **J. Moran**
44 **GOLDEN ALPHA (IRE)**, 11, b g Alphabatim (USA)—Gina's Love **D. A. Johnson**
45 **GONE FAR (USA)**, 8, b g Gone West (USA)—Vallee Dansante (USA) **Mr Matt Archer & Miss Jean Broadhurst**
46 **GREEN PROSPECT (FR)**, 5, b g Green Tune (USA)—City Prospect (FR) **S. M. Mercer**
47 **HE'S A LEADER (IRE)**, 6, b g Supreme Leader—Raise The Bells **Mr Matt Archer & Miss Jean Broadhurst**
48 **HEADLINER (IRE)**, 6, ch g Topanoora—Fairy River **D. A. Johnson**
49 **HEART MIDOLTIAN (FR)**, 8, gr g Royal Charter (FR)—Pride of Queen (FR) **Mrs S. Neville**
50 **HENRIETTA (IRE)**, 7, b m Hushang (USA)—Jennie's First **B. A. Kilpatrick**
51 **HEVER ROAD (IRE)**, 6, ch g Anshan—The Little Bag **Dr D. Silk & Mrs Heather Silk**
52 **HONAN (FR)**, 6, b g College Chapel—Medical Times (IRE) **Eminence Grise Partnership**
53 **HORUS (IRE)**, 10, b g Teenoso (USA)—Jennie's First **B. A. Kilpatrick**
54 **IDAHO D'OX (FR)**, 9, b br g Bad Conduct (USA)—Queseda (FR) **The Dionysius Partnership**
55 **ILNAMAR (FR)**, 9, b g Officiel (FR)—Quillemare (FR) **J. Moran**
56 **IRIS BLEU (FR)**, 9, ch g Beyssac (FR)—Dear Blue (FR) **D. A. Johnson**
57 **ISARD III (FR)**, 9, gr g Royal Charter (FR)—Aurore D'ex (FR) **C. M., B. J. & R. F. Batterham II**
58 **IT TAKES TIME (IRE)**, 11, b g Montelimar (USA)—Dysart Lady **D. A. Johnson**
59 **IT'S MUSIC (IRE)**, 5, b g Accordion—Leadon Lady **D. A. Johnson**
60 **ITSMYBOY (IRE)**, 5, br g Frimaire—Hawkfield Lass (IRE) **D. A. Johnson**
61 **IZNOGOUD (FR)**, 9, b br g Shafoun (FR)—Vancia (FR) **The County Stores and Avalon Surfacing**
62 **JIVATY (FR)**, 8, b g Quart de Vin (FR)—Tenacity (FR) **D. A. Johnson**
63 **JURANCON II (FR)**, 8, b g Scooter Bleu (IRE)—Volniste (FR) **D. A. Johnson**
64 **JUST CLASSIC**, 5, gr g Classic Cliche (IRE)—Misty View **D. A. Johnson**
65 **KINGSTON TOWN (USA)**, 5, ch g King of Kings (IRE)—Lady Ferial (FR) **J. L. Guillambert**
66 **KORELO (FR)**, 7, b g Cadoudal (FR)—Lora du Charmil (FR) **D. A. Johnson**
67 **LA LAMBERTINE (FR)**, 4, b f Glaieul (USA)—Mesoraca (IRE) **D. A. Johnson**
68 **LAGO NAM (FR)**, 6, gr g Cardoun (FR)—Rivalago (FR) **D. A. Johnson**
69 **LATITUDE (FR)**, 6, b m Kadalko (FR)—Diyala III (FR) **N. J. Edwards**
70 **LEGATUS (IRE)**, 8, ch g Alphabatim (USA)—Take A Guess (IRE) **B. A. Kilpatrick**
71 **LIBERMAN (IRE)**, 7, br g Standiford (USA)—Hail To You (USA) **D. A. Johnson**
72 **LIRTA (FR)**, 6, gr g Art Francais (USA)—Sirta (FR) **P. A. Newey**
73 **LOCKSMITH**, 5, b br g Linamix (FR)—Zenith **D. A. Johnson**
74 **LORD OSCAR (IRE)**, 6, b g Oscar (IRE)—Americo Rose (IRE) **B. A. Kilpatrick**
75 **LOTUS DES PICTONS (FR)**, 6, b g Grand Tresor (FR)—
Ballaway (FR) **Lord Donoughmore & Countess Donoughmore**
76 **LOUGH DERG (FR)**, 5, b g Apple Tree (FR)—Asturias (FR) **W. F. Frewen**
77 **LUNAR CRYSTAL (IRE)**, 7, b g Shirley Heights—Solar Crystal (IRE) **Teddington Racing Club**
78 **LUTEA (IRE)**, 5, ch g Beneficial—Francie's Treble **D. A. Johnson**
79 **MADE IN FRANCE (FR)**, 5, b g Luchiroverte (IRE)—Birgonde (FR) **T. Neill**
80 **MALDOUN (IRE)**, 6, b g Kaldoun (FR)—Marzipan (FR) **The Dionysius Partnership**
81 **MANX ROYAL (FR)**, 6, b g Cyborg (FR)—Badj II (FR) **James and Antoinette Kennedy**
82 **MARCEL (FR)**, 5, b g Bateau Rouge—Une Risette (FR) **D. A. Johnson**
83 **MARK EQUAL**, 9, b g Nicholas Bill—Dissolution **Heeru Kirpalani Racing**
84 **MAXIMIZE (IRE)**, 11, b g Mandalus—Lone Run **D. A. Johnson**
85 **MEDISON (FR)**, 5, b br g Video Rock (FR)—Colombia III (FR) **D. A. Johnson**
86 **MEGA D'ESTRUVAL (FR)**, 5, ch m Garde Royale—Vocation (FR) **D. A. Johnson**
87 **MILORD LESCRIBAA (FR)**, 5, b g Cadoudal (FR)—Mona Lisaa (FR) **Mr M. C. Pipe, C.B.E.**
88 **MIOCHE D'ESTRUVAL (FR)**, 5, bl g Lute Antique—Charme d'estruval (FR) **J. Moran**
89 **MONDIAL JACK (FR)**, 6, ch g Apple Tree (FR)—Cackle (USA) **C. M., B. J. & R. F. Batterham II**
90 **MONTREAL (FR)**, 8, b br g Chamberlin (FR)—Massada (FR) **D. A. Johnson**
91 **MR COOL**, 11, b g Jupiter Island—Laurel Diver **N. G. Mills**
92 **MUJALINA (FR)**, 7, b g Mujadil (USA)—Talina's Law (IRE) **Mr & Mrs M. Bovingdon & Mr C. Langley**
93 **MURAT (FR)**, 5, b g Useful (FR)—La Marianne (FR) **P. A. Deal**
94 **NABIR (FR)**, 5, gr g Linamix (FR)—Nabagha (FR) **J. R. W. Weeden**
95 **NEW CURRENCY (USA)**, 5, b br g Touch Gold (USA)—
Ceirseach (IRE) **Mr Matt Archer & Miss Jean Broadhurst**
96 **NICK THE SILVER**, 4, gr g Nicolotte—Brillante (FR) **Four Men And A Liver Bird**
97 **NORTHERN MADRIK (FR)**, 4, b br g Useful (FR)—
Belle Des Belles (FR) **The County Stores and Avalon Surfacing**

MR M. C. PIPE, C.B.E.—continued

98 **NOT LEFT YET (IRE)**, 4, b br g Old Vic—Dalus Dawn **D. A. Johnson**
99 **OASIS BANUS (IRE)**, 4, b g Shaamit (IRE)—Summit Else **D. A. Johnson**
100 **OASIS BLUE (IRE)**, 4, gr g Norwich—Mini Fashion (IRE) **D. A. Johnson**
101 **OUR VIC (IRE)**, 7, b g Old Vic—Shabra Princess **D. A. Johnson**
102 **OVER THE CREEK**, 6, br g Over The River (FR)—Solo Girl (IRE) **D. A. Johnson**
103 **PAPILLON DE IENA (FR)**, 5, ch g Varese—Belle Du Chesne (FR) **J. Moran**
104 **PENNY PICTURES (IRE)**, 6, b g Theatrical—Copper Creek **T. Neill**
105 **PERFECT STORM**, 6, b g Vettori (IRE)—Gorgeous Dancer (IRE) **The Newchange Syndicate**
106 **PHILIPPA YEATES (IRE)**, 6, b m Hushang (IRE)—Miss Bobby Bennett **B. A. Kilpatrick**
107 **POLAR RED**, 8, ch g Polar Falcon (USA)—Sharp Top **Lady Hilda Clarke**
108 **PUNCHY (IRE)**, 9, b br g Freddie's Star—Baltimore Fox (IRE) **G-Force Partnership**
109 **PUNTAL (FR)**, 9, b g Bering—Saveur **T. Neill**
110 **QUICK**, 5, b g Kahyasi—Prompt **Kinsford Champagne Partnership**
111 **RAVENSWOOD (IRE)**, 8, b g Warning—Green Lucia **D. A. Johnson**
112 **ROBBIE ON TOUR (IRE)**, 6, b g Oscar (IRE)—Mystery Woman **D. A. Johnson**
113 **ROSE OF THE HILL (IRE)**, 6, gr g Roselier (FR)—Golden Leaf **T. Neill**
114 **ROSEMAUVE (FR)**, 5, b g Cyborg (FR)—Sweet Jaune (FR) **Mr M. C. Pipe, C.B.E.**
115 **ROVERETTO**, 10, b g Robellino (USA)—Spring Flyer (IRE) **Swanvista Limited**
116 **ROYAL HECTOR (GER)**, 6, b g Hector Protector (USA)—Rudolfina (CAN) **Three Counties Racing 2**
117 **RUN OF KINGS (IRE)**, 7, b g King's Ride—Arctic Tartan **D. A. Johnson**
118 **SAMSAAM (IRE)**, 8, b g Sadler's Wells (USA)—Azyaa **Mr Matt Archer & Miss Jean Broadhurst**
119 **SARDAGNA (FR)**, 5, gr m Medaaly—Sarda (FR)
120 **SAY WHAT YOU SEE (IRE)**, 5, b h Charnwood Forest (IRE)—Aster Aweke (IRE) **Sharp Minds Betfair Syndicate**
121 **SCARFACE**, 8, ch g Hernando—Scarlatine (IRE) **Three Counties Racing**
122 **SCARLET MIX (FR)**, 4, gr g Linamix (FR)—Scarlet Raider (USA) **D. A. Johnson**
123 **SEEBALD (GER)**, 10, b g Mulberry (FR)—Spartina (USA) **The Macca & Growler Partnership**
124 **SHINING LIGHTS (IRE)**, 6, b m Moscow Society (USA)—Orwell Rose (IRE) **D. A. Johnson**
125 **SHOWER OF HAIL (IRE)**, 5, b g Luso—Hail To Home (IRE) **D. A. Johnson**
126 **SIMOUN (IRE)**, 7, b g Monsun (GER)—Suivez (FR) **The Macca & Growler Partnership**
127 **SINDAPOUR (IRE)**, 7, b g Priolo (USA)—Sinntara (IRE) **Mrs M. Burke**
128 **SIXO (IRE)**, 8, gr g Roselier (FR)—Miss Mangaroo **Mr Matt Archer & Miss Jean Broadhurst**
129 **STORMEZ (FR)**, 8, b g Ezzoud (IRE)—Stormy Scene (USA) **D. A. Johnson**
130 **SYLVIE D'ORTHE (FR)**, 4, b f Saint Preuil—Paola Santa (FR) **D. A. Johnson**
131 **TAMARINBLEU (FR)**, 5, b g Epervier Bleu—Tamainia (FR) **The Arthur White Partnership**
132 **TANGO ROYAL (FR)**, 9, gr g Royal Charter—Nazia (FR) **B. A. Kilpatrick**
133 **TANTERARI (IRE)**, 7, b g Safety Catch (USA)—Cobblers Crest (IRE) **D. A. Johnson**
134 **TARXIEN**, 11, b g Kendor (FR)—Tanz (IRE) **B. A. Kilpatrick**
135 **TEAM TASSEL (IRE)**, 7, b g Be My Native (USA)—Alcmena's Last **Mr Matt Archer & Miss Jean Broadhurst**
136 **TELL THE TREES**, 4, br f Tamure (IRE)—Bluebell Copse **S. M. Mercer**
137 **THE THREE BANDITS (IRE)**, 5, b g Accordion—Katie Baggage (IRE) **D. A. Johnson**
138 **THEREALBANDIT (IRE)**, 8, b g Torus—Sunrise Highway VII **D. A. Johnson**
139 **TIME TO ROAM (IRE)**, 5, br g Darshaan—Minstrels Folly (USA) **Mrs M. Burke**
140 **TIUTCHEV**, 12, b g Soviet Star—Cut Ahead **The Liars Poker Partnership**
141 **TIZI OUZOU (IRE)**, 4, ch f Desert Prince (IRE)—Tresor (USA) **Mr A. R. West**
142 **TONIC DU CHARMIL (FR)**, 5, b g Mansonnien (FR)—Thrusting (FR) **Roger Stanley & Yvonne Reynolds**
143 **TRESOR DE MAI (FR)**, 11, ch g Grand Tresor (FR)—Lady Night (FR) **Partnership**
144 **TRY CATCH PADDY (IRE)**, 7, ch g Safety Catch (USA)—Blackwater Rose VII **D. A. Johnson**
145 **UPGRADE**, 11, b g Be My Guest (USA)—Cantanta **Mr Matt Archer & Miss Jean Broadhurst**
146 **VILLA**, 9, b g Jupiter Island—Spoonhill Wood **Mr Matt Archer & Miss Jean Broadhurst**
147 **VISIBILITY (FR)**, 6, gr g Linamix (FR)—Visor (USA) **J. R. W. Weeden**
148 **VIVID IMAGINATION (IRE)**, 6, b g Moonax (USA)—Sezu (IRE) **D. A. Johnson**
149 **WARDASH (GER)**, 5, b g Dashing Blade—Warusha (GER) **D. A. Johnson**
150 **WELL CHIEF (GER)**, 6, ch g Night Shift (USA)—Wellesiena (GER) **D. A. Johnson**
151 **WESTENDER (FR)**, 9, b g In The Wings—Trude (GER) **Mr Matt Archer & Miss Jean Broadhurst**
152 **WHISPERED SECRET (GER)**, 6, b g Selkirk (USA)—
Wells Whisper (FR) **David Manasseh Daniel Evans Dan Levine**
153 **WILL OF THE PEOPLE (IRE)**, 10, b g Supreme Leader—
Another Partner **Drs' D. Silk, M. Gillard, P. Walker, R. Purkis**
154 **WOOD LORD (FR)**, 4, b g Lord of Men—Genevieve des Bois (FR) **D. A. Johnson**
155 **YES MY LORD (IRE)**, 6, b g Mister Lord (USA)—Lady Shalom (IRE) **D. A. Johnson**
156 **YOUR SO COOL**, 8, ch g Karinga Bay—Laurel Diver **Mr Matt Archer & Miss Jean Broadhurst**

MR M. C. PIPE, C.B.E.—continued

157 **YOURMAN (IRE)**, 5, b g Shernazar—Lantern Lover **D. A. Johnson**
158 **ZETA'S RIVER (IRE)**, 7, ch g Over The River (FR)—Laurebon **D. A. Johnson**

Other Owners: Mrs Jane Reiss, Mr Michael Shufflebotham, Mr D. Sloan, Mr C. McKenna, Gill Nevin, Ron Middleton, Stuart Middleton, Mr N. A. Brimble, Mr N. Scanlan, Joshua Apiafi, Avalon Surfacing and Construction Co Ltd, S. Barnes, Mrs L. Barnes, T. W. Benson, B. E. Case, County Stores (Somerset) Holdings Ltd, R. Fowler, R. B. Gray, Mrs J. Kirpalani, H. L. Kirpalani M.B.E., Mrs S. J. Ling, S. McManaman, A. Perkins, B. V. Sangster, G. E. Sangster, G. T. Scanlon, Mr M. Stone, J. Wright.

Assistant Trainer: David E Pipe

Jockey (NH): R. Greene, T. J. Murphy, J. E. Moore, G. Supple. **Conditional:** T. J. Malone, C. Bonhoff. **Amateur:** Mr A. Glassonbury.

471 MR M. A. PITMAN, Upper Lambourn
Postal: **Weathercock House, Upper Lambourn, Hungerford, Berkshire, RG17 8QT.**
Contacts: **YARD** (01488) 73311 **FAX** (01488) 71065 **MOBILE** (07836) 792771
E-MAIL mark.pitman@markpitmanracing.com **WEBSITE** www.markpitmanracing.com

1 4, B g Synefos (USA)—Almost Regal (IRE) **P. A. Bancroft**
2 **AUBURN DUKE**, 5, ch g Inchinor—Dakota Girl **B. Perkins**
3 **BAY ISLAND (IRE)**, 9, b g Treasure Hunter—Wild Deer **B. Perkins**
4 **BELUGA (IRE)**, 6, gr g John French—Mesena **M. C. Denmark**
5 **BEST ACTOR (IRE)**, 6, b g Oscar (IRE)—Supreme Princess (IRE) **S. D. Hemstock**
6 **BOHEMIAN BOY (IRE)**, 7, gr g Roselier (FR)—Right Hand **S. D. Hemstock**
7 **BRADLEY BOY (IRE)**, 4, ch g Presenting—Mistric **S. D. Hemstock**
8 **BUDDHI (IRE)**, 7, b g Be My Native (USA)—Paean Express (IRE) **Mrs T. Brown**
9 **CAPTAIN CORELLI**, 8, b g Weld—Deaconess **P. A. Bancroft**
10 **CAPTAIN MADUCK (IRE)**, 7, b g Distinctly North (USA)—Avril's Choice **S. D. Hemstock**
11 **CLAIM TO FAME**, 4, b g Selkirk (USA)—Loving Claim (USA) **G. Pascoe & S. Brewer**
12 **COUNT CAMPIONI (IRE)**, 11, br g Brush Aside (USA)—Emerald Flair **J. F. Garrett**
13 **DEMPSEY (IRE)**, 7, b g Lord Americo—Kyle Cailin **Mrs T. Brown**
14 **DEO GRATIAS (POL)**, 5, b h Enjoy Plan (USA)—Dea (POL) **D. Brown & M. Pitman**
15 4, B g Supreme Leader—Divine Comedy (IRE) **M. C. Denmark**
16 **DOMART (POL)**, 5, gr g Baby Bid (USA)—Dominet (POL) **H. J. Jarvis**
17 **DONALD (POL)**, 5, b g Enjoy Plan (USA)—Dahira (POL) **J. F. Garrett**
18 4, B g Fourstars Allstar (USA)—Except Alice (IRE) **M. C. Denmark**
19 **FINELY TUNED (IRE)**, 6, b g Lord Americo—Gusserane Princess **M. C. Denmark**
20 **FIREBALL MACNAMARA (IRE)**, 9, b g Lord Americo—Glint of Baron **J. C. Hitchins**
21 5, B g Needle Gun (IRE)—Flapping Freda (IRE) **Mrs E. Pearce**
22 **FLY FOR PADDY**, 7, b g Michelozzo (USA)—Tirley Pop Eye **B. Perkins**
23 **FLYING TRIX (IRE)**, 9, b g Lord Americo—Bannow Drive (IRE) **P. A. Bancroft**
24 4, B g Accordion—Gaye Humour (IRE) **M. C. Denmark**
25 **GENUINE ARTICLE (IRE)**, 9, ch g Insan (USA)—Rosemount Rose **M. C. Denmark**
26 4, B g Zaffaran (USA)—Gilston Lass **M. C. Denmark**
27 **GODFATHER (IRE)**, 7, ch g Insan (USA)—Lady Letitia **M. C. Denmark**
28 **GOOD SAMARITAN (IRE)**, 6, ch g Insan (USA)—Ballymave (IRE) **M. C. Denmark**
29 4, B g Supreme Leader—Guess Twice **M. C. Denmark**
30 **HOT SHOTS (FR)**, 10, b g Passing Sale (FR)—Uguette IV (FR) **Mrs Jill Eynon & Mr Robin Eynon**
31 **IRONMAN MULDOON (IRE)**, 8, gr g Roselier (FR)—Darjoy **Mrs M. J. Bone**
32 **JOHNNY WILKIE**, 6, b g Shambo—Kelly's Maid **North Farm Stud**
33 **JUMP FOR PADDY**, 6, b g Michelozzo (USA)—Tudor Spartan **B. Perkins**
34 **KING OF THE JUNGLE (IRE)**, 4, ch g Accordion—What It Takes (IRE) **Mrs E. Pearce**
35 4, B gr g Cloudings (IRE)—Knight Ryde **M. C. Denmark**
36 4, B g Keen—Knowing **M. C. Denmark**
37 **LIMITED EDITION (IRE)**, 7, b g Parthian Springs—Rosemount Rose **M. C. Denmark**
38 **MONSIGNOR (IRE)**, 11, ch g Mister Lord (USA)—Dooney's Daughter **M. C. Denmark**
39 5, B g Alflora (IRE)—Northwood May **M. C. Denmark**
40 **PADRE (IRE)**, 6, b g Mister Lord (USA)—Lee Valley Lady (IRE) **M. C. Denmark**
41 **PATRIARCH (IRE)**, 9, b g Alphabatim (USA)—Strong Language **M. C. Denmark**
42 **PIPER HALL (UAE)**, 4, ch g Gulch (USA)—Ines Bloom (USA) **M. C. Denmark**
43 **PROUD PEER (IRE)**, 7, ch g Mister Lord (USA)—Raffeen Pride **G. C. Stevens**
44 **RAPALLO (IRE)**, 4, b g Luso—Sheeba Queen **Mrs Jill Eynon & Mr Robin Eynon**
45 **RED DAHLIA**, 8, b m Alflora (IRE)—Redgrave Devil **Mr J. Goodman**
46 **ROLL ALONG (IRE)**, 5, b g Carroll House—Callmartel (IRE) **B. R. H. Burrough**

MR M. A. PITMAN—continued

47 **RUN FOR PADDY**, 9, b g Michelozzo (USA)—Deep Selection (IRE) **B. Perkins**
48 **SCHUMANN**, 4, b c Rainbow Quest (USA)—Dance Sequence (USA) **Something In The City Partnership**
49 **SMART (SLO)**, 6, b g Glenstal (USA)—Satyra (POL) **M. C. Denmark**
50 **SMARTY (IRE)**, 12, b br g Royal Fountain—Cahernane Girl **Mrs T. Brown**
51 **SNAKEBITE (IRE)**, 5, gr g Taipan (IRE)—Bee In The Rose (IRE) **M. C. Denmark**
52 **SOLDIER OF ROME (IRE)**, 8, b g Satco (FR)—Queens Tricks **Mr M. A. Pitman**
53 **SPIKE JONES (NZ)**, 7, br g Colonel Collins (USA)—Gloss (NZ) **R. J. Pascoe**
54 4, B br g Presenting—Steel Grey Lady (IRE) **M. C. Denmark**
55 **SYDNEY (IRE)**, 5, b g Saddlers' Hall (IRE)—Magic Gale (IRE) **M. C. Denmark**
56 **SZEROKI BOR (POL)**, 6, b g In Camera (IRE)—Szuana (POL) **G Pascoe, S Brewer, J Newton & I Mcewen**
57 **TOO FORWARD (IRE)**, 9, ch g Toulon—One Back (IRE) **Mr T. L. Gibson & Mr D. Mathias**
58 **TOP OF THE AGENDA**, 6, b g Michelozzo (USA)—Expensive Lark **The Leaflet Company Ltd**
59 6, Ch g Executive Perk—Will I Or Wont I (IRE) **M. C. Denmark**
60 **WITHOUT A DOUBT**, 6, b g Singspiel (IRE)—El Rabab (USA) **M. C. Denmark**
61 **ZAFFRE D'OR (IRE)**, 8, b g Zaffaran (USA)—Massinetta **Mrs D. A. T. Salmon**

Other Owners: Mr D. Ellis, Mr J. Barson, Mr P. J. Dixon, Mr M. Crossley, Mrs Teresa Hilborn, Mr Mark Tracey, Mr Daniel Watkins, Mrs Sue Venton, Mrs Toni S. Tipper, Mr Andrew Harding, Mrs H. Bancroft, S. J. Brewer, D. A. Brown, Mrs J. M. Eynon, R. A. F. Eynon, T. L. Gibson, D. C. A. Mathias, David J. Muir, Mrs A. Muir, G. J. Pascoe.

Assistant Trainer: Paul Price

Jockey (NH): B. J. Crowley, S. Durack, T. J. Murphy. **Conditional:** C. Leveque.

---

472 MR C. T. POGSON, Newark
Postal: **Allamoor Farm, Mansfield Road, Farnsfield, Nottinghamshire, NG22 8HZ.**
Contacts: **PHONE (01623) 882275 MOBILE (07966) 725102**

1 **BRUSH A KING**, 10, b g Derrylin—Colonial Princess **Mr C. T. Pogson**
2 **DERRY DICE**, 9, b g Derrylin—Paper Dice **Mr C. T. Pogson**
3 **GAMMA-DELTA (IRE)**, 10, b g Alphabatim (USA)—Hardy Polly **Mr C. T. Pogson**
4 **OSCARDEAL (IRE)**, 6, b g Oscar (IRE)—Sleepy Bye Byes (IRE) **Mr C. T. Pogson**
5 **RAVENSCAR**, 7, b g Thethingaboutitus (USA)—Outcrop **Mr C. T. Pogson**
6 **REEL MISSILE**, 6, b g Weld—Landsker Missile **Mr C. T. Pogson**

Assistant Trainer: Mrs K J Pogson

Conditional: A. Pogson.

---

473 MR M. J. POLGLASE, Newark
Postal: **The Training Centre, Southwell Racecourse, Rolleston, Nottinghamshire, NG25 0TS.**
Contacts: **PHONE (01636) 816717 FAX (01636) 819127 MOBILE (07813) 103490**
E-MAIL polglaseracing@aol.co.uk

1 **BEAUTEOUS (IRE)**, 6, ch g Tagula (IRE)—Beauty Appeal (USA) **P. J. Dixon**
2 **BOLD BLADE**, 4, b g Sure Blade (USA)—Golden Ciel (USA) **P. J. Dixon**
3 **KING PRIAM (IRE)**, 10, b g Priolo (USA)—Barinia **Mr M. J. Polglase**
4 **MARENGO**, 11, b g Never So Bold—Born To Dance **Miss P. D. Insull**
5 **NICHOLAS NICKELBY**, 5, gr g Fayruz—Alasib **P. J. Dixon**
6 **NO TIME (IRE)**, 5, b h Danetime (IRE)—Muckross Park **P. J. Dixon**
7 **PARK AVE PRINCESS (IRE)**, 4, b f Titus Livius (FR)—Satinette **P. J. Dixon**
8 **PICCLEYES**, 4, b g Piccolo—Dark Eyed Lady (IRE) **P. J. Dixon**
9 **PICKPOCKET**, 5, ch g Paris House—Sabo Song
10 **SACCHARINE**, 4, b f Whittingham (IRE)—Sweet And Lucky **P. J. Dixon**
11 **SOLOMON'S MINE (USA)**, 6, b g Rahy (USA)—Shes A Sheba (USA) **P. J. Dixon**
12 **TALLY (IRE)**, 5, ch g Tagula (IRE)—Sally Chase **General Sir G. H. W. Howlett**

THREE-YEAR-OLDS

13 **ALPAGA LE JOMAGE (IRE)**, b c Orpen (USA)—Miss Bagatelle
14 **DANEHILL ANGEL**, ch f Danehill Dancer (IRE)—Ace Girl **P. J. Dixon**
15 **ELLIS CAVE**, gr g Diktat—Cole Slaw
16 **HAMBURG SPRINGER (IRE)**, b g Charnwood Forest (IRE)—Kyra Crown (IRE) **Bosco Racing**
17 **ITSA MONKEY (IRE)**, b g Merdon Melody—Gracious Imp (USA) **Mr G. M. Kinnersley**

MR M. J. POLGLASE—continued

18 **MINDFUL**, b c Mind Games—Blushing Victoria **P. J. Dixon**
19 **MISS MALONE (IRE)**, b f Daggers Drawn (USA)—Queen Molly **P. J. Dixon**
20 **MISTY PRINCESS**, gr f Paris House—Miss Whittingham (IRE) **Mrs M. Tanner**
21 **NEXT TIME (IRE)**, b f Danetime (IRE)—Muckross Park **P. J. Dixon**
22 **SMALL TIME BLUES (IRE)**, b f Danetime (IRE)—Barinia **Mr B. Green**
23 **WITTY GIRL**, b f Whittingham (IRE)—Zando's Charm **P. J. Dixon**

TWO-YEAR-OLDS

24 B f 20/3 Montjeu (IRE)—Castara Beach (IRE) (Danehill (USA)) (10060)
25 **DASHEENA**, b f 9/3 Magic Ring (IRE)—Sweet And Lucky (Lucky Wednesday)
26 Br f 26/3 Brave Act—Faypool (IRE) (Fayruz) (8718)
27 Gr c 28/3 Beckett (IRE)—Marathon Maid (Kalaglow) (5000)
28 **VERITE**, b c 22/3 Foxhound (USA)—Blushing Victoria (Weldnaas (USA))

Other Owners: T. Burton, Mr S. R. James, G. A. Lucas, Mrs D. E. Sharp.

Assistant Trainer: Jim Bird

Apprentice: Dawn Watson.

---

474 **MR B. N. POLLOCK, Market Harborough**
Postal: **18 Old Holt Road, Medbourne, Market Harborough, Leicestershire, LE16 8DY.**
Contacts: MOBILE (07968) 565225 MOBILE (07968) 032774
E-MAIL ben@bnpracing.com WEBSITE www.bnpracing.com

1 **A GLASS IN THYNE (IRE)**, 7, br g Glacial Storm (USA)—River Thyne (IRE) **J. B. Dale**
2 **BRIGHT PRESENT (IRE)**, 7, b br g Presenting—Bright Rose **The Gifted Girls**
3 **DERAMORE (IRE)**, 8, b g Hollow Hand—Leaney Kamscort **Medbourne Racing Club**
4 **EARL OF MERCIA**, 5, b g Mistertopogigo (IRE)—Lady Godiva **Partnership**
5 **GAME ON (IRE)**, 9, b g Terimon—Nun So Game **Mrs S. E. M. Platt**
6 **INCOADY**, 7, gr g Aydimour—Fallonetta **Lake House Partnership**
7 **NEVER AWOL (IRE)**, 8, ch g John French—Lark Lass **Charles And Rachel Wilson**
8 **PARSON'S ROSE**, 8, ch m Lancastrian—Sexton's Service **Medbourne Racing Club**
9 **REBEL RAIDER (IRE)**, 6, b g Mujadil (USA)—Emily's Pride **S. G. B. Morrison**

Other Owners: Mrs J. R. Dale, C. A. Green, Mrs A. Richardson, Mr I. T. Stevens, K. Thompson, Mrs E. Townsend, L. Turnbull, C. M. Wilson, Mrs R. E. Wilson.

Jockey (flat): J. Quinn. **Jockey (NH):** J. P. McNamara, A. Thornton. **Amateur:** Mr T. Messenger.

---

475 **MR N. J. POMFRET, Tilton-on-the-Hill**
Postal: **Red Lodge Farm, Marefield Lane, Tilton-on-the-Hill, Leicester.**
Contacts: PHONE (0116) 259 7537

1 **BALLARDS BOY (FR)**, 6, b g Sleeping Car (FR)—Anita (FR) **Mrs E. M. Deacon**
2 **COOL CHILLI**, 7, gr g Gran Alba (USA)—Miss Flossa (FR) **R. P. Brett**
3 **FRENCH BEY (IRE)**, 5, b m Beyssac (FR)—Cerise de Totes (FR) **J. R. Millington**
4 **INTREPID SAMSON**, 7, br g Terimon—Jasmin Path **J. N. Cheatle**
5 **SMART THINKER**, 4, gr f Silver Patriarch (IRE)—Smart Rhythm **R. H. Woodward**

---

476 **MR C. L. POPHAM, Taunton**
Postal: **Bashford Racing Stables, West Bagborough, Taunton, Somerset, TA4 3EF.**
Contacts: PHONE (01823) 432769 MOBILE (07967) 506430

1 **FU FIGHTER**, 4, b g Unfuwain (USA)—Runelia **The Boyz R Uz Partnership**
2 **LESCER'S LAD**, 8, b g Perpendicular—Grange Gracie **The Four Bucks**
3 **PURPLE PATCH**, 7, b m Afzal—My Purple Prose **Mrs C. C. Scott**

Other Owners: L. A. Heard, P. Lazenby, P. Littlejohns, A. S. Skidmore, G. T. Watson, R. J. Weeks.

Assistant Trainer: Mr J Scott

Amateur: Mr Saul McHugh.

477 MR J. G. B. PORTMAN, Compton
Postal: **Hamilton Stables, Hockham Road, Compton, Newbury, Berkshire, RG20 6QJ.**
Contacts: OFFICE (01635) 578031 FAX (01635) 579323 MOBILE (07798) 824513
E-MAIL portman.hamiltonstables@virgin.net

1 ARIMERO (GER), 5, b g Monsun (GER)—Averna **A. R. Boswood**
2 ASK FOR LUCK (IRE), 8, b g Camden Town—French Thistle **A. R. Boswood**
3 BODFARI CREEK, 8, ch g In The Wings—Cormorant Creek **Pump Technology Limited**
4 BULLYRAG, 4, b g Makbul—Dusk In Daytona **A. S. B. Portman**
5 CHARLIE'S CROSS (IRE), 7, gr g Roselier (FR)—Estuary View **Mrs E. J. Tice**
6 CREATE A STORM (IRE), 5, b br m Bob Back (USA)—Elag **M. J. Vandenberghe**
7 DASH FOR COVER (IRE), 5, b g Sesaro (USA)—Raindancing (IRE) **Eddis, Buchanan And Kottler**
8 EMPHATIC (IRE), 10, ch g Ela-Mana-Mou—Sally Rose **Hockham Racing**
9 FRAMBO (IRE), 4, b f Fraam—Wings Awarded **The Naughty Boys**
10 HIERS DE BROUAGE (FR), 10, b g Neustrien (FR)—Thalandrezienne (FR) **Seddon - Brown Partnership**
11 KING OF SPARTA, 12, b g Kefaah (USA)—Khaizaraan (CAN) **Mrs S. J. Portman**
12 LYNRICK LADY (IRE), 9, b m Un Desperado (FR)—Decent Lady **Milady Partnership**
13 MEASURELESS, 10, ch g Lion Cavern (USA)—Magnetic Point (USA) **Mr J. G. B. Portman**
14 RIDICULE, 6, b g Piccolo—Mockingbird **Pump Technology Limited**
15 SAFFRON FOX, 4, ch f Safawan—Fox Oa (FR) **The Hon Mrs R. Pease**
16 SAUCYNORWICH (IRE), 7, b g Norwich—Kelly Gales (IRE) **Mrs E. J. Tice**
17 VARUNI (IRE), 4, b f Ali-Royal (IRE)—Sauvignon (IRE) **Mr J. G. B. Portman**
18 WASTED TALENT (IRE), 5, b m Sesaro (USA)—Miss Garuda **Wasted Talent Partnership**

THREE-YEAR-OLDS

19 ARCH FOLLY, b g Silver Patriarch (IRE)—Folly Fox **S. J. Skinner**
20 CINDER MAID, b f Piccolo—Bella Helena **Mrs F. A. Veasey**
21 B g Atraf—E Sharp (USA)
22 GHAILL FORCE, b g Piccolo—Coir 'a' Ghaill **Mr J. T. Habershon-Butcher**
23 ISABELLA ROSSINI, b br f Rossini (USA)—Misty Rain **Out To Grass Partnership**
24 MARIANIS, b f Lujain (USA)—Without Warning (IRE) **Coriolan Partnership IV**
25 MISS PATRICIA, b f Mister Baileys—Zoena **Mrs J. N. Edwards-Heathcote**
26 SPINNING COIN, b f Mujahid (USA)—Cointosser **Hockham Racing**
27 SWEENEY TODD (IRE), ch g Raise A Grand (IRE)—Optional **M. J. Vandenberghe**

TWO-YEAR-OLDS

28 Br c 9/3 Zilzal (USA)—Bob's Princess (Bob's Return (IRE)) (5000)
29 Ch c 15/4 Mark of Esteem (IRE)—Flavian (Catrail (USA)) (4200)
30 GRAND SEFTON, br g 29/1 Pivotal—Nahlin (Slip Anchor) (10000) **T. D. Rootes**
31 Ch c 30/4 Tagula (IRE)—Mousseux (IRE) (Jareer (USA)) (8047) **Wasted Talent Partnership**
32 RETINA (SWI), b f 29/4 Xaar—Razida (IRE) (Last Tycoon) (5000)
33 SARA MANA MOU, b f 11/4 Medicean—Sarabah (IRE) (Ela-Mana-Mou) (17000) **A. H. Robinson**

Other Owners: J Hawkins-Byass, Mrs J. Alton, Mrs G. Powell, Mr J. Brownlee, Mr C. Curtis, Mrs J Garvin, I. Flooks, Mrs P. Thorman, Mr M. Shilling, Mrs T. Brudenell, T. Edwards, Miss J. Kempsey, Mr S. R. Hope, Mr R. Simmons, Mr D. Prior, Mr C. Elkins, Mr M. McMenemy, Mr K. Clarke, G. Greaves, Mr G. Clarke, Mr G. Wordsworth, The Hon J Deedes, Mr P. Deal, Mr W. L. Simmons, Mrs D. Farmer, Mrs N Haywood-Cole, E. Benson, R. C. Dollar, Mr M. Edwards, Mr D. Powell, Mrs M. Roberts, Lt Cdr N. S. Seddon-Brown, O. F. Waller.

Assistant Trainer: Sophie Portman

478 MR J. C. POULTON, Newmarket
Postal: **Meddler Racing Stables, Meddler Stud, Kentford, Newmarket, Suffolk, CB8 7PT.**
Contacts: PHONE (01638) 751504 FAX (01638) 751602 MOBILE (07779) 229827
E-MAIL meddlerstud@aol.com

1 ALI ZANDRA, 4, b f Prince Sabo—Priceless Fantasy
2 ANISETTE, 4, b f Abou Zouz (USA)—Natural Gold (USA)
3 BERTIES CONNECTION, 6, b g Danzig Connection (USA)—Bertie's Girl
4 BOOGARBAROO (IRE), 7, gr g Turtle Island (IRE)—Lingdale Lass
5 DAGGERS CANYON, 4, ch g Daggers Drawn (USA)—Chipewyas (FR)
6 DANCING BEAR, 4, b g Groom Dancer (USA)—Sickle Moon
7 DANCING DOLPHIN (IRE), 6, b m Dolphin Street (FR)—Dance Model
8 DUCKETT (IRE), 5, b h Charnwood Forest (IRE)—Lovat Spring (USA)

MR J. C. POULTON—continued

9 **DUMNONI**, 4, b f Titus Livius (FR)—Lamees (USA)
10 **EJAY**, 6, b br m Emperor Jones (USA)—Lough Erne
11 **EUROLINK ARTEMIS**, 8, b m Common Grounds—Taiga
12 **FUBOS**, 4, b g Atraf—Homebeforemidnight
13 **GRAND IDEAS**, 6, br g Grand Lodge (USA)—Afrafa (IRE)
14 **HAMMER OF THE GODS (IRE)**, 5, ch g Tagula (IRE)—Bhama (FR)
15 **INDIAN STEPPES (FR)**, 6, b m Indian Ridge—Ukraine Venture
16 **ITALIAN MIST (FR)**, 6, b g Forzando—Digamist Girl (IRE)
17 **JATH**, 4, b f Bishop of Cashel—Night Trader (USA)
18 **LEGALITY**, 5, b m Polar Falcon (USA)—Lady Barrister
19 **LIKE TO GO**, 4, b g Meadowbrook—Never Been VII
20 **MALAAH (IRE)**, 9, gr g Pips Pride—Lingdale Lass
21 **MISHKA**, 7, b g Mistertopogigo (IRE)—Walsham Witch
22 **MR UPPITY**, 6, b g Shareef Dancer (USA)—Queenfisher
23 **OH DANNY BOY**, 4, b g Cadeaux Genereux—Final Shot
24 **PRIVATE SEAL**, 10, b g King's Signet (USA)—Slender
25 **RAFTERS MUSIC (IRE)**, 10, b g Thatching—Princess Dixieland (USA)
26 **RED CONTACT (USA)**, 4, b g Sahm (USA)—Basma (USA)
27 **REPENT AT LEISURE**, 5, b g Bishop of Cashel—Sutosky
28 **SAUVE BERTIE**, 7, b h Suave Dancer (USA)—Bertie's Girl
29 **SIRAJ**, 6, B G Piccolo—Masuri Kabisa (USA)
30 **TALE OF THE TIGER**, 4, ch g Bijou d'inde—La Belle Dominique
31 **TEE JAY KASSIDY**, 5, b g Petong—Priceless Fantasy
32 **TRUE THUNDER**, 8, b g Bigstone (IRE)—Puget Dancer (USA)
33 **ZAC'S SPREE**, 6, b g Dancing Spree (USA)—Zac's Desire

THREE-YEAR-OLDS

34 B f Easycall—As Mustard
35 **ELRAFA MUJAHID**, b f Mujahid (USA)—Fancier Bit
36 **LOVE AND HONOUR**, b f Silver Patriarch (IRE)—Fox Star (IRE)
37 **OPENING LINE**, ch c Opening Verse (USA)—Denton Lady
38 B c Opening Verse (USA)—Philarmonique (FR)
39 **PRECIOUS SAMMI**, b g Mark of Esteem (USA)—Night Over Day
40 **TICKI TORI (IRE)**, b f Vettori (IRE)—Lamees (USA)
41 **TIPSY LILLIE**, ch f Tipsy Creek (USA)—Belle de Nuit (IRE)
42 **URABANDE**, b f Tipsy Creek (USA)—La Belle Mystere

TWO-YEAR-OLDS

43 B f 1/1 Most Welcome—Bertie's Girl (Another Realm)
44 B c 9/5 Robellino (USA)—Blue Fiction (IRE) (Bluebird (USA)) (4000)
45 B f 12/4 Distant Music (USA)—Distant Music (Darshaan) (10000)
46 Ch f 1/4 Arkadian Hero (USA)—Dunloe (IRE) (Shaadi (USA))
47 Ch c 28/4 Bertolini (USA)—Fancier Bit (Lion Cavern (USA)) (7000)
48 B c 11/3 Groom Dancer (USA)—Fox Star (IRE) (Foxhound (USA))
49 B f 28/4 Mister Baileys—Furry Dance (Nureyev (USA)) (3500)
50 **GRAND ASSAULT**, b c 29/3 Mujahid (USA)—As Mustard (Keen)
51 **HUGGLE**, b c 13/3 Groom Dancer (USA)—Perle de Sagesse (Namaqualand (USA))
52 Gr c 14/3 Most Welcome—Kinraddie (Wuzo (USA))
53 Ch f 10/3 Foxhound (USA)—La Belle Dominique (Dominion) (4500)
54 B c 20/4 Foxhound (USA)—La Belle Mystere (Lycius (USA)) (1600)
55 **WELCOME RELEAF**, ch c 25/3 Most Welcome—Mint Leaf (IRE) (Sri Pekan (USA))
56 B f 1/1 Most Welcome—Zac's Desire (Swing Easy (USA))

Owners: Headquarters Partnership, Mr Peter Webb, Mr Ray Jackson, Jason Thompson, Mr T. Gilligan, Mr P. Jenkins, Alan Price, B & B Hygiene, Eugene Lismonde, Sutton Oil (Bermuda) Leasing, Meddler Racing, Mr R. Favarulo, Exors of the Late Mrs T. A. Kemp, Tony Taylor, John Porteous, George & Jane Papps, Eileen & Peter Hutchinson, M. Robinson, Mr & Mrs Alan Shaw, Mrs A. C. Guinle, C. R. Withers, Meddler Bloodstock, S. M. Kemp, S. P. Shore, M. F. T. Sullivan, Neil Mitchell, Mrs Nikki Hillman, At Leisure Racing, Mr K. D. Berry, J. E. S. Colling, Mrs F. R. Colling, F. Cook, Gryffindor (www.racingtours.co.uk), K. A. Ingram, R. C. Kerry, Ormonde Racing, R. W. Reed, Mrs E. J. Reed, The Beare Family, Miss A. Thompson.

Assistant Trainer: Mrs Elizabeth Reed & Mr John Ryan

Jockey (flat): G. Faulkner, N. Callan, I. Mongan. **Jockey (NH):** A. Proctor, C. Bolger. **Conditional:** H. Poulton. **Apprentice:** Marc Halford. **Amateur:** Mr Anmole Chahal.

479 MR J. R. POULTON, Lewes

Postal: **White Cottage, Stud Farm, Telscombe, Lewes, East Sussex, BN7 3HZ.**
Contacts: **HOME (01273) 300127 YARD (01273) 302486 MOBILE (07980) 596952**
E-MAIL jamiepoulton@yahoo.co.uk

1 **CORRIB ECLIPSE**, 6, b g Double Eclipse (IRE)—Last Night's Fun (IRE) **M. Ioannou**
2 **DANGEROUS DAVE**, 6, b g Superpower—Lovely Lilly **Mr J. R. Poulton**
3 **DOLPHINELLE (IRE)**, 9, b g Dolphin Street (FR)—Mamie's Joy **C. R. Steward**
4 **DOUBLE MAGNUM**, 5, b g Double Trigger (IRE)—Raise The Dawn **R. W. Huggins**
5 **EXPECTED BONUS (USA)**, 6, b br g Kris S (USA)—Nidd (USA) **T. D. Racing**
6 **LAND 'N STARS**, 5, b g Mtoto—Uncharted Waters **K. Wilkinson**
7 **MYSTIC LAD**, 4, gr g Magic Ring—Jilly Woo **Mrs J. Wotherspoon**
8 **PIPSSALIO (SPA)**, 8, b g Pips Pride—Tesalia (SPA) **C. R. Steward**
9 **PRIVATE BENJAMIN**, 5, gr g Ridgewood Ben—Jilly Woo **Mrs J. Wotherspoon**
10 **RIVER BUG (IRE)**, 11, ch g Over The River (FR)—Fiona's Wish **Ormonde Racing**
11 **SUMMER CHERRY (USA)**, 8, b g Summer Squall (USA)—Cherryrob (USA) **Mr J. R. Poulton**
12 **THEATRE (USA)**, 6, b g Theatrical—Fasta (USA) **C. R. Steward**
13 **TIGER TIGER (FR)**, 4, b c Tiger Hill (IRE)—Adorable Emilie (FR) **R. W. Huggins**
14 **TOMMY CARSON**, 10, b g Last Tycoon—Ivory Palm **J. A. A. S. Logan**

THREE-YEAR-OLDS

15 **DOUBLE KUDOS (FR)**, gr c Highest Honor (FR)—Black Tulip (FR) **The 4th Middleham Partnership**
16 **DOUBLE MARGIN (USA)**, b g Boundary (USA)—Maniches Slew (USA) **R. W. Huggins**
17 **FABULOUS EMPEROR (IRE)**, b c Imperial Ballet (IRE)—Al Cairo (FR) **The Fabulous Emperor Syndicate**
18 **LINDEN LIME**, ch f Double Trigger (IRE)—Linden Grace (USA) **R. C. Moules**
19 **LORD OF ADVENTURE (IRE)**, b c Inzar (USA)—Highly Fashionable (IRE) **Barrie & Shirley Sancto**

TWO-YEAR-OLDS

20 B br c 28/3 Imperial Ballet (IRE)—Blue Dream (USA) (Irish River (FR)) (7000) **Mr J. R. Poulton**
21 B c 20/2 Gorse—Last Night's Fun (IRE) (Law Society (USA)) **M. Ioannou**
22 B f 1/5 In The Wings—Mosquera (GER) (Acatenango (GER)) (30000) **R. W. Huggins**

Other Owners: L. A. Bolingbroke, G. J. Bush, J. H. Bush, T. G. Dorrington, T. L. Gray, Dr C. A. Hey, G. P. Howard, K. A. Ingram, J. McGuigan, G. J. Price, J. M. Rands, M. L. Wakefield.

Assistant Trainer: Mrs C D Poulton

Jockey (flat): P. Doe, J. F. Egan. **Conditional:** C. Bolger, H. Poulton. **Amateur:** Mrs C. Poulton.

480 MR B. G. POWELL, Winchester

Postal: **Morestead Stables, Morestead, Twyford, Winchester, Hampshire, SO21 1JD.**
Contacts: **HOME (01962) 717705 FAX (01962) 717706 MOBILE (07768) 390737**

1 **ANALYZE (FR)**, 7, b g Anabaa (USA)—Bramosia **The Arkle Bar Partnership**
2 **APOLLO VICTORIA (FR)**, 8, b g Sadler's Wells (USA)—Dame Solitaire (CAN) **R. J. T. 290 Limited**
3 **ARUBA DAM (IRE)**, 7, br m Be My Native (USA)—Arumah **Mrs K. A. Stuart**
4 **BACKPACKER (IRE)**, 8, b g Petoski—Yellow Iris **C R H Racing**
5 **BALLYAAHBUTT (IRE)**, 6, b g Good Thyne (USA)—Lady Henbit (IRE) **Mrs A. Ellis**
6 **BEBOPSKIDDLY**, 4, b g Robellino (USA)—Adarama (IRE) **A. Head**
7 **BIG ROB (IRE)**, 6, b g Bob Back (USA)—Native Shore (IRE) **P. H. Betts**
8 **BLUEBERRY ICE (IRE)**, 7, b br m Glacial Storm (USA)—Call Me Honey **Mrs B. A. M. Studd**
9 **BUBBLE BOY (IRE)**, 6, ch g Hubbly Bubbly (USA)—Cool Charm **Exors of the Late J. G. Plackett**
10 **CHATEAU NICOL**, 6, b g Distant Relative—Glensara **Basingstoke Commercials**
11 **CHEVALIER BAYARD (IRE)**, 12, br g Strong Gale—Flying Pegus **J. Adam**
12 **COLONEL FRANK**, 8, b g Toulon—Fit For Firing (FR) **The Hambledon Hunters**
13 **COURT AWARD (IRE)**, 8, b g Montelimar (USA)—Derring Lass **A. Ayers and B. Belchem**
14 **CRUISE THE FAIRWAY (IRE)**, 9, b g Insan (USA)—Tickhill **R. J. T. 290 Limited**
15 **EURO AMERICAN (GER)**, 5, br g Snurge—Egyptale **Shore Property Developments**
16 **FINBAR'S REVENGE**, 10, b g Gildoran—Grotto Princess **K. Price**
17 **GLANAMANA (IRE)**, 9, b g Be My Native (USA)—Brides Choice **Mrs M. O'Kelly**
18 **GRACEFUL DANCER**, 8, b m Old Vic—Its My Turn **The Fairway Connection**
19 **GROVE JULIET (IRE)**, 6, ch m Moscow Society (USA)—Cloona Lady (IRE) **P. H. Betts**
20 **HEADINGLEY (IRE)**, 6, b g Supreme Leader—Wild Venture (IRE) **Mrs J. R. Bishop**
21 **INDIGO SKY (IRE)**, 4, gr c Adieu Au Roi (IRE)—Urban Sky (FR) **Hilton & Lyn Ramseyer**

MR B. G. POWELL—continued

22 **IT'S JUST SALLY**, 8, b m Kylian (USA)—Hush It Up **N. Stafford**
23 **JAY GEE'S CHOICE**, 5, b g Barathea (IRE)—Llia **A. Head**
24 **JUBBA'S JESTER (USA)**, 6, b g St Jovite (USA)—Wisecrack (USA) **J. Vail**
25 **JUST TOUCH WOOD**, 4, ch g Fraam—Versaillesprincess **Mrs J. I. Lankshear**
26 **KILLENAULE (IRE)**, 5, b g Bob Back (USA)—Party Woman (IRE) **Mrs J. R. Bishop**
27 **KIROV KING (IRE)**, 5, b h Desert King (USA)—Nymphs Echo (IRE) **Hop-Pickers**
28 **L'ESCALOU (FR)**, 8, b g Big John (FR)—Lescale (FR) **W. M. Smith**
29 **LAHINCH LAD (IRE)**, 5, ch g Bigstone (IRE)—Classic Coral (USA) **R. H. Gunn**
30 **LATIN PLAYER (IRE)**, 6, b g Vestris Abu—Legal Minstrel (USA) **B. M. Belcham**
31 **LINENS FLAME**, 6, ch g Blushing Flame (USA)—Atlantic Air **D & J Newell**
32 **LITTLE EDWARD**, 7, gr g King's Signet (USA)—Cedar Lady **J. Mursell**
33 **LORDINGTON LAD**, 5, br g Terimon—Fit For Firing (FR) **Dr M. Evans**
34 **LUCKY SINNA (IRE)**, 9, b br g Insan (USA)—Bit of A Chance **Exors of the Late J. G. Plackett**
35 **MAGNESIUM (USA)**, 5, ch h Kris S (USA)—Proflare (USA) **C. Harrington**
36 **MEN OF DESTINY (IRE)**, 4, b g Sadler's Wells (USA)—Caladira (IRE) **L. Gilbert**
37 **MESMERIC (IRE)**, 7, b g Sadler's Wells (USA)—Mesmerize **FF Racing Services XI Syndicate**
38 **MIDNIGHT SPUR (IRE)**, 6, b g Flying Spur (AUS)—Faramisa (USA) **D & J Newell**
39 **MINERS DANCE (IRE)**, 12, b g Miner's Lamp—Prudent Birdie **J. Studd**
40 **MONSTER MICK (FR)**, 7, b g Turgeon (USA)—The Dream I Dream (USA) **P. O'Donnell**
41 **MOON RIVER WONDER (IRE)**, 9, b g Doyoun—Bayazida **P. O'Donnell**
42 **MUMBLING (IRE)**, 7, ch g Dr Devious (IRE)—Valley Lights (IRE) **R. H. Gunn**
43 **MUTTLEY MAGUIRE (IRE)**, 6, b g Zaffaran (USA)—Alavie (FR) **Mrs J. R. Bishop**
44 **MY GALLIANO (IRE)**, 9, b g Muharib (USA)—Hogan Stand **J. Kavanagh**
45 **OBAY**, 4, ch g Kingmambo (USA)—Parade Queen (USA) **FF Racing Services Partnership XVIII**
46 **OFF THE SEAL (NZ)**, 9, b g Imperial Seal—Grand Countess (NZ) **Miss S. Harrison**
47 **POGGENIP**, 6, b m Petoski—Princess Tria **The Poggen Partners**
48 **RANDOM PRECISION (IRE)**, 6, ch g Presenting—Rendezvous **J. Studd**
49 **REASONABLE RESERVE (IRE)**, 8, ch g Fourstars Allstar—Alice O'malley **S. Mannion**
50 **REDHOUSE CHEVALIER**, 6, b g Pursuit of Love—Trampolo (USA) **Mrs J. M. Penney**
51 **SATTELIGHT**, 5, b m Fraam—Ajig Dancer **Sideways Racing II**
52 **SCARRABUS (IRE)**, 4, b g Charnwood Forest (IRE)—Errazuriz (IRE) **I. Smith**
53 **SISTER PHOEBE (IRE)**, 6, b br m Germany (USA)—Elea Victoria (IRE) **Mrs R. Powell**
54 **SITTING DUCK**, 6, b g Sir Harry Lewis (USA)—Fit For Firing (FR) **Mr M. D. Powers**
55 **SUNGIO**, 7, b g Halling (USA)—Time Or Never (FR) **Mrs R. Powell**
56 **TACIN (IRE)**, 8, b br g Supreme Leader—Nicat **Mrs J. R. Bishop**
57 **TAP DANCER (IRE)**, 7, b g Sadler's Wells (USA)—Watch Out (USA) **Mrs R. Powell**
58 **THE LORDOF MYSTERY (IRE)**, 7, b g Mister Lord (USA)—Coolline Mist (IRE) **A. Ayers and B. Belcham**
59 **THYNE'S OPTIMIST**, 6, b g Good Thyne (USA)—Sweet Optimist **Mrs P. Glenn**
60 **WALTZING BEAU**, 4, ch g Dancing Spree (USA)—Blushing Belle **David Cliff and Philippa Clunes**
61 **WELL ACTUALLY (IRE)**, 5, b g Luso—Lake Garden Park **Mrs A. Ellis**
62 **WHO'S WINNING (IRE)**, 4, ch g Docksider (USA)—Quintellina **Tony Head and Caroline Andrus**
63 **XCENTRA**, 4, b g Docksider (USA)—Dicentra **Favourites Racing Ltd**
64 **ZALKANI (IRE)**, 5, ch g Cadeaux Genereux—Zallaka (IRE) **J. W. Mursell**

THREE-YEAR-OLDS

65 **ATACAMA STAR**, ch g Desert King (IRE)—Aunty (FR) **R.H. Gunn**
66 **WEMBURY POINT (IRE)**, gr c Monashee Mountain (USA)—Lady Celina (FR) **Mr & Mrs D. A. Gamble**

Other Owners: T. H. Blackman, Mr A. J. Cork, Mr P. S. Dove, Mrs G. Elliott, G. M. Flood, Mrs S. R. Garratt, G. L. C. Hodgson, C. R. Holden, Mr S. M. Little, D. N. McLiesh, Mrs C. M. Poland, Miss J. A. Self, C. H. Shankland, K. Sobey, Mrs M. E. Topham-Holden, P. R. Webb, Mrs D. V. C. Whittingham.

Assistant Trainer: Rachel Powell

Jockey (NH): J. Tizzard. **Conditional:** J. Davies. **Apprentice:** A. Hindley. **Amateur:** Mr W. P. Kavanagh, Mrs R. Powell, Charles Studd.

---

481 **SIR MARK PRESCOTT BT, Newmarket**
Postal: Heath House, Newmarket, Suffolk, CB8 8DU.
Contacts: PHONE (01638) 662117 FAX (01638) 666572

1 **CORDIAL (IRE)**, 5, gr g Charnwood Forest (IRE)—Moon Festival **Mrs L. Burnet - Osborne House**
2 **ELUSIVE DREAM**, 4, b g Rainbow Quest (USA)—Dance A Dream **Cheveley Park Stud**
3 **FALL IN LINE**, 5, gr g Linamix (FR)—Shortfall **Neil Greig - Osborne House II**

SIR MARK PRESCOTT BT—continued

4 **FOREIGN AFFAIRS**, 7, ch h Hernando (FR)—Entente Cordiale (USA) **Charles C. Walker - Osborne House**
5 **INCROYABLE**, 4, gr f Linamix (FR)—Crodelle (IRE) **Lady C. J. O'Reilly**
6 **MASAFI (IRE)**, 4, b g Desert King (IRE)—Mrs Fisher (IRE) **G. D. Waters**
7 **PEDRILLO**, 4, b g Singspiel (IRE)—Patria (USA) **Hesmonds Stud Ltd**
8 **RED DAMSON (IRE)**, 4, b g Croco Rouge (IRE)—Damascene (IRE) **W. E. Sturt-Osborne House V**
9 **TEMPSFORD (USA)**, 5, b g Bering—Nadra (IRE) **Syndicate 2001**

THREE-YEAR-OLDS

10 **ALVARITA**, gr f Selkirk (USA)—Alborada **Miss K. Rausing**
11 **AMORIST (IRE)**, b g Anabaa (USA)—Moivouloirtoi (USA) **W. E. Sturt - Osborne House IV**
12 **ANNIBALE CARO**, b c Mtoto—Isabella Gonzaga **Cyril Humphris**
13 **COMIC STRIP** b g Marju (IRE)—Comic (IRE) **Neil Greig - Osborne House**
14 **CUPID'S GLORY**, b c Pursuit of Love—Doctor's Glory (USA) **Hesmonds Stud Ltd**
15 **EMPIRE CITY (USA)**, b g Carson City (USA)—Teeming Shore (USA) **Timothy J. Rooney**
16 **EPICES**, b g Mtoto—French Spice **C. J. Spence**
17 **ESPRIT DE CORPS**, b c Hernando (FR)—Entente Cordiale (USA) **W. E. Sturt - Osborne House II**
18 **HEREDITARY**, ch c Hernando (FR)—Eversince (USA) **Eclipse Thoroughbreds - Osborne House**
19 **HYPNOTIC**, ch c Lomitas—Hypnotize **Cheveley Park Stud**
20 **INTRIGUED**, gr f Darshaan—Last Second (IRE) **Faisal Salman**
21 **KANGRINA**, b f Acatenango (GER)—Kirona **Faisal Salman**
22 **KEY TIME (IRE)**, b f Darshaan—Kasota (USA) **G. Moore - Osborne House**
23 **KISWAHILI**, ch f Selkirk (USA)—Kiliniski **Miss K. Rausing**
24 **OBLIQUE (IRE)**, b f Giant's Causeway (USA)—On Call **Lady C. J. O'Reilly**
25 **PIVOTAL ROLE**, ch f Pivotal—Heckle **Cheveley Park Stud**
26 **RED PEONY**, b f Montjeu (IRE)—Red Azalea **Cheveley Park Stud**
27 **SAFE HARBOUR**, b f Docksider (USA)—Number One Spot **Mrs S. Thomson Jones**
28 **SONGERIE**, b f Hernando (FR)—Summer Night **Miss K. Rausing**
29 **SPECTAIT**, b g Spectrum (IRE)—Shanghai Girl **Mr E. S. A. Belcher**
30 **STAR APPLE**, b f Barathea (IRE)—Apple Town **Dr C. M. H. Wills**
31 **SUCCESSION**, ch f Groom Dancer (USA)—Pitcroy **Dr C. M. H. Wills**
32 **SUNLIT SKIES**, b f Selkirk (USA)—Shimmering Sea **Miss K. Rausing**
33 **TANGIBLE**, b f Hernando (FR)—Trinity Reef **Cheveley Park Stud**
34 **VAGARY (IRE)**, gr f Zafonic (USA)—Vadsagreya (FR) **Lady Roborough**
35 **VARENKA (IRE)**, b f Fasliyev (USA)—Castara Beach (IRE) **Lady Roborough**
36 **VIZ (IRE)**, b f Darshaan—For Example (USA) **Mrs S. M. Rogers**

TWO-YEAR-OLDS

37 **ACCENT (IRE)**, b g 18/1 Beckett (IRE)—Umlaut (Zafonic (USA)) (12742) **L. A. Larratt - Osborne House**
38 **ALAMBIC**, gr f 9/2 Cozzene (USA)—Alexandrine (IRE) (Nashwan (USA)) (180000) **Lady C. J. O'Reilly**
39 **ALMA MATER**, b f 9/1 Sadler's Wells (USA)—Alouette (Darshaan) **Miss K. Rausing**
40 **ARCHIMBOLDO (USA)**, ch c 6/3 Woodman (USA)—Awesome Strike (USA) (Theatrical) **Lady C. J. O'Reilly**
41 **ASPEN FALLS (IRE)**, ch f 3/2 Elnadim (USA)—Esquiline (USA) (Gone West (USA)) (73775) **Sir E. J. Loder**
42 **BRIDAL PATH**, gr b f 1/4 Groom Dancer (USA)—Doctor's Glory (USA) (Elmaamul (USA)) **Cheveley Park Stud**
43 **CAPTIVATE**, ch f 22/3 Hernando (FR)—Catch (USA) (Blushing Groom (FR)) **Miss K. Rausing**
44 **CARMONA**, b f 28/2 Rainbow Quest (USA)—El Opera (IRE) (Sadler's Wells (USA)) **Faisal Salman**
45 **CHESS BOARD**, b c 3/3 Vettori (IRE)—Cruinn A Bhord (Inchinor) **Lord Derby**
46 Ch f 16/1 Theatrical—Chitka (USA) (Jade Hunter (USA)) (106411) **Faisal Salman**
47 **CITY CHANCER (IRE)**, b c 17/3 Kalanisi (IRE)—Rachrush (IRE) (Sadler's Wells (USA)) (29000) **Ne'er Do Wells II**
48 **CONFIDENTIAL LADY**, b f 4/4 Singspiel (IRE)—Confidante (USA) (Dayjur (USA)) **Cheveley Park Stud**
49 **DAMOCLES SWORD (USA)**, ch c 14/2 Diesis—
                              Greek Myth (IRE) (Sadler's Wells (USA)) (85000) **Byrne Bros (Formwork) Limited**
50 **DREAM FANTASY (IRE)**, b g 11/3 Barathea (IRE)—
                              Night Mirage (USA) (Silver Hawk (USA)) (20120) **P. J. McSwiney-Osborne House**
51 **EL ALAMEIN (IRE)**, ch c 26/4 Nashwan (USA)—
                              El Rabab (USA) (Roberto (USA)) (70421) **Charles C. Walker - Osborne House II**
52 **EN FAMILLE**, gr f 2/3 Hernando (FR)—Entente Cordiale (USA) (Affirmed (USA)) **Miss K. Rausing**
53 **ENTHRALLED**, br b f 24/1 Zafonic (USA)—Artifice (Green Desert (USA)) **Dr C. M. H. Wills**
54 **FLOR Y NATA (USA)**, b f 24/3 Fusaichi Pegasus (USA)—
                              Rose of Zollern (IRE) (Seattle Dancer (USA)) **Miss K. Rausing**
55 **GENTIAN**, ch f 19/4 Generous (IRE)—French Spice (Cadeaux Genereux) **C. J. Spence**
56 **IRIDESCENCE**, b f 17/2 Daylami (IRE)—Eilean Shona (Suave Dancer (USA)) **Dr C. M. H. Wills**
57 **LIBERATE**, ch c 2/5 Lomitas—
                              Eversince (USA) (Foolish Pleasure (USA)) (52000) **Eclipse Thoroughbreds-Osborne House III**
58 **NATIONAL DRESS**, b f 8/5 Singspiel (IRE)—National Treasure (Shirley Heights) **Cheveley Park Stud**
59 **OUTLOOK**, ch c 7/2 Observatory (USA)—Area Girl (Jareer (USA)) (5000) **Neil Greig - Osborne House III**

SIR MARK PRESCOTT BT—continued

60 **PHONE IN,** b c 19/3 Sinndar (IRE)—Patria (USA) (Mr Prospector (USA)) **Hesmonds Stud Ltd**
61 **PICADOR,** b c 4/5 Pivotal—Candescent (Machiavellian (USA)) **Cheveley Park Stud**
62 **PLUSH,** ch c 5/2 Medicean—Glorious (Nashwan (USA)) **Cheveley Park Stud**
63 **PRINCE PICASSO,** b c 5/2 Lomitas—Auspicious (Shirley Heights) (50000) **Syndicate 2004**
64 **QUOTE UNQUOTE,** ch f 4/3 Allied Forces (USA)—Quiz Time (Efisio) (5500) **Lady Fairhaven**
65 **RED BEGONIA,** b f 24/3 Pivotal—Red Azalea (Shirley Heights) **Cheveley Park Stud**
66 **RIVETTING,** b g 6/4 Vettori (IRE)—Frog (Akarad (FR)) **B. Haggas**
67 **ROYAL CURTSY,** b f 26/4 Pivotal—Fen Princess (IRE) (15000) **Hesmonds Stud Ltd**
68 **SATIN SMOOTH (USA),** ch f 19/4 Giant's Causeway (USA)—
                        Louve Mysterieuse (USA) (Seeking The Gold (USA)) (159616) **Faisal Salman**
69 **SECRET LIAISON,** gr c 15/5 Medicean—Courting (Pursuit of Love) (50000) **W. E. Sturt - Osborne House**
70 **SKALA (IRE),** b f 13/3 Hernando (FR)—Apple Tree (Warning) **Dr C. M. H. Wills**
71 **SOUVENANCE,** b f 3/5 Hernando (FR)—Summer Night (Nashwan (USA)) **Miss K. Rausing**
72 **SPASIBA,** b f 21/1 Pivotal—Skimra (Hernando (FR)) **Miss K. Rausing**
73 **TARANIS,** b c 3/4 Lomitas—Woodbeck (Terimon) (70000) **Lady K. M. Watts**
74 **VIOLETTE,** b f 31/3 Observatory (USA)—Odette (Pursuit of Love) **C. G. Rowles Nicholson**
75 **WARSAW PACT (IRE),** b g 4/4 Polish Precedent (USA)—
                        Always Friendly (High Line) (45606) **J. Fishpool - Osborne House**
76 **WICKED DAZE,** ch g 6/4 Generous (IRE)—Thrilling Day (Groom Dancer (USA)) (38000) **R. T. Ferris**

Other Owners: Mr J. M. Brown, Mr Patsy Byrne, Mr Thomas Carroll, Mr Nigel Cobby, Mrs Lindsay Douglas-Hughes, The Hon. Mrs Gillie Greenwood, Mr Michael Le Quesne Herbert, Mr Chris Jenkins, Mrs Margaret Latham, Mrs Jennifer Lambert, Mr E. J. Williams, Mr Kevin Wilde, Mr Ian Spearing, Mrs Joan Rock, Mrs Jane Rimmer, Mr F. A. R. Packard, Mrs Sara Metherell, Mr Donald Mackenzie, Mr David Lowrey, Mrs Judy Le Quesne Herbert, Mr David Harding, Mr Fred Done, Mrs Megan Dennis, Mr Yagnish Chotai, Mr P. G. Goulandris, Robert Aird, J. J. Durkin, The Hon Pearl Lawson Johnston, Sir Mark Prescott Bt, Skymarc Farm Inc., Tessona Racing Ltd, Mrs S. L. Warman.

Assistant Trainer: William Butler

Jockey (flat): J. Mackay, S. Sanders. **Apprentice:** Simon Archer. **Amateur:** Mr M. J. Harvey.

---

482 MRS A. PRICE, Presteigne
Postal: **The Meeting House, Norton, Presteigne, Powys, LD8 2HA.**
Contacts: **PHONE (01544) 267221**

1 **GET THE VET,** 5, b g Thowra (FR)—Profit And Loss **Mrs A. Price**
2 **HUNTERSWAY (IRE),** 8, ch g Treasure Hunter—Dunmanway **Mrs A. Price**
3 **LET'S ROCK,** 7, b g Rock City—Sizzling Sista **Mrs A. Price**
4 **NORTON WOOD (IRE),** 9, ch g Shardari—Colligan Forest **Mrs A. Price**
5 **TUFF JOINT (IRE),** 7, b br g Good Thyne (USA)—The Furnituremaker **Mrs A. Price**

Jockey (NH): J. Goldstein. **Amateur:** Mr R. Hodges, Miss E. James.

---

483 MR A. E. PRICE, Leominster
Postal: **Eaton Hall Farm, Leominster, Herefordshire, HR6 0NA.**
Contacts: **PHONE (01568) 611137 MOBILE (07729) 838660**
E-MAIL price.eaton@tinyworld.co.uk

1 **CASTANET,** 6, b m Pennekamp (USA)—Addaya (IRE) **Mrs C. Davis**
2 **COMMANCHE GUN,** 5, b g Commanche Run—Busy Girl **M. G. Racing**
3 **CRAOBH RUA (IRE),** 8, b g Lord Americo—Addies Lass **Sastastic Partnership**
4 **GOLDEN TINA,** 7, ch m Tina's Pet—Gold 'n Soft **Mrs J. P. V. Baldwin**
5 **MIDNIGHT GUNNER,** 11, b g Gunner B—Light Tonight **M. G. Racing**
6 **PITHY'S FRIEND,** 5, gr g Terimon—Take The Veil **Mr B. Owen**
7 **STOLEN GIFT,** 5, b m Zahran (IRE)—Stolen Owl **Lea Hall Lodge Racing 2**

THREE-YEAR-OLDS

8 B c f Fraam—Flakey Dove **Mrs M. Price**
9 B f Atraf—Flossy Dove **Mrs M. Price**

Other Owners: J. Penfold, Miss S. Bather, A. G. Bathurst, E. J. Bywater, B. S. Jones, R. Smith.

Assistant Trainer: Mrs H L Price

484 **MR C. J. PRICE, Leominster**
Postal: **Brockmanton Hall, Brockmanton, Leominster, Herefordshire, HR6 0QU.**
Contacts: **PHONE (01568) 760695**

1 DANCING PEARL, 7, ch m Dancing Spree (USA)—Elegant Rose **John Heymans**
2 GEORGIE GIRL DOVE, 5, b m Busy Flight—Emerald Dove **M. J. Low**
3 MASTER MONEYSPIDER, 6, b g Regal Embers (IRE)—Mis-E-Fishant **H. Turberfield**
4 SCRATCH THE DOVE, 8, b m Henbit (USA)—Coney Dove **Mr C. J. Price**
5 WIZ THE DOVE, 4, b f Wizard King—Deadly Dove **Mr C. J. Price**

485 **MR J. K. PRICE, Ebbw Vale**
Postal: **41 Beaufort Terrace, Ebbw Vale, Gwent, NP23 5NW.**
Contacts: **PHONE (01495) 306113 MOBILE (07870) 475156**

1 SARAGANN (IRE), 10, b g Danehill (USA)—Sarliya (IRE) **Mr J. K. Price**

Assistant Trainer: A J Price

486 **MR RICHARD J. PRICE, Hereford**
Postal: **Criftage Farm, Ullingswick, Hereford, Herefordshire, HR1 1JG.**
Contacts: **PHONE (01432) 820263 FAX (01432) 820785 MOBILE (07929) 200598**

1 BAUDOLINO, 8, br g Bin Ajwaad (IRE)—Stos (IRE) **S. J. Fletcher**
2 BOBSBEST (IRE), 9, b g Lashkari—Bobs **R. A. Jefferies**
3 BUSINESS TRAVELLER (IRE), 5, ch g Titus Livius (FR)—Dancing Venus **Karl And Patricia Reece**
4 DAY ONE, 4, ch c Daylami (IRE)—Myself **A. Gray, P. McNeil, G. Court**
5 DOLLAR LAW, 9, ch g Selkirk (USA)—Western Heights **The Cleobury Partnership**
6 FARNBOROUGH (USA), 4, b g Lear Fan (USA)—Gretel **David Prosser & Keith Warrington**
7 FLITE OF ARABY, 8, b g Green Desert (USA)—Allegedly Blue (USA) **E. J. Whilding**
8 LILAC, 8, ch m Alhijaz—Fairfield's Breeze **Derek & Cheryl Holder**
9 LORD ON THE RUN (IRE), 6, b g Lord Americo—Polar Crash **Mrs A. M. O'Sullivan**
10 ONASSIS, 8, b g Roselier (FR)—Jack's The Girl (IRE) **Englands Gate Limited**
11 RADNOR LAD, 5, ch g Double Trigger (IRE)—Gabibti (IRE) **The Ever Hopeful Partnership**
12 RED LANCER, 4, ch g Deploy—Miss Bussell **Fox and Cub Partnership**
13 REFLEX BLUE, 8, b g Ezzoud (IRE)—Briggsmaid **Fox and Cub Partnership**
14 STARRY MARY, 7, b m Deploy—Darling Splodge **Dick's Neighbours**

THREE-YEAR-OLDS

15 GALLEGO, br c Danzero (AUS)—Shafir (IRE) **My Left Foot Racing Syndicate**
16 WOTCHALIKE (IRE), ch c Spectrum (IRE)—Juno Madonna (IRE) **Fox and Cub Partnership**

Other Owners: Mrs N. J. V. Barrett, A. J. Chance, Mr G. J. Court, R. A. Davies, Mrs P. A. Hill, B. S. Hill, S. S. Hill, P. J. Hoare, D. C. Holder, Mrs C. R. Holder, P. J. McNeil, Mr N. J. Panniers, Mr R. T. R. Price.

Assistant Trainer: Jane Price

Conditional: Richard Spate. **Amateur:** Miss V. Price.

487 **DR P. L. J. PRITCHARD, Purton**
Postal: **Timber Pond House, Purton, Berkeley, Gloucestershire, GL13 9HY.**
Contacts: **PHONE (01453) 811989 FAX (01453) 521557**
E-MAIL jockeysdoc@msn.com WEBSITE www.timberpondracing.com

1 ASHGAN (IRE), 12, br g Yashgan—Nicky's Dilemma **The Shooting Stars**
2 BLAZING BATMAN, 12, ch g Shaab—Cottage Blaze **Jumping Jokers**
3 CYANARA, 9, b m Jupiter Island—Shamana **Mr S. R. Hanney**
4 DAMIEN'S CHOICE (IRE), 13, b g Erin's Hope—Reenoga **Timber Pond Racing Club**
5 DAVOSKI, 11, b g Niniski (USA)—Pamela Peach **Lady Maria Coventry**
6 DISPOL ROCK (IRE), 9, b g Ballad Rock—Havana Moon **Dr P. L. J. Pritchard**
7 FAST KING (FR), 7, b g Housamix (FR)—Fast Girl (FR) **Docs'R'Us**
8 FRANCOLINO (FR), 12, b g Useful (FR)—Quintefeuille II (FR) **B. R. Marsden**
9 GET THE POINT, 11, b g Sadler's Wells (USA)—Tolmi **Norwester Racing Club**
10 HAPPY HUSSAR (IRE), 12, b g Balinger—Merry Mirth **Dr. J. J. Kabler & Mrs T. Pritchard**

DR P. L. J. PRITCHARD—continued

11 **HI TECH**, 6, b g Polar Falcon (USA)—Just Speculation (IRE) **Juro Antiques**
12 **JAYBEEDEE**, 9, b g Rudimentary (USA)—Meavy **Lady Maria Coventry**
13 **KNOCKRIGG (IRE)**, 11, ch g Commanche Run (USA) **Timber Pond Racing Club**
14 **QUEENS HARBOUR (IRE)**, 11, b g Brush Aside (USA)—Queenie Kelly **Timber Pond Racing Club**
15 **SUNDAY HABITS (IRE)**, 11, ch g Montelimar (USA)—Robertina (USA) **The It's My Job Partnership**

Other Owners: R. H. Brookes, Mrs J. A. George, Mr C. D. Hazelwood, Dr J. P. Heathcock, Mr R. H. Hughes, J. J. Kabler, P. Nurcombe, Mrs M. Phillips, Miss C. J. Shearer.

Assistant Trainer: Mrs T. Pritchard

Jockey (NH): R. Greene, J. Mogford. **Conditional:** O Dayman. **Amateur:** Dr P. L. J. Pritchard.

---

488 MR G. PRODROMOU, East Harling
Postal: **Georges Farm, Bryants Bridge, East Harling, Norfolk, NR16 2JR.**
Contacts: **OFFICE** (01953) 717224 **FAX** (01953) 717317 **MOBILE** (07899) 071001

1 **ARK ADMIRAL**, 6, b g Inchinor—Kelimutu **What R U Like Partnership**
2 **CANARYLOVE**, 4, b g Pursuit of Love—Lyssage **M. M. Foulger**
3 **GRAN DANA (IRE)**, 5, b g Grand Lodge (USA)—Olean **Mr Ericos Costopoulos & Mr P. Prodromou**
4 **GREY PRINCE**, 4, gr g Samraan (USA)—Scallys Queen Jay **Mr F. & Mrs A. Butler**
5 **KING OF KNIGHT (IRE)**, 4, gr g Orpen (USA)—Peace Melody (IRE) **M. M. Foulger**
6 **KING OF MEZE (IRE)**, 4, b g Croco Rouge (IRE)—Cossack Princess (IRE) **Mr F. & Mrs A. Butler**
7 **KING OF MUSIC (USA)**, 4, ch g Jade Hunter (USA)—Hail Roberta (USA) **Mrs B. A. Macalister**
8 **MR HICKMAN (IRE)**, 8, b g Montelimar (USA)—Cabin Glory **A. R. Macalister**
9 **SOUL PROVIDER (IRE)**, 4, ch f Danehill Dancer (IRE)—Wing And A Prayer (IRE) **Mr F. & Mrs A. Butler**
10 **SRIOLOGY (IRE)**, 4, b g Sri Pekan (USA)—Sinology **A. R. Macalister**

THREE-YEAR-OLDS

11 **KALHMERA (IRE)**, b f Gone Fishin—Biddy Widdy (IRE)

TWO-YEAR-OLDS

12 **AL RAYANAH**, b f 13/4 Almushtarak (IRE)—Desert Bloom (FR) (Last Tycoon) **F. Al-Nassar**

Other Owners: Mrs A. Butler, F. Butler, Mr E. Costopoulos, Mr P. Prodromou.

Assistant Trainer: Alan Macallister

Jockey (flat): O. Urbina. **Jockey (NH):** R. Thornton. **Conditional:** Mathew Smith. **Amateur:** Mr Paul Fergunson.

---

489 MRS H. PUDD, Taunton
Postal: **Pyleigh Court Farm, Lydeard St Lawrence, Taunton, Somerset, TA4 3QZ.**
Contacts: **PHONE** (01984) 667229 **FAX** (01984) 667428

1 **ARCTIC GLOW**, 6, ch m Weld—Arctic Mission **Mrs H. Pudd**
2 **ARDROE HILL**, 6, b g Weld—Kathleen Callaghan **R. C. Pudd**
3 **COOL WAGER**, 13, br g Arctic Lord—Gamblingway **R. C. Pudd**
4 **JULES LEVINE**, 7, b g Karinga Bay—Miss Tullulah **Mrs H. Pudd**
5 5, B m Double Trigger (IRE)—Scarlet Dymond **Mrs H. Pudd**

---

490 MR P. D. PURDY, Bridgwater
Postal: **Fyne Court Farm, Broomfield, Bridgwater, Somerset, TA5 2EQ.**
Contacts: **PHONE/FAX** (01823) 451632 **MOBILE** (07860) 392786

1 **COURT EMPRESS**, 8, ch m Emperor Fountain—Tudor Sunset **Mr P. D. Purdy**
2 **COURT FINALE**, 4, ch g One Voice (USA)—Tudor Sunset **Mr P. D. Purdy**
3 **COURT NANNY**, 11, ch m Nicholas Bill—Tudor Sunset **Mr P. D. Purdy**
4 **COURT OLIVER**, 7, ch g One Voice (USA)—Tudor Sunset **Mr P. D. Purdy**
5 **COURT SENOR**, 9, gr g Gran Alba (USA)—Tudor Sunset **Mr P. D. Purdy**
6 **GREY COURT**, 10, ro g Gran Alba (USA)—Tudor Sunset **Mr P. D. Purdy**
7 **SUNRISE COURT**, 6, ch g One Voice (USA)—Tudor Sunset **Mr P. D. Purdy**
8 **SUTTON BALLAD**, 11, b m Emperor Fountain—Crescent Cottage **Mr P. D. Purdy**

MR P. D. PURDY—continued

9 **SUTTON LION**, 13, b g Lyphento (USA)—Crescent Cottage **Mr P. D. Purdy**
10 **TUDOR NICKOLA**, 13, ch m Nicholas Bill—Cottage Melody **Mr P. D. Purdy**

TWO-YEAR-OLDS

11 **COURT HUMOUR**, b g 27/6 Joligeneration—Tudor Sunset (Sunyboy) **Mr P. D. Purdy**

Assistant Trainer: Alison J Purdy

Conditional: Mr R. Lucey-Butler. **Amateur:** Miss A. Purdy.

---

491 MR M. QUINLAN, Newmarket
Postal: **Athnid Stables, Hamilton Road, Newmarket, Suffolk, CB8 7JQ.**
Contacts: **OFFICE (01638) 603530 FAX (01638) 603488 MOBILE (07815) 072946**

1 **BULBERRY HILL**, 4, b g Makbul—Hurtleberry (IRE) **Mrs J Johnson, Mrs P Dunne**
2 **FRANK SONATA**, 4, b c Opening Verse (USA)—Megdale (IRE) **W. P. Flynn**
3 **HUXLEY (IRE)**, 6, b g Danehill Dancer (IRE)—Biddy Mulligan **L. Mulryan**
4 **SIERA SPIRIT (IRE)**, 4, b f Desert Sun—Jay And-A (IRE) **P. Ashmore & Mrs J. Quinlan**

THREE-YEAR-OLDS

5 B f Tagula (IRE)—Black Jack Girl (IRE) **Mrs J. M. Quinlan**
6 **DAYGAR**, b c Spectrum (IRE)—Milly Ha Ha **A. J. Del-Giudice**
7 **HERES THE PLAN (IRE)**, b f Revoque (IRE)—Fanciful (IRE) **L. Mulryan**
8 **RUDAKI**, ch g Opening Verse (USA)—Persian Fountain (IRE) **The Avalon Group**
9 **SUBTLE AFFAIR (IRE)**, b f Barathea (IRE)—Uncertain Affair (IRE) **L. Cashman & M. C. Fahy**

TWO-YEAR-OLDS

10 B f 14/2 Fasliyev (USA)—Aiming Upwards (Blushing Flame (USA)) (35000) **Mr L. Cashman**
11 B f 24/4 Revoque (IRE)—Alexanders Way (FR) (Persian Heights) (18000)
12 B c 4/5 Montjeu (IRE)—An Mosey (USA) (Royal Academy (USA)) (25485) **Dr Angelo Macchi**
13 **ARMENIAN HERITAGE**, b f 6/3 Bluebird (USA)—Blueberry Walk (Green Desert (USA)) **A. Pettinari**
14 B c 27/4 Alhaarth (IRE)—Bee Off (IRE) (Wolfhound (USA)) (10000) **G. Manfredini**
15 **CASTELLANO**, b c 22/4 Mujahid (USA)—Megdale (IRE) (Waajib) (31000) **Mrs N. J. McGreavy**
16 **CENTRINO**, b c 21/4 Bertolini (USA)—Celestina (IRE) (Priolo USA) **Paolo Benedetti**
17 B br c 25/2 Louis Quatorze (USA)—Conectis (IRE) (River Falls) (34875) **O'Connor Racing**
18 **DIXIE BELLE**, b f 18/2 Diktat—Inspiring (IRE) (Anabaa (USA)) (10000) **Burns Farm Racing**
19 B c 14/2 Mujadil (USA)—Dusky Virgin (Missed Flight) (26827)
20 B c 28/2 Dansili—Ellie Ardensky (Slip Anchor) (5200)
21 B c 28/1 Peintre Celebre (USA)—Fearless (Groom Dancer (USA)) (20000)
22 **FUSILI (IRE)**, ch f 3/2 Silvano (GER)—Flunder (Nebos (GER)) (22000) **Mr W. P. Flynn**
23 B c 2/2 Gorse—General Jane (Be My Chief (USA)) (11000) **Dr Angelo Macchi**
24 B c 5/3 Key of Luck (USA)—Hang Fire (Marju (IRE)) (8000) **G. Manfredini**
25 B f 17/4 Barathea (IRE)—High Flying Adored (In The Wings) **Mr L. Cashman**
26 **HOSIVA (GER)**, b f 28/1 Silvano (GER)—Hosianna (GER) (Surumu (GER)) (18779)
27 B c 26/3 Night Shift (USA)—In Your Dreams (IRE) (Suave Dancer (USA)) (46000) **L. Mulryan**
28 B c 18/4 Robellino (USA)—Laugharne (Known Fact (USA)) (14000)
29 B f 1/4 Groom Dancer (USA)—Marbella Beach (IRE) (Bigstone (IRE))
30 B f 21/4 Danehill Dancer (IRE)—Mary Hinge (Dowsing (USA)) (38000) **L. Mulryan**
31 Ch c 17/4 Carrowkeel (IRE)—Mauras Pride (IRE) (Cadeaux Genereux) (13413)
32 B f 11/3 Mujahid (USA)—Nashkova (Nashwan (USA))
33 B c 22/2 Mull of Kintyre (USA)—Never End (Alzao (USA)) (800) **Mrs R. A. Smith**
34 Gr c 5/3 Bertolini (USA)—Paris Mist (Paris House) **Mrs J. M. Quinlan**
35 Ch c 16/2 In The Wings—Polygueza (FR) (Be My Guest (USA)) (40000) **L. Mulryan**
36 B c 18/4 Desert Style (IRE)—Snoozy (Cadeaux Genereux) (3000)
37 B c 4/2 Tagula (IRE)—Sodfahh (Lion Cavern (USA)) (8000)
38 B c 22/4 Desert Prince (IRE)—Swan's Loop (Caerleon (USA)) (2011)
39 **TASKA**, b f 1/4 Lomitas—Tarnaka (Formidable) (USA) (15000) **Mr W. P. Flynn**
40 B c 19/2 Pivotal—Tatanka (IRE) (Lear Fan (USA))
41 **THE BUCK (IRE)**, ch c 10/4 Quws—Erin Anam Cara (IRE) (Exit To Nowhere (USA)) (1428) **Miss M. Archdeacon**
42 B f 28/4 Namid—Vintage Escape (IRE) (Cyrano de Bergerac) (25485) **L. Mulryan**

MR M. QUINLAN—continued

43 B br f 3/3 Raise A Grand (IRE)—Where's The Money (Lochnager) (9389)
44 B c 7/4 Piccolo—Yesterday's Song (Shirley Heights) (7500)

Other Owners: Mr J. O'Connor, Mr B. Sigurdsson, Mr & Mrs J. Moore, Mr V. T. Vilhjalmsson, Mr J. de Selincourt, Mr A. Panetta, Mr D. Jordan, Mr W. Adams, Mr W. R. Asquith, Mr D. Flynn.

Assistant Trainer: N Quinlan

Jockey (flat): T. P. Queally, R. L. Moore. **Conditional:** Tim Bailey. **Apprentice:** Nicol Polli.

---

492 **MR J. J. QUINN**, Malton
Postal: **Bellwood Cottage Stables, Settrington, Malton, North Yorkshire, YO17 8NR.**
Contacts: **PHONE** (01944) 768370 **FAX** (01944) 768261 **MOBILE** (07899) 873304
E-MAIL jjq@quinn-settrington.freeserve.co.uk

1 A BIT OF FUN, 4, ch g Unfuwain (USA)—Horseshoe Reef **The Fun Seekers**
2 ADJAWAR (IRE), 7, b g Ashkalani (IRE)—Adjriyna **Mrs M. Taylor**
3 ALERON (IRE), 7, b g Sadler's Wells (USA)—High Hawk **G. Liles**
4 ARCHIE BABE (IRE), 9, ch g Archway (IRE)—Frensham Manor **Bowett Lamb & Kelly**
5 BASINET, 7, b g Alzao (USA)—Valiancy **Tara Leisure**
6 BELLANEY JEWEL (IRE), 6, b m Roselier (FR)—Sister of Gold **J. W. Rosbotham**
7 CARIBBEAN CORAL, 6, ch g Brief Truce (USA)—Caribbean Star **Dawson, Green, Quinn, Roberts**
8 CD EUROPE (IRE), 7, ch g Royal Academy (USA)—Woodland Orchid (IRE) **Mr L. Neill and Mr G. Flitcroft**
9 CROW WOOD, 6, b g Halling (USA)—Play With Me (IRE) **Mrs M. Taylor & Mrs J. Stone**
10 DONT CALL ME DEREK, 4, b g Sri Pekan (USA)—Cultural Role **Camisgate Racing Club**
11 EVERY NOTE COUNTS, 5, b g Bluegrass Prince (IRE)—Miss Mirror **Tara Leisure**
12 FANTASY BELIEVER, 7, b g Sure Blade (USA)—Delicious **The Fantasy Fellowship B**
13 HANDY STATION (IRE), 4, b f Desert Style (IRE)—Art Age **Mr Brian Donovan**
14 HILLTIME (IRE), 5, b g Danetime (IRE)—Ceannanas (IRE) **Mrs S. Quinn**
15 ICENASLICE (IRE), 4, b f Fayruz—Come Dancing **Miss D. A. Johnson**
16 INTO BATTLE, 11, b g Daring March—Mischievous Miss **Lady Anne Bentinck**
17 JAKE BLACK (IRE), 5, b g Definite Article—Tirhala (IRE) **G. A. Lucas**
18 JANORAMIC (FR), 8, b g Panoramic—Victoire V (FR) **Richard Brown & Jane Dwyer**
19 KING'S CREST, 7, b g Deploy—Classic Beauty (IRE) **The Kings Crest Partnership**
20 KIRKHAM ABBEY, 5, b g Selkirk (USA)—Totham **Mrs M Taylor & Mrs J Stone**
21 LETS GET IT ON (IRE), 4, b f Perugino (USA)—Lets Clic Together (IRE) **The Usual Suspects**
22 LOW CLOUD, 5, b g Danehill (USA)—Raincloud **Maxilead Limited**
23 POLAR KINGDOM, 7, b g Pivotal—Scarlet Lake **Millie and Poppy Squire**
24 POMFRET LAD, 7, b g Cyrano de Bergerac—Lucky Flinders **Maxilead Limited**
25 SMART DANNY, 4, gr g Danzero (AUS)—She's Smart **Bernard Shaw**
26 TELLITLIKEITIS, 4, b g Defacto (USA)—Chimes of Peace **Mrs Lingwood & Mrs S. Quinn**
27 THUNDERCLAP, 6, b br g Royal Applause—Gloriana **The Wednesday Club**
28 TIME TO RELAX (IRE), 4, b f Orpen (USA)—Lassalia **B Selective**
29 WINTHORPE (IRE), 5, b g Tagula (IRE)—Zazu **G. A. Lucas**

THREE-YEAR-OLDS

30 BIGALOS BANDIT, ch c Compton Place—Move Darling **Ian Buckley**
31 FANTASY DEFENDER (IRE), b g Fayruz—Mrs Lucky **The Fantasy Fellowship D**
32 GRAZE ON, b g Factual (USA)—Queens Check **J. R. Rowbottom**
33 HARRYS HOUSE, gr g Paris House—Rum Lass **N. Bulmer**
34 KASHTANKA (IRE), ch c Ashkalani (IRE)—Spark (IRE) **The Most Wanted Partnership**
35 LESLINGTAYLOR (IRE), b g Orpen (USA)—Rite of Spring **D. Bloy**
36 LODGICIAN (IRE), b c Grand Lodge (USA)—Dundel (IRE) **J. Henderson**
37 MELALCHRIST, b g Almaty (IRE)—Lawless Bridget **Timothy Woods**
38 NEVSKY BRIDGE, b f Soviet Star (USA)—Pontressina (USA)
39 STREET DANCER (IRE), b g Imperial Ballet (IRE)—Life On The Street **G. Liles**
40 TARAGAN, b f Kayf Tara—Morgannwg (IRE) **Mrs J. M. Bletsoe**
41 TARAS KNIGHT (IRE), b g Indian Danehill (IRE)—Queen of Art (IRE) **Tara Leisure**
42 ZOMERLUST, b g Josr Algarhoud (IRE)—Passiflora **P. J. Carr**

TWO-YEAR-OLDS

43 B c 28/3 Mujadil (USA)—Break For Peace (IRE) (Brief Truce (USA)) (16766) **Timothy Woods**
44 Ch f 19/4 Danehill Dancer (IRE)—Dubai Lady (Kris) (12000) **Mr F. Green & Mr G. Roberts**
45 B f 22/2 Bertolini (USA)—Early Call (Kind of Hush) (16096) **Tara Leisure**

MR J. J. QUINN—continued

46 **KATIES HOUSE**, gr f 27/2 Paris House—Rum Lass (Distant Relative) (10000) **N. Bulmer**
47 **MARTHARUM**, ch f 3/3 Muhtarram (USA)—
        Needwood Truffle (IRE) (Brief Truce (USA)) (3000) **The New Century Partnership**
48 **MAXOLINI**, ch g 12/2 Bertolini (USA)—Evening Falls (Beveled (USA)) (31000) **Maxilead Limited**
49 B c 27/4 Monashee Mountain (USA)—Miss Butterfield (Cure The Blues (USA)) (7000) **Mrs K. M. Thomas**
50 B c 9/4 Josr Algarhoud (USA)—Search Party (Rainbow Quest (USA)) (12000) **Timothy Woods**
51 Ch f 26/3 Sugarfoot—She's A Breeze (Crofthall) (2600) **Miss D. A. Johnson**
52 **SPITZENSPARKES (IRE)**, ch f 7/3 Tagula (IRE)—Danita (IRE) (Roi Danzig (USA)) (4158) **Spitzensparkes Racing**
53 B f 23/3 Mujahid (USA)—Stygian (USA) (Irish River (FR)) (800) **Bellwood Cottage Partnership I**
54 Ch c 8/3 Paris House—Thalya (Crofthall) (6800) **J. R. Rowbottom**
55 B f 15/4 Beckett (IRE)—Wicken Wonder (IRE) (Distant Relative) (9054) **G. Flitcroft**
56 B f 13/3 Distant Music (USA)—Yellow Ribbon (IRE) (Hamas (IRE)) (14083) **Tara Leisure**
57 B c 29/3 Imperial Ballet (IRE)—Zapata (IRE) (Thatching) (5500) **Mrs S. Quinn**
58 B c 22/4 Compton Place—Zinzi (Song) (6500) **Fantasy Fellowship**

Other Owners: S. V. Barker, A. M. Blewitt, S. J. Bowett, P. Coll, Miss V. C. Frith, W. E. Gruber, Mr D. P. Kelly, R. A. Lamb, Mr D. P. McEvoy, M. W. Paley, Mr A. P. Reed, J. E. Stringer, J. Waddington.

Jockey (flat): D. Holland, R. Winston. **Jockey (NH):** R. Garritty. **Conditional:** Douglas Costello. **Apprentice:** Krisnaduth Ghunowa.

---

493   MRS J. R. RAMSDEN, Thirsk
Postal: **J. R. Racing Ltd, Breckenbrough House, Sandhutton, Thirsk, North Yorkshire, YO7 4EL.**
Contacts: **PHONE (01845) 587226 FAX (01845) 587443**
E-MAIL jackr.ramsden@virgin.net

1 **BISHOPS COURT**, 11, ch g Clantime—Indigo
2 **DISTANT COUNTRY (USA)**, 6, b g Distant View (USA)—Memsahb (USA)
3 **DOUBLE VODKA (IRE)**, 4, b br g Russian Revival (USA)—Silius
4 **FAVOUR**, 5, b m Gothenberg (IRE)—Prejudice
5 **GREENWICH MEANTIME**, 5, b g Royal Academy (USA)—Shirley Valentine
6 **KANGARILLA ROAD**, 6, b g Magic Ring (IRE)—Kangra Valley
7 **POLYGONAL (FR)**, 5, b g Octagonal (NZ)—Sectarine (FR)
8 **TROJAN FLIGHT**, 4, ch g Hector Protector (USA)—Fairywings

THREE-YEAR-OLDS

9 **ALONG THE NILE**, b g Desert Prince (IRE)—Golden Fortune
10 **FERRANDO**, b g Hernando (FR)—Oh So Misty
11 **HALLA SAN**, b g Halling (USA)—St Radegund
12 **MUSARDIERE**, b f Montjeu (IRE)—Majestic Image
13 **TANFORAN**, b g Mujahid (USA)—Florentynna Bay
14 **TURNAROUND (GER)**, gr g Highest Honor (FR)—Tamacana

TWO-YEAR-OLDS

15 **ANDORRAN (GER)**, b c 9/4 Lando (GER)—Adora (GER) (Danehill (USA)) (20120)
16 **BRANSTON BERTIE**, b c 21/2 Bertolini (USA)—Kauri (USA) (Woodman (USA)) (16000)
17 **CATEGORICAL**, b c 17/2 Diktat—Zibet (Kris) (36000)
18 **CONSENT**, ch f 31/1 Groom Dancer (USA)—Preference (Efisio)
19 B c 3/4 Diktat—Formida (FR) (Highest Honor (FR)) (28839)
20 **MALELANE (IRE)**, b f 4/2 Prince Sabo—Indigo (Primo Dominie)
21 **MONTE MAJOR (GER)**, ch c 12/5 Trempolino (USA)—Monbijou (GER) (Dashing Blade) (21462)
22 **RAINBOW PRINCE**, b c 11/2 Desert Prince (IRE)—Eve (Rainbow Quest (USA)) (16000)
23 **ROYAL BOROUGH**, ch c 23/4 Compton Place—Norpella (Northfields (USA)) (26000)
24 **SHANGAZI (USA)**, ch f 9/5 Miswaki (USA)—Gran Ole Flag (USA) (El Gran Senor (USA)) (31000)

Other Owners: D. R. Brotherton, M. R. Charlton, J. D. Martin, Mrs A. Iles, J. Musgrave, Manor Farm Stud (Rutland), R. Morecombe, P. C. Thompson, J. Gompertz, T. J. O'Gram, R. C. Thompson, J. D. Abell, P. J. Carr, A. Mallen, N. R. Munton, Mrs K. S. Pratt, Mrs J. R. Ramsden, SP Racing Investments S.A., L. C. Sigsworth, Mrs A. E. Sigsworth.

494 MR W. T. REED, Hexham
Postal: Moss Kennels, Haydon Bridge, Hexham, Northumberland, NE47 6NL.
Contacts: PHONE/FAX (01434) 344016 MOBILES (07889) 111885 or (07703) 270408
E-MAIL timreed8@aol.com

1 DETROIT STORM, 6, b m Detroit Sam (FR)—Gale Storm **Mr W. T. Reed**
2 FASTER SWEEP (IRE), 8, ch g Phardante (FR)—Sweeping Brush (IRE) **The Hot Chestnuts Club**
3 HELVETIUS, 9, b g In The Wings—Hejraan (USA) **Mrs Anthony, Mrs Craggs, Mrs Huddlestone**
4 KIDITHOU (FR), 7, b g Royal Charter (FR)—De Thou (FR) **Roman Wall Racing**
5 THE MILECASTLE (IRE), 6, b g Oscar (IRE)—Kiladante (IRE) **Roman Wall Racing**
6 THORNTOUN HOUSE (IRE), 12, b g Durgam (USA)—Commanche Song **W. M. Johnstone**
7 THREE SPIRES, 10, ch g Minster Son—Mystic Music **Mrs P. Pattinson & Mr W. T. Reed**

THREE-YEAR-OLDS
8 SILIVRI, gr f Silver Patriarch (IRE)—Riviere **Dr R. G. Fairs**

Other Owners: F. A. B. Burn, G. F. Burn, P. R. Crawfurd, Mrs S. D. Dean, M. C. Hind, J. K. Huddleston, J. A. Ogle.

Assistant Trainer: Mrs C. J. Reed

Jockey (NH): Bruce Gibson. **Conditional:** Peter Buchanan.

495 MR D. REES, Haverfordwest
Postal: The Grove Yard, Clarbeston Road, Haverfordwest, Pembrokeshire, SA63 4SP.
Contacts: PHONE (01437) 731308 MOBILE (07831) 800172/(07775) 662463
E-MAIL davidreesfencing@lineone.net

1 BONNY BOY (IRE), 10, b g Bustino—Dingle Bay **Mr D. Rees**
2 CRESSWELL GOLD, 8, b m Homo Sapien—Running For Gold **Mr D. A. Rees & Mr P. Harris**
3 CRUISING HOME, 7, b g Homo Sapien—Fast Cruise **P. Harris**
4 LADY SHANAN (IRE), 5, b m Anshan—Cothill Lady (IRE) **Mr D. A. Rees & Mr P. Harris**
5 RUNNING LORD (IRE), 7, b g Mister Lord (USA)—Craic Go Leor **Mr D. A. Rees & Mr P. Harris**
6 SCARLET DAWN (IRE), 7, b m Supreme Leader—Dawn Appeal **Mr D. Rees**
7 SMALLTOWN CHARLIE, 5, b g Silver Owl—Downhill Racer **Mr T. J. F. Morris**
8 SUPREMELY RED (IRE), 8, b g Supreme Leader—Her Name Was Lola **Mr D. A. Rees & Mr P. Harris**
9 TIP AWAY (IRE), 7, b g Broken Hearted—Jesse Twist (IRE) **Mr D. Rees**

THREE-YEAR-OLDS
10 SKISTORM, b f Petoski—Dai-Namic-Storm (IRE) **Mr D. Rees**

Assistant Trainer: Miss D J Green

Amateur: Mr Paul Sheldrake.

496 MRS H. E. REES, Dorchester
Postal: Distant Hills, Chalmington, Dorchester, Dorset, DT2 0HB.
Contacts: PHONE (01300) 320683 MOBILE (07715) 558289
E-MAIL rupertandhelenrees@distanthills.freeserve.co.uk

1 SHOTACROSS THE BOW (IRE), 8, b g Warning—Nordica **Mrs H. E. Rees**
2 STAKEHOLDER (IRE), 7, ch g Priolo (USA)—Island Goddess **Mrs H. E. Rees**

Assistant Trainer: Mr Rupert Rees

497 **MR A. S. REID, Mill Hill, London**
Postal: **Highwood Lodge, Highwood Hill, Mill Hill, London.**
Contacts: **PHONE (0208) 9061255 MOBILE (07836) 214617**

1 **BARTON SANDS (IRE),** 8, b g Tenby—Hetty Green **Mr A. S. Reid**
2 **BULAWAYO,** 8, b g Prince Sabo—Ra Ra Girl **Mr A. S. Reid**
3 **CERTIFIABLE,** 4, b g Deploy—Gentle Irony **Mr A. S. Reid**
4 **ECCENTRIC,** 4, ch g Most Welcome—Sure Care **Mr A. S. Reid**
5 **INDIAN BLAZE,** 11, ch g Indian Ridge—Odile **Mrs I. L. Clifford**
6 **MAD,** 4, br f Pursuit of Love—Emily-Mou (IRE) **Mr A. S. Reid**
7 **MOON SPINNER,** 8, b m Elmaamul (USA)—Lunabelle **Mr A. S. Reid**
8 **PHRENOLOGIST,** 5, gr g Mind Games—Leading Princess (IRE) **Mr A. S. Reid**
9 **RISE,** 4, b f Polar Falcon (USA)—Splice **Mr A. S. Reid**
10 **TAYIF,** 9, gr g Taufan (USA)—Rich Lass **Mr A. S. Reid**
11 **TROTTERS BOTTOM,** 4, b g Mind Games—Fleeting Affair **Mr A. S. Reid**
12 **TROUSERS,** 6, b g Pivotal—Palo Blanco **Mr A. S. Reid**
13 **VENDORS MISTAKE (IRE),** 4, b f Danehill (USA)—Sunspangled (IRE) **Mr A. S. Reid**
14 **WILLHECONQUERTOO,** 5, ch g Primo Dominie—Sure Care **Mr A. S. Reid**

THREE-YEAR-OLDS

15 **AGGRAVATION,** b g Sure Blade (USA)—Confection **Mr A. S. Reid**
16 **DEPRESSED,** ch f Most Welcome—Sure Care **Mr A. S. Reid**
17 **MANIC,** br f Polar Falcon (USA)—Gentle Irony **Mr A. S. Reid**
18 **QUESTION MARK,** b g Polar Falcon (USA)—Frankie Fair (IRE) **Mr A. S. Reid**
19 **RONNIES LAD,** b g Lake Coniston (IRE)—Lycius Touch **Mr A. S. Reid**
20 **WRIT (IRE),** ch g Indian Lodge (IRE)—Carnelly (IRE) **Mr A. S. Reid**

TWO-YEAR-OLDS

21 Gr c 22/3 Zilzal (USA)—Arantxa (Sharpo) (2000) **Mr A. S. Reid**
22 **IN HOPE,** b f 13/2 Most Welcome—Frankie Fair (IRE) (Red Sunset) **Mr A. S. Reid**
23 **LETHAL,** ch c 26/2 Nashwan (USA)—Ipanema Beach (Lion Cavern (USA)) **Mr A. S. Reid**

Other Owners: Ms C. Bithell, Dr David Myres.

Jockey (flat): J. Egan.

498 **MRS J. G. RETTER, Swindon**
Postal: **Foxhill Farm Stables, Foxhill, Swindon, Wiltshire, SN4 0DS.**
Contacts: **PHONE/FAX (01793) 791515**

1 **BICKWELL,** 7, br m Afzal—Flying Cherub **Mrs J. G. Retter**
2 **DEVON BLUE (IRE),** 6, ch m Hubbly Bubbly (USA)—Tuney Blade **Mrs J. G. Retter**
3 5, B g El Conquistador—Flying Cherub **Mrs J. G. Retter**
4 **NADDERWATER,** 13, br g Arctic Lord—Flying Cherub **Mrs J. G. Retter**
5 **REDDE (IRE),** 10, ch g Classic Memory—Stoney Broke **Mrs J. G. Retter**

499 **MR K. G. REVELEY, Saltburn**
Postal: **Groundhill Farm, Lingdale, Saltburn-by-the-Sea, Cleveland, TS12 3HD.**
Contacts: **OFFICE (01287) 650456 FAX (01287) 653095 MOBILE (07971) 784539**

1 **ACCORDELLO (IRE),** 4, b f Accordion—Marello **Mr & Mrs W. J. Williams**
2 **ALETHEA GEE,** 7, b m Sure Blade (USA)—Star Flower **W. Ginzel**
3 **ALFIE'S CONNECTION,** 4, ch g Danzig Connection (USA)—Lady Warninglid **A. Flannigan**
4 **ALPHECCA (USA),** 4, b c Kingmambo (USA)—Limbo (USA) **Mr P. D. Savill**
5 **BACKGAMMON,** 4, b g Sadler's Wells (USA)—Game Plan **J. J. G. Good & C. Anderson**
6 **BAYSIDE,** 4, ch g Docksider (USA)—Sister Sophie **Mrs R. E. Savill**
7 **BIRDWATCH,** 7, b g Minshaanshu Amad (USA)—Eider **Jeremy Mitchell and Janet Powney**
8 **BLACKERGREEN,** 6, b g Zaffaran (USA)—Ballinderry Moss **P. England**
9 **BORDER ARTIST,** 6, ch g Selkirk (USA)—Aunt Tate **F. F. Racing Services Partnership V**
10 **BRAVE REBELLION,** 6, b g Primitive Rising (USA)—Grand Queen **Cristiana's Crew**
11 **CAKE IT EASY (IRE),** 5, ch m Kendor (FR)—Diese Memory (USA) **Lightbody Celebration Cakes Ltd**
12 **CELTIC LEGEND (FR),** 6, br g Celtic Swing—Another Legend (USA) **Jemm Partnership Limited**
13 **CELTIC SKY,** 7, b m Celtic Swing—Southern Sky **H. G. W. Brown**

MR K. G. REVELEY—continued

14 **CHAMACCO (FR)**, 5, b g Cadoudal (FR)—Awentina (FR) **Sir Robert Ogden C.B.E., LLD**
15 **CHOMOLUNGA (FR)**, 5, b g Video Rock (FR)—Siesta (FR) **Sir Robert Ogden C.B.E., LLD**
16 **CLOUDING OVER**, 5, gr m Cloudings (IRE)—Wellwotdouthink **W. D. Hockenhull**
17 **CROWNFIELD**, 6, b g Blushing Flame (USA)—Chief Island **H. G. W. Brown**
18 **DARAZARI BAY (IRE)**, 4, b g Darazari (IRE)—Conna Dodger (IRE) **11 O'clock Club**
19 **DIKLERS ROSE (IRE)**, 6, gr m Roselier (FR)—Diklers Run **The Mary Reveley Racing Club**
20 **FAIRLIE**, 4, b g Halling (USA)—Fairy Flax (IRE) **Reveley Farms**
21 **FORMAL CLICHE**, 6, b g Classic Cliche (IRE)—Formal Affair **Mr and Mrs J. D. Cotton**
22 **GAY KINDERSLEY (IRE)**, 7, ch g Roselier (FR)—Ramble Bramble **W. J. Smith and M. D. Dudley**
23 **GOLDEN ODYSSEY (IRE)**, 5, ch m Barathea (IRE)—Opus One **Sir Robert Ogden C.B.E., LLD**
24 **GRAND MANNER (IRE)**, 5, b g Desert Style (IRE)—Reacted **M. E. Foxton**
25 **HERNANDO'S BOY**, 4, b g Hernando (IRE)—Leave At Dawn **Crack of Dawn Partnership**
26 **HIDDEN BOUNTY (IRE)**, 9, b g Generous (IRE)—Sought Out **M. E. Foxton**
27 **I GOT RHYTHM**, 7, gr m Lycius (USA)—Eurythmic **G. M. Thomson**
28 **ICY RIVER (IRE)**, 8, ch g Over The River (FR)—Icy Lou **A. J. Peake**
29 **IL CAVALIERE**, 10, b g Mtoto—Kalmia **The Thoughtful Partnership**
30 **INTO THE SHADOWS**, 6, ch m Safawan—Shadows of Silver **Mr R. C. Mayall**
31 **ISLAND LIGHT (USA)**, 5, ch g Woodman (USA)—Isla Del Rey (USA) **FF Racing Services Partnership VIII**
32 **JUNKANOO**, 9, ch g Generous (IRE)—Lupescu **The Scarth Racing Partnership**
33 **LE ROYAL (FR)**, 6, b g Garde Royale—Caucasie (FR) **Mrs S. A. Smith**
34 **LET IT BE**, 4, ch f Entrepreneur—Noble Dane (IRE) **A. Frame**
35 **LOOP THE LOUP**, 9, b g Petit Loup (USA)—Mithi Al Gamar (USA) **Mr and Mrs J. D. Cotton**
36 **LORD LAMB**, 13, gr g Dunbeath (USA)—Caroline Lamb **Reveley Farms**
37 **MACEO (GER)**, 11, ch g Acatenango (GER)—Metropolitan Star (USA) **L. De La Haye**
38 **MALEK (IRE)**, 9, b g Tremblant—Any Offers **Mrs J. W. Furness & Lord Zetland**
39 **MINSTER MISSILE**, 7, b g Minster Son—Manettia (IRE) **G. G. Stevenson**
40 **MORITZ (FR)**, 5, b g Video Rock (FR)—Nivernaise (FR) **Sir Robert Ogden C.B.E., LLD**
41 **MOUNT VETTORE**, 4, br g Vettori (IRE)—Honeyspike (IRE) **Mrs E. A. Murray**
42 **NOBRATINETTA (FR)**, 6, b m Celtic Swing—Bustinetta **Reveley Farms**
43 **NORTHERN SHADOWS**, 6, b m Rock Hopper—Shadows of Silver **M J Hutton, Mrs M Laing, Mrs G Waters**
44 **OCTOBER MIST (IRE)**, 11, gr g Roselier (FR)—Bonny Joe **Mrs E. A. Murray**
45 **OUR JASPER**, 5, ch g Tina's Pet—Dawn's Della **K. Benson**
46 **OUR TEES COMPONENT (IRE)**, 4, b f Saddlers' Hall (IRE)—Shaiymara (IRE) **Tees Components Ltd**
47 **OVERSTRAND (IRE)**, 6, b g In The Wings—Vaison La Romaine **F. F. Racing Services Partnership IV**
48 **POLISH FLAME**, 7, b g Blushing Flame (USA)—Lady Emm **O'Brien Kent Racing**
49 **POWDER CREEK (IRE)**, 8, b g Little Bighorn—Our Dorcet **T. M. Mckain**
50 **RAMBLING MINSTER**, 7, b g Minster Son—Howcleuch **The Lingdale Optimists**
51 **ROBBO**, 11, b g Robellino (USA)—Basha (USA) **The Scarth Racing Partnership**
52 **ROUGE ET NOIR**, 7, b g Hernando (FR)—Bayrouge (IRE) **The Mary Reveley Racing Club**
53 **RUBY LEGEND**, 7, b g Perpendicular—Singing High **Mrs J. M. Grimston**
54 **SADDLERS' HARMONY (IRE)**, 4, b g Saddlers' Hall (IRE)—
Sweet Mignonette **The Home And Away Partnership 1**
55 **SPITTING IMAGE (IRE)**, 5, ch m Spectrum (IRE)—Decrescendo (IRE) **The Mary Reveley Racing Club**
56 **TEES COMPONENTS**, 10, b g Risk Me (FR)—Lady Warninglid **Tees Components Ltd**
57 **TIME MARCHES ON**, 7, b g Timeless Times (USA)—Tees Gazette Girl **Mrs M. B. Thwaites**
58 **TOMASINO**, 7, br g Celtic Swing—Bustinetta **Mr P. D. Savill**
59 **TOTALLY SCOTTISH**, 9, b g Mtoto—Glenfinlass **The Phoenix Racing C.O.**
60 **WELCOME TO UNOS**, 8, ch g Exit To Nowhere (USA)—Royal Loft **J. W. Andrews**

THREE-YEAR-OLDS

61 **AZAHARA**, b f Vettori (IRE)—Branston Express **Mr J. Stevenson**
62 **CELTIC CARISMA**, b f Celtic Swing—Kathryn's Pet **H. G. W. Brown**
63 **JASS**, b g Robellino (USA)—Iota **The Scarth Racing Partnership**
64 **SHEKAN STAR**, b f Sri Pekan (USA)—Celestial Welcome **Star Alliance**
65 **SMART STREET**, b g Silver Patriarch (IRE)—Smart Spirit (IRE) **Mrs S. A. Smith**

MR K. G. REVELEY—continued

TWO-YEAR-OLDS

66 B c 8/5 Celtic Swing—Smart Spirit (IRE) (Persian Bold) **Mrs S. A. Smith**
67 B f 13/4 Poliglote—Southern Sky (Comedy Star (USA) **H. G. W. Brown**
68 Ch c 21/2 Danzig Connection (USA)—Trevorsninepoints (Jester) **Mr Child**

Other Owners: Mrs M. S. Mayall, C. Anderson, M. Bailey, Mrs J. Bailey, G. M. Barnard, K. E. Bodenham, M. J. Bradley, Mr A. J. Cork, M. Dunbar, J. A. Evans, B. W. Goodall, David A. Green, J. L. Maclean, S. J. Mitchell, Mr P. Morrison, Mrs D. A. Oliver, D. C. Renton, J. Scarth, J. Shack, G. S. Slater, J. J. Snaith, K. Sobey, J. Struth, R. Whitehead, Major J. C. K. Young.

Assistant Trainer: Fiona Reveley

Jockey (NH): R. McGrath. **Apprentice:** Neil Brown.

---

500 MR P. M. RICH, Usk
Postal: **Cwrt-y-Mwnws Farmhouse, Allt-yr-Yn, Newport, Gwent, NP20 5EL.**
Contacts: **PHONE (01291) 690864/(01633) 262791 FAX (01633) 262791 MOBILE (07971) 218286**
E-MAIL **paul@m-rich.freeserve.co.uk**

1 GRANRICH, 5, ch m Alflora (IRE)—Weareagrandmother **Mr P. M. Rich**
2 RANDRICH, 8, b m Alflora (IRE)—Randama **Mr P. M. Rich**
3 RICHWAY, 6, ch g Nomadic Way (USA)—Weareagrandmother **Mr P. M. Rich**
4 SEVERN MAGIC, 12, b m Buckley—La Margarite **R. Packer**

Assistant Trainer: Mr D Thomas

Amateur: Mr J. Cook.

---

501 MRS LYDIA RICHARDS, Chichester
Postal: **Lynch Farm, Hares Lane, Funtington, Chichester, West Sussex, PO18 9LW.**
Contacts: **HOME (01243) 574882 YARD (01243) 574379 MOBILE (07803) 199061**
E-MAIL **lydiarichards.racing@zoom.co.uk**

1 ASHSTANZA, 4, gr g Ashkalani (IRE)—Poetry In Motion (IRE)
2 ATLANTIC CITY, 4, ch g First Trump—Pleasuring **The Atlantic City Partnership**
3 DOUBLE M, 8, ch g First Trump—Girton Degree **B. M. Mathieson**
4 KAPPELHOFF (IRE), 8, b g Mukaddamah (USA)—Miss Penguin **Mrs Lydia Richards**
5 KING ALFRED (IRE), 5, b g Doubletour (USA)—Society Girl **L. Howard**
6 KINGLEY VALE, 11, br g Neltino—Altaghaderry Run **B. L. F. Seal**
7 MANQUE NEUF, 6, b g Cadeaux Genereux—Flying Squaw **B. L. F. Seal**
8 TROOPER KIT, 6, b g Petoski—Rolling Dice **L. Howard**

Other Owners: M. E. Thompsett, E. T. Wright.

---

502 MR N. G. RICHARDS, Greystoke
Postal: **The Old Rectory, Greystoke, Penrith, Cumbria, CA11 0UJ.**
Contacts: **HOME (01768) 483160 OFFICE (01768) 483392 FAX (01768) 483933**
MOBILE (07771) 906609 E-MAIL **n.g.richards@virgin.net**

1 AL MABROOK (IRE), 10, b g Rainbows For Life (CAN)—Sky Lover **Hale Racing Limited**
2 ANOTHER BARGAIN (IRE), 6, b g Mister Lord (USA)—Flashy Treasure **It's a Bargain Syndicate**
3 BEDLAM BOY (IRE), 4, br g Broken Hearted—Evening Fashion (IRE) **Mr Tony Ambler**
4 BOB'S GONE (IRE), 7, ch g Eurobus—Bob's Girl (IRE) **Team Cobra Racing Syndicate**
5 BROKEN KNIGHTS (IRE), 8, ch g Broken Hearted—Knight's Row **The Broken Knights**
6 CARRIAGE RIDE (IRE), 7, b g Tidaro (USA)—Casakurali **Mr James Callow & Mr David Wesley Yates**
7 CORDILLA (IRE), 7, b g Accordion—Tumble Heather **Mr Trevor Hemmings**
8 DIRECT ACCESS (IRE), 10, ch g Roselier (FR)—Spanish Flame (IRE) **The Direct Access Partnership**
9 EMPEROR ROSS (IRE), 10, b br g Roselier (FR)—Gilded Empress **Mr James Callow**
10 EVER PRESENT (IRE), 7, ch g Presenting—My Grand Rose (IRE) **Mr Ramsey Brown**
11 FAASEL (IRE), 4, b g Unfuwain (USA)—Waqood (USA) **Mr Jim Ennis**
12 FUNNY TIMES, 4, b f Silver Patriarch (IRE)—Elegant City **Mr E. Briggs**
13 GLINGER (IRE), 12, b g Remainder Man—Harilla **Mr James Westoll**

MR N. G. RICHARDS—continued

14 **HARMONY BRIG (IRE)**, 6, ch g Accordion—Bridges Daughter (IRE) **It's a Bargain Syndicate**
15 **JAZZ D'ESTRUVAL (FR)**, 8, gr g Bayolidaan (FR)—Caro d'estruval (FR) **Ashleybank Investments Limited**
16 **JOE MALONE (IRE)**, 6, br g Rashar (USA)—Bucktina **Foreneish Racing**
17 **JUST SOOTY**, 10, br g Be My Native (USA)—March Fly **Mr David Wesley-Yates**
18 **JUSTUPYOURSTREET (IRE)**, 9, b g Dolphin Street (FR)—Sure Flyer (IRE) **David A. Harrison**
19 **LORD JACK (IRE)**, 9, ch g Mister Lord (USA)—Gentle Gill **Mr Trevor Hemmings**
20 **MARLBOROUGH SOUND**, 6, b g Overbury (IRE)—Dark City **Ashleybank Investments Limited**
21 **MAZZAREME (IRE)**, 7, b g Supreme Leader—Mazza **Ashleybank Investments Limited**
22 **MINNIGAFF (IRE)**, 5, b g Supreme Leader—Across The Pond (IRE) **Pike R. H. & Mrs E. A. Pike**
23 **MONET'S GARDEN (IRE)**, 7, gr g Roselier (FR)—Royal Remainder (IRE) **Mr David Wesley-Yates**
24 **MONTE ROSA (IRE)**, 6, b m Supreme Leader—Green Thorn (IRE) **E. H. Birkbeck and A. D. Stewart**
25 **MOSSLANE (IRE)**, 5, b g Taipan (IRE)—Shallow Run **Mr Trevor Hemmings**
26 **MR WOODENTOP (IRE)**, 9, b g Roselier (FR)—Una's Polly **Hale Racing Limited**
27 **MUCKLE FLUGGA (IRE)**, 6, ch m Karinga Bay—Dancing Dove (IRE) **Dr K. S. Fraser**
28 **NATIVE CORAL (IRE)**, 7, ch g Be My Native (USA)—
                                            Deep Coral (IRE) **M. Futter, K. Elliott, A. Armstrong & R. Don**
29 **NEAGH (FR)**, 4, b g Dress Parade—Carlie II (FR) **Mr Duncan Davidson**
30 **NEXT TO NOTHING (IRE)**, 8, b g Bob's Return (IRE)—Shuil Abhaile **D. E. Harrison**
31 **NOBEL (FR)**, 4, gr g Dadarissime (FR)—Eire Dancer (FR) **Mr Duncan Davidson**
32 **PAPERPROPHET**, 7, b g Glory of Dancer—Living Legend (ITY) **The Jockeys Whips**
33 **POSSEXTOWN (IRE)**, 7, b g Lord Americo—Tasse du The **Mr Trevor Hemmings**
34 **PRINCE AMONG MEN**, 8, b g Robellino (USA)—Forelino (USA) **Mr Jim Ennis**
35 **SAMARIA (GER)**, 4, b br f Acatenango (GER)—Suanita (GER) **Dr St John Collier & Mrs Sherry Collier**
36 **SEEKING SHELTER (IRE)**, 6, b m Glacial Storm (USA)—Seeking Gold (IRE) **Kinneston Racing**
37 **SERGIO COIMBRA (IRE)**, 6, b g Moscow Society (USA)—
                                            Across The Pond (IRE) **Ashleybank Investments Limited**
38 **SHANNON'S PRIDE (IRE)**, 9, gr g Roselier (FR)—Spanish Flame (IRE) **J. R. Hales**
39 **SOBRAON (IRE)**, 6, b g Topanoora—Anniepepp (IRE) **Mrs Julia Young & Mrs Sarah Walsh**
40 **SPARROW HAWK (FR)**, 5, b m Hawker's News (IRE)—In Memoriam (IRE) **Mr Richard Haggas**
41 **SWEET ARD (IRE)**, 5, b m Zaffaran (USA)—Ard Ri (IRE) **A. Clark/W. B. Morris/J. Dudgeon**
42 **TELEMOSS (IRE)**, 11, b g Montelimar—Shan's Moss **Ashleybank Investments Limited**
43 **THE FRENCH FURZE (IRE)**, 11, ch g Be My Guest (USA)—Exciting
44 **TOPANBERRY (IRE)**, 6, ch m Topanoora—Mulberry (IRE) **Mrs Doreen Mcgawn**
45 **TURPIN GREEN (IRE)**, 6, b g Presenting—Coolshamrock (IRE) **Mr Trevor Hemmings**
46 **VIC THE PILER (IRE)**, 6, ch g Old Vic—Strong Gale Pigeon (IRE) **Taranto De Pol**
47 **WESTMEATH FLYER**, 10, b g Deploy—Re-Release **Mr Jim Ennis**
48 **WHISPERING MOOR**, 6, br g Terimon—Larksmore **Mrs D. Stanistreet**
49 **WINDY HILLS**, 5, bl g Overbury (IRE)—Chinook's Daughter (IRE) **Lord Cavendish, Lord Reay & Mrs T Riley**
50 **ZAFFARAN EXPRESS (IRE)**, 6, b m Zaffaran (USA)—Majestic Run **A. Clark/W. B. Morris/J. Dudgeon**

Other Owners: Mr Jamie Alexander, Mrs R. S. Alexander, Mr A. Armstrong, Mr A. Clark, Mr K. Elliott, Mrs G. Fairbairn, Mr Kevin Johnston, Mr I. Lightfoot, Mr P. McMahon, Mr O. McGann, Mr S. J. Simpson, Mr B. Robb, Mr A. Quinn, Mr W. Peacock, Mr C. P. Norbury, Mr D. Neale, Mr W. Morris, Mr Edward Melville, Mr C. West, Mr T. Uprichard, Mr D. Stevenson, Mrs C. Stephenson, Mr W. McNeish, Mr S. Leece, Mr M. Futter, Mr N. Endor, Mr Jimmy Dudgeon, Mr R. Donn, Mr E. Coppel, MR N. W. Alexander, Mr Jamie Alexander, Mrs S. R. Alexander, E. H. Birkbeck, J. R. Callow, Lord Cavendish, A. Clark, Mr M. Clementson, Mr A. Dick, Direct Sales UK Ltd, Mr A. Duckworth, J. A. Dudgeon, J. M. Elliott, Mr J. M. Elliott, J. T. Ennis, Mrs E. M. Fairbairn, Dr D. J. Forecast, Greystoke Stables Ltd, Miss L. J. Hales, Mr S. A. Henshaw, S. Leece, P. McMahon, W. B. Morris, C. P. Norbury, R. H. Pike, Mrs E. A. Pike, Lord H. W. M. Reay, Mrs A. T. Riley, Mrs E. M. K. Roosmalecocq, S. J. Simpson, A. D. Stewart, Lady P. M. Talbot of Malahide, Mrs P. D. Turner, Mrs S. E. Walsh, Mrs J. R. L. Young.

Jockey (NH): A. Dobbin, B. Harding, P. Robson. **Conditional:** S. Marshall, G. Thomas. **Amateur:** Mr C. Callow, Mr F. Davis, Mr E. Whillans.

---

503 | **MRS S. L. RICHARDSON, Cheltenham**
Postal: **Owdeswell Manor, Andoversford, Cheltenham, Gloucestershire, GL54 4LD.**
Contacts: **PHONE (01242) 820297/(01242) 820505**

1 **BORN TO DREAM (IRE)**, 7, b m Supreme Leader—Ethel's Dream **R. Fairbarns**
2 **FLASH GORDON**, 11, ch g Gildoran—Florence May **R. Fairbarns**
3 **LORD MAX**, 13, br g Arctic Lord—Thames Air **Mrs S. L. Richardson**
4 5, B g Primitive Rising (USA)—Thames Air **Mrs S. L. Richardson**

Jockey (NH): O. McPhail. **Amateur:** Mr James Richardson.

504 MR M. G. RIMELL, Witney
Postal: **Fairspear Racing Stables, Fairspear Road, Leafield, Witney, Oxfordshire, OX29 9NT.**
Contacts: **PHONE (01993) 878551 FAX (01993) 878551**
MOBILES (07778) 648303 or (07973) 627054
E-MAIL mrimell@aol.com WEBSITE www.rimellracing.com

1 CROSSBOW CREEK, 7, b g Lugana Beach—Roxy River **Mrs M. R. T. Rimell**
2 CULLYBACKY KING (IRE), 9, b g Roi Guillaume (FR)—Maison Blanche **Mr M. G. Rimell**
3 ELA JAY, 6, b m Double Eclipse (IRE)—Papirusa (IRE) **J & L Wetherald - M & M Glover**
4 GENERAL OLIVER (IRE), 5, b g General Monash (USA)—Sea Idol (IRE)
5 HORCOTT BAY, 5, b m Thowra (FR)—Armagnac Messenger **The Posties Partnership**
6 MIND THE GATE, 12, b g Ardross—Mulloch Brae **Mr M. G. Rimell**
7 NESNAAS (USA), 4, ch g Gulch (USA)—Sedrah (USA) **Wychwood Racing Partnership**
8 ONEWAY (IRE), 8, b g Bob's Return (IRE)—Rendezvous **Mr M. G. Rimell**
9 SUN PAGEANT, 4, ch f Double Trigger (IRE)—Summer Pageant **J & L Wetherald - M & M Glover**
10 THE MAIN MAN, 4, b g Double Trigger (IRE)—Papirusa (IRE)

Other Owners: A. J. Collins, Mrs S. H. Jones, Mr K. J. Mustow, R. F. Shepherd.

Assistant Trainer: Anne Rimell

Jockey (NH): J. Moore, M. Foley, G. Lee. **Amateur:** Mr M. G. Rimell.

505 MR P. C. RITCHENS, Tidworth
Postal: **'Hillview', 91 Parkhouse Road, Shipton Bellinger, Tidworth, Hampshire, SP9 7YE.**
Contacts: **HOME (01980) 843088 YARD (01264) 781140 MOBILE (07932) 474005**

1 FORTANIS, 6, gr m Alflora (IRE)—Sister's Choice **Mrs K. M. Blackman**
2 FOX 'N' GOOSE (IRE), 5, ch g Ashmolean (USA)—Creative Flight (IRE) **J. F. Pearl**
3 FOXMEADE DANCER, 7, b g Lyphento (USA)—Georgian Quickstep **Mrs A. E. Morton**
4 HASHID (IRE), 5, b g Darshaan—Alkaffeyeh (IRE) **R. G. Catton**
5 HISAR (IRE), 12, br g Doyoun—Himaya (IRE) **R. G. Catton**
6 HORIZON (FR), 8, ch g Arctic Tern (USA)—Furtchella (FR) **J. F. Pearl**
7 OLD HARRY, 5, b g Case Law—Supreme Thought **D. L. W. Simester**
8 TRUST SMITH, 9, b m Greensmith—Loch Chastity **T. W. Newton**

Assistant Trainer: John Pearl

Amateur: Mr David Turner.

506 MISS V. C. ROBERTS, Upper Lambourn
Postal: **Frenchmans Stables, Upper Lambourn, Hungerford, Berkshire, RG17 8QT.**
Contacts: **PHONE (01488) 72132 FAX (01488) 73364 MOBILE (07768) 366935**
E-MAIL frenchmans.stables@virgin.net WEBSITE www.victoriarobertsracing.co.uk

1 BLUETORIA, 4, b f Vettori (IRE)—Blue Birds Fly **Mr D. C. Roberts**
2 COSTA DEL SOL (IRE), 4, ch g General Monash (USA)—L'harmonie (USA) **The Ola Partnership**
3 DEALER'S CHOICE (IRE), 11, gr g Roselier (FR)—Cam Flower VII **The Champetre Partnership**
4 DIAMOND DARREN (IRE), 6, ch g Dolphin Street (FR)—Deerussa (IRE) **Mr A. Smith**
5 FOUR OF DIAMONDS (IRE), 6, b g Fourstars Allstar (USA)—
Wine Rock Diamond (IRE) **Paul Duffy Diamond Partnership**
6 MIXED MARRIAGE (IRE), 7, ch g Indian Ridge—Marie de Flandre (FR) **Miss L. Ricci**
7 PERIWINKLE LAD (IRE), 8, b g Perugino (USA)—Bold Kate **Mr D. C. Roberts**
8 PERSIAN EMBERS, 6, gr m Blushing Flame (USA)—Podrida **Isle Of Wight Bloodstock And Racing**

THREE-YEAR-OLDS

9 LAMBRIGGAN LAD, b g Mazurek—Alfs Classic (FR) **Mr J. D. & Mrs J. A. Smeaden**

Other Owners: M. Graves, N. Harris, D. P. Duffy, A. P. Hartley, Mr J. A. Howarth, Mr J. R. Letham, E. C. Matthews.

Jockey (flat): V. Slattery. **Jockey (NH):** T. J. Murphy. **Conditional:** S. J. Craine.

507 MRS P. ROBESON, Newport Pagnell
Postal: **Fences Farm, Tyringham, Newport Pagnell, Buckinghamshire, MK16 9EN.**
Contacts: **PHONE/FAX** (01908) 611255 **MOBILE** (07831) 579898
E-MAIL robesons@attglobal.net

1 **CETTI'S WARBLER**, 7, gr m Sir Harry Lewis (USA)—Sedge Warbler **Mrs P. Robeson**
2 **CHOCSTAW (IRE)**, 8, b g Mtoto—Cwm Deri (IRE) **Sir Evelyn de Rothschild**
3 **CORALBROOK**, 5, b g Alderbrook—Coral Delight **Mrs P. Robeson**
4 **GORDON HIGHLANDER**, 6, ch m Master Willie—No Chilli **T. E. Short**
5 **HYLIA**, 6, ch m Sir Harry Lewis (USA)—Lady Stock **Mrs P. Robeson**
6 **MARCH NORTH**, 10, b g Petoski—Coral Delight **R. A. Collins**
7 **OLNEY LAD**, 6, b g Democratic (USA)—Alipampa (IRE) **The Tyringham Partnership**
8 **PINTAIL**, 5, b g Petoski—Tangara **Mrs P. Robeson**
9 **STOCK DOVE**, 7, ch m Deploy—Lady Stock **Mrs P. Robeson**

Other Owners: Mr N. J. Brown, Mrs A. A. Garratt, D. Yates.

508 MR A. ROBSON, Hawick
Postal: **Windyknowes, 7 Burnflat Brae, Hawick, Roxburghshire, TD9 0DJ.**
Contacts: **PHONE** (01450) 376886 **FAX** (01450) 376886 **MOBILE** (07721) 605131

1 4, B g Courtship—Raymylettes Niece (IRE) **A. Robson**
2 **SUPERIOR WEAPON (IRE)**, 11, b g Riverhead (USA)—Ballytrustan Maid (IRE) **A. Robson**

Jockey (NH): Brian Harding. **Conditional:** P. Robson.

509 MISS P. ROBSON, Capheaton
Postal: **Kidlaw Farm, Capheaton, Newcastle Upon Tyne.**
Contacts: **PHONE** (01830) 530241 **MOBILE** (07721) 887489
E-MAIL pauline.robson@virgin.net

1 **EMMASFLORA**, 7, b m Alflora (IRE)—Charlotte's Emma **Mrs A. C. D. Goodfellow**
2 **HALLRULE (IRE)**, 11, ch g Be My Native (USA)—Phantom Thistle **Mr & Mrs Raymond Anderson Green**
3 **HARROVIAN**, 8, b g Deploy—Homeoftheclassics **Major & Mrs Ivan Straker**
4 **ON THE LUCE**, 8, b g Karinga Bay—Lirchur **Mrs J. M. Crawfurd**
5 **SIMON'S HEIGHTS**, 4, b g Weldnaas (USA)—Star Thyme **R. M. Mitchell**
6 **THE RILE (IRE)**, 11, ch g Alphabatim (USA)—Donna Chimene **Mr & Mrs Raymond Anderson Green**
7 **THOSEWERETHEDAYS**, 12, b g Past Glories—Charlotte's Festival **D. Parker**

Assistant Trainer: David Parker

Jockey (NH): R. McGrath. **Amateur:** Mr Luke Morgan, Miss P. Robson.

510 MR FRANCOIS ROHAUT, France
Postal: **26, Rue Du Bearn, Sauvagnon, France, 64230.**
Contacts: **PHONE** +33 (0) 5 59 38 44 58 **FAX** +33 (0) 5 59 68 46 58
E-MAIL rohaut@wanadoo.fr

1 **BENZOLINA (IRE)**, 4, br f Second Empire (IRE)—Balouchina (IRE) **Mr M. Cordero**
2 **BEYNAC (FR)**, 7, b g Noblequest (FR)—Madrange (FR) **Mr J. M. Cledat**
3 **CABORIG (FR)**, 4, b f Entrepreneur—Troyes **Mr P. Connolly**
4 **DARTIGAN (FR)**, 6, b g Grape Tree Road—More Anchor (FR) **Mr B. Bargues**
5 **DOTTORE VETTORI (IRE)**, 4, ch g Vettori (IRE)—Lady Golconda (FR) **Mr B. Van Dalfsen**
6 **HASTA LUEGO (FR)**, 5, b g Saumarez—Magarance (FR) **Mr B. Bargues**
7 **HOWARD LE CANARD (FR)**, 4, b g Hamas (IRE)—No Exit (FR) **Mr B. Lalemant**
8 **JERSEY BOUNCE (IRE)**, 4, b c Septieme Ciel (USA)—Marcotte **Mr B. Lalemant**
9 **LOUVA (USA)**, 4, b f Atticus (USA)—Louve Bleue (USA) **Mr J. Gispert**
10 **LOVE GREEN (FR)**, 4, br f Green Tune (USA)—Love For Ever (FR) **Mr J. E. Strauss**
11 **NERIOLO (IRE)**, 4, b g Priolo (USA)—Neriella (USA) **Mme M. Daugreilh**
12 **SADLER'S GIRL (FR)**, 4, b f Sadler's Wells (USA)—Taffety **Mr E. De Rothschild**
13 **SARDOUM (FR)**, 9, b g Dounba (FR)—Sargasse (FR) **Mr M. Daugreilh**
14 **SERANDOR (FR)**, 4, b g Entrepreneur—Seranda (IRE) **Mr B. Barsi**
15 **SERMENT**, 4, b g Unfuwain (USA)—Silicon Girl (USA) **Mme M. Daugreilh**
16 **SIGN OF THE WOLF**, 5, b h Loup Solitaire (USA)—Sign of The Vine (FR) **B. Van Dalfsen**

MR FRANCOIS ROHAUT—continued

17 **TRAINER CHOICE (USA),** 4, b f Woodman (USA)—Ispirata (IRE) **Mr J. Gispert**
18 **WHORTLEBERRY (FR),** 5, ch m Starborough—Rotina (FR) **Mr T. Yoshida**
19 **YOUNG TIGER (FR),** 4, b g Tiger Hill (IRE)—Youngolina (IRE) **Mr J. Gispert**

THREE-YEAR-OLDS

20 **ALCHIMIE (IRE),** b f Sri Pekan (USA)—Arctic Winter (CAN) **Haras de Beauvoir**
21 **BESCAME (FR),** b c Astair (FR)—Bescate (FR) **Mr M. Cordero**
22 **BISK (FR),** b c Grape Tree Road—Balioka (FR) **Mr F. Rohaut**
23 **BOYAKA (FR),** b f Key of Luck (USA)—Bengalie (FR) **Mr F. Rohaut**
24 **CHALUSSET (FR),** b c Noblequest (FR)—Madrange (FR) **Mr J. M. Cledat**
25 **CHAUKAO (FR),** ch f Inchinor—Cravatte Noire (USA) **Skymarc Farm**
26 **DANSE D'AMOUR,** br f Dansili—Young Rozy (FR) **Mr B. Bargues**
27 **DOM JARO (FR),** b c Sendawar (IRE)—John Quatz (FR) **Mr J. Biraben**
28 **FAST STYLE (FR),** b f Fasliyev (USA)—Style For Life (IRE) **Mr J. Gispert**
29 **FLOWER BOWL (FR),** b f Anabaa (USA)—Lady Vettori **Mr B Van Dalfsen**
30 **GRAPEFRUIT (FR),** b f Grape Tree Road—Kakouetta (FR) **Mr J. Segunotte**
31 **I SAW STARS (FR),** b f Baryshnikov (AUS)—Basie Blues **Mr B. Lalemant**
32 **IA ORANA (FR),** b f Lost World (IRE)—Miss Vaya (FR) **Mr B. Barthe**
33 **IMPERIAL SECRET (IRE),** b c Imperial Ballet (IRE)—Ron's Secret **Mr R. Temam**
34 **IRISH SPRING (IRE),** b c Anabaa (USA)—Irish Source **Mr B. Van Dalfsen**
35 **KENDORINA (FR),** ch f Kendor (FR)—Infiltrate (USA) **Mr B. Bargues**
36 **MAGIC DES GALAS (FR),** b c Sagamix (FR)—Gisborne (FR) **Mr J. Gispert**
37 **MARGHELAN (FR),** b f Soviet Star (USA)—Marcotte **Mr B. Lalemant**
38 **MATJA (FR),** b f Montjeu (IRE)—Rabea (USA) **Mr J. Biraben**
39 **MEADOW LODGE (IRE),** ch f Grand Lodge (USA)—Meadowlark (FR) **Mr J. Gispert**
40 **MOUTANEXO (FR),** ro c Muhtathir—Nexia (FR) **Mr J. Biraben**
41 **MUGUET (FR),** b c Alamo Bay (USA)—Adios Chica (FR) **Mr B. Barthe**
42 **MY FOOLISH HEART (FR),** b f Baryshnikov (AUS)—No Exit (FR) **Mr B. Lalemant**
43 **OLYMPIC GIRL (IRE),** b f Darshaan—Lille Hammer **Mr E. De Rothschild**
44 **OMANA PETRA (FR),** b f Sendawar (IRE)—France Rodney (FR) **Mr P. Moen**
45 **OPEN WAY (IRE),** ch f Giant's Causeway (USA)—Aspiration (FR) **Aleyrion Bloodstock**
46 **PRINCE D'ORANGE (FR),** b c Dyhim Diamond (IRE)—Sign of The Vine (FR) **Mr B. Van Dalfsen**
47 **PRINCE SOLOR (FR),** ch c Baryshnikov (AUS)—Lady Vivienne **Mr B. Lalemant**
48 **RAINBOY (IRE),** b c Darshaan—Rain Dancer (IRE) **Aleyrion Bloodstock**
49 **RICINE (FR),** b f Titus Livius (FR)—Rince Deas (IRE) **Mr F. Rohaut**
50 **SENDBACK LADY (USA),** b f Elusive Quality (USA)—Carrie Free (USA) **Aleyrion Bloodstock**
51 **SUMMER SEA,** b f Bahhare (USA)—Sea Ring (USA) **Mr P. Jeanneret**
52 **TEMPTATION (FR),** ch f Lando (GER)—Cure The Blues (IRE) **Mr B. Lalemant**
53 **TOUPIE,** ch f Intikhab (USA)—Turpitude **Mr J. Gispert**
54 **TRITICALE (FR),** b c Dyhim Diamond (IRE)—Trelakari (FR) **Mr B Van Dalfsen**
55 **TURTLE BOWL (IRE),** b c Dyhim Diamond (IRE)—Clara Bow (FR) **Mr B. Van Dalfsen**
56 **YES MY LOVE (FR),** b f Anabaa (USA)—Green Field Park **Mr J. Gispert**

TWO-YEAR-OLDS

57 **AMODIA (FR),** b br c 16/4 Grape Tree Road—Aquae (FR) (Tel Quel (FR)) **Mr H. Chamarty**
58 **BAIE DES FLEURS (FR),** b f 4/4 Chelsea Manor—Baie des Roses (IRE) (Hamas (IRE)) **Mme M. Rohaut**
59 B f 31/1 Fasliyev (USA)—Baronne Volante (IRE) (Fairy King (USA)) (46948) **Mr B. Van Dalfsen**
60 B f 19/2 Dansili—Batchelor's Button (FR) (Kenmare (FR)) (20120) **Mme M. Daugreilh**
61 **BOBTAIL (FR),** b c 15/5 Dyhim Diamond (IRE)—Bengalie (FR) (Lesotho (USA)) **Mr F. Rohaut**
62 **BRIERE (FR),** b f 6/4 Kahyasi—Balioka (FR) (Tourangeau (FR)) **Mr F. Rohaut**
63 **CHRISTMAS CRACKER (FR),** ch f 29/4 Alhaarth (IRE)—Cravatte Noire (USA) (Black Tie Affair) **Skymarc Farm**
64 B c 22/4 Xaar—Cozzene's Pride (USA) (Cozzene (USA)) **Mr B. Van Dalfsen**
65 B c 3/4 Cadeaux Genereux—Danseuse Indienne (IRE) (Danehill (USA)) **Mr E. De Rothschild**
66 **DIAMOND COAT,** ch f 21/2 Diesis—Double Platinum (Seeking The Gold (USA)) **Skymarc Farm**
67 Ch f 27/2 Cadeaux Genereux—Epistolienne (Law Society (USA)) **Mr E. De Rothschild**
68 B f 9/4 Cape Cross (IRE)—Ever In Love (FR) (Neverneyev (USA)) (6706) **Mr J. Biraben**
69 B c 25/3 Anabaa (USA)—Fouesnantaise (FR) (Hernando (FR)) **Mr E. De. Rothschild**
70 **HAPPY LODGE (IRE),** b f 12/2 Grand Lodge (USA)—Bonheur (IRE) (Royal Academy (USA)) (67069) **Mr J. Gispert**
71 B f 10/5 Night Shift (USA)—Irish Source (Irish River (FR)) **Mr B. Van Dalfsen**
72 **LOVE MAR (FR),** b f 21/2 Marathon (USA)—Love And Kiss (FR) (Astair (FR)) **Mme M. Daugreilh**
73 **LOVOCEANE,** ch f 13/2 Ocean of Wisdom (USA)—Septieme Element (Bering) (21462) **Mr J. E. Strauss**
74 **MAKISARDE (FR),** b f 17/2 Xaar—Makila (IRE) (Entrepreneur) (28169) **Mr B. Bargues**
75 **MIRACLE CARD (FR),** ch f 4/4 Green Tune—Poudriere (FR) (Trempolino (USA)) (63715) **Skymarc Farm**
76 **PIVOLINE (FR),** gr f 14/5 Pivotal—Lady Glitters (FR) (Homme de Loi (IRE)) (67069) **Mr J. Gispert**

MR FRANCOIS ROHAUT—continued

77 **POCKET MONEY (FR)**, b f 24/4 Kahyasi—Romanche (FR) (Galetto (FR)) (20791) **Mr G. Pariente**
78 **PRAY FOR SUN (IRE)**, b f 27/2 Fantastic Light (USA)—
Karakia (IRE) (Sadler's Wells (USA)) (134138) **Aleyrion Bloodstock**
79 Ch c 15/4 Cadeaux Genereux—Rosereine (USA) (Slew O' Gold (USA)) (38229) **Mr B. Lalemant**
80 B f 18/4 Fusaichi Pegasus (USA)—Royal Ballerina (IRE) (Sadler's Wells (USA)) (67068) **Mr B. Barsi**
81 **SABASHA (FR)**, b f 6/2 Xaar—Saba (ITY) (Kris) (31522) **Mr G. Pariente**
82 Gr f 12/4 Marathon (USA)—Saraxa (Linamix (FR)) **Mr F. Bayrou**
83 **SESAME STREET (FR)**, b f 27/3 Night Shift (USA)—
Exit To Ville (FR) (Exit To Nowhere (USA)) (13413) **Mr B. Lalemant**
84 B c 13/5 Poliglote—Sign of The Vine (FR) (Kendor (FR)) **Mr B. Van Dalfsen**
85 **SIREMAR (IRE)**, b c 12/3 Sinndar (IRE)—Rain Dancer (IRE) (Sadler's Wells (USA)) (20120) **Aleyrion Bloodstock**
86 **SOPRAN GALLOW (IRE)**, ch f 4/2 Galileo (IRE)—Wooderine (USA) (Woodman (USA)) (73775) **Mr B. Bargues**
87 **SOPRAN MARPIONE (ITY)**, b c 26/3 Orpen (USA)—Sopran Martha (IRE) (Thatching) (26827) **Mr B. Bargues**
88 B c 24/2 Sadler's Wells (USA)—Taffety (Last Tycoon) **Mr E. De Rothschild**
89 **THE HIGHEST MAJOR (IRE)**, ch c 17/3 Majorien—
Highest Nobles (FR) (Highest Honor (FR)) (9389) **Mr M. Perret**
90 **TIE BLACK (IRE)**, b f 18/3 Machiavellian (USA)—Tender Is Thenight (IRE) (Barathea (IRE)) (221327)
91 Ch c 27/4 Dyhim Diamond—Trelakari (FR) (Lashkari) **Mr B. Van Dalfsen**
92 **VIAL DE KERDEC (FR)**, b c 25/2 Poliglote—Love For Ever (FR) (Kaldoun (FR)) **Mr J. E. Strauss**

---

511 MR W. M. ROPER, Curragh
Postal: **French Furze, Maddenstown, The Curragh, Co. Kildare, Ireland.**
Contacts: **HOUSE & YARD** (045) 441821 **FAX** (045) 441821 **MOBILE** (086) 8234279

1 **ABOVE (NZ)**, 7, b g Yamanin Vital (NZ)—Arena (NZ) **Bellevue Ltd**
2 **ARBORETA (IRE)**, 7, b m Charnwood Forest (IRE)—Blazing Glory (IRE)
3 **BELLEVUE HERO (NZ)**, 8, b g Heroicity (AUS)—Rummage (NZ) **Bellevue Ltd**
4 **BELLEVUE SUNRISE (NZ)**, 8, ch g Beau Zephyr (AUS)—Dubra Crown (NZ) **Bellevue Ltd**
5 **BOOK BINDER (IRE)**, 5, b g Perugino (USA)—Dulceata (IRE) **Mr M. Roper**
6 **EDIRNELI (IRE)**, 8, b g Ela-Mana-Mou—Eviyrna (USA)
7 **HAWKFIELD LAD (IRE)**, 7, b g Shernazar—Auction Piece (IRE) **Mr G. Connors**
8 **HONOR'S STAG (USA)**, 11, ch g Blushing John (USA)—Bobbinette (USA) **Mr M. Wyley**
9 **KITCHENCOOK**, 9, b m Domitor (USA)—Dawn O'er Kells (IRE) **Mr A. Cook**
10 4, B f Idris (IRE)—Marqueterie (USA) **M. J. Keogh**
11 **QUINTUSARIUS (NZ)**, 4, b g Val d'arno (USA)—Let's Hula (NZ) **P. J. Burke**
12 5, B g Shardari—Somerset Pride (IRE) **Philip Quigley**

THREE-YEAR-OLDS

13 **MISS KINGSDALE (IRE)**, ch f Bold Fact (USA)—Pleasant Outlook (USA) **Mrs J. Devey**

---

512 MR N. I. M. ROSSITER, Somerton
Postal: **Springfield Farm, Kingsdon, Somerton, Somerset, TA11 7LA.**
Contacts: **PHONE** (01935) 841595/841191 **FAX** (01935) 841090 **MOBILE** (07779) 542671
E-MAIL horseswithattitude@horseswithattitude.com WEBSITE www.horseswithattitude.com

1 **BORDER SAINT**, 4, b g Selkirk (USA)—Caramba **Mr N. I. M. Rossiter**
2 **CHORUS BEAUTY**, 4, b f Royal Applause—Happy Lady (FR) **Stibbs Cross Partnership**
3 **CRANMER**, 6, ch g Machiavellian (USA)—True Glory (IRE) **Diabloz Owners Group**
4 **FRONTLINEFINANCIER**, 5, b g Bluegrass Prince (IRE)—Bunny Gee **Mrs E. R. Rossiter**
5 **HARBOUR KING**, 6, b br h Darshaan—Zinarelle (FR) **Diabloz Owners Group**
6 **HARPS HALL (IRE)**, 11, ch g Yashgan—Parsons Glen (IRE) **Ann Hughes & Liza Pern**
7 **LOUVE HEUREUSE (IRE)**, 4, ch f Peintre Celebre (USA)—Louve Sereine (FR) **Mr A. Whitton**
8 **MAWAZEEN (IRE)**, 4, b f Unfuwain (USA)—Atnab (USA) **Stibbs Cross Partnership**
9 **SALISBURY PLAIN**, 4, b c Mark of Esteem (IRE)—Wild Pavane **Diabloz Owners Group**
10 **SEEMMA**, 5, b m Romany Rye—Shepani **J. A. G. Meaden**
11 **SOLIPSIST (IRE)**, 4, ch c Grand Lodge (USA)—Mijouter (USA) **Stibbs Cross Partnership**
12 **SWORN IN (USA)**, 4, ch c Kingmambo (USA)—Under Oath (USA) **Mr & Mrs R. Turner**
13 **THREE COUNTIES (IRE)**, 4, b c Danehill (USA)—Royal Show (IRE) **Diabloz Owners Group**
14 **TRACE CLIP**, 7, b g Zafonic (USA)—Illusory **Stibbs Cross Partnership**

MR N. I. M. ROSSITER—continued

THREE-YEAR-OLDS

15 Ch f Bandmaster (USA)—Double Or Bust **Mr A. Whitton**
16 MAGPIE BRIDGE, b f Bandmaster (USA)—Peapod **Mr A. Whitton**

Other Owners: Major R. Paruin, Mrs C. Paruin, Miss L. Titterington, Mr E. Garrett, Mr M. Sheppard, Mr J. Higgins.

Assistant Trainer: Miss R A Duke

Jockey (flat): E. Ahern, A Culhane, J. Quinn, V. Slattery. **Jockey (NH):** E. Ahern, V. Slattery. **Amateur:** Miss R. Duke.

---

513   MR B. S. ROTHWELL, Nawton
Postal: **Arthington Barn, Little Manor Farm Stables, Highfield Lane, Nawton, York.**
Contacts: **HOME (01439) 770168 OFFICE (01439) 770437 FAX (01439) 770437
MOBILE (07968) 848724 E-MAIL rothwellb@freeuk.com**

1 ALWAYS RAINBOWS (IRE), 7, b g Rainbows For Life (CAN)—Maura's Guest (IRE) **J. Eddings**
2 BALLINRUANE (IRE), 6, br g Norwich—Katie Dick (IRE) **Mr B. S. Rothwell**
3 CELTIC BLAZE (IRE), 6, b m Charente River (IRE)—Firdaunt **Mr M. C. Saunders**
4 CEOL NA SRAIDE (IRE), 6, b m King's Theatre (IRE)—My Lady's Key (USA) **J. Eddings**
5 HALLAHOISE HYDRO (IRE), 4, ch g Lake Coniston (IRE)—Flo Bear (IRE) **J. Eddings**
6 LITTLE ALFIE (IRE), 8, b g Shahanndeh—Debbies Scud (IRE) **J. M. Gosse**
7 PASSIONATE KNIGHT (IRE), 6, ch g Semillon—Knight's Maid **R. J. A. Macdonald**
8 SHELIAK, 4, b f Binary Star (USA)—Flo's Choice (IRE) **Mrs H. M. Godfrey**
9 SONOMA (IRE), 5, ch m Dr Devious (IRE)—Mazarine Blue (USA) **D. J. Coles**
10 THORNTON CHARLOTTE, 4, b f Defacto (USA)—Lindrick Lady (IRE) **S. P. Hudson**

THREE-YEAR-OLDS

11 Ch f Keen—Auntie Fay (IRE) **S. P. Hudson**
12 B f Kayf Tara—Lindrick Lady (IRE) **S. P. Hudson**
13 ZANDERIDO, b g Forzando—Triple Concerto **M. S. Whitehead**

TWO-YEAR-OLDS

14 B f 11/5 Darnay—Kissimmee Bay (IRE) (Brief Truce (USA))
15 B g 24/5 Great Palm (USA)—Kuuipo (Puissance)
16 B f 10/4 Most Welcome—Princess Emily (IRE) (Dolphin Street (FR)) **Ms D. S. Doyle**
17 Ch c 16/4 Most Welcome—Triple Concerto (Grand Lodge (USA)) (2011)

Other Owners: J. H. Price.

Jockey (flat): M. Fenton. **Jockey (NH):** A. Ross. **Conditional:** P. A. Aspell. **Apprentice:** P. A. Aspell.

---

514   MR J-C ROUGET, France
Postal: **Chemin de la Foret Bastard, 64000 Pau, France.**
Contacts: **PHONE +33 (0) 5 59 33 27 90 FAX +33 (0) 5 59 33 29 30 MOBILE +33 (0) 6 10 270335
E-MAIL societe.entrainement.rouget@wanadoo.fr**

1 ALWAYS KING (FR), 4, b c Desert King (IRE)—Always On Time **Mr J. F. Gribomont**
2 BROTHER BUCK (USA), 6, b h Private Terms (USA)—Miss Buck Trout (USA) **Mr L. Di Saro**
3 CHUNKY MONKEY, 4, b g Millkom—Pearl of Dubai (USA) **Havana Horse (UK) Ltd**
4 DE PHAZZ (IRE), 5, ch h Barathea (IRE)—Fizz Up **Mr D. Treves**
5 DUIJKER (FR), 4, ch c Dr Fong (USA)—L'arrosee (USA) **Mr J. L. Tepper**
6 ELEUSIS (USA), 4, b f Diesis—Balancing Act (USA) **Mr G. Tanaka**
7 GENEVALE (FR), 4, ch f Unfuwain (USA)—Femme de Fer (FR) **Mme F. Levesque-Liboire**
8 GURSKY (USA), 4, gr ro c Red Ransom (USA)—Super Sheila (AUS) **Mr D. Treves**
9 KAZIMIERSKI (USA), 4, b c Silver Hawk (USA)—Party Cited (USA) **Mr G. Tanaka**
10 LE PRINCE CHARMANT (FR), 4, ch c Priolo (USA)—La Petite Danseuse (USA) **Mr R. Bousquet**
11 LES ANNEES POP (FR), 4, ch c Green Tune (USA)—La Popesse (USA) **Mme J. F. Dupont**
12 LORD DU SUD (FR), 4, gr c Linamix (FR)—Marseillaise (FR) **Mme B. Hermelin**
13 MADANI (FR), 4, b c Royal Applause—First Served (FR) **Mr A. Caro**
14 MARBEUF (USA), 4, b c Bahri (USA)—Salon Prive (USA) **Mr D. Treves**
15 MASSIZAL (FR), 5, b h Zilzal (USA)—Massatixa (FR) **Mr P. Lapique**
16 MISTER SACHA (FR), 4, b c Tiger Hill (IRE)—Miss Sacha (IRE) **S N C Lagardere Elevage**

MR J-C ROUGET—continued

17 **MONSELET BASTILLE (USA)**, 4, ch c Gulch (USA)—Elafonissos (FR) **Mr J. Seche**
18 **OLIVIANE**, 4, b gr f Cardoun (FR)—Nuit d'opale (IRE) **Mr Baguenault de Puchesse**
19 **POLITIES (USA)**, 6, b h Atticus (USA)—Spectacular Face (USA) **Ecurie I. M. Fares**
20 **POLY DANCE (FR)**, 4, br c Le Triton (USA)—Dancing Machine (FR) **Mme L. Rabineau**
21 **POPEE (FR)**, 4, br f Take Risks (FR)—Pop Out (FR) **Mme J. F. Dupont**
22 **REVE D'EMPIRE (IRE)**, 5, b h Emperor Jones (USA)—Imaginaire **Mr F. Bayrou**
23 **RONNIE GAUCHO (USA)**, 4, b c Lear Fan (USA)—Byre Bird (USA) **Mr D. Treves**
24 **SEIGNEUR JONES**, 6, br h Emperor Jones (USA)—Miss Up N Go **Mr A. Bidart**
25 **SIXELA (FR)**, 4, b c Septieme Ciel (USA)—Kadouville (FR) **Mme J. F. Dupont**
26 **STAR VALLEY (FR)**, 5, b h Starborough—Valleyrose (IRE) **Mr A. Caro**
27 **STENDHAL (IRE)**, 5, b h Polish Precedent (USA)—Kenmist **Mr J. L. Tepper**
28 **XIMB (FR)**, 4, gr c Septieme Ciel (USA)—Tambura (FR) **Mr N. Forgeard**
29 **ZILZOOM**, 5, ch h Zilzal (USA)—Sinking **Comte L De Quintanilla**

THREE-YEAR-OLDS

30 **ALDO L' ARGENTIN (USA)**, b br c Anabaa (USA)—Soubrette (USA) **Mr J. Seche**
31 **ALL HEART (FR)**, ch f Alhaarth (IRE)—Life On The Road (IRE) **Mr F. Bayrou**
32 **AMOUAGE (IRE)**, ch f Groom Dancer (USA)—Idle Chat (USA) **Mr R. Bousquet**
33 **ANTARTIS**, ch c Barathea (IRE)—Atlantic Blue (IRE) **Mr R. Bousquet**
34 **AZUCAR (FR)**, b f Marathon (USA)—Alabala (FR) **Comte L De Quintanilla**
35 **BACK THE WINNER (IRE)**, b f Entrepreneur—Good To Dance (IRE) **Mr J. F. Gribomont**
36 **BAINO RIDGE (FR)**, b f Highest Honor (USA)—Baino Bluff **Ecurie I. M. Fares**
37 **BANDIAMIR (FR)**, b c Keos (USA)—Suadif (FR) **Mr J. C. Weill**
38 **BARCHAVEZ (FR)**, b c Anabaa (USA)—Baiser Vole (USA) **Mr N. Radwan**
39 **BIENS NANTI (IRE)**, b c Montjeu (IRE)—Trexana **Marquesa de Moratalla**
40 **BREATH OF LOVE (USA)**, ch f Mutakddim (USA)—Breath Taking (FR) **Mr N. Radwan**
41 **BRUNOY**, b c Spectrum (IRE)—Timing (FR) **Mr D. Treves**
42 **CATSTONE (FR)**, b c Grindstone (USA)—Catskill Mountains (USA) **S N C Lagardere Elevage**
43 **CAVOUR (FR)**, b c Entrepreneur—Catalane (USA) **Mr N. Radwan**
44 **COOLGRAPE (IRE)**, gr b c Grape Tree Road—Coolgrape (IRE) **Mr A. Caro**
45 **CRISTAL ROSE (IRE)**, b f Montjeu (IRE)—Little Italy (IRE) **Mr Cheng**
46 **ELODIE DES CHARMES (FR)**, b f Diesis—Gontcharova (IRE) **Ecurie des Monceaux**
47 **FAUSSAIRE (IRE)**, b br c Fasliyev (USA)—Chalosse **Marquesa de Moratalla**
48 **FORMAX (FR)**, gr c Marathon (USA)—Fortuna (FR) **Mr J. F. Gribomont**
49 **FRAMBROISE**, ch f Diesis—Applaud (FR) **Mr Salman**
50 **GAIMIX (FR)**, gr c Linamix (FR)—Gueridia (IRE) **Mr Dubois**
51 **HABIT TAKEN (IRE)**, b c Take Risks (FR)—Habidancer (IRE) **Haras d'Etreham**
52 **HEAVENLY (FR)**, ch f Sendawar (IRE)—Alcove (USA) **Mr Dundon**
53 **HOCKNEY**, br c Zafonic (USA)—Doliouchka **Mr D. Treves**
54 **INCENTIVE (FR)**, b br c Machiavellian (USA)—Seductrice (USA) **Mr J. L. Tepper**
55 **IONALY (IRE)**, ch c Septieme Ciel (USA)—Mercedes (GER) **Mme L. Rabineau**
56 **ISIDORO (FR)**, ch c Sendawar (USA)—Verzasca (IRE) **Mr J. L. Tepper**
57 **ISNELDONE**, b c Nashwan (USA)—Milly of The Vally **Mr N. Forgeard**
58 **KARLABRUNUM (IRE)**, b f Spectrum (IRE)—Kartabula (FR) **Haras d'Etreham**
59 **LAXLOVA (FR)**, gr f Linamix (FR)—Labour of Love (USA) **S N C Lagardere Elevage**
60 **LONE REEF (FR)**, b c Lone Bid (FR)—Wavy Reef **Mme De Sangosse**
61 **LONG LOST (FR)**, b f Priolo (USA)—Lost Ring (FR) **Mr R. Bousquet**
62 **MAHIMA (FR)**, b f Linamix (FR)—Macellum (USA) **Mme J. F. Dupont**
63 **MELANOSPORUM (FR)**, b c Royal Anthem (USA)—Innes (USA) **Mr Holmes**
64 **MIGUEL DO BRAZIL**, b c Spectrum (IRE)—L'animee (USA) **Mr J. Seche**
65 **MISTER ALEXIS (FR)**, b c Bering—Albiatra (USA) **Mme L. Rabineau**
66 **MONTMARIN (FR)**, b c Dansili—Monacita (FR) **Mr Pariente**
67 **MOON WEST (USA)**, b f Gone West (USA)—June Moon (USA) **Mr Costa**
68 **MOVING DAY**, b c Grand Lodge (USA)—Star of Akkar **Marquesa de Moratalla**
69 **MULETA (IRE)**, b c Daggers Drawn (USA)—Undercover **Team Havana**
70 **MUTRAH (FR)**, b c Barathea (USA)—Perellina (IRE) **Mr R. Bousquet**
71 **NAMBAN**, b c Anabaa (USA)—Nany's Affair (USA) **Mr R. Bousquet**
72 **NATURALLY (IRE)**, b f Mtoto—Tamnia **Prince A. A. Faisal**
73 **OLAYA (USA)**, b f Theatrical—Solaia (USA) **Mr Salman**
74 **OLGA BERE (FR)**, b f Broadway Flyer (USA)—Known Alibi (USA) **Mr D. Treves**
75 **OMBLE CHEVALIER (FR)**, b f Astair (FR)—Lake Annecy (USA) **Mme J. F. Dupont**
76 **OUR ZIGA (FR)**, gr f Linamix (FR)—Zigaura (USA) **S N C Lagardere Elevage**
77 **OUVRIER (FR)**, ch c Inchinor—Nuit d'opale (IRE) **Baron Guy de Rothschild**
78 **PAOLI (FR)**, b c Dr Fong (USA)—Paola (FR) **Mr F. McNulty**
79 **PATAMAX (FR)**, gr c Linamix (FR)—Pats Martini (USA) **S N C Lagardere Elevage**

MR J-C ROUGET—continued

80 **PEGMATITE (USA)**, ch f Fusaichi Pegasus (USA)—Pleaseelookatmenow (USA) **Mr N. Radwan**
81 **PELLEAS (FR)**, b c Take Risks (FR)—Queen Emilie (FR) **Mr J. L. Tepper**
82 **PERIDIUM (IRE)**, ch c Barathea (IRE)—Padua (IRE) **Mr J. L. Tepper**
83 **PINSON (IRE)**, b c Halling (USA)—Tadorne (FR) **Baron Guy de Rothschild**
84 **PRETTY SOON (FR)**, b f Zafonic (USA)—Bocanegra (FR) **Baron Guy de Rothschild**
85 **RAFANA (FR)**, gr f Linamix (FR)—Restifia (FR) **S N C Lagardere Elevage**
86 **RED HAPPY (USA)**, b f A P Indy (USA)—Red Cat (USA) **Finsbury Bloodstock**
87 **REVE DE PAIX (FR)**, b c Selkirk (USA)—Vivre En Paix **Mr N. Forgeard**
88 **ROSE VOLAGE (FR)**, b f Vettori (IRE)—Happy Rose (IRE) **Baron Guy de Rothschild**
89 **ROSEWATER (GER)**, b f Winged Love (IRE)—River Patrol **Ecurie des Monceaux**
90 **RUWI**, b c Unfuwain (USA)—Ma Paloma (FR) **Mr R. Bousquet**
91 **SAN REAL (FR)**, b c Smadoun (FR)—Al Kicks (FR) **Mr J. C. Solhonne**
92 **SEED PEARL**, b gr f Lordmare (FR)—Top Seed (FR) **Baron Guy de Rothschild**
93 **SHEBANA (FR)**, b f Go Between (USA)—Birsheba (FR) **Mr H. Morin**
94 **SHORT LIST (IRE)**, b f Xaar—Always Glitter (FR) **Mr J. L. Tepper**
95 **SLAMY (USA)**, b f Grand Slam (USA)—Accountable Lady (USA) **Mr R. Bousquet**
96 **SLEDMERE (FR)**, bl c Dansili—Elacata (GER) **Mr D. Treves**
97 **SOCIANDO (IRE)**, ch c Loup Sauvage (USA)—Panorama **Mr D. Treves**
98 **STARPIX (FR)**, gr c Linamix (FR)—Star's Proud Penny (USA) **S N C Lagardere Elevage**
99 **SUNRISE NEVEES (FR)**, ch f Kaldounevees (FR)—Sauzet (FR) **Mme L. Rabineau**
100 **SUR SA MINE (FR)**, ro f Sevres Rose (FR)—Un Peu Grise (FR) **Baron Guy de Rothschild**
101 **SWAINY (FR)**, b c Swain (IRE)—Markale (FR) **Mr J. L. Tepper**
102 **TANDORI (FR)**, b c Loup Solitaire (USA)—Tamaziya (FR) **Mr A. Caro**
103 **TATOUFO (FR)**, b c Sendawar (IRE)—Hersande (FR) **Mr J. F. Gribomont**
104 **TEXAS REGENT (FR)**, b f Emperor Jones (USA)—Texarika (USA) **Ecurie I. M. Fares**
105 **TRUFFLE PRINCE (IRE)**, ch c Desert Prince (IRE)—Mamara Reef **Mr D. Treves**
106 **TULIPE DE CHARME (USA)**, b f Boundary (USA)—Relasure (USA) **Ecurie des Monceaux**
107 **VIANE ROSE (FR)**, b f Sevres Rose (FR)—Princesse de Viane (FR) **Mr A. Caro**
108 **WINDYA (FR)**, gr f Linamix (FR)—Windy Gulch (USA) **S N C Lagardere Elevage**
109 **YANKO (FR)**, gr c Sendawar (IRE)—Tambura (FR) **Mr J. L. Tepper**
110 **YASDANA (FR)**, b f Octagonal (NZ)—First Served (FR) **Mme G. Forien**
111 **YOLA BELLA (FR)**, b f King's Best (USA)—Liver De Saron (USA) **Mr A. Caro**
112 **YVOLINO (FR)**, b c Valanour (IRE)—Helen's Gamble (IRE) **Mr A. Caro**

TWO-YEAR-OLDS

113 **AMBER STAR (FR)**, ch c 28/2 Starborough—Infiltrate (IRE) (Bering) (20120) **Mr A. Caro**
114 B c 19/4 Red Ransom (USA)—Armure Royale (USA) (Woodman (USA)) (18000) **Mr D. Treves**
115 **ASHAMIKA (FR)**, gr f 27/3 Linamix (FR)—Ashaninka (USA) (Woodman (USA)) **S N C Lagardere Elevage**
116 **ASK FOR LOVE (IRE)**, b f 18/1 Montjeu (IRE)—Flyamore (FR) (Sanglamore (USA)) (70422) **Mr D. Treves**
117 B c 20/4 Groom Dancer (USA)—Baileys On Line (Shareef Dancer (USA)) (20120) **Marquesa de Moratalla**
118 **BARASTRAIGHT**, ch c 7/4 Barathea (IRE)—Straight Lass (IRE) (Machiavellian (USA)) (60362) **S. Boucheron**
119 Ch c 4/4 Elusive Quality (USA)—Better Be Sure (USA) (Diesis) (50545) **Mr J. L. Tepper**
120 Ch c 18/4 Theatrical—Bloomin Thunder (USA) (Thunder Gulch (USA)) (53205) **Mr J. Seche**
121 **BOCAROSA (IRE)**, b f 2/4 Linamix (FR)—Bocanegra (FR) (Night Shift (USA)) **Baron Guy de Rothschild**
122 **CHEVAL DE TROIS (IRE)**, ch c 4/4 Spectrum (IRE)—
               Grand Empress (IRE) (Grand Lodge (USA)) (7000) **Mme F. Levesque-Liboire**
123 **CHILENO (FR)**, b c 17/2 Alhaarth (IRE)—Waking Redhead (USA) (Miswaki (USA)) (23474) **Mr D. Treves**
124 **DOOSELINDE (USA)**, b f 24/3 Cozzene (USA)—Solaia (USA) (Miswaki (USA)) **Mr Salman**
125 **DOUBLE BRANDY (USA)**, b br c 22/4 Hennessy (USA)—
               Millie's Choice (IRE) (Taufan (USA)) (47885) **Mr D. Treves**
126 **DOUBNOV (FR)**, b c 17/5 Linamix (FR)—Karmitycia (FR) (Last Tycoon) (53655) **Mr D. Treves**
127 **ELEUTHERE (USA)**, b f 1/2 Elusive Quality (USA)—
               Irish Moment (USA) (Irish Tower (USA)) (31923) **Mr R. Bousquet**
128 **EPIMETHEE (IRE)**, ch c 16/1 Barathea (IRE)—Saskya's Dream (IRE) (Ashkalani (IRE)) (40241) **Mr R. Bousquet**
129 **EUMENE (FR)**, ch c 5/3 Grand Lodge (USA)—Pelagic (Rainbow Quest (USA)) (83836) **Mr R. Bousquet**
130 **EVE'S GARDEN**, b f 1/4 Boundary (USA)—
               Elafonissos (FR) (Exit To Nowhere (USA)) (32193) **Mr J. L. Tepper**
131 **FASCINATING (FR)**, b c 25/4 Starborough—Flaming Back (USA) (Shahrastani (USA)) (21462) **Mr A. Caro**
132 B f 15/4 Silver Hawk (USA)—Gaily Tiara (USA) (Caerleon (USA)) (106411) **Mr N. Radwan**
133 **GALATEE (FR)**, b f 22/2 Galileo (IRE)—Altana (USA) (Mountain Cat (USA)) (268276) **Ecurie Diablo**
134 **GLATIT**, b c 4/4 Grand Lodge (USA)—Messina (IRE) (Sadler's Wells (USA)) (57008) **Mr R. Bousquet**
135 **GRAND MASSA (FR)**, gr f 26/2 Grand Lodge (USA)—Massatixa (FR) (Linamix (FR)) **S N C Lagardere Elevage**
136 **GREY MYSTIQUE (IRE)**, gr f 29/1 Linamix (FR)—Atnab (USA) (Riverman (USA)) (40000) **Mr Salman**
137 **GUAJIRA (FR)**, ch f 31/3 Mtoto—Femme de Fer (FR) (Iron Duke (FR)) (51643) **Mr Soriano**
138 **HAPPY GO LUCKY (FR)**, ro f 24/3 Kendor (FR)—Happy Rose (IRE) (Linamix (FR)) **Baron Guy de Rothschild**

MR J-C ROUGET—continued

139 **HERALD ANGEL (FR)**, b c 30/4 Priolo (USA)—
Heavenly Music (USA) (Seattle Song (USA)) (36887) **Mr R. Bousquet**
140 **HIROPON (FR)**, gr f 22/4 Linamix (FR)—Sameerza (FR) (Akarad (FR)) (60362) **Mr J. L. Tepper**
141 **KABOOLTI (FR)**, b f 5/2 Kabool—Kalti (Kaldoun (FR)) (10731) **Mr S. Boucheron**
142 **KALKEN (FR)**, b c 14/5 Kendor (FR)—Super Vite (USA) (Septieme Ciel (USA)) (30181) **Mr J. L. Tepper**
143 B f 6/4 Alhaarth (IRE)—Karenaragon (Aragon) (12000) **Mr J. L. Tepper**
144 B f 26/4 Crafty Prospector (USA)—Karmifira (FR) (Always Fair (USA)) (63846) **Mr N. Radwan**
145 **KENKAYE (FR)**, b c 30/1 Kendor (FR)—River Ballade (Irish River (FR)) (32193) **Mr J. F. Gribomont**
146 **KING FASLIEV (IRE)**, b c 3/4 Fasliyev (USA)—Open Air (GER) (Nebos (GER)) (26827) **Mme B. Hermelin**
147 **KYA GULCH (USA)**, b f 11/4 Thunder Gulch (USA)—Luna Kya (FR) (Kendor (FR)) **S N C Lagardere Elevage**
148 **LANDLOVE (FR)**, b f 18/3 Septieme Ciel (USA)—Landless (Theatrical) (3353) **Mme F. Levesque-Liboire**
149 Gr c 3/2 Linamix (FR)—Lit (IRE) (Danehill (USA)) (83836) **Mr Dubois**
150 Ch f 3/2 Rahy (USA)—Lochlin Slew (Seattle Slew (USA)) (6384) **Mr Holmes**
151 **LOOK TO THE KING (FR)**, ch f 16/2 Kingmambo (USA)—
Laughing Look (USA) (Damascus (USA)) **Mr Stuart S. Janey III**
152 **LOW BUDGET (FR)**, b c 5/4 Kaldounevees (FR)—Spring Of Passion (FR) (Zieten (USA)) (20120) **Mr J. P. Rios**
153 **LUNATTORI**, b f 30/4 Vettori (IRE)—Ombre de Lune (IRE) (Polish Precedent (USA)) **Baron Guy de Rothschild**
154 **MADEMOISELLE SISSI (IRE)**, b f 17/2 Sadler's Wells (USA)—
Sister Dot (USA) (Secretariat (USA)) (268276) **Ecurie Diablo**
155 B f 3/2 Dansili—Makara (Lion Cavern (USA)) (20000) **Mr D. Treves**
156 **MAMITADOR**, br f 31/3 Anabaa (USA)—Lanasara (Generous (IRE)) (83836) **Mr J. L. Tepper**
157 **MARCEAU (FR)**, ch c 22/2 Starborough—Vadlaviria (IRE) (Bering) (28169) **Mr D. Treves**
158 **MARSEILLAIS (FR)**, b c 3/4 Linamix (FR)—Marseillaise (FR) (Esprit du Nord (USA)) **Mme B. Hermelin**
159 B f 24/5 War Chant (USA)—Megan's Leprechaun (USA) (Green Dancer (USA)) (58526) **Mr Dubois**
160 **MINEMA (FR)**, gr f 4/5 Linamix (FR)—You Be Mine (USA) (Arazi (USA)) **S N C Lagardere Elevage**
161 Ch c 7/3 Tale of The Cat (USA)—Miss U Fran (USA) (Brocco (USA)) (13301) **Mr C. Gour**
162 **MOONAMIX (FR)**, b c 5/4 Linamix (FR)—Evening Moon (USA) (Dayjur (USA)) **S N C Lagardere Elevage**
163 Gr f 17/3 Highest Honor (FR)—Mouriyana (IRE) (Akarad (FR)) (30000) **Marquesa de Moratalla**
164 **NAGEUR**, b c 20/3 Celtic Swing—Tadorne (FR) (Inchinor) **Baron Guy de Rothschild**
165 B f 4/3 Lear Fan (USA)—Narasimha (USA) (Nureyev (USA)) **S N C Lagardere Elevage**
166 B f 10/3 Daylami (IRE)—Nasaieb (IRE) (Fairy King (USA)) (41000) **Mr N. Radwan**
167 **NENDI (FR)**, ch c 13/1 Spinning World (USA)—Tanabata (FR) (Shining Steel) (77129) **Mr J. L. Tepper**
168 B c 2/6 Highest Honor (FR)—Numidie (FR) (Baillamont (USA)) (53655) **Ecurie I. M. Fares**
169 **OH SO AWESOME (USA)**, b c 21/1 Awesome Again (CAN)—Identify (IRE) (Persian Bold) (47885) **Mr Seche**
170 **ONE TWO OH THREE (USA)**, ch f 2/1 Diesis—
Life's An E Ticket (USA) (Deposit Ticket (USA)) (55865) **Mr Holmes**
171 Ch c 8/3 Mr Greeley (USA)—Palinisa (FR) (Night Shift (USA)) (63846) **Mr J. L. Tepper**
172 **PALMERO (USA)**, b c 26/2 Hennessy (USA)—Fifth High (USA) (Quiet American (USA)) **Mr J. Soriano**
173 **PENNE (FR)**, b f 10/3 Sevres Rose (IRE)—Une Pensee (FR) (Kenmare (FR)) **Baron Guy de Rothschild**
174 **PHENICIEN (FR)**, bl c 3/3 Sevres Rose (IRE)—Pharisienne (FR) (Kendor (FR)) **Baron Guy de Rothschild**
175 **POUND FOOLISH**, b f 5/3 Peintre Celebre (USA)—Bazbina (FR) (Highest Honor (FR)) **Marquesa de Moratalla**
176 B f 23/3 Marathon (USA)—Princesse de Viane (FR) (Kaldoun (FR)) **Mr A. Caro**
177 **RANSACKED (FR)**, gr c 18/5 Kendor (FR)—Little Emily (Zafonic (USA)) (28169) **Mr M. Parrish**
178 **RESLENAMIX (IRE)**, gr c 6/4 Linamix (FR)—
Resless Rain (Rainbow Quest (USA)) **S N C Lagardere Elevage**
179 **ROYAL FLUSH (FR)**, b c 12/2 Highest Honor (FR)—Art Fair (FR) (Fairy King (USA)) (34875) **Mr C. Gour**
180 **SIGNS OF LOVE (FR)**, b c 28/3 Poliglote—Severina (Darshaan) (26827) **Mme L. Rabineau**
181 **SOL MI FA (IRE)**, b f 21/3 Distant Music (USA)—Sil Sila (FR) (Marju (IRE)) (40241) **Mr J. P. Dubois**
182 B c 2/4 Aptitude (USA)—Sonja's Faith (IRE) (Sharp Victor (USA)) (31923) **Mr D. Treves**
183 B c 27/1 Grand Slam (USA)—Spankin' (USA) (A P Indy (USA)) (29263) **Mr R. Bousquet**
184 B f 26/4 Fasliyev (USA)—Sparkling Isle (Inchinor) (32000) **Mr J. L. Tepper**
185 **STADORE (FR)**, b f 13/1 Kendor (FR)—Stamingala (IRE) (Alzao (USA)) (16767) **Mr Dubois**
186 B c 28/3 Spinning World (USA)—Stellar Empress (IRE) (Star de Naskra (USA)) (20000) **Mr J. L. Tepper**
187 **TALIESYN (FR)**, b c 18/2 Baratinea (IRE)—Princess d'orange (FR) (Anabaa (USA)) (20120) **Mr De Moussac**
188 **TEMPRANILLO (GER)**, b c 5/4 Dashing Blade—Tepana (GER) (Polish Precedent (USA)) (53655) **Mr Dubois**
189 **TILLSITT**, b c 2/5 Grand Lodge—Lacatena (GER) (Acatenango (GER)) (32000) **Mr D. Treves**
190 **TRASIMENE**, br f 28/2 Sinndar (IRE)—Dame d'harvard (USA) (Quest For Fame) (53655) **Mr R. Bousquet**
191 **UT MAJEUR (FR)**, b c 22/2 Brahms (USA)—Bundle Up (USA) (Miner's Mark (USA)) (10000) **Mme J. F. Dupont**
192 **VADAZING (FR)**, ch f 11/2 Spinning World (USA)—Vadaza (FR) (Zafonic (USA)) **S N C Lagardere Elevage**
193 **VAL VERT (FR)**, b c 4/6 Kahyasi—Valverda (Irish River (USA)) (13413) **Mr Ciampi**
194 **VALAIN (IRE)**, b br c 15/4 Grand Lodge (USA)—Literary (Woodman (USA)) (36000) **Mr J. L. Tepper**
195 **VERSATILE (FR)**, bc 6/2 Vettori (IRE)—Direcvil (Top Ville) (6706) **Mme G. Forien**
196 **VIVARTIC (FR)**, gr f 18/3 Verglas (IRE)—Artic Bride (USA) (Arctic Tern (USA)) (24144) **Mr J. F. Gribomont**
197 **WINNING TEAM (FR)**, b c 30/4 Kaldounevees (FR)—
Lady Stapara (IRE) (Lead On Time) (16096) **Mr J. F. Gribomont**
198 **WORCHESTER**, ch c 24/4 Spinning World (USA)—Sea Vixen (Machiavellian (USA)) (10000) **Mme J. F. Dupont**

MR J-C ROUGET—continued

199 ZAIKEN (FR), gr c 26/3 Kendor (FR)—Miss Bedouine (FR) (Bering) (46948) **Mr J. L. Tepper**
200 Br f 12/3 Royal Academy (USA)—Zappeuse (USA) (Kingmambo (USA)) (42000) **Mme A. Doyle**

Other Owners: M. C. Moutray-Read, A. J. Smith.

---

515 **MR R. ROWE, Pulborough**
Postal: **Ashleigh House Stables, Sullington Lane, Storrington, Pulborough, West Sussex, RH20 4AE.**
Contacts: **PHONE (01903) 742871 FAX (01903) 740110 MOBILE (07831) 345636**
E-MAIL **r.rowe.racing@virgin.net**

1 **ACERTACK (IRE)**, 8, b g Supreme Leader—Ask The Madam **K. Hunter**
2 **ADELPHI THEATRE (USA)**, 8, b g Sadler's Wells (USA)—Truly Bound (USA) **The Encore Partnership**
3 **ALPHA GAMBLE (IRE)**, 5, ch g Alphabatim (USA)—Caher Cross (IRE) **Capt A. Pratt**
4 **AMBER STARLIGHT**, 7, b m Binary Star (USA)—Stupid Cupid **The Exclusive Partnership**
5 **ANNA GAYLE**, 4, ch f Dr Fong (USA)—Urban Dancer (IRE) **Alleynian Racing Partnership (jdrp)**
6 **APOLLO THEATRE**, 7, b g Sadler's Wells (USA)—Threatening **The Encore Partnership II**
7 **BEST OF GLORY (FR)**, 5, b g Medaaly—Glorieuse Shadows (FR) **K. Hunter**
8 **BLUE TUNE (FR)**, 4, b g Green Tune (USA)—Anvers (FR) **R. Meredith**
9 **CELTIC RUFFIAN (IRE)**, 7, b g Celio Rufo—Candid Lady **Mrs N. K. Crocker**
10 **CHARLESTON**, 4, ch g Pursuit of Love—Discomatic (USA) **Capt A. Pratt**
11 **CITIUS (IRE)**, 9, b g Supreme Leader—Fancy Me Not (IRE) **T. J. Perkins**
12 **EDGAR WILDE (IRE)**, 7, b g Invited (USA)—Ou La La (IRE) **The Bone Idol Partnership**
13 **FINE ENOUGH (IRE)**, 6, br g Florida Son—Lodge Party (IRE) **Mr & Mrs Robin Lamb**
14 **FLINDERS**, 10, b m Henbit (USA)—Stupid Cupid **Leith Hill Chasers**
15 **FRENCH DIRECTION (IRE)**, 6, ch g John French—Shelikesitstraight (IRE) **Mrs P. E. Proctor**
16 **GLOW IN THE PARK**, 7, gr m Darkwood Bay (USA)—Thames Glow
17 **HELM (IRE)**, 4, b g Alhaarth (IRE)—Pipers Pool (IRE) **Richard Rowe Racing Partnership**
18 **HEY PRESTO**, 5, b g Piccolo—Upping The Tempo **Robert Young**
19 **I'LLEVEIT TOU (IRE)**, 5, b g King Luthier—Shady Jumbo **T. Thompson**
20 **ICE COOL LAD (IRE)**, 11, b g Glacial Storm—My Serena **The Reality Partnership**
21 **KING COAL (IRE)**, 6, b br g Anshan—Lucky Trout **A. D. Kerman**
22 **KING LOUIS (FR)**, 4, b g Nikos—Rotina (FR) **Capt A. Pratt**
23 **KING'S MINSTREL (IRE)**, 4, b g Cape Cross (IRE)—Muwasim (USA) **Richard Rowe Racing Partnership**
24 **LEITH HILL STAR**, 9, ch m Comme L'etoile—Sunnyday **Mrs J. Maltby**
25 **LORD 'N' MASTER (IRE)**, 9, b g Lord Americo—Miss Good Night **Dr W. B. Alexander**
26 **MAGIC OF SYDNEY (IRE)**, 9, b g Broken Hearted—Chat Her Up **Ann & John Symes**
27 **MARRON PRINCE (FR)**, 5, ch g Cyborg (FR)—Colombine (USA) **Mrs C. J. Rayner**
28 5, ch f Accordion—Place Stephanie (USA) **Capt A. Pratt**
29 **PREMIER CHEVAL (USA)**, 6, ch g Irish River (FR)—Restikarada (FR) **R. C. Stillwell**
30 **PREMIER ESTATE (IRE)**, 8, b g Satco (FR)—Kettleby (IRE) **Mrs J. A. Field**
31 **SIR TOBY (IRE)**, 12, br g Strong Gale—Petite Deb **Capt A. Pratt**
32 **SIX OF ONE**, 7, b g Kahyasi—Ten To Six **Mrs P. E. Proctor**
33 **STATLEY RAJ (IND)**, 6, b g Mtoto—Donna Star **The Colonial Partnership**
34 **TOUCH OF FATE**, 6, b g Sovereign Water (FR)—Coral Delight **Richard Rowe Racing Partnership**
35 **TUDOR STAR**, 10, b g Comme L'etoile—Tudor Lilly **Leith Hill Chasers-Star Partnership**
36 **UP AT MIDNIGHT**, 5, b m Midnight Legend—Uplift **D. R. L. Evans**

THREE-YEAR-OLDS

37 **DONT CALL ME BABE**, b g Easycall—Ok Babe **D. W. Simpson**

Other Owners: A. L. Abrahams, A. Blades, Lady E. K. Blaker, Mr D. M. Bradshaw, Mrs H. C. G. Butcher, D. G. Coe, Mr S. Davies, D. T. Ellingham, G. M. Flood, Mrs G. S. Knight, R. A. Lamb, Mrs R. J. Lamb, Mr N. F. Maltby, N. J. Mckibbin, Mrs S. M. Murdoch, P. A. Naret-Barnes, Lady B. M. P. Neville, W. Packham, C. W. D. Poore, B. J. Reid, Mr J. Smee, Mrs A. Symes, J. Symes, A. Taylor, C. G. Turner, G. Ware.

Jockey (NH): B. Fenton.

---

516 **MISS M. E. ROWLAND, Lower Blidworth**
Postal: **Kirkfields, Calverton Road, Lower Blidworth, Nottingham, Nottinghamshire, NG21 0NW.**
Contacts: **PHONE (01623) 794831 MOBILE (07768) 224666**

1 **ANY NEWS**, 8, ch g Karinga Bay—D'egliere (FR) **Good Days Out Partnership**
2 **EXECUTIVE PROSPECT (IRE)**, 6, b m Executive Perk—Spring Trix (IRE) **Miss M. E. Rowland**

MISS M. E. ROWLAND—continued

3 **HUMMING**, 8, b g Bluebird (USA)—Risanda **Miss M. E. Rowland**
4 **INDIAN SIOUX (IRE)**, 6, b m Little Bighorn—Pepper Cannister **Miss M. E. Rowland**
5 **MISS JESSICA (IRE)**, 5, b br m Woodborough (USA)—Sarah Blue (IRE) **Mr K. Hopkin, Mr S. Deeman**
6 4, B g Forzando—Oh So Misty **Miss M. E. Rowland**
7 **REAL CHIEF (IRE)**, 7, b g Caerleon (USA)—Greek Air (IRE) **Miss M. E. Rowland**
8 **SEA DRIFTING**, 8, b g Slip Anchor—Theme (IRE) **J. Taqvi**
9 **TORZAL**, 5, br g Hector Protector (USA)—Alathezal (USA) **S. M. Deeman**
10 5, B br m Dover Patrol (IRE)—Up The Creek (IRE) **Miss M. E. Rowland**
11 **WATERCRESS**, 5, b m Slip Anchor—Theme (IRE) **J. Taqvi**
12 **XSYNNA**, 9, b g Cyrano de Bergerac—Rose Ciel (IRE) **C. A. McKechnie**
13 5, B m Moonax (IRE)—Zertxuna **Miss M. E. Rowland**

Other Owners: T. Sleath, M. Stirland.

Jockey (flat): A Culhane. **Jockey (NH):** J. Mogford. **Conditional:** A. Pogson. **Amateur:** Mrs K. Darmody.

---

517 MR A. DE ROYER-DUPRE, Chantilly
Postal: **3 Chemin des Aigles, 60500 Chantilly, France.**
Contacts: **PHONE +33 (0) 4 4580303 FAX +33 (0) 4 4573938 MOBILE +33 (0) 613 011009**

1 **DARKARA (IRE)**, 4, b f Halling (USA)—Daralbayda (IRE) **Princess Zahra Aga Khan**
2 **DEYNIZI (IRE)**, 4, ch c Kris—Denizliya (IRE) **Mr Beniamino Arbib**
3 **DIYAPOUR (FR)**, 5, b br h Alhaarth (IRE)—Diyawara (IRE) **S. A. Aga Khan**
4 **KALAJORANN (FR)**, 7, b h Salse (USA)—Kalajana (USA) **Mr Antoine Fontaine**
5 **KARANI (FR)**, 6, b h Distinctly North (USA)—Karikata (IRE) **S. A. Aga Khan**
6 **KIERAMON (FR)**, 5, b h Kendor (FR)—Kiera Marie (IRE) **Mr Beniamino Arbib**
7 **LE CARRE (USA)**, 7, gr ro g Miswaki (USA)—Dibs (USA) **Mr J. R. de Aragao Bozano**
8 **MIDSOU (FR)**, 4, b c Midyan (USA)—Queensouth (USA) **Mr Henri Philippart**
9 **MOORE'S MELODY (IRE)**, 4, b f Marju (IRE)—Liege (IRE) **Mr Francois Jean-Louis Branere**
10 **PAMPALALA (FR)**, 4, gr f Verglas (IRE)—Sirella (FR) **Mr Beniamino Arbib**
11 **PRIDE (FR)**, 5, b m Peintre Celebre (USA)—Specificity (USA) **N P Bloodstock Ltd**
12 **TASTE THE STARS (USA)**, 6, b br h Benny The Dip (USA)—Sassy Bird (USA) **Madame Didier Ricard**
13 **TCHIKALA**, 4, b f Inchinor—Tajrebah (USA) **6 C Racing Limited**
14 **VALENTINO (FR)**, 6, b h Valanour (IRE)—Rotina (FR) **Mr Eduardo Fierro**
15 **ZANJAN (FR)**, 4, d b c Indian Ridge—Zainta (IRE) **S. A. Aga Khan**

THREE-YEAR-OLDS

16 **AFSOUN (FR)**, b c Kahyasi—Afragha (IRE) **S. A. Aga Khan**
17 **ALALUNGA (USA)**, ch f Machiavellian (USA)—Classic Reign (CAN) **6 C Racing Limited**
18 **ART (IRE)**, b c In The Wings—Skew **Mr Jack Preston**
19 **ASTALANDA (FR)**, ch f Sendawar (IRE)—Ashkara (IRE) **S. A. Aga Khan**
20 **BALANKIYA (IRE)**, b f Darshaan—Balanka (IRE) **S. A. Aga Khan**
21 **BAYAZID (IRE)**, b c Grand Lodge (USA)—Bayrika (IRE) **S. A. Aga Khan**
22 **BEHNASAN (IRE)**, b c Darshaan—Behariya (IRE) **S. A. Aga Khan**
23 **CATALAN HILL (IRE)**, b f Danehill (USA)—Catalonia Express (USA) **Avv. E. Balbo Di Vinadio**
24 **DARAYBAD (IRE)**, b c Octagonal (NZ)—Daraydala (IRE) **S. A. Aga Khan**
25 **DARGASH (IRE)**, b c Darshaan—Darata (IRE) **S. A. Aga Khan**
26 **DARIYINIA (IRE)**, b c King's Best (USA)—Darariyna (IRE) **S. A. Aga Khan**
27 **DASHTAKI (FR)**, b c Night Shift (USA)—Darashandeh (IRE) **S. A. Aga Khan**
28 **GALE FORCE (IRE)**, b c Sinndar (IRE)—On Fair Stage (IRE) **N P Bloodstock Ltd**
29 **HAMALI (IRE)**, b c Muhtarram (USA)—Haladiya (IRE) **S. A. Aga Khan**
30 **JUST AERDEE (FR)**, gr f Kahyasi—Aerdee (FR) **Melle Michele Bliard**
31 **KALAWOUN (FR)**, b c Highest Honor (FR)—Kalajana (USA) **S. A. Aga Khan**
32 **KASSALIAN (FR)**, ch c Ashkalani (IRE)—Kassariya (FR) **S. A. Aga Khan**
33 **KERASHA (FR)**, b f Daylami (IRE)—Keraka (USA) **S. A. Aga Khan**
34 **KERIMBA (IRE)**, b f Sinndar (IRE)—Kerita **S. A. Aga Khan**
35 **KHALIMIA (IRE)**, b f Sendawar (IRE)—Khalisa (IRE) **S. A. Aga Khan**
36 **KHAYLAMA (FR)**, b f Dr Devious (IRE)—Khaytada (IRE) **S. A. Aga Khan**
37 **LAY DAYS (IRE)**, b f Daylami (IRE)—Just For Fun (IRE) **Marquesa de Moratalla**
38 **MANDARAKA (FR)**, ch f Ashkalani (IRE)—Mandalara (IRE) **Princess Zahra Aga Khan**
39 **MANNSAR (FR)**, ch c Sendawar (IRE)—Mannsara (IRE) **S. A. Aga Khan**
40 **NADIRANA (FR)**, gr f Kendor (FR)—Nadira (IRE) **S. A. Aga Khan**
41 **ON THE WIND (IRE)**, ch f Machiavellian (USA)—Lettre de Cachet (USA) **Marquesa de Moratalla**
42 **RIDAFANA (FR)**, b f Bahhare (USA)—Ridiyla (IRE) **S. A. Aga Khan**

MR A. DE ROYER-DUPRE—continued

43 **RIDIYR (IRE),** b c Indian Ridge—Ridaiyma (IRE) **S. A. Aga Khan**
44 **SANAGORA (IRE),** b f Mujadil (USA)—Sanariya (IRE) **S. A. Aga Khan**
45 **SAREKALA (FR),** bl f Desert King (IRE)—Sarekat (IRE) **S. A. Aga Khan**
46 **SARLISA (FR),** gr f Rainbow Quest (USA)—Sarliya (IRE) **S. A. Aga Khan**
47 **SERAYA (FR),** b f Danehill (USA)—Sendana (FR) **S. A. Aga Khan**
48 **SHAKANDARA (FR),** ch f Sendawar (IRE)—Sharakanda (USA) **S. A. Aga Khan**
49 **SHAMALANA (IRE),** b f Sinndar (IRE)—Shamaniya (IRE) **S. A. Aga Khan**
50 **SHAMAYOUN (FR),** b c Kahyasi—Shamanara (IRE) **S. A. Aga Khan**
51 **SHAMDALA (IRE),** b f Grand Lodge (USA)—Shamadara (IRE) **S. A. Aga Khan**
52 **SHARDAKHAN (IRE),** b c Dr Devious (IRE)—Sharamana (IRE) **S. A. Aga Khan**
53 **SHAWANDA (IRE),** b f Sinndar (IRE)—Shamawna (IRE) **S. A. Aga Khan**
54 **SHAYMAR (FR),** bl c Sendawar (IRE)—Shamatiya (IRE) **S. A. Aga Khan**
55 **SHEDARIAN (FR),** b c Grand Lodge (USA)—Shezerma (IRE) **S. A. Aga Khan**
56 **SHEKANA (FR),** b f Docksider (USA)—Sheshawa (IRE) **S. A. Aga Khan**
57 **SHEMRIYNA (IRE),** b f King of Kings (IRE)—Shemaya (USA) **S. A. Aga Khan**
58 **SHERZADA (IRE),** gr f Daylami (IRE)—Sherana (FR) **S. A. Aga Khan**
59 **SHEZAN (IRE),** br c Darshaan—Shemaka (IRE) **S. A. Aga Khan**
60 **SHIRLEY MOON (IRE),** b f Montjeu (IRE)—Greek Moon (IRE) **6 C Racing Limited**
61 **STASH THE ICE (IRE),** ch f Daylami (IRE)—Valley Quest (IRE) **Marquesa de Moratalla**
62 **TABARANA (IRE),** b f Cape Cross (IRE)—Tabariya (IRE) **S. A. Aga Khan**
63 **TARALAN (IRE),** b c Kahyasi—Tarabaya (IRE) **S. A. Aga Khan**
64 **TARKAR (IRE),** ch c Priolo (USA)—Tarakana (USA) **S. A. Aga Khan**
65 **TASHIGAR (IRE),** b c Darshaan—Tashiriya (IRE) **S. A. Aga Khan**
66 **VILLALIER (FR),** b c Medaaly—Vouivre (FR) **T. G. Holdcroft**
67 **WHY WORRY (FR),** b f Cadeaux Genereux—Seltitude (IRE) **N P Bloodstock Ltd**
68 **WINTER CORAL (FR),** ch f Pennekamp (USA)—Winter Water (FR) **Mme O. Bryant**
69 **YSOLDINA (FR),** b f Kendor (FR)—Rotina (FR) **Mme G. Forien**
70 **ZALAIYMA (FR),** b f Rainbow Quest (USA)—Zalaiyka (FR) **S. A. Aga Khan**
71 **ZANADI (FR),** bl c Cape Cross (IRE)—Zanakiya (USA) **S. A. Aga Khan**
72 **ZANAKARA (FR),** gr f Octagonal (NZ)—Zankara (FR) **S. A. Aga Khan**
73 **ZARKALIA (IRE),** b f Red Ransom (USA)—Zarkiya (IRE) **S. A. Aga Khan**
74 **ZARKIYNA (FR),** b f Sendawar (IRE)—Zarkana (IRE) **S. A. Aga Khan**

TWO-YEAR-OLDS

75 Bl c 25/3 Xaar—Afragha (IRE) (Darshaan) **S. A. Aga Khan**
76 Bl f 27/3 Diktat—Ashara (IRE) (Kahyasi) **S. A. Aga Khan**
77 B f 29/3 Kalanisi (IRE)—Bayrika (IRE) (Kahyasi) **S. A. Aga Khan**
78 B c 29/4 Selkirk (USA)—Behariya (IRE) (Sadler's Wells (USA)) **S. A. Aga Khan**
79 **COMME CI (IRE),** b f 1/5 Fasliyev (USA)—La Pointe (Sharpo) (87189) **Marquesa de Moratalla**
80 **DALEELA (IRE),** b f 15/5 Grand Lodge (USA)—Dalara (IRE) (Doyoun) **S. A. Aga Khan**
81 Gr f 19/5 Kalanisi (IRE)—Daltawa (IRE) (Miswaki (USA)) **S. A. Aga Khan**
82 **DALTAYA (FR),** b f 10/2 Anabaa (USA)—Daltaiyma (IRE) (Doyoun) **S. A. Aga Khan**
83 Gr c 23/1 Highest Honor (FR)—Darakiyla (IRE) (Last Tycoon) **S. A. Aga Khan**
84 **DARAMSAR (FR),** b c 5/3 Rainbow Quest (USA)—Daryaba (IRE) (Night Shift (USA)) **S. A. Aga Khan**
85 B c 2/5 Anabaa (USA)—Darata (IRE) (Vayrann) **S. A. Aga Khan**
86 **DARSI (FR),** b c 12/4 Polish Precedent (USA)—Darashandeh (IRE) (Darshaan) **S. A. Aga Khan**
87 **DILEK (FR),** bl c 17/4 Sendawar (IRE)—Diyawara (IRE) (Doyoun) **S. A. Aga Khan**
88 B c 20/3 Royal Academy (USA)—Gulf Cyclone (USA) (Sheikh Albadou) (53655) **Mr Jack Preston**
89 **HOLD THE THOUGHT,** ro f 27/2 Galileo (IRE)—Joyeuse Entree (Kendor (FR)) **Marquesa de Moratalla**
90 B c 14/5 Anabaa (USA)—Irtifa (Lahib (USA)) (16000) **6 C Racing Limited**
91 B f 23/1 Grand Lodge (USA)—Kadaka (IRE) (Sadler's Wells (USA)) **S. A. Aga Khan**
92 **KASIMALI (IRE),** b c 6/3 Soviet Star (USA)—Kassiyda (Mill Reef (USA)) **S. A. Aga Khan**
93 **KENTUCKY DYNAMITE (USA),** b c 3/2 Kingmambo (USA)—
Chelsey Flower (His Majesty (USA)) (133014) **Mr Viktor Timoshenko**
94 **KHAIYALA (FR),** b f 2/1 Kahyasi—Khaliyna (IRE) (Danehill (USA)) **S. A. Aga Khan**
95 **KHAZAR (FR),** b c 14/2 Anabaa (USA)—Khalisa (IRE) (Persian Bold) **S. A. Aga Khan**
96 **KOZAKA (FR),** b f 6/3 Mark of Esteem (IRE)—Kozmina (IRE) (Sadler's Wells (USA)) **S. A. Aga Khan**
97 **MANDESHA (FR),** b f 27/3 Desert Style (IRE)—Mandalara (IRE) (Lahib (USA)) **Princess Zahra Aga Khan**
98 Ch f 21/2 Polish Precedent (USA)—Nasriyda (FR) (Darshaan) **S. A. Aga Khan**
99 Ch c 17/3 Rahy (USA)—Premiere Creation (FR) (Green Tune (USA)) **Mr Jack Preston**
100 **RATIBOR (USA),** gr ro c 6/4 Cozzene (USA)—
Avie's Fancy (Lord Avie (USA)) (438946) **Mr Viktor Timoshenko**
101 **RIGHT STUFF (FR),** b c 19/5 Dansili—Specificity (USA) (Alleged (USA)) **Madame Didier Ricard**
102 B f 26/3 Barathea (IRE)—Sanariya (IRE) (Darshaan) **S. A. Aga Khan**
103 **SARANI (FR),** b c 18/4 Sendawar (IRE)—Sarekat (IRE) (Cadeaux Genereux) **S. A. Aga Khan**

MR A. DE ROYER-DUPRE—continued

104 B br c 2/5 Fantastic Light (USA)—Sassy Bird (USA) (Storm Bird (CAN)) (200000) **6 C Racing Limited**
105 B c 5/2 Daylami (IRE)—Shawara (IRE) (Barathea (IRE)) **S. A. Aga Khan**
106 **SHEMIYRA (IRE),** b f 22/2 In The Wings—Shemaka (IRE) (Nishapour (FR)) **S. A. Aga Khan**
107 B c 9/3 Spectrum (IRE)—Sherana (IRE) (Alleged (USA)) **S. A. Aga Khan**
108 **SHEREF (FR),** bl c 7/3 Benny The Dip (USA)—Shereda (IRE) (Indian Ridge) **S. A. Aga Khan**
109 B c 28/4 Lujain (USA)—Sheriya (USA) (Green Dancer (USA)) **S. A. Aga Khan**
110 B f 16/2 Inchinor—Tarabaya (IRE) (Warning) **S. A. Aga Khan**
111 **TASHAN (FR),** ch c 18/3 Sendawar (IRE)—Tashiriya (IRE) (Kenmare (FR)) **S. A. Aga Khan**
112 **USURPATOR (USA),** gr ro c 14/2 Unbridled's Song (USA)—
Zoftig (USA) (Cozzene (USA)) (345836) **Mr Viktor Timoshenko**
113 B f 9/1 Kahyasi—Veyara (IRE) (Ashkalani (IRE)) **S. A. Aga Khan**
114 Ch f 3/5 Giant's Causeway (USA)—Woodyousmileforme (USA) (Woodman (USA)) (65000) **6 C Racing Limited**
115 **ZAFIRAN (IRE),** gr c 3/3 Daylami (IRE)—Zafayana (IRE) (Mark of Esteem (IRE)) **S. A. Aga Khan**
116 **ZAKANIA (IRE),** b f 14/4 Indian Ridge—Zarkiya (IRE) (Catrail (USA)) **S. A. Aga Khan**
117 B f 17/2 Sinndar (IRE)—Zanadiyka (FR) (Akarad (FR)) **S. A. Aga Khan**
118 B f 2/4 Sinndar (IRE)—Zanakiya (FR) (Doyoun) **S. A. Aga Khan**
119 B c 9/4 Sinndar (IRE)—Zarabaya (IRE) (Doyoun) **S. A. Aga Khan**
120 **ZARIYAN (FR),** b c 20/5 Anabaa (USA)—Zarkana (IRE) (Doyoun) **S. A. Aga Khan**
121 **ZAYAFA (FR),** b f 3/1 Kalanisi (IRE)—Zayannda (IRE) (Alzao (USA)) **S. A. Aga Khan**
122 B f 30/3 King's Best (USA)—Zayana (IRE) (Darshaan) **S. A. Aga Khan**
123 Bl f 20/2 Mark of Esteem (IRE)—Zaydana (IRE) (Rainbow Quest (USA)) **S. A. Aga Khan**

Jockey (flat): C. Soumillon.

---

518 **MRS L. V. RUSSELL, Kinross**
Postal: **Arlary House Stables, Milnathort, Kinross, Tayside, KY13 9SJ.**
Contacts: **OFFICE (01577) 862482 YARD (01577) 865512 FAX (01577) 861171
MOBILE (07970) 645261**
E-MAIL lucinda@arlary.fsnet.co.uk

1 **AMBITION ROYAL (FR),** 5, ch g Cyborg (FR)—Before Royale (FR) **J. Petterson**
2 **BROADBAND,** 6, ch g Minster Son—Sound Bite **D. V. St Clair**
3 **BRORA SUTHERLAND (IRE),** 6, b g Synefos (USA)—Downtotheswallows (IRE) **W. Powrie**
4 **CAESAR'S PALACE (GER),** 8, ch g Lomitas—Caraveine (FR) **P. J. S. Russell**
5 **CATCH THE PERK (IRE),** 8, b g Executive Perk—Kilbally Quilty (IRE) **A. A. Bissett**
6 **CLAUDIA MAY,** 4, gr f Cloudings (IRE)—Princess Maxine (FR) **Mrs L. R. Joughin**
7 **DOTTIE DIGGER (IRE),** 6, b m Catrail (USA)—Hint-of-Romance (IRE) **Dig In Racing**
8 **DRUMS MUTYPSY,** 4, b g Mutamarrid—Drums Girl
9 **DUKE ORSINO (IRE),** 5, b g Old Vic—Deselby's Choice **P. K. Dale**
10 **DUNCRIEVIE GALE,** 8, gr g Gildoran—The Whirlie Weevil **D. Futong**
11 **FAIRWOOD NICKLE (IRE),** 6, b g Shernazar—Hop Picker (USA) **D. G. Pryde**
12 **FIRST ADARE (IRE),** 5, ch g Un Desperado (FR)—First Mistake **Mrs C. G. Greig**
13 **GLENFARCLAS BOY (IRE),** 9, b g Montelimar (USA)—Fairy Blaze (IRE) **Mrs I. M. Grant**
14 **GRAFTON TRUCE (IRE),** 8, gr g Brief Truce (USA)—Grafton Street (GER) **A. A. Bissett**
15 **HUGO DE PERRO (FR),** 10, b g Perrault—Fontaine Aux Faons (FR) **J. W. D. Campbell**
16 **JEFERTITI (FR),** 8, ch g Le Nain Jaune (FR)—Nefertiti (FR) **W. Powrie**
17 **JEROM DE VINDECY (FR),** 8, ch g Roi de Rome (USA)—Preves du Forez (FR) **R. H. Affleck**
18 **JOFI (IRE),** 6, b g Shernazar—Giolla Donn **Mr J. R. Adam**
19 **JUSTALITTLEMORE,** 5, b g Newsteadgoldenmorn VII—Just Pretend **A. R. Trotter**
20 **KERRY LADS (IRE),** 10, ch g Mister Lord (USA)—Minstrel Top **Mrs C. G. Greig**
21 **KILLER (FR),** 7, ch g Cupidon (FR)—Kaoutchka (FR) **Miss J. A. Buchanan**
22 **LAUDERDALE,** 9, b g Sula Bula—Miss Tullulah **Kelso Members Lowflyers Club**
23 **LEOPARD SPOT (IRE),** 7, b g Sadler's Wells (USA)—Savoureuse Lady **R. McAllister**
24 **MASTER FARRIER,** 5, br g Milieu—Nikwill (IRE) **P. J. S. Russell**
25 **MASTER SEBASTIAN,** 6, ch g Kasakov—Anchor Inn **Mrs J. M. Grimston**
26 **MISTER SMITH (IRE),** 6, b g Mister Lord (USA)—Just A Swop (IRE) **Mrs L. R. Joughin**
27 **MUMARIS (USA),** 11, br g Capote (USA)—Barakat **De Montfort Management Limited**
28 **NEVEN,** 6, b g Castedduu—Rose Burton **White Horse Racing Club**
29 **NOLIFE (IRE),** 9, b g Religiously (USA)—Garnerstown Lady **Dig In Racing**
30 **OLIVERJOHN (IRE),** 8, ch g Denel (FR)—Graeme's Gem **Thoroughbred Leisure Racing Club**
31 **RATHFRILAND (IRE),** 7, b m Supreme Leader—Tassagh Lady **Boysaday Racing**
32 **SCRAPPIE (IRE),** 5, b g Fourstars Allstar (USA)—Clonyn **John R. Adam & Sons Ltd**
33 **SEA FERRY (IRE),** 9, b g Ilium—Nicholas Ferry **D. G. Pryde**
34 **SEE YOU THERE (IRE),** 6, br g Religiously (USA)—Bye For Now
35 **SEEYAAJ,** 5, b g Darshaan—Subya **Brahms & Liszt**

MRS L. V. RUSSELL—continued

36 **SPORTS EXPRESS**, 7, ch m Then Again—Lady St Lawrence (USA) **Powrie,Valentine,Hawkins & McManus**
37 **STRONG RESOLVE (IRE)**, 9, gr g Roselier (FR)—Farmerette **Fair City Flyers**
38 **TETRAGON (IRE)**, 5, b g Octagonal (NZ)—Viva Verdi (IRE) **W. Powrie**
39 **THE ASSOCIATE (IRE)**, 8, b br g Religiously (USA)—Stormy Trip **Miss J. A. Buchanan**
40 **VANDAS CHOICE (IRE)**, 7, b g Sadler's Wells (USA)—Morning Devotion (USA) **J. Petterson**
41 **WAINAK (USA)**, 7, b g Silver Hawk (USA)—Cask **W. Powrie**
42 **WEE SEAN (IRE)**, 5, b g Rashar (USA)—Mrs Blobby (IRE) **Lothian Recycling Limited**
43 **WINTER GARDEN**, 11, ch g Old Vic—Winter Queen **A. A. Bissett**
44 **YOUR ADVANTAGE (IRE)**, 5, b g Septieme Ciel (USA)—Freedom Flame **Mr & Mrs T. P. Winnell**

Other Owners: Mr Thomas Boyle, Mrs P. A. M. McNeill, Mr G. Watson, Mr James Christie, Mr W. Ross, Mr W. Agnew, Mrs Kay Owens, Mrs Edith Russell, Mr W. Freerson, Mr D. Waters, Mrs M. Rees, Mr D. McIntosh, Mr K. N. R. MacNicol, Miss G. Joughin, Mr H. Gettings, Mr T. A. Boyle, I. Crole, T. D. Hawkins, Ms B. J. Johnston, R. S. Macdonald, A. McManus, D. McManus, K. Milne, B. Valentine.

Assistant Trainer: Magnus Nicholson & Jaimie Duff

Jockey (NH): P. Buchanan, R. Johnson.

---

519 **MR B. J. M. RYALL, Yeovil**
Postal: **Higher Farm, Rimpton, Yeovil, Somerset, BA22 8AD.**
Contacts: PHONE/FAX (01935) 850222
E-MAIL johnryall@rimpton.freeserve.co.uk

1 **ALCATRAS (IRE)**, 8, b br g Corrouge (USA)—Kisco (IRE) **Mr I. & Mrs K. G. Fawcett**
2 **BRONZESMITH**, 9, b g Greensmith—Bronze Age **Mrs M. E. Ash**
3 **COUNTRY KRIS**, 13, b g Town And Country—Mariban **Mr B. J. M. Ryall**
4 **IL CAPRICCIO (IRE)**, 5, b g Windsor Castle—Brogeen View **Mrs G. C. Pritchard**
5 **MICHIGAN D'ISOP (FR)**, 5, b g Cadoudal (FR)—Julie Du Berlais (FR) **Mr B. J. M. Ryall**
6 **PEWTER LIGHT (IRE)**, 8, gr g Roselier (FR)—Luminous Light **Mr I. & Mrs K. G. Fawcett**
7 **QUIZZLING (IRE)**, 7, b g Jurado (USA)—Monksville **Mr I. & Mrs K. G. Fawcett**
8 **SIR FROSTY**, 12, ch g Arctic Lord—Snowy Autumn **J. F. Tucker**
9 **TIN SYMPHONY**, 7, ch m Opera Ghost—Bronze Age **The Wessex Cornflower Partnership**

Other Owners: Miss G. N. Pope, Mrs J. Standen.

Assistant Trainer: Mrs R C Ryall

---

520 **MR K. A. RYAN, Hambleton**
Postal: **Hambleton Lodge, Hambleton, Thirsk, North Yorkshire, YO7 2HA.**
Contacts: HOME (01845) 597010 YARD (01845) 597622
FAX (01845) 597622 MOBILE (07768) 016930
E-MAIL kevin.hambleton@virgin.net

1 **ALWAYS ESTEEMED (IRE)**, 5, b g Mark of Esteem (IRE)—Always Far (USA) **Sunpak Potatoes**
2 **ARRAN SCOUT (IRE)**, 4, b g Piccolo—Evie Hone (IRE) **Thamer Al Daihani**
3 **BAYLAW STAR**, 4, b g Case Law—Caisson **T C Racing Partnership**
4 **BLUE PATRICK**, 5, gr g Wizard King—Great Intent **Mr S. R. H. Turner**
5 **BRIDGEWATER BOYS**, 4, b g Atraf—Dunloe (IRE) **Bishopthorpe Racing**
6 **CARDINAL VENTURE (IRE)**, 7, b g Bishop of Cashel—Phoenix Venture (IRE) **A. R. Fawcett**
7 **CLIMATE (IRE)**, 6, ch g Catrail (USA)—Burishki **J Nattrass M Howard R Fawcett T Fawcett**
8 **CLOUD DANCER**, 6, b br m Bishop of Cashel—Summer Pageant **Mrs G. O'Driscoll**
9 **DILSAA**, 8, ch g Night Shift (USA)—Llia **Yorkshire Racing Syndicate**
10 **DUNE RAIDER (USA)**, 4, b c Kingmambo (USA)—Glowing Honor (USA) **Mr T. Al Nisf**
11 **GRALMANO (IRE)**, 10, b g Scenic—Llangollen (IRE) **Coleorton Moor Racing**
12 **ISKANDER**, 4, b g Danzero (AUS)—Amber Mill **Mrs M. Forsyth**
13 **JOE COOLEY (IRE)**, 5, b g Accordion—My Miss Molly **Mr I. Bray**
14 **KARELIAN**, 4, gr g Linamix (FR)—Kalikala **J. Duddy**
15 **LADY KIA (IRE)**, 6, b m Petorius—Trapped (IRE) **Mr M. Casey**
16 **LOUISIADE (IRE)**, 4, b g Tagula (IRE)—Titchwell Lass **Whitestoncliffe Racing Partnership**
17 **MISTER REGENT**, 4, b g Mind Games—River of Fortune (IRE) **W. R. Hammond**
18 **MY PARIS**, 4, b g Paris House—My Desire **J & A Spensley**
19 **MY YORKSHIRE ROSE**, 5, b m Bishop of Cashel—Gloriana **Yorkshire Racing Syndicate**
20 **MYSTIC MAN (FR)**, 7, b g Cadeaux Genereux—Shawanni **R J H Limited**
21 **NORTHERN GAMES**, 6, b g Mind Games—Northern Sal **R. E. Robinson**

MR K. A. RYAN—continued

22 **PARADISE FLIGHT (IRE)**, 4, ch f In The Wings—Aloft (IRE) **Iona Equine & Mr J. Brown**
23 **PETRULA**, 6, ch g Tagula (IRE)—Bouffant **Peter & Richard Foden Racing Partnership**
24 **POPPYS FOOTPRINT (IRE)**, 4, ch f Titus Livius (FR)—Mica Male (ITY) **Kimian Barfly**
25 **QUIET TIMES (IRE)**, 6, ch g Dolphin Street (FR)—Super Times **Yorkshire Racing Club and Francis Moll**
26 **RAYMOND'S PRIDE**, 5, b g Mind Games—Northern Sal **R. E. Robinson**
27 **RESIDENTIAL**, 4, ch g Zilzal (USA)—House Hunting **Yorkshire Racing Syndicate**
28 **RIVER GEORGE**, 6, ch g River Falls—Suffolk Girl **Mrs V. C. Sugden**
29 **ROMAN EMPIRE**, 5, b g Efisio—Gena Ivor (USA) **Yorkshire Racing Syndicate**
30 **ROXANNE MILL**, 7, b m Cyrano de Bergerac—It Must Be Millie **J. Billson**
31 **SLAVONIC (USA)**, 4, ch g Royal Academy (USA)—Cyrillic (USA) **Mrs C. J. Reilly**
32 **SOYUZ (IRE)**, 5, ch g Cadeaux Genereux—Welsh Mist **The Fishermen**
33 **SUPER SAMMY**, 9, br m Mesleh—Super Sue **Whitestonecliffe Racing Partnership**
34 **TEDSTALE (USA)**, 7, ch g Irish River (FR)—Carefree Kate (USA) **Yorkshire Racing Syndicate**
35 **TICERO**, 4, ch g First Trump—Lucky Flinders **Mr J. Duddy**
36 **UHOOMAGOO**, 7, b g Namaqualand (USA)—Point of Law **Mr J. Duddy & Mr T. Fawcett**
37 **UP TEMPO (IRE)**, 7, b g Flying Spur (AUS)—Musical Essence **Yorkshire Racing Club & Derek Blackhurst**
38 **WESTCOTE (USA)**, 4, b f Gone West (USA)—Kingscote **Mrs J. Ryan**
39 **WINCHESTER**, 10, ch g Gunner B—Tracy Jack **Mr & Mrs K. Hughes**

THREE-YEAR-OLDS

40 **BLADES BOY**, ch g Paris House—Banningham Blade **Crown Select**
41 **COLEORTON DANCER**, ch g Danehill Dancer (IRE)—Tayovullin (IRE) **Coleorton Moor Racing**
42 **COLEORTON DANE**, gr g Danehill Dancer (IRE)—Cloudy Nine **Coleorton Moor Racing**
43 **DELTA SHAMROCK**, b c Montjoy (USA)—Miss Paradiso (IRE) **Miss Emma Shalley**
44 **DISTINCTLY GAME**, b g Mind Games—Distinctly Blu **Mr & Mrs Julian Richer**
45 **GIFTED GAMBLE**, b c Mind Games—Its Another Gift **Margaret's Partnership**
46 **KELLY NICOLE (IRE)**, b f Rainbow Quest (USA)—Banquise (IRE) **Mrs M. O'Keeffe**
47 **LINZIS LAD**, ch g Magic Ring (IRE)—Come On Katie **L. E. Neill**
48 **MAC COIS NA TINE**, b g Cois Na Tine (IRE)—Berenice (ITY) **Mrs G. M. Quinn**
49 **MISS TRENDSETTER (IRE)**, b f Desert Style (IRE)—Chummy's Friend (IRE) **Yorkshire Racing Syndicate**
50 **MISSPERON (IRE)**, b f Orpen (USA)—Secret Hideaway (USA) **Mrs Angie Bailey**
51 **ORPENDONNA (IRE)**, b f Orpen (USA)—Tetradonna (IRE) **Mrs C. Reilly & Mrs J. Ryan**
52 **RED LIGHT RUNNER**, gr c Mind Games—Sweet Whisper **Mr M. Casey**
53 **SUFFOLK HOUSE**, b g Paris House—Suffolk Girl **Mrs V. C. Sugden**
54 **THROW THE DICE**, b c Lujain (USA)—Euridice (IRE) **Pendle Inn Partnership**
55 **TOM FOREST**, b c Forest Wildcat (USA)—Silk Masque **B & K Systems Ltd**
56 **TYRONE SAM**, b g Mind Games—Crystal Sand (GER) **B. T. McDonald**
57 **WIGWAM WILLIE (IRE)**, b g Indian Rocket—Sweet Nature (IRE) **Neil & Anne Dawson Partnership**

TWO-YEAR-OLDS

58 **AMBER GLORY**, b f 10/3 Foxhound (USA)—Compton Amber (Puissance) (14500) **Wooster Partnership**
59 Ch f 2/4 Bertolini (USA)—Banningham Blade (Sure Blade (USA)) (1800) **Crown Select**
60 **BECKTARA (IRE)**, b c 3/3 Beckett (IRE)—
　　　　　Northern Tara (IRE) (Fayruz) (15000) **Crewe And Nantwich Racing Club**
61 B c 11/5 Woodman (USA)—Class Skipper (USA) (Skip Trial) (30180) **John Roundtree Ltd**
62 **COLEORTON FOXE (IRE)**, ch f 10/4 Foxhound (USA)—
　　　　　Tayovullin (IRE) (Shalford (IRE)) (3000) **Coleorton Moor Racing**
63 B c 26/4 Fasliyev (USA)—Copious (IRE) (Generous (IRE)) (25000) **Crewe And Nantwich Racing Club**
64 **COUNTRYWIDE BELLE**, b f 13/4 Josr Algarhoud (IRE)—
　　　　　Dancing Bluebell (IRE) (Bluebird (USA)) (800) **Countrywide Racing**
65 B f 24/3 Xaar—Dark Hyacinth (IRE) (Darshaan) (28000) **Mrs A. Bailey**
66 B c 18/4 Zilzal (USA)—Devastating (Bluebird (USA)) (8500) **Mr Pedro Rosas**
67 **EL BARCO (IRE)**, b g 20/4 Carrowkeel (IRE)—
　　　　　Life On The Street (Statoblest) (10500) **R.J.H. Ltd, G.Pickering & J.P.Hames**
68 B c 25/2 Danehill Dancer (IRE)—Elton Grove (IRE) (Astronef) (30000) **Yorkshire Racing Syndicate**
69 **FANGORN FOREST (IRE)**, b f 16/2 Shinko Forest (IRE)—
　　　　　Edge of Darkness (Vaigly Great) (6000) **R.J.H. Ltd, D. Hale, P. Saxton, J. P. Hames**
70 B f 7/5 Polar Prince (IRE)—Fisher Island (IRE) (Sri Pekan (USA)) (800) **The C H F Partnership**
71 **GUTO**, b g 30/4 Foxhound (USA)—Mujadilly (Mujadil (USA)) (3500) **H. B. Hughes**
72 B f 15/4 Classic Cliche (IRE)—Indian Summer (Young Generation) **Mr N. Warburton**
73 B f 9/4 Arkadian Hero (USA)—Inya Lake (Whittingham (IRE)) (8000) **Crown Select**
74 **KAYRATI**, b f 4/5 Cayman Kai (IRE)—Emmajoun (Emarati (USA)) **Maria Myco**
75 **KING ALFIE**, gr c 19/1 Foxhound (USA)—Its All Relative (Distant Relative) (4000) **Mrs M. Forsyth**
76 **KING ORCHISIOS (IRE)**, ch c 9/2 Tagula (IRE)—
　　　　　Wildflower (Namaqualand (USA)) (35000) **Mr & Mrs Julian Richer**

MR K. A. RYAN—continued

77 **LASTING LOVE**, ch f 16/2 Primo Valentino (IRE)—
Miss Beverley (Beveled) (USA)) (3047) **Mr & Mrs T. G. Holdcroft**
78 **MARGARETS CHOICE**, ch f 29/1 Foxhound (USA)—
Its Another Gift (Primo Dominie) (12000) **Margaret's Partnership**
79 B c 13/3 Montjeu (IRE)—Nwaahil (IRE) (Nashwan (USA)) (44000) **Limerick Lads Partnership**
80 **PANTANI (IRE)**, ch c 25/2 Bertolini (USA)—
Grand Splendour (Shirley Heights) (24144) **Pendle Inn Too Partnership**
81 **PETRICHAN (IRE)**, b c 12/1 Medicean—
Numancia (IRE) (Alzao (USA)) (35000) **Peter & Richard Foden Racing Partnership**
82 B f 29/3 Mind Games—Sioux Lady (Petong) **Mr N. Warburton**
83 **SNAKE SKIN**, ch f 27/3 Golden Snake (USA)—
Silken Dalliance (Rambo Dancer (CAN)) (1142) **The C H F Partnership**
84 Ch c 31/3 Compton Place—Souadah (USA) (General Holme (USA)) (30000) **Mr M. Casey**
85 **SPIRITUAL PEACE (IRE)**, b c 26/2 Cadeaux Genereux—
Emerald Peace (IRE) (Green Desert (USA)) (38000) **Mr M. Burke**
86 Ch f 30/1 Piccolo—Sunfleet (Red Sunset) **Mr Pedro Rosas**

Other Owners: Dr O. Butting, S. N. Cordingley, Miss V. Hall, P. Hampshire, A. C. Henson, M. P. Higson, D. Holgate, A. Holmes, B. Hutchinson, P. Morrell, Mr N. J. O'Brien, Denis O'Flynn, Miss P. M. O'Flynn, Mr M. Pavlovic, Mr P. Ringer, A. Speight, B. Tuer, Mr S. R. Wildsmith, A. Yates, Mrs S. J. Yates.

Assistant Trainer: M Birch

Jockey (flat): N. Callan. **Jockey (NH):** G. Lee. **Apprentice:** Andrew Mullen, Donna Caldwell.

---

521   **MR M. A. SALAMAN, Marlborough**
Postal: **Oaktree, Russley Park, Baydon, Marlborough, Wiltshire, SN8 2JY.**
Contacts: **PHONE (01672) 541048**

THREE-YEAR-OLDS

1 **MOUNT ARAFAT**, b br g Erhaab (USA)—Cache **Falcon Friends**
2 **SIRNANDO**, b c Hernando (FR)—Rynechra **M. J. Lewin**
3 **SPEEDY SPIRIT**, ch f Wolfhound (USA)—Ansellady **Falcon Friends**

TWO-YEAR-OLDS

4 **THREE FEATHERS**, b c 23/3 Averti (IRE)—Jane Grey (Tragic Role (USA)) (1904) **Falcon Friends**

Other Owners: A. M. Hession, R. H. Brookes.

Assistant Trainer: M B Salaman

---

522   **MISS B. SANDERS, Epsom**
Postal: **Chalk Pit Stables, Headley Road, Epsom, Surrey, KT18 6BW.**
Contacts: **PHONE (01372) 278453 FAX (01372) 276137**

1 **A WOMAN IN LOVE**, 6, gr m Muhtarram (USA)—Ma Lumiere (FR) **High & Dry Racing**
2 **ANOTHER GLIMPSE**, 7, b g Rudimentary (USA)—Running Glimpse (IRE) **E. Hyde**
3 **BLACKMAIL (USA)**, 7, b g Twining (USA)—Black Penny (USA) **P. D. Crate**
4 **CANTRIP**, 5, b m Celtic Swing—Circe **A. C. Verdie**
5 **FRANKSALOT (IRE)**, 5, ch g Desert Story (IRE)—Rosie's Guest (IRE) **Peter Crate And Jane Byers**
6 **INTRIGUING GLIMPSE**, 4, b br f Piccolo—Running Glimpse (IRE) **E. Hyde**
7 **JAYANJAY**, 6, b g Piccolo—Morica **P. D. Crate**
8 **KATIYPOUR (IRE)**, 8, ch g Be My Guest (USA)—Katiyfa **P. D. Crate**
9 **LARA FALANA**, 7, b m Tagula (IRE)—Victoria Mill **Exors of the Late R. Lamb**
10 **MINIMUM BID**, 4, b f First Trump—La Noisette **Exors of the Late R. Lamb**
11 **MUYASSIR (IRE)**, 10, b g Brief Truce (USA)—Twine **J. M. Quinn**
12 **PAPEETE (GER)**, 4, b f Alzao (USA)—Prairie Vela **M. L. Champion**
13 **POYLE JENNY**, 6, b m Piccolo—Poyle Amber **Miss A. J. Wiggins**
14 **SUPERCHIEF**, 10, b g Precocious—Rome Express **E. Hyde**

MISS B. SANDERS—continued

THREE-YEAR-OLDS

15 **ALL BEING WELL**, ch g Bien Bien (USA)—Princess Moodyshoe **Mrs Alison Farrant & Mr Frank Farrant**
16 **ATTISHOE**, b f Atraf—Royal Shoe **W. Saye and Friends**
17 **COSMIC APOLLO**, ch c Pennekamp (USA)—Windmill Princess **Mr R. Young**
18 **POYLE CAITLIN (IRE)**, b f Bachir (IRE)—Poyle Fizz **Miss A. J. Wiggins**

Other Owners: A. Laycock, Mrs F. J. Byers, P. D. Crate.

---

523 MRS J. A. SAUNDERS, Teeton
Postal: **Teeton Grange Farm, Teeton, Northampton.**
Contacts: **PHONE (01604) 505739 MOBILE (07970) 667852**

1 **HOMELIFE (IRE)**, 7, b g Persian Bold—Share The Vision **Mr & Mrs N. Ewbank & Ms L. Cross**
2 **YUKON JACK**, 7, b g Tharqaam (IRE)—Spanish Mermaid **Mr J. & Miss L. Cross**

Other Owners: Mr J. D. Cross, Miss L. A. Cross, Mr N. J. Ewbank, Mrs N. Ewbank, Mrs J. A. Saunders.

---

524 MR M. S. SAUNDERS, Wells
Postal: **Blue Mountain Farm, Wells Hill Bottom, Haydon, Wells, Somerset, BA5 3EZ.**
Contacts: **OFFICE/FAX (01749) 841011 MOBILE (07771) 601035**
E-MAIL **malcolm@malcolmsaunders.co.uk** WEBSITE **www.malcolmsaunders.co.uk**

1 **CAUSTIC WIT (IRE)**, 7, b g Cadeaux Genereux—Baldemosa (FR) **Mrs S. D. Jones**
2 **CRAIC SA CEILI (IRE)**, b m Danehill Dancer (IRE)—Fay's Song (IRE) **Charles Saunders Ltd**
3 **DEVISE (IRE)**, 6, b g Hamas (IRE)—Soreze (IRE) **David Naylor**
4 **INDIAN MAIDEN (IRE)**, 5, br m Indian Ridge—Jinsiyah (USA) **Chris Scott & Peter Hall**
5 **LOCKSTOCK (IRE)**, 7, b g Inchinor—Risalah **B. C. Scott**
6 **MY GIRL PEARL (IRE)**, 5, b m Sri Pekan (USA)—Desert Bloom (FR) **T. A. Godbert**
7 **SELDEMOSA**, 4, br f Selkirk (USA)—Baldemosa (FR) **B. J. Tutin**
8 **SOCKS FOR GLENN**, 5, ch g Factual (USA)—Payvashooz **Mrs H. F. Mahr**
9 **SPLIFF**, 4, b c Royal Applause—Snipe Hall **Mr M. S. Saunders**

THREE-YEAR-OLDS

10 **FISBERRY**, gr c Efisio—Elderberry **Charles Saunders Ltd**
11 **MAKTU**, ch g Bien Bien (USA)—Shalateeno **G. J. & Mrs M. Palmer**
12 **PATRICIAN DEALER**, br g Millkom—Double Fault (USA) **P.B.Finnegan I.M.Donnelly M.Prytherch**
13 **SATURDAY'S CHILD (FR)**, ch f Hamas (IRE)—Pleasant Whisper (FR) **J. A. Gent**

TWO-YEAR-OLDS

14 Ch g 14/2 Daggers Drawn (USA)—Fay's Song (IRE) (Fayruz) (10060) **Mr M. S. Saunders**
15 Ch g 24/3 Titus Livius (FR)—Stridhana (Indian Ridge) (8382) **Mr M. S. Saunders**

Other Owners: Mrs M. M. Godbert.

Amateur: Miss K Jones.

---

525 MRS H. D. SAYER, Penrith
Postal: **Town End Farm, Hackthorpe, Penrith, Cumbria, CA10 2HX.**
Contacts: **PHONE (01931) 712245 MOBILE (07980) 295316**

1 **BRAVE EFFECT (IRE)**, 9, br g Bravefoot—Crupney Lass
2 **GETINBYBUTONLYJUST**, 6, b g King's Ride—Madame President (IRE) **J. A. Sayer**
3 **GREENFIRE (FR)**, 7, ch g Ashkalani (IRE)—Greenvera (USA) **J. A. Sayer**
4 **I'M YOUR MAN**, 6, gr g Bigstone (IRE)—Snowgirl (IRE) **Mrs H. D. Sayer**

Other Owners: Mr Arthur Slack, Mrs Evelyn Slack.

Assistant Trainer: Mr Andrew Sayer

526 DR J. D. SCARGILL, Newmarket
Postal: **Red House Stables, Hamilton Road, Newmarket, Suffolk, CB8 0TE.**
Contacts: **PHONE (01638) 663254 MOBILE (07785) 350705**

1 **ABSOLUTELY SOAKED (IRE)**, 4, b f Alhaarth (IRE)—Vasilopoula (IRE) **The Four April Fools**
2 **ASBO**, 5, b m Abou Zouz (USA)—Star **JPT Partnership**
3 **BOBBY CHARLES**, 4, ch g Polish Precedent (USA)—Dina Line (USA) **Silent Partners**
4 **BRONX BOMBER**, 7, ch g Prince Sabo—Super Yankee (IRE) **R. A. Dalton**
5 **RED SAIL**, 4, ch f Dr Fong (USA)—Manhattan Sunset (USA) **The Hadley Woodnot Partnership**
6 **SCARLETT ROSE**, 4, b f Royal Applause—Billie Blue **R. A. Dalton**

THREE-YEAR-OLDS

7 **GENERATOR**, ch c Cadeaux Genereux—Billie Blue **R. A. Dalton**
8 **SON ALTESSE**, b c Tipsy Creek (USA)—Fabulous Night (FR) **Rightbetter Partnership**
9 **TACID**, b f Diktat—Defined Feature (IRE) **Derek W. Johnson**

TWO-YEAR-OLDS

10 B c 17/4 Royal Applause—Billie Blue (Ballad Rock) **R. A. Dalton**
11 B f 2/4 Observatory (USA)—Jade Vine (IRE) (Alzao (USA)) (2000) **Stag Racing Partnership**

Other Owners: G. A. Brigford, Mrs M. Coppitters, R. A. Gladdis, E. Gibb-Low, Mrs E. Goudge, D. Mielton, Mrs M. Stanton, B. Watson, S. Wrightson, Mrs R. Watson, I. Wagstaffe, K. Ruttle, P. Mason, M. W. Bacon, G. F. L. Robinson, Mrs S. M. Scargill.

527 MR D. D. SCOTT, Minehead
Postal: **East Lynch, Minehead, Somerset, TA24 8SS.**
Contacts: **PHONE (01643) 702430**

1 **BESUTO (IRE)**, 8, br g Fourstars Allstar (USA)—Mabbots Own **Mrs D. D. Scott**
2 **IMPORTANT BOY (ARG)**, 8, ch g Equalize (USA)—Important Girl (ARG) **Mrs D. D. Scott**

528 MISS V. SCOTT, Newcastle Upon Tyne
Postal: **Soppitt Farm, Elsdon, Newcastle upon Tyne.**
Contacts: **PHONE (01830) 520038 OR (01830) 520930 FAX (01830) 520176**
WEBSITE www.scottracing@lineone.net

1 **AFTER GALWAY (IRE)**, 9, b g Camden Town—Money For Honey **A. Butler**
2 **BOX ON (IRE)**, 8, b br g Un Desperado (FR)—Party Dancer **A. Rice**
3 **DAWN DEVOY (IRE)**, 6, b g Supreme Leader—Dawn Hunt (IRE) **Miss V. Scott**
4 **DISPOL FOXTROT**, 7, ch m Alhijaz—Foxtrot Pie **Miss V. Scott**
5 **GROVE HOUSE**, 9, b g Hatim (USA)—Camden Grove
6 **I'M ROCK (IRE)**, 8, ch g Executive Perk—Give Me A Name **Mrs V. Scott**
7 **KINGSBURY (IRE)**, 6, b g Norwich—Glen Na Mban (IRE) **Miss V. Scott**
8 **LAZERITO (IRE)**, 7, b g Shernazar—Nemova (IRE) **A. Butler**
9 **LITTLE FLORA**, 9, ch m Alflora (IRE)—Sister's Choice **Mrs V. Scott**
10 **LITTLE SPORT (IRE)**, 8, ch g Moscow Society (USA)—Ath Dara **Mrs V. Scott**
11 **LOY'S LAD (IRE)**, 9, b g Glacial Storm (USA)—Missing Note **Miss V. Scott**
12 **MIDNIGHT CREEK**, 7, br g Tragic Role (USA)—Greek Night Out (IRE) **A. Butler**
13 **MY WEE WOMAN**, 6, ch m Alflora (IRE)—Just A Tipple (IRE) **Mrs V. Scott**
14 **ONTOS (GER)**, 9, b br g Super Abound (USA)—Onestep (GER) **Miss V. Scott**
15 **PENRIC**, 5, b g Marju (IRE)—Nafhaat (USA) **A. Butler**
16 **RAISE YOUR GLASS (IRE)**, 6, b br g Namaqualand (USA)—Toast And Honey (IRE) **Miss V. Scott**
17 **RATHLIN ISLAND**, 7, b g Carroll House—Mermaid Bay
18 **SENOR GIGO**, 7, b g Mistertopogigo (IRE)—Lady Carol **Mrs V. Scott**
19 **SNOOPY LOOPY (IRE)**, 7, ch g Old Vic—Lovely Snoopy (IRE) **Miss V. Scott**
20 **SUPREME DESTINY (IRE)**, 7, b g Supreme Leader—Shuil Le Gaoth (IRE) **A. Butler**
21 **TOUCH CLOSER**, 8, b g Inchinor—Ryewater Dream **Miss V. Scott**

Other Owners: Mr M. Abercrombie.

Assistant Trainer: Mr Craig Wanless

Jockey (NH): C. Williams, P. Flynn. **Conditional:** T. Davidson, T. Hamilton.

529 **MRS J. E. SCRASE, Pulborough**
Postal: **Scrase Farms, Pulborough, West Sussex, RH20 1DF.**
Contacts: PHONE **(01403) 700525 MOBILE (07789) 888013**

1 NELTINA, 9, gr m Neltino—Mimizan (IRE) **Mrs J. E. Scrase**
2 TINARANA GALE (IRE), 7, b m Mister Lord (USA)—Dozing Gal (IRE) **Mrs J. E. Scrase**

530 **MR B. SCRIVEN, Taunton**
Postal: **Cogload Farm, Durston, Taunton, Somerset, TA3 5AW.**
Contacts: PHONE **(01823) 490208**

1 JANDAL, 11, ch g Arazi (USA)—Littlefield **Mr B. Scriven**
2 PRINCE ON THE TER, 10, b g Terimon—Princess Constanza **Mr B. Scriven**

Assistant Trainer: Miss Kay Scriven

531 **MR M. J. SCUDAMORE, Hoarwithy**
Postal: **Eccleswall Court, Bromsash, Ross-On-Wye, Herefordshire, HR9 7PP.**
Contacts: PHONE **(01989) 750844 FAX (01989) 750281**
E-MAIL peter.scu@ic24.net

1 AFZAL ROSE, 5, b m Afzal—Fortria Rosie Dawn **M. J. and W. J. Fenn**
2 AMADEUS (AUS), 8, ch g Brief Truce (USA)—Amazaan (NZ) **Miss S. A. Howell**
3 ANGIE'S DOUBLE, 5, ch m Double Trigger (IRE)—Arch Angel (IRE) **Peter H. Wafford**
4 ARUMUN (IRE), 4, b g Posidonas—Adwoa (IRE)
5 ASTONVILLE (FR), 11, b g Top Ville—Astonishing (BRZ) **F. G. Wilson**
6 AUTUMN MIST (IRE), 10, br g Phardante (FR)—Sprinkling Star **Mrs N. M. Watkins**
7 BEAUCHAMP PRINCE (IRE), 4, gr g Beauchamp King—Katie Baggage (IRE) **The "Yes" - "No" - "Wait"....Sorries**
8 BOLLITREE BOB, 4, b g Bob's Return (IRE)—Lady Prunella (IRE) **Mrs P. de W. Johnson**
9 CABALLE (USA), 8, ch m Opening Verse (USA)—Attirance (FR) **Bernard S. Hicks**
10 CHINA MISS, 5, b m Thowra (FR)—Sherdon Hutch **The Flying Temple Partnership**
11 CLASSIC QUART (IRE), 4, b f Classic Cliche (IRE)—Ganpati (IRE) **Harpers Brook Racing**
12 COOLOURKID (IRE), 5, b g Zaffaran (USA)—Vintage Classic (IRE) **The Creative Tops Partnership**
13 DARK RUM, 9, b g Hubbly Bubbly (USA)—Rose Sauvage **Mrs J. McLaughlin**
14 FINZI (IRE), 7, b g Zaffaran (USA)—Sporting Talent (IRE) **The Meld Partnership**
15 FRIXOS (IRE), 5, ch g Barathea (IRE)—Local Lass **The "Yes" - "No" - "Wait"....Sorries**
16 GAYE DREAM, 7, b g Gildoran—Gaye Fame **Mrs S. I. Tainton**
17 GRACE DIEU, 4, gr f Commanche Run—Race To The Rhythm **Run For Fun**
18 HELTORNIC (IRE), 5, ch m Zaffaran (USA)—Majestic Run **S. W. Molloy**
19 IDLE JOURNEY (IRE), 4, b g Mujadil—Camassina (IRE) **Mrs N. M. Watkins**
20 4, b g Fayruz—Iva's Flyer (IRE) **Mrs N. M. Watkins**
21 JANBRE (IRE), 6, br g Zaffaran (USA)—Black Gayle (IRE) **Granite By Design Ltd**
22 JIVER (IRE), 6, b g Flemensfirth (USA)—Choice Brush (IRE) **Mrs S. I. Tainton**
23 JOURNAL PRINCESS (IRE), 6, b m Zaffaran (USA)—Bramble Hatch **Hereford Journal Racing Club**
24 JUST TEN MINUTES, 5, ch g Atraf—Sabeel **S. W. Molloy**
25 LADY OF SCARVAGH (IRE), 6, b m Zaffaran (USA)—Dim Drums **The Meld Partnership**
26 MYSTIC KING, 4, b g Rakaposhi King—Just Lynn **E. W. Moss**
27 NORSEMAN CATELINE (FR), 4, b g Poplar Bluff—Dame Jaune (FR) **The "Yes" - "No" - "Wait"....Sorries**
28 NOTANOTHERDONKEY (IRE), 5, b g Zaffaran (USA)—Sporting Talent (IRE) **N. J. Ponting**
29 OLD GINGER (IRE), 5, ch g Zaffaran (USA)—Most Effective (IRE) **Mrs S. I. Tainton**
30 OUI EXIT (FR), 4, b g Exit To Nowhere (USA)—Forest Hills (FR) **Mr F. J. Mills & Mr W. Mills**
31 PRESENT BLEU (FR), 10, b g Epervier Bleu—Lointaine (FR) **F. G. Wilson**
32 RETRO'S GIRL (IRE), 4, ch f Zaffaran (USA)—Highland Chain **Retro's Again**
33 SCHOOL CLASS, 5, b m Classic Cliche (IRE)—School Run **Mrs S. I. Tainton**
34 SHAAMIT THE VAAMIT (IRE), 5, b g Shaamit (IRE)—Shocker (IRE) **Mrs S. I. Tainton**
35 SILLY MISS OFF (IRE), 4, b f Clerkenwell (USA)—Little Hulton **The "Yes" - "No" - "Wait"....Sorries**
36 SOLARIUS (FR), 8, ch g Kris—Nouvelle Lune (FR) **F. G. Wilson**
37 SOME TIMBERING (IRE), 6, b g Accordion—Hard Buns (IRE) **Mrs N. M. Watkins**
38 SOUTH SANDS (IRE), 4, b f Shaamit (IRE)—Mariners Mirror **The Select Few Syndicate**
39 SPEEDY RICHARD (IRE), 5, ch g Zaffaran (USA)—Chadandy (USA) **S. W. Molloy**
40 STAR TIME (IRE), 6, b g Fourstars Allstar (USA)—Punctual **successracing.com**
41 SUMMIT UP (IRE), 5, b g Zaffaran (USA)—Summit Else **Mrs S. I. Tainton**
42 THE VILLAGER (IRE), 9, br g Zaffaran (USA)—Kitty Wren **Mrs S. I. Tainton**
43 TORCHE (IRE), 7, b g Taos (IRE)—Orchette (IRE) **Mrs S. I. Tainton**
44 TURNIUM (FR), 10, b br g Turgeon (USA)—Royal Mia (FR) **F. G. Wilson**

MR M. J. SCUDAMORE—continued

45 **VIVRE AIMER RIRE (FR)**, 4, b f Cyborg (FR)—Badj II (FR) **Mr F. J. Mills & Mr W. Mills**
46 **WILD TEMPO (FR)**, 10, ch g Irish River (FR)—Fast Queen **F. G. Wilson**
47 **ZAFFAS MELODY (IRE)**, 5, ch g Zaffaran (USA)—Orchette (IRE) **Mrs S. I. Tainton**

Other Owners: Mr E. J. Arthey, A. Brush, W. R. Chudley, C. S. J. Coley, M. Court, A. M. E. Davis, Mrs P. A. Dawson, Mr J. A. Driver, Mrs S. J. Faulks, Mr N. J. Faulks, Mr P. Henchoz, D. M. Hussey, Mr N. R. Lawrence, Mr T. R. Lowe, C. D. Osborne, Ms N. J. Overton, J. M. Robinson, Mrs L. J. Sluman, W. E. Smith.

Assistant Trainer: Peter Scudamore

Jockey (NH): T. Scudamore. **Amateur:** Mr John Kington.

---

532 **MR I. SEMPLE, Carluke**
Postal: Belstane Racing Stables, Belstane Road, Carluke, Strathclyde, ML8 5HN.
Contacts: **PHONE (01555) 773335 FAX (01555) 772243 MOBILE (07788) 150969**

1 **APPALACHIAN TRAIL (IRE)**, 4, b g Indian Ridge—Karinski (USA) **G L S Partnership**
2 **BANDOS**, 5, ch g Cayman Kai (IRE)—Lekuti **J. O. Hall, Ken Topham, Linda Straker**
3 **BESSEMER (JPN)**, 4, b g Carnegie (IRE)—Chalna (IRE) **C. Boon**
4 **BIJOU DAN**, 4, ch g Bijou d'inde—Cal Norma's Lady **Belstane Racing - Greens Commitee**
5 **CHERISHED NUMBER**, 6, b g King's Signet (USA)—Pretty Average **Joseph Leckie & Sons Ltd**
6 **CHOOKIE HEITON (IRE)**, 7, br g Fumo di Londra (IRE)—Royal Wolff **Hamilton Park Members Syndicate**
7 **EASIBET DOT NET**, 5, gr g Atraf—Silvery **www.easibet.net Limited**
8 **JORDANS ELECT**, 5, ch g Fleetwood (IRE)—Cal Norma's Lady (IRE) **I. Crawford**
9 **JORDANS SPARK**, 4, ch g Opening Verse (USA)—Ribot's Pearl **Ian Crawford & Brian Jordan Jnr**
10 **KALANI STAR (IRE)**, 5, b h Ashkalani (IRE)—Bellissi **Ecosse Racing**
11 **MILLAGROS (IRE)**, 5, b m Pennekamp (USA)—Grey Galava **J. A. Cringan**
12 **MISTER MARMADUKE**, 4, b g Marju (IRE)—Lalique (IRE) **Mrs J. Delaney**
13 **MORNIN RESERVES**, 6, b g Atraf—Pusey Street Girl **W. G. Harrison**
14 **SAAMEQ (IRE)**, 4, b g Bahhare (USA)—Tajawuz **D. Irvine**
15 **SARRAAF (IRE)**, 9, ch g Perugino (USA)—Blue Vista (IRE) **G. McDowall**
16 **TEMPLET (USA)**, 5, b g Souvenir Copy (USA)—Two Step Trudy (USA) **J. and J. Hunter**
17 **THE NUMBER**, 4, gr g Silver Wizard (USA)—Elite Number (USA) **The Greens Committee**
18 **TRICKSTEP**, 4, b g Imperial Ballet (IRE)—Trick of Ace (USA) **Market Avenue Racing Club Ltd**
19 **ULYSEES (IRE)**, 6, b g Turtle Island (IRE)—Tamasriya (USA) **The Farmer Boys (Jock, Danny & Ally)**
20 **VIEWFORTH**, 7, b g Emarati (USA)—Miriam **G. McDowall**
21 **WEST HIGHLAND WAY (IRE)**, 4, b g Foxhound (USA)—Gilding The Lily (IRE) **Laumar Racing**

THREE-YEAR-OLDS

22 **DEFI (IRE)**, b c Rainbow Quest (USA)—Danse Classique (IRE) **G. McDowall**
23 **HANDSOME LADY**, ch f Handsome Ridge—Il Doria (IRE) **D. A. Platt**
24 **HOWARDS PRINCESS**, gr f Lujain (USA)—Grey Princess **G. McDowall**
25 **KAMES PARK (IRE)**, b g Desert Sun—Persian Sally (IRE) **Mrs J. Delaney**
26 **MINTLAW**, b f Mujahid (USA)—Rynavey **The Duchess of Sutherland**
27 **REAL QUALITY (USA)**, b g Elusive Quality (USA)—Pleasant Prize (USA) **D. L. McKenzie**
28 **TAYSIDE MOVER**, b g Namaqualand (USA)—Pretty Average **Mr W. Robinson**
29 **TOSHI (USA)**, b c Kingmambo (USA)—Majestic Role (FR) **G L S Partnership**

TWO-YEAR-OLDS

30 B c 29/4 Josr Algarhoud (IRE)—Belle de Nuit (IRE) (Statoblest) (11000) **Mrs J. M. MacPherson**
31 B g 2/4 Easycall—Bouchra (IRE) (Inchinor) **G. McDowall**
32 B g 20/4 Shinko Forest (IRE)—Dashing Rocksville (Rock City) (7377) **Robin Galbraith**
33 B f 21/3 Royal Applause—Elegant Lady (Selkirk (USA)) **D. A. Platt**
34 Gr g 16/3 Bertolini (USA)—Grey Princess (IRE) (Common Grounds) (32000) **G. McDowall**
35 B g 27/3 Mister Baileys—Inimitable (Polish Precedent (USA))
36 B f 7/3 Diktat—Jay Gee Ell (Vaigly Great) (6000) **Raeburn Brick Limited**
37 B f 28/4 Danetime (IRE)—Jellybeen (IRE) (Petardia) (7377) **G L S Partnership**
38 B g 20/3 Lake Coniston (IRE)—
          Lady of Windsor (IRE) (Woods of Windsor (USA)) **Hamilton Park Members Syndicate**

MR I. SEMPLE—continued

39 B f 18/4 Diktat—Pearl Venture (Salse (USA)) (10500) **Mrs J. M. MacPherson**
40 B f 10/4 Beckett (IRE)—Romangoddess (IRE) (Rhoman Rule (USA)) (4694)

Other Owners: J. F. Allan, W. Brand, I. M. Buchan, P. J. Burns, W. Docherty, Mr A. Fletcher, L. H. Gilmurray, Mr B. Johnstone, B. Jordan, Mr G. R. Leckie, P. H. Marron, A. C. Mathieson, Mrs H. G. Peplinski, Mrs R. C. Platt, Mr G. Pritchard, J. M. Raeburn, D. G. Savala, J. Smith, Mr R. K. Walkinshaw.

Jockey (flat): P. Hanagan, R. Winston. **Apprentice:** T. Eaves. **Amateur:** Mr J. McShane.

533　**MR A. SENIOR, Macclesfield**
Postal: **The Stables, Oak Lane, Kerridge, Macclesfield, Cheshire, SK10 5AP.**
Contacts: **PHONE (01625) 575735 FAX (01625) 575735 MOBILE (07837) 083285**
E-MAIL asenior99@tesco.net

1 BRANTWOOD (IRE), 5, b g Lake Coniston (IRE)—Angelic Sounds (IRE) **Mr A. Senior**
2 EXPULSION (USA), 4, b f Expelled (USA)—Solar Beam (USA) **Mr A. Senior**
3 MISTBLACK, 5, b m Wizard King—Dear Heart **C. C. Etridge**
4 RAETIHI, 4, b f Wizard King—Foreno **Miss S. L. Fagg**

THREE-YEAR-OLDS

5 FLY ME TO DUNOON (IRE), b f Rossini (USA)—Toledana (IRE) **Mr A. Senior**

TWO-YEAR-OLDS

6 B f 15/3 Mujahid (USA)—Arctic Guest (IRE) (Arctic Tern (USA)) (1000) **Mr A. Senior**
7 Br f 7/4 Averti (IRE)—Prima Venture (Pursuit of Love) (800) **Mr A. Senior**

Other Owners: Mr D. McGarvey, Elliot and Jackson Partnership, M. Duffy, George Maher.

534　**MRS N. S. SHARPE, Abergavenny**
Postal: **Penbiddle Farm, Penbidwal, Pandy, Abergavenny, Gwent, NP7 8EA.**
Contacts: **PHONE/FAX (01873) 890957 MOBILE (07977) 753437**
E-MAIL nikki@penbiddle.fsnet.co.uk WEBSITE www.penbiddleracing.co.uk

1 ARNBI DANCER, 6, b g Presidium—Travel Myth **P. T. Evans**
2 BUCKSKIN LAD (IRE), 10, b br g Buckskin (FR)—Loverush **Mr & Mrs P. Evans**
3 CONNEMARA MIST (IRE), 10, ch g Good Thyne (USA)—Rainys Run **Thomas Healy**
4 ETERNAL NIGHT (FR), 9, b g Night Shift (USA)—Echoes of Eternity (USA) **J. Pritchard**
5 HELL OF A TIME (IRE), 8, b g Phardante (FR)—Ticking Over (USA) **T. I. Thomas**
6 ILLINEYLAD (IRE), 11, b g Whitehall Bridge—Illiney Girl **The Illiney Group**
7 MCMAHON'S BROOK, 6, br g Alderbrook—McMahon's River **Mrs M. E. Gittings-Watts**
8 RED ACER (IRE), 4, ch g Shinko Forest (IRE)—Another Baileys **Mrs M. E. Gittings-Watts**
9 THE CROPPY BOY, 13, b g Arctic Lord—Deep Cut **Mrs N. S. Sharpe**
10 THE PECKER DUNN (IRE), 11, b g Be My Native (USA)—Riversdale Shadow **The Illiney Group**
11 TRICKY THYNE (IRE), 6, b g Good Thyne (USA)—Cuban Vacation **T. M. T. Racing**

THREE-YEAR-OLDS

12 Ch g Classic Cliche (IRE)—McMahon's River **Mrs S. Davenport**

Other Owners: Mr E. A. McGuinness, Mr J. Rawling, J. V. C. Davenport, Mr D. Wallis, Mr M. J. Dent, D. P. Stanton, Mr A. Treanor.

Jockey (flat): Joanna Badger. **Jockey (NH):** J. Mogford.

535　**MR D. SHAW, Newark**
Postal: **Stubby Nook Lodge, Danethorpe Lane, Danethorpe, Newark, Nottinghamshire, NG24 2PD.**
Contacts: **PHONE (01636) 605683 MOBILE (07721) 039645**
E-MAIL derek.shaw@tiscali.co.uk

1 A BID IN TIME (IRE), 4, b f Danetime (IRE)—Bidni (IRE) **Danethorpe Racing Ltd**
2 ARCTIC BURST (USA), 5, b br g Royal Academy (USA)—Polar Bird **Danethorpe Racing Ltd**
3 CHARNWOOD STREET (IRE), 6, b g Charnwood Forest (IRE)—La Vigie **Danethorpe Racing Ltd**

MR D. SHAW—continued

4 **DESERT LIGHT (IRE)**, 4, b c Desert Sun—Nacote (IRE) **Danethorpe Racing Ltd**
5 **HAITHEM (IRE)**, 8, b g Mtoto—Wukk (IRE) **Century Racing**
6 **LADIES KNIGHT**, 5, b g Among Men (USA)—Lady Silk **Danethorpe Racing Ltd**
7 **LONG WEEKEND (IRE)**, 7, b g Flying Spur (AUS)—Friday Night (USA) **The Marlow Lewin Partnership**
8 **LUCIUS VERRUS (USA)**, 5, b g Danzig—Magic of Life (USA) **Danethorpe Racing Ltd**
9 **MUKTASB (USA)**, 4, b g Bahri—Maghaarb **Danethorpe Racing Ltd**
10 **MUTARAFAA (USA)**, 6, b g Red Ransom (USA)—Mashaarif (USA) **Simon Mapletoft Racing I**
11 **OASES**, 4, ch g Zilzal (USA)—Markievicz (IRE) **The Whiteman Partnership**
12 **PARK STAR**, 5, b m Gothenberg (IRE)—Miriam **S. J. Woods**
13 **PARKVIEW LOVE (USA)**, 4, b br c Mister Baileys—Jerre Jo Glanville (USA) **Danethorpe Racing Ltd**
14 **PHAROAH'S GOLD (IRE)**, 7, b g Namaqualand (USA)—Queen Nefertiti (IRE) **The Whiteman Partnership**
15 **PRINCE OF PERLES**, 4, b g Mind Games—Pearls **N. P. Franklin**
16 **SAHARA SILK (IRE)**, 4, b f Desert Style (IRE)—Buddy And Soda (IRE) **Danethorpe Racing Ltd**
17 **SEA THE WORLD (IRE)**, 5, b g Inzar (USA)—Annie's Travels (IRE) **Danethorpe Racing Ltd**
18 **SIR ERNEST (IRE)**, 4, b g Daggers Drawn (USA)—Kyra Crown (IRE) **G. A. Lucas**
19 **SO SOBER (IRE)**, 7, b g Common Grounds—Femme Savante **Danethorpe Racing Ltd**
20 **STATE DILEMMA (IRE)**, 4, b c Green Desert (USA)—Nuriva (USA) **Danethorpe Racing Ltd**
21 **STATOYORK**, 12, b g Statoblest—Ultimate Dream **N. P. Franklin**
22 **TATWEER (IRE)**, 5, b g Among Men (USA)—Sandystones **Danethorpe Racing Ltd**
23 **TROPICAL SON**, 6, b g Distant Relative—Douce Maison (IRE) **Danethorpe Racing Ltd**
24 **WITCHCRAFT**, 4, b g Zilzal (USA)—Witch of Fife (USA) **Mrs B. E. Wilkinson**

THREE-YEAR-OLDS

25 **BAHAMIAN SPRING (IRE)**, b g Danehill Dancer (IRE)—Siana Springs (IRE) **N. P. Franklin**
26 **BENTLEY**, b c Atraf—Prim Lass **Danethorpe Racing Ltd**
27 **CLOANN (IRE)**, b f Danetime (IRE)—Rustic Lawn **Danethorpe Racing Ltd**
28 **COOL SANDS (IRE)**, b c Trans Island—Shalerina (USA) **P. Swann**
29 **CUT BACK**, ch f Factual (USA)—Mamoda **M. C. Wainman**
30 **DANETHORPE LADY (IRE)**, b f Brave Act—Annie's Travels (IRE) **Mrs B. E. Wilkinson**
31 **ICE RUBY**, b f Polar Prince (IRE)—Simply Style **Danethorpe Racing Ltd**
32 **MADAM BIJOU**, b f Atraf—Madame Sisu **N. P. Franklin**
33 **MYTORI**, ch f Vettori (IRE)—Markievicz (IRE) **The Whiteman Partnership**
34 **ROKO**, b g Komaite (USA)—Robert's Daughter **K. Nicholls**
35 **SAHARA MIST (IRE)**, b f Desert Style (IRE)—Tereed Elhawa **Danethorpe Racing Ltd**
36 **SAHARA SUNSET (IRE)**, b f Desert Style (IRE)—Ervedya (IRE) **Danethorpe Racing Ltd**
37 **TARTATARTUFATA**, b f Tagula (IRE)—It's So Easy **Danethorpe Racing Ltd**

TWO-YEAR-OLDS

38 B f 5/5 Celtic Swing—Acicula (IRE) (Night Shift (USA))
39 B f 19/2 Revoque (IRE)—Buddy And Soda (IRE) (Imperial Frontier (USA)) (3500) **Danethorpe Racing Ltd**
40 Ch c 25/3 Forest Wildcat (USA)—Dahlia's Krissy (USA) (Kris S (USA)) (18000) **Danethorpe Racing Ltd**
41 B f 14/4 King's Best (USA)—Filly Mignonne (IRE) (Nashwan (USA)) (21000) **Danethorpe Racing Ltd**
42 Br f 22/3 Averti (IRE)—Island Mead (Pharly (FR)) (16000) **N. P. Franklin**
43 Ch c 27/3 Allied Forces (USA)—Kildine (IRE) (Common Grounds) (2000) **Danethorpe Racing Ltd**
44 B c 22/4 Imperial Ballet (IRE)—Kurfuffle (Bluebird (USA)) (21000) **Danethorpe Racing Ltd**
45 B c 2/3 Royal Applause—La Caprice (Housebuster (USA)) (40000) **Mrs B. E. Wilkinson**
46 B c 28/3 Cape Cross (IRE)—There's Two (IRE) (Ashkalani (IRE)) (24000) **Danethorpe Racing Ltd**
47 B c 16/4 Bertolini (USA)—Tight Spin (High Top) (16000) **Mrs B. E. Wilkinson**
48 B c 28/4 Monashee Mountain (USA)—Waroonga (IRE) (Brief Truce (USA)) (17000) **Danethorpe Racing Ltd**

Other Owners: Mr R. A. Hill, Mr A. Hurst, Mr G. M. Langthorne, Mr D. A. Lees, R. Lewin, S. A. Mapletoft, Mrs J. Mapletoft, Mrs D. A. Marlow, P. A. Whiteman, S. A. Whiteman.

Jockey (flat): N. Callan, J. Fanning, S. Whitworth, Darren Williams. **Amateur:** Mrs M. Morris.

---

536 | **MR M. I. SHEPPARD, Ledbury**
Postal: **Home Farm Cottage, Eastnor, Ledbury, Herefordshire, HR8 1RD.**
Contacts: **FAX (01531) 634846 MOBILE (07770) 625061**
E-MAIL matthew.sheppard1@btopenworld.com

1 **CRUSTY MISS**, 6, b m Chaddleworth (IRE)—Miss Crusty **L. H. Ballinger**
2 **DELICEO (IRE)**, 12, br g Roselier (FR)—Grey's Delight **The Blues Partnership**
3 **DESERT CITY**, 6, b g Darnay—Oasis **G. C. Jones**
4 **GREENAWN (IRE)**, 6, ch g Anshan—Arctic Bead (IRE) **S. J. D. Gegg**

MR M. I. SHEPPARD—continued

5　**MR TENPERCENT**, 9, gr g Gran Alba (USA)—Chatty Corner **Mr H. J. Pugh**
6　**SMILE PLEEZE (IRE)**, 13, b g Naheez (USA)—Harkin Park **Miss S. Troughton**
7　**SOLEIL D'HIVER**, 4, b f Bahamian Bounty—Catriona **Out Of Bounds Racing Club**
8　**WELSH DANE**, 5, b g Chaddleworth—Dane Rose **K. Jones**

Other Owners: M. R. Bown, Mr M. E. Harris, Mr C. A. Jarman, Mr P. Turner.

537　**MR O. M. C. SHERWOOD, Upper Lambourn**
Postal: **Rhonehurst House, Upper Lambourn, Hungerford, Berkshire, RG17 8RG.**
Contacts: **PHONE (01488) 71411 FAX (01488) 72786 MOBILE (07979) 591867**
E-MAIL oliver.sherwood@virgin.net WEBSITE www.oliversherwood.com

1　**ARMAGEDDON**, 8, b g Deploy—Arusha (IRE) **R. C. Tooth**
2　**ARRAYOU (FR)**, 4, b g Valanjou (FR)—Cavatine (FR) **J. P. Ledwidge**
3　**BEL OMBRE (FR)**, 5, b g Nikos—Danse du Soleil (FR) **P. A. Deal, J. Tyndall, M. St Quinton**
4　**CELESTIAL HEIGHTS (IRE)**, 6, b g Fourstars Allstar (USA)—Aon Dochas (IRE) **Ledwidge Best Fforde**
5　**CLAYMORE (IRE)**, 9, b g Broadsword (USA)—Mazza **B. T. Stewart-Brown Esq**
6　**CONQUEROR**, 5, b g Supreme Leader—Call of The Night (IRE) **R. C. Tooth**
7　**CREINCH**, 4, b g Overbury (IRE)—Kingsfold Blaze **B. T. Stewart-Brown Esq**
8　**DANBURY (FR)**, 5, b g Lost World (IRE)—Dany Ohio (FR) **The St Joseph Partnership**
9　**EARL OF SPECTRUM (GER)**, 4, b g Spectrum (IRE)—Evry (GER) **The Second Kennet Partnership**
10　**ERIC'S CHARM (FR)**, 7, b g Nikos—Ladoun (FR) **M. St Quinton & P. A. Deal**
11　**FANTASMIC**, 9, ch g Broadsword (USA)—Squeaky Cottage **A. L. Cohen**
12　**FARNAHEEZVIEW (IRE)**, 7, b g Naheez (USA)—Sweet View **Mccarthy Keogh Booth & Ray Partnership**
13　4, B f Master Willie—General Comment (IRE) **P. A. Deal**
14　**GENEROUS SPIRIT (IRE)**, 4, ch g Cadeaux Genereux—Miss Rossi **J. Palmer-Brown**
15　**HARPASGON DE L'OMBRE (FR)**, 10, b g Mbaiki (FR)—Undress (FR) **It Wasn't Us**
16　**JENGA**, 8, ro m Minster Son—Maybe Daisy **Mr J. Loudon**
17　**KAUSSE DE THAIX (FR)**, 7, ch g Iris Noir (FR)—Etoile de Thaix (FR) **A. L. Cohen**
18　**KOHINOR**, 6, b m Supreme Leader—Always Shining **The Kohinor Partnership**
19　4, B f Hernando (FR)—Lemon's Mill (USA) **Roger Waters**
20　**LYON**, 5, ch g Pivotal—French Gift **R. C. Tooth**
21　**MANORSON (IRE)**, 6, ch g Desert King (IRE)—Familiar (USA) **Byrne Bros (Formwork) Limited**
22　**MINI DARE (IRE)**, 8, b g Derrylin—Minim **Furrows Ltd,Mr A. Douglas & Mrs S.Bridge**
23　**MISTLETOE (IRE)**, 11, gr m Montelimar (USA)—Nancy's Sister **Mrs E. M. F. Loudon**
24　**MONTY'S DOUBLE (IRE)**, 8, b g Montelimar (USA)—Macamore Rose **W. S. Watt**
25　4, B c Silver Patriarch (USA)—Mossy Fern **Roger Waters**
26　**ONCE SEEN**, 5, b g Celtic Swing—Brief Glimpse (IRE) **R. Fallon & Associates**
27　**REASONABLY SURE (IRE)**, 5, b g Presenting—No Reason **Million in Mind Partnership**
28　**RODALKO (FR)**, 7, b g Kadalko (FR)—Darling Rose (FR) **J. Palmer-Brown**
29　**SADLER'S LAMP (IRE)**, 6, b g Pierre—Kyle Lamp (IRE) **Martin Collins And Andrew Collins**
30　**SAMBY**, 7, ch g Anshan—Mossy Fern **Roger Waters**
31　**SECRET DRINKER (IRE)**, 9, b g Husyan (USA)—Try Le Reste (IRE) **I. Harfitt**
32　**SUPER ROAD TRAIN**, 6, b g Petoski—Foehn Gale (IRE) **D. B. Knox**
33　**SUPERROLLERCOASTER**, 5, b g Classic Cliche (IRE)—Foehn Gale (IRE) **D. B. Knox**
34　**SURPRISING**, 10, b g Primitive Rising (USA)—Ascot Lass **M. St Quinton**
35　**THE LYME VOLUNTEER (IRE)**, 8, b m Zaffaran (USA)—Dooley O'brien **The Chamberlain Addiscott Partnership**
36　5, Ch m Un Desperado (FR)—The Vine Browne (IRE) **J. P. Ledwidge**
37　**TIK-A-TAI (IRE)**, 10, b g Alphabatim (USA)—Carrig Ross **The Chamberlain Addiscott Partnership**
38　5, Br g Supreme Leader—Tullahought **Mr O. M. C. Sherwood**
39　**TYTHEKNOT**, 4, b g Pursuit of Love—Bundled Up (USA) **R Fallon & Associates**
40　**VALLEYOFTHEKINGS (IRE)**, 4, b g Beauchamp King—Nell Valley **Chris Munro**
41　**WINSLEY**, 7, gr g Sula Bula—Dissolve **Absolute Solvents Ltd**

Other Owners: Mr W. J. Bridge, Mr J. Ferraud, Mr M. Hartley, Mrs D. L. Addiscott, G. Addiscott, R. J. Bassett, J. C. Best, C. G. R. Booth, A. R. Bromley, Mrs P. C. Chamberlain, N. J. Chamberlain, P. Chapman, J. M. Dougall, J. G. Ferrand, G. F. Goode, T. C. Hartley, R. A. Keogh, Mrs A. T. Lambert, J. McCarthy, W. D. C. Minton, David Nicholson, MR J. O'Keeffe, H. M. J. Pope, Mr G. Ray, Mrs A. Ray, A. Walker, V. J. Walsh.

Jockey (NH): J. A. McCarthy. **Conditional:** O. Nelmes.

538   MR S. E. H. SHERWOOD, Bromyard
Postal: **The Day House, Bredenbury, Bromyard, Herefordshire, HR7 4TL.**
Contacts: **OFFICE (01885) 488567 FAX (01885) 488677 MOBILE (07836) 215639**
E-MAIL seh.sherwood@virgin.net

1 **ALL THINGS EQUAL (IRE)**, 6, b g Supreme Leader—Angel's Dream **J. R. Hales**
2 **IL'ATHOU (FR)**, 9, b g Lute Antique (FR)—Va Thou Line (FR) **Lady Thompson**
3 **ISARD DU BUARD (FR)**, 9, b g April Night (FR)—Upsala du Buard (FR) **Lady Thompson**
4 **LAURIER D'ESTRUVAL (FR)**, 8, ch g Ragmar (FR)—Grive d'estruval (FR) **T. N. Siviter**
5 **LUMYNO (FR)**, 6, b g Lute Antique (FR)—Framboline (FR) **Ms Y. S. Kennedy**
6 **MISTER BANJO (FR)**, 9, b g Mister Mat (FR)—Migre (FR) **J. R. Hales**
7 **ON THE OUTSIDE (IRE)**, 6, ch m Anshan—Kate Fisher (IRE) **G. C. Vos**
8 **PENDIL'S PRINCESS**, b m Afzal—Pendil's Delight **N. F. Williams**
9 **ROBBIE'S RETURN**, 6, b g Bob's Return (IRE)—Si-Gaoith **J. R. Hales**
10 **SHUFFLING PALS (IRE)**, 8, b g Roselier (FR)—Penny Shuffle (IRE) **Strachan,Boyne & Farrar**

Other Owners: Miss L. J. Hales.

Jockey (NH): J. Tizzard. **Amateur:** Mr R. Hodges.

539   MR S. H. SHIRLEY-BEAVAN, Hawick
Postal: **Gatehousecote, Bonchester Bridge, Hawick, Roxburghshire, TD9 8JD.**
Contacts: **PHONE (01450) 860210**

1 **JUNIOR DES ORMEAUX (FR)**, 8, b g Baby Turk—Chic d'estruval(FR) **Mrs P. M. Shirley-Beavan**
2 **MANOUCHKY (FR)**, 5, b br g Lute Antique (FR)—Olga Melody (FR) **Mrs P. M. Shirley-Beavan**
3 **MINOUCHKA (FR)**, 5, b br m Bulington (FR)—Elbury (FR) **Mrs P. M. Shirley-Beavan**
4 **THEMANFROMCARLISLE**, 9, br g Jupiter Island—Country Mistress **Mrs P. M. Shirley-Beavan**

540   MISS L. C. SIDDALL, Tadcaster
Postal: **Stonebridge Farm, Colton, Tadcaster, North Yorkshire, LS24 8EP.**
Contacts: **PHONE (01904) 744291 FAX (01904) 744291 MOBILE (07778) 216692/4**

1 **BENEFIT**, 11, b g Primitive Rising (USA)—Sobriquet **Mrs D. Ibbotson**
2 **CANTYS BRIG (IRE)**, 8, gr g Roselier (FR)—Call Catherine (IRE) **Mrs D. Ibbotson**
3 **CARMARTHEN BELLE**, 5, b m Merdon Melody—Woodland Steps **Stonebridge Racing**
4 **DAY DU ROY (FR)**, 7, b g Ajdayt (USA)—Rose Pomme (FR) **Norman Webb & Geoff Kennington**
5 **EXPLODE**, 8, b g Zafonic (USA)—Didicoy (USA) **Lynn Siddall Racing II**
6 **GRENADIER (IRE)**, 8, b g Sadler's Wells (USA)—Sandhurst Goddess **Podso Racing**
7 **LAZY LENA (IRE)**, 6, b m Oscar (IRE)—Magnum Gale (IRE) **Mrs T. O'Toole**
8 **LEAHSTAR**, 6, ch m In The Wings—Moondance **Mrs D. J. Morris**
9 **MERLIN'S CITY**, 5, b m Merdon Melody—Sharp Ego (USA) **Stonebridge Racing**
10 **MONTE ROUGE (IRE)**, 8, ch g Montelimar (USA)—Drumdeels Star (IRE) **The Full Monte**
11 **MR CHRISTIE**, 13, b g Doulab (USA)—Hi There **Lynn Siddall Racing**
12 5, B m Brief Truce (USA)—Perfect Answer **Mrs T. O'Toole**
13 **PLUMIER (FR)**, 7, b g Beyssac (FR)—Plume Rose (FR) **Kennington And Quorn**
14 **SILENT SNIPE**, 12, ch g Jendali (USA)—Sasol **Mrs D. Ibbotson**
15 **SUPER BOSTON**, 5, b g Saddlers' Hall (IRE)—Nasowas (IRE) **M. K. Oldham**

Other Owners: Miss S. Vinden, Miss S. Lythe, I. Grice, D. McGhee, A. Buxton, Mrs P. J. Clark, Mrs E. W. Cooper, A. J. Emmerson, Mrs P. M. Hornby, D. Mann.

Assistant Trainer: Stephen Hackney

Jockey (NH): T. Siddall.

541 MR D. M. I. SIMCOCK, Newmarket

Postal: **The Office, Trillium Place, Birdcage Walk, Newmarket, Suffolk, CB8 0NE.**
Contacts: **PHONE/FAX (01638) 662968 MOBILE (07808) 954109**
E-MAIL davidsimcock@ukonline.co.uk

1 **CUT AND DRIED,** 4, ch g Daggers Drawn (USA)—Apple Sauce
2 **DARK SHAH (IRE),** 5, b g Night Shift (USA)—Shanjah
3 **ENSEMBLE,** 5, b g Polish Precedent (USA)—Full Orchestra
4 **SILVER CHIME,** 5, gr m Robellino (USA)—Silver Charm

THREE-YEAR-OLDS

5 **CAUSEWAY GIRL (IRE),** br f Giant's Causeway (USA)—Darbela (IRE)
6 **CAYENNE (GER),** ch f Efisio—Carola Rouge
7 **DAISY BUCKET,** b f Lujain (USA)—Masrora (USA)
8 **DAMBURGER XPRESS,** b c Josr Algarhoud (IRE)—Upping The Tempo
9 **ELISHA (IRE),** ch f Raise A Grand (IRE)—Social Butterfly (USA)
10 **KATY JEM,** b f Night Shift (USA)—Top Jem
11 **ROBESON,** br g Primo Dominie—Montserrat
12 **VALIANT ACT (IRE),** b f Brave Act—Jungle Story (IRE)
13 **XTRA TORRENTIAL (USA),** b c Torrential (USA)—Offering (USA)

TWO-YEAR-OLDS

14 Ch c 2/2 Elusive Quality (USA)—Big Blue Bird (USA) (Storm Bird (CAN)) (48000)
15 B c 20/4 Alzao (USA)—Deft Touch (IRE) (Desert Style (IRE)) (15500)
16 B f 28/2 Singspiel (IRE)—Jaljuli (Jalmood (USA)) (15000)
17 B c 13/2 Lujain (USA)—Licence To Thrill (Wolfhound (USA)) (30000)
18 B f 2/4 Dixieland Band (USA)—Long View (USA) (Damascus (USA))
19 Ch f 5/3 Magic Ring (IRE)—Lyssage (Lycius (USA)) (3200)
20 **OMNEYA,** b f 3/2 Mister Baileys—Silent Miracle (IRE) (Night Shift (USA))
21 **PARK LANE PRINCESS (IRE),** ch f 17/3 King of Kings (IRE)—Heated Debate (USA) (Woodman (USA)) (11500)
22 Ch c 20/4 Dr Fong (USA)—Preceder (Polish Precedent (USA)) (10000)
23 B c 6/4 Distant Music (USA)—Snowspin (Carwhite) (10000)
24 B c 17/4 Piccolo—Whistfilly (First Trump) (19000)
25 Ch f 4/3 Piccolo—Zabelina (USA) (Diesis) (7000)

Jockey (flat): M. J. Dwyer.

---

542 MRS P. M. SLY, Peterborough

Postal: **Singlecote, Thorney, Peterborough, Cambridgeshire, PE6 0PB.**
Contacts: **PHONE (01733) 270212 MOBILE (07850) 511267**

1 **ALLSTARS BLAZING (IRE),** 5, b g Fourstars Allstar (USA)—Heather Blazing (IRE) **Mr J. Sargeant**
2 **BEULAH,** 4, b f Perpendicular—Ewe Lamb **Mrs P. M. Sly**
3 **BONNET'S PIECES,** 6, b m Alderbrook—Chichell's Hurst **The Stablemates II**
4 **COULTHARD (IRE),** 12, ch g Glenstal (USA)—Royal Aunt **Mrs P. M. Sly**
5 **DELIGHTFUL CLICHE,** 4, b g Classic Cliche (IRE)—Ima Delight **Mrs P. M. Sly**
6 **DHEHDAAH,** 4, b g Alhaarth (IRE)—Carina Clare **D. Bayliss, T. Davies, G. Libson & Mrs P. M. Sly**
7 **FILLE DETENTE,** 5, b g Double Trigger (IRE)—Matoaka **D. L. Bayliss**
8 **FULLARDS,** 7, b g Alderbrook—Milly Kelly **M. H. S. Sly**
9 **GRIFFENS BROOK,** 5, b g Alderbrook—Ima Delight **Messrs G.A.Libson,D.L.Bayliss & G.Taylor**
10 **HARLEY,** 7, ch g Alderbrook—Chichell's Hurst **Thorney Racing Club**
11 **HARRYCONE LEWIS,** 7, b g Sir Harry Lewis (USA)—Rosie Cone **The Craftsmen**
12 **HAWTHORN PRINCE (IRE),** 10, ch g Black Monday—Goose Loose **Messrs G.A.Libson,D.L.Bayliss & G.Taylor**
13 **ORCHARD FIELDS (IRE),** 5, ch m Double Trigger (IRE)—Art Lover (IRE) **P. J. Turner**
14 **PARABLE,** 9, b g Midyan (USA)—Top Table **R. P. G. Sturgess**
15 **ROSECHARMER,** 8, ch m Charmer—Rosie Cone **Mrs P. M. Sly**
16 **SAIDA LENASERA (FR),** 4, b f Fasliyev (USA)—Lanasara **D. L. Bayliss**
17 **SAN ANTONIO,** 5, b g Efisio—Winnebago **S. W. R. Brazier**
18 **STANDING BLOOM,** 9, ch m Presidium—Rosie Cone **The Stablemates**
19 **TEESWATER,** 5, b g Alderbrook—Ewe Lamb **Mrs P. M. Sly**
20 **UPRIGHT IMA,** 6, b m Perpendicular—Ima Delight **Mrs P. M. Sly**
21 **VERTICAL BLOOM,** 4, b f Perpendicular—Rosie Cone **Mrs P. M. Sly**

MRS P. M. SLY—continued

THREE-YEAR-OLDS

22 **VIABLE**, b g Vettori (IRE)—Danseuse Davis (FR) **Thorney Racing Club**

Other Owners: Mrs S. E. Godfrey, T. E. Kerfoot, A. Robinson, Derek Sly.

Jockey (flat): A. Culhane. **Jockey (NH):** Paul Moloney, W. Marston. **Amateur:** Miss Louise Allan.

---

543 | MR D. SMAGA, Lamorlaye
Postal: **17 Voie de la Grange des Pres, 60260 Lamorlaye, France.**
Contacts: PHONE +33 (0) 3 44 21 50 05 FAX +33 (0) 3 44 21 53 56

1 **ALCINOS (FR)**, 4, b c Highest Honor (FR)—Alshazam (IRE) **Baron T. Van Zuylen**
2 **BUBBLY MOLLY (FR)**, 4, b f Wagon Master (FR)—Shining Molly (FR) **Alain Morice**
3 **FAIRY NOTE (FR)**, 5, b h Victory Note (USA)—Catherine Schratt **Ecurie Chalhoub**
4 **GRANDES ILLUSIONS (FR)**, 4, ch f Kendor (FR)—Largesse (FR) **Baron T. Van Zuylen**
5 **IN THE DARK (FR)**, 5, b h Akarad (FR)—Petard Express (IRE) **Baron T. Van Zuylen**
6 **KASLIK (FR)**, 4, b f Desert Prince (IRE)—Mrs Ting (USA) **Ecurie Chalhoub**
7 **LE COMTE EST BON (USA)**, 4, br c King of Kings (IRE)—Navratilovna (USA) **Mme Ades-Hazan**
8 **LOCKOUT (IRE)**, 5, b h Spectrum (IRE)—Luvia **Claude Darty**
9 **MAREXA (FR)**, 6, b m Saumarez—Exclusivity (FR) **Baron T. Van Zuylen**
10 **MARIE VISON (IRE)**, 4, ch f Entrepreneur—Metisse (USA) **Mr M. Parrish**
11 **MARILDO**, 18, b g Romildo—Marike **David Smaga**
12 **PRENDS TON TEMPS (FR)**, 8, b h Exit To Nowhere (USA)—Sarooh's Love (USA) **Ecurie Chalhoub**
13 **SNOW GAP (FR)**, 6, b h Bering—Girl of France **Baron T. Van Zuylen**
14 **SPECIAL KALDOUN (IRE)**, 6, b h Alzao (USA)—Special Lady (FR) **Ecurie Chalhoub**
15 **VOIX DU NORD (FR)**, 4, b c Valanour (IRE)—Dame Edith (FR) **Baron T. Van Zuylen**

THREE-YEAR-OLDS

16 **BONNE FOI**, ch c Bering—Consolation **Ecurie Chalhoub**
17 **CELERE (FR)**, ch f Kabool—Flying Past (FR) **Baron T. Van Zuylen**
18 **CLOCKWORK (FR)**, b f Octagonal (NZ)—Timely Lady (FR) **Baron T. Van Zuylen**
19 **DYONISIENNE**, b f Groom Dancer (USA)—Direcvil **Haras d'Etreham**
20 **ESTAFILADE (FR)**, b f Gold Away (IRE)—Estava (FR) **Baron T. Van Zuylen**
21 **GOLD CHARM (GER)**, b f Key of Luck (USA)—Goldkatze (GER) **Mr M. Parrish**
22 B c Highest Honor (FR)—Green Rose (USA) **Mme G. Aoudai**
23 **IRISH WAY (FR)**, ch c Giant's Causeway (USA)—Irish Arms (FR) **Mme R. Ades**
24 **JANJAN (IRE)**, ch c Highest Honor (FR)—Fay Wray (FR) **Ecurie Chalhoub**
25 **LE SINDBAD (IRE)**, bl c Xaar—Fantastic Charm (USA) **R. Bellaiche**
26 **MIYAZAKI (IRE)**, b f Spectrum (IRE)—Zelah (IRE) **Mme Dominique Smaga**
27 **NEFEROUN (FR)**, bl f Sicyos (USA)—Largesse (FR) **Baron T. Van Zuylen**
28 **NON SONO SOLO (IRE)**, b c Montjeu (IRE)—Margi (USA) **Ecurie Chalhoub**
29 **ORESME (FR)**, b f Bering—Glivana (FR) **Baron T. Van Zuylen**
30 **PERFIDIE (IRE)**, b f Monsun (GER)—Pelagic **Haras d'Etreham**
31 **ROSE BURG (FR)**, b f Bering—Dancing Rose (FR) **Mr Thierry Roland**
32 **SATIE (IRE)**, b f Fasliyev (USA)—Sao (IRE) **Mr Marc de Chambure**
33 **SEA SCAN (IRE)**, b c Dr Fong (USA)—Sea Picture (IRE) **Succession Weinstock**
34 **SECOND TOUR (FR)**, b c Highest Honor (FR)—Girl Of France **Baron T. Van Zuylen**
35 **SEVEN NO TRUMP (FR)**, ro f Highest Honor (FR)—Colour Scheme (FR) **Baron T. Van Zuylen**
36 **SUR MA VIE (USA)**, b f Fusaichi Pegasus (USA)—Boubskaia **Mr Maurice Lagasse**
37 **TREE OF LIFE (FR)**, ch c Grape Tree Road—Avellaneda (FR) **Ecurie Seutet**
38 **ZENON (FR)**, b c Sendawar (IRE)—Glebe Place (FR) **Baron T. Van Zuylen**

TWO-YEAR-OLDS

39 **ELVARD (FR)**, gr c 4/3 Highest Honor (FR)—Dame Edith (FR) (Top Ville) **Baron T. Van Zuylen**
40 B f 13/2 Deputy Minister (CAN)—Firm Friend (IRE) (Affirmed (USA)) **Mr Maurice Lagasse**
41 B c 28/3 Fasliyev (USA)—Hermite (USA) (St Jovite (USA)) (80482) **Ecurie Chalhoub**
42 **KABOURA (FR)**, b c 28/3 Kabool—Colour Scheme (FR) (Perrault) **Baron T. Van Zuylen**
43 **LOOSE END (FR)**, b c 28/3 Sendawar (IRE)—Luvia (Cure The Blues (USA)) (13413) **Mme Bokobsa**
44 B c 6/4 Kaldounevees (FR)—Loyola (FR) (Sicyos (USA)) (23474) **Mr M. Parrish**
45 **MAGGY SHAN (FR)**, b f 3/2 Grape Tree Road—
                Eastern Myth (USA) (Housebuster (USA)) (11401) **Mme M. De Chambure**
46 **MARATIKA (IRE)**, ch c 7/3 Grape Tree Road—Metisse (USA) (Kingmambo (USA)) (34875) **Mr M. Parrish**

MR D. SMAGA—continued

47 **MISS SINDBAD (FR)**, ch f 3/4 Peintre Celebre (USA)—
                                Zalamalec (USA) (Septieme Ciel (USA)) (57008) **Mr R. Bellaiche**
48 **RAKIA (FR)**, ch f 9/4 Kabool—Sangrilla (FR) (Sanglamore (USA)) **Baron T. Van Zuylen**
49 **RIVERSPIANE (FR)**, ch c 31/1 River Bay (USA)—Gospellianne (FR) (Machiavellian (USA)) **Ecurie Chalhoub**
50 **SENDAMI (FR)**, b c 8/3 Sendawar (IRE)—Miss Afrique (FR) (African Song) **Ecurie Seutet**
51 **SENDNOWAR (FR)**, b f 28/1 Sendawar (IRE)—Glebe Place (FR) (Akarad (FR)) **Baron T. Van Zuylen**
52 **TOP SEVEN (IRE)**, ch f 2/4 Highest Honor (FR)—Sporades (USA) (Vaguely Noble) (34875)

Jockey (flat): D. Boeuf.

---

544   MR B. SMART, Thirsk
Postal: **Hambleton House, Sutton Bank, Thirsk, North Yorkshire, YO7 2HA.**
Contacts: **PHONE (01845) 597481 FAX (01845) 597480 MOBILE (07748) 634797**
E-MAIL vicky.smart@virgin.net

1 **ATLANTIC ACE**, 8, b g First Trump—Risalah **R. A. Page**
2 **BEADY (IRE)**, 6, b g Eagle Eyed (USA)—Tales of Wisdom **Mr B. Smart**
3 **BOND BECKS (IRE)**, 5, ch g Tagula (IRE)—At Amal (IRE) **R. C. Bond**
4 **BOND BOY**, 8, b g Piccolo—Arabellajill **R. C. Bond**
5 **BOND DOMINGO**, 6, b g Mind Games—Antonia's Folly **Mr B. Smart**
6 **BOND MILLENNIUM**, 7, ch g Piccolo—Farmer's Pet **R. C. Bond**
7 **BOND MOONLIGHT**, 4, ch g Danehill Dancer (IRE)—Interregnum **P. M. Rose**
8 **BOND PLAYBOY**, 5, b g Piccolo—Highest Ever (FR) **R. C. Bond**
9 **BONNE DE FLEUR**, 4, b f Whittingham (IRE)—L'estable Fleurie (IRE) **Miss N. A. Jefford**
10 **BOOK MATCHED**, 4, b g Efisio—Princess Latifa **P. A. Darling**
11 **COMMANDER BOND**, 4, b g Piccolo—Lonesome **R. C. Bond**
12 **CRESKELD (IRE)**, 6, b g Sri Pekan (USA)—Pizzazz **Creskeld Racing**
13 **DIFFERENTIAL (USA)**, 8, b br g Known Fact (USA)—Talk About Home (USA) **Mr B. Smart**
14 **KINTORE**, 4, ch g Inchinor—Souadah (USA) **Mr Bill Hall,Mr Bill Fraser,Mr E.Rennie**
15 **MON SECRET (IRE)**, 7, b g General Monash (USA)—Ron's Secret **Pinnacle Monash Partnership**
16 **REDWOOD ROCKS (IRE)**, 4, b g Blush Rambler (USA)—Crisp and Cool (USA) **D. A. Hall**
17 **SAROS (IRE)**, 4, b br g Desert Sun—Fight Right (FR) **Pinnacle Desert Sun Partnership**
18 **SENOR BOND (USA)**, 4, ch g Hennessy (USA)—Troppa Freska (USA) **R. C. Bond**
19 **SIR BOND (IRE)**, 4, ch g Desert Sun—In Tranquility (IRE) **R. C. Bond**
20 **VADEMECUM**, 4, br g Shinko Forest (IRE)—Sunshine Coast **EKOS Pinnacle Partnership**

THREE-YEAR-OLDS

21 **AEGEAN DANCER**, b g Piccolo—Aegean Flame **Pinnacle Piccolo Partnership**
22 **BEN CASEY**, b c Whittingham (IRE)—Hot Ice (IRE) **R. A. Page**
23 **BOND BABE**, b f Forzando—Lindfield Belle (IRE) **R. C. Bond**
24 **BOND CAT (IRE)**, ch f Raise A Grand (IRE)—Merrily **R. C. Bond**
25 **BOND CITY (IRE)**, b g Trans Island—Where's Charlotte **R. C. Bond**
26 **BOND FINESSE (IRE)**, b f Danehill Dancer (IRE)—Funny Cut (IRE) **R. C. Bond**
27 **BOND PUCCINI**, b g Piccolo—Baileys By Name **R. C. Bond**
28 **BOND ROCKERFELLA**, b c Lend A Hand—Highest Ever (FR) **R. C. Bond**
29 **CHINA BOND (IRE)**, ch c Shahrastani (USA)—At Amal (IRE) **R. C. Bond**
30 **GINGER COOKIE**, ch f Bold Edge—Pretty Pollyanna **Mrs F. Denniff**
31 **HANNAH'S TRIBE (IRE)**, b f Daggers Drawn (USA)—Cala-Holme (IRE) **Harlequin Pinnacle Partnership**
32 **JUST BOND (IRE)**, b g Namid—Give Warning (IRE) **R. C. Bond**
33 **MARY READ**, ch f Bahamian Bounty—Hill Welcome **S. J. F. Racing**
34 **MIDNIGHT TYCOON**, b g Marju (IRE)—Midnight Allure **Pinnacle Marju Partnership**
35 **MISS BEAR (IRE)**, b f Orpen (USA)—The Poachers Lady (IRE) **Pinstripe Partners Two**
36 **MONKEY MADGE**, br f Cape Cross (IRE)—Runelia **P. A. Darling**
37 **OUT OF INDIA**, b f Marju (IRE)—Tide of Fortune **Mrs J. M. T. Martin**
38 **PICK A NICE NAME**, ch f Polar Falcon (USA)—Opuntia **Mr John W. Ford**
39 **RAINBOW IRIS**, b br f Mister Baileys—Kastaway **Mr Paul K. Spencer**
40 **REAL BOND**, b g Mind Games—Bond Girl **R. C. Bond**
41 **SHANKLY BOND (IRE)**, b g Danehill Dancer (IRE)—Fanellan **R. C. Bond**
42 **SKIDDAW WOLF**, ch f Wolfhound (USA)—Stealthy **Mr John Wills**
43 **VILLA CHIGI (IRE)**, ch g Pistolet Bleu (IRE)—Musical Refrain (IRE) **Mr Paul J. Dixon**
44 **WESTLAKE BOND (IRE)**, b f Josr Algarhoud (IRE)—Rania **R. C. Bond**

MR B. SMART—continued

TWO-YEAR-OLDS

45 **AGNES PEARL**, b f 17/4 Agnes World (USA)—Paris Babe (Teenoso (USA)) (19000) **Mason Gill Partnership**
46 **ANGARIC (IRE)**, ch c 17/4 Pivotal—Grannys Reluctance (IRE) (Anita's Prince) (55000) **A. D. Gee**
47 B f 2/4 Polish Precedent (USA)—Arabellajill (Aragon) (15000) **Mr B. Smart**
48 B c 20/2 King's Best (USA)—Arabis (Arazi (USA)) (21000) **R. C. Bond**
49 **BETH'S MATE**, b f 13/3 Fleetwood (IRE)—Resemblance (State Diplomacy (USA)) (2500) **Mr B. Smart**
50 B f 28/4 Imperial Ballet (IRE)—Birthday Belle (Lycius (USA)) (5000) **L. A. Bolingbroke**
51 Br f 27/2 Diktat—Bond Girl (Magic Ring (IRE)) (800) **R. C. Bond**
52 Ch c 17/3 Night Shift (USA)—Cartesian (Shirley Heights) **Pinnacle Night Shift Partnership**
53 **COUNTERFACTUAL (IRE)**, br c 20/3 Key of Luck (USA)—
Wakayi (Persian Bold) (40240) **EKOS Pinnacle Partnership**
54 B c 10/5 Shinko Forest (IRE)—Creese (USA) (Diesis) (24144) **H.E. Sheikh R. Al Maktoum**
55 B f 18/4 Mozart (IRE)—Dance By Night (Northfields (USA)) (70000) **H.E. Sheikh R. Al Maktoum**
56 B c 10/5 Miswaki (USA)—Dippers (Polish Numbers (USA)) (22000) **Bigwigs Bloodstock**
57 **DISTINCTLY JIM (IRE)**, ch c 26/2 City On A Hill (USA)—
Bucaramanga (IRE) (Distinctly North (USA)) (12000) **Harlequin Pinnacle Partnership**
58 **GIZMO**, b c 21/3 Fasliyev (USA)—Sly Baby (IRE) (Dr Devious (IRE)) (32000) **EKOS Pinnacle Partnership**
59 B f 18/4 Namid—Gold Prospector (IRE) (Spectrum (IRE)) (6706) **R. C. Bond**
60 **GUALLATIRI**, ch f 28/1 Selkirk (USA)—Guaranda (Acatenango (GER)) (50000) **H.E. Sheikh R. Al Maktoum**
61 **JACK FROST NIPPING (USA)**, b c 1/2 Miswaki (USA)—Sulalat (Hamas (IRE)) (38000) **Mr M. Rashid**
62 Ch c 18/3 Allied Forces (USA)—Karameg (Danehill (USA)) (2000) **D. A. N. Ross**
63 Br c 5/2 Indian Danehill (IRE)—Lady Stalker (Primo Dominie) (12000) **Pinnacle Danehill Partnership**
64 B c 26/4 Danehill Dancer (IRE)—Lime Hill Honey (IRE) (Topanoora) (60000) **H.E. Sheikh R. Al Maktoum**
65 B f 26/2 Trans Island—Miss Game Plan (Hector Protector (USA)) (2700) **R. C. Bond**
66 **MISS SURE BOND (IRE)**, ch f 17/4 Danehill Dancer (IRE)—
Desert Rose (Green Desert (USA)) (60361) **R. C. Bond**
67 **MISU BOND (IRE)**, b c 22/4 Danehill Dancer (IRE)—Hawala (IRE) (Warning) (60361) **R. C. Bond**
68 **OUR SHEILA**, ch f 10/4 Bahamian Bounty—Shifting Mist (Night Shift (USA)) (32000) **A. D. Gee**
69 B c 30/4 Diktat—Princess Latifa (Wolfhound (USA)) (16000) **P. A. Darling**
70 **QUEEN'S COMPOSER (IRE)**, b c 3/2 Mozart (IRE)—
Queen Leonor (IRE) (Caerleon (USA)) (25000) **Pinnacle Mozart Partnership**
71 **RIOTOUS ASSEMBLY**, b g 19/3 Dansili—Pretty Pollyanna (General Assembly (USA)) (3000) **L. A. Bolingbroke**
72 Ch f 8/2 City On A Hill (USA)—Royal Musical (Royal Abjar (USA)) **P. A. Mason**
73 Br f 9/4 Shinko Forest (IRE)—Sawaki (Song) (8718) **R. C. Bond**
74 B f 28/1 Bertolini (USA)—Skiddaw Bird (Bold Owl) (4200) **J. Howse & D. Elders**
75 Ch c 21/3 Danehill Dancer (IRE)—Slayjay (IRE) (Mujtahid (USA)) (18500) **R. C. Bond**
76 B f 25/3 Dr Fong (USA)—Speedybird (Danehill (USA)) (19449) **R. C. Bond**
77 **STARTORI**, b f 16/3 Vettori (FR)—Celestial Welcome (Most Welcome) (14500) **Star Alliance (I)**
78 Ch c 1/3 Titus Livius (FR)—Swan Sea (Sea Hero (USA)) (5364) **David Allan**
79 B c 5/4 Elnadim (USA)—Titania (Fairy King (USA)) (21461) **C. A. Lynch**
80 Ch f 6/5 City On A Hill (USA)—Trinida (Jaazeiro (USA)) (13413) **L. A. Bolingbroke**
81 **WORLDLY PURSUIT**, ch f 19/2 Spinning World (USA)—
Final Pursuit (Pursuit of Love) (30000) **The Gardner Eden Partnership**

Other Owners: Sue Johnson, Nigel Gravett, J. Gill, S. Pailor, J. Laughton, G. Gardner, Hon. R. Eden, M. H. A. Broke, J. A. Evans, M. F. Ford, Mrs J. A. Hyde, Exors of the Late Mr J. H. Hyde, D. R. Martin, J. P. Massy-Collier, Miss E. Shepherd, R. H. Shepherd, G. S. Slater, Mrs V. Smart, N. H. Tritton, Mr A. Worrall.

Assistant Trainer: Mrs V R Smart

Jockey (flat): F. Lynch, D. McGaffin. **Amateur:** Mrs V. Smart.

---

545 MR A. D. SMITH, Westward Ho
Postal: **Duckhaven Stud, Cornborough Road, Westward Ho, Bideford, Devon, EX39 1AA.**
Contacts: **PHONE/FAX (01237) 478648**
E-MAIL duckhavenstud@btinternet.com

1 5, Ch m Dancing Spree (USA)—Cinderella Derek
2 **JOB SHOP**, 4, b c Dancing Spree (USA)—Kathy Fair (IRE) **Pertemps Ltd**
3 5, B h Double Trigger (IRE)—Kathy Fair (IRE)
4 **MAID THE CUT**, 4, ch f Silver Wizard (USA)—Third Dam **Duckhaven Stud**
5 **PERTEMPS JOB**, 4, b c First Trump—Happy And Blessed (IRE) **Pertemps Ltd**
6 **PERTEMPS RED**, 4, ch c Dancing Spree (USA)—Lady Lullaby (USA) **Pertemps Ltd**
7 **PERTEMPS STYLE**, 4, b br f Double Trigger (IRE)—Peristyle **Pertemps Ltd**

MR A. D. SMITH—continued

8 **THE JOB**, 4, ch c Dancing Spree (USA)—Bay Bianca (IRE) **Pertemps Ltd**
9 **YORK DANCER**, 4, ch f Dancing Spree (USA)—York Street (USA) **Duckhaven Stud**

THREE-YEAR-OLDS

10 **DAVALA**, b c Lake Coniston (IRE)—Velvet Heart (IRE) **Duckhaven Stud**
11 **HYGIEIA**, b c Silver Wizard (USA)—Defy Me **Duckhaven Stud**
12 **KATHYS JOB**, b f Silver Wizard (USA)—Kathy Fair (IRE) **Pertemps Ltd**
13 **NIP NIP (IRE)**, b f Royal Applause—Rustie Bliss **Duckhaven Stud**
14 B f Dancing Spree (USA)—Total Rach (IRE) **Miss K. L. Pluess**

Other Owners: MR A. D. Smith, Mrs J. M. Smith.

Assistant Trainer: Mat Druce

Amateur: Mr Gavin Hall.

---

546 **MR G. J. SMITH, Melton Mowbray**
Postal: **Fox Covert Farm, Narrow Lane, Wymeswold, Loughborough, Leicestershire, LE12 6SD.**
Contacts: **PHONE (01509) 881250 MOBILE (07831) 531765**

1 **BROUGHTON BOY**, 5, br g Alhaatmi—Metabolic Melody **Kenneth George Kitchen**
2 **JACKS HELEN**, 8, b m Lancastrian—Troublewithjack **Mr A. W. Bult**
3 **JEANIE'S LAST**, 6, b m Primitive Rising (USA)—Jean Jeanie **T. Evans**
4 **RED NOSE LADY**, 8, b m Teenoso (USA)—Red Rambler **Slow Donkey Partnership**
5 **REDVIC**, 5, b g Alhaatmi—Sweet Fortune **Kenneth George Kitchen**
6 **SADLER'S SECRET (IRE)**, 10, b g Sadler's Wells (USA)—Athyka (USA) **Slow Donkey Partnership**

Other Owners: Mrs D. Key, Mrs H. Renshaw.

Assistant Trainer: R J Smith

---

547 **MR JULIAN SIMON SMITH, Tirley**
Postal: **Tirley Court, Tirley, Gloucester.**
Contacts: **PHONE (01452) 780461 FAX (01452) 780461 MOBILE (07880) 732337**

1 **BRUSH THE ARK**, 11, b m Brush Aside (USA)—Expensive Lark **D. E. S. Smith**
2 **GLEN WARRIOR**, 9, b g Michelozzo (USA)—Mascara VII **D. E. S. Smith**
3 **GOLDEN KEY**, 4, b g Rainbow Quest (USA)—Keyboogie (USA) **R. P. Taylor**
4 **LOGIES LASS**, 6, b m Nomadic Way (USA)—Random Select **R. P. Taylor**
5 **SWISS ROSE**, 8, ch m Michelozzo (USA)—Tic-On-Rose **Grand Jury Partnership**
6 **TIRLEY STORM**, 10, b g Tirley Gale—Random Select **D. E. S. Smith**
7 **VALLEY WARRIOR**, 8, b g Michelozzo (USA)—Mascara VII **Mrs J. A. Benson**

Other Owners: Miss S. N. Benson, A. W. Brookes, R. Brookes.

Assistant Trainer: Mrs Nicky Smith

Jockey (NH): T. J. Murphy, W. Marston. **Conditional:** Antony Evans.

---

548 **MRS NADINE SMITH, Pulborough**
Postal: **Hillside Cottage Stables, Hillside Fruit Farm, Bury, Pulborough, West Sussex, RH20 1NR.**
Contacts: **PHONE (01798) 831206**

1 **ALASIL (USA)**, 5, b br g Swain (IRE)—Asl (USA) **Tony Hayward and Barry Fulton**
2 **FOREST DANE**, 5, b g Danetime (IRE)—Forest Maid **The Ember Partnership**
3 **MISTER PUTT (USA)**, 7, b br g Mister Baileys—Theresita (GER) **Tony Hayward and Barry Fulton**
4 **WHIST DRIVE**, 5, ch g First Trump—Fine Quill **Tony Hayward and Barry Fulton**

Other Owners: A. P. King, M. A. King.

Assistant Trainer: A M Smith

549

MISS S. SMITH, Lewes
Postal: **County Stables, The Old Racecourse, Lewes, East Sussex, BN7 1UR.**
Contacts: **PHONE (01273) 477173 MOBILE (07970) 550828**
E-MAIL suzy@racing951.fsnet.co.uk WEBSITE www.suzysmithracing.co.uk

1 **CRAFTY LADY (IRE)**, 6, b br m Warcraft (USA)—Kilmana (IRE)
2 **DADS LAD (IRE)**, 11, b g Supreme Leader—Furryvale **Miss S. Smith**
3 5, Gr g Rock Hopper—Hop Picker (USA) **R. F. Smith**
4 **JIM JAM JOEY (IRE)**, 12, ch g Big Sink Hope (USA)—Ascot Princess **The Risk Assessors**
5 **MATERIAL WORLD**, 7, b m Karinga Bay—Material Girl **Southern Bloodstock**
6 **PRINCE OF ARAGON**, 9, b g Aragon—Queens Welcome **Miss S. Smith**
7 4, Ch f Keen—Ropsley High Style **Mr T. J. Absolom**
8 4, Gr f Clerkenwell (USA)—Rosy Posy **Miss S. Smith**
9 **TEEN HOUSE**, 6, b m Teenoso (USA)—Last House **Mr S. E. & J. M. Gordon-Watson**

Other Owners: J. A. A. S. Logan, Mr M. J. Sealey, Mrs V. J. Smith, R. F. Smith, M. W. Woolveridge.

Assistant Trainer: Mr S E Gordon-Watson

Conditional: C. Bolger. **Amateur:** Mr S. Gordon-Watson.

550

MS SUE SMITH, Gentleshaw
Postal: **Coldwell Cottage, Gentleshaw, Rugeley, Staffordshire, WS15 4NJ.**
Contacts: **PHONE (01543) 686587 MOBILE (07791) 347860**

1 **CELTIC ROMANCE**, 6, b m Celtic Swing—Southern Sky **Ms Sue Smith**
2 **DESLA'S DEVIL**, 13, b g Devil To Play—Miss Desla **J. P. Smith**
3 **DUNSTON DURGAM (IRE)**, 11, b g Durgam (USA)—Blazing Sunset **Ms Sue Smith**
4 **FOUR KISSES (IRE)**, 5, b m Supreme Leader—Danjo's Lady (IRE) **J. P. Smith**

551

MR V. SMITH, Newmarket
Postal: **Exeter Stables, Church Street, Exning, Newmarket, Suffolk, CB8 7EH.**
Contacts: **PHONE/FAX (01638) 608542 MOBILE (07780) 853232**
E-MAIL vince.smith@virgin.net

1 **ALI DEO**, 4, ch g Ali-Royal (IRE)—Lady In Colour (IRE) **Jinquera Partnership**
2 **AMERICAN EMBASSY (USA)**, 5, b h Quiet American (USA)—Foreign Courier (USA) **Mrs C. Gilliar**
3 **ARMORINE (FR)**, 5, b m Jeune Homme (USA)—Motzki (FR) **The Lamprell Partnership**
4 **ARRAN**, 5, ch g Selkirk (USA)—Humble Pie **The Humble Partnership**
5 **ASK THE CLERK (IRE)**, 4, b g Turtle Island (IRE)—Some Fun **Mrs Joanne Baines**
6 **BAYADERE (GER)**, 5, br m Lavirco (GER)—Brangane (IRE) **The Small World Partnership**
7 **CHILLY MILLY**, 4, b f Shambo—Phrase'n Cold (IRE) **Gumbrills Racing Partnership**
8 **CORONADO'S GOLD (USA)**, 4, ch c Coronado's Quest (USA)—
                                                    Debit My Account (USA) **Studio Club Partnership**
9 **EXPLOSIVE FOX (IRE)**, 4, ch c Foxhound (USA)—Grise Mine (FR) **L. M. Power**
10 **FABULOSO**, 4, b f Dr Fong (USA)—Shafir (IRE) **Mrs J. M. Davie**
11 **HARRYCAT (IRE)**, 4, b g Bahhare (USA)—Quiver Tree **The S.I.R. Partnership**
12 **KINGSTON HARBOUR (IRE)**, 4, b g Danehill (USA)—Kallavesi (USA) **J. L. Guillambert**
13 **MAC'S TALISMAN (IRE)**, 5, ch h Hector Protector (USA)—Inherent Magic (IRE) **Mr V. Smith**
14 **MAEVEEN (IRE)**, 5, b m Flying Spur (AUS)—Cool Gales **Metropolitan Properties Ltd**
15 **MAGICAL WIT (IRE)**, 5, ch m Bahhare (USA)—Saleemah (USA) **Seeking The Gold**
16 **PACHARAN QUEEN**, 4, b f Terimon—Persian Fountain (IRE) **K. R. M. Racing**
17 **SEMPER PARATUS (USA)**, 6, b g Foxhound—Bletcha Lass (AUS) **Mrs Jenny Moore**
18 **SHARADI (IRE)**, 4, b g Desert Sun—Sharadiya (IRE) **R. J. Baines**
19 **SILVER SILENCE (JPN)**, 4, b br g Sunday Silence (USA)—Island of Silver (USA) **Jinquera Partnership**
20 **THE COBBLER**, 6, b g Glory of Dancer—Lady Eccentric (IRE) **L. M. Power**
21 **TOLEDO SUN**, 5, b g Zamindar—Shafir (IRE) **Monkey a Month Racing**
22 **VRUBEL (IRE)**, 6, ch g Entrepreneur—Renzola **Mr V. Smith**

THREE-YEAR-OLDS

23 **BIBI HELEN**, b f Robellino (USA)—Tarry **Mr J. Pearce**
24 **CASINO (IRE)**, b g Desert Sun—Go Indigo (IRE) **R. J. Baines**
25 **CONSCRIPT (IRE)**, b c Mujadil (USA)—Battle Queen **R. J. Baines**
26 **DEVIL'S DISGUISE**, b g Atraf—Dunloe (IRE) **R. J. Baines**

MR V. SMITH—continued

27 **ELAALA (USA)**, ch f Aljabr (USA)—Nufuth (USA) **Mr Tony Stafford**
28 **THREE PENNIES**, b f Pennekamp (USA)—Triple Zee (USA)

TWO-YEAR-OLDS

29 B f 25/1 King Charlemagne (USA)—Amneris (IRE) (Alzao (USA)) (9724)
30 **BLITZKRIEG (IRE)**, b c 8/3 Barathea (IRE)—Eman's Joy (Lion Cavern (USA)) (35000) **R. J. Baines**
31 B c 7/3 King Charlemagne (USA)—Lady Peculiar (CAN) (Sunshine Forever (USA)) (15000) **Mr A. Downes**
32 **LENOIR (GER)**, b c 9/2 Lujain (USA)—Luna de Miel (Shareef Dancer (USA)) (8000) **Mrs J. J. Dye**
33 **RED TSARINA**, b f 12/4 Russian Red—Tudor Bay Lady (Faustus (USA)) **Mrs Eileen Graham**
34 B c 19/2 Spectrum (IRE)—Tanasie (Cadeaux Genereux)

Other Owners: Mr M. M. Bloomquest, Mr K J Curson, Mr Vincent Armstrong, Mr David Clayton, Mrs Toots Cowen, Mr J. Dalton, Mrs D. Dawes, Mr W. Doherty, Miss Susan Gostick, Mr John S. C. Fry, Mr David Metcalfe, Mr J. Lovat, Mrs A Lovat, Mr I. Lewis, Mr V. A. Jenkins, Mr David Jenkins, Mrs Clarissa Howkins, Mr & Mrs Brian Hind, Mr John Turner, Mr M. J. Tate, Mr Keith Spriggs, Mr Dai Smith, Mr C. L. Small, Mr Roger Patchin, Mr W. Parkinson, Mr & Mrs David Odell, Mr Marcus McKinley, Mr Frank McDermott, Mr Mark Heaton, Mr Mike Dawes, Mr Stephen Dartnell, Mr David Cummins, Mr Malcolm Clifford, Mr David Cheeson, H. G. Newell.

Jockey (flat): N. Callan, D. Holland, J. Quinn, M. A. Tebbutt. **Jockey (NH):** P. Hide. **Apprentice:** Rory Moore.

---

552 **MR G. R. I. SMYLY, Broadway**
Postal: **Garden Cottage, Wormington Grange, Broadway, Worcestershire, WR12 7NJ.**
Contacts: **PHONE** (01386) 584085 **FAX** (01386) 584085 **MOBILE** (07747) 035169

1 **CALGARY JOCK**, 4, ch g Rakaposhi King—Lily of The West
2 **DAISY FAY**, 10, b m Broadsword—Lily of The West **Mr P. McCanlis**
3 **NORTH PASS**, 7, b g North Col—Nunswalk **B. Eccles**
4 **STAR WONDER**, 5, b m Syrtos—Galava (CAN) **Mr M. K. Deakin**

Amateur: Mr H. Dowty.

---

553 **MISS J. A. SOUTHCOMBE, Chard**
Postal: **Holemoor Farm Bungalow, Combe St Nicholas, Chard, Somerset, TA20 3AE.**
Contacts: **PHONE** (01460) 68865 **MOBILE** (07968) 178121
E-MAIL jane@southcomberacing.co.uk **WEBSITE** www.southcomberacing.co.uk

1 **BAYONET**, 9, b m Then Again—Lambay **M. Savill**
2 **BENJAMIN (IRE)**, 7, b g Night Shift (USA)—Best Academy (USA) **M. Savill**
3 **EASTER OGIL (IRE)**, 10, ch g Pips Pride—Piney Pass **M. Savill**
4 **GIKO**, 11, b g Arazi (USA)—Gayane **V. R. V. Partnership**
5 **INNCLASSIC (IRE)**, 4, b f Stravinsky (USA)—Kyka (USA) **Mr K. S. Howard**
6 **MASTER RATTLE**, 6, b g Sabrehill (USA)—Miss Primula **The Master Rattles Partnership**
7 **MEELUP (IRE)**, 5, ch g Night Shift (USA)—Centella (IRE) **Mr K. S. Howard**
8 **SALFORD FLYER**, 9, b g Pharly (FR)—Edge of Darkness **P. L. Southcombe**
9 **TYRO'S BID**, 7, b g Greensmith—Two Hearts **M. Savill**

THREE-YEAR-OLDS

10 **LUCIFEROUS (USA)**, ch f Devil's Bag (USA)—Vital Laser (USA) **M. Savill**

TWO-YEAR-OLDS

11 Ch f 22/3 Foxhound (USA)—Le Pin (Persian Bold) (476)
12 B f 8/4 Lahib (USA)—Perfect Poppy (Shareef Dancer (USA)) (3000)
13 B f 28/4 Night Shift (USA)—Peshawar (Persian Bold) (14000) **Mr K. A. Parr**

Other Owners: Mrs R. G. H. Vivian, Miss V. Vivian.

Jockey (flat): V Slattery. **Jockey (NH):** V Slattery. **Amateur:** Miss W. Southcombe.

554 MR M. E. SOWERSBY, York

Postal: Southwold Farm, Goodmanham Wold, Market Weighton, York, East Yorkshire, YO43 3NA.
Contacts: PHONE (01430) 810534 MOBILE (07855) 551056

1 **BOWLING ALONG**, 4, b f The West (USA)—Bystrouska **Keith Brown Properties (Hull) Ltd**
2 **CLUB OASIS**, 4, b f Forzando—Tatouma (USA) **Keith Brown Properties (Hull) Ltd**
3 **COMMEMORATION DAY (IRE)**, 4, b g Daylami—Bequeath (USA) **A. H. Milner**
4 **DEL TROTTER (IRE)**, 10, b g King Luthier—Arctic Alice **The Wolds Partnership**
5 **FRENCHGATE**, 4, br g Paris House—Let's Hang On (IRE) **R & E Hall & Son**
6 **GAME FLORA**, 4, b f Mind Games—Breakfast Creek **The Southwold Set**
7 **GLENSAN (IRE)**, 8, b g Insan (USA)—Strikes Glen **C. N. Richardson**
8 **JACK FLUSH (IRE)**, 11, b g Broken Hearted—Clubhouse Turn (IRE) **B. Walker**
9 **KARATHAENA (IRE)**, 5, b m Barathea (IRE)—Dabtara (IRE) **The Southwold Set**
10 **MAMORE GAP (IRE)**, 7, b h General Monash (USA)—Ravensdale Rose (IRE) **The Southwold Set**
11 **MEGAN'S MAGIC**, 5, b m Blue Ocean (USA)—Hot Sunday Sport **R. D. Seldon**
12 **MIND PLAY**, 4, b f Mind Games—Diplomatist **Mr M. E. Sowersby**
13 **MY SUNSHINE (IRE)**, 4, b f Alzao (USA)—Sunlit Ride **J. A. Featherstone**
14 **SCHOOLHOUSE WALK**, 7, b g Mistertopogigo (IRE)—Restandbejoyful **Lord Manton**
15 **SPITFIRE BOB (USA)**, 6, b g Mister Baileys—Gulf Cyclone (USA) **A. H. Milner**
16 **WARIF (USA)**, 4, ch c Diesis—Alshoowg (USA) **Racing Ladies**

THREE-YEAR-OLDS

17 **HUNIPOT**, ch f Aragon—Acinom **Mr M. E. Sowersby**
18 **JUST ELIZABETH**, b f Aragon—Collison Lane **Mr S. J. Crawford**
19 **RAVEN (IRE)**, b f Alzao (USA)—Eman's Joy **R & E Hall & Son**

TWO-YEAR-OLDS

20 B f 19/3 Daggers Drawn (USA)—Exhibit Air (IRE) (Exhibitioner) (2000) **Mr M. E. Sowersby**
21 Ch c 26/2 Atraf—Forbidden Monkey (Gabitat) (7500) **J. Morris**
22 B c 12/4 Wizard King—High Stepping (IRE) (Taufan (USA)) (1600) **Mr M. E. Sowersby**
23 B f 30/4 Mujahid (USA)—Stolen Melody (Robellino (USA)) **R. S. Cockerill (Farms) Ltd**

Other Owners: T. J. Stubbins, M. E. Stubbins, Lady Manton, K. Townend, M. Townend, Janet Cooper, S. Evans, J. Vincent, E. Bailey, P Laverack, S. Watson, P. Featherstone, D. Hall, R. Waite, E. Mudd, Miss F. K. Mudd, Mrs D. McNulty, Mrs J. Breen, Mrs J. Crawford, A. West.

Assistant Trainer: Mary Sowersby

Jockey (flat): P. Hanagan. **Jockey (NH):** G. Lee. **Conditional:** F. King. **Apprentice:** T. Eaves. **Amateur:** Mr G. Brewer.

555 MR J. L. SPEARING, Kinnersley

Postal: Kinnersley Racing Stables, Kinnersley, Severn Stoke, Worcestershire, WR8 9JR.
Contacts: PHONE (01905) 371054 FAX (01905) 371054 MOBILE (07801) 552922
E-MAIL caroline@johnspearinghorseracing.com

1 **ANGEL DELIGHT**, 9, gr m Seymour Hicks (FR)—Bird's Custard **Croome Cavaliers**
2 **ARMENTIERES**, 4, b f Robellino (USA)—Perfect Poppy **Mr J. L. Spearing**
3 **BOLD WOLF**, 4, b g Wolfhound (USA)—Rambold **R. A. Collins**
4 **BOREHILL JOKER**, 9, ch g Pure Melody (USA)—Queen Matilda **Miss H. M. Newell**
5 **BORZOI MAESTRO**, 4, ch g Wolfhound (USA)—Ashkernazy (IRE) **The Square Milers**
6 **CASHEL MEAD**, 5, b m Bishop of Cashel—Island Mead **Masonaires**
7 **CHINA CHASE (IRE)**, 6, b g Anshan—Hannies Girl (IRE) **T. N. Siviter**
8 **DORINGO**, 4, b c Prince Sabo—Mistral's Dancer **Robert Heathcote**
9 **FLYING TREATY (USA)**, 8, br h You and I (USA)—Cherie's Hope (USA) **R. J. Buxton**
10 **GAYE TRIGGER**, 7, ch g Karinga Bay—Gaye Memory **Mrs Mercy Rimell**
11 **GRAND RAPIDE**, 4, ch f Grand Lodge (USA)—Vax Rapide **Mr A. J. & Mrs L. Brazier**
12 **HAKIM (NZ)**, 11, ch g Half Iced—Topitup (NZ) **T. N. Siviter**
13 **HOP FAIR**, 6, ch m Gildoran—Haraka Sasa **Mrs S. M. Newell**
14 **HOPBINE**, 9, ch m Gildoran—Haraka Sasa **Miss S. A. Howell**
15 **HOWGREENISMYVALLEY**, 6, b m Executive Perk—Macklette (IRE) **Mrs R. Evans**
16 **INNSTYLE**, 4, b f Daggers Drawn (USA)—Tarneem (USA) **The Square Milers**
17 **JACKS CRAIC (IRE)**, 6, b g Lord Americo—Boleree (IRE) **BBB Computer Services Limited**
18 **JONQUIL LAD**, 6, b g Superlative—Daffodil Express (IRE) **Mrs D. Jones**
19 **KITTY JOHN (IRE)**, 8, gr m Safety Catch (USA)—La Baladina **Masonaires**
20 **KNIGHT'S EMPEROR (IRE)**, 8, b g Grand Lodge (USA)—So Kind **Mrs P. Joynes**

MR J. L. SPEARING—continued

21 LADY LIESEL, 5, b m Bin Ajwaad (IRE)—Griddle Cake (IRE) **Mr J. L. Spearing**
22 MONTANA, 5, b h Puissance—Mistral's Dancer **Robert Heathcote**
23 ONE WILD NIGHT, 5, b m Rakaposhi King—Teenero **R. E. Bailey**
24 OSCARS LAW, 4, b f Oscar (IRE)—Eloquent Lawyer **A. J. Brazier**
25 PAUNTLEY GOFA, 9, b g Afzal—Gotageton
26 PINTLE, 5, b m Pivotal—Boozy **Robert Heathcote**
27 ROVING VIXEN (IRE), 4, b f Foxhound (USA)—Rend Rover (FR) **Mr J. L. Spearing**
28 SEVERN AIR, 7, b m Alderbrook—Mariner's Air **Mrs W. M. Badger**
29 SPARKLINSPIRIT, 6, b g Sovereign Water (FR)—Emilys Trust **K. Young**
30 STOKESIES BOY, 5, gr h Key of Luck (USA)—Lesley's Fashion **B. J. Stokes**
31 STOKESIES WISH, 5, ch m Fumo di Londra (IRE)—Jess Rebec **B. J. Stokes**
32 THIHN (IRE), 10, ch g Machiavellian (USA)—Hasana (USA) **The Square Milers**
33 TOM'S PRIZE, 10, ch g Gunner B—Pandora's Prize **Mrs P. Joynes**
34 4, b f Oscar (IRE)—Vi's Delight
35 WATERSPRAY (AUS), 7, ch g Lake Coniston (IRE)—Forain (NZ) **Bache Silk**

THREE-YEAR-OLDS

36 BINTY, b f Prince Sabo—Mistral's Dancer **Robert Heathcote**
37 ISLAND SWING (IRE), ch f Trans Island—Farmers Swing (IRE) **Mr J. L. Spearing**
38 LEGAL BELLE, ch f Superpower—Legal Sound **Mrs J. E. Young**
39 MILLSY, b f Pursuit of Love—Jucea **A. A. Campbell and G. M. Eales**
40 MISTER ELEGANT, b c Fraam—Risky Valentine **M. Lawrence & W. Cooper**
41 PETITE GIRL, gr f Daylami (IRE)—Pagoda (FR) **Jackie & George Smith**
42 SAXON LIL (IRE), b f Second Empire (IRE)—Salva **T. N. Masonaires**
43 TOP PURSUIT, b g Pursuit of Love—Top of The Parkes **Masonaires**

TWO-YEAR-OLDS

44 B f 10/4 Averti (IRE)—Adeptation (USA) (Exceller (USA)) (5000)
45 Ch f 10/3 Tomba—Ashkernazy (IRE) (Salt Dome (USA)) (1904) **The Square Milers**
46 B f 11/2 Zilzal (USA)—Jucea (Bluebird (USA)) **G. M. Eales**
47 B f 4/4 Josr Algarhoud (IRE)—Vax Rapide (Sharpo) **A. J. Brazier**

Other Owners: P. A. Bache, B. A. Beale, Mrs S. L. Beale, J. H. A. Bennett, S. J. Court, Countess Coventry, W. J. Goddard, P. L. Jackson, Mr G. H. Silk., D. A. Thorpe.

Assistant Trainer: Miss T Spearing

Jockey (flat): Lisa Jones, S. Drowne. **Jockey (NH):** A. Evans, A. P. McCoy, H. Oliver, R. Thornton. **Amateur:** Mr J. Evans.

---

556 **MR P. SPOTTISWOOD, Hexham**
Postal: **Cleugh Head, Greenhaugh, Tarset, Hexham, Northumberland, NE48 1PT.**
Contacts: **PHONE (01434) 240336 MOBILE (07977) 502281**

1 THE ROOKEN (IRE), 6, b g Fourstars Allstar (USA)—Be My Sweetheart (IRE) **Mr P. Spottiswood**

Assistant Trainer: Anne Spottiswood

---

557 **MR T. STACK, Golden**
Postal: **Thomastown Castle, Golden, Co. Tipperary, Ireland.**
Contacts: **PHONE +353 (0) 62 54129 FAX +353 (0) 62 54399**
E-MAIL tommystack@eircom.net

1 ENFIELD CHASE (IRE), 4, b c Foxhound (USA)—Melinte
2 GOLDEN BASKET (IRE), 5, ch m College Chapel—Touche-A-Tout (IRE)
3 HIT THE NET (IRE), 8, b g Be My Native (USA)—Thetravellinglady (IRE)
4 KERRY WAY (IRE), 6, b h Dolphin Street (FR)—Fairy Highlands (IRE)
5 OTHERWISE (IRE), 4, ch f Dr Devious (IRE)—Touche-A-Tout (IRE)
6 SEROV (IRE), 7, ch h Mujtahid (USA)—Title Roll (IRE)
7 TINQUEST, 6, b m Rainbow Quest (USA)—Tizona
8 TOLPUDDLE (IRE), 5, b h College Chapel—Tabdea (USA)

MR T. STACK—continued

THREE-YEAR-OLDS

9 **BOWERMAN**, ch c Dr Fong (USA)—Itqan (IRE)
10 **DILLONS DILEMMA (IRE)**, ch c Monashee Mountain (USA)—God Speed Her
11 **GREAT QUEST (IRE)**, b f Montjeu (IRE)—Paparazzi (IRE)
12 **HOFFMAN (IRE)**, ch c Dr Devious (USA)—Morale
13 **KING OF MERLIA (USA)**, ch c High Yield (USA)—Fardus (IRE)
14 **LIVE IN FEAR (IRE)**, b c Fasliyev (USA)—Fear And Greed (IRE)
15 **MONSUSU (IRE)**, b f Montjeu (IRE)—Susun Kelapa (USA)
16 **MURANI (IRE)**, b f Marju (IRE)—Tafrah (IRE)
17 **PERCE ROCK**, b c Dansili—Twilight Secret
18 **PREFONTAINE**, gr c Nashwan (USA)—Ashjaan (USA)
19 **QUASIMODO (IRE)**, b c Night Shift (USA)—Daziyra (IRE)
20 **RAMAYNA (IRE)**, b f Entrepreneur—Fruition
21 **WOMAN'S CHAT (IRE)**, b f Montjeu (IRE)—Shesadelight
22 B c Entrepreneur—Zing Ping (IRE)

TWO-YEAR-OLDS

23 B f 9/5 Mull of Kintyre (USA)—Basin Street Blues (IRE) (Dolphin Street (FR))
24 B f 16/4 Danehill (USA)—Dance Date (IRE) (Sadler's Wells (USA)) (26827)
25 **DISCLOSURE (IRE)**, b c 1/5 Desert Style (IRE)—Blazing Soul (IRE) (Common Grounds) (12072)
26 Ch f 7/4 Galileo (IRE)—Fear And Greed (IRE) (Brief Truce (USA))
27 **FINAL QUEST (IRE)**, ch f 5/2 King Charlemagne (USA)—Tuscaloosa (Robellino (USA)) (6706)
28 **KATCHATURIAN (IRE)**, b c 21/3 Spectrum (IRE)—On Air (FR) (Chief Singer)
29 **LIGHTNING HIT (IRE)**, b c 18/3 Orpen (USA)—Starring Role (IRE) (Glenstal (USA))
30 **LITHICA (IRE)**, b f 25/2 Orpen (USA)—Vespers (IRE) (Perugino (USA))
31 B c 1/3 Mull of Kintyre (USA)—Mepa Discovery (USA) (Clever Trick (USA)) (18779)
32 Ch c 24/2 Spectrum (IRE)—Missie Madam (IRE) (Kenmare (FR)) (3353)
33 B f 26/3 Montjeu (IRE)—Paparazzi (IRE) (Shernazar) (40240)
34 B c 24/3 Randy Regent (CAN)—Penda (USA) (Pioneering (USA))
35 Ch f 18/5 Galileo (IRE)—Silver Skates (IRE) (Slip Anchor)
36 B f 15/3 Brave Act—Silver Venture (USA) (Silver Hawk (USA)) (5364)
37 B f 25/1 Orpen (USA)—Some Fun (Wolverlife)
38 **STOLEN SUMMER (IRE)**, ch c 1/5 Spectrum (IRE)—Touche-A-Tout (IRE) (Royal Academy (USA)) (9389)
39 **THE CONTENDER (IRE)**, b c 22/1 Spectrum (IRE)—Tabdea (USA) (Topsider (USA))
40 **WHOOSH (IRE)**, b f 14/1 Barathea (IRE)—Gift Box (IRE) (Jareer (USA)) (10060)
41 B c 12/2 Fasliyev (USA)—Young Affair (IRE) (Mukaddamah (USA)) (28000)

Owners: Ms Anja Geselbracht, Mr T. V. Magnier, Mr M. A. Begley, Mr P. A. Byrne, Mr T. Corden, Ms W. Cousins, Arthur Finnan, Pearse Gately, Miss C. Lynch, Mrs John Magnier, Mr J. P. McManus, Mrs Diane Nagle, Mrs Wendy O'Leary, Mr Peter Piller, Mr R. E. Sangster, Ms K. Vaughan.

Jockey (flat): W. M. Lordan. **Apprentice:** M. A. Cleere, W. J. Lee.

---

558 **MR J. T. STIMPSON, Newcastle-under-Lyme**
Postal: **Park House, Park Road, Butterton, Newcastle-under-Lyme, Staffordshire, ST5 4DZ.**
Contacts: **PHONE (01782) 636020**

1 **ICE AND FIRE**, 6, b g Cadeaux Genereux—Tanz (IRE) **Mr J. T. Stimpson**
2 **MONSTER JAWBREAKER (IRE)**, 6, b g Zafonic (USA)—Salvora (USA) **Mr J. T. Stimpson**
3 **MR EYE POPPER (IRE)**, 6, b g Sadler's Wells (USA)—Tipperary Tartan **Mr J. T. Stimpson**
4 **MR FREEZE (IRE)**, 5, b g Silver Hawk (USA)—Iviza (IRE) **Mr J. T. Stimpson**
5 **MR JAWBREAKER (IRE)**, 6, b g Sadler's Wells (USA)—Abury (IRE) **Mr J. T. Stimpson**
6 **ROYALTEA**, 4, ch f Desert King (IRE)—Come To Tea (IRE) **Mr J. T. Stimpson**

559 **MRS M. K. STIRK, Ripon**
Postal: **Fountains Farm, Aldfield, Ripon, North Yorkshire, HG4 3EB.**
Contacts: **PHONE (01765) 606000 MOBILE (07759) 295989**
E-MAIL **maxinestirk@lineone.net** WEBSITE **www.chaserstore.co.uk**

1 ATTICUS FINCH (IRE), 8, b g Witness Box (USA)—Dramatic Loop (IRE) **Mrs M. K. Stirk**
2 CLEVER NORA (IRE), 5, b br m Topanoora—Mona Curra Gale (IRE) **Mrs M. K. Stirk**
3 THE BIG BREAKFAST (IRE), 5, b g Rashar (USA)—Aokay (IRE) **Mrs M. K. Stirk**

Assistant Trainer: A J Stirk

Jockey (NH): B. Harding. **Conditional:** R. Walford. **Amateur:** Mr G. Brewer, Mr M. Walford.

560 **MR D. R. STODDART, Towcester**
Postal: **Highfields, Adstone, Towcester, Northamptonshire, NN12 8DS.**
Contacts: **PHONE (01327) 860433 FAX (01327) 860305 MOBILE (07793) 983921**

1 KILLONE MOONLIGHT (IRE), 6, b m Moonax (IRE)—Killone Brae **Mr D. R. Stoddart**
2 OFF SPIN, 5, b g Petoski—Re-Spin **Mr D. R. Stoddart**
3 QUAINTON HILLS, 11, b g Gildoran—Spin Again **Mr D. R. Stoddart**
4 SERIOUS POSITION (IRE), 10, ch g Orchestra—Lady Temba **Mr D. R. Stoddart**

561 **MR W. STOREY, Consett**
Postal: **Grange Farm Stables, Muggleswick, Consett, Co. Durham, DH8 9DW.**
Contacts: **PHONE (01207) 255259 FAX (01207) 255607 MOBILE (07860) 510441**
E-MAIL **wlstorey@dsi.pipex.com** WEBSITE **www.wilfstorey.com**

1 BARGAIN HUNT (IRE), 4, b g Foxhound (USA)—Atisayin (USA) **Gremlin Racing**
2 COLWAY RITZ, 11, b g Rudimentary—Million Heiress **Mrs M. Tindale & Mr Tom Park**
3 COPPLESTONE (IRE), 9, b g Second Set (IRE)—Queen of The Brush **J. D. Wright**
4 DARK SHADOWS, 10, b g Machiavellian (USA)—Instant Desire (USA) **D. O. Cremin**
5 DIMPLE CHAD, 6, b g Sadler's Wells (USA)—Fern **Tony Stafford Racing Partnership II**
6 DR BILLY (IRE), 11, b g Dry Dock—Carrigconeen **Mr W. Storey**
7 KILLOCH PLACE (IRE), 4, b g Compton Place—Hibernica (IRE) **A. J. Stafford**
8 MINSTER ABBI, 5, b m Minster Son—Elitist **D. Swan**
9 MISS WIZZ, 5, b m Wizard King—Fyas **A. McCormick**
10 RACING NIGHT (USA), 5, b g Lear Fan (USA)—Broom Dance (USA) **Tony Stafford Racing Partnership I**
11 SIR EDWARD BURROW (IRE), 7, b g Distinctly North (USA)—Alalja (IRE) **Mr W. Storey**
12 SUGGEST, 10, b g Midyan (USA)—Awham (USA) **Mrs M. Tindale**
13 THE WIZARD MUL, 5, br g Wizard King—Longden Pride **Gremlin Racing**
14 TIZ WIZ, 4, b f Wizard King—Dannistar **Thistle And Rose Racing**
15 WEAVER GEORGE (IRE), 15, b g Flash of Steel—Nephrite **Regent Decorators Ltd**

THREE-YEAR-OLDS

16 EKATERINA, b f Merdon Melody—Hsian **A. J. Stafford**
17 HIMIST (IRE), b g Lahib (USA)—Tara View (IRE) **The Friendly Racing Partnership**

Other Owners: Mr A. J. Cork, Mr S. J. Howard, Mrs K. J. Hutchinson, T. Park, Mr T. Peters, K. Sobey, A. J. Stafford, Mrs M. Tindale.

Assistant Trainer: Miss S Storey

562 **SIR M. STOUTE, Newmarket**
Postal: **Freemason Lodge, Bury Road, Newmarket, Suffolk, CB8 7BY.**
Contacts: **PHONE (01638) 663801 FAX (01638) 667276**

1 ALMURAAD (IRE), 4, b c Machiavellian (USA)—Wellspring (IRE) **Hamdan Al Maktoum**
2 ARAKAN (USA), 5, b h Nureyev (USA)—Far Across **The Niarchos Family**
3 BORDER CASTLE, 4, b c Grand Lodge (USA)—Tempting Prospect **Her Majesty The Queen**
4 CHIC, 5, ch m Machiavellian (USA)—Exclusive **Cheveley Park Stud**
5 COVER UP (IRE), 8, b g Machiavellian (USA)—Sought Out (IRE) **Ballymacoll Stud Farm Ltd**
6 DESERT STAR, 5, b g Green Desert (USA)—Phantom Gold **Her Majesty The Queen**
7 DISTINCTION (IRE), 6, b g Danehill (USA)—Ivy Leaf (IRE) **Highclere Thoroughbred Racing Ltd**

SIR M. STOUTE—continued

8 **EDEN ROCK (IRE)**, 4, b c Danehill (USA)—Marlene-D **The Celle Syndicate Incorporated**
9 **FAVOURABLE TERMS**, 5, b m Selkirk (USA)—Fatefully (USA) **Maktoum Al Maktoum**
10 **FORT DIGNITY (USA)**, 4, b c Seeking The Gold (USA)—Kitza (IRE) **Britton House Stud**
11 **GAMUT (IRE)**, 6, b h Spectrum (IRE)—Greektown **Mrs G. K. Smith**
12 **IMPERIAL STRIDE**, 4, b c Indian Ridge—Place de L'opera **Saeed Suhail**
13 **LORD MAYOR**, 4, b g Machiavellian (USA)—Misleading Lady
14 **MARAAHEL (IRE)**, 4, b c Alzao (USA)—Nasanice (IRE) **Hamdan Al Maktoum**
15 **MENOKEE (USA)**, 4, b c Cherokee Run (USA)—Meniatarra (USA) **Mrs S. Al Maktoum**
16 **NORTH LIGHT (IRE)**, 4, b c Danehill (USA)—Sought Out (IRE) **Ballymacoll Stud Farm Ltd**
17 **NOTABLE GUEST (USA)**, 4, b c Kingmambo (USA)—Yenda **K. Abdulla**
18 **PEERESS**, 4, ch f Pivotal—Noble One **Cheveley Park Stud**
19 **POISE (IRE)**, 4, b f Rainbow Quest (USA)—Crepe Ginger (IRE) **Cheveley Park Stud**
20 **PROMOTION**, 5, b g Sadler's Wells (USA)—Tempting Prospect **Her Majesty The Queen**
21 **QUIFF**, 4, b f Sadler's Wells (USA)—Wince **K. Abdulla**
22 **RED BLOOM**, 4, b f Selkirk (USA)—Red Camellia **Cheveley Park Stud**
23 **STREAM OF GOLD (IRE)**, 4, b c Rainbow Quest (USA)—River Dancer **Ballymacoll Stud Farm Ltd**

THREE-YEAR-OLDS

24 **ALAMIYAN (IRE)**, b c King's Best (USA)—Alasana (IRE) **H. H. Aga Khan**
25 **ALDABRA**, b c Green Desert (USA)—Krisalya **Mrs S. Al Maktoum**
26 **ANTOINETTE (USA)**, b f Silver Hawk (USA)—Excellentadventure (USA) **Highclere Thoroughbred Racing XXIV**
27 **ARTURIUS (IRE)**, b c Anabaa (USA)—Steeple **The Celle Syndicate Incorporated**
28 **ASAWER (IRE)**, b f Darshaan—Sassy Bird (USA) **Hamdan Al Maktoum**
29 **AVIEMORE**, b c Selkirk (USA)—Film Script **Her Majesty The Queen**
30 **BLUE TRAIN (IRE)**, b c Sadler's Wells (USA)—Igreja (ARG) **The Celle Syndicate Incorporated**
31 **BOLD EAGLE (IRE)**, ch c Rainbow Quest (USA)—Britannia (GER) **Ammerland Verwaltung GmbH & Co.KG**
32 **CARISOLO**, b f Dubai Millennium—Solo de Lune (IRE) **Britton House Stud**
33 **CELTIQUE**, b f Celtic Swing—Heart's Harmony **Mrs D. M. Haynes**
34 **CHORALIST**, b f Danehill (USA)—Choir Mistress **Cheveley Park Stud**
35 **DISCUSS (USA)**, b f Danzig (USA)—Private Line (USA) **K. Abdulla**
36 **DUBAI VENTURE**, b c Rainbow Quest (USA)—Bombazine (IRE) **Saeed Suhail**
37 **ECHELON**, b f Danehill (USA)—Exclusive **Cheveley Park Stud**
38 **EXHIBIT ONE (USA)**, b f Silver Hawk (USA)—Tsar's Pride **K. Abdulla**
39 **FLAG LIEUTENANT**, b c Machiavellian (USA)—Fairy Godmother **Her Majesty The Queen**
40 **FRONT STAGE (IRE)**, b br c Grand Lodge (USA)—Dreams **Saeed Suhail**
41 **GALA EVENING**, b c Daylami (IRE)—Balleta (USA) **K. Abdulla**
42 **GALLANTRY**, b c Green Desert (USA)—Gay Gallanta (USA) **Cheveley Park Stud**
43 **GAMBLE OF THE DAY (USA)**, ch c Cozzene (USA)—Sue Warner (USA) **Saeed Suhail**
44 **GLISTENING**, b c Sadler's Wells (USA)—Shining Water **K. Abdulla**
45 **HARD TOP (IRE)**, b c Darshaan—Well Head (IRE) **Ballymacoll Stud Farm Ltd**
46 **HIGHINDI**, b f Montjeu (IRE)—Lalindi (IRE) **Lady Bamford**
47 **HIGHLAND DIVA (IRE)**, ch f Selkirk (USA)—Drama Class (IRE) **Ballymacoll Stud Farm Ltd**
48 **HOME AFFAIRS**, b c Dansili—Orford Ness **K. Abdulla**
49 **HORNPIPE**, b c Danehill (USA)—Dance Sequence (USA) **Cheveley Park Stud**
50 **INCH LODGE**, ch c Grand Lodge (USA)—Legaya **Maktoum Al Maktoum**
51 **KALAMKAR (IRE)**, gr c Daylami (IRE)—Kalamba (IRE) **H. H. Aga Khan**
52 **KARLIYNA (IRE)**, br f Rainbow Quest (USA)—Karliyka (IRE) **H. H. Aga Khan**
53 **KERASHAN (IRE)**, b c Sinndar (IRE)—Kerataka (IRE) **H. H. Aga Khan**
54 **KING'S KAMA**, b c Giant's Causeway—Maid For The Hills **Saeed Suhail**
55 **KING'S MAJESTY (IRE)**, b c King's Best (USA)—Tiavanita (USA) **Saeed Suhail**
56 **KINGDOM OF DREAMS (IRE)**, b c Sadler's Wells (USA)—Regal Portrait (USA) **Saeed Suhail**
57 **KUBA (IRE)**, b f Sadler's Wells (USA)—Key Change (IRE) **Lady Clague**
58 **LINNGARI (IRE)**, ch c Indian Ridge—Lidakiya (IRE) **H. H. Aga Khan**
59 **LYSANDRA (IRE)**, b f Danehill (USA)—Oriane **Lady Clague**
60 **MARITIMA**, b f Darshaan—Armeria (USA) **K. Abdulla**
61 **MASTER OF THE RACE**, ch c Selkirk (USA)—Dust Dancer **Saeed Suhail**
62 **MORDOR (FR)**, b c Sadler's Wells (USA)—Moon Driver (USA) **The Niarchos Family**
63 **MOSTASHAAR (FR)**, b c Intikhab (USA)—Nasanice (IRE) **Hamdan Al Maktoum**
64 **MOUNTAIN HIGH (IRE)**, b c Danehill (USA)—Hellenic **Mrs S. Magnier**
65 **MUTAJAMMEL (FR)**, b c Kingmambo (USA)—Irtifa **Hamdan Al Maktoum**
66 **NATIONAL TRUST**, b c Sadler's Wells (USA)—National Treasure **Cheveley Park Stud**
67 **NOTNOWCATO**, ch c Inchinnor—Rambling Rose **Anthony & David De Rothschild**
68 **PUBLIC FORUM**, b c Rainbow Quest (USA)—Valentine Girl **K. Abdulla**
69 **PYRAMID**, ch c Pivotal—Mary Cornwallis **Cheveley Park Stud**
70 **QUICKFIRE**, b f Dubai Millennium—Daring Miss **K. Abdulla**

SIR M. STOUTE—continued

71 **RAIDER OF THE EAST (IRE)**, b c Darshaan—Convenience (IRE) **Saeed Suhail**
72 **RAZE**, ch f Halling (USA)—Rive (USA) **K. Abdulla**
73 **READ FEDERICA**, ch f Fusaichi Pegasus (USA)—Reading Habit (USA) **Mrs R. J. Jacobs**
74 **REGINA**, b f Green Desert (USA)—Dazzle **Cheveley Park Stud**
75 **ROB ROY (USA)**, b br c Lear Fan (USA)—Camanoe (USA) **Mr P. Newton**
76 **ROHAANI (USA)**, ch c High Yield (USA)—Strawberry's Charm (USA) **Hamdan Al Maktoum**
77 **SANTA FE (IRE)**, b c Green Desert (USA)—Shimna **The Celle Syndicate Incorporated**
78 **SEVEN MAGICIANS (USA)**, b br f Silver Hawk (USA)—Mambo Jambo (USA) **The Niarchos Family**
79 **SHANGHAI LILY (IRE)**, b f King's Best (USA)—Marlene-D **Cheveley Park Stud**
80 **SHARP REPLY (USA)**, b c Diesis—Questonia **K. Abdulla**
81 **STAMFORD**, b br c Darshaan—Silver Lane (USA) **Mrs S. Al Maktoum**
82 **STELLAR BRILLIANT (USA)**, b br f Kris S (USA)—Subeen **Maktoum Al Maktoum**
83 **THUNDER ROCK (IRE)**, b c King's Best (USA)—Park Express **The Celle Syndicate Incorporated**
84 **TOMOOHAT (USA)**, b f Danzig (USA)—Crystal Downs (USA) **Hamdan Al Maktoum**
85 **TRIBE**, b c Danehill (USA)—Leo Girl (USA) **Highclere Thoroughbred Racing XXII**
86 **VILLARRICA (USA)**, ch f Selkirk (USA)—Melikah (IRE) **Maktoum Al Maktoum**
87 **ZALONGO**, ch c Zafonic (USA)—Tamassos **A. Christodoulou**
88 **ZARABAD (IRE)**, b c King's Best (USA)—Zarannda (IRE) **H. H. Aga Khan**
89 **ZAYNIYA (IRE)**, b f Machiavellian (USA)—Zayana (IRE) **H. H. Aga Khan**

TWO-YEAR-OLDS

90 Ch f 8/2 Sinndar (IRE)—Adaiyka (IRE) (Doyoun) **H. H. Aga Khan**
91 B c 18/4 Kalanisi (IRE)—Alasana (IRE) (Darshaan) **H. H. Aga Khan**
92 B f 4/4 Machiavellian (USA)—All Grain (Polish Precedent (USA)) **R. Barnett**
93 **ALLEGRETTO (IRE)**, ch f 31/1 Galileo (IRE)—Alleluia (Caerleon (USA)) (415000) **Cheveley Park Stud**
94 **ARMADA**, b c 4/2 Anabaa (USA)—
    Trevillari (USA) (Riverman (USA)) (70000) **Highclere Thoroughbred Racing XXVIII**
95 B c 3/2 Danehill (USA)—Arrive (Kahyasi) **K. Abdulla**
96 B c 12/3 Fantastic Light (USA)—Barboukh (Night Shift (USA)) (90000) **The Duke of Devonshire**
97 **BAYYAAN (USA)**, br f 19/4 Dixieland Band (USA)—Najiya (Nashwan (USA)) **Hamdan Al Maktoum**
98 **BELANAK (IRE)**, b c 14/4 Sinndar (IRE)—Balanka (IRE) (Alzao (USA)) **H. H. Aga Khan**
99 **BEST ALIBI (IRE)**, b c 25/2 King's Best (USA)—
    Chauncy Lane (IRE) (Sadler's Wells (USA)) (190000) **Maktoum Al Maktoum**
100 **BEST WAY (IRE)**, ch c 12/2 King's Best (USA)—Green Jannat (USA) (Alydar (USA)) **Saeed Suhail**
101 **BOOK OF MUSIC (IRE)**, b c 7/5 Sadler's Wells (USA)—Novelette (Darshaan) (200000) **Maktoum Al Maktoum**
102 B f 9/2 Sadler's Wells (USA)—Borgia (GER) (Acatenango (GER)) **Ammerland Verwaltung GmbH & Co.KG**
103 Ch f 14/4 Galileo (IRE)—Britannia (GER) (Tarim) **Ammerland Verwaltung GmbH & Co.KG**
104 **CHAMINADE (USA)**, b f 2/2 Danzig (USA)—Flute (Seattle Slew (USA)) **K. Abdulla**
105 **CLAFOUTIS (USA)**, ch f 26/2 Unbridled's Song (USA)—
    Sous Entendu (USA) (Shadeed (USA)) **Maktoum Al Maktoum**
106 **DANCE SEQUEL**, ch f 18/3 Selkirk (USA)—Dance Sequence (USA) (Mr Prospector (USA)) **Cheveley Park Stud**
107 **DANKOVA (IRE)**, b c 19/2 Danehill (USA)—
    Born Beautiful (USA) (Silver Deputy (CAN)) (280000) **Maktoum Al Maktoum**
108 B c 23/4 Alhaarth (IRE)—Darariyna (IRE) (Shirley Heights) **H. H. Aga Khan**
109 B f 20/3 Spinning World (USA)—Dawala (IRE) (Lashkari) **H. H. Aga Khan**
110 **DAYROSE**, ch f 18/3 Daylami (USA)—Blush Rambler (USA) (Blushing Groom (FR)) **Sir Evelyn de Rothschild**
111 **DEAN'S YARD**, b c 27/3 Machiavellian (USA)—Abbey Strand (USA) (Shadeed (USA)) **Her Majesty The Queen**
112 **DIWALI**, b c 25/3 Fantastic Light (USA)—Zandaka (FR) (Doyoun) **Maktoum Al Maktoum**
113 **DREAM PRIZE (IRE)**, b c 6/3 Peintre Celebre (USA)—Night Teeny (Platini (GER)) (170000) **Saeed Suhail**
114 **DUKEDOM**, gr c 12/4 Highest Honor (FR)—
    Rose Noble (USA) (Vaguely Noble) (140000) **Highclere Thoroughbred Racing XXXI**
115 **DUTY (IRE)**, b c 18/3 Rainbow Quest (USA)—
    Wendylina (IRE) (In The Wings) (105000) **Highclere Thoroughbred Racing XXX**
116 **DYNACAM (USA)**, b f 10/5 Dynaformer (USA)—Najecam (USA) (Trempolino) (199521) **Saeed Suhail**
117 **ELISE**, b f 16/4 Fantastic Light (USA)—Napoleon's Sister (IRE) (Alzao (USA)) **Normandie Stud Ltd**
118 **ERYTHEIS (USA)**, b f 27/1 Theatrical—Enthused (USA) (Seeking the Gold (USA)) **The Niarchos Family**
119 **EXCELLENT**, ch f 26/6 Grand Lodge (USA)—Exclusive (Polar Falcon (USA)) **Cheveley Park Stud**
120 **FINAL VERSE**, b c 22/2 Mark of Esteem (IRE)—Tamassos (Dance In Time (CAN)) **Mr Athos Christodoulou**
121 **FLEETING MEMORY**, b f 31/1 Danehill (USA)—Flight of Fancy (Sadler's Wells (USA)) **Her Majesty The Queen**
122 **FUSILIER**, ch c 11/2 Medicean—Fearless Revival (Cozzene (USA)) **Cheveley Park Stud**
123 **GALACTIC STAR**, bc 9/3 Galileo (IRE)—Balisada (Kris) (700000) **Saeed Suhail**
124 **GATHERING LIGHT**, b c 14/5 Fantastic Light (USA)—
    Woodland Melody (USA) (Woodman (USA)) **Maktoum Al Maktoum**
125 **GLAMIS CASTLE (USA)**, b c 2/3 Selkirk (USA)—Fairy Godmother (Fairy King (USA)) **Her Majesty The Queen**
126 **GRAIN OF TRUTH**, b f 1/2 Gulch (USA)—Pure Grain (Polish Precedent (USA)) (270000) **Maktoum Al Maktoum**

SIR M. STOUTE—continued

127 **GRAND PALACE (IRE)**, b c 24/1 Grand Lodge (USA)—
Pocket Book (IRE) (Reference Point) (220000) **Saeed Suhail**
128 **GREAT HAWK (USA)**, b c 19/4 El Prado (IRE)—Laser Hawk (USA) (Silver Hawk (USA)) (212822) **Saeed Suhail**
129 **GRECIAN AIR (FR)**, b f 28/2 King's Best (USA)—Greek Air (IRE) (Ela-Mana-Mou) (107310) **Saeed Suhail**
130 **GREEK WELL (IRE)**, b c 19/4 Sadler's Wells (USA)—Hellenic (Darshaan) **Ballymacoll Stud Farm Ltd**
131 **GREEN CALIBRE**, b c 31/3 Green Desert (USA)—
Air of Distinction (IRE) (Distinctly North (USA)) (150000) **Saeed Suhail**
132 **GREEN DOLLAR**, b f 20/3 Kingmambo (USA)—
Strawberry Roan (IRE) (Sadler's Wells (USA)) (122372) **Saeed Suhail**
133 B c 17/2 Barathea (IRE)—Hasainiya (IRE) (Top Ville) **H. H. Aga Khan**
134 **HEAVEN SENT**, ch f 4/2 Pivotal—Heavenly Ray (Rahy (USA)) **Cheveley Park Stud**
135 B f 28/1 Diesis—High Walden (USA) (El Gran Senor (USA)) **K. Abdulla**
136 **INNER VOICE (USA)**, gr c 23/4 Cozzene (USA)—
Miss Henderson Co (USA) (Silver Hawk (USA)) (252726) **Maktoum Al Maktoum**
137 **JEREMY (USA)**, b c 2/3 Danehill Dancer (IRE)—Glint In Her Eye (USA) (Arazi (USA))
138 **JUROR (USA)**, gr ro c 17/3 Royal Academy (USA)—
Paper Princess (USA) (Flying Paster (USA)) (95770) **Highclere Thoroughbred Racing XXVII**
139 **KALANDARA (IRE)**, b f 1/4 Rainbow Quest (USA)—Kalamba (IRE) (Green Dancer (USA)) **H. H. Aga Khan**
140 B br c 16/4 Fantastic Light (USA)—Karliyka (IRE) (Last Tycoon) **H. H. Aga Khan**
141 **LEMON DROP LAD (USA)**, ch c 14/3 Lemon Drop Kid (USA)—
April Starlight (USA) (Storm Bird (CAN)) (58526) **Saeed Suhail**
142 **LIGHT SENTENCE**, b c 20/1 Fantastic Light (USA)—Almela (IRE) (Akarad (FR)) (130000) **Maktoum Al Maktoum**
143 **LOVINGLY**, b f 14/1 Grand Lodge (USA)—Easy To Love (USA) (Diesis) **Lordship Stud Limited**
144 **MAGIC PEAK (IRE)**, b f 23/2 Danehill (USA)—
Magic Cove (USA) (Kingmambo (USA)) (230000) **Cheveley Park Stud**
145 **MATHOOR**, ch c 20/1 Fantastic Light (USA)—
Madame Dubois (Legend of France (USA)) (230000) **Hamdan Al Maktoum**
146 **MIGHTY**, ch c 3/5 Pivotal—Miswaki Belle (USA) (Miswaki (USA)) **Cheveley Park Stud**
147 B c 28/3 Stravinsky—Mimbet (USA) (Raise A Native) **Ammerland Verwaltung GmbH & Co.KG**
148 **MUTAMARRES**, b c 17/4 Green Desert (USA)—Inajad (Machiavellian (USA)) **Hamdan Al Maktoum**
149 **NASTRELLI (IRE)**, b c 25/4 Mozart (IRE)—Dawnsio (IRE) (Tate Gallery (USA)) **Lady Clague**
150 **NAUGHTY BY NATURE**, b c 7/5 Machiavellian (USA)—
Rumpipumpy (Shirley Heights) (160000) **Maktoum Al Maktoum**
151 **OGEE**, ch c 17/2 Generous (IRE)—Aethra (USA) (Trempolino (USA)) (85000) **Sir Evelyn de Rothschild**
152 **ORANGE STRAVINSKY**, b c 16/3 Stravinsky (USA)—
Orange Sunset (IRE) (Roanoke (USA)) (150000) **Newsells Park Stud Limited**
153 B f 22/2 Sadler's Wells (USA)—Orford Ness (Selkirk (USA)) **K. Abdulla**
154 **PEARLY KING (USA)**, br c 18/4 Kingmambo (USA)—
Mother of Pearl (IRE) (Sadler's Wells (USA)) (106411) **Maktoum Al Maktoum**
155 B f 23/1 Sadler's Wells (USA)—Prove (Danehill (USA)) **K. Abdulla**
156 **QUEEN'S BEST**, b f 15/1 King's Best (USA)—Cloud Castle (In The Wings) (310000) **Cheveley Park Stud**
157 **RAINBOW FLING (IRE)**, b c 18/2 Spectrum (IRE)—Naval Affair (IRE) (Last Tycoon) **Ballymacoll Stud Farm Ltd**
158 **RANDOM CALL (USA)**, b f 12/3 War Chant (USA)—
Lignify (ARG) (Confidential Talk (USA)) **Maktoum Al Maktoum**
159 **RED GALA**, b c 21/4 Sinndar (IRE)—Red Camellia (Polar Falcon (USA)) **Cheveley Park Stud**
160 **REGAL ROYALE**, b c 22/1 Medicean—Regal Rose (Danehill (USA)) **Cheveley Park Stud**
161 B c 22/3 Sadler's Wells (USA)—Request (Rainbow Quest (USA)) **
162 B f 24/4 Selkirk (USA)—Riyafa (IRE) (Kahyasi) **H. H. Aga Khan**
163 **SAND SPRITE (IRE)**, b f 3/5 Green Desert (USA)—Fleet Amour (USA) (Afleet (CAN)) **Mr & Mrs Denis Haynes**
164 **SCOTTISH STAGE (IRE)**, ch f 25/2 Selkirk (USA)—
Drama Class (IRE) (Caerleon (USA)) **Ballymacoll Stud Farm Ltd**
165 **SCYLLA CADEAUX (IRE)**, ch f 21/4 Cadeaux Genereux—
She's Classy (USA) (Boundary (USA)) (70000) **Newsells Park Stud Limited**
166 **SEEKING STRAIGHT (IRE)**, b c 13/4 Rainbow Quest (USA)—
Alignment (IRE) (Alzao (USA)) **Ballymacoll Stud Farm Ltd**
167 **SHADOW ASPECT**, b c 19/3 Nashwan (USA)—Hedonic (Gone West (USA)) **Maktoum Al Maktoum**
168 **SHORT SKIRT**, br f 16/3 Diktat—Much Too Risky (Bustino) **J. M. Greetham**
169 Br f 24/5 Kalanisi (IRE)—Sinndiya (IRE) (Pharly (FR)) **H. H. Aga Khan**
170 **SLEEP TALK (USA)**, br c 21/3 Theatrical—Sleep Easy (USA) (Seattle Slew (USA)) **K. Abdulla**
171 **SOMERSAULT**, ch f 24/3 Pivotal—Rash (Pursuit of Love) **Cheveley Park Stud**
172 Br f 6/5 Kalanisi (IRE)—Sought Out (IRE) (Rainbow Quest (USA)) **Ballymacoll Stud Farm Ltd**
173 **STAGE GIFT (IRE)**, ch c 25/4 Cadeaux Genereux—
Stage Struck (IRE) (Sadler's Wells (USA)) **Ballymacoll Stud Farm Ltd**
174 **STRAWBERRY LOLLY**, b f 21/2 Lomitas—
Strawberry Morn (CAN) (Travelling Victor (CAN)) **Newsells Park Stud Limited**
175 **SUMPTUOUS**, b f 9/3 Pivotal—Fabulous (Fabulous Dancer (USA)) **Cheveley Park Stud**

SIR M. STOUTE—continued

176 **TAMINOS LOVE,** b c 17/2 Lomitas—
      Tamise (USA) (Time For A Change (USA)) (42000) **Newsells Park Stud Limited**
177 **TAWAASSOL (USA),** b c 18/2 War Chant (USA)—
      Montecito (USA) (Seeking The Gold (USA)) (345836) **Hamdan Al Maktoum**
178 **UPPERMOST,** b f 24/2 Montjeu (IRE)—Zenith (Shirley Heights) **Her Majesty The Queen**
179 B c 25/1 Sadler's Wells (USA)—Valentine Girl (Alzao (USA)) **K. Abdulla**
180 **VALIANT,** b c 17/3 King's Best (USA)—Choir Mistress (Chief Singer) **Cheveley Park Stud**
181 **VELVET VALLEY (USA),** ch c 6/2 Gone West (USA)—Velvet Morning (USA) (Broad Brush (USA)) **K. Abdulla**
182 **VIRTUOSITY,** ch f 14/4 Pivotal—Virtuous (Exit To Nowhere (USA)) **Cheveley Park Stud**
183 **VISIBLE,** b c 28/2 Fantastic Light (USA)—Summer Dance (Sadler's Wells (USA)) **Cheveley Park Stud**
184 **VIVAT,** b f 9/3 Sadler's Wells (USA)—Dazzle (Gone West (USA)) **Cheveley Park Stud**
185 **WEDAAD,** ch f 10/1 Fantastic Light (USA)—My First Romance (Danehill) (240000) **Hamdan Al Maktoum**
186 **WELL HIDDEN,** b f 13/2 Sadler's Wells (USA)—Phantom Gold (Machiavellian (USA)) **Her Majesty The Queen**
187 B f 26/1 Zafonic (USA)—Winter Solstice (Unfuwain (USA)) **K. Abdulla**
188 **WULIMASTER (USA),** b br c 16/3 Silver Hawk (USA)—
      Kamaina (USA) (Mr Prospector (USA)) **The Niarchos Family**
189 **ZAM ZAMMAH,** b c 2/5 Agnes World (USA)—Krisalya (Kris) (160000)

Jockey (flat): K. Fallon.

563
MR R. M. STRONGE, Newbury
Postal: **Woods Folly, Beedon Common, Newbury, Berkshire, RG20 8TT.**
Contacts: **PHONE/FAX (01635) 248710 MOBILE (07887) 521333**
E-MAIL **robert@stronge4380.freeserve.co.uk**

1 **CORAL ISLAND,** 11, b g Charmer—Misowni **Mrs Bernice Stronge**
2 **COUSTOU (IRE),** 5, b g In Command (IRE)—Carranza (IRE) **A. P. Holland**
3 **GOLDEN FITZ (ARG),** 6, ch g Fitzcarraldo (ARG)—Good Last (ARG) **Mrs Bernice Stronge**
4 **INDUCEMENT,** 9, ch g Sabrehill (USA)—Verchinina **A. P. Holland**
5 **LEIGHTON (IRE),** 5, b g Desert Story (IRE)—Lady Fern **A. P. Holland**
6 **PORTICHOL PRINCESS,** 5, b m Bluegrass Prince (IRE)—Barbrallen **Peter J. Allen**
7 **STORM A BREWING,** 9, ch g Glacial Storm (USA)—Southern Squaw **Mrs Bernice Stronge**
8 **SURE FUTURE,** 9, b g Kylian (USA)—Lady Ever-So-Sure **The Test Valley Partnership**
9 **WATER KING (USA),** 6, b g Irish River (FR)—Brookshield Baby (IRE) **Hellyer, Clark, St Quinton**

Other Owners: N. Charlton, M. A. Clark, C. G. Hellyer, M. G. St Quinton.

Assistant Trainer: Bernice Stronge

Jockey (NH): B. Fenton, S. Stronge.

564
MRS L. STUBBS, Malton
Postal: **Beverley House Stables, Beverley Road, Malton, North Yorkshire, YO17 9PJ.**
Contacts: **PHONE (01653) 698731 FAX (01653) 698724 MOBILES (07747) 613962/(07801) 167707**

1 **DOUBLE RANSOM,** 6, b g Bahamian Bounty—Secrets of Honour **Tyme Partnership**
2 **EASTERN HOPE (IRE),** 6, b g Danehill Dancer (IRE)—Hope And Glory (USA) **T. C. Chiang**
3 **PAGAN STORM (USA),** 5, ch g Tabasco Cat (USA)—Melodeon (USA) **Mrs L. Stubbs**
4 **PRINCE PROSPECT,** 9, b g Lycius (USA)—Princess Dechtra (IRE) **Mrs L. Stubbs**
5 **SIR FRANCIS (IRE),** 7, b g Common Grounds—Red Note **The Champagne Club**
6 **SMARTER CHARTER,** 12, br g Master Willie—Irene's Charter **O. J. Williams**
7 **ZOOM ZOOM,** 5, b h Abou Zouz (USA)—Iltimas (USA) **H. Conlon**

THREE-YEAR-OLDS

8 **BEVERLEY BEAU,** b g Inchinor—Oriel Girl **Mrs K. J. Clappison**
9 **CABOPINO LAD (USA),** b g Comic Strip (USA)—Roxanne (USA) **H. Conlon**
10 **IL COLOSSEO (IRE),** b g Spectrum (IRE)—Valley Lights (IRE) **D. M. Thurlby**
11 **KEEPASHARPLOOKOUT (IRE),** b g Rossini (USA)—Zoyce **D. M. Smith**
12 **NEXT TIME AROUND (IRE),** b br g Namid—In Due Course (USA) **T. T. G. Osborne**
13 B f Brave Act—Queen Sigi (IRE) **C. A. McKechnie**
14 **RAPID RIVER,** b f Lahib (USA)—Cast A Spell **M. Sharkey**

MRS L. STUBBS—continued

TWO-YEAR-OLDS

15 **ACE BABY**, b g 12/3 First Trump—Mise En Scene (Lugana Beach) (2500) **D. M. Thurlby**
16 B c 10/3 Lujain (USA)—Bella Helena (Balidar) (2500) **The Champagne Club**
17 B c 25/3 Zilzal (USA)—Bring On The Choir (Chief Singer) (5000) **H. Conlon**
18 B g 9/3 Primo Valentino (IRE)—Cast A Spell (Magic Ring (IRE)) (6706) **B. Butt**
19 B g 14/4 Bold Fact (USA)—Heart of The Ocean (IRE) (Soviet Lad (USA)) (9000) **The Champagne Club**
20 Ch g 5/1 Arkadian Hero (USA)—Nashville Blues (IRE) (Try My Best (USA)) (2500) **The Champagne Club**
21 **RARE BREED**, b c 6/3 Foxhound (USA)—Rare Indigo (Timeless Times (USA)) (9000) **Rare Breeders**

Other Owners: Mrs J. Cummings, C. Barker, Mrs L. P. Beharrell, I. J. Blakey, Mr R. R. Irvine, M. S. Martin, T. T. G. Osborne, Mrs V. J. Pittman, P. G. Shorrock.

Jockey (flat): E. Ahern, K. Fallon. Jockey (NH): B. Fenton, A. P. McCoy. Apprentice: Kristin Stubbs.

---

565 **MR J. A. SUPPLE, Woodbridge**
Postal: The Dower House, Worlingworth Hall, Worlingworth, Woodbridge, Suffolk, IP13 7NS.
Contacts: PHONE (01728) 628554 MOBILE (07775) 943623

1 **ANOTHER PROMISE (IRE)**, 6, b g Presenting—Snape (IRE) **Geoff Hubbard Racing**
2 **ASK THE CHIEF**, 4, b g Silver Patriarch (IRE)—Kev's Lass (IRE) **Geoff Hubbard Racing**
3 **DAMASK DANCER (IRE)**, 6, b g Barathea (IRE)—Polish Rhythm (IRE) **Geoff Hubbard Racing**
4 **DON'T TELL JR (IRE)**, 11, b g Mister Lord (USA)—Middle Third **Geoff Hubbard Racing**
5 **GLORY OF LOVE**, 10, b g Belmez (USA)—Princess Lieven **Miss Lorna Preston**
6 **IMPS REFLECTION**, 8, gr g Terimon—Carousella **Mrs S. R. Bailey**
7 **LEVEL PAR (IRE)**, 5, ch g Cadeaux Genereux—Howaida (IRE) **Geoff Hubbard Racing**
8 **LITTLE SAXTEAD (IRE)**, 5, ch g Anshan—Snape (IRE) **Geoff Hubbard Racing**
9 **MESSAGER (FR)**, 5, ch g Brier Creek (USA)—Contessina (FR) **Geoff Hubbard Racing**
10 **NELLIE BROWNE (IRE)**, 5, ch m Presenting—Kev's Lass (IRE) **Geoff Hubbard Racing**
11 **PALES (GER)**, 4, ch g Secret 'n Classy (CAN)—Parlez Moi D'amour (FR) **Geoff Hubbard Racing**
12 **POLISH RHAPSODY (IRE)**, 4, b f Charnwood Forest (IRE)—Polish Rhythm (IRE) **Geoff Hubbard Racing**
13 **RICHIE'S DELIGHT (IRE)**, 12, br g Phardante (FR)—Johnstown Love (IRE) **Geoff Hubbard Racing**
14 **SUMMER STOCK (USA)**, 7, b g Theatrical—Lake Placid (USA) **Five Bells Racing**

Other Owners: Mr D. Johnson, Mrs J. Reader, Mrs S. Rodwell, Mr S. Taylor.

Assistant Trainer: Miss Lorna Preston

Jockey (flat): W. Supple. Jockey (NH): G. Supple. Conditional: S. Walsh. Amateur: Mr A. Merriam.

---

566 **MR CHARLIE SWAN, Cloughjordan**
Postal: Modreeny, Cloughjordan, Co. Tipperary, Ireland.
Contacts: HOME +353 (0) 505 42221 OFFICE/FAX +353 (0) 505 42128
MOBILE +353 (0) 862 573194
E-MAIL cswan@iol.ie

1 **AHEADOFHISTIME (IRE)**, 6, br g Supreme Leader—Timely Run (IRE) **Mrs T. Hyde**
2 **AMUIGH FEIN SPEIR (IRE)**, 5, br g Accordion—Spur of The Moment **Mr J. P. McManus**
3 **ANN AND TONIC (IRE)**, 4, b f Saddlers' Hall (IRE)—Any Dream (IRE) **Ann Medlock**
4 **ANNO JUBILO (GER)**, 8, b g Lando (GER)—Anna Maria (GER) **Mr Noel O'Flaherty**
5 **ANXIOUS MOMENTS (IRE)**, 10, b g Supreme Leader—Ms Brooks (IRE) **Mr J. P. McManus**
6 **ARELLANO (IRE)**, 7, ch g Erins Isle—Volnost (USA) **Mr J. P. McManus**
7 **ASTON (USA)**, 5, b g Bahri (USA)—Halholah (USA) **Tap Dancers Syndicate**
8 **BALINDOOLEY (FR)**, 5, b g Sheyrann—Rose des Ifs (FR) **P. G. Connolly**
9 **BALLYGUIDER BRIDGE (IRE)**, 5, b m Accordion—Shannon Dee (IRE) **Mrs Seamus Burns**
10 **BOG OAK (IRE)**, 5, b g Accordion—Miss Amy (IRE) **Mr J. P. McManus**
11 **BRAVERY (IRE)**, 6, b g Zaffaran (USA)—Carrick Shannon **Gigginstown House Stud**
12 **CAVALRY CHARGE (IRE)**, 4, b g War Hero—Desert Oasis **Capt D. G. Swan**
13 **COLONEL BRADLEY (IRE)**, 11, b g Un Desperado (FR)—Dora Frost **Mr J. P. McManus**
14 **CONTEMPO SUITE (IRE)**, 8, b g Lord Americo—Kintullagh **Mr Dermot Brennan**
15 **CORNIE O'CONNOR (IRE)**, 6, br g Roselier (FR)—Colleen Glen **Mr Michael Ryan**
16 **CROOKED THROW (IRE)**, 6, br g Anshan—Mary's View (IRE) **Hogan Woods Whelan Syndicate**
17 **DEBOMAR (IRE)**, 6, b g Taos (IRE)—Crimson Mary **Miss Rebecca Camlin**

MR CHARLIE SWAN—continued

18 **DIDUBACKIT (IRE)**, 6, b m Oscar (IRE)—Princess Henry (IRE) **Smith & Moorehead Syndicate**
19 **FAR MORE SERIOUS (IRE)**, 5, b br g Needle Gun (IRE)—Womans Heart (IRE) **Mr Fergus Byrne**
20 **GALTEEMOUNTAIN BOY (IRE)**, 5, b g Oscar (IRE)—Shantalla Bay **Charlie McCarthy**
21 **GLENBOGLE**, 6, b g Saddlers' Hall (IRE)—Great Exception **Mr J. P. McManus**
22 **GROUND BALL (IRE)**, 8, b g Bob's Return (IRE)—Bettyhill **Mr J. P. McManus**
23 **HASANPOUR (IRE)**, 5, b g Dr Devious (IRE)—Hasainiya (IRE) **Mr Derrick Smith**
24 **HE'S MY MAN (IRE)**, 7, b g Be My Native (USA)—That's The Bonus (IRE) **Mr J. P. McManus**
25 **HEROIC (IRE)**, 9, b g War Hero—Happy Patter **Mr J. P. McManus**
26 **INGRES**, 5, b g Sadler's Wells (USA)—Bloudan (USA) **Mr Dermot Cox**
27 **JUNIOR JURASIC (IRE)**, 5, b br g Un Desperado (FR)—Kalifornia Katie (IRE) **Howmuchamonth Syndicate**
28 **KIT CARSON (IRE)**, 5, b g Dr Massini (IRE)—Roses Niece (IRE) **Mrs Sue Magnier**
29 **LACKELLY BLAZE (IRE)**, 7, b m Eurobus—Dancing Melba **Lackelly Syndicate**
30 **LAKIL BOY (IRE)**, 5, b g Presenting—Tinerana Noble **Pat Droney**
31 **LAURA STAR (IRE)**, 7, b g Erins Isle—Lyphard Abu (IRE) **Mr Gerry McManus**
32 **LINCAM (IRE)**, 9, b g Broken Hearted—Nanogan **Miss Rebecca Camlin**
33 **LORDOFOUROWN (IRE)**, 7, b h Mister Lord (USA)—Twinkling **Mr G. M. Bourke**
34 **LOVE SUPREME (IRE)**, 5, b m Supreme Leader—Tri Folene (FR) **Mr Derek Mossop**
35 **MAMA JAFFA (IRE)**, 5, ch m In The Wings—Harir **Michael & Karina Healy**
36 **MARIA PIA (IRE)**, 8, b m Bob's Return (IRE)—Blackwater Mist (IRE) **Il Conte di Montefalco Syndicate**
37 **MASTER OFTHE CHASE (IRE)**, 7, b g Norwich—Beglawella **Mr Tom Keane**
38 **MIDFIELD (IRE)**, 7, br g King's Ride—Celio Lucy (IRE) **Mr J. P. McManus**
39 5, B g Alflora (IRE)—Miss Redlands **Mr Derrick Smith**
40 **MISSINDEPENDENCE (IRE)**, 6, b m Executive Perk—Bonnies Glory **Mr Seamus Mannion**
41 **MOCHARAMOR (IRE)**, 7, b g Distinctly North (USA)—Oso Sure (IRE) **Anne & Andrew Wishant**
42 **MOKORA (IRE)**, 5, b m Moscow Society (USA)—Dinghy (IRE) **Lady Virginia Petersham**
43 **OFFSHORE ACCOUNT (IRE)**, 5, b g Oscar (IRE)—Park Breeze (IRE) **Mr Brian Polly**
44 **OH BE THE HOKEY (IRE)**, 7, b g Be My Native (USA)—Lucky Perk **Mr J. P. McManus**
45 **OLD FLAME (IRE)**, 6, b g Oscar (IRE)—Flameing Run **Mr Peter Reilly**
46 **OLD IRONSIDE (IRE)**, 5, ch g Fresh Breeze (USA)—Right Love **Mr Donal Kenneally**
47 **ON THE OTHER HAND (IRE)**, 5, b g Oscar (IRE)—Coumeenoole Lady **Mr J. P. McManus**
48 **ONE MORE MINUTE (IRE)**, 5, ch g Zaffaran (USA)—Wollongong (IRE) **Mr Robert Butler Racing Ltd**
49 **OODACHEE**, 6, b g Marju (IRE)—Lady Marguerrite **Modreeny Syndicate**
50 **OVER THE FIRST (IRE)**, 10, b g Orchestra—Ruby Lodge **Mr Michael McKeon**
51 **PILLAR ROCK (USA)**, 9, b g Alysheba (USA)—Butterscotch Sauce (USA) **Mr D. J. Sharkey**
52 **PROFESSOR HEGARTY (IRE)**, 5, b g Dr Massini (IRE)—Preview Days (IRE) **Mrs T. Hyde**
53 **RANSBORO (IRE)**, 6, b g Needle Gun (IRE)—Moylena **Mr Noel Elliott**
54 **RORY SUNSET (IRE)**, 7, b g Lord Americo—Dunany Star (IRE) **E. Kavanagh**
55 **RORY'S SISTER (IRE)**, 4, b f Little Bighorn—Dunany Star (IRE) **E. Kavanagh**
56 **ROSSCLARE (IRE)**, 5, b g Warcraft (USA)—Ivory Queen **Mr Andrew Whisart**
57 **ROWLANDS DREAM (IRE)**, 5, b m Accordion—Bettyhill **Mr Dermot Brennan**
58 **SADDLERS JEWEL (IRE)**, 5, b m Saddlers' Hall (IRE)—Fontaine Jewel (IRE) **David Brosnan**
59 **SAINTLY RACHEL (IRE)**, 7, b m Religiously (USA)—Ursha (IRE) **The Whitethorn Syndicate**
60 **SORRY AL (IRE)**, 5, ch g Anshan—Just A Second **Mr Donal Carey**
61 **SOUNDS GOOD (IRE)**, 5, b g Oscar (IRE)—Wild Venture (IRE) **Mr J. P. McManus**
62 **STELWONG (IRE)**, 5, b g Blues Traveller (IRE)—Monterana **Long West Syndicate**
63 **STRONG PROJECT (IRE)**, 9, ch g Project Manager—Hurricane Girl (IRE) **Mr J. J. Buckley**
64 **TEDEEN (FR)**, 5, b g Saint Cyrien (FR)—Miss Lady (FR) **Mr Michael Connolly**
65 **TEEMING RAIN (IRE)**, 6, b g Supreme Leader—Lady Graduate (IRE) **Mr J. P. McManus**
66 **THANKS A MIL (IRE)**, 5, b g Charnwood Forest (IRE)—Lundylux
67 **THE DARK FLASHER (IRE)**, 8, b g Lucky Guest—Perpignan **Mr Noel O'Flaherty**
68 **THIS IS SERIOUS (IRE)**, 11, ch g Broken Hearted—Lady Virtue **Mrs Marie Byrne**
69 **TODAYSMYDAY**, 7, b g Home Sapien—Tuesdaynightmare **Mr Eugene Kavanagh**

THREE-YEAR-OLDS

70 **ALL WOMAN**, ch f Groom Dancer (USA)—Flight Soundly (IRE) **Carol Hyde**
71 **OPTIMISE (IRE)**, b f Danehill (USA)—Sifaara (IRE) **Jack of Trumps Racing Club**

Assistant Trainer: Mr Danny Barry (Mobile (0866) 179282)

Jockey (NH): D. J. Casey. **Conditional:** D. G. Hogan, J. F. Levins. **Amateur:** Mr L. Flynn, Mr Eoin Ryan, Miss Louisa Williams.

567 MRS H. SWEETING, Marlborough
Postal: **White Barn Farm, Lockeridge, Marlborough, Wiltshire, SN8 4EQ.**
Contacts: **PHONE (01672) 861424 FAX (01672) 861049 MOBILE (07736) 366158**

1 **CHARLIE KENNET**, 7, b g Pyramus (USA)—Evaporate **The Northleach Kennet Connection**
2 **DAINTREE AFFAIR (IRE)**, 5, b g Charnwood Forest (IRE)—Madam Loving **P. Sweeting**
3 **ERRACHT**, 7, gr m Emarati (USA)—Port Na Blath **P. Sweeting**
4 **FREE STYLE (GER)**, 5, ch m Most Welcome—Furiella **P. Sweeting**
5 **HIGHLAND LASS**, 4, b f Nicolotte—Portvasco **Ned MacKay**
6 **PLAYTIME BLUE**, 5, b g Komaite (USA)—Miss Calculate **P. Sweeting**
7 6, Ch g Nomadic Way (USA)—Ruby Rheims **P. Sweeting**
8 **SAVERNAKE BRAVE (IRE)**, 4, b g Charnwood Forest (IRE)—Jordinda (IRE) **P. Sweeting**
9 **STAGNITE**, 5, ch g Compton Place—Superspring **P. Sweeting**
10 **SWIFT ALCHEMIST**, 5, b m Fleetwood (IRE)—Pure Gold **The Kennet Connection**
11 **WOODBURY**, 6, b m Woodborough (USA)—Jeewan **P. Sweeting**
12 **YAMATO PINK**, 4, ch f Bijou d'inde—Time Or Never (FR) **P. Sweeting**

THREE-YEAR-OLDS
13 **ABERDEEN PARK**, gr f Environment Friend—Michelee **The Kennet Connection**
14 **BLUE OTIS (IRE)**, ch f Docksider (USA)—Minstrel's Gift **P. Sweeting**
15 **CLIPPER HOY**, ch c Bahamian Bounty—Indian Flag (IRE) **P. Sweeting**
16 **DANE'S ROCK (IRE)**, b g Indian Danehill (IRE)—Cutting Ground (IRE) **P. Sweeting**
17 **PRALIN STAR (IRE)**, ch g Daggers Drawn (USA)—Polaregina (FR) **Paul Sweeting & John Thompson**

TWO-YEAR-OLDS
18 Br f 13/4 Timeless Times (USA)—Belltina (Belfort (FR)) (1000)
19 B f 12/3 Desert Story (IRE)—Conspire (IRE) (Turtle Island (IRE)) (2700)
20 Ch c 23/2 Bahamian Bounty—Indian Flag (IRE) (Indian Ridge) **P. Sweeting**
21 B c 6/3 Mull of Kintyre (USA)—Maura's Pet (IRE) (Prince of Birds (USA)) (2500)
22 B c 4/4 Josr Algarhoud (IRE)—Pink Champagne (Cosmonaut) (4200)
23 B f 8/3 Imperial Ballet (IRE)—Quiver Tree (Lion Cavern (USA)) (2500)
24 B c 27/4 Tomba—Trinity Hall (Hallgate) (2000)

Other Owners: R. W. Floyd, J. M. Robson.

Jockey (flat): George Baker.

568 MR G. A. SWINBANK, Richmond
Postal: **Thorndale Farm, Melsonby, Richmond, North Yorkshire, DL10 5NJ.**
Contacts: **PHONE (01325) 377318 PHONE (01325) 377318 FAX (01325) 377796**
MOBILE (07860) 368365/(07711) 488341
E-MAIL info@alanswinbank.com

1 **ARCTIC ECHO**, 6, b g Alderbrook—Arctic Oats **R. P. D. T. Dineen**
2 **AWAKEN**, 4, b f Zafonic (USA)—Dawna **Miss T. Waggott**
3 **BLUE ETTE (IRE)**, 5, b g Blues Traveller (IRE)—Princess Roxanne **Elsa Crankshaw & G. Allan II**
4 **CAMPESINO (IRE)**, 6, b g Entrepreneur—Campestral (USA) **D. Buckle**
5 **CHA CHA CHA DANCER**, 5, ch g Groom Dancer (USA)—Amber Fizz (USA) **Scotnorth Racing Ltd**
6 **COLLIER HILL**, 7, ch g Dr Devious (IRE)—Polar Queen **Mr R. H. Hall & Mr Ashley Young**
7 **DARK CHARACTER**, 6, b g Reprimand—Poyle Jezebelle **A. Cairns**
8 **FAR PAVILIONS**, 6, b g Halling (USA)—Flambera (FR) **J. D. Abell**
9 **GO SOLO**, 4, b g Primo Dominie—Taza **Mrs M. Jayne**
10 **GOLDEN MEASURE**, 5, b g Rainbow Quest (USA)—Dawna **R. H. Hall**
11 **GRACILIS (IRE)**, 8, b g Caerleon (USA)—Grace Note (FR) **Regency Racing**
12 **HARTSHEAD**, 6, b g Machiavellian (USA)—Zalitzine (USA) **B. Valentine**
13 **JONNYEM**, 4, b g Emarati (USA)—Deerlet **B. Valentine**
14 **LINDBERGH LAW (USA)**, 5, b g Red Ransom (USA)—Not So Shy (USA) **Mrs F. H. Crone & Mrs J. A. Lawson**
15 **LUCKY JUDGE**, 8, b g Saddlers' Hall (IRE)—Lady Lydia **Mrs I. Gibson**
16 **MANHATTAN JACK**, 4, ch g Forzando—Manhattan Diamond **Mr. Terry Andrews**
17 **MULLIGAN'S CHOICE (IRE)**, 4, b g Kahyasi—Babs Mulligan (IRE) **Scot North**
18 **NORTHERN NEWS (IRE)**, 5, b g Saddlers' Hall (IRE)—Some News (IRE)
19 **OUNINPOHJA (IRE)**, 4, b g Imperial Ballet (IRE)—Daziyra (IRE) **Am No Havin That**
20 **PEARSON GLEN (IRE)**, 6, ch g Dolphin Street (FR)—Glendora **Miss S. R. Haynes**
21 **POP UP AGAIN (IRE)**, 5, ch m Bahamian Bounty—Bellair **Mrs P. M. Robinson**
22 **PRIMITIVE COVE**, 4, b g Primitive Rising (USA)—Katie-A (IRE) **Mr. D. Souley**

MR G. A. SWINBANK—continued

23 **PRINCE OF SLANE**, 6, b g Prince Daniel—Singing Slane **J. H. Richardson**
24 **RED ROMEO**, 4, ch g Case Law—Enchanting Eve **J. Yates**
25 **SPECIAL BALLOT (IRE)**, 4, br f Perugino (USA)—Election Special **Miss K. T. Thompson**
26 **SPECULIGHT**, 5, b g Spectrum (IRE)—Sprite **Brandsby Racing**
27 **TANNENBERG (IRE)**, 4, b g Polish Precedent (USA)—Upper Strata **Mr A. Young**
28 **THE MUSIC QUEEN**, 4, ch f Halling (USA)—Sadly Sober (IRE) **Mrs M. Jones**
29 **THEGEORDIEDUCHESS (IRE)**, 4, b f Revoque (IRE)—Tirhala (IRE) **McBonif Partnership**
30 **VIRGIN SOLDIER (IRE)**, 9, ch g Waajib—Never Been Chaste **J. D. Abell**

THREE-YEAR-OLDS

31 **ALISDANZA**, b f Namaqualand (USA)—Enchanting Eve **Mr J. Yates & Mrs A. Yates**
32 **BARTON BELLE**, b f Barathea (IRE)—Veronica **Mr C. Bellwood**
33 **BEAUMONT GIRL (IRE)**, ch f Trans Island—Persian Danser (IRE) **Mr G. Stephenson**
34 **BRONZE DANCER (IRE)**, b g Entrepreneur—Scrimshaw **Mr J. Yates & Mrs A. Yates**
35 **CHARTERS TOWERS**, b g Polish Precedent (USA)—Gay Fantastic **J. D. Abell**
36 **CHATEAU (IRE)**, ch c Grand Lodge (USA)—Miniver (IRE) **Mr. A. Flower**
37 **DANCEINTHEVALLEY (IRE)**, b c Imperial Ballet (IRE)—Dancing Willma (IRE) **Mr D. G. Williams**
38 **DESERT EXPRESS (IRE)**, b g Shinko Forest (IRE)—Perfect Guest **Mr L. Ferdinand**
39 **DOLLY PEEL**, b f Josr Algarhoud (IRE)—Transylvania **J. Hamilton**
40 **ETTRBEE (IRE)**, b br f Lujain (USA)—Chief Ornament (USA) **Miss Sally Haynes**
41 **FIGURATIVE (IRE)**, b c Machiavellian (USA)—Marble Maiden **Mr J. P. Ryder**
42 **IGNOTUS**, b g Vitus—Linns Heir **James Nelson**
43 **MOUNT USHER**, br g Polar Falcon (USA)—Division Bell **Mr A. Young**
44 **PROGRAMME GIRL (IRE)**, ch f Definite Article—Targhyb (IRE) **D. C. Young**
45 **QUEENS HAND (IRE)**, b f Lend A Hand—Winchester Queen **A. R. Barnes**
46 **TAJ INDIA (USA)**, b br c Gone West (USA)—Circle of Gold (IRE)
47 **THESPIAN (FR)**, b c Daylami (IRE)—Stage Manner **Mr L. Fernadanod**

TWO-YEAR-OLDS

48 B c 17/2 Aljabr (USA)—Afkaar (USA) (Unbridled (USA)) (7377)
49 B f 4/4 Indian Danehill (IRE)—Catfoot Lane (Batshoof) (4359)
50 B c 23/1 Indian Danehill (IRE)—Cory Everson (IRE) (Brief Truce (USA)) (8718)
51 B c 17/4 Royal Anthem (USA)—Given Moment (USA) (Diesis) (13413)
52 Br g 10/4 Orpen (USA)—Kayrava (Irish River (FR)) (5499)
53 Ch c 6/3 Piccolo—Starfleet (Inchinor) (9389)
54 **TURBO LINN**, b f 26/5 Turbo Speed—Linns Heir (Leading Counsel (USA)) **James Nelson**

Other Owners: Mr. Tim Hawkins, Mrs Sue Soley, Mr & Mrs McGee, Mrs Angela Young, J. P. Ryder, G. Allan, Mrs S. E. Barclay, Mrs A. Cairns, Mr S. E. Chappell, Mrs F. H. Crone, Mr C. E. Davies, J. A. Kavanagh, Mrs J. A. Lawson, M. D. Noble, Mrs A. Yates.

Assistant Trainer: Miss T Waggott & Mr W W Haigh

Jockey (flat): K. Fallon, Dean McKeown, R. Winston. **Jockey (NH):** J. P. McNamara. **Conditional:** J. Crowley. **Apprentice:** D. C. Costello.

---

569 **MR W. R. J. SWINBURN, Berkhampsted**
Postal: **Church Farm, Station Road, Aldbury, Tring, Hertfordshire, HP23 5RS.**
Contacts: **PHONE (01442) 851134 (01442) 851328 FAX (01442) 851063**
WEBSITE www.walterswinburnracing.co.uk

1 **ALINDA (IRE)**, 4, b f Revoque (IRE)—Gratclo
2 **ALPINE REEL (IRE)**, 4, b g Danehill Dancer (USA)—Alpine Flair (IRE)
3 **ANNA PALLIDA**, 4, b f Sadler's Wells (USA)—Masskana (IRE)
4 **BARATHEA BLUE**, 4, ch c Barathea (IRE)—Empty Purse
5 **BAROLO**, 6, b g Danehill (USA)—Lydia Maria
6 **BEST BE GOING (IRE)**, 5, b g Danehill (USA)—Bye Bold Aileen (IRE)
7 **CHARNWOOD PRIDE (IRE)**, 4, gr g Charnwood Forest (IRE)—Pride of Pendle
8 **CLIPPERDOWN (IRE)**, 4, b g Green Desert (USA)—Maroussie (FR)
9 **COOL HUNTER**, 4, ch g Polar Falcon (USA)—Seabound
10 **CUTTING CREW (USA)**, 4, ch c Diesis—Poppy Carew (IRE)
11 **DANZOLIN**, 4, b f Danzero (AUS)—Howlin' (USA)
12 **HILLS SPITFIRE (IRE)**, 4, b br g Kahyasi—Questina (FR)

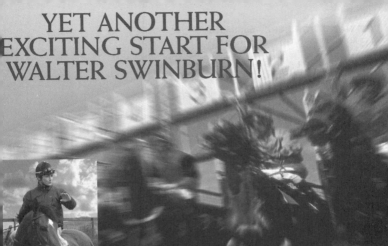

MR W. R. J. SWINBURN—continued

13 **KERNEL DOWERY (IRE)**, 5, b g Sri Pekan (USA)—Lady Dowery (USA)
14 **LEPORELLO (IRE)**, 5, b h Danehill (USA)—Why So Silent
15 **MAGIC MERLIN**, 4, b g Magic Ring (IRE)—St James's Antigua (IRE)
16 **MAJESTIC VISION**, 4, ch g Desert King (IRE)—Triste Oeil (USA)
17 **MASTERMAN READY**, 4, b g Unfuwain (USA)—Maria Isabella (FR)
18 **MISS POLARIS**, 4, b f Polar Falcon (USA)—Sarabah (IRE)
19 **MISTER MUJA (IRE)**, 4, gr g Mujadil (USA)—Remiss (IRE)
20 **NORDWIND (IRE)**, 4, b c Acatenango (GER)—Narola (GER)
21 **NORTHSIDE LODGE (IRE)**, 7, b g Grand Lodge (USA)—Alongside
22 **OASIS STAR (IRE)**, 4, b f Desert King (IRE)—Sound Tap (IRE)
23 **PALAMEDES**, 6, b g Sadler's Wells (USA)—Kristal Bridge
24 **PERSIAN MAJESTY**, 5, b h Grand Lodge (USA)—Spa
25 **POLISH EMPEROR (USA)**, 5, ch g Polish Precedent (USA)—Empress Jackie (USA)
26 **REZZAGO (USA)**, 5, b g Night Shift (USA)—Western Friend (USA)
27 **SERBELLONI**, 5, b g Spectrum (IRE)—Rose Vibert
28 **SERRE CHEVALIER (IRE)**, 4, b g Marju (IRE)—Ski Lodge (IRE)
29 **SHERGAEL (IRE)**, 4, b g Barathea (IRE)—Shergress
30 **SHOT TO FAME (USA)**, 6, b g Quest For Fame—Exocet (USA)
31 **SILK FAN (IRE)**, 4, b f Unfuwain (USA)—Alikhlas
32 **SKY QUEST (IRE)**, 7, b g Spectrum (IRE)—Rose Vibert
33 **STORMY NATURE (IRE)**, 4, b br f Mujadil (USA)—Ossana (USA)
34 **ZILMY (IRE)**, 4, ch g Zilzal (USA)—My Lewicia (IRE)

THREE-YEAR-OLDS

35 **ARBELLA**, ch f Primo Dominie—Kristal Bridge
36 **BIRIYANI (IRE)**, b f Danehill (USA)—Breyani
37 **BOXHALL (IRE)**, b c Grand Lodge (USA)—March Hare
38 **CROWN OF MEDINA**, ch g Fraam—Medina de Rioseco
39 **DAHLIYEV (IRE)**, b g Fasliyev (USA)—Thaidah (CAN)
40 **FAIRMILE**, b g Spectrum (IRE)—Juno Marlowe (USA)
41 **FOLLOW THE GAME**, b c Mind Games—Play The Game
42 **GRAND SHOW**, b c Efisio—Christine Daae
43 **HOPE AN GLORY (IRE)**, ch c Nashwan (USA)—Susi Wong (IRE)
44 **IRISH BALLAD**, b g Singspiel (IRE)—Auenlust (GER)
45 **KALAHARI DREAM (IRE)**, b f Desert Story (IRE)—Hope And Glory (USA)
46 **LORELEI BROWN**, b f Primo Dominie—Martha Stevens (USA)
47 **MAGGIE TULLIVER (IRE)**, b f Spectrum (IRE)—Eliza Acton
48 **MAKE IT SNAPPY**, b f Mujadil (USA)—Snap Crackle Pop (IRE)
49 **MAPLEDURHAM (IRE)**, ch c Grand Lodge (USA)—Gold Mist
50 **MARCHETTA**, b f Mujadil (USA)—My Lewicia (IRE)
51 **MISS PROVVIDENCE (IRE)**, b f Grand Lodge (USA)—My Southern Love (ITY)
52 **NOD OF APPROVAL**, b g Mark of Esteem (IRE)—Fetlar
53 **PERSIAN RUBY (IRE)**, b f Grand Lodge (USA)—Spa
54 **PHANTASMAGORIA**, b f Fraam—Magic Moment
55 **PHOEBE WOODSTOCK (IRE)**, ch f Grand Lodge (USA)—Why So Silent
56 **PINPOINT (IRE)**, b g Pivotal—Alessia (GER)
57 **PRINCESS OF SOUL**, b f Royal Applause—Alarming Motown
58 **PROPINQUITY**, b c Primo Dominie—Lydia Maria
59 **ROCK HAVEN (IRE)**, b g Danehill Dancer (IRE)—Mahabba (USA)
60 **SCAMPERDALE**, br g Compton Place—Miss Up N Go
61 **SOVEREIGN SPIRIT (IRE)**, b g Desert Prince—Sheer Spirit (IRE)
62 **SPIRITED DANCER (IRE)**, b f Sadler's Wells (USA)—Petroleuse
63 **SWEET SIOUX**, ch f Halling (USA)—Mohican Girl
64 **TYBALT**, b g Polar Falcon (USA)—Once Removed
65 **VIKING SPIRIT**, b c Mind Games—Dane Dancing (IRE)

TWO-YEAR-OLDS

66 Gr f 31/1 Alhaarth (IRE)—Alphilda (Ezzoud (IRE)) (12072)
67 Ch f 19/2 Pivotal—Annette Vallon (IRE) (Efisio)
68 **BLANDFORD FLYER**, b c 23/3 Soviet Star (USA)—Vento Del Oreno (FR) (Lando (GER)) (8000)
69 **BOLDINOR**, b c 22/2 Inchinor—Rambold (Rambo Dancer (CAN))
70 Ch c 26/1 Spinning World (USA)—Bright Hope (IRE) (Danehill (USA))
71 B c 11/2 Primo Valentino (IRE)—Bullion (Sabrehill (USA)) (42000)
72 **DANSA QUEEN**, gr f 17/3 Dansili—Pericardia (Petong) (38000)
73 B f 26/4 Green Desert (USA)—Dora Carrington (IRE) (Sri Pekan (USA))

MR W. R. J. SWINBURN—continued

74 Ch f 17/3 Dr Fong (USA)—Dorothea Brooke (IRE) (Dancing Brave (USA))
75 Ch f 21/4 Selkirk (USA)—Dubious (Darshaan) (50000)
76 **EASTERN EMPRESS**, b f 6/4 Mujadil (USA)—Noble One (Primo Dominie) (28000)
77 B c 27/4 Barathea (IRE)—Eliza Acton (Shirley Heights)
78 B c 1/3 Sinndar (IRE)—Eurobird (Ela-Mana-Mou) (80000)
79 B c 3/4 Royal Applause—Fantasy Ridge (Indian Ridge) (15000)
80 B f 28/4 In The Wings—Feather Bride (Groom Dancer (USA)) (46947)
81 B f 28/1 Selkirk (USA)—Firecrest (IRE) (Darshaan) (53655)
82 B f 4/3 Xaar—Flowering (Deploy) (30180)
83 B c 28/3 Night Shift (USA)—Frippet (IRE) (Ela-Mana-Mou) (17437)
84 **GATELAND**, b br c 1/4 Dansili—Encorenous (USA) (Diesis) (16000)
85 Ch c 7/3 Grand Lodge (USA)—Genoa (Zafonic (USA)) (80482)
86 B c 28/2 Anabaa (USA)—Glen Rosie (IRE) (Mujtahid (USA)) (110000)
87 B c 30/3 Royal Applause—Googoosh (IRE) (Danehill (USA)) (40240)
88 B f 25/3 Dansili—Housekeeper (IRE) (Common Grounds) (52000)
89 B c 28/2 Cape Cross (IRE)—Jemalina (USA) (Trempolino (USA)) (110000)
90 B c 9/3 Royal Applause—Juno Marlowe (IRE) (Danehill (USA))
91 Ch c 1/4 Singspiel (IRE)—Kristal Bridge (Kris)
92 Ch c 2/4 Danehill Dancer (IRE)—La Limite (IRE) (Dr Devious (IRE)) (25000)
93 B c 30/3 Intikhab (USA)—Mauradell (IRE) (Mujadil (USA)) (13000)
94 **MELODY MAKER**, br f 17/1 Diktat—First Musical (First Trump) (12000)
95 B f 7/2 Medicean—Miss Castaway (Selkirk (USA))
96 B c 27/4 Piccolo—Miss Dangerous (Komaite (USA)) (20000)
97 Ch f 26/3 Primo Dominie—My Lewicia (IRE) (Taufan (USA))
98 B c 24/1 Mind Games—Our Josie (First Trump) (30000)
99 **PERSIAN WARRIOR (IRE)**, b c 19/4 Desert Prince (IRE)—Viscaria (IRE) (Barathea (IRE)) (33534)
100 B f 15/2 Spinning World (USA)—Poppy Carew (IRE) (Danehill (USA))
101 B br c 21/2 Diktat—Possessive Artiste (Shareef Dancer (USA))
102 Ch c 16/3 Spinning World (USA)—Rainbow Dream (Rainbow Quest (USA)) (20120)
103 B f 10/5 Fasliyev (USA)—Raindancing (IRE) (Tirol) (33534)
104 B c 10/5 Fasliyev (USA)—Scenaria (IRE) (Scenic) (30180)
105 B f 20/3 Diktat—Southern Psychic (USA) (Alwasmi (USA)) (15000)
106 B c 20/2 Xaar—Summer Dreams (IRE) (Sadler's Wells (USA)) (57008)
107 B c 21/4 Desert Prince (IRE)—Sunsetter (USA) (Diesis) (40240)
108 Ch c 22/4 In The Wings—Tallahassee Spirit (THA) (Presidential (USA)) (33534)
109 B f 24/5 Danehill (USA)—Thaidah (CAN) (Vice Regent (CAN)) (60361)
110 **THE ART BIDDER**, b f 20/1 Primo Valentino (IRE)—Valldemosa (Music Boy) (11000)
111 Ch c 17/3 Desert Prince (IRE)—Valluga (IRE) (Ashkalani (IRE)) (16096)
112 **VERY AGREEABLE**, b f 12/3 Pursuit of Love—Oomph (Shareef Dancer (USA))
113 Ch c 18/5 Grand Lodge (USA)—Why So Silent (Mill Reef (USA))

Assistant Trainer: P. W. Harris

---

570 MR T. P. TATE, Tadcaster
Postal: **Castle Farm, Hazelwood, Tadcaster, North Yorkshire, LS24 9NJ.**
Contacts: **PHONE** (01937) 836036 **FAX** (01937) 530011 **MOBILE** (07970) 122818
E-MAIL tomtate@castlefarmstables.fsnet.co.uk

1 **ANOTHER BOTTLE (IRE)**, 4, b g Cape Cross (IRE)—Aster Aweke (IRE) **J. Hanson**
2 **CANUSEUS (USA)**, 4, b c Theatrical—Charmer's Gift (USA) **Mr T. P. Tate**
3 **DR SHARP (IRE)**, 5, ch g Dr Devious (IRE)—Stoned Imaculate (IRE) **The Ivy Syndicate**
4 **GRAND DAUM (FR)**, 4, b br g Double Bed (FR)—Maousse (FR) **Mr A. R. Trotter**
5 **MISSION AFFIRMED (USA)**, 4, ch g Stravinsky—Affirmed Legacy (USA) **Mr T. P. Tate**
6 **THE BUTTERWICK KID**, 12, ch g Interrex (CAN)—Ville Air **R. T. A. Tate**
7 **THE DUKE'S SPEECH (IRE)**, 4, b g Saddlers' Hall (IRE)—Dannkalia (IRE) **The Ivy Syndicate**
8 **WELSH EMPEROR (IRE)**, 6, b g Emperor Jones (USA)—Simply Times (USA) **Mrs Sylvia Clegg & Mr T. P. Tate**

THREE-YEAR-OLDS

9 **DANCER'S SERENADE (IRE)**, b g Almutawakel—Dance Serenade (IRE) **S. M. Racing**
10 **GARDASEE (GER)**, gr g Dashing Blade—Gladstone Street (IRE) **Mr T. P. Tate**
11 **HILL FAIRY**, ch f Monsun (GER)—Homing Instinct **S. M. Racing**
12 **LAST PIONEER (IRE)**, b g New Frontier (IRE)—Toordillon (IRE) **S. M. Racing**

MR T. P. TATE—continued

13 **NOWADAY (GER)**, b g Dashing Blade—Notre Dame (GER) **Mr T. P. Tate**
14 **VISION VICTORY (GER)**, b g Dashing Blade—Val d'isere (GER) **S. M. Racing**
15 **XAARIST (IRE)**, b g Xaar—Can Can Lady **Mr T. P. Tate**

TWO-YEAR-OLDS

16 Br f 19/3 Diktat—Alpine Time (IRE) (Tirol) (12500) **Mr T. P. Tate**
17 B c 14/5 Medicean—Bird of Time (IRE) (Persian Bold) (13000) **Mr T. P. Tate**
18 B c 1/3 Elnadim (USA)—Blue Satin (IRE) (Bluebird (USA)) (8000) **Mr T. P. Tate**
19 B g 27/3 Dansili—In Love Again (IRE) (Prince Rupert (FR)) (16000) **Mr T. P. Tate**
20 B f 18/3 Xaar—Lanelly (GER) (Shining Steel) (17437) **Mr T. P. Tate**
21 Ch c 4/2 Vettori (IRE)—Robin Lane (Tenby) **Mr T. P. Tate**
22 **WIND SHUFFLE (GER)**, b c 11/4 Big Shuffle (USA)—Wiesensturmerin (GER) (Lagunas) (17437) **Mr T. P. Tate**

Other Owners: D. M. W. Hodgkiss, Mrs S. A. Hodgkiss, J. Krieger.

Assistant Trainer: Mrs F H Tate

Jockey (flat): Robert Winston. **Jockey (NH):** J. M. Maguire. **Amateur:** Mr R T A Tate.

571	**MRS L. C. TAYLOR, Upper Lambourn** Postal: **Uplands, Upper Lambourn, Hungerford, Berkshire, RG17 8QJ.** Contacts: **HOME (01488) 670046 FAX (01488) 670047 MOBILE (07778) 780592** E-MAIL lavinia@uplandsracing.com

1 **GINGEMBRE (FR)**, 11, ch g Le Nain Jaune (FR)—Teuphaine (FR) **Mrs L. C. Taylor**
2 **IDIOME (FR)**, 9, b g Djarvis (FR)—Asterie L'ermitage (FR) **Mrs L. C. Taylor**
3 **JALOUX D'ESTRUVAL (FR)**, 8, b g Kadalko (FR)—Pommette III (FR) **Mrs P. V. E. Morrell**
4 **JAMEROSIER (FR)**, 8, b g The Wonder (FR)—Teuphaine (FR) **Mrs L. C. Taylor**
5 **JONCHEE (FR)**, 8, ch m Le Thuit Signol (FR)—Dame d'onze Heures (FR) **Miss M. Talbot**
6 **LASKARI (FR)**, 6, b g Great Palm (USA)—Hatzarie (FR) **Mrs L. C. Taylor**
7 **MISTRAL DE LA COUR (FR)**, 5, bl g Panoramic—Gracieuse Delacour (FR) **Miss M. Talbot**
8 **MONTE CRISTO (FR)**, 7, ch g Bigstone (IRE)—El Ouahirah (FR) **Mrs L. C. Taylor**
9 **MONTGERMONT (FR)**, 5, b g Useful (FR)—Blowin'in The Wind (FR) **Mrs L. C. Taylor**
10 **NOVICE D'ESTRUVAL (FR)**, 4, gr g Kadalko (FR)—Caro d'estruval (FR) **Mrs L. C. Taylor**
11 **TARONGO (FR)**, 7, b g Tel Quel (FR)—Rainbow Rainbow **Mrs L. C. Taylor**
12 **YVANOVITCH (FR)**, 7, b g Kaldounevees (FR)—County Kerry (FR) **R. N. Frosell**

Assistant Trainer: A J Taylor

Jockey (NH): M. Bradburne, A. Thornton.

572	**MR COLIN TEAGUE, Wingate** Postal: **Bridgefield Farm, Trimdon Lane, Station Town, Wingate, Co. Durham, TS28 5NE.** Contacts: **PHONE (01429) 837087 MOBILE (07967) 330929** E-MAIL colin.teague@btopenworld.com

1 **CHRISTY JNR (IRE)**, 11, b g Andretti—Rare Currency **Collins Chauffeur Driven Executive Cars**
2 **FORREST GUMP**, 5, ch g Zilzal (USA)—Mish Mish **Collins Chauffeur Driven Executive Cars**
3 **HIBERNATE (IRE)**, 11, ch g Lahib (USA)—Ministra (USA) **Collins Chauffeur Driven Executive Cars**
4 **MERLINS PROFIT**, 5, b g Wizard King—Quick Profit **C P T W Racing**
5 **MIKES MATE**, 4, b g Komaite (USA)—Pitcairn Princess **M. N. Emmerson**
6 **SILVER JADE**, 4, b f Silver Patriarch (IRE)—Kinraddie **Richardson Kelly O'Gara Partnership**
7 **TRANSYLVANIA**, 10, b m Wolfhound (USA)—Slava (USA) **Collins Chauffeur Driven Executive Cars**

THREE-YEAR-OLDS

8 **ROSS IS BOSS**, gr g Paris House—Billie Grey **R. Richardson**

MR COLIN TEAGUE—continued

TWO-YEAR-OLDS

  9 B f 22/3 King Charlemagne (USA)—Bint Alreeys (Polish Precedent (USA)) (3353) **M. N. Emmerson**
10 Ch c 30/4 Tipsy Creek (USA)—Jeethgaya (USA) (Critique (USA)) (800) **Collins Chauffeur Driven Executive Cars**
11 Ch c 11/3 Night Shift (USA)—Mountain Bluebird (USA)
               (Clever Trick (USA)) (2500) **R. Richardson & Collins Chauffeur Driven Executive Cars**
12 B c 8/4 Easycall—Regal Academy (IRE)
               (Royal Academy (USA)) (500) **R. Richardson & Collins Chauffeur Driven Executive Cars**

Other Owners: T. N. Kelly, P. O'Gara.

Amateur: Mr L Bates.

573
MRS P. A. TETLEY, Cranleigh
Postal: **Norley Farm, Horsham Road, Cranleigh, Surrey, GU6 8EH.**
Contacts: **PHONE (01483) 274013 MOBILE (07711) 867030**
E-MAIL btetley@btopenworld.com

  1 ABRAXAS, 7, b g Emperor Jones (USA)—Snipe Hall **B. R. Tetley**
  2 AMATEUR DRAMATICS, 9, b g Theatrical Charmer—Chaconia Girl **Mrs P. A. Tetley**

Jockey (NH): P. Hide.

574
MRS D. THOMAS, Bridgend
Postal: **Pen-Y-Lan Farm, Aberkenfig, Bridgend, Mid Glam.**
Contacts: **PHONE (01656) 720254 FAX (01656) 720254 MOBILE (07989) 462130**
E-MAIL philjones1226@aol.com

  1 KADLASS (FR), 10, b g Kadounor (FR)—Brave Lass **Mrs D. Thomas**
  2 PERTEMPS MISSION, 11, b g Safawan—Heresheis **Mrs D. Thomas**
  3 SAYEH (IRE), 13, b g Fools Holme (USA)—Piffle **Mrs D. Thomas**
  4 TIMIDJAR (IRE), 12, b g Doyoun—Timissara (USA) **Mrs D. Thomas**

Assistant Trainer: Miss D C Thomas

Conditional: C. Bolger.

575
MR K. S. THOMAS, Carlisle
Postal: **Murray Holme, Roadhead, Bewcastle, Carlisle, CA6 6PJ.**
Contacts: **PHONE (01697) 748157 FAX (01697) 748159 MOBILE (07770) 462839**
E-MAIL keiththomas@equilaw.co.uk WEBSITE www.equilaw.co.uk

  1 DAYTIME ARRIVAL (IRE), 7, ch g Lucky Guest—Daymer Bay **Mrs M. A. Holt**
  2 NORTHERN ECHO, 8, b g Pursuit of Love—Stop Press (USA) **Mr K. S. Thomas**

THREE-YEAR-OLDS

  3 DOUBLE RUNNER, b f Doubletour (USA)—Running Frau **Partnership**

Assistant Trainer: Ann Holt

Conditional: G. Thomas. **Amateur:** Mr M. McAlister.

576
MR D. W. THOMPSON, Darlington
Postal: **South View Racing, Ashley Cottage, South View, Bolam, Darlington, Co. Durham, DL2 2UP.**
Contacts: **PHONE (01388) 835806 FAX (01325) 835806 MOBILE (07795) 161657**

  1 ABUELOS, 6, b g Sabrehill (USA)—Miss Oasis **Mrs S. Armstrong & Mr C. Dickinson**
  2 BOOK'S WAY, 9, br g Afzal—In A Whirl **J. A. Moore**
  3 CADEAUX ROUGE (IRE), 4, ch f Croco Rouge (IRE)—Gift of Glory (FR) **D. Morland**
  4 CHARLIE CASTALLAN, 5, gr g Wace (USA)—Castle Cary **Mrs A. C. Davis**
  5 CROC EN BOUCHE (USA), 6, b g Broad Brush (USA)—Super Cook (USA) **J. A. Moore**

MR D. W. THOMPSON—continued

6 **DURAID (IRE)**, 13, ch g Irish River (FR)—Fateful Princess (USA) **A. Suddes**
7 **FIFTH COLUMN (USA)**, 4, b g Allied Forces (USA)—Miff (USA) **J. J. Greenbank**
8 **LAKE 'O' GOLD**, 6, ch m Karinga Bay—Ginka **D. Morland**
9 **PILGRIMS PROGRESS (IRE)**, 5, b g Entrepreneur—Rose Bonbon (FR) **South View Winning Ways**
10 **PINK PEARLS (IRE)**, 5, gr m Arzanni—Castle Ceile (IRE) **Mrs A. C. Davis**
11 **RUDI'S CHARM**, 8, b g Rudimentary (USA)—Irene's Charter **J. A. Moore**
12 **SOVEREIGN STATE (IRE)**, 8, b g Soviet Lad (USA)—Portree **J. J. Greenbank**
13 **STEP IN LINE (IRE)**, 13, gr g Step Together (USA)—Ballycahan Girl **Mrs A. C. Davis**
14 **THREE TIMES A LADY**, 5, b m Syrtos—Pure Formality
15 **WILD TIDE**, 6, b m Runnett—Polly Two **Michael Howitt and R C Davison**
16 **WIZARDS PRINCESS**, 5, b m Wizard King—Chalice **D. Paterson**

THREE-YEAR-OLDS

17 **DREAM THE DREAM**, b f Rock City—Celestial Ridge (IRE) **J. A. Moore**
18 **STERLING SUPPORTER**, b f Josr Algarhoud (IRE)—Riyoom (USA) **D. A. J. Bartlett**

TWO-YEAR-OLDS

19 **COORIE DOON**, ch c 23/5 Cayman Kai (IRE)—Camorra (My Chopin) **Arthur B. Graham**
20 **ZAHARA JOY**, ch f 11/5 Cayman Kai (IRE)—Enjoy (IRE) (Mazaad) **Arthur B. Graham**

Other Owners: W. N. Smith.

Assistant Trainer: J A Moore

Jockey (flat): T. Williams. **Jockey (NH):** C. Rafter.

---

577 MR RONALD THOMPSON, Doncaster
Postal: **No 2 Bungalow, Haggswood Racing Stable, Stainforth, Doncaster, South Yorkshire, DN7 5PS.**
Contacts: **PHONE (01302) 845904 FAX (01302) 845904 MOBILE (07713) 251141**

1 **KALUSH**, 4, b g Makbul—The Lady Vanishes **Mrs Janet Macabe**
2 **LAURA LEA**, 5, b g Bishop of Cashel—Kirriemuir **B. Bruce**
3 **TWINKLE TOE TITCH (IRE)**, 6, ch m Hubbly Bubbly (USA)—Hill Ranger **J. G. McGuinness**
4 **TYNDARIUS (IRE)**, 14, b g Mandalus—Lady Rerico **G. A. Shaw**

THREE-YEAR-OLDS

5 **BELTON**, b c Lujain (USA)—Efficacious (IRE) **B. Bruce**
6 **BEYOND THE RAINBOW**, b f Mind Games—Skyers Flyer (IRE) **A. Bell**
7 **CHICAGO NIGHTS (IRE)**, ch f Night Shift (USA)—Enclave (USA) **Mr Ronald Thompson**
8 **DIMASHQ**, b f Mtoto—Aqwaas (IRE) **Mr Ronald Thompson**
9 **FRENCH KISSES**, b f Paris House—Clashfern **Mr Barry Bryce**
10 **MAUREEN'S LOUGH (IRE)**, b f Bachir (IRE)—Tadjnama (USA) **Mrs Amanda Harrison**
11 **ROYALSILVERCHERRY**, b f Silver Patriarch (IRE)—Royal Hanina **Mrs S. Thrower**
12 **SKIPPIT JOHN**, b g Abou Zouz (USA)—Lady Quinta (IRE) **Mr J. P. Thompson**

TWO-YEAR-OLDS

13 B br c 11/5 Titus Livius (FR)—Regal Fanfare (IRE) (Taufan (USA)) (2000)
14 B c 6/2 Orpen (USA)—Scapula (Elmaamul (USA)) (1500)
15 Ch c 9/2 Atral—Star Dancer (Groom Dancer (USA)) (2200)
16 B g 16/2 Soviet Star (USA)—Why Worry Now (IRE) (College Chapel) (2400)

Other Owners: Mr Keith Manlove, Mr Alan Watson, Mr Gary Alexander, J. Bradwell.

Jockey (flat): D. McKeown, N. Callan, F. Lynch. **Conditional:** L. Vickers.

---

578 MR V. THOMPSON, Alnwick
Postal: **Link House Farm, Newton By The Sea, Embleton, Alnwick, Northumberland, NE66 3ED.**
Contacts: **PHONE (01665) 576272**

1 **ANOTHER WITNESS (IRE)**, 6, b g Witness Box (USA)—Another Plus (IRE) **Link House Farm Ltd**
2 **ARCTIC STAR**, 10, b g Polar Falcon (USA)—Three Stars **Link House Farm Ltd**

MR V. THOMPSON—continued

3 **BOARDSMILL RAMBLER (IRE)**, 6, b g Persian Mews—Trimmer Wonder (IRE) **Link House Farm Ltd**
4 **CREGG LORD (IRE)**, 6, b g Lord Americo—Philips River (IRE) **Link House Farm Ltd**
5 **DECENT BOND (IRE)**, 8, b g Witness Box (USA)—Decent Skin (IRE) **Link House Farm Ltd**
6 4, B g Commanche Run—Eastwell Star **Link House Farm Ltd**
7 **ERTE**, 4, ch g Vettori (IRE)—Cragreen **Mr V. Thompson**
8 **FALCON'S FLAME (USA)**, 12, b br g Hawkster (USA)—Staunch Flame (USA) **Mr V. Thompson**
9 **HANGAMASTERPIECE (IRE)**, 6, b m Master Willie—Dunnoholm **Link House Farm Ltd**
10 **KNOCK DAVRON (IRE)**, 6, ch g Beneficial—Chestnut Shoon **Link House Farm Ltd**
11 **MARAKASH (IRE)**, 6, b g Ashkalani (IRE)—Marilaya (IRE) **Link House Farm Ltd**
12 **SHOTGUN RIDER (IRE)**, 6, b g Aristocracy—Canute Princess **Link House Farm Ltd**
13 **SPRINGVALE (IRE)**, 6, b g Oscar (IRE)—Decent Skin (IRE) **Link House Farm Ltd**
14 **THE PREACHER MAN**, 10, b g Be My Native (USA)—Frankford Run **Link House Farm Ltd**
15 **TOP TENOR (IRE)**, 5, b g Sadler's Wells (USA)—Posta Vecchia (USA) **Mr V. Thompson**

Assistant Trainer: M Thompson

Amateur: Mr M. Thompson.

---

579 **MRS B. K. THOMSON, Duns**
Postal: **Lambden Burn, Greenlaw, Duns, Berwickshire, TD10 6UN.**
Contacts: **PHONE (01361) 810514 MOBILE (07890) 120066**
E-MAIL billiethomson@lineone.net

1 **CIACOLE**, 4, b f Primo Dominie—Dance On A Cloud (USA) **Mrs B. K. Thomson**
2 **INTERDIT (FR)**, 9, b br g Shafoun (FR)—Solaine (FR) **Mrs B. K. Thomson**
3 **JAVELOT D'OR (FR)**, 8, b br g Useful (FR)—Flika d'or (FR) **Mrs B. K. Thomson**
4 **ROSES ARE WILD (IRE)**, 7, gr m Roselier (FR)—Wild Bramble (IRE) **Mrs B. K. Thomson**
5 **TEMPLE DOG (IRE)**, 9, ch g Un Desperado (FR)—Shower **Mrs B. K. Thomson**

Jockey (NH): K. Renwick. **Conditional:** T. Greenway. **Amateur:** Mr D. E. Greenway.

---

580 **MR R. W. THOMSON, Hawick**
Postal: **Millcourt, Cavers, Hawick, Roxburghshire, TD9 8LN.**
Contacts: **PHONE (01450) 372668 PHONE (01450) 372473 FAX (01450) 372473**
MOBILE (07801) 594336
E-MAIL rennie.thomson@btopenworld.com

1 **BALLISTIC BOY**, 8, ch g First Trump—Be Discreet **Mr R. W. Thomson**
2 **MULLER (IRE)**, 5, gr g Bigstone (IRE)—Missie Madam (IRE) **Mr R. W. Thomson**
3 **SON OF ROSS**, 11, b g Minster Son—Nancy Ardross **Mr R. W. Thomson**

Conditional: D. C. Costello. **Amateur:** Miss P. Robson, Mr E. Whillans.

---

581 **MR C. W. THORNTON, Leyburn**
Postal: **Dale House, Rectory Garth, Wensley, Leyburn, North Yorkshire, DL8 4HS.**
Contacts: **HOME (01969) 623350 YARD (01969) 625446 FAX (01969) 624374**
MOBILE (07976) 648965
E-MAIL christopher.thornton@talk21.com
WEBSITE www.chris-thornton.com & www.luxury-villa-disney.com

1 **CUSP**, 5, b m Pivotal—Bambolona **The Challengers**
2 **EASBY MANDARIN**, 4, b g Emperor Fountain—Beijing (USA) **G. R. Orchard**
3 **GLIMPSE OF GLORY**, 5, b g Makbul—Bright-One **The Challengers**
4 **INTAVAC BOY**, 4, ch g Emperor Fountain—Altaia (FR) **Mr B. J. Kellett**
5 **INTAVAC FLIGHT**, 5, b g Tamure (IRE)—Mossfield **Mr B. J. Kellett**
6 **LE MINO (FR)**, 6, b g Noblequest (FR)—Minouche (FR) **G. R. Orchard**
7 **LETS ROLL**, 4, b g Tamure (IRE)—Miss Petronella **A. Crute and Partners**
8 **POWER AND DEMAND**, 8, b g Formidable (USA)—Mazurkanova **Mrs D. Wilkinson**
9 **QUICKS THE WORD**, 5, b g Sri Pekan (USA)—Fast Tempo (IRE) **Pegasus Team A**
10 **REDDITZIO**, 4, b f J B Quick—Ladys Regret (IRE) **Mr I. Townsend**
11 **RENO**, 5, ch m Efisio—Los Alamos **The Reno Partnership**

MR C. W. THORNTON—continued

THREE-YEAR-OLDS

12 **AMMIRARE**, b f Diktat—Mathaayl (USA) **D. B. Dennison**
13 **AU REVOIR**, ch f Efisio—Blow Me A Kiss **Guy Reed**
14 **COOLA TAGULA (IRE)**, b g Tagula (IRE)—Second Craft (IRE) **Chris Thornton Racing Ltd**
15 **CRUX**, b g Pivotal—Penny Dip **Team 30**
16 **DANZATRICE**, b f Tamure (IRE)—Miss Petronella **D. B. Dennison**
17 **DEVILS DELIGHT (IRE)**, b f Desert King (IRE)—Devil's Crown (USA) **G. B. Turnbull Ltd**
18 **DREAMALONGWITHME**, b g Dansili—Dream Baby **Mrs M. A. Blacker**
19 **FELLBECK FRED**, gr c Paris House—Wyse Folly **Tommy Dod Syndicate**
20 **FRESCHEZZA**, b f Tamure (IRE)—Minigale **D. B. Dennison**
21 B f Tamure (IRE)—Mossfield **Mr T. Grice**
22 **NAMKING**, b g Namid—Kingdom Queen (IRE) **G. B. Turnbull Ltd**

TWO-YEAR-OLDS

23 **AUTOMATION**, b f 3/4 Tamure (IRE)—Anatomic (Deerhound) (USA) **The Rollettes**
24 **INTAVAC GIRL**, b f 22/2 Sinndar (IRE)—Messila Rose (Darshaan) (4000) **Mr B. J. Kellett**
25 Ch f 3/5 Dancing Spree (USA)—Peggotty (Capricorn Line) (800) **Mr C. W. Thornton**
26 **ROLL EM OVER**, b f 7/5 Tamure (IRE)—Miss Petronella (Petoski) **The Rollettes**
27 **TAMMY**, b f 27/2 Tamure (IRE)—Heather Honey (Insan (USA)) **The Rollettes**
28 **VERTIGO BLUE**, b g 11/5 Averti (IRE)—Soft Colours (Presidium) (1200) **Team 30**

Other Owners: F. Fantoni, H. Lodge, Mr E. Goodall, Mr A. Cairns, K. Blakeson, Peter Barley, Miss J. Steenson, Mr B. Gauld, Mrs A. Cairns, Brian Dodsworth, Mr L. Miernik, Mrs R. M. Peck, Mrs J. Stringer-Calvert, J. E. Tennant, K. Zanft.

Jockey (flat): T. Eaves, Dean McKeown. **Jockey (NH):** F. Keniry. **Conditional:** G. Berridge. **Apprentice:** Paul Mulrennan.

---

582 **MRS A. M. THORPE, Carmarthen**
Postal: Felinfach, Bronwydd, Carmarthen, Carmarthenshire, SA33 6BE.
Contacts: PHONE (01267) 253509 or (01267) 253783 MOBILE (07795) 832004 or (07901) 528500
E-MAIL amthorpe@racingstables.freeserve.co.uk

1 **ASK ME WHAT (IRE)**, 8, b m Shernazar—Laffan's Bridge (IRE) **Miss P. M. Hearn**
2 **BEN THE BRAVE**, 6, b g Ridgewood Ben—Shoot The Dealer (IRE) **Just Maybe Club**
3 **CARPENTERS BOY**, 5, b g Nomination—Jolly Girl **Mel Davies**
4 **CLONEYBRIEN BOY (IRE)**, 5, ch g Mister Lord (USA)—Lougheagle **Mrs A. M. Thorpe**
5 **CRISTOPHE**, 7, b g Kris—Our Shirley **Formula One Racing**
6 **CYINDIEN (FR)**, 8, b br g Cyborg (FR)—Indiana Rose (FR) **Formula One Racing (2)**
7 **EASTWELL VIOLET**, 5, b m Danzig Connection (USA)—Kinchenjunga **D. Jenkins**
8 **FADDAD (USA)**, 9, b g Irish River (FR)—Miss Mistletoes (IRE) **D. Jones**
9 **GERI ROULETTE**, 3, b f Perpendicular—Clashfern **Mr Ron Stepney**
10 **ITSALLUPINTHEAIR**, 9, b g Lion Cavern (USA)—Flora Wood (IRE) **Miss A. Meakins and Mr L. Sloyan**
11 **JEEPERS CREEPERS**, 5, b g Wizard King—Dark Amber **D. Jenkins**
12 **LADY ROANIA (IRE)**, 5, b m Saddlers' Hall (IRE)—Ahead of My Time (IRE) **Mrs T. S. P. Stepney**
13 **LYRICAL LILY**, 7, b m Alflora (IRE)—Music Interpreter **G. Mills**
14 **MADAM MOSSO**, 9, b m Le Moss—Rochestown Lass **A. R. Evans**
15 **MAIDSTONE MONUMENT (IRE)**, 10, b g Jurado (USA)—Loreto Lady **D. Jenkins**
16 **MR DON (IRE)**, 6, b g Mister Lord (USA)—Paradiso (IRE) **D. Jones**
17 **ORBICULARIS (IRE)**, 9, b g Supreme Leader—Liffey Travel **D. Jones**
18 **REMINGTON (IRE)**, 7, ch g Indian Ridge—Sea Harrier **S. A. Douch**
19 **SHELU**, 7, b g Good Thyne (USA)—Nearly Married **D. Jones**
20 **SKIBEREEN (IRE)**, 5, b g Ashkalani (IRE)—Your Village (IRE) **J. H. Lee**
21 **SPIRIT OF TENBY (IRE)**, 8, b g Tenby—Asturiana **Miss P. M. Hearn**
22 4, B f Silver Patriarch (IRE)—Streaker
23 **TEA'S MAID**, 5, b m Wizard King—Come To Tea (IRE) **Mrs A. M. Thorpe**
24 **VALLICA**, 6, b m Bishop of Cashel—Vallauris **A. T. Bailey**

Other Owners: W. J. Hunter, Miss H. W. Spellman, Mrs J. Taylor.

Amateur: Miss P. M. Hearn.

583 MR C. TINKLER, Compton
Postal: **Uplands Stables, Downs Road, Compton, Newbury, Berkshire, RG20 6RE.**
Contacts: **PHONE (01635) 579090 FAX (01635) 578000 MOBILE (07717) 885204**
E-MAIL **uplands.stables@zen.co.uk** WEBSITE **www.uplandsstables.com**

1 **BOB AR AGHAIDH (IRE)**, 9, b g Bob Back (USA)—Shuil Ar Aghaidh **George Ward**
2 **BOBERELLE (IRE)**, 5, gr m Bob Back (USA)—Zephyrelle (IRE) **George Ward**
3 **CALL OSCAR (IRE)**, 6, b g Oscar (IRE)—Athy Princess (IRE) **George Ward**
4 **CRASHTOWN LEADER (IRE)**, 6, b g Supreme Leader—Crashtown Lucy **George Ward**
5 4, B c Saddlers' Hall (IRE)—Crashtown Lucy
6 4, B g King's Theatre (IRE)—Dance Alone (IRE)
7 **DESERT IMAGE (IRE)**, 4, b c Desert King (IRE)—Identical (IRE) **George Ward**
8 **DOMINICAN MONK (IRE)**, 6, b g Lord Americo—Ballybeg Katie (IRE) **George Ward**
9 **DR CERULLO**, 4, b g Dr Fong (USA)—Precocious Miss **Doubleprint**
10 **GLACIAL SUNSET (IRE)**, 10, ch g Glacial Storm (USA)—Twinkle Sunset **George Ward**
11 4, B br c Bob Back (USA)—Honey Mountain
12 **ITS ONLY POLITE (IRE)**, 9, gr g Roselier (FR)—Decent Debbie **Bonusprint Ltd**
13 4, B g Oscar (IRE)—Millers Run
14 **MUSICAL CHORD (IRE)**, 6, ch g Accordion—Slieveglagh Queen
15 **NATIVE IVY (IRE)**, 7, b g Be My Native (USA)—Outdoor Ivy **George Ward**
16 **NORTHAW LAD (IRE)**, 7, ch g Executive Perk—Black Tulip **J. E. Fishpool**
17 **OSCAR FOXBOW (IRE)**, 6, b br g Oscar (IRE)—Miss Fox Bow (IRE) **George Ward**
18 **OSCAR PARK (IRE)**, 6, b g Oscar (IRE)—Parkavoureen **George Ward**
19 **PLAY THE MELODY (IRE)**, 4, b br g Revoque (IRE)—Dumayla **Doubleprint**
20 **PRESENT GLORY (IRE)**, 6, br g Presenting—Prudent Rose (IRE) **George Ward**
21 **RIVER HEIGHTS (IRE)**, 4, b br g Kotashaan (FR)—Mrs Cullen
22 4, B c King's Theatre (IRE)—Shuil Ar Aghaidh
23 **SHUIL BOB (IRE)**, 5, b br m Bob Back (USA)—Shuil Ar Aghaidh
24 **SOUND ACCORD (IRE)**, 4, br g Accordion—Shuil Na Lee (IRE)
25 **STORMY MOMENT (IRE)**, 5, b m Glacial Storm (USA)—Golden Moment (IRE)
26 **SUNGATES (IRE)**, 9, ch g Glacial Storm (USA)—Live It Up **Team George II**
27 4, B br f Bob Back (USA)—Sunset Leader (IRE)
28 **SUNSET LIGHT (IRE)**, 7, b g Supreme Leader—Game Sunset **George Ward**
29 **SWINGIT LAD**, 5, b g Alflora (IRE)—Promitto
30 **VALLEY RIDE (IRE)**, 5, b br g Glacial Storm (USA)—Royal Lucy (IRE) **George Ward**

THREE-YEAR-OLDS

31 **GEORGIE BELLE (USA)**, ch f Southern Halo (USA)—Saabikah (USA) **George Ward**

TWO-YEAR-OLDS

32 B c 17/2 Mujahid (USA)—Bajan Blue (Lycius (USA)) (30000)
33 Ch f 11/1 Shinko Forest (IRE)—Between The Winds (Diesis) (7000)
34 B c 26/3 Orpen (USA)—Blue Heights (IRE) (Persian Heights)
35 Ch f 21/2 Soviet Star (USA)—Dumayla (Shernazar)
36 B f 28/4 Fantastic Light (USA)—Fabulous Account (USA) (Private Account (USA)) (40000)
37 B c 2/3 Desert Sun—Sea of Time (USA) (Gilded Time (USA)) (31000)
38 B c 24/4 Night Shift (USA)—Taysala (IRE) (Akarad (FR)) (14000)
39 B c 9/3 Intikhab (USA)—Tropical Dance (USA) (Thorn Dance (USA))

Other Owners: D. D. P. Burnett, Mel Davies, R. T. Ferris, R. L. C. Hartley, Mrs L. M. Ward, F. T. Ward.

Assistant Trainer: Heidi Leach

584 MR W. H. TINNING, York
Postal: **High Street Farm, Thornton-Le-Clay, York.**
Contacts: **PHONE (01653) 618996 MOBILE (07812) 098524**

1 **COMPTON PLUME**, 5, ch g Compton Place—Brockton Flame **W. H. & Mrs J. A. Tinning**
2 **RIGHTY HO**, 11, b g Reprimand—Challanging **W. H. & Mrs J. A. Tinning**
3 **SIMPLY SID**, 4, b g Presidium—Chadwick's Ginger **W. H. & Mrs J. A. Tinning**

MR W. H. TINNING—continued

THREE-YEAR-OLDS

4 CHRISJEN, ch f Wolfhound (USA)—Chadwick's Ginger W. H. & Mrs J A Tinning
5 SCARLET ROMANCE, ch f Pursuit of Love—Scarlet Livery W. H. & Mrs J. A. Tinning

Assistant Trainer: Mrs J A Tinning

Jockey (flat): Dale Gibson, R. Winston.

---

585 | MR C. TIZZARD, Sherborne
Postal: **Venn Farm, Milborne Port, Sherborne, Dorset, DT9 5RA.**
Contacts: PHONE (01963) 250598 FAX (01963) 250598 MOBILE (07976) 778656

1 BELSKI, 12, b g Arctic Lord—Bellekino **The Butterwick Syndicate**
2 BLAKENEY COAST (IRE), 8, b g Satco (FR)—Up To More Trix (IRE) **The Jam Boys**
3 BOB BOB BOBBIN, 8, gr g Bob Back (USA)—Absalom's Lady **Mrs S. L. Tizzard**
4 BRAVE SPIRIT (FR), 7, b g Legend of France (USA)—Guerre Ou Paix (FR) **The Con Club**
5 CLASSIC CLOVER, 5, ch g Classic Cliche (USA)—National Clover **Mr & Mrs J. W. Snook**
6 COUNTESS POINT, 7, ch m Karinga Bay—Rempstone **Mrs J. E. Purdie**
7 DEAR DEAL, 12, b g Sharp Deal—The Deer Hound **J. A. G. Meaden**
8 EARL'S KITCHEN, 8, ch g Karinga Bay—Rempstone **Mrs J. E. Purdie**
9 EASIBROOK JANE, 7, b m Alderbrook—Relatively Easy **R. G. Tizzard**
10 FIELD OF BLUE, 6, b g Shambo—Flashing Silks **Mr A. Russell**
11 FREEDOM NOW (IRE), 7, b g Sadler's Wells (USA)—Free At Last **A. C. W. Knott**
12 GAROLSA (FR), 11, b g Rivelago (FR)—Rols du Chatelier (FR) **R. G. And C. L. Tizzard**
13 JUST REUBEN (IRE), 10, gr g Roselier (FR)—Sharp Mama VII **A. J. M. Trowbridge**
14 KARAWA, 6, ch m Karinga Bay—Lady Buck **R. E. Dimond**
15 KIWI RIVERMAN, 5, b g Alderbrook—Kiwi Velocity (NZ) **Executors of the late M. L. Stoddart**
16 L'ORPHELIN, 10, ch g Gildoran—Balula **Mrs John Pope And Friends**
17 LORD KILLESHANRA (IRE), 6, b g Mister Lord (USA)—Killeshandra Lass (IRE) **G. F. Gingell**
18 LY'S WEST, 5, ch g The West (USA)—Lysithea **Mr R. Hedditch**
19 MATTHEW MUROTO (IRE), 6, b g Muroto—Glenmore Star (IRE) **A. J. M. Trowbridge**
20 MISTER QUASIMODO, 5, b g Busy Flight—Dubacilla **Dare, Hamlin, Snook**
21 MOORLANDS MILLY, 4, b f Sooty Tern—Sandford Springs (USA) **Mrs L. M. Williams**
22 MOORLANDS RETURN, 6, b g Bob's Return (IRE)—Sandford Springs (USA) **Mrs L. M. Williams**
23 4, Ch f Karinga Bay—Ower Farm **Mrs J. E. Purdie**
24 PASS ME A DIME, 6, b g Past Glories—Hand Out **Cherry Bolberry Partnership**
25 PETERSON'S CAY (IRE), 7, b g Grand Lodge (USA)—Columbian Sand (IRE) **Mr C. Tizzard**
26 PORT SODRICK, 4, b br g Young Ern—Keepsake (IRE) **A. C. W. Knott**
27 RED CANYON (IRE), 8, b g Zieten (USA)—Bayazida **Miss Jayne Brace & Mr Gwyn Brace**
28 UNCLE MICK (IRE), 10, b g Ikdam—Kandy Kate **D. J. Hinks**

Other Owners: 1st The Queens Dragoon Guards, Mr A. J. Callow, R. Dibble, Mr M. G. Hatcher, Mr E. J. Highnam, Mrs E. B. Pope, J. A. Pope, C. Raymond, E. R. Vickery.

Assistant Trainer: Mrs K. Gingell

Jockey (NH): J. Tizzard. **Conditional:** K Burke.

---

586 | MR D. M. TODHUNTER, Penrith
Postal: **The Park, Orton, Penrith, Cumbria, CA10 3SD.**
Contacts: PHONE (01539) 624314 FAX (01539) 624811 MOBILE (07976) 440082

1 ALFY RICH, 9, b g Alflora (IRE)—Weareagrandmother **The Carlisle Cavaliers**
2 BAAWRAH, 4, ch g Cadeaux Genereux—Kronengold (USA) **J. D. Gordon**
3 BE MY MANAGER (IRE), 10, b g Be My Native (USA)—Fahy Quay **B. L. Murfin**
4 BENRAJAH (IRE), 8, b g Lord Americo—Andy's Fancy (IRE) **B. L. Murfin**
5 BRIGHT STEEL (IRE), 8, gr g Roselier (FR)—Ikeathy **Mrs J. Mandle**
6 COUNT FOSCO, 7, b g Alflora (IRE)—Carrikins **Murphy's Law Partnership**
7 DALBLAIR (IRE), 6, b g Lake Coniston (IRE)—Cartagena Sand (IRE) **Abbadis Racing Club**
8 FLORRIES SON, 10, b g Minster Son—Florrie Palmer **Mrs F. M. Gray**
9 JUST IN DEBT (IRE), 9, b br g Montelimar (USA)—No Debt **J. W. Hazeldean**
10 MANOUBI, 6, b g Doyoun—Manuetti (IRE) **FF Racing Services Partnshsip XII**
11 MICKEY CROKE, 8, b g Alflora (IRE)—Praise The Lord **J. W. Hazeldean**

MR D. M. TODHUNTER—continued

12 OSTFANNI (IRE), 5, b m Spectrum (IRE)—Ostwahl (IRE) **FF Racing Services Partnership XVI**
13 PROVOCATIVE (FR), 7, b br g Useful (FR)—All Blue (FR) **Sir Robert Ogden C.B.E., LLD**
14 QUARRY ISLAND (IRE), 4, b f Turtle Island (IRE)—Last Quarry **B. Batey**
15 RAW SILK, 7, b g Rudimentary (USA)—Misty Silks **The Cartmel Syndicate**
16 ROCKERFELLA LAD (IRE), 5, b g Danetime (IRE)—Soucaro **Mrs K. Hall**
17 ROSIE'S RESULT, 5, ch g Case Law—Precious Girl **Mrs J. Mandle**
18 SILVER JACK (IRE), 7, gr g Roselier (FR)—Consharon (IRE) **B. Batey**
19 SPAINKRIS, 6, b g Kris—Pennycairn **Mr M. A. Wainwright**
20 SULLY SHUFFLES (IRE), 10, b g Broken Hearted—Green Legend (IRE) **Murphy's Law Partnership**
21 TARBOLTON MOSS, 10, b m Le Moss—Priceless Peril **Mrs A. G. Marshall**
22 VERY TASTY (IRE), 8, ch g Be My Native (USA)—Jasmine Melody **Mr F. G. Steel**
23 VIGOROUS (IRE), 5, b m Danetime (IRE)—Merrily **FF Racing Services Partnership IX**
24 WOODWIND DOWN, 8, b m Piccolo—Bint El Oumara **Domino Racing**
25 ZOFFANY (IRE), 8, b g Synefos (USA)—Shining Green **Sir Robert Ogden C.B.E., LLD**

THREE-YEAR-OLDS

26 ALMATY EXPRESS, b g Almaty (IRE)—Express Girl **P. G. Airey**

Other Owners: Mrs S. E. Barclay, Mrs L. Bell, P. M. Clarkson, P. W. Clement, Mr A. J. Cork, P. A. Dawson, W. Downs, R. E. Jackson, D. Musgrave, W. B. Parkinson, Mrs J. B. Pye, K. Sobey.

Jockey (flat): G. Duffield. **Jockey (NH):** A. Dobbin, G. Lee. **Conditional:** S. Gagen, C. Thompson. **Amateur:** Mr C. Thompson.

---

587 MR J. A. R. TOLLER, Newmarket
Postal: **Eve Lodge Stables, Hamilton Road, Newmarket, Suffolk, CB8 0NY.**
Contacts: **PHONE (01638) 668918 FAX (01638) 669384 MOBILE (07887) 942234**
E-MAIL james.toller@virgin.net

1 CAUTIOUSLY (USA), 4, b f Distant View (USA)—Curiously **J. R. Drew**
2 FLAMJICA (USA), 4, ch f Real Quiet (USA)—Fiamma (IRE) **The Cadagan Partnership**
3 FLARAN, 5, b g Emarati (USA)—Fragrance **Miss F. R. E. Dakers**
4 HANAZAKARI, 4, b c Danzero (AUS)—Russian Rose (IRE) **G. B. Partnership**
5 ISLAND RAPTURE, 5, b m Royal Applause—Gersey **Hants and Herts**
6 LINDOP, 5, ch h Nashwan (USA)—Footlight Fantasy (USA) **Lady Sophia Topley**
7 PAGAN MAGIC (USA), 4, b g Diesis—Great Lady Slew (USA) **The Gap Partnership**
8 PAGAN SKY (IRE), 6, ch g Inchinor—Rosy Sunset (IRE) **The Gap Partnership**
9 PEAK PARK (USA), 5, br g Dynaformer (USA)—Play Po (USA) **Lady Celina Carter**
10 SFORZANDO, 4, b f Robellino (USA)—Mory Kante (USA) **P. C. J. Dalby**
11 ST AUSTELL, 5, ch g Compton Place—Paris Joelle (IRE) **Miss J. Staughton**
12 SWINBROOK, 4, ch g Stravinsky (USA)—Dance Diane (USA) **Lady Sophia Topley**
13 TRUMAN, 4, b c Entrepreneur—Sabria (USA) **The Truman Syndicate**

THREE-YEAR-OLDS

14 ANATOLIAN STAR (USA), ch c Rahy (USA)—Rosebrook (USA) **Mr Y. Gelgin**
15 CAPTAIN GENERAL, br c In The Wings—Sea Quest (IRE) **Michael E. Wates**
16 FLEURANCE, br f High Estate—Fragrance **Miss F. R. E. Dakers**
17 B f Spectrum (IRE)—Juvenilia (IRE) **G. B. Partnership**
18 MEDORA LEIGH (USA), ch f Swain (IRE)—Gaily Tiara (USA) **Thoroughbred Farms Ltd**
19 PAGAN QUEST, b c Lujain (USA)—Rohita (IRE) **The Gap Partnership**
20 PERFECT SOLUTION (IRE), ch f Entrepreneur—Pearl Barley (IRE) **The Perfect Partnership**
21 PERFECT STORY (IRE), b f Desert Story (IRE)—Shore Lark (USA) **Mr John Drew and Dr Bridget Drew**
22 PERFECTIONIST, b f In The Wings—Lady Donatella **Mr John Drew and Dr Bridget Drew**
23 PERUVIAN PRINCE (USA), b c Silver Hawk (USA)—Inca Dove (USA) **P. C. J. Dalby**
24 RAMSGILL (USA), b c Prized (USA)—Crazee Mental **Lady Celina Carter**
25 RIGHT TO ROAM (IRE), b g Namid—Lloc **Lady Sophia Topley**
26 TRIBAL CHIEF (IRE), b c Desert Prince (IRE)—Lehua (IRE) **P. C. J. Dalby**

TWO-YEAR-OLDS

27 Br f 15/3 Nashwan (USA)—Bedara (Barathea (IRE)) (30000) **J Charrington & Partners**
28 B f 2/4 Mozart (IRE)—Belize Tropical (IRE) (Baillamont (USA))
29 DELORAIN (IRE), b c 6/2 Kalanisi (IRE)—Lady Nasrana (FR) (Al Nasr (FR)) (40000) **P. Dalby & R. Schuster**
30 GRECIANETTE (IRE), b f 22/3 Night Shift (USA)—Alexandria (IRE) (Irish River (FR)) **Thoroughbred Farms Ltd**

MR J. A. R. TOLLER—continued

31 **PAGAN ISLAND**, b c 14/4 Polish Precedent (USA)—Dodo (IRE) (Alzao (USA)) (64000) **The Gap Partnership**
32 **PINK PYJAMAS**, ch f 16/2 Compton Place—Pagan Princess (Mujtahid (USA)) **G. D. P. Materna**
33 **RIVER THAMES**, b c 23/3 Efisio—Dashing Water (Dashing Blade) (70000) **Mr John Drew and Dr Bridget Drew**
34 B f 3/4 Royal Applause—See You Later (Emarati (USA)) (75000) **Mr John Drew and Dr Bridget Drew**
35 **ST FRIS**, gr c 20/1 Silver Patriarch (IRE)—Fragrance (Mtoto) **Miss F. R. E. Dakers**
36 B c 26/3 Mark of Esteem (IRE)—Success Story (Sharrood (USA)) (25000) **M. A. Whelton**
37 **WOODNOOK**, b f 26/2 Cadeaux Genereux—Corndavon (USA) (Sheikh Albadou) **Mrs J. Scott**

Other Owners: D. Dennis, P. R. Anders, J. J. Corden, Mrs S. J. Glasgow, Mr H. I. Gurel, M. G. H. Heald, D. A. Poole, R. Santilli, Mrs Olivia Staughton, L. G. Straszewski, G. H. Toller, Mr D. H. Webb, Mrs J. B. Williams.

Assistant Trainer: Miss J Staughton

588

MR M. H. TOMPKINS, Newmarket
Postal: **Flint Cottage Stables, Rayes Lane, Newmarket, Suffolk, CB8 7AB.**
Contacts: **PHONE (01638) 661434 FAX (01638) 668107**
E-MAIL mht@marktompkins.co.uk WEBSITE www.marktompkins.co.uk

1 **ASTROCHARM (IRE)**, 6, b m Charnwood Forest (IRE)—Charm The Stars **Mystic Meg Limited**
2 **ASTROMANCER (USA)**, 5, b br m Silver Hawk (USA)—Colour Dance **Mystic Meg Limited**
3 **BABODANA**, 5, ch h Bahamian Bounty—Daanat Nawal **M. P. Bowring**
4 **BUMPTIOUS**, 4, b c Mister Baileys—Gleam of Light (IRE) **Mrs B. Lockey**
5 **CONNECT**, 8, b g Petong—Natchez Trace **Mrs P. R. Bowring**
6 **CROCIERA (IRE)**, 4, b g Croco Rouge (IRE)—Ombry Girl (IRE) **Roalco Ltd**
7 **FRANKLINS GARDENS**, 5, b h Halling (USA)—Woodbeck **Mrs M. J. Barwell**
8 **ICE DRAGON**, 4, b f Polar Falcon (USA)—Qilin (IRE) **I. C. Lochhead**
9 **INCHPAST**, 4, ch c Inchinor—Victor Ludorum **Marcoe Racing Welwyn**
10 **JAMES CAIRD (IRE)**, 5, ch g Catrail—Polish Saga **Kenneth MacPherson**
11 **LANGFORD**, 5, ch g Compton Place—Sharpening **Marlborough Electronics**
12 **MARSHMAN (IRE)**, 6, ch g College Chapel—Gold Fly (IRE) **J. H. Ellis**
13 **MIKAO (IRE)**, 4, b g Tagula (IRE)—Oumaladia (USA) **B. R. Allen**
14 **PATRIXPRIAL**, 4, gr c Linamix (FR)—Magnificent Star (USA) **P. H. Betts**
15 **PHONE TAPPING**, 4, b c Robellino (USA)—Miss Party Line (USA) **The LevelsyouDevils Partnership**
16 **RAJAYOGA**, 4, ch g Kris—Optimistic **Mystic Meg Limited**
17 **RETIREMENT**, 6, b g Zilzal (USA)—Adeptation (USA) **B. R. Allen**
18 **ROYAL CHALLENGE**, 4, b g Royal Applause—Anotheranniversary **Killarney Glen**
19 **SAND AND STARS (IRE)**, 4, ch f Dr Devious (IRE)—Charm The Stars **Pollards Bloodstock**
20 **ST PETERSBURG**, 5, ch g Polar Falcon (USA)—First Law **P. J. Heath**
21 **STEENBERG (IRE)**, 6, ch g Flying Spur (AUS)—Kip's Sister **Kenneth MacPherson**
22 **TOPARUDI**, 4, b g Rudimentary (USA)—Topatori (IRE) **M. P. Bowring**
23 **TREW CLASS**, 4, ch f Inchinor—Inimitable **Russell Trew Roofing Ltd**

THREE-YEAR-OLDS

24 **BEN BACCHUS (IRE)**, b g Bahhare (USA)—Bodfaridistinction (IRE) **Mrs M. Gallop**
25 **DIAMONDS AND DUST**, c Mister Baileys—Dusty Shoes **Mrs S. Ashby**
26 **DOLLS HOUSE**, b f Dancing Spree (USA)—Kip's Sister **Mrs M. H. Tompkins**
27 **DUDLEY DOCKER (IRE)**, b g Victory Note (USA)—Nordic Abu (IRE) **Kenneth MacPherson**
28 **HAWKES BAY**, b c Vettori (IRE)—Nordico Princess **Mrs C. E. Heath**
29 **HELEN HOUSE**, b f Tipsy Creek (USA)—Tiempo **Mrs M. H. Tompkins**
30 **MANEKI NEKO (IRE)**, b g Rudimentary (USA)—Ardbess **David Boyce And Partners**
31 **MINERAL STAR (IRE)**, b c Monashee Mountain (USA)—Summit Talk **Mineral Star Partnership**
32 **MONASH LAD (IRE)**, ch g General Monash (USA)—Story Time (IRE) **The Monash Partnership**
33 **MRS CHIPPY (IRE)**, ch f Docksider (USA)—Pile (USA) **Mr M. H. Tompkins**
34 **RINGAROOMA**, b f Erhaab (USA)—Tatouma (USA) **Mr N. Hodgkinson**
35 **RIVER CARD**, ch f Zaha (CAN)—Light Hand **R. M. Levitt**
36 **ROWAN LODGE (IRE)**, ch c Indian Lodge (IRE)—Tirol Hope (IRE) **The Rowan Stud and Clique Partnership**
37 **SELIKA (IRE)**, ch g Daggers Drawn (USA)—Hint-of-Romance (IRE) **Mrs B. Lockey**
38 **SHINGLE STREET (IRE)**, b g Bahhare (USA)—Sandystones **R. R. Flatt**
39 **STANCOMB WILLS (IRE)**, b c Trans Island—First Nadia **Kenneth MacPherson**
40 **TIAMO**, ch c Vettori (IRE)—Speed To Lead (IRE) **P. A. & D. G. Sakal**
41 **TOMOBEL**, b f Josr Algarhoud (IRE)—Eileen's Lady **Ray Smith and Partners**
42 **TOPATO**, ch f Bahamian Bounty—Topatori (IRE) **Mrs P. R. Bowring**
43 **TREW FLIGHT (USA)**, b c Rahy (USA)—Magdala (IRE) **R. D. Trew**
44 **TREW STYLE**, ch c Desert King (IRE)—Southern Psychic (USA) **R. D. Trew**

MR M. H. TOMPKINS—continued

45 TURKS WOOD (IRE), b g Charnwood Forest (IRE)—Nairasha (IRE) **Mrs P. M. Rickett**
46 VINIYOGA, b g Cadeaux Genereux—Optimistic **Mystic Meg Limited**

TWO-YEAR-OLDS

47 ANTICA (IRE), ch f 19/2 Raise A Grand (IRE)—Travel Tricks (IRE) (Presidium) (3353) **Phil Green and Partners**
48 ASTROBELLA, ch f 15/4 Medicean—Optimistic (Reprimand) **Mystic Meg Limited**
49 ASTRONOVA, ch f 7/4 Bahamian Bounty—Astrolove (IRE) (Bigstone (IRE)) **Mystic Meg Limited**
50 BILLANROY (IRE), ch c 23/4 Inchinor—Charm The Stars (Roi Danzig (USA)) (58000) **Mrs M. J. Barwell**
51 DEEP SLEEP, b c 13/5 Tipsy Creek (USA)—Tiempo (King of Spain) **Mrs M. H. Tompkins**
52 B c 26/3 Spectrum (USA)—Dixieline City (USA) (Dixieland Band (USA)) (13413)
53 DON'TCALLMEGINGER (IRE), ch c 7/4 Fruits of Love (USA)—
                                    Scotia Rose (Tap On Wood) (9389) **Jenkins, Knight and Trott**
54 B c 2/3 Bahhare (USA)—Eastern Star (IRE) (Sri Pekan (USA)) (7041)
55 EMILY'S PLACE (IRE), b f 27/3 Mujadil (USA)—Dulcinea (Selkirk (USA)) **Mr B. Brewster**
56 B f 3/5 Namid—Fifth Avenue (Unfuwain (USA))
57 GEE DEE NEN, b c 6/4 Mister Baileys—Special Beat (Bustino) (12000) **Mr D. Noblett**
58 B f 7/2 Tagula (IRE)—Ghana (GER) (Bigstone (IRE)) (5364)
59 B f 15/2 Tipsy Creek (USA)—Grove Dancer (Reprimand)
60 B f 24/4 City On A Hill (USA)—Kaliningrad (IRE) (Red Sunset) (4560)
61 KINSYA, ch c 29/4 Mister Baileys—Kimono (USA) (Machiavellian (USA)) (11000) **Roalco Ltd**
62 LAHEEN (IRE), b f 13/3 Bluebird (USA)—Ashirah (USA) (Housebuster (USA)) (59020) **Pollards Stables**
63 MIGHTY OBSERVER (IRE), b c 24/4 Observatory (USA)—
                                    Staff Approved (Teenoso (USA)) (23473) **The Mighty Empire Partnership**
64 MISSOULA (IRE), b f 9/3 Kalanisi (IRE)—Medway (IRE) (Shernazar) (13413) **Pollards Bloodstock**
65 Br f 28/4 Xaar—Mixremember (FR) (Linamix (FR)) (14083)
66 Ch f 14/2 Zilzal (USA)—No Islands (Lomond (USA)) (5000)
67 PENMARA, b f 16/1 Mtoto—Pendulum (Pursuit of Love) (5000) **B. R. Allen**
68 ROWAN VIEW (IRE), ch c 26/2 Observatory (USA)—Be Decisive (Diesis) **Rowan Stud Partnership**
69 RUBENSTAR (IRE), b c 3/2 Soviet Star (USA)—Ansariya (USA) (Shahrastani (USA)) (8000) **B. R. Allen**
70 SHORE THING (IRE), b c 25/3 Docksider (USA)—Spicebird (IRE) (Ela-Mana-Mou) (14754) **Roalco Ltd**
71 SIENNA STORM (IRE), b c 9/4 Peintre Celebre (USA)—
                                    Saint Ann (USA) (Geiger Counter (USA)) (50300) **Mrs B. Lockey**
72 B c 29/3 Atraf—Silvery (Petong) (13413)
73 Gr c 1/4 Mister Baileys—Sky Red (Night Shift (USA)) (6500)
74 SUMMER LODGE, b c 1/2 Indian Lodge (IRE)—Summer Siren (FR) (Saint Cyrien (FR)) (16000) **Roalco Ltd**
75 TOP SHOT, ch c 20/4 College Chapel—Topatori (IRE) (Topanoora) **J. H. Ellis**
76 Ch f 2/4 Fantastic Light (USA)—True Joy (IRE) (Zilzal (USA)) (57000) **Mr Frank Cosgrove**

Other Owners: B. Joyce, Mrs D. J. Arstall, Mr L. Arstall, J. Barrett, G. Eaton, Mr M. J. Greenwood, N. H. Hanger, K. A. A. Hodges, Ms S. Kelly, Mr P. I. King, R. B. Kolien, Mr D. Latter, C. B. Lockey, S. R. Powell, Mr B. W. Price, Mrs R. Ridout, Mr R. J. Thornalley, Mr D. Ward, M. Wilkinson.

Assistant Trainer: Steven Avery

Apprentice: Saleem Golam.

---

589 **MRS P. TOWNSLEY, Godalming**
Postal: **Mendips, The Common, Dunsfold, Godalming, Surrey, GU8 4LA.**
Contacts: PHONE (01483) 200849 FAX (01483) 200055 MOBILE (07887) 726363
E-MAIL pruetownsley@classicsecurity.co.uk

1 ESCOBAR (POL), 4, b g Royal Court (IRE)—Escola (POL) **Pole to Pole Partnership**
2 GRAFT, 6, b g Entrepreneur—Mariakova (USA) **P. Townsley**
3 GRUMPYINTMORNING, 6, b g Magic Ring—Grecian Belle **Classic Security UK Ltd**
4 LAGO DI COMO, 8, b g Piccolo—Farmer's Pet **Mr M. J. Caldwell**
5 LITTLETON ZEPHIR (USA), 6, b m Sandpit (BRZ)—Miss Gorgeous (IRE) **Classic Security UK Ltd**
6 NOSTROMO (POL), 4, b g Don Corleone—Novara (POL) **Pole to Pole Partnership**
7 SECAM (POL), 6, gr g Alywar (USA)—Scytia (POL) **Jamie Butler & Paul Townsley**
8 SIDONIUS (POL), 5, b h Special Power—Solera (POL) **The Pole to Pole Partnership**
9 SKINSEY FINNEGAN (IRE), 11, b g Fresh Breeze (USA)—Rose of Solway **Mrs P. Townsley**
10 TIRAILLEUR (IRE), 5, b m Eagle Eyed (USA)—Tiralle (IRE) **Jamie & Charlotte Thompson**

Other Owners: Mr S. F. Johnstone.

Assistant Trainer: C Thompson

Jockey (flat): A. Culhane. **Jockey (NH):** M. Batchelor, C. Bolger. **Amateur:** Mrs C Thompson.

590 **MR M. P. TREGONING, Lambourn**
Postal: Kingwood House Stables, Lambourn, Berkshire, RG17 7RS.
Contacts: PHONE (01488) 73300 FAX (01488) 71728 MOBILE (07767) 888100
E-MAIL enquiries@kingwood-stables.co.uk WEBSITE www.kingwood-stables.co.uk

1 ALKAADHEM, 5, b h Green Desert (USA)—Balalaika **Hamdan Al Maktoum**
2 BIENVENUE, 4, ch f Bien Bien (USA)—Mossy Rose **Stanley J. Sharp**
3 BUSTAN (IRE), 6, b g Darshaan—Dazzlingly Radiant **Hamdan Al Maktoum**
4 HIGH ACCOLADE, 5, b h Mark of Esteem (IRE)—Generous Lady **Lady Tennant**
5 MESHAHEER (USA), 6, b h Nureyev (USA)—Race The Wild Wind (USA) **Hamdan Al Maktoum**
6 MUBTAKER (USA), 8, ch h Silver Hawk (USA)—Gazayil (USA) **Hamdan Al Maktoum**
7 MUTAMARED (USA), 5, ch h Nureyev (USA)—Alydariel (USA) **Hamdan Al Maktoum**
8 ORIENTAL WARRIOR, 4, b c Alhaarth (IRE)—Oriental Fashion (IRE) **Hadi Al-Tajir**
9 PRIORS LODGE (IRE), 7, br h Grand Lodge (USA)—Addaya (IRE) **Lady Tennant**
10 SEVEN YEAR ITCH (IRE), 5, b g Danehill (USA)—Itching (IRE) **Greenbay Stables Ltd**
11 TAHTHEEB (IRE), 4, b f Muhtarram (USA)—Mihnah (IRE) **Hamdan Al Maktoum**

THREE-YEAR-OLDS

12 ACTUALITY, b g So Factual (USA)—Cottage Maid **Stanley J. Sharp**
13 ALMAMOORAH (IRE), ch f Sinndar (IRE)—Alkaffeyeh (IRE) **Hamdan Al Maktoum**
14 ALSHAMATRY (USA), ch f Seeking The Gold (USA)—Mehthaaf (USA) **Hamdan Al Maktoum**
15 ALSHARQ (IRE), b f Machiavellian (USA)—Balaabel (USA) **Hamdan Al Maktoum**
16 ALSHIMAAL (IRE), b f Namid—Bold As Love **Hamdan Al Maktoum**
17 AMEEQ (USA), b c Silver Hawk (USA)—Haniya (IRE) **Hamdan Al Maktoum**
18 AWAASER (USA), ch f Diesis—Forest Storm (USA) **Hamdan Al Maktoum**
19 BATTLEDRESS (IRE), b g In The Wings—Chaturanga **Jumeirah Racing**
20 BLA SHAK (IRE), b c Alhaarth (IRE)—Really Gifted (IRE) **Sheikh Ahmed Al Maktoum**
21 BLACK VELVET, b g Inchinor—Three Owls (IRE) **Lady Tennant**
22 BLUE LULLABY (IRE), b f Fasliyev—Whispering (IRE) **Greenbay Stables Ltd**
23 CASH ON (IRE), ch g Spectrum (IRE)—Lady Lucre (IRE) **Mr M. Calvert and Mr Colin E. Lewis**
24 CHANDRA, b f Cape Cross (IRE)—Dom Pennion **Mr A. Krishnan**
25 CLAMBAKE (IRE), ch f Grand Lodge (USA)—Sometime (IRE) **Greenbay Stables Ltd**
26 DAND NEE (USA), b f Kabool—Zobaida (USA) **Sheikh Ahmed Al Maktoum**
27 DANZARE, b f Dansili—Shot of Redemption **R. C. C. Villers**
28 DEFINITE DANCER (IRE), b g Definite Article—Greeba **Geoffrey and Miss Joan Hayes**
29 DISPATCHES, br g Diktat—Petriece **Jumeirah Racing**
30 EMILE ZOLA, b c Singspiel (IRE)—Ellie Ardensky **Jumeirah Racing**
31 FALEH, ch f Silver Hawk (USA)—Marasem **Hamdan Al Maktoum**
32 FLAUNT N FLIRT, b f Erhaab (USA)—Lets Fall In Love (USA) **Miss N. G. Sexton**
33 GAWAIN (USA), ch g Horse Chestnut (SAF)—Maid of Camelot **A. E. Oppenheimer**
34 HUBOOB (FR), b g Almutawakel—Atnab (USA) **Hamdan Al Maktoum**
35 IMPERIAL RULE (IRE), b g Second Empire (IRE)—Alikhlas **Imperial Rule Partnership**
36 ISLE DE MAURICE, b c Sinndar (IRE)—Circe's Isle **A. E. Oppenheimer**
37 ITQAAN (IRE), b f Danzig (USA)—Sarayir (USA) **Hamdan Al Maktoum**
38 JAAFI (IRE), b c Celtic Swing—Bustinetta **Hamdan Al Maktoum**
39 JACK ROLFE, b g Polish Precedent (USA)—Haboobti **Mrs S. Diamandis**
40 JALWADA, b f Cadeaux Genereux—Wedoudah (IRE) **Sheikh Ahmed Al Maktoum**
41 KATHEER, b c Anabaa (USA)—Elhida (IRE) **Hamdan Al Maktoum**
42 KAWN, b f Cadeaux Genereux—Khubza **Hamdan Al Maktoum**
43 MAGHAZI (IRE), b c Fasliyev (USA)—Dalayil (IRE) **Hamdan Al Maktoum**
44 MAYADEEN (IRE), b c King's Best (USA)—Inaaq **Hamdan Al Maktoum**
45 MEGGIDO (IRE), b c Green Desert (USA)—No Win No Deal **Sheikh Ahmed Al Maktoum**
46 MERAYAAT (IRE), b f Darshaan—Maddelina (IRE) **Hamdan Al Maktoum**
47 MOGAAMER (USA), b c Dixieland Band (USA)—Dolly Talbo (USA) **Hamdan Al Maktoum**
48 MOHAFAZAAT (IRE), b f Sadler's Wells (USA)—Wijdan (USA) **Hamdan Al Maktoum**
49 MOLLZAM (IRE), b c Danehill (USA)—Matilda Bay (IRE) **Sheikh Ahmed Al Maktoum**
50 MONDAREJ (IRE), b g Sinndar (IRE)—Masharik (IRE) **Hamdan Al Maktoum**
51 MUSHAJER, gr g Linamix (FR)—Luxurious **Hamdan Al Maktoum**
52 NIGHT HOUR (IRE), b c Entrepreneur—Witching Hour (IRE) **Greenbay Stables Ltd**
53 NOUBIAN (USA), ch c Diesis—Beraysim **Sheikh Ahmed Al Maktoum**
54 OONAGH MACCOOL (IRE), ch f Giant's Causeway—Alidiva **Greenbay Stables Ltd**
55 PASSEPARTOUT, b g Entrepreneur—Passe Passe (USA) **A. E. Oppenheimer**
56 PERFECT IMAGE, b f Makbul—Perfect Timing **Wild Beef Racing**
57 QADAR (IRE), b c Xaar—Iktidar **Hamdan Al Maktoum**
58 REMAAL (IRE), ch f Unfuwain—Marah **Hamdan Al Maktoum**
59 SAREM (USA), b br c Kingmambo (USA)—Storm Beauty (USA) **Hamdan Al Maktoum**

MR M. P. TREGONING—continued

60 **SEASONS PARKS**, b f Desert Prince (IRE)—Fantazia **Seasons Holidays**
61 **SHOHRAH (IRE)**, ch f Giant's Causeway (USA)—Taqreem (IRE) **Hamdan Al Maktoum**
62 **SOLWAY FIRTH**, b c Mark of Esteem (IRE)—Whitehaven **Jumeirah Racing**
63 **TAKHLEED (USA)**, b g Stravinsky (USA)—Bold Threat (CAN) **Hamdan Al Maktoum**
64 **UMTHOULAH (IRE)**, b f Unfuwain (USA)—Susquehanna Days (USA) **Hamdan Al Maktoum**
65 **WAR AT SEA (IRE)**, b c Bering—Naval Affair (IRE) **Ballymacoll Stud Farm Ltd**
66 **WELLING (IRE)**, b br c Darshaan—Felona **Sheikh Ahmed Al Maktoum**
67 **WHISPERING BLUES (IRE)**, b f Sadler's Wells (USA)—Will Be Blue (IRE) **Mr P. Newton**
68 **ZEENA**, b f Unfuwain (USA)—Forest Fire (SWE) **Mrs Mette Campbell-Andenaes**

TWO-YEAR-OLDS

69 Br c 28/2 Singspiel (IRE)—Abyaan (IRE) (Ela-Mana-Mou) **Sheikh Ahmed Al Maktoum**
70 B c 31/1 Alhaarth (USA)—Alhufoof (USA) (Dayjur) (95000) **Hamdan Al Maktoum**
71 **AND I**, b f 4/2 Inchinor—Fur Will Fly (Petong) (95000) **Mrs Mette Campbell-Andenaes**
72 **ASAASI (USA)**, b c 21/5 Danzig (USA)—Bashayer (USA) (Mr Prospector (USA)) **Hamdan Al Maktoum**
73 B c 9/3 Singspiel (IRE)—Atamana (Lahib (USA)) **Sheikh Ahmed Al Maktoum**
74 **AZMAAN (USA)**, b f 19/4 Bahri (USA)—Nasaayem (USA) (Gulch (USA)) **Hamdan Al Maktoum**
75 B f 6/2 Mark of Esteem (IRE)—Baaderah (IRE) (Cadeaux Genereux) **Sheikh Ahmed Al Maktoum**
76 **BABCARY**, b f 23/3 Bertolini (USA)—
        Midnight Break (Night Shift (USA)) (5000) **Major & Mrs R. B. Kennard & Partner**
77 B c 4/2 Theatrical—Bahr Alsalaam (USA) (Riverman (USA)) **Sheikh Ahmed Al Maktoum**
78 **BURKINA FASO**, b c 20/2 Green Desert (USA)—Ya Tarra (Unbridled (USA)) **Saeed Maktoum Al Maktoum**
79 B f 31/1 Daylami (USA)—Cambara (Dancing Brave (USA)) **Sheikh Ahmed Al Maktoum**
80 **CHAPEL CORNER (IRE)**, b f 18/4 Alhaarth (IRE)—
        Sheppard's Cross (Soviet Star (USA)) **Major & Mrs R. B. Kennard & Partner**
81 **CULTURE QUEEN**, b f 28/2 King's Best (USA)—
        Cultured Pearl (IRE) (Lammtarra (USA)) **Mr W. Carson & Mr C. Wright**
82 **DAHAALEEZ (USA)**, b c 22/2 Red Ransom (USA)—Raajiya (USA) (Gulch (USA)) **Hamdan Al Maktoum**
83 B c 20/4 Distant Music (USA)—Dance Ahead (Shareef Dancer (USA)) (55000) **Sheikh Ahmed Al Maktoum**
84 **DAWALEEB**, b f 18/4 Alhaarth (IRE)—Summerhill (Habitat) (75000) **Hamdan Al Maktoum**
85 **DHURWAH (IRE)**, b f 19/2 Green Desert (USA)—Bintalbawadi (IRE) (Diesis) **Hamdan Al Maktoum**
86 **ENLIGHTENED WAY (FR)**, ch f 19/2 Indian Ridge—Golden Way (IRE) (Cadeaux Genereux) **Maktoum Al Maktoum**
87 **ENTISAAR (USA)**, b f 2/5 Gulch (USA)—Manwah (USA) (Lyphard (USA)) **Hamdan Al Maktoum**
88 **GLENROWAN (USA)**, b f 11/5 Danzig (USA)—Pricket (USA) (Diesis) **Hamdan Al Maktoum**
89 **GRANDMA MOSES**, gr f 15/3 Linamix (FR)—Picture Princess (Sadler's Wells (USA)) **Hamdan Al Maktoum**
90 **GREEK RENAISSANCE (IRE)**, b c 27/4 Machiavellian (USA)—
        Athene (IRE) (Rousillon (USA)) **Ballymacoll Stud Farm Ltd**
91 B c 4/4 Silver Hawk (USA)—Guerre Et Paix (USA) (Soviet Star (USA)) (266028) **Hamdan Al Maktoum**
92 Ch c 7/3 Silver Hawk (USA)—Hamasah (USA) (Irish River (FR)) **Hamdan Al Maktoum**
93 **IN DUBAI (USA)**, ch f 26/4 Giant's Causeway (USA)—Bahr (Generous (IRE)) **Sheikh Ahmed Al Maktoum**
94 Ch c 3/4 Inchinor—Jersey Lillie (IRE) (Hector Protector (USA)) (33000) **R. C. C. Villers**
95 **JEWAAR (USA)**, b f 15/2 Diesis—Ringshaan (FR) (Darshaan) (239425) **Hamdan Al Maktoum**
96 **JUMPSHIP**, ch f 13/4 Night Shift (USA)—Flagship (Rainbow Quest (USA)) **M. H. Dixon**
97 **KIAWAH ISLAND**, ch c 18/4 Indian Ridge—Amusing Time (IRE) (Sadler's Wells (USA)) **Maktoum Al Maktoum**
98 B f 31/1 Alhaarth (IRE)—Kronengold (USA) (Golden Act (USA)) **Sheikh Ahmed Al Maktoum**
99 **LIFE PEER**, b c 18/2 Mark of Esteem (IRE)—Sadaka (USA) (Kingmambo (USA)) (25000) **Mark Five Racing**
100 B c 25/1 Desert Prince (USA)—Lionne (Darshaan) (220000) **Sheikh Ahmed Al Maktoum**
101 B c 18/2 Dansili—Love And Affection (USA) (Exclusive Era (USA)) (42000) **Byculla Thoroughbreds**
102 B c 8/1 Sadler's Wells (USA)—Lurina (IRE) (Lure (USA)) (200000) **Sheikh Ahmed Al Maktoum**
103 **MAAL (IRE)**, b c 28/3 Mozart (IRE)—Dalayil (IRE) (Sadler's Wells (USA)) **Hamdan Al Maktoum**
104 **MAHFADHA**, b f 30/1 Erhaab (USA)—Eljariha (Unfuwain (USA)) **Hamdan Al Maktoum**
105 **MAKDERAH (IRE)**, b f 27/3 Danehill (USA)—Wijdan (USA) (Mr Prospector (USA)) **Hamdan Al Maktoum**
106 **MASAAR (USA)**, b c 18/2 Aljabr (USA)—Awtaan (USA) (Arazi (USA)) **Hamdan Al Maktoum**
107 **MOON VALLEY**, ch f 1/4 Halling (USA)—Crescent Moon (Mr Prospector (USA)) **Hamdan Al Maktoum**
108 **MOWAZANA (IRE)**, ch f 31/1 Galileo (IRE)—Taqreem (IRE) (Nashwan (USA)) **Hamdan Al Maktoum**
109 **MUKAABER**, ch c 19/2 Pivotal—Placement (Kris) (115000) **Hamdan Al Maktoum**
110 **MULAAZEM**, b c 21/2 King's Best (USA)—Harayir (USA) (Gulch (USA)) **Hamdan Al Maktoum**
111 **MULTAKKA (IRE)**, b c 20/3 Alhaarth (IRE)—Elfaslah (IRE) (Green Desert (USA)) **Hamdan Al Maktoum**
112 **MUNTADA**, b f 18/2 King's Best (USA)—Inaaq (Lammtarra (USA)) **Hamdan Al Maktoum**
113 **MUSTAMMER**, b c 14/4 Fasliyev (USA)—Alazima (USA) (Mujtahid (USA)) **Hamdan Al Maktoum**
114 **NAHAAR (IRE)**, b c 26/3 Royal Applause—Elhida (IRE) (Mujtahid (USA)) **Hamdan Al Maktoum**
115 Ch f 14/3 Gilded Time (USA)—Nasmatt (Danehill (USA)) **Sheikh Ahmed Al Maktoum**
116 **NAWAADI**, b c 22/4 Intikhab (USA)—Elhilmeya (IRE) (Unfuwain (USA)) **Hamdan Al Maktoum**
117 **OSCAR SNOWMAN**, b c 26/2 Selkirk (USA)—Chilly Start (USA) (Caerleon (USA)) **Saeed Maktoum Al Maktoum**
118 B c 27/1 Mark of Esteem (IRE)—Percy's Lass (Blakeney) (16000) **A. E. Pakenham**

MR M. P. TREGONING—continued

119 B c 7/3 Compton Place—Polished Up (Polish Precedent (USA)) (50000) **Sheikh Ahmed Al Maktoum**
120 B f 14/2 Lujain (USA)—Rateeba (IRE) (Green Desert (USA)) **Sheikh Ahmed Al Maktoum**
121 REALLY GIVEN (IRE), b f 15/2 Alhaarth (IRE)—Really Gifted (IRE) (Cadeaux Genereux) (24000) **Mr R. Barnett**
122 B c 3/5 Sadler's Wells (USA)—Rebecca Sharp (Machiavellian (USA)) (300000) **A. E. Oppenheimer**
123 REMELLURI (FR), ch f 28/2 Nashwan (USA)—

                   La Genereuse (Generous (IRE)) (18779) **Mrs Mette Campbell-Andeneas**
124 ROSE OF INCHINOR, b f 23/1 Inchinor—Rosa Canina (Bustino) **The Hopeful Partnership**
125 B c 5/4 Diesis—Roseate Tern (Blakeney) **Hamdan Al Maktoum**
126 B f 6/3 Lujain (USA)—Saleyma (Mtoto) **Sheikh Ahmed Al Maktoum**
127 SATIN DOLL, b f 15/4 Diktat—Unconditional Love (IRE) (Polish Patriot (USA)) (48000) **Itchen Valley Stud**
128 B c 18/3 Bahri (USA)—Sayedah (IRE) (Darshaan) **Hamdan Al Maktoum**
129 SEAL OF HOPE, b c 29/4 Cape Cross (IRE)—

                  Heavenly Waters (Celestial Storm (USA)) (15000) **The Hopeful Partnership**
130 SEBAAQ (USA), ch c 27/2 Rahy (USA)—

                  Malibu Karen (Seeking The Gold (USA)) (212822) **Hamdan Al Maktoum**
131 SHAHIN (USA), b c 31/1 Kingmambo (USA)—

                  String Quartet (IRE) (Sadler's Wells (USA)) (505453) **Hamdan Al Maktoum**
132 B f 31/1 Lujain (USA)—Shallat (IRE) (Pennekamp (USA)) **Sheikh Ahmed Al Maktoum**
133 SILVERHILLS (IRE), b f 4/3 Peintre Celebre (USA)—

                  Litchfield Hills (USA) (Relaunch (USA)) **Greenbay Stables Ltd**
134 B f 15/4 Alhaarth (IRE)—

            Susquehanna Days (USA) (Chief's Crown (USA)) **Mrs C. F. van Straubenzee and Partners**
135 THE MOON AND BACK (USA), ch f 26/4 Sky Classic (CAN)—

               Fly To The Moon (Blushing Groom (FR)) **Saeed Maktoum Al Maktoum**
136 WICKER PARK (IRE), b c 13/4 Galileo (IRE)—Green Field Park (Akarad (FR)) (114017) **Maktoum Al Maktoum**
137 WINGS OF DAWN, b f 26/2 In The Wings—Petit Point (IRE) (Petorius) **Lady Tennant**
138 B f 23/3 Fasliyev (USA)—Witching Hour (IRE) (Alzao (USA)) (13413) **Greenbay Stables Ltd**
139 B c 21/2 Red Ransom (USA)—Zobaida (IRE) (Green Desert (USA)) **Sheikh Ahmed Al Maktoum**

Other Owners: Mrs C. Woollett, Mr J. Wallis, Lady Allendale, Mr N. Peppiatt, Capt. T. Luckock, Mr J. Bernstein, Mr N. Wrigley, Sir Philip Payne-Gallwey, Mrs E. Brown, Mrs H. Dalgety, Mr G. Blomfield, Lady M. Fortescue, R. F. U. Gaskell, Mrs A. J. Hamilton, A. Maccioni, Mr J. Owen, Tessona Racing Ltd, Mr J. G. Tregoning, N. H. T. Wrigley.

Assistant Trainer: Patrick Macewan

Jockey (flat): M Dwyer, A. Daly, R. Hills, W. Supple.

---

591   **MR J. C. TUCK, Didmarton**
     Postal: **Manor Farm, Oldbury-On-The-Hill, Didmarton, South Gloucestershire.**
     Contacts: **PHONE (01454) 238236 FAX (01454) 238488 MOBILE (07971) 789069**

1 ARMAGH SOUTH (IRE), 6, ch g Topanoora—Mogen **Matthew Tuck**
2 BEKSTAR, 10, br m Nicholas Bill—Murex **Mrs J. Chapman**
3 BIG SMOKE (IRE), 5, gr g Perugino (USA)—Lightning Bug **J. R. Tuck**
4 COUNSEL, 10, ch g Most Welcome—My Polished Corner (IRE) **Mr J. C. Tuck**
5 ESS OF NORWAY (FR), 6, gr g Linamix (FR)—Tres de Cem (NOR) **Mr J. C. Tuck**
6 FINAL COMMAND, 8, ch g Gildoran—Fine Fettle **The Fine Gild Racing Partnership**
7 INDIAN STAR (GER), 7, br g Sternkoenig (IRE)—Indian Night (GER) **D. J. Neale**
8 JOHN JORROCKS (FR), 6, br g Chamberlin (FR)—Caryatide (FR) **The Cat & Custard Pot**
9 JUMPTY DUMPTY (FR), 8, b b g Chamberlin (FR)—Caryatide (FR) **Matthew Tuck**
10 KING GEORGES (FR), 7, b g Kadalko (FR)—Djoumi (FR) **The Try-Line Partnership**
11 LANCIER D'ESTRUVAL (FR), 6, ch g Epervier Bleu—Pommette III (FR) **Lord Huffington-Smythe Racing**
12 LORAMORE, 8, ch m Alflora (IRE)—Apsimore **Mrs E. J. Griffiths**
13 LOVELY LULU, 7, b m Petrizzo—The Green Girls (USA) **Mr J. C. Tuck**
14 MEGA CHIC (FR), 5, b g Useful (FR)—Pampachic (FR) **D. J. Neale**
15 MR BANKER, 10, b g Cashwvn—Flaming Fox **Mrs C. Y. Clift**
16 SPREEWALD (GER), 6, b g Dulcero (USA)—Spartina (USA) **Seven Star Racing Club**
17 SUNNYARJUN, 7, ch g Afzal—Hush Tina **Matthew Tuck**

Other Owners: M. Boothright, M. R. Brooks, Mr G. P. Golbey, K. M. Grey, Mrs M. Griffiths, Dr Lesley-Anne Hatter, Dr J. P. Heathcock, J. H. Knight, P. H. Watts.

Assistant Trainer: Matthew Tuck

Jockey (NH): R. Farrant, F. Keniry, R. Wakley. **Amateur:** Miss F J Jones.

592 MR F. G. TUCKER, Wedmore
Postal: **Mudgley Hill Farm, Mudgley, Wedmore, Somerset, BS28 4TZ.**
Contacts: **PHONE (01934) 712684 MOBILE (07989) 713264**

1 DUNNICKS FIELD, 9, b g Greensmith—Field Chance **Mr F. G. Tucker**

Assistant Trainer: Mrs C Tucker

---

593 MR E. W. TUER, Northallerton
Postal: **Home Farm, Great Smeaton, Northallerton, North Yorkshire, DL6 2EP.**
Contacts: **PHONE (01609) 881214 FAX (01609) 881214 MOBILE (07808) 330306**
E-MAIL ewtuer@clara.co.uk

1 ARCTIC MOSS (IRE), 6, ch m Moscow Society (USA)—Arctic Match **Yarm Skip Alliance**
2 AWWAL MARRA (USA), 5, ch m King of Kings (IRE)—Secretariat Lass (USA) **Far Distant Partnership**
3 BAMBINO ROSSI, 4, ch f Classic Cliche (IRE)—Leading Note (USA) **Mr E. W. Tuer**
4 COMMANCHE WIND (IRE), 10, b g Commanche Run—Delko **Mr E. W. Tuer**
5 FISHKI'S LAD, 10, b g Casteddu—Fishki **Mr E. W. Tuer**
6 LADY STRATAGEM, 6, gr m Mark of Esteem (IRE)—Grey Angel **Mr E. W. Tuer**
7 NORMA SPEAKMAN (IRE), 5, ch m Among Men (USA)—Bride Bank (IRE) **Mr E. W. Tuer**
8 SIMLET, 10, b g Forzando—Besito **Mr E. W. Tuer**
9 TERIMONS DAUGHTER, 6, b m Terimon—Fun While It Lasts **Mr E. W. Tuer**
10 THROUGH THE RYE, 9, ch g Sabrehill (USA)—Baharlilys **Nice to See You Euro-Racing**
11 WENDYS COMET, 8, b g Sea Raven (IRE)—Welsh Orbit **W. & W. Tarren**

Other Owners: T. Bosomworth, E. Carr, I. C. Forsyth, P. Lancaster, M. J. Molloy, R. Pawson, W. Tarren.

Assistant Trainer: G F Tuer

Amateur: Mr G. F. Tuer.

---

594 MR ANDREW TURNELL, Malton
Postal: **Highfield Stables, Beverley Road, Malton, North Yorkshire, YO17 9PJ.**
Contacts: **PHONE (01653) 699555 FAX (01653) 699333 MOBILE (07973) 933450**

1 AGGI MAC, 4, b f Defacto (USA)—Giffoine **Mr & Mrs P. France**
2 BISHOP'S BRIDGE (IRE), 7, b g Norwich—River Swell (IRE) **S. Kimber**
3 BUYING A DREAM (IRE), 8, ch g Prince of Birds (USA)—
    Cartagena Lady (IRE) **Robinson Webster (Holdings) Ltd**
4 DOWER HOUSE, 10, ch g Groom Dancer (USA)—Rose Noble (USA) **Mrs J. Hollowood**
5 DUBONAI (IRE), 5, ch g Peintre Celebre (USA)—Web of Intrigue **Mr G. R. Jewson**
6 JIGSAW JUMPER (IRE), 5, b m Shahrastani (USA)—Cockney Bug **Robinson Webster (Holdings) Ltd**
7 KEW JUMPER (IRE), 6, b g Mister Lord (USA)—Pharisee (IRE) **Robinson Webster (Holdings) Ltd**
8 NOBLE PASAO (IRE), 8, b g Alzao (USA)—Belle Passe **Mrs J. Hollowood**
9 RIVER TOP (IRE), 6, b g Norwich—River Swell (IRE) **Mr L. G. Kimber**
10 SADLER'S PRIDE (IRE), 5, b g Sadler's Wells (USA)—Gentle Thoughts **Paradime Ltd**
11 SIX PACK (IRE), 7, ch g Royal Abjar (USA)—Regal Entrance **J. J. Canny**
12 THE NAMES BOND, 7, b g Tragic Role (USA)—Artistic Licence **Mrs J. Hollowood**

THREE-YEAR-OLDS

13 B g Classic Cliche (IRE)—Bakers Daughter **Active Leisure.com Ltd**
14 BLUE BAJAN (IRE), b g Montjeu (IRE)—Gentle Thoughts **Dr J. Hollowood**
15 SHAANBAR (IRE), b f Darshaan—Barbara Frietchie (IRE) **Paradime Ltd**

TWO-YEAR-OLDS

16 B f 6/3 Foxhound (USA)—Celandine (Warning) **Mrs Claire Hollowood**
17 PREMIER CRU, b c 27/3 King's Best (USA)—No Rehearsal (FR) (Baillamont (USA)) **Paradime Ltd**

Other Owners: D. Murray.

595 MR D. C. TURNER, Plymouth
Postal: **Higher Collard Farm, Wotter, Plymouth, Devon, PL7 5HU.**
Contacts: **PHONE (01752) 839231**

1 DUKE'S VIEW (IRE), 4, b g Sadler's Wells (USA)—Igreja (ARG) **Mrs M. E. Turner**
2 RICCARTON, 12, b g Nomination—Legendary Dancer **Mrs M. E. Turner**
3 SILVER MAN, 11, gr g Silver Owl—What An Experiance **Mrs M. E. Turner**
4 SOVIET SPIRIT, 4, ch f Soviet Star (USA)—Kristina **Mrs M. E. Turner**
5 ZORALO (IRE), 9, gr g Toulon—Another Yankee **Mrs M. E. Turner**

Assistant Trainer: Sally Palmer

Jockey (NH): R. Greene. **Amateur:** Mrs A. Hand.

596 MR D. T. TURNER, Spalding
Postal: **West View, Tydd Road, West Pinchbeck, Spalding, Lincolnshire, PE11 3QA.**
Contacts: **PHONE (01775) 640300**

1 MEMORY'S MUSIC, 13, b g Dance of Life (USA)—Sheer Luck **Mrs A. W. Turner**
2 TORY BOY, 10, b g Deploy—Mukhayyalah **Mrs A. W. Turner**

Amateur: Miss Angela Turner.

597 MR J. R. TURNER, Helperby
Postal: **Mayfield Farm, Norton-le-Clay, Helperby, York, YO61 2RS.**
Contacts: **PHONE (01423) 322239 FAX (01423) 322239**

1 AIR OF AFFECTION, 4, b f Air Express (IRE)—Auntie Gladys **Miss S. J. Turner**
2 FILEY FLYER, 5, ch m Weldnaas (USA)—Chasers' Bar **J. E. Swiers**
3 KEEN TO GO, 5, b m Keen—Popping On **R. C. Shedden**
4 5, B m Glacial Storm (USA)—Menelave (IRE) **R. N. Ellerbeck**
5 5, B m Un Desperado (FR)—Naar Chamali **R. N. Ellerbeck & G. W. Turner**
6 OCTAVIO, 4, ch g Efisio—Lassoo **J. Binks**
7 4, B g Keen—Popping On **Mr J. A. Lee**
8 ROSIE REDMAN (IRE), 8, gr m Roselier (FR)—Carbia's Last **Miss S. J. Turner**
9 WHITFIELD WARRIOR, 7, ch g Husyan (USA)—Valentines Day **Yarm Racing Partnership**
10 ZIPADEA (IRE), 6, b g Florida Son—Prudent Princess **G. Towersey**

Other Owners: R. Spilman, Mrs V. Robinson, R. A. Brown, J. H. Madden, MR J. R. Turner.

Assistant Trainer: Oliver J Turner

Jockey (NH): David O'Meara. **Conditional:** P. Whelan. **Amateur:** Mr R. Wakeham.

598 MRS K. J. TUTTY, Northallerton
Postal: **Trenholme House Farm, Osmotherley, Northallerton, North Yorkshire, DL6 3QA.**
Contacts: **PHONE (01609) 883624 MOBILE (07967) 837406**

1 DARAK (IRE), 9, b g Doyoun—Dararita (IRE) **Mr N. Tutty**
2 DRACAENA, 8, b m State Diplomacy (USA)—Jay-Dee-Jay **Mr N. Tutty**
3 LILLY BEACH, 9, b m Milieu—Marlowvous **Mr N. Tutty**

Amateur: Mr N. Tutty.

599 MR N. A. TWISTON-DAVIES, Cheltenham
Postal: **Grange Hill Farm, Naunton, Cheltenham, Gloucestershire, GL54 3AY.**
Contacts: **PHONE (01451) 850278 FAX (01451) 850101 MOBILE (07836) 664440**
E-MAIL nigel@nigeltwistondavies.co.uk WEBSITE www.nigeltwistondavies.co.uk

1 ARDAGHEY (IRE), 6, b br g Lord Americo—Mrs Pepper **D. J. & S. A. Goodman**
2 ARDASHIR (FR), 6, b g Simon du Desert (FR)—Antea (FR) **Mrs C. M. Mould**
3 BABY RUN (FR), 5, b g Baby Turk—Run For Laborie (FR) **Mr & Mrs Peter Orton**

MR N. A. TWISTON-DAVIES—continued

4 **BARNEYS LYRIC**, 5, ch g Hector Protector (USA)—Anchorage (IRE) **Mr & Mrs Peter Orton**
5 **BARON WINDRUSH**, 7, b g Alderbrook—Dame Scarlet **The Double Octagon Partnership**
6 **BINDAREE (IRE)**, 11, ch g Roselier (FR)—Flowing Tide **H. R. Mould**
7 **BOB THE BUILDER**, 6, b g Terimon—True Clown **Mr & Mrs Peter Orton**
8 **BORDER TALE**, 5, b g Selkirk (USA)—Likely Story (IRE) **Chadwick, Dyer & Flynn**
9 **CHAMPAGNE HARRY**, 7, b g Sir Harry Lewis (USA)—Sparkling Cinders **H. R. Mould**
10 **CO OPTIMIST**, 8, b g Homo Sapien—Tapua Taranata (IRE) **The Co-optimistic Partnership**
11 **DANTE'S BACK (IRE)**, 7, b g Phardante (FR)—Jordans Pet (IRE) **The "Yes" - "No" - "Wait"....Sorries**
12 **DARNAYSON (IRE)**, 5, b g Darnay—Nakuru (IRE) **The Son Partnership**
13 **DD'S GLENALLA (IRE)**, 8, b m Be My Native (USA)—Willowho Pride **Mrs C. Beresford-Wylie**
14 **DEDRUNKNMUNKY (IRE)**, 6, b br m Rashar (USA)—Rostoonstown Lass (IRE) **The Inebriated Apes**
15 **EATON HALL (IRE)**, 5, b br g Saddlers' Hall (IRE)—Lady Bow **Turf Club Racing Syndicate (2004)**
16 **FLORIDA DREAM (IRE)**, 6, b g Florida Son—Ice Pearl **D. J. & S. A. Goodman & T.Puffett**
17 **FUNDAMENTALIST (IRE)**, 7, b g Supreme Leader—Run For Shelter **Gripen**
18 **GAZUMP (FR)**, 7, b g Iris Noir (FR)—Viva Sacree (FR) **H. R. Mould**
19 **GIGONDAS (IRE)**, 7, b g Zaffaran (USA)—Summit Else **Mr H. E. Coombs**
20 **GOLDEN DUCK (IRE)**, 5, b g Turtle Island (IRE)—Mazeeka (IRE) **Mrs Sally & Miss Isobel Noott**
21 **GRUMPY STUMPY**, 10, ch g Gunner B—Moaning Jenny **The "Yes" - "No" - "Wait"....Sorries**
22 **GULABILL**, 6, b g Safawan—Gulsha **Mrs J. K. Powell**
23 **HANOVER SQUARE**, 9, b g Le Moss—Hilly-Down Lass **The Oriental Partnership III**
24 **ICY PROSPECT (IRE)**, 7, ch g Glacial Storm (USA)—Prospect Lady (FR) **D. M. Mason**
25 **ITS CRUCIAL (IRE)**, 5, b g Beneficial—Balda Girl (IRE) **Mrs C. Beresford-Wylie**
26 **JACKIE BOY (IRE)**, 6, b g Lord Americo—Riverpauper (IRE) **J. F. Bance**
27 **KIRBY'S VIC (IRE)**, 5, b g Old Vic—Just Affable (IRE) **Mr and Mrs P. & V. Kirby**
28 **LADY DE PARIS**, 5, b m Paris of Troy—Kitty Bank VII **J. C. De Lisle Wells**
29 **LADY ZEPHYR (IRE)**, 7, b m Toulon—Sorimak Gale (IRE) **D. J. Langdon**
30 **LORD BROCK**, 6, b g Alderbrook—Mariner's Air **Graham and Alison Jelley**
31 **MASTER PAPA (IRE)**, 6, bl g Key of Luck (USA)—Beguine (USA) **The Alchemists 2**
32 **MAXIE MCDONALD (IRE)**, 12, b g Homo Sapien—Lovely Sanara **Mrs J. E. Meek**
33 **NEEDLE PRICK (IRE)**, 4, b g Needle Gun (IRE)—Emerson Supreme (IRE) **Mr N. A. Twiston-Davies**
34 **NO GUARANTEES**, 5, b g Master Willie—Princess Hotpot (IRE) **Mrs M. Slade and Mr G. MacEchern**
35 **OLLIE MAGERN**, 7, b g Alderbrook—Outfield **R. Nicholls**
36 **PETITE MARGOT**, 6, b m Alderbrook—Outfield **R. Nicholls**
37 **PRESENT COMPANY (IRE)**, 7, ch m Presenting—Calmount (IRE) **Mr F. J. Mills & Mr W. Mills**
38 **PRESTBURY KNIGHT**, 5, ch g Sir Harry Lewis (USA)—Lambrini (IRE) **Cheltenham Racing Ltd**
39 **PROMINENT PROFILE (IRE)**, 12, ch g Mazaad—Nakuru (IRE) **The Son Partnership**
40 **RANDOLPH O'BRIEN (IRE)**, 7, b g Zaffaran (USA)—Gala's Pride **Geoffrey & Donna Keeys**
41 **RED GEORGIE (IRE)**, 7, ch g Old Vic—Do We Know **M. P. Wareing**
42 **REDEMPTION**, 10, b g Sanglamore (USA)—Ypha (USA) **Mr John Duggan & Mr Michael Purtill**
43 **RESONANCE**, 4, b f Slip Anchor—Music In My Life (USA) **Mr N. A. Twiston-Davies**
44 **SCOTCH CORNER (IRE)**, 7, b g Jurado (USA)—Quennie Mo Ghra (IRE) **H. R. Mould**
45 **SOMMELIER**, 5, gr g Tamure (IRE)—Dissolve **The New Club Partnership 2**
46 **STAGE FRIENDLY (IRE)**, 6, ch g Old Vic—Just Affable (IRE) **I. F. Guest**
47 **STAR DOUBLE (ITY)**, 5, ch g Bob Back (USA)—Among The Stars **Mrs L. M. Berryman**
48 **SWAZI PRINCE**, 6, b g Rakaposhi King—Swazi Princess (IRE) **Mrs S. Orchart**
49 **SYNCOPATED RHYTHM (IRE)**, 5, b g Synefos (USA)—Northern Elation (IRE) **Mrs C. Beresford-Wylie**
50 **TATES AVENUE (IRE)**, 7, b g Zaffaran (USA)—Tate Divinity (IRE) **S. P. Tindall**
51 **THE COOL GUY (IRE)**, 5, b g Zaffaran (USA)—Frostbite **Frosty's Four**
52 **THE GANGERMAN (IRE)**, 5, ch g Anshan—Ivy Lane (IRE) **Agetur (UK) Ltd**
53 **THE NEEDLER (IRE)**, 5, b g Needle Gun (IRE)—Monteanna (IRE) **Mr & Mrs Peter Orton**
54 **TIVERTON TRYER**, 7, b g Gran Alba (USA)—Chester Belle **C. W. Jenkins**
55 **VA VAVOOM (IRE)**, 7, b g Supreme Leader—Shalom Joy **H. R. Mould**
56 **WELLPOT ONE (IRE)**, 5, b g Taipan (IRE)—Emily Bishop (IRE) **M. K. F. Seymour**
57 **WHAT DO'IN (IRE)**, 7, b br g Good Thyne (USA)—Della Wee (IRE) **Mr C. Cornes**
58 **WHEREAREYOUNOW (IRE)**, 8, ch g Mister Lord (USA)—Angie's Delight **H. R. Mould**
59 **WILLY FURNLEY (IRE)**, 5, b g Synefos (USA)—Random Bay **Mrs M. Curran**

Other Owners: C. J. Barker, D. Blake, J. S. Cantrill, J. P Carrington, Mr J. W. Clark, C. S. J. Coley, J. Duggan, I. Dunbar, J. A. R. R. French, T. R. Gittins, Mrs N. J. Gittins, Mrs F. E. Griffin, W. G. Hinshelwood, D. M. Hussey, Mrs C. M. Keeys, Mrs S. A. MacEchern, P. R. Noott, E. J. R. Noy, T. H. Ounsley, Mrs C. M. Pennell, R. G. Perry, O. D. Plunkett, G. W. Sanders, Mrs J. Scott, H. B. Shouler, Mrs H. I. Slade, N. J. Whitfield, A. P. Wyer.

Assistant Trainer: Gemma Emtage

Jockey (NH): J. Goldstein, C. Llewellyn. **Conditional:** Antony Evans, Mark Goldstein. **Amateur:** Mr David England.

600 **MR J. W. UNETT, Shrewsbury**
Postal: Preston Farm, Preston-on-Severn, Uffington, Shrewsbury, Shropshire, SY4 4TB.
Contacts: PHONE (01743) 709037 FAX (01743) 709529 MOBILE (07587) 534753
E-MAIL unettjames@aol.com

1 **CLASSIC ROCK**, 6, b g Classic Cliche (IRE)—Ruby Vision (IRE) **G. J. G. Roberts**
2 **CLOUDLESS (USA)**, 5, b br m Lord Avie (USA)—Summer Retreat (USA) **P. Bourchier**
3 **DANCES WITH ANGELS (IRE)**, 5, b m Mukaddamah (USA)—Lady of Leisure (USA) **Miss C. H. Jones**
4 **DOCDUCKOUT**, 5, b g Bluegrass Prince (IRE)—Fayre Holly (IRE) **P. Bourchier**
5 **ENDLESS PEACE (IRE)**, 4, ch f Russian Revival (USA)—Magical Peace (IRE) **Mr J. Malone**
6 **FIGHT THE FEELING**, 7, ch g Beveled (USA)—Alvecote Lady **T. Morning**
7 **GILLY'S GENERAL (IRE)**, 5, ch g General Monash (USA)—Good Aim (IRE) **J. E. Price**
8 **GREEN OCEAN**, 5, gr m Environment Friend—Northern Swinger **Mr J. W. Unett**
9 **NOBLE LOCKS (IRE)**, 7, ch g Night Shift (USA)—Imperial Graf (USA) **Mr J. W. Unett & T. Morning**
10 **PEACE EMBLEM (IRE)**, 4, b f Bahhare (USA)—Beseeching (IRE) **Mr J. Malone**
11 **RADMORE SPIRIT**, 5, b m Whittingham—Ruda (FR) **J. R. Salter**
12 **SHERIFF'S DEPUTY**, 5, b g Atraf—Forest Fantasy **T. Morning D. Auburn + A.G.S.**
13 **SPARK UP**, 5, b m Lahib (USA)—Catch The Flame (USA) **'Come And Join Us'**
14 **URBAN CALM**, 4, b f Cadeaux Genereux—Silver Sun **Mr P. Morrison**
15 **URBAN ROSE**, 4, b f Piccolo—Blue Lamp (USA) **Mr P. Morrison**
16 **WHITE O' MORN**, 6, gr m Petong—I'm Your Lady **J. E. Price**

THREE-YEAR-OLDS

17 **PRINCESS KARLA (IRE)**, b f Fayruz—Mystique Air (IRE) **P. Rosas**
18 **RAUL SAHARA**, br g Makbul—Sheraton Heights **P. Bourchier**

Other Owners: R. Ashford, A. W. Black, C. Chell, S. J. High, Mrs J. Kerr.

Assistant Trainer: Miss C. H. Jones

601 **MR J. R. UPSON, Towcester**
Postal: Glebe Stables, Blakesley Heath, Maidford, Towcester, Northamptonshire, NN12 8HN.
Contacts: PHONE (01327) 860043 FAX (01327) 860238

1 **AGINCOURT (IRE)**, 9, b g Alphabatim (USA)—Miss Brantridge **Middleham Park Racing XXI**
2 **ANOTHER GRADUATE (IRE)**, 7, ch g Naheez (USA)—Another Daisy **The Nap Hand Partnership**
3 **BACKSCRATCHER**, 11, b g Backchat (USA)—Tiernee Quintana **The Fourways Partnership**
4 **BEAU COUP**, 8, b g Toulon—Energance (IRE) **Mrs A. F. Key**
5 **BLUNHAM HILL (IRE)**, 7, ch g Over The River (FR)—Bronach **I. N. Mallett**
6 **CLEYMOR HOUSE (IRE)**, 7, ch g Duky—Deise Lady **The Reserved Judgment Partnership**
7 **DONNABELLA**, 8, b m Bustino—Howanever **Mrs B. A. Tate**
8 **GAINING GROUND (IRE)**, 5, ch g Presenting—Lorglane Lady (IRE) **Mrs D. Upson**
9 **GOLDEN AMBER (IRE)**, 6, ch g Glacial Storm (USA)—Rigton Angle **The Peter Partnership**
10 **GRITTI PALACE (IRE)**, 5, b g Duky—Glittering Grit (IRE) **Sir Nicholas Wilson**
11 **LORD OF THE PARK (IRE)**, 8, b g Lord Americo—Wind Chimes **Middleham Park Racing V**
12 **MISS SIRIUS**, 5, ch m Royal Vulcan—Star Shell **S. J. Smith**
13 **OVER ZEALOUS (IRE)**, 13, ch g Over The River (FR)—Chatty Di **Middleham Park Racing X**
14 **REACH THE CLOUDS (IRE)**, 13, b g Lord Americo—Dusky Stream **The Three Horseshoes Sporting Club**
15 **REFLEX COURIER (IRE)**, 13, b g Over The River (FR)—Thornpark Lady **Mrs D. Upson**
16 **REGAL RIVER (IRE)**, 8, b g Over The River (FR)—My Friend Fashion **Middleham Park Racing XIX**
17 **STROLLING VAGABOND (IRE)**, 6, ch g Glacial Storm (USA)—Found Again (IRE) **J. F. Bath**
18 **THE RIVER JOKER (IRE)**, 9, ch g Over The River (FR)—Augustaeliza (IRE) **G. P. McPherson**

Other Owners: M. H. Beesley, M. Chapman, G. D. Dalrymple, D. Deveney, F. Fountain, Ms S. M. Gilmore, J. D. Horgan, S. Massey, T. S. Palin, C. G. Wallis, M. E. White.

Conditional: M. Mello.

602 **MR M. D. I. USHER, Lambourn**
Postal: **Saxon House Stables, Upper Lambourn, Hungerford, Berkshire, RG17 8QH.**
Contacts: PHONE (01488) 72598 FAX (01488) 72646 MOBILE (07831) 873531
E-MAIL mark@markusherracing.freeserve.co.uk

1 AMONG THIEVES (IRE), 5, b m Among Men (USA)—Abbesingh **Mr M. D. I. Usher**
2 AUBURN SPIRIT, 10, ch g Teamster—Spirit of Youth **G. A. Summers**
3 GOLDEN QUEEN, 4, b f Unfuwain (USA)—Queen Linear (USA) **I. J. Sheward**
4 MR MISCHIEVOUS, 4, b g Magic Ring (IRE)—Inya Lake **Mr M. D. I. Usher**
5 MRS PICKLES, 10, gr m Northern Park (USA)—Able Mabel **Midweek Racing**
6 SCOTTISH RIVER (USA), 6, b g Thunder Gulch (USA)—Overbrook **Mr M. D. I. Usher**
7 SUCCESSOR, 5, ch g Entrepreneur—Petralona (USA) **G. A. Summers**
8 SWEETEST REVENGE (IRE), 4, ch f Daggers Drawn (USA)—Joza **Bryan Fry & The Ridgeway Partnership**

THREE-YEAR-OLDS

9 MAYA'S PRINCE, b g Easycall—Delciana (IRE) **Partnership**
10 RULING REEF, b f Diktat—Horseshoe Reef **Midweek Racing**
11 SAUCEPOT, ch f Bold Edge—Apple Sauce **The Goodracing Partnership**

TWO-YEAR-OLDS

12 B f 3/3 Indian Lodge (IRE)—Faraway Moon (Distant Relative) **Mr M. D. I. Usher**
13 LADY DUXYANA, b f 13/3 Most Welcome—Duxyana (IRE) (Cyrano de Bergerac) (17000) **B. Fry**
14 MISS REDACTIVE, b f 20/4 Whittingham (IRE)—
                    Gold And Blue (IRE) (Bluebird (USA)) **Redactive (Publishing) Limited**
15 Ch c 30/3 Woodborough (USA)—Pure Gold (Dilum (USA)) **The Ridgeway Partnership**
16 SAXON SAINT, b g 22/2 Josr Algarhoud (IRE)—Antithesis (IRE) (Fairy King (USA)) **Saxon House Racing**
17 SAXON STAR (IRE), b g 5/2 Vettori (IRE)—Thicket (Wolfhound (USA)) (5000) **Saxon House Racing**

Other Owners: Miss D. G. Kerr, J. A. Stansfield, C. West-Meads.

Jockey (NH): W Hutchinson. Amateur: Mr L. Newnes.

603 **MR E. F. VAUGHAN, Newmarket**
Postal: **The Fillies Yard, Warren Place, Moulton Road, Newmarket, Suffolk, CB8 8QQ.**
Contacts: PHONE (01638) 667411 FAX (01638) 667452
E-MAIL edvaughan@efvaughan.com WEBSITE www.efvaughan.com

1 DAY TO REMEMBER, 4, gr c Daylami (IRE)—Miss Universe (IRE) **Racing For Gold**
2 MR VELOCITY (IRE), 5, b g Tagula (IRE)—Miss Rusty (IRE) **A. M. Pickering**
3 NAMROC (IRE), 4, b c Indian Ridge—Hesperia **B. Corman**
4 PREMIER ROUGE, 4, b g Croco Rouge (IRE)—Petit Point (USA) **M. J. C. Hawkes & P. T. Saunders**
5 TIZZY'S LAW, 4, b f Case Law—Bo' Babbity **North Cheshire Trading & Storage Ltd**

THREE-YEAR-OLDS

6 CATSKILL, ch g Inchinor—Manhattan Sunset (USA) **Mrs M. E. Domvile**
7 COSMIC DESTINY (IRE), b f Soviet Star (USA)—Cruelle (USA) **A. M. Pickering**
8 FOREHAND (IRE), b f Lend A Hand—Set Trail (IRE) **Gibson, Goddard, Hamer & Hawkes**
9 NEW REALM (USA), b c Red Ransom (USA)—Mystery Rays (USA) **P. Webb**
10 NOBLE FUTURE, b g Averti (IRE)—Gold Luck (USA) **Paterson, Saunders, Kinge & Fine**

TWO-YEAR-OLDS

11 COMMAND RESPECT, b f 26/3 Commands (AUS)—
                    The Blade (GER) (Sure Blade (USA)) (12000) **Racing For Gold**
12 SUNNY DISPOSITION (IRE), b c 8/2 Desert Sun—Madam Waajib (IRE) (Waajib) (21000) **A. M. Pickering**

604 **MR CHRISTIAN VON DER RECKE, Weilerswist**
Postal: **Rennstall Recke, Hovener Hof, D-53919, Weilerswist, Germany.**
Contacts: HOME (0049 22 54) 84 53 14 FAX (0049 22 54) 84 53 15 MOBILE (0049 17 15) 42 50 50
E-MAIL recke@t-online.de WEBSITE www.rennstall-recke.de

1 AESOP (GER), 4, ch c Green Tune (USA)—Alisa (USA) **H. Kronseder**
2 AKEBONO (GER), 6, b h Surako (GER)—Alpha Sum (GER) **H. Kronseder**
3 ALL THEATRICAL (USA), 5, b m Theatrical—Slew All (USA) **H. Krouseder**

MR CHRISTIAN VON DER RECKE—continued

4 **ANISSINA (GER)**, 5, b m Second Set (IRE)—Amabossa (GER) **Stall Chevalex**
5 **ANSCO (GER)**, 5, b h Silver Hawk (USA)—All An Angel (CAN) **Gestut Hony-Hof**
6 **ARC LEMANIQUE (GER)**, 5, b h Hernando (FR)—Arkona (GER) **Gestut Ebbesloh**
7 **AVENCHES (GER)**, 5, ch m Dashing Blade—Altja (GER) **Gestut Ebbesloh**
8 **AVERA (GER)**, 4, br f Monsun (GER)—Anna Leone **Stall Weissenhof**
9 **AZEEM (GER)**, 4, ch g Devil River Peek (USA)—Arpege (GER) **Stall Maraunenhof**
10 **BARITO (GER)**, 8, b g Winged Love (IRE)—Blumme (CHI) **Gestut Am Schlossgarten**
11 **BARRICHELLO (GER)**, 5, ch h Waky Nao—Bandira (GER) **Gestut Park Wiedingen**
12 **BEANNEY (ARG)**, 5, gr h Handsome Halo (ARG)—Little Wing (ARG) **Gestut Am Schlossgarten**
13 **BIG PAUL (GER)**, 4, b g Tiger Hill (IRE)—Birell (GER) **E. A. Wahler**
14 **DON BERNARDO (GER)**, 5, ch h Monsun (GER)—Daydream (GER) **Stall Topigal**
15 **DOUBLE FUN (HOL)**, 6, b g Bretigny (FR)—Rising Stream **M. P. Himmelsbach**
16 **DUBAI KING (GER)**, 4, b g Dashing Blade—Depeche Toi (GER) **Quadriga GmbH**
17 **EIGHT DELIGHTS (JPN)**, 4, b f Spinning World (USA)—Metaphor (USA) **Stall Alexa**
18 **EXOTIC QUEEN (GER)**, 4, b f Tannenkonig (IRE)—Eurydike (GER) **Stall Four Friends**
19 **FARALLON (GER)**, 6, ch g Lando (GER)—Flunder **Frau I. Horlemann**
20 **FIEPES SHUFFLE (GER)**, 5, b g Big Shuffle (USA)—Fiepe (EG) **Stall Jenny**
21 **FYODOR (GER)**, 4, b g Stravinsky (USA)—Cox Girl (USA) **Stall Chevalex**
22 **GOLDEN MILLENIUM (GER)**, 4, b c Monsun (GER)—Gluckskind (GER) **BMK Racing**
23 **GOLDHANS (GER)**, 4, b g Kornado—Goldsamt (GER) **Stall Jenny**
24 **HILLTOPPER (IRE)**, 9, b g Mandalus—Thistletopper **R. Grimminger**
25 **IRISH TIMES (GER)**, 4, ch g Second Set (IRE)—Irish Fritter (USA) **P. Chodaert**
26 **ISHIKA (GER)**, 4, b f Lagunas—Ibidem (GER) **Frau R.u.A. Hacker**
27 **LA UTOPIA (GER)**, 4, b f Unfuwain (USA)—Lara (GER) **Gestut Rangau Stall Fairy Tale**
28 **LARSSARTO (GER)**, 7, b h Lomitas—Lady Shepard (GER) **P. Cnockaert**
29 **LEVIRAT (GER)**, 6, ch h Lomitas—Laurier d'or **Stall Jenny**
30 **MARIELLA (GER)**, 4, b br f Zinaad—Morgenrote (EG) **R. Paulick**
31 **MISS MONARIA (GER)**, 5, br m Alkalde (GER)—Monaria (GER) **Stall Karlshorst**
32 **NIGHT LOOM (GER)**, 4, ch f Lomitas—Night Music (GER) **Stall Blankenese**
33 **NIZZOLINO (GER)**, 6, b g Pennekamp (USA)—Shallop **Gestut Hony-Hof**
34 **NOCEUR (GER)**, 8, b h Second Set (IRE)—Noble Princesse (GER) **Stall Mydlinghoven**
35 **NOCINO (IRE)**, 4, b c Orpen (USA)—Nethanya (GER) **Stall Blau-Weiss**
36 **NOTHING TO LOOSE (GER)**, 4, b f Winged Love (IRE)—New Berlin (IRE) **Gestut Am Schlossgarten**
37 **ORIENTAL ROCK (GER)**, 4, b g Acatenango (GER)—Oriental Flower (GER) **P. J. Vogt**
38 **PARASSIA (FR)**, 4, ch f Halling (USA)—Patricia (USA) **W. Bischoff**
39 **PRATO (GER)**, 5, ch g Kornado—Prairie Lila (GER) **Stall Mydlinghoven**
40 **PRINCE NICO (GER)**, 6, ch g Lagunas—Princess Liberte (GER) **Stall Rafra**
41 **QUIRINO (GER)**, 4, b g Lagunas—Queen's Diamond (GER) **Quadriga GmbH**
42 **ROSENBRIEF (GER)**, 4, b g Brief Truce (USA)—Roseraie (GER) **Frau Dr A. Grimminger**
43 **SCHNIPP SCHNAPP (FR)**, 4, b g Acatenango (GER)—Selva (IRE) **Stall Jenny**
44 **SIBERION (GER)**, 4, b g Acambaro (GER)—Siberian's Image **Stall Jenny**
45 **SIBERIUS (GER)**, 7, ch h Lomitas—Siberian's Image **Stall Jenny**
46 **SUNSHINE STORY (IRE)**, 5, b m Desert Story (IRE)—Sweet Tern (GER) **J. Horlemann**
47 **TO ALL (FR)**, 5, b h Alwuhush (USA)—The Mood (GER) **U. Giesgen**
48 **TOTAL FORCE (IRE)**, 4, b g Night Shift (USA)—Capegulch (USA) **Stall Karlshorst**
49 **TRANSLUCID (GER)**, 7, b h Woodman (USA)—Gossamer (USA) **BMK Racing**
50 **TROPICAL WIND (GER)**, 4, b c Monsun (GER)—Tomasa (GER) **A. C. Herrmann**
51 **VEGANO (FR)**, 4, bl g Waky Nao—Vega Sicilia **H. Kagel**

THREE-YEAR-OLDS

52 **A PRIORI (GER)**, b f General Assembly (USA)—Algebra (GER) **Frau S. Putensen**
53 **ACT GOLD (GER)**, b g Slip Anchor—Alisa (GER) **Gestut Ebbesloh**
54 **ACTION SPIRIT (GER)**, b c Dashing Blade—Action Art (IRE) **P. J. Vogt**
55 **ADELA (GER)**, b f Tannenkonig (IRE)—Adora (GER) **M. E. Veeck**
56 **ALBARINO (GER)**, b c Platini (GER)—Anna Leone **Stall Weissenhof**
57 **CHARLOTT (GER)**, b f Alwuhush (USA)—Cordona (GER) **G. Schmitz**
58 **CLASSIC NIGHT (GER)**, b f Erminius (GER)—Classic Light (IRE) **Biesdeel Stud**
59 **CONGRIO DORADO (USA)**, b c Real Quiet (USA)—Cox Girl (USA) **Stall Chevalex**
60 **ESPOSITO**, ch c Inchinor—Celebrate (IRE) **Stall Blau-Gelb**
61 **EVENING SUN (GER)**, b f Dashing Blade—East Society (GER) **Gestut Monchhof**
62 **FANTASTIC FLEUR (GER)**, b f Winged Love (IRE)—Fleurie (GER) **Stall Gelb-Blau**
63 **FEDERSTAR (GER)**, b c In A Tiff (IRE)—Federspiel **R. Paulick**
64 **FORETTO (GER)**, b c Lavirco (GER)—Fairwind (GER) **Stall Margarethe**
65 **FURSTENBERG (IRE)**, b c Monashee Mountain (USA)—Flagny (FR) **Stall Blau-Weiss**

MR CHRISTIAN VON DER RECKE—continued

66 **GLENAKA (GER)**, b f Turtle Island (IRE)—Giralda (IRE) **Frau M. Munchow-Eskens**
67 **HEXI GIRL (GER)**, b f Sharp Prod (USA)—Herbstrose (EG) **R. Paulick**
68 **IRISH HAWK (GER)**, ch c Platini (GER)—Irish Fritter (USA) **Gestut Romerhof**
69 **ISEIA (GER)**, b c Kornado—Isadora (GER) **Gestut Schattauer Hof-Granum Zuc**
70 **LANSON (GER)**, b c Goofalik (USA)—Libertad (GER) **U. und H. Alcke**
71 **LINDSTROEM (GER)**, b br c Kendor (GER)—Lindenblute **Stall Terry**
72 **LOUP GAROU (GER)**, b c Benny The Dip (USA)—Prickly Pear (USA) **Stall Blau-Gelb**
73 **MAIMONIDES (FR)**, ch c Saratoga Springs (CAN)—Moskovskaya (USA) **Stall Mohlenberg**
74 **MASHINU (GER)**, b c Sharp Prod (USA)—Mondalita (GER) **L. Paulick**
75 **MONDEGO (GER)**, b c Big Shuffle (USA)—Molto In Forma (GER) **Stall Hanse**
76 **MR XAAR (IRE)**, b c Xaar—Maegashira (GER) **Gestut Katharinenhof**
77 **NEXT LORD (GER)**, b c Lord of Men—Next Victory (FR) **K. Kremer**
78 **NUVOLINA (GER)**, b f Platini (GER)—Nova (GER) **Gestut Am Schlossgarten**
79 **PLACEBO (GER)**, b c Foxhound (USA)—Pat's River (FR) **Quadriga GmbH**
80 **PURPLE STORM (GER)**, b c Monsun (GER)—Purple Dream (IRE) **H. Bartelt W. Molitor**
81 **QUADRUPA (GER)**, ch f Big Shuffle (USA)—Queen's Diamond (GER) **Quadriga GmbH**
82 **RASCACIO (GER)**, b br c Big Shuffle (USA)—Royal Wind (GER) **Stall Blankenese**
83 **RICING SUN (GER)**, br f Lavirco (GER)—Rapid Starlight **Gestut Hof Ahorn**
84 **RUBY STAR (GER)**, b g Alwuhush (USA)—Roxette (GER) **Stall Roxette**
85 **SPECIAL EDITION (GER)**, b c Big Shuffle (USA)—Safrane (GER) **Stall Tommy**
86 **STRAIGHT AHEAD (GER)**, ch c Cadeaux Genereux—Shining High **H. Bartelt w. W. Molitor**
87 **SULTANA (GER)**, b br f Law Society (USA)—Sweet Second (IRE) **Quadriga GmbH**
88 **TRENDY TOUCH (GER)**, b c Bretigny (FR)—Teri Belle (HOL) **Biesdeel Stud**
89 **ZAIANA (IRE)**, b f Desert Story (IRE)—Zauberwelt **Joachim Erhardt**

TWO-YEAR-OLDS

90 **ALINGA (GER)**, br f 19/4 Platini (GER)—Anna Leone (Caerleon (USA)) **Stall Weissenhof**
91 **ALRAUNE (GER)**, b br f 30/4 Platini (GER)—Avanti Adda (GER) (Law Society (USA)) **Gestut Katharinenhof**
92 **CHELLO (GER)**, b g 1/1 Esclavo (FR)—Courtoisie (FR) (Frere Basile (FR)) **Frau I. Horlemann**
93 **FESTERO (GER)**, b g 28/2 Silvano (GER)—Freni (Primo Dominie) **A. C. Herrmann**
94 **GLANWORTH MILL (GER)**, ch f 16/3 Monsun (GER)—Giralda (IRE) (Tenby) (14755) **Frau R.u.A. Hacker**
95 **B f** 12/3 Acatenango (GER)—Hesperia (Slip Anchor) (27000) **Mr CHRISTIAN VON DER RECKE**
96 **KING'S LAND (GER)**, b c 18/4 Devil River Peek (USA)—Karuma (GER) (Surumu (GER)) (24144) **Frau A. Lippert**
97 **LIBERTY LU (GER)**, b c 6/3 Waky Nao—Lunar Lu (GER) (Marignan (USA)) **G. u. U. Fischer**
98 **MONTICELLO (GER)**, b c 15/4 Perugino (GER)—Molto In Forma (GER) (Surumu (GER)) (6371) **Stall Hanse**
99 **PERSONAL POWER (GER)**, b c 28/2 Dashing Blade—Personal Hope (GER) (Great Lakes) **F. Zech**
100 **ROMANZE RHEINBERG (GER)**, ch f 15/3 Perugino (GER)—Ruby Lady (GER) (Master Willie) **Stall Chevalex**
101 **ROYAL EMPIRE (GER)**, b f 13/2 Second Empire (IRE)—
                                                    Royal Polish (Polish Precedent (USA)) **Gestut Katharinenhof**
102 **SPAGATO (GER)**, b c 20/5 Platini (GER)—Sweet Second (IRE) (Second Set (IRE)) (6371) **Quadriga GmbH**
103 **SWING TIME (GER)**, b f 19/4 Lando (GER)—Safrane (GER) (Mister Rock's (GER)) **Stall Tommy**
104 **TARANA (GER)**, bl f 4/2 Zinaad—Tarnfarbe (EG) (Shepard (GER)) **R. Paulick**
105 **VEGA'S LORD (GER)**, ch c 6/3 Lord of Men—Vega Sicilia (Environment Friend) **H. Kagel**
106 **ZOOM (GER)**, ch f 10/4 Lomitas—Zizi Top (Robellino (USA)) **Stall Hanse**

Assistant Trainer: Mrs Conny Kaiser

Jockey (flat): Adrie De Vries, Andrasch Starke, Andreas Suborics. **Jockey (NH):** Dirk Fuhrmann, A. P. McCoy, Lukas Sloup.
Conditional: P A Johnson. **Apprentice:** Mr Rene Piechulek, Mrs Julia Arlie, Mrs Carolin Lippert. **Amateur:** Miss M. Sauer,
Mr O. Sauer, Mr Thierry Steeger, Miss K. Schlick.

605 **MR J. WADE, Aycliffe**
Postal: **Howe Hills, Mordon, Sedgefield, Cleveland, TS21 2HF.**
Contacts: **PHONE (01325) 313129/315521 FAX (01325) 320660 MOBILE (07831) 686968**

1 **ARGY BARGY (IRE)**, 8, b g Lord Americo—Bargy Fancy **Mr J. Wade**
2 **COUNT THE COST (IRE)**, 6, ch g Old Vic—Roseaustin (IRE) **Mr J. Wade**
3 **DARK BUCCANEER**, 7, b g Sovereign Water (FR)—Some Cherry **Mr J. Wade**
4 **DEVIL'S RUN (IRE)**, 9, b g Commanche Run—She Devil **Mr J. Wade**
5 **EISENHOWER (IRE)**, 6, b g Erins Isle—Lyphard Abu (USA) **Mr J. Wade**
6 **EMPEROR'S MONARCH**, 5, b g Emperor Fountain—Shalta (FR) **Mr J. Wade**
7 **FLEET ADMIRAL**, 4, ch g Fleetwood (IRE)—Dame du Moulin **Mr J. Wade**
8 **GENERAL HARDI**, 4, b g In Command (IRE)—Hardiprincess **Mr J. Wade**
9 **GUNNER ROYAL**, 7, b g Gunner B—Loadplan Lass **Mr J. Wade**

MR J. WADE—continued

10 **IMPACT CRUSHER (IRE)**, 5, b g Sri Pekan (USA)—Costume Drama (USA) **Mr J. Wade**
11 **IRON TROOPER (IRE)**, 7, ch g Glacial Storm (USA)—Iron Star **Mr J. Wade**
12 **KING OF THE ARCTIC (IRE)**, 7, b g Arctic Lord—Ye Little Daisy **Mr J. Wade**
13 **LOVE THAT BENNY (USA)**, 5, ch g Benny The Dip (USA)—Marie Loves Emma (USA) **Mr J. Wade**
14 **MANDHOOR (IRE)**, 5, b g Flying Spur (AUS)—Moy Water (IRE) **Mr J. Wade**
15 **OVER BOOKED**, 6, b g Overbury (IRE)—Miss Arc **Mr J. Wade**
16 **PAROLE OFFICER**, 6, b g Priolo (USA)—Twosixtythreewest (FR) **Mr J. Wade**
17 **POLAR GALE (IRE)**, 5, b g Anshan—Ali-Kin **Mr J. Wade**
18 **RECENT EDITION (IRE)**, 7, b g Roselier (FR)—Hi Millie **Mr J. Wade**
19 **RED CEDAR (USA)**, 5, ch g Woodman (USA)—Jewell Ridge (USA) **Mr J. Wade**
20 **ROLLING RIVER (IRE)**, 8, b g Over The River (FR)—Paddy's Dancer **Mr J. Wade**
21 **RUNNING QUILL (IRE)**, 9, ch g Commanche Run—Quilty Rose **Mr J. Wade**
22 **RYMINSTER**, 6, ch g Minster Son—Shultan (IRE) **Mr J. Wade**
23 **SHADY BARON (IRE)**, 6, b g Lord Americo—Glint of Baron **Mr J. Wade**
24 **SHARP EXIT (IRE)**, 6, ch g Fourstars Allstar—Dipper's Gift (IRE) **Mr J. Wade**
25 **SHULMIN**, 5, ch m Minster Son—Shultan (IRE) **Mr J. Wade**
26 **STORMY LORD (IRE)**, 9, br g Lord Americo—Decent Shower **Mr J. Wade**
27 **TALEBAN**, 10, b g Alleged (USA)—Triode (USA) **Mr J. Wade**
28 **THE RECIPIENT (IRE)**, 6, b g Eurobus—Saxa Princess (IRE) **Mr J. Wade**
29 **THE SWOPPER**, 7, b g Sovereign Water (FR)—Strathrusdale **Mr J. Wade**
30 **TRADING TROUBLE**, 8, b g Petoski—Marielou (FR) **Mr J. Wade**
31 **VICTOR ONE (IRE)**, 5, b g Victory Note (USA)—Another Baileys **Mr J. Wade**
32 **WILFUL LORD (IRE)**, 8, b g Lord Americo—Dotties Girl (IRE) **Mr J. Wade**

Assistant Trainer: Mrs Maria Myco

606	**MRS L. A. M. WADHAM, Newmarket** Postal: **The Trainer's House, Moulton Paddocks, Newmarket, Suffolk, CB8 7PJ.** Contacts: **PHONE (01638) 662411 FAX (01638) 668821 MOBILE (07980) 545776**

1 **BARNEYS REFLECTION**, 5, b g Petoski—Annaberg (IRE) **Mrs C. Bailey**
2 **BOUND**, 7, b g Kris—Tender Moment (IRE) **Hebomapa**
3 **BRIGADIER DU BOIS (FR)**, 6, gr g Apeldoorn (FR)—Artic Night (FR) **Hebomapa**
4 **CHARLEY BROWN (IRE)**, 5, b g Muroto—Ballinure Girl **Miss K. J. Austin**
5 **DEEP REFLECTION**, 5, b g Cloudings (IRE)—Tudor Thyne **Mr J. J. M. Bailey**
6 **EURO BLEU (IRE)**, 7, b g Franc Bleu Argent (USA)—Princess Card (FR) **Hebomapa**
7 **EXECUTIVE DECISION (IRE)**, 11, ch g Classic Music (USA)—Bengala (FR) **Miss K. J. Austin**
8 **FENIX (GER)**, 6, b g Lavirco (GER)—Frille (FR) **P.A.Philipps,T.S.Redman & J.S.Redman**
9 **HEIR TO BE**, 6, b g Elmaamul (USA)—Princess Genista **R. B. Holt**
10 **HIGHPOINT (GER)**, 7, b m Acatenango (GER)—Holly (GER) **J. J. M. Bailey & Mrs C. Bailey**
11 **KING'S MILL (IRE)**, 8, b g Doyoun—Adarika **First Millennium Racing**
12 **KOPECK (IRE)**, 7, ch g Moscow Society (USA)—Cashla (IRE) **P. H. Betts**
13 **LOS SAINOS (GER)**, 6, b g Winged Love (IRE)—La Sierra **The Not Over Big Partnership**
14 **MIGWELL (FR)**, 5, b g Assessor (IRE)—Uguette IV (FR) **DGM Partnership**
15 **NAKED OAT**, 10, b g Imp Society (USA)—Bajina **The Dyball Partnership**
16 **PRINCESS PEA**, 5, b m Shareef Dancer (USA)—Super Sol **Miss I. McMillan**
17 **RESPLENDENT STAR (IRE)**, 8, b g Northern Baby (CAN)—Whitethroat **Waterhall Racing**
18 **RUBY HARE**, 4, ch g Classic Cliche (IRE)—Five And Four (IRE) **Campbell Gray Partnership**
19 **SECOND PAIGE (IRE)**, 8, b g Nicolotte—My First Paige (IRE) **Coronation Partnership**
20 **SIR CULAR**, 6, b g Sir Harry Lewis—Puki Puki **Miss S. Wilson**
21 **THE DARK LORD (IRE)**, 8, b g Lord Americo—Khalkeys Shoon **A. E. Pakenham**
22 **UNITED (GER)**, 4, b f Desert King (IRE)—Una Kasala (GER) **R. B. Holt**

Other Owners: W. F. Bottriell, Mrs C. P. Campbell, Mr C. Campbell, G. Charlesworth, D. Charlesworth, Mrs J. A. Cross, R. A. Smith, R. M. Venn, J. J. W. Wadham.

Jockey (NH): L. Aspell. **Conditional:** N. Walker.

607	**MR N. WAGGOTT, Spennymoor** Postal: **Ingledene, Vyners Close, Merrington Lane, Spennymoor, Co. Durham, DL16 7HB.** Contacts: **PHONE (01388) 819012**

1 **DELFINIA**, 4, b f Kingsinger (IRE)—Delvecchia **Miss T. Waggott**
2 **FRED'S IN THE KNOW**, 10, ch g Interrex (CAN)—Lady Vynz **Mr N. Waggott**

MR N. WAGGOTT—continued

3 **IPLEDGEALLEGIANCE (USA)**, 9, b g Alleged (USA)—Yafill (USA) **Mrs J. Waggott**
4 **LUKE AFTER ME (IRE)**, 5, b g Victory Note (USA)—Summit Talk **Miss T. Waggott**
5 **MISS MIA**, 5, b m Merit (IRE)—Alisa Bower **Mrs J. Waggott**
6 **MISS OCEAN MONARCH**, 5, ch m Blue Ocean (USA)—Faraway Grey **Mrs J. Waggott**
7 **SCIPPIT**, 6, ch g Unfuwain (USA)—Scierpan (USA) **Mrs J. Waggott**

Assistant Trainer: Miss T. Waggott

---

608 **MR J. S. WAINWRIGHT, Malton**
Postal: **Hanging Hill Farm, Kennythorpe, Malton, North Yorkshire, YO17 9LA.**
Contacts: **PHONE** (01653) 658537 **FAX** (01653) 658658 **MOBILE** (07798) 778070

1 **BARON RHODES**, 4, b f Presidium—Superstream **Mr I Barran & Mr P Rhodes**
2 **BEYOND THE CLOUDS (IRE)**, 9, b g Midhish—Tongabezi (IRE) **S. E. Pedersen**
3 **CATCH THE CAT (IRE)**, 6, b g Catrail (USA)—Tongabezi (IRE) **T. W. Heseltine**
4 **CLOUDS OF GOLD (IRE)**, 4, b f Goldmark (USA)—Tongabezi (IRE) **S. E. Pedersen**
5 **CUT RIDGE (IRE)**, 6, b m Indian Ridge—Cutting Ground (IRE) **Mrs C. Harrington**
6 **DORMY TWO (IRE)**, 5, b m Eagle Eyed (USA)—Tartan Lady (IRE) **A. D. Copley**
7 **EDDIES JEWEL**, 5, b g Presidium—Superstream **Denison Arms**
8 **FAIRGAME MAN**, 7, ch g Clantime—Thalya **Mrs P. D. Wake**
9 **JEDEYDD**, 8, b g Shareef Dancer (USA)—Bilad (USA) **Miss S. L. Iggulden**
10 **JOYCE'S CHOICE**, 6, b g Mind Games—Madrina **Mrs J. Neilson**
11 **LITTLE TASK**, 7, b g Environment Friend—Lucky Thing **K. Jackson**
12 **LITTLE TOBIAS (IRE)**, 6, ch g Millkom—Barbara Frietchie (IRE) **Mrs J. Neilson**
13 **LORD WISHINGWELL (IRE)**, 4, b g Lake Coniston (IRE)—Spirito Libro (USA) **Mrs L. D. O'Sullivan**
14 **ONIZ TIPTOES (IRE)**, 4, ch g Russian Revival (USA)—Edionda (IRE) **drawn2win.co.uk Partnership**
15 **RINCOOLA (IRE)**, 6, br m Warcraft (USA)—Very Tense (IRE) **A. Nicholls**
16 **STAVROS (IRE)**, 5, b g General Monash (USA)—Rivers Rainbow **S. E. Pedersen**
17 **TIME TO REGRET**, 5, b g Presidium—Scoffera **Denison Arms**
18 **TOMMY SMITH**, 7, ch g Timeless Times (USA)—Superstream **T. W. Heseltine**
19 **TRAVELLING TIMES**, 6, ch g Timeless Times (USA)—Bollin Sophie **S. E. Pedersen**

THREE-YEAR-OLDS

20 **FINAL OVERTURE (IRE)**, b f Rossini (USA)—Two Magpies **Miss S. L. Iggulden**
21 **FOREST VIKING (IRE)**, b g Orpen (USA)—Berhala (IRE) **P. W. Cooper**
22 **LA BELLA ROSA (IRE)**, b f Revoque (IRE)—Tempesta Rossa (IRE) **Hurn Racing Club**
23 **LADY INDIANA (IRE)**, b f King's Theatre (IRE)—Najeyba **Mr M. W. Syme & Mr Simon James**
24 **MOONLIGHT APPEAL (IRE)**, ch f Bahamian Bounty—Divine Appeal **Miss S. L. Iggulden**
25 **OUR LOUIS**, b f Abou Zouz (USA)—Ninfa of Cisterna **Whitestonecliffe Racing Partnership**
26 **PAULA JO**, b f Factual (USA)—Superstream **Mr I Barran & Mr P Rhodes**
27 **TIME TO SUCCEED**, b g Pennekamp (USA)—Ivory League **B Selective Partnership**
28 **WAGGLEDANCE (IRE)**, b g Mujadil (USA)—Assertive Lass (USA) **D. I. Perry**

TWO-YEAR-OLDS

29 B f 27/4 Mujadil (USA)—Desert Gem (Green Desert (USA)) (3889) **T. W. Heseltine**
30 B f 2/3 Orpen (USA)—Ervedya (IRE) (Doyoun) (5364) **T. W. Heseltine**
31 B f 22/2 Bluebird (USA)—Fun Board (FR) (Saumarez) (5364) **Denison Arms**
32 **SILVER SAILS**, gr f 20/3 Daylami (IRE)—Fiveofive (IRE) (Fairy King (USA)) (10000) **Miss S. L. Iggulden**
33 B g 24/4 Beckett (IRE)—Tara View (IRE) (Wassl) (5029) **A. Brown**

Other Owners: Mr W. C. Bavill, Mr A. J. McClymont, Mr A. D. Renham, N. A. Ryall, MR J. S. Wainwright, Mr P. R. Walker.

Jockey (flat): T. Eaves, R. Winston. Conditional: L Vickers.

---

609 **MR R. B. WALEY-COHEN, Banbury**
Postal: **18 Gilston Road, London, SW10 9SR.**
Contacts: **PHONE** (0207) 2446022 **MOBILE** (07831) 888778
E-MAIL rwc@alliance.co.uk

1 **KERRES NOIRES (FR)**, 7, b g Noir Et Or—Viagara (FR) **Mr R. B. Waley-Cohen**
2 **MEL IN BLUE (FR)**, 7, b g Pistolet Bleu (IRE)—Calligraphie (FR) **Mr R. B. Waley-Cohen**

MR R. B. WALEY-COHEN—continued

3 **SOMETHING SMALL**, 5, br g Supreme Leader—Rachel C (IRE) **Mr R. B. Waley-Cohen**
4 **STORMING BACK**, 6, b g Bob Back (USA)—Prussian Storm (IRE) **Mr R. B. Waley-Cohen**

Assistant Trainer: Kate Mawle

Amateur: Mr S. Waley-Cohen.

610

MR T. D. WALFORD, Sheriff Hutton
Postal: **Cornborough Manor, Sheriff Hutton, York, YO60 6QN..**
Contacts: PHONE **(01347) 878382** FAX **(01347) 878547** MOBILE **(07904) 237676**
E-MAIL **g_walford@hotmail.com** WEBSITE **www.timwalford.co.uk**

1 **BROX BOUFACTO**, 4, b g Defacto (USA)—Boulevard Girl
2 **BROXNOTANOTHERONE**, 5, ch m Defacto (USA)—Boulevard Girl
3 **HURRICANE FRANCIS**, 5, ch g Minster Son—Joe's Fancy
4 **MASTER JACKSON**, 6, b g Jendali (USA)—Fardella (ITY) **P. S. Spencer**
5 **MISS PROSS**, 5, b m Bob's Return (IRE)—Lucy Manette **D. Coates**
6 **PASS ME BY**, 5, b g Balnibarbi—Errol Emerald **Mrs M. Cooper**
7 **ROSE OF YORK (IRE)**, 5, b m Emarati (USA)—True Ring **Mrs S. A. York**
8 **WAYDALE HILL**, 6, ch m Minster Son—Buckby Folly **Mrs S. A. York**
9 **WESTON ROCK**, 6, b g Double Eclipse (IRE)—Mossberry Fair **Mrs H. P. Spath**

Other Owners: J. R. Burns, Mrs R. Conway, G. E. Dempsey, D. J. Dickson, Mrs B. A. Lockwood, Mr C. Moss, A. T. Preston, Mrs G. B. Walford.

Assistant Trainer: Mrs G B Walford

Conditional: R. Walford. **Amateur:** Mr M. Walford.

611

MR C. F. WALL, Newmarket
Postal: **Induna Stables, Fordham Road, Newmarket, Suffolk, CB8 7AQ.**
Contacts: HOME **(01638) 668896** OFFICE **(01638) 661999**
FAX **(01638) 667279** MOBILE **(07764) 940255**
E-MAIL **christian.wall@btopenworld.com**

1 **ACE OF HEARTS**, 6, b g Magic Ring (IRE)—Lonely Heart **Lady Stuttaford & Mr W. G. Bovill**
2 **ASHDOWN EXPRESS (IRE)**, 6, ch g Ashkalani (IRE)—Indian Express **Mr W. J. P. Jackson**
3 **CIMYLA (IRE)**, 4, b c Lomitas—Coyaima (GER) **Peter Botham**
4 **COUNSEL'S OPINION (IRE)**, 8, ch g Rudimentary (USA)—Fairy Fortune **Mrs S. P. Roberts**
5 **CRAIL**, 5, b g Vettori (IRE)—Tendency **The Crail Partnership**
6 **DIDNT TELL MY WIFE**, 6, ch g Aragon—Bee Dee Dancer **Mr G. D. Newton**
7 **GABANA (IRE)**, 4, br f Polish Precedent (USA)—Out West (USA) **Mr S. Fustok**
8 **GENERAL FLUMPA**, 4, b g Vettori (IRE)—Macca Luna (IRE) **Mrs L. N. Smith**
9 **HABSHAN (USA)**, 5, ch g Swain (IRE)—Cambara **Alan & Jill Smith**
10 **KEYAKI (IRE)**, 4, b f Shinko Forest (IRE)—Woodie Dancer (USA) **Hintlesham SPD Partners**
11 **LITTLE VENICE (IRE)**, 5, b m Fumo di Londra (IRE)—Petrine (IRE) **Hintlesham SPD Partners**
12 **PANSHIR (FR)**, 4, ch g Unfuwain (USA)—Jalcamin (USA) **Mr E. Landi**
13 **PARADISE ISLE**, 4, b f Bahamian Bounty—Merry Rous **The Equema Partnership**
14 **SHAMARA (IRE)**, 5, b m Spectrum (IRE)—Hamara (FR) **Lady Juliet Tadgell**
15 **SUNSHINE ON ME**, 4, ch f Kris—Degannwy **Mrs Celia Miller**
16 **TANCRED TIMES**, 10, ch m Clantime—Mischievous Miss **Hintlesham Thoroughbreds**
17 **ZANGEAL**, 5, ch g Selkirk (USA)—Generous Lady **Mr S. Fustok**

THREE-YEAR-OLDS

18 **ALEYAH**, ch f Bachir (IRE)—Silver Peak (FR) **The WEB Partnership**
19 **ASHDOWN PRINCESS (IRE)**, b f King's Theatre (IRE)—Indian Express **W. J. P. Jackson & Dwayne Woods**
20 **BONNABEE (IRE)**, b f Benny The Dip (USA)—Samhat Mtoto **Mr T. J. Wells**
21 **BUNDITTEN (IRE)**, gr f Soviet Star (USA)—Felicita (IRE) **Thoroughbred Farms Ltd**
22 **CARVOEIRO**, ch f Compton Place—Shoshone **Thoroughbred Farms Ltd**
23 **CAVARADOSSI**, gr c Lake Coniston (IRE)—Floria Tosca **Mrs Yoshiko Allan**
24 **CUYAMACA (IRE)**, b f Desert King (IRE)—Surprise Visitor (USA) **Mr M. Sinclair/ Mrs C. J. Walker**
25 **DEEDAY BAY (IRE)**, b f Brave Act—Skerries Bell **Mr Peter Botham**
26 **DESERT GOOGLE**, b f Green Desert (USA)—Khambani (IRE) **Mr S. Fustok**

MR C. F. WALL—continued

27 **HORNINGSHEATH**, b f Royal Applause—Pacifica **Mr T. J. Wells**
28 **LEKKA DING (IRE)**, b br f Raise A Grand (IRE)—Non Dimenticar Me (IRE) **Mr M. Tilbrook**
29 **MON PLAISIR**, br f Singspiel (IRE)—Mademoiselle Chloe **Mr S. Fustok**
30 **NEW WAVE**, b g Woodman (USA)—Vanishing Point (USA) **Mr S. Fustok**
31 **ROSAPENNA (IRE)**, b f Spectrum (IRE)—Blaine (USA) **Thoroughbred Farms Ltd**
32 **SIEGLINDE**, b f High Estate—Carinthia (IRE) **Hintlesham DS Partners**
33 **STAMBAH**, b f Pivotal—Double Top (IRE) **Lady Juliet Tadgell**
34 **UNRESTRICTED**, ch f Mark of Esteem (USA)—Generous Lady **Mr S. Fustok**
35 **ZOWINGTON**, gr c Zafonic (USA)—Carmela Owen **Mr O. Pointing**

TWO-YEAR-OLDS

36 **AIR BISCUIT (IRE)**, b f 19/4 Galileo (IRE)—
  Surprise Visitor (IRE) (Be My Guest (USA)) (30000) **Mr M. Sinclair/ Mr J. Sims**
37 B f 9/3 Definite Article—Atmospheric Blues (IRE) (Double Schwartz) (8500) **Mr David Crichton-Watt**
38 Ch c 29/1 Night Shift (USA)—Baileys Cream (Mister Baileys) (20120) **Hintlesham Thoroughbreds**
39 **DESERT MASTER**, b c 3/3 Green Desert (USA)—Khambani (IRE) (Royal Academy (USA)) (30000) **Mr S. Fustok**
40 **EXPENSIVE**, b f 3/3 Royal Applause—Vayavaig (Damister (USA)) (40000) **Mr M. Tilbrook**
41 Ch c 4/3 Pivotal—Femme Savante (Glenstal (USA)) **The Boardroom Syndicate**
42 **FINSBURY**, gr c 5/2 Observatory (USA)—Carmela Owen (Owington) **Mr O. Pointing**
43 **FOXYSOX**, ch f 5/3 Foxhound (USA)—Triple Tricks (IRE) (Royal Academy (USA)) (13000) **Mr Peter Botham**
44 **FRAXINUS**, gr g 27/4 Muhtarram (USA)—Ancestry (Persepolis (FR)) (10000) **Mr Peter Botham**
45 B f 20/2 Robellino (USA)—Greek Dream (USA) (Distant View (USA)) (23000) **Stourbank Racing**
46 **INDIGO DANCER**, b c 16/3 Groom Dancer (USA)—
  Violet (IRE) (Mukaddamah (USA)) (32000) **Induna Racing Partners (Two)**
47 **JULIETS FOLLY (USA)**, b br f 2/4 Black Minnaloushe (USA)—
  Just Juliet (USA) (What A Pleasure (USA)) (7500) **Lady Juliet Tadgell**
48 **MARKET GIRL**, b f 11/1 Mark of Esteem (USA)—It Girl (Robellino) (USA) **Mr S. Fustok**
49 **MASTER PEGASUS**, b c 17/2 Lujain (USA)—Seeking Utopia (Wolfhound (USA)) (USA) **Mr & Mrs J. Roberts**
50 B c 4/3 Florida's Son (ARG)—Maureen's Hope (USA) (Northern Baby (CAN)) **Mr S. Fustok**
51 B c 15/4 Zafonic (USA)—Midnight Allure (Aragon) (10000) **The Countryside Alliance Racing Partnership**
52 **MIDNIGHT MOONLIGHT**, ro f 21/2 Bahamian Bounty—Magnolia (Petong) (26000) **Mr P. J. Smith**
53 **NIGHT CRU**, b c 29/3 Night Shift (USA)—Jouet (Reprimand) (35000) **Geoffrey Bovill & John Bridge**
54 **POWER ASSISTED**, ch f 1/2 Observatory (USA)—Caribbean Star (Soviet Star (USA)) **Thoroughbred Farms Ltd**
55 **SALONGA (IRE)**, b f 11/2 Shinko Forest (IRE)—Alongside (Slip Anchor) (4694) **Mr David Allan**
56 B f 6/1 Diktat—Slave To The Rythm (IRE) (Hamas (IRE)) (800) **Mr M. Ayers**

Other Owners: P. W. Brown, Mr P. S. Burnett, R. G. R. Chapman, J. F. Chapman, Mrs S. E. Cunningham, Mrs J. E. Dobie, Miss P. M. E. Ede, R. Fraiser, Mrs E. J. Kerr-Smiley, Mrs R. M. S. Neave, Mrs G. M. Park, Mr A. B. S. Webb.

Assistant Trainer: Adrian Rogers

Apprentice: S O'Hara.

---

612 **MRS S. WALL, Dallington**
Postal: **Little Pines, Bakers Lane, Dallington, Heathfield, East Sussex, TN21 9JS.**
Contacts: **PHONE/FAX (01435) 831048**
E-MAIL jeremywall60@btinternet.com

1 **ACUTEANGLE (IRE)**, 9, b br m Cataldi—Sharp Mama VII **J. P. C. Wall**
2 **TALLOW BAY (IRE)**, 10, b g Glacial Storm (USA)—Minimum Choice (IRE) **Mrs S. Wall**
3 **TOMCAPPAGH (IRE)**, 14, br g Riberetto—Shuil Suas **Mrs S. Wall**

Assistant Trainer: Jeremy Wall

Conditional: Anthony Honeyball.

---

613 **MR T. R. WALL, Church Stretton**
Postal: **Harton Manor, Harton, Church Stretton, Shropshire, SY6 7DL.**
Contacts: **PHONE (01694) 724144 FAX (01694) 724144 MOBILE (07815) 813789**

1 **BUBBLING FUN**, 4, b f Marju (IRE)—Blushing Barada (USA) **Mr Derek & Mrs Marie Dean**
2 **E MINOR (IRE)**, 6, b m Blushing Flame (USA)—Watch The Clock **Mr Derek & Mrs Marie Dean**
3 **EXPECTEDTOFLI (IRE)**, 7, b m Mujadil (USA)—Zurarah **Eric Young**

MR T. R. WALL—continued

4 **LITTLE VILLAIN (IRE),** 7, b g Old Vic—Party Woman (IRE) **M. Doocey**
5 **MARGARETS WISH,** 5, gr m Cloudings (IRE)—Gentle Gain **A. H. Bennett**
6 **POTTER'S WHEEL,** 6, b g Elmaamul (USA)—Bewitch **D. B. Roberts**
7 **SOME OPERATOR (IRE),** 11, b g Lord Americo—Rathvilly Flier **M. Doocey**
8 **SPRING BEE,** 5, b m Parthian Springs—First Bee **D. Pugh**
9 **SPY GUN (USA),** 5, ch g Mt Livermore—Takeover Target (USA) **Mr Derek & Mrs Marie Dean**
10 6, B m Overbury (IRE)—Starch Brook **Fairy Hill Partnership**
11 **THE RANDY BISHOP,** 5, b g Bishop of Cashel—Fly South **Wenlock Edge Optimists**

Other Owners: MR T. R. Wall.

Assistant Trainer: Mr D B Roberts

Jockey (NH): R. Greene. **Amateur:** Mr L. P. Edwards, Mr M. Wall.

MR MARK WALLACE, Newmarket

614

Postal: **Woodland Stables, The Severals, Newmarket, Suffolk, CB8 7BS.**
Contacts: PHONE **(01638) 560752** FAX **(01638) 561387** MOBILE **(07771) 532422**
E-MAIL mwallace.racing@virgin.net

1 **ATHBOY,** 4, ch g Entrepreneur—Glorious
2 **BENBAUN (IRE),** 4, b g Stravinsky (USA)—Escape To Victory **Ransley Birks**
3 **ERRACHIDIA (IRE),** 5, b m King of Kings (USA)—Sunset Reigns (IRE) **Kilboy Estate**
4 **MY ONLY SUNSHINE,** 6, b g First Trump—Fiveofive (IRE) **Mrs T. A. Foreman**
5 **WEST END WONDER (IRE),** 6, b g Idris (IRE)—Miss Plum **Lucayan Stud Ltd**

THREE-YEAR-OLDS

6 **AIM FOR THE SKY (IRE),** b g Namid—Mamma's Too **Favourites Racing Ltd**
7 **ARIADAEUS (USA),** b f Thunder Gulch (USA)—Rills (USA) **Mr E. Irwin**
8 **ATHBOY NIGHTS (IRE),** b f Night Shift (USA)—Missing Love (IRE) **D. Mcgovern**
9 **BE LUCKY LADY (GER),** br f Law Society (USA)—Ballata (GER) **Franconson Partners**
10 **BROTHER EDWARD (IRE),** b c Desert Story (IRE)—Alchiea **Mr J. A. Ward**
11 **CHALET,** b f Singspiel (IRE)—Douce Maison (IRE) **M. Woodall**
12 **CHEHALIS MIST (IRE),** b c Orpen (USA)—Classic Heights **H. Shepherd**
13 **COVIE LAD (USA),** ch g Royal Anthem (USA)—Lyphard's Starlite (USA) **B. Walsh**
14 **CRAZY FLIRT (IRE),** b f King's Best (USA)—Itab (USA) **Birchwood Stud Ltd**
15 **ELSIE WAGG (USA),** b br f Mt Livermore (USA)—Hoedown Honey (CAN) **Mr P. K. O'Rourke**
16 **GLINSK (IRE),** ch c Namid—Kilshanny **Mrs Maeve Queally, Mr R. G. Hillen & Mr Mark Wallace**
17 **INAGH,** b f Tipsy Creek (USA)—Compton Amber **The Inagh Partnership**
18 **MISS RANI (IRE),** b f Xaar—Bea's Ruby (IRE) **Dr K. Sanderson**
19 **MY RASCAL (IRE),** b g Imperial Ballet (USA)—Derena (FR) **W. Ward**
20 **NEW DANCER,** b c Zafonic (USA)—Paradise Soul (USA) **P. Rosal & Mr R. G. Hillen**
21 **ROCK FEVER (IRE),** ch f Desert Sun—Icefern **Bermuda Wrectangle Ltd**
22 **RUBYANNE (IRE),** b f Fasliyev (USA)—Phyliel (USA) **Sheikh Rashid Bin Mohammed**
23 **WHITE BEAR (FR),** ch g Gold Away (IRE)—Danaide (FR) **G. M. McGuinness**
24 **WOOLACOMBE DREAM,** b f Orpen (USA)—Cadeau Elegant **Mrs T. A. Foreman**

TWO-YEAR-OLDS

25 Ch f 22/1 King's Best (USA)—Annieirwin (IRE) (Perugino (USA)) (23473)
26 B c 20/4 Princely Heir (IRE)—Another Rainbow (IRE) (Rainbows For Life (CAN)) (6036)
27 Ch f 8/3 Observatory (USA)—Aravonian (Night Shift (USA)) (23000)
28 Ch c 12/2 Bold Edge—Berenice (ITY) (Maroube) (23000)
29 B f 29/4 Xaar—Caer Mecene (FR) (Caerwent)
30 Ch c 17/2 King Charlemagne (USA)—Delta Blues (IRE) (Digamist (USA)) (31000) **B. Walsh**
31 B f 3/4 Josr Algarhoud (IRE)—Double Fault (IRE) (Zieten (USA)) (4000)
32 B c 12/5 Danehill (USA)—Double Grange (IRE) (Double Schwartz)
33 Ch f 12/4 Night Shift (USA)—Flush Rush (Zilzal (USA)) (11500) **Mrs R. G. Hillen**
34 B br f 23/2 Xaar—Foolish Fun (Fools Holme (USA)) (67068)
35 B br f 15/2 Danetime (IRE)—Forget Paris (IRE) (Broken Hearted) (12000) **Mr Mark Wallace**
36 Ch c 27/3 Diesis—Future Act (USA) (Known Fact (USA)) (31923)
37 B br c 12/5 Rahy (USA)—Grab The Prize (USA) (Green Dancer (USA)) (35000)
38 Ch f 31/3 Dr Fong (USA)—Intercede (Pursuit of Love) (20000)
39 B f 22/4 Fasliyev (USA)—Kentucky Starlet (USA) (Cox's Ridge (USA)) (10000)
40 **LUCKY SIS (USA),** b br f 5/2 King of Kings (IRE)—Crafty Nan (USA) (Crafty Prospector (USA)) (10641)

MR MARK WALLACE—continued

41 B f 25/3 Mozart (IRE)—Marlene-D (Selkirk (USA)) (46000)
42 **MARY DELANEY (USA)**, b f 24/2 Hennessy (USA)—Crafty Emerald (USA) (Crafty Prospector (USA)) (45224)
43 B f 6/2 Royal Applause—Mazarine Blue (Bellypha) (65000)
44 Ch f 7/3 Observatory (USA)—Musianica (Music Boy) (90000)
45 B c 4/3 Soviet Star (USA)—Ordinate (Nashwan (USA)) (33000) **D. McGovern**
46 B c 29/3 Xaar—Raw Diamond (IRE) (Roi Danzig (USA))
47 **RUSSIAN MIST (IRE)**, gr c 28/3 Xaar—Cape Mist (USA) (Lure (USA)) (16000)
48 Ch f 10/2 Raise A Grand (IRE)—Somers Heath (IRE) (Definite Article) (6000)
49 B f 24/4 Galileo (IRE)—Strutting (IRE) (Ela-Mana-Mou) (30180)
50 B f 12/5 Grand Lodge (USA)—Sweeping (Indian King (USA)) (33534)

Other Owners: J. Browne, P. J. Towell.

Assistant Trainer: Brendan Walsh

Jockey (flat): K. Fallon. **Apprentice:** D. Corey, T. Howell.

---

615 **MRS K. WALTON, Middleham**
Postal: **Sharp Hill Farm, Middleham, Leyburn, North Yorkshire, DL8 4QY.**
Contacts: **PHONE (01969) 622250 MOBILE (07718) 909356**

1 **CLEVER FELLA**, 6, ch g Elmaamul (USA)—Festival of Magic (USA) **Mrs K. Walton**
2 **DAJAZAR (IRE)**, 9, b g Seattle Dancer (USA)—Dajarra (IRE) **P. R. Aynsley & Mrs T. Aynsley**
3 **FANTASTICO (IRE)**, 5, b m Bahhare—Minatina (IRE) **The Suffolk Punch Syndicate**
4 **FUSION OF TUNES**, 7, b m Mr Confusion (USA)—Daleria (IRE) **Jeffrey McCarthy**
5 **GALWAY BREEZE (IRE)**, 10, b g Broussard (USA)—Furena **The White Liners**
6 **GAY OSCAR (IRE)**, 6, b g Oscar (IRE)—Deep Inthought (IRE) **Percy Vere Partnership**
7 **ONLY ONE MATTY (IRE)**, 8, b g Satco (FR)—Poundworld (IRE) **The White Liners**
8 **OYSTER POINT (IRE)**, 6, br g Corrouge (USA)—Ross Gale **Mrs K. Walton**
9 **PINNACLE RIDGE**, 5, ch g Bob's Return (USA)—Canal Street **Mrs C. E. Holroyd**
10 **SIKASSO (USA)**, 9, b br g Silver Hawk (USA)—Silken Doll (USA) **Stableline.com Ltd**
11 **WILDFIELD RUFO (IRE)**, 10, b g Celio Rufo—Jersey Girl **Mrs C. E. Holroyd**

Other Owners: Mr J. Edwards, Mr P. Groom, G. Lansbury, Mr G. Pearson, Mr B. Smith, Mr G. M. Spall, Mr R. Squirrel, M. White.

Jockey (NH): R. McGrath. **Conditional:** R. Utley.

---

616 **MRS BARBARA WARING, Welford-on-Avon**
Postal: Rumer Farm Stables, Long Marston Road, Welford on Avon, Warwickshire, CV37 8AF.
Contacts: **PHONE (01789) 750786 MOBILE (07787) 516723**

1 **BRONHALLOW**, 12, b g Belmez (USA)—Grey Twig **Davies, Nicholls, Parker, Holman, Field**
2 **ETTRICK (NZ)**, 10, b g Hereward The Wake (USA)—Kardinia (NZ) **Mrs Barbara Waring**
3 **MARTHA REILLY (IRE)**, 9, ch m Rainbows For Life (CAN)—Debach Delight **Hodgekinson Goode Owen Vickers**
4 **MURAQEB**, 5, ch g Grand Lodge (USA)—Oh So Well (IRE) **B. W. Parren**
5 **SMILEAFACT**, 5, b g So Factual (USA)—Smilingatstrangers **Williams Waggott Chakko Connelly Cullen**
6 **SMILING APPLAUSE**, 6, b g Royal Applause—Smilingatstrangers **Eddys A Team**
7 **SOUTHERNCROSSPATCH**, 14, ch g Ra Nova—Southern Bird **E. S. Chivers**
8 **STUNNING MAGIC**, 5, b g Magic Ring (IRE)—Absolutelystunning **J. Macrae, S. Gillett, H. Shapter**
9 **TAKEACHANCEONHIM**, 7, b g Dilum (USA)—Smilingatstrangers **A. G. Gibbs**

Other Owners: P. F. Chakko, B. Conneely, Mr A. M. Cullen, E. A. Davies, Mrs R. A. Field, Mrs E. D. Holman, L. Nicholls, R. G. Parker, J. W. Waggott, Mrs P. C. E. Williams.

Assistant Trainer: H Chisman

Jockey (flat): Lisa Jones, T. Quinn. **Jockey (NH):** M. A. Fitzgerald, B. Hitchcott. **Conditional:** J. Pritchard. **Apprentice:** S Hitchcott.

617 MR L. WARING, Bridgwater
Postal: **Culverwells Stables, Lower Merridge, Spaxton, Bridgwater, Somerset, TA5 1AS.**
Contacts: **PHONE (01278) 671750**

1 DUAL STAR (IRE), 10, b g Warning—Sizes Vary **Mrs Jennifer Waring**

Assistant Trainer: Jenny Waring

Jockey (NH): O. Nelmes.

618 LADY S. WATSON, Bossall
Postal: **Bossall Hall, Bossall, York, North Yorkshire, YO60 7NT.**
Contacts: **PHONE (01904) 468315**

1 FRANCKEN (ITY), 6, ro g Petit Loup (USA)—Filicaia **Lady S. Watson**
2 JUST FLUSTER, 9, ch g Triune—Flamber **Lady S. Watson**
3 KISMET, 7, b m Tirol—Belamcanda **Lady S. Watson**
4 TRIPLE PLAY (IRE), 6, br g Tagula (IRE)—Shiyra **Lady S. Watson**

619 MRS S. A. WATT, Richmond
Postal: **Rosey Hill Farm, Scorton Road, Brompton on Swale, Richmond, North Yorkshire, DL10 7EQ.**
Contacts: **PHONE (01748) 812064 FAX (01748) 812064 MOBILE (07970) 826046**
E-MAIL wattfences@aol.com

1 FEANOR, 7, b m Presidium—Nouvelle Cuisine **Mrs S. A. Watt**
2 NOW THEN AUNTIE (IRE), 4, gr f Anshan—Tara's Lady **Mrs S. A. Watt**
3 NOW THEN SID, 6, ch g Presidium—Callace **Mrs S. A. Watt**
4 TOP THE BILL (IRE), 5, b g Topanoora—Rio Star (IRE) **Mrs S. A. Watt**

Conditional: K. Mercer. **Amateur:** Miss T. Jackson.

620 MR P. R. WEBBER, Banbury
Postal: **Cropredy Lawn, Mollington, Banbury, Oxfordshire, OX17 1DR.**
Contacts: **PHONE (01295) 750226 FAX (01295) 758482 MOBILE (07836) 232465**
E-MAIL paul@paulwebberracing.com WEBSITE www.paulwebberracing.com

1 ABALVINO (FR), 11, ch g Sillery (USA)—Abalvina (FR) **I. M. S. Racing & Noel Cronin**
2 APPLEADAY (IRE), 4, gr g Beneficial—Hello Aris (FR) **D. C. R. Allen**
3 ATUM RE (IRE), 8, br g Be My Native (USA)—Collopy's Cross **P. C. Green**
4 AUTUMN RED (IRE), 5, ch g Zaffaran (USA)—Ballygullen River (IRE) **Richard Dodson & Partners**
5 BARONS KNIGHT, 4, ch g Lahib (USA)—Red Barons Lady (IRE) **D. C. R. Allen**
6 BODFARI SAUVAGE, 5, b g Loup Sauvage (USA)—Petite Sonnerie **Bodfari Stud Ltd**
7 BONNYJO (FR), 6, br g Cyborg (FR)—Argument Facile (FR) **The Branners & Guido Partnership**
8 BUCKBY LANE, 9, b g Nomadic Way (USA)—Buckby Folly **Mrs A. P. Starkey**
9 CALLMECOZMO (IRE), 7, ch g Zaffaran (USA)—Call Me Connie (IRE) **Mollington House Racing**
10 CATCHATAN (IRE), 10, b g Cataldi—Snowtan (IRE) **Mr D. A. Yardy**
11 CHAPLIN, 4, b c Groom Dancer (USA)—Princess Borghese (USA) **Mr P. R. Webber**
12 5, B g Tamure—Clodaigh Gale **B. Nielsen**
13 CLOUDY CLUB (IRE), 5, b g Moscow Society (USA)—Glenpatrick Peach (IRE) **Mrs W. J. Sherwood**
14 COOLDINE KING (IRE), 6, b g Germany—Tara's Serenade (IRE) **Mrs M. B. O'Connor**
15 DE SOTO, 4, b g Hernando (FR)—Vanessa Bell (IRE) **P. A. Deal**
16 DECISIVE, 6, b g Alhaarth (IRE)—Alys **P. S. Jensen**
17 DOUBLE LAW, 5, ch g Double Trigger (IRE)—Sister-In-Law **Mrs P. Scott-Dunn**
18 DUKE OF BUCKINGHAM (IRE), 9, b g Phardante (FR)—Deselby's Choice **The Dream On Partnership**
19 ELLANDSHE (IRE), 5, b br g Topanoora—Fox Glen **E. E. Williams**
20 EMERALD EXPRESS, 6, b m Bigstone (IRE)—Nashkara **Economic Security**
21 FIZZYWIZ, 5, b m Wizard King—Edina (IRE) **Mr D. A. Yardy**
22 FREELINE FURY, 5, b g Sir Harry Lewis—Queen's Favourite **I. Struel**
23 FROSTY'S COUSIN (IRE), 6, b g Arctic Lord—Farojina (IRE) **Mrs W. J. Sherwood**
24 FULL HOUSE (IRE), 6, br g King's Theatre (IRE)—Nirvavita (FR) **The Chamberlain Addiscott Partnership**
25 GIFT VOUCHER (IRE), 4, ch g Cadeaux Genereux—Highland Gift (IRE) **R. M. Kirkland**
26 GINGKO, 8, b g Pursuit of Love—Arboretum (IRE) **Four Counties Partnership**
27 GOLANO, 5, gr g Linamix (FR)—Dimakya (USA) **Mr D. A. Yardy**

MR P. R. WEBBER—continued

28 **HIGH BIRD HUMPHREY**, 6, ch g Nomadic Way (USA)—Miss Kewmill **Mr P. R. Webber**
29 **JAOKA DU GORD (FR)**, 8, b g Concorde Jr (USA)—Theorie du Cochet (FR) **R. W. Barnett**
30 **JUSTALFRED (IRE)**, 7, b g Rashar (USA)—Forthetimebeing **Mollington House Racing**
31 **KATE'S GIFT**, 4, b g Supreme Leader—Ardentinny **Mr & Mrs M. J. Dowd**
32 **KEW GREEN (USA)**, 7, b br g Brocco (USA)—Jump With Joy (USA) **P. S. Jensen**
33 **LITTLE CHARTRIDGE**, 7, b m Anshan—Auntie Dot **Mrs D. J. Webber**
34 **LITTLE ED**, 7, b g Shambo—Edina (IRE) **Mr D. A. Yardy**
35 **LUGO ROCK (IRE)**, 5, b br g Luso—Rocher Lady (IRE) **G. M. Powell**
36 **MAIDEN VOYAGE**, 7, b m Slip Anchor—Elaine Tully (IRE) **R. J. McAlpine**
37 5, Ch m Anshan—Mid Day Chaser (IRE) **Mrs J. Webber**
38 **MODAFFAA**, 5, b g Darshaan—Irish Valley (USA) **Mrs C. Ridley**
39 **MOLLY'S SPIRIT (IRE)**, 4, br f Anshan—Native Success (IRE) **Mr & Mrs M. J. Dowd**
40 **MUSICAL STAGE (USA)**, 6, b g Theatrical—Changed Tune (USA) **N. Ruddell & D. Heath**
41 **NORMA DESMEND**, 4, ch f Deploy—Toi Toi (IRE) **N. D. Cronin**
42 5, B g Beneficial—On The Bridle (IRE) **B. Nielsen**
43 **ONE OF THE BOYS (IRE)**, 4, ch g Shernazar—Easter Morning (FR) **D. E. Czarnetzki**
44 5, Ch g Topanoora—Phar Bolder (IRE) **Raymond Anderson Green & D. Taglight**
45 4, B g Shambo—Rent Day **D. I. Bare**
46 **RHAPSODY ROSE**, 4, b f Unfuwain (USA)—Haboobti **D. Allen**
47 **SALT CELLAR (IRE)**, 6, b g Salse (USA)—Athene (IRE) **Auctionair Racing Partnership**
48 **SHUHOOD (USA)**, 5, b g Kingmambo (USA)—Nifty (USA) **Mr & Mrs M. J. Dowd**
49 4, B f Overbury (IRE)—Snowdon Lily **Mrs P. A. Starkey**
50 **SONIC SOUND**, 6, b g Cosmonaut—Sophiesue **Skeltools Ltd**
51 **SPACE STAR**, 5, b g Cosmonaut—Sophiesue **Skeltools Ltd**
52 **SPINAROUND**, 7, gr g Terimon—Re-Spin **M. Stoddart & D. R. Stoddart**
53 **SPINOFSKI**, 10, b g Petoski—Spin Again **Mr D. R. Stoddart**
54 **STATE OF PLAY**, 5, b g Hernando (FR)—Kaprice (GER) **Mrs C. A. Waters**
55 **TEELIN**, 8, gr g Neltino—Slieve League (IRE) **J. A. Jenkins**
56 **TIGHE CASTER**, 6, b g Makbul—Miss Fire **Mr D. P. Barrie & Mr M. J. Rees**
57 **UNCLE WALLACE**, 9, b g Neltino—Auntie Dot **Mrs D. J. Webber**

THREE-YEAR-OLDS

58 **EKTISHAAF**, b f Mujahid (USA)—Tahnee **Mr P. R. Webber & Partners**
59 **LORD RAFFLES**, b g Zafonic (USA)—Dawna **J. A. Jenkins**
60 **MEASURED RESPONSE**, ch c Inchinor—Seal Indigo (IRE) **Mr P. R. Webber & Partners**

Other Owners: M. H. D. Barlow, Mrs D. Barnett, Mr P. A. Branigan, G. Bridgford, D. P. Cassidy, N. J. Chamberlain, P. M. Clarkson, J. M. Dougall, D. J. Greenall, D. A. Hibbert, D. W. Higgins, Mrs S. J. Jensen, A. S. Lancaster, I. Magee, Prof D. H. Metcalf, M. L. Pepper, Mrs S. C. Ross, Mrs I. M. Steinmann, J. D. Steinmann, Mrs C. J. Sunderland, N. J. Titcombe, W. S. Watt, Mrs R. M. Wilson.

Jockey (NH): J. Davies, T. Doyle, A. Thornton. **Conditional:** Mark Nicolls.

621 **MR M. J. WEEDEN, Weymouth**
Postal: **Highfield, Fleet, Weymouth, Dorset, DT3 4EB.**
Contacts: **PHONE (01305) 776822 MOBILE (07866) 313914**
E-MAIL highfield.fleet@lineone.net

1 **CHANTILLY LADY**, 12, ch m Rising—Ladiz **Just Racing**
2 **DUSTY CARPET**, 7, ch g Pivotal—Euridice (USA) **Chickerellites**
3 **JAZZ JUNIOR**, 6, ch g Romany Rye—Rising's Lass (IRE) **Chickerellites**
4 **MADAM FLORA**, 8, b m Alflora (IRE)—Madam's Choice **T. J. Swaffield**
5 **PITCHER PERFECT**, 4, b f Relief Pitcher—Rising's Lass (IRE) **Mr M. J. Weeden**
6 **SKYE BLUE (IRE)**, 8, b g Blues Traveller (IRE)—Hitopah **Mr D. Coombe**

TWO-YEAR-OLDS

7 Ch c 3/4 Classic Cliche (IRE)—Happy Go Lucky (Teamster)
8 B c 19/4 Emperor Fountain—Rising's Lass (IRE) (Rising)

Other Owners: Mrs E. A. Haycock, Mr R. Mowlam, Mr A. J. Welch, Mrs M. C. M. Walters, C. R. Borries, Mrs W. M. Pope.

Assistant Trainer: Mrs S Weeden

622 MR P. WEGMANN, Gloucester
Postal: **Maisemore Park, Maisemore, Gloucester, GL2 8HX.**
Contacts: **PHONE (01452) 301332 FAX (01452) 505002 MOBILE (07785) 242857**

1 COPYERSELFON (IRE), 6, b br g Right Win (IRE)—Cedarbelle (IRE) **J. Mcgrath**
2 CULLEN ROAD (IRE), 7, b g Wakashan—My Wings **Mr P. Wegmann**
3 LANOS (POL), 7, ch g Special Power—Lubeka (POL) **Mr P. Wegmann**
4 LEGALIS (USA), 7, ch g Gone West (USA)—Loyalize (USA) **Mr P. Wegmann**
5 MONTY'S THEME (IRE), 11, b br g Montelimar (USA)—Theme Music **Mr P. Wegmann**
6 PARSIFAL, 6, b g Sadler's Wells (USA)—Moss (USA) **Mr P. Wegmann**
7 POLISH LEGEND, 6, b g Polish Precedent (USA)—Chita Rivera **Mr P. Wegmann**
8 ROYAL ALLEGIANCE, 10, ch g Kris—Wilayif (USA) **R. Koniger**
9 TEENAGER, 5, b m Young Ern—Washita **Mr P. Wegmann**

Assistant Trainer: Miss V Williams

623 MR MARK WELLINGS, Bridgnorth
Postal: **Broad Acre Stables, Broadlanes, Quatt, Bridgnorth, Shropshire, WV15 6EG.**
Contacts: **PHONE (01746) 781019 MOBILE (07973) 763469**
E-MAIL mark@broadacre.fsnet.co.uk

1 BEN'S REVENGE, 5, b g Emperor Jones (USA)—Bumble Boogie (IRE) **J. W. Da Costa**
2 BLAZING FIRE, 8, b g Derrylin—Shean Deas **Mrs M. James**
3 ESPERE D'OR, 8, b g Golden Heights—Drummer's Dream (IRE) **Ricochet Management Limited**
4 HI BLUE, 6, b g Weld—Winnie Lorraine **Mrs M. James**
5 LITTLE RICHARD (IRE), 6, b g Alhaarth (IRE)—Intricacy **Mark Wellings Racing**
6 OLD GOLDEN BAY, 5, b g Meqdaam (USA)—Modina April **Stephen Williams**
7 PLATINUM BAY (IRE), 5, b g Goldmark (USA)—Brown Foam **Mark Wellings Racing**
8 SUPRENDRE ESPERE, 5, b g Espere d'or—Celtic Dream **Ricochet Management Limited**
9 TEYAAR, 9, b g Polar Falcon (USA)—Music In My Life (IRE) **Mark Wellings Racing**
10 UN AUTRE ESPERE, 6, b g Golden Heights—Drummer's Dream (IRE) **Ricochet Management Limited**

Other Owners: A. Tranter.

Assistant Trainer: Mrs L A Wellings

624 MR L. WELLS, Billingshurst
Postal: **Pallingham Manor Farm, Wisborough Green, Billingshurst, West Sussex, RH14 0EZ.**
Contacts: **HOME (01403) 700679 OFFICE (01403) 700119 FAX (01403) 700899**
MOBILE (07977) 144949
E-MAIL pmf@btinternet.com WEBSITE www.lawrencewells.co.uk

1 ALL BART NATIVE (IRE), 10, gr g Be My Native (USA)—Bissie's Jayla **Mrs C. J. Zetter-Wells**
2 CLASSIC ROLE, 6, b g Tragic Role (USA)—Clare Island **Pillar To Post Racing**
3 COWBOYBOOTS (IRE), 7, b g Lord Americo—Little Welly **D. I. Gower**
4 EL VIEJO (IRE), 8, b g Norwich—Shuil Na Gale **Mrs C. J. Zetter-Wells**
5 ESTUPENDO (IRE), 8, b g Tidaro (USA)—Spendapromise **W. A. Scott**
6 GALE FORCE ONE, 7, b g Elbio—Brief Gale **P. Zetter**
7 IMTOUCHINGWOOD, 4, b f Fleetwood (IRE)—Shanuke (IRE) **R. Howitt**
8 JUST ANVIL (IRE), 7, ch g Baron Blakeney—Amy Just (IRE) **D. W. Cox**
9 KING TRITON (IRE), 8, br g Mister Lord (USA)—Deepwater Woman **Selsey Clubbers**
10 LEASE BACK (FR), 6, b g Sleeping Car (FR)—Salse Pareille (FR) **P. Zetter**
11 LORD NORMAN (IRE), 4, b g Norwich—Sue's A Lady **Mrs C. J. Zetter-Wells**
12 MULTI TALENTED (IRE), 9, b g Montelimar (USA)—Boro Glen **D. W. Cox**
13 NOVI SAD (IRE), 7, ch g Norwich—Shuil Na Gale **Mrs C. J. Zetter-Wells**
14 ONE CORNETTO (IRE), 6, b g Eurobus—Costenetta (IRE) **Mrs C. J. Zetter-Wells**
15 RHAPSODY IN BLOOM, 4, b g Botanic (USA)—Jazzy Refrain (IRE) **P. Zetter**
16 RUSINGA, 7, gr g Homo Sapien—Royal Blaze **P. Evans**
17 SMOKIN GREY, 5, gr m Terimon—Wollow Maid **The Disciples**
18 SPIRITUAL DANCER (IRE), 10, b g King's Ride—Arctic Tartan **Mr D. W. Cox & Mr Paul Zetter**
19 5, B br g Norwich—Sue's A Lady **Mrs C. J. Zetter-Wells**
20 THE STAFFORD, 4, b g Selkirk (USA)—Bint Zamayem (IRE) **Sir Eric Parker**
21 THE WOODEN SPOON (IRE), 7, b g Old Vic—Amy's Gale (IRE) **Hills, Smith and Wearne**
22 TOP DOG (IRE), 6, b g Topanoora—Dun Oengus (IRE) **Mrs C. J. Zetter-Wells**

MR L. WELLS—continued

 23 VICTREE (IRE), 6, b g Old Vic—Boro Glen P. Zetter
 24 YLANG, 4, b f Fleetwood (IRE)—Ulla Laing **Mrs C. J. Zetter-Wells**

Other Owners: Mr C. Cole, A. J. Cousins, J. Dwight, W. Harlow, M. J. Hills, J. P. Smith, Mr A. Stanton, P. Thwaites, G. H. Tizzard, G. Tustin, P. Wearne, MR L. Wells.

Assistant Trainer: Mrs C J Zetter-Wells

Amateur: Miss Claire Milne, Mr J. Morgan.

MR J. R. WEYMES, Middleham
Postal: **Ashgill, Coverham, Leyburn, North Yorkshire, DL8 4TJ.**
Contacts: **PHONE (01969) 640420 FAX (01969) 640505 MOBILE (07753) 792516**
E-MAIL johnweymes@aol.com WEBSITE www.johnweymes.co.uk

 1 ATTACCA, 4, b g Piccolo—Jubilee Place (IRE) **Mr Gibblet & Mr Pratt**
 2 BLUE VIKING (IRE), 4, b g Danetime (IRE)—Jenny Spinner (IRE) **J. J. Crosier**
 3 CROSBY DON, 10, b g Alhijaz—Evening Star **Don Raper**
 4 CROSBY DONJOHN, 8, ch g Magic Ring (IRE)—Ovideo **Don Raper**
 5 CROSBY JUBILEE (IRE), 4, b g Shinko Forest (IRE)—Quicksand (IRE) **Don Raper**
 6 DANAKIM, 8, b g Emarati (USA)—Kangra Valley **Miss Kirsty Buckle**
 7 DO KEEP UP, 8, b g Missed Flight—Aimee Jane (USA) **W. R. Hornby**
 8 FOXIES FUTURE (IRE), 4, b f General Monash (USA)—Indescent Blue **Dandyjack Racing**
 9 GRACEFUL AIR (IRE), 4, b f Danzero (AUS)—Samsung Spirit **T. A. Scothern & N. Wellock**
 10 GRAND VIEW, 9, ch g Grand Lodge (USA)—Hemline **Sporting Occasions**
 11 LINDEN'S LADY, 5, b m Compton Place—Jubilee Place (IRE) **T.H.E. Racing**
 12 MYANNABANANA, 4, ch g Woodborough (USA)—Raging Storm **T. A. Scothern & N. Wellock**
 13 ROYAL GRAND, 5, ch h Prince Sabo—Hemline **Sporting Occasions**
 14 VALIANT AIR (IRE), 4, b g Spectrum (IRE)—Shining Desert (IRE) **Mr J. R. Weymes**

THREE-YEAR-OLDS

 15 DUCAL DIVA, b f Bahamian Bounty—Lucky Thing
 16 JEFFSLOTTERY, b g Rock City—Thieves Welcome **Mr Isteed & K. Buckle**
 17 MORNING WORLD, b c Bahamian Bounty—Snap Cracker **N. Palamountain**
 18 SIMPLY ST LUCIA, b f Charnwood Forest (IRE)—Mubadara (IRE) **Sporting Occasions**
 19 SPINNAKERS GIRL, b f Bluegrass Prince (IRE)—Brac Princess (IRE) **Sporting Occasions**
 20 WHITE STAR MAGIC, ch c Bluegrass Prince (IRE)—Bless **White Star Racing**

TWO-YEAR-OLDS

 21 B c 15/4 Agnes World (USA)—Aegean Blue (Warning) (27000)
 22 Ch f 18/4 Rambling Bear—Bayrami (Emarati (USA))
 23 DRINK TO ME ONLY, b c 18/4 Pursuit of Love—Champenoise (Forzando) (5000)
 24 Ch c 24/4 Woodborough (USA)—Evaporate (Insan (USA)) (1000)
 25 LINTON DANCER (IRE), b f 28/3 Mujadil (USA)—Daisy Grey (Nordance (USA)) (6036)
 26 B c 14/2 Bertolini (USA)—Mark of Respect (Mark of Esteem (IRE)) (2200)
 27 B f 13/2 Forzando—Martha P Perkins (Fayruz) (900)
 28 MYTASS, b c 11/4 Averti (IRE)—Emerald Dream (IRE) (Vision (USA)) (4000)
 29 B f 13/4 Rossini (USA)—Raging Storm (Horage) (2346)
 30 Ch f 12/3 Barathea (IRE)—Samsung Spirit (Statoblest)
 31 SECRET TENDER (IRE), ch c 14/3 Beckett (IRE)—Mystery Bid (Auction Ring (USA)) (10500)
 32 TALLYHOBYE, b c 2/3 Foxhound (USA)—Bebe de Cham (Tragic Role (USA)) (7500)
 33 Ch f 12/4 Fruits of Love (USA)—Tana Mana (Alzao (USA)) (1005)

Other Owners: Mrs J. A. Buckle, Mrs D. Catlow, Mel Catlow, Mr I. A. Gregg, A. W. Hornby, Mr C. A. Watson, Mr P. Wyatt.

Assistant Trainer: Kirsty Buckle

Jockey (flat): P. Hanagan, R. Winston. **Jockey (NH):** J. Crowley. **Conditional:** P. Whelan. **Apprentice:** D Fentiman.

626 MR E. A. WHEELER, Pangbourne
Postal: **Coombe Park Stables, Whitchurch on Thames, Pangbourne, Oxfordshire, RG8 7QT.**
Contacts: **PHONE (01189) 841317 FAX (01189) 841924 MOBILE (07712) 880966**

1 **APPOLONIOUS,** 4, b g Case Law—Supreme Thought **D. L. W. Simester**
2 **BATCHWORTH BEAU,** 4, ch g Bluegrass Prince (IRE)—Batchworth Belle **Mrs D. T. M. S. Price**
3 **CATCHTHEBATCH,** 9, b g Beveled (USA)—Batchworth Dancer **Four Of A Kind Racing**
4 **DANCING GIPSY,** 4, ch f Young Ern—Batchworth Dancer **Mrs U. Deaner**
5 **DANCING MYSTERY,** 11, b g Beveled (USA)—Batchworth Dancer **Astrod Limited TA Austin Stroud & Co**
6 **DANGEROUS BEANS,** 5, b gr g Bluegrass Prince (IRE)—A Little Hot **G. W. Witheford**
7 **DIAPHANOUS,** 7, b m Beveled (USA)—Sharp Venita **Mr E. A. Wheeler**
8 **FIREWORK,** 7, b g Primo Dominie—Prancing **Miss L. Simmons**
9 **HELLO MOLLY,** 4, b f Young Ern—Treasurebound **Mrs U. Deaner**
10 **MASTER MCGHEE,** 6, ch g Beveled (USA)—Sandra Dee (IRE) **Mr E. A. Wheeler**
11 **RATHMULLAN,** 6, ch g Bluegrass Prince (IRE)—National Time (USA) **Mr E. A. Wheeler**

THREE-YEAR-OLDS

12 **CLUSOES MYSTERY,** b f Fraam—Clued Up **Four Of A Kind Racing**
13 **B g Almaty (IRE)—Supreme Thought **D. L. W. Simester**
14 **WAR DANCER,** b g Wolfhound (USA)—Batchworth Dancer **Astrod Limited TA Austin Stroud & Co**

TWO-YEAR-OLDS

15 B f 1/1 Woodborough (USA)—Another Jade (Beveled (USA)) **G. W. Witheford**
16 **BATCHWORTH FLEUR,** b f 6/5 Little Jim—Batchworth Belle (Interrex (CAN)) **Mrs D. T. M. S. Price**
17 B f 1/1 Little Jim—Treasurebound (Beldale Flutter (USA)) **Mrs D. T. M. S. Price**

Other Owners: A. M. Tatum.

Jockey (flat): S. Carson. **Amateur:** Miss C. Nosworthy.

627 MR A. C. WHILLANS, Hawick
Postal: **Esker House, Newmill-On-Slitrig, Hawick, TD9 9UQ.**
Contacts: **PHONE (01450) 376642 MOBILE (07771) 550555**

1 **ANOTHER TAIPAN (IRE),** 5, b g Taipan (IRE)—Sheeghee (IRE) **Mrs S. Scott**
2 **BRAVE VISION,** 9, b g Clantime—Kinlet Vision (IRE) **Mrs S. Harrow**
3 **CHIVVY CHARVER (IRE),** 8, ch g Commanche Run—Claddagh Pride **Mrs L. M. Whillans**
4 **CRYSTAL GIFT,** 13, b g Dominion—Grain Lady (USA) **Mrs L. M. Whillans**
5 **EASTERN TRIBUTE (USA),** 9, b g Affirmed (USA)—Mia Duchessa (USA) **J. J. Elliot**
6 **FIVE GOLD (IRE),** 4, b g Desert Prince (IRE)—Ceide Dancer (IRE) **Jethart Justice**
7 **GOFAGOLD,** 10, ch g Tina's Pet—Golden Della **Mrs L. M. Whillans**
8 **GOSPEL SONG,** 13, ch g King Among Kings—Market Blues **C. N. Whillans**
9 **GRAND SLAM (IRE),** 10, b g Second Set (IRE)—Lady In The Park (IRE) **7 Up Partnership**
10 **HELLO BABY,** 5, b g Jumbo Hirt (USA)—Silver Flyer **Miss J. Gibson**
11 **KIWIJIMBO (IRE),** 5, b g Germany (USA)—Final Touch (IRE) **W.Scott,K.Creighton,O.Hogg,J.Mckinnon**
12 **KRACK DE L'ISLE (FR),** 7, b g Kadalko (FR)—Ceres de L'isle (FR) **J. J. Elliot**
13 4, Gr g Aahsaylad—Moenzi (IRE) **Partnership**
14 **NEIDPATH CASTLE,** 6, b g Alflora (IRE)—Pennant Cottage (IRE) **B.McKie G.Harrow, K.Creighton, W.Scott**
15 **PAPER CLASSIC,** 5, ch m Classic Cliche (IRE)—Kiniohio (FR) **C. N. Whillans**
16 **SCURRA,** 6, b g Spectrum—Tamnia **Mrs L. M. Whillans**
17 **SOUND LEADER (USA),** 5, ch g Diesis—Colledge Leader (USA) **Mrs H. Greggan**
18 **SPYCATCHER (USA),** 5, b g Dixieland Band (USA)—Secret Seeker (USA) **Mrs L. M. Whillans**

Other Owners: C. Bird, G. L. Harrow, W. Mckie, W. J. E. Scott, W. Telfer, MR A. C. Whillans.

628 MR R. M. WHITAKER, Scarcroft
Postal: **Hellwood Racing Stables, Hellwood Lane, Scarcroft, Leeds, West Yorkshire, LS14 3BP.**
Contacts: **PHONE (0113) 892265 FAX (01132) 893680 MOBILE (07831) 870454**

1 **ACCA LARENTIA (IRE),** 4, gr f Titus Livius (FR)—Daisy Grey **K. Lewis**
2 **AIREDALE LAD (IRE),** 4, b g Charnwood Forest (IRE)—Tamarsiya (USA) **In Memory of Mary Syndicate**
3 **ALCHEMIST MASTER,** 6, b g Machiavellian (USA)—Gussy Marlowe **G. F. Pemberton**
4 **CARIBBEAN BLUE,** 4, b f First Trump—Something Blue **Mr R. M. Whitaker**

MR R. M. WHITAKER—continued

5 **HARRINGTON BATES**, 4, ch g Wolfhound (USA)—Fiddling **P. Davies**
6 **JAKEAL (IRE)**, 6, b g Eagle Eyed (USA)—Karoi (IRE) **Mr James Marshall & Mrs Susan Marshall**
7 **KAYMICH PERFECTO**, 5, b g Sheikh Albadou—Manhattan Diamond **G. B. Bedford**
8 **MYND**, 5, b g Atraf—Prim Lass **Derek and Jean Clee**
9 **NECKAR VALLEY (IRE)**, 6, b g Desert King (IRE)—Solar Attraction (IRE) **G. Morrill**
10 **NEON BLUE**, 4, b br g Atraf—Desert Lynx (IRE) **Country Lane Partnership**
11 **NEVADA DESERT (IRE)**, 5, b g Desert King (IRE)—Kayanga **J. B. Pemberton**
12 4, Ch g Wolfhound (USA)—Parfait Amour **Mr R. M. Whitaker**
13 **STEEL BLUE**, 5, b g Atraf—Something Blue **Country Lane Partnership**
14 **VICIOUS PRINCE (IRE)**, 6, b g Sadler's Wells (USA)—Sunny Flower (FR) **Joint Ownership Terminated**
15 **VICIOUS WARRIOR**, 6, b g Elmaamul (USA)—Ling Lane **Mr A. S. Crossan**

THREE-YEAR-OLDS

16 **AFRICAN BREEZE**, b f Atraf—Luanshya **G. F. Pemberton**
17 **AUTUMN DREAM**, b f Primo Dominie—Red Cascade (IRE) **G. Morrill**
18 **CHINGOLA**, b f Atraf—Sulaka **T. L. Adams**
19 **DANCING DEANO (IRE)**, b g Second Empire (IRE)—Ultimate Beat (USA) **Craig and Amanda Harrison**
20 **DESERTINA (IRE)**, b f Spectrum (IRE)—Kayanga **J. B. Pemberton**
21 **FILEY BUOY**, b g Factual (USA)—Tugra (FR) **The Barflys**
22 **JUST WAZ (USA)**, ch g Woodman (USA)—Just Tops (USA) **Mrs L. Ziegler**
23 **LUCKY LIL**, ch f Cadeaux Genereux—Amalia (IRE) **Mrs L. Ziegler**
24 **MR MAJESTIC**, b g Vettori (IRE)—Alacrity **W. M. Ellis**
25 **MR MAXIM**, ch g Lake Coniston (IRE)—White Hare **The Maxim Group Limited**
26 **PARIS HEIGHTS**, gr g Paris House—Petra Nova **W. M. Ellis**

TWO-YEAR-OLDS

27 **EBONY LADY**, br f 20/2 Vettori (IRE)—Keen Melody (USA) (Sharpen Up) **W. M. Ellis**
28 Ch c 2/5 Desert Story (IRE)—Fairy Free (Rousillon (USA)) (9500) **Mr R. M. Whitaker**
29 **JAKEINI (IRE)**, b c 10/3 Rossini (USA)—Talita Kumi (IRE) (High Estate) (14000) **Mr M. W. Crane**
30 B c 8/5 Foxhound (USA)—Ling Lane (Slip Anchor) (5000) **Mr R. M. Whitaker**
31 B f 20/4 Observatory (USA)—Majalis (Mujadil (USA)) (5000) **Mr R. M. Whitaker**
32 B f 4/3 Primo Valentino (IRE)—Sulaka (Owington) **T. L. Adams**
33 **TABARET**, ch g 28/2 Bertolini (USA)—Luanshya (First Trump) **T. L. Adams**

Other Owners: M. Charles, J. Devine, C. D. Harrison, Mrs A. J. Harrison, Mrs R. M. Whitaker.

Assistant Trainer: Simon R Whitaker

Jockey (flat): V. Halliday, Dean McKeown.

MR A. J. WHITEHEAD, Craven Arms
Postal: Lawn Farm, Beambridge, Aston on Clun, Craven Arms, Shropshire, SY7 0HA.
Contacts: PHONE (01588) 660424

1 **CITIMAN (AUS)**, 8, b g Citidancer—Taimian (NZ) **Mr A. J. Whitehead**
2 **LORD DAL (FR)**, 12, b g Cadoudal (FR)—Lady Corteira (FR) **Mr A. J. Whitehead**
3 **MEILLEUR (NZ)**, 7, ch g Mellifont (NZ)—Petite Cheval (NZ) **Mr A. J. Whitehead**

Jockey (NH): O. McPhail. **Conditional:** W. Kennedy.

MR M. S. WILESMITH, Dymock
Postal: Bellamys Farm, Dymock, Gloucestershire, GL18 2DX.
Contacts: PHONE (01531) 890410 FAX (01684) 893428 MOBILE (07970) 411638
E-MAIL martin@m.s.wilesmith.com

1 5, B m Alflora (IRE)—Annicombe Run **Mr M. S. Wilesmith**
2 **COTTON ON**, 8, b g Henbit (USA)—Linen Leaf **Mr M. S. Wilesmith**
3 **MOUNTAIN SINGER (IRE)**, 6, b g Carroll House—Mountain Grove **Mr M. S. Wilesmith**
4 **THIS ONE IS A BOY (IRE)**, 9, b g Executive Perk—Belinda Vard **Mr M. S. Wilesmith**

Assistant Trainer: Miss E C Wilesmith

Amateur: Mr M. Wilesmith.

631 MR D. L. WILLIAMS, Hungerford

Postal: **Hillside Stud, Great Shefford, Hungerford, Berkshire, RG17 7DL.**
Contacts: **HOME (01488) 638636 FAX (01488) 638121 MOBILE (07879) 403160 (07879) 403595**
E-MAIL gcheshire@hotmail.com

1 AUTUMN RAIN (USA), 8, br g Dynaformer (USA)—Edda (USA) **Hillside Stud Racing**
2 BOLD LEADER, 8, b g Tragic Role (USA)—Swift Messenger **Mr D. L. Williams**
3 CANACHAM, 6, ch m Beveled (USA)—Austral Jane **All On Top Racing**
4 CLOUDINGSWELL, 4, b ro f Cloudings (IRE)—L'ancressaan **Symbol Of Success Racing**
5 COMPTON EXPERT (IRE), 5, b g Cadeaux Genereux—Samira **Mr D. L. Williams**
6 FLOODGATE, 8, b g Bin Ajwaad (USA)—Miss Haversham **Gareth Cheshire**
7 GILDORANS SPICE, 7, gr m Gildoran—Sea Spice **Mr E. Davies**
8 GOLLY (IRE), 9, b g Toulon—Tor-Na-Grena **Reliance Car Hire Services Ltd**
9 JOINT AUTHORITY (IRE), 10, b g Religiously (USA)—Highway's Last **Miss L. Horner**
10 LUNARDI (IRE), 7, b g Indian Ridge—Gold Tear (USA) **Miss L. Horner**
11 MACGYVER (NZ), 9, b g Jahafil—Corazon (NZ) **Miss L. Horner**
12 MISS KOEN (IRE), 6, b m Barathea (IRE)—Fanny Blankers (IRE) **Mr D. L. Williams**
13 MR COSPECTOR, 8, b g Cosmonaut—L'ancressaan **The Eight Prospectors Syndicate**
14 RELIANCE LEADER, 9, ch g Weld—Swift Messenger **Reliance Car Hire Services Ltd**
15 SPARKLING WATER (USA), 6, b h Woodman (USA)—Shirley Valentine **Miss L. Horner**

Other Owners: Major Simon Robinson, Fred Marden, M. G. Wooldridge, R. J. Barker, Mrs P. M. Colson, R. J. Darby, Mrs N. C. Diment, K. L. Pollington.

Assistant Trainer: Miss Victoria Flood

Jockey (NH): James Diment. **Amateur:** Miss V. Flood, Miss L. Horner.

632 MR EVAN WILLIAMS, Llancarfan

Postal: **Aberogwrn Farm, Llancarfan, Vale of Glamorgan.**
Contacts: **PHONE (01446) 754045 MOBILE (07950) 381227**

1 BANGALORE, 9, ch g Sanglamore (USA)—Ajuga (USA) **M. V. Dawson**
2 BLUE YONDER, 5, b m Terimon—Areal (IRE) **The Blue Yonder Partnership**
3 CALLED TO THE BAR, 12, b g Legal Bwana—Miss Gaylord **Mr L. W. Meadmore**
4 CANNON FIRE (FR), 4, ch c Grand Lodge—Muirfield (FR) **M. J. Haines**
5 COOLING CASTLE (FR), 9, ch g Sanglamore (USA)—Syphaly **K. J. Glastonbury**
6 FLYING DRUID (FR), 5, b g Celtic Swing—Sky Bibi (FR) **Mr and Mrs Glynne Clay**
7 FOREST CHIEF (IRE), 9, b g Forest Wind (USA)—Cryptic Gold **Dapper Racing Syndicate**
8 HARBOUR BOUND (IRE), 6, b g Sadler's Wells (USA)—Argon Laser **Fox And Hounds Racing**
9 ICE RAIN (IRE), 5, gr g Zaffaran (USA)—Turbet Lass (IRE) **Mr & Mrs R. J. Thomas**
10 INDIBAR (IRE), 4, b g Indian Ridge—Barbara Frietchie (IRE) **Lewis Racing**
11 JO'S SALE (IRE), 6, b g Germany (USA)—Clonmeen Lodge (IRE) **R. A. Mason**
12 KERRY ZULU WARRIOR, 8, ch g Aspect (USA)—Kerry Blue Nun **Mike Teague & Graeme Price**
13 KOUMBA (FR), 7, b g Luchiroverte (IRE)—Agenore (FR) **Mr and Mrs Glynne Clay**
14 MISS MUSCAT, 5, b m Environment Friend—Fisima **Red & Black Racing**
15 MR NEMO (IRE), 9, b g Doubletour (USA)—Snowdrifter **M. V. Dawson**
16 NORTHERN DEAL (IRE), 10, b g Top of The World—Amberley **The Robin Raceline Syndicate**
17 PERUVIAN BREEZE (IRE), 4, b g Foxhound (USA)—Quietly Impressive (IRE) **Dead Loss Racing**
18 PETANQUE (IRE), 9, b g King's Ride—Phargara (IRE) **The Blue Yonder Partnership**
19 SHE'S OUR NATIVE (IRE), 7, b m Be My Native (USA)—More Dash (IRE) **I. C. Brice**
20 SILVER CHARTER (USA), 6, b g Silver Hawk (USA)—Pride of Darby (USA) **J. Tudor**
21 SPRING LUNAR (IRE), 7, b g Parthian Springs—Orospring **W. J. Evans**

Other Owners: E. J. Chapman, P. Collins, Mr P. M. Cooper, W. A. Edgington, J. G. Huckle, M. Jenkins, Mr P. Lewis, Mr P. Maloney, Mr J. R. Millard, Mrs S. M. Millard, D. P. Pope, J. Pritchard, Miss E. A. Saunders, D. J. Wallis, W. E. Wilde.

Assistant Trainer: Mrs C. Williams

Conditional: C. Williams.

633 **MR IAN WILLIAMS, Alvechurch**
Postal: **Dominion Racing Stables, Seafield Lane, Portway, Birmingham, B48 7HL.**
Contacts: **PHONE** (01564) 822392 **FAX** (01564) 829475
E-MAIL info@ianwilliamsracing.com **WEBSITE** ianwilliamsracing.com

1 **ALAGON (IRE)**, 5, b g Alzao (USA)—Forest Lair **ROA Red Alligator Partnership**
2 **ALF'S SPINNEY**, 5, ch g Anshan—Netherdrom **Mrs J. Tredwell**
3 **ARABIE**, 7, b g Polish Precedent (USA)—Always Friendly **G. Ferrigno**
4 **ARGONAUT**, 5, b g Rainbow Quest (USA)—Chief Bee **The Five Nations Partnership**
5 **AT YOUR REQUEST**, 4, gr g Bering—Requesting **Cockbury Court Partnership**
6 **BAIKALINE (FR)**, 6, b m Cadoudal (FR)—Advantage (FR) **JSM Fabrications Ltd**
7 **BAMBI DE L'ORME (FR)**, 6, gr g True Brave (USA)—Princesse Ira (FR) **Mr & Mrs John Poynton**
8 **BARNEY BLUE (IRE)**, 5, ch g Presenting—Six of Spades (IRE) **Mrs A. Tincknell**
9 **BATMAN SENORA (FR)**, 9, b g Chamberlin (FR)—Cartza (FR) **G. Polinski**
10 **BEAU DE TURGEON (FR)**, 4, b g Turgeon (USA)—Beluda (FR) **Mr and Mrs J. D. Cotton**
11 **BIRCHALL (IRE)**, 6, b g Priolo (USA)—Ballycuirke **Trump Card Racing**
12 **BLACK FALCON (IRE)**, 5, ch g In The Wings—Muwasim (USA) **C. N. Barnes**
13 **BOB'S THE BUSINESS (IRE)**, 11, b g Bob Back (USA)—Kiora **Mr C. I. K. Harris**
14 **BREWSTER (IRE)**, 8, b g Roselier (FR)—Aelia Paetina **Mr & Mrs John Poynton**
15 **BROOKLYN'S GOLD (USA)**, 10, b g Seeking The Gold (USA)—Brooklyn's Dance (FR) **J. T. Warner**
16 **CALIBAN (IRE)**, 7, ch g Rainbows For Life (CAN)—Amour Toujours (IRE) **J. Edmunds**
17 **CAUCASIAN (IRE)**, 7, gr g Leading Counsel (USA)—Kemal's Princess **Mr Ian Williams**
18 **CHRISTMAS TRUCE (IRE)**, 6, b g Brief Truce (USA)—Superflash **M. Murphy**
19 **COLWYN JAKE (IRE)**, 6, b br g Jolly Jake (NZ)—Maggie's Beauty **C. M. Kinane**
20 **DAD'S ELECT (GER)**, 6, b g Lomitas—Diamond Lake (USA) **A. L. R. Morton**
21 **DALLAS ALICE**, 5, ch m Sir Harry Lewis (USA)—Run On Stirling **J. L. Rowsell**
22 **DOWNPOUR (USA)**, 7, b g Torrential (USA)—Juliac (USA) **Favourites Racing Ltd**
23 **EVEON (IRE)**, 5, b m Synefos (USA)—Lovely Grand **Mrs R. W. Paterson**
24 **FULWELL HILL**, 7, b m Anshan—Finkin **J. Tredwell**
25 **GREGORIAN (IRE)**, 8, b g Foxhound (USA)—East River (FR) **NewmarketConnections.com**
26 **GREGORIO (FR)**, 11, b br g Passing Sale (FR)—Apside (FR) **Miss Anna Bramall**
27 **HAWKES RUN**, 7, b g Hernando (FR)—Wise Speculation (USA) **The Baron Rouge Partnership**
28 **HI FI**, 7, b g Homo Sapien—Baroness Orkzy **Mrs R. W. Paterson**
29 **HORS LA LOI (FR)**, 9, ch g Exit To Nowhere (USA)—Kernia (IRE) **The Not So Risky Partnership**
30 **IDEALKO (FR)**, 9, b g Kadalko (FR)—Belfaster (FR) **Mrs M. A. Bull**
31 **JACKEM (IRE)**, 11, b br g Lord Americo—Laurence Lady **The Duck Racing Partnership**
32 **JARDIN DE BEAULIEU (FR)**, 8, ch g Rough Magic (FR)—Emblem (FR) **Mr & Mrs John Poynton**
33 **JORIS DE VONNAS (FR)**, 8, ch g Dear Doctor (FR)—Carine de Neuvy (FR) **Miss Anna Bramall**
34 **KILGOWAN (IRE)**, 6, b g Accordion—Gaiety Lass **The Ferandlin Peaches**
35 **KORAKOR (FR)**, 11, ch g Nikos—Aniflore (FR) **Mr and Mrs J. D. Cotton**
36 **LE GRAND ROCHER**, 8, ch g Factual (USA)—Honey Bridge **JSM Fabrications Ltd**
37 **LODESTAR (IRE)**, 8, br g Good Thyne (USA)—Let's Compromise **Sir Robert Ogden C.B.E., LLD**
38 **LUCKY LEO**, 5, b g Muhtarram (USA)—Wrong Bride **B and S Vaughan**
39 **MADGIK DE BEAUMONT (FR)**, 5, b br g Sleeping Car (FR)—Matalie (FR) **M. Murphy**
40 **MAJESTIC (IRE)**, 10, b g Belmez (USA)—Noble Lily (USA) **P. Kelly**
41 **MASSIMO (FR)**, 5, b g Gunboat Diplomacy (FR)—Gitaine de L'allier (FR) **J. J. Boulter**
42 **MAZILEO**, 12, b g Mazilier (USA)—Embroglio (USA) **Mr T. J. & Mrs H. Parrott**
43 **MEADOW HAWK (IRE)**, 5, ch g Spinning World (USA)—Sophonisbe **Mr Ian Williams**
44 **MISTER MUSTARD (IRE)**, 8, b g Norwich—Monalma (IRE) **Favourites Racing Ltd**
45 ** **, 5, b g Safety Catch (USA)—Monalma (IRE) **Favourites Racing Ltd**
46 **NAGANO (FR)**, 7, b g Hero's Honor (USA)—Sadinskaya (FR) **Allan Stennett & Terry Warner**
47 **NAVARONE**, 11, b g Gunner B—Anamasi **A. J. Cresser**
48 **NEM CON**, 7, b g Afflora (IRE)—Poppy's Pride **Mr & Mrs John Poynton**
49 **NORWEGIAN**, 4, b g Halling (USA)—Chicarica (USA) **Mr Ian Williams**
50 **OSCATELLO (USA)**, 5, b br g Woodman (USA)—Galea des Bois (FR) **R. M. Braune**
51 **PARISH OAK**, 10, b g Rakaposhi King—Poppy's Pride **Mrs M. Mann**
52 **PILLAR OF FIRE (IRE)**, 11, gr g Roselier (FR)—Cousin Flo **Paul Robson**
53 **PILLAR TO POST**, 6, b g Bluegrass Prince (IRE)—Parisana (FR) **Mr T. J. & Mrs H. Parrott**
54 ** **, 4, Ch g Classic Cliche (USA)—Poussetiere Deux (FR) **Mr & Mrs John Poynton**
55 **RESEDA (GER)**, 6, b m Lavirco (GER)—Reklame (EG) **R. J. Turton**
56 **RISK FACTOR**, 6, b g Classic Cliche (USA)—Easy Risk **Mr W. Gibber**
57 **RIVER PHANTOM (IRE)**, 8, b g Over The River (FR)—Cathilda (IRE) **G. Ketley**
58 **ROYAL TRIGGER**, 5, b g Double Trigger (IRE)—Jeronime (USA) **Lady Caffyn-Parsons & Mrs E. E. Dedman**
59 **ROYALEETY (IRE)**, 6, b g Garde Royale—La Grive (FR) **Mr & Mrs John Poynton**
60 **SHARMY (IRE)**, 9, b g Caerleon (USA)—Petticoat Lane **B. Vaughan S. Vaughan D. Allwood**
61 **THE BATTLIN BISHOP**, 6, br g Bishop of Cashel—Angel Drummer **Mr T. J. & Mrs H. Parrott**
62 **THE PRINCE**, 11, b g Machiavellian (USA)—Mohican Girl **P. Kelly**

MR IAN WILLIAMS—continued

63 TURNNOCARD (IRE), 6, b m Air Display (USA)—Night Blade **Mrs B. B. Whitehorn**
64 UNGARETTI (GER), 8, b g Law Society (USA)—Urena (GER) **B. L. Hiskey**
65 WAR OWL (USA), 8, gr g Linamix (FR)—Ganasheba (USA) **Mrs G. Braune**
66 WHITE DOVE (FR), 7, b m Beaudelaire (USA)—Hermine And Pearls (FR) **Creme de la Creme**

Other Owners: R. D. Allen, Ms D. S. Brown, Lady Caffyn-Parsons, G. J. Clinton, Mrs J. E. Clinton, D. G. Conyers, J. D. Cotton, Mrs B. Cotton, Mrs S. Dedman, A. C. Eaves, W. Edwyn-Jones, P. V. Harris, Ms R. J. Harris, H. R. Johnstone, A. S. Johnstone, G. J. King, Mrs M. E. Kirk, T. C. Marshall, Mrs C. Mitchener, J. A. Nash, T. Neill, R. J. Newbery, Dr R. D. P. Newland, R. F. Pavey, P. A. Rose, W. C. Tincknell, J. Tredwell, S. R. Trow.

Assistant Trainer: Chris Kinane

Jockey (NH): D R Dennis. **Conditional:** J. Doab, W. A. Worthington. **Apprentice:** D. Nolan. **Amateur:** Mr B. Gallagher.

---

634   MR N. S. L. WILLIAMS, South Molton
Postal: **Culverhill Farm, George Nympton, South Molton, Devon, EX36 4JE.**
Contacts: **HOME (01769) 574174 FAX (01769) 573661 MOBILE (07855) 450379**

1 BLANDINGS CASTLE, 4, ro g Cloudings (IRE)—Country House **Mr J. D. Cox & Mrs J. R. Williams**
2 4, B c Flemensfirth (USA)—Cheryls Pet (IRE) **Mrs J. R. Williams**
3 COMPLETE OUTSIDER, 4, b g Opera Ghost—Alice Passthorn **M. W. Ford**
4 4, B c Oscar (IRE)—Cush Maid **Mrs J. R. Williams**
5 DEAD-EYED DICK (IRE), 9, b g Un Desperado (FR)—Glendale Charmer **Mrs J. R. Williams**
6 DOM D'ORGEVAL (FR), 5, b g Belmez (USA)—Marie D'orgeval (FR) **Mrs J. R. Williams**
7 FEAR SIUIL (IRE), 12, b g Strong Gale—Astral River **Mr J. D. Cox & Mrs J. R. Williams**
8 HE'S THE BIZ (FR), 6, b g Nikos—Irun **Mrs J. R. Williams**
9 KINGS BROOK, 5, br g Alderbrook—Kins Token **Mr A. P. Gale**
10 LADY LOVEDAY, 4, b br f Panoramic—Cadal Queen (FR) **Mrs J. R. Williams**
11 MR CRAWFORD, 6, b g Opera Ghost—Alice Passthorn **Gale Force Two**
12 PHILSON RUN (IRE), 9, b g Un Desperado (FR)—Isis **Gale Force One**
13 4, Br c Supreme Leader—Stormy Miss (IRE) **Mrs J. R. Williams**
14 THE REAL DEAL (IRE), 4, b g Taipan (IRE)—Forest Mist **Mrs J. R. Williams**
15 THEOCRITUS (GER), 4, b g Trempolino (USA)—Thyatira (FR) **Gale Force Three**
16 TRAVEL DEHOUCHE, 5, b m Defacto (USA)—Travel Mystery **M. H. D. Madden**

THREE-YEAR-OLDS

17 DIZZY LIZZY, gr f Sendawar (IRE)—Black Velvet (FR) **Mrs J. R. Williams**

TWO-YEAR-OLDS

18 Ch c 24/4 Double Trigger (IRE)—Cadal Queen (FR) (Cadoudal (FR)) **Mrs J. R. Williams**

Other Owners: J. G. Storey.

Assistant Trainer: Mrs Jane Williams

---

635   MR S. C. WILLIAMS, Newmarket
Postal: **Diomed Stables, Hamilton Road, Newmarket, CB8 0PD.**
Contacts: **HOME (01638) 560143 YARD (01638) 663984**
FAX (01638) 560143 MOBILE (07730) 314102
E-MAIL scwilliams@ntlworld.com

1 BINAA (IRE), 4, b f Marju—Hadeb **James G. Thom**
2 BOLD BUNNY, 4, b f Piccolo—Bold And Beautiful **Freedom Farm Stud**
3 FILLAMEENA, 5, b m Robellino (USA)—Lotus Moon **John & Linda Godfrey**
4 FULVIO (USA), 5, b g Sword Dance—One Tuff Gal (USA) **J. L. Guillambert**
5 KILLMOREY, 4, ch g Nashwan (USA)—Zarma (FR) **Wood Farm Stud (Waresley) Partnership**
6 KOOL ACCLAIM, 4, b f Royal Applause—Carrie Kool **Carol Shekells & Associates**
7 PORTMEIRION, 4, b f Polish Precedent—India Atlanta **Usk Valley Stud**
8 PRETTY KOOL, 5, b m Inchinor—Carrie Kool **Carol Shekells & Associates**
9 SENDINTANK, 5, ch g Halling (USA)—Colleville **Steve Jones and Phil McGovern**
10 TREVIAN, 4, ch g Atraf—Ascend (IRE) **The Little Trev Partnership**
11 TYCHY, 6, ch m Suave Dancer (USA)—Touch of White **Mr P. Ellinas**
12 WONKY DONKEY, 4, b g Piccolo—Salinas **The Wonky Donkey Partnership**

MR S. C. WILLIAMS—continued

THREE-YEAR-OLDS

13 **ANOTHER MISK**, ch g Storm Boot (USA)—Pure Misk **The Another Misk Partnership**
14 **BLAZING BAILEY**, b g Mister Baileys—Wannaplantatree **Mr M. C. North**
15 **DAISYS GIRL**, b f Inchinor—Andbell **Mr S. J. Day**
16 **DROOPYS JOEL**, b g Primo Dominie—Zaima (IRE) **Tom Dorrington**
17 **EXPONENTIAL (IRE)**, b g Namid—Exponent (USA) **The Exponential Partnership**
18 **HIGH RHYTHM**, b f Piccolo—Slave To The Rythm (IRE) **Mr M. L. Ayers**
19 **HOLIDAY COCKTAIL**, b g Mister Baileys—Bermuda Lily **The B52's**
20 **IDYLL**, b f Dansili—Serene View (USA) **Alastair Simpson**
21 **JOSEAR**, b c Josr Algarhoud (IRE)—Real Popcorn (IRE) **The Nomads**
22 **LANKAWI**, ch g Unfuwain (USA)—Zarma (FR) **Four Winds Racing**
23 **LASTING IMAGE**, br f Zilzal (USA)—Minsden's Image **Mr I. A. Southcott**
24 **LITTLE LORD TOM (IRE)**, b g Fasliyev (USA)—Gan Ainm (IRE) **Mr J. W. Parry**
25 **MAMBAZO**, b c Dansili—Kalindi **Mr D. G. Burge**
26 **NODINA**, gr c Primo Dominie—Princess Tara **Throcking Racing**
27 **PRETTY WOMAN (IRE)**, ch f Night Shift (USA)—Kind of Cute **Mr A. A. Lyons**
28 **SMOOTH MOVER**, b g Mister Baileys—Dancing Heights (IRE) **Sacks Partnership**
29 **SPEEDIE ROSSINI (IRE)**, b g Rossini (USA)—Skatt **The Lager Khan**
30 **SWEET ROYALE**, b f Royal Applause—Sorara **Sandy & Lucille Bone**
31 **TYCHEROS**, b g Polar Falcon (USA)—Marie de Flandre (FR) **Mr S. C. Williams**

TWO-YEAR-OLDS

32 B f 20/1 Dansili—Colleville (Charly (FR)) (1500) **Mr P. McGrane**
33 B c 21/4 Primo Valentino (IRE)—Drudwen (Sayf El Arab (USA)) (4200) **Mr E. Lloyd**
34 B f 9/2 Zafonic (USA)—Fairlee Mixa (FR) (Linamix (FR)) (30000) **Four Winds Racing**
35 B f 28/3 Bertolini (USA)—Glensara (Petoski) (5000) **The Countryside Alliance Racing Partnership**
36 B c 3/3 Singspiel (IRE)—Heuston Station (IRE) (Fairy King (USA)) **Four Winds Racing**
37 **HOGMANEIGH (IRE)**, b c 22/4 Namid—
   Magical Peace (IRE) (Magical Wonder (USA)) (18000) **Sandy & Lucille Bone**
38 Ch f 4/3 Mark of Esteem (IRE)—Intervene (Zafonic (USA)) **Four Winds Racing**
39 **JAMES THE THIRD**, b c 18/3 Diktat—Attention Seeker (USA) (Exbourne (USA)) (16000) **Mr J. W. Parry**
40 **LORIINAE**, b f 20/2 Generous (IRE)—Courtain (USA) (Diesis) (1000) **Mrs A. R. Ruggles**
41 **MUCKLE**, ch f 14/4 Muhtarram (USA)—Crackle (Anshan) (2200) **Simon Tindall**
42 B f 11/3 Beckett (IRE)—Native Force (IRE) (Indian Ridge) (4000)
43 **NOBLE MINSTREL**, ch c 23/2 Fantastic Light (USA)—
   Sweetness Herself (Unfuwain (USA)) (45000) **Mr J. W. Parry**
44 Ch c 27/4 Halling (USA)—Panache Arabelle (Nashwan (USA)) (11000)
45 **RATIONALE (IRE)**, b c 15/2 Singspiel (IRE)—Logic (Slip Anchor) (17000) **Alastair Simpson**
46 **STEVE AUSTIN**, b c 11/4 Zafonic (USA)—Deegee (Warning) **Mr D. A. Shekells**

Other Owners: Mrs M. North, Mr C. Harper, Mr G. Dowler, Mr K. Childs, Mr M. Wakefield, A. G. Axton, J. L. W. Bicknell, A. L. Clarke, W. E. Enticknap, D. J. Evans, P. S. M. Geoghan, D. Alastair Hodge, T. Jacobs, J. M. Lamont, Mrs J. R. Lamont, Ms V. J. Lawson, Ms A. L. Osgood, Mrs J. M. Power, B. H. Prebble, G. D. Thompson, T. A. H. Wake, Mr G. V. Williams.

Assistant Trainer: Michael Hammond

---

636 **MRS S. D. WILLIAMS, South Molton**
Postal: Hilltown Farm, Mariansleigh, South Molton, Devon, EX36 4NS.
Contacts: PHONE (01769) 550291 FAX (01769) 550291 MOBILE (07969) 992152
E-MAIL sarahwilliams@hotmail.com WEBSITE www.sarahwilliamsracing.co.uk

1 **BALLY BOLSHOI (IRE)**, 5, b m Bob Back (USA)—Moscow Money (IRE) **Mrs Rowena Cotton**
2 **BARUM BELLE**, 5, b m Thowra (FR)—La Belle Shyanne **Barnstaple Racing Club**
3 **BOBBY GAYLE (IRE)**, 5, ch m Bob Back (USA)—Élite **W. N. Peto**
4 **DOUBLE HEADER (IRE)**, 6, b g Old Vic—Ballybeggan Lady (IRE) **F. R. Williamson**
5 **ECCENTRICITY**, 7, b m Emarati (USA)—Lady Electric **Mr C. P. Frampton & Miss P. A. Matthews**
6 **HOLLAND PARK (IRE)**, 8, gr g Roselier (FR)—Bluebell Avenue **B. M. Yin**
7 **MASTER BILLYBOY (IRE)**, 7, b g Old Vic—Clonodfoy **W. N. Peto**
8 **ONE FOR TERRY**, 5, b m Saddlers' Hall (IRE)—Crosschild (IRE) **Berry Racing**
9 **REPLACEMENT PET (IRE)**, 8, b m Petardia—Richardstown Lass (IRE) **Beck And The Boys**
10 **RYDON LANE (IRE)**, 9, br g Toca Madera—Polocracy (IRE) **D. C. Coard**

MRS S. D. WILLIAMS—continued

11 **SOVEREIGN'S GIFT,** 9, ch m Elegant Monarch—Cadeau d'aragon **B. W. Gillbard**
12 **SWORD LADY,** 7, b m Broadsword (USA)—Speckyfoureyes **Berry Racing**

Other Owners: J. M. Barlow, Mr C. P. Frampton, Mr C. J. James, Mr A. J. Kingdon, Miss P. Mathews, Mr P. Saxby, J. L. Whitten, Mrs A. Whitten.

---

637 **MISS V. M. WILLIAMS, Hereford**
Postal: **Aramstone, Kings Caple, Hereford, HR1 4TU.**
Contacts: **PHONE (01432) 840646 FAX (01432) 840830 MOBILE (07770) 627108**

1 **AFTER EIGHT (GER),** 5, br g Sir Felix (FR)—Amrei **Let's Live Racing**
2 **AGOSTINI (GER),** 4, ch c Platini (GER)—Ariostea (FR) **Mrs R. C. Hartley & Mr P. A. H. Hartley**
3 **ALCOPOP,** 6, b g Alderbrook—Albacyna **P. S. & B. M. Willcocks**
4 **ALMAH (SAF),** 7, b m Al Mufti (USA)—Jazz Champion (SAF) **P. A. Deal & Tweenhills Racing**
5 **ASHGREEN,** 8, b g Afzal—Space Kate **C. J. Green**
6 **AVITTA (IRE),** 6, b m Pennekamp (USA)—Alinova (USA) **P.A.Deal, A.Hirschfeld & M.Graham**
7 **BANKER COUNT,** 13, b g Lord Bud—Gilzie Bank **Mrs P. Brown & O. P. Darkin**
8 **BEWLEYS GUEST (IRE),** 6, b g Presenting—Pedigree Corner **Mr M. Davies**
9 **BLEU SUPERBE (FR),** 10, b g Epervier Bleu—Brett's Dream (FR) **P.A. Deal, A. Hirschfeld & J. Tyndall**
10 **BRAMBLEHILL DUKE (IRE),** 13, b g Kambalda—Scat-Cat **Mel Davies**
11 **CANADIAN STORM,** 4, gr g With Approval (CAN)—Sheer Gold (USA) **Direct Sales UK Ltd**
12 **CHIEF YEOMAN,** 5, br g Machiavellian (USA)—Step Aloft **B. Moore & E. C. Stephens**
13 **CITY POSER (IRE),** 10, b g Posen (USA)—Citissima **The Plum Merchants**
14 **CLEAR THINKING,** 5, b g Rainbow Quest (USA)—Coraline **Derek and Jean Clee**
15 **COACH LANE,** 4, b c Barathea (IRE)—Emplane (USA) **B. Moore & E. C. Stephens**
16 **DE BLANC (IRE),** 5, b m Revoque (IRE)—Queen's Share **Mrs K. A. Stuart**
17 **DICKENS (USA),** 5, ch g King of Kings (IRE)—Dellagrazia (USA) **P. Ryan & G. Houghton**
18 **DOOR OF KNOWLEDGE (USA),** 5, b br g Theatrical—Mynador **Lets Live Racing**
19 **FABULOUS JET (FR),** 5, ch g Starborough—Jetty (FR) **Mr M. Edwards**
20 **FAIR QUESTION (IRE),** 7, b g Rainbow Quest (USA)—Fair of the Furze **The MerseyClyde Partnership**
21 **FANTASTIC ARTS (FR),** 5, b g Royal Applause—Magic Arts (IRE) **Knightsbridge Business Centre (Glos) Ltd**
22 **FLYING ENTERPRISE (IRE),** 5, b g Darshaan—Flying Kiss (IRE) **Mr M. Edwards**
23 **GAN EAGLA (IRE),** 6, b g Paris House—Mafiosa **T. H. Jones**
24 **GRAND FINALE (IRE),** 8, b h Sadler's Wells (USA)—Final Figure (USA) **T. H. Jones**
25 **HIS NIBS (IRE),** 8, b g Afflora (IRE)—Mrs Jennifer **J. Galvanoni**
26 **IDOLE FIRST (IRE),** 6, b g Flemensfirth (USA)—Sharon Doll (IRE) **Direct Sales UK Ltd**
27 **IMAGINAIRE (USA),** 10, b g Quest For Fame—Hail The Dancer (USA) **Miss J.Davies,Mr L.Jakeman,Mr W.Fenn**
28 **INDALO (IRE),** 10, b g Lord Americo—Parson's Princess **ROA Arkle Partnership**
29 **ISMENE (IRE),** 9, b m Bad Conduct (USA)—Athena de L'isle (FR) **A. G. Parker & J. H. Parker**
30 **ITSONLYME (IRE),** 12, b g Broken Hearted—Over The Arctic **Mel Davies**
31 **JARRO (FR),** 9, b g Pistolet Bleu (IRE)—Junta (FR) **Mrs R. C. Hartley & Mr P. A. H. Hartley**
32 **JIMMY TENNIS (FR),** 8, b br g Video Rock (FR)—Via Tennise (FR) **Derek and Jean Clee**
33 **JOLLY BOY (FR),** 6, b g Franc Bleu Argent (USA)—Lady Charrecey (FR) **Favourites Racing Ltd**
34 **JURADO EXPRESS (IRE),** 9, b g Jurado (USA)—Express Film **Gallant Denco Wallace Whittle**
35 **JUST MAYBE (IRE),** 11, b g Glacial Storm (USA)—Purlace **W. E. Prichard**
36 **KELLY (SAF),** 8, b g Ethique (ARG)—Dancing Flower (SAF) **P. A. Deal**
37 **KELREV (FR),** 7, ch g Video Rock (FR)—Bellile II (FR) **Len Jakeman, Flintham, King & Roberts**
38 **KING ON THE RUN (IRE),** 12, b g King's Ride—Fly Run **Lady Harris**
39 **KOCK DE LA VESVRE (FR),** 7, b g Sassanian—Csardas (FR) **O. P. Dakin**
40 **KRAKOW BABA (FR),** 5, b g Sleeping Car (FR)—Babacha (FR) **Flintham, King, Jakeman & Roberts**
41 **LA CUENTA (IRE),** 5, b g Accordion—Foyle Wanderer (IRE) **J. Galvanoni**
42 **LIMERICK BOY (GER),** 7, b g Alwuhush (USA)—Limoges (GER) **Favourites Racing Ltd**
43 **LORD OLYMPIA (IRE),** 6, b g Lord Americo—Mooreshill (IRE) **Mrs S. A. Ryan**
44 **LORIENT EXPRESS (FR),** 6, b g Sleeping Car (FR)—Envie de Chalamont (FR) **Let's Live Racing**
45 **MA YAHAB,** 4, ch g Dr Fong (USA)—Bay Shade (USA) **M. J. Pilkington & M. Stewart**
46 **MALETTON (FR),** 5, b g Bulington (FR)—Reine Dougla (FR) **Mr M. Edwards**
47 **MAMBO DES MOTTES (FR),** 5, b g Useful (FR)—Julie des Mottes (FR) **John Nicholls (Trading) Ltd**
48 **MARATHEA (FR),** 4, b f Marathon (USA)—Shahmy (USA) **Sir Clement Freud**
49 **MISTY DANCER,** 6, gr g Vettori (IRE)—Light Fantastic **Pinks Gym & Leisure Wear Ltd**
50 **MOBASHER (IRE),** 6, b g Spectrum (IRE)—Danse Royale (IRE) **The 1961 Partnership**
51 **MOHAWK STAR (IRE),** 4, ch g Indian Ridge—Searching Star **Richard Abbott & Mario Stavrou**
52 **MON MOME (FR),** 5, b g Passing Sale (FR)—Etoile du Lion (FR) **Mrs V. A. Bingham**
53 **MONITA DES BOIS (FR),** 5, b m Snurge—Fauvette Grise (FR) **Vulkan Partners**
54 **MR PRESIDENT (GER),** 6, br g Surako (GER)—Mostly Sure (FR) **J M Boodle, A H M White, P M Shawyer**
55 **MY LADY LINK (FR),** 6, bl m Sleeping Car (FR)—Cadoudaline (FR) **Six Diamonds Partnership**

MISS V. M. WILLIAMS—continued

56 **NEPHITE (NZ)**, 11, b g Star Way—Te Akau Charmer (NZ) **Mrs H. Spencer & Mrs S. Thomas**
57 **NETHERLEY (FR)**, 6, gr g Beyssac (FR)—Lessons In Love (FR) **P. Ryan**
58 **NOISETINE (FR)**, 7, ch m Mansonnien (FR)—Notabilite (FR) **Mrs J. Yeomans**
59 **OUR PRIMA DONNA (IRE)**, 7, ch m Be My Native (USA)—Stage Debut **GPS Racing**
60 **POUGATCHEVA (FR)**, 6, ch m Epervier Bleu—Direct Sales **Direct Sales UK Ltd**
61 **RADCLIFFE (IRE)**, 8, b g Supreme Leader—Marys Course **M. L. Shone**
62 **REAL CRACKER (IRE)**, 6, b g Lahib (USA)—Loreo (IRE) **The Juggins Partnership**
63 **RESEARCHER**, 6, ch m Cosmonaut—Rest **Mrs K. A. Stuart**
64 **RIDERS REVENGE (IRE)**, 7, b g Norwich—Paico Ana **Dr M. A. Hamlin**
65 **RISINGTON**, 7, b g Afzal—Barton Rise **Dragon Racing**
66 **RUDOLF RASSENDYLL (IRE)**, 10, b g Supreme Leader—Chantel Rouge **Mrs Caroline Wilson**
67 **RUNNING MACHINE (IRE)**, 8, b g Classic Memory—Foxborough Lady **Favourites Racing Ltd**
68 **SCHUH SHINE (IRE)**, 8, gr g Roselier (FR)—Naar Chamali **Mrs Gill Harrison**
69 **SIR CUMFERENCE**, 9, b g Sir Harry Lewis (USA)—Puki Puki **Mrs N. L. M. Moores**
70 **SONEVAFUSHI (FR)**, 7, b g Ganges (USA)—For Kicks (FR) **Mr B. C. Dice**
71 **SPARTACUS BAY (FR)**, 4, b g Simply Great (FR)—Decent Slave **You Can Be Sure**
72 **SPRING LOVER (FR)**, 6, b g Fijar Tango (FR)—Kailasa (FR) **Mr M. Edwards**
73 **SWEET OONA (FR)**, 6, gr m Kendor (FR)—Poplife (FR) **The Leadenhall Partnership**
74 **THE OUTLIER (IRE)**, 7, gr g Roselier (FR)—Shuil A Cuig **Mr P. J. Murphy**
75 **THE RISEN LARK (IRE)**, 5, b m Celtic Swing—May Hills Legacy (IRE) **John Williams**
76 **THESIS (IRE)**, 7, ch g Definite Article—Chouette **The 1961 Partnership**
77 **TRIBAL DANCER (IRE)**, 11, ch g Commanche Run—Cute Play **You Can Be Sure**
78 **TRIGGERLINO**, 5, b m Double Trigger (IRE)—Voolino **Mrs V. E. Nock-Sampson**
79 **TROUBLE AHEAD (IRE)**, 14, b g Cataldi—Why 'o' Why **Mrs S. C. Nelson**
80 **VENICE ROAD (IRE)**, 4, ch g Halling (USA)—Croeso Cynnes **T. W. Bloodstock Ltd**
81 **WILD SPICE (IRE)**, 10, b g Mandalus—Curry Lunch **M. Crabb**
82 **WISCALITUS (GER)**, 6, b g Lead On Time (USA)—Wiscaria (GER) **Direct Sales UK Ltd**
83 **WOODY VALENTINE (USA)**, 4, ch g Woodman (USA)—Mudslinger (USA) **Favourites Racing Ltd**

THREE-YEAR-OLDS

84 Gr c Almutawakel—Hariyana (IRE) **Mr B. C. Dice**

Jockey (NH): S. Thomas. **Conditional:** L. Treadwell, L. Stephens, A. O'Keeffe, P. C. O'Neill.

---

638 **MRS L. V. WILLIAMSON, Chester**
Postal: **Saighton Hall, Saighton, Chester, Cheshire, CH3 6EE.**
Contacts: **PHONE (01244) 314254 MOBILE (07970) 437679**

1 **ALNEY ISLAND**, 7, b g Puget (USA)—Queen of The Nile **Mrs L. V. Williamson**
2 **CELTIC STAR (IRE)**, 7, b g Celtic Swing—Recherchee **Partnership**
3 **CITY SPRINGS**, 5, b m Parthian Springs—City's Sister **Please Hold UK**
4 **COLLIERS COURT**, 8, b g Puget (USA)—Rag Time Belle **The Castle Bend Syndicate**
5 **HAREM SCAREM (IRE)**, 14, b g Lord Americo—River Rescue **Colin Mather & Stephen Tomkinson**
6 **HOW RAN ON (IRE)**, 14, b brg Mandalus—Kelly's Bridge **Halewood International Ltd**
7 **KILT (FR)**, 7, ch g Luchiroverte (IRE)—Unite II (FR) **Halewood International Ltd**
8 **LADY LAMBRINI**, 5, b m Overbury (IRE)—Miss Lambrini **Mrs L. V. Williamson**
9 **LAMBRINI BIANCO (IRE)**, 7, br g Roselier (FR)—Darjoy **Mrs L. V. Williamson**
10 **LAMBRINI MIST**, 7, gr g Terimon—Miss Fern **Halewood International Ltd**
11 **MORGAN BE**, 5, b g Alderbrook—Vicie **Mr S. Breakspeare**
12 **RED ALERT MAN**, 7, ch g Sharp Charter—Tukurua **Halewood International Ltd**
13 **RED SQUARE LAD (IRE)**, 9, ch g Toulon—Tempestuous Girl **Mrs L. V. Williamson**
14 **SANDAL SAPHIRE**, 6, b m Danzig Connection (USA)—Mudflap **W. J. Dobson**
15 **SHERANI**, 5, b m Cigar—Aquainted **V. de Lanerolle**
16 **TOP OF THE DEE**, 8, ch m Rakaposhi King—Lavenham's Last **M. S. Williamson**

THREE-YEAR-OLDS

17 **ALL A DREAM**, br f Desert Story (IRE)—Alioli **J. Riley**
18 **ALPHONSINA**, b f Josr Algarhoud (IRE)—Club Elite **W. J. Dobson**

TWO-YEAR-OLDS

19 **LA BOMBA VELOCE**, b f 14/2 Tomba—Charleigh Keary (Sulaafah (USA)) (1000) **Mr C. T. O'Donnell**
20 **MIDNIGHT DIAMOND (IRE)**, b c 1/5 Alzao (USA)—Derena (FR) (Crystal Palace (FR)) (6500) **Miss J. M. Eaton**

MRS L. V. WILLIAMSON—continued

21 NAVAL HERO (IRE), b c 11/3 Arkadian Hero (USA)—Isla Negra (IRE) (Last Tycoon) (800) **J. Riley**
22 Ch f 14/5 Piccolo—Nevita (Never So Bold) (1000) **Mrs L. V. Williamson**

Other Owners: J. P. Clarke, Mrs K. J. Hughes, Mr C. W. Mather, K. L. Mullett, Mr G. L. Reed, S. H. Tomkinson.

Assistant Trainer: Mark Williamson

Jockey (NH): O. McPhail. **Amateur:** Mr D. Gater.

639

MR A. J. WILSON, Cheltenham
Postal: **Glenfall Stables, Ham, Charlton Kings, Cheltenham, Gloucestershire, GL52 6NH.**
Contacts: **PHONE** (01242) 244713 **FAX** (01242) 226319 **MOBILE** (07932) 157243
E-MAIL ajwglenfall@aol.com

1 BOB'S TEMPTATION, 6, br g Bob's Return (IRE)—Temptation (IRE) **The Cotswold Partnership**
2 CERULEAN, 7, ch g Polar Falcon (USA)—Billie Blue **J. A. Cover**
3 5, Ch g Bandmaster (USA)—Letitica **Mrs M. J. Wilson**
4 LORD THOMAS (IRE), 7, b g Grand Lodge (USA)—Noble Rocket **E. T. D. Leadbeater**
5 PERFECT VENUE (IRE), 12, b g Danehill (USA)—Welsh Fantasy **Mrs M. J. Wilson**
6 SALLIEMAK, 7, b m Makbul—Glenbrook Fort **E. T. D. Leadbeater**
7 SHARP RALLY (IRE), 4, ch g Night Shift (USA)—La Pointe **H. J. Fentum**
8 VIVANTE (IRE), 7, b m Toulon—Splendidly Gay **P. A. Deal**
9 WIZARD LOOKING, 4, b g Wizard King—High Stepping (IRE) **J. A. Cover**

Other Owners: Ms J. Baker, J. W. Griffin, B. J. Hughes, Mrs T. D. Pilkington, D. A. Smyth.

640

MR C. R. WILSON, Darlington
Postal: **Manor Farm, Manfield, Darlington, Co. Durham, DL2 2RW.**
Contacts: **PHONE** (01325) 374595 **MOBILES** (07815) 952306/(07721) 379277
E-MAIL wilsoncracing@ad.com

1 CELTIC FLOW, 7, b m Primitive Rising (USA)—Celtic Lane **Exors of the late W. R. Wilson**
2 COTTAGE HILL, 6, b m Primitive Rising (USA)—Celtic Lane **Exors of the late W. R. Wilson**
3 ELTRINGHAM, 5, b m Milieu—Whosgotsillysense **Mrs S. Martin**
4 QUARTERSTAFF, 11, b g Charmer—Quaranta **Mrs J. Wilson**
5 ROYAL FRIEND, 6, b g Environment Friend—La Princesse **Mrs J. Wilson**
6 SEA MAIZE, 7, b m Sea Raven (IRE)—Dragons Daughter **Exors of the late W. R. Wilson**
7 ZEYDNAA (IRE), 5, b g Bahhare (USA)—Hadawah (USA) **A. E. Lea**

THREE-YEAR-OLDS

8 SO INDEPENDENT, b f Tipsy Creek (USA)—So Bold **S. R. Bainbridge**

TWO-YEAR-OLDS

9 Br f 22/5 Hunting Lion (IRE)—Dragons Daughter (Mandrake Major) **Mrs J. Wilson**

Assistant Trainer: Julie Wilson

641

MR N. WILSON, York
Postal: **Grange Farm, Upper Helmsley, York, YO41 1NA.**
Contacts: **HOME/WORK** (01759) 372331 **OFFICE** (01759) 371395 **MOBILE** (07808) 162631
E-MAIL noelwilsonracing@virginnet.com **WEBSITE** www.noelwilsonracing.com

1 ACOMB, 5, b g Shaamit (IRE)—Aurora Bay (IRE) **I. W. Glenton**
2 AIR MAIL, 8, b g Night Shift (USA)—Wizardry **Ian W Glenton John Watson Steven Downes**
3 ALWAYS FLYING (USA), 4, ch g Fly So Free (USA)—Dubiously (USA) **I. W. Glenton**
4 BELTER, 5, b g Terimon—Bellinote (FR) **Five Boys**
5 BEST FLIGHT, 5, gr g Sheikh Albadou—Bustling Nelly **I. W. Glenton**
6 CAPTAIN SAIF, 5, b h Compton Place—Bahawir Pour **Nosredla**
7 DANIAN (IRE), 6, b g Fourstars Allstar (USA)—Ruby Belle (IRE) **Mr H. Beggs**
8 DOUBLE BLADE, 10, b g Kris—Sesame **Razor Sharp Partnership**
9 EXIT FAST (USA), 4, ch g Announce (USA)—Distinct Beauty (USA) **Mrs N. C. Wilson**
10 GOLDEN BOUNTY, 6, b g Bahamian Bounty—Cumbrian Melody **I. W. Glenton**

MR N. WILSON—continued

11 **JBALLINGALL**, 6, b g Overbury (IRE)—Sister Delaney **W R S**
12 **LATALOMNE (USA)**, 11, ch g Zilzal (USA)—Sanctuary **Alderclad Roofing/Mr K. M. Everitt**
13 **LOCOMBE HILL (IRE)**, 9, b g Barathea (IRE)—Roberts Pride **I. W. Glenton**
14 **LOVES TRAVELLING (IRE)**, 5, b g Blues Traveller (IRE)—Fast Love (IRE) **Mrs K. A. Ridley**
15 **MAD MAX TOO**, 6, gr g Environment Friend—Marnworth **Mrs K. A. Ridley**
16 **MINIBULE (FR)**, 5, ch m Funambule (USA)—Mipour (FR) **John Watson & Ian W. Glenton**
17 **MONSIEUR DELAGE**, 5, b g Overbury (IRE)—Sally Ho **G. Griffin**
18 **NICOZETTO (FR)**, 5, b g Nicolotte—Arcizette (FR) **M. Wilson**
19 **PAGAN CEREMONY (USA)**, 4, ch g Rahy (USA)—Delightful Linda (USA) **I. W. Glenton**
20 **SANTIBURI LAD (IRE)**, 8, b g Namaqualand (USA)—Suggia **Mrs K. A. Ridley**
21 **SEYED (IRE)**, 5, b g Desert Prince (IRE)—Royal Bounty (IRE) **I. W. Glenton**
22 **STALLONE**, 8, ch g Brief Truce (USA)—Bering Honneur (USA) **Mrs K. A. Ridley**
23 **STERLING GUARANTEE (USA)**, 7, b g Silver Hawk (USA)—
Sterling Pound (USA) **Ian W Glenton Peter Whinham Keith Benson**
24 **UNITED NATIONS**, 4, ch g Halling (USA)—Congress (IRE) **Mrs K. A. Ridley**
25 **YENALED**, 8, gr g Rambo Dancer (CAN)—Fancy Flight (FR) **Watson Wilson Mckinnon**
26 **ZANJEER**, 5, b g Averti (IRE)—Cloudslea (USA) **M. Wilson**

TWO-YEAR-OLDS

27 B f 14/3 Forzando—Fly South (Polar Falcon (USA)) (3800)
28 Ch c 8/5 Titus Livius (FR)—Orange Royale (IRE) (Exit To Nowhere (USA)) (1800)
29 B f 26/3 Desert Style (IRE)—Osprey Point (IRE) (Entrepreneur) (1200)
30 Ch c 7/4 Titus Livius (FR)—Torrmana (IRE) (Ela-Mana-Mou) (3600)
31 Ch f 15/4 Inchinor—Zaragossa (Paris House) (2200)

Other Owners: T. Alderson, E. Bell, John Chapman, Mr A. Duffy, J. Hope, S. J. Laverick, P. M. Lodge, Mrs V. McGee, Mr K. A. Millar, A. J. Nevison, P. D. Price, Mr R. Price, I. Robinson, M. G. Shepherd, Brian Womersley.

Assistant Trainer: Mrs N C Wilson

Jockey (NH): P. Robson, A. Ross. **Apprentice:** T. Hamilton, P. Mulrennan, D. Tudhope. **Amateur:** Mr N. Wilson.

---

642 MISS S. J. WILTON, Stoke-on-Trent
Postal: **Round Meadow Racing Stables, Rownal Road, Wetley Rocks, Stoke-On-Trent, Staffordshire, ST9 0BP.**
Contacts: **HOME (01782) 550861 OFFICE (01782) 550115 FAX (01782) 551548
MOBILE (07771) 650010**

1 **ARAGLIN**, 6, b g Sadler's Wells (USA)—River Cara (USA) **John Pointon and Sons**
2 **BARON DE PICHON (IRE)**, 9, b g Perugino (USA)—Ariadne **John Pointon and Sons**
3 **BOING BOING (IRE)**, 5, b g King's Theatre (IRE)—Limerick Princess (IRE) **John Pointon and Sons**
4 **COUNT DE MONEY (IRE)**, 10, b g Last Tycoon—Menominee **John Pointon and Sons**
5 **CRIMSON DANCER**, 5, b m Groom Dancer (USA)—Crimson Rosella **John Pointon and Sons**
6 **DANTON (IRE)**, 7, ch g Cadeaux Genereux—Royal Circle **John Pointon and Sons**
7 **FINE FRENZY (IRE)**, 5, b m Great Commotion (USA)—Fine Project (IRE) **John Pointon and Sons**
8 **FIRST DYNASTY (USA)**, 5, br b h Danzig (USA)—Willow Runner (USA) **John Pointon and Sons**
9 **FORTY FORTE**, 9, b g Pursuit of Love—Cominna **John Pointon and Sons**
10 **IMPREVUE (IRE)**, 11, ch m Priolo (USA)—Las Bela **P. W. Saunders**
11 **KHALADJISTAN (IRE)**, 7, gr g Tirol—Khaladja (IRE) **John Pointon and Sons**
12 **MELLEDGAN (IRE)**, 8, b m Catrail (USA)—Dark Hyacinth (IRE) **John Pointon and Sons**
13 **NZAME (IRE)**, 7, b g Darshaan—Dawnsio (IRE) **John Pointon and Sons**
14 **RELATIVE HERO (IRE)**, 5, ch g Entrepreneur—Aunty (FR) **John Pointon and Sons**
15 **REVELINO (IRE)**, 6, b g Revoque—Forelino (USA) **John Pointon and Sons**
16 **SOFISIO**, 8, ch g Efisio—Legal Embrace (CAN) **John Pointon and Sons**
17 **THE FLYER (IRE)**, 8, b g Blues Traveller (IRE)—National Ballet **John Pointon and Sons**
18 **THE RENDERER**, 9, b g Homo Sapien—Kingsley **John Pointon and Sons**
19 **TWO OF CLUBS**, 4, b g First Trump—Sulaka **John Pointon and Sons**
20 **VITELUCY**, 6, b m Vettori (IRE)—Classic Line **John Pointon and Sons**

Conditional: T. Burrows. **Amateur:** Mr A. Swinswood.

643 MR P. L. WINKWORTH, Chiddingfold

Postal: Robins Farm Racing Stables, Fisher Lane, Chiddingfold, Surrey, GU8 4TB.
Contacts: PHONE (01428) 685025 FAX (01483) 200878 MOBILE (07968) 799950
E-MAIL peter.winkworth@cbcf.com

1 **ARKHOLME**, 4, b g Robellino (USA)—Free Spirit (IRE) **Mr I. Russell, Mr B. J. Malone**
2 **AT THE DOUBLE**, 9, b g Sure Blade (USA)—Moheli **Mr P. Winkworth**
3 **BANDIT BROWN (IRE)**, 9, b g Supreme Leader—Parkroe Lady (IRE) **R. D. Barber & R. J. B. Blake**
4 **CHAMPAGNE SUNDAE (IRE)**, 7, b g Supreme Leader—Partners In Crime **Sundae Best**
5 **CHART TOPPER (IRE)**, 5, b m Glacial Storm (USA)—Divine Affair (IRE) **N H Bloodstock Limited**
6 **CONCERT PIANIST**, 10, b g Rakaposhi King—Divine Affair (IRE) **Ms J. P. Segal, Mrs C. Barber**
7 **DERVALLOC (IRE)**, 8, b g Zaffaran (USA)—Keeping Company **Mr P. Winkworth**
8 **DRY OLD PARTY (IRE)**, 6, ch g Un Desperado (FR)—The Vine Browne (IRE) **Mr P. Winkworth**
9 **DUNSFOLD DUKE**, 5, b g Cloudings (IRE)—Rositary (FR) **Mr P. Winkworth**
10 **GOLD TARIFF (IRE)**, 5, b g Good Thyne (USA)—Ashville Lady (IRE) **Mr Victor Martin**
11 **GROUSE MOOR (IRE)**, 6, b g Distant View (USA)—Caithness (USA) **Mr P. Winkworth**
12 **INAKI (FR)**, 8, b g Dounba (FR)—Incredule (FR) **Robert Scott & Partners**
13 **INSTANT APPEAL**, 8, gr g Terimon—Free Travel **G. Clark, C. Haycock, M. Rogerson**
14 **JUST A TOUCH**, 9, ch g Rakaposhi King—Minim **R N Scott, R G Robinson, Peter Broste**
15 **KEN SCOTT (FR)**, 7, b g Kendor (FR)—Scottish Bride (FR) **Mr P. Winkworth**
16 **LEVALLOIS (IRE)**, 9, b g Trempolino (USA)—Broken Wave **Mr & Mrs James Hayman-Joyce**
17 **MANITOU SPRINGS**, 8, br g Mandalus—Swift Conveyance (IRE) **Mr P. Winkworth**
18 **MOUNT KIMBLE (IRE)**, 9, b g Montelimar (USA)—Sweet Thunder **Mrs T. A. Winkworth**
19 **NOBEL BLEU DE KERPAUL (FR)**, 4, b g Pistolet Bleu (IRE)—Gecika de Kerpaul (FR) **Brilliant By You**
20 **ROZNIC (FR)**, 7, b g Nikos—Rozamie (FR) **Mr P. Winkworth**
21 **SHERIFF ROSCOE**, 5, b g Roscoe Blake—Silva Linda **The Ten Gallon Partnership**
22 **SIGNATURE TUNE (IRE)**, 6, b g Gothland (FR)—Divine Affair (IRE) **Mr S. Martyn**
23 **SOSSUS VLEI**, 9, b g Inchinor—Sassalya **Mr P. Winkworth**
24 **SUPER TIP (IRE)**, 7, b g Supreme Leader—Tip Marie (IRE) **Mr P. Winkworth**
25 **TUCK IN**, 8, b g Good Thyne (USA)—Always Shining **Help-Yourself**
26 **WALTER (IRE)**, 6, ch g Presenting—Siberian Princess **Mr P. Winkworth**
27 **WENGER (FR)**, 5, b g Unfuwain (USA)—Molly Dance **Mr P. Winkworth**

THREE-YEAR-OLDS

28 **IT'S A HOTTIE**, b g Bahamian Bounty—Laser Light Lady **Mr P. Winkworth**
29 **RIDE SAFARI**, b g Fraam—Vocation (IRE) **Mr M. Gould**
30 **SAFARI ADVENTURES (IRE)**, b g King's Theatre (IRE)—Persian Walk (FR) **Team Safari**
31 **SAFARI SUNSET (IRE)**, b g Fayruz—Umlani (IRE) **Mr P. Winkworth**

TWO-YEAR-OLDS

32 **BRAZILIAN STYLE**, br f 9/4 Exit To Nowhere (USA)—
                     Cosmic Star (Siberian Express (USA)) (1523) **Mrs J. J. Muddle**
33 **DANISH EXPRESS (IRE)**, b c 15/3 Danetime (IRE)—Jungle Story (IRE) (Alzao (USA)) (22000) **Pay And Play**
34 **FLOATING BANKER**, b c 22/3 Zieten (USA)—Form At Last (Formidable (USA)) (3800) **Mr P. Winkworth**
35 **KARSHAAN (FR)**, b c 31/3 Kahyasi—Mon Petitnamour (IRE) (Darshaan) (8048) **The Ten Gallon Partnership**
36 **MIC AUBIN (FR)**, b c 11/4 Broadway Flyer (USA)—Patney (FR) (Hasty Tudor (USA)) (7377) **Mr P. Winkworth**
37 **MY LADY VALENTINE**, b f 23/2 Bahamian Bounty—
                     Laser Light Lady (Tragic Role (USA)) (1047) **Mrs Pam MacMillan, Mr Richard Muddle**
38 **OCEAN FURY**, b g 19/2 Lujain (USA)—Constant Delight (Never So Bold) (10000) **Mr C. Ryan, Mr M. Gould**
39 **SAFARI MISCHIEF**, b c 26/3 Primo Valentino (IRE)—Night Gypsy (Mind Games) (24000) **Team Safari**
40 **SUNRISE SAFARI (IRE)**, b c 16/2 Mozart (USA)—Lady Scarlett (Woodman (USA)) (30000) **Team Safari**

Other Owners: Mr Patrick Allen, Mr Rob Brook, Mr D. E. Chambers, Mr Simon N. Champ, Mr Greg Chamberlain, Mr Angus Donaldson, Mrs Lois Eadie, Mr Rupert Fleming, Mr Andy Goodsir, Mr N. Fyler, Mrs Sal Marks, Mrs Victoria Lowrie, Mr Alex Lowrie, Mr Tom Little, Mrs Gillian Hayward, Mrs Lottie Hayman-Joyce, Mrs Jennie Hardless, Mr Peter Hall, Mrs Uschi Williams, Mr J. Waterlow, Mrs Camilla Waterlow, Mr Matthew Turner, Mrs Y. C. Timberlake, Mr Rupert Taylor, Mrs Rhona Reynolds, Mr D. Redvers, Mr Chris Poltera, Mr D. R. Obank, Mr Jamie Moyes, Mr Carl Morris, Mr Keith Marsden, Mrs Rosemary Gourlay, Mrs Jo Farrant, Mrs Cax Du Pon, J. Palmer-Brown, C. C. Shand Kydd, B. T. Stewart-Brown Esq, A. J. Viall.

Assistant Trainer: Anton Pearson

Jockey (flat): P. Doe. **Jockey (NH):** L. Aspell, P. Hide.

644 MR D. J. WINTLE, Cheltenham

Postal: **Lavender Hill Stud, Naunton, Cheltenham, Gloucestershire, GL54 3AZ.**
Contacts: **PHONE (01451) 850182/850893 FAX (01451) 850187 MOBILE (07798) 822477**
E-MAIL info@lavenderhillstud.co.uk WEBSITE www.lavenderhillstud.co.uk

1 **BAMBY (IRE)**, 5, b m Glacial Storm (USA)—Ardfallon (IRE) **Mrs S. Granger**
2 **BUSTISU**, 8, b m Rakaposhi King—Tasmin Gayle (IRE) **J. W. Egan**
3 **CAMILLE PISSARRO (USA)**, 5, b g Red Ransom (USA)—Serenity **J. W. Egan**
4 **CEOPERK (IRE)**, 6, ch m Executive Perk—Golden Mela **J. W. Egan**
5 **HEATHERLEA SQUIRE (NZ)**, 7, b g His Royal Highness (NZ)—Misty Gleam (NZ) **Mrs R. K. Wilkerson**
6 **KEY PHIL (FR)**, 7, ch g Beyssac (FR)—Rivolie (FR)
7 **MEAD (IRE)**, 8, b g Mujadil (USA)—Sweetest Thing (IRE) **Lyonshall Racing**
8 **MUSICAL MAYHEM (IRE)**, 12, b g Shernazar—Minstrels Folly (USA) **Mr A. Wintle**
9 **PEARL ISLAND (USA)**, 4, b g Kingmambo (USA)—Mother of Pearl (IRE) **Mr D. J. Wintle**
10 **REAL DEFINITION**, 6, gr g Highest Honor (FR)—Segovia **Lady Blyth**
11 **ROYAL NIECE (IRE)**, 6, b m Rakaposhi King—Sister Stephanie (IRE) **Mr M & J Gent, Mr C White, Mrs M Turner**
12 **SEVENEIGHTSIX (IRE)**, 5, ch m Old Vic—Necochea **S. Bell**
13 **SILK APPEAL**, 5, b m Lord of Appeal—Amazing Silks **Mick Coulson, John Bull, John Gent**
14 **STORM CLEAR (IRE)**, 6, b g Mujadil (USA)—Escape Path **Mr Derek Boocock and Mrs Joan Egan**
15 **TOO POSH TO SHARE**, 7, b m Rakaposhi King—Two Shares **Mr D. J. Wintle**
16 **WEARERICH**, 8, ch m Alflora (IRE)—Weareagrandmother **Mr D. J. Wintle**
17 **YASSAR (IRE)**, 10, b g Yashgan—Go Hunting (IRE) **Lavender Hill Stud L.L.C.**

Other Owners: R. O. Addis, R. R. Jones.

Assistant Trainer: Mr Michael Finn, Mr Graham McCourt

Jockey (NH): W. Marston, J. Mogford. Conditional: R. Cummings. Amateur: Mr A. Wintle.

645 MR I. A. WOOD, Upper Lambourn

Postal: **Neardown Stables, Upper Lambourn, Hungerford, Berkshire, RG17 8QP.**
Contacts: **PHONE (01488) 72324 FAX (01488) 72877 MOBILE (07775) 508111**

1 **BJORLING**, 4, ch c Opening Verse (USA)—Pola Star (IRE) **Miss P. J. C. Watson**
2 **CATCH THE WIND**, 4, b f Bahamian Bounty—Tinkerbird **C. S. Tateson**
3 **CICATRICE**, 4, ch g Wolfhound (USA)—Capricious Lady (IRE) **Miss J. E. Reed**
4 **CORNISH GOLD**, 4, b f Slip Anchor—Sans Diablo (IRE) **L. Lockwood, S. Marsh, M. Burne**
5 **DESERT DAISY (IRE)**, 4, gr f Desert Prince (IRE)—Pomponette (USA) **Neardown Stables**
6 **HEARTBEAT**, 4, b f Pursuit of Love—Lyrical Bid (USA) **Neardown Stables**
7 **MORAG**, 4, b f Aragon—Minnehaha **D. Miller**
8 **MOST-SAUCY**, 9, br m Most Welcome—So Saucy **Mrs A. M. Riney**
9 **PHRED**, 5, ch g Safawan—Phlirty **Neardown Stables**
10 **RED SOVEREIGN**, 4, b f Danzig Connection (USA)—Ruby Princess (IRE) **Miss Jacqueline Goodearl**
11 **STYLISH SUNRISE (IRE)**, 4, b g Desert Style (IRE)—Anita At Dawn (IRE) **Neardown Stables**
12 **SWEET REPLY**, 4, ch f Opening Verse (USA)—Sweet Revival **C. S. Tateson**
13 **THAAYER**, 10, b g Wolfhound (USA)—Hamaya (USA) **Mrs J. Wood**

THREE-YEAR-OLDS

14 **ACKNOWLEDGEMENT**, b c Josr Algarhoud (IRE)—On Request (IRE) **Woodhaven Racing Syndicate**
15 B f Bahhare (USA)—Another Rainbow (IRE) **Kilnamaragh Stud**
16 **BARNBROOK EMPIRE (IRE)**, b f Second Empire (IRE)—Home Comforts **Mr H. Barnbrook**
17 **BEAU MARCHE**, b g My Best Valentine—Beau Dada (IRE) **C. H. Shankland**
18 **BEE STINGER**, b c Almaty (IRE)—Nest Egg **Neardown Racing Club**
19 **BERHAM MALDU (IRE)**, b f Fraam—Corniche Quest (IRE) **Richard Lewis**
20 **BRENDAN'S SURPRISE**, b g Faustus (USA)—Primrose Way **Mrs A. M. Riney**
21 **BRIAR GHYLL**, ch f Zaha (CAN)—Charlotte Penny **Miss P. J. C. Watson**
22 **CARIBBEAN DIAMOND (IRE)**, b f Imperial Ballet (IRE)—Bebe Auction (IRE) **Sporting Occasions**
23 **CHANTELLE'S DREAM**, ch f Compton Place—Polar Peak **Neardown Stables**
24 **DISPOL IN MIND**, b f Mind Games—Sans Diablo (IRE) **Thomas & Susan Blane**
25 **DYNAMIC BEMMY**, ch f Fleetwood (IRE)—Wigit **Neardown Stables**
26 B c Imperial Ballet (IRE)—Firedancer **Neardown Stables**
27 **JAMAICAN (UAE)**, ch c Timber Country (USA)—Notting Hill **A1 Racing, Binks & Sellers**
28 **JUSTAQUESTION**, b f Pursuit of Love—Queenbird **C. H. Shankland**
29 **KERESFORTH**, b g Mind Games—Bullion **Neardown Stables**
30 **KING OF STING**, ch c Compton Place—Dance of The Swans (IRE) **A1 Racing**

MR I. A. WOOD—continued

31 **LADY ALGARHOUD (FR)**, b f Josr Algarhoud (IRE)—Lady of Limerick (IRE) **Neardown Racing Club**
32 **LARA'S GIRL**, b f Tipsy Creek (USA)—Joe's Dancer **Sporting Occasions**
33 **MA'AM (USA)**, ch f Royal Anthem (USA)—Hide the Bride (USA) **Neardown Racing Club**
34 **MEDITATION**, ch f Inchinor—Trojan Desert **P. E. Barrett**
35 **MICKEHAHA**, b c Lake Coniston (IRE)—Minnehaha **D. Miller**
36 B f Spectrum (IRE)—Pirouette **Lewis Caterers**
37 **PRINCELYWALLYWOGAN**, b c Princely Heir (IRE)—Dublivia **Neardown Racing Club**
38 **ROYAL MISS**, b f Royal Applause—Foreign Mistress **Mr H. Duery**
39 **SAPPHIRE PRINCESS**, b f Namaqualand—Breakfast Creek **Sporting Occasions**
40 **SHE'S MY OUTSIDER**, b f Docksider (USA)—Solar Flare (IRE) **Lewis Caterers**
41 B c Fraam—Silk Daisy **Richard Lewis**
42 **SILVER CREEK**, gr c Tipsy Creek (USA)—Silver Wedding **The Dirty Dozen Partnership**
43 **STAN'S GIRL**, b f Fraam—Gigetta (IRE) **The Stan James Winners**
44 **TAKEMETOYOURHEART**, ch f Zaha (CAN)—Mother Molly **Neardown Stables**
45 **ZIZZLE**, ch c Zaha (CAN)—Maria Cappuccini **D. Bass**

TWO-YEAR-OLDS

46 **ALEXANDRITE**, b c 9/3 Mind Games—Millie's Lady (IRE) (Common Grounds) (5200) **Thomas & Susan Blane**
47 B c 6/3 Montjeu (IRE)—Breakfast Bay (IRE) (Charnwood Forest (IRE)) (10000) **Lewis Caterers**
48 B f 4/4 Groom Dancer (USA)—Bron Hilda (IRE) (Namaqualand (USA)) (800) **J. Purcell**
49 Ch f 15/5 Piccolo—Cayla (Tumble Wind) (5700) **Neardown Racing Club**
50 B c 20/4 Vettori (IRE)—Desert Nomad (Green Desert (USA)) (7000) **Graham Bradbury**
51 B f 24/3 Bertolini (USA)—Edgeaway (Ajdal (USA)) (1142) **Neardown Racing Club**
52 B f 2/5 Cyrano de Bergerac—Exit (Exbourne (USA)) (380) **Neardown Racing Club**
53 **FASHION CHIC**, b f 18/3 Averti (IRE)—Fashion Bride (IRE) (Prince Rupert (FR)) (476) **C. H. Shankland**
54 Ch c 24/4 Most Welcome—Glenfinlass (Lomond (USA)) (7500) **Neardown Racing Club**
55 Br f 8/3 Bahhare (USA)—Habla Me (IRE) (Fairy King (USA)) (9523) **Neardown Racing Club**
56 **HAITI DANCER**, b f 7/3 Josr Algarhoud (IRE)—
    Haitienne (FR) (Green Dancer (USA)) (7500) **Belmore Lane Stud Racing Partnership**
57 B f 11/3 Mujahid (USA)—Heavens Above (FR) (Pistolet Bleu (IRE)) (5500) **Neardown Racing Club**
58 **JAZZ LADY (IRE)**, b f 20/4 Mujahid (USA)—La Fija (USA) (Dixieland Band (USA)) (6666) **C. H. Shankland**
59 Ch c 6/2 Spinning World (USA)—Mar Blue (FR) (Marju (IRE)) **Richard Lewis**
60 Ch f 10/2 Golden Snake (USA)—Minette (Bishop of Cashel) (800) **E. Dafydd**
61 B f 13/4 College Chapel—Minnehaha (Be My Chief (USA)) (6000) **Neardown Racing Club**
62 B c 14/4 Spectrum (IRE)—Pirouette (Sadler's Wells (USA)) **Richard Lewis**
63 B f 31/1 Lugana Beach—Polgwynne (Forzando) (5200) **Neardown Racing Club**
64 B c 5/3 Indian Lodge (IRE)—Sandy Fitzgerald (IRE) (Last Tycoon) (6000) **Neardown Racing Club**
65 **TOUR D'AMOUR (IRE)**, b f 28/4 Fruits of Love (USA)—Touraneena (Robellino (USA)) (4500) **C. H. Shankland**
66 B f 26/2 Mujadil (USA)—Widows Walk (Habitat) (3500) **Neardown Racing Club**
67 **WOODLANDS BELLE**, ch f 27/2 Woodborough (USA)—
    Blushing Belle (Local Suitor (USA)) (952) **C. H. Shankland**

Other Owners: Mr M. C. Binks, Mrs D. Catlow, Mel Catlow, Mr S. D. Fisher, Mrs A. P. Fisher, C. A. Leafe, Mrs P. Leavett-Shenley, S. A. McCallum, S. J. Pembroke, Mr M. D. Sellers, MR I. A. Wood.

Assistant Trainer: Kevin Frost

Jockey (flat): N. Callan, I. Mongan. **Apprentice:** D. Fox. **Amateur:** Mr C. Martin, Mr R. Pooles.

---

646 MR R. D. E. WOODHOUSE, York
Postal: **Teal House Racing Stables, Chestnut Avenue, Welburn, York.**
Contacts: **PHONE (01653) 618637 FAX (01653) 619481 MOBILE (07885) 651348**

1 **BARRYSCOURT LAD (IRE)**, 11, b g Glacial Storm (USA)—Clonana **Roseberry Racing**
2 **DONNYBROOK (IRE)**, 12, ch g Riot Helmet—Evening Bun **Mr R. D. E. Woodhouse**
3 **ELLIE BEE**, 6, b m Primitive Rising (USA)—Hutcel Loch **Mr R. D. E. Woodhouse**
4 **IRON BAY**, 7, b g Karinga Bay—Misowni **Mr R. D. E. Woodhouse**
5 **MR MAHDLO**, 11, b g Rakaposhi King—Fedelm **Mr R. D. E. Woodhouse**
6 **TICKATEAL**, 5, ch g Emperor Fountain—Mary Hand (IRE) **Mr R. D. E. Woodhouse**

Other Owners: J. Dwyer, P. J. Finn.

Jockey (flat): R. Winston. **Jockey (NH):** Tony Dobbin. **Conditional:** D. Harold, P. Whelan.

647 MRS A. M. WOODROW, High Wycombe
Postal: **Crookswood Stud Farm, Horsleys Green, High Wycombe, Buckinghamshire, HP14 3XB.**
Contacts: **PHONE (01494) 482557**

1 **MUALLAF (IRE)**, 13, b g Unfuwain (USA)—Honourable Sheba (USA) **Mrs A. M. Woodrow**
2 **SIR PELINORE**, 10, b g Caerleon (USA)—Soemba **Mrs A. M. Woodrow**

Other Owners: J. G. Woodrow.

Assistant Trainer: John Woodrow

Jockey (NH): S. Durack, J. A. McCarthy. **Conditional:** S. Elliott.

648 MR G. WOODWARD, Tickhill
Postal: **Moorhouse Farm Racing Stables, Blyth Road, Tickhill, Doncaster, South Yorkshire, DN11 9EY.**
Contacts: **WORK (07739) 382052 HOME (01709) 866276**
E-MAIL garry@garrywoodward.co.uk WEBSITE www.garrywoodward.co.uk

1 **ALI D**, 7, b g Alhijaz—Doppio **Mr G. Woodward**
2 **TYPHOON GINGER (IRE)**, 10, ch m Archway (IRE)—Pallas Viking **Mr G. Woodward**

THREE-YEAR-OLDS

3 **GYPSY ROYAL (IRE)**, b f Desert Prince (IRE)—Menominee **R. W. Empson**

TWO-YEAR-OLDS

4 B c 29/1 Lahib (USA)—Cupid Miss (Anita's Prince) (12000) **R. W. Empson**
5 B c 6/5 Killer Instinct—Eternal Triangle (USA) (Barachois (CAN)) (3500) **Sunday Session**
6 B c 7/2 Nashwan (USA)—Ghay (USA) (Bahri (USA)) (800) **R. W. Empson**
7 **MOORHOUSE LAD**, b c 17/2 Bertolini (USA)—Record Time (Clantime) (32000) **Ron Hull**

Other Owners: Mr A. Lloyd, Mr M. Hill, Mr R. Russem, Mr C. Mclelland, Mr A. Watson, Mr C. Bonnett.

Jockey (flat): D. Sweeney.

649 MISS J. WORMALL, Ibstock
Postal: **Ibstock Grange, Ibstock, Leicester.**
Contacts: **PHONE (01530) 260224 MOBILE (07761) 947524**

1 **JAFFA**, 13, ch g Kind of Hush—Sip of Orange **Mrs R. Wormall**
2 **MAKANDY**, 6, b g Makbul—Derring Floss **Mrs R. Wormall**
3 5, B m Gildoran—Notinhand **Mrs R. Wormall**
4 6, B g Alflora (IRE)—Red Dust **Mrs R. Wormall**

650 MR GEOFFREY WRAGG, Newmarket
Postal: **Abington Place, Bury Road, Newmarket, Suffolk, CB8 7BT.**
Contacts: **OFFICE (01638) 662328 FAX (01638) 663576**
E-MAIL gwragg@btclick.com

1 **ACCIACATURA (USA)**, 4, gr f Stravinsky (USA)—Lady In Waiting (USA) **Trevor Stewart**
2 **ASIAN HEIGHTS**, 7, b h Hernando (FR)—Miss Rinjani **J. L. C. Pearce**
3 **AUTUMN GLORY (IRE)**, 5, b h Charnwood Forest (IRE)—Archipova (IRE) **Mollers Racing**
4 **COQUETERIA (USA)**, 4, b f Cozzene (USA)—Miss Waikiki **Miss K. Rausing**
5 **GRAHAM ISLAND**, 4, b g Acatenango (GER)—Gryada **Mollers Racing**
6 **GRAND PASSION (IRE)**, 5, b g Grand Lodge (USA)—Lovers' Parlour **Mr & Mrs H. H. Morriss**
7 **HIDDEN HOPE**, 4, ch f Daylami (IRE)—Nuryana **Mrs S. Lussier**
8 **JACK OF TRUMPS (IRE)**, 5, b h King's Theatre (IRE)—Queen Caroline (USA) **Mollers Racing**
9 **LARKWING (IRE)**, 4, b c Ela-Mana-Mou—The Dawn Trader (USA) **Mollers Racing**
10 **LOCHBUIE (IRE)**, 4, b c Definite Article—Uncertain Affair (IRE) **Mollers Racing**
11 **MR MISTRAL**, 6, b g Zilzal (USA)—Miss Sancerre **Howard Spooner and Partners (II)**
12 **THE WHISTLING TEAL**, 9, b g Rudimentary (USA)—Lonely Shore **Mrs F. A. Veasey & Mr J. Porteous**

MR GEOFFREY WRAGG—continued

THREE-YEAR-OLDS

13 **ALTESSE**, br f Highest Honor (FR)—All Is Fair **Miss K. Rausing**
14 **BARATARIA**, ch c Barathea (IRE)—Aethra (USA) **Mollers Racing**
15 **BON NUIT (IRE)**, b f Night Shift (USA)—Pray (IRE) **Mr Howard Spooner**
16 **ELLE NINO**, b f Inchinor—Robellino Miss (USA) **The Eclipse Partnership**
17 **FAIRY DANCE (IRE)**, b f Zafonic (USA)—Oh So Well (IRE) **Dr A. J. F. Gillespie**
18 **HIDDENAWAY (IRE)**, b f In The Wings—Dananira **Ali Saeed**
19 **LOCHRANZA (IRE)**, b c a Fasliyev (USA)—Mysistra (FR) **Mollers Racing**
20 **MARLION (FR)**, gr c Linamix (FR)—Marzipan (IRE) **Mollers Racing**
21 **MISS INCH**, b f Inchinor—Twitcher's Delight **A. E. Oppenheimer**
22 **MISS KATMANDU (IRE)**, ch f Rainbow Quest (USA)—Miss Rinjani **J. L. C. Pearce**
23 **MONT SAINT MICHEL (IRE)**, b c Montjeu (IRE)—Band of Angels (IRE) **J. L. C. Pearce**
24 **NEVERLETME GO (IRE)**, b f Green Desert (USA)—Cassandra Go (IRE) **Trevor Stewart**
25 **TAYMAN (IRE)**, b br c Sinndar (IRE)—Sweet Emotion (IRE) **Mollers Racing**
26 **TURKANA GIRL**, ch f Hernando (FR)—Miss Penton **A. E. Oppenheimer**

TWO-YEAR-OLDS

27 **DISCO BALL**, ch f 4/2 Fantastic Light (USA)—Danceabout (Shareef Dancer (USA)) **Bloomsbury Stud**
28 **DRAGON DANCER**, b c 16/2 Sadler's Wells (USA)—Alakananda (Hernando (FR)) (200000) **J. L. C. Pearce**
29 **EAGLE EYE**, br c 21/3 Capote (USA)—Bitwa (USA) (Conquistador Cielo (USA)) (25000) **Mollers Racing**
30 **EMINENCIA**, ch f 12/4 Sadler's Wells (USA)—My Emma (Marju (IRE)) (320000) **Miss K. Rausing**
31 **GIVING**, br f 18/2 Generous (IRE)—Madiyla (Darshaan) **The Sporting Partnership**
32 **HOTEL DU CAP**, br c 14/2 Grand Lodge (USA)—Miss Riviera Golf (Hernando (FR)) **J. L. C. Pearce**
33 **INCHMAHOME**, b f 8/5 Galileo (IRE)—Inchmurrin (Lomond (USA)) **A. E. Oppenheimer**
34 **IVY CREEK (USA)**, b c 23/3 Gulch (USA)—Ivy Leaf (IRE) (Nureyev (USA)) (85000) **Mollers Racing**
35 **LADY AGNES**, b f 14/3 Singspiel (IRE)—St Radegund (Green Desert (USA)) **A. E. Oppenheimer**
36 **MANNIKKO (IRE)**, gr c 7/4 Green Desert (USA)—Cassandra Go (IRE) (Indian Ridge) (170000) **Trevor Stewart**
37 **MISS PROVENCE**, b f 28/1 Hernando (FR)—Miss Beaulieu (Northfields (USA)) **J. L. C. Pearce**
38 **MISS THAILAND**, b f 3/2 Grand Lodge (USA)—Miss Amanpuri (Alzao (USA)) **J. L. C. Pearce**
39 **MONTCHARA (IRE)**, b f 4/4 Montjeu (IRE)—Mochara (Last Fandango) (120000) **Mollers Racing**
40 **NYARHINI**, b f 15/3 Fantastic Light (USA)—Nuryana (Nureyev (USA)) **Mrs Arabella Morris**
41 **PRINCESS LAVINIA**, ch f 25/5 Fraam—Affaire de Coeur (Imperial Fling (USA)) **Mr D. R. Hunnisett**
42 **ROAD HOME**, ch c 6/5 Grand Lodge (USA)—Lady In Waiting (Kylian (USA)) (130000) **Mr Howard Spooner**
43 **SANT ELENA**, ch f 1/2 Efisio—Argent du Bois (USA) (Silver Hawk (USA)) **The Eclipse Partnership**
44 **TELEGONUS**, b c 24/3 Fantastic Light (USA)—Circe's Isle (Be My Guest (USA)) (30000) **A. E. Oppenheimer**
45 **THE LADY MANDARIN**, b f 26/5 Groom Dancer (USA)—Lonely Shore (Blakeney) **Mrs F. A. Veasey**
46 **WISSAHICKON**, ch f 4/3 Grand Lodge (USA)—
                                                     Deep Ravine (USA) (Gulch (USA)) **The Snailwell Stud Company Limited**

Other Owners: James Charrington, Stuart Richmond Watson, Anthony Richmond Watson, Lady de Ramsey, Ian Macnicol, G. Strahan, Patrick Ramsay, Anthony Cane, D. W. Dennis, N. J. Forman Hardy, C. G. Hellyer, Mrs M. D. Morriss, Mrs A. M. Oppenheimer.

---

651 **MR R. H. YORK, Cobham**
Postal: **Newmarsh Farm, Horsley Road, Cobham, Surrey, KT11 3JX.**
Contacts: **PHONE (01932) 863594 FAX (01932) 860703 MOBILE (07808) 344131**
E-MAIL ray.york@virgin.net

1 **BLAZE ON**, 6, ch g Minster Son—Clova **Mr R. H. York**
2 6, B m Alderbrook—Bridepark Rose (IRE) **Mr R. H. York**
3 **CHARANGO STAR**, 7, b g Petoski—Pejawi **Mr R. H. York**
4 4, B g New Frontier (IRE)—Drumkilly Lilly (IRE) **Mr R. H. York**
5 **LADY MORDAUNT (IRE)**, 7, b m Mister Lord (USA)—Castle Flame (IRE) **Mr R. H. York**
6 4, ch g Paris of Troy—Perryline **Mr R. H. York**
7 **PIERRE DE LUNE**, 5, b g Double Eclipse (IRE)—Rowlandsons Charm (IRE) **J. A. Gillett**
8 **SECOND RESOLUTION**, 4, b g Superpower—Peggotty **S. Cargill**
9 **STAR GLOW**, 11, b g Dunbeath (USA)—Betrothed **Mr R. H. York**

Amateur: Mr N. Kinnon, Mr P. York.

652 MR W. G. YOUNG, Carluke

Postal: **Overton Farm, Crossford, Carluke, Lanarkshire, ML8 5QF.**
Contacts: PHONE **(01555) 860226** MOBILE **(07889) 442584**
E-MAIL **wgyoung@fsbdial.co.uk**

1 **GALA QUEEN**, 5, gr m Accondy (IRE)—Miss Jedd **Mr W. G. Young**
2 **LISDANTE (IRE)**, 12, b g Phardante (FR)—Shuil Eile **Mr W. G. Young**
3 **LORD OF THE LOCH (IRE)**, 14, b br g Lord Americo—Loughamaire **Mr W. G. Young**
4 **NUZUM ROAD MAKERS (IRE)**, 14, b g Lafontaine (USA)—Dark Gold **Mr W. G. Young**
5 **RAB CEE**, 5, b br g Tragic Role (USA)—Hilltop Lady **Mr W. G. Young**
6 **STARBRIGHT**, 4, b g Polar Falcon (USA)—Treasure Hunt **Mr W. G. Young**
7 **SUNSET BLUES (FR)**, 5, ch g Green Tune (USA)—Sunset Reef **Mr W. G. Young**
8 **TURBO MOWER**, 7, b g Turbo Speed—Fruids Park **Mr W. G. Young**

Assistant Trainer: W G Young Jnr

Conditional: T. Davidson, B Orde-Powlett.

INDEX TO HORSES

The Figure before the name of the horse refers to the number of the team in which it appears and **The Figure after** the horse supplies a ready reference to each animal. Horses are indexed strictly alphabetically, e.g. THE CARROT MAN appears in the T's, MR BUSBY in the MR's, ST MELLION WAY in the ST's etc.

ALROYAL (GER) 3
ALSHAMATRY (USA) 14
ALSHARQ (IRE) 15
ALSHIMAAL (IRE) 16
ALTA PETERS (GB) 9
ALTAIR (USA) C 48
ALTAMIRA (FR) C 82
ALTAREJOS (IRE) 37
ALTAWEELAH (IRE) F 89
ALTAY (GB) 7
ALTESSA (IRE) 25
ALTESSE (GB) 13
ALTESSE DE SOU (FR) 3
ALTITUDE DANCER (IRE) 2
ALTO FICO (IRE) 1
ALTO VERTIGO (GB) 46
ALUMNI (GB) 12
ALVA GLEN (USA) 1
ALVARINHO LADY (GB) 10
ALVARITA (GB) 10
ALVARO (IRE) 2
ALVECOTE LADY F 1
ALWAYS BELIEVE (USA) 1
ALWAYS ESTEEMED (IRE) 2
ALWAYS FLYING (USA) 3
ALWAYS IN DEBT (IRE) 4
ALWAYS KING (FR) 1
ALWAYS MINE (GB) 33
ALWAYS ON MY MIND (GB) F 49
ALWAYS OPTIMISTIC (GB) 28
ALWAYS RAINBOWS (IRE) 1
ALWAYS TRUE (USA) C 22
ALWAYS WAINING (IRE) 2
ALYZEA (IRE) 65
AMADEUS (AUS) 2
AMAETHON (USA) 32
AMALFI COAST (GB) 1
AMALFI STORM (GB) 1
AMALIE (IRE) 17
AMANDA'S LAD (IRE) 1
AMANDERICA (IRE) 16
AMARULA RIDGE (IRE) 5
AMARYLLIS (IRE) C 33
AMATEUR DRAMATICS (GB) 2
AMAYA SILVA (GB) 17
AMARAZON (GB) 28
AMAZING GRACE MARY (GB) 18
AMAZONE DU BERLAIS (FR) 2
AMBER GLORY (GB) 58
AMBER GO GO (GB) 1
AMBER LEGEND (GB) 1
AMBER ROSE (IRE) F 19
AMBER STAR (FR) 113
AMBER STARLIGHT (GB) 4
AMBER WARRIOR (FR) 1
AMBERLEIGH HOUSE (IRE) 1
AMBERSONG (GB) 2
AMBITION ROYAL (FR) 1
AMEEQ (USA) 17
AMEERAT JUMAIRA (GB) F 53
AMELLNAA (IRE) C 47
AMEN DESERT (FR) 90
AMERAS (IRE) 1
AMERICA LONTANA (IRE) C 53
AMERICAN COUSIN (GB) 2
AMERICAN EMBASSY (USA) 2
AMERICAN PRESIDENT (IRE) 2
AMERICAN TRUST (USA) 2
AMERIGO VESPUCCI (GB) 10
AMES SOUER (IRE) 29
AMETHYST (IRE) F 50
AMETHYST ROCK (GB) 1
AMICA (GB) 102
AMICELLI (GER) 2
AMID THE STARS (GB) F 20
AMIGRA (IRE) 5
AMIR ZAMAN (GB) 1

AMIRA (GB) 13
AMMIRARE (GB) 12
AMMO (IRE) 12
AMMONIAS (GER) 4
AMNERIS (IRE) F 29
AMNESTY (GB) 7
AMODIA (FR) 57
AMONG DREAMS (GB) 1
AMONG FRIENDS (IRE) 1
AMONG THIEVES (GB) 1
AMONG WOMEN (GB) C 34
AMORIST (IRE) 11
AMOROSO BRI (GB) 1
AMOUAGE (IRE) 32
AMOURALLIS (IRE) 1
AMPOULE (GB) 2
AMUIGH FEIN SPEIR (IRE) 2
AMUSEMENT (GB) 1
AMWELL BRAVE (GB) 2
AMY G (IRE) F 8
AMY LOUISE (IRE) 51
AMYROSEISUPPOSE (GB) 1
AN MOSEY (USA) C 12
ANAAMIL (IRE) 15
ANABAA BOY (IRE) 19
ANABAA INDY (IRE) 46
ANABAA REPUBLIC (FR) 1
ANABAA'S MUSIC (GB) C 34
ANAKA FLIGHT (GB) 1
ANALOGICAL (GB) G 2
ANALOGY (FR) 5
ANALYZE (FR) 1
ANASTASIA STORM (GB) 48
ANASTASIA VENTURE (GB) C 31
ANATAR (IRE) 4
ANATASE (GB) 2
ANATOLIAN STAR (USA) 14
ANCHOR DATE (GB) 14
ANCIENT SECRET (GB) C 26
AND AGAIN (USA) 69
AND I (GB) 71
ANDALUZA (IRE) 1
ANDORRAN (IRE) 15
ANDRE CHENIER (GB) 1
ANDREAS (FR) 7
ANDRONIKOS (GB) 25
ANDROS DAWN (IRE) G 1
ANDURIL (GB) 3
ANDY GIN (FR) 1
ANDY MAL (GB) 64
ANEFEW (USA) 16
ANEMONE (GB) 55
ANESTASIA (IRE) 14
ANFIELD DREAM (GB) 33
ANFLORA (GB) 3
ANGARIC (IRE) 46
ANGEL DELIGHT (GB) 1
ANGEL SPRINTS (GB) 6
ANGEL VOICES (IRE) 51
ANGEL WING (GB) 29
ANGELA SERRA (FR) 61
ANGELITA (GB) 97
ANGELO'S PRIDE (GB) 1
ANGELOFTHENORTH (GB) 14
ANGHIARA (FR) 1
ANGIE'S DOUBLE (GB) 3
ANGLONA (IRE) 47
ANISETTE (GB) 4
ANISSATI (GB) 18
ANISSINA (GB) 4
ANKA BRITANNIA (USA) C 91
ANKLES BACK (IRE) 2
ANKUDHEPLAY (GB) 6
ANN AND TONIC (IRE) 3
ANN'S ANNIE (IRE) C 24
ANN'S DELIGHT (IRE) 19
ANNA DEESSE (FR) 62
ANNA FRANCESCA (FR) 11

ANNA GAYLE (GB) 5
ANNA KARIETTA C 35
ANNA MONA (GER) 28
ANNA OG (IRE) 4
ANNA PALLIDA (GB) 3
ANNAKITA (GB) 1
ANNALS (GB) 13
ANNAPURNA (IRE) F 56
ANNE BONNY (GB) C 25
ANNE'S BAND (GB) 2
ANNEE LUMIERE (IRE) 15
ANNENKOV (IRE) 38
ANNETTE VALLON (IRE) F 67
ANNETTES STAR (GB) 2
ANNIBALE CARO (GB) 12
ANNICOMBE RUN F 1
ANNIE HALL (GB) G 57
ANNIE'S GLEN (IRE) G 2
ANNIEIRWIN (IRE) F 25
ANNIES THEME (GB) 1
ANNIVERSARY (GB) F 64
ANNO JUBILO (GER) 4
ANOTHER BARGAIN (IRE) 2
ANOTHER BOTTLE (IRE) 1
ANOTHER CHANCE (IRE) 1
ANOTHER CHOICE (IRE) 1
ANOTHER CON (IRE) 1
ANOTHER CONQUEST (GB) 1
ANOTHER DECKIE (IRE) 1
ANOTHER DIAMOND (IRE) 1
ANOTHER DOLLAR (IRE) 1
ANOTHER DUDE (IRE) 7
ANOTHER GENERAL (IRE) 5
ANOTHER GLIMPSE (IRE) 1
ANOTHER GRADUATE (IRE) 2
ANOTHER GROUSE F 2
ANOTHER JADE (GB) F 15
ANOTHER JOKER (IRE) 1
ANOTHER MISK (GB) 13
ANOTHER NATIVE (IRE) 6
ANOTHER PROMISE (IRE) 1
ANOTHER RAINBOW (IRE) F 26
ANOTHER RAINBOW (IRE) F 15
ANOTHER RALEAGH (IRE) 1
ANOTHER TAIPAN (IRE) 1
ANOTHER WITNESS (IRE) 1
ANOUKIT (GB) F 48
ANOUSA (IRE) 3
ANSCO (GB) 5
ANSELLS JOY (GB) 32
ANSELLS LEGACY (IRE) 25
ANSELLS PRIDE (IRE) 33
ANSHABIL (IRE) 6
ANTARTIS (GB) 33
ANTHEMION (IRE) 1
ANTICA (GB) 47
ANTICS (USA) F 34
ANTIGONE'S FIRE (GB) 3
ANTIGONI (FR) 80
ANTIGUAN JANE (GB) F 54
ANTINOMY (GB) 4
ANTIOQUIA (IRE) 2
ANTIQUARIAN (IRE) 5
ANTIQUE (IRE) 20
ANTOINETTE (USA) 26
ANTONIA'S CHOICE (GB) F 30
ANTONIA'S DOUBLE (GB) F 24
ANTONIA'S FOLLY (GB) C 48
ANTONIA'S MELODY (GB) C 22
ANURA (IRE) 17
ANUVASTEEL (GB) 1
ANXIOUS MOMENTS (IRE) 5
ANY NEWS (GB) 1
ANYNAME (IRE) 22
ANYTIME BABY (GB) C 20
AOIFE (IRE) C 29
AONACH MOR (GB) F 45
AONINCH (GB) 1

551 **ASK THE CLERK** (IRE) 5
45 **ASKWITH** (IRE) 15
124 **ASMARADANA** (GB) 61
232 **ASNIERES** (USA) F 51
125 **ASO ROCK** (IRE) 2
481 **ASPEN FALLS** (IRE) 41
432 **ASPIRING ACTOR** (IRE) 11
115 **ASSAILANT** (IRE) 19
357 **ASSASSINO** (FR) 41
265 **ASSERTIVE** (GB) 74
383 **ASSERTIVE DANCER** (USA) F 21
265 **ASSET** (IRE) 75
408 **ASSOON** (GB) 9
252 **ASSUMETHEPOSITION** (FR) 3
467 **ASSUMPTALINA** (GB) 8
517 **ASTALANDA** (FR) 19
318 **ASTEEM** (GB) 4
566 **ASTON** (USA) 7
264 **ASTON LAD** (GB) 3
531 **ASTONVILLE** (FR) 5
335 **ASTORMYDAYISCOMING** (GB) 1
340 **ASTRAC** (FR) 2
372 **ASTRAL DANCER** (IRE) 3
88 **ASTRILLE** (IRE) 1
588 **ASTROBELLA** (GB) 48
588 **ASTROCHARM** (IRE) 1
588 **ASTROMANCER** (USA) 2
319 **ASTRONOMIC** (GB) 10
287 **ASTRONOMICAL** (IRE) 17
588 **ASTRONOVA** (GB) 4
72 **ASTUTI** (IRE) F 58
282 **ASTYANAX** (IRE) 8
59 **ASWAN** (GB) 3
306 **AT THE BAR** (IRE) 34
643 **AT THE DOUBLE** (GB) 2
192 **AT THE MONEY** (GB) 27
633 **AT YOUR REQUEST** (GB) 5
480 **ATACAMA STAR** (GB) 65
341 **ATAHUELPA** (GB) 7
590 **ATAMANA** (IRE) C 73
383 **ATAVUS** (GB) 1
268 **ATELIOS** (USA) 3
165 **ATEMME** (GB) F 6
233 **ATH DARA** G 3
614 **ATHBOY** (GB) 1
614 **ATHBOY NIGHTS** (IRE) 8
333 **ATHENS** (IRE) 13
457 **ATHNOWEN** (IRE) 1
339 **ATHOLLBROSE** (USA) 1
349 **ATICA** (IRE) 21
32 **ATLANDO** (IRE) 3
544 **ATLANTIC ACE** (GB) 1
501 **ATLANTIC CITY** (GB) 2
8 **ATLANTIC JANE** 1
87 **ATLANTIC QUEST** (USA) 2
16 **ATLANTIC TERN** (GB) 1
431 **ATLANTIC VIKING** (IRE) 5
408 **ATLANTIS** (HOL) 10
611 **ATMOSPHERIC BLUES** (IRE) F 37
218 **ATOMIC BREEZE** (IRE) 1
336 **ATRIFFIC STORY** (GB) 27
625 **ATTACCA** (GB) 2
319 **ATTACHMENT** (USA) F 123
307 **ATTACK MINDED** (GB) 1
559 **ATTICUS FINCH** (IRE) 1
32 **ATTIMA** (GB) 63
279 **ATTIRINA** (GB) 25
522 **ATTISHOE** (GB) 16
341 **ATTITUDE** (GB) 8
271 **ATTORNEY** (GB) 1
449 **ATTORNEY GENERAL** (IRE) 2
463 **ATTRACTIVE CROWN** (USA) F 35
396 **ATTUNE** (GB) 1
620 **ATUM RE** (IRE) 3
148 **ATWIRL** (GB) 20
419 **AU LAC** (GB) 2
581 **AU REVOIR** (GB) 13
471 **AUBURN DUKE** (GB) 2

602 **AUBURN SPIRIT** (GB) 2
287 **AUCTION ROOM** (USA) 84
32 **AUDELA** (IRE) 64
1 **AUDIENCE** (GB) 1
271 **AUDIOSTREETDOTCOM** (GB) 2
308 **AUDITION** (GB) F 10
465 **AUDITORIUM** (GB) 1
409 **AUDRINA** F 7
213 **AUENTRAUM** (GB) 2
23 **AUGUST ROSE** (IRE) 1
265 **AUNT JULIA** (GB) 29
513 **AUNTIE FAY** (IRE) F 11
182 **AURAZORE** (IRE) 3
232 **AUSTRALIE** (IRE) 1
393 **AUTHENTICATE** (GB) 11
283 **AUTHORITY** (IRE) 2
581 **AUTOMATION** (GB) 23
628 **AUTUMN DREAM** (GB) 17
650 **AUTUMN GLORY** (IRE) 3
396 **AUTUMN LEAF** (USA) C 58
531 **AUTUMN MIST** (IRE) 6
199 **AUTUMN PROMISE** (GB) 93
631 **AUTUMN RAIN** (USA) 1
620 **AUTUMN RED** (IRE) 4
465 **AUTUMN WEALTH** (IRE) 2
400 **AUWITESWEETHEART** (GB) 19
146 **AVADI** (FR) 2
44 **AVALANCHE** (FR) 1
425 **AVANTI** (GB) 1
34 **AVANTI TIGER** (IRE) 1
5 **AVAS DELIGHT** (IRE) 1
116 **AVEIRO** (IRE) 1
253 **AVELIAN** (IRE) 49
604 **AVENCHES** (GER) 7
59 **AVENTURA** (IRE) 4
125 **AVENUE MONTAIGNE** (FR) 3
604 **AVERA** (GER) 8
299 **AVERARD** (IRE) 8
154 **AVERELINE** (GB) 1
115 **AVERSHAM** (GB) 2
177 **AVERTIBLE** (GB) 80
436 **AVESA** (GB) 3
173 **AVESOMEOFTHAT** (IRE) 1
456 **AVESSIA** (GB) 11
562 **AVIEMORE** (GB) 29
275 **AVIGAIL** (FR) F 19
234 **AVIT** (FR) 2
637 **AVITTA** (IRE) 6
420 **AVOCA MIST** (IRE) 5
115 **AVONBRIDGE** (GB) 3
110 **AVONTUUR** (FR) 17
590 **AWAASER** (USA) 18
431 **AWAKE** (GB) 6
568 **AWAKEN** (GB) 2
425 **AWARDING** (GB) 1
104 **AWASH** (USA) 7
593 **AWWAL MARRA** (USA) 2
119 **AXE CREEK** (USA) F 30
309 **AYAM ZAMAN** (IRE) 16
124 **AYLMER ROAD** (IRE) 26
137 **AYMARA** (GB) F 56
193 **AZA WISH** (IRE) 12
499 **AZAHARA** (GB) 61
357 **AZALEE** (IRE) 99
202 **AZAROLE** (IRE) 2
357 **AZAY LE RIDEAU** (USA) 42
357 **AZAZELLO** (IRE) 43
604 **AZEEM** (GER) 9
393 **AZEEZAH** (GB) 7
45 **AZERLEY** (IRE) 23
432 **AZERTYUIOP** (FR) 12
72 **AZIME** (IRE) 59
112 **AZIZAM** (GB) 10
590 **AZMAAN** (USA) 74
306 **AZREME** (GB) 1
347 **AZTEC WARRIOR** (IRE) 3
198 **AZTURK** (FR) 8
514 **AZUCAR** (FR) 34

202 **AZUCAR** (IRE) 31
18 **AZURE WINGS** (IRE) 2
432 **AZZEMOUR** (FR) 13
109 **BA FOXTROT** (GB) 91
590 **BAADERAH** (FR) F 75
586 **BAAWRAH** (GB) 2
310 **BABA GHANOUSH** (GB) 12
220 **BABABULLAH** (GB) 1
279 **BABBLING ON** (FR) 26
590 **BABCARY** (GB) 76
287 **BABE MACCOOL** (IRE) 18
220 **BABODANA** (GB) 3
125 **BABOUCHE** (FR) 4
599 **BABY RUN** (FR) 3
209 **BACHARACH** (IRE) 20
310 **BACHELOR AFFAIR** (GB) 13
449 **BACK AMONG FRIENDS** (GB) 3
271 **BACK AT DE FRONT** (IRE) 3
357 **BACK BACK BERO** (FR) 4
130 **BACK DE BAY** (IRE) 1
377 **BACK IN ACTION** (GB) 1
441 **BACK IN FRONT** (IRE) 5
393 **BACK IN SPIRIT** (GB) 1
152 **BACK IN THE GAME** (GB) 1
5 **BACK NINE** (IRE) 2
221 **BACK ON CONCORDE** (IRE) 2
514 **BACK THE WINNER** (IRE) 35
282 **BACK TO BEN ALDER** (IRE) 9
186 **BACKBEAT** (IRE) 2
441 **BACKFOREMORE** (IRE) 6
499 **BACKGAMMON** (GB) 5
98 **BACKLASH** (GB) 3
480 **BACKPACKER** (IRE) 4
601 **BACKSCRATCHER** (GB) 3
268 **BACKSIDEUP** (IRE) 4
400 **BACKSTREET LAD** (GB) 20
172 **BADDAM** (GB) 23
268 **BADGERLAW** (IRE) 5
368 **BAFFLING SECRET** (FR) 5
381 **BAGAN** (FR) 7
463 **BAGO** (FR) 2
316 **BAHAMA BELLE** (GB) 1
369 **BAHAMAMIA** (GB) 2
73 **BAHAMIAN BAY** (GB) 9
87 **BAHAMIAN DUKE** (GB) 53
431 **BAHAMIAN PIRATE** (USA) 7
535 **BAHAMIAN SPRING** (IRE) 25
72 **BAHAR SHUMAAL** (IRE) 20
251 **BAHIA BREEZE** (GB) 14
72 **BAHIANO** (IRE) 3
590 **BAHR ALSALAAM** (USA) C 77
287 **BAIE DES FLAMANDS** (USA) 19
510 **BAIE DES FLEURS** (FR) 58
196 **BAIE DES SINGES** (GB) 2
633 **BAIKALINE** (FR) 6
311 **BAILANDA** (GER) 13
169 **BAILAORA** (IRE) 1
174 **BAILEYS APPLAUSE** (GB) 15
611 **BAILEYS CREAM** (GB) C 38
429 **BAILEYS HONOUR** (GB) 30
514 **BAILEYS ON LINE** (GB) C 117
363 **BAILEYS PRIZE** (USA) 4
431 **BAILIEBOROUGH** (IRE) 8
413 **BAILY BREEZE** (IRE) 2
413 **BAILY MIST** (IRE) 3
54 **BAINO BLUFF** C 25
514 **BAINO RIDGE** (FR) 36
583 **BAJAN BLUE** (GB) C 32
97 **BAJAN PARKES** (GB) 36
228 **BAK TO BILL** (GB) 1
86 **BAKER OF OZ** (GB) 1
199 **BAKERMAN** (GB) 22
594 **BAKERS DAUGHTER** (GB) G 13
102 **BAKKE** (GB) 13
396 **BAKLAWA** (GB) 59
161 **BALAKIREF** (GB) 2
137 **BALALAIKA** (GB) C 57
220 **BALALAIKA TUNE** (IRE) 2

94 **BAYLEAF** (GB) F 15
553 **BAYONET** (GB) 1
24 **BAYOSS** (IRE) 1
625 **BAYRAMI** (GB) F 22
237 **BAYREUTH** (GB) 29
517 **BAYRIKA** (IRE) F 77
499 **BAYSIDE** (GB) 9
562 **BAYYAAN** (USA) 97
32 **BAZART** (GB) 10
349 **BAZATHA** (GB) 68
102 **BDELLIUM** (GB) 1
432 **BE BE KING** (IRE) 15
42 **BE BOP ALOHA** (GB) 11
614 **BE LUCKY LADY** (GB) 9
407 **BE MY BETTER HALF** (IRE) 2
447 **BE MY CITIZEN** (GB) 4
290 **BE MY GUIDE** (GB) 6
214 **BE MY LEADER** (IRE) 5
586 **BE MY MANAGER** (IRE) 3
231 **BE MY ROYAL** (IRE) 3
220 **BE OFF WITH YOU** (GB) 3
164 **BE POSITIVE** (GB) 3
142 **BE TELLING** (IRE) 1
421 **BE UPSTANDING** (GB) 5
98 **BE WISE GIRL** (GB) 4
544 **BEADY** (IRE) 2
409 **BEAMISH PRINCE** (GB) 9
161 **BEAMSLEY BEACON** (GB) 3
604 **BEANNEY** (ARG) 12
146 **BEARAWAY** (IRE) 1
88 **BEAT IT** (USA) C 42
442 **BEAT THE HEAT** (IRE) 1
319 **BEAU ARTISTE** (GB) 13
601 **BEAU COUP** (GB) 4
633 **BEAU DE TURGEON** (FR) 10
153 **BEAU JAZZ** (GB) 1
153 **BEAU LARGESSE** (GB) 7
645 **BEAU MARCHE** (GB) 7
164 **BEAU SUPREME** (IRE) 3
233 **BEAU'S DELIGHT** (USA) G 4
319 **BEAUCHAMP GIGI** (IRE) 14
531 **BEAUCHAMP PRINCE** (IRE) 7
241 **BEAUCHAMP QUEST** (GB) 1
106 **BEAUCHAMP RIBBON** (GB) 1
306 **BEAUFORT** (GB) 2
252 **BEAUGENCY** (NZ) 4
568 **BEAUMONT GIRL** (IRE) 33
288 **BEAUSITE** (GB) 8
473 **BEAUTEOUS** (IRE) 1
124 **BEAUTIFUL MARIA** (IRE) 27
288 **BEAUTIFUL MOVER** (USA) 9
370 **BEAUTIFUL NIGHT** (FR) 128
199 **BEAUTY OF A TIGER** (GER) 95
109 **BEAUTY OF DREAMS** (GB) 3
272 **BEAUTY ONE** (GB) 47
252 **BEAVER** (AUS) 5
71 **BEAVER DIVA** (GB) 6
318 **BEAVER PATROL** (IRE) 5
224 **BEBE FACTUAL** (GER) 2
357 **BEBESEC** (IRE) 5
480 **BEBOPSKIDDLY** (GB) 6
209 **BECKERMET** (GB) 12
520 **BECKTARA** (IRE) 60
232 **BECOLINA** (USA) F 52
357 **BEDAMIX** (FR) 46
587 **BEDARA** (GB) F 27
310 **BEDLAM** (GB) 14
502 **BEDLAM BOY** (IRE) 3
272 **BEDOUIN BLUE** (IRE) 48
238 **BEDTIME BLUES** (GB) 3
231 **BEE AN BEE** (IRE) 4
193 **BEE MINOR** (GB) 2
491 **BEE OFF** (IRE) C 14
311 **BEE SHARP** (GB) 14
645 **BEE STINGER** (GB) 18
71 **BEECHES THEATRE** (IRE) 13
259 **BEECHY BANK** (IRE) 1
299 **BEEF OR SALMON** (IRE) 9

432 **BEEHAWK** (GB) 16
124 **BEEJAY** (GB) 3
316 **BEENABOUTABIT** (GB) 2
171 **BEEPING** (GB) 47
38 **BEETHOVENS FIFTH** (IRE) 52
196 **BEETLE BUG** (GB) 3
451 **BEFITTING** (GB) 12
429 **BEFORE THE DAWN** (GB) 31
172 **BEFORE TIME** (GB) 1
401 **BEFORE YOU GO** (IRE) 35
53 **BEFRIEND** (USA) 5
517 **BEHARIYA** (IRE) C 78
455 **BEHAVINGBADLY** (IRE) 1
517 **BEHNASAN** (IRE) 22
591 **BEKSTAR** (GB) 2
537 **BEL OMBRE** (FR) 3
562 **BELANAK** (IRE) 98
451 **BELIEVING** (GB) F 53
420 **BELINKIN** (GB) 10
370 **BELISAMA** (FR) 6
177 **BELISARIO** (IRE) 3
174 **BELISCO** (USA) 2
587 **BELIZE TROPICAL** (IRE) F 28
341 **BELL LANE LAD** (IRE) 11
309 **BELLA BERTOLINI** (GB) 57
564 **BELLA HELENA** (GB) C 16
437 **BELLA LIANA** (IRE) 6
71 **BELLA PAVLINA** (GB) 7
71 **BELLA PLUNKETT** (IRE) 81
12 **BELLA TUTRICE** (IRE) 1
184 **BELLALINI** (GB) 18
93 **BELLALOU** (GB) 3
451 **BELLAMANDA** (IRE) 13
199 **BELLAMY CAY** (IRE) 3
158 **BELLAMY ROAD** (USA) 18
492 **BELLANEY JEWEL** (IRE) 6
318 **BELLANORA** (GB) 18
425 **BELLAPORT GIRL** (GB) 4
426 **BELLASSINI** (GB) 2
60 **BELLE CHANSON** (GB) 19
93 **BELLE DE CADIX** (IRE) C 23
532 **BELLE DE NUIT** (IRE) 3
308 **BELLE ENCORE** (GB) 11
109 **BELLE GENIUS** (USA) C 92
153 **BELLE LARGESSE** (GB) 8
439 **BELLE SULTANE** (USA) C 51
32 **BELLEROPHON** (USA) 66
511 **BELLEVUE HERO** (NZ) 3
511 **BELLEVUE SUNRISE** (NZ) 4
362 **BELLINO EMPRESARIO** (IRE) 1
301 **BELLS BEACH** (IRE) 4
567 **BELLTINA** (GB) F 18
124 **BELLY DANCER** (IRE) 28
12 **BELMONT PRINCESS** (IRE) F 9
332 **BELMOUNT STAR** (IRE) G 12
585 **BELSKI** (GB) 1
153 **BELTANE** (GB) 2
641 **BELTER** (GB) 4
577 **BELTON** (GB) 5
471 **BELUGA** (IRE) 4
588 **BEN BACCHUS** (GB) 24
544 **BEN CASEY** (GB) 22
71 **BEN HUR** (GB) 8
216 **BEN KENOBI** (GB) 3
169 **BEN LOMAND** (GB) 2
582 **BEN THE BRAVE** (IRE) 2
370 **BEN VETO** (FR) 7
623 **BEN'S REVENGE** (GB) 1
341 **BEN'S TURN** (IRE) 2
614 **BENBAUN** (IRE) 2
99 **BENBYAS** (GB) 1
42 **BENEDICT** (GB) 12
229 **BENEDICT BAY** (GB) 57
540 **BENEFIT** (GB) 1
107 **BENELLINO** (FR) 39
154 **BENGO** (IRE) 2
186 **BENIGHTED** (GB) 30
102 **BENISON** (GB) 17

553 **BENJAMIN** (IRE) 2
89 **BENNANABAA** (GB) 3
400 **BENNY BATHWICK** (IRE) 5
361 **BENNY THE BALL** (USA) 2
125 **BENODET** (IRE) 26
586 **BENRAJAH** (IRE) 4
306 **BENS GEORGIE** (IRE) 23
168 **BENT AL FALA** (IRE) F 18
396 **BENTINCK** (IRE) 21
535 **BENTLEY** (GB) 26
53 **BENTLEY BROOK** (IRE) 47
265 **BENTLEY'S BUSH** (IRE) 31
418 **BENTYHEATH LANE** (GB) 1
369 **BENWILT BREEZE** (IRE) 36
369 **BENWILT GOLD** (IRE) 3
510 **BENZOLINA** (IRE) 1
89 **BERENGARIO** (IRE) 4
614 **BERENICE** (ITY) C 28
306 **BERESFORD BOY** (GB) 2
185 **BERGAMO** (GB) 3
252 **BERGERAC** (NZ) 6
40 **BERGLIOT** (GB) F 51
645 **BERHAM MALDU** (IRE) 19
199 **BERINGOER** (FR) 96
119 **BERINGS EXPRESS** (FR) 31
349 **BERISSIMO** (FR) 3
96 **BERKELEY HEIGHTS** (GB) 2
451 **BERKHAMSTED** (IRE) 14
308 **BERLIESE** (IRE) F 31
199 **BERNABEU** (USA) 25
155 **BERNARDON** (GER) 1
282 **BERNINI** (IRE) 10
361 **BERRY RACER** (IRE) 3
401 **BERTI BERTOLINI** (GB) 36
312 **BERTIE ARMS** (GB) 3
478 **BERTIE'S GIRL** F 43
470 **BERTIEBANOO** (IRE) 6
478 **BERTIES CONNECTION** (GB) 3
383 **BERTOCELLI** (IRE) 3
172 **BERTROSE** (GB) 25
400 **BERYL** (GB) C 37
510 **BESCAME** (FR) 21
87 **BESEECHING** (IRE) F 54
200 **BESEIGED** (USA) 5
209 **BESPOKE TRADER** (IRE) 22
532 **BESSEMER** (JPN) 3
214 **BESSINA** (IRE) 6
319 **BEST ACCOLADE** (GB) 15
471 **BEST ACTOR** (IRE) 5
562 **BEST ALIBI** (GB) 99
293 **BEST AWAY** (IRE) 1
569 **BEST BE GOING** (IRE) 6
197 **BEST BEFORE** (GB) 2
162 **BEST BELOVED** (FR) 4
44 **BEST DESERT** (IRE) 2
641 **BEST FLIGHT** (GB) 5
441 **BEST GREY** (GB) 7
287 **BEST LADY** (GB) 85
188 **BEST LEAD** (GB) 2
347 **BEST MATE** (IRE) 6
398 **BEST OF FRIENDS** (GB) 12
515 **BEST OF GLORY** (IRE) 7
370 **BEST OF THE WEST** (FR) 187
562 **BEST WAY** (IRE) 100
64 **BESTAM** (GB) 1
237 **BESTBYFAR** (IRE) 30
446 **BESTSELLER** (GB) 1
527 **BESUTO** (IRE) 1
370 **BET ON ME** (GER) 188
544 **BETH'S MATE** (GB) 49
345 **BETHANIA** (GB) F 42
185 **BETHANYS BOY** (IRE) 4
514 **BETTER BE SURE** (USA) C 119
325 **BETTERWARE BOY** (GB) 1
40 **BETWEEN FRIENDS** (GB) 26
583 **BETWEEN THE WINDS** (USA) F 33
542 **BEULAH** (GB) 2
72 **BEVEL** (GB) F 60

291 **CHANCE FLIGHT** (GB) 2
417 **CHANCE FOR ROMANCE** (GB) 2
178 **CHANCEL** (USA) F 96
421 **CHANCERS DANTE** (IRE) 14
386 **CHANCY GAL** G 6
590 **CHANDRA** (GB) 24
157 **CHANGE AGENT** (GB) 6
199 **CHANGEABLE** (GB) 29
32 **CHANGER TOUT CA** (FR) 71
137 **CHANGING PARTNERS** (GB) C 60
229 **CHANGIZ** (GB) 68
157 **CHANNAHRLIE** (IRE) 7
370 **CHANT DE LUNE** (FR) 130
20 **CHANTACO** (USA) 36
370 **CHANTEGRIL** (FR) 15
345 **CHANTELLE** (IRE) 2
645 **CHANTELLE'S DREAM** (GB) 23
18 **CHANTICLIER** (GB) 6
621 **CHANTILLY LADY** (GB) 1
237 **CHANTRY FALLS** (IRE) 2
146 **CHAPEL BAY** (GB) 8
590 **CHAPEL CORNER** (GB) 80
447 **CHAPEL CROSS** (IRE) 8
386 **CHAPEL HILL** (GB) F 7
620 **CHAPLIN** (GB) 11
265 **CHAPTER** (IRE) 35
313 **CHARA** (GB) 3
309 **CHARADE** (IRE) 18
651 **CHARANGO STAR** (GB) 3
112 **CHARDANIA** (IRE) C 45
408 **CHARING CROSS** (IRE) 19
55 **CHARIOT** (IRE) 3
392 **CHARITABLE** (IRE) C 6
85 **CHARLECOTE** (IRE) F 15
515 **CHARLESTON** (GB) 10
606 **CHARLEY BROWN** (IRE) 4
241 **CHARLIE BEAR** (GB) 3
576 **CHARLIE CASTALLAN** (GB) 4
71 **CHARLIE CHAPEL** (GB) 17
36 **CHARLIE DELTA** (GB) 29
406 **CHARLIE GEORGE** (GB) 5
185 **CHARLIE GIRL** (GB) C 44
567 **CHARLIE KENNET** (GB) 1
301 **CHARLIE MASTERS** (GB) 6
418 **CHARLIE PARKES** (GB) 4
265 **CHARLIE TOKYO** (IRE) 85
477 **CHARLIE'S CROSS** (IRE) 5
408 **CHARLIEMOORE** (GB) 20
40 **CHARLIES BRIDE** (IRE) C 27
44 **CHARLIES DOUBLE** (GB) 5
89 **CHARLIES FUTURE** (GB) 6
177 **CHARLIES MEMORY** (GB) 11
393 **CHARLLEN** (GB) 2
604 **CHARLOTT** (GER) 57
264 **CHARLOTTE VALE** (GB) 5
120 **CHARLOTTEBUTTERFLY** (GB) 3
305 **CHARLOTTEVALENTINA** (IRE) F 19
421 **CHARLY JACK** (GB) 15
214 **CHARM LOOT** (IRE) 8
247 **CHARM OFFENSIVE** (GB) 1
88 **CHARMED FOREST** 2
148 **CHARMED LADY** (GB) C 8
199 **CHARMINAMIX** (IRE) 106
347 **CHARMING FELLOW** (IRE) 13
178 **CHARMING LOTTE** (GB) F 97
33 **CHARMING PRINCESS** (GB) 18
178 **CHARNOCK BATES ONE** (IRE) 7
569 **CHARNWOOD PRIDE** (IRE) 7
535 **CHARNWOOD STREET** (IRE) 3
643 **CHART TOPPER** (GB) 5
568 **CHARTERS TOWERS** (GB) 35
178 **CHASE THE ACE** (GB) 98
347 **CHASE THE SUNSET** (IRE) 14
340 **CHASING THE DREAM** (IRE) 3
56 **CHASTE** (GB) 3
72 **CHASTE** (USA) F 63
467 **CHASTLETON BOY** (IRE) 17
568 **CHATEAU** (IRE) 36

480 **CHATEAU NICOL** (GB) 10
351 **CHATEAU ROSE** (IRE) 6
98 **CHATSHOW** (USA) 8
510 **CHAUKAO** (IRE) 25
282 **CHAUVINIST** (IRE) 22
429 **CHAYANEE'S ARENA** (IRE) C 40
396 **CHEAP N CHIC** (GB) 65
353 **CHEEKY GIRL** 2
267 **CHEEKY LAD** (GB) 2
467 **CHEEKY TRUCKER** (GB) 18
451 **CHEEKY WEEKY** (GB) C 55
111 **CHEENEY BASIN** (IRE) 3
53 **CHEERFUL GROOM** (GB) 8
309 **CHEERLEADER** (GB) 19
427 **CHEERY MARTYR** (GB) 1
408 **CHEESE 'N BISCUITS** (GB) 21
368 **CHEF DE COUR** (FR) 12
432 **CHEF TARTARE** (FR) 26
614 **CHEHALIS MIST** (IRE) 12
604 **CHELLO** (GER) 92
497 **CHELSEA** (USA) F 56
347 **CHELSEA BRIDGE** (IRE) 15
97 **CHENEY HILL** (GB) 39
370 **CHEPSTOW** (FR) 16
61 **CHERGAN** (IRE) 6
251 **CHERISH** (GB) 33
532 **CHERISHED NUMBER** (GB) 5
408 **CHEROKEE BAY** (GB) 22
294 **CHERRY'S ECHO** (GB) 3
444 **CHERUB** (GB) 2
634 **CHERYLS PET** (IRE) C 2
481 **CHESS BOARD** (GB) 45
297 **CHESTALL** (GB) 4
325 **CHESTMINSTER GIRL** (GB) 16
514 **CHEVAL DE TROIS** (GB) 122
480 **CHEVALIER BAYARD** (IRE) 11
299 **CHEVAUX LOCO** (IRE) 13
304 **CHEVERAK FOREST** (IRE) 2
319 **CHEVET BOY** (IRE) 22
200 **CHEVON** (GB) 10
465 **CHEVIOT HEIGHTS** (GB) 77
362 **CHEVRONNE** (GB) 2
275 **CHIA** (IRE) 20
562 **CHIC** (GB) 4
421 **CHICAGO BREEZE** (IRE) 16
341 **CHICAGO BULLS** (IRE) 7
577 **CHICAGO NIGHTS** (IRE) 7
166 **CHICHELE COLLEGE** (GB) 1
275 **CHICKADO** (IRE) 3
386 **CHICKAPEAKRAY** (GB) 8
297 **CHICKASAW TRAIL** (GB) 5
451 **CHICKEN SOUP** (GB) 16
453 **CHICKS BABE** (GB) 17
453 **CHICKS GIRL** (GB) 18
470 **CHICUELO** (FR) 18
385 **CHIEF DIPPER** (GB) 8
396 **CHIEF SCOUT** (GB) 27
637 **CHIEF YEOMAN** (GB) 12
192 **CHIGORIN** (GB) 1
265 **CHILD STAR** (FR) F 86
514 **CHILENO** (FR) 123
310 **CHILLIN OUT** (GB) 15
290 **CHILLING PLACE** (IRE) 11
297 **CHILLY CRACKER** (GB) 33
551 **CHILLY MILLY** (GB) 7
72 **CHILTERN COURT** (USA) C 64
60 **CHIMALI** (IRE) 3
279 **CHIMICHANGA** (FR) 85
213 **CHINA BEACH** (IRE) 5
544 **CHINA BOND** (IRE) 29
555 **CHINA CHASE** (IRE) 7
165 **CHINA JACK** (IRE) 1
531 **CHINA MISS** (GB) 15
199 **CHINA MOON** (USA) F 107
265 **CHINA PEARL** (GB) 87
133 **CHINALEA** (IRE) 10
431 **CHING CHING** (IRE) 79
628 **CHINGOLA** (GB) 18

370 **CHINKAPIN** (GB) 131
357 **CHIP AND CHARGE** (FR) 7
125 **CHIQUELINA** (FR) C 49
396 **CHIRACAHUA** (IRE) 28
390 **CHISEL** (GB) 2
87 **CHISELLED** (IRE) 30
89 **CHITA'S FLIGHT** (GB) 7
481 **CHITKA** (USA) F 46
319 **CHIVALRY** (GB) 23
290 **CHIVITE** (IRE) 12
627 **CHIVVY CHARVER** (IRE) 3
148 **CHLOE** (IRE) F 23
432 **CHOCKDEE** (FR) 27
394 **CHOCOLATCHANT** (GB) 3
184 **CHOCOLATE** (IRE) F 20
408 **CHOCOLATE BOY** (IRE) 23
465 **CHOCOLATE CARAMEL** (USA) 40
507 **CHOCSTAW** (IRE) 2
384 **CHOICE CONNECTION** (GB) 9
253 **CHOIR LEADER** (GB) 4
277 **CHOISTY** (IRE) 1
499 **CHOMOLUNGA** (FR) 15
532 **CHOOKIE HEITON** (IRE) 6
467 **CHOPINEYEV** (FR) 19
197 **CHORAL DANCER** (USA) C 50
562 **CHORALIST** (GB) 34
200 **CHOREOGRAPHIC** (IRE) 70
38 **CHOREOGRAPHY** (GB) 54
417 **CHORISTAR** (GB) 3
400 **CHORUS** (GB) 6
169 **CHORUS** (USA) F 12
512 **CHORUS BEAUTY** (GB) 2
25 **CHOYSIA** (GB) 24
437 **CHRIS AND RYAN** (IRE) 11
38 **CHRIS CORSA** (GB) 55
584 **CHRISJEN** (GB) 3
510 **CHRISTMAS CRACKER** (FR) 63
633 **CHRISTMAS TRUCE** (IRE) 18
425 **CHRISTON CANE** (GB) 6
290 **CHRISTOPHER** (GB) 1
572 **CHRISTY JNR** (IRE) 1
343 **CHROMBOY** (GER) 1
109 **CHRYSANDER** (GB) 27
514 **CHUNKY MONKEY** (GB) 3
299 **CHURCH ISLAND** (IRE) 14
579 **CIACOLE** (GB) 2
125 **CIARA MO GRA** (IRE) 6
409 **CIARA'S RUN** (IRE) 12
645 **CICATRICE** (GB) 3
310 **CICCONE** (GB) 37
287 **CIEL BLEU** (GB) 29
400 **CIEL DE FEU** (USA) F 39
108 **CIGARILLO** (IRE) 3
451 **CIGGI** (GB) 57
85 **CILLA'S SMILE** (GB) 11
50 **CILLAMON** (GB) 3
470 **CIMMAROON** (IRE) 19
611 **CIMYLA** (IRE) 3
477 **CINDER MAID** (GB) 20
545 **CINDERELLA DEREK** F 1
276 **CINDY'S BABY** (GB) C 17
133 **CINDY'S STAR** (IRE) C 27
60 **CINNAMON GIRL** (GB) 28
356 **CINNAMON LINE** (GB) 6
35 **CIONN MHALANNA** (IRE) 2
36 **CIRCE** G 30
88 **CIRCE'S MELODY** (IRE) 3
171 **CIRCLE OF LIGHT** (GB) F 53
40 **CIRCUIT DANCER** (IRE) 3
272 **CIRCUMSPECT** (IRE) 20
629 **CITIMAN** (AUS) 1
515 **CITIUS** (IRE) 11
164 **CITY AFFAIR** (GB) 4
481 **CITY CHANCER** (IRE) 47
87 **CITY FOR CONQUEST** (IRE) 56
410 **CITY GENERAL** (IRE) 3
464 **CITY MISS** (GB) 26
242 **CITY PALACE** (GB) 6

566 **DIDUBACKIT** (IRE) 18
408 **DIEGO CAO** (IRE) 30
420 **DIEGO GARCIA** (IRE) 22
216 **DIEQUEST** (USA) 3
451 **DIFFERENT** (IRE) 62
272 **DIFFERENTGEAR** (GB) 3
544 **DIFFERENTIAL** (USA) 13
253 **DIG DEEP** (IRE) 24
109 **DIGITAL** (GB) 5
202 **DIK DIK** (GB) 80
499 **DIKLERS ROSE** (IRE) 19
20 **DIKTATORIAL** (GB) 40
371 **DIL** (GB) 4
199 **DILAG** (IRE) 37
287 **DILALA** (IRE) 37
517 **DILEK** (FR) 87
5 **DILETIA** (GB) 10
557 **DILLONS DILEMMA** (IRE) 10
115 **DILMOUN** (IRE) 26
520 **DILSAA** (GB) 9
577 **DIMASHQ** (GB) 8
186 **DIMELIGHT** (GB) 60
561 **DIMPLE CHAD** (GB) 5
470 **DINARELLI** (FR) 28
429 **DINE 'N' DASH** (GB) 4
253 **DINNER DANCE** (GB) 53
310 **DINNER DATE** (GB) 16
369 **DIOSPER** (USA) 38
47 **DIPADOR** (FR) F 2
227 **DIPLOMATIC DAISY** (IRE) 3
172 **DIPPED WINGS** (IRE) 90
544 **DIPPERS** (GB) C 56
502 **DIRECT ACCESS** (IRE) 8
38 **DIRECT DEBIT** (IRE) 61
108 **DIRECT FLIGHT** (IRE) 7
557 **DISCLOSURE** (IRE) 25
650 **DISCO BALL** (GB) 27
301 **DISCO DIVA** (GB) 6
238 **DISCOMANIA** (GB) 5
92 **DISCORD** (GB) 3
562 **DISCUSS** (GB) 35
310 **DISEUSE** (GB) 38
287 **DISGUISE** (GB) 38
109 **DISOBEY** (GB) 33
590 **DISPATCHES** (GB) 29
110 **DISPOL CHARM** (IRE) 19
528 **DISPOL FOXTROT** (GB) 4
645 **DISPOL IN MIND** (GB) 24
30 **DISPOL ISLE** (IRE) 35
188 **DISPOL KATIE** (GB) 3
487 **DISPOL PETO** (GB) 5
30 **DISPOL ROCK** (IRE) 6
71 **DISPOL VELETA** (GB) 3
213 **DISPOL VERITY** (GB) 20
213 **DISSIDENT** (GB) 6
493 **DISTANT COUNTRY** (USA) 2
85 **DISTANT COUSIN** (GB) 5
287 **DISTANT DRUMS** (IRE) 90
478 **DISTANT MUSIC** (GB) F 45
20 **DISTANT PROSPECT** (IRE) 11
152 **DISTANT ROMANCE** (GB) 3
5 **DISTANT THUNDER** (IRE) 11
178 **DISTANT TIMES** (GB) 11
562 **DISTINCTION** (IRE) 7
520 **DISTINCTLY GAME** (GB) 44
544 **DISTINCTLY JIM** (IRE) 57
74 **DISTRACTING** (GB) 1
461 **DIVANI** (IRE) 12
261 **DIVET HILL** (GB) 1
264 **DIVEX** (GB) 9
412 **DIVIDEND** (GB) 1
471 **DIVINE COMEDY** (IRE) G 15
309 **DIVINE GIFT** (GB) 1
32 **DIVINE PROPORTIONS** (USA) 16
32 **DIVINE REINE** (USA) 17
161 **DIVINE SPIRIT** (GB) 6
112 **DIVINELY DECADENT** (IRE) 16
465 **DIVISION BELL** (GB) C 80

137 **DIVO NERO** (IRE) 65
562 **DIWALI** (GB) 112
177 **DIX BAY** (GB) 15
319 **DIX HUIT CYBORG** (FR) 34
491 **DIXIE BELLE** (GB) 1
94 **DIXIE FAVOR** (USA) F 17
287 **DIXIEANNA** (GB) 39
588 **DIXIELINE CITY** (GB) C 52
517 **DIYAPOUR** (FR) 3
112 **DIZZY DREAMER** (IRE) 48
310 **DIZZY FUTURE** (GB) 17
320 **DIZZY IN THE HEAD** (GB) 2
634 **DIZZY LIZZY** (GB) 17
268 **DJANGO** (IRE) 22
224 **DMITRI** (GB) 5
625 **DO KEEP UP** (GB) 7
290 **DO L'ENFANT D'EAU** (FR) 19
184 **DO THE RIGHT THING** (GB) F 21
353 **DOBERMAN** (IRE) 4
600 **DOCDUCKOUT** (GB) 4
341 **DOCE VIDA** (GB) 23
49 **DOCK COPPER'S GIRL** (GB) 4
288 **DOCK TOWER** (IRE) 14
394 **DOCKERSBOY** (USA) 5
109 **DOCTOR BAILEY** (GB) 34
186 **DOCTOR DASH** (GB) 61
461 **DOCTOR DENNIS** (IRE) 1
232 **DOCTOR DINO** (FR) 20
54 **DOCTOR ICE** (FR) 12
72 **DOCTOR'S CAVE** (IRE) 25
197 **DOCTORED** (GB) 8
199 **DOCUMENTARY** (USA) 38
178 **DOE NAL RUA** (IRE) 12
335 **DOES IT MATTER** (GB) 3
200 **DOITNOW** (IRE) 15
370 **DOLCE DU BERLAIS** (FR) 19
396 **DOLCE PICCATA** (GB) 5
486 **DOLLAR LAW** (GB) 5
193 **DOLLIVIUS** (IRE) 4
588 **DOLLS HOUSE** (GB) 26
178 **DOLLY BROWN** (GB) 104
221 **DOLLY OF DUBLIN** (IRE) 4
568 **DOLLY PEEL** (GB) 39
361 **DOLLY WOTNOT** (IRE) 8
119 **DOLMA** (FR) 1
421 **DOLMUR** (IRE) 20
88 **DOLPHIN BAY** (IRE) 4
357 **DOLPHIN STAR** (FR) 50
479 **DOLPHINELLE** (IRE) 3
414 **DOLYDILLE** (IRE) F 67
408 **DOLZAGO** (GB) 31
634 **DOM D'ORGEVAL** (FR) 6
510 **DOM JARO** (FR) 27
471 **DOMART** (POL) 16
313 **DOMENICO** (IRE) 6
439 **DOMINATING VISTA** (GB) 18
583 **DOMINICAN MONK** (IRE) 8
319 **DOMINUET** F 108
45 **DOMIRATI** (GB) 1
370 **DOMIROME** (FR) 20
89 **DOMPTEUR** (FR) 29
303 **DON AMECHIE** (IRE) 15
58 **DON ARGENTO** (GB) 4
604 **DON BERNARDO** (GER) 14
345 **DON PELE** (GB) 23
138 **DON PIETRO** (GB) 13
470 **DON'T ASK ME** (IRE) 29
323 **DON'T MATTER** (GB) 3
444 **DON'T PUSH IT** (IRE) 22
166 **DON'T SMILE** (GB) C 5
565 **DON'T TELL JR** (IRE) 4
287 **DON'T TELL SUE** (IRE) 91
410 **DON'T TELL TRIGGER** (IRE) 17
588 **DON'TCCALLMEGINGER** (IRE) 53
345 **DONA VITORIA** (GB) 48
471 **DONALD** (POL) 17
20 **DONASTRELA** (IRE) 12
96 **DONEGAL SHORE** (IRE) 7

168 **DONIA DUBAI** (IRE) 19
147 **DONIE DOOLEY** (IRE) 3
396 **DONNA BLINI** (GB) 69
180 **DONNA'S DOUBLE** (GB) 2
601 **DONNABELLA** (GB) 7
646 **DONNYBROOK** (IRE) 2
252 **DONOVAN** (NZ) 17
515 **DONT CALL ME BABE** (GB) 37
492 **DONT CALL ME DEREK** (GB) 10
410 **DONT DILI DALI** (GB) 28
401 **DONT WORRY BOUT ME** (IRE) 2
84 **DONTNOCK'ER** (IRE) 4
137 **DONYA** C 66
137 **DONYA ONE** (GB) 24
309 **DONYANA** (GB) 21
470 **DOOF** (IRE) 30
104 **DOOIE DANCER** (GB) 10
253 **DOONEQ** (GB) 25
637 **DOOR OF KNOWLEDGE** (USA) 18
514 **DOOSELINDE** (USA) 124
569 **DORA CARRINGTON** (IRE) F 73
297 **DORA CORBINO** (GB) 9
52 **DORA'S GREEN** (GB) 24
115 **DORABIL** (IRE) 63
447 **DORAN'S DAY** (IRE) 11
71 **DORANS LANE** (GB) 21
270 **DORAZINE** (GB) G 3
424 **DORCHESTER** (GB) 5
185 **DORIC** (USA) 12
555 **DORINGO** (GB) 3
265 **DORIS SOUTER** (IRE) 8
319 **DORIS'S GIFT** (GB) 35
608 **DORMY TWO** (IRE) 6
25 **DORN DANCER** (IRE) 13
259 **DORN HILL** (GB) 9
569 **DOROTHEA BROOKE** (IRE) F 74
115 **DOROTHY'S FRIEND** (GB) 6
518 **DOTTIE DIGGER** (IRE) 7
510 **DOTTORE VETTORI** (IRE) 5
172 **DOUBLE AGENT** (IRE) 91
430 **DOUBLE AGENT** (GB) 3
444 **DOUBLE ASPECT** (IRE) 23
641 **DOUBLE BLADE** (GB) 8
514 **DOUBLE BRANDY** (USA) 125
162 **DOUBLE CREME** (FR) 8
154 **DOUBLE DAWN** (GB) 18
84 **DOUBLE DIZZY** (GB) 5
451 **DOUBLE EIGHT** (IRE) C 63
312 **DOUBLE ELLS** (GB) 39
220 **DOUBLE EMBLEM** (IRE) 6
614 **DOUBLE FAULT** (GB) F 31
162 **DOUBLE FIL** (FR) 68
604 **DOUBLE FUN** (HOL) 15
114 **DOUBLE GEM** (IRE) 4
7 **DOUBLE GIN** (GB) 4
614 **DOUBLE GRANGE** (IRE) C 32
636 **DOUBLE HEADER** (IRE) 4
290 **DOUBLE HONOUR** (FR) 20
479 **DOUBLE KUDOS** (FR) 15
620 **DOUBLE LAW** (GB) 17
421 **DOUBLE LEO** (FR) 21
501 **DOUBLE M** (GB) 3
479 **DOUBLE MAGNUM** (GB) 4
479 **DOUBLE MARGIN** (USA) 16
512 **DOUBLE OR BUST** (GB) F 15
564 **DOUBLE RANSOM** (GB) 1
301 **DOUBLE ROCK** (GB) G 26
575 **DOUBLE RUNNER** (GB) 3
418 **DOUBLE SPREAD** (GB) 6
162 **DOUBLE TONIC** (FR) 9
71 **DOUBLE TURN** (GB) 3
493 **DOUBLE VODKA** (IRE) 3
239 **DOUBLE YOU CUBED** (GB) 3
514 **DOUBNOV** (FR) 126
215 **DOUCEUR DES SONGES** (FR) 3
370 **DOUZE DOUZE** (FR) 21
346 **DOVE COTTAGE** (IRE) 8
259 **DOVEDALE** (GB) 3

478 FOX STAR (IRE) C 48
282 FOXCHAPEL QUEEN (IRE) 35
107 FOXHAVEN (GB) 26
625 FOXIES FUTURE (IRE) 8
505 FOXMEADE DANCER (GB) 1
282 FOXTON BROOK (IRE) 36
227 FOXTROT PIE (GB) F 6
342 FOXTROT YANKEE (IRE) 3
145 FOXTROTROMEOYANKEE (GB) 3
214 FOXY FRED (IRE) 14
20 FOXY GWYNNE (GB) 43
611 FOXYSOX (GB) 43
405 FRABROFEN (GB) 42
199 FRACASSANT (IRE) 9
438 FRAGILE WITNESS (GB) 16
72 FRAGRANT STAR (GB) 5
199 FRALOGA (IRE) 42
477 FRAMBO (IRE) 9
514 FRAMBOISE (GB) 49
112 FRAMILY LOVE (GB) 18
143 FRAMLINGHAM (GB) 5
357 FRANC BOURGEOIS (FR) 52
304 FRANCESCHIELLA (ITY) 5
618 FRANCKEN (ITY) 1
487 FRANCOLINO (GB) 8
268 FRANK MOSS BENNETT (IRE) 28
491 FRANK SONATA (GB) 2
276 FRANK'S QUEST (IRE) 2
366 FRANKINCENSE (IRE) 2
588 FRANKLINS GARDENS (GB) 7
420 FRANKLINS TRAIL (GB) 28
348 FRANKLY NATIVE (IRE) F 1
217 FRANKLY NATIVE (IRE) F 8
522 FRANKSALOT (IRE) 5
137 FRANNY (GB) 28
272 FRANSISCAN (GB) 26
67 FRATT'N PARK (IRE) 18
611 FRAXINUS (GB) 44
351 FREAK OCCURENCE (IRE) 9
162 FRED ASTOR (FR) 12
607 FRED'S IN THE KNOW (GB) 7
46 FREDDIE ED 5
237 FREDDIE FRECCLES (GB) 6
277 FREDERICK JAMES (GB) 3
115 FREE LIFT (GB) 29
424 FREE OPTION (IRE) 9
108 FREE RETURN (IRE) 9
404 FREE STRIKE (NZ) 6
567 FREE STYLE (GER) 4
139 FREE SURFING (FR) 6
20 FREE TO AIR (GB) 94
1 FREE WHEELIN' (IRE) 11
272 FREEDOM FLYING (GB) 53
585 FREEDOM NOW (IRE) 11
620 FREELINE FURY (GB) 22
288 FREELOADER (GB) 4
221 FREEMANTLE DOCTOR (IRE) 7
237 FREEST (GB) 42
368 FREETOWN (IRE) 20
253 FREGATE ISLAND (IRE) 56
431 FREMEN (USA) 23
475 FRENCH BEY (IRE) 3
515 FRENCH DIRECTION (IRE) 15
432 FRENCH EXECUTIVE (IRE) 42
186 FRENCH GIFT (GB) C 65
4 FRENCH GIGOLO (GB) 1
577 FRENCH KISSES (GB) 9
263 FRENCH MANNEQUIN (IRE) 2
451 FRENCH OPERA (IRE) 65
71 FRENCH RISK (IRE) 29
257 FRENCH TUNE (FR) 1
554 FRENCHGATE (GB) 5
414 FRENCHMAN'S CREEK (GB) 12
62 FRENCHMANS LODGE (GB) 11
581 FRESCHEZZA (GB) 20
313 FRESH FRUIT DAILY (GB) G 40
242 FREYDIS (IRE) 8
464 FRIAR TUCK (GB) 4

138 FRIDA (GB) 9
433 FRIEDHELMO (GER) 9
407 FRIENDLY CONFLICT (IRE) 11
273 FRIENDLY GIRL (IRE) 2
53 FRIENDS HOPE (GB) 14
349 FRIGILIANA (GB) 30
29 FRIMLEY'S MATTERRY (GB) 6
569 FRIPPET (IRE) C 83
287 FRITH (IRE) 45
531 FRIXOS (IRE) 15
409 FROGS' GIFT (GB) 38
290 FROM DAWN TO DUSK (GB) 31
421 FROM LITTLE ACORNS (IRE) 26
400 FROMSONG (GB) 8
18 FRONT RANK (IRE) 10
562 FRONT STAGE (IRE) 40
363 FRONTIER (GB) 10
512 FRONTLINEFINANCIER (IRE) 4
369 FROOT LOOP (IRE) 3
620 FROSTY'S COUSIN (IRE) 23
313 FRUIT OF GLORY (GB) 9
447 FRUITFULL CITIZEN (IRE) 15
476 FU FIGHTER (GB) 1
478 FUBOS (GB) 12
30 FUDGE (GB) C 58
265 FUEL CELL (IRE) 11
370 FUELA PASS (IRE) 191
162 FUJAIRAH (SWI) 51
148 FULFILL (GB) 24
18 FULGERE (IRE) 11
431 FULL AS A ROCKET (IRE) 24
620 FULL HOUSE (IRE) 24
368 FULL IRISH (IRE) 21
465 FULL OF ZEST (GB) 45
256 FULL ON (GB) 2
314 FULL PITCH (GB) 3
62 FULL SPATE (GB) 12
542 FULLANIS (GB) 11
635 FULVIO (USA) 4
633 FULWELL HILL (GB) 24
608 FUN BOARD (FR) F 31
177 FUN TO RIDE (GB) 2
444 FUNDAMENTAL (GB) 29
599 FUNDAMENTALIST (IRE) 17
172 FUNDRAISER C 96
465 FUNFAIR (GB) 8
431 FUNFAIR WANE (GB) 25
199 FUNMAKER (GB) 115
502 FUNNY TIMES (GB) 2
40 FUREUR DE VIVRE (IRE) F 58
478 FURRY DANCE (USA) F 49
178 FURS N GEMS (GB) 107
604 FURSTENBERG (IRE) 65
306 FURTHER OUTLOOK (USA) 6
491 FUSILI (IRE) 22
562 FUSILIER (GB) 122
366 FUSILLADE (IRE) 7
615 FUSION OF TUNES (GB) 4
310 FUSS (GB) 2
409 FUTOO (IRE) 13
171 FUTUH (USA) C 72
137 FUTUN (GB) 72
614 FUTURE ACT (USA) C 36
449 FUTURE LEGEND (GB) 14
604 FYODOR (GER) 21
253 FYODOR (IRE) 6
171 FYVIE (GB) 73
214 G V A IRELAND (IRE) 15
463 GABACHA (USA) C 42
611 GABANA (GB) 7
252 GABANA (NZ) 20
408 GABOR (GB) 39
199 GABRIELI (GB) 116
225 GAELIC COLLEEN (GB) 12
108 GAELIC FLIGHT (IRE) 10
400 GAELIC FORAY (GB) F 25
114 GAELIC JIG (GB) 5
63 GAELIC MUSIC (IRE) 4

429 GAELIC PRINCESS (GB) 8
311 GAELIC ROULETTE (IRE) 4
116 GAILY ROYAL (IRE) C 13
514 GAILY TIARA (USA) F 132
514 GAIMIX (GB) 50
601 GAINING GROUND (IRE) 8
562 GALA EVENING (GB) 41
652 GALA QUEEN (GB) 1
88 GALA STYLE (IRE) 22
177 GALA SUNDAY (USA) 21
562 GALACTIC STAR (GB) 123
425 GALANDORA (GB) 7
324 GALANT EYE (IRE) 3
432 GALAPIAT DU MESNIL (FR) 43
420 GALARINI (IRE) 29
514 GALATEE (GB) F 133
171 GALAXY BOUND (GB) 74
233 GALAXY SAM (USA) 8
369 GALDO (IRE) 39
437 GALE (GB) G 18
437 GALE (GB) G 19
437 GALE (GB) G 43
517 GALE FORCE (IRE) 28
624 GALE FORCE ONE (GB) 6
65 GALE STAR (IRE) 7
265 GALEOTA (IRE) 43
319 GALERO (GB) 41
309 GALIENT (IRE) 67
199 GALILANO (GB) 43
287 GALILEO'S STAR (IRE) 95
440 GALINE (GB) C 4
182 GALLANT APPROACH (IRE) 11
197 GALLANT BOY (IRE) 10
202 GALLANT GUEST (IRE) 42
562 GALLANTRY (GB) 42
486 GALLEGO (GB) 15
53 GALLERY BREEZE (GB) 15
178 GALLERY GIRL (IRE) 108
163 GALLERY GOD (FR) 4
134 GALLEY LAW (GB) 1
183 GALLIC FLAME (GB) G 1
296 GALLIK DAWN (GB) 3
41 GALLOPING HOME (IRE) 6
440 GALLOWAY MAC (GB) 1
566 GALTEEMOUNTAIN BOY (IRE) 20
369 GALWAY ADVERTISER (IRE) 9
615 GALWAY BREEZE (IRE) 5
265 GAMBLE IN GOLD (IRE) 96
562 GAMBLE OF THE DAY (USA) 43
97 GAMBLING SPIRIT (GB) 20
412 GAME DOMINO (GB) F 6
554 GAME FLORA (GB) 2
53 GAME GURU (GB) 16
178 GAME LAD (GB) 64
178 GAME OF LOVE (GB) 109
474 GAME ON (IRE) 3
71 GAMESTERS LADY (GB) 98
472 GAMMA-DELTA (IRE) 3
562 GAMUT (IRE) 1
637 GAN EAGLA (IRE) 23
107 GANACHE (GB) 27
279 GANAGO (FR) 39
202 GANDALF (GB) 43
349 GANDIA (IRE) 31
437 GANDILOO GULLY (GB) 20
303 GANDY (IRE) 20
354 GANE MARIE (IRE) 6
455 GANGSTERS R US (IRE) 6
381 GAORA BRIDGE (IRE) 25
570 GARDASEE (GER) 10
421 GARDE BIEN (GB) 27
414 GARDEN FOLLY (USA) C 69
108 GARDEN SHED REBEL (GB) 11
234 GARDEN SOCIETY (IRE) 6
437 GARGOYLE GIRL (GB) 4
171 GARHOUD (GB) 19
186 GARIBALDI (GER) 36
40 GARNOCK VENTURE (IRE) 7

581 GLIMPSE OF GLORY (GB) 3
502 GLINGER (IRE) 13
614 GLINSK (IRE) 16
148 GLINTING DESERT (IRE) 11
562 GLISTENING (GB) 44
116 GLOBAL ACHIEVER (GB) 2
116 GLOBAL BANKER (IRE) 8
444 GLOBAL CHALLENGE (IRE) 30
287 GLOBAL GENIUS (IRE) 97
396 GLOBAL GUARDIAN (GB) 73
423 GLOBE PEARL (IRE) 7
405 GLOBE TREKKER (USA) 21
565 GLORY OF LOVE (GB) 5
336 GLORY QUEST (USA) 10
237 GLOVED HAND (GB) 44
515 GLOW IN THE PARK (GB) 16
151 GLOWING DAWN (IRE) 4
454 GLOWING EMBER (GB) 2
470 GNILLISH (GB) 42
256 GO CLASSIC (GB) 3
282 GO FOR BUST (GB) 38
9 GO GARUDA (IRE) 4
131 GO GO GIRL (GB) 1
197 GO GREEN (GB) 11
467 GO HARVEY GO (IRE) 36
251 GO LIKE THE WIND (GB) 21
345 GO MO (IRE) 26
11 GO NOMADIC (GB) 1
129 GO ON AHEAD (IRE) 1
208 GO ON JACK (GB) 2
370 GO ON MY SON (FR) 24
252 GO PETE (NZ) 23
441 GO ROGER GO (IRE) 20
568 GO SOLO (GB) 4
238 GO TALLY-HO (GB) F 10
178 GO TECH (GB) 19
436 GO THUNDER (GB) 8
63 GO WHITE LIGHTNING (IRE) 5
197 GO YELLOW (GB) 12
432 GOBLET OF FIRE (USA) 47
471 GODFATHER (IRE) 27
265 GODFREY STREET (GB) 98
627 GOFAGOLD (GB) 7
225 GOGETTER GIRL (GB) 10
177 GOHH (GB) 2
453 GOJO (IRE) 8
356 GOLA SUPREME (IRE) 9
620 GOLANO (GB) 27
137 GOLBAND (GB) 29
184 GOLCONDA (GB) C 24
108 GOLD AGAIN (IRE) 12
543 GOLD CHARM (GB) 21
310 GOLD DRAGON (GB) 40
440 GOLD EXPRESS (GB) 5
71 GOLD FERVOUR (IRE) 31
97 GOLD FLAME (GB) 46
470 GOLD FOR ME (IRE) 43
99 GOLD GUEST (GB) 5
309 GOLD GUN (USA) 23
109 GOLD MAJESTY (GB) 41
396 GOLD MIST (GB) G 74
544 GOLD PROSPECTOR (IRE) F 59
109 GOLD QUEEN (GB) 42
229 GOLD RING (GB) 19
349 GOLD SOUND (FR) 32
390 GOLD STRIKE (GB) 9
643 GOLD TARIFF (IRE) 10
272 GOLDA SEEK (USA) 54
71 GOLDBRICKER (GB) 32
291 GOLDBROOK (GB) 5
265 GOLDEN ACER (IRE) 99
470 GOLDEN ALPHA (IRE) 44
601 GOLDEN AMBER (IRE) 9
461 GOLDEN ANTHEM (USA) 14
340 GOLDEN APPLAUSE (FR) 13
93 GOLDEN ASHA (GB) 10
557 GOLDEN BASKET (IRE) 2
229 GOLDEN BAY (GB) 20

17 GOLDEN BOOT (GB) 8
641 GOLDEN BOUNTY (GB) 10
351 GOLDEN CHALICE (IRE) 11
71 GOLDEN COIN (GB) 33
229 GOLDEN CREW (GB) 21
419 GOLDEN CRUSADER (GB) 13
88 GOLDEN DEW (IRE) 23
178 GOLDEN DIAMONT (IRE) F 110
174 GOLDEN DIXIE (IRE) 12
599 GOLDEN DUCK (IRE) 20
265 GOLDEN DYNASTY (GB) 45
96 GOLDEN FIELDS (IRE) 11
563 GOLDEN FITZ (ARG) 3
370 GOLDEN FLIGHT (FR) 25
172 GOLDEN FURY (GB) 41
38 GOLDEN GATE (IRE) 22
287 GOLDEN GRIMSHAW (IRE) 46
201 GOLDEN GROOM (GB) 16
117 GOLDEN HAWK (USA) 1
288 GOLDEN ISLAND (IRE) 5
547 GOLDEN KEY (GB) 3
274 GOLDEN LEAP (GB) C 9
200 GOLDEN LEGACY (IRE) 75
568 GOLDEN MEASURE (GB) 10
604 GOLDEN MILLENIUM (GER) 22
499 GOLDEN ODYSSEY (IRE) 3
279 GOLDEN PALACE (USA) 40
184 GOLDEN PANDA G 25
34 GOLDEN PARACHUTE (IRE) 15
602 GOLDEN QUEEN (GB) 3
444 GOLDEN RAMBLER (IRE) 31
92 GOLDEN SNOOPY (GB) 7
431 GOLDEN SPECTRUM (IRE) 27
178 GOLDEN SQUAW (GB) 65
265 GOLDEN SURF (IRE) 100
157 GOLDEN TAMESIS (GB) 9
483 GOLDEN TINA (GB) 4
463 GOLDEN WINGS (USA) C 43
217 GOLDENAVOUR (FR) 9
125 GOLDENPHEE (FR) 10
297 GOLDEVA (GB) 12
604 GOLDHANS (GER) 23
65 GOLDHORN (IRE) 8
279 GOLDINA (USA) 41
89 GOLDSEAM (GER) 11
369 GOLDSTAR DANCER (IRE) 40
631 GOLLY (IRE) 8
309 GOLO GAL (GB) 24
246 GOLOVIN (GER) 10
408 GONCHAROVA (USA) C 118
78 GONDOLIN (IRE) 3
214 GONE DANCING (IRE) 18
470 GONE FAR (USA) 45
309 GONE FISHING (IRE) 25
406 GONE TOO FAR (GB) 8
9 GONE WITH THE WIND (IRE) F 16
303 GONEFORALLTIME (IRE) 21
325 GOOD ARTICLE (GB) 6
231 GOOD CITIZEN (IRE) 16
135 GOOD FRIEND (GB) 3
171 GOOD GOING GRACIE (USA) C 78
272 GOOD INVESTMENT (GB) 28
444 GOOD JUDGEMENT (IRE) 32
268 GOOD NICK (GB) 30
217 GOOD OUTLOOK (IRE) 10
471 GOOD SAMARITAN (IRE) 28
370 GOOD SPIRIT (FR) 136
389 GOODANDPLENTY (GB) 6
389 GOODBADINDIFERENT (IRE) 7
6 GOODBYE MR BOND (GB) 5
342 GOODENOUGH MOVER (GB) 4
346 GOODLEIGH GENERAL (GB) 9
420 GOODNIGHT DICK (IRE) 32
178 GOODTIME GIRL (IRE) 111
172 GOODWOOD MARCH (GB) 98
172 GOODWOOD SPIRIT (GB) 42
429 GOODY FOUR SHOES (GB) F 42
569 GOOGOOSH (IRE) C 87

38 GOOSE CHASE (GB) 23
507 GORDON HIGHLANDER (GB) 4
258 GORDY'S JOY (GB) 7
234 GORGEOUS BOY (IRE) 11
109 GORGEOUS DANCER (IRE) C 111
432 GORTNAVARNOGUE (IRE) 48
206 GORTUMBLO (GB) 14
97 GOSLAR (GB) 5
627 GOSPEL SONG (GB) 8
444 GOSS (GB) 33
444 GOSS HAWK (NZ) 34
277 GOT ALOT ON (USA) 4
343 GOT NO SHADOW (GB) 5
71 GOT TO BE CASH (GB) 34
463 GOTABLUSH (IRE) 14
5 GOTHAM (IRE) 18
5 GOTTA GET ON (GB) 19
111 GOVERNMENT (IRE) 7
186 GOWER SONG (GB) 66
614 GRAB THE PRIZE (USA) C 37
531 GRACE DIEU (GB) 17
109 GRACECHURCH (IRE) 112
625 GRACEFUL AIR (IRE) 9
480 GRACEFUL DANCER (GB) 18
20 GRACEFUL EXIT (IRE) 97
398 GRACEFUL FLIGHT (GB) 11
272 GRACIE'S GIFT (IRE) 29
568 GRACILIS (IRE) 11
168 GRACIOUS IMP (USA) F 20
589 GRAFT (GB) 2
45 GRAFTON (IRE) 25
518 GRAFTON TRUCE (IRE) 14
650 GRAHAM ISLAND (GB) 5
562 GRAIN OF TRUTH (GB) 126
520 GRALMANO (IRE) 11
213 GRAMADA (IRE) 20
237 GRAMPIAN (GB) 7
191 GRAN CLICQUOT (GB) 3
488 GRAN DANA (IRE) 3
453 GRANARY AIR (GB) 21
478 GRAND ASSAULT (GB) 50
199 GRAND BAHAMA (IRE) 44
88 GRAND CARE (IRE) 24
251 GRAND COURSE (IRE) 22
570 GRAND DAUM (FR) 4
182 GRAND ENTRANCE (IRE) 37
637 GRAND FINALE (IRE) 24
169 GRAND GIRL (GB) 8
478 GRAND IDEAS (GB) 13
499 GRAND MANNER (IRE) 24
514 GRAND MASSA (FR) 135
357 GRAND OPENING (GB) 53
169 GRAND OPTION (GB) 9
562 GRAND PALACE (IRE) 127
650 GRAND PASSION (IRE) 6
408 GRAND PRAIRIE (SWE) 42
555 GRAND RAPIDE (GB) 11
477 GRAND SEFTON (GB) 30
569 GRAND SHOW (GB) 42
627 GRAND SLAM (GB) 9
199 GRAND VADLA (FR) 118
625 GRAND VIEW (GB) 10
432 GRANDE CREOLE (FR) 49
282 GRANDE JETE (SAF) 39
32 GRANDE MELODY (IRE) 76
287 GRANDE ROCHE (IRE) 47
543 GRANDES ILLUSIONS (FR) 4
246 GRANDFIELD (IRE) 41
99 GRANDMA LILY (IRE) 6
590 GRANDMA MOSES (GB) 89
42 GRANDMA RYTA (GB) 16
251 GRANDMA'S GIRL (GB) 23
178 GRANDOS (IRE) 66
108 GRANGE PARK (IRE) G 13
214 GRANGEBEG (IRE) 19
421 GRANIT D'ESTRUVAL (FR) 28
52 GRANITA (GB) 11
421 GRANITE STEPS (GB) 29

272 LUCKY BAMBLUE (IRE) 60
3 LUCKY BRUSH (IRE) 5
319 LUCKY DAISY (GB) C 69
157 LUCKY DO (GB) 27
261 LUCKY DUCK (GB) 3
453 LUCKY EMERALD (IRE) 23
568 LUCKY JUDGE (GB) 15
464 LUCKY LARGO (IRE) 5
403 LUCKY LEADER (IRE) 4
633 LUCKY LEO (GB) 38
628 LUCKY LIL (GB) 23
72 LUCKY LINEAGE (USA) F 81
184 LUCKY LUCKY (IRE) 12
18 LUCKY LUK (IRE) 20
349 LUCKY NAME (IRE) 26
217 LUCKY NOMAD (GB) 14
119 LUCKY NORWEGIAN (IRE) 15
327 LUCKY PETE (GB) 3
201 LUCKY PISCEAN (GB) 3
480 LUCKY SINNA (IRE) 34
614 LUCKY SIS (GB) 40
265 LUCKY SPIN (GB) 17
369 LUCKY SPIRIT (IRE) 20
407 LUCKY STAR (FR) 25
171 LUCKY TOKEN (FR) 92
408 LUCKY VALENTINE (GB) 55
104 LUCKY WISH (GB) 45
577 LUCKYCHARM (FR) 28
439 LUCY IN THE SKY (IRE) C 70
1125 LUDERE (IRE) 4
162 LUDRE (IRE) 20
304 LUFERTON LANE (IRE) 7
351 LUFTIKUS (GER) 19
21 LUGANA POINT (GB) 45
268 LUGANTE (IRE) 48
153 LUGNASAD (GB) 9
620 LUGO ROCK (GB) 35
124 LUIS MELENDEZ (USA) 42
40 LUISA DEMON (GB) F 64
414 LUJAIN ROSE (GB) 50
232 LUJEANNE (FR) 78
607 LUKE AFTER ME (IRE) 4
441 LULLABY (FR) 35
119 LUMINOSITY (GB) F 34
432 LUMINOUS GIRL (IRE) G 77
538 LUMYNO (FR) 5
470 LUNAR CRYSTAL (IRE) 77
283 LUNAR EXIT (IRE) 9
426 LUNAR FOX (GB) 9
86 LUNAR LORD (GB) 4
196 LUNAR LORD (GB) 5
308 LUNAR PROMISE (IRE) 19
441 LUNAR SEA (IRE) 36
72 LUNAR SKY (USA) 58
631 LUNARDI (IRE) 10
514 LUNATTORI (GB) 153
432 LUNCH WAS MY IDEA (IRE) 78
72 LUNDA (FR) F 82
429 LUNDY LADY (GB) F 44
232 LUNE D'OR (FR) 6
432 LUNERAY (FR) 79
98 LUPIN (FR) 26
228 LURID AFFAIR (FR) 4
590 LURINA (IRE) C 102
370 LUSAKA DE PEMBO (FR) 51
93 LUSCINIA (GB) 33
226 LUSHES RUN (GB) 1
69 LUSHPOOL (IRE) 16
229 LUSIMUS (GB) 28
282 LUSTRAL DU SEUIL (FR) 60
470 LUTEA (IRE) 78
319 LUTHELLO (FR) 70
32 LUTIKAI (GB) 28
368 LUTIN DU MOULIN (FR) 32
437 LUTINE BELL (IRE) 44
421 LUZCADOU (FR) 45
585 LY'S WEST (GB) 18
36 LYES GREEN (GB) 7

279 LYFORDMIX (FR) 48
336 LYGETON LAD (GB) 15
439 LYNA (GB) C 71
178 LYNDALEE (IRE) 118
369 LYNNESEEMEPLEASE (USA) F 62
232 LYNNWOOD CHASE (USA) 31
477 LYNRICK LADY (IRE) 12
537 LYON (GB) 20
417 LYPHARDEN (FR) C 39
72 LYRIC (GB) C 83
311 LYRIC DANCE (FR) 16
202 LYRICAL DANCE (USA) C 88
582 LYRICAL LILY (GB) 13
107 LYRICAL WAY (GB) 8
305 LYSANDER'S QUEST (IRE) 6
562 LYSANDRA (FR) 59
541 LYSSAGE (GB) F 19
441 LYSTER (IRE) 37
201 M FOR MAGIC (GB) 4
229 M'LORD (GB) 29
40 MA BELLA LUNA (GB) F 65
236 MA BURLS (GB) 7
347 MA FURIE (FR) 45
637 MA YAHAB (GB) 45
645 MA'AM (USA) 33
590 MAAL (FR) 103
191 MAAREES (GB) 7
287 MABADI (USA) 108
369 MABEL (FR) 63
355 MABEL RILEY (FR) 4
400 MABELLA (FR) 28
520 MAC COIS NA TINE (GB) 48
444 MAC HINE (IRE) 48
1 MAC LOVE (GB) 16
421 MAC'S SUPREME (IRE) 46
551 MAC'S TALISMAN (IRE) 13
310 MACARONI GOLD (IRE) 4
115 MACAULAY (IRE) 39
442 MACCA LUNA (IRE) C 22
391 MACCHIATO (GB) 7
410 MACEDON (GB) 33
499 MACEO (FR) 37
356 MACGEORGE (IRE) 13
631 MACGYVER (NZ) 11
32 MACHINALE (USA) 29
431 MACHINIST (IRE) 18
161 MACHUDI (GB) F 36
339 MACKENZIE (IRE) 3
408 MACLEAN (GB) 56
5 MACMAR (FR) 28
356 MACNANCE (IRE) 14
368 MACONNOR (IRE) 33
411 MACREATER (GB) 16
420 MACS GILDORAN (GB) 51
268 MACS JOY (IRE) 49
93 MACS RANSOM (USA) 34
52 MACVEL (IRE) 26
497 MAD (GB) 6
308 MAD ANNIE (USA) C 36
408 MAD CAREW (GB) 57
370 MAD EO (FR) 52
152 MAD LOUIE (GB) 8
77 MAD MARTY WILDCARD (GB) 16
142 MAD MAURICE (GB) 5
641 MAD MAX TOO (GB) 15
99 MADAM BAILEYS (IRE) C 33
535 MADAM BIJOU (GB) 32
129 MADAM FLEET (GB) 1
621 MADAM FLORA (GB) 7
396 MADAM MAC (IRE) 85
582 MADAM MOSSO (GB) 14
199 MADAME ARCATI (GB) 130
395 MADAME BAVARDE (GB) 1
318 MADAME CLAUDE (GB) C 22
442 MADAME FATALE (IRE) 19
164 MADAME LUSO (GB) 19
246 MADAME MARJOU (IRE) 16
104 MADAME MOGAMBO (USA) 22

166 MADAME ROUX (GB) 2
514 MADANI (FR) 13
313 MADDIE'S A JEM (GB) 17
470 MADE IN FRANCE (FR) 79
290 MADE IN JAPAN (JPN) 52
432 MADE IN MONTOT (FR) 80
287 MADEMOISELLE (GB) 18
178 MADEMOISELLE CHLOE C 119
514 MADEMOISELLE SISSI (IRE) 154
633 MADGIK DE BEAUMONT (FR) 39
265 MADHAVI (GB) 54
301 MADIBA (GB) 11
328 MADISON AVENUE (GER) 4
351 MADISON DE VONNAS (FR) 20
370 MADISON DU BERLAIS (FR) 53
464 MADRA RUA (IRE) 6
128 MADRID PLEASE (IRE) 6
551 MAEVEEN (IRE) 14
88 MAFIOSA F 30
332 MAGALINA (IRE) 25
71 MAGARI (GB) 41
256 MAGDELAINE (GB) 16
370 MAGE D'ESTRUVAL (FR) 54
287 MAGENKO (FR) 12
72 MAGGI FOR MARGARET (GB) F 84
396 MAGGIE JORDAN (USA) 36
569 MAGGIE TULLIVER (IRE) 47
543 MAGGY SHAN (FR) 45
590 MAGHAZI (FR) 43
313 MAGIC AMIGO (GB) 18
344 MAGIC BENGIE (GB) 2
148 MAGIC BRACELET (GB) 13
442 MAGIC CHARM (GB) 6
510 MAGIC DES GALAS (FR) 36
77 MAGIC GLADE (GB) 7
214 MAGIC MARK (IRE) 26
569 MAGIC MERLIN (GB) 15
282 MAGIC MISTRESS (GB) 61
515 MAGIC OF SYDNEY (IRE) 26
562 MAGIC PEAK (IRE) 144
72 MAGIC SISTER (GB) F 85
38 MAGIC STING (GB) 4
109 MAGIC TREE (UAE) 52
222 MAGIC WARRIOR (GB) 8
314 MAGICAL LIAISON (IRE) 5
109 MAGICAL MUSIC (GB) 127
396 MAGICAL ROMANCE (FR) 37
551 MAGICAL WIT (IRE) 15
276 MAGICO (GB) 4
252 MAGICO (NZ) 28
44 MAGIDENE (GB) 49
279 MAGIE FRANCAISE (FR) 97
377 MAGNATE (IRE) 7
480 MAGNESIUM (USA) 35
102 MAGNETIC POLE (GB) 9
347 MAGNIFICENT SEVEN (IRE) 46
199 MAGNUM OPUS (IRE) 55
5 MAGOT DE GRUGY (FR) 29
512 MAGPIE BRIDGE (GB) 16
423 MAGS TWO (GB) 13
270 MAGUIRE (GER) 10
290 MAHARAAT (USA) 53
282 MAHARBAL (FR) 62
177 MAHBOB DANCER (FR) F 94
407 MAHDI DE COEUR (FR) 26
590 MAHFADHA (GB) 104
514 MAHIMA (FR) 62
109 MAHMJRA (GB) 53
132 MAID FOR LOVE (GB) 28
226 MAID OF GLENDURAGH (IRE) F 2
149 MAID OF GLENDURAGH (IRE) G 27
309 MAID OF KASHMIR (IRE) F 73
545 MAID THE CUT (GB) 4
620 MAIDEN VOYAGE (GB) 28
287 MAIDS CAUSEWAY (IRE) 59
582 MAIDSTONE MONUMENT (IRE) 15
432 MAIFUL (FR) 81
88 MAIGUE VIOLET (IRE) 31

1	**MARNIE** (GB) 17
33	**MAROMITO** (IRE) 4
329	**MARON** (GB) 16
272	**MAROUSSIES WINGS** (IRE) 61
511	**MARQUETERIE** (USA) F 10
515	**MARRON PRINCE** (FR) 27
370	**MARS DES OBEAUX** (FR) 58
1	**MARSAD** (GB) 18
514	**MARSEILLAIS** (FR) 158
34	**MARSH ORCHID** (GB) 17
177	**MARSH RUN** (GB) 31
200	**MARSHALLSPARK** (IRE) 33
588	**MARSHMAN** (IRE) 12
420	**MARTATOMIC** (IRE) 57
625	**MARTHA P PERKINES** (IRE) F 27
616	**MARTHA REILLY** (IRE) 3
149	**MARTHA'S KINSMAN** (IRE) 29
492	**MARTHARUM** (GB) 47
325	**MARTIAN MELODY** F 23
353	**MARTIN'S SUNSET** (GB) 7
32	**MARTINES** (IRE) 31
18	**MARTOVIC** (IRE) 22
132	**MARY CARLETON** (GB) 6
614	**MARY DELANEY** (USA) 42
491	**MARY HINGE** (GB) F 30
197	**MARY MAGDALENE** (GB) F 57
544	**MARY READ** (GB) 33
88	**MARYLOU WHITNEY** (USA) F 48
171	**MARYMAS** (GB) 96
21	**MARYSIENKA** (GB) 12
590	**MASAAR** (USA) 106
481	**MASAFI** (IRE) 6
239	**MASAKIRA** (GB) C 35
68	**MASALARIAN** (IRE) 5
522	**MASHAAHED** (GB) 111
287	**MASHAAIR** (IRE) 112
604	**MASHINU** (GER) 74
172	**MASHONA** (GB) 55
370	**MASKA** (FR) 59
488	**MASKED** (IRE) 7
369	**MASHIYKN'S HEIRESS** (IRE) 21
137	**MASSARO PAPE** (IRE) 32
186	**MASSIF CENTRALE** (IRE) 19
633	**MASSIMO** (FR) 41
114	**MASSIZAL** (FR) 15
309	**MASSKANA** (IRE) F 75
137	**MASTER AT ARMS** (GB) 81
200	**MASTER BEAR** (IRE) 5
636	**MASTER BILLYBOY** (IRE) 7
44	**MASTER BREW** (GB) 15
1	**MASTER COBBLER** (IRE) 27
437	**MASTER CORROUGE** (IRE) 26
290	**MASTER D'OR** (FR) 54
518	**MASTER FARRIER** (GB) 24
231	**MASTER FOX** (GB) 26
610	**MASTER JACKSON** (GB) 4
109	**MASTER JOSEPH** (GB) 56
291	**MASTER MAHOGANY** (GB) 11
626	**MASTER MCGHEE** (GB) 10
370	**MASTER MINDED** (FR) 195
484	**MASTER MONEYSPIDER** (GB) 3
429	**MASTER OF STAFFORD** (GB) 14
562	**MASTER OF THE RACE** (GB) 61
566	**MASTER OFTHE CHASE** (IRE) 37
599	**MASTER PAPA** (GB) 31
611	**MASTER PEGASUS** (GB) 49
553	**MASTER RATTLE** (GB) 6
154	**MASTER REX** (GB) 10
109	**MASTER ROBBIE** (GB) 13
149	**MASTER SAM** (IRE) 30
518	**MASTER SEBASTIAN** (GB) 25
266	**MASTER SPEAKER** (GB) 9
408	**MASTER T** (USA) 58
175	**MASTER TANNER** (GB) 5
290	**MASTER THEO** (IRE) 4
45	**MASTER WELLS** (IRE) 6
244	**MASTER WOOD** (GB) 6
569	**MASTERMAN READY** (GB) 17
414	**MASTEROFTHECOURT** (USA) 79
162	**MATELOT** (FR) 22
417	**MATERIAL WITNESS** (IRE) 6
549	**MATERIAL WORLD** (GB) 5
32	**MATERNELLE** (FR) 32
465	**MATH** (GB) C 90
199	**MATHEMATICIAN** (IRE) 56
384	**MATHMAGICIAN** (IRE) 1
562	**MATHOOR** (GB) 145
178	**MATIKANEHANAFUBUKI** (IRE) C 121
32	**MATINEE** (GB) C 88
510	**MATJA** (FR) 38
124	**MATLOCK GREEN** (IRE) 43
136	**MATMATA DE TENDRON** (FR) 6
112	**MATOURAKA** (FR) 2
232	**MATTAHORN** (GB) 79
173	**MATTEROFACT** (IRE) 21
585	**MATTHEW MURITO** (IRE) 19
423	**MATTHEW MY SON** (IRE) 14
21	**MATTY TUN** (GB) 13
115	**MATURIN** (GB) 75
272	**MAUNBY RAVER** (GB) 7
272	**MAUNBY REVELLER** (GB) 35
411	**MAUNBY ROLLER** (GB) 18
368	**MAUNSELL'S ROAD** (IRE) 36
567	**MAURA'S PET** (GB) C 21
569	**MAURADELL** (IRE) C 93
491	**MAURAS PRIDE** (IRE) C 31
611	**MAUREEN'S HOPE** (USA) C 50
577	**MAUREEN'S LOUGH** (IRE) 10
302	**MAUREENA** (IRE) F 14
256	**MAURO** (IRE) 17
299	**MAVERICK DANCER** (IRE) 40
357	**MAVIALEVA** (IRE) 67
512	**MAWAZEEN** (IRE) 8
345	**MAXAMILLION** (IRE) 31
599	**MAXIE MCDONALD** (IRE) 32
151	**MAXILLA** (IRE) 5
354	**MAXIME** (FR) 24
376	**MAXIMINUS** (GB) 8
470	**MAXIMIZE** (IRE) 84
232	**MAXIMO** (GER) 80
492	**MAXOLINI** (GB) 48
279	**MAXWELL** (FR) 7
2	**MAY MORNING** (IRE) 60
602	**MAYA'S PRINCE** (GB) 9
590	**MAYADEEN** (FR) 44
265	**MAYARO BAY** (GB) G 114
157	**MAYBESEVEN** (GB) 29
162	**MAYEUL** (FR) 23
2	**MAYNOOTH PRINCE** (IRE) 11
431	**MAYS DREAM** (GB) 69
415	**MAYTPLEASETHECOURT** (IRE) C 12
34	**MAYYAS** (GB) 8
614	**MAZARINE BLUE** (GB) F 43
199	**MAZARINI** (GB) 131
349	**MAZEA** (IRE) 47
633	**MAZILEO** (GB) 42
123	**MAZINDAR** (GB) 7
391	**MAZRAM** (GB) 9
72	**MAZUNA** (IRE) 6
602	**MAZZAREME** (IRE) 21
290	**MCBAIN** (GB) 55
97	**MCCALL** (USA) F 50
264	**MCCORMACK** (GB) 36
217	**MCCRACKEN** (IRE) 15
339	**MCCRINKLE** (IRE) 4
534	**MCMAHON'S BROOK** (GB) 7
534	**MCMAHON'S RIVER** (GB) G 12
138	**MCNAIROBI** (GB) 14
146	**MCQUEEN** (IRE) 19
419	**MCSNAPPY** (GB) 23
112	**ME** (GB) 18
268	**ME TOO SAN** (IRE) 50
644	**MEAD** (IRE) 7
633	**MEADOW HAWK** (USA) 43
510	**MEADOW LODGE** (IRE) 39
171	**MEADOW MISCHIEF** (FR) 97
446	**MEANDMRSJONES** (GB) 14
620	**MEASURED RESPONSE** (GB) 60
477	**MEASURELESS** (GB) 13
25	**MECCA'S MATE** (GB) 4
162	**MEDAILLE** (FR) 56
73	**MEDALLA** (FR) 4
199	**MEDIA BARON** (GB) 132
413	**MEDIANOCHE** (IRE) 11
2	**MEDIC** (IRE) 4
44	**MEDINA DE BIOSECO** (GB) C 50
470	**MEDISON** (FR) 85
645	**MEDITATION** (GB) 34
329	**MEDKHAN** (IRE) 19
232	**MEDNAYA** (IRE) 81
587	**MEDORA LEIGH** (USA) 18
120	**MEDUSA** (GB) 12
232	**MEDUSE** (FR) G 82
151	**MEEHAN** (IRE) 6
553	**MEELUP** (IRE) 7
30	**MEESON TIMES** (GB) C 67
591	**MEGA CHIC** (FR) 14
470	**MEGA D'ESTRUVAL** (FR) 86
174	**MEGABOND** (GB) 9
33	**MEGALO MANIAC** (GB) 21
514	**MEGAN'S LEPRECHAUN** (USA) F 159
554	**MEGAN'S MAGIC** (GB) 11
108	**MEGAPAC** (IRE) 22
590	**MEGGIDO** (GB) 45
29	**MEHMAAS** (GB) 9
422	**MEIJIN** (GB) 8
115	**MEIKLE BARFIL** (GB) 41
70	**MEIKLECANTLY CHARM** (GB) 5
629	**MEILLEUR** (NZ) 3
370	**MEISIR DU LUC** (FR) 60
309	**MEKYAAS** (GB) 76
609	**MEL IN BLUE** (FR) 1
465	**MEL'S MOMENT** (USA) 52
373	**MELAINA** (GB) 11
492	**MELALCHRIST** (GB) 37
73	**MELANDRE** (GB) 12
514	**MELANOSPORUM** (USA) 63
347	**MELFORD** (FR) 49
384	**MELFORD RED** (GB) 4
642	**MELLEDGAN** (IRE) 12
319	**MELMOUNT STAR** (IRE) 71
73	**MELODIAN** (GB) 5
197	**MELODY KING** (GB) 17
569	**MELODY MAKER** (GB) 94
319	**MELODY QUE** (GB) 110
95	**MELOGRANO** (IRE) 4
284	**MELROSE** (GB) 9
284	**MELTONBY** (GB) F 20
30	**MELVINO** (GB) 42
343	**MEM SCYLLA** (GB) 7
72	**MEMBERSHIP** (USA) 7
445	**MEMORIES OF GOLD** (IRE) 5
596	**MEMORY'S MUSIC** (IRE) 1
480	**MEN OF DESTINY** (IRE) 36
209	**MENAI STRAIGHTS** (GB) 5
282	**MENCHIKOV** (FR) 66
89	**MENDIP MANOR** (GB) 16
597	**MENELAVE** (FR) F 4
279	**MENEUR** (FR) 49
72	**MENHOUBAH** (USA) 8
323	**MENINA** (GB) 5
297	**MENNA** (GB) 41
562	**MENOKEE** (USA) 15
149	**MEMPHIS BEURY** (FR) 31
71	**MEOLE BRACE** (GB) 43
557	**MEPA DISCOVERY** (USA) C 31
319	**MEPHISTO** (FR) 72
13	**MEPHISTOS KICK** (GB) 9
368	**MER BIHAN** (FR) 37
369	**MER D'ARAL** (FR) 22
192	**MERANIE GIRL** (IRE) C 36
590	**MERAYAAT** (IRE) 46
409	**MERCARI** (GB) 39

105 **MISS ARAGONT** (GB) 6
152 **MISS ARK ROYAL** G 9
544 **MISS BEAR** (IRE) 35
162 **MISS BEHAVIOUR** (FR) 28
40 **MISS BODY** (IRE) F 67
202 **MISS BRUSH** (GB) 89
116 **MISS BUSSELL** (GB) C 14
492 **MISS BUTTERFIELD** C 49
569 **MISS CASTAWAY** (GB) F 95
240 **MISS CAVO** (GB) C 4
240 **MISS CAVO** (GB) C 8
240 **MISS CAVO** (GB) F 11
250 **MISS CEYLON** (GB) 4
250 **MISS CHANCELOT** (GB) 5
231 **MISS CHIPPY** (IRE) 28
32 **MISS CLEM'S** (FR) 92
315 **MISS COLMESNIL** (FR) 4
92 **MISS COSPECTOR** (GB) 9
415 **MISS CUE** (GB) 8
197 **MISS CUISINA** (GB) 43
569 **MISS DANGEROUS** (GB) C 96
143 **MISS DEFYING** (GB) 14
419 **MISS DOUBLET** (GB) 26
339 **MISS ELLIE** (GB) 5
134 **MISS FLEURIE** (GB) 3
119 **MISS FRIME** (IRE) 14
544 **MISS GAME PLAN** (IRE) F 65
448 **MISS GLORY BE** (GB) 3
436 **MISS HOSTESS** F 24
650 **MISS INCH** (GB) 21
251 **MISS INKHA** (GB) 8
516 **MISS JESSICA** (IRE) 5
417 **MISS JUDGEMENT** (IRE) 7
650 **MISS KATMANDU** (IRE) 22
288 **MISS KINABALU** (GB) C 40
511 **MISS KINGSDALE** (IRE) 13
631 **MISS KOEN** (GB) 12
451 **MISS LACEY** (GB) 72
394 **MISS LAKELAND** G 8
224 **MISS LEHMAN** (IRE) 19
164 **MISS LEWIS** (GB) 21
87 **MISS LOPEZ** (IRE) 65
279 **MISS LORILAW** (FR) F 101
449 **MISS MAILMIT** (GB) 21
473 **MISS MALONE** (IRE) 19
453 **MISS MAXI** (IRE) 28
302 **MISS MERCY** (IRE) F 15
607 **MISS MIA** (GB) 5
604 **MISS MONARIA** (GER) 31
143 **MISS MUIRE** F 7
632 **MISS MUSCAT** (GB) 14
54 **MISS NELLA** (FR) 16
180 **MISS NUTWOOD** (IRE) C 11
607 **MISS OCEAN MONARCH** (GB) 6
287 **MISS PARTICULAR** (IRE) 62
477 **MISS PATRICIA** (GB) 25
569 **MISS POLARIS** (GB) 18
112 **MISS PORCIA** (GB) 3
337 **MISS PRIM** (GB) 3
610 **MISS PROSS** (GB) 5
650 **MISS PROVENCE** (GB) 37
569 **MISS PROVVIDENCE** (IRE) 51
614 **MISS RANI** (IRE) 18
268 **MISS RANOVA** F 51
602 **MISS REDACTIVE** (GB) 14
566 **MISS REDLANDS** G 39
78 **MISS RIDEAMIGHT** (GB) 5
202 **MISS RIMEX** (IRE) F 90
178 **MISS ROSIE** (GB) 73
261 **MISS ROYELLO** (GB) 3
251 **MISS RUBY** (GB) 25
414 **MISS SABRE** (GB) F 80
357 **MISS SIBERIA** (GB) 115
360 **MISS SIHAM** (IRE) C 32
473 **MISS SINDBAD** (FR) 47
601 **MISS SIRIUS** (GB) 12
429 **MISS SKIPPY** (GB) 16
275 **MISS SUDBROOK** (GB) 14

544 **MISS SURE BOND** (IRE) 66
650 **MISS THAILAND** (GB) 38
172 **MISS THE BOAT** (GB) 56
307 **MISS TIDDLYPUSH** (GB) 4
520 **MISS TRENDSETTER** (IRE) 49
329 **MISS TROOPER** (GB) 18
38 **MISS TRUANT** (GB) 30
465 **MISS TWINKLETOES** (IRE) F 53
514 **MISS U FRAN** (USA) C 161
30 **MISS U MAMA** (USA) C 68
112 **MISS UP N GO** C 59
310 **MISS WILLOW BEND** (GB) C 42
176 **MISS WIZADORA** (GB) 4
561 **MISS WIZZ** (GB) 9
224 **MISS WOODPECKER** (GB) 20
148 **MISSATACAMA** (IRE) 15
81 **MISSATTITUDE** (GB) 8
52 **MISSED A BEAT** (GB) 14
247 **MISSED A NOTE** (GB) 5
420 **MISSED THAT** (GB) 59
192 **MISSED TURN** (GB) 15
186 **MISSIE BAILEYS** (GB) 3
557 **MISSIE MADAM** (IRE) C 32
193 **MISSIN MARGOT** (GB) 18
566 **MISSINDEPENDENCE** (IRE) 40
570 **MISSION AFFIRMED** (USA) 5
442 **MISSION TO BE** (GB) 7
280 **MISSION TO MARS** (GB) 5
421 **MISSOUDUN** (FR) 48
588 **MISSOULA** (IRE) 24
520 **MISSPERON** (IRE) 50
310 **MISSTURNER** (IRE) 24
265 **MISSUS LINKS** (USA) 18
272 **MIST OPPORTUNITY** (IRE) 38
533 **MISTBLACK** (GB) 3
514 **MISTER ALEXIS** (FR) 65
185 **MISTER ARJAY** (USA) 24
192 **MISTER AZIZ** (IRE) 16
538 **MISTER BANJO** (FR) 6
446 **MISTER BELL** (GB) 33
264 **MISTER BUZZ** (GB) 37
333 **MISTER CHALK** (GB) 3
290 **MISTER CHATTERBOX** (IRE) 57
306 **MISTER CLINTON** (IRE) 15
44 **MISTER COMPLETELY** (IRE) 19
555 **MISTER ELEGANT** (GB) 40
435 **MISTER FELIX** (IRE) 5
290 **MISTER FLINT** (GB) 58
417 **MISTER GENEPI** (GB) 21
122 **MISTER GRAHAM** (GB) 6
157 **MISTER KINGSTON** (GB) 30
406 **MISTER MAGNUM** (IRE) 14
226 **MISTER MAMBO** (GB) 3
532 **MISTER MARMADUKE** (GB) 12
99 **MISTER MINTY** (GB) 27
569 **MISTER MUJA** (IRE) 19
633 **MISTER MUSTARD** (IRE) 44
357 **MISTER PACHA PACHA** (FR) 17
548 **MISTER PUTT** (USA) 3
585 **MISTER QUASIMODO** (GB) 20
4 **MISTER QUICKSAND** (USA) 2
520 **MISTER REGENT** (GB) 17
206 **MISTER RIGHT** (FR) 4
514 **MISTER SACHA** (FR) 16
518 **MISTER SMITH** (GB) 26
99 **MISTER SWEETS** (GB) 11
157 **MISTER TRICKSTER** (IRE) 31
229 **MISTER TROUBRIDGE** (IRE) 63
268 **MISTER VIRGINIAN** (IRE) 52
237 **MISTERS SISTER** (IRE) 48
419 **MISTIFIED** (FR) 27
72 **MISTLE SONG** (GB) F 87
537 **MISTLETOE** (IRE) 23
72 **MISTOOK** (USA) C 88
370 **MISTRAL BOY** (FR) 66
571 **MISTRAL DE LA COUR** (FR) 7
360 **MISTRAL SKY** (GB) 4
341 **MISTRESS BANJO** (GB) 63

359 **MISTRESS NELL** (GB) 6
30 **MISTRESS TWISTER** (GB) 10
637 **MISTY DANCER** (GB) 49
386 **MISTY JOY** F 22
205 **MISTY MAN** (GB) 9
237 **MISTY MOON** (GB) F 81
473 **MISTY PRINCESS** (GB) 7
544 **MISU BOND** (IRE) 67
172 **MISWADAH** (IRE) 112
405 **MITCHELLAND** (GB) 22
171 **MITH HILL** (GB) 6
370 **MITHRA DES OBEAUX** (FR) 67
506 **MIXED MARRIAGE** (IRE) 6
310 **MIXING** (GB) 25
588 **MIXREMEMBER** (FR) F 65
24 **MIXSTERTHETRIXSTER** (USA) 2
543 **MIYAZAKI** (IRE) 26
178 **MIZZ TEE** (IRE) 74
235 **MNASON** (FR) 2
287 **MO CHROI** (GB) 113
310 **MO STOPHER** (GB) C 26
361 **MOAYED** (GB) 17
200 **MOBANE FLYER** (GB) 34
637 **MOBASHER** (IRE) 50
291 **MOBO-BACO** (GB) 12
171 **MOBSIR** (GB) 98
123 **MOCCA** (IRE) 4
125 **MOCHAM GLEN** (FR) 15
566 **MOCHARAMOR** (IRE) 41
620 **MODAFFAA** (GB) 38
104 **MODENA** (USA) F 48
307 **MODULOR** (FR) 5
627 **MOENZI** (IRE) G 13
437 **MOFFIED** (FR) 27
590 **MOGAAMER** (USA) 47
590 **MOHAFZAAT** (IRE) 48
637 **MOHAWK STAR** (IRE) 51
370 **MOKA DE L'ISLE** (FR) 68
172 **MOKARABA** (GB) 57
566 **MOKORA** (FR) 42
98 **MOKUM** (FR) 28
246 **MOLASSES** (GB) F 66
414 **MOLDAVIA** (GER) 19
283 **MOLEM** (GB) 19
360 **MOLINIA** (GB) 17
109 **MOLLY DANCER** (GB) 58
187 **MOLLY MAY** (GB) 4
620 **MOLLY'S SPIRIT** (IRE) 39
202 **MOLLYPUTTHEKETELON** (USA) 14
590 **MOLLZAM** (IRE) 49
237 **MOLOMO** (GB) C 82
435 **MOLOSTIEP** (FR) 6
391 **MOLOTOV** (GB) 10
451 **MOMENT OF CLARITY** (GB) 29
210 **MOMENT OF MADNESS** (IRE) 6
268 **MOMMA MIA** (IRE) 53
310 **MOMTIC** (IRE) 5
637 **MON MOME** (FR) 52
9 **MON PETITE AMOUR** (IRE) 18
611 **MON PLAISIR** (GB) 29
544 **MON SECRET** (IRE) 15
357 **MONA DES SABLES** (FR) 68
166 **MONAD** (IRE) 3
633 **MONALMA** (IRE) G 45
317 **MONASH GIRL** (IRE) 3
588 **MONASH LAD** (IRE) 32
44 **MONASHEE PRINCE** (IRE) 42
410 **MONASHEE ROSE** (IRE) 20
371 **MONASHEEMINI** (IRE) 21
590 **MONDAREJ** (IRE) 50
604 **MONDEGO** (GER) 75
6 **MONDELLO** (IRE) 20
470 **MONDIAL JACK** (FR) 89
270 **MONDIAL** (IRE) 11
502 **MONET'S GARDEN** (IRE) 23
50 **MONGER LANE** (GB) 11
270 **MONGINO** (GB) 12
161 **MONICA GELLER** (GB) 10

137 **NEWNHAM** (IRE) 15
265 **NEWPORT BOY** (IRE) 119
146 **NEWS MAKER** (IRE) 20
309 **NEWSROUND** (GB) 35
370 **NEWTON D'AVELOT** (FR) 88
456 **NEWTONIAN** (USA) 5
270 **NEWTOWN** (GB) 14
293 **NEWTOWN DANCER** (IRE) 10
104 **NEWTOWN VILLA** (GB) 23
29 **NEXT FLIGHT** (IRE) 10
604 **NEXT LORD** (IRE) 77
209 **NEXT NESS** (IRE) 26
473 **NEXT TIME** (IRE) 21
564 **NEXT TIME AROUND** (IRE) 12
502 **NEXT TO NOTHING** (IRE) 30
42 **NGAURUHOE** (IRE) 80
420 **NIAMH CINN OIR** (GB) F 90
32 **NIBBANA** (USA) 95
184 **NIBBLES** (IRE) 13
369 **NICE SPICE** (IRE) C 25
72 **NICE TUNE** (GB) 43
473 **NICHOLAS NICKELBY** (GB) 5
470 **NICK THE SILVER** (GB) 96
86 **NICK'S CHOICE** (GB) 5
370 **NICKEL DU COCHET** (FR) 89
177 **NICO'S GIRL** (GB) 97
641 **NICOZETTO** (FR) 18
12 **NID D'ABEILLES** (IRE) 38
171 **NIDHAAL** (IRE) 103
447 **NIGHT BILLIARDS** (IRE) 25
303 **NIGHT BUSKER** (IRE) 43
611 **NIGHT CRU** (GB) 53
451 **NIGHT CRUISE** (IRE) 75
246 **NIGHT CRY** (IRE) 46
32 **NIGHT DHU** (GB) 39
206 **NIGHT EXPLOSION** (IRE) 10
246 **NIGHT FAIRY** (IRE) 20
465 **NIGHT FAX** (USA) C 94
29 **NIGHT GUEST** (IRE) 17
109 **NIGHT HAVEN** (GB) F 135
590 **NIGHT HOUR** (IRE) 52
604 **NIGHT LOOM** (GER) 42
309 **NIGHT OF JOY** (IRE) 36
64 **NIGHT OUT** (FR) 7
272 **NIGHT OWL** (GB) F 62
6 **NIGHT PEARL** (IRE) 11
274 **NIGHT PRAYERS** (IRE) 6
458 **NIGHT PROSPECTOR** (GB) 5
359 **NIGHT RAINBOW** (IRE) 11
99 **NIGHT RHAPSODY** (IRE) C 34
115 **NIGHT SCENT** (IRE) C 76
163 **NIGHT STORM** (GB) 8
213 **NIGHT WARRIOR** (IRE) 12
87 **NIGHTINGALE SONG** (GB) F 68
115 **NIGHTSPOT** (GB) 9
97 **NIGHTSTRIKE** (IRE) 52
282 **NIGHTWATCHMAN** (IRE) 70
20 **NIGHTWING** (GB) 55
370 **NIKAIDO** (FR) 90
439 **NIKITA MOON** (USA) C 76
6 **NIKITA SUNRISE** (IRE) 21
282 **NIKOLAIEV** (FR) 71
319 **NILE MOON** (IRE) 77
201 **NIMBLE STAR** (GB) 17
429 **NIMELLO** (USA) 20
172 **NIMRANA FORT** (IRE) 118
400 **NINA FONTENAIL** (FR) 11
62 **NINAH** (GB) 17
162 **NINAS** (FR) 33
119 **NINGFIELD** (FR) 2
370 **NINI MALTA** (FR) 91
408 **NINJA STORM** (FR) 113
319 **NINTH WONDER** (USA) C 133
519 **NIOBE'S WAY** (GB) 12
545 **NIP NIP** (IRE) 13
275 **NIPPING** (IRE) 34
129 **NIPPY** (FR) 54
432 **NIPPY DES MOTTES** (FR) 91

370 **NIRVANA SWING** (FR) 92
458 **NISR** (GB) 6
178 **NISTAKI** (USA) 31
146 **NITE FOX** (IRE) 21
125 **NITE TRIPPA** (FR) 16
451 **NITELITE** (GB) 34
162 **NITRAT** (FR) 34
265 **NIVELLE** (GB) 120
97 **NIVERNAIS** (GB) 8
604 **NIZZOLINO** (GB) 33
126 **NO CHANCE TO DANCE** (IRE) 8
347 **NO COLLUSION** (IRE) 54
209 **NO COMMISSION** (IRE) 17
279 **NO DANZIG** (USA) 55
463 **NO EXIT** (FR) 47
293 **NO FRONTIER** (IRE) 11
433 **NO GLOATING** (IRE) 11
199 **NO GREATER LOVE** (FR) 59
6 **NO GROUSE** (GB) 12
599 **NO GUARANTEES** (GB) 34
61 **NO HESITATION** (GB) 9
588 **NO ISLANDS** (GB) F 66
114 **NO KIDDING** (GB) 7
460 **NO MERCY** (GB) 6
61 **NO PICNIC** (GB) 10
319 **NO REFUGE** (IRE) 78
282 **NO REGRETS** (FR) 72
356 **NO REMORSE** (GB) 16
89 **NO SAM NO** (GB) 20
398 **NO SHAME** (GB) C 19
282 **NO SHENANIGANS** (IRE) 73
41 **NO TAILS TOLD** (IRE) 10
473 **NO TIME** (IRE) 6
413 **NO TOAST** (IRE) 13
108 **NO TURNING BACK** (IRE) 27
351 **NO WAY BACK** (IRE) 22
407 **NOADIBOU** (FR) 35
288 **NOBBLER** (GB) 16
502 **NOBEL** (FR) 31
643 **NOBEL BLEU DE KERPAUL** (FR) 19
202 **NOBELIX** (FR) 51
133 **NOBLE BARON** (GB) 6
291 **NOBLE CALLING** (FR) 14
603 **NOBLE FUTURE** (GB) 10
168 **NOBLE HOUSE** (GB) 5
600 **NOBLE LOCKS** (GB) 9
422 **NOBLE MIND** (GB) 9
635 **NOBLE MINSTREL** (GB) 43
276 **NOBLE MOUNT** (GB) 5
594 **NOBLE PASAO** (IRE) 8
29 **NOBLE PURSUIT** (GB) 11
379 **NOBLE REEF** 4
290 **NOBLE REQUEST** (FR) 65
325 **NOBLE SOUL** G 20
325 **NOBLE SOUL** C 25
7 **NOBLE TEVIOT** (GB) 6
61 **NOBLE TIGER** (IRE) 11
368 **NOBLEFIR** (GB) 44
421 **NOBODYS PERFECT** (IRE) 50
499 **NOBRATINETTA** (FR) 42
272 **NOCATEE** (IRE) 11
604 **NOCEUR** (GER) 34
370 **NOCINO** (IRE) 35
162 **NOCTAMBULE** (FR) 35
150 **NOCTURNALLY** (GB) 13
569 **NOD OF APPROVAL** (GB) 52
635 **NODINA** (GB) 26
139 **NOELEEN'S DELIGHT** (IRE) C 24
370 **NOIR SUR BLANC** 93
637 **NOISETINE** (FR) 58
171 **NOJOOM** (IRE) 104
432 **NOLAND** (GB) 92
518 **NOLIFE** (GB) 29
370 **NOLWENN** (FR) 94
197 **NOM FRANÇAIS** (GB) C 59
162 **NOMAD** (FR) 36
11 **NOMADIC BLAZE** (GB) 4
431 **NOMADIC DANCER** (IRE) G 70

370 **NOMINALE** (FR) 95
401 **NON DIMENTICAR ME** (IRE) C 38
282 **NON SO** (FR) 74
543 **NON SONO SOLO** (IRE) 28
215 **NONA'S LASS** (GB) 6
63 **NONANTAIS** (FR) 10
351 **NONE SO PRETTY** (GB) 23
178 **NOODLES** (GB) 75
268 **NOONEWANTSME** (IRE) 60
173 **NOOR EL HOUDAH** (IRE) F 22
310 **NOORA** (FR) 7
371 **NOPLEAZINU** (GB) 9
202 **NOR'WESTER** (GB) 52
109 **NORAKIT** (GB) 136
369 **NORBORNE BANDIT** (IRE) 26
234 **NORDESTA** (IRE) C 16
289 **NORDESTA** (IRE) C 9
446 **NORDIC PRINCE** (IRE) 17
161 **NORDICO PRINCESS** (GB) C 37
569 **NORDWIND** (IRE) 20
620 **NORMA DESMEND** (GB) 41
297 **NORMA HILL** (GB) 19
593 **NORMA SPEAKMAN** (IRE) 7
324 **NORMAN'S DELIGHT** (IRE) F 19
186 **NORSE DANCER** (IRE) 21
531 **NORSEMAN CATELINE** (FR) 27
420 **NORTH ATLANTIC** (IRE) 65
562 **NORTH LIGHT** (IRE) 16
341 **NORTH LODGE** (GER) 67
552 **NORTH PASS** (GB) 3
143 **NORTH POINT** (IRE) 8
265 **NORTH SHORE** (IRE) 55
583 **NORTHAW LAD** (IRE) 16
56 **NORTHERN BIRD** (GB) F 9
632 **NORTHERN DEAL** (IRE) 16
285 **NORTHERN DESERT** (IRE) 14
575 **NORTHERN ECHO** (IRE) 2
154 **NORTHERN ENDEAVOUR** (GB) 12
278 **NORTHERN FLASH** (GB) 3
252 **NORTHERN FRIEND** (GB) 32
520 **NORTHERN GAMES** (GB) 21
81 **NORTHERN LINK** (GB) 9
470 **NORTHERN MADRIK** (FR) 97
423 **NORTHERN MINSTER** (GB) 18
107 **NORTHERN MOON** F 43
568 **NORTHERN NEWS** (IRE) 18
297 **NORTHERN NYMPH** (GB) 20
20 **NORTHERN SECRET** (GB) 56
499 **NORTHERN SHADOWS** (GB) 43
436 **NORTHERN SVENGALI** (IRE) 15
176 **NORTHERN VALENTINE** (GB) 5
438 **NORTHERNER** (IRE) 22
569 **NORTHSIDE LODGE** (IRE) 21
139 **NORTHSIDER** (IRE) 14
471 **NORTHWOOD MAY** (GB) G 39
401 **NORTON** (IRE) 8
210 **NORTON ROSE** (GB) 17
236 **NORTON SAPPHIRE** (GB) 10
482 **NORTON WOOD** (IRE) 4
177 **NORTONTHORPE LAD** (IRE) 70
633 **NORWEGIAN** (GB) 49
119 **NORWEGIAN PRIDE** (IRE) 16
465 **NOS FERATU** (IRE) 95
88 **NOSE ONE'S WAY** (IRE) 32
589 **NOSTROMO** (POL) 6
61 **NOT A TRACE** (IRE) 12
369 **NOT CRAFTY** (USA) 45
146 **NOT FOR DIAMONDS** (IRE) 22
470 **NOT LEFT YET** (IRE) 98
378 **NOT SO DUSTY** (GB) 6
157 **NOT TO BE MISSED** (GB) 34
186 **NOTA BENE** (GB) 41
309 **NOTABILITY** (IRE) 37
562 **NOTABLE GUEST** (USA) 17
531 **NOTANOTHERDONKEY** (IRE) 28
266 **NOTAPROBLEM** (IRE) 11
370 **NOTEZ LE** (FR) 96
604 **NOTHING TO LOOSE** (GER) 36

107 **ONEIRO WAY** (IRE) 30
429 **ONETHREESIXSQADRON** (GB) 22
504 **ONEWAY** (IRE) 8
370 **ONIGHT** (FR) 151
370 **ONIX** (FR) 152
608 **ONIZ TIPTOES** (IRE) 14
53 **ONLINE INVESTOR** (IRE) 28
268 **ONLY ALYMER** (GB) 64
346 **ONLY FOR SUE** (GB) 5
199 **ONLY HIM** (GB) 138
53 **ONLY IF I LAUGH** (GB) 29
124 **ONLY IN DREAMS** (GB) F 69
405 **ONLY MILLIE** (GB) 14
319 **ONLY ONCE** (GB) 80
615 **ONLY ONE MATTY** (IRE) 7
347 **ONLY VINTAGE** (USA) 55
366 **ONLY WORDS** (USA) 4
319 **ONLY YOURS** (GB) C 134
431 **ONLYTIME WILL TELL** (GB) 43
528 **ONTOS** (IRE) 14
18 **ONYOURHEADBEIT** (IRE) 27
153 **ONYX** (GB) 3
370 **ONYX BRUERE** (FR) 153
566 **OODACHEE** 9
590 **OONAGH MACCOOL** (IRE) 54
127 **OPAL'S HELMSMAN** (USA) 8
72 **OPARI** (IRE) F 92
340 **OPEN ARMS** (GB) 9
308 **OPEN VERDICT** (GB) 22
510 **OPEN WAY** (IRE) 45
169 **OPENIDE** (GB) 5
347 **OPENING HYMN** (GB) 56
478 **OPENING LINE** (GB) 37
308 **OPERA BELLE** (GB) 23
345 **OPERA CAPE** (GB) 57
149 **OPERA HALL** (GB) 33
200 **OPERA SINGER** (GB) 40
178 **OPERA WRITER** (GB) 129
408 **OPERASHAAN** (GB) 67
345 **OPHISTROLIE** (IRE) 34
349 **OPHTALMO** (IRE) 51
370 **OPIPARO** (FR) 51
370 **OPIUM DE COTTE** (FR) 155
71 **OPPORTUNE** (GB) 51
273 **OPPORTUNITY KNOCKS** (GB) 10
566 **OPTIMISE** (GB) 71
408 **OPTIMO** (GER) 68
171 **OQUAWKA** (USA) 106
370 **OR EN BARRE** (FR) 156
432 **ORACLE DES MOTTES** (FR) 94
370 **ORAGE DE COTTE** (FR) 157
198 **ORANG OUTAN** (FR) 12
414 **ORANGE DANCER** (GB) 81
641 **ORANGE ROYALE** (IRE) C 28
562 **ORANGE STRAVINSKY** (GB) 152
465 **ORANGE TOUCH** (GB) 13
72 **ORANGES AND LEMONS** (FR) 93
255 **ORANGINO** (GB) 7
287 **ORANMORE CASTLE** (GB) 64
582 **ORBICULARIS** (IRE) 17
199 **ORBIT O'GOLD** (USA) 62
192 **ORCADIAN** (GB) 5
542 **ORCHARD FIELDS** (GB) 13
299 **ORCHESTRAL DREAM** (IRE) 47
98 **ORCHESTRATION** (IRE) 32
614 **ORDINATE** (GB) C 45
543 **ORESME** (FR) 29
562 **ORFORD NESS** (GB) F 153
370 **ORGANIZ** (FR) 158
370 **ORGUEIL DES DIMES** (FR) 159
43 **ORIEL GIRL** (GB) F 39
357 **ORIENTAL LADY** (IRE) 121
288 **ORIENTAL MYSTIQUE** C 43
604 **ORIENTAL ROCK** (GER) 37
43 **ORIENTAL STYLE** (IRE) 4
590 **ORIENTAL WARRIOR** (GB) 8
107 **ORIENTAL WAY** (GR) 31
239 **ORIENTOR** (GB) 20

80 **ORIGINAL SIN** (IRE) 2
154 **ORIGINAL THOUGHT** (IRE) 13
369 **ORIHUELA FELLA** (IRE) 48
361 **ORINOCOVSKY** (IRE) 19
177 **ORION EXPRESS** (GB) 41
451 **ORLAR** (IRE) 35
162 **ORMELLO** (FR) 57
421 **ORNELLA SPEED** (FR) 51
70 **ORO STREET** (IRE) 6
370 **OROCK** (FR) 160
205 **ORPEN ANNIE** (IRE) 16
111 **ORPEN WIDE** (IRE) 18
520 **ORPENDONNA** (IRE) 51
87 **ORPHAN** (IRE) 42
370 **ORPHEE DE VONNAS** (FR) 161
370 **ORPHICA DE THAIX** (FR) 162
371 **ORPHIR** (GB) 22
226 **ORREZZO** (GER) 4
290 **ORSWELL CREST** (GB) 69
408 **ORTHODOX** (GB) 69
69 **ORTICA** (IRE) 28
162 **OSANA** (FR) 58
583 **OSCAR FOXBOW** (IRE) 17
583 **OSCAR PARK** (IRE) 18
84 **OSCAR PERFORMANCE** (IRE) 15
590 **OSCAR SNOWMAN** (GB) 117
312 **OSCAR THE BOXER** (IRE) 23
370 **OSCARD MALTA** (FR) 163
472 **OSCARDEAL** (FR) 4
555 **OSCARS LAW** (GB) 24
169 **OSCARS VISION** (IRE) 6
633 **OSCATELLO** (USA) 50
107 **OSIRIS WAY** (GB) 32
71 **OSORNO** (GB) 52
641 **OSPREY POINT** (USA) F 29
268 **OSSIANA** (IRE) 111
218 **OSSMOSES** (IRE) 5
357 **OSTANKINO** (FR) 18
586 **OSTFANNI** (IRE) 12
451 **OSTRUSA** (AUT) F 76
44 **OTAGO** (IRE) 22
439 **OTELCALIFONI** (USA) 77
557 **OTHERWISE** (IRE) 5
297 **OTTER'S FIELD** (IRE) F 49
132 **OTYLIA** (GB) 7
370 **OUBLIES CA** (FR) 105
370 **OUBLIONS LES** (FR) 164
162 **OUED** (FR) 39
57 **OUH JAY** (GB) 12
531 **OUI EXIT** (FR) 30
171 **OUIJA BOARD** (GB) 7
303 **OULART** (GB) 46
236 **OULTON BROAD** (GB) 11
308 **OUMALADIA** (IRE) C 39
112 **OUMALDAAYA** (USA) F 60
568 **OUNINPOHJA** (IRE) 19
238 **OUR AISLING** (GB) F 7
252 **OUR ARMAGEDDON** (NZ) 33
420 **OUR BEN** (GB) 17
88 **OUR BLUEBUTTON** (IRE) 35
361 **OUR CHOICE** (IRE) 39
98 **OUR DESTINY** (GB) 33
214 **OUR FELLA** (IRE) 30
303 **OUR HANDYMAN** (IRE) 47
96 **OUR IMPERIAL BAY** (USA) 16
69 **OUR JAKE** (GB) 29
499 **OUR JASPER** (GB) 45
419 **OUR JOLLY SWAGMAN** (GB) 28
569 **OUR JOSIE** (GB) C 98
301 **OUR KES** (IRE) 22
40 **OUR LITTLE SECRET** (IRE) 40
608 **OUR LOUIS** (GB) 25
216 **OUR MAN DENNIS** (GB) 9
182 **OUR MEN** (GB) 18
36 **OUR MONOGRAM** (GB) 8
637 **OUR PRIMA DONNA** (IRE) 59
408 **OUR SAMSON** (IRE) 70
156 **OUR SEAFARER** (IRE) 4

544 **OUR SHEILA** (GB) 68
281 **OUR SION** (GB) 5
499 **OUR TEES COMPONENT** (IRE) 46
470 **OUR VIC** (GB) 101
256 **OUR WILDEST DREAMS** (GB) 18
389 **OUR WILMA** (GB) F 11
514 **OUR ZIGA** (FR) 76
45 **OURS** (IRE) 31
162 **OUSTE** (FR) 59
133 **OUT AFTER DARK** (GB) 7
544 **OUT OF INDIA** (GB) 37
370 **OUT OF REACH** (IRE) 165
393 **OUT THE ORDINARY** (GB) 24
481 **OUTLOOK** (GB) 59
268 **OUTONACALL** (IRE) 65
424 **OUTSIDE HALF** (IRE) 32
33 **OUTWARD** (USA) 7
514 **OUVREUR** (FR) 77
370 **OUVRONS LE FEU** (FR) 166
370 **OUZBEK** (FR) 167
107 **OVATION WAY** (GB) 33
605 **OVER BOOKED** (GB) 15
323 **OVER BRIDGE** (GB) 6
244 **OVER FLO** (GB) 8
441 **OVER THE BAR** (GB) 45
365 **OVER THE CLOUDS** (GB) 2
470 **OVER THE CREEK** (GB) 102
566 **OVER THE FIRST** (IRE) 50
465 **OVER THE LIMIT** (GB) 54
244 **OVER TO JOE** (GB) 9
291 **OVER TO YOU BERT** (GB) 16
601 **OVER ZEALOUS** (IRE) 13
426 **OVERAMOROUS** (GB) 11
441 **OVERBURY AFFAIR** (GB) 46
451 **OVERDRAWN** (IRE) 8
107 **OVERJOY WAY** (GB) 34
20 **OVERLOOK** (GB) 106
107 **OVERLORD WAY** (GB) 35
455 **OVERSERVED** (GB) 14
199 **OVERSHADOW** (IRE) 139
499 **OVERSTRAND** (IRE) 47
107 **OVERTOP WAY** (GB) 36
186 **OVIDEO** (GB) C 74
357 **OVIDIE** (FR) 71
370 **OVOMALTHINE** (FR) 168
370 **OWARD** (FR) 169
585 **OWER FARM** (GB) F 23
284 **OWN LINE** (GB) 10
17 **OXFORD STREET PETE** (IRE) 25
615 **OYSTER POINT** (IRE) 8
332 **OYSTERHAVEN** (IRE) 27
72 **OZENA** (USA) F 94
162 **OZYMANDIAS** (FR) 60
87 **PAB SPECIAL** (IRE) 69
309 **PACE SHOT** (IRE) 39
289 **PACE STALKER** (USA) 4
232 **PACHANGA** (GB) 34
551 **PACHARAN QUEEN** (GB) 16
199 **PACHELLO** (IRE) 63
357 **PACIENCIA** (IRE) 72
311 **PACIFIC BREEZE** (IRE) 17
437 **PACIFIC HIGHWAY** (IRE) 29
369 **PACKIE TAM** (IRE) 49
60 **PACKIN EM IN** (GB) 11
158 **PADDINGTON** (USA) 8
414 **PADDINGTON GREEN** (GB) 22
60 **PADDY BOY** (IRE) 12
366 **PADDY GEORGE** (IRE) 5
237 **PADDY MOON** (GB) 85
86 **PADDY THE OPTIMIST** (GB) 4
368 **PADDY THE PIPER** (IRE) 45
52 **PADDY'S PLACE** (IRE) 29
16 **PADDY'S TERN** (GB) 15
425 **PADDYS COCKTAIL** (IRE) F 20
110 **PADDYWACK** (GB) 9
471 **PADRE** (IRE) 40
641 **PAGAN CEREMONY** (USA) 19
465 **PAGAN CREST** (GB) 97

557 **PENDA** (CAN) C 34
538 **PENDIL'S PRINCESS** (GB) 8
200 **PENDLE FOREST** (GB) 41
32 **PENDRAGON** (USA) 97
53 **PENEL** (FR) 30
36 **PENKENNA PRINCESS** (IRE) 20
588 **PENNA** (GB) 67
53 **PENNAUTIER** (GB) 59
514 **PENNE** (FR) 173
334 **PENNEECK** (GB) 5
229 **PENNETHORNE PLACE** C 33
229 **PENNETHORNE PLACE** F 77
229 **PENNEYROSE BAY** (GB) 34
389 **PENNILLION** (GB) 12
416 **PENNY CHASE** (GB) 3
177 **PENNY HASSET** (GB) C 98
341 **PENNY ISLAND** (IRE) 106
470 **PENNY PICTURES** (IRE) 104
293 **PENNY RICH** (IRE) 13
351 **PENNY STALL** (IRE) 26
393 **PENNY THOUGHTS** (GB) 25
202 **PENNY WEDDING** (IRE) 53
258 **PENNY'S CROWN** (GB) 12
268 **PENNYHILL THYNE** (IRE) 68
24 **PENNYS FROM HEAVEN** (IRE) 3
528 **PENRIC** (GB) 15
186 **PENRYN** (GB) 75
464 **PENSATA** (GB) 30
300 **PENSTRUMBLY FLOWER** (GB) 2
439 **PENT** (USA) F 79
137 **PENTATONIC** (GB) 86
20 **PENTHESTER** (GB) 19
291 **PENTHOUSE MINSTREL** (GB) 17
370 **PENVERN** (FR) 198
301 **PENWAY** (GB) 16
30 **PENWELL HILL** (USA) 17
341 **PENZANCE** (GB) 73
52 **PEONY** (GB) C 30
62 **PEOPLETON BROOK** (GB) 39
33 **PEPPER ROAD** (GB) 8
38 **PEPPERMINT TEA** (IRE) 35
66 **PEPPERNICK** (GB) 4
191 **PEPPERSHOT** (GB) 8
202 **PEPPERTREE** (GB) 92
557 **PERCE ROCK** 17
53 **PERCHERON** (IRE) 60
227 **PERCIPIENT** (GB) 12
319 **PERCUSSIONIST** (GB) 81
314 **PERCY BECK** (GB) 3
314 **PERCY JAY** (NZ) 7
590 **PERCY'S LASS** C 118
112 **PERDICULA** (GB) C 61
357 **PEREDOVO** (FR) 74
343 **PERERIN** (GB) 9
540 **PERFECT ANSWER** (GB) F 12
287 **PERFECT BLEND** (GB) 66
396 **PERFECT CHOICE** (IRE) 41
32 **PERFECT CROSS** (FR) 42
347 **PERFECT FELLOW** (GB) 57
247 **PERFECT HINDSIGHT** (IRE) 7
590 **PERFECT IMAGE** (GB) 56
5 **PERFECT LIAISON** (GB) 35
108 **PERFECT MATCH** (IRE) 28
357 **PERFECT MURDER** (IRE) 75
451 **PERFECT PLUM** (IRE) C 79
553 **PERFECT POPPY** (GB) F 12
379 **PERFECT PORTRAIT** (GB) 7
587 **PERFECT SOLUTION** (IRE) 20
470 **PERFECT STORM** (GB) 105
587 **PERFECT STORY** (IRE) 21
377 **PERFECT TONE** (USA) 8
639 **PERFECT VENUE** (IRE) 5
587 **PERFECTIONIST** (GB) 22
543 **PERFIDIE** (GB) 30
60 **PERFIDIOUS** (USA) 14
112 **PERFORMING ART** (GB) 29
151 **PERHAPS THIS TIME** (IRE) 7
514 **PERIDIUM** (IRE) 82

171 **PERIQUITUM** (GB) C 108
506 **PERIWINKLE LAD** (IRE) 7
253 **PERLE D'OR** (IRE) 10
282 **PERLE DE PUCE** (FR) 78
186 **PERMANEX PRIDE** (IRE) 76
432 **PEROUSE** (GB) 98
651 **PERRYLINE** (GB) 6
376 **PERSEPHONE HEIGHTS** (GB) 10
172 **PERSIAN CONQUEROR** (IRE) 121
172 **PERSIAN DAGGER** (IRE) 14
506 **PERSIAN EMBERS** (GB) 8
177 **PERSIAN FLOWER** (GB) F 99
302 **PERSIAN FORTUNE** (GB) G 16
384 **PERSIAN FORTUNE** (GB) G 10
229 **PERSIAN GENIE** (IRE) 35
451 **PERSIAN KHANOOM** (IRE) 36
172 **PERSIAN LIGHTNING** (IRE) 15
569 **PERSIAN MAJESTY** (IRE) 24
205 **PERSIAN MISTRESS** (IRE) F 23
219 **PERSIAN POINT** (GB) 9
451 **PERSIAN ROCK** (IRE) 37
569 **PERSIAN RUBY** (GB) 53
451 **PERSIAN SONG** (GB) C 80
569 **PERSIAN WARRIOR** (IRE) 99
202 **PERSIAN WATERS** (IRE) 16
439 **PERSONA** (IRE) 33
444 **PERSONAL ASSURANCE** (GB) 59
604 **PERSONAL POWER** (GER) 99
357 **PERSTROVKA** (IRE) 123
268 **PERSUE A HEAD** (IRE) 69
545 **PERTEMPS JOB** (GB) 5
200 **PERTEMPS MAGUS** (GB) 42
574 **PERTEMPS MISSION** (GB) 1
545 **PERTEMPS RED** (GB) 6
545 **PERTEMPS STYLE** (GB) 7
312 **PERTINO** (GB) 24
93 **PERUGIA** (GB) C 35
632 **PERUVIAN BREEZE** (IRE) 17
587 **PERUVIAN PRINCE** (USA) 23
335 **PERUVIAN PRINCESS** (GB) 12
361 **PERUVIAN STYLE** (IRE) 20
553 **PESHAWAR** (GB) F 13
184 **PETANA** (GB) 2
632 **PETANQUE** (IRE) 18
174 **PETARDIAS MAGIC** (IRE) 10
403 **PETER PARKGATE** (GB) 6
124 **PETER PAUL RUBENS** (USA) 16
40 **PETER ROUGHLEY** (IRE) 41
231 **PETER'S DEBT** (GB) 31
40 **PETER'S IMP** (IRE) 16
200 **PETERS DELITE** (GB) 82
333 **PETERS PLOY** (GB) 9
585 **PETERSON'S CAY** (IRE) 25
232 **PETIT CALVA** (FR) 7
370 **PETIT PRINCE SUN** (FR) 199
41 **PETITE GIRL** (GB) 41
265 **PETITE LIQUEURELLE** (IRE) C 122
37 **PETITE MARGOT** (GB) 36
520 **PETRICHAN** (IRE) 81
357 **PETROGRAD** (IRE) 19
405 **PETROLERO** (ARG) 18
463 **PETRONILLA** (GB) C 48
242 **PETROVKA** (IRE) 17
520 **PETRULA** (GB) 23
422 **PETWICK** (IRE) 11
85 **PEVENSEY** (IRE) 14
229 **PEVERIL PRIDE** (GB) 36
519 **PEWTER LIGHT** (IRE) 6
569 **PHANTASMAGORIA** (GB) 54
168 **PHANTOM RING** (GB) F 28
199 **PHANTOM ROSE** (GB) 140
451 **PHANTOM SONG** (IRE) 38
81 **PHAR BLEU** (FR) 13
620 **PHAR BOLDER** (IRE) G 44
84 **PHAR CITY** (IRE) 18
227 **PHAR FAR AWAY** (GB) 13
291 **PHAR JEFFEN** (IRE) 18
351 **PHAR OUT PHAVORITE** (IRE) 27

71 **PHAR RIVER** (IRE) 54
339 **PHARAGON** (IRE) 6
349 **PHARATTA** (IRE) F 90
396 **PHARMACIST** (IRE) C 91
535 **PHAROAH'S GOLD** (IRE) 14
284 **PHASE EIGHT GIRL** (GB) 11
163 **PHAT PEOPLES BEACH** (GB) 9
137 **PHEBE** (GB) 87
62 **PHECKLESS** (GB) 20
514 **PHENICIEN** (FR) 174
251 **PHI PHI** (IRE) 26
303 **PHIL'S THUNDER** (IRE) 48
357 **PHILADELPHIE** (IRE) 76
478 **PHILHARMONIQUE** (FR) C 38
200 **PHILHARMONIC** (GB) 43
470 **PHILIPPA YEATES** (IRE) 106
438 **PHILLY ATHLETIC** F 6
150 **PHILOMENA** (GB) 14
634 **PHILSON RUN** (IRE) 12
318 **PHLAUNT** (GB) 13
318 **PHLUKE** (GB) 1
569 **PHOEBE WOODSTOCK** (IRE) 55
418 **PHOENIX EYE** (GB) 14
40 **PHOENIX NIGHTS** (IRE) 17
20 **PHOENIX REACH** (IRE) 20
408 **PHONE BACK** (IRE) 74
481 **PHONE IN** (GB) 60
588 **PHONE TAPPING** (GB) 15
32 **PHONE WEST** (USA) F 98
645 **PHRED** (GB) 9
497 **PHRENOLOGIST** (GB) 8
254 **PHYLELLA** F 7
465 **PHYSICAL** (IRE) 56
449 **PHYSICAL GRAFFITI** (USA) 24
451 **PIANO PLAYER** (GB) 81
481 **PICADOR** (GB) 61
378 **PICCANTE** (GB) F 29
6 **PICCOLED** (GB) 13
473 **PICCLEYES** (GB) 8
6 **PICCOLO PRINCE** (GB) 14
276 **PICCOSTAR** (GB) 20
544 **PICK A NICE NAME** (GB) 38
313 **PICK OF THE CROP** (GB) 21
318 **PICKAPEPPA** (GB) 14
473 **PICKPOCKET** (GB) 9
192 **PICOT** (GB) C 37
42 **PICOT DE SAY** (GB) 21
17 **PICTINA** (GB) C 34
376 **PIE CORNER** (GB) 17
251 **PIE IN THE SKY** (GB) F 40
357 **PIERRE BONNARD** (USA) 20
651 **PIERRE DE LUNE** (GB) 7
232 **PIETEN BERE** (FR) 7
431 **PIETER BRUEGHEL** (USA) 45
115 **PIKE BISHOP** (IRE) 8
28 **PIKESTAFF** (USA) 4
391 **PILCA** (FR) 12
6 **PILGRIM PRINCESS** (IRE) 15
576 **PILGRIMS PROGRESS** (IRE) 9
633 **PILLAR OF FIRE** (IRE) 52
566 **PILLAR ROCK** (USA) 51
633 **PILLAR TO POST** (GB) 53
172 **PILLARS OF WISDOM** (GB) 64
347 **PIN HIGH** (IRE) 58
414 **PINAFORE** (GB) 54
35 **PINCH** (GB) F 22
20 **PINCH OF SALT** (IRE) 108
341 **PINE CONE** (GB) 107
229 **PINE MARTEN** (GB) 37
246 **PINE VALLEY** (IRE) 22
253 **PINGUS** (GB) 34
346 **PINK BAY** (GB) 14
567 **PINK CHAMPAGNE** (IRE) C 22
386 **PINK HARBOUR** (GB) 24
576 **PINK PEARLS** (IRE) 10
587 **PINK PYJAMAS** 32
137 **PINK SHOES** (IRE) 37
615 **PINNACLE RIDGE** (GB) 9

44 **SHEILA'S SECRET** (IRE) C 54
300 **SHEILAS DREAM** (GB) C 15
499 **SHEKAN STAR** (GB) 64
517 **SHEKANA** (FR) 56
7 **SHELEVEN** (IRE) 8
513 **SHELIAK** (GB) 8
582 **SHELU** (GB) 19
252 **SHEM DYLAN** (NZ) 44
517 **SHEMIYRA** (IRE) 106
232 **SHEMRANA** (USA) 8
517 **SHEMRIYNA** (IRE) 57
517 **SHERANA** (GB) C 107
638 **SHERANI** (GB) 15
420 **SHERBERRY** (GB) 78
517 **SHEREF** (FR) 108
569 **SHERGAEL** (IRE) 29
643 **SHERIFF ROSCOE** (GB) 21
337 **SHERIFF STAR** (GB) 7
600 **SHERIFF'S DEPUTY** (GB) 12
517 **SHERIYA** (GB) C 109
444 **SHERKIN ISLAND** (IRE) 72
178 **SHERNA GIRL** (IRE) C 143
449 **SHERNATRA** (IRE) 29
309 **SHEROOG** (USA) C 90
177 **SHERRINGTON** (GB) C 103
517 **SHERZADA** (IRE) 58
309 **SHESASMARTLADY** (IRE) C 91
202 **SHESTHEBISCUIT** (GB) 57
517 **SHEZAN** (IRE) 59
414 **SHI SHI** (GB) C 86
336 **SHIELALIGH** (GB) 21
200 **SHIFTING SHADOW** (IRE) G 85
99 **SHIFTY** (GB) 18
221 **SHIMINNIE** (IRE) 17
40 **SHIMLA** (GB) C 74
109 **SHIMLA** (GB) C 151
588 **SHINGLE STREET** (IRE) 38
319 **SHINING DESERT** (IRE) C 136
470 **SHINING LIGHTS** (IRE) 124
282 **SHINING STRAND** (GB) 88
39 **SHINING TYNE** (GB) 4
53 **SHINJIRU** (USA) 36
341 **SHINY THING** (USA) 111
341 **SHIPMASTER** (GB) 119
32 **SHIPPING LANE** (GB) 52
227 **SHIRAZI** (GB) 21
186 **SHIRE** (IRE) 46
453 **SHIRLEY BLUE** (IRE) F 29
517 **SHIRLEY MOON** (IRE) 60
152 **SHIRLEY OAKS** (IRE) 12
214 **SHIVERMETIMBER** (IRE) 35
341 **SHOGUN PRINCE** (IRE) 120
590 **SHOHRAH** (IRE) 61
404 **SHOLAY** (IRE) 14
396 **SHONA** (GB) C 104
588 **SHORE THING** (GB) 70
441 **SHORT AND SWEET** (IRE) 55
21 **SHORT CHORUS** (GB) 17
287 **SHORT DANCE** (USA) 131
514 **SHORT LIST** (IRE) 94
199 **SHORT PAUSE** (GB) 15
562 **SHORT SKIRT** (GB) 168
172 **SHORTBREAD** (GB) 68
396 **SHOSOLOSA** (IRE) 47
569 **SHOT TO FAME** (USA) 30
496 **SHOTACROSS THE BOW** (IRE) 1
202 **SHOTFIRE RIDGE** (GB) 100
163 **SHOTGUN ANNIE** (GB) 13
578 **SHOTGUN RIDER** (IRE) 12
432 **SHOTGUN WILLY** (GB) 107
115 **SHOUT** (GB) 97
409 **SHOW NO FEAR** (GB) 31
446 **SHOW OF HANDS** (IRE) 20
439 **SHOW WINNER** (GB) 83
443 **SHOWBIZ FLOOZIE** (GB) 1
470 **SHOWER OF HAIL** (IRE) 125
253 **SHOWERING** (GB) F 79
17 **SHOWTIME ANNIE** (GB) 16

17 **SHOWTIME FAYE** (GB) 26
72 **SHRINE MOUNTAIN** (USA) 49
538 **SHUFFLING PALS** (IRE) 10
620 **SHUHOOD** (USA) 48
172 **SHUHRAH** (USA) F 126
583 **SHUIL AR AGHAIDH** C 22
583 **SHUIL BOB** (IRE) 23
136 **SHUIL SHELL** (IRE) G 9
312 **SHUIL TSARINA** (IRE) 31
605 **SHULMIN** (GB) 25
72 **SHUSH** (GB) 11
287 **SHY PRINCESS** (USA) C 132
64 **SIANEMA** (GB) F 13
604 **SIBERION** (GER) 44
604 **SIBERIUS** (GER) 45
287 **SICILIAN** (IRE) 133
246 **SIDECAR** (GB) 26
87 **SIDELOADER SPECIAL** C 73
449 **SIDNEY CHARLES** (IRE) 43
589 **SIDONIUS** (POL) 8
111 **SIEGFRIEDS NIGHT** (IRE) 13
611 **SIEGLINDE** (GB) 32
396 **SIENA GOLD** (GB) 48
57 **SIENA STAR** (IRE) 16
588 **SIENNA STORM** (IRE) 71
71 **SIENNA SUNSET** (IRE) 67
491 **SIERA SPIRIT** (IRE) 4
72 **SIERRA** (GB) 12
25 **SIERRA VISTA** (GB) 7
274 **SIGHTSEER** (USA) 8
124 **SIGN HERE** (GB) C 74
72 **SIGN OF LUCK** (IRE) 50
510 **SIGN OF THE VINE** (GB) C 84
510 **SIGN OF THE WOLF** (GB) 71
643 **SIGNATURE TUNE** (IRE) 22
97 **SIGNOR PELTRO** (GB) 55
109 **SIGNORA PANETTIERA** (FR) 19
72 **SIGNS AND WONDERS** (GB) F 104
514 **SIGNS OF LOVE** (IRE) 180
211 **SIGWELLS CLUB BOY** (GB) 3
615 **SIKASSO** (USA) 10
370 **SIKI** (FR) 116
38 **SILBER MOND** (GB) 41
109 **SILCA'S SISTER** (GB) 152
432 **SILENCE REIGNS** (GB) 108
341 **SILENCIO** (IRE) 89
242 **SILENT AGE** (IRE) 25
224 **SILENT GUEST** (IRE) 27
342 **SILENT GUNNER** (GB) 7
279 **SILENT NAME** (JPN) 64
540 **SILENT SNIPE** (GB) 35
287 **SILENT SPRING** (USA) 76
441 **SILENT SUPREME** (IRE) C 56
27 **SILENT VOICE** (IRE) 4
463 **SILHOUETTING** (GB) 50
463 **SILICON LADY** (F 51
316 **SILISTRA** (GB) 15
494 **SILIVRI** (GB) 8
182 **SILJAN** (GER) 23
644 **SILK APPEAL** (GB) 13
645 **SILK DAISY** (GB) C 41
569 **SILK FAN** (IRE) 31
396 **SILK LAW** (IRE) F 105
32 **SILK ROAD** (GB) 53
467 **SILK ROPE** (IRE) 59
420 **SILK SCREEN** (IRE) 79
237 **SILK SUIVANTE** (IRE) 22
372 **SILK TRADER** (GB) 18
465 **SILKEN ACT** (CAN) 103
368 **SILKEN PEARLS** (GB) 52
123 **SILKEN SKY** (GB) 12
403 **SILKIE PEKIN** (GB) 8
153 **SILKSTONE LADY** (GB) C 11
150 **SILKWOOD TOP** (IRE) 16
94 **SILKY HEIGHTS** (IRE) F 13
439 **SILKY OAK** (IRE) 84
124 **SILLY GOOSE** (IRE) C 75
369 **SILLY IMP** (IRE) F 67

283 **SILLY MID-ON** (GB) G 27
531 **SILLY MISS OFF** (IRE) 35
349 **SILVA** (FR) 97
333 **SILVALINE** (GB) 10
319 **SILVER ARROW** (USA) C 137
102 **SILVER BEAN** (GB) 15
432 **SILVER BIRCH** (IRE) 100
265 **SILVER BLUE** (IRE) 134
312 **SILVER BOW** (GB) 32
345 **SILVER CHARM** (GB) F 61
300 **SILVER CHARMER** (GB) 3
632 **SILVER CHARTER** (USA) 20
541 **SILVER CHIME** (GB) 4
645 **SILVER CREEK** (GB) 42
393 **SILVER CREST** (GB) 28
273 **SILVER CRYSTAL** (IRE) 16
287 **SILVER DIP** (GB) 134
319 **SILVER DOLLARS** (IRE) 89
300 **SILVER DREAMER** (IRE) 7
279 **SILVER FASHION** (IRE) 65
20 **SILVER FLING** (USA) C 115
63 **SILVER GHOST** (GB) 12
208 **SILVER GIFT** (GB) 5
20 **SILVER HIGHLIGHT** (CAN) 67
201 **SILVER HILL LAD** (GB) 10
5 **SILVER INNGOT** (IRE) 38
132 **SILVER ISLAND** (GB) 11
586 **SILVER JACK** (IRE) 18
572 **SILVER JADE** (GB) 6
432 **SILVER JEWEL** (IRE) 110
595 **SILVER MAN** (GB) 3
168 **SILVER MONT** (IRE) 29
276 **SILVER MORGAN** (GB) 13
178 **SILVER NUN** (GB) 144
23 **SILVER PEARL** (GB) 3
279 **SILVER POINT** (IRE) 114
306 **SILVER PRELUDE** (GB) 18
55 **SILVER PROPHET** (IRE) 14
279 **SILVER RAIN** (FR) 15
229 **SILVER REIGN** (GB) 45
87 **SILVER RHYTHM** (GB) 22
608 **SILVER SAILS** (GB) 32
76 **SILVER SAMUEL** (NZ) 8
38 **SILVER SASH** (GB) 8
551 **SILVER SILENCE** (JPN) 19
224 **SILVER SISTER** (GB) 28
557 **SILVER SKATES** (FR) F 35
34 **SILVER SNITCH** (IRE) 23
172 **SILVER SONG** (GB) 9
298 **SILVER STYX** (GB) 3
120 **SILVER TIARA** (GB) 18
109 **SILVER TOUCH** (IRE) 153
557 **SILVER VENTURE** (USA) F 36
205 **SILVER VISAGE** (IRE) 19
222 **SILVER WOOD** (GB) 12
30 **SILVERHAY** (GB) 22
590 **SILVERHILLS** (IRE) 133
368 **SILVERTOWN** (GB) 53
588 **SILVERY** (GB) C 72
93 **SIMACOTA** (GER) C 37
254 **SIMLA BIBI** (GB) F 9
593 **SIMLET** (GB) 8
125 **SIMON LE MAGICIEN** (FR) 18
245 **SIMON THE POACHER** (GB) 8
299 **SIMON VAUGHAN** (IRE) 52
509 **SIMON'S HEIGHTS** (GB) 5
301 **SIMON'S SEAT** (USA) 19
193 **SIMONA** (CHI) F 25
465 **SIMONDA** (GB) 18
89 **SIMONOVSKI** (USA) 4
264 **SIMONSTOWN** (GB) 23
470 **SIMOUN** (IRE) 126
157 **SIMPLE GLORY** (IRE) 41
304 **SIMPLE IDEALS** (USA) 9
349 **SIMPLEX** (FR) 11
87 **SIMPLIFY** (GB) 44
444 **SIMPLY GIFTED** (GB) 73
433 **SIMPLY MYSTIC** (GB) 12

449 **STEVE THE FISH** (IRE) 34
400 **STEVEDORE** (IRE) 16
299 **STEVIE JAY** (IRE) 55
238 **STEVMARIE STAR** (GB) 8
290 **STICKY WICKET** (GB) 88
335 **STILETTO LADY** (IRE) 17
323 **STILL RUNS DEEP** (GB) 7
332 **STILLBYHERSELF** (IRE) G 35
177 **STING IN HER TAIL** (IRE) 105
239 **STING LIKE A BEE** (IRE) 25
124 **STINGRAY** (IRE) 52
507 **STOCK DOVE** (GB) 9
351 **STOCKS 'N SHARES** (GB) 38
209 **STOIC LEADER** (GB) 8
555 **STOKESIES BOY** (GB) 30
555 **STOKESIES WISH** (GB) 31
417 **STOLEN** (GB) 26
483 **STOLEN GIFT** (GB) 7
1 **STOLEN HOURS** (USA) 23
554 **STOLEN MELODY** (GB) F 23
433 **STOLEN MOMENTS** (FR) 13
557 **STOLEN SUMMER** (IRE) 38
178 **STONE COLD** (GB) 38
184 **STONEACRE GIRL** (IRE) 31
184 **STONEACRE LAD** (IRE) 32
184 **STONEACRE LIL** (IRE) 33
217 **STONED** (IRE) 24
55 **STONESFIELD CONEY** (GB) 15
444 **STONEWALL GEORGE** (NZ) 77
178 **STONEWARE** (GB) C 149
347 **STONEY DROVE** (FR) 73
81 **STONEY ROAD GIRL** (IRE) 15
242 **STONEYFOND BEN** (IRE) 26
98 **STOOP TO CONQUER** (GB) 38
199 **STOP MAKING SENSE** (GB) 76
414 **STOP OUT** (GB) C 88
316 **STOPWATCH** (IRE) 17
563 **STORM A BREWING** (GB) 7
279 **STORM AVERTED** (USA) 70
20 **STORM CENTRE** (GB) 70
308 **STORM CHASE** (USA) 18
644 **STORM CLEAR** (IRE) 14
290 **STORM OF APPLAUSE** (IRE) 89
265 **STORM ON THE RUN** (IRE) 138
349 **STORM WATCH** (IRE) 98
319 **STORM WEST** (USA) C 140
119 **STORM'S STORY** (GB) 22
203 **STORMDANCER** (IRE) 7
470 **STORMEZ** (FR) 129
609 **STORMING BACK** (GB) 4
398 **STORMING NORMAN** (GB) 22
73 **STORMVILLE** (FR) 7
277 **STORMWORTHY MISS** (IRE) F 13
158 **STORMY ARCTIC** (IRE) 12
322 **STORMY BEECH** (GB) 13
605 **STORMY LORD** (IRE) 26
634 **STORMY MISS** (GB) C 13
583 **STORMY MOMENT** (IRE) 25
288 **STORMY MONDAY** (GB) 48
569 **STORMY NATURE** (GB) 33
408 **STORMY SKYE** (IRE) 86
124 **STORMY SQUAB** (USA) F 76
370 **STOWAY** (FR) 177
279 **STRADIVARI** (GB) 71
431 **STRAFFAN** (IRE) 74
604 **STRAIGHT AHEAD** (GB) 86
300 **STRAIGHT TALKER** (IRE) 4
268 **STRAIGHT'N'NARROW** (IRE) 88
442 **STRAIT TALKING** (FR) 13
156 **STRATCO** (IRE) 6
124 **STRATEGIC MOUNT** (IRE) 77
124 **STRATEGIC PRINCE** (IRE) 78
124 **STRATEGIC QUEST** (GB) 53
256 **STRATHCLYDE** (IRE) 11
385 **STRATHSPEY** (GB) 6
40 **STRATHTAY** (GB) 45
297 **STRAVMOUR** (GB) 26
436 **STRAVONIAN** (GB) 20

297 **STRAVSEA** (GB) C 52
45 **STRAWBERRY DALE** (IRE) 20
115 **STRAWBERRY LEAF** (GB) 51
562 **STRAWBERRY LOLLY** (GB) 174
464 **STRAWBERRY PATCH** (GB) 7
319 **STRAWBERRY SPLIT** G 90
335 **STRAWMAN** (GB) 18
582 **STREAKER** (GB) F 22
562 **STREAM OF GOLD** (IRE) 23
109 **STREAM OF PASSION** (GB) 73
492 **STREET DANCER** (IRE) 39
69 **STREET GAMES** (GB) 24
424 **STREET LIFE** (IRE) 20
29 **STRENSALL** (GB) 14
279 **STRETCHING** (USA) 72
45 **STRETTON** (FR) 11
85 **STRICTLY COOL** (USA) G 16
77 **STRICTLY SPEAKING** (FR) 12
109 **STRIDE HOME** (IRE) F 158
197 **STRIDER** (GB) 21
524 **STRIDHANA** (GB) G 15
268 **STRIKE BACK** (IRE) 89
345 **STRIKE GOLD** (GB) 38
378 **STRIKE LUCKY** (GB) 9
214 **STRIKE RATE** (GB) 37
431 **STRIKE UP THE BAND** (GB) 84
115 **STRIKING AMBITION** (GB) 16
20 **STRING BAND** (USA) 71
202 **STROLLER** (IRE) 28
296 **STROLLING** (GB) 7
601 **STROLLING VAGABOND** (IRE) 17
432 **STRONG FLOW** (IRE) 115
177 **STRONG HAND** (GB) 50
130 **STRONG MAGIC** (IRE) 10
441 **STRONG PROFIT** (GB) G 59
566 **STRONG PROJECT** (IRE) 63
518 **STRONG RESOLVE** (IRE) 37
119 **STROUDY** (FR) 42
115 **STRUT** (GB) 91
614 **STRUTTING** (IRE) F 49
268 **STUDMASTER** (GB) 90
616 **STUNNING MAGIC** (GB) 8
492 **STYGIAN** (USA) F 53
232 **STYLE FOR LIFE** (GB) C 99
246 **STYLISH BID** (IRE) 55
106 **STYLISH DANCER** (GB) 10
645 **STYLISH SUNRISE** (IRE) 11
349 **STYLUS** (IRE) 58
200 **SUALDA** (IRE) 53
162 **SUAVE** (GB) 83
439 **SUAVE LADY** (FR) C 87
386 **SUBADAR MAJOR** (GB) 33
370 **SUBEHARGUES** (FR) 117
491 **SUBTLE AFFAIR** (IRE) 9
429 **SUBTLE ONE** (GB) C 37
112 **SUBYAN DREAMS** (GB) 35
587 **SUCCESS STORY** (GB) C 36
481 **SUCCESSION** (GB) 31
602 **SUCCESSOR** (GB) 7
329 **SUCHWOT** (GB) 23
119 **SUCRE BRUN** (FR) 43
357 **SUDAN** (IRE) 132
97 **SUDDEN EDGE** (GB) 31
197 **SUDDEN FLIGHT** (IRE) 27
624 **SUE'S A LADY** G 19
346 **SUE'S SYMPHONY** (GB) 20
520 **SUFFOLK HOUSE** (GB) 53
109 **SUFFRAGETTE** (GB) 74
60 **SUGAR** (GB) F 33
561 **SUGGEST** (GB) 12
253 **SUGGESTIVE** (GB) 13
41 **SUIL NA STOIRME** (IRE) 16
193 **SUITCASE MURPHY** (IRE) 9
354 **SUITS ME FINE** (IRE) 14
112 **SUIVEZ MOI** (IRE) 36
463 **SUKAR** (FR) 27
20 **SUKUMA** (GB) 72
628 **SULAKA** (GB) F 32

332 **SULAPUFF** (GB) C 36
137 **SULARINA** (IRE) 95
586 **SULLY SHUFFLES** (IRE) 20
604 **SULTANA** (GER) 87
329 **SUMMER BOUNTY** (GB) 24
199 **SUMMER BREEZE** (GB) F 151
310 **SUMMER CHARM** (GB) 31
479 **SUMMER CHERRY** (USA) 11
569 **SUMMER DREAMS** (IRE) C 106
186 **SUMMER FASHION** F 82
306 **SUMMER JOY** (GB) 19
588 **SUMMER LODGE** (GB) 14
62 **SUMMER RECLUSE** (USA) 28
510 **SUMMER SEA** (GB) 51
71 **SUMMER SHADES** (GB) 70
200 **SUMMER SILKS** (GB) 87
25 **SUMMER SPECIAL** (GB) 8
61 **SUMMER SPECIAL** (GB) 16
137 **SUMMER STAGE** (GB) 96
565 **SUMMER STOCK** (USA) 14
186 **SUMMER STYLE** (IRE) F 83
97 **SUMMER'S EVE** (IRE) 56
4 **SUMMERISE** (GB) 4
221 **SUMMERTIME BLUES** (IRE) 18
97 **SUMMERTIME PARKES** (GB) 57
531 **SUMMIT UP** (IRE) 41
237 **SUMMITVILLE** (IRE) 26
562 **SUMPTUOUS** (GB) 175
20 **SUN BIAN** (GB) 73
265 **SUN CATCHER** (IRE) 139
20 **SUN FIRE** (GB) 118
378 **SUN GOD** (GB) 22
504 **SUN PAGEANT** (GB) 9
109 **SUNAMI STORM** (IRE) 82
349 **SUNANA** (GB) 59
109 **SUNBLUSH** (UAE) 75
30 **SUNBOLT** (IRE) 78
109 **SUNCAR** (GB) 159
168 **SUNCLIFF** (GB) 14
126 **SUNDANCE** (IRE) 19
412 **SUNDAWN LADY** (IRE) 17
487 **SUNDAY HABITS** (IRE) 15
285 **SUNDRIED TOMATO** (GB) 18
520 **SUNFLEET** (GB) 7
583 **SUNGATES** (IRE) 26
480 **SUNGIO** (GB) 55
282 **SUNLEY FUTURE** (IRE) 95
109 **SUNLEY SINNER** (GB) 160
205 **SUNLIT RIDE** F 24
481 **SUNLIT SKIES** (GB) 32
603 **SUNNY DISPOSITION** (IRE) 12
173 **SUNNY HAZE** (GB) 25
418 **SUNNY PARKES** (GB) 7
210 **SUNNY SLOPE** (GB) C 23
458 **SUNNY TIMES** (IRE) 16
591 **SUNNYARJUN** (GB) 17
237 **SUNNYDALE** (IRE) 58
290 **SUNNYLAND** (GB) 90
33 **SUNNYSIDE ROYALE** (IRE) 11
490 **SUNRISE COURT** (GB) 7
162 **SUNRISE HAVELI** (FR) 66
514 **SUNRISE NEVEES** (FR) 99
643 **SUNRISE SAFARI** (IRE) 40
591 **SUNRISE SPIRIT** (FR) 43
652 **SUNSET BLUES** (FR) 7
404 **SUNSET DREAMER** (USA) 15
354 **SUNSET ISLAND** (FR) 21
222 **SUNSET KING** (USA) 13
583 **SUNSET LEADER** (FR) F 27
583 **SUNSET LIGHT** (IRE) 28
254 **SUNSET PARK** (IRE) F 11
251 **SUNSET RIDGE** (IRE) 43
109 **SUNSET STRIP** (GB) 76
569 **SUNSETTER** (USA) C 107
246 **SUNSHINE GUEST** (IRE) 32
611 **SUNSHINE ON ME** (GB) 1
604 **SUNSHINE STORY** (IRE) 46
240 **SUNY HENRY** (GB) 5

256 **WAGES** (GB) 15
608 **WAGGLEDANCE** (IRE) 28
171 **WAGTAIL** (GB) 118
337 **WAHCHI** (IRE) 5
648 **WAHIBA SANDS** (GB) 10
30 **WAHOO SAM** (USA) 27
119 **WAIA** (IRE) 40
280 **WAIMEA BAY** (GB) 9
449 **WAIN MOUNTAIN** (GB) 40
518 **WAINAK** (USA) 41
53 **WAINWRIGHT** (IRE) 41
408 **WAIT FOR THE WILL** (USA) 94
268 **WAKE UP HENRY** (GB) 99
351 **WAKEUP SMILING** (IRE) 45
407 **WAKI BAKI** (IRE) 44
246 **WAKRIA** (IRE) F 74
190 **WALCOT LAD** (IRE) 8
354 **WALK IN MY SHADOW** (IRE) 17
162 **WALK ON SEAS** (IRE) 45
214 **WALK OVER** (IRE) 43
150 **WALKERS LADY** (IRE) F 19
303 **WALKIN AISY** (GB) 61
18 **WALKING SUNDAY** (IRE) 37
456 **WALKMILL** (IRE) 7
353 **WALL STREET RUNNER** (GB) 13
33 **WALLY WONDER** (IRE) 14
345 **WALNUT LADY** (GB) C 65
643 **WALTER** (IRE) 2
402 **WALTER'S DESTINY** (GB) 3
411 **WALTHAM DOVE** (GB) 26
480 **WALTZING BEAU** (GB) 60
23 **WALTZING WIZARD** (GB) 42
431 **WANCHAI LAD** (GB) 62
336 **WANDERING ACT** (IRE) 32
349 **WANDERING SPIRIT** (GER) 102
157 **WANNA SHOUT** (GB) 47
172 **WANNABE POSH** (GB) 136
109 **WANSDYKE LASS** (GB) 81
318 **WAQOOD** (USA) C 27
590 **WAR AT SEA** (IRE) 65
626 **WAR DANCER** (GB) 14
413 **WAR OF ATTRITION** (GB) 27
633 **WAR OWL** (USA) 65
109 **WAR PENNANT** (GB) 82
470 **WARDASH** (GER) 149
109 **WARDAT ALLAYL** (IRE) F 166
357 **WARDEN** (GB) 138
87 **WARES HOME** (IRE) 25
554 **WARIF** (USA) 16
301 **WARLINGHAM** (IRE) 22
72 **WARNING SHADOWS** (IRE) C 113
357 **WARNING SIGN** (IRE) 92
87 **WARNING STAR** (GB) C 78
283 **WARNINGCAMP** (GER) 15
535 **WAROONGA** (GB) C 48
284 **WARREN PLACE** (GB) 16
420 **WARRENS CASTLE** (IRE) 87
379 **WARRIORS PATH** (IRE) 10
72 **WARRSAN** (IRE) 15
481 **WARSAW PACT** (IRE) 75
336 **WASALAT** (USA) 33
264 **WASHBROOK** (GB) 31
244 **WASHINGTON PINK** (IRE) 12
172 **WASNAH** (USA) C 137
477 **WASTED TALENT** (IRE) 18
378 **WATAMU** (IRE) 10
171 **WATCH ME** (IRE) F 119
101 **WATCH ME DOODLE** (GB) 7
376 **WATCH OUT JESS** (GB) 18
199 **WATCH WHAT HAPPENS** (IRE) 158
425 **WATCHFUL WITNESS** (IRE) 18
200 **WATCHING** (GB) 57
343 **WATCHMYEYES** (IRE) 42
347 **WATER JUMP** (IRE) 84
563 **WATER KING** (USA) 9
465 **WATER PISTOL** (GB) 68
270 **WATER QUIRL** (GB) 25
420 **WATER STORM** (IRE) 88

421 **WATER TAXI** (GB) 62
149 **WATERBERG** (IRE) 49
516 **WATERCRESS** (GB) 11
44 **WATERFRONT DANCER** (GB) 43
268 **WATERLILY** (GB) 100
197 **WATERLINE LOVER** (GB) 49
134 **WATERLOO CORNER** (GB) 10
229 **WATERLOO LILY** (GB) 53
149 **WATERLOO SON** (IRE) 50
32 **WATERPAINT** (GB) 109
134 **WATERPARK** (GB) 7
408 **WATERSIDE** (IRE) 95
555 **WATERSPRAY** (AUS) 35
30 **WATHBAT MTOTO** (GB) C 81
286 **WAVE BACK** (IRE) 7
98 **WAVE ROCK** (GB) 43
414 **WAVERLEY** (IRE) 33
376 **WAVERLEY ROAD** (GB) 15
186 **WAVERTREE BOY** (IRE) 27
186 **WAVERTREE ONE OFF** (GB) 52
361 **WAVERTREE WARRIOR** (IRE) 43
171 **WAVESKI** (GB) 120
461 **WAVET** (GB) 9
232 **WAVY KRIS** (IRE) F 106
112 **WAVY UP** (IRE) C 69
20 **WAY TO THE STARS** (IRE) 127
610 **WAYDALE HILL** (GB) 8
408 **WAYWARD MELODY** (GB) 96
177 **WAYWARD SHOT** (IRE) 75
414 **WAZIRI** (IRE) 34
380 **WE HAVE TIME** (IRE) 7
408 **WE'LL MAKE IT** (IRE) 97
177 **WE'LL MEET AGAIN** (GB) 59
178 **WE'RE JOKEN** (GB) F 153
139 **WE'VE JUST BEGUN** (USA) F 26
6 **WEAKEST LINK** (IRE) 18
644 **WEARERICH** (GB) 16
561 **WEAVER GEORGE** (IRE) 15
244 **WEB MASTER** (IRE) 13
360 **WEBBSWOOD LAD** (IRE) 25
52 **WEBSTER** (GB) 19
562 **WEDAAD** (GB) 185
465 **WEDDING PARTY** (GB) 69
16 **WEDNESDAY CLUB** (GB) 13
109 **WEDOUDAH** (IRE) F 167
109 **WEE CHARLIE CASTLE** (IRE) 168
345 **WEE DINNS** (IRE) 16
233 **WEE ROBBIE** (GB) 25
518 **WEE SEAN** (IRE) 42
40 **WEE ZIGGY** (GB) 77
4 **WEECANDOO** (IRE) 5
297 **WEET A HEAD** (IRE) 31
297 **WEET FOR YOU** (GB) 53
53 **WEET FOR YOU** (GB) 67
53 **WEET N MEASURES** (GB) 65
53 **WEET WATCHERS** (GB) 42
451 **WEFT** (GB) 97
465 **WEIGHTLESS** (GB) 28
478 **WELCOME RELEAF** (GB) 55
192 **WELCOME STRANGER** (GB) 6
499 **WELCOME TO UNOS** (GB) 60
372 **WELKINO'S BOY** (GB) 22
480 **WELL ACTUALLY** (IRE) 61
345 **WELL BOUGHT** (GB) C 66
470 **WELL CHIEF** (GB) 150
309 **WELL ESTABLISHED** (IRE) 48
182 **WELL GUARDED** (IRE) 41
562 **WELL HIDDEN** (GB) 186
268 **WELL PRESENTED** (IRE) 101
199 **WELL SPOKEN** (IRE) 84
115 **WELL WARNED** (GB) F 95
290 **WELLBEING** (GB) 100
590 **WELLING** (IRE) 66
112 **WELLINGTON HALL** (GER) 8
599 **WELLPICT ONE** (IRE) 56
349 **WELLSAID** (FR) 62
191 **WELSH ASSEMBLY** (GB) 10
536 **WELSH DANE** (GB) 8

20 **WELSH DRAGON** (GB) 128
219 **WELSH DREAM** (GB) 18
570 **WELSH EMPEROR** (IRE) 8
234 **WELSH GALAXY** (IRE) 13
329 **WELSH MAIN** (GB) 29
205 **WELSH TOUCH** (IRE) 20
76 **WELSH WHISPER** (GB) 10
480 **WEMBURY POINT** (IRE) 66
347 **WENCESLAS** (IRE) 85
184 **WENDY'S GIRL** (IRE) 5
593 **WENDYS COMET** (GB) 11
137 **WENGE** (USA) F 103
643 **WENGER** (FR) 27
30 **WENSLEYDALE STAR** (GB) 82
432 **WERE IN TOUCH** (IRE) 123
33 **WERE NOT STOPPIN** (GB) 15
86 **WESLEY'S LAD** (IRE) 12
33 **WESSEX** (USA) 43
388 **WEST ASIDE** (IRE) 7
428 **WEST BAY STORM** (GB) 45
279 **WEST DAKOTA** (USA) C 125
287 **WEST DEVON** (USA) F 146
133 **WEST END PEARL** (GB) 9
614 **WEST END WONDER** (IRE) 5
532 **WEST HIGHLAND WAY** (IRE) 21
386 **WEST HILL** (IRE) 40
150 **WEST HILL GAIL** (IRE) 20
32 **WEST INDIAN** (IRE) 110
264 **WEST POINT** (GB) 32
214 **WEST WICKLOW** (IRE) 44
281 **WESTCORK** (IRE) 6
520 **WESTCOTE** (USA) 38
177 **WESTCOURT DREAM** (GB) 60
177 **WESTCOURT PEARL** (GB) C 109
190 **WESTCRAFT** (IRE) 9
470 **WESTENDER** (FR) 151
192 **WESTER LODGE** (IRE) 24
408 **WESTERN** (IRE) 98
246 **WESTERN BRAVE** (IRE) 60
371 **WESTERN COMMAND** (GER) 17
214 **WESTERN FLYER** (IRE) 45
439 **WESTERN HEIGHTS** (GB) F 90
158 **WESTERN RANSOM** (USA) 15
407 **WESTERN ROAD** (GER) 47
391 **WESTERN ROOTS** (GB) 20
357 **WESTERNER** (GB) 31
361 **WESTFIELD BOY** (GB) 44
544 **WESTLAKE BOND** (IRE) 44
465 **WESTLAND** (USA) 70
313 **WESTMEAD ETOILE** (GB) 31
502 **WESTMEATH FLYER** (GB) 47
465 **WESTMORELAND ROAD** (USA) 29
610 **WESTON ROCK** (GB) 9
370 **WESTOS** (FR) 125
157 **WESTSIDE FLYER** (GB) F 51
363 **WHALEEF** (IRE) 17
408 **WHAT A MAN** (IRE) 99
37 **WHAT A MONDAY** (GB) 10
262 **WHAT A NIGHT** (GB) 2
599 **WHAT DO'IN** (IRE) 57
407 **WHAT PERK** (IRE) 48
252 **WHAT'S A FILLY** (GB) 52
317 **WHAT'S THE COUNT** (GB) 8
361 **WHAT-A-DANCER** (IRE) 29
38 **WHATATODO** (GB) 45
287 **WHAZZAT** (GB) 82
410 **WHENWILLITWIN** (GB) 14
20 **WHERE'S CHARLOTTE** (GB) C 129
491 **WHERE'S THE MONEY** F 43
599 **WHEREAREYOUNOW** (IRE) 58
418 **WHERETHERES A WILL** (GB) 27
25 **WHINHILL HOUSE** (GB) 11
141 **WHIPLASH** (IRE) 3
44 **WHIPPASNAPPER** (GB) 33
125 **WHIPPER** (USA) 23
113 **WHIPPERS DELIGHT** (IRE) 5
237 **WHIRLING** (GB) 64
465 **WHIRLY BIRD** (GB) 30

LOCATION OF TRAINING QUARTERS

References show squares as on map

IN SEVERAL CASES THE NEAREST MAIN CENTRE IS SHOWN TO LOCATE SITUATION OF STABLES

TRAINERS' VAT NUMBERS

TRAINER	REG NUMBER
JONATHAN AKEHURST	563964796
C. N. ALLEN	637912028
AUVRAY, JEAN-RENE	797413783
N. M. BABBAGE	650825538
K. C. BAILEY	314664563
A. M. BALDING	199094119
J. BALDING	457758887
D. W. BARKER	633223080
M. A. BARNES	621400401
T. D. BARRON	772206343
A. K. BARROW	129915054
R. BASTIMAN	482127648
P. BEAUMONT	171124988
R. M. BECKETT	724510267
J. C. DE P BERRY	638100758
J. D. BETHELL	323421206
R. N. BEVIS	713204777
M. T. W. BLANSHARD	314339869
M. R. BOSLEY	685442802
MRS A. J. BOWLBY	569925283
S. R. BOWRING	509278724
J. M. BRADLEY	274664333
M. F. BRADSTOCK	491470535
G. G. BRAVERY	571294237
G. G. BRIDGWATER	650994018
C. E. BRITTAIN	102592304
M. A. BRITTAIN	599146977
R. H. BUCKLER	398770975
M. A. BUCKLEY	721353368
W. D. BURCHELL	540651465
N. A. CALLAGHAN	102933011
A. M. CAMPION	587879646
HENRY D. N. B. CANDY	200880890
A. W. CARROLL	704885219
B. I. CASE	739507017
P. R. CHAMINGS	537571819
N. T. CHANCE	724408546
M. CHANNON	189661117
DAVID W. CHAPMAN	168959983
M. C. CHAPMAN	344208574
P. W. CHAPPLE-HYAM	823354737
J. I. A. CHARLTON	746465407
G. C. H. CHUNG	711369745
P. F. I. COLE	314293378
H. J. COLLINGRIDGE	1042548907
J. R. CORNWALL	745692595
C. G. COX	718184818
R. CRAGGS	602268958
L. M. & MRS S. CUMANI	285323550
P. D. CUNDELL	614824055
T. A. K. CUTHBERT	330488857
L. A. DACE	712064377
P. T. DALTON	616881224
H. D. J. DALY	713143671
DECLAN DALY	754612921
V. R. A. DARTNALL	631092665
B. DE HAAN	314859934
R. DICKIN	650226565
M. J. K. DODS	257933133
S. L. DOW	413544574
C. A. DWYER	638198012
M. W. EASTERBY	169069725
C. R. EGERTON	569752780
BRIAN ELLISON	660293245
D. R. C. ELSWORTH	355785023
A. E. EMBIRICOS	637949092
G. P. ENRIGHT	435943923
J. M. P. EUSTACE	521219779
P. D. EVANS	489174986
R. A. FAHEY	598892254
C. W. FAIRHURST	602285861
J. R. FANSHAWE	521042309
J. D. FEILDEN	776710308

TRAINER	REG NUMBER
G. FIERRO	536880711
M. E. D. FRANCIS	314910188
JOHN GALLAGHER	754510246
J. A. GEORGE	286221849
T. R. GEORGE	571312270
J. A. GLOVER	570900256
J. S. GOLDIE	556428423
R. H. GOLDIE	264621953
R. GUEST	521042211
W. J. HAGGAS	442932451
J. S. HALDANE	271440773
S. E. HALL	602277467
G. A. HARKER	829155316
PATRICK HASLAM	199936189
N. J. HAWKE	679656268
J. C. HAYNES	621426962
P. R. HEDGER	503611295
N. J. HENDERSON	314065590
LADY HERRIES	321820494
J. HETHERTON	598972355
P. W. HIATT	119746644
B. W. HILLS	385437325
J. W. HILLS	569940094
P. J. HOBBS	357220859
R. J. HODGES	379438207
R. HOLLINSHEAD	100714234
H. S. HOWE	763022162
DON E. INCISA	602257083
A. P. JARVIS	569954274
M. A. JARVIS	344445361
W. JARVIS	410611119
J. M. JEFFERSON	347619039
J. R. W. JENKINS	321802888
W. P. JENKS	632098837
J. H. JOHNSON	532645354
R. F. JOHNSON HOUGHTON	199189886
MISS G. M. KELLEWAY	703016686
A. L. M. KING	398488080
J. S. KING	195142948
MISS H. C. KNIGHT	200516720
MRS S. LAMYMAN	128334771
B. J. LLEWELLYN	691545413
J. A. LOCKWOOD	317079458
L. LUNGO	292955317
MRS N. J. MACAULEY	520735078
W. J. W. MACKIE	390480447
P. J. MAKIN	194790518
C. J. MANN	614848525
G. G. MARGARSON	632698317
T. P. MCGOVERN	620849049
M. K. MILLIGAN	633271164
B. R. MILLMAN	570248055
T. G. MILLS	564116061
G. M. MOORE	602113509
H. MORRISON	614830161
WILLIAM R. MUIR	569865572
J. W. MULLINS	504372669
F. MURPHY	634496811
F. G. MURPHY	775931488
F. P. MURTAGH	686608000
W. J. MUSSON	213080024
A. G. NEWCOMBE	320610613
D. NICHOLLS	613401686
L. B. NORMILE	751407546
W. A. O'GORMAN	521157284
J. J. O'NEILL	257253650
J. A. B. OLD	501801302
MRS J. K. M. OLIVER	270373273
J. A. OSBORNE	537599888
BRYN PALLING	588023523
ANDREW PARKER	416021696
J. W. PAYNE	521068184
J. PEARCE	443013104

TRAINER	REG NUMBER
R. T. PHILLIPS	614622855
M. C. PIPE, C.B.E.	794117903
M. A. PITMAN	614846825
M. J. POLGLASE	637800631
B. N. POLLOCK	800263871
C. L. POPHAM	131287782
J. G. B. PORTMAN	642435647
P. D. PURDY	529855403
J. J. QUINN	647217923
J. R. RAMSDEN	754555901
A. S. REID	511129591
B. S. ROTHWELL	599172585
R. ROWE	397611812
MISS M. E. ROWLAND	684046620
O. M. C. SHERWOOD	363042676
MISS L. C. SIDDALL	431044695
P. M. SLY	486255319
B. SMART	450209482
MISS S. SMITH	793750002
M. E. SOWERSBY	698398155
J. L. SPEARING	275942326
R. M. STRONGE	757205428
L. STUBBS	685582192
L. C. TAYLOR	623648926
RONALD THOMPSON	591076039
C. W. THORNTON	755350234

TRAINER	REG NUMBER
C. TIZZARD	768814579
J. A. R. TOLLER	684781191
M. H. TOMPKINS	334108488
J. C. TUCK	618276525
E. W. TUER	721823061
ANDREW TURNELL	734554526
N. A. TWISTON-DAVIES	713747237
J. R. UPSON	623653839
J. WADE	602275669
C. F. WALL	496701221
T. R. WALL	682132153
MARK WALLACE	811681052
P. WEGMANN	681808804
J. R. WEYMES	734217450
A. C. WHILLANS	663893882
R. M. WHITAKER	170674459
M. S. WILESMITH	771353725
S. C. WILLIAMS	637792789
S. D. WILLIAMS	631020504
MISS V. M. WILLIAMS	655596100
A. J. WILSON	286154441
I. A. WOOD	562221667
GEOFFREY WRAGG	102855589

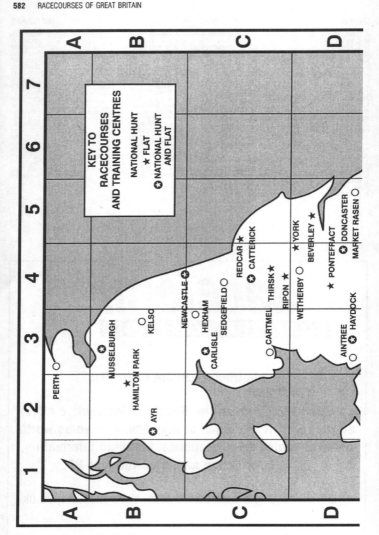

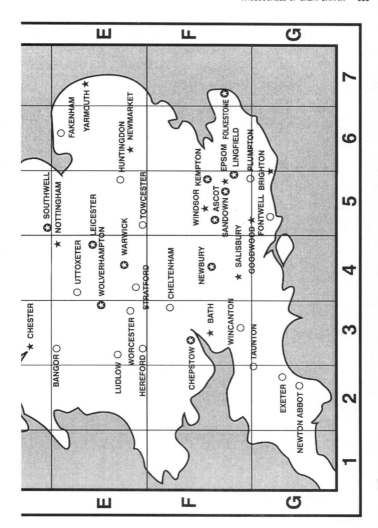

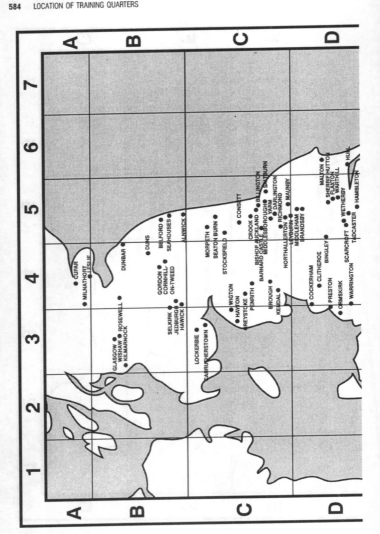

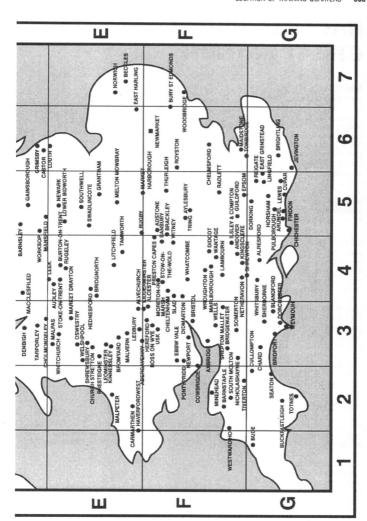

RACECOURSES OF GREAT BRITAIN

AINTREE (L.H)

Grand National Course: Triangular, 2m 2f (16) 494y run-in with elbow. Perfectly flat. A severe test for both horse and rider, putting a premium on jumping ability, fitness and courage, although some of the fences were recently modified.

Mildmay Course: Rectangular, 1m 4f (8) 260y run-in. A very fast course with sharp bends.

Address: Aintree Racecourse, Aintree, Liverpool, L9 5AS Tel: (0151) 523 2600 Fax: (0151) 522 2920

E-mail: aintree@rht.net www.aintree.co.uk

Clerk Of The Course: Mr A Tulloch

Managing Director: Mr C. H. Barnett

Going Reports: (0151) 523 2600.

Stabling: 176 boxes allocated in strict rotation. Facilities are available on the course for up to 100 stable staff. (0151) 523 2600.

By Road: North of the City, near the junction of the M57 and M58 with the A59 (Preston).

By Rail: Aintree Station is adjacent to the Stands, from Liverpool Central.

By Air: Liverpool (Speke) Airport is 10 miles. Helicopter landing facility by prior arrangement.

ASCOT (R.H)

Flat: Right-handed triangular course of 1m 6f 34y, with a run-in of two and half furlongs. Ascot is galloping and stiff, slightly undulating with easy turns. All races up to 7f take place on the straight course.

N.H. Triangular, 1m 6f (10) 240y run-in mostly uphill. A galloping course with an uphill finish, Ascot provides a real test of stamina. The fences are stiff and sound jumping is essential, especially for novices.

Address: Ascot Racecourse, Ascot, Berkshire SL5 7JN Tel: (01344) 622211 Fax: (01344) 628299

www.ascot.co.uk

Clerk Of The Course: TBA

Chief Executive: Mr D. Erskine-Crum.

Going Reports: Day: (01344) 874567

Stabling: Free, with shavings, straw or paper provided. Tel: (01344) 625630 Fax: (01344) 873751

By Road: West of the town on the A329. Easy access from the M3 (Junction 3) and the M4 (Junction 6). Car parking adjoining the course and Ascot Heath.

By Rail: Regular service from Waterloo to Ascot (500y from the racecourse).

By Air: Helicopter landing facility at the course. London (Heathrow) Airport 15 miles, White Waltam Airfield 12 miles.

AYR (L.H)

Flat: A left-handed, galloping, flat oval track of 1m 4f with a 4f run-in. The straight 6f is essentially flat.

N.H. Oval, 1m 4f (9) 210y run-in. Relatively flat and one of the fastest tracks in Great Britain. It is a well-drained course and the ground rarely becomes testing. Suits the long-striding galloper.

Address: Ayr Racecourse, Whitletts Road, Ayr KA8 0JE Tel: (01292) 264179 Fax: (01292) 610140

Internet: www.ayr-racecourse.com

Clerk Of The Course: Mrs A Morshead Tel: (01292) 264179. Mobile: (07789) 697241

General Manager: Mr W Gorol

Going Reports: Contact Clerk of the Course as above.

Stabling: Free stabling and accommodation for lads and lasses. Tel: (01292) 264179.

By Road: East of the town on the A758. Free parking for buses and cars.

By Rail: Ayr Station (trains on the half hour from Glasgow Central). Journey time 55 minutes. Buses and taxis also to the course.

By Air: Prestwick International Airport (10 minutes), Glasgow Airport (1 hour).

BANGOR-ON-DEE (L.H)

N.H. Circular, 1m 4f (9) 325y run-in. Apart from some 'ridge and furrow', this is a flat course notable for three sharp bends, especially the paddock turn. Suits handy, speedy sorts and is ideal for front-runners.
Address: Bangor-On-Dee Racecourse, Overton Road, Bangor-On-Dee, Wrexham. LL13 0DA
Tel: (01978) 780323, Fax: (01978) 780985
Clerk of the Course: Mr E Gretton Tel: (01978) 780323 or Mobile (07855) 807718. Fax: (01978) 780985.
Chief Executive: Mr R Thomas.
Going Reports: Contact Clerk of the Course as above.
Stabling: 84 stables, allotted on arrival. Shavings (straw on request). Applications to the Manager.
Tel: (01978) 780323.
By Road: 5 miles South-East of Wrexham, off the B5069.
By Rail: Wrexham Station (bus or taxi to the course).
By Air: Helicopters may land by prior arrangement with Clerk of the Course at entirely their own risk.

BATH (L.H)

Flat: Galloping, left-handed, level oval of 1m 4f 25y, with long, stiff run-in of about 4f which bends to the left. An extended chute provides for races over 5f 11y and 5f 161y.
Address: The Racecourse, Lansdown, Bath. (01225) 424609 Fax: (01225) 444415.
Internet: www.bath-racecouse.co.uk
Clerk Of The Course: Mr T Long Tel: (01255) 424609 (Office), (07966) 893531 (Mobile).
General Manager: Mr J Williams
Managing Director: Mr R Street.
Going Reports: Contact Clerk of the Course as above.
Stabling: Free stabling and accommodation for lads and lasses. Tel: (01225) 444274
By Road: 2 miles North-West of the City (M4 Junction 18) at Lansdown. Unlimited free car and coach parking space immediately behind the stands. Special bus services operate from Bath to the racecourse.
By Rail: Bath Station (from Paddington), regular bus service from Bath to the course (3 miles).
By Air: Bristol or Colerne Airports. (no landing facilities at the course).

BEVERLEY (R.H)

Flat: A right-handed oval of 1m 3f, generally galloping, with an uphill run-in of two and a half furlongs. The 5f course is very stiff.
Address: Beverley Race Co. Ltd., York Road, Beverley, Yorkshire HU17 9QZ Tel: (01482) 867488/882645.
Clerk Of The Course: Mr J. M. Hutchinson. Tel: (01765) 602156. Mobile (07860) 679904.
Racecourse Manager: Sally Iggulden (07850) 458605
Going Reports: Tel: (01482) 867488/882645 or Head Groundsman (Mr. S Jessop) mobile 07885 678186
Stabling: Free stabling. Accommodation available for lads and lasses Tel: (01482) 867488/882645.
By Road: 7 miles from the M62 (Junction 38) off the A1035. Free car parking opposite the course. Owners and Trainers use a separate enclosure.
By Rail: Beverley Station (Hull-Scarborough line). Occasional bus service to the course (1 mile).
By Air: Helicopter landings by prior arrangement. Light aircraft landing facilities at Linley Hill, Leven airport.

BRIGHTON (L.H)

Flat: Left-handed, 1m 4f horseshoe with easy turns and a run-in of three and a half furlongs. Undulating and sharp, the track suits handy types.
Address: Brighton Racecourse, Brighton, Sussex BN2 2XZ Tel: (01273) 603580 Fax: (01273) 673267.
Clerk Of The Course: Mr Geoffrey Stickels Tel: (01273) 603580. Mobile: (07973 737006)
General Manager: Mr M Hudson
Going Reports: Available on brighton-racecourse.co.uk or contact main office/Clerk Of Course as above
Stabling: Stabling & accommodation: Tel: (01273) 603580, available on request.
By Road: East of the city on the A27 (Lewes Road). There is a car park adjoining the course.

By Rail: Brighton Station (from Victoria on the hour, London Bridge or Portsmouth). Special bus service to the course from the station (approx 2 miles).
By Air: No racecourse facilities.

CARLISLE (R.H)

Flat: Right-handed, 1m 4f pear-shaped track. Galloping and undulating with easy turns and a stiff uphill run-in of three and a half furlongs. 6f course begins on an extended chute.
N.H.: Pear-shaped, 1m 5f (9) 300y run-in uphill. Undulating and a stiff test of stamina, ideally suited to the long-striding thorough stayer. Three mile chases start on a chute, and the first fence is only jumped once. Ground tends to be either very fast or very soft.
Address: Carlisle Racecourse, Durdar Road, Carlisle CA2 4TS Tel: (01228) 554700 Office: (01228) 554747 www.carlisle-races.co.uk
Clerk Of The Course: Mr J. E. Fenwicke-Clennell. Tel: Office (01228) 554700. Home (016974) 76589. Mobile: (07860) 737729.
General Manager: Mr J Baker
Going Reports: (01228) 554700 (recorded) or contact Clerk Of The Course above
Stabling: Stabling and accommodation available on request. Please phone Head Groundsman on (01228) 546188, or Stable Office on (01228) 549489 from 3pm day before racing.
By Road: 2 miles south of the town (Durdar Road). Easy access from the M6 (Junction 42). The car park is free (adjacent to the course). Trackside car parking £3 (except Saturdays & Bank Holidays £5).
By Rail: Carlisle Station (2 miles from the course).
By Air: Helicopter landing facility by prior arrangement.

CARTMEL (L.H)

N.H.: Oval, 1m 1f (6) 800y run-in. Almost perfectly flat but very sharp, with the longest run-in in the country, approximately half a mile. The fences are stiff but fair.
Address: Cartmel Racecourse, Cartmel, nr Grange-Over-Sands, Cumbria LA11 6QF Tel: (015395) 36340. Out of season (015395) 33335 Fax: (01539) 536004
Clerk Of The Course: Mr A. J. A. Tulloch Tel: (0151) 523 2600 Fax: (0151) 522 2920 Car: (0411) 880123 Racedays: (01539) 536340.
General Manager: Mr C Barnett
Club Secretary: Mrs Bray (015395) 33434
Going Reports: (015395) 36340 or contact Clerk Of Course as above.
Stabling: Boxes and accommodation for lads and lasses is limited. Prior booking is advisable.
By Road: 1 mile West of the town, 2 miles off the B5277 (Grange-Haverthwaite road). M36 (Junction 36).
By Rail: Cark and Cartmel Station (2½ miles) (Carnforth-Barrow line).
By Air: Light aircraft facilities available at Cark Airport (4 miles from the course). Helicopter landing facility at the course, by prior arrangement only.

CATTERICK (L.H)

Flat: A sharp, left-handed, undulating oval of 1m 180y with a downhill run-in of 3f.
N.H.: Oval, 1m 1f (9) 240y run-in. Undulating, sharp track that favours the handy, front-running sort, rather than the long-striding galloper.
Address: The Racecourse, Catterick Bridge, Richmond, North Yorkshire DL10 7PE Tel: (01748) 811478 Fax: (01748) 811082
Clerk Of The Course (Flat): International racecourse management (07831) 457453
Clerk of the Course (jumps): Mr C.M.Tetley. Manor Farm, Little Habton, Malton, N.Yorkshire YO17 OUA. Tel: (01302) 320066 (racedays), Home (01904) 489669. Mobile (07860) 919661.
Going Reports: Contact Clerk Of Course as above
Stabling: Boxes are allotted on arrival.
By Road: The course is adjacent to the A1, 1 mile North-West of the town on the A6136. There is a free car park.

By Rail: Darlington Station (special buses to course - 14 mile journey).
By Air: Helicopters can land by prior arrangement. Fixed wing planes contact RAF Leeming
Tel: 01677 423041

CHELTENHAM (L.H)

Old Course: Oval, 1m 4f (9) 350y run-in. A testing, undulating track with stiff fences. The ability to stay is essential.
New Course: Oval, 1m 5f (10) 220y run-in. Undulating, stiff fences, testing course, uphill for the final half-mile.
Address: Cheltenham Racecourse, Prestbury Park, Cheltenham, Gloucestershire GL50 4SH
Tel (01242) 513014 Fax: (01242) 224227 Internet: http://www.cheltenham.co.uk
Managing Director: Mr E. W. Gillespie
Clerk Of The Course: Mr S. J. Claisse
Going Reports: Available from 6 days before racing (01242) 517900
Stabling: Ample stabling and accommodation for lads. Apply to the Stable Manager (01242) 513014
or 521950.
By Road: 1.5 miles North of the town on the A435. M5 (Junction 10 or 11).
By Rail: Cheltenham (Lansdowne) Station. Buses and taxis to course.
By Air: Helicopter landing site to the North-East of the stands.

CHEPSTOW (L.H)

Flat: A left-handed, undulating oval of about 2m, with easy turns, and a straight run-in of 5f. There is a straight track of 1m 14y.
N.H. Oval, 2m (11) 240y run-in. Many changing gradients, five fences in the home straight. Favours the long-striding front-runner, but stamina is important.
Address: Chepstow Racecourse, Chepstow, Gwent NP6 5YH Tel: (01291) 622260 Fax: (01291) 627061
Internet: www.chepstow-racecourse.co.uk
Clerk Of The Course: Mr T Long Tel: (01283) 711233 (Office), (07966) 893531 (Mobile).
General Manager: Mr S Lee
Going Reports: Contact Clerk of the Course as above.
Stabling: 40 boxes, allotted on arrival. Limited accommodation for lads and lasses. Apply: (01291)
623414.
By Road: 1 mile North-West of the town on the A466. (1 mile from Junction 22 of the M4 (Severn Bridge).
There is a Free public car park opposite the Stands entrance.
By Rail: Chepstow Station (from Paddington, change at Gloucester or Newport). The course is 1 mile from
station.
By Air: Helicopter landing facility in the centre of the course.

CHESTER (L.H)

Flat: A level, sharp, left-handed, circular course of 1m 73y, with a short run-in of 230y.
Chester is a specialists track which generally suits the sharp-actioned horse.
Address: The Racecourse, Chester CH1 2LY Tel: (01244) 304600 Fax: (01244) 304649
www.chester-races.co.uk
Clerk Of The Course: Mr E Gretton (07855) 807710
Chief Executive: Mr R Thomas
Going Reports: Contact Main Office (01244) 304600
Stabling: (175 boxes) and accommodation. Tel: (01244) 324880
By Road: The course is near the centre of the city on the A548 (Queensferry Road). The Owners and
Trainers car park is adjacent to the County Stand. There is a public car park in the centre of the course.
By Rail: Chester Station ¾ mile from the course). Services from Euston, Paddington and Northgate.
By Air: Hawarden Airport (2 miles).

DONCASTER (L.H)

Flat: A left-handed, flat, galloping course of 1m 7f 110y, with a long run-in which extends to a straight mile.
N.H. Conical, 2m (11) 247y run-in. A very fair, flat track ideally suited to the long-striding galloper.
Address: Doncaster Racecourse, Leger Way, Doncaster DN2 6BB Tel: (01302) 304200,
Fax: (01302) 323271 E-mail: info@britishracing.com, Internet: www.britishracing.com
Chief Executive & Clerk of Course (Flat): Mr J. Sanderson.
Clerk of the Course: Mr J Pullin
Director Of Racing: Mr I Renton
General Manager: Mr S Clarke
Going Reports: Contact Clerk of the Course as above.
Stabling: Free stabling and accommodation. Mr M Taylor Tel: (01302) 349337
By Road: East of the town, off the A638 (M18 Junctions 3 & 4). Club members car park reserved. Large public car park free and adjacent to the course.
By Rail: Doncaster Central Station (from King's Cross). Special bus service from the station (1 mile).
By Air: Helicopter landing facility by prior arrangement only.

EPSOM (L.H)

Flat: Left-handed and undulating with easy turns, and a run-in of just under 4f. The straight 5f course is also undulating and downhill all the way, making it the fastest 5f in the world.
Address: The Racecourse, Epsom Downs, Surrey, KT18 5LQ. Tel: (01372) 726311, Fax (01372) 748253
www.epsomderby.co.uk
Clerk Of The Course: Mr A. J. Cooper. Tel: (01372) 726311, Mobile (07774) 230850.
Managing Director: Mr Stephen Wallis
Going Reports: Contact Clerk of the Course as above.
Stabling: Free stabling and accommodation. Tel: (01372) 460454
By Road: 2 miles South of the town on the B290 (M25 Junctions 8 & 9). For full car park particulars apply to: The Club Secretary, Epsom Grandstand, Epsom Downs, Surrey KT18 5LQ. Tel: (01372) 726311.
By Rail: Epsom, Epsom Downs or Tattenham Corner Stations (trains from London Bridge, Waterloo, Victoria). Regular bus services run to the course from Epsom and Morden Underground Station.
By Air: London (Heathrow) and London (Gatwick) are both within 20 miles of the course. Heliport (Derby Meeting only) apply to Hascombe Aviation. Tel: (01279) 680291.

EXETER (R.H)

N.H.: Oval, 2m (11) 300y run-in uphill. Undulating with a home straight of half a mile. A good test of stamina, suiting the handy, well-balanced sort.
Address: Exeter Racecourse, Kennford, Exeter, Devon EX6 7XS Tel: (01392) 832599 Fax: (01392) 833454
Email: exeter-racecourse@eclipse.co.uk. Internet: www.exeter-racecourse.co.uk
Clerk Of The Course: Mr Barry Johnson
Managing Director: Mr G. K. Billson
Raceday Manager: Mr B. W. Soper
Club Secretary: Mrs Robinson
Going Reports: Contact Clerk of the Course as above.
Stabling: 81 loose boxes on the course. Sleeping accommodation and canteen for both lads and lasses by prior arrangement. Apply to Mrs J. Browning. Tel: (01392) 832816 or (01392) 832599.**By Road:** The course is at Haldon, 5 miles South-West of Exeter on the A38 (Plymouth) road, 2 miles East of Chudleigh.
By Rail: Exeter (St Davids) Station.
By Air: Helicopters can land by prior arrangement.

FAKENHAM (L.H)

N.H. Square, 1m (6) 200y run-in. On the turn almost throughout and undulating, suiting the handy front-runner. The going rarely becomes heavy.

Address: The Racecourse, Fakenham, Norfolk NR21 7NY Tel: (01328) 862388 Fax: (01328) 855908 email: info@fakenhamracecourse.co.uk Internet: www.fakenhamracecourse.co.uk

Clerk of the Course & Racecourse Manager: Mr D. J. Hunter Tel: (01328) 862388 Mobile (07767) 802206.

Going Reports: Contact Clerk of the Course as above.

Stabling: 68 boxes available. Tel: (01328) 862388 Fax (01328) 855908.

By Road: 1 mile South of the town on the B1146 (East Dereham) road.

By Rail: Norwich Station (26 miles) (Liverpool Street line), King's Lynn (22 miles) (Liverpool Street).

By Air: Helicopter landing facility in the centre of the course.

FOLKESTONE (R.H)

Flat: Right-handed, undulating, circuit of 1m 3f, with a two and a half furlong run-in. There is a straight 6f course.

N.H. Oval, 1m 3f (8) chases 220y run-in, hurdles 250y run-in. An undulating course with easy fences, not particularly suitable for the long-striding galloper.

Address: Folkestone Racecourse, Westenhanger, Hythe, Kent CT21 4HX Tel (0870) 2200023 Fax: (01303) 260185 Internet: www.folkestone-racecourse.co.uk

Director of Racing: Mr I Renton Tel: (01753) 498442

Clerk Of The Course: Mr C Stickels Tel: (01342) 831720.

General Manager: Mr C Stephens

Going Reports: Contact Clerk Of The Course as above

Stabling: 90 boxes allotted in rotation. Advance notice required for overnight accommodation, from 2pm on the day prior to racing. (01303) 266407 or 268449 (racedays).

By Road: 6 miles West of town at Westenhanger. Easy access from Junction 11 of the M20. Car park adjoins stands. (Free, except course enclosure £4).

By Rail: Westenhanger Station adjoins course. Trains from Charing Cross.

By Air: Helicopter landing facility by prior arrangement.

FONTWELL (Fig. 8)

N.H. 2m (7) 230y run-in with left-hand bend close home. The figure-of-eight chase course suits handy types and is something of a specialists' track. The hurdle course is oval, one mile round with nine hurdles per two and a quarter miles.

Address: Fontwell Park Racecourse, nr Arundel, West Sussex BN18 0SX Tel: (01243) 543335 Fax: (01243) 543904 www.fontwellpark.co.uk

Clerk Of The Course: Mr Geoffrey Stickels Tel: (01273) 603580. Mobile: (07973) 737006

General Manager: P Bell

Going Reports: (01243) 543335 during office hours.

Stabling: 77 boxes. Limited accommodation. If arriving the day before the meeting, contact: Tel: (01243) 543370.

By Road: South of village at the junction of the A29 (Bognor) and A27 (Brighton-Chichester) roads.

By Rail: Barnham Station (2 miles). Brighton-Portsmouth line (access via London Victoria).

By Air: Helicopter landing facility by prior arrangement with the Clerk of the Course.

GOODWOOD (R.H)

Flat: A sharp, undulating, essentially right-handed track with a long run-in. There is also a straight six furlong course.

Address: Goodwood Racecourse Ltd., Goodwood, Chichester, West Sussex PO18 0PX Tel: (01243) 755022, Fax: (01243) 755025 www.goodwood.co.uk

Clerk of the Course and Managing Director: Mr R. N. Fabricus Tel: Mobile (07836) 321254

Raceday Clerk: Mr S Buckley (07774) 100223

Going Reports: (01243) 755022 (recorded message)

Stabling: Free stabling and accommodation for runners (115 well equipped boxes at Goodwood House). Subsidised canteen and recreational facilities. Tel: (01243) 755022/755036.
By Road: 6 miles North of Chichester between the A286 & A285. There is a car park adjacent to the course. Ample free car and coach parking.
By Rail: Chichester Station (from Victoria or London Bridge). Regular bus service to the course (6 miles).
By Air: Helicopter landing facility by prior arrangement with Martin Fiddler. Tel: (01279) 850750.
Fax (01279) 850459 Goodwood Airport 2 miles (taxi to the course).

HAMILTON (R.H)

Flat: Sharp, undulating, right-handed course of 1m 5f with a five and a half furlong, uphill run-in. There is a straight track of 6f.
Address: Hamilton Park Racecourse, Bothwell Road, Hamilton, Lanarkshire ML3 0DW Tel: (01698) 283806
Fax: (01698) 286621 www.hamilton-park.co.uk
Racing Manager & Clerk Of The Course: Mrs Hazel Peplinski (01698) 283806. Mobile (07774) 116733.
Fax (01698) 286621
Chief Executive: Mr A Warwick Tel: (01698) 283806
Going Reports: Head Groundsman: (07850) 609037 (mobile).
Stabling: Free stabling (120 boxes) and accommodation on request. Tel: (01698) 248892 or Office.
By Road: Off the A74 on the B7071 (Hamilton-Bothwell road). (M74 Junction 5). Free parking for cars and buses.
By Rail: Hamilton West Station (1 mile).
By Air: Glasgow Airport (20 miles).

HAYDOCK (L.H)

Flat: A galloping, almost flat, oval track, 1m 5f round, with a run-in of four and a half furlongs and a straight six furlong course.
N.H. Oval, 1m 5f (10) 440y run-in. Flat, galloping chase course with stiff drop fences. The hurdle track, which is sharp, is inside the chase course and has some tight bends.
Address: Haydock Park Racecourse, Newton-le-Willows, Merseyside WA12 0HQ Tel: (01942) 725963
Fax: (01942) 270879 www.haydock-park.co.uk
Clerk Of The Course: Mr W. K. Tellwright.
Managing Director: Mr A. J. P. Waterworth.
Going Reports: Contact Clerk Of The Course as above
Stabling: Applications to be made to the Racecourse for stabling and accommodation. Tel (01942)
725963 or (01942) 402615 (racedays).
By Road: The course is on the A49 near Junction 23 of the M6.
By Rail: Newton-le-Willows Station (Manchester-Liverpool line) is 2.5 miles from the course. Earlstown 3 miles from the course. Warrington Bank Quay and Wigan are on the London to Carlisle/ Glasgow line.
By Air: Landing facilities in the centre of the course for helicopters and planes not exceeding 10,000lbs laden weight. Apply to the Sales Office.

HEREFORD (R.H)

N.H. Square, 1m 4f (9) 300y run-in. The turns, apart from the final one that is on falling ground, are easily negotiated, placing the emphasis on speed rather than stamina. A handy position round the home turn is vital, as winners rarely come from behind. The hurdle track is on the outside of the chase course. The fences have a reputation of being pretty stiff, but at the same time fair.
Address: Hereford Racecourse, Roman Road, Holmer, Hereford HR4 9 QU Tel: (01432) 273560, Fax (01432) 352807 Internet: www.hereford-racecourse.co.uk
Clerk of the Course and Secretary: Mr M Jones
General Manager: Mrs Katie Langdell
Managing Director: Mr R Street
Going Reports: (01432) 352807 (Recorded) or web site as listed above
Stabling: 90 boxes allocated on arrival. Apply to the Stabling Manager, The Racecourse House, Roman Road, Holmer, Hereford. Tel: (01432) 273560.

By Road: 1 mile North West of the City centre off the A49 (Leominster) road.
By Rail: Hereford Station (1 mile from the course).
By Air: Helicopter landing facility in the centre of the course by arrangement with the Clerk of the Course, and entirely at own risk.

HEXHAM (L.H)

N.H.: Oval, 1m 4f (10) 220y run-in. An undulating course that becomes very testing when the ground is soft, it has easy fences and a stiff uphill climb to the finishing straight, which is on a separate spur.
Address: Hexham Racecourse, The Riding, Hexham, Northumberland NE46 4PF Tel: (01434) 606881 Fax (01434) 605814, Racedays (01434) 603738. Email: hexrace@aol.com Internet: www.hexham-racecourse.co.uk
Clerk of the Course, Managing Director, Secretary: Mr C. Enderby
Going Reports: Contact Clerk Of The Course as above
Stabling: Boxes allocated in rotation. Tel: (01434) 603738.
By Road: 1.5 miles South-West of the town off the B6305.
By Rail: Hexham Station (Newcastle-Carlisle line). Free bus to the course.
By Air: Helicopter landing facility in centre of course (by special arrangement only).

HUNTINGDON (R.H)

N.H.: Oval, 1m 4f (9) 200y run-in. Perfectly flat, galloping track with a tricky open ditch in front of the stands. The two fences in the home straight can cause problems for novice chasers. Suits front runners.
Address: The Racecourse, Brampton, Huntingdon, Cambridgeshire PE18 8NN Tel: (01480) 453373 Fax: (01480) 455275 www.huntingdon-racecourse.co.uk
Clerk Of The Course: Mrs F Needham Tel: (01638) 675559 (mobile)
Manager: Mrs T Dawson
Going Reports: Tel: (01480) 453373
Stabling: 100 boxes available. Allotted on arrival. Tel Racecourse Office.
By Road: The course is situated at Brampton, 2 miles West of Huntingdon on the A14. Easy access from the A1 (½ mile from the course).
By Rail: Huntingdon Station. Buses and taxis to course.
By Air: Helicopter landing facility by prior arrangement.

KELSO (L.H)

N.H.: Oval, 1m 3f (9) 440y run-in uphill. Rather undulating with two downhill fences opposite the stands, Kelso suits the nippy, front-running sort, though the uphill run to the finish helps the true stayer. The hurdle course is smaller and very sharp with a tight turn away from the stands.
Address: Kelso Racecourse, Kelso, Roxburghshire TD5 7SX Tel: (01573) 224767 www.kelso-races.co.uk
Clerk Of The Course: Mr J. E. Fenwicke-Clennell. The Grandstand Office, The Racecourse, Durdar Road, Carlisle, CA2 4TS. Tel: Office (01228) 554700. Home (016974) 76589. Mobile: (07860) 737729.
Secretary: Mr Richard M. Landale, c/o Sale & Partners, 18-20 Glendale Road, Wooler, Northumberland NE71 6DW. Tel: (01668) 280800. Fax: (01668) 281113
Going Reports: Racecourse: (01573) 22767 Groundsman Tel: (07774) 172527
Stabling: Boxes allotted in rotation. Reservations for stabling and accommodation for lads and lasses at the racecourse. Please phone Head Groundsman Tel: (01573) 224767 or
Racecourse stables: (01573) 224822 from 3pm the day before racing.
By Road: 1 mile North of the town, off the B6461.
By Rail: Berwick-upon-Tweed Station. 23 mile bus journey to Kelso.
By Air: Helicopters can land at course by arrangement, fixed wing aircraft Winfield, regular aircraft Edinburgh

KEMPTON (R.H)

N.H. Triangular, 1m 5f (10) 175y run-in. Practically flat; sharp course where the long run between the last obstacle on the far side and the first in the home straight switches the emphasis from jumping to speed.
Address: Kempton Park Racecourse, Sunbury-on-Thames, Middlesex TW16 5AQ Tel: (01932) 782292 Fax: (01932) 782044 Raceday Fax: (01932) 779525 Internet: www.kempton.co.uk Email: kempton@rht.net
Clerk Of The Course: Mr B Clifford Mobile (07880) 784484
Managing Director: Mr J Thick
Going Reports: (01932) 782292 if unavailable contact Clerk Of The Course as above
Stabling: Allocated on arrival. Prior booking required for overnight stay. Tel: (01932) 783334
By Road: On the A308 near Junction 1 of the M3. Main car park £2, Silver Ring and centre car park free.
By Rail: Kempton Park Station (from Waterloo).
By Air: London (Heathrow) Airport 6 miles.

LEICESTER (R.H)

Flat: Stiff, galloping, right-handed oval of 1m 5f, with a 5f run-in. There is a straight course of seven furlongs.
N.H. Rectangular, 1m 6f (10) 250y run-in uphill. An undulating course with an elbow 150y from the finish, Leicester can demand a high degree of stamina, for the going can become extremely heavy and the last three furlongs are uphill.
Address: Leicester Racecourse, Oadby, Leicester LE2 3QH. Tel: (0116) 2716515 Fax (0116) 2711746
www.leicester-racecourse.com
Clerk Of The Course: Mr J Stevenson (0116) 2712115
Racecourse Manager & Company Secretary: Mr R Parrott (0116) 2716515
Going Reports: Recorded message (0116) 2710875 or contact Head Groundsman (0116) 2712115 (07774) 497281 (mobile).
Stabling: Allocated on arrival. canteen opens at 7.30a.m. tel: (0116) 271 2115.
By Road: The course is 2.5 miles South-East of the City on the A6 (M1, Junction 21). The car park is free.
By Rail: Leicester Station (from St Pancras) is 2.5 miles.
By Air: Helicopter landing facility in the centre of the course.

LINGFIELD (L.H)

Flat, Turf: A sharp, undulating left-handed circuit, with a 7f 140y straight course.
Flat, Polytrack: The left-handed all-weather polytack is 1m 2f round, with an extended chute to provide a 1m 5f start. It is a sharp, level track with a short run-in.
N.H. Conical, 1m 5f (10) 200y run-in. Severely undulating with a tight downhill turn into the straight, the chase course suits front runners and those of doubtful resolution.
Address: Lingfield Park Racecourse, Lingfield, Surrey RH7 6PQ Tel: (01342) 831720 Fax: (01342) 832833
www.lingfield-racecourse.co.uk
Director of Racing: Mr I Renton Tel: (01753) 498442
Clerk Of The Course: Mr C Stickels Tel: (01342) 831720.
General Manager: Mr C Stephens
Going Reports: Contact Clerk Of The Course as above
Stabling: 180 boxes. For details of accommodation tel (01342) 831720. Advance notice for overnight accommodation required before 12 noon on the day before racing.
By Road: South-East of the town off the A22 (M25 Junction 6). Ample free parking. Reserved car park £3.
By Rail: Lingfield Station (regular services from London Bridge and Victoria). ½m walk to the course.
By Air: London (Gatwick) Airport 10 miles. Helicopter landing facility south of wind-sock.

LUDLOW (R.H)

N.H. Oval, 1m 4f (9) 185y run-in. The chase course is flat and has quite sharp bends into and out of the home straight, although long-striding horses never seem to have any difficulties. The hurdle course is on the outside of the chase track and is not so sharp.

Address: Ludlow Race Club Ltd, The Racecourse, Bromfield, Ludlow, Shropshire SY8 2BT

Tel: (01584) 856221 (Racedays) or see below.

Secretary & Clerk Of The Course: Mr B. R. Davies. Tel: (01981) 580260 (Home), Mobile (07970) 861533, Fax (01981) 580181 (home), 01584 856217 (course) Email: bobdavies@ludlowracecourse.co.uk
www.ludlowracecourse.co.uk

Going Reports: Contact Clerk Of Course as above or Groundsman Tel: (01584) 856269

Stabling: Free and allocated on arrival. 100 stables, mainly shavings with a limited number of paper and straw. Tel: (01584) 856269.

By Road: The course is situated at Bromfield, 2 miles North of Ludlow on the A49.

By Rail: Ludlow Station (Hereford-Shrewsbury line) 2 miles.

By Air: Helicopter landing facility in the centre of the course by arrangement with the Clerk of the Course and entirely at own risk.

MARKET RASEN (R.H)

N.H. Oval, 1m 2f (8) 250y run-in. A sharp, undulating course with a long run to the straight, Market Rasen favours the handy, front-running type. The fences are not as easy as they used to be.

Address: Market Rasen Racecourse, Legsby Road, Market Rasen, Lincolnshire LN8 3EA

Tel: (01673) 843434 Fax: (01673) 844532

Clerk Of The Course: Mr N Patton Tel: (07775) 704822

Racecourse Manager: Miss P Adams

Going Reports: Contact Clerk Of The Course as above.

Stabling: 90 boxes at the course, allocated on arrival. Accommodation for lads and lasses is by reservation only. Tel: (01673) 842307 (racedays only)

By Road: The town is just off A46, and the racecourse is one mile East of the town on the A631. Free car parks and racecards.

By Rail: Market Rasen Station 1 mile (King's Cross - Cleethorpes line).

By Air: Helicopter landing facility by prior arrangement only.

MUSSELBURGH (R.H)

Flat: A sharp, level, right-handed oval of 1m 2f, with a run-in of 4f. There is an additional 5f straight course.

N.H. Rectangular, 1m 3f (8) 150y run-in (variable). A virtually flat track with sharp turns, suiting the handy, front-running sort. Drains well.

Address: Musselburgh Racecourse, Linkfield Road, Musselburgh, East Lothian EH21 7RG

Tel: (0131) 665 2859 (Racecourse) Fax: (0131) 653 2083

Clerk Of The Course & General Manager: Mr W Farnsworth

Raceday Clerk: Mrs A Morshead

Going Reports: Contact main office as above.

Stabling: Free stabling. Accommodation provided. Tel: (0131) 665 4955, Stables (racedays) (0131) 665 2796.

By Road: The course is situated at Musselburgh, 5 miles East of Edinburgh on the A1. Car park, adjoining course, free for buses and cars.

By Rail: Waverley Station (Edinburgh). Local Rail service to Musselburgh.

By Air: Edinburgh (Turnhouse) Airport 30 minutes

NEWBURY (L.H)

Flat: Left-handed, oval track of about 1m 7f, with a slightly undulating straight mile. The round course is level and galloping with a four and a half furlong run-in. Races over the round mile and 7f 60y start on the adjoining chute.

N.H. Oval, 1m 6f (11) 255y run-in. Slightly undulating, wide and galloping in nature. The fences are stiff and sound jumping is essential. One of the fairest tracks in the country.

Address: The Racecourse, Newbury, Berkshire RG14 7NZ Fax: (01635) 528354

Managing Director & Clerk Of The Course: Mr M. Kershaw Racecourse Office (01635) 40015 or 550354.

Raceday Clerk: Mr R Osgood

Going Reports: Clerk of the Course as above.

Stabling: Free stabling and accommodation for lads and lasses. Tel: (01635) 40015.

By Road: East of the town off the A34 (M4, Junction 12 or 13). Car park, adjoining enclosures, free.

By Rail: Newbury Racecourse Station, adjoins course.

By Air: Light Aircraft landing strip East/West. 830 metres by 30 metres wide. Helicopter landing facilities.

NEWCASTLE (L.H)

Flat: Galloping, easy, left-handed oval of 1m 6f, with an uphill 4f run-in. There is a straight course of 1m 8y.

N.H. Oval, 1m 6f (11) 220y run-in. A gradually rising home straight of four furlongs makes this galloping track a true test of stamina, especially as the ground can become very heavy. The fences are rather stiff.

Address: High Gosforth Park, Newcastle-Upon-Tyne NE3 5HP Tel: (0191) 236 2020 Fax 0191 236 7761

Clerk Of The Course: Mr J Armstrong (07801) 166820

General Manager/Executive Director: Mr D Williamson

Stabling: Stabling Free. It is essential to book accommodation in advance. Apply via the Racecourse Office.

Going Reports: Contact Clerk of the Course as above.

By Road: 4 miles North of city on the A6125 (near the A1). Car and coach park free.

By Rail: Newcastle Central Station (from King's Cross), a free bus service operates from South Gosforth and Regent Centre Metro Station.

By Air: Helicopter landing facility by prior arrangement. The Airport is 4 miles from the course.

NEWMARKET (R.H)

Rowley Mile Course: There is a straight ten furlong course, which is wide and galloping. Races over 12f or more are right-handed. The Rowley course has a long run-in and a stiff finish.

July Course: Races up to a mile are run on the Bunbury course, which is straight. Races over 10f or more are right-handed, with a 7f run-in. Like the Rowley course, the July track is stiff.

Address: Newmarket Racecourse, Newmarket, Suffolk CB8 0TG Tel: (01638) 663482 (Main Office), (01638) 663762 (Rowley), (01638) 662752 (July) Fax: Rowley (01638) 675340. Fax: July (01638) 667839 www.newmarketracecourse.co.uk

Clerk Of The Course: Mr M. Prosser, Westfield House, The Links, Newmarket. Tel: (01638) 662933

Managing Director: Mrs Lisa Hancock

Going Reports: Contact main office or Clerk Of Course as above

Stabling: Free accommodation available at the Links Stables. Tel: (01638) 662200

By Road: South-West of the town on the A1304 London Road (M11 Junction 9). Free car parking at the rear of the enclosure. Members car park all days; Free courtesy bus service from Newmarket Station, Bus Station and High Street, commencing 90 minutes prior to the first race, and return trips up to 60 minutes after the last race.

By Rail: Infrequent rail service to Newmarket Station from Cambridge (Liverpool Street) or direct bus service from Cambridge (13 mile journey).

By Air: Landing facilities for light aircraft and helicopters on racedays at both racecourses. See Flight Guide. Cambridge Airport 11 miles.

NEWTON ABBOT (L.H)

N.H. Oval, 1m 2f (7) 300y run-in. Flat with two tight bends and a water jump situated three fences from home. The nippy, agile sort is favoured. The run-in can be very short on the hurdle course.
Address: Newton Abbot Races Ltd., Kingsteignton Road, Newton Abbot, Devon TQ12 3AF
Tel: (01626) 353235 Fax: (01626) 336972 www.newtonabbotracing.com
Clerk Of The Course/Estate Manager: Mr J Loosemoore (07788) 463207
Managing Director: Mr P. G. Masterson. Tel: (01626) 353235 Fax: (01626) 336972 Mobile: (07778) 463207.
Going reports: Clerk of the Course as above, or Head Groundsman: (0374) 914403
Stabling: 90 boxes, allocated on arrival. Tel: (07467) 264796
By Road: North of the town on the A380. Torquay 6 miles, Exeter 17 miles.
By Rail: Newton Abbot Station (from Paddington) ¾ mile. Buses and taxis operate to and from the course.
By Air: Helicopter landing pad in the centre of the course.

NOTTINGHAM (L.H)

Flat: Left-handed, galloping, oval of about 1m 4f, and a run-in of four and a half furlongs. Flat with easy turns.
Address: Nottingham Racecourse, Colwick Park, Nottingham NG2 4BE Tel: (0115) 958 0620
Fax: (0115) 958 4515 www.nottinghamracecourse.co.uk
Clerk Of The Course: Mr N Patton (07775) 704822
Going Reports: Contact main office as above
Racecourse Manager: Miss Nina Coverley
Stabling: 120 boxes allotted on arrival. Hostel for lads and lasses. Tel: (0115) 950 1198
By Road: 2 miles East of the City on the B686. The car park is free. Silver Ring Picnic Car Park £12 (admits car and four occupants).
By Rail: Nottingham (Midland) Station. Regular bus service to course (2 miles).
By Air: Helicopter landing facility in the centre of the course.

PERTH (R.H)

N.H. Rectangular, 1m 2f (8) 283y run-in. A flat, easy track with sweeping turns. Not a course for the long-striding galloper. An efficient watering system ensures that the ground rarely gets hard.
Address: Perth Racecourse, Scone Palace Park, Perth PH2 6BB Tel (01738) 551597 Fax: (01738) 553021
Internet: www.perth-races.co.uk
Clerk Of The Course: Mrs Anthea Morshead Tel: (07789) 697241
General Manager: Mr S. R. Morshead Tel: (01738) 551597 Mobile: (07768) 868848 Home: (01764) 652658.
Secretary: Mrs Lucy Normile
Going Reports: Groundsman: (07899 034 012) or contact Clerk of the Course as above.
Stabling: 96 boxes and accommodation for lads and lasses Tel: (01738) 551597. Stables
Tel: (01738) 621604 (racedays only).
By Road: 4 miles North of the town off the A93.
By Rail: Perth Station (from Dundee) 4 miles. There are buses to the course.
By Air: Scone Airport (3.75 miles). Edinburgh Airport 45 minutes.

PLUMPTON (L.H)

N.H.: Oval, 1m 1f (7) 200y run-in uphill. A tight, undulating circuit with an uphill finish, Plumpton favours the handy, fast jumper. The ground often gets heavy, as the course is based on clay soil.
Address: Plumpton Racecourse, Plumpton, East Sussex, BN7 3AL Tel: (01273) 891550/890383
Fax: (01273) 891557 www.plumpton-racecourse.co.uk
Clerk Of The Course: Mr M Comford
Chief Executive: Mr P Davis
Going Reports: Tel: (01273) 891550, or (07771) 660115.
Stabling: 75 boxes. Advance notice required for overnight arrival. Tel: (01273) 890522

By Road: 2 miles North of the village off the B2116.
By Rail: Plumpton Station (from Victoria) adjoins course.
By Air: Helicopter landing facility by prior arrangement with the Clerk of the Course.

PONTEFRACT (L.H)

Flat: Left-handed oval, undulating course of 2m 133y, with a short run-in of 2f. It is a particularly stiff track with the last 3f uphill.
Address: Pontefract Park Race Co. Ltd., The Park, Pontefract, West Yorkshire Tel: (01977) 703224 (Admin Office) (01977) 702210 (Racedays)
Clerk of the Course, Managing Director & Secretary: Mr J. N. Gundill, 33 Ropergate, Pontefract, West Yorkshire. WF8 1LE. Tel: (01977) 703224 (Office), (01977) 620649 (Home), (01977) 702210 (racedays)
Going Reports: Contact Admin Office as above, or Racedays number
Stabling: Stabling and accommodation must be reserved. They will be allocated on a first come-first served basis. Tel: (01977 702323)
By Road: 1 mile North of the town on the A639. Junction 32 of M62. Free car park adjacent to the course.
By Rail: Pontefract Station (Tanshelf, every hour to Wakefield), 1½ miles from the course. Regular bus service from Leeds.
By Air: Helicopters by arrangement only. (Nearest Airfields: Doncaster, Sherburn-in-Elmet, Yeadon (Leeds/Bradford))

REDCAR (L.H)

Flat: Left-handed, level, galloping, oval course of 14f with a straight run-in of 5f. There is also a straight 8f.
Address: Redcar Racecourse, Redcar, Cleveland TS10 2BY Tel: (01642) 484068 Fax: (01642) 488272
Clerk of the Course & General Manager: Mr J. N. Gundill Tel: (01642) 484068 Mobile (07770) 613049
Going Reports: Contact main office as above
Stabling: 142 Boxes available. Tel Stables (01642) 484068 or racedays only (01642) 484254).
By Road: In town off the A1085. Free parking adjoining the course for buses and cars.
By Rail: Redcar Station (¼ mile from the course).
By Air: Landing facilities at Turners Arms Farm (600y runway) Yearby, Cleveland. 2 miles South of the racecourse - transport available. Teeside airport (18 miles west of Redcar).

RIPON (R.H)

Flat: A sharp, undulating, right-handed oval of 1m 5f, with a 5f run-in. There is also a 6f straight course.
Address: Ripon Racecourse, Boroughbridge Road, Ripon, North Yorkshire HG4 1UG Tel: (01765) 602156 Fax: (01765) 690018 E-mail: cwpy@hutchbutch.co.uk Internet: www.ripon-races.co.uk
Clerk Of The Course: Mr J. Hutchinson, 77 North Street, Ripon HG4 1DS. Tel: (01765) 602156, Mobile (07860) 679904. Racedays (01765) 603696
Managing Director: Mr M. Hutchinson
Going Reports: Tel: (01765) 603696
Stabling: Trainers requiring stabling (104 boxes available) are requested to contact Stable Manager prior to 11a.m. the day before racing. Tel: (01765) 604135/603696
By Road: The course is situated 2 miles South-East of the city, on the B6265. There is ample free parking for cars and coaches. For reservations apply to the Secretary.
By Rail: Harrogate Station (11 miles), or Thirsk (15 miles). Bus services to Ripon.
By Air: Helicopters only on the course. Otherwise Leeds/Bradford airport.

SALISBURY (R.H)

Flat: Right-handed and level, with a run-in of 4f. There is a straight 8f track. The last half mile is uphill, providing a stiff test of stamina.
Address: Salisbury Racecourse, Netherhampton, Salisbury, Wiltshire SP2 8PN Tel: (01722) 326461 Fax: 01722 412710 www.salisburyracecourse.co.uk
Clerk Of The Course & General Manager: Mr J Martin (07880) 744999 mobile
Going Reports: Contact main office as above
Stabling: Free stabling (112 boxes) and accommodation for lads and lasses, apply to the Stabling

Manager (01722) 327327.
By Road: 3 miles South-West of the city on the A3094 at Netherhampton. Free car park adjoins the course.
By Rail: Salisbury Station is 3.5 miles (from London Waterloo). Bus service to the course.
By Air: Helicopter landing facility near the ten furlong start.

SANDOWN (R.H)

Flat: An easy right-handed oval course of 1m 5f with a stiff straight uphill run-in of 4f. Separate straight 5f track is also uphill. Galloping.
N.H. Oval, 1m 5f (11) 220y run-in uphill. Features seven fences on the back straight, the last three (Railway Fences) are very close together and can often decide the outcome of races. The stiff uphill climb to the finish puts the emphasis very much on stamina, but accurate-jumping, free-running sorts are also favoured. Hurdle races are run on the Flat course.
Address: Sandown Park Racecourse, Esher, Surrey KT10 9AJ Tel: (01372) 463072 Fax: (01372) 470427
www.sandown.co.uk
Clerk Of The Course & Director Of Racing: Mr A. J. Cooper, Sandown Park, Esher, Surrey.
Tel: (01372) 463072 Mobile (0374) 230850.
Managing Director: Mr D Morris
Going Reports: (01372) 461212.
Stabling: Free stabling and accommodation for lads and lasses. Tel: (01372) 463511.
By Road: 4 miles South-West of Kingston-on-Thames, on the A307 (M25 Junction 10). The members' car park in More Lane £2. All other car parking is free.
By Rail: Esher Station (from Waterloo) adjoins the course.
By Air: London (Heathrow) Airport 12 miles.

SEDGEFIELD (L.H)

N.H. Oval, 1m 2f (8) 200y run-in: Hurdles 200y run-in. Undulating with fairly tight turns and does not suit the big, long-striding horse.
Address: Sedgefield Racecourse, Sedgefield, Stockton-on-Tees, Cleveland TS21 2HW
Tel: (01740) 621925 (Office) Fax: (01740) 620663
Clerk Of The Course: Major C Moore Tel: (01287) 711233, (07764) 255500 mobile
Racecourse Manager/Secretary: Mr J Allan
Managing Director: Mr Simon Clarke
Going Reports: Tel: (01740) 621925 or contact Clerk Of Course as above
Stabling: 115 boxes filled in rotation. No forage. Accommodation for horse attendants: Tel: (01740) 621925
By Road: ¾ mile South-West of the town, near the junction of the A689 (Bishop Auckland) and the A177 (Durham) roads. The car park is free.
By Rail: Darlington Station (9 miles). Durham Station (12 miles).
By Air: Helicopter landing facility in car park area by prior arrangement only.

SOUTHWELL (L.H)

Flat, Turf: Tight left-handed track.
Flat, Fibresand: Left-handed oval, Fibresand course of 1m 2f with a 3f run-in. There is a straight 5f. Sharp and level, Southwell suits front-runners.
N.H. Oval, 1m 1f (7) 220y run-in. A tight, flat track with a short run-in, suits front-runners.
Address: Southwell Racecourse, Rolleston, Newark, Nottinghamshire NG25 0TS Tel: (01636) 814481
Fax: (01636) 812271 www.southwell-racecourse.co.uk
Clerk Of The Course: Mr J Pullin (07775) 943341
General Manager: Mr N Corden
Going Reports: Contact Clerk Of The Course as above.
Stabling: 110 boxes at the course. Applications for staff and horse accommodation to be booked by noon the day before racing on (01636) 814481.

By Road: The course is situated at Rolleston, 3 miles South of Southwell, 5 miles from Newark.
By Rail: Rolleston Station (Nottingham-Newark line) adjoins the course.
By Air: Helicopters can land by prior arrangement with Mr David Williams Tel: (07968) 306373

STRATFORD-ON-AVON (L.H)

N.H. Triangular, 1m 2f (8) 200y run-in. Virtually flat with two tight bends, and quite a short home straight. A sharp and turning course, Stratford-on-Avon suits the well-balanced, handy sort.
Address: Stratford Racecourse, Luddington Road, Stratford-upon-Avon, Warwickshire CV37 9SE
Tel: (01789) 267949 Fax: (01789) 415850 www.stratfordracecourse.net
Clerk Of The Course: Mr Stephen Lambert. Mobile (07836) 384932. Home (01608) 674354
Going reports: Contact main office as above or Head Groundsman Tel: (07770) 623366.
Stabling: Allotted on arrival. Advance notice must be given for overnight stays. Tel: (01789) 267949.
By Road: 1 mile from the town centre, off the A429 (Evesham road).
By Rail: Stratford-on-Avon Station (from Birmingham New Street or Leamington Spa) 1 mile.
By Air: Helicopter landing facility by prior arrangement.

TAUNTON (R.H)

N.H. Elongated oval, 1m 2f (8) 150y run-in uphill. Sharp turns, especially after the winning post, with a steady climb from the home bend. Suits the handy sort.
Address: Taunton Racecourse, Orchard Portman, Taunton, Somerset TA3 7BL
Tel: (01823) 337172 (Office) Fax: (01823) 325881 www.tauntonracecourse.co.uk
Clerk Of The Course: Mr M. Trickey, The Racecourse, Taunton, Somerset TA3 7BL.
Tel: (01823) 337172 (07774) 620717 mobile
Racecourse Secretary & Manager: Mr J Hills
Going reports: Contact Clerk of the Course as above, or head Groundsman (after 4.30pm) (07971) 695132.
Stabling: 98 boxes allotted on arrival. Advance bookings for long journeys. Apply to the Stable Manager, c/o The Racecourse (01823) 337172
By Road: 2 miles South of the town on the B3170 (Honiton) road (M5 Junction 25). Free car park for Members. The public car parks are free or £3 on course.
By Rail: Taunton Station 2½ miles. There are buses and taxis to course.
By Air: Helicopter landing facility by prior arrangement.

THIRSK (L.H)

Flat: Left-handed, oval of 1m 2f with sharp turns and an undulating run-in of 4f. There is a straight 6f track.
Address: The Racecourse, Station Road, Thirsk, North Yorkshire YO7 1QL Tel: (01845) 522276
Fax: (01845) 525353.
Clerk Of The Course: Mr C.M. Tetley (07860) 919661 mobile
Going reports: Contact main office as above
Club Secretary: Mr D. Whitehead
Stabling: For stabling and accommodation apply to the Racecourse Tel: (01845) 522276
or (01845) 522096 (racedays).
By Road: West of the town on the A61. Free car park adjacent to the course for buses and cars.
By Rail: Thirsk Station (from King's Cross). 1/2 mile from the course.
By Air: Helicopters can land by prior arrangement. Tel: Racecourse (01845) 522276. Fixed wing aircraft can land at RAF Leeming. Tel: (01677) 423041. Light aircraft at Bagby. Tel: (01845) 597385 or (01845) 537555.

TOWCESTER (R.H)

N.H. Square, 1m 6f (10) 200y run-in uphill. The final six furlongs are uphill. One of the most testing tracks in the country with the emphasis purely on stamina.

Address: The Racecourse, Easton Neston, Towcester, Northants NN12 7HS Tel: (01327) 353414
Fax: (01327) 358534 www.towcester-racecourse.co.uk

Clerk Of The Course: Mr D. Henson, Tel: (01327) 861061 Mobile (07740) 853170

Racecourse Manager: Mr P Robinson.

General Manager/Trainee Clerk: Mr K Ackerman.

Chief Executive: Mr C Palmer.

Going Reports: Tel: (01327) 353414 or contact Clerk Of The Course as above.

Stabling: Being re-built at time of going to press. Contact racecourse office for details

By Road: 1 mile South-East of the town on the A5 (Milton Keynes road). M1 (Junction 15) (from the South), M1 (Junction 16) (from the North).

By Rail: Northampton Station (Euston) 9 miles, buses to Towcester; or Milton Keynes (Euston) 12 miles, taxis available.

By Air: Helicopters can land by prior arrangement with the Racecourse Manager.

UTTOXETER (L.H)

N.H. Oval, 1m 2f (8) 170y run-in. A few undulations, easy bends and fences and a flat home straight of over half a mile. Suits front-runners, especially on the two mile hurdle course.

Address: The Racecourse, Wood Lane, Uttoxeter, Staffordshire ST14 8BD Tel: (01889) 562561
Fax: (01889) 562786 Internet: www.uttoxeter-racecourse.co.uk

Clerk Of The Course/Manager: Mr K Ottensen (07813) 043453

General Manager: Mrs Julie Emery

Managing Director: Mr R Street

Going Reports: Contact main office or Clerk of the Course, as above.

Stabling: 90 boxes, allotted on arrival. Tel: (01889) 562561.

By Road: South-East of the town off the B5017 (Marchington Road).

By Rail: Uttoxeter Station (Crewe-Derby line) adjoins the course.

By Air: Helicopters can land by prior arrangement with the raceday office.

WARWICK (L.H)

Flat: Left-handed, sharp, level track of 1m 6f 32y in circumference, with a run-in of two and a half furlongs. There is a dog-leg 5f course.

N.H. Circular, 1m 6f (10) 240y run-in. Undulating with tight bends, five quick fences in the back straight and a short home straight, Warwick favours handiness and speed rather than stamina.

Address: Warwick Racecourse, Hampton Street, Warwick CV34 6HN Tel: (01926) 491553
Fax: (01926) 403223 www.warwickracecourse.co.uk

Clerk Of The Course: Mrs F Needham

Racecourse Manager: Mrs Vicky Parris

Going Reports: Contact main office as above

Stabling: 112 boxes allocated on arrival or by reservation (01926) 493803.

By Road: West of the town on the B4095 adjacent to Junction 15 of the M40. Free parking (except the Members' Car Park, £5 to Daily Club Members).

By Rail: Warwick or Leamington Spa Station.

By Air: Helicopters can land by prior arrangement with the Clerk Of The Course.

WETHERBY (L.H)

N.H. Oval, 1m 4f (9) 200y run-in slightly uphill. A flat, very fair course which suits the long-striding galloper.
Address: The Racecourse, York Road, Wetherby, LS22 5EJ Tel: (01937) 582035 Fax: (01937) 588021
www.wetherbyracing.co.uk
Clerk Of The Course: Mr C. M. Tetley (07860) 919661 mobile
Chief Executive: Mr T Betteridge
Going reports: Tel: (01937) 582035, or Course Foreman: (07880) 722586
Stabling: 98 boxes allocated on arrival. Accommodation available. Tel: (01937) 582035 or from 2pm day before racing (01937) 582074.
By Road: East of the town off the B1224 (York Road). Adjacent to the A1. Excellent bus and coach facilities. Car park free.
By Rail: Leeds Station 12 miles. Buses to Wetherby.
By Air: Helicopters can land by prior arrangement

WiNCANTON (R.H)

N.H. Rectangular, 1m 3f (9) 200y run-in. Good galloping course where the going rarely becomes heavy. The home straight is mainly downhill.
Address: Wincanton Racecourse, Wincanton, Somerset BA9 8BJ Tel: (01963) 32344 Fax: (01963) 34668
www.wincantonracecourse.co.uk
Clerk Of The Course: Mrs Rebecca Morgan (07767) 612931
Racecourse Manager: Mr S Higgins
Going Reports: Contact Racecourse Office as above.
Stabling: 92 boxes allocated on arrival, overnight accommodation must be booked in advance. Apply to the Stable Manager, Wincanton Racecourse. Tel: (01963) 32344.
By Road: 1 mile North of the town on the B3081.
By Rail: Gillingham Station (from Waterloo) or Castle Cary Station (from Paddington). Buses and taxis to the course.
By Air: Helicopter landing area is situated in the centre of the course.

WINDSOR (Fig. 8)

Flat: Figure eight track of 1m 4f 110y. The course is level and sharp with a long run-in. The 6f course is essentially straight.
N.H.: Figure-of-eight course, sharp and flat with a circuit of 1m 4f
Address: Royal Windsor Racecourse, Maidenhead Road, Windsor, Berkshire SL4 5JJ Tel: (01753) 498400 Fax: (01753) 830156. Internet: www.windsor-racecourse.co.uk
Clerk Of The Course/Racecourse Manager: Mr D Mackinnon Mobile: (07776) 135965
Going Reports: Contact Clerk Of The Course as above.
Stabling: 120 boxes available. Reservation required for overnight stay and accommodation only.
Tel: (01753) 498400 or (01753) 498405 (racedays).
By Road: North of the town on the A308 (M4 Junction 6). Car parks adjoin the course (£1, £1.50, £2).
By Rail: Windsor Central Station (from Paddington) or Windsor & Eton Riverside Station (from Waterloo).
By Air: London (Heathrow) Airport 15 minutes
By Road: via the M4. Also White Waltham Airport (West London Aero Club) 15 minutes.
River Bus: 7mins from Barry Avenue promenade at Windsor £2 fare each way

WOLVERHAMPTON (L.H)

Flat: Left-handed oval of 1m, with a run-in of 380y. A level track with sharp bends, the Polytrack surface, in use since October 2004, generally rides slower than that at Lingfield.
Address: Wolverhampton Racecourse, Dunstall Park, Gorsebrook Road, Wolverhampton WV6 0PE
Tel: (01902) 421421 Fax: 0870 220 0107 www.wolverhampton-racecourse.co.uk
Clerk Of The Course: Mr F Cameron Mobile (07971) 531162
General Manager: Mr D Roberts
Going Reports: Contact Main Office as above
Stabling: 100 boxes allotted on arrival. Applications for lads and lasses, and overnight stables must be made to Racecourse by noon on the day before racing. Tel: (01902) 421421. Fax: (01902) 421621.
By Road: 1 mile North of city on the A449 (M54 Junction 2 or M6 Junction 12). Car parking free of charge.
By Rail: Wolverhampton Station (from Euston) 1 mile.
By Air: Halfpenny Green Airport 8 miles.

WORCESTER (L.H)

N.H. Elongated oval, 1m 5f (9) 220y run-in. Flat with easy turns, Worcester is a very fair, galloping track.
Address: Worcester Racecourse, Pitchcroft, Worcester WR1 3EJ Tel: (01905) 25364 (racedays)
Fax: (01905) 617563 www.worcester-racecourse.co.uk
Clerk Of The Course: Mr F Cameron, Wolverhampton Racecourse. Tel: (07971) 531162.
Manager: Mr D. Roberts Tel: (01905) 25364.
Going Reports: Contact Clerk of the Course as above, or (01905) 25364.
Stabling: 100 boxes allotted on arrival. Overnight accommodation for lads and lasses in Worcester.
Tel: (01905) 25364.
By Road: West of the city off the A449 (Kidderminster road) (M5 Junc 8).
By Rail: Foregate Street Station, Worcester (from Paddington) ¾ mile.
By Air: Helicopter landing facility in the centre of the course, by prior arrangement only.

YARMOUTH (L.H)

Flat: Left-handed, level circuit of 1m 4f, with a run-in of 5f. The straight course is 8f long.
Address: The Racecourse, Jellicoe Road, Great Yarmouth, Norfolk NR30 4AU Tel: (01493) 842527 Fax: (01493) 843254 www.greatyarmouth-racecourse.co.uk
Clerk Of The Course: Major Charlie Moore, Mr G Stickels or Mrs Katharine Self
General Manager: Mrs Katharine Self
Going Reports: Contact Main Office as above
Stabling: Allocated on arrival. Tel: (01493) 855651.
By Road: 1 mile East of town centre (well sign-posted from A47 & A12). Large car park adjoining course £1.
By Rail: Great Yarmouth Station (1 mile). Bus service to the course.
By Air: Helicopter landing available by prior arrangement with Racecourse Office

YORK (L.H)

Flat: Left-handed, level, galloping track, with a straight 6f. There is also an adjoining course of 6f 214y.
Address: The Racecourse, York YO23 1EX Tel: (01904) 620911 Fax: (01904) 611071
Clerk of the Course and Chief Executive: Mr W Derby
Going Reports: Contact Main Office as above
Stabling: 200 boxes available Tel: (01904) 706317 (Racedays).
By Road: 1 mile South-East of the city on the A1036.
Car parking: Car Park 'D': £5 per space, available all meetings bar May & August. Car Park 'D2': £2 per space. All other parking is free.
By Rail: 1½ miles York Station (from King's Cross). Special bus service from station to the course.
By Air: Light aircraft and helicopter landing facilities available at Rufforth aerodrome (5,000ft tarmac runway). £20 landing fee-transport arranged to course. Leeds/Bradford airport (25 miles).

THE VODAFONE DERBY STAKES (CLASS A)
EPSOM, SATURDAY, JUNE 4th

HORSE	TRAINER	HORSE	TRAINER
ABERDEEN (IRE)		BLUE TRAIN (IRE)	Sir Michael Stoute
ADAWAAT (IRE)		BOLD EAGLE (IRE)	Sir Michael Stoute
ADMIRAL'S CRUISE (USA)	B. J. Meehan	BOLLIN MICHAEL	T. D. Easterby
AFRICANUS (IRE)		BONANZA (IRE)	A. P. O'Brien, Ireland
AGE OF KINGS (USA)	J. H. M. Gosden	BOOK FAIR (USA)	D. R. Loder
AIR COMMODORE (USA)	H. R. A. Cecil	BORACAY DREAM (IRE)	P. W. Chapple-Hyam
AKRAM (IRE)	John M. Oxx, Ireland	BOROUJ (IRE)	J. H. M. Gosden
ALAMIYAN (IRE)	Sir Michael Stoute	BOXHALL (USA)	W. R. Swinburn
ALBERT HALL	A. P. O'Brien, Ireland	BRAHMINY KITE (USA)	
ALFAASIL	M. A. Jarvis	BRAVEMORE (USA)	B. J. Meehan
ALFIE NOAKES	Mrs A. J. Perrett	BRECON BEACON	P. F. I. Cole
ALFRED THE GREAT (IRE)	M. Johnston	BRINKMANSHIP (USA)	John M. Oxx, Ireland
ALJIWAAR (USA)		BULLSEYE	P. W. D'Arcy
AL KURDI (USA)		BURGUNDIAN (USA)	
ALL THAT AND MORE (IRE)	B. W. Hills	BUSHWALK	John M. Oxx, Ireland
ALMANSHOOD (USA)	J. H. M. Gosden	CAHEERLOCH (IRE)	
ALMANSOOR (IRE)	B. W. Hills	CAMPLI (IRE)	L. M. Cumani
ALMANSOORA (USA)		CAPE GREKO	J. A. R. Toller
ALMIGHTY (USA)	A. P. O'Brien, Ireland	CARPET RIDE	E. A. L. Dunlop
ALQAAHIR (USA)		CARTE COEUR (IRE)	M. Johnston
ALRAFIDAIN (IRE)	M. Johnston	CARTE ROYALE	
ALTENBURG (IRE)		CASHIER	J. H. M. Gosden
AMAZING VALOUR (IRE)		CASH ON (IRE)	M. P. Tregoning
AMEEQ (USA)	M. P. Tregoning	CASTLE HOWARD (IRE)	A. Fabre, France
AMORIST (IRE)	Sir Mark Prescott	CENTAURUS	
AMPELIO (IRE)		CHAPTER (IRE)	R. Hannon
AMSTERDAM (IRE)	A. P. O'Brien, Ireland	CHARISMATIC CAT (USA)	A. P. O'Brien, Ireland
ANCIENT EGYPT	J. H. M. Gosden	CHASM	
ANNA WI'YAAK (JPN)		CHATEAU (IRE)	
ARAFAN (IRE)	John M. Oxx, Ireland	CHINA BEACH (IRE)	
ARAGORN (IRE)	John M. Oxx, Ireland	CHINA BOND (IRE)	
ARNO RIVER		CHINESE DRAGON (IRE)	A. P. O'Brien, Ireland
ARPETCHEEO (USA)	John M. Oxx, Ireland	CHOCOLATE CARAMEL (USA)	Mrs A. J. Perrett
ARRIMAN	J. A. Geake	CLASSICISM (USA)	
ART ELEGANT	B. W. Hills	CLUELESS	W. J. Haggas
ART ROYAL (USA)	Mrs A. J. Perrett	COLOURS FLYING (IRE)	
ARTURIUS (IRE)	Sir Michael Stoute	COLWYN BAY (IRE)	A. P. O'Brien, Ireland
ASAATEEL (IRE)	J. L. Dunlop	COMMUNICATION	M. Johnston
ASHARON	C. E. Brittain	CONCERT PARTY (IRE)	John M. Oxx, Ireland
ASHKAL WAY (IRE)	B. Ellison	CONSTANTINOPLE (IRE)	A. P. O'Brien, Ireland
ATHENS (IRE)	T. Keddy	CONSULAR	M. A. Jarvis
AUSTRALIAN	J. H. M. Gosden	CONTRALTO (IRE)	
AUTUMN MELODY (FR)		COOL AS A MOOSE	N. Tinkler
AVALON	A. P. O'Brien, Ireland	COPPER BAY (IRE)	A. King
AVIEMORE	Sir Michael Stoute	CORKER	G. A. Butler
AWAKENING	C. Laffon-Parias, France	COSMIC STRING (IRE)	D. K. Weld, Ireland
AWASH (USA)	H. R. A. Cecil	COST ANALYSIS (IRE)	M. A. Jarvis
BABE MACCOOL (IRE)	B. W. Hills	COUNCELLOR (FR)	R. Hannon
BAG OF GOLD		COUNT KRISTO	C. G. Cox
BAHAR SHUMAAL (IRE)	C. E. Brittain	COUNTRY RAMBLER (USA)	
BAIE DES FLAMANDS (USA)	B. W. Hills	COUNTRYWIDE SUN	
BAKERMAN	A. Fabre, France	COVIE LAD (USA)	M. J. Wallace
BALANCE OF POWER	R. Charlton	CRAFT FAIR (IRE)	A. Fabre, France
BALDASSARE	J. Noseda	CRETE (IRE)	W. J. Haggas
BANCHIERI		CRIMSON AND GOLD	A. Fabre, France
BANJO PATTERSON	G. A. Huffer	CROON	L. M. Cumani
BANKALAN (IRE)	John M. Oxx, Ireland	DABHANI (IRE)	John M. Oxx, Ireland
BANK ON BENNY	J. H. M. Gosden	DAFARABAD (IRE)	John M. Oxx, Ireland
BANZINE (IRE)	M. Johnston	DAHMAN	
BARONIAL	A. Fabre, France	DANIEL O'DONNELL	C. E. Brittain
BATTLEDRESS (IRE)	M. P. Tregoning	DANIEL THOMAS (IRE)	Mrs A. J. Perrett
BATTLESTAR		DARAMAS (IRE)	John M. Oxx, Ireland
BAYARD (USA)		DARGASH (IRE)	A. de Royer Dupre, France
BAY HAWK	A. M. Balding	DARK MONARCH	
BAY STORY (USA)	M. Johnston	DARTH VADER	N. P. Littmoden
BEFORE TIME	J. L. Dunlop	DARWAZ (IRE)	John M. Oxx, Ireland
BEHNASAN (IRE)	A. de Royer Dupre, France	DASHTAKI (FR)	A. de Royer Dupre, France
BELENUS (IRE)		DATA FLOW (USA)	
BELLAMY CAY	A. Fabre, France	DEEP SPELL (USA)	R. Charlton
BENEDICT	John Berry	DE LAURENTIIS (IRE)	A. P. O'Brien, Ireland
BENTINCK (IRE)	B. J. Meehan	DESCARTES	
BERNABEU (USA)	A. Fabre, France	DESERT DEMON (IRE)	B. W. Hills
BEST OF THE LOT (USA)	Rupert Pritchard-Gordon, France	DESERT LYNX (USA)	
BILKIE (IRE)	John Berry	DESIDERATUM	A. Fabre, France
BLACK DIAMOND (IRE)	A. P. O'Brien, Ireland	DHAULAR DHAR (IRE)	B. W. Hills
BLUE BAJAN (IRE)	Andrew Turnell	DILMOUN (USA)	R. Charlton
BLUE GIANT (USA)		DINNER DATE	W. Jarvis

HORSE	TRAINER	HORSE	TRAINER
DOCTOR'S CAVE	C. E. Brittain	GRAND SEIGNEUR (IRE)	D. R. Loder
DOCTOR BAILEY	M. R. Channon	GREAT BUSTARD (IRE)	D. Wachman, Ireland
DOOIE DANCER	H. R. A. Cecil	GREAT LOOP (USA)	P. Bary, France
DORRATI (USA)		GRECIAN GROOM (IRE)	J. E. Hammond, France
DOWN MEXICO WAY (IRE)	A. P. O'Brien, Ireland	GREGS GIRL	
DRAMATIC ART	John M. Oxx, Ireland	GROSVENOR SQUARE (IRE)	
DREAM ALONG	Mrs A. J. Perrett	GUADIARO (USA)	B. W. Hills
DREAMSCAPE		GYPSY KING (IRE)	A. P. O'Brien, Ireland
DR GNOME		HADDAAF (USA)	J. L. Dunlop
DUBAI VENTURE	Sir Michael Stoute	HADEETH	
DUBAWI (IRE)		HADRIAN (IRE)	M. Johnston
EARL'S COURT	A. Fabre, France	HALKIN (USA)	J. H. M. Gosden
EBTIKAAR (IRE)	J. L. Dunlop	HALLE BOP	
ECCOLLO (IRE)		HAMALI (IRE)	A. de Royer Dupre, France
ECHO OF LIGHT	L. M. Cumani	HANSEATIC LEAGUE (USA)	M. Johnston
EDAS		HARD TOP (IRE)	Sir Michael Stoute
EEEYORE		HATTAN (IRE)	C. E. Brittain
EHSAN (IRE)	John M. Oxx, Ireland	HAUNTING MEMORIES (IRE)	M. A. Jarvis
ELATED (IRE)	W. J. Haggas	HAWK ARROW (IRE)	H. Morrison
ELTIZAAM (USA)		HAWKSBURY HEIGHTS	Mme C. Head-Maarek, France
EMILE ZOLA	M. P. Tregoning	HAWKSMOOR (IRE)	A. Fabre, France
ENGLISH VICTORY	T. G. Mills	HAWKS TOR (IRE)	
ESPRIT DE CORPS	D. K. Weld, Ireland	HEARTHSTEAD WINGS	M. Johnston
ESTATE		HELVETIO	D. K. Weld, Ireland
ETIHAAD		HEREDITARY	Sir Mark Prescott
ETIJAHAAT (IRE)		HER OWN KIND (JPN)	
ETLAALA	B. W. Hills	HIDDENSEE (IRE)	M. Johnston
EUPHRATES (IRE)	A. P. O'Brien, Ireland	HIGGYS PRINCE	D. Flood
EYE OF PARIS (IRE)	J. E. Hammond, France	HIGHEST RETURN (USA)	M. Johnston
FAIRMILE	W. R. Swinburn	HILLS OF ARAN	A. P. O'Brien, Ireland
FALSTAFF (IRE)	A. P. O'Brien, Ireland	HINTERLAND (IRE)	M. A. Jarvis
FAMCAPII (IRE)		HIPPODROME (IRE)	A. P. O'Brien, Ireland
FANTORINI (USA)	J. H. M. Gosden	HITAAF (IRE)	
FATUR		HOME AFFAIRS	Sir Michael Stoute
FEN GAME (IRE)	J. H. M. Gosden	HUBOOB (FR)	M. P. Tregoning
FIEFDOM (IRE)	M. Johnston	HUMBLE OPINION	
FIGARO'S QUEST (IRE)	P. F. I. Cole	HUMOUROUS (IRE)	
FINNEGANS RAINBOW	P. F. I. Cole	HURRICANE RUN (IRE)	A. Fabre, France
FIRST ROW (IRE)	B. J. Meehan	ICE OF BATTLE (USA)	Mrs A. J. Perrett
FIRST SHOW	J. Noseda	I HAVE DREAMED (IRE)	T. G. Mills
FLAG LIEUTENANT	Sir Michael Stoute	IMLAAK	J. Noseda
FLAME BEARER (USA)	Charles O'Brien, Ireland	INCH LODGE	Sir Michael Stoute
FLAMING WEAPON	J. W. Hills	INDIAN PASSAGE	B. J. Meehan
FONRAZADE (IRE)		INDIAN PIPE DREAM (IRE)	J. H. M. Gosden
FOOTSTEPSINTHESAND	A. P. O'Brien, Ireland	INDIGO CAT (USA)	A. P. O'Brien, Ireland
FOR A DANCER (IRE)	R. Charlton	INDONESIA	M. Johnston
FORGERY (IRE)	G. A. Butler	IN EXCELSIS (USA)	A. P. O'Brien, Ireland
FORT ASSOS	W. Jarvis	INSAANI (IRE)	
FORT AUGUSTUS (USA)	E. A. L. Dunlop	INTEND TO LEAVE (IRE)	
FORTUNATE ISLE (USA)	B. W. Hills	INTISHAAR (IRE)	
FRACAS (IRE)	D. Wachman, Ireland	JAAFI (IRE)	M. P. Tregoning
FRANCHISE		JACK THE GIANT (IRE)	B. W. Hills
FRANCIS DRAKE	John M. Oxx, Ireland	JAGUAR ON THE RUN (USA)	A. P. O'Brien, Ireland
FRITH (IRE)	B. W. Hills	JAMAAR	J. R. Fanshawe
FRONT STAGE (IRE)	Sir Michael Stoute	JAMEHIR (IRE)	J. Noseda
GABANNA (USA)		JELLICLE CAT (USA)	A. P. O'Brien, Ireland
GALA EVENING	Sir Michael Stoute	JONQUIL (IRE)	J. H. M. Gosden
GAMBLE OF THE DAY (USA)	Sir Michael Stoute	JUNGLE DRUMS (IRE)	J. L. Dunlop
GANDALF	J. R. Fanshawe	KABIS AMIGOS	H. R. A. Cecil
GARHOUD	E. A. L. Dunlop	KADDASAN	
GARIBALDI (IRE)		KALAMKAR (IRE)	Sir Michael Stoute
GATO GRANDE (USA)	A. P. O'Brien, Ireland	KANDIDATE	C. E. Brittain
GEOMETRIC		KARNAK (IRE)	A. P. O'Brien, Ireland
GERMANICUS	R. Charlton	KARRNAK	M. A. Jarvis
GESTURE		KASNANI (IRE)	John M. Oxx, Ireland
GHARIR (IRE)	J. E. Hammond, France	KERASHAN (IRE)	Sir Michael Stoute
GIANT EAGLE (IRE)	A. P. O'Brien, Ireland	KEY OF SOLOMON (IRE)	H. Morrison
GIFTED MUSICIAN	J. L. Dunlop	KEY TIME (IRE)	Sir Mark Prescott
GLEN IDA	M. L. W. Bell	KICKAHEAD (USA)	Mme C. Head-Maarek, France
GLISTENING	Sir Michael Stoute	KING'S ADMIRAL (USA)	Sir Michael Stoute
GLORY (IRE)	A. P. O'Brien, Ireland	KING'S JESTER (IRE)	Rupert Pritchard-Gordon, France
GOLD CONVENTION		KING'S KAMA	Sir Michael Stoute
GOLDEN DYNASTY	R. Hannon	KING'S MAJESTY (IRE)	Sir Michael Stoute
GOLDEN GATE (IRE)	M. L. W. Bell	KINGDOM OF DREAMS (IRE)	Sir Michael Stoute
GOLDEN GRIMSHAW (IRE)	B. W. Hills	KING FOREVER	J. Noseda
GOLDFINGER (IRE)	A. P. O'Brien, Ireland	KING MARRAKECH (IRE)	M. R. Channon
GOLD HERITAGE (USA)		KING OF LOVE	M. Johnston
GOODBYE BEN	J. H. M. Gosden	KING OF THE SUN (USA)	
GRAND BAHAMA (USA)	A. Fabre, France	KINGSBARNS (USA)	Charles O'Brien, Ireland
GRAND CENTRAL (IRE)	A. P. O'Brien, Ireland	KINGS EX (USA)	
GRANDE ROCHE (IRE)	B. W. Hills	KINGSHOLM	A. M. Balding
GRAND OCEAN (IRE)	Sir Michael Stoute	KINGS QUAY	R. Hannon
GRAND SEA (IRE)		KIRIN	J. E. Pease, France
		KOCAB	

HORSE	TRAINER
KONG (IRE)	J. L. Dunlop
LAKE VOSTOCK (IRE)	D. K. Weld, Ireland
LAMA ALBARQ (USA)	
LATEST DREAM (FR)	F. Head, France
LAYMAN (USA)	A. Fabre, France
LEGAL FIGHT	
LIAKOURA (GER)	Mrs A. J. Perrett
LINNGARI (IRE)	Sir Michael Stoute
LIVING FOR GOLD (USA)	
LOCH QUEST (IRE)	Mrs A. J. Perrett
LORD NELSON (IRE)	A. P. O'Brien, Ireland
LOVE ANGEL (USA)	M. Johnston
LOVE BEAUTY (USA)	M. Johnston
LOVE PALACE (IRE)	M. Johnston
LOYALTY LODGE (IRE)	J. D. Bethell
LUTIKAI	P. Bary, France
MACABRE	
MACDUFF	John M. Oxx, Ireland
MACHISMO	
MAGNUM OPUS (IRE)	
MAJESTIC MONARCH (USA)	
MAKAASED (IRE)	
MANRIQUE (USA)	
MANTA RAY	
MAPLEDURHAM (IRE)	W. R. Swinburn
MARINE LIFE	P. Bary, France
MARLOWE (IRE)	J. Noseda
MASTER OF THE RACE	Sir Michael Stoute
MATHEMATICIAN (IRE)	A. Fabre, France
MAYADEEN (IRE)	M. P. Tregoning
MCCORMACK (IRE)	
MEL'S MOMENT (USA)	Mrs A. J. Perrett
MELROSE AVENUE (USA)	M. Johnston
MENWAAL (FR)	
MERRIMACK (IRE)	John M. Oxx, Ireland
MIDDLE EARTH (USA)	A. M. Balding
MIGHTYMULLER (IRE)	
MILESIUS (IRE)	A. P. O'Brien, Ireland
MILLE	
MIRABEAU	J. S. Bolger, Ireland
MIXING	W. Jarvis
MOHAYER (IRE)	
MOKTABES (USA)	
MOLLOOK (USA)	
MONDAREJ (IRE)	M. P. Tregoning
MONSOON RAIN (USA)	
MONT JOUX (FR)	F. Head, France
MONTECARMELO (USA)	C. Laffon-Parias, France
MONT SAINT MICHEL (IRE)	G. Wragg
MORDOR (FR)	Sir Michael Stoute
MOSAIC	
MOSTANAD	
MOSTAQEEM (USA)	
MOTAFARRED (IRE)	
MOTIVATOR	M. L. W. Bell
MOUNTAIN HIGH (IRE)	Sir Michael Stoute
MT DESERT	J. H. M. Gosden
MUJAZAF	M. R. Channon
MUNADDAM (USA)	
MURAABET	J. L. Dunlop
MUSHAJER	M. P. Tregoning
MUTAJAMMEL (FR)	Sir Michael Stoute
MUTAMAASEK (USA)	Lady Herries
MY IMMORTAL	J. H. M. Gosden
MY TIGER (IRE)	A. P. O'Brien, Ireland
NASRAWY	L. M. Cumani
NATIONAL TRUST	Sir Michael Stoute
NAVY LARK	R. Charlton
NEUTRINO	L. M. Cumani
NEW LEGEND (USA)	Mme C. Head-Maarek, France
NEWSPRINT	J. H. M. Gosden
NEW YEAR'S DAY (USA)	A. Fabre, France
NIGHT HOUR (IRE)	M. P. Tregoning
NINTH HOUSE (USA)	J. H. M. Gosden
NOBEL PRIZE (IRE)	A. P. O'Brien, Ireland
NOBLE CONCORDE	D. K. Weld, Ireland
NOBLE DUTY (USA)	
NORTHANGER ABBEY (IRE)	
NOTABILITY (IRE)	M. A. Jarvis
NOTNOWCATO	Sir Michael Stoute
NOVEMBER BIRTHDAY	
NUBIAN DIGNITARY (FR)	A. Fabre, France
NUWARA ELIYA	
OBERON'S PRIZE	

HORSE	TRAINER
OFF COLOUR	
ONE GOOD THING (USA)	
ONEIRO WAY (IRE)	P. R. Chamings
ONLY MAKE BELIEVE	J. S. Bolger, Ireland
OPTIMUM (IRE)	D. R. Loder
ORANMORE CASTLE (IRE)	B. W. Hills
ORATORIO (IRE)	A. P. O'Brien, Ireland
ORBIT O'GOLD (USA)	A. Fabre, France
ORIENTALIST (USA)	
ORION BELL	M. Johnston
OSIRIS WAY	P. R. Chamings
OTRANTO (USA)	
OUDE (USA)	Saeed bin Suroor, U.A.E.
PACE SHOT (IRE)	M. A. Jarvis
PACHELLO (IRE)	A. Fabre, France
PADRAO (IRE)	D. R. Loder
PAGAN SWORD	Mrs A. J. Perrett
PALOMAR (USA)	P. Bary, France
PAPER TALK (USA)	B. W. Hills
PARAMOUNT (FR)	Mme C. Head-Maarek, France
PARTY BOSS	C. E. Brittain
PATRONAGE	M. L. W. Bell
PEARL KING (IRE)	M. A. Jarvis
PEKAN ONE	
PERFECT CHOICE (IRE)	B. J. Meehan
PERFECTPERFORMANCE (USA)	
PERFORMING ART	P. W. Chapple-Hyam
PHI (USA)	D. Sepulchre, France
PHOENIX HILL (USA)	
PHYSICAL (IRE)	Mrs A. J. Perrett
PICKWICKIAN (USA)	J. H. M. Gosden
PITTSBURGH	A. M. Balding
PLAINTIFF	
PLANET (IRE)	M. L. W. Bell
PLEA BARGAIN	J. H. M. Gosden
PLIGHT (IRE)	J. H. M. Gosden
POCKETWOOD	Jean-Rene Auvray
POIROT	J. Howard Johnson
POLISH EAGLE	E. A. L. Dunlop
POLITICAL INTRIGUE	H. R. A. Cecil
PORTSMOUTH (USA)	A. P. O'Brien, Ireland
POSTMASTER	B. W. Hills
PREDATORY (USA)	
PRESSGANG	
PRIMONDO (IRE)	J. R. Fanshawe
PRINCE VECTOR	A. King
PRIZE FIGHTER (IRE)	
PROCLAMATION (IRE)	J. Noseda
PSEUDONYM (IRE)	
PUBLIC FORUM	Sir Michael Stoute
QASSAS	K. Prendergast, Ireland
QUICK MOVE	H. R. A. Cecil
QUIET ISLE (IRE)	A. Fabre, France
QUIZZENE (USA)	M. Johnston
RAIDER OF THE EAST (IRE)	Sir Michael Stoute
RANELAGH (FR)	Mme C. Head-Maarek, France
RANSACKER	C. E. Brittain
RATHOR (IRE)	H. R. A. Cecil
RAYDAN (IRE)	John M. Oxx, Ireland
REACH FOR GOLD	A. P. O'Brien, Ireland
RED ADMIRAL (USA)	
RED CHAIRMAN	D. R. Loder
RED MORNING SKY (USA)	J. S. Bolger, Ireland
RED OPERA	Sir Mark Prescott
RED RACKETEER (USA)	E. A. L. Dunlop
RED RIOT (USA)	
REFERENCE (IRE)	
REGALLE (IRE)	
REGAL SILK	
RESTORATION (FR)	J. H. M. Gosden
RETURN OF THE KING	L. M. Cumani
RICHELIEU	
RIGHTFUL RULER	B. W. Hills
RIVER STREET	
ROB ROY (USA)	Sir Michael Stoute
ROCK MUSIC	D. R. Loder
ROSECLIFF	A. M. Balding
ROSSBEIGH (IRE)	D. R. Loder
ROWAN TREE	A. P. O'Brien, Ireland
ROYAL ISLAND (IRE)	M. Johnston
ROYAL WEDDING	D. R. Loder
RUSSIAN BLUE (IRE)	A. P. O'Brien, Ireland
RUSSIAN CONSORT (IRE)	A. King
RUSSIAN REVOLUTION	

HORSE	TRAINER	HORSE	TRAINER
SAILOR KING (IRE)	A. Fabre, France	TASIS (IRE)	
SALFORD ARTIST	D. R. C. Elsworth	TAVALU (USA)	
SALINJA (USA)	Mrs A. J. Perrett	TAWAAZUN (USA)	
SALTBURN LAD (IRE)	J. W. Hills	TAWQEET (USA)	J. L. Dunlop
SAMURAI WAY		TAXMAN (IRE)	C. E. Brittain
SANCHI (IRE)		TERMINATE (GER)	N. A. Callaghan
SAND SEEKER		TEST THE BEST	
SANOR (FR)	P. Bary, France	THEATRE SCHOOL (IRE)	
SANTA FE (IRE)	Sir Michael Stoute	THEBESTISYETTOCOME	T. G. Mills
SARABAN (IRE)	John M. Oxx, Ireland	THE COOIE (IRE)	J. D. Bethell
SAYWAAN (USA)		THE GEEZER	D. R. C. Elsworth
SCALE THE HEIGHTS (IRE)		THE IRON GIANT (IRE)	A. P. O'Brien, Ireland
SCORPION (IRE)	A. P. O'Brien, Ireland	THORN	
SCRIPTWRITER (IRE)		THUNDER ROCK (IRE)	Sir Michael Stoute
SEAGROVE BAY (IRE)		TIBET (IRE)	A. P. O'Brien, Ireland
SEA KESTREL (USA)	M. Johnston	TIGER DANCE (USA)	A. P. O'Brien, Ireland
SEA OF MOYLE (IRE)	A. P. O'Brien, Ireland	TILLANDS (USA)	D. R. Loder
SEARCH FOR ROYALTY	D. K. Weld, Ireland	TILT	J. R. Fanshawe
SEA WALL	R. Charlton	TIMIAS (USA)	P. Bary, France
SECRET FORCE		TIMISVAR (IRE)	John M. Oxx, Ireland
SEEKING AN ALIBI (USA)		TIMOTHEUS (USA)	L. M. Cumani
SERVE TIME		TOMBOLA (FR)	
SHALAPOUR (IRE)	John M. Oxx, Ireland	TONY JAMES (IRE)	C. E. Brittain
SHAMARDAL (USA)	Saeed bin Suroor, U.A.E.	TOP GEAR	D. R. C. Elsworth
SHAMAYOUN (FR)	A. de Royer Dupre, France	TOP MARK	H. Morrison
SHANEHILL (IRE)	D. R. Loder	TORRENS (IRE)	S. P. Griffiths
SHANNON SPRINGS (IRE)	B. W. Hills	TOSHI (USA)	I. Semple
SHARDAKHAN (IRE)	A. de Royer Dupre, France	TOUT ROUGE (USA)	Mme C. Head-Maarek, France
SHAREB (USA)	B. W. Hills	TRAFALGAR SQUARE	R. Guest
SHARE OPTION	A. Fabre, France	TRAGEDIAN (USA)	J. H. M. Gosden
SHEDARIAN (FR)	A. de Royer Dupre, France	TRAPRAIN (IRE)	
SHEZAN (IRE)	A. de Royer Dupre, France	TREW FLIGHT (USA)	M. H. Tompkins
SHOWDANCE (USA)	A. P. O'Brien, Ireland	TRIBE	Sir Michael Stoute
SHY GLANCE (IRE)	J. H. M. Gosden	TRUCKLE	C. W. Fairhurst
SIGNATORY (USA)	J. H. M. Gosden	TRUEHEART (USA)	A. P. O'Brien, Ireland
SILBER MOND	M. L. W. Bell	TSAROXY (IRE)	J. Howard Johnson
SILENT JO (JPN)		TUVALU (GER)	A. M. Balding
SILVER COURT		TWAIN (IRE)	A. P. O'Brien, Ireland
SILVER SONG	J. L. Dunlop	UHLAN	C. Laffon-Parias, France
SINNOMORE (IRE)	M. A. Magnusson	UNDERGRADUATE (IRE)	
SMEMI AN NADA		UNFURLED (IRE)	J. L. Dunlop
SNOW PLOUGH (IRE)		UREDALE (IRE)	Mrs A. Duffield
SOLAR HEIGHT (USA)	J. H. M. Gosden	USTAD (IRE)	J. L. Dunlop
SOLEMNITY (USA)		VELVET HEIGHTS (IRE)	J. L. Dunlop
SOLWAY FIRTH	M. P. Tregoning	VINERY	
SOUTHERN AIR	J. S. Bolger, Ireland	VIP	
SOUTH WIND RISING (IRE)	A. P. O'Brien, Ireland	WAR AT SEA (IRE)	M. P. Tregoning
SOVEREIGN SPIRIT (IRE)	W. R. Swinburn	WATCHTOWER (IRE)	
SOVEREIGNTY (JPN)	D. R. Loder	WATER PISTOL	Mrs A. J. Perrett
SPANISH RIDGE (IRE)	J. L. Dunlop	WAVERTREE WARRIOR (IRE)	N. P. Littmoden
SPEAR (IRE)	D. R. Loder	WELL ESTABLISHED (IRE)	M. A. Jarvis
SPEAR THISTLE	J. H. M. Gosden	WELLSAID (FR)	C. Laffon-Parias, France
SPEIGHTSTOWN	P. F. I. Cole	WESTERN HOUSE (USA)	M. Johnston
STAGELIGHT (IRE)	J. Noseda	WESTLAND (USA)	Mrs A. J. Perrett
STAMFORD	Sir Michael Stoute	WHERE WITH ALL (IRE)	
STATUTE	K. Prendergast, Ireland	WICKLOW (USA)	A. P. O'Brien, Ireland
STETCHWORTH PRINCE	D. R. Loder	WILD SAVANNAH	J. H. M. Gosden
STOCKBROKER (IRE)	A. Fabre, France	WINDHOVER	M. Johnston
STORM BREAKER (IRE)	A. P. O'Brien, Ireland	WINDSOR KNOT (IRE)	
STORMY LOVE (IRE)	M. Johnston	WINGMAN (IRE)	J. W. Hills
STREETS OF GOLD (IRE)	A. P. O'Brien, Ireland	WINGSPEED (IRE)	
SUGITANI (USA)		WINTER PALACE (IRE)	A. P. O'Brien, Ireland
SUMEIA (IRE)		WISE OWL	M. Johnston
SUN AND SHOWERS (IRE)	J. H. M. Gosden	WIJOOD	H. Morrison
SUN BOAT	A. Fabre, France	WUTHERING HEIGHTS (JPN)	A. P. O'Brien, Ireland
SUNDAY SYMPHONY		YANKEY	
SUN KISSED (JPN)		YEHUDI (IRE)	A. P. O'Brien, Ireland
SWAINS BRIDGE (USA)	L. M. Cumani	ZABEEL PALACE	D. R. Loder
SWIFT TIGER (USA)		ZADALRAKIB	
SWISS COTTAGE	John M. Oxx, Ireland	ZAILANN (IRE)	A. de Royer Dupre, France
SWORD OF DAMASCUS (IRE)	D. R. Loder	EX DAROURA (USA)	
TAJ INDIA (USA)		EX FALAFIL (USA)	J. E. Hammond, France
TAKAFU (USA)	W. J. Haggas	EX MASKUNAH (USA)	
TAMATAVE (IRE)		EX MISTLE SONG	
TANZANI (USA)	C. E. Brittain	EX POLAR QUEEN	
TARALAN (IRE)	A. de Royer Dupre, France	EX SEARCH COMMITTEE (USA)	D. K. Weld, Ireland
TARRAMAN (USA)	M. Johnston	EX SUPERB INVESTMENT (IRE)	
TASHIGAR (IRE)	A. de Royer Dupre, France	EX WELL BEYOND (IRE)	

EUROPEAN FREE HANDICAP
NEWMARKET CRAVEN MEETING 2005
(ON THE ROWLEY MILE COURSE)
WEDNESDAY, APRIL 13TH

The Free Handicap (Class A) (Listed race) with total prize fund of £28,000 added for two-years old only of 2004 (including all two-year-olds in the 2004 European two-year-old Thoroughbred Racehorse Rankings), to run as three-year-olds; lowest weight 7st 12lb; highest weight 9st 7lb.

Penalty for winner after December 31, 2004, 5lb. Seven furlongs.

Rating		st	lb	Rating		st	lb
123	SHAMARDAL (USA)	9	7	110	MYSTICAL LAND (IRE)	8	8
122	AD VALOREM (USA)	9	6	110	SCANDINAVIA (USA)	8	8
122	DUBAWI (IRE)	9	6	110	WALK IN THE PARK (IRE)	8	8
120	REBUTTAL (USA)	9	4	110	WINDSOR KNOT (IRE)	8	8
119	WILKO (USA)	9	3	109	GOLDEN LEGACY (IRE)	8	7
117	DIVINE PROPORTIONS (USA)	9	1	109	JOSH (GB)	8	7
117	MOTIVATOR (GB)	9	1	109	POLLY PERKINS (IRE)	8	7
117	ORATORIO (IRE)	9	1	109	SLIP DANCE (IRE)	8	7
116	BERENSON (IRE)	9	0	108	BLUE DAKOTA (IRE)	8	6
116	EARLY MARCH (GB)	9	0	108	CUPID'S GLORY (GB)	8	6
116	ICEMAN (GB)	9	0	108	MOTH BALL (GB)	8	6
116	LAYMAN (USA)	9	0	107	ABRAXAS ANTELOPE (IRE)	8	5
116	MONTGOMERY'S ARCH (USA)	9	0	107	DANCE NIGHT (IRE)	8	5
114	DAMSON (IRE)	8	12	107	DIKTATORIAL (GB)	8	5
114	ETLAALA (GB)	8	12	107	DRAMATICUS (GB)	8	5
114	LIBRETTIST (USA)	8	12	107	DUBAI SURPRISE (IRE)	8	5
114	SATCHEM (GB)	8	12	107	ELLIOTS WORLD (IRE)	8	5
113	FRALOGA (IRE)	8	11	107	LUAS LINE (IRE)	8	5
113	GALEOTA (IRE)	8	11	107	SOMETHING EXCITING (GB)	8	5
113	HELIOS QUERCUS (FR)	8	11	107	WHERE WITH ALL (IRE)	8	5
113	PERFECTPERFORMANCE (USA)	8	11	106	AFRASHAD (IRE)	8	4
113	PLAYFUL ACT (IRE)	8	11	106	CAPABLE GUEST (IRE)	8	4
113	RUSSIAN BLUE (IRE)	8	11	106	COMIC STRIP (GB)	8	4
113	SOAR (IRE)	8	11	106	CRIMSON SUN (USA)	8	4
113	TITIAN TIME (USA)	8	11	106	FOX (GB)	8	4
112	ALBERT HALL (IRE)	8	10	106	HEARTHSTEAD WINGS (GB)	8	4
112	INTRIGUED (GB)	8	10	106	JEWEL IN THE SAND (IRE)	8	4
112	MAGICAL ROMANCE (IRE)	8	10	106	MISTER GENEPI (GB)	8	4
112	MANDURO (GER)	8	10	106	OUDE (USA)	8	4
112	PORTRAYAL (USA)	8	10	106	VISIONIST (IRE)	8	4
112	YEHUDI (IRE)	8	10	105	COURS DE LA REINE (IRE)	8	3
111	ANDRONIKOS (GB)	8	9	105	DON PELE (IRE)	8	3
111	LAVEROCK (IRE)	8	9	105	ECHELON (GB)	8	3
111	MAIDS CAUSEWAY (IRE)	8	9	105	EMBOSSED (IRE)	8	3
111	PAITA (GB)	8	9	105	JOINT ASPIRATION (GB)	8	3
111	QUEEN OF POLAND (GB)	8	9	105	MERCHANT (GB)	8	3
111	SUEZ (GB)	8	9	105	SACRED NUTS (IRE)	8	3
111	TONY JAMES (IRE)	8	9	105	SALSA BRAVA (IRE)	8	3
111	TREMAR (GB)	8	9	105	SANTA FE (IRE)	8	3
110	CAESAR BEWARE (IRE)	8	8	105	SHOHRAH (IRE)	8	3
110	CAPTAIN HURRICANE (GB)	8	8	105	SILVER WRAITH (IRE)	8	3
110	CENTIFOLIA (FR)	8	8	105	SONGERIE (GB)	8	3
110	CHATEAU ISTANA (GB)	8	8	105	STAGBURY HILL (USA)	8	3
110	COUGAR CAT (USA)	8	8	105	TOURNEDOS (IRE)	8	3
110	COUNCIL MEMBER (USA)	8	8	104	CHEROKEE (USA)	8	2
110	DASH TO THE TOP (GB)	8	8	104	DESTINATE (IRE)	8	2
110	FOOTSTEPSINTHESAND (GB)	8	8	104	IN EXCELSIS (USA)	8	2
110	GORELLA (FR)	8	8	104	KINGS QUAY (IRE)	8	2
110	HENRIK (GB)	8	8	104	PROPINQUITY (GB)	8	2
110	MONA LISA (GB)	8	8				

104	**SQUAW DANCE** (GB)	8	2
104	**TURNKEY** (GB)	8	2
104	**WHAZZAT** (GB)	8	2
103	**DISTINCTLY GAME** (GB)	8	1
103	**MARY READ** (GB)	8	1
103	**MOSCOW MUSIC** (GB)	8	1
103	**ROWAN TREE** (GB)	8	1
103	**SUMORA** (IRE)	8	1
102	**BERKHAMSTED** (IRE)	8	0
102	**BRAHMINY KITE** (USA)	8	0
102	**BRECON BEACON** (GB)	8	0
102	**CAPE GREKO** (GB)	8	0
102	**CORNUS** (GB)	8	0
102	**FRITH** (IRE)	8	0
102	**GRAND MARQUE** (IRE)	8	0
102	**LEO'S LUCKY STAR** (USA)	8	0
102	**NORTHERN SPLENDOUR** (USA)	8	0
102	**PENKENNA PRINCESS** (IRE)	8	0
102	**SHANGHAI LILY** (IRE)	8	0
101	**BAHIA BREEZE** (GB)	7	13
101	**CASTELLETTO** (GB)	7	13
101	**FAVOURITA** (GB)	7	13

101	**HARVEST WARRIOR** (GB)	7	13
101	**KAY TWO** (IRE)	7	13
101	**NANABANANA** (IRE)	7	13
101	**SPIRIT OF CHESTER** (IRE)	7	13
101	**STETCHWORTH PRINCE** (GB)	7	13
101	**YAJBILL** (IRE)	7	13
100	**BEAVER PATROL** (IRE)	7	12
100	**BECKERMET** (IRE)	7	12
100	**BLACK VELVET** (GB)	7	12
100	**JOHNNY JUMPUP** (IRE)	7	12
100	**KAMAKIRI** (IRE)	7	12
100	**NUFOOS** (GB)	7	12
100	**OBE GOLD** (GB)	7	12
100	**SHANNON SPRINGS** (IRE)	7	12
100	**SKYWARDS** (GB)	7	12

Last Year: Brunel (IRE) 8-13 (D Holland)
W N Haggas 9/1 11 ran 1m 26.40

Compile your own horse comments, ratings and lists to follow and form your OWN opinion.

Become Interactive and get what you want.

For details of our free trial offer see page 736.

WORLD THOROUGHBRED HORSERACE RANKINGS

For three-year-olds rated 110 or greater by the International Federation of Horseracing Authorities

Rating		Trained
128	**SMARTY JONES** (USA)	USA
126	**BAGO** (FR)	FR
125	**CHERRY MIX** (FR)	FR
124	**HAAFHD** (GB)	GB
123	**AZAMOUR** (IRE)	IRE
123	**GREY SWALLOW** (IRE)	IRE
122	**KITTEN'S JOY** (USA)	USA
122	**LUCKY STORY** (USA)	GB
122	**NORTH LIGHT** (IRE)	GB
120	**ACROPOLIS** (IRE)	IRE
120	**BIRDSTONE** (USA)	USA
120	**OUIJA BOARD** (GB)	GB
120	**RULE OF LAW** (USA)	GB
120	**TYCOON** (GB)	IRE
119	**SHIROCCO** (GER)	GER
118	**ATTRACTION** (GB)	GB
118	**BACHELOR DUKE** (USA)	GB
118	**ELECTROCUTIONIST** (USA)	ITY
118	**LET THE LION ROAR** (GB)	GB
118	**SNOW RIDGE** (IRE)	GB
118	**WHIPPER** (USA)	FR
117	**ANTONIUS PIUS** (USA)	IRE
117	**ASHADO** (USA)	USA
117	**COSMO BULK** (JPN)	JPN
117	**DIAMOND GREEN** (FR)	FR
117	**EGERTON** (GER)	GER
117	**KING KAMEHAMEHA** (JPN)	JPN
117	**LATICE** (IRE)	FR
117	**LION HEART** (USA)	USA
117	**QUIFF** (GB)	GB
117	**VOIX DU NORD** (FR)	FR
116	**ALEXANDER GOLDRUN** (IRE)	IRE
116	**BLUE CANARI** (FR)	FR
116	**DELTA BLUES** (JPN)	JPN
116	**GREY LILAS** (IRE)	FR
116	**INTENDANT** (GER)	GER
116	**MILLEMIX** (FR)	FR
116	**MISTER MONET** (IRE)	GB
116	**VALIXIR** (IRE)	FR
115	**AMERICAN POST** (GB)	FR
115	**ARTIE SCHILLER** (USA)	USA
115	**CACIQUE** (IRE)	FR
115	**GROOM TESSE** (GB)	ITY
115	**LUNE D'OR** (FR)	FR
115	**MARAAHEL** (IRE)	GB
115	**MIKADO** (GB)	IRE
115	**MILLIONAIA** (IRE)	GB
115	**PERCUSSIONIST** (IRE)	GB
115	**PROSPECT PARK** (FR)	FR
115	**PURGE** (USA)	USA
115	**READ THE FOOTNOTES** (USA)	USA
115	**SOCIETY SELECTION** (USA)	USA
115	**THE CLIFF'S EDGE** (USA)	USA
114	**BULL RUN** (IRE)	GB
114	**LORD DU SUD** (FR)	FR

Rating		Trained
114	**ONE COOL CAT** (USA)	IRE
114	**PASTORAL PURSUITS** (GB)	GB
114	**PEPPERSTORM** (GER)	GER
114	**REEFSCAPE** (GB)	FR
114	**SUNDROP** (JPN)	GB
114	**TORRESTRELLA** (FR)	FR
113	**BOOK OF KINGS** (USA)	IRE
113	**DARSALAM** (IRE)	CHR
113	**DAY FLIGHT** (GB)	GB
113	**DAYANO** (GER)	GER
113	**DELFOS** (FR)	FR
113	**DENEBOLA** (USA)	FR
113	**HATHRAH** (IRE)	FR
113	**SALFORD CITY** (IRE)	GB/USA
112	**BRUNEL** (IRE)	GB
112	**BYRON** (GB)	GB
112	**CASTLETON** (GB)	GB
112	**DOLMA** (FR)	FR
112	**GO FOR GOLD** (IRE)	IRE
112	**LEITRIM HOUSE** (GB)	GB
112	**MALINAS** (GER)	GER
112	**MISTER SACHA** (FR)	FR
112	**NECKLACE** (GB)	IRE
112	**PUNCTILIOUS** (USA)	GB
112	**THREE VALLEYS** (USA)	GB/USA
112	**YEATS** (IRE)	IRE
111	**ACE** (IRE)	IRE
111	**ART MASTER** (USA)	FR
111	**ASSIUN** (GER)	GER
111	**HAZARISTA** (IRE)	IRE
111	**INTO THE DARK** (GB)	GB
111	**MAJESTIC DESERT** (GB)	GB
111	**PEAK TO CREEK** (GB)	GB
111	**RED BLOOM** (GB)	GB
111	**SILVERSKAYA** (USA)	FR
110	**AFRICAN DREAM** (GB)	GB
110	**AGATA** (FR)	FR
110	**ALL TOO BEAUTIFUL** (IRE)	IRE
110	**ALWAYS FIRST** (GB)	GB
110	**ASK FOR THE MOON** (FR)	FR
110	**BALMONT** (USA)	GB
110	**CAIRDEAS** (IRE)	IRE
110	**DUKE OF VENICE** (USA)	GB
110	**ERSHAAD** (USA)	FR
110	**HAZYVIEW** (GB)	GB
110	**ILLUSTRIOUS MISS** (USA)	GB
110	**LAZIO** (GER)	GER
110	**LOVE AND BUBBLES** (USA)	FR
110	**MAC LOVE** (GB)	GB
110	**MOSS VALE** (IRE)	GB
110	**RAFFELBERGER** (GER)	GER
110	**SALDENTIGERIN** (GER)	GER
110	**SIMPLE EXCHANGE** (IRE)	IRE
110	**SPIRIT OF DESERT** (IRE)	ITY
110	**SUPER BOBBINA** (IRE)	ITY

FOUR-YEAR-OLDS 2004

For four-year-olds and up rated 110 or greater by the Federation of Horseracing Authorities

Rating	Age	Trained	Rating	Age	Trained
130 GHOSTZAPPER (USA)	4	USA	116 STRONG HOPE (USA)	4	USA
127 DOYEN (IRE)	4	GB	116 TSURUMARU BOY (JPN)	6	JPN
126 PLEASANTLY PERFECT (USA)	6	USA	115 ADMIRE DON (JPN)	5	JPN
124 MEDAGLIA D'ORO (USA)	5	USA	115 ASHDOWN EXPRESS (IRE)	5	GB
123 PICO CENTRAL (BRZ)	5	USA	115 BAHAMIAN PIRATE (USA)	9	GB
123 RAKTI (GB)	5	GB	115 BLUESTHESTANDARD (USA)	7	USA
123 ROSES IN MAY (USA)	4	USA	115 CALSTONE LIGHT O (JPN)	6	JPN
123 SULAMANI (IRE)	5	GB	115 CAPE OF GOOD HOPE (GB)	6	HK
122 SOUTHERN IMAGE (USA)	4	USA	115 DESIGNED FOR LUCK (USA)	7	USA
122 SPEIGHTSTOWN (USA)	6	USA	115 DYNEVER (USA)	4	USA
122 ZENNO ROB ROY (JPN)	4	JPN	115 EMA BOVARY (CHI)	5	USA
121 BETTER TALK NOW (USA)	5	USA	115 EVEN THE SCORE (USA)	6	USA
121 NORSE DANCER (IRE)	4	GB	115 EVENING ATTIRE (USA)	6	USA
121 REFUSE TO BEND (IRE)	4	UAE/GB	115 EXECUTE (FR)	7	FR
120 DURANDAL (JPN)	5	JPN	115 FILM MAKER (USA)	4	USA
120 HARD BUCK (BRZ)	5	USA	115 FIREBREAK (GB)	5	GB
120 POWERSCOURT (GB)	4	IRE	115 INGRANDIRE (JPN)	5	JPN
120 TAP DANCE CITY (USA)	7	JPN	115 INTERCONTINENTAL (GB)	4	USA
120 WARRSAN (IRE)	6	GB	115 ISLAND FASHION (USA)	4	USA
119 PAPINEAU (GB)	4	GB	115 KALAMAN (IRE)	4	GB/HK
119 PEACE RULES (USA)	4	USA	115 LINCOLN (JPN)	4	JPN
119 PERFECT DRIFT (USA)	5	USA	115 LUNDY'S LIABILITY (BRZ)	4	USA
119 SAINT LIAM (USA)	4	USA	115 MIDWAY ROAD (USA)	4	USA
119 SOVIET SONG (IRE)	4	GB	115 MY COUSIN MATT (USA)	5	USA
119 VINNIE ROE (IRE)	6	IRE	115 NARITA CENTURY (JPN)	5	JPN
118 AZERI (USA)	6	USA	115 NOTHING TO LOSE (USA)	4	USA
118 BANDARI (IRE)	5	GB	115 OUR NEW RECRUIT (USA)	5	USA
118 GAMUT (IRE)	5	GB	115 PAOLINI (GER)	7	GER
118 KELA (USA)	6	USA	115 PASSING GLANCE (GB)	5	GB
118 MIDAS EYES (USA)	4	USA	115 PATAVELLIAN (IRE)	6	GB
118 NAYYIR (GB)	6	GB	115 PHOENIX REACH (IRE)	4	GB
118 SIGHTSEEK (USA)	5	USA	115 PIVOTAL POINT (GB)	4	GB
118 SINGLETARY (USA)	4	USA	115 POHAVE (USA)	6	USA
118 SOMNUS (GB)	4	GB	115 POLISH SUMMER (GB)	7	FR
118 WESTERNER (GB)	5	FR	115 REQUEST FOR PAROLE (USA)	5	USA
117 ANCIENT WORLD (USA)	4	GB	115 SABIANGO (GER)	6	USA
117 CHIC (GB)	4	GB	115 SALSELON (GB)	5	GB
117 CHORIST (GB)	5	GB	115 SENEX (GER)	4	GER
117 EPALO (GER)	5	GER	115 STAR OVER THE BAY (USA)	6	USA
117 KICKEN KRIS (USA)	4	USA	115 SWEET RETURN (GB)	4	USA
117 MAGISTRETTI (USA)	4	GB/USA	115 TANTE ROSE (IRE)	4	GB
117 MILLENARY (GB)	7	GB	115 TELEGNOSIS (JPN)	5	JPN
117 MR DINOS (IRE)	5	GB	115 TEN MOST WANTED (USA)	4	USA
117 MUBTAKER (USA)	7	GB	115 THE TATLING (IRE)	7	GB
117 RUSSIAN RHYTHM (USA)	4	GB	115 TIME PARADOX (JPN)	6	JPN
117 SIMONAS (IRE)	5	GER	115 VALLEE ENCHANTEE (IRE)	4	FR
117 SPECIAL RING (USA)	7	USA	115 WONDER AGAIN (USA)	5	USA
117 TOTAL IMPACT (CHI)	6	USA	114 ALKAADHEM (GB)	4	GB
117 TOUCH OF LAND (FR)	4	FR	114 AUTUMN GLORY (IRE)	4	GB
117 VAR (USA)	5	GB	114 BRIAN BORU (GB)	4	IRE
116 ADORATION (USA)	5	USA	114 DARASIM (IRE)	6	GB
116 ALTIERI (GB)	6	ITY	114 FIRST CHARTER (GB)	5	GB
116 BAYAMO (IRE)	5	USA	114 FORESTIER (FR)	4	FR
116 FUNNY CIDE (USA)	4	USA	114 HIGH ACCOLADE (GB)	4	GB
116 IKHTYAR (GB)	4	GB	114 HURRICANE ALAN (IRE)	4	GB
116 METEOR STORM (GB)	5	USA	114 KASTHARI (IRE)	5	GB
116 MR O'BRIEN (IRE)	5	USA	114 LE VIE DEI COLORI (GB)	4	ITY/GB
116 POLICY MAKER (IRE)	4	FR	114 MAMOOL (IRE)	5	GB
116 PRINCE KIRK (FR)	4	ITY	114 MONSIEUR BOND (IRE)	4	GB
116 SILK FAMOUS (JPN)	5	JPN	114 MY RISK (FR)	5	FR
116 SOLDIER HOLLOW (GB)	4	GER	114 NEBRASKA TORNADO (USA)	4	FR
116 STROLL (USA)	4	USA	114 PORLEZZA (FR)	5	FR

Rating	Age	Trained
114 **SCOTT'S VIEW** (GB)	5	GB
114 **SIGHTS ON GOLD** (IRE)	5	GB
114 **THE TRADER** (IRE)	6	GB
114 **VANGELIS** (USA)	5	FR/USA
113 **ALKAASED** (USA)	4	GB
113 **AVONBRIDGE** (GB)	4	GB
113 **CRIMSON PALACE** (SAF)	5	UAE/GB
113 **EAGLE RISE** (IRE)	4	GER
113 **FAIR MIX** (IRE)	6	FR
113 **FAVOURABLE TERMS** (GB)	4	GB
113 **FRIZZANTE** (GB)	5	GB
113 **GATEMAN** (GB)	7	GB
113 **IMPERIAL DANCER** (GB)	6	GB
113 **MARTILLO** (GER)	4	GER
113 **MUQBIL** (USA)	4	GB
113 **OSTERHASE** (IRE)	5	IRE
113 **PERSIAN MAJESTY** (IRE)	4	GB
113 **SIX PERFECTIONS** (FR)	4	FR
113 **SYSTEMATIC** (GB)	5	GB
113 **TILLERMAN** (GB)	8	GB
112 **ALBANOVA** (GB)	5	GB
112 **ALCAZAR** (IRE)	9	GB
112 **BOWMAN'S CROSSING** (IRE)	5	HK
112 **DANCING BAY** (GB)	7	GB
112 **DUBAI SUCCESS** (GB)	4	GB
112 **MARBYE** (IRE)	4	ITY
112 **NYSAEAN** (IRE)	5	GB
112 **OLASO** (GER)	5	GER
112 **ORIENTOR** (GB)	6	GB
112 **PRIDE** (FR)	4	FR
112 **RAZKALLA** (USA)	6	UAE/GB
112 **ROTTECK** (GER)	4	GER
112 **ROYAL MILLENNIUM** (IRE)	6	GB
112 **SELF DEFENSE** (GB)	7	GB
112 **SHORT PAUSE** (GB)	5	FR
112 **SILENCE IS GOLDEN** (GB)	5	GB
112 **VALENTINO** (FR)	5	FR
112 **VESPONE** (IRE)	4	UAE/GB
112 **WHORTLEBERRY** (FR)	4	FR
111 **ARAKAN** (USA)	4	GB
111 **BRIGHT SKY** (IRE)	5	FR
111 **CHECKIT** (IRE)	4	GB
111 **CUT QUARTZ** (FR)	7	FR
111 **D'ANJOU** (GB)	7	IRE
111 **DISTINCTION** (IRE)	5	GB

Rating	Age	Trained
111 **FAYR JAG** (IRE)	5	GB
111 **MILLSTREET** (GB)	5	GB
111 **NONNO CARLO** (IRE)	4	ITY
111 **POLAR BEN** (GB)	5	GB
111 **RYONO** (USA)	5	GER
111 **SHOT TO FAME** (USA)	5	GB
111 **STORM TROOPER** (GER)	4	GER
111 **WALKAMIA** (GB)	4	FR
110 **ACTRICE** (IRE)	4	FR
110 **AUBONNE** (GER)	4	FR
110 **BAROLO** (GB)	5	GB
110 **BEHKARA** (IRE)	4	FR
110 **BENEVENTA** (GB)	4	GB
110 **BIG BAD BOB** (IRE)	4	GB
110 **CHANCELLOR** (IRE)	6	GB
110 **CHARMING GROOM** (FR)	5	FR
110 **CRYSTAL CASTLE** (USA)	6	FR/USA
110 **FRUHLINGSSTURM** (GB)	4	GB
110 **GOLD MEDALLIST** (GB)	4	GB
110 **LE CARRE** (USA)	6	FR
110 **LEPORELLO** (IRE)	4	GB
110 **LOOK HONEY** (IRE)	4	FR
110 **LUCKY STRIKE** (GB)	6	GER
110 **MAKTUB** (ITY)	5	GB
110 **MARTALINE** (GB)	5	FR
110 **MKUZI** (GB)	5	IRE
110 **NEW SOUTH WALES** (GB)	4	GB
110 **ORANGE TOUCH** (GER)	4	GB
110 **PEPPERCORN** (GER)	7	GER
110 **POLAR WAY** (GB)	5	GB
110 **RED FORT** (IRE)	4	GB
110 **RISK SEEKER** (GB)	4	FR
110 **ROYAL REBEL** (GB)	8	GB
110 **SONGLARK** (GB)	4	GB
110 **SPECIAL KALDOUN** (IRE)	5	FR
110 **STAR VALLEY** (FR)	4	FR
110 **STEENBERG** (IRE)	5	GB
110 **STRIKING AMBITION** (GB)	4	GB
110 **SUGGESTIVE** (GB)	6	GB
110 **SWEET STREAM** (ITY)	4	FR
110 **THE WHISTLING TEAL** (GB)	8	GB
110 **TRADE FAIR** (GB)	4	GB
110 **WITH REASON** (USA)	6	GB
110 **WITHOUT CONNEXION** (IRE)	5	FR/ITY

Owners names are shown against their horses where this information is available. In the case of Partnerships and Syndicates, the nominated owner is given alongside the horse with other owners listed below the team.

GODOLPHIN HORSES IN THE WORLD THOROUGHBRED RACEHORSE RANKINGS

TWO-YEAR-OLDS

SHAMARDAL (USA)	Giant's Causeway (USA) - Helsinki	123
DUBAWI (IRE)	Dubai Millennium - Zomaradah	122
LAYMAN (USA)	Sunday Silence - Laiyl (IRE)	116
LIBRETTIST (USA)	Danzig (USA) - Mysterial (USA)	114
SATCHEM (IRE)	Inchinor - Mohican Princess	114
PERFECTPERFORMANCE (USA)	Rahy (USA) - Balistroika (USA)	113
QUEEN OF POLAND	Halling (USA)- Polska (USA)	111
SUEZ	Green Desert (USA) - Repeat Warning	111
COUNCIL MEMBER (USA)	Seattle Slew - Zoe Montana (USA)	110
WINDSOR KNOT (IRE)	Pivotal - Triple Tie (USA)	110
DUBAI SURPRISE (IRE)	King's Best - Toujours Irish (USA)	107
WHERE WITH ALL (IRE)	Montjeu (IRE) - Zelding (IRE)	107
AFRASHAD (USA)	Smoke Glacken (USA) - Flo White (USA)	106
CRIMSON SUN (USA)	Danzig (USA) - Crimplene (IRE)	106
OUDE (USA)	Dubai Millennium - Chosen Lady (USA)	106
NORTHERN SPLENDOUR (USA)	Giant's Causeway (USA) - Ribbonwood (USA)	102

THREE-YEAR-OLDS

CHERRY MIX (FR)	Linamix (FR) - Cherry Moon (USA)	125
RULE OF LAW (USA)	Kingmambo (USA) - Crystal Crossing (IRE)	120
SNOW RIDGE (IRE)	Indian Ridge (IRE) - Snow Princess (IRE)	118
BULL RUN (IRE)	Daylami (IRE) - Bulaxie	114
SUNDROP (JPN)	Sunday Silence (USA) - Oenothera (IRE)	114
BYRON	Green Desert (USA) - Gay Gallanta (USA)	112
PUNCTILIOUS	Danehill (USA) - Robertet (USA)	112
INTO THE DARK	Rainbow Quest (USA) - Land of Dreams	111
DUKE OF VENICE (USA)	Theatrical (IRE) - Rihan (USA)	110

FOUR-YEAR-OLDS AND UP

DOYEN (IRE), 4	Sadler's Wells (USA) - Moon Cactus	127
SULAMANI (IRE), 5	Hernando (FR) - Soul Dream (USA)	123
REFUSE TO BEND (IRE), 4	Sadler's Wells (USA) - Market Slide (USA)	121
PAPINEAU, 4	Singspiel (IRE) - Early Rising (USA)	119
ANCIENT WORLD (USA), 4	Spinning World (USA) - Headline	117
FIREBREAK, 5	Charnwood Forest (IRE) - Breakaway	115
MAMOOL (IRE), 5	In The Wings - Genovefa (USA)	114
SIGHTS ON GOLD (IRE), 5	Indian Ridge (IRE) - Summer Trysting (USA)	114
CRIMSON PALACE (SAF), 5	Elliodor (FR) - Perfect Guest (SAF)	113
RAZKALLA (USA), 6	Caerleon (USA) - Larrocha (IRE)	112
VESPONE (IRE), 4	Llandaff (USA) - Vanishing Prairie (USA)	112
MILLSTREET, 5	Polish Precedent (USA) - Mill Path	111
NEW SOUTH WALES, 4	In The Wings - Temora (IRE)	110
SONGLARK, 4	Singspiel (IRE) - Negligent (IRE)	110
WITH REASON (USA), 6	Nashwan (USA) - Just Cause (IRE)	110

AIDAN O'BRIEN-TRAINED HORSES IN THE WORLD THOROUGHBRED RACEHORSE RANKINGS

TWO-YEAR-OLDS

AD VALOREM (USA)	Danzig (USA) - Classy Women (USA)	122
ORATORIO (IRE)	Danehill (USA) - Mahrah (USA)	117
RUSSIAN BLUE (IRE)	Danehill (USA) - Soviet Artic (FR)	113
ALBERT HALL	Danehill (USA) - Al Theraab (USA)	112
YEHUDI (IRE)	Sadler's Wells (USA) - Bella Vitessa (IRE)	112
COUGAR CAT (USA)	Storm Cat (USA) - Excellent Meeting (USA)	110
FOOTSTEPSINTHESAND	Giant's Causeway (USA) - Glatisant	110
MONA LISA	Giant's Causeway (USA) - Colorsnap	110
SCANDINAVIA (USA)	Fusaichi Pegasus (USA) - Party Cited (USA)	110
SILK AND SCARLET	Sadler's Wells (USA) - Danilova (USA)	109
DARK CHEETAH (USA)	Storm Cat (USA) - Layounne (USA)	108
IN EXCELSIS (USA)	Fusaichi Pegasus (USA) - Lakeway (USA)	104
ROWAN TREE	Singspiel (IRE) - Dashing Water	103
CARNEGIE HALL (IRE)	Danehill (USA) - Bolshaya	102
AMSTERDAM (IRE)	Danehill (USA) - Dathiyna (IRE)	100

THREE-YEAR-OLDS

ACROPOLIS (IRE)	Sadler's Wells (USA) - Dedicated Lady (IRE)	120
TYCOON	Sadler's Wells (USA) - Fleeting Glimpse	120
ANTONIUS PIUS (USA)	Danzig (USA) - Catchascatchcan	117
MIKADO	Sadler's Wels (USA) - Free At Last	115
ONE COOL CAT (USA)	Storm Cat (USA) - Tacha (USA)	114
BOOK OF KINGS (USA)	Kingmambo (USA) - Honfleur (IRE)	113
GO FOR GOLD (IRE)	Machiavellian (USA) - Kithanga (IRE)	112
NECKLACE	Darshaan - Spinning The Yarn	112
YEATS (IRE)	Sadler's Wells (USA) - Lyndonville (IRE)	112
ACE (IRE)	Danehill (USA) - Tea House (IRE)	111
ALL TOO BEAUTIFUL (IRE)	Sadler's Wells (USA) - Urban Sea (USA)	110

FOUR-YEAR-OLDS AND UP

POWERSCOURT, 4	Sadler's Wells (USA) - Rainbow Lake	120
BRIAN BORU, 4	Sadler's Wells (USA) - Eva Luna (USA)	114

RACEFORM CHAMPIONS 2004
THREE-YEAR-OLDS AND UP

5f-6f

PICO CENTRAL	128
SILENT WITNESS	127

SPEIGHTSTOWN	126
SOMNUS	124
CAJUN BEAT	123

7f-9f

SMARTY JONES	131
PLEASANTLY PERFECT	128
ROSES IN MAY	128
LUCKY STORY	127
NAYYIR	126
AZERI	124
PERFECT DRIFT	124
SOVIET SONG	124
WHIPPER	124

ATTRACTION	123
CHIC	123
FIREBREAK	123
LEROIDESANIMAUX	123
LION HEART	123
SIGHTSEEK	123
SINGLETARY	123
SNOW RIDGE	123

10f-12f

GHOSTZAPPER	133
DOYEN	131
BAGO	129
HAAFHD	129
RAKTI	129
CHERRY MIX	128
MEDAGLIA D'ORO	127
SULAMANI	127
AZAMOUR	126
GREY SWALLOW	126
KITTEN'S JOY	126
REFUSE TO BEND	126
WARRSAN	126
BIRDSTONE	125
KING KAMEHAMEHA	125
NORSE DANCER	125

NORTH LIGHT	125
BETTER TALK NOW	124
BULLISH LUCK	124
MISTER MONET	124
OUIJA BOARD	124
POWERSCOURT	124
ZENNO ROB ROY	124
ACROPOLIS	123
BANDARI	123
EGERTON	123
HARD BUCK	123
HEART'S CRY	123
KICKEN KRIS	123
ORIENTAL MAGIC	123
TOUCH OF LAND	123
TOTAL IMPACT	123

13f+

VINNIE ROE	126
MAKYBE DIVA	123

Owners names are shown against their horses
where this information is available. In the case of
Partnerships and Syndicates, the nominated owner
is given alongside the horse with other owners listed
below the team.

RACEFORM CHAMPIONS 2004
TWO-YEAR-OLDS

5f-6f

AD VALOREM	121
REBUTTAL	119
DIVINE PROPORTIONS	117
CENTIFOLIA	114
RUSSIAN BLUE	113
CAESAR BEWARE	112
SALUT THOMAS	112

7f+

SHAMARDAL	125
DUBAWI	122
PROUD ACCOLADE	120
WILKO	120
AFLEET ALEX	119
ORATORIO	119
SWEET CATOMINE	119
MONTGOMERY'S ARCH	118
MOTIVATOR	118
SUN KING	118
EARLY MARCH	117
ETLAALA	117
ICEMAN	117
LAYMAN	117
CONSOLIDATOR	115
LIBRETTIST	115
BERENSON	115
PLAYFUL ACT	113
CULINARY	112
FOOTSTEPSINTHESAND	112
HELIOS QUERCUS	112
MONA LISA	112
PERFECTPERFORMANCE	112
ROMAN RULER	112

RACEFORM FASTEST PERFORMERS THREE-YEAR-OLDS AND UP 2004

5f-6f Turf

BAHAMIAN PIRATE	117
OSTERHASE	117
VAR	117
FRIZZANTE	116
LOYAL TYCOON	116
TANTE ROSE	116
THE TATLING	116
ASHDOWN EXPRESS	115
AVONBRIDGE	115
CARIBBEAN CORAL	115
DOLMA	115
FANTASY BELIEVER	115
PTARMIGAN RIDGE	115
ROYAL MILLENNIUM	115
RUM SHOT	115
SILVER PRELUDE	115
STRIKING AMBITION	115

5f-6f AW

NO TIME	117
SPEED COP	116
JUSTALORD	115

7f-9f Turf

SOVIET SONG	121
ATTRACTION	120
RAKTI	120
AUTUMN GLORY	119
AZAMOUR	119
LUCKY STORY	119
PUTRA PEKAN	119
COURT MASTERPIECE	118
DIAMOND GREEN	118
MARTILLO	118
WHIPPER	118
ANTONIUS PIUS	117
DUCK ROW	117
NAYYIR	117
POLAR WAY	117
REFUSE TO BEND	117
SARRE	117
SIX PERFECTIONS	117
SOMNUS	117
UHOOMAGOO	116
ART MASTER	116
BLUE SPINNAKER	116
BRUNEL	116
CASTLETON	116
DENEBOLA	116
EL COTO	116
ETTRICK WATER	116
FIREBREAK	116
GATEMAN	116
MAXWELL	116
MINE	116
MONSIEUR BOND	116
ACE	115
ALMOND MOUSSE	115
BAQAH	115
BYRON	115
CHRISTAVELLI	115
HURRICANE ALAN	115
KHELEYF	115
KING'S DRAMA	115
KRATAIOS	115
LE VIE DEI COLORI	115
MAJESTIC DESERT	115
MY RISK	115
NEW SEEKER	115
PHANTOM WIND	115
RED BLOOM	115
RUSSIAN RHYTHM	115
SHOT TO FAME	115
TOLPUDDLE	115
TORRESTRELLA	115

7f-9f AW

VORTEX	115

10f-12f Turf

13f+ turf

RACEFORM FASTEST PERFORMERS TWO-YEAR-OLDS OF 2004

5f-6f Turf

5f-6f AW

7f+ Turf

MEDIAN TIMES 2004

The following Raceform median times are used in the calculation of the Split Second speed figures. They represent a true average time for the distance, which has been arrived at after looking at the winning times for all races over each distance within the past five years, except for those restricted to two or three-year-olds.

Some current race distances have been omitted as they have not yet had a sufficient number of races run over them to produce a reliable average time.

ASCOT

5f	1m 01.93	1m Straight	1m 41.92	2m 4f	4m 24.53
6f	1m 15.99	1m 2f	2m 08.73	2m 6f 34yds	4m 56.57
7f	1m 29.67	1m 4f	2m 33.56		
1m Round	1m 43.04	2m 45yds	3m 34.84		

AYR

5f	1m 00.43	1m	1m 43.12	1m 5f 13yds	2m 55.85
6f	1m 13.72	1m 1f 20yds	1m 54.21	1m 7f	3m 22.47
7f	1m 29.38	1m 2f	2m 12.19	2m 1f 105yds	3m 54.77
7f 50yds	1m 32.47	1m 2f 192yds	2m 23.32		

BATH

5f 11yds	1m 02.50	1m 2f 46yds	2m 11.00	1m 5f 22yds	2m 51.30
5f 161yds	1m 11.14	1m 3f 144yds	2m 30.30	2m 1f 34yds	3m 49.60
1m 5yds	1m 41.00				

BEVERLEY

5f	1m 04.00	1m 100yds	1m 47.30	1m 4f 16yds	2m 39.30
7f 100yds	1m 34.30	1m 1f 207yds	2m 07.20	2m 35yds	3m 39.40

BRIGHTON

5f 59yds	1m 02.27	6f 209yds	1m 22.60	1m 1f 209yds	2m 2.54
5f 213yds	1m 10.10	7f 214yds	1m 35.00	1m 3f 196yds	2m 32.10

CARLISLE

5f	1m 1.50	7f 200yds	1m 40.00	1m 6f 32yds	3m 7.30
5f 193yds	1m 14.20	1m 1f 61yds	1m 58.03	2m 1f 52yds	3m 49.90
6f 192yds	1m 27.10	1m 3f 206yds	2m 32.40		

CATTERICK

5f	1m 00.60	7f	1m 27.50	1m 4f 44yds	2m 39.70
5f 212yds	1m 14.00	1m 3f 214yds	2m 39.00	1m 5f 175yds	3m 04.50
				1m 7f 177yds	3m 31.40

CHEPSTOW

5f 16yds	59.50	1m 14yds	1m 35.90	2m 49yds	3m 39.10
6f 16yds	1m 12.20	1m 2f 36yds	2m 9.60	2m 2f	4m 0.20
7f 16yds	1m 23.20	1m 4f 23yds	2m 38.50		

CHESTER

5f 16yds	1m 01.98	1m 2f 75yds	2m 12.55	1m 7f 195yds	3m 33.78
6f 18yds	1m 15.88	1m 3f 79yds	2m 25.49	2m 2f 147yds	4m 05.38
7f 2yds	1m 28.29	1m 4f 66yds	2m 40.52		
7f 122yds	1m 34.75	1m 5f 89yds	2m 55.39		

DONCASTER

5f	1m 01.42	7f	1m 27.81	1m 4f	2m 35.70
5f 140yds	1m 08.09	1m Round	1m 40.55	1m 6f 132yds	3m 09.74
6f	1m 14.28	1m Straight	1m 41.60	2m 110yds	3m 41.96
6f 110yds	1m 20.48	2f 60yds	2m 11.76	2m 2f	3m 57.93

EPSOM

5f	55.68	7f	1m 23.95	1m 2f 18yds	2m 8.70
6f	1m 10.63	1m 114yds	1m 45.74	1m 4f 10yds	2m 38.72

FOLKESTONE

5f	1m 00.70	7f	1m 27.80	1m 7f 92yds	3m 27.20
6f	1m 13.60	1m 1f 149yds	2m 5.16	2m 93yds	3m 40.60
6f 189yds Round	1m 25.70	1m 4f	2m 40.40		

GOODWOOD

5f	59.05	1m1f	1m 56.86	2m	3m 30.66
6f	1m 12.84	1m 1f 192yds	2m 07.68	2m 4f	4m 20.89
7f	1m 28.03	1m 4f	2m 38.93		
1m	1m 40.27	1m 6f	3m 03.75		

HAMILTON

5f 4yds	1m 01.26	1m 1f 36yds	1m 59.60	1m 4f 17yds	2m 39.20
6f 5yds	1m 13.10	1m 3f 16yds	2m 26.50	1m 5f 9yds	2m 53.40
1m 65yds	1m 49.30				

HAYDOCK

5f	1m 02.07	1m 30yds	1m 45.55	1m 6f	3m 06.15
6f	1m 14.89	1m 2f 120yds	2m 17.73	2m 45yds	3m 37.90
7f 30yds	1m 32.16	1m 3f 200yds	2m 35.16		

KEMPTON

5f	1m 01.21	1m Jubilee	1m 40.47	1m 3f 30yds	2m 23.05
6f	1m 13.07	1m	1m 39.62	1m 4f	2m 35.00
7f Jubilee	1m 27.27	1m 1f	1m 54.33	1m 6f 92yds	3m 10.66
7f	1m 26.61	1m 2f Jubilee	2m 06.14	2m	3m 30.36

LEICESTER

5f 2yds	1m 00.93	7f 9yds	1m 26.10	1m 1f 218yds	2m 08.40
5f 218yds	1m 13.40	1m 9yds	1m 42.60	1m 3f 183yds	2m 34.68

LINGFIELD (TURF)

5f	58.87	7f 140yds	1m 31.46	1m 3f 106yds	2m 29.52
6f	1m 11.65	1m 1f	1m 55.29	1m 6f	3m 06.92
7f	1m 24.21	1m 2f	2m 09.60	2m	3m 33.19

LINGFIELD (AW)

5f	59.78	1m	1m 39.55	1m 5f	2m 48.08
6f	1m 12.92	1m 2f	2m 07.58	2m	3m 28.58
7f	1m 25.94	1m 4f	2m 34.08		

MUSSELBURGH

5f	1m 00.40	1m 1f	1m 53.20	1m 6f	3m 05.60
7f 30yds	1m 29.53	1m 4f	2m 38.02	2m	3m 33.70
1m	1m 42.70				

NEWBURY

5f 34yds.......................... 1m 02.65	1m Straight........................ 1m 40.83	1m 3f 5yds.......................... 2m 22.81
6f 8yds............................ 1m 14.37	1m 7yds Round 1m 38.73	1m 4f 5yds.......................... 2m 36.29
7f.................................... 1m 27.22	1m 1f.............................. 1m 54.35	1m 5f 61yds........................ 2m 50.99
7f 64yds Round................ 1m 31.26	1m 2f 6yds........................ 2m 08.71	2m.................................... 3m 35.43

NEWCASTLE

5f.................................... 1m 01.53	1m Round........................ 1m 43.48	1m 2f 32yds........................ 2m 11.60
6f.................................... 1m 15.04	1m 3yds.......................... 1m 41.20	1m 4f 93yds........................ 2m 43.30
7f.................................... 1m 28.02	1m 1f 9yds...................... 1m 57.80	2m 19yds.......................... 3m 35.03

NEWMARKET (ROWLEY)

5f.................................... 1m 00.41	1m.................................. 1m 39.40	1m 4f.................................. 2m 33.46
6f.................................... 1m 13.09	1m 1f.............................. 1m 51.91	1m 6f.................................. 3m 00.32
7f.................................... 1m 26.47	1m 2f.............................. 2m 05.69	2m.................................... 3m 26.52
		2m 2f.................................. 3m 52.62

NEWMARKET (JULY)

5f..59.65	1m.................................. 1m 40.48	1m 6f 175yds...................... 3m 10.76
6f.................................... 1m 13.32	1m 2f.............................. 2m 06.46	2m 24yds.......................... 3m 26.99
7f.................................... 1m 26.77	1m 4f.............................. 2m 32.96	

NOTTINGHAM

5f 13yds.......................... 1m 01.80	1m 54yds........................ 1m 46.40	1m 6f 15yds........................ 3m 07.20
6f 15yds.......................... 1m 14.80	1m 1f 213yds.................. 2m 09.50	2m 9yds............................ 3m 33.50

PONTEFRACT

5f.................................... 1m 03.80	1m 2f 6yds........................ 2m 13.91	1m 7f 216yds...................... 4m 03.00
6f.................................... 1m 17.40	1m 4f 8yds........................ 2m 40.05	2m 5f 122yds...................... 4m 57.60
1m 4yds.......................... 1m 45.60	2m 1f 22yds.................... 3m 50.50	

REDCAR

5f..58.70	1m 1f.............................. 1m 53.40	1m 6f 19yds........................ 3m 05.00
6f.................................... 1m 11.70	1m 2f.............................. 2m 06.80	2m.................................... 3m 31.50
7f.................................... 1m 24.90	1m 3f.............................. 2m 21.00	
1m.................................. 1m 37.70		

RIPON

5f.................................... 1m 00.20	1m 1f.............................. 1m 53.85	1m 4f 60yds........................ 2m 39.90
6f.................................... 1m 12.90	1m 2f.............................. 2m 08.00	2m.................................... 3m 33.50
1m.................................. 1m 41.10		

SALISBURY

5f.................................... 1m 01.57	1m.................................. 1m 42.97	1m 4f.................................. 2m 36.35
6f.................................... 1m 14.94	1m 1f 198yds.................. 2m 08.32	1m 6f 15yds........................ 3m 06.00
6f 212yds........................ 1m 29.00		

SANDOWN

5f 6yds............................ 1m 02.22	1m1f................................1m 56.11	1m 6f.................................. 3m 04.37
7f 16yds.......................... 1m 31.09	1m 2f 7yds........................ 2m 10.18	2m 78yds.......................... 3m 38.23.
1m 14yds........................ 1m 43.92	1m 3f 91yds...................... 2m 28.07	

SOUTHWELL (TURF)

6f.................................... 1m 15.80	1m 2f.............................. 2m 13.90	2m.................................... 3m 37.20
7f.................................... 1m 29.20	1m 4f.............................. 2m 40.30	

SOUTHWELL (AW)

5f	1m 00.40	1m	1m 44.60	1m 6f	3m 09.70
6f	1m 16.90	1m 3f	2m 28.90	2m	3m 52.40
7f	1m 30.80	1m 4f	2m 42.10		

THIRSK

5f	59.90	7f	1m 27.10	1m 4f	2m 35.20
6f	1m 12.50	1m	1m 39.70	2m	3m 31.20

WARWICK

5f	1m 00.20	1m 22yds	1m 39.30	1m 4f 134yds	2m 43.30
6f 21yds	1m 12.30	1m 2f 188yds	2m 19.40	2m 39yds	3m 31.80
7f 26yds	1m 24.90				

WINDSOR

5f 10yds	1m 01.20	1m 67yds	1m 45.60	1m 3f 135yds	2m 30.10
6f	1m 13.84	1m 2f 7yds	2m 08.30		

WOLVERHAMPTON (AW)

5f 20yds	1m 02.77	1m 141yds	1m 51.78	1m 5f 194yds	3m 07.85
5f 216yds	1m 15.74	1m 1f 103yds	2m 02.57	2m 119yds	3m 41.80
7f 32yds	1m 30.54	1m 4f 50yds	2m 42.88		

YARMOUTH

5f 43yds	1m 02.70	1m 3yds	1m 39.70	1m 6f 17yds	3m 05.20
6f 3yds	1m 13.60	1m 2f 21yds	2m 07.97	2m	3m 33.00
7f 3yds	1m 26.50	1m 3f 101yds	2m 27.40	2m 2f 51yds	4m 06.90

YORK

5f 3yds	58.74	7f 205yds	1m 37.74	1m 3f 198yds	2m 28.86
6f 3yds	1m 11.07	1m 208yds	1m 49.96	1m 5f 197yds	2m 56.40
6f 217yds	1m 23.31	1m 2f 88yds	2m 09.44	1m 7f 198yds	3m 23.25

If an entry is incorrect or has been omitted, please notify the editor by January 3rd, 2006.

This will ensure it appears correctly in the 2006 edition.

RACEFORM RECORD TIMES (FLAT)

ASCOT

DISTANCE	TIME	AGE	WEIGHT	GOING	HORSE	DATE		
5f	59.7 secs	2	8-8	Good To Firm	LYRIC FANTASY	Jun	17	1992
5f	59.1 secs	3	8-8	Firm	ORIENT	Jun	21	1986
6f	1m 13.6	2	8-12	Good To Firm	THREE VALLEYS	Jun	17	2003
6f	1m 12.1	4	9-6	Firm	FAYR JAG	Jun	21	2003
6f	1m 12.1	5	9-3	Firm	RATIO	Jun	21	2003
7f	1m 27.2	2	8-11	Good To Firm	CELTIC SWING	Oct	8	1994
7f	1m 25.8	4	8-2	Good To Firm	MASTER ROBBIE	Sep	27	2003
1m (Rnd)	1m 40.8	2	8-10	Good To Firm	RED BLOOM	Sep	27	2003
1m (Str)	1m 38.0	4	7-8	Good To Firm	COLOUR SERGEANT	Jun	17	1992
1m (Rnd)	1m 38.5	3	9-0	Good To Firm	RUSSIAN RHYTHM	Jun	20	2003
1m 2f	2m 02.7	4	9-3	Good To Firm	FIRST ISLAND	Jun	18	1996
1m 4f	2m 26.5	4	8-9	Firm	DOYEN	Jun	19	2004
2m 45y	3m 25.2	3	8-11	Good To Firm	LANDOWNER	Jun	17	1992
2m 4f	4m 15.3	5	9-0	Good To Firm	ROYAL GAIT (DISQ)	Jun	16	1988
2m 6f 34y	4m 47.8	5	8-9	Firm	COVER UP	Jun	23	2003

AYR

DISTANCE	TIME	AGE	WEIGHT	GOING	HORSE	DATE		
5f	56.9 secs	2	8-11	Good	BOOGIE STREET	Sep	18	2003
5f	57.2 secs	4	9-5	Good To Firm	SIR JOEY	Sep	16	1993
6f	1m 09.7	2	7-10	Good To Firm	SIR BERT	Sep	17	1969
6f	1m 08.9	7	8-8	Good To Firm	SOBERING THOUGHTS	Sep	18	1993
7f 50y	1m 28.9	2	9-0	Good	TAFAAHUM	Sep	19	2003
7f 50y	1m 28.2	4	9-2	Good To Firm	FLU NA H ALBA	Jun	21	2003
1m	1m 39.2	2	9-0	Good To Firm	KRIBENSIS	Sep	17	1986
1m	1m 36.0	4	7-13	Firm	SUFI	Sep	16	1959
1m 1f 20y	1m 50.3	4	9-3	Good	RETIREMENT	Sep	19	2003
1m 2f	2m 04.0	4	9-9	Good To Firm	ENDLESS HALL	July	17	2000
1m 2f 192y	2m 13.3	4	9-0	Good To Firm	AZZAAM	Sep	18	1991
1m 5f 13y	2m 45.8	4	9-7	Good To Firm	EDEN'S CLOSE	Sep	18	1993
1m 7f	3m 13.1	3	9-4	Good	ROMANY RYE	Sep	19	1991
2m 1f 105y	3m 45.0	4	6-13	Good	CURRY	Sep	16	1955

BATH

DISTANCE	TIME	AGE	WEIGHT	GOING	HORSE	DATE		
5f 11y	1m 00.1	2	8-11	Firm	DOUBLE FANTASY	Aug	25	2000
5f 11y	59.9 secs	6	9-2	Firm	CAUDA EQUINA	Aug	25	2000
5f 161y	1m 09.1	2	8-7	Firm	SIBLA	Aug	25	2000
5f 161y	1m 08.1	6	9-0	Firm	MADRACO	May	22	1989
1m 5y	1m 40.3	2	8-12	Good To Firm	KHASSAH	Sep	9	1999
1m 5y	1m 37.2	5	8-12	Good To Firm	ADOBE	Jun	17	2000
1m 2f 46y	2m 05.6	2	9-0	Good To Firm	CONNOISSEUR BAY	May	29	1998
1m 3f 144y	2m 26.1	3	8-12	Firm	ANTICIPATE	Sep	10	2001
1m 5f 22y	2m 47.2	4	10-0	Firm	FLOWN	Aug	13	1991
2m 1f 34y	3m 43.4	6	7-9	Firm	YAHESKA	Jun	14	2003

BEVERLEY

DISTANCE	TIME	AGE	WEIGHT	GOING	HORSE	DATE		
5f	1m 01.0	2	8-2	Good To Firm	ADDO	July	17	2001
5f	1m 00.1	4	9-5	Firm	PIC UP STICKS	Apr	16	2003
7f 100y	1m 31.1	2	9-0	Firm	MAJAL	July	30	1991
7f 100y	1m 29.5	3	7-8	Firm	WHO'S TEF	July	30	1991
1m 100y	1m 43.3	2	9-0	Firm	ARDEN	Sep	24	1986
1m 100y	1m 42.2	3	8-4	Firm	LEGAL CASE	Jun	14	1989
1m 1f 207y	2m 01.3	3	9-7	Firm	ROSE ALTO	July	5	1991
1m 3f 216y	2m 30.8	3	8-1	Hard	COINAGE	Jun	18	1986
2m 35y	3m 29.5	4	9-2	Good To Firm	RUSHEN RAIDER	Aug	14	1996

BRIGHTON

DISTANCE	TIME	AGE	WEIGHT	GOING	HORSE	DATE		
5f 59y	1m.00.1	2	9-0	Firm	BID FOR BLUE	May	6	1993
5f 59y	59.3 secs	3	8-9	Firm	PLAY HEVER GOLF	May	26	1993
5f 213y	1m 08.1	2	8-9	Firm	SONG MIST	July	16	1996
5f 213y	1m 07.3	3	8-9	Firm	THIRD PARTY	Jun	3	1997
5f 213y	1m 07.3	5	9-1	Good To Firm	BLUNDELL LANE	May	4	2000
6f 209y	1m 19.9	2	8-11	Hard	RAIN BURST	Sep	15	1988
6f 209y	1m 19.4	4	9-3	Good To Firm	SAWAKI	Sep	3	1991
7f 214y	1m 32.8	2	9-7	Firm	ASIAN PETE	Oct	3	1989
7f 214y	1m 30.5	5	8-11	Firm	MYSTIC RIDGE	May	27	1999
1m 1f 209y	2m 04.7	2	9-0	Good To Soft	ESTEEMED MASTER	Nov	2	2001
1m 1f 209y	1m 57.2	3	9-0	Firm	GET THE MESSAGE	Apr	30	1984
1m 3f 196y	2m 25.8	4	8-2	Firm	NEW ZEALAND	July	4	1985

CARLISLE

DISTANCE	TIME	AGE	WEIGHT	GOING	HORSE	DATE		
5f	1m 00.1	2	8-5	Firm	LA TORTUGA	Aug	2	1999
5f	59.3 secs	5	8-12	Firm	FRIAR TUCK	July	21	2000
5f 207y	1m 12.8	2	8-9	Hard	PARFAIT ARMOUR	Sep	10	1991
5f 193y	1m 11.7	5	8-6	Good To Firm	CHAIRMAN BOBBY	Jun	15	2003
6f 206y	1m 26.5	2	9-4	Hard	SENSE OF PRIORITY	Sep	10	1991
6f 206y	1m 25.3	4	9-1	Firm	MOVE WITH EDES	July	6	1996
7f 214y	1m 44.6	2	8-8	Firm	BLUE GARTER	Sep	9	1980
7f 214y	1m 37.4	4	9-8	Good To Firm	GIFTED FLAME	Jun	15	2003
1m 1f 61y	1m 53.8	3	9-0	Firm	LITTLE JIMBOB	Jun	14	2004
1m 3f 206y	2m 29.4	8	8-13	Firm	SILVERTOWN	Jun	26	2003
1m 6f 32y	3m 02.2	6	8-10	Firm	EXPLOSIVE SPEED	May	26	1994

CATTERICK

DISTANCE	TIME	AGE	WEIGHT	GOING	HORSE	DATE		
5f	57.7 secs	2	9-0	Good To Firm	VERDE ALITALIA	Sep	21	1991
5f	57.1 secs	4	8-7	Firm	KABCAST	July	6	1989
5f 212y	1m 11.4	2	9-4	Good To Firm	CAPTAIN NICK	July	11	1978
5f 212y	1m 09.8	9	8-13	Good To Firm	SHARP HAT	May	30	2003
5f 212y	1m 10.4	3	8-8	Firm	TRIAD TREBLE	May	31	1984
7f	1m 24.1	2	8-11	Firm	LINDAS FANTASY	Sep	18	1982
7f	1m 22.5	6	8-7	Firm	DIFFERENTIAL	May	31	2003
1m 3f 214y	2m 30.5	3	8-8	Good To Firm	RAHAF	May	30	2003
1m 5f 175y	2m 54.8	3	8-5	Firm	GERYON	May	31	1984
1m 7f 177y	3m 20.8	4	7-11	Firm	BEAN BOY	July	8	1982

CHEPSTOW

DISTANCE	TIME	AGE	WEIGHT	GOING	HORSE	DATE		
5f 16y	57.6 secs	2	8-11	Firm	**MICRO LOVE**	July	8	1986
5f 16y	56.8 secs	3	8-4	Firm	**TORBAY EXPRESS**	Sep	15	1979
6f 16y	1m 09.4	2	9-0	Good To Firm	**ROYAL FIFI**	Sep	9	1989
6f 16y	1m 08.8	4	8-6	Good To Firm	**AFRICAN REX**	May	12	1987
7f 16y	1m 20.8	2	9-0	Good To Firm	**ROYAL AMARETTO**	Sep	12	1996
7f 16y	1m 19.3	3	9-0	Firm	**TARANAKI**	Sep	18	2001
1m 14y	1m 33.1	2	8-11	Good To Firm	**SKI ACADEMY**	Aug	28	1995
1m 14y	1m 31.6	3	8-13	Firm	**STOLI**	Sep	18	2001
1m 2f 36y	2m 04.1	5	8-9	Hard	**LEONIDAS**	July	5	1983
1m 2f 36y	2m 04.1	5	7-8	Good To Firm	**IT'S VARADAN**	Sep	9	1989
1m 2f 36y	2m 04.1	3	8-5	Good To Firm	**ELA ATHENA**	July	23	1999
1m 4f 23y	2m 31.0	3	8-9	Good To Firm	**SPRITSAIL**	July	13	1989
1m 4f 23y	2m 31.0	7	9-6	Hard	**MAINTOP**	Aug	27	1984
2m 49y	3m 27.7	4	9-0	Good To Firm	**WIZZARD ARTIST**	July	1	1989
2m 2f	3m 56.4	5	8-7	Good To Firm	**LAFFAH**	July	8	2000

CHESTER

DISTANCE	TIME	AGE	WEIGHT	GOING	HORSE	DATE		
5f 16y	1m 00.2	2	9-0	Good To Firm	**MAJESTIC MISSILE**	July	11	2003
5f 16y	59.2 secs	3	10-0	Firm	**ALTHREY DON**	July	10	1964
6f 18y	1m 13.2	2	8-11	Good To Firm	**ACE OF PARKES**	July	11	1998
6f 18y	1m 12.7	3	8-3	Good To Firm	**PLAY HEVER GOLF**	May	4	1993
6f 18y	1m 12.7	6	9-2	Good	**STACK ROCK**	Jun	23	1993
7f 2y	1m 26.2	2	8-4	Good To Firm	**BY HAND**	Aug	31	1991
7f 2y	1m 24.5	3	8-11	Good To Firm	**MONNAVANNA**	May	9	2001
7f 122y	1m 35.0	2	9-0	Firm	**DOUBLE VALUE**	Sep	1	1972
7f 122y	1m 31.5	3	8-12	Good To Firm	**STEAL 'EM**	July	12	1996
1m 2f 75y	2m 7.9	3	8-10	Good To Firm	**BENEFICIAL**	May	6	1993
1m 3f 79y	2m 22.5	3	8-9	Good To Firm	**ROCKERLONG**	May	9	2001
1m 4f 66y	2m 34.2	3	8-11	Good To Firm	**OLD VIC**	May	9	1989
1m 5f 89y	2m 45.4	5	8-11	Firm	**RAKAPOSHI KING**	May	7	1987
1m 7f 195y	3m 24.5	7	7-11	Good To Firm	**MOONLIGHT QUEST**	July	30	1995
2m 2f 147y	4m 00.6	4	9-0	Good To Firm	**RAINBOW HIGH**	May	5	1999

DONCASTER

DISTANCE	TIME	AGE	WEIGHT	GOING	HORSE	DATE		
5f	58.4 secs	2	9-5	Firm	**SING SING**	Sep	11	1959
5f	57.2 secs	6	9-12	Good To Firm	**CELTIC MILL**	Sep	9	2004
5f 140y	1m 07.2	2	9-0	Good To Firm	**CARTOGRAPHY**	Jun	29	2003
5f 140y	1m 05.6	9	9-10	Good	**HALMAHERA**	Sep	8	2004
6f	1m 09.6	2	8-11	Good	**CAESAR BEWARE**	Sep	8	2004
6f	1m 09.7	3	8-9	Good To Firm	**ILTIMAS**	July	26	1995
6f 110y	1m 17.9	2	8-13	Good To Firm	**SWAN NEBULA**	Sep	8	2004
7f	1m 22.6	2	9-1	Good To Firm	**LIBRETTIST**	Sep	8	2004
7f	1m 21.6	3	9-4	Good To Firm	**PASTORAL PURSUITS**	Sep	9	2004
1m Str	1m 36.5	2	8-6	Good To Firm	**SINGHALESE**	Sep	9	2004
1m Rnd	1m 35.4	2	9-0	Good To Firm	**PLAYFUL ACT**	Sep	9	2004
1m Str	1m 36.6	7	9-9	Good To Firm	**INVADER**	Jun	29	2003
1m Rnd	1m 36.7	3	8-10	Good To Firm	**MUSHAHID**	July	17	1996
1m 2f 60y	2m 13.4	2	8-8	Good	**YARD BIRD**	Nov	6	1981
1m 2f 60y	2m 05.4	3	8-8	Good To Firm	**CARLITO BRIGANTE**	July	26	1995
1m 4f	2m 27.7	3	8-12	Good To Firm	**TAKWIN**	Sep	9	2000
1m 6f 132y	3m 02.2	3	8-3	Good To Firm	**BRIER CREEK**	Sep	10	1992
2m 110y	3m 34.4	4	9-12	Good To Firm	**FARSI**	Jun	12	1992
2m 2f	3m 52.1	4	9-0	Good To Firm	**CANON CAN**	Sep	11	1997

EPSOM

DISTANCE	TIME	AGE	WEIGHT	GOING	HORSE	DATE		
5f	55.0 secs	2	8-9	Good To Firm	**PRINCE ASLIA**	Jun	9	1995
5f	53.6 secs	4	9-5	Firm	**INDIGENOUS**	Jun	2	1960
6f	1m 07.8	2	8-11	Good To Firm	**SHOWBROOK**	Jun	5	1991
6f	1m 07.3	5	8-12	Good	**LOYAL TYCOON**	Jun	7	2003
7f	1m 21.3	2	8-9	Good To Firm	**RED PEONY**	July	29	2004
7f	1m 20.1	4	8-7	Firm	**CAPISTRANO**	Jun	7	1972
1m 114y	1m 42.8	2	8-5	Good To Firm	**NIGHTSTALKER**	Aug	30	1988
1m 114y	1m 40.7	3	8-6	Good To Firm	**SYLVA HONDA**	Jun	5	1991
1m 2f 18y	2m 03.5	5	7-13	Good	**CROSSBOW**	Jun	7	1967
1m 4f 10y	2m 32.3	3	9-0	Good To Firm	**LAMMTARRA**	Jun	10	1995

FOLKESTONE

DISTANCE	TIME	AGE	WEIGHT	GOING	HORSE	DATE		
5f	58.4 secs	2	9-2	Good To Firm	**PIVOTAL**	Nov	6	1995
5f	58.65 secs	3	9-0	Good To Firm	**ZARZU**	Jun	28	2002
6f	1m 10.8	2	8-9	Good	**BOOMERANG BLADE**	July	16	1998
6f	1m 09.5	4	8-12	Good To Firm	**DOUBLE OSCAR**	July	14	1997
6f 189y	1m 23.7	2	8-11	Good	**HEN HARRIER**	July	3	1996
6f 189y	1m 22.0	4	10-0	Firm	**NEUWEST**	Jun	28	1996
7f	1m 21.4	3	8-9	Firm	**CIELAMOUR**	Aug	9	1988
1m 1f 149y	1m 59.7	3	8-6	Good To Firm	**DIZZY**	July	23	1991
1m 4f	2m 33.2	4	8-8	Hard	**SNOW BLIZZARD**	Jun	30	1992
1m 7f 92y	3m 23.1	3	9-11	Firm	**MATA ASKARI**	Sep	12	1991
2m 93y	3m 34.9	3	8-12	Good To Firm	**CANDLE SMOKE**	Aug	20	1996

GOODWOOD

DISTANCE	TIME	AGE	WEIGHT	GOING	HORSE	DATE		
5f	57.5 secs	2	8-12	Good To Firm	**POETS COVE**	Aug	3	1990
5f	56.0 secs	5	9-0	Good To Firm	**RUDI'S PET**	July	27	1999
6f	1m 09.8	2	8-11	Good To Firm	**BACHIR**	July	28	1999
6f	1m 09.5	4	8-3	Firm	**FOR THE PRESENT**	July	30	1994
7f	1m 24.9	2	8-11	Good To Firm	**EKRAAR**	July	29	1999
7f	1m 23.8	3	8-7	Firm	**BRIEF GLIMPSE**	July	25	1995
1m	1m 38.5	2	8-11	Good To Firm	**SELKIRK**	Sep	14	1990
1m	1m 35.6	3	8-13	Good To Firm	**ALJABR**	July	28	1999
1m 1f	1m 52.8	3	9-6	Good	**VENA**	July	27	1995
1m 1f 192y	2m 04.5	3	8-9	Firm	**AZOUZ PASHA**	July	30	1999
1m 2f	2m 04.9	3	8-6	Firm	**KARTAJANA**	Aug	4	1990
1m 3f	2m 23.0	3	8-8	Good To Firm	**ASIAN HEIGHTS**	May	22	2001
1m 4f	2m 31.5	3	8-10	Firm	**PRESENTING**	July	25	1995
1m 6f	2m 58.5	4	9-2	Good To Firm	**MOWBRAY**	July	27	1999
2m	3m 21.63	5	9-2	Good To Firm	**JARDINES LOOKOUT**	Aug	1	2002
2m 4f	4m 11.7	3	7-10	Firm	**LUCKY MOON**	Sep	2	1990

HAMILTON

DISTANCE	TIME	AGE	WEIGHT	GOING	HORSE	DATE		
5f 4y	58.0 secs	3	7-8	Firm	**FAIR DANDY**	Sep	25	1972
5f 4y	58.0 secs	5	8-6	Firm	**GOLDEN SLEIGH**	Sep	6	1972
6f 5y	1m 10.0	2	8-12	Good To Firm	**BREAK THE CODE**	Aug	24	1999
6f 5y	1m 09.3	4	8-7	Firm	**MARCUS GAME**	July	11	1974
1m 65y	1m 45.8	2	8-11	Firm	**HOPEFUL SUBJECT**	Sep	24	1973
1m 65y	1m 42.7	6	7-7	Firm	**CRANLEY**	Sep	25	1972
1m 1f 36y	1m 54.1	3	9-4	Good To Firm	**JEDI KNIGHT**	Aug	24	1999
1m 3f 16y	2m 20.7	8	9-9	Firm	**DESERT FIGHTER**	July	9	1999
1m 3f 16y	2m 20.7	5	9-8	Good To Firm	**WADI**	July	20	2000
1m 4f 17y	2m 32.0	4	7-4	Firm	**FINE POINT**	Aug	24	1981
1m 5f 9y	2m 45.1	6	9-6	Firm	**MENTALASANYTHIN**	Jun	14	1995

HAYDOCK

DISTANCE	TIME	AGE	WEIGHT	GOING	HORSE	DATE		
5f	59.2 secs	2	9-4	Firm	MONEY FOR NOTHING	Aug	21	1964
5f	58.5 secs	6	8-9	Good To Firm	WHISTLER	Aug	9	2003
6f	1m 09.9	4	9-0	Good To Firm	IKTAMAL	Sep	7	1996
7f 30y	1m 29.4	2	9-0	Good To Firm	APPREHENSION	Sep	7	1996
7f 30y	1m 27.2	4	9-4	Firm	INDIAN KING	Jun	5	1982
1m 30y	1m 40.6	2	8-12	Good To Firm	BESIEGE	Sep	7	1996
1m 30y	1m 40.1	3	9-2	Firm	UNTOLD RICHES	July	11	1999
1m 2f 120y	2m 08.5	3	8-7	Good To Firm	FAHAL	Aug	5	1995
1m 3f 200y	2m 26.4	5	8-2	Firm	NEW MEMBER	July	4	1970
1m 6f	2m 59.5	3	8-3	Good To Firm	CASTLE SECRET	Sep	30	1989
2m 45y	3m 27.0	4	8-13	Firm	PRINCE OF PEACE	May	26	1984
2m 1f 130y	3m 55.0	3	8-12	Good	CRYSTAL SPIRIT	Sep	8	1990

KEMPTON

DISTANCE	TIME	AGE	WEIGHT	GOING	HORSE	DATE		
5f	58.3 secs	2	9-0	Firm	SCHWEPPESHIRE LAD	Jun	3	1978
5f	57.4 secs	4	9-3	Good To Firm	ALMATY	May	31	1997
6f	1m 10.6	2	8-10	Good To Firm	DON PUCCINI	May	29	1999
6f	1m 09.5	3	8-11	Good To Firm	INDIAN TRAIL	Jun	25	2003
7f	1m 26.7	2	8-8	Good	EXCLUSIVE	Sep	10	1997
7f	1m 24.7	2	9-0	Good To Firm	CANONS PARK	Jun	28	1995
7f	1m 23.5	3	9-2	Good To Firm	WILD RICE	Aug	2	1995
7f	1m 23.6	3	9-0	Good To Firm	SHAHEEN	May	31	1997
1m	1m 43.4	2	7-0	Good	FASCINATING	Nov	5	1956
1m	1m 38.7	2	9-0	Good To Firm	TAVERNER SOCIETY	Sep	22	1997
1m	1m 35.8	4	9-1	Firm	COUNTY BROKER	May	23	1984
1m	1m 35.3	3	8-12	Good To Firm	PRIVATE LINE	Jun	28	1995
1m 1f	1m 50.0	4	9-11	Good To Firm	BAHRQUEEN	Jun	25	2003
1m 2f	1m 59.5	4	9-6	Firm	BATSHOOF	Apr	6	1990
1m 3f 30y	2m 16.2	4	9-2	Firm	SHERNAZAR	Sep	6	1985
1m 4f	2m 30.1	6	8-5	Firm	GOING GOING	Sep	7	1985
1m 6f 92y	3m 06.5	4	9-8	Good To Firm	RENZO	Sep	21	1997
2m	3m 24.3	4	8-9	Good To Firm	EMINENCE GRISE	May	29	1999

LEICESTER

DISTANCE	TIME	AGE	WEIGHT	GOING	HORSE	DATE		
5f 2y	58.4 secs	2	9-0	Firm	CUTTING BLADE	Jun	9	1986
5f 2y	58.0 secs	3	7-13	Good To Firm	EMERALD PEACE	Sep	5	2000
5f 218y	1m 10.1	2	9-0	Firm	THORDIS	Oct	24	1995
5f 218y	1m 09.4	3	8-12	Good To Firm	LAKELAND BEAUTY	May	29	1990
7f 9y	1m 22.8	2	8-6	Good	MISS DRAGONFLY	Sep	22	1997
7f 9y	1m 20.8	3	8-7	Firm	FLOWER BOWL	Jun	9	1986
1m 8y	1m 34.5	2	8-9	Firm	LADY CARLA	Oct	24	1995
1m 8y	1m 33.6	5	7-13	Good To Firm	DERRYQUINN	Aug	13	2000
1m 9y	1m 39.2	4	8-11	Firm	NASHAAB	May	28	2001
1m 1f 218y	2m 05.3	2	9-1	Good To Firm	WINDSOR CASTLE	Oct	14	1996
1m 1f 218y	2m 02.4	3	8-11	Firm	EFFIGY	Nov	4	1985
1m 1f 218y	2m 02.4	4	9-6	Good To Firm	LADY ANGHARAD	Jun	18	2000
1m 3f 183y	2m 27.1	5	8-12	Good To Firm	MURGHEM	Jun	18	2000

LINGFIELD (TURF)

DISTANCE	TIME	AGE	WEIGHT	GOING	HORSE	DATE		
5f	57.1 secs	2	8-9	Good	EMERALD PEACE	Aug	6	1999
5f	56.2 secs	3	9-1	Good To Firm	EVENINGPERFORMANCE	July	25	1994
6f	1m 08.6	2	9-3	Firm	THE RITZ	Jun	11	1965
6f	1m 08.2	6	9-10	Firm	AL AMEAD	July	2	1986
7f	1m 21.3	2	7-6	Firm	MANDAV	Oct	3	1980
7f	1m 20.1	3	8-7	Good To Firm	ZELAH	May	13	1998
7f 140y	1m 29.9	2	8-12	Firm	RATHER WARM	Nov	7	1978
7f 140y	1m 26.7	3	8-6	Good To Firm	HIAAM	July	11	1987
1m 1f	1m 52.4	4	9-2	Good To Firm	QUANDARY	July	15	1995
1m 2f	2m 04.6	3	9-3	Firm	USRAN	July	15	1989
1m 3f 106y	2m 23.3	3	8-5	Firm	NIGHT-SHIRT	July	14	1990
1m 6f	2m 59.1	5	9-5	Firm	IBN BEY	July	1	1989
2m	3m 23.7	3	9-5	Good To Firm	LAURIES CRUSADOR	Aug	13	1988

LINGFIELD (A.W)

DISTANCE	TIME	AGE	WEIGHT	GOING	HORSE	DATE		
5f	58.6 secs	2	9-7	Standard	CLASSY CLEO	Nov	28	1997
5f	57.3 secs	4	9-5	Standard	NO TIME	Mar	20	2004
6f	1m 11.5	2	8-8	Standard	TWO STEP KID	Oct	27	2003
6f	1m 10.4	4	8-4	Standard	DESERT LORD	Dec	18	2004
7f	1m 24.0	2	8-12	Standard	SCOTTISH CASTLE	Nov	2	1990
7f	1m 22.9	3	9-3	Standard	CONFRONTER	July	18	1992
1m	1m 35.86	4	9-0	Standard	ECCENTRIC	Feb	1	2005
1m	1m 36.5	2	9-5	Standard	SANPIER NICETO	Nov	30	1989
1m 2f	2m 02.6	3	8-10	Standard	COMPTON BOLTER	Nov	18	2000
1m 4f	2m 29.2	6	8-13	Standard	URSA MAJOR	Dec	28	2000
1m 5f	2m 42.9	3	9-7	Standard	GLOBAL DANCER	Dec	7	1994
2m	3m 20.0	3	9-0	Standard	YENOORA	Aug	8	1992

MUSSELBURGH

DISTANCE	TIME	AGE	WEIGHT	GOING	HORSE	DATE		
5f	57.7 secs	2	8-2	Firm	ARASONG	May	16	1994
5f	57.3 secs	3	8-12	Firm	CORUNNA	Jun	3	2000
7f 30y	1m 28.4	2	8-8	Firm	SAND BANKES	Jun	26	2000
7f 30y	1m 27.1	5	8-12	Good	DIAMOND DECORUM	Jun	18	2001
1m	1m 40.3	2	8-12	Good To Firm	SUCESSION	Sep	26	2004
1m	1m 38.8	6	9-4	Good To Firm	SEA STORM	May	29	2004
1m	1m 39.2	4	8-4	Firm	SWYNFORD ELEGANCE	Sep	4	2001
1m 1f	1m 51.7	4	9-7	Firm	KID'Z'PLAY	Jun	3	2000
1m 4f	2m 33.7	3	9-11	Firm	ALEXANDRINE	Jun	26	2000
1m 5f	2m 51.1	9	8-6	Good To Firm	COSMIC CASE	July	28	2004
1m 6f	2m 59.2	3	9-7	Firm	FORUM CHRIS	July	3	2000
2m	3m 28.1	3	8-1	Good To Firm	WARRING KINGDOM	Sep	13	1999

NEWBURY

DISTANCE	TIME	AGE	WEIGHT	GOING	HORSE	DATE	
5f 34y	59.1 secs	2	8-6	Good To Firm	SUPERSTAR LEO	July	22 2000
5f 34y	59.2 secs	3	9-5	Good To Firm	THE TRADER	Aug	18 2001
6f 8y	1m 11.4	2	8-8	Good To Firm	ASCENSION	July	22 2000
6f 8y	1m 09.8	3	8-12	Good To Firm	AUENKLANG	July	22 2000
7f	1m 24.1	2	8-11	Good To Firm	HAAFHD	Aug	15 2003
7f	1m 21.5	3	8-4	Good To Firm	THREE POINTS	July	21 2000
7f 64y	1m 28.8	2	8-10	Good To Firm	DUTY TIME	Aug	14 1993
7f 64y	1m 26.1	4	9-12	Good To Firm	GREEN PERFUME	July	19 1996
1m	1m 37.7	2	8-10	Good	ETHMAAR	Sep	17 1999
1m	1m 35.1	3	8-11	Good To Firm	DANCING TRIBUTE	Sep	23 1989
1m 7y	1m 37.2	3	8-11	Firm	MASTER WILLIE	Oct	1 1979
1m 7y	1m 34.9	3	8-9	Good To Firm	PHILIDOR	May	16 1992
1m 1f	1m 49.6	3	8-0	Good To Firm	HOLTYE	May	21 1995
1m 2f 6y	2m 1.2	3	8-7	Good To Firm	WALL STREET	July	20 1996
1m 3f 5y	2m 16.5	3	8-9	Good To Firm	GRANDERA	Sep	22 2001
1m 4f 5y	2m 29.2	4	8-9	Hard	VIDI VIC	Jun	21 1951
1m 5f 61y	2m 44.9	5	10-0	Good To Firm	MYSTIC HILL	July	20 1996
2m	3m 25.4	8	9-12	Good To Firm	MOONLIGHT QUEST	July	19 1996

NEWCASTLE

DISTANCE	TIME	AGE	WEIGHT	GOING	HORSE	DATE	
5f	58.8 secs	2	9-0	Firm	ATLANTIC VIKING	Jun	4 1997
5f	58.0 secs	4	9-2	Firm	PRINCESS OBERON	July	23 1994
6f	1m 12.3	2	9-0	Good To Firm	CROSSPEACE	Sep	29 2004
6f	1m 10.6	8	9-5	Firm	TEDBURROW	July	1 2000
7f	1m 24.2	2	9-0	Good To Firm	ISCAN	Aug	31 1998
7f	1m 23.3	4	9-2	Good To Firm	QUIET VENTURE	Aug	31 1998
1m	1m 38.9	2	9-0	Good To Firm	STOWAWAY	Oct	2 1996
1m	1m 38.9	3	8-12	Firm	JACAMAR	July	22 1989
1m 3y	1m 37.1	2	8-3	Good To Firm	HOH STEAMER	Aug	31 1998
1m 3y	1m 37.3	3	8-8	Good To Firm	ITS MAGIC	May	27 1999
1m 1f 9y	2m 03.2	2	8-13	Soft	RESPONSE	Oct	30 1993
1m 1f 9y	1m 58.4	3	8-8	Good To Firm	INTRODUCING	Aug	6 2003
1m 2f 32y	2m 06.5	3	8-11	Good To Firm	MISSIONARY RIDGE	July	29 1990
1m 4f 93y	2m 37.3	5	8-12	Firm	RETENDER	Jun	25 1994
1m 6f 97y	3m 06.4	3	9-6	Good To Firm	ONE OFF	Aug	6 2003
2m 19y	3m 24.3	4	8-10	Good	FAR CRY	Jun	26 1999

NEWMARKET (ROWLEY)

DISTANCE	TIME	AGE	WEIGHT	GOING	HORSE	DATE	
5f	58.76 secs	2	8-5	Good To Firm	VALIANT ROMEO	Oct	3 2002
5f	56.8 secs	6	9-2	Good To Firm	LOCHSONG	Apr	30 1994
6f	1m 09.61	2	8-11	Good To Firm	OASIS DREAM	Oct	3 2002
6f	1m 10.2	4	9-8	Good To Firm	LAKE CONISTON	Apr	18 1995
7f	1m 22.9	2	8-11	Good To Firm	GROSVENOR SQUARE	Sep	21 2004
7f	1m 22.2	4	9-5	Good To Firm	PERFOLIA	Oct	17 1991
1m	1m 35.7	2	9-0	Good To Firm	FORWARD MOVE	Sep	21 2004
1m	1m 34.54	4	9-0	Good To Firm	DESERT DEER	Oct	3 2002
1m 1f	1m 47.28	4	9-5	Firm	BEAUCHAMP PILOT	Oct	5 2002
1m 2f	2m 04.6	2	9-4	Good	HIGHLAND CHIEFTAIN	Nov	2 1984
1m 2f	2m 01.0	3	8-10	Good	PALACE MUSIC	Oct	20 1985
1m 4f	2m 27.1	5	8-12	Good To Firm	EASTERN BREEZE	Oct	3 2003
1m 6f	2m 54.3	5	8-6	Good To Firm	TUDOR ISLAND	Sep	30 1994
2m	3m 19.5	5	9-5	Good To Firm	GREY SHOT	Oct	4 1997
2m 2f	3m 47.5	3	7-12	Hard	WHITEWAY	Oct	15 1947

NEWMARKET (JULY)

DISTANCE	TIME	AGE	WEIGHT	GOING	HORSE	DATE		
5f	58.5 secs	2	8-10	Good	**SEDUCTRESS**	July	10	1990
5f	57.3 secs	6	8-12	Good To Firm	**RAMBLING BEAR**	Jan	1	1999
6f	1m 10.6	2	8-10	Good To Firm	**MUJTAHID**	July	11	1990
6f	1m 09.5	3	8-13	Good To Firm	**STRAVINSKY**	July	8	1999
7f	1m 24.1	2	8-11	Good	**MY HANSEL**	Aug	27	1999
7f	1m 22.5	3	9-7	Firm	**HO LENG**	July	9	1998
1m	1m 39.0	2	8-11	Good	**TRACEABILITY**	Aug	25	1995
1m	1m 35.5	3	8-6	Good To Firm	**LOVERS KNOT**	July	8	1998
1m 110y	1m 44.1	3	8-11	Good	**GOLDEN SNAKE**	Apr	15	1999
1m 2f	2m 00.9	4	9-3	Good To Firm	**ELHAYQ**	May	1	1999
1m 4f	2m 25.2	4	9-2	Good	**CRAIGSTEEL**	July	6	1999
1m 6f 175y	3m 04.2	3	8-5	Good	**ARRIVE**	July	11	2001
2m 24y	3m 20.2	7	9-10	Good	**YORKSHIRE**	July	11	2001

NOTTINGHAM

DISTANCE	TIME	AGE	WEIGHT	GOING	HORSE	DATE		
5f 13y	57.9 secs	2	8-9	Firm	**HOH MAGIC**	May	13	1994
5f 13y	57.9 secs	9	9-1	Good	**BAHAMIAN PIRATE**	Mar	31	2004
5f 13y	58.4 secs	6	8-8	Good	**MINSTREL KING**	Mar	29	1960
6f 15y	1m 11.4	2	8-11	Firm	**JAMEELAPI**	Aug	8	1983
6f 15y	1m 10.0	4	9-2	Firm	**AJANAC**	Aug	8	1988
1m 54y	1m 40.8	2	9-0	Good To Firm	**KING'S LOCH**	Sep	2	1991
1m 54y	1m 39.6	4	8-2	Good To Firm	**BLAKE'S TREASURE**	Sep	2	1991
1m 1f 213y	2m 02.3	2	9-0	Firm	**AYAABI**	July	21	1984
1m 6f 15y	2m 57.8	3	8-10	Firm	**BUSTER JO**	Oct	1	1985
2m 9y	3m 24.0	5	7-7	Firm	**FET**	Oct	5	2036
2m 2f 18y	3m 55.1	9	9-10	Good To Firm	**PEARL RUN**	May	1	1990

PONTEFRACT

DISTANCE	TIME	AGE	WEIGHT	GOING	HORSE	DATE		
5f	1m 01.1	2	9-0	Firm	**GOLDEN BOUNTY**	Sep	20	2001
5f	1m 00.8	4	8-9	Firm	**BLUE MEAVE**	Sep	29	2004
6f	1m 14.0	2	9-3	Firm	**FAWZI**	Sep	6	1983
6f	1m 12.6	3	7-13	Firm	**MERRY ONE**	Aug	29	1970
1m 4y	1m 42.8	2	9-13	Firm	**STAR SPRAY**	Sep	6	1970
1m 4y	1m 41.3	7	8-9	Firm	**NIGRASINE**	Sep	20	2001
1m 2f 6y	2m 12.8	2	9-0	Good To Firm	**WARBROOK**	Oct	2	1995
1m 2f 6y	2m 08.2	4	7-8	Hard	**HAPPY HECTOR**	July	9	1979
1m 4f 8y	2m 34.1	3	9-5	Good To Firm	**HIGH ACTION**	Aug	6	2003
2m 1f 22y	3m 42.1	3	9-2	Firm	**NIGHT EYE**	Sep	6	1983
2m 1f 216y	3m 51.1	3	8-8	Firm	**KUDZ**	Sep	9	1986
2m 5f 122y	4m 47.8	4	8-4	Firm	**PHYSICAL**	May	14	1984

REDCAR

DISTANCE	TIME	AGE	WEIGHT	GOING	HORSE	DATE		
5f	56.9 secs	2	9-0	Firm	MISTER JOEL	Oct	24	1995
5f	56.5 secs	3	9-7	Firm	NAZELA	Aug	10	1980
6f	1m 08.8	2	8-3	Good To Firm	OBE GOLD	Oct	2	2004
6f	1m 08.6	3	9-2	Good To Firm	SIZZLING SAGA	Jun	21	1991
7f	1m 21.9	2	8-11	Firm	NAGWA	Sep	27	1975
7f	1m 21.0	3	9-1	Firm	EMPTY QUARTER	Oct	3	1995
1m	1m 36.1	2	7-11	Good To Soft	MASTER SODEN	Nov	1	1999
1m	1m 33.1	3	9-5	Firm	NIGHT WINK	Oct	24	1995
1m 1f	1m 52.4	2	9-0	Firm	SPEAR	Sep	13	2004
1m 1f	1m 48.5	5	8-12	Firm	MELLOTTIE	July	25	1990
1m 2f	2m 10.1	2	8-11	Good	ADDING	Nov	10	1989
1m 2f	2m 01.4	5	9-2	Firm	ERADICATE	May	28	1990
1m 3f	2m 17.2	3	8-9	Firm	PHOTO CALL	Aug	7	1990
1m 5f 135y	2m 54.7	6	9-10	Firm	BRODESSA	Jun	20	1992
1m 6f 19y	2m 59.9	3	8-7	Firm	TRAINGLOT	July	25	1990
2m 4y	3m 24.9	3	9-3	Good To Firm	SUBSONIC	Oct	8	1991

RIPON

DISTANCE	TIME	AGE	WEIGHT	GOING	HORSE	DATE		
5f	57.8 secs	2	8-8	Firm	SUPER ROCKY	July	5	1991
5f	57.6 secs	5	8-5	Good	BROADSTAIRS BEAUTY	May	21	1995
6f	1m 10.9	2	8-11	Good	KAHIR ALMAYDAN	Aug	28	1995
6f	1m 09.8	4	9-8	Good To Firm	TADEO	Aug	16	1997
6f	1m 09.8	5	7-10	Firm	QUOIT	July	23	1966
1m	1m 41.1	2	9-0	Good To Firm	RAPHAEL	Sep	1	2001
1m	1m 37.0	4	7-10	Firm	CROWN WITNESS	Aug	25	1980
1m 1f	1m 50.4	3	9-2	Good To Firm	BOLD WORDS	Apr	9	1997
1m 2f	2m 02.6	3	9-4	Firm	SWIFT SWORD	July	20	1990
1m 4f 60y	2m 32.2	6	8-7	Firm	CHOLO	Sep	27	1941
2m	3m 27.8	6	9-0	Good To Firm	SAMAIN	Aug	31	1993

SALISBURY

DISTANCE	TIME	AGE	WEIGHT	GOING	HORSE	DATE		
5f	59.8 secs	2	8-5	Good To Firm	TARF	Aug	17	1995
5f	59.4 secs	3	8-11	Firm	BELLSABANGING	May	5	1993
6f	1m 12.1	2	8-0	Good To Firm	PARISIAN LADY	Jun	10	1997
6f	1m 11.5	4	8-7	Good To Firm	PRINCE SKY	Jun	25	1986
6f 212y	1m 25.9	2	9-0	Firm	MORE ROYAL	Jun	29	1995
6f 212y	1m 24.9	3	9-7	Firm	HIGH SUMMER	Sep	5	1996
1m	1m 40.48	2	8-13	Firm	CHOIR MASTER	Sep	17	2002
1m	1m 38.6	4	8-8	Firm	TAKE HEART	July	14	1990
1m 1f 198y	2m 04.9	3	8-6	Good To Firm	ZANTE	Aug	12	1998
1m 4f	2m 31.6	3	9-5	Good To Firm	ARRIVE	Jun	27	2001
1m 6f 15y	2m 59.4	3	8-6	Good To Firm	TABAREEH	Sep	2	1999

SANDOWN

DISTANCE	TIME	AGE	WEIGHT	GOING	HORSE	DATE		
5f 6y	59.4 secs	2	9-3	Firm	**TIMES TIME**	July	22	1982
5f 6y	58.8 secs	6	8-9	Good To Firm	**PALACEGATE TOUCH**	Sep	17	1996
7f 16y	1m 27.8	2	8-12	Good To Firm	**RED CAMELLIA**	July	25	1996
7f 16y	1m 26.3	3	9-0	Firm	**MAWSUFF**	Jun	14	1983
1m 14y	1m 41.1	2	8-11	Good To Firm	**REFERENCE POINT**	Sep	23	1986
1m 14y	1m 39.0	3	8-8	Firm	**LINDA'S FANASTY**	Aug	19	1983
1m 1f	1m 54.6	2	8-8	Good To Firm	**FRENCH PRETENDER**	Sep	20	1988
1m 1f	1m 52.6	3	8-9	Good To Firm	**DARNELLE**	Aug	19	1988
1m 2f 7y	2m 02.1	4	8-11	Firm	**KALAGLOW**	May	31	1982
1m 3f 91y	2m 21.6	4	8-3	Good To Firm	**AYLESFIELD**	July	7	1984
1m 6f	2m 56.9	4	8-7	Good To Firm	**LADY ROSANNA**	July	19	1989
2m 78y	3m 29.9	6	9-2	Firm	**SADEEM**	May	29	1989

SOUTHWELL (TURF)

DISTANCE	TIME	AGE	WEIGHT	GOING	HORSE	DATE		
6f	1m 15.6	2	8-11	Good To Firm	**YASELDA**	July	4	2001
6f	1m 14.1	4	9-12	Good To Firm	**MISS HAGGIS**	July	26	1993
7f	1m 29.1	2	9-0	Good To Firm	**DULCET SPEAR**	July	4	2001
7f	1m 26.5	3	9-5	Good To Firm	**SEA STORM**	July	5	2001
1m 2f	2m 10.0	3	9-4	Good	**BRONZE MAQUETTE**	July	26	1993
1m 4f	2m 34.4	5	9-3	Good To Firm	**CORN LILY**	Aug	10	1991
2m	3m 34.1	5	9-1	Good To Firm	**TRIPLICATE**	Sep	20	1991

SOUTHWELL (A.W)

DISTANCE	TIME	AGE	WEIGHT	GOING	HORSE	DATE		
5f	58.5 secs	2	8-1	Standard	**PRIMROSE AND ROSE**	Apr	4	2001
5f	57.4 secs	4	9-4	Standard	**WOODLAND BLAZE**	May	8	2003
6f	1m 14.0	2	8-5	Standard	**PANALO**	Nov	8	1989
6f	1m 13.3	3	9-2	Standard	**RAMBO EXPRESS**	Dec	18	1990
7f	1m 27.1	2	8-2	Standard	**MYSTIC CRYSTAL**	Nov	20	1990
7f	1m 26.8	5	8-4	Standard	**'AMENABLE**	Dec	13	1990
1m	1m 38.0	2	8-9	Standard	**ALPHA RASCAL**	Nov	13	1990
1m	1m 38.0	2	8-10	Standard	**ANDREW'S FIRST**	Dec	30	1989
1m	1m 37.2	3	8-6	Standard	**VALIRA**	Nov	3	1990
1m 3f	2m 21.5	4	9-7	Standard	**TEMPERING**	Dec	5	1990
1m 4f	2m 33.9	4	9-12	Standard	**FAST CHICK**	Nov	8	1989
1m 6f	3m 01.6	3	7-7	Standard	**QUALITAIR AVIATOR**	Dec	1	1989
1m 6f	3m 01.6	3	7-8	Standard	**EREVNON**	Dec	29	1990
2m	3m 37.6	9	8-12	Standard	**OLD HUBERT**	Dec	5	1990

THIRSK

DISTANCE	TIME	AGE	WEIGHT	GOING	HORSE	DATE		
5f	57.2 secs	2	9-7	Good To Firm	**PROAD BOAST**	Aug	5	2000
5f	56.1 secs	7	8-0	Firm	**SIR SANDROVITCH**	Jun	26	2003
6f	1m 09.2	2	9-6	Good To Firm	**WESTCOURT MAGIC**	Aug	25	1995
6f	1m 08.8	6	9-4	Firm	**JOHAYRO**	July	23	1999
7f	1m 23.7	2	8-9	Firm	**COURTING**	July	23	1999
7f	1m 22.8	4	8-5	Firm	**SILVER HAZE**	May	21	1988
1m	1m 37.9	2	9-0	Good To Firm	**SUNDAY SYMPHONY**	Sep	4	2004
1m	1m 34.8	4	8-13	Firm	**YEARSLEY**	May	5	1990
1m 4f	2m 29.9	5	9-12	Firm	**GALLERY GOD**	Jun	4	2001
2m	3m 22.3	3	8-10	Firm	**TOMASCHEK**	Aug	1	1964

WARWICK

DISTANCE	TIME	AGE	WEIGHT	GOING	HORSE	DATE		
5f	58.4 secs	2	9-7	Good To Firm	PRENONAMOSS	Oct	9	1990
5f	57.8 secs	5	9-4	Good To Firm	ANOTHER EPISODE	Aug	29	1994
5f 110y	1m 03.6	8	8-6	Good To Firm	DIZZY IN THE HEAD	Jun	27	2004
6f 21y	1m 10.6	2	9-0	Good To Firm	VIKING SPIRIT	Sep	6	2004
6f 21y	1m 09.6	6	9-2	Firm	PARKSIDE PURSUIT	Jun	20	2004
6f 21y	1m 12.1	3	8-6	Good To Firm	GEMTASTIC	Jun	18	2001
7f 26y	1m 22.9	2	9-3	Good To Firm	COUNTRY RAMBLER	Jun	20	2004
7f 26y	1m 21.2	3	8-11	Good To Firm	LUCKY SPIN	Jun	19	2004
1m 22y	1m 37.1	3	8-11	Firm	ORINOCOVSKY	Jun	26	2002
1m 2f 188y	2m 16.2	6	7-12	Good To Firm	SCENTED AIR	Apr	21	2003
1m 4f 134y	2m 39.5	3	8-13	Good To Firm	MAIMANA	Jun	22	2002
1m 6f 135y	3m 07.5	3	9-7	Good To Firm	BURMA BAY	July	2	1999
2m 39y	3m 30.6	5	8-1	Good To Firm	RENAISSANCE LADY	Jun	27	2001

WINDSOR

DISTANCE	TIME	AGE	WEIGHT	GOING	HORSE	DATE		
5f 10y	58.9 secs	2	9-0	Firm	STRICTLY PRIVATE	July	22	1974
5f 10y	59.1 secs	4	8-13	Good	BEYOND THE CLOUDS	July	17	2000
5f 217y	1m 09.0	2	8-7	Good To Firm	OPTIONS OPEN	July	25	1994
5f 217y	1m 10.1	3	8-4	Firm	SWEET RELIEF	Sep	11	1978
6f	1m 10.5	2	9-5	Good To Firm	CUBISM	Aug	17	1998
6f	1m 10.3	4	8-12	Good To Firm	CARLTON	Jun	22	1998
1m 67y	1m 44.4	2	9-0	Good To Firm	TEMPLE PLACE	Sep	29	2003
1m 67y	1m 40.6	7	9-8	Good To Firm	GATEMAN	Jun	26	2004
1m 2f 7y	2m 03.0	3	9-1	Firm	MOOMBA MASQUERADE	May	19	1990
1m 3f 135y	2m 21.5	3	9-2	Firm	DOUBLE FLORIN	May	19	1980

WOLVERHAMPTON (A.W)
COURSE SWITCHED TO POLYTRACK IN OCTOBER 2004, INSUFFICIENT DATA AVAILABLE OVER THE NEW DISTANCES

YARMOUTH

DISTANCE	TIME	AGE	WEIGHT	GOING	HORSE	DATE		
5f 43y	1m 00.4	2	8-6	Good To Firm	EBBA	July	26	1999
5f 43y	1m 00.2	3	8-11	Firm	CHARM BIRD	Sep	15	1988
6f 3y	1m 10.4	2	9-0	Good To Firm	LANCHESTER	Aug	15	1988
6f 3y	1m 10.0	3	8-10	Good To Firm	TIPSY CREEK	Aug	10	1997
7f 3y	1m 22.2	2	9-0	Good To Firm	WARRSHAN	Sep	14	1988
7f 3y	1m 22.2	3	8-7	Firm	CIELAMOUR	Sep	15	1988
1m 3y	1m 36.3	2	8-2	Good To Firm	OUTRUN	Sep	15	1988
1m 3y	1m 33.9	3	8-8	Firm	BONNE ETOILE	Jun	27	1995
1m 2f 21y	2m 03.1	4	8-9	Good To Firm	SUPREME SOUND	Aug	9	1998
1m 3f 101y	2m 23.1	3	8-9	Firm	RAHIL	July	1	1993
1m 6f 17y	2m 57.8	3	8-2	Good To Firm	BARAKAT	July	24	1990
2m	3m 26.7	4	8-2	Good To Firm	ALHESN	July	26	1999
2m 2f 51y	3m 56.8	4	9-10	Firm	PROVENCE	Sep	19	1991

YORK

DISTANCE	TIME	AGE	WEIGHT	GOING	HORSE	DATE		
5f 3y	58.4 secs	2	8-11	Good To Firm	HOWICK FALLS	Aug	20	2003
5f 3y	56.2 secs	3	9-9	Good To Firm	OASIS DREAM	Aug	21	2003
6f 3y	1m 10.6	2	9-0	Good To Firm	CARRY ON KATIE	Aug	21	2003
6f 3y	1m 09.4	3	8-2	Good To Firm	DAZZLING BAY	Jun	14	2003
6f 217y	1m 22.6	2	9-0	Good To Firm	MOONLIGHT MAN	Oct	9	2003
6f 217y	1m 22.0	4	9-0	Good To Firm	VANDERLIN	Aug	21	2003
7f 202y	1m 37.2	2	9-4	Good To Firm	THE WIFE	Sep	2	1999
7f 205y	1m 36.0	5	8-7	Good To Firm	FAITHFUL WARRIOR	July	11	2003
1m 205y	1m 52.4	2	8-1	Good To Firm	ORAL EVIDENCE	Oct	6	1988
1m 208y	1m 48.9	4	8-5	Good To Firm	KRUGERRAND	Jun	14	2003
1m 2f 88y	2m 06.5	4	9-4	Good To Firm	FAR LANE	July	12	2003
1m 3f 198y	2m 27.4	4	9-4	Good To Firm	ISLINGTON	Aug	20	2003
1m 5f 197y	2m 52.5	4	8-9	Good To Firm	MAMOOL	May	15	2003
1m 7f 195y	3m 18.4	3	8-0	Good To Firm	DAM BUSTERS	Aug	16	1988

TOP FLAT JOCKEYS IN BRITAIN 2004

WINS-RUNS	%	JOCKEY	2ND	3RD	TOTAL PRIZE	WIN PRIZE
200-1109	18%	K FALLON	166	136	4,948,877	3,486,742
195-850	23%	L DETTORI	132	89	4,655,372	3,564,350
165-1003	16%	S SANDERS	120	87	1,836,076	1,345,911
152-1177	13%	D HOLLAND	137	137	2,383,260	1,280,027
132-1009	13%	R L MOORE	125	107	1,488,267	879,223
126-1030	12%	N CALLAN	117	103	997,969	608,605
114-1008	11%	R WINSTON	105	114	1,175,674	811,531
111-1016	11%	E AHERN	99	108	1,187,251	721,808
111-1048	11%	A CULHANE	104	108	923,280	571,041
101-829	12%	P HANAGAN	70	100	1,066,847	777,202
99-1115	9%	S DROWNE	93	103	1,289,499	810,323
97-787	12%	J FANNING	72	70	1,045,851	718,972
85-822	10%	K DARLEY	97	89	1,777,012	1,194,899
82-848	10%	MARTIN DWYER	90	77	1,109,601	665,627
77-574	13%	J P MURTAGH	57	60	1,877,451	1,221,703
76-688	11%	T QUINN	79	75	1,267,906	751,221
74-974	8%	DANE O'NEILL	73	97	946,890	572,656
73-662	11%	R HUGHES	76	70	1,067,192	639,569
72-615	12%	J FORTUNE	87	76	1,316,689	813,559
72-1016	7%	J QUINN	103	96	773,257	427,306
68-792	9%	I MONGAN	85	78	474,042	279,770
67-552	12%	P ROBINSON	58	67	1,464,505	988,137
66-454	15%	R HILLS	49	65	1,665,768	1,110,992
66-510	13%	M HILLS	60	42	982,855	559,989
66-748	9%	T P QUEALLY	65	52	614,264	348,534
63-711	9%	J F EGAN	75	61	811,777	391,574
62-569	11%	F NORTON	64	67	575,794	340,728
62-932	7%	C CATLIN	75	58	613,272	368,874
60-709	8%	M FENTON	60	66	555,657	320,575
55-801	7%	S W KELLY	81	71	481,923	285,346
54-605	9%	D SWEENEY	48	44	356,369	229,322
52-387	13%	N MACKAY	41	35	572,173	440,817
52-619	8%	W SUPPLE	74	64	871,571	501,444
51-537	9%	DARREN WILLIAMS	51	51	319,925	202,505
49-590	8%	D ALLAN	65	60	458,346	289,739
48-447	11%	F LYNCH	35	48	469,877	296,958
47-666	7%	LISA JONES	45	46	310,388	196,912
45-569	8%	R FFRENCH	60	43	439,151	281,957
45-606	7%	T EAVES	31	40	303,557	210,046
44-322	14%	K MCEVOY	30	32	1,347,681	650,439
42-423	10%	P MAKIN	30	35	258,066	171,665
41-477	9%	J MACKAY	38	34	325,293	212,405
41-552	7%	DALE GIBSON	37	52	277,573	164,386
40-407	10%	G BAKER	37	31	226,933	154,492
40-589	7%	T E DURCAN	60	43	729,766	323,437
39-470	8%	B SWARBRICK	36	36	201,533	125,093
38-440	9%	N POLLARD	36	22	203,682	134,181
35-310	11%	W RYAN	19	26	326,601	199,051
35-361	10%	R MILES	32	33	287,744	195,893
35-457	8%	S HITCHCOTT	43	49	440,059	247,261

TOP FLAT TRAINERS IN BRITAIN 2004

TRAINER	LEADING HORSE	WINS-RUNS	2ND	3RD	4TH	TOTAL PRIZE	WIN PRIZE
SAEED BIN SUROOR	Rule Of Law	115-455	75	43	38	4,320,171	3,057,921
SIR MICHAEL STOUTE	North Light	87-400	49	46	50	2,926,327	2,301,032
M JOHNSTON	Attraction	119-797	111	76	70	2,437,238	1,726,936
M R CHANNON	Obe Gold	98-1039	124	100	82	1,737,728	899,749
B W HILLS	Haafhd	81-635	76	61	53	1,553,830	1,096,634
R HANNON	Hurricane Alan	113-1201	123	127	113	1,464,125	795,942
M A JARVIS	Rakti	65-371	49	44	34	1,310,666	943,371
J H M GOSDEN	Playful Act	66-458	64	59	32	1,273,375	741,368
J R FANSHAWE	Soviet Song	43-294	39	33	33	1,185,481	860,798
J L DUNLOP	Let The Lion Roar	55-513	51	62	53	1,168,926	636,040
L M CUMANI	Mephisto	42-293	45	35	32	1,058,417	636,887
T D EASTERBY	Fayr Jag	62-738	86	71	55	919,052	561,783
D NICHOLLS	Bahamian Pirate	55-681	50	54	48	874,519	614,422
B J MEEHAN	Magical Romance	60-505	47	54	40	857,247	554,323
E A L DUNLOP	Ouija Board	48-392	45	47	37	808,841	567,923
A P O'BRIEN	Ad Valorem	4-60	8	7	5	804,447	246,894
D R C ELSWORTH	Norse Dancer	37-315	25	30	37	795,074	438,139
MRS A J PERRETT	Polar Way	52-392	47	43	34	750,271	435,802
R A FAHEY	Tagula Sunrise	77-647	61	72	42	740,641	504,814
C E BRITTAIN	Warrsan	28-315	32	20	22	711,908	397,725
A M BALDING	Pentecost	48-542	59	57	41	680,579	389,774
P F I COLE	Peter Paul Rubens	41-366	37	37	37	644,931	314,575
K A RYAN	Distinctly Game	67-489	55	57	30	640,558	371,622
M L W BELL	Motivator	55-420	48	47	37	622,226	421,571
M P TREGONING	High Accolade	26-190	27	23	22	616,166	323,476
R CHARLTON	Tante Rose	36-230	24	26	25	604,569	452,664
W J HAGGAS	Chorist	46-304	29	25	25	603,365	322,153
N P LITTMODEN	Moayed	44-514	60	47	33	554,311	358,453
J M BRADLEY	The Tatling	40-710	55	52	43	540,705	299,757
P W HARRIS	Shot To Fame	42-335	36	37	19	534,192	370,290
SIR MARK PRESCOTT	Comic Strip	66-234	30	15	13	529,519	426,235
H MORRISON	Pastoral Pursuits	34-335	39	40	24	517,954	332,507
J NOSEDA	Two Step Kid	34-215	34	29	20	497,050	272,012
M H TOMPKINS	Babodana	34-317	35	34	30	489,151	278,924
T D BARRON	Raccoon	59-447	39	55	40	485,635	336,165
H CANDY	Caesar Beware	23-190	21	21	21	484,776	317,281
G A BUTLER	Nayyir	30-296	34	36	36	467,697	180,396
D R LODER	Illustrious Miss	45-342	36	36	38	459,573	272,847
G WRAGG	Autumn Glory	23-174	19	19	16	451,750	259,027
S KIRK	Salamanca	35-384	47	26	25	448,141	322,551
P D EVANS	Nashaab	62-693	61	67	54	412,921	259,826
P W CHAPPLE-HYAM	African Dream	30-163	19	20	9	392,111	280,422
K R BURKE	Party Ploy	64-487	53	51	34	390,580	263,900
W R MUIR	Material Witness	20-295	38	21	22	350,571	190,990
G L MOORE	Cold Turkey	48-474	50	38	34	343,608	207,994
N A CALLAGHAN	Hazyview	35-285	24	21	17	340,075	202,243
B A MCMAHON	Castelletto	28-236	18	19	17	335,077	226,601
J J QUINN	Fantasy Believer	30-332	28	24	24	331,147	188,225
A BERRY	Simianna	37-571	40	46	36	328,432	196,802
J A OSBORNE	Morse	40-425	38	47	28	326,374	205,680

TOP FLAT OWNERS IN BRITAIN 2004

OWNER	LEADING HORSE	WINS-RUNS	2ND	3RD	4TH	TOTAL PRIZE	WIN PRIZE
GODOLPHIN	Rule Of Law	115-455	75	43	38	4,320,171	3,057,921
HAMDAN AL MAKTOUM	Haafhd	73-464	46	66	57	1,753,484	1,179,555
CHEVELEY PARK STUD	Chic	58-218	29	29	16	1,144,217	713,694
K ABDULLA	Quiff	54-328	45	38	27	923,500	523,383
BALLYMACOLL STUD	North Light	8-28	3	2	3	916,889	908,579
MAKTOUM AL MAKTOUM	Favourable Terms	33-235	32	29	29	775,738	568,110
SHEIKH MOHAMMED	Suez	52-311	42	38	33	685,442	403,317
ELITE RACING CLUB	Soviet Song	16-64	7	6	6	560,885	409,126
SHEIKH AHMED AL MAKTOUM	Mandobi	36-266	49	26	30	492,645	254,088
DUKE OF ROXBURGHE	Attraction	3-5	1	0	0	487,018	443,018
H H AGA KHAN	Azamour	11-42	6	6	5	464,507	276,073
L NEIL JONES	Let The Lion Roar	4-13	1	5	1	379,139	166,187
GARY A TANAKA	Rakti	3-12	0	1	1	368,282	356,932
SAEED MANANA	Warrsan	8-87	12	6	6	364,713	199,799
J C SMITH	Norse Dancer	5-108	11	16	19	350,404	77,125
MRS JOHN MAGNIER & M TABOR	Five Dynasties	2-22	3	4	1	328,838	123,938
SANGSTER FAMILY	Playful Act	8-30	8	1	3	320,953	210,089
LUCAYAN STUD	Bahamian Pirate	20-164	21	14	16	307,680	215,015
MRS JOHN MAGNIER	Ad Valorem	1-14	1	1	1	278,361	110,606
NIGEL SHIELDS	Moayed	36-200	23	33	13	277,679	197,500
H R H SULTAN AHMAD SHAH	Anak Pekan	11-66	8	10	4	259,152	170,135
P D SAVILL	Celtic Heroine	16-114	13	10	8	247,006	144,740
ABDULLA BUHALEEBA	Lucky Story	11-67	9	5	6	229,592	122,859
LORD DERBY	Ouija Board	2-2	0	0	0	220,400	220,400
THE QUEEN	Promotion	15-82	18	11	6	212,182	98,131
JABER ABDULLAH	Majestic Desert	6-78	11	7	6	207,457	51,354
HESMONDS STUD	Two Step Kid	14-73	6	10	11	203,308	150,369
MRS J HOPPER & MRS E GRUNDY	Frizzante	2-5	1	1	0	196,000	174,000
FITTOCKS STUD	Pongee	6-33	9	2	3	194,946	104,465
B E NIELSEN	Tante Rose	4-13	2	1	3	190,524	185,312
DAB HAND RACING	The Tatling	4-28	3	7	1	190,410	118,331
MRS P W HARRIS	Cutting Crew	15-105	14	16	10	190,251	141,378
MOLLERS RACING	Autumn Glory	13-53	3	6	8	188,974	134,209
PAUL J DIXON	No Time	23-309	30	26	21	186,567	114,906
M TABOR & MRS JOHN MAGNIER	All Too Beautiful	2-19	3	2	1	185,534	27,327
MRS ANGIE SILVER	Mephisto	4-6	0	0	0	184,528	183,778
MILL HOUSE PARTNERSHIP	Caesar Beware	3-3	0	0	0	184,017	184,017
BDR PARTNERSHIP	Obe Gold	2-26	3	3	6	182,882	142,218
M J DAWSON	Mine	5-65	8	9	6	176,054	111,419
FRANCONSON PARTNERS	African Dream	6-34	1	5	1	168,684	136,102
J C FRETWELL	Castelletto	13-102	8	11	6	166,203	123,626
TEAM VICTORY	Hard Buck	0-1	1	0	0	165,000	0
ANDREA & GRAHAM WYLIE	Arcalis	6-38	6	4	4	160,138	117,946
RAYMOND TOOTH	Whistler	9-134	12	15	14	158,681	93,630
RIDGEWAY DOWNS RACING	Tournedos	7-40	9	8	3	157,847	75,777
SAEED SUHAIL	First Charter	5-57	7	5	9	156,577	104,149
GAINSBOROUGH STUD	Shamardal	1-9	0	3	0	154,497	152,772
MRS SUSAN ROY	Wilko	14-97	11	16	12	153,994	65,296
WOOD STREET SYNDICATE	Salamanca	2-5	0	0	1	152,577	151,766
F C T WILSON	Magical Romance	6-20	2	1	1	151,758	133,463

TOP FLAT HORSES IN BRITAIN & IRELAND 2004

HORSE (AGE)	WIN & PLACE £	W-R	TRAINER	OWNER	BREEDER
NORTH LIGHT (3)	1,049,150	2-3	Sir M Stoute	Ballymacoll Stud	Ballymacoll Stud
ATTRACTION (3)	680,398	4-6	M Johnston	Duke Of Roxburghe	Floors Farming
RULE OF LAW (3)	679,532	2-5	S Bin Suroor	Godolphin	R E Sangster & B Sangster
AZAMOUR (3)	675,796	2-5	J M Oxx	H H Aga Khan	H H Aga Khan
GREY SWALLOW (3)	603,274	2-5	D K Weld	Mrs Rochelle Quinn	Mrs C L Weld
DOYEN (4)	571,200	2-5	S Bin Suroor	Godolphin	Sheikh Mohammed
SOVIET SONG (4)	542,124	4-8	J R Fanshawe	Elite Racing Club	Elite Racing Club
HAAFHD (3)	430,874	3-5	B W Hills	Hamdan Al Maktoum	Shadwell Estate Co. Ltd.
REFUSE TO BEND (4)	418,990	2-6	S Bin Suroor	Godolphin	Moyglare Stud Farm Ltd
SULAMANI (5)	388,800	1-4	S Bin Suroor	Godolphin	The Niarchos Family
OUIJA BOARD (3)	387,442	3-3	E A L Dunlop	Lord Derby	Stanley Estate & Stud Co
RAKTI (5)	361,380	2-4	M A Jarvis	Gary A Tanaka	Az Agricola Rosati Colarieti
NORSE DANCER (4)	350,088	1-10	D R C Elsworth	J C Smith	R Ergnist & B Faust
POWERSCOURT (4)	263,422	1-4	A P O'Brien	Mrs John Magnier	Juddmonte Farms
QUIFF (3)	256,851	2-4	Sir M Stoute	K Abdulla	Juddmonte Farms
WARRSAN (6)	245,980	1-4	C E Brittain	Saeed Manana	Saeed Manana
DAMSON (2)	234,605	4-5	D Wachman	Mrs J Magnier & M Tabor	Epona Bloodstock Ltd
CHORIST (5)	233,735	2-4	W J Haggas	Cheveley Park Stud	Cheveley Park Stud Ltd
CAESAR BEWARE (2)	232,725	3-4	H Candy	Sheikh Rashid	Glending Bloodstock
LET THE LION ROAR (3)	225,024	1-6	J L Dunlop	L Neil Jones	Abergwaun Farms
PAPINEAU (4)	212,999	3-3	S Bin Suroor	Godolphin	Exors Of The Late P Winfield
PUNCTILIOUS (3)	212,666	2-5	S Bin Suroor	Godolphin	Bjorn E Nielsen
FAVOURABLE TERMS (4)	200,200	2-3	Sir M Stoute	Maktoum Al Maktoum	Gainsborough Stud
ORATORIO (2)	198,824	3-6	A P O'Brien	Mrs J Magnier & M Tabor	Barronstown Stud/Orpendale
SHAMARDAL (2)	198,819	3-3	M Johnston	Godolphin	Brilliant Stable
FRIZZANTE (5)	196,000	2-5	J R Fanshawe	Mrs J Hopper & Mrs E Grundy	Mrs J Hopper & Mrs E Grundy
MEPHISTO (5)	184,528	4-6	L M Cumani	Mrs Angie Silver	Shadwell Estate Co. Ltd.
OBE GOLD (2)	180,108	3-10	M R Channon	BDR Partnership	Mrs M Mason
TANTE ROSE (4)	176,900	3-3	R Charlton	B E Nielsen	Addison Racing Ltd Inc
MILLENARY (7)	174,000	3-5	J L Dunlop	L Neil Jones	Abergwaun Farms
THE TATLING (7)	174,000	2-7	J M Bradley	Dab Hand Racing	P J Power
PLAYFUL ACT (2)	165,255	3-4	J H M Gosden	Sangster Family	Swettenham Stud
HARD BUCK (5)	165,000	0-1	K McPeek	Team Victory	Haras Old Friends
BACHELOR DUKE (3)	164,225	1-3	J A R Toller	Exors of Duke of Devonshire	Airlie Stud
ALEXANDER GOLDRUN (3)	162,507	2-4	J S Bolger	Mrs N O'Callaghan	Dermot Cantillon
TROPICAL LADY (4)	157,158	5-9	J S Bolger	George J Kent	J Boden & W Kane
DUBAWI (2)	152,962	3-3	S Bin Suroor	Godolphin	Darley
SALAMANCA (2)	152,141	2-3	S Kirk	Wood Street Syndicate	D P Martin
BAHAMIAN PIRATE (9)	148,919	4-14	D Nicholls	Lucayan Stud	Trackside/Liberation/Seelbinder
PONGEE (4)	148,807	2-5	L M Cumani	Fittocks Stud	Fittocks Stud
AD VALOREM (2)	145,066	3-3	A P O'Brien	Mrs J Magnier	Calumet Farm
FAYR JAG (5)	145,000	1-4	T D Easterby	Jonathan Gill	Canice M Farrell Jnr
PIVOTAL POINT (4)	143,295	3-7	P J Makin	R A Bernard & J E Perry	T R Lock
TYCOON (3)	142,531	0-4	A P O'Brien	Mrs J Magnier	Juddmonte Farms
ORIENTAL MAGIC (4)	138,740	2-5	D Hayes	Larry Yung	HH The Aga Khan's Studs S C
CHIC (4)	136,950	2-6	Sir M Stoute	Cheveley Park Stud	Cheveley Park Stud Ltd
CHELSEA ROSE (2)	136,140	2-3	C Collins	Mrs A J Donnelly	Airlie Stud
GATWICK (3)	135,351	4-11	M R Channon	W H Ponsonby	M J Dargan
BEAVER PATROL (2)	134,986	3-10	R Johnson Houghton	G C Stevens	Kevin B Lynch
ALL TOO BEAUTIFUL (3)	134,412	2-5	A P O'Brien	M Tabor & Mrs J Magnier	Sunderland Hold./Abbey Bloo
VINNIE ROE (6)	132,183	1-3	D K Weld	Seamus Sheridan	Mrs Virginia Moeran

TOP NH JOCKEYS IN BRITAIN 2003/04

WINS-RUNS	%	JOCKEY	2ND	3RD	TOTAL PRIZE
209-800	26%	A P MCCOY	144	111	2,032,216
186-891	21%	R JOHNSON	158	107	1,974,603
94-625	15%	G LEE	87	69	1,356,757
89-499	18%	A DOBBIN	61	45	660,681
86-528	16%	A THORNTON	68	64	832,736
73-521	14%	R THORNTON	59	70	699,160
65-420	15%	C LLEWELLYN	48	37	715,967
62-294	21%	R WALSH	66	41	1,463,043
61-470	13%	J TIZZARD	69	54	625,678
58-367	16%	J CULLOTY	48	49	1,055,994
57-411	14%	T J MURPHY	53	41	737,791
52-377	14%	N FEHILY	54	41	452,138
51-338	15%	M A FITZGERALD	29	47	754,644
49-230	21%	D ELSWORTH	26	29	475,555
49-396	12%	J A MCCARTHY	36	49	394,286
48-372	13%	T DOYLE	38	41	399,251
48-411	12%	J E MOORE	53	42	478,586
47-298	16%	J M MAGUIRE	33	36	345,210
47-337	14%	S THOMAS	48	37	445,658
47-541	9%	L ASPELL	67	65	396,739
45-285	16%	L COOPER	30	22	733,740
43-263	16%	A TINKLER	17	18	252,018
40-360	11%	R MCGRATH	30	42	359,548
39-328	12%	J P MCNAMARA	40	44	310,644
39-394	10%	S DURACK	34	28	318,911
39-402	10%	M BRADBURNE	37	55	481,435
38-488	8%	JAMES DAVIES	38	50	238,275
36-380	9%	P FLYNN	31	30	249,029
34-322	11%	D R DENNIS	31	39	267,390
33-441	7%	W MARSTON	50	61	293,775
30-261	11%	B FENTON	28	20	263,378
30-492	6%	R GREENE	34	45	334,984
29-206	14%	L MCGRATH	26	22	242,801
28-207	14%	D N RUSSELL	28	24	182,653
27-249	11%	P MOLONEY	17	12	184,153
27-268	10%	J CROWLEY	19	18	179,337
27-361	7%	T SCUDAMORE	37	31	250,028
25-199	13%	T SIDDALL	18	17	178,133
25-266	9%	A O'KEEFFE	35	34	191,737
24-216	11%	CHRISTIAN WILLIAMS	31	26	233,318
23-173	13%	ANTONY EVANS	12	15	129,221
23-264	9%	R GARRITTY	36	41	224,962
23-323	7%	B HITCHCOTT	27	26	176,691
23-337	7%	B HARDING	26	28	235,882
21-176	12%	B J CROWLEY	19	25	265,076
21-188	11%	M FOLEY	20	19	279,292
21-232	9%	R WALFORD	24	37	157,941
21-261	8%	A DEMPSEY	32	39	202,758
20-217	9%	W HUTCHINSON	22	17	179,478
20-272	7%	H OLIVER	30	25	217,210

TOP NH TRAINERS IN BRITAIN 2003/04

TRAINER	LEADING HORSE	WINS-RUNS	2ND	3RD	4TH	TOTAL PRIZE	WIN PRIZE
M C PIPE	Well Chief	173-1055	121	106	71	2,299,984	1,458,964
P F NICHOLLS	Azertyuiop	126-646	128	78	47	2,100,809	1,313,712
JONJO O'NEILL	Clan Royal	102-631	72	50	45	1,543,697	1,034,435
P J HOBBS	Rooster Booster	121-704	119	81	51	1,501,870	810,153
N J HENDERSON	Isio	79-369	35	49	28	1,186,814	870,073
MISS VENETIA WILLIAMS	Thesis	88-560	86	72	49	930,577	594,207
MISS H C KNIGHT	Best Mate	42-256	38	29	20	820,796	646,481
N A TWISTON-DAVIES	Shardam	79-383	47	41	24	758,330	560,101
MRS S J SMITH	Simply Supreme	67-424	54	75	33	732,992	469,489
A KING	Crystal D'Ainay	46-259	32	31	25	519,389	344,035
J HOWARD JOHNSON	Grey Abbey	42-196	28	16	13	475,449	354,627
R C GUEST	Our Armageddon	46-401	48	48	23	426,817	306,909
R H ALNER	Sir Rembrandt	28-280	34	42	23	424,288	193,809
D MCCAIN	Amberleigh House	8-133	7	7	11	421,107	380,194
MRS M REVELEY	Robbo	41-353	56	47	28	416,981	242,737
T R GEORGE	Bee An Bee	50-302	49	38	27	409,557	244,140
P BOWEN	Ballycassidy	38-126	16	10	7	395,670	344,878
H D DALY	Hand Inn Hand	43-207	30	28	14	391,517	269,556
C J MANN	Keltic Bard	37-231	34	28	22	365,425	239,304
P R WEBBER	Tidour	35-224	28	26	10	343,884	238,908
IAN WILLIAMS	Mantilla	50-357	41	35	26	338,217	231,257
G L MOORE	Tikram	36-233	48	22	21	327,925	197,498
N G RICHARDS	The French Furze	38-170	27	13	7	309,572	210,347
L LUNGO	Paddy The Piper	47-303	32	23	12	295,215	218,867
F DOUMEN	Baracouda	7-23	4	1	2	249,314	137,595
FERDY MURPHY	Dominikus	31-318	37	36	23	231,833	132,735
C L TIZZARD	Dear Deal	22-190	30	21	23	213,712	117,629
G B BALDING	Accipiter	18-117	11	11	3	205,291	158,573
K C BAILEY	Longshanks	24-235	24	38	15	196,441	108,406
O SHERWOOD	Eric's Charm	22-152	27	16	10	195,136	107,118
D T HUGHES	Hardy Eustace	2-7	1	0	0	193,681	179,681
M PITMAN	Hot Shots	22-117	14	8	7	189,607	145,215
J W MULLINS	Kentford Grebe	22-218	26	23	11	182,622	117,836
T D EASTERBY	Turgeonev	18-121	20	17	9	178,214	91,301
MISS LUCINDA V RUSSELL	Kerry Lads	14-201	29	27	19	164,595	60,982
MRS JOHN HARRINGTON	Moscow Flyer	2-10	0	0	0	154,500	147,250
M W EASTERBY	Minster Glory	24-175	26	17	8	152,401	107,029
B ELLISON	Zibeline	15-103	17	14	8	147,358	92,657
R J HODGES	Penthouse Minstrel	17-128	11	13	16	139,306	99,279
G M MOORE	Sir Storm	16-189	25	21	15	136,088	78,154
R A FAHEY	Altay	15-102	16	10	11	134,674	92,815
MISS E C LAVELLE	Self Defense	13-113	17	7	11	133,498	83,667
R LEE	Mythical Ridge	20-163	15	15	15	133,483	97,407
P MONTEITH	Jordan's Ridge	17-142	12	19	14	132,033	84,847
M TODHUNTER	Be My Manager	22-131	12	9	8	131,615	96,188
R DICKIN	Channahrlie	18-186	19	19	12	130,561	79,005
G MACAIRE	Jair Du Cochet	3-16	5	5	0	129,368	98,540
B G POWELL	Miners Dance	20-216	16	20	17	126,373	85,139
W P MULLINS	Rule Supreme	1-28	1	2	1	125,900	81,200
S A BROOKSHAW	Cassia Heights	9-79	11	12	9	122,041	83,267

TOP NH OWNERS IN BRITAIN 2003/04

OWNER	LEADING HORSE	WINS-RUNS	2ND	3RD	4TH	TOTAL PRIZE	WIN PRIZE
D A JOHNSON	Well Chief	48-285	37	33	20	908,843	574,544
JOHN P MCMANUS	Clan Royal	36-264	30	17	19	834,430	369,302
SIR ROBERT OGDEN	Iris Royal	35-152	16	14	12	449,432	363,765
TREVOR HEMMINGS	Southern Star	30-164	18	19	13	447,988	335,992
JIM LEWIS	Best Mate	8-28	10	3	0	444,757	377,018
HALEWOOD INTERNATIONAL LTD	Amberleigh House	4-70	3	7	6	387,599	358,206
J HALES	Azertyuiop	5-28	5	3	0	247,499	192,734
C G ROACH	Thisthatandtother	13-30	5	3	0	199,278	149,225
B C MARSHALL	Strong Flow	8-22	2	1	3	194,743	161,931
LAURENCE BYRNE	Hardy Eustace	1-2	1	0	0	185,000	174,000
ANDREA & GRAHAM WYLIE	Inglis Drever	16-45	7	2	2	181,086	125,785
TERRY WARNER	Rooster Booster	2-26	6	0	2	178,912	26,826
SIR PETER AND LADY GIBBINGS	Isio	3-8	1	0	0	168,450	134,200
H R MOULD	Bindaree	12-42	6	3	3	166,025	131,589
MR & MRS MARK WOODHOUSE	Rigmarole	6-11	2	0	1	163,713	142,605
MRS J STEWART	Cenkos	8-51	7	6	11	157,931	63,960
N B MASON	Tyneandthyneagain	11-97	15	15	8	152,247	102,968
MRS JOHN MAGNIER	Rhinestone Cowboy	3-8	0	3	0	151,803	122,653
THE LIARS POKER PARTNERSHIP	Tiutchev	1-5	1	1	1	151,200	87,000
BRIAN KEARNEY	Moscow Flyer	2-3	0	0	0	147,250	147,250
MR & MRS R. ANDERSON GREEN	Paddy The Piper	18-118	7	24	9	140,803	98,502
A HORDLE	Sir Rembrandt	2-7	2	0	0	128,564	32,914
ASHLEYBANK INVESTMENTS LTD.	Skippers Cleuch	15-133	18	10	7	125,430	74,086
B A KILPATRICK	Tango Royal	9-51	7	8	4	116,570	78,362
KEITH NICHOLSON	Gottabe	12-78	13	17	6	115,620	69,926
ROBERT LESTER	Iris's Gift	2-3	1	0	0	114,160	110,200
M G ST QUINTON	Monkerhostin	5-12	2	2	1	114,095	80,713
R OWEN	Ballycassidy	7-10	0	1	0	108,060	106,780
INTERSKYRACING.COM & MRS J J O'NEILL	Intersky Falcon	1-6	1	2	1	106,800	46,400
TERRY EVANS	Made In Japan	3-9	1	4	0	104,873	69,998
M ARCHER & MISS J BROADHURST	Upgrade	5-42	5	4	2	103,078	38,839
THE 1961 PARTNERSHIP	Thesis	6-12	3	2	0	102,460	91,080
LESLIE JOHN GARRETT	Our Armageddon	7-17	2	1	1	102,052	94,692
W J BROWN	Fondmort	1-16	2	3	2	98,660	63,800
K ROPER,E M ROPER,N FURNESS	Grey Abbey	3-4	0	0	0	94,991	94,241
KEITH MIDDLETON	Cill Churnain	12-38	7	6	2	94,431	75,108
M A RYAN	Al Eile	2-4	1	0	0	92,052	76,652
MILLION IN MIND PARTNERSHIP	Garde Champetre	7-22	3	5	2	91,567	63,527
MRS F MONTAUBAN	Jair Du Cochet	2-3	0	0	0	91,400	91,400
LET'S LIVE RACING	Mondul	7-43	4	1	3	88,445	68,431
THURLOE FINSBURY	Geos	2-9	1	0	0	88,247	77,934
P BURLING DEVELOPMENTS LTD	Hand Inn Hand	1-9	2	2	1	87,514	59,500
JOHN P LYNCH	Rule Supreme	1-3	0	1	0	87,250	81,200
MISS B SWIRE	Accipiter	5-11	1	1	0	85,994	82,866
M CHARLTON AND R SARGENT	Tikram	3-9	3	1	1	85,361	57,817
J E BROWN	Bear On Board	8-22	3	1	2	82,791	51,576
THE EARL CADOGAN	Jakari	7-25	1	6	1	82,012	63,246
F F RACING SERVICES P'SHIP III	Hasty Prince	2-8	1	2	0	81,800	58,000
MRS S M RICHARDS	Ei Ei	3-25	4	5	6	80,654	25,567
PETER BOWLING	Swansea Bay	4-5	0	0	0	79,743	79,743

TOP NH HORSES IN BRITAIN & IRELAND 2003/04

HORSE (AGE)	WIN & PLACE £	W-R	TRAINER	OWNER	BREEDER
AMBERLEIGH HOUSE (12)	365,935	1-6	D McCain	Halewood Int'l Ltd	Robert McCarthy
BEST MATE (9)	277,311	2-3	Miss H C Knight	Jim Lewis	Jacques Van't Hart
AZERTYUIOP (7)	225,300	2-5	P F Nicholls	J Hales	P De Maleissye Melun
HARDY EUSTACE (7)	199,239	1-5	D T Hughes	Laurence Byrne	Patrick Joyce
MOSCOW FLYER (10)	189,457	4-6	Mrs J Harrington	Brian Kearney	Edward Joyce
EDREDON BLEU (12)	179,207	5-5	Miss H C Knight	Jim Lewis	Lucien Chevrollier
CLAN ROYAL (9)	178,500	1-2	Jonjo O'Neill	John P McManus	Ctsse B De Tarragon
ROOSTER BOOSTER (10)	169,175	1-6	P J Hobbs	Terry Warner	Mrs E Mitchell
RIGMAROLE (6)	166,021	6-14	P F Nicholls	Mr & Mrs M Woodhouse	Juddmonte Farms
ISIO (8)	165,051	2-4	N J Henderson	Sir Peter & Lady Gibbings	J Bedu & Vcte R De Soultrait
WELL CHIEF (5)	162,546	4-5	M C Pipe	D A Johnson	Gestut Norina
TIUTCHEV (11)	162,303	1-6	M C Pipe	The Liars Poker P'ship	Exors Of Mrs D De Rothschild
PUNTAL (8)	149,170	5-10	M C Pipe	Terry Neill	Aylesfield Farms Stud Co
INTERSKY FALCON (7)	149,007	2-7	Jonjo O'Neill	Interskyracing.com & Mrs O'Neill	Fulling Mill Farm & Stud
RULE SUPREME (8)	144,710	3-9	W P Mullins	John J Fallon	Ms M A & Mrs H T Murphy
JURANCON II (7)	132,202	2-6	M C Pipe	D A Johnson	Mme Monique Trinquet
RHINESTONE COWBOY (8)	130,903	3-5	Jonjo O'Neill	Mrs John Magnier	Mrs Frances Whelan
STRONG FLOW (7)	130,702	5-6	P F Nicholls	B C Marshall	Peter McCarthy
BARACOUDA (9)	129,400	3-4	F Doumen	John P McManus	R Dupuis
FLAGSHIP UBERALLES (10)	125,480	1-5	P J Hobbs	John P McManus	Miss E C Holdsworth
FIRST GOLD (11)	121,687	1-4	F Doumen	John P McManus	Roger Chaignon
BALLYCASSIDY (8)	120,160	7-11	P Bowen	R Owen & P Fullagar	Michael Griffin
SIR REMBRANDT (8)	119,450	1-6	R H Alner	A Hordle	F Warren
IRIS ROYAL (8)	117,868	3-5	N J Henderson	Sir Robert Ogden	J And Mrs Besnouin
IRIS'S GIFT (7)	114,160	2-3	Jonjo O'Neill	Robert Lester	Mrs R Crank
CENKOS (10)	113,211	3-8	P F Nicholls	Mrs J Stewart	Gerard Samama
BRAVE INCA (6)	110,613	4-4	C A Murphy	Novices Syndicate	D W Macauley
NEWMILL (6)	109,727	4-8	T G O'Leary	Mrs Mary T Hayes	Mrs Veronica O'Farrell
HI CLOY (7)	108,751	4-11	M Hourigan	Mrs S McCloy	Mrs Paul Finegan
MONKERHOSTIN (7)	106,043	3-8	P J Hobbs	M G St Quinton	Mme D Steverlynck
CLOUDY BAYS (7)	102,038	3-11	C Byrnes	Cloudy Bay Syndicate	J L Rothwell
OUR ARMAGEDDON (7)	99,202	6-10	R C Guest	Leslie John Garrett	L W Bowater & C Marchant
SPORAZENE (8)	96,285	2-6	P F Nicholls	G Mason & D Jackson	Haras Du Mezeray
GREY ABBEY (10)	94,991	3-4	J H Johnson	K Roper,E M Roper,N Furness	Francis Small
JAIR DU COCHET (7)	91,400	2-3	G Macaire	Mrs F Montauban	C De Chambord
AL EILE (4)	90,885	3-5	J Queally	M A Ryan	Michael Ryan
PIZARRO (7)	90,481	3-6	E J O'Grady	Edward Wallace	John Farrar
FONDMORT (8)	90,050	1-6	N J Henderson	W J Brown	Hubert Carion
SABADILLA (10)	89,509	3-8	P M Verling	W Coleman	John C And Mrs Mabee
BEEF OR SALMON (8)	88,863	2-5	MHourigan	B J Craig	John Murphy
KICKING KING (6)	88,616	2-6	T J Taaffe	Conor Clarkson	Sunnyhill Stud
MADE IN JAPAN (4)	88,194	2-5	P J Hobbs	Terry Evans	Darley Stud
HAND INN HAND (8)	86,748	1-7	H D Daly	P Burling Developments Ltd	P Burling
THISTHATANDTOTHER (8)	86,442	4-8	P F Nicholls	C G Roach	Mrs Joerg Vasicek
ACCIPITER (5)	85,994	5-8	G B Balding	Miss B Swire	Miss B Swire
FLORIDA PEARL (12)	85,528	2-3	W P Mullins	Mrs Violet O'Leary	P Mackean
TIKRAM (7)	85,361	3-8	G L Moore	M Charlton & R Sargent	Buckram T'bred Ent. Inc
GRANIT D'ESTRUVAL (10)	84,897	1-6	Ferdy Murphy	W J Gott	Bernard Le Gentil
BACK IN FRONT (7)	83,246	2-5	E J O'Grady	Nelius Hayes	Miss Noreen Hayes
FOREMAN (6)	82,556	1-4	T Doumen	John P McManus	Mrs B Neumann

LEADING SIRES OF 2004 IN GREAT BRITAIN AND IRELAND

STALLION	BREEDING	RNRS	WNRS	WINS	WIN MONEY	PLACES	PLACE MONEY	TOTAL
SADLER'S WELLS (USA) (1981)	by Northern Dancer	199	83	104	2540633	269	1506186	4046819
DANEHILL (USA) (1986)	by Danzig (USA)	132	67	105	2102739	197	932227	3034966
PIVOTAL (GB) (1993)	by Polar Falcon (USA)	93	53	89	1059544	171	454649	1514192
EFISIO (1982)	by Formidable (USA)	81	39	61	1049598	145	289658	1339256
KINGMAMBO (USA) (1990)	by Mr Prospector (USA)	61	26	36	728811	84	531315	1260126
NIGHT SHIFT (USA) (1980)	by Northern Dancer	111	40	50	873299	189	359148	1232447
BARATHEA (IRE) (1990)	by Sadler's Wells (USA)	112	39	67	885911	161	331721	1217632
CAPE CROSS (IRE) (1994)	by Green Desert (USA)	77	37	56	874894	114	269184	1144078
SELKIRK (USA) (1988)	by Sharpen Up	101	46	70	805454	201	335910	1141365
MARJU (IRE) (1988)	by Last Tycoon	78	30	52	868894	130	252566	1121460
MACHIAVELLIAN (USA) (1987)	by Mr Prospector (USA)	106	40	70	737118	157	323947	1061066
INDIAN RIDGE (1985)	by Ahonoora	101	43	56	483231	204	504718	987948
GRAND LODGE (USA) (1991)	by Chief's Crown (USA)	163	46	71	612431	215	333199	945631
DAYLAMI (IRE) (1994)	by Doyoun	55	22	34	766561	77	176553	943115
CADEAUX GENEREUX (1985)	by Young Generation	119	49	79	583016	228	352915	935931
POLAR FALCON (USA) (1987)	by Nureyev (USA)	83	37	63	553303	139	339173	892475
HALLING (USA) (1991)	by Diesis (USA)	69	19	37	330124	103	532424	862547
POLISH PRECEDENT (USA) (1986)	by Danzig (USA)	62	14	21	610182	85	243104	853286
GREEN DESERT (USA) (1983)	by Danzig (USA)	93	37	51	485055	179	361329	846384
ALHAARTH (IRE) (1993)	by Unfuwain (USA)	60	18	28	663464	73	98416	761880

LEADING BRITISH AND IRISH BASED SIRES OF 2004 (GREAT BRITAIN, IRELAND AND OVERSEAS)

STALLION	BREEDING	DOMESTIC WNRS	DOMESTIC WINS	WIN MONEY	OVERSEAS WNRS	OVERSEAS WINS	WIN MONEY	TOTAL
DANEHILL (USA) (1986)	by Danzig (USA)	67	105	2102739	52	95	2537594	4640333
SADLER'S WELLS (USA) (1981)	by Northern Dancer	83	104	2540633	34	45	1212231	3752864
MARJU (IRE) (1988)	by Last Tycoon	30	52	868894	55	97	1212405	2081299
DESERT KING (IRE) (1994)	by Danehill (USA)	25	38	355998	28	50	1724610	2080608
PIVOTAL (GB) (1993)	by Polar Falcon (USA)	53	89	1059544	24	42	777564	1837108
MACHIAVELLIAN (USA) (1987)	by Mr Prospector (USA)	40	70	737118	47	71	1096518	1833636
POLISH PRECEDENT (USA) (1986)	by Danzig (USA)	14	21	610182	22	45	942547	1552728
CHARNWOOD FOREST (IRE) (1992)	by Warning	21	35	304211	37	79	1238578	1542788
ALHAARTH (IRE) (1993)	by Unfuwain (USA)	18	28	663464	20	42	847833	1511297
BARATHEA (IRE) (1990)	by Sadler's Wells (USA)	39	67	885911	45	77	597856	1483766
NIGHT SHIFT (USA) (1980)	by Northern Dancer	40	50	873299	54	95	580419	1453718
CAPE CROSS (IRE) (1994)	by Green Desert (USA)	37	56	874894	20	28	551210	1426104
SELKIRK (USA) (1988)	by Sharpen Up	46	61	805454	30	45	608267	1413721
EFISIO (1982)	by Formidable (USA)	39	61	1049598	29	48	312779	1362377
SRI PEKAN (USA) (1992)	by Red Ransom (USA)	30	54	431737	79	138	923117	1354853
CADEAUX GENEREUX (1985)	by Young Generation	49	79	583016	27	46	743976	1326992
HERNANDO (FR) (1990)	by Niniski (USA)	18	25	458327	32	54	861867	1320194
NASHWAN (USA) (1986)	by Blushing Groom (FR)	21	27	197366	16	23	1087317	1284683
SINGSPIEL (IRE) (1992)	by In The Wings	28	36	480792	35	59	735042	1215834
GRAND LODGE (USA) (1991)	by Chief's Crown (USA)	46	71	612431	54	91	601624	1214055

LEADING TWO-YEAR-OLD SIRES OF 2004 IN GREAT BRITAIN AND IRELAND

STALLION	BREEDING	RNRS	WNRS	WINS	WIN MONEY	PLACES	PLACE MONEY	TOTAL
DANEHILL (USA) 1986	by Danzig (USA)	35	19	24	327303	44	274217	601520
PIVOTAL (GB) (1993)	by Polar Falcon (USA)	37	21	36	401317	57	114086	515403
SADLER'S WELLS (USA) (1981)	by Northern Dancer	44	11	15	343073	23	40304	383377
DANEHILL DANCER (IRE) (1993)	by Danehill (USA)	40	18	27	168980	81	182218	351198
ENTREPRENEUR (GB) (1994)	by Sadler's Wells (USA)	30	10	14	273290	21	75485	348774
TAGULA (IRE) (1993)	by Taufan (USA)	32	10	19	229622	39	61336	290958
MUJADIL (USA) (1988)	by Storm Bird (CAN)	42	14	21	173060	70	98134	271194
BARATHEA (IRE) (1990)	by Sadler's Wells (USA)	24	11	15	208303	35	58771	267074
DAGGERS DRAWN (USA) (1995)	by Diesis	19	2	4	186608	16	60548	247156
MIND GAMES (GB) (1992)	by Puissance	38	15	21	82713	62	148904	231617
ZAFONIC (USA) (1990)	by Gone West (USA)	38	13	17	131730	60	98851	230582
XAAR (GB) (1995)	by Zafonic (USA)	30	10	13	137842	36	92101	229943
ROYAL APPLAUSE (GB) (1993)	by Waajib	45	16	22	131877	69	90411	222288
NAMAQUALAND (USA) (1990)	by Mr Prospector (USA)	9	4	10	178471	19	42395	220866
DANZIG (USA) (1977)	by Northern Dancer	11	6	10	186699	9	29363	216063
CAPE CROSS (IRE) (1994)	by Green Desert (USA)	29	9	13	144080	42	63910	207990
GRAND LODGE (USA) (1991)	by Chief's Crown (USA)	37	10	15	157665	27	39700	197366
KEY OF LUCK (USA) (1991)	by Chief's Crown (USA)	17	7	10	138004	30	57352	195356
DESERT KING (IRE) (1994)	by Danehill (USA)	21	7	8	157832	19	36364	194196
BLUEBIRD (USA) (1984)	by Storm Bird (CAN)	26	7	10	96234	35	70951	167184

LEADING FIRST CROP SIRES OF 2004 IN GREAT BRITAIN AND IRELAND

STALLION	BREEDING	RNRS	WNRS	WINS	WIN MONEY	PLACES	PLACE MONEY	TOTAL
MONTJEU (IRE) (1996)	by Sadler's Wells (USA)	35	14	19	238512	25	49216	287728
GIANT'S CAUSEWAY (USA) (1997)	by Storm Cat (USA)	43	12	18	365000	43	125330	490330
DUBAI MILLENNIUM (GB) (1996)	by Seeking The Gold (USA)	18	10	12	211641	19	43737	255378
DIKTAT (GB) (1995)	by Warning	34	11	15	178508	48	63401	241909
NAMID (GB) (1996)	by Indian Ridge	42	16	23	157712	65	79326	237038
KING'S BEST (USA) (1997)	by Kingmambo (USA)	46	19	23	172007	33	45020	217028
MONASHEE MOUNTAIN (USA) (1997)	by Danzig (USA)	39	8	12	100536	58	90912	191448
DANSILI (GB) (1996)	by Danehill (USA)	39	12	12	47291	43	138588	185879
TRANS ISLAND (GB) (1995)	by Selkirk (USA)	30	10	20	113931	35	62625	176556
ROSSINI (USA) (1997)	by Miswaki (USA)	41	7	11	87192	54	87776	174968
LUJAIN (USA) (1996)	by Seeking The Gold (USA)	49	15	15	62344	44	48921	111265
ALMUTAWAKEL (GB) (1995)	by Machiavellian (USA)	19	7	8	36867	30	69685	106552
JOSR ALGARHOUD (IRE) (1996)	by Darshaan	39	9	10	44965	47	55378	100343
BOLD FACT (USA) (1995)	by Known Fact (USA)	18	5	9	33344	30	54962	88306
FUSAICHI PEGASUS (USA) (1997)	by Mr Prospector (USA)	12	7	7	47985	11	39706	87691
SINNDAR (IRE) (1997)	by Grand Lodge (USA)	21	3	3	15517	17	68745	84262
MUJAHID (USA) (1996)	by Danzig (USA)	29	11	11	42563	38	40053	82616
LEND A HAND (GB) (1995)	by Great Commotion (USA)	14	5	7	30871	24	42262	73133

LEADING MATERNAL GRANDSIRES OF 2004 IN GREAT BRITAIN AND IRELAND

STALLION	BREEDING	RNRS	WNRS	WINS	WIN MONEY	PLACES	PLACE MONEY	TOTAL
RAINBOW QUEST (USA) (1981)	by Blushing Groom (FR)	118	42	60	1881034	159	759666	2640701
DARSHAAN (1981)	by Shirley Heights	135	46	75	857320	184	513895	1371214
SADLER'S WELLS (USA) (1981)	by Northern Dancer	179	59	89	878916	231	486631	1365547
SHIRLEY HEIGHTS (1975)	by Mill Reef (USA)	156	72	105	841509	274	468479	1309987
ROYAL ACADEMY (USA) (1987)	by Nijinsky (CAN)	89	26	39	585636	131	550954	1136589
KRIS (1976)	by Sharpen Up	122	35	49	814916	129	237691	1052607
SOVIET STAR (USA) (1984)	by Nureyev (USA)	39	16	26	750195	102	269729	1019924
NIGHT SHIFT (USA) (1980)	by Northern Dancer	131	48	64	505132	215	504620	1009751
LEAR FAN (USA) (1981)	by Roberto (USA)	39	11	18	704128	47	236960	941088
WARNING (1985)	by Known Fact (USA)	93	44	67	653967	164	268534	922501
GREEN DESERT (USA) (1983)	by Danzig (USA)	138	57	79	567967	204	294077	862044
DANCING BRAVE (USA) (1983)	by Lyphard (USA)	61	21	37	385512	93	475833	861345
THE MINSTREL (CAN) (1974)	by Northern Dancer	53	20	28	683646	83	150444	834090
ALLEGED (USA) (1974)	by Hoist The Flag (USA)	55	19	25	499355	62	300377	799731
PURSUIT OF LOVE (GB) (1989)	by Groom Dancer (USA)	29	5	9	667302	23	129129	796431
CAERLEON (USA) (1980)	by Nijinsky (CAN)	133	53	76	549682	178	234564	784246
MACHIAVELLIAN (USA) (1987)	by Mr Prospector (USA)	60	28	37	549910	95	200253	750163
LAST TYCOON (1983)	by Try My Best (USA)	117	37	61	479499	162	212047	691546
BLUSHING GROOM (FR) (1974)	by Red God	40	15	23	571593	69	117777	689370
ELA-MANA-MOU (1976)	by Pitcairn	79	23	36	434854	99	253125	687979

STALLIONS EARNINGS FOR 2004

(includes every stallion who sired a winner on the flat in Great Britain and Ireland in 2004)

STALLIONS	RNRS	STARTS	WNRS	WINS	PLACES	TOTAL
ABOU ZOUZ (USA)	15	109	2	3	17	19922.24
ACAMBARO (GER)	1	8	1	1	2	4517.00
ACATENANGO (GER)	14	71	4	7	20	72055.59
ADIEU AU ROI (IRE)	2	7	1	1	2	6007.05
AFFIRMED (USA)	4	24	1	1	8	14398.00
AIR EXPRESS (IRE)	11	57	4	5	18	104305.70
ALHAARTH (IRE)	60	279	18	28	73	761879.97
ALHIJAZ (GB)	6	43	1	3	11	23333.45
ALI-ROYAL (IRE)	47	296	15	23	61	334972.83
ALJABR (USA)	9	22	3	3	7	21539.55
ALKALDE (GER)	1	8	1	1	1	3235.25
ALMATY (IRE)	4	21	2	3	11	20506.50
ALMUTAWAKEL (GB)	19	80	7	8	30	106551.55
ALNASR ALWASHEEK (GB)	1	9	1	1	1	1967.00
ALYDEED (CAN)	1	18	1	1	1	2790.50
ALZAO (USA)	70	339	15	28	84	396124.13
AMFORTAS (IRE)	3	9	2	2	3	9323.25
AMONG MEN (USA)	27	133	3	3	19	24614.25
ANABAA (USA)	26	145	7	13	43	145673.03
ANITA'S PRINCE (GB)	10	69	4	5	14	62416.59
ANSHAN (IRE)	7	30	1	1	10	10835.33
A P INDY (USA)	8	22	1	2	5	25348.13
ARAGON (GB)	15	101	5	7	15	33652.50
ARAZI (USA)	5	29	1	1	8	14603.50
ARCH (USA)	5	26	4	7	9	161345.17
ARCHWAY (IRE)	9	39	3	4	8	24364.01
ARDKINGLASS (GB)	5	23	1	2	7	17503.00
ASHKALANI (IRE)	52	292	12	15	70	201341.17
ATRAF (GB)	66	389	21	41	97	277576.60
ATTICUS (USA)	5	19	2	2	2	18413.15
AVERTI (IRE)	35	233	11	16	61	128101.87
AWESOME AGAIN (CAN)	4	19	1	2	12	62729.50
BACHIR (IRE)	13	54	7	9	13	56341.52
BAHAMIAN BOUNTY (GB)	57	364	20	35	87	465694.87
BAHHARE (USA)	65	319	20	33	67	375579.71
BAHRI (USA)	25	147	9	11	50	102016.96
BAL HARBOUR (GB)	6	29	1	1	6	7613.50
BALLA COVE	5	29	2	6	6	64513.56
BANDMASTER (USA)	5	46	3	3	10	13717.00
BAND ON THE RUN	1	11	1	1	2	4211.25
BARATHEA (IRE)	112	636	39	67	161	1217632.12
THE BART (USA)	1	4	1	1	1	7093.66
BAY TERN (USA)	1	12	1	1	2	5375.20
BELONG TO ME (USA)	7	27	3	6	13	94488.65
BE MY CHIEF (USA)	8	76	5	6	16	40436.05
BE MY GUEST (USA)	26	147	9	16	44	171269.13
BE MY NATIVE (USA)	7	23	2	2	5	14131.72
BENNY THE DIP (USA)	24	96	3	7	19	88603.06
BERING	25	134	8	11	41	157535.68
BEVELED (USA)	23	204	7	15	50	137213.73
BIEN BIEN (USA)	21	119	6	13	25	62319.95
BIG SHUFFLE (USA)	11	33	3	5	9	101134.32
BIGSTONE (IRE)	22	132	7	8	25	65011.89
BIJOU D'INDE (GB)	25	137	8	9	26	42444.16
BIN AJWAAD (IRE)	21	156	9	16	47	136907.79
BISHOP OF CASHEL (GB)	37	239	18	25	56	259086.11
BLUEBIRD (USA)	65	383	17	21	93	375604.64
BLUEGRASS PRINCE (IRE)	38	238	10	15	55	149931.83
BLUE OCEAN (USA)	8	61	2	3	17	24384.03
BLUES TRAVELLER (IRE)	13	72	5	5	17	59269.24

STALLIONS	RNRS	STARTS	WNRS	WINS	PLACES	TOTAL
BLUSHING FLAME (USA)	7	37	2	3	9	20106.00
BLUSH RAMBLER (USA)	1	6	1	1	1	11895.60
BOB BACK (USA)	10	18	3	3	3	28342.26
BOLD EDGE (GB)	23	102	5	5	31	40040.05
BOLD FACT (USA)	18	88	5	9	30	88305.79
BOTANIC (USA)	6	38	2	4	6	31925.68
BOUNDARY (USA)	11	58	6	6	17	45748.17
BRAVE ACT (GB)	15	53	3	3	11	24193.76
BRIEF TRUCE (USA)	22	140	8	15	30	164009.29
BROCCO (USA)	1	1	1	1	0	3460.60
BRUNSWICK (USA)	1	12	1	1	6	7436.00
CADEAUX GENEREUX	119	742	49	79	228	935931.01
CAERLEON (USA)	13	82	3	5	24	310287.82
CAPE CROSS (IRE)	77	368	37	56	114	1144077.72
CAPE TOWN (USA)	2	10	2	3	2	22199.50
CAPOTE (USA)	5	29	2	4	9	35536.60
CARNEGIE (IRE)	5	22	2	2	7	16640.15
CASE LAW	17	114	5	8	26	59999.95
CASTEDDU (GB)	2	24	1	2	7	11727.25
CATRAIL (USA)	27	205	9	20	55	136452.65
CAT'S CAREER (USA)	2	5	1	1	1	6069.75
CAYMAN KAI (IRE)	14	72	2	4	18	28881.60
CELTIC SWING (GB)	26	126	8	18	39	320879.60
CHADDLEWORTH (IRE)	1	16	1	1	5	4242.70
CHARNWOOD FOREST (IRE)	70	401	21	35	89	424914.32
CHEROKEE RUN (USA)	2	6	1	1	4	22444.30
CHIEF'S CROWN (USA)	1	17	1	5	4	15457.80
CIGAR	4	35	2	6	6	81836.37
CITIDANCER (USA)	1	10	1	1	4	27734.60
CLANTIME	15	150	8	10	32	75459.68
CLASSIC CLICHE (IRE)	17	61	1	2	4	10457.61
CLOUDINGS (IRE)	15	76	6	6	14	35635.65
COIS NA TINE (IRE)	5	39	1	1	12	15627.08
COLLEGE CHAPEL (GB)	45	253	13	15	47	217887.58
COMMON GROUNDS	28	180	8	15	32	101734.66
COMPTON PLACE (GB)	83	548	33	44	139	457031.98
CONQUISTADOR CIELO (USA)	1	4	1	1	0	1277.50
COOL JAZZ (GB)	2	7	1	1	0	3220.00
COSMONAUT (GB)	5	12	1	1	2	1942.50
COZZENE (USA)	14	56	5	6	13	52932.55
CRAFTY PROSPECTOR (USA)	2	15	2	2	1	10765.00
CROCO ROUGE (IRE)	23	141	13	17	46	190083.83
CRYPTOCLEARANCE (USA)	3	35	2	2	12	18315.51
CYRANO DE BERGERAC	16	91	3	3	27	35118.55
DAGGERS DRAWN (USA)	55	335	13	18	71	348731.70
DANCING DISSIDENT (USA)	4	32	1	2	11	25819.62
DANCING SPREE (USA)	30	165	4	4	28	24109.05
DANEHILL (USA)	132	620	67	105	197	3034966.13
DANEHILL DANCER (IRE)	105	644	37	53	189	760784.31
DANETIME (IRE)	69	435	14	24	107	340654.43
DANSILI (GB)	39	141	12	12	43	185878.60
DANZERO (AUS)	46	271	11	15	61	187461.09
DANZIG (USA)	26	113	11	17	35	402124.01
DANZIG CONNECTION (USA)	35	206	9	13	43	87163.83
DARNAY (GB)	9	30	2	2	2	11126.06
DARSHAAN	58	221	11	17	82	251806.85
DAYJUR (USA)	8	45	5	6	13	45247.10
DAYLAMI (IRE)	55	210	22	34	77	943114.76
DEFACTO (USA)	8	44	1	1	6	6312.95
DEFENSIVE PLAY (USA)	1	7	1	1	2	7077.11
DEFINITE ARTICLE (GB)	60	282	16	29	66	439391.85
DELTA DANCER (GB)	1	18	1	2	5	19585.72
DEMOCRATIC (USA)	2	15	1	2	5	6734.25
DEPLOY	31	170	11	26	53	251355.89

STALLIONS	RNRS	STARTS	WNRS	WINS	PLACES	TOTAL
DEPUTY MINISTER (CAN)	5	10	1	1	2	8170.00
DESERT KING (IRE)	82	388	25	38	109	548145.60
DESERT PRINCE (IRE)	92	426	22	29	113	587056.81
DESERT STORY (IRE)	58	280	12	15	72	124077.04
DESERT STYLE (IRE)	72	427	22	30	111	398090.17
DESERT SUN (GB)	63	354	21	39	91	324157.20
DIESIS	49	188	12	16	56	227324.78
DIKTAT (GB)	34	142	11	15	48	241908.73
DILUM (USA)	4	21	1	1	4	5779.50
DISTANT RELATIVE	17	168	11	21	52	138151.42
DISTANT VIEW (USA)	46	256	16	24	61	167989.10
DISTINCTLY NORTH (USA)	17	90	3	3	16	15205.95
DIXIELAND BAND (USA)	10	35	1	2	14	43640.00
DIXIE UNION (USA)	2	7	1	1	3	9916.39
DOCKSIDER (USA)	47	243	16	27	71	296538.08
DOLPHIN STREET (FR)	27	163	10	18	43	143978.87
DON CORLEONE (GB)	2	20	2	2	3	6749.30
DOUBLE BED (FR)	2	6	1	1	0	2975.00
DOUBLE ECLIPSE (IRE)	3	10	1	2	4	33320.60
DOUBLE TRIGGER (IRE)	11	36	2	2	2	6929.00
DOWSING (USA)	2	24	1	2	11	15561.95
DOYOUN	11	55	4	5	16	37645.18
DRACULA (AUS)	11	51	4	6	8	23555.05
DR DEVIOUS (IRE)	52	277	16	26	60	270319.48
DREAMS END (GB)	2	13	1	1	0	3926.00
DR FONG (USA)	79	418	29	42	138	536153.25
DR MASSINI (IRE)	3	12	2	2	0	8392.45
DUBAI MILLENNIUM (GB)	18	34	10	12	19	255377.60
DUMAANI (USA)	1	7	1	1	2	7284.00
DUSHYANTOR (USA)	7	19	1	1	2	67816.91
DYNAFORMER (USA)	6	40	3	4	15	64971.65
EAGLE EYED (USA)	50	343	13	16	84	160697.05
EARL OF BARKING (IRE)	1	11	1	1	5	8942.95
EFISIO	81	519	39	61	145	1339256.22
ELA-MANA-MOU	10	62	6	8	21	113627.27
ELBIO	9	58	3	3	16	35412.65
EL GRAN SENOR (USA)	4	32	2	4	9	49525.07
ELLIODOR (FR)	1	2	1	1	1	31100.00
ELMAAMUL (USA)	27	193	10	18	52	176191.46
EL PRADO (IRE)	9	54	1	1	13	32144.14
ELUSIVE QUALITY (USA)	4	19	1	1	6	7970.50
EMARATI (USA)	36	280	11	21	63	144963.48
EMPEROR JONES (USA)	42	308	12	21	79	160018.97
ENTREPRENEUR (GB)	95	475	29	39	102	552636.61
ENVIRONMENT FRIEND (GB)	14	84	4	5	22	24767.35
ERINS ISLE	15	48	4	6	11	41349.43
EXECUTIVE MAN	1	19	1	2	5	9977.85
EXIT TO NOWHERE (USA)	7	41	3	3	10	14773.65
EXPELLED (USA)	2	11	1	1	4	6904.00
EXPLOIT (USA)	3	9	1	1	1	2041.60
EZZOUD (IRE)	11	67	2	5	23	57624.25
FACTUAL (USA)	11	49	3	4	9	32534.85
FAIRY KING (USA)	6	48	1	2	12	20680.65
FALTAAT (USA)	1	6	1	3	1	52036.60
FARFELU	2	9	1	1	1	2935.00
FASLIYEV (USA)	87	405	21	26	120	305297.21
FAYRUZ	60	399	17	24	102	372258.92
FIRST TRUMP (GB)	58	385	20	32	87	209254.69
FITZCARRALDO (ARG)	2	21	1	1	8	7999.00
FLEETWOOD (IRE)	29	163	11	15	42	94481.45
FLYING SPUR (AUS)	33	205	8	18	47	260512.87
FLY SO FREE (USA)	1	12	1	1	3	6808.70
FORESTRY (USA)	3	10	1	2	0	12711.40
FOREST WILDCAT (USA)	4	14	3	3	5	83612.85

STALLIONS	RNRS	STARTS	WNRS	WINS	PLACES	TOTAL
FORTY NINER (USA)	1	2	1	1	0	8272.54
FORZANDO	60	342	15	24	79	215197.90
FOURSTARS ALLSTAR (USA)	7	16	1	3	1	14818.67
FOXHOUND	72	438	17	26	108	209792.63
FRAAM (GB)	65	368	19	24	78	243348.13
FRENCH DEPUTY (USA)	2	9	2	2	1	7384.40
FRIMAIRE (GB)	2	5	1	1	1	5426.76
FRIUL (ARG)	1	18	1	2	4	7116.20
.FUMO DI LONDRA (IRE)	18	87	5	6	14	52596.11
FUSAICHI PEGASUS (USA)	12	23	7	7	11	87691.47
GENERAL MONASH (USA)	66	371	14	19	60	102583.13
GHAZI (USA)	4	24	2	4	5	48073.38
GIANT'S CAUSEWAY (USA)	43	116	12	18	43	490330.41
GILDED TIME (USA)	5	26	2	2	13	80254.05
GLORY OF DANCER (GB)	5	53	3	6	23	61754.20
GOLD AWAY (IRE)	3	11	2	3	3	168215.04
GOLDEN HEIGHTS	4	24	2	3	2	6491.00
GOLDMARK (USA)	27	129	7	10	20	89997.96
GONE WEST (USA)	30	115	7	9	33	163090.72
GOOD THYNE (USA)	2	7	1	1	1	11961.27
GOTHENBERG (IRE)	10	63	1	3	12	44957.70
GRAN ALBA (USA)	1	10	1	1	2	5078.75
GRAND LODGE (USA)	163	826	46	71	215	945630.79
GRAND SLAM (USA)	5	16	1	1	6	8051.36
GREAT COMMOTION (USA)	13	81	5	6	18	51701.16
GREAT DANE (IRE)	11	85	2	4	19	45415.41
GREEN DANCER (USA)	3	12	1	1	3	2408.50
GREEN DESERT (USA)	93	528	37	51	179	846383.86
GREENSMITH	6	41	2	3	10	39440.81
GREEN TUNE (USA)	3	11	1	2	4	43264.48
GREY DAWN II	1	21	1	4	2	9263.75
GREY DESIRE	6	36	1	2	8	12071.85
GROOM DANCER (USA)	89	427	31	41	119	384262.80
GULCH (USA)	24	114	6	10	26	72982.85
HALLING (USA)	69	306	19	37	103	862547.20
HAMAS (IRE)	18	99	5	8	21	56143.34
HANDSOME RIDGE (GB)	4	20	1	1	3	5391.20
HANDSOME SAILOR	2	13	1	1	7	6804.00
HECTOR PROTECTOR (USA)	48	234	14	19	48	126275.85
HENNESSY (USA)	5	16	1	1	3	4650.25
HERNANDO (FR)	43	213	18	25	72	712207.89
HIGH ESTATE	7	32	2	2	1	45490.49
HIGHEST HONOR (FR)	20	90	3	4	25	75728.66
HIGH KICKER (USA)	2	11	1	2	3	6594.00
HOLY BULL (USA)	2	16	1	2	1	5363.20
HONOUR AND GLORY (USA)	4	9	1	1	3	9664.00
HORSE CHESTNUT (SAF)	6	22	3	3	9	36367.25
HOUMAYOUN (FR)	6	19	2	2	2	12767.60
HOUSEBUSTER (USA)	3	26	1	4	7	149964.05
HURRICANE SKY (AUS)	6	84	4	18	27	144790.43
IDRIS (IRE)	17	88	5	8	16	62037.86
IMPERIAL BALLET (IRE)	69	355	18	29	73	326110.10
IMPERIAL FRONTIER (USA)	7	41	1	1	7	11958.37
IMP SOCIETY (USA)	5	19	1	1	6	6338.55
INCHINOR (USA)	102	561	32	50	164	543218.37
IN COMMAND (IRE)	9	41	2	3	8	24288.75
INDIAN DANEHILL (IRE)	19	91	3	5	26	46387.71
INDIAN LODGE (IRE)	22	105	3	7	26	50666.14
INDIAN RIDGE	101	601	43	56	204	987948.47
INDIAN ROCKET (GB)	24	164	9	14	42	140597.93
INSAN (USA)	3	19	2	3	6	36180.99
IN THE WINGS	75	283	24	30	80	517064.68
INTIDAB (USA)	2	13	2	2	3	12385.90
INTIKHAB (USA)	49	280	20	34	97	469247.60

STALLIONS	RNRS	STARTS	WNRS	WINS	PLACES	TOTAL
INZAR (USA)	13	73	4	5	13	47874.48
IRISH RIVER (FR)	11	89	5	5	21	47277.66
JADE HUNTER (USA)	2	18	2	2	5	8751.40
JAMBALAYA JAZZ (USA)	1	7	1	1	1	14364.20
JOSR ALGARHOUD (IRE)	39	152	9	10	47	100342.85
JUMBO HIRT (USA)	3	7	1	1	0	1449.00
JURADO (USA)	3	11	1	1	2	3756.00
KABOOL (GB)	2	10	1	1	6	13399.25
KADEED (IRE)	2	7	1	1	1	3840.75
KAHYASI	35	144	6	8	35	135629.47
KASAKOV (GB)	3	16	1	1	0	9074.00
KAYRAWAN (USA)	1	3	1	1	0	3347.50
KEY OF LUCK (USA)	55	272	18	23	58	295794.96
KINGMAMBO (USA)	61	224	26	36	84	1260126.03
KING OF KINGS (IRE)	43	191	8	10	39	100206.04
KING'S BEST (USA)	46	111	19	23	33	217027.64
KINGSINGER (IRE)	13	65	3	3	16	30265.81
KING'S SIGNET (USA)	12	108	4	6	43	128569.35
KING'S THEATRE (IRE)	46	239	15	24	60	219786.54
KIRKWALL (GB)	7	44	3	4	9	47482.75
KOMAITE (USA)	63	456	24	43	124	349148.26
KRIS	38	157	9	15	26	142876.43
KRIS S (USA)	13	73	6	6	34	180339.67
KYLIAN (USA)	5	25	2	2	9	20163.92
LABEEB (GB)	3	21	1	1	9	19023.50
LAHIB (USA)	28	163	10	12	42	146645.15
LAKE CONISTON (IRE)	54	341	18	27	68	194165.58
LANDO (GER)	5	15	1	2	9	41473.40
LARGESSE (GB)	4	20	1	2	4	13162.25
LAST TYCOON	5	31	3	4	4	15886.27
LAW SOCIETY (USA)	3	23	2	5	7	20947.25
LEADING COUNSEL (USA)	5	11	1	1	3	4850.15
LEAR FAN (USA)	32	116	10	12	36	227167.14
LEND A HAND (GB)	14	63	5	7	24	73133.44
LIL'S BOY (USA)	22	68	3	4	14	49954.21
LINAMIX (FR)	44	180	16	26	61	298406.59
LION CAVERN (USA)	28	185	14	23	52	167517.08
LIT DE JUSTICE (USA)	2	22	1	3	2	10273.60
LITTLE BIGHORN	2	13	1	3	3	22814.79
LOCHNAGER	1	5	1	1	0	4379.58
LOMITAS (GB)	14	68	3	5	13	41262.50
LOUP SAUVAGE (USA)	13	54	5	8	9	47387.25
LOUP SOLITAIRE (USA)	1	6	1	1	1	4531.80
LUCKY GUEST	8	38	2	3	13	25605.62
LUGANA BEACH	16	122	4	12	20	64368.22
LUHUK (USA)	1	4	1	1	1	3272.50
LUJAIN (USA)	49	222	15	15	44	111264.89
LURE (USA)	8	47	1	1	7	8849.15
LYCIUS (USA)	18	136	6	11	37	64058.63
LYPHARD (USA)	1	12	1	1	5	7471.00
MACHIAVELLIAN (USA)	106	500	40	70	157	1061065.61
MAGICAL WONDER (USA)	9	28	2	2	4	16042.24
MAGIC RING (IRE)	65	452	19	37	106	294587.69
MAKBUL	29	204	14	24	48	231407.27
MANGO EXPRESS	1	6	1	1	0	1463.00
MANHAL (GB)	1	13	1	2	3	5859.00
MARIA'S MON (USA)	1	2	1	1	1	32338.03
MARJU (IRE)	78	416	30	52	130	1121460.00
MARK OF ESTEEM (IRE)	83	393	29	41	95	548324.19
MARQUETRY (USA)	2	7	1	2	1	13680.15
MASTER WILLIE	5	23	1	1	5	14639.00
MERDON MELODY	16	124	2	7	20	44563.88
MIDHISH (GB)	16	87	4	6	12	57159.25
MIDYAN (USA)	6	29	2	4	9	21958.00

STALLIONS	RNRS	STARTS	WNRS	WINS	PLACES	TOTAL
MILLKOM (GB)	17	125	10	16	40	115823.58
MIND GAMES (GB)	94	629	29	47	159	417159.48
MINSHAANSHU AMAD (USA)	5	33	2	3	12	15861.00
MISSED FLIGHT (GB)	4	23	2	4	7	10734.70
MISTER BAILEYS (GB)	45	207	14	17	65	165687.67
MISWAKI (USA)	21	107	5	5	34	231115.14
MIZORAM (USA)	2	12	1	1	2	4169.00
MONASHEE MOUNTAIN (USA)	39	182	8	12	58	191448.07
MONSAGEM (USA)	1	5	1	1	2	3604.00
MONSUN (GER)	7	23	1	1	7	12394.32
MONTJEU (IRE)	35	110	14	19	25	287727.82
MON TRESOR	5	34	1	1	10	12791.39
MOST WELCOME	35	246	15	37	69	299313.52
MR GREELEY (USA)	2	6	2	2	4	78518.07
MR PROSPECTOR (USA)	1	8	1	2	4	6008.25
MT LIVERMORE (USA)	12	73	2	4	21	52366.96
MTOTO	53	238	13	16	66	152112.45
MUHTARRAM (USA)	34	194	12	19	36	133807.30
MUJADIL (USA)	116	716	42	68	175	592445.24
MUJAHID (USA)	29	114	11	11	38	82615.60
MUJTAHID (USA)	10	61	1	1	16	37049.72
MUKADDAMAH (USA)	29	224	10	13	56	202804.55
MY BEST VALENTINE (GB)	12	74	2	2	11	10328.00
MYSTIKO (USA)	4	18	1	1	3	2599.50
NAMAQUALAND (USA)	31	216	14	29	58	386981.27
NAMID (GB)	42	185	16	23	65	237038.00
NASHWAN (USA)	51	237	21	27	70	345394.05
NEVER SO BOLD	6	45	1	2	8	7368.50
NICHOLAS (USA)	3	29	2	5	9	21000.20
NICOLOTTE (GB)	22	109	4	8	25	61906.33
NIGHT SHIFT (USA)	111	743	40	50	189	1232447.19
NOBLE PATRIARCH	2	6	1	1	0	3571.75
NOTEBOOK (USA)	1	1	1	1	0	5954.00
NUREYEV (USA)	11	46	7	10	13	131113.82
OCTAGONAL (NZ)	15	94	4	8	25	43625.95
OLD TRIESTE (USA)	3	10	1	1	2	10482.96
OLD VIC	6	16	1	1	6	9005.28
OPENING VERSE (USA)	18	104	5	7	11	74525.81
ORPEN (USA)	88	488	37	54	157	525809.87
OSCAR (IRE)	4	17	1	2	5	14635.92
OUT OF PLACE (USA)	1	4	1	1	1	6098.50
OVERBURY (IRE)	8	73	3	4	14	17270.00
OWINGTON (GB)	3	20	1	2	9	132050.80
PARADE MARSHAL (USA)	1	7	1	1	1	2004.00
PARIS HOUSE (GB)	43	264	18	26	58	178832.26
PEINTRE CELEBRE (USA)	46	201	14	21	60	296002.15
PENNEKAMP (USA)	38	224	9	10	53	111387.66
PERSIAN BOLD	16	73	5	7	23	52348.55
PERSIAN BRAVE (IRE)	2	9	1	2	3	16365.85
PERUGINO (USA)	68	411	13	25	100	367745.62
PETARDIA (GB)	27	176	7	10	33	97572.45
PETIONVILLE (USA)	1	8	1	1	4	7881.00
PETONG	33	215	8	17	36	104607.70
PETORIUS	11	57	2	3	8	15411.45
PETOSKI	1	12	1	2	4	12511.28
PHARLY (FR)	10	51	1	1	13	14109.30
PICCOLO (GB)	105	698	34	50	159	454629.36
PIPS PRIDE (GB)	8	80	1	1	15	16512.50
PISTOLET BLEU (IRE)	6	18	2	2	3	8253.50
PIVOTAL (GB)	93	536	53	89	171	1514192.34
PLATINI (GER)	1	18	1	4	4	18910.00
PLEASANT TAP (USA)	2	4	2	2	2	20189.47
POLAR FALCON (USA)	83	462	37	63	139	892475.25
POLAR PRINCE (IRE)	18	129	9	17	30	78224.70

STALLIONS	RNRS	STARTS	WNRS	WINS	PLACES	TOTAL
POLIGLOTE (GB)	2	11	1	2	1	11771.00
POLISH PRECEDENT (USA)	62	269	14	21	85	853286.12
POYLE GEORGE	1	14	1	2	3	6799.00
PRESIDIUM	32	235	11	15	60	130697.47
PRIMO DOMINIE	70	438	22	31	112	390505.17
PRINCELY HEIR (IRE)	12	80	7	11	18	59861.79
PRINCE OF BIRDS (USA)	11	79	5	9	23	55620.05
PRINCE SABO	31	205	9	18	38	117695.32
PRIOLO (USA)	24	133	8	13	34	151002.88
PRIVATE TERMS (USA)	1	3	1	1	1	5681.50
PUISSANCE	24	164	5	6	35	70103.60
PULPIT (USA)	3	9	1	1	2	8362.00
PURSUIT OF LOVE (GB)	63	463	24	38	120	315306.68
PYRAMUS (USA)	10	51	1	1	11	12565.17
QUEST FOR FAME	8	55	3	8	17	120694.75
QUIET AMERICAN (USA)	7	30	1	3	9	16843.90
RAHY (USA)	29	136	12	17	34	207292.19
RAINBOW QUEST (USA)	76	285	23	40	82	625315.74
RAINBOWS FOR LIFE (CAN)	11	38	2	3	7	25658.69
RAISE A GRAND (IRE)	30	141	7	8	26	59436.73
RAMBO DANCER (CAN)	3	27	2	8	9	42579.15
RAPHANE (USA)	11	61	2	4	7	55603.90
RED RANSOM (USA)	36	144	13	15	45	166357.83
RED SUNSET	6	38	3	5	15	87355.41
RELIGIOUSLY (USA)	2	8	1	2	3	21971.83
REPRIMAND	13	75	6	7	26	84642.72
REVOQUE (IRE)	79	391	28	42	110	351562.28
RHYTHM (USA)	2	12	1	1	4	10211.27
RIDGEWOOD BEN (GB)	8	40	2	3	7	17589.34
RISK ME (FR)	6	32	1	2	8	14216.10
ROBELLINO (USA)	61	337	18	23	78	204422.70
ROCK HOPPER	7	29	2	2	6	7496.85
ROMANOV (IRE)	1	8	1	2	3	13460.75
ROSELIER (FR)	2	2	1	1	0	3740.75
ROSSINI (USA)	41	183	7	11	54	174967.50
ROYAL ABJAR (USA)	16	113	5	10	24	102766.16
ROYAL ACADEMY (USA)	50	270	14	20	69	323131.74
ROYAL ANTHEM (USA)	5	21	1	1	6	6730.20
ROYAL APPLAUSE (GB)	124	709	41	56	200	677480.88
RUDIMENTARY (USA)	23	146	7	8	41	130999.31
RUN SOFTLY (USA)	1	5	1	1	1	5503.25
RUSSIAN REVIVAL (USA)	9	65	2	6	10	37661.29
RYMER	1	10	1	1	5	7765.70
SABREHILL (USA)	20	146	7	10	41	72740.83
SADDLERS' HALL (IRE)	14	80	2	5	8	36355.36
SADLER'S WELLS (USA)	199	738	83	104	269	4046819.11
SAFAWAN	8	81	2	3	33	79648.94
SAHM (USA)	5	18	3	4	6	36518.28
SAINT BALLADO (CAN)	3	4	1	1	1	7263.00
SAINT PREUIL (FR)	1	2	1	1	0	3308.50
SALSE (USA)	19	131	3	4	29	142218.85
SALT DOME (USA)	2	10	1	1	2	9022.54
SALT LAKE (USA)	3	16	1	1	4	8262.40
SANDPIT (BRZ)	2	22	2	6	3	25308.60
SANGLAMORE (USA)	6	39	3	4	12	44002.40
SAUMAREZ	3	10	1	1	1	16970.77
SAVAHRA SOUND	3	41	2	2	5	8463.50
SCENIC	9	42	3	6	10	41198.85
SEA RAVEN (IRE)	3	31	2	3	7	41616.46
SEATTLE SLEW (USA)	5	16	2	2	4	49625.75
SECOND EMPIRE (IRE)	43	207	15	26	61	206717.43
SECOND SET (IRE)	5	54	2	2	13	24014.90
SEEKING THE GOLD (USA)	35	136	7	13	42	223286.26
SELKIRK (USA)	101	539	46	70	201	1141364.72

STALLIONS	RNRS	STARTS	WNRS	WINS	PLACES	TOTAL
SEPTIEME CIEL (USA)	3	14	1	2	3	7241.35
SESARO (USA)	30	180	8	9	30	54743.14
SEYMOUR HICKS (FR)	1	9	1	3	2	4997.50
SHAAMIT (IRE)	9	51	2	4	14	32163.70
SHAHRASTANI (USA)	5	20	1	1	1	5475.58
SHALFORD (IRE)	6	39	3	5	6	30102.11
SHAREEF DANCER (USA)	13	94	5	10	26	118595.19
SHEIKH ALBADOU (GB)	12	93	4	7	26	73323.74
SHERNAZAR	7	29	1	1	6	67066.91
SHINKO FOREST (IRE)	45	243	10	17	57	248447.64
SHY GROOM (USA)	1	5	1	2	1	9491.50
SILLERY (USA)	5	39	2	2	14	18873.55
SILVER DEPUTY (CAN)	1	10	1	1	4	10357.50
SILVER HAWK (USA)	31	134	8	10	39	180270.60
SILVER PATRIARCH (IRE)	18	63	1	1	7	6860.20
SILVER WIZARD (USA)	6	25	1	2	7	12650.85
SIMPLY GREAT (FR)	7	35	3	4	7	34579.78
SINGSPIEL (IRE)	69	299	28	36	104	630063.36
SINNDAR (IRE)	21	59	3	3	17	84261.59
SKY CLASSIC (CAN)	4	38	2	4	14	28917.15
SLIP ANCHOR	20	79	6	12	18	86480.10
SMART STRIKE (CAN)	2	24	2	4	5	38270.25
SMOKE GLACKEN (USA)	1	1	1	1	0	4303.00
SO FACTUAL (USA)	17	113	4	7	22	44175.85
SON PARDO (GB)	2	10	1	2	1	8732.00
SORBIE TOWER (IRE)	1	21	1	4	5	13012.40
SOUTHERN HALO (USA)	15	81	5	6	23	46909.55
SOUVENIR COPY (USA)	2	21	1	1	11	14514.10
SOVIET LAD (USA)	6	16	1	1	2	4773.40
SOVIET STAR (USA)	57	265	18	22	75	286531.45
SPECIAL POWER	2	9	1	1	1	1848.50
SPECTRUM (IRE)	138	676	32	49	182	683352.96
SPINNING WORLD (USA)	19	84	6	9	27	251905.24
SRI PEKAN (USA)	84	580	30	54	156	661090.67
STANDIFORD (USA)	4	12	1	1	2	6416.90
STARBOROUGH (GB)	9	53	3	5	5	34863.95
STATOBLEST	3	23	2	2	6	6444.50
STORM CAT (USA)	29	93	12	13	36	371411.26
STORM CREEK (USA)	4	18	2	2	4	16815.37
STORMIN FEVER (USA)	3	4	1	1	1	7606.35
STORMY ATLANTIC (USA)	1	3	1	1	1	7836.00
STRAVINSKY (USA)	48	232	10	14	66	188208.42
SUAVE DANCER (USA)	5	37	3	3	17	105532.00
SUBORDINATION (USA)	1	3	1	1	0	4348.50
SULTRY SONG (USA)	1	2	1	1	1	18150.00
SUNDAY SILENCE (USA)	9	35	5	6	14	135408.61
SUPERLATIVE	2	19	1	1	6	6675.00
SUPERPOWER	11	64	2	3	15	11390.25
SUPREMO (USA)	1	6	1	1	1	1670.00
SURE BLADE (USA)	12	82	7	14	14	130403.36
SWAIN (IRE)	28	108	7	8	37	111457.39
TAGULA (IRE)	71	518	29	58	135	651498.18
TAKE RISKS (FR)	3	6	1	1	0	9169.01
TALE OF THE CAT (USA)	6	28	1	1	8	10842.80
TAMURE (IRE)	5	26	2	3	9	55101.06
TANNENKONIG (IRE)	2	18	1	1	7	9940.00
TAUFAN (USA)	3	19	1	4	6	17073.55
TEMPORAL (GER)	1	7	1	1	5	8570.07
TENBY (GB)	8	32	4	5	8	128999.82
TERIMON	10	52	3	3	8	23068.50
THATCHING	8	68	1	4	18	39020.88
THEATRICAL	38	155	9	15	52	298951.20
THUNDER GULCH (USA)	7	38	2	6	11	28243.12
TIGER HILL (IRE)	2	13	1	3	4	27735.00

STALLIONS	RNRS	STARTS	WNRS	WINS	PLACES	TOTAL
TIMBER COUNTRY (USA)	9	18	1	1	5	10896.65
TIMELESS TIMES (USA)	32	209	7	9	40	66838.95
TIPSY CREEK (USA)	26	132	3	4	23	27040.75
TIROL	3	15	1	1	0	3571.75
TITUS LIVIUS (FR)	60	346	21	24	89	213010.74
TOMBA (GB)	12	52	2	2	11	17107.40
TOPANOORA	6	16	2	2	4	8510.70
TOP OF THE WORLD	1	5	1	1	2	5165.47
TORRENTIAL (USA)	1	2	1	1	1	10319.00
TOULON (GB)	9	20	2	4	5	65385.92
TRAGIC ROLE (USA)	13	61	1	1	15	15711.70
TRANS ISLAND (GB)	30	134	10	20	35	176555.96
TREMPOLINO (USA)	9	39	1	1	12	20420.47
TURTLE ISLAND (IRE)	74	383	17	25	99	230583.75
TWINING (USA)	2	14	1	1	4	4762.25
UNBLEST (GB)	4	33	2	2	9	40957.11
UNBRIDLED'S SONG (USA)	4	7	1	1	2	7847.50
UNFUWAIN (USA)	75	344	30	42	125	594258.22
UP AND AT 'EM (GB)	18	116	7	14	24	78187.84
VETTORI (IRE)	84	429	20	24	105	209501.92
VICTORY NOTE (USA)	61	334	15	21	80	210604.18
WAAJIB	1	2	1	1	0	18338.03
WAR CHANT (USA)	3	11	3	3	5	22527.75
WARNING	11	108	4	7	31	80967.61
WELDNAAS (USA)	8	47	1	1	10	16388.20
THE WEST (USA)	11	69	1	1	8	7651.70
WHITTINGHAM (IRE)	23	166	10	21	37	115722.49
WINNING GALLERY	1	15	1	1	4	12974.83
WITH APPROVAL (CAN)	3	10	1	1	1	4445.25
WIZARD KING (GB)	49	267	11	19	42	93619.00
WOLFHOUND (USA)	58	421	11	16	96	139268.74
WOODBOROUGH (USA)	56	362	19	28	75	185202.82
WOODMAN (USA)	38	208	10	12	58	113324.62
XAAR (GB)	30	106	10	13	36	229942.75
YES IT'S TRUE (USA)	2	2	1	1	1	4728.85
YOUNG ERN (GB)	16	102	6	9	21	50306.45
ZABEEL (NZ)	2	14	1	1	5	7151.95
ZAFONIC (USA)	89	437	26	39	142	632985.39
ZAHA (CAN)	12	38	1	2	3	6904.00
ZAMINDAR (USA)	25	102	3	5	17	67075.83
ZIETEN (USA)	11	92	7	8	25	83344.60
ZILZAL (USA)	44	279	19	26	92	275116.99

BY KIND PERMISSION OF WEATHERBYS

Foaling dates are shown for two-year-olds where these are provided, and the purchase price (in guineas) as a yearling.

NH STALLIONS EARNINGS FOR 2004

(includes every stallion who sired a winner over jumps in Great Britain and Ireland in 2003/2004)

STALLIONS	RNRS	STARTS	WNRS	WINS	PLACES	TOTAL
AAHSAYLAD	11	67	3	4	19	41537.65
ABEDNEGO	5	6	1	1	1	9263.75
ABSALOM	6	24	1	1	3	6513.25
ACATENANGO (GER)	9	45	3	3	14	40495.63
ACCESS SKI	2	26	1	4	9	36819.75
ACCORDION	74	209	8	12	54	198474.04
ACCOUNTANT (NZ)	1	12	1	1	7	9571.35
ACTINIUM (FR)	6	24	1	1	8	9486.00
AELAN HAPI (USA)	2	5	1	1	1	3857.00
AFFIRMED (USA)	3	13	1	1	3	6008.18
AFZAL	29	107	5	6	24	41487.48
AGENT BLEU (FR)	7	21	4	5	9	47172.02
AJDAYT (USA)	3	24	1	2	10	29647.50
AJRAAS (USA)	7	32	2	2	7	13918.62
ALA HOUNAK	8	30	1	1	10	15027.75
ALDERBROOK (GB)	51	170	12	26	40	216861.51
ALESSO (USA)	1	4	1	3	1	129400.00
ALFIE DICKINS	1	14	1	1	4	6072.25
ALFLORA (IRE)	101	359	25	34	90	389969.59
ALHAARTH (IRE)	8	37	5	9	9	42755.75
ALHIJAZ (GB)	10	24	2	2	6	8592.50
ALI-ROYAL (IRE)	25	84	7	9	11	96607.80
ALLEGED (USA)	8	41	4	7	15	36062.75
ALL HASTE (USA)	5	16	1	1	7	11391.90
AL NASR (FR)	2	5	1	1	1	4579.45
ALPHABATIM (USA)	59	205	13	20	58	185430.76
ALWUHUSH (USA)	1	6	1	1	0	29000.00
ALZAO (USA)	20	62	3	7	16	124999.08
AMONG MEN (USA)	8	18	1	1	3	5985.50
ANABAA (USA)	11	45	1	2	17	32735.07
ANDRETTI	5	25	1	1	2	6167.38
ANSHAN	75	214	10	14	46	142452.18
APELDOORN (FR)	6	28	1	3	12	73965.70
APPLE TREE (FR)	5	25	3	9	6	67181.76
APRIL NIGHT (FR)	4	10	1	1	1	6251.38
ARAZI (USA)	5	23	1	1	7	19061.57
ARCHITECT (USA)	3	11	1	2	0	12346.20
ARCHWAY (IRE)	12	52	4	7	14	295418.29
ARCTIC CIDER (USA)	9	34	3	8	10	87564.42
ARCTIC LORD	78	306	16	26	72	247102.65
ARCTIC TERN (USA)	4	18	1	1	3	8473.00
ARDROSS	10	46	4	4	18	46915.01
ARISTOCRACY	38	145	7	9	35	67003.56
ART FRANCAIS (USA)	3	15	1	2	4	7063.33
ARZANNI	16	55	4	5	8	34725.83
ASHKALANI (IRE)	19	57	2	4	11	53457.80
ASIR	7	39	1	1	16	16512.22
ASSESSOR (IRE)	2	6	1	1	2	5656.50
ATRAF (GB)	7	22	2	2	5	9621.80
BABY TURK	6	24	5	6	12	287947.11
BACKCHAT (USA)	1	10	1	1	1	3218.00
BAD CONDUCT (USA)	4	20	1	3	6	31212.83
BAHHARE (USA)	10	36	4	6	9	32895.37
BAL HARBOUR (GB)	5	26	1	4	5	16374.00
BALINGER	3	17	1	1	3	6292.00
BALLACASHTAL (CAN)	3	16	1	1	3	4048.50
BALLA COVE	13	35	3	4	11	27395.55

STALLIONS	RNRS	STARTS	WNRS	WINS	PLACES	TOTAL
BALLAD ROCK	3	4	1	1	1	5321.60
BALLEROY (USA)	4	16	3	4	8	59291.50
BALLET ROYAL (USA)	7	51	4	6	21	39913.75
BALNIBARBI (GB)	5	22	1	2	3	10346.25
BARATHEA (IRE)	36	116	8	13	25	181559.67
BARON BLAKENEY	12	37	1	1	9	11567.05
THE BART (USA)	9	63	4	6	13	45195.96
BATSHOOF	9	46	2	3	12	18030.25
BEAUDELAIRE (USA)	4	12	1	1	2	4975.27
BEAU SHER	23	127	9	14	34	159591.13
BEAU ZEPHYR (AUS)	1	3	1	1	1	3541.00
BEDFORD (USA)	10	38	2	2	5	10614.50
BELMEZ (USA)	7	17	1	1	5	8455.25
BE MY CHIEF (USA)	17	52	2	2	12	25027.88
BE MY GUEST (USA)	21	87	7	13	32	175098.96
BE MY NATIVE (USA)	262	974	70	101	301	1523154.10
BENEFICIAL (GB)	40	139	10	15	40	144225.83
BEREG (USA)	1	12	1	2	3	17785.24
BERING	17	78	7	14	34	216682.34
BEVELED (USA)	16	72	6	6	17	38285.22
BEYSSAC (FR)	9	47	3	3	11	29185.29
BIEN BIEN (USA)	3	19	1	3	12	27864.30
BIGSTONE (IRE)	34	143	10	16	43	155299.64
BIJOU D'INDE (GB)	8	24	2	3	2	10430.30
BIN AJWAAD (IRE)	10	33	2	2	6	10646.55
BISHOP OF CASHEL (GB)	7	28	1	1	7	8141.75
BLACK MINSTREL	7	37	1	1	7	19375.98
BLACK MONDAY	12	60	3	6	19	83762.40
BLUEBIRD (USA)	21	73	6	7	13	47108.68
BLUES TRAVELLER (IRE)	19	50	2	2	4	22590.12
BLUFFER	1	8	1	1	2	6450.00
BLUSHING FLAME (USA)	13	33	3	3	5	13558.46
BOB BACK (USA)	70	248	24	34	74	437384.84
BOB'S RETURN (IRE)	46	162	13	24	31	160738.16
BOJADOR (FR)	1	8	1	4	4	23836.43
BOLD FOX	8	20	2	2	0	9457.62
BOWLING PIN	1	11	1	2	1	10470.78
BOYNE VALLEY	9	28	3	3	4	19499.25
BRAVEFOOT (GB)	9	36	2	2	7	23301.24
BRIEF TRUCE (USA)	32	137	4	5	43	56462.01
BROADSWORD (USA)	11	46	4	9	13	91560.98
BROKEN HEARTED	59	209	10	16	47	248049.91
BRUSH ASIDE (USA)	8	31	2	2	11	24287.21
BUCKLEY	7	35	1	1	10	15205.15
BUCKSKIN (FR)	33	124	9	10	40	477416.23
BULINGTON (FR)	2	9	1	1	1	3218.38
BUSTINO	12	37	2	2	5	13028.00
BUSY FLIGHT (GB)	5	11	1	1	0	1988.00
CADEAUX GENEREUX	26	97	5	9	22	73830.94
CADOUDAL (FR)	30	112	14	17	36	208185.46
CAERLEON (USA)	13	57	6	7	10	48373.23
CAJETANO (USA)	2	10	1	3	3	164919.97
CALLER I D (USA)	1	9	1	2	2	7747.00
CALLERNISH	1	3	1	1	1	5981.00
CAMDEN TOWN	38	137	6	8	36	84208.54
CAPOTE (USA)	3	16	1	3	9	29013.35
CARDINAL FLOWER	6	30	1	2	8	19764.69
CARDOUN (FR)	3	9	1	1	3	14088.73
CARLINGFORD CASTLE	18	60	2	3	16	27707.00
CARLTON (GER)	2	11	1	1	4	5073.00
CARROLL HOUSE	38	103	2	3	29	58151.44
CASE LAW	6	24	1	2	5	9473.12
CASHEL COURT	1	9	1	1	0	8272.54
CASTEDDU (GB)	4	19	1	1	4	15596.00
CASTLE KEEP	10	35	4	5	8	41327.80
CATALDI	16	55	3	4	12	41761.62

STALLIONS	RNRS	STARTS	WNRS	WINS	PLACES	TOTAL
CATRAIL (USA)	13	48	4	6	13	62257.62
CELIO RUFO	19	96	9	15	32	153579.61
CELTIC SWING (GB)	9	34	3	3	9	16483.00
CHADDLEWORTH (IRE)	3	11	1	1	4	7342.19
CHAMBERLIN (FR)	9	22	3	3	6	34968.40
CHARENTE RIVER (IRE)	8	24	1	3	8	45320.95
CHARMER	13	47	2	5	10	40150.27
CHARNWOOD FOREST (IRE)	30	88	2	2	24	25537.32
CHEF DE CLAN II (FR)	3	10	1	1	4	181323.98
CHIEF'S CROWN (USA)	2	15	2	2	5	10132.05
CHILIBANG	1	6	1	2	2	14592.90
CLANTIME	5	14	1	1	4	5366.40
CLASSIC CLICHE (IRE)	21	47	4	4	7	14921.50
CLASSIC MEMORY	4	18	1	1	6	8315.00
CLASSIC SECRET (USA)	5	26	2	3	7	32135.18
CLEARLY BUST	8	26	2	2	7	16587.75
CLOUDINGS (IRE)	10	27	1	1	4	8030.90
COLLEGE CHAPEL (GB)	24	63	3	3	12	18594.44
COLON (GER)	1	7	1	3	2	50245.00
COLONEL COLLINS (USA)	1	7	1	1	2	2618.50
COMMANCHE RUN	86	316	16	19	86	243416.83
COMME L'ETOILE	1	8	1	3	3	15208.50
COMMON GROUNDS	18	56	2	3	9	23807.06
COMTE DU BOURG (FR)	1	10	1	1	0	2842.00
CONQUERING HERO (USA)	3	13	1	1	1	5292.21
CONTRACT LAW (USA)	12	35	2	2	4	8974.10
CONVINCED	5	22	1	3	7	19234.26
CORROUGE (USA)	18	55	1	1	8	10672.19
COSMONAUT (GB)	11	30	3	5	7	36344.04
COUNTRY PINE (USA)	1	7	1	2	2	7629.85
COZZENE (USA)	4	17	2	2	7	58516.25
CRAFTY PROSPECTOR (USA)	2	15	1	2	6	13741.75
CRAGADOR	1	11	1	1	1	6324.00
CRESTED LARK	5	17	1	1	6	9734.88
CYBORG (FR)	24	101	10	12	30	199115.34
DAHAR (USA)	1	2	1	2	0	7725.25
DANCING DISSIDENT (USA)	9	34	1	1	7	6062.89
DANCING HIGH	11	32	2	2	9	9002.00
DANCING SPREE (USA)	12	33	3	3	6	30773.00
DANEHILL (USA)	22	71	5	7	27	77883.60
DANEHILL DANCER (IRE)	22	56	1	1	7	18984.11
DANETIME (IRE)	3	8	1	2	1	8780.75
DANZIG CONNECTION (USA)	21	55	3	5	6	28484.05
DARNAY (GB)	11	21	1	1	4	9195.66
DARSHAAN	34	104	8	11	29	123976.36
DASHING BLADE	7	20	3	3	2	15732.00
DEFINITE ARTICLE (GB)	38	149	13	18	49	199386.63
DEHERE (USA)	1	6	1	1	1	7720.78
DELTIC (USA)	3	5	1	1	0	3368.30
DEMOCRATIC (USA)	6	20	1	2	8	11363.25
DENEL (FR)	19	69	6	8	21	61309.51
DENHAM RED (FR)	1	10	1	1	3	9506.50
DEPLOY	27	94	7	9	23	80471.67
DERRYLIN	20	90	4	7	25	58805.56
DESERT KING (IRE)	13	40	3	3	11	34253.25
DESERT OF WIND (USA)	2	8	1	2	4	39100.51
DESERT PRINCE (IRE)	4	13	1	1	1	3558.00
DESERT STORY (IRE)	8	27	3	3	3	17793.26
DESERT STYLE (IRE)	8	35	1	6	10	54849.96
DESTROYER	3	13	1	1	3	6931.50
DIESIS	15	61	5	5	12	36677.44
DILUM (USA)	5	24	1	1	11	8907.29
DISTANT RELATIVE	6	26	2	2	4	9061.98
DISTANT VIEW (USA)	8	27	2	4	5	21821.71
DISTINCTLY NORTH (USA)	30	95	4	6	18	42749.35
DIXIELAND BAND (USA)	2	5	1	1	1	6212.18

STALLIONS	RNRS	STARTS	WNRS	WINS	PLACES	TOTAL
DJARVIS (FR)	2	15	1	1	9	15067.08
DOLPHIN STREET (FR)	30	134	6	6	40	70602.12
DOM ALCO (FR)	3	10	2	3	3	33475.60
DOMITOR (USA)	1	6	1	3	1	13912.25
DOUBLE BED (FR)	4	11	1	1	3	5369.15
DOUBLE ECLIPSE (IRE)	9	43	4	5	15	42264.12
DOUBLETOUR (USA)	12	38	1	1	9	11883.65
DOUBLE TRIGGER (IRE)	6	18	2	3	4	20497.70
DOUNBA (FR)	1	2	1	1	1	6036.25
DOYOUN	18	99	7	12	31	111304.38
DR DEVIOUS (IRE)	23	89	10	11	16	100450.80
DRESS PARADE	1	5	1	1	1	4279.50
DROMOD HILL	6	26	2	5	9	27545.66
DRY DOCK	8	20	3	3	2	36684.54
DUKE VALENTINO (GB)	2	10	1	2	2	8011.50
DUKY	7	26	1	1	3	4579.16
DURGAM (USA)	3	6	1	1	1	3613.00
DYNAFORMER (USA)	7	27	2	3	14	36414.01
EAGLE EYED (USA)	33	130	8	13	31	81277.22
EFISIO	16	51	1	1	11	10810.75
ELA-MANA-MOU	17	78	7	8	23	66130.53
ELBIO	10	32	2	3	4	19914.86
EL CONQUISTADOR	16	40	2	3	7	12342.65
ELEGANT MONARCH	3	8	1	1	2	5311.20
ELMAAMUL (USA)	14	40	1	2	8	12300.44
EL PRADO (IRE)	5	15	1	2	6	12127.66
EMPEROR FOUNTAIN	8	31	1	1	9	13385.00
EMPEROR JONES (USA)	23	114	6	10	35	132595.84
EN CALCAT (FR)	3	19	2	6	8	48806.95
ENDOLI	4	15	1	1	2	2190.50
ENTREPRENEUR (GB)	21	69	4	4	22	33278.19
ENVIRONMENT FRIEND (GB)	24	92	5	11	20	84875.24
EPERVIER BLEU	11	52	7	9	16	57968.35
EQUALIZE (USA)	2	11	1	1	2	5365.50
ERDELISTAN (FR)	2	11	1	1	1	7601.28
ERINS ISLE	45	180	12	17	43	159569.48
ESPRIT DU NORD (USA)	1	7	1	1	4	6326.55
ESTEEM BALL (FR)	1	2	1	1	0	3444.00
EUROBUS	30	92	5	7	21	62735.23
EVE'S ERROR	11	40	1	1	3	6138.21
EXECUTIVE PERK	95	335	20	24	76	233891.49
EXIT TO NOWHERE (USA)	14	66	6	8	25	115595.65
EZZOUD (IRE)	12	37	3	4	8	37137.80
FAIRY KING (USA)	8	49	3	9	16	226131.67
FARHAAN	11	36	3	3	11	22415.73
FARMA WAY (USA)	1	7	1	1	3	11357.32
FAUSTUS (USA)	13	53	2	2	16	32514.45
FAVOURED NATIONS (IRE)	1	5	1	1	4	10948.25
FAYRUZ	13	49	1	1	18	20162.03
FIESTA STAR (AUS)	1	6	1	1	3	6494.80
FIJAR TANGO (FR)	5	23	2	2	8	19253.25
FILL MY HOPES (FR)	2	8	1	2	2	14630.13
FIRST TRUMP (GB)	19	56	2	3	9	10123.00
FLEETWOOD (IRE)	10	37	4	5	7	26002.00
FLEMENSFIRTH (USA)	28	80	6	10	14	85277.01
FLORIDA SON	11	37	2	3	8	108116.03
FLYING SPUR (AUS)	20	74	5	6	16	43197.18
FOREST WIND (USA)	14	36	1	1	13	9770.74
FORZANDO	14	52	3	5	19	32479.07
FOURSTARS ALLSTAR (USA)	72	252	18	29	49	269699.75
FOXHOUND (USA)	13	50	5	8	9	41227.55
FRAAM (GB)	11	32	1	1	5	7483.75
FREDDIE'S STAR	1	9	1	2	2	12779.00
FRENCH DEPUTY (USA)	1	15	1	2	5	9116.80
FRESH BREEZE (USA)	9	30	1	1	11	16464.16
FRIMAIRE (GB)	6	23	4	4	8	31957.25

STALLIONS	RNRS	STARTS	WNRS	WINS	PLACES	TOTAL
FUJI KISEKI (JPN)	1	6	1	3	1	18972.73
FULL EXTENT (USA)	1	4	1	1	0	1834.00
GARDE ROYALE	21	78	11	18	33	368167.90
GARGOOR	1	7	1	1	3	8380.50
GENERAL ASSEMBLY (USA)	1	5	1	2	1	8267.00
GENERAL MONASH (USA)	8	20	2	3	8	34379.03
GENEREUX GENIE	3	7	1	1	2	4685.75
GENEROUS (IRE)	15	74	6	10	22	107145.73
GERMANY (USA)	24	86	3	3	24	43622.30
GILDORAN	47	148	7	8	32	53967.70
GLACIAL STORM (USA)	133	473	27	44	128	466080.16
GLAIEUL (USA)	1	7	1	3	2	54017.60
GLORY OF DANCER (GB)	3	8	1	2	1	31503.00
GODS SOLUTION	2	8	1	1	1	6223.00
GOLD AND IVORY (USA)	2	7	1	2	3	10924.35
GOLDEN HEIGHTS	8	36	1	1	9	10655.00
GOLDMARK (USA)	30	117	6	8	27	100556.13
GONE FISHIN	11	34	1	1	0	4928.57
GOOD THYNE (USA)	129	405	23	33	90	435246.36
GOTHLAND (FR)	18	59	2	3	13	17608.38
GOVERNOR GENERAL	3	15	2	8	4	28759.15
GRAN ALBA (USA)	8	16	1	1	5	8393.55
GRAND LODGE (USA)	32	112	6	6	31	51043.72
GRAND PLAISIR (IRE)	28	81	4	10	18	78319.19
GRAND TRESOR (FR)	8	53	4	10	21	223637.73
GREAT COMMOTION (USA)	10	39	1	1	8	11384.37
GREAT MARQUESS	11	39	2	2	7	11986.08
GREAT PALM (USA)	3	13	1	2	6	21785.25
GREEN DANCER (USA)	10	42	4	6	17	33991.40
GREEN DESERT (USA)	11	28	1	1	5	8747.00
GREENSMITH	13	57	5	13	15	62053.49
GREEN TUNE (USA)	4	18	2	2	7	47069.40
GROOM DANCER (USA)	14	53	1	1	15	14224.63
GROSVENOR (NZ)	1	7	1	1	0	3623.75
GUNNER B	38	128	10	13	41	282069.00
HALF ICED (USA)	1	2	1	1	1	4455.00
HALLING (USA)	6	30	2	3	9	86584.25
HAMAS (IRE)	11	38	2	4	9	28971.82
HANSEL (USA)	2	15	1	3	4	25468.34
HATIM (USA)	10	27	1	2	4	12458.55
HAWKSTONE (IRE)	3	9	1	1	1	6449.50
HAZAAM (USA)	1	4	1	1	1	5501.80
HECTOR PROTECTOR (USA)	10	43	1	2	15	19836.48
HENBIT (USA)	20	73	2	3	31	45925.89
HERNANDO (FR)	22	80	7	8	31	131596.93
HIGHEST HONOR (FR)	12	57	5	10	25	121631.60
HIGH KICKER (USA)	4	18	2	3	5	13320.50
HOLLOW HAND	18	47	1	2	15	34024.55
HOMO SAPIEN	38	173	9	12	45	87250.05
HOUMAYOUN (FR)	11	31	1	1	9	19236.03
HUBBLY BUBBLY (USA)	19	67	2	5	15	116366.27
HULA TOWN (NZ)	2	19	2	8	5	68083.50
HURRICANE SKY (AUS)	3	11	1	1	4	6495.75
HUSHANG (IRE)	5	19	1	3	6	16680.00
HUSYAN (USA)	33	130	7	11	35	99406.05
IDIOT'S DELIGHT	4	27	3	4	8	33303.25
IDRIS (IRE)	9	29	1	1	5	6378.00
IKDAM	13	74	2	2	22	27354.83
ILE DE CHYPRE	1	3	1	1	1	1790.00
ILIUM	5	18	1	1	2	4912.00
IMPERIAL FRONTIER (USA)	6	19	1	1	2	7363.42
IMP SOCIETY (USA)	8	26	2	2	7	13066.70
INCA CHIEF (USA)	1	2	1	1	1	3343.00
INCHINOR (GB)	18	62	5	6	19	40471.30
INDIAN RIDGE	21	98	5	9	27	60024.37
INFANTRY	7	20	2	2	4	8351.00

STALLIONS	RNRS	STARTS	WNRS	WINS	PLACES	TOTAL
INSAN (USA)	43	163	10	17	45	256693.72
INTERREX (CAN)	5	43	4	6	22	46424.89
IN THE WINGS	28	113	12	22	35	294080.87
INZAR (USA)	7	31	1	1	10	28732.48
IRISH PROSPECTOR (FR)	1	10	1	3	4	11582.00
IRISH RIVER (FR)	13	50	5	6	12	29285.33
IRIS NOIR (FR)	3	8	1	1	1	3548.00
JACKSON'S DRIFT (USA)	4	10	1	2	1	12017.93
JALLAD (USA)	1	3	1	1	1	4256.50
JAMESMEAD	5	23	1	1	7	13156.62
JAPE (USA)	3	14	1	1	6	16197.49
JENDALI (USA)	9	39	2	5	12	22815.08
JOHN FRENCH	14	57	3	3	12	26736.15
JOLLY JAKE (NZ)	32	126	7	10	48	112863.18
JUMBO HIRT (USA)	14	65	4	6	20	36451.68
JUPITER ISLAND	22	100	4	6	33	84417.87
JURADO (USA)	79	333	20	32	71	291532.84
KADALKO (FR)	13	49	7	11	15	83510.40
KADROU (FR)	2	4	1	1	1	4843.00
KAHYASI	41	181	12	19	61	168770.30
KALA SHIKARI	1	4	1	1	2	1671.00
KALDOUNEVEES (FR)	4	20	2	3	11	19390.50
KAMBALDA	5	20	1	1	4	11999.75
KARINGA BAY	75	271	24	35	65	233150.60
KARLINSKY (USA)	1	4	1	1	2	6770.20
KASMAYO (GB)	3	13	1	1	5	7487.04
K-BATTERY	2	6	1	1	2	3670.00
KEEN	15	57	3	8	13	44347.84
KEFAAH (USA)	1	3	1	1	0	4082.00
KEY OF LUCK (USA)	17	72	4	4	23	42997.59
KIND OF HUSH	1	2	1	1	0	4036.50
KING AMONG KINGS	3	14	2	3	3	18194.30
KING LUTHIER	8	34	2	2	6	13598.56
KINGMAMBO (USA)	4	28	2	3	11	53082.67
KING OF KINGS (IRE)	9	33	2	2	4	13133.19
KING PERSIAN	3	14	1	1	5	9630.09
KING'S RIDE	89	292	14	19	74	165042.01
KING'S SIGNET (USA)	6	31	1	1	9	13084.91
KING'S THEATRE (IRE)	27	127	13	19	43	218628.66
KLIMT (FR)	1	5	1	1	3	10430.00
KNOWN FACT (USA)	3	18	1	1	6	10354.00
KOMAITE (USA)	5	13	1	1	2	7188.25
KRIS	32	146	10	13	43	116574.96
KRIS S (USA)	2	7	1	1	3	11448.79
LAFONTAINE (USA)	10	38	3	3	17	60434.83
LAHIB (USA)	18	66	2	3	17	39258.89
LAKE CONISTON (IRE)	13	52	5	5	17	37643.17
LANCASTRIAN	22	85	3	6	17	26842.05
LANDO (GER)	5	13	1	3	2	38466.55
LANDYAP (USA)	6	25	1	2	8	20200.45
LAPIERRE	5	33	1	1	5	8476.00
LASHKARI	15	64	4	6	14	47604.20
LAST TYCOON	6	24	3	4	4	19794.89
LAVIRCO (GER)	3	11	1	1	4	15338.44
LAW SOCIETY (USA)	6	28	4	4	7	26506.35
LEADING COUNSEL (USA)	44	206	18	26	54	216053.13
LEAR FAN (USA)	13	53	4	8	11	51157.96
LE BALAFRE (FR)	1	5	1	1	2	7451.50
LE BAVARD (FR)	8	25	1	1	1	5187.57
LE COQ D'OR	2	10	1	1	5	8449.50
LE MOSS	16	57	3	3	16	37560.90
LE RIVERAIN (FR)	3	10	1	1	3	5249.75
LESOTHO (USA)	3	13	1	1	4	30149.39
LIGHTER	7	26	2	2	9	17265.35
LIGHTS OUT (FR)	3	17	1	1	10	13974.25
LINAMIX (FR)	19	80	11	16	22	164426.31

STALLIONS	RNRS	STARTS	WNRS	WINS	PLACES	TOTAL
LION CAVERN (USA)	13	39	3	3	7	19502.66
LITHGIE-BRIG	2	11	1	1	3	5145.05
LITTLE BIGHORN	18	48	2	4	5	23977.73
LOMITAS (GB)	8	27	3	3	12	21567.00
LORD AMÉRICO	161	634	37	52	181	500417.27
LORD AT WAR (ARG)	1	4	1	2	1	6680.75
LORD BUD	7	37	2	2	10	14296.10
LUCHIROVERTE (IRE)	6	19	2	2	6	12286.81
LUCKY GUEST	8	41	2	2	12	18424.67
LUGANA BEACH	5	18	2	2	5	11649.00
LURE (USA)	5	15	2	4	4	30415.77
LUTE ANTIQUE (FR)	13	43	4	5	11	113829.29
LUTH DANCER (USA)	1	5	1	1	1	6691.50
LYCIUS (USA)	14	59	4	7	16	108041.87
LYPHENTO (USA)	12	48	3	3	9	15506.00
MACHIAVELLIAN (USA)	14	64	6	10	31	140929.56
MACMILLION	2	4	1	1	2	6454.60
MAGICAL STRIKE (USA)	7	22	1	1	3	9592.92
MAGICAL WONDER (USA)	28	123	4	11	35	179426.25
MAGIC RING (IRE)	12	32	2	2	5	8967.25
MAKBUL	9	21	1	1	6	9508.30
MALASPINA	1	1	1	1	0	2576.00
MANDALUS	73	297	19	30	78	383339.14
MANHAL (GB)	2	8	1	1	0	2408.00
MANSONNIEN (FR)	5	36	4	6	18	76991.21
MARJU (IRE)	27	110	10	21	25	145596.14
MARK OF ESTEEM (IRE)	9	41	2	4	6	43255.56
MAZAAD	10	40	2	3	11	37211.67
MEADOWBROOK	5	8	1	1	* 1	2934.00
MERDON MELODY	5	24	2	5	5	15108.25
MERRYMOUNT	1	8	1	2	5	23344.16
MICHELOZZO (USA)	11	35	3	3	8	17943.15
MIDHISH (GB)	12	38	3	3	5	16802.15
MIDNIGHT LEGEND (GB)	9	36	2	2	12	13185.00
MIDYAN (USA)	8	38	5	7	9	29274.25
MIESQUE'S SON (USA)	1	3	1	1	1	3657.00
MILIEU	11	44	2	4	8	16022.50
MILLE BALLES (FR)	1	8	1	2	5	12954.00
MILLFONTAINE	2	22	1	1	10	25485.72
MILLKOM (GB)	5	15	2	2	3	5758.00
MINER'S LAMP	6	19	1	2	4	19788.75
MINSTER SON	53	218	12	18	55	122131.77
MIRROR BOY	2	23	1	1	9	12172.30
MISTER BAILEYS (GB)	7	27	2	3	7	18677.63
MISTER LORD (USA)	99	387	23	38	106	526638.86
MISTER MAT (FR)	4	21	3	6	4	50742.80
MISTERTOPOGIGO (IRE)	6	12	1	1	1	3749.00
MONDRIAN (GER)	1	13	1	5	3	22260.90
MONSUN (GER)	9	28	3	4	10	103271.29
MONTELIMAR (USA)	127	541	37	48	152	708118.68
MONTORSELLI	1	4	1	1	2	9178.50
MOONAX (IRE)	10	26	1	2	7	14367.27
MORPETH (GB)	12	48	4	4	15	30612.02
MOSCOW SOCIETY (USA)	77	295	24	38	83	509517.49
MOST WELCOME	16	42	6	6	6	35295.21
MOTIVATE	1	2	1	1	0	3347.50
MR CONFUSION (IRE)	6	18	2	2	4	15833.39
MTOTO	33	155	9	13	35	105215.15
MUHARIB (USA)	10	46	4	4	19	32916.97
MUHTARRAM (USA)	9	29	4	6	7	38190.20
MUJADIL (USA)	24	92	3	3	26	30720.98
MUJTAHID (USA)	9	53	4	8	16	72898.93
MULBERRY (FR)	1	9	1	1	4	48357.20
MUROTO	5	21	1	3	5	17911.31
MUSIC BOY	1	4	1	2	0	6523.25
MYSTIKO (USA)	5	15	1	1	3	3603.00

STALLIONS	RNRS	STARTS	WNRS	WINS	PLACES	TOTAL
NAHEEZ (USA)	22	74	3	5	15	39120.96
NALCHIK (USA)	6	10	1	1	2	4391.00
NAMAQUALAND (USA)	25	132	10	13	53	95002.26
NASHAMAA	1	4	1	2	1	13818.00
NASHWAN (USA)	16	57	3	7	12	63123.90
NEARLY A HAND	6	18	2	2	1	24127.30
NEEDLE GUN (IRE)	13	34	4	5	5	24100.41
NELTINO	11	32	2	2	9	20763.50
NESHAD (USA)	7	16	1	2	2	11387.00
NESTOR	1	4	1	3	1	94991.50
NICHOLAS BILL	18	71	7	10	27	63383.70
NICOLOTTE (GB)	8	28	2	6	9	66853.99
NIGHT SHIFT (USA)	17	66	6	10	20	203560.82
NIKOS	15	76	6	13	35	196630.30
NINISKI (USA)	7	28	3	4	6	32517.81
NOBLE PATRIARCH	4	18	3	4	11	25452.95
NOMADIC WAY (USA)	27	114	7	12	30	105486.67
NOMINATION	4	11	1	2	6	12669.65
NONONITO (FR)	1	1	1	1	0	6073.94
NORDANCE (USA)	2	5	1	2	0	5173.00
NORTH BRITON	3	24	1	1	15	58205.70
NORTHERN FLAGSHIP (USA)	4	13	2	2	8	21087.60
NORWICH	58	206	15	23	46	247368.99
NUCLEON (USA)	7	25	1	1	6	11696.56
NUREYEV (USA)	1	8	1	3	0	20638.50
OLD VIC	98	329	21	29	72	331933.51
OMNICORP (NZ)	3	9	2	2	9	14088.47
OPERA GHOST	4	10	1	1	2	3698.00
ORCHESTRA	19	87	4	7	25	115544.86
ORE	7	33	4	14	8	138042.19
ORFANO (GER)	1	4	1	1	2	18752.50
OSCAR (IRE)	44	122	9	13	35	127574.23
OSCAR SCHINDLER (IRE)	4	8	1	1	1	2911.99
OUR ACCOUNT (USA)	1	5	1	3	0	18014.50
OVAC (ITY)	1	10	1	3	1	20648.00
OVERBURY (IRE)	36	112	4	5	15	30193.75
OVER THE RIVER (FR)	72	264	19	29	72	408662.32
OWINGTON (GB)	4	32	2	3	12	30023.44
THE PARSON	2	5	1	1	1	3969.00
PASSING SALE (FR)	10	41	4	6	10	103649.55
PAST GLORIES	11	38	3	3	8	15575.83
PEACOCK (FR)	9	33	1	2	7	13205.80
PELDER (IRE)	2	12	1	2	3	11369.50
PENNEKAMP (USA)	16	59	1	1	16	23634.04
PERPENDICULAR (GB)	23	92	6	9	20	59959.20
PERRAULT	10	47	5	6	15	55351.28
PERSIAN BOLD	31	114	5	11	29	107342.71
PERSIAN MEWS	12	58	4	7	17	59041.89
PERUGINO (USA)	41	147	10	12	46	110818.42
PETARDIA (GB)	21	61	1	2	14	19340.45
PETIT LOUP (USA)	5	20	1	2	5	19070.83
PETIT MONTMORENCY (USA)	1	6	1	1	0	8482.50
PETONG	8	28	1	1	7	10203.87
PETORIUS	8	14	1	1	0	2471.00
PETOSKI	43	118	3	4	24	29788.75
PHARDANTE (FR)	205	798	44	70	219	634087.72
PICCOLO (GB)	11	21	2	2	3	14084.93
PICEA	3	12	1	1	1	7100.90
PIERRE (GB)	8	22	1	1	5	6569.83
PINE BLUFF (USA)	2	10	1	2	3	14304.15
PIPS PRIDE (GB)	3	7	1	1	0	6099.58
PISTOLET BLEU (IRE)	14	50	5	6	16	143046.88
PIVOTAL (GB)	10	35	2	3	6	16799.25
PLEASANT COLONY (USA)	5	24	2	3	7	17404.97
PLEASANT TAP (USA)	3	20	3	5	9	105221.63
POLAR FALCON (USA)	22	79	8	20	21	297026.17

STALLIONS	RNRS	STARTS	WNRS	WINS	PLACES	TOTAL
POLIGLOTE (GB)	2	7	1	2	5	46387.83
POLISH PRECEDENT (USA)	22	100	6	10	28	70638.28
POLITICAL MERGER (USA)	1	12	1	1	2	8732.10
POPLAR BLUFF (GB)	1	4	1	1	3	8736.50
PORT ETIENNE (FR)	3	13	1	1	7	23835.75
PORT LUCAYA (GB)	7	22	3	3	6	17208.67
PRAIRIE	1	6	1	1	1	3945.00
PRESENTING (GB)	90	293	18	23	61	202599.50
PRESIDIUM	30	122	7	9	23	45294.03
PRIMITIVE RISING (USA)	53	178	10	13	35	83664.55
PRIMO DOMINIE	9	27	1	3	6	20797.75
PRINCE FERDINAND (GB)	1	3	1	1	0	12870.00
PRINCE OF BIRDS (USA)	15	50	3	4	7	26958.81
PRINCE OF PRAISE (NZ)	1	12	1	2	6	12583.00
PRINCE ROONEY (IRE)	4	22	1	1	4	7354.27
PRIOLO (USA)	19	62	4	4	15	27835.22
PROFESSIONAL (IRE)	3	15	1	1	1	3246.00
PROJECT MANAGER	5	18	1	1	8	19577.14
PUISSANCE	7	18	1	1	3	7173.00
PURSUIT OF LOVE (GB)	24	73	1	1	13	10195.20
PUSH ON	2	10	2	2	4	12778.90
PYRAMUS (USA)	1	5	1	1	1	10983.09
QUART DE VIN (FR)	4	15	3	3	6	96687.70
QUEST FOR FAME	8	36	2	3	12	16982.11
QUIET AMERICAN (USA)	1	6	1	1	0	6496.75
RAGMAR (FR)	4	12	1	1	0	3828.50
RAHOTEP (FR)	4	13	3	6	6	150550.25
RAHY (USA)	3	10	1	1	4	13106.00
RAINBOW QUEST (USA)	22	72	6	6	19	34759.90
RAINBOWS FOR LIFE (CAN)	24	98	5	9	32	75308.72
RAKAPOSHI KING	53	193	7	11	41	67033.66
RAMBO DANCER (CAN)	6	33	1	1	14	28513.32
RANGOON (FR)	1	6	1	1	0	6740.00
RA NOVA	7	44	3	5	14	25808.15
RASHAR (USA)	29	76	4	6	12	76489.31
RED RANSOM (USA)	2	12	1	4	3	39365.49
RED SUNSET	7	29	2	2	9	16418.67
REGAL EMBERS (IRE)	4	10	1	1	0	4290.00
REGAL INTENTION (CAN)	1	7	1	2	3	12279.70
RELIGIOUSLY (USA)	29	120	9	19	30	263804.45
REMAINDER MAN	2	5	1	1	2	10258.50
REPRIMAND	21	73	5	6	10	52328.11
REVOQUE (IRE)	28	87	7	11	33	91735.22
RIBERETTO	5	16	1	1	5	5550.65
RIDGEWOOD BEN (GB)	14	51	3	3	7	18089.31
RISING	3	10	1	1	4	5747.00
RISK ME (FR)	14	65	6	7	22	49360.88
RIVELAGO (FR)	1	9	1	2	3	11097.50
RIVER FALLS (GB)	6	25	2	2	5	12643.74
RIVER GOD (USA)	3	13	1	1	4	6564.75
RIVERHEAD (USA)	6	20	2	2	8	18593.70
RIVER MIST (USA)	2	8	1	1	2	7797.54
RIVERWISE (USA)	10	42	2	2	17	202374.20
ROBELLINO (USA)	31	110	4	5	46	108224.57
ROCK HOPPER	22	67	2	3	11	24453.25
RODRIGO DE TRIANO (USA)	1	11	1	2	6	23848.06
ROI DE ROME (USA)	5	22	1	1	8	35195.86
ROI GUILLAUME (FR)	3	9	1	1	5	18285.75
ROLFE (USA)	3	8	1	1	2	3218.50
ROMANY RYE (GB)	4	13	1	1	1	2469.00
ROSCOE BLAKE	8	26	3	4	4	21494.24
ROSELIER (FR)	255	1050	60	104	276	1156228.32
ROUGH MAGIC (FR)	1	7	1	2	2	22886.05
ROYAL ABJAR (USA)	10	23	1	1	3	6964.00
ROYAL ACADEMY (USA)	22	52	2	3	2	9120.80
ROYAL CHARTER (FR)	16	67	5	10	21	124659.06

STALLIONS	RNRS	STARTS	WNRS	WINS	PLACES	TOTAL
ROYAL FOUNTAIN	16	35	1	1	6	17333.50
ROYAL MATCH	2	7	1	1	0	2436.00
RUDIMENTARY (USA)	27	111	10	13	30	96737.00
SABREHILL (USA)	29	110	5	9	29	87319.79
SADDLERS' HALL (IRE)	32	98	6	6	20	71818.60
SADLER'S WELLS (USA)	75	318	31	49	107	507519.42
SAFAWAN	12	32	1	1	5	6893.85
SAFETY CATCH (USA)	15	51	6	7	14	51778.84
SAINT ESTEPHE (FR)	3	11	1	2	5	12448.63
SAINT PREUIL (FR)	9	41	4	6	21	143552.24
SALSE (USA)	18	67	6	8	15	55196.10
SANGLAMORE (USA)	10	57	5	9	21	103698.17
SASSANIAN	6	37	2	4	14	59843.05
SATCO (FR)	36	185	15	27	50	245489.24
SAUMAREZ	8	20	1	3	5	17194.32
SAVAHRA SOUND	2	7	1	1	2	3604.00
SAYAARR (USA)	3	14	2	2	7	13871.75
SCALLYWAG	9	25	1	1	11	17610.70
SCENIC	12	53	3	4	12	34235.16
SCOOTER BLEU (IRE)	1	6	1	2	3	132202.00
SEA RAVEN (IRE)	9	21	2	2	2	6406.00
SECLUDE (USA)	5	15	1	2	1	10211.06
SECOND SET (IRE)	9	30	2	2	9	34193.51
SECRET HAUNT (USA)	1	4	1	1	1	5165.00
SECRET 'N CLASSY (CAN)	2	14	2	3	4	16350.00
SECRET OF SUCCESS	1	7	1	2	2	14660.00
SELKIRK (USA)	23	83	6	7	25	101768.20
SEMILLON (GB)	13	72	4	5	20	41921.92
SEPTIEME CIEL (USA)	4	18	2	2	1	6397.61
SESARO (USA)	9	31	1	1	7	8363.61
SEVEN HEARTS	1	12	1	4	5	37893.21
SEYMOUR HICKS (FR)	11	39	2	2	11	14264.10
SHAAB	5	32	1	1	14	16852.80
SHAAMIT (IRE)	12	32	2	3	4	14523.00
SHAFOUN (FR)	3	26	2	4	10	133083.05
SHAHANNDEH	7	13	2	2	3	11574.75
SHAHRASTANI (USA)	4	14	1	1	2	3791.16
SHALFORD (IRE)	13	45	4	5	5	31242.25
SHARDARI	47	208	13	17	55	193743.47
SHAREEF DANCER (USA)	18	74	5	7	18	77172.44
SHARIFABAD (IRE)	15	58	1	1	12	13212.12
SHARP DEAL	4	22	1	2	14	57149.88
SHARP VICTOR (USA)	4	23	1	1	8	10625.54
SHEIKH ALBADOU (GB)	4	14	2	3	2	15544.50
SHERNAZAR	69	200	13	16	47	146703.89
SHINING STEEL	4	29	3	5	10	123321.69
SHUAILAAN (USA)	1	8	1	1	4	6372.00
SIGNE DIVIN (USA)	2	8	2	2	5	16173.00
SILLY PRICES	4	27	1	1	8	13381.54
SILVER KITE (USA)	1	8	1	2	4	14714.50
SILVER RAINBOW (GB)	8	32	3	6	11	228212.28
SIMON DU DESERT (FR)	2	15	2	3	6	19603.00
SIMPLY GREAT (FR)	21	86	4	8	27	96822.69
SINGSPIEL (IRE)	4	10	1	1	0	3584.42
SIR FELIX	1	4	1	1	3	19327.25
SIR HARRY LEWIS (USA)	40	164	14	25	41	177150.29
SIRSAN (IRE)	2	11	1	3	3	18344.16
SKY CHASE (NZ)	1	10	1	6	3	99202.50
SKY CLASSIC (CAN)	5	18	1	2	6	24354.60
SLEEPING CAR (FR)	7	21	1	1	6	8158.75
SLIP ANCHOR	34	120	10	16	22	119462.41
SNURGE	6	32	3	4	9	34485.53
SOLID ILLUSION (USA)	1	7	1	1	0	2317.00
SOLIDOUN (FR)	1	4	1	1	2	3248.75
SONGLINES (FR)	1	8	1	1	2	3640.40
SON OF SHARP SHOT (IRE)	7	19	1	2	1	8711.00

STALLIONS	RNRS	STARTS	WNRS	WINS	PLACES	TOTAL
SON OF SILVER	1	6	1	2	3	12807.50
SON PARDO (GB)	5	28	2	6	8	32034.64
SOVEREIGN WATER (FR)	15	48	1	1	5	6019.56
SOVIET LAD (USA)	12	50	4	6	16	35719.25
SOVIET STAR (USA)	2	9	1	1	6	164065.90
SPANISH PLACE (USA)	12	56	2	3	8	52411.86
SPECTRUM (IRE)	32	115	6	8	25	94889.33
SRI PEKAN (USA)	29	94	9	12	25	101969.64
STANDIFORD (USA)	5	18	1	1	8	6491.99
STARK SOUTH (USA)	2	16	1	1	1	3307.50
STAR WAY	2	22	2	2	7	12828.30
STETCHWORTH (USA)	1	5	1	1	0	6569.37
ST JOVITE (USA)	5	16	1	1	0	2023.00
ST NINIAN	5	13	1	2	3	6204.00
STRONG GALE	48	204	21	30	69	464000.46
SUAVE DANCER (USA)	11	37	3	4	6	43543.57
SULA BULA	21	94	7	14	28	98466.48
SUMMER SQUALL (USA)	2	8	2	3	4	23248.57
SUNLEY BUILDS	4	11	1	1	4	4526.50
SUNNY'S HALO (CAN)	1	4	1	1	2	2924.00
SUPERLATIVE	3	12	1	2	3	11132.50
SUPREME LEADER	301	972	75	107	244	1265447.68
SURUMU (GER)	3	12	1	1	4	8076.21
SYLVAN EXPRESS	2	8	1	1	2	10930.83
SYMBOLI HEIGHTS (FR)	6	21	3	5	6	28716.87
SYNEFOS (USA)	22	64	6	6	18	47805.63
SYRTOS	16	70	2	5	21	35122.25
TAGULA (IRE)	6	22	1	1	7	11607.70
TAKE RISKS (FR)	6	29	3	3	7	28419.46
TAMURE (IRE)	3	9	1	1	4	5663.50
TANAOS	2	8	1	1	1	3876.63
TAOS (IRE)	4	19	1	1	4	5513.55
TAUFAN (USA)	3	19	1	1	2	3364.20
TEAMSTER	15	59	7	10	23	100787.28
TEENOSO (USA)	37	139	13	16	41	162856.48
TEL QUEL (FR)	8	20	1	1	6	13007.19
TENBY (GB)	9	29	3	4	8	27516.25
TERIMON	48	198	13	16	54	124145.97
THEATRICAL	12	44	3	3	13	19043.55
THEATRICAL CHARMER	4	18	1	1	5	6840.80
THEN AGAIN	8	41	2	2	11	12938.00
THOWRA (FR)	10	23	2	2	0	7585.00
THUNDER GULCH (USA)	1	8	1	1	3	6046.25
TIDARO (USA)	16	92	5	7	32	74029.54
TIMELESS TIMES (USA)	8	25	2	2	1	7026.50
TINA'S PET	11	64	4	8	27	50548.15
TIP MOSS (FR)	2	8	1	2	1	6418.75
TIRLEY GALE (GB)	1	7	1	1	4	6560.00
TIROL	13	34	3	4	4	15747.58
TITUS LIVIUS (FR)	14	50	4	5	10	33360.07
TOCA MADERA	8	35	3	5	13	38671.15
TOPANOORA	54	139	11	16	34	140019.70
TOPSIDER (USA)	1	3	1	1	2	5295.68
TOP VILLE	2	5	1	1	3	3680.00
TORRENTIAL (USA)	2	4	1	1	0	6870.50
TORUS	38	167	11	17	40	191508.02
TOULON (GB)	74	295	18	28	80	353548.06
TOUT ENSEMBLE	2	10	1	2	1	11372.40
TRAGIC ROLE (USA)	17	85	6	12	19	78292.44
TREASURE HUNTER	31	151	9	17	47	205568.95
TREBROOK (FR)	2	10	1	1	2	7993.51
TREMBLANT	14	51	5	6	15	63941.65
TREMPOLINO (USA)	10	45	4	7	19	92471.39
TROPULAR	1	3	1	1	0	2213.40
TRUE BRAVE (USA)	2	6	2	2	4	12496.25
TRY TO STOP ME	2	17	1	2	7	12581.00

STALLIONS	RNRS	STARTS	WNRS	WINS	PLACES	TOTAL
TUDOR DIVER	2	4	1	1	0	2261.00
TURGEON (USA)	5	21	1	2	6	57477.39
TURTLE ISLAND (IRE)	47	175	14	19	47	145024.76
UN DESPERADO (FR)	120	451	36	55	110	857009.54
UNFUWAIN (USA)	26	98	4	6	29	53544.58
UP AND AT 'EM (GB)	14	36	1	2	6	21457.80
USEFUL (FR)	16	75	3	4	23	29264.50
VAGUELY PLEASANT (FR)	1	5	1	1	1	11738.50
VALANOUR (IRE)	2	11	2	2	4	12616.62
VALVILLE (FR)	3	13	1	2	7	15412.75
VAN DER LINDEN (FR)	2	8	1	1	0	7785.92
VARESE (FR)	1	3	1	1	1	3927.50
VESTRIS ABÚ	5	17	1	2	4	11010.80
VETTORI (IRE)	16	62	4	5	17	31035.92
VICTORY NOTE (USA)	12	49	6	6	9	38070.02
VIDEO ROCK (FR)	18	89	7	11	34	141898.09
VILLEZ (USA)	8	40	4	7	10	62686.05
WAAJIB	6	25	1	4	9	29928.14
WAKASHAN (GB)	6	12	1	1	2	6201.50
WALL STREET DANCER (USA)	1	10	1	2	4	16425.32
WARCRAFT (USA)	31	92	3	4	14	32845.90
WAR HERO	2	4	1	1	1	7584.41
WARNING	7	29	3	6	8	74401.89
WARRSHAN (USA)	5	25	2	2	4	14732.68
WELD	31	101	6	9	19	65095.72
WELDNAAS (USA)	4	17	2	2	7	12087.50
WELSH TERM	18	58	4	4	13	49580.39
WEST CHINA	2	6	1	1	0	4480.52
WESTMINSTER (NZ)	1	16	1	4	7	28528.25
WHITEHALL BRIDGE	2	6	1	1	1	5241.00
WHITTINGHAM (IRE)	7	11	1	2	1	8897.80
WINGED LOVE (IRE)	5	21	3	4	7	88006.93
WITNESS BOX (USA)	19	95	6	12	29	107173.26
WIZARD KING (GB)	20	59	2	2	9	10944.75
WOLFHOUND (USA)	8	31	3	4	9	38956.25
WOODBOROUGH (USA)	22	59	2	2	10	10459.65
WOODMAN (USA)	11	29	2	2	11	13857.63
YASHGAN	28	99	4	8	24	67673.00
ZABEEL (NZ)	1	2	1	2	0	12288.25
ZAFFARAN (USA)	82	279	19	27	75	239495.88
ZAFONIC (USA)	14	25	1	1	3	5853.00
ZAIZOOM (USA)	1	9	1	3	5	17894.00
ZAMBRANO	2	12	1	1	6	6869.20
ZAYYANI	2	5	1	1	1	2433.00
ZIETEN (USA)	4	22	1	1	7	6948.90
ZILZAL (USA)	15	70	2	4	23	49874.93

BY KIND PERMISSION OF WEATHERBYS

HIGH-PRICED YEARLINGS OF 2004 AT TATTERSALLS' SALES

The following yearlings realised 105,000 guineas and over at Tattersalls' Sales in 2004:-

Name and Breeding	Vendor	Purchaser	Guineas
BR G C DANEHILL (USA) - BORDIGHERA (USA)	TRICKLEDOWN STUD	D O'BYRNE	1150000
B C DANEHILL (USA) - ROCKERLONG (GB)	HASCOMBE STUD	D O'BYRNE	750000
B C SADLER'S WELLS (USA) - BEX (USA)	CAMAS PARK STUD, IRELAND	NOBUTAKA TADA	700000
GALACTIC STAR (GB) CH C GALILEO (IRE) - BALISADA (GB)	HASCOMBE STUD	C GORDON-WATSON BS	700000
B C DANEHILL (USA) - HEAVENLY WHISPER (IRE)	HIGHCLERE STUD	D O'BYRNE	580000
B C SADLER'S WELLS (USA) - SUMOTO (GB)	WATERSHIP DOWN STUD	D O'BYRNE	580000
B F DANEHILL (USA) - HOTELGENIE DOT COM (GB)	CATRIDGE FARM STUD	BBA (IRELAND)	520000
B F DANEHILL (USA) - BRIGITTA (IRE)	WATERSHIP DOWN STUD	BBA (IRELAND)	500000
B C KINGMAMBO (USA) - VALENTINE WALTZ (IRE)	ROUND HILL STUD, IRELAND	VENDOR	480000
B F SADLER'S WELLS (USA) - SHOUK (GB)	CAMAS PARK STUD, IRELAND	BBA (IRELAND)	420000
B C GALILEO (IRE) - CHILD PRODIGY (IRE)	CAMAS PARK STUD, IRELAND	D O'BYRNE	420000
ALLEGRETTO (IRE) CH F GALILEO (IRE) - ALLELUIA (GB)	AIRLIE STUD, IRELAND	CHEVELEY PARK STUD	415000
B F GREEN DESERT (USA) - LADY MILETRIAN (IRE)	LODGE PARK STUD, IRELAND	J GOSDEN	400000
NOBLE GENT (IRE) B C DANEHILL (USA) - BLANCHE DUBOIS (GB)	CAMAS PARK STUD, IRELAND	JOHN FERGUSON BS	400000
IRISH BLARNEY (GB) CH F HALLING (USA) - SPINNING THE YARN (GB)	CAMAS PARK STUD, IRELAND	JOHN FERGUSON BS	400000
B F WAR CHANT (USA) - GOSSAMER (USA)	AIRLIE STUD, IRELAND	M O'TOOLE	400000
HUMUNGOUS (IRE) CH C GIANT'S CAUSEWAY (USA) - DOULA (USA)	CAMAS PARK STUD, IRELAND	C EGERTON	380000
B F GALILEO (IRE) - ZIBILENE (GB)	BAROUCHE STUD (IRELAND) LTD	M JARVIS	360000
EXTREME MEASURES (GB) B C MONTJEU (IRE) - FADE (GB)	HIGHCLERE STUD	JOHN FERGUSON BS	360000
B C SADLER'S WELLS (USA) - MOSAIQUE BLEUE (GB)	HIGHCLERE STUD	D O'BYRNE	350000
DANCE TO THE BAND (USA) B F KINGMAMBO (USA) - DANCE DESIGN (IRE)	BUGLEY STUD	BBA (IRELAND)	340000
EMINENCIA (GB) B F SADLER'S WELLS (USA) - MY EMMA (GB)	STAFFORDSTOWN, IRELAND	MEAD. GOODBODY	320000
B C MONTJEU (IRE) - MIDNIGHT FEVER (IRE)	KILDARAGH STUD, IRELAND (AGENT)	ANTHONY STROUD BS	320000
B C DANEHILL (USA) - DANCING MIRAGE (IRE)	HIGHCLERE STUD	D O'BYRNE	310000
QUEEN'S BEST (GB) B F KING'S BEST (USA) - CLOUD CASTLE (GB)	ABBEVILLE & MEADOW COURT STUDS, IRELAND	CHEVELEY PARK STUD	310000
HONOUR BRIGHT (IRE) B F DANEHILL (USA) - DABILIYA	BARROMSTOWN STUD, IRELAND	BBA (IRELAND)	300000
THERMIDOR (USA) CH C GIANT'S CAUSEWAY (USA) - LANGOUSTINE (AUS)	HIGHCLERE STUD	C GORDON-WATSON BS	300000
JAMRAH (IRE) B F DANEHILL (USA) - PIPALONG (IRE)	OAKS FARM STABLES	BBA (IRELAND)	300000
B C SADLER'S WELLS (USA) - REBECCA SHARP (GB)	HASCOMBE STUD	SHADWELL ESTATE	300000
CHAMBORD (IRE) GR C GREEN DESERT (USA) - KENMIST (GB)	EUROPEAN SALES MANAGEMENT	M TREGONING	300000
B F MOZART (IRE) - SARAH-CLARE (GB)	CAMAS PARK STUD, IRELAND	VENDOR	290000
B F SADLER'S WELLS (USA) - AIM FOR THE TOP (USA)	ASHTOWN HOUSE STUD, IRELAND	D O'BYRNE	290000
DANKOVA (IRE) B C DANEHILL (USA) - BORN BEAUTIFUL (USA)	LYNN LODGE STUD, IRELAND (AGENT)	J DELAHOOKE	280000
GRAIN OF TRUTH (IRE) B F GULCH (USA) - PURE GRAIN (GB)	JAMIE RAILTON, AGENT	JOHN FERGUSON BS	280000
B F SADLER'S WELLS (USA) - BRIGID (USA)	OAKS FARM STABLES	PEGASUS FARMS	270000
CH C RAINBOW QUEST (USA) - BALLET SHOES (IRE)	AIRLIE STUD, IRELAND	NOBUTAKA TADA	265000
GR/RO C WAR CHANT (USA) - LA GANDILE (FR)	SWORDLESTOWN STUD, IRELAND	C GORDON-WATSON BS	260000
MEKYAS (IRE) B C DANEHILL (USA) - WELSH LOVE	THE CASTLEBRIDGE CONSIGNMENT	SHADWELL ESTATE	260000
CH C GALILEO (IRE) - WELSH LOVE	KILCARN STUD, IRELAND	SHADWELL ESTATE	255000
AQUARIST (GB) CH F CORONADO'S QUEST (USA) - OYSTER CATCHER (IRE)	BRITTON HOUSE STUD	D O'BYRNE	250000
B C GIANT'S CAUSEWAY (USA) - BRIGHTEST STAR (GB)	MEON VALLEY STUD	JOHN FERGUSON BS	250000
WEDAAD (GB) CH F FANTASTIC LIGHT (USA) - MY FIRST ROMANCE (GB)	BEARSTONE STUD	SHADWELL ESTATE	250000
B F SADLER'S WELLS (USA) - MASSKANA (IRE)	WHATTON MANOR STUD	ANTHONY STROUD BS	240000
GREEN EYES (IRE) BR F GREEN DESERT (USA) - KARLAFSHA	BAROUCHE STUD (IRELAND) LTD	ANTHONY STROUD BS	230000

Name	Vendor	Buyer	Price
MAGIC PEAK (IRE) B F DANEHILL (USA) - MAGIC COVE (USA)	AIRLIE STUD, IRELAND	CHEVELEY PARK STUD	230000
CH C GALILEO (IRE) - ARCTIC HUNT (IRE)	ROUND HILL STUD, IRELAND	M JARVIS	230000
B C CAPE CROSS (IRE) - CAPE MERINO (GB)	JAMIE RAILTON, AGENT	J GOSDEN	230000
B C GALILEO (IRE) - LOVE DIVINE (GB)	WATERSHIP DOWN STUD	JOHN WARREN BS.	230000
B F DANEHILL (USA) - DEMURE (GB)	CASTLETON GROUP	D O'BYRNE	230000
MATHOOR (GB) CH C FANTASTIC LIGHT (USA) - MADAME DUBOIS	NEW ENGLAND STUD	SHADWELL ESTATE	230000
PAWTUCKET (IRE) B C CAPE CROSS (IRE) - MANCHOLA (FR)	YEOMANSTOWN STUD, IRELAND	JOHN FERGUSON BS.	220000
GRAND PALACE (IRE) B C GRAND LODGE (USA) - POCKET BOOK (IRE)	PARKWAY FARM, IRELAND	C GORDON-WATSON BS.	220000
B C GALILEO (IRE) - LIONNE (GB)	LODGE PARK STUD, IRELAND	D O'BYRNE	220000
B C GALILEO (IRE) - ABTARA (IRE)	CASTLETOWN STUD, IRELAND (AGENT)	D O'BYRNE	220000
BR C FANTASTIC LIGHT (USA) - OUT WEST (USA)	DEERFIELD FARM	JOHN FERGUSON BS.	220000
B C DANEHILL (USA) - ZARAWA (IRE)	TULLAMAINE CASTLE STUD, IRELAND	G ARMENGOL	210000
B C SADLER'S WELLS (USA) - ROSE PALLE (FR)	JOHN TROY, AGENT	D O'BYRNE	200000
PARIS WINDS (IRE) CH F GALILEO (IRE) - LILS JESSY (FR)	PEGASUS FARMS LTD, IRELAND	BBA (IRELAND)	200000
BOOK OF MUSIC (IRE) B C SADLER'S WELLS (USA) - NOVELETTE (GB)	BARRONSTOWN STUD, IRELAND (AGENT)	J GOSDEN	200000
WANNABE POSH (IRE) B F GRAND LODGE (USA) - WANNABE (GB)	GLENVALE STUD, IRELAND (AGENT)	C GORDON-WATSON BS.	200000
B C PIVOTAL (GB) - ZIARA (FR)	YEOMANSTOWN STUD, IRELAND	J GOSDEN	200000
B C CAPE CROSS (IRE) - TEE CEE (GB)	STAFFORDSTOWN, IRELAND	JOHN FERGUSON BS.	200000
DRAGON DANCER (GB) B C SADLER'S WELLS (USA) - ALAKANANDA (GB)	GENESIS GREEN STUD	G WRAGG	200000
LAITH (IRE) B C ROYAL APPLAUSE (GB) - DANIA (GER)	YEOMANSTOWN STUD, IRELAND	SHADWELL ESTATE.	200000
KING'S POET (IRE) B C SADLER'S BEST (USA) - TEGWEN (USA)	LOUGHBROWN STUD, IRELAND	JOHN FERGUSON BS.	200000
B/BR C FANTASTIC LIGHT (USA) - SASSY BIRD (IRE)	HARAS DE MONTAIGU, FRANCE	VENDOR.	200000
B C MOZART - DON'T WORRY ME (IRE)	CROOM HOUSE STUD, IRELAND	D O'BYRNE	200000
B C KING CHARLEMAGNE (USA) - TADKYRA (IRE)	NEWTOWN STUD, IRELAND	JOHN WARREN BS.	200000
B C SADLER'S WELLS (USA) - LURINA (IRE)	ROUND HILL STUD, IRELAND	M TREGONING	200000
B F MACHIAVELLIAN (USA) - GOLD FIELD (IRE)	WATERSHIP DOWN STUD	JOHN FERGUSON BS.	200000
OTELCALIFORNI (GB) GR F GULCH (USA) - IVE GOTA BAD LIVER (USA)		R GODEN	200000
PENTATONIC (GB) B F GIANT'S CAUSEWAY (USA) - FASCINATING RHYTHM (GB)	MEON VALLEY STUD	VENDOR	200000
KASSIOPEIA (IRE) B F GALILEO (IRE) - BRUSH STROKES (IRE)	FURNACE MILL STUD.	VENDOR.	195000
BEST ALIBI (IRE) B C KING'S BEST (USA) - CHAUNCY LANE (IRE)	YEOMANSTOWN STUD, IRELAND	JOHN FERGUSON BS.	190000
B C DANEHILL (USA) - PAPER MOON (IRE)	ASHTOWN HOUSE STUD, IRELAND	D O'BYRNE	190000
B C NIGHT SHIFT (USA) - BELLE DE CADIX (IRE)	GLENVALE STUD IRELAND (AGENT)	D O'BYRNE	190000
B F GALILEO (IRE) - TROIS GRACES (USA)	MARSTON STUD	MCKEEVER ST LAWRENCE BS.	180000
B C KINGMAMBO (USA) - SHERIKYA (IRE)	WATERSHIP DOWN STUD	VENDOR.	180000
ALAMBIC (GB) GR F COZZENE (USA) - ALEXANDRINE (IRE)	STAFFORDSTOWN, IRELAND	CBA.	180000
B C SADLER'S WELLS (USA) - WANNABE GRAND (IRE)	DAYLESFORD STUD.	J GOSDEN.	180000
ERMINE SEA (USA) B G RAINBOW QUEST (USA) - BINT PASHA (USA)	RATHBARRY STUD, IRELAND	JOHN FERGUSON BS.	180000
BOLD ALASKA (USA) B C CAPE CROSS (IRE) - DRAMATIC ENTRY (IRE)	MEON VALLEY STUD	JOHN FERGUSON BS.	180000
PHILANTHROPIST (GB) B C FANTASTIC LIGHT (USA) - SOMEONE SPECIAL	ENNISTOWN STUD, IRELAND	C GORDON-WATSON BS.	180000
CH F ROYAL ACADEMY (USA) - WHITE WISTERIA (GB)	OLD CARHUE STUD, IRELAND	D WELD	180000
PERSIAN LIGHT (GER) B F FANTASTIC LIGHT (USA) - PRIVATE LIFE (FR)	UNION STUD, GERMANY	SHADWELL ESTATE	175000
DREAM PRIZE (IRE) CH C PENTIRE CELEBRE (USA) - NIGHT TEENY (GB)	YEOMANSTOWN STUD, IRELAND	C GORDON-WATSON BS.	170000
WELL GUARDED (IRE) B C SADLER'S WELLS (USA) - EN GARDE (USA)	ASHTOWN HOUSE STUD, IRELAND	CHARLES EGERTON BS.	170000
MANNIKKO (IRE) GR C GREEN DESERT (USA) - CASSANDRA GO (IRE)	BALLYHIMIKIN STUD, IRELAND	VENDOR.	170000
B F HALLING (USA) - MARIENBAD (FR)	NEW ENGLAND STUD	J GOSDEN	170000
GREEN DESERT (USA) - PRIORY BELLE (IRE)	BALLYLINCH STUD, IRELAND	MCKEEVER ST LAWRENCE BS.	160000
B C MACHIAVELLIAN (USA) - RUMPUMPUMPY (GB)	STRADBALLI MANOR STUD	JOHN FERGUSON BS.	160000
NAUGHTY BY NATURE B C ROYAL APPLAUSE (GB) - GORGEOUS DANCER (IRE)	TRICKLEDOWN STUD	G RICHARDSON.	160000

Breeding	Vendor	Purchaser	Price
B C DANEHILL (USA) - LOIRE VALLEY (IRE)	VOUTE SALES, AGENT	C EGERTON	160000
ZAM ZAMMAH (GB) B C AGNES WORLD (USA) - KRISALYA	COLLIN STUD	D WOODS	160000
MAYSOOR (GB) CH C SELKIRK (USA) - JUST DREAMS (GB)	YEOMANSTOWN STUD, IRELAND (AGENT)	SHADWELL ESTATE	160000
B C GALILEO (IRE) - VALLEE DES REYES (USA)	MARSTON STUD	J GOSDEN	160000
MOTARAQEB (GB) B C GRAND LODGE (USA) - PINK CRISTAL (GB)	DAYLESFORD STUD	SHADWELL ESTATE	155000
B C MOZART (IRE) - KARDELLE (GB)	FLOORS STUD	G RICHARDSON	150000
B F ALHAARTH (IRE) - FRAPPE (IRE)	NORELANDS STUD, IRELAND	J GOSDEN	150000
GREEN CALIBRE (GB) B C GREEN DESERT (USA) - AIR OF DISTINCTION (IRE)	NORMANDIE STUD	C GORDON-WATSON BS	150000
ROMANTIC TOUCH (IRE) CH F KING'S BEST (USA) - GLANCING TOUCH (GB)	RATHBARRY STUD, IRELAND	MCKEEVER ST LAWRENCE BS	150000
MASHAAHED (GB) B C IN THE WINGS - PATACAKE PATACAKE (USA)	EUROPEAN SALES MANAGEMENT	SHADWELL ESTATE	150000
B C MULL OF KINTYRE (USA) - RESURGENCE (GB)	ASHTOWN HOUSE STUD, IRELAND	A O NERSES	150000
CRITICAL LIGHT (IRE) B C FANTASTIC LIGHT (USA) - CAERLINA (IRE)	BALLYLINCH STUD, IRELAND	MURAYAMA BS	150000
SULARINA (IRE) BR F ALHAARTH (IRE) - QUIET COUNSEL (IRE)	CAMAS PARK STUD, IRELAND	C GORDON-WATSON BS	150000
POMPEY GIRL (GB) B F RAINBOW QUEST (USA) - INCHIRI (GB)	WOODCOTE STUD	VENDOR	150000
WONDERFUL ONE (IRE) CH F NASHWAN (USA) - RING THE RELATIVES (GB)	JOCKEY HALL STUD, IRELAND (AGENT)	KERVI/LLINGSTON ASS.	150000
RUSSIAN LULLABY (IRE) CH F GALILEO (IRE) - RUSSIAN BALLET (USA)	BARODA STUD, IRELAND	VENDOR	150000
MARINA GAMBA (IRE) B F GALILEO (IRE) - APPRECIATIVELY (USA)	CROOM HOUSE STUD, IRELAND	JOHN FERGUSON BS	150000
GOLD HORIZONS (IRE) B C GRAND LODGE (USA) - DAZZLING PARK (IRE)	LODGE PARK STUD, IRELAND	JOHN FERGUSON BS	150000
PARADISE STREET (IRE) B F MACHIAVELLIAN (USA) - TAN (USA)	CASTLETON GROUP	VENDOR	150000
SOFT CENTRE (IRE) B C ZAFONIC (USA) - FOODBROKER FANCY (IRE)	NORMANDIE STUD	MEAD, GOODBODY.	150000
INTERACTIVE (IRE) B C KING'S BEST (USA) - FORENTIA (GB)	BALLYMONEY PARK STUD, IRELAND	JOHN FERGUSON BS	150000
PERFECT BEAT (IRE) B F FASLIYEV (USA) - DANCING DROP (GB)	GERRARDSTOWN HOUSE STUD, IRELAND	JOHN FERGUSON BS	150000
MOBSIR (GB) B C MOZART (IRE) - PRETTY SHARP (GB)	FURNACE MILL STUD	SHADWELL ESTATE	150000
B C SINGSPIEL (IRE) - ELEGANT (IRE)	ASHTOWN HOUSE STUD, IRELAND	BIG RED FARM	150000
ORANGE STRAVINSKY (GB) B C STRAVINSKY (USA) - ORANGE SUNSET (IRE)	VOUTE SALES, AGENT	ANTHONY STROUD BS	150000
ROYAL INTRIGUE (IRE) B.C. ROYAL APPLAUSE (GB) - CONGRESS (IRE)	BEECHGROVE STUD	NEWMARKET INT.	150000
CH F GRAND LODGE (USA) - DEBBIE'S NEXT (USA)	EYERFIELD HOUSE STUD, IRELAND	VENDOR	145000
B F MR GREELEY (USA) - MYSTIC LURE (GB)	WATERSHIP DOWN STUD	BBA (IRELAND)	145000
INDIAN BALLET (GB) CH F INDIAN RIDGE - BOLSHAYA (GB)	FURNACE MILL STUD	CHEVELEY PARK STUD	140000
PRESERVA (IRE) B C DANEHILL (USA) - LA PITIE (USA)	CAMAS PARK STUD, IRELAND	C GORDON-WATSON BS	140000
WELLSATA (FR) B F SADLER'S WELLS (USA) - MISS SATAMIXA (FR)	HARAS D'OUILLY, FRANCE	D O'BYRNE	140000
B C MONTJEU (IRE) - LUCY IN THE SKY (IRE)	GLENALE STUD, IRELAND	JOHN WARREN BS	140000
CH F DANEHILL DANCER (IRE) - JUNO MADONNA (IRE)	CAMAS PARK STUD, IRELAND	D O'BYRNE	140000
B C GRAND LODGE (USA) - SOVIET ARTIC (FR)	STAFFORDSTOWN, IRELAND	BBA (IRELAND)	140000
ART DECO (IRE) CH C PEINTRE CELEBRE (USA) - SOMETIME (IRE)	MOUNT COOTE STUD, IRELAND	C EGERTON	140000
MARMOOQ (GB) CH C CADEAUX GENEREUX - PORTELET (GB)	RATHBARRY STUD, IRELAND	SHADWELL ESTATE	140000
DUKEDOM (GB) GR C HIGHEST HONOR (FR) - ROSE NOBLE (USA)	RATHBARRY STUD, IRELAND	JOHN WARREN BS	140000
CH C GRAND LODGE (USA) - RIVER FANTASY (USA)	CAMAS PARK STUD, IRELAND	MCKEEVER ST LAWRENCE BS	135000
EKTIMAAL (GB) CH C BAHAMIAN BOUNTY (GB) - SECRET CIRCLE (GB)	TALLY-HO STUD, IRELAND	SHADWELL ESTATE	135000
B C DANEHILL DANCER (IRE) - FILLE DANSANTE (IRE)	CAMAS PARK STUD, IRELAND	D O'BYRNE	135000
PUNTA GALERA (IRE) BR C ZAFONIC (USA) - KOBALT SEA (FR)	GLENALE STUD, IRELAND	PETER DOYLE BS	135000
B C AGNES WORLD (USA) - CRIME OFTHECENTURY (GB)	STRATFORD PLACE STUD	M A JARVIS	130000
GALAXY BOUND (IRE) B G MARK OF ESTEEM (IRE) - DINER DE LUNE (IRE)	MOUNT COOTE STUD, IRELAND	MCKEEVER ST LAWRENCE BS	130000
MUSICAL ROMANCE (IRE) B F MOZART (IRE) - DEAR GIRL (IRE)	KNOCKTORAN STUD, IRELAND	JOHN FERGUSON BS	130000
B C HALLING (USA) - PLACE DE L'OPERA (GB)	NEW ENGLAND STUD	M JARVIS	130000
GR C FANTASTIC LIGHT (USA) - CREPE GINGER (GB)	WATERSHIP DOWN STUD	M JARVIS	130000
RASAMAAT (IRE) B F DANEHILL (USA) - SHINING HOUR (USA)	CAMAS PARK STUD, IRELAND	MCKEEVER ST LAWRENCE BS	130000
B C PIVOTAL (GB) - SEA DRIFT (FR)	VOUTE SALES, AGENT	SHADWELL ESTATE	130000
MONTPELLIER (IRE) B F MONTJEU (IRE) - RING OF ESTEEM (GB)	TRICKLEDOWN STUD	JOHN FERGUSON BS	130000

Name	Consignor	Buyer	Price
LIGHT SENTENCE (GB) B C FANTASTIC LIGHT (USA) - ALMELA (IRE).	THE CASTLEBRIDGE CONSIGNMENT	JOHN FERGUSON BS.	130000
ROAD HOME (GB) CH C GRAND LODGE (USA) - LADY IN WAITING (GB)	KIRTLINGTON STUD.	C GORDON-WATSON BS	130000
B/BR C GIANT'S CAUSEWAY (USA) - THEORETICALLY (USA).	CASTLEMARTIN STUD, IRELAND.	LA BAHIA STUD.	130000
EDAARA (IRE) CH F PIVOTAL (GB) - ARABIAN LASS (SAF)	GENESIS GREEN STUD.	SHADWELL ESTATE	125000
TOPJEU (IRE) B C MONTJEU (IRE) - ARABIAN LASS (SAF)	CAMAS PARK STUD, IRELAND.	C GORDON-WATSON BS	125000
B C PIVOTAL (GB) - SEDNA (FR)	CORDUFF STUD, IRELAND.	JOHN WARREN BS.	120000
B/BR C GIANT'S CAUSEWAY (USA) - WOODLAND ORCHID (IRE)	AIRLIE STUD, IRELAND.	C GORDON-WATSON BS	120000
CH F GRAND LODGE (USA) - TRUE CRYSTAL (IRE)	ROUND HILL STUD, IRELAND.	JOHN FERGUSON BS	120000
ANYAAB (IRE) CH C HALLING (USA) - FEMME FATALE (GB)	BALLYHIMIKIN STUD, IRELAND.	SHADWELL ESTATE	120000
B C GALILEO (IRE) - HIGHSHAAN (GB)	JOHN OSBORNE, AGENT.	D O'BYRNE	120000
WAGTAIL (GB) B F CAPE CROSS (IRE) - DANCING FEATHER (GB)	STOWELL HILL STUD.	HESMONDS STUD.	120000
MONTCHARA (IRE) B C MONTJEU (IRE) - MOCHARA.	ASHTOWN HOUSE STUD, IRELAND.	B OLSSON.	120000
DORELIA (IRE) B F EFISIO - DOMINO (IRE).	BALLYLINCH STUD, IRELAND (AGENT)	P WEBBER.	115000
MATTAHORN (IRE) B C IN THE WINGS - FRANCFURTER (GB)	CAMAS PARK STUD, IRELAND.	VENDOR.	115000
SNOW GRETEL (IRE) B F GREEN DESERT (USA) - SNOW PRINCESS (IRE)	ASHTOWN HOUSE STUD, IRELAND.	ANTHONY STROUD BS.	115000
B F KING'S BEST (USA) - TROPICANA (IRE)	EUROPEAN SALES MANAGEMENT.	C GORDON-WATSON BS	115000
B C RAHY (USA) - KITZA (IRE)	BRITTON HOUSE STUD, IRELAND.	D O'BYRNE	115000
B/BR F ZAFONIC (USA) - BANK ON HER (USA)	ROUND HOUSE STUD, IRELAND.	EAST WIND RACING.	115000
CH F KING'S BEST (USA) - PARTY DOLL.	WATERSHIP DOWN STUD.	CBA.	115000
MUKAABER (GB) CH C PIVOTAL (GB) - PLACEMENT (GB)	LANGTON STUD.	SHADWELL ESTATE.	115000
CAPTAIN STIRLING (IRE) B C IN THE WINGS - ROSES FROM RIDEY (IRE)	ARLIE STUD, IRELAND.	VENDOR.	115000
B C SADLER'S WELLS (USA) - DALAWARA (IRE)	BARRONSTOWN STUD, IRELAND.	R GIBSON.	110000
STRATEGIC PRINCE (IRE) B C ANABAA (USA) - MISS PARTY LINE (USA)	CORDUFF STUD, IRELAND.	C GORDON-WATSON BS	110000
B C KING'S BEST (USA) - LYRICAL DANCE (USA)	BAROUCHE STUD, IRELAND) LTD	VENDOR.	110000
B C SINNDAR (IRE) - ZIVANIA (GB)	KILDARAGH STUD, IRELAND (AGENT)	MCKEEVER ST LAWRENCE BS.	110000
B F SADLER'S WELLS (USA) - ANTIGUAN JANE (GB)	CAMAS PARK STUD, IRELAND.	ANTHONY STROUD BS.	110000
ROYAL ENVOY (IRE) B C ROYAL APPLAUSE (GB) - SEVEN NOTES (GB)	YEOMANSTOWN STUD, IRELAND.	PETER DOYLE BS.	110000
B C CAPE CROSS (IRE) - JEMALINA (USA)	YEOMANSTOWN STUD, IRELAND.	C GORDON-WATSON BS	110000
CH F HALLING (USA) - RED RITA (IRE)	GLENALA STUD, IRELAND.	JOHN FERGUSON BS.	110000
B C FRAAM (GB) - PERIQUITUM (GB)	VOUTE SALES, AGENT.	C GORDON-WATSON BS	110000
NIKOLENKA (IRE) B F INDIAN RIDGE - LADY OF KILDARE (IRE)	JOCKEY HALL STUD, IRELAND (AGENT)	EMERALD BS.	110000
B C GREEN DESERT (USA) - PURE MISK (GB)	OLD MILL STUD LTD.	WILL EDMEADES BS.	110000
B C MARJU (IRE) - SHIMNA (GB)	NEW ENGLAND STUD.	G RICHARDSON.	105000
FUTURE'S DREAM (GB) B C BERTOLINI (USA) - BAHAWIR POUR (USA)	REDPENDER STUD, IRELAND.	C GORDON-WATSON BS	105000
GR F DAYLAMI (IRE) - KALIMAR (IRE)	CORDUFF STUD, IRELAND.	T EASTERBY.	105000
BRABAZON (IRE) B C IN THE WINGS - AZURE LAKE (USA)	GLENALA STUD, IRELAND.	B O'RYAN.	105000
B C CAPE CROSS (IRE) - MONARCHY (IRE)	JOHN OSBORNE, AGENT.	JOHN WARREN BS.	105000
B C BARATHEA (IRE) - LIGHTHOUSE (GB)	RATHBARRY STUD, IRELAND.	MRS A SKIFFINGTON.	105000
KAPELLMEISTER (IRE) B C MOZART - MARCH HARE (GB)	WATERSHIP DOWN STUD.	WAI SIU KEE.	105000
DUTY (IRE) B C RAINBOW QUEST (USA) - WENDYLINA (IRE)	GLENALA STUD, IRELAND.	MRS A SKIFFINGTON.	105000
	HAWTHORN VILLA STUD, IRELAND.	C GORDON-WATSON BS	105000
		JOHN WARREN BS.	105000

HIGH-PRICED YEARLINGS OF 2004 AT GOFFS' SALES

The following yearlings realised 53,000 Euros and over at Goffs' Sales in 2004:-

Name and Breeding	Vendor	Purchaser	Euros
B F GREEN DESERT (USA) - SIMAAT (USA)	CAMAS PARK STUD	J MAGNIER	650000
DAWN ATTACK (IRE) B F FANTASTIC LIGHT (USA) - SABAAH (USA)	IRISH NATIONAL STUD	JOHN FERGUSON BS.	550000
GR C MONTJEU (IRE) - SALLANCHES (USA)	ASHFORD HOUSE STUD	D O'BYRNE.	520000
CITY OF POETS (IRE) B C ALHAARTH (IRE) - CASTLE QUEST (IRE)	CROOM HOUSE STUD	J FERGUSON.	360000
RADIANT MONARCH (IRE) B C ROYAL APPLAUSE (GB) - YARA (IRE)	CASTLEMARTIN STUD	JOHN FERGUSON BS.	340000
B C SADLER'S WELLS (USA) - COPPER CREEK	AIRLIE STUD	D O'BYRNE.	310000
CH C GIANT'S CAUSEWAY (USA) - MUSIC HOUSE (USA)	MR JOHN OSBORNE.	H JOHNSON.	300000
BLUE MIRAGE (IRE) B C KING'S BEST (USA) - CATCH THE BLUES (IRE)	BALLYBIN STUD	RICHARD O'GORMAN BS.	270000
B C CAPE CROSS (IRE) - NINTH WONDER (USA)	LYNN LODGE STUD	J H JOHNSON.	260000
YANDINA (IRE) B F DANEHILL (USA) - LIGHZ (USA)	CROOM HOUSE STUD	BBA (IRELAND).	250000
TOMMY TOOGOOD (IRE) B C DANEHILL (USA) - ON THE NILE (IRE)	BARRONSTOWN STUD	BBA (IRELAND).	240000
B C STRAVINSKY (USA) - STORM WEST (USA)	ASHTOWN HOUSE STUD	H JOHNSON.	230000
B F FANTASTIC LIGHT (USA) - SPIRIT OF TARA (IRE)	KILCARN STUD	ENNISTOWN STUD.	225000
B C GALILEO (IRE) - MOOD SWINGS (IRE)	BALLYHIMIKIN STUD	MRS A SKIFFINGTON	225000
CINNAMON TREE (IRE) GR F BARATHEA (IRE) - LA SUSIANE	RATHBARRY STUD (AGENT).	D WELD	225000
B C SADLER'S WELLS (USA) - CALADIRA (IRE)	BARRONSTOWN STUD	D L O'BYRNE.	220000
B C DANEHILL (USA) - DEAREST (USA)	KILCARN STUD	D O'BYRNE.	200000
CH C CADEAUX GENEREUX - AOIFE (IRE)	ROUNDHILL STUD	HONG KONG JOCKEY CLUB.	200000
PRAY FOR SUN (IRE) B F FANTASTIC LIGHT (USA) - KARAKIA (IRE)	SWORDLESTOWN STUD.	F SAUQUE.	200000
B C XAAR (GB) - COMMON RUMPUS (IRE)	CAMAS PARK STUD	VENDOR.	200000
B C DANEHILL (USA) - DATHYNA (IRE)	GLENVALE STUD (AGENT)	MRS A SKIFFINGTON	190000
B C KING CHARLEMAGNE (USA) - RIHAN (USA)	FORENAGHTS STUD.	D O'BYRNE.	180000
COUNTING HOUSE (IRE) CH C K'ING'S BEST (USA) - INFORAPENNY (GB)	REDPENDER STUD.	C GORDON-WATSON BS	180000
GIGANTICUS (USA) CH C GIANT'S CAUSEWAY (USA) - SHY PRINCESS (USA)	ASHTOWN HOUSE STUD	BBA (IRELAND).	180000
GR C CAPE CROSS (IRE) - ESPANA (GB)	MEADOWLANDS STUD.	HONG KONG JOCKEY CLUB.	180000
GOLDEN ARROW (IRE) B C DANEHILL (USA) - CHEAL ROSE (IRE)	ABBEVILLE & MEADOW COURT STUDS.	D WELD	180000
B C SELKIRK (USA) - PUMP (USA)	AIRLIE STUD	JOHN FERGUSON BS	180000
B C CAPE CROSS (IRE) - DAFTYNA (IRE)	WOODTOWN HOUSE STUD	JOHN FERGUSON BS	180000
ICE PRINCESS (IRE) B F GRAND LODGE (USA) - GHANA (IRE)	CAMAS PARK STUD	DE BURGH/FARRINGTON	170000
B F SADLER'S WELLS (USA) - SWEET JUSTICE	LODGE PARK STUD.	D L O'BYRNE	170000
CH C SPINNING WORLD (USA) - CLASSIC PARK (GB)	CROOM HOUSE STUD	JOHN WARREN BS.	165000
TAJNEED (IRE) B C ALHAARTH (IRE) - INDIAN EXPRESS (GB)	BALLYLINCH STUD (AGENT)	PETER DOYLE BS	165000
B F CAPE CROSS (IRE) - TRIM STAR (GB)	BALLYBIN STUD (AGENT)	SHADWELL ESTATE.	160000
COSMOLOGIST (USA) B C GALILEO (IRE) - FONTEMAR (ARG)	GLENEALE STUD	C EGERTON	150000
I KEY (IRE) B C FASLIVEY (USA) - TAMMANY HALL (IRE)	ASHTOWN HOUSE STUD.	BBA (IRELAND).	150000
B F KING'S BEST (USA) - MISS MISTLETOES (IRE).	GERRARDSTOWN HOUSE STUD	ENNISTOWN STUD.	150000
CH C GALILEO (IRE) - OCEAN VIEW (USA)	GERRARDSTOWN HOUSE STUD	MAB AGENCY	150000
B C ALHAARTH (IRE) - ACTUALITE (GB)	CAMAS PARK STUD	C GORDON-WATSON BS	150000
CH C FANTASTIC LIGHT (USA) - OBSCURA (USA)	CAMAS PARK STUD	RICHARD FRISBY BS	145000
IGRAND ENTRANCE (IRE) B C GRAND LODGE (USA) - ALESSIA (GER)	ASHTOWN HOUSE STUD	C EGERTON	140000
B/BR F WOODMAN (USA) - ELEGANT RIDGE (IRE)	CROOM HOUSE STUD	H JOHNSON	140000
GREAT HOPE (IRE) B F HALLING (USA) - ASPIRATION (IRE)	CROOM HOUSE STUD.	CBA.	140000
CH C DR FONG (USA) - HECKLE (GB)	CORDUFF STUD.	J H JOHNSON.	140000
B C GALILEO (IRE) - PHARMACIST (IRE)	BALLYLINCH STUD (AGENT)	MCKEVER ST LAWRENCE BS.	130000

Yearling	Vendor	Purchaser	Price
CHEROKEE STREAM (IRE) B F INDIAN RIDGE - MOY WATER (IRE)	IRISH NATIONAL STUD	D WELD	130000
B F CADEAUX GENEREUX - MIRAGE	J K THOROUGHBREDS	G RICHARDSON	130000
CARAVINO (IRE) B C INDIAN RIDGE - DANSE ROYALE (IRE)	KILCARN STUD	J OXX	130000
PRINCE OF LIGHT (IRE) CH C FANTASTIC LIGHT (USA) - MISS QUEEN (USA)	TIPPER HOUSE STUD	CASH	130000
TALWIN (IRE) B F ALHAARTH (IRE) - LADY WINDLEY (GB)	GLDAWN STUD	SHADWELL ESTATE	120000
CH C GRAND LODGE (USA) - GENOA (GB)	MOUNT COOTE STUD	W SWINBURN	120000
B/BR F DANEHILL DANCER (IRE) - MISS CHAMPAGNE (FR)	CORDUFF STUD	BBA (IRELAND)	120000
B F MOZART (IRE) - ANTINNAZ (IRE)	NEWBOROUGH STUD	JOHN FERGUSON	120000
BR C KALANISI (IRE) - OSKARBERG (GB)	MOUNTAIN VIEW STUD	BIG RED FARM	120000
SAPPHIRE STONE (IRE) B C NTIKHAB (USA) - MARJU GUEST (IRE)	BROGLESTOWN STUD	D WELD	115000
B C MEDICEAN (GB) - LISHAWAY (FR)	RISH NATIONAL STUD	A CHOONG	115000
SHALLIKA (IRE) B F ALHAARTH (IRE) - ALKHLAS (GB)	ABBEVILLE & MEADOW COURT STUDS	B O'RYAN	110000
ASPEN FALLS (IRE) CH C FLNADIM (USA) - ESQUILINE (USA)	RATHMORE STUD	SHEEHY BROS	110000
B C DANEHILL DANCER (IRE) - PIRIE (USA)	ASHTOWN HOUSE STUD	M JOHNSTON	110000
B C SADLER'S WELLS (USA) - ORIENTAL MYSTIQUE	CASTLETON GROUP	MCKEEVER ST LAWRENCE BS	110000
B C FANTASTIC LIGHT (USA) - ITAB (USA)	TAROKA STUD (AGENT)	RICHARD O'GORMAN BS	110000
B C NAMID (GB) - TILLER GIRL (IRE)	CORDUFF STUD	C COX	110000
DUNELIGHT (IRE) CH C DESERT SUN (GB) - BADEFA (IRE)	BALLYHAMPSHIRE STUD	KERI/LLINGSTON ASS.	110000
B F REVOQUE (IRE) - SHAJARA (FR)	LODGE PARK STUD	G RICHARDSON	110000
BUSY SHARK (IRE) GR C SHINKO FOREST (IRE) - FELICITA (IRE)	FORENAGHTS STUD	SIR M PRESCOTT	105000
EL ALAMEIN (IRE) CH C NASHWAN (USA) - EL RABAB (USA)	ASHTOWN HOUSE STUD	J GIVEN	105000
B C DANEHILL (USA) - FLOOD (USA)	OWENSTOWN STUD	T COLLINS	105000
FREE ROSES (IRE) B F XAAR (GB) - CRYSTAL BLUE (IRE)	HANLON STUD FARM	SKYMARC/CASTLEMARTIN	105000
B C GREEN DESERT (USA) - GHANAJ (GB)	CASTLEMARTIN STUD	MRS A SKIFFINGTON	105000
B C NAMID (GB) - FLYING CLOUDS (GB)	RATHBARRY STUD	D K WELD	105000
B C DANEHILL (USA) - REGENT GOLD (USA)	LYNN LODGE STUD (AGENT)	VENDOR	105000
HOPEFUL PURCHASE (IRE) CH C GRAND LODGE (USA) - FUNOON (IRE)	BARRONSTOWN STUD	C GORDON-WATSON BS	105000
BEST LADY (IRE) B F KING'S BEST (USA) - SASSENACH (IRE)	NEWTOWN STUD	BBA (IRELAND)	105000
LOYAL ROYAL (IRE) B C KING CHARLEMAGNE (USA) - SUPPORTIVE (IRE)	BROADFIELD STUD	D ELSWORTH	100000
DANISH MERMAID (GB) B F DANEHILL DANCER (IRE) - DALTAK (USA)	HAWTHORN VILLA STUD	BBA (IRELAND)	100000
B C ZAFONIC (USA) - TARZYANA (USA)	FORENAGHTS STUD	BBA (IRELAND)	100000
JAMIESON GOLD (IRE) B C DESERT STYLE (IRE) - PRINCESS OF ZURICH (IRE)	YEOMANSTOWN STUD	VENDOR	100000
B F BERTOLINI (USA) - INCENDIO (GB)	MR JOHN OSBORNE	AGENCE FPS	100000
B F FUSAICHI PEGASUS (USA) - ROYAL BALLERINA (IRE)	ABBEVILLE & MEADOW COURT STUDS (AGENT)	G BUTLER	100000
B C RED RANSOM (USA) - REALLY FANCY (USA)	YEOMANSTOWN STUD (AGENT)	STEPHEN HILLEN BS	100000
B/BR F XAAR (GB) - FOOLISH FUN (GB)	CAMAS PARK STUD	VENDOR	100000
B F BERTOLINI (USA) - FRENCH RIVER (GB)	MEADOWLANDS STUD	M O'TOOLE	100000
B F DANEHILL (USA) - GREEK MOON (IRE)	ROUNDHILL STUD	RICHARD O'GORMAN BS	100000
B F BERTOLINI (USA) - JEWEL (IRE)	BALLYMONEY PARK STUD	J OXX	100000
CH C DIESIS - SUPER SUPREME (IND)	AIRLIE STUD	MCKEEVER ST LAWRENCE BS	100000
CH C STRAVINSKY (USA) - MISS DYNA CHRIS (USA)	LYNN LODGE STUD	M GRASSICK	95000
DEISE HOPE (IRE) B F GALILEO (IRE) - OUR HOPE (GB)	GERRARDSTOWN HOUSE STUD	BISHOPSTOWN STUD	95000
B F INDIAN RIDGE - ALASSIO (USA)	NEWTOWN STUD	H JOHNSON	95000
WHO HA (USA) B C STRAVINSKY (USA) - I DON'T KNOW (USA)	ASHTOWN HOUSE STUD	W SWINBURN	95000
B F DANEHILL (USA) - THAIDAH (CAN)	CAMAS PARK STUD	VENDOR	90000
HEATSEEKER (IRE) CH C GIANT'S CAUSEWAY (USA) - RUSTY BACK (USA)	ABBEVILLE & MEADOW COURT STUDS	C GORDON-WATSON BS	90000
B C CAPE CROSS (IRE) - WINTER TERN (USA)	GERRARDSTOWN HOUSE STUD	VENDOR	90000
B C MARJU (IRE) - ELA CASSINI (IRE)	GERRARDSTOWN HOUSE STUD	C GORDON-WATSON BS	90000
	LANDSCAPE STUD (AGENT)	HONG KONG JOCKEY CLUB	90000

Yearling	Vendor	Purchaser	Price
MIST AND STONE (IRE) B F XAAR (GB) - DAUNTING LADY (IRE)	DEERPARK STUD.	PETER DOYLE BS.	90000
MT WEATHER (IRE) B C NAMID (GB) - IT TAKES TWO (IRE)	LISIEUX STUD.	MR & MRS B FRESTONE.	90000
WADDON (IRE) B C GREEN DESERT (USA) - BALDEMARA (FR)	BALLYSHEEHAN STUD LTD	C COX.	90000
ALEXANDER ALLIANCE (IRE) B F DANETIME (IRE) - GEHT SCHNELL	TALLY-HO STUD.	M H TOMPKINS.	88000
LAHEEN (IRE) B F BLUEBIRD (USA) - ASHRAH (USA)	CREGG STUD.	F BARRY.	87000
B/GR C DAYLAMI (IRE) - ELEGANT BLOOM (IRE)	TARA STUD.	EAST WIND RACING.	85000
CH F BARATHEA (IRE) - MUSCHANA (GB)	MOUNT COOTE STUD.	F BARRY.	85000
B F BARATHEA (IRE) - CALAMANDER (IRE)	CAHERASS STUD.	W SWINBURN.	85000
B C XAAR (GB) - SUMMER DREAMS (IRE)	LYNN LODGE STUD.	C GORDON-WATSON BS.	80000
DAYS OF MY LIFE (IRE) B C DAYLAMI (IRE) - TRULY YOURS (IRE)	EYREFIELD LODGE STUD.	JOHN WARREN BS.	80000
PLUM PUDDING (IRE) B C ELNADIM (USA) - KARAYB (IRE)	YEOMANSTOWN STUD.	MR & MRS B FRESTONE.	80000
RESIDE (IRE) B F MONTJEU (IRE) - DARKLING (IRE)	GRANGEMORE STUD.	A M BALDING.	80000
FLY BY JOVE (IRE) B C FASLIYEV (USA) - FLYLEAF (FR)	ABBEVILLE EADOW COURT STUDS.	W SWINBURN.	80000
B F SELKIRK (USA) - FIRECREST (IRE)	ARLIE STUD.	MRS A SKIFFINGTON.	80000
B F GRAND LODGE (USA) - POSTA VECCHIA (USA)	BARRONSTOWN STUD.	J H JOHNSON.	80000
GR F MOZART (IRE) - ATTACHMENT (USA)	IRISH NATIONAL STUD.	M A JARVIS.	80000
BR C KEY OF LUCK (USA) - MUSIC KHAN (GB)	CORDUFF STUD.	J QUINN.	80000
B C MUJADIL (USA) - ADVANCING (IRE)	PORTLESTER STUD.	BBA (IRELAND).	75000
B C STRAVINSKY (USA) - POSSIBLE CONSORT (USA)	MR JOHN OSBORNE (AGENT).	VENDOR.	75000
CELTIC TRIUMPH (IRE) B F MONTJEU (IRE) - TWICE THE EASE (GB)	CAMAS PARK STUD.	MRS A SKIFFINGTON.	75000
VEBA (USA) CH CH C BLACK MINNALOUSHE (USA) - MAKE OVER (USA)	YEOMANSTOWN STUD.	EQUINE SERVICES.	75000
SIENNA STORM (IRE) B C PEINTRE CELEBRE (USA) - SAINT ANN (USA)	AIRLIE STUD.	M H TOMPKINS.	75000
PUSKAS (IRE) B C KING'S BEST (USA) - CHIQUITA LINDA (IRE)	KILDARAGH STUD (AGENT).	G RICHARDSON.	75000
B C NIGHT SHIFT (USA) - THERMOPYLAE (GB)	TALLY-HO STUD.	P COLE.	75000
B F FANTASTIC LIGHT (USA) - MAJESTIC SISTER (IRE)	THE COTTAGE STUD.	JOCKEY HALL STUD.	75000
MAJESTIC CONCORDE (IRE) B C DEFINITE ARTICLE (GB) - TALINA'S LAW (IRE)	KILLADOON STUD.	D K WELD.	75000
B F JESIS - SILVER TOP HAT (USA)	RATHBARRY STUD (AGENT).	M O'TOOLE.	72000
B C MONTJEU (IRE) - ZARYSHA (IRE)	LYNN LODGE STUD (AGENT).	MRS A SKIFFINGTON.	72000
B F FASLIYEV (USA) - SERVA (GER)	SWORDLESTOWN STUD.	C O'BRIEN.	70000
MY LOVELY LADY (IRE) B F CAPE CROSS (IRE) - LACE FLOWER (GB)	DEERPARK STUD.	KERN/LILLINGSTON ASS.	70000
CH C DAYLAMI (IRE) - PHARAOHS DELIGHT	BALLYINCH STUD.	SHADWELL ESTATE.	70000
B F IN THE WINGS - FEATHER BRIDE (IRE)	ABBEVILLE & MEADOW COURT STUDS.	MCKEEVER ST LAWRENCE BS.	70000
B C INDIAN RIDGE - TAFRAH (IRE)	GLENVALE STUD.	W SWINBURN.	70000
B F XAAR (GB) - JET CAT (IRE)	RATHMORE STUD.	PETER DOYLE BS.	70000
B C TAGULA (IRE) - EASY POP (IRE)	GLOSTER COTTAGE STUD.	MCKEEVER ST LAWRENCE BS.	70000
B C GRAND LODGE (USA) - KYLEMORE (IRE)	SWORDLESTOWN STUD.	PETER DOYLE BS.	70000
CH F INCHINOR (GB) - PRESENT IMPERFECT (GB)	AIRLIE STUD.	C MARNANE.	70000
B C SADLER'S WELLS (USA) - GHOST TREE (IRE)	MARLHILL HOUSE STUD.	J W HILLS.	70000
B C FANTASTIC LIGHT (USA) - DAY FAIRY (IRE)	GROVE STUD.	T HOGAN.	70000
CH C FRUITS OF LOVE (USA) - ALPINE FLAIR (IRE)	ENNISTOWN STUD.	B O'RYAN.	70000
B C MARJU (IRE) - MUNEERA (USA)	MR. JOHN OSBORNE.	C GORDON-WATSON BS.	70000
JUST LOGIC (IRE) B/BR C DESERT PRINCE (IRE) - TIAVANITA (USA)	KILCORAN HOUSE STUD.	RATHBARRY STUD.	70000
BOLD ALASKA (IRE) B C CAPE CROSS (IRE) - DRAMATIC ENTRY (IRE)	PIERCETOWN STUD.	G FONOS.	68000
CH C DANEHILL DANCER (IRE) - IMPERIAL GRAF (USA)	CROOM HOUSE STUD.	FERNHAM FARM.	68000
B C TITUS LIVIUS (FR) - EXCITING	NEWLANDS HOUSE STUD.	SIR M PRESCOTT.	68000
WARSAW PACT (IRE) B G POLISH PRECEDENT (USA) - ALWAYS FRIENDLY (GB)	RINGFORT STUD (AGENT).	BBA (IRELAND).	68000
MOONE CROSS (IRE) B C CAPE CROSS (IRE) - CANNIKIN (IRE)	RATHBARRY STUD (AGENT).	MRS A SKIFFINGTON.	65000
B F MARJU (IRE) - BRAARI (USA)	MOORPARK STUD.		65000

B F KINGMAMBO (USA) - ISLE DE FRANCE (USA)	OAKS FARM STABLES (AGENT)	A STROUD	65000
PORTICCIO (IRE) CH C LOMITAS (GB) - REKINDLED AFFAIR (IRE)	BEER FOREST STUD (AGENT)	F SAUQUE	65000
B F XAAR (GB) - ADULTRESS (IRE)	MIRLIE STUD	CORMAC MCCORMACK ASS	65000
ITRIMWAKI (USA) B C MISWAKI (USA) - MY TRIM (USA)	OAKS FARM STABLES	G RICHARDSON	65000
B F SPECTRUM (IRE) - PARK CHARGER (GB)	LODGE PARK STUD	BAROUCHE STUD	65000
CH C INDIAN RIDGE - BYE BOLD AILEEN (IRE)	IRISH NATIONAL STUD	MCKEEVER ST LAWRENCE BS	65000
CH C PEINTRE CELEBRE (USA) - SNOW HOUSE (IRE)	LOUGHBROWN STUD	M JOHNSON	65000
THEY ALL LAUGHED (GB) CH C ZAFONIC (USA) - ROYAL FUTURE (IRE)	WOODTOWN HOUSE STUD	T G MILLS	65000
B/BR F KALANISI (IRE) - HAWKSBILL SPECIAL (USA)	BROGUESTOWN STUD	PETER DOYLE BS	65000
WHITE LADDER (IRE) BR C MARJU (IRE) - LADY RACHEL (IRE)	DUNDERRY STUD	D WELD	65000
KILLYBEGS (IRE) B C ORPEN (USA) - BELSAY (GB)	BROGUESTOWN STUD	P COLE	65000
B C SWAIN (IRE) - NIJINSKY'S BEAUTY (USA)	LYNN LODGE STUD	BBA (IRELAND)	65000
B C NAMID (GB) - TYCOON ALY (IRE)	MR. JOHN OSBORNE	C O'BRIEN	62000
GR F GREEN DESERT (USA) - FLOURISHING WAY (GB)	J K THOROUGHBREDS (AGENT)	HONG KONG JOCKEY CLUB	62000
SOUTHPORT STAR B C KING'S BEST (USA) - SISTER GOLDEN HAIR (IRE)	MOUNT COOTE STUD	BELJAR BS	62000
B C NAMID (GB) - NIGHT SCENT (IRE)	SWORDLESTOWN STUD (AGENT)	B O'RYAN	62000
OUR SUE (GB) CH F DR FONG (USA) - EVENING CHARM (IRE)	MEADOWLANDS STUD (AGENT)	J BRUMMITT	60000
B C INDIAN RIDGE - PERFECT PLUM (IRE)	PIER HOUSE STUD	PETER DOYLE BS	60000
B C SINNDAR (IRE) - SOEUR TI (FR)	GRAIGUESHONEEN STUD	R O'RYAN	60000
B C ROYAL APPLAUSE (GB) - GOOGOOSH (IRE)	EYREFIELD LODGE STUD	MRS A SKIFFINGTON	60000
B C CITY ON A HILL (USA) - FAHAN (IRE)	KNOCKTORAN STUD	J OXX	60000
B C KEY OF LUCK (USA) - CHERRY FALLS (IRE)	GLENEALE STUD	W SWINBURN	60000
FANTASTISCH (IRE) B F FANTASTIC LIGHT (USA) - ALEXANDRA S (IRE)	MANISTER HOUSE STUD	I ALLAN	60000
B C SADLER'S WELLS (USA) - RAIN FLOWER (IRE)	BALLYBRENNAN STUD	CASTLEMARTIN/SKYMARC	60000
RAVISH (GB) B F EFISIO - LOOKS SENSATIONAL (USA)	CRONE STUD	M MCNEILLY	60000
B C DESERT PRINCE (IRE) - LIBERTY SONG (IRE)	CAMAS PARK STUD	M JOHNSON	60000
B C DESERT PRINCE (IRE) - SUNSETTER (USA)	GROVE STUD	J WARREN	60000
KALANTERA (IRE) B C KALANISI (IRE) - TINTERA (IRE)	MOORPARK STUD	RINGFORT STUD	60000
NIHAL (IRE) B F SINGSPIEL (IRE) - KATIE MCLAIN (USA)	NIGHTINGALE STUD	W SWINBURN	60000
DUKE OF MILAN (IRE) CH C DESERT PRINCE (IRE) - ABYAT (USA)	PIER HOUSE STUD	A BALDING	60000
B F KING CHARLEMAGNE (USA) - JOYFULLNESS (USA)	SPRINGBANK WAY	M JOHNSON	60000
DIKTATORSHIP (IRE) B C DIKTAT (GB) - POLKA DANCER (GB)	IRISH NATIONAL STUD	BRIAN GRASSICK BS	60000
B C STRAVINSKY (USA) - FIFE (IRE)	CREGG STUD	M HALFORD	58000
B C MONTJEU (IRE) - MINIVER (IRE)	KNOCKLONG HOUSE STUD	BLANDFORD BS	58000
B C KING CHARLEMAGNE (USA) - GOLDEN CONCORDE	ASHLEIGH HOUSE STUD	PETER DOYLE BS	58000
GR C ELNADIM (USA) - BEAUHARNAIS (FR)	LISIEUX STUD (AGENT)	F BARRY	58000
B C TITUS LIVIUS (FR) - JAMEELA (IRE)	TAROKA STUD	B O'RYAN	55000
B C STRAVINSKY (USA) - SIGN HERE (USA)	WOODTOWN HOUSE STUD	D WELD	55000
ZIZOU (IRE) B C FANTASTIC LIGHT (USA) - SEARCH COMMITTEE (USA)	GLENEALE STUD (AGENT)	J WHOLLEY	55000
B C DESERT STYLE (IRE) - PLATSHAW (GB)	FORENAGHTS STUD	O COLE	55000
CH C DANEHILL DANCER (IRE) - ALCADIA (IRE)	YEOMANSTOWN STUD	HONG KONG JOCKEY CLUB	55000
B C DANETIME (IRE) - COTTON GRACE (IRE)	OAKS FARM STABLES	BBA (IRELAND)	55000
	GLENEALE STUD	MRS A SKIFFINGTON	53000

HIGH-PRICED YEARLINGS OF 2004 AT DONCASTER SALES

The following yearlings realised 25,000 Guineas and over at Doncaster Sales in 2004:-

Name and Breeding	Vendor	Purchaser	Euros
B C DISTANT MUSIC (USA) - ITKAN (IRE)	YEOMANSTOWN STUD, IRELAND	A JARVIS	125000
B C STRAVINSKY (USA) - SPIRIT IN THE SKY (USA)	JOHN TROY (AGENT)	G RICHARDSON	110000
B C NIGHT SHIFT (USA) - IKTIDAR (IRE)	BALLYORCHID HOUSE, IRELAND	H JOHNSON	110000
B C ANABAA (USA) - GLEN ROSIE (IRE)	VOUTE SALES, AGENT	W SWINBURN	110000
QUTANG (GB) CH C DR FONG (USA) - RAVINE (GB)	HIGHCLERE STUD	W HAGGAS	105000
B F DIKTAT (GB) - HILL WELCOME (GB)	DENHIFF FARMS	DARLEY	90000
B F BERTOLINI (USA) - CONN FUTURES (GB)	LIMESTONE AND TARA STUDS	DARLEY	90000
B C COMPTON PLACE (GB) - ONLY YOURS (GB)	WHITSBURY MANOR STUD	H JOHNSON	88000
SCOT LOVE (IRE) B C DANSILI (GB) - FASHION (GB)	CAMAS PARK STUD, IRELAND	PETER DOYLE BS	85000
GR C MARJU (IRE) - PURPLE RISKS (FR)	GLENEAL STUD (AGENT), IRELAND	N CALLAGHAN	85000
B F DANEHILL DANCER (IRE) - SWAN RIVER (USA)	JAMIE RAILTON (AGENT)	G BUTLER	75000
B/BR C MT LIVERMORE (USA) - FALSE SPRING (IRE)	ROSSENARRA STUD, IRELAND	T HYDE	70000
GR F DANEHILL DANCER (IRE) - MERRILY (GB)	CAMAS PARK STUD, IRELAND	HAVANA HORSE UK LTD	70000
B C MULL OF KINTYRE (USA) - WINNING GIRL (GB)	KILMINFOYLE HOUSE STUD, IRELAND	N CALLAGHAN	70000
BR/GR C KALANISI (IRE) - PERUGIA (IRE)	FURNACE MILL STUD (AGENT)	JOHN FERGUSON BS	66000
B C CAPE CROSS (IRE) - DRAMATIC MOOD (GB)	HEDSOR STUD	PETER DOYLE BS	65000
ENVISION (GB) B C PIVOTAL (GB) - ENTWINE (GB)	HEDSOR STUD	SHADWELL ESTATE	62000
ESDARAAT (GB) CH F PIVOTAL (GB) - DAHLAWISE (IRE)	FOXFIELD STUD (AGENT), IRELAND	B HILLS	60000
LISFANNON (GB) CH F BAHAMIAN BOUNTY (GB) - AMAZED (GB)	YEOMANSTOWN STUD, IRELAND	MRS A SKIFFINGTON	58000
SONNY SANTINO (USA) B C BERTOLINI (USA) - IRISH IMPULSE (USA)	JOHN OSBORNE, IRELAND	PETER DOYLE BS	55000
B/BR C KING CHARLEMAGNE (USA) - SHINING DESERT (IRE)	RATHARRY STUD, IRELAND	H JOHNSON	54000
B C SHINKO FOREST (IRE) - CHANGING PARTNERS (GB)	YEOMANSTOWN STUD, IRELAND	GEOFFREY HOWSON BS	52000
B C DESERT STYLE (IRE) - DOUBLE EIGHT (IRE)	YEOMANSTOWN STUD, IRELAND	MRS A SKIFFINGTON	52000
PLUM PUDDING (IRE) B C ELNADIM (USA) - KARAYB (IRE)	NEWLANDS HOUSE STUD, IRELAND	PETER DOYLE BS	52000
LAYAZAAL (IRE) B C ORPEN (USA) - LAW REVIEW (IRE)	RANWAY STUD (AGENT)	SHADWELL ESTATE	50000
MR EXCEL (IRE) B C ORPEN (USA) - COLLECTED (IRE)	ASH TREE FARM	MRS A SKIFFINGTON	50000
BR C MOZART (IRE) - IN FULL CRY (USA)	OAKS FARM STABLES	VENDOR	50000
B/BR C DAYJUR (USA) - RAYA (USA)	JOHN OSBORNE, IRELAND	B ELLISON	50000
B C MUJADIL (USA) - SILVER ARROW (USA)	HIGHCLERE STUD	H JOHNSON	50000
COLLETTE'S CHOICE (GB) B F ROYAL APPLAUSE (GB) - BRILLIANCE (GB)	FURNACE MILL STUD	R O'RYAN	50000
B C DANEHILL DANCER (IRE) - PRICE OF PASSION (GB)	MEADOWLANDS STUD, IRELAND	MCKEEVER ST LAWRENCE BS	50000
CH C TITUS LIVIUS (FR) - HARABAH (USA)	CATRIDGE FARM STUD	G BUTLER	50000
B C LEAR SPEAR (USA) - FRENCH GIFT (GB)	FURNACE MILL STUD	D ELSWORTH	50000
FIKRI (GB) B C BERTOLINI (USA) - WELCOME HOME (GB)	CATRIDGE FARM STUD	SHADWELL ESTATE	48000
RYDAL MOUNT (IRE) B C CAPE CROSS (IRE) - POOKA (USA)	GALTE VIEW STABLES, IRELAND	S KITTOW	46000
THOMAS A BECKETT (IRE) B C BECKETT (IRE) - KENEMA (IRE)	RATHARRY STUD (AGENT), IRELAND	A JENKINS	46000
B C NIGHT SHIFT (USA) - IN YOUR DREAMS (IRE)	LYNN LODGE STUD, IRELAND	DAVID MCGREAVY BS	46000
CH C PIVOTAL (GB) - STARRING (FR)	GLENEAL STUD (AGENT), IRELAND	D BARRON	46000
RUNDEAR (GB) B F DANEHILL DANCER (IRE) - COMPREHENSION (USA)	JAMIE RAILTON (AGENT)	G RICHARDSON	44000
CRIMSON (IRE) B F FASLIYEV (USA) - FEY LADY (IRE)	TALLY-HO STUD, IRELAND	JOHN WARREN BS	44000
ROYAL ENGINEER (GB) B C ROYAL APPLAUSE (GB) - IRIS MAY (GB)	MANOR HOUSE STUD	A JARVIS	44000
CH C BECKETT (IRE) - VILLA NOVA (IRE)	FURNACE MILL STUD	HIGHFLYER BS	44000
IMPERIAL SWORD (GB) B C DANEHILL DANCER (IRE) - HAJAT (GB)		D BARRON	42000

Horse	Farm	Buyer	Price
STRIKE UP THE BAND (GB) B C CYRANO DE BERGERAC - GREEN SUPREME (GB)	MANOR HOUSE FARM.	A A BS.	42000
B C DAGGERS DRAWN (USA) - WINGED VICTORY (IRE)	REDPENDER STUD, IRELAND.	R O'RYAN.	42000
B C BERTOLINI (USA) - NIGHTINGALE (GB)	PENMARRIC STUD, IRELAND.	DARLEY STUD.	42000
DONA VITORIA B C PRIMO VALENTINO (IRE) - BULLION (GB)	GLENALE STUD, IRELAND.	W SWINBURN.	42000
B C DIKTAT (GB) B F DIKTAT (GB) - SALANKA (IRE)	BALLYHIMIKIN STUD, IRELAND.	S KIRK.	42000
INCIDENTALLY (GB) CH C INCHINOR (GB) - TOP SAUCE (GB)	CATRIDGE FARM STUD.	PETER DOYLE BS.	40000
B C SINGSPIEL (IRE) - LOVE SONG (GB)	TRICKLEDOWN STUD.	N LITTMODEN.	40000
B F FANTASTIC LIGHT (USA) - FABULOUS ACCOUNT (USA)	GLIDAWN STUD, IRELAND.	C TINKLER.	40000
JOHNNY ALPHA (IRE) B C NAMID (GB) - GREEN'S MAUD EARL (GB)	CORRIN STUD, IRELAND.	BLANDFORD BS.	40000
PREJUDICIAL (GB) CH C EFSIOO - QUEENIE (GB)	WHITSBURY MANOR STUD.	C TINKLER.	40000
CHEAP N CHIC (GB) CH F PRIMO VALENTINO (IRE) - AMBER MILL (GB)	BEARSTONE STUD.	McKEEVER ST LAWRENCE BS.	40000
B F NAMID (GB) - PREPONDERANCE (IRE)	BALLYHAMPSHIRE STUD, IRELAND.	McKEEVER ST LAWRENCE BS.	40000
MORETASTIC (USA) CH G MT LIVERMORE (USA) - BRAVE NEW BOUNDARY (USA)	GLENALE STUD, IRELAND.	MRS S KIRK.	40000
BL/GR C DANSILI (GB) - ARISTOCRATIQUE (GB)	THROCKMORTON COURT STUD.	N DUFFIELD.	40000
SIR ALFONS (FR) B C PIVOTAL (GB) - LA CAPRICE (FR)	GOLDFORD STUD.	J H JOHNSON.	40000
B C ROYAL APPLAUSE (GB) - LA CAPRICE (FR)	FURNACE MILL STUD.	McKEEVER ST LAWRENCE BS.	40000
RIVER KINTYRE (GB) B C MULL OF KINTYRE (USA) - OUR PLEASURE (IRE)	GLENALE STUD, IRELAND.	J BERRY.	40000
PEEL HOUSE (GB) CH C GRAND LODGE (USA) - ICE HOUSE	GLENALE STUD, IRELAND.	B HILLS.	40000
GOLDEN SURF (IRE) B F GOLD AWAY (IRE) - SILVERY SURF (USA)	CAMAS PARK STUD, IRELAND.	C EGERTON.	40000
MEMPHIS MAN (GB) B C BERTOLINI (USA) - SOMETHING BLUE (GB)	MANOR FARM STUD (RUTLAND).	PETER DOYLE BS.	40000
CH C INDIAN ROCKET (GB) - LA FILLE DE CIRQUE (GB)	ROUNDHILL STUD, IRELAND.	J FRETWELL.	40000
B F XAAR (GB) - MISS MERCY (IRE)	THE WHITWORTH STUD.	M JARVIS.	40000
B C CITY ON A HILL (USA) - VICTORIA'S SECRET (IRE)	BALLYHANE STUD, IRELAND.	ALAN BRAZIL RACING.	39000
B C ORPEN (USA) - SIRAKA (FR)	CAMAS PARK STUD, IRELAND.	H JOHNSON.	38000
SIR ORPEN (IRE) GR C ORPEN (USA) - YALOYNA.	CAMAS PARK STUD, IRELAND.	H JOHNSON.	38000
B F DANEHILL DANCER (IRE) - MARY HINGE (GB)	HAWTHORN VILLA STUD, IRELAND.	DAVID McGREAVY BS.	38000
FANTASY LEGEND (IRE) CH C BECKETT (IRE) - SIANISKI (GB)	TRICKLEDOWN STUD.	D BARRON.	38000
SIRBRIT (GB) B C CADEAUX GENEREUX - EVENING PROMISE (GB)	TEMPLEHILL STUD, IRELAND.	NERVEND LTD.	38000
B C FASLIYEV (USA) - GREY AGAIN (GB)	VOUTE SALES, AGENT.	D MALONEY.	38000
SUN CATCHER (USA) B C CAPE CROSS (IRE) - TALLUF (USA)	FERNHAM FARM.	H JOHNSON.	37000
ELLCON (IRE) B F ROYAL APPLAUSE (GB) - CARRANITA (IRE)	MEADOWLANDS STUD, IRELAND.	PETER DOYLE BS.	37000
CH F PIVOTAL (GB) - NOTTURNA.	TALLYHO STUD, IRELAND.	A BAILEY.	36000
ASSERTIVE (GB) CH C BOLD EDGE (GB) - TART AND A HALF (GB)	COBHALL COURT STUD.	W BROWNE.	36000
B C DANEHILL DANCER (IRE) - ROXY (GB)	RAFFIN STUD.	PETER DOYLE BS.	36000
TALBOT STREET (GB) CH C COMPTON PLACE (GB) - ROXY (GB)	CATRIDGE FARM STUD.	J FRETWELL.	36000
MONTZANDO (GB) B C FORZANDO - CLASHFERN (GB)	THROCKMORTON COURT STUD.	R MILLMAN.	36000
B C EFSIO - ZOENA (GB).	MEADOWLANDS STUD, IRELAND.	PETER DOYLE BS.	36000
CH F BERTOLINI (USA) - ALKARIYA (USA)	WOODTOWN HOUSE STUD, IRELAND.	B ELLISON.	36000
FIRE OF LOVE (GB) GB) CH F ALLIED FORCES (USA) - PRINCESS MINNIE (GB)	FURNACE MILL STUD.	A JARVIS.	36000
ONE FELL SWOOP (IRE) B C DANEHILL DANCER (USA) - AGLAIA (SWI)	BEECHGROVE STUD.	P WEBB.	36000
KING ORCHISIOS (IRE) CH C TAGULA (IRE) - WILDFLOWER (GB)	CAMAS PARK STUD, IRELAND.	D WACHMAN.	35000
FISOLA (GB) B F FASLIYEV (USA) - AFSIAK (GB)	RATHBARRY STUD (IRE).	G RICHARDSON.	35000
PETRICHAN (IRE) B C MEDICEAN (GB) - NUMANCIA.	GLENALE STUD (AGENT), IRELAND.	CLIVE COX SYNDICATE.	35000
CH F DR FONG (USA) - LOST IN LUCCA (GB).	TRICKLEDOWN STUD.	G RICHARDSON.	35000
B C IMPERIAL BALLET (IRE) - TWO MAGPIES.	GROVE STUD, IRELAND.	J BUMMITY.	35000
B F DAGGERS DRAWN (USA) - VITALITY.	MEADOWLANDS STUD, IRELAND.	MRS A SKIFFINGTON.	35000
SUNNY SOLITAIRE (GB) B F FANTASTIC LIGHT (USA) - DIAMOND WHITE (GB)	VOUTE SALES, AGENT.	D JOHNSTON.	35000

1000 GUINEAS STAKES (3y fillies) Newmarket-1 mile

Year	Owner	Winner and Price	Jockey	Trainer	Second	Third	Ran	Time
1964	Beatrice, Lady Granard's	POURPARLER (11/2)	G Bougoure	P J Prendergast	Gwen	Royal Danseuse / Petite Gina	18	1 38.82
1965	L Holliday's	NIGHT OFF (9/2)	W Williamson	W Wharton	Yami	Mabel	16	1 45.43
1966	Mrs J Mills's	GLAD RAGS (100/6)	P Cook	V O'Brien	Berkeley Springs	Miliza	21	1 40.30
1967	R Boucher's	FLEET (11/2)	G Moore	N Murless	St Pauli Girl	Jacquer	16	1 44.76
1968	Mrs N Murless's	CAERGWRLE (4/1)	A Barclay	N Murless	Photo Flash	Sovereign	14	1 40.38
1969	R Moller's	FULL DRESS (7/1)	R Hutchinson	H Wragg	Hecuba	Motionless	13	1 44.53
1970	Jean, Lady Ashcombe's	HUMBLE DUTY (3/1)	L Piggott	N Murless	Gleam	Black Satin	12	1 42.13
1971	F Hue-Williams's	ALTESSE ROYALE (25/1)	Y Saint Martin	N Murless	Super Honey	Catherine Wheel	10	1 40.90
1972	Mrs R Stanley's	WATERLOO (8/1)	E Hide	J W Watts	Marsaila	Rose Dubarry	10	1 40.90
1973	G Pope's	MYSTERIOUS (11/1)	G Lewis	R Hern	Jacinth	Shellshock	14	1 39.49
1974	The Queen's	HIGHCLERE (12/1)	J Mercer	S Murless	Polygamy	Mrs Tiggywinkle	14	1 42.12
1975	Mrs D O' Kelly's	NOCTURNAL SPREE (14/1)	J Roe	R Hern	Girl Friend	Joking Apart	15	1 40.32
1976	D Wildenstein's	FLYING WATER (2/1)	Y Saint Martin	A Penna	Konata	Kesar Queen	16	1 41.65
1977	Mrs E Kettlewell's	MRS McARDY (16/1)	E Hide	M W Easterby	Freeze The Secret	Sanedtki	18	1 37.83
1978	R Bonnycastle's	ENSTONE SPARK (35/1)	E Johnson	B Hills	Fair Salinia	Seraphima	16	1 40.07
1979	Helena Springfield Ltd's	ONE IN A MILLION (evens)	J Mercer	J Dunlop	Abbeydale	Yanuka	17	1 41.56
1980	O Phipps's	QUICK AS LIGHTNING (12/1)	B Rouse	J Dunlop	Our Home	Mrs Penny	23	1 43.06
1981	H Joel's	FAIRY FOOTSTEPS (6/4)	L Piggott	H Cecil	Tolmi	Go Leasing	14	1 41.89
1982	Sir P Oppenheimer's	ON THE HOUSE (33/1)	J Reid	H Wragg	Time Charter	Dione	15	1 40.43
1983	Maktoum Al-Maktoum's	MA BICHE (5/2)	F Head	C Brittain	Favoridge	Habibti	18	1 40.45
1984	M Lemos's	PEBBLES (8/1)	W Robinson	C Brittain	Meis El-Reem	Desirable	15	1 41.71
1985	Sheikh Mohammed's	OH SO SHARP (2/1)	S Cauthen	H Cecil	Al Bahathri	Bella Colora	17	1 38.18
1986	H Ranier's	MIDWAY LADY (10/1)	R Cochrane	B Hanbury	Maysoon	Sonic Lady	15	1 36.85
1987	S Niarchos's	MIESQUE (15/8)	F Head	F Boutin	Milligram	Interval	14	1 41.54
1988	E Aland's	RAVINELLA (4/5)	G W Moore	Mme C Head	Dabaweyaa	Diminuendo	12	1 38.48
1989	Sheikh Mohammed's	MUSICAL BLISS (7/2)	W R Swinburn	M Stoute	Kerrera	Aldbourne	7	1 40.88
1990	Hamdan Al-Maktoum's	SALSABIL (6/4)	W Carson	J Dunlop	Heart of Joy	Negligent	10	1 42.69
1991	Hamdan Al-Maktoum's	SHADAYID (4/6)	W Carson	J Dunlop	Kooyonga	Crystal Gazing	14	1 38.06
1992	Maktoum Al-Maktoum's	HATOOF (5/1)	W R Swinburn	Mme C Head	Marling	Kenbu	14	1 38.18
1993	Mohamed Obaida's	SAYYEDATI (4/1)	W R Swinburn	C Brittain	Niche	Ajfan	12	1 39.45
1994	R Sangster's	LAS MENINAS (12/1)	J Reid	T Stack	Balanchine	Coup de Genie	15	1 37.34
1995	Wafic Said's	HARAYIR (5/1)	R Hills	Major W R Hern	Aqaarid	Moonshell	14	1 36.72
1996	Greenbay Stables Ltd's	BOSRA SHAM (10/11)	Pat Eddery	H Cecil	Matiya	Bint Shadayid	13	1 36.71
1997	Godolphin's	SLEEPYTIME (5/1)	L Dettori	H Cecil	Oh Nellie	Dazzle	15	1 37.75
1998	K Abdulla's	CAPE VERDI (100/30)	L Dettori	S Bin Suroor	Shahtoush	Exclusive	16	1 37.86
1999	Godolphin's	WINCE (4/1)	K Fallon	H Cecil	Wannabe Grand	Valentine Waltz	22	1 37.91
2000	Hamdan Al-Maktoum's	LAHAN (14/1)	R Hills	J Gosden	Princess Ellen	Petrushka	18	1 36.38
2001	Sheikh Ahmed Al Maktoum's	AMEERAT (11/1)	P Robinson	M Jarvis	Muwakleh	Tonca	15	1 38.36
2002	Godolphin's	KAZZIA (14/1)	L Dettori	S Bin Suroor	Snowfire	Alaska	17	1 37.85
2003	Cheveley Park Stud's	RUSSIAN RHYTHM (12/1)	K Fallon	Sir M Stoute	Six Perfections	Intercontinental	19	1 38.43
2004	Duke of Roxburghe's	ATTRACTION (11/2)	K Darley	M Johnston	Sundrop	Hathrah	16	1.36.70

2000 GUINEAS STAKES (3y) Newmarket-1 mile

Year	Owner	Winner and Price	Jockey	Trainer	Second	Third	Ran	Time
1964	Mrs H. Jackson's	BALDRIC (20/1)	W Pyers	E Fellows	Faberge	Balustrade	27	38.44
1965	H Harvey's	NIKSAR (100/8)	D Keith	W Nightingall	Silly Season	Present	22	43.31
1966	P Butler's	KASHMIR (7/1)	J Lindley	M Bartholomew	Great Nephew	Celic Song	25	40.63
1967	H Joel's	ROYAL PALACE (100/30)	G Moore	N Murless	Taj Dewan	Missile	18	39.37
1968	R Guest's	SIR IVOR (11/8)	L Piggott	V O'Brien	Petingo	Jimmy Reppin	10	39.26
1969	J Brown's	RIGHT TACK (15/2)	G Lewis	J Sutcliffe	Tower Walk	Welsh Pageant	18	41.54
1970	C Engelhart's	NIJINSKY (4/7)	L Piggott	V O'Brien	Yellow God	Roi Soleil	13	41.65
1971	Mrs J Hislop's	BRIGADIER GERARD (11/2)	J Mercer	R Hern	Mill Reef	My Swallow	14	41.54
1972	Sir J Thorn's	HIGH TOP (85/40)	W Carson	B Van Cutsem	Roberto	Sun Prince	6	39.20
1973	Mrs R B Davis's	MON FILS (50/1)	F Durr	R Hannon	Noble Decree	Sharp Edge	18	40.82
1974	Mme M Berger's	NONOALCO (19/2)	Y Saint Martin	F Boutin	Giacometti	Apalachee	12	42.97
1975	C d'Alessio's	BOLKONSKI (33/1)	G Dettori	H Cecil	Grundy	Dominion	24	39.53
1976	C d'Alessio's	WOLLOW (evens)	G Dettori	H Cecil	Vitiges	Thieving Demon	17	39.53
1977	N Schibbye's	NEBBIOLO (20/1)	G Curran	K Prendergast	Tachypous	The Minstrel	18	38.09
1978	J Hayter's	ROLAND GARDENS (28/1)	F Durr	D Sasse	Remainder Man	Weh Nan	19	38.54
1979	A Shead's	TAP ON WOOD (20/1)	S Cauthen	B Hills	Kris	Young Generation	20	47.33
1980	K Abdulla's	KNOWN FACT (14/1)	W Carson	J Tree	Posse	Night Alert	14	43.60
	(Nureyev fin first disqualified)							40.46
1981	Mrs A Muinos's	TO-AGORI-MOU (5/2)	G Starkey	G Harwood	Mattaboy	Bel Bolide	19	41.43
1982	G Oldham's	ZINO (9/1)	F Head	F Boutin	Wind and Wuthering	Tender King	26	37.13
1983	R Sangster's	LOMOND (9/1)	Pat Eddery	V O'Brien	Tolomeo	Muscatite	16	43.87
1984	R Sangster's	EL GRAN SENOR (15/8)	Pat Eddery	V O'Brien	Chief Singer	Lear Fan	9	37.41
1985	Maktoum Al Maktoum's	SHADEED (4/5)	L Piggott	M Stoute	Bairn	Supreme Leader	14	37.41
1986	K Abdulla's	DANCING BRAVE (15/8)	G Starkey	G Harwood	Green Desert	Huntingdale	15	40.00
1987	K Abdulla's	DON'T FORGET ME (9/1)	W Carson	R Hannon	Bellotto	Midyan	13	36.74
1988	H H Aga Khan's	DOYOUN (4/5)	W R Swinburn	M Stoute	Charmer	Bellefela	9	41.73
1989	Hamdan Al-Maktoum's	NASHWAN (3/1)	W Carson	R Hern	Exbourne	Danehill	14	36.44
1990	John Horgan's	TIROL (9/1)	M Kinane	C Britain	Machiavellian	Anshan	14	35.84
1991	Lady Beaverbrook's	MYSTIKO (13/2)	M Roberts	C Brittain	Lycius	Ganges	14	37.83
1992	R Sangster's	RODRIGO DE TRIANO (6/1)	L Piggott	P Chapple-Hyam	Lucky Lindy	Pursuit of Love	16	38.37
1993	K Abdulla's	ZAFONIC (5/6)	Pat Eddery	A Fabre	Barathea	Bin Awaad	14	35.32
1994	G R Bailey Ltd's	MISTER BAILEYS (16/1)	J Weaver	M Johnston	Grand Lodge	Colonel Collins	23	35.08
1995	Sheikh Mohammed's	PENNEKAMP (8/1)	T Jarnet	A Fabre	Celtic Swing	Bahri	14	35.16
1996	Godolphin's	MARK OF ESTEEM (8/1)	L Dettori	S bin Suroor	Even Top	Bijou D'Inde	13	37.59
1997	M Tabor & Mrs J Magnier's	ENTREPRENEUR (11/2)	M Kinane	M Stoute	Revoque	Poteen	16	35.64
1998	M Tabor & Mrs J Magnier's	KING OF KINGS (7/2)	M Kinane	A O'Brien	Lend A Hand	Border Arrow	18	39.25
1999	Godolphin's	ISLAND SANDS (10/1)	L Dettori	S Bin Suroor	Enrique	Mujahid	16	37.14
2000	Saeed Suhail's	KINGS BEST (13/2)	K Fallon	Sir M Stoute	Giant's Causeway	Barathea Guest	27	37.77
2001	Lord Weinstock's	GOLAN (11/1)	K Fallon	Sir M Stoute	Tamburaine	Frenchmans Bay	18	37.48
2002	Sir A Ferguson & Mrs J Magnier's	ROCK OF GIBRALTAR (9/1)	J Murtagh	A O'Brien	Hawk Wing	Redback	22	36.50
2003	Moyglare Stud Farm's	REFUSE TO BEND (9/2)	P J Smullen	D Weld	Zafeen	Norse Dancer	20	1 37.98
2004	Hamdan Al Maktoum's	HAAFHD (11/2)	R Hills	B Hills	Snow Ridge	Azamour	14	1 36.60

DERBY STAKES (3y) Epsom-1 mile 4 furlongs 10 yards

Year	Owner	Winner and Price	Jockey	Trainer	Second	Third	Ran	Time
1963	F Dupre's	RELKO (5/1)	Y Saint Martin	F Mathet	Merchant Venturer	Ragusa	26	2 39.40
1964	J Ismay's	SANTA CLAUS (15/8)	A Breasley	M Rogers	Indiana	Dilettante	17	2 41.98
1965	J Ternynck's	SEA-BIRD (7/4)	P Glennon	E Pollet	Meadow Court	I Say	22	2 38.41
1966	Lady Z Wernher's	CHARLOTTOWN (5/1)	A Breasley	G Smyth	Pretendre	Black Prince	25	2 37.63
1967	H Joel's	ROYAL PALACE (7/4)	G Moore	N Murless	Ribocco	Dart Board	22	2 38.36
1968	R Guest's	SIR IVOR (4/5)	L Piggott	V O'Brien	Connaught	Mount Athos	13	2 38.73
1969	A Budgett's	BLAKENEY (15/2)	E Johnson	A Budgett	Shoemaker	Prince Regent	26	2 40.30
1970	C Engelhard's	NIJINSKY (11/8)	L Piggott	V O'Brien	Gyr	Stintino	11	2 34.68
1971	P Mellon's	MILL REEF (100/30)	G Lewis	I Balding	Linden Tree	Irish Ball	21	2 37.14
1972	J Galbreath's	ROBERTO (3/1)	L Piggott	V O'Brien	Rheingold	Pentland Firth	22	2 36.09
1973	A Budgett's	MORSTON (25/1)	E Hide	A Budgett	Cavo Doro	Freefoot	25	2 35.92
1974	Mrs N Phillips's	SNOW KNIGHT (50/1)	B Taylor	P Nelson	Imperial Prince	Giacometti	18	2 35.04
1975	Dr C Vittadini's	GRUNDY (5/1)	Pat Eddery	P Walwyn	Nobiliary	Hunza Dancer	18	2 35.35
1976	N B Hunt's	EMPERY (10/1)	L Piggott	M Zilber	Relkino	Oats	23	2 35.69
1977	R Sangster's	THE MINSTREL(5/1)	L Piggott	V O'Brien	Hot Grove	Blushing Groom	22	2 36.44
1978	Lord Halifax's	SHIRLEY HEIGHTS (8/1)	G Starkey	J Dunlop	Hawaiian Sound	Remainder Man	25	2 35.30
1979	Sir M Sobell's	TROY (6/1)	W Carson	R Hern	Dickens Hill	Northern Baby	23	2 36.59
1980	Mrs A Plesch's	HENBIT (7/1)	W Carson	R Hern	Master Willie	Rankin	24	2 34.77
1981	H H Aga Khan's	SHERGAR (10/11)	W Swinburn	M Stoute	Glint of Gold	Scintillating Air	18	2 44.21
1982	R Sangster's	GOLDEN FLEECE (3/1)	Pat Eddery	V O'Brien	Touching Wood	Silver Hawk	18	2 34.27
1983	E Moller's	TEENOSO (9/2)	L Piggott	G Wragg	Carlingford Castle	Shearwalk	21	2 49.07
1984	L Miglitti's	SECRETO (14/1)	C Roche	D O'Brien	El Gran Senor	Mighty Flutter	17	2 39.12
1985	Lord H. de Walden's	SLIP ANCHOR (9/4)	S Cauthen	H Cecil	Law Society	Damister	14	2 36.23
1986	H H Aga Khan's	SHAHRASTANI (11/2)	W Swinburn	M Stoute	Dancing Brave	Mashkour	17	2 37.13
1987	H H Aga Khan's	REFERENCE POINT (6/4)	S Cauthen	H Cecil	Most Welcome	Bellotto	19	2 33.90
1988	H H Aga Khan's	KAHYASI (11/1)	R Cochrane	L Cumani	Glacial Storm	Doyoun	14	2 33.84
1989	Hamdan Al-Maktoum's	NASHWAN (5/4)	W Carson	R Hern	Terimon	Cacoethes	12	2 34.90
1990	K Abdulla's	QUEST FOR FAME (7/1)	Pat Eddery	R Charlton	Blue Stag	Elmaamul	18	2 34.00
1991	F Salman's	GENEROUS (9/1)	A Munro	P Cole	Marju	Star of Gdansk	13	2 34.00
1992	Sidney H Craig's	DR DEVIOUS (8/1)	J Reid	P Chapple-Hyam	St Jovite	Silver Wisp	18	2 36.19
1993	K Abdulla's	COMMANDER IN CHIEF (15/2)	M Kinane	H Cecil	Blue Judge	Blues Traveller	16	2 34.51
1994	Saeed Maktoum Al Maktoum's	ERHAAB (7/2)	W Carson	J Dunlop	King's Theatre	Colonel Collins	25	2 34.16
1995	K Dasmal's	LAMMTARRA (14/1)	L Dettori	S Bin Suroor	Tamure	Presenting	15	2 32.31
1996	L Knight's	SHAAMIT (12/1)	M Hills	W Haggas	Dushyantor	Shantou	20	2 35.05
1997	K Knight's	BENNY THE DIP (11/1)	W Ryan	J Gosden	Silver Patriarch	Romanov	13	2 35.77
1998	Sheikh Mohammed Obaid Al Maktoum's	HIGH-RISE (20/1)	O Peslier	L Cumani	City Honours	Border Arrow	15	2 33.88
1999	Thoroughbred Corporation's	OATH (13/2)	K Fallon	H Cecil	Daliapour	Beat All	16	2 37.43
2000	H H Aga Khan's	SINNDAR (7/1)	J Murtagh	J Oxx	Sakhee	Beat Hollow	15	2 36.75
2001	M Tabor & Mrs J Magnier's	GALILEO (11/4)	M Kinane	A O'Brien	Golan	Tobougg	12	2 33.27
2002	M Tabor & Mrs J Magnier's	HIGH CHAPARRAL (7/2)	J Murtagh	A O'Brien	Hawk Wing	Moon Ballad	12	2 39.45
2003	Saeed Suhail's	KRIS KIN (6/1)	K Fallon	Sir M Stoute	The Great Gatsby	Alamshar	20	2 33.35
2004	Ballymacoll Stud's	NORTH LIGHT (7/2)	K Fallon	Sir M Stoute	Rule Of Law	Let The Lion Roar	14	2 33.70

OAKS STAKES (3y fillies) Epsom-1 mile 4 furlongs 10 yards

Year	Owner	Winner and Price	Jockey	Trainer	Second	Third	Ran	Time
1970	Mrs S Joel's	LUPE (100/30)	A Barclay	N Murless	State Pension	Arctic Wave	16	2 41.46
1971	F Hue-Williams's	ALTESSE ROYALE (6/4)	G Lewis	N Murless	Maina	La Manille	11	2 36.95
1972	C St George's	GINEVRA (8/1)	A Murray	R Price	Regal Exception	Arkadina	17	2 39.35
1973	G Pope's	MYSTERIOUS (13/8)	G Lewis	N Murless	Where You Lead	Aureoletta	10	2 36.31
1974	L Freedman's	POLYGAMY (3/1)	Pat Eddery	P Walwyn	Furioso	Matuta	15	2 39.39
1975	J Morrison's	JULIETTE MARNY (12/1)	L Piggott	J Tree	Val's Girl	Moonlight Night	12	2 39.10
1976	D Wildenstein's	PAWNEESE (6/5)	Y Saint Martin	A Penna	Roses for the Star	African Dancer	14	2 35.25
1977	The Queen's	DUNFERMLINE (6/1)	W Carson	R Hern	Freeze the Secret	Vaguely Deb.	13	2 36.53
1978	S Hanson's	FAIR SALINIA (8/1)	G Starkey	M Stoute	Dancing Maid	Suni	15	2 36.82
1979	J Morrison's	SCINTILLATE (20/1)	Pat Eddery	J Tree	Bonnie Isle	Britannia's Rule.	14	2 43.74
1980	R Hollingsworth's	BIREME (9/2)	W Carson	R Hern	Vielle	The Dancer	11	2 34.33
1981	Mrs B Firestone's	BLUE WIND (3/1)	L Piggott	D Weld	Madam Gay.	Leap Lively	12	2 40.93
1982	R Barnett's	TIME CHARTER (12/1)	W Newnes	H Candy	Slightly Dangerous	Last Feather	13	2 34.21
1983	Sir M Sobell's	SUN PRINCESS (6/1)	W Carson	R Hern	Acclimatise	New Coins	15	2 40.98
1984	Sir R McAlpine's	CIRCUS PLUME (4/1)	L Piggott	J Dunlop	Media Luna	Poquito Queen	15	2 38.97
1985	Sheikh Mohammed's	OH SO SHARP (6/4)	S Cauthen	H Cecil	Triptych.	Dubian.	12	2 41.37
1986	H Ranier's	MIDWAY LADY (15/8)	R Cochrane	B Hanbury	Untold.	Maysoon.	15	2 35.60
1987	Sheikh Mohammed's	UNITE (11/1)	W R Swinburn	M Stoute.	Bourbon Girl.	Three Tails.	11	2 38.17
1988	Sheikh Mohammed's	DIMINUENDO (7/4)	S Cauthen	H Cecil	Sudden Love	Animatrice.	11	2 35.02
1989	S M Al Maktoum's	SNOW BRIDE (13/2)	S Cauthen	H Cecil	Roseate Tern.	Mamaluna.	9	2 34.22

(Aliysa finished first but was disqualified)

Year	Owner	Winner and Price	Jockey	Trainer	Second	Third	Ran	Time
1990	Hamdan Al-Maktoum's	SALSABIL (2/1)	W Carson	J Dunlop	Game Plan	Knight's Baroness	8	2 38.70
1991	Maktoum Al-Maktoum's	JET SKI LADY (50/1)	C Roche	J Bolger	Shamshir.	Shadayid	9	2 37.30
1992	W J Gredley's	USER FRIENDLY (5/1)	G Duffield	C Brittain	All At Sea	Pearl Angel	7	2 39.77
1993	Sheikh Mohammed's	INTREPIDITY (5/1)	M Roberts	A Fabre.	Royal Ballerina.	Oakmead	14	2 34.19
1994	Godolphin's	BALANCHINE (6/1)	L Dettori	H Ibrahim.	Wind In Her Hair.	Hawajiss	10	2 40.37
1995	Maktoum Al Maktoum/	MOONSHELL (3/1)	L Dettori	S Bin Suroor	Dance A Dream.	Pure Grain.	10	2 35.44

Year	Owner	Winner and Price	Jockey	Trainer	Second	Third	Ran	Time
1996	Wafic Said's	LADY CARLA (100/30)	Pat Eddery.	H Cecil	Pricket.	Mezzogiorno.	11	2 35.55
1997	K Abdulla's	REAMS OF VERSE (5/6)	K Fallon	H Cecil	Gazelle Royale.	Crown of Light.	12	2 35.59
1998	Mrs D Nagle & Mrs J Magnier's	SHAHTOUSH (12/1)	M Kinane	A O'Brien	Bahr	Midnight Line	8	2 38.23
1999	F Salman's	RAMRUMA (3/1)	K Fallon	H Cecil	Noushkey.	Zahrat Dubai.	10	2 38.72
2000	Lordship Stud's	LOVE DIVINE (9/4)	T Quinn.	H Cecil	Kalypso Katie.	Melikah.	16	2 43.11
2001	Mrs D. Nagle & Mrs J Magnier's	IMAGINE (3/1)	M Kinane	A O'Brien.	Flight Of Fancy	Relish The Thought	14	2 36.70
2002	Godolphin's	KAZZIA (100/30)	L Dettori	S Bin Suroor	Quarter Moon	Shadow Dancing	14	2 44.52
2003	W S Farish III's	CASUAL LOOK (10/1)	M Dwyer	A Balding	Yesterday	Summitville	15	2 38.07
2004	Lord Derby's	OUIJA BOARD (7/2)	K Fallon	E Dunlop	All Too Beautiful	Punctilious	7	2 35.40

ST LEGER STAKES (3y) Doncaster-1 mile 6 furlongs 132 yards

Year	Owner	Winner and Price	Jockey	Trainer	Second	Third	Ran	Time
1963	J Mullion's	RAGUSA (2/5)	G Bougoure	P J Prendergast	Star Moss	Fighting Ship	7	3 5.40
1964	C Engelhard's	INDIANA (100/7)	J Lindley	J Watts	Pati	Soderini	15	3 5.40
1965	J Astor's	PROVOKE (28/1)	J Mercer	R Hern	Meadow Court	Solstice	11	3 18.60
1966	R Sigtia's	SODIUM (7/1)	F Durr	G Todd	Charlttown	David Jack	9	3 9.80
1967	C Engelhard's	RIBOCCO (7/2)	L Piggott	R Houghton	Hopeful Venture	Ruysdael	9	3 5.40
1968	C Engelhard's	RIBERO (100/30)	L Piggott	R Houghton	Canterbury	Cold Storage	8	3 19.80
1969	G Oldham's	INTERMEZZO (7/1)	R Hutchinson	H Wragg	Ribofilo	Prince Consort	11	3 11.80
1970	C Engelhard's	NIJINSKY (2/7)	L Piggott	V O'Brien	Meadowville	Politico	8	3 6.40
1971	Mrs J Rogerson's	ATHENS WOOD (5/2)	L Piggott	H T Jones	Homeric	Falkland	9	3 14.90
1972	O Phipps's	BOUCHER (3/1)	L Piggott	V O'Brien	Our Mirage	Ginevra	8	3 28.71
1973	W Behrens's	PELEID (28/1)	F Durr	W Elsey	Buoy	Duke of Ragusa	13	3 8.21
1974	Lady Beaverbrook's	BUSTINO (11/10)	J Mercer	R Hern	Giacometti	Riboson	13	3 9.02
1975	C St George's	BRUNI (9/1)	A Murray	R Price	King Pellinore	Libra's Rib	12	3 9.02
1976	D Wildenstein's	CROW (9/1)	Y Saint-Martin	A Penna	Secret Man	Scallywag	15	3 13.17
1977	The Queen's	DUNFERMLINE (10/1)	W Carson	R Hern	Alleged	Classic Example	13	3 5.17
1978	R Lemos's	JULIO MARINER (28/1)	E Hide	C Brittain	Le Moss	M-Lolshan	14	3 4.94
1979	A Rolland's	SON OF LOVE (20/1)	A Lequeux	R Collet	Soleil Noir	Niniski	17	3 9.02
1980	H Joel's	LIGHT CAVALRY (3/1)	J Mercer	H Cecil	Water Mill	World Leader	11	3 11.48
1981	Sir J Astor's	CUT ABOVE (28/1)	J Mercer	H Cecil	Glint of Gold	Bustomi	7	3 11.60
1982	Maktoum Al Maktoum's	TOUCHING WOOD (7/1)	P Cook	H T Jones	Zilos	Diamond Shoal	15	3 53
1983	Sir M Sobell's	SUN PRINCESS (11/8)	W Carson	H Cecil	Esprit du Nord	Carlingford Castle	10	3 16.65
1984	I Allan's	COMMANCHE RUN (7/4)	L Piggott	L Cumani	Baynoun	Alphabatim	11	3 9.93
1985	Sheikh Mohammed's	OH SO SHARP (8/11)	S Cauthen	H Cecil	Phardante	Lanfranco	6	3 7.13
1986	Duchess of Norfolk's	MOON MADNESS (9/2)	Pat Eddery	J Dunlop	Celestial Storm	Untold	8	3 5.03
1987	L Freedman's	REFERENCE POINT (4/11)	S Cauthen	H Cecil	Mountain Kingdom	Dry Dock	8	3 5.91
1988	Lady Beaverbrook's	MINSTER SON (15/2)	W Carson	N A Graham	Diminuendo	Sheriff's Star	7	3 6.80
1989	C St George's	MICHELOZZO (6/4)	S Cauthen	H Cecil	Sapience	Roseate Tern	8	3 20.72
1990	M Arbib's	SNURGE (7/2)	T Quinn	P Cole	Hellenic	River God	8	3 8.78
1991	K Abdulla's	TOULON (5/2)	Pat Eddery	A Fabre	Saddlers' Hall	Micheletti	10	3 3.12
1992	W J Gredley's	USER FRIENDLY (7/4)	G Duffield	C Brittain	Sonus	Bonny Scot	7	3 5.48
1993	Mrs G A E Smith's	BOB'S RETURN (3/1)	P Robinson	M Tompkins	Armiger	Edbaysaan	9	3 7.85
1994	Sheikh Mohammed's	MOONAX (40/1)	Pat Eddery	B Hills	Broadway Flyer	Double Trigger	8	3 4.19
1995	Godolphin's	CLASSIC CLICHE (100/30)	L Dettori	S Bin Suroor	Minds Music	Istidaad	10	3 9.74
1996	Sheikh Mohammed's	SHANTOU (8/1)	L Dettori	J Gosden	Dushyantor	Samraan	11	3 5.10
1997	P Winfield's	SILVER PATRIARCH (5/4)	Pat Eddery	J Dunlop	Vertical Speed	The Fly	10	3 6.92
1998	Godolphin's	NEDAWI (5/2)	J Reid	S Bin Suroor	High and Low	Sunshine Street	9	3 5.61
1999	Godolphin's	MUTAFAWEQ (11/2)	R Hills	S Bin Suroor	Ramruma	Adair	9	3 2.75
2000	N Jones'	MILLENARY (11/4)	T Quinn	J Dunlop	Air Marshall	Chimes At Midnight	11	3 2.58
2001	M Tabor & Mrs J Magnier's	MILAN (13/8)	M Kinane	A O'Brien	Demophilos	Mr Combustible	10	3 5.16
2002	Sir Neil Westbrook's	BOLLIN ERIC (7/2)	K Darley	T Easterby	Highest	Bandari	8	3 2.92
2003	Mrs J Magnier's	BRIAN BORU (5/4)	J P Spencer	A O'Brien	High Accolade	Phoenix Reach	12	3 4.64
2004	Godolphin's	RULE OF LAW (3/1)	K McEvoy	S Bin Suroor	Quiff	Tycoon	9	3 6.20

(Run at Ayr)

KING GEORGE VI AND QUEEN ELIZABETH STAKES Ascot-1 mile 4 furlongs

Year	Owner	Winner and Price	Jockey	Trainer	Second	Third	Ran	Time
1965	G Bell's	MEADOW COURT 3-8-7 (6/5)	L Piggott	P J Prendergast	Soderini	Oncidium	12	2 33.27
1966	J Hornung's	AUNT EDITH 4-9-4 (7/2)	L Piggott	N Murless	Sodium	Prominer	5	2 35.06
1967	S Joel's	BUSTED 4-9-7 (4/1)	G Moore	N Murless	Salvo	Ribocco	9	2 33.64
1968	H Joel's	ROYAL PALACE 4-9-7 (7/4)	A Barclay	N Murless	Felicio	Topyo	7	2 33.22
1969	Duke of Devonshire's	PARK TOP 5-9-4 (9/4)	L Piggott	B van Cutsem	Crozier	Hogarth	9	2 32.46
1970	C Engelhard's	NIJINSKY 3-8-7 (40/85)	L Piggott	V O'Brien	Blakeney	Crepellana	6	2 36.16
1971	P Mellon's	MILL REEF 3-8-7 (8/13)	G Lewis	I Balding	Ortis	Acclimatization	10	2 32.56
1972	Mrs J Hislop's	BRIGADIER GERARD 4-9-7 (8/13)	J Mercer	R Hern	Parnell	Riverman	9	2 32.91
1973	N B Hunt's	DAHLIA 3-8-4 (10/1)	W Pyers	M Zilber	Rheingold	Our Mirage	12	2 30.43
1974	N B Hunt's	DAHLIA 4-9-4 (15/8)	L Piggott	M Zilber	Highclere	Dankaro	10	2 33.03
1975	D C Vitadini's	GRUNDY 3-8-7 (4/5)	P Eddery	P Walwyn	Bustino	Dahlia	11	2 26.98
1976	D McCall's	PAWNEESE 3-8-5 (9/4)	Y Saint Martin	A Penna	Bruni	Orange Bay	10	2 29.36
1977	R Sangster's	THE MINSTREL 3-8-8 (7/4)	L Piggott	V O'Brien	Orange Bay	Exceller	11	2 30.48
1978	Sir M Sobell's	ILE DE BOURBON 3-8-8 (12/1)	J Reid	F Houghton	Hawaiian Sound	Montcontour	14	2 30.53
1979	Sir M Sobell's	TROY 3-8-8 (2/5)	W Carson	R Hern	Gay Mecene	Ela-Mana-Mou	7	2 33.75
1980	H H Aga Khan's	ELA-MANA-MOU 4-9-7 (11/4)	W Carson	R Hern	Mrs Penny	Gregorian	10	2 35.39
1981	A Ward's	SHERGAR 3-8-8 (2/5)	W Swinburn	M Stoute	Madam Gay	Fingals Cave	10	2 35.40
1982	E Moller's	KALAGLOW 4-9-7 (13-2)	G Starkey	G Harwood	Assert	Glint of Gold	9	2 31.58
1983	E Moller's	TIME CHARTER 4-9-4 (5/1)	J Mercer	H Candy	Diamond Shoal	Sun Princess	9	2 30.78
1984	Lady Beaverbrook's	TEENOSO 4-9-7 (13/2)	L Piggott	G Wragg	Sadler's Wells	Tolomeo	13	2 27.61
1985	K Abdulla's	PETOSKI 3-8-8 (12/1)	W Carson	R Hern	Oh So Sharp	Rainbow Quest	12	2 29.49
1986	L Freedman's	DANCING BRAVE 3-8-8 (6/4)	Pat Eddery	G Harwood	Shardari	Triptych	9	2 34.63
1987	Sheikh Ahmed Al Maktoum	REFERENCE POINT 3-8-8 (11/10)	S Cauthen	A C Stewart	Celestial Storm	Triptych	9	2 37.33
1988	Hamdan Al-Maktoum's	MTOTO 5-9-7 (4/1)	M Roberts	R Hern	Unfuwain	Tony Bin	10	2 37.33
1989	Sheikh Mohammed's	NASHWAN 3-8-8 (2/9)	W Carson	R Hern	Cacoethes	Top Class	7	2 32.27
1990	Sheikh Mohammed's	BELMEZ 3-8-9 (15/2)	M Kinane	H Cecil	Old Vic	Assatis	11	2 30.76
1991	F Salman's	GENEROUS 3-8-9 (4/6)	A Munro	P Cole	Sanglamore	Rock Hopper	8	2 28.99
1992	Mrs V K Payson's	ST JOVITE 3-8-9 (4/5)	S Crane	J Bolger	Saddlers' Hall	Opera House	8	2 30.85
1993	Sheikh Mohammed's	OPERA HOUSE 5-9-7 (8/1)	M Roberts	M Stoute	White Muzzle	Commander in Chief	10	2 33.94
1994	Sheikh Mohammed's	KING'S THEATRE 3-8-9 (12/1)	M Kinane	H Cecil	White Muzzle	Wagon Master	12	2 28.92
1995	Saeed Maktoum	LAMMTARRA 3-8-9 (9/4)	L Dettori	S Bin Suroor	Pentire	Strategic Choice	9	2 31.01
1996	Mollers Racing's	PENTIRE 4-9-7 (100/30)	M Hills	G Wragg	Classic Cliche	Shaamit	8	2 28.11
1997	Godolphin's	SWAIN 5-9-7 (16/1)	J Reid	S Bin Suroor	Pilsudski	Helissio	8	2 36.45
1998	Godolphin's	SWAIN 6-9-7 (11/2)	L Dettori	S Bin Suroor	High-Rise	Royal Anthem	8	2 29.06
1999	Godolphin's	DAYLAMI 5-9-7 (3/1)	L Dettori	S Bin Suroor	Nedawi	Fruits Of Love	8	2 29.95
2000	M Tabor's	MONTJEU 4-9-7 (1/3)	M Kinane	J Hammond	Fantastic Light	Daliapour	7	2 29.98
2001	Mrs J Magnier & M Tabor's	GALILEO 3-8-9 (1/2)	M Kinane	A O'Brien	Fantastic Light	Hightori	12	2 27.71
2002	Exors of the late Lord Weinstock's	GOLAN 4-9-7 (13/2)	K Fallon	Sir M Stoute	Nayef	Zindabad	9	2 29.70
2003	H H Aga Khan	ALAMSHAR 3-8-9 (13/2)	J Murtagh	J Oxx	Sulamani	Kris Kin	12	2 33.26
2004	Godolphin's	DOYEN 4-9-7 (11/10)	L Dettori	S Bin Suroor	Hard Buck	Sulamani	11	2.33.10

PRIX DE L'ARC DE TRIOMPHE Longchamp-1 mile 4 furlongs

Year	Owner	Winner and Price	Jockey	Trainer	Second	Third	Ran	Time
1963	Baron G de Rothschild's	EXBURY 4-9-6 (36/10)	J Deforge	G Watson	Le Mesnil	Misti	15	2 34.90
1964	R Ellsworth's	PRINCE ROYAL 3-8-10 (16/1)	R Poincelet	G Bridgland	Santa Claus	La Bamba	22	2 35.50
1965	J Ternynck's	SEA-BIRD 3-8-10 (6/5)	P Glennon	E Pollet	Reliance	Diatome	20	2 35.50
1966	W Burmann's	BON MOT 3-8-10 (53/10)	F Head	W Head	Sigebert	Lionel	24	2 39.80
1967	Mme S Volterra's	TOPYO 3-8-10 (82/1)	W Pyers	M Bartholomew	Salvo	Ribocco	30	2 38.20
1968	Mrs W Franklyn's	VAGUELY NOBLE 3-8-10 (5/2)	W Williamson	M Bartholomew	Sir Ivor	Carmarthen	17	2 35.20
1969	S McGrath's	LEVMOSS 4-9-6 (52/1)	W Williamson	S McGrath	Park Top	Grandier	24	2 29.00
1970	A Plesch's	SASSAFRAS 3-8-10 (19/1)	Y Saint Martin	F Mathet	Nijinsky	Miss Dan	15	2 29.70
1971	P Mellon's	MILL REEF 3-8-10 (7/10)	G Lewis	I Balding	Pistol Packer	Cambrizzia	18	2 28.30
1972	Countess M Batthyany's	SAN SAN 3-8-7 (37/2)	F Head	A Penna	Rescousse	Homeric	19	2 28.30
1973	Zeisel's	RHEINGOLD 4-9-6 (77/10)	L Piggott	B Hills	Allez France	Hard to Beat	27	2 35.80
1974	D Wildenstein's	ALLEZ FRANCE 4-9-3 (1/2)	Y Saint Martin	A Penna	Comtesse de Loir	Margouillat	20	2 36.90
1975	W Zeitelhack's	STAR APPEAL 5-9-6 (119/1)	G Starkey	T Grieper	On My Way	Comtesse de Loir	24	2 33.60
1976	J Wertheimer's	IVANJICA 4-9-1 (7/10)	F Head	A Head	Crow	Youth	20	2 39.40
1977	R Sangster's	ALLEGED 3-8-11 (38/10)	L Piggott	V O'Brien	Balmerino	Crystal Palace	26	2 30.60
1978	R Sangster's	ALLEGED 4-9-4 (7/5)	L Piggott	V O'Brien	Trillion	Dancing Maid	18	2 36.10
1979	Mme G Head's	THREE TROIKAS 3-8-8 (88/10)	Head	Mme C Head	Le Marmot	Troy	22	2 28.90
1980	R Sangster's	DETROIT 3-8-8 (67/10)	Pat Eddery	O Douieb	Argument	Ela-Mana-Mou	20	2 28.00
1981	J Wertheimer's	GOLD RIVER 4-9-1 (53/1)	G W Moore	A Head	Bikala	April Run	24	2 35.20
1982	H H Aga Khan's	AKYDA 3-8-8 (43/4)	Y Saint Martin	F Mathet	Ardross	Awaasif	17	2 37.00
1983	D Wildenstein's	ALL ALONG 4-9-1 (173/10)	W Swinburn	P Biancone	Sun Princess	Luth Enchantee	26	2 28.10
1984	D Wildenstein's	SAGACE 4-9-4 (29/10)	Y Saint Martin	P Biancone	Northern Trick	All Along	22	2 39.10
1985	K Abdulla's	RAINBOW QUEST 4-9-4 (71/10)	Pat Eddery	J Tree	Sagace	Kozana	15	2 29.50
1986	K Abdulla's	DANCING BRAVE 3-8-11 (11/10)	Pat Eddery	G Harwood	Bering	Triptych	15	2 27.70
1987	P de Moussac's	TREMPOLINO 3-8-11 (20/1)	Pat Eddery	A Fabre	Tony Bin	Triptych	11	2 26.30
1988	Mrs V Gaucci del Bono's	TONY BIN 5-9-4 (14/1)	J Reid	L Camici	Mtoto	Boyatino	24	2 27.30
1989	A Balzarini's	CARROLL HOUSE 4-9-4 (19/1)	M Kinane	M Jarvis	Behera	Saint Andrews	19	2 30.80
1990	B McKall's	SAUMAREZ 3-8-11 (15/1)	G Mosse	N Clement	Epervier Bleu	Snurge	21	2 29.80
1991	J Chalhoub's	SUAVE DANCER 3-8-11 (37/10)	C Asmussen	J Hammond	Magic Night	Pistolet Bleu	14	2 31.40
1992	O Lecerf's	SUBOTICA 4-9-4 (88/10)	T Jarnet	A Fabre	User Friendly	Vert Amande	18	2 39.00
1993	O Tsui's	URBAN SEA 4-9-1 (37/1)	E Saint Martin	J Lesbordes	White Muzzle	Opera House	23	2 37.90
1994	Sheikh Mohammed's	CARNEGIE 3-8-11 (3/1)	T Jarnet	A Fabre	Hernando	Apple Tree	20	2 31.10
1995	Saeed Maktoum Al Maktoum's	LAMMTARRA 3-8-11 (2/1)	L Dettori	S Bin Suroor	Freedom Cry	Swain	16	2 31.80
1996	S Sarasola's	HELISSIO 3-8-11 (18/10)	O Peslier	E Lellouche	Pilsudski	Oscar Schindler	16	2 29.90
1997	J Wildenstein's	PEINTRE CELEBRE 3-8-11 (22/10)	O Peslier	A Fabre	Pilsudski	Borgia	18	2 24.60
1998	J-L Lagardère's	SAGAMIX 3-8-11 (5/2)	O Peslier	A Fabre	Leggera	Tiger Hill	14	2 34.50
1999	M Tabor's	MONTJEU 3-8-11 (6/4)	M Kinane	J Hammond	El Condor Pasa	Croco Rouge	14	2 38.50
2000	H H Aga Khan's	SINNDAR 3-8-11 (6/4)	J Murtagh	J Oxx	Egyptband	Volvoreta	10	2 25.80
2001	Godolphin's	SAKHEE 4-9-5 (22/10)	L Dettori	S Bin Suroor	Aquarelliste	Sagacity	17	2 36.10
2002	Godolphin's	MARIENBARD 5-9-5 (158/10)	L Dettori	S Bin Suroor	Sulamani	High Chaparral	16	2 26.70
2003	H H Aga Khan's	DALAKHANI 3-8-11 (9/4)	C Soumillon	A DeRoyer-Dupre	Mubtaker	High Chaparral	13	2 32.30
2004	Niarchos Family's	BAGO 3-8-11 (10/1)	T Gillet	J E Pease	Cherry Mix	Ouija Board	13	2 25.00

GRAND NATIONAL STEEPLECHASE Aintree-4m 4f

Year	Winner and Price	Age & Weight	Jockey	Second	Third	Ran	Time
1962	KILMORE (28-1)	12 10 4	F T Winter	Wyndburgh	Mr What	32	9 50.00
1963	AYALA (66-1)	9 10 0	P Buckley	Carrickbeg	Hawa's Song	47	9 35.80
1964	TEAM SPIRIT (18-1)	12 10 3	G W Robinson	Purple Silk	Peacetown	33	9 47.00
1965	JAY TRUMP (100-8)	8 11 5	Mr C Smith, jun	Freddie	Mr Jones	47	9 30.60
1966	ANGLO (50-1)	8 10 0	T Norman	Freddie	Forest Prince	47	9 52.80
1967	FOINAVON (100-1)	9 10 0	J Buckingham	Honey End	Red Alligator	44	9 49.60
1968	RED ALLIGATOR (100-7)	9 10 0	B Fletcher	Moidore's Token	Different Class	45	9 28.60
1969	HIGHLAND WEDDING (100-9)	12 10 4	E Harty	Steel Bridge	Rondetto	30	9 30.80
1970	GAY TRIP (15-1)	8 11 5	P Taaffe	Vulture	Miss Hunter	28	9 38.00
1971	SPECIFY (28-1)	9 10 13	J Cook	Black Secret	Astbury	38	9 34.20
1972	WELL TO DO (14-1)	9 10 1	G Thorner	Gay Trip	Black Secret	42	10 08.40
1973	RED RUM (9-1)	8 10 5	B Fletcher	Crisp	L'Escargot	38	9 01.90
1974	RED RUM (11-1)	9 12 0	B Fletcher	L'Escargot	Charles Dickens	42	9 20.30
1975	L'ESCARGOT (13-2)	12 11 3	T Carberry	Red Rum	Spanish Steps	31	9 31.10
1976	RAG TRADE (14-1)	10 10 12	J Burke	Red Rum	Eyecatcher	32	9 20.90
1977	RED RUM (9-1)	12 11 8	T Stack	Churchtown Boy	Eyecatcher	42	9 30.30
1978	LUCIUS (14-1)	9 10 9	B R Davies	Sebastian V	Drumnan	37	9 33.90
1979	RUBSTIC (25-1)	10 10 0	M Barnes	Zongalero	Rough & Tumble	34	9 52.90
1980	BEN NEVIS (40-1)	12 10 12	Mr C Fenwick	Rough & Tumble	The Pilgarlic	30	10 17.40
1981	ALDANITI (10-1)	11 10 13	R Champion	Spartan Missile	Royal Mail	39	9 47.20
1982	GRITTAR (7-1)	9 11 5	Mr D Saunders	Hard Outlook	Loving Words	39	9 12.60
1983	CORBIERE (13-1)	8 11 4	B de Haan	Greasepaint	Yer Man	41	9 47.04
1984	HALLO DANDY (13-1)	10 10 2	N Doughty	Greasepaint	Corbiere	40	9 21.04
1985	LAST SUSPECT (50-1)	11 10 5	H Davies	Mr Snugfit	Corbiere	40	9 42.70
1986	WEST TIP (15-2)	9 10 11	R Dunwoody	Young Driver	Classified	40	9 33.00
1987	MAORI VENTURE (28-1)	11 10 13	S C Knight	The Tsarevich	Lean Ar Aghaidh	40	9 19.30
1988	RHYME N'REASON (10-1)	9 11 0	B Powell	Durham Edition	Monanore	40	9 53.50
1989	LITTLE POLVEIR (28-1)	12 10 3	J Frost	West Tip	The Thinker	40	10 06.80
1990	MR FRISK (16-1)	11 10 6	Mr M Armytage	Durham Edition	Rinus	38	8 47.80
1991	SEAGRAM (12-1)	11 10 6	N Hawke	Garrison Savannah	Auntie Dot	40	9 29.90
1992	PARTY POLITICS (14-1)	8 10 7	C Llewellyn	Romany King	Laura's Beau	40	9 06.30
1993	Race Void						
1994	MINNEHOMA (16-1)	11 10 8	R Dunwoody	Just So	Moorcroft Boy	36	10 18.80
1995	ROYAL ATHLETE (40-1)	12 10 6	J Titley	Party Politics	Over The Deel	35	9 04.00
1996	ROUGH QUEST (7-1)	10 10 7	M Fitzgerald	Encore Un Peu	Superior Finish	27	9 00.80
1997	LORD GYLLENE (14-1)	9 10 0	A Dobbin	Suny Bay	Camelot Knight	36	9 05.80
1998	EARTH SUMMIT (7-1)	10 10 5	C Llewellyn	Suny Bay	Samlee	37	10 51.40
1999	BOBBYJO (10-1)	9 10 0	P Carberry	Blue Charm	Call It A Day	32	9 14.00
2000	PAPILLON (10-1)	9 10 12	R Walsh	Mely Moss	Niki Dee	40	9 09.70
2001	RED MARAUDER (33-1)	11 10 11	R Guest	Smarty	Blowing Wind	40	11 00.10
2002	BINDAREE (20-1)	8 10 4	J Culloty	What's Up Boys	Blowing Wind	40	9 09.00
2003	MONTY'S PASS (16-1)	10 10 7	B J Geraghty	Supreme Glory	Amberleigh House	40	9 21.70
2004	AMBERLEIGH HOUSE (16/1)	12-10-10	G Lee	Clan Royal	Lord Atterbury	39	9 20.30

WINNERS OF GREAT RACES

LINCOLN HANDICAP
Doncaster-1m
1995	**ROVING MINSTREL** 4-8-3	23
1996	**STONE RIDGE** 4-8-7	24
1997	**KUALA LIPIS** 4-8-6	24
1998	**HUNTERS OF BRORA** 8-9-0	23
1999	**RIGHT WING** 5-9-5	24
2000	**JOHN FERNELEY** 5-8-10	24
2001	**NIMELLO** 5-8-9	23
2002	**ZUCCHERO** 6-8-13	23
2003	**PABLO** 4-8-11	24
2004	**BABODANA** 4-9-10	24

GREENHAM STAKES (3y)
Newbury-7f
1995	**CELTIC SWING** 9-0	9
1996	**DANEHILL DANCER** 9-0	8
1997	**YALAIETANEE** 9-0	6
1998	**VICTORY NOTE** 9-0	6
1999	**ENRIQUE** 9-0	7
*2000	**BARATHEA GUEST** 9-0	7
2001	**MUNIR** 9-0	7
2002	**REDBACK** 9-0	10
2003	**MUQBIL** 9-0	8
2004	**SALFORD CITY** 9-0	10

* Run at Newmarket

JOHN PORTER STAKES
Newbury-1m 4f 5yds
1995	**STRATEGIC CHOICE** 4-8-11	10
1996	**SPOUT** 4-8-8	9
1997	**WHITEWATER AFFAIR** 4-8-8	13
1998	**POSIDONAS** 6-8-12	12
1999	**SADIAN** 4-8-11	11
*2000	**YAVANA'S PACE** 8-9-1	11
2001	**LUCIDO** 5-8-12	13
2002	**ZINDABAD** 6-8-12	10
2003	**WARRSAN** 5-8-12	9
2004	**DUBAI SUCCESS** 4-8-11	17

* Run at Haydock

EUROPEAN FREE HANDICAP (3y)
Newmarket-7f
1995	**DIFFIDENT** 9-5	12
1996	**CAYMAN KAI** 9-7	8
1997	**HIDDEN MEADOW** 9-3	11
1998	**DESERT PRINCE** 9-5	9
1999	**BERTOLINI** 9-7	6
2000	**CAPE TOWN** 9-2	8
2001	**CLEARING** 9-6	10
2002	**TWILIGHT BLUES** 9-5	8
2003	**INDIAN HAVEN** 9-1	6
2004	**BRUNEL** 8-13	11

CRAVEN STAKES (3y)
Newmarket-1m
1995	**PAINTER'S ROW** 8-12	5
1996	**BEAUCHAMP KING** 9-0	5
1997	**DESERT STORY** 8-12	8
1998	**XAAR** 8-12	6
1999	**COMPTON ADMIRAL** 8-9	7
2000	**UMISTIM** 8-9	6
2001	**KING'S IRONBRIDGE** 8-9	8

2002	**KING OF HAPPINESS** 8-9	6
2003	**HURRICANE ALAN** 8-9	7
2004	**HAAFHD** 8-9	5

VICTORIA CUP
Ascot-7f
1995	**JAWAAL** 5-8-6	25
1996	**YEAST** 4-8-9	24
1997	**TREGARON** 6-8-13	25
1998	ABANDONED	
1999	**GREAT NEWS** 4-7-12	18
2000	**BOLD KING** 5-8-9	21
2001	**CLEARING** 9-6	10
2002	**SCOTTY'S FUTURE** 4-8-11	28
2003	**CAMP COMMANDER** 4-8-10	28
2004	**MINE** 6-9-7	20

JOCKEY CLUB STAKES
Newmarket-1m 4f
1995	**ONLY ROYALE** 6-8-11	7
1996	**RIYADIAN** 4-8-9	9
1997	**TIME ALLOWED** 4-8-6	10
1998	**ROMANOV** 4-8-9	8
1999	**SILVER PATRIARCH** 5-9-0	11
2000	**BLUEPRINT** 5-8-9	11
2001	**MILLENARY** 4-9-0	7
2002	**MARIENBARD** 5-8-9	9
2003	**WARRSAN** 5-8-9	6
2004	**GAMUT** 5-8-9	7

CHESTER VASE (3y)
Chester-1m 4f 66yds
1995	**LUSO** 8-10	7
1996	**HIGH BAROQUE** 8-10	6
1997	**PANAMA CITY** 8-10	5
1998	**GULLAND** 8-10	5
1999	**PESHTIGO** 8-10	8
2000	**MILLENARY** 8-10	8
2001	**MR COMBUSTIBLE** 8-10	7
2002	**FIGHT YOUR CORNER** 8-10	8
2003	**DUTCH GOLD** 8-10	4
2004	**RED LANCER** 8-10	6

CHESTER CUP
Chester-2m 2f 147yds
1995	**TOP CEES** 5-8-8	18
1996	**MERIT** 4-7-10	18
1997	**TOP CEES** 7-8-11	12
1998	**SILENCE IN COURT** 7-9-0	18
1999	**RAINBOW HIGH** 4-9-0	16
2000	**BANGALORE** 4-7-10	18
2001	**RAINBOW HIGH** 6-9-13	17
2002	**FANTASY HILL** 6-8-9	18
2003	**HUGS DANCER** 6-8-11	16
2004	**ANAK PEKAN** 4-8-2	17

ORMONDE STAKES
Chester-1m 5f 89yds
1995	**ZILZAL ZAMAAN** 4-8-11	4
1996	**OSCAR SCHINDLER** 4-8-11	7
1997	**ROYAL COURT** 4-8-11	7
1998	**STRETAREZ** 5-9-2	6
1999	**SADIAN** 4-9-0	7

2000	**DALIAPOUR** 4-8-11	9
2001	**ST EXPEDIT** 4-8-11	5
2002	**ST EXPEDIT** 5-8-11	6
2003	**ASIAN HEIGHTS** 5-9-0	7
2004	**SYSTEMATIC** 5-8-11	9

OAKS TRIAL (3y fillies)
Lingfield-1m 3f 106yds

1995	**ASTERITA** 8-8	5
1996	**LADY CARLA** 8-8	4
1997	**CROWN OF LIGHT** 8-8	6
1998	**BRISTOL CHANNEL** 8-8	6
1999	**RAMRUMA** 8-8	7
2000	**FILM SCRIPT** 8-8	7
2001	**DOUBLE CROSSED** 8-8	3
2002	**BIRDIE** 8-8	7
2003	**SANTA SOPHIA** 8-8	8
2004	**BARAKA** 8-8	5

DERBY TRIAL (3y)
Lingfield-1m 3f 106yds

1995	**MUNWAR** 8-7	7
1996	**MYSTIC KNIGHT** 8-7	6
1997	**SILVER PATRIARCH** 8-7	6
1998	**HIGH-RISE** 8-7	5
1999	**LUCIDO** 8-7	5
2000	**SADDLER'S QUEST** 8-7	8
2001	**PERFECT SUNDAY** 8-7	8
2002	**BANDARI** 8-7	6
2003	**FRANKLINS GARDENS** 8-7	6
2004	**PERCUSSIONIST** 8-7	4

MUSIDORA STAKES (3y fillies)
York-1m 2f 85yds

1995	**PURE GRAIN** 8-10	5
1996	**MAGNIFICENT STYLE** 8-8	5
1997	**REAMS OF VERSE** 8-11	10
1998	**BAHR** 8-8	4
1999	**ZAHRAT DUBAI** 8-8	6
2000	**KALYPSO KATIE** 8-8	9
2001	**TIME AWAY** 8-8	11
2002	**ISLINGTON** 8-8	5
2003	**CASSIS** 8-8	8
2004	**PUNCTILIOUS** 8-8	6

DANTE STAKES (3y)
York-1m 2f 85yds

1995	**CLASSIC CLICHE** 8-11	8
1996	**GLORY OF DANCER** 8-11	7
1997	**BENNY THE DIP** 8-11	8
1998	**SARATOGA SPRINGS** 8-11	8
1999	**SALFORD EXPRESS** 8-11	6
2000	**SAKHEE** 8-11	8
2001	**DILSHAAN** 8-11	5
2002	**MOON BALLAD** 8-11	9
2003	**MAGISTRETTI** 8-11	10
2004	**NORTH LIGHT** 8-11	10

YORKSHIRE CUP
York-1m 5f 194yds

1995	**MOONAX** 4-9-0	7
1996	**CLASSIC CLICHE** 4-9-0	5
1997	**CELERIC** 5-8-9	9
1998	**BUSY FLIGHT** 5-8-9	6
1999	**CHURLISH CHARM** 4-8-9	9
2000	**KAYF TARA** 6-9-0	9
2001	**MARIENBARD** 4-8-9	8

2002	**ZINDABAD** 6-8-9	7
2003	**MAMOOL** 4-8-9	8
2004	**MILLENARY** 7-8-13	10

DUKE OF YORK STAKES
York-6f

1995	**LAKE CONISTON** 4-9-4	7
1996	**VENTURE CAPITALIST** 7-9-0	12
1997	**ROYAL APPLAUSE** 4-9-0	10
1998	**BOLLIN JOANNE** 5-8-11	10
1999	**SAMPOWER STAR** 3-8-5	14
2000	**LEND A HAND** 5-9-5	10
2001	**PIPALONG** 5-9-6	14
2002	**INVINCIBLE SPIRIT** 5-9-5	12
2003	**TWILIGHT BLUES** 4-9-2	15
2004	**MONSIEUR BOND** 4-9-2	15

LOCKINGE STAKES
Newbury-1m

1995	**SOVIET LINE** 5-9-0	5
1996	**SOVIET LINE** 6-9-0	7
1997	**FIRST ISLAND** 5-9-0	10
1998	**CAPE CROSS** 4-9-0	10
1999	**FLY TO THE STARS** 5-9-0	10
2000	**ALJABR** 4-9-0	7
2001	**MEDICEAN** 4-9-0	7
2002	**KELTOS** 4-9-0	10
2003	**HAWK WING** 4-9-0	6
2004	**RUSSIAN RHYTHM** 4-8-11	15

HENRY II STAKES
Sandown-2m 78yds

1995	**DOUBLE TRIGGER** 4-8-13	7
1996	**DOUBLE TRIGGER** 5-9-5	5
1997	**PERSIAN PUNCH** 4-8-10	7
1998	**PERSIAN PUNCH** 5-9-1	10
1999	**ARCTIC OWL** 5-9-3	11
2000	**PERSIAN PUNCH** 7-8-12	7
2001	**SOLO MIO** 7-9-1	11
2002	**AKBAR** 6-9-0	11
2003	**MR DINOS** 4-9-3	10
2004	**PAPINEAU** 4-8-12	9

PREDOMINATE STAKES (3y)
Goodwood-1m 2f

1995	**PENTIRE** 9-0	6
1996	**DON MICHELETTO** 8-8	9
1997	**GRAPESHOT** 8-11	6
1998	**RABAH** 8-8	6
1999	**DUBAI MILLENNIUM** 8-8	6
2000	**ROSCIUS** 8-8	8
2001	**ASIAN HEIGHTS** 8-8	11
2002	**COSHOCTON** 8-8	6
2003	**HIGH ACCOLADE** 8-8	7
2004	**MANYANA** 8-8	7

LUPE STAKES (3y)
Goodwood-1m 2f

1995	**SUBYA** 8-11	9
1996	**WHITEWATER AFFAIR** 8-8	8
1997	**MAID OF CAMELOT** 8-8	7
1998	**NAPOLEON'S SISTER** 8-8	8
1999	**CLAXON** 8-11	8
2000	**LOVE DIVINE** 8-8	6
2001	**FOODBROKER FANCY** 8-8	9

2002	**MELLOW PARK** 8-8	6
2003	**OCEAN SILK** 8-8	8
2004	**HALICARDIA** 8-8	7

TEMPLE STAKES
Sandown-5f 6yds

1995	**MIND GAMES** 3-8-8	5
1996	**MIND GAMES** 4-9-7	9
1997	**CROFT POOL** 6-9-3	10
1998	**BOLSHOI** 6-9-3	8
1999	**TIPSY CREEK** 5-9-3	8
2000	**PERRYSTON VIEW** 8-9-3	9
2001	**CASSANDRA GO** 5-9-0	10
2002	**KYLLACHY** 4-9-3	11
2003	**AIRWAVE** 3-9-0	7
*2004	**NIGHT PROSPECTOR** 4-9-4	12

* Run at Epsom

BRIGADIER GERARD STAKES
Sandown-1m 2f 7yds

1995	**ALRIFFA** 4-8-10	7
1996	**PILSUDSKI** 4-8-10	11
1997	**BOSRA SHAM** 4-9-0	6
1998	**INSATIABLE** 5-8-10	9
1999	**CHESTER HOUSE** 4-8-10	6
2000	**SHIVA** 5-9-0	8
2001	**BORDER ARROW** 6-8-10	5
2002	**POTEMKIN** 4-8-10	4
2003	**SIGHTS ON GOLD** 4-8-10	8
2004	**BANDARI** 5-8-10	9

DIOMED STAKES
Epsom-1m 114yds

1995	**MR MARTINI** 5-9-4	7
1996	**BLOMBERG** 4-9-4	8
1997	**POLAR PRINCE** 4-9-4	9
1998	**INTIKHAB** 4-9-4	10
1999	**LEAR SPEAR** 4-9-4	6
2000	**TRANS ISLAND** 5-9-9	5
2001	**PULAU TIOMAN** 5-9-4	8
2002	**NAYYIR** 4-9-4	9
2003	**GATEMAN** 6-9-4	10
2004	**PASSING GLANCE** 5-9-9	11

CORONATION CUP
Epsom-1m 4f 10yds

1995	**SUNSHACK** 4-9-0	7
1996	**SWAIN** 4-9-0	4
1997	**SINGSPIEL** 5-9-0	5
1998	**SILVER PATRIARCH** 4-9-0	7
1999	**DAYLAMI** 5-9-0	7
2000	**DALIAPOUR** 4-9-0	4
2001	**MUTAFAWEQ** 5-9-0	6
2002	**BOREAL** 4-9-0	6
2003	**WARRSAN** 5-9-0	9
2004	**WARRSAN** 6-9-0	11

JOHN OF GAUNT STAKES
Haydock-7f 30yds

1995	**MUTAKDDIM** 4-8-12	8
1996	**INZAR** 4-9-5	9
1997	**DECORATED HERO** 5-9-3	4
1998	**NIGRASINE** 4-8-12	7
1999	**WARNINGFORD** 5-9-5	6
2000	**ONE WON ONE** 6-9-3	10
2001	**MOUNT ABU** 4-9-5	10
2002	**WARNINGFORD** 8-9-5	7

2003	**WITH REASON** 5-8-12	7
2004	**SUGGESTIVE** 6-8-12	11

WILLIAM HILL TROPHY (HANDICAP) (3y)
York-6f

1995	**BOLD EFFORT** 8-8	15
1996	**MALLIA** 7-10	18
1997	**RETURN OF AMIN** 7-7	19
1998	**FRIAR TUCK** 8-11	22
1999	**PEPPERDINE** 8-3	23
2000	**COTTON HOUSE** 8-13	23
2001	**ORIENTOR** 9-2	20
2002	**ARTIE** 7-10	20
2003	**DAZZLING BAY** 8-2	19
2004	**TWO STEP KID** 8-9	20

QUEEN ANNE STAKES
Ascot-1m

1995	**NICOLOTTE** 4-9-2	7
1996	**CHARNWOOD FOREST** 4-9-2	9
1997	**ALLIED FORCES** 4-9-5	11
1998	**INTIKHAB** 4-9-2	9
1999	**CAPE CROSS** 5-9-7	8
2000	**KALANISI** 4-9-2	11
2001	**MEDICEAN** 4-9-7	10
2002	**NO EXCUSE NEEDED** 4-9-2	12
2003	**DUBAI DESTINATION** 4-9-0	10
2004	**REFUSE TO BEND** 4-9-0	16

PRINCE OF WALES'S STAKES
Ascot-1m 2f

1995	**MUHTARRAM** 6-9-8	6
1996	**FIRST ISLAND** 4-9-3	12
1997	**BOSRA SHAM** 4-9-5	6
1998	**FAITHFUL SON** 4-9-3	8
1999	**LEAR SPEAR** 4-9-3	8
2000	**DUBAI MILLENNIUM** 4-9-0	6
2001	**FANTASTIC LIGHT** 5-9-1	9
2002	**GRANDERA** 4-9-0	12
2003	**NAYEF** 5-9-0	10
2004	**RAKTI** 5-9-0	10

ST JAMES'S PALACE STAKES (3y)
Ascot-1m

1995	**BAHRI** 9-0	9
1996	**BIJOU D'INDE** 9-0	9
1997	**STARBOROUGH** 9-0	8
1998	**DR FONG** 9-0	8
1999	**SENDAWAR** 9-0	11
2000	**GIANT'S CAUSEWAY** 9-0	11
2001	**BLACK MINNALOUSHE** 9-0	11
2002	**ROCK OF GIBRALTAR** 9-0	11
2003	**ZAFEEN** 9-0	11
2004	**AZAMOUR** 9-0	11

COVENTRY STAKES (2y)
Ascot-6f

1995	**ROYAL APPLAUSE** 8-12	13
1996	**VERGLAS** 8-12	15
1997	**HARBOUR MASTER** 8-12	15
1998	**RED SEA** 8-12	17
1999	**FASILIYEV** 8-12	18
2000	**CD EUROPE** 8-12	12
2001	**LANDSEER** 8-12	20
2002	**STATUE OF LIBERTY** 8-12	16
2003	**THREE VALLEYS** 8-12	13
2004	**ICEMAN** 8-12	13

KING EDWARD VII STAKES (3y)
Ascot-1m 4f

1995	**PENTIRE** 8-8	8
1996	**AMFORTAS** 8-8	7
1997	**KINGFISHER MILL** 8-8	5
1998	**ROYAL ANTHEM** 8-8	10
1999	**MUTAFAWEQ** 8-8	10
2000	**SUBTLE POWER** 8-8	7
2001	**STORMING HOME** 8-8	12
2002	**BALAKHERI** 8-10	4
2003	**HIGH ACCOLADE** 8-11	8
2004	**FIVE DYNASTIES** 8-11	5

JERSEY STAKES (3y)
Ascot-7f

1995	**SERGEYEV** 8-10	16
1996	**LUCAYAN PRINCE** 8-10	16
1997	**AMONG MEN** 8-13	20
1998	**DIKTAT** 8-10	16
1999	**LOTS OF MAGIC** 8-11	12
2000	**OBSERVATORY** 8-11	19
2001	**MOZART** 8-11	18
2002	**JUST JAMES** 8-11	15
2003	**MEMBERSHIP** 8-10	14
2004	**KHELEYF** 8-10	15

QUEEN MARY STAKES (2y fillies)
Ascot-5f

1995	**BLUE DUSTER** 8-8	12
1996	**DANCE PARADE** 8-8	13
1997	**NADWAH** 8-8	18
1998	**BINT ALLAYL** 8-8	17
1999	**SHINING HOUR** 8-8	13
2000	**ROMANTIC MYTH** 8-8	20
2001	**QUEEN'S LOGIC** 8-8	20
2002	**ROMANTIC LIASON** 8-8	19
2003	**ATTRACTION** 8-10	14
2004	**DAMSON** 8-10	17

CORONATION STAKES (3y fillies)
Ascot-1m

1995	**RIDGEWOOD PEARL** 9-0	10
1996	**SHAKE THE YOKE** 9-0	6
1997	**REBECCA SHARP** 9-0	6
1998	**EXCLUSIVE** 9-0	9
1999	**BALISADA** 9-0	9
2000	**CRIMPLENE** 9-0	9
2001	**BANKS HILL** 9-0	13
2002	**SOPHISTICAT** 9-0	11
2003	**RUSSIAN RHYTHM** 9-0	9
2004	**ATTRACTION** 9-0	11

ROYAL HUNT CUP
Ascot-1m

1995	**REALITIES** 5-9-10	32
1996	**YEAST** 4-8-6	31
1997	**RED ROBBO** 4-8-6	32
1998	**REFUSE TO LOSE** 4-7-11	32
1999	**SHOWBOAT** 5-8-6	32
2000	**CARIBBEAN MONARCH** 5-8-10	32
2001	**SURPRISE ENCOUNTER** 5-8-9	30
2002	**NORTON** 5-8-9	30
2003	**MACADAMIA** 4-8-13	32
2004	**MINE** 6-9-5	31

QUEENS VASE (3y)
Ascot-2m 45yds

1995	**STELVIO** 8-11	11
1996	**GORDI** 8-11	14
1997	**WINDSOR CASTLE** 8-11	11
1998	**MARIDPOUR** 8-11	8
1999	**ENDORSEMENT** 8-6	11
2000	**DALAMPOUR** 8-11	13
2001	**AND BEYOND** 8-11	16
2002	**MAMOOL** 8-11	14
2003	**SHANTY STAR** 8-11	12
2004	**DUKE OF VENICE** 8-11	10

GOLDEN JUBILEE STAKES
Ascot-6f
(formerly Cork and Orrery Stakes)

1995	**SO FACTUAL** 5-8-13	11
1996	**ATRAF** 3-8-6	17
1997	**ROYAL APPLAUSE** 4-9-3	23
1998	**TOMBA** 4-9-0	19
1999	**BOLD EDGE** 4-9-0	19
2000	**SUPERIOR PREMIUM** 6-9-0	16
2001	**HARMONIC WAY** 9-0	21
2002	**MALHUB** 4-9-4	20
2003	**CHOISIR** 4-9-4	17
2004	**FAYR JAG** 5-9-4	14

NORFOLK STAKES (2y)
Ascot-5f

1995	**LUCKY LIONEL** 8-12	9
1996	**TIPSY CREEK** 8-12	10
1997	**TIPPITT BOY** 8-12	6
1998	**ROSSELLI** 8-12	15
1999	**WARM HEART** 8-12	13
2000	**SUPERSTAR LEO** 8-7	11
2001	**JOHANNESBURG** 8-12	10
2002	**BARON'S PIT** 8-12	12
2003	**RUSSIAN VALOUR** 8-12	8
2004	**BLUE DAKOTA** 8-12	9

GOLD CUP
Ascot-2m 4f

1995	**DOUBLE TRIGGER** 4-9-0	7
1996	**CLASSIC CLICHE** 4-9-0	7
1997	**CELERIC** 5-9-2	13
1998	**KAYF TARA** 4-9-0	16
1999	**ENZELI** 4-9-0	17
2000	**KAYF TARA** 6-9-2	11
2001	**ROYAL REBEL** 5-9-2	12
2002	**ROYAL REBEL** 6-9-2	15
2003	**MR DINOS** 4-9-0	11
2004	**PAPINEAU** 4-9-0	13

RIBBLESDALE STAKES (3y fillies)
Ascot-1m 4f

1995	**PHANTOM GOLD** 8-8	7
1996	**TULIPA** 8-8	10
1997	**YASHMAK** 8-8	9
1998	**BAHR** 8-8	9
1999	**FAIRY QUEEN** 8-8	12
2000	**MILETRIAN** 8-8	9
2001	**SAHARA SLEW** 8-8	14
2002	**IRRESISTIBLE JEWEL** 8-8	15
2003	**SPANISH SUN** 8-11	9
2004	**PUNCTILIOUS** 8-11	9

HARDWICKE STAKES

Ascot-1m 4f

1995	BEAUCHAMP HERO 5-8-9	6
1996	OSCAR SCHINDLER 4-8-9	8
1997	PREDAPPIO 4-8-12	10
1998	POSIDONAS 6-8-9	7
1999	FRUITS OF LOVE 4-8-12	8
2000	FRUITS OF LOVE 5-8-12	9
2001	SANDMASON 4-8-9	7
2002	ZINDABAD 6-8-12	7
2003	INDIAN CREEK 5-8-9	9
2004	DOYEN 4-8-9	6

WOKINGHAM STAKES

Ascot-6f

1995	ASTRAC 4-8-7	30
1996	EMERGING MARKET 4-8-13	29
1997	SELHURSTPARK FLYER 6-8-9	30
1998	SELHURSTPARK FLYER 7-9-7	29
1999	DEEP SPACE 4-8-7	30
2000	HARMONIC WAY 5-9-6	29
2001	NICE ONE CLARE 5-9-3	30
2002	CAPRICHO 5-8-11	28
2003	RATIO 5-9-3 dead heated with	
	FAYR JAG 4-9-6	29
2004	LAFI 5-8-13	29

KING'S STAND STAKES

Ascot-5f

1995	PICCOLO 4-9-6	10
1996	PIVOTAL 3-8-10	17
1997	DON'T WORRY ME 5-8-13	18
1998	BOLSHOI 6-9-2	19
1999	MITCHAM 3-8-10	17
2000	NUCLEAR DEBATE 5-9-2	23
2001	CASSANDRA GO 5-8-13	22
2002	DOMINICA 3-8-7	15
2003	CHOISIR 4-9-7	20
2004	THE TATLING 7-9-2	19

NORTHUMBERLAND PLATE

Newcastle-2m 19yds

1995	BOLD GAIT 4-9-10	17
1996	CELERIC 4-9-4	13
1997	WINDSOR CASTLE 3-8-10	18
1998	CYRIAN 4-7-13	20
1999	FAR CRY 4-8-10	20
2000	BAY OF ISLANDS 8-8-4	18
2001	ARCHDUKE FERDINAND 3-8-4	18
2002	BANGALORE 6-9-5	16
2003	UNLEASH 4-8-11	20
2004	MIRJAN 8-8-3	19

CRITERION STAKES

Newmarket-7f

1995	PIPE MAJOR 3-8-8	8
1996	GABR 6-9-10	9
1997	RAMOOZ 4-9-2	9
1998	MUCHEA 4-9-7	10
1999	DIKTAT 4-9-7	6
2000	ARKADIAN HERO 5-9-1	9
2001	SHIBBOLETH 4-9-2	6
2002	ATAVUS 5-9-2	6
2003	TRADE FAIR 3-8-7	11
2004	ARAKAN 4-9-2	8

ECLIPSE STAKES

Sandown-1m 2f 7yds

1995	HALLING 4-9-7	8
1996	HALLING 5-9-7	7
1997	PILSUDSKI 5-9-7	5
1998	DAYLAMI 4-9-7	8
1999	COMPTON ADMIRAL 3-8-10	8
2000	GIANT'S CAUSEWAY 3-8-10	8
2001	MEDICEAN 4-9-7	8
2002	HAWK WING 3-8-10	5
2003	FALBRAV 5-9-7	15
2004	REFUSE TO BEND 4-9-7	12

OLD NEWTON CUP

Haydock-1m 3f 200yds

1995	LOMBARDIC 4-8-12	10
1996	KEY TO MY HEART 6-10-0	8
1997	ZARALASKA 6-9-8	16
1998	PERFECT PARADIGM 4-9-2	8
1999	CELESTIAL WELCOME 4-8-10	15
2000	RADA'S DAUGHTER 4-8-11	14
2001	HANNIBAL LAD 5-8-8	14
2002	SUN BIRD 4-7-12	16
2003	COLLIER HILL 5-8-10	16
2004	ALKAASED 4-9-1	15

LANCASHIRE OAKS (fillies and mares)

Haydock-1m 3f 200yds

1995	FANJICA 3-8-4	5
1996	SPOUT 4-9-6	10
1997	SQUEAK 3-8-4	9
1998	CATCHASCATCHCAN 3-8-4	6
1999	NOUSHKEY 3-8-4	7
2000	ELA ATHENA 4-9-3	11
2001	SACRED SONG 4-9-6	8
2002	MELLOW PARK 3-8-5	6
2003	PLACE ROUGE 4-9-3	12
2004	PONGEE 4-9-3	8

CHERRY HINTON STAKES (2y)

Newmarket-6f

1995	APPLAUD 8-9	8
1996	DAZZLE 8-9	9
1997	ASFURAH 8-9	12
1998	WANNABE GRAND 8-9	10
1999	TORGAU 8-9	12
2000	DORA CARRINGTON 8-9	9
2001	SILENT HONOR 8-9	7
2002	SPINOLA 8-9	9
2003	ATTRACTION 8-12	8
2004	JEWEL IN THE SAND 8-9	10

BUNBURY CUP HANDICAP

Newmarket-7f

1995	CADEAUX TRYST 3-9-1	19
1996	CRUMPTON HILL 4-8-12	16
1997	TUMBLEWEED RIDGE 4-9-6	20
1998	HO LENG 3-9-7	20
1999	GRANGEVILLE 4-9-3	19
2000	TAYSEER 4-9-9	19
2001	ATAVUS 4-8-9	19
2002	MINE 4-8-12	16
2003	PATAVELLIAN 5-9-1	20
2004	MATERIAL WITNESS 7-9-3	19

PRINCESS OF WALES'S STAKES
Newmarket-1m 4f

1995	**BEAUCHAMP HERO** 5-9-5	9
1996	**POSIDONAS** 4-9-7	8
1997	**SHANTOU** 4-9-7	7
1998	**FRUITS OF LOVE** 3-8-3	8
1999	**CRAIGSTEEL** 4-9-2	8
2000	**LITTLE ROCK** 4-9-2	6
2001	**MUTAMAM** 6-9-2	9
2002	**MILLENARY** 5-9-2	9
2003	**MILLENARY** 6-9-2	6
2004	**BANDARI** 5-9-2	8

JULY STAKES (2y)
Newmarket-6f

1995	**TAGULA** 8-10	9
1996	**RICH GROUND** 8-10	9
1997	**BOLD FACT** 8-10	8
1998	**BERTOLINI** 8-10	7
1999	**CITY ON A HILL** 8-13	6
2000	**NOVERRE** 8-13	9
2001	**MESHAHEER** 8-10	5
2002	**MISTER LINKS** 8-10	10
2003	**NEVISIAN LAD** 8-10	9
2004	**CAPTAIN HURRICANE** 8-10	7

FALMOUTH STAKES (fillies)
Newmarket-1m

1995	**CARAMBA** 3-8-6	5
1996	**SENSATION** 3-8-6	9
1997	**RYAFAN** 3-8-6	7
1998	**LOVERS KNOT** 3-8-6	13
1999	**RONDA** 3-8-6	8
2000	**ALSHAKR** 3-8-6	10
2001	**PROUDWINGS** 5-9-4	11
2002	**TASHAWAK** 3-8-6	9
2003	**MACADAMIA** 4-9-1	8
2004	**SOVIET SONG** 4-9-1	7

JULY CUP
Newmarket-6f

1995	**LAKE CONISTON** 4-9-6	9
1996	**ANABAA** 4-9-5	10
1997	**COMPTON PLACE** 3-8-13	9
1998	**ELNADIM** 4-9-5	17
1999	**STRAVINSKY** 3-8-13	17
2000	**AGNES WORLD** 5-9-5	10
2001	**MOZART** 3-8-13	18
2002	**CONTINENT** 5-9-5	14
2003	**OASIS DREAM** 3-8-13	16
2004	**FRIZZANTE** 5-9-2	20

JOHN SMITH'S CUP
York-1m 2f 85yds

1995	**NAKED WELCOME** 3-8-4	16
1996	**WILCUMA** 5-9-2	17
1997	**PASTERNAK** 4-8-3	21
1998	**PORTO FORICOS** 3-8-3	20
1999	**ACHILLES** 4-8-11	15
2000	**SOBRIETY** 3-8-8	22
2001	**FOREIGN AFFAIRS** 3-8-6	19
2002	**VINTAGE PREMIUM** 5-9-9	20
2003	**FAR LANE** 4-9-4	20
2004	**ARCALIS** 4-9-2	21

PRINCESS MARGARET STAKES (2y)
Ascot-6f

1995	**BLUE DUSTER** 9-0	7
1996	**SEEBE** 8-9	8
1997	**EMBASSY** 8-9	7
1998	**MYTHICAL GIRL** 8-9	6
1999	**SAINTLY SPEECH** 8-9	8
2000	**ENTHUSED** 8-9	9
2001	**LEGGY LOU** 8-9	8
2002	**RUSSIAN RHYTHM** 8-9	6
2003	**RIVER BELLE** 8-9	9
2004	**SOAR** 8-9	6

BEESWING STAKES
Newcastle-7f
(from 2000 run as a Handicap)

1995	**SHAHID** 3-8-7	7
1996	**IKTAMAL** 4-9-0	9
1997	**WIZARD KING** 6-9-4	8
1998	**DECORATED HERO** 6-9-7	4
1999	**JOSR ALGARHOUD** 3-8-7	5
2000	**TONY TIE** 4-9-12	11
2001	**SLOANE** 5-9-11	14
2002	**MILLENNIUM FORCE** 4-9-7	14
2003	**QUITO** 6-9-6	8
2004	**TRUE NIGHT** 7-9-4	13

STEWARDS' CUP
Goodwood-6f

1995	**SHIKARI'S SON** 8-8-13	27
1996	**COASTAL BLUFF** 4-9-5	30
1997	**DANETIME** 3-8-10	30
1998	**SUPERIOR PREMIUM** 4-8-12	29
1999	**HARMONIC WAY** 4-8-6	30
2000	**TAYSEER** 6-8-11	30
2001	**GUINEA HUNTER** 5-9-0	30
2002	**BOND BOY** 5-8-2	28
2003	**PATAVELLIAN** 5-8-11	29
2004	**PIVOTAL POINT** 4-8-11	28

GORDON STAKES (3y)
Goodwood-1m 4f

1995	**PRESENTING** 8-10	7
1996	**ST MAWES** 8-10	12
1997	**STOWAWAY** 8-10	10
1998	**RABAH** 8-10 dead heated with	
	NEDAWI 8-10	6
1999	**COMPTON ACE** 8-10	6
2000	**MILLENARY** 8-13	10
2001	**ALEXIUS** 8-10	11
2002	**BANDARI** 8-13	4
2003	**PHOENIX REACH** 8-10	10
2004	**MARAAHEL** 8-10	8

OAK TREE STAKES
Goodwood-7f

1995	**BRIEF GLIMPSE** 3-8-7	10
1996	**THRILLING DAY** 3-8-13	14
1997	**DAZZLE** 3-8-7	8
1998	**BERAYSIM** 3-8-7	9
1999	**SELFISH** 5-9-0	6
2000	**DANCEABOUT** 3-8-7	11
2001	**MAURI MOON** 3-8-7	13
2002	**DESERT ALCHEMY** 3-8-6	7
2003	**TANTINA** 3-8-7	13
2004	**PHANTOM WIND** 3-8-6	12

SUSSEX STAKES
Goodwood-1m
1995	SAYYEDATI 5-9-4	6
1996	FIRST ISLAND 4-9-7	10
1997	ALI-ROYAL 4-9-7	9
1998	AMONG MEN 4-9-7	10
1999	ALJABR 3-8-13	8
2000	GIANT'S CAUSEWAY 3-9-0	10
2001	NOVERRE 3-9-0	10
2002	ROCK OF GIBRALTAR 3-8-13	5
2003	REEL BUDDY 5-9-7	9
2004	SOVIET SONG 4-9-4	11

RICHMOND STAKES (2y)
Goodwood-6f
1995	POLARIS FLIGHT 8-11	6
1996	EASYCALL 8-11	7
1997	DAGGERS DRAWN 8-11	6
1998	MUQTARIB 8-11	4
1999	BACHIR 8-11	7
2000	ENDLESS SUMMER 8-11	8
2001	MISTER COSMI 8-11	8
2002	*REVENUE 8-11	9
2003	CARRIZO CREEK 8-11	7
2004	MONTGOMERY'S ARCH 8-11	8
* Elusive City disqualified from first place

KING GEORGE STAKES
Goodwood-5f
1995	HEVER GOLF ROSE 4-9-5	11
1996	RAMBLING BEAR 3-8-10	14
1997	AVERTI 6-9-0	15
1998	LAND OF DREAMS 3-8-7	15
1999	RUDI'S PET 5-9-0	15
2000	CASSANDRA GO 4-8-10	13
2001	DIETRICH 3-8-12	15
2002	AGNETHA 3-8-7	14
2003	THE TATLING 6-9-0	9
2004	RINGMOOR DOWN 5-8-11	13

WILLIAM HILL MILE HANDICAP
Goodwood-1m
1995	KHAYRAPOUR 5-7-13	21
1996	MOSCOW MIST 5-7-10	18
1997	FLY TO THE STARS 3-9-6	20
1998	FOR YOUR EYES ONLY 4-9-6	22
1999	LONESOME DUDE 4-9-7	20
2000	PERSIANO 4-9-6	22
2001	RIBERAC 5-8-12	21
2002	SMIRK 4-9-5	21
2003	LADY BEAR 5-8-6	21
2004	ANCIENT WORLD 4-9-10	21

GOODWOOD CUP
Goodwood-2m
1995	DOUBLE TRIGGER 4-9-5	9
1996	GREY SHOT 4-9-0	7
1997	DOUBLE TRIGGER 6-9-0	10
1998	DOUBLE TRIGGER 7-9-5	9
1999	KAYF TARA 5-9-7	7
2000	ROYAL REBEL 4-9-0	8
2001	PERSIAN PUNCH 8-9-5	12
2002	JARDINES LOOKOUT 5-9-2	9
2003	PERSIAN PUNCH 10-9-4	9
2004	DARASIM 6-9-4	9

MOLECOMB STAKES (2y)
Goodwood-5f
1995	ALMATY 9-3	7
1996	CARMINE LAKE 8-7	7
1997	LADY ALEXANDER 8-12	13
1998	INYA LAKE 8-7	9
1999	MISTY MISS 8-7	10
2000	MISTY EYED 8-10	9
2001	WHITBARROW 9-1	14
2002	WUNDERS DREAM 8-7	13
2003	MAJESTIC MISSILE 8-12	9
2004	TOURNEDOS 8-12	13

NASSAU STAKES (fillies and mares)
Goodwood-1m 2f
1995	CARAMBA 3-8-9	6
1996	LAST SECOND 3-8-6	8
1997	RYAFAN 3-8-9	7
1998	ALBORADA 3-9-9	9
1999	ZAHRAT DUBAI 3-8-6	8
2000	CRIMPLENE 3-8-6	7
2001	LAILANI 3-8-6	7
2002	ISLINGTON 3-8-6	10
2003	RUSSIAN RHYTHM 3-8-6	8
2004	FAVOURABLE TERMS 4-9-2	6

HUNGERFORD STAKES
Newbury-7f 64yds
1995	HARAYIR 3-8-13	9
1996	BIN ROSIE 4-9-0	8
1997	DECORATED HERO 5-9-0	10
1998	MUHTATHIR 3-8-8	9
1999	LEND A HAND 4-9-0	7
2000	ARKADIAN HERO 5-9-2	8
2001	ATAVUS 4-8-13	7
2002	REEL BUDDY 4-8-13	10
2003	WITH REASON 5-8-13	11
2004	CHIC 4-8-11	13

GEOFFREY FREER STAKES
Newbury-1m 5f 61yds
1995	PRESENTING 3-8-5	6
1996	PHANTOM GOLD 4-9-3	7
1997	DUSHYANTOR 4-9-6	4
1998	MULTICOLOURED 5-9-3	4
1999	SILVER PATRIARCH 5-9-9	4
2000	MURGHEM 5-9-3	6
2001	MR COMBUSTIBLE 3-8-6	5
2002	MUBTAKER 5-9-3	7
2003	MUBTAKER 6-9-3	5
2004	MUBTAKER 7-9-3	4

JUDDMONTE INTERNATIONAL STAKES
York-1m 2f 85yds
1995	HALLING 4-9-6	6
1996	HALLING 5-9-5	6
1997	SINGSPIEL 5-9-5	4
1998	ONE SO WONDERFUL 4-9-2	6
1999	ROYAL ANTHEM 4-9-5	12
2000	GIANT'S CAUSEWAY 3-8-11	6
2001	SAKHEE 4-9-5	8
2002	NAYEF 4-9-5	7
2003	FALBRAV 5-9-5	8
2004	SULAMANI 5-9-5	9

GREAT VOLTIGEUR STAKES (3y)
York-1m 3f 195yds
1995	PENTIRE 8-12	4
1996	DUSHYANTOR 8-9	6
1997	STOWAWAY 8-9	5
1998	SEA WAVE 8-9	6
1999	FANTASTIC LIGHT 8-9	7
2000	AIR MARSHALL 8-9	5
2001	MILAN 8-9	9
2002	BANDARI 3-8-9	6
2003	POWERSCOURT 8-9	9
2004	RULE OF LAW 8-9	7

YORKSHIRE OAKS (fillies and mares)
York-1m 3f 195yds
1995	PURE GRAIN 3-8-8	8
1996	KEY CHANGE 3-8-8	9
1997	MY EMMA 4-9-4	8
1998	CATCHASCATCHCAN 3-8-8	6
1999	RAMRUMA 3-8-8	11
2000	PETRUSHKA 3-8-8	6
2001	SUPER TASSA 5-9-4	9
2002	ISLINGTON 3-8-8	11
2003	ISLINGTON 4-9-4	8
2004	QUIFF 3-8-8	8

EBOR HANDICAP
York-1m 5f 194yds
1995	SANMARTINO 3-7-11	21
1996	CLERKENWELL 3-7-11	21
1997	FAR AHEAD 5-8-0	21
1998	TUNING 3-8-7	21
1999	VICIOUS CIRCLE 5-8-4	21
2000	GIVE THE SLIP 3-8-8	22
2001	MEDITERRANEAN 3-8-4	22
2002	HUGS DANCER 5-8-5	22
2003	SAINT ALEBE 4-8-8	22
2004	MEPHISTO 3-8-6	19

GIMCRACK STAKES (2y)
York-6f
1995	ROYAL APPLAUSE 9-0	5
1996	ABOU ZOUZ 8-11	9
1997	CARROWKEEL 8-11	7
1998	JOSR ALGARHOUD 8-11	8
1999	MULL OF KINTYRE 8-11	10
2000	BANNISTER 8-11	10
2001	ROCK OF GIBRALTER 9-0	9
2002	COUNTRY REEL 8-11	11
2003	BALMONT 8-11	9
2004	TONY JAMES 8-11	11

NUNTHORPE STAKES
York-5f
1995	SO FACTUAL 5-9-6	8
1996	PIVOTAL 3-9-7	8
1997	YA MALAK 6-9-9 dead heated with COASTAL BLUFF 5-9-9	15
1998	LOCHANGEL 4-9-6	17
1999	STRAVINSKY 3-9-7	16
2000	NUCLEAR DEBATE 5-9-9	13
2001	MOZART 3-9-7	10
2002	KYLLACHY 4-9-11	17
2003	OASIS DREAM 3-9-9	8
2004	BAHAMIAN PIRATE 9-9-11	12

PERSIMMON HOMES HANDICAP
York-7f 205yds
(formerly Bradford and Bingley Handicap and Ariva Trains Handicap)
1995	CAP JULUCA 3-8-11	15
1996	CONCER UN 4-8-10	18
1997	CONCER UN 5-8-7	14
1998	SUGARFOOT 4-8-9	14
1999	SUGARFOOT 5-9-7	20
2000	PEARTREE HOUSE 6-8-2	16
2001	TOUGH SPEED 4-9-7	17
2002	FUNFAIR 3-8-1	18
2003	TERFEL 4-8-12	15
2004	AUDIENCE 4-8-11	15

PRESTIGE STAKES (2y)
Goodwood-7f
1995	BINT SHADAYID 8-9	6
1996	RED CAMELLIA 8-12	6
1997	MIDNIGHT LINE 8-9	6
1998	CIRCLE OF GOLD 8-9	9
1999	ICICLE 8-9	9
2000	FREEFOURRACING 8-9	6
2001	GOSSAMER 8-9	6
2002	GEMINIANI 8-9	8
2003	GRACEFULLY 8-9	6
2004	DUBAI SURPRISE 8-9	12

CELEBRATION MILE
Goodwood-1m)
1995	HARAYIR 3-8-12	6
1996	MARK OF ESTEEM 3-9-1	7
1997	*AMONG MEN 3-8-9	4
1998	MUHTATHIR 3-8-9	7
1999	CAPE CROSS 5-9-7	5
2000	MEDICEAN 3-8-9	6
2001	NO EXCUSE NEEDED 3-8-9	6
2002	TILLERMAN 6-9-1	7
2003	PRIORS LODGE 5-9-1	6
2004	CHIC 4-8-12	7
*Cape Cross disqualified from first place

SOLARIO STAKES (2y)
Sandown-7f 16yds
1995	ALHAARTH 9-2	4
1996	BRAVE ACT 8-11	7
1997	LITTLE INDIAN 8-11	5
1998	RAISE A GRAND 8-11	7
1999	BEST OF THE BESTS 8-11	7
2000	KING'S IRONBRIDGE 8-11	7
2001	REDBACK 9-0	10
2002	FOSS WAY 8-11	11
2003	BARBAJUAN 8-11	8
2004	WINDSOR KNOT 8-11	8

SPRINT CUP
Haydock-6f
1995	CHEROKEE ROSE 4-8-11	6
1996	IKTAMAL 4-9-0	11
1997	ROYAL APPLAUSE 4-9-0	7
1998	TAMARISK 3-8-12	13
1999	DIKTAT 4-9-0	16
2000	PIPALONG 4-8-11	13
2001	NUCLEAR DEBATE 6-9-0	12
2002	INVINCIBLE SPIRIT 5-9-0	14
2003	SOMNUS 3-8-12	10

2004 **TANTE ROSE** 4-8-11................................19

SEPTEMBER STAKES
Kempton-1m
1995 **BUROOJ** 5-9-0.....................................7
1996 **SACRAMENT** 5-9-5...............................7
*1997 **MAYLANE** 3-8-5..................................6
*1998 **CRIMSON TIDE** 4-9-5..........................5
*1999 **YAVANA'S PACE** 7-9-0........................5
2000 **MUTAMAM** 5-9-0.................................7
2001 **MUTAMAM** 6-9-8.................................4
2002 **ASIAN HEIGHTS** 4-9-3.........................6
2003 **MUBTAKER** 6-9-8.................................5
2004 **MAMOOL** 5-9-3...................................4
* Run at Epsom

MAY HILL STAKES (2y)
Doncaster-1m
1995 **SOLAR CRYSTAL** 8-9...........................11
1996 **REAMS OF VERSE** 8-9.........................11
1997 **MIDNIGHT LINE** 9-0.............................9
1998 **CALANDO** 8-9....................................10
1999 **TEGGIANO** 8-9..................................12
2000 **KARASTA** 8-9....................................12
2001 **HALF GLANCE** 8-9.............................10
2002 **SUMMITVILLE** 8-9...............................9
2003 **KINNAIRD** 8-10..................................10
2004 **PLAYFUL ACT** 8-10..............................8

PORTLAND HANDICAP
Doncaster-5f 140yds
1995 **HELLO MISTER** 4-8-7...........................22
1996 **MUSICAL SEASON** 4-8-5......................21
1997 **DASHING BLUE** 4-9-12.........................22
1998 **CADEAUX CHER** 4-8-7.........................21
1999 **ASTONISHED** 3-9-6.............................21
2000 **COMPTON BANKER** 3-8-8....................22
2001 **SMOKIN BEAU** 4-9-4...........................22
2002 **HALMAHERA** 7-8-13............................22
2003 **HALMAHERA** 8-9-4..............................22
2004 **HALMAHERA** 9-9-10............................22

PARK HILL STAKES (fillies and mares)
Doncaster-1m 6f 132yds
1995 **NOBLE ROSE** 4-9-3...............................8
1996 **EVA LUNA** 4-9-3..................................6
1997 **BOOK AT BEDTIME** 3-8-5......................7
1998 **DELILAH** 4-9-6....................................9
1999 **MISTLE SONG** 3-8-5...........................10
2000 **MILETRIAN** 3-8-10..............................11
2001 **RANIN** 3-8-5......................................13
2002 **ALEXANDER THREE D** 3-8-5...................9
2003 **DISCREET BRIEF** 3-8-5..........................8
2004 **ECHOES IN ETERNITY** 4-9-3.................10

G.N.E.R. PARK STAKES
Doncaster-1m
(formerly Kiveton Park Stakes)
1995 **BISHOP OF CASHEL** 3-8-9......................8
1996 **BISHOP OF CASHEL** 4-9-4......................8
1997 **ALMUSHTARAK** 4-9-0............................8
1998 **HANDSOME RIDGE** 4-9-4.......................6
1999 **SUGARFOOT** 5-9-0.............................10
2000 **DISTANT MUSIC** 3-8-9...........................5
2001 **TOUGH SPEED** 4-9-0...........................11
2002 **DUCK ROW** 7-9-0.................................6
2003 **POLAR BEN** 4-9-0.................................9

2004 **PASTORAL PURSUITS** 3-8-10..................8

DONCASTER CUP
Doncaster-2m 2f
1995 **DOUBLE TRIGGER** 4-9-7........................6
1996 **DOUBLE TRIGGER** 5-9-7........................6
1997 **CANON CAN** 4-9-0................................5
1998 **DOUBLE TRIGGER** 7-9-5........................6
1999 **FAR CRY** 4-9-0....................................6
2000 **ENZELI** 5-9-7......................................9
2001 **ALLELUIA** 3-7-11................................11
2002 **BOREAS** 7-9-1.....................................8
2003 **PERSIAN PUNCH** 10-9-4........................6
2004 **MILLENARY** 7-9-4 deadheated with
          KASTHARI 5-9-1...............................8

CHAMPAGNE STAKES (2y)
Doncaster-7f
1995 **ALHAARTH** 9-0.....................................3
1996 **BAHHARE** 8-10....................................4
1997 **DAGGERS DRAWN** 9-0..........................5
1998 **AUCTION HOUSE** 8-10..........................6
1999 **DISTANT MUSIC** 8-10...........................6
2000 **NOVERRE** 9-0.....................................8
2001 **DUBAI DESTINATION** 8-10.....................8
2002 **ALMUSHAHAR** 8-10............................11
2003 **LUCKY STORY** 9-0................................6
2004 **ETALAAL** 8-10....................................10

FLYING CHILDERS STAKES (2y)
Doncaster-5f
1995 **CAYMAN KAI** 8-12................................8
1996 **EASYCALL** 9-3.....................................7
1997 **LAND OF DREAMS** 8-7..........................7
1998 **SHEER VIKING** 8-12............................13
1999 **MRS P** 8-7.......................................14
2000 **SUPERSTAR LEO** 8-12.........................11
2001 **SADDAD** 8-12....................................13
2002 **WUNDERS DREAM** 8-12........................14
2003 **HOWICK FALLS** 8-12...........................13
2004 **CHATEAU ISTANA** 8-12........................11

AYR GOLD CUP
Ayr-6f
1995 **ROYALE FIGURINE** 4-8-9......................29
1996 **COASTAL BLUFF** 4-9-10.......................28
1997 **WILDWOOD FLOWER** 4-9-3...................29
1998 **ALWAYS ALIGHT** 4-8-7.........................29
1999 **GRANGEVILLE** 4-9-0...........................28
2000 **BAHAMIAN PIRATE** 5-8-0......................28
2001 **CONTINENT** 4-8-10.............................28
2002 **FUNFAIR WANE** 3-9-3..........................28
2003 **QUITO** 6-8-6.....................................26
2004 **FUNFAIR WANE** 5-8-6..........................24

SELECT STAKES
Goodwood-1m 2f)
1995 **TRIARIUS** 5-9-0....................................6
1996 **SINGSPIEL** 4-9-3..................................4
1997 **FAHRIS** 3-8-7......................................5
1998 **MUTAMAM** 3-8-10.................................4
1999 **LEAR SPEAR** 4-9-5...............................7
2000 **EKRAAR** 3-8-10...................................3
2001 **NAYEF** 3-8-10.....................................3
2002 **MOON BALLAD** 3-8-12..........................6

2003 **LEPORELLO** 3-8-10 5
2004 **ALKAADHEM** 4-9-0 7

MILL REEF STAKES (2y)
Newbury-6f 8yds
1995 **KAHIR ALMAYDAN** 8-12 6
1996 **INDIAN ROCKET** 8-12 10
1997 **ARKADIAN HERO** 8-12 7
1998 **GOLDEN SILCA** 8-12 5
1999 **PRIMO VALENTINO** 8-12 4
2000 **BOUNCING BOWDLER** 8-12 7
2001 **FIREBREAK** 9-1 10
2002 **ZAFEEN** 8-12 8
2003 **BYRON** 8-12 10
2004 **GALEOTA** 8-12 9

CUMBERLAND LODGE STAKES
Ascot-1m 4f
1995 **RIYADIAN** 3-8-6 8
1996 **WALL STREET** 3-8-6 8
1997 **KINGFISHER MILL** 3-8-11 8
1998 **CAPRI** 3-8-7 9
1999 ABANDONED
2000 **MUTAMAM** 5-9-3 6
2001 **NAYEF** 3-8-9 7
2002 **SYSTEMATIC** 3-8-6 5
2003 **HIGH ACCOLADE** 3-8-11 5
2004 **HIGH ACCOLADE** 4-9-0 9

THE FILLIES' MILE (2y fillies)
Ascot-1m
1995 **BOSRA SHAM** 8-10 6
1996 **REAMS OF VERSE** 8-10 8
1997 **GLOROSIA** 8-10 8
1998 **SUNSPANGLED** 8-10 8
1999 **TEGGIANO** 8-10 6
2000 **CRYSTAL MUSIC** 8-10 9
2001 **GOSSAMER** 8-10 7
2002 **SOVIET SONG** 8-10 10
2003 **RED BLOOM** 8-10 7
2004 **PLAYFUL ACT** 8-10 9

DIADEM STAKES
Ascot-6f
1995 **COOL JAZZ** 4-9-0 15
1996 **DIFFIDENT** 4-9-0 12
1997 **ELNADIM** 3-8-12 14
1998 **BIANCONI** 3-8-12 9
1999 **BOLD EDGE** 4-9-4 11
2000 **SAMPOWER STAR** 4-9-0 11
2001 **NICE ONE CLARE** 5-8-11 15
2002 **CRYSTAL CASTLE** 4-9-0 11
2003 **ACCLAMATION** 4-9-0 14
2004 **PIVOTAL POINT** 4-9-0 12

QUEEN ELIZABETH II STAKES
Ascot-1m
1995 **BAHRI** 3-8-11 6
1996 **MARK OF ESTEEM** 3-8-11 7
1997 **AIR EXPRESS** 3-8-11 9
1998 **DESERT PRINCE** 3-8-11 7
1999 **DUBAI MILLENNIUM** 3-8-11 4
2000 **OBSERVATORY** 3-8-11 12
2001 **SUMMONER** 4-9-1 8
2002 **WHERE OR WHEN** 3-8-11 5
2003 **FALBRAV** 5-9-1 8
2004 **RAKTI** 5-9-1 11

ROYAL LODGE STAKES (2y)
Ascot-1m
1995 **MONS** 8-11 8
1996 **BENNY THE DIP** 8-11 8
1997 **TEAPOT ROW** 8-11 8
1998 **MUTAAHAB** 8-11 6
1999 **ROYAL KINGDOM** 8-11 8
2000 **ATLANTIS PRINCE** 8-11 8
2001 **MUTINYONTHEBOUNTY** 8-11 9
2002 **AL JADEED** 8-11 9
2003 **SNOW RIDGE** 8-11 10
2004 **PERFECTPERFORMANCE** 8-11 8

CHEVELEY PARK STAKES (2y fillies)
Newmarket-6f
1995 **BLUE DUSTER** 8-11 5
1996 **PAS DE REPONSE** 8-11 8
1997 **EMBASSY** 8-11 8
1998 **WANNABE GRAND** 8-11 9
1999 **SEAZUN** 8-11 14
2000 **REGAL ROSE** 8-11 13
2001 **QUEEN'S LOGIC** 8-11 6
2002 **AIRWAVE** 8-11 8
2003 **CARRY ON KATIE** 8-11 10
2004 **MAGICAL ROMANCE** 8-11 7

MIDDLE PARK STAKES (2y)
Newmarket-6f
1995 **ROYAL APPLAUSE** 8-11 5
1996 **BAHAMIAN BOUNTY** 8-11 11
1997 **HAYIL** 8-11 7
1998 **LUJAIN** 8-11 7
1999 **PRIMO VALENTINO** 8-11 6
2000 **MINARDI** 8-11 10
2001 **JOHANNESBURG** 8-11 7
2002 **OASIS DREAM** 8-11 10
2003 ***BALMONT** 8-11 13
2004 **AD VALOREM** 8-11 9
* Three Valleys disqualified from first place

SUN CHARIOT STAKES
(fillies and mares)
Newmarket-1m 2f
1995 **WARNING SHADOWS** 3-8-8 7
1996 **LAST SECOND** 3-8-11 9
1997 **ONE SO WONDERFUL** 3-8-8 8
1998 **KISSOGRAM** 3-8-8 5
1999 **LADY IN WAITING** 4-8-13 9
2000 **DANCEABOUT** 3-8-9 9
2001 **INDEPENDENCE** 3-8-10 16
2002 **DRESS TO THRILL** 3-8-10 10
2003 **ECHOES IN ETERNITY** 3-8-10 10
2004 **ATTRACTION** 3-8-11 5

CAMBRIDGESHIRE
Newmarket-1m 1f
1995 **CAP JULUCA** 3-9-10 39
1996 **CLIFTON FOX** 4-8-2 38
1997 **PASTERNAK** 4-9-1 36
1998 **LEAR SPEAR** 3-7-13 35
*1999 **SHE'S OUR MARE** 6-7-12 33
2000 **KATY NOWAITEE** 4-8-8 35
2001 **I CRIED FOR YOU** 6-8-6 35
2002 **BEAUCHAMP PILOT** 4-9-5 30
2003 **CHIVALRY** 4-8-1 34
2004 **SPANISH DON** 6-8-7 32
* Run over 1m 2f

JOCKEY CLUB CUP
Newmarket-2m
1995	**FURTHER FLIGHT** 9-9-3	8
1996	**CELERIC** 4-9-0	8
1997	**GREY SHOT** 5-9-5	7
1998	**ARCTIC OWL** 4-9-5	7
1999	**RAINBOW HIGH** 4-9-0	3
2000	**PERSIAN PUNCH** 7-9-5	9
2001	**CAPAL GARMON** 3-8-4	7
2002	**PERSIAN PUNCH** 9-9-0	8
2003	**PERSIAN PUNCH** 10-9-0	6
2004	**MILLENARY** 7-9-5	11

SUPREME STAKES
Goodwood-7f
1995	**INZAR** 3-8-8	10
1996	**TAGULA** 3-8-9	9
1997	**DECORATED HERO** 5-9-2	6
1998	**DECORATED HERO** 6-9-5	8
1999	ABANDONED	
2000	**MOUNT ABU** 3-8-9	8
2001	**LATE NIGHT OUT** 6-8-12	4
2002	**FIREBREAK** 3-8-9	10
2003	**WITH REASON** 5-9-2	7
2004	**MAC LOVE** 3-8-9	11

PRINCESS ROYAL STAKES
Ascot-1m 4f
1995	**LABIBEH** 3-8-6	5
1996	**TIME ALLOWED** 3-8-7	11
1997	**DELILAH** 3-8-7	7
1998	**SILVER RHAPSODY** 3-8-7	7
1999	**SIGNORINA CATTIVA** 3-8-7	12
*2000	**SACRED SONG** 3-8-7	15
2001	**HEAD IN THE CLOUDS** 3-8-7	11
2002	**LOVE EVERLASTING** 4-9-0	4
2003	**ITNAB** 3-8-7	9
2004	**MAZUNA** 3-8-6	8

* Run at Newmarket

CORNWALLIS STAKES (2y)
Ascot-5f
1995	**MUBHIJ** 8-12	7
1996	**EASYCALL** 9-4	11
1997	**HALMAHERA** 8-12	13
1998	**SHOW ME THE MONEY** 8-8	12
1999	**KIER PARK** 8-12	13
*2000	**DANEHURST** 8-7	17
2001	**DOMINICA** 8-7	11
2002	**PEACE OFFERING** 8-12	11
2003	**MAJESTIC MISSILE** 9-1	11
†2004	**CASTELLETTO** 8-9	11

* Run at Newbury
† Run at Newmarket

DEWHURST STAKES (2y)
Newmarket-7f
1995	**ALHAARTH** 9-0	4
1996	**IN COMMAND** 9-0	8
1997	**XAAR** 9-0	7
1998	**MUJAHID** 9-0	7
1999	**DISTANT MUSIC** 9-0	5
2000	**TOBOUGG** 9-0	10
2001	**ROCK OF GIBRALTAR** 9-0	8
2002	**TOUT SEUL** 9-0	16
2003	**MILK IT MICK** 9-0	12
2004	**SHAMARDAL** 9-0	9

ROCKFEL STAKES (2y)
Newmarket-7f
1995	**BINT SALSABIL** 8-12	8
1996	**MOONLIGHT PARADISE** 8-12	6
1997	**NAME OF LOVE** 8-12	12
1998	**HULA ANGEL** 8-9	14
1999	**LAHAN** 8-9	12
2000	**SAYEDAH** 8-9	16
2001	**DISTANT VALLEY** 8-9	10
2002	**LUVAH GIRL** 8-9	11
2003	**CAIRNS** 8-9	10
2004	**MAIDS CAUSEWAY** 8-12	8

CHALLENGE STAKES
Newmarket-7f
1995	**HARAYIR** 3-8-12	8
1996	**CHARNWOOD FOREST** 4-9-4	8
1997	**KAHAL** 3-8-12	12
1998	**DECORATED HERO** 6-9-4	10
1999	**SUSU** 6-8-11	10
2000	**LAST RESORT** 3-8-9	9
2001	**MUNIR** 3-8-12	14
2002	**NAYYIR** 4-9-0	17
2003	**JUST JAMES** 4-9-0	11
2004	**FIREBREAK** 5-9-4	12

TWO-YEAR-OLD TROPHY (2y)
Redcar-6f
1995	**BLUE IRIS** 8-2	26
1996	**PROUD NATIVE** 8-7	25
1997	**GRAZIA** 8-2	26
1998	**PIPALONG** 7-13	22
1999	**KHASAYL** 8-8	26
2000	**DIM SUMS** 8-4	23
2001	**CAPTAIN RIO** 8-10	25
2002	**SOMNUS** 8-12	18
2003	**PEAK TO CREEK** 9-0	23
2004	**OBE GOLD** 8-3	24

CHAMPION STAKES
Newmarket-1m 2f
1995	**SPECTRUM** 3-8-10	8
1996	**BOSRA SHAM** 3-8-8	6
1997	**PILSUDSKI** 5-9-2	7
1998	**ALBORADA** 3-8-8	10
1999	**ALBORADA** 4-8-13	13
2000	**KALANISI** 4-9-2	15
2001	**NAYEF** 3-8-11	12
2002	**STORMING HOME** 4-9-2	11
2003	**RAKTI** 4-9-2	12
2004	**HAAFHD** 3-8-11	11

CESAREWITCH
Newmarket-2m 2f
1995	**OLD RED** 5-7-11	21
1996	**INCHCAILLOCH** 7-7-3	26
1997	**TURNPOLE** 6-7-10	31
1998	**SPIRIT OF LOVE** 3-8-8	29
1999	**TOP CEES** 9-8-10	32
2000	**HEROS FATAL** 6-8-1	33
2001	**DISTANT PROSPECT** 4-8-8	31
2002	**MISS FARA** 7-8-0	36
2003	**LANDING LIGHT** 8-9-4	36
2004	**CONTACT DANCER** 5-8-2	34

HORRIS HILL STAKES (2y)
Newbury-7f 64yds
1995	**TUMBLEWEED RIDGE** 8-9	9
1996	**DESERT STORY** 8-9	8
1997	**LA-FAAH** 8-9	8
1998	**BRANCASTER** 8-9	6
1999	**UMISTIM** 8-9	9
2000	**CLEARING** 8-9	8
2001	**RAPSCALLION** 8-9	10
2002	**MAKHLAB** 8-9	10
2003	**PEAK TO CREEK** 8-9	9
2004	**CUPID'S GLORY** 8-9	13

ST SIMON STAKES
Newbury-1m 4f 5yds
1995	**PHANTOM GOLD** 3-8-9	12
1996	**SALMON LADDER** 4-9-0	12
1997	**KALIANA** 3-8-4	10
*1998	**DARK MOONDANCER** 3-8-7	5
1999	**SIGNORINA CATTIVA** 3-8-7	10
2000	**WELLBEING** 3-8-7	5
*2001	**HIGH PITCHED** 3-8-7	5
2002	**THE WHISTLING TEAL** 6-9-0	13
2003	**IMPERIAL DANCER** 5-9-0	9
2004	**ORCADIAN** 3-8-7	8

* Run at Newmarket

RACING POST TROPHY (2y)
Doncaster-1m
1995	**BEAUCHAMP KING** 9-0	4
1996	**MEDAALY** 9-0	5
1997	**SARATOGA SPRINGS** 9-0	8
1998	**COMMANDER COLLINS** 9-0	6
1999	**ARISTOTLE** 9-0	9
2000	**DILSHAAN** 9-0	10
2001	**HIGH CHAPARRAL** 9-0	6
2002	**BRIAN BORU** 9-0	9
2003	**AMERICAN POST** 9-0	9
2004	**MOTIVATOR** 9-0	8

NOVEMBER HANDICAP
Doncaster-1m 4f
1995	**SNOW PRINCESS** 3-8-2	18
1996	**CLIFTON FOX** 4-8-10	22
1997	**SABADILLA** 3-7-8	24
1998	**YAVANA'S PACE** 6-9-10	23
1999	**FLOSSY** 3-7-7	16
2000	**BATSWING** 5-8-8	20
2001	**ROYAL CAVALIER** 4-7-10	24
2002	**RED WINE** 3-8-1	23
2003	**TURBO** 4-9-2	24
2004	**CARTE DIAMOND** 3-9-6	24

WINNERS OF PRINCIPAL RACES IN IRELAND

IRISH 2000 GUINEAS (3y)
The Curragh-1m
1995	**SPECTRUM** 9-0	9
1996	**SPINNING WORLD** 9-0	10
1997	**DESERT KING** 9-0	12
1998	**DESERT PRINCE** 9-0	7
1999	**SAFFRON WALDEN** 9-0	10
2000	**BACHIR** 9-0	9
2001	**BLACK MINNALOUSHE** 9-0	12
2002	**ROCK OF GIBRALTAR** 9-0	7
2003	**INDIAN HAVEN** 9-0	16
2004	**BACHELOR DUKE** 9-0	8

TATTERSALLS GOLD CUP
The Curragh-1m 2f 110yds
1995	**PRINCE OF ANDROS** 4-8-12	7
1996	**DEFINITE ARTICLE** 4-8-12	8
1997	**DANCE DESIGN** 4-9-1	7
1998	**DAYLAMI** 4-9-4	5
1999	**SHIVA** 4-8-11	6
2000	**MONTJEU** 4-9-0	5
2001	**FANTASTIC LIGHT** 5-9-0	6
2002	**REBELLINE** 4-8-11	8
2003	**BLACK SAM BELLAMY** 4-9-0	8
2004	**POWERSCOURT** 4-9-0	6

IRISH 1000 GUINEAS (3y fillies)
The Curragh-1m
1995	**RIDGEWOOD PEARL** 9-0	10
1996	**MATIYA** 9-0	12
1997	**CLASSIC PARK** 9-0	10
1998	**TARASCON** 9-0	13
1999	**HULA ANGEL** 9-0	17
2000	**CRIMPLENE** 9-0	13
2001	**IMAGINE** 9-0	16
2002	**GOSSAMER** 9-0	15
2003	**YESTERDAY** 9-0	8
2004	**ATTRACTION** 9-0	15

IRISH DERBY (3y)
The Curragh-1m 4f
1995	**WINGED LOVE** 9-0	13
1996	**ZAGREB** 9-0	13
1997	**DESERT KING** 9-0	10
1998	**DREAM WELL** 9-0	10
1999	**MONTJEU** 9-0	10
2000	**SINNDAR** 9-0	11
2001	**GALILEO** 9-0	12
2002	**HIGH CHAPARRAL** 9-0	9
2003	**ALAMSHAR** 9-0	9
2004	**GREY SWALLOW** 9-0	10

IRISH OAKS (3y fillies)
The Curragh-1m 4f
1995	**PURE GRAIN** 9-0	10
1996	**DANCE DESIGN** 9-0	6
1997	**EBADIYLA** 9-0	11
1998	**WINONA** 9-0	9
1999	**RAMRUMA** 9-0	7
2000	**PETRUSHKA** 9-0	10
2001	**LAILANI** 9-0	12
2002	**MARGARULA** 9-0	12

2003	**VINTAGE TIPPLE** 9-0	11
2004	**OUIJA BOARD** 9-0	7

PHOENIX STAKES (2y)
Leopardstown-6f

1995	**DANEHILL DANCER** 9-0	10
1996	**MANTOVANI** 9-0	9
1997	**PRINCELY HEIR** 9-0	9
1998	**LAVERY** 9-0	11
1999	**FASLIYEV** 9-0	6
2000	**MINARDI** 9-0	10
2001	**JOHANNESBURG** 9-0	11
2002	**SPARTACUS** 9-0	9
2003	**ONE COOL CAT** 9-0	7
2004	**DAMSON** 8-11	6

IRISH CHAMPION STAKES
Leopardstown-1m 2f

1995	**PENTIRE** 3-8-11	8
1996	**TIMARIDA** 4-9-1	6
1997	**PILSUDSKI** 5-9-4	7
1998	**SWAIN** 6-9-4	8
1999	**DAYLAMI** 5-9-4	7
2000	**GIANT'S CAUSEWAY** 3-8-11	7
2001	**FANTASTIC LIGHT** 5-9-4	7
2002	**GRANDERA** 4-9-4	7
2003	**HIGH CHAPARRAL** 4-9-4	7
2004	**AZAMOUR** 8-11	8

IRISH CAMBRIDGESHIRE
The Curragh-1m

1995	**THE BOWER** 6-7-8	15
1996	**RAIYOUN** 3-9-8	16
1997	**QUWS** 3-9-2	11
1998	**LADY ORANSWELL** 4-7-3	21
1999	**SEEFINN** 4-7-7	14
2000	**SILVERWARE** 4-7-11	24
2001	**OSPREY RIDGE** 8-8-13	22
2002	**MASANI** 3-9-7	21
2003	**DEFINITE BEST** 5-8-5	15
2004	**DUE RESPECT** 5-8-10	18

MOYGLARE STUD STAKES (2y fillies)
The Curragh-7f

1995	**PRIORY BELLE** 8-11	13
1996	**BIANCA NERA** 8-11	10
1997	**TARASCON** 8-12	12
1998	**EDABIYA** 8-11	13
1999	**PRESELI** 8-11	12
2000	**SEQUOYAH** 8-11	10
2001	**QUARTER MOON** 8-11	17
2002	**MAIL THE DESERT** 8-11	9
2003	**NECKLACE** 8-11	11
2004	**CHELSEA ROSE** 8-11	12

NATIONAL STAKES (2y)
The Curragh-7f
(8f between 1997 and 1999)

1995	**DANEHILL DANCER** 9-0	7
1996	**DESERT KING** 9-0	10
1997	**KING OF KINGS** 9-0	9

1998	**MUS-IF** 9-0	9
1999	**SINNDAR** 9-0	9
2000	**BECKETT** 9-0	9
2001	**HAWK WING** 9-0	7
2002	**REFUSE TO BEND** 9-0	7
2003	**ONE COOL CAT** 9-0	8
2004	**DUBAWI** 9-0	7

IRISH ST LEGER
The Curragh-1m 6f

1995	**STRATEGIC CHOICE** 4-9-8	7
1996	**OSCAR SCHINDLER** 4-9-8	9
1997	**OSCAR SCHINDLER** 5-9-8	7
1998	**KAYF TARA** 4-9-8	7
1999	**KAYF TARA** 5-9-8	5
2000	**ARCTIC OWL** 6-9-8	8
2001	**VINNIE ROE** 3-8-12	8
2002	**VINNIE ROE** 4-9-9	8
2003	**VINNIE ROE** 5-9-9	6
2004	**VINNIE ROE** 6-9-9	13

IRISH CESAREWITCH
The Curragh-2m

1995	**MONTELADO** 8-8-9	14
1996	**MILTONFIELD** 7-8-6	26
1997	**WINGED HUSSAR** 4-8-9	20
1998	**SWEETNESS HERSELF** 5-9-6	15
1999	**MILTONFIELD** 10-9-6	13
2000	**TRAGIC LOVER** 4-9-7	24
2001	**RAPID DEPLOYMENT** 4-8-13	19
2002	**AMERICAN GOTHIC** 4-9-0	18
2003	**ZIMBABWE** 3-8-0	17
2004	**ESSEX** 4-7-9	20

THE PIERSE HURDLE
Leopardstown-2m
(formerly The Ladbroke Hurdle)

1996	**DANCE BEAT** 5-9-12	22
1997	**MASTER TRIBE** 7-10-4	23
1998	**GRAPHIC EQUALISER** 6-10-0	20
1999	**ARCHIVE FOOTAGE** 7-11-8	25
2000	**MANTLES PRINCE** 6-9-12	14
2001	**GRINKOV** 6-10-7	24
2002	**ADAMANT APPROACH** 8-11-1	26
2003	**XENOPHON** 7-10-11	28
2004	**DROMLEASE EXPRESS** 6-10-4	19
2005	**ESSEX** 5-10-8	21

HENNESSY COGNAC GOLD CUP
Leopardstown-3m

1996	**IMPERIAL CALL** 7-12-0	8
1997	**DANOLI** 9-12-0	8
1998	**DORANS PRIDE** 9-12-0	8
1999	**FLORIDA PEARL** 7-12-0	7
2000	**FLORIDA PEARL** 8-12-0	7
2001	**FLORIDA PEARL** 9-12-0	7
2002	**ALEXANDER BANQUET** 9-12-0	5
2003	**BEEF OR SALMON** 7-12-0	5
2004	**FLORIDA PEARL** 12-11-12	7
2005	**RULE SUPREME** 9-11-12	7

WINNERS OF PRINCIPAL RACES IN FRANCE

PRIX GANAY
Longchamp-1m 2f 110yds
1995	**PELDER** 5-9-2	10
1996	**VALANOUR** 4-9-2	10
1997	**HELISSIO** 4-9-2	8
1998	**ASTARABAD** 4-9-2	4
1999	**DARK MOONDANCER** 4-9-2	5
2000	**INDIAN DANEHILL** 4-9-2	4
2001	**GOLDEN SNAKE** 5-9-2	9
2002	**AQUARELLISTE** 4-8-13	7
2003	**FAIR MIX** 5-9-2	9
2004	**EXECUTE** 7-9-2	8

POULE D'ESSAI DES POULAINS (3y)
Longchamp-1m
1995	**VETTORI** 9-2	8
1996	**ASHKALANI** 9-2	10
1997	**DAYLAMI** 9-2	6
1998	**VICTORY NOTE** 9-2	12
1999	**SENDAWAR** 9-2	15
2000	**BACHIR** 9-2	7
2001	***VAHORIMIX** 9-2	12
2002	**LANDSEER** 9-2	13
2003	**CLODOVIL** 9-2	10
2004	**AMERICAN POST** 9-2	7

* Noverre disqualified from first place

POULE D'ESSAI DES POULICHES (3y)
Longchamp-1m
1995	**MATIARA** 9-2	16
1996	**TA RIB** 9-0	9
1997	**ALWAYS LOYAL** 9-0	7
1998	**ZALAIYKA** 9-0	14
1999	**VALENTINE WALTZ** 9-0	14
2000	**BLUEMAMBA** 9-0	11
2001	**ROSE GYPSY** 9-0	15
2002	**ZENDA** 9-0	17
2003	**MUSICAL CHIMES** 9-0	12
2004	**TORRESTRELLA** 9-0	13

PRIX LUPIN (3y)
Longchamp-1m 2f 110yds
1995	**FLEMENSFIRTH** 9-2	6
1996	**HELISSIO** 9-2	5
1997	**CLOUDINGS** 9-2	5
1998	**CROCO ROUGE** 9-2	5
1999	**GRACIOSO** 9-2	4
2000	**CIRO** 9-2	7
2001	**CHICHICASTENANGO** 9-2	5
2002	**ACT ONE** 9-2	7
2003	**DALAKHANI** 9-2	7
2004	**VOIX DU NORD** 9-2	5

PRIX SAINT-ALARY (3y fillies)
Longchamp-1m 2f
1995	**MUNCIE** 9-2	5
1996	**LUNA WELLS** 9-0	6
1997	**BRILLIANCE** 9-0	7
1998	**ZAINTA** 9-0	9
1999	**CERULEAN SKY** 9-0	10

PRIX JEAN PRAT (3y)
Chantilly-1m 1f
1995	**TORRENTIAL** 9-2	7
1996	**LE TRITON** 9-2	6
1997	**STARBOROUGH** 9-2	5
1998	**ALMUTAWAKEL** 8-11	6
1999	**GOLDEN SNAKE** 9-2	6
2000	**SUANCES** 9-2	7
2001	**OLDEN TIMES** 9-2	5
2002	**ROUVRES** 9-2	8
2003	**VESPONE** 9-2	8
2004	**BAGO** 9-2	8

PRIX D'ISPAHAN
Longchamp-1m 1f 55yds
1995	**GREEN TUNE** 4-9-2	9
1996	**HALLING** 5-9-2	4
1997	**SASURU** 4-9-2	6
1998	**LOUP SAUVAGE** 4-9-2	7
1999	**CROCO ROUGE** 4-9-2	8
2000	**SENDAWAR** 4-9-2	5
2001	**OBSERVATORY** 4-9-2	5
2002	**BEST OF THE BESTS** 5-9-2	4
2003	**FALBRAV** 5-9-2	8
2004	**PRINCE KIRK** 4-9-2	5

PRIX DU JOCKEY-CLUB (3y)
Chantilly-1m 4f
1995	**CELTIC SWING** 9-2	11
1996	**RAGMAR** 9-2	15
1997	**PEINTRE CELEBRE** 9-2	14
1998	**DREAM WELL** 9-2	13
1999	**MONTJEU** 9-2	8
2000	**HOLDING COURT** 9-2	14
2001	**ANABAA BLUE** 9-2	14
2002	**SULAMANI** 9-2	7
2003	**DALAKHANI** 9-2	7
2004	**BLUE CANARI** 9-2	15

PRIX DE DIANE (3y fillies)
Chantilly-1m 2f 110yds
1995	**CARLING** 9-2	12
1996	**SIL SILA** 9-0	12
1997	**VEREVA** 9-0	12
1998	**ZAINTA** 9-0	11
1999	**DARYABA** 9-2	14
2000	**EGYPTBAND** 9-0	14
2001	**AQUARELLISTE** 9-0	12
2002	**BRIGHT SKY** 9-0	15
2003	**NEBRASKA TORNADO** 9-0	10
2004	**LATICE** 9-0	17

PRIX JEAN PRAT (3y)

(continued at top right)

2000	**REVE D'OSCAR** 9-0	7
2001	**NADIA** 9-0	7
2002	**MAROTTA** 9-0	12
2003	**FIDELITE** 9-0	9
2004	**ASK FOR THE MOON** 9-0	7

GRAND PRIX DE PARIS (3y)

Longchamp-1m 2f
1995	**VALANOUR** 9-2	10
1996	**GRAPE TREE ROAD** 9-2	10
1997	**PEINTRE CELEBRE** 9-2	7
1998	**LIMPID** 9-2	7
1999	**SLICKLY** 9-2	8
2000	**BEAT HOLLOW** 9-2	7
2001	**CHICHICASTENANGO** 9-2	5
2002	**KHALKEVI** 9-2	6
2003	**VESPONE** 9-2	11
2004	**BAGO** 9-2	4

GRAND PRIX DE SAINT-CLOUD

Saint-Cloud-1m 4f
1995	**CARNEGIE** 4-9-8	8
1996	**HELISSIO** 3-8-8	9
1997	**HELISSIO** 4-9-9	4
1998	**FRAGRANT MIX** 4-9-8	9
1999	**EL CONDOR PASA** 4-9-8	4
2000	**MONTJEU** 4-9-8	9
2001	**MIRIO** 4-9-9	9
2002	**ANGE GABRIEL** 4-9-8	6
2003	**ANGE GABRIEL** 5-9-9	10
2004	**GAMUT** 5-9-9	10

PRIX MAURICE DE GHEEST

Deauville-6f 110yds
1995	**CHEROKEE ROSE** 4-8-13	10
1996	**ANABAA** 4-9-2	9
1997	**OCCUPANDISTE** 4-8-13	8
1998	**SEEKING THE PEARL** 4-8-13	12
1999	**DIKTAT** 4-9-2	10
2000	**BOLD EDGE** 5-9-2	11
2001	**KING CHARLEMAGNE** 3-8-12	9
2002	**MAY BALL** 5-8-13	9
2003	**PORLEZZA** 4-8-12	12
2004	**SOMNUS** 4-9-2	18

PRIX JACQUES LE MAROIS

Deauville-1m
1995	**MISS SATAMIXA** 3-8-8	9
1996	**SPINNING WORLD** 3-8-11	9
1997	**SPINNING WORLD** 4-9-4	6
1998	**TAIKI SHUTTLE** 4-9-4	8
1999	**DUBAI MILLENNIUM** 3-8-11	5
2000	**MUHTATHIR** 5-9-4	11
2001	***VAHORIMIX** 3-8-13	8
2002	**BANKS HILL** 4-9-1	8
2003	**SIX PERFECTIONS** 3-8-9	12
2004	**WHIPPER** 3-8-11	10

*Proudwings disqualified from first place

PRIX MORNY (2y)

Deauville-6f
1995	**TAGULA** 9-0	8
1996	**BAHAMIAN BOUNTY** 9-0	5
1997	**CHARGE D'AFFAIRES** 8-13	7
1998	**ORPEN** 9-0	13
1999	**FASLIYEV** 9-0	7
2000	**BAD AS I WANNA BE** 9-0	6
2001	**JOHANNESBURG** 9-0	11
2002	**ELUSIVE CITY** 9-0	6
2003	**WHIPPER** 9-0	8
2004	**DIVINE PROPORTIONS** 8-11	9

PRIX DU MOULIN DE LONGCHAMP

Longchamp-1m
1995	**RIDGEWOOD PEARL** 3-8-8	8
1996	**ASHKALANI** 3-8-11	9
1997	**SPINNING WORLD** 4-9-2	9
1998	**DESERT PRINCE** 3-8-11	7
1999	**SENDAWAR** 3-8-11	9
2000	**INDIAN LODGE** 4-9-2	8
2001	**SLICKLY** 5-9-2	8
2002	**ROCK OF GIBRALTAR** 3-8-11	7
2003	**NEBRASKA TORNADO** 3-8-8	14
2004	**GREY LILAS** 3-8-8	11

CRITERIUM INTERNATIONAL (2y)

Saint-Cloud-1m
(Prix de la Salamandre, run over
7f at Longchamp prior to 2001)
1995	**LORD OF MEN** 8-11	7
1996	**REVOQUE** 9-0	5
1997	**XAAR** 9-0	8
1998	**ALJABR** 9-0	6
1999	**GIANT'S CAUSEWAY** 9-0	5
2000	**TOBOUGG** 9-0	4
2001	**ACT ONE** 9-0	6
2002	**DALAKHANI** 9-0	5
2003	**BAGO** 9-0	7
2004	**HELIOS QUERCUS** 9-0	8

PRIX VERMEILLE (fillies and mares)

Longchamp-1m 4f
(for 3yo fillies only prior to 2004)
1995	**CARLING** 9-2	10
1996	**MY EMMA** 9-0	10
1997	**QUEEN MAUD** 9-0	9
1998	**LEGGERA** 9-0	11
1999	**DARYABA** 9-0	11
2000	**VOLVORETA** 9-0	11
2001	**AQUARELLISTE** 9-0	12
2002	**PEARLY SHELLS** 9-0	11
2003	**MEZZO SOPRANO** 9-0	11
2004	**SWEET STREAM** 4-9-2	13

PRIX DU CADRAN

Longchamp-2m 4f
1995	**ALWAYS EARNEST** 7-9-2	6
1996	**NONONITO** 5-9-2	10
1997	**CHIEF CONTENDER** 4-9-2	7
1998	**INVERMARK** 4-9-2	9
1999	**TAJOUN** 5-9-2	8
2000	**SAN SEBASTIAN** 6-9-2	9
2001	**GERMINIS** 7-9-2	9
2002	**GIVE NOTICE** 5-9-2	16
2003	**WESTERNER** 4-9-2	10
2004	**WESTERNER** 5-9-6	8

PRIX DE L'ABBAYE DE LONGCHAMP

Longchamp-5f
1995	**HEVER GOLF ROSE** 4-9-7	12
1996	**KISTENA** 3-9-8	10
1997	**CARMINE LAKE** 3-9-8	12
1998	**MY BEST VALENTINE** 8-9-10	14
1999	**AGNES WORLD** 4-9-10	14
2000	**NAMID** 4-9-11	11
2001	**IMPERIAL BEAUTY** 5-9-8	19
2002	**CONTINENT** 5-9-11	20
2003	**PATAVELLIAN** 5-9-11	19
2004	**VAR** 5-9-11	15

PRIX MARCEL BOUSSAC (2y fillies)
Longchamp-1m
1995	**MISS TAHITI** 8-11	11
1996	**RYAFAN** 8-11	13
1997	**LOVING CLAIM** 8-12	10
1998	**JUVENIA** 8-11	11
1999	**LADY OF CHAD** 8-11	11
2000	**AMONITA** 8-11	10
2001	**SULK** 8-11	9
2002	**SIX PERFECTIONS** 8-11	10
2003	**DENEBOLA** 8-11	16
2004	**DIVINE PROPORTIONS** 8-11	10

PRIX JEAN LUC LAGARDERE (2y)
(formerly Grand Criterium)
Longchamp-1m
1995	**LOUP SOLITAIRE** 8-11	7
1996	**REVOQUE** 9-0	9
1997	**SECOND EMPIRE** 9-0	5
1998	**WAY OF LIGHT** 9-0	7
1999	**CIRO** 9-0	3
2000	**OKAWANGO** 9-0	7
2001	**ROCK OF GIBRALTAR** 9-0	5
2002	**HOLD THAT TIGER** 9-0	14
2003	**AMERICAN POST** 9-0	6
2004	**ORATORIO** 9-0	6

PRIX DE LA FORET
Longchamp-7f
1995	**POPLAR BLUFF** 3-9-0	10
1996	**A MAGICMAN** 4-9-2	11
1997	**OCCUPANDISTE** 4-8-13	10
1998	**TOMBA** 4-9-2	9

1999	**FIELD OF HOPE** 4-8-12	11
2000	**INDIAN LODGE** 4-9-2	11
2001	**MOUNT ABU** 4-9-2	11
2002	**DEDICATION** 3-8-11	10
2003	**ETOILE MONTANTE** 3-8-11	10
2004	**SOMNUS** 4-9-2	7

PRIX ROYAL-OAK
Longchamp-1m 7f 110yds
1995	**SUNSHACK** 4-9-4	7
1996	**RED ROSES STORY** 4-9-1	5
1997	**EBADIYLA** 3-8-7	11
1998	**TIRAAZ** 4-9-4	7
1999	**AMILYNX** 3-8-9	7
2000	**AMILYNX** 4-9-4	7
2001	**VINNIE ROE** 3-8-9	13
2002	**MR DINOS** 3-8-9	7
2003	**WESTERNER** 4-9-4	14
2004	**WESTERNER** 5-9-4	8

CRITERIUM DE SAINT-CLOUD (2y)
Saint-Cloud-1m 2f
1995	**POLARIS FLIGHT** 9-0	5
1996	**SHAKA** 9-0	10
1997	**SPECIAL QUEST** 9-0	7
1998	**SPADOUN** 9-0	6
1999	**GOLDAMIX** 8-10	10
2000	**SAGACITY** 9-0	8
2001	**BALLINGARRY** 9-0	10
2002	**ALBERTO GIACOMETTI** 9-0	10
2003	**VOIX DU NORD** 9-0	10
2004	**PAITA** 8-11	7

WINNERS OF OTHER OVERSEAS RACES

DUBAI WORLD CUP
Nad Al Sheba-1m 2f dirt
1996	**CIGAR** 6-8-13	11
1997	**SINGSPIEL** 5-9-0	12
1998	**SILVER CHARM** 4-9-0	9
1999	**ALMUTAWAKEL** 4-9-0	8
2000	**DUBAI MILLENNIUM** 4-9-0	11
2001	**CAPTAIN STEVE** 4-9-0	12
2002	**STREET CRY** 4-9-0	11
2003	**MOON BALLAD** 4-9-0	11
2004	**PLEASANTLY PERFECT** 6-9-0	12

KENTUCKY DERBY
Churchill Downs-1m 2f dirt
1995	**THUNDER GULCH** 9-0	19
1996	**GRINDSTONE** 9-0	19
1997	**SILVER CHARM** 9-0	13
1998	**REAL QUIET** 9-0	15
1999	**CHARISMATIC** 9-0	19
2000	**FUSAICHI PEGASUS** 9-0	19
2001	**MONARCHOS** 9-0	17
2002	**WAR EMBLEM** 9-0	18
2003	**FUNNY CIDE** 9-0	16
2004	**SMARTY JONES** 9-0	18

BREEDERS' CUP TURF
Various-courses-1m 4f
1995	**NORTHERN SPUR 5** 4-9-0	13
1996	**PILSUDSKI** 5-9-0	14
1997	**CHIEF BEARHEART** 4-9-0	11
1998	**BUCK'S BOY** 5-9-0	13
1999	**DAYLAMI** 5-9-0	14
2000	**KALANISI** 4-9-0	13
2001	**FANTASTIC LIGHT** 5-9-0	11
2002	**HIGH CHAPARRAL** 3-8-9	8
2003	**JOHAR** 4-9-0 dead heated with	
	HIGH CHAPARRAL 4-9-0	9
2004	**BETTER TALK NOW** 5-9-0	8

BREEDERS' CUP CLASSIC
Various courses-1m 2f dirt
1995	**CIGAR** 5-9-0	11
1996	**ALPHABET SOUP** 5-9-0	13
1997	**SKIP AWAY** 4-9-0	9
1998	**AWESOME AGAIN** 4-9-0	10
1999	**CAT THIEF** 3-8-10	14
2000	**TIZNOW** 3-8-10	13
2001	**TIZNOW** 4-9-0	13
2002	**VOLPONI** 4-9-0	12

| 2003 | **PLEASANTLY PERFECT** 5-9-0 | 10 |
| 2004 | **GHOSTZAPPER** 4-9-0 | 13 |

MELBOURNE CUP
Flemington-2m

1995	**DORIMUS** 5-8-8	21
1996	**SAINTLY** 4-8-9	22
1997	**MIGHT AND POWER** 4-8-11	22
1998	**JEZABEEL** 6-8-0	24
1999	**ROGAN JOSH** 7-7-12	24
2000	**BREW** 6-7-10	22
2001	**ETHEREAL** 3-8-2	22
2002	**MEDIA PUZZLE** 5-8-4	23
2003	**MAKYBE DIVA** 4-8-0	23
2004	**MAKYBE DIVA** 7-8-11	24

JAPAN CUP
Tokyo-1m 4f

1995	**LANDO** 5-9-0	14
1996	**SINGSPIEL** 4-9-0	15
1997	**PILSUDSKI** 4-9-0	14
1998	**EL CONDOR PASA** 3-8-5	15
1999	**SPECIAL WEEK** 4-9-0	14
2000	**T.M. OPERA** 4-9-0	16
2001	**JUNGLE POCKET** 3-8-10	15
2002	**FALBRAV** 4-9-0	16
2003	**TAP DANCE CITY** 6-9-0	18
2004	**ZENNO ROB ROY** 4-9-0	16

WINNERS OF PRINCIPAL NATIONAL HUNT RACES

PADDY POWER GOLD CUP H'CAP CHASE
Cheltenham-2m 4f 110yds
(formerly Mackeson Gold Cup, Murphy's Gold Cup and Thomas Pink Gold Cup)

1995	**DUBLIN FLYER** 9-11-8	12
1996	**CHALLENGER DU LUC** 6-10-2	12
1997	**SENOR EL BETRUTTI** 8-10-0	9
1998	**CYFOR MALTA** 5-11-3	12
1999	**THE OUTBACK WAY** 9-10-0	14
2000	**LADY CRICKET** 6-10-13	15
2001	**SHOOTING LIGHT** 8-11-3	14
2002	**CYFOR MALTA** 9-11-9	15
2003	**FONDMORT** 7-10-13	9
2004	**CELESTIAL GOLD** 6-10-2	14

HENNESSY COGNAC GOLD CUP H'CAP CHASE
Newbury-3m 2f 110yds

1995	**COULDN'T BE BETTER** 8-10-8	11
1996	**COOME HILL** 7-10-0	11
1997	**SUNY BAY** 8-11-8	14
1998	**TEETON MILL** 9-10-5	16
1999	**EVER BLESSED** 7-10-0	13
2000	**KING'S ROAD** 7-10-7	17
2001	**WHAT'S UP BOYS** 7-10-12	14
2002	**BE MY ROYAL** 8-10-0	25
2003	**STRONG FLOW** 6-11-0	21
2004	**CELESTIAL GOLD** 6-10-5	14

BONUSPRINT.COM GOLD CUP H'CAP CHASE
Cheltenham-2m 4f

1995	ABANDONED	
1996	**ADDINGTON BOY** 8-11-10	10
1997	**SENOR EL BETRUTTI** 8-11-3	9
1998	**NORTHERN STARLIGHT** 7-10-1	13
1999	**LEGAL RIGHT** 6-10-13	9
2000	**GO ROGER GO** 8-11-0	12
2001	ABANDONED	
2002	**FONDMORT** 6-10-5	9
2003	**IRIS ROYAL** 7-10-13	17
2004	**MONKERHOSTIN** 7-10-2	13

PERTEMPS CHRISTMAS HURDLE
Kempton-2m

1995	ABANDONED	
1996	ABANDONED	
1997	**KERAWI** 4-11-7	5
1998	**FRENCH HOLLY** 7-11-7	5
1999	**DATO STAR** 8-11-7	4
2000	**GEOS** 5-11-7	7
2001	**LANDING LIGHT** 6-11-7	5
2002	**INTERSKY FALCON** 5-11-7	6
2003	**INTERSKY FALCON** 6-11-7	6
2004	**HARCHIBALD** 5-11-7	7

PERTEMPS KING GEORGE VI CHASE
Kempton-3m

1995	**ONE MAN** 8-11-10 (RUN AT SANDOWN)	11
1996	**ONE MAN** 8-11-10	5
1997	**SEE MORE BUSINESS** 7-11-10	8
1998	**TEETON MILL** 9-11-10	9
1999	**SEE MORE BUSINESS** 9-11-10	9
2000	**FIRST GOLD** 7-11-10	9
2001	**FLORIDA PEARL** 9-11-10	8
2002	**BEST MATE** 7-11-10	10
2003	**EDREDON BLEU** 11-11-10	12
2004	**KICKING KING** 6-11-10	13

CORAL WELSH NATIONAL H'CAP CHASE
Chepstow-3m 6f

1995	ABANDONED	
1996	ABANDONED	
1997	**EARTH SUMMIT** 9-10-13	14
1998	**KENDAL CAVALIER** 8-10-0	14
1999	**EDMOND** 7-10-0	16
2000	**JOCKS CROSS** 10-9-4	19
2001	**SUPREME GLORY** 8-10-0	13
2002	**MINI SENSATION** 9-10-4	16
2003	**BINDAREE** 9-10-9	14
2004	**SILVER BIRCH** 7-10-5	17

VICTOR CHANDLER H'CAP CHASE
Ascot-2m
1996	**BIG MATT** 9-10-4	11
1997	**ASK TOM** 8-10-10 (RUN AT KEMPTON)	8
1998	**JEFFELL** 8-10-11	9
1999	**CALL EQUINAME** 9-11-3 (RUN AT KEMPTON)	7
2000	**NORDANCE PRINCE** 9-10-0	10
2001	**FUNCTION DREAM** 9-10-11	10
2002	**TURGEONOV** 7-10-4	8
2003	ABANDONED	
2004	**ISIO** 8-10-5	13
2005	**WELL CHIEF** 6-11-10	10

TOTE GOLD TROPHY H'CAP HURDLE
Newbury-2m 110yds
1995	**MYSILV** 5-10-8	8
1996	**SQUIRE SILK** 7-10-12	18
1997	**MAKE A STAND** 6-11-7	18
1998	**SHARPICAL** 6-11-1	14
1999	**DECOUPAGE** 7-11-10	18
2000	**GEOS** 5-11-3	17
2001	**LANDING LIGHT** 6-10-2	20
2002	**COPELAND** 7-11-7	16
2003	**SPIRIT LEADER** 7-10-0	27
2004	**GEOS** 9-10-9	25

RACING POST H'CAP CHASE
Kempton-3m
1995	**VAL D'ALENE** 8-11-2	9
1996	**ROUGH QUEST** 10-10-8	9
1997	**MUDAHIM** 11-10-2	9
1998	**SUPER TACTICS** 10-10-10	7
1999	**DR LEUNT** 8-11-5	8
2000	**GLORIA VICTIS** 6-11-10	13
2001	**YOUNG SPARTACUS** 8-11-3	15
2002	**GUNTHER MCBRIDE** 7-10-3	14
2003	**LA LANDIERE** 8-11-7	12
2004	**MARLBOROUGH** 12-11-12	11

IRISH INDEPENDANT ARKLE CHALLENGE TROPHY (NOVICES' CHASE)
Cheltenham-2m
1995	**KLAIRON DAVIS** 6-11-8	11
1996	**VENTANA CANYON** 7-11-8	16
1997	**OR ROYAL** 6-11-8	9
1998	**CHAMPLEVE** 5-11-0	16
1999	**FLAGSHIP UBERALLES** 5-11-0	14
2000	**TIUTCHEV** 7-11-8	12
2001	ABANDONED	
2002	**MOSCOW FLYER** 8-11-8	11
2003	**TRAVADO** 7-11-8	8
2004	**WELL CHIEF** 5-11-3	16

SMURFIT CHAMPION HURDLE
Cheltenham-2m 110yds
1995	**ALDERBROOK** 6-12-0	14
1996	**COLLIER BAY** 6-12-0	13
1997	**MAKE A STAND** 6-12-0	17
1998	**ISTABRAQ** 6-12-0	14
1999	**ISTABRAQ** 7-12-0	18
2000	**ISTABRAQ** 8-12-0	12
2001	ABANDONED	
2002	**HORS LA LOI III** 7-12-0	15
2003	**ROOSTER BOOSTER** 9-12-0	17
2004	**HARDY EUSTACE** 7-11-10	14

QUEEN MOTHER CHAMPION CHASE
Cheltenham-2m
1995	**VIKING FLAGSHIP** 8-12-0	10
1996	**KLAIRON DAVIS** 7-12-0	7
1997	**MARTHA'S SON** 10-12-0	6
1998	**ONE MAN** 10-12-0	8
1999	**CALL EQUINAME** 9-12-0	13
2000	**EDREDON BLEU** 8-12-0	9
2001	ABANDONED	
2002	**FLAGSHIP UBERALLES** 8-12-0	12
2003	**MOSCOW FLYER** 9-12-0	11
2004	**AZERTYUIOP** 7-11-10	8

ROYAL & SUNALLIANCE NOVICES' CHASE
Cheltenham-3m
1995	**BRIEF GALE** 8-10-13	13
1996	**NAHTHEN LAD** 7-11-4	12
1997	**HANAKHAM** 8-11-4	14
1998	**FLORIDA PEARL** 6-11-4	10
1999	**LOOKS LIKE TROUBLE** 7-11-4	14
2000	**LORD NOELIE** 7-11-4	9
2001	ABANDONED	
2002	**HUSSARD COLLONGES** 7-11-4	19
2003	**ONE KNIGHT** 7-11-4	9
2004	**FUNDAMENTALIST** 6-11-7	15

JCB TRIUMPH HURDLE (4Y)
Cheltenham-2m 1f
1995	**KISSAIR** 11-0	26
1996	**PADDY'S RETURN** 11-0	29
1997	**COMMANCHE COURT** 11-0	28
1998	**UPGRADE** 11-0	25
1999	**KATARINO** 11-0	23
2000	**SNOW DROP** 10-9	28
2001	ABANDONED	
2002	**SCOLARDY** 11-0	28
2003	**SPECTROSCOPE** 11-0	27
2004	**MADE IN JAPAN** 11-0	23

TOTESPORT CHELTENHAM GOLD CUP
Cheltenham-3m 2f 110yds
1995	**MASTER OATS** 9-12-0	15
1996	**IMPERIAL CALL** 7-12-0	10
1997	**MR MULLIGAN** 9-12-0	14
1998	**COOL DAWN** 10-12-0	17
1999	**SEE MORE BUSINESS** 9-12-0	12
2000	**LOOKS LIKE TROUBLE** 8-12-0	12
2001	ABANDONED	
2002	**BEST MATE** 7-12-0	18
2003	**BEST MATE** 8-12-0	15
2004	**BEST MATE** 9-11-10	10

MARTELL CUP CHASE
Aintree-3m 1f
1995	**MERRY GALE** 7-11-9	6
1996	**SCOTTON BANKS** 7-11-5	6
1997	**BARTON BANK** 11-11-5	5
1998	**ESCARTEFIGUE** 6-11-13	8
1999	**MACGEORGE** 9-11-5	5
2000	**SEE MORE BUSINESS** 10-12-0	4
2001	**FIRST GOLD** 8-12-0	7
2002	**FLORIDA PEARL** 10-11-12	6
2003	**FIRST GOLD** 10-11-12	7
2004	**TIUTCHEV** 11-11-12	8

MARTELL AINTREE HURDLE
Aintree-2m 4f

1995	**DANOLI** 7-11-7	6
1996	**URUBANDE** 6-11-7	8
1997	**BIMSEY** 7-11-7	7
1998	**PRIDWELL** 8-11-7	6
1999	**ISTABRAQ** 7-11-7	7
2000	**MISTER MOROSE** 10-11-7	10
2001	**BARTON** 8-11-7	8
2002	**ILNAMAR** 6-11-7	14
2003	**SACUNDAI** 6-11-7	11
2004	**RHINESTONE COWBOY** 8-11-7	11

GALA GROUP SCOTTISH GRAND NATIONAL (H'CAP CHASE)
Ayr-4m 1f

1995	**WILSFORD** 12-10-12	22
1996	**MOORCROFT BOY** 11-10-2	20
1997	**BELMONT KING** 9-11-10	17
1998	**BARONET** 8-10-0	18
1999	**YOUNG KENNY** 8-11-10	15
2000	**PARIS PIKE** 8-11-0	18
2001	**GINGEMBRE** 7-11-2	30
2002	**TAKE CONTROL** 8-10-6	18
2003	**RYALLUX** 10-10-5	19
2004	**GREY ABBEY** 10-11-12	28

betfred GOLD CUP (H'CAP CHASE)
(formerly Whitbread Gold Cup)
Sandown-3m 5f 110yds

1995	**CACHE FLEUR** 9-10-1	14
1996	**LIFE OF A LORD** 10-11-10	17
1997	**HARWELL LAD** 8-10-0	9
1998	**CALL IT A DAY** 8-10-10	19
1999	**EULOGY** 9-10-0	19
2000	**BEAU** 7-10-9	20
2001	**AD HOC** 7-10-4	25
2002	**BOUNCE BACK** 6-10-9	20
2003	**AD HOC** 9-10-10	16
2004	**PUNTAL** 8-11-4	18

MEREWOOD HOMES SWINTON H'CAP HURDLE
Haydock-2m

1995	**CHIEF MINISTER** 6-11-6	13
1996	**TRAGIC HERO** 4-10-9	19
1997	**DREAMS END** 9-11-11	19
1998	**RAINBOW FRONTIER** 4-10-0	16
1999	**SHE'S OUR MARE** 6-10-0	22
2000	**MIRJAN** 4-10-6	22
2001	**MILLIGAN** 6-11-4	23
2002	**INTERSKY FALCON** 5-11-10	11
2003	**ALTAY** 6-10-0	14
2004	**MACS JOY** 5-10-0	19

Foaling dates are shown for two-year-olds where these are provided, and the purchase price (in guineas) as a yearling.

DATES OF PRINCIPAL RACES

(SUBJECT TO ALTERATION)

JANUARY

Cantor Sport "Dipper" Novices' Chase (Cheltenham) 1st
Junior Standard Open Bumper (Cheltenham) 1st
Slaney Novices' Hurdle (Naas) 2nd
Sandown Ladbroke Hurdle (Sandown Park) 8th
Gerrard Wealth Management Tolworth Novices' Hurdle (Sandown Park) 8th
Pierse Hurdle (Leopardstown) 9th
Paddy Fitzpatrick Memorial Novices' Chase (Leopardstown) 9th
Leopardstown Handicap Chase (Leopardstown) 9th
totescoop6 Lanzarote Handicap Hurdle (Kempton Park) 15th
Leamington Novices' Hurdle (Warwick) 15th
totesport Classic Gold Cup Handicap Chase (Warwick) 15th
Juvenile Hurdle (Punchestown) 16th
Normans Grove Chase (Fairyhouse) 20th
Thyestes Handicap Chase (Gowran Park) 20th
Galmoy Hurdle (Gowran Park) 20th
Victor Chandler Lightning Novices' Chase (Uttoxeter) 22nd
Bet Direct Peter Marsh Chase (Limited Handicap) (Haydock Park) 22nd
Red Square Reloaded Champion Trial Hurdle (Haydock Park) 22nd
Premier Hurdle (Haydock Park) 22nd
Woodlands Park Naas Novices' Chase (Naas) 22nd
AIG Champion Hurdle (Leopardstown) 23rd
Arkle Novices' Chase (Leopardstown) 23rd
Golden Cygnet Novices' Hurdle (Leopardstown) 23rd
Anaglogs Daughter Mares Novices' Chase (Thurles) 27th
Kinloch Brae Chase (Thurles) 27th
Victor Chandler Chase (Handicap) (Cheltenham) (from Ascot) 29th
Byrne Bros Cleeve Hurdle (Cheltenham) 29th
Pillar Property Chase (Cheltenham) 29th
Wragge & Co Finesse Juvenile Novices' Hurdle (Cheltenham) 29th
Ladbroke Trophy Chase (Handicap) (Cheltenham) 29th
Listed Novices' Hurdle (Cheltenham) 29th
River Don Novices' Hurdle (Doncaster) 29th
Skybet Handicap Chase (Doncaster) 29th
Novice Hurdle Series (Punchestown) 30th
National Trial Chase (Punchestown) 30th
Tied Cottage Chase (Punchestown) 30th

FEBRUARY

totesport Scilly Isles Novices' Chase (Sandown Park) 5th
totescoop6 Sandown Hurdle (Handicap) (Sandown Park) 5th
Agfa Diamond Chase (Handicap) (Sandown Park) 5th
Gerrard Wealth Management Rossington Main Novices' Hurdle (Wetherby) 5th
Towton Novices' Chase (Wetherby) 5th
Hennessy Gold Cup (Leopardstown) 6th
Dr P J Moriarty Novices' Chase (Leopardstown) 6th
Deloitte Novices' Hurdle (Leopardstown) 6th
Spring 4yo Hurdle (Leopardstown) 6th
Michael Page International Kingmaker Novices' Chase (Warwick) 12th
totepool Game Spirit Chase (Newbury) 12th
AON Chase (Newbury) 12th
AON Standard Open Bumper (Newbury) 12th
totesport Gold Trophy (Handicap Hurdle) (Newbury) 12th
Red Mills Trial Hurdle (Gowran Park) 12th
Red Mills Chase (Gowran Park) 13th
Flyingbolt Novices' Chase (Navan) 13th
Boyne Hurdle (Navan) 13th
Ten Up Novices' Chase (Navan) 13th
Ritz Club Ascot Chase (Ascot at Lingfield) 19th
Amlin Reynoldstown Novices' Chase (Ascot at Lingfield) 19th
De Vere Prestige Novices' Chase (Haydock Park) 19th
Haydock Park Gold Cup (Handicap Chase) (Haydock Park) 19th
Singer & Friedlander National Trial (Handicap Chase) (Uttoxeter) 19th
Axminster Kingwell Hurdle (Wincanton) 19th
Country Gentleman's Association Chase (Wincanton) 19th

Bobbyjo Chase (Fairyhouse) 19th
Winning Fair Juvenile Hurdle (Fairyhouse) 19th
INHSO Series Final   (Novices' Handicap Hurdle) (Fairyhouse) 19th
Newlands Chase (Naas) 20th
Collins Stewart National Spirit Hurdle (Fontwell Park) 20th
Johnstown Novices' Hurdle (Naas) 20th
Nas Na Riogh Novices' Chase (Naas) 20th
Rendlesham Hurdle (Kempton Park) 25th
Gerrard Wealth Management Dovecote Novices' Hurdle (Kempton Park) 25th
Michael Page International Standard Open Bumper (Warwick) 25th
Pendil Novices' Chase (Kempton Park) 26th
Adonis Juvenile Novices' Hurdle (Kempton Park) 26th
Racing Post Chase (Handicap) (Kempton Park) 26th
Bet Direct from Littlewoods Winter Derby Trial Stakes (Lingfield Park) 26th
totesport Eider Handicap Chase (Newcastle) 26th

MARCH

toteexacta Premier Kelso Novices' Hurdle (Kelso) 5th
Vodafone Gold Cup Chase (Newbury) 5th
EBF Novices' Handicap Chase Final (Navan) 5th
EBF/Doncaster Bloodstock Sales Mares Bumper Final (Sandown Park) 12th
European Breeders Fund National Hunt Novices' Hurdle Final (Handicap) (Sandown Park) 12th
Sunderlands Imperial Cup (Handicap Hurdle) (Sandown Park) 12th
Littlewoods Bet Direct Lincoln Trial Handicap Stakes (Wolverhampton) 12th
Smurfit Champion Hurdle Challenge Trophy (Cheltenham) 15th
Irish Independent Arkle Challenge Trophy Novices' Chase (Cheltenham) 15th
Letheby & Christopher Supreme Novices' Hurdle (Cheltenham) 15th
William Hill Trophy Handicap Chase (Cheltenham) 15th
Fred Winter Juvenile Novices' Handicap Hurdle (Cheltenham) 15th
Queen Mother Champion Chase (Cheltenham) 16th
Royal & SunAlliance Novices' Chase (Cheltenham) 16th
Royal & SunAlliance Novices' Hurdle (Cheltenham) 16th
Weatherbys Champion Bumper (Cheltenham) 16th
Coral Cup (Handicap Hurdle) (Cheltenham) 16th
Ladbrokes World Hurdle (Cheltenham) 16th
Fulke Walwyn Kim Muir Challenge Cup (Handicap Chase) (Cheltenham) 16th
Daily Telegraph Festival Trophy Chase (Cheltenham) 17th
Mildmay of Fleet Handicap Chase (Cheltenham) 17th
Pertemps Hurdle Final (Handicap) (Cheltenham) 17th
Jewson Novices' Handicap Chase (Cheltenham) 17th
NH Steeple Chase Challenge Cup (Amateur Riders Novices' Chase) (Cheltenham) 17th
totesport Cheltenham Gold Cup Chase (Cheltenham) 18th
JCB Triumph Novices' Hurdle (Cheltenham) 18th
Spa Novices' Hurdle (Cheltenham) 18th
Vincent O'Brien County Hurdle (Handicap) (Cheltenham) 18th
Johnny Henderson Grand Annual Challenge Cup Chase (Handicap) (Cheltenham) 18th
Christie's Foxhunter Challenge Cup Chase (Cheltenham) 18th
Littlewoods Bet Direct Winter Derby Stakes (Lingfield Park) 19th
Spring Cup (Lingfield Park) 19th
John Smith's Midlands Grand National Chase (Handicap) (Uttoxeter) 19th
EBF Tattersalls (Ireland) Mares Final Novices' Chase (Handicap) (Uttoxeter) 19th
Dawn Run Mares Novices' Chase (Limerick) 20th
Blue Square Easter Stakes (colts & geldings) (Kempton Park) 26th
Blue Square Masaka Stakes (fillies) (Kempton Park) 26th
Snowdrop Stakes (fillies) (Kempton Park) 26th
Magnolia Stakes (Kempton Park) 26th
Coral Eurobet Rosebery Handicap Stakes (Kempton Park) 26th
Moore Memorial Handicap Chase (Fairyhouse) 27th
Festival Novices' Hurdle (Fairyhouse) 27th
EBF Mares Hurdle Final (Fairyhouse) 27th
Irish Grand National   (Handicap Chase) (Fairyhouse) 28th
Menolly Homes Novices' Hurdle (Fairyhouse) 29th
Powers Gold Cup Novices' Chase (Fairyhouse) 29th
Menolly Homes Handicap Hurdle (Fairyhouse) 29th
Doncaster Mile (Doncaster) 31st

APRIL

Freephone Stanley Spring Mile (Handicap) (Doncaster) 1st
Cammidge Trophy (Doncaster) 2nd
Freephone Stanley Lincoln Handicap (Doncaster) 2nd
EBF Crandon Park Stud Mares 'NH' Novices' Hurdle Final (Handicap) (Newbury) 2nd
An Uaimh Chase (Navan) 2nd

MAY

UltimateBet.com 1000 Guineas Stakes (fillies) (Newmarket) 1st
UltimateBet.com Jockey Club Stakes (Newmarket) 1st
Dahlia Stakes (fillies) (Newmarket) 1st
R.L. Davison Pretty Polly Stakes (fillies) (Newmarket) 1st
Jubiliee Handicap Stakes (Kempton Park) 2nd
John Smiths Durham National (Handicap Chase) (Sedgefield) 2nd
Tetrarch Stakes (Curragh) 2nd
Mooresbridge Stakes (Curragh) 2nd
Victor Chandler Chester Vase (Chester) 4th
UPM-Kyemmene Cheshire Oaks (fillies) (Chester) 5th
totesport Chester Cup (Handicap) (Chester) 5th
Betfair.com Ormonde Stakes (Chester) 6th
Philip Leverhulme Dee Stakes (Chester) 6th
Breitling Watches & Waltons of Chester Huxley Stakes (Chester) 6th
Merewood Homes Swinton Handicap Hurdle (Haydock Park) 7th
Merewood Homes Spring Trophy Stakes (Haydock Park) 7th
Derby Trial Stakes (colts & geldings) (Lingfield Park) 7th
Oaks Trial Stakes (fillies) (Lingfield Park) 7th
totesport Chartwell Stakes (fillies) (Lingfield Park) 7th
totescoop6 Sprint Handicap Stakes (Lingfield Park) 7th
Derrinstown Derby Trial (Leopardstown) 8th
Derrinstown 1000 Guineas Trial (Leopardstown) 8th
Murphys Hurdle (Killarney) 8th
Royal Windsor Stakes (Windsor) 9th
Duke of York Stakes (York) 11th
Tattersalls Musidora Stakes (fillies) (York) 11th
totesport Dante Stakes (York) 12th
totepool Middleton Stakes (fillies) (York) 12th
Bank of Scotland Business Banking Hambleton Rated Handicap Stakes (York) 12th
Braveheart Rated Stakes (Hamilton Park) 13th
Swettenham Stud Fillies' Trial Stakes (Newbury) 13th
Yorkshire Cup (York) 13th
Michael Seely Memorial Glasgow Stakes (York) 14th
Juddmonte Lockinge Stakes (Newbury) 14th
Aston Park Stakes (Newbury) 14th
Carnarvon Stakes (Newbury) 14th
Kilvington Stakes (fillies) (Nottingham) 14th
Letheby & Christopher Predominate Stakes (colts & geldings) (Goodwood) 18th
Victor Chandler Lupe Stakes (fillies) (Goodwood) 19th
Festival Stakes (Goodwood) 20th
European Breeders Fund Conqueror Stakes (fillies) (Goodwood) 20th
Blue Wind Stakes (Cork) 20th
EBF Pinnacle Stakes (fillies and mares) (Haydock Park) 21st
Dunwoody Sports Marketing Sandy Lane Rated Stakes (Haydock Park) 21st
totesport Silver Bowl Handicap Stakes (Haydock Park) 21st
Heron Stakes (Kempton Park) 21st
Achilles Stakes (Kempton Park) 21st
King Charles II Stakes (Newmarket) 21st
Haven and British Holidays Fairway Stakes (Newmarket) 21st
Coral Sprint Handicap Stakes (Newmarket) 21st
Intrum Justitia Cup Champion Hunter Chase (Stratford-on-Avon) 21st
Irish 2000 Guineas Stakes (Curragh) 21st
Ridgewood Pearl Stakes (Curragh) 21st
Greenlands Stakes (Curragh) 21st
Prix St-Alary (Longchamp) 22nd
Prix Isaphan (Longchamp) 22nd
Irish 1000 Guineas Stakes (Curragh) 22nd
Tattersalls Gold Cup (Curragh) 22nd
Gallinule Stakes (Curragh) 22nd
On The House Stakes (Goodwood) 27th
totesport Zetland Gold Cup (Handicap) (Redcar) 30th
Bonusprint Henry II Stakes (Sandown Park) 30th
National Stakes (Sandown Park) 30th
Brigadier Gerard Stakes (Sandown Park) 31st

JUNE

Hilary Needler Trophy (fillies) (Beverley) 1st
Vodafone Oaks (fillies) (Epsom Downs) 3rd
Vodafone Coronation Cup (Epsom Downs) 3rd
Temple Stakes (Epsom Downs) 3rd

Princess Elizabeth Vodafone Stakes (fillies) (Epsom Downs)..3rd
Vodafone Surrey Stakes (Epsom Downs)..3rd
Vodafone Derby (colts & fillies) (Epsom Downs)..4th
Vodafone Diomed Stakes (Epsom Downs)..4th
Vodafone 'Dash' Rated Stakes (Epsom Downs)..4th
Vodafone Woodcote Stakes (Epsom Downs)..4th
Betfair.com John of Gaunt Stakes (Haydock Park)..4th
Stanley Racing Cecil Frail Stakes (fillies) (Haydock Park)..4th
City of Perth Gold Cup (Handicap Chase) (Perth)..5th
Prix du Jockey-Club (Chantilly)..5th
Pipalong Stakes (fillies and mares) (Pontefract)..6th
Ballycorus Stakes (Leopardstown)..8th
Leicester Mercury Stakes (Leicester)..11th
Axminster Carpets Cathedral Stakes (Salisbury)..12th
Prix de Diane Hermes (Chantilly)..12th
Ballyogan Stakes (Cork)..12th
St James's Palace Stakes (colts) (Royal Ascot at York)..14th
Queen Anne Stakes (Royal Ascot at York)..14th
King's Stand Stakes (Royal Ascot at York)..14th
Coventry Stakes (Royal Ascot at York)..14th
Windsor Castle Stakes (Royal Ascot at York)..14th
Ascot Handicap Stakes (Royal Ascot at York)..14th
Prince of Wales's Stakes (Royal Ascot at York)..15th
Queen Mary Stakes (fillies) (Royal Ascot at York)..15th
Windsor Forest Stakes (fillies and mares) (Royal Ascot at York)..15th
Jersey Stakes (Royal Ascot at York)..15th
Sandringham Rated Handicap Stakes (Royal Ascot at York)..15th
Royal Hunt Cup (Heritage Handicap) (Royal Ascot at York)..15th
Ballymacoll Stud Stakes (Newbury)..16th
Gold Cup (Royal Ascot at York)..16th
Ribblesdale Stakes (fillies) (Royal Ascot at York)..16th
Norfolk Stakes (Royal Ascot at York)..16th
Hampton Court Stakes (Royal Ascot at York)..16th
King George V Stakes (Heritage Handicap) (Royal Ascot at York)..16th
Britannia Heritage Handicap Stakes (colts & geldings) (Royal Ascot at York)..16th
Coronation Stakes (fillies) (Royal Ascot at York)..17th
King Edward VII Stakes (colts & geldings) (Royal Ascot at York)..17th
Queen's Vase (Royal Ascot at York)..17th
Albany Stakes (Royal Ascot at York)..17th
Wolferton Rated Stakes (Royal Ascot at York)..17th
Buckingham Palace Handicap Stakes (Royal Ascot at York)..17th
Golden Jubilee Stakes (Royal Ascot at York)..18th
Hardwicke Stakes (Royal Ascot at York)..18th
Chesham Stakes (Royal Ascot at York)..18th
Duke of Edinburgh Stakes (Heritage Handicap) (Royal Ascot at York)..18th
Wokingham Stakes (Heritage Handicap) (Royal Ascot at York)..18th
Queen Alexandra Stakes (Royal Ascot at York)..18th
Eternal Stakes (fillies) (Warwick)..18th
Crowther Homes Carlisle Bell Stakes (Handicap) (Carlisle)..22nd
toteplacepot Cumberland Plate (Handicap) (Carlisle)..22nd
Noblesse Stakes (Naas)..22nd
Kronenbourg 1664 Chipchase Stakes (Newcastle)..25th
EBF Hoppings Stakes (fillies) (Newcastle)..25th
Foster's Lager Northumberland Plate (Handicap) (Newcastle)..25th
Criterion Stakes (Newmarket)..25th
Fred Archer Stakes (Newmarket)..25th
Empress Stakes (fillies) (Newmarket)..25th
Gala Bingo Berkshire Stakes (Windsor)..25th
totescoop6 Leisure Stakes (Windsor)..25th
totepool Midsummer Stakes (Windsor)..25th
Curragh Cup Stakes (Curragh)..25th
Pretty Polly Stakes (Curragh)..25th
Britannia Building Society English Summer National (Handicap Chase) (Uttoxeter)..26th
Grand Prix de Saint-Cloud (Saint-Cloud)..26th
Irish Derby Stakes (Curragh)..26th
Railway Stakes (Curragh)..26th

JULY

Gala Stakes (Sandown Park)..1st
Dragon Stakes (Sandown Park)..1st
Lancashire Oaks (fillies) (Haydock Park)..2nd
Old Newton Cup (Handicap) (Haydock Park)..2nd

Coral Eclipse Stakes (Sandown Park) 2nd
Porcelanosa Sprint Stakes (Sandown Park) 2nd
Distaff Stakes (fillies) (Sandown Park) 2nd
Esher Stakes (Sandown Park) 2nd
totescoop6 Handicap Stakes (Sandown Park) 2nd
Brownstown Stakes (Leopardstown) 2nd
Prix Jean Prat (Chantilly) 3rd
Falmouth Stakes (fillies) (Newmarket) 5th
Princess of Wales's UAE Equestrian & Racing Federation Stakes (Newmarket) 5th
Cherry Hinton Stakes (fillies) (Newmarket) 5th
TNT July Stakes (colts & geldings) (Newmarket) 6th
Bahrain Trophy (Newmarket) 6th
Darley July Cup (Newmarket) 7th
Weatherbys Superlative Stakes (Newmarket) 7th
Ladbrokes Bunbury Cup (Handicap) (Newmarket) 7th
Cuisine de France Summer Stakes (fillies) (York) 8th
Michael Page International Silver Trophy (Ascot at Lingfield) 9th
City Wall Stakes (Chester) 9th
Webster's Silver Cup (Rated Handicap Stakes) (York) 9th
John Smith's Cup (Handicap) (York) 9th
Grand Prix de Paris (Longchamp) 14th
Manchester Evening News July Trophy (colts & geldings) (Haydock Park) 16th
totescoop6 Summer Plate Handicap Chase (Market Rasen) 16th
totesport Summer Hurdle (Market Rasen) 16th
Shadwell Stud Rose Bowl Stakes (Newbury) 16th
Steventon Stakes (Newbury) 16th
David Wilson Homes Hackwood Stakes (Newbury) 16th
Weatherbys Super Sprint (Newbury) 16th
Food Brokers Aphrodite Stakes (fillies) (Newmarket) 16th
International Stakes (Curragh) 16th
Anglesey Stakes (Curragh) 17th
Minstrel Stakes (Curragh) 17th
Irish Oaks (Curragh) 17th
Daily Record Scottish Derby (Ayr) 18th
Land O'Burns Stakes (fillies) (Ayr) 18th
Star Stakes (fillies) (Sandown Park) 21st
Weatherbys EBF Valiant Stakes (fillies) (Ascot at Newbury) 22nd
Oakgrove Stud Golden Daffodil Stakes (fillies) (Chepstow) 22nd
King George VI and Queen Elizabeth Diamond Stakes (Ascot at Newbury) 23rd
Princess Margaret Stakes (fillies) (Ascot at Newbury) 23rd
totesport International Handicap Stakes (Ascot at Newbury) 23rd
Meld Stakes (Leopardstown) 23rd
Hong Kong Jockey Club Sprint Handicap Stakes (Ascot at Newbury) 24th
Prix Robert Papin (Maisons-Laffitte) 24th
Richmond Stakes (colts & geldings) (Goodwood) 26th
Theo Fennell Lennox Stakes (Goodwood) 26th
Peugeot Gordon Stakes (Goodwood) 26th
Cantor Odds Sussex Stakes (Goodwood) 27th
Veuve Cliquot Vintage Stakes (Goodwood) 27th
totesport Gold Trophy (Handicap Stakes) (Goodwood) 27th
Galway Plate (Handicap Chase) (Galway) 27th
Lady O Goodwood Cup (Goodwood) 28th
King George Stakes (Goodwood) 28th
Betfair Molecomb Stakes (Goodwood) 28th
Galway Hurdle (Handicap) (Galway) 28th
Oak Tree Stakes (fillies) (Goodwood) 29th
Glorious Rated Stakes (Goodwood) 29th
William Hill Mile (Handicap) (Goodwood) 29th
Stewards' Sprint Handicap Stakes (Goodwood) 29th
Vodafone Nassau Stakes (fillies) (Goodwood) 30th
Vodafone EBF Lily Langtree Stakes (fillies and mares) (Goodwood) 30th
Vodafone Thoroughbred Stakes (Goodwood) 30th
Vodafone Stewards' Cup (Handicap) (Goodwood) 30th
Stubbs Stakes (Newmarket) 30th
Queensferry Stakes (Chester) 31st
EBF Chalice Stakes (fillies) (Newbury) 31st

AUGUST

Petros Rose of Lancaster Stakes (Haydock Park) 6th
Sweet Solera Stakes (fillies) (Newmarket) 6th
Phoenix Sprint (Curragh) 7th
Debutante Stakes (Curragh) 7th

Phoenix Stakes (Curragh) 7th
Royal Whip Stakes (Curragh) 7th
Phoenix Sprint (Leopardstown) 8th
Phoenix Stakes (Leopardstown) 8th
European Breeders Fund Upavon Stakes (fillies) (Salisbury) 10th
Stonehenge Stakes (Salisbury) 10th
Sovereign Stakes (colts & geldings) (Salisbury) 11th
Newbury Racecourse Washington Singer Stakes (Newbury) 12th
Stan James Geoffrey Freer Stakes (Newbury) 13th
Stan James Hungerford Stakes (Newbury) 13th
Stan James St Hugh's Stakes (fillies) (Newbury) 13th
William Hill Great St Wilfrid Handicap Stakes (Ripon) 13th
EBF Dick Hern Stakes (Bath) 14th
Slatch Farm Stud Flying Stakes (fillies) (Pontefract) 14th
Prix Jacques Le Marois (Deauville) 14th
Desmond Stakes (Leopardstown) 14th
Juddmonte International Stakes (York) 16th
Great Voltigeur Stakes (colts & geldings) (York) 16th
Weatherbys Insurance Lonsdale Cup (York) 16th
Acomb Stakes (York) 16th
Aston Upthorpe Yorkshire Oaks (fillies) (York) 17th
Scottish Equitable Gimcrack Stakes (colts & geldings) (York) 17th
Costcutter Roses Stakes (colts & geldings) (York) 17th
totesport Ebor Handicap (York) 17th
Victor Chandler Nunthorpe Stakes (York) 18th
Peugeot Lowther Stakes (fillies) (York) 18th
European Breeders Fund Galtres Stakes (fillies) (York) 18th
City of York Stakes (York) 18th
Beverley Bullet Sprint Stakes (Beverley) 20th
Bet Direct Chester Stakes (Rated) (Chester) 20th
Iveco Daily Solario Stakes (Sandown Park) 20th
Sunley Atalanta Stakes (fillies) (Sandown Park) 20th
Futurity Stakes (Curragh) 20th
Prix Morny (Deauville) 21st
Flower of Scotland Stakes (fillies and mares) (Hamilton Park) 22nd
Winter Hill Stakes (Windsor) 22nd
Saltwell Signs Virginia Rated Stakes (fillies) (Yarmouth) 24th
Denny Handicap Chase (Tralee 25th
totesport Celebration Mile (Goodwood) 27th
San Miguel March Stakes (Goodwood) 27th
Hopeful Stakes (Newmarket) 27th
August Stakes (Windsor) 27th
Prestige Stakes (fillies) (Goodwood) 28th
Betfair.com Ripon Champion Two Years Old Trophy (Ripon) 29th
Strensall Stakes (York) 31st

SEPTEMBER

EBF Dick Poole Stakes (fillies) (Salisbury) 1st
Stanleybet Sprint Cup (Haydock Park) 3rd
Stanleybet Superior Mile Stakes (Haydock Park) 3rd
stanleybet.com Old Borough Cup (Haydock Park) 3rd
Pentax September Stakes (Kempton Park) 3rd
Pentax Sirenia Stakes (Kempton Park) 3rd
Prix de Moulin de Longchamp (Longchamp) 4th
Moyglare Stud Stakes (Curragh) 4th
Flying Five (Curragh) 4th
Round Tower Stakes (Curragh) 4th
Park Hill Stakes (fillies) (Doncaster) 7th
£200,000 St Leger Yearling Stakes (Doncaster) 7th
totesport Portland Handicap Stakes (Doncaster) 7th
GNER Doncaster Cup (Doncaster) 8th
GNER Park Stakes (Doncaster) 8th
May Hill Stakes (fillies) (Doncaster) 8th
JRA London Office's Kyoto Sceptre Stakes (fillies) (Doncaster) 8th
Scarbrough Stakes (Doncaster) 8th
Fortune Stakes (Epsom Downs) 8th
Champagne Stakes (colts & geldings) (Doncaster) 9th
Amco Corporation Troy Stakes (Doncaster) 9th
DBS St Leger Yearling Stakes (Doncaster) 9th
totesport Henry Gee Stakes (fillies and mares) (Chester) 10th
St Leger (colts & fillies) (Doncaster) 10th
Polypipe Flying Childers Stakes (Doncaster) 10th

OCTOBER

Beresford Stakes (Curragh) 9th
Munster National (Handicap Chase) (Limerick) 9th
EBF Boadicea Stakes (fillies and mares) (Newmarket) 13th
Lanwades Stud Severals Stakes (fillies) (Newmarket) 13th
Bentinck Stakes (Newmarket) 14th
Listed Novices' Hurdle (Kempton Park) 15th
Charisma Gold Cup Chase (Handicap) (Kempton Park) 15th
Emirates Airline Champion Stakes (Newmarket) 15th
Darley Dewhurst Stakes (colts & fillies) (Newmarket) 15th
Victor Chandler Challenge Stakes (Newmarket) 15th
Owen Brown Rockfel Stakes (fillies) (Newmarket) 15th
Newmarket Darley Stakes (Newmarket) 15th
Jockey Club Cup (Newmarket) 15th
totesport Cesarewitch Handicap Stakes (Newmarket) 15th
totesport Silver Tankard Stakes (Pontefract) 17th
DBS October Yearling Stakes (Doncaster) 21st
Vodafone Horris Hill Stakes (colts & geldings) (Newbury) 21st
Molyneux Novices' Chase (Aintree) 22nd
Persian War Novices' Hurdle (Chepstow) 22nd
Racing Post Trophy (colts & fillies) (Doncaster) 22nd
Doncaster Stakes (Doncaster) 22nd
St Simon Stakes (Newbury) 22nd
Swettenham Stud Radley Stakes (fillies) (Newbury) 23rd
Fieldspring Old Roan Chase (Limited Handicap) (Aintree) 23rd
Prix Royal-Oak (Longchamp) 25th
Lady Godiva Stakes (fillies and mares) (Yarmouth) 28th
James Seymour Stakes (Newmarket) 28th
EBF Bosra Sham Stakes (fillies) (Newmarket) 29th
United House Handicap Chase (Lingfield Park) 29th
Ben Marshall Stakes (Newmarket) 29th
Zetland Stakes (Newmarket) 29th
European Breeders Fund Montrose Stakes (fillies) (Newmarket) 29th
Peterhouse Group Charlie Hall Chase (Wetherby) 29th
John Smith's West Yorkshire Hurdle (Wetherby) 29th
Stanley Racing Wensleydale Juvenile Novices' Hurdle (Wetherby) 29th
Brown Lad Handicap Hurdle (Naas) 29th
EBF Fleur de Lys Stakes (Lingfield Park) 30th
Ballybrit Novices' Chase (Galway) 30th
Killavullan Stakes (Leopardstown) 31st

NOVEMBER

Williamhill.co.uk Haldon Gold Cup (Limited Handicap Chase) (Exeter) 1st
Willie Park Trophy (Musselburgh) 3rd
EBF Gillies Stakes (fillies and mares) (Doncaster) 5th
CIU Serlby Stakes (Doncaster) 5th
Charles Sidney Mercedes Benz Wentworth Stakes (Doncaster) 5th
totescoop6 November Handicap (Doncaster) 5th
K J Pike & Sons Elite Hurdle (Limited Handicap) (Wincanton) 5th
Badger Brewery Handicap Chase (Wincanton) 5th
Nicholson Chase (Down Royal) 5th
Killultagh Properties Chase (Down Royal) 5th
Cork National (Cork) 6th
Gerrard Wealth Management Sharp Novices' Hurdle (Cheltenham) 11th
Open Juvenile Novices' Hurdle (Cheltenham) 12th
Paddy Power Gold Cup (Handicap Chase) (Cheltenham) 12th
Open Trophy (Handicap Chase) (Cheltenham) 12th
Lombard Properties Handicap Hurdle (Cheltenham) 12th
Criterium de Saint-Cloud (Saint-Cloud) 12th
Poplar Square Chase (Naas) 12th
Independent November Novices' Chase (Cheltenham) 13th
Greatwood Handicap Hurdle (Cheltenham) 13th
Betfair Open Bumper (Cheltenham) 13th
Fortria Chase (Navan) 13th
Lismullen Hurdle (Navan) 13th
For Auction Novices' Hurdle (Navan) 13th
Clonmel Oil Chase (Clonmel) 17th
PricewaterhouseCoopers Ascot Hurdle (Windsor) 18th
Clonmel Chase (Clonmel) 18th
Edward Hanmer Memorial Chase (Limited Handicap) (Haydock Park) 19th
BBA Peterborough Chase (Huntingdon) 19th
Littlewoods Bet Direct Churchill Stakes (Lingfield Park) 19th
First National Gold Cup Chase (Limited Intermediate Handicap) (Windsor) 19th

Morgiana Hurdle (Punchestown)..19th
Craddockstown Novices' Chase (Punchestown)..19th
totesport Becher Handicap Chase (Aintree)...20th
Sussex National Chase (Handicap) (Plumpton)...20th
Irish Field Novices' Chase (Punchestown)...20th
RBI Promotions Newbury Novices' Chase (Newbury)..26th
RBI Promotions Long Distance Hurdle (Newbury)...26th
Systems by Design Fulke Walwyn Novices' Chase (Newbury)..26th
Hennessy Cognac Gold Cup (Handicap Chase) (Newbury)...26th
Stan James Gerry Feilden Hurdle (Limited Intermediate Handicap) (Newbury).............................26th
Pertemps 'Fighting Fifth' Hurdle (Newcastle)..26th
Troytown Handicap Chase (Navan)..26th
Monksfield Novices' Hurdle (Navan)...27th

DECEMBER

Winter Novices' Hurdle (Sandown Park)..2nd
John Hughes Rehearsal Chase (Limited Handicap) (Chepstow)..3rd
Listed Novices' Hurdle (Haydock Park)...3rd
Mitsubishi Shogun Tingle Creek Trophy Chase (Sandown Park)..3rd
Extraman Trophy Henry VIII Novices' Chase (Sandown Park)..3rd
William Hill Handicap Hurdle (Sandown Park)...3rd
Sun "King of the Punters" Mildmay Cazalet Memorial Handicap Chase (Sandown Park)................3rd
New Stand Handicap Hurdle (Fairyhouse)..3rd
Porterstown Handicap Chase (Fairyhouse)...3rd
Juvenile Hurdle (Fairyhouse)..3rd
Drinmore Novices' Chase (Fairyhouse)...4th
Royal Bond Novices' Hurdle (Fairyhouse)...4th
Hattons Grace Hurdle (Fairyhouse)..4th
totesport Bula Hurdle (Cheltenham)...10th
Tripleprint Bristol Novices' Hurdle (Cheltenham)...10th
Tripleprint Gold Cup (Handicap Chase) (Cheltenham)..10th
Arena Racing December Novices' Chase (Lingfield Park)...10th
Summit Novices' Hurdle (Lingfield Park)...10th
Barry & Sandra Kelly Memorial Novices' Hurdle (Navan)...10th
Hilly Way Chase (Cork)...11th
Cork Stayers Novices' Hurdle (Cork)...11th
John Durkan Memorial Chase (Punchestown)..11th
Cantor Sport Long Walk Hurdle (Windsor)...16th
Kennel Gate Novices' Hurdle (Windsor)..16th
Tommy Whittle Chase (Haydock Park)...17th
Cantor Sport Noel Novices' Chase (Windsor)..17th
Silver Cup Handicap Chase (Windsor)...17th
Tara Hurdle (Navan)...18th
Rowland Meyrick Handicap Chase (Wetherby)...26th
Stan James King George VI Chase (Kempton Park)..26th
Stan James Christmas Hurdle (Kempton Park)...26th
Stan James Feltham Novices' Chase (Kempton Park)..26th
Juvenile Hurdle (Leopardstown)...26th
Novices' Chase (Leopardstown)..26th
Greenmount Park Novices' Chase (Limerick)...26th
Castleford Chase (Wetherby)...27th
Finale Juvenile Hurdle (Chepstow)...27th
Coral Eurobet Welsh National (Handicap Chase) (Chepstow)..27th
Wayward Lad Novices' Chase (Kempton Park)...27th
Future Champion Novices' Hurdle (Leopardstown)...27th
Paddy Power Handicap Chase (Leopardstown)...27th
Dial A Bet Chase (Leopardstown)...27th
Neville Novices' Chase (Leopardstown)...28th
Christmas Hurdle (Leopardstown)..28th
Lexus Chase (Leopardstown)...28th
Dorans Pride Novices' Hurdle (Limerick)...28th
TFM Cyntergy Challow Hurdle (Newbury)..29th
Championship" Standard Open Bumper (Newbury)...29th
December Hurdle (Leopardstown)...29th

The information contained within this section is kindly supplied by the BHB and is provisional. In all cases, the dates, venues and names of sponsors are correct at the time of going to press but subject to possible alteration.

LEADING TRAINERS ON THE FLAT: 1896-2004

1896 A Hayhoe	1933 F Darling	1970 C F N Murless
1897 R Marsh	1934 Frank Butters	1971 I Balding
1898 R Marsh	1935 Frank Butters	1972 W Hern
1899 J Porter	1936 J Lawson	1973 C F N Murless
1900 R Marsh	1937 C Boyd-Rochfort	1974 P Walwyn
1901 J Huggins	1938 C Boyd-Rochfort	1975 P Walwyn
1902 R S Sievier	1939 J L Jarvis	1976 H Cecil
1903 G Blackwell	1940 F Darling	1977 M V O'Brien
1904 P P Gilpin	1941 F Darling	1978 H Cecil
1905 W T Robinson	1942 F Darling	1979 H Cecil
1906 Hon G Lambton	1943 W Nightingall	1980 W Hern
1907 A Taylor	1944 Frank Butters	1981 M Stoute
1908 C Morton	1945 W Earl	1982 H Cecil
1909 A Taylor	1946 Frank Butters	1983 W Hern
1910 A Taylor	1947 F Darling	1984 H Cecil
1911 Hon G Lambton	1948 C F N Murless	1985 H Cecil
1912 Hon G Lambton	1949 Frank Butters	1986 M Stoute
1913 R Wootton	1950 C H Semblat	1987 H Cecil
1914 A Taylor	1951 J L Jarvis	1988 H Cecil
1915 P P Gilpin	1952 M Marsh	1989 M Stoute
1916 R C Dawson	1953 J L Jarvis	1990 H Cecil
1917 A Taylor	1954 C Boyd-Rochfort	1991 P Cole
1918 A Taylor	1955 C Boyd-Rochfort	1992 R Hannon
1919 A Taylor	1956 C F Elsey	1993 H Cecil
1920 A Taylor	1957 C F N Murless	1994 M Stoute
1921 A Taylor	1958 C Boyd-Rochfort	1995 J Dunlop
1922 A Taylor	1959 C F N Murless	1996 Saeed bin Suroor
1923 A Taylor	1960 C F N Murless	1997 M Stoute
1924 R C Dawson	1961 C F N Murless	1998 Saeed bin Suroor
1925 A Taylor	1962 W Hern	1999 Saeed bin Suroor
1926 F Darling	1963 P Prendergast	2000 Sir M Stoute
1927 Frank Butters	1964 P Prendergast	2001 A O'Brien
1928 Frank Butters	1965 P Prendergast	2002 A O'Brien
1929 R C Dawson	1966 M V O'Brien	2003 Sir M Stoute
1930 H S Persse	1967 C F N Murless	2004 Saeed bin Suroor
1931 J Lawson	1968 C F N Murless	
1932 Frank Butters	1969 A M Budgett	

CHAMPION JOCKEYS ON THE FLAT: 1894-2004

1894 M Cannon	167	1917 S Donoghue	42	1939 G Richards	155
1895 M Cannon	184	1918 S Donoghue	66	1940 G Richards	68
1896 M Cannon	164	1919 S Donoghue	129	1941 H Wragg	71
1897 M Cannon	145	1920 S Donoghue	143	1942 G Richards	67
1898 O Madden	161	1921 S Donoghue	141	1943 G Richards	65
1899 S Loates	160	1922 S Donoghue	102	1944 G Richards	88
1900 L Reiff	143	1923 S Donoghue	89	1945 G Richards	104
1901 O Madden	130	1923 C Elliott	89	1946 G Richards	212
1902 W Lane	170	1924 C Elliott	106	1947 G Richards	269
1903 O Madden	154	1925 G Richards	118	1948 G Richards	224
1904 O Madden	161	1926 T Weston	95	1949 G Richards	261
1905 E Wheatley	124	1927 G Richards	164	1950 G Richards	201
1906 W Higgs	149	1928 G Richards	148	1951 G Richards	227
1907 W Higgs	146	1929 G Richards	135	1952 G Richards	231
1908 D Maher	139	1930 F Fox	129	1953 G Richards	191
1909 F Wootton	165	1931 G Richards	145	1954 D Smith	129
1910 F Wootton	137	1932 G Richards	190	1955 D Smith	168
1911 F Wootton	187	1933 G Richards	259	1956 D Smith	155
1912 F Wootton	118	1934 G Richards	212	1957 A Breasley	173
1913 D Maher	115	1935 G Richards	217	1958 D Smith	165
1914 S Donoghue	129	1936 G Richards	174	1959 D Smith	157
1915 S Donoghue	62	1937 G Richards	216	1960 L Piggott	170
1916 S Donoghue	43	1938 G Richards	206	1961 A Breasley	171

1962 A Breasley 179	1977 Pat Eddery 176	1992 M Roberts.................... 206
1963 A Breasley 176	1978 W Carson 182	1993 Pat Eddery 169
1964 L Piggott.................... 140	1979 J Mercer 164	1994 L Dettori 233
1965 L Piggott.................... 160	1980 W Carson 166	1995 L Dettori 211
1966 L Piggott.................... 191	1981 L Piggott 179	1996 Pat Eddery 186
1967 L Piggott.................... 117	1982 L Piggott 188	1997 K Fallon.................... 202
1968 L Piggott.................... 139	1983 W Carson 159	1998 K Fallon.................... 204
1969 L Piggott.................... 163	1984 S Cauthen 130	1999 K Fallon.................... 201
1970 L Piggott.................... 162	1985 S Cauthen 195	2000 K Darley.................... 152
1971 L Piggott.................... 162	1986 Pat Eddery 176	2001 K Fallon.................... 167
1972 W Carson 132	1987 S Cauthen 197	2002 K Fallon.................... 151
1973 W Carson 164	1988 Pat Eddery 183	2003 K Fallon.................... 221
1974 Pat Eddery 148	1989 Pat Eddery 171	2004 L Dettori 192
1975 Pat Eddery 164	1990 Pat Eddery 209	
1976 Pat Eddery 162	1991 Pat Eddery 165	

LEADING OWNERS ON THE FLAT: 1894-2004

1894 Mr H. McCalmont	1931 Mr J A Dewar	1969 Mr D Robinson
1895 Ld de Rothschild	1932 H.H. Aga Khan	1970 Mr C Engelhard
1896 Ld de Rothschild	1933 Ld Derby	1971 Mr P Mellon
1987 Mr J Gubbins	1934 H.H. Aga Khan	1972 Mrs J Hislop
1898 Ld de Rothschild	1935 H.H. Aga Khan	1973 Mr N B Hunt
1899 Duke of Westminster	1936 Ld Astor	1974 Mr N B Hunt
1900 H.R.H. The Prince	1937 H.H. Aga Khan	1975 Dr C Vittadini
of Wales	1938 Ld Derby	1976 Mr D Wildenstein
1901 Sir G Blundell Maple	1939 Ld Rosebery	1977 Mr R Sangster
1902 Mr R S Sievier	1940 Lord Rothermere	1978 Mr R Sangster
1903 Sir James Miller	1941 Ld Glanely	1979 Sir M Sobell
1904 Sir James Miller	1942 His Majesty	1980 S Weinstock
1905 Col W Hall Walker	1943 Miss D Paget	1981 H.H. Aga Khan
1906 Ld Derby (late)	1944 H.H. Aga Khan	1982 Mr R Sangster
1907 Col W Hall Walker	1945 Ld Derby	1983 Mr R Sangster
1908 Mr J B Joel	1946 H.H. Aga Khan	1984 Mr R Sangster
1909 Mr "Fairie"	1947 H.H. Aga Khan	1985 Sheikh Mohammed
1910 Mr "Fairie"	1948 H.H. Aga Khan	1986 Sheikh Mohammed
1911 Ld Derby	1949 H.H. Aga Khan	1987 Sheikh Mohammed
1912 Mr T Pilkington	1950 M M Boussac	1988 Sheikh Mohammed
1913 Mr J B Joel	1951 M M Boussac	1989 Sheikh Mohammed
1914 Mr J B Joel	1952 H. H. Aga Khan	1990 Mr Hamdan Al-Maktoum
1915 Mr L Neumann	1953 Sir Victor Sassoon	1991 Sheikh Mohammed
1916 Mr E Hulton	1954 Her Majesty	1992 Sheikh Mohammed
1917 Mr "Fairie"	1955 Lady Zia Wernher	1993 Sheikh Mohammed
1918 Lady James Douglas	1956 Maj L B Holliday	1994 Mr Hamdan Al-Maktoum
1919 Ld Glanely	1957 Her Majesty	1995 Mr Hamdan Al-Maktoum
1920 Sir Robert Jardine	1958 Mr J McShain	1996 Godolphin
1921 Mr S B Joel	1959 Prince Aly Khan	1997 Sheikh Mohammed
1922 Ld Woolavington	1960 Sir Victor Sassoon	1998 Godolphin
1923 Ld Derby	1961 Maj L B Holliday	1999 Godolphin
1924 H.H. Aga Khan	1962 Maj L B Holliday	2000 H.H. Aga Khan
1925 Ld Astor	1963 Mr J R Mullion	2001 Godolphin
1926 Ld Woolavington	1964 Mrs H E Jackson	2002 Mr Hamdan Al-Maktoum
1927 Ld Derby	1965 M J Ternynck	2003 K Abdullah
1928 Ld Derby	1966 Lady Zia Wernher	2004 Godolphin
1929 H.H. Aga Khan	1967 Mr H J Joel	
1930 H.H. Aga Khan	1968 Mr Raymond R Guest	

LEADING SIRES ON THE FLAT: 1894-2004

1894 St Simon	1901 St Simon	1908 Persimmon
1895 St Simon	1902 Persimmon	1909 Cyllene
1896 St Simon	1903 St Frusquin	1910 Cyllene
1897 Kendal	1904 Gallinule	1911 Sundridge
1898 Galopin	1905 Gallinule	1912 Persimmon
1899 Orme	1906 Persimmon	1913 Desmond
1900 St Simon	1907 St Frusquin	1914 Polymelus

1915 Polymelus	1945 Hyperion	1975 Great Nephew
1916 Polymelus	1946 Hyperion	1976 Wolver Hollow
1917 Bayardo	1947 Nearco	1977 Northern Dancer
1918 Bayardo	1948 Big Game	1978 Mill Reef (USA)
1919 The Tetrarch	1949 Nearco	1979 Petingo
1920 Polymelus	1950 Fair Trial	1980 Pitcairn
1921 Polymelus	1951 Nasrullah	1981 Great Nephew
1922 Lemberg	1952 Tehran	1982 Be My Guest (USA)
1923 Swynford	1953 Chanteur II	1983 Northern Dancer
1924 Son-in-Law	1954 Hyperion	1984 Northern Dancer
1925 Phalaris	1955 Alycidon	1985 Kris
1926 Hurry On	1956 Court Martial	1986 Nijinsky (CAN)
1927 Buchan	1957 Court Martial	1987 Mill Reef (USA)
1928 Phalaris	1958 Mossborough	1988 Caerleon (USA)
1929 Tetratema	1959 Petition	1989 Blushing Groom (FR)
1930 Son-in-Law	1960 Aureole	1990 Sadler's Wells (USA)
1931 Pharos	1961 Aureole	1991 Caerleon (USA)
1932 Gainsborough	1962 Never Say Die	1992 Sadler's Wells (USA)
1933 Gainsborough	1963 Ribot	1993 Sadler's Wells (USA)
1934 Blandford	1964 Chamossaire	1994 Sadler's Wells (USA)
1935 Blandford	1965 Court Harwell	1995 Sadler's Wells (USA)
1936 Fairway	1966 Charlottesville	1996 Sadler's Wells (USA)
1937 Solario	1967 Ribot	1997 Sadler's Wells (USA)
1938 Blandford	1968 Ribot	1998 Sadler's Wells (USA)
1939 Fairway	1969 Crepello	1999 Sadler's Wells (USA)
1940 Hyperion	1970 Northern Dancer	2000 Sadler's Wells (USA)
1941 Hyperion	1971 Never Bend	2001 Sadler's Wells (USA)
1942 Hyperion	1972 Queen's Hussar	2002 Sadler's Wells (USA)
1943 Fairway	1973 Vaguely Noble	2003 Sadler's Wells (USA)
1944 Fairway	1974 Vaguely Noble	2004 Sadler's Wells (USA)

LEADING BREEDERS ON THE FLAT: 1909-2004

1909 Mr "Fairie"	1942 National Stud	1974 Mr N B Hunt
1910 Mr "Fairie"	1943 Miss D Paget	1975 Overbury Stud
1911 Ld Derby (late)	1944 Ld Rosebery	1976 Dayton Ltd
1912 Col. W Hall Walker	1945 Ld Derby	1977 Mr E P Taylor
1913 Mr J B Joel	1946 Lt- Col H Boyd-Rochfort	1978 Cragwood Estates Inc
1914 Mr J B Joel	1947 H.H. Aga Khan	1979 Ballymacoll Stud
1915 Mr L Neumann	1948 H.H. Aga Khan	1980 P Clarke
1916 Mr E Hulton	1949 H.H. Aga Khan	1981 H.H. Aga Khan
1917 Mr "Fairie"	1950 M M Boussac	1982 Someries Stud
1918 Lady James Douglas	1951 M M Boussac	1983 White Lodge Stud
1919 Ld Derby	1952 H. H. Aga Khan	1984 Mr E P Taylor
1920 Ld Derby	1953 Mr F Darling	1985 Dalham Stud Farms
1921 Mr S B Joel	1954 Maj L B Holliday	1986 H.H. Aga Khan
1922 Ld Derby	1955 Someries Stud	1987 Cliveden Stud
1923 Ld Derby	1956 Maj L B Holliday	1988 H. H. Aga Khan
1924 Lady Sykes	1957 Eve Stud	1989 Mr Hamdan Al- Maktoum
1925 Ld Astor	1958 Mr R Ball	1990 Capt. Macdonald- Buchanan
1926 Ld Woolavington	1959 Prince Aly Khan and the late	1991 Barronstown Stud
1927 Ld Derby	H.H. Aga Khan	1992 Swettenham Stud
1928 Ld Derby	1960 Eve Stud Ltd	1993 Juddmonte Farms
1929 Ld Derby	1961 Eve Stud Ltd	1994 Shadwell Farm & Estate Ltd
1930 Ld Derby	1962 Maj L B Holliday	1995 Shadwell Farm & Estate Ltd
1931 Ld Dewar	1963 Mr H F Guggenheim	1996 Sheikh Mohammed
1932 H.H. Aga Khan	1964 Bull Run Stud	1997 Sheikh Mohammed
1933 Sir Alec Black	1965 Mr J Ternynck	1998 Sheikh Mohammed
1934 H.H. Aga Khan	1966 Someries Stud	1999 H. H. The Aga Khan's Studs
1935 H.H. Aga Khan	1967 Mr H J Joel	2000 H. H. The Aga Khan's Studs
1936 Ld Astor	1968 Mill Ridge Stud	2001 Shadwell Farm & Estate Ltd
1937 H.H. Aga Khan	1969 Lord Rosebery	2002 Gainsborough Stud
1938 Ld Derby	1970 Mr E P Taylor	Management Ltd
1939 Ld Rosebery	1971 Mr P Mellon	2003 Juddmonte
1940 Mr H E Morriss	1972 Mr J Hislop	2004 Juddmonte
1941 Ld Glanely	1973 Claiborne Farm	

LEADING TRAINERS OVER JUMPS: 1945-2004

1945-46 T Rayson	1966-67 H R Price	1987-88 D R C Elsworth
1946-47 F T T Walwyn	1967-68 Denys Smith	1988-89 M C Pipe
1947-48 F T T Walwyn	1968-69 T F Rimell	1989-90 M C Pipe
1948-49 F T T Walwyn	1969-70 T F Rimell	1990-91 M C Pipe
1949-50 P V F Cazalet	1970-71 F T Winter	1991-92 M C Pipe
1950-51 T F Rimell	1971-72 F T Winter	1992-93 M C Pipe
1951-52 N Crump	1972-73 F T Winter	1993-94 D Nicholson
1952-53 M V O'Brien	1973-74 F T Winter	1994-95 D Nicholson
1953-54 M V O'Brien	1974-75 F T Winter	1995-96 M C Pipe
1954-55 H R Price	1975-76 T F Rimell	1996-97 M C Pipe
1955-56 W Hall	1976-77 F T Winter	1997-98 M C Pipe
1956-57 N Crump	1977-78 F T Winter	1998-99 M C Pipe
1957-58 F T T Walwyn	1978-79 M H Easterby	1999-00 M C Pipe
1958-59 H R Price	1979-80 M H Easterby	2000-01 M C Pipe
1959-60 P V F Cazalet	1980-81 M H Easterby	2001-02 M C Pipe
1960-61 T F Rimell	1981-82 M W Dickinson	2002-03 M C Pipe
1961-62 H R Price	1982-83 M W Dickinson	2003-04 M C Pipe
1962-63 K Piggott	1983-84 M W Dickinson	
1963-64 F T T Walwyn	1984-85 F T Winter	
1964-65 P V F Cazalet	1985-86 N J Henderson	
1965-66 H R Price	1986-87 N J Henderson	

CHAMPION JOCKEYS OVER JUMPS: 1900-2004

Prior to the 1925-26 season the figure relates to racing between January and December

1900	Mr H S Sidney	53	1936-37 G Wilson	45	1971-72 B R Davies	89
1901	F Mason	58	1937-38 G Wilson	59	1972-73 R Barry	125
1902	F Mason	67	1938-39 T F Rimell	61	1973-74 R Barry	94
1903	P Woodland	54	1939-40 T F Rimell	24	1974-75 T Stack	82
1904	F Mason	59	1940-41 G Wilson	22	1975-76 J Francome	96
1905	F Mason	73	1941-42 R Smyth	12	1976-77 T Stack	97
1906	F Mason	58	1942-43 No racing		1977-78 J J O'Neill	149
1907	F Mason	59	1943-44 No racing		1978-79 J Francome	95
1908	P Cowley	65	1944-45 H Nicholson	15	1979-80 J J O'Neill	117
1909	R Gordon	45	T F Rimell	15	1980-81 J Francome	105
1910	E Piggott	67	1945-46 T F Rimell	54	1981-82 J Francome	120
1911	W Payne	76	1946-47 J Dowdeswell	58	P Scudamore	120
1912	I Anthony	78	1947-48 B Marshall	66	1982-83 J Francome	106
1913	E Piggott	60	1948-49 T Moloney	60	1983-84 J Francome	131
1914	Mr J R Anthony	60	1949-50 T Moloney	95	1984-85 J Francome	101
1915	E Piggott	44	1950-51 T Moloney	83	1985-86 P Scudamore	91
1916	C Hawkins	17	1951-52 T Moloney	99	1986-87 P Scudamore	123
1917	W Smith	15	1952-53 F Winter	121	1987-88 P Scudamore	132
1918	G Duller	17	1953-54 R Francis	76	1988-89 P Scudamore	221
1919	Mr H Brown	48	1954-55 T Moloney	67	1989-90 P Scudamore	170
1920	F B Rees	64	1955-56 F Winter	74	1990-91 P Scudamore	141
1921	F B Rees	65	1956-57 F Winter	80	1991-92 P Scudamore	175
1922	J Anthony	78	1957-58 F Winter	82	1992-93 R Dunwoody	173
1923	F B Rees	64	1958-59 T Brookshaw	83	1993-94 R Dunwoody	197
1924	F B Rees	108	1959-60 S Mellor	68	1994-95 R Dunwoody	160
1925	E Foster	76	1960-61 S Mellor	118	1995-96 A P McCoy	175
1925-26 T Leader		61	1961-62 S Mellor	80	1996-97 A P McCoy	190
1926-27 F B Rees		59	1962-63 J Gifford	70	1997-98 A P McCoy	253
1927-28 W Stott		88	1963-64 J Gifford	94	1998-99 A P McCoy	186
1928-29 W Stott		65	1964-65 T Biddlecombe	114	1999-00 A P McCoy	245
1929-30 W Stott		77	1965-66 T Biddlecombe	102	2000-01 A P McCoy	191
1930-31 W Stott		81	1966-67 J Gifford	122	2001-02 A P McCoy	289
1931-32 W Stott		77	1967-68 J Gifford	82	2002-03 A P McCoy	256
1932-33 G Wilson		61	1968-69 B R Davies	77	2003-04 A P McCoy	157
1933-34 G Wilson		56	T Biddlecombe	77	
1934-35 G Wilson		73	1969-70 B R Davies	91	
1935-36 G Wilson		57	1970-71 G Thorner	74	

LEADING OWNERS OVER JUMPS: 1945-2004
(Please note that prior to the 1994-95 season the leading owner was determined by win prizemoney only)

1945-46 Mr J Morant	1967-68 Mr H S Alper	1989-90 Mrs Harry J Duffey
1946-47 Mr J J McDowell	1968-69 Mr B P Jenks	1990-91 Mr P Piller
1947-48 Mr J Proctor	1969-70 Mr E R Courage	1991-92 Whitcombe Manor
1948-49 Mr W F Williamson	1970-71 Mr F Pontin	Racing Stables Ltd
1949-50 Mrs L Brotherton	1971-72 Capt T A Forster	1992-93 Mrs J Mould
1950-51 Mr J Royle	1972-73 Mr N H Le Mare	1993-94 Pell-Mell Partners
1951-52 Miss D Paget	1973-74 Mr N H Le Mare	1994-95 Roach Foods Limited
1952-53 Mr J H Griffin	1974-75 Mr R Guest	1995-96 Mr A T A Wates
1953-54 Mr J H Griffin	1975-76 Mr P B Raymond	1996-97 Mr R Ogden
1954-55 Mrs W H E Welman	1976-77 Mr N H Le Mare	1997-98 Mr D A Johnson
1955-56 Mrs L Carver	1977-78 Mrs O Jackson	1998-99 Mr J P McManus
1956-57 Mrs Geoffrey Kohn	1978-79 Snailwell Stud Co Ltd	1999-00 Mr R Ogden
1957-58 Mr D J Coughlan	1979-80 Mr H J Joel	2000-01 Sir R Ogden
1958-59 Mr J E Bigg	1980-81 Mr R J Wilson	2001-02 Mr D A Johnson
1959-60 Miss W H Wallace	1981-82 Sheikh Ali Abu Khamsin	2002-03 Mr D A Johnson
1960-61 Mr C Vaughan	1982-83 Sheikh Ali Abu Khamsin	2003-04 Mr D A Johnson
1961-62 Mr N Cohen	1983-84 Sheikh Ali Abu Khamsin	
1962-63 Mr P B Raymond	1984-85 T Kilroe and Son Ltd	
1963-64 Mr J K Goodman	1985-86 Sheikh Ali Abu Khamsin	
1964-65 Mrs M Stephenson	1986-87 Mr H J Joel	
1965-66 Duchess of Westminster	1987-88 Miss Juliet E Reed	
1966-67 Mr C P T Watkins	1988-89 Mr R Burridge	

LEADING AMATEUR RIDERS OVER JUMPS: 1945-2004

1945-46 Mr A B Mildmay 11	1965-66 Mr C Collins 24	1985-86 Mr T Thomson Jones ...25
1946-47 Ld Mildmay 32	1966-67 Mr C Collins 33	1986-87 Mr T Thomson Jones ...19
1947-48 Ld Mildmay 22	1967-68 Mr R Tate 30	1987-88 Mr T Thomson Jones ...15
1948-49 Ld Mildmay 30	1968-69 Mr R Tate 17	1988-89 Mr P Fenton 18
1949-50 Ld Mildmay 38	1969-70 Mr M Dickinson 23	1989-90 Mr P McMahon 15
1950-51 Mr P Chisman 13	1970-71 Mr J Lawrence 17	1990-91 Mr K Johnson 24
1951-52 Mr C Straker 19	1971-72 Mr W Foulkes 26	1991-92 Mr M P Hourigan 24
1952-53 Mr A H Moralee 22	1972-73 Mr R Smith 56	1992-93 Mr A Thornton 26
1953-54 Mr A H Moralee 22	1973-74 Mr A Webber 21	1993-94 Mr J Greenall 21
1954-55 Mr A H Moralee 16	1974-75 Mr R Lamb 22	1994-95 Mr D Parker 16
1955-56 Mr R McCreery 13	1975-76 Mr P Greenall 25	1995-96 Mr J Culloty 40
Mr A H Moralee 13	Mr G Jones 25	1996-97 Mr R Thornton 30
1956-57 Mr R McCreery 23	1976-77 Mr P Greenall 27	1997-98 Mr S Durack 41
1957-58 Mr J Lawrence 18	1977-78 Mr G Sloan 23	1998-99 Mr A Dempsey 47
1958-59 Mr J Sutcliffe 18	1978-79 Mr T G Dun 26	1999-00 Mr P Flynn 41
1959-60 Mr G Kindersley 22	1979-80 Mr O Sherwood 29	2000-01 Mr T Scudamore 24
1960-61 Sir W Pigott-Brown 28	1980-81 Mr P Webber 32	2001-02 Mr D Crosse 19
1961-62 Mr A Biddlecombe 30	1981-82 Mr D Browne 28	2002-03 Mr C Williams 23
1962-63 Sir W Pigott-Brown 20	1982-83 Mr D Browne 33	2003-04 Mr O Nelmes 14
1963-64 Mr S Davenport 32	1983-84 Mr S Sherwood 28	
1964-65 Mr M Gifford 15	1984-85 Mr S Sherwood 30	

LEADING SIRES OVER JUMPS: 1985-2004

1985 Deep Run	1992-93 Deep Run	2000-01 Be My Native (USA)
1986 Deep Run	1993-94 Strong Gale	2001-02 Be My Native (USA)
1987 Deep Run	1994-95 Strong Gale	2002-03 Be My Native (USA)
1988 Deep Run	1995-96 Strong Gale	2003-04 Be My Native (USA)
1989 Deep Run	1996-97 Strong Gale	
1989-90 Deep Run	1997-98 Strong Gale	
1990-91 Deep Run	1998-99 Strong Gale	
1991-92 Deep Run	1999-00 Strong Gale	

JOCKEY AGENTS

Jockeys Agents and their Contact Details

Agent	Telephone	Mobile	Fax
N M ADAMS	(01488) 72004	(07778) 032906	
NEIL ALLAN	(01903) 883797	(07895) 311141	
W ADAMS	(01656) 734416 welshwizard@wadams.fsbusiness.co.uk	(07767) 847025	(01656) 731915
NEIL ALLAN	(01903) 883797	(07985) 311141	
KEITH BRADLEY	(01638) 666350 keith.bradley2@ntlworld.com	(07754) 690050	
PAUL BRIERLEY	(01577) 830330	(07977) 934655	
C D BROAD	(01452) 760482/447 c.j.broad@talk21.com	(07836) 622858	(01452) 760394
MRS RUTH BURCHELL	(01495) 352464	(07816) 450026	(01495) 302551
MRS G S CHARNOCK	(01653) 695004/690097	(07951) 576912	
RAY COCHRANE	(01223) 812008	(07798) 651247	
R T DODDS	(02380) 222985	(07952) 226092	
S T DODDS	(01273) 487092	(07974) 924735	

Agent	Telephone	Mobile	Fax
SHIPPY ELLIS	(01638) 668484 shippy.jockeys@virgin.net	(07860) 864864	(01638) 660946
CLAIRE FITZPATRICK	(01793) 845254	(07789) 758558	
P G FORSTER	(01434) 684754	(07786) 001344	(01434) 604779
JOHN W FORD	(01954) 261122	(07860) 390904	(01954) 261565
D M FOX	(01302) 562992 dmfox@blueyonder.co.uk	(07710) 430454	(01302) 562992
MARK GILCHRIST	(01903) 883356	(07810) 821787	
W P GRUNDY	(01845) 597850/597532 (2nd pref)	(07973) 817634	(01845) 597945
RICHARD A HALE	(01768) 886990/887320	(07909) 520542	
JOHN HANMER	(01235) 762450	(07715) 565488	
ALAN HARRISON	(01969) 625006/623788	(07740) 530298	(01969) 625006
R T HARRISON	(01325) 732186/182		
MIKE HAWKETT	(01844) 202120	(07836) 206127	
TONY HIND	(01922) 501588	(07779) 208430	(01638) 723157
G J HORNE	(01823) 661371	(07833) 697987	

Agent	Telephone	Mobile	Fax
RICHARD HUNTER	(01377) 259123	(07801) 248644	
L R JAMES	(01653) 699466	(07947) 414001	(01653) 691455
G D JEWELL	(01672) 861231 guy.jewel@talk21.com	(07765) 248859	(01672) 861231
J LEES	(01306) 888318	(07711) 972643	
GEOFF LESTER	(01635) 253150	(07771) 832788	
MRS E LUCEY-BUTLER	(01273) 890124	(07973) 873846	
G MACDONALD	(01628) 770766	(07770) 262686	
BARRIE MELROSE	(01835) 863411	(07746) 332022	
TERRY J NORMAN	(01279) 304844	(07900) 525033	(01279) 306304
G R OWEN	(01638) 669968 gareth.owen@ntlworld.com	(07958) 335206	
DAVID A POLLINGTON	(01751) 477142	(07850) 015711	
JONATHAN RAMSDEN	(01423) 564178	(07715) 167693	
DAVE ROBERTS	(01737) 761369	(07860) 234342	
B J ROBERTSON	(01284) 850805/850807	(07860) 235151	(01284) 850807

Agent	Telephone	Mobile	Fax
J B SIMPSON	(01765) 688535	(07734) 112941	
R W STUBBS	(01653) 698731	(07747) 613962/(07801) 167707 (car)	
HUGH TAYLOR	(01483) 858023	(07736) 635459	
S C TURNER	(01782) 327697 scott@jockeyagent.co.uk	(07803) 619968	
K P WARBUTON	(01609) 779256	(07843) 281212	
I P WARDLE	(01761) 453555	(07831) 865974	
A WATERWORTH	(0113) 2174396 trueprofessional2002@yahoo.co.uk	(07968) 911848	
L H WAY	(01704) 834488	(07775) 777494	
BOB WILLIAMS	(01638) 750032	(07774) 662278	
JULIAN WILLIAMS	(01904) 521117 julianjwilliams@netbreeze.co.uk	(07867) 656899	

FLAT JOCKEYS

Riding weights and their contact details.
An Index of Agents appears on page 723

AHERN, E	8-2	J Lees
ALLAN, D	8-2	Mrs G S Charnock
BADGER, MISS J	7-12	Richard Hunter
BAKER, G	8-7	G D Jewell
BASTIMAN, H	9-9	D M Booth/(01423) 359397
BRADLEY, P	8-2	D M Fox
BRISLAND, R	7-12	D M Booth
CALLAN, N	8-5	S T Dodds
CARROLL, J	8-5	Tony Hind
CARSON, S	8-2	Keith Bradley
CARTER, G	8-4	Shippy Ellis
CATLIN, C	7-12	N M Adams
CHIN, S	8-3	K Warbuton
COGAN, C	8-0	Richard Hunter
COSGRAVE, P	8-4	G R Owen
CROWLEY, J	9-5	C Broad
CULHANE, A	8-6	Mark Gilchrist
DALY, A	8-0	G D Jewell
DARLEY, K	8-4	Shippy Ellis
DAY, N	8-2	(0771) 911346
DETTORI, L	8-6	R Cochrane
DOBBS, P	8-4	Tony Hind
DOE, P	8-3	Mark Gilchrist
DOWLING, W	9-4	Richard Hale
DOYLE, B	8-5	G D Jewell
DROWNE, S	8-4	I P Wardle
DUFFIELD, G	8-2	Keith Bradley/(01677) 450303
DURCAN, T	8-4	Mrs L H Way
DWYER, M	8-0	G R Owen
EDDERY, PAUL	8-2	Mike Hawkett
EDMUNDS, J	8-2	(01302) 719734
EGAN, J	8-0	I P Wardle
FALLON, K	8-4	David A Pollington
FANNING, J	8-2	W P Grundy
FAULKNER, G	8-4	Alan Harrison/(01638) 663984
FENTON, M	8-5	Mrs L H Way
FERRIS, F	7-12	N M Adams
FESSEY, P	7-12	Richard Hale
FFRENCH, R	8-0	Richard Hale
FITZPATRICK, R	8-2	G Horne
FITZSIMONS, P	8-1	G D Jewell
FORTUNE, J	8-6	Tony Hind
FOWLE, J	7-12	I P Wardle
GIBBONS, G	8-1	Mrs L H Way
GIBSON, D	7-12	W P Grundy
GONCALVES, L	8-0	c/o (01845) 587226
GREAVES, MISS A	8-12	(01845) 501470
HALLIDAY, V	8-5	L R James
HANAGAN, P	8-0	Richard Hale
HANNON, G	8-4	R T Dodds
HAVLIN, R	8-4	I P Wardle
HENRY, M	8-0	G D Jewell
HILLS, M	8-5	B J Robertson
HILLS, R	8-3	B J Robertson
HIND, G	8-4	(01638) 561096
HOLLAND, D	8-5	Terry Norman
HUGHES, R	8-6	Geoff Lester
JONES, LISA	7-9	Richard Hunter
KELLY, S	8-5	Richard Hunter
KINANE, M J	8-4	John Hanmer

KINSELLA, D.	7-12	I P Wardle
LAPPIN, R.	8-5	Alan Harrison
LOWTHER, C.	8-5	Miss F J Enefer
LUCAS, T.	8-5	(07770) 812011
LYNCH, F.	8-5	W P Grundy
MACKAY, A.	8-0	(01761) 453555
MACKAY, J.	7-12	Keith Bradley
MCCARTHY, A.	7-12	N Allan
MCAULEY, J.	7-12	G D Horne
MCCABE, D.	8-1	Mrs G S Charnock
MCCABE, P.	8-9	R T Harrison
MCEVOY, K.	8-3	Hugh Taylor
MCGAFFIN, D.	8-4	Richard Hale
MCKEOWN, D.	8-3	S T Dodds
MCLAUGHLIN, T.	8-8	(01638) 660214
MERNAGH, D.	7-12	Richard Hale
MONGAN, I.	8-6	S T Dodds
MOORE, RYAN	8-4	Tony Hind
MOSSE, G.	8-10	Shippy Ellis
MULLEN, R.	8-2	G R Owen
MURPHY, T J	9-7	C Broad
MURTAGH, J P	8-9	R Cochrane
NICHOLLS, A	7-12	N M Adams
NORTON, F.	7-12	I P Wardle
O'DONOHOE, D	8-2	c/o Godolphin
O'NEILL, D	8-5	N M Adams
PARKIN, G.	8-6	Richard Hale
PESLIER, O	8-5	Shippy Ellis
POLLARD, N	8-2	Alan Harrison
PRICE, R	8-4	Mrs Ruth Burchell
PROCTER, A.	9-0	(07919) 521773
QUEALLY, T	8-1	Keith Bradley
QUINN, J	7-12	Keith Bradley
QUINN, P M	7-12	Mrs G S Charnock
QUINN, T	8-6	G D Jewell
RIGHTON, S	7-12	L R James/(07787) 748712
ROBINSON, P	8-3	Shippy Ellis
SANDERS, S	8-5	Keith Bradley/(01284) 735410
SLATTERY, V	8-9	(01242) 820907/(07831) 545789
SMITH, J D	8-6	Mrs Ruth Burchell
SMITH, R	8-0	N Allan
SOUMILLON, C	8-6	Shippy Ellis
SPENCER, J P	8-6	Jonathan Ramsden
STACK, E	8-4	R T Harrison
STOKELL, MRS A	8-7	(01748) 811873
STEVENS, GARY	8-4	Terry Norman
SUPPLE, W	8-0	Mrs L H Way
SWEENEY, D	8-5	N M Adams
TATE, J	8-0	Mrs Ruth Burchell
TEBBUTT, M	8-6	N Allan
TINKLER, MRS K	7-12	(01653) 658245
TOPPER, MISS N	7-12	c/o (01969) 624351
URBINA, O	8-4	G D Jewell
VICKERS, L	9-0	L R James
WHITWORTH, S	8-2	N M Adams
WILLIAMS, C	8-1	I P Wardle
WILLIAMS D	8-6	Richard Hunter
WILLIAMS, T	8-0	J J Williams
WINSTON, R	8-4	Richard Hale
WORRELL, M	8-3	Bob Williams

APPRENTICES

Their employers and contact details.
An Index of Agents appears on page 723

ADAMS, MISS S (G Margarson)	7-1	c/o (01638) 668043
ARCHER, S (Sir Mark Prescott)	8-2	(07786) 160812/(01638) 666350
ASPELL, P (Mrs M Reveley)	9-0	Richard Hale
BAKER, Miss A (Mrs Nerys Dutfield)	7-6	c/o (01297) 553560
BARTLEY, G (P C. Haslam)	8-2	A Harrison
BASHTON MISS D (A Charlton)	8-2	(01264) 852789
BEECH, A (D R Loder)	8-6	N Allan
BENSON, P J (D. Nicholls)	7-12	A Harrison
BIRD, MISS R (Mr C. F. Wall)	8-0	(01638) 668896
BOWMAN, K (M. J. Wallace)	8-0	c/o (01638) 560752
BROWN, N (K. G. Reveley)	8-0	A Harrison
BURKE, K (C L Tizzard)	8-12	c/o (01963) 250598
BURTON, W (R Hannon)	8-2	c/o (01264) 850254
BUSHBY, S (J Balding)	7-12	J J Williams
CAETANO, MISS C (Philip Mitchell)	8-0	c/o (01372) 273729
CALDWELL, MISS D (K. A. Ryan)	7-7	c/o (01845) 597622
CAVANAGH, C (Henry Candy)	8-2	c/o (01367) 820276
CAVANAGH, J S (J D Bethell)	8-1	Gavin Horne
CHALMERS, N (A M Balding)	8-0	N M Adams
CHEUNG, M (Mel Brittain)	7-6	c/o (01759) 371472
COFFILL-BROWN, J (S Dow)	8-7	c/o (01372) 721490
CORBY, D (M J Wallace)	8-2	N M Adams
COSTELLO, MISS R (Miss Gay Kelleway)	7-12	c/o (01342) 837100
COUMBE, M (J Akehurst)	8-3	c/o (01372) 745880
CRAWFORD, MISS L (T D Barron)	8-7	c/o (01845) 587435
CRAWFORD, S (J A Osborne)	8-12	c/o (01488) 73139
CURRIE, J (J S Goldie)	7-10	c/o (01505) 850212
DALY, J (S Kirk)	8-5	R Harrison
DAVIES, C J (J M Bradley)	8-12	c/o (01291) 626939
DAVIES, MISS S J (M Brisbourne)	8-0	c/o (01743) 741536
DE SOUZA, N (P F. I. Cole)	8-0	c/o (01488) 638433
DEAN, T C (M. Channon)	7-3	N Allan
DEVERSON, MISS D (W. J. Haggas)	8-0	c/o (01638) 667013
DONOHOE, S (P D Evans)	8-3	Keith Bradley
DOYLE, J (Miss J. S. Doyle)	7-12	(01488) 72223
EAVES, T (Brian Ellison)	8-3	Richard Hale
EDWARDS, G J (M C Chapman)	8-0	c/o (01673) 843663
ELLIOTT, A (K R Burke)	7-5	c/o (01969) 625088
ELY, C (P. A. Blockley)	8-0	c/o (01636) 819082
ENSTONE, L (D W Barker)	8-3	Alan Harrison
FAIRLEY, G (M Johnston)	8-2	c/o (01969) 622237
FELLOWS, H (R Hollinshead)	7-10	c/o (01543) 490298
FENTIMAN, D (J Weymes)	7-5	Alan Harrison
FLETCHER, L (H. Morrison)	8-4	L R James/(01635) 281678
FLYNN, M (Alan Berry)	8-0	A Harrsion
FOX, D (C A Dwyer)	7-7	G D Jewell
FRANCE, MISS S (Andrew Turnell)	8-2	c/o (01653) 699555
GALLAGHER, P (J. A. Geake)	8-7	N Allan
GEMBERLU, H (J W Hills)	8-5	(07947) 775688
GEMELOVA, MISS N (I W McInnes)	7-5	L R James
GHUNOWA, K (J J Quinn)	7-12	A Harrison
GOLAM, S (M H Tompkins)	8-0	Richard Hunter
GORDON, R (Richard Rowe)	8-10	c/o (01903) 742871
GUILLAMBERT, J-P (Nick Littmoden)	8-4	Simon Dodds
HADDON, C (W G M Turner)	7-4	N Allan
HADDON, S M (W G M Turner)	8-2	c/o (01963) 220523
HALFORD, M (Julian Poulton)	7-6	N Allan
HAMBLETT, A (L. M. Cumani)	8-0	c/o (01638) 665432
HAMBLETT, J (Sir Michael Stoute)	8-0	c/o (01638) 663801
HAMILTON, T (R. A. Fahey)	8-0	Richard Hale

HANN, MISS F (Mr Dean Ivory)	8-2	c/o (01923) 855337
		N Allan
HARMAN, L (M. Channon)	7-12	c/o (01264) 772278
HARPER, MISS F (J Geake)	8-0	c/o (01746) 789288
HARRIS, MISS K (W. Jenks)	7-5	Richard Hunter
HARRISON, S J (Nick Littmoden)	8-0	
HASSALL, MISS N (A Bailey)	7-4	c/o (01829) 760762
HESLOP D (A. M. Balding)	7-7	c/o (01635) 298210
HILL, MISS V J (J. C. Fox)	8-2	c/o (01264) 850218
HINDLEY, A (B G Powell)	8-2	N Allan
HITCHCOTT, S (M Channon)	8-1	N M Adams
HOGG, W (Mark Johnston)	8-2	N Allan
HOLLINSHEAD, MISS S (R Hollinshead)	7-12	A Harrison
HORTON, MISS A (M. D. I. Usher)	7-10	R Harrison
HOWARD, M (John Akehurst)	8-3	John Ford
HOWELL, T (M. J. Wallace)	7-8	c/o (01638) 560752
JACKSON, K (P. J. McBride)	7-7	c/o (01638) 667841
JANKIEWICZ, MISS N (Mr C. F. Wall)	8-4	c/o (01638) 668896
JEFFREY, J (J. R. Jenkins)	7-5	John Ford
JONES, J J (G L Moore)	7-0	c/o (01273) 620405
JONES, L (J Jay)	7-7	Richard Hunter
JONES, S (J M Bradley)	7-11	c/o (01291) 622486
KENIRY, L (A M Balding)	8-2	N M Adams
KENNEMORE, R (R Hollinshead)	7-12	c/o (01543) 490298
KEOGH, R (J A Osborne)	7-12	c/o (01488) 73139
KERSHAW, MISS L (Jedd O'Keeffe)	7-5	Alan Harrison
KILLORAN, R (A M Balding)	8-2	Simon Dodds
KINGSCOTE, R (R J Charlton)	8-2	Gavin Horne
KIRBY, A (M Wigham)	7-7	Keith Bradley
LAWES, N (R A Fahey)	7-0	c/o (01653) 698915
LAWLOR, G (N I M Rossiter)	8-11	c/o (01409) 231433
LAWSON, M (I McInnes)	8-2	A Harrison
LOVERIDGE, J (Roger Ingram)	9-0	c/o (01372) 748505
LUCEY-BUTLER, R (P Butler)		Dave Roberts
MACKAY, N (L M Cumani)	7-7	Mrs L H Way
MAKIN, P (T D Barron)	8-0	Mark Gilchrist
MARSHALL, MISS J (G L Moore)	8-5	N Allan
MARSHALL, S (N Richards)	9-2	Richard Hale
MATHERS, P (Alan Berry)	8-2	A Harrison
MAY, K (B W Hills)	7-6	(01488) 71548
MCCREERY, MISS D (Mr D. Carroll)	8-0	c/o (01759) 373586
MCDONALD, J (B. J. Meehan)	7-7	I P Wardle
MCGANN, D (D. W. Thompson)	9-0	J J Williams
MEDEIROS, A (B. W. Hills)	7-7	c/o (01488) 71548
MILCZAREK, MISS K (Miss J. Feilden)	7-12	John Ford
MILLS, R (R Guest)	8-0	c/o (01638) 661508
MITCHELL, MISS S (M J Polglase)	7-12	c/o (01636) 816717
MOORE, RORY (V. Smith)	7-11	Alan Harrison
MULLEN, A (K. A. Ryan)	7-12	Richard Hale
MULLINEAUX, MISS K (M Mullineaux)	8-7	(01829) 261440
MULRENNAN, P (M W Easterby)	8-4	Richard Hale
MUYA, H W (J. L. Dunlop)	7-4	c/o (01903) 882194
MYATT, MISS A L (P D. Evans)	7-0	c/o (01873) 890837
NEM, M (Polglase)	7-2	c/o (01636) 816717
NOLAN, DAVID (Ian Williams)	8-9	Gavin Horne
NOLAN, DEREK (J S Moore)	8-2	Gavin Horne
O'BRIEN, T (M Channon)	7-12	c/o (01635) 281166
O'HARA, S (C F Wall)	8-0	Bob Williams
O'NEILL, B (M Channon)	8-0	c/o (01653) 281166
O'REILLY, J (J O'Reilly)	8-2	c/o (01226) 711123
PARSONS, MISS A (J. S. Moore)	7-7	John Ford
PARSONS, S (M P Tregoning)	8-2	c/o (01488) 73300
PEIPPO, MISS K (B G Powell)	7-7	c/o (01488) 638433
PICKARD, MISS F (P C. Haslam)	7-7	A Harrison
PICKARD, P (J M Jefferson)	7-7	c/o (01653) 697225
PIERREPONT, K (John Balding)	8-7	A Harrison
PIKE, MISS L (W J Musson)	7-12	Richard Hunter
POLLI, N (M G Quinlan)	7-10	c/o (01638) 603530
POULTON, H (G L Moore)	8-10	c/o 01273 620405

Are your contact details missing or incorrect?
If so please update us by email:
simon.turner@mgn.co.uk
or leave a message on 0500 007071

JUMPS JOCKEYS

Riding weights and their contact details.
An Index of Agents appears on page 723

An Index of Agents appears on page 723

ASPELL, L.	10-0	N M Adams/(01903) 893323/(0797) 1675127
BATCHELOR, M.	10-0	Dave Roberts
BRADBURNE, M.	10-0	L R James/(01337) 810325 (07773) 327377
BUCHANAN, P.	10-0	Richard Hale
COYLE, A.	10-0	L R James
CROWLEY, B J.	10-0	Dave Roberts
CROWLEY, J.	10-0	Richard Hale/(01274) 564930
CULLOTY, J.	10-0	C D Broad
CUMMINS, L.	10-0	Dave Roberts
CURRAN, S.	10-0	W Adams
DEMPSEY, A.	10-0	Richard Hale/(01969) 622750
DENNIS, D.	10-0	C D Broad
DOBBIN, A.	10-0	Richard Hale
DOWLING, W.	10-0	Richard Hale
DOYLE, T.	10-0	Dave Roberts
DURACK, S.	10-0	Dave Roberts
ELSWORTH, D.	10-0	Richard Hale
FEHILY, N.	10-0	C D Broad
FENTON, B.	10-0	Dave Roberts
FITZGERALD, M A.	10-4	Dave Roberts/(01235) 751695/(07771) 768368
FLETCHER, L.	10-0	L R James
FLYNN, P.	10-0	Dave Roberts/(01782) 327697/(07803) 619968
FOLEY, M.	10-0	Dave Roberts/(07884) 054921
FOX, S.	10-4	W Adams
GALLAGHER, D.	10-0	Dave Roberts
GARRITTY, R.	10-7	G MacDonald
GERAGHTY, B.	10-0	Dave Roberts
GIBSON, B.	10-2	Richard Hale
GICQUEL, B.	10-0	c/o 00 33 6088 31272
GOLDSTEIN, J.	10-0	L R James
GREENE, R.	10-0	L R James/(01323) 509086
GRIFFITHS, P.	10-2	G Horne
HARDING, B.	10-0	Richard Hale
HARRIS, J.	10-0	(01458) 223922
HIDE, P.	10-0	L R James/(01903) 877323/(07768) 233324
HITCHCOTT, B.	10-0	Dave Roberts/(07881) 633099
HOBSON, R.	10-4	L R James
HOLLEY, P.	10-4	(01297) 553560
HOURIGAN, P.	10-0	(045) 530080
JOHNSON, K.	10-0	L R James
JOHNSON, R.	10-0	Dave Roberts
KEANE, V.	10-0	Richard Hale
KENIRY, F.	10-0	Richard Hale
LEE, G.	10-0	Richard Hale/(01642) 763500/(07885) 888020
LLEWELLYN, C.	10-3	C D Broad/(07236) 783223
MAGUIRE, J M.	10-0	Dave Roberts
MARSTON, W.	10-0	C D Broad/(01451) 821553/(07831) 664745
MCCARTHY, J.	10-0	L R James/(07860) 905017
MCCOY, A P.	10-0	Dave Roberts
MCGRATH, L.	10-0	P Forster
MCGRATH, R.	10-0	Richard Hale/(07775) 680895
MCNALLY, R.	10-0	L R James/(07958) 475171
MCNAMARA, J P.	10-5	Dave Roberts
MCPHAIL, O.	10-0	L R James
MOGFORD, J.	10-0	Dave Roberts/(01451) 810165/(07808) 799959
MOLONEY, P.	10-0	C D Broad
MOORE, J.	10-0	Dave Robers
MURPHY, T J.	10-0	C D Broad/(07866) 681565
O'MEARA, D.	10-0	Richard Hale
OLIVER, H.	10-0	c/o (0191) 373 5220

PROCTER, A	10-0	John Ford
RAFTER, C	10-0	L R James/(07919) 008041
RENWICK, K	10-0	Richard Hale
RICOU, J	10-0	00 33 6804 19253
ROSS, A	10-0	L R James
RUSSELL, D	10-5	Richard Hale
SCHOLES, A	10-0	Mrs Ruth Burchell
SCUDAMORE, T	10-0	Dave Roberts/(07809) 131121
SIDDALL, T	10-0	Dave Roberts
SLATTERY, V	10-0	(01242) 820907 or (07831) 545789
STRONGE, S	10-2	L R James/(07775) 727 778
STUDD, C	10-0	L R James
SUPPLE, G	10-0	L R James
THORNTON, A	10-2	Dave Roberts/(07831) 102065
THORNTON, R	10-0	Dave Roberts
TIZZARD, J	10-2	Dave Roberts
VERCO, D	10-4	Miss L V Davis (01785) 284371
VICKERS, L	10-0	L R James
WALSH, R	10-4	Jennifer Walsh
WHELAN, P	10-0	L R James
YOUNG, R	10-0	L R James

CONDITIONALS

Their employers and contact details.
An Index of Agents appears on page 723

ASPELL, P (B Rothwell)	9-7	Richard Hale
BAILEY, T (M G Quinlan)	10-0	John Ford
BERRIDGE, G (L Lungo)	10-0	Richard Hale/(01387) 840361/(07970) 041568
BERRIDGE, L (L Lungo)	9-7	c/o (01387) 840361
BEST, T (J A Geake)	10-0	Dave Roberts/(01264) 772278
BOLGER, C (Miss Suzy Smith)	9-9	N M Adams/(01273) 300127
BONHOFF, C (M C Pipe)	9-11	c/o (01884) 840715
BRENNAN, P (P J Hobbs)	9-9	C D Broad
BRIMBLE, A (A Crook)	9-7	(01969) 640303
BURKE, K (C Tizzard)	9-7	Dave Roberts
BURTON-PYE, T (P Haslam)	9-7	c/o (01969) 624351
BYRNE, J (H Daly)	9-9	Dave Roberts/(07974) 262246
CARENZA, G (Mrs S Smith)	10-0	L R James
CAREY, S (O Brennan)	9-4	c/o (01909) 473950
CARTER, N (J G M O'Shea)	9-7	Dave Roberts
CLARE, J (R Fahey)	10-0	c/o (01653) 698915
COOK, D (B Leavy)	9-7	c/o (01782) 398591
COOPER, E (Jonjo O'Neill)	10-0	c/o (01386) 277202
COSGRAVE, D (B De Haan)	9-7	L R James
COSTELLO, D (J J Quinn)	9-4	Richard Hale
CRAINE, S J (C Mann)	9-7	C D Broad
CROSSE, D (C Mann)	9-7	Dave Roberts/(07775) 920489
CRAWFORD S J (J Osborne)	9-2	L R James
CUMMINGS, R (D J Wintle)	9-7	c/o (01451) 850893
CURLING, S (N J Henderson)	9-7	Dave Roberts
DAVEY, P (R Buckler)	9-7	c/o (01308) 710772
DAVIDSON, J (Alan Swinbank)	10-2	c/o (01325) 377318
DAVIES, J (B G Powell)	9-7	Dave Roberts
DAYMAN, O (Dr P Pritchard)	9-7	c/o (01453) 811989
DEHDASHTI, E (G L Moore)	9-7	L R James
DIXON, M (G Harker)	9-7	c/o (01969) 116412
DOAB, J (Jonjo O'Neill)	10-0	c/o (01386) 584209
EDDERY, C (R Johnson)	9-12	L R James
ELLIOTT, S (J A Geake)	9-7	L R James
EVANS, A (N A Twiston-Davies)	10-0	C D Broad/(07789) 936986
FLAVIN, D (L Normile)	9-12	P Brierley
GAGAN, S (M Todhunter)	9-7	c/o (01539) 624314
GOLDSTEIN, M (N A Twiston-Davies)	9-7	C D Broad
GORDON, R (Richard Rowe)	9-7	Wayne Hardie
GRAY, J (J R Best)	9-7	c/o (01622) 880276
GROGAN, G (D McCain)	9-7	c/o (01829) 720352
HALLIDAY, J (R C Guest)	8-12	c/o (01913) 735220
HALLIDAY, T (Mrs S Smith)	9-10	c/o (01274) 564930
HANNITY, N (G A Harker)	10-2	Richard Hale
HAROLD, D (R C Guest)	9-3	c/o (01913) 735220
HONEYBALL, A (R H Buckler)	9-11	Dave Roberts
HONOUR, C (J D Frost)	9-12	L R James
HORNER, G (J R Cornwall)	9-4	c/o (01644) 444453
HURLEY, MISS C (R Ford)	9-7	c/o (01829) 760095
HUTCHINSON, W (A King)	9-11	C D Broad/(01793) 815009
JENKINS, J (H J Manners)	10-0	Dave Roberts
JOHNSON, S (D G Bridgwater)	9-10	c/o (01242) 609086
JONES, W (Jonjo O'Neill)	9-7	c/o (01386) 584209
KENNEDY, W (N Chance)	9-7	Dave Roberts
KING, F (J M Jefferson)	10-0	Richard Hale
KINGTON, J (M Scudamore)	9-7	c/o (01989) 750844
LAVERTY, D (L Dace)	9-7	L R James/(07905) 697061
LAWLOR, G (N I M Rossiter)	9-0	c/o (01409) 231433
LUCEY-BUTLER, R (P Butler)	9-7	Dave Roberts
MADDEN, P (Mrs S Smith)	9-7	c/o (01274) 564930

Name	Trainer	Weight	Contact
MALONE, T J (M C Pipe)		9-7	Dave Roberts
MARSHALL, MISS J (G L Moore)		8-4	c/o (01273) 620405
MARSHALL, S (Nicholas G Richards)		9-4	c/o (01768) 483392
MCCARTHY, W (T R George)		10-0	C D Broad
MCGANN, D (Miss Kariana Key)		9-2	J J Williams
MELLO, M (J R Upson)		10-0	Adam Waterworth
MERCER, K (Ferdy Murphy)		9-7	Richard Hale
MERRIGAN, P (Mrs H Dalton)		9-7	c/o (01952) 73032
MOORMAN, J (R C Guest)		9-7	c/o (01913) 735220
MULHOLLAND, N (F Murphy)		9-11	Richard Hale
MURRAY, C (T P McGovern)		10-0	L R James
NELMES, O (O M C Sherwood)		9-11	L R James
NICOLLS, M (P Webber)		9-7	L R James
NOLAN, D (Ian Williams)		9-7	G Horne
O'KEEFFE, A (Miss V M Williams)		9-11	Dave Roberts
O'NEILL, P (Miss V M Williams)		9-10	Dave Roberts
ORDE-POWLETT, B (M Harris)		9-7	L R James
OWEN, MISS Z (T R George)		9-7	(07866) 460939
PHELAN, T (Jonjo O'Neill)		9-7	Dave Roberts
POGSON, A (C T Pogson)		9-13	J Ford
POSTE, C (C W Moore)		9-7	G Horne
POULTON, H (G L Moore)		9-7	c/o (01273) 620405
PRITCHARD, J (R Dickin)		9-7	S C Turner/(01789) 450052
QUINTIN, J (P G Murphy)		10-2	c/o (01488) 648473
ROBSON, P (N G Richards)		10-0	Richard Hale
ROE, M (C Fairhurst)		10-0	c/o (01969) 622039
RYAN, J (Mrs S Smith)		9-7	c/o (01274) 564930
SESTON, M (J M Jefferson)		10-0	Richard Hale
SHARKEY, C (P F I Nicholls)		9-7	C D Broad
SPATE, R (R J Price)		9-7	L R James
STEPHENS, L (Miss V M Williams)		9-12	Mrs Ruth Burchell
STEPHENS, R (P Hobbs)		9-7	Dave Roberts
STEVENSON, J (Robin Dickin)		9-4	c/o (01789) 450052
STRINGER, P (Alan King)		9-0	L R James
STUDD, C (B G Powell)		9-4	c/o (01962) 717705
SWAN, D (M Chapman)		9-7	c/o (01673) 843663
THOMAS, G (R Ford)		9-12	Richard Hale
THOMAS, S (Miss V Williams)		10-0	Dave Roberts
THOMPSON, C D (M Todhunter)		9-7	c/o (01539) 624314
THORNTON, A P (J Howard Johnson)		9-7	c/o (01388) 762133
TINKLER A (N J Henderson)		9-11	Dave Roberts/(07812) 134077
TREADWELL, L (Miss V Williams)		9-7	Dave Roberts
UTLEY, R (Mrs K Walton)		9-9	c/o (01969) 622250
WALFORD, R (R Alner)		9-7	Dave Roberts
WALSH, B (K G Reveley)		9-7	c/o (01287) 650456
WALSH, S (Miss E C Lavelle)		9-7	L R James
WHARFE, B (T H Caldwell)		9-7	c/o (01565) 777275
WILEMAN, MISS S (C N Kellett)		9-7	c/o (01283) 226046
WILLIAMS, C R (P F Nicholls)		9-11	Dave Roberts/(07815) 774306
WORTHINGTON, W (Ian Williams)		10-0	C D Broad

Are your contact details missing or incorrect?
If so please update us by email:
simon.turner@mgn.co.uk
or leave a message on 0500 007071

AMATEUR RIDERS
Riding weights and contact details.
An Index of Agents appears on page 723

ADAMS, A R 9-0 ....
AITCHISON, S R 10-2 ....
AKEHURST, J N 9-6 ....
ALERS-HANKEY, D 11-9 .... (07811) 335979
ALEXANDER, A A 9-7 ....
ALEXANDER, J F 11-0 .... (0131) 3328850
ALLAN, MISS L 9-0 ....
ALLISON, MISS J 10-0 .... (01488) 73656
ALLMAN, MISS D 9-10 ....
ANGELL, D 10-0 ....
ARMITAGE, MISS A 9-0 ....
ARMSON, R 10-7 .... (01332) 865293
ARNOLD, MISS S N 8-10 ....
ARTHUR, F 9-10 .... (07815) 057729
AYRES, S M 9-7 ....
BAGGALEY, MISS C 8-6 ....
BAINES, G 9-7 ....
BALDOCK, M 10-0 .... (07796) 260429
BALDWIN, MISS L C 8-0 ....
BANDEY, R J 11-0 ....
BANKS, J B 8-10 ....
BARBER, M 10-2 .... Dave Roberts/
.... (01437) 763772/(07977) 778172
BARFOOT-SAUNT, G 10-7 ....
BARLOW, A M E 11-0 ....
BARLOW, J R 11-0 ....
BARNES, J 10-0 .... (07763) 384169
BARNETT, MISS A L 8-7 ....
BARR, F J A 9-10 ....
BARR, MISS V G 10-7 ....
BARRETT, RAY 9-7 ....
BARRETT, RICHARD 10-7 ....
BASHTON, MISS D M 8-3 ....
BASTIMAN, MISS R 9-7 .... (01423) 359397
BATES, LEE 10-5 .... (01429) 837087
BEDDOES, MISS S 9-0 .... c/o (01273) 620106
BELL, MRS D 7-7 ....
BENSTEAD, N R 10-12 ....
BERRY, A J 10-0 ....
BERRY, MRS M L 9-12 ....
BEST, JAMES 9-7 ....
BEST, MRS L A 10-0 ....
BEVAN, MISS A 8-7 .... (01531) 634846
BISHOP, T H B 10-7 ....
BISSESSUR, S 9-0 ....
BLISS, R K A 10-0 ....
BLOOM, N M 11-4 ....
BOEDER, MS A L 9-0 ....
BOLTON, MISS R M 8-4 ....
BOSLEY, MRS S 9-0 .. (01367) 820115/(07778) 938040
BOYD, MISS H L 7-10 ....
BOYNTON, J E 10-5 ....
BRADBURNE, MISS L 9-4 .... (01337) 810325
BRAITHWAITE, A J 10-0 ....
BRAMLEY, MISS F H 8-7 ....
BREWER, G C 10-12 .... (01653) 648166
BREWER, MISS L J 8-10 .... (07974) 765506
BRIDGES, MISS L H DOVETON 8-8 .. (01747) 852825
BRIGGS, M J 9-7 ....
BRINT, M 9-10 .... (01534) 481461

BRITTON, MISS M 8-12 ....
BROOKE, A D 10-3 ....
BROOKE, MISS L R 9-0 ....
BROTHERTON, MISS S 9-0 .... c/o (01653) 618620
BROWN, A C 9-7 .... (01544) 267322
BROWN, MISS F C 9-0 .... (01638) 577470
BROWN, MRS J 9-7 ....
BRYAN, MISS H G 8-12 ....
BRYANT, MISS M P 10-0 ....
BUCK, MISS J M 10-0 ....
BULL, MISS M J 9-0 .... (01636) 816717
BULL, P .... (01634) 235253
BURKE, MISS K A 8-7 ....
BURROWS, M 9-13 .... (07773) 317775
BURROWS, T J 9-7 ....
BURTON, R P L 10-10 .... (01743) 709697
BUXTON, J 11-0 ....
COLLINSON, R E 9-7 ....
CALLAGHAN, P G 9-7 ....
CALLAGHAN, S A 10-0 .... (01638) 664040
CAMPBELL, M T P 9-5 ....
CAREY, R D 10-10 ....
CARRY, P M 10-0 ....
CARTER, M R 10-0 ....
CASEY, MISS V 9-7 ....
CASSIDY, MISS S C 9-0 .... (07985) 296945
CAVE, MISS T C 9-0 ....
CHAHAL, A S 9-4 ....
CHARLES-JONES, A 10-0 .... (01993) 823265
CHAPMAN, N A B 10-0 ....
CHILTON, MISS K N 9-12 .... (01743) 741536
CLARK, MISS R L 10-4 ....
CLARK, R S 11-5 .... (01347) 810700/(07989) 805873
CLEARY, A 9-7 .... (01327) 860043
CLEMENTS, MISS H A 9-3 ....
CLUBB, MRS H 8-12 .... R Harrison
COE, A R 10-6 ....
COLE, O N I 10-6 ....
COLERIDGE, R J D 11-7 ....
COLES, T B P 10-6 ....
COLLIER, D G 9-7 ....
COLLIER, T JADE 8-2 ....
COLLINGTON, P M 9-0 .... (07946) 516070
COLLINS, C M P 9-0 ....
COLLINSON, R E 10-2 ....
COLTHERD, W S 11-0 ....
COOGAN, V L 10-4 ...... (01488) 73065/(07977) 236699
COOK, J R F 10-0 .... (01281) 690864
CORCORAN, MRS S L 9-10 ....
CORNFORTH, P J 11-7 ....
COTTLE, D G G 9-7 ....
COTTRILL, MISS V L 9-0 .... (01829) 760095
COURIER, MISS L A 9-0 ....
COURNANE, J K 10-2 ....
COWARD, MISS J M 9-3 ....
COWDREY, MRS M 9-7 ....
COWLEY, P E 10-4 .... (07775) 943346
CRAGGS, T G 9-0 .... (01740) 620239
CROSS, S P B 9-12 ....
CROW, A H 11-10 ....

CULLIGAN, K T 9-7 ....(01403) 700911
CULLOTY, MISS S L 9-0 ....(01235) 751507
CULLY, C J 9-12
CUMANI, MISS F 9-11 ....c/o (01638) 665432
CUMANI, MISS S D 9-6 ....c/o (01638) 665432
CUTHBERT, MISS H E 9-0 ....(01228) 560822
CUTHBERTSON, MISS K M 9-0
D'ARCY, MISS R E 8-0
DA SILVA, D B B 10-0 ....(01887) 830354
DAINTON, MISS D 8-10
DARMODY, MRS K L 8-4
DAVIDSON, J T 10-4
DAVIDSON, MISS R P 9-0 ....Richard Hale
DAVIES, C W 9-1
DAVIES, J J 10-9
DAVIES, J M A 9-7 ....(01635) 298210
DAWSON, C T 11-5
DEADY, M C 9-5 ....(01488) 73436
DEAKIN, A G 8-8
DEAN, P D 11-4
DE BEST, MRS I 8-7 ....(07836) 799919
DE FERRARI, MISS C 7-10
DENIEL, MISS A J 9-3 ....(0795) 1102441
DENNIS, T 10-5 ....(01288) 352849
DENVIR, G A J 9-0 ....(01608) 674492
DEWSE, MISS C H 9-7
DICKENSON, D J 10-7
DIMENT, J B 9-12 ......(01488) 638636/(07970) 015911
DOAK, MISS C A 8-10
DOBSON, S 9-7 ....A Harrison
DOCKER, J M 10-7
DODD, K 10-7 ....(01451) 850496
DONNELLY, MISS B P 10-3
DORAN, C G 9-13
DOWTY, H G 9-7
DOYLE, MISS S 8-0 ....(01488) 72223
DREAPER, J 10-5 ....Richard Hale
DREW, MISS P 8-7 ...(01954) 250772/(07986) 325921
DUARTE, A P 9-3
DUGUID, W A 9-7
DUNCAN, MISS J C 9-0 ....(01638) 663375
DUNSDON, D H 10-0 .....(01433) 277605/(07885) 110826
DURMAN, MISS S-J   8-5. c/o Jimmy Fox (01264) 850218
DURRANS, MISS J K 9-0
DYSON, MISS C 9-7..(01527) 821493/(0780) 3720183
DZIECIOLOWSKA, MISS T G 10-4
EDDERY, MRS S 9-0
EDE, A10-7..(01258) 817271
EDWARDS, D 10-2 ....(01643) 831549/(07811) 898002
EDWARDS, S J 10-7
EDWARDS, T W C 11-0
ELLIOTT, R J 10-0
ELLINGHAM, C 9-4
ELLIS, MISS J B 8-5 ....(07766) 256918
ELLIS, T J 10-7
ELLISON, MISS L L 8-2 ....(01653) 690005
ELLWOOD, M E 9-1
ELSEY, MISS A F 8-7
EMBIRICOS, MS A E 10-10
ENGLAND, D R 9-0
ENRIGHT, MRS M 8-7 ....(01273) 479183
EVANS, P 9-7 ....(07850) 752957
EVATT, D B 11-9
EWART, J P L 10-2 ....(07971) 857068
FAULKNER, T P 10-7 .(01633) 870769/(07813) 921316
FEILDEN, MISS J D 9-0
FERGUSON, MISS J M 8-5
FERGUSON, P K 9-6 ....(01953) 717224

FRENCH, MRS G 8-10
FINDLAY, A J 10-7
FISHER, MISS B J 9-0
FLOOD, MISS V M L 10-7 ....(01235) 835888/
                                                            (01488) 638636
FLYNN, MISS R E 9-4
FOLEY, MISS D M 8-4
FOLKES, MISS E 9-0 ....(01743) 741536
FOORD, B R 9-7
FORD, MRS C-A 9-7 ....(0976) 522768
FORD, K R 9-12 ....(01432) 820604
FOSTER, B R J P 10-7
FOSTER, MISS J E 8-4
FOX, MISS H 8-7
FRATER, MISS C R 7-12
FRIEZE, MISS A S 9-2
FROUD, H C 11-0
GAGAN, S P 9-7
GAISFORD, MISS S L 9-7 ....(01364) 642219/
                                                            (07890) 633323
GALLAGHER, B J 10-0
GALLAGHER, G R P 10-0
GALLAGHER, MISS L 9-10
GARDNER, MISS L J 9-12 ....(07971) 660190
GARNER, MISS A J 9-0
GARRETT, W G T 9-7
GASCOYNE, S 9-0
GEE, JAMES R 9-6
GEORGE, MISS E S 9-0
GIBSON, G E 10-9
GIBSON, L 9-7
GIBSON, MISS W 8-0
GILLIGAN, MRS V J 9-12
GILLON, C 10-12 ....Barrie Melrose
GLASS, C T 11-7
GLASSONBURY, A 9-3 ....(01364) 642267
GOAD, MS D J 8-4 ....(01273) 621303
GOLDIE, W O D 10-8
GOLDIE, G D 11-2
GOLLINGS, MRS J 9-0 ....(0507) 343204
GORDON, C E 11-0
GORDON, MRS J L 10-0
GORDON, R D 9-7
GORDON-WATSON, S E 10-0 ....(01273) 477173/
                                                            (07812) 525411
GOSCHEN, MISS A B 10-9 ....(07719) 611301
GOSWELL, S G 9-7 ....(01635) 298210
GRACEY-DAVISON, MISS G D 9-7
GRAINGER, MISS E 9-7 ....(01905) 381077
GRAHAM, MISS E E 8-5 ....(01635) 298210
GORMAN, M S 11-7
GRAHAM, SCOTT 9-7
GRAHAM, S J 10-2
GRAY, S R 10-12
GREEN, MISS R A 9-0 ....(01258) 817271
GREEN, R M 11-0 ....(01258) 817271
GREENALL, O C 10-5
GREENALL, HON T E 10-3 ....A Waterworth/
                                                            (07773) 771895
GREENWAY, D E 10-0 ....Griffiths, Miss L C 8-4

GRIME, MISS C A 9-0
GRISSELL, MISS H R A 9-7
GUILLAMBERT, MISS F I 8-0
GUNDRY, MISS P-A B 9-11 ....W Adams
GUNSTONE, MISS M J 9-5 ....(01488) 73007
HAIGH, MISS V 10-0 ....(01302) 710235

HALEY, J 9-7 ....(01969) 622289
HALL, G 9-0 ....(07956) 281440
HALL, MISS S K 9-0 ....
HALLIDAY, J L 8-12 ....
HAMILTON, L 10-10 ....
HAMILTON, MS S 8-4 ....
HAMMOND, M A 9-0 ....
HAMPTON, T J 9-10 ....
HAND, MRS A J 10-0 ....(01882) 855406
HANDLEY, MISS D M 10-4 ....(01428) 722528
HANDLEY, M J 10-7 ....
HANDLEY, J P 10-7 ....
HANLY, A F P 10-7 ....(01584) 874064
HANNA, MISS K L 9-5 ....(01638) 663375
HANNAFORD, MISS C 9-1 ....(01271) 858647
HANNAFORD, MISS J A 8-4 ....
HARBOUR, MISS E-J 9-5 ....
HARDING, THE HON MISS D M 9-2 ....
HARDISTY, G W 10-9 ....
HARLER, MISS S E 8-13 ....
HARRIS, MRS A 10-2 ....
HARRIS, G P 9-0 ....
HARRIS, J A 10-0 ....
HARRIS, M C M 10-10 ....
HARRIS, NEIL J 10-7 ....
HARRISON, MISS K C 8-4 ....Alan Harrison
HARRISON, S 9-0 ....
HARRISON, MISS T S 9-4 ....
HARVEY, M J 9-0 .....(01638) 66457/(01638) 662117
HARWOOD, MISS L J 8-7 ....(01798) 873011
HASLAM, B M R 10-10 ....c/o (01969) 624351
HATFIELD, MISS F J 9-7 ....
HAYNES, M Y 9-7 ....(01372) 722664
HAYNES, M F 9-5 ....(01793) 762437
HEARD, L 10-0 ....
HEARN, MISS P M 8-0 ....(01269) 850805/
                                                                        (07747) 056917
HENNESSY, MR R 10-0 ....(045) 521490
HICKS, L W 11-4 ....(07961) 1557720
HICKS-LITTLE, MISS E M 8-7 ....
HILL, M D 10-10 ....
HILL, MRS J M 9-0 ....
HILL, MISS V J 8-11 ....
HILLS, MRS K M 9-0 ....
HISLOP, MISS L 9-7 ....
HOCKLEY, MISS A L 9-2 ....
HODGE, MRS S A 9-7 ....
HODGES, R J 10-3 ....
HODGSON, MISS G 8-10 ....
HODSON, R K 9-0 ....
HOLLANDS, MISS J M 10-7 ....
HOLLEY, MRS D 8-0 ....
HOLMES, MISS J F 9-10 ....
HOPE, MISS A K 9-7 ....
HORN, MISS R A 10-0 ....
HORNER, MISS L V 9-3 ....(01235) 835888/
                                                                        (01488) 638636
HORSFALL, MISS L J 7-12 ....
HOWELL, MRS R 10-10 ....
HUGGAN, S T 10-8 ....
HUGHES, MISS J A 9-7 ....
HUGHES, R S 10-0 ....
HUGHES, S M 10-0 ....(01829) 760095
HUMPHREY, A R 10-10 ....
HURLEY, MISS C R 9-7 ....
HUTCHINSON, MISS A L 9-2 ....(01638) 577288
HUTCHINSON, D 9-2 ....(01372) 721490
HUTSBY, F A 11-0 ....(01789) 740241

ILLMAN, MISS R 9-0 ....(01428) 722528
IMELOV, E P 10-0 ....
IRVING, MISS H M O 10-0 ....
IRVING, S A 9-10 ....
JACOB, D A 9-10 ....
JACKSON, MISS T 9-7 ....
JACKSON, MRS V S 10-0 ....(01830) 530218
JAMES, MISS K A 9-2 ....
JARRETT, J H 10-5 ....
JARVIS, P J 10-0 ....
JEFFERSON, MISS N R 8-7 ....
JEFFORD, L D B 10-0 .(01884) 35839/(01884) 266320
JENKINS, M C 11-4 ....
JENKINSON, J 10-0 ....
JESSOP, MISS C 7-12 ....(01638) 667870
JEWELL, MISS K C 8-10 ....(01622) 842788
JEWETT, D J 11-0 ....(01768) 484649
JOHNSON, S M 9-7 ....
JOHNSON, P 10-9 ....(091) 2674464
JOHNSON HOUGHTON, MISS E A 9-7 ....
                                                    (01235) 850500/(07721) 622700
JOHNSON HOUGHTON, G F 10-7 ....
JONES, A M E 9-9 ....
JONES, D 11-0 ....(07831) 641434
JONES, MISS E J 9-3 ....Mrs Ruth Burchell
JONES, Q R 9-6 ....
KAVANAGH, W P J 9-7 ....Dave Roberts
KEDDY, MRS H E 8-2 ....(07710) 450982
KEITH, MISS L D 8-0 ....(01372) 721490
KELLEWAY, MISS S G 7-12 ....(01638) 664292
KEMP, D J 11-0 ....
KEMP, MISS E 9-0 ....
KENDALL, MISS B 9-5 ....
KENDALL, MISS L 10-0 ....
KENT, J N 10-4 ....
KERR, G R 11-1 ....
KESTER, C 9-7 ....
KINCHIN, H J 10-0 ....
KING, B A 9-10 ....L R James/(01865) 361260
KING, J A 9-9 ....(01974) 640532
KING, J J 9-12 ....(01403) 700911
KING, N B 10-12 ....
KING, MRS M J 9-0 ....
KINGTON, J R 9-0 ....
KINNON, N C 10-0 ....
KINSELLA, P D 9-10 ....(07970) 673351
KIRKBRIDE, P 8-0 ....
KIRKPATRICK, P J 12-0 ....
KNAPP, MISS L A 9-0 ....
KNOTT, A C W 10-7 ....
KWIATKOWSKI, J W 11-8 ....
LAWLESS, J A 9-9 ....
LEAHY, MISS S. J. 8-8 ....(063) 90676
LAMB, MISS S K 9-7 ....(01665) 720251
LANGLEY, R G 10-4 ....(07866) 532722
LE BROCQ, J 9-13 ....(01534) 481461
LEON PENATE, E 9-6 ....
LEWIS, D W 9-10 ....
LEWIS-PRICE, MISS D A 9-0 ....(01488) 72324
LEWIS, MISS H M 9-2 ....
LIDDIARD, MRS S A 8-10 ....(07887) 991292
LIDSTER, C 9-0 ....
LILLY, MISS Z E 8-12 ....
LINDSAY, T M 10-9 ....
LITTMODEN, MISS E P 9-2 ....(01638) 663375
LLEWELLYN, J L 10-5...(0685) 841259/(0685) 843467
LLOYD, MISS N E 10-10 ....
LOUGHRAN, R 10-0 ....(045) 521490

LOWE, D J 9-7.....................................
LUFF, D 11-0.....................................(01934) 733341
LURCOCK, MR J 10-9...........................
LUND, B V 10-0.................................
MACDONALD-WAGSTAFFE, M 8-12.......
MACKLEY, M R 10-4............................
MACLEAN, MISS S L 8-10.....................
MACTAGGART, J 11-07........................(01450) 860314
MANN, P R 10-4.................................
MANN, MRS S M 9-3......... c/o (01488) 73118/71717
MANSELL, D 10-4................................
MANSER, MRS K 8-5............................
MARCH, J 9-7.....................................
MARSHALL, MISS J E 8-12....................
MARTIN, C J 8-12...............................
MARTIN, L 8-12..................................
MASKILL, A P 9-6...............................
MASON, P W 10-12.............................
MASTORAS, C 9-10.............................
MAXSE, J J I 9-12...............................
MACTAGGART, J 11-07........................(01450) 860314
MCALISTER, M J 10-2...........................Richard Hale/
............................(01387) 840361/(0774) 5954000
MCCARTHY, DR H 9-12........................
MCCARTHY, MISS M A 9-4.....................
MCCAUL, R M 9-2...............................
MCCAVANA, C 10-0.............................(01488) 71411
MCCOURT, T M 9-6....(01235) 867453/(01451) 850182
MCCUBBIN, D 10-0....(01748) 825272 (07970) 982338
MCGEORGE, SD 9-5.............................(01638) 663375
MCGLINCHEY, B J 10-0.........................
MCHUGH, S S 11-0..............................(07904) 089322
MCINTOSH, MISS L S 8-7.......................
MCKEE, N B 10-0................................
MCKENNA, D A 10-7............................
MCKIM, B L 10-2.................................
MCKIM, MISS N A 9-7...........................
MCLAUGHLIN, W 10-0...........................(01515) 200299
MCSHANE, J A 9-4...............................
MEAD, J H 10-8..................................
MEAKINS, MISS A M 10-0......................
MERRIAM, A G L 11-7..........................
MESSENGER, C B 9-0...........................
MESSENGER, T H 9-7...........................(07977) 279026
METCALFE, MISS C 10-0.......................(0191) 3736277
MICHAEL, CAPT A H L 10-10..................
MIDDLETON, A 11-0.............................
MILLMAN, P R 8-12.............................(01884) 266620
MILNE, MISS C P 9-0............................(01403) 700911
MINTON, MISS R P 9-7..........................
MITCHELL, N R 11-4.............................(01258) 880633
MOLLHALL, MRS S 9-7.........................(01638) 668503
MOONEY, MISS C R 10-0.......................
MOORE, MISS H J 9-10.........................
MOORE, MRS N 9-0..............................
MOORE, MRS S J 8-0............................(01488) 648822
MOORE, N P 10-7................................
MOORE, R V 9-7..................................
MOREAN, MR J 10-0............................(01403) 700911
MORGAN, J J 9-7.................................(01403) 700911
MORGAN, L 9-7...................................(07813) 944107
MORGAN-EVANS, R D E 9-12.................
MORGAN-MURPHY, MISS Z M 9-8............
MORLEY, J 9-7....................................
MORRIS, MISS G 9-0.............................
MORRIS, MRS M A 8-10........................(01400) 273930/
............................(07702) 719902
MORRIS, R C 9-0.................................

MORRIS, S W 10-7...............................(07771) 922808
MOULSON, L M F 9-3............................(07789) 681512
MUIR, J F W 12-0.................................
MULHALL, MRS C A 10-9.......................
MULHALL, MRS S M 9-0.........................(01904) 691510
MULLINEAUX, MISS M J L 8-7..........(01829) 261440
MURPHY, B 10-0.................................
MURPHY, M 11-9.................................
MUSGRAVE, C B 10-2...........................
NASH, J 10-7......................................(086) 8259787
NAYLOR, MISS K S 8-10.........................
NEALE, B 10-0.....................................(01905) 381077
NEEDHAM, MRS F E 9-7.........................(01638) 750546
NEWBOLD, J D 10-0..............................(01327) 361733
NEWMAN, E 9-0...................................
NEWNES, L A 9-3.........R T Harrison/(07879) 630324
NOSWORTHY, MISS C C 8-5....................(07971) 106044
O'BRIEN, MISS D J E 9-5........................
O'BRIEN, T J 9-7..................................Dave Roberts
O'DONOGHUE, D E 9-0..........................(07900) 477863
O'KEEFFE, A CH 9-5.............(01969) 622289/625006/
............................(0776) 1106485

O'NEILL, MISS C J 9-7...........................
OWEN, MRS C E 10-0............................
OWEN, MRS E J 8-0...............................
OWEN, J P 10-4...................................
OWEN, MRS S J 8-9..............................
PAGE, A 10-12....................................(01638) 664669
PAGE, D J 10-0....................................
PAINTER, D W 10-0..............................
PATTINSON, M I 8-12............................(01372) 748800
PAYNE, PIP 9-7....................................(07850) 133116
PAYTER, L R 9-7...................................(01327) 860043
PEARCE, S 7-10...................................(01638) 664669
PEARCE, N A 9-10................................
PEARSON, K D 10-0..............................
PEARSON, M J 9-7................................
PEBODY, D M 9-7.......(01295) 750807/(07909) 834113
PEIPPO, MISS K L 8-0............................
PELTELL, S A 9-12................................Wayne Hardie
PEMBERTON, J 9-7...............................Wayne Hardie
PEOPLES, B O 9-10...............................
PERRY, MISS S J 9-0.............................
PETERS, J F 9-0...................................
PETTITT, N J 10-0.................................
PEWTER, G R 10-2...............................
PHILLIPS, N J 10-10..............................
PHIZACKLEA, MISS S J 9-0.....................
PICKARD, MISS F I 8-0..........................
PIDCOCK, MISS D M 7-8........................
PITMAN, MISS T 8-0.............................
PLEDGE, MISS J A 8-8...........................(01638) 663371
POOLES, R L 10-0.......(01488) 73032/(07977) 099953
POWELL, MISS J 10-0............................
POWELL, MRS R A 9-0...........................
PRENDERGAST, K M 9-10.......................
PRICE, A S O 9-5..................................(07771) 608475
PRICE, MRS C J 9-4..............................
PRICE, MISS V J 9-7.............................
PRITCHARD-GORDON, P A 10-5..............
PRITCHARD, J M 11-0...........................
PRITCHARD, DR P L J 9-9..............(01453) 811881/
............................(01453) 811989

PRITCHARD, MISS S 9-0.........................
PROCTER, MISS S 8-7............................
PURDY, MISS A. J. 9-0..........................(01823) 350311/
............................(07970) 803706
QUAYLE, MISS K G 8-0...........................(01235) 835888

QUINTIN, J S 9-7 ....
QUIRK, S P 10-7 ....
RAMSAY, W B 11-10 ....
RAMSDEN, MISS E L 8-7 ....c/o (01845) 587226
RANKIN, MISS D 8-5 ....
RAVENSCROFT, D J 11-0 ....
REES, J 9-12 ....(01635) 281678
REES, MISS J M 9-0 (01488) 639100/(07881) 821500
REES, S P 8-10 ....(01638) 577470
RENNEY, D J 11-5 ....
RENWICK, MISS S L 8-0 ....
RICH, W D 9-11 ....
RICHARDSON, J A 10-4 ....(0498) 584711
RIDING, MISS J E 9-0 ....
RIMELL, M G 10-7 ... (01451) 820819/(07778) 648303
ROCKEY, MISS K C 9-8 ....(01743) 741536
ROBERTS, MRS M S 9-7 ....(01305) 761745/
(07803) 752831
ROBINSON, S C 12-0 ....
ROBINSON, MISS S E 9-7 ....
ROBINSON, S J 11-0 ....
ROBSON, MISS P 9-3 ....(01830) 530241,
(01484) 608000/(07721) 887489
RODDA, M G 10-0 ....
RODDICK, MISS C 9-7 ....(0773) 4543439
ROGERS, R J 11-2 ....
ROSS, R B 10-7 ....
ROSS, S I 10-5 ....
ROTHERY, MISS A C 7-5 ....
ROWSELL, MRS L A 10-0 ....(07814) 148932
RUSSELL, MISS K 10-0 ....
RUSSELL, W 9-1 ....
RUTTY, MISS L A 8-0 ....(01969) 640330
SAINT, M C 8-4 ....
SALAMAN, M B 10-0 .. (01672) 541048/(01488) 72324
SANDERCOCK, MISS M-A 8-2 ....
SANSOME, A D 11-2 ....
SANTANA, K 10-0 ....
SAVILLE, N S 10-7 ....
SAWYER, MISS S J 9-6 ....
SCALES, M N 9-7 ....
SCHERER, MISS M J 9-0 ....(07740) 255588/
(01302) 539090/(01638) 661999
SCOTT, MISS E L 9-0 ....
SCRASE, MRS A M 8-10 ....
SEARBY, MISS K E 9-7 ....
SHARRATT, MISS S 10-4 ....(07966) 467879
SHAW, B T 10-10 ....
SHEEN, MISS L J 9-0 ....(07788) 122942
SHELDRAKE, P G 9-7 ....
SHERWOOD, MISS S I 10-0 ....
SIMMS, D A 9-10 ....
SIMPSON, MISS V J 10-0 ....
SKIDMORE, MISS N E 8-4 ....
SMART, MRS V R 9-0 (01845) 597481/(07780) 673520
SMITH, MISS A J 9-7 ....
SMITH, MISS K L 8-7 ....
SMITH, M J J 10-0 ....
SMITH, M K 10-0 ....
SMITH, N M 9-7 ....
SNOWDEN, J E 10-8 ....
SOARES, N M 8-10 ....
SOLE, J D 10-0 ....
SOUTHCOMBE, MISS W L 8-5 ....(0797) 1225621
SOWERBY, MISS M N 8-10 ....(01635) 298210
SPEARING, MISS T S 9-7 ....(01789) 772639
STEARN, R R P 10-6 ....
STEDMAN, MISS A C 9-0 ....

STEPHENS, MISS V A 10-0 ....
STIRLING, MISS N C 10-0 ....
STOCK, MS L J 10-0 ....
STOKES, MISS S-J 7-0 ....
STONE, MISS T N 10-0 ....
STOREY, C 10-0 ...... (01573) 420615/(07976) 587315
STOREY, N J 9-7 ....Richard Hale
STRATTON, MISS J A 7-5 ....
STUCLEY, MISS C C 9-7 ....
STURGIS, MISS V C 9-0 ....
SWAN, MISS G T 8-13 ....
SWEETLAND, M S 10-5 ....
SWINSWOOD, A 9-7 ....
TATE, R T A 10-7 ....(01937) 835774
TATE, J J S 10-8 ....(01937) 836036
TATE, DR M P 10-5 ....
THOMAS, T N 8-4 ....(01638) 664348
THOMPSON, MRS C A 9-0 ....(01483) 200135/
(0836) 205579
THOMPSON, M 10-6 ....(01665) 76272
THOMPSON, T W 10-0 ....
THOROGOOD, MISS G M 9-0 ....
TIERNEY, R R 9-0 ....
TIZZARD, MISS C A 9-7 ....(01258) 817271
TOMPSETT, MISS I G 10-0 ....
TORY, MISS E C 10-5 ....
TRICE-ROLPH, J C 11-2 ....
TROTTER, R J 10-0 ....(07802) 427351
TUCK, MISS E J 8-10 ....
TUCKER, MISS E A 9-7 ....
TUCKER, MISS J L 8-4 ....
TUDOR, J E 10-0 ....
TUMELTY, G A 9-7 .... C D Broad
TUNNICLIFFE, MISS V C 9-3 ....
TURBUTT, MISS K L 9-0 ....
TURNER, MISS A L 9-0 ....(07939) 585 526/
(01664) 464 351
TURNER, D I 9-5 .... (01722) 337399/(07768) 094908
TURNER, MISS F K 9-0 ....(07788) 541106
TUTTY, N D 10-11 ....(01609) 883624
VAUGHAN, T E 10-12 ....
VERBURG, MS E J L 9-7 ....
VOLLARO, M L 8-7 ....
WADLOW, A G 10-10 ....
WAKEHAM, R T H 10-0 ....(0771) 697452
WALLACE, MISS A 8-4 ....Wayne Hardie
WALEY-COHEN, S B 10-5 ....(07887) 848425/
(0131) 440 2309
WALFORD, M T 10-7 (01653) 648166 (07734) 265687
WALKER, N M 9-7 ....(01638) 663375
WALKER, S A 9-7 ....
WALL, M J 9-10 ....
WALLACE, MISS A L 8-5 ....(07721) 785503
WALLING, MISS K-J 9-3 ....
WALSH, J P 9-4 ....
WATERS, T 9-7 ....(01634) 668088
WALTON, A E 9-7 ....(01400) 50531
WARD, L C 9-0 ....
WARD, MISS S M 10-2 ....
WARING, MISS J L 8-9 ....(01969) 640330
WARREN, S M 9-0 ....
WATSON, MAJOR M R 11-2 ....
WATTERSON, S T 9-10 ....
WAUGH, A R G 11-7 ....
WEBB, MISS D F 9-0 ....
WEBB-BOWEN, COL R I 11-7 ....
WEBSTER, MISS H J 9-5 ....(01638) 668115
WEEKES, D T 9-0 ....(07977) 599596

WELLS, MISS L C 8-6 ....
WEST, MISS S 10-0 ....
WHARFE, MRS P 9-7 .... (01565) 777275
WHEELER, G F 11-7 ....
WHILLANS, E A 9-9 .... Richard Hale
WHILLANS, G D 8-7 ....
WHITE, J A 9-8 ....
WILLIAMS, O R 10-4 ....
WICKENS, MISS J H 9-2 ....
WIGLEY, G J 10-7 ...... (01903) 872226/(07790) 614037
WILESMITH, M. C. 10-9 .... (01531) 890410/
(07768) 431894
WILKINSON, MRS D S 7-7 ....
WILLEY, J P 9-0 ....
WILLIAMS, MS C A 8-12 .... Alan Harrison
WILLIAMS, C R P 9-7 .... (07815) 774306
WILLIAMS, D F 9-7 ....
WILLIAMS, MISS J C 8-10 ....
WILLIAMS, N 9-7 .... Dave Roberts

WILLOUGHBY, GUY N J 10-4**WILMOT-SMITH, MISS J
B** 9-2 ....
WILSON, MISS D Y 8-6 .... (01242) 519008
WILSON, MISS F 9-0(01642) 784587**WILSON, MRS N
C** 8-13 .... (01759) 368249
WILSON, N 11-0 .... (01759) 368249
WINTLE, A A 11-0 .... (07767) 351144
WISE, MISS F C R 9-10 .... (01296) 655255
WITHEFORD, C W 9-11 ....
WOOD, MISS K M 9-7 ....
WOODHOUSE, B R 11-7 ....
WOODMAN, MISS R E 8-7 .... (01903) 871421
WOODSIDE, T F 8-10 ....
WOOLLACOTT, R M 10-0 ....
WORMALL, MISS J 9-7 ....
WORTHINGTON, W A 9-9 ....
YOUNG, A 10-0 ....
YORK, P 10-4 .... (01372) 457102/(07774) 962168
YOUNG, MISS S E M 10-0 ....

NOTES

NOTES

NOTES

THE
HOLIDAYS
SURVIVAL
GUIDE

THE HOLIDAYS SURVIVAL GUIDE

Jim Eldridge

Illustrated by David Mostyn

BEAVER BOOKS

A Beaver Book
Published by Arrow Books Limited
62–5 Chandos Place, London WC2N 4NW

An imprint of Century Hutchinson Ltd

London Melbourne Sydney Auckland
Johannesburg and agencies throughout the world

First published 1989

Set in Century Schoolbook
by JH Graphics Ltd, Reading

Printed and bound in Great Britain by
Courier International Ltd, Tiptree, Essex

ISBN 0 09 965620 5

CONTENTS

INTroDUCTION

This book is to show you how to survive holidays. All sorts of holidays: holidays by the seaside when the weather's terrible; holidays when your parents insist on dragging you around ancient ruins and art galleries; holidays where you get sent to stay with terrible relatives who don't like you; holidays where you just stay at home and try to avoid getting lumbered with doing all the heavy housework (like cleaning the kitchen floor, or washing up, or vacuuming).

If you've ever been in that sort of situation, then buy this book NOW, and it need never happen to you again!

HOLidays ABROAD

Holidays abroad are great, providing you go somewhere really hot and sunny and you can lie on the beach all day and eat ice cream. But how often are you allowed to do this? Hardly ever! And why? Because your adult(s) will insist on taking you 'Sight-Seeing'! And when you point out that you can Sight-See perfectly well while lying on the beach, they just force you into your clothes and drag you off with them!

If you are in Italy, for example, this often means being taken to look at a pile of old broken rocks, which your adults will tell you are the remains of a Roman building. Your witty quip — 'If that's how bad their buildings were, no wonder the Roman Empire collapsed' — will just get you stern looks and, if there are other tourists in the area, a hand over your mouth to stop you saying any more.

So, here is how to deal with Sight-Seeing Abroad:

RULE 1: It is easier to get out of something if you don't get into it in the first place. In this case, that means Not Going To Wherever It Is Your Parents Want To Take You.

If this fails and you are dragged off there, then Rule 2 applies:

RULE 2: Cause havoc and upset for all concerned once you get to the Sight to See. This will make sure your family do not take you to it, or anything similar, again.

We can now look at how to apply rules 1 and 2 in specific countries:

France

France is full of places called Chateaux. These are enormous palaces about 100 kilometres long, which take about ten days to walk around. They are full of boring paintings of all the people who used to live there since the year dot, old suits of armour and velvet chairs that you aren't allowed to sit on. They also have enormous gardens about the size of London, full of plastic flowers (at least they look as if they're plastic) which you're not

allowed to touch or even breathe on. These places cost trillions and trillions of francs to run, which is why they charge you a fortune to go in. Frankly, they are to be avoided at all costs, but adults insist on going to look at them because they are of 'historical interest'.

So, here is how to deal with Chateaux Sight-Seeing:

RULE 1: *(Getting out of going)*

- 'All those flowers in the gardens will affect my hay fever.'

- 'I might break something.'

- 'They're so big we might not find our way out again. I heard of a family who went into one and were found still wandering around, lost, three years later.'

- 'I don't think it's a good idea for me to be taken to a place where the rich lived in luxury while outside the poor starved to death. I think it shows very bad taste.'

- 'I heard the woman in the Tourist Office tell someone else that it shuts on Wednesdays (or Saturdays, or Tuesdays, or whichever day your parents intend to go).'

- 'We've already seen a Chateau. They're all the same; see one, you've seen them all.'

RULE 2: *(Being a nuisance once you get there)*

- Knock on the suits of armour and call 'Anyone in there?'

- Comment loudly on how tired you are (e.g. 'My feet hurt'). When your family continue to ignore you (as they will) sit down on one of the velvet chairs. This will lead to all of you being thrown out.

- Drop marbles on the floor. The floors of Chateaux are so highly polished that your marbles will travel for ages and it will take the attendants and your family hours to find them all.

- As the floors are so highly polished, and the rooms so long, use them as a slide.

Italy

Italy is where the Romans came from, and you can see why. If you lived there you'd go somewhere else as well. Most of it is full of old ruined Roman Remains, and it is to these that your adult will insist on dragging you, instead of letting you lie somewhere nice and sunny on a beach. Nearly all Roman Remains have a Roman Bath, which is just like a small swimming pool filled with dirty hot water. Why adults feel they need to go and look at this is baffling. For a lot less money they could go into their own bathroom after one of their children has had a bath and look at water that is a lot hotter and a lot dirtier.

Italy is also full of ancient tombs, where dead Romans are buried. (See why they're called Roman Remains?) Why on earth people should want to spend their holidays in a sunny country wandering around old graveyards is impossible to understand, but that is what some adults want to do.

To avoid Roman Remains here's what to say and do:

Tombs

RULE 1

- 'I don't want to go and look at a load of dead people.'

- 'There will be ghosts there.'

- 'We could catch some ancient Roman disease.'

- 'You won't let me watch horror films but now you want me to go and look at real skeletons! You're potty!'

- 'I've heard that these tombs are in tunnels and are like underground mazes. We might get lost in them.'

- 'This will be a horrifying experience for me and I could end up suffering from nightmares.'

RULE 2

- If you see a skeleton or a mummy (the sort that's wrapped up in old cloth, not your mother) give out a piercing scream, and faint.

- Keep saying things like, 'I saw that one move.'

- Keep complaining: 'I think this is a very disrespectful thing to do, walking around looking at people's tombs. We should respect the dead.'

- Say loudly, 'These graves are thousands of years old. Haven't they got any new ones?'

- Say loudly, 'I hear that all these people died of Bubonic Plague. Did you know that Bubonic Plague germs live for over two thousand years?'

Other Roman Ruins
(including **Roman Baths**)

RULE 1

- 'What do we need to go and look at a pile of broken bricks for?'
- 'My teacher says all Roman Ruins are haunted by terrible spirits who seek revenge on anyone who disturbs their rest by visiting these places.'
- 'One of us might fall in the Roman Bath and drown. And I've heard of several cases of people catching terrible diseases from the water.'

RULE 2

- 'I reckon these are fake ruins. We've been conned.'
- 'Did a load of Roman football supporters do all this damage?'
- 'Something moved in that water! It looked like a monster!'

(*See also* GREECE *for further excuses.*)

Greece

Greece is also full of old ruins, even more than Italy. The parts that aren't full of old ruins are full of huge, broken statues of the Greek Gods and Goddesses who used to live in the old ruins. In between the old ruins and the statues are the goats. See one old ruin, one broken statue, and a goat, and you have seen all there is to see of Greece.

However, adults, being as gullible as ever, will insist on dragging you all over the country looking at even more ruins, statues and goats. If they want to do that and wear their feet out, fine, but if they insist on dragging young people along with them *this has to be put a stop to*. For one thing, you owe it to your adults to prevent them from being fooled. (After all, in reality no country can have that many old ruins and broken statues. We support the theory that there is really only one ruin and one statue, and that they are trundled around Greece on wheels during the night so that tourists pay to go and look at them somewhere different the next day, and think they are looking at a new lot of ruins.)

RULE 1

- 'I think it would be dangerous to go there. The ruins look as if they could fall down any moment and harm us.' (To this your adults will reply: 'Nonsense, they've been standing there for thousands of years.' There is only one sensible answer to this: 'In that case they are even more dangerous than I thought. They will definitely collapse tomorrow.')

- 'It is against my religion to visit those statues of Pagan Gods and Goddesses.'

RULE 2

- If one of the statues is of an animal (e.g. a lion), climb on its back and shout, 'Hi Ho, Silver!' or 'Yoicks, tally-ho.'

- Say loudly, 'All these statues are broken! We ought to demand our money back.'

Switzerland

When you get to Switzerland you will notice that there is a marked lack of sun, sand and sea in the area. This is because you have been taken there by your adults under False Pretences. Any thoughts of surfing in Switzerland will have to be pushed to the back of your mind, because Switzerland Does Not Have A Sea. You will therefore be forced to go Sight-Seeing, and the best you can hope for if you manage to get out of it is to lie by the hotel or camp-site swimming pool. (Don't try the lakes – they're freezing.)

What Switzerland has a lot of is mountains, especially The Alps. This is what your adults have come to Sight-See – a load of mountains. And not content with looking at them from the bottom, they will insist on climbing up them to the top. And what will they see when they get to the top? Another mountain. All pretty pointless, isn't it? So, here is how to deal with such a predicament:

RULE 1

- 'It's cold up there.'

- 'There's no oxygen up there. I won't be able to breathe properly.'

- 'I hear that the Abominable Snowman is in these mountains. I think it'd be dangerous to go up there in case we met it.'

16

- 'There was an avalanche in those mountains last week, and they reckon there'll be another one any moment now.'

- 'We might fall off.'

- 'We haven't got the right equipment. I saw this television programme and they said that people who go up mountains need ropes and axes and things, otherwise they're risking their lives.'

- 'The weather forecast said there's a mist due to come down and no one should go out on a mountain in weather like that.'

RULE 2

Actually there is not a lot you can do when you are halfway up a mountain. Not safely, anyway. So the best thing to do under Rule 2 is to complain constantly. Here are some helpful suggestions:

- 'How far is it now?'

- 'My legs ache.'

- 'I'm getting dizzy from lack of oxygen.'

The trouble is, it's difficult to keep up a constant stream of complaints while you're walking up a mountain because you run out of breath, so in the end your adult wins. The best thing to do, therefore, is make sure you don't go in the first place. If your adults tell you that you're all going to have a fun family holiday swimming in the Swiss Alps, *you have been warned,* this is a Con Trick. Catch measles and stay at home watching TV instead.

17

Spain

Spain is wonderful because it's very sunny (usually). All that sun, sand, and warm sea to swim in – just what you and your family need for a really good holiday – you'd think. But you'd be wrong. Your adults have other ideas. They will want to go as far away from the sea as possible right into the middle of a huge city slap bang in the middle of the country and look at it. Why? Because they are idiots. Here is how to avoid getting involved in such idiocy:

RULE 1

- 'Did you know that the traffic fumes in these Continental cities are more poisonous than at home? The lead in the petrol and the fumes from the diesel could damage me permanently.'

- 'They've got the same shops there as they have at home. It's a waste of money to come all the way here and then do the same things we do at home.'

- 'We'll get lost. They only speak Spanish in the cities so we'll never find our way out.'

- 'They have bullfighting in Spanish cities. As a member of the RSPCA, the League Against Cruel Sports and the Vegetarian Society I couldn't possibly support such a thing – and going to that city would be giving my support to it.'

- 'Do you know how high the poverty and homelessness rate is in Spanish towns? Do you really want to expose us to such misery and ruin our holiday?'

- 'We might get mugged and lose all our money.'

RULE 2

- Complain constantly: (e.g. 'My feet hurt', 'It's so hot I can't breathe', etc).

- Keep asking what the time is, and when you are leaving.

- Point out horrible things: (e.g. 'Oh, look, isn't that a dead dog/pigeon in the gutter?')

- Say that the traffic is too frightening for you to dare to cross any road.

- Embarrass your adults by trying to talk in terrible Spanish, very loudly.

North Africa (Morocco, Tunisia, etc)

Just like Spain, North Africa is great because it is hot. The beaches are huge with proper sand, and the sea is warm. Ideal, you would think, for a holiday. But what do adults do? Do they want to sit on the beach and relax and swim and things? No they do not. Instead they insist on going huge distances inland and walking around markets full of snake charmers and people selling baskets.

As if they couldn't do the same thing at home (except for the snake charmers). Even worse, they also insist on going out into the desert, usually the Sahara.

Now one thing that any young person with half a brain could tell an adult about the desert is this: it doesn't have any sea with it. Sand by the lorryload, yes, but the nearest bit of sea is usually about twenty-seven days' camel ride away. What is the point of going on holiday with all that sand, but no sea? You might just as well spend two weeks in a sand factory.

So, in order to make sure that you spend your North African holiday where you should (i.e. by the sea), here's what to say and do:

Sight-seeing trip to a local market

RULE 1

- 'One of the snakes might bite us.'

- 'Those places are full of thieves. We could have all our money and belongings stolen.'

- 'We might get kidnapped.'

- 'Everyone knows you get cheated in those markets.'

- 'These markets have all kinds of dangerous germs and diseases floating around in them. We could catch something and be ill in bed for the rest of our holiday.'

- 'These old markets are built in mazes. We might get lost and never get out again.'

RULE 2

- Say you'll buy everything; then point at your parents and say, 'They're paying.'

- Fall against a stall and knock something over, which your adult will then have to pay for.

- Scream, hold your leg and yell, 'Something's just bitten me!'

- Say loudly, 'I'm sure that man's a wanted criminal. I'm sure I've seen his face on a police "Wanted" poster back home.'

- Ask a stallholder (making sure your adult is near enough to hear): 'Do you have any stolen ancient valuables for sale? I want to buy a pyramid.'

A trip to the desert

RULE 1

- 'It's so hot in the desert we could fry to death.'

- 'We might get attacked by a camel.'

- 'We might get taken prisoner, like in the films.'

- 'We might get lost.'

- 'We might get caught in a sandstorm.'

- 'People have sunk in that sand and never been seen again. It could happen to us.'

- 'I hear they've been testing nuclear weapons in that desert, and it's been declared a danger area because of the radiation.'

RULE 2

- Faint 'due to the heat', and have to be carried everywhere by your adult.

- Keep saying, 'I can see a mirage!' Then, when they all look, say, 'Oh no it isn't. Sorry.'

- As soon as you reach the desert, fall to your knees and cry out, 'Water! Water!'

- Say loudly, 'Well, this beach looks okay, but where's the sea?'

No, General is not a country. Here we look at a typical holiday problem that is the same (well, similar anyway) in all the above countries plus a few more that haven't been mentioned.

Visiting Art Galleries and Museums

Sooner or later your adult will turn a corner, lead you up some wide stone steps on the pretext of taking you somewhere exciting, and you will find

yourself in an Art Gallery or a Museum. Argh! As if you don't suffer enough of this at home, what with your school dragging you along to such places, you now have to suffer it while you're supposed to be on holiday enjoying yourself. And this time it's going to be in a foreign language!

Because adults are getting wise to young people's aversions to Art Galleries and Museums, they tend not to alert them in advance when they plan one of these trips. It can therefore be difficult to use Rule 1 (getting out of going). However, there are tell-tale signs that adults betray. These include looking at maps of whichever city you are in and marking places on it. Check if you see them doing this. If the place they have just marked is called something like a musée, museo, or Kunstgallerie, then apply Rule 1 immediately:

RULE 1

- 'It's odd, you know, but lately I've started to have this overpowering urge to punch paintings. It started to happen at school last term. That's why they've banned me from going on any of the school trips to Art Galleries or Museums. Let's hope we don't go to one here.'

- 'My friend's dad bet me that you'd be stupid enough to want to go to an Art Gallery or Museum while we were on holiday. I said you weren't that stupid.'

- 'Did you know that they issued a warning just this morning about the Art Galleries and Museums in this place? Apparently the air in

24

them is infected with something called Legionnaires' Disease.'

RULE 2

- Complain loudly: 'When you said we were going to see some pictures, I thought you meant we were going to the cinema.'

- Go up to a really ugly statue and say loudly, 'My heavens, it looks just like Grandma!'

- Go up to one of the attendants, peer closely at him, and then say loudly, 'What's this sculpture supposed to be of? It's pretty ugly, isn't it?'

- Try testing to see if the Art Gallery or Museum has an echo, by shouting. This should get you thrown out immediately.

- Say loudly and contemptuously, 'I can paint a better picture than that with my Paint By Numbers outfit.'

SEaside
HOLIDAYS

Holidays by the seaside are great. They are even
better if your parents keep you supplied with bags
and bags of money so that you can: (1) play all the
machines in the amusement arcades; (2) buy loads
and loads of ice cream and soft drinks; (3) buy
loads of chips and crisps.

Unfortunately adults don't see it this way.
Their idea of a great holiday by the sea is sitting
in a deckchair and falling asleep.

In Britain, particularly, this often has terrible,
consequences. Because the weather is what we
politely call 'changeable' in Britain, the chances
are that when your adults fall asleep the sky will
be overcast and the sun will be obscured by
clouds. What happens then is this: as soon as they
Zzzzzzz into slumberland, the clouds vanish and
the sun comes out with a vengeance. The result is
they get terrible sunburn and the next day they
look like something out of a Horror Movie (*The
Thing from the Fried Planet*). It is then totally
embarrassing for you to be seen walking along
the street with them. If this happens, offer them
large paper bags to put their heads in as they
walk along with you.

Anyway, here is how to get money from your

adults for the essentials of a seaside holiday
(amusement machines, candy floss, ice cream):

- 'I need some more spending money so that I can send postcards home.'

- 'I need more spending money because Auntie/Gran said she'd like me to bring her a souvenir back as a present.'

  (Note: more about both of these in *Postcards and Presents for Relatives* (pages 30−35).)

- 'I'm thirsty/hungry.'

- 'Would you like me to go and get you a drink/candy floss/ice cream? I haven't got any money myself, but if you give me some change I'll get it for you.'

- 'They've got a new flavour ice cream on sale here that I've never tried before, and I'm collecting the tastes of ice creams. So far I've tried 357 different types. It would be a tragedy if I missed out on this one, especially as this is the only town in the whole wide world where they sell it.'

- 'They've got a new educational machine in that Amusement Arcade. My teacher said if I saw one, I ought to have a go on it.'

- 'That man selling those ice creams looks so poor and unhappy. I think we ought to cheer him up by buying something off him. You're always saying that we should help those less fortunate than ourselves.'

- 'I need some money to buy a special sun-tan cream. It's very expensive, but you wouldn't want me to get sunburned because you only let me have the money to buy a very cheap sun-tan cream, would you?'

Persuading your adult to buy you a snorkel, flippers, wet suit or surfboard

- 'Everyone else has got one.'

- 'Everyone can see that I'm a deprived child because I haven't got one.'

- 'Everyone must think we're very, very poor as I'm the only child without one.'

- 'It's good exercise and will help me get healthy and strong.'

- 'Snorkelling is educational because you can learn all about fishes and underwater plants.'

- 'I need a wet suit because the water is freezing cold.'

- 'If I learned to surf properly I could appear on films and television and earn us a lot of money.'

- 'Not only do flippers help you swim farther and better, they stop your feet getting hurt on the pebbles as you walk down to the sea.'

- 'If I wear flippers I won't get bitten by a crab.'

- 'If I got swept out to sea while swimming then if I was wearing flippers I'd be able to swim back to the shore more safely.'

Postcards and presents for relatives

Another nasty trick adults play when on holiday is giving you hardly any pocket money at all, and then expecting you to send postcards to half the people in the Northern Hemisphere of the Planet Earth and also buy presents for every relative who bears some kind of loose connection with your family. ('Don't forget to take a little something back for your Gran. You know how she looks forward to getting something that shows that you haven't forgotten her.' How can you forget someone who tells you off every time you walk into their house/flat and tread the tiniest bit of mud on their carpet?)

It is very unfair of adults to expect you to fork out the few measly pennies that they grudgingly give you on wasteful items such as postcards to relatives when it is needed for vital things like ice creams and chips. To be able to send the number of postcards your adults want you to send, let alone buy the number of presents they want you to buy, you'd need a bag of money the size of Buckingham Palace. So, here's how to get out of spending your hard-won money on these things:

How to save money on postcards

Appeal to your adult's good nature (if they've got one):

● 'I would much prefer to be included in the postcards you send. It makes us seem more like a close family. If I send my postcards separately everyone might think we're not talking to each other and it would start rumours about us.'

● 'I think it's unfair to the postman to give him all this extra weight to carry, when we could make his job so much easier by just sending one card from all of us.'

31

- 'There aren't any postcards here that really show the beauty of this place. I think it would be unfair to our holiday to send something that didn't show just how wonderful this place is.'

If none of these work and your adults insist on you sending postcards on your own, then try these dodges:

- Find an old postcard that has already been used. Stick a piece of paper over the address already on it and write the address of whoever you want to send it to. Then add your own name to the message that's already on it.

  For example, if the post card that you have found is to Doris Higgins, High Street, Manchester, and says, 'Having a lovely time. Weather good. The kippers we had for breakfast at the hotel are wonderful. Love, Mary and John'; when you have altered it it will read:

  To (your Gran, Whichever Street of Whatever Town): 'Having a lovely time. Weather good. The kippers we had for breakfast at the hotel are wonderful. Love, Mary and John and Ian (or Amanda, or whatever your name is).'

- To save money on stamps, put different stickers on instead (e.g. 'BMX for ever,' 'Support British Ballet'). Alright, your relatives will have to pay the postage at the other end, but it serves them right for insisting that you send them a postcard in the first place.

- Make your own postcards by cutting a photo out and sticking it on a piece of cardboard. It doesn't *have* to be a photo of where you are staying. Make your relatives wonder — send them a photograph of an elephant or a block of flats in Addis Ababa.

How to save money on souvenir gifts

The sort of souvenirs your adults expect you to buy as presents for your ten million or so relatives are things like jars of coloured sand, model boats made out of bits of wood, or sea-shells stuck together so they look (vaguely) like a mermaid. These are all enormously expensive, and look suspiciously as if they were made in Taiwan or the Antarctic, or somewhere at least two Continents away.

Because of this it would be an absolute insult to your relatives to buy something like this for them. Why not give them a *real* souvenir of the seaside instead? After all, as they are fond of telling you when it comes to their turn to buy something for you, 'It's not what it costs; it's the thought that counts.' (This is why the things they buy for you always break after you've used them once.)

The great advantage of real souvenirs is that they don't cost any money at all. Things like:

- A piece of seaweed. (Useful for telling what the weather's going to be like, according to Ancient Myths and Legends. If it's wet, it's raining; if it's dry, it isn't. The fact that this must be obvious to even the dimmest person seems to have escaped the people who made up these Ancient Legends.)

- A pebble from the beach.

- A bag of sand. (Why pay all that money in a Gift Shop for it when there are about twelve million tonnes lying around on the beach?)

- A shell (or even two, let's be generous).

- A dead crab.

- A dead fish.

- A lump of driftwood that looks like a boat if you hold it at a certain angle.

- A piece of broken deck-chair.

- An empty ice-cream cone.

- A lump of rock (real rock, as found on beaches, as opposed to that pink and white stuff that you eat. That pink and white stuff is bad for your adult's teeth. It also costs money, which rocks found on the beach don't.)

Exploring

Sooner or later your adult will decide to go 'exploring'. This means clambering over rocks along the shore, walking into deep, dark caves that smell of rotting seaweed and seagull poo, or just going for a twenty-kilometre 'ramble' that takes in most of the little villages around and about the resort where you are staying.

Such activities are to be avoided at all costs, because sooner or later:

1. When climbing over rocks, you or your adult will fall and hurt yourself.

2. While in the cave, the tide will come in and you will be trapped.

3. All the shops/cafés in the small villages will be shut and you will get ill from exhaustion walking around with nothing to eat, or die of thirst because you can't get a drink.

Point out all these facts to your adults in an effort to persuade them to avoid taking such unnecessary risks. Adults being basically idiots, they will ignore you and insist on going. If they must, they must. Do not go with them, however. Just wait for about six hours or so after they have gone, then send out the Air Sea Rescue, the Army, the Navy, Uncle Tom Cobbley and all to look for them. They will be found stranded: (1) on the nearest rock, or (2) in the nearest caves, or (3) in the smallest village.

How to beat your adult at __ Crazy (or Obstacle) Golf __

One thing you can be sure of when on holiday by the seaside is that your adult will want to play a game of Crazy Golf (also known as Obstacle Golf). This is like ordinary golf, except you have to bash your ball around different obstacles (e.g. in and out of toy castles, over model roller-coasters) before it drops into the hole. The reason that adults love playing this game is that they can show off to their children.

We will now show you how you can beat your adult at this game. (IMPORTANT NOTE: However, we would advise leaving your victory until the last day of your holiday. This is because if you beat adults early on they get really mad and miserable and angry with you, which makes it a lot harder for you to get any extra money out of them. If you play them at this or any other game early in the holiday, LOSE.)

However, on that last day, WIN. And here's how to do it.

As your adult is about to hit the ball with her/his golf club, say something distracting such as:

- 'Careful!'
- 'Is your ball in the right place?'
- 'My shadow's not disturbing you, is it?'
- 'There's an ant by your foot. Don't tread on it.'
- 'Is that a spot on your face?'
- 'Look out!'
- 'You're holding the golf club the wrong way.'

- 'Wow, look at that helicopter up there!'

- 'Watch out for that dog just behind you.'

- 'Do you know you've got your shoes on upside down?'

As the game continues you can carry on putting your adult off the game with each swing by using the suggestions above.

After quite a few holes have been played, question how many points your adult has scored. For example, after the ball has gone in the hole, your adult may proudly announce, 'That makes me 15.' Quickly, you say 'I think it's 16.' This will upset your adult. He/she will count the scores up again and say, 'No, it's definitely 15.' You then challenge the score on an earlier hole. The reason you choose an early one is because it will be difficult for your adult to prove definitely how many strokes were played that long ago in the game.

There will then be a short argument between you, which will end in one of two ways:

1. Your adult will say, 'All right, to stop you going on about it, even though you're wrong, we'll call it 16, if it makes you feel better.'

2. Your adult will insist that his/her score really is 15, in which case you sigh and say, 'All right, if you feel you need to cheat to win.'

Whichever of the two it is, your adult will be angry and will start to lose his/her temper. Once this hapens he/she will be a lot less accurate when hitting the ball. From here on you can continue to upset him/her further by questioning the score as the game continues (e.g. 'That was definitely a 4 that time, wasn't it?').

To further put your adult off, when you come to a *really* hard obstacle, say, 'This is a really easy one. My friend's Dad/Mum did it in one go, three times!' This will put your adult off straight away.

When he/she starts to make lots of mistakes (which is almost certain to happen once he/she begins to get flustered), you can upset him/her even more by offering 'helpful' advice:

- 'Try hitting the ball nearer the bottom.'

- 'Count to 10 before hitting the ball.'

- 'Perhaps it would help if you kept your eye on the ball.'

Beating your adult at other _____ seaside games _____

This same method for putting your adult off can also be used for the following seaside games: BEACH CRICKET, BEACH TENNIS, THROWING A FRISBEE, and BOULES with the following additions or variations:

Beach cricket

If you are bowling at your adult, shout 'Howzat!' every time you throw the ball at him/her, whether he/she hits it or not. If he/she has hit it you can justify yourself by claiming 'Leg Before Wicket'. If he/she didn't hit it you can say it would have hit the wicket if there had been a real wicket.

If you are batting, keep hitting the ball into the sea. This will mean your adult will get very very wet and will soon give up the game, in which case you will be the winner.

If they ban the ball from going in the sea (i.e. by saying something like, 'If the ball goes in the sea, then you're out,') then keep hitting the ball so that it lands right in the middle of other family parties on the beach. Your adult will then have to keep apologizing every time he/she goes to collect the ball.

Beach tennis

Make sure that the sun is always in your adult's eyes so that he/she can't see the ball.

If he/she does managed to hit it, claim that it was 'Out' and that it is your point every time, even if it is a long way In. As your adult can't see because of the sun, he/she won't be able to dispute your call.

If your adult insists that you change ends so that *you* now have the sun in your eyes, complain bitterly that he/she is being unfair. Do this in a very loud voice. 'It's bad enough that you have to take on a child like me, but to cheat in this way, by putting me where the sun is in my eyes, is very, very unsporting!' This will shame your adult in the eyes of everyone on the beach and he/she will go back to having the sun in his/her eyes.

Throwing a frisbee

Whenever your adult throws it at you, deliberately miss it. This will mean that the frisbee will go past you and bash into some poor unfortunate holidaymaker sitting nearby. They will not blame you but your adult for 'not throwing it properly'.

After a few more glares and insults from the other holidaymakers on the beach, your adult will decide to give up, and you will have won.

Boules

This is a French version of bowls. It involves throwing lots of big heavy balls at one little one. Whoever gets their big ball nearest the small one, wins. It can be difficult to win at boules by cheating, but you can still have a lot of fun with your adult while playing this game. For a start, you can chuck your big ball so that it lands on someone's sandcastle. When they look around in anger to see who did it, look at your adult accusingly.

When it comes to your turn to throw the little ball, throw it as far as you can. This is bound to cause trouble as you and your adult attempt to chuck a ball (that is as heavy as a brick) about ten kilometres along a crowded beach. Someone is bound to get hit by something.

Sand and beaches

We could not write about holidays by the seaside without giving a special mention to beaches and sand. Sand (or what passes for it) on British beaches comes in different sorts and sizes:

1. **Mud.** This is brown and horrible and bears no relation to sand whatsoever. However it can be

found by the sea on some beaches, and some people think it is sand, so they lie on it and sunbathe. They usually then sink into it.

2. **Fine sand.** This is great and soft and nice to walk on, except that you keep sinking in it as you walk along the beach. Also, if you walk across a beach of fine sand wearing flip-flops, then it keeps coming up in great clouds, covering everyone as you pass near them. The answer to this is to walk on it barefoot. The trouble is, if it's sunny it's like walking on red hot coals.

3. **Pebbles.** A pebbly beach is one where the sand hasn't broken down properly into grains, but is still in the form of small stones. (Well,

that's what they tell you, anyway.) Because the stones are small it makes it even harder to walk on them than if they were big. In fact, try walking across a beach made of these stones barefooted, and you'll be crippled for life.

4. **Rocks.** Rocky beaches have hardly any sand on them at all, but are mostly strewn with huge rocks. Fall over on a beach like this and you'll break every bone in your body.

If you *are* on a sandy beach, then there are various fun things you can do:

1. **Make a sandcastle.** This is easy providing you have a Degree in Engineering and Design, which it seems every other child's grown-up has, because their sandcastles always look brilliant and perfect and like a life-sized model of the Tower of London.

   The sandcastle that you and your adult will build, however, always looks as if it was built by a blind dog with one leg. It will also fall down at the first tremor caused by someone walking past it. Our advice is: while on holiday by the seaside, swap your adult for one better at building sandcastles if you don't want to be completely shown up.

2. **Bury your adult.** This is also good fun. One important thing to bear in mind, however: always remember where you buried them. Leave a flag or a bucket marking the spot. This is essential because when it gets to the time to have something to eat you can dig them up and ask them for the money.

AdveNTuRe HoliDAYS

Adventure holidays are great as an idea. The one big trouble with them is that they are Just Like School. What happens is that your parents dump you in a cabin in the middle of a huge jungle and then disappear, glad to see the back of you for one week or two weeks.

'Great!' you think. 'I can have fun at this place!'

And you set off to enjoy yourself, but no, it's not that simple. You'll be just about to jump into a canoe, or saw down a huge tree, when the people in charge appear and start to Order You About, just like in school or at home. So instead of getting to do the things that you *want* to do, you get told to do something else instead, which you absolutely hate. This is most unfair. But, of course, adults being adults, that is the way they work things out, calculated to upset all young people. What you have to do, therefore, is Take Control of the situation.

As with the first section of this book, *Holidays Abroad,* you apply two basic rules:

RULE 1: Get out of the activity before it even begins.

45

RULE 2: If you can't, make such a mess of it that you won't have to do it again.

These are the sort of things you will find on an adventure holiday, and here is how to get out of doing them if you don't like them:

Ballooning

RULE 1

- 'I don't like heights.'

- 'Balloons always go "Pop!" and burst when I get near them.'

- 'I'm jinxed. Every car I've ever been in has crashed, and every house I've lived in has fallen down. Are you really sure you want me to go up in this balloon?'

RULE 2

Once you are up in the basket of this balloon, hovering zillions of kilometres above the Earth, the safest thing to do is nothing. This is because if you do something that ruins either the balloon or the basket underneath it, remember that you are in the basket, i.e. if it drops, you drop. Therefore apply Rule 1 with even greater determination. If that fails, then hide before they can find you and take you up. If they do take you up, then there is only one aspect of Rule 2 that you can apply: be sick in the basket. All right, you'll

have to live with the smell until you come down, but so will everyone else, and that should stop them taking you up again.

Birdwatching

This *could* be a very pleasant occupation because you don't really have to do anything except sit and watch birds, and therefore you use up no physical energy whatsoever. I stress 'could', because once the adults get involved in it, they make it hard work. They insist on you writing down what birds you've seen, and then tell you off if you've identified them wrongly. So:

RULE 1

- 'I'm shortsighted, I can't see anything if it's more than two metres away.'

- 'I've been afraid of birds ever since I was bitten by a canary.'

- 'Can I bring my shotgun/catapult?'

- 'I think it's an intrusion on the birds' privacy. We wouldn't like it if someone hid outside our houses and watched us for hours.'

- 'Because I'm colour blind I can't recognize the birds' different colours, so it's a waste of time my going.'

RULE 2

- Whatever sort of bird turns up, write down the same species each time. The more outrageous the better. Keep writing down 'vulture' every time you see any bird, from a chaffinch to a sparrow or a robin, or whatever.

- Point at other moving things, like insects, rabbits, horses, or tractors and ask, 'Is that a bird?'

- Say, 'My pencil's broken/My pen's run out.'

- Call loudly to the instructor: 'What bird is that?' This will frighten all the birds away for miles around.

- Sneeze loudly and often, and keep saying, 'Sorry, I've got a terrible cold.'

Canoeing

This is a fine activity, providing you don't mind being dragged along upside down over waterfalls at 1000kph in something made of papier-mâché. If you do mind such things being done to you, then:

RULE 1

- 'I shrink if I get wet.' (Also applicable to *Sailing*, *Scuba diving* and *Windsurfing*.)

- 'This canoe's got a hole in it.'

- 'I get seasick easily.' (This also can be used for *Sailing* and *Windsurfing*.)

- 'Because I've got a cold my parents have said that I'm not to go near the water.'

RULE 2

- Bash into everyone else's canoes.

- Put your foot through the bottom of the canoe as you get into it. This will cause it to sink immediately, but at least you will be in shallow water.

Climbing
___(incl. **Mountaineering**)___

Climbing is: (a) hard work; (b) dangerous; and (c) pointless, because when you get to the top you have to come all the way down again, which defeats the object of having gone up in the first place. Therefore:

RULE 1

- 'I can't stand heights.'

- 'I can't go higher than a few metres above sea level unless I have an oxygen mask.'

- 'I get a nose bleed if I get too high off the ground.' (Can also be used for *Ballooning*.)

- 'I can't possibly go climbing unless I have my own equipment, and unfortunately I've left it all at home.'

RULE 2

- As with ballooning, once they've got you doing it, it is not a good idea to mess around, because if you fall off a mountain halfway up you tend to go downwards due to Gravity. If this happens you could get hurt. The best thing,

therefore, is to apply RULE 1 and make sure you don't go up the mountain or rock wall in the first place.

However, there is one way of using RULE 2 in this situation, which is Getting Stuck Halfway Up. Simply stop halfway up and say that you can't go up, or back down. This will mean they have to bring out the Army, the Navy, Air-Sea Rescue, Lifeboats, etc, to rescue you. (See also *Orienteering* for another variation of this dodge.)

Cycling

If this was just riding around on a BMX it would be alright, but nearly aways 'cycling' means a 100-kilometre ride on a bike with a dodgy saddle. Either it's loose and keeps swivelling round all the time, so that you end up facing the way you've come, or it's made from solid wood, and after one ride you're unable to sit down again for the next ten days. So, the dodges:

RULE 1

● 'I've got cramp in my leg.'

● 'I've got an ear infection which means that I can't balance properly on a bike.'

● 'I never ever go on a bike nowadays, not since I was knocked off one by a car when I was small.'

● 'Because my back hurts I can't bend over, so that prevents me from riding a bicycle.'

- 'My religion prevents me from cycling anywhere in case I crush an insect beneath my tyres.'

- 'I've got a boil on my bottom.'

RULE 2

- 'The brakes on this bike don't work.'

- 'The chain's come off!'

- Get a puncture after the first half kilometre. Tell everyone to go on while you fix it 'rather than hold everyone up'. As soon as they're out of sight, just go back to the camp and have a rest.

- Work the saddle loose, which will mean you have to stop.

- Go slower and slower, which will mean everyone will have to keep stopping for you to catch up with them.

Hiking

Do not be fooled by the interesting-sounding name, this means 'walking'. Even worse, it means walking with heavy boots on over rough ground where only sheep and goats were ever intended to walk. You also have to carry a heavy pack on your back filled with everything anyone would ever need to survive in a wilderness: e.g. maps, food, ropes, tents, a bed, kitchen sink, a do-it-yourself table, a complete central heating unit, etc. The

whole lot weighs about two tonnes, and even though Arnold Schwarzenegger would have difficulty lifting it, you're expected to walk about fifty kilometres up and down mountains carrying it. This activity needs to be got out of at all costs.

RULE 1

- 'My leg/ankle hurts.'

- 'This is not my real leg, it's made of plastic and it's likely to give way after I've walked two kilometres or so. I'm sorry, because I really would have loved to go on this hike.'

- 'I really can only wear my own walking boots. That's because my feet are two different sizes. And unfortunately I've left them at home.'

- 'I've been told by my doctor not to walk too far in case it brings on my asthma/bronchitis/bubonic plague.'

- 'I've got a sore place on my shoulders which means I can't carry a rucksack.'

RULE 2

- Keep stopping to untie and re-tie your bootlaces.

- Keep stopping because you think you've got a blister coming on your foot.

- Every few minutes stop and say, 'Isn't that a lovely view. Let's sit down and look at it for a bit.'

- Start limping as soon as you set off.

- Tell really terrible jokes non-stop as you walk along. Either that or boast constantly about what a truly wonderful person you are. It will use up a lot of breath, but it will be worth it, because no one will want to go walking with you again.

Orienteering
(incl. **Map Reading**)

This is for SAS-type people only. What happens is that you get dumped blindfolded in the middle of nowhere, with only a compass and two sticks so that you can make a fire. Then the organizers take the blindfold off you, hurtle off in their helicopter, and you have to find you own way back to camp. Frankly it has always seemed to me like a very unsubtle way of telling somebody that they are not wanted back at camp. It is like hiking, only worse. At least with hiking you knew where you were to start with. With orienteering you could be going hopelessly in the wrong direction, especially if (a) you can't read a compass; and (b) you haven't spent your young life watching films where lost cowboys find their way by using the sun and the stars. Definitely an 'adventure' to be avoided at all costs, and here's how:

RULE 1:

- 'My uncle is a Mafia Don. If I get lost and fall over a cliff, the Mafia will seek revenge on whoever is responsible.'

- 'I can't read at all, let alone maps and signposts.'

- 'I've left my contact lenses at home.'

- 'I've got a metal bone in my nose which affects the Magnetic North of compasses.'

- 'I've heard that there's a werewolf out there on the prowl.'

RULE 2:

Do nothing. Sit tight and send up a distress signal (e.g. a flare). The whole combined Emergency Rescue Teams will then turn out: Mountain Rescue, RAF helicopters, police with tracker dogs, the Army, the Navy, the Boys' Brigade, the Girl Guides, the Brownies, etc, etc. After causing all this fuss they'll never let you go orienteering again.

Rafting

Rafting is similar to canoeing, except that you are supposed to stay on top of the water rather than in it. To achieve this you are put on a raft and given a pole. Even worse, at many adventure camps you are expected to *build* your own raft.

Frankly, to those who have seen a raft, it must be obvious that being on one in raging water is not a very good idea. If it was such a good way of moving across water, why isn't it in standard use today? Why has it been superseded by the ocean liner, the yacht, the submarine, and every other known form of boat? Because the raft sinks, that's why.

Also, before it sinks, it moves very fast and out of control. What the designers of the raft seem to have forgotten is: the raft does not have brakes!

Here is how to avoid putting yourself at risk in this dubious activity:

RULE 1

- 'I've had an allergy to things made of wood ever since I got a splinter in my finger when I was four.'

- 'The ropes holding the raft together look loose.'

- 'I am a member of the Save The Trees Campaign, and this forbids me from riding on anything made of chopped-down trees or wood in any form.'

- 'I cannot do this because this kind of thing causes pollution of rivers.'

- 'My granny made me promise her that I'd never ever go on a raft. I must honour that promise.'

RULE 2

- Put a skull and crossbones flag on the flagpole.

- While using the pole to move the raft along, get the pole stuck in the muddy bottom of the river. BUT make sure that you don't let go of the pole once you have done this, otherwise you will just hurtle out of control down the river and possibly disappear over a waterfall. The point about this dodge is that the organizers will have to come out to the middle of the river to rescue you, which will annoy them intensely.

- Shout, 'Look out, there's a crocodile in the water!'

Riding

This involves getting on a horse. That, alone, is enough to mark this activity down as one to be avoided. For one thing, horses are very tall. For another thing, they move while you are on them, whether you want them to or not. And for a third thing, as with the raft, they don't have any brakes, so you can't stop them once they are moving.

RULE 1

- 'The RSPCA has banned me from going anywhere near animals.'

- 'I think riding horses is cruel.'

- 'My mum told me you can catch diseases from animals – things like distemper and hardpad. I'm not to go near them.'

- 'Have you got one with pedals?'

- 'I've got a sore bottom.'

RULE 2

It is important that whatever you do, you do *not* hurt the horse. After all, it's not the horse's fault that it's stuck with this job of carrying you around.

Therefore, the best way to get out of riding, once the organizers have got you as far as the horse, is not actually to get on the horse. The way to do this is to tell the people in charge that you can't mount properly. You then prove it to them by falling over on the ground every time you put your foot in the stirrup.

If they do manage to get you on the horse, then fall off the other side. Keep repeating this until

(a) they get fed up, or

(b) it begins to hurt you, by which time they will have to admit that you are in no fit shape to go riding after all.

If you should actually get on the horse, then fall off it straight away and lie on the ground moaning.

The big problem with all this falling off is that if you don't fall properly you might hurt yourself and then you'll be moaning for real. There are two ways round this problem:

1. Choose a very small horse to fall off.

2. Take a mattress with you to fall on to.

Sailing

For sailing, see also *Canoeing* and *Rafting*. The principle is the same: you are totally out of control on something that floats on water, without either an engine or a brake. An additional hazard in this case is that it has large sheets of cloth attached to it, called sails. It only needs one small puff of wind even to touch these things, and you are off across the lake (or wherever you are) at about 200kph. Then, when you are in the middle of the lake (or ocean, or sea, or whatever), the wind will suddenly drop. And there you will have to stay for the next trillion years until a hurricane appears and blows you completely out of the lake and deposits you and the yacht on the roof of someone's house. So here are some helpful tips to keep your feet firmly on dry land when you are threatened with this 'adventure':

RULE 1

- 'My family have always forbidden me to have anything to do with boats because my grandfather was in the Navy and the boat he was on sank.'

- 'My parents won't let me go sailing in case the boom swings round and hits me and knocks me overboard.'

- 'I'm sure I saw a mine floating out there in the water. If we go out we might all get blown up.'

- 'The bottom of the boat might hit a fish. As a member of the Friends of Fish Organization that would always be on my conscience.'

- 'I'm a World Champion at sailing. I don't want to go out because I'd show you up, and I'd hate to make you all feel so embarrassed.'

RULE 2

- Be sick all over the boat.

- Get in everyone's way.

- Scream, 'There's a torpedo coming towards us!'

- Tell the sailing instructors, 'You're doing it all wrong. My dad says you should do it the other way.' Then offer to show them the other way, and ruin everything.

- Shout, 'We're sinking!'

Scuba diving/Snorkelling

Two very dodgy occupations indeed, since they involve spending all your time under water. The major drawbacks are: (1) it's wet; (2) the other occupants of the water might take a dislike to you (i.e. sharks, giant eels, octopuses, piranha fish, etc). This may be fun for people like James Bond, but for any normal person the best activity around water is lying on the beach looking at it. So, here is how to make sure that you don't get involved with this underwater action:

RULE 1

- 'I'm afraid of fish.'

- 'I was once attacked by an octopus/shark/piranha fish.'

- 'I can't swim.' (Also can be used for *Canoeing, Sailing, Rafting* and *Windsurfing*).

- 'A man was attacked by a shark/shoal of jellyfish in these waters just two weeks ago. I wonder if they're still here?'

- 'I can't wear a face mask because it won't fit over my glasses.'

- 'I suffer from an ear infection so my doctor's told me that I can't go under water.'

RULE 2

As with ballooning, it is best if you don't do anything to mess things up, mainly because *you* will be at risk. This is because you will be under water. It is therefore extra important that you do your best to make RULE 1 work so that you don't get involved in this activity in the first place. However, if you do get dragged into this 'adventure':

- Turn up wearing a plaster cast on your leg or arm.

- Take a tin of red paint with you and open it when you are underwater. The adults watching on the shore will think you have been attacked by a shark or some similar dangerous sea creature.

- Take along a fake jellyfish or octopus and pretend it has attacked you.

Skiing

What can you say about an activity that consists of you hurtling at thousands of kph down a slope with your feet tied to long skates. One for stunt people and idiots only.

RULE 1

- 'I can't go anywhere near snow because it brings on my bronchitis/asthma/pneumonia.'

- 'Because my dad wants me to be a dancer/footballer, my legs are insured for a million pounds each. So, if I damage them whoever is responsible will get sued for all that money by the insurance company.'

- 'I thought it was water skiing. I'm no good at skiing down hills, only skiing on water.' (However, before using this excuse, check first that the particular Adventure Camp you are at does not also have water skiing, otherwise you will have landed yourself with another 'Adventure' to get out of.)

- 'I can't do anything that involves going downhill at speed because I'm allergic to Gravity.'

RULE 2

- Fall over immediately and lie in the snow, groaning.

- Crash into the adult in charge and knock him/her over (making sure not to injure yourself).

- Start a snowball fight.

- Build a snowman on the ski slope.
- Keep putting your skis on wrongly (e.g. upside down).

Windsurfing

Yet another 'adventure activity' that involves water. All the arguments against all the other water activities apply here, because it combines the worst of each one. It's like standing on a narrow raft, or an upside-down canoe, with a sail on it. Sooner or later you will fall in and then be underwater, but without a snorkel. Do not hesitate, get out of it immediately! This way:

RULE 1

- 'I hear there's a gale/hurricane forecast for today.' (This excuse can also be used for *Canoeing, Climbing, Orienteering, Rafting* and *Sailing*).

- 'I catch pneumonia if water goes up my nose.'

- 'I've just recovered from tonsillitis and my doctor's told me I'm not supposed to go near water.'

- Keep insisting that the board is an alien spaceship in disguise and that you're afraid to go near it.

RULE 2

- 'Accidentally' set the surfboard going on the water before you can get on it. If it is done on an outgoing tide, the board will never be seen again.

- Fall off and swim underwater to a place where you can hide (e.g. a bush by the edge of the lake, a moored boat). This will cause panic among the people in charge.

- Fall off as soon as you get on it. Keep falling off.

BEING SENT TO STAY WITH RELATIVES IN THE COUNTRY

'What a wonderful idea!' you may think. 'I'd love to be sent to stay with relatives in the country.' Well, this depends on the relatives. It also depends on the country. If it was full of things like video arcades and cinemas and beaches, yes, but it is noticeable that most of these things are markedly lacking out in the country.

In fact, the country seem to consist of the following things: trees, grass, mud, animals. Also, the relatives who usually live in these places look and act like they're made from the same ingredients.

So how come you get sent to the country in the first place? Your parents will tell you:

1. You deserve a break in the fresh air of the country.

2. Your relatives are desperately keen for you to stay with them.

Everyone knows that these are lies. The real reasons are:

1. Your parents want a break from you.

2. It's cheaper than sending you on an adventure holiday.

You, you will notice, have no choice in the matter. You are tied, bound and gagged and bundled, with your case, on to a train or coach and sent off, with a label tied to your clothing saying something like, 'To be collected by Uncle Mike and Auntie Dorothy.'

If you like Uncle Mike and Auntie Dorothy (or whoever else it is you are sent to stay with), or you like being in the countryside surrounded by trees, grass, mud and animals, fine. Do not bother to read the rest of this chapter. If, however, the mere idea of it strikes more fear and horror into you than Count Dracula and Frankenstein combined, then here is how to change the situation.

The Method is in Three Parts:

PART 1: Reasons for not going in the first place.

PART 2: How to avoid getting put on the coach or train.

PART 3: If you do get sent there, how to get sent back very quickly. (This also includes, *And Making Sure You Will Never Be Allowed Back There Again.*)

Reasons for not going in the first place

- 'My clothes will get ruined with all that mud.'

- 'They' [your relatives] 'don't like me.'

- 'I don't like them.'

- 'All those flowers/crops will make me ill with hay fever.'

- 'I could get stung by a bee.'

- 'I could get trodden on by a horse/cow/sheep/pig/rabbit/hedgehog.'

- 'I could get caught up in a fox hunt and torn to bits.'

- 'I could get attacked by birds.'

- 'I'm frightened of scarecrows.'
- 'I could catch terrible diseases from the farm animals.'
- 'I'll miss you.'
- 'I can't bear to be parted from you.'
- 'Their cooking is terrible; I might catch food poisoning.'

How to avoid getting put
_____ on the coach or train _____

- Hide until it's gone.

- Faint.

- Get your parents to take you to the bus/train station buffet so that you can wait for the coach or train 'in the warm'. Keep them talking there until the coach or train has gone.

- Go to the toilet, and don't come out until after the train or coach has gone.

Say:

- 'I get travel sick on coaches/trains.'

- 'The driver is drunk.'

- 'The driver looks like a notorious crook. I'm sure I've seen his face on *Crimewatch*.'

- 'I'm sure this train/coach is the wrong one.'

- 'Oh dear, I've left my bag at home with all my money/toothbrush and flannel/pyjamas.'

- 'I don't like the look of those other passengers. I'm sure it's not safe for me to be in the same coach/train as them.'

_____ How to get sent back _____

Rude comments

- 'Good heavens, a cow has got into the house! Oh, I'm sorry, Cousin Freda.'

- 'I suppose, living on a farm, you get used to your house smelling like cow dung.'

- 'Isn't it fascinating how people look like their animals. Funny you living on a pig farm.'

- 'My dad says people who live in the country are as thick as planks.'

- 'Will you do some fish impressions for me? The reason I ask is because my mum says you drink like a fish.'

- 'Have you ever thought of taking cooking lessons?'

- 'Is this house safe? It looks as if it's about to fall down.'

- 'I suppose you're forced to live in the country because you're so very poor.'

- 'Which one of you is the village idiot?'

Using local animals

While in the country you will notice a lot of living beings wandering around the countryside on all fours. Some of these will be your relatives scrabbling around looking for their lost contact lenses. The others will be animals.

Animals in the country come in two sizes:

BIG: e.g. horses, cows, sheep.

SMALL: e.g. cats, mice, rats, frogs, toads, hedgehogs, snails, various insects.

With animals in such abundance it seems a pity to waste them in your quest to be sent back home. So, what you do is, you use them to your advantage by placing them at strategic points around the house to shock and surprise your relatives.

NOTE: This last paragraph refers, of course, to SMALL animals. This is because it is much easier, for example, to place an animal the size of a lizard in the cutlery drawer in the kitchen than it is to try to squeeze a horse into one. There is room in this scheme for using BIG animals, but that comes only if using the smaller ones fails.

Small animals (big insects, frogs, mice, snails, etc) can be placed in a variety of places around the house, all of which will lead to your relatives screaming and falling over in a faint when the animal is discovered. Good places include:

- Any drawer or cupboard in the kitchen.

- In the bath.

- In the toilet.

- In their bed (especially if hidden under their sheets. Their screams when they pull the covers back to get into bed will be heard at least two towns away.)

- In a handbag or briefcase.

- In the clothes they are about to put on.

If all else fails, as we said before, then you may have to resort to using a big animal. Alright, it's harder to get a horse or a cow or a bull into a living room or kitchen, but it's very effective. You will, of course, have a hard time explaining what on earth made you bring an animal of that size into the house. Reply that it looked cold and lonely outside.

Mud

This is another useful commodity. For one thing there's always a lot of it lying around in the country. It is also easy to collect – just walk in it and it will stick to your boots. To use it to get sent

home, just walk across your relatives' best carpet
wearing boots with mud on them.

Trees, etc

Another thing to remember is to use all the
country-type stuff that is lying around all over
the countryside: e.g. trees, hedges, etc. Tell your
relatives that your teacher wants you to do a

project on the country while you're away, to show that you have taken a keen interest in rural matters. To do this project means collecting bits of the country so that you can take them home with you.

The bits of the country that you will then start to collect will include: huge fallen branches, cow pats, hay, horse troughs, bits of old rusty farm machinery that aren't used any more, loads and load of flowers and weeds (complete with roots and earth clinging to them). Fill every room in your relatives' house with them. With a bit of luck, within a day they should be packing you off home.

Wild plants and berries

Everyone knows that many of these are dangerous and must not be eaten, so do not do it. However, tell your relatives that you have. When you are all sitting around reading books, or watching the telly, suddenly clutch your stomach and fall on the floor, groaning. When your relatives ask you what the matter is, croak, 'I think it must be those red and blue striped berries/purple toadstools/deadly nightshade, that I ate while I was out walking today.' This will cause much panic and consternation among your relatives.

Offering to 'help'

Offer to help while you are staying with them, and do everything wrong:

- Help with the washing up and break all the plates.

- Help vacuum clean the house, but switch the machine to 'blow' instead, and so cover the whole house with dust and dirt.

- Paint the outside of the house a really awful colour. When they find out what you've done they will scream and faint. When they regain consciousness, tell them that you were only trying to help because the outside of their house looked so terrible.

- If they live on a farm, offer to help with the animals. Then put all the animals in the wrong fields (e.g. put the sheep or cows, or other grazing animals, in the field where their crops are growing).

- Offer to park their tractor in the barn. This will mean attempting to drive it through the large doors. Miss, and knock the barn down.

- Chop up wood in the living room on their best carpet.

- Take the farm animals for a walk (e.g. the herd of cows), and come back without them, saying that you lost them.

HOLIDAYS WITH THE SCHOOL

This means Going Somewhere With Your School. School trips and holidays would actually be really terrific things to go on, if it wasn't for one thing: the teachers.

The big problem when dealing with teachers is that they are completely cold-hearted and unsympathetic. You can crawl along a floor towards a teacher, lie there groaning at his/her feet and say, 'I'm ill, Sir/Miss,' but what do they do? Do they scoop you up in their arms and rush you to the nearest Casualty Department for urgent treatment (i.e. sweets and ice creams). No they do not, they just glare down at you and say things like, 'Don't be ridiculous! Get up at once!' And then they walk over you and carry on as if nothing had happened.

The trouble is that teachers (certainly the ones who've been teaching since the Stone Age) have become immune to children's excuses, believing all children to be: (1) liars; (2) dodgers; (3) dedicated to upsetting teachers.

This goes to show how unnecessarily suspicious teachers are.

New teachers are different. Most of them still believe that children are all right really. It follows that new teachers are the only ones who can be appealed to and reasoned with. The best thing you can hope for on a school holiday, therefore, is that all the teachers going with you are new ones. However, this rarely happens, and instead of the school holiday being all fun it nearly always becomes just like school, because the crabby old rotten teachers in charge of you insist on making sure that it is 'Educational'.

Because the teachers in charge of you will either be experienced or mean as ferrets, the excuses and dodges in Chapters One, Two, Three and Four of this book will just be treated by them with total contempt. You will have to use Other Methods if you're going to have fun, and the best Other Method is:

Get Rid of Your Teachers

Here's how to do it:

Phone up the local police and tell them that you are giving them a tip-off about a notorious gang of English crooks who have just arrived in their country, disguised as school teachers. Give the police the descriptions of all your teachers. The police will then round them up and lock them away. After a day or so your teachers will eventually be released, after they have called in the British Consul. However, this will give you a bit of time without them.

Find out where the washroom of your hotel is, or find a room in your hotel where no one ever goes.

Tell one of your teachers (the one you want to get rid of most) that somebody has heard voices coming from this room calling for help. Follow your teacher (at a discreet distance so that you aren't spotted) as he/she goes to investigate. Once Sir/Miss is in the room, lock them in. Then stick a sign on the door saying 'Out of Order'. (*Note:* Make sure that the sign is in the language of the country you are in, otherwise people will get suspicious.)

Slip itching powder in their clothes. When they start to scratch frantically, say sympathetically, 'Oh dear, you've caught it.' When they say 'What?' tell them that there's an epidemic of Mediterranean Measles in this particular town, and that the first symptom is a terrible itching. Tell them that the only known cure is for them to stay in bed in their room for at least two days.

Put mustard (or something similar) in their hot drink. After a while they will feel sick. Encourage them in this by telling them how ill they look. Persuade them to spend a day or two in bed to recover.

When you are off on one of your sight-seeing trips, try and lose the teacher with your party. (*Important Note*: You must all do this together, however, otherwise there is a serious danger of YOU being the one who gets lost.) Once you are all out of sight of your teacher, rush back to the hotel (or wherever you are staying). Your teacher will be worried about what has happened to you all (even teachers have some concern) and will spend the rest of the day looking for you.

If you go to the beach or swimming with your teachers, hide their clothes. They will then have to spend the rest of that day (and possibly the next day as well) looking for them.

When you are walking around a town or city with your teacher, rush up to a passer-by and plead urgently: 'Help us! We are English schoolchildren and we have been kidnapped by this bad man/woman. He/she is taking us to sell us as child slaves!' Then nip off to join the school party again. With a bit of luck your teacher will be grabbed by the local gendarmes or polizei within a few minutes and you can all rush off somewhere and enjoy yourselves.

If all this fails and you are still stuck with them for the rest of the School Holiday, then try appealing to their Good Nature. Even ancient teachers have one somewhere deep down inside. If you can get them to feel sympathetic towards you then they might start to allow you to go off on your own and do the things you really want to do (e.g. lie on the beach and eat ice creams until you feel sick).

The sort of flattering phrases that some teachers can be suckered by include:

- 'You're the best teacher I've ever had.'

- 'You are my inspiration.'

- 'Has anyone ever told you you look like. . . .' (Name a famous pop star or film star, but *not* someone like Dracula or Lassie the Wonder Dog.)

- 'I bet when you were my age you went off on your own. It gives you such a feeling of adventure and excitement.'

- 'I've always said how lucky we are to have you as our teacher because you are so forward-looking and you treat us as grown up enough to look after ourselves.'

- 'I think it's most unfair for you to have to look after us all the time while we're here, especially as you've worked so hard all this year at school.'

- 'I think teachers are terribly underpaid and I've written to my MP demanding that teachers' salaries are increased by 100%.'

- 'You deserve a rest. Why don't you have one tomorrow. We can look after ourselves just for one day.'

- 'You look ill. You ought to be careful in this foreign country, with the different climate and the different water.'

- 'Let us prove to you how grown up we can be, just to show you that your teaching us how to behave abroad has worked. Let us go out on our own tomorrow, in your honour.'

Teachers and foreign languages

Another thing about teachers abroad: they like their pupils to think that they can speak the language of whichever country they are in fluently. Either this is true (which is very rare) or they are just pretending.

If it is true, then you can embarrass your teacher by trying to talk in that foreign language, and deliberately saying things wrongly.

If, on the other hand, they are just pretending, then you can embarrass them by showing them up in public for their lack of knowledge.

How to embarrass your teacher in foreign languages by using the wrong words

French

Quelle heure est-il? Il est six fromages. (*Trans:* What time is it? It is six cheeses.)

Garçon, apportez-nous un éléphant, s'il vous plaît. (*Trans:* Waiter, bring me an elephant, please.)

J'ai une douleur dans l'armoire. (*Trans:* I have a pain in my wardrobe.)

Spanish

Quiero comer los neumáticos, por favor. (*Trans:* I would like to eat the tyres, please.)

¿Donde puedo comprar un prohibido el paso? (*Trans:* Where can I buy trespassers will be prosecuted?)

Me duele la cacerola. (*Trans:* I have a pain in my saucepan.)

German

Können Sie mir den Kamel reparieren? (*Trans:* Can you mend my camel for me?)

Bringen Sie mir noch ein Messer, eine Gabel, einen Löffel, einen Teller und ein Autobus. (*Trans:* Bring me another knife, fork, spoon, plate and a bus.)

Ich habe Schmerzen in meinem Winker. (*Trans:* I have a pain in my indicator.)

Italian

Mangiamo la minestra colla porta. (*Trans:* We eat soup with a door.)

Non ho ne caldo, ne freddo, ho dodici. (*Trans:* I am neither hot nor cold, I am twelve.)

Siamo ammalati con spinosi. (*Trans:* We are ill with hedgehogs.)

How to embarrass your teachers when they don't really know the foreign language

Rush up to them looking as if you are in great pain, and say, 'Please, Sir/Miss, what's the French/German/Spanish/Italian for toilet, only I'm dying to go?!'

'That restaurant owner was laughing at you behind your back. I think you must have said a word wrong.'

'You pronounced that word wrongly. If it's said that way it means "overcoat" and not "potatoes". You've just ordered a fried egg and peas with roast overcoat.'

'We're lost. How are we going to find our way back to the bus when you don't know the language?'

'How much is that in English money, Miss/Sir?'

Worksheets

While on School Holidays, teachers will insist on issuing you with Worksheets all the time. As if it's not enough that they drag you around hot streets looking at castles, ancient ruins, etc, etc, they make it worse by giving you a sheet of paper with about ten trillion questions on it.

These questions include things like:

● How many bricks are there in the East Wall of the South Wing of the West Tower?

- Where was the Treaty of Paris signed? (To a question like this always answer, 'At the bottom of the page.' It's guaranteed to drive teachers mad.)

- What can you see if you stand at the edge of the harbour and look East? (Answer: water.)

There are two ways of dealing with these worksheets:

1. Get rid of them before the teachers have issued them to you all.

2. Get rid of them *after* the teachers have collected them in, but *before* they have had a chance to look at them properly and found out that you haven't filled yours in.

Number One (getting rid of them before they are issued) is always difficult. This is because teachers know how cunning their pupils can be and so they always make a point of keeping the worksheets hidden until the last moment. Some teachers even use Security Firms to carry the Worksheets and prevent them from being stolen. If this is the case it might be worth contacting the Intelligence Service of the country you are in (e.g. CIA in the USA, KGB in Russia) and offering them a bribe if they will find the worksheets for you. Tell them all they have to do is to discover where they are, and you will do the rest (i.e. destroy them).

However, because of the enormously tight security that teachers use to keep the worksheets away from pupils (huge locks and chains tied around cases; burglar-proof steel safes in the hotel, etc), the best bet is to get rid of them *after* they've been handed out to you, the pupils. There are different ways of doing this:

- Just simply lose them.

- Pour ink or dye over them so that no one can read the questions.

- Give them to the hotel owner to put in the hotel boiler.

- Drop them in the sea so that they float away and are never seen again.

- Take them with you when you visit somewhere high (e.g. the Eiffel Tower, the Leaning Tower of Pisa, Mount Everest). 'Accidentally' drop them when you reach the top and let them be blown away by the wind.

- Make paper hats out of them and wear them in the rain.

The journey home

This is a wonderful opportunity to get rid of your teacher. You may wonder why we only deal with this possibility on the journey *home,* and not on the way to the holiday. There is a very simple reason for this: your teacher is the one who has all the tickets and the money for the hotel, so it is important that your teachers are with you when you arrive at your holiday destination.

However, once the holiday is over it is almost your duty to get rid of your teachers so that you do not have to put up with them (nor they with you) when you get back to school.

There will be various points on the journey home when opportunities will arise. If they do not, you can make them arise by using these dodges:

The coach journey

- Say, 'Excuse me, Sir/Miss. I think we've got a puncture.' When your teacher gets out to check the tyres, shut the door of the coach immediately and say to the driver, 'Quick! Drive on! That man/woman is mad and we've been trying to get rid of him/her!'

- When you stop at a café for refreshments on the journey, lock your teacher in the toilet.

- Again at the refreshment stop, switch the destination name on your coach with that of another coach. Your teacher will get on the wrong coach and won't realize it until it's too late.

The boat

Tell the captain of the boat that your teacher is actually a stowaway you found hiding in a lifeboat. The captain will then stop the boat and send your teacher back.

Lock your teacher away somewhere on the boat as it is coming in to harbour (e.g. an empty cabin, a toilet or washroom, a store room).

Customs

This is the perfect place to get rid of your teacher. Plant any of the following items in your teacher's suitcase:

- Beer, whisky, etc.

- Towels and knives and forks and spoons from the hotel.

- Books from the local library of the town you have been staying in.

Tip the Customs Officers off that a well-known English crook is going to try to smuggle all this stuff past them, and give them a good description of your teacher.

You can be pretty sure your teacher will not be able to get out of the country.

The 'RAINY DAY FUN' CHAPTER

I thought this was a good title, because I stole it from a book called The Rainy Day Fun Book. (Although you have to agree that the author – a certain I. M. Wett – must be an idiot, because how you could call a rainy day 'fun' is beyond imagining.)

The point about these books is that they are supposed to be full of things you can make or do to entertain and amuse yourself while you're on holiday or at home and it's too wet to go outside. The real trouble comes when you try actually to make or do the things they suggest. You follow the instructions absolutely word for word, but it never works out like it does in the book. Building a model of St Paul's Cathedral out of matches, for example. How many kids have ever made one that looks like either the picture in the book or the real St Paul's? The answer: *None.* And we bet there aren't many adults who could make one like it, either.

The truth is these books are a fraud. They are like these TV programmes for kids, where some presenter produces a lump of cardboard, a washing-up liquid bottle and a ball of string, and

proceeds to make a nuclear missile out of it. After tying themselves up with the string and dropping the rest of it on the floor, they beam at the camera and say, 'And here's one we made earlier!' They then produce an absolutely perfect piece of machinery that must have taken 47 years and about 1000 people to make.

So, if you're going to have a fraud, have a Good Fraud. All the things in this chapter are therefore Absolutely Impossible to make, and if you attempt to do so you will drive yourself mad, as well as get yourself covered in paint, glue and cardboard. You will also annoy your neighbours.

Tie and Dye

Have you ever admired the interesting patterns that decorate some of your friends' T-shirts! You have! Then here's how YOU can have an interesting T-shirt too, using Tie and Dye.

This is so called because you TIE up whatever you want patterned, and then you put it in DYE to make it different colours. It's LOTS OF FUN and VERY EASY to do.

Here's what you do:

First, mix up some dye. You can do this in the bath in your house. Just pour in some water, and then add the following ingredients:

    coal dust
    mud (made very simply with earth)
    indelible ink
    a bottle of blackcurrant juice
    a lump of rusty metal
    three tins of gloss paint of different colours

Take the T-shirt that you want to dye and tie it up very tightly with string. Drop it into the mixture. Leave it for about two hours. That's all you have to do. At the end of that time, just pull

95

out the plug and let the water run away and just see what you are left with.

You will now have:

1. A T-shirt that is ruined and will have to be thrown away because you can't wear it any more.

2. A bath that will be so stained that the marks will never come out. The staining will also quite likely have spread to the rest of the bathroom, the tiles, the wash-basin, etc. Your family will now have to buy a new bathroom (about £6000).

So, instead of spending £5.99 to buy a tie-and-dye T-shirt, you have tied and dyed your own, for a mere £6005.99! (The additional £5.99 is what it will cost to replace your ruined T-shirt.)

__Paper Folding (Origami)__

Have you ever gazed in awe and wonder at a friend as he or she has taken an ordinary piece of paper and, with a few simple folds, turned it into a beautiful bird or an angry lion? Of course you have. Well, here's how you, too, can learn the art of Origami, the ancient Japanese art of paper folding.

1. Take a sheet of paper.

2. Fold it in half.

3. Fold it in half again.

4. Fold it in half again.

5. Fold it in half another time.

6. Fold it in half one more time.

7. Fold it in half yet again.

8. Fold it in half again.

9. Fold it in half again.

10. Fold it in half one more time.

Finished! You now have a small but thick piece of paper. Simple, isn't it!

Having mastered that, we'll try another one:

Making a Giraffe

1. Take a piece of paper.

2. Fold along Line AB.

3. Fold along Line CD.

4. Fold along Line CABD.

5. Fold Line XZ and ABCD/CBAD.

6. Fold Lines TSB, HGV, KGB and CIA.

7. Fold the forward bits back and the back bits forward.

8. Connect NOP to PON and SOCK to FOOT.

9. Fold MUB through 180 degrees so that it becomes BUM.

10. Do the same with MUM, DAD and GAG.

There, finished! Does it look like a giraffe? No? Neither did mine.

___ Make your own music ___

Did you know that you can make your own musical instruments very cheaply indeed? In fact some can be made for only a few pennies! For example:

Making a guitar in three easy steps

1. First find a tree. Dig it up, cut off all the branches, and then drag the trunk into your

living room. The tree trunk needs to be guitar sized. (If you were making a double bass then you would need a bigger tree.)

2. Get a chain saw, and cut the tree trunk into a guitar shape.

3. Stick some strings on it.

There, simple!

If you want to make an electric guitar, this is easily achieved by adding a Fourth Step:

4. Plug it in.

Drums

For a simple set of drums, borrow your family's saucepans. Just turn them upside down and hit them with something.

Drums can also be made by hitting any other object: e.g.

> your neighbour's front door
> your head
> a double-decker bus
> your best friend
> a brick
> a Complete Set of Encyclopaedias

Wind instruments

A wind instrument is any instrument that uses wind. Therefore you can make a good wind instrument from any of the following ordinary common

or garden things you would find in the ordinary
house:

- a vacuum cleaner
- a jet engine
- a bicycle pump
- a balloon
- a Space Shuttle

Just simply connect them all together, and then
blow down one end. You can get different notes
by putting your fingers over the different holes.
All you need for this are three hands that are
twenty-seven metres wide with forty-five fingers
on each.

Cooking

Who said cooking was hard! Cooking is easy, and
it can be a lot of fun! Why not try the following
simple recipes, and then invite your friends round
for a scrumptious tea-time treat!

Roast Camels' feet in garlic

Ingredients
15 camels' feet
12 cloves of garlic
peel from 2 large melons
3 tablespoons olive oil
2 tonnes flour
pinch of salt
1 crushed egg
1 litre of 20/30 engine oil

Method

Stick all the ingredients in a cement mixer, switch on and mix. Then pour the mixture into a lightly greased bucket.

This dish can be served hot or cold, as a starter, or simply to poison people.

To follow, why not try this delicious sweet:

Telephone directory surprise

Ingredients

4 halves telephone directories
1 litre sand and cement
small bucket raspberry jam
2kg mud from the garden

Method

Put all the ingredients on the best carpet in the house and tread on them so that they are all mixed well in. Then leave for an hour or two. (Or even longer, depending on when your parents come home.) The 'Surprise' bit comes when your parents say, *'Who did this?!'* Their second surprise is when they ask, 'Have you seen the telephone directory?'

Collecting

Stamps

Lie in wait by your local post box. When the postman comes to open the box and collect the letters, leap out on him, push his cap over his eyes, and run off with his sack.

Simple!

Fossils

Why make do with boring old second-hand fossils when you can so easily *make your own fossil*! All you need is a lump of clay and a Prehistoric Animal such as a Pterodactyl or a Tyrannosaurus Rex. Stick the clay all over the Prehistoric Beast, then just sit and wait for the clay to harden and the Prehistoric Beast to die out and turn completely into dust, bones and all. This will take about 20 million years or so.

When that's done, just crack open the clay (which by now will have turned to stone) and Hey Presto! Your very own Fossil!

Simple!

Trains

The collecting of train numbers is an interesting hobby, popularly known as 'train spotting'. But why stop there?! Why should you have to make do with a boring list of train numbers when you could have the real thing!

Start collecting trains now!

For this you need:

(a) a huge railway station,
(b) lots of trains.

Simple!

Indoor gardening

Growing beans

This is very easy indeed. First, dig up the floor of your living room until you get down to Good Soil. This will mean digging up the foundations of your house.

Plant the beans, and then move next door. This last bit is important because without proper foundations, your house will fall down.

After your house has fallen down, search around the ruins to see if any of your beans have come up yet.

Growing vegetables in jars

Most books that urge children to grow vegetables in jars and on saucers suggest that they use bits of small vegetables (e.g. the top of a carrot, the top of an onion). Nonsense! Go for the big ones:

Oak trees

Put an acorn into a little bit of earth, stick it in a jar, and place it on your window sill for 200 years. You will know when it is ready to be taken out of the jar, because it will fall over and demolish your kitchen.

Marrows

Find a glass jar about fifteen metres long, big enough to take a full grown marrow. Stick a small marrow in it. If it hasn't grown any bigger in two days, attach a bicycle pump to it and pump it up.

An alien from the planet vegetable

These are creatures who are half-potato, half-banana and they come from Outer Space. They can be grown very easily because their natural habitat on their home planet of Vegetable is inside a glass jar.

First, find out where their spaceship has landed. Then catch a small one and put it in a glass jar on your kitchen shelf. You will soon know when it is big enough because it will leap out of the glass jar, bash you over the head, and run off with your house under its arm.

Ten games you
_____can play indoors_____

1. Indoor football

First, knock down all the inside walls of your house. Then find another 21 people who also want to play with you. Divide yourselves into two teams of 11, and then . . . *play the game!*

2. Indoor hockey

The same as *Indoor football,* except you need sticks as well as a ball. Chair legs are always easily available about the home, and make excellent hockey sticks if sawn off neatly and gripped correctly.

3. Draughts

Keep opening all the doors and windows. Your adults will keep shutting them. As soon as they have shut them, open them again. When they yell at you: 'What do you think you're playing at?' reply, 'Draughts!' You have then won the game.

4. Snakes and ladders

For this game you will need the following: one boa constrictor, one python, one viper, one adder, one king cobra, one rattlesnake, one grass snake, one anaconda, one ladder, and one spot.

The object of the game is to spot the grass snake.

Holding the spot in one hand, you approach the snakes. Work out which one is the grass snake, and place the spot on it. As soon as you have done this, run quickly up the ladder. However, this will not do you a lot of good as snakes can climb ladders.

5. Treasure hunt

For this you need a shipload of pirates and a load of shovels. Tell the pirates that there is a chest full of treasure hidden somewhere beneath your kitchen. Give them each a shovel, then stand back and watch your adults' reaction when they get home. How they will laugh!

6. Battleships

For this you need a rather large room, one big enough to take a couple of huge grey battleships, each about 2km long. Put the two of them in the same room with their guns facing each other, and then blow a whistle for them to begin firing.

7. Noughts and crosses

Find a marker pen and go all over the house writing 'NOUGHT' all over the walls. You can do this in your own house or in a neighbour's house.

When you have finished find the adult whose house it is (either your parent or your neighbour) and show them what you have done. They will get very CROSS.

At this point the game ends.

8. Musical chairs

Take all the chairs in your house and stuff them inside the nearest piano.

9. Hide and seek

This game is named after the famous novel by Robert Louis Stephenson, *Dr Hide and Mr Seek*. What you have to do is drink a magic potion that will turn you into a hideous monster who runs around the house frightening everybody. 'Who is this hideous monster?' your family will scream in fear. The monster is, of course, Your Granny.

10. Snap

Most people think this is a game played with cards, but they are wrong. For this game, take a long piece of elastic. Nail one end to your living room wall. Pull the other end. One of two things will happen: either the wall will come out and you will be covered in bricks and wallpaper, or the elastic will break and go SNAP!

The 'Rainy Day Fun' Quiz and Puzzle

When you are stuck inside on a rainy day, there is nothing like a nice fun quiz to pass away those long wet hours. And this is nothing like a nice fun quiz.

1. What do the following have in common? CHIMPANZEE; TELEPHONE; LIBRARY BOOK; MOUNT EVEREST; RADIATOR.
(*Answer:* They are all different from each other.)

2. What is the difference between an encyclopaedia and a packet of washing powder?
(*Answer:* About 5cm.)

3. What is the name given to the unit for measuring electricity?
(*Answer:* Watt.)

How do you measure electricity?
(*Answer:* Watt.)

How do you measure electricity?
(*Answer:* Watt.)

How do you measure electricity?
(*Answer:* Watt.)

Look, are you deaf or something? I've already asked you loads of times: How do you measure electricity?

4. What do the following abbreviations stand for?

(a) MP; (b) UK; (c) HGV; (d) LBW; (e) BA; (f) AA;
(g) OBE; (h) H$_2$O; (i) RSPCA; (j) PTO.
(*Answers:* (a) My Potato; (b) Useful Knickers; (c)
Hot Green Vest; (d) Little Brown Wellingtons; (e)
Busted Axle; (f) Arthur Aardvark; (g) Ordinary
Butter Eaten; (h) Heat Twice Only; (i) Rotten Suet
Pudding Cracks Apart; (j) Push Ted Over.

5. What is the Capital of Australia?
(*Answer:* X.)

6. Can you name four other countries where
Chinese is the national language, apart from
China?
(*Answer:* Yes.)

7. Name two different sorts of horse.
(*Answer:* Dobbin I and Dobbin II.)

8. What was a dodo?
(*Answer:* It was a thing on a string that went up
and down until it died out.)

9. Where did the Romans come from?
(*Answer:* They caught the 11.15 train from Kings
Cross.)

10. What is the exact temperature of the human
body in centimetres?
(*Answer:* Lukewarm.)

There you are, that's the end of the 'Rainy Day
Fun' chapter. Frankly, if you want our advice –
go and watch the TV or a video instead.

YOUNGER BROTHERS and SISTERS (and FAMILY PETS)

OUR ~~CAT~~

There is one major obstacle to enjoying your holiday, and that is your younger brothers and sisters. Because you are not at school, your parents will do their very best to use you as an unpaid childminder. ('Look after Darren for a minute,' they say as they exit at speed through the front door, just as *you* are about to go out to the park. And that is it for the rest of the day. They finally arrive back ten hours later, and you have missed everything good.)

There are two ways of dealing with this problem:

1. Come up with excuses for getting out of it.

2. Make use of your younger brother and/or sister (or family pet).

Here's how:

Excuses for getting out of looking after your younger brother or sister (or your family pet)

- 'I'm far too young to be given such a responsibility.'

- 'Say he/she/it fell ill?'

- 'The neighbours will report you to the National Society for the Prevention of Cruelty to Children/the RSPCA.'

- 'He/she/it doesn't like me.'

- 'I don't like him/her/it.'

- 'He/she/it will fret and worry all the time you're not here. They'll miss you.'

- 'I've arranged to go and see my friend.'

- 'I've offered to do voluntary work with the tramps and drunks in the Community Centre. Surely you wouldn't want me to shirk my social responsibilities.'

- 'If I don't go to the Community Centre to help the tramps and drunks there, they'll have to come here instead.'

- 'I'm sure I heard him/her/it cough a few minutes ago. If they do it again while you're out I'll have to phone 999, because I'm too young to know what to do in such an emergency.'

- 'The doctor at school has discovered that I suffer from claustrophobia and I need to be outside all the time. I can't be outside if I'm looking after (whichever one it is).'

- 'I saw the vicar/Mayor/local Member of Parliament yesterday, and he/she said to tell you that he/she will be calling on you today.'

- 'I've got a splinter in my finger so I won't be able to look after him/her/it.'

- 'I don't feel very well. You wouldn't want me to pass on whatever disease it is I'm catching, would you? You know how susceptible small children/animals are to germs.'

Making use of your younger brother or sister ____ (or your family pet)____

All right, all those excuses failed. However, here are a few ways that you can turn this unfortuante situation that you are in to your advantage. Here is how to earn a little bit of extra money from your rotten predicament:

Advertising (child)

Hire him/her out as a model. Advertising firms are always looking for laughing little kids to promote small kids' things like nappies, tiny toys, etc. If your little brother or sister doesn't laugh, stick a few feathers inside his/her clothes.

Advertising (animal)

Advertising firms are always looking for animals to promote things like dog food and cat food, not to mention paint, toilet rolls, cornflakes, etc. Take your pet along to the advertising firm and offer it to them. If they refuse, set your animal on them and refuse to order it off them until they have signed a contract worth zillions of pounds. (*Note:* this really only works with animals such as Big Dogs (e.g. Dobermans, Alsatians). Somehow it doesn't have the same frightening effect if you aim a canary at someone and say, 'Attack that man, Tweety!')

Ventriloquism

Phone up the local theatre and tell them you are a ventriloquist. Take along your little brother/ sister. Sit him/her on your knee and just do your act. This will be much cheaper than using a dummy. (*Note:* you can also try this with your family pet, but it's usually not as effective. For one thing, it's a lot more difficult to make your family pet stay still on your knee.)

Begging

Put very ragged, old and dirty clothes on your younger brother/sister and wheel him/her in a pram to the local shopping precinct. Stick on a sign saying: 'Poor children. Please give generously.' This is not really a lie because you are not using the word 'poor' to mean you have no money, but 'poor' because your parent has gone off and lumbered you with your younger brother or sister for the day (or the hour, or whatever).

Pram testing

Phone up the local pram company and offer your brother's/sister's services as a pram tester.

Toy testing

Similar to pram testing. Persuade toy manufacturers that your brother or sister will soon test if their toys are unbreakable or not, which will save them thousands of pounds if they should get sued for damages for toys that break/harm people.

Food testing

As with *Pram* and *Toy testing*: phone up the local baby food firm and offer to try out their foods on your brother and sister.

If it is the family pet you are lumbered with, phone up the local pet food company and offer to test their foods on your pet. However, make sure you get it right: small children are not too keen on cat and dog food or bird seed. (Most pets, however, will eat *anything*.)

Shops

Take your little brother or sister into a large shop or showroom (e.g. the Electricity or the Gas Board). Wait until they start crying. When the manager comes up to you and asks you to take him/her out, say pitifully: 'I would love to. I wanted to take him/her to a café and buy him/her a drink of milk, but I have no money. That is why I am forced to seek shelter from the cold winds in here.' All the adults around will then fuss and coo over your young bro or sis and will then have a whip round to give you the necessary funds for a 'drink of milk'. With a bit of luck you should get enough cash this way to be able to buy a whole café.

You can do this with pets although not so effectively. In fact the only pets it is effective with are big ones: e.g. dogs or horses, and then only because the manager will be worried in case they do something on the floor.

'THE DIARY OF X' ..... ON HOLIDAY

Yes, it's me again, 'X'. After bits of my diary were published in those other books, *How To Handle Grown-Ups, What Grown-Ups Say*, etc, with immense success, you may remember that the people at BBC Television offered me money if I put my adventures on television. Because of that my name was revealed as Bryan Boyes (or, to give me my full title, Bryan Arthur Derek Boyes — BAD Boyes).

At the time I thought that was a great idea, but there was one major drawback. After those programmes went out ALL OVER THE WORLD, everyone knew all about my dodges, which made being a brilliant dodger much harder. I can't even go to Spain now without some hotel owner recognizing me and saying 'It's the Bryan Boyes! Lock up all the cups and saucers and everybody hide!'

So, as a result of that, I have decided that Enough is Enough! I shall go back to being 'X', so

116

that no one knows that I am really Bryan . . . Curses!

Anyway, as this book is about Holidays, let me tell you what happened to me and my mum and dad one year when we went camping (Ugh!).

Yours . . . X (a.k.a Bryan Arthur . . . Ssshh)

_____ Saturday 3rd August _____

Today we set off for our annual family holiday, Mum driving, Dad navigating, me complaining. The reason why I was complaining is because we are headed for the Isle of Wight. Everyone else in my class is going somewhere wonderful and exciting: America, Africa, Spain, where the sunshine is hot and blistering and they'll all come back looking like baked potatoes. (Except for Joanne Suss, because she's going to Iceland. Try and sunbathe on Iceland and you'll get covered in ice. But even Iceland is more interesting and exciting than the Isle of Wight!)

'Why the Isle of Wight?' I moaned at Mum and Dad before we left.

'Because we like it,' they said.

'Yes, but I don't and I'm going on holiday as well. Couldn't you go to the Isle of Wight and send me to Greece, or somewhere hot?'

Dad said he could think of one hot place I'd be suited for, but he didn't say where it was. He also said that it wasn't safe for me to travel on my own to places like Greece because the plane I would be

flying on might be hijacked by terrorists. Mum
said, 'In that case I pity the poor terrorists.'

'I can't see why we can't go abroad,' I said.

'We are going abroad,' said Dad. 'We have to go
across the sea in a boat.'

'That's not really crossing the sea,' I protested.

'You try walking across it,' said Mum.

Actually I bet you could at low tide, the place is
that near to the mainland.

'Anyway,' said Mum, 'we can't afford a holiday
abroad. Your Dad doesn't earn enough money.'

'Oh yes I do,' retorted Dad indignantly. 'It's just
that you spend too much of it.'

'I suppose you'd prefer us to starve,' said Mum.

'I only ever buy things for the house, like food.'

'I suppose that new coat you bought is food, is it?' said Dad bitingly.

'Oh!' said Mum. 'I suppose you'd like us all to walk around with no clothes on!'

And then they were away, at it hammer and tongs. So, with them arguing like this, we arrived at Southampton and caught the car ferry over to the Isle of Wight. This ferry was the oldest boat I have ever seen. I expect it was a left-over from the invasion of William the Conqueror. I kept expecting it to sink all the way across. For such a short journey it seemed to take hours. Various kids on the boat were sea-sick, helped by the fact that whenever I saw a kid looking a little green about the gills, I went and stood next to them and pretended to eat a dead frog. (It was actually a rubber one that I got from a joke shop, but very life-like. Well, as life-like as a dead frog can be.)

This made them throw up. I then offered to take their sweets off them at a bargain price.

When we arrived at the Isle of Wight, we drove out to this camp site in the middle of nowhere, and Dad and Mum started to put up the tent.

We've got one of these big frame tents, like a big Wendy House, and you need a Degree in Engineering, plus a complete team of pyramid builders to be able to work out where all the different bits go. An hour later and the tent is still lying in a heap of metal framework, and Mum and Dad are shouting at each other again, and it's just starting to rain, so I'm going off to the Clubhouse on the site to play the video games and let them get on with it. This will teach them for not taking me on holiday to Ibiza.

119

Sunday 4th August

Still raining. Tent up, but crooked and wet. My only sight of the sea so far has been from inside the car in a car park as Gale Force Winds blew our car all over the place.

Monday 5th August

Still raining.

Conversations between Mum and Dad are of the following sort:

MUM: Typical. Our holidays are always a washout.

DAD: It was you who wanted to come here.

MUM: I didn't want to come here. I just knew we couldn't afford anywhere else.

DAD: And whose fault is that?

MUM: Certainly not mine. How is it that John and Maureen next door go to France every year, and they earn less than you do?

DAD: I thought we'd agreed to have a holiday in England this year.

MUM: We have a holiday in England *every* year. And *you* agreed it, *I* didn't.

DAD: You said 'Yes'.

MUM: That was so you wouldn't sulk. It wouldn't be so bad if we weren't camping.

Actually, I have to agree with Mum on this. I can't see why we have to stay in a tent while everyone else stays in hotels or guest houses. Mum and Dad claim it is my fault, and that no respectable hotel or guest house would want me anywhere near their premises. I think this is a lie and the truth is that they can't afford it.

Meanwhile we sleep in something that looks like a team of builders with one arm between them assembled it. It leans over every time the wind blows, and it lets in the rain. I think I ought to leave my parents and find a more successful family to live with.

_____ **Thursday 8th August** _____

No diary entries for the last two days because the rain stopped, so we went down to the beach.

Actually they call it a beach but I've seen more attractive building sites with more sand on them. The 'grains' of sand are at least a metre across each, which makes them rocks in my book. Mum and Dad, trying to make the best of it, lay down on this gravel and said, 'Lovely beach, isn't it? And it's not at all crowded.'

I pointed out that the reasons for it not being crowded were:

1. It would be more comfortable lying on the M1.

2. There was a 40kph icy wind blowing in off the freezing sea.

3. There was a big oil slick lying out on the 15-metre-high waves, waiting to be thrown up on to the beach.

4. It was so cold that even a penguin with half a brain wouldn't be idiot enough to venture out on the beach.

They just said that I ought to be grateful that I was on holiday. Some children, they said, wouldn't get to lie on a beach like this.

Lucky children, is what I say.

One thing that's interested me. As we've been driving around this island I've been noticing the other cars. There are loads and loads of these cars that rich people have: big Porsches and BMWs and stuff, all 150kph jobs. Strikes me as a crackpot thing to own a car like that on an island of this size, which is about 5km long by 5km wide. By the time you've put one of these superfast cars into gear and got up speed, you've driven over a cliff. Ridiculous.

_____Friday 9th August_____

Rained again, so we spent the day 'sight-seeing'. The one thing the Isle of Wight is short of, in my opinion, is sights to see. There's the odd cow in a field, or shops selling glass jars full of coloured sand, and that's about it. Not exactly the Taj Mahal or the Great Wall of China.

Still, Mum and Dad were impressed. Mind you, they're so desperate to convince me that this is a wonderful holiday that they'd say they were impressed by the sight of grass growing.

_____Saturday 10th August_____

An interesting thing happened today. A new family arrived on our site and pitched their tent near to ours. Or, rather, they started to pitch their tent near to ours, but had to stop when they found out they'd left their tent pegs behind.

This started a right royal row, and the row got even worse when the family found out that the shop on the site didn't sell tent pegs (which just shows what a real backwoods site this is! It's lucky they even sell matches, I half expected them to sell you two bits of wood and tell you to rub them together.)

Anyway, I saw a way to make a bit of spare money here, so I went to the teenage son (who was getting most of the stick from the rest of the family) and offered to sell him a set of secondhand tent pegs for a pound. He agreed, gave me a pound, and I went round the camp site and removed one peg from every other tent. Not enough to cause anyone to comment on it, but enough to earn me a pound.

This has given me An Idea.

____Sunday 11th August____

Drizzle weather today. Mum and Dad gloomy, expecting me to start moaning about the place again.

Instead I said: 'What does a little rain matter. Let's go sight-seeing.'

They looked at one another suspiciously, and I could see from Mum's expression that she was wondering whether to take my temperature in case I was sickening for something.

'Is there anywhere special you'd like to go?' asked Dad.

'I thought it might be interesting to look at

other camp sites,' I said. 'Who knows, there may be one we like the look of better than this. At least it will give us a chance to see other parts of the island.'

After their initial surprise, Mum and Dad said they thought it was a good idea, mainly because they think that anything that keeps me from moaning about this God-forsaken place is a relief. So off we went on a tour of the island's camp sites, and visited six. I managed to collect a total of twenty-four tent pegs in all, which wasn't bad.

When we got back to our camp site I went off for a stroll around the site, and stopped at each tent where I'd removed a peg yesterday. I pointed out to the people that they had a tent peg missing, and told them that I had a couple of spare pegs, and that I could sell them one for ten pence. Everyone paid up.

It's lucky that the British don't talk to each other, or they would have found out that a few other people also had tent pegs missing. Also, some of the campers were from abroad, quite a few Germans and Dutch, and we all know how rotten the British are about talking to people from other countries (fortunately for me).

(*Thought:* Why do these people want to waste their precious holidays coming to England, and especially a place like the Isle of Wight? If this is their idea of a fun place, it shows what terrible places Germany and Holland must be!)

_____ Tuesday 13th August _____

It rained again.

To ease the boredom we went into the nearest town, where we had a cream tea each (a scone with jam and real cream). Actually I had two cream teas. I asked Mum and Dad if they'd buy me a second helping (with jam and real cream), but being so tight-fisted that when they open their wallets moths fly out and gasp for air, they refused. So I worked the old 'fly in the food' dodge.

To explain how this works: catch a fly. Personally I find it easier to find a fly that's already dead because it saves you a lot of jumping around trying to catch one. If you can't get a fly, any other small dead insect will do. Keep this small dead insect on you (say, in a matchbox) until the opportunity to use it arises.

In my case, I waited until I'd nearly finished my scone (I'd certainly finished the jam, and real cream), then I took out the fly , and stuck it in the

125

bit of scone that was left. A quick scream of horror and revulsion from me, a yell of 'Urgh! There's a dead fly in my scone!', and the waitress, the owner of the tea rooms, and Uncle Tom Cobbley and all came rushing over to find out what all the fuss was about.

The result: I got another scone (with an even bigger helping of jam and real cream than before) to make up for 'the fly in the first scone'.

Apart from that, nothing much happened today.

Thursday 15th August

Still raining. That makes it nearly constant rain since we've been here, except for those two days last week, when there was no rain but just sub-zero temperatures instead.

I saw a poster on a wall today which said: 'Why not have a holiday in England?'

As no one was looking, I wrote on it: 'Because of the rotten weather.'

Saturday 17th August

Still raining. In fact it hasn't stopped at all.

Today Mum said to Dad, 'I am fed up with this. I came here to lie on the beach, and I'm going to lie on it.'

'But it's raining,' Dad pointed out.

'I don't care if it's the monsoon season, I am not going to go back home without having had one day lying on the beach.'

'We had a day on the beach last week,' said Dad.

'And I want one this week,' said Mum. 'Two days in two weeks shouldn't be too much to ask.'

So we drove to the famous layer of gravel again (see *Thursday 8th August*), and Mum and Dad lay down on it in the pouring rain and got soaked.

I sheltered in a cave and watched them as the rain came down in buckets. There they were, in rainmacs and wellington boots, lying on the ground, getting soaking wet. I am convinced that they are both going mad. I wonder if I can have them both certified insane? And if so, I wonder if I'd be allowed to keep the house?

Sunday 18th August

Today we drove home. We wrung out the tent and packed it up, and did the journey back to the mainland on the ferry. The ferry this time went up and down like a roller coaster, and even I felt a bit queasy, so this time I laid off the dead frog dodge.

As we drove out of Southampton it stopped raining. A few kilometres more and the sun came out. Soon there was really hot sunshine. Mum and Dad looked sick. I was going to say, 'I told you so,' but decided against it because the expressions on their faces told me that if I said such a thing there was a very good chance of them putting me out of the car and leaving me by the side of the motorway.

The last ten kilometres of our motorway journey home, we got stuck in a tail-back, and that ten kilometres took us four and a half hours! What a great advert for cars and motorways: 'Buy a new car and travel slower than you do when walking!'

When we got home Dad wanted me to help unload the tent from the car. I got out of this by walking into the house, collapsing on the settee, and pretending to fall asleep. I expected at least one of them to say, 'Ah, the poor dear. That terrible journey back must have worn him out.' Then they would unpack the car, and I would 'wake up' after it was all over, and be very apologetic that I hadn't been awake to help.

Instead I heard Dad mutter, 'Lazy rotten kid,' and he actually kicked the settee as he went past with the tent! This man has no sensitivity and I shall definitely write and complain to the NSPCC about him.